HANDBOOK OF RESEARCH

ON

TEACHER EDUCATION

Second Edition

HANDBOOK OF RESEARCH

ON

TEACHER EDUCATION

Second Edition

A Project of the Association of Teacher Educators

John Sikula
National University
Senior Editor

Thomas J. Buttery
East Carolina University
Editor

Edith Guyton
Georgia State University
Editor

Macmillan LIBRARY Reference USA
Simon & Schuster Macmillan
New York

Prentice Hall International
London   Mexico City   New Delhi   Singapore   Sydney   Toronto

Macmillan Library Reference USA
Simon & Schuster Macmillan
1633 Broadway
New York, NY 10019

Library of Congress Catalog Card Number: 95-7504
ISBN: 0-02-897194-9

Printed in the United States of America

Printing number
1 2 3 4 5 6 7 8 9 10

Library of Congress Cataloging-in-Publication Data

Handbook of research on teacher education: a project of the
    Association of Teacher Educators / John Sikula, senior editor;
    Thomas Buttery, Edith Guyton, editors.—2nd ed.
        p. cm.
    Includes bibliographical references and index.
    ISBN 0-02-897194-9
    1. Teachers—Training of—United States.   I. Sikula, John P.
II. Buttery, Thomas J.   III. Guyton, Edith.   IV. Association of
Teacher Educators.
LB1715.H274   1996
370'.71'072073—dc20   95-7504
                                                 CIP

This paper meets the requirements of ANSI/NISO Z39.48-1992 (Permanence of Paper).

CONTENTS

Part I
TEACHER EDUCATION AS A FIELD OF STUDY   1

Part II
RECRUITMENT, SELECTION, AND INITIAL PREPARATION   65

Part III

CONTEXTUAL INFLUENCES ON TEACHER EDUCATION 211

Part IV

TEACHER EDUCATION CURRICULUM 321

Part
VII

EMERGING DIRECTIONS IN TEACHER EDUCATION   867

FOREWORD

Philosopher George Santayana's oft-quoted axiom, "Those who forget the past are doomed to relive it," is appropriate in teacher education. The short lives of innovations and movements, practices based almost entirely on personal experience or political decisions rather than supported by solid research, and the nominal mutations in professional language that defy analysis across strategies or concepts are indicative of the need not only for syntheses of research and professional literature, but also for their use in improving the education of teachers.

Short Life of Programs

Twenty years ago a movement called competency-based teacher education (CBTE) or performance-based teacher education (PBTE) consumed teacher education. The movement was based on the behavioral objectives movement but declined to embrace behavioral objectives because of their links to behaviorism. Schools, textbooks, state department of education regulations, and the public itself also supported the competency-based movement, and it swept across the United States. Within a few years, more than 400 teacher education programs in the nation were based on CBTE; at the same time, charges of ineffectiveness, irrelevancy, and lack of vision sparked a growing counter movement. As the term became tarnished, the name was changed to outcomes-based education and/or proficiency-directed education; and now that these terms are also decried, results-based education, standards, and criteria are in vogue. The name changed, but the general concept remains the same.

Sixteen years ago, B. O. Smith (1980), in a cogent analysis of teacher preparation, charged that programs were very similar to those of 50 years earlier. Although the rhetoric of journal articles and papers delivered at scholarly meetings convey the impression of considerable action and euphoric effective change, most of America's teachers still are prepared using the same basic framework employed six decades ago. The lack of a sound basis for making changes and the short life of programs has led to stagnation of the system. Program changes have been watered down and nullified so effectively in the caldron of bureaucratic practices that changes seldom affect the basic fabric of teacher education.

Programs Based on Lore, Not Research

During the past few years, I have interviewed dozens of teacher educators from institutions across America. In describing their teacher preparation programs, they emphasized innovations and conceptual models. Each recognized the importance placed on program models by most states and the National Council for Accreditation of Teacher Education (NCATE). Yet, program changes over the previous years, although appearing to be significant, were actually quite modest when the actual experiences of students were analyzed. Course and program requirements remained basically the same, and the content and experiences tended to be based primarily on traditional course content, instructors' personal experiences, and textbooks rather than on programmatic models.

An interesting phenomenon occurs—the rapid changes without institutionalization lead to the cult of change, but the results are stagnation and lack of change. After brief periods of experimentation, usually externally funded and involving small groups of people (often brought in from the outside to complete a project), programs tend to return to their original states. The famed "double-speak" applies where a word or term is defined one way in the dictionary but is used in selected practice to mean just the opposite. Educators often describe change but do not change.

Evaluations of the effectiveness of such programs are virtually nonexistent. Even the content of programs often is poorly chronicled. The "black box" of professional preparation experiences decries comparison. As one example, consider the distinction between traditional teacher education and experience-based (field-based) teacher education. Traditional teacher preparation is based on the premise that students study and master the fundamental concepts of teaching prior to gradual introduction to practice and finally a capstone experience in student teaching. In an alternate form, prospective teachers first experience schools, then explore the theoretical concepts related to their experiences. These two paradigms dominate educational debate today; yet, neither has been adequately tested nor compared. A second example involves the distinction between *process* and *substance* in teacher preparation. Are there differences between outcomes of inquiry-based teacher preparation in which students are taught to reflect on their experience and to improve their practice (process oriented) and programs in which concepts and skills related to teacher education are central (substance oriented)?

Need for Programmatic Research

The *Handbook of Research on Teacher Education* was conceptualized as a way to ferment change based on solid evidence. The first handbook, published in 1990, included a synthesis of the knowledge base of teacher education organized in 48 chapters written by some of America's foremost educational researchers. As the senior editor of the first handbook, I was privileged to read critically all of those chapters, and in so doing, to strengthen my own understanding of teacher education research and theory. The handbook has been used in dozens of research seminars since 1990, with similar reactions from doctoral students and faculty. It has provided a resource for those conceptualizing new programs and needing research. It has stimulated considerable debate about the merits of various movements and has been referenced widely in the literature.

The second handbook builds on the first. Experience with the first handbook indicated a number of fields that required further and more extensive exploration and others in which developments had been so rapid that they required additional attention. The two handbooks complement each other and, thus, may be used in tandem. The authors and editors hope teacher educators will continue to use both handbooks as resources that encourage systemic, research-based reform. The editors and authors of the second handbook are to be commended for their care in selecting content and communicating vital concepts that are directed to the improved education of teachers.

Both handbooks are based on the premise that improving teaching is critical to improving schooling in America, and that the education of professionals is a lifelong process, from initial preparation through induction into the profession, to regular continuing development of career professionals. The audience of the handbooks is composed of professionals in schools, universities, state agencies, private industries, and other areas who are involved in improving the knowledge and skills of prospective and practicing teachers.

Rapid Societal and Technological Change

The culture of informed inquiry in professional education remains a challenge. Technological and sociological changes re-

shaping our country are occurring so rapidly that the education of future generations in schools and the preparation of their teachers have not kept pace.

Changes in technology have been so rapid that they segregate generations of Americans (e.g., the ease with which children play computer games as compared to their parents) and increasingly separate those families with computers in the home from those without computers. (Are we generating a new type of segregation based on economic grounds that ultimately will limit future generations' access to better jobs?) In teacher education, technological innovations provide potential but generally untapped means for improving the preparation of prospective teachers (e.g., CD-roms; computers' increased power and availability, decreased size, and decreased cost; access through electronic mail and the telecommunications super highway to encyclopedias and galleries of European art museums; ERIC collections of research; personal interactions with others in the field). Today's technological innovation is tomorrow's antique. For example, by the time this handbook is published, the computer on which this Foreword is being composed will be far outdated. Those preparing teachers must continually update our knowledge and skills in using technology and drawing on software to strengthen programs.

Society, too, is rapidly changing. Population centers are shifting from north to south, from east to west, and from rural to urban centers. Characteristic of social problems are drugs, violence, poverty, crowded living conditions, and unemployment among young minorities. Family patterns have changed from traditional nuclear families to a range of arrangements, particularly single-parent families and a majority of mothers of school-age children who work outside the home. Immigrants entering the United States, particularly those unable to speak English and who have few job skills and little or no formal education, have increased from a trickle to a torrent. Governmental social service agencies have increased rapidly, and local businesses are challenged by international cartels with assets in the billions of dollars, some larger than that of many countries.

The education of students and of their teachers has fallen behind the power curve of change. I believe that schools are more effective today than a half century ago and that teacher education is more effective than a half century ago, but that neither are effective enough for the changing world. They are more effective in preparing students and teachers for the world of 1950 and 1960 than the radically different world of 2001, only a few years away! The school of 30 years ago may have been relevant for its time, but what was appropriate and effective then is outdated today.

Teacher education needs to reassess its effectiveness for the new reality—a reality that will continue to change at an accelerated rate. Criticized for its ineffectiveness, monitored by governmental sructures and strictures, and mired in bureaucracy, teacher education has not kept pace with rapidly changing America. The major hope for real restructuring lies in programs based on research and best practice, with processes of experimental and innovative programs carefully monitored to document what is occurring, and effectiveness assessed in terms of outcomes for diverse learners. The handbooks are important tools in this process because with them teacher educators can readily find relevant related research, conceptual models, and practices that have been tested. From these descriptions and from the detailed references in each chapter, teacher educators can design and test programs that build on previous successes and failures rather than whim or intuition.

W. Robert Houston
University of Houston
Editor, *Handbook of Research on Teacher Education*

Reference

Smith, B. O. (1980). *A design for a school of pedagogy.* Washington, DC: U.S. Government Printing Office.

PREFACE

Serving as editors of the second edition of the *Handbook of Research on Teacher Education* has been one of the highlights of our professional careers. The opportunity to work with recognized leaders in different and critical areas of teacher education research has broadened our own understanding and appreciation of the complexities of the field. Similarly, readers who carefully examine this volume will find a kaleidoscope of significant information to process that will contribute to their own knowledge base about learning and teaching.

The second edition of the handbook is very different, by design, from the first edition published in 1990. Significant new developments, changing content, and emerging new authorities made feasible the publication of a second edition 6 years after the first edition. Some of the important new chapters in the second edition include research analyses on early childhood, elementary, middle level, and secondary education; classroom management; teacher empowerment and site-based management; authentic assessment; case methods in teacher education; moral responsibilities; collaborative education; alternatives to public schooling; rural teacher education; international teacher education; and an entire section of eight chapters on diversity and equity issues.

VALUABLE RESOURCE

The editors hope that readers find this volume useful. We believe that some very significant contributions to the advancement of knowledge in the field are contained herein. Please use the handbook as it is intended, as a resource and reference point for improving understanding and practice in not only educational institutions but also among individual educators. Similar to the first edition, this second edition of the *Handbook of Research on Teacher Education* is committed to the belief that the improvement of teacher education is integral to the improvement of schools. Both editions were conceptualized and developed to provide a basis for improving the education of teachers at every level, from recruitment and initial preparation through the induction of beginners, to continued development as career professionals. The handbook is dedicated to and is designed for people responsible for preservice and in-service teacher education who would benefit from a critical synthesis

and careful interpretation of research, while improving their own practice.

CONCEPTUAL FRAMEWORK

The conceptual framework for the second edition is both similar to and different from the first edition. The opening sections on the field of study are similar, as are the sections on curriculum; however, the first edition contained sections on governance and processes, whereas the second edition has new sections on diversity and equity and emerging directions.

The second edition attempts to place teacher education and professional development within a framework for taking a novice in the field to the developmental point of being an expert, one open to new ideas, fresh approaches, and emerging challenges. By definition, education is a process of change. As one works through this publication from beginning to end, one can gain significant insight about career educators who first learn something about the field of study, become initially involved in it, learn about contextual influences as they develop, then become expert and experienced in some curricular area, seek personal and professional growth and development, learn to appreciate diversity and equity issues, and, finally, seek new and better answers to lingering questions. The framework is not flawless and is not intended to be; it is offered for those who look for logic, order, and/or reason in a world that often has little.

How the second edition topics and treatment differ from those in the first edition informs readers about issues and changes in teacher education today, 6 years later. Chapters are not a rehash of the same topics, but, rather, they present fresh new analyses of important research affecting teacher education.

HANDBOOK DEVELOPMENT AND CONTENT

The second edition represents the efforts of more than 200 people from all 50 states and many countries who contributed as editors, advisory council members, authors, and critical reviewers.

Initial development of the second edition began in December 1992, when the senior editor received phone calls asking him to consider heading the effort. During January 1993, discussions between the three editors began, and the national office of ATE negotiated a contract with Macmillan. The senior editor then organized an advisory council consisting of

Gloria Chernay
Carl Grant
Martin Haberman
Fay Haisley
Francisco Hidalgo
Jean Houck
W. Robert Houston
Peggy Ishler
Howard Macauley
Elaine McNiece

These people are all highly respected teacher educators with long careers, established reputations, and interest in advancing knowledge in the field via handbook production.

The advisory council met during the 1993 annual meeting of ATE in Los Angeles. Members reviewed an initial outline, discussed chapter topics and authors, and made suggestions on how to broaden input into the second edition. The outline was revised to reflect an analysis of the needs of educators, and some topic and author suggestions were made to include chapter presentations by respected authors on emerging areas of research.

The three editors met later during the 1993 annual meeting to review advisory council input and to develop plans for soliciting further input and refining the effort. Later, the editors sought author/reviewer nominations from across the nation in identifying persons with the greatest expertise related to specified topics.

In April 1993, the editors discussed further written input from the advisory council and from four formal reviews of the handbook outline commissioned by Macmillan. Another iteration of the content and authors was circulated to advisory council members.

In May, the senior editor began inviting authors to contribute to the volume. He discussed the purpose of the handbook, its audience, the need for current and readable manuscripts, and he answered many of their questions. He spoke personally to prospective authors and sent them complete packets of material containing a letter of invitation, an outline of chapter topics and authors, short scope statements about each chapter, an information collection sheet, a production schedule, "Guidelines for Preparing Manuscripts," a description of the "Process for Handling Manuscripts," and an editor assignment. In the directions for preparing their chapters, authors were asked not only to synthesize the most important research in their areas but also to place it within a conceptual framework, to analyze trends, and to summarize new directions. Authors were required to verify each and every reference used via photocopy. Chapters were to be submitted on disk as well as hard copy. Deadlines were established.

The two editors followed authorship confirmation with calls and/or letters identifying or confirming at least two critical reviewers for each chapter. Reviewers played an important role in ensuring validity and comprehensiveness of materials, and they were decided upon with care. The editors not only considered expertise, but also they paid attention to equity concerns, including sex, race, state, institutional affiliation, and professional membership(s).

In terms of content, the second edition is divided into 48 chapters organized into seven parts.

Part I	Teacher Education as a Field of Study
Part II	Recruitment, Selection, and Initial Preparation
Part III	Contextual Influences on Teacher Education
Part IV	Teacher Education Curriculum
Part V	Continuing Professional Growth, Development, and Assessment
Part VI	Diversity and Equity Issues
Part VII	Emerging Directions in Teacher Education

Chapters were placed within sections and sequenced with the professional development framework in mind. In several cases, chapters could be placed in one of two or more sections; and in some cases, section headings were developed well after chapter sequencing. The editors decided not to worry excessively about chapter location, but rather to concentrate their efforts on high-quality chapter content.

ACKNOWLEDGMENTS

The editors wish to acknowledge the work of several people. The prodigious efforts of authors, who ultimately are responsible for the content and quality of chapters, deserve special attention. The handbook is only as good as its authors. The critical reviewers also made important contributions, and they are often acknowledged at the beginning of each chapter.

The editors wish to thank the Association of Teacher Educators and Macmillan for their confidence in this editorial team. More specifically, Gloria Chernay, ATE Executive Director, and Philip Friedman, President and Publisher, Macmillan Reference, are acknowledged for their significant efforts and assistance.

Lastly, editor Guyton wants to thank Brenda Moss Galina, chair of the Department of Early Childhood Education at Georgia State University, for her professional support; her husband Narl Davidson for his personal support; and Trish Levitt for her excellent help in checking references. Editor Buttery knows that time is a precious commodity, especially in a family. Much appreciation is extended to his children Katie, Tommy, and Ashley Claire for sharing their time during the preparation of this handbook, and in memory of Nancy Caldwell Buttery, who as a wife supported him in his work with ATE. A special thank you is extended to Brenna Horne and Teresa LaBiche who spent much of their time as graduate assistants providing editorial assistance. Senior editor Sikula wishes to acknowledge three people for their personal support during the 3-year period of handbook development: his mother Anna Sikula, identical twin brother Andy Sikula, and he also wants to provide a very special note of appreciation for Belen Estrada, his secretary and friend for 12 years.

John Sikula
National University
Thomas J. Buttery
East Carolina University
Edith Guyton
Georgia State University

INTRODUCTION

For the last 3 years I have spent considerable time and effort gathering and editing chapters for the second edition of the *Handbook of Research on Teacher Education*. Sponsored by the national Association of Teacher Educators (ATE) and the Macmillan Publishing Company, this resource aggregates some of the most recent and best analyses of teaching and teacher education available today. This experience has allowed me to attain an informed perspective on issues facing schooling and teacher education in America. Also, delivering the Distinguished Educator Lecture at the ATE annual meeting in St. Louis in February 1996 (where the handbook second edition will be released) seemed to be a good opportunity to synthesize and present some critical points from the 3-year handbook effort.

What follows are some important points and observations for teacher educators and others living in this critical period of our nation's educational history. In addition to handbook chapters, material for this introduction draws heavily from two other sources that I have relied on in 12 years of touring for Phi Delta Kappa and talking to groups in the United States and 17 countries about teacher education and schooling in America. The first source, not popularly known or used among educators, is the paperback *We're Number One*, written by Andrew Shapiro and published as a Vintage paperback in May 1992. The second important resource is *Knowledge Revolution for All Americans, Winning the War Against Ignorance: Empowering Public Schools*, published by The Knowledge Network for All Americans in 1992 and first introduced to me at the annual meeting of the American Association of Colleges for Teacher Education (AACTE) 4 years ago.

The material in this introduction also draws on my 27 years of experience as a teacher educator, the last 12 1/2 years of which were spent in California where firsthand awareness of educational problems has been heightened while watching and experiencing a fading vision of educational excellence in America.

This material is not intended to be entertaining or uplifting; examination of educational progress in recent years is somewhat uncomfortable. Yet, the information and impressions shared here may be seen as challenging, thought provoking, and worthy of further analysis and discussion.

This analysis focuses on a few disturbing observations, each of which is discussed in detail.

1. Schooling and teacher preparation in America are *not* high-priority items.
2. Educational reform efforts in America are disjointed, uncoordinated, and often contradictory.
3. The prospects for educational improvement in America in the near future are bleak.
4. In recent history, Americans have been unwilling to invest adequate dollars for high-quality public education.

THE CURRENT CONDITION OF TEACHER EDUCATION

Few of the several hundred professions have as little of a consensus about a common knowledge base as does the teaching profession. This condition has been improving in recent years with attention from ATE, AACTE, the National Council for Accreditation of Teacher Education (NCATE), the Teacher Education Council of State Colleges and Universities (TECSCU), and other professional groups associated with teacher education in the United States. There is a growing consensus today about the need to move the profession of teaching in the direction of a more common knowledge base. There is much less consensus about other matters, such as the specific direction that a reform effort should take, or even whether or not schooling and teacher education are important enough topics to attract the priority attention and resources of this country as a whole.

The fact of the matter is that schooling and teacher education are not high-priority items in this country generally and in state institutions of higher education specifically. In fact, many people in the United States today have written off schooling and education as being unimportant to them personally in achieving their own goals. For example, 65% of all youth in the United States work during the school year, as compared with 2% of Japanese students (see Corrigan & Udas, chap. 41). Schooling and work and earning a living are not necessarily connected in the minds of many youths and other people today. In addition, it is obvious that many reformers have discounted teacher preparation programs in institutions of higher education for being incapable of making the dramatic changes being called for by education critics today. For example, witness the growing number of current school reform efforts with no connections whatsoever with institutions of higher education. In Los Angeles, for example, a person can become licensed to teach without taking any education coursework in a school, college, or department of education.

In weighing the issues and evidence, we need to be philosophical, yet realistic. Sometimes we lose perspective and think that our concerns as teacher educators are shared as priority items by others in this country. Generally, they are not. Our concerns are not burning issues with most people in America. Health care, violence, the economy, and a host of other issues are much higher priority items with most Americans. National concerns shift, with no single item holding center stage for very long; clearly rising violence and health care costs are national priorities in the 1990s. Also, considering that less than 5% of the world's population lives in the United States, it becomes clear what a small piece these concerns are in the overall course of human events. Nonetheless, each of us has a sphere of influence and a chance to make some difference at something in this world, and teacher education is the arena where we have chosen to try to make a difference.

Let us start with a look at California. California contains 33 million people, more than most countries of the world, and 12% of the U.S. population. One out of every seven school-age youth in the United States lives in California, and the state prepares 1 out of every 10 teachers. The latest census shows that California, Texas, Florida, and New York account for half of the growth in the nation's population since the mid-1980s.

Such growth is not necessarily an asset. The growth primarily has been among immigrants and the undereducated who need a variety of educational support that costs additional dollars during a time when they are not available. California schools are the most crowded in the nation; California state budgets for schooling and teacher education have been declining for years; and the state is being asked to do more and more with fewer and fewer resources.

It is also important to realize that only about 20% of this nation's adults have children in school today. There are more people over age 65 than teenagers. The fastest growing population group in the United States is people over 85 (see Corrigan & Udas, chap. 41), and because this population is living on fixed incomes, retired, requiring increasing health care, and becoming more conservative, these people are not inclined to support local education initiatives at the polls in California, Florida, Texas, or anywhere else. The American Association of Retired Persons is now the largest individual member organization in the country (see Kohl & Witty, chap. 39), and retirees are increasingly influencing policies and practices through their collective power at election time.

Local and state dollars for schooling and teacher education will continue to be scarce. National dollars for education have declined over more than a decade. The Clinton administration made a very modest reversal of the trend, but additional resources are needed to implement successful educational reform. This point is elaborated later.

The current condition of teacher education also finds teacher educators continuing to experiment will all kinds of reforms. Many of these are not only unrelated, disjointed, and uncoordinated, but also they are often contradictory. There are limita-

tions to how thoroughly this topic can be addressed here, but the following six dilemmas and contradictions in American educational reform efforts give a sense of how educational reform efforts in America are often counterproductive.

Conformity versus Diversity

For years teacher educators have been in a testing-assessment frenzy. Teacher testing, basic skills testing, subject-matter knowledge testing, professional skills testing, and, more recently, authentic assessment, portfolio assessment, and case study examinations have dominated many reform discussions. These latter three types of assessment have emerged to help address the real problem that one cannot promote more traditional testing and embrace diversity simultaneously. Diversity is one of our strengths, but it cannot be promoted via increased state and national testing, which contribute to homogeneity. Some (especially traditional) testing discriminates against minorities. This is a complex issue that will require much more analysis and work in the years ahead, but more testing based on state and national standards and the idea of promoting diversity are extremely difficult, if not impossible, to support simultaneously. One cannot standardize and individualize at the same time. Several chapters in this handbook address this problem.

Local versus National Control

Equally difficult is to support the traditional American notion of local control and neighborhood schools, while at the same time supporting efforts to devise national certification exams for teachers, national standards for curriculum, and state and national examinations for teachers in training and in-service teachers. Local teachers, students, parents, and administrators who want influence over their own lives and situations are justly concerned about reform efforts initiated top-down by people unfamiliar with local conditions and personalities. The U.S. Constitution delegates responsibility for education to the states, which in turn have traditionally relied on local school districts to control what happens in schools. Site-based management is designed to place control of each school's curriculum, policies, processes, and personnel in the hands of local communities and the local school staff. Yet, state and national trends in centralized curriculum are based on standards, test specifications, and achievement assessments, which, when combined with media events that publicize how each school performs on such tests, promote centralized control. The growing trend to look nationally for educational solutions will surely meet some stiff resistance from state and local communities in the years ahead.

Partnership/Collaboration versus Empowerment

There has been much discussion about site-based management and teacher empowerment in the reform literature. At the same time, reformers talk about the necessity for "partnerships" and "collaboration." Yet, these are very much opposite notions that logically cannot be pursued simultaneously. Generally, when one group (e.g., teachers) is empowered, the position or authority of another is weakened. Ten states now have professional standards boards empowering teachers to have more control over state licensing. This number has doubled in recent years. It is also known that a "partnership/collaboration" works best when different groups come to the bargaining table as equals. It is clear that it is not possible to move in both directions at the same time; they are basically mutually exclusive.

This dilemma may present more of a false dichotomy than the others. If empowerment is thought of as enfranchisement, then Americans might be able to be more inclusive and less exclusive than others have been in the educational decision-making process. Again, this is a complex issue worthy of much more extensive analysis, which is beyond the purpose and scope here (see Clark, Hong, and Schoeppach, chap. 27, which provides several specific examples of how empowering teachers, for example, has had some negative effects for principals). It is not possible to empower one group and promote collaboration simultaneously without jeopardizing the balance of power and often dooming a reform effort to failure.

Product/Content versus Process Solutions

Recent reforms have swayed back and forth on issues related to content/product and process solutions to educational problems. Today it is popular to think that "less is more"; that, for example, more thorough analysis of a few subject-matter topics is superior to less extensive content coverage of more topics. Others believe that the process involved in decision making is more important then the content or result of the process. Still others believe that the end result justifies the means, that process is not just less important but is insignificant. Such arguments back and forth have influenced reform efforts for years; and little real agreement exists beyond a small group of people doing things in a similar way in some specific locality. This unresolved and often unanalyzed conflict results in failure of many educational reform efforts.

This reform dilemma illustrates the sometimes noted differences between an educational generalist and a specialist. A generalist is a person who learns less about specific topics and more about general topics; he or she learns a little bit about everything to the point where he or she ends up knowing absolutely nothing about everything. Equally disturbing is the specialist who learns more about a specific topic and less about topics in general; he or she learns a great deal about a very small area to the point where he or she ends up knowing absolutely everything about nothing.

Home versus School Cultures

The reform literature is replete with descriptions of conflicts between the cultures of the home and the school. Examples abound. Most schools expect students to be quiet, respectful, on time, passive, clean, healthy, fed, and rested. The list goes on and on. The culture in the home and/or community often encourages opposite characteristics. Schools prohibit cigarettes, drugs, weapons, violence, sex, alcohol, guns, loud music, cer-

tain clothing, and a host of other things often prized in cultures and among people out of school. The constant clash of cultures creates enormous problems for formal educational institutions, problems that, for the most part, still have been inadequately addressed. This culture clash programs many reform efforts for failure because they often fail to recognize, appreciate, and make accommodations for differing values and positions that may have equal validity. Several chapters in this handbook address this issue, including Chapter 33 by Hidalgo, Chávez-Chávez, and Ramage.

Equity versus Access

Providing equal access for everyone to formal educational institutions in America and treating everyone equally are ideals generically at odds. The playing field is not level, and people come to situations with unequal skills, experiences, and abilities to cope and succeed. Affirmative action policies often require preferential treatment to correct historical patterns of discrimination. Backlashes of all types and reversions to previous policies and practices are becoming more common in America. For example, we are returning to mainstreaming students with special educational problems into regular classrooms. Why? Inclusion is being supported popularly today because we have found, for example in New York City in 1991 (see York & Reynolds, chap. 38) and elsewhere, that as much as 25% of total school expenditures was tied to a very small percentage of special education students. Almost everyone today can point to instances where positions and promotions went to candidates often considered by their peers to be less than fully qualified. Actions were designed to meet affirmative action or other political requirements. In trying to promote equal access, some people inadvertently, unintentionally, and unwittingly have engaged in reverse discrimination and have treated others unequally or unfairly. Accounts and court cases are legion in this area. This is a topic too controversial for full elaboration here. It is covered in several handbook chapters, including Chapter 39 by Kohl and Witty. Suffice it now to say that it is often very difficult to promote equity or equal treatment and equal access simultaneously.

These are but six of the dilemmas evident in educational reform efforts in America today. The end result of all these different reform efforts headed in so many different directions simultaneously is that, on the whole, much less has been accomplished than generally meets the eye. In addition, there has generally been a standoff, with little sustained movement in any one consistent reform direction. The end result tends to perpetuate the status quo, and the current status is chaotic and undesirable.

WHY ARE THE PROSPECTS FOR EDUCATIONAL IMPROVEMENT BLEAK?

When comparing the United States with other industrialized countries of the world, we can find some very disturbing results. Andrew Shapiro reports in *We're Number One* (1992) that when comparing the United States with 17 other industrial nations, we find that the United States is number one in

- Single-parent families
- Marriage and divorce
- Unequal wealth distribution
- Homelessness
- Murders
- Gun ownership
- Incarceration
- Capital punishment
- Lawyers
- High-paid athletes
- Budget deficit
- Defense spending
- Children and elderly in poverty
- Infant mortality
- Cars
- Televisions
- Garbage

Looking at other factors that affect or have an impact on schooling and education even more directly, Shapiro reports that among the 17 major industrialized nations, the United States is ranked

- First in television watching
- First in fewest homework hours
- Fifteenth in days spent in school
- Last in rewarding teachers
- Last in public spending on education

Students in the United States spend more time watching television than attending school (see Jones, chap. 24). Youth work habits, respect for authority, and punctuality are relatively poor. Work force skills are not being developed in many of our schools. Fewer and fewer students and workers are drug free, willing to work, able to follow directions, respect others, and are honest.

In the United States today we are spending more and more time, effort, and resources on simply trying to maintain a safe and orderly environment, which was once taken for granted in most parts of this country. As our economy has faltered in the 1980s and 1990s, as the dollar has slipped in value, and as our social problems have escalated, less money and fewer resources have been available for traditional American priority areas such as education. As a result, the American schools and educational system continue to fail in many respects.

A real crisis exists in American education today, but this crisis is not so much an academic one as it is a social one. Our priorities and spending are out of line with our historical traditions and previous values. *Prisons have replaced schools as high-priority items.* Nowhere is this more evident than in California where 18 prisons and only one senior university were built in the last 25 years. California is not alone in this regard. In 1990, 11 states spent at least 24 times more on corrections and prisons than was spent on the care and education of children (see Corrigan & Udas, chap. 41).

This country is not the same one that it was 50 years ago. American priorities have changed, as well as the composition of the American people. In 1940, 70% of U.S. immigrants came from Europe. In 1992, 15% came from Europe, 37% from Asia, and 44% from Latin America and the Caribbean. Thirteen percent of Americans and one seventh of all school-age children in the United States speak a language other than English at home. Most of these students enter school with limited English proficiency (see Garcia, chap. 36). In Los Angeles, for example, 21% of the youths under 18 years of age are foreign born.

Economic conditions have changed as well, making the prospects for educational improvement bleak. In 1950, 16 workers contributed to social security for every retiree drawing social security benefits; in 1960, the ratio was 5 to 1; in 1990, 3 to 1; and by 2020 the ratio is predicted to be approximately 2.2 to 1 (see Corrigan & Udas, chap. 41). California's education problems are complicated by no- or low-income people flooding the state while high salaried workers are leaving. Young families in the United States now can expect to spend as many years taking care of dependent parents as they spend taking care of dependent children.

So the situation has changed. Old solutions will not work. Neither becoming more efficient nor returning to the past will be effective. We could look to other countries and models for potential ideas and practices, but our culture is different from theirs, and their solutions are not likely to be effective here.

The real issue is the need for adequate resources during an era of heightened educational need and lowered educational resources. Educational institutions in the United States can no longer do more with less; the point of diminishing returns has long passed. We can restructure, but effective restructuring requires resources.

WHAT EVIDENCE SUPPORTS THE NEED FOR MORE RESOURCES?

Can spending American dollars differently really make any difference? Yes, it can. Let us examine a few ways how it can, but first let it be known that if someone claims that money makes no difference in quality educational outcomes, they either know very little about schooling or they are making a political statement. Such people generally have little if any current or practical experience in a classroom.

Berliner (1993) has helped to dispel this and other myths about education when he reported in the *Phi Delta Kappan* that "academically more proficient teachers, who are more experienced, who are better educated, and who work with smaller classes, are associated with students who demonstrate significantly higher achievement" (pp. 636–637). Also, of course, money is associated with educating and developing teacher proficiency and experience and with providing smaller classes. Common sense and practical experience also explain that well-educated teachers are superior to untrained ones in effecting positive results with students, and funding is associated with developing these positive teacher attributes of being better educated and experienced. Good (see chap. 28) further reports that several studies show a positive relationship between school resources and student achievement. Money also is associated with attracting high-quality students into the profession, keeping them there, and developing their productivity on the job.

Research tells us that most teenagers decide what they do *not* want to be by 14 years of age, and most of the brightest youth in the United States today do *not* want to be teachers. They see the stress, the low pay, and the working conditions, and they decide early not to become educators. Those who do begin to teach frequently drop out. It is not uncommon to lose 50% of a staff in an urban school within 5 years.

The working conditions of American teachers are among the worst in the industrialized world. This is particularly true of secondary teachers who have low pay, high risks, and little status. The Association for Supervision and Curriculum Development (ASCD) conducted a study of its membership and reported in 1990 that the status of teaching and, as a result, morale remains at an all-time low.

The shortage of teachers in the United States is a result of a shortage of dollars attracting people to the profession. There are a few geographic exceptions, but the shortage is general and pervasive. The dilution of financial support for educational institutions so common in the 1980s and 1990s has contributed directly to not enough qualified teachers being willing to take positions in schools. More than 50,000 emergency licenses are issued each year to "teachers," some of whom are substandard. All kinds of less expensive alternative certification programs are being tried in at least 31 states, and 46 states are issuing emergency licenses, sometimes with as little as 2–3 weeks of training. In 1990–1991, more than one in four new hires held either substandard certificates or none at all (see Darling-Hammond & Sclan, chap. 5). Clearly, money is related to who teaches where. Economically poor schools have more teachers with substandard certificates and experience, and the dichotomy is growing. The economically poor are getting poor teachers, whereas the rich get the better teachers. The discrepancy in quality between rich and poor schools is worse today than ever (see Darling-Hammond & Sclan, chap. 5), a condition that has led the Supreme Court to intervene in Texas, Michigan, and several other states.

American teacher working conditions are poor by comparison to other nations. Compare the average American teacher's workday, generally from 7:30 A.M. to 3:30 P.M., often with little time to even go to the restroom, with the workday in Japan, China, or Germany, where the typical high school teacher teaches only 15–20 hours out of a 40–45-hour school week, with the other hours being available for rest, preparation, joint curriculum planning, tutoring, and consultation with parents, students, and colleagues (see Darling-Hammond & Sclan, chap. 5).

Inadequate funding currently is affecting all levels of education. In institutions of higher education, teacher education programs are typically underfunded, with conditions having worsened considerably during the late 1980s and early 1990s. Between 1980 and 1989, funding for schools, colleges and departments of education (SCDEs) deteriorated because of flat or declining budgets and inflation. SCDEs also lost ground in their ability to secure resources relative to other departments, for example, physical and biological sciences, business and management, engineering, and psychology (see Monk & Brent, chap. 12). Several studies have concluded that SCDEs and

teacher education progress are treated poorly in the resource allocation process (see Monk & Brent, chap. 12). Even within SCDEs, teacher education programs frequently are underfunded. Studies show that approximately 10% of the resources generated by teacher education are used to subsidize other SCDE programs (see Monk & Brent, chap. 12).

The evidence supporting the need for more resources for schools and teacher education is clear. Having been an education dean for 20 years in two states has certainly taught me that educational problems in America cannot be resolved without additional resources, that reform efforts to be successful require financial support, and that money is related to quality educational outcomes. The fact of the matter is that people and society can simply learn to pay or invest in education early in the process of a young person's life or plan to support the consequences later. Studies show, for example, that every dollar invested in preschool education saves $4.75 that otherwise would be spent on future costs of special education, crime, and welfare (see Corrigan & Udas, chap. 41). Furthermore, studies show that each year of poverty increases the likelihood of being below expected grade level by 2% (see Corrigan & Udas, chap. 41). Bredekamp (see chap. 16) notes that $7.16 is returned for every $1.00 invested in a high-quality preschool in which the curriculum facilitates active learning and promotes decision making and parent involvement. Yet, in 1990, half of the states spent less than $25 annually per child on the education of its youngest children (see Corrigan & Udas, chap. 41).

It is, therefore, imperative to support educational investment up front. Why? Because we simply cannot afford to keep building more and more prisons and incarcerating more and more of our citizenry. It costs $20,000–$30,000 per year to keep an adolescent in a penal or reform institution (see Corrigan & Udas, chap. 41). In addition, we know that 82% of our prisoners are high school dropouts (see Corrigan & Udas, chap. 41). Educators are simply going to have to do a better job of convincing others of the wisdom of investing now in prevention rather than later in spurious "cures."

The resources needed to improve schooling and teacher education in this country are available and are best invested locally. Clearer connections need to be established among local educational institutions and state and national initiatives, standard setting, and reform efforts. In addition, local schools and local teacher education programs need to be renewed *simultaneously,* a theme that AACTE has been promoting for several years. This simultaneous renewal is best accomplished when and where there is stability and continuity in educational leadership. With superintendents changing positions every 2.5 years, education deans changing jobs every 3–4 years, and teachers dropping out often at the rate of 20% within the first year after graduation, sustaining quality reform efforts will continue to be difficult. As a personal example, I can report that in my first 10 years as Education Dean in California, I served under five different presidents and five different vice presidents for academic affairs. Additional resources can serve to improve on this loss of talent and experience.

Where do we start? We start at the top and with the federal government leading the way. The federal government needs to assume more responsibility for improving public schools. This has begun to happen with the Clinton administration, but our president has very little money with which to work. Educators are encouraged that federal funds for education increased significantly for the first time in many years during the first year of the Clinton administration. Even though there appears to be improved leadership in the Department of Education, still little significant improvement will take place until society as a whole demands more of its schools and teachers. We can do better than we are; however, the majority of Americans are satisfied with their local schools. Where there is low expectation and satisfaction, mediocrity will prevail. If we know anything in education, we know that performance follows expectation. Expect little and you will get it; expect and demand more and your chances improve tremendously!

Of course, because the federal government supplies only about 7% of the budgets of elementary and secondary schools, major educational reform will have to rely primarily on state and local funds and initiatives to improve. With the help of private organizations, business, and key individuals, such a turnaround is possible and very much needed.

Americans can afford to invest a much larger proportion of their gross national product in education; other countries do. Funding and investing can follow if citizens change their will, their resolve, their values, and simply require more.

The next question to be addressed is "Why has this will to improve been lacking?" We know that there is no other public investment that can match education for significantly improving the standard of living of all Americans. So why is educational improvement not happening to any large degree?

WHY IS THE AMERICAN WILL TO IMPROVE EDUCATION CURRENTLY LACKING?

Where there is a will, there is a way. When the ways are confused, the will is unresolved and torn in different directions. The fact of the matter is that our country and society have changed so much and have embraced so much diversity, technology, and instant communication that the core fabric is unsettled and insecure. Societal change has been so rapid in the last 30 years that the very foundation of traditional American life has been shaken and shattered. People today are becoming more desperate and unsure as basic institutions deteriorate before their eyes. Given the crises in so many vital areas of our lives today, it is difficult to focus upon one basic institution, education, when others also need so much attention. The problem is not so much that we lack the will to improve education in the United States as it is that so many other areas of our lives also need increased attention that there simply is not enough time, effort, energy, or money for systemic reform.

The following are a few commonly publicized statistics comparing, for example, the 1960s with the 1990s.

Social Ill	1960	1990
Single-parent families	9.1%	28.6%
Children on welfare	3.5%	12.9%
Out-of-wedlock births	5.3%	28.0%

During this same period, the divorce rate doubled, teen suicide tripled, the crime rate tripled, and violent crimes in-

creased 500%, but the average time served in prison declined by one third. Clearly, social ills are undercutting efforts to improve schooling and teacher education, and we are in the midst of three decades of decline.

With state and national debts continuing to increase, there are simply few new dollars to address successfully major issues, and only some reshuffling is possible for the groups most vocal and organized around their individualistic concern.

Historically, educators have not been organized in addressing issues related to resource allocation. In fact, splintered control in education is a defining characteristic of the American educational system with governors, legislators, licensing commissions, lay school boards, a variety of professional associations, superintendents, teachers, university professors, and a host of others constantly vying for power and a little more say in how education is to be conducted.

The real issue boils down to the fact that American priorities are going to have to change before schooling and teacher education will improve significantly. Money follows priorities. Furthermore, primarily, educators will have to effect this change; nobody will do it for us. Other pressing issues of poverty, minority rights, special accommodations, women parity, violence, and so forth, should have to be shown to be related to quality education before attention and resources are paid to them. Such constitutes much of the research agenda needed in the decades ahead.

Let us return to the main question facing teacher educators. Why is the American will to improve education currently lacking? Because social ills in American society today are diverting our attention and resources. These resources are being spent to address but not resolve social problems that better education could correct or prevent. An ounce of prevention is worth a pound of cure here. Educators must become more proactive in educating the public and legislators about the relationships that exist between poor and inadequate education and social problems. Accomplishing this constitutes the bulk of the needed educational research agenda for the rest of the 1990s and beyond.

The information in the second edition of the *Handbook of Research on Teacher Education* can go a long way in promoting such a research agenda. The following are a few examples of social problems, demographic shifts, and societal changes discussed in chapters and therein related to schooling and teacher education.

We learn from the handbook that:

- Twenty-five percent of all 5-year-old children live below the federal poverty line (see Ishler, Edens, & Berry, chap. 17).

- Between 1975 and 1991 the percentage of employed mothers with children under 6 years increased from 39% to 58% (see Bredekamp, chap. 16).

- More than half of the mothers of infants under age one were employed in 1990 (see Bredekamp, chap. 16).

- Unmarried women account for an increasing number of births, rising from 18.4% in 1980 to 28% in 1990 (see Williamson, chap. 18).

- Child abuse cases increased 31% from 1985 to 1990 (see Corrigan & Udas, chap. 41).

- Women head one third of all family households in the United States, and single female-headed families have high poverty rates—47% among whites, 72% among blacks. Without a high school diploma, the rates are 77% among whites and 87% among blacks (see Kohl & Witty, chap. 39).
- The violent crime rate increased 48% from 1986 to 1991 (see Corrigan & Udas, chap. 41).
- The number of firearm-related deaths among youth 4–19 years of age nearly doubled between 1985 and 1990 (see Williamson, chap. 18).
- More teenage males die of gunshot wounds than all natural causes combined. Gunshot deaths among teen males increased by 40% from 1984 to 1988 (see Corrigan & Udas, chap. 41).

The improvement of schooling and teacher education in America in the years ahead will be successful to the degree that research establishes clearer and more widely known connections between problems like those just listed and schooling. Strategies for change need to be identified and implemented. For example, professional development schools can more clearly link teacher education, public schooling, and a host of societal impacts such as parent involvement, pupil attendance and graduation rates, teacher satisfaction, graduate employment rates, and so forth. Research in this area is just beginning (see Book, chap. 10).

Special interests and narrow concerns must be put aside if we are to improve schooling and teacher education more generally. We cannot continue to support narrow interests while allowing the basic educational system to deteriorate. And scrapping the whole public school system as we know it is not the answer. This is impractical, wasteful, expensive, traditionally un-American, and ill advised for a host of reasons beyond the scope of discussion here.

The simultaneous renewal of schooling and teacher education in America needs to be centered around changing social problems facing all of us today. The connections and lines must be more clearly drawn and publicized. Educators must become more willing to serve as advocates and change agents, no longer merely accepting the roles of impartial observers and transmitters of culture. Teacher educators in particular need to become, similar to pioneers, *reconstructioneers of culture*, change agents, and people willing to risk, to strive for higher ideals, and to be dissatisfied with current conditions and the status quo. *American reconstructioneers of culture* (ARCs) are needed to work to improve schooling and teacher education, fashioning new approaches to subject matter and trying out novel methods of learning both traditional and nontraditional content. ARCs would work to iron out issues and problems; bridge gaps between the past and the future, practice and theory, and the real and the ideal; and address the six dilemmas indicated earlier as counterproductive trends within our current educational reform efforts. Only with improved vision and mobilization by educators will the desired changes in funding and conditions be realized. The goal is worthy of the massive effort required. The result could be not only educational improvement, but societal and lifestyle enhancement as well.

Americans need to be convinced that positive change can happen. Educators need to lead the way, not be followers, if the will and priorities of the American public and their purse strings are to change. People individually and collectively are capable of significant change, sometimes within short periods of time. Although in the United States today education is not the top national priority, this could change as individual local communities and some states move assertively to demonstrate how investing in education pays off in the short and long runs in the quality of life afforded to citizen-investors.

The resource mentioned at the beginning of this analysis, *Knowledge Revolution for All Americans, Winning the War Against Ignorance: Empowering Public Schools* (1992), states that in the United States we have been giving away the American dream. We have been content to produce the first generation of Americans with a lower standard of living than their parents. Are we going to continue to allow this to happen?

CONCLUSION

Educational funding provides a barometer of society's level of commitment to the educational enterprise, and the barometer has been going down during the 1980s and the early 1990s. We want the barometer to rise again, for conditions in the United States to get better, and for our standard of living to rise. Is this just naive and wishful thinking? Or can we turn improved vision, dissatisfaction with mediocrity, and heightened expectations into improved reality in our schools and society? Working together, I believe that we can effect this change. I would not be spending my life's work in this arena if I did not believe that this were the case.

We need new solutions to new problems. We cannot afford to treat symptoms anymore or to invest in often-failed reform efforts such as vouchers and merit pay that offer trinkets and band-aids, but too often are top-down conceived and implemented. And constantly finding new ways of testing, assessing, measuring, evaluating, and critiquing the educational system without investing in it will not produce the desired effects either. Accountability that is narrow and unsupported by resources will not work. Mary Diez in her AACTE 1994 presidential address said that "You don't fatten a pig by weighing it more often." In a unique way, this is a profound statement. We must avoid more nonsolutions during this era when we have been so critical of our educational institutions and so unwilling to support or invest in them.

We need to change the image of schooling and teacher education in America by establishing more clearly via research and reported experience the clear connections between formal education and citizenship behavior. We need to popularize relationships between education and quality of life. For example, in 1991, among white male workers in the United States between 25 and 34 years of age, the earnings of college graduates were 47% greater than those of high school graduates (National Center for Education Statistics, 1994).

Changing our image from reactive or status quo educational institutions to more proactive positioning and functioning will not be easy, but it is absolutely necessary if we want any additional resources to be directed our way. Changing societal priorities and the flow of dollars that follow could produce results that would speak for themselves. Yet, starting the flow will require unrelenting efforts. But we must try. Let's try investing in education on a grand scale for once in America and just see how it works. Education has always been and still is a good investment in this country, but we have largely neglected it for years. In the United States we have more opportunities throughout our lives for more diverse people and working adults, particularly women, than any other country in the history of the world. We want to keep it this way.

The time has come to put aside self-interest and to concentrate on our educational system as a whole. The forgotten masses of students in our educational institutions deserve a chance at the American dream of a better life through education.

Educators working alone cannot accomplish what needs to be done. American public schools can prepare students for successful futures only if they have the cooperation and support of other basic institutions—families, churches, businesses, government, medicine, and the economy. Educators cannot do it alone, and we must convince the key players of the merits of our proposals. The political elite must be engaged as well.

In advancing the cause of educational improvement, we must be careful to maintain and to nourish what is working well and to change what is not. Our local-based system of education needs to be reinforced, not replaced; its flexibility allows the innovation necessary without the heavy hand of state or national control. This is not to say that the federal and state roles are not important as well.

I began this presentation with four observations; I conclude with two declarations.

1. Improvement in schooling and teacher education in the United States will be successful to the extent that educators establish via research and make known to the public and to budget controlling authorities the clear relationships that exist between investment in education and productive citizenship.
2. Until educators become more proactive, demanding, political, and willing to serve as *American Reconstructioneers of Culture* (ARCs), our educational institutions will continue to drift with the tide of mediocrity as resources flow to other more visible and vocal areas.

Is There Hope?

There is hope that our educational system will change in a positive direction. This change will require more enlightened and proactive teacher educators if the direction of the observations made at the beginning of this analysis is to change. With time, additional research of the type suggested, and a change of will and priorities by the American people, not only could our educational system improve dramatically, but so could the quality of life in America. Our economy cannot continue to be depressed forever, and when the time comes for educators to advocate for additional resources, they must be ready. Further, balancing the budget cannot be accepted as an excuse for nonsupport of educational programs.

I am happy to say that I can point to some positive developments. The second edition of the *Handbook of Research on Teacher Education* can help to move us in the direction described here. With a better understanding of how resources and education and quality of life are related, the citizens of this country could mobilize quite rapidly. I see as very positive the growing interest in the moral dimensions of schooling, education, and teacher education, which was largely stimulated by John Goodlad and his associates at the beginning of the decade (Goodlad, Soder, & Sirotnik, 1990). Our nation's educators and educational institutions could well engage in the late 1990s in a reinvestment and revitalization of education.

The time has come to reopen the discussion and analysis of the social purpose or role of the school in American society. With today's discussions of and interest in "school choice" and various "alternatives," surely not all schools will or should have the same purpose, will subscribe to the same values, or will follow the same practices. But educational institutions need to stand for something, something clearly explicated and understood, if they are to provide meaningful and useful experiences and are to demonstrate responsibility for specified outcomes.

It is within such a context that educational improvement needs to be pursued in this country. Concepts such as *school choice, alternative education,* and *educational improvement* can be developed simultaneously by teacher preparation programs and public and private schools. These are ideas favored by the public in general, who, with proper encouragement and enlightenment, could be taught and convinced to support such ideas with resources. Operationalizing and implementing these concepts in a manner that makes sense locally will require the participation of many people.

Today, the traditional role of the school to transmit prevailing values has been deemphasized, particularly during the last two decades as demographic changes literally have transformed the nature of the population in educational institutions. Today's educational institutions need to be places where diversity is staunchly supported, but commonality of institutional values and operating principles cannot be simply laid aside, as has happened in at least some cases. Where this has happened, against the wishes of the majority, perhaps an alternative form of education is in order. The point here is that our educational institutions need to reexamine their roles and purposes and not serve as a melting pot, but rather as a smorgasbord from which parents, students, and educators alike can choose, each according to his or her own values, goals, and expectations.

This is only beginning to happen as educators such as Goodlad and his colleagues (1990) and Strike (see chap. 40) have encouraged us to explore options and the moral dimensions of teaching much further than we have to date. The ethical and moral responsibilities of teachers and teacher educators need much more explicit attention and development if our nation's formal educational institutions are expected to produce productive citizens capable of living successfully and effectively in a rapidly changing society.

John Sikula
Dean
School of Education and Human Services
National University
San Diego, California

References

Berliner, D. C. (1993). Mythology and the American system of education. *Phi Delta Kappan,* 74 (8), 632–640.

Diez, M. E. (1994). Presidential address at the annual meeting of the American Association of Colleges for Teacher Education, Chicago.

Goodlad, J. I., Soder, R., & Sirotnik, K. A. (1990). *The moral dimensions of teaching.* San Francisco: Jossey-Bass.

Knowledge revolution for all Americans, winning the war against igno-rance: Empowering public schools. (1992). Arlington, VA: Knowledge Network for All Americans.

National Center for Education Statistics. (1994, March). *Annual earnings of young adults.* (NCES 94-407). Washington, DC: U.S. Department of Education, Office of Educational Research and Improvement.

Shapiro, A. L. (1992). *We're number one.* New York: Vintage Books, Random House.

ABOUT THE CONTRIBUTORS

Beverly J. Armento is Research Professor of Social Studies Education and Director of the Center for Economic Education at Georgia State University where she directs the middle childhood teacher education program. She is interested in teachers' knowledge and attitudes about diversity and about multicultural issues in the curriculum as well as in teachers' social studies pedagogical content knowledge. Previous chapters by Dr. Armento on the research on teaching social studies appeared in the *Handbook of Research on Teaching* (3rd ed.) and in the *Handbook of Research on Teaching and Learning Social Studies*. She has served as President of the National Association of Economic Educators.

Steven F. Arvizu, Provost at California State University, Monterey Bay, has worked with California State University for the past 23 years in a variety of faculty and administrative assignments in Sacramento, Bakersfield, and most recently at the chancellor's office as an Executive Fellow. Dr. Arvizu is an educational anthropologist with a masters of arts and a doctorate from Stanford University. Dr. Arvizu conducted postdoctoral study at the University of Michigan and the Institute for Educational Management at Harvard. He has been an Executive Fellow, a Kellogg Fellow with the Academic Leadership Academy (American Association of State Colleges and Universities), and a scholar at the Tomas Rivera National Policy Center at the Claremont Graduate School. He served as a presidential appointee to the National Advisory Council on Historic Preservation under Presidents Carter and Reagan. He has published numerous scholarly articles, chapters, monographs, and books on multicultural education, organizational change, and community relations. He is past president of the Council on Anthropology and Education and President Elect of the Association of Latina-Latino Anthropologists, affiliate organizations of the American Anthropology Association.

H. Prentice Baptiste, Jr. is Professor and Associate Director of the Center for Science Education, College of Education, Kansas State University. His research interest includes the conceptualization of multiculturalizing educational entities and culturally diversifying science and math instruction. Dr. Baptiste has authored or edited six books and numerous articles, papers, and chapters in multicultural and science education. He works extensively with urban and rural schools and school districts in designing and implementing comprehensive multicultural plans in science, math, and other curriculum areas.

Thomas Barone is an Associate Professor in the Division of Curriculum and Instruction, College of Education, Arizona State University. He received his doctorate in education from Stanford University. His writings explore, conceptually through examples, the possibilities of a variety of journalistic and arts-based approaches to contextualizing and theorizing about fundamental curriculum issues. Recent publications can be found in *Theory into Practice, Educational Leadership, Phi Delta Kappan, Journal of Curriculum Studies,* and *Qualitative Inquiry in Education: The Continuing Debate.*

Weldon Beckner is Professor and Vice President for Academic and Student Affairs at Wayland Baptist University, Plainview, Texas. Prior to assuming this position in January 1992, he was Professor and Chair of Educational Administration in the College of Education at Texas Tech University. His special interests in applying theories of leadership and school change to curriculum development and teacher effectiveness, particularly in rural schools, attracted a substantial private grant to establish a center to conduct research, conferences, and special projects related to smaller schools. His publications include five textbooks and numerous journal articles.

David C. Berliner is Professor of Curriculum and Instruction and Professor of Psychology in Education at the College of Education, Arizona State University. He received his doctor of philosophy degree from Stanford University. He has authored or edited 20 books and written more than 150 articles and chapters on educational psychology, research on teaching, teacher education, and educational policy. He is past president of both the Division of Educational Psychology of the American Psychological Association and the American Educational Research Association. He is a fellow of the Center for Advanced Study in the Behavioral Sciences and a member of the National Research Council/National Academy of Sciences Board on Testing and Assessment.

Barnett W. Berry, an Assistant Professor of Educational Leadership and Policies at The University of South Carolina, earned his doctor of philosophy degree in 1984 in educational administration and policy studies from the University of North Carolina–Chapel Hill. Dr. Berry has worked in a variety of roles supporting school reform and teacher professionalism. He has worked as a social studies teacher in an inner-city high school; a social scientist for the RAND Corporation; a consultant to a range of foundations, research centers, and professional associations; and as associate director of the South Carolina Educational Policy Center. In 1991, he served as a Senior Executive Assistant for Policy at the South Carolina State Department of Education. Much of his current work involves research on and policy development for the transformation of both the public schools and teacher education.

Jay Blanchard is an Associate Professor in the Division of Curriculum and Instruction, College of Education, Arizona State University. He received his doctor of philosophy degree from the University of Georgia. His research interests include teacher education, technology in education, and reading education.

Cassandra L. Book is Associate Dean of the College of Education, Professor of Teacher Education, and Adjunct Professor of Communication at Michigan State University. She has authored or co-authored seven books and more than 40 chapters and articles in communication and teacher education. She is the past chairperson of the Educational Policy Board of the Speech Communication Association, past chairperson of ATE's Research Committee, Executive Secretary of the Michigan Association of Colleges for Teacher Education, and past president of the Michigan Association of Speech Communication. She has been recognized for outstanding teaching by Michigan State University, Central States Speech Association, and the Speech Communication Association.

James J. Bosco is a professor in the Department of Education and Professional Development and Director of the Office of Educational Technology in the College of Education at Western Michigan University in Kalamazoo. He earned a bachelor's degree at Duquesne University, master's degree from the University of Pittsburgh, and a doctorate from Columbia University. Recently he has been involved with major corporations in the development of interactive video, multimedia, and transfer technology. His current work is focused on technology and school reform. He is principal investigator for the Great Lakes Collaborative Star Schools Project evaluation sponsored by the U.S. Department of Education, co-director of a Kellogg Foundation project to restructure a secondary school, member of the "Telecity USA" board of directors, and Director of a State of Michigan project to develop a computer network for schools.

James B. Boyer is professor of Curriculum and American Ethnic Studies at Kansas State University (Manhattan) where he has been active with multicultural education institutes and doctoral studies on curriculum and cultural understandings. His most recent research efforts are focused on African-American males in classrooms and the dynamics of cross-racial, cross-ethnic teaching and learning. He has authored or edited *Curriculum Materials for Ethnic Diversity, Teaching the Economically Poor,* and several checklists, including the "Collegiate Instructional Discrimination Index" and the "Multicultural Instructional Inventory for Enhancing College–University Curriculum." He also coordinates the urban master's program in curriculum in Kansas City.

Sue Bredekamp is the Director of Professional Development for the National Association for the Education of Young Children (NAEYC). Her major contributions to the work of NAEYC have been developing and directing a national, voluntary accreditation system for early childhood programs. Dr. Bredekamp also researched and wrote NAEYC's position statements on early childhood teacher education, developmentally appropriate practice, and appropriate curriculum and assessment. Bredekamp's professional experience includes teaching and directing early childhood programs, serving on a 4-year college faculty, and working in the Head Start Bureau at the Administration for Children, Youth, and Families.

Brian O. Brent is an advanced candidate for the doctor of philosophy degree at Cornell University where he works as a lecturer in the Department of Agricultural, Resource, and Managerial Economics. Mr. Brent is a Certified Public Accountant, with a specialty in issues of public school finance.

Thomas J. Buttery is currently a Professor of Elementary and Middle Grades Education at East Carolina University. He was the 1994–1995 President of the Association of Teacher Educators. As a researcher, he was the 1982 and 1988 recipient of ATE's Distinguished Research Award in Teacher Education. He is a two time recipient (1986 and 1988) of the University of Alabama's Academic Excellence Award for Faculty, the Outstanding Researcher Award for the College of Education at Northeast Louisiana University (1982), and he was named The Distinguished Alumnus of Kean College for 1988. As an author, he has written more than 150 articles on teaching and teacher education and has served as one of the three editors for the *Handbook of Research on Teacher Education* (2nd ed.). In addition, he serves on the editorial boards of six national and regional journals. In program development, he has been directly involved with teacher education programs that have received state, regional, and national awards. His academic degrees are from Kean College (B.A., 1968) and Indiana University (M.S. Rec., 1970; M.S. Ed., 1971; and Ed.D., 1972). He has taught elementary school in New Jersey and at the Indiana University Laboratory School. His higher education work was with the University of Georgia, Northeast Louisiana University, and the University of Alabama prior to East Carolina University.

David M. Byrd is an Associate Professor and Director of the Office of Teacher Education at the University of Rhode Island and has a long-term professional and research interest in the preparation of teachers. Dr. Byrd is a graduate of the doctoral program in teacher education at Syracuse University. He has authored or co-authored more than 20 articles in professional journals. Recently, he co-authored the textbook *Methods for Effective Teaching* published by Allyn & Bacon. He presently sits on the editorial board of the ATE Teacher Education Yearbook and will serve as co-editor of Yearbooks IV–VI.

Kathy Carter is Associate Professor in the Department of Teaching and Teacher Education in the College of Education at the University of Arizona. She is an associate editor of *Teaching and Teacher Education* and serves on the editorial boards of the *Journal of Teacher Education* and the *Elementary School Journal.* Her publications have addressed issues in teacher education, classroom processes, classroom management, and expertise in teaching. Her present research focuses on the narrative structure of novice teachers' knowledge and the development of a case literature in teacher education.

Ursula Casanova is an Associate Professor in the Division of Educational Leadership and Policy Studies at the College of Education, Arizona State University. She received her doctor of philosophy degree from Arizona State University. Her publications include *Bilingual Education: Politics, Practice and Research* (1993 Yearbook of the National Society for the Study of Education) and *School Children At-Risk* (a study of urban schools). She is currently editor of the Research News & Comments section of the *Educational Researcher.* She has a long-term commitment to the preparation of teachers and administrators for contemporary schools.

Rudolfo Chávez-Chávez is the Associate Department Head in the Department of Curriculum and Instruction at New Mexico State University. He teaches and coordinates the multicultural education courses at both the undergraduate and graduate levels and teaches curriculum theory and multicultural education courses at the doctoral level. In 1980, he earned his doctorate of education in Curriculum and Instruction with emphasis in bilingual education from New Mexico State University. He holds a master of arts degree and a bachelor of science degree in Bilingual/Bicultural Education and Elementary Education with a minor in Music Education. His first 9 years in academe were spent at the California State University, Bakersfield. Currently, he serves on the editorial board of *The Journal of Educational Issues of Language Minority Students,* is on the Board of Examiners for the National Council for Accreditation of Teacher Education, and has completed a 3-year term on the International Committee of the American Association for Colleges of Teacher Education. He has co-edited two books, *The Leaning Ivory Tower: Latino Professors in American Universities* and *Ethnolinguistic Issues in Education.* His publications span "cross-border" curricular and multicultural issues such as classroom climate research, second language acquisition, computer-assisted instruction, as well as bilingual and multicultural education. International appointments include positions as Senior Fulbright Scholar to Colombia, U.S.A.I.D. Lecturer to Honduras, and Educational Specialist to El Salvador.

Doran Christensen is Dean, School of Education and Professional Studies at Salisbury State University in Maryland. After 20 years of teaching school in North Dakota and Minnesota, he joined the staff of NCATE as deputy director for 13 years. He holds a doctorate in philosophy from the University of Maryland and has served in teacher education in many roles, such as professor, department chair, and dean. His major research interest is in alternative classroom teaching models about which he has presented and published both nationally and internationally. He has served as a consultant to institutions, schools, education organizations, and developing countries.

Richard W. Clark is a senior associate with the Center for Educational Renewal at the University of Washington. He also works as a team leader on the School Change Study with the Coalition of Essential Schools and serves as an external evaluator for school reform projects financed by the Pew Charitable Trusts in Philadelphia. Clark served 12 years as the deputy superintendent for the Bellevue (Washington) Public Schools. He has taught at three universities; has worked nationally as a consultant on school-based management and teacher and program evaluation; and has written language arts textbooks, articles, and book chapters on various topics related to educational reform.

Charles R. Coble is Dean, School of Education at East Carolina University, Greenville, North Carolina. He is author or co-author of 10 books and dozens of published articles in the area of science education. Dr. Coble is currently Director of the North Carolina Scope, Sequence and Coordination Project, which is focused on redesigning middle school and high school science in cooperation with the National Science Teachers Association's SS&C Project. Dr. Coble has received numerous awards from science organizations, including NSTA, AETS, Sigma Xi, and the North Carolina Science Teachers Association.

Dean C. Corrigan served as Dean of the College of Education at Texas A&M University from 1980 to 1989. The Board of Regents of Texas A&M appointed him as the first holder of the Ruth Harrington Endowed Chair in Educational Leadership in 1991. He serves as Director of Commitment to Education, a program that involves the university, the public schools, and the private sector. He chairs the Association of Teacher Educators Commission on Leadership in Interprofessional Education. Dr. Corrigan is a past president of the American Association of Colleges for Teacher Education and the National Association of Colleges and Schools of Education in State Universities and Land Grant Colleges. He was a member of the executive committee and a vice president of the Holmes Group from 1986 to 1990.

Dr. Corrigan's vita includes a list of more than 100 scholarly publications. The Texas Society of College Teachers awarded him the Ted Booker Memorial Award as Outstanding Educator in Texas in 1984. In June 1989, he was presented the Texas A&M University Association of Former Students Faculty Distinguished Achievement Award. In this same year he was presented the Robert B. Howsam Award for Educational Leadership by the Texas Association of Colleges for Teacher Education and was selected as one of the top educators for recognition at the 70th Anniversary Conference of the Association of Teacher Educators. Most recently he received the University Faculty Scholar/Artist Award from the Phi Kappa Phi Honor Society and was presented the Pomeroy Award for Outstanding Contributions to Teacher Education by AACTE.

Linda Darling-Hammond is William F. Russell Professor of Education and Co-Director of the National Center for Restructuring Education, Schools, and Teaching at Teachers College, Columbia University. Her research and policy work focus on issues of teaching quality, educational equity, and school restructuring. Among her recent books are *Professional Development Schools: Schools for Developing a Profession, Authentic Assessment in Action: Studies of Schools and Students at Work,* and *A License to Teach: Building a Profession for the 21st Century Schools.*

Vicky S. Dill is the writer of The Commissioner's Critical Issue Analysis Series, a sequence of whitepapers developed for The Texas Education Agency (Austin). In this context, she has examined issues such as student achievement, school violence, restructuring, and bilingual education. She was also the Director of Student Teaching and Early Field Experiences at St. Cloud State University. Her research has included many projects exploring the nature of student and teacher culture, teacher pedagogy for students in poverty or from violent environments, and increasing teacher diversity. In addition to an extensive list of publications and grants, she has founded the Hill Country Center for Professional Development and Technology at Schreiner College in Kerrville, Texas.

Walter Doyle is Professor in the Department of Teaching and Teacher Education in the College of Education at the University of Arizona. He was on the faculty of North Texas State University and served as Research Scientist in the Research and Development Center for Teacher Education at the University of Texas at Austin. He is United States co-editor of the *Journal of Curriculum Studies.* He has published in the areas of classroom management, teaching effectiveness, teacher education, and curriculum theory. His most recent work focuses on curriculum events in classrooms and teachers' subject-matter theories.

Edward R. Ducharme is the Ellis and Nelle Levitt Distinguished Professor of Education at Drake University. He currently co-chairs the Department of Teaching and Learning at Drake University. He has published widely on teacher education, higher education, faculty development, and public education. In addition to more than 40 articles, he has authored or co-authored five chapters and co-edited collections of writing on teacher education. He is the author of *The Lives of Teacher Educators,* published by Teachers College Press. Ducharme has been a member of the Board of Examiners of the National Council for Accreditation of Teacher Education since 1988. He serves as co-editor of the *Journal of Teacher Education.*

Mary K. Ducharme is associate professor of education at Drake University. She currently co-chairs the Department of Teaching and Learning at Drake University. She has authored

or co-authored numerous articles, monographs, and chapters on teacher education students, faculty, and programs. Ducharme was a Kellogg National Fellow from 1988 to 1990. She serves as co-editor of the *Journal of Teacher Education.*

Rose M. Duhon-Sells is currently Professor of Teacher Education at McNeese State University, specializing in educational administration, curriculum development, and multicultural education. Dr. Duhon-Sells's most recent publications include "Parental Skills for Children of Color," "Multicultural Education Is Essential for the Academic Success of Schools in the 21st Century," and "The Impact of Family Violence on the Developmental Process of Young Children." She serves as President of the Association of Teacher Educators during the 1995–1996 year.

Penelope M. Earley is a senior director with the American Association of Colleges for Teacher Education. At AACTE she is responsible for federal and state governmental relations, issue analysis, policy studies, and public and affiliate relations. In 1986 she established AACTE's State Issues Clearinghouse, a nationally recognized information source on state government policies relative to teacher education. Dr. Earley's areas of research include federal education policy, state education policy, public policy regarding teacher education, and gender issues. Her undergraduate degree is from the University of Michigan, her master's degree is from the University of Virginia, and her doctorate of philosophy is from Virginia Tech.

Kellah M. Edens is an Assistant Clinical Professor in the Department of Educational Psychology, College of Education, University of South Carolina. She received her doctor of philosophy degree from the University of South Carolina, and, in addition to teaching at the undergraduate and graduate level, is active in the College's Professional Development School initiative. Her current interests include designing case studies and simulated materials/videodisc to enhance clinical experiences, developing rubrics for scoring writing tasks, evaluating the use of spatial-verbal displays in the college classroom, and measuring the effects of advertising on young people.

Carol J. Fisher is a Professor at the University of Georgia in Athens and head of the Language Education Department. Prior to completing her doctorate at The Ohio State University, she taught upper elementary grades, high school English and French, and foreign language in the elementary grades. She is co-author of *Children's Language and the Language Arts: A Literature-Based Approach,* 3rd edition (Allyn & Bacon, 1990), and her research interests are in poetry for children. She teaches both undergraduate and graduate language arts and literature classes for elementary and middle school teachers.

Dana L. Fox currently serves as an Assistant Professor in the Department of Language, Reading and Culture at the University of Arizona where she teaches courses in reading and writing processes, literary theory, qualitative research methods, teacher research, and gender and literacy. Her research focuses on teacher preparation and professional development in secondary English, teacher beliefs and teacher knowledge, professional coursework in teacher education, and case methods in teacher education. She has received two national awards for her research with preservice teachers in secondary English, including a 1992 Award for Outstanding Scholarship on Teacher Education.

Susan M. Foxx received her doctor of philosophy degree in curriculum and instruction with a specialization in teacher education and supervision from Southern Illinois University at Carbondale in 1991. Her research interests include reflective teaching, issues related to beginning teacher programs, and mentoring programs. Dr. Foxx has been a member of ATE since 1987 and has served on the Resolutions Committee, on the Professional Journal Committee, and on the Planning Committee for the 1995 conference. She currently balances being a full-time mother with part-time teaching at Penn State University–Harrisburg.

Eugene E. Garcia is Director of the Office of Bilingual Education and Minority Languages Affairs of the U.S. Department of Education in Washington, DC. Dr. Garcia is former Dean of the Division of Social Sciences and Professor of Education and Psychology at the University of California, Santa Cruz. He is on leave from this post. He earned his bachelor's degree in Psychology from the University of Utah and his doctor of philosophy degree in Human Development from the University of Kansas. He has published extensively in the areas of language teaching and bilingual development, authoring and/or co-authoring some 100 journal articles and book chapters along with seven book-length volumes. His most recent research is in the areas of language and education as they relate to linguistically and culturally diverse children and their families.

Yvonne Gold is a professor in the Department of Teacher Education, California State University, Long Beach and a psychotherapist in private practice in Los Alamitos, California. Her research interests and publications focus on teacher stress and burnout, psychological support, and beginning teacher support programs. She has worked extensively with local district and university teacher induction programs and graduate programs in education. She has published numerous articles, book chapters, and monographs on these and related areas, including *Teachers Managing Stress and Preventing Burnout: The Professional Health Solution* (co-authored with Robert A. Roth). She was recognized as Distinguished Faculty Scholar (1990–1991), named University Outstanding Professor (1991–1992), and received the Distinguished Faculty Teaching Award (1992–1993) from California State University, Long Beach.

Thomas L. Good is Professor and Head of the Department of Educational Psychology at The University of Arizona, Tucson. He has served as the editor of the *Elementary School Journal* for more than a decade. His textbooks include *Looking in Classrooms,* 6th edition, and *Contemporary Educational Psychology,* 5th edition (both with Jere Brophy). His textbooks have been translated into German, Spanish, Japanese, and Chinese. He has published numerous articles and book chapters, and his professional research has been sup-

ported by various agencies, including NSF and NIMH. His present research interests include the study of teacher and student performance expectations, the informal curriculum, and citizens' expectations for schooling.

Douglas A. Grouws is Professor of Mathematics Education at the University of Iowa where he teaches undergraduate and graduate courses in mathematics education. His research interests include mathematics teaching, small-group instruction, and mathematical problem solving. His research has been supported by several agencies including NSF, the U.S. Office of Education, Monsanto Foundation, and Eisenhower funds. He is editor of the *Journal for Research in Mathematics Education* monograph series. His publications include more than 50 articles and chapters and three books. He is co-author of *Active Mathematics Teaching* and co-editor of *Effective Mathematics Teaching.* He is past president of the Missouri Council of Teachers of Mathematics, past chairman of the editorial panel of the *Journal for Research in Mathematics Education,* and former member of the executive committee of the AERA Special Interest Group for Research in Mathematics Education. He is a recipient of a William T. Kemper Fellowship for Outstanding Teaching.

Edith Guyton is Associate Professor of Early Childhood Education at Georgia State University. She has served on the Executive Board of the Association of Teacher Educators and as President of the Georgia and Southeastern Association of Teacher Educators. She was chairperson of the National Field Directors Forum and received their Outstanding Service Award in 1991. She was co-author of the chapter on field experiences in teacher education in the first *Handbook of Research on Teacher Education.* Her many articles in teacher education journals include five articles in *Action in Teacher Education* and three articles in the *Journal of Teacher Education.* Her current research and writing focus is on teacher socialization, diversity in teacher education, and constructivist teacher education. She is editor of the Georgia Association of Teacher Educators journal, *GATEways to Teacher Education.*

Martin Haberman is a Distinguished Professor at the University of Wisconsin–Milwaukee. Professor Haberman serves on eight editorial boards. He holds numerous awards for his writing, a Standard Oil Award for Excellence in Teaching, a special award from The Corporation for Public Broadcasting, AACTE Medals for offering a Hunt Lecture, and the Pomeroy Award (1990). In January 1989, Rhode Island College awarded him an honorary doctorate. He is a distinguished member of the Association of Teacher Education and a Laureate member of Kappa Delta Pi. In 1993, the Wisconsin Board of Regents named him a Distinguished Professor. The most widely known of his programs are The National Teacher Corps and his current Milwaukee program for preparing teachers for teaching children in poverty. His interview for selecting teachers and principals is used in cities throughout the country.

Kenneth T. Henson is Professor and Dean of the College of Education at Eastern Kentucky University. A Fulbright Fellow and National Science Foundation Academic Year Institute recipient, he is one of ATE's 70 Leaders in Teacher Education. His grant proposals have produced $2 million. He has authored or co-authored several books, including *Methods and Strategies for Teaching in Secondary and Middle Schools* (2nd ed.), *Education: An Introduction* (4th ed.), *Case Studies of Beginning Teachers, Curriculum Development for Educational Reform,* and *The Art of Writing for Publication.*

Francisco Hidalgo is Dean of the College of Education at Texas A&M University–Kingsville. Formerly Professor of Education Foundations at California State University, San Bernardino, he directed a $2 million defense-conversion New Careers Project and co-directed a joint master of arts degree program with the Universidad Autonoma de Baja California. He was founding Chair of the Department of Secondary & Vocational Education and directed an Exxon-funded Learning Community Project through the Tomas Rivera Center. At CSU, Long Beach, Dr. Hidalgo was Professor of Teacher Education, founder and administrator of major bilingual teacher programs, and Chair of Mexican-American Studies. He previously served as Lecturer of Education at Loyola-Marymount University, and taught in public schools in rural California as a Teacher Corps Intern. Dr. Hidalgo has been a board member for ATE and the California Council on the Education of Teachers and President of California's ATE. He is current president-elect of ATE and was Board President of Project INFO Community Services, Inc., dedicated to substance abuse prevention. Professor Hidalgo holds a doctor of philosophy degree in Education and a master's of science in education degree from the University of Southern California, and a bachelor of arts degree in History from Loyola-Marymount University.

Karen Hoeft is a doctoral student in the Department of Curriculum and Instruction at the University of Wisconsin–Madison. She has taught in secondary public schools, participated on curriculum projects at the local school district and state levels, and facilitated preservice and in-service teacher education opportunities across Wisconsin, Minnesota, and Nebraska. Her doctoral research is aimed at exploring issues of context and the necessary conditions for teacher service. Her current interests are family life and teacher education.

Laraine K. Hong has been an Assistant Professor in Education at the University of Colorado at Denver during 1993–1994 and at Whitman College (Washington) from 1978 to 1981. Her areas of emphasis have been elementary language arts and children's literature. She began teaching in Bellevue, Washington in 1985. During her 8 years of teaching there she taught grades second through fifth, including multiage classes. Beginning in 1994–1995, she began work establishing the Northwest Center for the Improvement of Teaching and Learning, a foundation-funded collaboration of school districts, higher education institutions, and reform agencies in the greater Seattle area. She is also serving as a Language Arts Curriculum Specialist for the Bellevue Schools. Dr. Hong has participated as a researcher with the 3-year School Change Study conducted by the Coalition of Essential Schools and has written *Surviving School Reform* (in press), a personal narrative of one school's experience with change.

W. Robert Houston is Professor and Executive Director, Texas Center for University School Partnerships, University of Houston. He has been principal investigator for 29 major multiyear externally funded research and development projects, primarily related to designing and implementing teacher education conceptual models based on research and building partnerships with teachers and schools.

He has authored or edited hundreds of journal articles, research reports, and 39 books, including being senior editor for the first edition of the *Handbook of Research on Teacher Education.* He has been invited to deliver major addresses in 42 states; consulted with schools, universities, and education ministries in 17 countries; and was President of the Association of Teacher Educators during 1985–1986.

Ken Howey is a Professor of Teacher Education at The Ohio State University. For more than a quarter of a century he has been involved in experimental efforts concerned with the improvement of teacher education. These activities have resulted in numerous books and more than 100 publications addressing all facets of teacher education. His latest book, edited with Nancy Zimpher, is *Informing Faculty Development for Teacher Educators.* Recently Dr. Howey served as the team leader for the longest running study of preservice teacher education in the United States (the 8-year RATE study supported by AACTE). He currently serves as the director of the Urban Network to Improve Teacher Education.

David G. Imig, Chief Executive Officer of the American Association of Colleges for Teacher Education, has more than 25 years of experience in educational practice, research, and policy. Beginning his professional career in 1961 as a teacher at the Nyakato Secondary School in Bukoba, Tanzania, Dr. Imig was a teaching assistant in the College of Education at the University of Illinois, Urbana from 1964 to 1966 while completing his graduate work in the Foundations of Education. In 1966, he became an education officer with the United States AID mission to Sierra Leone, later transferring to the AID mission in Liberia. He joined AACTE in 1970 as program director for international activities. Dr. Imig was promoted to special assistant to the AACTE executive director in 1974, was appointed director of governmental relations in 1975, and was named associate director in 1979. In 1980, he was selected in a nationwide search to be executive director of AACTE. Dr. Imig is the author of several educational policy and research publications and articles.

Richard E. Ishler is Professor and Dean of the College of Education at the University of South Carolina. Previously he served as Dean of Education at Texas Tech University and Emporia State University and as Associate Dean at the University of Toledo. He received his doctorate of education degree from Pennsylvania State University. His primary research interests are in the area of teacher education, professional development schools, and accreditation. He has published more than 100 articles in scholarly journals. Also, he has served on the Board of Directors of the Association of Teacher Educators, American Association of Colleges for Teacher Education, and the Holmes Group. During 1981–1982 he was president of the Teacher Education Council of State Colleges and Universities. In addition, he has been president of three state AACTE units: Ohio, Kansas, and Texas.

He was recognized by ATE in 1990 as one of the 70 Leaders in Teacher Education and in that same year was named a Distinguished Member of ATE. In 1988, the Texas Association of Teacher Educators presented him with the Ben E. Coody Distinguished Service Award.

Elaine Jarchow is Dean of the College of Education at Texas Tech University. Her major research area is international education, specifically curriculum decision making in emerging democracies and cultural awareness in international student teaching and faculty exchange settings. She has served as a consultant in China, Thailand, Egypt, Ghana, New Zealand, Australia, Mexico, Belize, Poland, and Honduras. She chairs the American Association of Colleges for Teacher Education's Committee on International Education and the International Service Committee of the Association of Teacher Education Council for International Affairs and is a member of ATE's Global Education Task Force and Publications Committee.

Vern Jones has been a teacher of students with serious emotional and behavioral problems and a junior high school vice principal. From 1986 to 1989, Dr. Jones was co-chairman of the American Educational Research Association Special Interest Group on Classroom Management. He is the author of *Comprehensive Classroom Management* and *Adolescents with Behavior Problems*. Dr. Jones has served as Scholar in Residence at Western Michigan State University and has visited the University of California, Riverside, as a Distinguished Scholar. He is currently professor of Teacher Education at Lewis and Clark College in Portland, Oregon where, in 1990, he won the Burlington Northern Award as Graduate School Teacher of the Year.

Thomas R. Koballa, Jr. is a professor of science education at the University of Georgia. After completing a master's degree at East Carolina University and a doctor of philosophy degree in curriculum and instruction/science education at the Pennsylvania State University, he served as a member of the faculty of the Science Education Center at the University of Texas at Austin until 1990. He is the recipient of research and training grants from the National Science Foundation and the U.S. Department of Education. He has authored or co-authored more than 50 articles and book chapters and currently serves as the editor of *The Georgia Science Teacher*. Dr. Koballa's research interest in persuasive communication design and attitude change are reflected in his recent contribution to the *Handbook of Research on Science Teaching and Learning* entitled "Research on the Affective Dimension of Science Learning."

Patrice LeBlanc Kohl is an Associate Professor in the School of Education at Barry University, Miami Shores, Florida. After receiving her doctorate in Educational Leadership from Boston University she became Director of the Educational Leadership Program at Barry University. She is currently teaching in both the master's and doctoral programs in leadership. She has spent 15 years in public schools in various positions, gaining much experience in the areas of special education and staff development. She has been an active member of the Association of Teacher Educators, most recently completing a term on the Board of Directors. Her current areas of interest for research are gender equity and school culture.

Okhee Lee is an Assistant Professor in the School of Education at the University of Miami. Her research interests include research on teaching and teacher education, science education, and culture and language issues in education. She was a National Academy of Education Spencer Postdoctoral Fellow during the 1993–1994 academic year. Professor Lee has a number of research and teacher training grants in science education, especially working with culturally and linguistically diverse students and their teachers.

Thomas McGowan is an Associate Professor in the Division of Curriculum and Instruction, College of Education, Arizona State University. His research interests include teacher education and social studies education. He received his doctor of philosophy degree from the University of Nebraska.

D. John McIntyre is Professor in the Department of Curriculum and Instruction and Director of the Teaching Skills Laboratory at Southern Illinois University at Carbondale. Dr. McIntyre is a former president of the Association of Teacher Educators, has received that organization's Outstanding Research in Teacher Education award, and has been named one of the Outstanding Leaders in Teacher Education. He has degrees from Otterbein College, The Ohio State University, and Syracuse University. Dr. McIntyre has published more than 60 articles and chapters on teacher education in professional journals and books.

Howard D. Mehlinger is Professor of Education and History at Indiana University. He served as Dean of the University's School of Education from July 1981 to July 1990, when he became Director of the Center for Excellence in Education, a research and development center whose mission is to explore appropriate applications of technology in education. During the time he was dean, he worked with others at Indiana University to conceive, fund, and build a new facility that would become a national showcase to demonstrate the use of technology for teaching and learning. He is the author or editor of nine books, more than a half dozen pamphlets and reports, approximately 40 articles, and two film series.

Katherine K. Merseth is Dean of Program Development at the Harvard Graduate School of Education and Executive Director of the Harvard Project on Schooling and Children. She began teaching at Harvard in 1983, her administrative positions including the Director of Teacher Education and the Director of the Roderick MacDougall Center for Case Development and Teaching. From 1988 to 1991, she was a member of the faculty at the University of California, Riverside, and Director of the Comprehensive Teacher Education Institute.

She is the author of *The Case for Cases* (1991) and her collection of cases on teacher education and decision making was published in 1995 by HarperCollins. She also is the author of numerous articles, chapters, and monographs on teacher education and case-based instruction.

David H. Monk is professor of educational administration at Cornell University. He earned his doctor of philosophy degree at the University of Chicago and has taught in a visiting capacity at the University of Rochester and the University of Burgundy in Dijon, France. Monk is the author of *Educational Finance: An Economic Approach,* as well as numerous articles in scholarly journals. He is a Senior Research Fellow for the Consortium for Policy Research in Education (CPRE) and serves on the editorial boards of *Educational Evaluation and Policy Analysis, The Economics of Education Review,* and the *Journal of Research in Rural Education.* He consults widely on matters related to educational productivity and the organizational structuring of schools and school districts, and he is a past president of the American Education Finance Association.

William E. Moore is Vice Chancellor for Academic Affairs at Southern University in Baton Rouge, Louisiana, a position he has held since 1989. During his 27 years of work in higher education, Dr. Moore has held a series of professorial and administrative positions at several universities. He has published more than 35 articles as a research chemist, science educator, and more recently in the broad area of testing and education of minorities. In 1994, Dr. Moore was invited to serve as a guest editor of *Education,* a 115-year-old international journal. Dr. Moore holds a bachelor of science degree in chemistry from Southern University and was the first African American to earn a doctor of philosophy degree in chemistry from Purdue University.

Alma Thornton Page received her bachelor of arts degree in 1971 from Northeast Louisiana State University in Monroe, Louisiana; her master of arts degree in 1973 from Southern University; and her doctor of philosophy degree in 1979 from Louisiana State University. Dr. Page's academic experience includes Director, Center for Social Research; Interim Chair, Sociology; Professor of Sociology; and Research Assistant, all at Southern University. Her publications include "Traditional and Contemporary Perspectives on Rural Women," "Rural Poverty," and "Determinants of Job Satisfaction among Indigenous Employees of a New Rural Industry."

Emilie Paille is an Assistant Professor in the Department of Early Childhood Education at Georgia State University in Atlanta, where she teaches and conducts research in English language arts, children's literature, and in teacher education. She received her doctorate from the Language Education Department at the University of Georgia. She is the co-director of a yearly state conference, Georgia Write Now, which focuses on writing in schools, preschool through college.

VerJanis A. Peoples is the Assistant Dean in the College of Education at Southern University. She has special expertise in staff, curriculum, and program development in teacher education and multicultural education. While at Southern University, she has made numerous presentations on teaching and learning and multicultural education.

She has written articles and chapters for monographs sponsored by various agencies. She holds the doctor of philosophy degree from Kansas State University.

Vito Perrone is currently a member of the faculty and Director of Teacher Education at Harvard Graduate School of Education. He served for 18 years prior to his Harvard tenure as Professor of History, Education and Peace Studies, and Dean of the Center for Teaching and Learning at the University of North Dakota. His most recent books are *101 Conversations with Your Child* (a series of books for parents), *Letters to Teachers,* and *Working Papers: Reflections on Schools and Communities.*

Nancy L. Quisenberry is Associate Dean for Academic Affairs in the College of Education at Southern Illinois University at Carbondale and Professor in the Department of Curriculum and Instruction. An early childhood educator, her major publications and research interests have been on the topics of language development, language arts, parent involvement, play as development, and all areas of teacher education. She has twice served on the board of Directors of the American Association of Colleges for Teacher Education and as Chair of AACTE's Advisory Council of State Representatives. She is on the Board of Directors and serves as North American Region Vice President of the International Council on Education for Teaching, chairs the International Research Committee of the Association of Teacher Educators' Council for International Affairs, and is the Folio Review Coordinator for the Association for Childhood Education International for the Elementary Education Guidelines for the National Council for Accreditation of Teacher Education. She is a member of the Board of Examiners for NCATE. She has presented papers and consulted with colleges of education and ministries of education in 17 countries. She is co-author of *Early Childhood Education, Developmental Objectives and Their Use,* and *Play as Development,* and author of *Elementary Education: Curriculum Folio Guidelines for the NCATE Review Process.*

Jean C. Ramage is Dean of the College of Education at University of Nebraska, Kearney. She has research interest, expertise, and experience in multicultural and bilingual teacher education, counseling, and school psychology. Her expertise in policy development has led to national involvement in protecting civil rights and in the restructuring of teacher education. Her publications and presentations focus on the rights of children and youth with a special focus on breaking down the barriers in the fields of science, mathematics, and technology. She continues her involvement with program development and accreditation to ensure that the professionals of tomorrow can prepare citizens for the twenty-first century.

Alan J. Reiman began his career in education as an elementary teacher in Georgia and North Carolina. During those 10 years he worked in both rural and urban settings. After completing his doctoral studies at North Carolina State University, Dr. Reiman's research turned to qualitative and quasi-experimental investigations of how role taking and reflection promote preservice and in-service teacher development. Dr. Reiman is a clinical assistant professor working jointly between the Wake County Public Schools and North Carolina State University. He has published numerous journal articles and book chapters, and he is a co-author with

Lois Thies-Sprinthall of a forthcoming book, *Developmental Supervision for Teachers.*

Maynard C. Reynolds retired as Professor of Educational Psychology, University of Minnesota, in the spring of 1989. From 1950 to 1957 he directed the Psychoeducational Clinic that served children (and families) who were experiencing school-related problems. Beginning in 1957 he chaired a department concerned with preparation of specialized teachers and research relating to disabled and gifted students. His publications, including 31 books (written and edited) and more than 100 articles, reflect this background in "special" education and school psychology. One of his books is a basic textbook for teachers and school principals on human "exceptionality." Another, published in the year of his retirement, is a volume edited for the American Association of Colleges for Teacher Education titled *Knowledge Base for Beginning Teachers.* He is a past president of the International Council for Exceptional Children (1965–1966) and received the highest award of that organization, the Wallin Award, in 1971.

Virginia Richardson is a Professor of Teaching and Teacher Education in the College of Education, University of Arizona. Prior to this position, Dr. Richardson was responsible for the division at the National Institute of Education that funded research on teaching, schooling, and teacher education. Her research interests include teacher beliefs and teacher change, staff development, at-risk students, and research methodology. She has recently edited a book that describes an OERI-funded study of teacher change in reading comprehension instruction, titled *Teacher Change and the Staff Development Process: A Case in Reading Instruction.*

Robert A. Roth is Professor of Education and Chair of the Department of Teacher Education at California State University, Long Beach. He is author of more than 100 publications and research studies. He is past national president of the Association of Teacher Educators (ATE), National Association of State Directors of Teacher Education and Certification, and the Interstate Certification Compact. He has been named Distinguished Leader in Teacher Education in the United States by ATE, Distinguished Teacher Educator by the California ATE, Distinguished Member by ATE, and University Distinguished Faculty Scholar at California State University, Long Beach. His areas of interest include teacher education program structure, interpersonal communication, new teacher induction, and teacher stress and burnout.

E. Joseph Schneider is Senior Associate Executive Director of the American Association of School Administrators (AASA) and is the former deputy executive director, Southwest Regional Laboratory (SWRL). From 1970 to 1989 he was executive director of the Council for Educational Development and Research, a Washington-based association. Schneider is a former newspaper reporter and editor. He has published extensively on educational issues, including the 1993 book *Exploding the Myths: Another Round in the Education Debate,* which he co-authored with Paul Houston, executive director of the AASA. Schneider has degrees from North Dakota State University and the University of Oregon.

Michael R. Schoeppach, a former high school social studies and English teacher, is currently the Executive Director of the Bellevue Education Association in Bellevue, Washington. Mr. Schoeppach is deeply involved in the school renewal activities of the district. Bellevue has a 40-year history of shared decision making and is now designated as a NEA Learning Laboratory site. In addition to representing certificated and classified employees in collective bargaining, Mr. Schoeppach serves nationally as a consultant on site-based management through SHO CONSULTANTS. He has written for *Collective Bargaining Quarterly* and for the NEA's Mastery Learning Project occasional paper series.

Karen A. Schultz is Research Professor of Mathematics Education at Georgia State University, where she also is Mathematics Coordinator and Director of the Mathematics and Science Education Research Group. She received her doctor of philosophy degree in mathematics education from Northwestern University. She is co-author of *Mathematics for Every Young Child* and senior author of *Mathematics Plus,* a Harcourt Brace and Company K–8 textbook series. She is past president of the Georgia Council of Teachers of Mathematics and former officer of the AERA Special Interest Group for Research in Mathematics Education and the North American Branch of the International Group for the Psychology of Mathematics Education. Currently she co-directs the Atlanta Math Project and the Georgia Initiative in Mathematics and Science at the Georgia State University site in the Georgia Statewide Systemic Initiative, both funded by the National Science Foundation. Schultz's interests focus on implementation of the NCTM standards and studying teacher change.

Henrietta Schwartz is State University Dean of Education for the California State University System. Formerly, she was Dean of the College of Education at San Francisco State University. She also has served as Education Dean at Roosevelt University and was on the faculty at the University of Chicago where she earned a doctorate in Anthropology and Education. She has been a teacher and administrator in Chicago public schools. Her research interests include the socialization function of schools, schools as cultures, and characteristics of collaboration. Dr. Schwartz has been a commissioner on the California Commission on Teacher Credentialing, representing the California State University System. She has authored seven books and a number of research articles and chapters.

Eileen Mary Sclan is a Research Consultant at the National Center for Restructuring Education, Schools, and Teaching at Teachers College, Columbia University. Prior to her work at Teachers College she was a classroom teacher. A grant from the National Center for Education Statistics supported her recent research on beginning teachers' commitment and workplace conditions. A paper that reported the results of this research won the Outstanding Paper Award for 1993 from the AERA SIG Advanced Study of National Databases. Her research interests include policy issues relating to teacher professionalization, workplace conditions, teacher evaluation, and beginning teacher induction.

Julie A. Sherrill is currently Assistant to the Dean, College of Education, The Ohio State University. In addition to her administrative appointment, she also teaches graduate level courses related to curriculum development. Dr. Sherrill completed her doctorate at The Ohio State University with an emphasis in the professional development of teachers, teacher education, and curriculum and instruction. Her dissertation focused on the implementation of pilot clinical educator roles for teacher leaders as part of the Professional Development School initiative between the College of Education and Franklin County Schools. While in graduate school, Dr. Sherrill served as a graduate research associate in both the University Provost's Office and College of Education Dean's Office. Before assuming her current position, Dr. Sherrill served as an administrator in Westerville City Schools where she provided leadership for vocational education, career education, and staff development. She also worked to develop a pilot school-to-work transition program after successfully obtaining external funding.

John Sikula is Dean of the School of Education and Human Services at National University since July 1995; just prior to that he was Dean of the College of Education at California State University, Long Beach since 1984. He graduated with honors from Hiram College with a bachelor of arts degree, and he received the master of arts and doctor of philosophy degrees from Case Western Reserve University where he was an N.D.E.A. Fellow. Dr. Sikula was President of ATE during 1989–1990. He received Presidential Awards for Service in 1986, 1993, and 1995. Dean Sikula was the founding president of the State of California Association of Teacher Educators (SCATE). He was founding editor of *Action in Teacher Education,* ATE's national journal, serving from 1978 to 1988. He was chairman of the ATE Blue Ribbon Task Force that analyzed commission reports in *Visions of Reform: Implications for the Education Profession,* published in 1986, and was editor of *Action in Teacher Education, Tenth-Year Anniversary Issue, Commemorative Edition,* published in 1988. He has authored or co-authored more than 200 publications, including nine books and monographs and 11 book chapters and research reports. His refereed works include some 70 journal articles in 35 different journals. Dr. Sikula was associate editor of the first edition of the *Handbook of Research on Teacher Education.*

Among Dean Sikula's honors are having been recognized with an Outstanding Teaching Award by the University of Toledo in 1976, as one of 75 Young Educational Leaders of America by Phi Delta Kappa in 1981, for Community Service by the *Gary Post-Tribune* in 1981, for Outstanding Service and Leadership by Indiana ATE in 1979 and 1984, and as the first recipient of the Distinguished Educator Award by SCATE in 1990. His publication awards include being recognized with Distinguished Achievement Awards from the Educational Press Association of America in 1971 and 1991. He became a Distinguished Member of ATE in 1994, and in 1996 he was recognized by ATE as Distinguished Educator. Phi Delta Kappa also honored Dr. Sikula with an Outstanding Educator Award in 1980, with a Service Key for Leadership, Service, and Research in 1984, and with opportunities to serve as chapter president in Toledo, Ohio, and Northwest Indiana.

Dean Sikula has been a consultant to schools, state departments, universities, and other education agencies in all 50 states and in 17 countries.

Norman A. Sprinthall received his doctor of education degree from Harvard University in 1963. His early research focused on the MAT program at Harvard with a colleague team of Mosher, Purpel, Weller, and others. These investigations examined teacher and counselor cognitive flexibility as predictors of performance. Gradually, as a result of colleagueship with Larry Kohlberg and Bill Perry, the framework shifted more toward cognitive developmental stage theory as a framework for intervention strategies for both adults and pupils. In the 1970s he moved to Minnesota and teamed with his wife Lois Thies in teacher supervision. More recently they moved to North Carolina State University and have continued to build theory, research, and practice for teaching, counseling, and supervision. He has co-authored *Educational Psychology: A Developmental Approach,* 6th edition, and *Adolescent Psychology: A Developmental View,* 3rd edition.

Kenneth A. Strike is Professor of Philosophy of Education at Cornell University where he has taught since 1971. He received his bachelor of arts degree from Wheaton College and his master of arts and doctor of philosophy degrees from Northwestern University. He has been a distinguished visiting professor at the University of Alberta, is a past president of the Philosophy of Education Society, and is a member of the National Academy of Education. His principal interests are professional ethics and political philosophy as they apply to matters of educational practice and policy. He is the author of several books and more than 100 articles. Recent works include *The Ethics of Teaching* (with Jonas Soltis), *The Ethics of School Administration* (with Jonas Soltis and Emil Haller), and *Liberal Justice and the Marxist Critique of Schooling.*

Thomas J. Switzer is Dean of the College of Education at the University of Northern Iowa in Cedar Falls. From 1971 to 1987, he served on the faculty and as Associate Dean of the School of Education at the University of Michigan at Ann Arbor. Prior to his university teaching experience, he was a design team member of the Sociological Resources for Social Studies curricular project and a social studies teacher in Waterloo, Iowa. While at the University of Michigan, he was involved in the education of social studies teachers and doctoral students in curriculum and instruction and conducted research on change and the change process. As Dean at Northern Iowa, he has been extensively involved in establishing school–university partnerships and in implementing instructional technology in education.

Dr. Switzer was instrumental in the formation of the Renaissance Group. He currently serves as President-Elect and as a member on the Executive Committee of TECSCU and as a member of the Board of Directors for AACTE. He is also a member of IBM's National Education Advisory Board.

Kip Tellez is an assistant professor in the College of Education at the University of Houston. His research interests include teacher education, second language acquisition, assessment issues, and the study of pragmatism. He has helped to initiate field-based teacher education programs, focusing on the development of urban teachers. A former ESL teacher, he is interested in the urban, multilingual, and multicultural issues that have an impact on teacher development. His recent publications include articles in the *Journal of Teacher Education, Journal of Education for Teaching, Urban Education,* and *Action in Teacher Education* and several book chapters on multicultural teacher education. He is currently at work on an introduction to education text centered on the progressive movement.

Lois Thies-Sprinthall began her career in education in the elementary classrooms in Iowa and Illinois in the 1950s and 1960s. It was her graduate work at Minnesota and at Northern Colorado, however, that created an interest in teacher education as innovative practice. She managed Project Sixty at Minnesota with a cadre of young assistant professors, including Ken Howey, David Pearson, and Roger Johnson. This was followed by appointments to St. Cloud State and more recently to North Carolina State University. Her work has continued to focus in supervision for student teachers and mentoring for beginning teachers. In 1987, the collaborative teacher education program she directed won the AACTE award for innovative practice in school–university collaboration. She has published numerous journal articles and book chapters detailing her applied research, and she is a co-author with Alan Reiman of the forthcoming book *Developmental Supervision for Teachers*.

Rob Traver is a member of the faculty of the Harvard Graduate School of Education and Associate Director of an NSF-sponsored Mathematics and Science Preservice Teacher Education Collaborative serving the Boston-Cambridge area. Formerly, he was Program Administrator for the Harvard/Radcliffe Undergraduate Teacher Education Program. Recent writings include "Prints from the Past" in *The Science Teacher* and *Science in a Sandbox: A Teacher's Guide to the Instructional Uses of Animal Tracks, Brown Tracking Boxes, and Stylized Track Diagrams in K–12 Science Education,* with Enid Irwin.

Ken Udas is a Research Associate in Commitment to Education, Texas A&M University, a program that involves the university, the public schools, and the private sector. He is completing his doctor of philosophy degree in Educational Administration, and he holds a master's of science degree in Management Information Systems, a master's of business administration, and a bachelor of science in biology. His research and teaching interests are in the areas of human services integration, participatory system design, general systems theory, and systems engineering. He received the New Professional of the Year Award from the Massachusetts College Personnel Association.

B. Bradley West is Professor of Teacher Education at Michigan State University. He has also been a secondary chemistry, physics, and mathematics teacher, guidance counselor, and clinical psychologist. Formerly, he was Assistant Director of the Division of Student Teaching and Professional Develop-

ment at Michigan State University. He was director of the Michigan Consortium for Overseas Student Teaching and founder of the National Consortium that subsequently became the ATE Council for International Affairs, which he continues to chair. He has taught in several foreign universities and is currently on the national staff of the Holmes Group. He is Michigan editor of the journal of the Michigan and Ohio Associations of Teacher Education and serves on the editorial board of two professional journals. His research interests include follow-up studies, international field experience research, and international studies focused on teaching behavior as related to values, cultural imperatives, attitudes, and beliefs.

Ronald D. Williamson is a Doctoral Fellow at Eastern Michigan University. He is the immediate past Executive Director of the National Middle School Association and was formerly Executive Director of Instruction with the Ann Arbor public schools. He previously served as a junior high and middle school teacher, team leader, assistant principal, and principal. Mr. Williamson is the author of several articles, monographs, and chapters, including "Planning for Success: Successful Implementation of Middle Level Reorganization" and "Scheduling the Middle Level School to Meet Early Adolescent Needs." He has written about middle-level leadership as well as interdisciplinary teaming and advisory programs. He is currently a member of NASSP's Middle Level Council and is a frequent speaker and consultant with school districts throughout the United States.

Jerry W. Willis is Professor of Curriculum and Instruction and Director of the Center for Information Technology in Education at the College of Education, University of Houston. He is also editor of the *Journal of Technology and Teacher Education* and the *Technology and Teacher Education Annual,* as well as author of more than 50 books on information technology and its role in education and society. He is the Founding President of the Society for Technology and Teacher Education and regularly publishes papers on research and practice in the emerging field of information technology and teacher education.

Elaine P. Witty is Dean of the School of Education at Norfolk State University. Since assuming this position in 1979, her professional interests have focused on the recruitment and preparation of minority teachers, multicultural education, and institution and program accreditation. She has sponsored 10 national conferences on minority teacher shortage, directed the Norfolk Teacher Corps Project, and sponsored and co-produced 18 community forums on education that were televised on local cable stations. Dr. Witty served two terms on the board of directors of AACTE and was the 1994 recipient of the Pomeroy Award.

Sam J. Yarger is a Professor and the Dean of the School of Education at the University of Miami. He has also served in the same position at the University of Wisconsin–Milwaukee. In addition, Professor Yarger served on the faculties of both Syracuse University and the University of Toledo. Although his graduate work is in educational psychology, Professor Yarger's scholarly interests have focused on preservice and in-service teacher education for many years. He also works in the area of education policy and higher education administration.

Jennifer Lowell York is an Associate Professor in the College of Education and Coordinator of Preservice Interdisciplinary Training for the Institute on Community Integration at the University of Minnesota. She holds a doctor of philosophy degree from the University of Wisconsin–Madison. She has written extensively on the topics of collaboration across disciplines and school inclusion, especially related to students with severe disabilities. Current research and service interests address the relationship of inclusive schooling with school restructuring and reform, role changes for general and special educators to accommodate diverse learners in integrated contexts, and creating collaborative school cultures. She teaches in Educational Psychology, Educational Policy and Administration training programs, and holds adjunct appointments in physical therapy and nursing.

Kenneth M. Zeichner is Hoefs-Bascom Professor of Teacher Education at the University of Wisconsin–Madison and a Senior Researcher in the National Center for Research on Teacher Education. His writings on teacher education have been published in North America, Europe, and Australia and include a chapter written with Jennifer Gore on "Teacher Socialization" in the first edition of *Handbook of Research on Teacher Education*.

Nancy L. Zimpher is currently professor and Dean for the College of Education at The Ohio State University. Her academic appointment is within the Department of Educational Policy and Leadership, with specialization in teacher education and the continuing professional development of teachers. After completing her doctorate at The Ohio State University, Dr. Zimpher assumed the position of director of laboratory experiences and coordinator of the undergraduate teacher education program. Dr. Zimpher has studied issues related to teacher education from multiple perspectives. Dr. Zimpher serves on a national research team to study the perceptions of teacher education programs from faculty, students, administrative leaders, and school-related personnel. This national longitudinal study is now in its eighth year.

Dr. Zimpher is the recipient of The Ohio State University Alumni Distinguished Teaching Award and has also been recognized by professional learned societies for her work in the field of teacher education.

TEACHER EDUCATION AS A FIELD OF STUDY

• 1 •

THE CHANGING NATURE OF
TEACHER EDUCATION

Henrietta Schwartz

CALIFORNIA STATE UNIVERSITY

TEACHER EDUCATION AS A FIELD OF STUDY

How do you make a teacher? This seemingly simple question hides a complex, contradictory, and constantly changing set of answers and, as some persons maintain, may not be the right question (Noddings, 1991). If teaching is an art, the selection and identification of creative talents and abilities may be at the core of the answer to this question; however, if teaching is a science, then tested and verifiable training experiences may be the answer instead. If, as Gage (1992) states, teaching is an instrumental art, then one may need a combined approach to produce good teachers. It is fair to say that no single, unifying theory of teacher education exists today, and, therefore, preparation and research modalities are flexible frameworks rather than tight conceptual models (Doyle, 1990).

Much of this uncertainty has to do with the way that the preparation of teachers evolved in the United States. During the 1900s, an organizational revolution took place in American education, during which schools shaped and were shaped by the transformation of the United States into an urban-industrial nation (Tyack, 1974). After the Civil War, in fact, there were major shifts in the role of schooling, the nature of teaching, and the country's demographics. Previously, from colonial days to the 1840s and 1850s, schools were literacy training and socialization centers where teachers were expected to impart to students the values of their community, church, and country, while also teaching enough of the three "R"s to satisfy the needs of an agrarian society. Public support for the common school was predicated on a need for an educated populace to preserve democracy. The community school board controlled the school, the curriculum, and, in particular, the teachers.

Post–Civil War years brought about an intense period of urbanization and the most significant wave of immigration in the United States's short history. Concurrently, administrators and other educational leaders began to professionalize teaching and to organize control of local community schools. In 1890, the prestigious National Education Association Committee of Twelve on Rural Schools called for professionally trained teachers, connection of the curriculum with the everyday life of the community, consolidation of schools, bus transportation, and expert supervision by county superintendents who would exercise leadership in the modern community (Cubberley, 1916). Normal schools that would prepare the new breed of teachers were established. Prior to this movement, elementary teachers were required to have only elementary and preferably some high school education, and high school teachers were expected to have completed high school and preferably some university training. The study of pedagogy was introduced with the advent of the normal teacher training establishment, which typically included a laboratory school. Tension among professionalism or standardization of practice and local community control is still a critical issue in the preparation of teachers, as Sikula points out in the preface of this handbook. Should the teacher be prepared to function in a unique community setting with a unique language or in the larger mainstream society where he or she can prepare students to do the same? How can the teacher be prepared for both?

In 1922, the typical requirements for a teacher, enforced by the state superintendent, were uniform and dull. The teacher "must maintain good order at all times; supervise playground; have her work well prepared; follow state course of study; take at least one educational journal; have daily program, approved

The author thanks John Sikula, Senior Editor, for his assistance with this chapter.

by county superintendent, posted in the room within the first month of school; keep register in good condition; be neat in attire" (Tyack, 1974, p. 24). Fortunately, the changing nature of the population (i.e., immigrants joining the teaching force; in 1914, 50% of American rural teachers were immigrants), along with increased urbanization, improved communication systems, and the advent of the automobile, prevented teacher education from becoming too uniform. Pluralism is any form prevents complete bureaucracy.

The normal school training initially took place at the high school level and may have included an additional year of practice teaching in the campus laboratory school before graduation. Classes were composed mostly of women, and they reflected the changing character of elementary school teaching since the early 1900s. Women comprised 30% of elementary teachers in 1840, 59% in 1870, and 70% in 1900. By 1920, 86% of the elementary teaching force was female (Tyack, 1974). This movement, along with the rise of the professional administrator who was, for the most part, male, resulted in the subordination of women in the educational structure of the United States. In fact, one male superintendent in 1911 said that it was idle for teachers to read professional books because they looked to him for proper methods. According to the dominant view, women worked for less money and were suited better to the narrow intellectual range and adaptability required of elementary teachers (Coffman, 1911). If women were the teachers and men the college professors and administrators who trained and supervised them, then the issue that faced teacher education at the turn of the century was whether preparation and on-the-job supervision should be geared toward the strengths that women bring to the role of teacher.

Before this issue could be resolved, World War I began and the "Roaring 20s" and the Great Depression visited America. The normal school responded to social and political changes by expanding the curriculum for teacher preparation to include additional work in the social sciences, in pedagogy, and in theories of learning. By the time World War II began, most normal schools had become 4-year state teachers' colleges that granted bachelor's degrees in education, with various subject matter or grade-level specializations.

One major development in transforming teacher preparation and its related institutions was the GI Bill, which was established for returning veterans of World War II. It literally forced a new male population on the state teachers' colleges. These new students were demanding and mature, and they clearly wanted more variety in the curriculum. Although most of the GIs who went to teachers' colleges after World War II either became secondary school teachers and administrators or used their training and degrees to enter other fields, most women continued to train as elementary teachers and tended to stay in teaching once they began their careers. During this period, teachers' colleges became part of the comprehensive state university system, and teacher preparation programs were incorporated into schools or colleges of education offering bachelor's, master's, and doctoral degrees.

Teacher preparation programs became similar to traditional arts and science programs with a general education component, a subject matter specialization, some methods and pedagogy courses, and a limited culminating clinical experience in the public schools. Depending on state licensure requirements and social and political support at the state legislative level, teacher preparation programs were primarily 4-year undergraduate programs and, in a few states such as California (Ryan Act, 1960), post-baccalaureate professional programs that led to the initial teaching credential. In the 1970s, however, universities increasingly closed their laboratory schools as a cost-cutting measure and as a response to the criticism that laboratory schools were not representative of the real world. It is interesting to note that medical schools did not close their research hospitals, although nursing programs did move into the university and away from the clinical setting of the hospital, except in their structured clinical experiences.

In summary, the forces that shaped schools, teachers, and teacher preparation in the 1800s stemmed from a need to build an American populace that valued egalitarianism and was capable of self-government, economic independence, and self-reliance, particularly on the frontier. Transmitting this cultural heritage and preparing generations for a difficult future as new Americans required the teacher to be literate, patriotic, of high moral character, and willing to work within the context of the local community, while modeling American core values. School teachers presumably did what was necessary to control behavior and ensure attention in the classroom, with support from the home.

In contrast, the twentieth century was characterized by urbanization, modernization, and immigration. The setting changed from the rural, one-room schoolhouse to the small city or urban model, from the farm to the factory, and from a monolingual community to a multicultural clientele. Typically, the secondary school teacher was a white male who knew the subject matter well, having been to a university, and who was a firm taskmaster. The elementary school teacher was a nurturing woman who could read, write, and cipher.

The twentieth century, however, with two world wars, several "police" actions, an information explosion, increasing diversity and mobility, widespread political unrest, economic gaps between rich and poor, struggles over civil rights, and expansion of public schools to include universal coverage, requires many different kinds of teachers and teacher preparation programs. The teacher of the 1980s and 1990s needs to have knowledge of the social, physical, emotional, and cognitive well-being of the child, as well as of pedagogy, subject matter content, and enactment strategies. In addition, the teacher should have a thorough understanding of educational theory and clinical practice.

How much of what we have learned about teaching and teacher preparation in the last 160 years is universal, and what is unique to the individual teacher? Are these knowledge bases sufficient to permit application of acceptable research models and enhance our general and specific knowledge? Along with the expansion of knowledge in the social science, the research base in education, particularly teacher education, has exploded and diversified. Multiple research methodologies have been employed to examine all aspects of preservice teacher preparation. According to Berliner (1985), the replication, validity, and reliability of this body of work is as sound and extensive as similar work in the physical sciences.

MAJOR RESEARCH MODALITIES IN TEACHER EDUCATION IN THE TWENTIETH CENTURY

For an extensive discussion of the major research modalities in teacher education in the twentieth century, the reader is referred to the first edition of the *Handbook of Research on Teacher Education* (Houston, Haberman, and Sikula, 1990), particularly Chapter 1 by Walter Doyle. The reader is also referred to Chapter 2 of this edition, written by Okhee Lee and Sam Yarger.

Since the days of Plato and Socrates, the question of effectiveness has been at the core of research on teaching and teacher education. Doyle (1990), for example, focuses on quality control, whereas other researchers describe outcomes, assessment, standards, and achievement. During the early years of teacher education, and particularly in the eighteenth and nineteenth centuries, the effectiveness of schools, teachers, and students was measured by what might be considered the anecdotal mode—the endorsement of parents, influential community members, the increasingly powerful administrative group, local school boards, and alumni. At the beginning of the twentieth century, however, with the advent of state licensure and its close relationship to normal school attendance, more formal measures to check the compliance of teacher preparation programs with state and local mandates were introduced. Increasingly, schooling and classroom practices identified as best by the professional group of administrators became the context for teacher education.

The quest for standardization and the need for generalizability to accommodate state licensure requirements dictated curricula and their treatment in the preparation programs of the normal schools. Later, individual objective tests were introduced, which candidates had to pass before entering teacher preparation programs and/or achieving a license to practice. The preparation programs, training models, and state requirements for practice were infinitely variable, thus making it difficult to create a reliable knowledge base for teacher education and for the semiprofession of teaching. In fact, curricula in the nineteenth and early twentieth centuries were validated only by common sense or common knowledge, or by an unwritten and uncodified knowledge based on mystery, mythology, and management's beliefs about what constituted effective teaching.

More recently, since the 1930s, a set of patterns that exhibits the characteristics of a profession has emerged in the research and literature on teacher education. There are identifiable values, both sacred and operant, that characterize good teacher education programs. Agreed-upon functions, typical structures, similar content, and successful enactments or implementation at the classroom level create recognizable patterns in the culture of teacher education. Doyle (1990) discusses acceptable patterns of teacher education, while mapping the culture of research in teacher education. He charts the conceptual underpinnings of research in teacher education and its patterns, and identifies the commonalities and uniquenesses present in the various models.

The shape of teacher education today in America confirms its current status as a mass profession or as a semiprofession.

There are 500,000 preservice teachers at 1,200 public and private institutions of higher education, not to mention the alternative and internship models that account for another 2,000 to 3,000 neophytes (National Center for Education Statistics [NCES], 1993). Each year 150,000 newcomers join the ranks of the 2 million or more in-service teachers in America's schools. There are a myriad of stakeholders with interests in teacher education, among them university professors, school administrators, in-service teachers, state credential boards, local school boards, state boards of education, professional accreditation associations, regional accrediting entities, community leaders, role specialists, reformers, legislators, and local businessmen. Teacher education is a complex production with many voices. In an attempt to gain some hold on this intricate undertaking and to give teacher education some substance and content, several scholars (Doyle, 1978, 1990; Joyce, 1975; Zeichner, 1983) have proposed five major profiles for the ideal teacher, with attendant implications for the elements of the teacher preparation program that produce them. This codification allows questions about effectiveness and quality control, as well as core research themes, to be framed across programs.

In the first major profile, the *good employee model,* the teacher education program prepares new teachers to behave like good teachers in schools and classrooms. They are prepared to cope with real-world problems, provided with technical skills, and taught both to value experiential knowledge and to maintain the status quo. This model is preferred by in-service practitioners and administrators for validation for their life's work and professional expertise.

In the second profile, the *junior professor model,* knowledge of the core subject matter discipline and additional courses in the academic field cause the teacher to behave like the subject matter-based professor. Methods and pedagogy courses are formalities to endure during the process of achieving the teaching credential. According to the advocates of this model, teacher education should be conducted in academic subject departments, and the novice should apprentice with a master teacher, such as the university professor in arts and sciences who has an excellent knowledge of the discipline. The university program should be selective, rigorous, and academically oriented, and it should be deserving of support from arts and science faculty, private school personnel, and elitist legislators.

In contrast, the *fully functioning person model* maintains that teacher education should be devoted to personal development, self-efficacy, clarification of one's values, discovery of meaning, and development of a unique and personal style of teaching. The confluent education movement of the early 1970s (Brown, 1971) is a prime example of this model and at its core has knowledge of human development and of techniques for creating positive learning environments. This model is a favorite of psychologists, counselors, and elementary educators.

The *innovator model* insists that teacher education programs provide a source of renewal and innovation for schools. Following Comer and Poussaint (1992), Goodlad (1991), Levin (1986), and others, advocates of this view assume that individual schools, classrooms, and teachers are the true reformers—proactive, trained in laboratory settings with new modalities, and not socialized to the outmoded mores of the traditional, backward school. Typically, social and behavioral scientists, educational researchers, curriculum reformers, and teacher education professors prefer this model.

The fifth profile, the *reflective practitioner* or the *practitioner/scholar model,* is intended to hone the reflective capabilities of observation, analysis, interpretation, and decision making in the potential teacher. Teachers are challenged to inquire into the nature of teaching, to think critically about the work of teaching, and to develop conceptual frameworks that allow them to determine when to use particular skills. Typically, the research related to this model is qualitative with thick descriptions, ethnographic methods, and case studies. Study samples are small. Education professors with qualitative or phenomenological orientations to research and theory favor this model (Schon, 1983).

Each of the profiles represents a set of research models and traditions that logically grow from its basic assumptions, but no single approach provides the ultimate answer to questions of program quality and the effectiveness of graduates.

As a result, the major questions in teacher education have centered around selection criteria for entry into teaching, indicators of appropriate content for the curriculum, efficacy of training methods, and procedures for evaluating candidates and programs. . . . Indeed, over the past several years, the content and pedagogy of teacher education and the evaluation of graduates have been increasingly integrated into a model grounded in conceptions of effective teaching practices. (Doyle, 1990, p. 7)

The contexts in which teacher education occurs are also important. Teacher education is an establishment act, but its content, governance, and contexts are severely fragmented. Teacher educators and school district staff development personnel are extraordinarily heterogeneous (Lanier & Little, 1986). In many universities, teacher preparation programs resemble arts and science programs that have an additional student teaching component. The low status of teacher preparation programs on university campuses has contributed to the willingness on the part of many teacher educators to mimic other respectable academic programs. Thus, the unique qualities that might define teacher preparation are often suppressed. The supply of potential teachers also varies according to market demands, the influence of salaries, working conditions, and career opportunities. If there is a shortage of qualified teachers, prospects for employment are good until the district or state decides to issue emergency credentials to fill teacherless classrooms. If there is an oversupply of teachers, promising candidates are discouraged from entering the teacher preparation programs for fear of a jobless future. As such, the size and quality of the teacher candidate pool are greatly determined by the behavior of state and local education agencies. Because of accreditation and licensure standards, program curricula cannot be site specific; as a result, beginning teachers may not be well prepared for local situations. Virtually every university-based teacher education program is torn between the demands of the academy and the practitioner community.

In addition to context, one must also consider what constitutes a profession. Unlike medicine, law, acting, and other traditional professions that rely upon specialized knowledge, individual judgment based upon experience, and extensive training in fields supported by public trust, teacher education evolved out of interest in increasing effectiveness and enhancing the relationship among teacher characteristics and practices and student achievement outcomes. Therefore, research was focused on building a technical core of knowledge that could be transmitted to all teachers, leading to success in the classroom and permitting teaching to become a profession in its own right. This approach provided effective administrative control over teaching, but it eliminated elements such as judgment and curricular or content wisdom, the hallmarks of a professional.

Common sense dictates that when one has professional knowledge, it will be applied; theory into practice is the sine qua non of a profession. Applying knowledge requires theories, strategies, and practices validated by research, time introspection, and leadership in the field. Education has such a body of theory. In the literature, research confirms approved practices found to be effective in the classroom. According to Berliner (1988), existing data on best practices in education are as comprehensive as those in the hard sciences. Professionals know of these practices. For example, giving students time to respond to questions has been found to be significantly related to gains in achievement. There is nothing secret about what works. Jackson (1991) wrote the following:

Good schools, unlike the manufacturers of perfumes or other exotic concoctions, have few, if any, secrets to divulge. What their teachers and administrators know about how to educate, most other educators know as well. The determination to act on that knowledge is another matter entirely, of course, and is surely one of the major qualities distinguishing truly outstanding schools from those that are less so. (p. 94)

The quality that Jackson describes—the ability to act on knowledge—is missing in many classrooms and teacher preparation programs. Teachers are not implementing what they know and recognize as sound pedagogy. Goodlad (1984) found that teachers tend to rely on a single method; they do not vary their teaching methods in accordance with the purposes and demands of the subject matter. The curricular, situational, and practical knowledge is present, but teachers do not use it. Furthermore, leaders at the school and at the university seldom challenge teachers or teacher education students to apply their unique sets of knowledge, skills, and personal attributes. Since the 1980s, most professions, including teaching, have begun to question the basic assumption that those who understand theoretical constructs, situational complexities, and desirable practices will make use of that knowledge. Knowing does not mean doing, whether in medicine, law, education, or any other profession. Professionalism, or research-based practice, is a much more complex problem than was first recognized. Eisner (1992) maintains that knowledge is not power until it is applied and that most teachers have no way of learning the extent of their knowledge because they receive so little feedback on their teaching during training or while on the job. The isolation of the classroom inhibits discovery of behavior that is inconsistent with knowledge; however, the stated code and apparent belief behind this view is that learning the right method is the key to becoming a good teacher, and research leads the way to the best method. The history of research influencing practice in teacher education and schooling reveals a sequence of enthusiastic beginnings and frustrating conclusions.

In the post–World War II era, psychometric methods were used extensively to measure process–product relationships. This line of research was very promising because it provided objective scientific data to ensure administrators and others that if teachers were trained in a particular method and if they applied it properly and consistently, then achievement goals could be reached successfully (Berliner, 1988; Bloom, 1976; Brophy, 1988; Evertson, 1987; Gage, 1992; Slavin, 1983). Teachers complained that this kind of teaching did not reflect the sum total of their knowledge, and they indicated that they knew much more about teaching and learning than the prescribed method allowed them to demonstrate in the classroom. Nevertheless, the process–product approach was successful because it met the effectiveness criteria of administrators, school board members, and legislators. However, it did discourage teachers from inventive, judgment-based behavior in the classroom.

Many teacher preparation programs were structured on the systems approach (Joyce & Showers, 1988), and they were expected to produce teachers with such abilities and knowledge as: assessment and evaluation of student behavior, planning of instruction, implementation of instructional plans, analysis of teaching and self-reflection, development of human relations skills, and development of positive student self-concepts (Broudy, 1972; Charters & Waples, 1929; Cruickshank, 1990; Dunkin, 1987; Flanders, 1963; Gage, 1972; Jackson, 1965; Medley, 1984). Because of status issues, however, the idea of training or learning how to conduct a classroom became very unpopular, and knowing about a process or a situation became the focus of teacher preparation instead. Clearly, both education and training are needed (Dewey, 1916; Schwab, 1983). In addition to theories of learning and teaching, teachers need knowledge about how to use behavioral modification in the classroom, how to apply the inquiry method, how to operationalize interaction analysis in the classroom, how to practice skills in microteaching situations, when and how to use simulations, and how to engage in reflective teaching (Cruickshank & Metcalf, 1994).

The teacher effectiveness model of research is important and will continue to add to the growing body of codified knowledge in teacher education literature (Stallings, 1984). This line of inquiry greatly influenced reform efforts in preservice and in-service programs and the wider educational reform movement of the 1980s. Again, processes and procedures, as well as specific methodological training and assessment, were emphasized rather than teachers' decision-making abilities. Generic competencies were captured in government documents such as *What Works* (U.S. Department of Education [USDE], 1992b), *First Lessons* (USDE, 1992a), *Second to None* (California Department of Education [CDE], 1993b), *Caught in the Middle* (CDE, 1993a), and others, and supported the *good employee model* of the teacher. This management tool approach, which reduced teaching to a set of indicators, was questioned by a group of scholars in the late 1980s and is still being questioned by Doyle (1978), Garrison (1988), Shulman (1986a, 1986b), Zumwalt (1982, 1988), and others. Some critics argued that this approach eliminates the artistic and moral dimensions of teaching (Noddings, 1988; Tom, 1987), favoring instead the *reflective practitioner model,* which suggests that a unique and individual artistic interpretation of what is to be taught is the true professional model of teaching. These contrasting views reveal that the same dilemma that has generated discussion for decades remains: Is teaching an art or a science?

One less successful line of research concentrated on teacher characteristics and selection studies. Scholars conducted career pattern studies (Koff, Laffey, Olson, & Cichon, 1981) and attempted to link various preparation elements in the programs to effective teaching, but with little or no predictive validity. Currently, case studies and ethnographic methods, such as naturalistic observations, interviews, and content analysis, as well as analysis of teacher-produced journals, are generating deeper understandings of the connections between preparation and performance (Shulman & Mesa-Bains, 1990, 1993). If pursued over time, seeking commonalities across cases and cultures and looking at studies of expert teachers in special settings should yield face validity and logical situational generalizability.

Another factor that has influenced the progress of teacher education research is the political nature of schooling. As long as public education is supported by public funds, many powerful voices will express opinions about teaching, schooling, and teacher education. Since the 1970s, and especially since *A Nation at Risk* (USDE, 1983) was published in 1983, policymakers have used isolated research studies to mandate program elements, despite objections from the research community. This is both good and bad news; it demonstrates that research can influence public policy, but it also shows how research can be used improperly (Fullan, 1985). Clearly, teacher education is complex, difficult to study, and in great need of codification and professional standards. The *Handbook of Research on Teacher Education* is an attempt to pull disparate elements together, and the fact that a second edition exists indicates some degree of success.

MAJOR PHILOSOPHICAL, THEORETICAL, AND SOCIAL ISSUES IN TEACHER EDUCATION

Other chapters in this handbook will report in much greater detail on most of the issues raised here, but it is necessary to at least acknowledge the issues within the larger matrix. The field of teacher education is undergoing massive transitions and is experiencing major controversies. Now and for the next few years, what teacher educators do and say will define the field for the next quarter century. We are on the verge of giving birth to our version of the Flexner Report (Flexner, 1910), which defined the modern medical education system. New programs and practices are being tested all over the country. Some threaten the traditional university-based teacher preparation model; others reinforce the academic and curricular focus of the *junior professor model.* Joyce A. Scott provided an excellent discussion of five major themes in her address, "Developments for Teacher Education and Policy Implications," delivered in Chicago at the winter conference of the Teacher Education Council of State Colleges and Universities in February 1994. Scott asserts that the changes instituted in teacher preparation programs in response to the reform frenzy of the 1980s constituted "little more than adjusting on the margins" and did not address the structural mismatch between what university-based programs provide and what schools indicate they need. Schools require more diversity in the teaching pool, and they need a much larger role in clinical and professional development school settings working in collaboration with higher education. They also need teacher education programs to support and implement outcome-based accountability systems for graduates of teacher preparation programs. Furthermore, they need more arts and sciences faculty at the university involved in reforming subject matter preparation for new teachers. Finally, schools need to support merit systems that recognize and reward those faculty who work extensively with public schools.

Following are some of the major issues facing teacher education; the list offered here is neither exhaustive nor prioritized.

- *Alternative tracks to teacher certification.* Programs such as Teach America, district-based internships, apprenticeships, and on-the-job training offer various ways other than the traditional university-based academic program to become a teacher. (See Dill, chap. 43, this volume.)

- *Teacher licensure and national certification and accreditation.* Every state has changed its criteria for licensure since the early 1990s, and most states have had heavy involvement from classroom teachers in developing new standards and acceptable practices. For example, the National Professional Teaching Standards Board, the National Council for Accreditation of Teacher Education, and the National Association of Teachers of Mathematics have had a direct impact on the structure, content, and processes of current teacher preparation programs. (See Roth, chap. 13, this volume.)

- *Outcomes assessment for licensure.* Outcomes assessment represents another route to licensure. Instead of completing approved university-based courses in accredited programs, students have the option of taking various written and performance tests to qualify for state licensure. (See Roth, chap. 13, this volume.)

- *Testing in teacher education.* Closely related to outcomes assessment, testing in teacher education is a response to calls for objective proof that teachers know what they are supposed to know and that they can help ensure students' increased achievement. Most states have instituted exams for entering and exiting teacher preparation candidates; the validity, cultural bias, and work relationship of most of these tests are being questioned in the literature and in the courts. (See Good, chap. 28, and Tellez, chap. 30, this volume.)

- *Teacher education as graduate level professional training.* Several reports and the Holmes Group agenda in the mid-1980s called for teacher preparation programs to join other high status professional programs by adopting the professional school model, a move that would enhance the status of teachers and the training program, thereby attracting better students and faculty.

- *Limitations by legislators.* Since the Ryan legislation was introduced in California in 1960, many states have placed limits in terms of semester hours, academic credits, and transfer of units on teacher preparation programs to reduce costs and eliminate elements deemed unnecessary, such as methods courses from the curriculum. As a result, in most states, less time is devoted to training a teacher than to training pharmacists, nurses, architects, accountants, and other professionals.

- *Assessment, accountability, and evaluation of teachers on the basis of student achievement.* Teacher education programs and teacher unions have rejected this outcomes orientation, which bases approval of programs and individual licensure on standards of student performance as developed by the state.

- *Arts and sciences faculty involvement.* Arts and science programs need to be more involved in planning and delivering teacher education programs at the undergraduate level and changing teacher education curricula to reflect what is commonly taught in the public schools.

- *Clinical schools and professional development centers as training sites.* This requires a collaborative partnership between university and school district that includes a common agenda and set of goals; agreed-upon procedures for the preparation of new teachers; explicit new roles and relationships for teachers, administrators, and university faculty; a willingness to accept joint responsibility for support of the field-based program and its products; acceptance of negotiation as the primary program process; extensive communication at all levels of involved agencies; and parity among the participants. Successful collaborative programs are expensive and difficult to maintain, and they have yet to demonstrate through research how the teachers they prepare are more effective, more reflective, or more enduring than traditionally prepared teachers. (See Book, chap. 10, this volume.)

- *Diversity.* The population in the public schools is becoming increasingly diverse ethnically, racially, socially, economically, and in terms of motivation to learn. The teaching force is still largely what it was 25 years ago; for example, of the 2.6 million teachers, 87% of female teachers and 90% of male teachers are white and non-Hispanic. This leaves a total of 13% who are minority teachers, a number that does not reflect the 30% of the 40 million students who are minorities (NCES, 1993). The curricula, materials, strategies, and models must become more diverse while maintaining excellence and access for all. (Part VI, this volume, explores related issues.)

In addition to these issues, we must focus our attention on efforts to renew both teacher preparation programs and schools, efforts like those mounted by such groups as Project 30, the Renaissance Group, the Holmes Group, the National Network for Educational Renewal, Goals 2000, and by associations such as the National Council for Accreditation of Teacher Education (NCATE), the American Association of Colleges for Teacher Education (AACTE), and American Association of State Colleges and Universities (AASCU). Although these issues are part of the context for teacher education, the search for a professional core based on research, theory, and best practice must continue.

Within the landscape of research in teacher education during the next decade, a need for a grand systems theory or a unifying field theory still exists. In a careful, straightforward, and conceptually compelling way, teacher education must find a set of constructs that will allow, if not be predictive of, at least descriptive ways of addressing the commonalities and uniquenesses, the beliefs and behaviors, and the mainstream culture of teacher education from the university to the individual classroom. Theory must generate worthwhile questions whose answers will enhance the knowledge and practice base of the profession.

Many of the data-based, conceptual underpinnings are already present in the literature, and the delay in applying this new knowledge to training programs is frustrating (Schwartz, 1988).

In education, this languishing of unapplied knowledge about teaching, learning, and schools is called the implementation or enactment problem. Assuming that preservice programs in teacher education do provide students with the best possible evidence and the most elegant theoretical paradigm, how can we be sure that this knowledge is applied in the classroom? What constructs do we use to study the classroom and to determine the teacher preparation program that is most compatible? The analytical tools of the anthropologist can provide some insight into this problem, perhaps to describe the commonalities and uniquenesses of the culture of teacher education—the beliefs, behaviors, and artifacts of a group of individuals that recognizes itself as a unique community. These research methodologies have been used to describe the culture of the schools (Erickson, 1982).

The nine universal cultural patterns described by anthropologist Melville J. Herskovits seem particularly useful because all schools and classrooms exhibit them (Schwartz, Olson, Ginsberg, & Bennett, 1983), and teacher education programs appear to have similar characteristics. All cultures and subcultures, for example, have a value system that indicates the preferred ways of doing things and specifies what is good and what is bad. In teacher education, the research clearly shows that effectiveness and quality control are regarded as core values. All cultures have a cosmology or world view that identifies beliefs concerning the relative position of man in the cosmos and the limits that individuals must accept in the larger school, community, church, or classroom culture. In the same way, most states have enacted laws against teacher-initiated corporal punishment or child abuse in the schools, and any student teacher engaging in this behavior would likely be eliminated from a preparation program. Each cultural unit also has some form of social organization that governs individual and group relationships, even to the point of determining forms of verbal address. Student-teacher orientation programs at the university and the school make it known quickly and explicitly what proper title is acceptable—Mrs. Smith, Mr. Jackson, Ms. Hernandez, Dr. Shapiro, and so forth.

Each cultural system also has a technology, a body of knowledge and skills used to perform the tasks necessary for the system to function and survive. Some schools and/or systems have adopted the whole language approach, or the Reading Recovery Method or Hooked on Phonics to teach reading, and they mandate that every teacher use the techniques and materials of the preferred method. It is this area that is receiving much attention in the literature. In teacher education, some of this technology has been codified as licensure requirements (e.g., student teaching as part of preservice programs).

Culture also relies on an economic system to regulate the allocation of goods and services. In a school, the economic system may be nothing more than having a key to the supply cabinet. In a teacher education program, the student : faculty ratio may be the key. Most programs have a much lower student : faculty ratio for supervision of student teaching than for lecture classes on campus. In fact, NCATE guidelines specify an appropriate student : faculty ratio in student teaching for accredited programs.

In addition, cultures depend on a form of governance or a political system regulating individual and institutional behavior to specify how decisions are made; how power, authority, and influence are acquired and used; and who participates in what decisions. Aside from the literature on collaborative and experimental programs and some of the governance literature in higher education, descriptions of how decisions are made in teacher preparation programs are rare.

Typically, cultural patterns also reveal a special language uniquely suited to particular processes and content. The language of teacher preparation has yet to be codified and could benefit from a glossary similar to the one Scriven (1988) produced for the field of educational evaluation. Cultures also have an aesthetic system that defines what is beautiful, creative, and artistic. Finally, there exists a socialization or educational process that regularizes the transmission of knowledge. Here, descriptions, mandates, and common collective wisdom in teacher preparation abounds. Any issue of *The Journal of Teacher Education* contains one or more articles describing the content and sequence of the curriculum and how the candidate moves through the preparation/socialization program under examination.

The most important lesson in comparing teacher education to cultural patterns, however, is that the beginning teacher finds that he or she must live up to norms of behavior or expectations determined by the university as well as the school culture in relation to these nine areas. For example, if the prevailing school values embrace professional improvement, new teachers will be socialized to accept this value. If the social organization favors teachers engaging in professional collaboration with one another, application of pedagogical knowledge may be the direct outcome. If the political system is such that principals and teachers are colleagues in professional activity, teachers are more likely to focus on their educational function instead of their custodial function. Each cultural universal and its unique patterns of interaction affects teachers' utilization of the pedagogical and other worthwhile knowledge that they acquire in their teacher preparation programs. Each universal provides a lens for approaching the problem of unapplied knowledge in a given school, classroom, and preparation program.

The prominence of case studies of teachers in training and experienced teachers since the mid-1980s is welcome for the same reasons. Even though case studies have existed in the teacher training literature (Kagan, 1993) since 1927, vignettes, protocols, simulations, and critical incidents are now becoming useful as qualitative data because they are what Eisner (1993) calls naturalistic, interpretative data that are expressive and attentive to the particular. Copeland, Birmingham, DeMeulle, D'Emidio-Caston, and Natal (1994) laud videotapes of exemplary teachers providing descriptive approaches to understanding teaching, content pedagogical processes, instructional purposes, and linkages; however, this approach can be carried too far. Personal histories are useful in conjunction with other data developed using multiple research methodologies, but they can lead one into the trap of the national profile school of history, which maintains that one knows a culture by studying its great leaders. Beyer (1987) presents an interesting discussion of the culture of teacher education in the chapter, "What Knowledge Is of Most Worth in Teacher Education?" in J. Smyth's *Educating Teachers: Changing the Nature of Pedagogical Knowledge*. Beyer maintains that teacher education in the United States today is dominated by technocratic rationality, or what Katz and Raths (1992) refer to as excessive realism, which trivializes the relationship between teacher and learner. Certainly, the quantity of literature on what might be called utilitarian teaching perspectives, or survival in the classroom, has separated teaching from its ethical, political, and social roots.

CODIFICATION OF GENERIC AND SPECIFIC KNOWLEDGE BASES

Do teacher preparation programs provide newcomers with the essential ingredients for competent practice, theory, and experiences? Are teacher preparation programs contributing to the profession? As Tanner and Tanner (1987) remind us in their work on supervision, "If you are prepared to do something, you see it as your area of competence and responsibility, and consequently, it becomes a professional responsibility" (p. 357). Unfortunately, this belief is not held widely by policymakers because teaching, perhaps more than any other profession, is regulated by outsiders to the field of education, such as legislators, commissioners, boards members, and the general public. Recent studies indicate that the quality of teacher preparation programs and the criteria for certification vary widely. Many states, such as New Jersey, California, and Texas, have approved alternative paths to certification that include no pedagogy or professional preparation and have granted teaching credentials on the basis of on-the-job training. These credentialing procedures detract from professional teaching efforts and signal both disbelief in a teaching knowledge base and lack of respect for schools of education on the part of legislators and/or the governor. Obviously, that portion of the teaching force whose preparation includes no pedagogy and no knowledge of research is ill prepared to implement theoretical ideas in the classroom (Feistreitzer, 1984). The situation created is a vicious circle. Because so many new teachers are unprepared, stylized teaching methods become the norm and supervision becomes increasingly bureaucratic. The nonpecuniary rewards of teaching have dwindled as teachers are viewed more and more as bureaucratic cogs rather than as practicing professionals. The National Board for Professional Teaching Standards is one important effort to counter this trend. As Darling-Hammond (1993) observes, however, lack of input into professional decision making, overly restrictive bureaucratic controls, and inadequate administrative support contribute to dissatisfaction and attrition, particularly among the most highly qualified members of the teaching force. The ultimate result is that the implementation gap between research-based knowledge and theory and practice widens.

In any profession, the practitioner uses codified knowledge, the wisdom of experience, intuition, and creativity in interventions with clients. Before this kind of organized behavior can become the standard for teacher education, the teaching force, in collaboration with teacher educators, scholars, and researchers, must address certain basic dilemmas in the profession. For example, does the profession seek equity or excellence in its teacher preparation programs? Most of the major reform reports of the 1980s and 1990s recommended raising entry standards for teachers, although historically teaching has had relatively flexible admission standards and has been the road to upward social and professional mobility for those previously excluded from the mainstream. How can the profession combine equity and excellence?

In a similar vein, another dilemma in teacher education stems from the core assumptions that "a teacher is a teacher is a teacher" and one teacher's opinions and contributions are as good as those of any other. Clearly, some teachers are better than others, and reform reports have called for differentiation among the teaching ranks in terms of status and salary. How will the profession reconcile the tradition of egalitarianism with calls for differentiation? More important, does differentiation signal acceptance of a situation in which some teachers are not expected to perform as well as other teachers?

A third dilemma resembles the nature-nurture paradox: Are good teachers born or trained? The literature is replete with examples of what good teachers are and what they do, but it fails to provide a resolution to the issue of whether education students can be trained to do what good teachers do and to be good teachers or whether some basic aptitudes must be present before training. Furthermore, how much of expert teaching is context specific, and is an expert teacher an expert in all settings?

A fourth dilemma arises out of a demand in recent reports and state legislation for more standardization in curricular content and delivery. A number of systemic reforms embrace the curriculum and instruction framework approach (Honig, 1994; Kirst, 1990; Smith, Silverman, Borg, & Fry, 1980), but teachers and university faculty have a long-standing tradition of academic freedom, that is, the right to teach without restraints, to develop curricula, and to structure delivery according to personal style within peer-determined limits. How can the curricula of teacher preparation programs, in-service activities, and the classroom accommodate standardization and individualization simultaneously? (Standardization of in-service activities has driven many experienced teachers from the profession.) Sikula also expounds on this dilemma in the preface of this handbook.

Finally, what shall be the focus of the teacher preparation program—the curriculum or the child? At the university level, curricular content takes precedence over the student as an individual. In the kindergarten class, the reverse is true. Although Dewey (1902) counseled that the child and the curriculum are part of the same process, they often continue to be pitted against one another in teacher education. Consider as one case in point the alternative routes to certification that include no pedagogy and no work in child growth and development: How do in-service teachers and teacher educators strike a balance and integrate both academic content and pedagogy?

These dilemmas are not impossible to resolve. Dualisms can be avoided through a "both/and" approach, but any attempt must include, above all, understanding of and appreciation for the central role of the teacher in any reform movement. Teacher preparation programs must look ahead to the future, engage in strategic planning, and distinguish between what is mandated and what preserves the creativity in each child. The reform movement since the mid-1980s has been a mixed affair, including both teacher-proof prescriptions and cries for more teacher judgment in the classroom. If we expect teachers in training to use the knowledge available in preparation programs, we must supervise them carefully during the induction period, point out helpful pedagogical methods, and show them how to incorporate new knowledge and ideas into their own teaching practices. Offering feedback and advice is essential; however, all this is irrelevant unless the system allows teachers to use their pedagogical methods, content, personal knowledge, and educated judgment.

Researchers in education during the next decade must present teachers and teacher educators with a deep description of the field, as well as encourage them to participate in the debate, dialogue, and decision making about what and how to teach and how to prepare individuals to teach well.

CONCLUSION

Where are we going and who will lead us should become clearer as serious students of schooling and teacher education in America work their way through different parts of this handbook. No single answer will emerge, and no single way is desirable. In a democratic country where individualism and diversity are highly valued, one should not look for or expect conformity in all situations. Yet, we know more today about best practice and what works than ever before, and this handbook synthesizes and effectively presents much of this information. Our job is to know what is available and where it has been and can be successfully applied, as well as to implement what we know works rather than to rely simply on the status quo, the easy way, or the road more traveled. The improvement of schooling and teacher education in America requires no less than this of us. This handbook makes it easier to understand the complexities of today's changing educational environment. No recipes for guaranteed success are offered; what is provided is the cumulative wisdom of many of our nation's most outstanding educators. Those who indulge heavily in the banquet offered here will surely gain significantly in their understanding of education in America. Such understanding is the basis for improved practice as the word is spread throughout the nation.

Most scholars, practitioners, and reformers agree that teachers need to be well educated, sensitive, intelligent, and capable

of learning from theory and example. They also need to be action researchers and amateur actors who like children and enjoy working with people and ideas. Teachers should be familiar with the principles of learning and other pedagogical theory, and they should possess skills in analysis, synthesis, and presentation. They should also have knowledge of their subject area and knowledge of the major studies in education bearing on their field or subject area. They should have opportunities—vast opportunities—to practice, train, and apply their knowledge and skills under the supervision of a variety of masters and under the tutelage of an experienced university faculty member. Their mentors must be able to communicate with student teachers and with faculty, and they must be able to demonstrate practical applications of the cumulative body of teaching knowledge.

Admittedly that is a tall order for any preparation program. It requires schools, colleges, and departments of education to do more with less while they are engaged in various renewal efforts. It is currently expected that teacher educators work closely with their colleagues in the public schools as they prepare preservice teachers. The most common complaint from teacher educators is their intensive work load and the lack of time for reflection and scholarship—a complaint very similar to that of teachers in the K–12 arena. However, attention must be given to several research questions raised by the issues of implementation. For example, how can more collaborative research and development be generated within faculties and with colleagues in the public schools across institutions of higher education to achieve more data-based structural changes? How can teacher education have more influence in the policy arena? How can professional development schools be persuaded to focus more on preservice education as well as in-service staff development? How can technology be truly integrated into teacher preparation programs in innovative and meaningful ways? How can priority status be given to cross-institutional research on the assessment of teacher preparation programs and a serious exploration of what types of teachers are needed? How can the research community assist in providing moral leadership to a discipline under siege from many quarters? Reform requires teachers/teacher educators to be and do everything. Although certainly a difficult task and an enormous responsibility, it is absolutely essential to our future. In sentiment, it is rather like the answer given by Margaret Mead. When asked where she would begin to educate people for world peace, she replied, "Why everywhere at once, of course, everywhere at once."

References

Berliner, D. (1985). Critical needs in teacher education. *Journal of Industrial Teacher Education, 22*(4), 5–11.

Berliner, D. C. (1988, April). *The development of expertise in pedagogy.* The Charles W. Hunt Memorial Lecture presented at the annual meeting of the American Association of Colleges for Teacher Education, New Orleans.

Beyer, L. (1987). What knowledge is of most worth in teacher education? In J. Smyth (Ed.), *Educating teachers: Changing the nature of pedagogical knowledge* (pp. 19–34). London: Falmer Press.

Bloom, B. S. (1976). *Human characteristics and school learning.* New York: McGraw-Hill.

Brophy, J. E. (1988). Research on teacher effects: Uses and abuses. *Elementary School Journal, 89,* 3–21.

Broudy, H. (1972). *The real world of the public schools.* New York: Harcourt Brace Jovanovich.

Brown, G. I. (1971). *Human teaching for human learning: An introduction to confluent education.* New York: Viking Press.

California Department of Education (CDE). (1993a). *Caught in the middle.* Sacramento: Author.

California Department of Education (CDE). (1993b). *Second to none.* Sacramento: Author.

Charters, W. & Waples, D. (1929). *The commonwealth teacher training study.* Chicago: The University of Chicago Press.

Coffman, L. D. (1911). *Contributions to education: The social composition of the teaching population, 41.* New York: Columbia University.

Comer, J. P., & Poussaint, A. F. (1992). *Raising black children. Two leading psychiatrists confront the educational, social, and emotional problems facing black children.* New York: Penguin Books.

Copeland, W. D., Birmingham, C., DeMeulle, L., D'Emidio-Caston, M., & Natal, D. (1994). Making meaning in classrooms: An investigation of cognitive processes in aspiring teachers, experienced teachers, and their peers. *American Educational Research Journal, 31*(1), 166–196.

Cruickshank, D. (1990). *Research that informs teaching and teacher preparation.* Bloomington, IN: Phi Delta Kappa.

Cruickshank, D. R., & Metcalf, K. K. (1994). Teacher education is not enough! *Teacher Education Quarterly, 21*(2), 115–128.

Cubberley, E. P. (1916). *The Portland surveyor.* Yonkers-on-Hudson: World Book.

Darling-Hammond, L. (1993, June). Reframing the school reform agenda: Developing capacity for school transformation. *Phi Delta Kappan,* 752–761.

Dewey, J. (1902). *The educational situation.* Chicago: The University of Chicago Press.

Dewey, J. (1916). *Democracy and education.* New York: Macmillan.

Doyle, W. (1978). Paradigms for research on teacher effectiveness. In L. S. Shulman (Ed.), *Review of research in education* (Vol. 5, pp. 163–198). Itasca, IL: F. E. Peacock.

Doyle, W. (1990). Themes in teacher education research. In W. R. Houston, M. Haberman, & J. Sikula (Eds.), *Handbook of research on teacher education* (pp. 3–24). New York: Macmillan.

Dunkin, M. (1987). Technical skills of teaching. In M. Dunkin (Ed.), *International encyclopedia of teaching and teacher education* (pp. 703–706). Oxford, England: Pergamon Press.

Eisner, E. W. (1992, April). The misunderstood role of the arts in human development. *Phi Delta Kappan,* 592.

Eisner, E. W. (1993a, October). Forms of understanding and the future of educational research. *Educational Researcher,* 5–11.

Eisner, E. W. (1993b). Why national performance standards won't do the trick. *Wingspan, 9*(1), 3–4.

Erickson, F. (1982). Taught cognitive learning in its immediate environment: A neglected topic in the anthropology of education. *Anthropology and Education Quarterly, 13,* 149–180.

Evertson, C. M. (1987). Creating conditions for learning: From research to practice. *Theory into Practice, 26*(1), 44–50.

Feistreitzer, C. E. (1984). *The making of a teacher.* Washington, DC: National Center for Educational Information.

Flanders, N. (1963). *Helping teachers change their behavior.* Project numbers 1721012 & 7-32-0560-171.0. Washington, DC: U.S. Office of Education.

Flexner, A. (1910). *Medical education in the United States and Canada: A report to the Carnegie Foundation for the Advancement of Teaching.* New York.

Fullan, M. G. (1985). Change processes and strategies at the local level. *Elementary Schools Journal, 85*(3), 391–421.

Gage, N. L. (1972). *Teacher effectiveness & teacher education: The search for a scientific basis.* Palo Alto, CA: Pacific Books.

Gage, N. L. (1992). Art, science, and teaching from the standpoint of an eclectic purist. *School of Education Review, 4,* 8–17.

Garrison, J. W. (1988). Democracy, scientific knowledge, and teacher empowerment. *Teachers College Record, 89,* 487–504.

Goodlad, J. I. (1984). *A place called school.* New York: McGraw-Hill.

Goodlad, J. I. (1991). Why we need a complete redesign of teacher education. *Educational Leadership, 49*(3), 4–10.

Honig, B. (1994). A decade of educational reform in California. *School of Education Review, 6,* 93–106.

Houston, W. R., Haberman, M., & Sikula, J. (Eds.). (1990). *Handbook of research on teacher education.* New York: Macmillan.

Jackson, P. (1965). The way teaching is. *NEA Journal, 54*(8), 10–13.

Jackson, P. W. (1991, Fall). Comprehending a well-run comprehensive: A report on a visit to a large suburban high school. *Daedalus,* 94–95.

Joyce, B. (1975). Conceptions of man and their implications for teacher education. In K. Ryan (Ed.), *Teacher education* (74th yearbook of the National Society for the Study of Education, Part II, pp. 111–145). Chicago: The University of Chicago Press.

Joyce, B., & Showers, B. (1988). *Student achievement through staff development.* New York: Longman.

Kagan, D. M. (1993). Contexts for the use of classroom cases. *American Educational Research Journal, 30*(4), 703–723.

Katz, L. G., & Raths, J. D. (1992). Six dilemmas in teacher education. *Journal of Teacher Education, 43*(5), 376–385.

Kirst, M. W. (1990). *Accountability: Implications for state and local policy makers* (policy perspectives series). Washington, DC: U.S. Department of Education, Office of Educational Research and Improvement.

Koff, R. H., Laffey, J. M., Olson, G. E., & Cichon, D. J. (1981). Stress and the school administrator. *National Association of Secondary Schools Principals Bulletin, 65*(449).

Lanier, J. E., & Little, J. W. (1986). Research on teacher education. In M. C. Wittrock (Ed.), *Handbook of research on teaching* (3rd ed., pp. 527–569). New York: Macmillan.

Levin, H. M. (1986). *Educational reform for disadvantaged students: An emerging crisis.* West Haven, CT: NEA Professional Library.

Medley, D. M. (1984). Teacher competency testing and the teacher educator. In L. G. Katz & J. D. Raths (Eds.), *Advances in teacher education* (Vol. 1, pp. 51–94). Norwood, NJ: Ablex.

National Center for Education Statistics (NCES). (1993a). *America's teachers: Profile of a profession* (NCES Publication No. NCES 93-025, pp. v–vi). Washington, DC: Author.

National Center for Education Statistics (NCES). (1993b). *Education in states and nations: Indicators comparing U.S. states with the OECD countries in 1988* (NCES Publication No. NCES 93-237). Washington, DC: Author.

National Center for Education Statistics (NCES). (1993c). *Statistical analysis report: New teachers in the job market, 1991 update: Contractor report* (NCES Publication No. NCES 93-392). Washington, DC: Author.

National Center for Education Statistics (NCES). (1994a). *Characteristics of stayers, movers, and leavers: Results from the teacher followup survey: 1991–92* (NCES Publication No. NCES 94-337). Washington, DC: Author.

National Center for Education Statistics (NCES). (1994b). *Overview of NAEP assessment frameworks* (NCES Publication No. NCES 94-412). Washington, DC: Author.

Noddings, N. (1988, February). An ethic of caring and its implications for instructional arrangements. *American Journal of Education, 96*(2), 215–230.

Noddings, N. (1991). Stories in dialogue: Caring and interpersonal reasoning. In C. Witherell & N. Noddings (Eds.), *Stories lives tell: Narrative and dialogue in education* (pp. 157–170). New York: Teachers College Press.

Ryan Act. (1960). California Education Code.

Schon, D. (1983). *The reflective practitioner: How professionals think in action.* New York: Basic Books.

Schwab, J. (1983). The practical 4: Something for curriculum professors to do. *Curriculum Inquiry, 13,* 240.

Schwartz, H. S. (1988). Unapplied curriculum knowledge. In L. N. Tanner (Ed.), *Critical issues in curriculum* (87th yearbook of the National Society for the Study of Education, Part 1, pp. 35–59). Chicago: The University of Chicago Press.

Schwartz, H. S., Olson, G., Ginsberg, R., & Bennett, A. (1983). *Schools as a workplace: The realities of stress* (NIE No. NIE-G-80-0011).

Scott, J. A. (1994, February 16). *Developments for teacher education and policy implications*. Address given at the winter conference of the Teacher Education Council of State Colleges and Universities, Chicago.

Scriven, M. (1988). *Evaluating teachers as professionals* (ERIC Document No. ED300882). Washington, DC: Clearinghouse on Teacher Education.

Shulman, J. H., & Mesa-Bains, A. (Eds.). (1990). *Teaching diverse students: Cases and commentaries* (Contract No. 40-86-0009). San Francisco: Far West Laboratory.

Shulman, J. H., & Mesa-Bains, A. (Eds.). (1993). *Diversity in the classroom: A case book for teachers and teacher educators* (Contract Nos. RP91002004 & RP91002006). San Francisco: Far West Laboratory.

Shulman, L. S. (1986a). Paradigms and research programs in the study of teaching: A contemporary perspective. In M. C. Wittrock (Ed.), *Handbook of research on teaching* (3rd ed., pp. 3–36). New York: Macmillan.

Shulman, L. S. (1986b). Those who understand: Knowledge growth in teaching. *Educational Researcher, 15*(2), 4–14.

Slavin, R. (1983). *Cooperative learning*. New York: Longman.

Smith, B. O., Silverman, S., Borg, J., & Fry, B. (1980). *A design for a school of pedagogy*. Washington, DC: U.S. Department of Education.

Stallings, J. A. (1984). Implications from the research on teaching for teacher preparation. In R. L. Egbert & M. M. Kluender (Eds.), *Using research to improve teacher education: The Nebraska Consortium* (Teacher Education Monograph No. 1) (pp. 128–145). Washington, DC: ERIC Clearinghouse on Teacher Education.

Tanner, D., & Tanner, L. (1987). *Supervision in education: Problems and practices*. New York: Macmillan.

Tom, A. R. (1987). Replacing pedagogical knowledge with pedagogical questions. In J. Smyth (Ed.), *Educating teachers: Changing the nature of pedagogical knowledge* (pp. 9–17). London: Falmer.

Tyack, D. B. (1974). *The one best system: A history of American urban education*. Cambridge, MA: Harvard University Press.

U.S. Department of Education (USDE). (1983). *A nation at risk*. Washington, DC: Author.

U.S. Department of Education (USDE). (1992a). *First lesson*. Washington, DC: Author.

U.S. Department of Education (USDE). (1992b). *What works*. Washington, DC: Author.

Zeichner, K. M. (1983). Alternative paradigms of teacher education. *Journal of Teacher Education, 34*(3), 3–9.

Zumwalt, K. K. (1982). Research on teaching: Policy implications for teacher education. In A. Lieberman & M. McLaughlin (Eds.), *Policy making in education* (81st yearbook of the National Society for the Study of Education, Part I, pp. 215–248). Chicago: University of Chicago Press.

Zumwalt, K. K. (1988). Are we improving or undermining teaching? In L. N. Tanner (Ed.), *Critical issues in curriculum* (87th yearbook of the National Society for the Study of Education, Part I, pp. 148–174). Chicago: The University of Chicago Press.

•2•

MODES OF INQUIRY IN RESEARCH ON TEACHER EDUCATION

Okhee Lee
UNIVERSITY OF MIAMI

Sam J. Yarger
UNIVERSITY OF MIAMI

Research on teacher education is becoming a burgeoning area of inquiry, complete with new developments and important advances. The expansion of substantive issues in teacher education, accompanied by methodological advances, has provided an opportunity for researchers in teacher education to explore many new areas (Kennedy, 1991a, 1991b; McDiarmid & Ball, 1988). Furthermore, the education research community continues to call for integration of research, practice, and policy in teacher education (e.g., National Academy of Education, 1991).

This chapter concerns modes of inquiry in teacher education. As a greater variety of modes of inquiry is employed in educational research, it is becoming increasingly important to have criteria for deciding the appropriate mode to use to maintain the quality of work in a particular study. This chapter helps researchers sort through these choices in the unique contexts of teacher education research. This chapter also provides a framework for better understanding the other chapters in this volume, many of which will be devoted to research in specific areas of teacher education. It should be noted that modes of measurement related to the assessment of teachers and students are described elsewhere in this volume.

This chapter consists of four sections. The first section briefly describes recent developments and current trends of methodological and substantive issues in research on teacher education. This section also addresses the problem of language and terminology in teacher education research. The second section discusses the context and settings in which teacher education research is conducted and how this context influences the research endeavor. The third section describes the different modes of inquiry commonly employed in teacher education research as well as the contextual issues for each mode of inquiry and examples of specific studies. The conclusion stresses the need for interdisciplinary approaches to teacher education research, the necessity for training researchers across varied modes of inquiry, and other suggestions for future research in teacher education.

There is surprisingly little discussion about modes of inquiry in teacher education (as an exception, see Kennedy, 1991b). This chapter provides a comprehensive, systematic review for both a general readership and one whose specific interest is in teacher education research. As a result of its broad purpose, this chapter is rather lengthy. Those without sufficient knowledge or active participation in educational research may benefit from reading the entire chapter, whereas experienced researchers may skip some parts (e.g., overview of each mode of inquiry in the "Modes of Inquiry in Teacher Education" section) without losing the continuity of thoughts.

The authors thank reviewers James Cooper and Robert Floden for their helpful suggestions. The first author acknowledges the support of the National Academy of Education Spencer Postdoctoral Fellowship.

RECENT DEVELOPMENTS AND
CURRENT TRENDS

Fueled by the national debate on education reform since the 1980s, teacher education has been a target of blame for the nation's education problems and has been the focus of renewed attention for improvement. After the wave of calls for teacher education reform subsided (e.g., Carnegie Forum on Education and the Economy, 1986; The Holmes Group, 1986; National Commission on Excellence in Education, 1983), a plethora of personal opinions and suggestions dominated the debate. For instance, during the mid-1980s scholarly journals specializing in teacher education devoted significant space to air the debate about the collaboration between professional education and liberal arts studies (e.g., Beineke, 1988; Gore, 1987; King, 1987; Reagan, 1990; Weaver, 1987).

Research efforts in teacher education are certainly not new. Research on teacher education occurred during the 1970s at, for example, the research and development center at the University of Texas at Austin and the teacher education center at Syracuse University, as well as in the volume on teacher education by the National Society for the Study of Education (Ryan, 1975) and the work of individual scholars (e.g, Gage, 1978). What distinguishes current research from previous research is the extent of interests and concerted efforts. The research also has branched into many new domains (e.g., cognitive psychology, sociocultural perspectives) and is proliferating at a rate unthought of in the 1970s. Current research tends to be more theoretically grounded and requires an analytical structure that was previously not needed.

Serious efforts have recently been undertaken to establish a knowledge base for teacher education. The publication of *Knowledge Base for the Beginning Teacher* (Reynolds, 1989) under the sponsorship of the American Association of Colleges for Teacher Education (AACTE) was an attempt to promote dialogue between the research community and the broader teacher education community. The Research About Teacher Education (RATE) project is an ongoing survey project that was initiated in 1985 by the AACTE (Galluzzo & Arends, 1989; Howey, 1989; Yarger, 1989; Zimpher, 1989). The RATE project has been establishing a national data base about teacher education programs and the perceptions of students and faculty. Furthermore, a systematic research agenda on teacher education programs and learning to teach has been initiated by the National Center for Research on Teacher Learning (formerly the National Center for Research on Teacher Education) at Michigan State University.

In recent years, research on teacher education increasingly has involved a range of alternative research methods, especially with the growing popularity of qualitative and narrative approaches. After a period of competition for methodological, paradigmatic, or even ideological dominance (Gage, 1989), these competing modes of inquiry now exist simultaneously, although not always comfortably, to respond to a much wider variety of research questions in teacher education (Kennedy, 1991b; Shulman, 1988).

Methodological alternatives enable new lines of inquiry in teacher education. Efforts in teacher education research since the late 1980s concern not only teacher education programs and their components but also changes in teachers' knowledge, skills, and dispositions that may occur through the interaction of a student with a teacher education program (Carter, 1990; National Center for Research on Teacher Education, 1988, 1991; Richardson, 1990). This research on learning to teach or teacher learning investigates the relationship among the opportunities offered through teacher education programs and changes in teachers' ideas and practices over time. The research has been facilitated by the greater use of qualitative modes of inquiry that enable rich descriptions about the process of teacher learning. Research programs or genres in teacher education are discussed in this chapter as they relate to major modes of inquiry in teacher education research.

Methodological and substantive advances in research on teacher education occur against a backdrop of the social, cultural, economic, and political climate of the nation's educational enterprise. Teacher education reform started to enhance the quality of teaching through collaboration among teacher educators in the schools or colleges of education, subject matter specialists of the colleges of arts and sciences, and teachers and administrators in school systems. As teacher education reform progresses, accountability demands are increasingly placed on teachers and teacher educators in the form of teacher assessment programs, certification, and licensure. Furthermore, teacher education as a national endeavor requires better communication among policymakers, researchers, practitioners, and the general public. Although these issues are not the focus of this chapter, they are discussed at one level or another in the other chapters in this volume.

Key Terms

Two key terms used in this chapter are *modes of inquiry* and *teacher education*. Modes of inquiry, as used in this chapter, refers to the intellectual strategy selected by the researcher to address research questions in teacher education. Several factors influence a researcher's decision to employ a specific mode of inquiry. Clearly, the researcher's prior educational experiences, often shaped by a particular world view or intellectual disposition, form a base for selecting a mode of inquiry. This intellectual base, however, must also accommodate other factors, such as the context in which the research takes place and the nature of the research question(s). (These factors are discussed in later sections of this chapter.) Although modes of inquiry are described in this chapter in their "pure" form, the interaction of the factors mentioned often lead to hybrid approaches. Thus, it is always necessary to take into account the interrelationship of these factors when judging research in teacher education.

The term *teacher education* is used to include preservice programs for prospective teachers, induction programs for beginning teachers, and in-service programs for practicing teachers. Regardless of whether a program is preservice, induction, or in-service in nature, a teacher education program indicates "a deliberate educational intervention designed to foster [teachers'] learning" (National Center for Research on Teacher Education, 1988, p. 28). A program includes various dimensions on three levels—the overall program, the individual component, and the specific learning opportunities within each given component. Furthermore, the learning opportunities embedded in a teacher education program are intended to contribute to changes in teachers' knowledge, skills, and dispositions across different settings and at different points in teachers' careers. In this sense, teacher education includes both teacher education programs and learning to teach.

Problems of Language

The task of defining terms is always risky in any area of research, including educational research (see the description about philosophical research in the "Modes of Inquiry in Teacher Education" section of this chapter). The problems of language and terminology are critical issues in research on teacher education, which has a rather short history of disciplined inquiry but has witnessed a burgeoning of substantive and methodological advances in recent years. In some cases one term may have multiple meanings, whereas in other cases different terms may have a single meaning. Houston, Haberman, and Sikula (1989) singled out language as a major problem in teacher education. The example they provided focused on terms to describe those teachers engaged in reflective inquiry, including reflective teachers; adaptive teachers; teachers as action researchers; teachers as applied scientists; teachers as moral craftsmen; teachers as problem solvers; teachers as hypotheses makers; teachers as clinical inquirers; self-teachers; teachers as radical pedagogues; teachers as political craftsmen; scholar-teachers; and teachers as reflective practitioners, critical thinkers, and improvisers. There undoubtedly are different meanings for these terms in someone's mind; yet, unfortunately, they are too often used interchangeably.

To make the matter more complicated, the terminology of research methods is equally laden with problems of language. One example concerns the terms *quantitative* and *qualitative* research perspectives. These two terms, although commonly used, are not favored by many researchers who often prefer more explicit terms (e.g., *positivistic* or *empirical* versus *naturalistic, interpretive,* or *phenomenological*) to connote a distinction that, to some, may seem unimportant. Another example involves the term *case study research,* which is interpreted differently by different researchers. Some researchers use this term interchangeably with qualitative/ethnographic research (another example of a language problem) (Erickson, 1986; Hamel, Dufour, & Fortin, 1993; Merriam, 1988), whereas others use it as a distinct mode of inquiry (Yin, 1993, 1994). This topic is discussed in more detail later in this chapter.

The point to be made is that although the debate on language and terminology may clarify the meanings of terms and improve the accuracy of communication, it may also be a critical impediment to our ability to conceptualize and to exchange dialogue. Houston et al. (1989) claimed that "without an agreed-upon, technical language, there can be no profession and no knowledge base" in teacher education (p. 21). This issue should be addressed by the educational research community. It is conceivable that the American Educational Research Association or the National Academy of Education could empower a task force to construct a glossary of terms on research in education and/or teacher education.

CONTEXT OF TEACHER EDUCATION RESEARCH

Research occurs within the larger context of social, political, cultural, financial, and interpersonal factors. These factors occur at different levels, including national, regional, state, school district, university, and school or department of education. The identification of contextual factors in teacher education is a major task itself, not to mention the examination of how these factors influence the enterprise of teacher education (Corrigan & Haberman, 1990). Considering the importance of the context in teacher education, it seems logical that this volume devotes substantial space to the discussion of contextual influences (see Part III, this volume). In this section, these authors discuss major issues about the context in which research on teacher education occurs. Contextual influences specific to each mode of inquiry are described in the "Modes of Inquiry in Teacher Education" section of this chapter.

Contextual Influences on Research Issues and Methods

Magnitude and complexity characterize the context of teacher education. There are more than 2 million teachers in the nation's schools. More than 1,200 higher education institutions offer teacher preparation programs, producing 100,000 new teachers each year (Kennedy, 1991a). In addition, numerous staff development programs for practicing teachers as well as induction programs for beginning teachers exist at higher education institutions, school districts, and various alternative education agencies or institutions. These various teacher education programs are designed with very different structural and conceptual orientations (Feiman-Nemser, 1990; Little, 1993). It is all too unclear what factors are considered in deciding the structural and conceptual orientations of programs, how the decisions are made, and who plays key roles in the decisions. Furthermore, teacher education as a social enterprise is largely influenced by political and financial conditions.

Context plays important roles for research on teacher education, although it may not seem as obvious as the roles that context plays for practice and policy making. First, the context determines what issues require careful examination. As much as research findings change or modify the configuration of the context, the context requires researchers to attend to certain issues. This reactive role is much greater in applied areas such as teacher education than in the basic disciplines. Funding priorities set by the federal or state government are an example of how the context dictates research agendas.

Second, the context of teacher education influences the research methods used in inquiry. Each mode of inquiry carries with it its own set of assumptions or conditions to achieve its intended purpose. When these assumptions are not met, knowledge claims from the inquiry are significantly weakened or subject to doubt. In a real-world situation it is very difficult to satisfy these assumptions. As a consequence, the researchers are forced to compromise between what is ideal and what is possible in a given research setting.

Let us take experimental research as a case in point, although similar scenarios apply to other modes of inquiry. To establish the "causality" claim in experimental research, three conditions are commonly held as necessary (Porter, 1988). First, changes in the independent variable should precede in time changes in the dependent variable (temporal precedence). Second, independent and dependent variables should be correlated; knowledge of the independent variable must be sufficient to predict the dependent variable. Finally, there must be no plausible third variable (confounding variable) that explains the relationship between the independent and dependent variables. In a given research setting, it is difficult to meet these conditions. Researchers often do not have direct control over the independent variable that they expect will create changes in the dependent variable. They may not be able to disentangle the multitude of variables that are interrelated or may not be allowed to include related variables for investigation. Researchers often cannot randomly assign subjects to treatment groups to rule out plausible confounding variables. Given the situation, the researchers have no other recourse but to try to make the most informed and sound decisions within the contextual confines.

Human Subjects and Interpersonal Relations

The context of teacher education research involves issues of human subjects and interpersonal relations, in addition to social, political, and financial influences. The Code of Federal Regulations for the Protection of Human Subjects (45 CFR 46) requires consent by human subjects to participate in research. The issue of informed consent has become a major concern in social science research. From the range of different modes of inquiry, experimental research and ethnography seem to be most affected by this regulation.

Experimental research requires random assignment of subjects from a given sample into different treatment groups. To avoid confounding the experimental effects by the interjection of human expectations (called Hawthorne effect), experimental research should keep the subjects unaware of any change in their environment (idealistically) or of the nature of treatment they are receiving (realistically). The requirement of informed consent, however, precludes some subjects in the given sample who decline participation. The resulting sample of volunteers limits the generalizability of the findings to the intended population. Furthermore, subjects often learn in advance what kinds of treatment they will be receiving. The subjects' knowledge and possibly their desire to benefit from certain treatments confound the effects that may result from the treatments without their knowledge. The tension between enhancing the rigor and quality of research, on the one hand, and protecting human rights and being ethical, on the other hand, is inevitable.

The regulation of informed consent also complicates qualitative research (Howe & Dougherty, 1993). Because qualitative research involves close interpersonal relationships between the researchers and participants (subjects), it is ethically charged and unpredictable from the outset. Also, because qualitative research is open-ended and research directions evolve and change over the course of inquiry, the informed consent form obtained at the outset of the research may become irrelevant over time. Furthermore, because qualitative research involves detailed descriptions of a specific group that can be easily identifiable, the threat to the confidentiality of the group and certain members of the group is high. Unless the group or individual members desire to become visible, protecting their anonymity is a major concern in qualitative research (Punch, 1986; Shulman, 1990).

In addition to issues of informed consent, teacher education research is also complicated with interpersonal relations involving researchers, subjects or participants, and audiences. Much of teacher education research conducted at higher education institutions concerns the performance of teacher education programs, teacher educators, and/or teacher education students. Because researchers are also associated with the programs and/or the institutions, the research often involves the study of one's *own* institutions, programs, colleagues, or students. When research is conducted at other higher education institutions or K–12 schools, the researchers are likely to have some connection with teacher educators at those institutions. This situation raises potential conflicts of interest in an academic, political, and interpersonal sense. Any negative findings will put the institutions, programs, or teacher educators under study at risk. If negative findings are intentionally eliminated for political and interpersonal reasons, the integrity of the research is compromised. These kinds of conflicts may raise concerns about the overall credibility of teacher education research.

Expectations of teacher educators in research activities seem to vary by type of institution. Whereas a potential conflict between knowledge production and student service (teaching and supervision) exists with all higher education professors, the conflict seems more acute with teacher education professors. This conflict is reflected in the historical development of teacher education from normal schools to colleges or schools of education within the university system (Urban, 1990). In response to the dual role between research and service, teacher education programs often have stressed one role over the other (Howey & Zimpher, 1989), and many teacher educators have expended their efforts in one area relative to or at the exclusion of the other (Ducharme, 1993). For teacher education to become a mature area of study, teacher educators from various types of institutions should engage in research activities and generate knowledge about teacher education in diverse situations.

Basic versus Applied Research

Traditionally there has been a distinction between basic and applied research. Basic research is conceived as building and testing theories or constructs in basic disciplines, whereas applied research is directed toward answering practical questions about real-life problems. Most teacher education research has been applied research, often concerned with program intervention and improvement. In teacher education research, the role of theory is often secondary, if it is existent at all. In place of theory, one often finds a conceptual framework or a knowledge base, which guides the design of new programs, materials, or strategies. Also important are the social, political, financial, and interpersonal factors that have an impact on program development. After a teacher education program or program component has been implemented, the primary concern is to evaluate whether it works, rather than to provide theoretical explanations for why it does or does not work.

Recently there has been an attempt to converge basic and applied research in education (Kaestle, 1993). This new effort tries to maximize both the rigor and utility of research with researchers field testing theories as they are implemented in real-world situations. Although this effort has brought about some success in certain areas (e.g., research on teaching), it is unclear how well it will work on research in teacher education.

Most teacher education programs, program components, and program activities did not derive from theory. Rather, in most cases teacher education has developed from historical perspectives, the wisdom of practice, and a good deal of trial and error on the part of teacher educators. Although it certainly is laudable to link theory and practice in teacher education, it is simply not always possible. In fact, the extent to which a "forced linking" is promoted is perhaps the extent to which a number of important questions concerning teacher education are not addressed. It is difficult to retrofit a construct to an activity that did not derive from a foundation of theory. At this stage of development in teacher education research, atheoretical and nontheoretical inquiry through careful observations by knowledgeable teacher educators is acceptable and needed. Based on the results of research, conceptual issues may emerge, and theories may even be generated.

Research Integrity

Thus far in this section the context of teacher education research has been presented as the interrelationship of social, political, financial, interpersonal, and theoretical factors. These contextual factors exert a range of constraints on research, requiring the researcher to be continually vigilant. The integrity of research refers to how well the researcher has accommodated all of these factors, including the setting where the research occurs. There is no absolute set of criteria for judging the integrity of a research study, rather the judgment must come from an understanding and consideration of the setting as well as the research methods being used. One might think of it as a continuum of research integrity based on settings.

Research integrity is different from research quality in that the former relates to the appropriate match of the research method with the setting, whereas the latter relates to the value of the research itself. If the setting where the research occurs can accommodate the research method being used, then the research project can be said to have high integrity. The human subjects laboratory, for example, is designed to accommodate experimental or quasi-experimental research. The microteaching laboratory, in many cases, also accommodates an experimental approach. The elementary or secondary classroom, however, because of the many distractions, interferences, and the inability to control the setting, would probably not serve well for an experimental study. In this instance, one would likely end up with "low integrity" research.

When a researcher is faced with the possibility of low integrity research, at least two choices can be made. First, the researcher can rethink the research question(s) and attempt to devise a study in which the mode of inquiry better accommodates the research setting. In this case, a correlational or narrative study might be better accommodated in a classroom than an experiment. It should be noted, however, that if the researcher selects this option, the research question(s) being addressed might be very different from the one(s) that was originally posed, eventually producing different kinds of answers resulting from a different mode of inquiry.

The researcher also has the choice of moving ahead with the original study even though it is flawed. This decision would be made based on how the results are to be used. For example, if the question relates to whether a particular instructional strategy works, it might be important to have the answer to that question even though the research has limitations. If a program decision must be made at a particular point in time, it is better to have some information, particularly if the limitations are well noted, than no information at all.

The importance of the concept of research integrity is that it recognizes that research in teacher education does not occur in a vacuum and often cannot take place under ideal circumstances. The fact that a proposed study has less than perfect integrity does not mean that it should not be carried out. Rather, it means that the researcher should explore every possibility and select the best option given the circumstances and the knowledge of how the results will be used.

The point of the discussion about the context of teacher education research is not to condone researchers who use contextual constraints as an excuse for low quality research. Instead, the point is that teacher education researchers should conduct realistic assessments of the nature of the context in which the research occurs and make the most informed decision within the confines of that context. Certainly realistic assessments of the context would also include consideration of probable costs and efforts on the one hand and likely outcomes on the other hand.

MODES OF INQUIRY IN TEACHER EDUCATION

The previous section discussed the complexity of the social, political, financial, and interpersonal contexts in which research on teacher education is conducted and reported. Teacher education research becomes more complicated by the diversity of issues in the field (Kennedy, 1991b). To make the situation more challenging and stimulating, research on teacher education must also contend with a range of alternative modes of inquiry. These factors require researchers to carefully select a mode of inquiry appropriate for their own clearly defined research question.

This section consists of three parts. The first concerns the debate between the quantitative and qualitative research paradigms and related issues in research on teacher education. Then, a range of modes of inquiry in teacher education research is described, including experimental and quasi-experimental, correlational, survey, case study, ethnographic, historical, and philosophical. Finally, general issues and concerns that go across modes of inquiry are discussed, including validity, reliability, generalizability, and practice-related and policy implications.

Research Paradigms and Related Issues in Teacher Education

It is commonly agreed that research questions dictate research methods. As discussed in the previous section, the context in which research is conducted also influences research methods. In addition, the researcher's world view, paradigm, or perspective often determines what questions to pursue, which subsequently necessitates a certain research method. The great debate between the proponents of quantitative and qualitative perspectives (other terms might be used, such as *positivistic* or *empirical* versus *naturalistic, interpretive,* or *phenomenological*) has dominated the educational research community since the 1980s as qualitative research became popular in educational research. For instance, *Educational Researcher,* the official forum of the American Educational Research Association, published more than 30 articles on this topic during the period between 1985 and 1993, and many of the feature articles are accompanied by responses and counterresponses (e.g., Firestone, 1987; Gage, 1989; Howe, 1985; Phillips, 1983; Rizo, 1991; Salomon, 1991; Schrag, 1992; Smith, 1983; Smith & Heshusius, 1986).

The debate between advocates of the two research paradigms has involved various issues at different phases. The first phase of the debate centered on philosophical and epistemological differences between the paradigms and hegemony or dominance by either paradigm in educational research (e.g., Howe, 1985; Phillips, 1983; Schrag, 1992; Smith, 1983). The second phase of the debate focused on compatibility or incompatibility of the two paradigms at both epistemological or methodological levels (e.g., Firestone, 1987; Smith & Heshusius, 1986). Gage (1989), declaring that " 'Paradigm Wars' had come to a sanguinary climax" (p. 4), projected three scenarios (i.e., confrontation, coexistence, and collaboration) of the educational research community 20 years later. Gage called for collaboration as a moral obligation, noting that the purpose of educational research is better education of the nation's children and youth. In his reaction to Gage, Rizo (1991) provided a historical context for this debate during the last two centuries and predicted that confrontation would continue at the epistemological level. In the meantime, other researchers have attempted to "transcend" the paradigmatic debate invoking practical as well as epistemological necessity to address real issues and problems in education (e.g., Salomon, 1991). The latest debate has concerned specific research issues between the two paradigms, including validity (Maxwell, 1992), reliability (Kirk & Miller, 1986), generalizability (Firestone, 1993), and subjectivity versus objectivity (Peshkin, 1988; Smith, 1988).

This chapter leaves the discussion on epistemological differences between advocates of the two research paradigms to textbooks and readings in educational research methods. It also leaves the discussion on compatibility or incompatibility to other sources (Firestone, 1987; Smith & Heshusius, 1986). This section addresses several major issues from the paradigmatic debate as they relate to research on teacher education.

One issue concerns the variety of disciplinary backgrounds possessed by researchers in teacher education. Because teacher education is an applied area, researchers come from a range of disciplines, including psychology, sociology, anthropology, history, philosophy, economics, and political science (Shulman, 1988). Not only do the researchers bring with them a set of research agendas and methods, but they also bring world views or research perspectives associated with their disciplines. It would be difficult, although not impossible, to imagine an educational anthropologist disposed to a quantitative perspective, as much as it would be difficult to find an experimental psychologist adopt a qualitative perspective. In addition to differences in their perspectives, researchers often do not share the necessary common language to communicate with each other. For example, some basic research issues from the quantitative perspective are addressed in terms different from those used by qualitative researchers, such as credibility (internal validity), dependability (reliability), transferability (external validity or generalizability), and confirmability (objectivity) (Lincoln & Guba, 1985). This variety of disciplinary backgrounds, associated with research perspectives and interests, can be interpreted differently depending on how one views the situation. Some may regard this variety as a valuable asset of teacher education research because it can provide diverse approaches to inquiry, verify findings from different research methods, or suggest alternative explanations to findings. Others may regard it as a serious liability because it can hinder communication or bring about a contest for dominance by certain groups within the teacher education community.

The debate on research paradigms is further complicated by the underlying issues of power and voice. The paradigmatic debate started with the qualitative researchers gaining power and asserting their voice to be heard in the education research community, which has been dominated by the researchers with quantitative orientations. One recent movement in educational research concerns the distinction between paradigmatic and narrative modes of inquiry and knowledge claims (Bruner, 1990; Eisner, 1993). Despite cautions and concerns about its legitimacy, narrative inquiry into the personal biography of teachers and teacher educators has gained acceptance in the educational research community (Carter, 1993; Connelly & Clandinin, 1990; Nespor & Barylske, 1991). With the growing use of narrative inquiry, teachers who have traditionally been silent are now interested in sharing their ideas with researchers. Teachers are telling their stories in their own voice. The idea of a teacher researcher has been recognized as a means of teacher growth or professional development by some in the education community (Cochran-Smith & Lytle, 1990).

Just as there is a range of perspectives and voices among researchers, there is also a range of differing positions and agendas in the various audiences. The immediate audience for research on teacher education consists of scholars who engage in establishing a body of knowledge. Some teacher educators follow closely because they are interested in implementing research findings in the design and delivery of teacher education programs and curricula. Teachers have an interest because they want to learn about research for their professional growth. School and district administrators incorporate research ideas for staff development activities. In addition to these interested parties within the education circle, research results reach the press; legislators and bureaucrats at the national, state, and local levels; and eventually the general public (McCarthy, 1990; McNergney, 1990, 1992).

The diversity of audiences makes the job of researchers much more complicated. In addition to producing knowledge, researchers must consider information dissemination across these various groups. This is especially the case for the policy-making and political arenas because research findings tend to be used in a way that is typically not intended by the researcher (Barone, 1992; Kaestle, 1993). Although inconsistent research results and opposing conceptual orientations help the research community to raise additional questions and recognize complexities, the situation can also give the impression of "no laws or rules" in teacher education to policymakers and the general public. This is a particularly acute concern for teacher education research, which is still in its infancy. Although teacher education institutions are held accountable by the public for the education of the nation's teachers and their students, it is unfortunately the case that teacher education research has not yet reached the level of maturity to assume the responsibility called for by the public.

The descriptions so far may sound like pitting one perspective, voice, or audience group against another. On the contrary, the trend seems to be in the direction of coexistence and even collaboration. Through collaborative inquiry, researchers from different disciplines are learning from each other (e.g, Crow, Levine, & Nager, 1992; Eisenhart & Borko, 1991). Researchers, mostly from the qualitative perspective, are trying to develop language and terminology compatible with the quantitative paradigm. While the paradigmatic debate on philosophical and epistemological differences continues, practicing researchers are becoming more knowledgeable about research perspectives and more eclectic in their choice of research methods. In addition, more teachers are joining in teacher education research collaboratively with researchers or even independently.

Modes of inquiry commonly used in teacher education research are described in this section, starting with the traditionally prominent modes of experimental, correlational, and survey research, followed by qualitatively based modes of case study research and ethnography, and ending with historical and philosophical research in teacher education. Modes of inquiry appropriate for studies on policy, finance and governance, curriculum, and critical theory in teacher education are not discussed. These modes of inquiry are described elsewhere in this volume.

Each mode of inquiry is described in three parts: (1) overview of its purpose, assumptions, strengths, and limitations; (2) contextual issues in teacher education; and (3) a specific example of relevant research. The intention here is not to give detailed descriptions and critiques of each mode (see Jaeger, 1988); instead, the focus is on key aspects within the context of teacher education research. Using example studies, the authors point out limitations of the studies due to the shortcomings in a particular study and/or the inherent constraints of the context in which the study was conducted. These studies were chosen as examples, not necessarily exemplary, each with unique sets of strengths and limitations in the context of teacher education research.

Experimental and Quasi-Experimental Research

Overview Originating from the natural sciences, experimental research is the prototype of the quantitative research perspective. The purpose of experimental research is to establish a theory or to test an already existing theory that explains the cause–effect relationship between an independent (or treatment) variable(s) and dependent (or outcome) variable(s). Experimentation attempts to control an infinite number of rival hypotheses through random assignment to treatments and later accounts for the plausibility of rival hypotheses using probability theory. The effectiveness of the treatment is supported or not supported (but never proved or disproved) through replication across subjects, settings, and times.

Quasi-experimentation is a less powerful model for testing hypotheses about cause–effect relationships. There are many varieties of quasi-experiments (Cook & Campbell, 1979). The key difference between experimental and quasi-experimental research involves random assignment. Quasi-experiments occur using random assignment of intact groups to treatment conditions and then use individual subjects as the unit of analysis. Quasi-experiments also occur without random assignment. A difficult problem in establishing the cause–effect relationship is to determine whether the outcome is due to the treatment, initial differences among intact groups prior to the treatment, or some other variable(s). Alternative methods for data analysis have been proposed, such as using groups as the unit of analysis rather than individuals (with the danger of losing statistical power due to a small sample size) or using the hierarchical linear model to analyze data at multilevels of relevant units (Bryk & Raudenbush, 1992).

Experimental research is the most powerful mode of inquiry capable of testing and establishing cause–effect relationships between variables. Considering that education is, in fact, intended to bring about change and improvement, experimental research is appealing because the results possess the possibility of prescribing general rules for educational intervention, such as "curriculum X results in better prepared teachers than curriculum Y or Z." Experimental research, however, often has limited applicability in "real life" social situations, including education. Experimental research is an attempt to isolate a few selected variables and to identify the cause–effect relationship between them. Because of its very nature of experimental control and manipulation, experimental research takes subjects out of their natural environments and often fails the test of the validity of findings in real-world situations. In the complexity of social contexts, it is often extremely difficult or even impossible to meet the fundamental assumptions of experimental research, such as random assignment of subjects to different treatments or the researcher's ability to directly control treatment conditions.

Teacher Education Context Experimental and quasi-experimental research have traditionally been dominant modes of inquiry in research on teacher education. Within the behavioral tradition of teacher education, experimental research has been used to train teachers in the use of specific teaching strategies and to examine the impact of training on teachers and teaching practices. Although the dominance of experimental research has declined due to the increased popularity of qualitative modes of inquiry, experimental research still has its place in teacher education research. Although microteaching has been the most common source of experiments (see Kennedy, 1991b, for summary), this inquiry mode has also been used for many other topics in teacher training research (see Joyce, 1988, for summary), such as the effects of behaviorally oriented instructional strategies (e.g., Metcalf, 1992), cognitively oriented instructional strategies (e.g., Hazareezingh & Bielawski, 1991), student teaching (e.g., Hoy & Woolfolk, 1990), induction programs (e.g., Klug & Saltzman, 1991), and research-based intervention for staff development (e.g., Griffin & Barnes, 1986).

There are several obvious limitations with many of the experimental studies in teacher education. Within the dynamic enterprise of a teacher education program, experimental research is usually conducted at a microlevel (i.e., with a set of highly defined and discrete skills, a short duration of treatment, and a very limited and short-term impact on teachers and teaching). When it is impossible to "force" subjects randomly into certain courses or programs, the researchers often settle for treatment groups of subjects through self-selection. Furthermore, some studies involve only the experimental group(s) (called "pre-experimental design" by Campbell & Stanley, 1963) when it is difficult to identify comparable control groups, the associated expenses are too high, the pool of participants is too small, or it is unethical to withhold programs perceived as desirable for all participants.

Experimental research design in teacher education can be strengthened by including random assignment of subjects to the extent possible and by including an adequate number of subjects for statistical power. Experimental research in teacher education can also be strengthened by choosing the right variables, by improving the quality of intervention programs, by expanding the scope of training beyond discrete skills, by providing a more substantial degree and duration of training, by following teacher participants for a longer period of time, and by extending outcome measures beyond specific teacher behaviors.

Example Study The study by Klug and Saltzman (1991) examined the comparative effects and outcomes of two induction programs—a formal induction program incorporating a team approach and an informal buddy system approach—on the teaching performance and attitudes toward teaching of novice teachers. During a 2-year period of the study, 26 novice elementary school teachers in their first or second year of teaching from two rural districts and one small city district participated. The 26 subjects were randomly assigned to two treatment groups during the academic year: 14 engaged in structured induction activities of the team approach, and 12 engaged in loosely structured induction activities of the buddy approach.

The pre-induction and postinduction program teaching performance was assessed through analysis of videotaped lessons using an existing observation instrument with two subscales. The preprogram and postprogram attitudes toward teaching were measured using an existing self-report instrument with 10 subscales. The data were analyzed using a series of analysis of variance techniques (ANOVAs) with mean difference scores between the two groups on each of the subscales of teaching performance and attitudes. The data analyses were conducted with 11 subjects in the team approach group and nine in the buddy system group.

The attitude results showed more positive postratings than preratings on 8 of the 10 subscales for both induction ap-

proaches. The ANOVA results showed more positive attitudes with the team approach on five subscales and more negative attitudes with one subscale. The teaching performance results, however, showed lower postratings on both subscales for both approaches. The ANOVA results showed no significant differences in teaching performance between the two groups.

In addition to quantitative analyses, the study conducted interviews with all novice teachers and their mentors at the end of the academic year. The study also included field notes of committee meetings in the team approach, but not in the buddy system group. Supplementing the quantitative results, the qualitative data provided insights into the reasons for the effectiveness of the team approach compared to the buddy system approach, as well as the elements and characteristics of effective induction models. Inconsistent with the quantitative results, however, the qualitative data indicated positive outcomes of teaching performance in the team approach over the course of the academic year.

Finally, the researchers discussed the quantitative and qualitative results of the study in relation to theoretical frameworks in the literature. The results of more positive attitudes with the team approach were consistent with findings from other studies. The quantitative results of teaching performance in the negative direction were inconsistent with qualitative results and also contradicted previous studies. The researchers provided explanations for these incongruent results. They closed the paper by calling for more research on this topic and by advocating structured induction programs to policymakers at the state and local district levels as well as to university teacher educators.

The study has many strengths. It achieved random assignment of subjects into two treatment groups and examined the effects on both teaching performance and attitudes during a time period of 1 academic year. The training procedures were adequately documented and the instruments seemed to be of high quality and appropriate for the study. The study used triangulation techniques by collecting qualitative data to supplement the primarily quantitative data and by considering multiple prespectives of novice teachers, mentors, and principals. The results were interpreted in relation to theoretical frameworks and previous studies. The study addressed an important topic in the field of teacher education, as the researchers stated, "While the literature provides extensive information outlining the needs of beginning teachers and lessons from exemplary programs, little empirical data exist regarding comparative effects and outcomes of different induction models" (Klug & Saltzman, 1991, p. 241).

The study also has limitations and concerns, some due to the shortcomings of this particular study and others due to the constraints of the context in which the research was conducted. Contextual limitations are discussed first. The absence of hypotheses at the start of the study might reflect the fledgling state of empirical research on this topic, a common phenomenon with many topics in teacher education research. Only a small number of the 26 subjects participated during the 2-year period, although the paper does not state the number of participants initially intended. A recruitment problem seemed to be inherent in this study conducted with a relatively small population in two rural districts and a small city. The fact that the study started with 26 subjects but ended with 20 subjects indicates natural attrition of subjects from training programs spanning an entire academic year. The small number of subjects in the two groups, however, is a serious limitation to statistical power.

Whereas some limitations might be beyond the control of the study, other limitations could have been avoided or minimized. The reported research failed to provide adequate information about the novice teachers and mentor teachers in the study. There was no information about the academic preparation of the novice teachers, the recruitment process, and the reasons for dropping out of the program. Neither was there information about the qualifications and the selection process of mentor teachers. It is unclear how novice teachers and mentors were assigned to each induction program, whether there was a one-on-one match between a novice teacher and a mentor or whether the same mentors were assigned to novice teachers from both programs (there is no mention of random assignment of mentors in the two programs). Although the researchers' control of these aspects in the research might not always be possible, the information would have been helpful in the interpretation and generalization of the results.

The study also suffered from methodological limitations. One of them concerned the experimental condition between the two groups. Whereas the novice teachers and masters in the buddy system were left alone to devise whatever plans deemed necessary, those in the team approach were supported by principals and university representatives. In addition, there was more attention and participation of the researchers in the team approach group (e.g., field notes of committee meetings). Thus, participants' expectations of the research could be a confounding variable. Another confounding variable could be the number of contact hours, which differed vastly between the two groups. Other methodological limitations concerned data collection and analysis procedures. One involved the use of videotaped lessons as samples of overall teaching performance, including the problem of inexpert videotaping procedures. The coding and analysis of teaching performance might be further confounded by a rather large number of observers. There was no information about the "nine trained observers" and the training procedures for data coding and analyses.

Correlational Research

Overview Correlational research is designed to establish relationships between or among variables in nonexperimental, natural settings. This approach may be the only one available in some situations that do not lend themselves to experimentation. In other situations, correlational research may be preferred over experimental research because the intent is to study natural or social phenomena as they naturally occur. There are many varieties of correlational research, ranging from a simple correlation between two variables to multivariate correlations among various combinations of three or more variables. For instance, multiple regression can include multiple variables and can compute how much each of the predictor variables accounts for the variance in the criterion (or outcome) variable. Going even further, path analysis can project potential cause–effect relation-

ships between three or more variables based on correlational information.

Correlational research identifies how variables are related to one another in naturally occurring situations. When experimentation is impossible or inappropriate, correlational information provides, with distinct limitations, some support for possible cause–effect relationships. Correlational information can also be used to design experimental studies for formal hypothesis testing of cause–effect relationships. In both cases, correlational information offers valuable insight that is not available otherwise, reduces effort and expense, increases the likelihood of conducting relevant experimental research, and/or increases the precision or power of experimental outcomes by focusing on significantly related variables.

A major limitation of correlational research is that one cannot introduce a multitude of variables into the analyses without a guiding theoretical framework. When that occurs, the result is mountains of correlation coefficients that are difficult to interpret, sometimes referred to as a "fishing expedition." With multivariate correlation methods, theoretical models may fail to include major variables that are related to the outcome variable. Another limitation is demonstrated when the relationship between two variables exists due to a third variable that is either unknown or unconsidered. There **are** many funny examples of correlations, such as the relationship between shoe size and height (developmental issue) or between water temperature and the death rate at beaches (there are fewer people at the beaches when it is cold). One must always be careful not to imply causality when interpreting correlational research, no matter how tempting it might be.

Teacher Education Context Correlational research can be applicable to some of the major issues in teacher education, as there certainly is no paucity of variables, many of which are beyond our manipulation. Researchers cannot even identify or measure them all, not to mention being able to control their influences. Surprisingly, correlational research in teacher education has been rather sparse. In some instances, particularly using a multiple regression technique, teacher characteristics have been explained, such as the factors contributing to teachers' job satisfaction (Culver, Wolfle, & Cross, 1990) or attrition (Heyns, 1988). Although these issues concern teachers, they are not issues of teacher education per se. Multiple regression has also been used to identify factors residing with teachers or teacher education that significantly contribute to student achievement (see Kennedy, 1991b for summary). These studies have examined such factors as teachers' verbal fluency, college major, education levels, years of teaching experience, number of hours of graduate course work, and recency of last educational experience. Correlational research examining issues of teacher education programs, teachers, or teacher educators is almost nonexistent.

Example Study The study by Smylie (1988) examined the relationships among organizational contexts of schools and classrooms, teachers' psychological states, and changes in teaching practices with individual teachers through staff development. Specifically, the study examined the relationships when the teachers voluntarily participated in a staff development program to improve their teaching practices without the resources, rewards, pressures, or group level orientation associated with school or district programs.

Drawing from several relevant areas of research, the study constructed a path model that considered three groups of antecedents to change in individual teacher practice: (1) teachers' pretraining psychological states, (2) the classroom environment, and (3) the interactive contexts of the school. The model hypothesized direct and/or indirect effects of each of these antecedents on teacher change in either a positive or negative direction.

The study tested the path model in the context of a staff development program offered for 56 elementary and secondary school teachers who voluntarily participated. The program was designed to help the teachers increase the amount of class time engaged in academic work. Throughout six 2 1/2 hour workshops over the course of an academic semester, the teachers completed four phases of staff development, including goal setting, development and implementation of strategies for effective use of class time, guided practice and feedback, and new goals of improvement.

The study collected data through a series of classroom observations, teacher surveys and interviews, and a classroom information questionnaire. As the outcome measure of teacher change, the study used the difference in pretraining and posttraining proportions of time teachers spent in interactive instruction during explanation, discussion and review of assignments, practice drill, and oral reading.

The results of path analysis indicated that individual teacher change is directly influenced by personal teaching efficacy and class size and indirectly influenced by teachers' certainty about practice, the concentration of low-achieving students in the classrooms, and interactions with colleague teachers about instruction. Thus, the results suggest that, in the absence of organizational emphases or pressures for change associated with school or district programs, teacher change resided in individual perceptions of self as influenced by experiences within the classrooms and colleague teachers. Various school-level factors, however, made little difference.

The study has many strengths. It dealt with an important topic for which practice and policy has been implemented with little empirical evidence. Specifically, the study examined an area that had been previously unexplored—the direct and indirect influences of the school context, classroom environment, and teachers' psychological factors on *individual* teacher change through staff development *unassociated* with school or district programs. The study was guided consistently by a theoretical framework from its inception, the construction of a path model, and the interpretation of results. The path analysis results indicated plausible cause–effect relationships between predictor variables and the outcome variable of teacher change. The researcher provided alternative explanations for results that were inconsistent with the path model or existing research. This study, which examined individual teacher change using a sophisticated path model, complements more recent research on individual teacher change from qualitative and descriptive approaches (see "Case Study Research" later in this section).

The most binding limitation of the study, although a unique opportunity for investigation, was the fact that the study was part of an existing staff development program. Because the staff development program concerned teachers' use of instructional time, the outcome variable in the path model was predetermined accordingly. In addition, the outcome variable was limited in terms of the amount of instructional time, but not the quality of the time. The study involved a relatively small sample size, based on voluntary participation. The duration of one academic semester might be insufficient to bring about significant change in teacher practice.

When a study is conducted as part of an existing research or intervention program, this situation provides a unique opportunity that may not otherwise be possible. The situation, however, sets the boundaries for the study. The greater the difference between the purpose and procedures of the program and those of the study, the more limitations with which the study has to contend. In any circumstance, it is important to provide sufficient information about the existing program as the context of the study.

Survey Research

Overview Survey research estimates characteristics or perceptions of a defined population about specific issues based on the information collected in a sample. The purpose of survey research is to generalize from the sample to the population within a certain margin of sampling error based on probability theory. A critical task in survey research involves reducing the error and increasing the accuracy of the inferences made about the population. Sources of error exist throughout the research process, especially in the sampling technique, sample size, return rate, response rate, and instruments. Survey research depends on the assumption that respondents are willing and capable of providing accurate and honest responses. Their tendency to give socially desirable responses is a common concern, especially with controversial or threatening topics, although there are techniques for minimizing this problem.

Survey research is intended to obtain information that will generalize to, and thus define, a relevant and logical population. Accurate description and understanding of what the people, objects, or institutions in specified populations resemble, think, and believe are the first steps to taking action. Survey research answers the questions "What is?" or "What exists?" This information is used as a basis for the design of policy decisions for teacher education at the institutional, local, state, and national levels. The primary benefit of survey research is that it can provide information about a population in a very economical manner.

One must be cautious about using survey research because of its apparent simplicity: "Just write some questions, ask some people (either directly or by mailing them a questionnaire), count their answers, and write a report" (Jaeger, 1988, p. 307). To obtain valid and reliable results in survey research, much expertise is required; otherwise, there may be little truth in the leap of faith from the sample to the population. One must also be cautious about the burden imposed on respondents by a survey questionnaire. The researcher often expects that respondents, usually strangers, are interested enough to provide accurate, complete, and honest responses. Before expecting such cooperation from respondents, the researcher should ensure that there is a high likelihood that the desired cooperation will be forthcoming. When research expertise and care are lacking, survey researchers may ask the wrong questions of the wrong people, select a biased sample, send out a poorly constructed instrument, fail to follow up on nonrespondents, employ an inappropriate data analysis technique, or, finally, make inaccurate inferences about the population.

Teacher Education Context Survey research has been commonly used in research on teacher education. Many of these studies are conducted by teacher education institutions, asking their own graduates to rate the quality or value of teacher education programs or certain program components (e.g., courses, field experiences, student teaching, advising). Teacher education institutions also survey their own students or graduates to assess their knowledge and skills at different points in the teacher education program or in their teaching careers. This information is valuable for the institution to assess how effectively the teacher education program meets the students' needs or provides students with the appropriate experiences. Yet, these survey studies have major limitations. The studies are highly localized, and their relevance is confined to particular institutions. Also, teachers' judgments of themselves or their teacher education programs are often subjective or biased. Furthermore, many of these studies suffer from inattention to the technicalities of survey research.

There have been several national survey studies in teacher education. Research About Teacher Education (RATE), to be described next, is an ongoing study that was initiated in 1985 by the American Association of Colleges for Teacher Education (AACTE). The National Center for Education Statistics (NCES) has been establishing a national data base on a range of education issues, including teacher education, for many years. The National Education Association surveyed its member teachers (K–12 and teachers with special assignments) concerning their views on the effectiveness of 14 different sources of knowledge about teaching (Smylie, 1989). Recently, the Association of Teacher Educators surveyed its members, including K–12 teachers and administrators, college professors and administrators, and others of various educational professions. The survey asked these self-identified teacher educators to rank the most critical issues in teacher education (Buttery, Haberman, & Houston, 1990).

Example Study AACTE established the RATE project to develop an ongoing data collection system capable of gathering accurate and reliable information about teacher education. The project was started in 1985 with the first wave of data collected in the spring of 1986. Subsequently, several more waves of data have been collected and the project is continuing. The example here focuses on the study conducted in the spring of 1986 because it was the first of the series and the most comprehensively documented.

This survey research project solicited data from three sources. First, institutional data were collected by a trained research associate on the campus of each of the institutions that was selected and agreed to participate in the study. To provide a more complete picture of teacher education, two additional instruments were developed to gain the perspectives of professors and students currently engaged in teacher education. In the 1986 data collection, these subjects were professors of secondary education and their students.

The population included 713 institutions that comprised the 1985 membership list of the AACTE, stratified by the highest degree offered within the school, college, or department of education. There was a strong belief that the characteristics that described and defined teacher education would be different between the various strata. Stratum 1 included those member institutions that offered only the baccalaureate degree. Stratum 2 consisted of those institutions that offered baccalaureate degrees, master's degrees, and sixth-year programs. Finally, stratum 3 consisted of those institutions that offered baccalaureate degrees, master's degrees, sixth-year programs, and doctorates. The researchers determined that if 30 institutions were randomly selected from each stratum for a total of 90 in the sample, then any numerical generalization would be considered accurate within ±.2 standard deviations. Finally, they determined that from the 90 institutions in the sample, data should be gathered from 360 professors and 900 students to ensure that inferences made from the data and generalized to the population would be accurate.

Particular attention was paid to the technicalities of survey research. The development of the instruments included the generation of an item pool, the use of a panel of experts, and the field testing of all the instruments. In addition, a research representative handbook was written and the research representatives were trained prior to data collection. Because each campus had provided a research representative, the distribution and retrieval of the instruments went smoothly. Approximately 85% of the sample returned all of the required instruments. The response rate within the questionnaires, assessed on an item-by-item basis, was well over 95%.

The analysis of the data led to many interesting and even a few unusual findings relevant to teacher education. For example, the quality of students enrolled in teacher education programs was very similar to the quality of all students enrolled in America's colleges and universities, including a fair share of the best and the brightest. In addition, teacher education students were quite realistic concerning the rigor of teacher education programs and clearly differentiated the level of rigor from the amount of work involved. In other cases, however, these data tended to confirm the conventional wisdom of the field: professors viewed themselves as underpaid and overworked; women did not achieve the tenure and salary level of their male counterparts; and students, who tended to come from middle class economic backgrounds, preferred to teach in schools very similar to those that they had attended.

The RATE study has many strengths to recommend it. It is an ongoing study that allows for comparisons on a year-by-year basis in specific areas. In addition, it accounted for the technicalities of survey research in the design and implementation. The series of RATE studies has produced accurate and reliable information that previously was not available. These studies can be described as having "high integrity" because the researchers took special care to focus the research questions on topics that were both relevant to and obtainable from a legitimate population using survey questionnaires.

The study also has its share of limitations. Similar to any survey research project, the data are often impossible to verify, and one is compelled to accept the perceptions of the respondents. It is also impossible to query respondents with follow-up questions. Thus, although the consumer of this research may have information that is accurate and reliable, there is surely a level of depth and richness that is missing. Because the project is sponsored by a professional association with a political agenda, it is likely that some consumers view the data with suspicion. Finally, the studies have yet to generate more in-depth information using different modes of inquiry.

Case Study Research

Overview Case study research, although prominent in recent educational research, is not clearly defined as a mode of inquiry. Three approaches to case study research are briefly discussed here. It should be noted that ethnographic or qualitative research (e.g., Hamel et al., 1993; Merriam, 1988) is not regarded as case study research in this chapter.

The first approach is the one advanced by Yin (1993, 1994). The popularity of his book, *Case Study Research: Design and Methods* (1994), is demonstrated by more than 13 additional printings to date. According to Yin (1989), "A case study is an empirical inquiry that: investigates a contemporary phenomenon within its real-life context; when the boundaries between phenomenon and context are not clearly evident; and in which multiple sources of evidence are used" (p. 23). A case is selected by the theoretical or conceptual framework to be examined in the research. As long as a study meets the above conditions, it is considered case study research, regardless of whether primarily quantitative or qualitative research techniques are employed. Yin's approach has been most commonly used in organizational and management studies.

The second approach to case study research comes from the cognitive science tradition. Instead of following any particular research methods, this approach utilizes variations of qualitative methods within cognitive science frameworks. Using systematic guidelines for data collection and analysis, in-depth descriptions about selected aspects of a sample of subjects are recorded. When different patterns occur among subgroups in the sample, these groups are identified and the subjects are classified into relevant groups. Then a typical case of each group is selected to represent common patterns of that group. The case of each group illustrates an underlying theory or construct. This approach is most commonly used for research on human cognition, knowledge, skills, dispositions, and beliefs.

The third approach emerges from the narrative inquiry tradition. Although narrative inquiry has had a long history in the social sciences and the humanities, it is a recent addition to educational research (Carter, 1993; Connelly & Clandinin, 1990). Whereas all other modes of inquiry in this chapter concern systematic ways of knowing, narrative inquiry often involves personal and subjective experiences. Unlike other modes of inquiry, narrative inquiry is not primarily concerned with theory. Narrative inquiry is "the study of the ways humans experience the world" (Connelly & Clandinin, 1990, p. 2), and it

describes stories of life experiences, both personal and social. In other words, narrative inquiry is a story of the history or biography of a person written by that person or others. Narrative inquiry involves both narrative as phenomenon (e.g., stories of experience) and narrative as method (e.g., narrative forms of research reports).

A most significant merit of case study research is that it is intended to be both rich in detail and explicit about contextual factors. Case study research produces rich descriptions about the case, be it an institution, program, person, or phenomenon. The results are based on multiple sources of data. The results also consider complex aspects of the context under investigation. From the perspective of readers, case study research invites the readers to refine the experiences or phenomena in a real-world context.

These strengths of case study research, however, can also be its major limitations. The need for in-depth understanding limits the researcher to dealing with one case or a small number of cases at a time. The case of one or a few has been the topic of debate about generalization and the general usefulness of results, which are discussed later in this section. The need to collect data from multiple sources is a demanding task in a practical sense. Theoretically, the need to consider complex aspects of the context in the sense-making process is very difficult and open to multiple interpretations. Case study research also suffers from its relative infancy in educational research. It needs considerable development and refinement, starting with a clear definition of what it is and what it is not, as well as how it is different from other modes of inquiry. Due to its seeming ease and simplicity, perhaps created by the lack of specific guidelines, some researchers conduct case study research in a haphazard manner. The danger of methodological abuse is much more likely with narrative inquiry than with the other two approaches to case study research.

Teacher Education Context Case study research has recently become a much more prominent mode of inquiry in teacher education research. In fact, case study research seems to be particularly relevant to the study of teacher education and teachers because of the obvious importance of understanding complexities and contextual factors. Considering that teacher education is usually perceived in terms of programs and institutions, Yin's approach is useful in describing and explaining teacher education programs or institutions across a wide range of conceptual, structural, and managerial issues (e.g., Howey & Zimpher, 1989). For a comprehensive understanding of programs or institutions, the research should include multiple sources of data from multiple perspectives of participants within the real-life context.

Researchers in teacher education, in recent times, have begun to investigate the impact of teacher education programs on the changes in teachers' knowledge, skills, and dispositions. Case study research from the cognitive science tradition enables the researcher to monitor carefully and describe changes in teachers across settings and at different points of their teaching careers. Based on conceptual frameworks, the results can provide explanations for the differential impact of programs on changes in teacher knowledge, skills, beliefs, and dispositions (e.g., Feiman-Nemser & Buchmann, 1989; Grossman, 1990; Hollingsworth, 1989).

Finally, narrative inquiry is the most recent development in teacher education research, emerging in the mid- to late-1980s. The act of teaching is intentional and personal. Teaching practices constitute the core knowledge that teachers have of teaching (i.e., for taking action as teachers in classrooms), and teachers' stories provide special access to that knowledge (Carter, 1993). Narrative inquiries have been conducted by teacher educators writing stories of their own teacher education efforts (e.g., Duckworth, 1986) or by researchers writing stories about teachers (e.g., Hollingsworth, Teel, & Minarik, 1992; Kagan, Dennis, Igou, Moore, & Sparks, 1993). There has also been more research jointly conducted and written by researchers and teachers (e.g., Cryns & Johnston, 1993). Furthermore, teachers find their voice as they tell their own personal stories about teaching (e.g., Paley, 1979). Teacher research has been proposed as a means for continuing professional development of teachers because it may promote reflection and analysis of their own teaching and provide the opportunities for communication and collaboration with colleague teachers and researchers (Cochran-Smith & Lytle, 1990).

Example Study The study entitled *Profiles of Preservice Teacher Education: Inquiry into the Nature of Programs* (Howey & Zimpher, 1989) involves case studies of elementary teacher education programs. The purpose of the study was to provide in-depth, yet personal, accounts of how preservice teacher education was conducted in different contexts of higher education institutions. Six research sites in the midwest were selected for two reasons. First, they represented different types of institutions preparing teachers, including research-oriented institutions, comprehensive state universities with a rich history of teacher education, and liberal arts institutions. Second, these institutions had reputations of having distinctive or exemplary programs in elementary teacher education. The researchers examined similarities and differences across these institutions and attempted to identify conditions and practices for effective preservice teacher education programs.

The design for the research was multiple case studies using naturalistic qualitative methods. During brief visits to each site, the researchers collected data from multiple sources and from multiple perspectives. Using guidelines for observations and interviews, the researchers talked with university faculty, preservice students, and university administrators, as well as school-based teachers and district administrators. The researchers also reviewed documents and written materials.

These guidelines for data collection were used as frameworks for developing case studies of the teacher education programs. After describing each program, the researchers presented cross-institutional analysis of common strengths and concerns. Various issues were addressed for cross-program analysis, including teacher education curricula, collaboration of education programs with the arts and sciences curricula, coordination of university courses with field experiences in public schools, and conceptions of teaching and learning by faculty and students. Finally, the researchers generated a list of conditions and practices that appeared to contribute to coherent

or effective teacher preparation programs across these institutions.

The research had many strengths. The study represented systematic initiatives to provide "a more in-depth picture than currently exists of how teachers are prepared in preservice programs" (Howey & Zimpher, 1989, p. 6). Subsequently, many descriptive studies of teacher education programs have been conducted, most notably in a series of studies about a dozen institutions of preservice, first-year, and in-service teacher education programs at the National Center for Research on Teacher Education (1991). This growing, descriptive literature fills a void in teacher education research that has been dominated traditionally by quantitative modes of inquiry.

The selection of cases represents different types of teacher education programs with distinct reputation and acclaim. Triangulation of multiple sources and perspectives, in addition to other techniques for verification, enhanced the validity and knowledge claims in the study. Whereas general guidelines for data collection were applied across the research sites, flexibility in data collection procedures was also evident, addressing the unique aspects of each site. In a similar manner, the results and conclusions highlighted common elements across programs, as well as singular aspects of each program. The study was also explicit about concerns of objectivity and limitations of generalizability.

The study also had limitations. One concern involved interpersonal relations between the researchers and the participants in the study, a common concern in the context of teacher education research (described earlier in this chapter). The research was conducted by two teacher educators concerned with the practices of colleague teacher educators and their programs within the same geographic area. Due to the nature of "known" programs and highly personal accounts, the researchers decided to identify the names of key informants, mostly teacher educators. The descriptions of each program in each chapter were highly complementary, and concerns and cautions were offered across the programs only later in the report.

Interpersonal and political issues posed a credibility question in this research. Less than positive portrayal of a program or less desirable comparison of a program to other programs would subject teacher educators and some university administrators to political hardship. Certainly, the situation would also sever the trust and confidence between the researchers and the research participants who might be friends or colleagues. To what extent could it be possible for the researchers to present a balanced picture of "good news" and "bad news" about a program without causing interpersonal and political trouble (Erickson, 1986)? The researchers were aware of this dilemma: "It remains to the reader to decide if the portrayals we present belie a kind of trustworthiness that could have been garnered by anonymity" (Howey & Zimpher, 1989, p. 13). The problem of interpersonal and political concerns, however, is inherent in teacher education research beyond the simple solution of anonymity.

Another limitation of the research involves resource constraints to conduct research in multiple sites. The researchers stated that although they designed the case studies carefully, "nonetheless we were limited by the brief periods of time we actually spent on each campus" (Howey & Zimpher, 1989, p. 9). Given more frequent visits and longer periods of stay, the study could have delved into the "why" of the practices and conditions, in addition to descriptions of practices and conditions in the report. A careful analysis of relative costs and likely outcomes is inevitable in any research, especially in this study that involved rich descriptions of multiple cases at different geographic locations.

Ethnography

Overview There are many approaches to qualitative research, including interpretative research, naturalistic inquiry, ethnography, sociological qualitative research, connoisseurship/criticism, symbolic interactionism, semiotics, cognitive anthropology, and ecological psychology (Erickson, 1986; Fetterman, 1988). These approaches are associated with different traditions of qualitative research from the disciplines of anthropology, sociology, and psychology (Atkinson, Delamont, & Hammersley, 1988; Buchmann & Floden, 1989; Jacob, 1987, 1988, 1989; Lincoln, 1989). It should be noted that there are substantial differences among qualitative research approaches and dangers in haphazardly mixing and matching elements of different approaches (Fetterman, 1988; Jacob, 1988). Because ethnography is regarded as the prototype of the qualitative research paradigm and because it has been the most dominant among the qualitative research approaches in education, it is selected to represent a distinct mode of inquiry in this chapter.

Ethnography is commmonly called fieldwork research in anthropology. Ethnography is an inquiry into the "way of life" or the culture of some identifiable group of people. As both a process and product of inquiry, ethnography portrays the concepts, beliefs, customs, norms, and rules of a socially interacting group of people in cultural contexts. To learn about the culture of a group, an ethnographer lives with the group for an extensive period of time. Understanding emerges as the ethnographer, both methodically and insightfully, makes sense of the culture through observing people and events, participating in daily activities, listening and talking with others, and reading documents and records. In this sense, the ethnographer is the key instrument of research. The process of sense-making requires an "objective" understanding of the culture as an object of inquiry through "subjective" experiences and insights as a member of the group. The product of ethnography involves not only the descriptions of people and events in the group but also the construction of a theory(ies) to explain ways of life in that group.

A primary strength of ethnography is the rich descriptions about social and cultural meanings from the insider's point of view. Unlike other research methods that are theory testing or confirming, ethnography is theory building that is inductively derived and grounded on the data about the culture or phenomenon (Glaser & Strauss, 1967; Strauss & Corbin, 1990). The variety of methods used in data collection, multiple sources of information, and the different perspectives of participants support the credibility of research findings (called triangulation). Credibility is also derived from the fact that the ethnographer portrays the culture as it naturally exists after a long period of interaction with the people in the group.

The unique strengths of ethnography are also its limitations. Practical problems of time, resources, and effort associated with the requirement for a long-term stay in research setting occur. Once in the setting, the ethnographer's task is to understand the culture by "making the familiar strange" or "making the strange familiar." There are both liabilities and benefits from being either a stranger (outsider) or a natural participant (insider). The ethnographer's own bias, beliefs, and expectations have to be constantly tested and verified against the data as they emerge. Furthermore, in coming to understand the culture from the insider's viewpoint, the ethnographer has to walk a fine line between maintaining distance and perspective (objectivity) and developing familiarity and empathy (subjectivity). Ethnographers end up with poorly conducted research if they either remain too aloof or "go native."

Teacher Education Context Considering that teacher education is a complex enterprise, ethnography can be a valuable tool in describing and understanding issues, groups, and participants in the field. Yet, the context of teacher education poses inherent challenges to ethnographic research. One challenge concerns familiarity; virtually everyone who grew up in the United States has had the long-term experience of being a student and having extensive exposure to teaching and teachers. The ethnographer has to strive to make the familiar strange or, in some cases, simply to not get bored. Another challenge concerns the prescriptive and normative nature of teacher education. The ethnographer, who understands the basic ethnographic premises of describing and understanding cultural meaning, may still find it difficult not to engage in evaluation or value judgment. The ethnographer's personal experiences and beliefs often will make it difficult to remain objective and analytical.

Ethnographic studies are sparse in teacher education. Even the small body of ethnographic studies that exist are not "doing ethnography," but "borrowing ethnographic techniques" in descriptive studies (Wolcott, 1988, p. 201). This situation is an interesting contrast to the popularity of ethnography in research on teaching and schooling. Whereas ethnographic research is rare in teacher education, other types of descriptive studies (mostly case study research) have recently become dominant in the literature of the field. It is not clear why ethnography has been slow to enter the field of teacher education research. Perhaps teacher education does not lend itself to this mode of inquiry, or perhaps teacher education is too familiar to render it for ethnographic research.

Example Study Ethnographic studies of teacher education are rare. The study, *The Lives of Teacher Educators* (Ducharme, 1993), is not what these authors (and perhaps the researcher himself) would consider ethnographic research in the true sense described in this chapter. Despite this concern, these authors chose this study as an example of ethnography because of the study's relevance and significance to the teacher education profession and because there is considerable overlap of research approaches and techniques with the traditional ethnographic research approach.

The purpose of the study was to understand the lives of teacher educators (i.e., their experiences, perceptions, beliefs, and views of the profession). The study attempted to develop a rich portrayal of these issues from the point of view of the people doing the work of teacher education. The researcher believed that a better understanding of teacher educators' roles and responsibilities is critical to the welfare and growth of teacher preparation programs in the nation's colleges and universities.

Based on the definition of a teacher educator presented in the study, the researcher selected 34 teacher educators across a range of 11 institutions of higher education. Despite this rather small sample size, he attempted to select a representative sample of teacher educators, approximating the population demographic data in terms of gender and professorial ranks. The researcher conducted in-depth interviews with each of the participants using an interview protocol developed by the researcher for this study.

The study presented the lives of teacher educators with regard to the following issues: reasons for teaching in elementary or secondary schools, reasons for leaving these lower schools and moving to higher education, influences of lower school teaching on university work, issues and problems of scholarly research and publication, mentoring and collaborating, and satisfaction and frustrations in the profession. For each of these issues, common patterns among the participants were identified and specific vignettes were provided as illustrations of the patterns. In addition, prominent patterns among subgroups of the sample were noted, such as the different perceptions and expectations of scholarly research and publication between older and younger faculty members, different experiences of mentoring and collaborating between males and females, and gender differences in job demands and responsibilities.

Interpretive commentaries by the researcher from the perspective of a fellow teacher educator complemented the descriptions of teacher educators' lives in their own words. References to the teacher education literature supplemented the descriptions and the personal commentaries. The researcher indicated how the results in the study were consistent or discrepant with his personal experience and knowledge as a teacher educator and/or the teacher education literature, and he offered explanations when there were discrepancies.

The researcher started the study with a rather gloomy, negative picture of teacher education faculty in higher education institutions based on his own research and the teacher education literature. However, he concluded the study with a positive picture of teacher educators with decency, integrity, commitment, and excitement in their professional lives. Ducharme stated, "It was pleasant to be proven wrong in at least the instances of the faculty in this study" (1993, p. 109).

The study has many merits. The research provides rich and detailed descriptions and insights into the lives of teacher educators. The study offers an opportunity for teacher educators to reflect on and analyze their own lives as teacher educators. For those outside the teacher education community, the study depicts the lives, satisfaction, and frustrations of teacher educators. The book can, therefore, stimulate conversation among teacher educators and help other educators and the general public to better understand teacher education.

The researcher demonstrated what an ethnographer should do with the concept of the researcher as the key instrument. In his effort to make sense of the culture of the teacher education profession, the researcher used his own personal experience as a faculty member and department chair, his own research-based knowledge, and the teacher education literature in general. The researcher constantly tested his biases, beliefs, and expectations against the data. He was open to notice discrepant events and disconfirming evidence and willing to change some of his fundamental beliefs and knowledge as warranted by the data in the study. Furthermore, the researcher used his insider's knowledge to help readers understand the lives of teacher educators. At the same time, he was acutely aware of the effect that his own experiences might have on his analyses and meaning making. He also cautioned that his status as an active, well-known teacher educator might have influenced the responses and reactions of the teacher educators in the study. In summarizing the findings of the study that were largely inconsistent with his personal knowledge and the literature, the researcher was cautious about the generalizability based on the sample characteristics in the study.

The study is not without limitations and concerns. A serious concern, as the researcher admitted, involved the fact that the study relied solely on the words of the participants but employed no mechanism to verify the validity of these words. The problem was exacerbated by the interpersonal relations between the participants and the researcher because, except for a few cases, some sort of personal connection or acquaintance existed. This problem, however, could have been lessened through triangulation of information from additional sources, such as the review of curriculum vitae (e.g., research productivity), course syllabi (e.g., teaching load and course activities), and official documents about the participants at their universities or departments. Certainly, the addition of these information sources would require some expenses and efforts on the part of the researcher. Because such costs did not seem prohibitive, the likely benefits could have outweighed the costs.

The book as a report fails to provide sufficient information about research methods, with little description about the development of the interview protocol, data analysis procedures, and organization of findings in the report. Although embedded in the text at various points, the researcher could have been more explicit about the problems as well as the strengths of being an insider, such as what he did to make the familiar strange, to be critical of his own personal knowledge and experience, to keep distance from the participants in the study, to maintain the balance between objectivity and subjectivity, and to avoid evaluation and value judgment. It is noted that although the researcher did not discuss these issues explicitly, he, to his credit, practiced some of them throughout the research process.

Finally, the study is rich in descriptions but short on underlying theories. The power of qualitative research is to explain why people act and believe the way they do, in addition to describing what they say or do. The study fails to build a theory grounded on the data in the study. Several themes seemed to emerge, such as gender inequality, differential demands and expectations of teaching versus research between old and new faculty members, and differences between research-oriented and teaching-oriented institutions. None of these themes, however, were fully developed as theoretical frameworks to explain the results. In all fairness, the study seems to be intended for general readership interested in knowing and learning about teacher education rather than for those concerned about technical qualities of inquiry or theoretical underpinnings in the education research community.

Historical Research

Overview The purpose of historical research is to understand the present by learning about the past. Historical research is based on the premise that the past is the origin of the present. Some historical research is directed toward knowing about the past for its own sake, whereas other research attempts, to a certain extent, to predict the future based on the knowledge of the past. The conduct of historical research is based solely on historical sources.

Unlike other modes of inquiry that are closely associated with certain disciplines and have distinct research techniques, historical research is eclectic in terms of both theoretical frameworks and research methods from other disciplines. In other words, diverse theories and research techniques are used in the service of the primary purpose of knowing about and making sense of the past in order to better understand the present. Traditionally, historical research is considered part of the qualitative research tradition with its emphasis on interpretation and "meaning making" of historical data. For the past 2 decades, the quantitative research tradition has charted a new approach to historical research. Whereas qualitatively oriented historical research has focused on historical events from a biographical perspective, quantitatively oriented research has studied various educational issues (e.g., school attendance, years of schooling, school expenditures) with a more class inclusive approach. The advent of quantitatively oriented historical research has allowed educational historians to explore new questions and to set new standards of evidence and argument (Kaestle, 1988).

Historical research also is eclectic in the choice of theories from diverse disciplines, including sociology, psychology, political science, anthropology, philosophy, and linguistics. Educational historians differ in terms of how much importance they assign to theories; some accept general theoretical frameworks, others are eclectic in using theories incidentally and selectively, and still others resist mixing theories with data. Regardless of one's position, the use of theories is an important issue in historical research, as much as the issue of research techniques. Although multiple perspectives may be valuable, unbridled eclecticism poses danger.

The single most significant strength of historical research lies in its ability to dig into the past and link the past to the present and, to some extent, to the future. In its attempt to see the patterns or meanings of historical sources, historical research is eclectic in the choice of research methods and/or theoretical frameworks. The fact that there is no single method or discipline is unique in historical research.

A key limitation of historical research involves its sole data source—historical sources. So much of historical research depends on the availability of historical sources. In a sense, sources dictate research questions in historical research, and a breakthrough occurs at the discovery of new sources of evidence. Even when historical sources are available, historians face other problems. One problem concerns whether a historical source is genuine or credible, whether the information in the source is accurate, and what individual or institutional biases might have affected the results. Another problem concerns whether the information is complete in terms of both cross-sectional samples and longitudinal periods.

Historical research has other limitations (Kaestle, 1988). Two common pitfalls associated with the problem of defining key terms involve vagueness and presentism. Some terms are too vague to have any analytical value; they need more precision in meaning. Presentism indicates the assumption or bias that terms have their current meanings in the past, and often the current terms did not exist or meant something else at the time in the past. Another limitation of historical research concerns the confusion of causality and correlation. Because certain historical events preceded subsequent events, there is always temptation to the argument of causality. Temporal precedence between variables (using statistical terms) is only one condition for causality; other conditions should be met. In addition to these limitations, historical research is also liable to many of the limitations of quantitative or qualitative research methods depending on the research method used in a particular study.

Teacher Education Context The histories of teaching, teachers, and teacher education have been inseparable (Warren, 1985). Although historical research on teacher education per se is not very active, historical research on issues of teaching and teachers as they relate to teacher education is active. After all, teacher education has existed for centuries, and teacher educators can learn a great deal from the mistakes and accomplishments of the past. This knowledge can help teacher educators make more informed decisions and project potential concerns and issues of teacher education (Urban, 1990; Warren, 1985). However, a caution always exists in drawing implications for the present from the past because of differences in the larger social, economic, and political contexts influencing teacher education.

Many issues have been topics of historical research in teacher education. Some studies examine the history of teaching and teachers (e.g., teacher contracts, teacher workplaces) as they relate to teacher education (Warren, 1989); others concern the history of teacher education curricula, programs, or institutions (Clifford & Guthrie, 1988; Herbst, 1989; Kliebard, 1987); and still others address specifically the history of teacher education reform against the backdrop of current teacher education reform (Johnson, 1987; Ziechner & Liston, 1990). Some studies are critical of the history of teacher education, whereas others come to its defense. There is much that teacher educators can learn from knowledge of the past.

Example Study *Ed School: A Brief for Professional Education* (Clifford & Guthrie, 1988) is not a book about the history of teacher education, but rather a book about the history of those institutions that house teacher education. The book is presented in a quasi-chronological framework, introduced by a chapter that defines the profession, attempts to place it in a cultural context, and explains many of the factors that have an impact on the profession (e.g., supply and demand, teacher salaries, teacher unions). The second section of the book explores the "formative years" of schools of education lasting from 1900 to about 1940. Using numerous examples, Clifford and Guthrie trace the birth and demise of normal schools and describe the development of schools of education in research universities. The authors then trace the proliferation of schools of education across America's colleges and universities, concluding that just prior to World War II education had, in fact, been "professionalized."

In the section that the authors title "Years of Maturity" (1955–1985), they describe the continued growth of schools of education across the university landscape, dealing with the various innovations and reforms that have occurred. They also include descriptions of the structural barriers to reform in teacher education, and in many ways, although not always explicitly, the authors explain why it is difficult for teacher education to survive and prosper in a university setting.

The authors continue to tell their story with a series of mini case studies about Peabody, Duke (which no longer has a school of education), the University of Michigan, Stanford, Teachers College–Columbia University, and The University of Chicago. It becomes abundantly clear that the foundation of schools and colleges of education in the United States came from a very limited number of institutions.

Toward the end of the book, the authors describe a comparative study of institutional cultures, comparing the School of Education at the University of California–Los Angeles (UCLA) with the School of Education at the University of California—Berkeley. The authors describe very different institutional cultures that allowed the programs at UCLA to grow and prosper while the programs at Berkeley faltered, went through very difficult periods, and nearly did not survive at one point. The authors were quick to draw meaning from their work and make that meaning very clear to the reader.

The book does not conclude with a prediction of the future. Rather, the authors attempted a variation on that theme, offering advice that they believe will strengthen schools of education in the future. It is at this point that critics of the book become more active, suggesting that although the authors are excellent educational historians, they are more limited in their ability to offer helpful advice.

Although the authors detail many of the real problems facing schools of education, such as a condition of intellectual ambivalence, limited technology, a feminized profession, a weak mission, and dysfunctional coping strategies, their advice does not appear to be particularly innovative or even necessarily reactive to the environment and problems they so eloquently describe.

Regardless of its shortcomings, *Ed School* is a good example of historical research in education. Although it does not focus on teacher education, the subject cannot be separated from the target of this investigation. It is a book of crucial importance to teacher educators because it tells a very important story about the institutional and organizational structures that are necessary for teacher education to exist in a college or university setting. The book is well conceptualized and extremely well documented. It is also very readable, written in an almost storylike

manner. It avoids the dull overproliferation of details that characterize so many historical works. The authors tend to "cut to the chase" and provide the meaning of their work as they see it rather than use tedious examples of the work they saw. This approach is justified based on the thorough documentation of the book, an obvious basic requisite for historical research.

Philosophical Research

Overview Unlike other modes of inquiry, it is difficult to explicate the mode(s) of philosophical inquiry because inquiry in this area does not adhere to the same "methods" and procedures. Philosophical inquiry is not a topic in most readings or textbooks on educational research. Written materials on how to conduct philosophical inquiry are rare. Whereas other modes of inquiry employ "data" in the development or testing theories, philosophical inquiry relies on logic. Because of its independence from the data in a research setting, philosophical research is largely free from the constraints residing in the research context.

Philosophical inquiry is not limited to philosophers; instead, it is a component of any research activity. Through every step of the research process, researchers should have a resonable level of competence in the analysis of concepts, clarity of language, and logic of arguments. Researchers address particular issues or problems based on their philosophical beliefs and convictions. They also employ particular research methods consistent with their beliefs in a particular research paradigm(s). These are matters of philosophical concern with any researcher.

There are two major approaches to philosophical inquiry. The first is inquiry concerned with normative questions and problems in education. Topics include ethics or issues of right and wrong (e.g., Is it right to provide sex education in schools?), values (e.g., Among a range of bilingual/ESOL programs, which is the most beneficial for students with limited English proficiency?), goals and aims (e.g., What is the goal of vocational education?), and normative theories about the ideal form of education (e.g., What is the best way to attain both excellence and equality of education for all students?).

The other approach is inquiry concerned with the analysis of concepts (Scriven, 1988). Essentially as a methodology, philosophy attempts to define and analyze abstract concepts and investigate different interpretations of the concepts. Dealing with ordinary language for a complex question, the researcher attempts to establish linguistic accuracy and conceptual clarity. For instance, a researcher may ask, "What is multicultural education?" The researcher defines the concept and also examines alternative interpretations. The researcher may even claim among many alternatives an interpretation that is deemed most appropriate. Philosophy also examines the logic and assumptions in an argument, policy, or practice. For example, a researcher may ask, "Is the current practice of multicultural education adequate?" The researcher tries to find logical flaws in current practice, defines the meaning of "adequacy," and eventually presents a new proposal for practice and policy.

Beyond the province of philosophers, all researchers can make use of analytic philosophy. As discussed earlier in this chapter, language and terminology are serious problems in educational research. Analytic philosophy reminds researchers of the importance of linguistic accuracy and logical clarity. In this sense, educational researchers can benefit from some training in philosophy.

Teacher Education Context Philosophical inquiry in teacher education is common compared to most other areas of education. Although pure philosophical inquiry is rare, most philosophical inquiry in teacher education has been conducted by nonphilosophers who have addressed philosophical questions and concerns. The substantial body of literature on philosophical inquiry by philosophers and nonphilosophers on a variety of topics reflects the fact that many of the issues in teacher education are value laden, controversial, and directly related to matters of practice and policy.

Floden and Buchmann, in the first edition of *Handbook of Research on Teacher Education* (1990), conducted a thorough review of philosophical research in teacher education in their chapter, "Philosophical Inquiry in Teacher Education." After a brief description about philosophical inquiry in general, they indentified four categories of philosophical research in teacher education and provided examples of philosophical works of each category.

The first category of philosophical research in teacher education involves inquiry that is exclusively philosophical, relying on linguistic and conceptual analysis. Floden and Buchmann described the works by John Wilson (1975), Israel Scheffler (1968), and Arthur Combs (1965, 1972), all of whom attempted to delineate the concept of teacher education. Their approaches, however, differed—Wilson conducted linguistic analysis, Scheffler examined implicit assumptions and found logical flaws in an argument, and Combs developed a conceptual argument as a basis of his recommendation for teacher education.

The second category involves philosophical arguments that are integrated with empirical claims. The strengths and limitations of the work depend on both the philosophical component and the empirical evidence. The examples provided by Floden and Buchmann contrast Gage's (1978, 1985) claim for teaching methods in teacher preparation with Buchmann's claim for subject matter knowledge. In developing their arguments, both authors combined analysis of meaning and logic with empirical educational research.

The third category involves recommendations for action in teacher education by reminding readers of their background knowledge, by appealing to shared ideas and values, and by referring to texts or insights of great educators (e.g., Dewey). Floden and Buchmann described the works by Maxine Greene (1981) and Kenneth Zeichner (1981/1982), who tried to convince readers by evoking shared ideas and common background knowledge rather than developing explicit arguments or logic.

Finally, some philosophical works in teacher education establish distinctions and category systems by separating different components or elements of a concept. Examples include Lee Shulman's (1986) work on multiple components of teacher knowledge and John Dewey's two ways of looking at classroom experience as part of teacher preparation.

Example Study Readers are advised to look at the examples provided in the Floden and Buchmann chapter. With each of these examples, they described what it was that the author tried to accomplish and how he or she carried out philosophical inquiry. At the end of each example, Floden and Buchmann provided assessments in terms of strengths and weaknesses. Readers will gain insights into various approaches to engaging in philosophical inquiry and different ways to judge the quality.

Common Issues in Modes of Inquiry

This section describes each of the modes of inquiry commonly used in research on teacher education. However different the purposes and methods of inquiry, all modes of inquiry share certain issues. Some issues concern the internal quality of research, including validity, reliability, and generalizability. Others concern the significance of the research for practice and policy making. The explication and examination of these issues in teacher education research are discussed next.

Internal Quality of Research The issues of validity, reliability, and generalizability are major topics of debate in the education research community. With the advent of various modes of qualitative research, the debate has become more complicated because of differences in language as well as philosophical/theoretical orientations. Some qualitative researchers use different terms (Goetz & LeCompte, 1984; Lincoln & Guba, 1985), whereas others regard these terms and related issues as irrelevant in qualitative research (see the debate in Eisner & Peshkin, 1990). Recently, some qualitative researchers have attempted to develop a common vocabulary that can be understood by researchers from various perspectives and yet convey differences among the perspectives (e.g., generalizability in Firestone, 1993; reliability and validity in Kirk & Miller, 1986; validity in Maxwell, 1992). The authors, without bias in favor of the quantitative research perspective, use the terms *validity, reliability,* and *generalizability* in concert with the traditional convention of the education research community.

Validity, reliability, and generalizability determine the quality of inquiry and the credibility of knowledge claims. Often, however, these three aspects of research are at odds with one another. Faced with such conflicts, each mode of inquiry tries to maximize its unique strengths while compromising with weaknesses in other aspects.

Although every mode of inquiry is concerned with various types of validity, each mode has its primary focus. For instance, experimental research is basically concerned with internal validity of causality between a treatment variable(s) and an outcome variable(s). Case study research is mainly concerned with construct validity—whether a case is indeed a case of a theoretical/conceptual construct of interest in a study (Yin, 1993, 1994). Ethnography, however, is concerned with different issues of validity—whether the descriptions about people and events are accurate, whether the ethnographer's interpretation or meaning making is valid against the evidence in the field, and whether a grounded theory adequately explains the phenomenon or culture in the field (Kirk & Miller, 1986; Maxwell, 1992).

Reliability involves consistency of results over settings or times of measurement. To obtain consistent results, it is necessary to develop clear definitions of key terms and specific procedures to follow for data collection and analysis. The modes of inquiry from the quantitative perspective, including experimental, correlational, survey, case study research to a large extent, and quantitatively oriented historical research, are all concerned with reliability of instruments and results.

Reliability has not been an issue of great concern from the qualitative perspective, including ethnography, qualitatively oriented historical research, and philosophical research. It would seem almost contradictory to specify procedures for data collection and analysis when so much of the nature of study depends on personal experiences of researchers and subjective meaning making of the phenomenon as the study progresses. For this reason, many qualitative researchers have regarded the reliability issue as irrelevant. Others, however, have expressed concerns over the need to establish some guidelines for reliability in qualitative research. Kirk and Miller (1986) expressed this concern, "Qualitative researchers can no longer afford to beg the issue of reliability. While the forte of field research will always lie in its capability to sort out the validity of propositions, its results will (reasonably) go ignored minus attention to reliability" (p. 72).

Finally, generalizability is an issue that all modes of inquiry are consistently concerned about—to what extent are the study findings applicable to other people or settings? Survey research is the most explicit about the generalizability issue, with its primary emphasis on random selection or sampling from the population to the sample in a study. Using probability theory, inferences about certain characteristics in the population can be drawn from the sample data with a certain level of confidence (or with a certain margin of error). This process is called statistical generalization.

Experimental research can seldom afford to select subjects randomly from the population because the process is too costly or simply not feasible. Although weak with statistical generalization, experimental research is mainly concerned with generalizing to a theory. This is called analytic generalization, the purpose of which is to provide evidence that supports or refutes the theory (Firestone, 1993). Like experimental research, case study research also is concerned with analytic generalizability. In case study research, a case is selected precisely to generalize a set of results to a broader theory (Yin, 1989, 1993).

Ethnography traditionally has been criticized for its relative inability to generalize from its findings. After all, it is assumed that each culture is unique with its own ways of living. Ethnography deals with the generalizability issue in terms of case-to-case transfer (Firestone, 1993). The ethnographer provides readers with rich and detailed descriptions about a broad range of background features, the processes of inquiry, and various aspects of outcomes. Then the transfer of findings from the case to other situations is done by the readers as they assess the extent of match between the situation under study and their own. For those studies specifically aiming to develop a grounded theory, the theory or a general theme, rather than specific results, can be generalizable to other situations.

Historical research has its own concerns with generalizability. As with survey research, historians usually study small samples of people, settings, events, or objects. These samples are determined by available records that may not be at all representative of the population. Working with small samples, historians sometimes collapse data from distinct categories into aggregated categories, with the result of losing generalizability to the distinct subgroups in the population. Qualitatively oriented historians work with cases of individuals or institutions. Interpretations of historical evidence in these cases share similar concerns of generalizability with ethnography.

External Quality of Research Poorly conducted research has little value for anything because one cannot trust the knowledge claims. High quality research, however, does not necessarily mean that the findings have practical value. Research findings have different relevance or significance to practitioners and to policymakers, respectively. These issues are now briefly discussed.

Experimental research, by its very nature, often has limited practical relevance. Because experimental research examines only a few variables at a time, these variables are taken away from the larger context. Experimental research is also faced with the problem of maintaining balance between rigorous scientific control (internal validity) and sufficient realism of natural environments (ecological validity). In general, experimental research results have suffered from poor communication with laypeople, including practitioners and policymakers who have little technical knowledge of experimental research and statistics. Often, statistically significant results are erroneously believed to possess practical or educational significance.

Experimental research, however, can have powerful value to practitioners and policymakers. When results from replication studies across people and across settings converge, the knowledge claims gain more credibility. These knowledge claims are often stated in simple, behavioristic, and prescriptive statements, such that a certain intervention or treatment results in improved outcomes. These rules or guidelines for action can be heuristically understood by practitioners and policymakers and can be used to guide practice and policy making across a range of settings. Regardless, a danger exists when experimental results are used uncritically or excessively.

Unlike experimental research, case study research examines a case as it naturally exists, considers various aspects of the case in a given context, and provides rich and detailed descriptions of the case. Narrative inquiry of teaching, teachers, and teacher education has a special value for practitioners because it includes stories of their own histories and biographies. In a different sense, ethnography also has a particular value in that the culture or phenomenon under study is portrayed with fresh eyes by an outsider who has learned the insider's ways of living. In addition to easy reading, reports of case study research and ethnography provide practitioners and policymakers with opportunities to reflect on and to analyze their own situations.

Both case study research and ethnography, however, suffer from the fact that there is so much variation from the case under study to other situations, and that practitioners often have difficulty determining the relevance of the research findings to their own situations. Case study research and ethnography can be problematic in the hands of policymakers. On the one hand, faced with the need to devise general rules or guidelines that apply across situations, they may ignore the results on the ground of their complexity and singularity in specific situations.

On the other hand, policymakers may be overly influenced by particular cases or anecdotes that ring true to them rather than more rigorous research findings.

Other modes of inquiry have their own strengths and weaknesses in regards to practical relevance. Survey research has special value for policymakers because the findings present overall, basic information about the population as a basis for policy decisions. However, information for various subgroups of the population or for certain issues is often missing. Survey research usually has little practical value to practitioners in specific situations because the information lacks details about local settings. Historical and philosophical research both have unique value for helping practitioners and policymakers understand the historical or philosophical underpinnings of contemporary issues. Both, however, suffer from lack of direct, immediate, and pragmatic relevance to practitioners or policymakers.

What is the significance of *teacher education research* to practice and policy making? As discussed earlier, most teacher education research is applied research concerned with intervention and improvement of practice and performance. Unfortunately, teacher education research has often benefited only those practitioners who have been involved in or informed of particular studies. Even with these practitioners, teacher change or teacher learning is demanding, diffuse, and complex. Although current interest in teacher research or teacher collaboration may alleviate this problem, the impact seems to be limited to a small circle of practitioners.

The relationship between research and policy making is equally complicated because policy decisions are often more driven by politics than by research. This is also a case where the perceived confusion in teacher education research complicates the situation, making it more likely that policymakers can be influenced by a single or small number of studies that make a point, while ignoring the context that provides for more accurate assessments.

CONCLUSION

This chapter addresses various issues of research on teacher education. The chapter starts with a brief introduction to methodological and substantive issues in teacher education research. It continues with a discussion of contextual influences on teacher education research and research integrity, which is, to a large extent, a function of the context. The bulk of the chapter is devoted to descriptions about commonly used modes of inquiry in teacher education research and contextual issues for each mode of inquiry. In this final section, the authors draw conclusions and offer suggestions for modes of inquiry in future research on teacher education.

Recent Developments in Research Methods and Issues

There are some noticeable developments in teacher education research. Methodologically, teacher education research has recently witnessed a dramatic, although not necessarily healthy, shift to qualitative and narrative modes of inquiry. Despite their predominance, a number of issues are unclear about these modes of inquiry in educational research generally and teacher education research in particular. Case study research is a case in point. As discussed earlier, case study research is not clearly defined, and different conceptions of case study research are employed by researchers with different conceptual and methodological orientations. It is necessary to clarify the confusion, such as what case study research is, what types or approaches to case study research exist, how one approach is different from another, and which approach is most appropriate for certain research topics. Qualitative researchers, in this instance, may learn a lesson from the quantitative traditions, which have clear distinctions among different modes of inquiry (experimental vs. quasi-experimental vs. correlational research) and the specifics of research techniques within each mode of inquiry (e.g., multiple regression, path analysis, and factor analysis within correlational research). Although some distinctions exist among qualitative research traditions, the distinctions are not yet clearly evident (Atkinson et al., 1988; Buchmann & Floden, 1989; Jacob, 1987, 1988, 1989; Lincoln, 1989).

Narrative inquiry is the most recent and unique development in teacher education research. Narrative inquiry raises an intriguing set of questions and issues. In a broad sense, narrative inquiry is a mode of inquiry. In a narrow sense, it is unclear whether narrative inquiry is a research activity. Narrative inquiry is the only mode of inquiry that does not carry the word "research." Fundamental issues of research, including validity, reliability, generalizability, knowledge claims, and evidence, are problematic with narrative inquiry (Carter, 1993; Connelly & Clandinin, 1990). The methodological development of narrative inquiry, in the final analysis, will determine the magnitude of its contribution to research on teacher education.

Narrative inquiry addresses issues of power and voice. Whereas research has existed in academic circles dealing with abstract theories and constructs, narrative inquiry originates from the world of practice and everyday experiences. Especially when narrative inquiries are written by teachers, the teachers find their voice as they tell their own stories of personal histories and biographies. Narrative inquiry has pragmatic and ideological merits. It recognizes the wisdom and knowledge of teachers in practice. Teachers' stories told to researchers for research purposes can inform the researchers and expand a knowledge base. Considering that teacher education is about teachers and teaching, researchers have much to learn from teachers about teaching. Teachers' stories told to other teachers, although thus far largely neglected, can educate other teachers and build a practical knowledge base. Furthermore, narratives of teaching and teachers can communicate easily with the public (Barone, 1992). Despite methodological problems and uncertainties, one cannot dispute the utility of narrative inquiry in teacher education.

The new developments in modes of inquiry have accompanied recent substantive issues in teacher education research. One such issue involves research on learning to teach or teacher learning, which examines how teacher education programs and activities relate with changes in teachers' knowledge, skills, and dispositions (Carter, 1990; Kennedy, 1991a; Richardson, 1990). This research interest seems to be supported by other developments in educational research. First, educational research has shifted its focus from product to process. Second, teacher education recognizes the need to examine interactive relationships among various forms of teacher education and the differential impact that these forms have on individuals. Finally, research on learning to teach is facilitated by qualitative and narrative modes of inquiry, which enable researchers or teachers to produce rich, detailed descriptions of how changes occur over time.

Another substantive issue involves the call for comprehensive investigation of teacher education, addressing the entire process of program design, implementation, and impact within the larger context (National Center for Research on Teacher Education, 1988; Yarger & Smith, 1990). Most teacher education research, in contrast, has examined segments of teacher education separately as program studies, implementation studies, or impact studies without consideration of contextual influences. To conduct comprehensive investigation of teacher education, multiple modes of inquiry from various theoretical perspectives need to be considered. This is related to the issue of interdisciplinary approaches to teacher education research to be discussed later.

Research, Theory, Practice, and Policy Making

Research builds a knowledge base grounded in theories to better understand and to improve practice and to assist with policy making. Teacher education research has its unique problems with the relationship between theory and research. Educational research of both quantitative and qualitative traditions has been charged with overemphasis on gathering empirical data about the phenomenon of interest and underemphasis on explicating theoretical and conceptual underpinnings (Martin & Sugarman, 1993). This problem is inherent in applied research in which the primary interest involves finding out what works and how it works rather than providing explanations for why it works. For teacher education research to grow into a mature field of study, theory development should accompany empirical and methodological advancements.

The relationships between research and practice also have been problematic in teacher education. The practical value of research in teacher education is ambiguous. One example is the debate concerning the extent to which research on teacher thinking can contribute to teacher preparation (Clark, 1988; Floden & Klinzing, 1990; Lampert & Clark, 1990). Whereas some researchers are more conservative and cautious about the applicability of research to practice, other are more optimistic. As discussed earlier, there are efforts to converge basic and applied research in real-world settings. In addition, narrative inquiry and teacher research will contribute to the effort to narrow the gap between research and practice. It remains to be seen whether these efforts will bear fruit.

The relationships between research and policy making further complicate teacher education research. Policymakers take research findings into consideration as a source of information, whereas more practical concerns of politics, finance, and public opinion dominate the decisions. Communicating research findings with policymakers presents a dilemma. If the research findings are presented in a manner too abstract and full of jargon, the findings will never be understood and thus will be disregarded. Yet, if the findings are presented as heuristically sensible and understandable, research findings may be perceived as no better than common sense. A more fundamental problem involves having policymakers seek and listen to research information in the first place. The importance of communication with legislators and bureaucrats, the press, and the general public has gained serious attention in the educational research community (Barone, 1992; Kaestle, 1993; McCarthy, 1990; McNergney, 1990).

Interdisciplinary Approach to Teacher Education Research

The need for interdisciplinary approaches to research in teacher education is evident for at least two reasons: (1) the disciplinary backgrounds of teacher education researchers are extremely varied, and (2) the complexities of the context in which teacher education research occurs demand expertise in various modes of inquiry. In a broad sense, interdisciplinary approaches to research are an extension of the notion of "triangulation," which can be conceived in terms of multiple data sources, multiple research methods, and multiple investigators (Mathison, 1988). Results of interdisciplinary research efforts begin to emerge, which conclude that the benefits to participant researchers and research products are greater than the problems encountered (Crow et al., 1992; Eisenhart & Borko, 1991).

Training teacher education researchers in different perspectives and various modes of inquiry also is needed. Many teacher educators have not developed adequate expertise for performing high quality research. Even those who have been actively engaged in research usually have training in certain research approaches, but not others. The training of researchers is a complicated issue because research involves not only methods or techniques but also world views or perspectives. The danger of knowing only one perspective and associated research methods is that this narrow view could prevent the researchers from seeing a range of issues and alternative approaches to inquiry about the phenomenon of interest. Interdisciplinary approaches to research seem to be an effective way to train researchers in teacher education.

Teacher education is at a time in the developmental stage of the field where it needs more research and fewer opinions, reactions, and debates. Although opinions, reactions, and debates can be helpful, it is difficult to derive much from these activities if teacher education does not have better and more grounded research. Furthermore, empirical research results need to be explained in terms of underlying theoretical frameworks.

Teacher education research recently has gained serious scholarly attention, and the education research community is calling for the integration of research, practice, and policy in teacher education (National Academy of Education, 1991). While systematic research agendas and major research genres in teacher education begin to emerge (Kennedy, 1991a, 1991b; McDiarmid & Ball, 1988) and national centers conduct systematic research on teacher education (e.g., National Center for Research on Teacher Learning and the RATE project by AACTE), the absence of discussion about modes of inquiry in teacher education research is striking. This chapter is an attempt to respond to this need. As teacher education research becomes more active and productive, more discussions about modes of inquiry will prevail.

References

Atkinson, P., Delamont, S., & Hammersley, M. (1988). Qualitative research traditions: A British response to Jacob. *Review of Educational Research, 58*(2), 231–250.

Barone, T. E. (1991). A narrative of enhanced professionalism: Educational researchers and popular storybooks about schoolpeople. *Educational Researcher, 21*(8), 15–24.

Beineke, J. A. (1988). Education's knowledge base and the liberal arts: Is collaboration possible? *Contemporay Education, 59*(4), 211–214.

Bruner, J. (1990). *Acts of meaning.* Cambridge, MA: Harvard University Press.

Bryk, A. S., & Raudenbush, S. W. (1992). *Hierarchical linear models: Applications and data analysis methods.* Thousand Oaks, CA: Sage Publications.

Buchmann, M., & Floden, R. E. (1989). Research traditions, diversity, and progress. *Review of Educational Research, 59*(2), 241–248.

Buttery, T. J., Haberman, M., & Houston, W. R. (1990). First annual ATE survey of critical issues in teacher education. *Action in Teacher Education, 12*(2), 1–7.

Campbell, D. T., & Stanley, J. C. (1963). *Experimental and quasi-experimental designs for research.* Chicago: Rand McNally College Publishing Company.

Carnegie Forum on Eduction and the Economy. (1986). *A nation prepared: Teachers for the 21st century.* Washington, DC: Author.

Carter, K. (1990). Teachers' knowledge and learning to teach. In W. R. Houston, M. Haberman, & J. Sikula (Eds.), *Handbook of research on teacher education* (pp. 291–310). New York: Macmillan.

Carter, K. (1993). The place of story in the study of teaching and teacher education. *Educational Researcher, 22*(1), 5–12.

Clark, C. M. (1988). Asking the right questions about teacher preparation: Contributions of research on teacher thinking. *Educational Researcher, 17*(2), 5–12.

Clifford, G. J., & Guthrie, J. W. (1988). *Ed school: A brief for professional education.* Chicago: The University of Chicago Press.

Cochran-Smith, M., & Lytle, S. L. (1990). Research on teaching and teacher research: The issues that divide. *Educational Researcher, 19*(2), 2–10.

Combs, A. W. (1965). *The professional education of teachers: A perceptual view of teacher preparation.* Boston: Allyn & Bacon.

Combs, A. W. (1972). Some basic concepts for teacher education. *Journal of Teacher Education, 23,* 286–290.

Connelly, F. M., & Clandinin, D. J. (1990). Stories of experience and narrative inquiry. *Educational Researcher, 19*(5), 2–14.

Cook, T. D., & Campbell, D. T. (1979). *Quasi-experimentation: Design and analysis issues for field settings.* Boston: Houghton Mifflin.

Corrigan, D. C., & Haberman, M. (1990). The context of teacher education. In W. R. Houston, M. Haberman, & J. Sikula (Eds.), *Handbook of research on teacher education* (pp. 195–211). New York: Macmillan.

Crow, G. M., Levine, L., & Nager, N. (1992). Are three heads better than one? Reflections on doing collaborative interdisciplinary research. *American Educational Research Journal, 29*(4), 737–753.

Cryns, T., & Johnston, M. (1993). A collaborative case study of teacher change: From a personal to a professional perspective. *Teaching and Teacher Education, 9*(2), 147–158.

Culver, B. M., Wolfle, L. M., & Cross, L. H. (1990). Testing a model of teacher satisfaction for blacks and whites. *American Educational Research Journal, 27*(2), 323–349.

Ducharme, E. (1993). *The lives of teacher educators.* Ithaca, NY: Teachers College Press.

Duckworth, E. (1986). Teaching as research. *Harvard Educational Review, 56*(4), 481–495.

Eisenhart, M. A., & Borko, H. (1991). In search of an interdisciplinary collaborative design for studying teacher education. *Teaching and Teacher Education, 7*(2), 137–157.

Eisner, E. W. (1993). Forms of understanding and the future of educational research. *Educational Researcher, 22*(7), 5–11.

Eisner, E. W., & Peshkin, A. (1990). *Qualitative inquiry in education: The continuing debate.* New York: Teachers College Press.

Erickson, F. (1986). Qualitative methods in research on teaching. In M. C. Wittrock (Ed.), *Handbook of research on teaching* (3rd ed.) (pp. 119–161). New York: Macmillan.

Feiman-Nemser, S. (1990). Teacher preparation: Structural and conceptual alternatives. In W. R. Houston, M. Haberman, & J. Sikula (Eds.), *Handbook of research on teacher education* (pp. 212–233). New York: Macmillan.

Feiman-Nemser, S., & Buchmann, M. (1989). Describing teacher education: A framework and illustrative findings from a longitudinal study of six students. *The Elementary School Journal, 89*(3), 365–378.

Fetterman, D. M. (1988). Qualitative approaches to evaluating education. *Educational researcher, 17*(8), 17–23.

Firestone, W. A. (1987). Meaning in method: The rhetoric quantitative and qualitative research. *Educational Researcher, 16*(7), 16–21.

Firestone, W. A. (1993). Alternative arguments for generalizing from data as applied to qualitative research. *Educational Researcher, 22*(4), 16–23.

Floden, R. E., & Buchmann, M. (1990). Philosophical inquiry in teacher education. In W. R. Houston, M. Haberman, & J. Sikula (Eds.), *Handbook of research on teacher education* (pp. 42–58). New York: Macmillan.

Folden, R. E., & Klinzing, H. G. (1990). What can research on teacher thinking contribute to teacher preparation? A second opinion. *Educational Researcher, 19*(4), 15–20.

Gage, N. L. (1978). *The scientific basis of the art of teaching.* New York: Teachers College Press.

Gage, N. L. (1985). *Hard gains in the soft sciences: The case of pedagogy.* Bloomington, IN: Center on Evaluation, Development, and Research, Phi Delta Kappa.

Gage, N. L. (1989). The paradigm wars and their aftermath. *Educational Researcher, 18*(7), 4–10.

Galluzzo, G. R., & Arends, R. I. (1989). The RATE project: A profile of teacher education institutions. *Journal of Teacher Education, 40*(4), 56–58.

Glaser, B., & Strauss, A. (1967). *The discovery of grounded theory.* Chicago: Aldine.

Goetz, J. P., & LeCompte, M. D. (1984). *Ethnography and qualitative design in educational research.* Orlando, FL: Academic Press.

Gore, J. (1987). Liberal and professional education: Keep them separate. *Journal of Teacher Education, 38*(1), 2–5.

Greene, M. (1981). Contexts, connections, and consequences: The matter of philosophical and psychological foundations. *Journal of Teacher Education, 32,* 31–37.

Griffin, G. A., & Barnes, S. (1986). Using research findings to change school and classroom practices: Results of an experimental study. *American Educational Research Journal, 23*(4), 572–586.

Grossman, P. L. (1990). *The making of a teacher: Teacher knowledge and teacher education.* New York: Teachers College Press.

Hamel, J., Dufour, S., & Fortin, D. (1993). *Case study methods* (Qualitative Research Methods Series, Vol. 32). Newbury Park, CA: Sage Publications.

Hazareezingh, N. A., & Bielawski, L. L. (1991). The effects of cognitive self-instruction on student teachers' perceptions of control. *Teaching and Teacher Education, 7*(4), 383–393.

Herbst, J. (1989). *And sadly teach: Teacher education and professionalization in American culture.* Madison: University of Wisconsin Press.

Heyns, B. (1988). Educational defectors: A first look at teacher attrition in the NLS-72. *Educational Researcher, 17*(3), 24–32.

Hollingsworth, S. (1989). Prior beliefs and cognitive change in learning to teach. *American Educational Research Journal, 26*(2), 160–189.

Hollingsworth, S., Teel, K., & Minarik, L. (1992). Learning to teach Aaron: A beginning teacher's story of literacy instruction in an urban classroom. *Journal of Teacher Education, 43*(2), 116–127.

The Holmes Group. (1986). *Tomorrow's teachers: A report of the Holmes Group.* East Lansing, MI: Author.

Houston, W. R., Haberman, M., & Sikula, J. (1989). Teacher education as a field of scholarly inquiry. *Action in Teacher Education, 11*(2), 19–24.

Howe, K. R. (1985). Two dogmas of educational research. *Educational Researcher, 14*(8), 10–18.

Howe, K. R., & Dougherty, K. C. (1993). Ethics, institutional review boards, and the changing face of educational research. *Educational Researcher, 22*(9), 16–21.

Howey, K. R. (1989). Research About Teacher Education: Programs of teacher preparation. *Journal of Teacher Education, 40*(6), 23–26.

Howey, K., & Zimpher, N. (1989). *Profiles of preservice teacher education: Inquiry into the nature of programs.* Albany: State University of New York Press.

Hoy, W. K., & Woolfolk, A. E. (1990). Socialization of student teachers. *American Educational Research Journal, 27*(2), 279–300.

Jacob, E. (1987). Qualitative research traditions: A review. *Review of Educational Research, 57*(1), 1–50.

Jacob, E. (1988). Clarifying qualitative research: A focus on traditions. *Educational Researcher, 17*(1), 16–24.

Jacob, E. (1989). Qualitative research: A defense of traditions. *Review of Educational Research, 59*(2), 229–239.

Jaeger, R. M. (Ed.). (1988). *Complementary methods for research in education.* Washington, DC: American Educational Research Association.

Johnson, W. R. (1987). Empowering practitioners: Holmes, Carnegie and the lessons of history. *History of Education Quarterly, 27*(2), 221–240.

Joyce, B. R. (1988). Training research and preservice teacher education: A reconsideration. *Journal of Teacher Education, 39*(5), 32–36.

Kaestle, C. F. (1988). Recent methodological developments in the history of American education. In R. M. Jaeger (Ed.), *Complementary methods for research in education* (pp. 61–71). Washington, DC: American Educational Research Association.

Kaestle, C. F. (1993). The awful reputation of education research. *Educational Researcher, 22*(1), 23–31.

Kagan, D. M., Dennis, M. B., Igou, M., Moore, P., & Sparks, K. (1993). The experience of being a teacher in residence. *American Educational Research Journal, 30*(2), 426–443.

Kennedy, M. M. (Spring, 1991a). *An agenda for research on teacher learning* (NCRTL Special Report). East Lansing: Michigan State University, National Center for Research on Teacher Learning.

Kennedy, M. M. (1991b). *Research genres in teacher education* (Issue Paper 91-1). East Lansing: Michigan State University, National Center for Research on Teacher Learning.

King, J. A. (1987). The uneasy relationship between teacher education and the liberal arts and sciences. *Journal of Teacher Education, 38*(1), 6–10.

Kirk, J., & Miller, M. L. (1986). *Reliability and validity in qualitative research* (Qualitative Research Methods, Vol. 1). Newbury Park, CA: Sage Publications.

Kliebard, H. M. (1987). *The struggle for the American curriculum, 1893–1958.* New York: Routledge & Kagan Paul.

Klug, B. J., & Saltzman, S. A. (1991). Formal induction vs. informal mentoring: Comparative effects and outcomes. *Teaching and Teacher Education, 7*(3), 241–251.

Lampert, M., & Clark, C. M. (1990). Expert knowledge and expert thinking in teaching: A response to Floden and Klinzing. *Educational Researcher, 19*(5), 21–23.

Lincoln, Y. S. (1989). Qualitative research: A response to Atkinson, Delamont, and Hammersley. *Review of Educational Research, 59*(2), 237–239.

Lincoln, Y. S., & Guba, E. G. (1985). *Naturalistic inquiry.* Newbury Park, CA: Sage Publications.

Little, J. W. (1993). Teachers' professional development in a climate of educational reform. *Educational Evaluation and Policy Analysis, 15*(2), 129–151.

Martin, J., & Sugarman, J. (1993). Beyond methodolatry: Two conceptions of relations between theory and research in research on teaching. *Educational Researcher, 22*(8), 17–24.

Mathison, S. (1988). Why triangulate? *Educational Researcher, 17*(2), 13–17.

Maxwell, J. A. (1992). Understanding and validity in qualitative research. *Harvard Educational Review, 62*(3), 279–300.

McCarthy, M. M. (1990). University-based policy centers: New actors in the education policy arena. *Educational Researcher, 19*(8), 25–29.

McDiarmid, G. W., & Ball, D. L. (1988). *"Many moons": Understanding teacher learning from a teacher education perspective* (Issue Paper 88-5). East Lansing: Michigan State University, National Center for Research on Teacher Learning.

McNergney, R. F. (1990). Improving communication among educational researchers, policymakers, and the press. *Educational Researcher, 19*(3), 20–23.

McNergney, R. F. (1992). *Educational research, policy, and the press: Research as news.* Needham Heights, MA: Allyn and Bacon.

Merriam, S. B. (1988). *Case study research in education: A qualitative approach.* San Francisco: Jossey-Bass.

Metcalf, K. K. (1992). The effects of a guided training experience on the instructional clarity of preservice teachers. *Teaching and Teacher Education, 8*(3), 275–286.

National Academy of Education. (1991). *Research and the renewal of education: A report from the National Academy of Education.* Stanford, CA: Author.

National Center for Research on Teacher Education. (1988). Teacher education and learning to teach: A research agenda. *Journal of Teacher Education, 39*(6), 27–32.

National Center for Research on Teacher Education. (1991). *Findings from the Teacher Education and Learning to Teach Study: Final report, The National Center for Research on Teacher Education* (Special Report 6/91). East Lansing: Michigan State University, National Center for Research on Teacher Learning.

National Commission on Excellence in Education. (1983). *A nation at risk: The imperative for educational reform.* Washington, DC: Government Printing Office.

Nespor, J., & Barylske, J. (1991). Narrative discourse and teacher knowledge. *American Educational Research Journal, 28*(4), 805–823.

Paley, V. G. (1979). *White teacher.* Cambridge, MA: Harvard University Press.

Peshkin, A. (1988). In search of subjectivity—One's own. *Educational Researcher, 17*(7), 17–21.

Phillips, D. C. (1983). After the wake: Postpositivistic educational thought. *Educational Researcher, 12*(5), 4–12.

Porter, A. C. (1988). Comparative experimental methods in educational research. In R. M. Jaeger (Ed.), *Complementary methods for research in education* (pp. 391–411). Washington, DC: American Educational Research Association.

Punch, M. (1986). *The politics and ethics of fieldwork* (Qualitative Research Methods Series, Vol. 3). Beverly Hills, CA: Sage Pulblications.

Reagan, G. M. (1990). Liberal studies and the education of teachers. *Theory into Practice, 29*(1), 30–35.

Reynolds, M. C. (1989). *Knowledge base for the beginning teacher.* Elmsford, NY: Pergamon Press.

Richardson, V. (1990). Significant and worthwhile change in teaching practice. *Educational Researcher, 19*(7), 10–18.

Rizo, F. M. (1991). The controversy about quantification in social research: An extension of Gage's " 'historical' sketch." *Educational Researcher, 20*(9), 9–12.

Ryan, K. (Ed.). (1975). *Teacher education* (The 74th Yearbook of the National Society for the Study of Education, Part II.) Chicago: The University of Chicago Press.

Salomon, G. (1991). Transcending the qualitative-quantitative debate: The analytic and systemic approaches to educational research. *Educational Researcher, 20*(6), 10–18.

Scheffler, I. (1968). University scholarship and the education of teachers. *Teachers College Record, 70*(1), 1–12.

Schrag, F. (1992). In defense of positivist research paradigms. *Educational Researcher, 21*(5), 5–8.

Scriven, M. (1988). Philosophical inquiry methods in education. In R. M. Jaeger (Ed.), *Contemporary methods for research in education* (pp. 131–183). Washington, DC: American Educational Research Association.

Shulman, J. H. (1990). Now you see them, now you don't: Anonymity versus visibility in case studies of teachers. *Educational Researcher, 19*(6), 11–15.

Shulman, L. S. (1986). Those who understand: Knowledge growth in teaching. *Educational Researcher, 15*(2), 4–14.

Shulman, L. S. (1988). Disciplines of inquiry in education: An overview. In R. M. Jaeger (Ed.), *Complementary methods for research in education* (pp. 3–17). Washington, DC: American Educational Research Association.

Smith, J. K. (1983). Quantitative vs. qualitative research: An attempt to clarify the issue. *Educational Researcher, 12*(3), 6–12.

Smith, J. K. (1988). The evaluator/researcher as person vs. the person as evaluator/researcher. *Educational Researcher, 17*(2), 18–23.

Smith, J. K., & Heshusius, L. (1986). Closing down the conversation: The end of the quantitative-qualitative debate among educational inquirers. *Educational Researcher, 15*(1), 4–12.

Smylie, M. A. (1988). The enhancement function of staff development: Organizational and psychological antecedents to individual teacher change. *American Educational Research Journal, 25*(1), 1–30.

Smylie, M. A. (1989). Teachers' views of the effectiveness of sources of learning to teach. *The Elementary School Journal, 89*(5), 543–558.

Strauss, A., & Corbin, J. (1990). *Basics of qualitative research: Grounded theory procedures and techniques.* Newbury Park, CA: Sage Publications.

Urban, W. (1990). Historical studies of teacher education. In W. R. Houston, M. Haberman, & J. Sikula (Eds.), *Handbook of research on teacher education* (pp. 59–71). New York: Macmillan.

Warren, D. (1985). Learning from experience: History and teacher education. *Educational Researcher, 14*(10), 5–12.

Warren, D. (Ed.). (1989). *American teachers: Histories of a profession at work.* New York: Macmillan.

Weaver, F. S. (1987). Teacher education, liberal education, and the liberal arts. *Action in Teacher Education, 9*(1), 1–7.

Wilson, J. (1975). *Educational theory and the preparation of teachers.* Windsor, England: National Foundation for Educational Research.

Wolcott, H. F. (1988). Ethnographic research in education. In R. M. Jaeger (Ed.), *Complementary methods for research in education* (pp. 187–206). Washington, DC: American Educational Research Association.

Yarger, S. J. (1989). Research About Teacher Education (RATE): Introduction to an ongoing study. *Journal of Teacher Education, 40*(4), 53–55.

Yager, S. J., & Smith, P. L. (1990). Issues in research on teacher education. In W. R. Houston, M. Haberman, & J. Sikula (Eds.), *Handbook of research on teacher education* (pp. 25–41). New York: Macmillan.

Yin, R. K. (1993). *Applications of case study research* (Applied Social Research Methods Series, Vol. 34). Newbury Park, CA: Sage Publications.

Yin, R. K. (1994). *Case study research: Design and methods* (2nd ed.) (Applied Social Research Methods Series, Vol. 5). Thousand Oaks, CA: Sage Publications.

Zeichner, K. M. (1981/1982). Reflective teaching and field-based experience in teacher education. *Interchange, 12*(4), 1–22.

Zeichner, K. M., & Liston, D. P. (1990). Traditions of reform in U.S. teacher education. *Journal of Teacher Education, 41*(2), 3–20.

Zimpher, N. L. (1989). The RATE project: A profile of teacher education students. *Journal of Teacher Education, 40*(6), 27–30.

THE PROFESSIONAL KNOWLEDGE-RESEARCH BASE FOR TEACHER EDUCATION

Doran Christensen

SALISBURY STATE UNIVERSITY

What must teachers know about teaching? What knowledge is essential to their work? Is there a lot to learn or just a little? Is it easy or difficult? How is such knowledge generated and confirmed? Indeed, dare we even call it knowledge in the strict sense of the term? Is so much of what guides the actions of teachers nothing more than opinion, not to say out-and-out guesswork? But even if that were so, what of the remainder? If *any* of what teachers claim to know about teaching qualifies as knowledge (and who dares deny that some does?), what can be said of its adequacy? How complete is it? Does much remain to be discovered or do the best of today's teachers already know most of what there is to learn? And whether the bulk of it is fully known or yet to be discovered, what, if anything, must be added to such knowledge to ready the teacher for his or her work? In other words, is there more to teaching than the skilled application of something called know-how? If so, what might that be? (Jackson, 1986, p. 1)

The questions raised in this quotation are among those that tantalize and plague teachers and teacher educators. What do we know about teaching and teacher education? If we do know something, do we make use of our knowledge? Or is teaching and/or teacher education driven by some combination of guesses, past practices, and "feeling our way"?

The matter of a knowledge-research base that has developed or is developing has interested many educators over time. Recently, however, the level of interest has reached unusually high levels. The American Association of Colleges for Teacher Education (AACTE) has provided leadership in addressing the question. A particular product of that leadership is the *Knowledge Base for the Beginning Teacher* (Reynolds, 1989) published by the AACTE. In the preface of that publication, Gardner (1989) identified assumptions about the knowledge base to the effect that "it is possible to say something at this time about what is known . . . , knowledge about teaching will never be complete . . . , the knowledge base for teaching takes a variety of forms and is drawn from many disciplines and other sources. . . ." (p. x).

In their landmark work, *Educating a Profession,* also published by AACTE, Howsam, Corrigan, and Denemark (1976)

The author wishes to acknowledge the helpful counsel and assistance of reviewers James Raths, University of Delaware, and Gene Hall, University of Northern Colorado; and the assistance of Arthur Wise, Donna Gollnick, and the rest of the NCATE staff.

stressed the importance of a professional knowledge base and the need for teachers to understand and apply research findings.

Yet the questions persist. Finkel (1984) raised the issue of the little faith and confidence that the general public and educators themselves have in educational research. Barnes (1991), in a thoughtful and persuasive commentary on the knowledge base concept, correctly pointed out the dilemmas of too narrowly defining knowledge bases, the danger of relying on the cumulative interest of specialists, and "distinctions necessary between what teachers need to know in order to foster valuable student learning . . . and what teacher educators need to consider in order to create a curriculum that will allow novices to gain such knowledge" (pp. 8–9).

In spite of the many questions and skepticisms, the world of teaching and teacher education has been proceeding on many fronts in its efforts to identify a knowledge base (Dill et al., 1990; Goodlad, Soder, & Sirotnik, 1990; Grossman, 1990; Johnstone, Spalding, Paden, & Ziffren, 1989). Whether such efforts are having any effect on teacher education programs, however, is another matter. Identifying sources for information about such effects provides a serious challenge; therefore, the reason for the design of this chapter.

The National Council for Accreditation of Teacher Education (NCATE) is the one agency that collects this kind of information. Because NCATE has been applying standards about the knowledge base for teacher education for some time, it seems logical to examine the information that has been submitted by institutions presenting for accreditation. NCATE does not evaluate all institutions because accreditation is voluntary; however, it is the one agency that applies given standards to a significant number of programs, and it is the only single focus for such information.

ACCREDITATION STANDARDS

Teacher education programs in many institutions are evaluated regularly in terms of national standards promulgated by the NCATE. The most recent revision of the standards contains very specific expectations that institutions demonstrate the knowledge base used for the development of teacher education programs.

The standards in question "were developed over a two-year period between 1983 and 1985 as part of the broad redesign of NCATE. The standards were ratified on October 12, 1985" (National Council for Accreditation of Teacher Education [NCATE], 1992, p. 11). The standards address five categories including: (1) knowledge base for professional education, (2) relationship to the world of practice, (3) students, (4) faculty, and (5) governance and resources. Within this collection of categories exist 18 standards and 94 criteria for compliance.

For the purposes of this chapter, the only categories, standards, and criteria to be considered are those that address the knowledge-research base for teacher education. They are found in only the first category of the NCATE standards—"Knowledge Bases for Professional Education." They read as follows:

Standard 1.A: Design of Curriculum

The unit ensures that its professional education programs are based on essential knowledge, established and current research findings, and sound professional practice. Each program in the unit reflects a systematic design with an explicitly stated philosophy and objectives. Coherence exists between (1) courses and experiences and (2) purposes and outcomes.

Criteria for Compliance:

1. The unit ensures that its professional education programs have adopted a model(s) that explicates the purposes, outcomes, and evaluation of the program. The rationales for the model(s) and the knowledge bases that undergird them are clearly stated along with goals, philosophy, and objectives.
2. The knowledge bases used in professional education are broad and include the traditional forms of scholarly inquiry as well as theory development related to professional practice.
4. The knowledge bases of the professional studies component(s) are reflected in curricular design and planning; course syllabi; instructional design, practice, and evaluation; students' work; use of major journals in the field by faculty and students; and faculty and students' (especially graduate students) participation in research and synthesis.

Standard 1.B: Delivery of the Curriculum

The unit ensures that knowledge bases and best practice in professional education are reflected in the instruction offered. The instructional practices and evaluation are fully congruent with the current state of knowledge about curriculum design, instruction, and evaluation.

Criteria for Compliance:

6. Instruction by faculty in the unit is congruent in content and process with best practice and current and established research.
7. Faculty instruction in the unit provides students with systematically varied models of instruction.
8. The institution as a whole regards the unit as one where instructional practice is constantly superior.
9. The unit maintains a rigorous, professional instructional quality control mechanism. (Reprinted from NCATE's *Standards, Procedures and Policies for the Accreditation of Professional Education Units* [February 1992]. Washington, DC: Author, pp. 47–48. Used by permission.)

The emphasis on employing a knowledge-research base in designing the curriculum for teacher education can be seen as a logical continuation of long-term efforts of NCATE to design programs with care and with specific outcomes in mind. Earl Armstrong (personal communication, December 15, 1986), the first director of NCATE, from 1954 to 1964, testified that the two most important and difficult expectations to implement in the early days of teacher education accreditation were those requiring a defined unit responsible for the teacher education programs and a program that was designed with certain outcomes in mind (many programs simply provided courses, often only student teaching, required for state or local certification). The 1960 version of the NCATE standards reads as follows: "Every institution maintaining a program of teacher education should have a written statement of its objectives. The statement should indicate the school positions for which the program prepares persons and should describe the entire scope of the effort being made by the institution to improve the quality of education in the schools. . . . The statement should also set forth the major beliefs and assumptions as to the most effective means of developing these desired personal and intellectual objectives" (NCATE, 1960, p. 3).

From the 1977 version of the NCATE standards we see a tightening of expectations regarding program design. "Curricula for teacher education programs are based upon a systematic approach. There is a conceptualization of roles to be performed which is followed by explicitly stated objectives. These roles and objectives reflect the results of research and the considered judgments of the teacher education faculty and staff, students, graduates of the programs, the profession as a whole, and national professional associations concerning the goals of education in our society" (NCATE, 1977, p. 3).

The genesis of the current standards, those that are the most explicit, seemed to demonstrate the need for ever increasing demands that institutions be responsive to the developed and developing knowledge base in teaching and learning. The primary purpose of this chapter is to review the institutional response to these more explicit standards.

Subsequent to this review, the standards of NCATE were modified, adopted by NCATE on May 19, 1994, and applied effective for fall 1995 visits. These newest standards, referred to as "NCATE Refined Standards" (NCATE, 1994, p. 1) seem to reflect a shift of emphasis away from a focus on knowledge bases and models to conceptual frameworks. Category I of the earlier standards, for example, are titled "Knowledge Bases for Professional Education," whereas this category in the newer standards is called "Design of Professional Education." In the text of the earlier standards the key concepts driving the expectations are knowledge bases as well as research findings and sound professional practice. The refined standards, by comparison, focus primarily on conceptual frameworks. There is still a reference to the role of knowledge bases in developing the frameworks; however, the prevalence of the knowledge base concept is substantially minimized. It will be interesting to observe the impact of the newer standards on institutional responses.

DESIGN FOR THE REVIEW

The information sources for this chapter are the self-study reports of institutions submitting programs for accreditation wherein the visits to campuses were completed during the spring semester of 1993. This sample was selected because all hard copy reports were available in the NCATE offices at the time of the review (December 1993), and decisions regarding accreditation had been rendered. NCATE had a total of 42 reports representing a cross section of private, public, regional, research, and large and small programs and institutions.

The only documents reviewed were those prepared by the institution; no effort was made to determine the degree of success each institution had experienced in its quest for accreditation. The board of examiners report was not reviewed. To have extended the review to subsequent levels of the process would have entailed a study of such depth as to go beyond the limits of this review. The quality of the Institutional Report (IR) and the apparent success of the institution in responding completely and specifically to the knowledge base standards and criteria were the criteria employed by this author in selecting the institutions to describe fully. Although space considera-

tions limited the number to three, many other reports were of similar quality and could have been reported as well.

GENERAL FINDINGS

The review of all documents began with an analysis of what institutions described as the "rationales for the model(s) and the knowledge bases that undergird them" (NCATE, 1992, p. 47) as well as an examination of the goals, philosophy, and objectives of the programs (criterion 1). The overwhelming impression gained from the review was the diversity of approaches reflected in the 42 institutions. Evidence of institutions following a similar model or approach toward this standard occurred in only four reports at the most.

In 31 instances the institution identified a theme statement that described its program design or conceptualization. Some of these were similar (see Table 3.1); yet, programs with similar theme statements had substantially different approaches. Four statements were characterized as some form of "teacher as decision maker." One of the four institutions listed 13 outcomes/dispositions (e.g., examine their own teaching, use a variety of teaching strategies, master subject-matter content) expected of their graduates. A second institution presented a belief statement (related to Christian doctrine); seven outcomes (e.g., learning the knowledge bases, ability to think critically, solve problems, good citizenship); proficiencies (technical, in-

TABLE 3.1. Program Design Themes

Becoming a complete professional
Constructivist reflective model
Education in a community of inquiry
Educators engaged in growth
Effective liberally educated teacher
Empowered person and professional
Head, heart, hand
Lifelong scholar
New novice teacher
Practicing professional
Professional educator
Professional development model
Reflective practitioners
Reflective practice
Reflective practitioner
Reflective decision maker
Skilled and reflective teacher
Targeting educational excellence
Teacher as a catalyst
Teacher as an active learner and decision maker
Teacher as a wise decision maker
Teacher as decision maker
Teacher as the developer of human potential
Teacher as decision maker
Teacher as an effective leader in a diversified society
Teacher: Catalyst for change
Teachers reflecting, engaging, collaborating
Teaching as reflective practice
Teaching and learning in a social context
The teacher as a reflective decision maker
The beginning teacher

structional, decoding classroom situations); roles (instructor, curriculum organizer, prescriber, counselor); and goals (knowledge of the role of education in our society, professional attitude, knowledge of the nature of teaching and learning, sound teaching principles) as the program design. Yet a third report with the same theme statement provided a long list for each of the following areas: (a) educational aims, (b) content knowledge, (c) knowledge of learners, and (d) knowledge of curriculum. The fourth institution provided a statement of philosophy and a list of seven broad-based outcomes. It was clear that each of the four were very different from each other in spite of virtually identical themes.

Many reports credited a certain scholar(s) as responsible for the knowledge base structure influencing the design of the programs. By a large margin, the most commonly cited work was that of Shulman (1987) who was credited in at least nine reports. Others who were identified by more than one institution included Brophy and Good (1986), Howey and Zimpher (1989), and Zeichner and Liston (1987). Other scholars influencing program designs included Barnes (1991); Boyer (1987); Bruner (1960); Dewey (1983); Gage (1984); Gagne (1985); Goodlad (1990); Grossman, Wilson, and Shulman (1989); The Holmes Group (1986); Katz and Raths (1988); and Schon (1983).

Terms employed to categorize the statements composing the design/conceptualization of the programs were also very broad. The most commonly used category terms were *goals, outcomes, beliefs, objectives, roles, philosophy, mission, assumptions,* and *components.* Other category terms were *dispositions, theme, requirements, proficiencies, purpose, commonalities, concepts, foci, guidelines, domains, aims, rationale,* and *characteristics.* The terms used to categorize the statements seemed to have little relationship to the kind of statements presented; for example, there was little distinction between goals, aims, outcomes, roles, or objectives.

Fifteen of the institutions presented some kind of graphic to explain better the design of the program. These also varied widely, with some resembling flow charts, others data charts, and still others maps or pictorials. (See Figures 3.1, 3.2, and 3.3.)

Criterion 2 requires the knowledge bases used in professional education to be broad and to include the traditional forms of scholarly inquiry as well as theory development related to professional practice. In most cases, once the reporting of criterion 1 was complete, the only additional description provided was the assertion that evidence for criterion 2 had been presented.

Scholars cited in all of the reports numbered more than 1,000; in the general program design alone, Indiana State University (1993) listed more than 750 scholars representing 856 citations. Except for six reports in which no scholarly works were referenced, all reports had developed a substantial knowledge-research base of scholarly works on which to build programs. Furthermore, it was apparent that the references were related appropriately to the specific components detailed in each case. That is, there was no evidence of institutions assembling a long list of references simply because they existed; the congruency of the knowledge base and the program design was apparent in each instance.

Criterion 4 requires the knowledge bases to be reflected in curricular design and planning; course syllabi; instructional

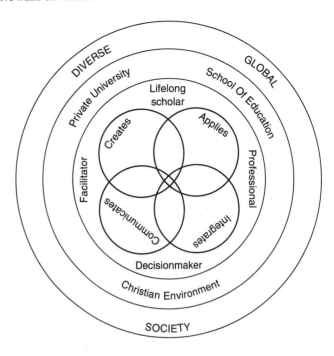

FIGURE 3.1. Teacher education design model.

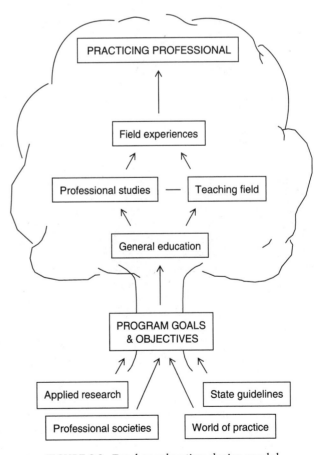

FIGURE 3.2. Teacher education design model.

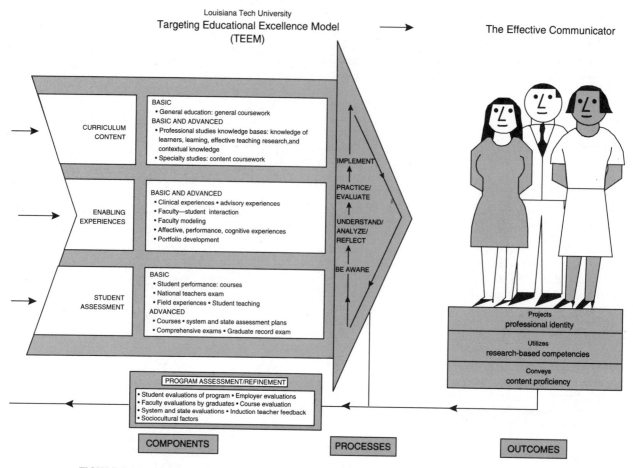

FIGURE 3.3. Targeting Educational Excellence Model (TEEM)—The effective communicator.

design, practice, and evaluation; students' work; and use of major journals. Many tables were employed to demonstrate meeting this criterion. The most common model showed goals, outcomes, competencies, and objectives on one axis and course offerings on the other, which formed a matrix with cells available to indicate the inclusion of each in the courses. Here, as in other sections of the reports, the overwhelming impression is that institutions took great care to describe fully the implementation of the knowledge base. A further study of subsequent levels of the accreditation process would require determining the degree to which the substance offered in the tables was carried out in the programs, such as the evaluation of student teaching based on the outcomes described by the institutions.

The criteria for Standard 1B, "Delivery of the Curriculum," relate to faculty performance and faculty evaluation. Reports for these criteria were somewhat alike in that institutions detailed the degree to which faculty were engaged in ongoing professional involvement and development, how they compared to other faculty members across campus, and the nature of the faculty evaluation processes employed. The most fascinating content was in terms of "systematically varied models of instruction" utilized by institutions. Eighty-three different

models were noted (see Table 3.2). In some instances, institutions not only identified instructional models, they also provided a knowledge base for each one. An example is "cooperative learning" (Johnson & Johnson, 1987; Slavin, 1983). As in so many other aspects of the reports, the diversity and originality evidenced was surprising.

Interestingly, an analysis conducted by Hall et al. (1994) for the Teacher Education Council of State Colleges and Universities (TECSCU) revealed equally diverse themes, models, and knowledge base domains. Based on a review of 44 reports voluntarily submitted by TECSCU insitutions, this analysis emphasized a review of themes, figures (graphics), and outcomes. A key finding was that the knowledge base descriptions fail to support the concept of a single generally accepted knowledge base undergirding teacher education; rather, teaching and learning are extremely complex phenomena that trigger a vast array of knowledge.

SPECIFIC EXAMPLES

The quality of most of the 42 institutional reports examined warranted their being reported in greater detail. It was apparent

TABLE 3.2. Knowledge-Based Instructional Models: Frequency of Identification by 42 Institutions

Advance Organizers (2)	Learning Styles
Audio-Visual (2)	**Lecture (20)**
Awareness Training	Lesson Plan (2)
Bibliography	Manipulatives
Brainstorming (3)	Mentoring
Case Study (13)	Microteaching (8)
Coaching Collaborative	Modeling (3)
Collaboration	Multicultural Education
Computer-aided Instruction (6)	Networking
Concept Mapping	Nondirective Teaching
Concrete—Abstract	Observations (2)
Constructivist Interactions	Observations (Guided)
Cooperative Learning (19)	Outcome-based Education
Creative Expression (2)	Panel Discussions (3)
Curriculum Writing (2)	**Peer Tutoring (10)**
Debates (4)	Performance Tasks Projects
Decision Making	Portfolio (3)
Demonstrations (8)	Problem Solving (8)
Discovery Learning (2)	Protocols
Discussion (14)	Questioning (5)
Distance Learning (2)	Questionnaires (2)
Drill/Practice	Readings/Critiques (4)
Exams/Quizzes	Recitation
Experiential Activities (5)	Reflective Practicum
Exploratory Activities	Reflective Thinking
Field Experience (8)	Reflective Teaching (2)
Field Trips (2)	Research (Action) (8)
Flexible Grouping	**Role Playing (13)**
Games	Semantic Mapping
Glasser Circle	Shock Therapy
Guest Speakers (7)	**Simulations (12)**
Guided Outline	Socratic Method
Independent Projects	Student Presentations (8)
Individualization (3)	Team Teaching (3)
Inquiry Projects (5)	Test Administration
Instructional Media (4)	Unit Planning
Integrated Content/Methods	Values Clarification
Integrated Units	Videotaping (6)
Interviewing (3)	Webbing
Journals (9)	Workshops (3)
Laboratory Exercises (14)	Writing Across the Curriculum
Learning Center Activities	

Note: Models identified by 10 or more institutions are listed in bold, by two to nine institutions are listed in italic, and by one institution are listed in regular type.

the institutions had responded to the standards pertinent to the knowledge-research base in such a way as to demonstrate an insightful knowledge of the standards, an impressive strategy for developing and implementing programs based on this knowledge, and a result that was clear and convincing.

Based on those criteria, the three reports selected for detailed reporting were Indiana State University, Louisiana Tech University, and the College of William and Mary. These reports not only met the criteria noted here but also represented diverse responses.

The report for each institution follows, as appropriate, the standards and criteria as they were reported by the institution. Also, even though each of the institutions presented many pro-

grams for accreditation, descriptions of only the basic (usually undergraduate) teacher education programs are reported here.

Indiana State University

Indiana State University (ISU) offers many programs at all degree levels, but has developed a common theme for all programs entitled "Becoming a Complete Professional." The theme was developed through a process of extended faculty study and development during a substantial period of time. ISU is a good example of the fascinating array of approaches used by the institutions.

Criteria (1) The theme, "Becoming a Complete Professional," drives the entire program and includes three broad areas, each of which includes four features of successful practice. The theme is broadly disseminated (the institution even distributes bookmarks with this design) and is apparently well understood by all persons involved in the programs (see Table 3.3).

Each of the 12 features of successful practice is described and rooted in a base of scholarly works. The first teacher outcome of basing practice on high but realistic expectations is described here. (Space limits this chapter to one example only.)

An essential feature of successful teaching is having high but realistic standards and goals for students and operating with the belief that students can meet those expectations. This means not simply placating less enthusiastic students and allowing, or even encouraging, them to believe that "getting by" is the objective. With students having low academic self-concepts, it means helping them develop confidence that they can achieve, partly by doing what is necessary to bring about that achievement. In general, teachers who exemplify this feature of teaching expertise communicate to students that they can be successful, and these teachers carry out their responsibilities with that assumption in mind.

For a myriad of interrelated reasons, Teacher Outcome 1 deserves the emphasis placed on it in Indiana State University's teacher education programs. Certainly the relationship between teacher expectations and student achievement is not as straightforward and powerful as some

TABLE 3.3. ISU Teacher Education Program Theme: "Becoming a Complete Professional"

A Teacher as a Mediator of Learning
1. Basing practice on high but realistic expectations
2. Helping individuals achieve their potential
3. Using professional strategies that actively engage individuals
4. Being open to change in professional service

A Teacher as a Person
5. Being an exemplar of lifelong learning
6. Being a model of effective communication
7. Demonstrating care for individuals as persons
8. Acknowledging one's influence on student values

A Teacher as a Member of Communities
9. Collaborating to achieve educational goals
10. Responding to the social context in which one works
11. Promoting social responsibility among students
12. Demonstrating commitment to the profession

educators concluded based on Rosenthal and Jacobson's (1968) *Pygmalion in the Classroom,* but the relationship is a crucially important one nevertheless. Among other research results on teacher expectations studies have yielded the finding that a teacher's belief that students will be academically successful in his or her [*sic*] classes is associated with the teacher's eventual success in fostering academic achievement by the students (Brophy & Evertson, 1976). The complex psychological and sociological dynamics which explain this type of finding are one reason this programmatic outcome receives the attention it does in the University's teacher education program.

One area of research and theory supporting this programmatic outcome focuses on the effect of teacher behaviors on student achievement. Some of the reports of scholarly work in this area suggest that teachers tend, often inadvertently, to create more favorable learning environments for the students for whom they have high expectations (Hamachek, 1971; Rosenthal, 1989; Smey-Richman, 1989), thus contributing to greater achievement by these students. On the other hand, at least one study found a tendency for teachers to give less attention to students for whom they expect high achievement and, instead, for the teachers to concentrate their instructional efforts on the students they consider less capable, resulting in unexpectedly low achievement for the more able ones (Goldenberg, 1992). Despite these seemingly conflicting findings, the broader conclusion is that teacher expectations for students can influence instruction and, in turn, student performance. The encouraging findings from other investigations are that teachers can be made sensitive to unintended differential treatment of students based on expectations and that improved student achievement can result when the teachers make appropriate adjustments in their instruction (Lindley & Keithley, 1991; Murphy, 1988; Smey-Richman, 1989).

Another reason for the importance of teacher expectations relates to the role teachers play in the formation of a student's self-image and the influence which self-image can have on achievement. The scholarly work in this area goes back at least to the efforts of Charles Cooley (1902) and George Mead (1934), who spoke of the "looking glass self." Most recent investigations of self-image and its relationship to school performance focus on what is known as academic self-concept, which is generally acknowledged to be an important educational variable (Byrne & Shavelson, 1986; Marsh, Byrne, & Shavelson, 1988; Strein, 1990). Research indicates that teachers can have an impact on students' academic self-concepts (Harris, Rosenthal, & Snodgrass, 1986). Moreover, studies reveal a statistical relationship between academic self-concept and academic achievement (Kelly & Jordan, 1990; Kershner, 1990; Mboya, 1986). Controversy exists, however, regarding the nature of any causality in that relationship. A number of investigators have concluded that academic self-concept can affect achievement (Marsh, 1990), though some of them argue the effect is an indirect one through other variables (Pottebaum, Keith, & Ehly, 1986). Research on the somewhat broader but related variable, self-esteem, gives a different picture; it suggests that school performance affects self-esteem, rather than vice versa (Rosenberg, Schooler, & Schenbach, 1989). Regardless of the nature of the relationship between self-image and academic achievement, teachers recognized for their expertise maintain that enhancing student self-image is an important role of educators (Maeroff, 1991). Indeed, this may be an especially significant role when teaching females in certain subject areas, such as mathematics and the sciences, and when teaching learning disabled and other handicapped students (Byrne & Shavelson, 1987; Chapman, 1988; Gregory, 1986). From another perspective, scholars who attempt to predict the skills and personal characteristics needed for success in the society of the future argue that self-confidence will be increasingly important (Carnevale, 1992). In other words, for a variety of reasons individuals being prepared as teachers need to understand the significance of student self-image and ways they can enhance it.

Teacher expectations can also have an important influence on students' motivation to achieve and on their aspirations. David McClelland

(1985) is responsible for some of the most significant research and theory on achievement motivation, and investigators and theorists today are continuing to emphasize the importance of this and related variables and their relationship to academic achievement (Brophy, 1983; Gottfried, 1985). Additionally, both theorists and teachers alike recognize the impact of teacher expectations on the intrinsic motivation of students to learn (Brophy & Kher, 1986; Whitlock & DuCette, 1989). Though influences on the educational and occupational aspirations of students have been examined less than have influences on self-image and achievement motivation, evidence does exist that teacher expectations have an effect on student aspirations as well (Saltiel, 1986).

With regard to student self-image, achievement motivation, and level of aspirations, there is reason to believe that a favorable impact by teachers results not primarily by believing students can be successful but by providing experiences in which students are successful and by making them aware of their role in that success. Some of the research leading to this conclusion has focused on a construct known as self-efficacy (Schunk, 1985; Schunk, 1989). Studies in this area offer convincing evidence that students' self-efficacy beliefs influence goals, effort, and achievement (MacIver, Stipek, & Daniels, 1991; Zimmerman, Bandura, & Martinez-Ponz, 1992). Other investigations on self-efficacy and ones on achievement motivation emphasize the role of teachers in encouraging student performance (Van Hecke & Tracy, 1987) and in helping students see how their ability and effort determine success (Black, 1992; Pintrich & Blumenfeld, 1985; Schunk & Rice, 1991). Research suggests these teaching functions are especially, but not exclusively, important with the less able and less advantaged students (Duckworth & Lind, 1989; Hilman & Golumbia, 1990; Teddlie & Whelan, 1989).

Implied in the preceding comments on self-efficacy is the assumption that the effectiveness of teachers depends on the use of instructional activities in which students have a reasonable probability of success. In other words, along with being high, teacher expectations must be realistic. In the language of self-efficacy theorists, communicating expectations which are not achievable can prevent a student from developing a sense of self-efficacy in the area of expectations (Bandura, 1989). Having expectations which are not unrealistically high seems especially important when working with at-risk, disadvantaged students (Alderman, 1990). With such students and particularly on certain types of tasks, a high success rate appears desirable (Brophy, 1986; Crawford, King, Brophy, & Evertson, 1975; Marliave, 1978). In general, however, to avoid having students conclude that success was inevitable, research and practical wisdom suggest that teachers should set standards which challenge students but which are not likely to be seen as unattainable (Burkman & Brezin, 1981; Clifford, 1990; Rogoff & Wertsch, 1984).

In addition to believing that students can perform at a high but realistic level, teachers must be prepared to hold students individually accountable for what is expected of them. Both critics (Jackson, 1985; Landfried, 1989) and researchers (Miller, Leinhardt, & Zigmond, 1988) point to a tendency of teachers and schools to too readily accept from students performance of lower quality than can be expected. In the context of concern about educational standards in the United States, observers of the educational scene argue that students should be expected to perform better and should be held accountable for putting forth appropriate effort (O'Neil, 1991; Tomlinson & Cross, 1991). Research suggests that this perspective can be justified. For example, evidence exists that teachers who are business-like and task-oriented tend to be more effective in nurturing student achievement than teachers who convey the impression that student performance is not of primary importance (Brophy, 1986). Holding students accountable for performance seems especially important in teachers of the gifted (Wendel & Heiser, 1989). The effectiveness of even an instructional approach as popular with students as cooperative learning has been found to depend on the accountability of individual students (Slavin, 1983, 1989). Research suggests that the teacher's role in holding students accountable can be a challenge when the students' task is difficult (Hughes, Sullivan, & Mosley, 1985) but that this role of evaluator does not have to bring about a decrease in students' persistence on such tasks (Hughes, Sullivan & Beaird, 1986). In sum, part of a teacher's success in having high but realistic expectations of students is holding students accountable for putting forth the effort necessary to meet those expectations.

If the teacher education faculty of Indiana State University believed this feature of successful teaching was easy to exemplify in practice, Teacher Outcome 1 would be different than it is. To the contrary, the faculty recognizes that circumstances operate against having high expectations and holding students accountable. One reason for the emphasis placed on this programmatic outcome is the evidence that, as they move through the grades, students tend to take less responsibility for their learning and to desire less personal challenge (Sullivan & Igoe, 1991). Also, researchers find that many students put forth less than diligent effort because they believe they might be less than successful despite the effort and would be labeled "dumb," or because they simply want to avoid being viewed as hard-working (Tomlinson, 1992). Critics contend, too, that the public tolerates massive employment of high school students and an undue emphasis on athletics, both of which compete with school work for student time (Sizer, 1992). Research indicates, as well, that, unlike in Japan, academic achievement by secondary students in the United States has little effect on the quality of the first jobs they obtain after graduating from high school (Rosenbaum & Kariya, 1991). Other scholars argue that the absence of national achievement tests used routinely in decisions regarding college admission and hiring allows students to focus on obtaining the grades they want rather than on learning as much as possible in school (Bishop, 1989). Studies by one research team indicate that whereas Chinese and Japanese parents place almost exclusive emphasis on effort in the achievement of academic success, American parents also see ability as a major contributor and, on the average, do not expect as much of their children academically. One consequence is that American parents do less than parents in these Asian cultures to foster academic achievement (Stevenson, 1992). In a more sweeping analysis of the challenge facing teachers, other critics say that motivating American students is difficult primarily because education in this country is not a scarce, expensive, highly valued, respected commodity, as it is in many countries (Heyneman, 1990). Of course, most students in Indiana State University's teacher education programs do not need to be informed of this difficult circumstance facing teachers. Instead, this challenge is discussed here because it is one reason having high but realistic expectations of pupils is a feature of teaching deemed important enough to be a programmatic outcome of the institution's teacher education programs. (Reprinted from Indiana State University. [1993]. *Institutional report for NCATE and Indiana Professional Standards Board*. Terre Haute, IN: Author, pp. 3–5. Used by permission.)

The institutional report provided a similar explanation for each of the other 11 outcomes with an equally rich grounding in scholarship. Each deserves the same attention as the first outcome, but space limitations prohibit such coverage.

Criteria (2) Following the explanations for each of the outcomes, the ISU report included a list of 856 citations by more than 750 authors supporting the explanation. Additional descriptions of individual specialty programs each included a similar grounding in scholarship and research.

Criteria (4) The programmatic theme, "Becoming a Complete Professional," as well as the programmatic outcomes were preceded by and evolved from an earlier document, "Principles and Guidelines for Undergraduate Teacher Education." The language of the outcomes, therefore, does not permeate all curricular documents, yet the important ideas were infused throughout the documents.

The report included a table for each program offered (12 for undergraduate teacher preparation) that listed each course offered and where each of the programmatic outcomes is addressed. Most of the cells in most of the matrices were filled.

Standard 1.B: Delivery of the Curriculum Whereas the classroom instruction of faculty members included information that went beyond the outcomes presented, the institution monitored most closely information that pertained directly to the outcomes. Course syllabi structure ensured attention to the outcomes.

Furthermore, faculty utilized an array of 13 teaching strategies to ensure adequate models were exemplified.

1. Lecture
2. Demonstration
3. Discussion/questioning
4. Viewing/listening
5. Practice/drill
6. Problem solving
7. Discovery
8. Laboratory
9. Practicum
10. Role playing/simulation
11. Games
12. Cooperative learning
13. Independent learning/self-instruction

A table for each of the 12 undergraduate programs with a list of the strategies and the courses offered shows where each of the strategies is practiced.

A listing of faculty who have received university honors for effective teaching was reported as well as a detailed description of the faculty evaluation model utilized by the school of education.

Louisiana Tech University

Louisiana Tech University (LTU) approached the challenge of developing a discrete knowledge-research base for programs by organizing the faculty to study the matter. They collaborated with the American Association of Colleges for Teacher Education (AACTE) in sponsoring, with a sister institution, a knowledge base workshop. The purposes of the workshop included opportunities to: (a) identify and work with scholars mapping the knowledge bases for teacher education, (b) increase the recognition and receptivity by the professoriate of the knowledge bases for program change, (c) translate the knowledge bases into practical methods of teacher education, (d) defend programs through rationales that include the knowledge bases, and (e) facilitate the change process among teacher education institutions.

Criteria (1) Continued faculty study following the workshop resulted in developing the unit-wide model "Targeting Educational Excellence Model—The Effective Communicator" (see Figure 3.3).

Faculty efforts also resulted in the formulation of the following philosophical principles and beliefs:

1. There is a scientific knowledge base for teaching and counseling which should be incorporated into the professional curriculum.
2. There is a theoretical and practical knowledge base for teaching and counseling which should be incorporated into the professional curriculum.
3. The curriculum should be designed utilizing adult cognitive development patterns as theoretical frameworks (Hunt, 1971, 1975; Sprinthall & Thies-Sprinthall, 1983).
4. Curriculum content should focus on categories of knowledge. Program graduates must possess proficiencies in declarative knowledge, procedural knowledge, and conditional or contextual knowledge (Shulman, 1987; Peterson & Comeaux, 1989; Bandura, 1986).
5. Curriculum processes should accommodate cognitive and affective development of professional educators.
6. Curriculum delivery systems should promote modeling; integrating experiences across declarative knowledge, procedural knowledge, and conditional or contextual knowledge; and active construction of meaning.
7. The curriculum content and processes should emanate from the adopted model. Courses and other experiences should emphasize development of communication skills necessary for effectiveness in roles of collaborators, problem solvers, consultants, and group process facilitators.
8. Faculty participants in the professional development of educators should model effective communicator roles (collaborators, problem solvers, consultants, and group process facilitators) and other attributes expected of students in the program. (Reprinted from Louisiana Tech University. [1993]. *A report to the NCATE*. Ruston: Author, p. 39. Used by permission.)

The works of theorists and researchers (Anderson, 1989; Bandura, 1986; Gagne, 1985; Peterson & Comeaux, 1989; Shulman, 1987; Zimpher, 1988) were synthesized to develop the knowledge base areas around which the professional curricula were constructed. The four areas of knowledge determined as forming the base for the model include: (1) knowledge of learners (theoretical base); (2) knowledge of learning (theoretical knowledge, research-based knowledge, wisdom of practice base); (3) effective teaching (research base); and (4) conditional or contextual knowledge (theoretical base, wisdom of practice, philosophical base).

The institution developed the following statement of goals and objectives for the programs.

Goal: To prepare excellent educators who are effective communicators of content, effective communicators through utilization of the research base on teaching and learning, and effective communicators of professionalism.

Objectives: The beginning teacher will develop and demonstrate communication expertise in three areas which integrate the essential knowledge base: content proficiency, research-based competencies, and professional identity. The specific objectives associated with each component area include the following:

Content Proficiency

A. General Education Objectives
   The program graduate will:

   1. Be aware of broad fields of knowledge which depict the human condition.

2. Be aware of the needs and responsibilities which people have in common.
3. Be an alert, cultivated, and responsible individual and citizen.
4. Demonstrate intellectual curiosity, a positive attitude toward learning, and a disposition to examine, inquire, and analyze.

B. Subject Matter Specialization Objectives
   The program graduate will:

   5. Demonstrate competence in academic major/minor areas.
   6. Be aware of the importance of research and the application of research findings to teaching and/or counseling situations.
   7. Practice use of the major ideas and reasoned inquiry and other intellectual skills of the respective discipline.
   8. Be aware of sources and resources, print and nonprint, available in the respective professional areas.

C. Professional Education Objectives
   The program graduate will:

   9. Be knowledgeable of human growth and development, theories of learning, and the application of psychosocial and physical learning environment principles to the instructional setting.
   10. Demonstrate knowledge of educational goals, educational contexts (social, political, historical, legal), and curriculum.
   11. Apply professional knowledge to teaching.

Research-Based Competencies
The program graduate will:

   12. Practice effective planning which accommodates individual differences.
   13. Implement formative and summative evaluation using various assessment strategies.
   14. Implement instruction effectively using appropriate sequences, strategies, materials, and content.
   15. Provide opportunities for active student involvement in the learning process.
   16. Organize and manage classrooms (including routine or other settings) to achieve optimal learning.

Professional Identity
The program graduate will:

   17. Understand diversity and interact successfully in diverse educational settings and professional circumstances.
   18. Implement effective interpersonal communication skills.
   19. Practice continuous professional development (commitment to the profession).
   20. Adapt and implement new ideas and research findings.
   21. Practice effective situational problem solving, critical thinking, and reflection.
   22. Demonstrate the ethic of caring. (Reprinted from Louisiana Tech University. [1993]. *A report to the NCATE*. Ruston: Author, pp. 40–42. Used by permission.)

An explication of the "Conceptual Framework for Professional Component" discussed the manner in which the program is structured based on adult cognitive theory and the integration and sequencing to promote both hierarchical and cyclical learning of content, the empirical bases for teaching and learning, and professional attributes. The scope and sequence model is based on adaptations of the works of Bloom, Englehart, Furst, Hill, and Krathwohl (1956) and Joyce and Showers (1982).

The components of the Targeting Educational Excellence Model (TEEM)—The Effective Communicator provided the basis for the roles of a communicator: collaborator, problem solver, consultant, and group process facilitator. Fully described are the four components of: (1) curriculum content, (2) enabling experiences, (3) student assessment, and (4) program assessment and refinement (Louisiana Tech University, 1993).

Characteristics of the effective communicator were those of: (1) professional identity, including problem-solving skills; decision-making skills; coping skills; beliefs about the profession; caring about content, learners, and the profession; professional ethics; (2) research-based competencies utilizing the research base on teaching and learning to foster optimal student achievement and research skills to solve problems; and (3) content proficiency conveying substantive knowledge of the subject and appropriate dispositions toward the subject (Louisiana Tech University, 1993).

Criteria (2) The institution demonstrated the knowledge base driving each of the following four areas: (1) knowledge of learners, (2) knowledge of learning, (3) research on effective practice, and (4) conditional or contextual knowledge (Louisiana Tech University, 1993). Shulman (1987) provided a comprehensive categorization of a knowledge base for teaching from which the TEEM model is drawn. Table 3.4 demonstrates the structure for the knowledge base on learners.

The specific courses incorporating the knowledge base on learners were identified next, including educational psychology, child psychology, adolescent psychology, human growth and development, introduction to exceptional students, foundations of education, education of exceptional students, and methods courses in each discipline for application in the content areas. Selected knowledge base references on learners cited specific works by the previously noted theorists in a bibliography with 21 citations (Louisiana Tech University, 1993, p. 50).

A similar explication of the knowledge base was then provided for each of the other three essential knowledge areas—learning, effective practice, and context of practice—each with its own list of key theories/concepts, key theorists/researchers, courses incorporating the knowledge base, and an accompanying bibliography. Table 3.5 provides a table for the knowledge base on learning.

Criteria (4) The essential knowledge bases pervaded the professional studies component as noted; they also undergird, develop, and promote TEEM outcomes. They informed curriculum design, course planning and sequencing, enabling experiences, and evaluation processes. Major works forming the knowledge bases were assembled in a central location for student and faculty access, and expected student performances were incorporated into course syllabi and program evaluation instruments.

Standard 1.B: Delivery of the Curriculum Described in this section is a process by which faculty were ensured access to expanding information bases and from which ongoing program development and delivery perpetually develop.

A broad variety of strategies for instruction (32) categorized in four different models (information processing model, behavioral model, social model, and personal model) were coded to the courses where each is demonstrated and practiced.

The college of education's faculty's range of activities and the earned awards both within the university and in the broader profession were provided as evidence of the institution's recognition of professional vitality. Student evaluation ratings were reported as further evidence of faculty superiority.

The College of William and Mary

The College of William and Mary emphasized a strong grounding in the liberal arts and sciences for prospective teachers.

TABLE 3.4. Knowledge Base on Learners:
Teaching Programs

Key Theories/Concepts	Key Theorists/Researchers
Stages of Development	Piaget, Havinghurst, Erikson, Kohlberg
Learning Styles	Gregorc, Dunn, Kolb, Moston
Whole Child	Dewey
Hierarchy of needs	Maslow
Psychomotor development	Montessori, Simpson, Nichols, Gallahue, Newell, Ulrich
Categorical/non-categorical exceptionalities	AAMD, APA, Gallagher, Lerner, Silver, Wang, Reynolds, Algozzine, Ysseldyke, Sigmond, Dunn, Kirk
Facets of intellect	Guilford, Gardener, Sternberg
Moral development	Kohlberg, Erikson

Source: From A *Report to the National Council for Accreditation of Teacher Education* (p. 50) by Louisiana Tech University, College of Education, 1993, Ruston, LA: Author. Reprinted with permission. The authors listed in this table may not appear in the references to this chapter.

TABLE 3.5. Knowledge Base on Learning:
Teaching Programs

Key Theories/Concepts	Key Theorists/Researchers
Learning domains	Bloom, Gagne
Cognitive development	Piaget, Wadsworth
Creativity	Didge, Torrance, Parnes
Learning styles	Gregorc, Dunn & Dunn; Carbo; Moston
Cooperative learning	Slavin, Johnson, & Johnson
Behaviorism	Thoresen, Skinner, Bandura, Watson, Thorndike
Maturation	Gesell
Humanism	Maslow, Charles, & French; McMurry
Motivation	Maslow, Berlyne, Brophy, Hunter
Discovery learning	Bruner, Moston
Empiricism	Locke
Conditions of learning	Gagne
Learning by exceptional students	Skinner, Lindsley, Dunn, Phillips, Kirk, Hewitt
Prior knowledge	Ausubel, Holmes, & Roser
Whole language	Goodman, Kiefer
Scaffolding theory	Vygotsky, Palinscar, & Brown
Student-centered learning	Rogers

Source: From A *Report to the National Council for Accreditation of Teacher Education* (p. 52) by Louisiana Tech University, College of Education, 1993, Ruston, LA: Author. The authors listed in this table may not appear in the references to this chapter.

What this college terms an *effective liberally educated teacher* must be a teacher who is well educated, knowledgeable about specific teaching domains and general principles of teaching and learning, and able to grasp content-specific pedagogy. The effective liberally educated teacher was prepared through three areas of study—general studies, a teaching specialty, and professional studies—by which teachers are expected to develop understandings, abilities, and values in six areas: individual autonomy, social responsibility, personal fulfillment, cultural literacy, political autonomy and responsible citizenship, and life and career enhancement.

In presenting the case for the undergirding of programs with a knowledge base, the institution provided a single response for Standard 1.A: Design of the Curriculum and Criteria 1, 2, and 3 combined.

Standard 1.A: Design of the Curriculum, Criteria 1, 2, and 3

The College of William and Mary cited Grossman, Wilson, and Shulman (1989) and Reynolds (1992) as major informers of the design for the general studies in the liberal arts. This component was cited as a major focus of the teacher education programs and was designed to help students achieve knowledge, skill, and attitude and value objectives. Knowledge objectives, of which there are six, include areas such as understanding the world of nature, understanding individual and social behavior, general historical knowledge, and general knowledge of masterworks of the arts. Skills included critical thinking, verbal, quantitative, scientific, aesthetic, historical inquiry, language, information acquisition, and computer skills. Some examples of attitudes and values were intellectual values; social and civic values; and values of a personal, moral, and identity nature. These were extensively described and rationalized.

Teacher education students are required to pursue their primary concentration in an academic discipline. Cited again were Grossman, Wilson, and Shulman (1989) and Reynolds (1992).

In professional studies in teacher education, the knowledge base in all teacher education programs was organized around the categories of knowledge cited by Shulman (1987). The foundation for general and specific pedagogical and curriculum knowledge was derived from the effective teaching research of Brophy and Good (1986), Gage (1984, 1985), Reynolds (1992), and Rosenshine and Stevens (1986). The programs developed three competency areas of preteaching, teaching, and postteaching as noted in Reynolds (1992). Additional scholars supported the three areas. A comprehensive bibliography of 60 citations supported the general descriptions of all programs.

Each program (elementary, secondary in each of its specialties, physical education, and special education) was developed based on the noted knowledge base but with distinct goals, objectives, and course requirements. Objectives for the secondary program in English, for example, include the following:

Students are expected to develop and demonstrate knowledge of:
1.1 Schools and schooling
1.2 Schools as changing social systems
1.3 The social, economic, political, and ethical factors that impinge on teaching
1.4 Concepts related to knowing and learning
1.5 Adolescence
1.6 Their academic specialization
1.7 Curriculum and instruction related to the subject matter of their academic specialization

Students are expected to develop and demonstrate the skills to:
2.1 Recognize and apply a code of ethics
2.2 Appreciate the functions and responsibilities of professional organizations
2.3 Interact effectively as individuals and group members
2.4 Communicate effectively
2.5 Make rational decisions about classroom instruction
2.6 Implement instructional skills
2.7 Employ a variety of classroom management techniques

Students are expected to develop and demonstrate attitudes that reflect:
3.1 Respect for the unique potential of each human being
3.2 Respect for students as individuals
3.3 Respect for individual differences
3.4 An ability to tolerate ambiguity
3.5 Respect for evidence as a measure of truth and for the use of reason, intuition, and creative intelligence
3.6 Excitement for intellectual life, learning, and professional development. (Reprinted from the College of William & Mary. [1993]. *Institutional report for the NCATE and the Virginia Department of Education.* Williamsburg, VA: Author, pp. 29–30. Used by permission.)

In addition to these unit objectives, students in English education must meet the specialty area guidelines and objectives of the National Council of Teachers of English. The objectives for the elementary education program have distinctions appropriate to that program as do objectives for all other programs.

Criterion (4) For each program, a table coded with course offerings and the degree to which each objective is addressed was presented. Further evidence was presented in course outlines and syllabi, examples of student work, faculty resumes, and materials in the Swem Library and the School of Education Learning Resource Center.

Standard 1.B: Delivery of the Curriculum Course outlines and descriptions in the institutional report demonstrated that instruction is current, varied, and congruent with best practices and established research. Furthermore, the institution listed 15 models of teaching (supported by appropriate research) and the courses in which each is studied and demonstrated. For example, the concept attainment model is found in Elementary Science Curriculum and Instruction, Social and Philosophical Foundations of Education, Child Development and Learning, Elementary Science Curriculum and Instruction, Literature for Adolescents, Curriculum and Instructional Methods—English, Curriculum and Instructional Methods—Science, Education and the Structure of Knowledge, and Child Psychology. Group investigation model is found in Elementary Science Curriculum and Instruction, Social and Philosophical Foundations of Education, Elementary Social Studies Curriculum and Instruction, Elementary Mathematics Curriculum and Instruction, Literature for Adolescents, Curriculum and Instructional Methods, Curriculum and Instructional Methods—Science, Seminar in Teaching—English, Education and the Structure of Knowledge, and Child Psychology.

The College of William and Mary presented an extensive report regarding the reputation for quality instruction in the professional education unit within and outside the institution. The report also provided a description of the faculty evaluation model employed by the school.

CONCLUSION

The 42 institutional reports in this analysis show that institutions take seriously their responsibilities to demonstrate a program based on a systematic design with explicitly stated philosophy and objectives. This facet of the NCATE standards received careful attention. The range and substance of the statements composing the systematic design often were surprising and impressive. Often the diversity of systematic designs that emerged was fascinating. Presuming each design has validity, one must conclude there are many different ways to design teacher education programs based on a selected knowledge-research base.

The NCATE standards ensured in many cases that institutions adopted models for their professional education programs, even though evidence relative to models was much more difficult to determine than for other requirements (e.g., themes, instructional models, appropriate citations). It may be the case that many institutions are not all sure what is meant by a model. Some institutions testified they had adopted a model(s) based on the work of certain scholars; that of Shulman (1987) was most frequently cited.

The Shulman (1987) proposal probably qualifies as a model in that it includes defined segments of the knowledge base in which the following categories are indentified: (1) content knowledge; (2) general pedagogical knowledge; (3) curriculum knowledge; (4) pedagogical content knowledge; (5) knowledge of learners and their characteristics; (6) knowledge of essential contexts; and (7) knowledge of educational ends, purposes, values, philosophical grounds, and historical grounds. It also identified the following sources for the teaching knowledge base: (1) scholarship in the content disciplines, (2) educational materials and structures, (3) formal educational scholarship, and (4) wisdom of practice. Shulman's model of pedagogical reasoning and action—comprehension, transformation, instruction, evaluation, reflection, and new comprehensions—is clear and persuasive. It is easy to understand why this approach is so popular with institutions.

The knowledge bases across all of the programs were very broad and diverse. In each case it seemed clear that the knowledge base was carefully designed and provided a solid basis for the models and program rationales. Across all of the reports, the number of individual works cited numbered 2,000 or more. One institution alone had nearly 900 citations for the basic design, not counting the references for each specialty program. Some institutions had no citations. It is probable that additonal citations were noted in documents available only on campus; these were not reviewed for this chapter.

In spite of the impressive number of scholars identified in the reports, some scholars whose works might be expected in such a broad knowledge base were not seen; for example, Stephen Brookfield's (1987) monumental contributions on critical thinking; Patricia Cross (1986) and her classroom action research initiatives that have influenced many classrooms; Stephen Gould (1981), who writes about mental measurements; Alfie Kohn's (1986) important work on the negative effects of competition; and Parker Palmer (1990), whose work on effective teaching is well known. This point is made not to reflect criticism of the selections but rather to emphasize that the breadth of the potential knowledge-research base is very extensive. Some exclusions are understandable.

An obvious question is whether the institutions were successful in meeting the knowledge base standards. A standard-by-standard review of NCATE actions revealed that 16 of the 42 institutions "met" both standards 1.A and 1.B, the highest rating possible. Two "met" 1.A and "met with weakness" 1.B; nine "met with weakness" 1.A and "met" 1.B; five "met with weakness" both 1.A and 1.B; three "Not met" 1.A and "met" 1.B; four "Not met" 1.A and "met with weakness" 1.B; and three "Not met" both 1.A and 1.B.

The knowledge bases found in this review included the traditional forms of scholarly inquiry and theory development. A broad array of quantitative and qualitative research studies was evident. There was also an impressive base of theoretical works representing a large number of scholars. Learning theories, cognitive psychological theories, measurement and evaluation theories, and many others were noted.

Also apparent was the broad range of scholarship reflected in curricular design and planning, course syllabi, instructional practice, and measurement and evaluation. The range of instructional models were all substantiated by a base of knowledge and research.

This review was conducted by examining the institutional reports only. The evidence, therefore, was self-reported and did not include the information that is provided in the reports of the teams visiting the campuses; team reports include a validation of the institution's self-study and evaluative judgments about program quality. It is possible, therefore, that the impressive evidence in the reports may not be reflected in the practices of the institutions. To revalidate each institutional report would have required some sort of replication of team visit and council action that would go well beyond the limits of this review. The three institutions chosen for more detailed reporting, however, had completed the NCATE process with standards met; this can reasonably be considered prima facie evidence that practices are reflective of assertions in at least those institutions.

This review indicates that the NCATE standard as they are now being applied seem to be having a substantial and positive effect on the knowledge base used by institutions seeking NCATE accreditation. This review also validates the variety of options available to institutions of higher education in the development and implementation of teacher education programs.

References

Alderman, M. K. (1990). Motivation for at-risk students. *Educational Leadership, 48*(1), 27–30.

Anderson, C. (1989). The role of education in the academic disciplines in teacher preparation. In A. Woolfolk (Ed.), *Research perspectives on the graduate preparation of teachers* (pp. 88–107). Englewood Cliffs, NJ: Prentice Hall.

Bandura, A. (1986). *Social foundations of thought and action: A social cognitive theory.* Englewood Cliffs, NJ: Prentice Hall.

Bandura, A. (1989). Human agency in social cognitive theory. *American Psychologist, 44*(9), 1175–1184.

Barnes, H. (1991). Reconceptualizing the knowledge base for teacher education. In M. Pugach, H. Barnes, & L. Beckum (Eds.), *Changing the practice of teacher education: The role of the knowledge base* (pp. 3–21). Washington, DC: American Association of Colleges for Teacher Education.

Bishop, J. (1989). *Incentives for learning: Why American high school students compare so poorly to their counterparts overseas* (Working Paper No. 89–09). Ithaca, NY: School of Industrial and Labor Relations, Cornell University. (ERIC Documentation Reproduction Service No. ED 325 558)

Black, S. (1992). In praise of judicious praise. *Executive Educator, 14*(10), 24–27.

Bloom, B., Englehart, M., Furst, E., Hill, W., & Krathwohl, D. (1956). *Taxonomy of educational objectives: The classification of education goals: Handbook I: Cognitive domain.* New York: David McKay.

Boyer, E. (1987). *The early years.* New York: Harper & Row.

Brookfield, S. D. (1987). *Developing critical thinkers.* San Francisco: Jossey-Bass.

Brophy, J. (1983). Conceptualizing student motivation. *Educational Psychologist, 18*(3), 200–215.

Brophy, J. (1986). Teacher influences on student achievement. *American Psychologist, 41*(12), 1069–1077.

Brophy, J., & Evertson, C. (1976). *Learning from teaching: A developmental perspective.* Boston: Allyn & Bacon.

Brophy, J. E., & Good, T. L. (1986). Teacher behavior and student achievement. In M. C. Wittrock (Ed.), *Handbook of research on teaching* (3rd ed., pp. 328–375). New York: Macmillan.

Brophy, J. E., & Kher, N. (1986). Teacher socialization as a mechanism for developing student motivation to learn. In R. Feldman (Ed.), *Social psychology of education: Current research and theory.* New York: Cambridge University Press.

Bruner, J. S. (1960). *The process of education: A searching discussion of school education opening new paths to learning and teaching.* Cambridge: Harvard University Press.

Burkman, E., & Brezin, M. (1981). Effects of expectation level on achievement in high school physical science courses (ISIS) employing a quasi mastery teaching method. *Journal of Educational Research, 75*(2), 121–126.

Byrne, B. M., & Shavelson, R. J. (1986). On the structure of adolescent self-concept. *Journal of Educational Psychology, 78*(6), 473–481.

Byrne, B. M., & Shavelson, R. J. (1987). Adolescent self-concept: Testing the assumption of equivalent structure across gender. *American Educational Research Journal, 24*(3), 365–385.

Carnevale, A. P. (1992). Skills for the new world order. *American School Board Journal, 179*(5), 28–30.

Chapman, J. W. (1988). Learning disabled children's self-concepts. *Review of Educational Research, 58*(3), 347–371.

Clifford, M. M. (1990). Students need challenge, not easy success. *Educational Leadership, 48*(1), 22–26.

The College of William & Mary, School of Education. (1993). *Institutional report for the National Council for Accreditation of Teacher Education and the Virginia Department of Education.* Williamsburg, VA: Author.

Cooley, C. H. (1902). *Human nature and the social order.* New York: Scribner's.

Crawford, W. J., King, C. E., Brophy, J. E., & Evertson, C. M. (1975, April). *Error rates and question difficulty related to elementary children's learning.* Paper presented at the annual meeting of the American Educational Research Association, Washington, DC. (ERIC Document Reproduction Service No. ED 147 275)

Cross, K. P. (1986). A proposal to improve teaching or what taking teaching seriously should mean. *AAHE Bulletin, 39*(1), 9–15.

Dewey, J. (1983). The child and the curriculum. In J. A. Boydston (Ed.), *John Dewey: The middle works, 1899–1924, Volume 2: 1902–1903* (pp. 271–292). Chicago: Southern Illinois University Press.

Dill, D. (Ed.). (1990). *What teachers need to know: The knowledge, skills, and values essential to good teaching.* San Francisco: Jossey-Bass.

Duckworth, K., & Lind, K. (1989, March). *Curricular tools and motivating strategies with non-college bound students in science and social studies.* Paper presented at the annual meeting of the American Educational Research Association, San Francisco. (ERIC Document Reproduction Service No. ED 307 112)

Finkel, L. (1984). Foreword. In *Using what we know about teaching* (1984 Yearbook, p. vii). Alexandria, VA: Association for Supervision and Curriculum Development.

Gage, N. L. (1984). What do we know about teaching effectiveness? *Phi Delta Kappan, 66*(2), 87–93.

Gage, N. L. (1985). *Hard gains in the soft sciences: The case of pedagogy.* Bloomington, IN: Phi Delta Kappa Center on Education and Research.

Gagné, R. (1985). *The conditions of learning.* New York: Holt, Rinehart and Winston.

Gardner, W. (1989). Preface. In M. Reynolds (Ed.), *Knowledge base for the beginning teacher* (p. x). New York: Pergamon.

Goldenberg, C. (1992). The limits of expectations: A case for case knowledge about teacher expectancy effects. *American Educational Research Journal, 29*(3), 517–544.

Goodlad, J. (1990). *Teachers for our nation's schools.* San Francisco: Jossey-Bass.

Goodlad, J., Soder, R., & Sirotnik, K. (1990). *The moral dimensions of teaching.* San Francisco: Jossey-Bass.

Gottfried, A. E. (1985). Academic intrinsic motivation in elementary and junior high school students. *Journal of Educational Psychology, 77*(6), 631–645.

Gould, S. J. (1981). *The mismeasure of man.* New York: W. W. Norton & Co.

Gregory, J. F. (1986, April). *A secondary analysis of HSB data related to special education.* Paper presented at the annual conference of the American Educational Research Association, San Francisco. (ERIC Document Reproduction Service No. ED 276 219)

Grossman, P. (1990). *The making of a teacher: Teacher knowledge and teacher education.* New York: Teachers College Press.

Grossman, P., Wilson, G., & Shulman, L. (1989). Teachers of substance: Subject matter knowledge for teaching. In M. C. Reynolds (Ed.), *Knowledge base for the beginning teacher* (pp. 23–36). New York: Pergamon.

Hall, G., Campbell, G., Galluzzo, G., Horn, J., Pankratz, R., & Vickers, C. (1994). *Analysis of teacher education knowledge base statements: The foundation for advancing teacher education into the 21st century.* Report of the Knowledge Base Committee presented at the annual meeting of the Teacher Education Council at State Colleges and Universities, Chicago.

Hamachek, D. (1971). *Encounters with self*. Fort Worth: Holt, Reinhart and Winston.

Harris, M. J., Rosenthal, R., & Snodgrass, S. E. (1986). The effects of teacher expectations, gender, and behavior on pupil academic performance and self-concept. *Journal of Educational Research, 79*(3), 173–179.

Heyneman, S. P. (1990). Education on the world market. *American School Board Journal, 177*(3), 28–30.

Hilman, S. B., & Golumbia, L. R. (1990, August). *A comparison of learning disabled and nondisabled adolescent motivational processes*. Paper presented at the annual meeting of the American Psychological Association, Boston. (ERIC Document Reproduction Service No. ED 328 036)

The Holmes Group. (1986). *Tomorrow's teachers: A report of the Holmes Group*. East Lansing, MI: Author.

Howey, K., & Zimpher, N. (1989). *Profiles of preservice teacher education: Inquiry into the nature of programs*. Albany: State University of New York Press.

Howsam, R., Corrigan, D., & Denemark, G. (1976). *Educating a profession*. Washington, DC: American Association of Colleges for Teacher Education.

Hughes, B. J., Sullivan, H. J., & Beaird, J. (1986). Continuing motivation of boys and girls under differing evaluation conditions and achievement levels. *American Educational Research Journal, 23*(4), 660–667.

Hughes, B. J., Sullivan, H. J., & Mosley, M. L. (1985). External evaluation, task difficulty, and continuing motivation. *Journal of Educational Research, 78*(4), 210–215.

Hunt, D. E. (1971). *Matching models in education: The coordination of teaching methods with student characteristics*. Toronto: Ontario Institute for Studies in Education.

Hunt, D. E. (1975). Person–environment interaction: A challenge found wanting before it was tried. *Review of Educational Research, 45*(2), 209–230.

Indiana State University, School of Education. (1993). *Institutional report for National Council for Accreditation of Teacher Education and Indiana Professional Standards Board*. Terre Haute, IN: Author.

Jackson, B. (1985). Lowered expectations: How schools reward incompetence. *Phi Delta Kappan, 67*(4), 304–305.

Jackson, P. (1986). *The practice of teaching*. New York: Teachers College Press.

Johnson, D., & Johnson, R. (1987). *Learning together and alone: Cooperative, competitive, and individualistic learning*. Englewood Cliffs, NJ: Prentice Hall.

Johnstone, J., Spalding, J., Paden, R., & Ziffren, A. (1989). *Those who can: Undergraduate programs to prepare arts and sciences majors for teaching*. Washington, DC: American Association of Colleges for Teacher Education.

Katz, L., & Raths, J. (1988, April). *Dilemmas in teacher education*. Paper presented at the annual meeting of the American Educational Research Association, New Orleans.

Kelly, K. R., & Jordan, L. K. (1990). Effects of academic achievement and gender on academic and social self-concept: A replication study. *Journal of Counseling and Development, 69*(2), 173–177.

Kershner, J. R. (1990). Self-concept and IQ as predictors of remedial success in children with learning disabilities. *Journal of Learning Disabilities, 23*(6), 368–374.

Kohn, A. (1986). *No contest: The case against competition*. Boston: Houghton Mifflin.

Landfried, S. E. (1989). Enabling undermines responsibility in students. *Educational Leadership, 47*(3), 79–83.

Lindley, H. A., & Keithley, M. E. (1991). Gender expectations and student achievement. *Roeper Review, 13*(4), 213–215.

Louisiana Tech University, College of Education. (1993). *A report to the National Council for Accreditation of Teacher Education*. Ruston, LA: Author.

MacIver, D. J., Stipek, D. J., & Daniels, D. H. (1991). Explaining within semester changes in student effort in junior high school and senior high school courses. *Journal of Educational Psychology, 83*(3), 201–211.

Maeroff, G. I. (Ed.). (1991). *Voices from the classroom: Exceptional teachers speak*. Cupertino, CA: Apple Computer. (ERIC Document Reproduction Service No. ED 331 787)

Marliave, R. (1978, March). *Academic learning time and achievement: The validation of a measure of ongoing student engagement and task difficulty*. Paper presented at the annual meeting of the American Educational Research Association, Toronto. (ERIC Document Reproduction Service No. ED 160 661)

Marsh, H. W. (1990). Causal ordering of academic self-concept and academic achievement: A multiwave, longitudinal panel analysis. *Journal of Educational Psychology, 82*(4), 646–656.

Marsh, H. W., Byrne, B. M., & Shavelson, R. J. (1988). A multifaceted academic self-concept: Its hierarchical structure and its relation to academic achievement. *Journal of Educational Psychology, 80*(3), 366–380.

Mboya, M. M. (1986). Black adolescents: A descriptive study of their self-concepts and academic achievement. *Adolescence, 21*(83), 689–696.

McClelland, D. C. (1985). *Human motivation*. Glenview, IL: Scott, Foresman.

Mead, G. H. (1934). *Mind, self, and society from the standpoint of a social behaviorist*. Chicago: The University of Chicago Press.

Miller, S. E., Leinhardt, G., & Zigmond, N. (1988). Influencing engagement through accommodation: An ethnographic study of at-risk students. *American Educational Research Journal, 25*(4), 465–487.

Murphy, J. A. (1988). Improving the achievement of minority students. *Educational Leadership, 46*(2), 41–42.

National Council for Accreditation of Teacher Education (NCATE). (1960). *Standards for the accreditation of teacher education*. Washington, DC: Author.

National Council for Accreditation of Teacher Education (NCATE). (1977). *Standards for the accreditation of teacher education*. Washington, DC: Author.

National Council for Accreditation of Teacher Education (NCATE). (1992). *Standards, procedures and policies for the accreditation of professional education units*. Washington, DC: Author.

National Council for Accreditation of Teacher Education (NCATE). (1994). *NCATE standards*. Washington, DC: Author.

O'Neil, J. (1991). Drive for national standards picking up steam. *Educational Leadership, 48*(5), 4–8.

Palmer, P. J. (1990). Good teaching: A matter of living the mystery. *Change, 22*(1), 11–16.

Peterson, P., & Comeaux, M. (1989). Assessing the teacher as a reflective professional: New perspectives on teacher evaluation. In A. E. Woolfold (Ed.), *Research perspectives on the graduate preparation of teachers* (pp. 132–152). Englewood Cliffs, NJ: Prentice Hall.

Pintrich, P. R., & Blumenfeld, P. C. (1985). Classroom experience and children's self-perceptions of ability, effort, and conduct. *Journal of Educational Psychology, 77*(6), 646–657.

Pottebaum, S. M., Keith, T. Z., & Ehly, S. W. (1986). Is there a causal relation between self-concept and academic achievement? *Journal of Educational Research, 79*(3), 140–144.

Reynolds, A. C. (1992). What is competent beginning teaching? A review of literature. *Review of Educational Research, 62*(1), 1–35.

Reynolds, M. C. (Ed.). (1989). *Knowledge base for the beginning teacher*. Oxford, England: Pergamon.

Rogoff, B., & Wertsch, J. (Eds.). (1984). *Children's learning in the "zone" of proximal development*. San Francisco: Jossey-Bass.

Rosenbaum, J. E., & Kariya, T. (1991). Do school achievements affect the early jobs of high school graduates in the United States and Japan? *Sociology of Education, 64*(2), 78–95.

Rosenberg, M., Schooler, C., & Schenbach, C. (1989). Self-esteem and adolescent problems: Modeling reciprocal effects. *American Sociological Review, 54*(6), 1004–1018.

Rosenshine, B., & Stevens, R. (1986). Teaching functions. In M. C. Wittrock (Ed.), *Handbook of research on teaching* (3rd ed., pp. 376–391). New York: Macmillan.

Rosenthal, R. (1989, August). *Experimenter expectancy, covert communication, and meta-analysis methods.* Paper presented at the annual meeting of the American Psychological Association, New Orleans. (ERIC Document Reproduction Service No. ED 317 551)

Rosenthal, R., & Jacobson, L. (1968). *Pygmalion in the classroom: Teacher expectation and pupils' intellectual development.* New York: Holt.

Saltiel, J. (1986). Segmental influence: The case of educational and occupational significant others. *Adolescence, 21*(83), 615–622.

Schon, D. A. (1983). *The reflective practitioner: How professionals think in action.* New York: Basic Books.

Schunk, D. H. (1985). Self-efficacy and classroom learning. *Psychology in the schools, 22*(2), 208–223.

Schunk, D. H. (1989). Self-efficacy and cognitive achievement: Implications for students with learning problems. *Journal of Learning Disabilities, 22*(1), 14–22.

Schunk, D. H., & Rice, J. M. (1991). Learning goals and progress feedback during reading comprehension instruction. *Journal of Reading Behavior, 23*(3), 351–364.

Shulman, L. S. (1987). Knowledge and teaching: Foundations of the new reform. *Harvard Educational Review, 57*(1), 1–22.

Sizer, T. R. (1992). *Horace's school: Redesigning the American high school.* Boston: Houghton Mifflin.

Slavin, R. E. (1983). *Cooperative learning.* New York: Longman.

Slavin, R. E. (1989). Research on cooperative learning: Consensus and controversy. *Educational Leadership, 47*(4), 52–54.

Smey-Richman, B. (1989). *Teacher expectations and low-achieving students.* Philadelphia: Research for Better Schools. (ERIC Document Reproduction Service No. ED 328 627)

Sprinthall, N. A., & Thies-Sprinthall, L. (1983). The need for theoretical frameworks in educating teachers: A cognitive-developmental perspective. In K. R. Howey & W. F. Garner (Eds.), *The education of teachers: A look ahead.* New York: Longman.

Stevenson, H. W. (1992). Learning from Asian schools. *Scientific American, 267*(6), 70–76.

Strein, W. (1990, August). *The high school and beyond data set: Academic self-concept measures.* Paper presented at the annual convention of the American Psychological Association, Boston. (Eric Document Reproduction Service No. ED 326 826)

Sullivan, H., & Igoe, A. R. (1991, April). *Gender and grade-level differences in student attributes related to school learning and motivation.* Paper presented at the annual meeting of the American Educational Research Association, Chicago. (ERIC Document Reproduction Service No. ED 333 044)

Teddlie, C., & Whelan, C. S. (1989, March). *Self-fulfilling prophecy and attribution of responsibility: Is there a causal link to achievement?* Paper presented at the annual meeting of the American Educational Research Association, San Francisco. (ERIC Document Reproduction Service No. ED 323 211)

Tomlinson, T. M. (1992). *Hard work and high expectations: Motivating students to learn* (Report No. PIP 92-1500). Washington, DC: U.S. Department of Education.

Tomlinson, T. M., & Cross, C. T. (1991). Student effort: The key to high standards. *Educational Leadership, 49*(1), 69–73.

Van Hecke, M., & Tracy, R. J. (1987). The influence of adult encouragement on children's persistence. *Child Study Journal, 17*(4), 251–268.

Wendel, R., & Heiser, S. (1989). Effective instructional characteristics of teachers of junior high school gifted students. *Roeper Review, 11*(3), 151–153.

Whitlock, M. S., & DuCette, J. P. (1989). Outstanding and average teachers of the gifted: A comparative study. *Gifted Child Quarterly, 33*(1), 15–21.

Zeichner, K., & Liston, D. (1987). Teaching student teachers to reflect. *Harvard Educational Review, 57*(1), 23–48.

Zimmerman, B. J., Bandura, A., & Martinez-Ponz, M. (1992). Self-motivation for academic attainment: The role of self-efficacy beliefs and personal goal setting. *American Educational Research Journal, 29*(3), 663–676.

Zimpher, M. (1988). A design for the professional development of teacher leaders. *Journal of Teacher Education, 39*(1), 53–60.

· 4 ·

TEACHERS AS RESEARCHERS

Kenneth T. Henson

EASTERN KENTUCKY UNIVERSITY

DEFINITIONS

The term *teacher as researcher* is polymorphous; it continuously changes and it stimulates about as many concepts as the number of individuals who consider it. Any attempt to study the subject requires attention to its many definitions.

The number of ways the term teacher as researcher has been defined is matched by the diversity among the definitions; some of the definitions are all encompassing, some are narrow and specific, but most are somewhere between these ranges (Bracey, 1991). The definition used at any particular time may be determined by the context in which the term is found (McKernan, 1988).

The differences among the definitions of research are more than accidental and can be of significant consequence because they reflect different sets of values and assumptions (Shannon, 1990). An examination of these differences can lead to a better understanding of the individual terms and of how they are interrelated.

Vockell (1983) used a general definition of research that can lead to a broad definition of teacher as researcher. According to Vockell, research has three levels: (1) descriptions of processes (what actually happens); (2) descriptions of relationships (what is associated with what); and (3) research supporting a causative relationship, even without relationship to an overall theory.

Those who define research so generally will probably agree with Shalaway (1990) who said that "(for many teachers) research is more a verb than a noun" (p. 34). Shalaway pointed out that the work of researchers is similar, regardless of whether teachers work alone or collaborate with a research team: "no matter where they work, teacher researchers all engage in the same basic process—systematic inquiry" (p. 34). Although Shalaway's definition is general, it does specify "systematic" behavior.

Classroom/Action Teacher Research

The Reading/Language in Secondary Schools Subcommittee of the International Reading Association's (IRA) (1989) perception of the term is reflected in the following passages:

Any time you try an experiment with one group in the classroom and set up another group as a control for comparison, you have the foundation for research. When you decide a method worked or didn't work as judged from the results, you have done some classroom research.

Classroom action research may be as formal or informal as the teacher chooses. It may be done alone in the privacy of the classroom or teachers may prefer to collaborate with a university educator or other members of their faculty or district staff. (p. 216)

Lytle and Cochran-Smith (1990) defined teacher research as "systematic, intentional inquiry by teachers" (p. 83). They say that this definition is consistent with the idea that to learn deliberately is research, with the notion that every lesson should be an inquiry for the teacher (see Goswami & Stillman, 1987, p. 15). Steinhouse (see McKernan, 1988) defined research as systematic, self-critical inquiry made public. McKernan (1988) said that this definition of teacher research is useful because "it suggests rigorous examination of one's own practice as a basis for professional development, the idea is that each school, and indeed each classroom, is a laboratory in which the curriculum and problems experienced as problems by teachers (not outside researchers) are subjected to empirical examination by practitioners" (p. 154). McCutcheon and Jung (1990) defined action research as "inquiry teachers undertake to understand and improve their own practice" (p. 144). Oberg and McCutcheon (1987) said that action research is "any systematic inquiry, large or small, conducted by professionals and focusing

Back-up readers for this chapter include Dr. David E. Kapel, Dean of the School of Education at Rowan College of New Jersey, and Dr. Jay Thompson, Professor of Educational Leadership, Teachers College at Ball State University.

on some aspect of their practice in order to find out more about it, and eventually to act in ways they see as better or more effective" (p. 117). McKernan (1988) listed four self-recommending features of action research over fundamental or traditionally defined research:

1. It assists participants in gaining and *increasing their own understanding* of personally experienced educational or curriculum problems.
2. Action research as opposed to fundamental research focuses on problems of *immediate concern*.
3. Research is geared toward practical short-term solutions—thus, it is a form of *operational* or *applied* research.
4. Action research often encourages (though it does not have to be collaborative) *collaboration* of a number of participants on an equal footing. It is for equality of partnership, not simply in engaging of participants in a cooperative research enterprise. (p. 155)

Carr and Kemmis (1986) defined action research as a form of self-reflective inquiry undertaken by participants in social situations in order to improve the rationality and justice of their own practices, their understanding of these practices, and the situations in which the practices are carried out (p. 162).

These definitions (Carr & Kemmis, 1986; McCutcheon & Jung, 1990; McKernan, 1988; Oberg & McCutcheon, 1987) create an image of action researchers as teachers who each day pursue relevant topics to improve their teaching.

HISTORY

Teacher Involvement with Research

The concept of classroom teachers as researchers is not new. As early as 1908 concerted efforts were being made to involve classroom teachers in research (Lowery, 1908). Two years later the topic appeared in a professional journal (Bagley, Bell, Seashore, & Whipple, 1910). As Olson (1990) said, "it is interesting to note that early in the twentieth century teachers were recognized as persons to identify educational problems pertinent to teaching. Furthermore, teachers were charged with investigating solutions to those problems, although the practice was never called research" (p. 3). Even with encouragement to become involved with research, the type and level of involvement was limited throughout the first half of the twentieth century. Initially teachers were not conductors of research, nor were they full investigative partners; rather they remained primarily recipients of research (Peik, 1938).

Teacher-conducted research in America accelerated in the 1920s (Olson, 1990) as a consequence of encouragement from several sources (Buckingham, 1926; Cushman & Fox, 1938; Dewey, 1929; Good, Barr, & Scates, 1936; Peik, 1938; Waples & Tyler, 1930). Initially teachers were encouraged to conduct action research as a means of curriculum development (McKernan, 1988). In the 1950s, Corey (1953) and Shumsky (1958) urged teachers to become researchers in their own classrooms. Stevens, Slanton, and Bunny (1992) cited several studies that have described classroom teachers performing the role of researchers (Allen, Combs, Hendricks, Nash, & Wilson, 1988; Busching & Rowls, 1987; Copenhaver, Byrd, McIntyre, & Norris,

1982; Fischer, 1988–1989; McDaniel, 1988–1989; Reading/Language in Secondary Schools Subcommittee of IRA, 1989).

TEACHER ATTITUDES

Some clear differences exist in the way teachers and university researchers view research. This disparity frequently serves as a major barrier to effective collaboration. J. Myron Atkin (1989) addressed the problem.

Teachers are at best peripheral to the conduct of educational research. They are often studied, but they are seldom encouraged to undertake systematic studies of educational problems. As a result, serious gaps exist in our understanding of schools, and a great many teachers and administrators believe—and say, with conviction—that educational research is irrelevant, wrong-headed, or both. (p. 200)

Hastie (1992) reported that university researchers are concerned that "teachers do not attempt to attain up-to-date information about research, while teachers suggest that the information provided by researchers does not transfer well to the teaching context" (p. 371). Teachers also often perceive researchers' topics as too theoretical or, conversely, too superficial (Chattin-McNichols & Loeffler, 1989). Cuban (1992) said that the teacher's usual world is characterized by action, concrete knowledge, and the ability to work in actual settings. Cuban attributed this difference in perceptions among teachers and researchers to the different cultures in their daily lives; a teacher's world is more concrete. For example, researchers are comfortable in exploring possibilities such as possible products to come from collaboration, whereas teachers ask questions to remove the uncertainty, such as "What should the products look like?", "What does the collaboration want?", or "When?".

The literature is replete with expressions of concern over the bases for teacher decisions. For example, Egbert (1984) said, "Teachers ignore research and overestimate the value of personal experience" (p. 14). Garrison (1988) noted, "If they could, many if not most teachers would ignore research on teaching entirely . . ." (p. 489). Brown (1990) said that teachers usually do not base their planning on the factors that affect achievement. When Marshall (1991) asked teachers why they teach as they do, they reported:

It's the way I was taught.
It's the way I learned.
It's the easiest way to cover the material. (p. 227)

Bellon, Bellon, and Blank (1992) attributed teachers' failure to develop effective teaching strategies to the absence of opportunities to develop an adequate research knowledge base. These authors reported:

We have found that the most able teachers do not want simple prescriptions that are intended to help them be more effective. They know teaching is a complex process that is individual and highly contextual. . . . Successful teachers want to have a broad knowledge base that will help them make the most appropriate instructional decisions. (p. 3)

Historically, the level of teacher involvement in research has been low (Olson, 1990). This low involvement is attributable, at least in part, to the failure of preservice programs to prepare and require students to conduct research. Another contributor is poor communications between teacher and researcher (Bain & Gooseclose, 1979; Odell, 1976; Rainey, 1972; Travers, 1976). Even when teachers were involved, they usually had little or no voice in the desired outcome (Atkin, 1989; Fenstermacher, 1987). Often research involved teachers who were reluctant subjects of studies (Glatthorn, 1993). Tyack (1990) pointed out that most of the important changes that have occurred in the schools since the 1960s have resulted from federal laws. Yet, many educators (Haberman, 1992; Kirk, 1988; Kowalski & Reitzug, 1993; Ravitch, 1992) agree that if the conceived changes are to be effectively implemented, teachers must be involved in their planning. Intrinsic motivators (e.g., involvement with the results of an innovation) are exceedingly more powerful than extrinsic motivators (Herzberg, Mausner, & Snyderman, 1959; Wright, 1985; Young, 1985).

A major barrier to teacher involvement is teachers' schedules. Put simply, today's teachers have so many responsibilities that they have little or no time left in their schedules for doing research. Through the years, noneducators have viewed teaching as an act that requires little planning. Darling-Hammond (1993) concluded that American teachers are denied time to plan because they are stereotyped as being relatively unimportant; however, teachers' behaviors significantly affect the quality and amount of learning that occurs in their classrooms (Bellon, Bellon, & Blank, 1992; Chimes & Schmidt, 1990; Good & Brophy, 1987).

Given the important influence that teachers have on student learning, teachers need to keep up with the latest developments in their fields, and they need to develop the deepest possible level of understanding of the important concepts in their content specialties (Doyle, 1990). This can be done effectively through involving teachers in action research. The expansion of research on teaching in recent years has made research consumerism more important for teachers. Bellon, Bellon, and Blank (1992) explained: "now there is so much current research available that we have to carefully select findings that are consistent across studies and which are based on sound research techniques" (p. 7). Many resources are available to those who wish to know more about the relationships between teaching and research. These include commercially published books (Bissex & Bullock, 1987; Schon, 1987), books published by professional associations (Curtis, 1932; Elliott, 1980; Monroe, 1938; Olson, 1990), theme issues of journals (Oberg & McCutcheon, 1987), university projects (Oja & Pine, 1983), clearinghouse publications (Myers, 1985), research and development center publications (Houston, 1979; Huling & Griffin, 1983; Tikunoff, Ward, & Griffin, 1979), and federal publications (U.S. Department of Education, 1987). Resources also are available on the case study method (Bissex & Bullock, 1987; Kowalski, Henson, & Weaver, 1994).

Involvement in conducting research provides teachers a means of reaching goals. After monitoring and evaluating the behavior of teachers who were involved in conducting research, Bennett (1993) reported:

Teachers-researchers viewed themselves as being . . . better informed than they had been when they began their research. They now saw themselves as experts in their field who were better problem solvers and more effective teachers with fresher attitudes toward education. (p. 69)

Involvement in research can improve teachers' understanding of why they behave as they do. Oberg (1990) reported that those teachers who are aware of the reasons underlying their behavior can make better choices of behavior.

Levels of Involvement

Although teachers have been slow to get involved with research, they have been involved at three levels. The levels reflect the teacher's degree of decision-making power throughout the research process and particularly with the identification of the problem, design of the study, and use of the data. As shown in Table 4.1, at level 1 the teacher's behavior can be described as that of helper. For example, at this level the teacher's main role is to provide a classroom and students to be studied by an outside researcher. Also at this level the teacher may gather data to give to a university researcher.

At level 2 the teacher is a junior research partner who has little or no involvement in decisions that guide the research process. At level 3 the teacher is either a full research partner (collaborator) who participates equally in the decision-making process or a lone researcher who makes all of the decisions.

Three areas of decision making are especially important to teachers who work with research: (1) identifying the problem (Tripp, 1990), (2) designing the study, and (3) using the data (see Table 4.2.). At level 1, the teacher has no input into the selection of the problem to be investigated; rather, an outside researcher, traditionally a university professor, selects the problem, sometimes using as the major criterion the type of problem that can help lead to tenure, promotion, or merit pay. At this level the teacher facilitates by providing the necessary subjects for the study (e.g., classroom, students). These arrangements do not require the teacher's input into the design of the study. At this level the teacher collects the data and turns them over to the researcher. The teacher may or may not see the results.

At level 2 the teacher's level of input into the selection of the problem is minimal and the senior researcher has the final word. The teacher may make suggestions about the design of the study, but the final decisions will be made by the senior partner. The level 2 teacher seldom has access to the results once the data are turned over to the research partner.

At level 3 the teacher has equal or total choice on the problem, choosing a problem that can help improve one of his or her classes. The teacher may design the study or may choose to rely on a research partner who has more expertise. The

TABLE 4.1. Levels of Teacher Involvement

Level 3	Teacher as researcher Lone researcher or collaborator (equal partner)
Level 2	Teacher as junior partner
Level 1	Teacher as a helper

TABLE 4.2. Levels of Teacher Involvement: A Comprehensive View

	Identifying the Problem	Conducting the Research	Use of Results
Level 3	The teacher, either alone or in cooperation with equal partners, identifies a current classroom problem.	Either alone or in cooperation with equal partners, the teacher chooses to design and conduct the study or to let a partner who has more expertise in research design the study.	Either alone or with equal partners, the teacher uses the results to improve teaching.
Level 2	The teacher provides minimal input into identifying the problem to be studied.	The teacher may make suggestions about the design of the study, but the ultimate decision is made by the senior partner.	At this level the teacher seldom sees the results.
Level 1	The teacher is excluded from the process used to identify the problem to be investigated.	The teacher offers a classroom and students to be studied. The teacher may or may not assist with the collection of data. The data are turned over to the "real" researcher.	At this level the teacher typically does not ever see the results.

results are returned to the teacher who uses them to improve the class. When partners are used, often they are university personnel, faculty, and doctoral students who may wish to use those same data to produce an article for publication. Usually the article is mutually written and becomes the joint property of all research team members.

In this chapter the terms *collaborator* and *collaboration* refer to the teacher as an equal partner in research. Throughout the remainder of this chapter, the term teacher as researcher refers to both the teacher as an equal partner in research and to the teacher as a lone researcher, but not to the teacher as assistant or junior partner.

EFFECTS OF TEACHER INVOLVEMENT WITH RESEARCH

Effects on Teachers

A review of the literature shows that concern about the removal of most teachers from research has been growing during the past decade. Atkin (1989) gave several reasons why teachers should be more highly involved with research.

Research is needed for educational improvement to occur, of course. Teachers need new knowledge to cope with the complex issues they face, and they are continually seeking information. For example, they want to know how they can use their instructional time most effectively, how students can learn more, how children can teach other children, and how students' educational progress can best be evaluated.

They also want a deeper understanding of how the various subjects taught in school relate to one another and to the lives of young people, of what subject matter is most worth teaching and when and how students might best be engaged in activities with long-term educational payoffs, of what classroom implications stem from the rapidly changing characteristics of the student body, of how schools themselves might change to take advantage of growing community interest in the purposes and effectiveness of public education, and of how to capitalize on local (and often unanticipated) events that have potential for enriching life in classrooms. (pp. 200–201)

The Reading/Learning in Secondary Schools Subcommittee of the IRA (1989) identified the following benefits of action research:

Helps solve classroom problems
Encourages effective change
Revitalizes teachers
Empowers teachers to make decisions in their classrooms
Identifies effective teaching and learning methods
Promotes reflective teaching
Promotes ownership of effective practices
Verifies what methods work
Widens the range of teachers' professional skills
Provides a connection between instructional methods and results
Helps teachers apply research findings to their own classrooms
Enables teachers to become change agents (p. 217)

During the 1980s, the expression "teacher as researcher" commanded a strong emphasis in the literature (Chall, 1986; Hanna, 1986; Santa, Isaacson, & Manning, 1987; Stansell & Patterson, 1988). The literature consistently reports that those teachers who participate in research bring from the experience a variety of positive changes in themselves (Boyer, 1990; Carr & Kemmis, 1986; Carson, 1990; Chattin-McNichols & Loeffler, 1989; Goswami & Stillman, 1987; Kirk, 1988; Lieberman, 1986a; Lytle & Cochran-Smith, 1990; Nixon, 1981; Rogers, Noblit, & Ferrell, 1990; Sardo-Brown, 1992; Shalaway, 1990; Stevens, Slanton, & Bunny, 1992). As previously mentioned, when teachers initially became involved in research, the typical teacher's role was to offer their classes to the study. Yet, teachers have moved from this passive role to become equal partners in research and, indeed, in many instances to identify the problems to be studied and either conduct or coconduct the studies. This shift in the role that teachers play in research has greatly increased the positive changes that teachers experience from being involved with research.

Effects on Teachers' Ability to Teach (Instructional Empowerment)

Does involvement in research really help teachers to improve their teaching? To find the answer to this question, Stevens,

Slanton, and Bunny (1992) administered a questionnaire to a group of teachers who had been participating in a research project for 1 year. These researchers reported that "When asked to complete a brief questionnaire about their first year with the research group, each classroom teacher stated that the membership in the group helped him/her do a better job" (p. 8). These researchers further concluded that this improved teaching resulted in part from an "increased awareness of effective instructional practice" (p. 8).

There is evidence that involvment in research expands teachers' commitment to developing a variety of teaching methods and to keeping abreast of new information. Dicker (1990), Fullan (1982), Santa (1990), and Santa, Isaacson, and Manning (1987) reported that involvement with research expanded the teachers' possible approaches. Sardo-Brown (1992) reported that involvement in research gave teachers a renewed desire to stay current.

Teacher burnout takes a major toll on teachers in every school. Involvement in action research offers teachers a rich source of vitality (Sucher, 1990). One teacher who became involved in a research project had the following to say about burnout and the effect of involvement in research on teacher burnout:

Teacher burnout is really feeling that you have stopped growing as a person in the classroom. Learning how to do research in my own classroom has started me growing again. (Chattin-McNichols & Loeffler, 1989, p. 25)

Another major change that involvement in research fosters is an openness toward learning more about everything in general and about teaching in particular. By conducting research, teachers become ongoing learners (Boyer, 1990; Brownlie, 1990). As Boyer (1990) explained, "As teachers become researchers they become learners" (p. 57).

Neilsen (1990) identified several changes that occur when teachers become more open and when they commit their energy to learning about teaching by becoming involved in research.

As an observer, guide, and sometimes confidante, I have seen teachers grow in wisdom and confidence, learn to be eloquent speakers and group leaders, become assertive and knowledgeable advocates for change, forge new and affirming relationships, create support groups, and produce magnificent pieces of writing. (p. 249)

Marriott (1990) reported on his personal growth experience, which involved opening up and taking on new challenges.

The drudgery of complacency has been replaced with a sense of mission. I have experienced more professional growth than at any other period in my career. (p. 2)

Rogers, Noblit, and Ferrell (1990), however, warned that this growth may not always be in directions that teachers prefer. The goal should be to prepare teachers to change their classrooms as they would like to have them. Consider, too, that while successful action researchers can decide to make the changes they perceive necessary, they also have the ability to hold those practices that they perceive important. Nixon (1981)

said that "Action research serves primarily to sharpen perceptions, stimulate discussion and energize questioning" (p. 9).

A professor who required graduate education students to complete an action research project (Bennett, 1993) reported a positive change in the students' attitudes toward themselves and toward research.

I noted that teachers went into the research component of the program feeling anxious, and hostile, but emerged feeling positive about the experiences and their newly formed identities as teacher-researchers . . . as teachers gained experience and success with research, their attitude toward research greatly improved . . . teachers-researchers viewed themselves as being more open to change, more reflective, and better informed than they had been when they began their research. (p. 69)

Obviously, action research affects different teachers in different ways. Furthermore, different people seek different benefits from action research. Rogers, Noblit, and Ferrell (1990) did not see this as a problem.

Action research is a vehicle to put teachers in charge of their craft and its improvement. Yet there is considerable variation in what people see action research accomplishing for teachers. These variations range from mundane technical improvement in classrooms to transforming a teacher's identity. (p. 179)

Involvement with research makes teachers more critical (in an analytical sense), causing them to question their own beliefs and the assertions of others (Goswami & Stillman, 1987; Neilsen, 1990). Neilsen (1990) said, "As teachers substantiate what they know through research, they typically develop keen observational powers and a critical sensibility and are less likely to accept, without question" (p. 249). In their book, *Reclaiming the Classroom: Teacher Research as an Agency for Change*, Goswami and Stillman (1987) described the effects of research on teachers who do research.

They collaborate with their students to answer questions important to both, driving on resources in new and unexpected ways.

Their teaching is transformed in important ways: They become theorists, articulating their intentions, testing their assumptions, and finding connections with practice.

Their perceptions of themselves as writers and teachers are transformed. They step up their use of resources; they form networks; and they become more active professionally.

They become rich resources who can provide the profession with information it simply doesn't have . . . teachers know their classroom and students in ways that outsiders can't.

They become critical, responsive readers and users of current research, less apt to accept uncritically others' assertions, less vulnerable to fads, and more authoritative in their assessment of curricula, methods, and materials.

Lytle and Cochran-Smith (1990) said,

As teachers begin to participate in the generation of knowledge about teaching, learning, and schooling, they become more critical of both university-based research and standard school practices. They challenge taken-for-granted assumptions about theory and practice. (p. 101)

Shalaway (1990) summed up the attitudinal change that involvement in research has on teachers by saying

That's a typical pattern of teacher researchers. Above all, they illustrate the fact that good teachers never stop learning to teach—and research provides the means to do so. (p. 36)

Allan and Miller (1990) and Bennett (1993) reported positive changes in teachers' problem-solving skills (after having been involved in an action research project). "They (the teachers) now saw themselves as experts in their field who were better problem solvers . . ." (p. 69).

Effects on Students

Reed, Mergendoller, and Horan (1992) suggested broadening the membership of action research teams. Involvement in action research increases all parties' awareness of student needs (Kirk, 1988; SooHoo, 1993). Haberman (1992) reported that teachers who are directly involved in curriculum development tend to shift their style from prescriptive to more interactive, enabling the teacher to increase the interaction with students and to more effectively evaluate student needs.

As teachers feel more involved in the development of curriculum, it is clear that their personal commitment will be a primary factor in motivating the student to be more interested in the material being presented. Further, improvements in teacher–student relationships will not only enhance teaching, but will be evidenced in student achievement as well. Thus, curriculum development becomes curriculum renewal as the chain of communication from student to teacher to curriculum committee becomes a continuous cycle of analysis and problem solving. (p. 15)

PREREQUISITES FOR SUCCESSFUL TEACHER RESEARCH

A prerequisite for teachers' research success is the opportunity to reflect on the consequences of findings. Clandinin (1992) said that teachers' stories are a powerful means of helping teachers reflect on their teaching practices. Collaboration in reflection offers additional advantages. Reporting on a study at the Professional Development Center in Palo Alto, California, a participant said, "Teachers in our study were encouraged to interact with other teachers . . . as they documented and reflected on their practice" (Shalaway, 1990, p. 38). The teachers reported that this interaction provided a wonderful growth opportunity. This participant concluded that "Perhaps one of the best ways for a teacher to grow is to get together with colleagues to talk about teaching" (p. 38). Neufeld (1990) referred to such growth as "an increased sense of professionalism" (p. 345). A Canadian teacher-researcher said, "The opportunity to contribute to educational research allows the teacher to become more confident and to grow in a very personal way toward a deeper understanding of what is meant by the act of teaching" (McConaghy, 1987, p. 631). Although collaboration itself does not constitute conducting action research, it enriches the benefits of action research.

Reporting on an action research project involving middle and secondary teachers conducted at Friends University in Wichita, Kansas, Schumm (1993) identified as a primary concern "the

need for a support group to help sustain and guide the process" (p. 449).

The Reading/Language in Secondary Schools Subcommittee of the IRA (1989) listed the following steps, which it says are necessary for classroom action research:

1. Identify the problem, the experimental and control groups, and the change or strategy to try.
2. Establish a baseline by testing data, checklists, observations, behaviors.
3. Implement the change or strategy.
4. Analyze results and other influences that affect the outcome.
5. Share results with students, teachers, administrators, and others. (p. 217)

MODELS

Classroom-Based Model

Some teachers initiate their own research in the perimeter of their classrooms (Marks, 1989; Reading/Language in Secondary Schools Subcommittee of the IRA, 1989; Shalaway, 1990). This type of action research gives almost immediate feedback on questions that teachers have about their instructional and management practices. The intent is not to get published in a professional journal, but to see if the altering of practices can improve classroom performance or behavior. This context-based, classroom-based model is needed to improve teacher education (Cardelle-Elawar, 1993; Cross, 1990; Cunningham & Shillington, 1990).

Having access to knowledge that otherwise would not be available seems justification enough for classroom research, but as McKernan (1988) pointed out, "It is not enough that classrooms be researched, they need to be researched by teachers" (p. 154).

Traditional Collaboration Model

Although not all teacher involvement with research involves collaboration with universities or other agencies, most of this research is through cooperative efforts. Such collaborations usually involve universities. Most collaborative studies are initiated by university researchers (Van Manen, 1990). Definite problems (see Bracey, 1991) and benefits result when teachers and professors collaborate. A lack of agreement on the roles of teachers and ownership of the results is common. According to Porter (1990), "The research base relative to collaborative efforts is relatively non-existent" (p. 78). Porter says that this conclusion is supported by Fox and Faver (1984), Hord (1986), and Houston (1979); however, as mentioned earlier in this chapter, teacher involvement with research can be traced back to the early 1900s. At the beginning of teacher research, teachers linked with others (usually university faculty members or personnel in federal, state, or local school departments or districts). Since its beginning, teacher research has focused on a broad topic that was generated externally and that often had little apparent significance to the local teacher or classroom (Atkin, 1989; Fenstermacher, 1987; Houser, 1990). In fact, teachers often perceive the topics as either too theoretical or too superficial or both (Chattin-McNichols & Loeffler, 1989).

In recent years this model has come under much criticism. Critics (Chattin-McNichols & Loeffler, 1989; Neilsen, 1990) say the harshest of these criticisms is that a research problem is seldom perceived by teachers as significant. Houser (1990) said that teachers were minimally informed about the research project.

Although this model has existed since the 1930s, its limitations have grown as teacher empowerment has expanded. In addition to having an outside agency identify the problems to be studied without teacher input into the selection, the agencies have used teachers to gather data without knowing how these data were being used. Atkin (1989) addressed this problem.

In turn, investigators in the research community watch teachers and listen to them—but only when the teachers are doing things that the researchers consider important or interesting. This condition dominates mainstream educational research. . . . The resulting loss is profound, both in our understanding of educational events and in the disheartening message sent to teachers that their role in educational change is simply discovering the site-level consequences of somebody else's ideas or implementing the classroom techniques that other people have devised. (p. 201)

The collaboration research model offers several advantages that come from the associations that teachers have with others outside their own classrooms. The degree to which these advantages will be realized (and therefore the level of effectiveness of each collaborative research program) is contingent on each teacher, researcher, school district, parent, and other outside agency correctly performing its role.

Collaboration forces teachers to expose their teaching practices to others (McElroy, 1990; Santa, 1990). A willingness to share their practices, classroom, and students is a prerequisite for success. Therefore, one of the first steps in the teacher's role in collaboration is to develop a willingness to share and a willingness to experiment at the cost of failing and having others become aware of these failures.

Collaboration also requires the ability to critically self-analyze, with the willingness to change when a change is warranted. This self-analytic evaluation process can take the form of keeping a portfolio or keeping a journal. Recording experiences in a journal helps teachers reflect on both their thoughts and their actions (Shalaway, 1990).

Student-Centered Problem-Solving Model

As early as the seventeenth century, John Locke (see Gay, 1964) developed the concept "tabula rasa," which proclaimed that the mind at birth is a blank slate that can be filled only through experiences. By the late nineteenth century, Europeans realized the motivational and retention benefits of active student involvement in lessons. Froebel, Herbart, Pestalozzi, and Montessori (see Ikenberry, 1974) were quick to design curricula around planned student experiences. By the beginning of the twentieth century, Colonel Francis Parker (see Campbell, 1967) had brought the concept of learner-centered education to America and implemented it in the Quincy, Massachusetts

schools. By the early 1920s with the help of Colonel Parker, John Dewey had introduced a revolution in American schools called *progressive education*. This student-centered system dominated American education for more than two decades. The effectiveness of student-centered education was carefully measured in a famous Eight-Year Study (Henson, 1994). The results were that when compared to traditional teacher-dominated teaching, learner-centered teaching was far more effective in cognitive gains and in a host of other areas. Students in learner-centered classes were more creative, exhibited superior leadership skills, displayed more intellectual curiosity, and were more highly motivated.

Student involvement is just one example of the many principles of learning that guide teacher behavior. An awareness of these principles alone is inadequate; students and teachers need to be involved in discovering knowledge. Teachers also need to possess the skills required to measure the effectiveness of those principles when they are applied in the classroom (Marks, 1989).

CASE STUDIES

One major benefit of teacher research is the knowledge that it generates (Houser, 1990; Learning from Children, 1988); case study development can contribute greatly. Shulman (1990) believes that a major goal of future education is to develop a collection of case studies.

Teachers need opportunities to learn to become independent thinkers (Cardelle-Elawar, 1993; Cross, 1990; Floden & Klinzing, 1990; Sagor, 1991). The case study method can provide opportunities for teachers to make judicious decisions, a skill that cannot be developed by traditional teaching methods (Kowalski, Henson, & Weaver, 1994). Cases developed by teachers can even become springboards for further teacher-conducted research (Atkin, 1989).

BARRIERS

Successful collaboration among teachers and researchers requires certain conditions (Gies, 1984; Hastie, 1992; Sanger, 1990). Reporting on a joint conference involving the Association International des Écoles Superieures d'Éducation Physique (AIESEP) and the National Association for Physical Education in Higher Education (NAPEHE), Hastie (1992) said that successful collaboration requires a reward system to encourage and reward success; yet, Gies (1984) warned teachers to first consider the significance the problem(s) under investigation has for them because no reward system is likely to be adequate enough to satisfy teachers who are not committed to the study. Other researchers and teachers have stressed the need for teachers to be involved in deciding the problems to be studied (Applebee, 1987; Kearney & Tashlik, 1985; Lieberman, 1986b; McKernan, 1988). Gill (1993) listed the following conditions as prerequisites to successful collaboration:

Adequate professional development, including a sufficient knowledge base and enough time

Support from the union

A credible leadership team

Support from the school administration—philosophically and materially

Continuing support by those who understand the new practice(s)

Regular opportunities for reflection and problem solving

Relief from the constraints of traditional evaluation and testing while new ways are learned

Hope that structural changes teachers begin to find necessary to sustain their efforts can indeed happen. (p. 41)

A major barrier for most teachers who wish to participate in collaborative projects is the time required of them (Gajewski, 1986; Houser, 1990; Schumm, 1993). The problem is exacerbated by schools' inflexible schedules (Arndt, 1984). Often teacher-researchers trade half of their teaching time for researching time. The responsibilities of both jobs can grow until the teacher has two full-time jobs (Porter, 1990). Projects should be designed so that they do not make extra demands on teachers' time (Hastie, 1992). The problem can be further ameliorated by making sure that all participants are organized and by clarifying the role of each participant (Stevens, Slanton, & Bunny, 1992).

Another barrier to teachers conducting research is lack of confidence. Many teachers believe that they do not possess the research and statistical skills needed to perform research. Some educators believe that this is more a perceived weakness than a true weakness (Winter, 1982; Woods, 1986). In reality, action research may involve the use of sophisticated research knowledge and skills, but teachers who lack such sophistication can design and conduct simpler studies.

Some teachers work in environments where research is not appreciated (McDaniel, 1988–1989). This introduces another barrier that seems to develop automatically—a status hierarchy that separates teachers and professors. In some collaborations, university partners are ranked above teachers (Gies, 1984). Where this hierarchy exists, teachers are relegated to the status of a second-class partner in the research process. This can lead to inferior expectations for teachers and even to inferior self-expectations. Ironically, the same teachers who suffer a loss of self-esteem can also suffer a deterioration in relationships among fellow teachers (Porter, 1990).

Sometimes the idea of the teacher as an inferior professional incapable of conducting research is just that—an idea in the minds of teachers (Avery, 1990). Participation in research can dispel this common misconception.

CONTRIBUTIONS TO EDUCATION REFORM

Needed Support

Effective schools have principals who are effective instructional leaders (Beck, 1990); yet teachers do not perceive their principals as instructional leaders (Hall, 1986).

Recent education reform practices are holding schools (teachers and administrators, and in some states, parents) accountable for preparing students to apply learned knowledge. To ensure that this goal is being reached, "performance evaluation" of student work has become common in states where education reform is extensive. Self-evaluation through portfolios has been introduced to help students learn how to record data and to measure progress. These practices reflect a broadening concept of evaluation. This change has been paralleled by a broadening concept of research strategies appropriate for education. Gitlin (1990) addressed this expansion by quoting Gage:

Over the last two decades, dramatic shifts have occurred in the research methods that can be legitimately employed in the field of education. Ethnography, once the primary method of anthropologists, for example, is now widely used and valued by the educational research community. And, more recently, it has been noted that "nothing about objective-quantitative research preclude(s) the description and analysis of classroom practices with interpretive-qualitative methods." (p. 443)

As the century and millennium approach their ends, Americans are excited about their schools on a new level. The current wave of school reform was simmering at the turn of the 1980s when the National Commission on Excellence in Education's report, *A Nation at Risk* (1983), shifted the reform activities from low to high gear.

An analysis of school events since the 1960s shows that curricula have been implemented that give teachers a secondary role (Darling-Hammond, 1993). This trend was made obvious at the beginning of the 1960s when local curricula were being replaced by preconstructed curricula that put the student in the center of instruction, excluding the teacher. Programs developed at research and development centers, such as programmed instruction, were being sent to the schools along with paraphernalia to be used by students to solve problems. These programs were designed to be teacher-proof. Yet, teaching is a highly complex, demanding, and difficult activity (Cornett, 1990; Samuels & Jones, 1990), and major school reform success relies on teachers (Consortium on Chicago School Research, 1993; Cuban, 1993).

One way to promote reform is by involving teachers in research (Allan & Miller, 1990; Casanova, 1989; Hovda & Kyle, 1984; McCutcheon, 1987; Sardo-Brown, 1992; Shalaway, 1990). By conducting research, teachers increase their self-efficacy regarding their ability to make a difference (Cardelle-Elawar, 1993; Sardo-Brown, 1992). This increased self-confidence is not empty emotions but results from increased ability to make important differences in the levels of learning occurring in their classrooms and in the school at large. Teachers who are involved with research become more reflective, critical, and analytical of their own teaching (Cardelle-Elawar, 1993; Carr & Kemmis, 1986). The process teachers use to develop theories from their classroom experiences and then modify those theories through further experiences is called praxis. As Houser (1990) expressed, "If the ultimate goal of research and curriculum development is improved learning, then praxis, in the form of teacher-research, makes perfect sense" (p. 58).

This view of the praxis process is oversimplified. Although learning from research may occur in a simple, linear process, it is more likely to occur following questioning, pondering, and discussing the results (Kearney & Tashlik, 1985). This view of teacher research reflects Bertrand Russell's (1958) conception of "scientific temper" versus "scientific technique." Scientific temper recognizes that the investigator's work is never complete and the conclusions are never absolutely certain. Whereas some may question the application of this incomplete and uncertain investigative process to explore teaching, in fact, these apparent weaknesses of the scientific method are just the opposite, they are important strengths. Garrison (1988) explained

Of all the instruments of inquiry thus far fashioned there can be no doubt that the scientific method imparts the greatest power for solving our practical problems and achieving our daily purposes. The scientific method of inquiry is, in our time at least, the supreme knowledge gathering tool and the supreme form taken by knowledge. Let me hasten to add that for a philosophical pragmatist such as Dewey, science is supreme not because it yields necessarily "truth" but rather, as Russell indicates, it is systematically correctable and improvable. (p. 491)

Intensifying the need for teacher involvement in research, many of the reform reports either ignore or understate the importance of pedagogy, espousing the belief that teacher education programs should require fewer methods courses and more courses in the content areas. Cuban (1993) explained

Worse still, curriculum reformers ignore the power of pedagogy. They believe that content is more important than teaching. They are wrong. At the heart of schooling is the personal relationship between teacher and students that develop over matters of content. (p. 184)

Through conducting research, teachers develop a deeper and clearer understanding about their content areas and about how they are learned.

Restructuring

Throughout the 1980s and continuing into the 1990s, many education reform programs have stressed the need to restructure schools. Indeed, *restructuring* has been associated so closely with *reform* that the two terms are often used interchangeably (Boe & Boruch, 1992). An integral part of the restructuring movement is accountability; schools (meaning administrators and teachers) and parents are being held accountable for student success (National Center for Education Statistics, 1993). Site-based decision-making councils have been a vehicle through which administrators, teachers, and parents are being held accountable.

Effective participation on site-based decision-making councils requires expertise of all members (Fullen & Stiegelbauer, 1990). Participation in research is a direct route to increased expertise (Atkin, 1989; Bennett, 1993; Kirk, 1988) and is a way for teachers to improve their self-confidence as professionals (Bennett, 1993; Neilsen, 1990; Sardo-Brown, 1992).

Constructivism

Increased student learning (the ultimate goal of education reform) depends on increased teacher expertise (Consortium on Chicago School Research, 1993). In fact, a purpose of all education is to enable people to think and to perform more effectively. Education is about learning how to deal with uncertainty and ambiguity (Eisner, 1992). "Its goal is for people to become more skilled, more dynamic, more vital" (Ayers, 1992, p. 260).

This skill enhancement requires developing new insights and learning new knowledge. The development of new insights and knowledge requires relating newly discovered knowledge to previous understandings. King and Rosenshine (1993) explained, "According to constructivist views, when presented with new information individuals use their existing knowledge and prior knowledge to help make sense of the new material" (p. 127). Constructivists describe learning in terms of building connections between prior knowledge and new ideas and claim that effective teaching helps students construct an organized set of concepts that relates old and new ideas (Markle, Johnston, Geer, & Meichtry, 1990).

Teachers who engage in research studies of their own instructional practices position themselves in permanent confrontation with new knowledge. Through praxis, teachers are provided with continuous opportunities to add clarity to their never complete or perfect understanding, thereby serving education reform by improving their own understanding of the education process.

CONCLUSION

The term teacher as researcher has many definitions and may vary as the teachers vary and as the context changes (McKernan, 1988). Many who have attempted to define it have agreed that it involves the teacher purposefully engaged in inquiry. Action research is a term used to refer to a teacher being engaged in inquiry for the purpose of understanding and improving his or her own practice (McCutcheon & Jung, 1990; Shalaway, 1990). The inquiry is into problems of immediate concern (McKernan, 1988).

As early as 1908, efforts have been made to involve teachers in research (Lowery, 1908). The types and level of teacher involvement with research have been limited (Peik, 1938). In essence, when teachers have been involved they have helped collect data, often without the benefit of even seeing the results of the study.

Teachers often perceive researchers' topics as too theoretical (Chattin-McNichols & Loeffler, 1989), saying that the results do not transfer well to the teaching context (Hastie, 1992), but today teachers are under fire for failure to use research (Hastie, 1992). Staying alert to and using research are necessary for teachers to stay current and to develop the important concepts in their fields (Doyle, 1990).

When teachers do become involved with research, several benefits accrue—they remain better informed in their fields (Bennett, 1993) and they gain a better understanding of why they behave as they do (Oberg, 1990), which prepares them to make better choices of behavior (Oberg, 1990). Furthermore, involvement with research revitalizes teachers (Reading/Learning in Secondary Schools Subcommittee of the IRA, 1989) and promotes continuous learning (Boyer, 1990; Shalaway, 1990) and self-confidence (Neilsen, 1990), leaving themselves feeling more positive toward themselves and toward research (Bennett, 1993).

Many of these benefits are contingent on a high level of involvement with research, a level where teachers either conduct the research independently or where teachers are equal partners in collaborative studies.

Teacher research responds positively to the current reform pleas for teachers to expand their professional roles beyond their immediate classroom walls. Involvement with research increases teachers' self-efficacy (Cardelle-Elawar, 1993; Sardo-Brown, 1992) and causes teachers to become more reflective, analytical, and critical of their own teaching (Cardelle-Elawar, 1993; Carr & Kemmis, 1986). Involvement with research sharpens teachers' problem-solving skills.

Educational reform efforts are expanding teachers' roles. For example, site-based decision-making committees place teach-ers in problem-solving roles. New assessment practices demand high levels of self-confidence from teachers. Many school districts are now requiring teachers to choose and use those practices that are research proven. Teachers must be able to use the current knowledge base to justify the methods or strategies they use in the classroom.

Future teachers will be expected to be problem solvers and more; they must be proactive problem solvers. They must use their problem-solving skills to predict and to plan to avoid future problems. Direct involvement in research is excellent preparation for becoming a proactive problem solver.

References

Allan, K. K., & Miller, M. S. (1990). Teacher-researcher collaborative: Cooperative professional development. *Theory into Practice, 29*(3), 196–202.

Allen, J., Combs, J., Hendricks, M., Nash, P., & Wilson, S. (1988). Studying change: Teachers who become researchers. *Language Arts, 65*(4), 379–387.

Applebee, A. M. C. (1987). Musings . . . teachers and the process of research. *Language Arts, 64*(7), 714–716.

Arndt, R. (1984). Adjusting to contrasting tempos. *IRT Communication Quarterly, 7*(1), 2.

Atkin, J. M. (1989). Can educational research keep pace with education reform? *Phi Delta Kappan, 71*(3), 200–205.

Avery, C. S. (1990). Learning to research: Researching to learn. In M. W. Olson (Ed.), *Opening the door to educational research* (pp. 32–44). Newark, DE: International Reading Association.

Ayers, W. A. (1992). The shifting ground of curriculum thought and everyday practice. *Theory into Practice, 31*(3), 259–263.

Bagley, W. C., Bell, J. C., Seashore, C. E., & Whipple, G. M. (1910). Editorial. *Journal of Educational Psychology, 1*(1), 1–3.

Bain, H. P., & Gooseclose, J. R. (1979). The dissemination dilemma and a plan for uniting disseminators and practitioners. *Phi Delta Kappan, 61*(2), 101–103.

Beck, J. J. (1990). Preparing principals for an educational research agenda in the schools. In M. W. Olson (Ed.), *Opening the door to classroom research* (pp. 97–111). Newark, DE: International Reading Association.

Bellon, J. J., Bellon, E. C., & Blank, M. A. (1992). *Teaching from a research knowledge base*. New York: Merrill.

Bennett, C. K. (1993). Teacher-researchers: All dressed up and no place to go. *Educational Leadership, 51*(2), 69–70.

Bissex, G. L., & Bullock, R. H. (Eds.). (1987). *Seeing for ourselves: Case study research by teachers of writing*. Portsmouth, NH: Heinemann.

Boe, E. E., & Boruch, R. F. (1992, December). *Unpacking the concept of educational restructuring with a focus on the entrepreneurial approach*. Research report No. 1992-ERI, Center of Research and Evaluation in Social Policy.

Boyer, E. (1990). *Scholarship reconsidered: Priorities of the professoriate*. Princeton, NJ: Carnegie Foundation for the Advancement of Teaching.

Bracey, G. W. (1991). Teachers as researchers. *Phi Delta Kappan, 72*(5), 404–405.

Brown, D. S. (1990). Middle level teachers' perceptions of action research. *Middle School Journal, 22*(1), 30–32.

Brownlie, F. (1990). The door is open. Won't you come in? In M. W. Olson (Ed.), *Opening the door to educational research* (pp. 21–31). Newark, DE: International Reading Association.

Buckingham, B. R. (1926). *Research for teachers*. New York: Silver, Burdett.

Busching, B., & Rowls, M. (1987). Teachers: Professional partners in school reform. *Action in Teacher Education, 9*(3), 13–23.

Campbell, J. K. (1967). *Colonel Francis W. Parker: The children's crusader*. New York: Teachers College Press.

Cardelle-Elawar, M. (1993). The teacher as researcher in the classroom. *Action in Teacher Education, 15*(1), 49–57.

Carr, W., & Kemmis, S. (1986). *Becoming critical: Education, knowledge, and action research*. London: Falmer.

Carson, T. (1990). What kind of knowing is critical to action research? *Theory into Practice, 29*(3), 167–173.

Casanova, V. (1989). Research and practice: We can integrate them. *NEA Today, 7*(6), 44–49.

Chall, J. S. (1986). The teacher as scholar. *Reading Teacher, 39*(8), 792–797.

Chattin-McNichols, J., & Loeffler, M. H. (1989). Teachers as researchers: The first cycle of the teachers' research network. *Young Children, 44*(5), 20–27.

Chimes, M., & Schmidt, P. (1990). What I read over my summer vacation: Readings on cultural diversity. *The Clearing House, 64*(1), 44–46.

Clandinin, D. J. (1992). Creating spaces for teachers' voices. *Journal of Educational Thought, 26*(6), 59–71.

Consortium on Chicago School Research. (1993). Chicago elementary school reform: A mid-term exam. *The Education Digest, 59*(3), 4–8.

Copenhaver, R. W., Byrd, D. M., McIntyre, D. J., & Norris, W. R. (1982). Synergistic public school and university research. *Action in Teacher Education, 4*(1), 41–44.

Corey, S. M. (1953). *Action research to improve school practices*. New York: Teachers College Bureau of Publications, Columbia University.

Cornett, J. W. (1990). Utilizing action research in graduate curriculum courses. *Theory into Practice, 29*(3), 185–195.

Cross, P. (1990). Making teaching more effective. *Journal of Freshman Year Experience, 2*(2), 59–74.

Cuban, L. (1992). Managing dilemmas while building professional communities. *Educational Researcher, 21*(1), 4–11.

Cuban, L. (1993). The lure of curricular reform and its pitiful history. *Phi Delta Kappan, 75*(2), 182–185.

Cunningham, R. C., & Shillington, N. M. (1990). Mentoring preservice teachers through interdisciplinary teams: A school-university partnership. *Action in Teacher Education, 11*(4), 6–12.

Curtis, F. D. (1932). Some contributions of educational research to the solution of teaching science. In *Thirty-first yearbook of the National Society for the Study of Education, Part 1* (pp. 77–90). Bloomington, IL: Public School Publishing.

Cushman, C. L., & Fox, G. (1938). Research and the public school curriculum. In G. M. Whipple (Ed.), *The scientific movement in education. Thirty-seventh yearbook of the National Society for the Study of Education, Part 2* (pp. 67–68). Bloomington, IL: Public School Publishing.

Darling-Hammond, L. (1993). Reframing the school reform agenda: Developing capacity for school transformation. *Phi Delta Kappan, 74*(10), 752–761.

Dewey, J. (1929). *The sources of a science of education.* New York: Liverright.

Dicker, M. (1990). Using action research to navigate an unfamiliar teaching assignment. *Theory into Practice, 29*(3), 203–208.

Doyle, W. (1990). Themes in teacher education research. In W. R. Houston (Ed.), *Handbook of research on teacher education* (pp. 3–24). New York: Macmillan.

Egbert, R. L. (1984). The role of research in teacher education. In R. L. Egbert & M. M. Kluender (Eds.), *Using research to improve teacher education: The Nebraska consortium* (pp. 9–21). Lincoln, NE: American Association of Colleges for Teacher Education.

Eisner, E. (1992). *The educational imagination: On the design and evaluation of school programs* (2nd ed.). New York: Macmillan.

Elliott, J. (1980). Implications of classroom research for professional development. In E. Hoyle & J. Megarry (Eds.), *World yearbook of education: 1980. Professional development of teachers* (pp. 308–324). London: Nichols.

Fenstermacher, G. D. (1987). On understanding the connections between classroom research and teacher change. *Theory into Practice, 26*(1), 3–7.

Fischer, R. L. (1988–1989). When schools and colleges work together. *Action in Teacher Education, 10*(4), 63–66.

Floden, R. E., & Klinzing, H. G. (1990). What can research on teacher thinking contribute to teacher preparation? A second opinion. *Educational Researcher, 19*(5), 15–20.

Fox, M. F., & Faver, C. A. (1984). Independence and cooperation in research: The motivations and costs of collaboration. *Journal of Higher Education, 55*(3), 347–359.

Fullan, M. G. (1982). *The meaning of educational change.* New York: Teachers College.

Fullan, M. G., & Stiegelbauer, S. (1990). *The new meaning of educational change* (2nd ed.). Toronto: Ontario Institute for Studies in Education.

Gajewski, J. (1986). Teachers as full partners in research. *IRT Communication Quarterly, 1*(4), 2.

Garrison, J. W. (1988). Democracy, scientific knowledge, and teacher empowerment. *Teachers College Record, 89*(4), 487–504.

Gay, P. (Ed.). (1964). *John Locke on education.* New York: Teachers College Bureau of Publications.

Gies, F. (1984). The efficacy of educational research. *American Education, 20*(6), 15–16.

Gill, A. J. (1993). Thinking mathematics. *Educational Leadership, 50*(6), 40–41.

Gitlin, A. D. (1990). Educative research, voice, and school change. *Harvard Educational Review, 60*(4), 443–466.

Glatthorn, A. A. (1993). *Learning twice: An introduction to the methods of teaching.* New York: HarperCollins.

Good, C. V., Barr, A. S., & Scates, D. E. (1936). *The methodology of educational research.* New York: Appleton-Century.

Good, T. L., & Brophy, J. E. (1987). *Looking in classrooms* (4th ed.). New York: Harper & Row.

Goswami, D., & Stillman, P. (1987). *Reclaiming the classroom: Teacher research as an agency for change.* Portsmouth, NH: Boynton Cook.

Haberman, M. (1992). The role of the classroom teacher as a curriculum leader. *NASSP Bulletin, 76*(547), 11–19.

Hall, G. (Ed.). (1986). *Beyond the looking glass: Recommendations and critical warnings for teacher education practitioners, policy makers,*

and researchers. Austin: Research and Development Center for Teacher Education, University of Texas.

Hanna, B. (1986). Improving student-teaching effectiveness through action research projects. *Action in Teacher Education, 8*(3), 51–56.

Hastie, P. A. (1992). Prospects for collaboration between teachers and researchers. *Clearing House, 65*(6), 371–372.

Hattrup, U., & Bickel, W. E. (1993). Teacher-researcher collaborations: Resolving the tensions. *Educational Leadership, 50*(6), 38–40.

Henson, K. T. (1994). *Curriculum development for education reform.* New York: HarperCollins.

Herzberg, F., Mausner, B., & Snyderman, B. (1959). *The motivation to work.* New York: Wiley.

Hord, S. M. (1986). A synthesis of research on organizational collaboration. *Educational Leadership, 43*(5), 22–26.

Houser, N. O. (1990). Teacher-researcher: The synthesis of roles for teacher empowerment. *Action in Teacher Education, 12*(2), 55–60.

Houston, W. R. (1979). Collaboration—See "treason." In G. E. Hall, S. M. Hord, & E. Brown (Eds.), *Exploring issues in teacher education: Questions for future research* (pp. 331–348). Austin: University of Texas, Research and Development Center for Teacher Education.

Hovda, R. A., & Kyle, D. W. (1984). Action research: A professional development responsibility. *Middle School Journal, 15*(3), 21–23.

Huling, L. L., & Griffin, G. A. (1983). Educators work together with interactive research and development (collaboration is not a four-letter word). *Research and Development Center for Teacher Education Review, 1*(3), 1–2.

Ikenberry, O. S. (1974). *American educational foundations: An introduction.* Columbus, OH: Charles E. Merrill.

Kearney, L., & Tashlik, P. (1985). Collaboration and conflict: Teachers and researchers learning. *Language Arts, 62*(7), 765–769.

King, A., & Rosenshine, B. (1993). Effects of guided cooperative questioning on children's knowledge construction. *The Journal of Experimental Education, 61*(2), 127–148.

Kirk, D. (1988). Ideology and school-centered innovation: A case study and a critique. *Journal of Curriculum Studies, 20*(5), 449–464.

Kowalski, T. J., Henson, K. T., & Weaver, R. A. (1994). *Case studies on beginning teachers.* New York: Longman.

Kowalski, T. J., & Reitzug, V. C. (1993). *Contemporary school administration.* New York: Longman.

Learning from children: Teachers do research. (1988). *The Harvard Education Letter, 4*(4), 1–5.

Lieberman, A. (1986a). Collaborative research: Working with, not working on . . . . *Educational Leadership, 43*(5), 28–32.

Lieberman, A. (1986b). Collaborative work. *Educational Leadership, 43*(5), 4–8.

Lowery, C. D. (1908). The relation of superintendents and principals to the training and professional improvement of their teachers. *Seventh yearbook of the National Society for the Study of Education, Part 1.* Chicago: The University of Chicago Press.

Lytle, S. L., & Cochran-Smith, M. (1990). Learning from teacher research: A working typology. *Teachers College Record, 92*(1), 83–103.

Markle, G., Johnston, J. H., Geer, C., & Meichtry, Y. (1990). Teaching for understanding. *Middle School Journal, 22*(2), 53–57.

Marks, M. B. (1989). Practice into theory: The teacher authenticates research findings. *Educational Research Quarterly, 13*(3), 17–25.

Marriott, V. (1990). *Transition.* Unpublished paper, Mount Saint Vincent University, Nova Scotia, Canada.

Marshall, C. (1991). Teachers' learning styles: How they affect student learning. *The Clearing House, 64*(4), 225–227.

McConaghy, T. (1987). Teachers as researchers: Learning through teaching. *Phi Delta Kappan, 68*(8), 630–631.

McCutcheon, G. (1987). Teachers' experience doing action research. *Peabody Journal of Education, 64*(2), 116–127.

McCutcheon, G., & Jung, B. (1990). Alternative perspectives on action research. *Theory into Practice, 29*(3), 144–151.

McDaniel, E. (1988–1989). Collaboration for what? Sharpening the focus. *Action in Teacher Education, 10*(4), 1–8.

McElroy, L. (1990). Becoming real: An ethic at the heart of action research. *Theory into Practice, 29*(3), 209–218.

McKernan, J. (1988). Teacher as researcher: Paradigm and praxis. *Contemporary Education, 59*(3), 154–158.

Monroe, W. W. (1938). General methods: Classroom experimentation. In G. M. Whipple (Ed.), *The scientific movement in education. Thirty-seventh yearbook of the National Society for the Study of Education, Part 2* (pp. 319–328). Bloomington, IL: Public School Publishing.

Myers, M. (1985). *The teacher-researcher: How to study writing in the classroom.* Urbana, IL: ERIC Clearinghouse on Reading and Communications Skills and the National Council of Teachers of English.

National Center for Education Statistics. (1993). *America's teachers: Profile of a profession.* Washington, DC: U.S. Department of Education, Office of Educational Research and Improvement.

National Commission on Excellence in Education. (1983). *A nation at risk: The imperatives for educational reform.* Washington, DC: U.S. Government Printing Office.

Neilsen, L. (1990). Research comes home. *The Reading Teacher, 44*(3), 248–250.

Neufeld, K. (1990). Preparing future teachers as researchers. *Education, 110*(3), 345–351.

Nixon, J. (1981). *A teacher's guide to action research.* London: Grant McIntyre.

Oberg, A. (1990). Methods and meanings in action research: The action research journal. *Theory into Practice, 29*(3), 214–221.

Oberg, A., & McCutcheon, G. (1987). Teachers' experience doing action research. *Peabody Journal of Education, 64*(2), 116–127.

Odell, L. (1976). The classroom teacher as researcher. *English Journal, 65*(1), 106–111.

Oja, S. N., & Pine, G. (1983). *A two-year study of teacher stage of development in relation to collaborative action research in schools.* Durham: University of New Hampshire, Collaborative Action Research Project Office.

Olson, M. W. (1990). The teacher as researcher: A historical perspective. In M. W. Olson (Ed.), *Opening the door to classroom research.* Newark, DE: International Reading Association.

Peik, W. E. (1938). A generation of research on the curriculum. In G. M. Whipple (Ed.), *The scientific movement in education. Thirty-seventh yearbook of the National Society for the Study of Education, Part 2* (pp. 53–66). Bloomington, IL: Public School Publishing.

Porter, A. C. (1990). Collaborating with teachers on research. In M. W. Olson (Ed.), *Opening the door to classroom research* (pp. 77–96). Newark, DE: International Reading Association.

Rainey, B. G. (1972). Whatever happened to action research? *The Balance Sheet, 53*(7), 292–295.

Ravitch, D. (1992). National standards and curriculum reform: A view from the Department of Education. *NASSP Bulletin, 76*(548), 24–29.

Reading/Language in Secondary Schools Subcommittee of the International Reading Association (IRA). (1989). Classroom action research: The teacher as researcher. *Journal of Reading, 33*(3), 216–218.

Reed, C., Mergendoller, J., & Horan, C. (1992). Collaborative research: A strategy for school improvement. *Crossroads: The California Journal of Middle Grades Research, 2*(1), 5–12.

Rogers, D. L., Noblit, G. W., & Ferrell, P. (1990). Action research as an agent for developing teachers' communicative competence. *Theory into Practice, 29*(3), 179–184.

Russell, B. (1958). *Religion and science.* Oxford: Oxford University Press.

Sagor, R. (1991). What Project LEARN reveals about collaborative action research. *Educational Leadership, 48*(6), 6–7, 9–10.

Samuels, S. J., & Jones, H. L. (1990). A model of teaching and instructional improvement. In M. W. Olson (Ed.), *Opening the door to classroom research* (pp. 126–140). Newark, DE: International Reading Association.

Sanger, J. (1990). Awakening a scream of consciousness: The critical group in action research. *Theory into Practice, 29*(3), 174–178.

Santa, C. M. (1990). Teaching as research. In M. W. Olson (Ed.), *Opening the door to classroom research* (pp. 64–76). Newark, DE: International Reading Association.

Santa, C. M., Isaacson, L., & Manning, G. (1987). Changing content instruction through action research. *The Reading Teacher, 40*(4), 434–438.

Sardo-Brown, D. (1992). Elementary teachers' perceptions of action research. *Action in Teacher Education, 14*(2), 55–59.

Schon, D. (1987). *Educating the reflective practioner: Toward a new design for teaching and learning in the professions.* San Francisco: Jossey-Bass.

Schumm, J. S. (1993). Action research: What do secondary teachers think? (Summary of research by D. S. Brown). *Journal of Reading, 36*(6), 449.

Shalaway, L. (1990). Tap into teacher research. *Instructor, 100*(1), 34–38.

Shannon, P. (1990). Commentary: Teachers as researchers. In M. W. Olson (Ed.), *Opening the door to classroom research* (pp. 141–154). Newark, DE: International Reading Association.

Shulman, J. H. (1990). Now you see them, now you don't: Anonymity versus visibility in case studies of teachers. *Educational Researcher, 19*(6), 11–15.

Shumsky, A. (1958). *The action research way of learning.* New York: Teachers College Press.

SooHoo, S. (1993). Students as partners in research and restructuring schools. *The Educational Forum, 57*(3), 386–393.

Stansell, J., & Patterson, L. (1988). Teacher researchers find the answers in their classrooms. *Texas Reading Report, 10*(6), 2–4.

Stevens, K. B., Slanton, D. B., & Bunny, S. (1992). A collaborative research effort between public school and university faculty members. *Teacher Education and Special Education, 15*(1), 1–8.

Sucher, F. (1990). Involving school administrators in classroom research. In M. W. Olson (Ed.), *Opening the door to classroom research* (pp. 112–125). Newark, DE: International Reading Association.

Tikunoff, W., Ward, B., & Griffin, G. (1979). *Interactive research and development on teaching: Final report.* San Francisco: Far West Laboratory for Educational Research and Development.

Travers, R. M. W. (1976). Impact of research on teaching. *Education Digest, 42*(4), 6–8.

Tripp, D. H. (1990). Socially critical action research. *Theory into Practice, 29*(3), 158–166.

Tyack, D. (1990). Restructuring in historical perspective: Tinkering toward Utopia. *Teachers College Record, 92*(2), 170–191.

U.S. Department of Education. (1987). *Teachers as researchers program.* Washington, DC: U.S. Department of Education, Office of Educational Research and Improvement.

Van Manen, M. (1990). Beyond assumptions: Shifting the limits of action research. *Theory into Practice, 29*(3), 152–157.

Vockell, E. (1983). *Educational research.* New York: Macmillan.

Waples, D., & Tyler, R. W. (1930). *Research methods and teachers' problems.* New York: Macmillan.

Winter, R. (1982). Dilemma analysis: A contribution to methodology for action research. *Cambridge Journal of Education, 12*(6), 161–174.

Woods, P. (1986). *Inside schools: Ethnography in educational research.* London: Routledge and Kegan Paul.

Wright, R. (1985). Motivating teacher involvement in professional growth activities. *The Canadian Administrator, 24*(5), 1–6.

Young, J. H. (1985). Participation in curriculum development: An inquiry into the responses of teachers. *Curriculum Inquiry, 15*(4), 387–414.

Part

·II·

RECRUITMENT, SELECTION, AND INITIAL PREPARATION

WHO TEACHES AND WHY

DILEMMAS OF BUILDING A PROFESSION FOR TWENTY-FIRST CENTURY SCHOOLS

Linda Darling-Hammond

TEACHERS COLLEGE, COLUMBIA UNIVERSITY

Eileen Mary Sclan

TEACHERS COLLEGE, COLUMBIA UNIVERSITY

This chapter describes who is entering, staying in, and leaving teaching in America today, and how the structure and conditions of the profession influence teachers' decisions, their work, and their capacity to teach. Today's teaching force is growing and changing in important ways; many new teachers are entering, often prepared in different ways than was true for entrants during the 1960s, the last era of substantial teacher hiring. This discussion of teaching force trends is framed by a broader view of the demands facing schools and teachers at a time of massive school reform and societal change. This chapter describes how school restructuring, teacher preparation and licensing requirements, workplace conditions, and salaries interact to influence the shape of the teaching force and the prospects for meeting current challenges for more successful and equal educational opportunities.

In the course of this analysis, we highlight a troubling trend that divides the children and teachers of this country and poses a national dilemma. While the fruits of reform in the teaching profession are apparent in the increasingly impressive qualifications and abilities of teachers in advantaged communities, a countervailing trend is growing in underserved areas (inner cities and rural areas) where many underprepared candidates who are armed with little knowledge about teaching and learning are entering classrooms to teach the nation's most vulnerable students.

Working conditions that conspire against teacher success are still too prevalent across the field, but they are sometimes overwhelming in low-income communities, which exacerbates the increasingly bimodal distribution of the teaching force. This reflects an ongoing tension between two contradictory policies toward entry into teaching: one approach attempts to upgrade educational standards and teacher knowledge to meet growing expectations of teachers. The other overrides such standards to recruit "warm bodies" into classrooms where students are less powerful and resources are scarce. The policy wedge that divides America's students in this way is rooted in the failure of federal, state, and local policymakers, as well as the profession as a whole, to address the need for an adequate supply and equal distribution of qualified teachers. This is a failure that must be overcome by all members of the education community if America's schools and children are to meet the challenges they now face.

A CHANGING SOCIETY AND A CHANGING OCCUPATION OF TEACHING

Efforts to restructure America's schools for the demands of a post-industrial, knowledge-based economy are redefining the mission of schooling and the job of teaching. Because the great masses of students now need to be educated for thinking work rather than low-skilled factory tasks, and educational success is a necessity rather than a luxury for a chosen few, schools are being asked to restructure themselves to ensure higher levels of success for all. Rather than merely "offering education," schools are now expected to ensure that all students learn

We would like to thank Jerry Malitz at NCES and Henry deLong of Pinkerton, who were instrumental in expediting the unpublished SASS tabulations.

and perform at high levels. Rather than merely "covering the curriculum," teachers are expected to find ways to support and connect with the needs of all learners (Darling-Hammond, 1990a). Furthermore, they are expected to prepare all students for thinking work—framing problems; finding, integrating, and synthesizing information; creating new solutions; learning on their own; and working cooperatively.

More than a decade's worth of reform proposals have highlighted the urgency of educational improvement and have increasingly recognized that educational change rests in large part on the quality of the teaching force (Carnegie Forum, 1986; Holmes Group, 1986; National Governors' Association, 1986). Reforms aimed at building the capacity of teachers differ from change efforts that mandated new programs (courses, tests, curricula, and management systems) without accounting for the quality of the teachers and the nature of the school workplace.

The new mission for education, however, clearly requires substantially more knowledge and radically different skills for teachers. The kind of teaching required to meet these demands for more thoughtful learning cannot be produced through teacher-proof materials or regulated curriculum. To create bridges between common, challenging curriculum goals and individual learners' experiences and needs, teachers must understand cognition and the many different pathways to learning. They must understand child development and pedagogy as well as the structures of subject areas and a variety of alternatives for assessing learning (Darling-Hammond, 1990b; Shulman, 1987).

New Challenges for Teachers and Teacher Education

There is another challenge that requires a more knowledgeable and highly skilled teaching force: the social setting for teaching is more demanding than ever before. Teachers are currently striving to address the needs of a growing number of low-income children (one out of four American children now lives in poverty), the largest wave of immigrants since the turn of the last century, and children who encounter a wide variety of stresses in their families and communities. Educators are striving to attain more ambitious goals at a time when schools are more inclusive than they have ever been before. More students stay in school longer, and more students with special needs—many of whom were unserved several decades ago—are served in more mainstreamed settings.

If all children are to be effectively taught, teachers must be prepared to address the substantial diversity in experiences that children bring with them to school, that is, the range of languages, cultures, exceptionalities, learning styles, talents, and intelligences that require, in turn, an equally rich and varied repertoire of teaching strategies. In addition, teaching for universal learning demands a highly developed ability to discover what children know and can do, how they think and how they learn, and to match learning and performance opportunities to the needs of individual children. This mission for teaching defies the single, formula approach to delivering lessons and testing results that has characterized the goals of much regulation of teaching, many staff development programs, and a number of teacher testing and evaluation instruments.

While these school reforms occur, major changes are taking place in teacher preparation programs across the country, ap-

proaches to licensing and induction are being reconsidered, and a new National Board for Professional Teaching Standards (NBPTS) is beginning to offer recognition to highly accomplished teachers. Deeper commitments to professionalism in teaching are being made by many educators and policymakers nationwide. There is increasing recognition that the capacities teachers need in order to succeed at the twenty-first century agenda for education can only be widely acquired throughout the teaching force by major reforms of teacher preparation and major restructuring of the systems by which states and school districts license, hire, induct, support, and provide for the continual learning of teachers (Wise & Darling-Hammond, 1987).

The traditional system of teacher licensing based on completion of specified courses in state-approved programs of study has left more practitioners, members of the public, and policymakers unconvinced that licensing standards separate those who can teach responsibly from those who cannot. Despite the fact that there are many examples to the contrary, the conventional wisdom among many veteran practitioners is that the teacher education courses they experienced were too often unhelpful to them in their practice. Most members of the public continue to think of professional training requirements for teachers as weaker than those of other professions, such as medicine (National Council for Accreditation of Teacher Education, 1993). Many policymakers' suspicions lead them to create special routes into teaching that avoid teacher education and standard licensing because they believe these are either unnecessary or ineffective (Darling-Hammond, 1992).

Efforts currently underway to develop and implement more meaningful standards for teaching include the move toward performance-based standards for teacher licensing (Interstate New Teacher Support and Assessment Consortium [INTASC], 1992); companion efforts to develop more sophisticated and authentic assessments for teachers; and the development and integration of national standards for teacher education, licensing, and certification (Darling-Hammond, Wise, & Klein, 1995). These national efforts are being led by the new National Board for Professional Teaching Standards (NBPTS), established in 1987 as the first professional body in teaching to set standards for the advanced certification of highly accomplished teachers; the Interstate New Teacher Assessment and Support Consortium (INTASC), a consortium of states working together on "National Board–compatible" licensing standards and assessments; and the National Council for Accreditation of Teacher Education (NCATE), which has been strengthening standards for teacher education programs that recently incorporated the performance standards developed by INTASC.

These initiatives have in common a view of teaching as complex, grounded in decisions that are contingent on students' needs and instructional goals, and reciprocal, that is, continually shaped and reshaped by students' responses to learning events. This view contrasts with that of the recent "technicist" era of teacher training and evaluation in which teaching was seen as the implementation of set routines and formulas for behavior that were standardized and disconnected from the diverse needs and responses of students. The new standards and assessments also take into explicit account the multicultural, multilingual nature of a student body that possesses multiple intelligences and approaches to learning. In so doing, these efforts seek to encourage teacher education that will address teachers' needs for deeper and more varied understandings of learners and learning so that they can be more effective in their work.

Ultimately, reformers hope that altering the process by which teachers are prepared, inducted, and selected into teaching can provide the impetus for deeper structural changes in the recruitment and responsibilities of teachers. As has occurred in other professions, teachers' voice, effectiveness, and responsibilities within schools may increase as they receive more rigorous and relevant preparation, and the public (including potential recruits) may recognize teaching as a challenging career requiring expertise and talent.

The Recurring Dilemma of Unequal Access

While these challenges and changes in teaching are being tackled, the profession is confronted with the perennial problem it has experienced for centuries—disparities in salaries and working conditions have recreated teacher shortages in central cities and poor rural areas. For a variety of reasons, the responses of many governments continues to be to lower or eliminate standards for entry rather than to create incentives that will attract an adequate supply of teachers. As a consequence, this era is developing an even more sharply bimodal teaching force than ever before. Whereas some children are gaining access to teachers who are more qualified and well prepared than in years past, a growing number of poor and minority children are being taught by teachers who are sorely unprepared for the task they face. This poses the risk of heightened inequality in opportunities to learn and in outcomes of schooling, with all of the social dangers that it implies, at the very time all students need to be prepared more effectively for the greater challenges they face.

If the new forms of schooling that are emerging in this school reform era are to succeed, teaching as an occupation must be able to recruit and retain able and well-prepared individuals for *all* classrooms, not just the most affluent. These entrants must be equipped with the knowledge, skills, and dispositions that will enable them to succeed with all students, and their workplaces must offer them the supports to do so and the tangible and intangible incentives that will enable them to develop a lifelong career in the profession.

Creating an Adequate Supply of Competent Teachers

It is clear that the shape of the teaching work force depends not only on the qualities and qualifications of individuals who enter, but also on how occupational and workplace factors affect teachers' decisions to enter, stay in, or leave the profession (Blase & Kirby, 1992; Bobbitt, Faupel, & Burns, 1991; Haggstrom, Darling-Hammond, & Grissmer, 1988; Johnson, 1990; McLaughlin & Talbert, 1993; Metropolitan Life, 1993; Rosenholtz, 1989; Sclan, 1993; Yee, 1990). For talented candidates to decide to teach and to remain in teaching, they must perceive opportunities for professional growth, advancement, and financial rewards.

These and other workplace conditions are all the more important as women and minorities, once a captive labor force

for teaching, now have alternative career options (Darling-Hammond, 1984). In fact, Sedlak and Schlossman (1986) believe that the effects of the women's movement have yet to be fully felt in education because relatively little hiring occurred between the early 1970s and the mid-1980s. A strong, stable teaching force will rely both on strengthened teacher preparation and improved professional conditions. Looking at teacher supply, demand, qualifications, teaching practices, and conditions as interrelated may offer more inclusive and, therefore, promising approaches to educational improvement. These interrelationships and their implications for policy development are explored in this chapter.

CHARACTERISTICS OF TODAY'S TEACHERS

The teaching force in the United States is growing. The number of full-time equivalent teachers increased from 2.5 million in 1980 to 2.8 million in 1991 and is projected to reach 3.3 million by the year 2002 (Gerald & Hussar, 1991). Because of this, the number and proportion of newly hired teachers are also increasing. How these teachers are changing the nature of the work force is described more fully later in this chapter.

Demographics

Gender In 1991, the average public school teacher was 42 years old, white, married to an employed spouse, and a parent. The large majority of teachers continue to be women—almost 90% at the elementary level and just over half (56%) at the secondary level (National Education Association [NEA], 1992). The concentration of women in teaching has increased from 67.7% in 1961 to 72.1% in 1991. Very few men teach in the elementary, English/language arts, special education, and bilingual/English as a second language fields, whereas men continue to outnumber women in mathematics, science, social sciences, and vocational education (Blank & Gruebel, 1993; Choy, Bobbitt, et al., 1993).

Race/Ethnicity Minority teachers are also underrepresented in teaching generally, and in the mathematics and science fields particularly (Blank & Gruebel, 1993). The percentage of African American and Hispanic college students who majored in education at the bachelor's degree level declined steadily between 1972 and 1987 (National Center for Education Statistics [NCES], 1989). Even with more recent increases, African Americans represented only 8% of public school teachers in 1991, approximately the same as two decades earlier (see Table 5.1). Other minorities increased their representation to 5% of public school teachers by 1991, although the numbers are still small. The 13% of the public school teaching force that is minority compares to about one third of all public school students who are members of minority groups (see Table 5.1).

Minority teachers are much more likely to teach in central cities and in schools with a large population of minorities. For example, African-American teachers comprise 16.1% of the teaching force in central cities and Hispanic teachers comprise 6.6% of urban teachers, substantially higher than their representation nationally (Choy, Henke, Alt, Medrich, & Bobbitt, 1993).

TABLE 5.1. Selected Characteristics of Public School Teachers (NEA, 1992)

	1961–1991						
	1961	1966	1971	1976	1981	1986	1991
Median age							
All teachers	41	36	35	33	37	41	42
Males	34	33	33	33	38	42	43
Females	46	40	37	33	36	41	42
Race[a]							
Black	[b]	[b]	8.1%	8.0%	7.8%	6.9%	8.0%
White	[b]	[b]	88.3	90.8	91.6	89.6	86.8
Other	[b]	[b]	3.6	1.2	0.7	3.4	5.2
Gender							
Male	31.3%	31.1%	34.3%	32.9%	33.1%	31.2%	27.9%
Female	68.7	68.9	65.7	67.1	66.9	68.8	72.1
Marital status							
Single	22.3%	22.0%	19.5%	20.1%	18.5%	12.9%	11.7%
Married	68.0	69.1	71.9	71.3	73.0	75.7	75.7
Widowed, divorced, separated	9.7	9.0	8.6	8.6	8.5	11.4	12.6

[a] Percents may not total 100 due to rounding.
[b] Data not available

Whereas one out of five public school teachers in the 1987-1988 school year taught in schools where more than half the students were minorities, the majority of Asian, African-American, and Hispanic teachers taught at schools with a predominantly minority student body (Choy, Bobbitt, et al., 1993; NEA, 1992).

Age The teaching force has aged considerably since the 1970s when the last major hiring boom occurred. The percentage of teachers under age 30 declined sharply from 37.1% in 1976 to 11.1% in 1986, where it has held steady since. Meanwhile the proportions of teachers in their 40s and 50s has increased since the mid-1980s. Nearly 23% were older than 50 in 1991 (NEA, 1992). This means that large numbers of teachers will be retiring around the turn of the century, many of them, such as the aging population of mathematics and science teachers, in fields where there are already shortages (Blank & Gruebel, 1993). This trend, along with rising student enrollments, contributes to the projection that during the end of the 1990s and the beginning of the twenty-first century, more than 200,000 teachers will need to be hired annually (Gerald & Hussar, 1991; Murnane, Singer, Willett, Kemple, & Olsen, 1991).

Level and Sector Approximately 92% of teachers taught in public schools in 1990 (Choy, Bobbitt, et al., 1993). About half teach at the elementary level and half at the secondary level. Forty-five percent of public school teachers work in rural areas or small towns, as compared to 25% in urban areas and 30% in suburban communities (NEA, 1992).

Preparation and Qualifications

Teachers' qualifications can be measured to some extent by their degrees, academic background, and licensing or certification status. By 1991, virtually all public school teachers had bachelor's degrees. This is a substantial change from 30 years earlier when nearly 15% of teachers lacked bachelor's degrees. However, the proportion of private school teachers with less than a bachelor's degree increased from 4% to 6% between 1987 and 1991 (Choy, Bobbitt, et al., 1993).

Meanwhile, the proportion of public school teachers holding master's degrees more than doubled between 1961 and 1991, from 23% to 52% (see Table 5.2). This trend may be partly due to the fact that an increasing number of states have passed legislation requiring teachers to obtain master's degrees within a few years after entry in order to be granted a continuing or permanent license. Teachers with master's degrees still tend to be concentrated at the secondary level (Choy, Bobbitt, et al., 1993). Whereas men once significantly outnumbered women in obtaining postgraduate degrees, the gap between men and women has significantly narrowed in recent years (NEA, 1992).

Table 5.2 also illustrates the increasing prevalence of licensing tests for teachers, a function of policy changes throughout the 1980s. By 1991, 35% of public school teachers had taken and passed state-level competency tests.

Increasingly, states are expecting teachers to major in a discipline while also preparing to teach. Across all fields, about 75% of teachers had a major in their primary area of assignment in 1988, ranging from a low of 55% for mathematics teachers to a high of 91% for music teachers (Bobbitt & McMillen, 1990). As standards have risen, these proportions have increased, but the extent to which this is the case still varies substantially from field to field and from state to state. By 1991, for example, about 63% of mathematics teachers had majored in their field, ranging from 25% in Alaska to 87% in Maryland. The proportion of science teachers who had majored in their field increased from 64% in 1988 to 70% in 1991, ranging from 41% in New Mexico to 85% in Connecticut (Blank & Gruebel, 1993). Across fields, the proportion of public elementary and secondary teachers who were certified and held a major or minor in their main assignment field varied from a high of 91% in physical education to a low of 65% in mathematics in 1991.

TABLE 5.2. Educational Attainment and Competency Testing of Public
School Teachers (NEA, 1992)

	1961–1991						
	1961	1966	1971	1976	1981	1986	1991
Highest degree held[a]							
Less than bachelor's	14.6%	7.0%	2.9%	0.9%	0.4%	0.3%	0.6%
Bachelor's	61.9	69.6	69.6	61.6	50.1	48.3	46.3
Master's or 6 years	23.1	23.2	27.1	37.1	49.3	50.7	52.6
Doctor's	0.4	0.1	0.4	0.4	0.3	0.7	0.5
Competency testing							
Teachers required to pass competency test	[b]	[b]	[b]	[b]	21.7%	19.4%	35.0%

[a] Figures for curriculum specialist or professional diploma based on 6 years of college study are not included.

[b] Data not available

Ninety-one percent of all public school teachers held a regular or advanced license in their main teaching field in 1991 (Choy, Bobbitt, et al., 1993). This means that nearly one tenth of all public school teachers were teaching without having fully met the licensing standards for their fields. This is a sizable number, especially when considered in light of the fact that no other profession allows individuals to practice without a license. Among private school teachers, about 60% held regular or advanced licenses (Choy, Bobbitt, et al., 1993). This is because some states require private school teachers to hold a license, whereas others do not.

What these figures mean in terms of teacher qualifications varies from state to state due to differences in licensing standards. For example, a number of states, such as Arizona, Connecticut, and New York, require at least a master's degree on top of a strong subject-matter degree for a full professional license. These requirements generally incorporate 40 credits of professional education coursework and a lengthy supervised practicum or internship in addition to subject-matter preparation. Yet, states such as New Jersey, Texas, and Virginia have reduced professional education coursework to no more than 18 credits at the undergraduate level, without requiring a master's degree or intensive internship experience to compensate for the reductions in professional preparation. Thus, the meaning of a teaching license, in terms of knowledge and skills represented

varies tremendously from state to state (Darling-Hammond, 1992).

In addition, teachers are still often asked to teach outside their licensing field. One out of five public school teachers reported in 1987–1988 that they were not teaching in the area in which they felt best qualified (Choy, Bobbitt, et al., 1993). One fourth of mathematics and science public school teachers reported that they were not teaching in the area in which they were best qualified. These findings may be partly explained by the emergency or provisional status of many licenses and endorsements that allow teachers to teach without preparation or experience. These are most prevalent in shortage fields and in locations experiencing teacher shortages. For example, the largest concentrations of mathematics and science teachers who had not majored in and who were not certified in their assigned fields are in inner cities with large proportions of minority children. Inner-city high school students in schools with a large minority population, for example, have only a 50% chance of being taught by fully licensed mathematics or science teachers (Oakes, 1990).

Public school teachers in the United States are very experienced. In 1991, 70% had more than 10 years of teaching experience and 35% had 20 years or more of teaching experience (see Table 5.3). The increase in median number of years of experience from 8 to 15 years between 1976 and 1991 is largely

TABLE 5.3. Years of Full-Time Teaching Experience for Public
School Teachers (NEA, 1992)

	1961–1991						
Teaching Experience	1961	1966	1971	1976	1981	1986	1991
1 year	8.0%	9.1%	9.1%	5.5%	1.6%	2.5%	2.8%
2 years	6.3	9.3	7.7	5.8	3.7	2.1	3.9
3–4 years	13.2	14.4	15.6	16.0	8.2	4.8	7.0
5–9 years	19.4	21.7	24.0	28.9	26.2	17.7	16.3
10–14 years	15.1	14.2	15.8	17.3	23.0	22.3	17.2
15–19 years	10.4	9.8	9.7	12.5	15.4	23.1	18.2
20 or more years	27.6	21.4	18.3	14.1	21.9	27.7	34.7
Mean	13 yr	12 yr	11 yr	10 yr	13 yr	15 yr	15 yr
Median	11	8	8	8	12	15	15

Percents may not total 100 due to rounding.

due to the low levels of hiring throughout the 1980s and the consequent aging of the teaching force. This is beginning to change as hiring again increases. Between 1986 and 1991, the proportion of teachers with fewer than 5 years of experience increased from 9% to 14%.

Professional Working Conditions

Elementary teachers worked an average of 44 hours per week and secondary teachers spent an average of 50 hours per week on all duties in 1991 (see Table 5.4). Regarding class size, the average elementary class size has consistently decreased since the 1960s from 29 in 1961 to 24 in 1991. Secondary class size has fluctuated, dropping to 23 in 1981 but increasing again to 26 in 1991. U.S. teachers teach 180 days and work an average of 5 nonteaching days per year, a policy that has not changed since the 1960s (NEA, 1992).

Despite a shorter school year, no other nation requires teachers to teach more hours per week than the United States. Japanese and most European teachers have substantial time for preparation, curriculum development, and one-on-one work with students, parents, or colleagues, generally teaching large groups of students only about 15–20 hours during a 40–45-hour work week (Darling-Hammond, 1990; Nelson & O'Brien, 1993). By contrast, most U.S. elementary teachers have 3 or fewer hours for preparation per week, and secondary teachers generally have five preparation periods per week (see Table 5.4).

Although nearly three fourths of public school teachers participated in workshops sponsored by their school systems during the 1991 school year, most other kinds of professional development continued to be much less widely available. About one third of teachers served on curriculum committees and 46% served on other kinds of committees. Approximately 20% took college courses in education and 35% participated in association-sponsored activities (NEA, 1992).

WHO IS ENTERING TEACHING?

Prospective Teachers

In 1991, fewer than 9% of college freshmen indicated an interest in preparing to become teachers. Although this is a substantial increase over the lowest point of interest in 1982, when only 5% of freshmen indicated an interest in teaching, overall statistics continue to reflect the shift in interest since the early 1970s away from fields in education, social science, arts and humanities, and toward fields in business, engineering, and computer services (Astin, 1992). The magnitude of this shift can be seen in the fact that in 1966 nearly 22% of freshmen were interested in preparing to teach (Astin, Green, & Korn, 1987). For many talented young women, who have always provided the bulk of the entering teaching force, teaching has recently had to compete with (and often has lost to) other professions as a career interest (Astin et al., 1987). The same trend has been

TABLE 5.4. Teaching Assignment of Public School Teachers: 1961–1991: Pupils and Hours (NEA, 1992)

	1961	1966	1971	1976	1981	1986	1991
Pupil load (mean number)							
Elementary teachers							
Mean number of pupils in class	29	28	27	25	25	24	24
Secondary teachers							
Mean number of periods taught per day	5	5	5	5	5	5	5
Mean number of pupils taught per day	138	132	134	126	118	94	93
Mean number of pupils per class	28	26	27	25	23	25	26
Mean number of hours per week spent on all duties							
All teachers	47	47	47	46	46	49	47
Elementary	49	47	46	44	44	47	44
Secondary	46	48	48	48	48	51	50
Preparation time per week[a]							
Elementary							
None	b	b	b	b	25.0%	17.5%	9.7%
Less than 1 hour	b	b	b	b	6.6	10.8	7.8
From 1 to less than 3 hours	b	b	b	b	33.7	33.4	36.0
From 3 to less than 5 hours	b	b	b	b	21.1	23.0	31.4
5 or more hours	b	b	b	b	13.5	15.4	15.0
Secondary							
No preparation periods	21.4%	22.9%	19.4%	19.4%	11.4%	13.7%	5.8%
1–4 preparation periods	9.5	7.3	5.5	11.0	10.5	9.3	9.4
5 or more preparation periods	69.1	69.8	75.0	69.5	78.0	77.0	84.9

[a] Percents may not total 100 due to omission of some subject areas for 1961 and 1991 or rounding for other years.
[b] Data not available

true for minority college freshmen since the early 1980s. However, signs of an upswing in the number and quality of recruits to teaching are increasingly apparent.

"Quality" Indicators During the 1980s, there was a widespread belief and some evidence that the "quality" of new entrants to teaching was declining. For example, during the lowest recruitment point in the early 1980s, education was one of the fields least selected by those students scoring highest on aptitude and achievement tests (Lanier & Little, 1986; Southern Regional Education Board [SREB], 1985; Vance & Schlechty, 1982a). Yet, many indicators were badly flawed and most reasonably solid data (derived from large-scale studies in the 1970s) are now quite out of date. Recent indicators suggest that these trends, to the extent they were true during the 1980s, have substantially changed since then.

Many claims about declining quality were based on data about the career intentions of high school seniors planning to go to college. These intentions bear only a tenuous relationship to students' actual career activities 5 or more years later. Other data are based on actual career paths of the class of 1972 high school seniors (the cohort for the National Longitudinal Study); however, we do not know how similar their experiences are to the changed conditions in teaching today. What seems true from the data available are the following conclusions:

- Through the 1970s and early 1980s, teaching became substantially less attractive as a career option for college students, especially those with high academic ability (as measured by SAT tests) and those who had taken college preparatory course work while in high school. This was particularly true for women and minority college students (Astin, 1992; Darling-Hammond, 1984).
- During the late 1970s and early 1980s, those who defected from teaching at each point after choosing an education major (i.e., failing to enter teaching and failing to remain) disproportionately comprised high test scorers (NCES, 1986; Vance & Schlechty, 1982a, 1982b). Murnane, Singer, & Willett (1989) found that teachers who scored highly on the National Teacher Exam (NTE) were more likely to leave teaching, to do so sooner, and to be less likely to return.
- During the early 1980s, entrants into teacher education programs were much more likely to have pursued a vocational education or general education curriculum in high school than was the case a decade earlier when nearly all education students had pursued a college preparatory curriculum prior to college (Carnegie Forum, 1986).

Although teacher "quality" is difficult to measure, all of these indicators suggest that fewer of the most academically well-prepared college students were attracted to teaching during the 1970s and early 1980s. In addition, those with higher test scores, and presumably greater employment opportunities, were more likely to leave teaching if they had entered.

Many of these indicators have changed substantially in the past 5–10 years. To ensure adequate preparation, many teacher education institutions began to require higher grade point averages (GPAs) and test scores for admission (Darling-Hammond & Berry, 1988; Howey & Zimpher, 1993). Consequently, the aca-

demic qualifications of prospective teachers are now stronger than they were during the 1980s and stronger than those of the average college graduate. For example, the GPAs of newly qualified teachers in 1990 were noticeably higher than those of other bachelor's degree recipients, with 50% of newly qualified teachers earning an average of 3.25 or better as compared to 40% of all graduates (Gray et al., 1993).

Demographics The average age of prospective teachers, 25.7 years, is slightly older than the typical college graduate at age 23 (American Association of Colleges for Teacher Education [AACTE], 1991). Compared to current teachers, the gender and racial/ethnic profile of prospective teachers currently enrolled in the subset of teacher education programs surveyed by the (Research About Teacher Education (RATE) project (1988-1992) is even less representative of men and minorities. Men represented only 19% of these teacher education students, and they were academically the least well prepared of teacher candidates (AACTE, 1992; Brookhart & Loadman, 1993; Howey & Zimpher, 1993).

The percentage of minorities enrolled in undergraduate teacher education programs (8%) in the RATE sample was substantially lower than the proportion enrolled in higher education overall and the proportion in the current teaching force (Goodlad, 1990; Howey & Zimpher, 1993) (see Table 5.5). In addition, a study conducted by the American Association of Colleges for Teacher Education (AACTE) (AACTE, 1992), African-American teacher education students who had enrolled in the fall of 1985 and 1986 had a higher attrition rate than white or Hispanic teacher education students.

At the same time, African Americans who were newly qualified to teach in 1985 were the most likely group to be certified but not teaching (Darling-Hammond, 1990c). Whereas 14,600 African-American 1984 degree recipients were eligible or certified to teach, only 8,500 of them were actually teaching a year later. For Hispanics, of 4,100 certified recent graduates, only 2,700 were employed in teaching (NCES, 1983, 1985). These data demonstrate that the decline in minority presence in teaching is not just due to failure to enter or complete teacher educa-

TABLE 5.5. Demographic Characteristics of Prospective Teachers (AACTE, 1991)

Characteristic	Percentage
Gender	
Male	19
Female	81
Race/Ethnicity	
White (not Hispanic origin)	92
Black (not Hispanic origin)	5
Hispanic	2
Asian or Pacific Islander	2
American Indian or Alaskan Native	<1
Enrollment	
Full Time	94
Part Time	6
Marital Status	
Married	33
Single	67

tion, but to other factors that dissuade candidates from entering and staying in teaching.

There are many reasons to be concerned about the growing shortages of minority teachers. The importance of minority teachers as role models for majority and minority students alike is one reason for concern. In addition, minority teachers often bring a special level of understanding to the experiences of their minority students and a perspective on school policy and practice that is critical for all schools and districts to include. Finally, with the exception of minority teachers, most prospective teachers do not prefer to teach in inner-city schools, even though there are a disproportionate number of new jobs in these schools (Howey & Zimpher, 1993). This also presents a challenge for teacher education programs, which need to better address all teachers' preparation for urban school teaching. To address minority teacher shortages, higher education institutions, in conjunction with states and districts, need to develop strategies to attract and keep minority candidates in teacher education programs and support their entry into the profession (Dilworth, 1990).

Support Financial assistance is not available in substantial amounts for teacher education students. Although teacher education students receive funds from several sources (loans, grants, employment, etc.), the predominant source of financial income through the 1980s came from family resources, not unlike other undergraduate students (Howey & Zimpher, 1993). Most preservice teacher education students report that they enroll in programs close to where they are living at the time, mainly for convenience sake and due to a belief that staying in the area will increase chances for getting a job when they complete their programs (AACTE, 1992; Goodlad, 1990; Howey & Zimpher, 1993). Goodlad (1990) found that more than 70% of the preservice students in his study commuted, and the large majority held part-time or full-time jobs.

Newly Hired Teachers

Sources of Newly Hired Teachers In recent years the number of newly hired teachers has been increasing once again, and the proportion of them drawn from the reserve pool of former teachers has been decreasing. "Newly hired" teachers comprised 11.3% of the teaching force in 1987–1988 and 12.2% in 1990–1991, a sign of the increased demand for teachers projected to continue throughout the decade (see Table 5.6). The proportion of these newly hired teachers who had not taught before increased from 38.6% in 1987–1988 to more than half (53.2%) in 1990–1991, whereas those returning to teaching after a break in service decreased from 42% in 1987–1988 to 31% in 1990–1991. The remainder were transferring from one school or district to another (see Table 5.7).

Although a preponderance of new hires in many fields are experienced teachers returning to the classroom, a recent report by the Council for Chief State School Officers indicates that a large majority of newly hired teachers in mathematics and science in 1990 were first-time teachers (Blank & Gruebel, 1993). This probably indicates a smaller reserve pool of potential reentrants in these particular fields than in others. This makes sense given the different labor market conditions for teachers in fields

TABLE 5.6. Percentage of Full-Time Teachers Who Were Newly Hired and Who Were First-Time Teachers by Sector: 1987–1988 and 1990–1991 (Choy, Henke, et al., 1993)

	Percent Newly Hired	Percent First-Time Teachers
1987–1988		
Total	11.3	3.1
Public	10.5	2.8
Private	17.1	5.2
1990–1991		
Total	12.2	4.0
Public	11.5	3.6
Private	17.7	6.8

such as mathematics and science where alternative career opportunities are more available and more financially attractive.

Demographic Characteristics New hires in 1987–1988 and 1990–1991 were similar in many respects to teachers in general, although slightly more likely to be female (see Tables 5.8 and 5.9). Although younger than the average teacher, new entrants are older than was once the case: newly minted (right out of college) entrants were 28 years old on average, delayed entrants averaged 31 years of age, and reentrants averaged nearly 38 years old. In 1991, most newly hired teachers (new entrants and reentrants) were older than 30 years of age.

About 10% of entrants in 1987–1988 and 12% in 1990–1991 were African American, American Indian, Asian American, or Latino. Interestingly, more minority public school teachers were represented in the delayed entrants pool (16.6%) in 1987–1988 than in the pools of newly minted or reentering teachers (both about 9%). This may confirm anecdotal evidence about would-be teachers who either could not find jobs in the tighter hiring years of the mid-1980s or who took the more popular route into business jobs at that time and are now motivated and able to find teaching employment.

Compensation Beginning teacher salaries remain relatively low. The base salaries of new teachers averaged around $17,000

TABLE 5.7. Percent of Newly Hired Public and Private School Teachers by Supply Source: 1987–1988 and 1990–1991 (Rollefson & Broughman, 1994)

Source	Public		Private	
	87–88	90–91	87–88	90–91
First time teachers	38.6%	53.2%	31.1%	41.6%
Newly minted	26.8	33.8	17.4	22.2
Delayed entrants	11.8	19.4	13.7	19.4
Transfers	19.9	16.3	23.6	21.9
Reentrants	41.5	30.5	45.3	36.5

Note: Newly hired teachers are defined as regular teachers who teach half time or more and who in the previous year did not hold regular teaching positions in that state and/or sector.

TABLE 5.8. Newly Hired Public School Teachers by Type and Selected Demographic
Characteristics: 1987–1988 (Rollefson, 1993)

Characteristic	Total	New Newly Minted	New Delayed Entrants	Transfers	Reentrants
Percent female	78.5	79.4	71.8	78.4	80.1
Percent minority	10.7	9.2	16.6	10.2	9.9
Age					
Mean total	33.9	28.0	31.1	36.0	37.8
Marital status					
Percent married	64.9	44.8	64.0	69.8	76.4
Income/salary					
Base year salary ($)	19,380	17,723	17,300	21,133	20,419
Total year round income ($)	21,392	19,552	19,644	22,701	22,615
Family income					
Percent less than $25,000	30.9	57.6	47.7	26.9	19.1
Percent $25,000 but less than $50,000	42.5	29.4	40.0	47.4	42.5
Percent $50,000 or more	26.6	13.0	12.3	27.9	33.9

in 1987–1988. Whereas the total family income of most delayed entrants was more than $25,000, that of most "newly minted" entrants was under $25,000 for 1987–1988 (see Table 5.8). This suggests that delayed entrants, who are older and much more likely to be married, may find teaching more affordable with the income of a spouse as a supplement to a relatively small teacher salary. In 1990–1991, the base salary of most new entrants and experienced reentrants combined was only $22,242 (NDRC, 1993). Understandably, 50% of first-year teachers in 1987–1988 were dissatisfied with their salaries, a finding that was similar to public school teachers in general, 63% of whom rated their salaries from fair to poor in 1990 (Carnegie Foundation, 1990).

In contrast to teachers in general, a large majority of first-year teachers tend to favor various forms of incentive pay (Choy, Henke, et al., 1993; Metropolitan Life, 1989; Sclan, 1993; Smylie & Smart, 1990). However, the proportion of newly hired teachers actually receiving incentive pay of any kind was small in 1990–1991—about 2% on average for each of several forms of incentive pay, such as individual merit pay, a schoolwide bonus, or additional pay for teaching in a shortage field or high priority location. More noticeable numbers received payment for serving as master or mentor teachers (9%) or for participating in a career ladder program (23%). (See Table 5.9.) These figures appear to confirm policy trends noted in the late 1980s; at that time, most states and districts had abandoned merit pay programs, but greater ongoing support was apparent for mentor teacher and career ladder programs (Darling-Hammond & Berry, 1988).

Induction An increasing number of first-year teachers are participating in programs that formally socialize them into teaching. Forty-eight percent of all teachers with fewer than 3 years of experience and 54% of public school teachers had experienced some kind of induction program during their first year. The number of teachers who participated in formal induction programs almost doubled during the decade 1981–1991 and has more than tripled since the early 1970s (Choy, Henke, et al., 1993). Depending on the nature of the programs, including the extent to which they focus on support as well as evaluation and the extent to which they help teachers address real problems of practice, these induction initiatives may make a substantial difference in teacher recruitment and retention.

Previous research on teacher induction programs shows that there are major differences in the strategies adopted by states during the 1980s. Whereas places such as California and Connecticut funded mentor programs, many of the first-wave induction programs focused more on evaluation than mentoring. They required new teachers to pass an observational evaluation prior to receiving a continuing license. Although these were called induction programs, most did not fund the work of mentors, and the mandated evaluation strategies typically looked for the demonstration of predetermined generic behaviors rather than for the development of contextually appropriate good practice (see, e.g., Darling-Hammond with Sclan, 1992; Macmillan & Pendlebury, 1985; Peterson & Comeaux, 1989; Wise, Darling-Hammond, & Berry, 1987).

Since then more states and districts have sought to create programs that support new teachers in the development of guided, collegial practice and inquiry likely to promote higher levels of efficacy and effectiveness (see, e.g., Darling-Hammond, with Sclan, 1992; Little, 1987; Rosenholtz, 1985). Further research will be needed to ascertain what kinds of induction programs most new teachers are experiencing and how they are affecting teachers' effectiveness and retention in the profession.

Qualifications Approximately four out of five newly minted teachers in the public sector and just over half in the private sector had a college major or minor in their main assignment field and were licensed in that assignment field in 1987–1988 (Rollefson, 1993). By 1990–1991, the proportion of newly minted teachers with these combined qualifications had declined to two thirds, although 80% were licensed (see Table 5.10). Delayed entrants were even less likely to hold a college major or minor or to be licensed in their main assignment field in both of these years. In 1990–1991, just under two thirds were licensed and fewer than half held a license plus a major or minor

TABLE 5.9. Demographic Characteristics of Newly Hired Public and Private School Teachers 1990–1991: A National Model (New and Reentrants) (National Data Resource Center, 1993)

Characteristic	Percentage
Gender	
Male	21.7
Female	78.3
Race/Ethnicity[a]	
American Indian, Alaskan Native	.8
Asian or Pacific Islander	1.3
Black	5.4
White	92.5
Hispanic origin	5.1
Age	
30 years or younger	47.1
31–39 years	25.9
40 years or more	27.0
Marital Status	
Married	58.1
Single	41.9
Income	
Base salary	
$20,000 or less	42.2
$20,001–$25,000	33.2
$25,001–$30,000	14.4
$30,001–$35,000	4.0
$35,001 or more	6.2
Combined family income	
Less than $10,000	.3
$10,000–$24,999	23.2
$25,000–$49,999	41.5
$50,000 or more	35.0
Received incentive pay	
Master or mentor teacher	9.1
Shortage field	2.2
High-priority location	1.4
Career ladder promotion	23.2
Merit pay bonus	2.8
Schoolwide bonus	2.3

[a] Does not add to 100% because a small percentage of those who responded yes to black or white also responded yes to being of Hispanic origin.

in their subject field. It is possible that the delayed entrants had satisfied some but not all of the license requirements earlier or that they had not initially prepared to teach and entered teaching through emergency hiring routes when other career avenues proved closed or unrewarding.

The qualifications of new hires in 1990–1991 were troubling. In addition to the 15% of newly hired public and private teachers (new and reentering) who held no license at all in 1990–1991, 12.5% held substandard licenses (temporary, provisional, or emergency) (see Table 5.11). Thus, more than one in four new hires were not fully licensed in 1990–1991. Although most unlicensed teachers were in private schools where licensing is not always required, fully 10% of first-year public school teachers had no license in their field in that year (see Table 5.12), and 17% more held only temporary, provisional, or emergency licenses (NDRC, 1993).

This suggests two interrelated problems. First, regardless of what one thinks about the meaning of licensure in terms of teachers' qualifications, it is an indicator of shortages in the public school sector. In virtually all states, public schools are legally precluded form hiring unlicensed candidates when those with licenses are available. Second, although the issue is hotly debated, the great preponderance of evidence demonstrates that fully prepared and licensed teachers are more effective than those whose background lacks one or more of the elements required for licensing (i.e., subject-matter background, knowledge about teaching and learning, and a period of guided clinical experiences) (see Darling-Hammond, 1992, for a review).

Whereas hiring statistics show more teachers entering with marginal qualifications, nearly one fourth of newly hired teachers in 1990–1991 held at least a master's degree. Among first-year teachers the proportion has been about one tenth for the last several years (see Table 5.12). This represents a substantial increase in preparation for a subset of entering teachers. Together these sets of statistics illustrate the dual standard increasingly characterizing entry to teaching, one that provides teachers of dramatically different qualifications to different students and that exacerbates growing educational inequalities between the rich and the poor (Darling-Hammond, 1995).

These trends are related to teacher labor markets and different policy choices made by states and districts about how to structure teacher supply in light of very different demand conditions. These factors and their implications for teaching and schooling are discussed later in this chapter.

TABLE 5.10. Percent of Newly Hired Public and Private School Teachers with Various Qualifications in Primary Assignment Field and Average Base Year Salary by Sources of Supply: 1990–1991 (Rollefson & Broughman, 1994)

Qualifications/Salary	Newly Minted		Delayed Entrants		Transfers		Reentrants	
	Public	Private	Public	Private	Public	Private	Public	Private
Major/minor and certified	67.4%	43.8%	48.9%	29.4%	62.4%	39.2%	67.2%	40.1%
Certified	79.9	54.4	65.4	37.4	76.4	49.5	84.7	54.0
Major or minor	81.4	71.1	66.5	52.7	79.6	75.2	77.4	69.8
Neither major/minor nor certified	6.1	18.3	17.0	39.2	6.3	14.5	5.1	16.3
Degree higher than BA/BS	8.5	11.8	12.6	14.6	38.5	33.2	45.6	32.1
Base year salary	$20,784	$14,227	$20,974	$14,634	$25,052	$18,094	$25,934	$16,197

TABLE 5.11. Main Teaching Assignment, Qualifications, and Out-of-Sector Experience for Newly Hired Teachers, 1990–1991 (New and Reentrants) (NDRC, 1993)

Characteristic	Percentage
Main assignment field	
Elementary (pre K–general elementary)	38.4
Math/science/computer	12.4
Humanities/social science	15.7
Remedial/special education	13.3
Other	20.2
Certified to teach main assignment field	85.1
Not certified	14.9
Type of certification	
None	14.9
Advanced professional	4.5
Regular or probationary	68.1
Temporary, provisional, or emergency	12.5
Degree	
At least a bachelor's	98.1
Less than bachelor's	1.9
At least a master's	23.5
Less than master's	74.6
No degree	1.9
Experience	
Taught in other sector (public or private)	13.4
Never taught in another sector	86.6

Note: Percentages based on 154,421 total new hires.

TABLE 5.12. Academic Background, Class Size, Sector, Specialty Field, and Level of Public and Private School First-Year Teachers

Characteristic	Percent Response of First-Year Teachers	
	1987–1988[a]	1990–1991[b]
At least a bachelor's degree	98	97
Less than a bachelor's degree	2	3
At least a master's degree	10	9
Less than a master's degree	90	88
Missing	—	3
Degree in a discipline	32[c]	n/a
Degree in education only	68[c]	n/a
Certified in area teaching	84	83
Not certified	16	17
Private certified in area	61[c]	52
Private not certified	39[c]	48
Public certified in area	92[c]	90
Public not certified	8[c]	10
Average class size		
32 or less	90[c]	n/a
More than 32 (recoded to include all class types)	10[c]	n/a
Satisfied with class size		
Agree	71	
Disagree	29	Item not included
Math/science/computer	13	13
Remedial/special education	11	11
Humanities/social science	22	16
Elementary (Pre-K, K, Elementary)	40	41
Other	13	19
Public Sector	78	81
Private Sector	22	19
Elementary Level (K–8)	57	63
Secondary Level (9–12)	43	26
Combined (Elementary and Secondary)	—	11
Elementary school (Pre-K, K–5)	35[c]	n/a
Middle school (6–8)	33[c]	n/a
High school (9–12)	32[c]	n/a

[a] Source: From Sclan, 1993.

[b] Source: From NDRC, 1993.

[c] Calculated from SASS 1987–1988 random sample (unweighted $n = 651$, weighted $n = 34,506$) (Sclan, 1993).

TEACHER SUPPLY AND DEMAND

This section discusses the major factors currently influencing teacher supply and demand. The growing demand for new teachers will continue throughout the next decade. Although slight rises in supply have followed a 15-year decline in entry rates, shortages currently exist in specific teaching fields and locations. Meanwhile, important changes are also occurring in the standards for preparing and licensing teachers. The prognosis for the future depends on how policies, teacher education programs, and professional working conditions together influence the qualifications, supply, and distribution of teachers.

Trends in the Demand for Teachers

Steady increases in teacher demand are expected for most of the next decade (Gerald & Hussar, 1990). There are three major components of teacher demand: pupil enrollments, pupil : teacher ratios, and turnover. Two of these components—enrollments and pupil : teacher ratios—are reasonably easy to forecast; however, the third and largest component—turnover—has been subject to much debate and is the source of substantial divergence in the numerical estimates used for projections. In all three cases, however, the signs point to significant increases in new demand for teachers.

Pupil enrollments have increased in recent years due to a rise in the annual number of U.S. births coupled with the largest wave of immigration the United States has experienced since the early 1900s. This "baby boomlet," which began to enter the schools in 1985, has increased enrollment since then from 44.9 million to 46.9 million in 1991, with continued projected increases throughout the next decade and beyond (NCES, 1991). This reversed the sharply declining enrollments from 1970 to 1985 that had substantially reduced the need for new teachers. The new wave of students is now winding its way through elementary and secondary schools. If substantial progress were to be made in stemming the high level of dropouts in American schools (currently in the range of about 25% of high school age youth), this would also have a substantial effect on the demand for secondary level teachers.

Pupil : teacher ratios have been declining slowly but steadily for many years (NCES, 1992). Recent reform initiatives, including some to reduce class sizes and to provide additional special services to students, will likely cause this trend to continue, thus boosting teacher demand. Reform efforts to increase student coursetaking in particular subject areas, for example, mathematics, science, and foreign languages, have also increased the demand for teachers.

Important as these trends are, the demand for additional teachers in any given year is largely a function of turnover, which usually comprises two thirds to three fourths of total new demand. Because most published turnover estimates have been based on very old data, and few projections have taken teacher retirement trends into account, widely differing estimates of projected teacher demand are available.

For example, the National Center for Education Statistics (NCES) in consecutive years published projected estimates of new teacher demand for the years of 1988 to 1995 ranging from a total of 1,230,000 (an average of 175,000 annually) to 2,021,000 teachers (an average of 290,000 annually) (NCES, 1987, 1988). In 1991, the number of new hires, excluding transfers, was about 230,000, just between the two estimates.

The lower of these estimates was implausible because it was based on the assumption that the turnover rates present in the early 1980s when retirements were at their lowest level in 20 years would continue in the coming years when retirement rates are certain to climb steeply. The higher estimate (which assumed a 7.5% turnover rate for elementary teachers and a 6.5% rate for secondary teachers) is more realistic for the long term given the current age composition of the teaching force. Half of current teachers were age 42 or over in 1991 (NEA, 1992). Given current retirement trends, virtually all of them will retire by the year 2015, most by 2005. Some analysts believe the aging of the teaching force, and the traditionally higher turnover rates of the young teachers who will be replacing those who retire, could boost turnover rates to as high as 9% or 10% in coming years (Grissmer & Kirby, 1987).

In summary, there is no doubt that teacher demand will continue to increase into the next century. Based on NCES's middle-level alternative projections, annual demand for new hiring of classroom teachers in public elementary and secondary schools is projected to increase from 187,000 in 1990, which already proved to be an underestimate, to 225,000 in 2001 (Gerald & Hussar, 1990). The most well-reasoned estimates would place the total demand for new entrants at 2–2.5 million between 1990 and 2000, averaging more than 200,000 entrants annually.

Trends in the Supply of Teachers

While demand is increasing, the supply of newly prepared teachers is also beginning to increase again after a dramatic decline from the early 1970s through the mid-1980s. Between 1972 and 1987, the number of bachelor's degrees conferred in education plummeted by more than 50% from 194,229 to 87,083 (American Council on Education [ACE], 1989; NCES, 1989). The declines were most pronounced for minority candidates, plummeting by more than 40% for Hispanic and Native-American candidates between 1975 and 1987 and by two thirds for African-American candidates (ACE, 1989; NCES, 1989). By 1987, only 8,019 minority candidates received bachelor's degrees in

education, representing 9% of all education degrees, a substantial drop from the 13% of a much larger number of degrees that had been awarded to minorities 10 years earlier (ACE, 1989). Since then, the total number of bachelor's degrees in education has increased to 111,000 in 1990–1991 (Snyder & Hoffman, 1993). This represents about three fourths of all newly trained teachers each year. The remainder receive degrees in their disciplines with a minor or certificate in education or receive master's degrees. At current rates of increase, this number could grow to between 150,000 and 170,000 annually by the year 2000. Beyond that, a range of policy choices yet unmade will determine future trends. Recall that this compares to an estimated demand of more than 200,000 annually. Obviously, teaching vacancies are being and will continue to be filled from other sources.

Sources of Teacher Supply

There are a number of sources of teacher supply. New entrants can come from (1) undergraduate teacher education programs, the traditional path to teaching and still the largest single group of entrants; (2) graduate level programs, which are considered alternate routes in some states and are treated as traditional paths in others; (3) other alternate routes (aside from graduate programs) recently created in a number of states; or (4) no formal teaching preparation at all. Another major source of supply is the "reserve pool," which includes individuals who prepared to teach and did not do so initially or who left teaching and later returned. They may be reentering from other occupations, from homemaking or child rearing, or from higher education.

In 1990, one third of all teachers who were newly hired by local districts were first-time teachers. They comprised 4% of all teachers. Most newly hired teachers (73% of those hired and 6% of all teachers) were transfers from other districts. Although transfers are part of the supply source for local districts, they are not considered part of the national supply market because they are merely moving within the market rather than entering the market from another sector. Only about one sixth of newly hired teachers (or 2% of all teachers) were reentrants from the reserve pool. These individuals had been engaged in a variety of activities the year before: more than one third had been working in another occupation, about one fourth had been caring for family, and nearly one fourth had been substitute teaching. Smaller proportions had been attending college, seeking work, or doing something else (Choy, Bobbitt, et al., 1993).

Newly Qualified Teachers In 1991, the total number of "newly qualified teachers" (who prepared to teach, were licensed or state-certified, or had taught within a year of their graduation) was 140,000; of these, 121,000 were eligible or certified for teaching and 19,000 had taught without a license (Gray et al., 1993).

Of those who prepare to teach, only about 60% to 70% actually enter teaching after graduation, and the proportion is even lower for minority teacher candidates (Choy, Bobbitt, et al., 1993; Darling-Hammond, 1990c; Haggstrom, et al., 1988). In 1985, about 74% of those newly qualified to teach applied for teaching jobs, and just fewer than 50% ended up teaching full time. Only 38% of the newly qualified minority candidates entered teaching full time. Continuing the trend, only 76% of newly qualified teachers in 1990 applied for teaching jobs and only 58% were employed as teachers in 1991 (Choy, Bobbitt, et al., 1993; Gray et al., 1993).

In 1991, of the 81,500 newly qualified teachers who did enter teaching, 72% had majored in education at the undergraduate level, most of the remainder had received an education certificate while also majoring in another discipline, and 9% had a master's degree (Choy, Henke, et al., 1993; Gray et al., 1993). The proportion of new teachers entering with master's degrees has doubled since 1980. In addition to some state policies requiring master's degrees for teachers before they receive a full regular certificate, many mid-career entrants who already have bachelor's degrees are attracted by master's level teacher preparation programs (Darling-Hammond, Hudson, & Kirby, 1989). Interestingly, the number and proportion of master's degree entrants was at its highest in 1975 when master of arts degrees in teaching programs were still prevalent as one of the initiatives that had emerged from efforts to stimulate teacher supply during the late 1960s.

Although 92% of newly qualified teachers who taught in 1991 were certified in some field, many were not eligible or certified for the fields to which they were assigned. One third or more of those assigned to teach one or more courses in art, music, mathematics, science, social studies, physical education, and special education were neither certified nor eligible for certification in those fields (Gray et al., 1993). In terms of their primary teaching assignments, more than 10% of those teaching English/language arts or reading, science, social studies, or special education were not eligible or certified in those fields.

Unprepared Entrants The Recent College Graduates Survey includes individuals who, although not eligible or licensed to teach, nonetheless did so since their graduation a year earlier (Gray et al., 1993). As noted earlier, about 19,000 of 140,000 "newly qualified teachers" (or about 15% of the total) fit this definition (Gray et al., 1993). By the time of the survey (1 year after graduation), however, only one third of these individuals (or 5% of all newly qualified teachers) were still engaged in teaching as their primary job.

As compared to other newly qualified teachers who received bachelor's degrees, those having taught without a license were younger and exhibited lower levels of academic achievement. Whereas most of those prepared for teaching (51%) had grade point averages *above* 3.25, most unlicensed entrants (57%) had grade point averages *below* 3.25 (and 20% had GPAs below 2.25). The unprepared entrants were also more likely to be male, married, and African American (Gray et al., 1993).

Reentrants and the Reserve Pool By some estimates, about one third of new teacher hires in the early 1980s came from the reserve pool. This was not surprising given the declining student enrollments and teacher oversupply of the late 1970s. These factors resulted in some prospective teachers not getting jobs and other young teachers being released during reductions in force, with subsequent difficulty finding another job in teaching. This, coupled with many districts' preferences to hire experienced teachers whenever possible, left many would-be teach-

ers waiting for opportunities to enter or reenter teaching when demand increased. As discussed earlier, roughly the same ratio was held in 1990; excluding transfers, about one third of new hires were reentrants whereas two thirds were new teachers. The key question for the future is the extent to which this heavy use of the reserve pool can and will be continued.

Some evidence suggests that the character and size of the reserve pool for teaching may be changing. Several indicators suggest that the pool is shallower now than it was at the start of the 1980s. First, and most obvious, the size of the reserve pool has been shrinking each year as the number of individuals preparing to teach declined as the demand increased. Second, a number of small-scale studies confirm what larger data bases hint at, which is that the vast majority of those who have left teaching have taken up other careers. It would be logical to assume that the most ready and eager members of the reserve pool from the era of teacher surpluses have already been hired. Those remaining would likely require greater inducements to switch from their current pursuits back to teaching. Third, according to many labor market forecasts, competition in the labor market for college graduates will grow more keen as economic growth in knowledge-related fields continues while the number of college-age youth (and probable college graduates) declines (Gerald & Hussar, 1990).

Finally, at this point in history, a major part of the traditional reserve pool—women who have stopped teaching to raise children and who plan to return—is disappearing. Murnane and his colleagues (1991) found that, throughout the 1970s, most teachers who left and then returned to teaching were women elementary school teachers who left temporarily to raise children. Those women who left teaching primarily went into homemaking. Fifty-seven percent of the women who left teaching between 1970 and 1979 were out of the labor force the following year, and 47% of them ultimately returned to teaching. Currently, however, very few teachers leave teaching for homemaking and intend to return. Most teachers who have children continue to work without breaks in service (Darling-Hammond, 1990c). Those who leave generally go into other occupations. Thus, only 30% of the women who left teaching between 1980 and 1986 were out of the labor force the following year, and only 36% of women who left teaching in the 1980s returned to teaching (Murnane et al., 1991). These factors suggest that rates of entry into the reserve pool will be lower in coming years than they were in the past.

Mid-Career Changes and Alternate Routes Another potential source of teachers is mid-career entrants from other fields. There have been many proposals and initiatives in this area, ranging from mid-career recruitment through teacher education programs at the graduate level (these are classified as alternate routes in some states, but are traditional or "regular" routes in others), to shorter term alternative certification routes that reduce the requirements for state licensure, to emergency hiring practices that fill vacancies in any way possible. Most states' alternate routes aimed at recruiting nontraditional entrants into teaching are actually graduate-level programs structured to ensure that those who have already received other degrees do not have to repeat their undergraduate coursework (Feistritzer, 1990). A few states, however, have authorized programs offered by school districts or the state itself; these tend to require little formal preparation and rely instead on on-the-job supervision, which, unfortunately, does not always materialize (Darling-Hammond, 1992).

In a RAND Corporation study of nontraditional recruits into teaching, two types of alternate route programs were compared. One category included graduate-level preservice preparation targeted to the needs of midcareer entrants, including carefully focused coursework, an intensive supervised internship or student teaching experience, and, in most cases, a master's degree as a result. The other category included short-term programs, usually lasting only a few weeks, which placed recruits directly into teaching as full-fledged teachers. Recruits in the more extended university-based programs were much more satisfied with the amount and quality of preparation they received, reported fewer difficulties when they entered classroom teaching, and were more likely to say they planned to stay in the profession (Darling-Hammond et al., 1989).

Data on alternate route entry into teaching are difficult to interpret in terms of either the nature of recruits or their qualifications. First, not all candidates who enter teaching through alternate routes are midcareer changers, and most midcareer changers do not enter teaching through alternate routes. In fact, the average teacher education student is older than was once the case, and many have entered from short or long stints in other occupations. This is especially true in master's degree programs. At the same time, as noted earlier, many individuals entering teaching without full preparation, including through the shorter term alternate routes, are younger than the average and are often straight out of college. Similar to the data on unlicensed recruits described earlier, some studies have found that alternative certification recruits have lower grade point averages than teacher education students, particularly those alternate route candidates in shortage fields such as mathematics and science (Darling-Hammond, 1992; Natriello, Zumwalt, Hansen, & Frisch, 1990; Stoddart, 1992).

In addition, the requirements for alternate route certification vary widely. Some states' alternate route requirements are more stringent than the requirements for regular certification in others. For example, the amount of professional education beyond a liberal arts degree required of alternate route candidates can vary from only 9 credit hours in Virginia to the 45 credit hours required for a full master's degree or its equivalent in Alabama or Maryland (Cornett, 1992; Feistritzer, 1990). Even among programs that require alternate route candidates to complete all regular certification requirements, there is a stark difference between the rigorous 12-month preparation program required *prior to* entry in Maryland (Maryland State Department of Education, 1990) and the Tennessee requirement that apparently allows candidates to enter teaching without professional preparation while earning credits toward certification at the leisurely rate of 6 hours every 5 years (Cornett, 1992). At that rate, a teacher could spend 25 years in the classroom before meeting the licensing requirements still on the books in most states and might take nearly 40 years to acquire as much training as the alternate route candidate in Maryland receives in 1 year.

At the same time, as noted earlier, some states have much lower expectations for candidates' academic ability and preparation than others; therefore, alternate route candidates in "high standards" states such as Maryland or Connecticut are subjected to higher selection standards and likely to receive a substantially more rigorous professional preparation than either "regular" or "alternative" certification candidates in "low standards" states such as New Jersey or Texas (Darling-Hammond, 1992), except for those preparation programs that exceed the state standards.

Keeping all of these ambiguities in mind, it may be instructive to note that one estimate places the number of recruits entering teaching through alternate routes at about 40,000 between 1985 and 1992 (Feistritzer, 1992). This constitutes less than 3% of new hires during those years.

Influences on Teacher Supply

The prognosis for teacher supply is complicated. On the one hand, heightened demand usually produces a lagged increase in supply. This is occurring now, and current recruitment initiatives may further support this effect. Salary hikes for teachers during the late 1980s have also helped increase the attractions to teaching. On the other hand, by 1992, these increases had raised teachers' salaries to the levels they had previously reached in 1972 (after the last major round of teacher shortages), leaving them 25% below those of other college graduates and 30% to 50% below those of graduates in scientific and technical fields (Gray et al., 1993; NEA, 1986). Of the 1990 college graduates working full time in 1991, teachers' earnings were near the bottom. Annual salaries ranged from $18,400 for those in service jobs and $19,100 for those in education to $31,000 for health professionals and $32,000 for engineers (Gray et al., 1993). Without further substantial boosts in both the financial and nonpecuniary attractions to teaching, it is likely that teaching will have difficulty competing in the contest for college-educated workers.

Other influences on teacher supply include general labor market conditions (the ease of gaining jobs in nonteaching occupations) and the relative attractions and costs of entering teaching as compared to other alternative occupations. Thus, candidates for whom nonteaching jobs are more plentiful and attractive, such as individuals with training in mathematics and science, are less likely to choose teaching when wage differentials and working conditions compare unfavorably.

For the long term, much depends on policies currently being proposed, or yet to be formulated, in response to existing and emerging teacher shortages.

INDICATORS OF TEACHER SHORTAGES

During the 1980s, a debate began to emerge concerning the extent and nature of teacher shortages. There are two major factors underlying these disputes. First, teacher labor markets are local. Shortages can exist in one market while surpluses exist in another. Perceptions of shortage depend on the localities, states, and/or regions being examined. Second, indicators of qualifications are most problematic in teaching. Because standards are often reduced or eliminated to fill vacancies, it is almost always possible to find enough warm bodies to staff classrooms. This causes differences in views about whether a shortage exists or not.

It is because of the confusion between labor market indicators and indicators of teacher quality that a debate has emerged as to whether teacher shortages are real or illusory. Although an increasing number of school districts have been unable to find certified (and, in their view, qualified) applicants for thousands of vacancies since the mid-1980s, some reports have made headlines with conclusions that shortages do not exist (Feistritzer, 1986; Hecker, 1986).

In a survey of state agencies, Feistritzer (1986) found that half of the 44 responding states reported shortages in fields such as mathematics, science, foreign languages, and special education, and two thirds said they issued emergency or temporary certificates to fill teaching vacancies. For the few states in Feistritzer's sample that maintained data on the numbers of such licenses issued, the total number issued in 1985–1986 was more than 30,000. By 1987, the number of temporary and emergency certificates issued by states that kept tallies totalled more than 56,000 (Feistritzer, 1988). Yet, by asserting that no measure of qualifications differentiates good from poor teachers, Feistritzer concluded, in contradiction with her own data, that there was no shortage of qualified teachers.

School principals, as well as state agencies, would take issue with this assertion. A recent National Science Foundation survey found that three quarters of U.S. principals reported having difficulty filling mathematics and science vacancies with qualified applicants (Weiss, 1987). These difficulties are most pronounced in high-minority schools, high-poverty schools, and inner-city schools where, at the secondary level, only about half of mathematics and science teachers are fully certified for the subjects they teach and even fewer have a major in their subject area (Oakes, 1990). The Council of Chief State School Officers' 1990 science and mathematics indicators show that at least 11 states are experiencing shortages of chemistry and physics teachers, and states with high population growth and many small rural districts have shortages of mathematics teachers (Blank & Gruebel, 1993).

The annual Association for School, College, and University Staffing (ASCUS) surveys of school district personnel officials and college placement officers have shown high levels of reported shortages throughout much of the decade in bilingual education, special education, physics and chemistry, mathematics, and computer science. More moderate levels of shortage have existed for teachers of the gifted, school psychologists, biology and general science teachers, elementary guidance counselors, and industrial arts teachers. Shortages have recently been increasing to noticeable levels in foreign languages, library science, and English (Akin, 1989; Association for School, College, and University Staffing [ASCUS], n.d.). In addition to Alaska and Hawaii, the regions showing the most widespread shortages throughout the 1980s were the Northeast and the South Central states (ASCUS, n.d.). The Northwestern and Great Lakes States had the lowest levels of shortage, in part because of declining student enrollments in many school districts throughout much of the decade (ASCUS, n.d.).

National Center for Educational Statistics' (NCES) data confirm that difficulty filling teaching positions varies by field and by locale of schools. Overall, 15% of all schools reported in 1991 that they had vacancies they could not fill with a qualified teacher. Nearly one fourth of central-city schools (23.4%) found

they could not fill vacancies with qualified persons. Schools with minority enrollments of more than 20%, whether in central cities, urban fringe, or rural areas, had the most difficulty filling vacancies (Choy, Henke, et al., 1993).

In 1990–1991, English as a Second Language and bilingual positions were the most difficult to fill—37% of schools reported they could not find qualified applicants for these vacant positions. Other fields where large numbers of schools reported that qualified applicants were difficult or impossible to find included foreign languages (27% of schools), special education (26%), and physical sciences (20%) (Choy, Henke, et al., 1993).

These shortages were presaged by the NCES survey on teacher demand and shortage as early as 1983 when demand for teachers was just beginning to increase once again. Based on measures of unfilled vacancies, many of these fields showed disproportionate shortages, and the hiring of unlicensed applicants in substantial numbers was already beginning to occur. Although only 2% of vacancies were left entirely unfilled due to shortages, 12.4% of new hires were not state licensed in their principal assignment fields (Haggstrom et al., 1988). Rates of unfilled vacancies and unlicensed hirees were significantly higher in central cities than in other communities (NCES, 1985).

Implications of Shortages

Counts of unfilled vacancies and unlicensed hires always underestimate the extent of teacher shortages. School districts respond in different ways to shortages of qualified applicants and leaving positions vacant or filling them with unlicensed applicants are generally the least favored options. Districts may reassign staff from other fields to cover courses in fields where candidates are scarce; they may increase teachers' course loads or class sizes; or they may cancel courses or programs and limit student enrollments in elective courses (e.g., upper-level mathematics or science courses). All of these strategies are being used in schools today to keep classrooms operating, if not always optimally.

In 1990–1991, administrators who had vacancies they could not fill with qualified teachers were most likely to use substitute teachers (48%), to hire less qualified teachers (26%), or to assign other teachers (23%). Such strategies are employed most frequently in central cities, especially where minority enrollment is 20% or more. Less frequently, course offerings are eliminated or class sizes are enlarged (Choy, Henke, et al., 1993).

The impact of teacher shortages is felt by students when they are offered less challenging coursework or a meager menu from which to choose, and when they are taught by people with less than adequate preparation to teach. What students experience now, society experiences later, as displayed by complaints about insufficient competence of graduates in the workplace.

The curricular implications of these shortages have not yet been fully addressed. It could be convincingly argued that the chronic shortages of mathematics and science teachers in our nation's schools since the 1950s and 1960s have created the current situation in which too few students are well enough prepared by high school to take advanced courses, and even if they were, too few qualified teachers would be available to offer such courses. Data presented earlier in this chapter illustrate the large proportion of mathematics and science teachers teaching without a major or minor and license in their fields (more than a third in each case). These statistics have held fairly steady since the 1960s.

Because of these chronic shortages over a long period of time, generations of students have received suboptimal instruction in these fields. Research indicates that out-of-field mathematics and science teachers are less effective with students (Druva & Anderson, 1983; Hawk, Coble, & Swanson, 1985). In addition, these shortages reduce students' access to higher level content in mathematics and science because qualified teachers are not available to teach such courses. International studies show that U.S. students receive less rigorous and less well-taught science and mathematics from at least the upper elementary grades throughout secondary school than do students in most other industrialized countries (McKnight et al., 1987). In any given year, one third of U.S. high schools do not even offer a physics course (Aldridge, 1987). In addition, only about 3% of American students have access to calculus, as compared to four or five times that ratio in other countries (McKnight et al., 1987).

Inequality and Access to Competent Teachers

All students are affected by teacher shortages, but those who reside in districts that offer fewer inducements to teaching suffer most. Shortages of qualified teachers translate into enlarged class sizes, lack of access to higher level courses, and lower quality teaching. Minority and low-income students in urban settings are most likely to find themselves in classrooms staffed by inadequately prepared, inexperienced, and ill-qualified teachers because funding inequities, distributions of local power, and labor market conditions conspire to produce teacher shortages of which they bear the brunt. The data confirm that these difficulties continue to be structural conditions of urban schooling.

- In 1990–1991, schools in central cities and schools with higher minority populations were twice as likely to have unfilled vacancies and much more likely to have to hire unlicensed teachers than those in other communities (Choy, Henke, et al., 1993).

- In 1987, shortages stimulated the issuance of more than 50,000 emergency and temporary teaching certificates in the few states that keep records on such matters (Feistritzer, 1988). The vast majority of these teachers were hired in central-city and poor rural school districts and placed in the most disadvantaged schools. The same is true of teachers recruited through alternative certification routes who have often had only minimal preparation (Darling-Hammond, 1990c).

- In 1992, 2,600 of New York City's new hires were not fully licensed, bringing the total number of such teachers in the city at that time to 9,600. Cancellation of the state and city mentoring programs due to budget cuts meant that most of these teachers were also unsupervised (New York State Education Department, n.d.).

- Teachers who work in large urban districts leave their positions sooner than do teachers who work in smaller suburban districts (Murnane et al., 1991). In New York City, more than 70% of new teachers leave the system within the first 5 years, usually to take positions in suburban districts (Feldman, 1991).

All of this means that districts with the greatest concentrations of poor children, minority children, and children of immigrants are also those where teachers are most likely to be both inexperienced and untrained. Many of these teachers have not had the opportunity to learn about up-to-date teaching methods, about how children grow, learn, and develop, or about what to do if students experience learning difficulties. Many children in central-city schools are taught by a parade of short-term substitutes, inexperienced teachers who leave before their first year is up, and beginners with minimal preparation, who teach without mentoring or support (Darling-Hammond, with Green, 1988).

Oakes's (1990) nationwide study of the distribution of mathematics and science opportunities across hundreds of schools found pervasive patterns of inequality. Based on teacher experience, certification status, preparation in the discipline they are teaching, higher degrees, self-confidence, and other teacher and principal perceptions of competence, it is clear that low-income and minority students have less contact with the best qualified science and mathematics teachers. Students in such schools have only a 50% chance of being taught by a mathematics or science teacher who is certified at all and an even lower chance of being taught by one who is fully qualified for their teaching assignment by virtue of the subject area(s) they are prepared to teach. Oakes (1990) concludes:

Our evidence lends considerable support to the argument that low-income, minority, and inner-city students have fewer opportunities. . . . They have considerably less access to science and mathematics knowledge at school, fewer material resources, less-engaging learning activities in their classrooms, and less-qualified teachers. . . . The differences we have observed are likely to reflect more general patterns of educational inequality. (pp. x–xi)

Just as Dreeben (1987) found in his study of early reading teaching, Oakes also discovered that "high-ability students at low-socioeconomic status, high-minority schools may actually have fewer opportunities than low-ability students who attend more advantaged schools" (p. vii). The pattern of systematic underexposure to good teaching tends to put all children in high-minority schools at risk.

There is substantial disagreement about the kind and amount of knowledge beginning teachers ought to have to practice effectively, or at least safely. In addition, there is disagreement about whether current state licensure standards, and many teacher education programs, adequately tap that knowledge. Consequently, everyone does not agree that hiring teachers without prior formal training is problematic. (The predominance of such hiring policies in central cities rather than more affluent communities may contribute to the level of unconcern.)

Policymakers have nearly always answered the problem of teacher shortages by lowering standards so that people who have had little or no preparation for teaching can be hired. These teachers have always been disproportionately assigned to teach minority and low-income children in central cities and poor rural districts. Although this practice is often excused by the presumption that virtually anyone can figure out how to teach, a number of reviews of research summarizing the results of more than 100 studies have concluded that fully prepared and licensed teachers are more highly rated and more successful with students than teachers without full preparation (Ashton & Crocker, 1986, 1987; Darling-Hammond, 1992; Druva & Anderson, 1983; Evertson, Hawley, & Zlotnik, 1985; Greenberg, 1983). Thus, policies that resolve shortages in poor districts by supporting the hiring of unprepared teachers serve only to exacerbate the inequalities low-income and minority children experience.

At a time when the emergence of a knowledge-based society demands that teachers focus on student learning, rather than merely "covering" the curriculum, they must know enough about pedagogy and learning that they can find and encourage students' strengths, diagnose students' difficulties, and respond with effective teaching strategies. To the extent that shortages are answered by strategies that avoid any requirements for new teachers to encounter and master this kind of knowledge, especially those teachers who are responsible for students most in need of skillful, analytic, and child-focused teaching, the goal will be lost or long postponed.

To the extent that teaching remains a revolving door occupation for many of its recruits, investments in their preparation and gains in their knowledge about teaching are lost to the children who would ultimately profit from them. In the long term, making good on the current mantra "all children can learn" will require expanding the capacity of the profession to recruit, prepare, and keep competent teachers in all schools and communities.

WHO LEAVES TEACHING?

The likelihood of leaving teaching differs by age, gender, years of experience, academic background, level, specialty field, salary, and workplace conditions (Darling-Hammond & Hudson, 1990; Haggstrom et al., 1988; Murnane et al., 1991; Sclan, 1993). Whereas overall teacher attrition rates provide a global picture of movement out of the profession, attrition rates of particular types of teachers provide more useful information to policymakers in their quest to improve the quality of the teaching work force. For policies to work, it is crucial to understand which types of teachers tend to leave or stay in teaching and why some teachers are more likely to leave than others.

Demographic Influences on Attrition

Traditionally, gender and age have been the strongest measured determinants of survival in teaching. Attrition rates show a U-shaped relationship with age and experience—it is highest for the youngest and oldest teachers, whereas midcareer teachers are least likely to leave (Bobbitt et al., 1991; Grissmer & Kirby, 1987; Murnane et al., 1991). Whereas most older teachers leave for retirement reasons, younger teachers are more likely to be reacting to conditions of the workplace or the profession.

Among beginning teachers, most estimates suggest that one third to one half leave within their first 5 years (Grissmer &

Kirby, 1987; Haggstrom et al., 1988; Mark & Anderson, 1985; Murnane et al., 1991; Schlechty & Vance, 1983). Many entering teachers do not plan to stay; for example, nearly one out of five (18%) newly qualified teachers who were teaching in 1987 said that they viewed their current job as temporary (Choy, Bobbitt, et al., 1993). Bobbitt, Faupel, and Burns' (1991) data show that 30% of teachers with 3 or fewer years of experience left teaching between the 1987–1988 and 1988–1989 school years, once again demonstrating the continuation of this predictable, long-standing pattern among new teachers.

In previous eras, younger women were more likely to leave than were men or older women, but they were also more likely to return to teaching later (Grissmer & Kirby, 1987; Murnane et al., 1991). As noted earlier, this is increasingly less true as women's labor force participation patterns now more closely resemble men's. Fewer women now leave teaching for full-time childcare than was the case 25 years ago; however, those who do leave are less likely to come back to teaching (Murnane et al., 1991). In 1987, women in their first year of teaching were no more likely to plan to stay in teaching than men (Sclan, 1993), and the overall attrition rate for men and women was equivalent (Bobbitt et al., 1991).

Similarly, minorities were once more likely to stay in teaching than whites, perhaps because fewer alternative career opportunities were available (Grissmer & Kirby, 1987). Yet, with an increase in their career options, minority recruits are both less plentiful and more likely to leave teaching. Murnane and his colleagues (1991) found that during the 1970s, black teachers were less likely to leave teaching than white teachers. A decade later, Bobbitt and her colleagues (1991) reported little difference between attrition rates of black (5.1%) and white (5.7%) teachers in 1987–1988 and 1988–1989. Similarly, Sclan (1993) found that among first-year teachers, blacks were not more likely to say they planned to stay in teaching than whites. Harris and Associates (Metropolitan Life, 1988) reported that a lower proportion of minority entrants plan to stay in teaching, especially in the inner cities.

Academic Background

Beginning teachers, the academically talented, and those with a disciplinary specialty in addition to their education degree have tended to leave teaching first (Darling-Hammond, 1984; Murnane, Singer, & Willett, 1989; Sclan, 1993). For both experienced and beginning teachers throughout the 1970s, those with higher NTE scores were less likely to remain in teaching than those with lower scores (Murnane et al., 1991; Singer, 1993). As these authors indicate, the National Teachers Examination (NTE) may not be an ideal measure of teaching effectiveness, but the scores do correlate highly with scores on standardized tests used to screen applicants for entry into other relatively high-paid fields.

The kind of preparation beginning teachers experience, even more than the number of degrees they hold, shapes their plans to stay in teaching. Beginning and experienced teachers alike with a degree in an academic discipline are more likely to plan to leave the field than those with a degree in education only (Darling-Hammond, 1984; Sclan, 1993). Those with solid education training are more likely to plan to stay than those without preparation (Darling-Hammond, Hudson, & Kirby, 1989; Darling-Hammond, 1992). Recent studies suggest that candidates prepared in new model 5- and 5th-year teacher education programs are more likely to enter and stay in teaching and to be highly rated as teachers than those prepared in 4-year undergraduate programs (Andrew, 1990; Andrew & Schwab, 1994). Grossman (1990) suggests that there is a connection between subject-matter knowledge, pedagogical knowledge, and pedagogical content knowledge; that is, teachers with a strong subject-matter background and strong teacher education training are more likely to develop the pedagogical content knowledge to teach effectively and creatively.

Teaching Fields

Perhaps largely because of the concentration of women in elementary school teaching, elementary school teachers were less likely to leave teaching and had longer first spells than did secondary school teachers during the 1970s (Murnane et al., 1991). Just as attrition rates appear to be increasingly similar across genders, Bobbitt and her colleagues (1991) also report an equalization of attrition rates between elementary and secondary teachers from 1987–1988 to 1988–1989 for a teaching force heavily comprised of midcareer veterans. Among first-year teachers, however, high school teachers are still more apt to say they will leave teaching than elementary school teachers (Sclan, 1993). This is not surprising given the generally wider availability of alternative career opportunities for individuals with disciplinary degrees at the high school level (Sclan, 1993).

Attrition rates tend to be higher for teachers in fields that have attractive nonteaching alternatives. For example, because mathematics and science teachers have tended to have a wider range of better paying job options outside of teaching, they have been more likely than teachers in other subject areas to leave teaching (Darling-Hammond, 1990c; Murnane et al., 1991; Murnane & Olsen, 1988, 1990; Murnane et al., 1989; Rumberger, 1985; Sclan, 1993). During the 1970s and early 1980s, chemistry and physics teachers, who had the best paying alternatives, tended to have the shortest careers in teaching (Murnane et al., 1989, 1991), whereas mathematics and biology teachers had somewhat longer initial spells in teaching, in part because nonteaching alternatives were not as plentiful or as high paying. Murnane and colleagues point out that the large numbers of newly hired mathematics teachers who had not majored in mathematics in college may have a longer duration in teaching because they may not have the technical skills that are marketable outside of teaching (Murnane et al., 1991).

The differential attrition rates between mathematics and science teachers and others did not appear in NCES cross-sectional attrition estimates in 1988–1989, however, which showed science and mathematics teachers leaving teaching at the same rates as other teachers (Bobbitt et al., 1991). This is probably because single-year attrition estimates depend greatly on the state of the overall economy in a given year and the age demographics of the teaching force. Because the teaching force had relatively few beginning teachers in 1987–1988, and because unemployment outside of teaching was relatively high, these early career attrition differentials were less likely to appear.

Some studies have also found higher than average attrition rates for special education teachers (see, e.g., Boe, Bobbitt, & Cook, 1993; Grissmer & Kirby, 1987; Haggstrom et al., 1988). This differs by special education subfield and may also be partly due to the concentration of special education teachers in city schools, which have larger numbers of special education students as well as poorer salaries and working conditions that contribute to attrition. In a 13-year large-scale longitudinal study, Singer (1993) found little difference between regular and special education teachers' career paths between 1972 and 1983. Similar to regular teachers, those who were paid higher salaries and those with lower opportunity costs for pursuing a career in teaching (as measured by NTE scores and salary levels) were more likely to remain in teaching. Also similar to regular education beginning teachers, beginning special education teachers were more likely to leave than were more experienced teachers. Nonteaching alternatives made a difference here as in the sciences and other fields. Those who provide support services, including counseling, guidance, and diagnostic evaluations, were most likely to leave. These special educators have skills that can be used in other settings, such as clinics or hospitals, where they are paid more. Special educators who teach students with learning and other disabilities were the least likely to leave.

RELATIVE ATTRACTIONS OF TEACHING AS AN OCCUPATION

The relative attractions of teaching as an occupation are both monetary and nonmonetary; salary, working conditions, intrinsic work satisfactions, and opportunities for professional growth are all factors that affect recruitment and retention as individuals weigh and balance occupations against one another. When considering a change of occupation, individuals generally also consider the human capital investments they have already made, the costs of retraining, and the likelihood of securing another job with the preferred attributes (Grissmer & Kirby, 1987; Haggstrom et al., 1988). Thus, all of these factors influence teachers' decisions to enter and to stay in teaching at different points in their careers.

Financial Remuneration

As noted, teachers' salaries are not high relative to those of college graduates in other occupations. Of all college graduates, those with education majors received the lowest average starting salary in 1987 (Choy, Bobbitt, et al., 1993). With an average of 20 years of teaching experience and attainment of a master's degree, the average annual salary was only $29,987 in 1990–1991, and it was substantially lower in private schools (Choy, Henke, et al., 1993) (see Table 5.13.).

However, there is a very large range in teacher salaries across districts and states. For example, average salaries in 1990–1991 ranged from $20,354 in South Dakota to $43,326 in Connecticut (Choy, Henke, et al., 1993). Even within a single labor market there is often a marked difference in teachers' salaries based on the wealth and spending choices of various districts. Typically,

TABLE 5.13. Average Amounts of Compensation that Full-Time Teachers Received and Average Principal Salary, by Selected School Characteristics: 1990–1991 (Choy, Henke, et al., 1993)

	Total Earnings	Basic Salary	Other School Year Compensation	Summer Supplement	Nonschool Income	Other Earned Income	Average Principal Salary
			Average Amount Teachers Received				
Total	$32,225	$29,987	$1,926	$1,978	$4,245	$1,680	$45,057
Public	33,578	31,296	1,942	1,993	4,404	1,754	49,603
Private	21,673	19,783	1,712	1,864	3,302	1,146	28,384

Note: The averages were computed using only teachers with that type of compensation; consequently, the average in total earnings does not equal sum of the averages for the various types of compensation.

teachers in affluent suburban districts earn more than those in central cities or more rural communities within the same area. These differences make a difference in teacher retention, especially early in a teacher's career. Better paid elementary and secondary school teachers throughout the 1970s tended to stay in teaching longer than those with lower salaries, especially during their first year of teaching (Murnane et al., 1991). Among midcareer teachers, however, salary had little effect. As Murnane and colleagues (1991) explain, switching to a new occupation becomes less attractive as teachers gain experience, and by midcareer, those whose opportunity costs were highest had generally already left the field.

The influence of salary on early career retention appears to continue. In 1987–1988, more highly paid first-year teachers were more likely to say they planned to stay in teaching than those who were paid less (Sclan, 1993); however, these same teachers' receipt of incentive pay had no significant impact on their plans to stay in the profession (Sclan, 1993). It may be that the additional pay in these kinds of programs is not large enough to increase commitment to work or career, or that teachers regard current incentive pay programs as peripheral to their conception of what is important to them about teaching.

In any event, it is clear that most teachers are not satisfied with their salaries. Only 8% of teachers strongly agreed that they were satisfied with their salaries in 1987–1988 and 32% somewhat agreed (Choy, Medrich, Henke, & Bobbitt, 1992). Half of the first-year teachers were dissatisfied with their salaries (Sclan, 1993). Although a large majority of prospective teachers in teacher education programs remained positive about teaching as a career throughout the late 1980s, almost 9 in 10 believe that current salaries are inadequate to support a family (Goodlad, 1990; Howey & Zimpher, 1993). These dissatisfactions are most likely to affect teachers' choices to enter and stay in teaching near the front end of the career.

The adequacy of teachers' salaries also affects their uses of time and the probability of taking on additional nonteaching employment. This, in turn, is likely to influence the extent to which teachers can focus on the continuous planning and follow-up required for good teaching. In 1990–1991, about one third of all teachers earned supplemental wages during the school year; one fourth of teachers held nonschool employment. Seventeen percent of teachers earned a supplemental summer salary for work associated with teaching (see Table 5.14).

Workplace Conditions

The changing nature of the labor market and salary levels only partly explain teacher attrition and commitment. Salaries interact with workplace conditions in determining career choices. In most occupations, individuals are willing to trade off, to some extent, nonpecuniary satisfactions with financial gains. Recent research points to the increased importance of workplace conditions in explaining teacher attrition and commitment to teaching (Blase & Kirby, 1992; Firestone & Rosenblum, 1988; Fullan, 1992; Reyes, 1990; Rosenholtz, 1989; Rosenholtz & Simpson, 1990; Sclan, 1993; Yee, 1990). For example, preferred workplace conditions are one reason many teachers say they are willing to teach in private schools where autonomy and professional growth opportunities are high, even though wages are lower than in public schools. Working conditions also appear to be strongly linked to retention within public schools, as described later in this chapter.

Research on teacher attrition is increasingly recognizing the social organizational role of schools in teachers' commitment and retention (Sclan, 1993). Perceived social organizational conditions capture teachers' views of the organization in which they work. Rosenholtz (1989) argued that teachers' shared perceptions of their environment reflect patterns of professional beliefs and behaviors, and that teachers' attitudes about teaching are related to their role in the social organization of the school. This approach helps to focus on the interaction between the teacher and the workplace. If workplace conditions interfere with teaching, they are negatively perceived by teachers; these perceptions can then become further obstacles to effective teaching and weaken teachers' commitment to their work and to the profession.

TABLE 5.14. Percentage of Full-Time Teachers Who Received Various Types of Compensation in Addition to Their Regular Salary, by Selected School Characteristics: 1990–1991 (Choy, Henke, et al., 1993)

	Other School-Year Compensation	Summer Supplemental Salary	Nonschool Income	Other Earned Income
Total	32.0	16.9	24.9	13.7
Public	33.6	16.7	24.1	13.5
Private	19.9	18.1	31.6	14.7

The reason most often cited by teachers for entering teaching is their desire to work with young people (Choy, Bobbitt, et al., 1993; NEA, 1992). So it is reasonable to expect that their greatest rewards (other than pecuniary) would come from success with their students. For teachers to remain in teaching, the rewards must outweigh the frustrations. Teachers who feel a sense of professional efficacy, that is, who feel successful in helping their students to learn, are less likely to leave (Litt & Turk, 1985; Rosenholtz, 1985).

The problems of teachers' workplace conditions have been well documented. In survey after survey, teachers consistently report that they do not have the time and resources to do their work, that they have too few opportunities to interact with colleagues and to influence school policies and practices, and that their efforts go unrecognized (Corcoran, 1990). The fact that teachers' work environments are not universally supportive is clear. In 1990–1991, only about half of public school teachers strongly agreed with the statement "I usually look forward to each working day at this school" (Choy, Henke, et al., 1993), and substantially more than half said that morale at their schools was only "fair" or "poor" (Carnegie Foundation, 1990).

The transformation in teachers' attitudes typically takes place quickly after they join the profession. In 1990–1991, a striking 94% of public and private school first-year teachers reported that they look forward to working each day at their schools (NDRC, 1993); however, within 2 years of entering teaching, one fifth of teachers in a Metropolitan Life Survey in 1992 said that it was likely that they would leave teaching within the next 5 years. This proportion was higher for teachers at the high school level and in central city schools (Metropolitan Life, 1992).

Interestingly, structural workplace conditions having to do with autonomy, decision-making authority, and administrative supports appear to exert much more influence over most teachers' views of teaching than such factors as student behavior, which is often trumpeted by the media as a major problem, sometimes *the* major problem, in schools. Although the stresses of contemporary life, particularly in urban communities, should not be minimized as an influence on students, families, and schools, teachers do not view student behavior as the most overwhelming difficulty in their work. In 1990–1991, small minorities of teachers saw student behavior as a serious problem, even in the central cities. The largest problem category—student absenteeism—was cited by only 13% of all teachers and only 20% of urban teachers. Such issues as drug abuse were cited by only 4% of teachers as a serious problem (see Table 5.15).

By contrast, large majorities of teachers were dissatisfied with working conditions having to do with how schools are structured and managed. Fewer than one fourth of public school teachers overall in 1987–1988 said they were highly satisfied with the "administrative support" they received (Choy, Bobbitt, et al., 1993). Nearly half of all teachers in 1990 (up from one fourth in 1987) said they were not satisfied with the control they had over their professional lives (Carnegie Foundation, 1990).

Teachers who leave the profession permanently are often those who are most dissatisfied with these kinds of workplace conditions (Darling-Hammond, 1984; Johnson, 1990). Johnson (1990) explains that many talented teachers leave teaching because their workplaces do not sustain teachers' adaptability,

individuality, and the autonomy that they need to teach. Of those teachers who left teaching in 1988–1989, one out of five cited dissatisfaction with teaching or the desire to pursue another career as their main reasons for leaving (Bobbitt et al., 1991). In a telling commentary about the state of the occupation of teaching, those public school teachers who left teaching in 1988–1989 were more satisfied with the following features of their new jobs: salaries, opportunities for advancement, support from supervisors, influence over policy decisions, control over their work, esteem of society for their profession, evaluation procedures for their work, and available resources (Choy, Bobbitt, et al., 1993).

These findings intersect with a growing body of research on teacher efficacy, retention, and commitment, which suggests that retaining and supporting effective teachers will require restructuring schools to provide teachers with greater administrative supports, more decision-making input and control over their work, more useful feedback and opportunities for collegial work, and provision of material resources and supports (Darling-Hammond, 1990b, 1990c; Huberman & Miles, 1984; Lieberman, 1988, 1990; Louis & Miles, 1990; McLaughlin, Pfeifer, Swanson-Owens, & Yee, 1986). In addition, school reforms can heighten teachers' commitment by restructuring teaching and learning so that students become more successful and teachers feel more efficacious and motivated. Recent research on the effects of restructuring on teacher satisfaction, commitment, and efficacy is reviewed next.

School Leadership and Teacher Efficacy

One workplace condition that encompasses most others is school leadership and culture. School culture is the single most powerful predictor of teachers' work, career, and organizational commitment, and leadership is a measure of the quality of the culture (Ashburn, 1989). School culture refers to the dominant ethos of the organization, its values and visions, and the everyday experiences of members of the school community. Teachers' perceptions of their principals are almost always found to be directly related to their perceptions of the school culture (Anderman, Belzer, & Smith, 1991).

Research on school leadership frequently distinguishes among differing management styles, variously described as "organic" versus "mechanistic" (Burns & Stalker, 1961), "commitment" versus "control" (Rowan, 1990), "symbolic" versus "technical" (Deal & Peterson, 1990), "transformational" versus "transactional" (Burns, 1978), or "professional" versus "bureaucratic" (Darling-Hammond & Berry, 1988). Virtually all of the most recent research on school leadership connects teacher commitment with a more collaborative and value-based style of leadership—one aimed at enhancing professional commitment, using symbolic and transformational values as touchstones.

Principals who support norms of collegiality and encourage teacher development and self-management raise individual and group commitment to teaching (Fullan, 1992; Sergiovanni, 1987, 1992). Collaborative leadership styles focus on developing a clarity of mission; cultural cohesion through shared norms, values, and beliefs; and reward systems that reinforce those cultural values (Peterson & Martin, 1990). In these studies,

TABLE 5.15. Percentage of Public School Teachers Who Perceived Serious Problems with Students, by Selected School Characteristics: 1990–1991 (Choy, Henke, et al., 1993)

	Student Absenteeism	Use of Alcohol	Tardiness	Drug Abuse	Verbal Abuse of Teachers
Total	14.1%	8.2%	11.2%	4.2%	7.5%
Central city	20.7	6.3	18.1	4.8	12.8
School level					
Elementary	11.8	0.9	11.2	1.0	11.4
Secondary	38.7	17.1	32.1	12.2	15.2
Combined	21.1	7.8	16.4	6.9	16.5
Minority enrollment					
Less than 20%	10.3	6.9	8.9	3.6	3.3
20% or more	24.0	6.1	21.0	5.1	15.7
Urban fringe/large town	13.0	6.6	10.5	3.7	6.4
School level					
Elementary	5.7	0.3	4.8	0.3	4.6
Secondary	25.0	16.4	19.5	8.6	8.9
Combined	13.1	12.6	14.0	13.5	12.3
Minority enrollment					
Less than 20%	8.5	6.6	7.3	2.7	3.5
20% or more	18.5	6.5	14.5	5.1	10.0
Rural/small town	10.6	10.7	7.1	4.3	4.7
School level					
Elementary	4.4	2.5	2.8	1.0	3.6
Secondary	20.6	23.1	13.9	9.3	6.3
Combined	10.8	16.1	8.2	5.6	6.4
Minority enrollment					
Less than 20%	8.9	10.8	5.6	3.6	3.3
20% or more	14.7	10.6	10.9	5.9	8.2

Note: Teachers and principals were defined as perceiving these issues as serious problems in their schools if they responded with a 1 on a 4-point scale of problem seriousness, with 1 representing a serious problem.

teachers who participate in creating the culture of the school and the values that drive that culture tend to be more committed to teaching and to the school organization.

Effective leadership is interactive. The "school shapes the principal as much as a principal shapes a school" (Lieberman & Miller, 1984, p. 79). Although successful schools have a clear mission and structure, their members also have collective autonomy to determine how to realize their mission (Sergiovanni, 1984). And while collaborative leaders value participation in decision making, they are also focused on organizational purpose and are strong influences on efforts to attain the school's mission (Deal & Peterson, 1990; Peterson & Martin, 1990).

From the teacher's point of view, principals who provide frequent feedback, convey high expectations, involve teachers in decision making, ensure opportunities for teacher learning, and provide necessary support and materials are ensuring the conditions that allow them to be effective; this, in turn, increases teachers' commitment to teaching (Blase & Kirby, 1992; Rosenholtz, 1989).

Teachers' feelings of efficacy and beliefs in their ability to help students learn are strongly and consistently related to teacher performance and to student outcomes (Armor et al., 1976; Berman & McLaughlin, 1977; Brookover, 1977; Rutter, Maughan, Mortimore, & Ouston, with Smith, 1979), as well as to teacher satisfaction and commitment (Rosenholtz, 1985; Rosenholtz & Simpson, 1990). Teachers who lack confidence

in their teaching skills have higher rates of absenteeism and attrition (Chapman, 1984; Litt & Turk, 1985).

Not only are teachers' commitment and their effectiveness with students strongly interwined, both are influenced by organizational conditions. Efficacy-producing organizations are those that exhibit many of the qualities described earlier. They feature shared, consensual goals; higher levels of interaction among staff; more flexibility in performing work; and input by staff into design of the work, as well as criteria for judging success (Darling-Hammond, Wise, & Pease, 1983; Fuller, Wood, Rapoport, & Dornbusch, 1982). Thus, it is not surprising that teachers' sense of self-efficacy is enhanced by teacher involvement in important decision making, by professional corroboration, and by feedback about the effects of their actions (Raudenbush, Rowan, & Cheong, 1992; Rosenholtz, 1989; Rosenholtz & Simpson, 1990).

Teacher Participation in Decision Making Research over the past 20 years informs us that most teachers want more opportunities to be involved in decision making, especially in areas of school policy that affect teaching, and this is related to their satisfaction, stress, and loyalty (Conley, 1991). Yet, in 1990–1991, fewer than 40% of all teachers (and an even smaller proportion of public school teachers) felt they had much influence in determining school policies such as curriculum, student grouping, content of in-service training, or discipline policy

(Choy, Henke, et al., 1993) (see Table 5.16). In the same year, one out of four first-year teachers reported that they had to follow rules that conflicted with their best professional judgment—a situation highly correlated with lower levels of commitment and planned retention in teaching (Sclan, 1993).

The level and type of school in which teachers teach makes a difference in their perceived opportunities for decision making and discretion. Public elementary school teachers are more likely than secondary school teachers to report substantial influence over school discipline, student grouping, and teacher in-service policies, whereas secondary school teachers feel they have more influence over establishing curriculum. This was true in 1987–1988 (Choy, Bobbitt, et al., 1993) and again in 1990–1991. Teachers in central city schools and those in schools with higher minority enrollments were least likely to report having influence on school policies in any category (see Table 5.17).

Teacher autonomy and discretion are important to all teachers, as they are perceived to enable the kind of flexibility needed to meet the distinctive needs of individual students. These features of the workplace are most important to those teachers who also tend to have the largest span of career options. Although all teachers care about having control over policy and practice decisions that affect their work, those with the highest levels of academic attainment care most deeply and are most likely to say they will leave if sufficient professional autonomy is absent (Darling-Hammond, 1984). Similarly, Hart and Murphy (1990) report that more academically able new teachers are the most likely to say they care about school-level autonomy, individual teacher initiatives, and substantial professional control of resources.

Sclan (1993) found that the ways in which schools structure decision making and collegial relations constitute important attributes of school organization affecting beginning teachers' commitment to the profession. Beginning teachers appear to evaluate school leadership by how effectively it creates a school culture that is collaborative and supportive. The more beginning teachers believe that they can actively participate in making important decisions in their schools, the more positive their view of school leadership; the more collaborative and support-

ive the school leadership, the more involved teachers appear to be. The extent to which schools provide opportunities for involvement in decision making, for collaborative work with other teachers, and for engagement in curriculum building and other professional tasks strongly determines whether beginning teachers feel their efforts are worthwhile and whether they plan to remain in the profession (Sclan, 1993). A systemic approach to changing the organizational patterns of collegial work and decision making within schools may strengthen teachers' sense of efficacy, satisfaction, and their plans to remain in teaching.

Given traditional school norms and structures, however, teachers' willingness to be involved in decision making cannot be taken for granted. Teachers must believe that their views will be taken seriously and that their time investments will pay off in real changes if they are to take on the additional work involved in participative management. Not surprisingly, administrative leadership styles and teacher participation are strongly related to one another. Smylie (1992) found that the principal–teacher relationship was the most powerful predictor of teachers' willingness to participate in personnel, curriculum, staff development, and administrative decision making. He also found that teachers' beliefs about teacher responsibility for student learning, peer judgment, teacher accountability, and professional outcome expectancy also shaped their willingness to participate in personnel decisions. Encouraging teacher decision making is a problem of individual and organizational change that cannot be promoted by fiat; change must also address normative beliefs and social conditions of teaching (Smylie, 1992).

Collaboration Teachers' commitment to teaching, to students, and to the school at large is associated not only with teacher involvement in decision making, but also with collegiality, task variety, remuneration, sense of purpose about work, administrative support, and mutual respect (Firestone & Rosenblum, 1988). Opportunities for teachers to work together strengthen collaborative norms, which, in turn, strengthen the school community. Teachers who perceive schools as strong communities show greater enjoyment in their work (Bryk & Driscoll, 1988). In fact, teachers are better able to adapt to students' needs if

TABLE 5.16. Percentage of Teachers Who Believed They Had a Great Deal of Influence on Educational Policies, by Sector 1987–1988 and 1990–1991 (Choy, Henke, et al., 1993)

	Determining Discipline Policy	Content of In-Service Training	Grouping Students in Classes by Ability	Establishing Curriculum
1987–1988				
Total	37.3%	31.8%	30.3%	37.5%
Public	34.8	31.1	28.1	35.0
Private	55.9	36.8	47.2	56.3
1990–1991				
Total	39.1	33.3	29.0	37.5
Public	37.0	32.9	26.7	35.2
Private	54.4	36.2	45.1	54.1

Note: Teachers were defined as believing they had a great deal of influence if they responded with a 5 or 6 on a 6-point scale of influence, with 6 representing a great deal of influence.

TABLE 5.17. Percentage of Public School Teachers Who Believed They Had a Great Deal of Influence on Educational Policies, by Selected School Characteristics: 1990–1991 (Choy, Henke, et al., 1993)

	Determining Discipline Policy	Content of In-Service Training	Grouping Students in Classes by Ability	Establishing Curriculum
Total	37.0%	32.9%	26.7%	35.2%
Central City	36.1	32.1	26.3	27.8
School level				
Elementary	41.6	33.6	30.9	26.2
Secondary	24.7	28.7	16.3	30.3
Combined	39.3	36.9	34.3	38.2
Minority enrollment				
Less than 20%	42.1	37.7	28.8	35.2
20% or more	34.3	30.4	25.5	25.6
Urban fringe/large town	38.3	34.2	29.0	35.7
School level				
Elementary	44.9	34.8	34.3	32.4
Secondary	26.5	33.2	19.8	40.7
Combined	49.1	35.5	34.9	43.6
Minority enrollment				
Less than 20%	38.9	33.6	29.8	38.0
20% or more	37.5	35.1	28.0	32.9
Rural/small town	37.3	32.3	25.9	39.8
School level				
Elementary	43.7	33.7	31.0	38.5
Secondary	27.2	30.4	17.6	42.4
Combined	35.1	31.2	25.8	36.8
Minority enrollment				
Less than 20%	38.9	33.3	27.5	42.8
20% or more	33.4	30.0	21.8	32.2

Note: Teachers were defined as believing they had a great deal of influence if they responded with a 5 or 6 on a 6-point scale of influence, with 6 representing a great deal of influence.

they work in strong professional communities in a department, school, network, or professional organization that are engaged in systemic reform efforts (McLaughlin & Talbert, 1993).

Despite the importance of teachers' collegial work, one recent survey of teachers (Carnegie Foundation, 1990) noted that 59% of those queried rated the quality of time for meeting with colleagues "poor" or "not regularly available." In 1987–1988, fewer than 10% of public school teachers said they were highly satisfied with the extent and quality of opportunities to collaborate with colleagues (Choy, Bobbitt, et al., 1993).

Even though opportunities for collegial work are sparse, teachers still look to each other for support. At all levels and sectors, regardless of age, gender, experience, or degrees held, teachers are more likely to report that other teachers, as opposed to principals, chairpersons, or other administrators, help them to improve their teaching and to solve instructional or management problems (Choy, Bobbitt, et al., 1993). At even greater rates, new teachers in urban settings say their biggest source of support is other teachers (Driscoll, 1993). Given that teachers generally learn from each other, it seems only reasonable that more time should be provided for professional interaction among colleagues.

Such opportunities are routinely available in many other countries, where teachers spend only about half of their time teaching large groups of students and the remainder meeting with colleagues for purposes of planning and developing curric-

ulum, deciding on school policies, and solving problems of practice (Darling-Hammond, 1990b).

Effects of School Restructuring on Teachers' Views A recent survey of teachers regarding the extent and effects of recent school reform illustrates how professional working conditions affect teachers' attitudes about their work as well as their practices. Those who reported that site-based management (SBM) had been introduced in their schools (about 50% of the total) were also much more likely to report that a whole series of other curriculum and organizational reforms had also had an impact on their schools. For example, 72% of teachers in SBM schools said that cooperative learning had had a major impact on their school, as compared to only 35% of those teachers in non-SBM schools. Also more prevalent in SBM schools were mixed ability group classrooms; tougher graduation standards; authentic assessment practices; emphasis on in-depth understanding rather than superficial content coverage; accelerated learning approaches; connections among classroom practices, home experiences, and cultures of students; and teacher involvement in decisions about how school funds are spent.

These kinds of changes in governance seem to be associated with other changes that provide teachers with the teaching circumstances they need to feel effective. Teachers in schools that have felt the impact of reform were much more likely to report that their schools had become much better in the previous 3 years at providing structured time for teachers to work with each other on professional matters, enabling them to observe each other in the classroom and provide feedback about their teaching, allowing teachers to work in teams, giving teachers more time to plan instruction, and being willing to counsel students in home visits.

These changes appear to affect teachers' views of their work. Teachers in reform-impacted schools felt they had more opportunity to adapt their instruction to the needs of their students and to invent more effective methods, rather than being constrained by district routines or standardized curricula. They were more optimistic about principal–teacher relationships, working conditions for teachers, the educational performance of students, the professional status of teachers, and their own job satisfaction. They were much more likely to report themselves very satisfied with their career as a teacher (61% as compared to 44%) and to see teachers as the agents of reform rather than as the targets of reform (LH Research, 1993).

In summary, teachers' career decisions differ depending on a host of variables: demographics, specialty fields, academic backgrounds, attitudes and experiences in teaching, and career stages—teachers, returnees, transfers, or veterans. Yet, all teachers are in remarkable agreement about what they need in their workplace to teach—administrative support for their work, opportunities for involvement in decision making, time for collaborative work with other teachers, and engagement in curriculum building and other professional tasks.

For these kinds of opportunities to be available on a broad scale, two major sets of changes in policy and practice need to occur. One critical area is the restructuring of school organizations and of teaching work, including a reallocation of personnel and resources so that a different set of roles, responsibilities, and relationships between and among teachers, other staff, and students is both possible and affordable. The second major area is the redesign of teacher preparation as well as entry and induction into teaching so that teachers are fully prepared for the kinds of new roles and responsibilities that await them and so that all students will have access to such fully prepared teachers.

These two areas of work are closely related to one another; it will be difficult to attract and retain the kinds of talented and well-prepared teachers needed for twenty-first century schools if the structure of teaching work does not support their participation in collaborative work and decision making. It will be equally difficult to persuade policymakers to support more involvement in decision making for teachers if not all are fully prepared to exercise that responsibility knowledgeably. Both restructured schools and enhanced teacher preparation linked to universal, high standards for entry are needed to support the development of a profession full of effective, committed teachers.

PREPARING SCHOOLS FOR TOMORROW'S TEACHERS

It is clear from the research reviewed in this chapter that the manner in which schools organize teachers' and students' work may have more of an impact on teachers' effectiveness and decisions to stay in teaching than many other factors. Teachers who leave as well as those who stay in teaching all identify improving professional conditions as an effective way for schools to encourage teachers to remain in the field (Bobbitt et al., 1991). The evidence strongly suggests that teachers want to break free from the constraints of bureaucratic regulations that prevent them from teaching effectively. When they have greater opportunities for collaboration, more say in important educational decisions, and greater flexibility in their teaching options, they tend to become more committed and, for recent entrants, more likely to stay in the profession (Blase & Kirby, 1992; Hart & Murphy, 1990; Johnson, 1990; Rosenholtz, 1989; Sclan, 1993).

Schools must find new ways to offer opportunities for teachers to work together, to stay abreast of the ever-expanding knowledge base of teaching, and to experiment with new job roles that engender effective teaching practices. Knowledge sharing, team planning and teaching, and collective reflection are the essential ingredients in creating professional cultures that sustain learning in schools. As described next, creating such structures will rely in part on reallocations of personnel and resources as well as restructuring of school schedules and courses.

Policies for Providing Professional Working Conditions

Building and sustaining a well-prepared teaching force will require local, state, and federal initiatives to strengthen the teaching profession. As part of this effort, states and localities will need to upgrade teachers' salaries to levels more nearly competitive with those of college graduates in other occupations who currently earn 25% to 50% more, depending on the field. Efforts to improve teachers' financial compensation should occur as part of a general restructuring effort, which places more resources as well as decision-making authority at the school level (Darling-Hammond, 1990b). Most teachers say that the amount of decision-making power at the school level is too little relative to the power at the federal, state, and local school board levels. Teachers who teach minority and low-income students and who teach in urban districts are most likely to believe that they have too little power at the school level (Metropolitan Life, 1993).

Teacher professionalism proposals almost always incorporate recommendations for increases in teacher salaries, often linked to changes in working structures for teachers. This is because attracting and retaining well-trained, knowledgeable individuals into an occupation generally requires compensation competitive with that they could receive if they entered other fields requiring similar levels of knowledge and training. In addition, proposals to provide intensive induction of teachers and time for professional discourse and problem solving have cost implications as well. Some critics believe that the public will never be willing or able to afford a system that compensates and supports teachers in a manner comparable to other professions. This is probably true if current school structures and modes of investment were to continue. To afford greater investments in teachers, school districts and states need to rethink the ways in which they spend their overall resources. As discussed earlier in this chapter, allocations of staff and time are substantially different in other countries.

The vision of teaching work as it is implemented in American schools is one where the teacher's job is to instruct large groups of students for most of the working day. The other tasks of teaching—preparation, planning, curriculum development, tutoring those in need of additional help, consulting with other professionals, seeking answers to student or classroom problems, and working with parents—are deemed so unimportant that little or no time is made available for these activities. With the exception of most teachers' daily "prep period," usually spent filling out forms and trying to get access to the copy machine, teachers have virtually no planned time to consult with their colleagues.

Other countries, including Japan, China, and Germany, structure teaching much differently (Darling-Hammond, 1990c). A typical high school teacher in one of these countries teaches standard-sized groups of students approximately 15–20 hours out of a 40–45-hour school week. The remainder of that time is used for preparation and joint curriculum planning; tutoring of individuals or small groups; and consultations with parents, students, and colleagues.

How can these countries afford such a "luxurious" schedule for teachers while spending virtually the same amount per pupil on education overall? The basic answer is that whereas U.S. schools have invested in a relatively smaller number of lower paid teachers directed and supervised by large numbers of inspectors, administrators, and officials populating several layers of bureaucratic structures, other countries have invested primarily in better paid, better educated teachers who comprise virtually all of the employees in schools and who make most of the teaching decisions. So, for example, whereas fewer than half of all public education employees in the United States are actually teachers, teaching staff comprise three fourths of all public education employees in Australia and Japan and more than 80% of all education employees in Belgium, Germany, the Netherlands, and Spain (Organization for Economic Cooperation and Development [OECD], 1992, p. 67).

What do all of these nonteachers in U.S. schools do? In 1986, more than 21% of elementary and secondary school employees were engaged in administrative functions and 58% were engaged in teaching and other professional specialties. Of these, only about half were classroom teachers. The remaining employees were engaged in service, maintenance, and transportation activities (U.S. Department of Labor, 1986). Thus, excluding service workers, school systems in 1986 employed approximately one administrative staff person for every 2 1/2 teachers. This suggests a very top-heavy approach to the management of schooling. Incentives are needed to redirect resources to the front lines of schooling, that is, teachers and classrooms in smaller, more personalized school settings, rather than bureaucrats and supervisors who manage large, impersonal structures that require other wasteful expenditures because the structures are inherently dysfunctional.

Professionalizing teaching suggests a redefinition of administrative structures and roles and, therefore, reallocation of educational dollars. If teachers assume many of the instructional tasks currently performed by administrative staff (e.g., curriculum development and supervision), the layers of bureaucratic hierarchy will be reduced. If teachers are more carefully selected and better trained and supported, expenditures for management systems to control incompetence should become less necessary. If investments are made in the beginning of the teaching career for induction support and pretenure evaluation, the costs of continually recruiting and hiring new entrants to replace the 40% to 50% who leave in the first few years should decline; the costs of band-aid approaches to staff development for those who have not learned to teach effectively should be reduced; and the costs of remediating or seeking to dismiss poor teachers, as well as compensating for the effects of their poor teaching on children, should decrease. Strategic investment in teacher competence frees up resources for innovation and learning.

Equity Considerations

Another conclusion from the research reviewed here is that both teacher qualifications and teaching conditions are unequally distributed across different types of schools and students. Moreover, these differences in teaching conditions influence teacher turnover and teaching quality. The lower fiscal capacity of inner-city schools to attract qualified teachers is further undermined by the nonprofessional working conditions they offer, ranging from lower levels of teacher participation in decision making to more dysfunctional organizational conditions. Meanwhile, reforms in teachers' workplace conditions are more evident in schools outside central cities. The uneven pace and distribution of reform across the public school system may contribute to the increasingly bimodal distribution of teachers.

Unequal access to learning opportunities creates a threat to the survival of democracy. Given the difficulties in adapting to a knowledge-based, postindustrial economy, it appears more important than ever to heed Dewey's (1916) warning:

Obviously a [democratic] society to which stratification into separate classes would be fatal, must see to it that intellectual opportunities are accessible to all on equable and easy terms. . . . A society which is mobile, which is full of channels for the distribution of a change occurring anywhere, must see to it that its members are educated to personal initiative and adaptability. Otherwise, they will be overwhelmed by the changes in which they are caught and whose significance or connections they do not perceive. (pp. 87–88)

What can we do about this state of inequity? The federal government could play a leadership role in providing an adequate supply of well-qualified teachers just as it has in providing an adequate supply of well-qualified physicians for the nation. When shortages of physicians were a major problem during the 1960s, Congress passed the 1963 Health Professions Education Assistance Act to support and improve the caliber of medical training, to create and strengthen teaching hospitals, to provide scholarships and loans to medical students, and to create incentives for physicians to train in shortage specialties and to locate in underserved areas.

Similarly, federal initiatives in education should seek to

1. Recruit new teachers, especially in shortage fields and in shortage locations, through scholarships and forgivable loans for high-quality teacher education.

2. Strengthen and improve teachers' preparation through improvement incentive grants to schools of education and supports for licensing reform.
3. Improve teacher retention and effectiveness by improving clinical training and support during the beginning teaching stage when so many drop out. This would include funding internship programs for new teachers in which they receive structured coaching and mentoring, preferably in professional development schools organized to provide state-of-the-art practice.

If, in fact, the interaction between teachers and students is the most important aspect of effective schooling, then reducing inequality in learning has to rely on policies that provide equal access to competent, well-supported teachers. The American public education system ought to be able to guarantee that every child who is forced by public law to go to school is taught by someone who is prepared, knowledgeable, competent, and caring.

As part of this commitment, incentives should be developed to recruit the most well-qualified teachers, those who have the necessary skills and knowledge to meet the more acute needs of at-risk students and to transform the workplace structure into environments conducive to learning, into the schools that need them the most. It is difficult enough to challenge the status quo structures of schools and teaching with a strong faculty in place; it is nearly impossible for novices and underprepared teachers who have yet to become familiar with the configurations of power that operate within schools and who have yet to master organizational and pedagogical approaches that work for their students to challenge these structures.

Some models are emerging that suggest how incentive structures might be reshaped to encourage the provision of highly qualified teachers to low-income and minority schools. For example, in Rochester, New York, master teachers who have been recognized for their demonstrated expertise can be called on, as part of their privilege and their obligation, to teach children and create new programs in the schools that currently need transforming. In such experiments, and in policy changes they incorporate, lies one part of the hope for equalizing opportunities to learn.

Recruitment, Hiring, and Evaluation

To ensure an adequate supply of qualified teachers, it is clear that the attractions to teaching will have to be greater than they are now and the disincentives fewer. As discussed earlier, raising salaries and improving working conditions can lower the opportunity costs of choosing teaching. Other state and local policies can support recruitment efforts as well. For example, recruitment and retention of teachers could be enhanced by pragmatic measures aimed at reducing some current sources of attrition from teaching. Greater reciprocity in state licensing requirements, transferability of retirement benefits, and offering appropriate credit for previous years of service to transferring teachers would keep some individuals in teaching who otherwise would leave due to procedural frustration rather than lack of interest in teaching.

The hiring process has an equally important influence on the quantity and quality of teachers in the labor market and on the distribution of teachers to different types of school systems. The most qualified and highly ranked teachers often are not the ones who are finally hired (Wise et al., 1987). School districts do not always hire the best available teachers due to inadequate management information systems and antiquated hiring procedures that discourage good applicants by unprofessional treatment and lack of budget and timely action. Some prospective teachers report that they decided not to enter teaching at all after experiencing unprofessional treatment in the hiring process, for example, having their files lost, interviews in which their qualifications were barely reviewed, lack of response to repeated requests for information, and late notification of job availability.

These problems are particularly evident in large urban districts. Reports of vacancies and information on candidates are not always accessible and equitably distributed across all district decision makers. Hiring procedures are cumbersome and bureaucratic. Union contracts requiring placement of all internal teacher transfers prior to hiring of new candidates often put off hiring decisions until August or September when qualified candidates have since decided to take other jobs. As a result of these inefficiencies, large urban districts often lose good candidates both to other districts and to nonteaching jobs. Thus, many districts that have attracted good candidates do not actually hire them, resulting in a loss of the very teachers they so desperately need (Wise et al., 1987).

The most successful efforts to prepare high-quality teachers may be undermined by inefficiency in the hiring process coupled with lack of attention to important professional qualifications. Schlechty (1990) argues that specific criteria for recruitment into teaching are essential for developing a distinctive occupational identity and socializing members so that they are apt to adopt that identity. Furthermore, he asserts that a consensus has yet to be developed on what constitutes a "teacher," and until that happens it is unclear who are the most desirable candidates for teaching.

This same concern occurs in the area of teacher evaluation, where competing conceptions of teaching and teacher learning are at play. Traditional forms of evaluation are guided by checklists administered in quick visits by school administrators or supervisors to check minimal competency as defined by routine behaviors. These do not support or guide a style of teaching responsive to student needs and grounded in expertise about subjects and learners. Procedures that focus on teacher compliance with regimented sets of behaviors do not foster teacher analysis of student needs or participation in continual collegial learning (Darling-Hammond, with Sclan, 1992; Macmillan & Pendlebury, 1985; Peterson & Lomeaux, 1989; Sclan & Darling-Hammond, 1992).

Part of professionalizing teaching will be a need to professionalize the ways in which teachers are recruited, screened, and evaluated so that the attributes of effective teachers are the ones that receive attention in decisions about who will teach and how. A substantial research agenda is before us with respect to developing meaningful assessments of teaching quality. Most current tools for evaluating teaching suffer from many shortcomings, including a lack of consideration of teaching content and context, a reliance on a conception of teaching as the implementation of fixed routines rather than decision making about which of a range of strategies might address the diverse needs of students, and a view that teaching consists largely of imparting information to students rather than constructing (and reconstructing) learning opportunities for them to pursue.

As hierarchical structures give way to environments that sustain collegial interactions, new forms of evaluation will need to take root in schools. These should emphasize peer review of practice and focus on a learner-centered approach to teaching.

Eisner (1992) conceives of evaluation as inherently part of the everyday work life of teachers, a key aspect of professional practice:

Evaluation is an aspect of professional educational practice that should be regarded as one of the major means through which educators can secure information they can use to enhance the quality of their work. Evaluation ought to be an ongoing part of their work. Evaluation ought to be an ongoing part of the process of education, one that contributes to its enhancement, not simply a means for scoring students and teachers. (p. 625)

Teachers who have access to educative and collegial forms of evaluation are more apt to develop an array of behaviors, attitudes, and skills that are inherently self-renewing. Thus, the workplace conditions that support effective teaching are the same workplace conditions that support evaluation approaches that ensure professional growth.

PREPARING TEACHERS FOR TOMORROW'S SCHOOLS

Schlechty's plea for consensus on what constitutes a "teacher" is one that the profession as a whole is actively engaged in answering. In recent years, several major reports calling for the strengthening of the teaching profession have noted that teachers must take hold of standard setting if teaching is to make good on the promise of competence that professions make to the public (Carnegie Forum, 1986; Holmes Group, 1986). Teacher education leaders recognize that teachers and teacher educators

. . . must take greater control over their own destiny. A powerful place where this can be done is in standards-setting . . . . Professionals must define high standards, set rigorous expectations, and then hold peers to these standards and expectations. (Imig, 1992, p. 14)

Such a consensus is beginning to be forged by the profession as new professional bodies, such as the National Board for Professional Teaching Standards and new state-level professional standards boards in 12 states, define what beginning and experienced teachers should know and be able to do. Similarly, the efforts of teacher educators through such organizations as the American Association of Colleges for Teacher Education, the Association of Teacher Educators, the Holmes Group of education deans, and NCATE have begun to define a knowledge base for teaching and a conception of teacher education practice that can successfully convey such knowledge to enter-

ing teachers. These initiatives will also help shape both the nature of teaching and the nature of the teaching force in years to come.

A legitimate question can be raised as to whether improving standards will exacerbate teacher shortages. Interestingly, the reverse has been true historically. Throughout the twentieth century, teacher shortages have been an impetus for upgrading salaries and standards within the profession. Shortages following World War I and World War II, and again in the 1960s, propelled substantial real increases in teacher salaries accompanied by increases in the educational requirements for teaching. As Sedlak and Schlossman (1986) note:

Contrary to what many modern-day educators tend to assume, teacher shortages have been commonplace throughout the twentieth century. Nonetheless, it has proved possible, time and again, to raise certification standards during periods of protracted shortage. Not only has the raising of standards not exacerbated teacher shortages, it may even—at least where accompanied by significant increases in teachers' salaries—have helped to alleviate them (and, at the same time, enhanced popular respect for teaching as a profession). (p. 39)

Their research demonstrated that teacher shortages generally followed periods of real income decline for teachers and that in most instances the shortages produced both salary gains and heightened standards for teaching.

The dilemma, however, is that while teacher shortages create a political climate within which standards and salaries may be raised, they also create conditions that work against the continuation of these initiatives. The effect of having standards, however high, with large loopholes available to satisfy demand pressures is that salaries will always remain somewhat depressed. In the past, although teacher salaries have always increased in times of short supply, they have never reached comparability with those of other professions requiring similar training, and they have tended to slip again when the supply crisis was "solved." If no substantial improvement occurs in the attractions to teaching, it will be difficult to improve overall teacher quality because the pool of potential candidates who can meet the standards will not be sufficiently enlarged. In circular fashion, the failure to attract sufficient numbers of well-qualified teachers will lessen teachers' claims for professional responsibility and autonomy and will increase the press for regulation of teaching, thus further decreasing the attractions to teaching for professionally oriented candidates.

Because education is a public service not only offered to all children by state governments, but required of them by law, classrooms cannot be left unstaffed when shortages of qualified teachers occur. However, for the same reasons, the state has the obligation of not only staffing classrooms but also doing so in a manner that does no harm to students. This argues against allowing exceptions to meaningful licensing standards. The problem is that states' current standards for licensure are not accepted as meaningful (i.e., related to desired knowledge and skill) by the profession, the public, or even state policymakers themselves (who are sometimes quick to sidestep the very standards they have created). Screens to the profession must be legitimized if they are to be respected and observed; solutions to shortages must be found that protect clients as well as the profession itself.

In considering the supply and standards dilemma it is important to remember three things. First, there is not an absolute shortage of teachers, but a shortage in particular fields and locations. In fact, nearly twice as many teachers are prepared as actually enter teaching each year. The most pressing need is to equalize resources and create incentives that will fill vacancies in places that are not now sufficiently attractive to these nonentrants. Second, with nearly half of all beginning teachers leaving within a few years of entry, strategies that keep teachers in the profession will greatly reduce the demand for new teachers over time.

Finally, the most important concern regarding standards is that they represent meaningful kinds of knowledge and skills for candidates to acquire and schools of education to develop. The goal in standard setting should not be to increase the failure rates of candidates seeking to enter but to provide clarity, incentives, and supports to ensure more adequately prepared candidates when they do enter. More educationally meaningful standard setting is critical to providing teachers with the knowledge and skills they will need to succeed in today's classrooms and to continue as committed members of the profession.

Professional Standards and Preparation

Professions set standards in three major ways: (1) by professional accreditation of preparation programs; (2) by state licensing, which enables entry into practice; and (3) by certification, which is a professional recognition of high levels of competence. (Although we have used the term "state certification" throughout this chapter, as it is commonly used in the field to refer to state licensing, professional certification is a separate matter now being undertaken by NBPTS. To avoid confusion, state controls should properly be termed licensing standards.) In teaching, these standard-setting mechanisms have been historically weak, although this is beginning to change. As standards become clearer about what good teaching is and what teachers should understand and be able to do, they hold promise for becoming a real touchstone for preparation and for practice.

Standard Setting in Progress

Professional accreditation, although recently strengthened by NCATE's revision of standards in 1988, is not required of all teacher education programs. Only about 500 of nearly 1,300 programs are professionally accredited at the national level. The remainder are state approved and are of widely varying quality (Dennison, 1992). Licensing (inaccurately called "certification" by most states) has been controlled by legislatures and state agencies rather than by representatives of the profession. Here, too, standards are both highly variable and erratically enforced. Professional certification had not existed in teaching until the advent of the National Board, which is comprised of a majority of highly respected teacher members and which began developing standards and assessments for advanced certification in 1987.

The National Board's standards and assessments place student learning at the center of the teaching enterprise. They articulate a strong knowledge base, and they acknowledge that good teaching is contingent on reciprocal considerations of students, goals, and contexts (National Board for Professional Teaching Standards [NBPTS], n.d.). The understandings codified in the National Board standards are a reflection of reforms elsewhere—in teacher education, staff development efforts, induction programs, and, increasingly, state licensing.

To achieve the kinds of highly accomplished teaching envisioned by the National Board on a broad scale, states must also strengthen teacher education and licensing. In almost all states, teacher education is more poorly funded than other university departments. It has long been used as a revenue producer for programs that train engineers, accountants, lawyers, and future doctors. Needed investments should be tied to standards that point toward desired practices.

Thus, the improvement of teacher education depends in turn on major changes in teacher licensing standards. Virtually no one believes that most current state licensing requirements provide meaningful standards of teacher knowledge and competence, not the public, not the profession, and not even the policymakers who are responsible for setting the requirements. Their willingness to avoid their own regulations by creating emergency, temporary, and alternative routes to licensing is the most obvious indictment of the system they have established. Meaningful standards must be created and then they must be met by all entrants to the profession. Shortages must be met by enhanced incentives to teach rather than by lowering standards, especially for those who teach children in central cities and poor rural schools.

The Interstate New Teacher Assessment and Support Consortium (INTASC), a group of state representatives and professional associations, has articulated performance-based standards for initial licensing of teachers that are compatible with the National Board's standards. They describe what entering teachers should know, be like, and be able to do to practice responsibly and to develop the kinds of deeper expertise that will later enable highly accomplished practice. The introduction to these model standards states:

The National Board and INTASC are united in their view that the complex art of teaching requires performance-based standards and assessment strategies that are capable of capturing teachers' reasoned judgments and that evaluate what they can actually do in authentic teaching situations. (INTASC, 1992, p. 1)

Already used as the basis for new standards adopted in more than a dozen states and under consideration in a dozen more, the INTASC principles were developed based on the National Board propositions, standards in several states, and the efforts of teacher educators, including the Holmes Group of education deans, the AACTE's knowledge base initiatives, and Alverno College's performance-based approach to teacher education.

As these new licensing standards and teacher preparation initiatives demonstrate, a reflective, student-centered, problem-solving orientation is increasingly understood as a fundamental part of professional life for all teachers. Rather than teachers being viewed as implementors of externally designed and prescribed curricula, they are acknowledged as curriculum developers, learning analysts, and instructional strategists who must possess the deep knowledge of teaching, learning, curriculum, and assessment once reserved for others "above" them in the educational hierarchy.

Preparation for Learner-Centered and Learning-Centered Teaching Transforming teaching and learning in American schools rests on an understanding of students, not only what they know but also how they think. This transformation calls for educating teachers so they have a rich knowledge base about learning and an array of tools for accessing student thinking, understanding students' prior knowledge and backgrounds, and connecting to their families and communities.

The shared agenda of school restructuring and teacher preparation involves helping teachers make the necessary connections between students' needs and curriculum goals. This understanding of learners and learning has historically been the most neglected aspect of teacher preparation in this country. Licensing and preparation have focused more on subject-matter knowledge and methods than on a strong theoretical and empirical understanding of students and their learning. This is especially true for secondary school teachers who have rarely been given access to knowledge about how students learn, develop, think, and perform.

In the past, teachers have rarely been prepared to evaluate critically students' progress and learning in light of knowledge about cognitive, social, physical, and psychological development, multiple intelligences, and diverse performance modes; to develop curriculum grounded in a deep understanding of learning theory and learning differences; or to create assessments that can reveal student strengths, needs, and understandings. Giving teachers access to such knowledge is a major part of the transformation of teacher preparation and licensing that is on the horizon. It is also an important element of preparing prospective teachers so that they can be successful with the diverse range of students they will be asked to teach. Supporting this success is critical to retaining them in the profession as well because it will enhance the sense of efficacy that motivates ongoing commitment to the profession.

Since the mid-1980s, many schools of education have made great strides in incorporating new understandings of teaching and learning in their curriculum for prospective teachers. More attention to learning theory, cognition, and learning strategies has accompanied a deepening appreciation for content pedagogy and constructivist teaching strategies. In addition, teacher preparation and teacher induction programs are increasingly introducing strategies that help teachers develop a reflective and problem-solving orientation. This is done by engaging prospective teachers and interns in teacher research, school-based inquiry, and learning about students' experiences so that they are building an empirical understanding of learners and a capacity to analyze and reflect on their practice.

These efforts to develop teachers as managers of their own inquiry stands in contrast to earlier assumptions about teacher induction and about teaching in general, which is that beginning teachers needed to focus only on the most rudimentary tasks of teaching with basic precepts and cookbook rules to guide them and that teachers in general should be the recipients of knowledge rather than the generators of knowledge and understandings about students. The function of teacher preparation is increasingly seen as empowering teachers to own, use, and develop knowledge about teaching and learning as sophisticated and powerful as the demands of such work require.

Preparation for Teaching Diverse Learners In addition to preparation that is rigorous and relevant to today's educational needs, teacher education programs should offer prospective teachers opportunities to work with effective guidance in diverse settings and underserved areas. Most teacher education students have had little or no experience working in low-income urban or rural schools and little prior experience working with students with greatly diverse learning needs. Although the great majority of newly qualified teachers (84%) felt adequately prepared to teach all of the subject(s) they were teaching, a much smaller number felt adequately prepared to teach the full range of diverse learners in their classrooms. Of those who taught limited English-proficient students, only 57% felt adequately prepared to do so, and of those who taught students requiring special education, about 60% felt adequately prepared (Gray et al., 1993). About one in five preservice students reported that they were inadequately prepared to teach students with culturally diverse backgrounds (Howey & Zimpher, 1993). This is an area where enhanced preparation could make a difference in new teacher effectiveness and, perhaps, continuation in the profession as well.

Induction Stronger induction programs are needed to offer the necessary support that is especially crucial for retaining new teachers, especially those faced with the most difficult challenges. In contrast to most other professions, which require structured, intensely supervised internships prior to licensing, teaching has traditionally offered prospective teachers little assistance in learning to teach beyond a relatively short and idiosyncratic student teaching experience. Beginning teachers are generally left to "sink or swim" during their first years of teaching (Wise et al., 1987).

Because the development of learner-centered practice is enormously difficult, untutored novices often fail at their early attempts. The application of knowledge about learning, teaching, curriculum building, development, motivation, and behavior to the individual needs of diverse students is a daunting task requiring skillful observation, diagnosis, and integration of many different concepts and abilities. Unless this occurs with the support of an able mentor, the effort can quickly become overwhelming. This is one of the reasons that knowledge acquired in preservice courses is often not put to use, and that beginning teachers' practices often become less sensitive to students' needs rather than more so over the course of the initial year in teaching.

Teachers of all experience levels agree on the importance of supervised induction. When asked what would have helped them in their first years of teaching, 47% said that a skilled, experienced teacher assigned to provide advice and assistance would have been helpful, and 39% said that more practical training, such as a year's internship before having their own classroom, would have been most helpful (Metropolitan Life, 1992). Evidence suggests that mentoring programs improve beginning teachers' effectiveness and decrease their typically high attrition (Huling-Austin & Murphy, 1987; Odell, 1986; Wright, McKibbon, & Walton, 1987).

Beginning teachers must develop the ability to apply knowledge appropriately in different contexts while handling the dozens of cognitive, psychological, moral, and interpersonal demands that simultaneously require attention in a classroom. Learning to manage the different personalities and needs of 25 or 30 children while prioritizing and juggling often conflicting goals does not happen quickly, automatically, or easily. These are skills that have to be developed. Clinical experiences must enable teachers to learn firsthand about the variability in students' cognitive development and approaches to learning while they are supported with guided instruction and opportunities for reflection on their teaching and its effects on learners. These educative complements to classroom work should assist novices in acquiring wider repertoires of teaching strategies and help them relate problems of teaching practice to research on teaching and human development. Having these kinds of opportunities available should encourage beginners to teach reflectively, to evaluate what they are doing, to assess whether what they are doing is working and why, to understand how to make better decisions, and to juggle the many concerns of teaching.

An important part of the current redesign of teacher preparation includes efforts to extend the concept of mentoring in more systematic ways within restructured school settings. A growing number of education schools are working with school systems to create institutions such as professional development schools and internship sites that will allow new teachers to be inducted into schools as they must *become*, not only schools as they *are*. Too often there is a disjunction between the conceptions of good practice beginning teachers learn in their preparation programs and those they encounter when they begin teaching. Typically, beginning teachers are placed in the most difficult schools, those with the highest rates of teacher turnover, the greatest numbers of inexperienced staff, and the least capacity to support teacher growth and development. In addition, these are often schools where the kinds of learner-centered practices we are seeking to develop are not well developed or well supported. Thus, it is difficult for beginning teachers to develop ways of really connecting what they know to what students know when there are so few supports in the school environment for learning to practice in this more challenging way. The conditions for thoughtful, learner-centered teaching must be well supported by expert, experienced staff in order to be emulated and instilled in beginning teachers.

Professional development schools, created recently in a number of states and districts, may be the best hope for addressing beginning teachers' needs and for providing a work environment that is conducive to professional growth in which new teachers are gradually introduced to the responsibilities of teaching and are given assistance from experienced colleagues. In such environments beginning teachers not only receive ongoing evaluation and feedback from other teachers about their teaching, but they are encouraged as well to participate in school decisions. During a formalized induction year, beginning teachers have opportunities for professional development that encourage collaboration and that provide the support that is

associated with stronger beginning teacher work and career choice commitment and plans to remain in teaching.

The professional development school offers promise for supporting beginning teachers in developing state-of-the-art practice in settings that model and support such practice and provide needed coaching and collaboration. Similar to teaching hospitals in the medical profession, such schools aim to model best practices and to foster the learning of professionals (for a review, see Darling-Hammond, 1994). There are at least 200 professional development schools across the country that have been launched as partnerships between schools and teacher education programs. These schools should be carefully examined during the next several years as they attempt to prepare teachers and develop their practices in vanguard settings with a common set of expectations that link preparation and practice.

In many reform models, such as those offered by the Holmes Group (1986, 1989), the Carnegie Forum on Education and the Economy (1986), and the RAND Corporation (Wise & Darling-Hammond, 1987), all prospective teachers would undertake their student teaching and a more intensive internship in professional development schools. The hope is that in these schools they would encounter state-of-the-art practice and a range of diverse experiences under intensive supervision so that they learn to teach diverse learners effectively, rather than merely to cope or even to leave the profession as so many do. Ideally, professional development schools will also provide serious venues for developing the knowledge base for teaching by becoming places in which practice-based and practice-sensitive research can be carried out collaboratively by teachers, teacher educators, and researchers.

Probably the most important recognition of these attempts to link school restructuring and teacher education redesign is that prospective teachers must be taught in the same ways in which they will be expected to teach. As their students must do, teachers also construct their own understandings by doing—by collaborating, inquiring into problems, trying and testing ideas, evaluating, and reflecting on the outcomes of their work. As teacher educators, beginning teachers, and experienced teachers work together on real problems of practice in learner-centered settings, they can develop a collective knowledge base, along with ownership and participation in developing a common set of standards for practice. This development promotes deep understanding that cannot be obtained in coursework alone, although the foundation may be laid in coursework that provides a broader, theoretical frame for developing and interpreting practice.

NEEDED RESEARCH

Supply and Demand Issues

To develop a more comprehensive picture of the status of the teaching force and an in-depth understanding of trends in teacher supply and demand, a number of different sources of knowledge must be integrated. Research is needed to further explain the manner in which local and state recruitment and hiring practices influence attractions to teaching, the status of the profession, and supply and demand trends, as well as how local and state recruitment and hiring policies enhance or undermine the success of promising recruitment policies and whether problems are more likely to show up in particular locales or schools.

Another dimension of the quality of the teaching force relates to school management and staffing procedures. Both qualitative and quantitative studies are needed to explore the relationships between local and state policies and teaching conditions. Qualitative studies are needed to explore more fully how teachers make decisions about whether to enter and remain in teaching.

On a more subtle note, differences must be teased out among programs that are labeled under the same reform rubrics, such as "incentive pay plans," "restructured schools," "mentoring," and "teacher decision making." Restructured schools may not resemble each other much at all; teacher participation in budget decisions may have very different consequences from participation in curricular or professional development decisions; and mentoring in one site may consist mainly of moral support, whereas in another site it may include a comprehensive set of instructional supports and professional growth opportunities (e.g., time to solve instructional problems with colleagues). Similarly, one type of incentive pay plan may offer more money to improve standardized test scores or require teachers to follow prescribed sets of teaching behaviors, whereas another type of incentive pay plan may create supports for pursuing professional certification and meeting rigorous standards of practice. To study the effects of reform approaches they must be more carefully defined and distinguished from one another. Then productive answers may be pursued to such questions as "What supports decrease the traditionally high attrition rate of beginning teachers?" or "Which programs tend to attract and keep more talented candidates, more committed candidates, more shortage field candidates, or more minority candidates?"

Regarding the unequal distribution of qualified teachers, research should examine how these distributional differences influence teacher turnover and teaching quality, as well as how teaching conditions and teacher qualifications are distributed across schools, students, and courses. Future research should also address how more- and less-qualified teachers are distributed by field, level, sector, and locale. To understand and improve national teacher distribution, we must understand what conditions contribute to imbalances.

Teacher Preparation Issues

Teacher preparation varies across types of teachers by field, sector, source of entry, type of license, type of students taught, teacher preparation institution, and state. A clearer picture of the differences is needed to determine how preparation for teaching currently varies and how these differences may relate to measures of teacher quality. Inevitably, research questions on teacher preparation intersect with questions related to teacher supply and demand as well. What are the effects, for example, of different forms of academic training, selection into programs, field experiences, or induction experiences on teacher recruitment, effectiveness, and retention?

Research on new approaches to teacher education and assessment must begin to take into account the kinds of knowledge teachers need to have to understand learners and to evaluate their strengths, styles, and needs, as well as to create good representations of subject-matter knowledge and to find an interface between the two. The assessments must find ways to evaluate teacher thinking, judgment, reflection, and decision-making ability as well as to observe teachers' skillfulness in action. They must begin to assess the effects that teachers' knowledge, judgments, and actions have on the long-term growth, development, and learning of students, not just their immediate scores on basic skills tests. Much of this research relies in turn on a vigorous program of research on teaching, which should build on and connect previously distinct bodies of teaching-related research, as well as recent research on learning, cognition, and the nature of human performance and intelligence.

Another major area of research should seek to evaluate the effects of different kinds of teacher preparation programs on teachers and their teaching. This research clearly relies on work in the area of teacher assessment. How can we understand what teachers learn under different circumstances if we have poorly developed tools for measuring the criterion variable? The current policy muddle on teacher preparation is a function not only of the low status and low investment in teacher education, but also of the deeply divergent views of what it is we expect teachers to do in classrooms and, thus, what it is we expect them to know. As we examine teacher education alternatives, we must look not only at what teachers know upon completing preservice education, but also what they are prepared to learn subsequently, given the conceptual framework and tools for research and reflection they have been given.

This program of research should look at teacher preparation abroad as well as in the United States, and it should document how the roles of teachers, the structures of schools, and the expectations of students are influenced by the kind, quality, and quantity of education teachers receive.

A final area of research should examine teacher preparation models as they influence teacher recruitment and retention and the distribution of differently qualified teachers to diverse students. Among the kinds of questions we should ask are whether some kinds of programs recruit different kinds of candidates than others. Do some kinds of programs result in longer or shorter investments in teaching on the part of their recruits? Are those that seem to prepare teachers better equally available to serve prospective minority teachers as well as majority teachers? Are their graduates equally available to serve children of color and children in low-income communities as they are to serve children of traditionally advantaged communities?

Ultimately, a greater understanding of how teacher preparation influences the nature and capabilities of the teaching force can help ensure a profession full of qualified and committed teachers. It is this possibility that can realize Dewey's goal of a just education for all students: "What the best and wisest parent wants for his own child, that must the community want for all of its children. Any other ideal for our schools is narrow and unlovely; acted upon, it destroys our democracy" (Dewey, 1915, p. 3). Such an education rests on professional development for teachers that leads to the development of a profession that can create and use an expanding base of knowledge to serve all students well. This shared goal of school reform and teacher preparation is one that we now have a genuine opportu-nity and a serious obligation to achieve on behalf of all of the nation's school children.

References

Akin, J. N. (1989). *Teacher supply and demand in the United States: 1989 report*. ASCUS Research Report. Addison, IL: Association for School, College and University Staffing.

Aldridge, W. (1987). What's being taught and who's teaching it. In *This year in school science: The 1986 science curriculum* (pp. 207–224). Washington, DC: American Association for the Advancement of Science.

American Association of Colleges for Teacher Education [AACTE]. (1991). *Rate IV. Teaching teachers: Facts and figures*. Washington, DC: Author.

American Association of Colleges for Teacher Education [AACTE]. (1992). *Academic achievement of white, black, and Hispanic students in teacher education programs*. Washington, DC: Author.

American Council on Education [ACE]. (1989). *Eighth annual status report on minorities in higher education*. Washington, DC: Author.

Anderman, E., Belzer, S., & Smith, J. (1991, April). *Teacher commitment and job satisfaction: The role of school culture and principal leadership*. Paper presented at the meeting of the American Educational Research Association, Chicago.

Andrew, M. D. (1990). Differences between graduates of 4-year and 5-year teacher preparation programs. *Journal of Teacher Education, 41*(2), 45–51.

Andrew, M. D., & Schwab, R. L. (1994). Has reform in teacher education influenced teacher performance? An outcome assessment of graduates of an eleven university consortium. Unpublished manuscript.

Armor, D., Conroy-Oseguera, P., Cox, M., King, N., McDonnell, L., Pascal, A., Pauly, E., & Zellman, G. (1976). *Analysis of the school preferred reading program in selected Los Angeles minority schools*. Santa Monica, CA: RAND Corporation.

Ashburn, E. A. (1989, April). *The nature of teachers' commitment and its relationship to school work-place conditions*. Paper presented at the annual meeting of the American Educational Research Association, San Francisco.

Ashton, P., & Crocker, L. (1986). Does teacher certification make a difference? *Florida Journal of Teacher Education, 3*, 73–83.

Ashton, P., & Crocker, L. (1987). Systematic study of planned variations: The essential focus of teacher education reform. *Journal of Teacher Education, 38*(3), 2–8.

Association for School, College, and University Staffing (ASCUS). (n.d.). *Teacher supply and demand*. Addison, IL: Author.

Astin, A. W. (1992). *What matters in college? Four critical years revisited*. San Francisco: Jossey-Bass.

Astin, A., Green, K., & Korn, W. (1987). *The American freshman: Twenty year trends*. Los Angeles: Cooperative Institutional Research Program.

Berman, P., & McLaughlin, M. W. (1977). *Federal programs supporting educational change. Vol. 7: Factors affecting implementation and continuation*. Santa Monica, CA: RAND Corporation.

Blank, R. K., & Gruebel, D. (1993). *State indicators of science and mathematics education 1993*. Washington, DC: Council of Chief State School Officers.

Blase, J., & Kirby, P. C. (1992). *Bringing out the best in teachers*. Newbury Park, CA: Corwin.

Bobbitt, S., Faupel, E., & Burns, S. (1991). *Characteristics of stayers, movers, and leavers: Results from the teacher followup survey, 1988–89*. Washington, DC: NCES, U.S. Department of Education.

Bobbitt, S. A., & McMillen, M. M. (1990, April). *Teacher training, certification, and assignment*. Paper presented at the annual meeting of the American Educational Research Association, Boston.

Boe, E. E., Bobbitt, S. A., & Cook, L. H. (1993, May). *Whither didst thou go? Retention, reassignment, migration, and attrition of special and general education teachers in national perspective*. Paper presented at the meeting of Council for Exceptional Children, San Antonio.

Brookhart, S. M., & Loadman, W. E. (1993, April). *Critical minority: Males entering elementary teacher education programs*. Paper presented at the annual meeting of the American Educational Research Association, Atlanta.

Brookover, W. (1977). *Schools can make a difference*. East Lansing: College of Urban Development, Michigan State University.

Bryk, A. S., & Driscoll, M. E. (1988). *The high school as community: Contextual influences and consequences for students and teachers*. Chicago: National Center on Effective Schools.

Burns, J. M. (1978). *Leadership*. New York: Harper & Row.

Burns, T., & Stalker, G. M. (1961). *The management of innovation*. London: Tavistock.

Carnegie Forum on Education and the Economy. (1986). *A nation prepared: Teachers for the 21st century*. New York: Carnegie.

Carnegie Foundation. (1990). *The condition of teaching. A state-by-state analysis*. Princeton: Author.

Chapman, D. W. (1984). Teacher retention: The test of a model. *American Educational Research Journal, 21*(3), 645–659.

Choy, S. P., Bobbitt, S. A., Henke, R. R., Medrich, E. A., Horn, L. J., & Lieberman, J. (1993). *America's teachers: Profile of a profession*. Washington, DC: NCES, U.S. Department of Education.

Choy, S. P., Henke, R. R., Alt, M. N., Medrich, E. A., & Bobbitt, S. A. (1993). *Schools and staffing in the United States: A statistical profile, 1990–91*. Washington, DC: NCES, U.S. Department of Education.

Choy, S. P., Medrich, E. A., Henke, R. R., & Bobbitt, S. A. (1992). *Schools and staffing in the United States: A statistical profile, 1987–88*. Washington, DC: NCES, U.S. Department of Education.

Conley, S. (1991). Review of research on teacher participation in school decisionmaking. In G. Grant (Ed.), *Review of research in education* (pp. 225–266). Washington, DC: American Educational Research Association.

Corcoran, T. B. (1990). Schoolwork: Perspectives on workplace reform in public schools. In M. W. McLaughlin, J. E. Talbert, & N. Bascia (Eds.), *The context of teaching in secondary schools* (pp. 142–166). New York: Teachers College Press.

Cornett, L. M. (1992). Alternate certification: State policies in the SREB states. *Peabody Journal of Education, 67*(3), 55–83.

Darling-Hammond, L. (1984). *Beyond the commission reports. The coming crisis in teaching*. Santa Monica, CA: RAND Corporation. (No. R-3177-RC)

Darling-Hammond, L. (1990a). Achieving our goals: Structural or superficial reforms? *Phi Delta Kappan, 72*(4), 286–295.

Darling-Hammond, L. (1990b). Teacher professionalism: Why and how. In A. Lieberman (Ed.), *Schools as collaborative cultures: Creating the future now* (pp. 25–50). Philadelphia: Falmer Press.

Darling-Hammond, L. (1990c). Teachers and teaching: Signs of a changing profession. In R. Houston, M. Haberman, & J. Sikula (Eds.), *Handbook of research on teacher education* (pp. 267–290). New York: Macmillan.

Darling-Hammond, L. (1992). Teaching and knowledge: Policy issues posed by alternate certification for teachers. *Peabody Journal of Education, 67*(3), 123–154.

Darling-Hammond, L. (Ed.). (1994). *Professional development schools: Schools for developing a profession.* New York: Teachers College Press.

Darling-Hammond, L. (1995). Inequality and access to knowledge. In J. Banks (Ed.), *Handbook of research on multicultural education* (pp. 465–483). New York: Macmillan.

Darling-Hammond, L., & Berry, B. (1988). *The evolution of teacher policy.* Santa Monica, CA: RAND Corporation.

Darling-Hammond, L., with Green, J. (1988). Teacher quality and educational equality. *The College Board Review, 148,* Summer, 16–23, 39–41.

Darling-Hammond, L., & Hudson, L. (1990). Pre-college science and mathematics teachers: Supply, demand and quality. In C. B. Cazden (Ed.), Review of research in education (pp. 223–264). Washington, DC: American Educational Research Association.

Darling-Hammond, L., Hudson, L., & Kirby, S. N. (1989). *Redesigning teacher education: Opening the door for new recruits to science and mathematics teaching.* Santa Monica, CA: RAND Corporation.

Darling-Hammond, L., with Sclan, E. (1992). Policy and supervision. In Carl Glickman (Ed.), *Supervision in transition* (pp. 7–29). Alexandria, VA: Association for Supervision and Curriculum Development.

Darling-Hammond, L., Wise, A. E., & Klein, S. (1995). *A license to teach: Building a profession for 21st century schools.* Boulder, CO: Westview Press.

Darling-Hammond, L., Wise, A. E., & Pease, S. R. (1983). Teacher evaluation in the organizational context: A review of the literature. *Review of Educational Research, 53*(3), 285–328.

Deal, T. E., & Peterson, K. D. (1990). *The principal's role in shaping school culture.* Washington, DC: Superintendent of Documents, U.S. Government Printing Office.

Dennison, G. M. (1992). National standards in teacher preparation: A commitment to quality. *The Chronicle of Higher Education, 39*(15), A40.

Dewey, J. (1915). *The school and society.* Chicago: The University of Chicago Press.

Dewey, J. (1916). *Democracy and education.* New York: Macmillan.

Dilworth, M. E. (1990). *Reading between the lines. Teachers and their racial/ethnic cultures.* Washington, DC: ERIC Clearinghouse on Teacher Education and American Association of Colleges for Teacher Education.

Dreeben, R. (1987). Closing the divide: What teachers and administrators can do to help black students reach their reading potential. *American Educator, 11*(4), 28–35.

Driscoll, M. E. (1993, April). *The conditions of work for beginning teachers: An urban portrait.* Paper presented at the annual meeting of the American Educational Research Association, Atlanta.

Druva, C. A., & Anderson, R. D. (1983). Science teacher characteristics by teacher behavior and by student outcome: A meta-analysis of research. *Journal of Research in Science Teaching, 20*(5), 467–479.

Eisner, E. W. (1992). Educational reform and the ecology of schooling. *Teachers College Record, 93*(4), 610–627.

Evertson, C., Hawley, W., & Zlotnick, M. (1985). Making a difference in educational quality through teacher education. *Journal of Teacher Education, 36*(3), 2–12.

Feistritzer, C. E. (1986). *Teacher crisis: Myth or reality: A state by state analysis, 1986.* Washington, DC: National Center for Educational Information.

Feistritzer, C. E. (1988). *Teacher supply and demand survey 1988.* Washington, DC: National Center for Education Information.

Feistritzer, C. E. (1990). *Alternative teacher certification: A state-by-state analysis.* Washington, DC: National Center for Education Information.

Feistritzer, C. E. (1992). *Who wants to teach?* Washington, DC: National Center for Education Information.

Feldman, S. (1991, November 7). New York City needs money for schools, but also for teachers [Letter to the editor]. *The New York Times,* p. A28.

Firestone, W. A., & Rosenblum, S. (1988). Building commitment in urban high schools. *Educational Evaluation and Policy Analysis, 10*(4), 285–299.

Fullan, M. (1992). Visions that blind. *Educational Leadership, 49*(5), 19–20.

Fuller, B., Wood, K., Rapoport, T., & Dornbusch, S. M. (1982). The organizational context of individual efficacy. *Review of Educational Research, 52*(1), 7–30.

Gerald, D. E., & Hussar, W. J. (1990). *Projections of education statistics to 2001. An update.* Washington, DC: NCES, U.S. Department of Education.

Gerald, D. E., & Hussar, W. J. (1991). *Projections of education statistics to 2002.* Washington, DC: NCES, U.S. Department of Education.

Goodlad, J. I. (1990). *Teachers for our nation's schools.* San Francisco: Jossey-Bass.

Gray, L., Cahalan, M., Hein, S., Litman, C., Severynse, J., Warren, S., Wisan, G., & Stowe, P. (1993). *New teachers in the job market, 1991 update.* Washington, DC: U.S. Department of Education, OERI.

Greenberg, J. D. (1983). The case for teacher education: Open and shut. *Journal of Teacher Education, 34*(4), 2–5.

Grissmer, D. W., & Kirby, S. N. (1987). *Teacher attrition: The uphill climb to staff the nation's schools.* Santa Monica, CA: RAND Corporation.

Grossman, P. L. (1990). *The making of a teacher: Teacher knowledge and teacher education.* New York: Teachers College Press.

Haggstrom, G. W., Darling-Hammond, L., & Grissmer, D. W. (1988). *Assessing teacher supply and demand.* Santa Monica, CA: RAND Corporation.

Hart, A. W., & Murphy, M. J. (1990). New teachers react to redesigned teacher work. *American Journal of Education, 98*(3), 224–250.

Hawk, P., Coble, C. R., & Swanson, M. (1985). Certification: It does matter. *Journal of Teacher Education, 36*(3), 13–15.

Hecker, D. (1986). Teachers' job outlook: Is chicken little wrong again? *Occupational-Outlook-Quarterly, 30*(4), 13–17.

Holmes Group. (1986). *Tomorrow's teachers: A report of the Holmes Group.* East Lansing, MI: Author.

Holmes Group. (1989). *Work in progress: The Holmes Group one year on.* East Lansing, MI: Author.

Howey, K. R., & Zimpher, N. L. (1993). Patterns in prospective teachers: Guides for designing preservice programs. Columbus: Ohio State University. Unpublished paper.

Huberman, A. M., & Miles, M. (1984). Rethinking the quest for school improvement: Some findings from the DESSI study. *Teachers College Record, 86*(1), 34–54.

Huling-Austin, L., & Murphy, S. C. (1987, April). *Assessing the impact of teacher induction programs: Implications for program development.* Paper presented at the annual meeting of the American Educational Research Association, Washington, DC.

Imig, D. G. (1992). *The professionalization of teaching: Relying on a professional knowledge base.* St. Louis: AACTE Knowledge-Base Seminar.

Interstate New Teacher Assessment and Support Consortium (INTASC). (1992). *Model standards for beginning teacher licensing and development: A resource for state dialogue.* Washington, DC: Council for Chief State School Officers.

Johnson, S. M. (1990). *Teachers at work. Achieving success in our schools.* New York: Basic Books.

Lanier, J. E., & Little, J. W. (1986). Research on teacher education. In M. C. Wittrock (Ed.), *Handbook of research on teaching* (3rd ed., pp. 527–569). New York: Macmillan.

LH Research. (1993). *A survey of the perspective of elementary and secondary school teachers on reform.* Prepared for the Ford Foundation. New York: LH Research.

Lieberman, A. (1988). Expanding the leadership team. *Educational Leadership, 45*(5), 4–8.

Lieberman, A. (Ed.). (1990). *Schools as collaborative cultures: Creating the future now.* New York: Falmer.

Lieberman, A., & Miller, L. (1984). *Teachers, their world, and their work.* Alexandria, VA: Association for Supervision and Curriculum Development.

Litt, M. D., & Turk, D. C. (1985). Sources of stress and dissatisfaction in experienced public high school teachers. *Journal of Educational Research, 78*(3), 178–185.

Little, J. W. (1987). Teachers as colleagues. In V. Richardson-Koehler (Ed.), *Educator's handbook. A research perspective* (pp. 491–518). New York: Longman.

Louis, K. S., & Miles, M. B. (1990). *Improving the urban high school: What works and why.* New York: Teachers College Press.

Macmillan, C. J., & Pendlebury, S. (1985). The Florida Performance Measurement System: A consideration. *Teachers College Record, 87*(1), 69–78.

Mark, J. H., & Anderson, B. D. (1985). Teacher survival rates in St. Louis, 1969–1982. *American Educational Research Journal, 22,* 413–421.

Maryland State Department of Education. (1990). *Maryland's alternative programs for teacher preparation.* Baltimore: Author.

McKnight, C., Crosswhite, F. J., Dossey, J. A., Kifer, E., Swafford, S. O., Travers, K. J., & Cooney, T. J. (1987). *The underachieving curriculum: Assessing U.S. school mathematics from an international perspective.* Champaign, IL: Stipes Publishing.

McLaughlin, M. W., Pfeifer, R. S., Swanson-Owens, D., & Yee, S. (1986). Why teachers won't teach. *Phi Delta Kappan, 67*(6), 420–426.

McLaughlin, M. W., & Talbert, J. E. (1993). *Contexts that matter for teaching and learning.* Stanford, CA: Stanford University.

Metropolitan Life. (1988). *The Metropolitan Life survey of the American teacher, 1988.* New York: Author.

Metropolitan Life. (1989). *The American teacher 1989. Preparing schools for the 1990's.* New York: Author.

Metropolitan Life. (1992). *The American teacher 1992. The second year: New teachers' expectations and ideals.* New York: Author.

Metropolitan Life. (1993). *The American teacher 1993.* New York: Author.

Murnane, R., & Olsen, R. J. (1988, April). *Factors affecting length of stay in teaching.* Paper presented at the annual meeting of the American Education Research Association, New Orleans.

Murnane, R. J., & Olsen, R. J. (1990). The effects of salaries and opportunity costs on length of stay in teaching. *The Journal of Human Resources, 25*(1), 106–124.

Murnane, R. J., Singer, J. D., & Willett, J. B. (1989). The influences of salaries and "opportunity costs" on teachers' career choices: Evidence from North Carolina. *Harvard Educational Review, 59*(3), 325–346.

Murnane, R. J., Singer, J. D., Willett, J. B., Kemple, J. J., & Olsen, R. J. (1991). *Who will teach?* Cambridge: Harvard University Press.

National Center for Education Statistics (NCES). (1983). *Condition of education 1983.* Washington, DC: U.S. Department of Education.

National Center for Education Statistics (NCES). (1985). *Recent college graduates survey* (Unpublished tabulations). Washington, DC: U.S. Department of Education.

National Center for Education Statistics (NCES). (1986). *The condition of education, 1986 edition.* Washington, DC: U.S. Department of Education.

National Center for Education Statistics (NCES). (1987). *The condition of education, 1987 edition.* Washington, DC: U.S. Department of Education.

National Center for Education Statistics (NCES). (1988). *1988 education indicators.* Washington, DC: U.S. Department of Education.

National Center for Education Statistics (NCES). (1989). *The condition of education, 1989 edition* (Vol. 2). Washington, DC: U.S. Department of Education.

National Center for Education Statistics (NCES). (1991). *Digest of education statistics 1990.* Washington, DC: U.S. Department of Education.

National Center for Education Statistics (NCES). (1992). *Digest of education statistics 1992.* Washington, DC: Author.

National Council for Accreditation of Teacher Education (NCATE). (1993). *NCATE public opinion poll.* Washington, DC: Author.

National Data Resource Center (NDRC). (1993). Unpublished tabulations. Washington, DC: NCES, U.S. Department of Education.

National Education Association (NEA). (1986). *Estimates of school statistics 1985–86* (Unpublished tabulations). Washington, DC: Author.

National Education Association (NEA). (1992). *Status of the American public school teacher 1990–91.* Washington, DC: Author.

National Governors' Association. (1986). *Time for results: The governors' 1991 report.* Washington, DC: Author.

Natriello, G., Zumwalt, K., Hansen, A., & Frisch, A. (1990, April). *Characteristics of entering teachers in New Jersey.* Revised version of a paper presented at the 1988 annual meeting of the American Educational Research Association, Boston.

Nelson, F. H., & O'Brien, T. (1993). *How U.S. teachers measure up internationally: A comparative study of teacher pay, training, and conditions of service.* Washington, DC: American Federation of Teachers.

New York State Education Department. (n.d.). *Memorandum on staffing, 1992.*

Oakes, J. (1990). *Multiplying inequalities: The unequal distribution of mathematics and science opportunities.* Santa Monica, CA: RAND Corporation.

Odell, S. (1986). Induction support of new teachers: A functional approach. *Journal of Teacher Education, 37,* 26–30.

Organization for Economic Cooperation and Development (OECD). (1992). *Education at a glance, OECD indicators.* Paris: Author.

Peterson, K. D., & Martin, J. L. (1990). Developing teacher commitment. The role of the administrator. In P. Reyes (Ed.), *Teachers and their workplace. Commitment, performance, and productivity* (pp. 225–240). Newbury Park, CA: Sage Publications.

Peterson, P. L., & Comeaux, M. A. (1989, April). *Evaluating the systems: Teachers' perspectives on teacher evaluation.* Paper presented at the annual meeting of the American Educational Research Association, San Francisco.

Raudenbush, S. W., Rowan, B., & Cheong, Y. F. (1992). Contextual effects on the self perceived efficacy of high school teachers. *Sociology of Education, 65*(4), 150–167.

Reyes, P. (1990). Organizational commitment of teachers. In P. Reyes (Ed.), *Teachers and their workplace* (pp. 143–163). Newbury Park, CA: Sage Publications.

Rollefson, M. (1993). *Teacher supply in the United States: Sources of newly hired teachers in public and private schools.* Washington, DC: NCES, U.S. Department of Education.

Rollefson, M., & Broughman, S. (1994, June). *NCES issue brief. Sources of newly hired teachers in public and private schools: 1988–91.* Washington, DC: National Center for Education Statistics.

Rosenholtz, S. J. (1985). Effective schools: Interpreting the evidence. *American Journal of Education, 93*(3), 352–388.

Rosenholtz, S. J. (1989). *Teacher's workplace. The social organization of schools.* New York: Longman.

Rosenholtz, S. J., & Simpson, C. (1990). Workplace conditions and the rise and fall of teachers' commitment. *Sociology of Education, 63*(4), 241–257.

Rowan, B. (1990). Commitment and control: Alternative strategies for the organizational design of schools. In C. B. Cazden (Ed.), *Review of research in education* (pp. 353–389). Washington, DC: American Educational Research Association.

Rumberger, R. (1985). The shortage of mathematics and science teachers: A review of the evidence. *Educational Evaluation and Policy Analysis, 7,* 355–369.

Rutter, M., Maughan, B., Mortimore, P., & Ouston, J., with Smith, A. (1979). *Fifteen thousand hours: Secondary schools and their effects on children.* Cambridge: Harvard University Press.

Schlechty, P. C. (1990). *Reform in teacher education: A sociological view.* Washington, DC: American Association of Colleges for Teacher Education.

Schlechty, P. C., & Vance, V. S. (1983). Recruitment, selection, and retention: The shape of the teaching force. *The Elementary School Journal, 83*(4), 470–487.

Sclan, E. M. (1993). The effect of perceived workplace conditions on beginning teachers' work commitment, career choice commitment, and planned retention. *Dissertation Abstracts International, 54,* 08A. (University Microfilms No. 9400594)

Sclan, E. M. (1994). *Performance evaluation for experienced teachers: An overview of state policies.* Washington, DC: ERIC Clearinghouse on Teacher Education, AACTE.

Sclan, E., & Darling-Hammond, L. (1992). *Beginning teacher performance evaluation: An overview of state policies.* Trends and Issues Paper No. 7. Washington, DC: ERIC Clearinghouse on Teacher Education, AACTE. (ED 341689)

Sedlak, M., & Schlossman, S. (1986). *Who will teach?* Santa Monica, CA: RAND Corporation. (R-3472CSTP)

Sergiovanni, T. J. (1984). Leadership and excellence in schooling. *Educational Leadership, 41*(5), 4, 6–13.

Sergiovanni, T. J. (1987). *The principalship.* Boston: Allyn & Bacon.

Sergiovanni, T. J. (1992). Why we should seek substitutes for leadership. *Educational Leadership, 49*(5), 41–45.

Shulman, L. (1987). Knowledge and teaching: Foundations of the new reform. *Harvard Educational Review, 57*(1), 1–22.

Singer, J. D. (1993). Are special educators' career paths special? Results from a 13-year longitudinal study. *Exceptional Children, 59*(3), 262–279.

Smylie, M. A. (1992). Teacher participation in school decision making: Assessing willingness to participate. *Educational Evaluation and Policy Analysis, 14*(1), 53–67.

Smylie, M. A., & Smart, J. C. (1990). Teacher support for career enhancement initiatives: Program characteristics and effects on work. *Educational Evaluation and Policy Analysis, 12*(2), 139–155.

Snyder, T. D., & Hoffman, C. M. (1993). *Digest of education statistics 1993.* Washington, DC: NCES, U.S. Department of Education.

Southern Regional Education Board (SREB). (1985). *Access to quality undergraduate education.* Atlanta: Author.

Stoddart, T. (1992). Los Angeles Unified School District intern program: Recruiting and preparing teachers for an urban context. *Peabody Journal of Education, 67*(3), 84–122.

U.S. Department of Labor. (1986). Current population survey, 1986–87. (Unpublished data). Washington, DC: Author.

Vance, V. S., & Schlechty, P. C. (1982a). The distribution of academic ability in the teaching force: Policy implications. *Phi Delta Kappan, 64*(1), 22–27.

Vance, V., & Schlechty, P. (1982b, February 25–27). *The structure of the teaching occupation and the characteristics of teachers: A sociological interpretation.* Paper presented at the NTE Conference at Airleigh House, Virginia.

Weiss, I. R. (1987). *Report of the 1985–86 national survey of science and mathematics education.* Raleigh, NC: Research Triangle Institute.

Wise, A. E., & Darling-Hammond, L. (1987). *Licensing teachers. Design for a teaching profession.* Santa Monica, CA: RAND Corporation.

Wise, A. E., Darling-Hammond, L., & Berry, B. (1987). *Effective teacher selection. From recruitment to retention.* Santa Monica, CA: RAND Corporation. (No. R-3462-NIE/CSTP)

Wright, D. P., McKibbon, M., & Walton, P. (1987). *The effectiveness of the teacher trainee program: An alternate route into teaching in California.* Sacramento: California Commission on Teacher Credentialing.

Yee, S. M. (1990). *Careers in the classroom: When teaching is more than a job.* New York: Teachers College Press.

· 6 ·

THE ROLE OF ATTITUDES AND BELIEFS IN LEARNING TO TEACH

Virginia Richardson

UNIVERSITY OF ARIZONA

Attitudes and beliefs are important concepts in understanding teachers' thought processes, classroom practices, change, and learning to teach. Although attitudes received considerable attention in teaching and teacher education research between the early 1950s and the early 1970s, teacher beliefs only recently gained prominence in the literature. Summaries of the research suggest that both attitudes and beliefs drive classroom actions and influence the teacher change process (Nespor, 1987; Pajares, 1992; Peck & Tucker, 1973; Richardson, 1994b). Teacher attitudes and beliefs, therefore, are important considerations in understanding classroom practices and conducting teacher education designed to help prospective and in-service teachers develop their thinking and practices. In such change programs, beliefs and attitudes of incoming preservice students and in-service teachers strongly affect what and how they learn and are also targets of change within the process.

This chapter examines two roles of beliefs and attitudes in the education of teachers: (1) as facets of individual preservice and in-service teachers that affect the way they process new information, react to the possibilities of change, and teach; and (2) as the focus of change in teacher education programs. Thus, this chapter examines the ways preservice students' and teachers' beliefs influence learning to teach and looks at teacher education programs that are designed to change beliefs and attitudes. This author would like to acknowledge several summaries of the research that precede this volume and that were helpful in developing the framework for this chapter. They include the learning to teach chapters of Borko and Putnam (in press), Carter (1990), and Feiman-Nemser (1983); the teacher thinking chapter by Clark and Peterson (1986); a chapter on the culture of teaching and its effects on learning to teach by Feiman-Nemser and Floden (1986); teacher beliefs summaries by Nespor (1987) and Pajares (1992); the socialization of teaching chapters by Brookhart and Freeman (1992) and Zeichner

and Gore (1990); and a chapter on teacher knowledge by Fenstermacher (1994a). These summaries and analyses of the literature suggest that although research on learning to teach is relatively new in the teaching and teacher education literature, it has spawned a growing body of sophisticated conceptual and empirical studies that are influencing thinking and practice in teacher education.

This chapter begins with a conceptual framework gleaned from current work on beliefs and learning to teach and from an analysis of the assumptions underlying the research. It includes definitions of beliefs and knowledge, as well as a discussion of the methodologies used in determining them. The framework section provides a way to interpret the findings of the research that are summarized in the subsequent section.

CONCEPTUAL FRAMEWORK

Attitudes and beliefs are a subset of a group of constructs that name, define, and describe the structure and content of mental states that are thought to drive a person's actions. Other constructs in this set include conceptions, perspectives, perceptions, orientations, theories, and stances. The heyday of studies that focused on teachers' attitudes occurred from the 1950s through the early 1970s. Whereas teacher attitudes are still examined from time to time, beliefs have taken over as a major construct of interest in studying teachers' ways of thinking and classroom practices. This shift from attitudes to beliefs is described next.

Attitudes

Following an examination of the various definitions of attitude, Allport (1967) developed his definition of attitude as "a mental and neural state of readiness, organized through experience, exerting directive or dynamic influence upon the individual's response to all objects and situations with which it is related" (p. 8). This sense of attitudes as predispositions that consistently affect actions strongly influenced teaching and teacher education research for a number of years.

Of particular interest in the study of teaching during the 1950s and 1960s were teachers' social attitudes toward students, other people and their cultures, learning, and the purposes of education. More particularly, a group of researchers interested in the development of democratic and integrated classrooms examined teacher attitudes that hinder or ensure this normative vision. The attitudes of interest in these studies were related to democratic and authoritarian attitudes (Rokeach, 1960), as well as attitudes toward other cultures and races. Peck and Tucker (1973) summarized a series of studies that examined the relationship among attitudes, personality factors, and classroom behaviors. Studies were conducted, for example, on how dogmatic versus open-minded student teachers and their cooperating teachers rated their classroom practices and whether the degree of dogmatism of the cooperating teacher affected dogmatism in the student teachers.

Other areas of interest included the attitudes and values of teachers who choose teaching as a career (summarized by Stern, 1963) and how attitudes affect teacher–student interactions (Brophy & Good, 1974). For example, Stern found that the various studies of incoming teacher education students indicated that they were "essentially cooperative, restrained, lacking in social boldness, friendly, anxious to please" (p. 417).

Shifts in research paradigms in both social psychology and educational psychology moved the study of attitudes in teaching and teacher education out of the limelight. The discipline of social psychology became more cognitively oriented, as represented by a separation of attitudes (affective) and beliefs (cognitive). For example, Rokeach's (1968) definition of attitudes included the concept of beliefs. An attitude set, he wrote, is "a relatively enduring organization of beliefs around an object or situation predisposing one to respond in some preferential manner" (p. 112). Fishbein (1967), however, narrowed the scope of the concept of attitude by separating it from beliefs. The notion that attitudes consist of three components—affective, cognitive, and conative (action)—led to conceptual confusion, he suggested, because the three components were not always correlated with each other in empirical studies of individual attitudes. To deal with this problem, Fishbein limited the term *attitude* to the affective component and designated the cognitive as beliefs about objects and the conative as beliefs about what should be done concerning the object. Attitudes, therefore, for Fishbein, became "learned predispositions to respond to an object or class of objects in a favorable or unfavorable way" (1967, p. 257).

The growing interest in cognition within the discipline of social psychology drew interest away from the affective (attitudes) and toward the cognitive (beliefs), although the difference between the two terms remained somewhat unclear in the empirical literature. For example, Harvey, Prather, White, and Hoffmeister (1968) studied teacher beliefs that varied in terms of concreteness and abstraction and examined the relationships of these beliefs to classroom atmosphere and student

behavior. However, in this study, beliefs, as constructs, resembled attitudes in other studies.

At the same time, behavior, rather than mental processes, reigned supreme in educational psychology. In the study of teaching, process-product studies dominated the literature (Brophy & Good, 1986), although teacher attitudes were often still considered as "presage" variables (Dunkin & Biddle, 1974). Even the study of attitudes took on a behavioral twist. Campbell (1967), for example, defined social attitudes as "consistency in response to social objects" (p. 175). Perhaps, though, the shift away from the study of attitudes and personality in research on teaching and teacher education could be attributed to an end in a cycle of findings, such that only a new way of looking at the concepts could reverse the trend. Getzels and Jackson (1963) described many of the findings in teacher attitudes research in the following manner:

The regrettable fact is that many of the studies so far have not produced significant results. Many others have produced only pedestrian results. For example, it is said after the usual inventory tabulation that good teachers are friendly, cheerful, sympathetic, and morally virtuous, rather than cruel, depressed, unsympathetic, and morally depraved. But when this has been said, not much that is especially useful has been revealed. (p. 579)

Beliefs

Anthropologists, social psychologists, and philosophers have contributed to an understanding of the nature of beliefs and their effects on actions. There is considerable congruence of definition among these three disciplines in that beliefs are thought of as psychologically held understandings, premises, or propositions about the world that are felt to be true. Goodenough (1963), for example, described beliefs as propositions that are held to be true and are "accepted as guides for assessing the future, are cited in support of decisions, or are referred to in passing judgment on the behavior of others" (p. 151). Eisenhart, Shrum, Harding, and Cuthbert (1988), however, added an element of attitude to Goodenough's definition: "a belief is a way to describe a relationship between a task, an action, an event, or another person and an attitude of a person toward it" (p. 53). Rokeach (1968) defined beliefs as heuristic propositions that may begin with the phrase "I believe that . . ." (p. ix). He was particularly interested in the structure of belief systems, which he believed were organized in a psychological but not necessarily logical form. He also wrote that some beliefs are more central than others and that central beliefs are more difficult to change.

Green's (1971) philosophical approach to a description of beliefs provided an understanding of how humans can hold incompatible or inconsistent beliefs. He suggested that people hold beliefs in clusters, and each cluster within a belief system may be protected from other clusters. In Green's formulation, there is little cross-fertilization among belief systems, and beliefs that are incompatible may be held in different clusters. As long as incompatible beliefs are never set side by side and examined for consistency, the incompatibility may remain.

Although there is considerable agreement across disciplines about the nature of beliefs, there are many other mentalist constructs that, if not synonymous with beliefs, are closely related. Pajares (1992) suggested that such concepts as attitudes, values, preconceptions, theories, and images are really beliefs in disguise. Yet, perhaps the most complex issue in current research on teaching and teacher education is the confusion between the terms *belief* and *knowledge*.

Beliefs and Knowledge In the traditional philosophical literature, knowledge depends on a "truth condition" that suggests that a proposition is agreed on as being true by a community of people (Green, 1971; Lehrer, 1990). Propositional knowledge has epistemic standing; that is, there is some evidence to back up the claim. Beliefs, however, do not require a truth condition. As Feiman-Nemser and Floden (1986) pointed out, "It does not follow that everything a teacher believes or is willing to act on merits the label 'knowledge'" (p. 515).

Such a differentiation between beliefs and knowledge is not evident in much of the teaching and teacher education literature. Fenstermacher (1994a) suggested that many scholars use the term knowledge as a grouping term. For example, Alexander, Schallert, and Hare (1991) described 26 terms that are used in the literature on literacy to denote different types of knowledge. They also equated beliefs and knowledge as follows: "*knowledge* encompasses all that a person knows or believes to be true, whether or not it is verified as true in some sort of objective or external way" (p. 317). Kagan (1990) also made the decision to use the terms beliefs and knowledge synonymously in her analysis of methodological issues inherent in studying teachers' knowledge. Her rationale for this formulation was that teachers' knowledge is subjective and, therefore, much like beliefs.

There is also considerable similarity between the terms knowledge and beliefs in the concept of teachers' personal practical knowledge. Practical knowledge, first explored in teaching practice by Elbaz (1983) and developed further by Clandinin and Connelly (1987), is an account of how a teacher knows or understands a classroom situation. Practical knowledge is gained through experience, is often tacit, and is contextual. This form of knowledge, however, is not synonymous with beliefs because it is thought of as embodied within the whole person, not just the mind (see also Hollingsworth, Dybdahl, & Minarik, 1993). Embodied knowledge is more than cognitive and relates to the way in which people physically interact with the environment (Johnson, 1987). It is this knowledge that Yinger (1987; Yinger & Villar, 1986) suggested is used by the teacher in an improvisational manner in the classroom. Yinger stated that this knowledge may be inseparable from a particular classroom action, a view that is similar to Schön's (1983) notion of knowledge-in-action. As Carter (1990) pointed out, this conception of understanding or personal knowledge does not separate the knower from the known. It is personalized, idiosyncratic, and contextual and, for Yinger (1987), emerges during action.

The term *belief,* as used in this chapter, is derived from Green (1971) and describes a proposition that is accepted as true by the individual holding the belief. It is a psychological concept and differs from knowledge, which implies epistemic warrant. However, many other terms that are close in meaning to beliefs are used in the teacher education literature. In these

cases, this author refers to the concepts in the same way as the authors. Thus, this chapter includes the terms *attitudes, beliefs, conceptions, theories, understandings, practical knowledge,* and *values* as used by the particular author whose work is being described.

Relationship Between Beliefs and Action

Conceptions of the relationship between teacher beliefs and teaching practice are related, in part, to the goals of the researchers. As Doyle (1990) pointed out, studies conducted until quite recently were meant to lead to predictions and to research findings that could be used for such decisions as entrance into the teaching profession. There was a clear sense in this research of cause (attitudes) and effect (classroom behaviors). The attitudes and personality factors thought to cause certain classroom behaviors were relatively stable and difficult to change and, therefore, were considered to be valid indicators of the future effectiveness of a teacher. There were also experimental studies that tested teacher education programs designed to change dysfunctional attitudes.

More recently, studies conducted within the hermeneutic tradition suggest a complex relationship between teachers' beliefs and actions. In fact, the concept of "relationship" is sometimes viewed with disfavor because the separation of thinking and action, although useful for research and analysis, may make little sense in practice. The purpose of these studies is to conduct research that leads to understandings of the complexities of the contexts of teaching and of teachers' thinking processes and actions within those contexts. An understanding of a teacher's practices is enhanced by research attention to both beliefs and actions through interview and observation. Furthermore, such attention may contribute to change in beliefs and practices, particularly if the research is conducted in a collaborative manner. Yet, these understandings are quite person and context specific; therefore, the number of individual case studies has increased dramatically in the literature.

In most current conceptions, the perceived relationship between beliefs and actions is interactive. Beliefs are thought to drive actions; however, experiences and reflection on action may lead to changes in and/or additions to beliefs. Examples of these complex interrelationships may be found in research dating from the 1970s. One of the first large-scale studies of teachers' beliefs in the modern hermeneutic tradition was conducted by Bussis, Chittenden, and Amarel (1976) who examined teachers' personal constructs of the curriculum and children. These personal constructions, they suggested, result from an individual's interpretation of the world, and they "are forerunners of action" (p. 17). Significant teacher change can only occur, they concluded, if teachers are engaged in "personal exploration, experimentation, and reflection" (p. 17). For Clandinin (1986), a teacher's experiences lead to the formation of images that are a part of personal practical knowledge; these, in turn, are elements of classroom practices such as routines and rhythms. "Teachers' practices [are] the embodiment and enactment of their personal practical knowledge . . . of which imagery is a part" (p. 36). Cochran-Smith and Lytle (1990) suggested that teachers' theories are "sets of interrelated conceptual frameworks grounded in practice" (p. 7). Whereas many researchers separate beliefs and actions for purposes of conducting research, they understand that these constructs operate together in praxis, defined by Schubert (1991) as "a union of theory and practice in reflective action" (p. 214).

Why Beliefs Are Important in Learning to Teach

Beliefs are thought to have two functions in learning to teach. The first relates to the constructivist theories of learning that suggest that students bring beliefs to a teacher education program that strongly influence what and how they learn. The second function relates to beliefs as the focus of change in the process of education.

Current cognitive theories view learning as an active and constructive process that is strongly influenced by an individual's existing understandings, beliefs, and preconceptions (Resnick, 1989). Existing knowledge and beliefs play a strong role in shaping what students learn and how they learn it.

Constructivist theories have also been used to understand the learning to teach process (see summary in Borko & Putnam, in press). For example, students come to teacher education programs with strong theories of teaching acquired during many years of being a student (Brookhart & Freeman, 1992). These theories have been shown to influence the way students approach teacher education and what they learn from it (e.g., Calderhead & Robson, 1991). In addition, the beliefs that practicing teachers hold about subject matter, learning, and teaching influence the way they approach staff development, what they learn from it, and how they change (Richardson, 1994b). These studies are described later in this chapter in the section "Findings."

Beliefs are also the focus for instruction. Green (1971), for example, suggested that teaching is concerned with the formation of beliefs, and one goal of teaching is to help students form belief systems that consist of a large proportion of beliefs based on evidence and reason.

Teaching has to do, in part at least, with the formation of beliefs, and that means that it has to do not simply with *what* we shall believe, but with *how* we shall believe it. Teaching is an activity which has to do, among other things, with the modification and formation of belief systems. (p. 48)

Teachers, Green submitted, should also help students minimize belief clusters and promote cross-fertilization among the clusters.

This concept of the purpose of education was extended to teaching and teacher education by Fenstermacher (1979). Fenstermacher argued that one goal of teacher education is to help teachers transform tacit or unexamined beliefs about teaching, learning, and the curriculum into objectively reasonable or evidentiary beliefs. The process by which this can happen is to help preservice and in-service students identify and assess their beliefs in relation to their classroom actions (Fenstermacher, 1994b).

A number of studies have examined preservice and in-service education programs that focus, in part, on the participants' beliefs (Richardson, 1994a). Evidence from these studies indicate that many of these programs have been successful in

changing teachers' beliefs, although in-service programs appear to be more successful than preservice. These studies are also described in the "Findings" section later in this chapter.

Where Do Teachers' Beliefs Come From?

In the literature on learning to teach, three categories of experience are described as influencing the development of beliefs and knowledge about teaching. These categories may not be mutually exclusive and, in fact, may be studied together, as is the case with many teacher biography and life history studies (Ball & Goodson, 1985; Bullough & Baughman, 1993; Crow, 1987; Goodson, 1992; Knowles, 1992; Woods, 1984). The three forms of experience begin at different stages of the individual's educational career. They are personal experience, experience with schooling and instruction, and experience with formal knowledge.

Personal Experience Personal experience includes aspects of life that go into the formation of world view; intellectual and virtuous dispositions; beliefs about self in relation to others; understandings of the relationship of schooling to society; and other forms of personal, familial, and cultural understandings. Ethnic and socioeconomic background, gender, geographic location, religious upbringing, and life decisions may all affect an individual's beliefs that, in turn, affect learning to teach and teaching.

A growing literature examines the relationship between personal experiences and how one approaches teaching. These are generally case studies of individual teachers. For example, in developing the theory of personal practical knowledge, Clandinin (1986) suggested that personal experience is encoded in images that affect practice. Images have moral, emotional, personal, private, and professional dimensions. Clandinin and Connelly (1991) wrote a case study of an elementary school principal, Phil Bingham, with whom they worked in constructing and reconstructing his narrative to understand his personal practical knowledge and actions as a principal. An important image in Bingham's narrative was community, which was developed from his experiences of growing up in a tightly knit community on Toronto Island. This image of community affected his approach to the involvement of the community in his school. Another example is Bullough and Knowles' (1991) case study of a beginning teacher, Barbara, whose initial metaphor for teaching—teaching as nurturing—was thought to come from years of parenting.

Experience with Schooling and Instruction Lortie's (1975) discussion of the apprenticeship of experience suggests that students arrive in preservice teacher education with a set of deep-seated beliefs about the nature of teaching based on their own experiences as students. It is speculated that these strong beliefs, in combination with the salience of the real world of teaching practice, create conditions that make it difficult for preservice teacher education to have an impact.

A number of studies have examined beliefs acquired from such experiences and how these beliefs affect teachers' conceptions of their role as teacher. In a study of teachers' theories of children's learning, for example, Anning (1988) concluded that the theories about children's learning held by the six teachers in her study were determined "by their own particular previous experiences of teaching and learning in their classrooms" (p. 131). Britzman's (1991) case studies of two student teachers indicated that they held powerful conceptions of the role of teachers, both positive and negative, gained from observing teaching models. Britzman suggested that these conceptions profoundly affected the student teachers' classroom behaviors.

Life history studies often conclude that combinations of the first two types of experience—personal and schooling—strongly affect preservice education students' and in-service teachers' beliefs. For example, Knowles (1992) conducted case studies of five preservice secondary teachers and found that family influences and previous teachers had influenced all five students' conceptions of the teacher role. Most researchers involved in life history and socialization research also agree that the experiential effects of personal life, previous schooling, and student teaching are more powerful in building conceptions of teaching than the formal pedagogical education received in teacher education programs (Brousseau, Book, & Byers, 1988; Feiman-Nemser, 1983).

Experience with Formal Knowledge Formal knowledge, as used here, is understandings that have been agreed on within a community of scholars as worthwhile and valid. When students enter kindergarten, and often before, depending on the nature of family and community life, they experience formal knowledge in their school subjects, outside readings, television, religion classes, and so forth. Of particular interest in the consideration of learning to teach is knowledge of subject matter, conceptions or beliefs about the nature of subject matter and how students learn it, and experiences with formal pedagogical knowledge that usually begin in preservice teacher education programs.

School Subjects. In an attempt to understand teachers' classroom actions, researchers have recently examined the form and structure of subject matter in the minds of preservice students and in-service teachers. Leinhardt (1988), for example, investigated a teacher's experiences with math texts as a student and as a teacher and how these experiences contributed to her beliefs and understandings of the nature of mathematics and affected her classroom instruction. John (1991) followed five British students through their student teaching to determine how their perspectives on planning changed with experience. He found differences between the math and geography teachers in terms of how they viewed planning. The math student teachers' concepts of their subject had a strong impact on their formation of ideas about planning, whereas the geography student teachers had little overall conception of their subject matter, which, therefore, had little effect on their planning.

John's (1991) geography example seems the more likely scenario for teachers of many school subjects in American schools. Summarizing the longitudinal Teacher Education and Learning to Teach (TELT) study conducted by researchers at Michigan State University, McDiarmid (in press) concluded "Elementary and high school teachers frequently lack connected, conceptual understandings of the subject matters they are expected to teach" (p. 1). Furthermore, teachers have few opportunities, even in college or in teacher education programs, to develop that connected understanding of their subject matter.

Knowledge of subject matter, in combination with understandings of how students learn the subject matter, combines to form what is called pedagogical content knowledge (Shulman, 1987). A number of case studies have examined this form of knowledge in teachers and its effects on classroom teaching (e.g., Grossman, 1990; Gudmundsdottir, 1991; Munby & Russell, 1992; Wilson & Wineburg, 1988).

Pedagogical Knowledge. Another type of formal knowledge that teachers experience is pedagogical knowledge, most often initially encountered in preservice teacher education courses taken prior to student teaching. Pedagogical knowledge relates to the practice of teaching and includes such topics as classroom management, models of teaching, and classroom environment. As mentioned earlier, experiences with formal pedagogical knowledge are seen as the least powerful factor affecting beliefs and conceptions of teaching and the teacher role. This does not mean, however, that the influence is negligible. Several sets of case studies examined the nature of pedagogical content knowledge and teaching actions on the part of subject matter specialists who have and have not experienced formal pedagogical knowledge (Grossman, 1990; Grossman & Richert, 1988). These studies indicate considerable differences between pedagogically and nonpedagogically educated teachers in terms of their pedagogical content knowledge and classroom actions. Clift (1987) found significant differences in the beliefs about teaching and learning between English majors not interested in teaching and English majors who had completed their student teaching in a certification program. The English majors saw the teacher as the authority on the interpretation of literature, whereas the future teachers were much more constructivist.

Crow (1987) conducted a case study of the formation of teacher role identity of preservice teachers. Using a life history approach, she found that models of former teachers and early childhood family experiences strongly influence teacher role identity; however, she also concluded that although there was no evidence of the influence of formal pedagogical knowledge in the first several months of teaching practice, there may be a "lag time" at which point the cognitive changes that took place during formal pedagogical training find their way into teaching practice (Crow, 1988). Featherstone (1993) also suggested that there may be a "sleeper effect" of teacher education. "The voices of teacher educators sometimes echo forward into these first years of teaching; the novice sometimes rehears, with a new ear, propositions which seemed to make little impact on them at the time they were offered" (p. 110).

Summary Studies of the origins of teachers' beliefs indicate that many different life experiences contribute to the formation of strong and enduring beliefs about teaching and learning. Within a constructivist learning and teaching framework, these beliefs should be surfaced and acknowledged during the teacher education program if the program is to make a difference in the deep structure of knowledge and beliefs held by the students.

Methodology for Examining Attitudes and Beliefs

The measurement of attitudes and beliefs in teaching and teacher education have undergone considerable change, which reflects the paradigmatic shift from positivist research strategies to a more hermeneutic approach (Doyle, 1990). The teacher-attitude research of the mid-century attempted to develop predictive understandings of the relationships between teacher attitudes and behaviors so that attitude inventories could be used in the selection of teachers. Most of this research was large scale and employed paper-and-pencil, multiple-choice attitude surveys. More recent research on teacher beliefs reflects a shift toward qualitative methodology and the attempt to understand how teachers make sense of the classroom. Interviews and observations are the two most widely employed data-gathering techniques in this research.

The Minnesota Teacher Attitude Inventory (MTAI), a popular and representative measure of teacher attitudes, was used in many studies of preservice education students and in-service teachers (see Khan & Weiss, 1973). The MTAI, a Likert scale, was designed to differentiate among teachers in terms of their relationships with students. The major attitude factors that were thought to distinguish between good and bad teachers were understanding, democratic values versus harsh authoritarian values, and progressive versus traditional orientations. The form of measurement and the research questions of interest led to large-scale correlational studies that examined differences in attitudes between elementary and secondary students and teachers and between males and females. Semi-experimental studies, using various Likert attitude measures also examined the effects of student teaching and other teacher education activities on education students' attitudes.

The purposes of a number of measures were disguised for the subjects who were not aware that attitudes were being measured. An example is the Thematic Apperception Test in which the subject writes (or talks) about an interpretation of pictures representing ambiguous scenes. These measures were summarized by Campbell (1967) but were not used as much in the teaching and teacher education literature as were the various attitude inventories.

For a number of years, beliefs were also measured by multiple-choice tests. For example, Wehling and Charters (1969), who defined attitudes as a complex organization of beliefs, developed a set of questionnaires of teacher beliefs. They then used factor analytic techniques to identify dimensions thought to characterize teachers' attitudes.

Current thinking in the measurement of teachers' beliefs is that multiple-choice measures are too constraining. Multiple-choice tests of beliefs are derived from the scholarly literature and are predetermined by the researcher. These theories may not map on to teachers' beliefs (Hoffman & Kugle, 1982). For example, Schmidt and Kennedy (1990) found that experienced teachers' theories are highly eclectic. An individual teacher can hold beliefs that are at both ends of a particular scholarly educational controversy. Pinnegar and Carter (1990) found that teachers' theories of learning did not match learning theories as explicated in three current educational psychology texts. Furthermore, teachers' beliefs combine elements that are considered separately in the scholarly literature. Duffy (1981) and

O'Brien and Norton (1991), for example, found that teachers' theories of reading were often conjoined with theories of classroom management. Thus, predetermined beliefs that are included in multiple-choice measures often do not validly represent teachers' beliefs.

More recently, qualitative methodologies, many borrowed from anthropology, have been used to examine teachers' beliefs inductively. Although several researchers advocate the determination of beliefs through observation alone (Thompson, 1992), most researchers use interviews in combination with observations. The goal of these studies is not to develop predictive indicators of teacher effectiveness but to understand the nature of teachers' thinking and world view. More structured approaches, such as the Kelly Repertory Grid (KRG) (Kelly, 1955) and the Heuristic Elicitation Methodology (HEM) (Steffle, Reich, & McClaran, 1971) have been used in studies with large numbers of teacher education students or teachers. For example, Corporaal (1991) examined teachers' conceptions of "good teaching" using the KRG technique, and Eisenhart et al. (1988) employed the HEM technique in their study of preservice student teachers' beliefs about teaching.

Less structured approaches involve extensive interviewing and/or practical arguments with individual teachers and students in which beliefs are determined from the transcription of the interviews (see, e.g., Richardson, Anders, Tidwell, & Lloyd, 1991). Elicitation of metaphors has also been used to determine teacher beliefs (e.g., Munby, 1986; Russell, Munby, Spafford, & Johnston, 1988; Tobin & Jakubowski, 1990), as well as narrative semiotic analyses (Kagan, 1991) and concept maps in which students and/or researchers develop diagrams of student thinking on a particular topic (Morine-Dershimer, 1989; Tochon, 1990). Kagan (1990) summarized and critiqued many of these procedures and concluded that multiple measures should be used in determining teachers' cognitions.

A significant trend in hermeneutic studies of teachers' beliefs is the use of the data for purposes of teacher change as well as research. Bullough (1993), for example, used journals and portfolios to learn about preservice teacher development at the same time as the tasks of writing these materials contributed to beginning teacher development. In the Reading Instruction Study, Anders and Richardson (1991) conducted belief interviews with teachers who were participating in staff development on the teaching of reading comprehension. During the first session, Anders and Richardson, who were the staff developers and researchers, presented the teachers with transcriptions of their interviews with their empirical premises highlighted. Many of the teachers later acknowledged that the interview, in combination with reading the transcription, significantly affected their approach to reflection and change. These and other trends in this area of research have led to the need to reconceptualize the nature of research and practice and to develop new understandings of warrantableness in the findings of such research. These issues are addressed in the conclusion on this chapter.

FINDINGS

This section summarizes the findings of the studies on teachers' beliefs and attitudes, beginning with a description of the beliefs of students who are entering their preservice programs. Studies examining the influence of beliefs on learning to teach are then reviewed, followed by descriptions of studies examining the effects of certification and staff development programs on pre-service students' and in-service teachers' beliefs and practices.

Attitudes and Beliefs of Entering Preservice Students

A common thread throughout the research on the attitudes and values of entering preservice students is the finding that these students exhibit optimism and confidence, public service orientation, and a general belief that experience is the best teacher. These results are consistent across time (1950s to mid-1990s), methodology (large-scale attitude survey or qualitative case study), and nations. Whereas some of the studies have examined the beliefs and attitudes of preservice students in general, others have explored differences among identifiable groups of students.

Entering Attitudes and Beliefs The possibility of engaging in public service and helping children are strong motivators for entering preservice students (Book & Freeman, 1986; Pigge & Marso, 1988). This finding has been replicated in other countries such as Malaysia (Kam, 1990) and Israel (Ben-Peretz, 1990). Extrinsic rewards, such as salary, play a much smaller role in the decision to enter teaching and in the motivation to improve teaching practice (Mitchell, Ortiz, & Mitchell, 1987).

Preservice students' philosophies of teaching are loosely formulated (Buchmann & Schwille, 1983). For example, in a study of prospective teachers' perceptions about ethnicity and gender, Avery and Walker (1993) found that the students' explanations for gender and ethnic differences in achievement were simplistic in nature. In fact, as described in the results of the TELT research program, preservice students believe that categorical differences among students—ethnicity, gender, and class—do not make a difference in teaching; however, they believe that students' personalities do affect teaching (National Center for Research on Teacher Education, 1991). In fact, Gomez and Tabachnick (1992) suggested that the views of the prospective teachers in their sample toward minority children and children from low-income families would limit the children's opportunities to learn and prosper from schooling. This view of ethnicity, class, and learning may relate to the preservice students' limited background. Surveys of teacher education faculty suggest that preservice students have had little contact with minorities, are parochial, and have not experienced other cultures (Zimpher & Ashburn, 1992).

Entering students hold strong images of teachers, both negative and positive, and these images strongly influence how they approach their teacher education program (Britzman, 1991; Calderhead & Robson, 1991). These students are, by and large, highly confident of their own abilities as teachers (Book & Freeman, 1986); in fact, Weinstein (1988, 1989) suggested that they are "unrealistically optimistic." They believe that there is not much they can learn in preservice teacher education except during their student teaching experiences (Book, Byers, & Freeman, 1983), and they hold strong beliefs that learning to teach can only be accomplished through experience (Richardson-Koehler, 1988).

The conceptions of schooling held by entering students are that the teacher hands knowledge to students and learning involves memorizing the content of the curriculum (Black & Ammon, 1992; McDiarmid, 1990). Conceptions of the content of the curriculum reflect a positivistic view as described in Erickson and MacKinnon's (1991) study of secondary science teachers and by Civil's (1993) study of elementary preservice students in her mathematics course. This conception suggests that one correct answer exists for every question and that the teacher's responsibility is to get all students to learn the propositions presented to them or develop strategies for obtaining the correct answers. Entering preservice students often believe that some elementary and secondary students are not capable of learning basic skills in reading and math (Brousseau & Freeman, 1988).

Entering Beliefs by Categories of Students A number of studies have examined differences in preservice students' beliefs depending on whether they are elementary or secondary majors, male or female, and traditional or nontraditional students. Book and Freeman (1986), for example, found that elementary preservice students were more child-oriented than secondary majors who were more interested in their subject-matter content (see, also, Kile, 1993; Newfeld, 1974). Elementary preservice majors were more tolerant toward behavior problems in students than secondary majors (Khan & Weiss, 1973), and, in a study of preservice students in Israel, secondary majors were higher in self-concept than elementary majors (Ben-Peretz, 1990). Silverman and Creswell (1982) found differences in cognitive developmental level between elementary and secondary majors in terms of their preferences for mathematical consistency in a mathematics system. They found that elementary and secondary majors exhibited different cognitive levels of development in mathematics and that elementary majors were more anxious about the subject. In Avery and Walker's (1993) study of teachers' beliefs about ethnic and gender differences in achievement, secondary majors located the rationale for differences in a broader societal context and their explanations were more complex than those of elementary majors.

Differences in entering beliefs by gender seem fewer in the literature than those between elementary and secondary majors, although there is a correlation between level of schooling and gender—a higher percentage of females teach at the elementary than at the secondary level. In their summary of the literature on teachers' attitudes, Khan and Weiss (1973) concluded that elementary and female teachers held more positive attitudes toward students than secondary and male teachers. Book and Freeman (1986) found males more likely than females to state that they selected teaching as a career because they had been unsuccessful in their first academic major.

A relatively new interest in research on initial conceptions involves nontraditional students—those students who have had a gap in their formal educational studies, either from having pursued another career or homemaking. Powell and Birrell (1992) found that many of the nontraditional students in their study were parents who framed their conceptions of teaching around their experiences with their own children. Whereas traditional students stated that their conceptions of teaching were related strongly to former schooling experiences, nontraditional students' conceptions were grounded in their former work experiences. Kile (1993) examined differences in conceptions and beliefs of a group of 22 elementary and secondary majors who also varied in terms of traditional and nontraditional status. He found differences in traditional and nontraditional students' beliefs about teaching and learning as they entered the program. Nontraditional students appeared to understand the complexities of teaching and learning more than the traditional students. For example, traditional students believed that they could determine whether or not students were learning from their classroom behavior; in their view if the students looked like they were enjoying the activity, they were learning what the teachers wanted them to learn. Nontraditional students believed that student learning could only be determined through an examination of student work. As compared to nontraditional students, traditional students were surprised at the academic diversity in classrooms and did not indicate a need to adapt instruction and materials for different students.

A strand of the research on differences in traditional and nontraditional students focuses on second-career teachers. Crow, Levine, and Nager (1990), for example, studied 13 students who were switching careers and entering a teacher certification program. They found that these students could be divided into three groups in terms of their motivation to switch careers and their approaches to transitions. The first group, homemakers, were people who had always dreamed of becoming teachers but had ended up doing something else. The second group was the converted who had successful careers but entered teaching because of a major life change such as the birth of a child. The third group, the unconverted, were those who had achieved high status in their previous occupation but became dissatisfied with an element of it and expressed a vague interest in education. The first two categories of students successfully negotiated the transition into teaching, but the third group did not. Novak and Knowles (1992), whose sample of preservice students pursuing their second career resembled Crow, Levine, and Nager's (1990) second variety, the converted, found that their past occupational experiences strongly affected their beliefs about teaching and learning.

These studies suggest that the beliefs about teaching and learning that preservice students bring with them to teacher education programs are powerful and relate to their previous life and schooling experiences. They also suggest, as have Brookhart and Freeman (1992), that entering candidates should not be considered as an undifferentiated group, but that attention should be paid to individual and group differences in conceptions and developmental levels. The most powerful group differences appear to be those between traditional and nontraditional students and between elementary and secondary majors.

Influence of Beliefs in Learning to Teach and Teaching

Although knowledge of entering teacher education students' beliefs is interesting, it becomes useful to the teacher education process only through an understanding of the relationship between these beliefs and learning to teach. A number of studies,

conducted at both the preservice and in-service levels, have explored the role of teachers' beliefs in learning to teach and classroom practice. These studies point to the importance of understanding students' and teachers' beliefs when engaging with them in a change process.

Preservice Teachers Many current studies of the relationship between preservice students' beliefs and learning to teach take place within programs that attempt to advance reflection and constructivist philosophies. For example, in a study that investigated preservice students' entering perspectives and their learning-to-teach processes, Ross and colleagues (Ross, Johnson, & Smith, 1991) examined students' perspectives and learning in their PROTEACH teacher education program at the University of Florida, which is designed to prepare teachers as reflective practitioners. They found a number of factors that influence how and what their students learned in the preservice program, but the most important were the students' entering perspectives on learning and teaching.

Holt-Reynolds (1992) provided an example of the effects of entering preservice students' beliefs on the processing of the material presented in a content-area reading course. In an interview with nine students, she found that they brought with them beliefs about teaching and learning derived through their life experiences. These beliefs contradicted the constructivist approaches that were being promoted by the professor, reducing the students' receptiveness to the professor's ideas. MacKinnon and Erickson (1992) also found that the positivist views of scientific knowledge held by a student teacher, Rosie, led to her strong verbal domination of the classroom. She had great difficulty understanding her constructivist-oriented cooperating teacher's critique of her teaching.

Hollingsworth (1989) examined the entering beliefs of 14 preservice students in a program designed to develop a constructivist perspective on teaching and learning. A number of the students held strong beliefs that the role of the teacher is to hand knowledge to students in a direct instruction manner. At the end of the program, although all students believed that students construct meaning, some held this belief in much greater depth than others.

In a study of student teachers within a teacher education program that encourages reflective teaching, Korthagen (1988) found that the student teachers varied in terms of their learning orientations from those who learn within an internal orientation (reflection) to those who have an external orientation (just tell me what I should do). These orientations, Korthagen suggested, may relate to their beliefs and implicit theories about how students learn. Many students, whose approaches were not reflective and therefore not in tune with the orientations represented in the program, dropped out after 1 year, suggesting to Korthagen that teacher educators should understand both their students' learning orientations and those of the program.

Crow, Levine, and Nager (1990) also found a group of students in their career changers sample who tended to grow less interested in teaching as the program progressed. Their third category of career-changing students, the unconverted, maintained business values and beliefs during preservice training. They were product oriented and were not happy with a group orientation.

Several studies have examined the images of self held by student teachers and the effect of these images on learning to teach, particularly during the student teaching experience. In a collaborative case study of two student teachers, Clift, Meng, and Eggerding (1994) found that one student teacher's image of self as a superior student interfered in her communication with the cooperating teacher. In a study of 27 student teachers, Calderhead (1988) found that they learned very different things from their teaching experience depending, in part, on their conceptions of professional learning and their own roles as student teachers.

Practicing Teachers Learning to teach at the in-service level involves the development of what has been called practical knowledge, which is gained through experience and is often tacit (Fenstermacher, 1994). Several recent longitudinal studies examined the learning-to-teach process to explicate how practical knowledge is acquired. Prior to a discussion of these studies, however, a foundational premise in the argument that beliefs are important in the learning-to-teach process needs to be addressed. This premise suggests a relationship between beliefs and practices.

Grossman, Wilson, and Shulman (1989) suggested that "teachers' beliefs about the subject matter, including orientation toward the subject matter, contribute to the ways in which teachers think about their subject matter and the choices they make in their teaching" (p. 27), an idea born out in a growing number of studies. For example, in an exploration of teacher beliefs and practices in reading comprehension, Richardson and colleagues (1991) were able to predict how a sample of teachers taught reading comprehension on the basis of analyses of extensive interviews of the teachers' beliefs about teaching and learning. Peterson, Fennema, Carpenter, and Loef (1989) found that teachers with a more cognitive perspective taught mathematics differently than those with a less cognitive perspective. The former taught more word problems, and their students did better on achievement tests than the latter group of teachers. Wilson and Wineburg (1988) studied four history teachers and found that their subject-matter knowledge and beliefs about the nature of history strongly affected their teaching of the subject.

An understanding of the relationship between beliefs and learning to teach, however, would be enhanced by longitudinal studies of teachers who move from preservice teacher education into teaching practice. Hugh Munby and Tom Russell at Queens University in Ontario, Canada, have conducted a number of these studies. In a chapter that summarizes some of the studies, Russell (1988) described the development of teachers' knowledge through an examination of their metaphors (see, also, Munby, 1986, 1987). Russell concluded that "the image one holds of the relationship between theory and practice can significantly influence understanding of the personal learning process at every stage in one's development of the professional knowledge of teaching" (1988, p. 15). Munby and Russell (1992) also examined how conceptions of subject matter affect learning to teach in the early years of teaching. They concluded that learning by experience involves the development of new frames (Schön, 1983) and that some students are more predisposed than others to reframe their conceptions of practice.

Changes in Beliefs and Attitudes

Since the mid-1980s, research on teaching and teacher education has shifted from a focus on teacher behaviors and skills to an emphasis on teacher thought processes. In fact, an examination of the goals of teacher education as well as national standards programs (e.g., Interstate New Teacher Assessment and Support Consortium [INTASC], 1993) reveals a considerable de-emphasis of skills and behaviors in favor of an emphasis on the formation or transformation of teacher thinking and reflective processes, dispositions, knowledge, and beliefs. This has led to numerous studies that examine changes in beliefs at the preservice and in-service levels, both as a natural process that accompanies the acquisition of teaching experience or as an outcome of systematic teacher education programs.

Perhaps the greatest controversy in the teacher change literature relates to the difficulty in changing beliefs and practices. For some scholars, beliefs are thought to be extremely difficult, if not impossible, to change. This apparent difficulty is often used as an explanation of the sense that teachers are recalcitrant and do not like to change. Another group of scholars and educators, however, are optimistic that teachers and teacher education students can change and, in fact, often do change their beliefs and practices, and that programs can help them do so in significant and worthwhile directions.

The following studies are grouped into two categories: (1) those that examine changes in belief and attitude as a general outcome of socialization and teaching experience, and (2) those that examine changes in belief as an outcome of specific teacher education or staff development programs.

Changes in Beliefs Through Socialization and Experience Much of the work on socialization has focused on student teachers because this period represents the transition from formal pedagogical education into teaching. Of considerable concern to teacher educators is student teachers' change in attitude concerning the role of the teacher vis-à-vis the students. The change in attitude involves what Hoy (1967) described as moving from the humanistic view often stressed in teacher education programs to becoming more custodial or seeing students less as friends and individuals and more as students to be controlled by the authoritarian teacher. Cochran-Smith (1991) suggested two rationales for the findings that student teachers become less humanistic and more custodial. One suggests that student teachers are affected by the conservative press of schooling, and the second is related to the students' years of experience in schools that powerfully affect their beliefs. Although they may express humanistic views in their formal pedagogical classes as the university, when the student teachers move into the classroom, their preexisting beliefs prevail. Thus, the formal teacher education program does little to affect the beliefs that they bring to the program.

Hoy and Woolfolk (1990) reexamined Hoy's (1967) findings by comparing changes in the pupil control ideology of student teachers with those who were taking a beginning educational psychology course. They found, again, that the custodial ideology increased for those students during student teaching. The authors attribute the changes in ideology to socialization within the context of schooling. Tabachnick and Zeichner (1984), however, suggested that student teachers may be able to resist changing their perspectives to become more custodial if the teacher preparation programs they attend are inquiry oriented and their cooperating teachers' perspectives are humanistic.

Brousseau, Book, and Byers (1988) examined the beliefs of teachers related to the culture of the school among four groups of teachers differing in classroom experience. They found that the more experienced teachers were likely to believe that their students were trustworthy. This suggests that although student teachers become more custodial, over time and with experience they eventually become less custodial. Yet, they also found that over time experienced teachers' sense of efficacy decreased.

Experience in the classroom also is thought to shape beliefs and practical knowledge; in fact, a teacher may only acquire practical knowledge through classroom experience (Carter, 1990; Fenstermacher, 1994). Black and Ammon (1992), for example, posited a developmental stage theory of conceptions concerning the nature of learning that develops with classroom experience. Through experience, teachers move from behaviorist conceptions toward more constructivist conceptions that are differentiated and integrated. John (1991) examined the perspectives on planning of five student teachers and how these changed with experience in the classroom. The changes were quite idiosyncratic and related to the initial beliefs that the students brought into their teacher education program.

Bullough, Knowles, and Crow (1992) also suggested that teachers' personal identities, as examined through their metaphors, develop and change with teaching experience. Their longitudinal study of a teacher, Kerrie, revealed that she initially thought of teaching metaphorically, as teacher, as mother; later, she developed a sense of teaching nonmetaphorically, as its own particular role (Bullough & Knowles, 1991). Bullough and Baughman (1993) concluded that Kerrie's new beliefs "grew out of her life experience generally and her teaching experience specifically" (p. 93).

Changes Attributed to Teacher Education Programs Some of the more exciting work in this field is research that assesses the effects of preservice and in-service teacher education and staff development programs on preservice students' and in-service teachers' beliefs. The results are complex. Some programs effect change and others do not; some programs affect certain types of students and not others; and some beliefs are more difficult to change than others. An analysis of this work begins to provide an understanding of programs that seem to effect positive change, as well as provide an understanding of the types of students who are affected.

PRESERVICE. A number of studies have examined conceptual change and changes in beliefs in preservice teacher education students. Hollingsworth (1989) explored changes in conceptions of learning within a constructivist preservice teacher education program. She found that student teachers' initial beliefs affected the changes in beliefs that occurred during the program and that students who were able to confront their beliefs developed deeper knowledge. Belief confrontation was aided by placing student teachers in classrooms in which the cooperating teachers held contrasting viewpoints. Feiman-Nemser, McDiarmid, Melnick, and Parker (1989) examined conceptual change

in 91 students enrolled in an introductory course designed to help students examine conceptions of teaching and learning. They found that the students' conceptions changed in four areas.

1. The nature of teaching was more complex than they had initially thought it to be.
2. They began to realize that there is a relationship between teaching and learning.
3. They became aware of the school and classroom contexts of teaching.
4. Their views of the nature of teacher knowledge expanded considerably.

In many cases, the studies indicate that some students change and others do not, or that they change in different ways. Morine-Dershimer (1989), for example, used concept maps to assess eight students' changes in concepts in a course in which they practiced models of teaching. She found that the students changed their conceptions of both planning and content and found differences in undergraduate seniors and graduate students. The undergraduates used their concept maps to look back at the lessons they had taught, and the graduate students looked to future possibilities. Richardson and Kile (1992) also looked at differences in changes in beliefs of traditional and nontraditional students enrolled in a beginning teacher education course in which students analyzed videocases three times during the semester. They found that the students' theories of learning shifted from traditional (teacher as knowledge giver and student as passive recipient) to a more open, active theory of learning. In a content analysis of the written work, they found that the nontraditional students' initial orientations to the videocases were focused on the teachers, and the traditional students were concerned with the students (see, also, Serow, Eaker, & Forrest, 1994). However, by the end of the class, the traditional students' orientations toward the teacher resembled those of the nontraditional students. Ben-Peretz (1990) summarized research conducted in Israel that suggested that more dogmatic students do not change toward a more progressive orientation to education, whereas the less dogmatic students do.

Korthagen (1988) found that students who came to a reflective teacher education program with a reflective orientation did well in the program. Those who did not have a reflective orientation either dropped out or changed orientations. Korthagen, however, warned that the changes measured in such studies may be at a surface level; these students may "simulate learning behaviour (*quasi-adaption* to the conceptions of learning of the educators)" (p. 48). Bolin (1990) also found that not all students benefit from a reflective teacher education program. In his case study of a student teacher, Bolin found that the student teacher did not become reflective, rather he seemed to resist developing reflective capacities. In fact, Tickle (1991) conducted research that suggests that novice teachers do not begin to develop reflective abilities until they have started teaching.

A number of studies indicate that the particular teacher education program being studied (and in which the researchers are often working as teacher educators) has little effect on students' beliefs and conceptions. Most of these studies involved programs designed to help preservice students become more reflective and/or to develop a constructivist learning theory. Zeichner, Tabachnick, and Densmore (1987) used classroom vignettes before and after a reflective student-teaching experience to examine the effects of socialization on student teachers' beliefs and perspectives. They found that the student teachers' perspectives tended to solidify rather than change during their student-teaching experience. In a case study of two preservice students, Olson (1993) found that students did not change their beliefs and assumptions about good teaching during the course of their teacher education program. Her explanation was that the students were not encouraged to confront their beliefs and, therefore, continued to hold them. McDiarmid (1992) examined changes in teacher trainees' beliefs following a series of presentations in multicultural education. Few changes were noted, and McDiarmid suggested that the content of the course confused the students. McDiarmid (1990) also studied changes in the conceptions of preservice students in a class that was designed to change students' misconceptions. Although he found some changes in conceptions, he stated that he remains skeptical about the changes. Preservice students' beliefs, he believes, are extremely difficult to change.

A number of other scholars question the possibilities of changing preservice teachers' conceptions in one course or even one program. Often conducting research on their own teacher education classes and programs, they found that many of their students' beliefs and conceptions did not shift in the desired directions (Ball, 1989; Civil, 1993; Simon & Mazza, 1993). Feiman-Nemser and Buchmann (1989) presented a case study of a student who

combined past experience with ideas she encountered in formal preparation in a way that reinforced earlier beliefs and reversed the intended message of her assigned readings on the inequitable distribution of school knowledge. (p. 371)

Wilcox, Schram, Lappan, and Lanier (1991) found that students in their program designed to develop preservice teachers' pedagogical content knowledge in math actually did change their thinking about mathematics; however, this change did not encompass their beliefs about how the elementary math curriculum should be presented. For these students, their beliefs about the school curriculum remained positivist rather than constructivist.

IN-SERVICE. Recent studies of the effects of in-service programs on teachers' changes in beliefs are quite encouraging. This may be because of the nature of the staff development programs that focus on the teachers' beliefs and life histories. For example, Tobin (1990) found that metaphors reveal teachers' beliefs, and an examination of the metaphors may be used to change beliefs and influence practice. In staff development programs that focused on teacher metaphors, teachers adopted new metaphors and teaching practices changed along with the metaphors.

Barnett and Sather (1992) worked with a group of teachers to examine the notion of students' misconceptions in mathematics. The staff development consisted of extensive group case discussions in which teachers revealed their beliefs. Sixteen of the

20 teachers changed their beliefs toward a more constructivist conception of teaching. Senger (1992) worked with five mathematics teachers in a constructivist process that involved group elements and individual conversations around actions in their classrooms and found that most of the teachers changed their conceptions of mathematics and teaching mathematics. Peterman (1993) participated with a group of teachers in a similar manner around notions of concept development and also found that the teacher with whom she was conducting a case study developed new understandings about teaching and learning.

Kelchtermans (1993) collected career stories of 10 experienced Flemish elementary school teachers. This process resulted in the reconstruction of professional self and a subjective educational theory. Freeman (1993) traced changes in the language used by two foreign language teachers enrolled in Master of Teaching (MAT) programs. He found that changes in conceptions of teaching accompanied the introduction into their vocabulary of current professional concepts and premises.

Of course, one wonders whether these changes in beliefs and conceptions affect teachers' practices. In a long-term study of teachers' beliefs and practices, Richardson (1994b) and colleagues examined the effects of a practical argument staff development process on changes in teachers' beliefs and practices in teaching reading comprehension as well as the effects on student achievement. This practical argument process (Fenstermacher, 1994b) consisted of group and individual elements designed to help teachers examine the empirical, value, and situational premises that relate to their classroom actions and to consider alternative premises and practices that are brought into the conversations by the staff developers and colleagues. The staff development process focused on teachers' beliefs about teaching and learning reading comprehension. They found that teachers changed their beliefs (Richardson, 1994a) as well as their practices in teaching reading comprehension (Tidwell & Mitchell, 1994). Furthermore, using an achievement measure that relates to constructivist views of the reading comprehension process (Valencia, Pearson, Reeve, & Shanahan, 1988), they found that the students' reading achievement in the participating teachers' classrooms improved in comparison to students whose teachers had not yet participated in the process (Bos & Anders, 1994). In a follow-up study of the teachers 2 years later, Valdez (1992) found that the teachers' beliefs had continued to change. In addition, they had developed an improvement orientation and felt more empowered.

Marx et al. (1994) presented case studies of four middle school teachers who were involved in a change process related to project-based science instruction and collaborative conversation. The teachers were involved in a staff development process that included cycles of collaboration, enactment, and reflection (Blumenfeld, Kracjik, Marx, & Soloway, 1994). The research team found that changes in beliefs and practices did occur and described how these changes were influenced by context and the teachers' existing beliefs and knowledge.

A remaining question concerns whether major changes in beliefs in one subject transfer to another subject. For example, if, during a staff development program, a teacher's beliefs about mathematics teaching and learning shift in a constructivist direction, will this influence the teaching of reading? Two studies have produced conflicting evidence of such transfer, leading to the conclusion that this is a ripe area for more research. Wood, Cobb, and Yakel (1991) worked with a teacher in changing the nature of mathematics teaching in the classroom. She changed her understandings of mathematics teaching and learning and her instructional practices in a constructivist direction; however, her conceptions of and practices in reading did not change. Yet, Ball and Rundquist (1993) found that Rundquist's changes in beliefs and practices in the teaching of mathematics transferred to other subjects, particularly science and language arts.

The conclusion from these studies is that staff development that focuses, in part, on teacher beliefs is important in changing instructional practices. This view is buttressed by several studies that found that teachers participating in staff development programs that advocated and taught about a particular teaching method accepted the new practices only if their beliefs matched the underlying assumptions of the new teaching method (Rich, 1990; Sparks, 1988).

Summary of Change Studies The research on changes in teachers' beliefs suggests that the context of schooling and classroom experiences exert powerful influences on teachers' developing beliefs and knowledge. It also implies that, depending on the staff development program, facilitating meaningful change in in-service teachers, that is change in both beliefs and practice, may be easier than promoting changes in beliefs at the preservice level.

The research on changing beliefs in staff development programs indicates that programs that approach learning to teach in a constructivist manner are successful in engaging their participants in examining and changing their beliefs and practices. An analysis of successful constructivist staff development programs yields the following characteristics (see also Richardson & Hamilton, 1994):

1. The participating teachers' beliefs and understandings are a major element of the content of the staff development process.
2. The goal of the process is not to introduce a specific method or curriculum to be implemented by the teachers. Instead, the goal is to facilitate conversations that allow the participants to understand their own beliefs and practices, consider alternatives, and experiment with new beliefs and practices.
3. Conversations about beliefs and practices are brought together with considerations of the moral dimensions of teaching and schooling.
4. During the course of the process, the discussions among staff developer and teachers move away from domination by the staff developer toward teacher control of the agenda, process, and content.
5. The staff developer is knowledgeable about current research and practice; however, he or she is not seen as the only "expert." A collaborative process is facilitated that allows the teachers to recognize and value their own expertise.
6. The staff development process is long term, and it is expected that teachers change at very different rates.

Preservice teacher education, however, poses challenges for those interested in changing students' beliefs and conceptions about teaching. The complications in preservice teacher educa-

tion are the lack of practical knowledge on the part of the students and the difficulty, if not impossibility, in helping students tie their beliefs to teaching practices. The beliefs they hold when they enter their programs have not been tested in the classroom, and they are not aware of the role that these beliefs will take in their actions as teachers. Perceived changes in preservice students' beliefs and conceptions may be transitory or artificial and turn out not to drive their actions when they become teachers. As Korthagen (1988) suggested, students are good at figuring out what the teacher educator wants to hear.

Nonetheless, a number of the characteristics listed for successful constructivist staff development programs could be replicated in preservice teacher education programs, particularly those related to the exploration of the students' own beliefs, as well as alternative beliefs and practices. In addition, preservice students should have the opportunity to engage extensively in the active exploration of classroom contexts, that is, in written and videocases, discussions with practicing teachers, and field work. This process may promote the first stages in the acquisition of practical knowledge.

CONCLUSION

The research on the role of attitudes and beliefs in learning to teach presents a picture of preservice students who enter their initial teacher preparation program with strong, or perhaps even central, beliefs (Rokeach, 1968) about teaching, learning, subject matter, and students. They hold images of teachers, both negative and positive, formed during their experiences as students. The entering preservice students are not, however, an undifferentiated group. Differences in entering beliefs have been observed between elementary and secondary majors, traditional and nontraditional students, and males and females.

Except for the student-teaching element, preservice teacher education seems a weak intervention. It is sandwiched between two powerful forces—previous life history, particularly that related to being a student, and classroom experience as a student teacher and teacher. Experience as a student is important in setting images of teaching that drive initial classroom practice, and experience as a teacher is the only way to develop the practical knowledge that eventually makes routine at least some aspects of classroom practice and provides alternative approaches when faced with dilemmas.

There is, however, some indication that the academic elements of preservice teacher education have an impact on teachers, although perhaps not recognized by them. Several studies highlight differences between teachers who went through pedagogical education and those who did not (e.g., Grossman, 1990), and others suggest a lag time between when teachers start their career and when conceptions acquired in preservice education begin to make an impact on practice (Crow, 1987). Furthermore, a growing number of studies point to changes in conceptions and beliefs on the basis of specific teacher education classes. Nonetheless, these changes do not appear to have an impact on teaching practice in as powerful a way as life experiences and teaching experience, which leads, perhaps, to the skepticism in the possibilities of changing beliefs expressed by Ball (1989) and McDiarmid (1990).

Changes in conceptions and beliefs may be easier to facilitate at the in-service than at the preservice level. Certain forms of staff development programs help teachers examine and assess their practical knowledge and beliefs and tie that knowledge to their classroom practices. The major factor in the difference in effects of preservice versus in-service programs would appear to be experience as a classroom teacher. The deep practical knowledge held by experienced teachers is closely tied to action, and it is this action that is understood by teachers to be the focus of change.

This conception of the learning-to-teach process does not lead directly to prescriptions for teacher education practice. In fact, it leaves many questions unanswered. The following are conceptual and research issues derived from an analysis of this work.

Conceptual Issue: Is Change Improvement?

Current research on teachers' and students' beliefs stems from the European hermeneutic tradition of social theorists such as Hans-George Gadamer (see McCarthy, 1981). The purpose of contemporary hermeneutic research is to explore the meaning constructed by individuals operating within a cultural tradition. It is understood that the person (researcher) who is attempting to understand how another person constructs meaning is actually constructing an interpretation of the other's interpretation. This is called the double hermeneutic by Giddens (1976). Thus, a number of scholars suggest that the narrative that elucidates a teacher's understandings should be co-constructed by the researcher and the teacher (Clandinin & Connelly, 1991; Schön, 1991).

The approach to research employed in the hermeneutic studies of teachers' beliefs and conceptions is relativistic. That is, nothing within the contemporary hermeneutic social science tradition provides for the possibility of a normative conception of teaching or a critique of the picture that emerges. As Habermas (1984) pointed out, this approach does not allow for the identification of distortions in the understandings held by the participants. Beliefs and conceptions that are interpreted by researchers are neutral, and, without a normative conception of teaching, a change in beliefs can be considered no more than change, not learning or improvement.

Yet, many educational researchers are interested in improvement and learning. Within the hermeneutic research tradition, however, researchers' normative conceptions are often hidden or, at least, not revealed. It may be understood by many readers of a particular hermeneutic study that certain beliefs about learning and teaching on the part of preservice and in-service teachers are not conducive to teaching in a certain way; however, the relationship between the beliefs of the participants in a study and the normative conceptions of the researcher is seldom made explicit. In fact, studies of "change" are often meant to imply change in a positive direction, but the worthiness of the change is seldom discussed. An example of equating change and learning or growth is provided by Kagan (1992): "*professional growth* is defined as changes over time in the behavior, knowledge, images, beliefs, or perceptions of novice teachers" (p. 131). What is it about the change that makes it growth?

For many, the solution to the dilemma created by research with an educative goal, but conducted within the hermeneutic tradition, is a move to critical theory (e.g., Carr & Kemmis, 1986; Zeichner, 1994). The goal of research in the critical tradition is emancipation through self-reflection, specifically reflection on the underlying assumptions that drive the system in which one operates. Whether or not research on teachers' beliefs heads in this direction, researchers will have to become more explicit about normative considerations if the research is to become truly educative. Is the change in beliefs and conceptions that took place during a staff development program or a teacher education course a valued change? If so, why? How do we know?

Research Issues

Beliefs and Actions Since the mid-1980s, research on teaching and teacher education shifted dramatically from a focus on behaviors to an interest in cognition. Researchers have developed interesting and useful ways of examining teacher beliefs and changes in beliefs, conceptions, and cognitive processes, and these are being used to examine the impact of teacher education on what and how teachers and preservice students think. Although empirical work has been conducted that links beliefs to practices, it cannot be assumed that all changes in beliefs translate into changes in practices, certainly not practices that may be considered worthwhile. In fact, a given teacher belief or conception could support many different practices or no practices at all if the teacher does not know how to develop or enact a practice that meshes with a new belief (Richardson et al., 1991).

This concern calls for research that examines both beliefs and actions and perhaps further develops the concept of praxis within teaching and teacher education. Furthermore, as educators, we should also be interested in understanding how changes in teachers' beliefs and practices affect student learning. This calls for research that moves beyond descriptions of preservice and in-service teachers' beliefs and conceptions and toward the observation of teachers' actions in the classroom and their students' developing understandings.

Research on Teacher Educators This chapter describes a large and robust area of research that focuses on preservice and in-service teachers' beliefs and practices. Missing from this body of research are similar studies of teacher educators. There are exceptions, however, and most represent high-risk activities— teacher educator as researcher studies. These researchers study themselves as teacher educators. Rene Clift studied herself as the teacher educator in a collaborative study of the student-teaching process (Clift, Meng, & Eggerding, 1994). Sandra Hollingsworth (1990) studied herself as a teacher educator and discovered profound changes in her beliefs and practices over time. Margaret Olson (1993) is one of the first to explore the personal practical knowledge of teacher educators in her own teacher education program. In addition, Tom Russell (Munby & Russell, 1993; Russell, 1994) is exploring his own beliefs and practices as he moves from teacher educator to high school physics teacher for one period a day. This field of research will continue to grow as evidenced by the large number of scholars who have instituted a special interest group on self-study in the American Educational Research Association.

Research on teacher educators' beliefs and practices will be particularly helpful in attempts at reform. This author believes, however, that teacher educators as researcher studies, particularly those conducted within a faculty of teacher education, will be particularly helpful in the improvement of teacher education practice.

Research and Practice Designs Conducting research on change programs that employ the constructivist aspects of teacher education described in the previous section of this chapter requires a unique set of design characteristics. These elements differ from those of the assessments of more traditional forms of teacher education (Sparks & Loucks-Horsley, 1990). The training model assessments generally employ quasi-experimental or process-product designs to assess whether the participating teachers changed classroom behaviors in directions that match the intent of the programs (Cruickshank, Lorish, & Thompson, 1979). Such a research design would violate the nature of the newer constructivist programs. These newer teacher education programs do not have specific behavioral or skills objectives to be attained by all participants; they focus on the participants' beliefs and practices, and each participant develops his or her own vision of change.

Richardson and Anders (1994) outlined a set of design characteristics that would be appropriate for examining changes in beliefs and practices in such constructivist teacher education programs. These characteristics include an open-ended, qualitative approach to research; the collection of rich data; and the use of multiple measures of cognition (see also Kagan, 1990).

Because the focus of change is decided on by each teacher and evolves during the process, the constructs of change that are examined also emerge during the course of the study. Most important, the research design, similar to the staff development process, is collaborative; that is, the teachers and researchers participate as equal colleagues in the process. Data that are collected during the course of the study become part of the content of the teacher education process. For example, a videotape of a staff development session may be shown at the next session to remind participants where the conversation was heading. Transcribed belief interviews may be returned to the participants and the results discussed in the group.

Given the nature of the change process and assumptions of change inherent in the constructivist model, it is questionable whether the use of a control group adds to understandings of teacher change. This leaves open the question of whether a research design using these characteristics can lead to valid conclusions concerning the effect of the teacher education or staff development process on changes in teachers' thoughts and practices. Without a control group, it may be difficult to attribute the changes observed in individual teachers to the particular process in which they participated. It is, therefore, essential that the changes in beliefs and practices be tied to the nature of the conversations that took place during the process.

These design characteristics constitute a very different approach to research on change, and many of the studies described in this chapter employed elements of them. It is critical that teacher educator/scholars allow well-conceptualized normative conceptions of teacher education to drive research rather than traditional research designs. In this way, teacher educators can conduct research that is truly educative for the reform of schooling in America.

References

Alexander, P., Schallert, D., & Hare, V. (1991). Coming to terms: How researchers in learning and literacy talk about knowledge. *Review of Educational Research, 61*(3), 315–343.

Allport, G. (1967). Attitudes. In M. Fishbein (Ed.), *Readings in attitude theory and measurement* (pp. 1–13). New York: John Wiley & Sons.

Anders, P., & Richardson, V. (1991). Research directions: Staff development that empowers teachers' reflection and enhances instruction. *Language Arts, 68*(4), 316–321.

Anning, A. (1988). Teachers' theories about children's learning. In J. Calderhead (Ed.), *Teachers' professional learning* (pp. 128–145). London: Falmer.

Avery, P., & Walker, C. (1993). Prospective teachers' perceptions of ethnic and gender differences in academic achievement. *Journal of Teacher Education, 44*(1), 27–37.

Ball, D. L. (1989). *Breaking with experience in learning to teach mathematics: What do they bring with them to teacher education?* Paper presented at the annual meeting of the American Educational Research Association, San Francisco.

Ball, D. L., & Rundquist, S. S. (1993). Collaboration as a context for joining teacher learning with learning about teaching. In D. K. Cohen, M. W. McLaughlin, & J. E. Talbert (Eds.), *Teaching for understanding: Challenges for policy and practice* (pp. 13–42). San Francisco: Jossey-Bass.

Ball, S., & Goodson, I. (1985). Understanding teachers: Concepts and contexts. In S. Ball & I. Goodson (Eds.), *Teachers' lives and careers* (pp. 1–26). London: Falmer.

Barnett, C., & Sather, S. (1992). *Using case discussions to promote change in beliefs among mathematics teachers.* Paper presented at the annual meeting of the American Educational Research Association, San Francisco.

Ben-Peretz, M. (1990). Research on teacher education in Israel: Topics, methods and findings. In R. Tisher & M. Wideen (Eds.), *Research in teacher education* (pp. 207–225). London: Falmer.

Black, A., & Ammon, P. (1992). A developmental-constructivist approach to teacher education. *Journal of Teacher Education, 43*(5), 323–335.

Blumenfeld, P. C., Kracjik, J. S., Marx, R. W., & Soloway, E. (1994). Lessons learned: How collaboration helped middle-grade science teachers learn project-based instruction. *Elementary School Journal, 94*(5), 539–551.

Bolin, F. (1990). Helping student teachers think about teaching: Another look at Lou. *Journal of Teacher Education, 41*(1), 10–19.

Book, C., Byers, J., & Freeman, D. (1983). Student expectations and teacher education traditions with which we can and cannot live. *Journal of Teacher Education, 34*(1), 9–13.

Book, C., & Freeman, D. (1986). Differences in entry characteristics of elementary and secondary teacher candidates. *Journal of Teacher Education, 37*(2), 47–51.

Borko, H., & Putnam, R. (in press). Learning to teach. In R. Calfee & D. Berliner (Eds.), *Handbook of educational psychology.* New York: Macmillan.

Bos, C., & Anders, P. (1994). The study of student change. In V. Richardson (Ed.), *Teacher change and the staff development process: A case in reading instruction* (pp. 181–198). New York: Teachers College Press.

Britzman, D. (1991). *Practice makes practice: A critical study of learning to teach*. Albany: State University of New York Press.

Brookhart, S., & Freeman, D. (1992). Characteristics of entering teacher candidates. *Review of Educational Research, 62,* 37–60.

Brophy, J., & Good, T. (1974). *Teacher–student relationships.* New York: Holt, Rinehart and Winston.

Brophy, J., & Good, T. (1986). Teacher behavior and student achievement. In M. Wittrock (Ed.), *Handbook of research on teaching* (3rd ed., pp. 328–375). New York: Macmillan.

Brousseau, B., Book, C., & Byers, J. (1988). Teacher beliefs and the cultures of teaching. *Journal of Teacher Education, 39*(6), 33–39.

Brousseau, B., & Freeman, D. (1988). How do teacher education faculty members define desirable teacher beliefs? *Teaching and Teacher Education, 4*(3), 267–273.

Buchmann, M., & Schwille, J. (1983). Education: The overcoming of experience. *American Journal of Education, 92*(1), 30–51.

Bullough, R. (1993). Case records as personal teaching texts for study in preservice teacher education. *Teaching and Teacher Education, 9*(4), 385–396.

Bullough, R., & Baughman, K. (1993). Continuity and change in teacher development: First year teacher after five years. *Journal of Teacher Education, 44*(2), 86–95.

Bullough, R., & Knowles, J. (1991). Teaching and nurturing: Changing conceptions of self as teacher in a case study of becoming a teacher. *Qualitative Studies in Education, 4,* 121–140.

Bullough, R., Knowles, J., & Crow, N. (1992). *Emerging as a teacher.* London and New York: Routledge.

Bussis, A., Chittenden, E., & Amarel, M. (1976). *Beyond the surface curriculum: An interview study of teachers' understandings.* Boulder, CO: Westview Press.

Calderhead, J. (1988). Learning from introductory school experience. *Journal of Education for Teaching, 14*(1), 75–83.

Calderhead, J., & Robson, M. (1991). Images of teaching: Student teachers' early conceptions of classroom practice. *Teaching and Teacher Education, 7,* 1–8.

Campbell, D. T. (1967). The indirect assessment of social attitudes. In M. Fishbein (Ed.), *Readings in attitude theory and measurement* (pp. 163–179). New York: John Wiley & Sons.

Carr, W., & Kemmis, S. (1986). *Becoming critical: Knowing through action research and prospects.* Victoria, Australia: Deakin University Press.

Carter, K. (1990). Teachers' knowledge and learning to teach. In W. Houston (Ed.), *Handbook of research on teacher education* (pp. 291–310). New York: Macmillan.

Civil, M. (1993). Prospective elementary teachers' thinking about teaching mathematics. *Journal of Mathematical Behavior, 12,* 79–109.

Clandinin, D. J. (1986). *Classroom practice: Teacher images in action.* London: Falmer.

Clandinin, D. J., & Connelly, F. (1987). Teachers' personal knowledge: What counts as personal in studies of the personal. *Journal of Curriculum Studies, 19*(6), 487–500.

Clandinin, D. J., & Connelly, F. (1991). Narrative and story in practice and research. In D. Schön (Ed.), *The reflective turn: Case studies in and on educational practice* (pp. 258–281). New York: Teachers College Press.

Clark, C., & Peterson, P. (1986). Teachers' thought processes. In M. Wittrock (Ed.), *Handbook of research on teaching* (3rd ed., pp. 255–296). New York: Macmillan.

Clift, R. (1987). English teacher or English major: Epistemological differences in the teaching of English. *English Education, 19,* 229–236.

Clift, R., Meng, L., & Eggerding, S. (1994). Mixed messages in learning to teach English. *Teaching and Teacher Education, 19*(3), 265–279.

Cochran-Smith, M. (1991). Reinventing student teaching. *Journal of Teacher Education, 42*(2), 104–118.

Cochran-Smith, M., & Lytle, S. L. (1990). Research on teaching and teacher research: The issues that divide. *Educational Researcher, 19*(2), 2–10.

Corporaal, A. (1991). Repertory grid research into cognitions of prospective primary school teachers. *Teaching and Teacher Education, 7*(4), 315–329.

Crow, G., Levine, L., & Nager, N. (1990). No more business as usual: Career changers who become teachers. *American Journal of Education, 98*(3), 197–223.

Crow, N. (1987). *Socialization within a teacher education program.* Unpublished doctoral dissertation, University of Utah, Salt Lake City.

Crow, N. (1988, April). *A longitudinal study of teacher socialization: A case study.* Paper presented at the annual meeting of the American Educational Research Association, New Orleans.

Cruickshank, D., Lorish, C., & Thompson, L. (1979). What we think we know about inservice education. *Journal of Teacher Education, 30*(1), 27–32.

Doyle, W. (1990). Classroom knowledge as a foundation for teaching. *Teachers College Record, 91*(3), 247–260.

Duffy, G. (1981). *Theory to practice: How does it work in real classrooms?* (Research Series 98). East Lansing: Institute for Research on Teaching, College of Education, Michigan State University.

Dunkin, M., & Biddle, B. (1974). *The study of teaching.* New York: Holt, Rinehart and Winston.

Eisenhart, M., Shrum, J., Harding, J., & Cuthbert, A. (1988). Teacher beliefs: Definitions, findings and directions. *Educational Policy, 2,* 51–70.

Elbaz, F. L. (1983). *Teacher thinking: A study of practical knowledge.* London: Croom Helm.

Erickson, G., & MacKinnon, A. (1991). Seeing classrooms in new ways: On becoming a science teacher. In D. Schön (Ed.), *The reflective turn: Case studies in and on educational practice* (pp. 15–37). New York: Teachers College Press.

Featherstone, H. (1993). Learning from the first years of classroom teaching: The journey in, the journey out. *Teachers College Record, 95*(1), 93–112.

Feiman-Nemser, S. (1983). Learning to teach. In L. Shulman & G. Sykes (Eds.), *Handbook of teaching and policy* (pp. 150–171). New York: Longman.

Feiman-Nemser, S., & Buchmann, M. (1989). Describing teacher education: A framework and illustrative findings from a longitudinal study of six students. *The Elementary School Journal, 89*(3), 365–377.

Feiman-Nemser, S., & Floden, R. (1986). The cultures of teaching. In M. Wittrock (Ed.), *Handbook of research on teaching* (3rd ed., pp. 505–526). New York: Macmillan.

Feiman-Nemser, S., McDiarmid, G., Melnick, S., & Parker, M. (1989). *Changing beginning teachers' conceptions: A description of an introductory teacher education course* (Research Report 89-1). East Lansing: National Center for Research on Teacher Education, College of Education, Michigan State University.

Fenstermacher, G. (1979). A philosophical consideration of recent research on teacher effectiveness. In L. S. Shulman (Ed.), *Review of research in education* (Vol. 6, pp. 157–185). Itasca, IL: Peacock.

Fenstermacher, G. (1994a). The knower and the known: The nature of knowledge in research on teaching. In L. Darling-Hammond (Ed.), *Review of research in education* (Vol. 20, pp. 1–54). Washington, DC: American Educational Research Association.

Fenstermacher, G. D. (1994b). The place of practical arguments in the education of teachers. In V. Richardson (Ed.), *Teacher change and the staff development process: A case in reading instruction* (pp. 23–42). New York: Teachers College Press.

Fishbein, M. (1967). A consideration of beliefs, and their role in attitude measurement. In M. Fishbein (Ed.), *Readings in attitude theory and measurement* (pp. 257–266). New York: John Wiley & Sons.

Freeman, D. (1993). Renaming experience/reconstructing practice: Developing new understandings of teaching. *Teaching and Teacher Education, 9*(5/6), 485–497.

Getzels, J., & Jackson, P. (1963). The teacher's personality and characteristics. In N. Gage (Ed.), *The handbook of research on teaching* (pp. 506–582). Chicago: Rand McNally.

Giddens, A. (1976). *New rules of socio-logical method.* London: Hutchinson & Co.

Gomez, M. L., & Tabachnick, B. R. (1992). Telling teaching stories. *Teaching Education, 4*(2), 129–138.

Goodenough, W. (1963). *Cooperation in change.* New York: Russell Sage Foundation.

Goodson, I. (1992). Studying teachers' lives: An emergent field of inquiry. In I. Goodson (Ed.), *Studying teachers' lives* (pp. 1–17). New York: Teachers College Press.

Green, T. (1971). *The activities of teaching.* New York: McGraw-Hill.

Grossman, P. (1990). *The making of a teacher: Teacher knowledge and teacher education.* New York: Teachers College Press.

Grossman, P., & Richert, A. (1988). Unacknowledged knowledge growth: A re-examination of the effects of teacher education. *Teaching and Teacher Education, 4*(1), 53–62.

Grossman, P., Wilson, S., & Shulman, L. S. (1989). Teachers of substance: Subject matter knowledge for teaching. In M. Reynolds (Ed.), *Knowledge base for the beginning teacher* (pp. 23–36). New York: Pergamon Press.

Gudmundsdottir, S. (1991). Story-maker, story-teller: Narrative structures in curriculum. *Journal of Curriculum Studies, 23*(3), 207–218.

Habermas, J. (1984). *The theory of communicative action: Reason and the rationalization of society: Vol. 1.* Boston: Beacon.

Harvey, O., Prather, M., White, B., & Hoffmeister, J. (1968). Teachers' beliefs, classroom atmosphere and student behavior. *American Educational Research Journal, 5,* 151–165.

Hoffman, J., & Kugle, C. (1982). A study of theoretical orientation to reading and its relationship to teacher verbal feedback during reading instruction. *Journal of Classroom Interaction, 18*(1), 2–7.

Hollingsworth, S. (1989). Prior beliefs and cognitive change in learning to teach. *American Educational Research Journal, 26*(2), 160–189.

Hollingsworth, S. (1990, April). *Studying attentional and theoretical shifts across contexts as evidence of learning to teach: Teacher-educator as researcher.* Paper presented at the annual conference of the American Educational Research Association, Boston.

Hollingsworth, S., Dybdahl, M., & Minarik, L. (1993). By chart and chance and passion: The importance of relational knowing in learning to teach. *Curriculum Inquiry, 23*(1), 5–35.

Holt-Reynolds, D. (1992). Personal history-based beliefs as relevant prior knowledge in coursework: Can we practice what we teach? *American Educational Research Journal, 29,* 325–349.

Hoy, W. (1967). Organizational socialization: The student teacher and pupil control ideology. *The Journal of Educational Research, 61,* 153–259.

Hoy, W., & Woolfolk, A. (1990). Socialization of student teachers. *American Educational Research Journal, 27*(2), 279–300.

Interstate New Teacher Assessment and Support Consortium (INTASC). (1993). *Model standards for beginning teacher licensing and development: A resource for state dialogue.* Washington, DC: Council of Chief State School Officers.

John, P. D. (1991). A qualitative study of British student teachers' lesson planning perspectives. *Journal of Education for Teaching, 17*(3), 310–320.

Johnson, M. (1987). *The body in the mind: The bodily basis of meaning, imagination, and mind.* Chicago: The University of Chicago Press.

Kagan, D. (1990). Ways of evaluating teacher cognition: Inferences concerning the Goldilocks principle. *Review of Educational Research, 60*(3), 419–469.

Kagan, D. (1991). Narrative semiotics and teachers' beliefs regarding the relevance of formal learning theory to classroom practice: A U.S. study. *Journal of Education for Teaching, 17*(3), 245–262.

Kagan, D. (1992). Professional growth among preservice and beginning teachers. *Review of Educational Research, 62*(2), 129–169.

Kam, H. W. (1990). Research on teacher education in Singapore. In R. Tisher & M. F. Wideen (Eds.), *Research in teacher education* (pp. 105–120). London: Falmer.

Kelchtermans, G. (1993). Getting the story, understanding the lives: From career stories to teacher's professional development. *Teaching and Teacher Education, 9*(6), 443–456.

Kelly, G. (1955). *The psychology of personal constructs* (Vols. 1 and 2). New York: Norton.

Khan, S., & Weiss, J. (1973). The teaching of affective responses. In R. M. W. Travers (Ed.), *Second handbook of research on teaching* (pp. 759–804). Chicago: Rand McNally.

Kile, R. (1993). *Preconceptions of elementary and secondary preservice teachers.* Unpublished doctoral dissertation, University of Arizona, Tucson.

Knowles, J. G. (1992). Models for teachers' biographies. In I. Goodson (Ed.), *Studying teachers' lives* (pp. 99–152). New York: Teachers College Press.

Korthagen, F. A. J. (1988). The influence of learning orientations on the development of reflective teaching. In J. Calderhead (Ed.), *Teachers' professional learning* (pp. 35–50). Philadelphia: Falmer.

Lehrer, K. (1990). *Theory of knowledge.* Boulder, CO: Westview Press.

Leinhardt, G. (1988). Situated knowledge and expertise in teaching. In J. Calderhead (Ed.), *Teachers' professional learning* (pp. 146–168). London: Falmer.

Lortie, D. (1975). *Schoolteacher: A sociological study.* Chicago: The University of Chicago Press.

MacKinnon, A., & Erickson, G. (1992). The roles of reflective practice and foundational disciplines in teacher education. In T. Russell & H. Munby (Eds.), *Teachers and teaching: From classroom to reflection* (pp. 192–210). London: Falmer.

Marx, R. W., Blumenfeld, P. C., Krajcik, J. S., Blunk, M., Crawford, B., Kelly, B., & Meyer, K. M. (1994). Enacting project-based science: Experiences of four middle-grade teachers. *Elementary School Journal, 94*(5), 498–517.

McCarthy, T. (1981). *The critical theory of Jürgen Habermas.* Cambridge, MA: The MIT Press.

McDiarmid, G. (1990). Tilting at webs: Early field experiences as an occasion for breaking with experience. *Journal of Teacher Education, 41*(3), 12–20.

McDiarmid, G. W. (1992). What to do about differences? A study of multicultural education for teacher trainees in the Los Angeles Unified School District. *Journal of Teacher Education, 43*(2), 83–93.

McDiarmid, G. W. (in press). Is more better? The arts and science as preparation for teaching. In K. Howey & N. Zimpher (Eds.), *Faculty development for improving teaching preparation.* Reston, VA: Association of Teacher Educators.

Mitchell, D., Ortiz, F., & Mitchell, T. (1987). *Work orientation and job performance: The cultural basis of teaching rewards and incentives.* Albany: State University of New York Press.

Morine-Dershimer, G. (1989). Preservice teachers' conceptions of content and pedagogy: Measuring growth in reflective, pedagogical decision-making. *Journal of Teacher Education, 40*(3), 46–52.

Munby, H. (1986). Metaphor in the thinking of teachers: An exploratory study. *Journal of Curriculum Studies, 18*(2), 197–209.

Munby, H. (1987). Metaphor and teachers' knowledge. *Research in the teaching of English, 21*(4), 377–397.

Munby, H., & Russell, T. (1992). Transforming chemistry research into chemistry teaching: The complexities of adopting new frames for experience. In T. Russell & H. Munby (Eds.), *Teachers and teaching: From classroom to reflection* (pp. 90–123). London: Falmer.

Munby, T., & Russell, T. (1993). The authority of experience in learning to teach: Messages from a physics methods class. *Journal of Teacher Education, 44*(4), 1–10.

National Center for Research on Teacher Education. (1991). *Final report: The teacher education and learning to teach study.* East Lansing: College of Education, Michigan State University.

Nespor, J. (1987). The role of beliefs in the practice of teaching. *Journal of Curriculum Studies, 19*(4), 317–328.

Newfeld, J. (1974). Who chooses the teaching profession? *Saskatchewan Journal of Educational Research and Development, 51*(1), 21–26.

Novak, D., & Knowles, J. (1992, April). *Life histories and the transition to teaching as a second career.* Paper presented at the annual meeting of the American Educational Research Association, San Francisco.

O'Brien, K., & Norton, R. (1991). Beliefs, practices, and constraints: Influences on teacher decision-making processes. *Teacher Education Quarterly, 18*(1), 29–38.

Olson, M. (1993, June). *Knowing what counts in teacher education.* Paper presented at the Canadian Association of Teacher Educators, Canadian Society of Studies in Education Conference, Ottawa.

Pajares, M. (1992). Teachers' beliefs and educational research: Cleaning up a messy construct. *Review of Educational Research, 62*(3), 307–332.

Peck, R. F., & Tucker, J. A. (1973). Research on teacher education. In R. M. Travers (Ed.), *Second handbook of research on teaching* (pp. 940–978). Chicago: Rand McNally.

Peterman, F. (1993). Staff development and the process of changing: A teacher's emerging constructivist beliefs about learning and teaching. In K. Tobin (Ed.), *The practice of constructivism in science education* (pp. 226–245). Washington, DC: AAAS Press.

Peterson, P., Fennema, E., Carpenter, T., & Loef, M. (1989). Teachers' pedagogical content beliefs in mathematics. *Cognition and Instruction, 6*(1), 1–40.

Pigge, F., & Marso, R. (April, 1988). *Cognitive, affective, and personal characteristics associated with motives for entering teacher training.* Paper presented at the annual meeting of the American Education Research Association, New Orleans. (ERIC Document Reproduction Service No. ED 293 799)

Pinnegar, S., & Carter, K. (1990). Comparing theories from textbooks and practicing teachers. *Journal of Teacher Education, 41*(1), 21–27.

Powell, R., & Birrell, J. (1992, April). *The influence of prior experiences on pedagogical constructs of traditional and nontraditional preservice teachers.* Paper presented at the annual meeting of the American Educational Research Association, San Francisco.

Resnick, L. (1989). Introduction. In L. Resnick (Ed.), *Knowing, learning, and instruction: Essays in honor of Robert Glaser* (pp. 1–24). Hillsdale, NJ: Lawrence Erlbaum Associates.

Rich, Y. (1990). Ideological impediments to instructional innovation: The case of cooperative learning. *Teaching and Teacher Education, 6*(1), 81–91.

Richardson, V. (1994a). The consideration of beliefs in staff development. In V. Richardson (Ed.), *Teacher change and the staff development process: A case in reading instruction.* New York: Teachers College Press.

Richardson, V. (Ed.). (1994b). *Teacher change and the staff development process: A case in reading instruction* (pp. 90–108). New York: Teachers College Press.

Richardson, V., & Anders, P. (1994). The study of teacher change. In V. Richardson (Ed.), *Teacher change and the staff development process: A case in reading instruction* (pp. 159–180). New York: Teachers College Press.

Richardson, V., Anders, P., Tidwell, D., & Lloyd, C. (1991). The relationship between teachers' beliefs and practices in reading comprehension instruction. *American Educational Research Journal, 28*(3), 559–586.

Richardson, V., & Hamilton, M. (in press). The practical argument staff development process. In V. Richardson (Ed.), *Teacher change and the staff development process: A case in reading instruction.* New York: Teachers College Press.

Richardson, V., & Kile, S. (1992, April). *The use of videocases in teacher education.* Paper presented at the annual meeting of the American Educational Research Association, San Francisco.

Richardson-Koehler, V. (1988). Barriers to the effective supervision of student teaching. *Journal of Teacher Education, 39*(2), 28–34.

Rokeach, M. (1960). *The open and closed mind: Investigations into the nature of belief systems and personality systems.* New York: Basic Books.

Rokeach, M. (1968). *Beliefs, attitudes and values: A theory of organization and change.* San Francisco: Jossey-Bass.

Ross, D., Johnson, M., & Smith, W. (1991, April). *Developing a professional teacher at the University of Florida.* Paper presented at the annual meeting of the American Educational Research Association, Chicago.

Russell, T. (1988). From pre-service teacher education to the first year of teaching: A study of theory into practice. In J. Calderhead (Ed.), *Teachers' professional learning* (pp. 13–34). London: Falmer.

Russell, T. (1994, April). *Teaching to better understand how a teacher learns to teach: Can the authority of personal experience be taught?* Paper presented at the annual meeting of the American Educational Research Association, New Orleans.

Russell, T., Munby, H., Spafford, C., & Johnston, P. (1988). Learning the professional knowledge of teaching. In P. Grimmett & G. Erickson (Eds.), *Reflection in teacher education* (pp. 67–90). New York: Teachers College Press.

Schmidt, W., & Kennedy, M. M. (1990). *Teachers' and teacher candidates' beliefs about subject matter and about teaching responsibilities* (Research Report 91-1). East Lansing: National Center for Research on Teaching Learning, College of Education, Michigan State University.

Schön, D. (1983). *The reflective practitioner.* New York: Basic Books.

Schön, D. (1991). Concluding comments. In D. Schön (Ed.), *The reflective turn* (pp. 343–360). New York: Teachers College Press.

Schubert, W. (1991). Teacher lore: A basis for understanding praxis. In C. Witherell & N. Noddings (Eds.), *Stories lives tell: Narrative and dialogue in education* (pp. 207–233). New York: Teachers College Press.

Senger, E. (1992). *Personalized staff development: The effect of reflective dialogue on the beliefs, values, and practices of three elementary school mathematics teachers.* Unpublished doctoral dissertation, University of Arizona, Tucson.

Serow, R. C., Eaker, D. J., & Forrest, K. D. (1994). "I want to see some kind of growth out of them": What the service ethic means to teacher-education students. *American Educational Research Journal, 31*(1), 27–48.

Shulman, L. (1987). Knowledge and teaching: Foundations of the new reform. *Harvard Educational Review, 57*(1), 1–22.

Silverman, F., & Creswell, J. (1982). Preservice teachers: A profile of cognitive development. *Texas Tech Journal of Education, 9*(3), 175–185.

Simon, M. A., & Mazza, W. (1993, March). *From learning mathematics to teaching mathematics: A case study of a prospective teacher in a reform-oriented program.* Paper presented at the annual meeting of the North American Chapter of the International Group for the Psychology of Mathematics Education, Monterey, CA.

Sparks, D., & Loucks-Horsley, S. (1990). Models of staff development. In R. Houston (Ed.), *Handbook of research on teacher education* (pp. 234–250). New York: Macmillan.

Sparks, G. (1988). Teachers' attitudes toward change and subsequent improvements in classroom teaching. *Journal of Educational Psychology, 80*(1), 111–117.

Steffle, V., Reich, P., & McClaran, M. (1971). Some eliciting and computational procedures for descriptive semantics. In P. Kay (Ed.), *Explorations in mathematical anthropology* (pp. 79–116). Cambridge, MA: MIT Press.

Stern, G. G. (1963). Measuring noncognitive variables in research on teaching. In N. Gage (Ed.), *Handbook of research on teaching* (pp. 398–447). Chicago: Rand McNally.

Tabachnick, B., & Zeichner, K. (1984). The impact of the student teaching experience on the development of teacher perspectives. *Journal of Teacher Education, 35*(6), 28–36.

Thompson, A. (1992). Teachers' beliefs and conceptions: A synthesis of the research. In D. Grouws (Ed.), *Handbook of research on mathematics teaching and learning* (pp.127–146). New York: Macmillan.

Tickle, L. (1991). New teachers and the emotions of learning teaching. *Cambridge Journal of Education, 21*(3), 319–329.

Tidwell, D., & Mitchell, J. (1994). Current teaching practices in reading comprehension. In V. Richardson (Ed.), *Teacher change and the staff development process: A case in reading instruction* (pp. 43–67). New York: Teachers College Press.

Tobin, K. (1990). Changing metaphors and beliefs: A master switch for teaching? *Theory into Practice, 29*(2), 122–127.

Tobin, K., & Jakubowski, E. (1990). *Cooperative teacher project: Final report*. Tallahassee: Florida State University.

Tochon, F. (1990). Heuristic schemata as tools for epistemic analysis of teachers' thinking. *Teaching and Teacher Education, 6*(2), 183–196.

Valdez, A. (1992). *Changes in teachers' beliefs, understandings, and practices concerning reading comprehension through the use of practical arguments: A follow-up study*. Unpublished doctoral dissertation, University of Arizona, Tucson.

Valencia, S. W., Pearson, P. D., Reeve, R., & Shanahan, T. (1988). *Illinois Goal Assessment Program: Reading*. Springfield: Illinois State Board of Education.

Wehling, L., & Charters, W. W. (1969). Dimensions of teaching beliefs about the teaching process. *American Educational Research Journal, 6,* 7–30.

Weinstein, C. (1988). Preservice teachers' expectations about the first year of teaching. *Teaching and Teacher Education, 4*(1), 31–41.

Weinstein, C. (1989). Teacher education students' preconceptions of teaching. *Journal of Teacher Education, 40*(2), 53–60.

Wilcox, S., Schram, P., Lappan, G., & Lanier, P. (1991). *The role of a learning community in changing preservice teachers' knowledge* (Research Report 91-1). East Lansing: National Center for Research on Teacher Learning, College of Education, Michigan State University.

Wilson, S., & Wineburg, S. (1988). Peering at history through different lenses: The role of disciplinary perspectives in teaching history. *Teachers College Record, 89*(4), 525–539.

Wood, T., Cobb, P., & Yakel, E. (1991). Change in teaching mathematics: A case study. *American Educational Research Journal, 28*(3), 587–616.

Woods, P. (1984). Teacher, self and curriculum. In I. Goodson & S. Ball (Eds.), *Defining the curriculum: Histories and ethnographies* (pp. 1–26). London: Falmer.

Yinger, R. (1987, April). *By the seat of your pants: An inquiry into improvisation in teaching*. Paper presented at the annual meeting of the American Educational Research Association, Washington, DC.

Yinger, R., & Villar, L. (1986, June). *Studies of teachers' thought-in-action: A progress report*. Paper presented at the meeting of the International Study Association on Teacher Thinking, Leuven, Belgium.

Zeichner, K. (1994). Educational reform and teacher knowledge. In S. Hollingsworth & H. Sockett (Eds.), *Teacher research and educational reform,* 97th Yearbook of the National Society for the Study of Education, (pp. 66–84). Chicago: The University of Chicago Press.

Zeichner, K., & Gore, J. (1990). Teacher socialization. In W. Houston (Ed.), *Handbook of research on teacher education* (pp. 329–348). New York: Macmillan.

Zeichner, K., Tabachnick, B., & Densmore, K. (1987). Individual, institutional, and cultural influences on the development of teachers' craft knowledge. In J. Calderhead (Ed.), *Exploring teachers' thinking* (pp. 21–59). London: Cassell.

Zimpher, N., & Ashburn, E. (1992). Countering parochialism in teacher candidates. In M. Dilworth (Ed.), *Diversity in teacher education: New expectations* (pp. 40–62). San Francisco: Jossey-Bass.

7

PERSONAL NARRATIVE AND LIFE HISTORY IN LEARNING TO TEACH

Kathy Carter
UNIVERSITY OF ARIZONA

Walter Doyle
UNIVERSITY OF ARIZONA

There is a distinction between learning to teach and becoming a teacher. Indeed, the significant albeit hidden work of learning to teach concerns negotiating with conflicting representations and desires. One must ferret out how multiple interpretations of the meanings of social experience come to position one's identity as a teacher. This involves scrutiny into how we come to know ourselves when we are trying to become a teacher. (Britzman, 1992, p. 24)

Women today read and write biographies to gain perspective on their own lives. Each reading provokes a dialogue of comparison and recognition, a process of memory and articulation that makes one's own experience available as a lens of empathy. We gain even more from comparing notes and trying to understand the choices of our friends. When one has matured surrounded by implicit disparagement, the undiscovered self is an unexpected resource. Self knowledge is empowering. (Bateson, 1989, p. 5)

This chapter charts the relatively new, certainly vigorous, and often quite diverse efforts to place biography at the center of teaching practice, the study of teachers, and the teacher education process (see, e.g., Ayers, 1989; Casey, 1993; Goodson, 1992b; Huberman, 1989; Knowles & Holt-Reynolds, 1994). Overall, work that is grounded in a biographical perspective involves intense and extended conversations with teachers (see Woods, 1985) and is based on the premise that the act of teaching, teachers' experiences and the choices they make, and the process of learning to teach are deeply personal matters inexorably linked to one's identity and, thus, one's life story. From this perspective, a central focus on teachers' personal lives is considered essential in designing and conducting research, interpreting data, and formulating policy regarding school reform and the education of teachers at all levels of schooling and stages of their careers.

An emphasis on personal narrative and life history in learning to teach represents the shift that has taken place since the early 1990s from an assumption that the teacher is simply an instrument in the production of school achievement to a view of the teacher as an intelligent agent in educating children (see Goodson, 1994). In the former view, research was to discover the "knowledge base" (i.e., verify what teachers were supposed to learn to be effective), and teacher education was to make sure candidates for teaching mastered this content efficiently and thoroughly regardless of their personal dispositions or commitments (Doyle, 1990). The implicit presumption here was that teachers learned very little from their actual experiences of teaching that could contribute to this knowledge base. From the new perspective of personal agency, this technical view of teaching and teacher development has been challenged by an emphasis on personal voice and empowerment and a view of the teacher him- or herself both as a source of practices and, indeed, as an educative medium.

The authors thank Anna Richert and Ivor Goodson, the editorial consultants for this chapter, for their helpful comments and suggestions. They also thank Donna Jurich, Gary Knowles, and Nedra Crow for providing essential materials and references.

SCOPE OF THIS CHAPTER

The content of this chapter is grounded in a selected number of major research and development programs in which a biographical or autobiographical orientation is most explicitly represented. Movement out from this core is made in the service of illuminating the origins, conceptual foundations, and applications of this overall approach to teaching and learning to teach. At the same time, the authors have attempted to steer clear of the closely related domains of teacher research, teachers' beliefs and attitudes, and teacher socialization that are covered more fully in other chapters in this handbook. Moreover, the discussion is focused on learning to teach in K–12 classrooms and, thus, omits autobiographical studies of pedagogical development among teacher educators (see, e.g., Thompson, 1993; Trumbull, 1990). The authors recognize, of course, that further analysis of the interconnections among these domains is needed, but found such an analysis to be beyond the scope of this chapter.

Finally, given the rapid emergence and growing pervasiveness of work in this area, this chapter is not meant to be exhaustive or even comprehensive. The intent, rather, is to represent the basic structure of biographical scholarship in teacher education and to make this work accessible to the teacher education community. Thus, the chapter focuses on a few major strands that tend to define the larger body of literature in this area and then concentrates on extended descriptions and analyses of these strands (for related reviews, see Kagan, 1992; Knowles, 1992; Zeichner & Gore, 1990).

Although widely used in this literature, the term *knowledge* is quite problematic (Fenstermacher, 1994) and, therefore, has been avoided whenever possible. A discussion of the differences among such terms as *knowledge, belief, attitude,* and so forth, which are also featured in the literature on learning to teach, also has been avoided, in part because these issues are covered quite thoroughly in Chapter 6 of this volume. These authors prefer the terms *interpretation* and *understanding* as vehicles for capturing what personal narrative and life history inquiries are all about. A narrative or life story is an interpretation of experiences or events that reflects, perhaps, a more general understanding of similar experiences and events. Presumably individuals draw their interpretations from a variety of remembered experiences, bits of information, beliefs, knowledge, dispositions, commitments, and cultural forms, as well as the tasks at hand.

Two complementary but somewhat distinct methods are used, with variations, in the research covered in this chapter (for a general discussion, see Denzin, 1989). The first approach centers largely on teachers' personal narratives. The basic assumption is that "education is the construction and reconstruction of personal and social stories" (Connelly & Clandinin, 1990, p. 2), and the emphasis is on the teacher's story as an authentic voice in the research discourse. Inquiry typically begins with an event and "the event's emotional, moral, and aesthetic qualities; we then ask why the event is associated with these feelings and what their origins might be" (Connelly & Clandinin, 1990, p. 11). Biography serves as a way of making sense of the personal meanings teachers associate with the incidents and circumstances of teaching practice.

Life-history methods share this grounding in teachers' personal stories, but emphasis is also placed on the social and historical contexts that influenced what values teachers hold and how teachers interpret educational issues and situations (see, e.g., Goodson, 1992a, 1994; Woods, 1984, 1985). "A life history is therefore a very personal document, yet at the same time, in its attention to the historical, social, political and economic context of that life, it offers a means for a fully contextualized view, one that is sensitive to the structures and patterns of events that have a general influence" (Woods, 1987, p. 131). In life history, that is, personal meaning is situated in a historical context, in part to establish a critical perspective on one's understanding of the forms of teaching practice. Britzman (1986), in particular, has argued that connecting life experience with history "allows the individual critical insight into both the nature of her/his relationships to individuals, institutions, cultural values, and political events, and the ways in which these social relationships contribute to the individual's identity, values, and ideological perspectives" (p. 452).

Structure of This Chapter

The core of this chapter is organized around two major strands within biographical work on learning to teach (for a related discussion, see Butt & Raymond, 1989). In the first strand, the focus is on teachers' personal understandings of their practice and on the acquisition of these understandings as "the result of a dynamic interaction between context and personal biography" (Raymond, Butt, & Townsend, 1992, p. 152). The emphasis, in other words, is on teachers' theorizing rather than theorizing about teachers or teaching. Advocates of this perspective argue that personal, situated understanding is fundamental to practice, unavailable through standard forms of research on teaching, and often ignored in conventional preservice and inservice programs.

In the second strand, attention is centered on teachers' work and careers (see Goodson, 1992a, 1994). In these analyses, biography is used to enrich understanding of "the contours and dynamics of the professional career cycle of teachers" (Huberman, 1989, p. 343; see, also, Kelchtermans & Vandenberghe, 1994). Knowledge of teachers' career patterns are, in turn, seen as indispensable in formulating personnel policies and planning staff development.

Once the major research programs are delineated, largely as portrayed by their authors, the discussion turns to the types of teacher education practices that flow from an acknowledgment of a fundamental link between personal and professional dispositions. In the final section, attention is directed to some of the special issues of research method and ethics associated with biographical approaches and to a general appraisal of the status of work in this area.

BIOGRAPHY AS A PERSPECTIVE IN LEARNING TO TEACH

A biographical perspective in teacher learning and development has roots in several converging lines of thinking in education.

These origins and sources are examined briefly as a general introduction to the work surveyed in this chapter.

Concerns and Apprenticeship

Two important precursors, one based on psychological constructs and one derived from a sociological study, have become part of the intellectual fabric of teacher education. The first evolved from the personalized teacher education program that developed in the 1960s around the ideas of Carl Rogers (1961) in counseling psychology and the work of Peck, Fuller, Bown, and their colleagues at the University of Texas at Austin (see Fuller, 1969, 1970; Fuller & Bown, 1975; Fuller, Bown, & Peck, 1967). The hypothetical "stages" of personal-professional "concerns" that emerged from this work—concern about self, concern about teaching task, and concern about impact—have defined in broad strokes how the field understands teacher development (see, e.g., Nias, 1989).

Second, a biographical perspective was also energized by the often-cited observation by Lortie (1975) that prospective teachers undergo, as K-12 students themselves, a protracted apprenticeship of observation prior to entering formal preparation for teaching practice and , furthermore, that this antecedent socialization overpowers most of the effects of formal teacher preparation, especially standard course work in teacher education programs. Learning to teach, in other words, is driven by the candidates' personal dispositions rather than the curriculum of teacher education (see Knowles, 1992). This interpretation has not only received widespread endorsement but has also deeply influenced much of the work on teacher socialization and development (e.g., Zeichner & Gore, 1990) and is a basic notion in much biographical inquiry (e.g., Britzman, 1986).

In many respects, the more explicit interest in teachers' biographies that has developed recently is a natural extension of these broadly influential approaches to teacher enculturation and development. At the same time, the modern work has acquired special vigor from at least five movements that have recently gained prominence: teacher cognition, personal knowledge revolution, the politics of teaching, feminist perspectives, and stories as a form of inquiry and pedagogy.

Teacher Cognition

The first significant area of activity is the emergence of a cognitive perspective in research on teachers and teaching (see Carter, 1990; Clark & Peterson, 1986). In recent years, this work has shifted from an emphasis on teachers' information processing and decisions to their knowledge structures and comprehension processes. With this shift has come an interest in the central role of preconceptions in teacher learning (see Feiman-Nemser & Buchmann, 1987; Hollingsworth, 1989; McDiarmid, 1990; Weinstein, 1990; Wubbels, 1992) and an emphasis on situation and personal construction in teachers' knowledge acquisition. As Knowles and Holt-Reynolds (1994) stated, "People construct ideas as they learn, and they use prior knowledge, experiences, and beliefs, as well as interpretations they generate in the moment, as the stuff out of which to build those ideas" (p. 6). Indeed, the work on biography can be viewed, in part,

as a dedicated effort to take preconceptions and knowledge construction seriously in teacher education.

Personal Knowledge Revolution

The second important movement that has influenced a biographical approach is the forceful emergence of an emphasis on teachers' personal knowledge (see Carter, 1990; Clandinin & Connelly, 1987; Louden, 1991; Ross, Cornett, & McCutcheon, 1992; Schubert & Ayers, 1992; Solas, 1992; Zeichner, Tabachnick, & Densmore, 1987). In part, this movement reflects a general reaction against the technical rationality that has characterized much of teacher education policy and practice, a rationality that stressed the acquisition and testing of research-validated teaching skills (see Garrison, 1988; Sparkes, 1993; Zumwalt, 1988). Biographical investigators argue that teachers learn a great deal from the actual practice of teaching in classrooms, that is, what Schön (1983) called the "epistemology of practice," and that these situated and personalized understandings are at the heart of teachers' work (see Clandinin & Connelly, 1987). As Kelchtermans and Vandenberghe (1994) observed, "When a teacher thinks about concrete teaching strategies, he or she always does so in terms of behaviours in concrete classroom situations" (p. 56).

An emphasis on personal knowledge pushes the locus of inquiry into teaching further away from a knowledge based in researchers' observations and closer to the persons who hold practical understandings of teaching. In other words, experience teaches a great deal about teaching, but experience is not an abstraction or an experimental treatment. Rather, persons have experiences, and thus every experience and its consequences are constructions from the interplay of a situation and the person who is experiencing that situation (see Aoki, 1993; Grumet, 1992; van Manen, 1990). To understand personal knowledge, therefore, one must examine the experiences of the individual teacher through personal narrative and life-history studies (Cole & Knowles, 1993b; Connelly & Clandinin, 1990).

One senses that a recognition of the deeply personal nature of their own teaching practice is, in part, responsible for the interest many investigators have in a biographical approach to research on teachers and teaching (e.g., Grumet, 1988; Holt-Reynolds, 1992; Knowles, 1994; Trumbull, 1990). Teaching is easy to study as an event "out there" (i.e., as something only other people do) if one has never taught in the K–12 sector or does not recognize one's own teaching practice in higher education as significant activity or as analogous to what one is studying as a classroom researcher. For a large number of today's classroom researchers, teaching is something they do, something "close up." Thus, an objectified stance toward teaching is unacceptable.

The Politics of Teaching

Recently the reaction against technical rationality and the remote control of teachers has expanded into a critique of the politics of teaching (i.e., the power relationships that govern who decides what teachers are to be held accountable for) (see Goodson, 1994). One manifestation of such politics is what Gitlin (1990) argued is the alienating relationship between researcher and teacher in most forms of classroom research, including ethnography. This relationship denigrates the personal knowledge of teachers, silences their voices, and conveys the impression that only researchers produce knowledge for teaching.

Goodson (1994) has argued that research on teachers' lives and how teachers experience their work can serve to raise consciousness about conditions of teaching in schools, empower teachers to make their resistance to government reforms (e.g., the national curriculum movement in England) more clear and powerful, and enlist teachers' voices in the radical reconstruction of schooling practices to make them more inclusionary and emancipatory. In this view, the study of teachers' lives is seen as an attempt to create a "counter-culture based upon a research mode that above all places teachers at the centre of the action and seeks to sponsor 'the teacher's voice' " (Goodson, 1994, p. 31; see also Ayers, 1989). By locating knowledge for teaching within teachers themselves and by demonstrating clearly the complexity of the enterprise of teaching, it is possible to deny outsiders—university-based researchers or government policymakers—access to a simplistic "knowledge base" for controlling teaching.

Feminist Perspectives

The third important development stimulating an interest in teacher biography is the growing prominence of feminist perspectives in teaching and teacher education (see, e.g., Gore, 1993; Middleton, 1992; Personal Narratives Group, 1989; Traver, 1987). With an expanding awareness that much of the actual work of teaching is carried out by women, there has been increasing attention to gender issues in the control of teaching practice. In addition to focusing on "voice" as a central theme (see Carter, 1993; Elbaz, 1991; Fox, 1993; Richert, 1992), feminist scholars often reject "grand theory," that is, broad generic formulations of rules or principles, in favor of biography precisely because the former evades personal, gendered understandings of human action. Grumet (1988) noted, as "we slide into the discourse of political theory, cognitive theory, and educational history . . . our experience as children, as women, and as parents gathers up its convictions and its questions and quietly leaves the room" (p. xvii). She further argued that if we do not acknowledge our own experience of childhood and parenting in discussing educational issues, "we would literally 'overlook' the ways that each of us is implicated in them and the ways that our own practices as educators are motivated by them" (Grumet, 1988, p. xvii).

Story

There has been a rapidly expanding interest within the teaching and teacher education community in narrative and story as forms of both inquiry and pedagogy, an interest that has been directed especially to questions of how teachers understand and know their work (see Carter, 1993; Elbaz, 1991; Gomez & Tabachnick, 1992; Gudmundsdottir, 1991). Two central assumptions underlie the work on story as related to teaching and teacher education. The first is that story represents a way

of knowing and thinking that is particularly suited to explicating the knowledge that arises from action (see Bruner, 1985; Mitchell, 1981; Polkinghorne, 1988). Thus, story is an especially relevant form for expressing teachers' practical understandings. More broadly, however, it is argued that people live storied lives, that is, "My acting-in-the-world . . . is the continuous plotting of a narrative, interpreting the past and projecting the future according to my image of myself" (Funkenstein, 1993, p. 22).

Summary

These origins and sources of a biographical outlook in learning to teach are obviously interconnected. Indeed, this discussion indicates clearly that an emphasis on biography is part of a larger movement toward the personal and the local in understanding human action and social policy. Next, the themes of personal construction, gendered experience, social control, and narrative are discussed as the major research programs in this area are examined and their implications for teacher education policy, research, and practice are discussed.

TEACHERS' PERSONAL NARRATIVES

This section examines a set of research programs or frameworks that are grounded in intensely biographical and autobiographical perspectives and that focus largely on classroom practice. Each framework is generally described in terms of (1) its basic premises and underlying theoretical assumptions, (2) illustrative applications of the approach in research or practice, and (3) key conceptualizations of the role of personal narrative and life stories in learning to teach.

The intent here is to represent these research programs as portrayed by their authors, with little consideration of possible limitations or outside critiques and with only minor attention to teacher education issues and practices that flow from these approaches. The analysis of issues and practices in teacher education raised by an emphasis on biography are taken up in the sections that follow.

Currere: An Autobiographical Method

Grumet (1978) was among the early advocates of autobiography in teacher preparation. Although her work is often cited in the current literature, it is seldom explicated. Given the intrinsic merits and historical importance of her work, an attempt is made here to sketch the basic features of her approach.

Grumet adapted a method for critical reflection on educational experience that she developed with Pinar (1975) called "currere," the root word of "curriculum," which is translated as "experience." The method, embracing both context and self-report (i.e., subjectivity and the impact of social milieu on it), was grounded in humanistic philosophy, phenomenology, and existentialism's emphasis on the dialectical relationship of a person to his or her situation (see Grumet, 1975, 1992). Grumet (1988) also added a feminist perspective to the interpretation of autobiographical texts.

Currere was originally created as an approach to curriculum inquiry that takes inquiry to the level of the experience of a particular individual, thus achieving a synthesis within the person, which is in contrast to the analytical separation characteristic of traditional empiricist paradigms.

To practice currere, a person uses the psychoanalytic technique of free association to construct a multidimensional biography synthesizing the existential meaning of past, future, and present educational experiences. The emphasis is on both intellectual and physical knowledge of these experiences and on the reconstruction of factors influencing present choices (see Salvio, 1994). It is a search for the "architecture of self" (Pinar, 1988).

Literature, as a true experience and a text outside of one's own subjectivity, is proposed as a foil for self-reflection. Grumet (1975) argued

As the reader voluntarily recreates that which the writer discloses, he too creates a fictive world, drawn from the substance of his experience and his fantasy. This participation in an aesthetic experience is one way of demonstrating the reciprocity of objectivity and subjectivity and their interdependence; it extends to the researcher the artist's awareness that his subjectivity transforms any objectivity it seeks to describe. (p. 13)

In addition to revealing a reader's experience, literature also serves to initiate a distancing from the everyday world in order to see its freshness and immediacy.

Grumet (1978) applied currere to instructional supervision and illustrated it with a case of supervision with a teacher in a nursing program. The focus was on the kinds of questions a teacher asks of her own work on the grounds that these questions shape the nature and meaning of what is seen. Grumet asserted that "the concept of teacher effectiveness requires that the teacher learn to hear, formulate and articulate her own questions about her experience of teaching and that the primary function of supervision is to establish a dialectic form of reflection upon experience that the teacher can then adapt to her own pedagogical practice" (1978, p. 26). The key, in other words, is to help a teacher "extract information from his own response to his situation" (Grumet, 1978, p. 27). The method, operating within a dialectic relationship, establishes the necessary distance from everyday events for the teacher to ask questions of his or her work and to find the patterns that give it meaning. The questions, of course, are to emerge from the teacher rather than the supervisor.

The process begins with the teacher writing an essay on the nature of educational experience focusing on her own specific experiences. The supervisor reads this text and offers questions about details and/or meanings to encourage clarification and reflection. These essays and questions ultimately lead to themes to be examined through classroom observation. At this point the teacher begins writing journal entries to record his or her responses to everyday events.

Grumet (1978) emphasized that these exchanges are to be written. At one level, this requirement serves to enable teachers to edit texts so they can control their own representations in the exchange. Moreover, writing creates a distancing that encourages fresh insight. Most important, however, the written text plays a key role in interpreting an experience because it can be examined as written text itself for patterns, meanings,

and other "shadows" (Grumet, 1989). As Grumet (1988) noted, "if the text is to display teacher thinking for the thought of the teacher, for her reflection and interpretation, rather than for someone else's utilization and marketing, then the gaps, the contradictions, the leaks and explosions in the text are invitations to her own self-interpreting and self-determining reading" (p. 67).

Currere, therefore, is a method of generating and reading autobiographical texts to achieve more understanding of the meaning of one's work, that is, "the dialectical interplay of our experience in the world and our ways of thinking about it" (Grumet, 1988, p. 67; for illustrative readings by Grumet of a teacher's texts, see pp. 66–74). The approach is grounded in the dialectics of subjectivity and objectivity and the person in a situation. The texts are multidimensional and can be read (and reread) from multiple perspectives, and this multiplicity is celebrated rather than lamented. Grumet (1988) noted that "Fidelity rather than truth is the measure of these tales" (p. 66). Indeed, "the literary narrative that is autobiography resembles the social event that is curriculum: Both function as mediating forms that gather the categorical and the accidental, the anticipated and the unexpected, the individual and the collective" (p. 67).

From the perspective of learning to teach, it is clear that currere does not focus simply on a teacher's classroom performances, although certainly such practices are part of a teacher's work. The frame, rather, is experience and the meanings or understandings one brings to and can extract from experience. As understanding evolves, the potential for action also evolves. Also, given Grumet's roots in curriculum, meaning is not limited simply to private or subjective understandings, but rather is informed by and contextualized in knowledge from educational theory and other branches of the academy.

Personal Practical Knowledge: A Narrative Perspective

A vigorous tradition has developed since the mid-1980s around the idea of teachers' "personal practical knowledge," that is, how individual teachers come to understand local, everyday events and decisions in their classrooms as part of their life narratives. Although Connelly and Clandinin (1985, 1990) are the most prominent spokespersons for this work, others have also adopted this perspective in their inquiry (e.g., Elbaz, 1983; Johnson, 1990; Trumbull, 1990).

Connelly and Clandinin (1990) are significant in the present context because they frame their research on personal practical knowledge in the tradition of narrative inquiry—"the study of the ways humans experience the world" (p. 2). They conceive of practice as living out one's narrative of experience and see education as "the construction and reconstruction of personal and social stories" (p. 2). From this perspective, personal narrative is foundational to how an individual comes to know teaching at the practical level of everyday events, that is, how formal knowledge, personal aspirations and goals, and cumulative experience are integrated in an understanding of immediate, local situations.

In the conduct of studies, Connelly and Clandinin (1990) work closely over long periods of time with a small number of teachers to achieve, through observation, journal writing, conversation, documents, and the mutual construction of narrative, an understanding of how they interpret and give meaning to practice and come to terms with the interplay of self and situation. Central to the process is the teacher's story. The researcher, however, is quite active in the process of constructing a collaborative narrative.

Narrative inquiry is . . . a process of collaboration involving mutual storytelling and restorytelling as the research proceeds. In the process of beginning to live the shared story of narrative inquiry, the researcher needs to be aware of constructing a relationship in which both voices are heard. (Connelly & Clandinin, 1990, p. 4)

A key notion is that of narrative unities, which underscores the coherence and continuity of an individual's experience (for a critique of this emphasis, see Elbaz, 1990; Willinsky, 1989). Connelly and Clandinin (1985) have argued that, from the perspective of schooling, a teaching act is a "narrative-in-action," that is, an "expression of biography and history . . . in a particular situation" (p. 184). Thus, for an individual teacher, theory and practice are integrated through his or her narrative unity of experience.

Connelly and Clandinin (1985) emphasized that teachers know teaching experientially through "images, rituals, habits, cycles, routines, and rhythms" (p. 195). Special attention in their work is given to "image" as a form of knowing that is nonpropositional, holistic, imbued with emotionality and morality, largely tacit, and continuously under revision (see also Elbaz, 1983, 1991). Examples include such teachers' images as Stephanie's "classroom as home" or Aileen's "planting the seed" (see Clandinin, 1985, 1986). In terms similar to those used by Grumet (1975), Clandinin (1989) argued that image is

connected with the individual's past, present, and future. Image draws both from the present and future in a personally meaningful nexus of experience focused on the immediate situation that called it forth. It reaches into the past, gathering up experiential threads meaningfully connected to the present, and it reaches intentionally into the future and creates new meaningfully connected threads as situations are experienced and new situations are anticipated from the perspective of the image. Image is the glue that melds together a person's diverse experiences, both personal and professional. (pp. 139–140)

This knowing embodied in images stands in sharp contrast to the conceptual frameworks exemplified in the formal academic disciplines (i.e., the paradigmatic mode of knowing) (see Bruner, 1985).

These investigators also hold that continuities, cycles, and rhythms are fundamental to narratives of experience, especially in schools and classrooms. As a result, time and the experience of school time are often central to their analyses of the personal practical knowledge of experienced and novice teachers (see Clandinin & Connelly, 1986). In a report of a study about learning to teach, for example, Clandinin (1989) described the case of Stewart, a first-year kindergarten teacher. Stewart's image of teaching was that of "teaching as relating to children." This image was grounded in his past experiences with children that led him to want to be a kindergarten teacher. Using this image as a standard, Stewart chose practices that increased opportuni-

ties for interacting with children (e.g., center time) and resisted activities that decreased such time (e.g., filling out records and making detailed observations of children). Indeed, he insisted on teaching kindergarten because he felt that this age level had less external pressures to cover content and thus provided him with maximum opportunities to relate to the children.

During his first year, Stewart's image was in tension with school cycles and demands (e.g., letting students and parents into his classroom prior to the official starting time put him in conflict with the principal) and with colleagues in a team situation (e.g., wanting to preserve center time at all costs delayed the overall schedule). These tensions created dilemmas for Stewart. Throughout the year, Stewart came to terms with school cycles and came to know his teaching rhythmically, thus reducing the imbalance of his image and the situation. At the same time, he became concerned that his adaptations to school cycles were in conflict with his initial image of centering his teaching on the children.

With respect to teacher education, these investigators naturally point to the importance of seeing practical understanding of teaching as grounded in biography (i.e., in one's life narrative) (Clandinin, 1989). Learning to teach is a fundamental process of reconstructing one's narrative of experience with special reference to classrooms, schools, and the demands of being a teacher. "Learning to teach means, in part, learning to live in a certain cultural, historical and uniquely defined cyclic situation with young children in each particular teacher's narrative of experience" (Clandinin & Connelly, 1986, p. 386). The difficult tasks of transformation and reconstruction a teacher faces, especially during times of contradiction and imbalance between his or her image and the demands of situations, require reflection within a caring and supportive setting.

Collaborative Autobiography

The concept of "collaborative autobiography" has grown out of the work of Butt and Raymond and their colleagues on teachers' perspectives regarding the unfolding of their practical professional knowledge and consciousness over time (see Butt, 1989; Butt & Raymond, 1989; Butt, Raymond, McCue, & Yamagishi, 1992; Raymond, Butt, & Townsend, 1992). They see a reciprocal relationship between person and context and underscore the importance of personal knowledge gained through immediate experience. Such knowledge is seen as a product, through reflection, of biography (i.e., the collection of beliefs, values, principles, intentions, feelings, etc.) and interaction within situations in classrooms and schools.

The authors also argue that teaching becomes more personal with experience and that teachers' personal knowledge not only guides interpretations of ongoing experience, but also motivates them to seek out experiences for their own development. "Thus biography does not only influence the teacher's response to context and opportunities, it can also help select and guide the search for particular professional development opportunities" (Raymond, Butt, & Townsend, 1992, p. 152).

The underlying questions in this work include those of substance and expression (e.g., What are the central components and forms of a teacher's knowledge? How is it expressed in action? What situations produce dilemmas or satisfactions?) and those of development (e.g., What are the sources, life experiences, and contexts that have shaped a teacher's knowledge?).

Collaborative autobiography involves having teachers write personal statements that cover "a depiction of the context of current working reality, a description of current pedagogy and curriculum-in-use, reflections on past personal and professional lives that might facilitate understanding present professional thoughts and actions, and finally, a projection into preferred futures through a critical appraisal of the previous three phases" (Butt and Raymond, 1989, p. 407). These statements are done in a group setting so that individuals hear other autobiographies, which can prod memory. On the one hand, the researchers then enter to assist the autobiographer in identifying major themes, patterns, issues, and events in his or her text, and, on the other hand, in charting independently the concepts, ideas, and categories that the research finds in the text. The products from these two interpretive activities are then brought together to construct a composite description and explanation. This composite is then read by the autobiographer for validation. The researchers also visit classrooms to see if the accounts accord with actual events.

Butt and Raymond (1989) focused primarily on two collaborative autobiographies (see also Butt et al., 1992; Raymond et al., 1992). Lloyd, who was 40 years old and a sixth-grade teacher in a lower socioeconomic area with 14 years of experience, grounded his knowledge in the concepts of "survival, safety and success" (p. 408). These concepts or aims permeated his personal life as well as his teaching and appeared to be outgrowths of his personal and cultural background. In his teaching, he emphasized the themes of social development, covering the basics in a planned and sequential manner, and a family atmosphere of warmth and friendship. Glenda was 44 years old, had taught for 9 years, and worked with immigrant and refugee children in a pull-out resource room for English as a second language. Her knowledge was grounded in her experiences in international contexts and in multicultural classrooms and was organized around themes of self-initiation and self-determination. She depicted her own development in terms of blossoming from the seed planted in early childhood through her experiences in Pakistan and now in her teaching.

The authors pointed out that these teachers' knowledge was influenced by their experiences as "children, parents, teachers, cultural backgrounds, personal and professional experiences, and peers" (Butt & Raymond, 1989, p. 413). Early experiences were especially powerful and tended to have a persistent effect (Raymond et al., 1992). They also noted that both teachers identified and were heavily influenced by their pupils. Overall, they underscored the connection between personal and professional development in teaching.

Much of the work reported by Butt and Raymond was based on autobiographies written by experienced teachers as part of graduate coursework or field seminars (see Butt, 1989). They argued that collaborative autobiography provided an important tool for increasing the relevance of such courses and enhancing professional development.

Personal Histories

A body of work under the general title "personal histories" has been recently generated, independently and together, by Knowles, Holt-Reynolds, and Cole (see Cole, 1990; Cole & Knowles, 1993a; Holt-Reynolds, 1992; Knowles, 1992, 1993; Knowles & Holt-Reynolds, 1991). Among members of this group, the term *personal history* is often used interchangeably with such terms as *life history* and *biography* to refer to personal accounts that are "constructed at the request of someone other than the person the life history describes" (Knowles, 1993, p. 72).

These investigators are principally interested in the early development of novice teachers, especially during initial teacher preparation coursework and field experiences, and in the construction of pedagogies that will address in powerful ways the robust personal beliefs systems that preservice teachers bring to their professional education (Cole & Knowles, 1993a; Holt-Reynolds, 1992; Knowles & Holt-Reynolds, 1991). Knowles has explored the notion of metaphor as a window to preservice and beginning teachers' personal histories (Knowles, 1994; see also Bullough, 1994; Bullough, with Stokes, 1994) and has related personal histories to the conceptualization of reflection in teacher education (Knowles, 1993). It can also be noted that this body of work is closely tied to the literature on teacher socialization and the development of teachers' coping and problem-solving strategies (Knowles, 1992).

At the center of their analyses is the internal dialogue in which teacher education candidates interpret their coursework and field experiences and construct their understandings of how they will behave as teachers (see Cole, 1990; Knowles, 1993; Knowles & Holt-Reynolds, 1991). This dialogue occurs within the coherent and cohesive belief systems that have accumulated from candidates' personal histories in families, peer groups, schools, and classrooms.

Crow (1987) established the pattern for personal history studies. Crow was interested in understanding the actual socialization processes involved in becoming a teacher. In an extensive review of the existing literature, Crow concluded that teacher education candidates were active agents in their own socialization through the perspectives they brought with them to teaching and through their acceptance or rejection of the values and beliefs they encountered in teacher education programs.

Crow (1987) then examined the socialization of four prospective secondary school teachers with observations and interviews that included university instructors and cooperating teachers. She concluded that each candidate carried into the program a strong "teacher role identity" around which their socialization into teaching revolved throughout their experiences in the program. They used these identities, especially prior to student teaching, to interpret quite selectively the program itself and to project themselves into "imaginary classroom contexts made up of students and other variables" (Crow, 1987, p. 192). As they entered student teaching, they were confronted with contextual pressures and demands that challenged their own sense of rightness and effectiveness and their views of pupils' willingness to be cooperative with the candidates' approaches. Yet, they still expressed, whenever possible, their teacher role identities and looked forward to their own classrooms in which their preferred approaches would work better.

Knowles (1992) used Crow's (1987) concept of teacher role identity to construct a general model to account for the interaction of biography on teaching practice. He argued that formative experiences, including those with families, in schools, in prior teaching experiences, and with significant others, and the meanings or interpretations assigned to these experiences lead to a schema (i.e., an organized way of thinking about teaching). A schema, in turn, is used to project a framework for action, which, in turn, coalesces into a teacher role identity (for a critique of the construct of "identity," see Britzman, 1992). This identity, or image of self as teacher, is carried into practice settings and influences in profound ways the coping and problem-solving decisions and actions of beginning teachers. Moreover, the strength and appropriateness of this identity in terms of the demands of classrooms predict success in dealing with the rigors of early teaching experiences.

Personal history studies suggest that teacher candidates use their own student experiences as prototypical and generalizable for interpreting and making decisions about the teaching practices they encounter in courses and field experiences. During coursework, they think about various practices by first imagining themselves using them in classrooms and then quickly switching to a student persona to judge how they and students they knew would react to the circumstances the practices would create. That is, they use their past experiences as students "to construct a virtual world where they can explore predictions about what their own teaching might look like" (Knowles & Holt-Reynolds, 1991, p. 91).

In general, candidates judged those practices they felt worked or would have worked for them as students as likely to work for them as teachers and rejected those that they did not like in the past. This does not mean that candidates simply copy the methods they witnessed as students; indeed, they often are quite critical of the teaching they have experienced. Rather, they actively construct judgments grounded in the "relatively sound personal and pragmatic truths" (Cole, 1990, p. 203) that have emerged from their past experiences. In the process, they often ignore cases of teaching that differ from their own previous experience and sidestep theoretical arguments by instructors. Their ideal images are also often based on narrow assumptions about the range and diversity of students' capabilities and interests and on unrealistic beliefs in the power of their own personalities to motivate students.

The candidates' principal criterion for these judgments was students' motivation, that is, their own sense of whether they or their friends would, as students, have found the situations interesting and enjoyable. Such situations tend to be characterized, at least for secondary school teacher candidates, by a personal sense of fun and comfort, and they normally attribute these reactions to teacher characteristics such as caring and interest in the subject matter. Indeed, the teachers in these imaginary scenarios are quite active in creating enjoyable, comfortable classrooms.

Holt-Reynolds (1992) has provided useful insights into the nature of this internal dialogue in her study of the personal history-based beliefs of nine secondary teacher education candidates enrolled in a course in reading in the content areas who had not yet participated in field experiences. Six interviews were conducted with each candidate focusing on personal background and the specific content of the course. Holt-Reynolds then wrote personal histories describing themes and

their connection to personal stories, and these were discussed with each participant to establish agreement.

The instructor in the course placed strong emphasis on the difficulties of classroom texts for many secondary school students, on the need for teachers to provide direct instruction in reading processes so that pupils could independently learn by reading, and on the limited value if not detrimental effects of teacher-led class discussions and lecturing as substitutes for learning from reading. The course, in other words, "was, in essence, one extended campaign for the adoption of student-centered, process-focused, constructivist practices in subject-matter secondary classrooms" (Holt-Reynolds, p. 330).

The nine candidates found many of the techniques advocated in the course attractive and exciting, but they rejected the instructor's premises regarding independent learning and teacher telling. Based on their experiences as high school students, they felt that students were not passive during lectures but would actively follow along and learn if the lectures were interesting and not boring. They also thought lecturing was necessary because the textbooks were too boring (e.g., history) or that the subject matter was too difficult to learn independently (e.g., math). During lectures the material could be made more interesting and intelligible and students could ask questions. In literature, however, they expected that high school students would not have difficulty reading novels and stories and getting something out of them. As a result, they saw no need for direct instruction in reading processes, arguing that good teachers believed their students were competent. They also asserted that in literature lecturing would be useful in fulfilling the teacher's responsibility to motivate students by making the content come alive. Finally, lecturing was justified on the grounds that it is useful in demonstrating subject-matter expertise, which they believed good teachers need to do.

Holt-Reynolds also noted a major difference between the instructor's definition of lecturing and that of the students. For the instructor, lecturing was any mode in which predigested information was conveyed to students. This definition included question-answer formats. For the students, sessions that included questions and answers were seen as discussions, which were much more highly valued than straight lectures. Moreover, the students saw the need for variety and, thus, saw some of the instructor's suggestions as not inherently more valuable but as useful variations in classroom formats.

Holt-Reynolds (1992) commented on the strength and tenacity of the candidates' personal history belief systems. When they encountered conflicts between their personal beliefs and those of an instructor, they questioned the validity of the instructor's beliefs rather than their own. In a related report, Holt-Reynolds (1994) described a case of one of the nine candidates who was enthusiastic about the practices advocated in the course but used very different rationales, grounded in her personal history, to justify these practices and saw no conflicts. Holt-Reynolds also noted that most of the fundamental differences between the instructor and the students with regard to learning, knowledge, students' capabilities, and the effectiveness of various instructional formats never came up for discussion in the class.

As candidates move into field experiences, practicums, and the first year of teaching, their beliefs grounded in personal histories come up against classroom and school contingencies (Knowles, 1992, 1994; Knowles & Holt-Reynolds, 1991; see also Bullough, 1989; Bullough, Knowles, & Crow, 1989; Bullough, with Stokes, 1994; Cole, 1990). Here, their ideal practices, expectations about how successful they will be, and especially their assumptions and beliefs about students, are tested. Moreover, feelings and images associated with their own prior experiences as students are evoked. The consequence, Cole and Knowles (1993a) argued, is often "shattered images," in part because their images are "frozen in time and context and lacking animation, much as a photographic representation . . . [and thus] shatter against the hard realities and complexities of schools, classrooms, and day-to-day teaching" (p. 459). This effect appeared to be strongest for those candidates with weak role identities and with images that are least congruent with the actual demands of teaching (Knowles, 1992).

As difficulties are encountered, they often abandon initial decisions, especially if they involve complex instructional arrangements, and adopt more traditional but familiar roles and procedures, although this pattern is not necessarily universal (see Beier, 1994; Bullough, with Stokes, 1994). Natalie, for example, initially thought about teaching as grounded in being a buddy to students. When this was rejected by students, she abandoned an intensive conversational approach to language teaching in favor of workbook exercises and tried to be more strict (Knowles, 1994). Others try to ignore problems by teaching only to those who respond to their approaches (Knowles & Holt-Reynolds, 1991).

In coping with difficulties, student teachers and beginning teachers often blame others (students, parents, colleagues, schools), isolate themselves from colleagues, and otherwise think about teaching in ways that do not promote development or appropriate problem solving. These patterns of coping also reflect their personal histories. In other words, they continue the internal dialogue about pedagogy, but now are facing the demanding problems of coping with immediate classroom situations.

As their personal beliefs fail to provide adequate problem-solving tools, they are often at a loss to understand what to do. In such circumstances, learning from experience can be a difficult endeavor (see Munby & Russell, 1994). Thus, beginning teachers often reach deeper into their pasts to pull up practices that seemed to have solved similar problems for teachers they knew (see Rust, 1994). At the same time, candidates may retain their commitment to their basic perspectives or conceptions of teaching even as they adjust their practice to match the demands of classrooms or schools (see Zeichner, Tabachnick, & Densmore, 1987).

Personal history investigators have talked at some length about the fragility of most teacher education interventions in the face of the power of personal history beliefs (see Cole & Knowles, 1993a; Holt-Reynolds, 1993; Knowles, 1993, 1994). They place particular emphasis on teacher education pedagogies, such as writing personal histories, dialogue journals, open discussions of beliefs, and close working relationships between candidates and teacher educators, in which preconceptions are "laid bare" (Knowles, 1993, p. 81) and interpersonal influences are heightened.

Critical Perspectives on Teachers' Life Stories

Several investigators who emphasize the key role of biography in teaching and learning to teach have emphasized the importance of teachers examining their life stories within a larger historical frame "to develop a wide intertextual and intercontextual mode of analysis" (Goodson, 1994, p. 36). Britzman (1986, 1991), in particular, has argued that learning to teach must be placed in a larger political and ideological framework. Consistent with the work on personal histories reviewed earlier, she agreed that student teachers' institutional biographies, as evoked by their return to the classroom setting, profoundly inform their negotiation of meaning in these complex environments and shape the formulation of their pedagogies. Yet, "the underlying values which coalesce in one's institutional biography, if unexamined, propel the cultural reproduction of authoritarian teaching practices and naturalize the contexts which generate such a cycle" (Britzman, 1986, p. 443). She further argued that this reproduction often occurs despite the best intentions of teaching candidates who often enter teacher education wanting to alter many of the conditions they experienced as students.

Using examples from her study of two secondary English student teachers, Britzman maintained that this reproduction happens because the student's perspective in classrooms is separated from the behind-the-scenes organizational and political processes. Thus, important structural and authority issues are made invisible and unproblematic, and teaching is seen almost exclusively as a performance by a seemingly autonomous teacher (i.e., a matter of individual effort rather than institutional policies and practices). They enter teacher education seeking technical answers to how to teach and find little value in their more theoretically informed coursework. In student teaching, this orientation is reinforced by the pressure to survive in demanding circumstances and by the atheoretical culture of school situations. They come to believe in three "cultural myths": (1) that everything depends on the teacher, (2) that the teacher is the expert, and (3) that teachers are self-made.

Britzman argued that to break this cycle teaching candidates must come to understand their institutional biographies and how these personal histories impede their ability to transform classroom life. "Prospective teachers need to participate in developing critical ways of knowing which can interrogate school culture, the quality of students' and teachers' lives, school knowledge, and the particular role biography plays in understanding these dynamics" (Britzman, 1986, p. 454). She acknowledged that this critical reflection on one's constructions of teacher and self is not an easy process but can become "a socially empowering occasion" (Britzman, 1992, p. 44).

Barone (1987) examined the preprofessional biography of a student he called Shelley Citoyen, who developed a progressive/critical ideology or platform for teaching in her early school experiences. During her teacher preparation for the elementary school, she spent a summer in England and took a course on language and learning in the British schools. This course enabled her to articulate the progressive ideas underlying her early school experience. For student teaching, she selected a progressive teacher working alone in a traditional setting, in part to learn how to develop strategies to maintain the integrity of her platform as she entered teaching. Barone used this case to argue for the deliberate selection of candidates for teacher education who have a reformist platform and the environmental competence to carry it out and then for the nurturing of this orientation during their programs. He suggested that traditional criteria for admissions to teacher education, grounded in grade point averages and test scores, may well exclude candidates with platforms similar to Shelley's.

From a critical perspective, therefore, personal narratives are seen as powerful instruments in either maintaining or transforming teaching practice. If left unexamined, they are likely to perpetuate conventional practice in spite of the best intentions of beginning teachers. Such narratives need to be made explicit by and to individual teacher candidates and, importantly, need to be understood as products of particular social and historical circumstances that limit their vision for educational possibilities.

Summary

This section examines in some detail five research programs or frameworks that embody a biographical approach to understanding teachers, teaching, and learning to teach. This work is centered on the practical understandings that teachers develop as they enter into and begin to teach and on the ways in which beginning and/or experienced teachers come to frame their understandings within their life stories or life experiences. These investigators not only emphasize the fundamental role of personal narrative in becoming a teacher but also place great value on making personal narrative the cornerstone for the education of teachers.

Before expanding on the implications of and issues surrounding this work on personal narrative, the next section discusses a second strand of research that is situated in an understanding of teachers' lives, namely, the study of teachers' work and career cycle. In this second strand, the focus shifts from teachers' deliberations about immediate classroom incidents or decisions about practices to broader conceptions of teachers' lives as teachers.

TEACHERS' WORK AND CAREER CYCLES

In the mid-1980s, Feiman-Nemser and Floden (1986) introduced their survey of research related to an understanding of the "cultures of teaching" by calling attention to the "striking . . . shift from trying to study the world of teaching as a public, social phenomenon to trying to understand how teachers define their own work situations" (p. 505). This trend is certainly evident in the recent research on teachers' understanding of their work and their sense of career. Indeed, until quite recently, teachers seldom were seen to have personal lives outside of their classroom lessons and, except for some broad notions of development within initial teacher preparation (particularly during student teaching), there was little sense of any differentiation among experienced practitioners (see Floden & Huberman, 1989; Huberman, 1989). As Lightfoot (1983) noted, teachers were traditionally seen "as strangely presentist characters—

without past or future—and without life beyond the classroom" (p. 242).

The driving force behind life-span research on teachers' work and careers is threefold. First, there is the realization that "the teacher is the ultimate key to educational change and school improvement" (Hargreaves, 1993, p. vii). It follows that reform efforts must take into account teachers. Second, there is the recognition that how teachers teach is "grounded in their backgrounds, their biographies, in the kinds of teachers they have become" (Hargreaves, 1993, p. vii). It is insufficient, therefore, to focus solely on classroom performance, teaching skills, or curriculum in achieving school change. Who teachers are as persons must also be accounted for. Finally, there is an awareness, inspired in part by popularized books on adult developmental phases (e.g., Levinson, 1978; Sheehy, 1976), that people intersect with their work in different ways at different stages of their lives. For staff development and school improvement efforts to be successful, therefore, it is argued that they must be aligned with the personal and professional life cycles of teachers.

This section covers four studies that emphasize, in varying ways, the personal dimensions of teachers' careers, namely, Huberman (1993); Nias (1989); Sikes, Measor, and Woods (1985); and Spencer (1986). The particular focus in reviewing these studies is to relate them to conceptualizations of learning to teach. For additional studies in this area, see Fessler (1994); Kelchtermans (1993); Kelchtermans and Vandenberghe (1994); Schempp, Sparkes and Templin (1993); the articles in Huberman (1989); the chapter on educational innovators by Smith, Kleine, Prunty, and Dwyer (1992); the chapters in Ball and Goodson (1985); and the review of studies by Burden (1990).

The Lives of Women Teachers in the United States

Spencer (1986) studied the lives of women teachers in the United States with a particular focus on issues involved in balancing school and home. She interviewed 50 women teachers, but she concentrated on eight case studies framed according to whether the teachers were married, had children, or taught at the elementary or secondary level. This latter group of teachers was interviewed several times, observed in home and at school, and asked to keep diaries. The cases are presented in terms of the teachers' personal histories, their teaching experiences, their home lives, and their involvement in staff development. The cases were then discussed with respect to the larger sample of the 42 other teachers, a discussion that was related to issues of the professionalization of teachers.

In general, Spencer found that, on the one hand, school demands affected home life primarily in terms of the hours spent doing school work at home and, to a lesser extent, meeting responsibilities for extracurricular duties. On the other hand, home demands affected school life, primarily in terms of personal problems and scheduling complications. On the surface, these are not surprising findings. Conditions similar to this have probably existed since the beginning of formal schooling (see Lanier, 1986).

Yet, the stories Spencer tells are often quite poignant. Many of the teachers had working class origins with quite difficult family histories and current situations. For these women, personal relationships, family problems, and illness often affected their moods in the classroom and their enthusiasm for their work. Women with children, married or not, had very complicated home lives and major demands on their energies, especially during illnesses. These home and family responsibilities were often exacerbated because husbands either were not present or were not involved much in family life. Single teachers, however, typically had responsibilities for parents, low incomes, and few opportunities for relaxation. At the same time, married and single teachers often worried about events and people at school. Poor working conditions in the schools, including low salaries, had a major impact on their lifestyles, especially for the single teachers. Thus, terms such as *exhaustion, complication,* and *demoralized* often appear in Spencer's text.

Self in the Work of Primary Teachers in England

Nias (1989) interviewed 99 British teachers—30 men and 69 women—who completed Post Graduate Certificate in Education (PGCE) courses for work in infant, junior, and middle schools. Her purposes were "to present an account of primary teaching as work, from the perspective of its practitioners" (Nias, 1989, p. 2) and to understand the interactions between personal and professional lives of teachers. The interviews took place first from 1975 to 1977 and again, with about half of the original sample, in 1985. She noted that, especially for the 1985 group, "Most of those who replied were succeeding, in career terms, or were enthusiastically resuming a career after childrearing" (p. 7).

One of the central arguments Nias made was that "the self is a crucial element in the way teachers themselves construe the nature of their job" (p. 13). She attributed this "personal" view to the intellectual traditions of primary education and teacher preparation for primary teaching (traditions grounded in Rousseau, Froebel, and Pestalozzi). She further argued that this personal view is also emphasized in the solitary and isolated nature of much primary teaching and the relative autonomy teachers at this level possess to pursue individual ideology in teaching. In addition, although teachers differ in the degree to which they identify with their profession, there is a constant invitation for heavy self-investment in teaching.

Nias (1989) pointed out that "not all teachers incorporate an occupational identity into their self-image; those who do not, either leave the profession or lose interest in it (some of them attempting to pursue parallel careers [outside of the classroom])" (p. 3).

In discussing the nature of the teachers' sense of self, Nias noted that many saw themselves as people with a strong concern for the welfare of others and especially for improving the lives of children. They had, in other words, strong social, moral, and sometimes religious ideals, and they defined themselves as crusaders. Thus, they took their jobs seriously, worked for children on several fronts in addition to schools, and espoused high professional standards.

Nias further argued that identification as a primary teacher grows slowly with experience on the job. Teachers initially see themselves as teaching but not necessarily as teachers. This suspension of identification was in part a strategy the teachers used to protect themselves from the self-absorbing nature of teaching. Moreover, the teachers had reference groups in and out of school to help with defining the self in teaching, but pupils were the key to a sense of identity and satisfaction. This effect of pupils increased with experience. Thus, teachers' satisfaction was associated with the work they did in classrooms and only remotely with outside conditions, except as these directly affected the work they did with pupils.

As shifts in self-conception take place with classroom experience, Nias found that teachers' personal concerns in relation to their work change in a manner similar to that proposed by Fuller (1969). Their initial preoccupations were with survival in the face of the harsh realities of teaching and, after the basic technical problems of teaching became manageable, a search for occupational identification ("self" concerns). In the latter part of this initial phase, teachers tested their career choice against their experience in the profession, searching in part for a match between self and the values of the school and for self-expression through their work. Next there was a phase of consolidation and extension of work-related skills ("task" concerns). The teachers typically found a reference group within a school, felt competent, and developed personal definitions of good practice in learning from others. This phase was followed by a search for greater influence ("impact" concerns) "within what has now become a personally-selected profession" (Nias, 1989, p. 3). The teachers in this phase developed and extended their competence, took on responsibilities and intellectual challenges, and had high standards for their work and that of others. Some sought to increase their influence outside the classroom.

Those who left the profession tended not to see themselves as teachers, could not find a compatible setting, or came to the end of a sense of personal growth. A few became "privatized workers" who wanted to leave but could not because of personal circumstances.

Nias found increased stress among the teachers from 1975 to 1985, in part because of declining support for education, increases in class sizes, and a loss of control over classroom practice and curriculum policies. The teachers worked hard with high standards and were often tired. They were aware that they were not necessarily valued or supported by the general public.

Life Histories and Cycles of High School Teachers in England

Sikes et al. (1985) focused their life history study of teachers' careers on 41 high school teachers of science and art from two regions of England. Three age categories were used in establishing the sample—3 years into teaching, mid-career, and retirement. The life-history interviews averaged from 1 to 1 1/2 hours in length and varied from two to seven interviews per teacher. These conversations began with a career map and then focused on filling in this broad sketch.

The goal of the study was to examine teacher careers from the standpoint of the individuals involved and to take a "whole life view" (Sikes et al., 1985, p. 1) of ongoing development and identity. Finally, the research was guided by interactionist principles. "We were interested in how individuals adapted to, or sought to change, situations; how they managed roles and constraints; and, as we have noted, *their* perceptions of their careers" (p. 11).

The study was framed around what the authors perceived was a crisis in teacher careers, a "disjuncture . . . between past and present career perceptions large enough to render the future problematic, to disturb teachers' sense of well-being and to threaten their teaching efficiency" (p. 3). The crisis involves growing centralization and demands for accountability, deep cuts in educational expenditures, sharply decreased opportunities for promotion or for changing schools, and the consolidation of secondary modern schools with the grammar schools in the comprehensive school. As a result, they paid particular attention to critical phases and incidents in the teachers' lives as turning points in their careers and to how the teachers coped with constraints and managed the teacher role. Finally, they looked at influences from the management sector of schools, from pupils, and from the subject perspectives and identities of the teachers.

The report begins with an overview of the life cycle of the teacher, that is, the common pattern that emerged among the individual biographies. In this analysis, the authors placed special emphasis on the aging of the individual teacher in the face of a fixed generation of students. The categories for presenting the life cycle of teachers were adapted from Levinson's (1978) phases of adult development.

The first phase in the life cycle of the teacher occurred, they argued, in the age range 21–28 years. The investigators noted that this phase was an exploratory one for many in teaching, one in which they were trying teaching out to see if they wanted to stay. The major task faced in this phase was that of coming to terms with the reality of the classroom situation, with their skills as a teacher, and with their subjects. There was high anxiety about maintaining discipline and facing up to the testing by the students. Many experienced a critical incident with respect to discipline during their first year, often in a form of a direct challenge to their authority and, thus, their professional identity. As they met these challenges, they became more confident and less intimidated. In part they also learned that older teachers did not necessarily have the control they imagined they did.

After discipline, the teachers were concerned about the subject and how to communicate it to pupils.

Usually they evolve their own pedagogy through a mixture of trial and error, from observing others (on the rare occasions when this is possible), by remembering their own teachers (who, incidentally often serve as models of bad practice), and from their own idea of what it should be like. The majority say that their professional training, apart from teaching practice, was of very limited practical value. (Sikes et al., 1985, p. 32)

During this time they were also learning the codes for conduct as a teacher (e.g., how to fit in) (for an examination of the "micropolitics" of this induction process, see Schempp et al., 1993). They realized, for instance, that it was best not to talk about problems in the staff room. Because such rules were often unstated and hidden, they could be difficult to learn. With the aging of the school staff and the limited number of new

teachers, younger teachers were being socialized most often by middle-age teachers.

Phase 2 covered the ages of 28–33 years. This was a transition period in which teachers typically became more serious about their careers. They were now more secure and relaxed in the teaching role in terms of classroom demands and had reached some understanding of the privileges and responsibilities of being a teacher. In addition, they were moving in age away from their students and the interests of young people. Issues of job satisfaction, childbearing, and promotion became important because options began to narrow, with pronounced gender differences with respect to these issues. Some teachers became disillusioned, but others took an interest in curriculum development and innovation, in part to achieve personal satisfaction and to maintain interest in their jobs. The teachers also had a greater interest in pedagogy rather than their subject.

Phase 3 was defined by the age range of 30–40 years. In this phase, teachers settled into their careers and often worked very hard to achieve their goals. For men, this often meant promotion to an administrative post. Many women by this time had responsibilities for their own children, which placed the heavy demands on their time and energy that Spencer (1986) described. Some teachers sought second jobs outside of teaching, such as establishing small publishing companies, travel agencies, and so forth, and juggled their responsibilities. Relationships with pupils were now at a distance for many, and adverse comments about pupil standards, attitudes, and behavior began to appear in their conversations. Teachers who were parents were often more sympathetic with pupils.

The fourth phase consisted of teachers in the age range of 40–50/55 years. Many of the teachers in this phase were in middle management positions as heads of departments and so forth (teachers in senior management positions were not included in the sample). Men who had not been promoted by this age were unlikely ever to be, and women were often finished with the immediate demands of childrearing and began to apply for senior posts. Relationships with students were generally parental, and these teachers' roles on staffs were often ones of guiding younger teachers and maintaining standards.

The last phase covered the age range of 50–55 or more years. Because of the number of early retirements offered, teachers in this phase were considered to be facing the major task of retirement. Many felt their energy and enthusiasm were declining, but also that they were freer in their attitudes toward students and in their concern for classroom discipline. They had often been in their schools for an extended period and many had taught the parents of their current pupils. Relationships with pupils were strained by the age difference, as were those with younger staff. Sikes et al. (1985) also examined critical phases and incidents in the lives of teachers. They identified six intrinsic critical phases within the careers of teachers: (1) choosing to enter the teaching profession, (2) the first teaching practice, (3) the first 18 months of teaching, (4) 3 years after taking the first job, (5) mid-career moves and promotion, and (6) pre-retirement.

As noted previously, discipline problems and the potential of a loss of control were often critical in the early phases of a teaching career. Many of these problems served to set teachers off on a particular path toward defining the type of teacher they became. Kelchtermans and Vandenberghe (1994) noted that a critical event in a teacher's life did not necessarily occur at a set stage or phase but was an especially memorable incident that could be retold in great detail.

Sikes et al. (1985) also looked at how teachers coped with constraints, including general social and economic events, institutional factors, and personal events in their lives. Many of these, especially the establishment of comprehensive schools and budget cuts, had an impact on career trajectories and promotion opportunities. Among personal factors, it was clear that teaching was, for older women, one of the few career options they had. Moreover, women teachers often had to assume, as Spencer noted, family responsibility for childrearing and for care of parents. They noted that teachers have increasingly used public strategies of group action for their goals in contrast to private strategies for adjusting to constraints.

Finally, these investigators found that pupils and the subject specialization play important roles in shaping teachers' identities as teachers and their rewards and satisfactions in the occupation. Pupils' reactions affected teachers' reputations (which, in turn, influence their opportunities for advancement in the profession) and shaped their ideas of lesson content and their manner in the classroom. Moreover, relationships with pupils changed over a teaching career as the age differences between teachers and pupils increased. At the same time, secondary school teachers were subject specialists, and their subject philosophies and commitments interplayed with their personal histories throughout their careers (see also Woods, 1984).

Career Cycles of High School Teachers in Geneva

Huberman (1993) also studied the career cycles of secondary school teachers but focused more on years in the career rather than the ages of the teachers. The study consisted of long, in-depth interviews (from 3 to 9 hours) with 160 male and female secondary school teachers in three sites: Geneva lower secondary (pupils 13–15 years old), Geneva high school, and Vaud high school. The teachers had from 5 to 39 years of experience and entered the profession between 1941 and 1971. In addition to open-ended questions, Huberman and his research team used three standardized instruments: (1) Rotter's locus of control scale, (2) a checklist of aspects of pedagogical proficiency, and (3) a semantic differential.

Several "passionate" questions framed this investigation into teachers' professional life cycles. Among these were the following (adapted from Huberman, 1993, pp. 2–3):

1. Are there phases or stages in teaching and how do these manifest themselves in a particular generation of teachers or in relation to particular historical moments or social trends?
2. How does a teacher perceive him- or herself as a classroom teacher at different moments of his or her career, and is a teacher aware of changes over time in style, organization, priorities, mastery, or interactions with pupils?
3. Do teachers perceive themselves as becoming more competent with years of experience, and, if so, in what areas?
4. Is a teacher more or less content with his or her career at certain moments of the career cycle? What are the best years? Would they choose teaching again?

5. Is there an inevitable disenchantment with the profession, and, if so, at what point in a career does it occur?
6. Do teachers gradually become more cautious and conservative with experience?
7. What events in teachers' private lives reverberate into the classroom and what are the effects?
8. What distinguishes teachers who turn bitter from those who become or remain serene, and can such a differentiation be predicted in advance?

This was a large and quite complicated study that is difficult to summarize adequately in a chapter such as this. This chapter discusses the general flavor of the findings, relying heavily on the author's own synthesis (Huberman, 1993). It is clear from the findings that the trajectories of professional lives differed for women and men and for teachers at different grades and levels of experience. At the same time, Huberman and his colleagues looked for common themes across the teachers. In this summary, common patterns are discussed with some attention, as necessary, to variations within the group.

Overall, Huberman and his team found that teaching careers appeared to begin with an entry phase characterized by either an easy beginning (associated with a sense of discovery and enthusiasm and good rapport with pupils) or a painful beginning (associated with pupils, exhaustion, and trial-and-error coping). A painful beginning was especially prevalent among the teachers with 5–10 years of experience, many of whom, in contrast to older teachers who began as elementary teachers, complained that their teacher education programs left them quite unprepared for teaching. For women, the entry phase was often complicated by the need to balance personal and professional demands; for men, entry issues were often related to feeling their lives were controlled unnecessarily by rules and regulations and by supervisory inspections.

The next phase, mentioned by virtually all teachers, involved stabilization, associated with consolidation, relaxation with pupils and colleagues, effectiveness as a teacher, and pedagogical mastery of basic routines. This was a generally positive phase, occurring some 4–10 years into a career, in which teachers felt a part of the profession and were becoming competent in individual expression. They achieved good relations with colleagues and students, found the management of their classes easier, and accomplished a balance between school and personal life. Satisfaction with teaching appeared to follow from this period of stabilization.

Beyond these two phases the picture was more complicated. Huberman (1993) said

One principal route leads to periods of experimentation or diversification [especially among the younger teachers]. For some teachers, these two phases represent an attempt to have more impact in the classroom, once stabilization is established. For others, the focus is more institutional: once stabilized, they go after the aberrations of the system that have reduced their instructional impact in class. Finally, this phase can entail the active pursuit of administrative responsibilities, in line with personal ambitions and with fear of encroaching routine in the classroom. (p. 245)

The experimentation/diversification phase was followed, for about 40% of the teachers in the sample, by a period of self-doubt or reassessment of varying degrees of severity. For some of these teachers, self-doubt was followed by a phase of serenity and affective distance. Yet, this period of self-doubt was not true for a majority of the teachers and especially not so for women, many of whom were employed on a part-time basis and who had external interests to balance against their school lives. However, for most of the teachers in the sample, the second half of their careers was characterized by a general displacement of energy, that is, "a tendency toward less activism and less commitment in pursuit of a greater serenity" (Huberman, 1993, p. 246). This effect was associated in part with a natural relational distance from students—"A teacher ages; her pupils stay eternally the same age" (Huberman, 1993, p. 246).

At career end, a general disinvestment or withdrawal occurred, but the patterns for the teachers in this study were quite varied. For some, there was a negative focusing or a sense of disenchantment, betrayal, and devaluation by colleagues and a dissatisfaction with the state of schooling. Yet, for a significant group, the tone is much more positive, with continuing enthusiasm and openness not always shown by younger colleagues. Huberman noted that the major reforms of the junior secondary school system in 1962, in which elementary teachers were brought into the middle school structure and coeducation was introduced in the high schools, profoundly influenced the sense of disillusionment of the older teachers in the sample.

As did Nias, Huberman found relationships with students were central to the teachers' satisfaction, dissatisfaction, and sense of development throughout their careers. This effect was especially apparent among middle school teachers and particularly women.

Finally, men appeared to place more emphasis on their careers than women, in part because women typically had outside investments throughout their professional lives. Men, therefore, had more uneven career progressions in terms of commitment and disillusionment. Women, however, had a more constant level of commitment throughout their careers.

Summary

This section samples the research on teachers' work and lives with an emphasis on their perspectives on the experience of being teachers. A clear commonality in career stages appeared across the four studies summarized here, and these results are consonant with those reported in earlier studies (see Burden, 1990). A teaching career appears to involve an initial survival stage as entrants face and accommodate the demanding realities of being teachers. Some of the difficulties encountered at this stage may, of course, result from the conditions under which many beginning teachers are hired and the situations in which they are placed (see Cole, 1990). Once these initial demands have been mastered, teachers appear to reach a sense of consolidation or security and relax into the routines of the work. With this sense of mastery and security, they often experiment with alternatives and seek a wider impact. Huberman, in particular, noted that disillusionment can, but does not often, occur among mature, committed teachers, and that the ending of teaching careers is sometimes characterized by bitterness, but often by serenity and disengagement.

Within these broad patterns of teachers' lives, an interesting and seldom acknowledged picture of teachers emerges. At one level, teaching is clearly a difficult, demanding undertaking that pulls the self in strongly and thus pervades a person's entire life in significant ways. Indeed, only one teacher in Spencer's (1986) intensive sample of eight teachers, a relatively affluent married woman without childrearing responsibilities, was able to compartmentalize teaching and home life. At the same time, it appears that teachers take teaching quite seriously and invest quite heavily intellectually and emotionally in their work, especially at mid-career.

Finally, the pressures of teaching, the restricted rewards and opportunities for career advancement or diversification within teaching, and the often intractable nature of many of the basic problems in teaching can lead to self-doubt and disillusionment for many teachers, especially in the face of public devaluing of their work. On balance, most teachers find their careers satisfying. Yet, it is not surprising that some teachers become cynical about the promises of research or the latest school reforms, especially if these are presented to them without some concomitant sensitivity to their situations. What is more surprising is that cynicism is not more prevalent among seasoned teachers.

Finally, only one of the studies reviewed in this section is based on the lives of teachers in the United States; the other three projects involved teachers from the United Kingdom and Switzerland. Indeed, there is a great deal of attention to teaching careers among British investigators (see, e.g., Ball & Goodson, 1985). In the United States, the interest in teachers' careers seems to be limited largely to matters of demographics and the characteristics of the labor pool for teaching (see, e.g., Darling-Hammond & Hudson, 1990; Sweet & Jacobson, 1983), and Lortie (1975) and Fuller and Bown (1975) remain the standard references on teachers' career attitudes and stages (see Burden, 1990; Feiman-Nemser & Floden, 1986; Lanier, 1986). Burden (1990) reviewed studies of teachers' development stages, most of which were conducted in the 1970s. In large measure Burden's interpretive framework was grounded in developmental psychology. As a result, the thrust of the analysis was often toward individual dispositions rather than career cycles. Lanier (1986) declared teaching a "careerless" occupation (p. 561), and, using data largely from the 1960s and 1970s, argued that teachers were often "dissatisfied with and alienated from their work" (p. 544). From this point of view, there would be little to learn from a study of teachers' careers.

LEARNING TO TEACH AND TEACHER EDUCATION FROM A BIOGRAPHICAL PERSPECTIVE

Having sketched the general contours of the research on personal narrative and life history, this section discusses the implications of this line of inquiry for a general understanding of learning to teach and for envisioning curriculum and pedagogy in teacher education, matters only touched on in passing up to this point. In this discussion, the authors attempt to bring together both strands of life-history inquiry, namely, that which focuses on decisions about immediate contingencies and that which is directed to teachers' work and careers.

Learning to Teach as Personal Narrative

What picture of learning to teach emerges from an intense focus on the personal narratives and career cycles of novice and experienced teachers? In these authors' reflection on this work, four basic themes emerge: (1) teaching is deeply personal, (2) personal understandings of teaching are profoundly systematic and theoretical, (3) learning to teach is fundamentally a negotiated process, and (4) a sense of mastery in teaching takes a long time to achieve. Each of these is discussed on the following pages.

Teaching Is Deeply Personal Biographical inquiry in teaching underscores the degree to which teaching and the understandings that grow up as a result of watching and practicing teaching are truly personalized (i.e., rooted in an individual's identity and sense of meaning). Moreover, the impact of personal narrative is not limited to initial preparation for teaching. As Kagan (1992) asserted, "the practice of classroom teaching remains forever rooted in personality and experience" (p. 163). Indeed, Raymond and colleagues (1992) maintained that "teacher development seems to become even more personal during the teacher's career" (p. 152). Unfortunately, such terms as *perspectives* or *preconceptions* can too easily cast these personalized understandings as ill-grounded opinions or viewpoints that can easily be changed by rational argument. Such an interpretation seriously underestimates the passion these ideas embody and the extent to which they penetrate teachers' lives.

Personal Understandings of Teaching Are Profoundly Systematic and Theoretical It is clear from biographical studies that the basic ideas novice and experienced teachers have about teaching are remarkably coherent and serve a powerful organizing and explanatory function in their thinking and decision making. Perhaps, as Elbaz (1990) has suggested, it is possible to overinterpret the unity of teachers' personal narratives and thoughts. Yet, there would appear to be robust organizing and explanatory images in teachers' understanding of their work. These images are the basic tools teachers use to come to terms with the complexity of their work. Moreover, these images function like paradigms in that they (1) define what is recognized as significant in the stream of experience, (2) stipulate how issues and problems can be thought about, and (3) resist modification even in the face of discrepant information (see Doyle, 1978). In addition, despite their simplicity and lack of animation, the images held by novice teachers can also be characterized in this way.

Learning to Teach Is Fundamentally a Negotiated Process Teachers are not simply formed or socialized by their life experiences prior to, during, or after initial teacher preparation. Rather, they are highly active participants in interpreting their experiences, searching for and constructing images that capture the essential features of their understanding of the tasks they encounter in teaching, grappling with the dilemmas and chal-

lenges of classroom life, seeking out experiences and exploring avenues that might prove fruitful, and otherwise navigating the difficult circumstances of their work. It is important to underscore that this description of active construction of meaning is not intended only for those who are exceptionally successful as teachers; the same negotiation of self in situations is found among all teachers, even those who fail to achieve either their own ideals or those of their supervising teachers (see Cole & Knowles, 1993a).

Studies of images and of the key role of self in teaching suggest that considerable emotion as well as intellectual work is associated with teachers' efforts to understand the particularities of their practice in classrooms. Teaching and, certainly, learning to teach are absorbing projects. This may well mean that, in a particular context of preservice or in-service teacher education, a novice or experienced teacher would appear inarticulate or apathetic when the issues at hand are not those he or she is currently working on in the personal struggle to come to terms with teaching. Any judgment about a teacher's intelligence or motivation to change cannot, therefore, assume that the outsider's perspective is necessarily the most important (see Gitlin, 1990).

A Sense of Mastery in Teaching Takes a Long Time to Achieve Studies of teachers' career cycles indicate that it takes, on average, from 4 to 7 years for teachers to achieve a sense of identity with teaching, gain a feeling of confidence and stabilization, and reach a balance between teaching demands and other interests. In addition, it seems that only after this relatively protracted investiture process do teachers begin to explore alternatives and experiment with new ideas and ways of teaching. Clearly, learning to be a teacher is, from this perspective, not something that happens during initial teacher preparation or even an induction year. Ironically, the level of mastery that appears to take several years to achieve is often implicit in expectations for preservice teacher education programs. One can also note that many teacher educators have not taught in the K–12 sector long enough to have gained mastery.

The more detailed studies of the negotiation of personal meaning in teaching reviewed in this chapter, as well as related studies of the growth of teacher thinking with respect to classroom tasks (see Copeland, Birmingham, DeMeulle, D'Emidio-Caston, & Natal, 1994; Jones & Vesilind, 1994), suggest that the conceptualizing of practice is an exacting process that takes repeated experiences and considerable reflection and deliberation. As Spiro and his associates (Spiro, Vispoel, Schmitz, Samarapungavan, & Boerger, 1987) have argued, understanding an ill-structured domain requires that one "criss-cross" that domain repeatedly from different vantage points. Furthermore, given the complexity of the conceptualizing of teaching and the exacting demands of everyday life in classrooms, teaching cannot be practiced for very long with unformed and highly pliable ideas or perspectives; rather, a teacher at each moment of development needs strong and stable images (i.e., personal "truths"), both to act in immediate circumstances and to negotiate an understanding of lived experience in classrooms.

Implications of a Strong View of Teachers' Understandings

This analysis suggests that biographical studies, whether focused on immediate contingencies of teaching practice or on broad cycles of teachers' careers, underscore the intense complexity of teaching practice and life as a teacher, the substantial understandings that such practice requires, and the prolonged experience needed to accomplish the formidable task of conceptualizing a teacher's practice. Such studies also indicate the functional value of strong and durable conceptualizations in helping teachers meet the harsh demands of both acting in complex settings and constructing an understanding of that action.

One suspects that this conception of the strength, tenacity, and functional value of teachers' personal understandings rests uneasily among preservice and in-service teacher educators. In the teacher education literature, it is not uncommon to read that teachers' understandings are defective on a variety of counts. Narratives of teachers' personal understandings can be seen as manifestations of a subjectivist, and thus an inferior, way of knowing that needs to be transformed so that teachers can learn to see through the lenses of the academic disciplines (McAninch, 1993). Or, teachers' personal understandings can be interpreted as carriers of traditional forms of schooling that need to be transformed by engaging in critical and emancipatory analysis (Britzman, 1991). Or, teachers' "knowledge" can be viewed as lacking the warrant of knowledge claims in science (Fenstermacher, 1994).

This uneasiness about teachers' knowledge may, in part, reflect the occupational interests of teacher educators who are in the business of changing teachers, as well as more popular images of the simplicity and malleability of educational institutions. If teachers' conceptions are robust and grounded in a hard-fought understanding of the realities of classroom life, then it is unlikely that teacher educators, or policymakers for that matter, can ever find the magic bullet that will enable them to change schooling practice quickly or to produce in two to four semesters what career studies suggest takes teachers 4–7 years to acquire. It may also be necessary for teacher educators to abandon the long-held belief that schools can be readily changed by infusing them with novices armed with the latest research-based practices. In turn, the profession might gain an appreciation for the practices of experienced teachers as reasonable solutions to the actual demands of teaching.

Biography in Teacher Education

The discussion now turns to the implications of a biographical perspective for curriculum and pedagogy in teacher education. As this survey of the field indicates, this topic is never far from the minds of investigators who examine teachers' personal narratives and life histories. Aside from some discussion of the timing of interventions, however, much of this section is based on the work that is focused on classroom contingencies; the literature on teacher career cycles is much less specific about what should be done to educate teachers. The authors have minimized the number of citations in this discussion, relying instead on the references to the literature made in the earlier survey. For related discussions of a biographical orientation to teacher education pedagogy, see Cole and Knowles (1993a), Holt-Reynolds (1992), Kagan (1992), and Knowles and Holt-Reynolds (1991).

Personal Narratives as Teacher Education Clearly, and not surprisingly, the most prominent and pervasive recommendation flowing from the biographical perspective is that the examination of one's personal narrative and/or life history should constitute the core of teacher education. In part this recommendation for personal narrative as pedagogy is based on the enthusiastic reports of teachers who have participated in personal narrative and life-history studies. Biographically oriented investigators are not the first to recommend that their methods become teacher education pedagogy. Classroom researchers have traditionally thought that their tools for looking closely at classroom life would be educative for teachers (e.g., Flanders, 1970; Florio-Ruane, 1989).

More formal rationales for personal narrative in teacher education are grounded in two arguments. The first is that cognizance of one's own personal narrative (i.e., knowing what accounts for one's outlooks and perspectives) can empower one to understand the meaning of experiences and to be open to broader and more emancipatory views and practices. Ayers (1989), for example, quoted Maxine Greene (1978) to the effect that "Persons are more likely to ask their own questions and seek their own transcendence when they feel themselves grounded in their personal histories, their lived lives" (p. 2). Along similar lines, Widdershoven (1993) has argued that narrative gives meaning to experience.

> Life has an implicit meaning, which is made explicit in stories. Such a process of explication presupposes that there is already something present. What is present is, however, not just there to be uncovered. It is shaped and structured in a process of articulation. A story about life presents us life as it is lived, and as such life is the foundation of the story. In presenting life, however, the story gives life a specific sense, and makes clear what it is about. Thus a story is based on life, but it is not determined by it because it is an articulation of life that gives it a new and richer meaning. (pp. 5–6)

A second argument was advanced by Knowles and Holt-Reynolds (1991), who are especially concerned about the fragility of initial teacher preparation pedagogies in the face of the strength and tenacity of candidates' personal understandings and beliefs, especially when these beliefs are left private and hidden from view. They argued that personal narrative not only assists candidates in coming to terms with their personal beliefs but also exposes these beliefs to teacher educators so that the latter can design pedagogies that deal more directly and powerfully with what candidates are really thinking about. Thus, the use of personal narrative in teacher education is seen as a way to strengthen the impact of preparatory experiences.

As the survey of this literature indicates, various methods have been proposed for doing personal narrative in teacher education. Commonly, the process begins with a concrete expression of one's life story, usually in the form of a written text, although, in a few cases, drama, art, or dance are suggested as possible idioms. Some have advocated the use of metaphors or images as especially powerful windows into the core structures of one's personal narrative. Career studies indicate that teachers can recall in considerable detail specific incidents that have been critical in the development of personal identity and an understanding of teaching, suggesting that well-remembered events may be particularly useful in teacher preparation (see Carter, 1994).

In nearly all cases, it is recommended that personal narratives be constructed collaboratively. Indeed, in many of the examples in the literature, personal narratives are produced as assignments in pre- or postcertification courses (see, e.g., Butt, 1989). This recommendation underscores the rigors of constructing and examining one's personal narrative, which is what Britzman (1992) called the "terrible problem of knowing thyself" (p. 23). A genuinely and intensely collaborative relationship is needed to provide a context that encourages remembering and a high degree of personal support in coming to understand one's life story. Needless to say, teacher education based on personal narrative is quite labor intensive and personalized with small groups of teacher educators and teachers working closely together.

Personal Narrative in Context To varying degrees and for varying reasons, almost everyone maintains that personal narratives should be contextualized. Teachers should, in other words, be grounded in their own life stories but not be prisoners of their own experiences. For many, this contextualizing means that teachers should focus on the interplay of self with the broader world of educational ideas (Grumet, 1988). In addition, personal narrative is seen as a starting point for developing a reflective capacity as a teacher and should thus be used in conjunction with other tools, such as dialogue journals, group discussions, and the development of personalized teaching texts (Bullough, with Stokes, 1994; Knowles, 1993).

Those who have worked with preservice teachers are the most explicit about the need for contextualization within educational theory. Holt-Reynolds (1992), for example, emphasized the importance of explicit discussions of personal understandings and their possible conflict with educational theories encountered in coursework (i.e., teaching candidates should confront their "misconceptions"). Britzman (1991) argued that candidates should understand their life stories as products of particular historical circumstances and cultural suppositions and extend their analysis to encompass more inclusive and emancipatory educational forms and ideals. Those who have studied experienced teachers (e.g., Butt & Raymond, 1989; Clandinin, 1985) are more likely to emphasize the natural contextualization of teachers' lives in classroom and school settings and the power of reflection.

Curiously, there is only limited attention in this area to learning from the personal stories of others (see Ayers, 1989; Ryan, 1992; Schubert & Ayers, 1992). Nor is there much explicit reference to technical issues of classroom management and instruction, codified versions of classroom knowledge, or other aspects of procedural knowledge for teaching (see Carter & Doyle, 1989). The emphasis, rather, tends to be on reform literatures that emphasize intellectual, moral, and political alternatives to current forms of classroom and school practice. This emphasis no doubt reflects the intensely personal focus of work on life

story and history and the general rejection of technical rationality and the power relations that characterize conventional schooling.

Effectiveness Does a personal narrative pedagogy in teacher education work? On the surface, of course, this question is too simplistic and probably cannot be answered. Yet, are there any indications that making life stories central in teacher preparation will address some of the weakness of current pedagogies with respect to personal understandings, reduce some of the personal costs associated with learning to teach, and empower teachers to learn more fruitfully from their experiences?

Understandably, there is not a great deal of research on these broad questions and, it appears, few efforts to actually address personal history in teacher education programs (Kagan, 1992). A recent study by Bullough and Stokes (1994), however, is instructive. These investigators reported an attempt during 1 year to assist a cohort of 22 secondary preservice teachers in coming to understand their life narratives and conceptions of teaching, especially as expressed in their personal teaching metaphors. The investigators found that nearly all the candidates changed their conceptions over the year, many showing increased complexity and sophistication and a move from naive optimism to a more mature self-confidence. Several actually became less traditional in their outlooks. Yet, there were dramatic differences among the students with respect to the changes they made and the value they found in focusing on personal metaphors. Only 9 of the 22 students actually "got it and used it"; that is, they were "enthusiastically engaged in the identification and exploration of metaphors" and showed a "willingness to confront conceptions of self squarely and openly" (Bullough, with Stokes, 1994, p. 215). Three of the students were placed in the category "never got it"; that is, they did not engage substantively in the exploration of personal teaching metaphors. Another three were categorized as "got it, but didn't like it"; that is, they understood the activity but did not value it or find it useful in learning to teach. The authors noted that these students had particularly strong and comfortable self-conceptions as teachers and saw little reason to explore these understandings. Finally, seven students "went along, but didn't work up a sweat." These students completed the assignments but seldom pushed the analysis beyond a surface level. They were very goal-directed students who had a procedural rather than a theoretical focus.

In the context of the strong conception of teachers' personal knowledge, these results are not altogether surprising. The program was most successful for those students whose personal narratives intersected most closely with the thrust of the curriculum and less successful for those who were working on other issues. Once again, however, personal understandings are the determining factor. It remains to be seen whether, over the long run, a focus on personal narrative during initial preparation will be of use to these teachers as they live out their careers. These results are disappointing only if the unreasonable assumption is made that somehow a preservice program can be designed that achieves in a few short semesters what appears to take some 4 to 7 years for real teachers to accomplish.

ISSUES IN PERSONAL NARRATIVE AND LIFE HISTORY APPROACHES

The authors conclude this chapter by standing back a bit and examining some of the more general issues that surround research and practice stemming from a biographical perspective. In this section the authors combine both their own reflections as well as those of others who have written in the field. In addition, the substantive points that can be raised about personal narrative and life history approaches are combined with considerations that are more directly related to research styles and methods. These issues are framed as overlapping and in some sense conflicting questions to suggest that they are enduring concerns that cannot be settled here.

Is Biographical Research Biographical?

Milburn (1989) raised an important question with respect to the work reviewed in this chapter: "How much life is there in life history?" His answer suggests that there is not very much. For the most part Milburn argued that teachers remain in the shadows, their voices muted by the researchers' fairly transparent political agendas and their interests in broad generalizations that smooth over the particular and the idiosyncratic in real teachers' lives. Along similar lines, Popkewitz (1994) maintained that researchers' voices are the loudest in the study of teachers' personal knowledge and thinking. Such research is the "reinterpretation of situated thought through cognitive psychology or symbolic interactionist perspectives" rather than "a naive cataloging of thought that 'naturally' exists" (p. 2n).

This criticism certainly applies to the work on teachers' career cycles. Although teachers are seen to have lives outside of classrooms, the accent is clearly directed toward broad patterns in teachers' lives and issues of public policy affecting education in general. Thus, very little is known about these teachers as differentiated individuals, about what they teach or how they teach it (Sikes et al., 1985, are somewhat of an exception), or about what they aspire to or are attempting to accomplish in their classrooms. Even in Spencer's (1986) work, which is closest to biography, the stories are quite brief and are told from an outsider's perspective. In addition, although Huberman (1993) attended to the multiple variations in career cycles, the thrust is toward common themes that can help inform personnel policy and staff development planning.

Oddly, a somewhat similar assessment can be made of the body of work more directly focused on the particulars of classroom practice. In contrast to the career literature, individual teachers are certainly more visible in this work. The available reports, however, are written by academics who have a variety of theoretical, political, and practical agendas that extend from sponsoring a teacher voice against educational interventions by conservative governments (Goodson, 1994) to transforming the traditional educational establishment into more emancipatory forms (Britzman, 1991), to increasing the power and impact of teacher education by laying bare the private thoughts of teachers (Knowles, 1993). It is sometimes difficult, therefore, to hear the teachers through these screens and filters or to imagine that the teachers' voices would be uniform or that they would always agree with researchers on the meanings of this work.

As the particulars of real teachers' lives fade to the background, a number of significant dimensions and issues can be easily neglected. For example, differences associated with the age of the preservice or in-service teachers are not prominent in this research tradition. Similarly, differences between elementary and secondary teachers or between preservice and in-service teachers tend to be ignored, although across studies these differences would seem to be striking. For example, the experienced elementary teachers in Clandinin and Connelly's studies would seem to have a different outlook on their lives and work than the novice secondary teachers in the reports by Holt-Reynolds or by Britzman.

It can also be noted that social class and gender are muffled in most of the reports. In contrast to the reform literatures of the late 1960s and early 1970s (McPherson, 1985), biographical researchers give little attention to the class origins of teachers; class differences between teachers and researchers; or the socialization with respect to values, voice, status, and gender that occurs in class contexts (see Tokarczyk & Fay, 1993). A similar point can be made with respect to ethnicity, culture, and language history (an exception is Zitlow and DeCoker, 1994, who analyzed cases of African-American preservice teachers). Moreover, the gendered patterns in personal narratives are masked. Gergen and Gergen (1993) have pointed out the differences between men's and women's stories. Men's stories tend to be singular and linear in form; however, women's stories have multiple and intermingled facets and paths and are recursive in nature. Also, in contrast to men's stories, the body is central in women's stories. These patterns, in part, provide social and cultural frames that individuals use in telling their stories (see, also, Conway, 1992). One can easily assume that these differences influence the stories teachers tell.

Is a Biographical Approach Too Personal?

The question of whether a biographical approach is too personal can be interpreted in at least two ways. One interpretation involves the personal intrusiveness of the inquiry and practice and the consequences of this intrusiveness. The second involves a question of scope, that is, what a focus on the personal excludes from research and practice.

Intrusiveness Cole and Knowles (1993b) have argued forcefully that all research on teacher development and on "the contexts in which practical and professional action reside" (p. 491) requires a dialectic perspective or partnership at each and every stage of the process—question formulation, information gathering, interpretation, and theory construction (see also Gitlin, 1990, on educative research). "Thus, researcher and teacher become engaged as joint theorists/researchers in a mutual apprehension and interpretation of meaning in action" (Cole & Knowles, 1993b, p. 491).

Yet, Cole and Knowles (1993b), as well as others (e.g., Denzin, 1989; Goodson, 1994; Kompf, 1993) have pointed to the serious ethical, political, and educational issues that deeply collaborative and intensely personal inquiry raises. Teachers are being asked to disclose private thoughts and feelings, which in itself can make them vulnerable to censure or derision, especially outside the particular context of the life history interview. Anonymity, confidentiality, and control of the information are especially problematic for teachers in this research context and become even more so as they assume co-investigators' responsibilities for data interpretation and theory construction related to their own personal narratives.

In addition, the intensely personal nature of the subject matter and the collaboration itself can create personal disruption and interpersonal dynamics that can extend far beyond what is usually thought about with respect to research relationships. This disruption can be particularly acute if the interviews bring difficult personal issues to the surface or, as often appears to be the case in published reports, the teaching experience is quite problematic. As Gass (1994) observed, "I know of nothing more difficult than knowing who you are, and then having the courage to share the reasons for the catastrophe of your character with the world" (p. 50). Typically the interpersonal support and sense of relationship are high during the interviews but abruptly stop when the project moves to another phase or ends. This can have painful consequences for the teachers.

In a recent paper, Cole (1994), who is a specialist in the personal history approach to research and teacher education, described her reactions to being a participant in a life-history study. Reflecting on her experience of being the researched, she was aware of her strong emotional reactions. She was quite anxious in anticipation of the interviews and found that they invaded her daily life in ways she, as an experienced researcher, had never anticipated. She also worried about the coherence, accuracy, and relevance of her interview responses, that is, the subjective feeling of incompleteness in her answers and the flat, oversimplified, and sometimes distorted version of her life that she seemed to be hearing in her own answers and in the tentative interpretations that the researcher found. These factors complicated the issues of authority over the information and its interpretation and made her especially sensitive to who saw this information and how it was understood. Finally, the experience stayed with her well beyond the interviews themselves. Looking back over this experience she became aware that most of the teachers she interviewed in the past were silent on these matters, suggesting that the private impact of being researched in this intensely personal way can be masked.

The same analysis would seem to apply with equal force to teacher education pedagogies that are grounded in personal narrative and life history. Novices and experienced teachers are being asked to expose their private thoughts to public scrutiny in a context in which the real agenda is to change them in some specified direction defined by the teacher educators. Unfortunately, the ethical issues associated with the pedagogical applications of personal narrative and life-history work are not often discussed.

Grumet's (1978) work is unique with regard to the issue of intrusiveness. She encourages dialectical relationships as helpful in assisting teachers to gain sufficient distance on their own experience to focus on the interplay of subjective and objective perspectives. Yet, she concentrates more on the teacher's own reading of the text than on the power of the teacher educator's pedagogy to transform the teacher's exposed understanding.

More is left, in other words, to the teacher than to the teacher educator.

Exclusion   To what extent is a biographical approach so personal that important considerations in teaching and teacher education are excluded? Goodson (1992a, 1994) raised this issue in terms of the focus and scope of a biographical approach. He argued that an exclusive focus on teachers' practice in biographical research and pedagogy is quite limiting in that it catches teachers at their most vulnerable point, and it is ultimately politically conservative because it ignores the policy context within which teachers' work is embedded and shaped. Thus teachers are exposed to public scrutiny, but they are not empowered to address the real contextual issues that govern their work. The research simply recounts the stories of the powerless. A more appropriate trading point between teachers and researchers is, according to Goodson, a focus on "not only a *narrative of action,* but also on a history or *genealogy of context*" (Goodson, 1994, p. 34). A similar assessment of the narrowness of a focus on only the personal and procedural and an emphasis on the importance of context and a critical perspective on political and cultural institutions is found in Britzman (1991).

The issue of scope can also be raised with respect to teacher education curriculum. It appears that the general rejection of technical rationality that informs biographical work has meant a devaluing of technical issues in teaching, such as classroom management and instructional procedures, and a disregard of knowledge that might inform these areas. As Kagan (1992) noted with respect to preservice teacher education, novices entering teaching with a concern for procedure all too often find only abstract theories about broad educational issues. Substituting epistemology or critical theory for behavioral psychology is not likely to improve the correspondence between novice teachers' personal narratives and the curriculum of teacher education. Moreover, it is not necessary to render procedural knowledge as a recipe. Recent work on classroom knowledge, for example, suggests that formal understandings useful for interpreting classroom situations and acting in these complex settings are available and can be used with advantage by beginning teachers (see Carter & Doyle, 1989). Clearly more attention needs to be given to the connections between personal narrative investigations and more conventional approaches to the construction of knowledge for teaching.

A final comment in this area relates to the tendency of biographical work to be individualistic. Most of the teachers we meet in biographical studies are alone, despite the fact that the same studies indicate that confidants and reference groups are quite significant to teachers. This individualistic stance is also ironic given the emphasis in biographical work on story. Story necessarily implies a community both as a source of narrative forms and as an audience (see Carter, 1993). It would seem that the tradition would be enriched by a more explicit appreciation of community in personal narrative and life history.

What Is a Finding in a Biographical Approach?

Research in the area of personal narrative and life history is generally designed to: (a) demonstrate the validity and importance of biography in teaching and teacher education, (b) give voice to teachers, (c) find patterns in the development/socialization of teachers, and (d) demonstrate the value of life-story methods as teacher education experiences.

The question of what constitutes a "finding" casts light on a range of vital issues related to knowledge, meaning, and conceptions of "truth" in any field. This question is especially important with respect to the use of biography, autobiography, and narrative as social science "data" (Carter, 1993; Denzin, 1989; Gass, 1994). Life stories are fundamentally interpretive and are shaped by the considerations at hand rather than by factual accounts of events (see Rosenthal, 1993). Indeed, self is a construction, too; therefore, stories of self must be viewed both respectfully and judiciously. Autobiography, in particular, is a fictional product of a divided self that is "able to throw a full beam upon the life already lived and see there a pattern, as a plowed field seen from a plane reveals the geometry of the tractor's path" (Gass, 1994, p. 51).

Kagan (1992) is optimistic that narrative or interpretive material can be aggregated across studies and given a hard interpretation. Others, such as Connelly and Clandinin (1990), are more cautious, arguing that criteria for narrative inquiry are just emerging within research practice. It is certainly clear that the traditional criteria of validity and reliability are not satisfactory as frames for information reduction and manipulation. In their place, attempts are being made to explore such notions as the "invitational quality" and "authenticity" of a text (Connelly & Clandinin, 1990, p. 7) or its verisimilitude (Polkinghorne, 1988). This movement suggests that a basic transformation of stances toward information and understanding is being required for many in teaching and teacher education.

CONCLUSION

From an outside perspective of program and policy, becoming a teacher is all too often seen as obtaining credentials and acquiring skills. From a biographical frame, however, becoming a teacher means (a) transforming an identity, (b) adapting personal understandings and ideals to institutional realities, and (c) deciding how to express one's self in classroom activity. As the literature reviewed in this chapter suggests, this far more complex picture of the essence of the teacher education experience promises to transform fundamentally how teachers are viewed and perhaps even how they are valued.

References

Aoki, T. T. (1993). Legitimating lived curriculum: Towards a curricular landscape of multiplicity. *Journal of Curriculum and Supervision, 8*(3), 255–268.

Ayers, W. (1989). *The good preschool teacher: Six teachers reflect on their lives.* New York: Teachers College Press.

Ball, S. J., & Goodson, I. F. (Eds.). (1985). *Teachers' lives and careers.* London: Falmer Press.

Barone, T. E. (1987). Educational platforms, teacher selection, and school reform: Issues emanating from a biographical case study. *Journal of Teacher Education, 38*(2), 12–17.

Bateson, M. C. (1989). *Composing a life.* New York: Atlantic Monthly Press.

Beier, C. A. (1994). *Changes in preservice teacher conceptualizations of the integrated curriculum.* Unpublished doctoral dissertation, University of Arizona, Tucson.

Britzman, D. P. (1986). Cultural myths in the making of a teacher: Biography and social structure in teacher education. *Harvard Educational Review, 56*(4), 442–456.

Britzman, D. P. (1991). *Practice makes practice: A critical study of learning to teach.* Albany: State University of New York Press.

Britzman, D. P. (1992). The terrible problem of knowing thyself: Toward a poststructural account of teacher identity. *Journal of Curriculum Theorizing, 9*(3), 23–46.

Bruner, J. (1985). Narrative and paradigmatic modes of thought. In E. Eisner (Ed.), *Learning and teaching the ways of knowing* (84th Yearbook of the National Society for the Study of Education, part 2, pp. 97–115). Chicago: The University of Chicago Press.

Bullough, R. V., Jr. (1989). *First year teacher: A case study.* New York: Teachers College Press.

Bullough, R. V., Jr. (1994). Personality history and teaching metaphors: A self-study of teaching as conversation. *Teacher Education Quarterly, 21*(1), 107–120.

Bullough, R. V., Jr., Knowles, J. G., & Crow, N. A. (1989). Teacher self-concept and student culture in the first year of teaching. *Teachers College Record, 91*(2), 209–233.

Bullough, R. V., Jr., with Stokes, D. K. (1994). Analyzing personal teaching metaphors in preservice teacher education as a means for encouraging professional development. *American Educational Research Journal, 31*(1), 197–224.

Burden, P. R. (1990). Teacher development. In W. Robert Houston (Ed.), *Handbook of research on teacher education* (pp. 311–328). New York: Macmillan.

Butt, R. L. (1989). An integrative function for teachers' biographies. In G. Milburn, I. F. Goodson, & J. Clark (Eds.), *Re-interpreting curriculum research: Images and arguments* (pp. 146–159). Barcombe: Falmer Press.

Butt, R. L., & Raymond, D. (1989). Studying the nature and development of teachers' knowledge using collaborative autobiography. *International Journal of Educational Research, 13*(4), 403–419.

Butt, R. L., Raymond, D., McCue, G., & Yamagishi, L. (1992). Collaborative autobiography and the teacher's voice. In I. F. Goodson (Ed.), *Studying teachers' lives* (pp. 51–98). New York: Teachers College Press.

Carter, K. (1990). Teachers' knowledge and learning to teach. In W. R. Houston (Ed.), *Handbook of research on teacher education* (pp. 291–310). New York: Macmillan.

Carter, K. (1993, January). The place of story in research on teaching and teacher education. *Educational Researcher, 22*(1), 5–12.

Carter, K. (1994). Preservice teachers' well-remembered events and the acquisition of event-structured knowledge. *Journal of Curriculum Studies, 26*(3), 235–252.

Carter, K., & Doyle, W. (1989). Classroom research as a resource for the graduate preparation of teachers. In A. Woolfolk (Ed.), *Research perspectives on the graduate preparation of teachers* (pp. 51–68). Englewood Cliffs, NJ: Prentice Hall.

Casey, K. (1993). *I answer with my life: Life histories of women teachers working for social change.* New York: Routledge.

Clandinin, D. J. (1985). Personal practical knowledge: A study of teachers' classroom images. *Curriculum Inquiry, 15*(4), 361–385.

Clandinin, D. J. (1986). *Classroom practice: Teacher images in action.* London: Falmer Press.

Clandinin, D. J. (1989). Developing rhythm in teaching: The narrative study of a beginning teacher's personal practical knowledge of classrooms. *Curriculum Inquiry, 19*(2), 121–141.

Clandinin, D. J., & Connelly, F. M. (1986). Rhythms in teaching: The narrative study of teachers' personal practical knowledge of classrooms. *Teaching and Teacher Education, 2*(4), 377–387.

Clandinin, D. J., & Connelly, F. M. (1987). Teachers' personal knowledge: What counts as "personal" in studies of the personal. *Journal of Curriculum Studies, 19*(6), 487–500.

Clark, C. M., & Peterson, P. L. (1986). Teachers' thought processes. In M. C. Wittrock (Ed.), *Handbook of research on teaching* (3rd ed., pp. 255–296). New York: Macmillan.

Cole, A. L. (1990). Personal theories of teaching: Development in the formative years. *Alberta Journal of Educational Research, 36*(3), 203–222.

Cole, A. L. (1994, April). *Doing life history research—in theory and in practice.* Paper presented at the annual meeting of the American Educational Research Association, New Orleans.

Cole, A. L., & Knowles, J. G. (1993a). Shattered images: Understanding expectations and realities of field experiences. *Teaching and Teacher Education, 9*(5/6), 457–471.

Cole, A. L., & Knowles, J. G. (1993b). Teacher development partnership research: A focus on methods and issues. *American Educational Research Journal, 30*(3), 473–495.

Connelly, F. M., & Clandinin, D. J. (1985). Personal practical knowledge and the modes of knowing: Relevance for teaching and learning. In E. Eisner (Ed.), *Learning and teaching the ways of knowing* (84th Yearbook of the National Society for the Study of Education, Part 2, pp. 174–198). Chicago: The University of Chicago Press.

Connelly, F. M., & Clandinin, D. J. (1990). Stories of experience and narrative inquiry. *Educational Researcher, 19*(5), 2–14.

Conway, J. K. (Ed.). (1992). *Written by herself: Autobiographies of American women. An anthology.* New York: Vintage Books.

Copeland, W. D., Birmingham, C., DeMeulle, L., D'Emidio-Caston, M., & Natal, D. (1994). Making meaning in classrooms: An investigation of cognitive processes in aspiring teachers, experienced teachers, and their peers. *American Educational Research Journal, 31*(1), 166–196.

Crow, N. A. (1987). *Socialization within a teacher education program: A case study.* Unpublished doctoral dissertation, University of Utah.

Darling-Hammond, L., & Hudson, L. (1990). Precollege science and mathematics teachers: Supply, demand, and quality. In C. B. Cazden (Ed.), *Review of research in education* (vol. 16, pp. 223–264). Washington, DC: American Educational Research Association.

Denzin, N. K. (1989). *Interpretive biography.* Qualitative Research Methods, Vol. 17. Newbury Park, CA: Sage Publications.

Doyle, W. (1978). Paradigms for research on teaching effectiveness. In L. S. Shulman (Ed.), *Review of research in education 5* (pp. 163–198). Itasca, IL: F. E. Peacock.

Doyle, W. (1990). Themes in teacher education research. In W. R. Houston (Ed.), *Handbook of research on teacher education* (pp. 3–24). New York: Macmillan.

Elbaz, F. (1983). *Teacher thinking: A study of practical knowledge.* London: Croom Helm.

Elbaz, F. (1990). Knowledge and discourse: The evolution of research on teaching thinking. In C. Day, M. Pope, & P. Denicolo (Eds.), *Insights into teachers' thinking and practice* (pp. 15–42). London: Falmer Press.

Elbaz, F. (1991). Research on teachers' knowledge: The evolution of a discourse. *Journal of Curriculum Studies, 23*(1), 1–19.

Feiman-Nemser, S., & Buchmann, M. (1987). When is student teaching teacher education? *Teaching and Teacher Education, 3*(4), 255–273.

Feiman-Nemser, S., & Floden, R. F. (1986). The cultures of teaching. In M. C. Wittrock (Ed.), *Handbook of research on teaching* (3rd ed., pp. 505–526). New York: Macmillan.

Fenstermacher, G. D. (1994). The knower and the known: The nature of knowledge in research on teaching. In L. Darling-Hammond (Ed.), *Review of research in education* (vol. 20, pp. 3–56). Washington, DC: American Educational Research Association.

Fessler, R. (1994, April). *Dynamics of teacher career stages.* Paper presented at the annual meeting of the American Educational Research Association, New Orleans.

Flanders, N. A. (1970). *Analyzing teaching behavior.* Reading, MA: Addison-Wesley.

Floden, R. E., & Huberman, M. (1989). Teachers' professional lives: The state of the art. *International Journal of Educational Research, 13*(4), 455–466.

Florio-Ruane, S. (1989). Social organization of classes and schools. In M. C. Reynolds (Ed.), *Knowledge base for the beginning teacher* (pp. 163–172). Oxford: Pergamon.

Fox, D. L. (1993). *The struggle for voice in learning to teach: Lessons from one preservice teacher's portfolio.* Paper presented at the International Qualitative Research in Education Conference, University of Georgia, Athens.

Fuller, F. F. (1969). Concerns of teachers: A developmental conceptualization. *American Educational Research Journal, 6*(2), 207–226.

Fuller, F. F. (1970). *Personalized education for teachers: An introduction for teacher educators.* Austin: Research and Development Center for Teacher Education, University of Texas at Austin. (ERIC ED 048 105)

Fuller, F. F., & Bown, O. H. (1975). Becoming a teacher. In K. Ryan (Ed.), *Teacher education* (74th Yearbook of the National Society for the Study of Education, part 2, pp. 25–52). Chicago: The University of Chicago Press.

Fuller, F. F., Bown, O. H., & Peck, R. F. (1967). *Creating climates for growth.* Austin: Research and Development Center for Teacher Education, University of Texas at Austin. (ERIC ED 013 989)

Funkenstein, A. (1993). The incomprehensible catastrophe: Memory and narrative. In R. Josselson & A. Lieblich (Eds.), *The narrative study of lives* (vol. 1, pp. 21–29). Newbury Park, CA: Sage Publications.

Garrison, J. W. (1988). Democracy, scientific knowledge, and teacher empowerment. *Teachers College Record, 89*(4), 487–504.

Gass, W. (1994). The art of self: Autobiography in the age of narcissism. *Harper's, 288*(1728), 43–52.

Gergen, M. M., & Gergen, K. J. (1993). Narratives of the gendered body in popular autobiography. In R. Josselson & A. Lieblich (Eds.), *The narrative study of lives* (vol. 1, pp. 191–218). Newbury Park, CA: Sage Publications.

Gitlin, A. D. (1990). Educative research, voice, and school change. *Harvard Educational Review, 60*(4), 443–466.

Gomez, M. L., & Tabachnick, B. R. (1992). Telling teaching stories. *Teaching Education, 4*(2), 129–138.

Goodson, I. F. (1992a). Sponsoring the teacher's voice: Teachers' lives and teacher development. In A. Hargreaves & M. G. Fullan (Eds.), *Understanding teacher development* (pp. 110–121). New York: Teachers College Press.

Goodson, I. F. (Ed.). (1992b). *Studying teachers' lives.* New York: Teachers College Press.

Goodson, I. (1994). Studying the teacher's life and work. *Teaching and Teacher Education, 10*(1), 29–37.

Gore, J. M. (1993). *The struggle for pedagogies: Critical and feminist discourses as regimes of truth.* New York: Routledge.

Greene, M. (1978). *Landscapes of learning.* New York: Teachers College Press.

Grumet, M. R. (1975, April). *Existential and phenomenological foundations of currere: Self-report in curriculum inquiry.* Paper presented at the annual meeting of the American Educational Research Association, Washington, DC.

Grumet, M. R. (1978, March). *Supervision and situation: A methodology of self-report for teacher education.* Paper presented at the annual meeting of the American Educational Research Association, Toronto.

Grumet, M. R. (1988). *Bitter milk: Women and teaching.* Amherst: University of Massachusetts Press.

Grumet, M. R. (1989). Feminism and the phenomenology of the familiar. In G. Milburn, I. F. Goodson, & R. J. Clark (Eds.), *Re-interpreting curriculum research: Images and arguments* (pp. 87–101). Barcombe: Falmer Press.

Grumet, M. R. (1992). Existential and phenomenological foundations of autobiographical methods. In W. F. Pinar & W. M. Reynolds (Eds.), *Understanding curriculum as phenomenological and deconstructed text* (pp. 28–43). New York: Teachers College Press.

Gudmundsdottir, S. (1991). Story-maker, story-teller: Narrative structures in curriculum. *Journal of Curriculum Studies, 23*(3), 207–218.

Hargreaves, A. (1993). Foreword. In M. Huberman (Ed.), *The lives of teachers.* New York: Teachers College Press.

Hollingsworth, S. (1989). Prior beliefs and cognitive change in learning to teach. *American Educational Research Journal, 26*(2), 160–189.

Holt-Reynolds, D. (1992). Personal history-based beliefs as relevant prior knowledge in course work. *American Educational Research Journal, 29*(2), 325–349.

Holt-Reynolds, D. (1994). When agreeing with the professor is bad news: Jeneane, her personal history, and coursework. *Teacher Education Quarterly, 21*(1), 13–35.

Huberman, M. (Ed.). (1989). Research on teachers' professional lives. *International Journal of Educational Research, 13*(4), 341–466.

Huberman, M. (1993). *The lives of teachers* (J. Neufeld, Trans.). New York: Teachers College Press.

Johnson, S. (1990). Understanding curriculum decision making through teacher images. *Journal of Curriculum Studies, 22*(5), 463–471.

Jones, M. G., & Vesilind, E. (1994, April). *Changes in the structure of pedagogical knowledge of middle school preservice teachers.* Paper presented at the annual meeting of the American Educational Research Association, New Orleans.

Kagan, D. M. (1992). Professional growth among preservice beginning teachers. *Review of Educational Research, 62*(2), 129–169.

Kelchtermans, G. (1993). Getting the story, understanding the lives: From career stories to teachers' professional development. *Teaching and Teacher Education, 9*(5/6), 443–456.

Kelchtermans, G., & Vandenberghe, R. (1994). Teachers' professional development: A biographical perspective. *Journal of Curriculum Studies, 26*(1), 45–62.

Knowles, J. G. (1992). Models for understanding pre-service and beginning teachers' biographies: Illustrations from case studies. In I. F. Goodson (Ed.), *Studying teachers' lives* (pp. 99–152). New York: Teachers College Press.

Knowles, J. G. (1993). Life-history accounts as mirrors: A practical avenue for the conceptualization of reflection in teacher education. In J. Calderhead & P. Gates (Eds.), *Conceptualizing reflection in teacher development* (pp. 70–92). London: Falmer Press.

Knowles, J. G. (1994). Metaphors as windows on a personal history: A beginning teachers' experience. *Teacher Education Quarterly, 21*(1), 37–66.

Knowles, J. G., & Holt-Reynolds, D. (1991). Shaping pedagogies through personal histories in preservice teacher education. *Teachers College Record, 93*(1), 87–113.

Knowles, J. G., & Holt-Reynolds, D. (Eds.). (1994). Special issue on personal histories as medium, method, and milieu for gaining insights into teacher development. *Teacher Education Quarterly, 21*(1), 5–175.

Kompf, M. (1993). Ethical considerations in teacher disclosure: Construing persons and methods. *Teaching and Teacher Education, 9*(5/6), 519–528.

Lanier, J. E. (1986). Research on teacher education. In M. C. Wittrock (Ed.), *Handbook of research on teaching* (3rd ed., pp. 527–569). New York: Macmillan.

Levinson, D. J. (1978). *The seasons of a man's life.* New York: Knopf.

Lightfoot, S. L. (1983). The lives of teachers. In L. S. Shulman & G. Sykes (Eds.), *Handbook of teaching and policy* (pp. 241–260). New York: Longman.

Lortie, D. C. (1975). *Schoolteacher.* Chicago: The University of Chicago Press.

Louden, W. (1991). *Understanding teaching: Continuity and change in teachers' knowledge.* New York: Teachers College Press.

McAninch, A. R. (1993). *Teacher thinking and the case method: Theory and future directions.* New York: Teachers College Press.

McDiarmid, G. W. (1990). Challenging prospective teachers' beliefs during early field experience: A quixotic undertaking? *Journal of Teacher Education, 41*(3), 12–20.

McPherson, G. H. (1985). Teacher bashing and teacher boosting: Critical views of teachers between 1965 and 1975. In L. Barton & S. Walker (Eds.), *Education and social change* (pp. 88–110). London: Croom Helm.

Middleton, S. (1992). Developing a radical pedagogy: Autobiography of a New Zealand sociologist of women's education. In I. F. Goodson (Ed.), *Studying teachers' lives* (pp. 18–50). New York: Teachers College Press.

Milburn, G. (1989). How much life is there in life history? In G. Milburn, I. F. Goodson, & R. J. Clark (Eds.), *Re-interpreting curriculum research: Images and arguments* (pp. 160–168). Barcombe: Falmer Press.

Mitchell, W. J. T. (1981). Foreword. In W. J. T. Mitchell (Ed.), *On narrative* (pp. vii–x). Chicago: The University of Chicago Press.

Munby, H., & Russell, T. (1994). The authority of experience in learning to teach: Messages from a physics methods class. *Journal of Teacher Education, 45*(2), 86–95.

Nias, J. (1989). *Primary teachers talking: A study of teaching as work.* New York: Routledge.

Personal Narratives Group. (1989). *Interpreting women's lives: Feminist theory and personal narratives.* Bloomington: Indiana University Press.

Pinar, W. F. (1975, April). *The method of "currere."* Paper presented at the annual meeting of the American Educational Research Association, Washington, DC.

Pinar, W. F. (1988). Autobiography and the architecture of self. *Journal of Curriculum Theorizing, 8*(1), 7–35.

Polkinghorne, D. E. (1988). *Narrative knowing and the human sciences.* Albany: State University of New York Press.

Popkewitz, T. S. (1994). Professionalization in teaching and teacher education: Some notes on its history, ideology, and potential. *Teaching and Teacher Education, 10*(1), 1–14.

Raymond, D., Butt, R., & Townsend, D. (1992). Contexts for teacher development: Insights from teachers' stories. In A. Hargreaves & M. G. Fullan (Eds.), *Understanding teacher development* (pp. 143–161). New York: Teachers College Press.

Richert, A. E. (1992). Voice and power in teaching and learning to teach. In L. Valli (Ed.), *Reflective teacher education: Cases and critiques* (pp. 187–197). Albany: State University of New York Press.

Rogers, C. R. (1961). *On becoming a person: A therapist's view of psychotherapy.* Boston: Houghton Mifflin.

Rosenthal, G. (1993). Reconstruction of life stories: Principles of selection in generating stories for narrative biographical interviews. In R. Josselson & A. Lieblich (Eds.), *The narrative study of lives* (vol. 1, pp. 59–91). Newbury Park, CA: Sage Publications.

Ross, E. W., Cornett, J. W., & McCutcheon, G. (1992). *Teacher personal theorizing: Connecting curriculum practice, theory, and research.* Albany: State University of New York Press.

Rust, F. O. (1994). The first year of teaching: It's not what they expected. *Teaching and Teacher Education, 10*(2), 205–217.

Ryan, K. (Ed.). (1992). *The roller coaster year: Essays by and for beginning teachers.* New York: HarperCollins.

Salvio, P. M. (1994). What can a body know? Refiguring pedagogical intention into teacher education. *Journal of Teacher Education, 45*(1), 53–61.

Schempp, P. G., Sparkes, A. C., & Templin, T. J. (1993). The micropolitics of teacher induction. *American Educational Research Journal, 30*(3), 447–472.

Schön, D. (1983). *The reflective practitioner: How professionals think in action.* New York: Basic Books.

Schubert, W., & Ayers, W. (Eds.). (1992). *Teacher lore: Learning from our own experience.* New York: Longman.

Sheehy, G. (1976). *Passages: Predictable crises of adult life.* New York: Dutton.

Sikes, P. J., Measor, L., & Woods, P. (1985). *Teacher careers: Crises and continuities.* London: Falmer.

Smith, L. M., Kleine, P., Prunty, J. J., & Dwyer, D. C. (1992). School improvement and educator personality: Stages, types, traits, or processes? In I. F. Goodson (Ed.), *Studying teachers' lives* (pp. 153–166). New York: Teachers College Press.

Solas, J. (1992). Investigating teacher and student thinking about the process of teaching and learning using autobiography and repertory grid. *Review of Educational Research, 62*(2), 205–225.

Sparkes, A. C. (1993). Challenging technical rationality in physical education teacher education: The problem of a life history approach. *Physical Education Review, 16*(2), 107–121.

Spencer, D. A. (1986). *Contemporary women teachers: Balancing school and home.* New York: Longman.

Spiro, R. J., Vispoel, W. P., Schmitz, J. G., Samarapungavan, A., & Boerger, A. E. (1987). Knowledge acquisition for application: Cognitive flexibility and transfer in complex domains. In B. C. Britton (Ed.), *Executive control processes* (pp. 177–199). Hillsdale, NJ: Lawrence Erlbaum Associates.

Sweet, J. A., & Jacobsen, L. A. (1983). Demographic aspects of supply and demand for teachers. In L. S. Shulman & G. Sykes (Eds.), *Handbook of teaching and policy* (pp. 192–213). New York: Longman.

Thompson, B. C. (1993). *Curriculum theory in action: A case of children's literature in teacher education.* Unpublished doctoral dissertation, University of Arizona, Tucson.

Tokarczyk, M. M., & Fay, E. A. (Eds.). (1993). *Working-class women in the academy: Laborers in the knowledge factory.* Amherst: University of Massachusetts Press.

Traver, R. (1987). Autobiography, feminism, and the study of teaching. *Teachers College Record, 88*(3), 443–452.

Trumbull, D. (1990). Evolving conceptions of teaching: Reflections of one teacher. *Curriculum Inquiry, 20*(2), 161–182.

van Manen, M. (1990). *Researching lived experience: Human science for an action sensitive pedagogy.* Albany: State University of New York Press.

Weinstein, C. S. (1990). Prospective elementary teachers' beliefs about teaching: Implications for teacher education. *Teaching and Teacher Education, 6*(3), 279–290.

Widdershoven, G. A. M. (1993). The story of life: Hermeneutic perspectives on the relationship between narrative and life history. In R. Josselson & A. Lieblich (Eds.), *The narrative study of lives* (vol. 1, pp. 1–20). Newbury Park, CA: Sage Publications.

Willinsky, J. (1989). Getting personal and practical with personal practical knowledge. *Curriculum Inquiry, 19*(3), 247–264.

Woods, P. (1984). Teacher, self and curriculum. In I. F. Goodson & S. J. Ball (Eds.), *Defining the curriculum: Histories and ethnographies* (pp. 239–261). London: Falmer.

Woods, P. (1985). Conversations with teachers: Some aspects of life-history method. *British Educational Research Journal, 11*(1), 13–26.

Woods, P. (1987). Life histories and teacher knowledge. In J. Smyth (Ed.), *Educating teachers: Changing the nature of pedagogical knowledge* (pp. 121–135). London: Falmer Press.

Wubbels, T. (1992). Taking account of student teachers' preconceptions. *Teaching and Teacher Education, 8*(2), 137–149.

Zeichner, K. M., & Gore, J. M. (1990). Teacher socialization. In W. R. Houston (Ed.), *Handbook of research on teacher education* (pp. 329–348). New York: Macmillan.

Zeichner, K. M., Tabachnick, B. R., & Densmore, K. (1987). Individual, institutional, and cultural influences on the development of teachers' craft knowledge. In J. Calderhead (Ed.), *Exploring teachers' thinking* (pp. 21–59). London: Cassell.

Zitlow, C. S., & DeCoker, G. (1994). Drawing on personal histories in teacher education: Stories of three African-American preservice teachers. *Teacher Education Quarterly, 21*(1), 67–84.

Zumwalt, K. K. (1988). Are we improving or undermining teaching? In L. N. Tanner (Ed.), *Critical issues in curriculum* (87th Yearbook of the National Society for the Study of Education, part 1, pp. 148–174). Chicago: The University of Chicago Press.

8

DESIGNING COHERENT AND EFFECTIVE
TEACHER EDUCATION PROGRAMS

Ken Howey

THE OHIO STATE UNIVERSITY

This chapter draws from several sources to illustrate attributes of coherent, and hopefully effective, programs of preservice teacher preparation. First the chapter examines briefly some major contextual factors and challenges to teacher education at this time, especially in the United States. Next the assumptions that guide this chapter are made explicit. The chapter operationally defines the constructs of *program* as a heuristic to further inquiry and development. In this regard it addresses first the cornerstone of a coherent program—a conceptual framework. Such a framework, when fleshed out, makes explicit conceptions of teaching, learning, schooling, and learning to teach. The chapter provides multiple examples of each of these, but it emphasizes competing orientations to how one learns to teach. A concise overview of some of the major P-12 reform initiatives is provided to illustrate alternative conceptions of schooling. Other external forces influencing program design, such as state program approval and national accreditation standards, are also briefly acknowledged. The craft knowledge of teachers as an important source informing preservice programs is underscored as well.

A conceptual framework of this nature when negotiated across appropriate parties assists in deciding on a reasonable number of derivative themes or core abilities for preservice teachers. Thus, both a sample conceptual framework and criteria for determining these related themes are shared. Then, examples of themes that meet those criteria are illustrated for the reader.

Coherent programs should also assist in determining activities that socialize preservice students in purposeful and positive ways; examples of these types of activities are also provided. Ultimately preservice programs manifest their coherence in the type of pedagogy modeled for and engaged in by preservice students. This chapter concludes by examining socialization experiences and types of laboratory preparation called for by contemporary conceptions of learning to teach.

This chapter addresses a triadic approach to program design and implementation: (1) the evolution of a defensible conceptual framework that grounds and guides a program, (2) the derivation of themes that provide continuity and coherence to the program, and (3) the development of socialization and educative experiences that allow the themes to be manifested and that have the power to educate prospective teachers in a more programmatic and potent manner than they typically are currently.

What is meant by the concept of *program* in terms of the professional preparation of teachers? To advance the quality of programs—*program approval* is the primary means by which institutions are legally authorized to prepare teachers—what this concept of program embraces needs to be clearer. It is toward this goal that this chapter is directed.

A series of loosely coupled courses in professional education culminating in an even more disconnected experience, commonly referred to as "student teaching," obviously cannot be the standard for professional preparation. Neither can the standard for assessment be the prevailing practice of examining the "outcomes" of these experiences months and even years later in "follow-up" surveys of graduates' perceptions. By then attitudes and abilities fostered in preservice preparation have been mediated by a powerful array of personal and contextual factors. High-quality, comprehensive evaluation of teacher preparation is sadly lacking.

To make advances in the preparation of teachers, teacher educators need to be much clearer about which particular aspects or attributes of a program contribute to which particular understandings, abilities, and dispositional behaviors, as well as the more general cumulative effects of such programs. A standards setting "reform" movement that emphasizes "outcomes" only is misguided, especially if teacher educators hope to learn anything about how specifically designed pedagogical strategies undertaken in distinctively different contexts contribute to learning to teach.

CONTEXT AND PERSPECTIVE: PROBLEMS TO BE ADDRESSED

In suggesting directions for the design of preservice programs, this chapter draws from several data sources. The Research About Teacher Education (RATE) studies sponsored by the American Association of Colleges for Teacher Education (AACTE) and conducted annually since the late 1980s have attempted to shed light on specific strengths and weaknesses, progress and problems, and trends and issues associated with teacher preparation nationally. This author has been an integral part of these studies since their inception. Insights have also derived from related field studies designed to buttress and assist in the further interpretation of the RATE survey findings (Howey & Zimpher, 1989). Beyond these inquiries, there are major studies of teacher education that can be drawn upon to inform the design of programs. These include the comprehensive inquiry into the education of teachers conducted by John Goodlad (1990) and his colleagues, and the multiple studies emanating from the National Center for Research on Teacher Learning at the Michigan State University College of Education.

Although teacher educators need to be more precise in describing and understanding the content and processes involved in teacher education and their multiple effects, they also need to be more forceful in addressing the sources of certain problems constraining teacher preparation. A number of these problems and constraints are readily identifiable; no further inquiry is needed to document them. It is known, for example, that schools, colleges, and departments of education *are* inadequately funded. In the current economic climate it is not uncommon in many state-supported institutions for the marginal resources that existed to support instruction for prospective teachers to have endured further retrenchments undertaken to meet shortfalls in revenue.

At the same time, many teacher education faculty report increased demands being placed on them, especially in terms of scholarly "productivity" and their contributions to P–12 schools (RATE V, 1991; RATE VI, 1992). These broadened or heightened institutional expectations for *individuals* often fly in the face of the *collaborative* efforts required to make programmatic improvements in teacher preparation.

It is also known that initial teacher preparation as it is practiced in most instances is an abbreviated endeavor; the formal aspects of learning to teach are seen as completed upon graduation and receipt of an initial license. Although there are those in the P–12 sector who bemoan what they perceive to be the quality of entering teachers, there is little support to continue teacher preparation in a sustained substantive manner into the early, critical, formative years of teaching.

This lack of continuity and cooperation in promoting needed teacher development between those in college teacher preparation and the P–12 school sector has, as well, broader negative consequences. Major improvements in teacher preparation cannot go forward without also addressing the changing nature of P–12 schools in this vast and diverse country. Simultaneous

renewal in preservice teacher education and P–12 schools, however logical this seems, is nonetheless rare. The teacher education community typically is *not* involved in the widely heralded school reform initiatives at this time (Sizer, 1991). The implications of school restructuring for teacher education, especially *initial* teacher preparation, are generally not a major concern for those in P–12 schools or, for that matter, in the teacher education community. The exclusion of the teacher education community in many school reform initiatives at this time can be attributed to several factors, not the least of which is the lack of a history of coordinated institutional contribution to school reform by the higher education and teacher education community.

Although national standards are evolving, there is no national design for the reform of either P–12 schools or schools of education, let alone in tandem. There are a growing number of voluntary networks of schools concerned with restructuring that share common characteristics. These have been promulgated by such scholar-activists as Sizer (1991), Levin (1991a, 1991b), and Comer (1992). There are similar consortium initiatives in teacher education as well that are focused on reform, including The Holmes Group (1990), The Renaissance Group (1992), and Goodlad's (1990) National Network for Educational Renewal. The former represent only a small portion of P–12 schools, and the latter are only in the initial phases of a long-range reform agenda. Strategic planning across reform initiatives has not occurred. Many of the innovations espoused in the "reform" literature, such as interdisciplinary curriculum or authentic assessment, remain essentially outliers; they do not represent model practice either in P–12 schools or in schools and colleges of education.

Finally, it should be underscored that there are no powerful legal, political, or economic incentives for those in schools and those in schools of education to collaborate in sustained interinstitutional arrangements that would simultaneously influence *parallel* changes in teacher preparation and P–12 schools. More common are policies that widen an already considerable schism. For example, several states are now providing modest venture capital to P–12 schools to engage in restructuring and to meet new curriculum standards, but with no incentive for them to cooperate with the teacher education community. A second common example is the nominal support for entry-year teachers provided by the state to local districts with no consideration of these teachers' initial preparation or any incentive to engage substantively higher education in what should be a critical transitional phase of teacher education. Rather, general orientation and enculturation to a specific school community interspersed with periodic assessments of the beginning teachers' effectiveness characterize these entry-year efforts.

TWO MAJOR CHALLENGES

In setting a context for thinking about how more potent programs of teacher preparation could be enabled, this author also deemed it necessary to underscore two additional overriding characteristics of schooling in the United States. First, elementary and secondary schools are not only very much influenced by local norms but also by very different sociodemographic factors. Schools are part of a very large and diverse "system" of schooling. In the United States there are almost 86,000 *public* schools in 15,000 plus school districts, which employ more than 3 million teachers (National Center for Education Statistics [NCES], 1993). Beyond this, there is a very sizable and myriad assortment of private schools and private school teachers embracing a host of religious and philosophical persuasions, as well as college preparation programs enrolling the offspring of many wealthier citizens. The history of state control and local autonomy in this country combined with the diversity of schools explains why site- or school-based management schemes are promoted as a form of school reform with the same if not more fervor than those promoting *national* education goals with the similar intent of educational reform.

Although the country's schools are often stratified by their private and public character, they are also very stratified *within* the public sector. The support provided to many wealthier suburban districts as opposed to their less well-to-do urban and rural counterpoints is substantial; disparities in funding characterize public schooling. For example, Chicago was recently supporting youngsters in its school at $5,000 per individual. Niles Township, but a few miles away from Chicago, was expending $15,000 per student. Needless to say, the racial and cultural character and per capita income of families in these two settings vary greatly. Although geographically proximate, the social distance between the two districts is as vast as is the difference in educational opportunities.

Thus, there is school reform and there is school *reform* as it pertains more directly to redressing these problems. From this perspective one should not employ the term *reform* unless it centrally addresses the shroud of poverty engulfing so many youngsters and the special challenges they face in pursuing an education. The position taken here is that the same must be said relative to reform in teacher preparation. We need to squarely address the central question of just what the role of public schools and teachers are relative to transforming society and *then* how to recruit, select, and prepare such teachers to meet this challenge.

There is a second challenge, which is also of great proportions. It is the question of how to fundamentally transform the character of much of what now passes for teaching and learning in all school contexts and at all levels. Teaching in far too many instances, and certainly far too often in the halls of academe, remains largely a lecture-recitation activity. "Learning," in turn, remains basically a passive and largely individual activity. This form of "learning" is massively reinforced as youngsters watch tens of thousands of hours of television out of school. A vicious cycle of mediocrity continues in teaching wherein teachers continue to teach as they are taught. From this perspective, the challenge in designing more potent programs of teacher preparation is not so much coming to agreement on the "knowledge bases" for and the content of preservice preparation, although surely there are knotty issues here, but rather how that curriculum is represented to and engaged in by prospective teachers in pedagogically powerful ways, that is, in contexts that are, in fact, conducive to learning to teach. Thus, the nature of pedagogy or instruction in teacher preparation is a central theme in this chapter.

One last point should be underscored in this brief contextual overview. Existing conditions do *not* excuse the several shortcomings in initial teacher preparation. There are bad teacher education practices in too many instances, irrespective of unenlightened or constraining policies and problematic working conditions. This contextual backdrop has been provided not as an apology but because it suggests directions where collective action is needed by the teacher education community.

GUIDING ASSUMPTIONS

This author embraces five assumptions in this treatise that examine what might contribute to more coherent programs of teacher preparation than are currently available. They were derived from reflection on the pervasive conditions briefly described in the introduction. First, programs of teacher preparation need to be guided by a critical perspective addressing issues of social justice in this country and in the larger global society. Second, although content in programs will vary from one licensure area to another, the nature of socialization provided to prospective teachers and the character of the pedagogy they interact with and eventually take on need to be altered in a dramatic fashion. Third, programs of teacher preparation need to intersect more fundamentally with and influence as well as be influenced by practice in P–12 schools. Fourth, the changes needed in programs of teacher education call for considerable coordination and collaboration within the higher education community, as well as within the P–12 sector. Finally, programs of teacher preparation need to be extended in a relatively seamless fashion into the early years of teaching; teacher preparation as currently construed is very much an unfinished agenda.

These assumptions undergird and guide this chapter. These guiding assumptions also assisted in deciding what not to include in the chapter. For example, this chapter does not address the structural location of programs, that is, whether programs should be positioned strictly at the baccalaureate level, begin there but extend beyond, operate as an independent fifth-year program, or be constructed as one of several variations of graduate level only preparation. "Life-space" or the amount of time that prospective teachers spend in initial preparation is an important design consideration; time on task is a critical variable in any learning. Also, the point at which a prospective teacher enters a program correlates with the scope and type of experience that he or she has had and with his or her general maturity. Nonetheless, quality time over time and student readiness, motivation, and maturity are factors that program design can to some degree account for regardless of where the program is located structurally. These considerations, although important, are not viewed as the primary determinants of coherent and effective programs. There are data to support this contention; for example, the National Center for Research on Teacher Learning (1992) conducted a study of more than 700 teachers and teacher candidates at 11 structurally diverse teacher education programs across the United States. This inquiry, known as the Teacher Education and Learning to Teach (TELT) study, concluded that

Although the debates in teacher education tend to be about the structure of teacher education programs, the TELT data suggest that the content and orientation of programs are more likely to influence teacher learning. Differences in beliefs and knowledge about teaching practices, diverse learners, and subject matter among teacher candidates at the end of the preservice programs studied were largely a function of their entering beliefs and knowledge of the *conceptual orientation* [italics added] of the program. Differences across program structures did not produce noticeable differences in teacher candidates' beliefs. (p. 6)

It is also apparent that the structural locations of programs are made for legitimate economic, political, and symbolic reasons. In examining the arguments put forth for postbaccalaureate teacher preparation at the inception of the Holmes Group, Howey and Zimpher (1986) observed

One of the more compelling arguments for embedding teacher preparation at the post-baccalaureate level is that preparation for teachers would begin to more closely resemble other professional training. This, it is argued, along with considerably revised curriculum and instruction will help to improve the image of teachers who at present are viewed as less than professional and of teacher preparation programs that are seen as less than adequate. (p. 44)

During this same period, Wise (1986) also spoke to the antecedents for such a move.

Too much may have been made of the idea that a special knowledge base is prerequisite to create a profession. A knowledge base is necessary, but it may not be the most important ingredient. Most early moves that other professions took could not be substantiated by research. Where were the multiple regression analyses to show the effects of going from no law school to one year, two years, or three? What research supports the idea that students be college graduates before they are allowed to enter law school? Why do you have to graduate from college before you are allowed to study medicine?

The important fact is that other occupations organized to become professions. They recognized that if anyone can "hang a shingle out" (or if anyone can "hang a shingle out" with minimal preparation), then no special status inheres to membership in the profession. (pp. 37, 38)

Most fundamentally the reason that these structural considerations are not the primary determinants of a program's efficaciousness is that a program can be moved from the baccalaureate to the post-baccalaureate level with little, if any, substantive change. Forty-five credits of coursework at one level can be adjusted slightly to become 45 credits of coursework at another level. Tom (1991) makes this point in lamenting the lack of consideration that university-based teacher educators give to the complex linkages of their content with school practice.

Thus, the professional part of teacher education is more likely to be thought of in terms of cognitive and curricular tasks than in such sociological terms as peer group, socialization, and so forth. Most teacher educators do not adequately appreciate the social nature of teaching and of professional training programs; nor do they comprehend the extent to which such programs are embedded in the politics and value structures of the contemporary university. Stated in different terms, teacher educators are too willing to accept existing intellectual and organizational structures—both in universities and in teacher education programs—as "givens" and direct their attention almost solely to what can be done within the context of those structures. (p. 55)

TOWARD THE CONSTRUCT OF A PROGRAM

What are factors that might speak more directly to the nature and quality of *programs* of preservice preparation? Howey and Zimpher (1989) offered the following tentative conceptualization of program as a heuristic for needed further inquiry into the kinds of contexts, activities, and experiences that could contribute to learning to teach:

Programs have one or more frameworks grounded in theory and research as well as practice; frameworks that explicate, justify, and build consensus around such fundamental conceptions as the *role* of the teacher, the *nature* of teaching and learning, and the *mission* of schools in this democracy. These frameworks guide not only the nature of curriculum as manifested in individual courses but, as well, questions of scope; developmental sequence; integration of discrete disciplines; and the relationships of pedagogical knowledge to learning how to teach in various laboratory, clinical, and school settings. Programs embedded in such frameworks clearly establish priorities in terms of key dispositional attitudes and behaviors enabled and monitored in repeated structured experiences. Programs reflect consideration of ethos and culture building and the critical socialization of the prospective teacher. The nature and function of collegial relationships is considered both between and among faculty and students as well as with those who assume responsibilities for teacher preparation in K–12 schools. Conceptually coherent programs enable needed and *shared* faculty leadership by underscoring collective roles as well as individual course responsibilities. Programs also contribute to more mutual endeavors in research and evaluation beyond the individual course level. Various student cohort arrangements and other temporary social systems such as inquiry teams, cooperative learning structures, or political action committees would be considered. Finally, programs provide considerable guidance both in terms of the nature and pattern of *pre*professional or *pre*education study and also extended experiences in schools in the nature of induction programs. (p. 242)

Progress Toward More Coherent Programs

The RATE studies annually probed into conditions and activities embedded in this definition in a broad sample of teacher preparation programs across the United States. Each year questions were revised and refined. The RATE VI study (1992), for example, examined what teacher educators in 50 institutions of various types preparing teachers reported relative to various attributes derived from the above conceptualization of program. The specific attributes in that study included the following:

1. The explication of a thoughtful *conceptual framework* to guide the programs
2. The manifestation of derivative *themes* that interrelate courses and key activities in the programs
3. The utilization of short-term student *cohorts* designed to promote skills best learned in a group and to promote positive socialization
4. The incorporation of early *diagnostic measures and continuing screening* of preservice teachers
5. The development of *pedagogical laboratories and clinics* in on-campus facilities

6. The employment of *student portfolios* to provide a basis both for systematic program evaluation and the tracking of student development over time

7. The development of a *core curriculum* about teaching, learning, and learning to teach undergirded by scientific studies and the best of practice.

Teacher education faculty members reported their progress since the late 1980s relative to these programmatic attributes as illustrated in Table 8.1. These data are reviewed because they provide some indices of where teacher education is, which is a priority consideration in deciding where it might go.

As Table 8.1 clearly shows, there is considerable variability across programs relative to progress in developing a thoughtful conceptual framework for programs of teacher preparation. For example, slightly more than one fifth of the sample report no or only marginal progress, another one fourth report moderate progress, and only a slight majority report good or excellent progress.

An explicit conceptual framework takes on significance for a number of reasons. In the related field studies, Howey and Zimpher (1989) found that when there was an explicit and thoughtful conceptual framework, there was also likely to be a reasonable number of core teaching abilities or teacher qualities derived from this framework that were addressed thematically over time in a variety of program activities. Thus, one would expect the development of identifiable program themes to be about as prevalent as the development of explicit conceptual frameworks, and this appears to be the situation.

There is less progress reported across all types of teacher preparation institutions when it comes to instituting a variety of student cohort arrangements. Slightly more than one fourth of the respondents report good or excellent programs, but more than 35% report little or no progress in these regards. How programs are structured for students to learn from one another is a very important consideration especially in terms of dispositions and abilities relative to equity and diversity.

Activities specifically structured to provide continuing diagnosis and screening of prospective teachers, the next program attribute examined, is more likely when desired student qualities or characteristics are clearly explicated. Howey (1994) advocates selection as an ongoing process that is educative in nature. Selection from this perspective involves a set of clearly defined personal qualities and communication skills viewed as enabling of teaching. They take on more of a selection than educative focus because these qualities often cannot be fostered easily in a preservice program, but they can be assessed in a variety of ways in the early stages of a program. These qualities can be articulated in the conceptual framework for a program when delineating a vision of the teacher, especially the teacher as person. These screening activities over a reasonable period of time can culminate in a multidimensional profile of the preservice student and can be used to counsel him or her for roles within as well as outside of teaching. These activities can be integrated within and greatly complement what is commonly considered the teacher preparation "curriculum." Such screening activities, however, are rare, as Table 8-1 clearly shows. Goodlad (1990) explains

Every campus wide teacher education council I interviewed was skittish about discussing the role in selecting and monitoring candidates for teaching beyond the academic. Their concerns with broadened criteria

TABLE 8.1. Progress on Program Attributes (RATE VI, 1992)

	No Progress	Marginal Progress	Moderate Progress	Good Progress	Excellent Progress
Faculty agreement on a thoughtful conceptual framework to guide the program	1.8%	18.4%	24.5%	38.6%	16.6%
The explication of a reasonable number of student goals thematically articulated across courses and related activities	4.3	22.2	28.4	35.2	9.9
A variety of cohort structures to assist in the socialization of students	10.3	26.3	35.3	21.8	6.4
The development of various diagnostic activities early in programs to assist in screening students	11.6	29.3	31.1	20.2	7.9
The development of laboratory facilities to enable pedagogical development	22.2	29.0	16.7	25.9	6.2
The development of student portfolios	30.7	25.2	20.2	15.3	8.6
The development of a core curriculum undergirded by scientific studies of teaching, learning, and schooling	4.9	14.1	25.8	39.3	15.9
Faculty cooperation in program design and assessment	3.1	12.3	28.8	41.1	14.7
The achievement of a systematic design for research into and evaluation of the program	9.8	28.2	38.6	18.4	4.9

centered on potential legal problems and fear of litigation. Two groups had recently broadened their selection criteria to include character traits, but they had reluctantly backed off. Others simply shrugged off the question as leading into a morass. Generally, too, these councils were reluctant to put forward an array of criteria against which to judge the progress of candidates toward some vision of teaching. Not only was there rarely agreement on a vision, but there was a hesitancy to impose a vision on individual faculty members—even though they were offered the opportunity to help determine it. A logistical complication was frequently noted: the difficulty of articulating the pieces of a program conducted by different groups of actors that were often not in very close communication. (pp. 218, 219)

The development of pedagogical laboratory facilities (a topic for later discussion) also presents problems for those in teacher education. More than one half of the institutions in the RATE survey report little or no progress in this regard. If computer labs were not included in the definition of laboratory facilities, the number of institutions reporting progress would be very small. Whereas other academic units on large research campuses expect multimillion dollar laboratories for faculty and their stable of graduate students, the prevailing view in teacher education is that one can learn to teach in lecture halls as long as this is integrated with or followed by student teaching. This author takes the position that schools and colleges of education everywhere are seriously discriminated against in internal budgeting matters in this regard. The teacher educators' community must shoulder a good share of the blame for the view that teachers can be educated cheaply. They simply have not advanced a clear and powerful vision of laboratory and clinical preparation. Among the laboratory facilities that can be found, but in limited numbers, are micro-teaching laboratories and isolated examples of interactive problem solving with computers. Teacher educators are unclear as to the nature and frequency of their use. Laboratories for the viewing of protocol materials, teaching clinics for the systematic analysis of instruction, facilities incorporating hypermediated instructional classes, and even conventional college classrooms with video cameras mounted to assist in analyzing teaching and learning episodes are virtually nonexistent.

Student portfolios, another program attribute considered, have considerable potential for altering the manner in which both programs and students are assessed; however, again only marginal progress is reported in most teacher preparation programs with less than one in four institutions reporting good progress. If teacher education is to move from an evaluative focus on discrete performance of preservice teachers to a focus on the *development* of core teaching abilities over time, then preservice student portfolios can assist considerably and their construction should be guided by, among other things, an explicit rendering of what these core abilities are and the evidence for deciding progress toward them.

The *core* for professional study includes subject matter and experience concerned with learners and learning, teachers and teaching, and schooling and community. Again, one of the major problems in teacher education has been the lack of professional consensus in terms of what, if anything, should constitute essential study by all teachers. Despite the problems to this point in defining and implementing core activities for all teachers, slightly more than half of the institutions reported

progress in this regard, likely abetted by the National Council for Accreditation of Teacher Education's (NCATE) emphasis on the knowledge base undergirding a professional core and the delineation of understandings and abilities essential to all teachers by the National Board for Professional Teaching Standards (NBPTS) and the Holmes Group's (1990) emphasis on a core curriculum.

TEACHER EDUCATION AS PROFESSIONAL EDUCATION

Teacher education should rightfully be viewed as professional education. This is an important distinction for a number of reasons, not the least of which is that professions are characterized by the nature of the preparation undertaken by members of that profession. In this regard Kennedy (1990) is instructive. She suggested that professional educators have devised two general strategies for responding to the question of how professional education will influence practice. The first of these is to codify knowledge and to give students as much understanding as possible about every conceivable situation they might ever encounter. The alternative strategy is to give students (in this instance, teachers) the kind of reasoning skills and strategies that will allow them to adapt to the wide variety of situations they are likely to encounter.

Kennedy described two fields—medicine and engineering—in which educators emphasize the first goal of providing students with as much codified knowledge as possible and two others—law and architecture—that rather embrace the clinical orientation. Kennedy noted that there are also professions that are ambivalent about whether they lean toward the codified knowledge orientation or more toward that of reasoning and problem solving. Teacher educators appear to fall within this group of more ambivalent professional educators. There is on the one hand a very considerable emphasis on the "knowledge base" for teacher education. The "knowledge base" is a center piece of the NCATE guidelines, for example, and it is incorporated into the title of a recent book sponsored by the AACTE titled *Knowledge Base for the Beginning Teacher* (Reynolds, 1989). There are also continuing demands from those responsible for the regulation of teacher educators at several states to make more fully explicit core or essential understandings (and abilities) for teachers.

However, there are many who position themselves on the side of teacher reasoning and decision making. The literature, for example, on teacher cognition and reasoning is diverse and growing, and, from this perspective, it is compelling in terms of factors to be considered in the preparation of teachers.

In reality, these two orientations to professional preparation are hardly mutually exclusive. Despite this, Kennedy (1990) observes that rarely does any group of professional educators entertain the possibility that providing more knowledge may actually facilitate problem solving or, conversely, that providing one with a set of clinical and diagnostic skills will help the professional eventually uncover and locate whatever knowledge is needed as the situation arises. Despite the tenuous premises underlying these two orientations, she points out that both from the standpoint of public perception and professional culture, agreeing on one position or another serves multiple purposes.

A coherent "package" of views, regardless of whether the view is that practice requires volumes of knowledge *or* that it requires independent thought and analysis, enables both educators and practitioners to share a coherent set of beliefs and values, and thereby to develop unified professional standards, guidelines and curricula. Even if their educational practices fail to provide students with the full complement of intellectual tools they need, they provide clear intellectual identities. These intellectual identities, in turn, generate a public perception that practitioners really do possess a special kind of expertise that justifies a special status. Professions without such strongly shared views do not have clear intellectual identities, and their work is often not perceived to have a particularly demanding intellectual character. The choice between providing volumes of knowledge and fostering independent thought and analysis is a hard one to make, for either option necessarily means that students do not receive all the intellectual tools they need. But the failure to choose denies students an intellectual identity and consequently all the social and personal benefits that accompany that identity. (Kennedy, 1990, p. 823)

A considerable challenge to those in the teacher education community is, in fact, to bridge the two orientations identified by Kennedy. It is essential given the complexity of teaching and learning and the number of years it takes for a teacher to fully mature as a professional that initial teacher education set a course wherein teachers learn to critically inquire into and reason about their practice throughout their career. This is the bedrock for learning to teach. Yet, to assume that one acquires these reasoning and decision-making abilities largely on the basis of apprenticeship and general experience over time is indeed incorrect from this perspective. Multiple domains of knowledge, including the core disciplines, undergird these reasoning abilities. There are myriad ways in which the disciplines contribute directly to learning to teach and eventually teaching. The following example from Howey (1994) illustrates this:

For example, our prospective teachers should view dozens of hours of video representing both principles which guide the teaching profession and the pervasive problems teachers encounter. As I indicated earlier they should examine teaching and learning episodes from the vantage point of and with the concomitant conceptual lenses provided by the psycholinguist, political scientist, social psychologist, cognitive scientist and cultural anthropologist, as well as, of course, the classroom teacher, student and parent. The multiple perspectives brought to bear on video representations of teaching and learning in a laboratory setting lead to informed *professional* judgment. Taking on critical, multiple perspectives of teaching and learning demonstrates applied research and theories in use and vividly illustrates the scholarly bases for separating professional judgment from conventional wisdom. What a physician sees, and *why,* is vastly different than what the lay person observes, even in cursory examinations. Similarly what a teacher sees, and *why,* should be very different from what the lay person observes in teaching/learning episodes. (p. 82)

It should also be noted that whereas these two departure points guide the nature of different professional training, others have provided a more manifold synthesis of the purposes of professional preparation generally. McGlothlin (1960), for example, examined general professional education aims from 16 professional fields and derived five common goals of profes-

sional programs including sufficient knowledge and skill to practice the profession, social understanding of sufficient breadth to place professional practice in the societal context and to provide professional leadership, personality characteristics for effective practice, zest for continued study that will steadily increase the professional's skill and knowledge, and competence in conducting or interpreting research that adds to human knowledge.

To underscore *both* the knowledge-based and clinical aspects of learning to teach and subsequently teaching, several conceptions of each are reviewed because these understandably drive how programs of teacher preparation are constructed.

THE NATURE OF A CONCEPTUAL FRAMEWORK

What are attributes of a program? Those examined here are embedded in the heuristic put forward earlier to provoke further thinking about what could contribute to more conceptually coherent and efficacious programs of preservice teacher education. The first of these attributes is a conceptual framework. Henrietta Barnes, the former chairperson of the Department of Teacher Education at Michigan State University, assumed a major leadership role in promulgating a set of conceptually coherent alternative teacher preparation programs at that institution. The decision to develop thematic approaches to teacher education at MSU emerged from a growing awareness that learning to teach, as with other complex learning, required building schemata on the part of prospective teachers. Such schemata necessarily include both theoretical and practical knowledge. The teacher education faculty concluded that programs would have to be designed to address how the commonplaces of education were understood by students; that is, what beliefs about teaching, learning, and schooling did they bring with them to the program that would have to be altered or discarded if not professionally warranted? Given these assumptions, Barnes (1987) defined a conceptual framework for a thematic program as follows:

The cornerstone of a thematic program is its conceptual framework. This framework is described in a document that presents the program's assumptions, philosophy, and research base and outlines the implications of that knowledge for teaching. In addition to explicating the purposes and goals of the program, the conceptual framework describes how the program is organized to achieve the desired outcomes. Thus, the theme of the program is clarified and elaborated in concrete operational terms. The particular theme of each program provides clear direction for the development of courses that are distinct in content from similar courses within other thematic programs. Similarly, the program's theme is used to guide the structuring of practicum experiences. Operational practices important in the day-to-day management of the program and monitoring of students' progress also stem from the program's theme. Of course, not all thematic programs incorporate the same kinds of experiences to achieve their goals. Rather, each program designs learning opportunities—both in campus and school settings—that are the logical extensions of the program's theme. (pp. 14–15)

Gary Griffin formerly chaired the Curriculum Committee for the Holmes Group, a national consortium of major schools and colleges of education concerned with making major improvements in the education of teachers. As Griffin struggled with how to guide a large consortium of institutions in rethinking the nature of preservice programs, he too reached the conclusion that discourse around a conceptual framework to guide these decisions was a reasonable course of action. He argued that if disparate schools and colleges of education and P–12 schools in partnership with them were to achieve some agreement around core conceptions of teaching-related phenomenon, this would greatly facilitate collaborative program development. He suggested that the program architects at each institution sign off on a set of agreed-upon statements about such matters as teaching, learning, and schooling. This process would allow each institution within the Holmes network to embrace Holmes principles but maintain a considerable degree of autonomy vis-à-vis their approach to the education of teachers. Griffin (1989) provided examples of these agreed-upon conceptions that could contribute to a conceptual framework in writing about the Holmes Group in 1990.

Clearly, teacher education programs need to deal with the issue of student learning. A conception of student learning that could be used to guide curriculum decision making is that *children and youth construct knowledge through meaningful experience.* If such a statement were adopted, it would lead us to help teacher candidates, for instance, understand students' developmental capabilities, see the social dimensions of learning, develop sophisticated and refined questioning (versus telling) strategies, invent rich learning environments, and link classroom experiences to out-of-school learning opportunities. The statement would not dictate the content of the teacher education curriculum, but it would delimit in a coherent way the options that might be considered appropriate. (p. 277)

There are also those who, rightfully, have raised questions and concerns relative to this advocacy for developing conceptual underpinnings intended to lead to more program coherence than exists typically. Buchmann and Floden (1990) suggest that program coherence could well be a futile press for certainty, especially when joined to short-sighted views of teacher learning. They fear that programs that attempt to tie together all loose ends and to interlace all the parts will indeed provide a misleading sense of order and security for prospective teachers. They remind teacher educators that teaching has endemic uncertainties; many of which can be managed but never wholly eliminated. They cautioned that

Being well-poised between the extremes is not coming down plump in the middle but depends on teacher education goals, instructors, students, and circumstances. While teaching and teaching teachers are enterprises committed in conceptual and practical terms, teacher education can hardly be more certain that teaching itself. Desirable program coherence is found where students can build connections among various areas of knowledge and skill, but where loose ends remain, inviting a reweaving of beliefs and ties to the unknown. (p. 8)

This point is well taken, but the advocacy for more coherence seems from this vantage point appropriate nonetheless given the number of preservice programs that superficially engage students in a large number of disparate and unconnected ideas and practices.

FLESHING OUT A CONCEPTUAL FRAMEWORK

There are numerous sources that inform the construction of programs and that should be attended to in a conceptual framework, including disciplinary content knowledge, conceptions of what professional practice entails, standards-setting activities focused on the commonplaces of schooling, models and theoretical constructs concerned with teaching and learning, craft wisdom and scholarship, and enlightened P–12 school reform initiatives. This chapter focuses on variant conceptions of teaching, learning, schooling, and learning to teach as undergirded by research, scholarship, and practical knowledge. This is not to deny the importance of these other sources, but given the constraints of space, these alternative conceptions should illustrate well how programs can reflect coherence in a variety of ways.

Tom (1991) employed the term *model* as this author uses the term *conception.* He suggested that models do not so much aim to describe or prescribe as to *orient.* Whereas models simplify, this is a legitimate means of highlighting what is viewed as important features or attributes of the construct. Highlighting these features also allows one to decide whether teacher educators are guided by the model or whether it needs to be revised or rejected over time. Conceptions, as with models, are intended to highlight what is important in a teacher preparation program and allow teacher educators to focus on whether and how certain features need to be revised or dropped over time.

CONTEMPORARY CONCEPTIONS OF TEACHING AND LEARNING

A clinical view of teaching has long been embraced, at least in the literature. Borko and Shavelson (1983) provide the following concise definition of teaching in this regard:

First, teaching is an activity which occurs in a complex, uncertain environment. Within this environment there are no absolutes, no right answers. Different approaches will work well for different teachers and in different situations. Because we cannot specify all situations in which teachers will find themselves and because we cannot identify all teacher or student characteristics that help determine the appropriateness of various approaches, we cannot train teachers to use the available skills and methods in a way that will guarantee effective teaching. Rather, teaching is best characterized as a situation in which professional judgment and decision making must be exercised in order to guide the provision of appropriate instruction. Certainly there are basic "tools of the trade"—knowledge, skills, and teaching techniques—which teachers are expected to have mastered. However, teaching is not the rote application of these tools in accord with a set of rules. Rather, effective teaching is a process in which teachers make reasonable judgments and decisions about the appropriate tools to use in any particular teaching situation. This decision process takes into account many factors including the characteristics of students, nature of the instructional task, and contextual constraints. Moreover, teachers' behavior is guided by these reason-based thoughts, judgments and decisions. (p. 216)

Although the literature is replete with advocates for teaching characterized as fundamentally a clinical, problem-oriented activity, the extent to which teaching in many classroom settings takes on such characteristics is nonetheless problematic. In this respect, Cohen (1988) cautions about romanticizing the clinical nature of teaching, especially given the paucity of resources many classroom teachers have to meet manifold demands. He characterizes such teaching as adventurous.

Adventurous instruction makes distinctive demands on teachers. It opens up uncertainty by advancing a view of knowledge as a developing human construction and of academic discourse as a process in which uncertainty and dispute play central parts. It increases the difficulty of academic work by replacing memorization of facts and rules with disciplined inquiry and argument. And it invites teachers to depend on students to produce an unusually large share of instruction . . . Such teaching can be done and done well. But to do so, ways to relinquish the old instruction must be found, and new strategies devised at the same time. Neither is easy. (p. 36)

Another common conception is that teaching and learning are highly transactional and are at times reciprocal activities. Good instruction involves teaching on the part of learners and learning on the part of teachers. These two activities are in a state of continuing interplay. Hence, how one construes teaching is obviously dependent on, and interdependent with how one views the nature of learning.

Learning in the literature is increasingly portrayed as active, conceptual, self-monitored, as well as group interdependent and group monitored with learning activities related as often as possible to "real-world" contexts. The Holmes Group (1990), in the principles set forth for the design of "Professional Development Schools," articulated both a view of learning and of a community of learners. They defined learning as an active, social, and highly participatory affair characterized by conversation, experience, interpretation, criticism, engagement, voice, participation, and purpose (p. 12). The Holmes Group (1990) further suggested that

Learning at all levels is an active process, in which children construct and reconstruct knowledge as they go along. To know something is not only to take in the bare information but to interpret it and relate it to other knowledge. Powerful learning, then, comes about when students can develop a mental scheme in which to frame their knowledge and then go on to make fresh knowledge and an even newer mental scheme. Much current cognitive research holds that there is no way to make real use of knowledge other than creating a personal intellectual apparatus that holds information together and allows the learner to play with it. Real knowledge is purpose-built, site-built, and infused with the learner's sense of purpose. (p. 13)

Whether or not one agrees with these particular conceptions, the position taken by this author is that dialogue and debate relative to conceptions of learning and, in turn, teaching should be promoted and sustained over time among those responsible for the design of programs of teacher preparation, including both university-based teacher educators and their counterparts in P–12 schools as Griffin (1989) suggested. Such sustained dialogue, however, is both uncommon and difficult. It is also susceptible to shallow "consensus," to downplaying legitimate differences that should be illuminated and shared with prospective teachers. Notwithstanding these challenges, when agreement does exist or where there is agreement not to agree, there are particular implications for the way programs are designed

and eventually manifested. When competing views of teaching and learning are held, explicit attention then needs to be given to just what *is* expected of the prospective teacher. The basic challenge in the discourse is a fuller illumination of what the conception(s) of teaching and learning connotes for learning to teach and how these beliefs are manifested pedagogically.

CONCEPTIONS OF LEARNING TO TEACH

Feiman-Nemser and Buchmann (1989) criticized most models of learning to teach because they tended to put their emphasis on a singular source of influence on teacher learning. They argued, for example, that programs that derive from a conception of teacher development (e.g., Fuller, 1969) focus on individual teacher's capacities and concerns. Programs embedded in conceptions of teacher socialization placed most of their emphasis on the influences of the workplace (e.g., Rosenholtz, 1989). Conceptions of teacher *training* invariably gave disproportionate emphasis to practice, feedback, and, in some instances, coaching (e.g., Joyce & Weil, 1980).

They argued instead that a theoretical (conceptual) framework for teacher education has to rest on a conception of the *central tasks* and the *distinctive work* of teaching as a starting point for the design of programs. They also argued that teacher preparation programs must use as a departure point the prior beliefs or preconceptions that prospective teachers have about the commonplaces of teaching, learning, schooling, and learning to teach. Finally, they also insisted on an understandable emphasis on what it means to teach in a multicultural society (Feiman-Nemser & Buchmann, 1989). This appears to be sound advice.

Colton and Sparks-Langer (1993) also derived a conceptual framework to guide their view of learning to teach. The theoretical underpinnings for their framework, as with Feiman-Nemser and Buchmann (1989), are again multiple and embedded in principles derived from cognitive psychology, critical theory, motivation theory, and a conception of caring. They identified seven types of knowledge needed to build the habits and abilities of a reflective practitioner. The first four of these (content, students, pedagogy, and context) are derived from Shulman's (1987) work. The fifth category is concerned with prior experiences and beliefs (Kennedy, 1989) and the final two, personal views and values, are drawn from the work of Van Manen (1977) and Zeichner and Liston (1987).

Pedagogical Content Knowledge

Pedagogical content knowledge and knowing can serve as a departure point for learning to teach. Pedagogical content knowledge has been a major focus in the Stanford Knowledge Growth and Teaching Project under the leadership of Lee Shulman (1987) and his colleagues. This means of knowing or reasoning differentiates *expert teachers* in subject areas from subject area experts. The emphasis in this view of learning to teach is on how subject-matter knowledge is related to pedagogical knowledge and, furthermore, how subject-matter knowledge is part of the process of pedagogical reasoning. The transformation of subject matter in the act of teaching occurs as teachers critically reflect on and interpret subject matter, finding appropriate ways to represent that subject matter in such means as analogies, metaphors, examples, problems, and demonstrations. The utility of this view of teaching and learning to teach appears manifold, not the least of which is conceptually bridging the unnecessarily dichotomous aims of professional preparation noted earlier by Kennedy.

Constructivist Perspectives

Cochran, DeRuiter, and King (1993) propose a modification of pedagogical content knowledge based on principles derived from *constructivist* views of learning and the application of this knowledge to teaching and teacher preparation. They refer to the integration as pedagogical content *knowing* as opposed to pedagogical content knowledge. Constructivist principles of learning are widely advocated. Lerman (1989) identifies two primary attributes of this view of learning. First, knowledge is actively created as opposed to passively received. Second, the processes of knowing and learning do not reveal an increasingly accurate, objective, or true understanding of an independent preexisting world outside the mind of the knower.

Teachers embracing constructivist assumptions and principles need to monitor how students construct and employ their understandings; the better the teacher understands how each student comes to know something, the more effective the teacher will be. Another major tenet of a constructivist conception of learning is that understanding is situated and context bound, and social interactions are deeply intertwined with the development of tools for understanding.

Thus, constructivist principles for learning to teach imply that very careful attention needs to be given to the various contexts in which teaching understandings and abilities are to be developed and that learning should be situated in a context as much as possible like the one in which the understandings are to be used. In this regard, Cochran et al. (1993) concluded that learning to teach often demands teaching specific content to specific students in specific situations. Thus, these scholars argue for extended use of case studies, peer coaching, cooperative classroom methods, microteaching, and team teaching. They contend that these methods involve students in realistic contexts in which "active" learning can occur and in which the social construction of knowledge can best be fostered.

Alkove and McCarty (1992) further articulate the implications of a constructivist perspective in developing a conceptual framework for teacher preparation.

The idea of professionalism found in the constructivist program asserts that significant education must present the learner with relevant problematic situations in which the learner can experiment, that is, manipulate objects to see what happens, question what is already known, compare findings and assumptions with those of others, and search for their own answers. Because learning is viewed as a life long process, students are encouraged, as teachers, to continue learning through observation, literature review, and reflection on their own practices. Reflection is particularly important since it plays an important role in a teacher's search for congruency between his/her beliefs and practice. (p. 21)

Teacher Reasoning

The aforementioned references capture some of the dominant thinking relative to what influences the nature of teachers' learning. The central tasks of teaching, cognitive psychology, critical theory, pedagogical content knowledge, and constructivist principles of learning have been advocated as viable departure points or conceptual frameworks for a program of preservice teacher education. Of course, a centerpiece in the growing literature on learning to teach is the body of scholarship concerned with the pedagogical or practical reasoning of teachers. There have been numerous reviews of this literature concerned, for example, with teacher thought and decision processes (Borko & Shavelson, 1990), variations on teacher cognition (Shulman, 1987), and teacher reasoning from a more philosophical perspective (Morine-Dershimer, 1987). Rentel (1992) has produced an excellent synthesis of the various lines of inquiry relative to the reasoning of teachers. He characterizes the growth of teaching knowledge and ability as "an extraordinary complex process, apparently organized as a web of abstract beliefs, principles, and justifications about the teaching of rather specific subjects. Yet this process of growth is deeply sensitive to students and the social and political contexts of classroom and school life. No simple description of subject mastery can capture how teachers become skilled in their craft" (pp. 32–33).

Rentel (1992) examines empirical data that reveal teacher decision making embedded in a complex dialectic of justifications, premises, evidence, and subtle warrants. If teaching effectiveness, as Rentel and others argue, is related to teachers' ability to develop data-based and morally defensible warrants for their teaching, what does this literature on teacher reasoning imply for preservice teacher preparation? Rentel (1992) is informative in this regard.

Careful analysis of evidence and experience may be far more important in the education of novice teachers than efforts to inculcate good methodology and sound technique. Student or novice teachers who teach and observe real children being taught, or who engage in the analysis of simulated teaching, that is, "cases" embodying the situated complexities of teaching, if required to analyze and reflect upon them, can begin to acquire knowledge of alternative teaching approaches, knowledge of children's typical levels of performance and achievement, and they can begin to develop and refine their analytical skills. Thus, it follows that the analysis of first- and second-hand cases should play a pivotal role in teacher preparation programs.

It seems equally clear that clinical experiences must be carefully articulated with case analysis. In clinical settings, where situational variables can be controlled, students can grapple productively with problems, dilemmas, action premises, and hypotheses formed in first- and second-hand case experiences. Such experiences can be reexamined, viewed from multiple perspectives, and connected with solutions whose utility is obvious, or whose usefulness can be underscored where issues are subtle or very complex. The literature [on teacher reasoning] suggests that linkages are best achieved by discussion and argument aimed at justifying problems, dilemmas, premises, and hypotheses identifed and clarified in clinical experiences. (p. 35–36)

Critical Perspectives

At the outset of this chapter it was underscored that teacher education should address the continuing problems attached to achieving social justice and the central role of education in this regard. Zeichner (1983) identified four alternative paradigms driving programs of teacher education. He defined these as the "behavioristic," the "personalistic," the "traditional craft," and those that are primarily "inquiry oriented." Zeichner acknowledges that whereas there are numerous variations and practical applications within each of these paradigms, each paradigm nonetheless seems to be held together by a set of core assumptions. The progressive perspective, long embraced by many educators, is embedded within the inquiry-oriented tradition and speaks to concerns regarding social justice. Zeichner (1983) summarized this orientation as follows:

The fundamental task of teacher education from this point of view is to develop prospective teachers' capacities for *reflective action* (Dewey, 1933) and to help them examine the moral, ethical and political issues, as well as the instrumental issues, that are embedded in their everyday thinking and practice. (p. 6)

Valli (1993) elaborated on this critical perspective. She argued that those engaged in moral reflection must enter sympathetically into opposing points of view, acknowledging the limitations of their own understanding. Approaches to teaching that embody this perspective are often called "moral reflection," and Valli, in turn, identifies three variations of moral reflection: the deliberative, the relational, and the critical. For Valli, the deliberative approach encourages thoughtful consideration of educational issues. The relational approach is rooted more in questions of relatedness and responsiveness. An example of this relationship perspective is Nel Noddings's (1984) *Caring: A Feminine Approach to Ethics and Moral Education*. Herein the focus is on the student as a person with full consideration of that person both within and outside the school context.

The third category of moral reasoning set forth by Valli is the critical. Proponents of this reasoning argue

that as social institutions, schools help reproduce unjust class, race and gender relations, and that teachers must reflect on and help change teaching practices and school structures which perpetuate such arrangements. The purpose of teacher preparation, for critical theorists, would be assisting prospective teachers in understanding how schools contribute to an unjust society as a basis for developing skills and dispositions for emancipatory action. (Valli, 1990, p. 7)

Giroux and McLaren (1986) are advocates of this latter form of reflection. They contend that the historical precedent for educating teachers is intellectual, wherein schools are democratic sites for social transformation. They suggest educating teachers as transformative intellectuals, employing the term *intellectual* in the manner depicted by Lentricchia (1983) as "one whose radical work of transformation, whose fight against repression is carried on at the specific institutional site where he finds himself on the terms of his own expertise, on the terms inherent to his own functioning as an intellectual" (pp. 6–7).

It is certainly not just the broader social contexts and the several inequities within this to which attention needs to be directed. Education and teacher education are moral enterprises with their own attendant issues and problems. Ginsburg (1988) reminds us that prospective teachers, when examining their own teacher education programs and practices, can find multi-

ple opportunities to address moral issues in a firsthand, personal manner:

The curriculum content of teacher education programs and other courses must become not only a purveyor of these and other relevant skills and tools, but also the focus of critical examination. This would entail instructors and students identifying and discussing what messages are evidenced, and those which are not evidenced or are only part of the taken-for-granted background, in a given reading, handout, lecture, school/community observation. Moreover, the content of any specific message in the formal curriculum would have to be analyzed in relation to other messages in the formal curriculum, as well as those in the "hidden" curriculum—that constituted by the social relations of the teacher education program, the university, and school/communities. Such a process, of course, is not likely to be a comfortable one for instructors or students. From the instructor's perspective, this makes what they say, what they may decide upon as curricular materials, and their routine practices—including admission decisions, grading, and interaction outside of class—subject to critical inquiry and reflection. For students, not only would they be placed in the awkward position of publicly discussing the contradictory elements of a program organized by instructors who may be gate-keepers for their projected careers in teaching, but they would also have to interrogate their own actions and statements and those of their peers. (pp. 211–212)

Multicultural Teacher Education

Infusing attention to diversity, equity, multiracial, multicultural, and global perspectives into programs of teacher preparation has been the focus of numerous teacher reform initiatives. It was the centerpiece of the AACTE Commission on Multicultural Education (1973), and it is a permeating concern in the standards set forth by the NCATE. Just as there are multiple variations of pedagogical content knowledge, constructivist principles of learning, and teacher reasoning, there are as well numerous conceptions of multicultural education and strategies for infusing a multicultural perspective into programs of teacher preparation. Milhouse and Henderson (1993), for example, have identified six models of multicultural education, including single group/ethnics studies, human relations training, social reconstruction, intercultural communications, global education, and historical/reflective thinking.

Single group/ethnic studies variations examine a particular group in depth, whether it is racial, ethnic, or religious, and draw on a variety of disciplines such as history, literature, psychology, anthropology, and sociology. Human relations training has many variations but invariably employs group processes and experiential activities to help individuals understand one another and ameliorate conflict. Social reconstructionist variations focus on relationships between those in and out of power. They stress active participation, case studies, historical films, and experiential activities. Intercultural communications models emphasize how to enhance communications and understanding among culturally different groups. Prospective teachers are taught nonoppressive ways of communicating across cultures. Global education models, which are elaborated on in the next section, are based on the premise that diversity is the foremost characteristic of global community, and, therefore, prospective teachers must interact in positive ways with people from many different cultures. Historical/reflective thinking models are designed to enable group relationships through examining conflicts from a historical perspective.

Certainly when addressing issues of equity and social justice, gender needs to be addressed, especially in the education context. Gender distinctions have permeated the history of American education. Grumet (1981) reminds teacher educators of the contradictions that female teachers, who made up the majority of the working force in the nineteenth century, faced in a difficult role contradiction between nurturance, which they viewed as appropriate to their gender, and the need for more strict and impersonal discipline, which was an expectation held forth for them in their role as teachers. Grumet argues that these contradictions contributed to the imbalance between their dominance in numbers on the one hand and their exclusion from leadership on the other hand, and that these contradictions are still present in the culture of schooling.

Maher and Rathbone (1986) contend that understanding this historical condition can provide female prospective teachers especially an opportunity for identification with one another and with their female forebearers. They suggest

Together with general information on women's careers, students may use this history of women as teachers to examine the relationship of schools to other patriarchal social structures and to see the pressures that these social structures have placed on women's experiences and the ways such social norms may have influenced their own behaviors, expectations, and career choices. In their caring, nuturing, low-status roles, women have socialized generations of children for different positions and roles in our society—notably, girls to be girls and boys to be boys. Awareness of these conflicting and sometimes self-destructive demands on teachers permits both male and female education students to reexamine their personal career goals. (p. 219)

Global Teacher Education

A major variation within and/or extension of the multicultural orientation are those teacher preparation programs that attempt to promote a more global perspective. An intensive experience in another country is often an integral aspect of the preparation of teachers in these instances. Such teacher preparation programs, unfortunately, are very limited at this time. Given modern communications technology and the ability to negotiate reasonable travel to most places on the globe, one can only hope that such experiences will proliferate in the future. It would appear to be more a matter of wanting to engage prospective teachers in other cultures than not being able to do so. Certainly such activities have tremendous educative power, especially if students are properly prepared for such experiences and are fully immersed in the culture of the country in which they assume their teaching responsibilities.

An exemplar in this regard has been the overseas student teaching project at Indiana University coordinated by Jim Mahan. Students from numerous U.S. universities and colleges have participated in this program for close to two decades now. In their preparation for these international experiences, prospective teachers must participate in an extended seminar in which they complete numerous reading and writing assignments. They learn about the country and cultures via film, video, and guest speakers. In addition, these participants must have completed student teaching before taking on their teaching assignment in another country. They not only assume full teaching duties in the school to which they are assigned but also must participate in many community activities in which they interview individuals having a variety of roles and responsibilities. Finally, they develop "reflective" reports addressing cultural values and issues in their particular setting.

Mahan and Stachowski (1985) have attempted to assess the impact of these experiences on their students during the course of several years. Not suprisingly, students report myriad positive learnings not only in terms of their abilities as teachers, but also changes in their personal perspective about and understanding of others generally as a result of teaching and living in another country.

Human Development

A core corpus of research and theory that informs both teaching and learning to teach is that concerned with dimensions of human development at all ages: early childhood, adolescent, and adult. Early childhood and elementary teacher preparation programs tend to be rooted in principles of child and preadolescent development. There have also been instances where constructs of *adult* cognitive development have guided programs of teacher education and the selection and matching of student teachers with their supervising teachers (Sprinthall & Thies-Sprinthall, 1983). Basic assumptions in this orientation are that humans, and in this instance teachers, move developmentally from less complex cognitive stages to more cognitively complex stages, and that these stages are associated with the ability to perform in more adaptive and complex ways in the classroom. These propositions have been supported through a number of empirical investigations across the helping professions.

Reiman and Parramore (1994) recently reported on a teacher preparation program that was grounded in a conceptual framework based on cognitive developmental theory. The teacher preparation program was designed to manifest properties that have been reported over time as promoting psychological development in the helping professions. In this regard the program overtly addressed the subject matter on human development in a thematic manner and asked the prospective teachers to: (1) participate in challenging new and complex helping roles, but with support offered for meeting these challenges; and (2) participate in guided reflection on these experiences so that there was a balance between action and reflection as well as challenge and support. The prospective teachers were required to live on campus and were housed in the same dormitory. Each year in summer internships they took on roles other than that of the classroom teachers. Every individual was required to participate in and report on multicultural experiences on a regular basis.

Reiman and Parramore (1994) predicted that students at higher stages of cognitive development would move more readily from an emphasis on concerns with themselves and the task at hand to concerns for student learning and the factors that contribute to such. In this regard, they report

These results, then, indicate that two independent assessments of developmental stage both correlate positively with movement on concerns measures. . . . The trend for first-year teachers at higher developmental stages is to express more concern for student learning and welfare. (p. 131)

Cognitive Instruction

Several scholars have advanced the understanding of cognitive instruction (Palincsar & Brown, 1987). Cognitive instruction draws heavily from both motivation and attribution theory (Paris & Oka, 1986). A fundamental premise in attribution theory is that students who believe their personal effort is instrumental in affecting their achievement are more likely to learn than those pupils who assume a number of external factors are the determinants of their success or failure. Attribution theory underscores that student success is not enough to sustain student learning or motivation to learn; rather, the key is understanding what students do that contributes to or distracts from their success. Students are taught a number of cognitive strategies to monitor their progress, to contribute to their learning, and to sustain their motivation for further learning. Brown, Palincsar, and Armbruster (1984) have identified six common functions of cognitive-instruction strategies in the area of reading: (1) understanding the purpose of the learning activity; (2) activating relevant background knowledge; (3) allocating attention to major content; (4) critically evaluating for internal consistency and compatibility with prior knowledge and common sense; (5) monitoring to evaluate whether or not learning is occurring (e.g., by engaging in self-questioning or paraphrasing); and (6) drawing and testing inferences through interpretation, prediction, and the forming of conclusions.

If cognitive strategy instruction is to be deeply embedded in the ongoing activities of teachers, then understandably teachers must assume a different orientation than they typically adopt in their own classroom instruction or learning to teach. Teacher educators would need to focus specifically on the types of problems that they present in instructional tasks and on the array of cognitive strategies that their preservice students will need to employ to solve these problems. Preservice teachers would need to apply their understandings of motivation and attribution theory to their own learning as a precondition to engaging their own pupils in these strategies. In this regard, in 1983 Cohen advocated motivation theory as a conceptual framework for teacher education.

> One goal of employing personal causation theory in teacher preparation classes is to provide an alternative structure for students' perceptions and instructors' expectations. Another goal is to enhance the teacher preparation process by furnishing a model of the teacher who incorporates principles of motivation into his or her teaching. (p. 11)

BEHAVIORISM AND BEHAVIOR ANALYSES

Obviously the staples of teacher preparation for many years have been activities and practices reflective of behaviorism, behavioral analysis, and, consistent with a strong research tradition, applied behavioristic psychology.

This research was especially dominant throughout the 1970s and into the 1980s in driving studies of teaching and influencing teacher education. Studies examining these relationships were referred to as process-product studies, and this line of inquiry contributed to the competency or performance-based teacher education movement.

Although not as prevalent in preservice teacher preparation today, the competency or outcomes orientation is nonetheless widespread in the P–12 sector and is a staple of standards-setting activities in many state and national endeavors. The decline of this orientation in programs of preservice teacher preparation is attributable to several factors. First, the results of these investigations, although capable of providing excellent guidance to teacher educators, were unfortunately misinterpreted and misapplied in several instances, often prescriptively. Second, disproportionate attention was directed to the teachers' responsibilities at the expense of the pupils' roles in and responsibilities for learning, especially in reciprocal and collaborative ways. Third, effective patterns of teacher behavior derived from studies across several classrooms became decontextualized, often "molecularized," routines to be acquired, applied, and assessed without consideration of the complexity of classroom life. Fourth, too often resultant "training" was atheoretical, not acknowledging how individuals learn individually and collectively. Fifth, and perhaps most fundamentally, when critical teacher functions were addressed in the competency-based teacher education era, too often it was with the most primitive teacher education technology. For example, Joyce and Showers's (1981) advocacy of a progression from theory to demonstration to guided practice and "coaching" in a classroom context was not then and is not now a characteristic of teacher preparation. The lack of potent teacher preparation technology, often limited to lecture/recitation formats followed by relatively unsupervised P–12 classroom experiences (RATE VI, 1992), continues to constrain many preservice teachers from developing a reasonable repertoire of teaching abilities.

The behavioral orientation today has been put into perspective by the critical insights derived from the burgeoning lines of inquiry into how teaching is mediated both by the sense that pupils make of the social context of the classroom—social mediation—and the pupils' and teachers' thinking—cognitive mediation. Nonetheless, pedagogical skill development, fully cognizant of the teaching-learning context and the cognitive and social processing of those involved, is perhaps a greater priority now than ever. Unfortunately, lost in the widespread advocacy in teacher education for reflection and reasoning, for decision making and problem solving, for the development of theories-in-use, and for instruction as social reconstruction, is sufficient attention to the necessary technical undergirding needed to teach effectively (recall the RATE survey on dominant conceptions of learning to teach). There is even less attention to how these abilities are best acquired. Abilities such as active listening, appropriate wait time, clarifying and extending an idea, paraphrasing, and perception check are hardly wholly indigenous to types of learner, topics, or subject under discussion. Staples of direct instruction from overview, advance organizers, and introduction to soliciting feedback and summarizing are core abilities that, although obviously adapted to a given situation, are nonetheless transcendent in their applicability. More encompassing pedagogical strategies such as cooperative learning or reciprocal teaching can be pursued thematically over time by preservice teachers in a number of contexts and with a variety of topics.

Peer and microteaching arrangements are designed for both learning to teach and learning to *learn*. Peer and microteaching provide a time, a place, and a culture wherein one can experiment with specific skills. These activities need not reflect a narrow unduly behavioristic focus, as they often did in early microteaching ventures. A laboratory setting can focus attention through video replay on the thinking of both teachers and students (other preservice teachers assuming a learner role) and the nature of the dynamics between them. Later in this chapter the author returns to examples of laboratories to promote pedagogical development. What has been learned about teaching from the line of inquiry undergirded by behavioral psychology should not be ignored in light of more recent research and teacher education paradigms that have provided a more encompassing view of teaching and learning. The contributions of behavioral psychology should not be lost but rather incorporated in a thoughtful manner in teacher preparation with other perspectives in a manner Shulman (1987) has referred to as disciplined eclecticism.

In summary, learning to teach can obviously be addressed from a variety of vantage points. The several conceptions of learning to teach briefly presented here are hardly mutually exclusive. Numerous creative syntheses of these conceptions of or orientations to learning to teach can and have been incorporated into programs such as those advocated earlier by Feiman-Nemser and Buchmann (1989), and Colton and Sparks-Langer (1993). There are several matters to ponder, however, in delineating a conception of learning to teach, whether more singular or synthetic in nature.

1. If a preservice student is to internalize fully and employ often complex understandings and pedagogical strategies embedded in a particular conception, then opportunities for understanding and use need to extend beyond a course and be manifested thematically throughout the program. The effects of discontinuity across courses relative to teacher development are unclear, but it would seem reasonable that they contribute to fragmentation and superficiality in practice and thought.

2. Different conceptions of learning to teach certainly represent different values and beliefs. Whatever degree of agreement or lack thereof regarding these values exists among the teacher education faculty, these differences should be addressed by the faculty in terms of how they will be represented to the students.

3. Of course, more and better studies are needed of both how one learns to teach over time and the effects of more coherent as well as more eclectic or disparate program approaches. These studies need to be extremely cautious of interpretations of preservice student "outcomes" without careful consideration of how the specific elements of a program relate to these.

It may well be that the primary pattern of activities in programs relative to how one views learning to teach in teacher education today is what Zeichner and Tabachnick (1982) found more than 10 years ago, which is basically an eclectic pattern. However, there is some evidence that at this time there is more attention to coherency and conceptual frameworks, especially because the NCATE standards call for a systematic design for programs of teacher education. The RATE IV (1990) study polled teacher education faculty and students as to whether there was a discernible, dominant conception of learning to teach that ran throughout their program and, if so, whether it was (a) skill or competency oriented; (b) clinical or problem solving in nature; (c) the concept of a well-rounded, liberally educated person; (d) humanistic and person oriented; or (e) inquiring and reflective in posture. Space was left for respondents to enter other dominant conceptions as well. Obviously several of the dominant orientations identified in this chapter were not included in this earlier study, but it is nonetheless instructive.

Almost 60% of the faculty (57%) and almost two thirds of the students (65%) reported that their program was framed by one of these conceptions of teaching. The faculty responses were fairly evenly divided between the liberal (25.5%), humanistic (23.4%), and skill (22%) orientations. About one in seven faculty members (15.6%) indicated the inquiring and reflective perspective, and less than one in 10 (9.9%) indicated a clinical or cognitive perspective. The great majority of students, 42.5%, viewed liberally educated orientation as the dominant theme. The percentage of those responding in this manner was much higher for students than for faculty. Percentages of students indicating the humanistic and inquiry perspectives were 18% and 16%, respectively. A little less than 1 in 10 (8.5%) of the students identified the cognitive perspective as pervasive or thematic, and surprisingly, only a little more than 1 in 10 (13.1%) gave the skill orientation preeminence.

EXTERNAL FORCES INFLUENCING PROGRAM DESIGN

This chapter forefronts different views of how one learns to teach as a primary matter to be considered in designing programs. Obviously other factors need to be considered as well. Yet, this chapter cannot possibly begin to address all of the forces that influence or attempt to influence the nature and character of preservice programs in the United States. A few, however, warrant mention. The influence of state rule in program approval or voluntary accreditation cannot be ignored. In this regard, almost 600 of the more than 1,200 institutions that prepare teachers in this country stand for voluntary accreditation by the NCATE. In terms of state approval, the Interstate New Teacher Assessment and Support Consortium (INTASC) initiated by the Council of Chief State School Officers (CCSSO) in the United States is examining how initial licensing across the states might be consistent with new standards evolving for *advanced teacher certification* as put forward by the National Board for Professional Teaching Standards (NBPTS).

There are at least four discernible areas in which NCATE (1993), under the leadership of Arthur Wise, has recently influenced schools and colleges of education in the design of programs of teacher preparation. Consistent with the discussion in this chapter, NCATE calls for faculty dialogue to provide grounding for and interrelatedness to a *program* of teacher preparation. Standard 1.A, concerned with the design of curriculum, requires that programs are based both on current research and sound professional practice. It calls for a systematic design for teacher education with an explicitly stated philosophy and for coherence between courses and experiences and goals and outcomes. Second, NCATE centrally addresses the multicultural nature of faculty, students, curriculum, and instruction. Third, this accrediting agency emphasizes the recency and relevancy of the bodies of knowledge that undergird teacher preparation. Fourth, and finally, its standards are concerned with the nature and quality of relationships with the world of practice. As NCATE standards have gone through periodic revisions, more attention is now being given to the systematic evaluation of *programs* over time, as well as to the assessment of preservice teachers graduating from these programs.

One of the major initiatives at this time concerned with teacher standards setting or outcome identification is the vanguard effort supported by the NBPTS (1991). This board is concerned with establishing standards that signify *accomplished* practice. The NBPTS's ambitious agenda calls for developing standards for accomplished practice in 20 of the 30 certificate fields that will comprise the National Board Certification System when it is fully operational. How teachers will be assessed against these evolving standards is a major challenge and pilot testing of multiple means of documentation and assessment relative to teacher certification is now underway. Portfolio assessment comprises one major phase of this evaluation and assessment centers another. The NBPTS intends to develop assessment procedures that are deeply rooted in self-reflection as well as classroom practice. There is a considerable emphasis on the professional development of teachers and the closer coupling or blending of instruction and assessment.

The CCSSO established a consortium in 1987 to focus on *initial* teacher licensing in a manner that would be consonant with the initiatives of the NBPTS relative to *advanced* certification. Thus, INTASC was established to enhance cooperation across states that were interested in rethinking teacher assessment for initial licensing relative to the standards evolving for advanced certification. INTASC shares the view with the National Board that teaching is highly complex and that assessment strategies will be required that are capable of capturing teachers' judgments or reasoning about teaching as well as their instructional performance in actual teaching situations.

The INTASC (1992) task force initially decided that it would articulate standards for a common or central core of teaching knowledge and skills applicable to all new teachers. Eventually standards will be established as well for the diciplinary areas and for the levels of schooling and types of student teachers, parallel to the plan of the NBPTS. The five major propositions that guide the NBPTS standards-setting and assessment activities, and, hence, the INTASC task force, are as follows:

1. Teachers are committed to students and their learning.
2. Teachers know the subjects they teach and how to teach those subjects to diverse learners.
3. Teachers are responsible for managing and monitoring student learning.
4. Teachers think systematically about their practice and learn from experience.
5. Teachers are members of larger communities. (NBPTS, 1991, pp. 13–15)

The INTASC initiatives, as NCATE's ongoing efforts, are briefly shared here because standard setting and assessment are the most discernible and pervasive activities in a myriad array of "reform" endeavors in both the P–12 and teacher education sectors at this time in the United States. They are a definite influence on program design. INTASC has the support of the CCSSO, and, therefore, the vision of teaching put forward by this group could very well permeate rules and regulations for program approval across many states. These standards will be further reinforced by the parallel National Board standards. The conceptual frame, or at least a conception of teaching, undergirding this work appears supported by contemporary notions of learning; that is, their assessment procedure shifts from a preoccupation with periodic evaluation of discrete teacher behaviors to multiple measures of teacher development over time, and they focus on *student* reasoning abilities in instructional activities with parallel increasing attention to preservice *teacher* reasoning. Thus, from this perspective there is considerable potential in this initiative to contribute to an important shift in how teachers are prepared in the future.

P–12 SCHOOL INITIATIVES: IMPLICATIONS FOR PROGRAM DESIGN

Just as one cannot ignore standards-setting and rule-setting activities in discussing the design of teacher education, neither can one ignore, as is argued at the outset, the context of P–12 schooling and especially major efforts to improve practice. Reform needs to proceed in an interrelated fashion in both sectors. Whereas the constraints of space in a chapter limit what can be addressed, a very brief review of some of the major reform activities in the P–12 sector in the United States allows some comparison and contrast with the conceptions of teaching and learning and learning to teach shared to this point. Recall, as stated at the outset, that the teacher education community has not assumed a major role in many of these change projects, nor have the architects of these reform efforts been much concerned with their implications for professional preparation initially.

The review of school reform and restructuring efforts that follow is hardly inclusive, but it does provide a sense of common priorities. The review includes The Edison Project, school reform efforts supported by the RJR Nabisco Next Century Schools, projects selected by the New American Schools Development Corporation, Success for All, Comer's School Development Program, The Higher Order Thinking Skills Program, Levin's Accelerated Schools Project, Reading Recovery, Sizer's Coalition of Essential Schools, Hirsch's Core Knowledge initiative, and the Foxfire Project. These are intended to illustrate both the diversity and commonality across these projects and to stimulate thinking about what this implies for designing programs of perservice preparation.

The Edison Project is a major research and development initiative managed by Chris Whittle. Whittle proposes to dismantle the general structure of schooling currently in place and to combine old parts, "many of which work quite well," with new parts and put it back together in some fundamentally different ways to invent the "new American school." Whittle has been joined in the project by Benno C. Schmitt, Jr., who gave up his post as president of Yale University to become the project's chief executive officer.

The project proposes to create a large-scale, for-profit, private school system operated nationally to serve student populations similar to those in the public schools and at per-pupil costs similar to those in public schools. The program aspires to offer a model that will be replicable in the public sector. The Edison schools plan to offer contract services to other private and public schools, develop software and hardware, and be an ongoing educational research laboratory. Mr. Whittle's intent is to open 200 schools nationwide, serving from 100,000 to 150,000 students.

Although still in the development stage, examples of what the "new American school" might look like are offered in literature advertising the project. These include longer days, peer learning groups, electronic learning systems (ELSs), at-school "jobs" for students, and time for teachers to spend an hour or more per week one-on-one with each student. Students will also have access to an ELS at home.

Next Century Schools (NCS) is a competitive grant program designed to stimulate "bold reforms" in elementary and secondary education. Grants of up to $250,000 for 3 years have been made to "educational entrepreneurs" in local public schools. The program was launched in 1989 at the initiative of Louis V. Gerstner, Jr., CEO of the RJR Nabisco Company.

Specifically, the grants are designed to test variations in the school day and year, foster multi-age groupings, break down fixed-block instructional periods, and enhance the involvement of parents and the use of contemporary technology.

In examining several reform proposals submitted to NCS, the following commonalities were indentified: collaborative teaching, teaming with counselors, thematic study, active learning with an emphasis on problem solving and asking questions, involving community organizations and social service providers more centrally and fully in schools, and having teachers work with same groups of students for up to 3 years.

New American Schools Development Corporation (NASDC) is a private, nonprofit organization of business leaders formed to support the design and establishment of new, "high-performance" learning environments that will "transform schools for the next generation of American children." NASDC is not intended to be an incremental change strategy. Rather, it seeks to make a "quantum leap" toward the creation of new schools and new ways of teaching and learning.

NASCD announced in the summer of 1992 that 11 project teams had been selected to develop and refine their "prototypes for the best schools in the world." Proposals were required to address three major challenges. They must first help students meet new national standards in five core subject areas, as well as prepare them for responsible citizenship, further learning, and productive employment. Second, they must operate on a budget comparable to conventional schools. Third, they must seek fundamental *institutional* change in American schooling.

NASCD is directly connected to the federal government's America 2000 (1992) initiative. The Rand Corporation is the research and analysis contractor for the project.

Proposals submitted to NASDC were also reviewed, and the Roots and Wings Proposal is briefly reviewed to illustrate the innovations being supported. Roots and Wings: Universal Excel-

lence in Elementary Education is a collaborative project among Robert E. Slavin of the Center for Research on Effective Schooling for Disadvantaged Students at Johns Hopkins University, the Maryland State Department of Education, and the St. Mary's County Public School District. This approach to schooling has two major overarching goals.

1. Every child, regardless of family background or disability, will achieve world class standards in reading, writing and language arts, mathematics, science, history, and geography.
2. Students will creatively and flexibly solve problems, understand their own learning processes, and connect knowledges from different disciplines. Higher order skills will be developed collaboratively as children work together to solve both simulated and real-life problems.

The foundation of the program is the "Success for All" program developed at Johns Hopkins, which combines early prevention, tutoring for at-risk children, and family support. The project is designed for children from birth to age 11. It employs extensive use of cooperative learning and integration across disciplines.

The main elements of the program include a nongraded organization in which students are grouped into "learning blocks" (birth to age 4, 4–6, 6–8, 8–11) according to skills and interests. Within each block, tutoring and family support services will be available to assist students.

The Worldlab Integrated Simulations for Global Understanding will also be incorporated into the curriculum. With these, students will engage in simulations to help them apply what they are learning to "real" contexts and to see the interconnectedness and usefulness of knowledge across cultures.

The project will feature tutoring with an emphasis placed on students who have problems with reading. These students will be tutored one-on-one by certified teachers. The position taken is that reading is most critical to success in other areas and therefore requires the most intensive instruction.

Finally, the Family Report and Integrated Services Component will include day care; adult education; assistance with food, rent, and heat; and health and mental health assistance. It will be coordinated by a family support team at each school.

In 1968, James Comer established the School Development Program (SDP) in two elementary schools in the New Haven School System in collaboration with the Yale University Child Study Center. The project focused on two inner-city schools that had poor attendance and where the pupils had the lowest level of achievement in the city. By 1992, the SDP model was being used in more than 150 schools. Although originally developed for elementary schools, it is now being used at the high school and middle school levels.

The SDP is a comprehensive approach to child development and education that seeks the best possible adaptation by the child from the home and community to the school environment. It is based on the fundamental assumption that the traditional school is ill equipped to deal with the underlying problems associated with poorly socialized children in low socioeconomic status neighborhoods. Contributing factors to poor school performance are stress and student underdevelopment of the family side and lack of organization, management, and child development knowledge and skill on the part of the school staff. The SDP's approach is to treat the child, and the family if necessary, socially and behaviorally as well as educationally.

The Mental Health Team, another feature of the SDP organizational structure, is composed of a classroom teacher, the special education teacher, a social worker, and a parent assistant. A psychologist also serves as a member of the team. The social worker in turn advises the Governance and Management (G&M) team and helps integrate in an ongoing manner mental health principles with academic goals.

The Accelerated Schools Project (ASP) was established by Henry Levin and his colleagues at Stanford with an emphasis on meeting the needs of disadvantaged youth. It is based on school effectiveness studies and emphasizes site-based governance. The accelerated school is a "transitional" elementary school. A basic goal is to bring at-risk students into the mainstream (performing at grade level) by the end of the sixth grade.

The ASP focuses on changes in human behavior as opposed to changes in the system. It assumes that at-risk students must learn faster than more privileged students, and, thus, major interventions for at-risk students must begin at the elementary level. Schools must be dedicated to preparing all children for high-quality work at the secondary level.

Among the strategies employed in the ASP are developing learning activities characterized by high expectations and high status as a student and as an individual. Activities are designed to capitalize on the interest and curiosity of the students' oral and artistic expression. The curriculum is fast paced, and instruction actively engages the students.

The application to everyday problems is a major feature of the schools and, when possible, a range of resources in the community are engaged. Parents are also broadly involved in the design and implementation of the school. Peer tutoring and cooperative learning are staples. A major emphasis is extending and improving the amount of student time "on task." Both teacher preparation time and the school day are extended. Performance profiles or portfolios are commonly employed in accelerated schools.

The Higher-Order Thinking Skills (HOTS) program emphasizes four major components: (1) the use of computers for problem solving, (2) emphasis on dramatization techniques that require students to verbalize and thereby stimulate language development, (3) the use of Socratic questioning techniques, and (4) employment of a thinking skills curriculum stressing metacognitive learning and other learning-to-learn strategies. HOTS was developed at the University of Arizona and is expanding from a focus on remedial reading to other elementary subjects.

Theodore Sizer began the Coalition of Essential Schools in 1984, building on his study of the American high school. What began as a research project with a few schools has considerably expanded in a relatively short period of time. By 1992, the coalition had grown to include more than 300 individual schools.

There is no one "model" for an essential school. Rather, each school develops within its own unique context while guided by a common philosophy that includes general education with an academic focus and an emphasis on the mastery of "essential skills" for all students, including the development of critical thinking and growth as autonomous learners. The Essential Schools have been secondary schools, but their core principles are now being adapted to elementary schools as well.

The Coalition of Essential Schools is based on nine common principles, including the premise that the school's goals should be simple. Each student should master a limited number of essential skills and areas of knowledge. The governing and guiding metaphor of the school is an emphasis on learning rather than on the more familiar metaphor of teacher-as-deliverer-of-instructional-services. Accordingly, a prominent pedagogy is coaching; the tone of an Essential School both explicitly and self-consciously stresses values of unanxious expectation, trust, and decency. Parents are treated as essential collaborators.

The view of curriculum is a movement from display-of-content to framing questions that ultimately provoke the content. This content, however, is related to knowledge in the academic core. Teachers need the ability to enable student "exhibitions." An emphasis is on the ability to utilize knowledge and skills in real-life situations. The act of learning is viewed as the act of socially creating understanding and knowledge. Learning is an active, often collaborative process.

Using linguistic theories elaborated in New Zealand by Marie Clay and further developed at The Ohio State University, the Reading Recovery Program (Pinnell, 1990) provides systematic help for first graders with serious problems learning to read. Students with reading problems receive individual tutoring every day for 12–20 weeks from a trained reading teacher. A major staff development focus allows prospective Reading Recovery teachers to observe this tutoring and to engage afterwards in a clinic in which the teaching is analyzed and defended. Eventually teachers tutor in a clinic setting as well. Emphasis in this tutoring is on pupils learning to read through oral and written expression, diagnosis and correction of individual learning problems, and the use of short paperback books. Reading Recovery has distinctive implications not only for pedagogy in other subjects but also for the professional development of teachers.

The Core Knowledge Foundation was founded in 1986 by E. D. Hirsch, professor of English at the University of Virginia, and traces its philosophical roots to his 1987 bestseller *Cultural Literacy: What Every American Should Know*. The foundation has developed and continues to develop a "carefully sequenced body of knowledge" for each grade level of *elementary* schooling. The books in which this core is outlined are written and distributed in a manner to make them accessible to parents as well as education professionals. Schools and school districts in 13 states have adapted some or all of the program. Several schools are fully committed to the content prescribed and serve as "model" programs.

Core Knowledge is defined as "an evolving model of a body of specific, sequenced knowledge that all American school children should share." Advocates suggest that generally about half the instructional time be required for this core curriculum, permitting a similar amount of time for local requirements and students' interests.

In terms of instructional methodology, Hirsch embraces an anthropological view of education with literacy as its central aim. His framework stresses the necessity that a human group needs "effective communications to function effectively" (Hirsch, 1987, p. xvii). He also stresses recent discoveries in schema theory and the importance of background knowledge and schemata, along with content, as key considerations in learning.

The Foxfire project was initiated in the early 1970s by Eliot Wigginton at Raven Gap High School in Georgia. Until his recent death, Wigginton served as president of the Foxfire Fund, Inc. The Foxfire Project began out of Wigginton's frustrations as an English teacher to make the subject matter relevant to adolescents. Building on what his students indicated would make learning meaningful for them, he began to revise his teaching in ways that eventually resulted in numerous books and magazines and professional development activities for teachers across the country. One example of this is to take on the same writing assignments as the students. A common theme of Foxfire is the mutual negotiation of teaching and learning projects with students. Teaching and learning projects should have connections with the real world. In Wigginton's initial project students opted to study their roots in the Appalachian Mountain range in northeast Georgia, and they began by interviewing the older members of the community. Thus, the original Foxfire books contained oral history reports derived from these interviews.

Although the curriculum of Foxfire is student driven, it is also carefully matched to the curriculum objectives of the local district. The educational philosophy that has evolved around Foxfire focuses on how teachers can help students move into more caring and active relationships with others and better understand the problems of a world outside of school, while at the same time maintaining rigorous academic standards.

This very brief review of selected school reform initiatives reveals several commonalities. Schools, for example, are characterized by the following:

1. Site-based management and shared decision making
2. Considerably expanded parental involvement
3. More formalized relationships with a variety of social service agencies
4. Learning communities or cohorts remaining together across multiple years
5. Electronic learning laboratories
6. Job-embedded professional development
7. Differentiated staffing and team teaching
8. Civic activities and rigorous investigation of local issues

Classrooms tend to be characterized by the following:

1. Learning stations and learning laboratories
2. Cooperative learning structures
3. Cross-age tutoring
4. Paraprofessional and parent volunteers
5. Hands-on materials

Curriculum is often construed as embracing the following:

1. Themes and interdisciplinary units
2. High, clear standards
3. Closely coupled, outcomes-based assessment

4. Interaction in multiple modes with the "real world"
5. Diminished reliance on texts and inert information

Teaching and instruction tend to be distinguished by the following:

1. Team planning and multimode instruction
2. A focus on inquiry and conceptual learning
3. Attention to personal and social development as well as cognitive learning
4. The use of aides and paraprofessionals
5. The use of electronic communications
6. A focus on individual and group monitoring or metacognitive abilities
7. Attention to beliefs, preconceptions, and misconceptions
8. Reciprocal teaching and learning by teachers and students

Learners and learning are characterized by the following:

1. Active, self-monitored learning
2. Group interdependence and accountability; cooperative learning
3. An emphasis on the strengths of diversity and heterogeneity
4. Interaction with the school community and tasks geared toward civic responsibility
5. Parent–child learning centers
6. Personal computers
7. Time periods set aside for the enablement of "learning communities"

What several influential scholar-activists conceive of as attributes of good schools, along with the conceptions of learning to teach reviewed earlier, provides grist for thought in the construction of programs of preservice preparation. What is either endorsed or contested in these "reform" efforts will surely vary from reader to reader of this chapter. Of course, there are those who will find major omissions. The extent to which programs of preservice teacher education at this time address the purposes and processes espoused by those assuming leadership in school reform efforts will also vary, often considerably. The perception here is that many of the ideas being promulgated in these reform networks are consonant with the more thoughtful conceptions of how one learns to teach, which were shared earlier, especially the emphasis on monitoring one's learning and how learning is enabled in a community and through the use of modern communications technology. No one would argue against more and better dialogue needing to be fostered to achieve greater agreement about how preservice teacher education can be reshaped and improved to meet the challenges posed in the education of youth and to contribute more fully to school improvement. As stated at the outset, of special concern is the education of children in urban and rural settings who are trapped in conditions characterized by poverty and the threats so often attendant to it. The following questions are posed in summary of this section of the chapter to stimulate dialogue about the intersection of teacher preparation and school reform:

1. What are the implications of site-based management arrangements for the preparation of teachers or the prepara-

tion of teachers in concert at times with other education professionals such as administrators? How can the politics of education at the school level be understood by beginning teachers and enabled by activities in preservice teacher preparation?

2. What are the implications of team-teaching arrangements for the education of teachers? What short-term cohort arrangements, for example, might be considered in the preparation of teachers to enable joint planning, problem solving, child study, and collaborative action research activities?

3. What are the implications of interdisciplinary planning and teaching of thematic units and projects for how teachers are prepared initially?

4. When and how should management skills in terms of directing paraprofessionals, volunteers, cross-age tutors, and parents in learning activities be developed?

5. What are the implications of a counseling role for teachers as they work with a cohort of students during several years?

6. How can the teacher education community engage in instruction so that prospective teacher learning is active, self-monitored, responsive to and responsible for members of a "learning community"?

7. To what extent should prospective teachers become familiar with the range of social, health, family, legal, and mental health services necessitated by many students and their families?

8. How in the limited "life space" of teacher preparation can prospective teachers both learn their subject(s) in depth so that they can, in turn, acquire needed pedagogical content knowledge and ability and at the same time learn enough about various cultural patterns and ethnic characteristics to teach all children well?

9. How can prospective teachers best acquire the understandings and abilities to employ a range of measurement and evaluation tools and strategies, including such widely advocated procedures as "outcomes based" standards, performance portfolios, student exhibitions, criterion-referenced assessments, and forms of "authentic" testing?

10. What are the profound and manifold implications of modern communications technology for the preparation of teachers not only in terms of their technical understanding abilities but also in terms of the questions these tools and processes raise for the social, political, and moral dimensions of schooling.

Craft Knowledge

In informing the design of preservice programs, it is clear that not all guiding principles are derived from scientific study or theory development. Neither are they the sole domain of reformists. *Individual* teachers provide the broadest repository of knowledge. Obviously there is much to be learned from the wisdom and scholarship of teachers themselves. Grimmett and MacKinnon (1992) reviewed the various literature that portray teaching as craft. They suggest, for example, that Shulman's (1987) formulation of pedagogical content knowledge is apropos to a craft conception of teaching because pedagogical content knowledge "is derived from a considered response to experience and the practice setting informed over time in the minds

of teachers through reflection" (p. 3). They argue, however, for an extension of Shulman's conception of pedagogical content knowledge and suggest an amalgam with knowledge of learners that they term *pedagogical learner knowledge*, which is defined as follows:

Whereas pedagogical content knowledge concerns itself with teachers' representations of subject matter content in terms of how it might be effectively taught, pedagogical learner knowledge revolves around procedural ways in which teachers deal rigorously and supportively with learners. Though the "maxims" of craft knowledge are useful in guiding practice, they cannot replace the role of experience in the *development* of craft. Thus, pedagogical learner knowledge can be defined as *pedagogical procedural information useful in enhancing learner-focussed teaching in the dailiness of classroom action*. (Grimmett & MacKinnon, 1992, p. 387)

Recalling the two major orientations that characterized professional programs as put forth by Kennedy earlier in this chapter, Grimmett and MacKinnon (1992) argue that their focus on craft knowledge, given the current emphasis on codified knowledge in teacher education by such groups as the Holmes Group, is not merely flying the flag of the counterculture. Rather, they argue that there are practical arts of inquiry present in all professions, including medicine and law. They provide numerous suggestions for how the wisdom of craft or craft knowledge can be more fully integrated into programs of teacher education beyond the uneven interactions between "student" teachers and their "cooperating" teachers during the cumulative stages of teacher preparation. They suggest including more writing and research of teachers in the reading materials of teacher education courses. They also recommend that prospective teachers develop their own credo for teaching that would enable them to "look in their own backyard" for useful ideas and strategies and to counter the tendency to turn to outside experts for guidance in learning to teach. This seems wholly consistent with the achievement-motivation and metacognitive strategies discussed earlier. Finally, Grimmett and MacKinnon suggest, consistent with a craft perspective, that much of what now passes for method instruction should take place in actual school settings with professors joining their students in instructing P–12 pupils.

THEMATIC PROPERTIES OF A CONCEPTUAL FRAMEWORK

To this point, prevalent conceptions of learning, teaching, and more specifically learning to teach have been reviewed. Contemporary conceptions or attributes of good schools were also examined, and the great repository of wisdom among individual teachers was noted. The position held relative to these forms a conceptual framework for teacher preparation. Reasoned discourse among those responsible for the education of teachers both in the school or college of education and in cooperating P–12 schools can result in some degree of agreement and clarity regarding what is a good school, what it means to teach successfully in such schools, and how to go about learning to teach this way. Such frameworks need not be narrow or closed, and they invariably embrace multiple perspectives. They assist in deciding what should and can be done well in a program of initial preparation. They assist in deciding on a *reasonable* number of understandings and abilities, perhaps even dispositional behaviors for prospective teachers, framed by a clear vision of teaching and schooling. They serve as a road map. They allow the design of an interrelated set of activities designed to enable the prospective teachers to acquire or refine these understandings and abilities. This triad of activities comprises the essence of program design: (1) evolving a conceptual framework, (2) deriving from this framework reasonable teacher understandings and abilities, and (3) designing a related set of activities to enable these to develop. The following is an example of a conceptual framework that briefly enunciates the author's beliefs about learning, teaching, schooling, and learning to teach.

Learning is first an active process. It calls for the ability to responsibly monitor and manage the various problem-solving activities that are embedded in learning tasks. Good learners can critically examine both the effort put forth and the specific procedures they employ in their learning. Documentation and evaluation are ongoing activities integrated into learning, just as they are integral aspects of teaching. Teaching and learning are *reciprocal,* with roles and responsibilities at times formally exchanged and at other times naturally blended. Learning, in academic settings especially, is a social and community endeavor. The community or the group as a whole is responsible for its members. Members of a learning community must not only understand what responsibility they have for their own learning but also their responsibility for assisting others in their learning. Learning and socially responsible behavior is monitored by the community as well as by the individual.

Teaching is a highly moral endeavor. It is an endeavor concerned with beliefs and values, and it is very much about changing behavior; therefore, a teacher is concerned with the consequences of his or her actions on others. Teachers are cognizant of their constituted powers and how they are used. Although teaching is very much a goal-oriented endeavor, it is also interactive and open, and the teacher often assumes the role of learner. Teachers thus seek out multiple perspectives and are open to negotiation. Teaching is a highly intellectual and clinical activity rooted in a definable set of pedagogical understandings and abilities. The hallmark of an effective teacher is the ability to justify his or her thinking and actions in a rigorous and morally defensible manner, employing scientifically supported principles when appropriate. Teaching is also a highly personal activity. Personal attributes of a good teacher include empathy, adaptability, ingenuity, and the patience to seek out and reflect on the perspectives of others. Teaching is anchored not only in a deep understanding of at least one subject and how to represent this to others but also in a genuine appreciation of others and a desire to interact with and assist them.

Schools are characterized by the nature of the aforementioned learning community—a learning community for adults as well as for youngsters. There is no one template for the good school; good schools are continually being recreated. They are collaborative and caring. They seep into the community in numerous ways, and, in turn, connections with the outside world permeate the school setting. Schools are directly concerned with their school community and the larger society. The culture in a good school is defined by the pervasive, *public*

nature of teaching and learning. The emphasis is on how the journey of learning unfolds and the mutual as well as individual responsibilities for this. The climate of a good school is characterized by pride in both its individual and collective accomplishments, by security and confidence, by respect for one another, and by its humanity and civility everywhere. A good school also reflects the spontaneity and playful characteristic of the "young." The organization of school is fluid and dynamic in terms of time and space and how various persons interact one with another.

Given these assertions, it is clear that learning to teach is a highly intellectual, complicated endeavor. It calls for not only a deep understanding of subject matter but also continuing experimentation with how subject matter can best be represented for and engaged in by others. It also calls for a genuine caring for and appreciation of others. There is a powerful intersection here. A teacher educator's continuing assessment of how others (students) are engaged with the subject matter under consideration is a powerful means of helping the teacher understand both students and the subject(s) taught. Teaching is a chosen profession and it demands not only examining in a continuing manner the consequences of one's behavior on others but also one's role as a teacher and the role of a school in a democratic society and especially in addressing injustices in that society. It is essential that a teacher have the understandings and abilities to develop a productive learning community. Learning several ways in which one can inquire into his or her practice and the school context is the cornerstone for learning to teach over time. The public nature of teaching and learning reinforces the continuing dialogue about teaching and learning both among teachers and between teachers and students.

Given a conceptual framework such as this, a set of themes (core preservice student learnings) can be derived. These themes or threads run throughout a program with learning activities attached like buttons to promote these understandings and abilities. A number of factors should be considered in determining these themes.

The first consideration is whether there is *logical consistency* with the conceptual framework that undergirds the program. For example, if a critical perspective in learning to teach is the dominant departure point, then appropriate themes for preservice students might include developing the habit of reflecting on the moral and ethical consequences of school policy and classroom practice or the disposition to relate reasonably school subject matter to issues of equity and social justice in the larger society.

Whatever are determined as the most critical learnings and abilities for perservice students, these are addressed in a repeated manner over time and in a variety of appropriate contexts and experiences. This is the *thematic* nature of a program. Certain courses, course components, or experiences will be designed to orient, others to clarify, extend, and apply, and still others to challenge or rebut. A thematic set of activities extends throughout the program, beyond a course. In this regard an instructor is not wholly independent in deciding course content and pedagogy. He or she must jointly construct a program with campus and school-based colleagues and the growing number of faculty who work in both contexts.

A second factor to consider in developing a thematic teacher preparation program is *clarity*. At the outset, core or essential understanding and abilities that prospective teachers are expected to acquire should be clear. Although deeper understanding of these will understandably only occur over time, the themes provide both a desired vision of teacher and teaching and how one can move toward fulfilling the vision—what it means to learn to teach. When expectations for preservice students are clear, along with the rationale behind these expectations, they guide preservice teachers' learning individually and as a member of a learning community. A clear and reasonable set of expectations speaks to one of the moral dimensions of teacher preparation. The prospective teacher should be able to disagree, challenge, and negotiate with his or her instructors. Such activities are obviously enabled when both teacher educators and students are clear about expectations and the reasoning behind them. Obviously such activity involves risk on the part of the student, but individual students can enlist the support of others in their learning community. A coherent program calls for cooperative activity not only among faculty but also among students. More careful consideration of short-term preservice student cohort or grouping arrangements to purposefully and actively promote positive, professional socialization is needed in designing programs of preservice preparation.

A third factor in addition to consistency and clarity in the themes that manifest themselves in a related set of activities or a program skeleton is *reasonableness*. On the one hand, rather eloquent mission statements or platforms can be found for most teacher education programs. Typically, however, these are very general in nature, and it is not clear to either faculty or students where and how the mission statement is made manifest in the program. On the other hand, many preservice programs encompass relatively discrete program components or courses wherein the overall number of purposes, goals, objectives, or "outcomes" is very large and far ranging in nature. In some instances they surpass what the faculty could achieve in the "life space" of a preservice program, let alone a prospective teacher. Katz and Raths (1985) advocate the "Goldilocks" principle. They suggest that just as in Goldilocks's search for the right chair, core goals for preservice students should not be too big in number, nor too small, but rather just about right. Just about right from this perspective is from 6 to 10 major core abilities and related understandings for an entry-level teacher. The following is an example of a "just about right" set; that is, eight dispositional behaviors that could thematically permeate a preservice program in the form of interrelated pedagogical activities designed to promote them. The preservice teacher will have understandings, abilities, and disposition to:

1. Understand and celebrate individual and cultural diversity.
2. Understand the subject matter to be taught and be able to represent it in multiple ways pedagogically.
3. Reflect on the moral and ethical consequences of school policy and classroom practice.
4. Analyze and justify teaching practice.
5. Engage in teaching as a shared responsibility.
6. Monitor student understanding and foster conceptual learning.
7. Engage learners in active, self-monitoring learning tasks.
8. Relate experiences in school to critical issues in society.

A fourth thematic consideration beyond consistency, clarity, and reasonableness is *balance*. As illustrated earlier, different themes reflect different conceptions, or perhaps better dimensions, of learning to teach. In examining the set of themes just provided, analyzing and justifying teaching practice speaks to the centrality of developing one's reasoning abilities as a teacher. Understanding and respecting cultural diversity extends beyond the classroom and speaks to an overriding concern of all professional educators. Engaging the learner in active, self-monitoring learning tasks addresses essential technical aspects of teaching and draws from a cognitive-instructional perspective. Finally, engaging in teaching as a shared responsibility fosters, among other things, an understanding of a learning community and the power of constructivist principles in learning. A reasonable balance avoids an unnecessarily narrow view of teacher and teaching and also underscores the need for prospective teachers to attend continually to multiple perspectives. Balance avoids the image of a reflective practitioner as one who lacks the technical skills to teach a lesson well on the one hand, or the technical proficient novice who has little concern over the consequences of his or her actions, on the other hand.

A fifth consideration in the thematic construction of a program is that of *preservice student development* over time. The themes should undergird and guide not only program but also student assessment. Preservice student portfolios, for example, could record prospective teacher development over time in terms of each of the major themes in a program. The themes provide the skeletal structure not only for the program but also for student portfolios. Preservice students and the structured documentation and assessment that they engage in over time also provide the most reasonable and comprehensive means of program evaluation.

Sixth, and finally, the themes should have the power to enable *articulation*. They can assist in course design and course selection in general studies and in preeducation courses, and they can also assist in designing related educative experiences continued into the first years of teaching. The INTASC core abilities referenced earlier provide an excellent example of understanding and abilities that can be thematically manifested in preservice, continued through an internship experience, and extended eventually into the first years of teaching. The INTASC project (1992) has derived the following set of core understanding and abilities for all teachers regardless of their major:

1. The teacher understands the central concepts, tools of inquiry, and structures of the discipline(s) he or she teaches and can create learning experiences that make these aspects of subject matter meaningful for students.
2. The teacher understands how children learn and develop and can provide learning opportunities that support their intellectual, social, and personal development.
3. The teacher understands how students differ in their approaches to learning and creates instructional opportunities that are adapted to diverse learners.

4. The teacher understands and uses a variety of instructional strategies to encourage students' development of critical thinking, problem solving, and performance skills.

5. The teacher uses an understanding of individual and group motivation and behavior to create a learning environment that encourages positive social interaction, active engagement in learning, and self-motivation.

6. The teacher uses knowledge of effective verbal, nonverbal, and media communication techniques to foster active inquiry, collaboration, and supportive interaction in the classroom.

7. The teacher plans instruction based upon knowledge of subject matter, students, the community, and curriculum goals.

8. The teacher understands and uses formal and informal assessment strategies to evaluate and ensure the continuous intellectual, social, and physical development of the learner.

9. The teacher is a reflective practitioner who continually evaluates the effects of his/her choices and actions on others (students, parents, and other professionals in the learning community) and who actively seeks out opportunities to grow professionally.

10. The teacher fosters relationships with school colleagues, parents, and agencies in the larger community to support students' learning and well-being. (pp. 10–29)

What is most essential in the development of a thematic program is that the theme guides the development of appropriate contexts and activities for learning to teach, taking into account growing understandings and abilities on the part of the prospective teacher. Figure 8.1 illustrates a variety of learning-to-teach activities that preservice teachers might engage in over time to acquire the *ability and disposition to critically inquire into their practice* (note the absence of typical college classroom didactic experiences in this illustration).

COHERENT PROGRAMS AND PURPOSEFUL TEACHER SOCIALIZATION

The ability of programs of teacher preparation to positively and powerfully socialize prospective teachers has long been questioned. Part—but only part—of the difficulty attached to teacher socialization is rooted in the long-standing tension between general professional preparation and the specific needs and norms of the organization in which teachers eventually work. Many corporations understand that although new employees are socialized first by the profession in their professional training, they nonetheless receive powerful secondary socialization or more precisely enculturation in the organization in which they are employed. Deal and Chatman (1989) caution, however, that

Part of the difficulty surrounding teacher socialization is rooted in the classic tension between professionals and organizations. A hospital, university, or any business that employs professionals must recognize that they are socialized by the profession first and receive secondary socialization or acculturation from the organization in which they work.

But teaching is a semi-profession and for a variety of reasons it is not clear that the professional socialization experiences they receive

are adequate. As a consequence the burden of adequately acculturating new teachers—or experienced teachers taking a new position—is left to the organization, that is, the local district or school. But as we have seen, the way teachers are brought into the culture of a district or school leaves much to be desired. (p. 26)

The literature on teacher socialization within preservice programs is very thin. As Zeichner and Gore (1990) observed in their review on teacher socialization, "one major problem with almost all the research that has focused on the role of pretraining influences on teacher socialization (functionalist and interpretive) is that they have focused almost extensively on *individual* characteristics, conceptions, skills, and dispositions that students bring to teacher education programs and have ignored the *collective* aspects of socialization into teaching" (emphasis added) (p. 334).

Goodlad (1990), in his major study of programs of teacher preparation, suggests that one reason this is such an unstudied phenomenon is that students are rarely put into structured group experiences to foster positive socialization and other goals. He observed

One would expect students enrolled with others in a teacher education program spreading across two to four years of college to develop strong interpersonal associations. It seems surprising, then, that over 30 percent of those we surveyed (from 25 percent in the elementary programs to 40 percent in the secondary) had made only some casual acquaintances by the near-end of the training. We had expected the small size of an institution to make a considerable favorable difference, but the direction of the correlation was in the opposite direction: 21 percent in the flagship public universities as contrasted with 34 percent in the private liberal arts colleges had made only casual acquaintances; 42 percent as contrasted with 32 percent, respectively, in these two types of institutions had many friends and acquaintances or knew most of their fellow students. (p. 209)

From this perspective the manner in which preservice students are structured into groups or short-term cohort arrangements and for what purposes should be a major consideration in the design of coherent programs of preparation. A number of goals are essential to teacher development and are best, and perhaps only, accomplished in group settings over time. Among the goals and functions that could be pursued in small structured groups of six to eight preservice students working closely together for varying periods of time are

1. Promoting interpersonal development
2. Planning as a team for instruction
3. Engaging in cooperative learning activities
4. Rotating assignments as teachers and learners in microteaching or teaching clinic arrangements
5. Pursuing collaborative action research projects
6. Forming political action committees to address specific issues on campus or in the community
7. Helping one another develop portfolios
8. Providing feedback collectively to faculty about the multiple effects of programs

Thoughtful program design should consider how, in a variety of ways, prospective teachers can come to understand that

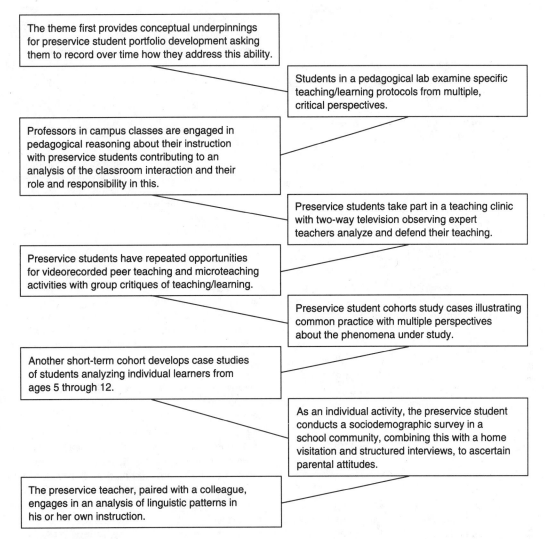

The theme first provides conceptual underpinnings for preservice student portfolio development asking them to record over time how they address this ability.

Students in a pedagogical lab examine specific teaching/learning protocols from multiple, critical perspectives.

Professors in campus classes are engaged in pedagogical reasoning about their instruction with preservice students contributing to an analysis of the classroom interaction and their role and responsibility in this.

Preservice students take part in a teaching clinic with two-way television observing expert teachers analyze and defend their teaching.

Preservice students have repeated opportunities for videorecorded peer teaching and microteaching activities with group critiques of teaching/learning.

Preservice student cohorts study cases illustrating common practice with multiple perspectives about the phenomena under study.

Another short-term cohort develops case studies of students analyzing individual learners from ages 5 through 12.

As an individual activity, the preservice student conducts a sociodemographic survey in a school community, combining this with a home visitation and structured interviews, to ascertain parental attitudes.

The preservice teacher, paired with a colleague, engages in an analysis of linguistic patterns in his or her own instruction.

FIGURE 8.1. Thematic activities to promote the ability and disposition to critically inquire into practice.

planning for and providing instruction collaboratively extend the richness and range of options available to students. Engaging in cooperative learning structures in a preservice program would appear an ideal means to dispose prospective teachers to utilize appropriately such practices as teachers. Learning how to form political coalitions and take an activist posture on social issues is obviously hinged on learning to negotiate with others and to reach compromises. These abilities and attitudes simply cannot be fostered well in textbooks or by operating as an individual student in pursuing one's teacher education studies. The powerful construct of a learning community obviously demands deep understanding and application of effective group dynamics.

Peer teaching arrangements allow multiple purposes to be served in an efficient manner and in a trusting environment. Although exemplary teaching often is characterized by its creative interplay and on-one's-feet clinical characteristics, such teaching is nonetheless undergirded by a base repertoire of instructional tactics and strategies. Teaching adaptability is hardly an inherent personality characteristic. Rather, it is deter

mined by the range of pedagogical options from which one can draw. Good instruction with learners of any age, in any classroom context, and with any subject matter is enhanced by the general pedagogical abilities one has developed; abilities that can be adapted for different children and with different subject matters.

A *learning community* from this perspective squarely addresses how a group enables learning not only for each individual within that group but also for the group or the community as a whole. In a teacher preparation program, a learning community addresses explicitly and repeatedly how members are responsible for one another, how they individually and collectively enable the teacher, and, of course, how they advance their own learning. In a peer teaching situation the responsibilities of *all* members for the success of a lesson is a central focus in subsequent video analysis. Cognitive-instructional strategies for individual learning pertain in similar but more powerful and manifold ways to learning in a group or a community as they address not only how one enables one's own learning but also that of others as well. Peer teaching would seem to be a centerpiece strategy for acquiring these abilities.

Every quarter or semester in every class or course component there are opportunities for thoughtfully organized group or short-term cohort activities. Such activities, when well conceived, are powerful catalysts for both the reform of how one learns to teach and, in turn, how one teaches. They also provide in a continuing manner opportunities for richer understanding and appreciation of diversity and for the continuing practice of equal access and fair treatment. The more heterogeneous the learning community, the more powerful the opportunity for learning and building community. The more one learns to listen, to seek out actively another's voice, and to learn to share, the more one begins to understand the nature of learning in a classroom—in a community.

A learning community does *not* occur when a professor finishes a lecture and then breaks the class up into discussion groups. It is what evolves over time in a *program* when structured work is undertaken in groups for a variety of purposes and when specific skills and attitudes practiced over time result in norms that define *community*. In a learning community there is active pursuit of learning, not performance or procedural display. Just as the public nature of teaching, that is, teaching that is observed and enabled by colleagues, is a powerful catalyst for improving teaching, so the public nature of learning, that is, learning that is observed and enabled by colleagues, is a powerful catalyst for improving learning. These long-standing, self-evident truths are widely ignored in the design and conduct of teacher preparation.

COHERENT PROGRAMS AND LABORATORY PREPARATION

How a theme manifests itself *pedagogically* speaks to the coherence and efficacy of a program. This is a challenge of considerable proportions as illustrated in Figure 8.1. It is not enough that prospective teachers have repeated opportunities to encounter key understandings and "core" concepts in a spiral *curriculum*. They must have that content represented for them in pedagogically powerful ways and, in turn, must represent it in multiple ways themselves, ways that are responsive to the abilities and interests of others. Additional contexts for learning to teach must evolve beyond the lecture hall or the P–12 classroom. There should be experimentation with a range of pedagogical laboratories. Berliner (1985) was one of the first to advocate this. He envisioned a fifth mature period in the history of teacher education wherein the field was research oriented and anchored in laboratory preparation.

The research base in the study of teaching is better and broader than it had been, and the methodology for studying teaching is both more sophisticated and more eclectic than ever before. The most obvious use of this research on teaching is as the content of programs of teacher education. What we face, however, is a problem of beliefs and reality out of phase with each other. Just as the reformers have given up on preservice pedagogical course work, educators have created the basis for a curriculum in preservice education. And, just as we see the possibility of creating pedagogical laboratories, we see reformers demanding arbitrary increases in student teaching and field-based experience. (p. 7)

Almost a decade later, little progress has been made in this regard. There has been no coordinated or concerted effort to "break the mold" in teacher education. For professors, courses—lecture and discussion—remain the coin of the realm. The abstract nature of much of this activity tends to reinforce in prospective teachers, and in a relatively nondiscriminating manner, the belief that P–12 classrooms are *the* place to learn to teach. Buchmann and Schwille (1983) explain

Firsthand experience is trusted implicitly as both means and content of education. It is "down to earth," personal, sensory, and practical. Ideas encountered in books are pale in contrast. Compared with life as a school of hard knocks, the school of hard books seems soft and ineffective. Immersion in the "real world" teaches people to think and act rightly. Those who want students to know the world of work firsthand often do not challenge limits set by occupations as they presently are. (p. 31)

From this perspective, novice teachers need to engage in learning-to-teach activities in well-conceived, distinctively laboratory contexts in which complex phenomena can be represented from multiple perspectives and in multiple forms and at a time, in a place, at a pace, and in a manner conducive to learning to teach. No one would condone pilots first learning to fly in real planes with actual passengers or defense attorneys beginning with real clients; yet, this is the nature of teacher preparation. Beyond this, after abbreviated forms of student teaching, prospective teachers are given the same assignment as far more experienced teachers. The current recourse is to suggest longer internships. From this perspective, a more prudent course of action would be developmental laboratory experiences. Viable laboratory alternatives have not been put forward to challenge the assumption that most teaching abilities are best acquired in situs. When the limited laboratory methods that do exist have been assessed with some rigor, the results are revealing. Metcalf (1993) examined the effects of three laboratory activities: microteaching, reflective teaching, and protocols. His data document efficiencies in the employment of such learning-to-teach activities, but more important they suggest that there is distinctive potency in these approaches that does not adhere easily to field settings. Metcalf (1993) concluded

It does not appear that the factors which students believe contribute most to the value of laboratory experiences are amenable to transfer to field-based experiences. More structure, organization, or instructor feedback regarding students' performance in field settings are not factors which students found most valuable. Implicit in these results is the importance of opportunities for limited but guided application of professional practices and relatively immediate, structured feedback from a small group of peers who witness the teacher's performance. Teacher educators could, perhaps, provide such opportunities in field-settings; however, it would be difficult and expensive to do so. (p. 172)

Metcalf's study supports an earlier study (Gliessman, 1984) that suggests that the power of laboratory training over time is in its ability to promote critical analysis and reflection. The seeds for the disposition to inquire into one's practice on a continuing basis and to support and guide increasingly that practice with decisions that are data based, theoretically grounded, and morally oriented are nurtured in laboratory settings. Those who argue that a technical base is antithetical to a clinical orientation have obviously never visited a teaching hospital. Just as the two major competing orientations to professional preparation elaborated on by Kennedy (1989) earlier in this chapter are not antithetical (clinical vs. codified knowledge), neither need to be technical and critical perspectives. Dreeban (1973) long ago put forth a compelling argument that teachers as opposed to other professionals are too easily and often unproductively influenced by their clients (students) because of the absence of a technical core of knowledge and skill that weakens their authority and forces reliance on personal and referential characteristics. Developing *complex* sets of abilities and patterns of diagnostic behavior appears to be less a result of practice, often unguided, and more a product of well-designed instruction and intervention. Although obviously practice in classrooms over time provides the ultimate laboratory for refinements and experimentation, well-conceived instructional and intervention variables when systematically introduced in laboratory contexts can effect complex changes in teacher behavior, changes that otherwise might not occur (Gliessman, 1984). Gliessman argued that there has been insufficient attention to how complex teacher skills are enabled. In reviewing what factors common to a variety of training methods, and often taking place in laboratory settings, appear to have the most potency, he concluded the following:

A major implication for teacher training is the desirability of reinstituting controlled conditions, such as the use of media- or computer-based, simulated training methods. Research on teacher training . . . should increasingly focus on the development of complex skills, especially those related to increased student learning. (p. 109)

Whereas the emphasis in teacher *preparation* should be on the development of a limited number of carefully selected but complex teaching abilities, the nature of laboratory settings themselves need not be that complicated. Designing a preservice program so that it comprises a developmental sequence of laboratory and clinical activities need not be constrained by a lack of sophisticated technology, such as the employment of visual reality, although the application of this to teacher education is obvious. The following are rather mundane examples of forms of pedagogical laboratories in which critical teaching abilities can be fostered:

1. Professional profile and portfolio development
2. Clinical diagnoses and child study employing one-way mirrors
3. Structured observation and analyses of videotaped teaching and learning
4. Simulations of a number of types
5. Case development and analyses
6. Interactive problem analyses employing computers
7. Micro/reflective teaching in peer groups
8. Remote viewing of teaching and learning with subsequent analysis
9. Teaching clinic (expert teacher analyzes teaching for novice)
10. Teaching clinic (novice teacher analyzes teaching for expert)

Space prohibits elaboration, but one can readily envision multiple facilities in a school or college of education that depart from the typical classroom arrangement. A video library with multiple carrels for both individual and small group viewing and with a giant screen for large groups could serve multiple purposes. Prospective teachers could observe children on videotape beginning with preschool children and proceeding through the teens to examine their developmental tendencies. Case studies of these children could, in fact, be undertaken by preservice student cohorts; this would contribute over time to a growing video bank. "Critical instances" of teaching and learning could be examined through various forms of secondary analyses using a number of sign and category systems rooted in social psychology, psycholinguistics, political science, or cultural anthropology. There has been a lack of creativity in applying conceptual lenses from core disciplines to the examination of teaching and learning; this should be a primary means of learning to teach. If there are limited hypermediated cases, one can begin with excellent narrative cases. The burgeoning literature on cases need not be referenced here to underscore their manifold potential in learning to teach. Microteaching facilities should exist where an entire section of 30–35 preservice students can regularly break into five or six peer groups for experimentation and practice employing video replay. Constructivist principles focusing on the monitoring and metacognitive responsibilities of the learners in the group, as well as the teacher, can be fostered in such activities. Given the centrality of teacher reasoning in learning to teach, numerous variations of teaching clinics on campus could be instituted. Preservice teachers should have multiple opportunities to observe professors and experienced teachers as they analyze and provide warrants for their teaching, again employing video. Designated classrooms could have multiple, remote-controlled cameras for later replay and analysis. At other times, one-way mirrors would provide perspectives not easily captured on camera. Eventually preservice students should be the focus in controlled teaching clinics.

Special mention needs to be made of a laboratory facility for the ongoing construction of student portfolios. These portfolios should mirror the skeletal framework of a well-conceived, coherent program of teacher preparation. This is to say that the themes of the program also serve as the roadmap for what is addressed in the portfolio. The manifold instructional activities, which in a repeated manner address these themes, serve as guideposts. Portfolios could be further guided by what is being learned about developmental patterns in immature teachers, such as changes in their beliefs over time or how their focus changes in clinical activities from a concentration on the nature of their appearance to the generation of hypotheses about causal antecedents of student behavior. A portfolio laboratory would facilitate various forms of documentation, including of course video documentation. It would take on aspects of the multimedia centers found in many P–12 schools. It would greatly facilitate how prospective teachers learn to document, analyze, and evaluate, as well as assist others in assessing their progress developmentally over time. Finally, this laboratory would contribute formative data on the effects of specific *program* activities as compiled by preservice students.

The nature of pedagogical activities and especially laboratory activities that are designed to address the program's themes—requisite entry-level teacher understandings and abilities—are the essence of a coherent program. The teacher education community needs to address the bedrock problem of teacher preparation—a narrow, relatively unexamined form of pedagogy that sustains a vicious cycle of mediocre instruction at all levels of education.

It is time to get on with this task of laboratory development, whether or not sophisticated technology is available. The power of modern communications technology for learning to teach should not be underestimated. Two contrasting scenarios can be examined to make this point. One of these was developed by Clifford and Guthrie (1988) in their examination of schools and colleges of education in a section of their book that they refer to as "Weak Technology."

Not only has instruction remained labor intensive and stylistically familiar, it carries no mystique of hard won, esoteric professional prowess. An unusually able classroom teacher may put forth the performing energy and creativity of a Laurence Olivier or Sarah Bernhardt, and do it day after day. To the unknowing public it all appears simple. Physicians and scientists display their shiny, "high-tech" tools and communicate in a baffling argot. Laypersons realize fully that they could not readily step up to an operating table, jetliner flight panel, or nuclear power plant control console and be anything less than hopelessly confused. Nevertheless, many people believe they could step into a public school classroom tomorrow and perform credibly, as well perhaps as the assigned teacher. (p. 327)

These authors suggest that teachers from the 1940s, upon returning to today's classroom, would not be shocked about what they would find because fundamental conceptions and components of instruction have in many respects remained the same. This is to say that teachers still mostly lecture and students still mostly listen. Now and then the instructional routine is punctuated by a film, videotape, or overhead projector, and occasionally students employ their computers at school and at home, but primarily for drill or practice. There has, they contend, been no major attempt to alter instruction in a dramatic fashion through the use of electronics.

Sizer (1992) portrays the counter scenario. He underscores the scope and impact of the television revolution. Cable offers the majority of families a far-reaching venue daily. Children typically watch television more hours per day than they spend in their classrooms. In fact, many of them spend more hours a day watching television than any other single activity, with the exception of sleeping. Television has indeed become the principal shaper of our culture—the biggest "school system" of all. Sizer's concern is whether this communication system can be altered so that television becomes more public and service oriented than private and profit oriented. He is concerned with whether we can change the very nature of what it means to watch television and whether the existing school system can be altered to accommodate and integrate this massive electronic "school" as something unique and powerful in its own right. The challenge is how actively to engage youth in experiences with television and other modern communications technology so they become a central aspect of schooling. Sizer (1992) states the challenge in the following manner:

Americans are but a decade from yet another technological leap forward, their connection by means of a nationwide fiber-optic network linking ever larger numbers of individuals, schools, homes, universities, and businesses to a massive national data base—in effect, giving the individual access to a vast library. And there is more: It may be possible for the individual to interact with that "library" in creative ways; that is, to be far more than just a passive recipient of what is "there to see." The computer, the telephone, and the television set will blend together—creating a yet more powerful "school" than even the ubiquitous TV set is today. (p. 26)

What will be the economics of this new system? What *public* interest will it serve, and how will that public interest be safeguarded? How will its existence change the purposes and shape of our schools? What measures can be taken to energize the education community, including the teacher education community to address these challenges? From this perspective, the first step in addressing this challenge of major proportion is for the teacher education community to demonstrate some evidence that it can, in fact, move beyond instruction typical of a half century ago.

CONCLUSION

In summary, this chapter examines what attributes of coherent, and hopefully potent, programs of preservice preparation might be. The chapter begins with an overview of the context in which teacher preparation finds itself today. Several problems are noted. It is a venture largely divorced from reform initiatives in P–12 schools. It is also an endeavor that is *not* preparing teachers for schools where the challenges are the greatest both in terms of numbers and ability. Serious reform initiatives in teacher education must address the stratification in schools that mirrors that in our society. Also, preservice preparation simply does not continue in any articulated, substantive manner into the early years of teaching. The most fundamental problem, however, remains the manner in which teachers are taught. Guiding assumptions are derived from this context and enable the selection of topics for the remainder of the chapter.

A robust definition of a *coherent* program is put forward. Among the attributes that it calls for are a conceptual framework, derivative themes, and laboratory contexts specifically designed for learning to teach. The conceptual framework results from dialogue and some degree of agreement by program architects about the commonplaces of formal education—the mission and nature of schools, the character of academic learning and teaching, and what these imply for learning to teach. The derivative themes are best thought of as a reasonable core of preservice student understandings and abilities embedded in a defensible vision of teaching. The themes, in turn, take on the nature of a skeletal structure for the program when they are manifested in a diverse and potent set of pedagogical activities, many of which are laboratory in nature.

In the main, the chapter provides multiple and contrasting examples for each of these triadic design functions: developing the conceptual framework, identifying reasonable derivation themes, and developing a *programmatic* structure through related socializing and educative activities. In terms of constructing a conceptual framework, multiple conceptions of learning, teaching, and, most fundamentally, learning to teach are put forward. The nature and mission of schools are examined in a brief review of various P–12 school reform initiatives. The essentiality of the wisdom of individual teachers is underscored. Examples of derivative themes and criteria for selecting these

are provided. The chapter culminates by examining a variety of ways in which learning communities could be established, positive socialization might occur, and learning to teach could take place in distinctive laboratory contexts to address these themes.

References

AACTE Commission on Multicultural Education. (1973). No one model America. *Journal of Teacher Education, 24,* 264–265.

Alkove, L. D., & McCarty, B. J. (1992). Plain talk: Recognizing positivism and constructivism in practice. *Action in Teacher Education, 14*(2), 16–21.

America 2000. (1992). *Community notebook* (GPO Publication No. 336-276/70591). Washington, DC: U.S. Government Printing Office.

Barnes, H. L. (1987). The conceptual basis for thematic teacher education programs. *Journal of Teacher Education, 38*(4), 13–18.

Berliner, D. C. (1985). Laboratory settings and the study of teacher education. *Journal of Teacher Education, 36*(6), 2–8.

Borko, H., & Shavelson, R. J. (1983). Speculations on teacher education: Recommendations from research on teachers' cognitions. *Journal of Education for Teaching, 9*(3), 210–224.

Borko, H., & Shavelson, R. J. (1990). Teacher decision making. In B. F. Jones & L. Idol (Eds.), *Dimensions of thinking and cognitive instruction* (pp. 311–346). Hillsdale, NJ: Lawrence Erlbaum Associates.

Brown, A. L., Palincsar, A. S., & Armbruster, B. B. (1984). Instructing comprehension-fostering activities in interactive learning situations. In H. Mandl, L. Stein, & T. Trabasso (Eds.), *Learning and comprehension of text* (pp. 255–285). Hillsdale, NJ: Lawrence Erlbaum Associates.

Buchmann, M., & Floden, R. E. (1990). *Program coherence in teacher education: A view from the United States.* East Lansing: Michigan State University, National Center for Research on Teacher Education.

Buchmann, M., & Schwille, J. (1983). Education: The overcoming of experience. *American Journal of Education, 92*(1), 31.

Clifford, G. J., & Guthrie, J. W. (1988). *Ed school: A brief for professional education.* Chicago: The University of Chicago Press.

Cochran, K. F., DeRuiter, J. A., & King, R. A. (1993). Pedagogical content knowing: An integrative model for teacher preparation. *Journal of Teacher Education, 44*(4), 263–272.

Cohen, D. K. (1988). *Teaching practice: Plus ça change* (Issue Paper 88-3). East Lansing, MI: National Center for Research on Teacher Education.

Cohen, M. W. (1983). Using motivation theory as a framework for teacher education. *Journal of Teacher Education, 34*(3), 11.

Colton, A. B., & Sparks-Langer, G. M. (1993). A conceptual framework to guide the development of teacher reflection and decision making. *Journal of Teacher Education, 44*(1), 50.

Comer, J. P. (1992). *A brief history and summary of the School Development Program.* New Haven, CT: Yale Child Study Center.

Deal, T. E., & Chatman, R. M. (1989). Learning the ropes alone: Socializing new teachers. *Action in Teacher Education, 11*(1), 21–29.

Dewey, J. (1933). *How we think.* Chicago: Henry Regnery Co.

Dreeban, R. (1973). The school as a workplace. In R. Travers (Ed.), *Second handbook of research on teaching.* Chicago: Rand McNally.

Feiman-Nemser, S., & Buchmann, M. (1989). Describing teacher education: A framework and illustrative findings from a longitudinal study of six students. *Elementary School Journal, 89,* 365–377.

Fuller, F. (1969). Concerns of teachers: A developmental conceptualization. *American Education Research Journal, 6*(2), 207–226.

Ginsburg, M. B. (1988). *Contradictions in teacher education and society: A critical analysis.* New York: Falmer.

Giroux, H. A., & McLaren, P. (1986). Teacher education and the politics of engagement: The case for democratic schooling. *Harvard Educational Review, 56*(3), 213–238.

Gliessman, D. H. (1984). Changing teaching performance. In L. G. Katz & J. D. Raths (Eds.), *Advances in teacher education* (Vol. 1, pp. 95–111). Norwood, NJ: Ablex.

Goodlad, J. I. (1990). *Teachers for our nation's schools.* San Francisco: Jossey-Bass.

Griffin, G. (1989). Coda: The knowledge-driven school. In M. Reynolds (Ed.), *Knowledge base for the beginning teacher* (pp. 277–286). Oxford: Pergamon Press.

Grimmett, P. P., & MacKinnon, A. M. (1992). Craft knowledge and the education of teachers. In G. Grant (Ed.), *Review of research in education, 18* (pp. 385–465). Washington, DC: American Educational Research Association.

Grumet, M. (1981). Pedagogy for patriarchy: The feminization of teaching. *Interchange on Educational Policy, 12*(2–3), 165–184.

Hirsch, E. D., Jr. (1987). *Cultural literacy: What every American should know.* New York: Vintage Books.

The Holmes Group. (1990). *Tomorrow's schools: Principles for the design of professional development.* East Lansing, MI: Author.

Howey, K. (1994). Partnerships in the laboratory and clinical preparation of teachers. In M. J. O'Hair & S. J. Odell (Eds.), *Partnerships in education: Teacher education yearbook II.* New York: Harcourt Brace.

Howey, K. R., & Zimpher, N. L. (1986). The current debate on teacher preparation. *Journal of Teacher Education, 37*(5), 44.

Howey, K. R., & Zimpher, N. L. (1989). *Profiles of preservice teacher education: Inquiry into the nature of programs.* Albany: State University of New York Press.

Interstate New Teacher Assessment and Support Consortium (INTASC). (1992). *Model standards for beginning teacher licensing and development: A resource for state dialogue.* Washington, DC: Council of Chief State School Officers.

Joyce, B., & Showers, B. (1981, April). *Teacher training research: Working hypotheses for program design and directions for future study.* Paper presented at the annual meeting of the American Education Research Association, Los Angeles.

Joyce, B., & Weil, M. (1980). *Models of teaching.* Englewood Cliffs, NJ: Prentice Hall.

Katz, L. G., & Raths, J. (1985). Dispositions as goals for teacher education. *Teaching and Teacher Education* (Vol. 1, pp. 301–307). New York: Pergamon.

Kennedy, M. (1989). *Means and ends in professional education* (Issue Paper 89-3). East Lansing: Michigan State University, National Center for Research on Teacher Education.

Kennedy, M. M. (1990). Choosing a goal for professional education. In W. R. Houston (Ed.), *Handbook of research on teacher education* (pp. 813–896). New York: Macmillan.

Lentricchia, F. (1983). *Criticism and school change.* Chicago: The University of Chicago Press.

Lerman, S. (1989). Constructivism, mathematics and mathematics education. *Educational Studies in Mathematics, 20,* 211–223.

Levin, H. M. (1991a). Accelerated schools for disadvantaged students. *Educational Leadership, 45*(7).

Levin, H. M. (1991b). *Accelerating the progress of all students.* (Rockefeller Institute Special Report, No. 31). Albany: State University of New York.

Mahan, J. M., & Stachowski, L. L. (1985). Overseas student teaching: A model, important outcomes, recommendations. *International Education, 15*(1), 9–28.

Maher, F. A., & Rathbone, C. H. (1986). Teacher education and feminist theory: Some implications for practice. *American Journal of Education, 217,* 219.

McGlothlin, W. J. (1960). *Patterns of professional education.* New York: G. P. Putnam's Sons.

Metcalf, K. K. (1993). Critical factors in on-campus clinical experiences: Perceptions of preservice teachers. *Teaching Education, 5*(2), 172.

Milhouse, V. H., & Henderson, G. (1993). Infusing a multicultural perspective into the basic communication course: An investigation. In M. J. O'Hair & S. J. Odell (Eds.), *Diversity and teaching: Teacher education yearbook I* (pp. 193–211). New York: Harcourt Brace Jovanovich.

Morine-Dershimer, G. (1987). Practical examples of the practical argument: A case in point. *Educational Theory, 37*(4), 395–407.

National Board for Professional Teaching Standards (NBPTS). (1991). *Toward high and rigorous standards for the teaching profession* (3rd ed.). Washington, DC: Author.

National Center for Education Statistics (NCES). (1993). *120 years of American education: A statistical portrait.* Washington, DC: U.S. Department of Education, Office of Educational Research and Improvement.

National Center for Research on Teacher Learning (NCATE). (1992). *Findings on learning to teach.* East Lansing, MI: Author.

National Council for Accreditation of Teacher Education (NCATE). (1993). *Quality teaching, 3*(1), 4–5.

Noddings, N. (1984). *Caring: A feminine approach to ethics and moral education.* Berkeley: University of California Press.

Palincsar, A. S., & Brown, A. L. (1987). Advances in improving the cognitive performance of handicapped students. In M. C. Wang, M. C. Reynolds., & H. J. Walberg (Eds.), *Handbook of special education: Research and practice: Vol. I. Learner characteristics and adaptive education* (pp. 93–112). Oxford: Pergamon.

Paris, S. G., & Oka, E. (1986). Self-regulated learning among exceptional children. *Exceptional Children, 53*(2), 103–108.

Pinnell, G. S. (1990). Success for low achievers through Reading Recovery, *Educational Leadership, 48*(1), 17–21.

RATE IV. (1990). *Teaching teachers: Facts & figures.* Washington, DC: American Association of Colleges for Teacher Education.

RATE V. (1991). *Teaching teachers: Facts & figures.* Washington, DC: American Association of Colleges for Teacher Education.

RATE VI. (1992). *Teaching teachers: Facts & figures.* Washington, DC: American Association of Colleges for Teacher Education.

Reiman, A. J., & Parramore, B. M. (1994). First-year teachers' assignments, expectations, and development: A collaborative investigation. In M. J. O'Hair & S. J. Odell (Eds.), *Partnerships in education: Teacher education yearbook II* (pp. 120–134). New York: Harcourt Brace Jovanovich.

The Renaissance Group. (1992). *Demonstration projects.* Cedar Falls, IA: Author.

Rentel, V. M. (1992, May). *Preparing clinical faculty: Research on teacher reasoning.* Paper presented at conference on faculty development, Washington, DC.

Reynolds, M. C. (Ed.). (1989). *Knowledge base for the beginning teacher.* New York: Pergamon Press.

Rosenholtz, S. J. (1989). *Teachers' workplace: The social organization of schools.* White Plains, NY: Longman.

Shulman, L. S. (1987). Knowledge and teaching: Foundations of the new reform. *Harvard Educational Review, 57*(1), 31.

Sizer, T. R. (1991). No pain, no gain. *Educational Leadership, 48*(8), 32–34.

Sizer, T. R. (1992, November). School reform: What's missing. *World Monitor,* 20–27.

Sprinthall, N., & Thies-Sprinthall, L. (1983). The teacher as an adult learner: A cognitive-development view. In G. A. Griffin (Ed.), *Staff development* (82nd Yearbook of the National Society for the Study of Education) (pp. 13–35). Chicago: The University of Chicago Press.

Tom, A. R. (1991, February 14–16). *Stirring the embers: Reconsidering the structure of teacher education programs.* Paper presented at the Conference on Teacher Development: The Key to Educational Change, Vancouver, British Columbia, Canada.

Valli, L. (1990). Moral approaches to reflective practice. In R. Clift, W. R. Houston, & M. Pugach (Eds.), *Encouraging reflective practice in education.* New York: Teachers College Press.

Valli, L. (1993). Reconsidering technical and reflective concepts in teacher education. *Action in Teacher Education, 15*(2), 35–44.

Van Manen, M. (1977). Linking ways of knowing with ways of being practical. *Curriculum Inquiry, 6,* 205–228.

Wise, A. E. (1986). Graduate teacher education and teacher professionalism. *Journal of Teacher Education, 37*(5), 36–38.

Zeichner, K. M. (1983). Alternative paradigms of teacher education. *Journal of Teacher Education, 34*(3), 3–9.

Zeichner, K. M., & Gore, J. M. (1990). Teacher socialization. In W. R. Houston (Ed.), *Handbook of research on teacher education* (pp. 329–348). New York: Macmillan.

Zeichner, K. M., & Liston, D. P. (1987). Teaching student teachers to reflect. *Harvard Educational Review, 57*(10), 23–48.

Zeichner, K., & Tabachnick, B. (1982). The belief systems of university supervisors in an elementary student teaching program. *Journal of Education for Teaching, 8,* 34–54.

• 9 •

FIELD AND LABORATORY EXPERIENCES

D. John McIntyre

SOUTHERN ILLINOIS UNIVERSITY AT CARBONDALE

David M. Byrd

UNIVERSITY OF RHODE ISLAND

Susan M. Foxx

HARRISBURG, PENNSYLVANIA

Recent reform movements have generally called for an increased amount of field or clinical experience for students during teacher preparation (Berliner, 1985). This broad-based appeal is not without support. Field-based experiences are often listed as the most important part of the educational program by teachers (Conant, 1963; Cruickshank & Armaline, 1986; Kuehl, 1979). However, the effectiveness of field experience, including student teaching, has come under increased scrutiny during the last few years. This is due in part to a belief that increased practice alone does not always lead to analysis, reflection, and growth on the part of the novice teacher (Armaline & Hoover, 1989; Feiman-Nemser, 1983; Griffin et al., 1983). The purpose of this chapter is to investigate the role of practicum and field- and laboratory-based experiences in the development of teachers in an attempt to bring some clarity to the discussion of field experience within teacher education programs. This is undertaken through an analysis of the literature on variables that can be utilized to examine field experience research. In essence, this chapter reveals the current state of field experience research and provides suggestions for future research to promote a better understanding of the field. Although several of the variables examined in this review are similar to those examined in the "Student Teaching and School Experiences" (Guyton & McIntyre, 1990) chapter in the 1990 edition of the *Handbook of Research on Teacher Education* (Houston, 1990), the goal of these authors is also to examine any progress that has been made with those variables and to assess those issues or variables that have emerged as important to field and laboratory experiences since the publication of the first handbook.

THEORETICAL FRAMEWORK FOR FIELD EXPERIENCES AND TEACHER EDUCATION

In 1990, Guyton and McIntyre lamented the lack of a theoretical framework or clear set of goals for the development and implementation of field experiences. At that time, teacher educators argued that field experiences had no agreed-upon definition of the purpose and goals for the field component of teacher education (McIntyre, 1983; Watts, 1987; Zeichner, 1987). This lack of focus and purpose for field experiences emanated from a similar problem existing in teacher education programs as a whole.

Goodlad, Soder, and Sirotnik's (1990) nationwide study of teacher education programs supported these assertions. Through a series of interviews and observations, they discovered that the typical teacher education program comprised a collection of courses, various field experiences, and student teaching. Each of these components appeared to be separate from the others and was taught by a variety of faculty who had little or no communication with each other. They stated that it was not uncommon for cooperating teachers not to have the slightest notion of the program's goals or to have any idea whether any existed.

This disjointedness of program goals and curriculum may be responsible for the historical ineffectiveness of teacher education because most preservice teachers are unable to grasp the whole while experiencing the myriad of disconnected parts of the curriculum. Many teacher education programs fail to challenge their students to understand how ideas are connected and/or related to field experiences. In addition, faculty often approach knowledge from a more technical view of what students should or must know rather than to encourage them to relate theory and practice (Lasley, Payne, Fuchs, & Egnor-Brown, 1993).

Emerging Unifying Theoretical Frameworks

Only recently has evidence emerged that theory and practice are becoming integrated in teacher education programs and that a set of goals and objectives are creating a common theme or model throughout these programs (Fullan, 1985). The impetus for this trend of creating goals that unify the teacher education curriculum certainly can be credited to those educators who focused on the need for a theoretical framework and goals that would guide the teacher education process. Yet, another major force in this evolution is the set of standards adopted by the National Council for Accreditation of Teacher Education (NCATE) in 1987. These standards require participating institutions to explicate a model and knowledge base that undergirds the purpose, processes, and outcomes of their teacher education program. The model and knowledge base adopted by the institutions must unify all components of a program, including campus courses and field and laboratory experiences.

Although the NCATE standards do not specify a common model to be adopted by all institutions, there does appear to be a trend emerging toward program goals and models that develop teachers who are reflective decision makers, not mere technicians. For example, Liston and Zeichner (1991) propose that the aims of teacher education programs should focus on developing teachers who are able to identify and articulate their purposes, who can choose the appropriate instructional strategies, who understand the social experiences and cognitive orientations of their students, and who can articulate their actions. Effective teachers must have an understanding of the activity of teaching and have a greater understanding of the political and social context of schooling. Farber, Wilson, and Holm (1989) support this framework for teacher education by asserting that teachers must be sensitized to the full range of social-political and personal consequences of student practice, examine the moral and professional ambiguities in the process of schooling, and critically examine the consequences of standard practice.

Constructivism and Reflective Teachers Alkove and McCarty (1992) argue that the trend toward developing a theoretical framework in teacher education is resulting in a movement away from a positivist orientation to a more constructivist approach to teacher preparation. Within a positivist teacher education program, a student teacher assumes that outside forces determine standards, that people conform to established practices, and that people follow mandates handed down by those in authority. The hidden curriculum within these programs is to create teachers who are followers, who do as they are told, and who communicate this to their students.

The constructivist framework emphasizes the growth of the prospective teacher through experiences, reflection, and self-examination. Constructivist programs recognize that teachers are primarily persons who enter the program processing values and beliefs that form the foundation from which they make professional choices. Student teachers within this framework view teaching as ongoing decision making rather than as a product or recipe. These student teachers learn that significant education must present learners with relevant problematic situations in which the learner can manipulate objects to see what happens, to question what is already known, to compare their findings and assumptions with those of others, and to search for their own answers. As a result, constructivist teacher education must provide prospective teachers with the same orientation and experiences in both coursework and field experiences.

This emergence of constructivist teacher education programs has resulted in the movement toward developing reflective teachers (i.e., Eby, 1992; Roth, 1989; Valli, 1992; Zeichner & Liston, 1987). McCullough and Mintz (1992) believe that all teachers are concerned with pedagogical skills throughout their careers but that the best teachers also understand that the decisions that are made concerning instruction and management are made in the complicated context of schooling and that the implications of these decisions go far beyond their own classroom.

Programs that focus on the development of reflective practitioners must create experiences in the field that enable preservice students not only to practice reflectivity but also to observe it being practiced by experienced teachers. Bullough (1989) asserts that the first priority in developing a reflective teacher education program is to restructure all field experiences so students can engage in reflective decision making and can act on their decisions in the spirit of praxis. He believes that reflective field experiences should begin during the first semester or quarter of the preservice teacher's program. Field experience students should study and critique the school and the cultural context within which they will be working. The emphasis of a reflective field experience program is to allow one to begin seeing through a teacher's eyes and to consider responses in light of practical, social, and ethical consequences. Changing the conditions of student teaching is of primary importance if reflectivity is to become a true objective of teacher education programs.

The notion of modifying the conditions of student teaching is a common theme among teacher educators who advocate the development of reflective teachers. For example, Britzman (1991) states that student teachers possess a personal biography that shapes their expectations of "real school life." The courses that these students take throughout their teacher education program are viewed as impractical and too theoretical. Student teaching is the opportunity to link theory and practice, but it too often serves to widen the gulf between the two. To modify the student teaching condition, McCaleb, Borko, and Arends (1992) suggest that student teaching placements must no longer be viewed as the "real world" and instead should be viewed as learning laboratories or studios where student teachers experience both the university and the school as the "real world." The student teaching experience would be characterized by continuing inquiry by the student teacher, cooperating teacher, and pupils rather than by the transmission and incorporation of predetermined information. In addition, Cinnamond and Zimpher (1990) note that the common practice of placing a student teacher with one cooperating teacher in one classroom limits the student's ability to become reflective and restricts learning about the multiple communities within the school and community. They believe that if a student teacher is to develop into a reflective practitioner then the prospective teacher must become caught up in interaction among all communities within the school. In addition to this modification, Rudney and Guillaume (1989–1990) suggest that teacher education programs can facilitate reflective teaching through field experience by assigning reflective activities to student teachers.

Ayers (1989) describes an experimental program in which students had three quarters of student teaching instead of one and in which experiences were created to enhance their students' reflectivity. In this program, student teachers developed a strong sense of efficacy and an ability to draw on personal as well as social resources in their efforts to create a successful learning environment. They were better able to consider a wider range of alternatives in the process of developing curriculum and were more willing to resist arbitrary directives from authority than were their peers in the traditional program. Students in the experimental program were more student oriented and tended to consider an array of teaching strategies to meet the particular needs of learners.

It is encouraging to note that there appears to be a movement toward defining the purpose of field experiences and toward clarifying the goals of teacher education. This action is assisting the profession in determining the kinds of teachers desired to prepare for future classrooms. What is missing, however, is quantifiable and qualitative data that will enable teacher educators to determine if these programs are, indeed, preparing more thoughtful, reflective teachers; that is, teachers who are more effective in the classroom than those prepared in more traditional, apprentice-type programs.

CONTEXT OF FIELD AND LABORATORY EXPERIENCES

In 1990, Guyton and McIntyre wrote that "available research . . . does not present the school context as a positive influence on student teacher development" (p. 518). This statement is especially important. Copeland (1977a) argues that the ecology of the school setting—pupils, physical environment, curriculum, and community—is the major influence on the student teacher's acquisition of skills. Bullough (1991) continues this discussion by claiming that the context of teaching, including the number of students in a class, the ability of students, the number of non-English speaking students, paperwork, and the length of class periods often make it difficult for student teachers to achieve their image of an effective teacher. As important as the school context is in the development of prospective teachers, Zeichner (1986b) believes that adequate attention has not been given to the impact of particular types of classrooms, schools, and communities on student teachers.

Although there have been some modifications in recent years, the common format for student teaching is still to limit a student teacher to one school, one classroom, and one teacher. Sedlak (1987) believes that this typical student teaching experience emphasizes imitation and subservience to the cooperating

teacher rather than emphasizing investigation, reflection, and problem solving. Lemlech and Kaplan (1990) continue the discussion on the context by stating that the commonly structured student teaching practice prepares teacher candidates for the loneliness of the classroom, not for reflection, networking, or collegiality. The one-on-one relationship of the student teacher and cooperating teacher, with an emphasis on observation and performance, tends to exaggerate the loneliness of classroom teaching. In the first *Handbook of Research on Teacher Education* (Houston, 1990), Zeichner and Gore provide an excellent review of the research in the socialization of student teachers and of the role played by the school context in that socialization.

Because most teacher candidates spend nearly 13 years in a public or private school setting, they are familiar with a school's classrooms and routines and, therefore, with the context of the field experience placement. This familiarity is often cited as a barrier to real professional growth during the field experience component. Feiman-Nemser and Buchmann (1986) cite familiar settings as the most salient and least amenable to inquiry. Students need assistance in seeing how their personal history and experience of schooling influence their perceptions of classrooms in a way that makes it difficult to appreciate alternatives. Armaline and Hoover (1989) support this notion that student teachers' familiarity with the context masks their potential vision of alternatives. They assert that the common structure of field experience prohibits thoughtful consideration of ideology and its language and actions, and it is necessarily reproductive, which is antithetical to empowering teacher candidates to find their own "teacher identity." Furthermore, they believe that the field experience context is where the potential for miseducation is as great as it is for education that transforms, depending on the way in which the phenomena of the sites are interpreted and acted on by students.

Effect of Placement and Cooperating Teacher

Teacher educators begin shaping future teachers by deciding where they will student teach; with whom they will student teach; what behaviors will be emphasized; and what theories, practices, and philosophies will be reinforced (Lemlech & Kaplan, 1990). Thus, the placement of the prospective teacher for both early field experience and student teaching is a crucial stage in teacher preparation. However, Applegate (1985) asserts that this placement process is often an institutional dilemma that can hamper teacher development. For example, Goodlad's (1990) national study revealed that many universities did not control the placement of student teachers and that placements were too often based on convenience rather than what would provide quality experience. Furthermore, Guyton, Paille, and Rainer (1993) found that some school principals place student teachers with weak teachers with the anticipation that the student teacher would provide assistance for the weaker teacher.

The influence of the cooperating teacher on the student teacher is covered more extensively in a later section of this chapter; however, it is clear that the cooperating teacher greatly influences the student teaching context and also the behavior and beliefs of novice teachers. In addition, research often depicts the influence of the cooperating teacher on the student teacher in negative terms (Guyton & McIntyre, 1990). For example, Winitsky, Stoddart, and O'Keefe (1992) found that when student teachers introduced a constructivist approach to teaching, the cooperating teacher quickly intervened and made the student teacher quickly conform to the cooperating teacher's didactic expectations. Applegate (1986) discovered that the interpersonal relationship between the cooperating teacher and student teacher focused primarily on pupils in the classroom. Virtually nothing is said about the curriculum. What is taught is either not noticed or is taken for granted in the given situation. Little is said between cooperating teacher and student teacher about instructional strategies. As a result, research challenges the assumption that any teacher who is effective with children in the classroom has the capacity to be a successful teacher trainer (Koerner, 1992).

Perhaps some or most of the responsibility for this problem rests with the lack of communication between most universities and school sites. Levin (1990) describes the typical communication process between university and schools as an engagement in reality without required dialogue. As a result, rather than a collaborative process, it becomes one of congeniality instead.

Transforming the Student Teaching Context

The preceding discussion reinforces the notion that the student teaching context, in general, remains a less than positive influence on the development of prospective teachers. Guyton and McIntyre's (1990) suggestion that the quality of student teaching programs depends too much on specific classroom sites that are not designed to prepare teachers and that are beyond the control of the institution remains true. However, Zimpher and Howey (1990) detect a vision beginning to evolve in terms of transforming the context of teacher preparation through the creation of a series of laboratory experiences throughout the student's program. This section describes several additional proposals for transforming the student teaching context in order for it to be more responsive to the development of novice teachers.

Perhaps the most recent major attempt to transform the context for the preparation of teachers has been the professional development school. Although professional development schools have existed in some form during the last two centuries, Stallings and Kowalski (1990) define them as a school setting focused on the professional development of teachers and the development of pedagogy. Professional development schools are places where teachers as well as pupils learn and where future teachers learn to teach in classrooms where their cooperating teachers are also students of teaching (Feiman-Nemser & Buchmann, 1986). A more complete compilation of research on professional development schools can be found in Stallings and Kowalski's (1990) chapter in the first *Handbook of Research on Teacher Education* and in Chapter 10 of this handbook.

Another recent approach to transforming the context of field experience is to develop cohort groups of students who proceed through their coursework and field experiences together. Bullough and Gitlin (1991) suggest that through sharing a placement, group members have increased opportunities to interact with one another but also have the opportunity to explore meanings and differences in meanings based on very similar, shared experiences. Sharing school placements and perhaps

pupils enables student teachers to locate problems and resources useful for resolving problems specific to a particular context. This encourages a more communal perspective and a weakening of the extreme form of individualism common to traditional approaches to student teaching placement. The notion of the communal perspective to teacher preparation through the use of cohort groups is supported by Winitsky, Stoddart, and O'Keefe's (1992) description of this approach in a collaborative program with the University of Utah and Salt Lake City schools.

In addition to professional development schools and cohort groups, other strategies are being utilized in an attempt to have a positive impact on the field experience context. One such attempt is to increase the number and variety of sites in which students are placed. Black and Ammon (1992) describe a program where students are placed in five different student teaching sites during a 2-year period. These prospective teachers are placed in several grades and in several socioeconomic and culturally diverse communities. Garibaldi (1992) believes that teacher education students must be exposed to a variety of students and schools as early as their first semester in college and should be assigned to different schools and classrooms every semester of their program. A purpose of increasing the number and variety of sites is to dilute the influence or impact of any one context.

Other strategies for transforming the context include the implementation of a reflective field experience program whose purpose is to develop teachers who are reflective about teaching and learning and the context in which it takes place (Pinar, 1989; Valli, 1992). (Reflective teacher education programs are described in more detail earlier in this chapter.) Finally, some teacher educators suggest modifying the roles of the participants within the student teaching context. For example, Goodlad (1990) suggests that field experience students become junior members of school faculties; Oja, Diller, Corcoran, and Andrew (1992) suggest making the cooperating teacher and university supervisors co-equals; and Killian and McIntyre (1986) suggest training the cooperating teachers as teacher educators and instructional supervisors.

There is evidence of a trend toward transforming the field experience context. How rapidly this transformation occurs most likely will depend on whether teacher educators can modify their own traditional paradigm for field experience. Although this trend is encouraging, it remains that quantitative and qualitative research on the effect of various components and various modifications of the student teaching context is minimal. Data are needed to validate the effectiveness of new paradigms for the student teaching context and to determine whether they are or are not more effective than their traditional contextual counterparts.

ORGANIZATION OF FIELD EXPERIENCES

Henry (1989) asserts that in spite of a lack of firm research data, the field experience component of teacher education continues to be the most popular aspect of teacher preparation programs. He lists the following factors as contributing to this continuing popularity: (1) field experiences link teacher candidates to the actual teaching setting; (2) field experiences exemplify the classical concept of learning through experience; (3) field experiences have a higher degree of emotional involvement, mostly positive; (4) field experiences are growth producing; (5) field experiences offer the opportunity for one-to-one teaching encounters; (6) goals are internally determined rather than externally imposed; and (7) prospective teachers are inducted into the existing school milieu. This universal popularity and acceptance of field experiences has persuaded many teacher educators and state legislators to support overwhelmingly recommendations to increase the number and length of field experience for preservice teachers. However, several researchers have pointed out the potential for field experiences to socialize novice teachers into the existing school milieu and have suggested limiting the length of early field experience and student teaching (Hoy & Rees, 1977; Liston & Zeichner, 1988; Popkewitz, 1985; Zeichner, 1986b, 1989). Fullan (1985) asserts that by extending field experiences, teacher education programs provide opportunities for students to adjust to the routines of teaching without advancing their knowledge base about the profession. This assertion is supported by Feiman-Nemser and Buchmann (1986) who believe that field experiences, as normally structured, encourage teacher candidates to learn things that are inappropriate in any teaching situation and that will be reinforced later in their teaching careers. They also believe that most classrooms are not set up for teaching teachers and that most field experiences mean learning things that are only part of the job of teaching.

Britzman (1991) states that student teachers who are committed to change learn that their intent to change classroom practices neither brings about effective transformation nor allows them to take up existing practices. If they attempt transformative practices, they may fail. If they adopt existing practices, they are critical of their capitulation into the socialized norm.

Structuring and Length of Field Experiences

Given this critical examination of the socialized tenor of field experience, what is known about the relationship between length of field experiences and the preparation of effective teachers? McIntyre's (1983) summary of research on field experiences reveals that the early field experience component does provide several benefits to prospective teachers and to the teacher education program. These benefits include: (1) allowing students to discover early if they like children and want to teach, (2) permitting programs to determine students' potential, (3) enabling students to practice instructional skills prior to student teaching, (4) developing the student's base of perceptions of classroom life, (5) improving communication between universities and public schools, and (6) accelerating passage through the stages from student to teacher. As positive as these data might appear, they still do not indicate that a longer period of early field experience is more effective than a shorter version.

Hudson, Bergin, and Chayst (1993) provide additional insight into this argument by listing five factors that serve to thwart effective early field experience programs. First, many early field experience programs lack quality control. As a result of the large numbers of preservice teachers that must be placed in classrooms during several semesters of early field experience,

teacher education programs often are unable to control the teachers with whom and the classrooms in which they are placed for their experience. Thus, it is not always possible to control the quality of the teachers with whom or classrooms in which students work. Second, cooperating teachers, college instructors, and early field experience students often lack common goals. The primary goal of classroom teachers is the education of their pupils. The preparation of a new teacher is secondary to the primary goal. Yet, the college instructor's goal is for the preservice teacher to have the opportunity to observe and to participate in activities that coincide with what is being taught on campus. Finally, preservice teachers can bring a myriad of goals to the early field experience site. These may include reinforcing their career choice, gaining more experience with a certain grade level, attempting new teaching strategies, and so forth. Third, preservice teachers have limited cognitive schemes for making sense of their observations in the field and hence learning from them. Because most of these students have little teaching experience, they often do not know what to look for or how to interpret what they see in the classroom. As a result, what they learn during an early field experience can be limited. Fourth, preservice teachers often observe practices in the classroom that contradict what college instructors consider appropriate practice. Thus, preservice teachers question the worthiness of what was learned on campus or of what they are observing in the classroom. Finally, too few multicultural classrooms exist to enhance a culturally sensitive pedagogy. In many instances, universities are located in geographical areas that lack a diverse population. Preservice students then are not able to observe and participate in classrooms that may be more representative of those where they might find employment.

In an effort to examine the effectiveness of extended programs, Thomson, Beacham, and Misulis (1992) described a year-long program that integrated traditional prestudent teaching coursework with an internship across a student's final college year. As a result of this extended experience, three factors were identified as critical by interns, cooperating teachers, university faculty, and principals. First, there was value in the extended time in the field. The extended experience helped the students develop confidence and self-esteem and heightened their awareness of the profession. Second, there was the value of the reflective model for mentoring and teaching practices. The extended experience provided the students with a better understanding of teachers' actions, curriculum, and student behavior. Third, there was the value of an intensive staff development component for clinical instructors.

Reiman and Parramore (1993) described an experimental program where students could volunteer for additional fieldwork as tutors during their sophomore and junior years. In addition, continuous reflection through careful, written feedback in coursework and journals was required of these students. Data indicate that these students developed increased dimensions of student justice, reasoning, conceptual complexity, and ego development.

Finally, Andrew (1990) assessed differences between graduates of 4- and 5-year teacher education programs. The data indicate that 5-year graduates were happier with their careers; were more likely to choose teaching again; were more positive about the school environment, school administrators, and students; were more confident at the conclusion of their teacher preparation programs; viewed colleagues more favorably; and viewed their teacher preparation programs as better than the 4-year program.

Despite the overwhelming positive feeling about the efficacy of field experiences, there does not exist enough data to determine that extending field experiences, whether at the early field experience or student teaching stage, will develop more effective, thoughtful teachers than those prepared in shorter field experience programs. Although there remains a great need for additional research in this area, it appears that what occurs during the field experience is more important than the length of that experience. Armstrong (1989–1990) states that more research is needed on this important component of teacher education. He believes that three broad areas in field experience are ripe for research. These are (1) What do students know about what they see?, (2) Do early field experiences adequately model the "reality" of teaching?, and (3) What is the effect of early field experiences on students' instructional behaviors? At this point, it is probably safe to say that a shorter field component with well-integrated experiences is more likely to produce effective teachers for the twenty-first century than a lengthier program whose major attribute is length.

INTERPERSONAL RELATIONS

Much of the early research on field experience centered on student teaching and the interpersonal relations among the student teacher, cooperating teacher, and university supervisor. Vickery and Brown (1967) discussed the demands on the student teacher and suggested that problems arise out of the conflicting philosophies of conservative cooperating teachers and liberal university supervisors. The student teacher, although often caught in the middle, is not surprised that conflict occurs. Peterson (1977) found that students, prior to student teaching, anticipate philosophical disagreement between university- and school-based educators.

Numerous studies have found differences in understanding among cooperating teachers, college supervisors, and student teachers about each other's role, expectations, decision making, and the process for policy formation (Castillo, 1971; Copas, 1984; Grimmett & Ratzlaff, 1986; Kapel & Sadler, 1978). There are even disagreements as to the student teacher's role (Gettone, 1980). These disagreements are, in part, based on the developmental nature of field experiences in which students' roles often change over time. This phenomenon is evidenced by the fact that Calderhead (1987) found that even student teachers' perceptions of their own roles shifted over the course of student teaching. Yet, there are also differences in opinion that go beyond each group having similar perspectives but different expectations relative to the speed with which student teachers develop a full range of abilities and dispositions. For example, cooperating teachers and student teachers perceived that the most important factor during student teaching was the development of self-confidence; however, college supervisors and school administrators considered application of theory into practice as the most important issue during student teaching (Tittle, 1974). Interestingly, student teachers rated experimenta-

tion during student teaching of much higher value than cooperating teachers, supervisors, or administrators; therefore, although triads of student teachers, cooperating teachers, and college supervisors work together in productive ways every day, their interactions are not without tension and some angst. A good portion of this tension seems to be caused by a lack of communication and agreement as to the responsibilities of each member of the triad.

Kagan (1990) provides additional insight into the phenomenon by suggesting that teacher and teacher educator attitudes and behaviors are a direct result of the norms of their workplace. She believes that schools can be low consensus (isolated and pluralistic) or high consensus (with agreement as to goals and desirable teaching methods), and that sharing a professional culture or sense of what its members hope to accomplish is an important characteristic of successful, or what Rosenholtz (1989) calls consensus, schools. University faculty, however, are described as a highly fragmented, pluralistic group, similar to teachers in low-consensus schools. Whereas academic freedom is central to being a professor, teacher educators and teacher education programs appear to define the term low consensus (Howey & Zimpher, 1989; Wisniewski & Ducharme, 1989). Yet, as stated previously, NCATE standards call for a common knowledge base for each teacher education unit to ensure

that its professional education programs are based on essential knowledge, established and current research findings, and sound professional practice. Each program in the unit reflects a systematic design with an explicitly stated philosophy and objectives. Coherence exists between 1) courses and experiences and 2) purposes and outcomes. (National Council for Accreditation on Teacher Education [NCATE], 1987, p. 37)

Yet, even with this requirement, too many teacher education programs are without a unifying focus or set of purposes. The lack of a coherent knowledge base is a major standard listed as not met in recent NCATE reviews.

A shared vision for teacher education is a fundamental point raised by Howey and Zimpher in their book *Profiles of Preservice Teacher Education* (1989). Their analysis of teacher education programs at six different types of institutions of higher education points to the need for "conceptually coherent programs [that] enable needed and *shared* faculty leadership to engage in more generative and continuing renewal by underscoring collective roles as well as individual course responsibilities" (1989, p. 242). As stated earlier in this chapter, there is often a lack of consensus on campuses relative to the goals for teacher education programs and their field components. Consequently, it is not surprising to find a lack of agreement between the campus and the field regarding goals, roles, and responsibilities expected of the triadic members. In a similar vein, Howey and Zimpher's interviews with cooperating teachers provide some evidence of the range of perceptions held by cooperating teachers. Cooperating teachers were asked "whether they believed the students today appear to be better prepared to teach than they were formerly" (p. 143). Most responded in a positive manner. For example, one teacher responded, "Of course, it depends upon the student teacher you work with in terms of how you see the program, but I've had excellent student teachers to work with. I'm amazed at how much know-how they have when they come into the classroom and how willing they are to try things" (p. 142). Yet, cooperating teachers also had concerns. Illustrative of these concerns is the following response:

I think the whole approach to training teachers is wrong. I think all people going into education should spend at least the first two years—or maybe more—in liberal arts . . . . My students don't always know some of the basics in American history. They don't know . . . they haven't read basic works of literature. And it's not because they don't want to, they haven't had the opportunity. (p. 144)

These exchanges provide some indication of the range and strength of opinions held by teachers on the issue of teacher preparation. Discussion of the content preparation of student teachers is a good example of the type of issue about which within-campus groups and campus and field groups may have differing opinions.

Within the profession, the importance of open communication and agreement as to the purposes, roles, and responsibilities of the triad are generally accepted in principle, yet under-achieved in reality. It appears that the perceived problem of students' content preparation will take a solution of more complexity than the addition of more liberal arts courses for teacher education students.

In addition to the call for a common knowledge base for teacher education programs there has also been discussion of the need for the delineation of the roles and responsibilities of each triad member. These roles and responsibilities have been outlined in college/university student teaching handbooks and in state teacher education program approval standards, such as those developed by the National Association of State Directors of Teacher Education and Certification (NASDTEC) and the national accreditation standards of NCATE. NCATE (1987) criterion 32 was clearly written to ensure an understanding among triad members about their functions and obligations: "The roles and responsibilities of education students, college-based supervisors and field-based supervisors who participate in field-based and clinical experiences are delineated in negotiated written agreements" (p. 42). Delineating roles and responsibilities, however, is only the first step toward ensuring that each member of the triad commits to fulfilling the outlined agreement. Without commitment to implementation, written agreements will not improve student teaching; however, many programs are beginning to address effectively the issues regarding the roles and responsibilities of cooperating teachers and university supervisors (Bennett, Ishler, & O'Loughlin, 1992; Cochran-Smith, 1991; Guyton, 1989; Wolfe, Schewel, & Bickman, 1989). Exemplary programs and practices are the necessary building blocks for establishing and maintaining collaborative relationships.

Cooperating Teachers

Teachers perceive that their cooperating teachers had the most significant influence on them during student teaching (Karmos & Jacko, 1977; Manning, 1977). The attitudes of student teachers are, perhaps, the variable most strongly shaped by cooperating teachers as the semester progresses (Dunham,

1958; Johnson, 1969; Price, 1961). Mahan and Lacefield (1976) found this specifically true of students' attitudes toward schooling. Where discrepancies existed between the attitudes of student teachers and cooperating teachers, the movement of the student was in the direction of the teacher. Student teacher attitudes seem to become more custodial and negative with a focus on classroom management, control, and lesson completion without concern for student progress (Dispoto, 1980; Iannacone, 1963).

Whereas recent studies have supported the general trend of movement of students' attitudes toward that of their cooperating teachers, there is a growing perception that the cooperating teacher alone is not responsible for this shift (Bryant, 1982). Zeichner (1979) points out that some student teachers do not adopt the attitudes of their cooperating teacher and that researchers should determine why some student teachers resist socialization while others do not.

The merging of the classroom behaviors of student teachers and their cooperating teachers has, to this point, been conflicting. Studies by Price (1961), Seperson and Joyce (1973), and Zevin (1974) have indicated adoption and movement of student teachers toward their cooperating teachers' classroom style; however, Seperson and Joyce found this influence pervasive only during the first few weeks of student teaching. McIntyre, Buell, and Casey (1979) reported that student teachers do not model the verbal behavior of their cooperating teacher.

Although the majority of the research on field placements has focused on attitudinal changes, there is a growing body of research concerned with other characteristics of the cooperating teacher. In a study to determine if characteristics of field placements had a relationship to students' final evaluations, Becher and Ade (1982) placed students in three settings: (1) teacher models good teaching, (2) teacher gives feedback to the student teacher, and (3) teacher allows the opportunity for innovation. They found that there was a lack of a strong relationship between the modeling of good practice by cooperating teachers and the final performance ratings of field-experience students. This finding is of major interest because the selection of cooperating teachers who are perceived as good role models is a pervasive criterion for placement of student teachers. It would seem that being a good role model, in and of itself, is not sufficient to bring about positive behaviors in students. Possible reasons for this finding might be that students could not recognize an effective model, cooperating teachers had little knowledge of the benefits of modeling (Joyce, Showers, & Rolheiser-Bennett, 1987; Joyce & Weil, 1986), or the cooperating teachers lacked expertise in guiding student practice. The results of feedback given to field experience students were mixed (highly positive for the last two semesters and negative for the first), whereas the results for innovation were highly positive in the first and last semester but not during the second semester. These results are more difficult to explain. Perhaps they were due to the perception by students and their cooperating teachers that students were to develop and practice but not imitate their teachers. In addition, one would expect that high-feedback teachers would provide additional feedback on the criterion used for the final evaluation and that this would aid student performance on the final evaluation.

Wright, Silvern, and Burkhater (1982) investigated whether cooperating teachers demonstrate or give direction on how to carry out activities that were perceived by university faculty and the cooperating teachers as instructionally important; that is (1) reading to class, (2) conducting an oral reading lesson with an audience situation, and (3) guiding pupils to more extensive reading. They found that more than half of the students did not recall receiving instruction to perform any of the listed tasks. Furthermore, teachers were much more likely to demonstrate an activity than to give directions. These studies on modeling point out that students need to observe and model the behaviors of cooperating teachers if they are to gain the maximum benefits from their cooperating teachers' experience and knowledge. Until cooperating teachers are trained to give directions and to demonstrate activities, their influence on the development of the student teachers' skills should be questioned. Perhaps this situation is best interpreted by Copeland (1977a) who suggested that the ecology of schooling is the major variable in the development of student teacher skills, rather than the influence of the cooperating teacher.

Killian and McIntyre (1986) found that teacher education students appear to have brief, impersonal interactions with their students and they avoid conflict and substantive discussion with cooperating teachers. In a study designed to overcome this phenomenon, McIntyre and Killian (1986) developed a course on instructional supervision for cooperating teachers and preservice students. A control group did not receive information on instructional supervision. In examining the differences in interactions of teacher education students and cooperating teachers, they found that teacher education students paired with trained cooperating teachers received significantly more feedback. In addition, the student teachers spent more time preparing and planning and interacting with their own students. They concluded that cooperating teachers need training in communication skills and that training should promote reflective thinking if teacher education students are to master this skill. Implied in this study is the assumption that representatives from the university must also promote an atmosphere of communication, feedback, and reflection if these factors are to be present during student teaching. In a related study, Hauwiller, Abel, Ausel, and Sparapani (1988–1989) found that a series of short-term in-service workshops provided by university supervisors for cooperating teachers appears to be an effective method for improving communication. Cochran-Smith (1991) suggests that student teachers can learn to be reformers if they are placed with experienced teachers who are attempting to reform their classrooms. This process of reform is maximized when there is a supportive linkage between the university and the schools.

University Supervisor

The university supervisor often has been criticized for not fulfilling the role of instructional leader (Diamonti, 1977). A number of studies have reported that the university supervisor has little measurable effect on student teachers' attitudes or behavior (Sandgren & Schmidt, 1956; Schueler, Gold, & Mitzel, 1962). Morris (1974) placed 96 student teachers in one of two groups— one with a university supervisor and a cooperating teacher and one with a cooperating teacher alone. She found no significant differences, as measured by the final evaluations of the student teachers, in classroom performance or adjustment between the group that had a university supervisor and the group that did not.

Additional data on university supervision do point to a level of influence by clinical faculty on student teachers. Bennie (1964) discovered that experienced teachers perceived that university supervisors improve student teachers' performance. In addition, Friebus (1977) found that university supervisors play a role as "coaches," providing suggestions and support about specific teaching problems; however, the most important role played by university supervisors results from the uncritical relationship between cooperating teachers and their student teachers. Zimpher, deVoss, and Nott (1980) found that cooperating teachers do not provide students with feedback and critical analyses of their teaching and that without the input of university supervisors, student teachers would be left to analyze their own teaching performance. In addition, this study reported that university supervisors provide needed support in defining and communicating program goals and in phasing the student into classroom activities. Corrigan and Griswold (1963) found those student teachers with certain university supervisors became more positive in their attitudes toward teaching, schools, and children. These students perceived their university supervisor as influencing their perceptions on these variables. One of the most comprehensive descriptive studies of student teaching was conducted by Griffin et al. (1983). A major finding was that the most significant characteristic of student teaching was the central role played by supervision, and that although the university supervisor plays a role in supervision, the cooperating teacher plays the most prominent role. The university supervisor is viewed as the more tolerant, secure, and independent member of the triad, and as more progressive and able to process a higher level of self-esteem than the cooperating teacher. An additional finding is that university supervisors and cooperating teachers do not apply a shared knowledge base during discussions or conferences. Perhaps this in turn leads to the perception by student teachers that although university supervisors could have been more helpful, they were perceived by student teachers as people they could talk to about both professional and personal issues (as opposed to cooperating teachers with whom they carried on only professional dialogue). Yet, whereas openness describes one major positive characteristic of university supervisors, research also points out the lack of an atmosphere for rigorous inquiry, which may limit the potential for increasing student analysis or what is often referred to in the literature as reflection. Future studies may do well to investigate the appropriate balance between openness and reflection. Koehler (1984) reported that university supervisors perceived that their primary duties centered on providing support for student teachers while facilitating growth and moderating conflict resolution between cooperating teachers and student teachers. Additional roles, in ascending order, included serving as a liaison between the university and the schools, providing a set of common expectations for cooperating teachers and student teachers, providing support for student teachers both professionally and personally, securing favorable placements, orienting student teachers to schools, evaluating student teachers relative to growth rather than specific skills or knowledge, providing feedback from observations, and conducting seminars. Most supervisors reported major problems, such as the breakdown of communication or working to ensure that the members of the triad worked together as a team.

University supervisors perceived effective supervisors in much the same way cooperating teachers and student teachers did, that is, as cooperative, flexible, hardworking, having a sense of humor, and able to work with others. Moreover, the university supervisors reported that they believed themselves pressed for time and overtaxed with a range of responsibilities.

Casey and Howson (1993) have called for an expansion of the triad to include methods course instructors. They believe that for students to become creative problem solvers able to "harness their creativity through organization and planning" (p. 361), the information and skills embedded in campus classes must be integrated during field experiences. Therefore, methods course professors should be encouraged to work closely with college supervisors and cooperating teachers in a "three person teaching team" (p. 365). They suggest that if student teachers are to problem solve and to teach their students to problem solve, they need to be part of an integrated campus and field system that models problem solving and reflection.

Additional research has been conducted on the concept of "clustering" student interns in schools and setting up what Oja (1988) calls Teacher Supervision Groups (TSGs) made up of cooperating teachers, the building principal, and the university supervisor. The groups met biweekly during the school day while the university interns were working independently in classrooms. TSGs focused on alternative models of supervision and the role that adult development plays in supervision. Action research projects appeared to assist the cooperating teachers in their investigation and understanding of supervision. Supervisors continued to meet with each intern and his or her cooperating teacher on a biweekly basis and to hold weekly seminars with cluster interns to get their impressions and to discuss a range of issues regarding their internships. Major outcomes centered on the benefits teacher educators and teachers gained by finding a professional way to talk with others about teaching and supervision.

In summary, a lack of clearly agreed-upon and delineated goals, roles, and responsibilities not only hampers teacher education programs in general but also more specifically hinders the effectiveness of the triad as a supportive alliance to advance the growth and development of the student teacher. During student teaching, a primary focus is on supervision; however, the potential for supervision to assist student teacher growth is not fully met due to problems of communication and delineation of roles and responsibilities of all participants. For example, if the student teaching experience is perceived as "not going well," then members of the triad can either begin to communicate or can retreat into silence. If the choice becomes one of silence, the student teacher can lose sight of the need for reflection and growth and simply focus on survival and graduation. The cooperating teachers may recognize that a problem exists, but they may not have a quick solution. Also, concern for the welfare of their own students often causes them to distance themselves from the student teacher's failure. The university supervisor, who by definition is not present on a daily or even weekly basis, may be viewed as a disconnected observer/evalu-ator, or worse yet, as an uninformed guest in the classroom. As such, the university supervisor may be considered an inappropriate choice to involve in assessing and facilitating solutions or interventions. Only by understanding each other's roles and through common understandings and open communication can cooperating teachers and university supervisors hope to promote an atmosphere of reflection in which problems can be solved.

Even given open communication, there is limited understanding of how supervisors influence changes in student teacher behaviors. Perhaps this is due to the subtle nature of the behaviors they hope to influence. For example, supervisors may attempt to influence decisions about when to use questions to probe student understanding, when to give feedback to students on their understanding of a concept or skill versus reteaching the concept or skill to students, or how to use long-term positive reinforcement to improve the ecology of the classroom. Perhaps as the field moves away from a reliance on quantitative models to analyze the interpersonal relationships of the student teaching triad and is recast in a naturalistic mode, the complexities of supervision will become better understood.

ADMINISTRATION OF FIELD EXPERIENCES

The administration of field experiences is most often centered within the college department of education and has the specific task of organizing and managing all field-based experiences. In 1990, Guyton and McIntyre found that most of the information regarding the administration of field experiences has been limited to results of descriptive research. The most comprehensive studies in this area have been conducted by Johnson and Yates (1982); Lamont (1993); and Morris, Pannell, and Houston (1985).

Currently, more than half of the administrators are female, 50 years old, and hold the position of Director of Student Teaching or Field Experiences. The director holds a doctoral degree and has 6–10 years of teaching experience. In addition, the majority of administrators has been cooperating teachers and university supervisors and has had some training in clinical supervision (Lamont, 1993). The administrator has professional rank and tenure, and his or her work is supported by secretarial and student assistance.

Approximately half of the administrator's work is administrative; the remainder is considered to be instructional. These duties include: (1) preparing the student teaching budget; (2) selecting, orienting, and providing in-service for college supervisors and cooperating teachers; (3) determining eligibility of and placement of student teachers; (4) maintaining records and preparing reports; (5) developing handbooks and forms used in student teaching; (6) handling public relations; (7) setting up seminars for and handling supervision of student teachers; and (8) making final decisions regarding student teachers. At public institutions, the administrator may also conduct research and experimental programs. In addition, administrators are highly satisfied with their role but are likely to feel somewhat dissatisfied with the qualifications and preparations of cooperating teachers and college supervisors (Guyton & McIntyre, 1990).

In 1993, Lamont discovered that private institutions provide a greater number of support services to student teachers than do public institutions, and those institutions with female directors of student teaching or field experiences provide a greater number of support services than institutions with male directors. In addition, institutions that require students to participate in more intense early field experiences had a greater number of support services for student teachers.

Currently there is no research that goes beyond the surface-level descriptions of the administrator's characteristics and responsibilities. This is the same situation discovered by Guyton and McIntyre in 1990. Indeed there continues to be a lack of in-depth analysis into the administrator's role and participation in the student teaching process. Further research is needed on the administrator's impact on field placements and relationship to other individuals involved in field experiences.

Policies Governing Field Experiences

There is tremendous variance in the policies and practices that govern field experiences (Johnson & Yates, 1982; Reyes & Isele, 1990; Simbol & Summers, 1984). In fact, the greatest commonality occurred in the admission requirements to student teaching. More than one half of all Schools, Colleges and Departments of Education (SCDEs) required a specific grade point average, English proficiency, test of basic skills, speech and voice screening, and advisor recommendations (Johnson & Yates, 1982; Lamont, 1993).

Policies governing field experiences have been developed by several external sources. The most influential are those of the NCATE. The most comprehensive set of standards are the Guidelines for Professional Experiences in Teacher Education (Association of Teacher Educators [ATE], 1986). The standards and guidelines of NCATE and the Association of Teacher Educators (ATE) are general enough to support great diversity in field experiences. The one exception is that both NCATE and ATE have made specific provisions regarding the preparation of college supervisors. McIntyre (1983) suggested that perhaps supervision skills may alter the existing pattern of a lack of college supervisor impact on the behavior of student teachers. Indeed, preparation in supervision does seem to have a meritorious effect on cooperating teachers (Killian & McIntyre, 1986; Thies-Sprinthall, 1984; Zeichner & Liston, 1987).

Morris, Pannell, and Houston (1985) reviewed state standards relating to professional field experiences in teacher education. Thirty-five states had standards for prestudent teaching experiences; student teaching is required by all 50 states. Common regulations pertain to substitutes for student teaching, design and length of student teaching, grade-level assignments, supervision, evaluation, and criteria for selection of a school or district. It is interesting to note that programs with NCATE accreditation had no systematic pattern for evaluation of student teachers (Reyes & Isele, 1990). Eighteen states provided criteria for being a cooperating teacher and five states provided criteria for college supervisors. Only two states provided for the evaluation of the cooperating teacher, and one state has standards for the performance evaluation of college supervisors.

Very little information is available regarding the costs of educational field programs. The limited information that does exist indicates that although programs are expanding with an increase of prestudent teaching experiences (Farris, Henniger, & Bischoff, 1991), the overall budgets for the program have decreased.

The existing literature on field experiences illustrates the problem of extreme diversity in standards, policies, and practices. Indeed, there appears to be a lack of a national perspective. There is a need for greater standardization across programs to ensure the quality of field experiences and a clear conceptualization of programs around a common knowledge base (Reyes & Isele, 1990).

Legal Aspects of Field Experiences

Morris and Curtis (1983) found the majority of states provide statutory authority for student teaching, and although statutes do differ in regard to specific issues, a review revealed a high level of commonality in the issues addressed. There have been very few lawsuits and court cases centered on student teaching. The most common causes of lawsuits are injury to a child by the student teacher, denial of entry to student teaching, negligence, and the grade given for student teaching. Most legal issues center around student teacher conduct in schools and SCDE policies governing student teaching (Johnson & Yates, 1982).

Although more and earlier field experiences are required, legal support systems relating to quality in field experiences are minimal (Morris & Curtis, 1983). Issues such as certification of cooperating teachers are more germane than tort issues to the interests of teacher education programs. Also SCDEs are required by law or by state standards to conduct student teaching experiences in teacher education programs. Yet, local education agencies do not have the same requirements.

LABORATORY EXPERIENCES

At one time in the history of teacher education, laboratory schools played a major role in the preparation of prospective teachers. Laboratory schools were developed on college campuses and were devoted to the preparation of future teachers as well as to the education of K–12 students. Students were able to observe teachers through one-way mirrors, observe demonstration lessons taught by university faculty, have access to the latest equipment and resources, and have the freedom to experiment with new educational ideas and strategies. During the late 1960s and early 1970s, the need for contact with "real" students in "real" classrooms and campus budgetary problems resulted in the elimination of the majority of these schools. In many respects, however, current professional development schools possess similar attributes.

Recently, universities have begun developing laboratory experiences and integrating them into their teacher education programs. These laboratory experiences are occasions during which students can practice specific instructional behaviors and skills in a controlled environment, such as a college teaching laboratory, and they are often designed to encourage prospective teachers to challenge their traditional beliefs about teaching and learning. Laboratory experiences are designed to support the methods and models espoused by the teacher education profession and to serve as a valuable link between methods courses and field experiences. These experiences may include microteaching, simulation and role playing, interactive computers, observing teacher demonstrations, and videotaped lessons.

Howey (1990) states that initial teacher preparation attempts to develop a disposition for intellectual discourse, logical analysis, formal critical thinking, and moral reasoning, and that the typical college classroom or K–12 classroom cannot accomplish this without major alterations. He believes that laboratory and clinical settings and experiences must be developed that facilitate this disposition in novice teachers. Howey envisions a teaching laboratory that permits small groups of prospective teachers to observe experienced teachers via one-way mirrors. This observation would be followed by a structured recall session or interview questions. This laboratory would also include a protocol library of many different teaching strategies illustrating propositional knowledge and its empirical and theoretical foundations, a laboratory for clinical observation and systematic analysis of classroom events, a microteaching laboratory, and interactive video stations.

Berliner (1985) also offers his vision of the ingredients of effective laboratory experiences in teacher education programs. These characteristics include computer simulations, videotape libraries of carefully chosen classroom interactions that students can analyze and code from a variety of perspectives, protocol materials, and microteaching opportunities. One will note that Berliner's recommendations for effective laboratory experiences are similar to Howey's.

Despite these recommendations, Howey and Zimpher (1989) report a paucity of well-conceived laboratory experiences. Their national survey of teacher education programs discovered that certain common conditions and practices seemed to exist in exemplary teacher education programs. These included a well-conceived laboratory component, as well as a theme that ran throughout the curriculum and linked a variety of courses, practices, and field experiences. They suggested, however, that expenditures for laboratory experiences cannot be justified until a better rationale is presented than currently exists.

Some teacher educators envision the concept of laboratory on a broader scale. For example, McNergney and Carrier (1981) advocate the classroom as a laboratory for teacher development. They realize that this requires the transformation of the contextual boundaries and histories of classrooms because traditional classrooms are not places for research, for improving teachers, or for outsiders to view instruction. Yet, Zeichner (1989) proposes including the community as a laboratory for teacher education programs. He believes that this notion is especially critical today because teachers are increasingly faced with educating children whose characteristics, cultural background, and values are different from their own. As a result, teacher education programs could do a better job of cultivating respect for human diversity and compassion for all children.

Much of the rationale for implementing laboratory experiences into teacher education programs must be found in research that supports laboratory experiences as promoting the development of effective teachers. Klinzing's (1990) summary

of the research conducted on teaching laboratories focuses on attempts to change personality characteristics, promote learner-supportive attitudes, improve abilities to improvise, and foster assertiveness through case studies, play, simulation, group encounters, and exercises in reacting to and interpreting educational situations. The research does not have clear findings regarding changes in attitudes, personality characteristics, and performances; however, students did report a favorable reception to laboratory experiences, stated that they learned a great deal, and were able to write satisfactory solutions to hypothetical critical incidents. It did appear that various laboratory experiences enhanced classroom skills in teacher indirectness, higher cognitive questioning and probing, management, lecturing, nonverbal communication, and counseling. Studies indicated that these programs were successful in attaining these skills and that they were maintained months after training.

The remainder of this section examines specific aspects of laboratory experience programs and the research that does or does not support these approaches.

Microteaching

Cruickshank (1988) defines microteaching as a brief teaching encounter in which teachers teach 5- to 20-minute lessons to a small group of pupils who are usually peers. The purpose of the microteaching lesson is to practice a specific teaching skill(s) until the teacher reaches an acceptable level of performance.

Although microteaching is popular in teacher education, the data to support its effectiveness are mixed. For example, Borg (1972) reported that questioning skills were significantly more evident following training and remained evident nearly 3 years later. Jensen and Young (1972) reported that students who completed microteaching presented more meaningful lessons and created better classroom climates during student teaching than those student teachers who did not experience microteaching. Yet, Copeland (1975, 1977b) and Copeland and Doyle (1973) reported that there were no significant differences between those students who had completed microteaching and those who had not.

This research seems to indicate that microteaching alone often will not produce the desired results. For example, Copeland (1977b) discovered that student teachers were more likely to utilize particular behaviors practiced in microteaching if their cooperating teachers also modeled the behavior. Also, Jerich (1989) reported that a preconference prior to microteaching contributed positively to the microteaching experience. A more thorough review of the research on microteaching can be found in the works of MacLeod (1987) and Cruickshank and Metcalf (1990).

Video Technology

Since the mid-1980s, the incorporation of video technology, with or without computer interactivity, into the teacher education curriculum has been greatly advocated, and to a lesser extent it has been incorporated into the mainstream teacher education curriculum. Robinson and West's (1989) characterization of the use of technology for educational purposes is that it has a relatively brief and unremarkable history. Although the cost of hardware and software is decreasing, it still poses limitations for many teacher education programs. As a result, Brooks and Kopp (1990) state that the current application of technology to teacher training is behind schedule, and beginning teachers cannot be expected to be creative and facile with technology unless they are exposed to it throughout their teacher education program.

One of the least expensive but useful uses of technology is the use of videotaped teaching demonstrations or models. Rowley and Hart (1993) assessed the effect of the use of a videotaped role play and videotaped expert teacher discussion in the thinking of preservice teachers. Their premise is that viewing videotaped representations of expert teacher thinking may serve to help beginning teachers move beyond propositional knowledge. They also assert that being exposed via video to expert teacher thinking may encourage beginning teachers to value more highly the need to resolve one's own teaching dilemmas through autonomous action or peer collaboration. The researchers discovered that viewing the videotapes resulted in preservice teachers demonstrating a more clinical approach to professional problem solving and that it seemed to aid in integrating expert teacher knowledge into the teacher education curriculum. Winitsky and Arends (1991) found that videotaped demonstrations were as effective as live ones, which is encouraging from a cost/benefit standpoint.

A more expensive but perhaps more valuable alternative to videotaped teacher demonstrations is the emerging use of interactive videodisk technology. The interactivity among student, videodisk, and computer allows the prospective teacher to view a critical event several times, view educational literature and research, intervene or propose a solution to the event without consequences to the pupils or themselves, have their response stored in the computer for future assessment by the college instructor, and/or view educational literature and research related to the event. This can all be done by pressing a computer key or touching the screen. The interactive videodisk concept permits students to "interact" with students and situations that may not be available to them in their field experience because of local demographics. Thus, for example, a prospective teacher at a rural campus can view classrooms and "interact" with students who are different from those in their locale. Rogers and Reiff (1989) state that computer-based interactive video simulations offer teacher education an alternative to traditional approaches by allowing a nonthreatening learning situation to be duplicated repeatedly with no variance of quality. The simulations provide prospective teachers with immediate feedback about their responses, and they encourage experimentation and risk taking, which might be suppressed by fear of failure in a live contact. In addition, the simulation or critical event is available at the student's convenience.

In 1990, Brooks and Kopp reviewed 72 studies concerning the use of technological enhancement of preservice teacher education. Only two studies reported on the use of interactive videodisk technology as a means of enhancing teacher preparation. Since 1990, several studies have been conducted on this topic and more teacher education programs are incorporating interactive videodisk technology into their programs.

McIntyre and Pape (1993) described the use of videodisk technology in the introduction to education course at Southern Illinois University at Carbondale. They discovered that students who had used the interactive videodisks component of the course were more descriptive in their analysis of critical classroom events and used more evidence to support their claims. At the conclusion of the course, students perceived that they were more reflective because of their interactive video experience. They stated that it gave them an opportunity to observe additional classroom teachers, grade levels, and situations that their peers in the traditional course did not have.

Goldman and Barron (1990) reported on a study that examined the use of interactive videodisk technology in a math methods course. Although students who had participated with the video examples and those who had studied without video illustrations performed equally well on test items, students found these videos to be valuable. They were more confident in presenting math lessons after having viewed and analyzed the video illustrations and more involved in the instruction when they had access to the information through the computer than when the class was conducted in a more traditional lecture format. The researchers also discovered that when video illustrations are used in the methods class to provide contexts for the topics studied and to demonstrate effective teaching techniques, students tend to incorporate these techniques into their own lessons.

Other studies examining the effectiveness of interactive video have described its use in skill analysis training in physical education (O'Sullivan, Stroot, Tannehill, & Chair, 1989) and in developing reflective clinical reasoning (Copeland, 1989). Copeland believes that clinical reasoning can be enhanced through interactive videodisk by providing valuable experiences to all students because certain situations occur during some field experiences but not during others. Reflection on these events can become more purposeful during these laboratory experiences because they can be viewed repeatedly by the student. In addition, the potential for disaster resulting from improper clinical behavior of novices during real field experience is reduced.

As technology becomes less expensive and provides additional opportunities to explore alternatives to the traditional approaches to teacher education, institutions will begin to incorporate more fully videotape simulations and interactive video into their programs. For example, programs at Cleveland State University, Indiana State University, Iowa State University, Luther College, Marywood College, Southern Illinois University at Carbondale, University of Minnesota at Duluth, University of Virginia, and Vanderbilt University, among others, have begun to integrate interactive video technology into their teacher education curriculum to varying degrees (McIntyre & Pape, 1993). Although there is not a plethora of research regarding this technology, there does appear to be a trend toward finding video technology useful in providing additional and richer "classroom" experiences and for enhancing prospective teachers' reflective thinking.

Case Studies

Another type of laboratory experience gaining in popularity and use throughout teacher education is the utilization of case studies. Case studies are provided to prospective teachers in a variety of formats ranging from written to video. The case method format provides the time, safety, and opportunity for the consideration of educational issues. Cases provide students of teaching with opportunities to begin to see the contextual specificity of teaching and learning and to understand that the practice of schooling is complex and problematic. Presenting classroom situations allows prospective teachers to consider the relevant factors, begin to draw together the different understandings developed through experience and formal preparation, assess political consequences of individual actions, and become aware of their preconceptions and misconceptions of teaching and learning (Harrington, 1990–1991; Kowalski, Weaver, & Henson, 1990; Richert, 1991). Chapter 31 of this handbook further addresses this topic.

Simulation

Cruickshank (1988) defines simulation as an instructional alternative whereby elements of real situations are presented to learners to provide them with awareness and with an opportunity to learn and practice responses. One of the difficulties in examining simulations is that there are many different approaches to and kinds of simulation, and that the purpose for the simulation varies depending on the program and its objectives. Cruickshank and Metcalf's chapter in the 1990 *Handbook of Research on Teacher Education* provides an excellent review of the research regarding the effects of simulation on improving teacher problem-solving ability.

Cruickshank and Metcalf report that much of the emphasis of the literature is on the development and description of the simulations rather than on their effectiveness. Briefly, however, they did discover that through simulations students can be reinforced to respond appropriately to classroom problems and to find the simulations to be timely and believable. In addition, students are perceived by their cooperating teachers as having fewer classroom problems (Cruickshank & Broadbent, 1968). Although these studies indicate a positive trend toward the effectiveness of simulations, additional research is needed to determine how simulations affect teacher development and the conditions necessary for success.

In summary, the utilization of laboratory experiences seem to be expanding in teacher education programs. In addition, available research appears to indicate a trend that many laboratory experiences are effective in improving skill acquisition and enhancing prospective teachers' ability to be reflective about the school context and about their preconceptions of teaching and learning. However, Lowriendee (1990) reported that there still does not appear to be any universal agreement as to how or when laboratory experiences should be incorporated into the curriculum. Thus, not only does it appear that additional research is required regarding the effectiveness of laboratory experiences, but also it seems that more discussion is required regarding the role of laboratory experiences in the teacher education curriculum.

MULTICULTURALISM AND DIVERSITY

Currently, the reality of schools in the United States is that the student population is becoming increasingly diverse while the teaching population remains homogeneous (Grant & Secada, 1990). In 1976, 24% of the total school-age population was nonwhite (Center for Education Statistics, 1987, p. 64); by the year 2000, experts predict this percentage will rise to 30% to 40% (Hodgkinson, 1985). Furthermore, the student population is increasingly poor and living in single-parent households. Yet, the teachers of these children remain now, and for the foreseeable future, white and female (Grant & Secada, 1990). These teachers will have to teach an increasingly diverse student population, a population "diverse in race, class, language, and sex-role socialization patterns" (Grant & Secada, 1990, p. 404).

Grant and Secada (1990), in their chapter in the first *Handbook of Research on Teacher Education,* investigated the research on diversity and teacher education. Their conclusions give focus to the issue of how field experiences help to prepare students to work in diverse environments. Surprisingly limited amounts of research have been completed on the important topic of preparing teachers to work with diverse populations; however, the authors reported that research has occurred in three key areas: teacher recruitment, preservice education of teachers, and in-service education of teachers. This discussion focuses on the second area of interest—preservice teacher education, specifically as it relates to field experiences. Recent research shows:

- Thirty percent to 40% of the student teachers showed a lack of empathy in regard to the effects of institutional racism and a lack of confidence in the ability of education to change the ways people think and act (Moultry, 1988).
- Although preservice programs focusing on multiculturalism did result in greater student awareness and understanding of multicultural concepts, there was little carryover to the use of these concepts in the classroom. When questioned, students reported that they did not use the concepts because of time constraints or because they were teaching in nonmulticultural teaching settings and did not see the need to use concepts for multicultural education (Grant & Koskela, 1986).
- Preservice teachers need to be encouraged to try the concepts and strategies they have learned in multicultural settings (e.g., use of a repertoire of teacher strategies and the importance of maintaining high expectations) and to critically think about the outcomes of their efforts. Without the opportunity to have direct contact with multicultural students and the opportunity for translation and interpretation of the results of this contact, programs will not be effective (Bennett, with Okinaka & Xiaoyang, 1988; Contreras, 1988; Wayson, 1988).

From these findings three conclusions can be drawn. First, preservice students do not enter teacher education programs with the skills, knowledge, and attitudes necessary to work successfully with a diverse population of students. Second, although students can be educated to have greater awareness and understanding of issues regarding multicultural education, they do not necessarily practice what they have learned. Third, preservice students need to be placed in schools where they have the opportunity to work with a diverse student body. Furthermore, they need to be encouraged and supported in their analysis of the decisions they and others make as teachers and the effects these decisions have on students.

Evaluation: How Student Teachers Learn to Teach and How They Are Assessed

It is charged that student teachers are not realistically evaluated during field experiences and that this relates to the question of why some fail during their first few years of teaching (Elliott & Mays, 1979). Concern about the competence of teacher candidates has resulted in increasing dissatisfaction with the state of teacher education. Suggested reforms have centered on three types: (1) increase the preparation in subject matter content knowledge, (2) increase field-based experiences, and (3) decrease hours in teaching methods and other pedagogical courses (Berliner, 1985). Interestingly, Berliner rejected the call for increased time committed to education courses. He reasoned that the evaluation of these experiences does not focus on aiding students in judging their work, but rather on imitation without reflection. During the mid-1980s the debate about the importance of subject matter courses as opposed to education coursework was a central issue in the literature. There was an outcry for adoption of accreditation standards and certification mandates requiring additional content preparation, in some cases at the expense of educational coursework. The authors of *A Nation at Risk* (National Commission on Excellence in Education, 1983) stated that teacher education programs included too many courses in the area of educational methods and not enough courses in content areas of subjects taught in public schools. This claim, never substantiated on empirical grounds, was continually reiterated by various groups and reports including the Holmes Group (1986), the Carnegie Forum on Education and the Economy (Carnegie Corporation, 1986), and other groups both within and external to education (Sikula, 1990).

A body of literature is growing around this issue and "the debate continues on ideological rather than empirical grounds" (Ferguson & Womack, 1993, p. 55). Investigation into the assessment of the importance and role of subject-matter coursework and education coursework on the preparation of successful teachers is an important area for current and future research. Darling-Hammond (1991), Ashton and Crocker (1987), and Evertson, Hawley, and Zlotnik (1985), in reviews of research, have found that teacher education coursework has a positive effect on teacher performance. Studies by Ball and McDiarmid (1990) support that knowledge of subject matter is important to teaching. Druva and Anderson's (1983) metaanalysis found both education and science courses were positively associated with successful teachers. Hawk, Coble, and Swanson (1985) provided additional support for the importance of content knowledge with their finding that mathematics teachers teaching outside their area of expertise were less successful. Veenman (1984), in a review of teacher education programs, found that those who emphasized subject matter training rather than education coursework were less effective at initial teacher preparation. Studies by Copley (1974), Denton and Lacina (1984), and Grossman (1990) comparing liberal arts majors to education graduates indicated that education majors had improved skills in the areas of classroom management, lesson introduction and summary, communication skills, pedagogical knowledge, and ability to meet the needs of students and to relate information in an interesting manner.

Yet, research provides little support for the notion that increasing the subject-area requirements for teachers beyond that typically required for certification increases the effectiveness of the teacher (Ashton & Crocker, 1987; Evertson et al., 1985).

Ferguson and Womack (1993) assessed, through a regression model, the extent education coursework, subject-matter coursework, and a test of subject knowledge (National Teacher Examination [NTE] Specialty Area Tests) predicted teaching performance of student teachers. They reported that grades from education courses are more powerful predictors of teaching effectiveness than grade point averages in liberal arts major or NTE specialty test scores. In addition, given the 2.5 grade point average as required by NCATE, no difference was found in the quality of instruction between students with lower and higher overall GPAs.

Ball (1990) adds clarity to this debate through her investigation of the subject-matter knowledge of preservice elementary and secondary mathematics teachers. Her data challenge common assumptions about evaluating content preparation of teacher candidates at the elementary or secondary level. Her research is outlined in some detail due to its important findings and its creative methodology; it is representative of emerging blends of quantitative and qualitative research techniques. To investigate this issue, Ball utilized questionnaires and interviews during which subjects were asked to solve problems and to explain how they might depict mathematical problems visually for students (e.g., represent 1¾ + ½ by pictures, models, stories, or real-world illustration). The first assumption her research challenges is that traditional mathematics content is not difficult. Throughout her interviews many college students had difficulty beyond simple use of rules and procedures. For example, they could remember to "invert and multiply" when using division with fractions, but they could not explain why this was being done. The second assumption her research challenges is that elementary and secondary mathematics classes provide teachers with much of what they need to know about mathematics. This assumption is implied by the fact that elementary education majors study very little mathematics as part of formal teacher preparation. Yet, the elementary and the secondary (mathematics majors) teacher candidates did not have "meaningful understanding or knowledge with which to figure out such understandings on the spot" (p. 463). The third assumption, that being a mathematics major (knowing mathematics) ensures the ability to teach mathematical understanding, is also questioned by this study. Ball states, "in mathematics . . . we find less difference in substantive understanding between elementary and secondary teacher education candidates than one might expect (or hope). Although the latter, because they are mathematics majors, had taken more mathematics, this did not seem to afford them substantial advantage in articulating and connecting underlying concepts, principles, and meanings" (p. 463). Ball goes on to explain that this was true for "good" mathematics students (majors) and for the mathematics students (majors) not planning to teach. In short, Ball found the preparation of mathematics teachers at the elementary and secondary levels to be inadequate; simply requiring a major in mathematics is not going to prepare teachers who can make sense of division of fractions, relate mathematical concepts to the real world, or explain concepts beyond a restatement of rules.

In summary, research seems to support that subject preparation is an important, although poorly understood, prerequisite for effective teaching. The issue perhaps centers on what Feiman-Nemser and Buchmann (1989) state simply as "teachers must know things worth teaching" (p. 366). This research also has major implications for the subject-matter preparation of teachers, the content and methodology utilized in methods courses, and the ways in which students are supported and evaluated during field experiences. Field experiences must be more than practice without reflection, rules without understanding.

Evaluation of Planning Activities: Preservice Students

Alexander et al. (1992), in a study of Australian preservice students' written reflections on lessons they had taught, found students had an orientation toward practicality. Their concerns were pragmatic, such as promotion of classroom discussion, questioning, and the intricacies of lesson planning. Schleuter (1991) found that music student teachers initially were most concerned with student enjoyment, but as they gained experience, student achievement became their primary goal. The importance of being able to relate to others was also shown to be an important variable in a study of student teachers in an English as a foreign language program in Israel (Kalekin-Fishman & Kornfeld, 1991). Results suggest that human relationships were the most important variable in determining the degree of success during student teaching. In a study of knowledge student teachers gain about students, Kagan and Tippins (1991) found that elementary teachers were intimately involved with students and were able to provide rich descriptions of students. Secondary student teachers, however, were judged to be more aloof and less attuned to students. Kagan and Tippins (1992) found that when elementary and secondary student teachers were given various linear lesson plan formats, they differed as to which aspects were most helpful. Secondary students used planning to help them remember material or facts. Their plans became more detailed and fact oriented as the semester progressed. Elementary students used plans to organize thoughts and material but never referred to the written plans while teaching. As the semester progressed, their plans became less detailed and served more as a supplement to teacher guides. Although planning is an important part of student teachers' lives, Ellwein, Graue, and Comfort (1990), in a study of student teachers' reflections on success and failure, found seven elements formed a multidimensional concept of student teachers' evaluation of their teaching. Interviews of student teachers revealed that in successful lessons and in those described as failures the following elements were often mentioned: student characteristics, implementation, planning, lesson uniqueness, management, student teacher characteristics, and lesson content. The reactions of students to lessons, lesson implementation, and the uniqueness of the lesson were all prominent in interns' descriptions. Student teachers appeared to judge successful lessons based on the level of "student interest, participation, and, to a lesser extent, learning" (p. 5). Although generally all elements were discussed by both elementary and secondary student teachers, there was some difference in frequency with which the elements were discussed. For example,

elementary teachers were more likely to mention planning as the cause of unsuccessful lessons, whereas secondary teachers often characterized problems related to their lesson implementation as reasons for failure. Elementary teachers were also more likely to mention lesson implementation and uniqueness of the lesson as elements of success.

Sparks-Langer, Simmons, Pasch, Colton, and Starko (1990) studied the ability of teacher education students to reflect on their performance. This study took place during a prestudent "block" that promoted reflection on issues of curriculum and methodology through linked campus classes and a field experience. Review of students' reflections indicated that students were able to think about successful and less successful lessons and describe what they thought contributed to the success or lack of success of lessons. In general, "students with lower course achievement . . . [had] more difficulty applying the course concepts and principles than . . . higher-achieving students" (p. 28). Higher achieving students (90% of all students) were able to analyze events that took place in their classrooms using pedagogical principles and contextual factors such as student characteristics, subject matter, or community factors. For example, student functioning at this level might relate a technique such as cooperative learning to the fact that it provides for "repeated positive experiences with children from different backgrounds" (p. 27).

In a related study, Rodreguez (1993) found that "student teachers entered teacher education programs with a revealing awareness of their beliefs, not only about teaching and learning but also about the possible barriers that may interfere in their professional growth" (p. 217). Students appreciated the usefulness of their university coursework but still wished that there were more attempts made to introduce content and procedures of a practical nature (i.e., discussion of videotaped school scenarios in which a teacher is working through a problem, such as classroom management, or using various instructional techniques to teach complex concepts to both receptive and unreceptive students).

In a study of two student teachers' well-remembered events, Carter and Gonzalez (1993) found a need for student teachers to have opportunities to relate theory to practice. The successful student teacher recalled events that point to orientation being focused on curriculum and the "process of enacting the curriculum with students." In particular, this student teacher appeared to recognize that enacting a curriculum in a classroom situation depended largely on students' interests and cooperation and that one's own actions were connected to how students reacted to content. The unsuccessful teacher, however, remembered her mistakes and feelings of being inadequate. Rather than focusing on the curricular or instructional implications of teaching, this student teacher focused on eliciting sympathy by mentioning inexperience and by using humor in relation to errors or problems perceived and made. In addition, this student teacher did not reflect on teaching but rather focused on gaining more experience and copying the behaviors of the cooperating teacher, but not on understanding how to merge what was observed into functional instructional activities. Carter and Gonzalez suggest that when using cases or videotape, university professors need to ensure that students have descriptions of teaching/learning and teachers' reflections about the same events. Moreover, cooperating teachers need to share their thoughts about lessons with students as a way for them to gain understanding of the decision-making process teachers use.

Reflection and Field Experiences

As stated earlier in this chapter, the goal of preparing reflective teachers has been adopted by many teacher education programs during the past decade. In this regard, Zeichner (1980) argued that teacher educators must have a better understanding of what actually occurred during the field experience component, from early field experience through student teaching, if there is going to be effective reform in teacher education. Existing studies suggest that students are engaged in a very limited and narrow range of classroom activities (Killian & McIntyre, 1986; Tabachnick, Popkewitz, & Zeichner, 1979–1980). As Howey (1986) charged

Many of the experiences that preservice students have in schools lie more in the direction of largely unchallenged pedestrian activities than in well-conceived activities where prospective teachers have opportunities to inquire, to experiment, and to reflect on the subtleties and complexities of the classroom including the moral as well as technical dimensions of teaching (p. 174).

John Dewey (1904) believed that too much emphasis on practice, without attention to the effects of practice on student learning, was nonproductive. Zeichner (1980, 1982) has supported this premise with a call for *reflective teaching,* a term used to refer to the analysis needed to bring understanding to the complex nature of classrooms. The central issue is how to improve evaluation during practicum experiences to ensure that students gain insights that will enable them to analyze their teaching and develop professionally now and in the future. In short, the goal is the development of lifelong, self-directed learners.

In response to the numerous criticisms of the practice and evaluation of field experience, analysis is needed of the evaluation of students' performance and its relationship to content learned throughout the teacher education curriculum and subsequent success as teachers. The evaluation of students is made more difficult by a number of factors, not the least of which is that evaluators seem to have personalized the act of evaluation (Tom, 1974). Although agreement on the criteria by which students should be judged during field experience exists, the relative importance of each criterion to successful teaching varies markedly from evaluator to evaluator. For example, in a study of directors of field experiences, there was serious disagreement as to whether classroom management was the most or least important variable in the evaluation of students (McIntyre & Norris, 1980).

A series of studies examined the role of university supervisors (Zeichner & Liston, 1987; Zeichner, Liston, Mahlios, & Gomez, 1988; Zeichner & Tabachnick, 1982) and aided in understanding how university supervisors conference with students. Zeichner and Tabachnick (1982) analyzed the belief system of a group of university supervisors and found that clinical supervision was interpreted in different ways and took on different meanings as it was filtered through the frame of reference each supervisor employed. Because the teacher education program had an orientation toward reflective teaching, this was expected to exert pressures on supervisors to raise questions (e.g., Why do you do certain practices in the classroom?) and to encourage student teachers to evaluate classroom practices in terms of moral as well as technical criteria. For example, students are encouraged to question classroom management activities (technical criteria), not only relative to whether they work in the short run, but also whether they are moral (e.g., using heavy sarcasm as a way to control children). In another study, Zeichner and Liston (1987) analyzed the form and substance of supervisory discourse in an "inquiry oriented" teacher education program. They found that roughly 20% of the discourse analyzed represented attention to reflective forms of discourse. In addition, student teacher conceptual level appeared to be linked to the level of reflective discourse. Student teachers functioning at high conceptual levels seem to promote higher levels of reflective discourse during post-conferences. The third study in this series (Zeichner et al., 1988) compared the structure and essence of conferences between student teachers and university supervisors in teacher education programs with two different philosophical approaches. One program had a "tradition-craft" orientation, the other had an "inquiry" approach. This research was an attempt to determine if differences in the goals of these two programs affected the form and substance of supervisory conferences. The researchers found a great deal of similarity in the supervisory discourse, regardless of program orientation. They suggest that the types of discourse they would like to see should focus on more complex discussions of how to improve schooling and the moral implications of educating children.

Given these data, the criticism that clinical faculty are unable to evaluate teaching takes on new meaning. The evaluations of students in practicum experiences are based on a limited knowledge base not unlike that which guides the evaluation of teaching in general. The criteria used to evaluate students are often based on some measure of the term *good teaching,* a term subject to various definitions and philosophical perspectives. For example, from an empirical perspective, good teaching could be perceived as the satisfactory delivery of a lesson with a direct instructional approach; from a philosophical perspective, good teaching could be helping students to internalize the concept of self-directed learning; and from an interpersonal relations perspective, good teaching could be whether the teacher is supportive and has a positive rapport with students (Griffin, 1986). This lack of a clear definition of good teaching has made the task of evaluation of field experience performance difficult for clinical faculty.

Evaluation: Two Paradigms for Arriving at Truth

An issue of major importance in any discussion of field experiences is how should teaching experience be evaluated or judged? Howey and Zimpher (1989) make the point that regardless of the introspection that many teacher education programs give to the issue of what is the nature or central essence of teaching and their teacher education programs' knowledge base,

far too great a reliance remains on behavioral psychology and skill and practice orientation to teaching others. "Student teaching" still is embedded in notions of assessing performance through periodic evaluative snapshots framed by debatable criteria of "teaching effectiveness." The conception of teaching as primarily cognitive and problem-oriented in a highly complex environment could receive more attention. (p. 217)

Past analysis of the field experience evaluation process reveals that it draws no clear distinction between outstanding and ineffective teaching and that there is a lack of distinction between degrees of teaching effectiveness resulting from a lack of agreement about the skills that comprise good teaching (Diamonti, 1977; Vittetoe, 1972). There is also considerable confusion as to whether the university supervisors exercise authority regarding evaluation or if they simply accept the evaluation of cooperating teachers as reported by Barrows (1979). Killian and McIntyre (1986), McIntyre and Killian (1986), and Zimpher et al. (1980) found that cooperating teachers are not especially critical or evaluative. Whereas cooperating teachers are often called upon to provide written evaluations of student teachers, they may not provide evaluations as an ongoing part of the student teaching experience, or as Howey and Zimpher (1989) indicate, they provide snapshots when called upon to do so.

Howey and Zimpher (1989) suggest that there is a contrast between "the demonstration of specific competencies" orientation and a view of professional competence embedded in practical reasoning. Koff (1986) explains this view of teaching as assuming that

Teachers can think and that in fact they do so while they are teaching. The actions these teachers take result from their practical arguments. A practical argument consists of a series of premises. It includes a value/belief premise (e.g., it is good/better to . . .), a set of empirical premises (e.g., if I do this, then x will result), and a situational/perceptive premise (e.g., this is the appropriate time/place to . . .), and culminates in action. Teachers can articulate these arguments. Specifically a competent teacher is one who can articulate the practical arguments on which his/her actions are based. (p. 4)

This concept of a professional teacher is not presently embedded in the culture of teacher education in respect to evaluation of student teachers; however, there are indications that the building blocks for this type of evaluation are becoming part of the culture of teacher education. These building blocks include the themes of reflection, as evidenced through journal writing and portfolio development.

Guba (1981, p. 76) refers to two discernible paradigms "for arriving at truth," each having had an impact on clinical evaluation (Zimpher & Ashburn, 1985). These paradigms or conceptual frameworks form two separate views of the standards, rules, and techniques of analyses for conducting research; therefore, two communities of researchers analyze teaching from different world views.

These paradigms not only enhance the knowledge base that guides practice but also the process or method by which supervisors analyze teaching. The concepts and techniques used by researchers to gain knowledge about teaching are used by supervisors to structure their interactions with students in clinical settings. Those who favor the empirical paradigm are apt to base their feedback on concepts related to research on teacher effectiveness (i.e., academic engagement, wait time,

structuring behavior, cooperative learning). Those with a more phenomenological or naturalistic perspective are apt to take a more holistic approach consistent with sociological groundings. Central to this perspective is the belief that supervision of teaching calls for an inquiry-oriented approach that "fosters a critical orientation on the part of student teachers toward both their teaching and the contexts that surround it" (Zeichner & Tabachnick, 1982, p. 41).

A blend of these approaches might produce supervisors and teachers who can use the strengths of both approaches to aid their teaching and to produce educators who could utilize the knowledge base or methodology of either paradigm to gain insight for supervisory feedback or self-analyses of teaching. Regarding evaluation, Patton (1980) stated, "there are two ways in which methodological mixes are achieved . . . in the study of the same phenomena or programs . . . . The first is through triangulation of data, investigator, theory, or methodology. . . ." The second "is to borrow and combine parts from pure methodological strategies, thus creating mixed methodological strategies" (pp. 110–111).

What strategies might a teacher or supervisor utilize in an attempt to draw from the strengths of such a model? They might utilize the results of empirical research (e.g., the results of positive time on task) as critical variables that may affect student performance (in much the same way Guba and Lincoln [1985] propose some prior investigation to aid in the development of questions for formal study). The open nature of phenomenological investigation calls for the collection of data on the studied topic from a number of sources. Thus, the supervisor would not rely solely on his or her own interpretation of a student's off-task behavior but might ask questions of the two key participants—the student teacher and the pupil who appears to be off task. There are, of course, many occasions in which the supervisor is free to move around the room during a lesson (i.e., during seatwork or small-group activities) and to question participants. If the constraints of classrooms should limit the ability to question participants immediately, videotape equipment could ensure the viewing of critical incidents. The importance of the context in which off-task behavior occurs could then be studied in relation to the student teachers' and the pupils' impressions of the event. This approach might give insight to the field-experience students and encourage a willingness to investigate students' perceptions of their behavior within the related contexts of curriculum, learning environment, motivational level, and home environment. Through analysis and reflection, a more realistic approach can be devised to deal with the problem of off-task behavior, one that is not viewed in isolation. In this way empiricism serves as a resource for the promotion of reflection about teaching; the former focusing attention, the latter providing a process for intervention. Patton (1980), in his review of evaluation design, might refer to this as using data from experimental design (use of quantitative data on off-task behavior of child and achievement), qualitative measurement observation, interviews of student teachers and pupils, and content analysis (of the patterns reported and observed).

This suggestion will not alleviate all problems associated with the evaluation of field experience. Reliability of evaluations provided by clinical faculty and cooperating teachers will still be of concern to those worried about the "subjective" nature of high inference data (Chiarelott, Davidman, & Muse, 1980); however, there seems to be a difference between the types of information presented in a low-inference form and the complexity of the classroom environment. Perhaps information on student teachers' ability to successfully recognize student off-task behaviors in a low-inference format would be cataloged during early field experiences. A developmental approach could be implemented in which low-inference measures are collected to ensure that students have the ability to recognize important variables. Intervention on the part of advanced field experience students requires more in-depth practice and experience with complex variables. This would entail feedback from trained personnel on performance and consequences for student motivation and learning.

CONCLUSION

The goal of this chapter is to analyze the research on field experience and to use this analysis to suggest areas for improvement. Research on field experience has not been conducted in a systematic fashion. Much of this problem is the result of a lack of a well-conceived theoretical base for field experience.

An examination of research on field experience brings forth certain factors that may help in this analysis. First, the realization that increased practice without analysis and reflection does not lead to professional growth. Research on the role of cooperating teachers and supervisors has reported some influence on student teachers' attitudes, but the larger question of their behaviors and how they might be shaped are largely unknown. Even such universally accepted notions as placing students with "good" role models have not been shown to be reflected in improved student evaluations. Perhaps a more open contextual approach is needed in research and evaluation. How field experiences are evaluated is of critical importance. Teacher educators must begin to utilize methodologies that allow them to understand the complex world of teaching and to present this world to field-experience students so that they may learn to better analyze the teaching-learning process.

The secondary purpose of this chapter is to examine any new trends or changes that have occurred in field and laboratory experiences since Guyton and McIntyre's 1990 chapter "Student Teaching and School Experiences." One obvious trend is the movement toward teacher education programs that are unified by a theme or model and an accompanying set of goals. This is an important trend for teacher education in general and field experiences specifically because the earlier chapter bemoaned the lack of a theoretical framework for both. The emergence of a theoretical framework results from an identifiable knowledge base in teacher education and provides the unifying force within the curriculum, linking campus courses and campus work and fieldwork. Although more needs to be accomplished in this area, this trend should strengthen the development and delivery of field experiences.

A second trend is the continuing application of qualitative methods to research and evaluation of field experiences. The data emanating from these studies have allowed teacher educators to have a richer understanding of some of the attitudes and behaviors of those involved in early field experiences and student teaching. The data also allow teacher educators to capture and analyze variables of students who engage in laboratory experiences. In 1990, Guyton and McIntyre referred to this research as the "new paradigm." Since that reference, it appears that this new approach has become more ingrained into the research mileu of field experiences.

Third, laboratory experiences and the utilization of technology appear to have become more integrated into teacher education programs as a supplement to field experiences. The use of microteaching continues to increase in many programs. In addition, interactive videodisk programs are allowing students to "interact" with teachers practicing a variety of teaching strategies not being implemented in their own field-experience context and/or with students of cultural, ethnic, or socioeconomic backgrounds different from those in their experience. Given the expense involved, it will be interesting to note the progress during the next decade of this aspect of teacher education.

Finally, there have been additional efforts to modify the field experience context during the past decade. Whether it be professional development schools or cohort groups, several teacher education programs are making an attempt to provide a different type of experience for their field-experience students. Whether this trend becomes a major force in education will depend on the commitment of teacher educators to change and their willingness to transcend the traditional field experience structure and format.

In closing, there appear to have been programmatic changes in field and laboratory experiences since Guyton and McIntyre's 1990 chapter. Professional judgment says that these transformations will improve teacher education; however, research efforts in this area still fall short of providing the profession with answers about what works best in field and laboratory experiences. Teacher educators continue to add to the length of field experiences without knowing if more is better, continue to modify programs without knowing if one type of program produces more effective teachers than others, and continue to modify the context of field and laboratory experiences without knowing if one method is more effective than another. Briefly, teacher educators need to continue to improve their research methods and the questions they ask to validate what they do in field and laboratory experiences.

References

Alexander, D., Muir, D., & Chant, D. (1992). Interrogating stories: How teachers think they learned to teach. *Teaching and Teacher Education, 8*(1), 59–68.

Alkove, L., & McCarty, B. (1992). Plain talk: Recognizing positivism and constructivism in practice. *Action in Teacher Education, 14*(2), 16–22.

Andrew, M. (1990). Differences between graduates of 4-year and 5-year teacher preparation programs. *Journal of Teacher Education, 41*(1), 45–51.

Applegate, J. (1985). Early field experiences: Recurring dilemmas. *Journal of Teacher Education, 36*(2), 60–64.

Applegate, J. (1986). Undergraduate students' perceptions of field experiences: Toward a framework of study. In J. Raths & L. Katz (Eds.), *Advances in teacher education* (Vol. 2, pp. 22–37). Norwood, NJ: Ablex.

Armaline, W., & Hoover, R. (1989). Field experiences as a vehicle for transformation: Ideology, education, and reflective process. *Journal of Teacher Education, 40*(2), 42–48.

Armstrong, D. (1989–1990). Early field experiences: Some key questions. *The Teacher Educator, 25*(3), 2–7.

Ashton, P., & Crocker, L. (1987). Systematic study of planned variations: The essential focus of teacher education reform. *Journal of Teacher Education, 38*(3), 2–8.

Association of Teacher Educators (ATE). (1986). *Guidelines for professional experiences in teacher education*. Reston, VA: Author.

Ayers, M. (1989). Headaches: On teaching and teacher education. *Action in Teacher Education, 11*(2), 1–7.

Ball, D. L. (1990). The mathematical understandings that prospective teachers bring to teacher education. *Elementary School Journal, 90*(4), 449–466.

Ball, D. L., & McDiarmid, G. L. (1990). The subject-matter preparation of teachers. In W. R. Houston (Ed.), *Handbook of research on teacher education* (pp. 437–449). New York: Macmillan.

Barrows, L. (1979, April). *Power relationships in the student teaching triad.* Paper presented at the annual meeting of the American Educational Research Association, San Francisco.

Becher, R., & Ade, W. (1982). The relationship of field placement characteristics and students potential field performance abilities to clinical experience performance rating. *Journal of Teacher Education, 33*(2), 24–30.

Bennett, C., with Okinaka, A., & Xiao-yang, W. (1988, April). *The effects of a multicultural education course on preservice teachers' attitudes, knowledge, and behavior.* Paper presented at the annual meeting of the American Educational Research Association, New Orleans.

Bennett, R., Ishler, M., & O'Loughlin, M. (1992). Effective collaboration in teacher education. *Action in Teacher Education, 14*(1), 52–56.

Bennie, W. (1964). Campus supervision of student teachers: A closer look. *Teachers College Journal, 36*(3), 131–133.

Berliner, D. (1985). Laboratory settings and the study of teacher education. *Journal of Teacher Education, 36*(6), 2–8.

Black, A., & Ammon, P. (1992). A developmental-constructivist approach to teacher education. *Journal of Teacher Education, 43*(5), 323–335.

Borg, W. (1972). The minicourse as a vehicle for changing teacher behavior: A three year follow-up. *Journal of Educational Psychology, 63*(6), 17–20.

Britzman, D. (1991). *Practice makes practice*. Albany: State University of New York Press.

Brooks, D., & Kopp, T. (1990). Technology and teacher education. In W. R. Houston (Ed.), *Handbook of research on teacher education* (pp. 498–513). New York: Macmillan.

Bryant, B. (1982, May). *Shaping teacher expectations for minority girls: A teacher training module*. Paper presented to Women's Educational Equity Act Program, Washington, DC.

Bullough, R. (1989). Teacher education and teacher reflectivity. *Journal of Teacher Education, 40*(2), 15–21.

Bullough, R. (1991). Exploring personal teaching metaphors in preservice teacher education. *Journal of Teacher Education, 42*(1), 43–51.

Bullough, R., & Gitlin, A. (1991). Educative communities and the development of the reflective practitioner. In R. Tabachnick & K. Zeichner (Eds.), *Issues and practices in inquiry-oriented teacher education* (pp. 33–55). London: Falmer Press.

Calderhead, J. (1987, April). *Cognition and metacognition in teachers' professional development*. Paper presented at the annual meeting of the American Educational Research Association, Washington, DC.

Carnegie Corporation of New York. (1986). *A nation prepared: Teachers for the 21st century*. New York: Carnegie Corporation of New York. (ERIC Document Reproduction Service No. ED 268 120)

Carter, K., & Gonzalez, L. (1993). Beginning teachers' knowledge of classroom events. *Journal of Teacher Education, 44*(3), 223–232.

Casey, B. M., & Howson, P. (1993). Educating preservice students based on a problem-centered approach to teaching. *Journal of Teacher Education, 44*(5), 361–369.

Castillo, J. B. (1971). *The role expectations of cooperating teachers as viewed by student teachers, college supervisors, and cooperating teachers*. Unpublished doctoral dissertation, University of Rochester.

Center for Education Statistics. (1987). *The conditions of education*. Washington, DC: U.S. Government Printing Office.

Chiarelott, L., Davidman, L., & Muse, C. (1980). Evaluating pre-service teacher candidates. *Clearing House. 53*(6), 295–299.

Cinnamond, J., & Zimpher, N. (1990). Reflectivity as a function of community. In R. Clift, W. R. Houston, & M. Pugach (Eds.), *Encouraging reflective practice in education: An analysis of issues and programs* (pp. 57–72). New York: Teachers College Press.

Cochran-Smith, M. (1991). Reinventing student teaching. *Journal of Teacher Education, 42*(2), 104–118.

Conant, J. (1963). *The education of American teachers*. New York: McGraw-Hill.

Contreras, A. R. (1988, April). *Multicultural attitudes and knowledge of education students at Indiana University*. Paper presented at annual meeting of the American Educational Research Association, New Orleans.

Copas, E. M. (1984). Critical requirements for cooperating teachers. *Journal of Teacher Education, 35*(6), 49–54.

Copeland, W. (1975). The relationship between microteaching and student teacher classroom performance. *Journal of Educational Research, 68*(8), 289–293.

Copeland, W. (1977a, April). *The nature of the relationship between cooperating teacher behavior and student teacher classroom performance*. Paper presented at the annual meeting of the American Educational Research Association, New York.

Copeland, W. (1977b). Some factors related to student teacher classroom performance following microteaching training. *American Educational Research Journal, 14*(1), 147–157.

Copeland, W. (1989). Technology-mediated laboratory experiences and the development of clinical reasoning in novice teachers. *Journal of Teacher Education, 40*(4), 10–18.

Copeland, W., & Doyle, W. (1973). Laboratory skill training and student teacher classroom performance. *Journal of Experimental Education, 42*(1), 16–21.

Copley, P. O. (1974). *A study of the effect of professional education courses on beginning teachers*. Springfield: Southeast Missouri State University. (ERIC Document Reproduction Service No. ED 098 147)

Corrigan, D., & Griswold, K. (1963). Attitude changes of student teachers. *Journal of Educational Research, 57*(2), 93–95.

Cruickshank, D. (1988). The uses of simulations in teacher preparation: Past present and future. *Simulations and Games, 19*(2), 133–156.

Cruickshank, D., & Armaline, W. (1986). Field experiences in teacher education: Considerations and recommendations. *Journal of Teacher Education, 37*(3), 34–40.

Cruickshank, D., & Broadbent, F. (1968). *The simulation and analysis of problems of beginning teachers* (Final report, Project No. 5-0798). Washington, DC: U.S. Department of Health, Education, and Welfare.

Cruickshank, D., & Metcalf, K. (1990). Training within teacher preparation. In W. R. Houston (Ed.), *Handbook of research on teacher education* (pp. 469–497). New York: Macmillan.

Darling-Hammond, L. (1991). Are our teachers ready to teach? *Newsletter of the National Council for Accreditation of Teacher Education, 1,* 6–7, 10.

Denton, J. J., & Lacina, L. J. (1984). Quantity of professional education coursework linked with process measures of education. *Teacher Education and Practice, 1*(1), 39–46.

Dewey, J. (1904). The relation of theory to practice in education. In National Society for the Study of Education (Ed.), *The relation of theory to practice in the education of teachers. Third yearbook. Part I*. Bloomington, IL: Public School Publishing Co.

Diamonti, M. (1977). Student teacher supervision. *Educational Forum, 41*(4), 477–486.

Dispoto, R. (1980). Affective changes associated with student teaching. *College Student Journal, 14*(2), 190–194.

Druva, C., & Anderson, R. D. (1983). Science teacher characteristics by teacher behavior and student outcome: A meta-analysis of research. *Journal of Research in Science Teaching, 20*(5), 467–479.

Dunham, D. (1958). Field attitudes of student teachers, college supervisors, and student teachers toward youth (Doctoral dissertation, Indiana University). *Dissertation Abstracts International, 19,* 1297.

Eby, J. (1992). *Reflective planning, teaching, and evaluation for the elementary school*. New York: Merrill.

Elliott, P. G., & Mays, R. E. (1979). *Early field experiences in teacher education* (Fastback 125). Bloomington, IN: Phi Delta Kappa Foundation.

Ellwein, M. C., Graue, M. E., & Comfort, R. E. (1990). Talking about instruction: Student teachers' reflections on success and failure in the classroom. *Journal of Teacher Education, 41*(4), 3–14.

Evertson, C. M., Hawley, W. D., & Zlotnik, M. (1985). Making a difference in educational quality through teacher education. *Journal of Teacher Education, 36*(3), 2–10.

Farber, P., Wilson, P., & Holm, G. (1989). From innocence to inquiry: A social reproduction framework. *Journal of Teacher Education, 40*(1), 45–50.

Farris, P., Henniger, M., & Bischoff, J. (1991). After the wave of reform, the role of early field experiences in elementary teacher education. *Action in Teacher Education, 13*(2), 20–24.

Feiman-Nemser, S. (1983). Learning to teach. In L. Shulman & G. Sykes (Eds.), *Handbook of teaching and policy* (pp. 150–170). New York: Longman.

Feiman-Nemser, S., & Buchmann, M. (1986). Pitfalls of experience in teacher education. In J. Raths & L. Katz (Eds.), *Advances in teacher education* (Vol. 2, pp. 61–73). Norwood, NJ: Ablex Publishing.

Feiman-Nemser, S., & Buchmann, M. (1989). Describing teacher education: A framework and illustrative findings from a longitudinal study of six students. *The Elementary School Journal, 89*(3), 365–377.

Ferguson, P., & Womack, S. T. (1993). The impact of subject matter and education coursework on teaching performance. *Journal of Teacher Education, 44*(1), 55–63.

Friebus, R. J. (1977). Agents of socialization involved in student teaching. *Journal of Educational Research, 70*(5), 263–268.

Fullan, M. (1985). Integrating theory and practice. In D. Hopkins & K. Reid (Eds.), *Rethinking teacher education* (pp. 195–211). London: Croom Helm.

Garibaldi, A. (1992). Preparing teachers. In M. Dilworth (Ed.), *Diversity in teacher education* (pp. 23–39). San Francisco: Jossey-Bass.

Gettone, V. G. (1980). Role conflict of student teachers. *College Student Journal, 14*(1), 92–100.

Goldman, E., & Barron, L. (1990). Using hypermedia to improve the preparation of elementary teachers. *Journal of Teacher Education, 41*(1), 21–31.

Goodlad, J. (1990). *Teachers for our nation's schools*. San Francisco: Jossey-Bass.

Goodlad, J., Soder, R., & Sirotnik, K. (1990). *Places where teachers are taught*. San Francisco: Jossey-Bass.

Grant, C., & Koskela, R. (1986). Education that is multicultural and the relationship between preservice and campus learning and field experiences. *Journal of Educational Research, 79*(4), 197–203.

Grant, C. A., & Secada, W. G. (1990). Preparing teachers for diversity. In W. R. Houston (Ed.), *Handbook of research on teacher education* (pp. 403–422). New York: Macmillan.

Griffin, G. (1986). Thinking about teaching. In K. Zumwalt (Ed.), *Improving teaching. 1986 ASCD Yearbook* (pp. 101–113). Alexandria, VA: Association for Supervision and Curriculum Development.

Griffin, G., Barnes, S., Hughes, R., O'Neal, S., Defino, M., Edwards, S., & Hukill, H. (1983). *Clinical preservice teacher education: Final report of a descriptive study*. Austin: Research in Teacher Education Program, Research and Development Center for Teacher Education, University of Texas at Austin. (ERIC Document Reproduction Service No. ED 240 101)

Grimmett, P. P., & Ratzlaff, H. C. (1986). Expectations for the cooperating teacher role. *Journal of Teacher Education, 37*(6), 41–50.

Grossman, P. (1990). *The making of a teacher: Teacher knowledge and teacher education*. New York: Teachers College Press.

Guba, E. G. (1981). Criteria for assessing the trustworthiness of naturalistic inquiries. *Educational Communication and Technology Journal, 29*(2), 75–91.

Guba, E. G., & Lincoln, Y. (1985). *Naturalistic inquiry*. San Francisco: Jossey-Bass.

Guyton, E. (1989). Guidelines for developing educational programs for cooperating teachers. *Action in Teacher Education, 11*(3), 54–58.

Guyton, E., & McIntyre, D. J. (1990). Student teaching and school experiences. In W. R. Houston (Ed.), *Handbook of research on teacher education* (pp. 514–534). New York: Macmillan.

Guyton, E., Paille, E., & Rainer, J. (1993). Collaborative field-based urban teacher education program. *Action in Teacher Education, 15*(3), 7–11.

Harrington, H. (1990–1991). The case as method. *Action in Teacher Education, 12*(4), 1–6.

Hauwiller, J., Abel, F., Ausel, D., & Sparapani, E. (1988–1989). Enhancing the effectiveness of cooperating teachers. *Action in Teacher Education, 10*(4), 42–46.

Hawk, P., Coble, C., & Swanson, M. (1985). Certification: It does matter. *Journal of Teacher Education, 36*(3), 13–15.

Henry, M. (1989). Change in teacher education: Focus on field experiences. In J. Braun (Ed.), *Reforming teacher education: Issues and new directions* (pp. 69–95). New York: Garland Press.

Hodgkinson, H. L. (1985). *All one system: Demographics of education—Kindergarten through graduate school*. Washington, DC: Institute for Educational Leadership.

The Holmes Group. (1986). *Tomorrow's teachers: A report of the Holmes Group*. East Lansing, MI: Author.

Houston, W. R. (1990). *The handbook of research on teacher education*. New York: Macmillan.

Howey, K. (1986). The next generation of teacher preparation programs. In T. Lasley (Ed.), *The dynamics of change in teacher education* (pp. 161–185). Washington, DC: American Association of Colleges for Teacher Education.

Howey, K. (1990). Changes in teacher education: Needed leadership and new networks. *Journal of Teacher Education, 41*(1), 3–9.

Howey, K., & Zimpher, N. (1989). *Profiles of preservice teacher education*. Albany: State University of New York Press.

Hoy, W., & Rees, R. (1977). The bureaucratic socialization of teachers. *Journal of Teacher Education, 28*(1), 23–26.

Hudson, L., Bergin, D., & Chayst, C. (1993). *Teacher Education Quarterly, 20*(3), 5–17.

Iannacone, L. (1963). Student teaching: A transitional stage in the making of a teacher. *Theory into Practice, 12*(2), 73–80.

Jensen, L., & Young, J. (1972). Effect of televised simulated instruction on subsequent teaching. *Journal of Educational Psychology, 63*(4), 368–373.

Jerich, K. (1989). Using a clinical supervision model for microteaching experiences. *Action in Teacher Education, 11*(3), 24–32.

Johnson, J. (1969). Change in student teacher dogmatism. *Journal of Educational Research, 62*(5), 224–226.

Johnson, J., & Yates, J. (1982). *A national survey of student teaching programs.* DeKalb: Northern Illinois University. (ERIC Document Reproduction Service No. ED 232 963)

Joyce, B., Showers, B., & Rolheiser-Bennett, C. (1987). Staff development and student learning: A synthesis of research on models of teaching. *Educational Leadership, 45*(2), 11–23.

Joyce, B., & Weil, M. (1986). *Models of teaching* (3rd ed.). Englewood Cliffs, NJ: Prentice Hall.

Kagan, D. M. (1990). Teachers' workplace meets the professors of teaching: A chance encounter at 30,000 feet. *Journal of Teacher Education, 41*(4), 46–53.

Kagan, D. M., & Tippins, D. J. (1991). Helping student teachers attend to student cues. *Elementary School Journal, 91*(4), 343–356.

Kagan, D. M., & Tippins, D. J. (1992). The evolution of functional lesson plans among twelve elementary and secondary student teachers. *Elementary School Journal, 92*(4), 477–489.

Kalekin-Fishman, D., & Kornfeld, G. (1991). Constructing roles: Co-operating teachers and student teachers in TEFL: An Israeli study. *Journal of Education for Teaching, 17*(2), 151–163.

Kapel, D. E., & Sadler, E. J. (1978, February). *How much involvement in student teaching: A study of cooperating teachers.* Paper presented at the annual meeting of the Association of Teacher Educators, Las Vegas.

Karmos, A., & Jacko, C. (1977). The role of significant others during the student teaching experience. *Journal of Teacher Education, 28*(5), 51–55.

Killian, J., & McIntyre, J. (1986). Quality in early field experiences: A product of grade level and cooperating teachers' training. *Teaching and Teacher Education, 2*(4), 367–376.

Klinzing, H. (1990). Research on teacher education in West Germany. In R. Tisher & M. Wideen (Eds.), *Research in teacher education: International perspectives* (pp. 89–103). London: Falmer Press.

Koehler, V. (1984, April). *University supervision of student teaching.* Paper presented at the annual meeting of the American Educational Research Association, New Orleans.

Koerner, M. (1992). The cooperating teacher: An ambivalent participant in student teaching. *Journal of Teacher Education, 43*(1), 46–56.

Koff, R. (1986). The socialization of a teacher: On metaphors and teaching. In *Tension and dynamism: The education of a teacher* (Conference proceedings). Ann Arbor: University of Michigan.

Kowalski, T., Weaver, R., & Henson, K. (1990). *Case studies on teaching.* New York: Longman.

Kuehl, R. (1979). *A taxonomy of critical tasks for evaluating student teaching.* Washington, DC: Association of Teacher Educators.

Lamont, W. (1993). *An analysis of support services provided to student teachers: The promotion of student teacher wellness by colleges of education.* Unpublished doctoral dissertation, Arizona State University.

Lasley, T., Payne, M., Fuchs, G., & Egnor-Brown, R. (1993). A hyphenated curriculum: A precondition for effective teacher education. *The Teacher Educator, 28*(3), 21–28.

Lemlech, J., & Kaplan, S. (1990). Learning to talk about teaching: Collegiality in clinical teacher education. *Action in Teacher Education, 12*(1), 13–19.

Levin, R. (1990). Recurring themes and variations. In J. Goodlad, R. Soder, & K. Sirotnik (Eds.), *Places where teachers are taught* (pp. 40–83). San Francisco: Jossey-Bass.

Liston, D., & Zeichner, K. (1988). Critical pedagogy and teacher education. *Journal of Education, 169*(3), 117–137.

Liston, D., & Zeichner, K. (1991). *Teacher education and the social conditions of schooling.* New York: Routledge.

Lowriendee, W. (1990). *An investigation of laboratory experiences offered in undergraduate teacher education programs in the United States.* Unpublished doctoral dissertation, Southern Illinois University at Carbondale.

MacLeod, G. (1987). Microteaching: Modeling. In M. J. Dunkin (Ed.), *The international encyclopedia of teaching and teacher education* (pp. 720–722). Oxford: Pergamon.

Mahan, J., & Lacefield, W. (1976). *Changes in preservice teachers value orientations toward education during year-long, cluster, student teaching placements.* Paper presented at the annual meeting of the American Educational Research Association, San Francisco. (ERIC Document Reproduction Service No. ED 124 534)

Manning, D. (1977). The influence of key individuals on student teachers in urban and suburban settings. *Teacher Educator, 13*(2), 2–8.

McCaleb, J., Borko, H., & Arends, R. (1992). Reflection, research, and repertoire in the masters certification program at the University of Maryland. In L. Valli (Ed.), *Reflection in teacher education* (pp. 40–64). Albany: State University of New York Press.

McCullough, L., & Mintz, S. (1992). Concerns of pre-service students in the USA about the practice of teaching. *Journal of Education for Teaching, 18*(1), 59–67.

McIntyre, D. J. (1983). *Field experiences in teacher education: From student to teacher.* Washington, DC: Foundation for Excellence in Teacher Education and ERIC Clearinghouse on Teacher Education.

McIntyre, D. J., Buell, M., & Casey, J. (1979). Verbal behavior of student teachers and cooperating teachers. *College Student Journal, 13*(3), 240–244.

McIntyre, D. J., & Killian, J. E. (1986). Students' interactions with pupils and cooperating teachers in early field experiences. *Teacher Educator, 22*(2), 2–9.

McIntyre, D. J., & Norris, W. (1980). The state of the art of pre-service teacher education programs and supervision of field experiences. *Action in Teacher Education, 2*(3), 67–69.

McIntyre, D. J., & Pape, S. (1993). Using video protocols to enhance teacher reflective thinking. *Teacher Educator, 28*(3), 2–10.

McNergney, R., & Carrier, C. (1981). *Teacher development.* New York: Macmillan.

Morris, J. R. (1974). The effects of the university supervisor on the performance and adjustment of student teachers. *Journal of Educational Research, 67*(8), 358–362.

Morris, J. E., & Curtis, F. (1983). Legal issues relating to field based experiences in teacher education. *Journal of Teacher Education, 34*(2), 2–6.

Morris, J. E., Pannell, S., & Houston, R. (1985). Standards for professional laboratory and field experiences: Review and recommendations. *Action in Teacher Education, 7*(3), 73–78.

Moultry, M. (1988, April). *Multicultural education among seniors in the College of Education at Ohio State University.* Paper presented at the annual meeting of the American Educational Research Association, New Orleans.

National Commission on Excellence in Education. (1983). *A nation at risk.* Washington, DC: Author.

National Council for Accreditation on Teacher Education (NCATE). (1987). *NCATE standards, procedures, and policies for the professional education units for the preparation of professional school personnel at basic and advanced levels.* Washington, DC: Author.

Oja, S. N. (1988). *A collaborative approach to leadership in supervision* (Final Report OERI 400-85-1056). Durham: University of New Hampshire, Department of Education.

Oja, S., Diller, A., Corcoran, E., & Andrew, M. (1992). Communities of inquiry, communities of support: The five year teacher education programs at the University of New Hampshire. In L. Valli (Ed.), *Reflective teacher education* (pp. 3–23). Albany, NY: State University of New York Press.

O'Sullivan, M., Stroot, S., Tannehill, D., & Chair, C. (1989). Interactive video technology in teacher education. *Journal of Teacher Education, 40*(4), 20–25.

Patton, M.Q. (1980). *Qualitative evaluation methods*. Beverly Hills: Sage Publications.

Peterson, G. (1977, October). *Belief and judgment policies in student teaching: Institutional differences and distribution of knowledge*. Paper presented at the annual meeting of the Midwestern Psychological Association, Chicago. (ERIC Document Reproduction Service No. ED 142 534)

Pinar, W. (1989). A reconceptualization of teacher education. *Journal of Teacher Education, 40*(1), 9–12.

Popkewitz, T. (1985). Ideology and social formation in teacher education. *Teaching and Teacher Education, 1*(2), 91–107.

Price, R. (1961). The influence of supervising teachers. *Journal of Teacher Education, 12*(1), 471–475.

Reiman, A., & Parramore, B. (1993). Promoting preservice teacher development through extended field experience. In M. O'Hair & S. Odell (Eds.), *Diversity and teaching: Association of Teacher Educators Yearbook I* (pp. 111–121). Ft. Worth: Harcourt Brace Jovanovich.

Reyes, D., & Isele, F. (1990). What do we expect from elementary student teachers? A national analysis of rating forms. *Action in Teacher Education, 12*(2), 8–13.

Richert, A. (1991). Case methods and teacher education: Using cases to teach teacher reflection. In R. Tabachnick & K. Zeichner (Eds.), *Issues and practices in inquiry-oriented teacher education* (pp. 130–150). London: Falmer Press.

Robinson, R., & West, P. (1989). Technology and teaching: Trends for the future. In J. Braun (Ed.), *Reforming teacher education: Issues and new directions* (pp. 97–116). New York: Garland Publishing.

Rodreguez, A. J. (1993). A dose of reality: Understanding the origin of the theory/practice dichotomy in teacher education from the students' point of view. *Journal of Teacher Education, 44*(3), 213–222.

Rogers, R., & Reiff, J. (1989). Developing computer-based interactive video simulations on questioning strategies. *Action in Teacher Education, 11*(3), 33–36.

Rosenholtz, S. J. (1989). *Teachers' workplace: The social organization of schools*. New York: Longman.

Roth, R. (1989). Preparing the reflective practitioner: Transforming the apprenticeship through the dialectic. *Journal of Teacher Education, 40*(2), 31–35.

Rowley, J., & Hart, P. (1993). Catching and releasing expert teacher thought: The effects of using videotaped presentations of expert teacher knowledge to promote preservice teacher thinking. In M. O'Hair & S. Odell (Eds.), *Diversity and teaching* (pp. 122–137). Ft. Worth: Harcourt Brace Jovanovich.

Rudney, G., & Guillaume, A. (1989–1990). Reflective teaching for student teachers. *The Teacher Educator, 25*(3), 13–19.

Sandgren, D. L., & Schmidt, L. G. (1956). Does practice teaching change attitudes toward teaching? *Journal of Educational Research, 50*(8), 673–680.

Schleuter, L. (1991). Student teachers' preactive and postactive curriculum thinking. *Journal of Research in Music Education, 39*(1), 46–63.

Schueler, R., Gold, B., & Mitzel, H. (1962). *Improvement of student teaching*. New York: City University of New York, Hunter College.

Sedlak, M. (1987). Tomorrow's teachers: The essential arguments of the report. In M. Sedlak (Ed.), *Reforming teacher education: The impact of the Holmes Group Report* (pp. 4–15). New York: Teachers College Press.

Seperson, M., & Joyce, B. (1973). Teaching styles of student teachers as related to those of their cooperating teachers. *Educational Leadership, 31*(1), 146–151.

Sikula, J. (1990). National commission reports of the 1980s. In W. R. Houston (Ed.), *Handbook of research on teacher education* (pp. 72–82). New York: Macmillan.

Simbol, M. A., & Summers, J. (1984). *Administrative policy and supervisory load for student teaching programs in Ohio, Indiana, Illinois, and Missouri*. Muncie: Indiana Unit of the Association of Teacher Educators.

Sparks-Langer, G. M., Simmons, J. M., Pasch, M., Colton, A., & Starko, A. (1990). Reflective pedagogical thinking: How can we promote it and measure it? *Journal of Teacher Education, 41*(4), 23–32.

Stallings, J., & Kowalski, T. (1990). Research on professional development schools. In W. R. Houston (Ed.), *Handbook of research on teacher education* (pp. 251–263). New York: Macmillan.

Tabachnick, B. R., Popkewitz, T., & Zeichner, K. M. (1979–1980). Teacher education and professional perspectives of student teachers. *Interchange on Educational Policy, 10*(40), 12–29.

Thies-Sprinthall, L. (1984). Promoting the developmental growth of supervising teachers: Theory, research, programs and implications. *Journal of Teacher Education, 35*(3), 53–60.

Thomson, S., Beacham, B., & Misulis, K. (1992). A university and public school collaborative approach to preparing elementary teachers. *The Teacher Educator, 28*(2), 46–51.

Tittle, C. (1974). *Student teaching: Attitude and research bases for change in school and university*. Metuchen, NJ: Scarecrow Press.

Tom, A. (1974). The case for pass/fail student teaching. *Teacher Educator, 10*(1), 2–8.

Valli, L. (Ed.). (1992). *Reflective teacher education: Cases and critiques*. Albany: State University of New York Press.

Veenman, S. (1984). The perceived problems of beginning teachers. *Review of Education Research, 54*(2), 143–178.

Vickery, T., & Brown, B. (1967, April). *Descriptive profiles of beliefs of teachers*. Paper presented at the annual meeting of the American Educational Research Association, New York.

Vittetoe, J. (1972). Evaluation of product—An essential first step. *Journal of Teacher Education, 23*(2), 129–133.

Watts, D. (1987). Student teaching. In M. Haberman & J. M. Backus (Eds.), *Advances in teacher education* (Vol. 3, pp. 151–167). Norwood, NJ: Ablex.

Wayson, W. (1988, April). *Multicultural education among seniors in the college of education at Ohio State University*. Paper presented at annual meeting of the American Educational Research Association, New Orleans.

Winitsky, N., & Arends, R. (1991). Translating research into practice: The effects of various forms of training and clinical experience on preservice students' knowledge, skill, and reflectiveness. *Journal of Teacher Education, 42*(1), 52–65.

Winitsky, N., Stoddart, T., & O'Keefe, P. (1992). Great expectations: Emergent professional development schools. *Journal of Teacher Education, 43*(1), 3–18.

Wisniewski, R., & Ducharme, E. (1989). Why study the education professorate? An introduction. In R. Wisniewski & E. Ducharme (Eds.), *The professors of teaching: An inquiry* (pp. 1–10). Albany: State University of New York Press.

Wolfe, D., Schewel, R., & Bickman, E. (1989). A gateway to collaboration: Clinical faculty programs. *Action in Teacher Education, 11*(2), 66–69.

Wright, P. J., Silvern, S.B., & Burkhater, B. B. (1982). An evaluation of teacher input in field-based instruction. *Journal of Research and Development in Education, 15*(2), 34–37.

Zeichner, K. (1979). *The dialectics of teacher socialization*. Paper presented at the annual meeting of the Association of Teacher Educators, Orlando.

Zeichner, K. (1980). Myths and realities: Field-based experiences in preservice teacher education. *Journal of Teacher Education, 31*(6), 45–49, 51–55.

Zeichner, K. (1982). Reflective teaching and field-based experience in teacher education. *Interchange, 12*(4), 1–21.

Zeichner, K. (1986b). Social and ethical dimensions of reform in teacher education. In J. Hoffman & S. Edwards (Eds.), *Clinical teacher education* (pp. 87–108). New York: Random House.

Zeichner, K. (1987). Toward an understanding of the role of field experiences in teacher development. In M. Haberman & J. M. Backus (Eds.), *Advances in teacher education* (Vol. 3, pp. 94–117). Norwood, NJ: Ablex.

Zeichner, K. (1989). Preparing teachers for democratic schools. *Action in Teacher Education, 11*(1), 5–10.

Zeichner, K., & Gore, J. (1990). Teacher socialization. In W. R. Houston (Ed.), *Handbook of research on teacher education* (pp. 329–348). New York: Macmillan.

Zeichner, K., & Liston, D. (1987). Teaching student teachers to reflect. *Harvard Educational Review, 57*(1), 23–48.

Zeichner, K., Liston, D. P., Mahlios, M., & Gomez, M. (1988). The structure and goals of a student teaching program and the character and quality of supervisory discourse. *Teaching and Teacher Education, 4*(4), 349–362.

Zeichner, K., & Tabachnick, B. R. (1982). The belief systems of university supervisors in an elementary student teaching program. *Journal of Education for Teaching, 8*(1), 35–54.

Zevin, J. (1974, April). *In the cooperating teachers image: Convergence of social studies of student teachers behavior patterns with cooperating teachers behavior patterns.* Paper presented at the annual meeting of American Educational Research Association, Chicago. (ERIC Documentation Reproduction Service No. ED 087 781)

Zimpher, N., & Ashburn, E. (1985). Studying the professional development of teachers: How conceptions of the world inform the research agenda. *Journal of Teacher Education, 36*(6), 16–26.

Zimpher, N. L., deVoss, G. G., & Nott, D. L. (1980). A closer look at university student teacher supervision. *Journal of Teacher Education, 31*(4), 11–15.

Zimpher, N., & Howey, K. (1990). Scholarly inquiry into teacher education in the United States. In R. Tisher & M. Wideen (Eds.), *Research in teacher education: International perspectives* (pp. 163–190). London: Falmer Press.

·10·

PROFESSIONAL DEVELOPMENT SCHOOLS

Cassandra L. Book

MICHIGAN STATE UNIVERSITY

The creation of professional development schools (PDSs) has been recommended by some educators as a means of attending to the calls for reform, particularly in the preparation of new and existing teachers, the way students are taught, and the way schools are structured to support these reforms. When preservice teacher education students in traditional teacher education programs are placed in K–12 schools for fieldwork or student teaching, relationships between universities and schools are generally directed by the universities and lacking in collaborative activities among K–12 teachers and university faculty. In contrast, when universities and schools enter into an agreement to create professional development schools, the expectations and roles for university and school personnel are significantly more complex and intertwined than in the traditional relationships. Creating such a new culture that relies on the collaboration of school and university transforms both institutions and the personnel within each.

This chapter reviews the research literature on professional development schools. It begins by defining PDSs according to criteria offered by several organizations and authors. In these definitions, recognition is given to the different labels used to refer to PDSs. Next, the methods used to conduct most of the research in PDSs is described along with cautions for future researchers in this context. The research emanating from PDSs focuses on: (1) teacher's attitudes within or about PDSs, (2) creating a new culture through collaboration, (3) new roles for the K–12 and university faculty involved in a PDS, (4) preservice education in PDSs, and (5) inquiry in PDSs. The chapter ends with concerns and benefits of research in and about professional development schools.

DEFINING THE PROFESSIONAL DEVELOPMENT SCHOOL

Schools that enter into relationships with universities to bring about reforms in education have been called different names by different organizations. The term *professional development school* was originated by the Holmes Group (1986) in the writing of *Tomorrow's Teachers* in which teacher educators created a vision about developing schools that

would provide superior opportunities for teachers and administrators to influence the development of their profession, and for university faculty to increase the professional relevance of their work, through (1) mutual deliberation on problems with student learning, and their possible solutions; (2) shared teaching in the university and schools; (3) collaborative research on the problems of educational practice; and (4) cooperative supervision of prospective teachers and administrators. (p. 56)

The Holmes Group (1990) further elaborated the concept of professional development schools in *Tomorrow's Schools* by explaining that they would be focused on providing professional development for both novice and experienced professionals as well as developing research about teaching. This vision for PDSs was influenced by the medical profession's teaching hospitals, which placed those who were in training with those who were providing medical service in real contexts augmented by interaction with medical researchers. The creation of such new relationships, and indeed new culture, within

The author gratefully acknowledges Nathalie Gehrke (University of Washington) for providing essential documents that were referenced in this chapter. In addition, Nathalie Gehrke and Renee Clift (University of Illinois) are sincerely appreciated for providing critical feedback on early drafts of this chapter. Finally, Jan Butler and Susan Clifford (Michigan State University) are to be credited with their assistance in the preparation of the typed manuscript.

the teaching hospitals became the model for the creation of professional development schools.

The Carnegie Forum on Education and the Economy (1986) in its report entitled *A Nation Prepared: Teachers for the 21st Century* also called for selected public schools to link with colleges of education and university arts and letters departments to prepare new teachers. These schools were called "clinical schools."

Similarly, the Ford Foundation (Anderson, 1993) provided program support to create teacher education's equivalent of medicine's teaching hospitals, which, in collaboration with higher education institutions, would train new teachers, focus on the instruction of students, and engage teachers in improving their own practice over a sustained period. Like the Carnegie Forum, the Ford Foundation referred to the sites in which such efforts took place as "clinical schools." The demonstration programs of the Ford Foundation Clinical Schools Project are reported in *Voices of Change* (Anderson, 1993).

The Rand Corporation (Wise & Darling-Hammond, 1987) called for "induction schools" in which prospective teachers would fulfill their internships. These schools would also be places where research about teaching practices could be conducted by teachers, teacher educators, and researchers in a collaborative mode. The American Federation of Teachers Task Force on Professional Practice Schools (Levine, 1992) identified what "professional practice schools" might look like, including support for student learning, professional practice, professional education of teachers, and inquiry directed at the improvement of practice. The Puget Sound Educational Consortium at first referred to schools in which reform of teaching and learning, teacher education, and school organization would occur as *professional development centers* and later as *partner schools* (Goodlad, 1993, p. 25). Whatever the name, the concept of these schools has remained relatively constant: (1) to improve the quality of instruction for K–12 students, the preparation of prospective teachers, and the continuing education of professional educators; (2) to provide a research base that informs the teaching profession; and (3) to encourage the school to undergo a structural reform that allows for the collaboration between school and university faculty and supports changes in teaching and learning. School- and university-based educators affiliated with these contexts are to develop and demonstrate exemplary practice in these areas and to disseminate the new knowledge gained about such practices.

Assumptions of a Professional Development School

To understand better research in or about professional development schools, it is important to clarify the nature of the context about which researchers are trying to gain new knowledge. The definition of PDSs and the assumptions that guide the unique work within them help to delineate the context. Murray's (1993) article, entitled "'All or None' Criteria for Professional Development Schools," provides a comprehensive statement about what defines a PDS and specifies that "the goals [of PDSs] are interconnected and that none can be achieved without the others" (p. 70). Murray's essay articulated the 11 features or goals that he believed characterize PDSs as follows:

1. Understanding the content by all students is the goal of the school.
2. It is the intention to teach important knowledge and for students to master that even if it means that they have exposure to less information.
3. The goals of the school apply to all pupils, including those who are often hard to teach.
4. Teachers use dialectical instruction, which is more responsive to the needs and understanding of the individual students.
5. Students are required to be active in their interaction with the knowledge because it is perceived "that understanding is dependent on, and critically shaped by, its context or its place" (p. 65).
6. Valid assessment is used to determine the students' abilities to use the information gained in real-world contexts.
7. The learning community that is established in a PDS models the community values students are to acquire, including those that are "inherent in the negotiated dialectical process that yields understanding" (p. 65).
8. The PDS values the professional teacher who continually is a learner and who seeks to collaborate with others to respond to the learning demands of the students and colleagues.
9. The school organization and finances are structured to allow teachers to have time for reflection, planning, and consultation necessary to respond to the demands of the dialectical environment.
10. The goal is to bring integrated support services to respond to the needs of the students.
11. The PDS research mission endorses the concept of the PDS being a "center of inquiry that contributes to the scholarly literature" and that works to solve "practical and theoretical problems so that knowledge can be more complete and coherent" (p. 67).

Apparently expanding on the assumptions of PDSs specified earlier by the Holmes Group in *Tomorrow's Schools* (1990) and those of the American Federation of Teacher's (AFT) Professional Practice Schools (Levine, 1992), Murray identified the key components of PDSs that prescribe an ambitious agenda for such schools and that also anticipate the difficulties in accomplishing the goals of these schools. In a similar way, Goodlad (1993) reported that 14 teacher preparation settings that formed the National Network for Educational Renewal committed themselves to 19 postulates that defined the commitments, levels of support, and nature of relationships among schools and universities as they collaborated in new partnerships. Whether part of the Holmes Group, Center for Educational Renewal, AFT Professional Practice Schools, or another network of PDSs, it is worthwhile to understand that the phenomenon called a PDS is compounded by political as well as intellectual agendas. If the researcher is not clear about the definition of the PDS or the assumptions such a school claims to fulfill, then he or she may draw uninformed or distorted conclusions about the PDS.

SCOPE OF THIS CHAPTER

In the first edition of the *Handbook of Research on Teacher Education,* Stallings and Kowalski (1990) comprehensively reviewed the forerunners to professional development schools (e.g., laboratory schools and portal schools). Thus, the historical context of these configurations of schools that also served as sites to prepare teachers is not repeated here.

This chapter is limited to research that occurs in or about professional development schools in which school and university faculty have joined together to try to restructure the learning that occurs for students, teachers, teacher educators, and administrators, and to bring about a new culture in the school. One problem with the literature is that some studies refer to the site as a PDS, but do not provide enough information to make it clear that it is indeed a PDS by meeting the assumptions or characteristics of a PDS. Other research appears to have taken place in a PDS, but the author does not indicate the impact of the context of the PDS on the subject of the research nor on the outcomes that were observed. Although there is an ever-present need to add to the research in teacher education and teaching and learning, it is important to bring a focus on research that is contributing to a PDS effort and to document the impact of the effect of the changes in teaching and learning that is occurring in the PDS setting.

Inasmuch as professional development schools are integrally tied to reforms in teacher education, reforms in teaching and learning, and reforms in the organization of schools, it is sometimes difficult to separate research in PDSs from these other more discrete reform efforts. Research about other school reform efforts external to professional development schools are not included in this review. For example, schools that have other missions or that are novel but do not meet the overall assumptions or characteristics of PDSs (e.g., charter schools) are not included in this chapter. Similarly, research on an aspect of teacher education or learning (e.g., collaborative action research or teaching for understanding) that is not conducted in a PDS is not included in this chapter. One of the recurrent problems in examining the research in and about professional development schools is that a PDS is an example of where the whole is indeed greater than the sum of its parts. It is extremely difficult for a researcher to capture or even reflect the complexity of the interactions that occur in a PDS and the impact of those interactions on the outcome of the variable(s) being studied. Thus, any summary of the research about PDSs may not provide a comprehensive representation of all of the many factors that make up a PDS and may not be the only viable vehicle for understanding the whole concept or process called a PDS.

SOURCES OF INFORMATION ON RESEARCH IN OR ABOUT PROFESSIONAL DEVELOPMENT SCHOOLS

Published sources of research in or about professional development schools are quite limited. At the time of the writing of this chapter, only three books were in print, two that directly discussed PDSs (Darling-Hammond, 1994; Levine, 1992) and one that included major chapters about research in professional development schools (Cohen, McLaughlin, & Talbert, 1993). At least three other books about PDSs are currently being written. Three journals had special issues devoted to the topic of PDSs (i.e., *Educational Policy,* 7[1], March, 1993; *Teaching Education 4*[2], Spring, 1992; and *Journal of Teacher Education, 43*[1], January–February, 1992). *Action in Teacher Education* (*15*[2], Summer, 1993) included several articles about PDSs. Although other articles have appeared in educational journals, most of the sources were in the form of convention papers, primarily from the conferences of the American Association of Colleges for Teacher Education (AACTE), the Association of Teacher Educators (ATE), and the American Educational Research Association (AERA). A small selection of dissertations indicated the study of professional development schools. The *Holmes Group Forum,* the newsletter of the Holmes Group, provided major coverage of information about PDSs, and local publications about PDS efforts comprised another fugitive source; however, these latter two sources generally did not include research summaries, but more anecdotal stories and reports about PDSs. In essence, the published literature about PDSs is sparse and the fugitive literature lacks accessibility as well as confidence in its rigor of reporting.

Professional development schools are such new institutions that most are in the process of evolving, and the research being conducted in these settings or about these settings is in very formative stages. Some of the research that has been conducted has not had time to appear in refereed journal articles and books, thus forcing reviews such as this to rely on research communicated in convention papers and locally published documents, many of which are available through ERIC. In addition, there may be a tension between creating the new cultures of PDSs and systematically studying and reporting on them. Also, some of the stories may be too personal or too painful for the people involved to publish at this formative stage. Although fugitive literature that may not be readily accessible to readers had not been included in this review, it is imperative to point out that many of the newsletters (both of a national scope, such as the *Holmes Group Forum,* and of a local focus, such as from individual schools) reveal keen insights into the actual workings, successes, failures, and inquiry of the professional development schools as described by the participants in those settings.

METHODOLOGY OF RESEARCH CONDUCTED IN PROFESSIONAL DEVELOPMENT SCHOOLS

The research that has been conducted in professional development schools has been primarily descriptive in nature and includes data collected by interviews, questionnaires, surveys, and journal writing by teachers and teacher educators, as well as document review, observational field notes, observations of classrooms, and conversations. Some of the studies are historical-ethnographic studies, and others reflect data that have been collected while the researcher was a participant observer in the classroom. Case studies of schools and teachers have been written. Triangulation of data and the constant comparative analysis have been used to verify the findings. Most of the research in PDSs has been conducted by university-based teacher education faculty and graduate students, often in collaboration with school-based practitioners; however, K–12 teachers have also been involved in action research in which they systematically inquired about their own school and classroom teaching and reported the findings about the impact of their own practice.

Descriptive methodologies dominate for a number of reasons. The complexity of the school and classroom and the interaction of factors there make it impossible to control each of the factors as might be done in an experimental study. Also, to reflect better the true nature of the school and classroom, it is desirable to try to describe the complexity of the interactions. In addition, the limited number of participants make case studies a valuable and even necessary methodology. Furthermore, the uniqueness of trying to document the evolution of the relationships between school and university personnel calls for descriptive research. Finally, the goal of encouraging collaboration between teachers and faculty in identifying and studying questions of interest to both, including the impact of their instruction, provides little opportunity for experimental research. Nonetheless, there are a few examples of research in PDSs that are of a quantitative nature.

CONSTRAINTS OF RESEARCH IN PROFESSIONAL DEVELOPMENT SCHOOLS

It is critical for data from professional development schools to be systematically collected and analyzed to be of most value now and in the future. Unfortunately, many of the studies lack sufficient description of the methodology used in collecting and analyzing the data, leaving the reader with questions about the validity of the findings, as well as the replicability of the studies. Collaborative reporting of data by classroom teachers and teacher educators/researchers poses a special problem in reporting because they must be particularly cautious not to report the event in a more positive manner than the actual experience. To counteract such a potential problem, Whitford (1994) had an uninvolved researcher conduct interviews with teachers who were in the PDS Whitford had written about to gather their reaction and criticisms of her case study about their school. She also had other university researchers examine her interpretations. The need exists to be accurate in the reporting of outcomes, yet sensitive to the multiple perspectives that construct the reality of the collaboration.

As Ruscoe, Whitford, Egginton, and Esselman (1989) pointed out, "The evaluative and judgmental conclusions of much traditional research would destroy the fragile partnership which ethnographic research attempts to foster" (p. 18). They went on to indicate that such ethnographic research encourages "reflection and self-evaluation . . . analysis of the data by the subjects themselves" (p. 18). Thus, whereas collaborative ethnography may be inviting to teachers and administrators who are being studied in the PDSs, it needs to be treated carefully.

The complex and often competing roles of university faculty in the PDSs compound the dilemma of reporting findings. Often university faculty are in the position of working with K–12

teachers to bring about changes in their teaching, as well as reporting the results of their work. Both participants (teachers and university faculty members) want the teachers to succeed and want the students to learn more and in new ways. The reporting of these activities may either be more positive than what actually occurred or may be reported in a more negative fashion than the participants wish to have revealed. There is often resistance in having their stories told publicly. In addition, the complication of reporting data that are about a particular person(s) in a particular site and of a personal nature makes it difficult for anonymity and confidentiality to be maintained.

Insights gained within these contexts are unique to the relationships developed among the participants and the particular circumstances; however, the goal should be for researchers to try to identify themes that might be useful or transferable to other PDS sites. For example, Wilson, with Miller and Yerkes (1993), provided an illustration of how such themes (e.g., the struggle of building collaborative relationships) might be identified and useful for others who are seeking to establish such relationships. Goodlad (cited in Shen, 1993) pointed out, "There are no blueprints to guide the building of school–university partnerships and partner schools, only a growing number of lessons from the field. The more careful the probe, the more useful the lesson" (p. iii). Thus, it is critical for researchers in the PDS to collect, analyze, and report their findings carefully so others may learn from their experiences.

Most of the studies that have been reported from PDSs focus on roles, relationships, creation of new institutions, teacher attitudes, and teacher education in the PDS contexts. There is a serious need for research questions to address the impact of the restructuring efforts on student learning. Such questions will mandate methodologies that allow for researchers to account for the impact of new modes of teaching and learning. In effect, the methods used in collecting data have fit the questions asked, but there are many more questions that need to be addressed in these schools and the methods will need to be adapted.

RESEARCH ABOUT CREATING THE NEW INSTITUTION

At the time of this writing, three studies reported the number of professional development schools. Drawing from the reform literature that called for the establishment of PDSs, Brainard (1989) constructed a list of 14 conditions that were perceived as necessary elements of a PDS. Brainard then interviewed administrators from 21 universities that were believed to have or soon have PDS sites. Twenty of these either were members of the Holmes Group or were recipients of Ford Foundation grants. Of those, Brainard found that "two partnerships have PDS projects that have been in operation for 10 years; one has been in operation for 2 years; and 3 were established in the fall of 1988" (p. 21). The respondents in Brainard's study generally confirmed the importance of these conditions, but their responses indicated that many of the fundamental elements were not included in the design or implementation of the PDS efforts. In fact, Brainard reported that "none of the projects included in this study appears to meet all or even most of the fourteen criteria . . . established for professional development schools"

(p. 49). Although now 5 years old, the same questions asked by Brainard are relevant today. There is little evidence that schools labeled as PDSs meet all or even most of the criteria that are to define a PDS. A measure of the number of schools claiming to be PDSs, as well as a description of the criteria they claim to fulfill, are needed. In addition, a school may fulfill different criteria or more or less of the criteria from year to year. Thus, sustainability of the qualities that constitute a PDS is fragile at best.

In 1990, Yinger and Hendricks reported a summary of reform efforts of 50 of the approximately 100 existing Holmes Group institutions described in *The Holmes Group Forum* from 1987 to 1989. At that time, 24 colleges or universities reported to have initiated PDSs. It should be noted, however, that this analysis was only reflective of those institutions included in the newsletter. Most recently, Darling-Hammond (1994, p. 2) reported that more than 100 PDS initiatives have been identified.

Several descriptions of the creation of individual PDSs have been documented (Darling-Hammond, 1994; Rosaen & Hoekwater, 1990; Sagmiller & Gehrke, 1992). Recommendations about how to create PDS sites and how to initiate conversations with appropriate school personnel about the concept have been elaborated (Bauer, 1991a, 1991b; Hendricks-Lee, 1993; Nystrand, 1991; Putnam, 1991; Zimpher, 1990). In addition, there are a plethora of articles that itemize issues in creating and maintaining PDSs (Darling-Hammond, 1994; Field, 1990, 1991; Jett-Simpson, Pugach, & Whipp, 1992; Mehaffy, 1992; Neufeld, with Boris-Schacter, 1991; Neufeld & Haavind, 1988; The Ohio State University, 1993; Pasch & Pugach, 1990; Pugach & Pasch, 1994). *The Holmes Group Forum* also provides descriptions of PDS activities, and *Changing Minds,* a serial publication of the Michigan Partnership for New Education located at Michigan State University, describes classroom activities and the experiences of teachers in PDSs in Michigan. These newsletters are valuable resources because they portray the complexity of the changing relationships within PDSs and offer insights into the collaborative work and changes in teaching of teachers and university professors; however, for the most part, they do not summarize research in or about the PDSs.

Although many of these articles appear to provide prescriptions for beginning a PDS, caution should be taken. The drawbacks for K–12 educators, as well as for university faculty, coupled with the expense of engaging in such new relationships should not be underestimated. Cultural differences between schools and universities interfere with the smooth enactment of the goals and underlying assumptions of a PDS. Nonetheless, there are advantages to be realized, including political agendas to be fulfilled. The initiation of a PDS should not be taken lightly, and as Goodlad (1993) cautioned, in spite of a political climate that celebrates these collaborative relationships, universities should guard against having a PDS for the sake of having a PDS. He cited Gehrke's (1991) warning "against the 'trophy mentality'—what counts is 'having' a professional development school" (Goodlad, 1993, p. 38).

TEACHERS' ATTITUDES IN PROFESSIONAL DEVELOPMENT SCHOOLS

One major area of study within professional development schools examined teachers' feelings about the effect of partici-

pating in a PDS on their sense of efficacy, involvement, and attitudes toward the goals of the PDS. Teachers' feelings of empowerment within PDSs merit examination because empowerment is part of the goal to be accomplished in these school reform efforts. Ruscoe et al. (1989) interviewed teachers and administrators within PDSs in Jefferson County, Kentucky, to determine the teacher's feelings of efficacy and empowerment. They reported

(1) a direct relationship between teachers' involvement in decision-making and their subsequent feelings of efficacy, (2) the importance of teaming in facilitating both increased teacher involvement in decision-making and increased feelings of efficacy, and (3) the importance of having a supportive faculty and administration as a basis for restructuring efforts. (p. 12)

The researchers concluded that "those who feel the most empowered also feel the most efficacious" (Ruscoe et al., 1989, p. 16). Ruscoe and Whitford (1991) reported that teachers' attitudes toward issues of their efficacy and influence and role in school decision making and the school learning climate remained fairly positive during a 3-year period. However, they qualified their positive conclusions by indicating "teachers' attitudes have become more 'realistic' as they have discovered that restructuring not only involves a lot of hard work but also provides little in the way of immediate, guaranteed results" (p. 3).

Ruscoe and Whitford (1991) considered the effects on teachers and schools when the teachers were participating in more than one reform effort at a time and found that the impact of individual schools affected the positive or negative sense of efficacy of teachers within those schools. Specifically, they found that teachers who were involved with more than one restructuring effort at a time were more positive than those only involved in one reform agenda. This finding has implications for those PDSs that are trying to address multiple goals at one time because it appears that teachers can work to bring about changes in multiple areas, particularly when there is school-wide support for the change efforts.

Stoddart (1993) described teachers' resistance to a top-down approach to staff development in PDSs. When university faculty members "lectured" on the constructivist theory as an underpinning of the teacher education program, the seminars were unsuccessful. Teachers found these lectures to be oppressive and irrelevant to their instructional practice. In effect, these attitudes reflected the importance of truly engaging the teachers and university faculty in collaborative contexts. As Stoddart pointed out, "the information was not made personally relevant to the PDS teacher/learners, they were not allowed to construct their own understanding and they never took ownership of the knowledge" (p. 10). The significance of enacting what is "preached" is evident in the resistance to learning by the teachers in these PDS contexts. Modeling ways to engage students in learning is particularly important if the goal of the PDSs is to alter the nature of instruction in the schools.

Moore, Hopkins, and Tullis (1991) examined the attitudes of 200 randomly selected teachers (who were not in a PDS) about their perceptions of the most important components of PDSs and the more important teaching skills needed by teachers in PDSs. The researchers found that these teachers generally supported the goals of PDSs and the characteristics that were desired for teachers in PDSs; however, they did not value planning and conducting research as part of the responsibilities of teachers, nor did they support the reward structure for university personnel. It appears that teachers who are not currently in a PDS are not generally interested in assuming the role of researcher in the PDS and may need to be motivated to participate and conduct research in the schools.

Karlsberger (1993) surveyed the attitudes of teachers within seven Ohio PDSs and found them to have a high degree of agreement with the Holmes Group goals. Yet, they reported an unfulfilled level of implementation of the goals within their PDSs. More than half of the teachers said that being out of the classroom for PDS activities was minimally problematic, but said that they needed more time for planning and reflection of their PDS work, as well as more resources to accomplish their goals. Teachers in these schools reported a high level of administrative and peer support for their work.

It behooves those who wish to implement PDSs to attend to teachers' attitudes about the goals of PDSs and their feelings of efficacy in their ability to enact the goals. It is also instructive that the best way to engage teachers, who on the surface may agree with the overall objectives of the PDS efforts, is to collaborate with the teachers rather than trying to direct their thinking. The engagement of teachers in problem-solving issues of teaching and learning that they perceive to be salient holds the best promise of engaging their work on the problems of practice, as well as conducting research about their attempts. It appears that teachers do not value, at least on first consideration, research being conducted in their schools, but over time they come to support the Holmes Group goals that include inquiry about practice.

CREATING A NEW CULTURE AND TRANSFORMING THE CULTURES OF THE SCHOOL AND UNIVERSITY THROUGH COLLABORATION

The goals of creating a professional development school include creating a new culture in which school and university faculty work together through collaborative efforts. The differences between the university and school cultures create problems. As Brookhart and Loadman (1992) declared, "There are four categories of assumptions that have posed problems for school–university collaboration: focus, tempo, rewards, and power" (p. 56). The focus of the university on theory contrasts with the focus of the school on practical matters. This "difference in focus creates culturally different perceptions of what is important to know" (Brookhart & Loadman, 1992, p. 56). Making time for collaboration is also a problem, especially given the different schedules the different cultures operate under and the rates at which teachers in the K–12 schools engage in activities and the length of time university faculty expect to take to examine an issue. Whereas the rewards for teachers are more likely to be intrinsic, the rewards for university faculty come primarily from "publication, recognition in an academic field, and academic rank"

(Brookhart & Loadman, 1992, p. 60). As Brookhart and Loadman pointed out, "Until members of the two cultures learn to appreciate what is rewarding and motivating to other collaborators, and until they build more rewards into their projects, collaboration will remain difficult" (p. 61). Finally, Brookhart and Loadman stated that "although there is also a personal, psychological dimension to these concepts [accomplishment, power, and efficacy], the culture creates and shapes expectations and norms for the effects of one's efforts" (p. 61). The way in which the two cultures promote a sense of efficacy and power can be quite different and it is imperative to diminish "one-upmanship" among either teachers or faculty. In fact, within the new culture it is desirable for all participants to have a sense of power and efficacy. Reaching this goal is difficult because the PDS calls for major alterations in the way in which participants are used to teaching, being organized, and being rewarded for their work.

In reporting their own experience in trying to change their practice and to collaborate within the context of a PDS, Wilson, with Miller and Yerkes (1993), described the difficulty.

We work in a professional development school, an environment in which there are financial and personal incentives, a great deal of intellectual and organizational support, and facilitative and supportive conditions. Yet with all these supports and resources, we have found the process of changing our practice to be difficult and slow. It is our collective experience that changing one's teaching practice, no matter what the conditions, is difficult work. (p. 86)

They explained that collaboration requires thinking about new ways to teach and changing the traditional habits of one's practice. They went on to say that four factors are critical in their ability to work together: "time, trust, courage, and communication" (p. 90).

These themes of a need for time, trust, and communication are recurrent in the literature. Wiseman and Nason (1993) analyzed the written responses of teachers, professors, administrators, graduate students, and preservice teachers who participated in meetings to evaluate the development of a PDS. Four themes emerged from the comments about the collaborative efforts: (1) personal and professional development focused heavily on the need for trust in the relationships, as well as opportunities to learn from one another and bond together; (2) communication and collaboration highlighted the value of their interaction and concern about the teachers' lack of communication among themselves; (3) curricular restructuring brought attention to the interdisciplinary goals they were trying to achieve; and (4) needed resources included time, money, and space to allow them to collaborate. Focusing the attention of the K–12 teachers and university faculty on the education of new teachers provided a common bond on which they could collaborate and a topic to which each person could legitimately bring his or her own expertise and experience. The focus on teacher education opened communication lines and allowed for the participants to begin to build a trusting relationship as long as each party was treated with respect.

These themes of a need for time, trust, and communication were evident in the stories of bringing about cultural change and collaboration in many of the PDSs. In her report of changing the school culture at Lark Creek Middle School in Washington

State, Grossman (1994) stated that teachers "cite greater collegiality, professional responsibility and communication . . . and their new understanding of their role as teacher educators and the rewards of working with student teachers" (p. 61) as the biggest changes in teachers' behaviors. She also pointed out that teachers reported "expanded vision of their professional roles and their awareness of broader issues in education" (p. 61).

Tensions in bringing about the changes in culture in the development of Fairdale High School were discussed by Whitford (1994). She explained that

Tensions about best practice within and among school and university faculties, kept sub rosa through isolation and disconnected through separation of work sites, are more exposed in a PDS . . . as school and university educators attempt fundamental change, the prevailing pattern of rules, roles, and relationships inside each organization is being challenged. If such changes are institutionalized beyond the current experimental stages, the cultures of both will be altered to include more perspectives. (p. 93)

By report of the teachers, it appears that teachers in PDSs are changing their behaviors and perceptions. Berry and Catoe (1994) reported that

Pontiac's PDS efforts are . . . leveraging a learning culture, for teachers, administrators, and interns. As a result of their PDS and restructuring efforts, over 70% of the teachers reported that they changed the way they reflect on practice while 61% reported they changed their conception of collegial work. Similarly, over one-half (55%) of the teachers reported that they have changed the way they teach and their conception of what needs to be known in order to teach . . . . The majority of teachers believe that the PDS efforts have forged changes regarding reflective practice (71%) and collegial work (61%). But far fewer believe that the PDS efforts have changed curriculum (41%) and conceptions of teaching (40%). (p. 184)

Such reports provide evidence that change in teachers' behaviors have occurred within PDSs; however, the collaborative nature of PDSs was expected to influence and change the behaviors of university teacher educators as well. Berry and Catoe (1994) reported that less than one fourth of the teacher educators believed they had changed the way they taught as a result of their participation in a PDS. However,

over 40% of the teacher education faculty noted that because of PDS efforts, they have changed the content of their courses and their concept of collegial work with K–12 teachers and they have noticed a change in the way their colleagues reflect upon their own practice . . . . [Also] COE faculty see more evidence of cultural changes (at least related to beliefs about teaching and learning) among PDS teachers than among their own university colleagues. (p. 190)

It is significant that Berry and Catoe surveyed both K–12 teachers and university faculty involved with the PDS to identify changes in their beliefs and practices that are inherent in the different cultures from which they operate. If this work is truly a collaboration, one would expect participants from both cultures to be changed as a result of their interactions in bringing about the new culture of the PDS.

Gehrke, Young, and Sagmiller (1991) analyzed the creation of a new culture in the Puget Sound Professional Development Center collaborative between the University of Washington and four middle schools. Because their goal was to sustain the PDC over a period of time, their reflection of the variables that contributed to longevity of the project provided insights to others as well. One variable, task distribution, led them to understand the value of sharing leadership responsibilities. The second variable they learned to handle over time was conflict resolution. Rather than evading problems, they developed means for dealing with the conflicts openly. Finally, during the years of working together, they learned to blur the boundaries between the roles of the participants. However, they noted that "as our numbers increased, a smaller percentage had been around since the very beginning, shared the vision and understanding of the center, and felt a commitment to the center rather than to their own school" (p. 9). They continued to have the need to find ways to help new participants move beyond their own boundaries. In essence, the participants in this PDC learned to anticipate factors that could impinge on their ability to create a new culture that brought participants from different cultures together to share a common vision.

Woloszyk (1992) studied the attitudes of teachers in the Holt (Michigan) High School PDS about their school climate and compared their attitudes before and after the school had become a PDS. Overall, the teachers reported that the school culture was overwhelmingly positive and that the PDS had had a powerful influence on the specific beliefs and attitudes of the high school faculty. They reported the climate was collegial and cooperative and one that encouraged teachers, principals, school district administrators, and university faculty to work together to enhance their professional growth. Woloszyk (1992) believed that

the professional development school has assisted the faculty in the development of new ways of thinking, improved teaching practices, provided time for reflection and inquiry, and fostered collaboration and cooperative endeavors between university and school faculty members. These activities have caused fundamental shifts in thinking and acting in the climate and culture of the high school. (p. 42)

Studies like this can be useful in verifying the shifts in attitudes and perceptions of school climate that occur in the establishment of PDSs; however, it is important for such studies to rigorously examine the culture of a PDS and to be careful not to appear to be only a public relations tool for the PDS.

NEW ROLES FOR TEACHERS

Part of the establishment of a new culture within a PDS is the evolution of the roles that K–12 teachers and university faculty play in the new institution of the PDS. Whereas previously reported studies have spoken of these changes in roles, other studies have focused directly on the roles teachers have assumed, particularly as they became empowered and shared leadership in the PDSs. In South Carolina, Berry and Catoe (1994) surveyed key participants in the PDS. Teacher education faculty overwhelmingly agreed that as part of their PDS efforts, teachers and college faculty had taken on new roles and responsibilities in teacher education, teachers had taken on research opportunities in partnership with university faculty, and PDS teachers and college faculty worked together to plan and conduct school in-service programs. However, it was not necessarily easy for participants in PDSs to overcome their traditional roles and views. Reporting on a different PDS, Snyder (1994) described that "all the participants had a difficult time transcending their historical roles, responsibilities, and perspectives" (p. 111). The problems with overcoming one's history included "the personal angst of taking on one's own institution" (p. 117), for as Snyder pointed out, often the obstacles faced were the systems to which people belonged. The change in roles for teachers and teacher educators, especially as viewed by their own colleagues, creates a serious challenge to the evolution of PDSs.

Rushcamp and Roehler (1992) analyzed professional development initiatives at a PDS and concluded that "role shifts of members on the central steering committee need careful nurturing" (p. 21). In this case, this nurturing occurred as the university facilitator and school principal sought ways to encourage teachers to assume leadership and to try out new ideas and roles. They also worked to act on teachers' ideas and initiatives and to nurture participatory decision making by teachers. They documented that teachers' participation and communication increased over the course of the year; however, they pointed out that "the teachers found their new roles as researchers and managers of professional development activities sometimes conflicted with norms, perspectives, and expectations of the teacher role" (p. 26). They went on to report that "by talking together about these conflicts and establishing shared understandings of the dilemmas and stress resulting from restructured roles, the participants resolved these impediments to change and built a stronger community of learners" (p. 26). Studies like this provide insight for those who struggle within a PDS to change roles and to enhance collaboration and provide illustrations of ways in which struggling with change can result in desired outcomes.

Brimhall (1993) examined teachers' perceptions of the roles they played in planning and implementing a PDS and the ways in which the teachers' sense of empowerment had been enhanced or diminished within this context. The results indicated that the teachers placed "a high priority on the freedom to use their expertise to make decisions about what to teach, when to teach, and how to teach in their own classrooms in order to meet the needs of the individuals and the group" (p. 15). In addition, although they desired to work collaboratively and to share ideas with their colleagues, they did not know how to reach this goal. It is likely that teachers in many schools and universities do not know how to work collaboratively (especially when doing so intrudes on their existing teaching plans and established behaviors) and will need guidance in reaching similar goals as they strive to establish a PDS. Several additional studies have revealed the ways in which participants from the schools and universities have learned to do collaborative teaching within PDSs (Hasbach & Hoekwater, 1993; Hohenbrink, 1993; Rosaen & Lindquist, 1992). These qualitative studies revealed personal struggles and successes in collaborative teaching.

Recognition of the need to empower teachers to take leadership roles was evident in the implementation of several PDSs. In the Puget Sound Educational Consortium, four middle schools were selected as sites for offering leadership development opportunities for teachers (McDaniel, Rice, & Romerdahl, 1990). Gehrke and Romerdahl (1992) in a later study examined the role personalization of teachers who assumed specific leadership roles in those PDSs. They examined the orientations of the teacher leaders in terms of task completion, relationship establishment, and knowledge development and the problems these teachers faced in fulfilling their new roles in the PDSs. Among concerns identified were problems with spending less time with students, fear of threatening the norms of collegiality with other teachers, concern for the hierarchical structure of the faculty, and a recognition of their ability to build closer relationships with the principals and university professors working in the building. As they pointed out,

within all organizations and institutions there is the need for participants to deal with things and tasks, people and relationships, and ideas or knowledge . . . . We suggest that how she [he] defines her [his] leadership role and where a teacher leader places emphasis will determine the satisfaction she [he] gets from the role. (p. 18)

The authors proposed that PDSs should benefit from understanding the ways in which different teachers react to the role of teacher leader and the satisfactions and dissatisfactions they might encounter in their orientation to the role.

Romerdahl and Gehrke (1993) examined the shared leadership of teacher leaders and principals in PDSs. Their preliminary findings, which analyzed the journals and interview responses of pairs of principals and teacher leaders throughout a 4-year period in the PDS, characterized the pairs as being primarily collegial/equal or as hierarchically differentiated. They pointed out that "collegial forms of leadership are more likely to arise over time and in contexts where decision-making is more inclusive" (p. 16). Next the researchers examined the pairs' views of the PDS as a total school transformation. They hypothesized that the pairs with broader visions for the PDS to accomplish multiple goals rather than a more narrow range of goals would be more successful. They found that

collegial leadership alone is not sufficient, but is required in combination with a broad vision for fuller implementation of the PDS ideal. The pair who exhibited collegial leadership and a narrower vision had implemented the PDS ideal only within preservice education, with little activity in the other domains. Further, only one of the two sites in which the leadership pairs held broad visions had had success in preservice and continuing professional growth as well as collaborative innovation and inquiry . . . The most broadly successful site is the site with the most collegial leadership and the broad vision; the second most successful has the moderately hierarchical leadership pattern. (pp. 20–21)

These researchers recognized the impact of contextual factors on the success of each site and pointed out that "the history, organizational structure and personalities of the school, and the district support for the broad vision of service appear to play crucial roles in the ability of the PDS to make progress on all goal areas" (p. 21).

Whereas the preparation of preservice teachers in the PDSs helped to bring about collegiality among the K–12 teachers and university faculty by giving them a common focus, the addition of becoming a teacher educator complicated the roles of the teachers. A review of what they had learned in their first year of implementing a PDS led Grossman and McDaniel (1990) to observe that "creating a professional development center entails redefining the role of a teacher to include the education of preservice teachers . . . [and that] adding the role of teacher educator to the already full role of a middle school teacher created a certain amount of role conflict for these teachers" (p. 6). Although the teacher leaders did not anticipate their own learning as a result of sharing their insights with student teachers, Grossman and McDaniel reported that "supervisors have begun to realize that their role in supervising student teachers has enabled them to learn more about teaching; in helping novices improve, they articulate more explicitly what they know and believe about teaching" (p. 7). Similarly, Berry and Catoe (1994) found strong support for the PDS teachers in South Carolina taking on the role of teacher educator because the teachers became more interested in their own professionalism as a result of being responsible for working with future educators.

A similar finding came from the research of Neufeld and Freeman (1993) at Arizona State University. PDS teachers were interviewed about their additional responsibilities of functioning as teacher educators in a PDS setting and reported that, in spite of difficulties, the added teacher education responsibilities increased their opportunities for personal reflection on their own teaching and their general views of teaching. However, the teachers especially expressed concern about the increased time commitment required of them in assuming this teacher education role. Neufeld and Freeman were surprised that few teachers saw a benefit to having these additional adults contribute to the instruction in the classroom. Nonetheless, the teachers in this PDS reinforced the preservice teachers' positive attributes rather than concentrate on the students' shortcomings. The researchers conjectured that because this PDS was somewhat unusual in that teachers were given the opportunity to choose to participate in the PDS or to transfer to another school, they may be unusual in their positive disposition. Nonetheless, these findings contribute to understanding the motivation of teachers in PDSs as they take on the additional role of teacher educator.

In New York City, Lythcott and Schwartz (1994) reported on a unique PDS in which they combined interdisciplinary curriculum, multidisciplinary teams of practicing and student teachers, and a team locus for all decision making. In this setting, the researchers reported that

it was clear that the teachers were not playing a traditional role with the student teachers. This was not a program in which 'experts' mentored 'apprentices'; rather everyone was learning together . . . . The student teachers were in some ways the proverbial extra pair of hands in the classroom, to help make the new activities work. But they were much more than this—their knowledge was valuable in that they actually created some of the most innovative ideas for activities. (pp. 136–137)

This report contrasted with the conclusions of Neufeld and Freeman (1993) because the New York PDS teachers seemed to embrace a more inclusive view of the role of the student teachers in their classrooms, rather than the more traditional view that student teachers were to learn from, rather than alongside, the classroom teachers.

Taking on the role of teacher educator in a PDS contributed to the teachers' opportunities to learn different things. Grossman (1992) reported that "this new role offers the opportunity to learn more about adult learning, about teacher education, about the world of educational policy and research in teacher education" (p. 186). According to Grossman,

emerging evidence from professional development schools and from restructured schools suggests that by fulfilling new roles within these sites, teachers can acquire new knowledge and understanding about teaching and broaden their sense of professional responsibility to include school governance and decision making or the preparation of tomorrow's teachers. (p. 193)

Indeed, one study by Nevins (1993) examined the way in which PDS teachers learned from their new role as a mentor of preservice teachers who were in field experiences and student teaching in the teachers' classrooms. Nevins documented differences in the kinds of learning, the vehicles for new learning, and the ways in which the mentors communicated with the preservice teachers. It was apparent that those teachers who most embraced the goals of constructivist learning and the goals of the PDS to include learning for all participants most faithfully modeled those beliefs in their mentoring of the preservice teachers.

New learning, however, was not unique to the K–12 teachers. Depending on the roles that university faculty assumed in the PDSs, they too have had opportunities for new learning. Lampert (1991), then a faculty member at Michigan State University, described the way in which she blurred the boundaries of institutions and roles when she taught in an elementary school (which soon thereafter became a PDS). She tried innovative practices with elementary children, but also worked with her preservice teachers and the teachers of the school to reflect on her practice. She maintained her responsibilities as a university faculty member and scholar in education. But even as she experienced these boundary-blurred roles, she pointed out that

these institutional reorganizations will not erase the tensions that have always existed between research and practice, between teaching as a profession and formal teacher education, and between researchers and teacher educators. These tensions will simply move from the institutional level to the level of the individuals who are trying to fill the boundary-blurring roles that restructured insititutions create. (p. 674)

Lampert's caution is instructive as university faculty and K–12 teachers seek to fulfill new roles and responsibilities within the PDSs.

PRESERVICE TEACHER EDUCATION IN PROFESSIONAL DEVELOPMENT SCHOOLS

One of the assumptions of a professional development school is that it is to serve as an exemplary site for the preparation of preservice teacher education students. Shen (1993) studied the school-based PDS faculty members' visions of the role of the

PDS in preservice teacher education and contrasted their views with what the literature identified to be the desired nature of preservice teacher education in the context of a PDS. The teachers' responses lacked innovation or vision for setting new exemplary practice and significantly differed from the goals described in the literature. In particular they did not recognize the goal of student teaching taking place in an exemplary setting. In addition, the school-based faculty members did not seem to recognize the role of inquiry in student teaching. Shen reported, however, that "the site supervisor's and teacher leadership coordinator's conceptions are closer to the literature, which means that the persons who have more opportunities to work with university people have developed conceptions which are closer to the literature" (p. 26). Thus, it appeared that the more school-based faculty have the opportunity to be involved with the university faculty in conceptualizing and enacting the role of teacher educator in the PDS, the more consistency there was in their understandings of the goals of the PDS as articulated in the literature.

The impact of student teaching in PDSs has been studied by several researchers. Teitel (1992) found that "assigning a cluster of PDS interns to work with a group of teachers . . . expands professional mentors for each student teacher and it reinforces the interdependence that grows among student teachers" (p. 79). Teitel also reported that having student teachers in a PDS affected positively the way in which university faculty thought about and worked with schools, cooperating teachers, and student teachers. These conclusions were echoed by Yerian and Grossman (1993) in their research, which contrasted students who completed their student teaching in one of the Puget Sound Professional Development Centers (PDCs) with those who were in traditional settings. Whereas they articulated many specific contrasts, the researchers found that those who had experienced student teaching in the PDCs felt better prepared than their counterparts to work with middle-level students during student teaching and were more positive about their preparation overall. Compared to the students in the traditional program, the PDC students were more knowledgeable about early adolescents and their needs, as well as about students with disabilities, including special education students. Although both groups "felt that their supervisors were helpful in their advice on instructional and management techniques, the PDC group was significantly more positive about the supervisor's feedback on the school environment, curriculum, teaching to multicultural groups, and integrating special education students into the regular classroom" (p. 11). PDC students consistently reported that they felt strongly supported throughout the program by school faculty, university faculty, and their peers. "PDC students, unlike the TEP students [students in the traditional program], continued to give credit to their preservice program for their ability to integrate theory and practice within the school environment" (Yerian & Grossman, 1993, p. 11). In essence, "PDC students felt empowered by their program" (p. 12). The analysis by Yerian and Grossman provided evidence that demonstrates the value of the goals of the PDS and the specific impact on the learning and attitudes of preservice teachers.

In a PDS related to the Center for Teacher Education at the University of Wisconsin–Milwaukee, Pasch and Pugach (1990) reported that they place up to 20 students in a single school to spend an averge of 7 hours each week in the building. Through regular meetings with cooperating teachers, student teachers, principals, and the university liaison person, they have managed to shift responsibility for placing student teachers from the university to the school. They noted that "it begins to create the expectation that student teachers are the responsibility of the entire school and not just of a single teacher. Their progress becomes a school-wide concern" (p. 140). Pasch and Pugach reported the benefits of having students in cohorts experience working in the inner-city schools and the value of these PDS sites in helping to overcome fears of teaching in the urban setting.

INQUIRY INTO PROFESSIONAL DEVELOPMENT SCHOOLS

Teachers have had the opportunity to participate in research in the contexts of the professional development school and often have generated their own questions to examine. Many teachers have asked questions about the impact of their instruction on students' learning of content or have become reflective about their role as a teacher educator. For example, Snyder (1994) reported

At I.S. 44, for instance, one teacher completed an action research investigation comparing hands-on and rote learning while another teacher worked with TC [Teachers College] personnel to document the January Experience. At the elementary school, two teachers wrote a history of the PDS project from a teacher's perspective, and another did library research on cooperative learning and teaching. (p. 108)

In some sites, university faculty have taken the lead in organizing teachers to participate in cooperative inquiry (Featherstone et al., 1993; Hunkins, 1990; White, Rainer, Clift, & Benson, 1994). Even in contexts in which there has been an effort to engage in collaborative research, the university faculty have still guided the research. For example,

an analysis of the Jane Long Partnership suggests that in the midst of complex collaboration, initiation of the research, establishment of the questions, and analysis of the results [are] still handled by the university in much the same way as usual. The analysis of inquiry in this partnership demonstrates that the initial planning, question formation, and analysis of data [are] generally directed by the university. The inquiry is conducted in the school setting and reporting often will involve school based and university faculty. (Wiseman, 1993, p. 12)

Wiseman (1993) reminded that

as we focus on true parity, the people who ask the questions may be different, different questions will be asked, analysis, and reporting systems may be expanded to include other outlets. New ethics for managing data must be considered. The results of the deliberations may be that interpretations are more inclusive to both schools and universities. (p. 14)

In a similar manner, Stoddart (1993) said, "What is needed is a collaborative staff development and research paradigm that respects the expertise and meets the needs of both public school teachers and university teacher educators and the development of a knowledge basis for teaching and teacher education" (p. 12). Accommodating the needs of both teachers and researchers is difficult at best and requires serious discussion and agreements early in the negotiations.

In other contexts, however, school administrators or teachers have taken the lead in asking and researching questions that are meaningful in their school context. For example, Soo-Hoo (1989) described a collaborative research project in which elementary teachers worked with a university faculty member to consider indicators of student achievement. An important point she made was "if teachers take on teacher research, this emerging role can have a powerful impact on how teachers see themselves as initiators of change in their individual classrooms and in schools" (p. 4). She concluded that it was valuable for teachers to engage in inquiry, reflection, and collaboration because it assumed

that the teacher is a professional, capable of examining his/her own teaching practice . . . . It positions the teacher in an ongoing process of intellectually engaging issues thus developing a community of thinkers . . . [and] it equips teachers with the skills to confront the critical issues facing public education . . . and develop the capacity of the school to respond as well. (p. 17)

In essence, SooHoo's example illustrated both that teachers are capable of participating in meaningful inquiry in their classrooms and that the benefits span well beyond the answers to their questions.

Many research studies with foci on curriculum reform, instructional practices with children, pedagogical content in specific subject areas, or learning to teach have been conducted in the context of PDSs. Attention to such goals as teaching for conceptual understanding and continuing learning by teachers, teacher educators, and administrators was highlighted by the Holmes Group (1990) and Murray (1993) as goals for PDSs. Researchers in the National Center for Research on Teacher Learning, the Center for the Learning and Teaching of Elementary Subjects, and the Institute for Research on Teaching at Michigan State University have conducted research in the areas of teaching mathematics (e.g., Peterson, 1992), social studies (e.g., Roth, Ligett, et al., 1993), literature (e.g., Cianciolo, 1991), and science (e.g., Roth, Hasbach, et al., 1993). Unfortunately, although these studies occurred in the context of a PDS, they seldom identified the impact of the PDS on their findings or the interaction of the factors that comprised the PDS on the teaching and learning of the subject matter.

Roth, Hasbach, et al. (1993) and Roth, Ligett, et al. (1993), in what was called the Literacy in Science and Social Studies Project of the Center for the Learning and Teaching Elementary Subjects at Michigan State University, worked with three classroom teachers in a PDS, two assistant professors, and three doctoral students in a collaborative model of reform. Their goal was to explore ways of engaging students in meaningful learning through different modes of classroom talk and writing primarily about science and social studies. They worked together in study groups, documented classroom observations, conducted interviews, and analyzed their own changing conceptions of teaching and learning science and social studies.

Their stories of their changes reflected the effect of a new professional development model and the effect of collaboration in changing each of them. Their stories gave insight into the connections they made in the subject areas, their new ways of teaching, and their value that all participants (teachers, students, and researchers) have the opportunities to think differently about teaching and learning. The authors at least indicated that the context of the PDS provided support for this kind of reform in teaching and learning, as well as for the collaboration of university faculty and K–12 teachers.

Peterson (1992) studied one third-grade teacher, whom she called Keisha, and documented how Keisha learned to think differently about teaching mathematics while in a PDS. Peterson detailed the impact on Keisha of a university professor who was teaching mathematics in the adjacent classroom in the PDS. Through discourse about teaching and by modeling the university professor's instruction, this teacher changed her instruction. Peterson said Keisha discovered the power of using student ideas. A further elaboration of the impact of Keisha's teaching on student learning can be found in Knapp and Peterson (1993). These authors provided an explanation of what they as researchers and teacher educators had learned about teaching for understanding from studying a teacher who was trying to implement the new form of instruction. This type of inquiry about specific instances of teaching is significant, but spans well beyond what can be summarized here. Some of this research could occur in any school and the PDS context is irrelevant to the outcomes with children. In some cases, the PDS classrooms simply provided an easy access for the researcher, but may not have necessarily affected the outcome of the research. However, as in the case of Peterson's study, it is important for researchers to identify the impact of the context of the PDS on the outcomes of their research.

CONCERNS ABOUT RESEARCH IN PROFESSIONAL DEVELOPMENT SCHOOLS

The operationalization of what is meant by a professional development school continues to plague researchers' ability to explain clearly what impact the activities of a PDS are having on teaching, learning, school organization, and teacher education. Researchers and teacher educators are often at a loss to define when a school is actually a PDS. Is it when the university and school district *label* it a PDS or make a commitment to create one? Is it when the *criteria* specified by the Holmes Group, another organization, or Frank Murray are met? Is it when there is *evidence* of the interacting effects of new forms of teaching on higher levels of learning that are studied and reported by K–12 teachers and university professors within the broader context of a reorganized school that also embraces teacher education? How sophisticated or developed must the relationships between goals and outcomes be to acknowledge a school as a PDS? If only a portion of the criteria are being embraced, can the school be considered a PDS? As Murray (1993) stated,

The emergent literature on professional development schools indicates that efforts to create these schools have proceeded to the point at which individual schools and universities have agreed to declare that a PDS has been initiated but not to the point where there have been documented improvements in student or teacher learning and understanding as a result of the PDS innovation. (p. 69)

Although some documentation of improvements in PDSs have been cited in this chapter, the overarching question is to what extent can the sites in which these improvements occurred be confirmed as PDSs in the full explanation of what a PDS is supposed to be? In other words, what evidence exists that the improvements resulted because of the interaction of the multitude of factors that make up a PDS, rather than, for example, individual teachers trying out innovative teaching practices? Houston (1992) pointed out the essence of the interaction of characteristics of a PDS when she said,

If we were to inspect a well-built professional practice school, we would find that research and experimentation have resulted in practices that truly enhance student learning and the life of the organization . . . . We would also find evidence that inquiry along these lines is valued . . . . This work should be important enough to warrant the systematic compilation of those problems and issues that individuals and teams have addressed through experimentation. From this, feedback loops of program evaluation should evolve that yield information about practices that tangibly improve instruction and learning. (p. 127)

Description of the systemic nature of the reform in PDSs is lacking from the literature at this time. Individual examples of experimentation with teaching methods, mentoring, or collaborative teaching provide very limited insight into the effect of the overall school organization or climate on the outcomes of the experimentation. Few of the studies reported to have taken place in PDSs described the impact of the context/culture of that reformed school on the outcome. Undoubtedly, there are many more studies that have occurred in PDSs in the literature, but they cannot be identified readily because there is no reference to the context of the PDS in the descriptors, perhaps suggesting that the researcher did not see the context of the PDS as significant in affecting the results. Peterson (1992) reflected this point when she stated that

While the "professional development" context of the school is important to Keisha Coleman, she believes that the principal and the teachers had established such a context through their own efforts at supporting and learning from one another well before last year, when the school officially became a "professional development school" associated with Michigan State University. (p. 174)

Although each school that is in the process of becoming a PDS is at a different stage of evolution, it would benefit readers of research to understand the context and the extent to which the participants are affected by the culture that supports the goals of a PDS. For example, it might be useful for the researcher to comment on the extent to which the following conditions exist in the school and their impact on the outcomes of the study. Houston (1992) identified four elements of a building code for professional practice school programs:

1. Students are provided opportunities to demonstrate their knowledge and skill in ways that are responsibly diverse and equitable, thus providing teachers, parents, policy makers, and students themselves with multiple and authentic indices of learning.
2. There is evidence of an orientation to educational problem solving and research that is experimental and collaborative in nature.
3. The induction of novice teachers into the teaching profession is structured to provide maximum opportunity for responsible experimentation and reflection on teaching and learning.
4. Educators understand the mission of the institution and their individual roles and responsibilities. (p. 129)

The complexity and cost of creating and maintaining PDSs may ultimately undermine the longevity of these innovations. There are many accounts of the difficulty in creating and maintaining PDSs (Berry & Catoe, 1994; Brennan & Simpson, 1993; Green, Baldini, & Stack, 1993; Murray, 1993; Neufeld, 1992; Snyder, 1994; Stoddart, 1993). The clash of the cultures of the schools and the universities and the difficulty in overcoming different goals, reward structures, time commitments, and perspectives on teaching and learning make collaboration difficult. Even after agreements have been reached, it is difficult to sustain the relationships over a long period of time; university faculty are drawn to other projects, teachers tire of having the added responsibilities of research and teacher education, and administrators change, thus taking away support.

The rewards for participating in a PDS are often very different than those with which K–12 teachers are familiar and comfortable. In fact, the very rewards for good K–12 teachers were often devalued or minimized in a PDS. Snyder (1994) commented on rewards for K–12 teachers, "Two of the major rewards they received were the pleasure of being with children, and the ability, when in their classrooms, to be the sole adult responsible for constructing classroom reality" (p. 115). The collaborative roles that are usually held in high regard in a PDS may, in fact, decrease the amount of time the teacher spends in the classroom with direct contact with children and usually brings several other adults into the classroom. In addition, K–12 teachers are generally not accustomed to spending time researching their practice or writing about their observations and generally have no built-in reward structure for publications. Whereas the teachers who participate in the activities of a PDS may be innovators or may find new forms of rewards in these new activities, collaborators need to be sensitive to the potential for this difference and ensure that the K–12 teachers are finding the activities to be satisfying as well.

In contrast to the reward structures of the K–12 teachers, promotion, tenure, and merit pay for university faculty typically relies on publications, grants, and professional presentations. These rewards are not immediately available from the hard work of building relationships, which are necessary precursors to conducting research in this collaborative context of a PDS. Snyder (1994) reiterated this point by saying, "At TC, as at most research universities, publish or perish is more than a cliché, it is an oppressive reality . . . [and] PDS-type projects are construed as service . . . . Participants were not, therefore, particularly well rewarded for their efforts with schools" (p. 114). Winitzky, Stoddart, and O'Keefe (1992) cautioned,

If university faculty conduct the field-based, applied research called for in the Holmes agenda and valued in the public schools, our research productivity and the perceived stature of the journals we publish may decline. It will take time for teachers to develop understanding of research, and every step taken collaboratively, from framing research questions, to data collection and analysis, to writing up the findings, will take longer . . . . Such collaborative research does not carry the stature of traditional educational research and is weighted accordingly in promotion, tenure, and merit pay decisions. (pp. 8–9)

For PDSs to survive, universities will have to take seriously this kind of research and count it in the reward structure for faculty.

Such an emphasis on standard research, however, is not always the result of administrative decisions. Berry and Catoe (1994) cite one university administrator from their study in South Carolina who claimed that "university faculty have not been willing to change to a reward system that could indeed support PDSs" (p. 193). In other words, it may require university faculty to broaden their view of the value of work in PDSs as well as the descriptive, generally qualitative, and often collaboratively written research that emerges from the work. Faculty may need to alter the criteria for tenure, promotion, and merit pay to include work in PDSs.

Harris and Harris (1994) explored the tangible and intangible cost and benefits of university–school partnerships. Tangible costs include time, services, and facilities; intangible costs include pressure, communication, and control; tangible benefits include time, service, and facilities; and intangible benefits include educational quality, communication, and empowerment. They assigned dollar values to many of the costs and benefits. Their formulation could be useful for those who wish to examine the costs and benefits of their PDSs. The financial burden of reallocating time for a teacher to participate in inquiry or teacher education is not easily borne by a school district. Similarly, the cost of rearranging faculty schedules to work in PDSs is generally difficult to absorb in a college budget. In addition, the activity of building collaborations and maintaining these relationships is labor intensive with many hours being spent in meetings that do not immediately reap a quantifiable benefit.

Evidence of the strain of supporting PDSs in their originally conceptualized form comes from the Puget Sound Professional Development Center (PDC) whose research contributed strongly to this chapter. In essence, the PDC has been phased out and those schools that had participated in the PDC have been invited to be partner schools with the University of Washington without the level of collaboration and inquiry that had epitomized the earlier relationships. In these new relationships, the focus of the activity will be on preservice teacher education rather than the multiple goals of the PDC and, rather than constructed through the balanced relationships of the PDS, will be directed by the university in a more traditional manner. Apparently the costs of maintaining the intensity of the relationships were too great and they outweighed the benefits.

If there are as many PDS efforts underway as claimed (Darling-Hammond, 1994, p. 2), it is unfortunate that the reports cited have come from only a small percentage of them. Unless a systematic research program in which many people are invested is developed and the outcomes of the research valued, educators may never know the possible benefits of a PDS. In essence, PDSs could be in jeopardy given the many factors that impinge on their probable success. The need to document the benefits of PDS efforts and specifically the outcomes that have been accomplished is great. Such documentation could provide the evidence to garner continued support from administrators who must justify the added expense of PDS participation as well as the support of private and governmental funding agencies that might be inclined to fund such educational innovations.

BENEFITS OF STUDYING PROFESSIONAL DEVELOPMENT SCHOOLS

The need to study professional development schools and the impact of their structure on improved teaching and learning extends beyond building a case for the financial support that might be mustered to continue PDSs. There are many benefits to studying PDSs; at this time of call for reform in education, the PDS movement provides a specific context in which to investigate efforts to restructure schools, empower teachers, and reform teaching and learning. Such examinations, however, need to focus on the complexities of the interactions of schooling, teaching, and learning, as well as the new roles and responsibilities called for in a PDS. Unlike other reform efforts that only approach one or two of the educational issues, the PDS effort brings together many issues and anticipates their interaction with each other to bring about the desired goals. One study by McCarthey and Peterson (1993) spoke to the issue of the interactions of components within the context affecting teaching. They stated

Our study demonstrated the complex interactions of individuals within contexts, suggesting that both individual differences within teachers as well as the layers of context within which teachers work affect their thinking and the ways that they create their practice . . . . Further, we suggest that supportive contexts for teacher learning include not only administrative support and a climate for risk-taking but also participation in and linkage among professional communities. (pp. 160–161)

More studies that point out and explain the impact of the various features of a PDS on the teaching and learning and school organization are needed. As Dana (1994) noted, "As our collaborative research project progressed, it became apparent that teacher change and school change were intricately intertwined with the development of a sense of teacher voice" (p. 15). The benefit of learning from teachers remains a unique contribution of research in PDSs.

The study of PDSs brings attention to teacher learning and provides an outlet for the teachers' voices in understanding the complexities of teaching. The National Center for Research on Teacher Learning has had as its primary objective examining how teachers learn to teach and change their practice given their beliefs, attitudes, and dispositions toward teaching, learning, schooling, and learners (Kennedy, 1991). However, the opportunity for teachers to work with university researchers augments the likelihood that the teachers' experiences in trying out new forms of teaching will be codified and made public. Teachers expressing their new understandings and experiences with the process of trying out new forms of teaching enhances the probability that other practitioners will identify with their experiences and potentially seek similar opportunities to improve their own practice. As evidenced from several articles (e.g., Ball & Rundquist, 1993; McCarthey & Peterson, 1993; Wilson, with Miller and Yerkes, 1993), teachers can significantly benefit from regular interaction with university faculty who are engaged in teaching in new ways and investigating the results of their practice. The benefit of bringing to light the teachers' perspectives on these learnings is that it expands their perspectives and provides a different expression of the complexities of teaching. Teachers and teacher educators can benefit from better understanding how teachers learn new information and how they unlearn some of the dispositions toward teaching and learning that may be in opposition to the goals of teaching for higher levels of understanding and learning by all students. Another benefit of studying PDSs is the opportunity to examine the impact of bringing university teacher educators into the schools with a new role. Much of the criticism of teacher education has focused on the "ivory tower" nature of the university faculty's perspective on how schools operate and what K–12 students are like. When university faculty are in the schools trying out new forms of teaching; documenting the impact of teaching methods on students' learning, motivation, and behavior; and evaluating the effectiveness of their learning theories, they are more likely to meaningfully adjust their own understandings and to be more credible in their own courses. The goal of improving both teacher education and in-service education for teachers can more readily be met when teacher educators have the reality base of being in the school and testing their ideas in the K–12 classroom. However, the PDS challenges teachers, teacher educators, university administrators, and school administrators to overcome traditional roles, to go beyond the familiar, and to seek new relationships as they collaborate to fulfill the goals of PDSs.

Again, the benefit of studying PDSs is that the results could provide a basis for helping to sustain this reform effort. Although the difficulties in creating PDSs are numerous, their documentation could be useful to others who are also struggling to form these new cultures. Although each school context and school–university–community collaboration provides unique dilemmas, those who strive to create PDSs should have the opportunity to learn from each others' experiences. Documentation of the development of PDSs potentially provides an opportunity to identify the barriers and facilitators of success in creating and sustaining PDSs. In addition, publication of research that confirms positive impacts of teaching, learning, school organization, role definition, and cultural change through the collaboration of schools and universities in PDSs provides a rationale for the continuation of such efforts. This kind of evidence can contribute to the argument for funding of PDSs and the motivation of administrators and faculty to support such activities.

The difficulty of explaining and studying the impact of all the forces that interact in a PDS poses a challenge to the research effort, both methodologically and pragmatically. The challenge is to ask important questions about the PDS and to collect and analyze systematically the data, giving as much clarity to the conclusions as possible. However, in the midst of enacting and embracing such changes in K–12 schools and universities, the caution about research in PDSs provided by Darling-Hammond (1992) should be central in the thinking by university and K–12 faculty. She stated

Experimentation can harm students, if it is conducted without care and appropriate safeguards. Too much innovation for its own sake can result in faddism and lack of a coherent philosophy over time and across classrooms in a school. Thus, research in the professional practice school must also be subject to careful faculty deliberation regarding its necessity, desirability, and likely effects on children; to monitoring while in progress; and to the informed consent of parents. (pp. 96–97)

CONCLUSION

PDSs hold much promise as a means of reforming teaching and learning in schools, the preparation of novice educators, and the organization of schools. The ambitious agenda of the Holmes Group and other reform efforts challenge teachers, administrators, teacher educators, and researchers to construct new ways of working together. Systematic research about their efforts to engage in these reforms and the outcomes is critically needed. Finally, dissemination of the positive results of their efforts to affect positively learning by all students and the professional development of all educators is needed if reform of education through the means of PDSs is to have an impact.

References

Anderson, C. R. (Ed.). (1993). *Voices of change: A report of the clinical schools project.* Washington, DC: American Association of Colleges for Teacher Education.

Ball, D. L., & Rundquist, S. R. (1993). Collaboration as a context for joining teacher learning with learning about teaching. In D. K. Cohen, M. W. McLaughlin, & J. E. Talbert (Eds.), *Teaching for understanding: Challenges for policy and practice* (pp. 13–42). San Francisco: Jossey-Bass.

Bauer, N. J. (1991a, April). *Professional development schools: A reflective analysis.* Paper presented at the annual spring conference of New York State Foundations of Education Association, Binghamton. (ERIC Document Reproduction Service No. ED 338 567)

Bauer, N. J. (1991b, April). *Professional development schools: Initiating a conversation.* Paper presented at the spring conference of Confederated Organizations for Teacher Education, Syracuse, NY. (ERIC Document Reproduction Service No. ED 339 681)

Berry, B., & Catoe, S. (1994). Creating professional development schools: Policy and practice in South Carolina's PDS initiative. In L. Darling-Hammond (Ed.), *Professional development schools: Schools for developing a profession* (pp. 176–202). New York: Teachers College Press.

Brainard, F. (1989). *Professional development schools: Status as of 1989* (Occasional Paper No. 9). Seattle: University of Washington, Institute for the Study of Educational Policy.

Brennan, S., & Simpson, K. (1993, Summer). The professional development school: Lessons from the past, prospects for the future. *Action in Teacher Education, 15*(2), 9–17.

Brimhall, P. A. (1993, April). *Restructuring and teacher empowerment.* Paper presented at the annual meeting of the American Educational Research Association, Atlanta.

Brookhart, S. M., & Loadman, W. E. (1992). School university collaboration: Across cultures. *Teaching Education, 4*(2), 53–68.

Carnegie Forum on Education and the Economy. (1986, May). *A nation prepared: Teachers for the 21st century.* New York: Author.

Cianciolo, P. J. (1991). *Teaching children to respond critically/aesthetically to picture books as literature* (Elementary Subjects Center Series No. 34). East Lansing: Michigan State University, Institute for Research on Teaching.

Cohen, D. K., McLaughlin, M. W., & Talbert, J. E. (Eds.). (1993). *Teaching for understanding: Challenges for policy and practice.* San Francisco: Jossey-Bass.

Dana, N. F. (1994). Building partnerships to effect educational changes: School culture and the finding of teacher voice. In M. J. O'Hair & S. J. Odell (Eds.), *Partnerships in education: Teacher education yearbook II* (pp. 11–26). Fort Worth, TX: Harcourt Brace College Publishers.

Darling-Hammond, L. (1992). Accountability for professional practice. In M. Levine (Ed.), *Professional practice schools: Linking teacher education and school reform* (pp. 81–104). New York: Teachers College Press.

Darling-Hammond, L. (1994). Developing professional development schools: Early lessons, challenge, and promises. In L. Darling-Hammond (Ed.), *Professional development schools: Schools for developing a profession* (pp. 1–27). New York: Teachers College Press.

Featherstone, H., Pfeiffer, L., Smith, S. P., Beasley, K., Corbin, D., Derksen, J., Pasek, L., Shank, C., & Shears, M. (1993). *"Could you say more about that?" A conversation about the development of a group's investigation of mathematics teaching* (Craft paper 93-2). East Lansing, MI: National Center for Research on Teacher Learning.

Field, T. T. (1990, April). *Establishing professional development schools: Forging school/university partnerships in West Virginia.* Paper presented at the annual meeting of the American Educational Research Association, Boston. (ERIC Document Reproduction Service No. ED 325 272)

Field, T. T. (1991, March). *Toward a shared vision of education reform: Establishing professional development schools.* Paper presented at the annual meeting of the American Association of Colleges for Teacher Education, Atlanta. (ERIC Document Reproduction Service No. ED 337 426)

Gehrke, N. (1991). Simultaneous improvement of schooling and the education of teachers: Creating a collaborative consciousness. *Metropolitan Universities, 2*(1), 43–50.

Gehrke, N. J., & Romerdahl, N. S. (1992, April). *Role personalization of teacher leaders in a professional development school.* Paper presented at the annual meeting of the American Educational Research Association, San Francisco.

Gehrke, N., Young, D., & Sagmiller, K. (1991, April). *Critical analysis of the creation of a new culture: A professional development center for teachers.* Paper presented at the annual meeting of the American Educational Research Association, Chicago.

Goodlad, J. I. (1993). School-university partnerships and partner schools. In P. G. Altbach, H. G. Petrie, M. J. Shujaa, & L. Weis (Eds.), *Educational policy: Volume 7, Number 1. Professional development schools* (pp. 24–39). Newbury Park, CA: Corwin Press.

Green, N., Baldini, B., & Stack, W. M. (1993, Summer). Spanning cultures: Teachers and professors in professional development schools. *Action in teacher education, 15*(2), 18–24.

Grossman, P. L. (1992). Teaching to learn. In A. Lieberman (Ed.), *The changing contexts of teaching: 91st NSSE yearbook* (pp. 179–196). Chicago: The University of Chicago.

Grossman, P. L. (1994). In pursuit of a dual agenda: Creating a middle level professional development school. In L. Darling-Hammond (Ed.), *Professional development schools: Schools for developing a profession* (pp. 50–73). New York: Teachers College Press.

Grossman, P. L., & McDaniel, J. E. (1990, April). *Breaking boundaries: Restructuring preservice teacher education as a collaborative school/university venture.* Paper presented at the annual meeting of the American Educational Research Association, Boston.

Harris, R. C., & Harris, M. F. (1994). University/school partnerships: Exploring tangible and intangible costs and benefits. In M. J. O'Hair & S. J. Odell (Eds.), *Partnerships in education: Teacher education yearbook II* (pp. 45–68). Fort Worth, TX: Harcourt Brace College Publishers.

Hasbach, C., & Hoekwater, E. (1993, February). *The smile, the journey, and the quilt: A story of collaborative teaching and learning in social studies* (Series No. 70). East Lansing: Michigan State University, The Center for the Learning and Teaching of Elementary Subjects, Institute for Research on Teaching.

Hendricks-Lee, M. S. (1993, April). *Creating professional practice schools: Collaboration as conversation.* Paper presented at the annual meeting of the American Educational Research Association, Atlanta.

Hohenbrink, J. (1993). *The influence of collaboratively teaching: University and school.* Unpublished doctoral dissertation, The Ohio State University. (University Microfilms No. 9316169)

The Holmes Group. (1986). *Tomorrow's teachers.* East Lansing, MI: Author.

The Holmes Group. (1990). *Tomorrow's schools.* East Lansing, MI: Author.

Houston, H. M. (1992). Institutional standard-setting in professional practice schools: Initial considerations. In M. Levine (Ed.), *Professional practice schools: Linking teacher education and school reform* (pp. 124–132). New York: Teachers College Press.

Hunkins, F. P. (1990, April). *Cooperative inquiry: Beginning attempts.* Paper presented at the annual meeting of the American Educational Research Association, Boston.

Jett-Simpson, M., Pugach, M. C., & Whipp, J. (1992, April). *Portrait of an urban professional development school.* Paper presented at the annual meeting of the American Educational Research Association, San Francisco. (ERIC Document Reproduction Service No. ED 351 285)

Karlsberger, H. C. P. (1993). *Perceptions of teachers involved in the creation of professional development schools.* Unpublished doctoral dissertation, The Ohio State University. (University Microfilms No. 9325523)

Kennedy, M. L. (1991, Spring). *An agenda for research on teacher learning* (NCRTL Special Report). East Lansing: Michigan State University, National Center for Research on Teacher Learning.

Knapp, N. F., & Peterson, P. L. (1993, March). *Understanding learners' understandings* (Series No. 97). East Lansing: Michigan State University, The Center for the Learning and Teaching of Elementary Subjects, Institute for Research on Teaching.

Lampert, M. (1991). Looking at restructuring from within a restructured role. *Phi Delta Kappan, 72*(9), 670–674.

Levine, M. (1992). A conceptual framework for professional practice schools. In M. Levine (Ed.), *Professional practice schools: Linking teacher education and school reform* (pp. 8–24). New York: Teachers College Press.

Lythcott, J., & Schwartz, F. (1994). Professional development in action: An idea with visiting rites. In L. Darling-Hammond (Ed.), *Professional development schools: Schools for developing a profession* (pp. 126–155). New York: Teachers College Press.

McCarthy, S. J., & Peterson, P. L. (1993). Creating classroom practice within the context of a restructured professional development school. In D. K. Cohen, M. W. McLaughlin, & J. E. Talbert (Eds.),

Teaching for understanding: Challenges for policy and practice (pp. 130–166). San Francisco: Jossey-Bass.

McDaniel, J. E., Rice, C., & Romerdahl, N. S. (1990, April). *Building teacher leadership in an emerging professional development center.* Paper presented at the annual meeting of the American Educational Research Association, Boston.

Mehaffy, G. L. (1992, February). *Issues in the creation and implementation of professional development school.* Paper presented at the annual meeting of the American Association of Colleges for Teacher Education, San Antonio.

Moore, K. D., Hopkins, S., & Tullis, R. (1991). Professional development schools: Classroom teacher perceptions. *Teacher Education and Practice, 7*(1), 45–50.

Murray, F. B. (1993). "All or none" criteria for professional development schools. In P. G. Altbach, H. G. Petrie, M. J. Shujaa, & L. Weis (Eds.), *Educational policy: Volume 7, Number 1. Professional development schools* (pp. 61–73). Newbury Park, CA: Corwin Press.

Neufeld, B. (1992). Professional practice schools in context: New mixtures of institutional authority. In M. Levine (Ed.), *Professional practice schools: Linking teacher education and school reform* (pp. 133–168). New York: Teachers College Press.

Neufeld, B., with Boris-Schacter, S. (1991, June). *Professional development schools in Massachusetts: Maintenance and growth.* Cambridge: The Massachusetts Field Center for Teaching and Learning.

Neufeld, B., & Haavind, S. (1988). *Professional development schools in Massachusetts: Beginning the process.* Cambridge: The Massachusetts Field Center for Teaching and Learning.

Neufeld, J., & Freeman, D. (1993, February). *Teachers as teacher educators within a professional development school context.* Paper presented at the annual meeting of the American Association of Colleges for Teacher Education, San Diego.

Nevins, R. J. (1993). *Classroom teachers as mentors: Their perspectives on helping novices learn to teach.* Unpublished doctoral dissertation, Michigan State University, East Lansing. (University Microfilms No. 9326750)

Nystrand, R. O. (1991). *Professional development schools: Toward a new relationship for schools and universities* (Trends and Issues Paper No. 4). Washington, DC: ERIC Clearinghouse on Teacher Education. (ERIC Document Reproduction Services No. ED 330 690)

The Ohio State University, Office of the Dean, College of Education. (1993, February). *Anatomy of a professional development school initiative.* A profile prepared for the annual meeting of the American Association of Colleges for Teacher Education, San Diego.

Pasch, S. H., & Pugach, M. C. (1990). Collaborative planning for urban professional development schools. *Contemporary Education, 61*(3), 135–143.

Peterson, P. L. (1992). Revising their thinking: Keisha Coleman and her third grade mathematics class. In H. H. Marshal (Ed.), *Redefining student learning* (pp. 151–176). Creskill, NJ: Ablex.

Pugach, M. C., & Pasch, S. H. (1994). The challenge of creating urban professional development schools. In R. Yinger & K. N. Borman (Eds.), *Restructuring education: Issues and strategies for communities, schools and universities.* Crèskill, NJ: Hampton Press.

Putnam, J. (1991). *Initiating conversation at a professional development school.* Paper presented at the annual meeting of the American Educational Research Association, Chicago.

Romerdahl, N., & Gehrke, N. (1993, April). *The shared leadership on teacher leaders and principals in professional development schools.* Paper presented at the annual meeting of the American Educational Research Association, Atlanta.

Rosaen, C. L., & Hoekwater, E. (1990). Collaboration: Empowering educators to take charge. *Contemporary Education, 61*(3), 144–151.

Rosaen, C. L., & Lindquist, B. (1992, November). *Collaborative teaching and research: Asking "what does it mean?"* (Series No. 73). East Lansing: Michigan State University, The Center for the Learning and Teaching of Elementary Subjects, Institute for Research on Teaching.

Roth, K. J., Hasbach, C., Hazelwood, C., Hoekwater, E., Ligett, C., Lindquist, B., Beasley, K., & Rosean, C. L. (1993, February). *Entryways into science and science teaching: Teacher and researcher development in a professional development school* (Series No. 84). East Lansing: Michigan State University, The Center for the Learning and Teaching of Elementary Subjects, Institute for Research on Teaching.

Roth, K. J., Ligett, C., Derksen, J., Hasbach, C., Hoekwater, E., Masters, J., & Woodhams, P. (1993, February). *Many voices: Learning to teach social studies* (Series No. 86). East Lansing: Michigan State University, The Center for the Learning and Teaching of Elementary Subjects, Institute for Research on Teaching.

Ruscoe, G. C., & Whitford, B. L. (1991, April). *Quantitative and qualitative perspectives on teacher attitudes: The third year.* Paper prepared for the annual meeting of the American Educational Research Association, Chicago. (ERIC Document Reproduction Service No. ED 336 351)

Ruscoe, G. C., Whitford, B. L., Egginton, W., & Esselman, M. (1989, March). *Quantitative and qualitative perspectives on teacher attitudes in professional development schools.* Paper prepared for the annual meeting of the American Educational Research Association, San Francisco. (ERIC Document Reproduction Service No. ED 310 068)

Rushcamp, S., & Roehler, L. R. (1992). Characteristics supporting change in a professional development school. *Journal of Teacher Education, 43*(1), 19–27.

Sagmiller, K., & Gehrke, N. (1992). *An historical-ethnographic study of an emerging professional development school.* Paper presented at the annual meeting of the American Educational Research Association, San Francisco.

Shen, J. (1993). *Voices from the field: School-based faculty members vision of preservice teacher education in the context of a professional development school* (Occasional Paper No. 16). Seattle: University of Washington, Center for Educational Renewal, Institute for the Study of Educational Policy.

Snyder, J. (1994). Perils and potentials: A tale of two professional development schools. In L. Darling-Hammond (Ed.), *Professional development schools: Schools for developing a profession* (pp. 98–125). New York: Teachers College Press.

SooHoo, S. (1989, March). *Teacher researcher: Emerging change agent.* Paper presented at the annual meeting of the American Educational Research Association, San Francisco.

Stallings, J. A., & Kowalski, T. (1990). Research on professional development schools. In W. R. Houston (Ed.), *Handbook of research on teacher education* (pp. 251–263). New York: Macmillan.

Stoddart, T. (1993). The professional development school: Building bridges between cultures. In P. G. Altbach, H. G. Petrie, M. J. Shujaa, & L. Weiss (Eds.), *Educational policy: Volume 7, Number 1. Professional development schools* (pp. 5–23). Newbury Park, CA: Corwin Press.

Teitel, L. (1992). The impact of professional development school partnerships on the preparation of teachers. *Teaching Education, 4*(2), 77–86.

White, A., Rainer, G., Clift, R., & Benson, S. (1994). School/university partners in research: The potential and the problems. In M. J. O'Hair & S. J. Odell (Eds.), *Partnerships in education: Teacher education yearbook II* (pp. 27–44). Fort Worth, TX: Harcourt Brace College Publishers.

Whitford, B. L. (1994). Permission, persistence, and resistance: Linking high school restructuring with teacher education reform. In L. Darling-Hammond (Ed.), *Professional development schools: Schools for developing a profession* (pp. 74–97). New York: Teachers College Press.

Wilson, S. M., with Miller, C., & Yerkes, C. (1993). Deeply rooted change: A tale of learning to teach adventurously. In D. K. Cohen, M. W. McLaughlin, & J. E. Talbert (Eds.), *Teaching for understanding: Challenges for policy and practice* (pp. 84–129). San Francisco: Jossey-Bass.

Winitzky, N., Stoddart, T., & O'Keefe, P. (1992). Great expectations: Emergent professional development schools. *Journal of Teacher Education, 43*(1), 3–18.

Wise, A. E., & Darling-Hammond, L. (1987). *Licensing teachers: Design for a teaching profession*. Santa Monica, CA: RAND Corporation.

Wiseman, D. L. (1993, April). *Inquiry processes in the Texas A&M University-Jane Long Middle School partnership*. Paper presented at the annual meeting of the American Educational Research Association, Atlanta.

Wiseman, D. L., & Nason, P. L. (1993, February). *School university partnerships: Patterns of interactions between participants*. Work-ing draft of a paper presented at the annual conference of American Association of Colleges for Teacher Education, San Diego.

Woloszyk, C. A. (1992, February). *A study of school climate in a second-ary professional development school*. Paper presented at the annual meeting of the American Association of Colleges for Teacher Educa-tion, San Antonio, TX. (ERIC Document Reproduction Service No. ED 346 026)

Yerian, S. Y., & Grossman, P. L. (1993, April). *Emerging themes on the effectiveness of teacher preparation through professional develop-ment schools*. Paper presented at the annual meeting of the American Educational Research Association, Atlanta.

Yinger, R. J., & Hendricks, M. S. (1990). An overview of reforms in Holmes Group institutions. *Journal of Teacher Education, 41*(2), 3–20.

Zimpher, N. L. (1990). Creating professional development school sites. *Theory Into Practice, 29*(1), 42–49.

CONTEXTUAL INFLUENCES ON TEACHER EDUCATION

·11·

CHANGING TEACHER EDUCATION PROGRAMS
RESTRUCTURING COLLEGIATE-BASED TEACHER EDUCATION

David G. Imig
AMERICAN ASSOCIATION OF COLLEGES FOR TEACHER EDUCATION

Thomas J. Switzer
UNIVERSITY OF NORTHERN IOWA

"Everywhere there is change; yet, there is nothing new under the sun!" So begins Michael Fullan's important work on educational change (Fullan, 1982, p. 2). Nowhere is this observation more forcefully directed than at collegiate-based teacher education. There is widespread belief that teacher education programs have changed little since their inception, have failed to keep pace with the profound sociopolitical changes in society, and have contributed little to the current efforts to dramatically restructure and reform American K–12 schools. Indeed, there is a perception that schools of education are almost impervious to change and lack the capacity to change even when confronted by a host of conditions that threaten their very existence.

Virtually every significant observer of teacher education during the past 150 years has written about the absence of "movement" within teacher education and has called for profound changes in the form and function of teacher education (see Conant, 1963; Howsam, Corrigan, Denemark, & Nash, 1976; Judge, 1982; Silberman, 1970; Smith, 1968, 1980). Seymour Sarason's *The Case for Change: Rethinking the Preparation of Educators* (1993) and John Goodlad's *Educational Renewal: Better Teachers, Better Schools* (1994) are two more recent efforts by both critics and friends of teacher education.

During the past 150 years, the United States has shifted from an agrarian economy to an industrial society, from a service economy to an information age. Yet, while these changes have occurred, many policymakers and journalists contend that teacher education in the United States has remained relatively the same. Many suggest that the form and function of teacher education in a New England Normal School of the 1840s differed little from the teacher education offered today in a large number of contemporary teacher education programs.

In "Business as Usual," David Ruenzel (1994) offers insight into the causes and conditions that predominate in "ed schools" that make change and transformation so difficult. He offers an insider's perspective on the struggles underway to transform teacher education at one large, comprehensive midwestern university. Reasons given for the sluggishness of teacher education programs and/or schools of education to respond include the fact that "professors . . . have little time to consider how they could change their own teaching, much less the philosophy of a vast institution. This is compounded by the constant pressure to publish" (p. 37). One of Ruenzel's informants complains that "We're too overpowered by numbers. There's constant demand to what consumers want you to do" (p. 37). He notes that another factor is that principals and teachers "are, for the most part, satisfied with the training . . . students receive . . . [consequently], there is little incentive for the ed school to change" (p. 37). Ruenzel concludes his article by writing that "renewing ed schools and schools is a Herculean task" (p. 37), but one that is absolutely essential.

John Goodlad, in his *Teachers for Our Nation's Schools* (1990), devotes several chapters to the constraints and barriers that cause education schools to be so impervious to meaningful change. From mission uncertainty to the instability of academic leadership, from the powerlessness of the faculty to the absence of sufficient resources, from the regulatory burdens imposed by the state to the fragmentation of programs (and the isolation of faculty), from scholarly expectations to reward and promotion systems that fail to recognize service to schools, the issues identified by Goodlad are not dissimilar to the observations of a host of scholars. Geraldine Clifford and James Guthrie offer similar observations and add to the list by noting the fact that

213

education school faculties are "politically impotent . . . marginal figures in institutional politics and naive about state political processes" (Clifford & Guthrie, 1988, p. 40).

"Hindering forces," as identified by Zaltman, Florio, and Sikorski (1977), or "barriers to change" are numerous and can be grouped according to their common characteristics. Among these are lack of time, lack of effective communication, lack of agreement about what is to be done, lack of money to do the necessary tasks, faculty turnover, lack of faculty interest and cooperation, lack of central-university support, and faculty apathy. The barriers or hindering forces can be categorized according to peer and authority relations (e.g., competition for prestige or norms that enforce privatism), personal attitudes (e.g., fear of evaluation and rejection or failure), characteristics of the practice (e.g., does not meet the needs of a class or the change "has already been tried and didn't work"), and physical and temporal arrangements not conducive to change (e.g., faculty does not have time to get together).

Today, the convergence of a series of conditions provides teacher educators and others associated with schools, colleges, and departments of education (SCDEs) with the need for sustained and meaningful change. These "facilitating forces" hold great possibility for teacher education; they also present real challenges to the future well being of the enterprise. They include changes in the environment, such as profound changes in the demographics, cultural norms and values, family structures, and workplace expectations and technologies, that have caused K–12 schools to adjust to accommodate them. They also include the efforts at school reform and transformation, the quest for teacher professionalism, the search for a knowledge base for teaching, and the need to find ways to educate all children in a dramatically different America.

As society changes to an information society where equity and excellence are valued, where there is an expectation that all children can learn, where schools are challenged to provide students with the knowledge and abilities for an uncertain future rather than maintaining existing systems and established ways of life, the demand for changes in teacher education will intensify (Imig, 1987).

What seems certain is that despite barriers or hindering forces, America's century-old experiment with collegiate-based teacher education is on the verge of a serious transformation, which is stimulated by the immense loss of confidence by the policy community and others in the ability or willingness of SCDEs to insist on quality in those they recommend to teach and to alleviate the frustration of beginning teachers in dealing with teaching and learning. Academic leaders, journalists and commentators, state and federal policymakers, and teacher leaders give impetus to the movement, as does added competition for scarce resources among a rising number of campus-based academic programs and other sectors and needs in society. In this climate, detractors issue tomes; congressional committees hear testimony; state legislatures appoint study commissions and draft legislation to realign, if not eliminate, SCDEs; governors propose alternative certification; teacher organizations decry the preparation of their members; and national and regional agencies and associations make recommendations for new standards (Watts, 1993).

What seems not to be widely understood is that teacher education has changed profoundly since the mid-1970s. When the "bottom" fell out of the market for beginning teachers in the 1970s, enrollments in teacher education programs plummeted (National Center for Education Statistics [NCES], 1993). The ensuing 10 years saw a "sea of change" in teacher education; every facet of teacher education was changed, including the following:

- Admission standards were raised and exit requirements were increased.
- Enrollments gradually increased even while budget allocations were flat.
- Faculty scholarship expectations increased and new forms of inquiry, including ethnographic and other qualitative forms of research, were developed.
- In many places, curricula were recast to give greater emphasis to multiculturalism and the creation of a culturally responsive pedagogy, often leading to the recruitment of minorities for faculty and teacher candidate positions.
- The attention to pedagogy and "good teaching" increased, and faculty took seriously the demands for more "relevant" but high quality content.
- More of the program for teacher education was "pushed" into the schools and into other learning environments using practitioners as "clinical faculty."
- Faculties struggled to create "communities of scholars," often including K–12 practitioners, that sought to identify a common mission and a strong commitment to a single conception of the "good teacher."
- Teacher candidates changed (as they became older, part-time, more serious, and often burdened with their own parenting and work responsibilities).
- Cohort groups emerged, instructional laboratories were built on campuses (better to videotape and analyze teaching performances), and professional development or partner schools or other forms of clinical practice were explored.
- Refashioned foundation courses and fundamentally reshaped tests and measurement expectations called attention to new knowledge about assessment and cognitive psychology.
- The call for school reform intensified, and all educators studied the emerging K–12 content standards to enable faculty to reshape their methods courses and the overall "framework" of their programs. (Imig, 1993)

Data provided in the Research About Teacher Education (RATE) reports confirm that leaders of schools of education and their faculty have mounted a host of initiatives to change their programs. Consistent across all strata of institutions have been efforts to create rigorous admission standards, set specific exit standards, create formal partnerships with local schools, and involve liberal arts faculty more directly in the preparation of teachers (American Association of Colleges for Teacher Education [AACTE], 1991).

Despite this, there remains an extraordinary amount of interest in changing teacher education (Pugach, 1991). Change in teacher education, according to Penelope Portman (1993), means "to alter or make different the organization, content, or personnel of an educational system designed to prepare teachers" (p. 14). A variety of social reformers, educational leaders, and political figures have called for profound changes in the way prospective teachers are educated in colleges, universities, and schools. As noted, the calls for change span virtually the entire 150-year history of teacher education in the United States and consist of admonishments that originate from within teacher education programs, as well as those that come from outside schools, colleges, and departments of education (Ginsburg, 1988; Tyson, 1994).

Change in teacher education is a topic of much debate. Those outside schools of education believe there is great need for change; those within schools of education suggest the need for much less change. Indeed, many teacher educators claim that the changes in all facets of teacher preparation programs have been so profound and far reaching that further change is unnecessary. In reality, there is limited understanding on the part of both insiders and outsiders that there are degrees, or orders, of change. Both "outsiders" and "insiders" are probably right. As noted many teacher education programs are responding to demands or outcries for change by implementing (if they have not already done so) a variety of improvement efforts. These efforts, however, are generally single purpose changes (e.g., raising admission standards, extending the student teaching experience), often implemented through the vigorous efforts of a particular dean or department chair. There have been relatively few major restructuring efforts (e.g., shifting the philosophic underpinnings of the program and its various components to adhere to the recommendations and philosophies of one or more reformers). As a result, it is commonplace to have policymakers and others describe the first of these types of changes as merely "tinkering at the margins" or as inconsequential. This chapter attempts to explore this issue of magnitude (or order) of change and to offer some understanding as to why "everywhere there is change; yet, there is nothing new under the sun."

Certainly, some change is easier to "come by" than other change. The RATE studies suggest that the reforms most easily adopted are those that "do not speak directly to the nature of the teacher education programs themselves" and are mandated by external agencies that regulate teacher education (AACTE, 1991, p. 37). Nancy Greenman reviews recent change literature and confirms the distinctions these authors are trying to make between *first-order change* (also labeled *surface change, alpha change,* and her own term, *intraparadigmatic change)* and change that she describes as *second order, change in principle, gamma change,* and *metamorphorphic change* (Greenman, 1994). Sarason (1993) distinguishes between *primary prevention* and *repair efforts* (pp. xii–xiii). Greenman offers explanations for the attractiveness of first-order change, "It focuses on maintaining the status quo; therefore modification, or rearranging the same elements, is the format" (p. 19). It is her contention that what makes this type of change so commonplace is the fact that it can so easily be justified with external audiences and the policy community.

Charles Handy (1989), in his book *The Age of Unreason,* reinforces the idea that there are different types of change—continuous change and discontinuous change. Continuous change is a sort of evolutionary change and is quite comfortable. The past is a reasonably good guide to the future. Handy contends that change today, however, is discontinuous. Discontinuous change in a society is not part of the normal pattern and results occasionally in history when major shifts in society make old patterns of interaction inappropriate. Handy argues that in periods of discontinuous change, "upside down thinking" is needed to deal with the changes occurring.

Whatever the merits of the assertion that the change that has occurred in teacher education programs is first order, surface change, or continuous change, it is fair to suggest that few scholars and/or reformers have looked critically at the change process and have attempted to understand the sources for changes or the dynamic interaction between those who would transform or change teacher education from outside the university and those internal forces that are altering the fabric and substance of the program. This chapter attempts to describe these forces for change and the interplay and interactions between and among these forces and their impact on university-based teacher education.

Originally influenced by sociological functionalism, the authors of this chapter have spent nearly 30 years attempting to understand education and teacher education in the context of a larger social system composed of interrelated parts. Influenced by Emile Durkheim, this concept of society-as-system offered a basis for their early exploration of the relationship of teacher education to the wider social system. A related consideration is the work of the developmental sociologists and anthropologists who struggled to understand institutional change in third-world settings. One such source is the work of Milton Esman and his colleagues at the University of Pittsburgh's Graduate School of Public and International Affairs (1962).

In that work, Esman and his colleagues advocate "social engineering" to change whole societies and to address ways that organizations "symbolize, promote, sustain and protect innovations" to both survive and change. They introduced these authors to the concept of "interactions" between organizations and their environments and to the "interdependencies" that exist between an institution and other relevant parts of society. They contend that "the institutionalized organization does not exist in isolation, it must establish and maintain a network of complementers in its environment to survive and to function. The environment, in turn, is not regarded as a generalized mass, but rather as a set of discrete structures with which the subject institution must interact" (p. 5). Esman made two points: (1) that institutions must maintain "a network of exchange relationships with a limited number of organizations and engage in transactions for the purposes of gaining support, overcoming resistance, exchanging resources, structuring the environment, and values"; and (2) institutions must "manipulate or accommodate to these linkage relationships" (p. 5). The concepts of linkage and interaction will continue to provide a frame for this analysis.

Understanding the organizational environment, that is, the multilayered atmosphere surrounding an institution, is at the heart of understanding the change process as it relates to teacher education (Zaltman et al., 1977, pp. 16–20). Those who want to promote change in schools of education need to consider a host of variables: the socioeconomic status of the teacher candidates; the strength and impact of professional organizations, governmental agencies, and disciplinary-based groups; the influence and history of support or criticism by (and accuracy of) the media when reporting about the teacher preparation program; and the resources available from a number of institutions and organizations (including the host college or university).

Since the early 1980s, these authors have also been influenced by scholars at the University of Wisconsin–Madison's College of Education who contend that change, rather than stability, is the central characteristic of society, and that the chief cause of change is continuing conflict among groups. Whereas post-modern conceptions of society are tempering this viewpoint, there remains strong evidence that teacher education is a "contest" in which a series of actors or participants are engaged to determine various outcomes.

In "An Eight-Country Study of Reform Practices in Teacher Education: An Outline of the Problematic," Popkewitz and Pereyra (1993) portray change in teacher education as largely the product of regulation. Using the theoretical work of Foucault on power and knowledge, they suggest that substantial change in teacher education occurs as a result of changing patterns of regulation and power. They contend that changes occur as a result of tensions and conflicts in the economic, demographic, cultural, and political organization of the states and suggest that change in teacher education is responsive to such tensions and conflicts (see also Kritzman, 1988). Later they assert that the new codes for regulating teacher education, the redefinitions of certification, and the program requirements of state departments of teacher education combine to offer systems of control as power is exercised (see also Popkewitz & Brennan, 1994).

Popkewitz and Brennan (1994) describe two types of regulation and present both a theoretical framework and a summary of eight cases of teacher education reform in Western Europe and the United States. The first is regulation that "prohibits and restrains" and is found in standards, rules, and administrative directions (p. 15); these represent "external restraints on practice". Popkewitz and Brennan view such regulation as "repressive" and suggest that these types of regulation are "owned" by groups, forces, or individuals. They suggest that to understand the source and ownership of such regulation, one must identify those who produce and implement these regulations. They view the concept of teacher education as a social arena with various social actors acting together and separately to cause change. The second and "more subtle notion of regulation" occurs through the definition and transmittal of "permissible boundaries to pedagogical practices through sanctioning of styles of reasoning and acting" "in the patterns of communication" and in "the categories and distinctions of research" (pp. 15–17). In this conception of regulation, actors combine their efforts to establish what is legitimate, reasonable, or important and impose it on teacher education. New research paradigms and methodologies create "standards of truth" (p. 293). It should be noted that Popkewitz and Brennan (1994) posit the thesis that there is considerable space for human agency; that is, individuals are able to operate on both spheres of regulation making. Ginsburg (1988) describes a similar "duality of structure" in which macropolitical, economic, and ideological spheres of influence constrain and enable human action and consciousness, while at the same time this context is reproduced, challenged, or sometimes transformed by human thought and action.

In the Popkewitz-Brennan model, change in teacher education occurs as a result of these regulations. Popkewitz and Brennan contend that in the United States "the federal government . . . philanthropic organizations, universities, teacher associations, and education research groups all operate within sets of relations through which the curriculum, organization and evaluation of teacher education are formed" (p. 267). They assert that "the arena of teacher education entails dynamic interactions, changing locations, and strategies that occur to produce regulations in teacher education" (p. 19). They add that "each actor is positioned within the arena and engages a variety of strategies to maintain or to gain resources" (p. 19).

For Popkewitz and Brennan, actors include "formal agencies of government that make policy decisions," as well as actors "outside of government that influence policy" (p. 41). Important to understanding contemporary change in teacher education in the United States, they suggest, is recognizing the role of both government and nongovernment bodies in organizing and steering the processes, finding common purpose, and working together to set regulations. It is important to consider that teacher education in this conception has instrumental purpose and is an instrument of the state. It has political purpose. Preparing teachers for schools run by the state, which have compulsory attendance laws and a regulated curriculum, creates civic expectations for teacher education. An extension of this argument is that because the state legitimately holds expectations for youngsters schooled in the public schools of the state, it has the right to hold similar expectations for individuals and institutions that prepare the teachers and principals who staff the schools.

In his preface to *Teacher Education Policy: Narratives, Stories, and Cases,* Gideonse (1993) offers an overview of teacher education policy making and makes use of the rubrics of stakeholders, actors, and agencies to describe the interplay between the policy community and teacher educators. His text describes policy developments in teacher education in 12 agencies and/or institutions in which the "complex interplay of climate, role, structure, assumptions, issues and players" are described and analyzed (pp. xi–xxxii). It is a rich description of conflict and competition between various external forces and those within institutions and agencies. Interestingly, Gideonse and his writers assume that the reader understands and accepts the interplay between the competing interests of the state bureaucrats and politicians and college faculties as a given not requiring analysis or description. Gideonse does suggest that policy is the "goals, criteria, standards, and accepted procedures impinging on performance" (p. xviii). He also suggests that teacher educators must become much more aware and sophisticated in the policy process "in hopes that they become, if not wholly in control of their destiny, much more effective in its determination" (p. xi).

Gideonse offers a set of cases in which regulation is imposed from outside teacher education and has both direct and indirect consequences. In virtually all of the cases, change is dictated through externally mandated regulations. Mandated competition with alternative providers in New Jersey and severe limitations on program flexibility and content in Texas are among the cases offered by Gideonse. He also cites cases in which teacher educators describe their attempts to influence policy and to manipulate the "control mechanisms" to better their condition, but this concept of duality is not central to the description or analysis.

Certainly a leading observer of educational change today is Michael Fullan. In a recent study of the change process (Fullan, 1993) in which he devotes an entire chapter to teacher education, Fullan is instructive about mandates. He contends that "policy makers have an obligation to set policy, establish standards and monitor performance" (p. 22). Yet, he asserts, "You cannot mandate what matters, because what really matters for complex goals of change are skills, creative thinking, and committed action" (p. 22). He then returns to the theme of linkage and interaction and suggests that the connection with the wider environment is "critical" and that "healthy organizations have to keep a proactive learning stance toward the environment" (p. 38).

Fullan continues that "to prosper, organizations must be actively plugged into their environments responding to and contributing to the issues of the day" (p. 39). Fullan concludes by suggesting that "seeing 'our connectedness to the world' and helping others to see it is a moral purpose and teaching learning opportunity to the highest order" (p. 39).

Regulation can be both externally imposed and professionally enacted. Regulations are constructed through deliberations between and among a series of social actors. The degree of their importance is in direct relationship to the power held or controlled by the actors, agencies, and so forth. These authors assert that successful change (second order, change in principle, gamma change, etc.) occurs (i.e., alteration occurs) when regulation is brought to bear on the organization, content, or personnel of "an educational system designed to prepare teachers" (Portman, 1993, pp. 15–16). It must be understood that such regulation must occur as a result of the continuing linkage and interaction among a number of social actors.

On the following pages, such changes as they have occurred and are occurring from outside and within schools, colleges, and departments of education are examined. The most common response to change is resistance. Although nearly everyone within a SCDE recognizes that change is inevitable, those same people usually perceive it as something needed by others. The impulse to deny the need for change is as strong in organizations as in individuals. Change in any organization will generate conflict; to argue that this conflict is healthy and positive does not alleviate the fact that it can be painful to all parties.

ENTITIES AFFECTING TEACHER EDUCATION

To bring about real and meaningful change in teacher education is the goal of many educators. Figure 11.1 illustrates 17 entities currently working to affect teacher education programs. Some have authority and influence derived from their status as legal authorities. Legislators, governors, state boards of education, and chief state school officers (and their national and regional organizations) constitute this set of participants. Although they have long held authority to "oversee" or regulate teacher educa-

tion, they have all tended to delegate such authority to state agency personnel responsible for teacher licensure and/or program approval. Not until the educational reform movement of the 1980s did they seek to exercise much greater authority over teacher education.

Through the passage of laws affecting teacher education, the revision of teacher education policy, and the issuance of positions regarding teacher education, the state policy community has had an enormous impact on teacher education since the early 1980s. Gideonse (1989) includes eight case studies of states that have embarked on serious efforts to reform or to restructure teacher education in the 1980s. Included are cases in New Jersey and Texas, the two most notorious examples of state control, but there are also other examples of state policymakers intruding into the near exclusive domain of the state licensing agency. (See also reports of AACTE's State Issues Clearinghouse (1989–1994) that tracked changes in state policy and practice since the early 1980s.)

Others derive their authority from their base of resources. They range from philanthropic foundations, such as the Ford Foundation and the Exxon Education Foundation, both of which have invested millions of dollars in attempting to transform teacher education, to the discretionary and categorical grants made by various federal agencies (Stone, 1970).

Other chapters in this handbook speak to the influence of the federal government on teacher education. Those influences extend back at least a century and have had influence on the form and substance of teacher education programs. Recent federal investments in knowledge generation and dissemination through research and development centers at the University of Texas at Austin and, more recently, at Michigan State University have influenced the direction taken by teacher education programs. Federal investments in particular program models and policy efforts to affect form and function have borne an impact on teacher education. The emergence of Goals 2000, with its extraordinary emphasis on systematic reform and "official knowledge," promises to hold many more implications for teacher education. (See Chapter 15 of this handbook.)

Specialized and general media that publish stories and editorial pieces regarding teacher education, and thereby influence the course or direction undertaken by a particular program or SCDE, can also be cited for the influence they are having on the form and function of teacher education. (See Fiske & Wells, 1992.)

The research establishment has had a substantial impact on teacher education through its "codification" of a knowledge base and its translation of that knowledge base into courses and experiences for teacher candidates (see Clift & Evertson, 1992; Condon, Clyde, Kyle, & Hovda, 1993; Hulsebosch, Koerner & Ball, 1994). The influence of a host of research scholars, the work of the National Center for Research on Teacher Education, the efforts of professional associations, and the accreditation process have helped to secure attention to the knowledge base as a means for transforming programs.

The influence of the standards-setting movement on the education of teachers is another facet of the movement to enlarge the number of entities affecting teacher education (see Chapter 13 of this handbook). As early as 1987, the National Board for Professional Teaching Standards (NBPTS) began de-

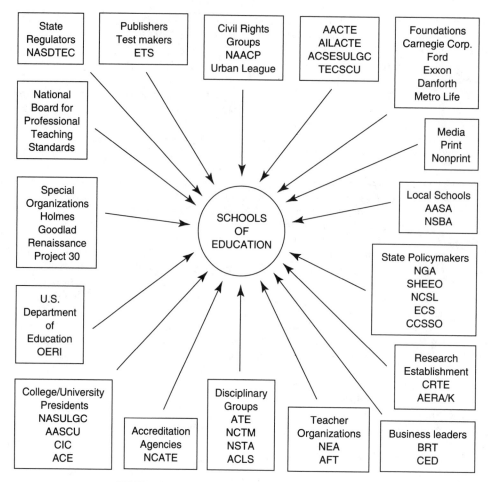

FIGURE 11.1. Entities affecting teacher education.

veloping standards and assessments for the certification of teachers (NBPTS, 1991). Although it is premature to assess the potential impact of the NBPTS standards and assessments on preservice or initial teacher education, a parallel movement to establish standards and assessments for the licensure of teachers is certain to have an immediate and profound impact. *Model Standards for Beginning Teacher Licensing and Development* is a statement intended to guide practice in teacher education. Set forth by the Interstate New Teacher Assessment and Support Consortium (1993), a unique network of state policymakers and professional association representatives, it is intended to change both the licensure practices of states and the program approval guidelines that regulate state-IHE relations.

Another powerful influence on teacher education is the effort of the two teacher organizations. Both the National Education Association (NEA) and the American Federation of Teachers (AFT) have supported a range of efforts to ground teacher education on a professional knowledge base and to fashion strong school–college partnership programs. NEA is currently sponsoring a major restructuring project that is investing in the change process for SCDEs, and AFT has launched a series of college–school partnerships and has recently announced its intention to offer graduate courses for practicing teachers in

both New York and Chicago. Both groups' involvement and leadership in national certification and accreditation, not to mention the NEA's strenuous efforts to support state-based professional practices or standards boards, indicate that the AFT and NEA are having a profound effect on teacher education.

The disciplinary-based groups (e.g., NCTM, NSTA, NCTE, IRA) are also having an important impact on teacher education, one that is likely to grow in importance as the emerging K–12 content standards for a number of subject matters are translated into frameworks or standards for teacher preparation. The sheer number of content areas for which standards are being developed and the expectation that beginning teachers will have mastered both appropriate content and the pedagogy to teach these subjects are certain to influence greatly teacher education in the coming decade (AACTE, 1994a, 1994b; Soper, 1994).

The National Council for Accreditation of Teacher Education (NCATE) has exerted a powerful influence on the content or substance of teacher education since the mid-1950s. Although less than one half of the 1,179 preparation programs currently are NCATE accredited, the standards used by NCATE influence state-based approval programs and help to determine what is important. Already evidence has been presented relative to the importance of the knowledge-base standard and its impact on "shaping" teacher education during the past decade. Similar documentation is available to show the importance of the NCATE process in influencing attention to multicultural education or a culturally responsive pedagogy. Emerging standards that pertain to professional development or partner schools are likely to affect all of teacher education in the future.

Those companies that have invested in writing and administering tests for beginning teachers are another powerful influence on teacher education programs. The Educational Testing Service is the most significant because of state usage of the National Teacher Examination (NTE) and now the PRAXIS series.

Groups of institutional presidents are offering their voices regarding teacher education. Although such groups have generally sought to limit or curtail the influence of accreditation or other external influences, their efforts to date have had minimal influence. More recently, the efforts of a number of "networks" of SCDEs are influencing teacher education. Although most of these networks are supported by philanthropic foundations, involve relatively few institutions, focus on a particular set of principles, and derive their "power" partly because of their exclusionary nature, they are having considerable influence on the universe of teacher preparation institutions (Sykes & Plastrik, 1993). The Holmes Group and the Renaissance Group are two such networks, but philanthropic efforts have spawned an array of other networks for institutional change, multicultural education, the infusion of context knowledge in teacher education, educational technology, school–college partnerships, and so forth. Other networks of similar institutions exist to promote dialogue and political action.

Clearly, the attention to "culturally responsive pedagogy" and to the recruitment of minorities to the teaching profession has been influenced by the various civil rights organizations. In combination with a host of other groups, these efforts are changing the character of teacher education. Perhaps the most evident result of these interventions has been to broaden or enlarge what Fenstermacher (1994) labels a traditional "decision context for teacher education," which characterized much of teacher education prior to the 1980s. Essentially, the most evident characteristic of that former or traditional context was the rather intimate relationship between the teacher education program and state authorities responsible for program approval. Fenstermacher and others suggest that the reform movement of the 1980s has dramatically changed this condition, driving decision making for teacher education from "a local (IHE)/state level to a local/state/national level, with diminishing emphasis on the local and increasing emphasis on the national" (Fenstermacher, in press). He concludes:

A consequence of the types of participants [entities] now involved in the decision context is an "upshifting" of the debate, wherein there is less discussion and decision making where [representatives of colleges and universities] meet the teacher education agencies in their own states, and more where these two parties meet with national organizations and associations, as well as the federal government.

TEACHER EDUCATION: FOCAL POINT FOR COMPETING CLAIMS AND EXPECTATIONS

Despite all of these efforts by various entities to promote change and new direction, the contention of many remains that higher

education teacher education is impervious to change. Some authors contend that the major change required by teacher education is to find its proper place within the structure of American higher education. As recently as the September 1993 issue of *AACTE Briefs,* John Mangieri, then President of Arkansas State University, titled his guest commentary, "Schools and Colleges of Education: The Unwelcome Visitor on Campus." His commentary, the landmark study of U.S. teacher education programs made by John Goodlad (1990), and a host of reports about the place of teacher education on the campus bemoan the fact that many institutions of higher education that once expressed strong commitment to and pride in their teacher education programs now make no mention of teacher education in their mission statements. The relatively recent formation of such organizations as the Renaissance Group and the Holmes Group can at least be partially explained by the desire of teacher educators on member campuses to ensure institutional commitment to their programs for the preparation of teachers. Provosts were expected to "sign off" on institutional involvement in the Holmes Group (1986), and the first guiding principle of the Renaissance Group (1993) is that teacher education is an all-campus responsibility. The Renaissance Group goes on to require full participation of the university president as the main criterion for membership. Even the work of Project 30, linking teacher education more closely with the liberal arts, can be seen in the context of building a campus-wide support base for teacher education (Murray & Fallon, 1989).

This effort to link teacher education more closely with other units on campus and thus build a support structure within the institution for the preparation of teachers is, of course, not a new phenomenon. It does reflect, however, an increasing awareness of the isolation of teacher education on many campuses and an appreciation that fundamental change in teacher education cannot occur unless the architecture of the university is prepared and willing to change to accommodate modern beliefs as to what must occur to strengthen teacher education programs.

It is the contention of the authors of this chapter that many teacher educators are trying to deal with change as if it were *first order* or *continuous* as contrasted to *second order* or *discontinuous,* and they believe that others will accept such tinkering. The authors believe that until there are fundamental efforts to transform every aspect of teacher education, including the basic philosophy that undergirds it, the changes will be seen merely as attempts to avoid serious engagement with societal demands and academic needs. The tendency to operate from existing paradigms is both self-imposed and results from existing within larger institutional arrangements that are not supportive of creative ways for the preparation of teachers (Switzer, 1994). Until teacher education breaks out of this frame of reference, the very existence of teacher education is in doubt. In effect, Clark and Astuto (1994) support this contention when they accuse teacher education and schools of education of lacking vision as they approach educational reform, and Switzer, in a report to the Renaissance Group, characterizes teacher education as operating from a closed-system mentality.

In the face of rapid technological and social change, we tend to operate with a stable state mentality. We need a system with open architecture.

Instead, we operate one with rigid boundaries. We hire faculty members on tenure track lines, provide them with limited opportunities for professional growth, and hope that they will be with us for the next 30 years. We place them in artificially defined departments and colleges and provide few opportunites for cross-departmental or college interaction. We assign them course schedules defined by contact hours with students, judge them by standard measures of productivity and tenure them when they have been around long enough to achieve success on standards of achievement determined by committee. In an age of discontinuous change we continue to perpetuate a closed system. It is secure. We understand it; we know how to manage it; we like it. In some cases the university we know and love has become our enemy. I am not suggesting, of course, that we dispense with everything that is good about the Academy as we know it. We must, however, be prepared to give serious consideration to alternative organizational patterns for getting the job done and we must be willing to engage in bold experimentation within these alternative models. The complexity of the solutions we create must at least equal the complexity of the problems we face. (Switzer, 1993)

Clark and Astuto support this contention that reform efforts in schools and in teacher education must be much more bold if they are to be successful.

The place of teacher education within the academy is likely to continue as a focus for discussion and debate both inside and outside the academy. College and university faculties and presidents have engaged in spirited debates for a century and a half regarding whether teacher education should be included as part of the academy (Atkin, 1987). John Goodlad is particularly pointed in his comments about college presidents who "rarely consider teacher education as a priority for themselves or their institutions. Many teacher education programs are tolerated merely because of economic or political expediency. These programs often have no organizational identity, no faculty with decision-making authority, and no constancy of budget and personnel" (Edmundson, 1990, p. 4). Such realities have prompted numerous efforts to "move" teacher education off the campus. These efforts have been sponsored by the federal government, philanthropic foundations, and a host of educational reformers who do not view teacher education as ever being accorded the funding, support, and promotion it so desperately needs (Denemark & Yff, 1974).

Goodlad's call for the creation of Centers of Pedagogy represents a response to the continuing neglect of teacher education in universities and colleges. He offers a definition and an illustration of what a center might consist of in both *Teachers for Our Nation's Schools* (1990) and *Educational Renewal: Better Teachers, Better Schools* (1994). His call for such centers is another form of an *alternative* to current academic structures for teacher education that Clifford and Guthrie caution have never been "institutionally viable." Clifford and Guthrie's (1988) contention that "academic departments, cross-campus teacher education committees, school districts, teacher corps, or whatever—none is sufficiently motivated, interested, capable, long lived, or trusted to conduct teacher preparation" (pp. 42–43) has been the predominant mindset. What Goodlad and others now contend is that such contrasts and barriers must be broken, that new forms, structures, and institutions must be created, nurtured, sustained, and evaluated.

Although it is unlikely that teacher education will be totally displaced on the campus, it is certain that the debate concerning the proper focus for teacher education will continue. What is obvious is that unless the preparation of teachers is given higher priority within institutions of higher education, there will be a continuing pressure to find alternative routes for the preparation of teachers; these alternatives are likely to lie outside of higher education (Hawley, 1992). Consequently, Goodlad's Centers of Pedagogy (or Smith's earlier *A Design for a School of Pedagogy*, [1980]) need to be examined carefully and critically by both teacher educators and policymakers.

CONNECTING TEACHER EDUCATION WITH THE WORLD OF PRACTICE

Part of the difficulty with finding the proper place for teacher education within higher education is the particular relationship that programs for the preparation of teachers have with the world of professional practice. More so than other professional schools that exist within the university, teacher education is closely tied to the schools and to the public perception of the quality of those schools. Although schools are at the same time seen as linked to the evils of society as well as the vehicles for making life better, teacher education is held responsible for the quality of teachers produced and for their performance in actual classroom practice.

The expectation that university preparation programs will work closely with schools is seen in the results of interviews with approximately 150 state legislators, governors' offices, and agency leaders conducted in 1991 and 1992 (Frazier, 1993). Among the several themes emerging from those interviews were the following:

- *Simultaneous renewal,* the renewal of teacher education, must occur in conjunction with the restructuring of K–12.
- Close relationships between higher education and the public schools have been too slow in developing.
- Clinical or professional development schools are a logical base for bringing the higher education faculty and public school staff together in a collaborative effort to improve teacher preparation opportunities while simultaneously advancing education programs for elementary and secondary students. (Frazier, 1993)

The call for school–college partnerships also comes from within the teacher education community itself (Bray, 1993; Darling-Hammond, 1994; Goodlad, 1994; Sirotnik & Goodlad, 1988). There is widespread acceptance of the belief that teacher preparation programs will be better to the extent that they are linked to schools and to those who practice in the schools. For instance, Principle Three of the Renaissance Group states that

Decisions concerning the education of teachers are the shared responsibility of the university faculty, practitioners, and other related professionals.

All segments of the education community share responsibility for the preparation of high quality professionals for the nation's schools. Although the college or university plays a key role in this process, decision making is shared with those who make up the larger education community. Those who practice in the schools are partners in conceptualizing, planning, developing, and delivering teacher education programs. (The Renaissance Group, 1993)

In response to those urging that teacher education be more closely linked to teachers, schools, and school reform, many programs for the preparation of teachers are now linked informally and/or formally to schools and school practitioners. These partnerships take many forms, but they may conform, at least in general terms, to the characteristics of a partner school or professional development school as defined by the National Network for Educational Renewal and the Holmes Group (Abdal-Haqq, 1991; Darling-Hammond, 1994; Goodlad, 1990, 1994; The Holmes Group, 1986).

Conceptually, such effort can be seen in Figure 11.2 being used by one preparation program. Figure 11.2 depicts the effort of one teacher preparation program to place teacher education clearly in the intersection of higher education and the N–12 school system (Switzer, 1993). Figure 11.2 also acknowledges the role played by state and federal policies and by the directives and standard setting of national organizations and accrediting bodies.

Less profound but equally important are efforts to bring practitioners more fully into the preparation of new teachers. The most obvious change is the increase in the clinical and field experience provided to teachers in training. Not only has the student teaching experience been extended to an academic semester, but that semester is being interpreted as the equivalent of a K–12 semester, often 2–3 weeks longer. Also important are the efforts to provide student experiences and efforts to have courses include school-based observation, tutoring, experimentation, and study. All of this is based on the assumption that such real-life school experiences will more fully prepare the teacher in training to cope with the realities of life in American schools while providing university faculty with an opportunity for field-based action research.

MAJOR CHANGES OCCURRING IN TEACHER EDUCATION

In addition to the internal debate regarding the "proper" place for teacher education and the external forces that are pulling teacher education into new partnerships or relationships with local or partner schools, there are a host of other forces that have an impact on teacher education. Among the most important of these is technology.

Technology and Teacher Education

A major development with an impact on teacher education, as on all other aspects of our society, is the rapid development in information technologies. Few people today would disagree with the statement that information technology has the potential to change fundamentally the current nature of teaching and schooling. If so, it also will fundamentally change the nature of teacher education. A large component of instruction involves interactions among students, teachers, and information. Technology alters the nature of those interactions because it alters

the ways that information can be obtained, manipulated, and displayed. Teachers and students in the future will have to learn how to adjust to new types of interactions, but equally important, teacher educators will also have to learn to cope. It is this process of change among teachers and teacher educators that will be the focus of research on technology and teacher education in years ahead.

There is, however, less agreement on the ability of teacher educators and others within schools, colleges, and departments of education to reach this potential.

As a field, teacher education has lagged behind many of the disciplines in higher education when it comes to integrating technology into the curriculum. In fact, in many parts of the country the local middle school has more technology and is putting it to better use than the local teacher education institution. (Willis & Willis, 1991)

Few studies exist to provide definitive evidence on (1) the degree to which instruction on the use of technology has been integrated into programs that prepare teachers, or (2) the best methods of achieving this objective. (An excellent analysis of this issue appears in Chapter 45 of this handbook.) Case reports and anecdotal evidence exist to suggest a considerable degree of infusion of technology into teacher education, but the degree to which such integration has occurred nationwide, or the effectiveness of such integration, remains undetermined (see Chapter 45 of this handbook). The research section of the *1991 Technology in Teacher Education Annual* (Willis & Willis, 1991) details research on strategies for integrating computers into teacher education and various reports on specific uses of technology in teacher education, but it does not provide evidence on the extent or effectiveness of integration.

These case reports and anecdotal evidence do suggest, however, that instruction through technology and instruction in the use of technology are becoming important components of programs that prepare teachers.

The process of infusing technology into programs that prepare teachers is also of great interest. Again, however, little definitive literature exists on how best to do this. Case reports, anecdotal evidence, and lessons learned from practice dominate the literature. Suggestions include the importance of (a) key institutional leadership, (b) saturating the environment with hardware and software, (c) providing technical assistance, and (d) focusing on institutional objectives (Waggoner & Switzer, 1991).

This last point deserves special mention because it suggests a somewhat different way of viewing efforts to infuse an innovation into a complicated social environment. The norm within the university has been to focus on the individual as the unit of adoption. A question frequently asked is, "How can we get Professor 'X' to use technology in his or her research?" This approach is consistent, of couse, with the view of these authors of the autonomous decision-making professor who may or may not decide to use a particular innovation depending on personal preference. This clearly puts the decision to adopt or not to adopt in the hands of the individual.

This approach can be contrasted with one that attempts to infuse technology into a system by making the technology an integral component of a solution to a larger institutional need. Technology does not then become an end in and of itself, but

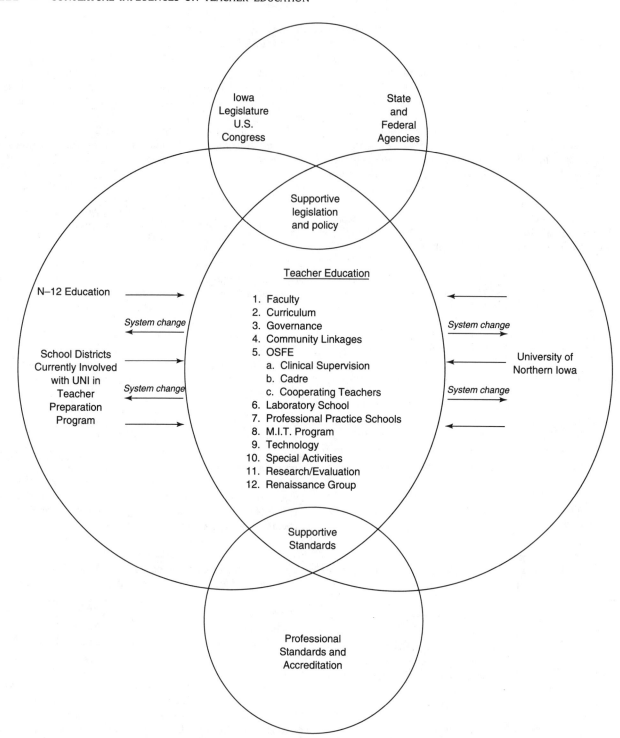

FIGURE 11.2. Forces affecting teacher education.

contributes to the solution of a problem. The most successful innovations involving technology include the participation of more than one person and evolve out of an identified organizational need and a general change or approach.

The impact of technology on teacher education may take yet another relatively unexplored direction in helping programs that prepare teachers achieve the dual objectives of (a) linking more closely with schools, and (b) changing the architecture of the university in ways that are supportive of teacher education. Handy, in his book *The Age of Unreason* (1989), forecasts that organizations in the future may find a considerable reduction in the number of core employees who are absolutely necessary to maintain the organizations. Increasingly, these core employees may be supplemented by other agencies contracted to provide a specific function for the core organization. These could be both long- and short-term relationships. A third level of service to the organization might be provided by people with specific expertise or people with portfolios who could come and go as needs of the organization dictate.

Technology has the potential to be a great facilitator of this type of organization through its ability to control the variables of time and space. Practitioners, once limited in their participation in the teacher education program, can now be full partners in delivery of the program. University resources can be allocated to their involvement. It is now possible to "teach into" the university through the use of technology and make more extensive use of contracted agencies and people with portfolios. With creative thinking, teacher educators could fundamentally change the architecture of the university (Switzer, 1993).

Achieving Diversity in Teacher Education

A persistent and yet unresolved problem in teacher education is how to achieve greater diversity within the teaching force (Dilworth, 1992). In spite of some exemplary efforts at achieving this objective, little progress has been made. In comparison to the percentage of minority students in the school population in many states, the percentage of minority representation in the teaching force is woefully inadequate. One can only conclude that current efforts to recruit minority students into the teacher education profession often are also inadequate. Part VI of this handbook presents related issues and research on this topic.

Emphasis on the Knowledge Bases

Another recent development in teacher education is the attempt to articulate clearly the knowledge base that serves as the foundation for, and drives the development of, a particular program. Howsam et al. (1976) describe the importance of a professional knowledge base and the potential it has for transforming teacher education. (See also Reynolds [1989] and Smith et al., [1983].) In part, this initiative has been "driven" by an NCATE standard requiring that each teacher program clearly articulate the knowledge base on which that program is constructed. The NCATE standard reads as follows:

Standard I.A.: Design of the Curriculum

The unit [e]nsures that its professional education programs are based on essential knowledge. Each program in that unit reflects a systematic design with an expressively stated philosophy and objectives. Coherence exists between (1) courses and experiences, and (2) purpose and outcomes.

This standard grows from the assumption that there is no single knowledge base for teacher education and that each program must identify the knowledge base that most fits its needs, the needs of its constituents, and the community it serves (Barnes, 1991; Gideonse, 1989). The result is the development of multiple knowledge bases in support of teacher education (Fenstermacher, 1994).

Until recently there has been no systematic study of the knowledge base statements prepared by institutions that prepare teachers. In January 1994, however, the Teacher Education Consortium of State Colleges and Universities released a statement from its knowledge base committee. The committee reviewed 44 knowledge base statements submitted by Teacher Education Council of State Colleges and Universities (TECSCU) institutions. (For an expanded discussion of this issue, refer to Chapter 3 of this handbook.)

Comprehensive or Integrated Services

Finally, a fourth significant force for change now being played out in teacher education is to focus on the needs of children in a more complex and challenging era. Although certainly not new, this effort is finding new voice in a host of organizational and governmental and foundation initiatives (e.g., see Ducharme & Ducharme, 1994; Lawser, 1994; Levin, 1994).

FUTURE DIRECTIONS FOR TEACHER EDUCATION

The Future of Teacher Education

It is difficult to document empirically the benefits of recent changes in teacher education. Raised admission standards, increased exit requirements, extended clinical practice, or the use of student cohorts intuitively should have changed the quality of teacher education. Whether, in fact, the quality of beginning teachers has changed significantly remains open to debate. These authors believe that these and other changes have had a positive and long-lasting effect, and that programs for the preparation of teachers are better today than at any time in the past.

The movement to identify the knowledge base for teacher education has required careful thought about the type of teachers an institution is trying to develop and the research base that undergirds that conception of the beginning teacher. These authors believe that this benefits the preparation program and brings coherence to the overall design and conduct of the program. At some colleges and universities, the campus-wide commitment to the preparation of teachers has brought education faculty into closer collaboration with their campus colleagues. This cooperation has been reinforced by the emphasis on quality teaching in all units of the university; that focus has provided proper modeling for students who will teach. The increased amount of clinical and field experiences in programs that prepare teachers and the development of cooperative relationships with schools have resulted in a reduction of the elusive theory-to-practice dilemma. Efforts to increase the diversity of students in programs that prepare teachers are beginning to have an impact on the overall character and substance of teacher preparation programs. In a few places, information technology is bringing exciting changes to universities and to their teacher education programs.

The fact that many of these changes have come only through the extraordinary efforts of faculty and deans will lead many to conclude that the changes that have occurred have been profound and will be long lasting. Others will be skeptical that such changes will fundamentally change the nature of teacher education. Until faculty are afforded the time to step back from the daily routines and to engage in a moral conversation about their responsibilities to create a just and caring society for all children, to hold a political conversation about the "regulations" in which they and their institution are willing to invest to benefit all children, to sponsor dialogue about the role of the public school in America and its purpose in preserving political democracy, and to debate the importance of beginning teachers being able to transform and restructure schools, we will continue to conduct teacher education in settings absent mission and genuine purpose. Faculties afforded opportunities to and empowered to debate the merits of John Goodlad's 19 postulates, the principles of the Holmes Group or the Renaissance Group, the standards for professional accreditation of NCATE, and the conceptual ideas of a host of other reformers will achieve much. Only when every facet of the structure, governance, funding, program, and staffing of teacher education programs is debated, analyzed, reconsidered, and "realigned" will there be truly significant change in teacher education.

The Dilemma of Predicting the Future of Schools and Teacher Education Reform

Change, of course, is not easy and the path to fundamental change in teacher education programs has resulted in some persistent problems. Teacher education remains chronically underfunded on most college and university campuses. Clini-cal- and field-based programs are extremely expensive and require differentiated staffing models if they are to be successful. Unfortunately, most colleges and universities have not yet accepted the costs associated with modern field-based programs that prepare teachers. They have not developed financial procedures to support these programs, and, with the exception of only a few, they have not developed a differentiated staffing model that recognizes and rewards faculty members who spend their time working with students in field settings. In spite of some dramatic changes in programs that prepare teachers, these programs continue, generally, to have low status on campus and low priority in the pecking order of the college and university.

School–university partnerships for the preparation of teachers, although holding great promise, have also been difficult to sustain. Where they exist on soft money, they frequently are not institutionalized into the college or university and, over time, tend to disappear. These relationships also need constant rebuilding, literally year by year, as key personnel change. Further complicating such relationships is the fact that the cultures of the university and the school are fundamentally different. Although these two institutional structures share a common goal of providing quality education for young people, the value systems that drive the two entities are unaligned, making collaborative work problematic.

Despite these reservations, these authors hold that schools, colleges, and departments of education have made significant progress in transforming every facet of their programs. They remain a focal point for a host of often competing forces and are marred by constant change; yet, they remain this nation's last hope for preparing leaders to meet the needs of American society and for educating a new generation of school personnel.

References

Abdal-Haqq, I. (1991). *Professional development schools and educational reform: Concepts and concerns.* Washington, DC: ERIC Clearinghouse of Teacher Education.

American Association of Colleges for Teacher Education (AACTE). (1991). *RATE V: Teaching teachers: Facts and figures.* Washington, DC: Author.

American Association of Colleges for Teacher Education (AACTE). (1994). *Setting standards and educating teachers: A national conversation.* Washington, DC: Author.

American Association of Colleges for Teacher Education (AACTE). (1994). *Teacher education policy in the states: A 50-state survey of legislative and administrative actions.* Washington, DC: Author.

Atkin, J. M. (1987). Reexamining the university's role in educating teachers. In *Strengthening teacher education* (pp. 12–21). San Francisco: Jossey-Bass.

Barnes, H. L. (1991). Reconceptualizing the knowledge base for teacher education. In *Changing the practice of teacher education* (pp. 3–19). Washington, DC: American Association of Colleges for Teacher Education.

Bray, C. (1993). *An American imperative: Higher expectations for higher education.* Kenosha, WI: The Johnson Foundation, Inc.

Clark, D. L., & Astuto, T. A. (1994). Redirecting reform. *Phi Delta Kappan, 75*(7), 512–520.

Clifford, G., & Guthrie, J. (1988). *Ed school: A brief for professional education.* Chicago: The University of Chicago Press.

Clift, R. T., & Evertson, C. M. (1992). Moving pictures, multiple frames. In *Focal points: Qualitative inquiries into teaching and teacher education* (pp. 117–123). Washington, DC: ERIC Clearinghouse on Teacher Education.

Conant, J. B. (1963). *The education of American teachers.* New York: McGraw-Hill.

Condon, M. W. F., Clyde, J. A., Kyle, D. W., & Hovda, R. A. (1993). A constructivist basis for teaching and teacher education: A framework for program development and research on graduates. *Journal of Teacher Education, 44*(4), 273–278.

Darling-Hammond, L. (1994). *Professional development schools: Schools for developing a profession.* New York: Teachers College Press.

Denemark, G. W., & Yff, J. (1974). *Obligation for reform: The final report of the higher education task force on improvement and reform in American education.* Washington, DC: American Association of Colleges for Teacher Education.

Dilworth, M. E. (1992). *Diversity in teacher education: New expectations.* San Francisco: Jossey-Bass.

Ducharme, E. R., & Ducharme, M. K. (1994). Teacher education: New societal challenges. *Journal of Teacher Education, 45*(1), 2–3.

Edmundson, P. J. (1990). *What college and university leaders can do to help change teacher education.* Washington, DC: American Association of Colleges for Teacher Education.

Esman, M. J. (1962). *The institution-building concept: An interim appraisal*. Pittsburgh: University of Pittsburgh, Graduate School of Public and International Affairs.

Fenstermacher, G. D. (1994). The knower and the known: The nature of knowledge in research and teaching. *Review of research in teacher education* (pp. 3–56). Washington, DC: American Educational Research Association.

Fenstermacher, G. D. (in press). *The decision context for the education of teachers, the knowledge base in teacher education*. San Francisco: Jossey-Bass.

Fiske, E. B., & Wells, A. S. (1992). A synthesis of the literature on education reporting. *Education research, policy, and the press* (pp. 31–52). Needham Heights, MA: Allyn and Bacon.

Frazier, C. (1993). *A shared vision: Policy recommendations linking teacher education to school reform*. Denver: Education Commission of the States.

Fullan, M. (1982). *The meaning of educational change*. Toronto: OISE Press.

Fullan, M. (1993). *Change forces: Probing the depths of educational reform*. Bristol, PA: The Falmer Press.

Gideonse, H. D. (1989). *Relating knowledge to teacher education: Responding to NCATE's knowledge base and related standards*. Washington, DC: American Association of Colleges for Teacher Education.

Gideonse, H. D. (1993). Preface. In *Teacher education policy: Narratives, stories, and cases* (pp. xi–xxxii). Albany: State University of New York Press.

Ginsburg, M. B. (1988). Teacher education in the United States: A critical review of historical studies. In *Contradications in teacher education and society: A critical analysis*. New York: The Falmer Press.

Goodlad, J. I. (1990). *Teachers for our nation's schools*. San Francisco: Jossey-Bass.

Goodlad, J. I. (1994). *Educational renewal: Better teachers, better schools*. San Francisco: Jossey-Bass.

Greenman, N. P. (1994). Not all caterpillars become butterflies: Reform and restructuring as educational change. In *Changing American education: Recapturing the past or inventing the future?* (pp. 3–31). Albany: State University of New York Press.

Handy, C. (1989). *The age of unreason*. Boston: Harvard Business School Press.

Hawley, W. D. (1992). *The alternative certification of teachers*. Washington, DC: ERIC Clearinghouse on Teacher Education.

The Holmes Group. (1986). *Tomorrow's teachers*. East Lansing, MI: Author.

Howsam, R. B., Corrigan, D. C., Denemark, G. W., & Nash, R. J. (1976). *Educating a profession*. Washington, DC: American Association of Colleges for Teacher Education.

Hulsebosch, P., Koerner, M., & Ball, E. (1994). Feminist pedagogy in teacher education. *Action in Teacher Education, 15*(4), ix–74.

Imig, D. (1987, October 16). *The challenge of change for teacher education*. An address delivered at the 20th Anniversary Convocation, College of Education, Georgia State University, Atlanta.

Imig, D. (1993, October 6). *A new beginning: Meeting the challenges of the 21st century*. An address delivered at the State University of New York at Oswego on the occasion of the inauguration of a new dean.

Interstate New Teacher Assessment and Support Consortium and the Council of Chief State School Officers. (1993). *Model standards for beginning teacher licensing and development: A resource for state dialogue*. Washington, DC: Author.

Judge, H. (1982). *American graduate schools of education*. New York: The Ford Foundation.

Kritzman, L. D. (1988). *Politics and reason in Michael Foucault: Interviews and other writings, 1977–1984*. New York: Routledge.

Lawson, H. A. (1994). Toward healthy learners, schools, and communities. *Journal of Teacher Education, 45*(1), 62–70.

Levin, R. A. (1994). *Greater than the sum: Professionals in a comprehensive services model*. Washington, DC: ERIC Clearinghouse on Teacher Education.

Mangieri, J. (1993, September 13). *Schools and colleges of education: The unwelcome visitor on campus*. Washington, DC: American Association of Colleges for Teacher Education.

Murray, F. B., & Fallon, D. (1989). *The reform of teacher education for the 21st century*. (Project 30 Year One Report). Newark: University of Delaware.

National Board for Professional Teaching Standards (NBPTS). (1991). *What teachers should know and be able to do*. Detroit: Author.

National Center for Education Statistics (NCES). (1993). *New teachers in the job market, 1991 update* (NCES 93-392). Washington, DC: U.S. Department of Education.

Popkewitz, T. B., & Brennan, M. (1994). Certification to credentialing: Reconstituting control mechanisms in teacher education. In *Changing American education* (pp. 33–70). Albany: State University of New York Press.

Popkewitz, T. B., & Pereyra, M. A. (1993). An eight-country study of reform practices in teacher education: An outline of the problematic. In *Changing patterns of power: Social regulation and teacher education reform* (pp. 1–52). Albany: State University of New York Press.

Portman, P. A. (1993). Barriers to change in teacher education. *Action in Teacher Education, 15*(1), 15–21.

Pugach, M. C. et al. (1991). *Changing the practice of teacher education: The role of the knowledge base*. Washington, DC: American Association of Colleges for Teacher Education.

The Renaissance Group. (1993). *Teachers for the new world*. Cedar Falls, IA: Author.

Reynolds, M. C. (Ed.). (1989). *Knowledge base for the beginning teacher*. Elmsford, NY: Pergamon Press.

Ruenzel, D. (1994). Business as usual. *Teacher, 5*(8), 32–37.

Sarason, S. B. (1993). *The case for change: Rethinking the preparation of educators*. San Francisco: Jossey-Bass.

Sikula, J., Buttery, T., & Guyton, E. (Eds.). (1996). *Handbook of research on teacher education* (2nd ed.). New York: Macmillan.

Silberman, C. E. (1970). *Crisis in the classroom*. New York: Random House.

Sirotnik, K. A., & Goodlad, J. I. (1988). *School-university partnerships in action: Concepts, cases, and concerns*. New York: Teachers College Press.

Smith, B. O. (1968). *Teachers for the real world*. Washington, DC: American Association of Colleges for Teacher Education.

Smith, B. O. (1980). *A design for a school of pedagogy*. Washington, DC: U.S. Department of Education.

Smith, D. C. et al, (1983). *Essential knowledge for beginning educators*. Washington, DC: AACTE.

Sopor, S. (1994). A standards primer. *Prespective of the Council of Basic Education, 6*(2), 1–3.

Stone, J. C. (1970). *Breakthrough in teacher education: A foundation goes to school*. San Francisco: Jossey-Bass.

Switzer, T. J. (1993, November 4). *Teacher education and the architecture of the university*. Paper presented at the Renaissance Group meeting, Huntsville, TX.

Sykes, G., & Plastrik, P. (1993). *Standard setting as educational reform*. Washington, DC: ERIC Clearinghouse on Teacher Education.

Tyson, H. (1994). *Who will teach the children? Progress and resistance in teacher education*. San Francisco: Jossey-Bass.

Waggoner, M. D., & Switzer, T. J. (1991). Using computer communication to enhance teacher education. In D. Carey, R. Carey, D. A. Willis, & J. Willis (Eds.), *Technology and teacher education annual* (pp. 135–139). Charlottesville, VA: Association for the Advancement of Computing in Education.

Watts, D. (1993). An interview with David Imig. *Teacher Education & Practice, 8*(2), 5–13.

Willis, J., & Willis, D. A. (1991). Preface. In *Technology and teacher education annual.* Charlottesville, VA: Association for the Advancement of Computing in Education.

Zaltman, G., Florio, D., & Sikorski, L. (1977). *Dynamic educational change: Models, strategies, tactics, and management.* New York: The Free Press.

·12·

FINANCING TEACHER EDUCATION AND PROFESSIONAL DEVELOPMENT

David H. Monk

CORNELL UNIVERSITY

Brian O. Brent

CORNELL UNIVERSITY

In 1983, *A Nation at Risk* (National Commission on Excellence in Education) informed the citizenry of the United States that its system of public education had placed the country at a competitive disadvantage in its market relationship with foreign industrial powers. Among the primary structural remedies suggested by the National Commission on Excellence in Education was the improvement of the quality of teachers and teaching. Many state boards of education responded by focusing attention on the reform of both teacher education and professional development. For example, one of the priorities identified in New York State's *A New Compact for Learning* is for institutions of higher education to develop preservice . . . and professional preparation programs for a new generation of elementary and secondary teachers . . . committed to achieving better results (New York State Department of Education, 1990). What the policy statement fails to address, however, is how, and the extent to which, such teacher education reform initiatives are ultimately to be funded.

State boards of education were not the only parties to neglect the fiscal dimensions of teacher education reform. Indeed the entire field of education finance was relatively quiet during the 1980s, particularly with respect to the fiscal implications of reform (Barro, 1989). An unfortunate consequence of this neglect is that numerous teacher education reform initiatives have moved forward with little explicit attention given to their financ-

ing. The resulting gaps have posed significant policy-making challenges for those seeking to implement ideas for reform.

Although the knowledge regarding the financing of teacher education is limited, there has been some progress, and it is the purpose of this chapter to report on and to interpret what is currently known. The emphasis here is on the most recent studies, although some attention is given to the larger context in which the research is embedded. Readers interested in the broader conceptual framework that guides most of this research, such as human capital theory and other key components of the economics of education, can find useful summaries in the previous edition of this handbook (Peseau, 1990) or in the *International Encyclopedia of Education*, 2nd edition (Husen & Postlethwaite, 1994).

This chapter is divided into three sections. The first examines research bearing on the fiscal aspects of teacher education. This section addresses equity concerns for preservice teacher education and continuing professional development. The second section shifts attention to matters of efficiency and productivity in the education of teachers. The third and final section addresses emerging practices with respect to the preservice and in-service education of teachers. This section of necessity is more speculative than the previous two because many of the reforms are at early stages of development. It is, nevertheless, important to consider the fiscal implications of these reforms

The authors would like to acknowledge and express their gratitude for the constructive and detailed reviews provided by Thomas J. Buttery (East Carolina University), Allan R. Odden (University of Wisconsin, Madison), Bruce A. Peseau (University of Alabama), and John Sikula (California State University, Long Beach).

if for no other reason than to prepare for the costs that are likely to be incurred.

EQUITY ISSUES

The extent to which resources are made available is presumed to be a critical determinant of the quality of existing teacher preparation programs and continuing professional development activities (Ebmeier, Twombly, & Teeter, 1991; Peseau, 1988; Theobald, 1992). Currently, however, much of the research on teacher education reform focuses primarily on program characteristics and delivery systems and neglects questions of funding and resource allocation (Denton & Smith, 1985; Ebmeier et al., 1991; Hawley, 1986; Nash & Ducharme, 1983; Peseau, 1990; Theobald, 1992). This section reviews the limited number of studies that have examined the fiscal implications of preservice and in-service teacher education activities.

Financing Preservice Teacher Education

The scarce resources of public institutions of higher education are allocated to departments and their respective programs through a series of administrative decisions, from the state legislature, to the university, to department officials. To aid legislatures in appropriating resources equitably among their many educational units, funding formulas are often employed. In this process, credit hours produced, the principal academic program productivity measure, are initially weighted to reflect the perceived differential complexity of the level (i.e., undergraduate, master's, and postmaster's) and major (e.g., English, education, business). Formulas are then constructed, based on tabulations of the number of credit hours produced for each discipline and level, and the resources appropriated accordingly (see Orr & Peseau, 1979; Peseau, 1988).

As Peseau (1990) pointed out, the fact that no a priori standard of adequacy exists makes it difficult to assess the extent to which resources currently allocated to schools, colleges, and departments of education (SCDEs) are sufficient to ensure the sound preparation of teachers. Analysts with interests in measuring equity in the provision of more resources for SCDEs and, more specifically, for teacher education, have instead conducted comparative examinations of *interinstitutional* (i.e., analyses of how well teacher education is funded in one institution compared to another), *intrainstitutional* (i.e., analyses of how well SCDEs are funded in comparison to other academic disciplines on the same campus), and *intradepartmental* resource allocations (i.e., analyses of how spending on teacher education compares with spending on other programs within the same SCDE).

Interinstitutional Resource Allocation The American Association of Colleges for Teacher Education (AACTE) annually gathers and compiles detailed information related to the financial activities of its member institutions. However, due to differences in accounting practices among the participating entities, the usefulness of the data base for purposes of designing comparative studies of resource allocation is significantly diminished (Ebmeier, et al., 1991; Peseau, 1990). Alternatively, researchers have conducted more microlevel interinstitutional comparisons of similar programs on peer campuses (Peseau, 1986, 1988; Peseau & Orr, 1980; Peseau & Tudor, 1989). (For a more comprehensive discussion of peer program analyses, see Brinkman & Teeter, 1987.) Peseau (1988), for example, used normalized data collected for the Association of Colleges and Schools of Education in State Universities and Land Grant Colleges and presented an intrastate comparison of teacher education programs in 15 states in three AACTE geographic regions. Large variations were found among teacher education programs within most of the 15 states as measured by several critical resource variables: funds for operations, total university funds per faculty member, ratio of support staff to faculty, and average graduate assistant salary. He concluded that because the funding for academic programs in a given state is derived from legislative appropriations based on credit hours produced and tuition, the financing differentials internal to several of the states can be attributed to the disparate value that officials within the universities place on these programs.

Peseau's results need to be interpreted with care. It would be interesting, for example, to assess the degree to which variation in funding levels characterizes the provision of other types of academic programs across the same institutions. Moreover, some portion of the differences is undoubtedly related to price levels. Nevertheless, Peseau's results, particularly those finding differences in program attributes such as the incidence of various types of professional personnel, suggest that there is little consensus regarding the "needed" level of resources to educate teachers.

Intrainstitutional Resource Allocation Researchers have also examined the funding of education programs relative to other academic offerings within the same institution. For many years it has been suspected that SCDEs are underfunded relative to other academic units (Orr & Peseau, 1979; Peseau, 1982; Peseau & Orr, 1980). For example, in a 1-year study of a single university, Peseau (1984) reported that teacher education, per weighted credit hour, was funded at 5% less than engineering and 14% less than business administration. Berliner (1984) revealed a similar expenditure pattern at another major research university. More recently, Ebmeier et al. (1991) collected financial data from six similar institutions (University of Kansas, University of Iowa, University of North Carolina, University of Oregon, University of Colorado, and University of Oklahoma) for the purpose of addressing the following questions: 1) Has funding for SCDEs changed during the last 10 years (i.e., 1980–1989)? 2) Where do schools of education stand relative to other academic units with respect to funding? and 3) Has this rank changed over time?

The Ebmeier et al. (1991) study began by aggregating instructional expenditures (salaries, equipment, supplies, computing, travel and other related expenses) by academic discipline and instructional level. Expenditures were then distributed among the levels of instruction (upper division undergraduate, lower division graduate, and upper division graduate) by "weights" that reflected differences in time and intensity of effort required to instruct the various types and levels of courses. The researchers noted that these weights were calculated using a complex procedure that incorporated, among other factors, weekly contact hours and class size.

With regard to longitudinal changes in SCDE funding, the study revealed that across all levels of instruction, expenditures per credit hour in education decreased by 1% in inflation-adjusted dollars during the period 1980–1989. Education, however, was not the only discipline to experience a real decline in available resources. Similarly, the following departments also recorded a relative decrease in support during the defined period: communications (2%), foreign languages (12%), letters (16%), and social science (1%). In contrast, the following academic units experienced a relative increase in support during the same period: biological sciences (10%), business and management (39%), engineering (23%), mathematics (5%), physical science (2%), and psychology (9%).

The study also found a considerable amount of cross-sectional variation in spending on education among program levels. To be specific, the upper undergraduate program in education expended $97 per credit hour in 1989, whereas programs at the lower graduate and upper graduate levels spent $106 and $350, respectively. Education's rankings relative to other academic areas are also revealing. Education placed consistently at or near the bottom rank in reference to other academic disciplines. For example, education ranked tenth out of 11 subject areas at the upper graduate level. Only business spent less ($346 compared to $350 for education), whereas the physical sciences ($1,072) and the biological sciences ($1,067) spent the most.

The examination of departmental expenditures across time revealed that during the 10-year period, education, compared to the relative ranking of other departments, dropped two ranks at the upper undergraduate level and one rank at the upper graduate level. Thus, during the period 1980–1989, SCDEs have not only lost ground to inflation, but also in their ability to secure resources relative to other departments.

Ebmeier and his colleagues did not study the effects of these funding trends on the quality of programs within SCDEs; however, it seems safe to assume that the effect will be negative and that it will develop over time. In other words, these well-established funding trends are likely to have lagged negative effects on the capacity of preservice teacher education programs to respond to the kinds of reform envisioned by education policymakers.

Intradepartmental Resource Allocation It is also possible to compare spending on teacher education per se with other types of programs within SCDEs. For example, Theobald (1992) developed a model for assessing the extent to which teacher education programs subsidize other SCDE activities. According to Theobald's model, changes in the number of students enrolled in teacher education programs affect the SCDE's satisfaction through their resultant impact on selectivity in choosing the respective students and the number of faculty that can be employed. More specifically, Theobald presumed that as a department dips deeper into a relatively fixed pool of applicants, student quality is likely to decline. Yet, he also recognized that increased enrollments are likely to have positive effects on the number of faculty employed with corresponding reductions in average class sizes. Therefore, a conflict develops between

the desire for larger SCDE enrollments that afford more credit hours, faculty, and research, and the desire for lower enrollments that permit smaller class sizes and higher student selectivity.

Theobald (1992) hypothesized that if an SCDE equally values student selectivity in its teacher education program and in other SCDE programs, then faculty resources per revenue unit allocated to the SCDEs by the university's budgeting process, which is a function of student credit hours, would be similar. If dissimilar, he reasoned that discrepancies between resource allocations and revenue sources would measure the extent to which cross-subsidization takes place within SCDEs. Information was collected about who delivered the SCDE's curriculum, the conditions under which they did so (e.g., class size), the salaries they were paid, the share of the budget each program comprised, and the share of the SCDE's student credit hours generated for the 1989–1990 and 1990–1991 academic years at a large public research university.

The results of the study indicated that students enrolled in teacher education programs were 36% and 126% *more* likely to be taught by an adjunct or assistant professor, respectively, and 21% and 41% *less* likely to be taught by an associate or full professor, respectively, than students enrolled in other SCDE programs (Theobald, 1992). In addition, the class size of teacher education courses averaged 29 students, compared with 13 for other SCDE courses. The most convincing evidence that cross-subsidization occurs, however, is the reported finding that the teacher education program generated 38% of the SCDE's total student credit hours, but secured only 20% of the revenue allocated to the SCDE by the university's budgeting process. Even when weighting factors are employed to adjust undergraduate and graduate credit hours, it appears clear that approximately 10% of the resources generated by teacher education are used to subsidize other SCDE programs.

Cost Implications of Prevailing Practices It is interesting to note that this review of the literature did not reveal any studies showing that SCDEs were overfunded relative to other academic units or that teacher education was overfunded relative to other educational disciplines. Indeed, all of these studies conclude that SCDEs and teacher education programs are treated unjustly in the resource allocation process. Although these studies are persuasive, caution must be exercised when interpreting their conclusions, particularly in the absence of agreed-upon standards of resource levels that are necessary to support sound programs. Regardless of the complexity of the cross-sectional comparisons made, these studies viewed the resource allocation process from the perspective of a single academic unit (i.e., SCDE, teacher education) without regard for the goals and priorities of the university as a collective entity. The budgetary process when viewed from an institutional perspective sheds light on the relative inability of SCDEs and teacher education programs to secure needed resources.

One of the more pressing concerns facing university administrators today is how to allocate scarce resources in a manner that best allows the institution to attain its goals. The resource allocation process is problematic in the sense that it involves a set of decisions that are typically unstructured, complex, and open-ended (Mintzberg, Raisinghani, & Theoret, 1976). The centrality of the budgetary function to the operational mission of the university has provoked many studies; several sought to determine whether budgeting is based on objective criteria, and therefore embody elements of a rational process (i.e., rational model). Others assessed the degree to which political power influenced administrative practice and, as a result, affected the outcome and nature of the resource allocation process (i.e., political model).

The rational model posits that throughout the budgetary process university officials use objective criteria to determine the most equitable and efficient allocation of resources. Administrators are constrained in their selection of criteria only to the extent that logical relationships exist between these objective measures and the budget categories to which they apply. Thus, the model suggests that budgeting is primarily a mechanistic activity involving only "rational" behavior and, as such, ignores the exercise of departmental power in budgetary decisions.

In contrast, the political model posits that resource allocations are the end result of internal power struggles among differentially powerful organizational subunits. Power may be derived from the position of the department or program within the organization's political structure for decision making, alliances with interest groups external to the organization, or the "centrality" of the unit to the university's prescribed mission (Ashar & Shapiro, 1988; Hackman, 1985; Hills & Mahoney, 1978). For example, Salancik and Pfeffer (1974) found that external funds correlated positively with unit power in decision making in such a way that departments that generated more external research funding gained seats on the university's resource allocation committee. Regardless of one's perception of what creates departmental power bases, the political model suggests that academic units pursue their own self-interests and seek to influence the resource allocation process by exercising unevenly distributed coercive power.

Utilizing these models, studies of the university resource allocation process have drawn contradictory conclusions. Cyert (1978), for example, asserts that resource scarcity promotes the need for joint decision making among organizational members and, therefore, the tendency for the use of power in the bargaining process. (See, also, Hills & Mahoney, 1978; Pfeffer & Moore, 1980; Pfeffer & Salancik, 1974; Salancik & Pfeffer, 1974.) In contrast, others reported that budgeting was essentially a rational process (Chaffee, 1983) and that administrators increased their use of objective criteria as resources became limited (Cameron, 1983; Rubin, 1977; Schick, 1985; Whetten, 1981).

A closer examination of the variables that were selected to designate a university's budget process as political or rational sheds some light on what initially appears to be a dubious body of research. For example, Chaffee (1983) found that a composite measure comprised of a department's national ranking, membership on university committees, and the amount of research funds generated explained more of the current year's budget than did student credit hours. She interpreted these findings to support her contention that the institutional budgeting process at Stanford University (1970–1979) followed a rational model. What permitted her to draw this conclusion was that Stanford's decisions about a department's share of the resource pool was dependent on the following defined objective criteria: 1) academic importance, 2) student interest, 3) possibility for excel-

lence in the program, and 4) funding potential. Thus, the elements of her rational model were similar to the measures of departmental power as defined in several of the political model studies. (See Hills & Mahoney, 1978; Pfeffer & Moore, 1980; Pfeffer & Salancik, 1974; Salancik & Pfeffer, 1974; Schick, Scherr, & Tuttle, 1982.) What is most central to the analysis in this chapter is that both models suggest that student credit hours do not serve as the controlling variable in the resource allocation process. Indeed, the convergence of the models toward the use of criteria that can be loosely interpreted as measuring "prestige" suggests that the relative amount of this attribute that a department or program possesses is critical to its ability to secure resources.

In any analysis of the resource allocation process, it is presumed that university officials are primarily concerned with an individual unit's departmental prestige only to the extent that it affects the overall prestige of the institution. The benefits that accrue to universities that increase their institutional prestige are well supported. In general, enhancing institutional prestige increases the number of students who apply to the institution, increases student selectivity, and decreases student sensitivity to tuition levels (Garvin, 1980). Therefore, to gain a favorable position in the allocation process, it is likely in the best interests of departments to increase those elements that the administration views as best contributing to prestige.

The discussion thus far focuses on how resources are allocated to departments through the university budgetary process. It is likely that a similar analytical framework can be applied to intradepartmental resource allocations. In general, the relative level of fiscal support for teacher education suggests that university officials and department administrators perceive that teacher preparation does not contribute to departmental and, in turn, institutional "prestige" (Gifford, 1984). As a result, teacher education programs do not have the power in the internal resource allocation processes to reap the full financial benefit of enrolling large numbers of students. (See also Twombly & Ebmeier, 1989.)

Examinations of the objective criteria used in budgetary processes also suggest that teacher education is deemed to be fiscally less demanding than other academic programs (Ebmeier et al., 1991; Peseau & Orr, 1980). (See also Allen & Topping, 1979; Berliner, 1984; Spence, 1978.) However, Peseau, Backman, and Fry (1987) assert that the weights used in funding formulas do not accurately reflect the complexity of current programs in education. Based on a study of eight university programs in Florida, they concluded that clinical teacher education activities encompassed several functions not generally characteristic of traditional didactic courses. Among these atypical functions were the following: program coordination, including student placement, travel, and communications; faculty expenditures budgeted for clinical supervision; support services and materials; simulation and microteaching expenditures; and payments to cooperating teachers. These additional expenditures were estimated to add an additional $40–$300 per credit hour. Applying these calculations to the eight Florida programs, the projected expenditures to the universities were estimated to be 106% greater than those amounts provided by the existing funding formulas. Accordingly, the authors recommended that classroom instruction be weighted 1.5 times, clinical observation 2 times, and clinical practice 2.5 times the cost of the university's general studies courses (Peseau et al., 1987).

If society views the production of quality teachers as a desired function of the university and the primary purpose of an SCDE, then it is likely to see classes in the teacher education programs instructed by the least senior faculty members and containing twice as many students as other department courses to be in conflict with its interests. Indeed, society is likely to question SCDEs that attempt to pursue internally generated goals (e.g., research) at the expense of activities that the public perceives to have greater value (e.g., teacher education). One must recall that the preparation of quality teachers, the purpose for which most SCDEs were founded, remains a source of legitimacy with much of the general public and, more important, with many legislators.

Financing Professional Development

Persuaded that preservice teacher education cannot provide adequately for a well-prepared work force singlehandedly, educational policymakers have sought support for accompanying programs of continuing professional development (Little, 1989). This section examines the extent to which fiscal support for staff development is currently provided at the federal, state, and local levels. It also considers cost implications of prevailing practices at the local level.

Federal Contributions Due to the myriad of federal agencies and programs that provide funds for professional development, it is difficult to determine the total aggregate support for in-service activities at the federal level. By examining several of the programs established to provide resources for such activities, however, insight can be gained into the federal government's commitment to professional development. For example, the Federal Coordinating Council for Science, Engineering and Technology (FCCSET) recently utilized this method and estimated that the federal government spent $369 million in fiscal year 1993 on core elementary and secondary programs focused on "teacher enhancement" in the science, mathematics, engineering, and technology areas (Federal Coordinating Council for Science, Engineering, and Technology [FCCSET], 1993). The report also notes that grants from the Eisenhower State Mathematics and Science Program totaled $246 million in fiscal year 1993 and served approximately 750,000 teachers (in 1991).

Additional opportunities for experienced teachers to learn more about science and math are provided through summer institutes sponsored by the National Science Foundation. In 1993, this agency allocated $99 million to be spent on in-service activities for approximately 21,800 "master" teachers (FCCSET, 1993). Other agencies, such as the Department of Energy, Department of Defense, and the Department of Health and Human Services, also contribute to specific in-service training programs; however, many of these programs serve a variety of purposes, which makes it difficult to isolate the contributions to teacher education and professional development.

Programs created to enhance the learning opportunities of designated classes of students also provide resources for in-service activities. For example, although expenditure figures are unavailable, according to a recent study of Chapter 1 imple

mentation supported by the U.S. Department of Education, the annual average number of days devoted in 1991–1992 to staff development for U.S. elementary and secondary school teachers is approximately 3 and 2.2 days, respectively (Millsap, Moss, & Gamse, 1993).

The current administration has also demonstrated its intent to support teachers' continuing professional development. For example, Section 308 of the Clinton administration's education bill, *Goals 2000: Educate America Act,* requires that states use a designated portion of the funds granted under Title III of the act for purposes of teacher training. Although the federal commitment to professional development is significant and appears to be growing, the greatest fiscal support for in-service training has been secured at the state and local levels.

State Contributions Provision for the delivery of state-supported professional development may take many forms. Although the type of delivery system may vary, in 1989 only 17 states (Alaska, Arizona, Colorado, Hawaii, Idaho, Indiana, Kansas, Louisiana, Maryland, Massachusetts, Michigan, Nevada, New Jersey, New York, North Dakota, Utah, and Washington) did *not* have some form of statute, mandate, or policy for professional development (Cooley & Thompson, 1990). However, like the 33 states that "officially" acknowledged a commitment to staff development, many of the 17 states did allocate resources for the provision of such activities (Cooley & Thompson, 1990).

The wide variation in the means employed to provide staff development is matched by the manner in which the activities are financed. The following provides a representative sample of the many funding mechanisms that were employed by the states in fiscal year 1990–1991 (for a comprehensive listing see Gold, Smith, Lawton, & Hyary, 1992):

State	Program/Mechanism
California	Mentor Teacher Program: The mentor program authorizes teachers with outstanding teaching ability to serve as "mentors" to other teachers, particularly new teachers, and provides for each mentor to receive a stipend of approximately $4,300 annually (adjusted for inflation) for performing additional work. In addition, a stipend of $2,150 per mentor teacher is provided to school districts to provide support, including travel funds, substitute teachers' time, and other support functions. Total program funding in 1990–1991 was $65.5 million (less than 1% of total school aid).
	School Development Plans: Thirteen million dollars for payment of up to 8 days for professional development during the regular school year.
Florida	Categorical Program: Categorical and special allocations are added to the Florida Education Finance Program (FEFP) funding formula and are distributed among eligible school districts. There were 28 categorical and special programs funded by the legislature in 1990–1991, including *instructional strategies enhancement* and *summer in-service institutes.* In fiscal year 1990–1991, funding for the programs was $27 million and $11.3 million, respectively.

Idaho   Innovative Teacher Grants: Individual teachers, or groups of teachers, submit applications describing various projects they would like to undertake that would enhance their teaching ability. A committee appointed by the State Department of Education screens the applications and determines those to be funded. Total program funding in 1990–1991 was $.25 million (less than 1% of total state school aid).

Louisiana Teacher Internship Program/Teacher Evaluation Program: The Teaching Internship Program provides for on-the-job assessment and team support of the beginning teacher. The Evaluation Program provides evaluation for experienced teachers every 5 years and provides feedback and professional assistance. Total program funding for 1990–1991 was $7.8 million (less than 1% of total state school aid).

South Dakota Three-day Curriculum and Staff Development: Funding is provided for teacher workshops prior to the start of the school year. School districts may distribute to teachers a $225 stipend in lump sum or spread the amount during the course of the year. Total program funding in 1990–1991 was $2 million (1.4% of total state school aid).

These programs are just a few examples of how different states currently support teacher staff development. As this listing suggests, states provide professional development through a variety of delivery systems and a comparably diverse mix of funding mechanisms. In addition to defined programs, if state aid is provided to districts when development activities take place during regularly scheduled class days (e.g., superintendent's conference days), states may also indirectly support staff development. It is therefore difficult to make interstate comparisons of the level of support that is currently provided; however, at least two generalizations can be made. First, the manner in which support is provided is more likely to be in the form of grants than formula funding. Second, in the majority of states, regardless of the funding mechanism employed, state support for professional development is less than 1% of total state aid (New York State Department of Education, 1993).

Local Contributions Research dealing with staff development in education has been dominated by descriptive studies and short-term evaluations of discrete programs. Although there have been a few exceptions in which analysts have dealt in passing with the costs of specific programs (see, e.g., Bass, 1978; Cady & Johnson, 1981; Conran & Chase, 1982; Leighty & Courter, 1984; Lytle, 1983; McIntyre, 1976; Runkel, Wyant, Bell, & Runkel, 1980; Thomas, 1978; Youngs & Hager, 1982), it remains the case that there is little generalizable information about the total amount of resources that are investigated in teachers' professional development (Orlich & Evans, 1990). Therefore, although one may look to federally legislated or state-mandated professional development programs to estimate the extent to which these levels provide support, the local contribution to such activities is often not readily discernible.

Moore and Hyde (1980, 1981) conducted one of the few general studies of the costs of in-service staff development.

The researchers focused their attention on three urban school districts and identified a range of activities that are not generally viewed as staff development (Moore & Hyde, 1980, 1981). For example, when an administrator observes a teacher, although the encounter may not result in staff improvement, Moore and Hyde assume that the activity is intended to achieve such a result and include it as a cost of staff development. Similarly, staff meetings, department meetings, workdays associated with the opening and closing of schools, early release for curriculum development, and preparation periods for training projects were also classified as staff development activities. Based on their findings, Moore and Hyde concluded that because many of these activities are embedded in the daily "routines" of the district, a substantial portion of staff development costs are borne at the local district level (Moore & Hyde, 1980, 1981).

During the 1980s, the Moore and Hyde model was used by several researchers to examine the local costs of staff development. For example, La Bolle (1983) used the model to estimate the total investment in staff development in four rural Alaskan school districts; Valiant (1985) used the model to study staff development costs in three moderate size school districts in the state of Washington. Similarly, Cole (1987) examined such costs in four smaller districts (1,000–5,000 students) in the state of Washington. All three studies corroborated Moore and Hyde's findings; that is, staff development often includes "hidden costs," which, when properly classified as staff development, are largely financed using locally generated funds (Orlich & Evans, 1990).

Table 12.1 provides a summary of these findings as reported by Orlich and Evans (1990). These contrast sharply with Houston and Freiberg's (1979) assertion that a school district with more than 1% of its budget allocated to professional development is an exception. All of the districts in Table 12.1 devoted a far greater portion of their budgeted resources to staff development.

Stern, Gerritz, and Little (1989) drew a dichotomy between resources invested by *participants* and resources invested by *taxpayers* and, thereby, developed a model for estimating the costs of staff development. In the model, participants are deemed to invest in their own staff development when they participate in such activities on their own time or without compensation. Accordingly, the resources invested by participants include both the value of time for which participants are not paid and the out-of-pocket expenses for which they are not reimbursed (e.g., cash payments to attend conferences, workshops, or courses). In contrast, the investment in staff development by taxpayers is comprised of the cost of participants' time and the cost of producing staff development activities. For example, if staff development requires payment of a stipend or a future salary increase, these costs are borne by the taxpayer. Similarly, when staff development takes place during regular workdays and a substitute must be hired or classes must be shortened (reallocated instructional time), these added costs of the participants' time are also properly classified as investments by taxpayers. With regard to the taxpayers' investment in producing staff development, these costs include the salaries of administrators or teachers whose job responsibilities include planning, organizing, or leading such activities; the fees paid

TABLE 12.1. Total Staff Development Costs as a Percentage of Total Operating Expenditures for Reported Years

District	Year	Staff Development Costs	Percentage of Total Expenditures	Study
Seaside	1977	$9,368,000	5.72%	Moore and Hyde (1980)
Riverview	1978	4,607,000	3.76	Moore and Hyde (1980)
Union	1978	3,953,000	3.38	Moore and Hyde (1980)
Baleen	1982	551,328	11.81	La Bolle (1983)
Beluga	1982	701,508	9.28	La Bolle (1983)
Scrimshaw	1982	280,693	6.26	La Bolle (1983)
Ptarmigan	1982	384,944	5.70	La Bolle (1983)
Fruitland	1983	463,801	3.10	Valiant (1985)
Orchard	1983	526,461	2.77	Valiant (1985)
Vineyard	1983	1,014,038	3.78	Valiant (1985)
Capital	1985	320,032	6.48	Cole (1987)
Newton	1985	943,144	5.67	Cole (1987)
Lake Shore	1985	613,433	5.74	Cole (1987)
Long Creek	1985	481,286	5.54	Cole (1987)

Source: Adapted from *Regression analysis: A novel way to examine staff development cost factors* by D. C. Orlich and A. Evans, 1990 (unpublished manuscript) (ERIC Reproduction Service Document No. ED 331 808).

to external consultants and presenters; and the costs of the facilities and materials used (Stern et al., 1989).

The Stern et al. study also presented four ways in which researchers can more accurately define the amount invested in staff development. Level I, the most restricted concept of investment, is current money outlays by taxpayers for staff development. This level includes only the costs of substitutes, stipends, and producing development activities. Level II, in addition to the current monetary investment by taxpayers, also includes the present value of future salary increases that are tied to current staff development. Level III includes both the monetary and nonmonetary investment by taxpayers in which the nonmonetary costs include the value of reduced instructional time when students are kept home on regularly scheduled class days (e.g., pupil free day). Finally, Level IV not only encompasses the investments detailed in the preceding levels, but also includes the personal investment by participants who undertake staff development on their own time and without compensation (see Stern et al., 1989).

Utilizing this conceptualization, these researchers surveyed more than 800 discrete staff development activities conducted in 30 public schools. On the basis of this survey, they estimated the investment in locally administered staff development in California for fiscal year 1986. Table 12.2 summarizes these findings.

As Little (1989) pointed out, bargained contracts affect staff development directly by designating the conditions under which employees might be granted leaves or apply earned credit for salary advancement; however, the most notable finding of the analysis is the percentage of the total investment in staff development attributed to the present value of future salary increases (i.e., 60.83%). As Stern and his colleagues noted, teachers in almost all school districts in the country receive automatic salary increases for development activities. Accordingly, the agreed-upon linkage between formal course credits and salaries in the standard teacher's compensation schedule

requires that future salary increases must be included as part of the total cost of staff development activities.

When examining the fiscal implications of in-service teacher education it is important to realize that many costs do not lend themselves to dollar metrics. For example, a potential cost that Stern et al. (1989) acknowledged but did not incorporate into the study was the value of the lost instructional time due to the hiring of less productive substitute teachers; that is, the cost of learning that is foregone because disparities exist between the instructional capabilities of regular and substitute teachers. Thus, it is important to look beyond traditional expenditure measures if one is to accurately assess the total cost of in-service teacher education activities that are borne by local districts.

Cost Implications of Prevailing Practices In a study of professional development in California, Little (1989) determined that directly or indirectly, districts control more than 80% of the resources flowing from the state that had been designated for staff development. (See also Little et al., 1987.) It follows that local districts are the primary provider of staff development. For example, in Little's (1989) study, teachers were found to be two to three times more likely to participate in a district-provided staff development program than to enroll in courses offered by a college or university. This finding corroborates data gathered by the National Education Association (NEA) (1987) that revealed a 15-year decline in teacher enrollment in university coursework and a corresponding increase in district-sponsored activities. Thus, the provision of teacher professional development most closely resembles an industrial model in which it is the employer that designs and conducts the job-related training.

The use of an industrial model has prompted districts to hire and retain specialists whose primary tasks are the design, delivery, and administration of staff development activities. This concentration of professional development resources at the district level (in terms of both program delivery and teacher

TABLE 12.2. Estimated Investment in Locally Administered Staff Development in California, 1986

	Percentage of Total Staff Development Costs	Percentage of Total Classroom Costs
Level I		
Substitutes	4.75%	0.24%
External providers	1.89	0.10
Facilities	1.25	0.06
Stipends	3.16	0.16
Leader's time for planning and delivery	9.79	0.50
Subtotal	20.83	1.06
Level II		
Present value of future salary increases	60.83	3.10
Subtotal	81.66	4.15
Level III		
Value of reallocated instructional time	7.24	0.37
Subtotal	88.90	4.52
Level IV	11.10	0.56
Investment by participants		
Combined investment by taxpayers and participants	100.00	5.09

Source: Adapted from "Making the Most of a School District's Two (or Five) Cents: Accounting for Investment in Teachers' Professional Development" by D. Stern, W. Gerritz, and J. W. Little, 1989, *Journal of Education Finance*, 14(3).

compensation) has fostered a tendency toward the specialization of staff development roles. For example, in a study of California's school districts, Little (1989) found that 92% of all participant hours in staff development were accounted for by full- or part-time central office administrators and development specialists who were charged with the design and delivery of the in-service activity. Although the Little (1989) study revealed that virtually all of the districts employed external consultants or presenters, the extent to which they were used and the cost devoted to such activities were not large. In particular, external presenters played a role in less than 20% of all participant hours at a cost of less than 10% of the average district's yearly monetary expenditures (Little, 1989).

Little's (1989) analysis permits educators to view staff development in terms of *leader* costs and *learner* costs. Leader costs include: 1) the salaries of administrators and specialists responsible for staff development, 2) the fees of external consultants or presenters, and 3) the additional compensation awarded to faculty members when they act as a planner or presenter. In contrast, learner costs include: 1) substitutes or release time; 2) stipends, registration fees, tuition subsidies; 3) materials available to teachers; and 4) travel reimbursement. Table 12.3 presents some of the key findings.

As Table 12.3 indicates, leader costs comprise the greatest share of the taxpayers' monetary investment in staff development. The modest role played by outside specialists is also revealed.

Resources expended on professional development are resources unavailable for other operating functions. As such, in periods of fiscal scarcity, educators will increasingly be required to provide comprehensive analyses of the costs and perceived benefits of in-service activities. This discussion presents several frameworks that are used to define and analyze the costs of staff development. As evidenced, there is a limited body of research that has adequately examined the fiscal implications of the escalating public investment in teachers' professional development. The importance of the topic would seem to require that it receive more attention than it has. Perhaps this chapter can help provoke interest in the issue.

EFFICIENCY/PRODUCTIVITY ISSUES

The Study of Educational Productivity

One of the major trends in education finance has involved a growing interest in the productivity of resources devoted to educational uses. Resources that are allocated to teacher education have been examined in this light, and the results have been frustrating for those convinced that well-educated teachers constitute a key ingredient of good schooling. Hanushek's review (1986) of productivity studies in education is perhaps the most often cited piece of research by those who question the wisdom of investing more dollars into conventional indicators of school quality, including the incidence of more highly trained teachers. According to Hanushek's metaanalysis, of the 106 productivity studies he examined that included a teacher education variable, 6 studies reported a statistically significant positive teacher effect, 5 reported a statistically significant negative effect, and 95 reported statistically insignificant effects.

Hanushek's findings need to be interpreted carefully. His evidence is not sufficient to claim that improving the quality of teacher education has little effect on pupil performance, nor does he draw this sort of conclusion. His actual conclusion is more narrow and questions the wisdom of simply providing more of the same kind of teacher education.

Recently, even this more narrowly drawn conclusion has been questioned. For example, Hedges, Laine, and Greenwald (1994) challenged the Hanushek analysis on methodological grounds. Questions can also be raised about the broadness of

TABLE 12.3. Current Monetary Investment in Professional Development for Teachers by Local School Districts[a]

Components of Current Monetary Expenditure	Percentage of Current Monetary Program Cost	Percentage of Total Classroom Cost
Substitutes	25%	0.23%
External providers	5	0.05
Facilities	4	0.04
Stipends	16	0.15
Leaders' time for planning and delivery	50	0.47
Total taxpayers' current monetary investment	100	0.94

Source: Adapted from "District Policy Choices and Teachers' Professional Development Opportunities" by J. W. Little, 1989, Educational Evaluation and Policy Analysis, 15(2).

[a] Based on costs associated with staff development in 30 California school districts in 1986.

the measures used to depict teacher education. The studies surveyed by Hanushek were focused on degree levels and thus failed to distinguish between teacher education per se and other types of education (e.g., liberal arts coursework, subject-specific education in the case of secondary teachers). Moreover, these early productivity studies had few if any direct measures of the quality of the coursework experienced by teachers.

Hanushek's pessimistic findings regarding the efficacy of existing teacher education need to be juxtaposed against the recurring findings within the productivity literature suggesting that measures of teachers' ability levels have positive effects on pupil performance. The Equality of Educational Opportunity (EEO) survey (Coleman et al., 1966) was one of the earliest studies to find positive relationships between measures of teachers' verbal abilities and pupil performance, although strictly speaking this study did not examine learning gains of pupils. Ehrenberg and Brewer (1993) recently reanalyzed the EEO data using modern statistical techniques and confirmed the earlier findings regarding the positive independent effects of teacher verbal ability on pupil performance.

Since publication of the EEO survey, a number of studies have revealed positive relationships between various measures of teachers' ability levels and the performance of their students (see, e.g., Bridge, Judd, & Moock, 1979; Hanushek, 1971; Murnane, 1975; Summers & Wolfe, 1977; Winkler, 1975). Levin (1976) was so impressed with the importance of teacher ability on pupil performance that he wrote

Virtually all of the studies that have measured teacher verbal aptitudes have found that variable to be significantly related to student achievement. Indeed, the consistency of this finding is buttressed by the fact that separate studies have been carried out at several grade levels and for samples of black, white, and Mexican-American students. (p. 152)

The sharpness of the difference in findings regarding the effectiveness of teacher education and teacher ability has prompted researchers to look more carefully at the teacher education input. Two strategies have been pursued. On the one hand, researchers have concentrated on more narrowly focused measures of what teachers know within various domains of knowledge. Ferguson (1991) contributed to this line of research by including a measure of teacher literacy in his assessment of educational quality in a study of Texas school

district productivity. He concluded that differences in his measure of the quality of schooling account for between one fourth and one third of the district variation in student test scores. Hanushek, Gomes-Neto, and Harbison (1992) had access to measures of teacher subject-matter knowledge in their Brazilian data and found evidence of positive relationships between how much a teacher knew about what was being taught and his or her students' subject-specific learning gains.

On the other hand, researchers have focused on measures of teacher preparation and have tried to gauge the effects of more or less of different types of educational activities. Druva and Anderson (1983), for example, conducted a metaanalysis of some 65 studies that involved estimating input–outcome relationships that pertain to teachers. These authors report "average" effects for selected input variables including teacher subject-matter preparation. They found positive but modest effects of such preparation on pupil performance. However, it is difficult to determine how well these studies controlled for the alignment between teachers' content preparation levels and the subject matter being taught. More refined measures of teacher preparation should be accompanied by comparably more refined measures of teachers' actual teaching assignments. After all, one presumes that more subject-matter training in chemistry has the largest impact when the teacher teaches chemistry.

Monk (1994) and Monk and King (1994) addressed these concerns by controlling for the subject being taught by teachers. They were able to assess the effects of teacher preparation in mathematics and science on pupil performance in the relevant subject area. Their evidence suggests that teacher subject-specific preparation has positive direct effects on pupil performance gains, although the magnitude of the effects they found were not large.

The positive effects found by Monk and King have several noteworthy attributes. First, they tend to be nonlinear. In mathematics, for example, the magnitude of the positive relationship between teachers' undergraduate coursework in the content area and pupil performance gains tends to diminish as teachers acquire more mathematics education. Second, there are contingencies that need to be considered. For example, there is evidence suggesting that teacher coursework that was completed in the recent past has a more powerful impact on pupil performance than does coursework completed in the more distant past. Finally, there is evidence suggesting that teachers' coursework preparation can have a cumulative positive effect on pupil performance.

Several points need to be kept in mind regarding the policy implications of these studies of educational productivity. First, the distinction between teacher ability and teacher education needs to be maintained. Researchers have had more success at demonstrating links between measures of teacher ability and pupil performance than they have had at establishing the effectiveness of teacher education per se. Second, the production function type of research program from which these studies are drawn has been notoriously undependable as a basis for social policy. The findings have a history of being inconsistent, particularly as the focus shifts to public policy options such as more or less of some type of teacher education (Monk, 1992). Third, effectiveness needs to be balanced against cost. Researchers may succeed at finding a highly productive input or treatment that is simply too costly to warrant widespread use. The following section of this chapter is devoted to an assessment of the progress analysts have made toward conceptualizing and estimating the costs of teacher education.

The Study of Educational Costs

It is impossible to divorce the study of educational costs from the study of educational productivity. According to economic theory, a cost is the best benefit foregone that is necessary to accomplish some result. If ignorance surrounds the question of what resources are required to accomplish given educational results (as the previous discussion about productivity research suggests), analysts are in a very difficult position with respect to the conceptualization, not to mention the estimation, of educational costs.

The problem is compounded by the widespread availability of budget and other types of expenditure data that pertain to education. As was made clear earlier, there is no shortage of summaries of what is "spent" on education. It is important, however, not to confuse "expenditures" with "costs." Suffice it to say that expenditures can far exceed real costs. Expenditures can also fall short of covering actual costs. The fact that funds were spent tells little if anything about the resources that were truly required for the obtained results.

In teacher education it is common for analysts to rely on budget data to make cross-sectional as well as longitudinal comparisons of expenditures. This practice risks inviting invidious and invalid comparisons because there are few controls on the outcomes being realized. As shown earlier in this chapter, such expenditure data can be used to assess equity or fairness in the provision of revenues. What these data do not permit is a calculation of the costs of teacher education. Instead, they provide a barometer of the society's level of commitment to the teacher education enterprise.

Yet, as Monk and King (1993) point out, ignorance of the underlying production regularities need not preclude the conduct of a cost analysis. What is typically required is a series of explicit assumptions about what resources are required to accomplish what results. Such heavy dependence on assump-

tions is troubling, but useful analyses can be conducted so long as the assumptions are clear.

Policymakers are seldom interested in cost estimates for their own sake. Frequently there is interest in assessing costs relative to measures of likely future economic benefits. This interest gives rise to what is often known as benefit-cost analysis. When the focus is on benefits relative to costs, not only does the analyst need to know what resources are required to accomplish what educational result, but there must also be an understanding of how educational results contribute to economic benefits over lengthy periods of time. Again, the requisite knowledge is typically not available (particularly with respect to the long-term economic consequences of having well-educated as opposed to poorly educated teachers), and analysts are often forced to make assumptions.

The net result is that cost and benefit-cost analyses of teacher education are heavily dependent on assumptions about both what resources are required to realize what educational results and how the educational results translate ultimately into economic benefits. Despite the difficulties, a few studies have gone forward and provided some insight into the likely costs and benefits of various types of teacher education.

For example, Hawley (1987) conducted a cost analysis of extending teacher education programs from 4 to 5 years. According to Hawley's calculations, the total cost of such an extension would amount to as much as $7 billion annually. His estimate reflects cost borne by individual teachers as well as those borne by the larger society. It reflects adjustments for additional tuitions and public subsidies that are made to higher education as well as the foregone earnings teachers would experience as a consequence of spending an additional year in school.

Hawley was skeptical about the benefits to be had from a simple expansion of existing programs from 4 to 5 years. He explicitly stated the assumptions that need to be made to think of the resource flows he anticipated as costs and then questioned the validity of each. He concluded that it is unlikely that prospective teachers will find the benefits of the fifth year encouraging relative to the costs they are likely to face. He finished his analysis by introducing an alternative approach that he believed had greater promise.

Lewis conducted a more focused cost analysis of adding a fifth year to teacher education programs as part of his benefit-cost evaluation of the University of Minnesota's new program of this type (Lewis, 1990). The cost components Lewis examined were similar to those utilized by Hawley. The main difference is that Lewis was able to incorporate the actual charges and foregone wages that faced prospective teachers within the University of Minnesota system at the time of his study. Lewis estimated the total costs of the fifth year at $30,754 per student. The bulk of these costs were accounted for by foregone wages during the year ($20,900), tuition ($2,475), and subsidies provided by society to cover the full costs of offering the program ($7,425).

Lewis reached a more optimistic conclusion about the viability of the fifth year program than did Hawley. He did so by calculating the benefits associated with the fifth year of training and found that they compared favorably with the anticipated costs from the perspective of the typical individual teacher.

The main difference between the Hawley and the Lewis analyses centers around their respective treatment of subsequent teacher wages. Lewis assumed that teachers graduating from the fifth-year program would realize the premium attached to 45 graduate credits currently enjoyed by teachers in three of the largest metropolitan districts that were representative of the districts currently hiring teacher graduates from the University of Minnesota. In effect, Lewis calculated the benefit associated with acquiring graduate credit and attributed that to the benefits offered to teachers by the fifth-year program. Hawley, in sharp contrast, recognized that there are other ways to acquire graduate credit than by attending a fifth-year program. He compared the benefits realized by teachers who completed the fifth-year program with those realized by teachers who reached comparable levels of training by taking part-time university classes. Not surprisingly, the benefits Hawley attributed to the fifth-year program are much smaller than those calculated by Lewis.

Denton and Smith (1985) examined two alternative approaches to teacher education, one based on a formal education major and the other structured around a major in a different subject area. Noneducation majors completed 22 semester hours of professional education coursework compared to 34 semester hours for majors. Both programs required students to take an additional 48 semester hours of teaching field coursework. The primary cost question that was addressed by Denton and Smith concerned the cost relative to the benefits of the additional 12 semester hours required of education majors.

This focus on the 12 semester hours created a difficulty for the cost portion of this study. Denton and Smith viewed costs from the perspective of the education college rather than from a more global perspective. The additional 12 semester hours do in fact constitute costs for the education college, but these need to be balanced against the costs associated with the 12 semester hours noneducation majors earned outside the college of education. For purposes of assessing the cost effectiveness of the 12 "extra" education semester hours, the focus needs to be on how the costs of education courses compare to the costs of courses elsewhere in the university, assuming the graduation semester hour requirements are the same across programs.

On the benefit side of their analysis, Denton and Smith gained access to information about actual differences in the experiences of teachers who passed through each of the two alternative programs. In other words, they were less dependent than either Hawley or Lewis on assumptions regarding the subsequent impact of the programs they examined. They did not go so far as to estimate economic effects; they focused instead on differences in various measures of the performance of these teachers' pupils. (Their type of analysis technically is known as cost-effectiveness analysis rather than the cost-benefit analyses conducted by Hawley and Lewis).

The Denton and Smith effects data revealed mixed results. No differences were found in teacher morale and there were mixed effects on supervisor ratings of the teachers' instructional skills across the two programs. In addition, there was evidence suggesting that the students of teachers with education majors learned more than students whose teachers majored in other subjects. The magnitude and robustness of these findings are difficult to assess from the published version of the Denton and Smith study.

There have also been several noteworthy attempts to consider cost and cost-benefit implications of selected aspects of teacher education, most especially assessments of the results of teacher preparation (Catterall, 1988; Shepard & Kreitzer, 1987; Solmon & Fagnano, 1988). The Shepard and Kreitzer (1987) study examined the costs associated with the ambitious attempt in Texas to measure the competencies of existing teachers. These analysts were particularly sensitive to the cost implications of the time teachers spent to prepare for the test and the resulting foregone opportunities for other activities, including additional instruction. According to Shepard and Kreitzer's estimates, these teacher time costs constituted 93.5% of their total $78,022,000 cost estimate.

Another important issue was raised by Solmon and Fagnano (1988) in connection with the Shepard and Kreitzer (1987) study. They argued that the relevant outcome measure is not the savings of dismissed teachers' salaries, but rather the subsequent differential labor market experiences of students taught by teachers who can and cannot pass the test. With a series of hypothetical assumptions linking exposure to teachers who were unable to pass the test to adverse labor market experiences (e.g., delayed job entry, unemployment, lowered earnings due to skills not learned), Solmon and Fagnano calculated a benefit (more than $1 billion) that compared favorably with Shepard and Kreitzer's estimate of costs ($78 million). Alternative assumptions about the relationships between exposure to non–test-passing teachers and subsequent labor market experiences would, of course, produce varying results.

Monk and King (1993) stress the importance of using cost analysis as a tool to give insight into sometimes subtle costs that might otherwise remain undetected until the actual implementation of a reform in question. Several of the cost analyses cited in this section succeed at this task. Hawley (1987), for example, goes beyond a simple totaling of tuition expenses, foregone salaries, and public subsidies to include the effects of an extended teacher education program on the quality and quantity of candidates in the applicant pool for teaching. Tom (1986) built on these insights and identified a series of what he called the "hidden costs" of extended teacher preparation. Shepard and Kreitzer (1987) also drew attention to more subtle types of cost by emphasizing the importance of the substantial opportunity costs associated with the time teachers spent preparing for their examinations. A more simplistic analysis would focus attention solely on the out-of-pocket expenses associated with the preparation, distribution, administration, and scoring of the test instruments, and would seriously underestimate the true costs associated with the teacher testing endeavor.

NEW DIRECTIONS

When schools are encouraged to offer "higher order thinking," "teaching for understanding," and so forth, educational policymakers have proposed an ambitious plan for enhancing pedagogy (Cohen & Barnes, 1993). Teachers must now expand their instructional role from merely providers of knowledge to one that helps students think as mathematicians, scientists, and historians. This hands-on, constructivist form of learning, however, requires that current and future teachers be prepared for a new approach to classroom instruction. That is, teachers must learn how to teach differently.

The most logical place to begin to train a new generation of teachers is at the preservice level. Currently, most colleges and universities do not permit undergraduates who intend to teach on the elementary level to major in an academic subject. Instead, they must major in teaching, learning, and other aspects of education. In contrast, those who seek positions on the secondary level concentrate on an academic subject area while only superficially studying learning and pedagogy (Cohen & Barnes, 1993). In the wake of a reform movement that requires teachers to possess a deeper knowledge of both the academic subject matter and the processes of learning and pedagogy, this finding has called into question the efficacy of existing teacher education programs. For example, Cohen and Barnes (1993) assert that most teacher preparation programs grant degrees to prospective elementary teachers despite their limited knowledge of the subjects they will teach and to prospective secondary teachers despite their limited knowledge of pedagogy and learning. If colleges and universities are to produce the type of "teaching" that reformers now envision, it appears that they must greatly expand the opportunities to study academic subjects, learning, and pedagogy currently available to prospective teachers.

Teacher education reform not only requires institutions of higher education to modify the selectivity of existing course offerings, but also to revise the manner in which the program is delivered. For example, as evidenced earlier, most prospective teachers are instructed by the least senior faculty members in classes that often contain twice as many students as other departments' courses. The classroom environment, therefore, is not conducive to the hands-on, interactive setting required to produce the pedagogical results desired by many education reformers. Although the outlays required to develop and introduce new preservice teacher education programs may eventually decline (e.g., start-up costs, curriculum development), the resources required to support smaller classes and increased student–teacher interaction will result in an ongoing additional fiscal commitment to the preservice education of teachers.

Many states have raised teacher education program admission and graduation requirements, several have mandated new 5-year degree programs, and several have undertaken major program reviews. Yet, based on a survey of State Higher Education Executive Officers, the new emphasis with regard to preservice teacher education appears to be in the recruitment of minority teachers (Lenth, 1990). Although continued efforts in this area are of great importance, the relative loss in the sense of urgency to improve teacher education per se makes it difficult to quantify the potential change in the costs of preservice teacher education that sufficiently incorporates teacher education reform initiatives. The difficulty does not result so much from the inability to assess the increase in expenditures by changing relative class sizes, but from the degree to which institutions of higher education, and more specifically SCDEs, alter their current programs to adopt the desired instructional changes.

It is unlikely that the onus for the reform of how teachers teach will fall solely on institutions of higher education. Rather, opportunities for continuing professional development must also be provided to practicing teachers to afford them the opportunity to understand and implement the reform movement's pedagogical objectives. It is doubtful that existing "quick-hit" in-service activities will provide the extended opportunities to enable teachers to conceive of and practice a very new and disparate pedagogy (Cohen & Barnes, 1993). What is required is that the existing training model for teachers' professional development be expanded to provide opportunities for practice, classroom consultation, and coaching to enable teachers to learn to use new ideas.

Among the suggested alternatives to the training model are teacher collaboratives, subject-matter associations, and special institutes and centers. Teacher collaboratives, such as PATHS (Philadelphia Alliance for Teaching Humanities in the Schools), seek to engage teachers directly in the modes of inquiry related to the respective discipline (Little, 1993). Through the program teachers are afforded the opportunity to interact with curators and other experts who acquire, maintain, and interpret the city's vast humanities collections. Mini grants in the amount of $300 are awarded for individual projects, whereas up to $3,000 can be secured for collaborations involving several teachers. The intent of the program is to provide teachers with the skills required to offer their students a "genuine" curriculum in the humanities (Little, 1993).

In addition to more traditional in-service activities (e.g., conferences, seminars, workshops), several states have adopted experimental programs that invest higher amounts of resources in smaller cadres of teachers. For example, the California Mentor Teacher program allocates approximately $6,000 per year to each selected mentor teacher, an amount that is nearly seven times the average per teacher expenditure (Little, 1993). The rationale behind this program is that by concentrating resources in 5% of the state's teachers, the remaining 95% will benefit through a ripple-type effect. To the extent the program is successful, the per teacher cost will be marginally lower than the per participant cost. That is, investments in such programs are defensible if they can meet one of the following three criteria (Little, 1993): 1) they can be credibly tied to a ripple effect, 2) one can claim the benefit linked to this program is far more certain than the benefit linked to conventional funding, or 3) the program contributes in demonstrable ways to increased organizational capacity in ways that transcend the impact on those individuals who participate directly in the program.

Like preservice teacher education, the extent to which current reform initiatives alter the existing cost structure of teachers' professional development is dependent on both the degree to which educators implement the desired pedagogical objectives and the availability of fiscal resources. In response to the latter, education reformers have proposed a myriad of plans that attempt to ensure the continued support for and maintenance of an adequate system of teacher professional development.

Odden (1993), for example, proposed investing 2% to 4% of the state's foundation formula in human resource development. He noted that Missouri is the first state to support ongoing professional development in this manner. As part of its 1993 school finance reform package, Missouri required that 1% of the foundation expenditure level be devolved to the site, where site-based professional development teams would decide how the money would be used. In addition, it created a pool equal to 1% of the foundation level times the number of students in the state and stipulated that the funds be used to improve student outcomes, teach the new curriculum program, administer new performance-based tests, involve parents in the school, or design school improvement programs. The result that up to 2% of the base spending per pupil will be spent each year on professional development has built ongoing training into the infrastructure of the Missouri public school system.

CONCLUSION

As the nation moves toward the twenty-first century, reform efforts will continue to focus on teachers' preservice education and continuing professional development. Although it may be ambiguous as to which teacher education venue is most effi-

cient, once determined it is clear that an adequate amount of resources must be secured if such efforts are to succeed. Indeed, what controls the ability of educators to alter their existing delivery systems in both institutions of higher education and local districts is their relative success in securing public support for the proposed activities. Therefore, both educators and legislators must grapple with how and the extent to which such activities are ultimately to be funded.

Both public universities and local districts are experiencing an ebb in the pool of available resources; therefore, it is likely that future proposals for the support of teacher education will have to be accompanied by evidence that the activity is both equitable and efficient. The intent of this chapter is to provide educators with an overview of the research that has attempted to address such issues. In a period when administrators on all levels are being held to higher standards of accountability, it may be those studies that address the costs and benefits of teacher education that are in the greatest demand by the ultimate providers of the resources required for education reform—the public.

References

Allen, R. H., & Topping, J. R. (Eds.). (1979). *Cost information and formula funding: New approaches.* Boulder: National Center for Higher Education Management Systems.

Ashar, H., & Shapiro, J. (1988). Measuring centrality: A note on Hackman's resource allocation theory. *Administrative Science Quarterly, 33*(2), 275–283.

Barro, S. (1989). Fund distribution issues in school finance: Priorities for the next round of research. *Educational Evaluation and Policy Analysis, 11*(1), 17–30.

Bass, G. V. (1978). *A study of alternatives in American Education, Vol. I: District policies and the implementation of change.* Santa Monica, CA: The Rand Corporation. (ERIC Document Reproduction Service No. ED 166 825)

Berliner, D. C. (1984). Making the right changes in pre-service teacher education. *Phi Delta Kappan, 62*(2), 94–96.

Bridge, R. G., Judd, C. M., & Moock, P. R. (1979). *The determinants of educational outcomes: The impact of families, peers, teachers, and schools.* Cambridge, MA: Ballinger.

Brinkman, P. T., & Teeter, D. J. (1987). Methods for selecting comparison groups. *New Directions for Institutional Research, 14*(1), 5–23.

Cady, L., & Johnson, L. (1981). *Perspectives on innovative delivery systems to meet school staffing needs.* (ERIC Document Reproduction Service No. ED 218 231)

Cameron, K. (1983). Strategic responses to conditions of decline: Higher education and the private sector. *Journal of Higher Education, 54*(4), 359–380.

Catterall, J. S. (1988, April). *Estimating the costs and benefits of large scale assessments: Lessons from past research.* Paper presented at the annual meeting of the American Educational Research Association, New Orleans. (ERIC Document Reproduction Service No. ED 293 856)

Chaffee, E. E. (1983). The role of rationality in university budgeting. *Research in Higher Education, 19*(4), 387–406.

Cohen, D. K., & Barnes, C. A. (1993). Conclusion: A new pedagogy for policy? In D. K. Cohen, M. W. McLaughlin, & J. E. Talbert (Eds.), *Teaching for understanding* (pp. 240–275). San Francisco: Jossey-Bass.

Cole, R. D. (1987). *A model to determine the fiscal impact of the Legislative Evaluation and Accountability Program (LEAP) on staff development in selected Washington school districts.* Unpublished doctoral dissertation, Washington State University.

Coleman, J. S., Campbell, E. Q., Hobson, C. J., McPartland, J., Mood, A. M., Weinfield, F. D., & York, R. L. (1966). *Equality of educational opportunity.* Washington, DC: U.S. Department of Health, Education and Welfare.

Conran, P. C., & Chase, A. (1982). The extended year program in suburban Chicago: A different approach to inservice training. *Phi Delta Kappan, 63*(6), 398–399.

Cooley, V. E., & Thompson, J. C., Jr. (1990). *Mandated staff development in the fifty states: A study of state activity 1983–1989.* A presentation for the National Council of States on Inservice Education. (ERIC Document Reproduction Service No. ED 327 495)

Cyert, R. M. (1978). The management of universities of constant or decreasing size. *Public Administration Review, 38*(4), 344–349.

Denton, J. J., & Smith, N. L. (1985). Alternative teacher preparation programs: A cost effectiveness comparison. *Educational Evaluation and Policy Analysis, 7*(3), 197–206.

Druva, C. A., & Anderson, R. D. (1983). Science teacher characteristics by teacher behavior and by student outcome: A meta-analysis of research. *Journal of Research in Science Teaching, 20*(5), 467–479.

Ebmeier, H., Twombly, S., & Teeter, D. J. (1991). The comparability and adequacy of financial support for schools of education. *Journal of Teacher Education, 42*(3), 226–239.

Ehrenberg, R., & Brewer, D. (1993). *Did teachers' race and verbal ability matter in the 1960s?: Coleman revisited.* Ithaca: New York State School of Industrial and Labor Relations, Cornell University, Department of Labor Economics.

Federal Coordinating Council for Science, Engineering and Technology (FCCSET). (1993). *The federal investment in science, mathematics, engineering and technology education: Where now? What next?* Washington, DC: Committee on Education and Human Resources.

Ferguson, R. F. (1991). Paying for public education: New evidence on how and why money matters. *Harvard Journal on Legislation, 28*(2), 465–498.

Garvin, D. (1980). *The economics of university behavior*. New York: Academic Press.

Gifford, B. R. (1984). Prestige and education: The missing link in school reform. *The Review of Education, 10*, 186–188.

Gold, S. D., Smith, D. M., Lawton, S. B., & Hyary, A. C. (1992). *Public school finance programs of the United States and Canada, 1990–91: Volumes 1 and 2*. Albany, NY: The Center for the Study of States.

Hackman, J. D. (1985). Power and centrality in the allocation of resources in colleges and universities. *Administrative Science Quarterly, 30*(1), 61–77.

Hanushek, E. A. (1971). Teacher characteristics and gains in student achievement: Estimation using micro data. *American Economic Review, 61*(2), 280–288.

Hanushek, E. A. (1986). The economics of schooling: Production and efficiency in the public schools. *Journal of Economic Literature, 24*(3), 1141–1178.

Hanushek, E. A., Gomes-Neto, J. B., & Harbison, R. W. (1992). *Self-financing educational investments: The quality imperative in developing countries*. Rochester, NY: University of Rochester.

Hawley, W. D. (1986). A critical analysis of the Holmes Group proposals for reforming teacher education. *Journal of Teacher Education, 37*(4), 47–51.

Hawley, W. D. (1987). The high costs and doubtful efficacy of extended teacher-preparation programs: An invitation to more basic reforms. *American Journal of Education, 95*(2), 275–298.

Hedges, L. V., Laine, R., & Greenwald, R. (1994). Does money matter? A meta-analysis of studies of the effects of differential school inputs on student outcomes. *Educational Researcher, 23*(3), 5–14.

Hills, F. S., & Mahoney, T. A. (1978). University budgets and organizational decision making. *Administrative Science Quarterly, 23*(3), 454–465.

Houston, R. W., & Freiberg, J. H. (1979). Perpetual motion, blindman's bluff, and inservice education. *Journal of Teacher Education, 30*(1), 7–9.

Husen, T., & Postlethwaite, T. N. (Eds.). (1994). *The international encyclopedia of education* (2nd ed.). Oxford, England: Pergamon Press.

La Bolle, L. D. (1983). *A model to determine the fiscal impact of staff development in selected Alaskan school districts*. Unpublished doctoral dissertation, Washington State University.

Leighty, C. A., & Courter, L. (1984). *Focus on effective teaching/staff development: District adoption of the changing teacher practice study, San Diego City Schools*. Austin, TX: Research and Development Center for Teacher Education. (ERIC Document Reproduction Service No. ED 246 039)

Lenth, C. S. (1990). *State priorities in higher education: 1990*. Denver: A Joint Project of the State Higher Education Executive Officers and the Education Commission of the States. (ERIC Document Reproduction Service No. ED 319 325)

Levin, H. M. (1976). Concepts of economic efficiency and educational production. In J. T. Froomkin, D. T. Jamison, & R. Radner (Eds.), *Education as an industry* (pp. 149–191). Cambridge, MA: Ballinger.

Lewis, D. R. (1990). Estimating the economic worth of a 5th-year licensure program for teachers. *Educational Evaluation and Policy Analysis, 12*(1), 25–39.

Little, J. W. (1989). District policy choices and teachers' professional development opportunities. *Educational Evaluation and Policy Analysis, 11*(2), 165–179.

Little, J. W. (1993). Teacher's professional development in a climate of educational reform. *Educational Evaluation and Policy Analysis, 15*(2), 129–151.

Little, J. W., Gerritz, W. H., Stern, D. S., Guthrie, J. W., Kirst, M. W., & Marsh, D. D. (1987). *Staff development in California: Public and personal investments, program patterns, and policy choices*. (ERIC Document Reproduction Service No. ED 300 342)

Lytle, J. H. (1983). Investment options for inservice teacher training. *Journal of Teacher Education, 34*(1), 28–31.

McIntyre, P. J. (1976). *Costs, benefits and/or liabilities model for the Western Washington State College Teachers Corps Teacher Designed Inservice Project*. Washington, DC: Office of Education, Teacher Corps. (ERIC Document Reproduction Service No. ED 129 805)

Millsap, M. A., Moss, M., & Gamse, B. (1993). *The Chapter 1 implementation study*. Washington, DC: Office of Policy and Planning. (ERIC Document Reproduction Service No. ED 351 420)

Mintzberg, H., Raisinghani, D., & Theoret, A. (1976). The structure of the unstructured decision processes. *Administrative Science Quarterly, 21*(2), 246–275.

Monk, D. H. (1992). Education productivity research: An update and assessment of its role in education finance reform. *Educational Evaluation and Policy Analysis, 14*(4), 307–332.

Monk, D. H. (1994). The content preparation of secondary mathematics and science teachers and pupil achievement. *Economics of Education Review*.

Monk, D., & King, J. (1993). Cost analysis as a tool for education reform. In S. L. Jacobson & R. Berne (Eds.), *Reforming education* (pp. 131–150). Newbury Park, CA: Corwin Press.

Monk, D. H., & King, J. A. (1994). Multi-level teacher resource effects on pupil performance in secondary mathematics and science: The role of teacher subject matter preparation. In R. G. Ehrenberg (Ed.), *Contemporary policy issues: Choices and consequences in education* (pp. 29–58). Ithaca, NY: Industrial and Labor Relations Press.

Moore, D., & Hyde, A. (1980). An analysis of staff development programs and their costs in three urban school districts. Washington, DC: National Institute of Education. (ERIC Document Reproduction Service No. ED 185 190)

Moore, D., & Hyde, A. (1981). *Making sense of staff development: An analysis of staff development programs and their costs in three urban districts*. Chicago: Designs for Change. (ERIC Reproduction Service Document No. ED 211 629)

Murnane, R. J. (1975). *The impact of school resources on the learning of inner city children*. Cambridge, MA: Ballinger.

Nash, R. J., & Ducharme, E. R. (1983). The paucity of the investment metaphor and other misunderstandings. *Journal of Teacher Education, 34*(1), 33–36.

National Commission on Excellence in Education. (1983). *A nation at risk*. Washington, DC: U.S. Government Printing Office.

National Education Association (NEA). (1987). *The status of the American teacher 1985–1986*. Washington, DC: Author.

New York State Department of Education. (1990). *A new compact for learning*. Albany: State University of New York Press.

New York State Department of Education. (1993). *A report on professional development*. Albany: State University of New York Press.

Odden, A. (1993). *Redesigning school finance in an era of national goals and systemic reform*. Madison, WI: Consortium for Policy Research in Education, The Finance Center.

Orlich, D. C., & Evans, A. (1990). *Regression analysis: A novel way to examine staff development cost factors*. Unpublished manuscript. (ERIC Reproduction Service Document No. ED 331 808)

Orr, P. G., & Peseau, B. A. (1979). Formula funding is not the problem in teacher education. *Peabody Journal of Education, 57*(1), 61–71.

Peseau, B. A. (1982). Developing an adequate resource base for teacher education. *Journal of Teacher Education, 33*(4), 13–15.

Peseau, B. A. (1984). *Resources allocated to teacher education in state universities and land grant colleges*. Report prepared for the National Commission on Excellence in Teacher Education. Tuscaloosa, AL: American Association of Colleges for Teacher Education. (ERIC Document Reproduction Service No. ED 250 297)

Peseau, B. A. (1986). *Funding and academic production of teacher education in state universities and land grant colleges* (8th Annual Study). Tuscaloosa, AL: Association of Colleges and Schools of Education in State Universities and Land Grant Colleges. (ERIC Document Reproduction Service No. ED 272 489)

Peseau, B. A. (1988). Funding teacher education in state universities. In K. Alexander & D. Monk (Eds.), *Attracting and compensating America's teachers* (8th annual Yearbook of the Education Finance Association) (pp. 179–208). New York: Ballinger.

Peseau, B. A. (1990). Financing teacher education. In R. W. Houston (Ed.), *Handbook of research on teacher education* (pp. 157–172). New York: Macmillan.

Peseau, B. A., Backman, C., & Fry, B. (1987). A cost model for clinical teacher education. *Action in Teacher Education, 9*(1), 21–34.

Peseau, B. A., & Orr, P. G. (1980). The outrageous underfunding of teacher education. *Phi Delta Kappan, 62*(2), 100–102.

Peseau, B. A., & Tudor, R. L. (1989). Peer teacher education programs. *Journal of Teacher Education, 40*(3), 42–48.

Pfeffer, J., & Moore, W. L. (1980). Power in university budgeting: A replication and extension. *Administrative Science Quarterly, 25*(4), 637–653.

Pfeffer, J., & Salancik, G. R. (1974). Organizational decision making as a political process: The case of a university budget. *Administrative Science Quarterly, 19*(2), 135–151.

Rubin, I. (1977). Universities in stress: Decision making under conditions of reduced resources. *Social Science Quarterly, 58*(2), 242–254.

Runkel, P. J., Wyant, S. H., Bell, W. E., & Runkel, M. (1980). *Organizational renewal in a school district: Self help through a cadre of organizational specialists.* Washington, DC: Center for Educational Policy and Management. (ERIC Document Reproduction Service No. ED 206 057)

Salancik, G. R., & Pfeffer, J. (1974). The bases and use of power in organizational decision making: The case of a university. *Administrative Science Quarterly, 19*(4), 453–473.

Schick, A. G. (1985). University budgeting: Administrative perspective, budget structure, and budget process. *Academy of Management Review, 10*(4), 794–802.

Schick, A. G., Sherr, L. A., & Tuttle, F. D. (1982). The bureaucratic model in university budgeting: An alternative explanation to power. *Journal of Management, 8*(1), 49–64.

Shepard, L. A., & Kreitzer, A. E. (1987). The Texas teacher test. *Educational Researcher, 16*(6), 22–31.

Solmon, L. C., & Fagnano, C. L. (1988, April). *Speculations on the benefits of large scale teacher assessment programs or how 78 million dollars can be considered a mere pittance.* Paper presented at the annual meeting of the American Educational Research Association, New Orleans.

Spence, D. S. (1978). *Formula funding in SREB states.* Atlanta: Southern Regional Education Board. (ERIC Document Reproduction Service No. ED 167 048)

Stern, D., Gerritz, W., & Little, J. W. (1989). Making the most of a school district's two (or five) cents: Accounting for investment in teacher's professional development. *Journal of Education Finance, 14*(3), 368–379.

Summers, A., & Wolfe, B. (1977). Do schools make a difference? *American Economic Review, 67*(4), 639–652.

Theobald, N. D. (1992). *How do we get from here to there? Allocating resources to renew teacher education.* Prepared for presentation at the annual conference of the American Educational Research Association, San Francisco. (ERIC Document Reproduction Service No. ED 346 056)

Thomas, M. A. (1978). *A study of alternatives in American education, Vol. II: The role of the principal.* Washington, DC: National Institute of Education. (ERIC Document Reproduction Service No. ED 163 591)

Tom, A. R. (1986). *The hidden costs of mandating extended teacher preparation.* (ERIC Document Reproduction Service No. ED 271 429)

Twombly, S., & Ebmeier, H. (1989). *Educational administration programs: The cash cows of universities?* (ERIC Document Reproduction Service No. ED 314 828)

Valiant, R. J. (1985). *The fiscal impact of staff development programs in selected Washington school districts.* Unpublished doctoral dissertation, Washington State University.

Whetten, D. A. (1981). Organizational responses to scarcity: Exploring the obstacles to innovative approaches to retrenchment in education. *Educational Administration Quarterly, 17*(3), 80–97.

Winkler, D. R. (1975). Education achievement and school peer group composition. *Journal of Human Resources, 10*(2), 189–205.

Youngs, B. B., & Hager, J. L. (1982). A cooperative plan for personal and professional growth in Lake Washington School District. *Phi Delta Kappan, 63*(6), 415–416.

·13·

STANDARDS FOR CERTIFICATION, LICENSURE, AND ACCREDITATION

Robert A. Roth

CALIFORNIA STATE UNIVERSITY, LONG BEACH

The domain encompassed by standards, accreditation, licensure, and certification is being reconstructed in fundamental ways. The impact is the creation of an entire historical era in the profession, equal in significance to other major periods in education history such as the development of normal schools. The standards movement is so pervasive and powerful that it appropriately may be termed the *Era of Standards*.

The movement in general may be characterized by several salient features. Among these are a deep-seated and growing distrust of teacher education; a change in the locus of control, with national policy emerging as a dominant influence; restructuring of licensing and governance; and reconceptualizing the nature of standards, with performance and outcomes assuming a preeminent role. The ferment is seething in the context of a tension between reformers who pursue standard setting as sheer accountability and those who view standards as a vehicle for revitalizing a withering system of preparation for an occupation and transforming it into a viable enterprise that educates for a profession. In essence, the latter group sees standards as an efficacious strategy to create a profession.

Analysis of the standards movement is in some respects a study of contrasts. The standards effort is intent on creating significant change, and change most often brings conflict. Yet, with a powerful reform underway in this licensure and accreditation domain, there has not been a commensurate level of controversy. The new agenda is being intensely pursued with little debate. There is such a compelling consensus that reform is seen as inevitable, and most of the literature simply addresses the point that it must be accomplished and with alacrity.

Attempting to capture the essential activities, nature, and spirit of the various components of the standards movement is quite an ambitious undertaking for a single chapter. Two basic approaches may be taken. One is to provide a status report that is primarily an overview and an update on the statistics of various activities of states or other programs. This is more descriptive in nature. Another approach is to identify the essential issues related to both the concept of standards and the means by which they are operationalized. This perspective is more analytical and tends to deal with issues such as underlying premises, forces, and influences that mold the development and practice of standards, as well as the various perspectives of the purposes, functions, and models of standards.

There are also three ways in which the purpose of this handbook may be viewed. One segment of the profession looks to this handbook as a source of statistical information related to the issues at hand. It looks for numbers, commonalities, exceptions, and emerging directions. There is an obligation to some extent to deal with this type of information to serve the needs of that particular audience. There is another segment of the profession that views this handbook as part of a group of resources that address issues of policy. It is this area that could have a significant influence on the development of future directions through analysis of the essential issues and underlying premises. A third audience looks to this handbook as a source of information in developing other professional publications and uses it as a basis for articles, chapters, and books to extend the knowledge base of the profession and to encourage and enhance thinking about these issues to generate additional stud-

The author is deeply appreciative of the insights and feedback provided by the chapter reviewers, Ted Andrews and Gary Sykes. Their suggestions made valuable contributions to the chapter. Also appreciated are the reviews of specific sections as follows: Art Wise, NCATE; Joan Baratz-Snowden, National Board for Professional Teaching Standards; Ted Andrews, NASDTEC.

ies. These purposes and audiences must be considered in the design of this chapter.

This chapter is designed to address the needs of each of these audiences, at least to a certain extent. It would not be possible to address all of these to the fullest extent possible, and thus an emphasis must be placed on one area more than is others. It also noted that other publications respond to some of these needs. For example, the National Association of State Directors of Teacher Education and Certification (NASDTEC) manual on certification contains a wealth of statistical information useful to the individual seeking a survey of the states in terms of their standards and practices. In addition, the National Council for Accreditation of Teacher Education (NCATE) publishes data on the numbers of programs accredited and related statistics. Various sources of information such as these can satisfy the need for statistical information that a particular segment of the profession seeks.

The purpose of this chapter is to provide an analysis of the concept of standards and implementation for the preparation of teachers. The issue of standards is the center of analysis; how it is operationalized in state or national systems is described to illustrate its application in specific contexts.

The essential aspects of the standards concept will be used as a template to present and to analyze how state certification systems, national accreditation, and national certification function. The template serves as an analytical framework for the identification and clarification of philosophical orientations, structures, and salient issues. These elements include the nature, development, governance, politics, implementation, and impact of standards in each setting. The intent is to delve into the substantive issues of standards and to use descriptions of the current status of these standards in the varied settings not only as an end in themselves, but also as a means of illuminating varied perspectives, commonalities, and differences in relation to the key elements.

Essential elements of the template include the purposes of standards, the development processes for standards, elements that influence standards and their development, the governance and financing of standards, how standards are implemented, the impact of or effectiveness of standards and implications for the profession, and unresolved issues. The manner in which these elements of standards are operationalized may vary from setting to setting. The settings to which the template is applied include state systems for licensing and program approval, national accreditation, and national board certification. The chapter concludes with sections on emerging perspectives and the legacy of standards.

DEFINITIONS

The issue of definitions would at first appear to be a fairly straightforward matter. Insightful treatments of the definition of standards have been prepared by Diez, Richardson, and Pearson (1994) and Sykes and Plastrik (1993). Diez, Richardson, and Pearson describe four categories of metaphors for standards: 1) those that connote identity, priorities, and core values (e.g., banner, vision); 2) those that connote direction or momentum (e.g., engine, mountain); 3) those that connote perfor-

mance or performance levels (e.g., high jump bar, rubric); and 4) those that connote transactions (e.g., responsibilities, rights).

Various types of standards have emerged with the current movement. These include content standards, performance standards, delivery standards, opportunity standards, assessment standards, instructional standards, and standards for standards themselves (Diez, 1994).

The issue of definition is not as simple as it may seem because of a renewed interest in the categorization of the various types of documents issued for those who are credentialed to teach in a particular state. The purpose here is not so much to provide the standard definitions, but to describe and clarify an emerging distinction among the labels and titles. It is believed that the categorization now underway will set the direction for the future. The primary distinction currently being made is between certification and licensure.

Until the mid-1980s the term *certification* was used consistently for the process of issuing a state validation of one's authority to teach in that particular state. Certification was "the education system's process for assuring that public school teachers possess minimum qualifications . . . . Certification is a process by which the state evaluates the credentials of prospective teachers to ensure that they meet the professional standards set by the state education agency" (American Association of Colleges for Teacher Education [AACTE], 1986, p. 1). Certification ratifies the quality of teachers' competence in subject area, educational methodology, teaching skills, and potential classroom management ability (Mastain & Roth, 1984). It is a legal process that is enacted by the respective states.

The literature on certification and accreditation has pointed out the often confusing and synonymous use of the terms *certification, licensure,* and *accreditation.* "These terms are frequently used interchangeably by practitioners, which leads to the increased confusion in application of each (Galbraith & Gilley, 1985, p. 12). "Educators blur and confuse the terms 'accreditation,' 'certification,' 'licensure,' and 'program review'" (Cronin, 1983, p. 173). The distinction became more evident, however, with the creation of the National Board for Professional Teaching Standards (NBPTS) as noted by Earley (1987).

Teacher credentialing has traditionally been a state responsibility with the terms *certification* and *licensure* used almost synonymously. The NBPTS is seen by many as a mechanism to sharpen the distinction between the two, with licensure limited to state recognition that an individual has met predetermined statutory qualifications for practice, and certification reserved to the Board as professional recognition that a person meets certain standards beyond those required to be licensed. (pp. 105–106)

Furthermore, if certification validates a person's skills as a teacher and licensure provides for a process that permits teaching (Shulman & Sykes, 1986), then licensing appropriately describes the process in most states (AACTE, 1986, p. 1). As noted by Kunkle, the developing definition of the word certification in the education field means something more than licensure, and the NBPTS certification is not being considered as an alternative to licensure, but a more specialized recognition as in other professions where board certification means qualifications beyond just those regulations required for license (Smith, 1990).

It was the Carnegie Task Force on Teaching as a Profession that promoted the distinction between licensure and certification in 1986. It defined licensure as a function of the state acting on its authority to protect and promote the general welfare, and it defined certification as a function of the profession acting to acknowledge those who demonstrate advanced capabilities (Carnegie Forum, 1986). Several other writers have continued this distinction (Fenstermacher, 1990; Goodlad, 1990; Jordan, 1988) and it is gaining wider acceptance in the literature and in the profession. The confounding factor is that state documents almost universally refer to certificates rather than licenses, and that terminology continues to be used in state agencies in an official capacity.

The terms *program approval* and *accreditation* also are often used synonymously. State program approval is a legal process in which the state agency recognizes the programs of an institution so that a person who successfully completes the program is issued a state license upon the recommendation of the preparing institution. Accreditation is a voluntary process in which a professional association provides recognition to programs for having met a particular set of standards developed by the profession.

These various terms need be distinguished on the basis of the agency providing the recognition, whether or not it is an individual, program, or institution being recognized, the level of expertise implied, and the required or voluntarily participation of the program or individuals. Table 13.1 provides for the distinction among the various terms in relation to the facts cited. It should be noted that the table reflects the definition of licensure as being a state agency function and certification being that of the external professional body, although these terms have not been universally accepted in the profession, as indicated in prior discussion.

CHARACTERISTICS AND ASSOCIATED ELEMENTS OF STANDARDS: A TEMPLATE

The purpose of this section is to provide an overview of the framework, or template, within which the chapter is designed. The elements of the template are described to identify their meaning and possible implications for how they can be applied in the analysis of each of the particular settings in which they are implemented, such as state systems and national accreditation. Another purpose here is to provide the reader with insights into the nature and functions of standards by understanding the varied components that shape the role and impact of standards. One may derive different and varied perspectives of how

they are operationalized in each of these different contexts. The template serves as a framework or matrix through which the standards for certification, licensure, and accreditation can be examined, and it enables greater options for comparing and contrasting these elements in the different contexts or settings.

Purposes

The purposes of standards can be viewed both in terms of general and specific intentions. These purposes differ depending on the function of the standards, such as for state licensure versus national program accreditation. Specific purposes are reviewed in each of the application areas later in the chapter. The nature, functions, and intended outcomes of standards may vary in several important ways; therefore, it is important to examine these purposes in each of the settings and to clarify what they are intended to achieve. Regardless of the specific setting, whether it be program accreditation, national individual certification, state licensure, or state program review, the ultimate purpose is to provide some assurance of qualification of individuals who are teaching in the schools in which children and youth are required to attend. Within this broader goal, other general purposes can be identified. Some of these include recruitment, screening, quality preparation, and legitimacy (Cronin, 1983).

Recruitment Recruitment involves encouraging literate, sensitive individuals to enter the teaching profession. The profession could be more attractive if it is known that it includes competent, student-oriented, scholarly individuals who have the proper training to teach in the schools. Thus, appropriate standards are enticing to individuals because they reflect a more highly regarded profession with a certain degree of selectivity.

Screening Standards can serve the function of ensuring that individuals with certain qualifications are allowed into the profession and are permitted to practice. This is a mechanism not only for protecting the public interest, but also the interests of the profession at large.

Quality Preparation Standards directly address the nature of the preparation that one must have to enter the profession and to achieve a license or certificate or to ensure that a program is of a reasonable degree of quality as specified.

Legitimacy Another important function of standards is to reassure the public that the teacher is competent, properly trained, and thoroughly reliable.

TABLE 13.1 State and National Functions

Agency	Program Recognition	Individual Credentialing	Expertise Level	Participation
State	Program approval	Licensure	Minimum level	Required
National	Accreditation	Certification	Higher professional level	Voluntary

It is important to know the role of standards in the profession. In many respects, standards define a profession. They set the gateways that determine who shall and shall not enter. They provide the parameters of the existence of a profession. The future of a profession depends to a large extent on the consent of the publics it serves, particularly in a public profession. For the public to understand how standards function and the degree to which their interests are protected, the standards must be visible and hold accountable those who practice and those who prepare the practitioners. This builds public trust and confidence in the profession through the vehicle of standards. In effect, standards must be accepted as a necessary part of the profession.

Perhaps the most widely held view of the function of standards is to guarantee some minimum level of competence or minimum level of program quality. Although this is perhaps the most simplistic, it is fundamental to the enterprise. Another perspective is that standards are intended to lead programs to improved levels of quality, and, thus, program improvement is a basic outcome. Related to this is the view that standards should or could lead programs and their candidates to new directions with higher levels of competence. The net result of this combination of both minimum and improved levels of quality leads to the purpose of elevating the status of the profession.

Standards play a fundamental role in transforming a domain of work or occupation into a profession. Standards could perform other related functions such as encouraging innovation and gathering data for purposes of establishing a normative base. Standards could be very prescriptive or they could provide parameters within which programs must operate. Accrediting agencies, for example, could require institutions to meet certain performance standards, but give the programs autonomy in setting the performance criteria and the method of assessment. This would ensure accountability, yet permit a certain degree of autonomy. A range of such options in the various standards are evident later in this chapter. Also of note is how these options have changed as a result of their implementation over time and as new directions emerge.

Once engaged in this inquiry, a number of questions surface that help reveal the nature of purposes. For example, it is probable that a purpose is to improve programs, but the subsequent question is "Is improvement in the most important areas?" or "How can improvement be ensured to be in the most important areas?" Related to this is "How can standards ensure that the really qualified individuals enter the profession and obtain a credential?"

Central to the purpose of standards is to determine the knowledge base that the candidate must bring to the credential process. Standards must rely on and be derived from this knowledge base to be a legitimate process. Related questions include: What knowledge is of most worth? What knowledge areas should be assessed? As an example, Shulman (1986) suggests that certification examinations should "measure deep knowledge of the content and structures of the subject matter, the subject and topic-specific pedagogical knowledge associated with the subject matter, and the curricular knowledge of the subject" (p. 10). He suggests that this would be a form of examination that "would be appropriate for assessing the capaci-

ties of a *professional*. It would not be a mere subject matter examination" (p. 10).

In relationship to accreditation, Wolff (1993) attempts to clarify the purpose of assuring minimum standards of quality. He asserts that "if one were to define 'minimum standards' in terms of demonstrated educational effectiveness of the institution and its educational programs, *all* institutions are equally challenged" (Wolff, 1993, p. B2). He maintains that the public is not interested in issues such as resources and governance when discussing quality programs, but rather issues such as the ability to write effectively, think critically, and be prepared for a professional career (Wolff, 1993). These issues and questions help in sharpening the meaning of minimum and help focus the purpose of standards.

Addressing the notion of minimum qualifications or standards, Cizek (1993) notes the issue comes down to the task of specifying how little is tolerable versus what aspirations are worthy. There continues to be a dichotomy between exciting programs to higher levels of excellence and requiring programs only to meet minimum levels. One purpose of standards in this respect is to serve as a catalyst for higher education institutions to focus on the contributions that they can best make to the profession. This involves outcomes that enable teachers to "have the capacity to appraise their actions, evaluate their work, anticipate and control classroom consequences, incorporate new theory and research into practice, and possess the skills and understanding needed to explain their work to other teachers, and to students and their parents" (Fenstermacher, 1990, p. 180). Pursuing this purpose of standards goes well beyond that of minimum expectations.

Developmental Processes

The developmental process can reveal much about standards. How standards are developed significantly affects their nature, effectiveness, and credibility. In the investigation of developmental processes, the following questions would be informative: Who was involved in their development? What process was used? How broad or extensive was the input? How representative of the constituent groups was the input in the development? What sources were used to define the standards, such as the professional research? How are standards reviewed or revised? How often does the revision process take place?

Cronin (1983) suggests that the developmental process should use a set of criteria with which to screen proposals for standards. These include the following:

1. Proven worth of the remedy: To what extent has the standard been tested and proven to be worthwhile?
2. Cost to each group affected: This entails a review of the costs to all involved constituents, such as candidates, the university faculty, the state, and so forth.
3. Access to the profession: Does the standard make it easier or more difficult for the candidate to enter the profession? What impact does it have on specific groups? How effective is the proposal as a screening device?
4. Provision for a balanced program: Does the proposal add to, decrease, or provide an important new element to the preparation or certification process?

5. Deregulation: Are there other requirements that can be eliminated at the same time the new proposals are adopted?

Reliance on an empirical base would appear to be logical and necessary. Diez et al. (1994) suggests examining standard developers for "commitment to evidence rather than to tradition, ideology, or political position" (p. 63).

Influences on Standards

Many factors can determine what standards ultimately will look like and identify aids in understanding how they are applied in different settings. The key question is "Who and what are the influences that determine the nature and direction of standards for that particular context?" The uninitiated might assume that standards and policy are derived from available research and input from the profession. Real-life experience suggests that "science does not settle policy questions, it contributes perspectives and information for use within the political process" (Sykes & Plastrik, 1993, p. 45). The development of standards clearly is not conducted in a vacuum; the process is subject to considerable pressures from a variety of sources. Accordingly, the eventual outcome is usually the one that most accords with the preferred values of the policymakers rather than the outcome that may be best supported by the available evidence (Fenstermacher, 1990).

Teacher education and the standards within which it operates are influenced by a number of different agencies, including the university governance structure and a group of influences outside the university, that is, foundations that make money available, the legislature and its appropriations, the State Board of Education, professional teacher educators, learned societies, various federal agencies, and the local districts that hire graduates (Schwank, 1982).

Of long-standing interest is the role of the federal government. Although the state function is legally constituted, the role of the federal government and its agencies is always a factor with which to contend. In an analysis of the governance of teacher education, it was concluded that "direct federal involvement in teacher education has been of modest proportion and limited duration" (Clark & McNergney, 1990, p. 101). It also has been surmised that "as federal involvement in teacher education diminishes, the role of the states increases greatly, and all other constituencies struggle to maintain or increase their influence in the face of these trends" (Schwank, 1982, p. 62). The recent movement in the development of alternative certification, however, appears to call for an increased role for the federal government. "This advocacy places the federal government in an arena in which it has not previously been involved, the preparation of classroom teachers" (Fenstermacher, 1990, p. 180). This is a trend in influence that bears watching.

Another area of influence that has recently gained in significance is that of the K–12 sector. The movement to set national standards for students has grown rapidly and has an increasing importance for the preparation of teachers. Efforts now are being made to note the linkage between the K–12 standards and teacher education standards. Thus, the role of the professional associations in the specialty areas (e.g., mathematics, science, English) is more of a factor and will continue to be so (Bradley, 1993b; Lieb, 1993). The development of "world class" standards for K–12 schools is now being moved to the design of world class standards for teacher education as well.

Other forces that in some sectors are viewed as barriers to the development of standards include the sociopolitical, practical-fiscal, and psychometric-evaluative domains. The sociopolitical influence is extremely strong from vested interest groups, the legislatures, and their constituencies. Sociopolitical influences include the politically correct, multicultural, and outcome-based standards protagonists. This is practically a given in the scenario of influences on standards, particularly in a public profession such as teaching. The practical-fiscal domain bears on the matter in terms of the degree to which standards can be reasonably set and within distinct fiscal parameters. Measurement or psychometric concerns are deeper and relate to the degree to which certain characteristics feasibly can be assessed. As standards move from simple pencil-and-paper tests, issues of fidelity, reliability, and validity become even more cogent.

Governance and Financing

There are many dimensions to the governance issue, and there are particular distinctions in governance among the different settings. State agencies primarily govern the legal processes in the states, but these are not always structured in the same way. Providing a greater role for the "profession" is of increasing interest, such as through the creation of professional practices boards at the state level and through a significant involvement on the NBPTS.

Hand in hand with governance is the issue of financing. No matter how great the intent or strong the standards, without sufficient resources to implement to an adequate level, the effectiveness of the standards is limited. In fact, in most cases the assessment that is needed to judge effectiveness is quite limited by cost constraints. An essential policy issue related to financing is whether or not the costs of the information obtained are justified by the benefit derived (Levin, 1980). Benefits would need to be defined in terms of the impact on the profession, clients, and society. In addition to the extent of financing, the control of finances can have an impact on the degree to which standards are implemented.

Implementation

Systems that utilize standards are only as effective as the process of implementation allows; therefore, an analysis of process is as important as standards in assessing the effectiveness of systems. General issues include the enforcement of standards, equal application of standards, and interpretation of standards. Specific concerns relate to factors such as training of observers for teams in accreditation. In terms of certification, a major element is the degree to which the standards are adhered. In some instances, for example, standards may be bypassed by emergency certification and alternative programs.

It is instructive to determine the principles that undergird the implementation process. Accreditation, for example, is based on the premise of self-regulation versus government control. One area that needs to be sorted out in each of the contexts reviewed is the difference among terms such as regulation, collegial peer review, consultation, and self-regulation. How these terms are interpreted in the development of the implementation process is informative in understanding how the process is operationalized.

Impact and Effectiveness

A review of studies and information on effectiveness is obviously essential. This includes assessing the impact on factors such as supply, quality, and equity as they relate to the profession at large and the needs of various client groups. Implications for the profession are a part of that analysis. The importance of assessing the impact and effectiveness is self-explanatory and, as noted by Darling-Hammond and Berry (1988), professionalization incorporates conditions of specialized knowledge, self-regulation, special attention to the unique needs of clients, autonomous performance, and a large dose of responsibility for client welfare. Thus, without evidence of impact and effectiveness, the issue of professionalization comes into question.

It may also be surmised that the issue of effectiveness is the sine qua non of standards. In general, this aspect of standards has come under great scrutiny and has not been looked upon very favorably. In relation to accreditation, for example, "there is no guarantee that schools will follow up on recommendations or that teacher competency will be achieved" (Cronin, 1983, p. 173). At issue here, however, is also the notion of expectations, as pointed out by Haberman (1986). The licensure examination for every other profession is arbitrary and "it makes no pretense of which candidates will be effective in practice" (Haberman, 1986, p. 722). This certainly adds an interesting twist to the discussion of program effectiveness and impact.

Unresolved Issues

Given the purposes of a set of standards, identifying ongoing or newly emerged problems provides an understanding of its current status and needed directions. Elements of standards, standard-setting activity, and each setting has ongoing problems of practice as well as emerging issues. An analysis of these would assist in providing an understanding of the status of the standards in that context.

Nature and Types of Standards

Standards come in various forms, such as individually focused, program focused, performance or outcome based, or combinations of these. A number of other variations occur in the form of standards with some of them primarily addressing content for preparation programs or certification, processes in which students are involved to achieve satisfactory levels (e.g., field experiences), or outcomes that define the competencies or abilities of the individual after having completed a specified program.

Content-based standards can have different emphases. Course-specific standards identify the particular courses one must have, such as teaching reading. Others relate to broad content areas such as classroom management, multicultural education, and so forth. Some standards also identify performance standards related to the particular content level. The outcome-focused standards may vary in that some have one or more performance levels associated with the particular outcome or level of competence. These differences among standards are used to characterize the particular set of criteria employed for accreditation or certification in the various contexts analyzed later in this chapter.

A surprising area of concern related to content of standards has been raised by Shulman (1986). He indicates that the area that should be the essence of content standards, subject matter, is noticeably absent from standards themselves. He notes the absence of focus on subject matter among the various research paradigms for the study of teaching and he refers to it as the "missing paradigm problem" (p. 6). Policymakers who have read the research and teaching literature "find little or no references to subject matter, so the resulting standards or mandates lack any reference to content dimensions of teaching. Similarly even in the research community, the importance of content has been forgotten" (Shulman, 1986, p. 6).

An emerging area of particular interest is the link between standards for K–12 schools and standards for teacher education. This coordination process is leading the standard-setting effort with discussion of "world class standards" and a proposed National Education Standards in Improvement Council (Viadero & West, 1993).

STATE SYSTEMS FOR LICENSING AND PROGRAM APPROVAL

This section reviews the status of the state programs for licensing and program approval. In addition, policy concerns, implementation strategies, and emerging issues are reviewed.

Purposes of State Systems

The purpose of state systems is primarily one of legal responsibility and public interest. The major function is to guarantee to the public through either state licensing or program approval that individuals admitted to practice have met the established requirements. It is intended that these individuals have a minimum level of knowledge and skills needed to function in the role designated by the state license. It is a form of public protection. A program approval's purpose is to ensure that the program meets state program approval criteria so that those successfully completing the program have the required minimum levels of knowledge and skills. Both of these processes are intended to protect the public interest and to ensure the following: (a) only qualified individuals enter the profession, (b) those not qualified are screened out, and (c) qualified practitioners are protected from competition with unqualified individuals (Watts, 1982).

A number of other related functions have been identified by Galbraith and Gilley (1985). These include: (1) promote professionalism, (2) enhance the prestige of the profession, (3) improve academic programs, (4) be an income producer,

(5) distinguish individuals from peers and colleagues, (6) encourage teachers to remain in the profession, (7) avoid external governmental regulations, (8) stabilize individual's job security, (9) protect clients/employers from incompetent practitioners, and (10) prevent cannibalism recruitment of individuals from other professional associations in order to strengthen one's own. Sykes (1989) identifies three functions of licensure systems as creating supply, constructing categories of competence (licensure designations such as science, English), and inventing conceptions of quality.

One means of clarifying the purposes of a state system is through the description of the premises of the system and standards. This may be presented through the design of the conceptual basis of the state system; yet, there appears to be little or no evidence that state systems are designed in this way, either explicitly or implicitly.

An example of system premises might include the following:

1. Licensing is designed around developmental levels of children (intellectual, social, psychological). For example, the state system requires study of two of the following: the pre-adolescent, early adolescent, and adolescent. The state licenses are issued to authorize the holder to teach children and/or youth in the grades that encompass the age ranges within the developmental levels (e.g., early adolescent: ages 10–13, grades five through eight). Study of two adjacent levels is required, and licenses only reflect combinations (i.e., pre-adolescent and early adolescent; early adolescent and adolescent).
2. The state licensing system provides for teacher options in employment in the schools. Licenses reflect a range of grade levels and/or subject areas in which the teacher is qualified and authorized to teach, but the first premise of teaching only in authorized developmental levels shall not be violated.
3. The state licensing system provides school districts and administrators with flexibility in teacher assignments to efficiently use resources through deployment of personnel. The first premise should not be violated through misassignment.
4. The appropriate integration of subject matter specialization and child orientation should be considered in terms of the grade level span of the license.
5. Professional renewal is an integral part of the licensing system. Professionals are required to engage in activities as specified in licensing regulations that provide for upgrading or extending knowledge and skills.

A similar set of premises could be devised for state program approval processes. This might include the principle of extensive field-based experiences in a variety of settings to enhance the integration of theory and practice. Another might relate to developing a firm foundation for practice in a rigorous knowledge base including research and theory. Also of value could be a premise that espouses the notion of a continuum of professional development, with preservice, new teacher induction, and continuing development integrated into a system.

A conceptual model would address the essential elements of a state system. One such model focuses on the professional continuum, the time devoted to each phase, and the role of the university and local schools. Figures 13.1 and 13.2 (Roth, 1982) illustrate the traditional state model and a proposed new model. Figure 13.1 shows a disjointed system with very little linkage between the separate stages, disproportionate time emphasis among the stages, and radically different role influences from one stage to another. The model in Figure 13.2 depicts a continuum with interrelated phases in teacher development. It proposes a more equal time emphasis across the phases in which the transition into teaching during the first few years is given as much emphasis as preservice preparation. It also illustrates a greater partnership between the university and local schools in each of the phases.

This type of framework provides a basis for the design of program approval standards that guide the development of teacher preparation programs. What notably appears to be lacking is the conceptualization of state licensing systems within which well-conceived, internally consistent licensure and program approval standards and processes can be devised.

State systems can develop and change in a haphazard fashion with little regard for guiding principles. State legislatures often simply add a requirement because of political convenience, pressure from special interest groups, or because it seems like the right thing to do. It would be naive to think that a state system conceptual model and premises would cause the system to be immune to legislative tampering, but it could be of some assistance in this regard as well as contributing in the other ways cited.

Types and Status of State Standards

Standards have been devised for various constituent groups and to address different functions. The primary group, of course, is colleges and universities and their programs for preparing teachers. Other groups include nonuniversity programs and related alternative teacher preparation programs. Local school districts are playing an increasing role in the preparation of teachers, and standards are being designed for programs related to these efforts. Standards have been developed to focus on preservice preparation, induction or new teacher support programs, substandard licenses, reciprocity, standards related to testing, and performance or outcome-based standards.

In general, there appears to be a great deal of discontent with the current procedures for state licensing and program approval. If the specific purposes of the state system are to ensure clients as well as society that those permitted to practice the profession are competent and that the approval/licensing process is meant to protect qualified practitioners, then "the present accreditation/certification processes for the teaching profession accomplishes neither of the above objectives" (Watts, 1982, p. 35). More specifically, Watts (1982) has suggested that in the early 1980s "the present teacher certification system is a catastrophe" (p. 37).

As context, it may be of value to recognize that there are usually five separate ways to obtain a basic teaching license in the states. The most common is the traditional teacher preparation program. In this process the programs of an institution are approved by the state agency; it is, therefore, sometimes referred to as the approved program approach. A second means is through the direct application to the state. In this instance

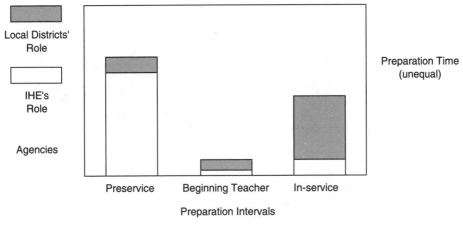

FIGURE 13.1.

the applicant submits documents verifying meeting all of the state requirements for a particular license or endorsement. This is submitted directly to the state for review and is followed by the issuance of a license if approved. Currently this only occurs for specialized situations such as out-of-state applicants, applicants for specific endorsements, or in some cases for advanced levels of certification.

A third means is through an emergency license that is issued to individuals or school districts for purposes of filling particular needs. Usually this is in the case of specific content areas such as science and mathematics or for areas such as urban schools in which there is an insufficient number of applicants for positions. A fourth approach is through alternative teacher certification programs. These are programs that may or may not be based in universities and do not follow the same requirements or time frames for completion of programs or for the issuance of a license. Requirements for these programs may not be as extensive as for programs of traditional teacher education preparation. A fifth mechanism for obtaining a state license is the "eminence" credential, which is available in some states. This is issued to an individual of particular distinction, reputation, or accomplishment in a specific field such as a great artist or musician. This license permits the person to teach in a particular area of expertise without having completed a preparation program.

The first and major area to be addressed in this section is the standards for university/college-based teacher preparation. These standards form the basis of the state program approval process.

Several concerns have been expressed regarding the status of either certification or program approval standards. These include the following:

1. Requirements are not well defined or based on research evidence (Watts, 1982).
2. The credit hours required in professional studies often are few in number (Watts, 1982).
3. In the main, program approval processes concentrate on reviewing course documents, avoid stipulating in great detail the content of coursework, and say little about how courses are to be delivered when students and faculty are face to face (Clark & McNergney, 1990).
4. Most states are plagued with numerous kinds, types, and levels of certificates (Watts, 1982).

Perhaps the most significant trend is the limitation scheme imposed on the number of professional education courses allowed for the preparation of teachers. In the past the focus had been on the number of courses required as a minimum, whereas some current efforts are now identifying the maximum number

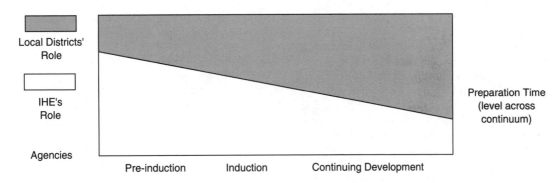

FIGURE 13.2. Proposed agency roles and preparation phases in a continuum.

of courses. The more notable examples of this activity are in the states of Texas, Virginia, and California (Roth, 1989). It is of greatest importance to note the rationale behind these efforts. Why would a state agency want to limit the amount of professional preparation required for those practicing any profession in their jurisdiction? This action clearly reflects a lack of confidence in the quality of the preparation program, including the professional education courses required for completion of the program. Although standards are intended to regulate the quality of the programs and the content, as well as determine that appropriate areas of study have been incorporated, some states have abandoned this guarantee process and even have placed limits to ensure that more damage will not be done through additional courses! This policy perspective is perhaps the most demeaning that can be adopted for any profession at any time. The underlying assumptions and forces that generate this type of action and the various ways in which it is manifest, including program limitations, are perhaps the most significant issue in the livelihood of teacher education as a profession. It is illustrative of the manner in which standards may actually deprofessionalize an occupation.

As an outcome of the lack of credibility in some of the existing teacher preparation programs and processes, alternative teacher education programs have emerged. This is discussed more extensively in Chapter 43 of this handbook; however, the relationship between standards and these programs is briefly discussed here.

Of particular interest are the nonuniversity based programs. The school-based teacher education alternative programs have grown in numbers and are becoming an important element in the teacher preparation system throughout the country (Feistritzer & Chester, 1993; Roth, 1994) (see also Dill, chap. 43, this volume).

A question of interest is what standards these programs must adhere to in order to be recognized as a teacher preparation program and to recommend candidates to the state for a state license. In each instance the state intends that these programs will meet certain quality criteria. The standards, however, are not necessarily the same as those applied to teacher preparation programs in institutions of higher education. There are obvious differences in the standards that would apply to each of these because they operate in different institutions and in different contexts. For example, standards related to governance, relationship to schools, and equality of treatment in relationship to other units on campus are not appropriate for school-based programs. Because these are not the issues of central importance in the preparation of teachers, much attention need not be focused on this discrepancy. It is in the areas of content and processes of preparation that do require an analysis to establish the application of standards to school-based programs in comparison with university-based programs. If the issues covered by the standards are deemed important for the preparation of teachers, then it should not make any difference if the preparation is taking place in the university or the school setting in the sense that both should meet the standards. School-based programs maintain that essentially the same content is indeed covered, with the possible exception of the area of foundations courses (e.g., social, political, historical). Furthermore, the proof is in the results rather than in the inputs and processes. The

issue of looking at outcomes or performance is examined both in this section and later in the chapter. Questions embedded in the issue of performance assessments are reviewed at those points.

A fundamental distinction between the school-based and university-based programs is in the early entry into schools in the school-based programs. Essentially this is the purpose of these programs, that is, to obtain candidates for positions in which there are no teachers available. It is thus necessary to place these candidates in full-time teaching positions as soon as possible. For this to occur, extended preparation in a preservice setting is not available. It is common to find program approval standards that require a certain degree of preparation prior to allowing candidates to assume responsibility for teaching in classrooms, such as student teaching. Where this is the case, standards clearly need to be different for school-based and university-based programs, at least on this particular dimension. If the principle of prior preparation is valid, then the question is on what grounds would this be violated in terms of differential standards or different application of standards. The response, of course, is one of expediency, which is the same criterion used to justify the issuance of emergency credentials or licenses. Therefore, either the validity of the principle must be questioned or the fact that standards are compromised to allow responses to particular contexts, situations, and needs must be recognized. This again reflects the understanding that standards are not derived from scientific principles, but rather for sociopolitical needs and interests.

California is one example of how such a dual system might operate. University-based teacher education programs are subject to a rather extensive and rigorous set of program approval standards. These are implemented through a self-study report, which is part of a 5-year, on-site process involving the traditional team review. This is a common format for program review procedures in the states. School-based programs, however, are not subject to the review by the state, although a voluntary review has been conducted. The governing body in this case is the Commission on Teacher Credentialing.

Local school involvement in the preparation of teachers extends beyond preservice education into the beginning years and advanced levels of licensing. Of particular interest in recent years is the development of more structured beginning teacher support programs. A comprehensive analysis of this movement is provided in Chapter 26 of this volume.

Although the need to provide support for new teachers is recognized by these beginning teacher induction programs, the opportunity for assessment is also incorporated into some of these approaches, such as in Florida, California, and Connecticut. What also is of significance to this chapter is that the assessment of performance may be integrated into the licensing process. Thus, new teachers in some of these states are issued a license valid for a limited period during which they must perform in accordance with evaluation criteria and instruments to obtain the next level state license. The inquiry here relates to the nature of standards for beginning teacher support programs and for the issuance of licenses based on assessment of these teachers new to the profession.

Although the assessment process and/or instruments can be quite formalized, as in Florida and Oklahoma, little is structured in terms of content as with preservice programs. Colorado, Minnesota, and Wyoming are considering more formal beginning teacher programs tied to specific state standards (Sclan & Darling-Hammond, 1992). The state of California has developed Draft Standards of Quality and Effectiveness for Beginning Teacher Support and Assessment Programs (Commission on Teacher Credentialing & California Department of Education, 1992). These address components such as program administration, design rationale, selection and preparation of support providers, design of training activities, and content presented. Minnesota has designed an internship program that is intended to be part of the licensing system as well. (Later in this section the initiatives related to state new teacher programs of the Interstate New Teacher Assessment and Support Consortium [INTASC] are reviewed.)

Designing standards for developing trends and new practices has also attracted attention. In view of this, NCATE at one point suggested that certain "emerging themes," such as professional development schools, might be substituted for an existing standard or standards. This option has not been implemented.

As schools and school-based programs for teacher preparation and licensure become an established part of the teacher preparation system, greater scrutiny of these programs is warranted and the issue of appropriate standards needs to be pursued. This is a vital link in the teacher education continuum. Program standards help to ensure the quality of these components and could strengthen their role in the profession rather than leave it to haphazard design and delivery. In reference to program approval or accreditation standards, it has been noted that "Such standards, particularly extended to internships and school-based practice, help build the capacity needed to improve the teaching of teachers and to bring new knowledge to bear on practice" (Sykes & Plastrik, 1993, p. 29).

The infusion of new knowledge is a key factor that must pervade the entire licensing sequence. Using the metaphor of the chain is only as strong as its weakest link, the characteristics of rigor, integration of new knowledge, and improvement of instructional practice must apply to each link in the licensing chain. Efforts such as those of INTASC and California warrant support and encouragement to the degree they can enhance these characteristics.

At the same time efforts are being made to extend the influence of standards beyond preservice programs, the problem of bypassing licensing requirements continues to plague the profession and to undermine the concept of standards. Substandard licenses, as they are referred to, include emergency permits and "intern" licenses that allow individuals without complete preparation to assume full instructional responsibilities in classrooms of their own. This chapter briefly looks at the extent of this practice and examines its impact on the profession.

The most recent summary of the status of nonstandard permits is provided by NASDTEC. This organization periodically publishes a manual that updates the state of the scene in a variety of areas related to licensure and other state functions.

The 1991 edition of the *Manual on Certification and Preparation of Educational Personnel in the United States* (NASDTEC, 1991) contains a section on substandard licenses. This should not be confused with the general term *alternative certification*,

which may or may not employ substandard licenses as part of their process (see Dill, chap. 43, this volume). The issue of concern here is the practice of permitting individuals to teach who are not fully prepared to assume legally full responsibility for their own classroom in grades K–12.

As indicated in the first part of this review of substandard licenses, this bypassing of licensing requirements undermines the entire concept of standards for the profession. As noted by Watts, "The practice by state education agencies of issuing temporary or emergency certificates to unqualified individuals is perhaps their most flagrant abuse of the licensure process" (Watts, 1982, p. 37).

There are several sides to the substandard license story. The teaching profession views this as clearly undermining the status of teaching as a profession. True professions would not tolerate such a practice; yet, in teaching it may be characterized as commonplace and in existence in almost every state. The K–12 school community, particularly administrators, see this as a necessary activity to have teachers in hard-to-staff schools, such as in urban and bilingual communities. The reality of their issue is that they are faced with simply not having a qualified, licensed teacher, yet being required to open the classroom. Even if they disagree with the practice philosophically, they see no reasonable alternative to meet their responsibilities. Policymakers such as government agencies and state legislatures are not hard pressed to be concerned from a policy perspective. In fact, with pressures from schools and antiteacher education constituencies, just the opposite may be the case.

Given this scenario, the issuance of nonstandard licenses must come to terms with the concept of standards. No matter how rigorous the standards, bypassing them undermines the entire system. The standards become an empty promise for the parents, children, and all others who rely on them for protection and quality of instruction. Emergency permits and other such licenses cast a long shadow over the profession.

Reciprocity

With an increasingly mobile society, the issue of reciprocity has become of great interest. Reciprocity exists through two vehicles. Many states will recognize licenses from other states on the basis of NCATE. In this system, teachers who have completed teacher preparation programs at NCATE-approved institutions are recognized for receiving a comparable license in another state. A formal, contractual system for reciprocity is conducted through the Interstate Certification Compact (ICC). In this system, states pass standard enabling legislation that permits state authorities to sign contracts with each other for certain categories of teachers (regular and special education), administrators, support professionals, or vocational educators. Teachers moving from one contract state to another automatically receive (under certain conditions), upon application, the initial regular, comparable license in the receiving state. This state system had its origins in the mid-1960s and has grown in number of participating states and types of activities since then. It is now affiliated with NASDTEC.

Currently 30 states participate by signing one or more contracts with one or more states. The contracts are revised and renewed every 5 years. NASDTEC and ICC do not compile overall statistics on the number of licenses issued on the basis of these reciprocal agreements, and there is no evidence of this record keeping being a common practice among the individual states.

States also use completion of a program accredited by NCATE as a basis for issuing a state license to an out-of-state applicant. It has been noted that this is not the same as true reciprocity in which states agree to accept *each other's* licenses or approved program graduates through the granting of a comparable, initial regular license. The NASDTEC manual reports that 21 states recognize NCATE accreditation to some extent to issue a license to an out-of-state applicant (NASDTEC, 1994).

A survey of states was conducted to answer specifically the question of whether or not NCATE accreditation would foster the transfer of teacher licensure from one state to another. It was found that "NCATE accreditation is the determining factor in interstate certification in only one state and for only one certificate. This is the superintendent's certificate in Missouri. In all other instances, NCATE accreditation is not necessary" (Raths, Zych, & Wojtaszek-Healy, 1985, p. 55). Furthermore, beyond this single exception, "graduates of institutions in states without reciprocity agreements would not be denied certification in other states solely on the basis that their preparing institution lacked NCATE accreditation. Eight certification officers suggested that NCATE accreditation is helpful to graduates in this category (Raths et al., 1985).

A separate study by Behling provided somewhat different conclusions, indicating that 25 jurisdictions will either grant automatic certification or automatic certification with conditions to an individual who has completed an NCATE-approved teacher preparation program. Seven of these jurisdictions will grant a certificate without transcript analysis, whereas the other 18 have certain conditions (Behling, 1986).

There is growing interest in a common basis for issuing state licenses and approving programs. Through the ICC and NASDTEC efforts, NCATE, and an emerging consortium of states collaborating on standards for new teachers, it is anticipated that this characteristic of the licensing process will become a more prominent feature. (This issue is discussed again later in this chapter in the section on a national system.)

State standards not only deal with the issuance of initial licenses, but also renewal and upgrading. Although permanent licensing was once commonplace, this practice has been virtually swept away with the reform movement. Currently, 23 states do not require a second-stage license, although 13 of these do offer a second-stage license. Only seven states do not have professional development requirements after the initial license. In six states the initial license is a permanent or life license (NASDTEC, 1994). Three states, Pennsylvania, New Jersey, and New York, are embroiled in political confrontations as they "have revived their statewide campaigns to replace lifetime teaching certificates with renewable licenses" (Richardson, 1993, p. 8).

On the surface this would appear to be a professional issue in which remaining current is an integral part of the notion of ongoing professional development. There are, however, considerable political undertones that are becoming more prominent in this scenario (Richardson, 1993). Consider, for example, the arguments presented by protagonists pushing for renewable licensure.

- It is a way to increase accountability for teachers.
- It requires teachers to engage in professional development.
- In-service would be focused on fields in which teachers are teaching.
- Local communities are strongly in favor of replacing lifetime certificates with renewable licenses.
- Lifetime licensing breeds mediocrity.

On the other side, teacher union representatives have provided a different perspective of a renewable license system, which includes:

- It shifts most of the burden for continuing education to teachers, rather than local districts assuming a reasonable share.
- It endangers job security by "politicizing" licensing procedures.
- Renewable license is another name for renewable tenure, which is just another name for no tenure; permanent licensure removes teaching from the political realm.
- Requiring teachers to renew their licenses is easier politically than questioning the competence of those who hire, evaluate, and remove teachers.
- The renewable system makes it easier for districts with fiscal problems to replace higher paid career teachers with inexperienced teachers hired at lower salaries (Richardson, 1993).

An issue related to the licensing of teachers appears to be a management–labor dispute. Licensing in other professions would hardly be characterized by the same type of rhetoric. Teaching is in the public service domain, and thus the dialogue moves out of the professional into the political arena.

Certification Testing

The reform movement initiated in the 1980s witnessed a resurgence of competency testing for state licensing, using either a state-developed or a national, commercially available test (Hawley, 1986). In the early 1990s, only six states reported not using some type of examination for teacher licensure (NASDTEC, 1994). In a 1990 survey of the states, 13 states in the preceding 5 years added testing to their requirements for entering or completing a teacher education program (Rothman, 1990). Although the movement almost reached a saturation point (39 states with some type of test in 1990, but little activity since then), interest has not waned, but rather has turned to examining the nature of testing. The focus has shifted from paper-and-pencil tests to performance assessments.

The fundamental issue is the impact or extent to which examinations can ensure competency or if teacher testing can result in better teaching (Nassif, 1992). This also raises questions regarding the impetus for this movement. According to one analyst, the impetus is marked by "the haste with which many people have become convinced of an epidemic of incompetence among teachers; and, second the rush to use tests to solve the problem" (Hathaway, 1980, p. 210). According to Cole (1979), it is a hollow means of judging the efficacy of teachers, "It can only whittle away at the edges of the problem; it has no power to cure, because it treats symptoms rather than causes . . . competency testing is nothing more than a search for victims" (p. 233). Furthermore, a comprehensive review by Schalock of the most frequently used national test found that "without exception . . . scores derived through the National Teacher Examination and performance as a teacher . . . [were] found to be unrelated" (Hathaway, 1980, p. 215).

A second issue revolves around the compatibility between tests and other related professional activities. "Around this topic a substantial gulf has always existed between, on the one hand, relatively narrow, instrumental conceptions of teaching represented in state licensure examinations, district evaluation schemes, and the content of inservice education, and, on the other, the more diffuse social and intellectual concerns of the university-based curriculum of teacher education" (Sykes & Plastrik, 1993, p. 39).

Of related interest is the disparate impact that testing might have on minorities, those underrepresented in the instructional work force. Elimination of cultural bias from such tests has been an issue of considerable concern (Anderson, 1991; Bentz, 1989; Hood & Parker, 1989; Murphy & Elliot, 1991). One study indicated that during the past decade more than 95,000 minorities in 35 states were denied entry into teaching because of restrictive teaching tests (Castenell & Soled, 1993).

A key issue is how tests are normed. Educational tests are normed for people without disabilities, and some aspects of tests such as use of scantron answer forms provide obstacles to those with disabilities. Furthermore, minorities are frequently overlooked in the norming of standards (Castenell & Soled, 1993). A recent example to address this is the test development process used by the Educational Testing Service (ETS) in the development of a new series of examinations referred to as Praxis. A question posed to ETS and its response follows:

To what extent have the Praxis Series tests been checked for cultural and racial bias? In the job analysis survey for Praxis I: Academic Skills Assessments, additional survey instruments were sent to members of minority groups to ensure that these groups were adequately represented in the results.

During the multistate validity studies, panelists were asked to judge each question's fairness. If even one person judged a question unfair to certain population groups, that question was reviewed by a special group of experts who recommended revisions to the question or elimination of it. This was all in addition to the regular sensitivity review process that is employed for every ETS test question and final test form. Items that suggest stereotyping, have potentially offensive language, or appear to discriminate against particular population group(s) are revised or dropped from the tests.

Following the multistate validity studies, states were asked to review the resulting documents. After reviewing these documents, states may move ahead to standard-setting studies. ETS is working closely with many states that are now establishing their qualifying scores through the standard-setting process. (Havrilesky, Dwyer, & Forbes, 1995)

Inherent in the use of tests for purposes of issuing a license is the question of establishing cutoff scores. This takes on considerable importance when recognized that such scores may be used to deny individuals or even groups access to the profes-

sion and possibly the need to defend the cutoff in court. Problems with setting such scores are not limited to psychometric concerns, but relate to the sociopolitical as well. To illustrate, if passing standards are set high enough to placate the public, substantial numbers of prospective teachers, particularly minority candidates, will be barred from the teaching profession. If passing standards are set low enough to allow a reasonable number of applicants to become teachers, then the public may rightfully dismiss teacher competency tests as empty rituals (Popham & Yalow, 1984). This puts policymakers in a quandary.

A common procedure for establishing cutoff scores is through field testing to gather normative data. A complication encountered here is that "in general, passing standards based on performance data (such as mean performance of field-test examinees) will be lower than the passing standards recommended by experts" (Popham & Yalow, 1984, p. 5).

Under certain conditions lower performance scores should influence standard setters to set cutoff scores lower than preference scores (scores determined by surveying several constituencies or experts in the field). These include gravity of mistakes and confidence factors (Popham & Yalow, 1984). If there is considerable danger associated with passing an individual with the lower score (e.g., airline pilot or brain surgeon), then the preference score should carry the burden of the rationale, not the mean score of field-test participants.

Confidence factors relate to the confidence placed in the score established through the preferences of the experts or practitioners. This degree of confidence relates to the competence of those rendering preferences (the more expert, the greater the confidence) and the extent to which there is a solid knowledge base in the subject matter being assessed (the more extensive the knowledge base, the greater the confidence in judgments of experts). All of this further substantiates the complexity of the business of testing for licensure.

Legal issues related to testing have emerged through the years in relation to five issues (McDonough & Wolf, 1988):

1. The arbitrary and capricious development or implementation of a test or employee selection procedure
2. The statistical and conceptual validity of a test or procedure
3. The adverse or disproportionate impact of a testing program or selection procedure on a "protected group"
4. The relevancy of a test or procedure to the identified requirements of the job (i.e., job-relatedness)
5. The use of tests or selection procedures to violate an individual's or group's civil rights

The courts have played an increasingly significant role in policy decision making related to teacher testing. There appear to be two trends in court decisions that policymakers would be prudent to be cognizant of in future actions regarding testing development and requirements. These include, "First, all teachers to be tested now have the opportunity to participate in a representative manner in test construction, test standard setting, and test interpretation. Second, all teachers who fail to meet test expectations at a particular time may pursue realistic alternatives in order to fulfill expectations at a later time" (McDonough & Wolf, 1988, p. 43).

Performance-Based Assessment

The shift to performance-based measures is gaining momentum. Some states, such as Mississippi, have considered using assessment of teaching performance during the beginning year as part of the data base to grant state program approval to teacher preparation institutions (Amos, Cheeseman, & Ward, 1986).

Measuring performance is a thread that runs through much of the reform movement in education (see Gough, 1991). It was the emphasis of President Bush's National Goals and World Class Standards. It carries with it the politically appealing notion of accountability. Some researchers maintain, however, that such a system may not be as practical as it is appealing due to the intricacies of assessment methods.

A study by Shavelson, Baxter, and Pine (1992) to evaluate the reliability and validity of science performance assessments provides some insights into the nature of the problem. Among their findings was that some students' scores depend on the particular science investigation (content) sampled and on the particular method used to assess performance. A conclusion was that each method provides different insights into what students know and can do. This translates into the need for multiple measures and multiple tasks, which generally have not been incorporated into teacher performance assessments. Their conclusion was that "we suspect that this nation may be placing far too much weight on accountability to achieve its reform agenda" (Shavelson, Baxter, & Pine, 1992, p. 26). An alternative or companion effort would be to put resources into teaching and learning.

A number of states have implemented beginning teacher evaluation systems. Their approach is either to establish general requirements for the local evaluation of new teachers or to create specific formal programs. In some instances states having general requirements expect the local districts to develop their own evaluation system compatible with state guidelines. These include Arizona, Colorado, Kansas, Maine, Missouri, New Mexico, Pennsylvania, Utah, and Washington. Other states (Alaska, Idaho, Illinois, Iowa, New Hampshire, New York, Oregon, South Dakota, and Wisconsin) require evaluation, but allow local districts to develop their own systems (Sclan & Darling-Hammond, 1992).

Twenty-two states have developed performance evaluation instruments, criteria, or guidelines with varying degrees of pre-scriptiveness as to their use. Connecticut and Kentucky require use of a state-developed instrument; Florida provides choice of the state instrument or a locally developed instrument. Ten states (Alabama, Connecticut, Florida, Georgia, Kentucky, Oklahoma, North Carolina, South Carolina, Tennessee, and Texas) have instruments that prescribe detailed generic teaching behaviors that all teachers must display (Sclan & Darling-Hammond, 1992).

In the fall of 1989 Connecticut introduced what many believe to be the nation's most rigorous assessment of beginning teachers' performance (Bradley, 1989). State legislation required a three-tier system of licensure that includes initial, provisional, and professional-educator licensure. Candidates for an initial license must pass a test on basic reading, writing, and mathematics skills called the Connecticut Competency Exam for Prospec-

tive Teachers (CONNCEPT). The test is required for admission to a Connecticut teacher preparation program and is a prerequisite for initial certification of all candidates.

Also required for initial certification is a test of the candidate's knowledge of their subject specialization, Connecticut Assessment of Content Competence (CONNTENT). This initial certification is valid for one year. During this year beginning teachers participate in the Beginning Educator Support and Training (BEST) program and are assessed on their performance. Successful completion of the BEST program leads to a provisional certificate valid for 8 years. To obtain a professional certificate, teachers must complete 30 hours of college-level study. Maintaining this provisional certificate requires nine units of continuing education every 5 years.

The BEST system contains 50 competencies that are assessed. The importance of context is emphasized and each assessor is given "contextual" information before beginning observations. Interviews are conducted both before and after the observation to clarify the lesson or explain changes made in the lesson plan and why. Professional judgment by the assessor plays an important role in this process.

Other evidence of the movement in performance assessment is provided by efforts of private organizations. National Evaluation Systems (NES), for example, published *Performance Assessment in Teacher Certification Testing* (National Evaluation Systems [NES], 1993), and Educational Testing Service (ETS) produced a series of new examinations that include Praxis III, Classroom Performance Assessments. This is a system of evaluating on-the-job performance.

Praxis III employs a system that incorporates observation with before and after interviews with teachers. It consists of three components: (1) a framework of knowledge and skills for beginning teachers, (2) various instruments (e.g., class profile, classroom observation record), and (3) a form to analyze and score teaching performance. Observers are trained on observation, interpretation, and scoring of the performance assessment data. Praxis is based on four domains: (1) organizing content knowledge for student learning, (2) teaching for student learning, (3) creating an environment for student learning, and (4) teacher professionalism (Dwyer & Villegas, 1992).

There are two other parts to the Praxis series. Praxis I deals with basic academic skills. It is available in a computer-based format and a paper-and-pencil format, which is the Pre-Professional Skills Tests (PPST). Praxis II assesses subject matter knowledge. The Praxis Series will replace the National Teacher Examinations (NTE) used by 33 states (Bradley, 1993a).

The essence of the performance assessment is to evaluate more accurately what teachers actually do. Models for evaluating performance are available in other professions, such as law, architecture, and medicine, but teacher assessments do not reflect the ways teachers make decisions and exercise professional judgment (Watkins, 1988). Although performance assessments are much more realistic than tests, according to Shulman they still leave out critical aspects of teaching. Structured portfolio documentation could augment the performance assessments (Watkins, 1988).

Together with performance assessments is the development of performance-based standards. Undoubtedly, this is the new wave in teacher licensure, replacing the previous emphasis on state testing that peaked around 1990 and has slowed since to a trickle. There is considerable interest in this at the national level, which is reviewed in subsequent sections. The state-level activity is equally intense, with leadership provided by NASDTEC, which has published the *NASDTEC Outcome-Based Standards and Portfolio Assessment* (1993). This document directly states that "the development of the NASDTEC outcome-based standards is a direct response to the emerging reform efforts throughout the United States" (p. 3). The standards are designed to provide a framework for review of college/university teacher education programs and alternative programs of preparation, to design licensure examinations, or to be used in conjunction with induction programs. These standards, along with those being developed by INTASC, will guide state standard setting in the coming years.

The format of the NASDTEC standards is to identify the client, teacher requirement, and purpose. This is followed by "authentic context," a description of the setting in which the outcome is demonstrated and verified. This context also provides a rationale for the standard. The last element is a description of sample portfolio entries, including research, video lessons, assessments, and resources.

The essence of a standard is the teacher requirement element. An example of this is as follows:

STANDARD 3.0 CURRICULUM
The beginning elementary level teacher in the certificated teaching assignment analyzes and organizes into daily, weekly, monthly, and yearly teaching units developmentally appropriate, culturally sensitive, basic and higher order, challenging, and integrated subject matter including, but not limited to, reading and language arts, mathematics, science, humanities, history, geography, and healthy lifestyles. (NASDTEC, 1993, p. 23)

The NASDTEC standards are cast within a client-service model of an agency. In trying to fit this mold, the format may be viewed as somewhat overstructured, such as through identification of "clients." Individuals served are obvious throughout the standards without such specification. It is indeed a significant change in approach by NASDTEC. (An analysis of the NASDTEC approach is provided in the context of performance/outcome-based standards in a later section of this chapter on emerging perspectives.)

Some states have already moved away from the course-counting approach to descriptions of performance expectations. K–12 student assessments are currently being developed in Kentucky, Connecticut, Vermont, California, and Maryland. The state of California standards for teacher preparation program approval, for example, contain the following:

Standard 23: Each candidate prepares at least one unit plan and several lesson plans that include goals, objectives, strategies, activities, materials and assessment plans that are well defined and coordinated with each other.

Standard 24: Each candidate prepares and uses instructional strategies, activities and materials that are appropriate for students with diverse needs, interests and learning styles. (Commission on Teacher Credentialing, 1992, pp. 24, 25)

In addition, for each standard there is a stated rationale and "Factors to Consider." There is a striking similarity between the California and NASDTEC standards. Other California standards include the additional dimensions cited in the NASDTEC standard, such as culturally sensitive and developmentally appropriate. In terms of statement of standards, NASDTEC may serve as a catalyst for operationalizing a movement that conceptually was well underway.

The Kentucky Education Professional Standards Board is developing standards to ensure that teachers can prepare elementary and secondary school students to master 75 skills required by the state (Lively, 1992). This is another aspect of the performance- or outcomes-based standards movement.

Performance- or outcome-based standards extend beyond state systems. The concept is rapidly becoming a significant force in the profession. This subject is reviewed from various perspectives as a major issue later in the chapter.

Influences on Design

Standards are not developed in a political vacuum. It is assumed also that the context is not an intellectual vacuum. One may cast the political and intellectual at either end of a continuum; the more the process is in one direction, the less it is in the other. Reality says that both influence design, and finding a reasonable balance becomes the objective.

Political Context and Sources

It is well known that standard setting is basically a political process. The political players, however, are found in different political arenas. One such group is the legislative and governmental constituent; another resides in educational politics.

As noted by one review of standards, requirements are often not well defined or based on research evidence (Watts, 1982). This is beginning to change as noted in previous sections, but research is still not the driving force. More often than not, licensure categories, such as specific roles or levels of instruction, reflect special interest groups.

Standards thus emerge from a myriad of forces, each vying for attention and a prominent place among the standards. Special interest groups, research, professional associations, NASDTEC, INTASC, private agencies, federal initiatives, current topics of public concern, and even legislative whims are caught up in a swirl of competing pressures to influence design. These forces may result in a patchwork of standards with no evident conception of the teacher's role. In a similar fashion, the recent emergence of K–12 standards "project a role for the teacher that is circumscribed largely by the classroom and the content of the curriculum" (Sykes & Plastrik, 1993, p. 39).

Other perspectives envision an expanded role that includes school leadership and community connections. "Such role conceptions potentially expand the terrain of standards beyond the academic requirements of effective instruction and have implications for teacher education and assessment" (Sykes & Plastrik, 1993, p. 39). The issue of role conceptions hardly enters the discussion of standards in the political arena.

Although federal funding has had some degree of influence in setting the teacher preparation and standards agenda, the federal role has not been perceived as intrusive. Some argue that federal efforts have been of little consequence with this role left to the states, and that the federal activity has been of modest proportion and limited duration. It exemplifies an ambivalent attitude of the federal government, and as the federal categorical aid stimulus has decreased there is a marked increase in state legislation (Clark & McNergny, 1990).

As testing for licensure became more prominent in the 1980s, the influence of private agencies increased accordingly. The two most influential are National Evaluation Systems (NES) and Educational Testing Service (ETS). NES has developed several state licensing exams. It has produced several volumes on various aspects of testing using state agency personnel or others with some knowledge of a particular aspect of assessment (e.g., legal considerations, cultural bias). Five of these volumes are listed in the references to this chapter (NES, 1989, 1990, 1991, 1992, 1993).

Role of NASDTEC

Professional association influence has been particularly notable through NASDTEC. "Although almost all states have developed their own standards, most have been influenced by the standards developed by NASDTEC" (Roth & Pipho, 1990, p. 127). NASDTEC has been developing standards for more than 20 years.

The purpose of the NASDTEC effort is not to establish national standards, but rather to "serve as guidelines or reference for individual states, not as mandates" (NASDTEC, 1976, p. 1). Furthermore, NASDTEC supports the belief that the role of government agencies and professional associations must be to provide leadership related to the outcomes of public education, but it also recognizes that the state has the fundamental responsibility for the certification/licensure of teachers (NASDTEC, 1993).

In addition to standards, NASDTEC has provided leadership in other related areas and offers certification-related services. One of the more notable areas is interstate certification reciprocity. The Interstate Certification Compact (ICC), described previously, is now part of NASDTEC, although it is governed by its own state representatives. Through the ICC, a central data base has been developed on individuals whose licenses have been denied or revoked.

A recent development is the NASDTEC Information Network (NIN). Certification information from all 50 states is available in a single software package. Answers to questions and information can be printed out, including applications for certification.

Development Process

The process used by states is one of consensus building. Use of democratic processes is the standard, although special interest group influence and legislative control have an impact on the ultimate outcome. The professional influence can be at odds with that of the public, which creates a dilemma for teacher policy to the extent public and professional forms of control over standard setting are in tension with each other (McDonnell, 1989).

One analysis of this current tension found that

attention to democratic control received greater emphasis than professionalism in the enactment of recent teacher policies. Performance standards were often defined through the political process, with limited input from teachers or the organizations representing them. Implicit in this emphasis was a belief that teacher quality had diminished and no longer met the electorate's performance expectations for a public institution. Therefore, rather than allowing the teaching profession to rejuvenate itself from within, state officials enacted policies requiring teachers to conform to performance criteria designed by public agencies and private test developers. (McDonnell, 1989, p. vi)

According to others this recent experience is contrary to a preferred democratic process where stakeholders freely engage in the standard setting. In the K–12 realm, it has been noted, "We have learned, as have others in standards-setting reform, that efforts . . . must build a comprehensive and consensus-generating framework in order to truly promote systematic reform" (Stewart, 1994, p. 45).

On the other side of the democratic process argument is the conclusion that democratic processes complicate and encumber standard setting (Chubb & Moe, 1990; Morone, 1990). As noted earlier in this chapter, development processes are more than a means for generating standards. They have significant political implications for "buy-in" of the results and setting a conducive context for implementation.

Financing Standards

It is generally recognized that the role of standards as a means of regulating or ensuring quality is fixed by the cost limits imposed by the fiscal agencies. As far as states are concerned, this has been a low level of investment, with virtually no efforts to test the limit.

Financing, as with most issues related to state standards, is a political issue. It may have little resemblance to the degree of support needed to meet the psychometric specifications, utility needs, or training requirements. Often it is predicated upon whatever is the simplest and easiest, and at the same time it generates the greatest accountability. This seemed to be an underlying premise on the minds of legislators during the wave of new tests for certification in the 1980s.

A question of considerable weight for policymakers is the effect of standards on the quality of the resultant pool of teachers admitted into the profession and costs associated with this outcome. It basically is an issue of cost benefits.

A related issue is identifying the criteria against which the benefits may be assessed. At its most basic level, a simple count of those who failed the test becomes the sum total of the benefit.

One such example is found in the experience of Texas in the mid-1980s. Legislators demanded a test in return for a tax to pay for a teacher's salary increase. Research showing the test was invalid or a poor choice did not enter into the dialogue in any meaningful way. The final passing rate was 99% with 1,199 teachers eliminated and another 1,000–2,000 forced out of the profession. These outcomes cost taxpayers $78 million (Roth & Pipho, 1990).

An analysis of cost benefits and a model for understanding the economics of information is proposed by Levin (1980). It is based on the premise that acquiring information has both a benefit and a cost, and the objective of an information system is to maximize benefits relative to cost. In certification and accreditation the public and profession assume that the benefits to society of maintaining high teacher standards will exceed the costs of acquiring information. One difficulty is measuring the benefits to society (e.g., citizenship, work behavior), particularly the benefits of any particular requirement. Although this is a constraint on the economics of information model in education, "it can definitely contribute in a heuristic way by forcing us to ask the question of whether any particular requirement is likely to yield benefits that exceed the costs of providing and meeting the standard that is set out" (Levin, 1980, p. 9).

Levin's economics of information model addresses the issue of the costs associated with gathering information and the resultant benefits. A corollary is the cost of not gathering sufficient or essential information in terms of the resultant consequences. For example, collecting information on individual candidate's effectiveness or qualifications for a license through performance assessments would require a costly process. An alternative is the program approval approach in which groups of candidates are issued licenses based on program completion. A question to consider is the consequences (cost in terms of lost benefits) of not obtaining individual performance assessment information.

There may be a certain threshold of information below which the system is virtually dysfunctional. As an example, if the state system allows a certain number of essentially incompetent individuals (e.g., 10%) to enter the profession (issued a license), that may be the level of tolerance for the system. Given that determination of acceptable "error" in the system, what are the associated cost savings and, conversely, what are the consequences of not providing the necessary financing?

It is this type of question and a myriad of others that need to be posed. The role of research is to provide the necessary information by which the economics of change in the data system can be determined.

Governance

State systems of licensure are governed in various ways. State legislatures, of course, have ultimate authority, and this is somewhat delegated to state boards of education or professional standards boards. Nevertheless, state legislatures continue to exercise their authority by passing statutes that prescribe specific requirements or even limit the number of units allowed in professional education (Roth, 1992).

Recent concern with governance by the states has been with overregulation (Association of Teacher Educators [ATE], 1991; Goodlad, 1990). There is a tension between the profession and state governing bodies and specifically between teacher education and state legislatures. Teacher education views the prescriptive mandates of government agencies as an intrusion into professional matters, although their graduates function in a public role as teachers. The basis for this appears to lie in a lack of credibility of teacher education, which motivates lawmakers to enter the scene and set matters straight. Many believe that the issue of credibility is the most critical problem facing the profession today, and it manifests itself in the standard-setting process.

The impact of state policy as enacted through standard setting needs careful scrutiny to ensure optimum results; yet, "In every state, public officials control the number and the quality of teachers without being held accountable" (Haberman, 1986, p. 720). The rationale for state control has been posed as follows: to protect the public, to be fair to those individuals seeking licenses, to raise the quality of a particular profession, and to limit the number of practitioners (Haberman, 1986).

An emerging locus of control in the states is the professional standards board. The purpose of such a board is to give the profession a role in self-governance by shaping and implementing the standards of the profession. Some forms of these state-level bodies have existed since the 1920s in New Jersey and since the 1940s in Indiana, Nebraska, South Carolina, and West Virginia (Jordan, 1988). The more recent impetus for this effort came through the National Education Association (NEA) and its interest in professional autonomy. Since the 1960s, the NEA has striven to establish autonomous boards that have the authority to determine standards for entry into teaching as well as related issues (Jordan, 1988). Some believe that such standards boards actually will not increase professional autonomy in schools. Public-professional democratic control such as this, it is argued, resulted in teachers' bureaucratic control in the first place. Others suggest that "current pressures for creating these bodies are coming from education reform advocates as well as state political figures" (Jordan, 1988, p. vii).

Professional standards boards (PSB) have varying degrees of authority and different membership composition. The existence of 18 national specialty boards in medicine suggests the possible degree of complexity involved (Jordan, 1988). One study reported that only three PSBs are autonomous, 21 give preliminary approval, and others are advisory only (Earley, 1987). A later study stated that in addition to four autonomous boards, 44 other states have PSBs with advisory prerogatives relative to setting licensure or certification standards and/or policing the conduct of teachers (Scanell, Andersen, & Gideonse, 1989). A report by the Connecticut Education Association (1993) indicates that eight states have established professional standards boards—California, Oregon, Minnesota, Nevada, Iowa, Kentucky, Georgia, and Indiana. Colorado also established a PSB in 1991. The American Association of Colleges for Teacher Education (AACTE) (AACTE, 1993) reports that twelve states appoint autonomous boards with duties ranging from complete responsibility for establishing standards and implementing procedures for licensure to partial responsibility. Two states are in transition, and one state has two boards, one for advising and the other for implementation. The boards are separate from state boards and are accountable directly to their state legislature. Among the groups represented in the PSBs, teachers are the largest group, although not necessarily a majority. In California, 6 of the 15 voting members are teachers, one other is from a teacher education institution. In Oregon, 8 of the 17 are teachers, two others are from teacher education institutions. In Minnesota, 6 of the 11 are teachers with one other from higher education.

A semiautonomous board exists in Nevada, with the State Board of Education having the authority, under certain conditions, to disapprove any regulation within 90 days of its adoption by the Professional Standards Board. The other seven boards are autonomous in matters related to standards.

INTASC

INTASC was created in 1987 by the Connecticut Commissioner of Education, Gerald Tirozzi, and California Superintendent of Public Instruction, Bill Honig, and is sponsored by the Council of Chief State School Officers. Its purpose is to enhance collaboration among states interested in rethinking teacher assessment for initial licensing, as well as to prepare and induct teachers into the profession. Its mission is to provide a forum for its members to learn about and collaborate in the development of new techniques to assess teacher performance and for new programs to enhance professional development. INTASC maintains a clearinghouse of the latest research on performance assessment and professional development for educators.

INTASC developed draft standards for licensing new teachers using representatives from the teaching profession and personnel from 17 state education agencies. The standards were developed to be compatible with the advanced certification standards of the National Board for Professional Teaching Standards (NBPTS). The initial document addresses the knowledge, dispositions, and performance deemed essential for all teachers regardless of their specialty area. Developing subject area standards for new teachers is the next step. The National Board Standards and accepted standards for student outcomes K–12 serve as reference points. As an integral part of this process, the Committee also works on the development of assessment prototypes for evaluating the achievement of these standards (Interstate New Teacher Assessment and Support Consortium [INTASC], 1992). This section first reviews the nature of these standards, examines their format, and then analyzes their impact in terms of purpose, influence, and connectedness to other standards efforts.

INTASC (1992) notes that "An important attribute of these proposed standards . . . is that they are *performance-based:* that is, they describe what teachers should know and be able to do rather than listing courses that teachers should take in order to be awarded a license" (p. 3), and "the complex art of teaching requires performance-based standards and assessment strategies that are capable of capturing teachers' reasoned judgments . . . that evaluate what they can actually do in authentic teaching situations" (p. 1).

The draft of INTASC standards are organized around 10 principles. For each principle there is a statement of knowledge required of teachers related to the principle, the dispositions needed by teachers, and the essential performances that demonstrate the teacher's ability to apply the principle in practice.

The following is one example from their draft document:

Principle #7
The teacher plans instruction based upon knowledge of subject matter, students, the community, and curriculum goals.
Knowledge. The teacher understands learning theory, subject matter, curriculum development, and student development and knows how to use this knowledge in planning instruction to meet curricular goals [other knowledge items are listed].

Dispositions. The teacher values both long- and short-term planning. The teacher believes that plans must always be open to adjustment and revision based on student needs and changing circumstances.
Performances. The teacher plans for learning opportunities that recognize and address variation in learning styles and performance modes. The teacher creates short-range and long-term plans that are linked to student needs and performance, and adapts the plan to ensure and capitalize on student progress and motivation [other items listed]. (INTASC, 1992, pp. 23–24)

How does INTASC see its standards fitting into the other standards initiatives in teacher education? INTASC cites two important issues in the development of their "board-compatible" standards. One is the difference between board certification and state licensing. They support the position that states issue licenses based on standards of minimal competence, whereas professional certification uses more advanced or exacting standards established by the profession itself. INTASC standards are intended to guide the state licensing standards.

A second issue has to do with how to distinguish between beginning and advanced level of performance. "We concluded that the appropriate distinctions between beginning and advanced practice are in the degree of sophistication teachers exhibit in the application of knowledge rather than in the kind of knowledge needed" (INTASC, 1992, p. 7). In essence, INTASC concluded that there were no certain kinds of classes of knowledge, understanding, commitment, or ability that an advanced practitioner might exhibit that would be wholly unnecessary for a beginning teacher.

One of the issues surrounding the INTASC effort is the role of INTASC standards in guiding state standards and the implications for the meaning of licensure. The practice of licensure in some states has come to mean not just a title change, but also performance assessment of candidates as a basis for issuing the license.

If INTASC perceives licensure in this manner, then its standards are meant to guide state performance standards for assessment. This would be consistent with its efforts to develop assessments as well. INTASC's standards, however, also may be to guide state standards for program approval purposes. This implies two different models, one in which states use assessment for licensure and one in which states both approve programs and assess candidates. The latter approach raises the question of the need for both processes. INTASC indicates its work is offered "as a resource to revisit state standards for training and licensing new teachers" (INTASC, 1992, p. 1). Because it is for both training and licensing, both functions are implied, although the emphasis is clearly on assessment, and INTASC leaves this to the discretion of each state.

A number of questions regarding INTASC are yet unanswered due to its early stage of development. For example: What influence will INTASC have on the development of performance-based, program-approval standards? Will INTASC serve as a catalyst for the design and development of state performance assessment systems for licensure? What will be the relationship between INTASC standards and the NASTDEC outcomes-based standards, and what will be the relative influence of each? How will INTASC standards ultimately interface with the National Board standards and assessments? How will INTASC standards guide the design of standards for new teacher assessment during or at the end of an induction period (e.g., standards being developed by California, an INTASC charter member)?

NATIONAL ACCREDITATION

National accreditation in teacher education is conducted by the National Council for Accreditation of Teacher Education (NCATE). As of November, 1993, 518 of the 1,279 teacher education institutions (40.5%) are NCATE accredited, although the 518 prepare a high percentage of licensed educational personnel.

Due to a number of concerns in the profession, the NCATE standards and process were redesigned during a 2-year period between 1983 and 1985. Implementation began on a pilot basis in 1987 and was started formally in 1988. In the summer of 1993, new revised standards were distributed for field review, representing the second major revision in only about 5 years. These were adopted in May 1994. The new NCATE standards have four standards categories: Design of Professional Education, Candidates in Professional Education, Professional Education Faculty, and the Unit for Professional Education (National Council for Accreditation of Teacher Education [NCATE], 1994b).

What is the purpose or role of accreditation in the profession? Some of the roles have been identified. They include to protect the profession from the unqualified (Watts, 1982), to assure the public that certain professional elements have been part of the training experience (Smith, 1990), to signify that peers value the program (Smith, 1990), to provide credibility to enhance professionalization of teaching and teacher education (Roth, 1992), to provide for quality control, and to assist institutions in improving programs through renewal.

NCATE identifies five broad benefits of NCATE accreditation.

- It assures the public and prospective students that the institution has met external standards that have been set by professionals in the field.
- It improves the quality of education units in higher education institutions as they modify requirements to reflect changes in knowledge and practice.
- It provides a common set of national standards for preparation of teachers and other school specialists.
- It strengthens institutional self-evaluation and spurs program improvement.
- It acts as a deterrent to undesirable decreases in resource allocations.

Assessing the capacity of institutions or their effectiveness is on the accreditation agenda. Two broad approaches have been identified relative to this task (Rowan, 1985). One is the goal-centered view that assesses an institution's attainment of its goals. The other is the natural system's view that maintains that an organization may be too large and complex to specify a manageable number of goals and is seen as oriented toward overall health and survival. In these instances in particular, the institutional process might relate to factors such as management procedures, organizational culture, market development, and innovation (Ewell, 1992).

Within these approaches, accreditation may base its judgments on three alternative approaches. An organization's performance may be compared to the performance of other similar organizations, to it previous performance to ascertain growth, or to independent standards of performance (Sykes & Plastrik, 1993).

NCATE primarily uses the third option through the NCATE standards against which institutions are measured. It should be noted that to some extent the standards are normative, derived from what a significant number of vanguard institutions are now doing, and thus are deemed reasonable expectations. In this sense institutions are compared to others, but not directly. Standards dealing with content of professional studies, faculty workloads, and student teacher supervision might be considered essentially normative. Some also are intended to lead institutions to ever higher levels of achievement. These might include standards related to multiculturalism (faculty, students, curriculum), and the knowledge base (conceptual model and explication of knowledge undergirding the curriculum). Others have no clear criteria for assessment of the standard, and more often than not they are interpreted in terms of normative experience. These include library holdings and use of part-time faculty.

NCATE standards may also be characterized in terms of the focus of the standard. These include input (resources, library, facilities), process (admissions, recruitment, advising, instruction), product (evaluation of graduates), and values (multicultural curriculum, culturally diverse faculty and students).

Effectiveness

There are various ways to view the effectiveness of NCATE, such as impact on program quality, denial-approval rates, and procedural efficiency. Each of these provides a different viewpoint.

The redesigned standards became effective in fall 1988. As of spring 1993, 364 institutions were reviewed (some twice, if denied and rescheduled). Of these, 73% (267) were accredited, 10% (35) were accredited with stipulations, and 17% (62) were denied accreditation (NCATE, 1993).

In the first 2 years of review, Standard I.A: Design of Curriculum was the standard most frequently unmet. This is now second to Standard IV.A: Faculty Qualifications and Assignments. The importance of this is that institutions did not have well-defined knowledge bases on which programs were designed. It may be surmised that NCATE has caused institutions to think through these essential issues and to design more carefully programs consistent with what is now known about the teaching-learning process and teacher education.

Procedural efficiency and effectiveness are under continual review as well. Four policy-making boards have committees making recommendations for procedural changes in their respective areas. These monitor performance and composition of the board of examiners (on-site review teams), review procedures and policies to ensure that processes emphasize critical factors, study development of standards for advanced programs, and examine the governance structure.

NCATE consists of 28 national organizations that are constituent members. These represent teacher organizations, teacher education associations, and specialty area groups. The four major governance groups are the Executive Board, the Unit Accreditation Board, the State Recognition Board, and the Specialty Area Studies Board.

An issue related to governance is the freedom of NCATE to exercise its role, as NCATE relies on dues from institutions it accredits for revenue (Cronin, 1983). Other sources of revenue, such as from constituent organizations, ameliorate this dilemma. The real test, however, is in the appropriate application of standards in an equitable manner and to effect meaningful evaluation. The strength of denial rates and changes made in programs are encouraging, suggesting little conflict with dependency on those who are the very subject of the evaluation.

A synthesis of studies on the effectiveness of NCATE is provided in a chapter on standards in the 1990 edition of this handbook (Roth & Pipho, 1990). This indicated that very few studies have been conducted. The first study of the new standards was conducted with the pilot institutions by Roth. Eleven categories of benefits were reported, including program cohesiveness, faculty team building, increased understanding of program, campus collaboration, practitioner linkage, improved image, and increased resources (Roth & Pipho, 1990). A study of 184 institutions reviewed by NCATE from spring 1989 through spring 1991 revealed the following rank order of benefits: cohesiveness of the professional unit; clarified goals, content, and program elements; collaboration on campus; cooperation with public and/or private schools; clarification of mission; improved status of professional programs on campus; improvement of faculty status; and increased resources (Jones, 1993). The striking similarity of findings reflects a consistent perspective of benefits of the new standards since their inception.

The study by Jones (1993) provides a comprehensive review of the various components of the NCATE process and the campus coordinators' views of the experience in particular. Three salient findings are of relevance here. One relates to the question, "Would you do it all over again?" Sixty-four percent of the campus coordinators responded "Yes," 33% said "We have no choice," and only 3% said "No." Notably, 46% of the coordinators from unsuccessful schools selected yes. In responding to the importance of NCATE, 53% chose the response indicating NCATE is valuable, and 38% selected the highest choice identifying NCATE as very important. Only 9% reported NCATE was not worth the effort (Jones, 1993). At the same time, however, 37% of the coordinators responding indicated NCATE had "very little impact . . . minimal changes" (Jones, 1993, p. 191).

NCATE's effectiveness may be assessed from several perspectives, including process, institutional change, and enhancement of the image of the profession. Although results thus far related to some of these perspectives are encouraging, more longitudinal studies of the impact on the profession are warranted.

Linkage to States

One of NCATE's goals is to increase collaboration with state departments of education. This is accomplished through a number of NCATE-state initiatives, such as joint state-NCATE program reviews, a state-NCATE partnership board, and a joint NCATE-NASDTEC committee.

A critical dimension of the NCATE link to states is a new partnership model adopted in fall 1992. The partnerships between NCATE and state agencies may now be individually negotiated according to one of the following three frameworks:

1. Use of NCATE unit standards and NCATE-approved curriculum guidelines
2. Use of NCATE unit standards and NCATE-approved state program standards
3. Use of NCATE unit standards and a performance-based state licensing system. (NCATE, 1994a)

As of August 4, 1994, 33 states are conducting joint reviews under the first two models. A few states require that all colleges and universities preparing teachers be reviewed by NCATE (either in addition to or instead of state review, such as Arkansas, North Carolina, and West Virginia), and Boards of Regents in 15 states require all public institutions be accredited by NCATE (NCATE, 1994a). The NASDTEC manual indicates that 24 states use NCATE as the source of standards utilized for the approval of teacher education institutions and programs (NASDTEC, 1994).

The use of NCATE unit standards and a performance-based state-licensing system is a new model; it is referrred to as a "radical departure" from current practice (NCATE, 1994a, p. 2). This arrangement has growing appeal among the states and is reviewed more thoroughly in the sections of this chapter on performance-based standards and national systems.

The national accreditation system, through NCATE, is becoming increasingly coordinated with other systems of standards. The relationship to state systems is a prime example. NCATE and the National Board for Professional Teaching Standards have a joint committee developing means for closer coordination between the two organizations. This includes discussion of possible alignment of national standards for teacher preparation and for advanced certification. A New Professional Teacher Project, funded by the Carnegie Corporation of New York, intends to make a three-way link between teacher education programs, licensing standards at state and national levels, and academic standards for students.

The newly proposed NCATE standards are an extension of the history of standards renewal by NCATE. Two studies have been conducted that summarize several aspects of the change process with NCATE standards. Sanders (1987) analyzed the relationship of NCATE accreditation decisions, major changes in standards, and the critical nature of certain standards during the period 1979–1986. This provides a context for the current revision process.

Sanders identified the critical standards as those that were more predictive or associated with denial of accreditation. Evaluation of graduates and modification of programs were critical for both basic and advanced programs. Long-range planning was also critical for basic programs, and the conditions under which advanced faculty work was a critical factor for advanced programs. The tension between scholarly activities and teaching loads was quite evident.

The relationship between time and major standard change was explored, as well as accreditation decisions. A conclusion was that "An institution considered for accreditation during a year when major revisions were occurring or being implemented was significantly more likely to be denied NCATE accreditation for one or more programs than institutions being considered in years when such changes were not occurring" (Sanders, 1987, p. 39). NCATE now expects to see change when reviewing programs.

An analysis of the forms of standards and how this may have changed since their inception in 1957 was conducted by Cruickshank, Cruz, McCullough, Reynolds, and Troyer (1991). This included review of 11 sets of standards from 1957 through 1990. They found that six major areas were addressed: (1) governance; (2) admission and retention of students; (3) faculty teaching, research, and service; (4) curriculum; (5) evaluation; and (6) the context and resources supporting professional programs (Cruickshank et al., 1991).

In terms of stability of standards, about half (55%) of the criteria contained in the original standards remain in the 1990 version and exactly half of the criteria introduced after 1957 remain. Criteria related to evaluation and faculty are most stable, whereas criteria related to curriculum and students are least stable (Cruickshank et al., 1991). The Cruickshank study also intended to provide an analysis of the overall, aggregate or collective wisdom of persons who framed the various sets of criteria. This is reported by the accumulated criteria under each of the six target categories of the standards previously cited. Conclusions included the following: (1) a large number of criteria have been seen to be appropriate to judge preparation programs; (2) about half the criteria survive over time; (3) criteria reflect beliefs and values (hence the criteria themselves); (4) the criteria seem to be given equal weight; (5) the criteria vary in their clarity, which creates a huge reliability problem; and (6) some seemingly important qualities of preparation programs are absent (Cruickshank et al., 1991).

The newly proposed standards in 1994 contain a variety of changes with focus on improved practice and developing trends in the following areas:

1. Greater attention to the assessment of individual candidates
2. Use of technology in K–12 and higher education
3. Opportunities to work in diverse classrooms (NCATE, 1993)

Philosophical underpinnings of the changes are described as professional conscience, intellectual vitality, and professional community. Professional conscience relates to five ethical foundations for teaching. These are commitment to inquiry, knowledge, competence, caring, and social justice. Intellectual vitality refers to reflection about current practices, both effective and problematic. Professional community entails a common vision that is shared by a school of education and collaborating schools. This is the conceptual framework in the program's knowledge base (NCATE, 1993). These interacting themes are elaborated on as creating a vision of quality in a monograph that "captures the vision" of NCATE (Gideonse et al., 1993).

Role of NCATE

NCATE plays a critical role in the making of a profession and in leading the reform movement. It is generally agreed that a strong accrediting body contributes significantly to the creation of a profession, the public supports it, and the profession looks to such an agency for leadership.

Many leaders for a long time have called for a strong national accreditation system (Gideonse, 1993; Roth, 1992; Sanders, 1993; Wise & Leibbrand, 1993). The leading, respected professions rely on their respective accrediting agencies to hold standards and to strengthen the credibility of their field. Without such a system a profession is considerably disadvantaged in a number of ways, several of which were specified in the identification of purposes of accreditation.

A survey of the public commissioned by NCATE in 1993 revealed public opinion strongly in favor of national accreditation standards for all schools, colleges, and departments of education. Seventy-eight percent of the respondents favored national accreditation, only 19% opposed it, and 4% were undecided. In addition, 68% of the public indicated that if teachers were required to meet higher professional training standards, it would improve student performances. Only 23% disagreed (Wise, 1993a).

The profession has demonstrated support for the concept of national accreditation, even though concerns have been expressed regarding NCATE's practices (Nicklin, 1992). A former president of AACTE, Richard Wisniewski, proposed that institutions not accredited by NCATE should have their AACTE membership status reduced. "We would be saying that national accreditation is a vehicle to quality that we believe in so strongly that we do not want to associate with those institutions that are not nationally accredited" (Bradley, 1994, p. 3). Although not adopted by AACTE, a commitment to encourage institutional pursuit of NCATE was made.

Serving as a vehicle to establishing quality programs, particularly through program renewal, is an essential role for NCATE. Institutions that view NCATE as a means of renewal, in contrast with just attempting to meet a set of external standards, take a much healthier approach and find the experience more productive. In this sense, NCATE has been a positive guide to the revision of programs.

A second question debated in the literature relates to the extent to which NCATE assists programs in creating and achieving a significant new vision. If one uses the 19 postulates in *Teachers for Our Nation's Schools* (Goodlad, 1990), for example, themes would include accepting moral responsibilities of teaching, developing a commitment to inquiry, confronting issues and dilemmas, embracing change, and so forth. According to one analysis, "No matter what organizational modifications an institution makes, what procedures it institutes, what models it adopts, unless these fundamental commitments form the bases of the programs to prepare teachers, the programs will not meet the spirit or intent of teacher education renewal coupled with ongoing renewal of K–12 schooling" (Edmundson, 1993, p. 174). The author also contends that if an institution is serious about making changes that matter, it "would do well to adopt a renewal agenda which . . . goes beyond accreditation standards" (Edmundson, 1993, p. 175).

The issues of meaningful renewal, restructuring, and revitalization are those with which NCATE is attempting to come to grips. Part of this relates to one perspective of the role of accreditation. Although the goals are laudable, they may not be within the purview of standards and accreditation. One could argue for at least three levels of criteria for change; these are a minimum level, an advanced level that embodies concepts such as intellectual vitality and professional conscience (NCATE), and an extended vision level that captures the essence of the postulates (Goodlad, 1990). Are there real differences between the last two levels as defined here? If so, is the third a prerogative of each institution consistent with its particular vision? Is the third level beyond the purview of accreditation? How can the third level, or even the second for that matter, be assessed through standards and accreditation processes? These are among the issues that NCATE and the profession will continue to probe in the never-ending quest to create a national accreditation system that is a cornerstone of the profession.

THE NATIONAL BOARD FOR PROFESSIONAL TEACHING STANDARDS

In *A Nation Prepared: Teachers for the 21st Century,* the Carnegie Forum on Education and the Economy (1986) recommended the creation of the National Board for Professional Teaching Standards (NBPTS). Initiated in 1987, the NBPTS is governed by a 63-member board of directors, the majority of whom are classroom teachers.

The mission or vision of the NBPTS is to establish high and rigorous standards for what accomplished teachers should know and be able to do. It intends to develop and operate a national voluntary system to assess and certify teachers. Its mission also includes advancing related education reforms intended to improve student learning in American schools.

The NBPTS policy position is based on five core propositions.

1. Teachers are committed to students and their learning.
2. Teachers know the subjects they teach and how to teach those subjects to students.
3. Teachers are responsible for managing and monitoring student learning.
4. Teachers think systematically about their practice and learn from experience.
5. Teachers are members of learning communities. (NBPTS, n.d., pp. 2–4)

The National Board has established a rather ambitious agenda involving three critical elements: standard setting, assessment instruments, and professional development. Standards and assessments are being established in 30 certification fields, primarily based on age levels and content areas, such as Early Childhood Generalist (ages 3–8) and Early Adolescence English Language Arts (ages 11–15).

The first field tests were initiated in fall 1993 and completed in spring 1995. Six certificates are expected to be available by fall 1996. In January 1995, 81 teachers were first to receive national certification.

The element receiving the greatest attention is that of assessment. The NBPTS is pursuing a significantly different, and costly, approach to assessing what teachers know and are able to do. As of spring 1994, the NBPTS had received up to $50 million to achieve its goals. With significant expenditures on assessment development, the NBPTS operates by funding external contractors for assessment design, such as the University of Pittsburgh, the Connecticut Education Department, and the University of Georgia.

The assessment component consists of two parts: a portfolio to be compiled at the teacher's own school and a set of exercises to be completed at an assessment center. Written responses are also required. The assessments differ somewhat by type of certification, but a portfolio might include curriculum guides, samples of student work, videotapes of lessons, and an analysis of the lesson by the teacher submitting the materials. The assessment centers focus on structured interviews, simulations, and the candidate's knowledge of content and pedagogy. Clearly this is a much more intensive and sophisticated approach than has ever been ventured in teacher education. In this respect alone it is quite a remarkable undertaking.

The NBPTS clearly distinguishes its function from the role of the states. The board policy states, "Offered on a voluntary basis, it will complement, not replace, state licensing. While state licensing systems set minimal standards for novice teachers, National Board Certification will establish advanced standards for experienced teachers" (NBPTS, n.d., p. 1).

The relation of the NBPTS to states can be viewed in a political context as well. One factor is the growth of professional practices boards and the emergence of the NBPTS. "Attention by state government to standards boards and the creation of the NBPTS are not coincidental" (Earley, 1987, p. 107). Earley cites new public understanding of the professional role of teachers and the NEA's professional self-governance interest as factors leading to these related movements. NEA "originally urged Carnegie to adopt a model for the national certification board that would link it to state standards boards" (Earley, 1987, p. 107). This arrangement, she contends, was much less desirable to the American Federation of Teachers (AFT), and thus the NBPTS is structurally unrelated to agencies of state government. Because state agencies will ultimately make decisions about the relationship between their state licenses and national board certification, the success of the board may be influenced to some extent by the structure and authority of the institutionalized state boards (Earley, 1987). A number of states and localities are providing incentives for national board-certified teachers, such as clearing time for staff development, providing reimbursement for the assessments, and providing release time for working or portfolios (J. Richardson, 1994).

Perhaps the most pressing issue is what impact the NBPTS intends to have and what promise it holds for the future of teaching and teacher education as elements of a profession. The board sees itself as "dedicated to bringing teaching the respect and recognition this important work deserves" (NBPTS, n.d., p. 1). The board also plans to release a policy paper explaining how national certification can fit into the entire course of a teacher's career (Bradley, 1993a). James A. Kelly, the NBPTS president, expects certification to improve public attitudes toward teachers and to provide greater rewards for teachers who are nationally certified (Watkins, 1993, p. A20). Another analysis suggests that the board's policies will broadly influence all levels of education, affecting teachers, administrators, teacher educators, and boards of education. National standards will reshape the teaching profession and teacher education, and colleges can be expected to revamp their teacher education programs. States could adopt national standards for state licensing and certification procedures or even waive license requirements for those already board certified (NBPTS, 1988). Activity by states in the policy domain is steadily growing (Baratz-Snowden, 1994).

There are, of course, critics of the effort and its potential effects. One report questions the board's ability to guarantee teacher quality based on concerns about the NBPTS requirements for public credibility, technical feasibility, and conceptual clarity (Edelfelt & Raths, 1992). Raths also expressed concern that only wealthy school districts will get board-certified teachers. This would create ill will between parents and schools when some children get a board-certified teacher and others do not (Watkins, 1993).

It is important to note that there are several historical concerns or myths about teacher education that the NBPTS could begin to dispel. It could demonstrate that there is such a thing as a professional teacher. The point is that many people believe that even at their very best, teachers are semiprofessionals or practitioners of a trade. If what a teacher can be and should be can be established, and this is a highly competent professional, then perhaps the public view of "teacher" could change dramatically. The notion is that not just anyone, such as those retiring from other occupations or simply those teaching as a temporary pastime, can be a professional educator overnight.

The board's activities could also counter the notion that teachers are born and thus do not need to be prepared. The differences between natural ability and professional training, or the contribution of each, could be more clearly contrasted. Also, the idea that providing a supervised internship is all that is necessary to produce a competent teacher could be dismissed.

Of critical importance to the concept of a profession is a body of knowledge. The board's standards and related assessments could add significantly to the belief in the existence of a body of knowledge, as well as competence in its application (pedagogy). This would be counter to the insistence by some that all one needs in order to teach effectively is to have a command of subject matter.

Finally, credibility of the entire enterprise may ultimately depend on the results it produces. It would be profitable to demonstrate that board-certified teachers actually produce specified levels of learning in their students. This may be a focus of research in the next decade.

EMERGING PERSPECTIVES OF STANDARDS

The preceding discussion describes a very extensive set of activities related to standards, certification, and accreditation. There are a number of significant issues embodied in these movements, many of which have been identified in the context of the respective area of activity. Two salient issues that encompass a variety of concerns and areas of inquiry are performance- or outcome-based standards and a national system. These two broad issues cut across each of the areas in the preceding sections of this chapter.

Performance- or Outcome-Based Standards

The area that has received the greatest attention in the new standards movement is development of performance- or outcome-based standards. This is a widespread effort touching the national and state level as well. An overview of the status of this activity would provide a context for subsequent identification and analysis of issues.

One of the more notable initiatives is the NASDTEC *Outcome-Based Standards and Portfolio Assessment* (1993) described previously. The "Teacher Requirement" element defines the necessary performance, along with context, context rationale, and sample portfolio entries. The significance of the NASDTEC outcome standards is the potential extensive impact they could have on state systems for licensure. NASDTEC standards have traditionally served as a guide to states for their program approval processes and standards. Thirty states use NASDTEC or NASDTEC-equivalent standards for approval of teacher education programs (NASDTEC, 1994). The NASDTEC document indicates that "the standards are designed to provide a framework for the approval of college and university teacher education programs" (NASDTEC, 1993, p. 4), as well as for other programs. NASDTEC's lead will undoubtedly influence a substantial number of states to adopt outcome- or performance-based standards.

INTASC also focused its efforts on performance, characterizing their standards as "performance-based: that is, they describe what teachers should know and be able to do rather than listing courses" (INTASC, 1992, p. 3). The influence of INTASC is yet untested, although its "goal is to create model standards for 'Board-Compatible' teacher licensing that can be reviewed by professional organizations and state agencies as a basis for their own standard-setting activities" (INTASC, 1992, p. 2). INTASC clearly envisions its work as providing a model for the states, and being a collaborative effort of states it is likely to influence state policy. This position is further strengthened by the deliberate link between the INTASC standards and the NBPTS standards, specifically identifying their standards as "board compatible." The intended sequence from INTASC to NBPTS performance standards provides a compelling rationale for states to either adopt INTASC standards or develop their own modeled after INTASC.

NASDTEC and INTASC standards share some similarities; there are differences as well. Both describe what candidates are expected to demonstrate and are intended to influence the states. NASDTEC is a client-centered approach and provides guidance to assessment through the section on "outcome documentation," which contains sample portfolio entries. INTASC does not directly relate standards to assessment in this way. Yet, it does describe the necessary knowledge underlying the performance; it also describes teacher "dispositions" that indicate the teacher has captured the spirit of the standard and thus is not only demonstrating the performance but also has a supporting belief system that is compatible. These are unique contributions and provide alternative perspectives of performance or outcome standards.

It is helpful to recognize a distinction between performance standards intended for program approval, such as NASDTEC's outcome-based standards, and performance standards designed for individual licensure, such as INTASC's standards. Ostensibly, performance standards developed for one purpose may be used for the other. In both instances, further delineation of the standards is necessary in order to operationalize them in practical application.

NCATE has identified emerging themes or trends in the profession for which it considered allowing institutions to substitute for an existing standard. One of these emerging areas is outcome-based programs. Although not implemented, NCATE clearly has recognized the performance movement.

In addition, embedded in the proposed revision of standards is greater attention to individual assessment of performance. This includes specifying criteria or outcomes for program exit and that "The unit's criteria/outcomes for exit are assessed through the use of multiple sources of data such as portfolios, interviews, videotaped and observed performance in schools, standardized tests and course grades" (Wise, 1993b, p. 14). NCATE also requested that curriculum guidelines submitted by the learned societies include attention to outcomes and adopted four such sets of standards in October, 1993 (Diegmueller, 1993). It is evident that performance and assessment of performance are integral to the NCATE process.

It is important to note another dimension of the NCATE stance on performance. It provides an opportunity for state performance standards to align with this element of NCATE's standards. This compatibility provides additional impetus to the performance-outcome movement.

Other national accrediting agencies also have adopted performance standards for their respective professionals. Although all such agencies identify general outcomes, some are specific as to what the program is expected to produce. The most extensive treatments of outcome criteria are in architecture, physical therapy, nursing, and social work (Yff, 1993).

The National Governors' Association has expressed a commitment to outcome-based systems as well. In a policy statement regarding state strategies for achieving the national education goals, the governors propose that states should "Develop an outcome-based system for preparation and licensure that is linked to the skills and knowledge needed for new roles in schools" (NCATE, 1991, p. 12). The statement also requires teachers to pass truly demanding performance examinations in all areas in which they teach, and that an outcomes-based system for preparation and licensure should include new forms of performance assessment for licensure.

In accordance with the National Governors' Association policy, and in response to individual state initiatives, states are developing their own performance- or outcome-based systems. Fourteen states report assessment of teaching performance as a requirement for the initial teaching certificate (NASDTEC, 1994, p. G2). Minnesota's legislature and state department of education have directed all teacher education programs to implement an outcome-based system of teacher education by 1995 (Towers, 1994). There is a growing network of collaborative relationships across the states and nationally that is expected to expand, strengthen, and increase in influence.

The teacher education outcome-based movement follows the extensive effort in establishing such standards for K–12 schools. The level of dialogue about outcome-based standards in teacher education is not at the level of sophistication of the K–12 sector. The K–12 community has more experience in a variety of approaches, settings, experiments, and time. Teacher education has yet to come to grips with many of the critical issues.

One teacher education program's experience in Minnesota led to identification of the following concerns with outcome-based teacher education: (1) it requires more time and effort; (2) faculty are required to further individualize their instruction; (3) remediation seems to take priority over enrichment, having a negative effect on the most capable students; and (4) the ability to select the most capable students for licensure is hampered in that with persistence, but not necessarily ability, practically any student could meet minimum competency requirements (Towers, 1994). Diez (1994) and others, however, have had positive experiences at Alverno College and have developed a model program.

Assessment Perhaps the most critical problem related to outcome-based standards is assessment. This standards approach relies on technical breakthroughs in assessment methods, and the design and implementation problems are formidable. This may require compromises that will have an effect on the overall strategy (Sykes & Plastrik, 1993). Furthermore, all too often the assessment instruments become the standards.

Outcome-based standards must rely on external assessments to safeguard the system. Otherwise, it would be difficult to discern any real differences between current assessment practices and assessment under outcome-based models. Consider, for example, the performance standards integrated into student teacher evaluation processes. These are assessed internally by program faculty with assistance from school personnel. With outcome-based standards the same procedure could be in operation. One scenario is that the state specifies performance standards and the teacher preparation institution conducts its own assessment and verifies to the state that the candidate has met the competencies. In essence, this scenario offers little real change.

NASDTEC suggests the use of portfolios in its outcome-based system. It also indicates that "determining criteria for the acceptability of the portfolio entries should most appropriately be based on professional judgment" (NASDTEC, 1993, p. 15). If it is presumed that professional judgment has always been exercised, then it might be difficult to discern a significant difference under the performance system.

Another perspective is that the identification of outcomes will raise awareness levels of institution personnel. The intended net result is a greater focus on demonstrated abilities. The advantage of this enhanced focus will be limited by the assessment capability. An underlying issue is the purpose of the assessment, which may be primarily accountability driven, improvement driven, or a combination of the two (Hinkle, 1993). Assessment of competence for professional growth holds greater promise for benefits of outcome-based standards than assessment for summative evaluation. To have an impact on improvement of education, evaluation must be explicitly linked to teaching and learning (Diez, 1993, p. 8).

An essential concern derived from the preceding discussion is that standards, particularly performance standards, must be part of a system with enhanced assessment capability. The concept of system as a major emerging force is analyzed in the next section of this chapter.

External assessment provides a safeguard from another perspective as well. States may not be fully aware of what they are entering into unless they project their assessment design and inquire as to what is lost by specification of outcomes alone. For example, by dropping content standards there is no assurance of an appropriate course of study or necessary experiences to gain insights into practice, or of a foundation of learning theory and child growth and development. In a performance-based model with no external assessment, candidates need only be deemed as having met outcomes as attested to internally by program faculty. In fact, currently there are nontraditional programs that operate in this way. Candidates may have minimal training, as little as 5 weeks, and participate in 1-hour workshops that they select with no required curriculum. The only assessment might be a portfolio submitted at the end of the experience, which is judged by "faculty" who have 1 or 2 years of teaching experience and no formal training. Of course, this is not the scenario envisioned by those who promote outcome-based preparation and licensure systems. Without an external assessment, such programs could co-exist with truly outstanding, performance-based programs with graduates of each of these receiving the same state license.

The experience of the K–12 sector can be looked at for insights on assessment. The work of the Mid-continent Regional Laboratory concluded that outcome-performance tasks in the K–12 school context have definite promise, but they cannot be used very frequently by classroom teachers and thus will not totally replace more traditional assessments. Furthermore, studies are needed on the validity of outcome-based performance tasks and the conditions under which high interrater reliabilities can be guaranteed (Marzano, 1994).

In a study of the implementation of the Kentucky Education Reform Act (KERA), it was concluded that performance-based assessments by themselves may be insufficient to bring about any significant change in the instructional practices of most classroom teachers. Furthermore, "bridging the chasm between authentic assessment and authentic classroom practice will require well-designed assessments, but it will also demand a substantial amount of additional time, resources, and training opportunities" (Guskey, 1994, p. 53).

States will need to be cognizant of these findings in terms of building program capacity to respond to performance assessment-driven systems. A policy issue is whether to embark on the change process even if supportive conditions do not exist, such as assessment technology and a resource base for program building.

Outcomes of Outcomes-Based Standards If a state develops an outcomes-based system that includes external assessment for licensure, is there a need to have program approval standards? If graduates of programs can demonstrate appropriate levels of expertise on state performance assessments, what is the value or need to shackle programs with input and process standards, such as resources and faculty, or even content requirements, such as curriculum specifications? This is particularly true as K–12 standards move to a performance-based curriculum.

Alternative programs are raising questions about program approval and accreditation standards. This also could lead to elimination of the inconsequential in standards.

NASDTEC suggests adoption of outcome-based standards. This does not preclude a state from maintaining existing rules and regulations related to program approval, such as admission requirements, grade point average, and length of student teaching (NASDTEC, 1993). NASDTEC also states, however, that "It is NASDTEC's strong belief that a solid set of outcome-based standards that can be used or adapted by individual states will eliminate or significantly reduce dictates to institutions of higher education related to resources, faculty, and curriculum" (1993, p. 7).

The danger in this approach was cited earlier. Without external assessment as a quality check, there is neither process nor outcome accountability. This opens the door to a variety of practices under the rubric of teacher education and presents a clear and present danger to the profession.

Omitting program standards also could raise provocative political issues. Those who shun regulation and take a more liberal position on standards would find an outcomes-only position refreshing. The issue may be cast in a different light, however, when some of the implications arise. What if a program indicates it does not have a culturally diverse faculty, yet graduates meet the multicultural performance standards? Would this suffice? Is there a necessity to give some attention to the nature of experience, principle, and values? A concept such as performance- or outcome-based standards cannot be viewed in the abstract because contextual, political, technical, and fiscal factors influence the overall system and its ultimate effectiveness and impact.

Genesis of Performance Standards Why the unrelenting pressure to adopt performance-based standards without pause to consider the attendant issues? Some might respond that the issue is accountability or lack thereof. Legislators, the public, and sectors of the profession itself demand more from the schools and place much of the responsibility for change squarely on the collective shoulders of teachers. One vehicle for moving this agenda is to hold teacher preparation more accountable for the quality of teacher it produces.

Behind the accountability drive, however, is a deeper issue of concern. The issue is one of trust, or more precisely mistrust, of schools and teacher education (Roth, 1992; Sykes & Plastrik, 1993). Dissatisfaction with public education breeds an ever deepening lack of confidence and trust in the profession. Further evidence of this is the analysis that performance standards were often defined through political processes, with limited input from teachers, emphasizing democratic control rather than professionalism (McDonnell, 1989). Some reformers recognize the seeds of discontent, but view the establishment of performance-based standards and licensure as a means of creating greater public confidence in the enterprise.

A profession-based perspective of performance-standards is that they engage the profession in addressing the character of teaching itself, the teacher's role, the norms and expectations that govern conduct, the process of learning to teach, and the advancement of teaching practice through research and development (Sykes & Plastrik, 1993). In essence, it provides a renewed emphasis on clarifying and better defining teaching and teacher education and leads to higher levels. As noted in the K–12 performance movement, "the most important reason to develop and implement performance assessment is that it provides an impetus to explore questions at the very heart of the purposes and processes of schooling" (Jamentz, 1994, p. 57).

Unresolved and Unexplored Issues Have outcome- or performance-based standards been tried? Why move with such certainty and force until more is known about the questions to ask and their answers? According to studies of outcome-based education (OBE) in the K–12 sector, "Despite the nationwide popularity of OBE, only a handful of studies provide meaningful answers to questions about its effect" (Evans & King, 1994, p. 12). Clearly, political expediency far outpaces empirical validation.

What is the nature of outcome- or performance-based standards? What are the differences among performance-, outcome-, and competency-based standards? Although some forms of the former competency-based teacher education (CBTE) outcomes were mechanized and too discrete, others are virtually identical to some of the current standards. What did we learn about CBTE that can be applied or avoided in the comtemporary performance movement? The extensive conceptualization of outcomes conducted in K–12 standards development provides a schema for outcomes, which includes discrete skills and structured tasks at the base, higher order competencies and unstructured task performances, and complex role performances at the highest level. Performances at lower levels are enabling outcomes for higher levels. Marzano (1994) describes a system in which each outcome has within it specific elements referred to as characteristics, proficiencies, indicators, attributes, or standards (p. 45). This type of analysis opens another dimension to the teacher education outcomes-based enterprise.

The test of a functional concept is how well it works or how well it can be operationalized. Operationally defining outcomes, as previously noted, is but one part of the puzzle. Just as teachers play a critical role in K–12 standards—"implementation requires innovation and experimentation . . . because their actions will literally construct the new standards" (Sykes & Plastrik, 1993, p. 47)—teacher education programs will provide accountability; however, unless programs have the necessary capacity, either large numbers will not pass licensure exams or standards will be lowered.

What are the limitations of performance standards? The literature and public pronouncements are particularly devoid of this type of discourse. Do performance standards and assessment get at the essence of teaching, particularly those elements the university claims to contribute? Critics of American education suggest that students are not doing well on thinking and reasoning. To address this, teachers must learn not only to teach differently, but also to teach a different kind of student (Kennedy, 1991). How can standards address or ensure this? Shulman and others have noted that performance assessment leaves out critical aspects (Watkins, 1988). One of these aspects, for example, is teacher thought processes and how they influence decision making in the classroom (Clark & Peterson, 1986). Is this beyond the role of standards?

The preceding questions do not assume that a sufficiently sophisticated system of outcome standards and assessment could not get at the critical elements of teaching. The NBPTS assessments are the best approximation thus far. The question is the likelihood of this high cost system being replicated for state licensure and teacher preparation program assessment. Fiscal constraints affect both the developmental and operational components, neither of which are currently feasible without an enormous investment. Diluted versions of performance assessment systems that might emerge may be little different from current performance assessments in student teaching as reviewed earlier.

Embedded in the present state of the movement is confusion regarding the nature of outcome statements and the levels to which they apply. Are the outcome standards intended only to address the performances teachers are expected to demonstrate, or are they intended to focus on the result of the teacher performance in terms of student outcomes as well? For example, NASDTEC outcome standard 4.0, Instruction, requires teachers to elicit learning levels expected of students by the local school district in subject matter (NASDTEC, 1993). Other NASDTEC standards require teacher performance, not student outcomes. California outcome Standard 28 also requires student data (Commission on Teacher Credentialing, 1992). If both types are to be employed, then a policy position relevant to this issue must be clearly articulated and the implications for assessment fully understood.

Assessment of teachers during the initial years of teaching for purposes of issuing a state license is still in an early stage of its implementation. Performance assessment for initial state licensure is only beginning to emerge. The convergence of these embryonic efforts has led to a degree of confusion regarding the specific level of experience or stage of teacher development to which standards apply. Distinctions between early stages of development for licensure and advanced levels for certification appear to be made more readily. According to INTASC, differences are more in terms of the degree to which competencies are performed at more sophisticated levels, rather than in additional competencies (INTASC, 1992).

It is at the levels of preservice and induction that the profession has not sufficiently clarified a continuum of competency levels. NASDTEC states its outcomes are "expected of prospective teachers completing state approved teacher education programs" (NASDTEC, 1993, p. 8). NASDTEC also indicates the outcome standards "could be used by states or school districts in conjunction with induction programs" (p. 4). INTASC (1992) also may be used in either context. Are there differences between expectations of teachers at exit from preservice programs and during induction? Are the beginning teacher standards applied the first year, at the end of the first year, or at another time during the second or third year? Performance standards have not yet provided clear distinctions in response to these issues.

An additional question has to do with one of the purposes of licensure systems—constructing categories of competence (Sykes, 1989). These categories determine the link between qualifications and assignments. The extent to which performance or outcome standards differentiate these role functions is yet to be analyzed. NASDTEC identifies outcome-based standards for the beginning elementary level teacher and a separate set of standards for the beginning middle level teacher. The middle level standards include an additional outcome that is related to organizing and operating a youth service program. All other standards are virtually identical with the elementary standards except that the terms *middle level teacher* and *young adolescent* are inserted. Contributions of performance standards to role differentiation may need further elaboration during the next several years.

A National System

The widespread effort to reform the profession is emanating from several sectors. One of the fundamental issues is how these can be linked. It may well be that the greatest leverage for reform can only come through some form of an integrated, well-articulated system. The prospects for such a system seem to be increasing in proportion to the demand for change and degree of political and fiscal influence. The purpose of this section is to explore how such a system might be fashioned.

First it is of value to identify the key elements that might be incorporated into a more unified national system. These include state licensure, national accreditation, national certification, state program approval, new teacher induction, preservice preparation programs, and continuing professional development. The New Professional Teacher Project seeks to link teacher education programs, state and national licensing standards, and academic standards for students in grades K–12.

Many of the agencies involved are already working together, even networking, to find common ground. NCATE and NASDTEC have a joint committee to find ways to collaborate and find ways in which standards and process can be shared to avoid duplication. In this situation, increased efficiency is one intended outcome. As noted earlier, NCATE has three types of relations with states and has entered into several agreements. The National Board and NCATE are also pursuing identification of relationships between their standards and how they might be forged for continuity (NCATE, 1992). INTASC standards were purposely designed to be board compatible, as well as to guide the development of state standards. This provides a somewhat direct link between the NBPTS certification and state licensure. NCATE also has integrated K–12 curriculum standards into the national accreditation process through the adoption of learned societies' standards (Lewis, 1993). To enhance the cross-referencing of standards, analyses have already been made to illustrate how sets of standards relate (Ingwerson, 1994). This includes how they are linked to assessment, such as Praxis III. What has emerged is a complex set of standards to guide the various components.

Induction program standards have been developed by a few states, and some sets of standards may be used for both preservice programs and new teacher programs. The INTASC standards and NASDTEC outcome-based standards are clear examples. Beyond induction, the National Board expects its standards to be a basis for continuing professional development.

The impact of these various standards on preservice teacher preparation can be staggering. Each has some relationship to these programs, either directly or indirectly. Teacher education institutions are caught in an intricate web of standards and assessments. This scenario places them in a seemingly contradictory situation, where on the one hand standards are restrictive by specifying the nature of the process and content and yet hold the institution responsible for outcomes for which it has little flexibility in determining how to achieve. On the other hand, institutions have a variety of sets of standards to choose from (except state mandated) and enjoy that degree of freedom. With selection of a given set of outcomes that have credence by way of their national visibility, the institution acquires the attendant credibility as well. There may be a greater degree of freedom in designing one's own outcomes, but the credibility-based freedom attached to national standards is quite compelling because it has dual benefits.

An initial set of questions that can be asked about a national system would include the following: How can educators systematically coordinate the various standards and systems? Should they? Taking this a step further, should they develop a national system with a formalized structure? Do they need such a system? What are the risks? What should it look like? These and other questions cause educators to glance frequently over their professional shoulders as they follow the relentless drive down the path of standards as the way to credibility.

Consider the need to coordinate standards. Certainly the nature of K–12 standards and those for the preparation of teachers should have some relationship. What is expected of K–12 students should be reflected in the knowledge and skills of teachers who guide their learning. How teachers fashion learning experiences, the way they construct the curriculum, is based on certain assumptions about learners and premises about what they should be able to do as a result of the curriculum and instructional experience. This concept of alignment of standards is somewhat of a breakthrough, and how it plays out will be of interest. Issues include how tightly these could or should be aligned and if or how they might provide a leadership role for both teaching and teacher learning. In recognition of this need for linkage, the Wingspread Conference in November, 1993 identified one of its objectives as "to establish ongoing lines of communication among the varied constituencies involved in the articulation between K–12 standards-setting efforts and teacher preparation" (Diez, 1994, p. 2).

The standard-setting process has a variety of options in terms of strategies. Four possibilities are as follows:

Democratic procedures to forge consensus . . . authority of experts and reference to research results to settle disputes and resolve questions . . . the force of law to impose agreements . . . and norm formation in the context of local community to build shared commitments. (Sykes & Plastrik, 1993, p. 44)

These approaches, or combinations thereof, are processes through which collaboration might transpire as a means of forging consensus. Certainly the cross-fertilization of standards has already begun, and exploration of more systematic and comprehensive mechanisms for integration could prove to be profitable. This issue needs to be an emerging priority on the reform agenda; it provides a possible role for the federal government and agencies.

Within the issue of coordination of standards is the question of duplication of efforts, particularly in terms of the same target group. The NBPTS is in a unique, even historic, role as it provides a vision of the highly competent professional reflected in its standards. The set of standards stands alone; there are no competing systems within the profession.

In the instance of those entering the profession, however, there may be as many as five or six sets of standards. These include NCATE; NASDTEC outcomes-based, state-developed standards; induction program standards; the ETS Praxis III; INTASC; as well as implications of the multitude of K–12 subject standards. Should these standards be consistent or even essentially the same to create a national conception of the new teacher? Some would argue that there is no one way to teach and a variety of standards is a healthy condition. Others maintain that there must be at least a common core that reflects a consensus or else there is not a true profession. In any event, generating agreement on a set of expectations may not be feasible due to philosophical, logistical, and political factors. Furthermore, the establishment of each set of these standards is intended primarily to further the interests of the initiating institution, not only in terms of its conceptions as an influential entity with respective jurisdiction, but in the profession at large as well. This latter role conceptualization may create irreconcilable differences, regardless of the feasibility for consensus. The linkage thus falls more in the domain of policy.

Scenario of National Systems A number of alternative structures, interrelationships, and sequential linkages may be devised. Although in an embryonic stage, elements of such a system are beginning to emerge. Potential confederations and coalitions are forming. There is clear evidence that the education field, in emulation of professions such as medicine, is beginning to explore a confederation model for licensure and accreditation, such as the INTASC model (Sykes & Plastrik, 1993). Coalitions represent another means of cooperation, possibly in combination with confederations. The development of coalitions is already underway, primarily within reform models (Sykes & Plastrik, 1993). In one sense NCATE already represents a coalition across reform areas in that school-related standards and the subject specialty organizations are part of the teacher education reform effort through NCATE.

Coalitions existing side by side with confederations is a likely scenario. As an example, states could form a confederation to adopt common licensure standards, an extension of what already exists with NASDTEC, ICC, and INTASC. This confederation could link to school-based confederations (e.g., Sizer and Comer in the NASDC project) through a coalition relationship. The possibilities are both intriguing and overwhelming due to the complexity of the enterprise.

A related issue is how these coalitions and confederations interact with the several professional communities that have been established to create or lead reform as well. These include Project 30, the Renaissance Group, the Goodlad initiative, and the Holmes Group. A set of policies need to be devised to create a support system as an adjunct to the dictates of regulations derived from standards and the standards themselves. The interplay among policy, standards, and voluntary professional leadership will be an interesting dynamic to observe.

System Models Models of future national systems are already being formulated beyond the confederations and coalitions.

These are structural models that would redefine the system of accreditation, licensure, and national certification. Indeed, these models would create more of an integrated system rather than the scenario of isolated components that now exists.

Before engaging in the task of constructing alternative models, it would do well for reformers to specify and clarify the ultimate purpose of a national system and the associated beneficial outcomes of their particular proposal. This is a responsibility they must assume. The value of solutions needs to be examined in light of the problems they intend to remedy. Is a national system ostensibly required to enhance the stature of the profession? If so, to what extent does a particular model contribute to that end?

As one means of framing the "professional conversation" regarding structural systems and standards, an attempt is made here to provide a framework for describing, analyzing, and discussing the essential characteristics of these issues. The framework consists of a set of premises, principles, or aspects of a system and its inherent standards. These are offered to initiate dialogue not only about specific systems, but also about the premises themselves.

The principles are not conceived to address all aspects of systems, standards, and related issues; this would require a lengthy treatise and a more comprehensive perspective. Issues addressed by these premises are selected in view of their contribution to the ongoing dialogue, relationship to current issues, and interests of the author. They are suggested as a seminal set of issues that if expanded, refined, and modified over time could lead to a more comprehensive and sophisticated framework for analysis.

PRINCIPLE OF SYSTEMIC SYNERGY. Standards are conceived of as being part of a system (this is detailed in a subsequent section). If all essential elements of that system perform their functions and interactions, the system operates smoothly, thus creating a whole that is greater than the sum of its individual parts (synergy). If one of those elements does not contribute adequately to the system, even if operational as a separate entity, then it could have a deleterious effect on the entire system, even rendering it dysfunctional. This is termed *systemic dysynergy,* in which the whole is actually less than the sum of its parts.

PRINCIPLE OF PARALLELISM. In a standards system presented later, there are three components. These three components are applied to each phase of the professional development continuum. The components must follow each other in a parallel fashion throughout the continuum or the system breaks down at one or more phases of the continuum.

PRINCIPLE OF SUFFICIENCY. In synergy each of the elements of the system is adequate on its own and each contributes to the entire system. If one or more of those elements is not sufficient on its own, or even is missing, the system is not sufficient. In essence, other elements cannot carry the system alone. The importance of this principle is particularly realized when the system recognizes that an element is missing.

THE PRINCIPLE OF CONGRUITY. Each part of the standards system must be congruent with the others in a mutually supportive fashion. If one part does not mesh with others, the system does not function as effectively.

THE PRINCIPLE OF THRESHOLD OF TOLERANCE. Systems are not perfect. To increase their effectiveness, usually there is an associated cost. As noted in the economics of information, there is a relationship among information, investment to acquire it, and benefits that result. The policymakers are not always willing to provide the financial support needed to construct a credible system. The question that they must be asked is how weak of a system can be tolerated given the politics, public demand, and other pressures. This is the threshold of tolerance.

THE PRINCIPLE OF OPERATIONAL FEASIBILITY. A concept that is related to function is only as useful as it can be operationalized for that function. If the procedures, development, or maintenance of the system is too costly or too complicated, then the concept is not feasible operationally. The assessment system frequently is a barrier to an adequately operational system, however well conceived the system.

THE PRINCIPLE OF SYSTEM-DERIVED VALUE. A system consists of component parts. The value of a particular component to the system is only as great as its role or contribution to the system meeting its purpose. This is viewed as its systemic function value.

THE PRINCIPLE OF VALUE-ADDED SIGNIFICANCE. A system is designed to achieve a pragmatic function, such as provide quality assurance for candidates entering a profession. Related outcomes that are realized are value added. These could include greater credibility of the profession, enhanced program design, and increased effort in research and development.

In addition to these eight system principles, there are at least six principles for standards or characteristics of standards that warrant consideration.

EFFICACY. Efficacy is the extent to which those who meet the standards achieve the ultimate purpose of the set of standards, such as effective performance.

THE PARAMETERS OF UTILITY. As with systems, standards are of value to the extent they can be used effectively. Their utility is framed by parameters that are defined by the degree to which the standards are operational. These parameters limit utility.

DEGREES OF FREEDOM. Degrees of freedom are extent to which standards allow flexibility or various ways to achieve the standards. The more precisely standards identify particular means as well as ends, for example, the fewer the degrees of freedom provided. There can be a tension between degrees of freedom and assessment utility.

LIMITS OF OMISSION. Limits of omission refer to the degree to which standard setters allow for insufficiencies or omissions in the standards. These limits are set by policies, contextual pressures, and so forth. Deficiencies may exist because of costs, concerns over value-embedded issues (e.g., in the outcome standards), lack of information, or just oversight (in which case it is not planned, yet it exists).

PRINCIPLE OF THE INCONSEQUENTIAL. Standards created through democratic processes may reflect developer attitudes, values, and intuitively known practices. These may not have a real relationship to the effectiveness of the standards. Standards derived through the authoritative-experts process are not likely to contain these, and norm-formation approaches provide a base through tested practice or shared commitments. The democratic process may yield some standards that are of little consequence to the intended outcomes of the standards. Inconsequential standards unnecessarily complicate the system, incur higher costs, and reduce credibility of the endeavor. Knowledge of state history for state licensure, for example, has been cited as one of the inconsequentials.

IMPLIED CONCEPTIONS. Embedded in standards are value judgments, perceptions of what is best practice, or what is politically desirable. Conceptions of teaching or teacher education are defined by standards. One of the NBPTS sets of standards, for example, requires demonstration of lessons using an integrated curriculum approach. The NCATE standards envision a teacher who is multiculturally sensitive and is able to effectively instruct a diverse student population. These are conceptions of teaching and teacher.

A Systemic Approach to Standards

Most of the effort in the reform through policy is centered on the development of standards. As has been noted, this is moving at a frenetic pace. Standards are clearly the central focus. Some attention is being given to assessment, such as Praxis, but it is a secondary issue on the agenda. To be effective as a system, each of three major components must be considered.

Standards-Capacity Model A standards-capacity model that provides for a comprehensive system is proposed here. The three components are standards, assessment, and capacity building. This is depicted in Figure 13.3.

Each of the three are essential for an effective system. Standards alone cannot constitute a system, and this is a shortcoming in much of the current standards movement. Standards are the core of the model; they represent the vision and provide a conception of teacher and teaching. They are part of the accountability factor in the system because programs are held accountable for the outcomes or elements of the standards. Standards also guide program design.

Assessment is the second element of the accountability factor, as it directs the way in which achievement of standards will be measured. Assessment is also an indicator of capacity

FIGURE 13.3 Standards-capacity model.

because it reflects the extent to which programs are capable of preparing professionals to meet the standards in the ways specified in the assessments. Another function of assessment is to provide feedback to the capacity component. Assessment reveals standards that are more problematic in relation to a particular program, providing insights as to where program modifications need to be made.

Capacity is the ability of programs to meet the standards. Requiring programs to be accountable without providing the wherewithal to respond to these is somewhat punitive. The public sector, in essence the states, has a responsibility to build a total system and, therefore, extend beyond a regulatory role. Standards and assessment alone create an accountability model, but a standards-capacity model is more productive to the profession. The Wingspread Conference deliberations underscored the need to "understand how education policy decisions on implementing new standards can move from a purely regulatory orientation to place more emphasis on developmental and support functions" (Diez, 1994, p. 12).

Capacity includes program resources, design, implementation, and evaluation factors. The fundamental question is "What is needed in terms of these factors in order to meet the standards?" Standards provide a guide for capacity building. This is one way in which the three components of the standards-capacity model operate in a mutually supportive and interactive mode.

The model also includes viewing the purpose of standard setting along a capacity-accountability axis. With increased capacity comes more cogent and higher levels of accountability. In turn, greater accountability leverages a comparable change in capacity to measure up to the standard. Each becomes a force in enhancing the efficacy of the other and potentially creates an ever-upward spiral of excellence. This "capacity-accountability dynamic" requires a recognition of implied capacity commitment in responsible accountability models. There is growing recognition of the need for an accountability-resources compact embedded in the standards movement. This is evidenced in the emergence of terms such as *delivery standards* and *opportunity standards,* and these relationships "are likely to dominate the standards discussion in the future" (Pearson, 1994, p. 41). In a sense, capacity becomes the medium of exchange in the accountability realm.

Extended Standards-Capacity Model Once the concept of a standards-capacity model is accepted, one soon comes to the realization that it must be applied throughout the professional development continuum. The phases of the continuum are broadly defined as preservice, induction, and professional development (Roth, 1982), with the last phase leading to National Board certification. This results in a most powerful conception and impact on the profession.

A first focus of analysis should be the standards. Standards are being developed for each phase of the continuum. From the perspective of the overall profession, the standards at each phase should have a relationship to precedent and antecedent standards where such phases exist (e.g., preservice only has antecedent standards). There should be a standards progressive sequence that articulates teacher development. For example, standards for induction, such as after 2 or 3 years of experience,

may require more complex demonstration of competencies than for preservice, and there also may be additional competencies required. A conception of teaching would be embedded in each, and the ways in which this conception is modified through the sequence would be important to note. Such a developmental sequence has been designed for trainers in business and industry by the American Society for Training and Development (ASTD) in their *Models for Excellence* document (1983). In this model, higher degrees of expertise are required at progressive levels on the same functions. California is also developing a continuum of knowledge (California Department of Education, 1992).

As with standards, assessments would also provide a sequence throughout the continuum. This should occur naturally if the standards describe increasingly complex competencies. The sequence of assessment should parallel the standards.

Capacity required to prepare professionals for each phase also should be sequenced. Presumably the program needed to prepare an individual for initial licensure would be significantly different from a program preparing a teacher for National Board certification. The capacity needed at each phase of the continuum should parallel the standards and assessment sequences.

The extended standards-capacity model requires a system that is congruent at each phase and throughout the continuum. It specifies compatibility across each of the three components at each phase (preservice, induction, advanced certification), as well as from one phase to the next. It is a natural system in which such compatibility and sequence would be expected to emerge as a logical outcome of the standards-building process. This is shown in Figure 13.4.

At the preservice level, K–12 standards could be added. At each point in the model the questions identified in the template introduced at the beginning of the chapter could be raised, including: Who is involved in designing each? What developmental process is used? What is the primary purpose? Who governs and finances? How can they be implemented? What is their ultimate impact?

It is of value to note how the standards-capacity model fits the premises of the standards system presented previously. This exercise would require a lengthy description, but a brief summary may be of interest here. Each principle is shown with a summary of how the model fits, as follows:

1. Systemic Synergy: The linkage among standards, assessment, and capacity, as well as the sequence across the continuum, creates mutually supportive elements and a total system.

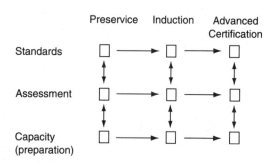

FIGURE 13.4. Extended standards-capacity model.

2. Parallelism: The three components parallel each other at each phase in the professional development continuum.
3. Sufficiency: All elements are present, including capacity building (but adequacy cannot be judged until developed).
4. Congruity: Matching each of the three components is specified as part of the model.
5. Threshold of Tolerance: This cannot be determined until each is designed.
6. Operational Feasibility: Assessment may be the most difficult.
7. System-Derived Value: Each component is essential to the system and derives significance in terms of its contributions to the system as a whole.
8. Value-Added Significance: The total system represented by the model goes well beyond its practical value, such as contributing to credibility and a long-term professional development model.

Credentialing Model Another system under discussion is a structural model that addresses the governance and licensing functions that utilize standards. This is called a credentialing model because it deals with credentialing candidates and programs. It includes licensing, certification, program approval, and accreditation.

An emerging model provides for a shift in function and control. Currently programs for preparation are approved by state agencies. National accreditation is voluntary. With NCATE's various arrangements with states, NCATE could become a major factor in program approval, with states using that process but within the legal jurisdiction of the state.

The state's primary role shifts to examining candidates for licensure in this model. The licensure examination could occur during the first few years, such as in induction programs. Graduates of programs could be given an intern license to be admitted into induction programs. Licensed teachers could subsequently pursue advanced certification, such as the National Board. This model is being advocated by some state officials, NCATE, and those involved in policy studies (Sanders, 1994; Wise, Darling-Hammond, Berry, & Klein, 1987).

State examinations for a license seem to be a feasible option, particularly with performance- or outcome-based standards and the increase in induction programs (see Chapter 26, this volume). Kentucky and NCATE are developing a performance-based testing program that all teacher candidates must pass to obtain a license. NCATE will then base its accreditation of an education school partially on how well its graduates perform on the test (Miller, 1994). Assessment technology may be the greatest barrier, but the work of the National Board and projected activity of INTASC in assessment may make greater strides in this domain.

This type of system could offer the profession a better structured and articulated system. If this is coupled with the standards-capacity model, it has significant potential. It may offer the benefits of systemic synergy, sufficiency, and congruency. The professional development continuum could be paralleled by the credentialing continuum to create a more unified professional system.

Implications of a National System The notion of national standards could be rendered ineffective if the principle of operational feasibility is violated. Standards will not work unless they are rigorously applied in preparation programs, states thoroughly enforce them, and systems (universities, states) empower programs with the necessary capacity. One pitfall is to follow the traditional pattern of teacher licensing standards, which vacillates with supply and demand. No matter how stringent the standards, if bypassed (emergency licenses, quick-entry alternative programs) the system offers an empty promise.

A national system with standards, if adopted, would define the profession. It would convey a concept of teacher never before agreed upon. Ostensibly, it would result in a stronger need for research to validate a universal system and standards, as well as provide for more focused research.

Other activities associated with licensing could also be affected. Interstate reciprocity could take on new meanings, and it has been suggested that National Board certification could contribute to this. This in turn could have some effect on supply-demand because teacher mobility would be enhanced.

The national credential model provides for realignment of professional governance. The most dramatic shift in policy at the state level is not licensure exams or performance-based standards; the salient shift is in restricting the state's role in program approval, a traditional and highly guarded function of the state. It is quite interesting for such a proposal to appear and even startling to witness the movement by states in this direction. This is more to the philosophy of the Council of Chief State School Officers than it is to NASDTEC.

An issue of consequence is the strategic approach to designing common standards and a national system. Four such strategies were cited previously (Sykes & Plastrik, 1993). To implement the credential model, the force of law strategy would be required for at least part of it. The force of law "both solves and creates problems" (Sykes & Plastrik, 1993, p. 46). One of the problems is mandating standards and assessment, an imposed accountability that could create great difficulty for programs. A buffer would be a phased-in approach with capacity building in the early stages to assist institutions as well as build the system.

THE LEGACY OF STANDARDS REFORM

The current standards movement in teacher education has attained historical significance in the development of teacher education in the United States and is emerging as the dominant force of the near future. The phenomenon is characterized in the professional literature as "a revolution is underway" (Miller, 1993, p. 7), a "little noticed revolution" (Shanker & Geiger, 1993), "the ambitions of many of the new standard setters are to revolutionize education in America" (Sykes & Plastrik, 1993, p. 1), a "modest revolution" (Lewis, 1993), and a "great adventure" (Sanders, 1987, p. 165).

This chapter begins with the introduction of a template as a means of describing and analyzing standards. The template is applied to varied contexts, such as state systems and national accreditation, to provide a perspective of how elements of the template are operationalized in each setting. In this concluding section the template is revisited, but in this instance it is applied to the overall standards reform movement itself, viewing its entirety. The template is engaged in the analysis through the lens of selected key issues that also provide a means of summarizing the status and legacy of the standards movement.

Role of Standards

The template suggests that delving into the purpose of standards is not only insightful but also necessary as an exercise in clarifying goals and devising means. It also can be productive in revealing agendas. In this domain the analysis revolves around the intended result and the underlying weaknesses in the existing system that standards are designed to resolve.

An overriding premise is that the purpose and beauty of the standards movement is dependent on the beholder. For those in the political arena the promise of accountability looms large and is quite compelling; therefore, moving forward with alacrity is paramount. Coming to grips with the problematic, such as assessment feasibility and costs, conceptions of teaching, and potential shallowness with abandonment of content and process in program review, are cast aside in the fervor to create the benchmarks to which programs and teachers will be held. Holding these standards and their accountability up to the public are ultimate outcomes. Tighter regulation, even greater constraints or limits on teacher education, is viewed by some in the political sector as a goal achievable through the vehicle of standards.

Institutions of higher education (IHE) involved in teacher education might view standards as externally imposed mandates with underlying agendas that are not directed entirely at improving schooling. Standards may be perceived as being prescriptive and interfering with professional autonomy. This is particularly true when both processes and outcomes are prescribed. In contrast, some IHEs may perceive performance-based licensure as a means to inspire public confidence in the enterprise. A more jaundiced view held by some critics is that IHEs are pursuing this purpose as an end in itself, with little regard for the supposed attendant improvement of practice in teacher education (Labaree, 1992a, 1992b).

Although the prevailing sentiment is one of a revolution, there are counterrevolutionists who perceive other opportunities emanating from the standards movement, particularly in the form of performance standards. This enclave is growing in numbers and influence and sees the new standards as a means of constructing an entire enterprise in teacher education that is not based in or even linked to the institutions of higher education. If they can prepare teachers who demonstrate the performance outcomes, what value is there in establishing all the accoutrements of an IHE program when the essence of standards can be accomplished in real-world settings in less time and at a lower cost? In this view, the standards effort is liberating, freeing up organizations to do things their way and outperform the establishment.

The consumer, or more broadly the public, most often views the standard-setting venture as a promise. Bombarded by the diatribes in the popular media, they are weary and wary of the teacher education establishment. The public both wants and expects change, and it holds onto the hope of standards; yet, it senses an empty promise.

Another constituent group may be identified as the profession at large, particularly its leadership. In their world the standards reform movement is intended not only to produce much-needed credibility, but also meaningful changes in how the business of preparing teachers is conducted. In essence, this view is one of shedding the mantle of a semiprofession and creating a true profession of teaching and teacher education. The "capacity-accountability dynamic" is perceived as an essential conceptual force.

Embedded in standards is the element of values. These are of varying types, such as moral, social, and professional. Setting standards is a way of virtually legislating these beliefs, such as cultural sensitivity, democratic processes, and teacher as continuous learner or reflective practitioner. This has led to conflicts, such as the struggle between fundamentalists and secular progressives (Sykes & Plastrik, 1993).

In summary, purposes of standard setting derive from agendas. These include accountability; political visibility; setting limits on programs; prescriptive mandates; the capacity-accountability dynamic; constraining, liberating, and inspiring public confidence and credibility; imparting values; providing the promise of quality; and creating a profession.

Developmental Processes

To what extent have all the stakeholders and those with expertise to contribute been involved? In pursuing the democratic process of standard setting, to what extent have all professional communities been involved? The notable absence of the research community in some of the standards-design efforts is both curious and understandable when the political context is noted. Questions raised and conclusions drawn about process in one analysis were as follows: "Which source does one turn to, who, and on which basis, makes these decisions? Not to deny the central role of the teaching profession, the teacher education community and especially the scholars and scholarship which inform teacher education appear underrepresented in several instances" (Howey & Zimpher, n.d.).

This also raises the question of the empirical base on which standards have been grounded. Such issues as the contrast between requiring demonstrations of teaching an integrated curriculum on the one hand and research on discipline-specific pedagogy on the other hand are yet to be reconciled. This is the tension between the philosophical and the empirical, with the former far outweighing the latter in the balance of standards design. As noted by Sykes and Plastrik (1993), however, "Science does not settle policy questions, it contributes perspectives and information for use within the political process" (p. 45).

Influences On and Governance of Standards

Standards have primarily been the purview of states, with local vested interest influencing the process and product. What is emerging is an overtone of national influence, which is manifest in collaboration, consensus, affiliation, confederation, and governance. There is a notable turn to national policy making, with efforts to seek a national consensus and aspirations of a national system with new standards that "require changes in our traditions and mechanisms of educational governance" (Sykes & Plastrik, 1993, p. 1).

Although legal authority remains vested in the states for licensure, changes in state governance models and the pervasive influence of national projects are clearly evident. There is a discernible movement to broadening participation in governance and linking education communities' perspectives across state boundaries through a professional network and within a national context. Just as teaching is moving away from teacher isolation in the classroom, teacher education standard setting is becoming less provincial and is developing a national conscience of standards.

A notable influence on the nature of standards is the emerging sense of a conception of teaching. There appears to be a well-established shift from a didactic model of instruction to one of reflective practice and active student engagement in learning. Standards attempt to capture more of the intellectual aspects of teaching, such as rationale based on theory and current state of knowledge about learners and curriculum. This is particularly true of the NBPTS standards, which require greater analysis of one's practice and evidence of an underlying knowledge base that supports curricular and instructional decision making.

This more intellectual conception of teaching is coupled with a similar theme in new K–12 standards. These requirements call for students to actively construct knowledge through immersion in authentic settings and tasks and to demonstrate their grasp of content interlaced with critical thinking. Thus, "Many of the standards projects seek to *change how teachers teach and children learn* by creating new visions of teaching" (Sykes & Plastrik, 1993, p. 9). A challenge in this respect is how standards can provide guidance to teach differently and to teach a different kind of student (Kennedy, 1991). These all are compelling influences on the design of new standards.

Implementation as System Boundary

The effectiveness of the standards movement will be determined to a great extent by the boundaries set by implementation constraints. The assessment issue forms part of that boundary as discussed previously. Some other issues are concerned with preciseness of form and integration of standards.

In order to transform standards into a functional form, a degree of specificity will most likely be required. For example, a standard such as "translates and aligns classroom expectations, climate, and instructional practices with children's stages of readiness and developmental characteristics" (NASDTEC, 1993, p. 21) can be assessed through high inference professional judgment or through greater specification of what "translates and aligns" means in the context cited. A step between the generic standard and assessment may be appropriate in order to bridge standards and assessment. Embedding this next step in the assessment process has the same effect as an intermediate standard. In general, "the degree of precision that is appropriate will vary according to the subject of the standard" (Sykes & Plastrik, 1993, p. 4). In this instance specificity is driven by other factors, such as reliance on assessment and purpose

(guidelines for program review or specifications for performance tests).

In some cases this may be accomplished by designating certain tasks that demonstrate evidence of ability in the performance standard. This assists in reliability of assessment; yet, too detailed of a specification could mechanize or trivialize the standard itself.

An example of how this problem is addressed in the K–12 sector is provided in the report of the 1993 Wingspread Conference (Diez, 1994). The Prince Elementary/Amphi Middle School Complex (PE/AMS) engaged in the process of identifying performance outcomes and assessments. In their "top priority" list they described five exit objectives (e.g., independent learner), and for each they identified criteria or indicators (e.g., independent learner: sets goals, is resourceful, is reflective). They also specified for each criterion what a student would do to indicate that he or she is achieving the criterion and what a teacher does to promote it.

In addition, the teachers designed eight benchmark tasks (to be used across grade levels) that teachers could use to measure multiple criteria and outcomes. One of these tasks was a research paper or project. Rubrics for assessing the tasks at six levels (six being high) were also developed. For the research paper benchmark, level six included one rubrics under content (e.g., topic clearly stated, sentence structure is precise and varied) and three mechanics rubrics (e.g., easy to read, uses complete sentences, uses paragraphs correctly). The need to further delineate standards or translate these into precise assessment rubrics is quite evident. If this process were to be transformed into teacher education outcomes, the resemblance to 1970s competency-based statements is striking. "The most notable difference is that standards, in contrast to the competency-based movement of the early seventies, are likely to bite pretty big 'competency chunks' " (Pearson, 1994, p. 60).

A review of types and specificity of standards in the K–12 sector indicated the following regarding content standards: "Depending on the language used and the curricular grain size used, these standards can resemble the well-worn (worn-out?) behavorial objectives of the mastery learning movement of the 1960's and 1970's or broad statements of goals or curricular intent" (Pearson, 1994, p. 43). In the domain of performance standards, the Standards Project for the Arts intends to employ a system with broad content standards (e.g., understanding how music relates to the other arts), followed by "achievement" standards at "proficient" and "advanced" levels (Pearson, 1994, p. 49).

Another analysis of the current teacher education outcomes efforts suggests that "What all of these efforts seem to have in common is the development of fairly broad and theoretically grounded guiding principles that are rendered increasingly more specific until they provide some guidance to answer the question 'What would count as evidence that the student (or teacher) has met the standard?' " (Pearson, 1994).

It is somewhat curious that there has been little debate about whether standards define a level of performance that is ideal, normative, or minimum. This has hardly been an issue because of the general nature of virtually all of the performance or outcome standards. For example, "The teacher plans for learning opportunities that recognize and address variation in learning styles and performance modes" (INTASC, 1992, p. 24) does not suggest that this is a minimum expectation, derived from consensus that reflects normative behavior, or ideal for the level of practitioner to which it is addressed. Indeed, INTASC's position is that these distinctions are in the "degree of sophistication teachers exhibit in the application of knowledge rather than in the kind of knowledge needed" (INTASC, 1992, p. 57).

The context of the analysis here is feasibility of implementation. In reference to the INTASC standards document, Richardson suggests "It is a lovely statement of desiderata . . . . Is it possible for a beginning teacher to attain the deep knowledge and understanding of classrooms, students, context, and subject matter implied in these principles?" (V. Richardson, 1994, p. 17). She references, as an example, "The teacher knows when and how to adjust plans based on student responses and other contingencies" (INTASC, 1992, p. 23).

Being attainable may not even be the right question. The standard and Richardson's analysis exemplify the point about the level of standard and preciseness of assessment. A candidate may be able to "adjust plans based on student responses" at a very basic or minimal level, such as slowing down the pace, repeating critical content, or using marker statements. The fundamental question is what is *meant* by adjusts plans? If the standard is not written into sublevels, then assessment certainly will define the meaning. Left to unsophisticated assessment techniques or an incomplete vision of the standard, the outcome could be vacuous and inconsequential. The need for meaningful external assessment, which has embedded in it a common view of the standard, becomes more evident through example.

The question of minimum or advanced performance levels as represented by the current form of standards may thus be a nonissue. This accounts for the dialogue void in the literature. It is at the assessment level that such distinctions are made. This places an additional burden on the assessment component, which has not always been up to the task; the Teacher Assessment Project at Stanford University documented the struggle to specify a vocabulary as basis for interpretation, in contrast to the creation of checklists to measure performance (Kerdeman, 1991). Further analysis reveals "Emerging professional standards for teaching, then, employ narrative, not numbers, to stimulate judgment rather than precise measurement" (Sykes & Plastrik, 1993, p. 33).

Of equal concern in terms of implementation is the prospect for integration of standards, both within teacher education and across domains (teacher education linked to K–12 standards). In an earlier section, some of the nuances and implications are reviewed. For this integration to proceed, there will need to be a context of shared meaning and values and the formation of consensus through political bargaining and negotiation (Sykes & Plastrik, 1993).

Educational Testing Service (ETS) has provided some leadership in this respect. "The CHART initiative at ETS seems especially helpful in terms of helping to understand the alignment or lack thereof between curriculum standards in various states, standards promulgated nationally by organizations such as the National Council for the Teaching of Mathematics (NCTM), and standards for preservice teachers and preservice programs" (Howey & Zimpher, n.d.). ETS has published a comparative view of the NBPTS, Praxis III, INTASC, and NASDTEC (Ingwer-

son, 1994). It is projected that such analyses will expand as the need for cross-referencing increases.

Implementation, including assessment, imposes considerable constraints. These may require tradeoffs and compromises to get the system up and running at a feasible level. The effect of this bartering on system effectiveness warrants careful observation.

Impact and Legacy

The most critical element of the template is impact. The remaining questions are: What difference will the standards movement make? What lasting impact will it have on the profession?

Teacher education programs and individual candidates are the prime focus in the teacher education standards-setting effort. Given the array of activities that focus on outcomes, it will be of interest to observe the nature of changes that emerge in response to the accountability of standards. If any significant changes are to occur at all, implementation strategies will need to be well conceived to avoid creating only the appearance of change. External assessment of candidates was cited earlier as one vehicle for achieving this.

Using standards for change is not consistently viewed as a sound strategy. As noted in the K–12 domain, "Many factors that most influence the outcomes of schooling may not be within the influencing reach of standard setting precisely because they lie outside of the education system" (Sykes & Plastrik, 1993, p. 54). The extent to which this premise applies to teacher education would be of interest to analyze.

The systems model previously delineated cited capacity building as the third essential element in a systems approach. Thus, the impact of the standards era on enhancing the capacity of teacher preparation programs bears watching. This well could be the most important value-added benefit.

Operating in a capacity-building mode requires recognition of and greater attention to the educative versus systemic purposes of standards in which the educative function promotes learning or program improvement and the systemic function is employed for comparison and accountability (V. Richardson, 1994).

Several standards factors have been noted for their possible or probable influence on teacher education programs. One relates to the proliferation of standards for the K–12 curriculum. How teachers can be prepared for this massive agenda is quite unclear. Curriculum integration and thematic approaches may be dictated by the pressures of the K–12 curriculum efforts. Finding common themes may be the ultimate path of reconciliation for the K–12 curriculum sector, which in turn would influence the teacher education curriculum. The NBPTS has already adopted presentation of integrated curriculum lessons as a policy for some of its assessments. In reference to the K–12 curriculum standards, "one can argue that their impact is likely to be greater in teacher education than on K–12 education" (Pearson, 1994, p. 58) due to the small size of teacher education compared to the teaching profession.

Hand in hand with curricular influences are those of assessment. If teachers are to use alternative assessments for performance outcomes of their students, they not only will need to be trained to use these, but also there will be considerable pressure on teacher preparation program faculty to model these and to employ them in the assessment of teacher candidates as well. The state of Vermont is developing an alternative assessment system for teacher education program approval. Faculty will be required to submit samples of work similar to portfolio assessment (Howey & Zimpher, n.d.).

Of particular interest is the ethos of the university and the manner in which it might be influenced by the variety of forces at work in this era of standards. Standards are but one of the factors. Performance assessment for licensure, national accreditation with an outcomes emphasis, and even the National Board activities could alter not only practice but also dispositions among teacher education faculty. Another view is that standards may be legislated through political processes, but ethos is socially constructed and its norms and standards evolve quite differently.

There again is the possibility that performance assessments for licensure will create a free market in the preparation of teachers, opening up to greater competition from private enterprise and expanded school-based preparation of teachers. The implications for university-based programs could be significant as performance assessment serves as a catalyst for an already rapidly growing alternative movement.

Although there are various perceived purposes of the standards-building effort, creating a viable profession with stature is one notable goal. Of concern here is whether the standards movement can capture the essence of teaching. This includes conceptions such as "for teachers to know when and how students are learning, a deep understanding of conceptual development within a subject matter context is critical" (Diez, 1994, p. 8); and providing "teachers at every grade level with considerable understanding of the cognitive and social theories that frame the realization of such tasks as 'research paper,' on ways of structuring the task, and criteria for assessing it" (V. Richardson, 1994, p. 22). One study concluded that at this juncture "neither the standards settings activities, in and of themselves, nor suggested structural alterations such as internships address the core questions of how one best learns to teach, where, and when" (Howey & Zimpher, n.d., p. 66).

An area overlooked in the push for standards is its impact on the educationally impoverished. A significant proportion of the concern regarding teacher education relates to its ability to serve the needs of children and youth in certain sectors of society that have been neglected, particularly areas of poverty, hard-to-staff schools, and the depths of urban and rural America. Responding to needs of these communities has allowed for lowering of standards on the one hand and calls for reform and more accountable preparation programs on the other hand.

To what extent will the standards movement have an impact on areas of need that opened doors to reduction in standards in the first place? Has anyone even seriously posed the question?

Related to this is the serious concern over the lack of diversity in the instructional work force. It is recognized that standards cannot remedy all problems of the system; yet, how standards could adversely affect the supply of underrepresented groups in the teaching profession has yet to be fully analyzed. The impact of standards on this issue bears careful scrutiny. It also has implications for capacity building cited previously. In the K–12 context, "the driving force behind the standards movement: the diverse student population in our schools" (Diez, 1994, p. 2) was clearly noted.

Finally, within the rubric of impact comes the question of how to know if the era of standards has made a difference? If so, how deep and significant will the change be and what will be the nature of that change? It is proposed that a comprehensive and systematic evaluation plan, executed at a national level to coincide with the drive for a national system, be designed now in the early stages of the movement.

An intriguing question is the matter of "onus probandi." Who is responsible for the burden of proof of impact? What are the consequences of not meeting the expectations of this massive effort? These issues and the various questions posed throughout are part of the legacy of this chapter and remain as subjects of inquiry for the next edition of this handbook. In the meantime, the profession will be observing with great interest as this chapter in its history unfolds.

The standard-setting activity has forged boldly and rapidly ahead and has left behind the necessary and more thoughtful, considered reflection as evidenced by the paucity of such dialogue in the literature. The necessity for these to be parallel processes is overshadowed by the political and social forces pressing for reform. Perhaps a slower pace, trial periods, and experimental efforts could provide time for these to become more in synch.

One such path is to encourage comparative reviews of the experiences of similar efforts in other professions or sectors of education; develop in-depth analyses of the myriad of underlying policy and implementation issues; conduct research on essential elements of standards and assessments; design evaluation of implementation strategies and effects; and pursue ongoing debate on process, policy, efficacy, and impact. This environment is imperative for the standards movement to leave a legacy of meaningful reform.

The impetus for reform through standards has emanated along an axis from accountability to creating a true profession. From this perspective, ultimately the era of standards must be held accountable for its contributions to creating a profession.

References

American Association of Colleges for Teacher Education (AACTE). (1986). *Teacher certification.* (Contract No. 400-83-0022). Washington, DC: ERIC Clearinghouse on Teacher Education.

American Association of Colleges for Teacher Education (AACTE). (1993, November). *Teacher education policy in the states: A 50-state survey of legislative and administrative actions.* Washington, DC: Author.

American Society for Training and Development (ASTD). (1983). *Models for excellence: The conclusions and recommendations of the ASTD training and development competency study.* Washington, DC: Author.

Amos, N., Cheeseman, B., & Ward, C. (1986, November 19–21). *An analysis of the Mississippi performance-based school accreditation* (pilot study). Paper presented at the 1986 annual meeting of the Mid-South Educational Research Association, Memphis.

Anderson, J. (1991). Meeting the challenges of the bias review process. In National Evaluation Systems (Ed.), *Teacher certification testing: Recent perspectives* (pp. 47–59). Amherst, MA: National Evaluation Systems, Inc.

Association of Teacher Educators (ATE). (1991). *Restructuring the education of teachers: Report of the Commission on the Education of Teachers into the 21st Century.* Reston, VA: Author.

Baratz-Snowden, J. (1994, Summer). NBPTS and teacher professional development: The policy context. *Portfolio, 3*(3), 4, 5.

Behling, H. E. (1986, June). *The use of NCATE-approved programs for automatic certification.* Unpublished manuscript. Maryland State Department of Education, Baltimore.

Bentz, S. (1989). Agency resources and policy development. In National Evaluation Systems (Ed.), *Program issues in teacher certification testing* (pp. 57–90). Amherst, MA: National Evaluation Systems, Inc.

Bradley, A. (1989, September 13). In Connecticut, moving past pencil and paper: Teachers evaluated on class behavior. *Education Week, 9*(1), 1, 22.

Bradley, A. (1993a, February 10). ETS unveils 3-stage assessment package for states to use in licensing new teachers. *Education Week, 12*(20), 13.

Bradley, A. (1993b, November 24). Teacher education and standards. *Education Week, 13*(12), 22, 23.

Bradley, A. (1994, March 2). Link between accreditation, status, in AACTE proposed. *Education Week, 13*(23), 3.

California Department of Education. (1992, May). A continuum of skills, knowledge, and attitudes from beginning to advanced levels of teaching. Sacramento: Author.

Carnegie Forum on Education and the Economy. (1986, May). *A nation prepared: Teachers for the 21st century.* New York: The Task Force on Teaching as a profession, Carnegie Forum on Education and the Economy.

Castenell, L. A., & Soled, S. W. (1993). Standards, assessments, and valuing diversity. In M. E. Diez et al. (Eds.), *Essays on emerging assessment issues* (pp. 43–48). Washington, DC: American Association of Colleges for Teacher Education.

Chubb, J. E., & Moe, T. M. (1990). *Politics, markets, and America's schools.* Washington, DC: The Brookings Institution.

Cizek, G. J. (1993, November 10). On the disappearance of standards. *Education Week, 13*(10), 32, 24.

Clark, C. M., & Peterson, P. L. (1986). Teachers' thought process. In M. C. Wittrock (Ed.), *Handbook of research on teaching* (3rd ed.) (pp. 255–296). New York: Macmillan.

Clark, D. L., & McNergney, R. F. (1990). Governance of teacher education. In W. R. Houston, M. Haberman & J. Sikula (Eds.), *Handbook of research on teacher education* (pp. 101–118). New York: Macmillan.

Cole, R. (1979, December). Minimum competency tests for teachers: Confusion compounded. *Phi Delta Kappan, 61,* 233.

Commission on Teacher Credentialing & California Department of Education. (1992, January 30). *Draft standards of quality and effectiveness for new teacher support and assessment programs.* Sacramento: Author.

Connecticut Education Association. (1993). *Characteristics of state teacher professional standards boards.* Hartford, CT: Author.

Cronin, J. M. (1983). State regulation of teacher preparation. In L. S. Shulman & G. Sykes (Eds.), *Handbook of teaching and policy* (pp. 171–190). New York: Longman.

Cruickshank, D. R., Cruz, J., Jr., McCullough, J. D., Reynolds, R. T., & Troyer, M. B. (1991, September 26). *The legacy of NCATE: An analysis of standards and criteria for compliance since 1957.* (Reports-Evaluative/Feasibility {142}). Washington, DC: Office of Educational Research and Improvement. (ERIC Document Reproduction Service No. ED 339 686)

Darling-Hammond, L., & Berry, B. (1988). *The evolution of teacher policy* (JRE-01). Santa Monica: The RAND Corporation. (ERIC Document Reproduction Service No. ED 298 599)

Diegmueller, K. (1993, October 13). NCATE moves forward in approving outcomes for preparation of teachers. *Education Week, 13*(6), 4.

Diez, M. E. (1994). Relating standards to systemic reform. In M. E. Diez, V. Richardson, & P. D. Pearson (Eds.), *Setting standards and educating teachers, a national conversation: A report from the Wingspread Conference, November 1-4, 1993.* (pp. 1–14). Washington, DC: American Association of Colleges for Teacher Education.

Diez, M. E. (1993). Probing the meaning of assessments. In *Essays on emerging assessment issues.* Washington, DC: American Association of Colleges for Teacher Education.

Dwyer, C., & Villegas, A. (1992, June). Guiding conceptions and assessment principles for The Praxis Series: Professional assessments for beginning teachers. *The Praxis Series.* Princeton, NJ: Educational Testing Services.

Earley, P. M. (1987, Summer). State and federal report: The importance of state-level activities. *Teacher Education Quarterly, 14*(3), 105–107.

Edelfelt, R., & Raths, J. (1992, May 20). National teacher certification: A quality guarantee? *Education Week, 11*(35), 26.

Edmundson, P. J. (1993, May–June). Renewal agendas and accreditation requirements: Contrasts and correspondence. *Journal of Teacher Education, 44*(3), 170–182.

Evans, K. M., & King, J. A. (1994, March). Research on OBE: What we know and don't know. *Educational Leadership, 51*(6), 12–17.

Ewell, P. (1992). Outcomes assessment, institutional effectiveness, and accreditation: A conceptual exploration. In Council on Postsecondary Accreditation (Eds.), *Accreditation, assessments and institutional effectiveness* (pp. 1–17). Washington, DC: Council on Postsecondary Accreditation.

Feistritzer, C. E., & Chester, D. T. (1993). *Alternative teacher certification: A state-by-state analysis 1993–94.* Washington, DC: National Center for Education Information.

Fenstermacher, G. D. (1990, Spring). The place of alternative certification in the education of teachers. *Peabody Journal of Education, 67*(3), 155–185.

Galbraith, M. W., & Gilley, J. W. (1985, October). An examination of professional certification. *Lifelong Learning, 9*(2), 12–15.

Gideonse, H. D. (1993, October). Appointments with ourselves: A faculty argument for NCATE. *Phi Delta Kappan, 75*(2), 174–179.

Gideonse, H. D., Ducharme, E. R., Ducharme, M. K., Gollnick, D., Lilly, M. S., Shelke, E. L., & Smith, P. (1993, February). *Capturing the vision: Reflections on NCATE's redesign five years after.* Washington, DC: American Association of Colleges for Teacher Education.

Goodlad, J. I. (1990). *Teachers for our nation's schools.* San Francisco: Jossey-Bass.

Gough, P. B. (1991, November). America 2000. *Phi Delta Kappan, 73*(3), 179.

Gusky, T. R. (1994, March). What you assess may not be what you get. *Educational Leadership, 51*(6), 51–54.

Haberman, M. (1986, June). Licensing teachers: Lessons from other professions. *Phi Delta Kappan, 67*(10), 719–722.

Hathaway, W. E. (1980, December). Testing teachers. *Educational Leadership, 38*(3), 210–215.

Havrilesky, C., Dwyer, C. A., & Forbes, E. (1993, November-December). Q&A on Praxis, the new teacher examination from ETS. *ATE Newsletter, 27*(2), 4–5.

Hawley, W. (1986). A critical analysis of the Holmes Group's proposals for reforming teacher education. *Journal of Teacher Education, 37*(4), 47–51.

Hinkle, D. E. (1993). Outcomes assessment and program evaluation: What are they—and for what purpose? In M. E. Diez et al. (Eds.),

Essays on emerging assessment issues (pp. 29–37). Washington, DC: American Association of Colleges for Teacher Education.

Hood, S., & Parker, L. (1989). Meaningful minority participation in the development and validation of certification testing systems: A comparison of the certification testing systems of Illinois and Pennsylvania. In National-Evaluation Systems (Ed.), *Program issues in teacher certification testing* (pp. 23–55). Amherst, MA: National Evaluation Systems, Inc.

Howey, K. R., & Zimpher, N. L. (n.d.). *Selected state initiatives in teacher education, standards setting and assessment, and professional practices boards.* Indianapolis, IN: Lilly Foundation.

Ingwerson, L. (1994, March). *A comparative view: National Board for Professional Teaching Standards, Praxis III performance assessment criteria, Interstate New Teacher Assessment and Support Consortium, and National Association of State Directors of Teacher Education and Certification.* Princeton, NJ: Educational Testing Service.

Interstate New Teacher Assessment and Support Consortium (INTASC) (1992, September 1). *Model standards for beginning teacher licensing and development: A resource for state dialogue.* Washington, DC: Council of Chief State School Officers.

Jamentz, K. (1994, March). Making sure that assessment improves performance. *Educational Leadership, 51*(6), 55–57.

Jones, D. W. (1993, January). *Final report: A longitudinal study of the impact of NCATE accreditation.* Muncie, IN: Ball State University.

Jordan, K. F. (1988). *State professional standards/practices commissions or boards: A policy analysis paper.* Washington, DC: American Association of Colleges for Teacher Education.

Kennedy, M. M. (1991, May). Policy issues in teacher education. *Phi Delta Kappan, 72*(9), 659–665.

Kerdeman, D. (1991). The 100 statements project: A study in the dynamics of teacher assessment. *Teacher Education Quarterly, 18*(3), 59–85.

Labaree, D. (1992a). Doing good, doing science: The Holmes Group reports and the rhetoric of educational reform. *Teachers College Record, 93*(4), 628–640.

Labaree, D. (1992b). Power, knowledge, and the rationalization of teaching: A genealogy of the movement to professionalize teaching. *Harvard Educational Review, 62*(2), 123–154.

Levin, H. M. (1980, July–August). Teacher certification and the economics of information. *Educational Evaluation and Policy Analysis, 2*(4), 5–18.

Lewis, A. C. (1993, April). The teaching 'profession' goes national. *Phi Delta Kappan, 74*(8), 588–589.

Lieb, B. (Ed.). (1993, March 22–24). *Achieving world class standards: The challenge for educating teachers.* Washington, DC: Office of Educational Research and Improvement, Study Group on Educating Teachers for World Class Standards.

Lively, K. (1992, December 9). More states back new standards for what teachers must know and be able to do in classrooms. *The Chronicle of Higher Education, 39*(16), A20.

Marzano, R. J. (1994, March). Lessons from the field about outcome-based performance assessments. *Educational Leadership, 51*(6), 44–50.

Mastain, R. K., & Roth, R. A. (Eds.). (1984). *The NASDTEC Manual: Manual on certification and preparation of educational personnel in the United States.* Sacramento: National Association of State Directors of Teacher Education and Certification.

McDonnell, L. M. (1989). *The dilemma of teacher policy.* Santa Monica: The RAND Corporation. (ERIC Document Reproduction Service No. ED 318 087)

McDonough, M. W., & Wolf, W. C. (1988, Spring). Court actions which helped define the direction of the competency-based testing movement. *Journal of Research and Development in Education, 21*(3), 37–43.

Miller, J. (1993, Spring). New trends in licensing: A revolution has begun. *NCATE Quality Teaching, 2*(3), 6–7.

Miller, L. (1994, October 6). Performance-based tests to determine licensure under Kentucky program. *Education Week, 14*(5), 15.

Morone, J. (1990). *The Democratic wish: Popular participation and the limits of American government.* New York: Basic Books.

Murphy, E. J., & Elliot, S. M. (1991). A sustained strategy for preventing potential bias in the TMTE. In National Evaluation Systems (Ed.), *Teacher certification testing: Recent perspectives* (pp. 99–117). Amherst, MA: National Evaluation Systems, Inc.

Nassif, P. M. (1992). Aligning assessment and instruction. In National Evaluation Systems (Ed.), *Current topics in teacher certification testing* (pp. 101–110). Amherst, MA: National Evaluation Systems, Inc.

National Association of State Directors of Teacher Education and Certification (NASDTEC). (1976, February 3). NASDTEC position statement: Approval/accreditation of programs to prepare professional educational personnel. In NASDTEC (Ed.), *Standards for state approval of teacher education* (1981 ed., rev. 1983) (Appendix B). Salt Lake City, UT: Author.

National Association of State Directors of Teacher Education and Certification (NASDTEC). (1993). *Outcome-based standards and portfolio assessment: Outcome-based teacher education standards for the elementary, middle and high school levels* (2nd ed.). Dubuque, IA: Kendall/Hunt.

National Association of State Directors of Teacher Education and Certification (NASDTEC). (1994). *Manual on certification and preparation of educational personnel in the United States* (2nd ed.). Dubuque, IA: Kendall/Hunt.

National Board for Professional Teaching Standards (NBPTS). (1988). (Contract No. 400-83-0022.) Washington, DC: Office of Educational Research and Improvement. (ERIC Document Reproduction Service No. Ed 304 444).

National Board for Professional Teaching Standards (NBPTS). (n.d.). *What teachers should know and be able to do.* Detroit, MI: Author.

National Council for Accreditation of Teacher Education (NCATE). (1991, fall). The governor's consensus on education reform. *NCATE Quality Teaching, 1*(1), 12.

National Council for Accreditation of Teacher Education (NCATE). (1992, Spring). NCATE Updates. *NCATE Quality Teaching, 1*(3), 9.

National Council for Accreditation of Teacher Education (NCATE). (1993, April). *Facts.* Washington, DC: Author.

National Council for Accreditation of Teacher Education (NCATE). (1994a, January). *Conditions & procedures for state/NCATE partnerships.* Washington, DC: Author.

National Council for Accreditation of Teacher Education (NCATE). (1994b, May 19). *NCATE standards.* Washington, DC: Author.

National Evaluation Systems, Inc. (NES). (1989). *Program issues in teacher certification testing.* Amherst, MA: Author.

National Evaluation Systems, Inc. (NES). (1990). *The assessment of teaching: Selected topics.* Amherst, MA: Author.

National Evaluation Systems, Inc. (NES). (1991). *Teacher certification testing: Recent perspectives.* Amherst, MA: Author.

National Evaluation Systems, Inc. (NES). (1992). *Current topics in teacher certification testing.* Amherst, MA: Author.

National Evaluation Systems, Inc. (NES). (1993). *Performance assessment in teacher certification testing.* Amherst, MA: Author.

Nicklin, J. L. (1992, May 6). Teacher-education programs debate the need for accrediting agency's stamp of approval. *The Chronicle of Higher Education, 38*(35), A19,22.

Pearson, P. D. (1994). Standards and teacher education: A policy perspective. In Diez, Richardson & Pearson, *Setting standards and educating teachers, a national conversation: A report from the Wingspread Conference, November 1–4, 1993* (pp. 37–67). Washington, DC: American Association of Colleges for Teacher Education.

Popham, W. J., & Yalow, E. S. (1984, April). *Standard-setting options for teacher competency tests*. Paper presented at a joint session of the American Educational Research Association and the National Council on Measurement in Education, New Orleans.

Raths, J., Zych, C., & Wojtaszek-Healy, M. (1985, September-October). NCATE and interstate certification: A status report. *Journal of Teacher Education, 36*(5), 53–55.

Richardson, J. (1993, December 8). Renewable teachers' licenses pushed in 3 states. *Education Week, 13*(14), 8.

Richardson, J. (1994). States offer incentives to teachers seeking national board certification. *Education Week, 14*(1), 14.

Richardson, V. (1994). Standards and assessments: What is their educative potential? In Diaz, Richardson, & Pearson. *Setting standards and educating teachers, a national conversation: A report from the Wingspread Conference, November 1–4, 1993* (pp. 15–36). Washington, DC: American Association of Colleges for Teacher Education.

Roth, R. A. (1982, spring/summer). Career phases of teachers as a continuum. *The Journal of the Michigan Association of Teacher Educators, 4*(1), 30–32.

Roth, R. A. (1989, December). The teacher education program: An endangered species? *Phi Delta Kappan, 71*(4), 319–323.

Roth, R. A. (1992, Spring). Dichotomous paradigms for teacher education: The rise or fall of the empire. *Action in Teacher Education, 14*(1), 1–9.

Roth, R. A. (1994). The university can't train teachers? The transformation of a profession. *Journal of Teacher Education, 45*(4), 261–268.

Roth, R. A., & Pipho, C. (1990). Teacher education standards. In W. R. Houston, M. Haberman, & J. Sikula (Eds.), *Handbook of research on teacher education* (pp. 119–135). New York: Macmillan.

Rothman, R. (1990, October 3). Survey shows expansion in programs to test students, teachers since 1985. *Education Week, 10*(5), 16.

Rowan, B. (1985). The assessment of school effectiveness. In R. Kyle (Ed.), *Reaching for excellence: An effective schools sourcebook* (pp. 99–116). Washington, DC: E. H. White.

Sanders, T. (1987). *The winds of change influence NCATE: An analysis of the NCATE accreditation process, 1979–1986*. Unpublished doctoral dissertation, University of Nevada, Reno.

Sanders, T. (1993, October). A state superintendent looks at national accreditation. *Phi Delta Kappan, 75*(3), 165–168.

Sanders, T. (1994, Winter). A new model: For quality assurance in teacher preparation. *NCATE Quality Teaching, 3*(2), 4–5.

Scanell, D., Andersen, D. G., & Gideonse, H. D. (1989, December). *The need for state professional standards and practices boards*. Las Vegas: Association of Colleges and Schools of Education in State Universities and Land Grant Colleges and Affiliated Private Universities.

Schwank, D. (1982, July–August). Who controls teacher education? *Journal of Teacher Education, 33*(4), 62–64.

Sclan, E., & Darling-Hammond, L. (1992, March). *Beginning teacher performance evaluation: An overview of state policies* (Trends and issues paper No. 7). Washington, DC: ERIC Clearinghouse on Teacher Education and American Association of Colleges for Teacher Education.

Shanker, A., & Greiger, K. (1993, Spring). A call for higher standards for teachers and teacher education. *NCATE Quality Teaching, 13*(23), 3.

Shavelson, R. J., Baxter, G., & Pine, G. (1992). Performance assessments: Political rhetoric and measurement reality. *Educational Researcher, 21*(4), 22–27.

Shulman, L. S. (1986, February). Those who understand: Knowledge growth in teaching. *Educational Researcher, 15*(2), 4–14.

Shulman, L. S., & Sykes, G. (1986, January). *A national board for teaching? In search of a bold standard*. A paper commissioned for the Task Force on Teaching as a Profession, Carnegie Forum on Education and the Economy.

Smith, D. C. (1990, September–October). Accreditation of teacher education institutions: An interview with Richard Kunkel. *Journal of Teacher Education, 41*(4), 3–6.

Stewart, D. M. (1994, February 9). Setting standards in a democracy: Filling the gap. *Education Week, 13*(20), 44–45.

Sykes, G. (1989, March 29). Examining the contradictions of licensure. *Education Week, 8*(27), 32.

Sykes, G., & Plastrik, P. (1993, May). *Standard setting as educational reform* (Trends and issues paper No. 8). Washington, DC: ERIC Clearinghouse on Teacher Education and American Association of Colleges for Teacher Education.

Towers, J. M (1994, April). The perils of outcome-based teacher education. *Phi Delta Kappan, 75*(8), 624–627.

Viadero, D., & West, P. (1993, June 16). Standards deviation: Benchmark-setting is marked by diversity. *Education Week, 12*(38), 1, 14–15.

Watkins, B. T. (1988, November 9). New tests expected to bring dramatic changes in the way prospective teachers are assessed. *The Chronicle of Higher Education, 35*(11), A1, A36.

Watkins, B. T. (1993, September 22). 1,000 schoolteachers sign up for evaluations that would lead to national certification. *The Chronicle of Higher Education, 40*(5), A19–21.

Watts, D. (1982, July–August). Can campus-based preservice teacher education survive? *Journal of Teacher Education, 33*(4), 35–39.

Wise, A. E. (1993a, spring). Public supports accreditation standards. *NCATE Quality Teaching, 2*(3), 1–2.

Wise, A. E. (1993b, June 16). Draft of the refinement of NCATE professional accreditation standards (p. 14). Washington, DC: NCATE Memorandum.

Wise, A. E., Darling-Hammond, L., Berry, B., & Klein, S. (1987, November). *Licensing teachers. Design for a teaching profession* (R-3576-CSTP). Santa Monica: The Rand Corporation. (ERIC Document Reproduction No. ED 293 794)

Wise, A. E., & Leibbrand, J. (1993, October). Accreditation and the creation of a profession of teaching. *Phi Delta Kappan, 75*(2), 133–157.

Wolff, R. A. (1993, June 9). Restoring the credibility of accreditation. *The Chronicle of Higher Education, 39*(40), B1, 2.

Yff, J. (1993, Winter). Accrediting agencies' standards share core elements. *NCATE Quality Teaching, 2*(2), 4–5.

·14·

PROFESSORS, TEACHERS, AND LEADERS IN SCDES

Nancy L. Zimpher
THE OHIO STATE UNIVERSITY

Julie A. Sherrill
THE OHIO STATE UNIVERSITY

This chapter uses as a point of departure the chapter "Professors and Deans of Education" (Howey & Zimpher, 1990) in the first *Handbook of Research on Teacher Education*. It reviews research on faculty members and deans/chairpersons who provide leadership in schools, colleges, and departments of education (SCDEs), and it extends beyond the previous chapter in several important ways. First, the earlier chapter embedded its analysis of education professors in the larger university context in order to assess how professors of education "measure up" to more generalizable conceptions of the professoriate. Although this context continues to be important, it is not appropriate to reiterate a foundation so recently drawn. Second, only 2 years of data from the American Association of Colleges for Teacher Education (AACTE) study on the teacher education professoriate, students, programs, and institutional context were available when the 1990 chapter was published. AACTE's Research About Teacher Education Project (RATE) (RATE I, 1987; RATE II, 1988; RATE III, 1989; RATE IV, 1990; RATE V, 1991; RATE VI, 1992; RATE VII, 1994; RATE VIII, 1995) provides an 8-year resource for analysis in this chapter.

A third important difference in the two chapters is the analysis in this chapter of the emerging role of classroom teachers as field-based teacher educators. This new role was referenced briefly in the 1990 chapter with regard to promoting more school-based engagement for education professors. This chapter addresses this role in two ways: (1) by providing previously unavailable RATE data on the backgrounds and perceptions of classroom teachers who supervise student teachers, traditionally recognized in the literature as cooperating teachers; and, more importantly, (2) by looking at the emergent clinical faculty

role, by whatever title, and its critical place in teacher preparation.

The section in this chapter on the deanship also follows on the 1990 work. At that time there had been no subsequent national study of the deanship since the study reported in Griffiths and McCarty's (1980) text on "The Dilemma of the Deanship," wherein Cyphert and Zimpher (1980) analyzed data from a national study of SCDE deans. With the publication of RATE V (1991), there is now a 10-year comparative base for understanding the role of the education deanship.

This chapter begins where the 1990 chapter (Howey & Zimpher) concludes.

Well-conceived studies of deans in different contexts should be complemented by more well-conceived personal profiles that portray the motivations, aspirations, wants and needs, successes and failures of real people in real places . . . to move from citing abstract principles of organizational change and leadership to rich descriptions of theory and practice and practicing new theories. A person-in-context perspective calls for, just as in studies of faculty, thoughtful selection of key presage and personal factors or variables as these interact with organizational and cultural ones. (p. 367)

Clearly the influence of school reform on the restructuring of SCDEs is causing a closer look at issues related to shared leadership and making more horizontal the traditional leadership hierarchy not only of schools but also of schools of education; therefore, the analysis of the education deanship reflects this perspective.

The chapter is organized into four sections. First, it describes dilemmas currently facing schools, colleges, and departments of education to enable a better understanding of "ed school" (Clifford & Guthrie, 1988) professors and classroom teachers and to frame an analysis of leadership roles of deans and heads of SCDEs. This terrain is explored through several historical and contemporary views of what a more effective SCDE might look like. The subsequent three sections cover professors in SCDEs, teachers in SCDEs, and leaders in SCDEs. A concluding section summarizes findings briefly and helps define needed research on the condition and capacity of professors, teachers, and deans as they collectively attempt to exercise leadership in SCDEs and in the profession writ large.

THE TERRAIN OF SCDES

This section delineates a "cultural portrait" (Goodlad, 1990) of teacher education as manifested in SCDEs. It draws on several landmark statements including B. O. Smith and colleague's (1980) "A Design for a School of Pedagogy"; the AACTE effort in 1976 to define the process of educating a profession (Howsam, Corrigan, Denemark, & Nash, 1976); Clifford and Guthrie's 1988 rendering of ed schools, subtitled "A Brief for Professional Education"; the trilogy of texts produced by John Goodlad (1990; Goodlad, Soder, & Sirotnik, 1990a, 1990b) and associates relative to the education of educators; and Harry Judge's (1982) *American Graduate Schools of Education: A View from Abroad.* Also, participation in the creation of the emerging text of the national Holmes Group, *Tomorrow's Schools of Education* (1995), has certainly influenced the authors' thinking on these issues. Some major themes appear crucial to an analysis of the roles of those who currently live within SCDEs. Essentially the attributes of greatest significance cluster around symptoms that have plagued teacher education for literally decades, such as low self-concept and status deprivation, failure to develop a knowledge base, underfunding, and lack of recognition of teacher education as central to the role and function of universities. These symptoms and missed opportunities have contributed to the subsequent denial by schools of education of their rightful professional status. The consequences of such role confusion have been the absence of a clear and purposeful focus, failed mission, lack of leadership, and certain internal and external forces that have mitigated against SCDEs achieving real professional status within the academy.

Denied Professional Status

In AACTE's Bicentennial Commission on Education for the Profession of Teaching called "Educating a Profession," Howsam et al. (1976) provide a conceptual definition of professions, which differentiates occupational categories across professional, semiprofessional, paraprofessional, skilled, and unskilled trade categories. They describe 12 characteristics of a profession charging that teaching meets some well, while falling far short on others. Although there is general agreement by teachers and professional educators that teaching belongs "in the company of the mature professions," there is similar agreement that it is still in the status-seeking mode. These authors recognize certain steps that will be necessary to claim full pro-

fessional status, including: (1) more rigorous criteria for professional competence, (2) longer periods of preparation, (3) continuing professional development, and (4) accountability for performance (Howsam et al., 1976, pp. 16–17).

Goodlad et al. (1990b) assert conditions necessary for teacher education to become a true profession, including

A reasonably coherent body of necessary knowledge and skills; a considerable measure of "professional" control over admissions to teacher education programs and of autonomy with respect to determining the relevant knowledge, skills, and norms; a degree of homogeneity in groups of program candidates with respect to expectations and curricula; and rather clear borders demarcating qualified candidates from the unqualified, legitimate programs of preparation free from shoddy and entrepreneurial fads, formed from innovation grounded in theory and research. With these conditions largely lacking, teacher education and the occupation of school-teaching have been at the mercy of supply and demand, pillages from without, and bulkanization from within. Even today, teaching remains the not-quite profession. (pp. 70–71)

Howey (1992) suggests achievements necessary to attain professional school status as follows: SCDEs must demonstrate that they can make direct contributions to improvements in K–12 schools and create a clinical faculty. There must be further development of a scientific knowledge base on teaching; a demonstration of pedagogical content knowledge as well as general pedagogical knowledge; and the creation of more coherent, interrelated, and "potent" programs of teacher preparation. SCDEs must create on-campus laboratory and clinical capacities. There must be evidence that beginning teachers can work with the growing plurality of those who attend America's public schools. Finally, teacher education must be continued through the entry years of teaching and beyond.

Rather than attempting to meet the preconditions of professionalization prescribed herein, schools of education have been diverted or embroiled in other issues more common to the goals and standards of colleges of arts and sciences than to that of a true professional school. Clifford and Guthrie (1988) caution

Schools of education, particularly located on the campuses of prestigious research universities, have become ensnared improvidently in the academic and political cultures of their institutions and have neglected their professional allegiances. They are like marginal-men, aliens in their own world. They have seldom succeeded in satisfying the scholarly norms of their campus letters and science colleagues and they are simultaneously estranged from their practicing professional peers. . . . The more forcefully they have rowed toward the shores of scholarly research, the more distant they have become from the public schools they are duty bound to serve. Conversely, systematic efforts at addressing the applied problems of public schools have placed schools of education at risk on their own campuses. (pp. 3–4)

In this context, Judge (1982) asserts the two-fold dilemma that as schools of education attempt to assert their place in the academy, they distance themselves from the field; ironically, they appear to gain no better stature by associating with the field. Furthermore, ed schools reflect the prestige of the professional for which they offer training and credentials. These clients are inevitably teachers. "Since they cannot achieve the autonomy or dignity of medicine or law," he asserts, "they seek another source of authority and acceptance. They have tuned into the values and habits of the graduate schools of arts and sciences, especially the social sciences. In the end, however, that does not help them. They remain professional schools aspiring to another status—and the more they aspire the more they are likely to alienate themselves from the world of schools and education" (p. 29).

In short, achievement of true professional status is linked to a host of barriers generated in part by a view of teacher education as, at the root of it, associated with a career unable to achieve professional status itself. The dilemma lies in breaking this "catch 22," such that ed schools create more rigorous and relevant programs, as invoked by Goodlad (1990) and Howey (1992), so that teachers can achieve greater status, in turn enabling ed schools to do the same. To the extent that those who manage the academic agenda of ed schools, the very personnel reviewed in this chapter, can follow the prescriptions suggested, they can become the architects of a better future. Much of this chapter is devoted to assessing their potential to do so.

Lack of an Intellectual Base

SCDEs in prestigious comprehensive research institutions continue to celebrate research over teaching and educational science over eclectic craft knowledge, according to Clifford and Guthrie (1988). No one would advocate that SCDEs disengage themselves from inquiry. On the contrary are advocates of more practice-centered research, with less reliance on a trial-and-error orientation to teaching, which is an elevation of craft knowledge to wisdom of practice. In the absence of this shift the legitimacy of ed schools is challenged because of their pedagogically weak technological underpinnings. Smith et al. (1980) bemoan that the problem of creating a profession of pedagogy has been dwarfed by the need for new knowledge relative to the nature and uses of pedagogy and the creation of viable teacher education programs. In his "design for a school of pedagogy," Smith charges that a crucial function for schools of education is to develop school clinics or a clinical complex for the training of personnel, almost all of which he sees as necessarily formulated in actual classroom settings. Furthermore, they point to the need to build a common point of view about the character and purposes of the professional school.

If, as pedagogical educators, we can get over our hang up with graduate studies; if we can end our love affair with ideologies and put them in proper perspective; if we can think of teaching as a noble profession and exalt teachers and the schools rather than treat them as objects of wholesale criticisms; if we can provide practitioners with workable procedures, techniques, and materials rather than with grandiose formulas for the correction of all educational ills; if we can end our preoccupation of how we are perceived in the academic community and turn our attention to how we perceive ourselves; if we can shed our masochistic attitudes and think positively about the schools, their personnel, and what a proper and adequate program of education for such personnel should be; if we can respect our own sources of empirical knowledge; if we can muster our courage to take the plight of pedagogical schools to the public with a firm conviction of what we must have to provide high quality personnel—yes, if we can do these things, there is hope that genuine professional schools of pedagogy can become a reality. (p. 14)

Hargreaves (in press) and Fullan (1993) observe of the American educational condition that teacher education is in the midst of profound change. Challenged by alternative routes to teacher certification that constitute a bypass of the conventional college or school of ed route and tempered by claims that teachers' work is craft work and therefore challenging the so-called development of the knowledge base or scientific basis for teaching, both authors acknowledge linkages between the worlds of theory and practice and the institutions of schooling and university training. Still, as Goodlad (1990) asserts,

The problem . . . is enormous. We don't have a learning profession. Teachers and teacher educators do not know enough about subject matter, they don't know enough about how to teach, and they don't know enough about how to understand and influence the conditions around them. Above all, teacher education—from initial preparation to the end of a career—is not geared toward continuous learning. (p. 108)

In short, do professors of education and expert teachers who enable collaborative teacher professional development have the conceptual capacity to put forward a knowledge base for teacher education? As many would argue, a substantial knowledge base exists already and is either underutilized or unrecognized by teacher educators in the academy or in the field. A closer look at the degree to which professors participate in the generation of new knowledge, the degree to which expert veteran teachers can engage in critical classroom inquiry, and the degree to which deans and leaders in SCDEs can create conditions to enable shifts from craft knowledge to the development of more scientific bases for teaching are discussed in subsequent sections of this chapter.

Failed Mission

At the culmination of their review of 29 SCDEs, Goodlad et al. (1990b) describe the peripheral assignment given by many academics to the place of professional schools in comprehensive institutions. "There is a good deal of space between medicine and law, at the one end, and journalism and social work at the other. Those who compare the professions readily separate the strong from the weak. Regrettably, education is usually ranked among the weakest of the weak" (p. 159). As Clifford and Guthrie (1988) observe, "Education schools have been unable either to establish the degree of academic prestige enjoyed by schools such as law and medicine or to obtain a perception of indispensability on the part of the education profession" (p. 324).

Goodlad et al. (1990b) characterize three conditions that exacerbate the perceived prestige deprivation of ed schools. One is the right of institutional passage from a time when institutions, namely those who were formerly normal schools, moved to other priorities and lowered the once substantial involvement of institutions in teacher education. Second, as previously observed, is the debilitating conditions that came out of the rising importance of research in major institutions. Third is the "low hanging cloud of prejudice toward school teaching and teacher education in both the field and by professors of education" (p. 157).

Clifford and Guthrie (1988) note that "continual attempts to compensate, supplicate, and acquire a higher status opinion on college campuses waste time and siphon energy from the more important task of preparing teachers and other professional educators in the most effective and profession-enhancing fashion possible" (p. 341). They assert that the major mission of schools of education should be "the enhancement of education for the preparation of educators, the study of the educative process, and the study of schooling as a social institution" (p. 349).

In short, schools of education, through their own self-perception and self-fulfilling actions, have invited the low status they have experienced. They have behaved as higher education's second-class citizens and have contributed to their own image problems. Thus a host of authors call for a reorientation of the ed school mission and specific strategies to enhance or make clear that mission. Cited is the clarity with which medical schools and law schools give emphasis to the practical application of research results and the high standards for preparing graduates. Through this pattern, they evolve their own professional amalgam and consider preparation a constructive element of their charge (Clifford & Guthrie, 1988). They remain qualified and engaged in the training of beginning professionals. This chapter assesses the capacity of the leadership of SCDEs to make this critical turn to a more focused mission and, to that end, a restructured school of education.

Size and Competition for Scarce Resources

Clifford and Guthrie (1988) report the size of the SCDE enterprise at the time of the publication of their text to be 1,287 teacher education programs with 645 of them in private institutions. They contrast accredited professional degree programs in business at 202, 243 engineering programs, 172 law schools, and 74 journalism and mass communication schools. "There are roughly 14 times as many ed schools as medical schools (about 127) in American higher education" (p. 39).

By any measure, teacher education is a sizable enterprise nationally, creating considerable density in many states. Goodlad et al. (1990b) observed considerable competition among types of institutions within states as to mission and jurisdiction and the competition for resources within an institution. Issues of size and resource recovery detract from the primary business of educating teachers and mitigate against the necessary resources to build capacity in a more limited but well-developed cohort of ed schools. This issue has a great impact on the capacity of heads of teacher education in their attempt to effect resource distribution both within the academy and within the state, as is observed in the subsequently reviewed data sets.

Moves Toward Restructuring

Within the past decade, reform agendas have surfaced that constitute necessary changes in the roles of teacher educators. At issue is the degree to which SCDEs can restructure themselves to meet the challenges of reform. The assistant secretary of the U.S. Department of Education's Office of Educational Research and Improvement frames the reform agenda by linking teacher education reform to school reform, identifying six ways that such reform might affect teacher education and the evolution of the profession. Accordingly, "re-formed" SCDEs will witness: (1) alignment of student standards and teacher standards; (2) teacher and teacher educator collaboration; (3) articulation and coordination across the professional continuum in teacher recruitment, preparation, licensing, induction, continuing development, and advanced certification; (4) development of a local capacity for rigorous inquiry and reflective action as the norm for continuous professional improvement; (5) creation of incentives and support for continuous professional learning and improvement, leadership, and client responsibilities; and (6) alignment of standards for licensing and advanced certification with the knowledge, skills, dispositions, and performances that contribute to the learning of a diverse student population (Robinson, 1994).

Each of these planks in the reform agenda will require commitment on the part of faculty and leaders in SCDEs, framing the direction personnel in ed schools can move this agenda. As Hargreaves (in press) observes, "Change in teacher education seems to be ubiquitous, relentless, and intensifying" (p. 17). He poses questions about the meaning of these changes, how to understand them, where they will take teacher education, and what stance teacher educators might best adopt toward them. At the heart of the reform claims is the quintessential dilemma, as Fullan (1993) notes, that "faculties of education should not be advocating things for teachers or schools that they are not capable of practicing themselves" (p. 114). As a consequence, he creates a metaphor for the "best" faculty of education, which would do the following:

1. Commit itself to producing teachers who are agents of educational and social improvement.
2. Commit itself to continuous improvement through program innovation and evaluation.
3. Value and practice exemplary teaching.
4. Engage in constant inquiry.
5. Model and develop lifelong learning among staff and students.
6. Model and develop collaboration among staff and students.
7. Be respected and engaged as a vital part of the university as a whole.
8. Form partnerships with schools and other agencies.
9. Be visible and valued internationally in a way that contributes locally and globally.
10. Work collaboratively to build regional, national, and international networks.

This is a tall order for ed school restructuring. Assessing capacity toward this direction is a central thesis of this chapter. Goodlad et al. (1990b) note

That the world of teacher education endures does not mean that it does not need changing or should not be changed . . . . As educators committed to the concept of the professional school of education and the centrality of educating educators, we become less concerned with enduring themes and more concerned with this question: Can we afford to endure them much longer? And if not, what must be changed? What endurance does suggest, of course, is that making the needed changes will be difficult, much like the progress of Sisyphus up the mount. The alternative, however, is to continue in a reactive and regressive mode until the historical weight of recurrent themes renders schools of education immovable and useless as units within institutions of higher education. (pp. 385–386)

In the face of these predominate themes of denied professional status, lack of intellectual development of the knowledge base, failed mission, constraints of size and resources, a restructured ed school appears both mandatory and inevitable. Culminating their studies of SCDEs, Goodlad and his colleagues (1990b) conclude:

We are arguing here that the reconstruction of schools of education is at least twofold: First, they must rediscover their mission as professional schools, built around the moral and ethical responsibilities of teaching and preparing to teach and all the scholarly and service activities that would be expected to support, nurture, and sustain this central purpose. (This may be the toughest of the two.) Second, they must learn well how to vie for power and resources, gain control of reward systems, form important coalition groups and negotiate successfully in their own best interests, grounded, of course, in their mission. (p. 400)

Goodlad et al. (1990a) portray a conception of the restructured school that challenges the ability of professors, clinical educators, and deans, who must mobilize the energy to direct the new ed school toward such a vision.

First, there must be a school or center of pedagogy committed solely to advancing the art and science of teaching and immersing educators in it. Second, this school or center must have its own budget, determined in negotiation at the highest level of budget approvals, and this budget must be immune to erosion by competing interests. Third, this unit must possess authority and responsibility over a student body of specified size and qualities, and over the personnel, materials, equipment, laboratories, and the like essential to the professional preparation of its members. Fourth, it must encompass the full complement of academic and clinical faculty members required for the development and renewal of a high quality curriculum. Fifth, this school or center of pedagogy must control the specification of prerequisites for admission and, in collaboration with school officials, the educational use of practice facilities. (p. 278)

Now this chapter takes a closer look at those who live in SCDEs: the education professoriate, clinical educators being invited to collaborate with ed school personnel, and those charged with providing the leadership necessary to restructure the house of teacher education. Such an agenda cannot be fashioned by one charismatic leader, the dean, alone. It must, by the sheer proportion and complexity of the challenge, be guided by and with professors and teachers; an agenda hopefully championed by the teaching profession at large and those who reside in universities outside of schools of education.

PROFESSORS IN SCDES

Descriptive data used to profile teacher education professors, deans, chairs, and school personnel who serve in roles as cooperating teachers are derived from several sources. A primary reference is the 8-year study of SCDEs as a part of the AACTE RATE studies. This initiative grew out of the need to create a more accurate data base describing the nature of programs in SCDEs and the condition of faculty service, the nature of the student population, the degree to which schools of education interact with the world of practice, and the general institutional profiles of institutions engaged in teacher education. The data typically are culled from an analysis of survey instruments administered annually, one of which is completed by a research representative who provides institutional profile data and other instruments that are randomly distributed to faculty, students, and participating school personnel.

Each year, institutions have been selected from a stratified random sample of the more than 700 member institutions of AACTE. Institutions have been sampled according to those offering only the baccalaureate degree; the baccalaureate, masters, and 6-year degree programs; and baccalaureate, masters, 6-year, and doctoral degree. Since the late 1980s, literally hundreds of education faculty members and students have been surveyed, as well as more limited samples of deans, chairs, and cooperating teachers. These data are hereafter identified by RATE number, reflecting the following foci:

RATE I	1987	Secondary Education
RATE II	1988	Humanistic Foundations
RATE III	1989	Elementary Education
RATE IV	1990	Laboratory, Clinical, Early Field, and Student Teaching Experiences
RATE V	1991	Leadership in SCDEs
RATE VI	1992	Reform in Teacher Education
RATE VII	1994	Teacher Education in Urban Institutions
RATE VIII	1995	Relationships with the World of Practice

With regard to the RATE studies of the faculty, early data analyses were prepared by Ducharme and Kluender who in 1990 published a 3-year summary of the faculty profile. The continuing RATE team added 5 more years to this analysis.

A second major source has been the Goodlad et al. study (1990b) during a 5-year period of carefully selected sampling of SCDE settings representing different types of colleges and universities that prepare teachers, including the flagship universities, major comprehensive universities, regional universities and colleges, and private liberal arts colleges, totaling 29 sites. The data were based on questionnaires filled out by thousands of prospective teachers, a broad sample of more than 1,200 faculty members, and field notes and impressions gleaned from visits to each site by two teams of experienced educational researchers, as well as case histories of the institutions. Hundreds of hours of interviews of presidents, provosts, deans, faculty members, students, and selected individuals in nearby school districts were also analyzed for this study.

Further, an in-depth analysis of the education professoriate, drawn from Wisniewski and Ducharme's (1989) edited text, has proven a useful resource, wherein the results of several data-based studies are analyzed. More recently, Ducharme (1993) has rendered a more qualitative view of the lives of education professors. This study was an intensive analysis of the work of 34 faculty members teaching full time at universities, among whom were 22 males and 12 females, 17 tenured professors, 10 tenured associate professors, and 7 untenured assistant professors. Using materials from these interviews, Ducharme described the personal lives and professional careers of teacher educators, their perceptions of their roles, and their own sense of their place in the institutional hierarchy.

The profiles rendered from these studies fall into two parts. The first part is a demographic profile of the faculty, including standard descriptive data on race and ethnicity, gender, rank, and age; followed by perceptions on faculty roles and responsibilities relative to SCDE mission, including the nature of their prior work experience; perceptions of workload, the relationship of faculty work to the world of practice, including student teaching supervision; and, finally, scholarly productivity. Second, several thematic issues also shed light on the professoriate, most notably related to definition of role, conceptions of self and career satisfaction, and goals for needed faculty professional development in light of challenges embedded in the restructuring of schools and SCDEs.

A Demographic Profile of Ed School Faculty

Common descriptions exist across research studies relative to the demographic profile of ed school faculty by race and ethnicity, gender, rank, and age, as well as projections of the demographic profile of the future professoriate from a review of those currently engaged in doctoral study.

Race and Ethnicity During the 8 years of the RATE study, the percentage of Anglo faculty has not varied considerably, holding at 91% to 93%. The population of Anglos is particularly high among secondary education professors and in the sampling of faculty members in RATE VIII; it never drops below 91%. Typically the distribution of the 8% minority assigns five percentage points to African Americans. In the Goodlad et al. (1990b) faculty study, minorities constituted 6.7% of the respondents, with percentages distributed as follows: 4.4% black, .9% Asian/Pacific Islander, .7% Hispanic, and .7% Native American.

Gender, Rank, and Age The gender of ed school professors has some considerable variability depending on the population surveyed, from a high of 70% to 72% male in the secondary and humanistic foundations area to 55% to 60% female in urban schools and in the culminating sample of RATE VIII. In the Goodlad et al. study (1990b), 40% of the respondents were female.

With regard to rank, there have been some continuing consistencies around the profile presented by Ducharme and Kluender (1990). They report a slightly higher percentage (45%) of full professors among foundations faculty than the approximate number of full professors among elementary and secondary faculty (40%). Doctoral institutions have consistently higher percentages of professors at the higher ranks. Most notably, for instance, in elementary education in doctoral institutions nearly 50% of the faculty are full professors as compared to 30% in bachelors' level institutions. The percentage of tenured faculty remains relatively constant over the years at 65% to 75%.

Relative to distribution of rank in the professoriate, men appear to dominate the rank of professor whereas women comprise the majority of those at the assistant professor rank. In the initial RATE surveys, four fifths of the faculty who held the rank of professor were males, whereas only two thirds

of the associate professors and less than half of the assistant professors were males. More women are likely to be promoted to the rank of professor concurrent with the retirement of male professors and associate professors, given that the average male professor's age is 53 and more women are in the lower professorial ranks and will be promoted in the future (RATE I, 1987, p. 26). Particularly important is the RATE VII (1994) urban sample, wherein more women were found in the ranks of the professoriate than in previous studies. It may well be the case that during the 8 years of RATE, unrelated to any particular sample, the demographic profile of women is truly shifting; this is witnessed by the highest number of females (60%) occurring in the RATE VIII (1995) sample.

Relative to perceptions of the ability to achieve promotion in rank as a result of changes in promotion standards in the 5-year period probed by RATE VI, teacher educators and deans responded consistently at almost 55% that promotion at the institutional level was either "much more or somewhat more difficult at present, and a slightly lower percentage of the respondents reported the same phenomenon at the unit level" (RATE VI, 1992, p. 13). The RATE authors observe, "Almost no one reports that promotion standards have made the ability to rise through the ranks easier than it has been in the past" (RATE VI, 1992, p. 13). Furthermore, as Goodlad et al. (1990b) observe, there is no diminution of faculty interest in promotion. In spite of the apparent differences among institutions of higher learning, "these are more of degree than kind . . . . Faculty rank—assistant/associate/and full professor—and progression up the ladder are extremely important in them all" (p. 109). Relative to the distribution of full-time faculty members by rank for all universities (The Almanac for Higher Education, 1992), 30% are full professors, 24% associate professors, 24% assistant professors, 11% instructors, and 11% other (p. 16).

The RATE data on age reflect a faculty age hovering around their early fifties, with little variation across the survey years. The distribution of full-time education faculty members by age and discipline according to The Almanac for Higher Education (1992) reflects ages 30–44 at 30%, 45–54 at 35%, and 55–64 at 30%, with the average age at 49 comparable to the average age of faculty in the humanities and engineering, as well as the all-university average of 47 years of age.

The Future Professoriate Relative to the demographic makeup of future education professors, the data show that women dominate doctoral programs in education at 57%. Thus, there is a greater proportion of women in doctoral programs than at the assistant professor rank. Relative to ethnicity, the trend line shows African Americans and Hispanics in doctoral programs at the rate of 8%, the minority trend line for most of the RATE studies. As Ducharme and Kluender (1990) observe, "the overwhelming 'maleness' of the faculty is likely to decrease, but the 'whiteness' factor will continue to grow . . . . Those concerned about the lack of correlation between the makeup of teacher education faculty and the nation's ethnic and racial makeup will find no comfort in this study" (p. 46).

Summary Data presented in the RATE studies can be compared with the newly produced AACTE "teacher education briefing book" (AACTE, 1993) wherein data from the RATE studies are compared to AACTE/NCATE joint data base collection systems (JDCS) and to the publication of "Teacher Education Pipeline III: Schools, Colleges and Departments of Education Enrollments by Race, Ethnicity, and Gender" (AACTE, 1994). These data reflect information about faculty in the field of education as contrasted to the fields of business and the arts and sciences, agriculture and home economics, engineering, the fine arts, health, humanities, natural sciences and the social sciences. In this instance, faculty in the field of education reflect a diversity higher than professors in any of these other program areas (approximately 12% minority and about 55% male). This is slightly in contrast to the percentages of minority faculty reflected in the RATE data of 8%. Relative to other comparisons of fields in postsecondary education, the age and rank distribution in education is similar to that in other fields.

With regard to compensation, it appears that education faculty may not be compensated as well as faculty in engineering and business, but they are on a par with faculty in the humanities and appear to have salaries somewhat higher than faculty in the fine arts. Relative to institutional type, faculty in private 2-year and research institutions appear to be best compensated, with faculty in public and private liberal arts institutions the least compensated.

The comprehensive summary of the ed school faculty as drawn from RATE VII (1994) suggests that the profile of teacher education faculty, regardless of their responsibilities, has remained quite stable. Teacher educators have been largely white (from 90% to 93% each year), and primarily male, with considerable variation by program affiliation. For example, almost three quarters of the foundation faculty members were male and almost one half (46%) of the elementary education faculty were female. These are middle-age faculty members with their mean ages in prior years ranging from 47 to 53 years. The considerable majority, more than 95%, have earned their doctorate degree. About two thirds of the sample tended to be tenured, and the greatest percentage were found at the level of full professor, followed in turn by those at the associate rank, with the fewest percentage (20%) at the assistant rank. They typically have been at their present institution between 12 and 15 years, and they have averaged almost 9 years of prior experience in one role or another in elementary or secondary schools. The typical faculty member in teacher education in the previous RATE was a white, middle-age male with some considerable experience in his present institution, as well as in an elementary or secondary school. Typically, he also was heavily invested in his students, engaged in a range of activities on- and off-campus, and had achieved only a modest publication record.

Throughout the 8-year history of RATE, the only significant deviation from this profile is among respondents in urban institutions (RATE VII, 1994). For instance, there is a slightly lower number of faculty at the rank of full professor and a slightly higher number at the rank of assistant professor. Here we find for the first time in RATE surveys, a majority of females in the professoriate at 55%, and a younger profile. The other departure from the cumulative profile of RATE surveys is relative to race or ethnicity. A 15% minority population was found among urban teacher educators, which exceeds by 5% any previous sample. Almost 10% of the total sample is African American, double that of any previous sample. The RATE VII (1994) studies also revealed a higher fluency among those who speak languages other than English; that is, almost 1 in 6 of the urban professors speak a language other than their native tongue.

Faculty Roles and Responsibilities

This section outlines faculty perceptions of their roles and responsibilities, including educational background and prior K–12 experience, faculty workload, relationships of the faculty to the world of practice, particularly in their role as field supervisors, and reports of faculty scholarly productivity.

Background and Prior K-12 Experience With regard to degree preparation, prior work experience, and time spent in elementary and secondary schools, the following profile emerges. Of the education professors studied in RATE across the years, more than 80% of the faculty typically and as high as 90% in one sample hold the doctoral degree. Relative to prior work experience, more than 80% of the education faculty have had primary experience in elementary and secondary schools, typically around 10 years on average. In contrast, only 27% of the faculty responding in the Goodlad et al. (1990b) study report prior elementary level experience and only 18% report experience at the secondary level. There is a degree of stability among education professors, as most professors have been in their current institution at least a dozen years, as is the case in the Goodlad et al. (1990b) study as well.

Faculty Work Load The typical work week of education professors reported in the early RATE studies was approximately 60% for teaching, 22% for service, and 15% for scholarship. Over the years, the RATE category system has expanded from teaching, service, and scholarship to a six-category system in RATE II (1988) of advising, teaching, scholarship, administration, course preparation, and community service, and then to a nine-category system in subsequent RATE studies. The eight-category system reflects the following framework for weekly distribution of faculty time: preparation for class, teaching undergraduates, research, administration, advising, committees, teaching graduate students, and in-service. As the response categories expanded, there was some reduction in the designation of hours spent specifically on teaching, only because student advising and course preparation were differentiated from teacher per se. Generally, a third of the responding faculty's time was devoted to these combined activities. Variations in faculty teaching load are accounted for largely by institutional stratification wherein teaching loads are somewhat heavier in bachelor's and master's level institutions than in doctoral level institutions (Ducharme & Kluender, 1990). Across institutional type, Howey and Zimpher (1989) observe, "One of the more lasting impressions we have from the study is the labor intensive nature of teacher preparation . . . . It was so evident on one campus that the *work ethic* became the major characteristic of our portrayal of their program" (p. 259).

Faculty Relationships to the World of Practice The view that university and college teacher educators "lack relevancy to the schools" (Ducharme & Kluender, 1990) may need reexamination. In repeated iterations of the RATE studies, faculty report a range of activities in their work with elementary and secondary schools from supervision of student teachers to consultative work with elementary and secondary school teachers. In the RATE VI (1992) studies, respondents were asked to reflect on the willingness of SCDEs to cooperate with elementary and secondary schools and vice-versa. Since the late 1980s, in general, faculty and leader respondents perceived little difference in the degree of participation of elementary and secondary schools with their ed schools. Nonetheless, 40% of the faculty and 50% of the deans clearly responded that they felt schools were interested in increased collaboration. As noted in the RATE VI (1992) studies, this could be "a function of elementary and secondary schools seeking more assistance in difficult times and of viewing prospective teachers as a means for gaining additional resources" (p. 2). When asked the degree to which faculty were solicited by elementary and secondary schools to assist in school restructuring or in teacher development efforts, less than 24% of the teacher education faculty reported a good deal or a great deal of solicitation on this count, which is further evidence that teacher education is often omitted from the reform loop.

The RATE VI (1992) inquiry focused not only on the relationship of SCDEs with schools but in particular relationships with school personnel. Most teacher educators and deans reported having sustained working relationships with urban and/or rural districts. However, less than half the deans and less than one fourth of the faculty perceive their contributions as good or effective; rather, they viewed their contributions somewhat modestly (RATE VI, 1992, p. 2).

RATE VI (1992) also probed the evolving partnership agreements between elementary and secondary schools and found them to be reciprocal in nature. Not only are those in schools and colleges of education asked to assist in the reform of elementary and secondary schools, but also individuals in these schools are often asked to assume a broadening role in the education of preservice teachers. About half of the teacher educators indicate a contribution by elementary and secondary teachers to recent changes in teacher preparation programs. Still teachers' roles tend to be characterized by "traditional cooperating teacher responsibilities, with little influence on program design or instructional innovation in the preparation of teachers" (RATE VI, 1992, p. 3). One in six teacher educators report that they are regularly involved in collaborative action research with elementary and secondary schools in spite of considerable discussion in the literature about the viability of this form of joint inquiry.

Relative to urban faculty members' work in school settings, there has been some assertion over time that many faculty members not only make little contribution to schools in urban districts, especially inner city schools, but also in fact have considerable apprehension about working in these schools. The RATE VII (1994) studies inquired into the facts of this situation and reported that although a limited number of teacher educators tend to have some apprehensions, only 4%, or 1 in 20, indicated that their reservations are considerable, with another one in five expressing a moderate amount of apprehension (RATE VII, 1994).

Rate VIII (1995) revisited the issue of the relationship of SCDEs with the world of practice as reported by methods faculty.

1. With regard to commitment of time to a variety of activities particularly relative to engagement in P–12 school related activities, considerable variability was observed. About one-third of the teacher educators report more time expended across each of the categories particularly relevant to considerably higher percentages of respondents indicating that their time increased relative to student teaching, supervision, working with P–12 schools generally, and engaging in joint research with school personnel specifically. Thus there is a trend for greater commitment of time, that time especially given over to program development and to school related activities.

2. Methods faculty were asked the degree to which they were sought out by school personnel to assist in school reform and restructuring initiatives. About a third of the faculty report that this happens occasionally and only 1 in 4 report that this happens a good or great deal of the time. The RATE studies observed that it appears that most methods faculty initiate school-related endeavors, as better than 4 in 5 teacher educators report that they regularly work with one or more P–12 schools. When estimating the number of hours they are engaged in school related functions, including supervising student teachers, teaching P–12 students, providing professional development for experienced teachers, engaging in both their own scholarly inquiry and that jointly negotiated with P–12 school personnel, assisting with school reform and restructuring and finally working in a follow up capacity with first year teachers, faculty members recorded about 27 hours a month or better than a day a week spent with in-school settings.

3. Methods faculty have taught full time in P–12 schools by virtue of their experience. A majority of the sample report that they occasionally do teach elementary and secondary youngsters while working in those schools currently.

4. One in five faculty members report that they have specific assignments in cooperatively sponsored professional development partnership for so designated schools.

5. About a third of the ed school faculty have a mailbox in a P–12 school and only about 1 in 10 have a desk or share an office space in a school setting.

6. When asked how they would characterize the responsibility of teachers in the school settings with whom they work today, almost three-fourths of the faculty report that teaching today is either more or much more difficult. Notwithstanding, one-fourth of the sample report that they are confident that they could be effective as a full time P–12 teacher today and a whopping 6 in 10 (61.8%) *very* confident of their ability to take on these responsibilities: responses that many would not expect.

Faculty members were also asked to rate their ability to assist prospective elementary and secondary teachers in a variety of activities. Faculty members were not only confident of their ability to teach in P–12 settings, but they were quite confident of their abilities to assist prospective teachers with regard to contemporary changes occurring in the schools, such as innovative practices in integrated/interdisciplinary curriculum, team teaching arrangements, site-based deicision making, cooperative learning, student portfolios, outcomes-based assessment, and technology-based learning. The responses of the faculty interviewed in RATE VIII (1995) revealed considerable confidence by methods faculty in their ability to address these topics and to assist prospective teachers to assume them effectively.

Student Teaching Supervision Relative to the amount of time spent on supervising student teachers, secondary methods faculty (RATE I, 1987) spend 90% more time supervising student teachers than do foundations faculty (RATE II, 1988). The latter group spends approximately 30% more time in scholarly activities, even though the distinctions are not reflected in lifetime publication rates (RATE II, 1988).

Relative to college-based faculty with particular responsibility for field supervision, they have similar demographic profiles to all professors in the RATE studies. They are primarily male, white, and middle-age, with the average age of 49. In the Goodlad et al. (1990b) study, female faculty were more consistently involved in supervision in higher percentages than male faculty. In fact, every statistic cited in this study reflects a greater female than male connection with the occupation of school teaching, particularly at the elementary level (p. 158). They are considerably experienced as teachers and have modest publication rates (RATE IV, 1990). Certain differences exist in academic rank and tenure that suggest that the role of supervision of student teachers may not engender the same status as professors of education generally. Whereas more than 40% of faculty in previous RATE studies hold the rank of full professor, only 24% of college-based supervisors hold that rank (RATE IV, 1990). In fact 26% of the student teacher supervisors are not full-time, tenure-track faculty. Student teaching supervisors are the only group in the RATE studies of education faculty where large percentages of individuals performing faculty functions are ineligible for tenure. This relates to the degree of self-esteem held by such individuals. Sixty-five percent of the respondents are concerned over the degree of esteem in which their roles are held (RATE IV, 1990).

Scholarly Productivity A number of years of analysis of the scholarly productivity of faculty in SCDEs (Ducharme & Agne, 1989; Guba & Clark, 1978) document that ed school faculty publish at a level of the professoriate generally. Ducharme and Kluender (1990) summarize the lifetime publication rate of ed school faculty in refered journals from none to more than 11, with the highest instances of publication in doctoral level institutions. Most of the differences in scholarly productivity reflect differences in institutional stratification as noted earlier. Clearly these variations relate to the degree to which time is provided in the institutional context for scholarship. For instance, Ducharme and Kluender (1990) observe that "the teaching mission of the bachelor's institution versus the teaching with research missions of doctoral level institutions" (p. 46) would likely explain this difference relative to institutional mission.

Goodlad et al. (1990b) confirm the propensities of ed school faculty in research institutions toward a mission of scholarship

as opposed to teaching. They describe a scenario observed while interviewing on various campuses.

There are two finalists for a position requiring a substantial commitment to the teacher education program. Both earned their doctorates at major research universities. One, the younger of the two, is fresh out of a three year post-doctoral fellowship with her major professor and has a substantial bibliography of papers published in refereed journals. She has not taught in elementary or secondary schools and is not particularly interested in teacher education, although she is well qualified academically for the course she would teach in the preparation program, and she is anxious to get on with her research career. The other has taught a subject (I varied the selection) in a secondary school (local circumstances sometimes cause me to choose elementary school teaching) for several years and taught for three years in the teacher education program during her doctoral studies. But she has a much shorter list of publications (focused primarily on teaching and teacher education). She wants the job in teacher education, is well prepared to teach the specific courses and hopes to get some time and support for scholarly work. (pp. 89–90)

They then recount several discussions about which of the two candidates current faculty would choose as their new colleagues. They note that with little hesitation faculty in the research oriented "beacon schools of education" felt that the first was clearly the choice of the two. Usually he notes after some exchange these same faculty would make room for a second kind of candidate. There would generally be some agreement with this point; however, the initial candidate remained the first choice. The discussion would invariably turn to the conditions of heavily research-oriented schools of education. They conclude, "Usually, faculty members agreed that participation in the teacher education program was good training for doctoral candidates, many of whom would teach in preparation programs, at least for a while. But most of these professors felt that working in teacher education programs was not for *their* graduate students" (p. 90). Thus they observe that whereas the institutional criteria for promotion are much the same, the balance among those criteria differs markedly by institutional type, and even between institutions of the same type.

Furthermore, as Ducharme and Kluender (1990) observe, "Men publish more frequently than women, regardless of rank, time at the institution or type of degree. Women do more field supervision and more teaching. Therefore, women may publish less because they are often asked to assume supervisory responsibilities at a disproportionate level, and they teach more" (p. 47). With respect to teacher education faculty, scholarly productivity relative to the higher ed professoriate in general reflects a sameness, including 50% in higher education and in ed schools who have published nothing.

In the Goodlad et al. (1990b) studies, most respondents placed a high value on teaching in the college or university, from 76% centrally important in the flagship public university to nearly 94% in the private liberal arts college. Essentially, however, conditions vary enormously across institutions. Goodlad et al. further observe that there has been a profound shift in the balance of institutional missions. Scholarly work has risen in preeminence at the expense of teaching and service. "Although the argument that research and teaching go hand in hand holds some water, the reality is that the box of academic work is finite: give more time and attention to scholarly activity and some must be taken from teaching and service" (p. 192).

Furthermore, Goodlad et al. (1990b) observe subtleties differentiating fields of study, kinds of publications, and awards. Recognition as a scholar is "exceedingly difficult" if one is connected with an SCDE. In the liberal arts institutions scholarship in teaching, particularly scholarship to support teaching, has always gone hand in hand. The assumption is that it is not necessarily true in the larger institutions.

Finally, there was revealed in these studies a considerable amount of bitterness, "often growing out of feelings of betrayal and entrapment and particularly shifts in status" (p. 194), from when faculty were really productive in teaching and service, which is now supplanted by new faculty more productive in research.

Summary In short the RATE studies have shown that "faculty have consistent backgrounds in demography, common experience in the lower schools, a continued commitment to field work, a publishing record similar to other higher education faculty, a commitment to teaching [and] a sense of self-satisfaction with their work" (Ducharme & Kluender, 1990, p. 48). Trend lines that can be observed about faculty role, based on the Ducharme and Kluender (1990) analysis and confirmed by other iterations of the RATE studies, include the following: (1) faculty observe a misfit between how they spend their time and how they perceive their institution would like them to spend their time, (2) scholarly productivity is unevenly distributed among institutional type, (3) there is a relatively lower scholarly productivity by gender, (4) there is a relative stability and tenure density of education faculty, and (5) pipeline data suggest that recruitment profiles by demographics will remain the same unless serious interventions occur (Ducharme & Kluender, 1990).

Themes About Conditions and Capacity of SCDE Faculty

This section characterizes several critical issues relative to faculty service, particularly in light of reform initiatives in teacher education and challenges to the professional status of the ed school wherein education professors reside. Particularly, the discussion centers on issues of role definition, conceptions of self and career satisfaction, and priorities in faculty development relative to the restructuring of ed schools.

Role Definition Relative to the preferred title of the education professor, secondary professors in RATE I (1987) were asked to identify the preferred choice. About half of those respondents preferred to be referred to as "professor" or "professor of education"; about one third prefer the title "teacher educator," whereas a smaller number would like their title attached to their discipline, such as "professor of social studies education" or "professor of educational psychology" (RATE I, 1987, p. 25). Ducharme (1993) confirms the reluctance of some education faculty to identify themselves as teacher educators, "even though they are much involved in teacher education" (p. 2). He offers a careful analysis of the problem of defining the

role of education faculty members. He notes that definitional problems are compounded by the structure of higher education and the difficulty of identifying exactly who among the faculty are teacher educators, compounded by the number and variety of people involved in teacher education.

The work of teacher education, Ducharme (1993) notes, is "done" by a wide variety of professionals—"cooperating teachers in the lower schools (elementary and secondary schools), faculty in arts and sciences who teach content courses to teacher education students, state department of education personnel who conduct workshops, and a number of others, virtually none of whom call themselves teacher educators" (p. 3).

To further compound problems of identification, there are many faculty in other related disciplines on whom teacher educators are dependent for their work, including sociology, psychology, anthropology, to name but a few of the foundational disciplines that inform teacher education. Ducharme further acknowledges that problems in the definition of the terms link to issues of status and poor reputation of education faculty, which has confounded the propensity of education faculty to self-identify.

Thus, Ducharme (1993) proposes the definition of teacher educators as "those who hold tenure line positions in teacher preparation in higher education institutions, teach beginning and advanced students in teacher education, and conduct research or engage in scholarly studies germane to teacher education" (p. 6). Still, as Wisniewski and Ducharme (1989) note,

Historically, functionally, and legally, the education professoriate is secure within the academic firmament. The preparation of teachers is as vital to society's perpetuation as any other professional preparation program. Schools, colleges, and departments of education are as much a part of the campus scene as departments of history, chemistry, or other disciplines. While their position within the academic pecking order is often questioned, professors of education enjoy all the privileges and opportunities of the academic community. Education is hardly a minor profession. Despite decades of both legitimate and unfounded criticism, the education professoriate has survived and thrived. (p. 147)

Wisniewski and Ducharme (1989) contrive a notion of the ideal education professor as

one who values and takes pride in the interrelationship among scholarship, teaching, and professional service. Such professors recognize that these activities nurture one another and cannot be separated. The ideal professor models behavior appropriate to these values and expects colleagues and students to behave similarly. The quality and reputation of colleges of education are largely determined by the degree to which we encounter this ideal in one another. (p. 144)

In their edited volume, Wisniewski and Ducharme (1989) conclude that "the study of teaching and learning and the preparation of teachers are our *raisons d'etre*. The preparation programs for other professional roles—principals, counselors, social workers, or librarians—are important but subsidiary to the prime task of preparing teachers. It is in the preparation of teachers that we fulfill or fail in our mission. Teachers in teaching are the foundation from which all other educational roles derive" (p. 149).

Conceptions of Self and Career Satisfaction Because so much has been said in review of ed schools about status issues, Ducharme and Agne (1989) revisit the issue of "second rated-ness" of professors of education, "for what purpose do we emphasize the sense of second ratedness in this discussion and whose second ratedness is it? We conjecture that the sense of second ratedness, perceived or otherwise, plays out in the lives of professors of education in a variety of ways" (p. 73).

They note that colleges of education are often assessed as second rate and therefore individuals cannot function effectively in such environments. They note that critics reason that ed school professors in fact do not take their work in higher education seriously enough, especially with regard to sustaining research and scholarship. Still others (Raths, Katz, & McAninch, 1989) argue that the complexity of the environment that exists in the academy creates different norms and cultures among fields, contrasted by a clinical mentality versus a scientific mentality. The authors note, "One of these cultures is associated with the world of the researcher, the scientist, who seeks to understand and generate new knowledge. The second has to do with the arena of the practitioner, the trainer, the developer, who applies knowledge to complex and demanding individual cases and in turn trains others to do the same" (p. 106).

Where clinicians may be prone to actions, scientist might be prone to more reflection; where clinicians are prone to more confidence, scientists are prone to more skepticism; where clinicians are prone to more pragmatism, scientists are prone to build theory; where clinicians are more empirical, relying on personal experiences, scientists are more likely to read the research of others; where clinicians believe in phenomena as complex, too complex to be lawful, scientists uncover laws to account for phenomena. What differentiates these mentalities apparently is "readiness to act, confidence, source of justifications, search for knowledge, and uses of knowledge" (Raths et al., 1989, p. 115) of scientific action. This stance blocks one's work, sense of efficacy, and reputation. As a consequence, "teacher educators must become bicultural," communicating with cultures with both mentalities and respecting the norms and cultures of both (p. 115). This rendering is provocative in its implications for ed school professors and may explain the difficulty of their assent in academia. Raths et al. (1989) note the "bicultural imperative" that exists for teacher educators to survive in an environment indifferent or even hostile to their work orientation. As Goodlad et al. (1990b) observe, "Professors in colleges and universities who engage seriously in preparing educators for the nation's school straddle two cultures: that of higher education and that of the K–12 educational system" (p. 154).

To the extent that these arguments render an explanation of uncertainty over status, they are rejoined by Giarelli (1990) in his critique of the Wisniewski and Ducharme volume, which he claims reflects this view of ed school professors. "They attend second rate institutions in pursuit of second rate education degrees in order to get second rate jobs as teachers, eventually pursuing second rate advance degrees through second rate part-time study in order to do second rate research and get a job in a second rate unit of a college or university" (p. 72). Giarelli (1990) cites no evidence to support this judgment in quality and the absence of empirical data in this argument and

concludes that social background and contrasting mentalities noted by Raths and others are not evidential and pose a lot of questions, and he simply concludes that "the data presented do not support any grand generalization about the 'second ratedness' of education faculty due to either their social backgrounds or their clinical mentalities" (p. 71). Given this confusion of terms, reliance upon perceptions, and misuse of evidence, some people say that the claims of a disproportionate dissatisfaction with the work and self-perceptions of education professors are ungrounded in the Wisniewski and Ducharme (1989) text.

Howey and Zimpher (1989) note that status arguments may emanate from the way in which teacher educators choose teaching as a career, their life in elementary and secondary schools, and continuing perceptions of their work, by others and by themselves relative to their chosen career. Ducharme (1993) draws a theory of the relative "chanciness" or randomness of career choice as reported by the faculty members he interviewed.

For some, the lives they have lived as teachers and teacher educators started out as half-chosen directions, as lukewarm alternatives to briefly considered careers in science and engineering, as casually made choices resulting in a lifetime of work. For some, the careers they chose and the lives they lived were the only ones they could see for themselves, given their economic and social status. Nearly all spoke of a sense of caring, and that teaching offered an opportunity not only to earn a living but also to contribute to society, an attitude they have carried into their present lives. Whatever the reasons, they found purpose and accomplishment in teaching. (p. 37)

Ducharme's (1993) work reflects, as other works have, the fact that entry into the teaching profession was in fact a point of entry into their professorial careers. Teacher educators report perceiving few alternatives and that their choices may have been a result in part of their social and economic class. This, readers are reminded, was certainly the proposition put forward a decade ago by Lanier and Little and their treatment of the profession in the third edition of the *Handbook of Research on Teaching* (Lanier & Little, 1986). Ducharme (1993) further observes that although teacher educators were like most teachers with respect to the manner with which they chose their careers, they were different in their subsequent decision to seek the doctorate and a position in higher education. As a matter of fact Ducharme (1993) reports that "with the routinized life and work come the lack of reward, differentiation for high performance, and the absence of personal freedom" (p. 41), which become important for teacher educators in their decision to leave teaching and go into advanced work in higher education. Ducharme (1993) also reports that most of the teacher educators whom he interviewed recorded a sense of excitement and fulfillment relative to the quality of life that generally runs through the remarks of all the interviewees. Numerous citations about the positive perspective of their work, their fondness for students, their praise for students with whom they work, capture certainly the essence of their continuing enthusiasm for their work. In contrast, there are a series of frustrations that Ducharme (1993) reports lace the lives of ed school professors. Clearly one observation has to do with the sense in which they feel powerless or impotent to influence or "vie for the soul of the student teacher" (p. 93). They feel a sense of a loss of input relative to student teachers' work with classroom teachers. They also report frustrations with their own accomplishments, for example, worrying about spending too much time teaching and not enough time publishing. They are also a cohort of faculty fraught with the lack of time to do the work they think is important, whether or not this work is viewed as important to the institution in which they reside. There are conflicting priorities set on their time. They also report differing job demands relative to gender; this has certainly been cited in the RATE studies as well. One female faculty member observed

I'm wondering if why I didn't get help in learning what it takes to succeed in higher education was because I'm a woman . . . . I'm wondering if the men that went through the program were inducted differently; you know, in terms of the informal kind of interactions that help one to succeed in a different way than I was. (Ducharme, 1993, p. 83)

Ducharme (1993) concludes that his interviews were laced with "high levels of satisfaction with life and work" (p. 101). Yet he cautions not to ignore negative perceptions, specifically those that are differentiated by gender. He concludes "the work *is* good and the faculty find immense fulfillment in it. I recall my intense enjoyment in conducting the interviews for the study and note that the enjoyment came in part from talking with individuals who were positive and affirming about their lives and their work. And these feelings were present across the various ages and in the different levels of experience within higher education" (p. 112).

Professional Development for Ed School Faculty In his review of restructuring initiatives in elementary and secondary schools, Howey (1994) makes note of several factors that emanate from a review of the very significant attributes of K–12 school restructuring initiatives. Although there are a host of attributes, easily 30 in number, that have profound implications for the way in which initial and continuing teacher preparation programs are constructed, there is also a selected set of variables that is important in looking at the future role of ed school professors and their own faculty development. These attributes, if evidenced in restructured elementary and secondary schools, will become a vital part of the professional development of ed school professors, including understanding (1) how to work effectively in shared decision-making contexts that undergird site-based management, (2) how to help teachers learn to work with other social agencies, (3) how to create learning communities and learning cohorts for students and for faculty, (4) how to use electronic and technological innovations, (5) how to use cooperative learning structures in decision making in curriculum and instruction, and (6) how to engage in team planning and multimode instruction that assumes instructional teams. These along with other profound curricular innovations will forever change the nature of faculty service in higher education and their subsequent ability to serve better K–12 schools both directly and through the preparation of future educators.

In a document prepared during the preparation of *Tomorrow's Schools of Education* (1995), a discussion guide for the Seventh Annual Meeting of the Holmes Group (in press) was prepared and several citations are linked to the nature of faculty service. These items underscore new needs for ed school faculty, including:

1. Faculty must be drawn in appropriate proportions from the many groups now established within American society so that multicultural issues and participation are focal rather than peripheral.
2. Faculty qualifications must be appropriate to those working in a graduate professional school in a research university. "Teaching for understanding" should be a qualification for faculty in Tomorrow's Schools of Education.
3. Many of the faculty must be engaged in research of nationally recognized quality, and much of that research needs to be embedded in the culture of a Professional Development School (PDS), carried out in collaboration with PDS faculty.
4. A clinical faculty recruited from among exemplary classroom teachers who also have extensive experience working with adult colleagues must be integrated into the school of education.
5. Criteria for the hiring, tenure, and promotion of faculty members in whatever category must be clearly specified and reflect differing demands and expectations (especially with regard to clinical faculty and faculty working in Professional Development Schools).
6. Faculty responsibilities will include leadership of and teaching within a student cohort in collaboration with other faculty members.
7. Close and continuing working relationships must be established by education faculty with appropriate faculty in the liberal arts and sciences and in other professional schools.
8. The structure of departments and other organizational units in the school or college of education should be examined and their aptness evaluated against other methods of cooperative working.
9. Workloads of all education faculty should be monitored and related to the changing and enlarging demands generated by fundamental changes of the ed school's mission. (pp. 12–13)

Finally, methods faculty in RATE VIII (1995) were asked whether they believed they would benefit from professional development activities designed to enable them and their colleagues in endeavors in P–12 schools. More than half the respondents indicated that a good or great deal of professional development would be in order, with another one third indicating that a moderate amount would be helpful (RATE VIII, 1995). Similarly, methods faculty were asked whether they should seek advanced certification from the National Board for Professional Teaching Standards (NBPTS) signifying that they are "an accomplished teacher" (RATE VIII, 1995, p. 19). At this time there was little support from these methods faculty for this concept. Less than one in five faculty members support the idea of faculty standing for NBPTS certification, another one fourth report they are unsure, and the remaining one fourth indicate they they are not familiar with the concept of board certification. "This last response suggests that there are a fair number of education faculty who are uninformed about a major standards setting, professional development and assessment activity in this country" (RATE VIII, 1995, p. 19).

Summary

Ducharme (1993) draws several conclusions in looking back on the findings of his interviews. He makes four observations:

1. Faculty in his study are individuals of great integrity who are committed to their work and hold respect for their col-

leagues and students, a concern for quality, and a fundamental belief in young people.

2. Faculty speak of the importance and value of their work and a sense of responsibility for their work in spite of several periods of growth and decline, intense criticism, and other questioning of their work.

3. With regard to research in the schools, there is a connectedness with elementary and secondary schools and the work that faculty do. This work in related activities "argue[s] that the faculty are knowledgeable about conditions in the schools, a necessary attribute for professional educators attempting to prepare young people to teach" (p. 109).

4. There is a broad range of activities, including conducting research in schools, that appears to be resulting in a manageable range of expectations.

5. The faculty appear to be content with their decision to choose higher education and college teaching of teachers as a career.

Although Ducharme (1993) observes he cannot generalize from these studies, "these faculty are generally actively involved in the life of higher education" (p. 110).

TEACHERS IN SCDES

Before attempting to illustrate and discuss the new conceptions of leadership roles evolving for classroom teachers within SCDEs, a brief reflection of teacher education programs and the roles that classroom teachers have played during the past century may be helpful.

During the past four decades, the most common form of practitioner involvement in teacher education programs has been through the utilization of cooperating teachers, most often experienced classroom practitioners assigned to take a student teacher under their wing for an extended period of time. The triadic relationship among classroom teacher, preservice student, and university supervisor has been the standard mode of operation in SCDEs for years and has served as a constant source of research and writing (Zimpher & Howey, 1987). Expectations have frequently clashed with reality as university supervisors, cooperating teachers, and student teachers attempted to carry out their individual roles. As well, graduate students and junior faculty have often been assigned the responsibilities of supervising preservice teachers because supervision has not been a role well suited to the college faculty career ladder (Meade, 1991). Standards used to select cooperating teachers have often been minimal, with those selected receiving token payment for their work (Zimpher & Howey, 1992). Furthermore, few institutions have offered comprehensive staff development to cooperating teachers or student teaching supervisors (Goodman, 1988).

More fundamentally, however, in spite of the obvious tensions inherent in the cooperating teacher role, new conceptions of how one learns to teach and emerging demands for school–university collaboration in initial and continuing teacher professional development are witness to a new ethic regarding teacher roles in SCDEs. Currently, there are calls to significantly alter the historical arrangements for teacher candidate supervision in SCDEs. Although not all of the teacher education reform

reports have contained the same recommendations, teacher leadership in school–university collaboration is assumed in reforms advocating postbaccalaureate teacher preparation (Clark, 1984; The Holmes Group, 1986), altering and extending undergraduate programming (Tom, 1986), streamlining the teacher preparation curriculum (Scannell, 1984; Smith, 1984), and improving conditions in schools before attending to teacher preparation.

Most notable in these reform agendas is the development of professional development schools (PDSs) as forwarded in the Holmes Group's *Tomorrow's Schools* (1987; see also Chapter 10, this volume). Such schools would recognize the interdependence of teaching and teacher education and the creation of a partnership to improve teaching and learning for both students in schools and for prospective teacher education candidates (Zimpher, 1990). An important component of the PDS vision is the notion of teachers serving as clinical faculty members, thus meeting the expectation of "career professional teacher" as outlined in *Tomorrow's Teachers* (The Holmes Group, 1986). Specific role definitions for university faculty and school-based teacher educators are critical to the successful operation of professional development school projects and the professional development activities undertaken in these sites. Particularly important is the selection of an organizing title and role definition that reflects some direct form of university affiliation for school-based teachers as teacher educators.

As Goodlad (1990) notes, teacher leaders are needed who are comfortable in both the K–12 system and in higher education, that is, teacher leaders who can provide the vision and the know-how for preparing a new breed of teachers and who can move the essential actors from dialogue to action. Without that crucial teacher leadership component, renewal in SCDEs is unlikely. What is fundamentally needed are highly competent leaders who reside where the problems primarily exist—in schools—and who can address such problems in a continuing, collective manner (Howey, 1988). Before focusing specifically on the emergence of clinical faculty in SCDEs, more traditional and recently initiated teacher leadership roles implemented prior to the current reform debate are explored to learn more about what characterizes the involvement of classroom teachers in teacher education programs.

More Traditional Roles for Teachers

This section summarizes traditional roles for teachers, including the cooperating teacher role, the emergence of mentor roles associated with entry-year or teacher induction programs that have evolved since the mid-1980s, and lead teacher roles as they have evolved in schools deeply involved in restructuring initiatives.

The Cooperating Teacher RATE data offer a profile of the long-acknowledged role of cooperating teachers in initial preparation. Relative to the demographic profile of cooperating teachers surveyed in RATE IV (1990), cooperating teachers are predominantly female (75%), white (96%), and experienced. Half of the teachers hold master's degrees and 10% hold certificates for advanced study or doctorates. Together these teachers average 16 years of teaching experience and have been in their same school about as long as professors have been in their current institution, that is, 12 years. Cooperating teachers have considerable experience supervising student teachers. The average age for cooperating teachers is 43 years (RATE IV, 1990). Cooperating teachers generally report that they are well prepared for their work with student teachers. More than 77% indicate that they are more than adequately prepared in terms of knowledge of effective teaching, classroom observation skills, holding conferences with student teachers, and providing feedback on performance. Typically, cooperating teachers receive materials and handbooks on their roles in the student teaching enterprise and they participate in some initial meetings relative to the initiation of their school-based supervision, although only one third report that they are engaged in any kind of coursework or extended formal degree programs relative to preparation for their role (RATE IV, 1990).

As with previous RATE studies, these data provide insights into the lives and views of teacher education faculty and cooperating teachers. As observed in RATE IV (1990), "the distributions of rank and tenure, the frequent use of graduate assistants and part time faculty for supervision, the lack of a feeling that the role of the college-based supervisor is valued by the institution, the consensus that teachers are not well prepared for at-risk students, these and other matters are clearly cause for concern" (p. 26). Also troubling is the institutional variation in terms of the value individuals feel is placed on their role as a supervisor, most strongly signaled in the doctoral degree granting institutions.

Many views previously held about cooperating teachers are confirmed by the RATE IV (1990) studies. The responses of cooperating teachers confirm that they are committed to their role in teacher preparation, that they view their role and their student teaching experience as the most important part of the teacher education process. Students confirm that they believe the practical experiences of observing expert teachers, receiving feedback, and practicing strategies are the most important factors in their growth. Cooperating teachers confirm this view. Although both parties are generally positive, college-based supervisors seem to be more satisfied generally with the preparation teacher candidates get in their field-based experiences and in their program as preparation for student teaching than do cooperating teachers. Finally, cooperating teachers perceive that they are consulted less by higher education colleagues than higher education believes itself to be consultative (RATE IV, 1990).

Koehler's (1984) study confirms RATE findings wherein university supervisors interviewed indicated that the cooperating teacher was the most important person in their student teaching experience. It is clear that their influence is extremely strong. Two important aspects stand out about the cooperating teacher role: the behaviors they exhibit or model and the process and content of feedback they provide to the student teacher. In a comparison of more and less effective cooperating teachers, Barnes and Edwards (1984) found that the more effective cooperating teachers provide clear and specific feedback to their student teachers, provide rationales for suggestions given, and exhibit self-reflection.

The caliber of many dedicated teachers who have served in this capacity, when considered within the structural context of where they serve, is truly remarkable. The student teaching practicum is not always a priority for either schools or universities. Cooperating teachers' roles have rarely been adjusted to accommodate for the added responsibilities of teacher education (Zeichner, 1992). Little or no recognition or compensation has been offered by the university for the teachers assuming these roles. Nonetheless, results of studies continue to reflect the degree to which teachers value opportunities to contribute to the profession by assisting with the preparation of preservice students; yet, they want recognition from the university for those contributions. Elementary education teachers as a group selected adjunct faculty status as frequently as the professional development and monetary categories in ranking their five top choices of incentives or recognition for serving as cooperating teachers (Korinek, 1989).

The shortcomings of the traditional cooperating teacher role have been well documented (Goodlad, 1990; Richardson-Koehler, 1988; Zeichner, 1990; Zimpher, 1987), including the lack of equitable treatment as true members of SCDE faculty, the competition between cooperating teachers and university supervisors in structuring the student teaching experience, and the general recognition on the part of teacher candidates and cooperating teachers that the university role in student teaching is secondary at best to that of the cooperating teacher. Professional development schools offer an opportunity to overcome some of the limitations of traditional student teacher and cooperating teacher relationships (Zeichner, 1992). The recent implementation of PDS projects has led to entire schools becoming involved in teacher preparation and induction (Abdal-Haqq, 1991), student teachers being placed in more than one school site for their practicum (Gomez & Tabachnick, 1991; Grant, Zeichner, & Gillette, 1988), cooperating teachers feeling responsible for all the university students in their building (Kroll, Rutherford, Bowyer, & Hauben, 1990), and student teachers being assigned to more than just a single individual in a school setting. As Pasch and Pugach (1990) point out when referring to a PDS initiative in Milwaukee, the intent is "that preservice students will see and value professional development and have the opportunity to participate in the process of changing schools as basic parts of their conceptions of teaching" (p. 138).

Teachers as Mentors Research on the beginning years of teaching describes the transition from preservice teacher training to becoming an experienced teacher as a period of chaos, often marked by a lack of support (Howey, 1988). New teachers struggle to master effective classroom control strategies, whereas concerns for learner growth and development are often overshadowed. In response to such concerns, entry year or induction programs for new teachers have evolved across the country. As a consequence, a number of teacher leadership roles focus specifically on emerging entry-year programs and other activities that support beginning-year teachers via mentor–inductee relationships. Whereas these designations have historically denoted a trusted guide and counselor or teacher-guardian (Galvez-Hjornevik, 1986), more contemporary designations have been derived that speak to more functional rather than "spiritual" mentor–inductee relationships. Anderson (1985) differentiates four such mentor titles and functions, including clinical mentor (an experienced classroom teacher who nurtures the growth and development of beginning teachers by systematically observing their classroom instruction and providing feedback to them on a regular basis); colleague mentor (an experienced classroom teacher who in addition to teaching full time, supports, encourages, and advises teachers as they carry out their day-to-day teaching responsibilities); consultant mentor (an experienced classroom teacher with expertise in the area of curriculum and instruction who is available to consult with beginning teachers and others as the need arises on classroom management, lesson development, and instructional strategies); and community mentor (a member of the community who on the basis of a certain specialization helps teachers develop professionally and/or personally).

Other titles given to mentor teacher roles include master teacher, teacher adviser, teacher specialist, teacher researcher-linker, and teacher consultant (Bird, 1985). An analysis of mentor titles by Borko (1986) adds colleague teacher, helping teacher, peer teacher, and support teacher. The notion of entitlement suggested in the initial Holmes report (The Holmes Group, 1986) together with the title of lead teacher employed by Carnegie (Carnegie Forum on Education, 1986) imply an ascending degree of competence and experience, willingness to assist other teachers, and a need for recognition of one's expertise, experience, and professional preparation. The purpose of reviewing this cadre of titles is not to suggest that one is more important or appropriate than another, but rather to illustrate that titles convey both meaning and function as well as a set of assumptions about roles within an organization.

A number of perspectives are represented in the literature regarding the attributes of teachers being considered for a mentoring role. Two of the selection criteria identified for mentors are particularly appropriate for the discussion of any teacher leadership role. First, there is the perspective that mentor teachers are selected because they are viewed as experts by their peers (Bird, 1985; Galvez-Hjornevik, 1986; Ward, 1986). Second, it is hoped that those selected have the ability to be reflective and analytic about their own teaching (Borko, 1986). Varah, Theune, and Parker (1986) also discuss selection criteria, underscoring two qualifications for the role as "a dedication to teaching and a willingness by the mentor to extend his or her teaching responsibility to include work with a new member of the profession" (p. 31).

In an analysis of the various criteria expected for the mentoring role, Zimpher and Reiger (1988) suggest that districts should establish selection criteria that (1) reflect a local definition of teacher expertise, including competence in the classroom and years of experience; (2) reflect evidence of commitment to the role, perhaps through a past history of professional involvement and willingness to serve and become prepared in the role; (3) reveal personal power, self-confidence, and ability to model integrity and empathy in relationships with other teachers; and (4) demonstrate expertise in the role. Similar criteria have been utilized by SCDEs in selecting teachers for new and expanded leadership roles relative to teacher education reform and school–university partnerships. Not all teachers will aspire to or ultimately be selected for these important leadership roles. To advance the development of colleagues through mentor leadership is a particular, honorific designation with considerable and uncommon responsibility (Howey & Zimpher, 1986).

For further exploration of mentoring and beginning teacher support, the reader is referred to Chapter 26 of this handbook.

Lead Teachers In Rosenholtz's (1986, 1989) studies of collaborative elementary schools, she found that "teachers from collaborative settings described their leaders as those who initiated new programs, tried new ideas, [and] motivated others to experiment and brainstorm solutions to teaching problems with those experiencing difficulty" (1986, p. 24). Relatedly, Howey and Zimpher (1986) have called for the preparation of highly selected experienced teachers for a variety of school-focused leadership roles to meet this vision of school leadership. Furthermore, for restructuring to occur in teacher preparation, similar restructuring has to occur in K–12 schools where teachers serve in leadership roles to enable beginning teacher and collegial professional development. Howey and Zimpher (1986) argue that placing uniquely trained teachers in a variety of leadership roles at the school site while maintaining instructional responsibilities will provide the credibility necessary for more effective and job-embedded professional development in contrast to staff development profiles of the past, which have been initiated largely external to the school site.

Wasley's (1989) study of teacher leadership raised important questions concerning how new leadership roles discussed in the current reform debate would be different from roles that currently exist for teachers in schools (i.e., department chairs, curriculum specialists, team leaders, and staff development trainers). The need for more time, the tension between structural changes and role changes, the lack of clarity about teacher leadership from national professional organizations, the varying support from administrators and colleagues, and the skills required to work collaboratively are but a few of the challenges that can plague these new positions. In addition, the teachers studied by Wasley wrestled with the many paradoxical questions raised by their new roles: Can there be shared leadership in hierarchical systems? How does a teacher leader deal with overt and covert colleague behaviors? Why is it that the members of a profession who advocate a love of lifelong learning have such difficulty learning from their colleagues?

The Emergence of Clinical Faculty

Historically, the clinical faculty role has consisted primarily, if not solely, of supervising student teachers. Rarely, too, has the role designation carried a title that would convey parity with their university counterparts, as witnessed by the titles summarized earlier. Little attention has been given to reconceptualizing teacher roles to reflect more reasonable spans of responsibility and more collaborative and equitable relationships in preservice programs. Today, the clinical faculty role is being interpreted more broadly to encompass bringing the experience of the school setting into the university, as well as working with the university at school sites (Cornbleth & Ellsworth, 1994).

The RATE VI (1992) study probed SCDE activity relative to the creation of alternative clinical roles for classroom teachers in the preparation of teachers. "At a time when professional development or partnership schools are becoming more common, albeit not as common as the literature might suggest, the strategy of teachers assuming broadened clinical roles in the preparation of teachers is also commonly advocated in the literature" (RATE VI, 1992, p. 4). As a consequence, leaders in SCDEs were asked the degree to which they employed experienced teachers who were at least partially released from their normal instructional responsibilities in elementary or secondary school settings to assume responsibilities beyond working with an individual preservice teacher. A little more than a third of the academic leaders indicated this to be the case. Thus, "as is the case with the partnership schools, the clinical faculty roles for school personnel appear to be expanding, but are a reality in only about one-third of the institutions in this study" (RATE VI, 1992, p. 4).

Reports of clinical educator efforts reviewed by Cornbleth and Ellsworth (1994) reveal three major forms of clinical faculty roles and relationships: (1) enhancement of the status of the traditional role of the cooperating teacher through title changes, increased preparation and perks, and role differentiation; (2) classroom teacher involvement in teaching university courses; and (3) broad classroom teacher participation in teacher education program planning, admission, and other program-related decisions.

Although it is premature to expect much in the way of formal research and current literature regarding these new roles, fugitive documentation of emerging roles is possible. Through informal surveys of institutional activity, the following designations have surfaced, reflecting degrees of responsibility as linked to differential titles. The variations across institutions and programs is significant, as is the varied degree of detail on the role definitions and functions, as the following titles and role descriptions indicate: (1) teacher-in-residence, visiting instructor, and faculty associate—roles quite similar to the traditional conception of cooperating teachers; (2) clinical supervisor and classroom teacher educator—roles with increased supervisory skills; (3) fellows, teachers-in-residence, visiting instructors, resident faculty, clinical supervisors, clinical professors, master teachers, faculty associates, clinical instructors, clinical faculty, and lead teachers—roles for those who teach or co-teach university courses for preservice teachers; and (4) clinical educators—roles designated to assume leadership in professional development school projects relative to program design and implementation, observation and feedback relative to professional preparation programs, and ongoing professional development at the school site.

Institutional Variations

Faculty Associates A faculty associate is a teacher or principal with whom university faculty work closely in the teacher education internship program. They assist the college in one or more of the following ways: (1) serving on admissions boards, (2) serving as supervisors of clinical/field experiences of the college's preservice teachers, (3) serving on the college's board of visitors or advisory council on teacher education, (4) serving as liaisons for public school–college partnerships, and/or (5) serving side by side in the delivery of methods instruction with university faculty. Faculty associates are appointed by the university and receive a token stipend (University of Tennessee, Knoxville). This term is also used in an alternative form at

Simon Fraser University (Vancouver, British Columbia) where classroom teachers are secunded for a 2-year term in which they rotate out of their K–12 classroom during this period and onto campus as temporary but full-time instructional staff. During this period, the faculty associates work with a regular faculty member in course planning. They also assume significant on-campus and site-based instructional responsibilities.

Hub Teachers The terms *hub* and *spoke* are currently being used to describe the level of involvement of classroom teachers who work in some capacity with preservice teachers. In this instance, regular faculty members, school teachers, and principals work together as peers in program development and supervision of teacher interns. Hub and spoke are specifically used to reflect direct interaction among respective staffs in collaborating schools and universities. Hub teachers are those who have assumed the mentoring role of a Master of Arts in Teaching (MAT) student for the year, along with the university liaison at the school in which the student has been assigned. Spoke teachers are teachers in that building who have made a commitment to work with the student in some capacity to fulfill specific teacher outcomes established for the students to be recommended for certification (University of Louisville).

Clinical Educator A clinical educator is a school-based teacher educator who continues a significant role in the classroom while also assuming responsibility for certain aspects of teacher development, including observation and feedback, program development and instruction relative to initial teacher preparation, entry-year support, continuing teacher professional development, shared inquiry, and school improvement. Service in this role is directly tied to professional development school projects within the college and appointment includes a 50% reduction in their school-based teaching load while serving to enable both initial teacher preparation and on-site collegial professional development (The Ohio State University, 1993).

Clinical Faculty The clinical faculty model includes a set of alternative titles for teachers working in field sites, which are educational settings where university students in education courses conduct structured observations, participate in supervised practical experiences, and conduct research. The various titles include: (1) clinical teacher who supervise observations and practicum experiences, participate in inquiry, seek advance training, and work with faculty; (2) clinical site coaches who coach student teachers, counselors, and administrative interns, and who work with faculty and supervise clinical students; (3) clinical adjunct practicing teachers who serve as lead site teachers, counselors, or administrators, and who supervise clinical students, work with faculty, and coordinate clinical experiences at the school site; and (4) clinical faculty who are university based and teach introductory methods courses, model excellent teaching, supervise clinical students, and work with faculty (University of South Carolina).

Although the literature is still limited with regard to specific illustrations of these various new roles and the research conducted on their implementation, several dissertations have focused on various aspects of professional development school projects and the clinical educator roles that have evolved as part of those projects (Hohenbrink, 1993; Karlsberger, 1993; Sherrill, 1993). To achieve a greater understanding of the daily challenges and successes experienced by teachers selected for these new leadership roles, as well as for the personal characteristics of teachers being selected for these roles, the following excerpt from a qualitative study on the implementation of clinical educator roles is provided.

Carol is an elementary teacher in a suburban school district and is a life-long resident of the state in which she resides. She attended a five-room rural elementary school and was one of the first of her family to pursue a college degree. Carol attended a branch campus for two years before moving to the main university which was located less than 100 miles from her family home. She has taught for a total of 18 years, 17 in the school district where she is currently employed.

It was after a course in action research at the university that Carol began to realize "I can do this and I can do it in my own classroom. I can attend to my own professional development." Having always been outspoken and involved in education association issues, Carol saw classroom inquiry as a way to bypass what she felt was a lack of progress in her district regarding teacher leadership and professional development. Her master's thesis explored cooperative learning as an action research intervention and the role of action research in teacher professional development.

Upon completion of the master's degree Carol became more involved in professional development teacher leadership within her district. She participated in a program taught by two university faculty members that enabled her to become a mentor for the district's entry-year program for beginning teachers. As a result of that involvement, Carol was selected to participate on university-school committees that were formed to explore the professional development school initiative. "I was on a subcommittee so I was in the loop of information. I knew professional development school projects were coming and I knew I wanted my school to be one of them. In fact, the very first time I heard about the possibility of clinical educators, I immediately placed myself in one of those positions. It was a goal I set for myself." (Sherrill, 1993, pp. 83–84)

Carol's role was multifaceted (Sherrill, 1993) and characterized by self-applied descriptive titles, such as "salesperson, school-based teacher educators, the PDS linchpin, and historian." Some of her responsibilities changed with each university quarter, whereas others remained constant throughout the year, such as writing funding grants; supervising student teachers at school sites through observations and conferencing; participating in a doctoral study on clinical educators; journaling with selected teachers at a school site; co-planning and implementing a student teacher retreat; planning, assisting, and participating in on-site PDS coursework; presenting at a national conference; assisting with the PDS project evaluation; evaluating the clinical educator role; writing conference and grant proposals; writing collaboratively for publication; and conducting collaborative inquiry on how engaging in classroom research affects teacher professional development.

Tensions that arose during the course of the initial implementation year involved communicating to parents that two half-time teachers (the release model used in this program) in the classroom would be as effective as, or more effective than, what everyone was used to. Tensions also arose around working with another professional educator to plan, deliver, and evaluate instruction for a combined classroom of fourth and fifth graders; convincing her school district of the value of being released

half time from teaching in order to work with the university and preservice students; and worrying about whether or not she was truly making a difference in her new role.

As Carol's first year in the clinical educator role drew to a close, she reflected that one of the more positive aspects of the experience was sharing her classroom with another professional. "I think there is always value in having to make your practice explicit to other people, and I have certainly had to a do that" (Sherrill, 1993, p. 96). In defining her clinical educator role at a national conference, this clinical educator stated,

A clinical educator is a person who values collaboration generally and school-university collaboration specifically and has demonstrated an ability to work toward professional development and instructional improvement; demonstrates that he/she is an expert classroom practitioner who can articulate his/her beliefs about children, teaching and learning; takes risks and works at the edge of his/her knowledge; has a strong commitment to his/her own professional development and is willing to engage in continuing preparation for the role. And by the way, they must be able to tolerate a high degree of ambiguity too. (Sherrill, 1993, p. 147)

Lessons can be learned relative to Goodlad's call for teacher leaders from the pilot clinical educator experiences described. Essentially these roles have evolved in large part because of the desire of competent teachers to seek new leadership roles and because of the needs made obvious through school–university collaboration in school improvement and professional development. Regarding the evolution of teacher leadership, Mertens and Yarger (1988) observe that

The challenge for teachers who have been promoted to the top is finding something for them to do that will distinguish them from their colleagues in such a way that their positions are respected, internally and externally. Whatever it is they do should be important, needed, and valued; require a high level of expertise; and have visibility beyond the classroom context. (p. 35)

Clearly, clinical educators who had experienced prior leadership development activities were better able to meet the challenge presented by Mertens and Yarger (1988). Barth (1991) points out that such leadership roles require special process skills of individuals forming collaborative groups. Running effective meetings, building consensus, securing and utilizing resources, developing action plans, and evaluating outcomes are skills not easily achieved. He observes that clinical educators who exhibit confidence in their ability to complete such tasks are those who have completed formal teacher leadership programs within their home school districts and in partnership with the university.

In the Sherrill study, none of the classroom teachers who served in these clinical educator roles felt as though they "fit" in any particular place. Not only does this relate to the importance of creating a supportive cohort of clinical educators, but also it represents how difficult it is to move, restructure, or change the field of education. It would be naive to think that all teachers, administrators, and university faculty would welcome new roles. It would be equally facile to think that teacher leaders could or should tackle on their own the indifference, detachment, and isolation experienced in the new roles without supportive professional development for this new role. The clinical educators survived these difficult aspects of change as their roles emerged because they were strong, committed teachers with a track record of innovation and experimentation, leadership skills built through practice, and individual support systems cultivated over time (Sherrill, 1993).

Summary

This section of the chapter reviews a host of teacher leadership roles, from the more traditional notion of teacher as cooperating teacher (with roles limited to student teacher and early field experience supervision) to clinical educator/clinical faculty roles (with formal attachment to universities and leadership responsibility not only for initial teacher preparation programs, courses, and field experiences, but also for school-based improvement and collegial continuing professional development). As with the emergence of the later roles, new issues evolve for SCDEs as these roles become more formalized.

The new issues include: (1) further clarification and experimentation with role definition; (2) probing the definition of the role and its implications for further leadership preparation; (3) programs of preparation to assist in the execution of multiple roles relative to both school improvement and professional development; (4) documented encounters through self-examination and other forms of inquiry to learn more about this new role; (5) exploring the relationship of informal professional development opportunities to formal advanced education programs for the role; (6) further refining the nature of initial teacher experiences, continuing professional development, and school improvement agendas to be influenced through these new roles; (7) how these new roles might be enabled through electronic communications systems and related technologies; and (8) responsibilities appropriately assigned to participating school districts and universities in support of these new roles.

LEADERS IN SCDES

This section summarizes the demographic profile of deans and chairs of SCDEs, as well as perceptions of role and governance from both administration and faculty. Also reviewed are issues in the SCDE deanship relative to perceptions of role and governance, mission, reform and restructuring, as well as a view of deans as leaders and the challenges of restructuring colleges of education as a function of the dean's role.

A Demographic Profile of Deans and Chairpersons

The focus of RATE V (1991) was on the leadership of department chairpersons and deans in SCDEs as taken from institutional questionnaires and a leadership questionnaire given to deans and faculty. This represents the first major national study of deans of education since the study conducted by Cyphert and Zimpher in 1980. The demographic profile of deans surveyed in RATE is described as follows by role (chairperson or dean) and by stratum (all degrees through the doctorate, baccalaureate and masters only, and baccalaureate only).

Deans in Doctoral Institutions Deans in this stratum are 88% male and 53 years old. All respondents are white. They have held their position for 5.4 years and have been faculty members for 9 years. Their annual 12-month salary is $73,800, with an additional $1,200 for consulting. They administer most of the time (79%), with 7% of their time for teaching, 6% for scholarship, and 8% for service. They are responsible for an average of 93 faculty members (with a range of 28–186). The major private research institutions in the sample reduce the mean, which is in the 125 faculty range in most institutions. Their efficacy rating is reported at 7.8 on a 10-point scale (10 = highly effective).

Deans in Masters Institutions Deans in this stratum are white males (91%, with one African-American respondent). They have been in the profession for 11 or more years. They receive a 12-month salary of $63,800, with $3,000 more from consulting. They administer 72% of their time, with 12% of the time devoted to teaching, 6% to scholarship, and 11% to service. They are responsible for an average of 50 faculty members (with a range of 6–120), and they report an efficacy rating of 7.8 on a 10-point scale.

Deans in Baccalaureate Institutions Deans in this stratum are white (only two from minority cultures) and male (64%). They are 51 years old, have held the position 6.7 years with the previous 10 years on the faculty, and earn a 12-month salary of $49,250. They add another $800 annually in consulting. Their time is spent predominantly on administrative duties (71%), then on teacher (10%), scholarship (5%), and service (14%) duties. They are responsible for an average of 29 faculty (with a range of 9–76), and they report their efficacy as 7.2 on a 10-point scale.

Chairpersons in Doctoral Institutions Chairpersons in this stratum are 85% white males; one respondent was Hispanic and two were Asian or Pacific Islander. They average slightly more than 50 years old. They have been in the role for 5.3 years and were professors for 13 years. Their annual 12-month salary is $60,250, with an additional $2,500 in consulting fees. Their time is consumed by administration (57%) and teaching (27%). They report 12% of their remaining time for scholarship and 9% for service. They are responsible for about 20 faculty. Their efficacy rating is 7.6 on a 10-point scale.

Chairpersons in Masters Institutions Chairpersons in this stratum are white (three are minorities), male (64%), and 52 years of age. They have been in the role 5.5 years, with 12 previous years in faculty rank. Their annual 12-month salary is $52,700 and they average an additional $2,100 from consulting. Administrative responsibilities consume one half of their time (52%), with lesser amounts devoted to teaching (29%), scholarship (9%), and service (10%). They are responsible for 12 faculty members. They rate themselves a 7.7 on a 10-point scale in terms of efficiency.

Chairpersons in Baccalaureate Institutions Chairpersons in this stratum are white males (64%) and 52 years old; only three respondents were from a minority culture. They have held their current position 7.6 years, with 9 previous years as a faculty member. They earn a 9-month salary of $36,800. They are on a 9-month contract. They rarely and barely augment their annual salaries, with an average of $1,000 in consulting income. They publish infrequently and spend 42% of their time on administrative duties, 46% on teaching, and 6% on scholarship and service. They are responsible for an average of eight faculty members and rate their efficacy in role as 7.5 on a 10-point scale.

In summary, the RATE profile of today's dean of education clearly reveals a cohort composed largely of white, middle-age males, with a tenure of 5–7 years, earning modest salaries from the mid-$40,000 range to the low-$70,000 range. They spend three quarters of their time executing administrative responsibilities, with less than 10% of their time devoted to scholarly activity. They find the job often to mostly satisfying, see themselves as moderately influential or at least as influential as others, and assign to themselves an efficacy rating of approximately 7.5 on a 10-point scale.

This is in many ways not unlike the profile of deans that emerged more than a decade ago (Cyphert & Zimpher, 1980).

Personally, American deans of education today are most commonly healthy and energetic, middle-aged, married, male, white, protestant, democratic, from a relatively non-college educated, lower middle class, non–professional-managerial, native-born, small town, multi-child family background.

Professionally, American deans of education today normally hold the doctorate degree, have had some training in educational administration, entered the profession through public school experiences, advanced from there to the university faculty, took the deanship directly from a position in higher education. Despite their administrative duties, they manage to engage in as much research and writing as do their professorial colleagues. They find that the deanship does constrain both their personal and professional activities, however. They do belong to several national and regional professional associations, and acknowledge the need for professorial self improvement, even though they engage in relatively little of it. (pp. 117–118)

Role and Governance

Perhaps more interesting than demographic profiles is the perception of leadership issues in SCDEs, as found in RATE V (1991), wherein faculty and administrators answered parallel questions about how they perceived the role of administrators and the extent to which administrators should assume responsibility for specific functions.

Specifically, deans and faculty were asked to compare perceptions on activities related to the faculty, programs, and external audiences in which deans and faculty essentially agree on the value of various administrative and leadership activities with some modest differences in emphasis in these activities. For instance, faculty believe that an administrator's highest priority should be to ensure conditions for faculty to perform at high levels. Administrators, however, do not rate this activity quite as high; their top priority is reported as contributing to program, curriculum, and instructional improvement. Faculty, however, did not place as much priority on program development activities. Faculty chose long-range planning and goal setting as their second priority. Administrators rated enabling high level faculty performance as their second priority. The third priority was

enabling a healthy organizational climate, which was only a fourth priority for faculty.

What emerged in these rankings is similar clusters of key activities with different emphases. It appears that faculty would prefer that administrators take a broader role in leadership relative to conditions of work, long-range planning, and then program improvement, which is the highest priority for deans. Whereas administrators are more likely to see themselves as having responsibility for personal leadership in program innovation and curriculum development, faculty expectations focus on quality of life issues such as enabling faculty to do their work while creating long-range planning agendas. These they rank as higher priorities than the dean's role in program innovation and curriculum development.

With regard to deans' and chairpersons' perceptions of governance and their influence in the governance process and changes in SCDEs, both parties were asked to describe governance mechanisms at their institutions against a framework that grew out of work of theorists and researchers who have studied organizational environments since the 1970s. These frameworks were summarized in the Howey and Zimpher (1990) chapter of the first handbook. Specifically, governance mechanisms can be characterized as collegial, bureaucratic, political, or anarchical. In collegial organizations, deans function as the first among equals in an organization of professionals; in bureaucratic organizations, operating goals are set by management and critical decisions are made by key executives at the top of the hierarchy; in the political organizational context, the dean's role is to function as a mediator; and in the anarchical organization, there are a variety of choices in dealing with and solving problems and there is no articulated strategy for decision making. Respondents from baccalaureate institutions believed that they existed predominantly in a collegial environment; master's institution respondents said they existed in a bureaucratic environment; and doctoral level respondents, like baccalaureate respondents, believed that they existed in a more collegial environment. However, in the doctoral institutions, the bureaucratic and anarchical aspects of organization are quite apparent.

When comparing deans with chairpersons, deans are more likely than chairpersons to view organizations as collegial. Chairpersons see organizations as more bureaucratic. In the same context, deans and chairpersons were asked which groups in the university they thought most important to the success of new ideas. On the whole, both types of leaders rely more heavily on trusted faculty than they do on the whole faculty, chairpersons, or their superiors. Superiors were a least preferred group and "whole faculty" and "entrusted faculty" were together more frequent choices of chairpersons, whereas deans report that they trusted chairpersons more than individual faculty or whole faculty groups. These differences in perspective may in fact be accounted for by the differences in the organizational position of deans and chairpersons. "Chairs in most instances work more directly with faculty on a day to day basis, where particularly in larger institutions deans work through and with their chairs" (RATE V, 1991, p. 32).

In summary of the RATE V observations about the administrative roles of chairpersons and deans, deans consume 70% of their time with administrative assignments whereas chairpersons report about half of their time as engaged in administration. Both deans and chairpersons report a high degree of satisfaction with their roles. Both deans and chairpersons see their role as demanding, the absence of resources making the role more difficult. On the whole deans reported that their leadership ability for enabling further programmatic improvements and faculty renewal in difficult times is good to outstanding. Leader respondents in RATE VI (1992) appear engaged in some degree of renewal effort wherein inroads are being made in several institutions on reconceptualizing core curriculum for teachers.

These abilities are largely substantiated by the faculty. As Ducharme (1993) observes, there are subtle ways in which SCDE leaders do influence what happens in their institutions. Certainly some of the faculty in his study expressed the idea that a dean's or a chairperson's influence played a significant part in their performance in research and publishing. For some, changes in leadership can make a difference in their perception about the value of scholarship. A male foundations professor expressed the idea that, even though he had been publishing regularly without much recognition, when the new dean and the chairperson came, "it made some difference. That kind of work is appreciated now."

Even though relatively positive relationships appear between deans and their faculty, little data are available to describe relationships between deans and their superiors, particularly in instances of financial support for desired changes at the college/school level. Leadership in central administration is reported as increasingly transient. Goodlad et al. (1990b) document considerable administrative instability at this level. A revolving syndrome is found from campus to campus wherein the number and tenure of administrators at the highest level from president to provost to dean rotates considerably. The job of provost or academic vice president had the highest turnover rate among the four positions reviewed in their studies, the average length of tenure in this position over 25 years was 4.7 years, the shortest of the four posts. Goodlad et al. (1990b) observed that

A dean with an average tenure of fewer than 7 years, reporting to a provost with an average tenure of fewer than 5 years, reporting to a president with an average of fewer than 8 years, creates a chain whose links are likely to be broken with greater frequency than these statistics by themselves suggest. A president in office for the past 8 years, deeply immersed in annual budget negotiations with the legislature, had just turned over internal academic responsibilities to the new provost, who had before him the promotion recommendations of the dean of education, who had just announced his resignation. (p. 130)

Yet another caution is the inability of deans to seek real relief from the heavy burdens of administrative role, and, most damagingly, those relative to teacher education. Goodlad and colleagues noted in their study that deans "delegated responsibility for teacher education to a director, who often carried the title of associate or assistant dean" (1990b, p. 135). It appears that deans have their attention diverted to other matters particularly in institutions moving toward increased attention to research. Unfortunately, the associate deans lack the authority over subdivision heads to move the teacher education program forward.

Furthermore, new faculty positions are difficult to come by. There has been little influence in the curriculum on changes through relationships with the arts and sciences. Likewise, criteria for promotion and tenure continue to be directed increasingly toward scholarship, wherein standards for promotion do not fully recognize practice-centered inquiry as a form of scholarship. Schools of education, and particularly deans, are faced with rules promulgated at the state level pertaining to teacher education, but deans report marginal influence on these policy and legal mandates. Finally, SCDEs might well be doing more with less but they are not necessarily doing better. As Goodlad (1991) observed about deans, "we are dealing with the perennial: the perennial world of principles, interests, ambition, resources, exchange, status, force, persuasion, negotiation, and compromise. In a word, *politics*" (p. 311).

Kagan's (1990) analysis of two texts, Rosenholtz's *Teachers' Workplace* (1989) and Wisniewski and Ducharme's "The Professors of Teaching" (1990) provides yet another provocative perspective on issues of governance and organizational context. In her analysis, Kagan (1990) summarizes Rosenholtz's thesis that teachers' attitudes and behaviors are a direct result of the social organization of their workplace in which "*low consensus schools,* where the many uncertainties in classroom teaching lead to isolation and pluralism, and *high consensus schools,* wherein teachers solve problems collaboratively and, in the process, define common goals and desirable teaching methods" (p. 46). Kagan (1990) contrasts this condition with the education faculty as described in the Wisniewski and Ducharme (1990) text in which they are described as "a highly fragmented, pluralistic group, strikingly similar to the teachers Rosenholtz (1989) describes in low consensus schools" (p. 46). Kagan goes on to note that although some degree of pluralism is inherent in the professoriate, ed school professors belong to a field that may itself be extremely ill structured. Thus, Kagan (1990) resolves "teacher educators, like K–12 teachers in low consensus schools, may be driven by the uncertainties of their work to the same coping mechanisms: isolation and self-defensiveness. The task of restructuring teacher education appears to entail transforming colleges of education into high consensus schools" (p. 46).

Kagan observes that the "connecting theme" of these two studies is the fragmented and ambiguous identity of professors of education. Others have noted as well the "collection of tensions," as Kagan (1990) refers to them, that affect schools of education—tension between the academic ethos of theory and research and the practice-oriented ethos of public schools; and tension between the lower-middle class, pragmatic socioeconomic background of most education faculty and the upper-middle class, theoretically oriented faculty in other colleges on a university campus (p. 48). She cites numerous studies to reflect these contrasting tensions. Thus she concludes, these texts share a single moral.

If we are to transform low consensus schools (including colleges of education) into places where 'virtuoso soloists arrange themselves into an ensemble' (Rosenholtz, 1989, p. 221), we may need to help policy makers (e.g., deans, college presidents, boards of regents) understand that workplace conditions promote consensus, collaboration, and certainty about a technical culture. Deans, like school principals, may have to relinquish most policy making decisions to faculty, who in the process of comparing and developing strategies, will define a common technical culture. (Kagan, 1990, p. 48)

She poses several strategies that if employed by deans might lead to a reconciled culture as follows: (1) effect genuine consensus among ed school faculty about subjective definitions of teaching and learning; (2) serve as instructional leaders in establishing norms of collegiality; (3) use some programs in preservice teacher education, which consists of sequences of courses and field experiences to create a common technical culture of a small group; and (4) stimulate applied research on the processes of teacher education wherein research can be a powerful vehicle for promoting professional growth, cohesiveness, and a feeling of effectiveness among teacher educators. To embrace research in this manner will resolve the collective identity crisis of ed school professors. Kagan (1990) concludes, "Perhaps it will also be a sign that teacher educators no longer perceive the ambiguities and uncertainties of their profession as fearful battlegrounds on which to defend their personal beliefs and practices" (p. 51). Central to the Kagan thesis, though, is the critical leadership role of deans.

The Reconceptualizing Mission

In the introductory section of this chapter, a summary of issues confronting SCDEs focuses on the need to reconceptualize mission. This position is confirmed by 15 years of experience in the deanship, in which Gardner (1992) observes that the major dilemma faced by ed school deans and faculties is how to resolve the confusion over mission. Such failure, he posits, weakens the authority and position of schools of education. "University administrators find ed schools harder to comprehend than other professional schools; they appear untidy in their organization, overextended in their programs and much too diverse (even schizoid) in their mission" (p. 357). This confusion over mission has resulted as ed schools have moved to prepare a broader range of school service people and moved into business training and a host of other program imperatives.

Goodlad et al. (1990b) confirm that statements of mission were rarely well articulated by deans, and, furthermore, when they were made they were rarely congruent with those of their faculty members. "The relationship between the two was often remote or even nonexistent" (p. 136). Articulation with central administration was not regularly evident either. "Rarely did deans successfully line up support of the president and provost for the joint pursuit of a major new thrust or for the resolution of one or more of the persistent problems we so frequently heard about" (p. 136).

Goodlad et al. (1990b) caution that most of the SCDEs in his sample had come through bumpy times in the 1970s and 1980s, bumpier times, for the most part, than were experienced by institutions as a whole.

There is a sense of crippling bitterness among the faculty and distrust on the part of education deans who remain isolated and aloof from their presidents and provosts. Although there was a lot of agitation for reform in schooling and teacher education, it was unclear on the part of central administrators, and deans and faculty for that matter, as to what schools of education could do about it or should do about it. This puzzlement is in direct proportion to the size and research orientation of the university. There seems to be a paucity of comprehensive planning in most of the SCDEs regarding growing enrollments, the reality or prospect of new positions, and pending retirements in an aging faculty—despite the eagerness of presidents and provosts to receive such plans. Interestingly the personal hopes and aspirations of ed school deans were in non-educator preparation areas, those least understood by central administrators and their colleagues in the arts and sciences including doctorates in comparative ed, leaps forward in ed tech, collaborative R&D abroad, and aggressive external research funds seeking. Rarely did they include a fundamental rethinking of teacher education or, for example, the establishment of strong links with surrounding school districts to establish professional development or 'teaching schools.' (pp. 134–135)

Gardner (1992) poses a series of questions about mission that question the viability of shifts in mission away from a focus on teaching, learning, and schooling as follows: (1) How should this change in definition of education be viewed in ed schools? (2) How much of an ed school's time, attention, and budget should these new needs receive? (3) Does training of "education managers" for businesses constitute a legitimate new market? (4) By mounting new programs in areas that do not serve the schools, are we denigrating our teacher education mission? (5) By moving aggressively in these directions, are we making the mission problem worse? (p. 60). Again, shifts in clientele signal distancing the ed school from its primary clients—teachers—and thus contributing to confusion on the part of central administrators as to the legitimate role of ed schools in the academic constellation.

The problem of achieving a focused mission is exacerbated as well by consistent messages from central administrations of all sizes relative to an emphasis on research. This research focus rarely focuses on clients or constituents, but, rather, on productivity. Here, too, confusion abounds in that messages of increased emphasis on research are not followed with any incentives, such as added resources or reduced teaching loads. In the Goodlad et al. studies (1990b), the research team was impressed by the conscientious attention by ed schools to students and teaching and to program revision. In contrast, administrative attention to research created anxiety and tension and "there was no sign of a helpful light at the end of the tunnel" (p. 136). In short "business was still being transacted as usual, but leadership appeared not to be transforming a potentially troublesome set of circumstances" (p. 136).

Goodlad et al. (1990b) bemoan the fact that in flagship and major research universities, faculty march to a different drummer.

An alternative drummer has largely replaced the president, provost, or dean, whatever his or her leadership style. This drummer is research. Its preeminent symbol is a grant; and its metaphors are couched in the language of personal recognition, power and independence from the institution and even colleagues (because the drumbeat is more compelling than colleagueship). It speaks scarcely at all to service and program development. The dean, meanwhile, cheers the dance on, massages the dancers, and blocks out the dissidence of other drumbeats. (p. 140)

There are, of course, variations on this theme. For instance, Goodlad et al. (1990b) observe from their sample that professors of education in all types of institutions are more deeply committed in spirit to teaching, teacher education, service, and the cause of improving schools than that often reflected in the observations drawn exclusively from faculty in schools of education at comprehensive research institutions. Still a central concern for ed school deans continues to be the dilemma of achieving a focused mission, particularly where ed school mission is at odds with university mission. In textbook fashion, Gardner (1992) forwards a dean's "to-do" list for achieving a well-articulated mission: (1) educating faculty and central administration to a more focused mission for schools of ed, (2) compiling data that will make the case in terms of the condition of or the doing of teacher education, (3) building development funds to enable outside resources where inside resources are declining, and (4) hiring faculty for this new mission.

Reform and Restructuring

Life in higher education during the balance of the 1990s will be something like it was during the great depression years—demands for retrenchment, angry confrontations between faculty and administrators, legislative demands for colleges to be more accountable. Faculty morale will decline, and administrators will be blamed for all kinds of unfortunate occurrences. In addition, control by central administration over the budget and decision making functions will continue to grow. Deans and other middle managers may be unable to maintain their ability to be influential as representatives of their faculties in the face of the recession problems and the organizational changes that lie ahead. All professional schools, but ed schools especially, will be called upon to demonstrate a heightened relevance to society. The clarion cry will be raised for organizational and structural change in ed schools at the same time that social and economic constraints are to increase. (Gardner, 1992, pp. 364–365)

Beyond Gardner's admonition, the challenges to deans as leaders of reform is enjoined as well in a recent RATE study report. "While SCDEs report progress on their programs, they have not collectively demonstrated the scientific advancements, moral vision, or political muscle necessary to assume a major leadership role in the plethora of reform efforts that dot the landscape of elementary and secondary schools today" (RATE VI, 1992, p. 28). Findings from both RATE V (1991) and RATE VI (1992) review deans' perspectives on their leadership in educational reform. Across the three institutional types, there was support for rigorous admissions and exit standards and recruitment of quality students into SCDE programs. Only in the doctoral institutions was there, in the top three reforms, support for formal partnerships with schools and more programs of research. The least support for deans and chairpersons came for extended preparation programs, grouping students into cohorts, and working more closely with liberal arts faculty (RATE V, 1991). Deans were asked to compare reforms reported out 3 years ago in the RATE studies and those reported in RATE V (1991). By far the most progress in the reports of deans is the 22% increase in activity in creating formal partnerships with schools and a 20% increase in efforts toward more rigorous admission standards.

Lawson (1990) sees increasing external service and collaboration as integral to the reform agendas for K–12 schools and SCDEs, citing a growing recognition of a need for college and university faculty to offer more service to external clientele. Most reform proposals he reviews call for increases in collaboration with K–12 schools. However, faculty service has been constrained by (1) more dominant models of theory and research; (2) the ethos of research universities in their quest for prestige, again mostly emanating around research productivity; (3) the recruitment of faculty who identify with these prestige factors; (4) reward systems as nested in universities that discourage service; and (5) missions of SCDEs that do not acknowledge the need for this kind of service. Still deans seem to view themselves as influential in the larger university context and report that the recent reform era in education has resulted in a more favorable view of SCDEs within the university than had previously been held by their central administration. Clearly of the externally influenced reform agendas, the most challenging for deans and faculty alike is working with schools, particularly with those where the challenges are the greatest.

Deans as Leaders

Goodlad et al. (1990b) observe that

The promise embedded in these data depends for its realization on unusually charismatic, transforming leaders capable of sensing the nature of the moral imperatives stemming from responsibilities outside of the university and reducing ambiguity, increasing predictability, and providing direction on the inside. It will help if these leaders are seen as being able to walk on water. (p. 142)

Geiger (1989) reflects on choices that confront deans relative to their leadership in SCDEs and suggests a collaborative approach, urging deans to cultivate input and craft harmony within and among the school, the university, and the organized teaching profession. He argues that collaboration offers the best opportunity to enhance recent successes and at the same time focus resources on correcting failure. He revisits the models of organizational administration visited earlier in RATE V (1991) and cautions that deans often have been called upon "to do more with less." He notes that deans have responded to these demands by overextending themselves and their faculties as well as their resources. The result, Geiger (1989) notes, has inevitably been disappointment and damage to the reputation of schools of education within the university and the larger educational community. Deans will also need to lead by learning when to 'say no' to university presidents and outside agencies when acquiescence would inhibit or prohibit the maintenance of successes and the overcoming of failures. Consequently, education deans will need to articulate clearly their vision of what teacher education can be, the reasons why on some occasions they must say no, and the significance of their role as a collaborative leader.

This observation brings us full circle to the Howey and Zimpher (1990) chapter that observed that leadership must be a shared activity involving deans, administrators, and faculty. Changes in organization involving the collectivity are possible, and deans are pivotal in bringing about these changes. As Gardner (1992) observes, "Ed schools are not rational, bureaucratic places capable of being led hierarchical; rather they are open systems with many layers of control and considerable autonomy for faculty" (p. 365). Gardner reminds teacher educators that the deanship must be seen as a key interactive role in a fluid and complex organization. Repeatedly Goodlad calls for a form of *transformational* leadership. As Goodlad et al. (1990a) define it, a leadership that attempts to draw out and improve on the best in its followers and, in the process, to transform the institution, best fits both the theological and religious traditions of the university and the emerging need for it to be a model of democracy.

Huffman-Joley (1992) agrees, observing that expectations for leaders in schools of education are changing away from traditional hierarchical models toward a transformation of organizational climate into teamwork and shared decision making, which have become watch words for organizational climate and change. Thus, deans of education must find new structures and strategies for enhancing the work of faculty, particularly relevant to teaching and scholarship, through dialogue and demonstration of teaching and learning. Huffman uses principals and findings from cognitive learning theorists who argue that knowledge is constructed, not transmitted, and that active engagement of learners depends on their own learning through team and group interaction in a climate and an environment where teaching and learning (and scholarship) are intertwined. This would be a compatible vision with that of others who argue that the dean's role is more interactive, or transformational, requiring new forms of leadership in teacher education to change the culture and the role of higher education and simultaneously link these changes to the change in culture of public schools. One must acknowledge the simultaneous renewal proposed by the Goodlad (1990) reforms. Huffman-Joley (1992) also reiterates that deans play a critical role in building vision among constituent groups about the college and the school and what they should look like in the future. Again she invokes cognitive learning principles to draw on the leader's role in helping faculty construct and work out their own meaning of change and how it relates to them. The problem of meaning is central to making sense of educational change and, consequently, encouraging others to embrace change.

This view of leadership is confirmed by Howey (1990) as he argues that it is a lack of *collective*, not individual, commitment to program change that severely constrains what might be in teacher education. Strong leadership is needed to achieve collective action. A fundamental principle in organizational change is to achieve a reasonable degree of consonance between individual and organizational goals. In his vision of needed leadership and new networks, Howey envisions the reciprocal benefits of faculty and leaders working interactively to encourage more teamwork not only within institutions but across institutions (Howey, 1990).

Networking, particularly across institutions, could be a leadership strategy that deans and others could employ in enabling the reform agenda in teacher education. At the heart of such networking, Howey observes, is a fundamental principle of leadership—identifying good people and then distributing power while maintaining reasonable focus. Whereas his charge is to broaden participation and create a more networked or teamed orientation to an agenda, particularly in reference to the Holmes agenda, such recommendations have viability for

leadership in SCDEs. As such, Howey (1990) views leadership the following way:

They [leaders] can support the conditions for change. They can unleash new ideas and talents, especially in groups (networks), but they cannot control the change process. Leadership to affect major changes exists (although more reflection about strategies is in order). Spread across campuses and school, the talent and energy to move forward with a little more joy and a lot more progress abound. (p. 9)

As Matczynski, Lasley, and Haberman observe (1989)

The deanship offers great challenges and opportunities. As someone in the middle, the dean must learn how to work with a range of interests, individuals and groups . . . that is, is the dean primarily a representative of central administration or is he or she the representative of the faculty . . . . Deans constantly feel the push and pull of all those individuals they report to and are responsible for in the academic setting. Individuals who assume the role of dean must be able to negotiate with a diverse set of constituents and must, as a consequence, possess consummate communication skills in order to be successful. (p. 12)

Thus, Goodlad et al. (1990b) observe that in view of the markedly longer tenure of presidents than provosts, "it is the canny dean who keeps the president fully informed as to visions and plans and who greets his or her successor early and warmly. It is the wise dean who builds the mission of the programs for which he or she is responsible into the fabric of the institution" (pp. 131–132).

Leadership in restructuring ultimately lies in leveraging faculty support in determining ed school prerequisites and in achieving support from school settings and practicing teaching in "revisioning" a restructured ed school. Goodlad et al. (1990b) observes that the farther down in a university's organizational structure teacher education finds itself, the less chance it has to obtain the conditions necessary to a healthy, dynamic existence.

In reference to an earlier observation of a drumbeat of research,

If faculty members' time and energies are to be mobilized for renewal, they must hear an alternative drumbeat and subsequently see progress toward the promises of the drumbeat: An elevation of teacher education to a central place in institutional mission, resources allocated via a formula that recognizes the high time and energy demands of a first rate teacher education program, an equitable share of scholarship funds and support services, additional funds for creating "teaching" schools and collaborating school districts, and faculty rewards geared to the nature of the required work. Unless it is clear that the work of planning and renewal are to be rewarded, there is little likelihood that it will begin. (Goodlad et al., 1990b, p. 195)

It is the dean, then, the "one in the middle," who must mediate competing interests and visions by instilling collective vision toward goals that bring recognition and success to the ed school.

CONCLUSION

This chapter provides a review of research focusing on those who serve in schools, colleges, and departments of education. Acknowledging that primary inhabitants are professors, it explores the movement by some SCDEs to establish closer link-ages with practitioners wherein teachers from local school set-tings are also attached to SCDEs as clinical faculty members. This distinction differs from previous designations of classroom teachers as cooperating teachers in that their supervisory re-sponsibilities are extended to include direct involvement in on-campus program development and delivery, as well as situated professional development for prospective and colleague teach-ers. Furthermore, the chapter characterizes research conducted on those who hold formal leadership roles in SCDEs, namely deans and chairpersons. Whereas larger SCDEs have chairper-sons who actually report to deans of education, the intent was to characterize primarily the leadership role of the head of the SCDE, be that designation chairperson or dean.

Although it is premature to designate a particular demo-graphic profile of those who would ultimately serve in emerging clinical faculty roles, it is certainly clear that faculty and deans reflect a cohort that is largely white (from 90% to 93%). There is little variation across institutional type, although there is a higher proportion of diversity (15% as opposed to 8%) in institu-tions located in urban settings. Deans reflect the same limited diversity. Whereas the majority of all professors (more than 60%) and deans (85%) are male, there is an emerging majority of females at the assistant professor rank and moving more quickly through the ranks in urban settings. Faculty are highly degreed, tenured, and ranked, and have served in their current institution for generally more than a dozen years. As would be expected, deans and faculty are generally middle-age, and deans have served in their current positions for about 5–7 years.

Faculty are generally characterized as extremely hard work-ing, serving well their instructional and advisory obligations while also generally committed to working with schools, if not always directly in field-based teacher education activity. They publish regularly and consider their work with the world of practice interesting both intellectually, as evidenced in their writings, and professionally. There is, however, disproportion-ate involvement in field-related activities by female faculty members, disproportionate research productivity among males, and considerable disproportion across both males and females by field; that is, several fields remain heavily dominated by one sex or the other (females in elementary education, males in secondary and humanistic foundations). Attitudinally, faculty report that they like their work, are committed to improved professional practice generally both in schools and in the acad-emy, and generally feel underappreciated for their efforts. This conclusion is attributed to a university reward system that ap-pears to favor traditional academic work in the face of a profes-sional agenda that encourages a kind of field involvement often not accountable to these traditional reward system measures.

Observations about the "role in the middle" are less easily concluded. A great deal is known, more than is needed, about the traditional role of the cooperating teacher. Many research syntheses, some noted earlier in the chapter, chronicle the work of teachers who have served over the years as field supervisors for early and culminating field experiences. Their struggle to clarify their responsibilities and negotiate parity in the assess-ment process, the negative and positive effects they appear to have on beginning teacher socialization, and their general commitment to fulfilling this role even in the absence of clearly

articulated relationships with faculty in SCDEs or adequate reim-bursement or acknowledgment for their services is known.

Much less is known about the emerging role of clinical educators, by whatever title, except to say in general that there is evidence that an increasing number of SCDEs are identifying roles and responsibilities for expert classroom teachers that far exceed traditional notions of field service. In large part, the curricular changes that signal this redefinition of role evolve out of the larger effort to unify the profession and particularly the gap that exists between the professoriate and the academy with that of teachers and others in elementary and secondary schools. An obvious manifestation of this more authentic collab-oration of professors and teachers is the recent creation of professional development schools, or teaching schools, fash-ioned by the national Holmes Group and other reform-minded groups. Teachers' roles in these entities will demand more comprehensive functioning, including program design, deliv-ery, and supervision among teacher candidates, as well as peer professional development toward more effective school re-newal. The full potential of these new teacher leadership roles has only begun to be uncovered.

Regarding deans, it is clear that their roles are becoming increasingly complex. Much of the introductory section of this chapter is devoted to an analysis of past and future directions of SCDEs. Past problems have revolved around low self-concept and status deprivation, failure to develop a significant knowl-edge base for teacher education, underfunding, and lack of recognition of teacher education as central to the role and function of universities. Although today's functions have not deviated much from these dilemmas, there is a comprehensive reform agenda evoked from several sources that guides the way toward restructuring the ed school. Much of the early section of this chapter, and the discussion around research on the deanship, provides a prescription for reform around which a number of important research questions can be posed for further study.

Restructuring arguments hinges on the recreation of colleges and schools of education as more identifiably "professional," that is, linked more fundamentally to the work and needs of practitioners. Does the background, preparation, and disposi-tion of faculty reflect an affinity toward working more closely and more effectively with school colleagues? Faculty attitudes toward a more unified profession need to be explored more fully and, concurrently, the disposition of expert teachers to-ward enjoining this agenda as clinical faculty. What are the implications, which are myriad, of teachers assuming clinical faculty roles? How are they selected, prepared, and released for service, and what are the implications for their service not only within the university, but also in the schools within which they serve? How do teachers maintain credibility with their school colleagues and also achieve parity with their faculty colleagues? What are the implications for reward systems over-haul, both in the academy and in schools?

Who will provide leadership for this more professionally focused agenda? Are today's deans and chairpersons so dis-posed? How do they view their leadership role in achieving a shared agenda for the ed school of the future? Do they have the capacity to assist in unifying the varying demands of an ed school for becoming more functionally successful in the academy and more effective in the larger profession? On what bases should the efficacy of deans and faculty be judged in the future? Can ed schools be held accountable for the success or failure of school renewal and renewed professional development agendas? What will be the measures of SCDE accountability and who will judge the success or failure of the ed school—clients (practitioners, students, parents, taxpayers), superiors (provosts and presidents), or peers (again, the profession)?

An assessment of research on faculty and deans reveals a relatively rich snapshot by demography and background, with some considerable exploration of attitudes of faculty through recently conducted qualitative studies. The research on clinical faculty is essentially nonexistent, or at best "in press," because the role is only recently emerging. Research on the deanship is plotted around several survey studies that have provided an array of demographic and role definition data and perceptions of responsibilities, dispositions toward reform, and sense of efficacy. As well, there are only minimal data on the interactions between deans and faculty. Next steps in expanding the research agenda around the roles of those who contribute to

SCDEs could focus on the questions posed earlier in more qualitative formats such as single and multiple case studies across institutional type, especially as the ed school continues to be deeply engaged in its own restructuring. Subsequent research should focus less on the individual in environment and more on the interactions of all parties in the transformation of SCDEs to more profession-oriented entities, especially focusing on the interaction of traditional academic residents with their practitioner colleagues. Explorations should also focus on the changing environment of higher education generally, as a number of reform-oriented initiatives are challenging current orientations in the academy, including continuous quality agendas, the reinvention of the service agenda of land grant institutions, and efforts to introduce measures of accountability and performance assessment into higher education evaluation. Essentially these agendas suggest a closer relationship between the role of academic units and the constituencies they serve. As SCDEs pursue a more profession-oriented status, they should be as well suited to "measure up" to such a standard as any other academic unit on the university campus.

References

Abdal-Haqq, I. (1991). *Professional development schools and educational reform: Concepts and concerns.* Washington, DC: American Association of Colleges for Teacher Education.

American Association of Colleges for Teacher Education (AACTE). (1993). *Briefing book.* Washington, DC: Author.

American Association of Colleges for Teacher Education (AACTE). (1994). *Teacher education pipeline III: Schools, colleges, and departments of education enrollments by race, ethnicity, and gender.* Washington, DC: Author.

Anderson, E. M. (1985). *Proposal for the development of a comprehensive program of mentoring beginning teachers.* Unpublished manuscript, University of Minnesota, College of Education.

Barnes, S., & Edwards, S. (1984). *Effective student teaching experience: A qualitative-quantitative study.* (Report No. 9060). Austin: Research and Development Center for Teacher Education, University of Texas.

Barth, R. S. (1991). Restructuring schools: Some questions for teacher and principals. *Phi Delta Kappan, 73*(2), 123–128.

Bird, T. (1985). *From teacher to leader: Training and support for mentor teachers, master teachers, and teacher advisors.* Unpublished manuscript, The Far West Regional Educational Laboratory, San Francisco.

Borko, H. (1986). Clinical teacher education: The induction years. In J. V. Hoffman & S. A. Edwards (Eds.), *Reality and reform in clinical teacher education* (pp. 45–63). New York: Random House.

Carnegie Forum on Education and the Economy's Task Force on Teaching as a Profession. (1986). *A nation prepared: Teachers for the 21st century.* Washington, DC: Author.

The Chronicle of Higher Education, Inc. (1992). *The Almanac for higher education.* Washington, DC: Author.

Clark, D. L. (1984). Transforming the structure for the professional preparation of teachers. In J. D. Raths & L. G. Katz (Eds.), *Advances in teacher education* (Vol. 2, pp. 1–20). Norwood, NJ: Ablex.

Clifford, G. J., & Guthrie, J. W. (1988). *Ed school: A brief for professional education.* Chicago: The University of Chicago Press.

Cornbleth, C., & Ellsworth, J. (1994). Clinical faculty in teaching education: Roles, relationships, and careers. In K. Howey & N. Zimpher (Eds.), *Informing faculty development for teacher educators* (pp. 213–248). Norwood, NJ: Ablex.

Cyphert, F., & Zimpher, N. (1980). The education deanship: What is the dean? In D. Griffiths & D. McCarty (Eds.), *The dilemma of the deanship* (pp. 91–122).

Ducharme, E. R. (1993). *The lives of teacher educators.* New York: Teachers College Press.

Ducharme, E. R., & Agne, R. M. (1989). Professors of education: Uneasy residents of academe. In R. Wisniewski & E. R. Ducharme (Eds.), *The professors of teaching: An inquiry* (pp. 67–86). Albany: State University of New York Press.

Ducharme, E. R., & Kluender, M. M. (1990). The RATE study: The faculty. *Journal of Teacher Education, 41*(4), 45–49.

Fullan, M. (1993). *Change forces: Probing the depths of educational reform.* New York: The Falmer Press.

Galvez-Hjornevik, C. (1986). Mentoring among teachers: A review of the literature. *Journal of Teacher Education, 37*(1), 6–11.

Gardner, W. E. (1992). Once a dean: Some reflections. *Journal of Teacher Education, 43*(5), 357–366.

Geiger, J. (1989). Education deans as collaborative leaders. *Journal of Teacher Education, 40*(6), 2–4.

Giarelli, J. M. (1990). The professors of teaching: An inquiry. *Journal of Teacher Education, 41*(4), 71–75.

Gomez, M., & Tabachnick, B. R. (1991, April). *Preparing preservice teachers to teach diverse learners.* Paper presented at the annual meeting of the American Educational Research Association, Chicago.

Goodlad, J. (1990). *Teachers for our nation's schools.* San Francisco: Jossey-Bass.

Goodlad, J. I. (1991). A study of the education of educators: One year later. *Phi Delta Kappan, 73*(4), 311–316.

Goodlad, J., Soder, R., & Sirotnik, K. A. (Eds.). (1990a). *The moral dimensions of teaching.* San Francisco, CA: Jossey-Bass.

Goodlad, J., Soder, R., & Sirotnik, K. A. (Eds.). (1990b). *Places where teachers are taught.* San Francisco, CA: Jossey-Bass.

Goodman, J. (1988). University culture and the problem of reforming field experiences in teacher education. *Journal of Teacher Education, 39*(5), 45–53.

Grant, C., Zeichner, K., & Gillette, M. (1988). *Preparing teachers to teacher diverse students in multicultural classrooms (final report).*

Washington, DC: U.S. Department of Education, Office of Educational Research and Improvement.

Griffiths, D., & McCarty, D. (1980). From here to there. In D. Griffiths & D. McCarty (Eds.), *The dilemma of the deanship* (pp. 285–294). Danville, IL: Interstate Printers and Publishers.

Guba, E., & Clark, D. (1978). Leads of R & D productivity in schools of education. *Educational Researcher, 7*(5), 3–9.

Hargreaves, A. (in press). Towards a social geography of teacher education. In N. K. Shimahara & I. Z. Howlowinsky (Eds.), *Teacher education in industrialized nations.* New York: Garland.

Hohenbrink, J. (1993). *The influence of collaboratively teaching: University and school.* Unpublished manuscript, The Ohio State University, Columbus.

The Holmes Group. (1986). *Tomorrow's teachers: A report of the Holmes Group.* East Lansing, MI: Author.

The Holmes Group. (1987). *Tomorrow's schools: Principles for the design of professional development schools.* East Lansing, MI: Author.

The Holmes Group. (1995). *Tomorrow's schools of education.* East Lansing, MI: Author.

Howey, K. R. (1988). Why teacher leadership? *Journal of Teacher Education, 39*(1), 28–31.

Howey, K. R. (1990). Changes in teacher education: Needed leadership and new networks. *Journal of Teacher Education, 41*(1), 3–9.

Howey, K. R. (1992). Teacher education in the United States: Trends and issues. *The Teacher Educator, 27*(4), 3–11.

Howey, K. R. (1994). *Recent reform and restructuring initiatives in elementary and secondary schools: Implications for preservice teacher education,* Unpublished manuscript, The Ohio State University, College of Education, Columbus.

Howey, K. R., & Zimpher, N. L. (1986). *Requisites for the teacher-mentor: Uncommon commitment and commonplace knowledges.* Unpublished manuscript, The Ohio State University, Columbus.

Howey, K. R., & Zimpher, N. (1989). *Profiles of preservice teacher education: Inquiry into the nature of programs.* Albany: State Library of New York Press.

Howey, K. R., & Zimpher, N. (1990). Professors and deans of education. In W. R. Houston, M. Haberman, & J. Sikula (Eds.), *Handbook of research on teacher education* (pp. 349–370). New York: Macmillan.

Howsam, R. B., Corrigan, D. C., Denemark, G. W., & Nash, R. J. (1976). *Educating a profession.* Report of the Bicentennial Commission on Education for the Profession of Teaching of the American Association of Colleges for Teacher Education. Washington, DC: AACTE.

Huffman-Joley, G. (1992, February). *The role of the dean: Fostering teaching as scholarship in the school of education learning community.* Paper presented at the annual meeting of the American Association of Colleges for Teacher Education, San Antonio, Texas.

Judge, H. (1982). *American graduate schools of education: A view from abroad.* New York: Ford Foundation.

Kagan, D. M. (1990). Teachers' workplace meets the professors of teaching: A chance encounter at 30,000 feet. *Journal of Teacher Education, 40*(4), 46–53.

Karlsberger, H. C. P. (1993). *Perceptions of teachers involved in the creation of professional development schools.* Unpublished manuscript, The Ohio State University, Columbus.

Koehler, V. (1984). *University supervision of student teaching* (Report No. 9061). Austin: University of Texas, Research and Development Center for Teacher Education.

Korinek, L. A. (1989). Teacher preferences for training and compensation for field supervision. *Journal of Teacher Education, 40*(6), 46–51.

Kroll, L., Rutherford, M., Bowyer, J., & Hauben, M. (1990, April). *The effect of a school–university partnership on the student teaching experience.* Paper presented at the annual meeting of the American Educational Research Association, Boston.

Lanier, J., & Little, J. (1986). Research on teacher education. In M. C. Wittrock (Ed.), *Handbook of research on teaching* (3rd ed., pp. 527–569). New York: Macmillan.

Lawson, H. A. (1990). Constraints on the professional service of education faculty. *Journal of Teacher Education, 41*(4), 57–70.

Matczynski, T., Lasley, T., & Haberman, M. (1989). The deanship: How faculty evaluate performance. *Journal of Teacher Education, 40*(6), 10–14.

Meade, E. J. (1991). Reshaping the clinical phase of teacher preparation. *Phi Delta Kappan, 72*(9), 666–669.

Mertens, S., & Yarger, S. J. (1988). Teaching as a profession: Leadership, empowerment, and involvement. *Journal of Teacher Education, 34*(1), 32–37.

The Ohio State University. (1993). *Tomorrow's schools in Franklin County.* Columbus: The Ohio State University, College of Education, Professional Development School Publication Series.

The Ohio State University. (1994). *What is different? What has changed?* Columbus: The Ohio State University, College of Education, Professional Development School Publication Series.

Pasch, S., & Pugach, M. (1990). Collaborative planning for urban professional development schools. *Contemporary Education, 61,* 135–143.

RATE I: Teaching teachers: Facts & figures. (1987). Washington, DC: American Association of Colleges for Teacher Education.

RATE II: Teaching teachers: Facts & figures. (1988). Washington, DC: American Association of Colleges for Teacher Education.

RATE III: Teaching teachers: Facts & figures. (1989). Washington, DC: American Association of Colleges for Teacher Education.

RATE IV: Teaching teachers: Facts & figures. (1990). Washington, DC: American Association of Colleges for Teacher Education.

RATE V: Teaching teachers: Facts & figures. (1991). Washington, DC: American Association of Colleges for Teacher Education.

RATE VI: Teaching teachers: Facts & figures. (1992). Washington, DC: American Association of Colleges for Teacher Education.

RATE VII: Teaching teachers: Facts & figures. (1994). Washington, DC: American Association of Colleges for Teacher Education.

RATE VIII: Teaching teachers: Facts & figures. (1995). Washington, DC: American Association of Colleges for Teacher Education.

Raths, J. L., Katz, L., & McAninch, A. (1989). A plight of teacher educators: Clinical mentalities in a scientific culture. In R. Wisniewski & E. R. Ducharme (Eds.), *The professors of teaching: An inquiry* (pp. 105–118). Albany: State University of New York Press.

Richardson-Koehler, V. (1988). Barriers to the effective supervision of student teaching: A field study. *Journal of Teacher Education, 32*(2).

Robinson, S. P. (1994). Linking school reform to teacher education reform. *Quality Teaching, The Newsletter of the National Council for Accreditation of Teacher Education, 3*(2).

Rosenholtz, S. J. (1986). Workplace conditions of teacher quality and commitment: Implications for the design of teacher induction programs. In G. A. Griffin & S. Millies (Eds.), *The first years of teaching: Background papers and a proposal* (pp. 15–34). Chicago: University of Illinois/Illinois State Board of Education.

Rosenholtz, S. J. (1989). *Teachers' workplace: The social organization of schools.* New York: Longman.

Scannell, D. P. (1984). The extended teacher education program at the University of Kansas. *Phi Delta Kappan, 66*(2), 130–133.

Sherrill, J. (1993). *A qualitative case study of the clinical educator role during a pilot year of implementation.* Unpublished manuscript, The Ohio State University, Columbus.

Smith, B. O., Silverman, S. H., Borg, J. M., & Fry, B. V. (1980). *A design for a school of pedagogy.* Washington, DC: U.S. Government Printing Office.

Smith, D. C. (1984). PROTEACH: Teacher preparation at the University of Florida. *Teacher Education and Practice, 1*(2), 5–12.

Tom, A. (1986). *The case for maintaining teacher education at the undergraduate level*. Paper prepared for the Coalition of Teacher Education Programs, St. Louis.

Varah, J., Theune, W. S., & Parker, L. (1986). Beginning teachers: Sink or swim? *Journal of Teacher Education, 35*(1), 30–34.

Ward, B. A. (1986). State and district structures to support initial year of teaching programs. In G. A. Griffin & S. Millies (Eds.), *The first years of teaching: Background papers and a proposal* (pp. 35–64). Chicago: University of Illinois/Illinois State Board of Education.

Wasley, P. (1989, April). *Lead teachers and teachers who lead: Reform rhetoric and real practice*. Paper presented at the annual meeting of the American Educational Research Association, San Francisco.

Wisniewski, R., & Ducharme, E. R. (1989). Where we stand. In R. Wisniewski & E. R. Ducharme (Eds.), *The professors of teaching: An inquiry* (pp. 147–162). Albany: State University of New York Press.

Wisniewski, R., & Ducharme, E. R. (Eds.). (1990). Book review: The professors of teaching: An inquiry. *Journal of Teacher Education, 41*(4), 71–75.

Zeichner, K. (1990). Changing directions in the practicum: Looking ahead to the 1990's. *Journal of Education for Teaching, 16,* 105–132.

Zeichner, K. (1992). Rethinking the practicum in the professional development school partnership. *Journal of Teacher Education, 43*(4), 296–307.

Zimpher, N. (1987). Current trends in research on university supervision of student teaching. In Haberman, M. & Backus, J. *Advances in teacher education,* Vol. 3, pp. 118–150.

Zimpher, N. (1990). Creating professional development school sites. *Theory into Practice, 29*(1), 42–49.

Zimpher, N. L., & Howey, K. R. (1987). Adapting supervisory practices to different orientations of teaching competence. *Journal of Curriculum and Supervision, 2*(2), 37–43.

Zimpher, N. L., & Howey, K. R. (1992). *Policy and practice toward the improvement of teacher education*. Oak Brook, IL: North Central Regional Educational Laboratory.

Zimpher, N., & Reiger, S. R. (1988). Mentoring teachers: What are the issues? *Theory Into Practice, 27*(3), 175–182.

FEDERAL POLICY AND TEACHER EDUCATION

Penelope M. Earley

AMERICAN ASSOCIATION OF COLLEGES FOR TEACHER EDUCATION

E. Joseph Schneider

SOUTHWEST REGIONAL EDUCATIONAL LABORATORY

Traditionally the federal government's interest in the preparation of teachers has been modest, generally limited, and of short duration (Jordan & Borkow, 1985). The authors of this chapter agree and add that, with only a few exceptions, federal attention to the recruitment, preparation, and continuing professional development of educators has been a policy instrument rather than the target of federal policy. That is, although programs related to special education, bilingual education, mathematics and science education, and vocational education include modest funds for educator recruitment, preparation, or retraining, the teacher education components of these programs are tools to achieve a broader policy objective, such as a more technologically literate work force, or to ease the transition of children with special needs into traditional elementary and secondary school settings. As a consequence, prior to the early 1990s, federal support for teacher education was characterized by a patchwork of programs that were small, categorical, of short duration, and peripheral to school improvement. In this chapter, these authors submit that consistent and coherent attention to teacher education by the federal government has been lacking. This occurred, in part, because of the categorical nature of federal support for education exacerbated by an unresolved policy conflict—what constitutes sound teacher preparation. Because this conflict was not addressed, federal programs tended to support training in the subject to be taught or how to teach a subject, but rarely favored an integrated approach that would address both.

Federal programs to subsidize educator preparation are found in the departments of agriculture, defense, energy, health and human services, interior, as well as education. The National Science Foundation, National Endowments for the Arts and for the Humanities, and National Aeronautics and Space Administration all provide some support for educator recruitment, prep-

aration, or professional development. In addition, the importance of federal support for research on teaching and learning to enhancing the teacher education curriculum in colleges and universities is noted. However, it is far beyond the scope of this chapter to describe and analyze all teacher education programs in every federal agency. In addition, discussion of the political and substantive impact of federally sponsored research on teacher education is a separate chapter in its own right. Rather, three initiatives authorized between 1958 and 1980 and three laws passed after 1990 that support teacher recruitment, preparation or professional development are reviewed: the National Defense Education Act (NDEA) (PL 85-864), Teacher Corps (PL 89-328), the Education Professions Development Act (EPDA) (PL 90-35), the 1992 Higher Education Amendments (PL 102-325), the Goals 2000: Educate America Act (PL 103-227), and Title II of the Elementary and Secondary Education Amendments of 1994 (PL 103-382).

Some argue that a program's policy significance is proportional to the level of federal funding it receives. In this chapter an alternative perspective is put forward. The federal education programs that are examined were selected because they illustrate government's uncertainty over its role in teacher education. A program that did not receive a federal appropriation, HEA Title V, is included in this discussion for its importance in setting the policy agenda for education initiatives in the 103rd Congress. The NDEA, Teacher Corps, and EPDA were selected because they are the federal education authorizations most often associated with teacher education policy. Also, these authorizations serve as useful illustrations of the different approaches the federal government has taken toward teacher education. A brief discussion of the influence of nongovernment policy voices of the 1980s in shaping the policy agenda of the 1990s establishes the link between past and current federal initiatives. Turning to the current decade, Title V of the 1992

Higher Education Amendments (PL 102-325), the Goals 2000: Educate America Act (PL 103-227), and reauthorization of the elementary and secondary amendments (PL 103-382) are reviewed and considered. The analysis of these measures centers on identifying policy conflicts. That is, did the federal authorization resolve policy conflicts, create new conflicts, or was it a neutral factor? Did the presence of unresolved policy conflicts affect the legislation's implementation? These authors suggest that the 1992 Higher Education Amendments (PL 102-325) and more recently Goals 2000 and reauthorization of the Elementary and Secondary Education Act signal a different approach to teacher education policy and address, at least in part, certain policy clashes that troubled earlier initiatives.

ANALYTIC FRAMEWORK

In his chapter for the 1990 *Handbook of Research on Teacher Education,* Hawley (1990) asserted that "most of the [public] policies being adopted are not burdened by their fit with available knowledge or systematically developed theory" (p. 136). These authors acknowledge Hawley's perspective and suggest that teacher education policy is further muddled because decisionmakers are confused by apparent differences within the teacher education field over what constitutes appropriate teacher preparation. This is not to suggest that no studies exist on methods to prepare teachers; to the contrary, there is a considerable body of research on the kind of professional knowledge teachers need and how it is translated into practice. Unfortunately, there has not been consensus among scholars on what the ideal teacher education program should look like (see Ball, 1987; Carter, 1990; Doyle, 1990; Fenstermacher, 1986; Gage, 1989; Pintrich, 1990; Richardson, 1990; Rosenshine & Stevens, 1986; Shulman, 1986; Tom & Valli, 1990). Collegiate-based teacher education is offered in large, small, public, and private institutions of higher learning. Program length varies and may be offered at the undergraduate and graduate levels. In some cases preparation to receive an initial teaching license is conducted by state or local education agencies. In these instances a teaching credential may be awarded, but no degree is confirmed. Most in the education community support the existence of a variety of approaches to preparing teachers; however, to those outside teacher education, this diversity is confusing. As a result, many policymakers have ignored existing research on teaching and relied instead on their personal experiences and anecdotal data to support government actions regarding education (Earley, 1994a; Gilley & Fulmer, 1986).

Airasian (1988) maintained that "because the wisdom and likely effects of educational innovations rarely are established before their adoption, the innovations must seek their legitimacy in nonempirical sources" (p. 301). He contended that many policies "find their way into practice by virtue of their potency as symbols of prevalent value orientations in the wider culture. Thus, innovations undergo a type of consensual, symbolic validation that determines their acceptability" (p. 301). Earley's (1994a) case studies of federal support for alternative licensure and the National Board for Professional Teaching Standards (NBPTS) found a similar pattern. She established that federal decisionmakers' support for or opposition to these two

teacher credentialling measures primarily was influenced by their personal perceptions or misperceptions about the quality of the current teaching force. Empirical research did not inform congressional decisions in regard to these two programs. In fact, Earley found that some policymakers simultaneously endorsed a federal program to alternatively license teachers (reducing the professional preparation educators receive) and a proposal to give federal funds to the NBPTS (increasing the professional preparation educators receive). A reasonable explanation for this behavior is that these policymakers valued privatization of education and saw both alternative licensure and the national certification of teachers as ways to deregulate the processes by which teachers earn an initial or continuing credential. This perspective notwithstanding, attention to deregulation of teacher education (a procedural or administrative issue) masked more fundamental matters: What standards should be used to license and certify teachers? Also, should the federal government set these standards?

In the legislation reviewed in this chapter, attention is given to the expectations members of the policy world held for the programs they created. This approach helps pinpoint friction that has confounded federal policy related to teacher education. This viewpoint is influenced by the work of Green (1983) who suggested that public policy regarding educational equity and access is befuddled when decisionmakers fail to address deep-seated societal ideals undergirding or associated with the policy in question.

Green (1983) advised that

A policy question is a request for a line of action to optimally resolve a conflict between different ideals, all of which must be accepted, but which taken together, cannot all be maximized. That is to say, we do not have a well-formed policy question, a fully formulated statement of a policy problem, until we are able to state the set of ideals from which the question arises, and state them so that their mutual inconsistency is evident. (p. 323)

Green concluded that because of these fundamental value conflicts, achieving both educational equity and access may not be possible. Conflicts of the kind Green identifies are found in teacher education policy as well. As a consequence, well-intended government initiatives may not have the desired or expected impacts.

With an eye to identifying policy conflicts that may have hampered successful federal interventions in the preparation of teachers, this chapter begins by turning to the past with the enactment of the National Defense Education Act, Teacher Corps, and the Education Professions Development Act.

NATIONAL DEFENSE EDUCATION ACT

The structure of federal policy to recruit or prepare teachers has mirrored that of other federal policy initiatives. Due to reluctance of policymakers to provide general federal aid to schools and other education institutions, since the 1950s the federal government has delivered support for education in a categorical manner. That is, most funding is tied to ameliorating specific conditions of particular categories of children. Programs such as Compensatory Education or assistance for limited-English proficient, disabled, or gifted children are examples of categorical federal aid. In a similar manner, support for teacher education also has been categorical in nature. Funds have been directed to promote certain teaching fields or to recruit individuals with specific characteristics into education careers. This categorical approach tempered the anxiety of those who oppose general aid to education and made it easier for program administrators to track federal dollars. The National Defense Education Act (NDEA) (PL 85-864) was an example of categorical assistance directed to educator recruitment and preparation.

NDEA was a multifaceted piece of legislation that established a number of categorical programs. It provided assistance to state and local education agencies to strengthen instruction in science, mathematics, modern foreign languages, and other critical services. The delivery of programs for teachers in these disciplines was through summer institutes, similar in structure to those offered by the National Science Foundation (PL 85-864) (1958; National Teacher Development Initiative [NTDI], 1978).

NDEA was enacted relatively quickly, in part because of the belief at the time that the nation's defense was in jeopardy following the Sputnik launch and in part because many of the programs that eventually became part of the act already were under consideration by Congress. One such program was support for high school guidance and counseling to stimulate preparation of counselors who then would identify talented students and track them into science and mathematics careers (Advisory Commission on Intergovernmental Relations [ACIR], 1981).

Amendments to the NDEA in 1964 increased its funding and broadened the base of the original institute program by adding new subject areas such as English, history, geography, economics, civics, and special education (Jordan & Borkow, 1985). According to an analysis of federal discretionary programs with professional development components (NTDI, 1978), the NDEA institutes almost exclusively provided short-term training for teachers already in the system. Title XI of the act's 1964 amendments consolidated NDEA programs under the Division of Educational Personnel Training. This unit provided a connection between the NDEA discipline-based programs and teacher training, a move that helped the federal government respond to requests by NDEA institute teachers for information on teaching strategies.

Kaestle and Smith (1982) provided an interesting perspective on NDEA. They pointed out that

Although Sputnik certainly caught the nation's attention and provided wonderful ammunition for critics of the schools, the causal connection is less than a half-truth. The myth is wrong on both sides: the Sputnik achievement was not the product of a superior school system; nor did it take a technological embarrassment to move academic critics of American progressive education into the spotlight. (p. 392)

They go on to submit that NDEA should be reviewed

in the context of a general trend back toward emphasis on cognitive skills and on academically talented children. It was another episode in a continuing dialogue—often acrimonious—between advocates of schooling for a variety of social activities and advocates of schooling for intellectual excellence. The latter tend to prevail during periods of heightened international competition. (p. 393)

For teacher education, NDEA often is recalled as the program that funded science and mathematics institutes for teachers. The idea of using institutes of one kind or another to upgrade individuals' skills in the subjects they will teach has been a common and powerful theme in federal teacher education policy. Yet, did these institutes really deliver on their promise?

In March 1984, the General Accounting Office (GAO) released a metaanalysis of the National Science Foundation (NSF) teacher institutes operated between the mid-1950s and the early 1970s. The GAO study found no evidence to link educators' attendance at these institutes to subsequent academic achievement of students in those teachers' classes. Acknowledging that an individual who does not know algebra or geometry cannot teach it, the GAO looked for studies that showed the additive value of the NSF institutes on performance of elementary or secondary school students. They concluded that "as a group, these studies fail to show any relationship between teacher knowledge and the knowledge gain of their students" (GAO, 1984, p. 33). The GAO authors observed in the executive summary,

Some observers link national economic prosperity to improved science and mathematics education aimed at achieving growth through technology, but others have opposing views of the goals of education and place different emphases on the educational needs of the future United States work force. The apparent national consensus on the need for educational reform thus obscures significant disagreement with regard to the dimensions and directions of that reform. Critics differ in their emphasis on mathematics and science as opposed to other subjects and on the education of the elite (or most able) as opposed to the education of all students. (p. i)

Notwithstanding the GAO analysis and these observations, in August 1984—just a few months after the GAO report was released—Congress passed the Education for Economic Security Act (PL 98-377), which was legislation to improve the quality of mathematics and science teaching and instruction in the United States. PL 98-377 again authorized the National Science Foundation to support institutes and workshops for supervisors and teachers to improve their skills in mathematics and science. Clearly, the belief that the summer institute model was the best way to deliver advanced instruction for mathematics and science teachers was more powerful than research to the contrary. The GAO study identified the presence of unresolved policy conflicts over the content in a teacher preparation program, the goals of the nation's education system, and whether government funds should be used for programs to advance the most able students or for the education of all students; however, discussion of these matters was not to be part of the debate. Passage of NDEA and similar programs supported through NSF reinforced the expectation that teacher training or retraining can be used as a tool to advance a broader societal goal—in this case economic development—without serious attention to what is meant by professional education.

The GAO could find no evidence that institutes operated through NSF or modeled after NSF programs actually promote student learning; however, this training institute approach has strong appeal in Congress. In 1992 when Congress reauthorized the Higher Education Act, it included a program of national teacher academies. This initiative was promoted by Rhode Island Senator Claiborne Pell and patterned on NSF institutes. Not to let a popular idea die, Senator Pell also included language to support these academies in the 1994 reauthorization of the Elementary and Secondary Education Act (PL 103-382). The reasons for such strong congressional support for teacher training institutes are not clear. Perhaps it is because the institutes are associated with core academic subjects. Or, policymakers may recall the "good old days" of the 1950s and assume, without evidence, that the NDEA and NSF programs must have been successful. Programs such as NDEA and professional development currently supported through the Eisenhower Mathematics and Science Act and NSF are examples of belief by decisionmakers that the measure of a good teacher is his or her depth of understanding of the field he or she will teach. The Teacher Corps program, enacted into law in 1965, reflects a different attitude toward teacher preparation.

TEACHER CORPS

In 1965 Congress enacted the Teacher Corps program as Part B of Title V of the Higher Education Act (PL 89-328). The initial purpose of Teacher Corps was not to promote a particular model of teaching but to advance an employment policy. In the 1960s the nation was facing a shortage of educators, and members of the Kennedy administration wanted to be sure jobs were available for returning Peace Corps volunteers (Earley, 1994a; Jordan & Borkow, 1985). Assuming that former Peace Corps volunteers would have special empathy for disadvantaged children, Teacher Corps provided incentives for individuals to enter teaching and to work with children in areas with high concentrations of low-income families. Teacher Corps interns completed the courses they needed to earn their baccalaureate degree and to qualify for a teaching credential. In addition, collegiate-based teacher education programs received funds to broaden their teacher preparation programs (NTDI, 1978).

By the 1970s when demographers reported a teacher surplus, not the shortage upon which the initial program was predicated, Teacher Corps' purpose had shifted to fund professional development for teachers working in high poverty areas. Regulations required local school staff to determine school improvement or staff development needs and to design programs to meet their requirements (Jordan & Borkow, 1985). Teacher Corps is an interesting illustration of federal attention to teacher preparation. Because government wanted to encourage persons to teach in certain schools, it linked higher education with elementary and secondary schools for initial teacher preparation and for professional development. Embedded in Teacher Corps, but not part of the law's initial design, is that colleges and universities receiving federal funds would revise their teacher preparation programs. Much like NDEA, Teacher Corps was created as an instrument to address a policy issue other than teacher education, in this case an employment imbalance—Peace Corps volunteers needed jobs and schools needed teachers. However, unlike NDEA, Teacher Corps built a link between higher education and K–12 schools.

When thinking about the impact of Teacher Corps, it is important to keep in mind that at various times Teacher Corps funds were awarded both to institutions of higher learning to

support teacher preparation programs and to local education agencies for teacher recruitment and induction. Yet, in 1972 when the Teacher Corps program was largest, fewer than 140 of the 16,730 school districts in the United States at that time were participants. In addition, only just over 100 institutions of higher education that prepared teachers, or roughly 9%, received Teacher Corps awards (Jordan & Borkow, 1985; National Center for Education Statistics [NCES], 1991, p. 93). These numbers represented a small portion of teacher preparation institutions and a smaller portion of school districts.

Originally, Teacher Corps was designed to recruit persons into teaching and to create jobs for returning Peace Corps volunteers. There is no evidence that the policy debate in the mid-1960s included serious discussion of whether the Teacher Corps model was the best teacher preparation model; rather it was seen as an expedient way to get persons into the classroom. Furthermore, although program changes in colleges and universities that participated in Teacher Corps were documented (Jordan & Borkow, 1985), this was not an initial purpose of the program. The idea that federal support may be sent in tandem to school districts and higher education institutions to improve the initial preparation of educators or their continuing professional development was an outgrowth of Teacher Corps, not its primary objective. Teacher Corps was a relatively modest program, funding a small percentage of school districts and higher education institutions. When it was assimilated into the Education Consolidation and Improvement Act of the Omnibus Budget Reconciliation Act of 1981 (PL 97-35), this model faded into policy history.

Because Teacher Corps funded only about 9% of the institutions that prepare teachers and less than 1% of local school districts, it operated almost as a demonstration or pilot program. Consequently, the policy and higher education communities did not become embroiled in matters of teacher education governance, such as (1) revising state program approval to correspond to guidelines for a federally supported teacher education program, (2) establishing mechanisms for states to award a common teaching license based on federal standards, or (3) shifting authority to award teaching licenses from state to local education agencies. If Teacher Corps had funded all teacher preparation institutions and school districts rather than just a few, it is likely the federal presence would have triggered a policy clash over the governance of teacher education. Would there have been a shift in program approval and licensure authority from the state to local districts or the federal government? If the federal government had used Teacher Corps to establish a common teacher education curriculum, could teacher education have survived in a collegiate environment that promotes institutional autonomy and spurns government intervention (Clark & McNergney, 1990; Green, 1983; Prestine, 1991)?

EDUCATION PROFESSIONS DEVELOPMENT ACT

It may be argued that the federal government made an attempt to address the stuggle between support for what a teacher will teach and how to teach it through the Education Professions

Development Act (EPDA) (PL 90-35). The EPDA became law in 1967 and encompassed educator recruitment and a variety of training programs. A National Advisory Council was established to oversee EPDA and impose some sense of order on its more than a dozen distinct programs, many with separate authorizations. At various times EPDA included initiatives such as vocational education, Teacher Corps, training for higher education personnel, and fellowships for elementary and secondary level educators. EPDA included a state grants program, but these funds were used for educator training rather than to coordinate the various categorical pieces administered through the Office of Education but conducted by local education agencies or higher education institutions.

Jordan and Borkow (1985) noted that EPDA never reached its potential, a perspective echoed by the National Advisory Council on Education Professions Development (1976). Among the problems they cited were (1) expectations for the programs were probably too high; (2) various "stakeholders" believed EPDA was a way to promote pet programs and as a result ignored other EPDA components; and (3) program managers saw the EPDA as a strategy to improve teacher quality, whereas Congress saw recruiting teachers as the law's primary goal. In the 1970s when the teacher supply and demand ratio began to balance out, original supporters felt EPDA's purpose was achieved (Jordan & Borkow, 1985; National Advisory Council on Education Professions Development, 1976).

The categorical nature of EPDA aggravated unresolved tension over what is necessary for good teaching. Furthermore, decisionmakers' expectations or values, teacher recruitment, clashed with expectations of program managers and many interest groups. In addition, some evidence indicated that the National Advisory Council on Education Professions Development viewed the various entities involved in teacher education—institutions of higher education, state agencies, and school districts—as competitors and attempted to structure EPDA programs and federal resources to force these clients to change behaviors without addressing structural and governance issues that impeded linkages between them (National Advisory Council on Education Professions Development, 1976, p. 5).

At various times during the 20 years from the late 1950s to the late 1970s, the federal government directed resources to teacher recruitment, preparation, and professional development. For the most part, teacher education was not the focus of this attention, but rather an instrument to achieve other policy goals. Employment and economic policy were to be advanced by NDEA and NSF institutes to stimulate science and mathematics study by vocational education programs and by Teacher Corps. In large authorizations such as the Elementary and Secondary Education Act and its subsequent amendments, minor provisions supported teacher preparation for those who would teach bilingual or Title I eligible children; however, educator recruitment, preparation, or professional development were not treated as integral parts of this legislation. Similarly, various categorical programs to support educator preparation were authorized as part of Title V of the Higher Education Amendments; however, few of these programs ever were funded. With the exception of Teacher Corps, most Title V programs existed only for a few years, and they treated teacher preparation as separate from other higher education policy.

For the Congress to engage in serious debate about teacher education policy would have forced decisionmakers to question the categorical nature of education funding and drawn them into discussions of what constitutes good teacher education. Should emphasis be on knowing the subject to be taught or how to teach the subject? What should teachers know and be able to do when they receive their initial teaching license? What should experienced teachers know and be able to do and how does this knowledge differ from that of the novice? What is the purpose of professional development—advanced skill training, remediation, or both? It should be noted that during the 1960s and 1970s much of the theoretical work on teaching was process-product research in which experimental studies attempted to isolate those teacher behaviors that would result in student achievement (Tom & Valli, 1990). This line of inquiry may have led those in the policy community to expect that a precise prescription for good teacher education was on the horizon. This expectation was not fulfilled. While researchers debated the merits of various research paradigms related to teaching, the policy world moved on. What on the surface appears to be decisionmakers' unwillingness to rely on teaching and learning research to inform federal policy more likely reflected the uncertainty of those who prepare teachers about best practice. This tension came to a head during the presidencies of Ronald Reagan and George Bush.

EXTERNAL INFLUENCES ON THE TEACHER EDUCATION POLICY AGENDA

At times in the history of the United States, the executive branch may not have behaved in a policy-initiating mode. Such was the case for education during the presidency of Ronald Reagan. Upon his election, President Reagan proposed that the Department of Education be eliminated and that the programs it administers be shut down or cut back (Finn, 1988; O'Neill & Simms, 1982). Congress never agreed to the first proposal but it did eliminate many education programs with passage of the Omnibus Budget Reconciliation Act (PL 97-35) in 1981. In his second term, Reagan's Department of Education took the stance that the federal government only had a limited role in education, which, they pointed out, was constitutionally a state responsibility (Finn, 1988). Congress did not concede this point and passed numerous pieces of legislation that actually saw some federal program expansion; however, little of this legislation focused on teacher education.

President Reagan's Department of Education was unwilling to advance new initiatives; yet, policy voices outside of the federal government were less reticent. Education interest groups, business organizations, and foundations, either on their own or through individuals and groups they funded, published educational reform reports. These documents, many supported by nonfederal funds, filled a void in the education policy world created by President Reagan's noninterventionist education agenda.

Kingdon (1984) wrote about the power of agenda setters on government policy. Individuals, organized groups, the media, or government agencies may play important roles in shaping policy arguments and direction before it begins the legislative process. The inability of President George Bush to receive a Texas teaching credential in the 1950s and the New Jersey "alternative route" promoted by former Governor Thomas Kean both helped move the alternative licensure of teachers onto the federal policy agenda (Earley, 1994a). In a similar manner, the various education reform documents published during the 1980s helped set the scene for federal initiatives during the 1990s.

It is worth mentioning that the report that produced the most attention was in fact the Department of Education document, *A Nation at Risk*. Published in 1983, the report included expressions of concern about the state of elementary and secondary education and urged action if the United States had any hope of retaining its economic standing among other industrialized nations (National Commission on Excellence in Education, 1983). Although the report generated extensive attention, particularly in the media, no major federal initiatives emerged to address the education problems described in *A Nation at Risk*.

The *Nation at Risk* report may not have led to new federal initiatives, but it did trigger activity outside government. Numerous education reports followed on its heels, including many that addressed teacher education, such as *A Call for Change in Teacher Education* (National Commission for Excellence in Teacher Education [NCETE], 1985), *A Nation Prepared: Teachers for the 21st Century* (Carnegie Forum on Education and the Economy, 1986), *A Place Called School* (Goodlad, 1984), *Time for Results* (National Governors' Association, 1986), and *Tomorrow's Teachers* (The Holmes Group, 1986). These documents and others raised issues related to the recruitment, preparation, and professional development of teachers.

Jordan (1986) pointed out that the advisory groups and authors involved in developing and writing these education reform documents tended to draw from a common intellectual pool. As a result it is not surprising that there are certain familiar recommendations regarding teacher preparation. There was general agreement that teachers should have "a full academic major in the discipline to be taught, supplemented by professional education courses and an internship that would develop professional knowledge and skills" (Jordan, 1986, p. 10). There were recommendations that colleges and universities extend teacher education students' clinical experiences and that public school teachers be involved in both the clinical supervision and the instruction of preservice teachers (Goodlad, 1984; The Holmes Group, 1986). Findings included in these reports began to make the link between good teaching and successful schools; yet, many recommendations conformed to the long-established pattern of independent and separate support for K–12 and higher education policy.

The education reform documents of the 1980s highlighted difficult issues and provided opportunity for debate on several unresolved policy conflicts regarding teacher education. What is the proper balance in teacher education between learning the subject to be taught and learning how to teach it? Can federal support for collegiate-based teacher education be considered independent of federal policy toward elementary and secondary schools? Can the federal government truly change teacher education without addressing matters of institutional program approval and teacher licensure, both functions reserved to state governments? Several reports addressed teacher education's

curriculum by recommending that teacher preparation be extended to 5 to 6 years (Carnegie Forum, 1986; The Holmes Group, 1986; NCETE, 1985). Authors of the reports suggested that this extension would allow students the opportunity to complete both coursework in teaching fields and professional preparation; however, most documents stayed clear of how these recommendations would have an impact on teacher licensure, salaries, or the teacher education program approval process.

Several somewhat modest federal education initiatives were considered by the Congress during the Bush administration, although none became law. The Educational Excellence Act (S. 695) attempted to fund school choice, alternative licensure of teachers, and other programs outlined in the President's America 2000 education strategy. The Democratic-controlled Congress advanced some education initiatives of its own. HR 5115, the Equity and Excellence in Education Act, HR 5932, the Educational Equity and Excellence Act, and S. 1676, the National Teacher Act each stressed improving student performance through federal assistance to states and school districts. The National Teacher Act would have created professional development institutes for educators based on content areas identified in the national education goals to upgrade skills of existing teachers. In an accommodation to the Bush administration, Senate legislation also would have given states awards to establish or maintain programs to alternatively license teachers. As noted, none of these education bills became law.

The legislation introduced in the last 2 years of the Bush presidency and the national debate on education generated by the reform reports of the 1980s served as powerful influences on the education policy agenda of the 1990s. Issues for teacher education included several questions. What should be the relationship between arts and sciences faculties and teacher education faculties in the preparation of educators? Should teacher preparation extend beyond the traditional 4 years? Can initial teacher preparation be offered by entities other than colleges and universities? Does the federal government have a role in licensing or certifying teachers? (Carnegie Forum, 1986; Goodlad, 1984; The Holmes Group, 1986; National Commission on Excellence in Education, 1983; National Governors' Association, 1986; NCETE, 1985). Lack of federal attention to education policy during the Reagan administrations and early years of the Bush administration presented an opportunity for those outside the federal government to suggest policy options in regard to educator recruitment, preparation, and professional development, and influencing the congressional agenda for reauthorization of the Higher Education Act.

HIGHER EDUCATION AMENDMENTS OF 1992

In 1990 the House and Senate of the United States began reauthorization of the Higher Education Act (HEA) (PL 102-325). This legislation authorized a system of financial aid for college students and other programs to support the mission of institutions of higher learning. Title V of HEA traditionally supported collegiate programs to prepare individuals to become teachers. By the time the act was passed and signed by President Bush in 1992, a new Title V had been created to support teacher recruitment, preparation, and professional development through awards to states, K–12 schools, and institutions of higher education. Title V did not receive an appropriation; yet, with this legislation Congress and the administration acknowledged that reform of higher education and K–12 schools could not be expected to proceed on parallel, yet independent, tracks. Title V of the 1992 Higher Education Amendments helped set the education policy agenda for consideration of education reform legislation that would occur 2 years later during the 103rd Congress.

The policy context for consideration of HEA, Title V began with the reform reports of the 1980s and calls for more systematic involvement between teacher preparation and elementary and secondary schools. Goodlad (1990) sets out this agenda, "The need for higher educational involvement in the schools is great. If we are to have good schools and good teachers for them, the simultaneous effort to improve both must proceed under conditions that make it possible for such a venture to succeed" (p. 181). The policy community picked up the idea of "simultaneous renewal" in K–12 schools and institutions of higher education. In Title V of the 1992 Higher Education Amendments, one of the purposes echoes Goodlad's theme, "to promote partnerships between institutions of higher education and local educational agencies for the purpose of promoting the simultaneous restructuring and renewal of elementary and secondary schools and college-based teacher education programs" (PL 102–325, Title V, Sec. 500 [b][8]).

Title V of the Higher Education Act authorized 18 programs. Most encouraged or required partnerships between colleges and universities and K–12 schools; however, the centerpiece of the legislation was the State and Local Programs for Teacher Excellence. Authorized at $350 million, this section would send funds to states on a formula basis. Fifty percent of a state's allocation was required to go to local school districts for teacher recruitment and professional development, with the districts encouraged to work with one or more colleges and universities to develop their programs.

Twenty-five percent of a state's funds would be made available to institutions of higher education with schools, colleges, or departments of education. These funds could be used to (1) establish professional development schools (called professional development academies in the legislation), (2) establish programs for persons moving to a career in education from another occupation, (3) provide teacher professional development, (4) implement changes in teacher education programs and curricula, and (5) improve training for pre-K and vocational educators.

The remaining 25% would be retained by the state to study teacher education, establish teacher and school leader professional academies, and implement recommendations of the teacher education study through grants to colleges and universities. The teacher education study would be conducted in consultation with higher education institutions, school districts, teachers, parents, the legislature, state boards of education, and others. Teacher academies would focus on knowledge and teaching of one or more "key academic subjects," with colleges and universities eligible to apply for funds to establish one of the teaching academies. Although authorized, this program was not funded.

In addition to the partnership programs, Title V created National Teacher Academies in English, mathematics, science, history, geography, civics and government, and foreign languages. Structured like the NSF summer institutes, each national academy would offer professional development for teachers. The Christa McAuliffe Fellowship Program, which provides awards to experienced teachers for sabbatical purposes, also was reauthorized. A new program of grants to institutions of higher education to develop model programs to train secondary school teachers to prepare students with disabilities for college also was created. Of these initiatives, only the Christa McAuliffe Fellowship Program received funding.

The Higher Education Amendments contained several programs to encourage persons to become teachers, most of which focused on recruiting minorities. The Paul Douglas Teacher Scholarship Program was reauthorized with a new requirement that priority consideration be given to persons from populations historically underrepresented in teaching and to individuals with disabilities. A new Teacher Corps program was established to provide scholarships to students who intend to become teachers, are from disadvantaged backgrounds, and intend to teach special needs children. A New Teaching Careers program to assist consortia of school districts and higher education institutions to design and implement programs to assist paraprofessionals working in schools to become teachers also was established. Finally, a program supported by President Bush to assist states to develop and implement alternative route programs to teacher licensure was created. Of these, only the Paul Douglas Teacher Scholar program received funding.

Title V authorized two programs to address the needs of pre-K children. Training in Early Childhood Education and Violence Counseling awards grants to colleges and universities to establish innovative programs to recruit and train students for careers in early childhood development and for careers as counselors of young children who have been affected by violence. Early Childhood Staff Training and Professional Enhancement provides competitive grants to states to review policies for the licensure of early childhood development staff and to provide professional development activities for these individuals. The Early Childhood Education and Violence Counseling Program received nearly $5 million in fiscal year 1993 and almost $15 million in fiscal year 1994. Title V included seven other relatively small programs. One such program allowed the Department of Education to award a series of grants to the NBPTS to develop teacher certification assessments.

Ultimately, few Title V programs received federal appropriations. Yet, the legislation is important because (1) it acknowledged the significance of K–12 and higher education partnerships; (2) it stressed both the necessity of knowing what to teach and how to teach it; and (3) the centerpiece program, State and Local Programs for Teacher Excellence, used a block grant rather than a categorical approach to distribute federal funds. In a political vein, Title V sent a message to college and university presidents that K–12 schools are important and alerted state education officials that they must find ways to involve teacher preparation institutions in K–12 policy. The same language in Part A of Title V promoting partnerships between K–12 schools and teacher preparation institutions would show up 2 years later in a new professional development initiative in the Elementary and Secondary Education Act (PL 103-382). More fundamentally, HEA, Title V moved the policy discussion from a higher education focus—how to redesign a collegiate-based teacher education program—to a broader education focus—how to redesign the lifelong education of educators.

The Higher Education Act (PL 102-325) was one of the last major pieces of legislation signed by President Bush, although little of Title V of HEA bore the imprimatur of his administration. Perhaps for this reason, Secretary of Education Alexander and others did not lobby the Congress to fund the Title V programs. The following November George Bush lost his bid for reelection to Bill Clinton. For the new Clinton administration, the 1992 Higher Education Amendments, including Title V, was seen as an artifact of the Bush presidency. Consequently, securing funds for Title V programs was not on the agenda for Richard Riley and new officials in the Department of Education.

THE CLINTON ADMINISTRATION

As Governor of Arkansas, Bill Clinton worked with then Tennessee Governor Lamar Alexander on the National Governors' Association report on education, *Time for Results* (1986), the governors' outline for education reform. He led the delegation of governors who met with President Bush in the fall of 1989 to adopt and ratify what were then six national education goals. During his presidential campaign Clinton relied on a number of education policy experts, among them Marshall Smith, dean of education at Stanford University. Smith served in the Office of Education during the Carter administration and when Clinton became president was nominated and confirmed as Undersecretary of Education, the number three position in the department.

Smith's writings while at Stanford and the University of Wisconsin reveal an education policy orientation that supports a common, although not federal, curriculum in K–12 schools and dismisses categorical approaches for the distribution of federal funds, such as the structure found in EPDA (Kaestle & Smith, 1982; Smith, O'Day, & Cohen, 1990). Smith proposed a systemic approach to education policy that would direct federal resources directly to school sites for reform and would link classrooms by a set of commonly held standards and commonly used assessments (Smith, O'Day, & Cohen, 1990). Unlike a rigidly centralized education system, the model Smith, O'Day, and Cohen suggested anticipates that national forces, such as standards-setting groups, will influence school systems to adopt nationally agreed upon, but not federally mandated, curriculum and assessments. This approach mirrors what eventually was considered by the Congress and signed by the president as the Goals 2000: Educate America Act. Embedded in this policy framework is the notion that educator professional development is necessary for school change and that higher education and K–12 schools have a responsibility to create a coherent system for teacher preparation and professional development.

This approach is not without its critics. Clune (1993) called the "statist-centralized version of systemic policy built around authoritative curriculum frameworks" flawed. He asserted that "A common curriculum is difficult, if not impossible to apply considering the immense diversity of American schooling, and a tolerable link between policy at the top and change at the bottom is all but unattainable" (p. 250). Similarly, when President Clinton announced the Goals 2000 initiative, it was not without its critics.

GOALS 2000: EDUCATE AMERICA ACT

On March 31, 1994, the Goals 2000: Educate America Act (PL 103-227) became law. Among the stated purposes of the law is to create a "template" or framework for other federal education legislation. This is, future federal policy will be linked to achieving one or more of the national education goals, and the framework laid out in the Goals 2000 legislation should be used in subsequent federal policy. The rationale for this approach is greater efficiencies in government spending and more focused federal policy.

The legislation adopted the original six national education goals and added two new ones: support for parental involvement in education and assurance that educators will receive high quality professional development. It authorized funds for K–12 school improvement and established a framework to encourage state and local educational agencies to develop comprehensive plans that will provide a coherent framework to integrate and implement federal education programs. Figure 15.1 describes Goals 2000 and includes the proposed authorization level for each of its parts.

Goals 2000 puts into place a system of common, but not federal, standards or benchmarks for student achievement and school system effort. Considerable controversy surrounded the legislation's provisions to create a federal body to identify voluntary "performance" and "opportunity-to-learn" standards. The law describes performance standards as what students must know and be able to do to demonstrate mastery of the skills and knowledge framed by content standards. Opportunity-to-learn standards are "the criteria for, and the basis of, assessing the sufficiency of quality for the resources, practices and conditions necessary at each level of the education system . . . to learn the materials in content standards" (PL 103-227, Sec. 2[7]). State and local officials argued that national standards such as these signaled federal intrusion into management of local school systems, a function reserved to the states by the Tenth Amendment to the U.S. Constitution. In response, Congress made adherence to the standards entirely voluntary. No state is required to meet nationally developed standards nor seek federal government endorsement of state or local standards to receive Goals 2000 funding.

The heart of Goals 2000 is Title III. In this title, the legislation establishes a mechanism for the federal government to support state and local school improvement efforts. Although institutions of higher education are not direct recipients of federal funds, they are intended to be key players in the school reform effort. The law states that

institutions of higher education should be encouraged to enter into partnerships with schools to provide information and guidance on the skills and knowledge graduates need in order to enter and successfully

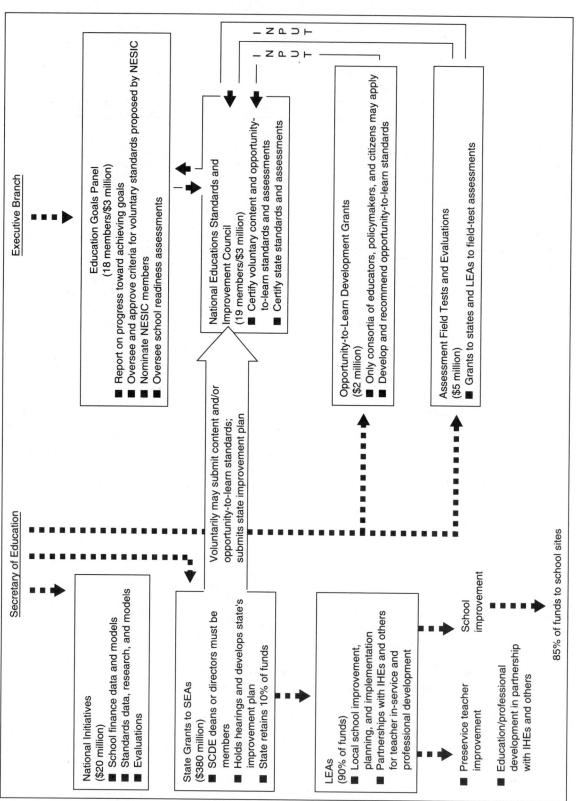

FIGURE 15.1. Goals 2000: Educate America Act (PL 103-227). (*Source:* From Goals 2000: Educate America Act Implications for Teacher Education (p. 6) byP. M. Earley, 1994, American Association of Colleges for Teacher Education. Copyright 1994 by the American Association of Colleges for Teacher Education. Reprinted by permission.) *Note:* Dashed lines indicate the flow of funds. Dollar amounts reflect the legislation's authorization level, not actual appropriations.

complete postsecondary education . . . schools should provide information and guidance to institutions on the skills, knowledge, and preservice training teachers need, and the types of professional development educators need. (PL 103-227, Sec. 301[12])

In fiscal year 1994, $104 million was available for Goals 2000 to use for program planning and initiation; however, for the following year, the Congress provided this program with funding of $403 million. Of this money, the secretary of education may reserve 5% for national projects. These include support for finance equalization efforts, technical assistance for states, research and evaluation of Goals 2000 programs, dissemination of model programs, special assistance to urban and to rural school districts, and a study of successful coordinated service programs. The remaining $380 million is available for states on a formula basis.

Each state must apply for its share of available Goals 2000 money. As part of the application process, the governor and chief state school officer must agree to develop and implement a state improvement plan for elementary and secondary education. The actual design of the plan is to be done by a state panel. The panel must include the governor and chief state school officer; the president of the state board of education and the chairs of appropriate state legislative committees; teachers; principals; administrators; deans or senior administrators of a college, school, or department of education; teacher education representatives; business and labor leaders; community-based organizations serving young children; local boards of education; and others. Priority will be given in these appointments to ensuring that individuals with some expertise or background in the education needs or assessments of at-risk, limited English-proficient, or disabled children serve on the state panel. The governor and chief state school officer each appoint half of the panel members who are required to conduct hearings and gather substantial public comment as the state plan is developed. The plan must include strategies to meet the national education goals by improving teaching and learning and mastery of basic and advanced skills. This includes a process for improving the state's system of teacher and school administrator preparation, the recruitment of persons into education careers, and the nature and delivery of educator professional development.

The state submits its plan to the secretary of education and voluntarily may submit performance, opportunity-to-learn standards, or both to the National Education Standards and Improvement Council for review. Not all states may choose to develop a state improvement plan. The governor and chief state school officer may request a waiver if they can demonstrate that a panel with essentially the same composition has developed a school improvement plan that was formulated with broad public and professional input. Once the plan is approved, a state will receive its Goals 2000 allocation. In the first year of the legislation, states may reserve 40% of their funds for initiating their state improvement plan; however, every year thereafter, the state share will be only 10%.

The state may use its money to work on development of standards; assist local schools and districts; support programs for minority, limited-English proficient, disabled, and female students; support innovative programs to upgrade teacher skills;

and other purposes. The remaining funds (90% of the state share) are reserved for local education agencies and schools. School districts may apply for and use their funds for local reform, educator professional development, or both. The legislation requires that both school improvement and educator professional development be supported, but the decision on the percent of funds spent on each is left to the state. As part of the state's school improvement plan, the school improvement panel will determine the percentage of its Goals 2000 money that will be used for each purpose. If a school district applies to the state for funds to support local reform efforts, it must submit a local improvement plan and agree that 85% of the funds it receives will flow through the local education agency to specific schools. At least half of these schools must be in need of special assistance. Indicators of this need may be low student achievement, large numbers of low-income families, or similar criteria developed by the school district. The local improvement plan must reflect the priorities of the state plan and include strategies that enhance teaching and learning, improve governance and management, strengthen parental and community involvement, and ensure a fair opportunity to learn for all students. The local improvement plan must be developed by a local improvement panel.

In addition, local education agencies or a consortium of school districts in cooperation with institutions of higher education, nonprofit organizations, or a combination of these groups may apply for awards to improve preservice teacher education or to support continuing, sustained professional development for educators. These are competitive grants to be awarded through a peer review process. Priority for awarding the grants is to be given to school districts that form partnerships with collegiate educators. These partnerships may establish professional development sites and focus on upgrading teachers' knowledge of content areas or may target the preparation and continued professional development of individuals who teach limited English-proficient students or students with disabilities. Funds received by these consortia must be used to improve preservice teacher education as it relates to educators' subject matter and pedagogical expertise or for the development and implementation of new and improved forms of continuing and sustained professional development opportunities for educators. Like the grants for local reform efforts, at least half of the professional development awards must go to schools in need of special assistance.

The focus of Goals 2000 is on improving student learning by establishing goals for students and schools, encouraging states and school districts to adopt rigorous standards for their education system, and improving the quality of teaching in K–12 schools. Institutions of higher education with schools, colleges, and departments of education and teacher educators are viewed as partners in this process; this is evidenced by the requirement that deans or other teacher education administrators must be part of the state panel to deisgn the school improvement plan. Moreover, if a local education agency intends to apply for funds to support educator preservice professional development, priority will be given to proposals in which school districts form partnerships with colleges and universities.

Goals 2000 presents new opportunities for schools, colleges, and departments of education; however, only those institutions that are committed to working in partnerships with K–12 schools, in particular schools with the most needy children, will be rewarded.

ELEMENTARY AND SECONDARY EDUCATION AMENDMENTS

Hearings on the reauthorization of the Elementary and Secondary Education Act (ESEA) began in 1992; however, Congress did not complete work on revisions to this legislation until after Goals 2000 became law. This time line reflected the strong commitment of the Clinton administration to use the Goals 2000 framework as a template for at least part of ESEA. The importance of the resulting revisions to ESEA cannot be underestimated. In the legislation, compensatory education programs are revised to stress schoolwide reform and improvement rather than the delivery of services to individual children. It is based on the assumption that all children will be able to meet challenging academic and performance standards. It encourages and in certain cases requires federal funds to be used for the professional development of teachers to improve both knowledge of the subject to be taught and how to teach the subject. In addition, it provides incentives for institutions of higher education to become partners with schools and school districts for the purpose of education reform (PL 103-382, 1994). With these provisions, a significant portion of federal support for education moved from allocation by a categorical approach (dollars targeted to children living in poverty) to distribution in a manner more like general aid (dollars targeted to schools with large numbers of children in poverty for schoolwide use). Moreover, the legislation identified educator professional development as central to school reform and defined professional development as encompassing both the teaching area and pedagogy. Whether by accident or design, Goals 2000 and the new ESEA legislation began to address policy conflicts that were created by the categorical nature of funding for education programs, by the establishment of arbitrary separations between elementary/ secondary and higher education programs, and by policy decisions that treated the subject to be taught independently of how to teach it.

Throughout the many programs in ESEA (PL 103-382), language is included that links their implementation to Goals 2000 and that supports educator professional development. However, most professional development programs are found in a new Title II, the Eisenhower Professional Development Program. The purposes of Title II include ensuring that (1) teachers and, where appropriate, other educators have access to sustained and intensive high-quality professional development aligned to challenging state content standards; (2) professional development reflects recent research on teaching and learning; and (3) professional development is part of the everyday life of the school and creates an orientation toward continuous improvement throughout the school (PL 103-382, Sec. 2002). Title II is structured in a manner similar to the state grant program in Goals 2000 and it is noted in the legislation that Title II programs should be linked to and coordinated with professional development supported through Goals 2000 (see Figure 15.2).

Title II allows the secretary of education to retain 6% of the total appropriation, which in fiscal year 1995 is $320,298,000, for a range of purposes, including (1) to provide grants to states, school districts, institutions of higher education, and others to develop their capacity to offer sustained, intensive, high-quality professional development; (2) to establish national clearinghouses in the core academic subjects; (3) to create professional development institutes; (4) to prepare teachers to effectively use technology; (5) to be used in up to 10 national teacher training institutes, each focusing on one of the core academic subjects; and (6) to support school improvement partnerships between school districts with very high poverty levels' institutions of higher education (IHEs), teachers' organizations, and others.

The bulk of the funds in Title II go to the state on a formula based on population and the state's Title I allocation. Of the state share, 84% is to be used by local education agencies for professional development; however, the school district may retain only 20% of these funds for district-wide activities. The remaining 80% must go directly to the school site for professional development that is tied to challenging state or local standards, that is based on recent research on teaching and learning, that includes strong academic and pedagogical components, and that is of sufficient intensity and duration to have a positive and lasting impact on the teachers' performance. Schools have wide latitude regarding use of their funds, including subsidizing the cost of release time for teachers and establishing partnerships between schools and IHEs (PL 103-382, 1994, Sec. 2210).

Institutions of higher education are eligible to apply to the state for awards to develop and deliver professional development for teachers; however, to compete for these funds, the IHE must demonstrate that it is working in partnership with one or more schools and that the application is a joint proposal of the school, college, or department of education and a department in one of the disciplines (e.g., mathematics, science, geography).

The new Title II was created by refocusing and refashioning the Eisenhower Mathematics and Science Act. This program supported advanced instruction in mathematics and science for secondary school teachers. The Clinton administration's initial proposal for Title II would have allowed funds to be used for professional development in any of the core academic subjects and how to teach them. However, some members of Congress were convinced that mathematics and science instruction should be a national priority and included provisions in the legislation requiring the first $250 million appropriated for Title II each year to be used for professional development in mathematics and science. There is an interesting irony in this action. As noted previously, in 1984 the GAO released a study of federal programs to aid mathematics and science teaching (GAO, 1984). In that study, they reported that there was virtually no relationship between knowledge gained by teachers enrolled in science and mathematics enhancement institutes and achievement by their students in these subjects. Nevertheless, later that year Congress passed the Education for Economic Security Act (PL 98-377), legislation that provided federal support for these institutes. During the summer of 1994, the GAO released another study of federal efforts to increase the mathematics and science

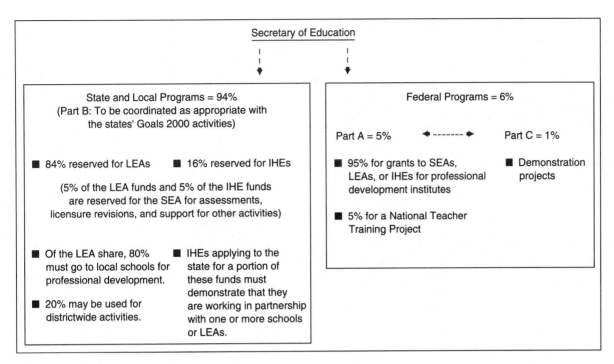

Secretary of Education

State and Local Programs = 94%
(Part B: To be coordinated as appropriate with
the states' Goals 2000 activities)

■ 84% reserved for LEAs   ■ 16% reserved for IHEs

(5% of the LEA funds and 5% of the IHE funds
are reserved for the SEA for assessments,
licensure revisions, and support for other activities)

■ Of the LEA share, 80%
must go to local schools for
professional development.

■ 20% may be used for
districtwide activities.

■ IHEs applying to the
state for a portion of
these funds must
demonstrate that they
are working in partnership
with one or more schools
or LEAs.

Federal Programs = 6%

Part A = 5%   ◄------►   Part C = 1%

■ 95% for grants to SEAs,
LEAs, or IHEs for professional
development institutes

■ 5% for a National Teacher
Training Project

■ Demonstration
projects

FIGURE 15.2. Elementary and Secondary Education Act, Title II (PL 103-382). (*Source:* From Goals 2000: Educate America Act Implications for Teacher Education by P. M. Earley, 1994, American Association of Colleges for Teacher Education. Copyright 1994 by the American Association of Colleges for Teacher Education. Reprinted by permission.)

ability of elementary and secondary school students (GAO, 1994). This study reviewed evaluations of teacher enhancement programs supported through the U.S. Department of Energy. Similar to their 1984 report, the GAO reported in 1994 that

In reviewing more recent studies, we found mixed results; in some instances, researchers found small yet statistically significant positive correlations between teacher knowledge and student achievements; in others, researchers failed to demonstrate any significant correlations. Conversely, current literature suggests that systemic reform measures, such as high-quality curriculum development, may hold the most promise for improving academic achievement and realizing the national math and science goals. (p. 5)

The GAO study suggests that the government's support of programs in the Department of Energy that are quite similar to those offered through the old Eisenhower mathematics and science program were not effective in promoting student achievement. This information notwithstanding, Congress moved forward and earmarked a significant part of the Title II program to replicate these mainly unsuccessful initiatives.

CONCLUSION

Prior to the early 1990s, teacher education was peripheral to the education policy agenda and generally was an instrument to advance a broader societal goal, such as economic develop-

ment. As a federal policy tool rather than a policy objective, the Congress and executive branch did not burden themselves with sorting out or even addressing deep and unresolved tensions regarding educator preparation, namely what constitutes good or appropriate preparation and professional development for educators, and the struggle between government and nongovernment entities for authority over teacher education programs. The lack of an opportunity for debate on these issues at the federal level had several consequences. Many congressional and executive branch decisionmakers took the default position of addressing teacher education policy ad hoc. Legislative or regulatory strategies were informed by anecdotal data rather than sound research. A systematic approach to federally sponsored teacher education policy was not in evidence and certain actions, such as support for both alternative licensure of teachers and their national certification, were contradictory to one another. Federal programs either supported training in the subject to be taught or how to teach a subject, as opposed to an integrated approach that would address both within the context of systemic school improvement. This exacerbated the assumption of many that there is not consensus on what should be included in the teacher education curriculum. In defense of government decisionmakers, they were not the cause of this apparent conflict over the meaning of good teaching. Rather, their somewhat paradoxical approach to teacher education policy may reflect a perception that there was and still is uncertainty in the field about the structure and content of initial teacher preparation and educators' continuing professional development.

Before 1990, federal policy targeted only a small percentage of teacher preparation institutions, such as those offering bilingual, vocational, or special education programs. As was noted, one of the largest programs to help finance teacher education—Teacher Corps—supported less than 10% of the nation's teacher preparation institutions. Consequently, debate over sticky policy issues regarding a federal role in the governance of teacher credentialling and teacher education program approval did not occur. Embedded in consideration of teacher education governance is the tension between the role of the state as an overseer of a large population of public employees—teachers—and the long-held tradition of college and university autonomy. Teacher education is caught in this struggle between government's need to be accountable to the public and powerful pressures to reject government intrusion by the colleges and universities that house teacher education programs. As Green (1983) indicated, conflicting policies, when taken together, "cannot all be maximized" (p. 323). At issue for teacher education has been the unwillingness of policymakers to confront these conflicting values and to determine if one is to be sacrificed for the health of the other.

Without question, the federal government's attitude toward teacher education began to change in the early 1990s. The reauthorization of the Higher Education Amendments (PL 102-325) signaled a different approach to teacher education policy. Teacher education continued to be a policy instrument, but in the HEA it was linked with K–12 schools toward the end of comprehensive school reform. The Higher Education Amendments were significant because they began to erode some of the traditional boundaries in the education system, namely the separation of policies directed to higher education and to K–12 schools. This legislation also took steps to address the matter of what should be included in the teacher education curriculum by noting that professional education should consider both the subject to be taught and how to teach it. Issues of teacher education program approval and educator licensure were touched only on the margin. Had Title V been funded, states receiving awards under the act would have been encouraged to look at teacher licensure policies toward the end of establishing credential portability among the states. Issues such as whether or not a partnership with a local school district should influence or alter the nature of a school, college, or department of education's program approval were not addressed in the legislation.

Building on the approach legislated in Title V, the Clinton administration included in Goals 2000 teacher education preservice and professional development as elements necessary for school reform. Because the Clinton administration has declared that Goals 2000 should be the template for future federal involvement in education, it is clear that the education of educators is considered important to achieving school reform. Goals 2000 and ESEA, Title II nudge the teacher education policy agenda further. Similar to HEA, Title V, they attempt to remove barriers between higher education and K–12 schools by encouraging the development of partnerships. In linking teacher preservice and professional development to the eight national education goals, both what and how to teach are tied to school reform. Finally, Goals 2000 sets in motion a framework to support teacher professional development, but not necessarily the evening or weekend in-service traditionally offered educators. The professional development implied in the Goals 2000 framework will enable teachers to be serious partners in school change, and by extension, it changes the way new teachers are prepared.

The staying power of the approach outlined in Goals 2000 will be tested when the newly revised and authorized programs in the Elementary and Secondary Education Act are implemented. In addition, the efficacy of this framework is likely to be questioned when Congress considers reauthorization of special education and vocational education programs. Policymakers may find it difficult to ensure that the legal projections afforded children with disabilities are maintained if targeted federal aid is replaced with a more general aid package. If there is a power shift in the Congress, members may be reticent to make major policy changes in other currently supported education initiatives. Adjusting federal policy to fund schoolwide reform and to involve both K–12 and higher education in the process may help resolve policy conflicts borne of very narrow targeting of federal aid without attention to how parts of the nation's complex education system are interrelated. However, this approach may create its own set of problems, such as ensuring that schoolwide reforms actually benefit those children who are most in need. Extensive evaluation of the impact of professional development to further states' Goals 2000 and ESEA will be needed to help decisionmakers and the education community determine if this approach warrants continuation and expansion to include other federally supported education efforts.

References

Advisory Commission on Intergovernmental Relations (ACIR). (1981). *The federal role in the federal system: The dynamics of growth.* Washington, DC: Author.

Airasian, P. W. (1988). Symbolic validation: The case of state-mandated, high-stakes testing. *Educational Evaluation and Policy Analysis, 10*(4), 301–313.

Ball, D. W. (1987). Some effects of training on competence of beginning teachers. *Journal of Educational Research, 80*(6), 343–347.

Carnegie Forum on Education and the Economy. (1986, May). *A nation prepared: Teachers for the 21st century.* Washington, DC: Author.

Carter, K. (1990). Teachers' knowledge and learning to teach. In W. R. Houston, M. Haberman, & J. Sikula (Eds.), *Handbook of research on teacher education* (pp. 291–310). New York: Macmillan.

Clark, D. L., & McNergney, R. F. (1990). Governance of teacher education. In W. R. Houston, M. Haberman, & J. Sikula (Eds.), *Handbook of research on teacher education* (pp. 101–118). New York: Macmillan.

Clune, W. H. (1993). The best path to systemic educational policy: Standard/centralized or differentiated/decentralized? *Educational Evaluation and Policy Analysis, 15*(3), 233–254.

Doyle, W. (1990). Themes in teacher education research. In W. R. Houston, M. Haberman, & J. Sikula (Eds.), *Handbook of research on teacher education* (pp. 3–24). New York: Macmillan.

Earley, P. M. (1994a). *Federal attention to teacher certification and licensure: Two policy case studies.* Unpublished doctoral dissertation, Virginia Tech.

Earley, P. M. (1994b). *Goals 2000: Educate America Act implications for teacher education*. Washington, DC: American Association of Colleges for Teacher Education.

Fenstermacher, G. (1986). Philosophy of research on teaching: Three aspects. In M. C. Whittrock (Ed.), *Handbook of research on teaching* (3rd ed., pp. 37–49). New York: Macmillan.

Finn, C. E., Jr. (1988). Education policy and the Reagan administration: A large but incomplete success. *Education Policy, 2*(4), 343–360.

Gage, N. L. (1989, October). The paradigm wars and their aftermath: A "historical" sketch of teaching since 1989. *Educational Researcher, 18*(7), 4–10.

Gilley, J. W., & Fulmer, K. A. (1986). *A question of leadership: Or, to whom are the governors listening?* Fairfax, VA: The Center for Policy Studies in Education, George Mason University.

General Accounting Office (GAO). (1984, March 6). *New directions for federal programs to aid mathematics and science teaching.* (GAO/PEMD-84-5). Washington, DC: Author.

General Accounting Office (GAO). (1994, September 13). *Precollege math and science education.* (GAO/HEHS-94-208). Washington, DC: Author.

Goodlad, J. I. (1984). *A place called school: Prospects for the future.* New York: McGraw-Hill.

Goodlad, J. I. (1990). *Teachers for our nation's schools.* San Francisco: Jossey-Bass.

Green, T. F. (1983). Excellence, equity, and equality. In L. S. Shulman & G. Sykes (Eds.), *Handbook of teaching and policy* (pp. 318–342). New York: Longman.

Hawley, W. D. (1990). Systematic analysis, public policy-making, and teacher education. In W. R. Houston, M. Haberman, & J. Sikula (Eds.), *Handbook of research on teacher education* (pp. 136–156). New York: Macmillan.

The Holmes Group. (1986). *Tomorrow's teachers.* East Lansing, MI: Author.

HR 5115, Equity and Excellence in Education Act. (1990).

HR 5932, Educational Equity and Excellence Act. (1990).

Jordan, K. F. (1986, July 18). *Teacher education recommendations in the school reform efforts.* (CRS Report No. 86-780 S). Washington, DC: Congressional Research Service.

Jordan, K. F., & Borkow, N. B. (1985). *Federal efforts to improve America's teaching force.* (CRS Report No. 85-644 S). Washington, DC: Congressional Research Service.

Kaestle, C. F., & Smith, M. S. (1982). The federal role in elementary and secondary education, 1940–1980. *Harvard Educational Review, 52*(4), 384–408.

Kingdon, J. W. (1984). *Agendas, alternatives, and public policy.* Boston: Little, Brown.

National Advisory Council on Education Professions Development. (1976). *National issues in education professions development.* Washington, DC: U.S. Department of Health, Education and Welfare.

National Center for Education Statistics (NCES). (1991). *Digest of Education Statistics.* Washington, DC: U.S. Department of Education, Office of Educational Research and Improvement.

National Commission for Excellence in Teacher Education (NCETE). (1985). *A call for change in teacher education.* Washington, DC: American Association of Colleges for Teacher Education.

National Commission on Excellence in Education. (1983). *A nation at risk: The imperative for educational reform.* Washington, DC: Author.

National Governors' Association. (1986). *Time for results.* Washington, DC: Author.

National Teacher Development Initiative (NTDI). (1978). *Analysis of U.S. Office of Education discretionary programs having a professional development of educational personnel component.* Report submitted to U.S. Commissioner of Education Ernest Boyer. Washington, DC: U.S. Office of Education.

O'Neill, J. A., & Simms, M. C. (1982). Education. In J. L. Palmer & I. V. Sawhill (Eds.), *The Reagan experiment: An experiment of economic and social policies under the Reagan administration* (pp. 329–359). Washington, DC: The Urban Institute Press.

Pintrich, P. R. (1990). Implications of psychological research on student learning and college teaching for teacher education. In W. R. Houston, M. Haberman, & J. Sikula (Eds.), *Handbook of research on teacher education* (pp. 826–857). New York: Macmillan.

Prestine, N. (1991, summer). Political system theory as an explanatory paradigm for teacher education reform. *American Educational Research Journal, 28*(2), 237–274.

Public Law 85-864, National Defense Education Act. (1958).

Public Law 89-328, Higher Education Amendments (Teacher Corps). (1965).

Public Law 90-35, Education Professions Development Act. (1967).

Public Law 97-35, Omnibus Budget Reconciliation Act. (1981).

Public Law 98-377, Education for Economic Security Act. (1984).

Public Law 102-325, Higher Education Amendments. (1992).

Public Law 103-227, Goals 2000: Educate America Act. (1994).

Public Law 103-382, Elementary and Secondary Education Amendments. (1994).

Richardson, V. (1990, October). Significant and worthwhile change in teaching practice. *Educational Researcher, 19*(7), 10–18.

Rosenshine, B., & Stevens, R. (1986). Teaching functions. In M. C. Whittrock (Ed.), *Handbook of research on teaching* (3rd ed., pp. 376–390). New York: Macmillan.

S. 695, Educational Excellence Act. (1989).

S. 1676, National Teacher Act. (1990).

Shulman, L. S. (1986). Paradigms and research programs in the study of teaching: A contemporary perspective. In M. C. Whittrock (Ed.), *Handbook of research on teaching* (3rd ed., pp. 3–36). New York: Macmillan.

Smith, M. S., O'Day, J., & Cohen, D. K. (1990, Winter). National curriculum American style. *American Educator, 14*(4), 10–17, 40–46.

Tom, A. R., & Valli, L. (1990). Professional knowledge for teachers. In W. R. Houston, M. Haberman, & J. Sikula (Eds.), *Handbook of research on teacher education* (pp. 373–392). New York: Macmillan.

U.S. Department of Education. (1991). *AMERICA 2000: An education strategy.* Washington, DC: U.S. Government Printing Office.

Part
·IV·

TEACHER EDUCATION CURRICULUM

·16·

EARLY CHILDHOOD EDUCATION

Sue Bredekamp

NATIONAL ASSOCIATION FOR THE EDUCATION OF YOUNG CHILDREN

Early childhood education is experiencing a period of tremendous public attention and growth. Major national reports recognize the value of early childhood education and call for improvements in the quality of early childhood programs and accessibility for our nation's children, especially children from low-income families (Committee for Economic Development, 1991, 1993; National Association of State Boards of Education, 1988, 1991; National Commission on Children, 1991). The National Education Goals Panel's (NEGP) first national goal (NEGP, 1991) targets the early childhood years, and, in fact, achievement of all the national goals has been said to depend on the progress made in achieving Goal 1 (Boyer, 1991). In the 1992 presidential election, all three major candidates' platforms called for full funding of Head Start to ensure that all eligible children gain access; the resulting expansion is the largest in the program's 30-year history. At the same time, elementary schools are serving younger children, with the majority of states now offering public school prekindergarten programs for 4-year-old children and some districts serving children as young as 3 years of age (Mitchell, Seligson, & Marx, 1989).

Bipartisan support for early childhood education by the President, the Congress, the nation's governors, and the business community is not matched by similar enthusiasm in the higher education community. As is described later in this chapter, for a variety of historical and political reasons, early childhood programs in institutions of higher education vary enormously in content and quality and continue to be understaffed, often with no more than one faculty member with primary assignments in early childhood (Bredekamp, 1990). Given the changing demographics of this country, the growing recognition that education begins at birth or at least well prior to what has traditionally been considered the beginning of formal schooling, and the continuing expansion in numbers of programs serving young children, institutions of higher education that do not support early childhood education programs are missing an opportunity, as well as failing to meet a responsibility, to ensure qualified teachers to meet the demand.

The primary purpose of this chapter is to introduce the broader field of teacher education to early childhood education. Early childhood education is a diverse field, encompassing a broad age span from birth through 8 years of age, various settings not limited to schools, diverse regulatory systems and standards, different professional roles requiring different kinds of preparation, and various levels and models of preparation. The unifying force for such a diverse field is shared knowledge. The knowledge bases of early childhood education can be variously described, but for the purpose of this chapter the joint position statement on standards for early childhood teacher certification developed by the Association of Teacher Educators (ATE) and the National Association for the Education of Young Children (NAEYC) (ATE & NAEYC, 1991, 1992) is used as the framework for describing the unifying knowledge bases of this diverse field.

In this chapter, early childhood education is defined and the diversity of the field and its history are briefly described. Then, research on the effects on children of participation in early childhood programs is summarized to demonstrate the importance of including early childhood education in state policies and institutions of higher education. The ATE/NAEYC certification standards are used as a framework for summarizing the research on the content of the early childhood teacher education curriculum and the effects of curriculum and teacher behaviors on children's development and learning. The chapter also summarizes research on the effectiveness of preparation, preservice, and in-service. Finally, the chapter identifies trends in early childhood education, such as the burgeoning professional development movement and the increasing connection with early childhood special education. The chapter concludes by identifying areas in need of further research.

Although earlier relevant reviews of the literature are available (Feeney & Chun, 1985; Powell, 1986; Spodek & Saracho, 1990; Stallings & Stipek, 1986), this chapter begins from the premise that there is insufficient research specifically addressing the issue of early childhood teacher education. The inadequacy of the literature has led other reviewers to conclude that an understanding of early childhood teacher education requires extrapolating from research on related areas (Goffin, 1989; Saracho, 1993). Although research on the effects of preservice education of teachers of young children is limited (Ott, Zeichner, & Price, 1990), there is a large body of research on program effects on children that has clear implications for teacher education. In other words, there is considerable literature, the more recent of which is reviewed in this chapter, from which to determine what an early childhood teacher should know and be able to do; this literature is useful in specifying the goals or expected outcomes of a teacher education program.

The decision to focus this chapter on research related to the potential outcomes of a teacher education program reflects the current trend toward outcome- or performance-based teacher education and licensure (Wise & Leibbrand, 1993). The debate over whether outcomes or performance indicators are the most appropriate mechanism for planning and evaluating programs is far from resolved (Elliot, 1993), and the decision to frame this chapter from the point of view of "outcomes" is not intended to reflect a resolution of that debate. In fact, the "outcomes" promoted here are not narrow behavioral objectives or competencies, but rather they are broad descriptors of what an early childhood teacher should know and be able to do that have been demonstrated to have a relationship to positive effects for children, also broadly defined, and they are not limited to academic achievement or standardized test scores.

The age span encompassed by early childhood education— birth through 8 years—overlaps in the primary grades with the topic of several other chapters in this handbook including elementary education, language arts and other curriculum content areas, and special education; therefore, the research cited here relevant to the primary grades is intended to be illustrative rather than comprehensive. To avoid redundancy, emphasis is placed on research applicable to programs for infants through kindergarten. This decision does not intend to lessen the importance of early childhood preparation across the full age span— birth through 8 years; instead, it reflects confidence in the growing research and philosophical base in general teacher education, especially in mathematics and literacy, that is congruent with the developmental and social-constructivist perspectives of early childhood education.

EARLY CHILDHOOD EDUCATION: DEFINED AND DESCRIBED

The National Association for the Education of Young Children (NAEYC), with 90,000 members in 1994, is the nation's largest professional organization exclusively focused on the educational and developmental needs of young children. Deriving its definition from a developmental perspective, NAEYC defines early childhood as birth through age eight. This definition is based on the assumption that the developmental needs and learning processes throughout this period of the lifespan are sufficiently similar to warrant consideration from a unified perspective. Obviously, this definition does not reflect other considerations such as the traditional structure of elementary schools (K–6) or the preexisting teacher certification (licensure)

standards of many states. Instead, the definition reflects the fact that children at this developmental period share certain characteristics, such as vulnerability, closeness to the family, dependence on adults, and concrete thinking, to name a few, that determine the type of relationships and experiences that are most appropriate for them. Experiences in the early years of life can be characterized as foundational and, therefore, viewing this period from a unified perspective can help to ensure that a positive foundation is laid for all children. Furthermore, early childhood is a valuable period of the lifespan in and of itself, necessitating that children be provided with the best possible environments. Young children's learning and development in the physical, social, emotional, aesthetic, and cognitive domains are also integrated and interrelated, thereby necessitating programs and services designed to meet the needs of the "whole child." Toward this goal, NAEYC promotes standards for early childhood program quality (Bredekamp, 1987; National Association for the Education of Young Children [NAEYC], 1991a) that are supported by congruent standards of other national education organizations (National Association of Elementary School Principals, 1990; National Association of State Boards of Education, 1988).

Such a broad definition of the age range of early childhood means that early childhood education by definition occurs under diverse auspices in diverse settings, including public and private centers and schools. The integrated nature of learning and development in early childhood prohibits the false distinction that is often made between care and education. NAEYC's position is that good quality programs for children from birth through age eight provide both care and education (ATE & NAEYC, 1991, 1992). The terminology that is sometimes used to distinguish these services, for example, child care versus preschool, is an artifact that more clearly reflects the length of the program day rather than the pedagogical experience provided for children in different programs.

Because the settings serving young children are so diverse, no one source of information can be consulted to gain a clear picture of where children are served and by whom. Nevertheless, the data that are available identify a large and growing component of educational service in America (Willer et al., 1991). Primarily the result of the large increase in numbers of mothers of young children in the labor force, the numbers of young children who are served in out-of-home programs has increased enormously. Between 1975 and 1991, the percentage of employed mothers with children under 6 years increased from 39% to 58%, and more than half the mothers of infants under age one were employed in 1991 (National Commission on Children, 1993). In the same time period, the number of child care centers in America tripled (Kisker, Hofferth, Phillips, & Farquhar, 1991). At the beginning of 1990, approximately 80,000 center-based early childhood programs capable of serving more than 5 million preschool-age children were operating in the United States (Kisker et al., 1991). Approximately two thirds of center-based programs are nonprofit organizations, including religious organizations, public schools, and Head Start; the remainder are private, for-profit, and often independently owned and operated. In addition, school-age children are served in before- and after-school programs. In 1991, 49,500 formal school-age child care programs served approximately 1.7 million children, 90% of whom were in the age range of prekindergarten through third grade (Seppanen, Kaplan de Vries, & Seligson, 1993).

By 1991, 28% of all 3-year-old children and 53% of all 4-year-old children were enrolled in a preschool program (National Center for Education Statistics [NCES], 1993). Growth of public school prekindergarten programs has been rapid. Between 1980 and 1983, three states instituted direct service public school programs for preschoolers; by 1989, 32 states offered such programs, with most states targeting programs to children identified as at risk for school failure (Mitchell et al., 1989). Kindergarten, which is now provided in every state, although attendance is rarely mandated, is almost a universal experience; virtually all children have attended kindergarten before starting first grade (NCES, 1993).

Despite the increase in publicly funded prekindergarten programs, participation in preschool continues to be related to family income. The National Center for Education Statistics (1993) reports that approximately 40% of 3- to 5-year-old children from families earning less than $20,000 per year attend preschool, whereas 75% of preschool children whose families earn more than $75,000 participate in a preschool program.

Preschool, child care, and before- and after-school programs, added to the existing public and private schools for children from kindergarten through third grade, indicate the need for a large work force of early childhood teachers. One might ask what the current work force looks like. Regulations for staff qualifications in child care programs vary from state to state and are generally quite minimal, with only 16 states requiring any preservice training for teachers in licensed child care centers (Morgan et al., 1993). Despite these low requirements and salaries that average approximately $11,500 per year, almost half (47%) of teachers in centers have a college degree and an additional 13% hold an associate-level degree (Willer et al., 1991). Public school related programs most often require a baccalaureate degree or teacher certification, and salaries in these programs average twice as much as child care salaries. Low salaries and lack of adequate benefits are found to be related to high levels of turnover in child care programs. In a random sample of child care centers in five major metropolitan areas in 1988, a staff turnover rate of 41% was found (Whitebook, Howes, & Phillips, 1989); a follow-up study found a lower rate of 26%, which is still significantly higher than the 5.6% turnover rate reported for public school teachers (Whitebook, Phillips, & Howes, 1993).

Given the inadequate compensation and high rates of turnover experienced in child care programs, as well as the projected growth in numbers of programs of all kinds, the early childhood profession is experiencing a staffing crisis of some proportion. An analysis of occupational trends to the year 2005 by the Bureau of Labor Statistics (Silvestri, 1993) identifies early childhood teachers in child care, preschool, and kindergarten as among the fastest growing occupations in America. Between 1992 and 2005, the number of child care teachers is expected to increase by at least 60%, more if overall economic growth is high. This trend is not only the result of anticipated growth in the number of young children, but also a projected change in the child care arrangements parents prefer, which are shifting from informal to more formal institutional settings. Similarly,

the numbers of preschool and kindergarten teachers are expected to increase by approximately 50% as a result of expected increases in student enrollments. Such trends clearly identify an opportunity and a challenge for institutions of higher education to ensure that these jobs are filled by qualified, knowledgable professionals.

Even such a brief description of types of programs and staffing issues confronting early childhood education reveals the complexity of the field. This complex field is perhaps best understood within some historical context, a brief description of which follows.

Historical Perspectives

A complete description of the history of early childhood education services in the United States is beyond the scope of this chapter and is available from other sources (see Williams & Fromberg, 1992). Part of the continuing tension between child care and preschool programs as well as the persistent dichotomy between care and education is the result of different historical origins. To oversimplify a relatively complex history, child care programs originally grew out of the social welfare movement and were provided as a service for parents who work; less emphasis was placed on the educational needs of children in such circumstances. On the contrary, preschool programs, formerly called nursery schools, grew out of the child study movement in university settings and were traditionally seen as providing enrichment, primarily social experiences, to children whose families could afford to pay for such services.

In some ways it could be said that the establishment of Head Start in the mid-1960s brought these two movements together. Head Start is a federally funded, usually half-day educational program that is designed to increase the likelihood of school success by providing educational and comprehensive health services for preschool-age children whose family incomes fall below the poverty level. The emphasis on children's cognitive development in Head Start and other experimental preschool programs in the 1960s led to a shift in all early childhood programs away from almost exclusive emphasis on social development to more emphasis on intellectual and academic achievement. Research on the lasting effects of such preschool experience, which is discussed in more detail later (Berrueta-Clement, Schweinhart, Barnett, Epstein, & Weikart, 1984; Lazar & Darlington, 1982; Miller & Bizzell, 1984), contributed to the expansion of Head Start as well as to the institutionalization of prekindergarten programs in public schools.

The kindergarten movement in the United States paralleled the nursery school movement to some extent. Beginning with the introduction of the Froebelian kindergarten from Germany in the mid-1800s, kindergartens gradually grew in numbers for a century. Until the 1960s most kindergartens were privately operated; during the 1960s and 1970s public schools began adding kindergarten at a rapid rate, with Mississippi, the last state to offer public kindergarten, doing so in 1987.

The development of professional preparation programs for early childhood personnel also reflects a complex history (Hewes, 1990). Teacher education programs in institutions of higher education tend to reflect the teacher licensure standards of the state. Because public schools were relatively late to add kindergarten and prekindergarten programs, it is not surprising that teacher licensure standards and preparation programs do not universally reflect this development. Teacher education programs most often emphasized an elementary focus, sometimes with an early childhood endorsement. If early childhood education was offered at all, it was usually defined as kindergarten through third grade (K–3) or nursery through third grade (N–3). Historically, curriculum addressing child development or services for children of preschool age and younger was more often found in what were formerly called home economics programs and what are now often found in departments of human development, human ecology, family studies, or under some other institutional structure and identity. As early childhood programs have expanded into colleges of education, some institutions have formed linkages with departments of child development, whereas others remain relatively autonomous and unrelated.

In addition to diversity at the program level in baccalaureate-level institutions, there is also diversity in levels of professional preparation available. Early childhood education is unique among teacher preparation programs in that degree programs in the field are available at the associate level. Associate degrees in early childhood education serve as terminal degrees for many people seeking employment in child care centers where 4-year degrees are not required for employment; however, associate degree holders also attempt to transfer to early childhood programs at senior-level institutions and usually find articulation of professional credits difficult, if not impossible (Morgan et al., 1993). In addition to formal preparation at institutions of higher education, the early childhood profession also supports a competency-based assessment and credentialing system, the Child Development Associate (CDA) credential. The CDA credentialing system was first developed for use in Head Start programs to provide a mechanism for assessing and recognizing the competence of individuals who have acquired knowledge and skills through informal, on-the-job, and in-service training, rather than through formal preservice preparation (Powell & Dunn, 1990).

Different levels of preparation in early childhood education create both an opportunity and a challenge. The opportunity is inherent in the potential for differentiated staffing models within agencies and the possibility for natural career ladders. The challenge lies in the reality that differentially qualified personnel earning vastly different amounts of compensation are responsible for groups of children. This situation is particularly apparent in different programs for 4-year-old children; the same young child may be enrolled in public school where a certified teacher is required, in a Head Start program where a CDA credentialed individual may teach, or in a child care center where no training may be required of the teacher. This situation is a product of the diverse regulatory systems that govern the field, a brief description of which follows.

Regulatory and Professional Standards

Another contributor to the diversity of early childhood programs and preparation for adults who work in them is the diverse standards that regulate the qualifications of personnel. As mentioned earlier, child care programs and most private preschools typically are regulated by state licensing standards administered by departments of health or social services. These standards dictate facility requirements and set a minimal standard for personnel training (Morgan et al., 1993). Even the states that require preservice training usually set a minimun number of clock hours of specialized training rather than semester hours or degrees. More states require ongoing in-service training for teaching staff, but again these requirements are in the form of clock hours, usually as few as 15 annually. One of the potentially positive effects of child care licensing standards is that they often identify more than one role with differing qualifications; for instance, standards for qualifications of program administrators are typically higher, usually requiring a baccalaureate degree in early childhood or a related field. Head Start programs set their own standards for personnel and now have a requirement that at least one teacher in each classroom must possess a CDA credential or other early childhood degree, and Head Start is working toward promoting a career ladder with a master teacher level. To be responsive to the needs and to take advantage of the situation created by such standards, higher education institutions could broaden the scope and content of the programs offered to prepare students for master teacher and administrative roles (Morgan et al., 1993).

Public schools, including public school prekindergartens, require teachers to have a baccalaureate degree and a teaching certificate. Whereas such a requirement ostensibly means that public school teachers are more qualified than personnel in other early childhood programs, the diversity of state teacher certification standards undermines such an outcome. Unlike other levels of teacher preparation, there is no uniform definition of early childhood applied by the states, and certification standards for early childhood vary considerably. A recent survey of state certification standards (Morgan et al., 1993) reveals that only half the states have a freestanding specialized early childhood certificate. Among these states, nine different definitions of the scope of early childhood can be found (McCarthy, 1988). Another 10 states have an add-on early childhood endorsement to an elementary education certificate. The amount of coursework and field experience specific to early childhood required by such endorsements varies considerably with some states requiring only two additional courses. Sixteen states have no early childhood certification or endorsement available. In addition, 30 states require no practicum experiences with children younger than kindergarten age (Morgan et al., 1993). The implication of these varying certification standards for teacher education is clear; because state certification standards virtually dictate program content in most teacher preparation programs, the scope and content of "early childhood education" programs vary enormously in baccalaureate programs.

In an attempt to improve the quality and consistency of early childhood teacher preparation programs, NAEYC (1991b) developed guidelines for baccalaureate and advanced degree programs in the 1980s that are approved by the National Council for Accreditation of Teacher Education (NCATE). As an associate member of NCATE, NAEYC reviews the early childhood curriculum folios for institutions seeking NCATE accreditation. From a decade of experience conducting folio review, NAEYC observed the impact of state certification standards on program content (Bredekamp, 1990). Despite the fact that NAEYC guidelines define early childhood as birth through age eight, programs tend to use the state's definition in defining the parameters of students' experience. One result, for example, is that very few baccalaureate programs address the educational and developmental needs of infants and toddlers in coursework, and field experiences with this age group are extremely rare. The lack of any preparation for working with infants and toddlers, the fastest growing age group in child care, is of real concern because the specific developmental needs and program requirements of this age group are different from those of older children (Robinson, 1990). Only half the states require any content relevant to critical dimensions of programs for young children (Morgan et al., 1993), such as working with families or health and safety, which is a major concern for children in group care (American Public Health Association & American Academy of Pediatrics, 1992).

Admittedly, covering the full range of birth through age eight may present challenges to teacher education programs that already find it difficult to adequately prepare teachers in the allotted number of credit hours. Nevertheless, the age span of birth through eight is no longer than the kindergarten through sixth- or eighth-grade span that elementary education has traditionally addressed, and it is far shorter than the K–12 age span possible with some certifications. Advocating for birth through eight programs assumes that some aspects of the preparation will be more integrated (courses in language and literacy development or working with families, for instance, can be adapted to cover the full age span), whereas some specialization will also be necessary. NAEYC's teacher education guidelines, for example, call for a broad base of knowledge in child development, learning, and curriculum across the full age span and more in-depth specialization and student teaching in two of three subperiods of that age-span—infants/toddlers, preschool, or primary grades (NAEYC, 1991b).

In recognition of the powerful influence of state certification standards on program content, NAEYC in collaboration with ATE targeted advocacy efforts at changing state standards. Toward this goal, the two organizations developed a joint position statement on early childhood teacher certification calling for specialized early childhood certification covering the full age span of birth through eight in every state (ATE & NAEYC, 1991). A supportive position statement was developed by the National Association of Early Childhood Teacher Educators (NAECTE) and the National Association of Early Childhood Specialists in State Departments of Education (NAECTE, 1993). A similar recommendation for specialized early childhood certification resulted from a survey of 100 teachers in Tennessee, approximately half of whom reported that their broad elementary education certification did not adequately prepare them for the age group they chose to teach, whether early or intermediate grades (Mitchell & Maar, 1986). Coincidentally, Tennessee was among the first states to approve a specialized early childhood certificate, for birth through age eight, following the dissemination of the ATE and NAEYC position statement. Other states, including Iowa, Connecticut, Delaware, Ohio, and New Mexico, approved new early childhood certificates guided by the ATE and NAEYC statement. These policy changes, as well as the growth in programs for young children, especially publicly funded programs, can be attributed at least in part to research on the lasting effects of such programs, which is summarized in the next section.

THE EFFECTIVENESS OF EARLY CHILDHOOD PROGRAMS: OUTCOMES FOR CHILDREN

Research on the lasting effects of early childhood programs on children not only has contributed to the increase in the numbers of such programs and the establishment of program standards, but also supports the need for adequate preparation of personnel. This research is primarily of two kinds: research on the effects of preschool programs for disadvantaged children and research on the effects of participation in child care programs of varying quality. Findings regarding the overall effects of participation in early childhood programs are reported here, whereas studies that address effects on children of specific curriculum implementation or teaching behaviors are reported later in the chapter as guidance for the content of the teacher education curriculum.

Research on the Lasting Effects of Early Childhood Education Programs

Expansion of Head Start and initiation of public school prekindergarten has been influenced by a relatively small number of longitudinal studies demonstrating long-term, positive consequences of participation in high quality early childhood programs for preschoolers and infants from low-income families. In the late 1970s, a consortium of 12 independent researchers who had conducted early intervention demonstration projects in the 1960s pooled their data to integrate findings of several studies and conducted a collaborative follow-up of subjects who then ranged in age from 9 to 19 years (Lazar & Darlington, 1982). The results demonstrated that early education programs for disadvantaged children demonstrated lasting, significant effects in four areas: "school competence, developed abilities, children's attitudes and values, and impact on the family" (Lazar & Darlington, 1982, p. 55). Children who participated in early childhood programs were significantly less likely than control group children to be assigned to special education or retained in grade. Experimental group children also performed better on measures of intelligence and achievement. Mothers of children who had participated in the early education programs were more likely to have positive attitudes about their children's performance in school and their future potential. The longitudinal studies in general suggested positive consequences for programs that stress child-initiated activities (Berrueta-Clement et al., 1984; Lazar & Darlington, 1982; Miller & Bizzell, 1984).

Among the 12 consortium participants was one research project, the Perry Preschool Project in Ypsilanti, Michigan, that has been highly influential for public policy related to early childhood education due to the demonstration of lasting results and the careful cost-benefit analysis included in the research. Similar to some other studies of preschool effects, the intelligence advantages of Perry Preschool graduates tended to fade by third grade (which may be more an effect of primary grade than preschool practices); however, by following the children over time and investigating outcomes with real-life consequences, the researchers were able to identify significant benefits of preschool participation at age 19 (Berrueta-Clement et al., 1984) and at age 27 (Schweinhart, Barnes, & Weikart, 1993). The sample consisted of 123 African-American children whose families were living in poverty and who were randomly assigned to participate in the program or to the control group. Data on both experimental and control groups have been collected annually from age 3 through 11 and at ages 14, 15, 19, and 27. At 19, the experimental group showed significant advantages in high school completion rate, fewer teen pregnancies, and lower rates of delinquency. At age 27, the preschool participants were significantly more likely to be earning at least $2,000 per month, to own their own homes, and to be in a stable marriage, and they were less likely to have been on welfare. Perhaps of greatest consequence for society were differences in crimes committed by control and experimental group members. Only 7% of those who had participated in the preschool program had been arrested five or more times, whereas 35% of those who had not attended preschool had such an extensive arrest record. The researchers concluded that $7.16 is returned for every $1.00 invested in a high quality preschool in which the curriculum facilitates active learning, promotes decision making, and involves parents.

The longitudinal studies cited have been influential in justifying ongoing and increased funding for Head Start despite the fact that they were not conducted in Head Start programs. No such longitudinal research exists for Head Start, nor would it be possible because random assignment to treatment is not feasible in a national program. The findings for lasting effects of Head Start are more modest, but nevertheless they do demonstrate positive effects, especially in the short-term. For example, a 1-year follow-up study (Lee, Brooks-Gunn, & Schnur, 1988) conducted in two regions of the country compared children who attended Head Start with those who attended other programs or no program. The study found that Head Start children, who began with greater deficits on most demographic and cognitive measures, showed significantly larger gains on measures of achievement adjusting for initial differences, with African-American Head Start children demonstrating the most progress. A synthesis of more than 200 separate evaluations of Head Start confirmed the program's effectiveness in improving cognition and social development as well as improving children's health and changing parents' attitudes about their children's abilities (McKey et al., 1985). One Head Start evaluation study, which emphasized that its results were based on "regular" rather than demonstration-quality program implementation, found significant and lasting positive results (Copple, Cline, & Smith, 1987). This study examined the impact of Head Start implemented in 33 different schools and its effects for children followed up in hundreds of schools within the Philadelphia area. The researchers found that achievement advantages diminished over time, but concluded that the long-term impact of Head Start is in reducing school failure; Head Start graduates were significantly less likely to be retained in grade from kindergarten through grade six, and their school attendance rates were better than non–Head Start students.

Sophisticated analysis of the effects of preschool participation on economically disadvantaged children (Reynolds, 1991) reveals that positive outcomes of preschool attendance are mediated by other factors, such as school mobility, parent involvement, and children's social and cognitive maturity. Nevertheless, Reynolds concludes that the effect of preschool should not be minimized, especially the immediate effect on cognitive readiness. None of the research cited here supports the overgeneralization that early childhood education is an inoculation against poverty or that it is the solution to school failure; however, a sufficient body of research does exist that demonstrates conclusively that high quality early childhood education plays an important role, along with other educational and social factors, in promoting success in school and in life for children who are at greatest risk of failure.

Very little research has been conducted to examine the lasting effects of preschool on middle-class children, who are at low risk. One such study (Larsen & Robinson, 1989) found significant effects on school achievement at second and third grade, especially in language-related areas, for low-risk males who attended preschool; no lasting effects were found for low-risk females. Ironically, despite the lack of data to support the lasting effects of early childhood education for advantaged children, preschool attendance rates increase as family income increases (NCES, 1993). Apparently, middle- and upper-income families are sufficiently convinced of the value of early childhood programs to invest their own money in programs in the absence of data to support lasting positive consequences.

Research on the Lasting Effects of Child Care Participation

Unlike the longitudinal preschool research cited previously, which is generalizable only to low-income populations, research on the effects of attending child care has been conducted primarily with middle-class children. Early studies of the effects of child care tended to compare attendance with nonattendance ("homerearing") and were designed to address the assumption that participation in child care was inevitably inferior to staying home with a parent. Such research was most often conducted in high quality demonstration sites and found no significant disadvantages for children who attended child care centers. The more recent waves of research on child care have asked more sophisticated questions. Specifically, research has attempted to provide answers about the effects of child care of varying quality and then, more recently, to "unpack" the variables that constitute child care experiences and examine the effects of specific dimensions of child care on children.

Not surprisingly, the findings of research on the long-term effects of child care indicate that children who attend good quality child care programs, even at very young ages, demonstrate positive outcomes, and children who attend poor quality programs show negative effects. One study (Field, Masi, Goldstein, Perry, & Parl, 1988) assessed 71 children in preschool who had attended a high quality, university-run infant child care center; some of the children had entered child care during the first 6 months of life and the rest had entered after 6 months of age. Results indicated that age of entry into the program had no significant effect on attachment to mother or on socialization skills observed in preschool. In fact, children who had attended more hours of a high quality infant day care program demonstrated more positive social behavior in preschool. These children were less likely to engage in solitary play, to watch, or to seek the teacher's attention or comfort. Moreover, they were more likely to engage in cooperative play, positive interaction with peers, and to demonstrate positive emotions and verbal interaction. The federal government's National Institute for Child Health and Human Development is engaged in a major longitudinal study of the effects of infant child care experiences on cognitive, linguistic, social, emotional, and physical development. The first data from the study that boasts a heterogeneous sample of 1,300 infants are available in 1995; the results will have important policy implications for infant child care, especially as publicly funded programs such as Head Start expand to serve younger children.

The long-term consequences of child care for school adjustment were also the subject of a study (Howes, 1988) that followed 87 children who had experienced high quality child care from age 3 years. After controlling for the effect of family characteristics, the results showed that high quality, stable child care experiences predicted academic success, adjustment to school, and lack of behavioral problems for both males and females in first grade.

A longitudinal study (Vandell, Henderson, & Wilson, 1988), which was actually a follow-up to an earlier study (Vandell & Powers, 1983), assessed 20 white, middle-class children who had attended low and high quality child care programs at third grade. High quality programs had well-trained teachers who engaged in positive interactions with children, more adults per child, more and varied equipment, and a stimulating program of activities. Controlling for family social class, at age 8 years children from better quality programs engaged in more friendly interactions with peers and were rated as more socially competent and happier. In the earlier study (Vandell & Powers, 1983), children from low quality programs engaged in fewer positive social interactions with adults and were more often found to wander aimlessly than children in higher quality programs. Social competence demonstrated at age four tended to be related to social skills demonstrated at age eight (Vandell et al., 1988). Children from high quality programs who had engaged in positive interactions with adults demonstrated more empathy and peer acceptance at age eight, whereas unoccupied behavior at age four among children in low quality programs was negatively related to social competence and negotiation of conflicts at age eight.

Similar results were found in another longitudinal study (Vandell & Corasanti, 1990) of the effects of varying levels of quality child care on children's social, emotional, and cognitive development at third grade. Children who had experienced poor quality early child care were rated more negatively by both parents and teachers on peer relationships, work habits, emotional health, and ability to get along with adults. Poor quality infant care was also related to lower report card grades and scores on standardized tests.

Although findings such as these are reassuring regarding the potential positive effects of high quality child care, some negative effects are disturbing in light of the fact that several large-scale evaluations of child care quality find that high quality experiences are not the norm. For instance, the National Child Care Staffing Study (Whitebook et al., 1989) found that on the Early Childhood Environmental Rating Scale (ECERS) developed by Thelma Harms and Richard Clifford, a widely used global measure of quality that ranks dimensions of programs on a seven-point scale, at least two thirds of the classrooms, observed in 227 centers serving children from infants through preschool in three different states, fell below a score of four (considered "barely adequate" quality) and only 12% scored in the "good" range. Another study (Howes, Phillips, & Whitebook, 1992) that examined the effects of quality of child care on social development of 414 children observed in different child care classrooms in three different metropolitan areas found that 70% of infants and 52% of toddlers were in classrooms that were rated "barely adequate" or "inadequate" for quality. Results such as these compared to the studies reported earlier indicate that whereas early childhood programs have the potential for producing positive and lasting effects on children, this potential will not be achieved unless more attention is paid to ensuring that all programs meet the highest standards of quality, the most important determinant of which is the teacher. Early childhood education, like all education, demands well-prepared teachers.

CONTENT OF THE EARLY CHILDHOOD TEACHER EDUCATION CURRICULUM

The diversity of the early childhood profession, with various settings and levels as described earlier, has been characterized by NAEYC as a career lattice rather than a career ladder (Bredekamp & Willer, 1992). What unifies this diverse field into a profession is shared knowledge. The shared knowledge of early childhood education constitutes the content of the early childhood teacher education curriculum. The ATE & NAEYC (1991, 1992) certification standards address five areas of the teacher education program: child development and learning (including health, safety, and nutrition); curriculum development, content, and implementation; family and community relations; professionalism; and field experiences and professional internship. Of these topic areas, content most specific to early childhood education, such as child development and learning, curriculum content and implementation, and family relations, is discussed here.

One of the primary tenets of early childhood education is that teachers need to understand and apply knowledge of child development and learning in all domains—physical, social, emotional, language, aesthetic, and cognitive (Peters & Klinzing, 1990). NAEYC has established standards for program practice that describe a high quality educational experience for children from birth through age eight (Bredekamp, 1987; NAEYC, 1991a). One of the criteria used to determine the quality of an early childhood program is the degree to which the various dimensions of the program are "developmentally appropriate," that is, the degree to which knowledge of children's development and learning in general (information about what is age appropriate) provides a framework within which adaptations are made for individual needs and interests of children (adjusting to ensure that children's experiences are individually appropriate). Implementation of "developmentally appropriate practices" presumes that teachers have a fundamental knowledge of child development theory and research and are able to apply that knowledge in planning and implementing curriculum and instruction. To achieve this goal, child development knowledge must be linked to pedagogical knowledge to ensure fully informed and skilled teachers (McCarthy, 1990). Child development knowledge and pedagogical knowledge are so closely linked in practice that it is very difficult to separate them conceptually, as becomes clear in discussing research on either area. What follows is a review of research on the effects of teacher behaviors and curriculum practices. This section concludes with a summary of the implications of this research for early childhood teacher education curriculum.

Research on the Effects of Teacher Behaviors on Children's Development

The most recent wave of research on the effects of early childhood programs attempted to analyze the effects on children of specific dimensions of their experience. Even a cursory reading of this research reveals that the tools that are used and the questions asked are rarely sensitive enough to draw neat conclusions. The "no significant differences" finding that often results (Dunn, 1993) may be due to the lack of precision of the measures; may be due to the fact that mediating variables have not been carefully examined; or may reflect the nonlinear, highly contextualized nature of development and learning during early childhood. To be more helpful, research in the future will need to address more fine-tuned questions such as which combinations of types of interactions and curriculum have which effects on different children, varying on a number of dimensions such as age, gender, cultural and linguistic diversity, and family background characteristics. Despite the limitations of the existing body of research, several studies that provide information about the relationships between teachers' and children's behaviors in early childhood programs have implications for teacher preparation.

One study (Phillips, Scarr, & McCartney, 1987) of the effects of child care quality drew on in-depth observations in nine child care centers in Bermuda, serving 166 children ranging in age from 36 to 68 months. Overall quality assessed using the ECERS and varying from poor to good was found to be related to child development, with children in better quality centers scoring higher on measures of language and social competence. More specifically, children's performance on measures of language and intellectual development was strongly predicted by the amount of verbal interaction with teachers. After controlling for family variables and amount of prior child care experience, children from centers with high levels of adult verbal interaction demonstrated better language development than children from centers with less adult verbal interaction (McCartney, 1984). On dimensions of social competence such as consideration, sociability, and task orientation, teachers' verbal interaction with children was a consistent predictor (Phillips, McCartney, & Scarr, 1987).

Not just the amount but the style of teacher interaction was examined in an observational study (Holloway & Reichhart-Erickson, 1988) of the free-play and problem-solving behavior

of a sample of 55 4-year-olds in 15 early childhood programs. This study examined the effects of numerous dimensions of quality, including the nature of the verbal interactions with teachers. Positive teaching style characterized as "being respectful, engaging, responsive, and democratic" (p. 49) was found to result in children being more prosocial in solving social problems.

Another study (Clarke-Stewart, 1987) examined both the forms of child care (e.g., in-home, family child care, center-based) and the various dimensions of the child care experience for their effects on 80 children's social and cognitive development. The results demonstrated the complexity of the relationships between features of the child's experiences in child care and developmental outcomes, with few linear relationships emerging from the data. Nevertheless, Clarke-Stewart drew some general conclusions relevant to teacher education. First, higher levels of a teacher's general education were related to more socially competent children, whereas specialized college training in child development predicted cognitive competence, but was inversely related to social competence. Clarke-Stewart speculates that the more specially trained teachers tended to be more directive, focusing on academic content to the exclusion of promoting the development of social skills. She found better cognitive and social results for children in situations in which they were "given the freedom to learn" (1987, p. 37). In such situations, teachers provided choices for children, read to them, and encouraged them to interact actively and independently with materials and other children. The more directive, controlling, and punishing teachers were, the worse children performed on tests of cognitive development and the less cooperative they were with adults. Teacher responsiveness, acceptance, and informative behavior were related to overall competence in children.

Studies such as these indicate how difficult it is to identify simple relationships between teacher behaviors and child development outcomes. Several descriptive studies of early childhood programs provide less information about effects on children but provide vivid pictures of children's experiences in early childhood programs. These descriptive studies describe specific behaviors of teachers that teacher education programs are designed to influence. For example, a naturalistic study (Innocenti et al., 1986) of teacher and child and peer interaction was conducted in six early childhood programs in which 53 3- through 5-year-old children were observed in four different activity contexts: free play, mealtime, teacher-directed individual activity, and teacher-directed group time. The findings revealed that peer interaction occurred most often during free play and less often as the context of the activity involved more direct interaction with teachers. The researchers concluded that teacher interaction actually retards peer interaction; moreover, teachers did little to facilitate peer interaction in any context.

Much more information about the relationship between teacher instructional practices and the social context experienced by children in early childhood programs was provided by a much larger observational study of 62 preschool and kindergarten programs enrolling children from poor and middle-income families (Stipek, Daniels, Galluzzo, & Milburn, 1992). This study used the ECERS and the Classroom Practices Inventory (Hyson, Hirsh-Pasek, & Rescoria, 1990) to assess the quality and developmental appropriateness of the programs and also used a protocol developed for the study to assess the social-motivational aspects of children's experiences. A typology emerged from the analysis that identified two strong program dimensions: (1) positive social climate, which included scores on child initiative, teacher warmth, and positive control; and (2) teacher-directed instruction, which included academic emphasis, performance pressure, and evaluation stress. Analysis of observations identified three different categories of preschool or kindergarten programs: (1) didactic, in which academic skill development was emphasized in a relatively negative social context; (2) child-centered, in which less emphasis was placed on academic skills but the social context was positive; and (3) intermediate programs, which were a blend of child-centered and teacher-directed characteristics. The researchers emphasized that although these three clusters emerged, programs fell at all points along a continuum on these variables. The most surprising finding from this study was that the programs that rated high on teacher directiveness invariably rated low on positive social context. The data were so consistent on this relationship, in fact, that the researchers concluded that for preschool and kindergarten, "A strong emphasis on academic achievement and teacher-directed instruction appeared to preclude a positive social context" (Stipek et al., 1992, p. 14). The study also found that income level of families was not related to the quality of program; in fact, preschoolers from poor families were more likely to be in programs that were rated higher on quality measures and were more child centered. The issue of teacher-directed versus child-centered instructional practices is one of ongoing debate in early childhood education. This study does not address the question of effects of type of instruction (as do other studies described later), but rather demonstrates that in practice more emphasis on academic instruction tends to be related to less emphasis on the kinds of positive social relationships between teachers and children that have been shown by other studies to have positive consequences. Finally, this study found that whereas teachers' beliefs about appropriate educational practices for children were related to their practices, teachers' educational levels and experience and the evaluation policies of the program, including testing and retention practices, were not related to the type of program delivered.

Stipek and her colleagues also identified the need for more research on the effects of various instructional practices on motivation and learning in children. In another study, Stipek and Daniels (1988) found that kindergarten children in classrooms that emphasized normative evaluation rated their own competence and their future attainment lower than children in kindergartens that did not stress evaluation and comparison with others; such a difference was not true of fourth graders. The early emphasis on competition in the educational environment appears to diminish motivation and is probably developmentally inappropriate for this age group. Other work on motivation questions the negative consequences of overreliance on external rewards, which tend to diminish children's intrinsic motivation to participate in learning tasks (Cannella, 1986). Clearly the issue of motivation must be considered in relation to other potential outcomes of teaching and learning behaviors.

Benham, Miller, and Kontos (1988) also used the ECERS to observe in 21 child care programs in Pennsylvania; the programs tended to be of average, rather than good, quality. Programs rated higher in quality had more variety of materials and more creative activities. Weaknesses in observed program quality were identified as areas in which better training is needed for teachers. The lowest rated aspect of the children's experience was the area of social development, especially in facilitating free play and providing for individual differences. Programs were very weak in supporting cultural awareness and individualizing for children with special needs. Even good quality centers were found to be weak in three key areas: (1) failing to plan for promoting language development, (2) providing play activities but not planning for learning experiences within the context of play, and (3) lack of teacher interaction with children to enhance or extend children's learning through play. The researchers conclude that teacher training (they emphasize in-service, but the findings are also applicable to preservice) needs to do a better job of preparing teachers to be sensitive to and plan for individual differences, to promote creativity (rather than art products), and to translate knowledge of child development gained through observational assessment of children into goals, planned projects, and activities.

Perhaps the most thorough observational study of early childhood programs in recent history was funded by the U.S. Department of Education (Layzer, Goodson, & Moss, 1993) to describe the experiences of disadvantaged 4-year-olds in three types of programs: Head Start, child care centers, and Chapter 1 funded prekindergartens. (Because programs were not randomly selected from among the population of these types of programs, results were not generalizable by program type; however, acceptable levels of quality were maintained in all three program types. On general measures of quality, Head Start programs rated highest and the level of quality was more consistent across Head Start programs than other types.) The sample included 199 randomly selected programs in five areas of the country; seven different observational measures were used to describe the classroom experiences of 4-year-old children from economically disadvantaged families and to identify the characteristics that influence the quality of the experiences provided. The observers spent 1 week in each classroom and collected a wealth of descriptive data from which to gain the clearest picture to date of "life in preschool." The study also included a substudy of 55 Chapter 1 prekindergarten classrooms in which cognitive and social outcome data were collected on 750 children; a randomly selected sample of 131 children was followed up in 48 kindergarten classrooms (Seppanen, Godin, Metzger, Bronson, & Cichon, 1993). The findings describe how children spend their day in preschool classrooms. More than half of children's time is spent in activities that are designed to foster cognitive growth; about one third of their time is spent in activities with more structured goals such as math and language arts, blocks, table games, books, or science activities. One quarter of children's time is spent in art and music or engaged in exploratory play (sand or water play or dramatic play). Another 20% of the time children are engaged in classroom routines such as transitions, eating, cleaning up, or toileting. The finding that one fifth of children's time is spent in routine activities identifies the need for teachers to be prepared to support learning during routines and also to be knowledgeable about promoting children's health, safety, and nutrition in group programs.

Although a wide variety of activities were generally available for children, the most surprising finding of the study was that some activities that are considered highly valuable learning experiences did not occur on a daily basis. For example, in the majority of classrooms children did not engage in science activities nor did they have sand or water play opportunities. In approximately one third of the classrooms, no block building or looking at books was observed. In 25% of the classrooms, no math or language activities were observed. Most surprisingly, more than 25% of the classrooms did not have a story time, either for the whole group or for smaller groups of children. Although there was substantial variation in the grouping patterns across classrooms, on average children spent approximately half their time in small groups or working individually, but about 40% of their time was spent in one large group.

This study also provided a picture of teacher and child behavior in preschool programs. Although teachers spent about two thirds of their time involved with children, just 25% of that time was spent in teaching activities and almost 20% was spent in controlling or managing children's behavior. Interacting with individual children was a rare behavior for teachers, who spent only 10% of their time in individual interaction and most of their time interacting with the whole class or large groups of children. More than 30% of all the children across all classrooms had no individual interaction with a teacher, although the number of children who failed to have individual interaction with teachers varied by classroom from a few to the majority. Perhaps the most disturbing finding was that "in 12% of the classrooms, more than half the children received no individual attention over two observational periods" (Layzer et al., 1993, p. 102). The content and techniques of teaching/managing interactions were also analyzed (pp. A42–A43). Approximately 58% of the interactions were considered "teaching" and 42% were considered management. The largest portion (25%) of teaching interactions was related to language/reading content with the remainder evenly divided between expressive/artistic skills, math/science, and developmental/self-help skills. More than 30% of the teachers' interactions with children related to classroom organization and management. Given this breakdown of the type and content of teachers' interactions, it is not surprising but still discouraging that the most common interaction technique used by teachers was to command (33.7%), followed by explain (33%) and question (16.3%).

The researchers devised two proxy outcome measures for children based on their observations of children's behavior, engagement in activities with goals, and use of higher level social strategies; these behaviors are generally related to success in school. The study found that children engaged in activities with goals approximately 40% of the time, usually by exploring materials rather than in more structured activities such as worksheets. About 25% of children's interactions involved higher level social strategies such as initiating and sustaining cooperative social activities, taking turns, or working with others to achieve a goal. The study found that each of these types of child behavior occurred under different classroom conditions, with goal-directed tasks more likely related to teacher-planned and guided activities, and higher level social strategies such as cooperation and organizing joint projects more likely to occur during dramatic play or informal, active play with peers. This finding is supportive of one of the more common standards of best practice in early childhood programs that calls for a balance of teacher-directed and child-initiated activity. From these extensive observations of children and teacher behavior in early childhood classrooms, it appears that children develop different, but equally important, skills from their experiences in the diverse activity contexts that are common to good early childhood programs. Moreover, in classrooms with more highly educated teachers (those with baccalaureate degrees, although no information was available about their experience with children) children tended to spend more time in activities with goals, indicating that such teachers were well prepared to "teach" but were less well prepared to support the kind of exploratory play that is needed for development of more sophisticated social skills.

The level of parent involvement in the program was found to be associated with not only overall program quality but also with more teacher involvement with children, more teaching behavior, and more attention to individual children. Parent involvement was highest in the Head Start programs and may account to some extent for better and more consistent quality demonstrated in those programs. Again, this finding has clear implications for teacher education programs, which should be preparing early childhood teachers to involve parents in the classroom.

In analyzing the implications of this study, Layzer et al. (1993, p. 104) conclude that within acceptable standards for overall quality such as staff:child ratio and group size, the most feasible approach to improving the quality of early childhood programs is to focus on training teachers to individualize the educational program, emphasize child-initiated learning, support children's development and use of higher level social strategies, and involve parents.

The substudy of Chapter 1 funded classrooms (Seppanen, Godin, et al., 1993) enabled the descriptive information of the larger study to be further examined in light of measured social and cognitive outcomes for children in prekindergarten. The description of life in these classrooms was similar to the main study, although there was a greater tendency in the Chapter 1 classrooms, all of which had teachers with baccalaureate degrees, for children to spend time in whole group, teacher-led activity and to have fewer opportunities for social interaction with peers; more than half of children's time was spent not interacting with peers or adults.

Short-term cognitive gains for children were related to teachers' spending time on cognitive concepts, and the amount of time spent teaching was related to children's engagement in tasks with goals and successful completion of tasks. The findings strongly supported the value of a positive teacher–child relationship; teacher warmth and responsiveness and positive interactions such as explaining, questioning, praising, and singing were related to short-term cognitive achievement and more involvement in tasks with goals. The picture emerging from these data was complex, indicating that teachers need multiple strategies for direct interaction and also need to know how to support children's independent functioning and social problem solving.

The kindergarten follow-up portion of the study was made extremely difficult by the wide dispersion of children to many different schools (children from 55 classrooms in 49 schools dispersed to 222 kindergartens in 84 schools) and prohibited measuring outcomes at kindergarten as desired. Yet, the study found that children tended to move from higher quality prekindergarten environments to kindergartens that ranged widely in quality, and few supports were in place to ease the transition for children, a finding that is consistent with the results of a larger study of kindergarten transition (Love, Logue, Trudeau, & Thayer, 1992). The researchers concluded that there is a need for more research on the effects of discontinuity on young children.

The studies described here reveal that the interactions among teachers and children in early childhood programs have important effects on children's social and cognitive development. The picture that emerges from even such a brief review of research on teacher behaviors in early childhood programs is that both cognitive and social development are influenced by teachers, but that different aspects of the environment and interaction seem to play different roles in the process. Another conclusion that can be drawn is that although social/emotional development has long been identified as a major goal of early childhood education (e.g., the overall goal of Head Start has always been the development of social competence), much work remains to be done to prepare teachers better to support the social development of children. The importance of this work cannot be overstated in light of research on the effects of early peer relations on later adjustment in school and in life (Parker & Asher, 1987), which finds that children who are neglected or rejected by peers are highly likely to experience long-term adjustment problems. There is a growing understanding from research that with teacher intervention and specific curriculum, early childhood teachers can greatly influence the development of positive peer relations and prosocial behavior (Battistich, Solomon, Watson, Solomon, & Schaps, 1989; Katz & McClellan, 1991; Kim & Stevens, 1987; Solomon, Watson, Delucchi, Schaps, & Battistich, 1988). For example, the authoritative style of interacting with children (nurturance with clearly stated expectations for behavior) is found to support the development of positive peer relations (Hartup & Moore, 1990). At the same time, there is evidence that teachers' understanding of children's social behavior and their attributions of the causes of misbehavior are unrelated to the teacher's having a degree in early childhood education (Scott-Little & Holloway, 1992). Teacher education, similar to early childhood education, needs to attend more to the development of positive social relationships. Research on the effects of curriculum on social/emotional development is addressed later in this chapter.

To summarize, research on teacher behaviors in early childhood classrooms supports the importance for children's development and learning of a responsive, positive, informative relationship between teachers and children; however, peer relationships are also found to be essential contributors to children's development and the teacher's ability to support peer relationships seems to be a real challenge. Finally, there appears to be a strong need for more attention to individualization of interaction and experiences.

Research on Curriculum and Teaching Practices

The ATE and NAEYC (1991, 1992) standards for early childhood teacher certification reflect current theoretical perspectives on how children learn, emphasizing that children construct knowledge through play and active manipulation of physical objects and interaction with other people (Piaget, 1970). They also stress the importance of the process of social construction of knowledge whereby children develop understanding through social interactions with peers and adults (Vygotsky, 1978, 1992). Operating from this theoretical perspective, the standards call for teachers to be able to develop, plan, and implement curriculum that promotes children's active construction of knowledge. In this section, research on curriculum and teaching practices is reviewed. More thorough reviews of research on early childhood curriculum are available (Seefeldt, 1992; Spodek, 1993).

The early curriculum comparison studies in the 1970s tended to support the importance of clearly defined curriculum goals without favoring any one specific curriculum approach. In other words, very different approaches could be found to result in academic gains for children as long as the approach was carefully planned and implemented. The later waves of research on curriculum effects have begun to go beyond simple academic gains, usually scores on standardized tests, to investigate social/emotional outcomes as well. The research tends to support the value of more active, hands-on, experiential approaches that promote some degree of child-initiated activity and social interaction, approaches that are considered by early childhood educators to be more "developmentally appropriate." Such approaches to curriculum and instruction include teacher-directed or teacher-guided instruction usually in small groups, but tend to reject formal, teacher-directed, predominantly large group instruction as the dominant teaching strategy.

One of the first studies to raise concerns about the long-term effects of highly didactic teacher-directed instruction models of early childhood education was a curriculum comparison study that followed graduates of some of the early demonstration projects to the age of 15 years (Schweinhart, Weikart, & Larner, 1986a, 1986b). The study compared the cognitive and social consequences of three curriculum models: a direct instruction model stressing academic skills (the DISTAR curriculum), a traditional nursery school model stressing social skills, and the High/Scope curriculum stressing child-initiated learning within a teacher-supported environment in which children engage in planning and evaluating their work. The results showed that although both the DISTAR and High/Scope curricula resulted in cognitive gains for children that were large at first and tended to fade over time, the two approaches had very different effects on social behavior. The DISTAR graduates at age 15 were found to engage in significantly more delinquent acts of behavior than the High/Scope or traditional nursery school groups. The researchers concluded that the social consequences of different curriculum approaches need to be weighed as heavily as the academic benefits. Not surprisingly, this research was met with considerable criticism by proponents of DISTAR (Bereiter, 1986; Gersten, 1986). The debate over the most appropriate degree of teacher direction (Schweinhart & Weikart, 1988) continues to be the source of some controversy within the field of early childhood education. Research, some of which is described later, is able to lend general support for constructivist approaches, whereas other questions remain to be addressed regarding which curriculum and teaching practices are most beneficial for which groups of individual children, especially children from diverse cultural and linguistic backgrounds and children with disabilities (Mallory & New, 1994).

The effect of different curriculum approaches on children's sociomoral development was the subject of an observational study in kindergartens employing direct instruction, constructivist, and eclectic approaches (DeVries, Haney, & Zan, 1991; DeVries, Reese-Learned, & Morgan, 1991). Results demonstrated significant differences in the interpersonal understanding of both teachers and children in each group, with differences in sociomoral development favoring children in the constructivist kindergartens. Although the studies by DeVries and her colleagues were also the subject of considerable criticism from advocates of direct instruction, the findings may explain some of the differences in social behavior at age 15 reported by Schweinhart and colleagues (1986a). DeVries and her colleagues also found a very negative atmosphere in teacher–child interactions in direct instruction kindergarten classrooms just as Stipek and her colleagues (1992) did.

The most controversial issue in the debate about direct instruction is whether children from low-income, culturally diverse backgrounds require a more didactic approach to succeed in school (Jipson, 1991). This debate is not limited to early childhood education as evidenced by the ongoing controversies about phonics instruction and whole language approaches, which are based on constructivist and social-constructivist theories of learning that are advocated by early childhood educators. A full discussion of the research on whole language is beyond the scope of this chapter; however, there is a growing number of studies that specifically identify the advantages of a more meaning-centered, holistic approach to literacy development among young children who are from low-income, minority group families (Manning, Manning, & Long, 1990; Roberts, 1991; Stice & Bertrand, 1990; Stice, Thompson, & Bertrand, 1991).

To address the question specifically for early childhood programs, there is some research to show that "developmentally appropriate" curriculum and instruction is beneficial for children identified as at risk. One study (Marcon, 1992) of preschool and kindergarten practices in the District of Columbia public schools, in which most of the children are African Americans and from low-income families, compared academic and social outcomes for children from classrooms described as predominantly child initiated, direct instruction, or "middle of the road," with the latter reflecting more of a hodgepodge of the two other approaches rather than a truly eclectic strategy. The results favored the child-initiated preschool program with children from these classrooms performing significantly better on mastery of basic skills than the direct instruction group in which academic achievement was more specifically stressed. The middle of the road group performed the worst raising concerns among school officials that mixed messages teachers get about appropriate instruction may result in their trying to accommodate both positions and failing to meet any of the children's

needs. The study (Marcon, 1990) continued to follow children into first grade and raised concerns about the impact of the direct instruction and middle-of-the-road approaches for children's social development. Whereas the child-initiated approach continued to have the most positive effect on academic achievement (children in these classrooms had an average grade of C in reading at the end of first grade, whereas the other children had an average grade of D), the direct instruction and middle-of-the-road approaches seemed actually to harm children's scores on measures of social development. The longer children spent in these classrooms, the worse their social skills became. Perhaps the social context of these classrooms was negative, as was found in the descriptive study conducted by Stipek and her colleagues (1992), but the findings lend support not only for the value of chlid-initiated learning to social development but also to academic achievement.

Another study evaluated the effects of developmentally appropriate public school prekindergarten on economically disadvantaged children's later academic achievement (Frede & Barnett, 1992). This study was larger scale, including an entire state system, that used the High/Scope curriculum. The researchers first evaluated the degree to which classrooms were effectively implementing the curriculum model and how well they met standards of developmentally appropriate practice. They found a range of implementation from low to high and removed children in the low implementation classrooms from the final analysis of effects. They found that implementation of a developmentally appropriate curriculum at high and moderate levels in prekindergarten contributed to increased academic achievement at first grade. The researchers also concluded that evaluation of a curriculum implementation is essential to an accurate determination of effects.

Evaluation of another curriculum approach designed to assist children at risk of school failure also demonstrated the positive effects of multiple instructional strategies (Slavin, Madden, Karweit, Livermon, & Dolan, 1990). The approach, called Success for All, was implemented at Baltimore city public schools. At the prekindergarten and kindergarten levels, the approach is described as employing "developmentally appropriate" curriculum emphasizing language, telling and retelling of stories read by teachers, and a balance of academic readiness with art, music, and movement. In the primary grades, the program stresses regrouping for intensive reading instruction, cooperative learning, and one-on-one tutoring for children who are not making progress. The first-year evaluation results indicated that the approach substantially enhanced language ability at prekindergarten and kindergarten levels and reading achievement at first, second, and third grade compared to a matched control group. An evaluation of various types of intervention programs for children at risk finds that one-on-one tutoring, or individualized instruction, is the most consistently effective strategy for increasing school success for children identified as at risk of school failure (Slavin, Karweit, & Madden, 1989).

A series of studies (Charlesworth, Hart, Burts, & DeWolf, 1993) was conducted by researchers at Louisiana State University to evaluate specifically the effectiveness of teaching practices described as developmentally appropriate and inappropriate according to NAEYC guidelines (Bredekamp, 1987); these studies also provide support for the importance of child development knowledge to early childhood teachers (Charlesworth, Burts, & Hart, 1994). One study (Charlesworth, Hart, Burts, Thomasson, et al., 1993) assessed principals' and kindergarten teachers' beliefs and teacher practices and found that the more important teachers believed appropriate practices to be, the more likely they were to use them. Beliefs and use of "inappropriate" practices were even more strongly related. Principals' beliefs also influenced practices, especially if principals believed in the value of highly directive, whole group instruction, teachers were more likely to practice it. Principals with early childhood certification or in-service training were more likely to believe in the value of developmentally appropriate practices than principals without such training.

Kindergarten classes rated as more developmentally appropriate included more variety of activity, were less tightly structured, and involved more participation by children in whole group activities; they also included learning centers, group story, whole group, and music time. The less appropriate kindergartens involved more teacher-directed small group workbook/worksheet activity, waiting, punishment, and transitions than more appropriate classes. Children in developmentally inappropriate classes exhibited more stress behaviors than children in appropriate classes; this finding was especially true for males (Burts, Hart, Charlesworth, & Kirk, 1990). There were no differences related to age of entry, which is interesting considering the trend to find younger children too immature for academic kindergarten programs. Black children and children from low-income families were more likely to be in less appropriate programs than white or middle-income children (Burts et al., 1992). Scores on standardized achievement tests were not different for children from appropriate and inappropriate kindergartens. Children from higher socioeconomic class (SEC) backgrounds in inappropriate classrooms scored higher on achievement tests than children from low SEC backgrounds in inappropriate classes; there were no differences by income level on test scores for children in appropriate classrooms (Burts, Charlesworth, & Fleege, 1991).

More than two thirds of the original sample of 204 children were followed into first and second grades (Charlesworth, Hart, Burts, & DeWolf, 1993). As indicated earlier, the two types of kindergarten experience did not affect standardized test scores at the end of kindergarten. At the end of first and second grade, there were also no significant differences in test scores for graduates of the two types of kindergarten. At the end of first and second grades, high SEC children from inappropriate classes scored higher than low SEC children from inappropriate classes. At the end of first grade, low SEC children in developmentally appropriate classes scored higher on reading comprehension than low SEC children from inappropriate kindergartens. An identical pattern was found in comparing report card grades, favoring the developmentally appropriate experiences. Finally, different social behaviors and conduct were reported by teachers in first grade for the two groups, with children from inappropriate kindergartens rated as more hostile and aggressive.

The LSU studies, although employing a rather global measure that does not actually assess specific teacher behaviors, do provide some indication of the potential benefits of child-initiated, active learning experiences for kindergartners. These findings are especially interesting in light of studies that show that developmentally appropriate curriculum and teaching practices are rare in kindergarten (Bryant, Clifford, & Peisner, 1991; Hatch & Freeman, 1988). For example, a study in which 103 kindergarten classrooms were randomly selected for observation from all the kindergartens in a large southern state found that only 20% of the classrooms met or exceeded the criterion of developmental appropriateness (Bryant et al., 1991). The quality of the classes as measured by the ECERS was predicted by principals' and teachers' scores on measures of beliefs and knowledge of developmentally appropriate practice, but was unrelated to teachers' or principals' education or experience. Of greatest concern was that 60% of classrooms fell below the adequate rating with extensive reliance on whole-group, worksheet-driven rote learning and little emphasis on small-group or individual instruction or hands-on, child-initiated activities. This study was conducted because of an alarming rise in kindergarten retention rate in the state, from .5% to 5.9%; the research was used to prevent a policy change that would have raised kindergarten entrance age to help prevent kindergarten failure. The conclusion was that children were failing kindergarten because kindergarten was failing to meet the individual and developmental needs of children.

These findings were supported by an observational study of reading instruction in 42 kindergarten classrooms in a midwestern state (Durkin, 1987). A large portion, 21.6%, of classroom time was devoted to reading and reading-related instruction with the content focusing on phonics instruction through workbooks and worksheets. Durkin was especially intrigued by the fact that although teachers emphasized using individual assessment of children with the Gesell test, differences in children's abilities had no effect on instruction, even at the end of the year when teachers knew the children much better. One method, whole-group class instruction, was used for reading, and children who did not learn using this method were judged "unready" and assigned to transition classes rather than promoted to first grade. Teachers demonstrated no recognition that their reliance on only one method of instruction, especially whole-group instruction, may have been related to the children's lack of progress.

Commercially available curriculum and materials are often a strong influence on teaching practices. Durkin (1990) evaluated the instructional materials available to kindergarten teachers and found that basal reading series designed for the kindergarten level presume whole class instruction, despite the trend toward the whole language approach and the need for greater individualization of instruction in general as children's experiences become more diverse. Hiebert and Papierz (1990) came to a similar conclusion in evaluating kindergarten reading curriculum materials. They found that widely used book series do not promote developmentally appropriate literacy experiences. Hiebert and Papierz (1990) raised serious concerns about the overreliance on worksheet-driven curriculum without any opportunities for meaningful interaction with literature and print. In their words, "Children who have had extensive literacy experiences in their home and environments may be able to make sense of such instruction. For children who depend on the school to learn to read, the complete separation of learning about words and listening comprehension from books undoubtedly makes the introduction to literacy formidable, if not impossible" (p. 332). The researchers concluded that such curriculum creates passivity in both teachers and children, and that teachers need to be able to make professional decisions about what is appropriate curriculum for children in order to avoid commercially available but inappropriate curriculum.

In a relatively new but growing dimension of the curriculum—the use of computers in preschool and kindergarten—a similar result was found in evaluating the effect of software on children's development. Haugland (1992) applied criteria of developmental appropriateness in evaluating computer software and found that more developmentally appropriate software that promotes active learning, problem solving, and decision making rather than rote learning of basic academic skills was related to enhanced cognitive development. The less appropriate software was not helpful and even harmful to children's development. The implications of these studies for teacher education are clear. Again, the need is for more emphasis on individualization and more specific training for teachers in how to be supportive of child-initiated activities and children's construction of knowledge and also for teachers to apply professional judgment in choosing appropriate curriculum materials and strategies.

Among the most valued of curriculum and teaching practices among early childhood educators is children's self-initiated play. The role of play in child development is not only a strong aspect of Piaget's theory of cognitive development, but also is reflected in Vygotsky's theories of language and cognitive development. Vygotsky (1978) believed that play leads development, with written language growing out of oral language through the vehicle of symbolic play, which promotes the development of symbolic representation abilities. (A complete discussion of the research on play is not possible and is available elsewhere [Fromberg, 1992].) Several studies cited previously have demonstrated the value of play, especially dramatic play and exploratory play, for children's social development, although play is also valuable for the development of academic skills (Gallegos, 1983).

A number of recent qualitative studies have identified the importance of play as a curricular tool for learning literacy, mathematics, social studies, and other curriculum content. Schrader (1990) conducted a case study of four teachers of 3-, 4-, and 5-year-old children to examine the teachers' participation in symbolic play and its use to support literacy development. Schrader found that young children incorporated literacy experiences and knowledge in their play; they wrote for real-life purposes, read what they had written, and discussed its meaning with teachers and peers. The teacher's involvement during children's play, intervening to extend the play and elaborate on children's ideas, was of particular importance in helping children move beyond their actual developmental level in literacy. This type of teacher interaction during children's play has been described as "teaching in the zone of proximal development" (Stremmel, 1993; Stremmel & Fu, 1993), which is based on Vygotsky's theory that there is a zone in which children are able to function beyond their current developmental level with the assistance of adults or more capable peers. This type of teaching is not traditional teacher direction, but it is more directive than what is often used in programs that emphasize a

traditional interpretation of Piagetian child-initiated learning. Although more research is needed, this type of supportive, interactive teacher behavior, what Stremmel and Fu (1993) call "responsive teaching," may be the answer to what has become a polarizing debate over child-initiated and teacher-directed learning. It may also be the most effective teaching strategy for promoting children's development and learning in both cognitive and social domains.

Inagaki (1992) further elaborates on a post-Piagetian view of development and, specifically, its implications for science education. From an analysis of children's cognitive development in relation to science curriculum, Inagaki concludes that even very young children can learn about some topics in depth if those topics are meaningful and involve them directly; children can be encouraged to engage in scientific experimentation in an intellectually honest way if the content is relevant to their everyday lives; and adults should not play a passive role but should actively assist the child's construction of knowledge. Inagaki suggests several roles for the teacher in this process: to set up situations in which children are able to engage in inquiry, to help children engage cognitively and metacognitively in the content, to organize intellectual peer interaction, and to intervene and sustain children's engagement and interaction (p. 129). Such teaching is similar to the strategy called *cognitively guided instruction* that has been used successfully in mathematics instruction with children in the primary grades (Carpenter, Fennema, Peterson, Chiang, & Loef, 1989; Fennema, Franke, Carpenter, & Carey, 1993). In this research, teachers were trained to understand children's thinking as well as to know mathematics content. They applied this knowledge during interactions with children while they solved relevant and meaningful mathematics problems in small groups. The children's progress in mathematics understanding not only surprised the teachers but also exceeded the curriculum standards of the National Council of Teachers of Mathematics.

To return to research on the value of play as a curriculum tool, Schrader (1989) also analyzed the functions of writing demonstrated by 5-year-olds during symbolic play. In realistic literacy environments set up by the teacher, such as an office, a post office, and a house, children demonstrated writing for several purposes, including instrumental, regulatory, interactional, personal, and informational. They demonstrated the imaginative function in other contexts of the classroom such as storytelling rather than in the realistic settings of their dramatic play. Schrader emphasized that children's functional writing skills were heavily influenced by the context of their experiences and that this context is directly controlled by teachers. Again, this research supports the importance of the teacher's role in establishing the environment for learning, providing the appropriate props, and promoting learning in context. Morrow (1990) also found that the physical environment had a powerful influence on children's behavior. Simply by providing writing tools in dramatic play settings, children's writing increased. Yet, by providing a thematic organization for the play (a veterinarian's office) as well as materials, more literacy experiences resulted and more reading occurred. When the teacher took a more active role in the play and made suggestions, children participated more. Again, research findings demonstrate the effectiveness of specific teacher behaviors that other research studies find occurring too seldom. Morrow's work strongly supports a more active, participatory rather than directive role for teachers in children's play, whereas other studies of children's play find that teachers tend not to become involved (Benham et al., 1988; Shin & Spodek, 1991).

Sociodramatic play has been found to be especially valuable for enhancing language abilities of preschool and kindergarten children. One study (Levy, Schaefer, & Phelps, 1986) that involved 28 three- and four-year-olds in a child care center found that participation in sociodramatic play was especially valuable for improving the language scores of males. Yet, most importantly, the researchers stressed the role of the teacher in "capturing" the participation of all the children in the play by organizing around a shared background of experiences (a theme); providing time, space, and props to enhance the play; and intervening appropriately to support and extend involvement in play. For example, prior to the teacher's intervention, only girls in the preschool engaged in sustained sociodramatic play. As a result, boys were missing this important learning opportunity and benefited most from the teacher's intervention. The teacher's provision of time for such play to develop should not be underestimated as an important strategy; research demonstrates that sufficient time (usually at least 45 minutes) is necessary for higher level social strategies to emerge in play (Christie & Wardle, 1992).

A case study/repeated measures design was used to assess experimentally the relationship between sociodramatic play and language development in kindergartners (Levy, Wolfgang, & Koorland, 1992). Baseline measures of language were taken during children's impromptu play. The experimental intervention consisted of enhanced sociodramatic play in which the teacher provided shared experiences (around a theme); more time, space, and props; and directly facilitated play by modeling, physically intervening, and scaffolding language development. The results revealed an increase in children's vocabulary and syntactical complexity.

In addition to demonstrating the value of teachers' supporting the learning experience while it is occurring, there is evidence that learning is enhanced when teachers support children's later reflection and "revisiting" of the experience. An interesting study explored 5- and 6-year-old children's learning about economics from a thematic study of "the shop" (Pramling, 1991). Several conditions were established with control groups; one situation mirrored a direct instruction approach in which the teacher told the children the economic content, whereas another mirrored a traditional nursery school approach in which the children had the concrete experiences of visiting the shop and playing shop in school. The experimental condition included the concrete experiences but added the dimension of teacher intervention to promote children's reflections about the experiences on the premise that learning is not just the result of having had concrete experiences, but is the result of thinking about the experiences. The results showed significant differences in both factual information and understanding of economic concepts, favoring the experimental group. Pramling (1991) offered the following descriptions of the teacher's role, which are strikingly similar to the teachers' behaviors found in the mathematics research cited earlier (Carpenter et al., 1989; Fennema et al., 1993): encourage children to talk and reflect,

be knowledgeable of the ways in which children conceptualize the content, use methods such as interviewing and planning, and create situations in which children are confronted with problems related to the content goals. Pramling's research also supports the value of the kind of teaching strategies used in 32 city-run early childhood programs in Reggio Emilia, Italy. Known as the Reggio Emilia approach, such strategies, including work on in-depth projects to solve problems, teachers' support of children "revisiting" their experiences, the use of several media to represent symbolically children's thinking, co-construction by teachers and children, and carefully documentation of children's thinking to support later reflection, are currently receiving considerable attention as well as adaptation in the early childhood community in the United States (Edwards, Gandini, & Forman, 1993).

Research on Family and Community Relations

A third area of the ATE/NAEYC standards for early childhood teacher preparation is not only applicable to early childhood but also to all levels of education, that is, the ability to work effectively with parents. The issue of family relationships is of particular importance in early childhood education because of the age group served. Young children are integrally connected to their families; moreover, the younger the child the more the roles of teacher and parent converge. In addition, the younger the child, the more essential it is that teachers communicate regularly with families about the child's care and education because the child is not yet able to communicate directly about his or her needs and desires. (For an excellent review of research on this topic, see Powell, 1989.) Most of the demonstration early childhood programs described here contained a strong element of parent involvement; likewise, the parent involvement component of Head Start is frequently cited as the major predictor of lasting effects for children. Despite the consistent recognition of the importance of parents to their children's care and education, preparation for working with parents remains a weakness in teacher education programs. Although there is some evidence that early childhood program graduates are provided more preparation for work with families than elementary graduates (Foster & Loven, 1992), most beginning and even experienced teachers report feelings of inadequacy about working with parents (Johnston, 1984a, 1984b; McBride, 1991; Swick & McKnight, 1989). McBride (1991) found that not only was coursework important in changing preservice teachers' attitudes about parent involvement, but also opportunities to interact with families during field work and student teaching were related to more positive attitudes about parent involvement. Preservice teachers were most favorably disposed to the basic obligational type of parent involvement (helping children with homework, volunteering for field trips) and were least positive about parents' direct involvement in the schools. The strongest barriers to parent involvement were identified as teachers having little knowledge of how to work with parents and no time for planning. One interesting finding of this study was that 76% of respondents thought that a class on parent involvement should be required in teacher preparation programs, but 78% had not had such a course.

Swick and McKnight (1989) found that kindergarten teachers who had early childhood degrees had more positive attitudes about parent involvement than those who had elementary degrees. They also found a significant relationship between teacher attitudes about parent involvement and their activity related to working with parents. One discouraging finding of this study was that class size and low socioeconomic levels of children were negatively related to teachers' attitudes toward parent involvement. This finding is ironic in that the larger the group size, the more potentially helpful parents could be if they were considered resources in the classroom. Likewise, children from low-income families have been found to benefit greatly from their parents' direct experience in schools as evidenced by considerable Head Start research.

Among the trends currently confronting early childhood education, discussed in more detail later in this chapter, is the growing trend toward inclusion of children with disabilities in all programs. Serving children with disabilities requires that early childhood educators increase their knowledge of early childhood special education, a discipline that goes beyond the construct of parent involvement to promote "family-centered services" (McCollum, 1987; Odom, 1987). McCollum (1987) surveyed early interventionists working with both preschoolers and infants to determine what knowledge they use in the performance of their jobs and compared these data to the content of teacher preparation programs. She found that the number of tasks involving working with families that infant interventionists perform was significantly higher than for preschool interventionists. Although preschool interventionists stressed the importance of working with families, they were more likely to stress the traditional teacher role of planning and implementing curriculum to meet the specific identified needs of children in a classroom setting. McCollum also reported that the content of preservice preparation programs did not reflect the needs of professionals working with infants and toddlers and their families, a conclusion that would also apply to early childhood education programs.

Research on Assessing and Adapting Programs for Individual Differences

A final area of the early childhood teacher education curriculum that has been alluded to before but needs additional study is the teacher's ability to assess individual children's needs and interests and to adapt curriculum and instruction to ensure the success of all children. The issue of appropriate assessment of young children is another area of considerable controversy within the field. Many early childhood practitioners oppose formal, standardized testing of young children because of the negative impact on curriculum and teaching and the tendency to use results of such measures to label, track, retain, or otherwise harm children at a young age (National Association for the Education of Young Children [NAEYC] and National Association of Early Childhood Specialists in State Departments of Education, 1992). Despite these concerns, the importance of accurate and useful assessment of children for the purpose of individualizing instruction and adapting curriculum to achieve "individual appropriateness" cannot be overstated. There is

some evidence, for instance, that use of systematic observation, assessment, and planning does benefit children (Bergen, Sladeczek, Schwarz, & Smith, 1991; Meisels, 1993; Schweinhart, 1993). Bergen and colleagues (1991) report that an observation-based measurement and planning system used with 838 kindergarten children resulted in higher scores in math, reading, and science and lower rates of retention and assignment to special education. Among the control group, one out of nearly four children was referred for special education and one out of five was placed in special education, whereas among the experimental group, one out of 17 children was referred and one out of 71 was placed in special education. There is also evidence that involving children in self-assessment and reflection is a valuable learning strategy for both children and teachers (Moxley, Kenny, & Hunt, 1990), and that teachers, especially beginning teachers, are not good observers of children's development and learning (Beyerbach, Smith & Swift, 1989).

Results such as these demonstrate the potential positive effects of using appropriate assessment mechanisms with young children and the need to prepare teachers adequately. Concerns remain, however, especially about the difficulties of accurately assessing young children from culturally and linguistically diverse backgrounds (Barona & Barona, 1991), which leads to another key aspect of professional preparation. The teacher preparation curriculum must prepare students to work with an increasing population of culturally diverse children. Some evidence (Aotaki-Phenice & Kostelnik, 1983; Reiff & Cannella, 1992) exists that specific content on working with multicultural/multiethnic populations can influence attitudes of preservice teachers, most of whom report feeling unprepared to work with cultures different from their own. Aotaki-Phenice and Kostelnik (1983) found that both preservice and experienced teachers agreed that knowledge of cultural diversity is important, but they differed in their understanding about children's knowledge of racial differences. These issues are not unique to early childhood education, but, again, the age of the client and the foundational nature of the learning experience necessitate some differences in how the issue is approached. For instance, bilingual education is an issue at all levels of education, but in early childhood the issue is somewhat more complex because young children are at the earliest stages of primary language acquisition. More research is needed on appropriate strategies for teaching young children whose primary language is not English, but some research suggests that "developmentally appropriate" practices that work for most children are perhaps the best context for teaching linguistically diverse young children (Pease-Alvarez, Garcia, & Espinosa, 1991; Wink & Garcia, 1992). Other research raises concerns that inappropriate emphasis on second language acquisition at too early an age can harm primary language proficiency and interfere with family communication and relationships (Fillmore, 1991). In general, there is a concern that child development research that is considered so important in guiding early childhood practice is dominated by studies of white, middle-class American children (Mallory & New, 1994). If child development knowledge is such an important part of the early childhood knowledge base, and if, when it is available, cross-cultural child development research does identify cultural differences (e.g., Rogoff, Mistry, Goncu, & Mosier, 1993), then more study of cultural differences and culturally appropriate practices must be incorporated in the teacher education curriculum.

Research on Issues of Professionalism

Although professionalism is applicable to all levels of teaching, the ATE/NAEYC standards stress the area of professional relations because the settings in which early childhood teachers work present specific challenges, especially in relationships with adults. Johnston (1984b) identified content needed for early childhood teacher education by surveying the frequent and bothersome problems encountered by practicing prekindergarten teachers. These problems, which tend to differ from those experienced by elementary teachers, are specific and unique to early childhood teachers: relationships with subordinates (teacher assistants and aides), relationships with supervisors, parent cooperation (because parent contact occurs on a daily basis in programs for young children), and management of routines (identified earlier as a unique problem for early childhood educators). Johnston concluded that these issues need to become part of the early childhood teacher education curriculum and, indeed, they are reflected in the ATE/NAEYC standards.

Summary

The content of the early childhood teacher education curriculum has been described from the point of view of what is known about the strengths and weaknesses of practices in programs for young children, a strategy for identifying areas where teacher education needs to do a better job. It is clear from the research on both teacher–child interactions and curriculum that knowledge of children's development and learning is an essential component of teacher education. Yet, knowledge is not enough unless the program also prepares the teacher to understand how to apply this knowledge in specific program planning and in assessing and adapting instruction to meet the needs of individual children. To achieve this goal, programs must also help teacher candidates do a better job of understanding and involving families and understanding and adapting instruction for children from diverse linguistic and cultural backgrounds. Of particular importance is that the teacher preparation program prepare teachers for the many different roles that they play to promote cognitive and social development of young children in a constructivist, child-initiated learning environment. For guidance in achieving the goal of improved teacher preparation programs, the next section discusses the research on the effectiveness of early childhood teacher education, both preservice and in-service.

RESEARCH ON THE EFFECTIVENESS OF EARLY CHILDHOOD TEACHER EDUCATION: PRESERVICE AND IN-SERVICE

This chapter begins with a strong statement lamenting the inadequate research base specifically related to early childhood teacher education. A search of the literature on this topic identifies very few studies specifically designed to evaluate programs that prepare early childhood teachers (Heidelbach, 1984; Saracho, 1987, 1988b) or to assess the recruitment and admission policies for early childhood teacher education (Dickerscheid, Briggs, & Gnezda, 1983). Saracho (1984) identifies various roles that early childhood teachers perform and evaluates an attempt to structure a teacher preparation program around those roles (Saracho, 1988a). Beyond these studies, little research can be identified that directly informs practice in early childhood teacher education programs.

Because of the diverse range of teacher qualifications permitted by regulatory standards in programs for young children, there is almost a natural experimental situation established in most studies about the effectiveness of early childhood teacher education. Typically program staff are differentially qualified with some staff holding baccalaureate degrees in early childhood education or other fields and other staff reflecting a range of diverse levels of qualifications. In reviewing the research on the effects of various dimensions of program quality on children, one of the most often cited predictive variables is the training of the teachers. In general, studies find that specialized teacher training in early childhood is related to higher levels of overall quality and specific positive effects on children from infancy through kindergarten.

In general, research supports the conclusion that training specifically related to child development and education of young children is an essential component of effective practice with all age groups (Arnett, 1989; Howes, 1987; Powell & Stremmel, 1989; Snider & Fu, 1990). For example, Howes (1983) found that the quality of care toddlers received in child care centers was related to teacher training; better trained teachers (half of the teachers in the study had baccalaureate degrees in child development or education) were more likely to play with children, mediate objects, express positive feelings, and respond positively to toddlers' behavior, and they were less likely to restrict toddlers' activity or ignore them. Dunn (1993) found that teachers' having a child development-related major was related to positive child development outcomes. Layzer and colleagues (1993) found that teacher education was strongly related to teacher behavior and interaction, with college degrees in early childhood education related to teachers' being more responsive to children, using positive techniques more often, and engaging in more interaction with and teaching of children. Teacher education was also related to children spending more time actively engaged in activities with goals and the frequency of developmentally appropriate teaching practices. One interesting finding of this study (Layzer et al., 1993) was that similar results were found in Head Start programs in which teachers lacked higher education; the researchers concluded that the preservice and in-service training provided by Head Start with the CDA credentialing system was able to achieve the same benefits as higher education degrees.

Similarly, the finding of positive effects for specialized training is not always supported by research. In the National Child Care Staffing Study (Whitebook et al., 1989), for instance, formal education and specialized college-level training were the most significant predictors of job performance, but formal education was more predictive than specialized knowledge. For all age groups, teachers with more formal education (college degrees) were more sensitive, less harsh, and less detached; specialized education predicted such behaviors for teachers of infants only. One explanation for the inconsistency of findings on positive effects of college-level teacher education is the variability in the content of teacher preparation programs as a result of diverse and sometimes nonexistent teacher certification standards, a situation described earlier in this chapter.

Powell and Stremmel (1989) surveyed the professional activity of child care teachers with differing amounts of preservice preparation. In general, they found low levels of involvement in professional development activities; however, the more training and experience (not just experience) teachers had, the more likely they were to be engaged in continuing professional development experiences.

The implementation of developmentally appropriate teaching practices appears to be dependent on professional preparation. Snider and Fu (1990) found that teachers' knowledge of appropriate practice was related to their use of such practices. Specifically, they found that coursework in five critical content areas, "planning, implementing, and evaluating developmentally appropriate content; creating, evaluating, and selecting materials; creating learning environments; curriculum models; and observing and recording (child) behaviors" (p. 75), in addition to supervised practice with children, was essential to teachers' knowledge of developmentally appropriate practice. They also found that practicum without specific early childhood course content was not valuable, nor was experience related to teachers' knowledge of developmentally appropriate practice. These findings are important in light of the fact that many state certification systems do not require a practicum with young children and few require specific early childhood curriculum content (Morgan et al., 1993).

One study was designed to address directly the question of the effectiveness of varying amounts of teacher preparation (Arnett, 1989). This study was conducted in 22 child care centers in Bermuda and evaluated the effect of different levels of training for 59 child care teachers. Four different levels of training existed in the sample: no training, two relevant courses, a four-course training program, and a 4-year college degree in early childhood education. The results demonstrated that the college degree made the biggest difference in positive interactions with children and was negatively related to teacher authoritarianism, detachment, and punitiveness. This study was also able to test the effect of specific child development training (the two course option) with no training and found that even that minimal amount of specific training in child development and communication with children resulted in teachers who were more positive, more involved, and less authoritarian than teachers with no training.

Several studies indicate that specific content related to child development and teaching practice is not sufficient to change practice; it is also necessary to influence teachers' attitudes and beliefs about children, what they think about how children learn (Beyerbach et al., 1989; Bondy, 1990; Levin, 1992; Robinson, 1990). Oakes and Caruso (1990) evaluated kindergarten teachers' use of developmentally appropriate practices in relation to their attitudes toward authority sharing. They found low levels of implementation of developmentally appropriate practices overall but did identify a relationship between teachers who were more open to sharing authority. They conclude that teacher education and other professional development strategies should focus less on prescriptions for practice and more on teacher attitudes and beliefs about children.

One well-designed study investigated the effects of a systematic in-service training program for early childhood teachers (Epstein, 1993). This study examined the relationship between in-service training and program quality in 366 programs employing the High/Scope curriculum, serving children from 2½ to 6 years of age. The design was unique in that it collected data from various sources in the training experience, including anecdotal data that were collected from the trainers and 793 participants in the training of trainers project, a survey of a random sample of trainers, interviews and observations of 244 High/Scope trained teachers and 122 nontrained teachers, and child assessments (97 children in High/Scope programs and 103 in comparison groups). Few studies of the effects of teacher education at any level follow the program to the level of outcomes for children despite the fact that this is the most appropriate level at which to evaluate a teacher training intervention. The findings are too extensive to discuss fully, but a few have important implications for early childhood teacher education. First, a relationship was found between both general education and specialized early childhood teacher education and program quality, with college degrees in general stronger predictors than specialized preparation. Teachers with college degrees implemented better quality programs (better physical, social/ emotional, and cognitive environments) than teachers without degrees, but teachers with early childhood degrees offered better quality than teachers who lacked such preparation. Teachers with early childhood degrees were better at supporting creative and social skills.

The results of assessment of the children found a relationship between program quality, specifically implementation of the High/Scope curriculum, and children's development. Overall children's language development was the area most affected by program quality. In analyzing the effects on children's development, there was a strong relationship among positive child outcomes and program quality, in-service training of teachers, and teachers' experience. The positive effect of experience in this study contradicts many other studies that find that teachers' experience alone is not helpful and may be harmful to quality. Epstein (1993) explained that in this study the teachers' experience was related to improved child outcomes because the experience occurred in high quality programs. Although preservice teacher education was related to program quality, it was not found to be related to children's language development or other areas of children's development. Access to diverse materials and a systematic approach to planning, implementing, and reviewing experiences (the High/Scope plan, do, review cycle) were related to children's development. In addition, children's language and creative representational abilities were most affected by program quality. This study supports the value of college degrees in early childhood education in general, but also supports the value of highly organized and consistently delivered in-service training for teachers working in high quality settings as an effective substitute for specialized preservice training. In fact, teachers in this condition actually produced better child development outcomes.

Until early childhood teacher education programs throughout the country achieve the highest standards of quality and consistency, as exemplified in the ATE/NAEYC position statement, research will undoubtedly continue to find mixed results for teacher education graduates. Nevertheless, the research that does exist provides a strong rationale for continued efforts to ensure wide access to early childhood teacher preparation and identifies the urgent need for specialized early childhood standards to support program content.

TRENDS IN EARLY CHILDHOOD TEACHER EDUCATION

Many of the trends that are influencing other areas of teacher education, such as mentor teacher programs and professional development schools, and new approaches, such as constructivist teacher education and case method, are having an impact on early childhood teacher education as well. A few trends have important implications for content and policy changes specific to early childhood teacher education. These trends include the convergence of the fields of early childhood and early childhood special education, the burgeoning professional development movement, and the increased demand for leadership/administrative preparation programs for the field.

Early Childhood and Early Childhood Special Education

Legislation, specifically PL 99-457 (Education of the Handicapped Act Amendments of 1986) and PL 101-336 (Americans with Disabilities Act), is driving the fields of early childhood education and early childhood special education closer together. Now that programs are no longer able to deny access to children with disabilities, personnel in all types of early childhood programs must be prepared to serve all children. The growing trend toward full inclusion of children with disabilities in early childhood programs requires that there be greater communication and clarity between personnel who are trained in the two relevant disciplines—early childhood and early childhood special education.

Research is also contributing to the convergence of the two fields as studies demonstrate that children with disabilities do better in mainstreamed settings and that practices that are considered developmentally appropriate for typically developing young children can be beneficial with adaptation for children with disabilities (Fox & Hanline, 1993; Guralnick, 1993; Hundert, Mahoney, & Hopkins, 1993). Yet, significant barriers still remain to the successful inclusion of children with disabilities (Odom & McEvoy, 1990). Among the most frequently cited barriers are the different philosophical and theoretical orientations of the fields, with early childhood heavily reflective of constructivist theories and early childhood special education still strongly influenced by behaviorism. Such differences are perpetuated by the fact that personnel preparation programs for the two fields are usually the products of separate certifications in separate departments; however, there is a growing recognition that inclusion of children with disabilities could be eased if preparation for professionals were more inclusionary and integrated (Burton, Hains, Hanline, McLean, & McCormick, 1992; Miller, 1992). Some states, including Kentucky, Massachusetts, New Mexico, and North Carolina, have adopted an integrated (early childhood and early childhood special education) certification, and successful program models are being implemented and studied (Stayton & Miller, 1993). One of the remaining challenges is the issue of the scope of the program. Heavily influenced by federal legislation, many early childhood special education programs prepare personnel for the age range of birth through five, whereas general early childhood educators advocate a broader span of birth through eight. The policy issues will be the subject of much debate as states and institutions reevaluate these programs to keep pace with the trends. Nevertheless, it is clear that the content and experiences provided in early childhood education programs must be infused with the knowledge bases of early childhood special education and must provide opportunities for direct experience in a variety of settings with children with disabilities.

Professional Development Movement

In the early 1990s, spurred by federal funding in the form of the Child Care and Development Block Grant, states began engaging in the process of state planning for early care and education systems. A large part of this work focused on the need for improvements in the training systems for early childhood personnel. State planning processes have targeted many of the problems confronting the early childhood work force that were briefly identified in the first section of this chapter. Most relevant here are the issues of early childhood certification and the growing demand for articulation between 2-year and 4-year institutions. The desire to articulate professional studies credits may be unique to early childhood education, but the need for greater articulation in teacher education programs in general is real. Currently, a large portion of college students, especially members of minority groups, begin their education in the 2-year college system. Failure to provide articulation agreements sets up a major barrier for these individuals to pursue careers in teacher education. For example, lack of articulation and other barriers such as financial resources prevent many African Americans in early childhood education from advancing beyond the entry levels of teacher assistant, a potentially serious problem in light of school demographics (National Black Child Development Institute, 1993). Due to the varying regulations for different sectors of the field, many people enter this field with little preservice education or after having acquired training in other fields. These individuals should pursue higher education, especially in light of research demonstrating the benefits for children of well-prepared teachers. The challenge for baccalaureate and advanced early childhood programs is to provide access to individuals who may not pursue the traditional route directly from high school to college, eliminate unnecessary bureaucratic barriers, and maintain standards of quality of preparation. Given the current and projected increases in numbers of early childhood teachers needed in the work force, institutions of higher education need to accept this challenge willingly.

Leadership/Administrative Development

One of the other effects of diverse delivery and regulatory systems for early childhood services is that there are a number of roles that early childhood professionals can serve in addition to classroom teacher that require the fundamental knowledge of early childhood education. Of the roles that require baccalaureate degrees or higher, administrative positions are the most common, but other types of positions are emerging as services become more varied; for example, child care resource and referral counselor or director, curriculum coordinator, program director, parent educator, and many more. One of the most pressing needs for the field is more and better training for administrators. Research supports the relationship between well-qualified directors and higher quality programs for children (Bloom & Sheerer, 1992); however, many directors were good teachers who were promoted to administrative positions with no administrative training and they often confront great challenges. Johnston (1984a) surveyed child care and prekindergarten program administrators and found that their most challenging problems arose in areas in which they had little or no training, such as establishing goals, fiscal management, efficiency and time management, personnel management, and relationships with parents. These findings provide guidance for the development of early childhood administrator preparation programs at both the baccalaureate and advanced degree levels. Recognizing that baccalaureate degree graduates will be likely candidates for administrative positions, early childhood "teacher" preparation programs should infuse some administrative content into the programs or at least offer administrative electives. Some creative institutions will offer specialized majors in early childhood program administration, although only one baccalaureate-level program was found (Morgan et al., 1993).

Each of the trends identified here presents both a challenge and an opportunity to institutions of higher education. To continue to prepare students for one narrowly defined role—classroom teacher in public school setting—is to ignore the growing needs for well-qualified professionals at various levels and in diverse settings. The programs of the future will need to preserve a common core of shared knowledge for all professionals, but will undoubtedly need to explore a variety of options for specialization at the baccalaureate as well as advanced levels.

CONCLUSION

This chapter begins and ends with the same premise; that is, there is inadequate research on early childhood professional development programs to provide clear guidance for policy at all levels. In the absence of such research, we continually attempt to explain the contradictory findings about the relationship between staff qualifications and quality for children. At the same time, there are intriguing findings (Epstein, 1993; Layzer et al., 1993) suggesting that various kinds of well-conceptualized and implemented in-service training programs produce the same or better outcomes than preservice degrees. Such findings have major implications for funding programs and demand additional study. In addition, more research is needed on how to prepare students for specific aspects of the early childhood teacher's role, such as working with parents and collaborating with colleagues and professionals from other disciplines.

A second major weakness in the current knowledge base relates to what teachers are being prepared to do. More research is clearly needed on the teacher's role and how to do a better job of individualizing learning experiences to ensure success for all children. Some of this research will evolve out of the convergence of early childhood education and early childhood special education, a field in which individualization is well studied; however, there is a need for an equal amount of attention on the subject of individualizing for typically developing children, especially those from diverse cultural and linguistic backgrounds. More research is needed on the concept of "teaching in the zone of proximal development," ways to prepare teachers for this type of responsive teaching, and how this teaching varies with the developmental level of the child. The issue of child-initiated learning needs more clarification and demands more carefully designed studies to address the controversial questions. Related to these issues is the need for better instruments and procedures for accurately assessing young children's learning and development, especially instruments that are culturally sensitive and are nonbiased.

Early childhood education is at a stage in its development that in some ways looks similar to other areas of education in the past, with diverse regulations, qualifications of personnel, and different levels of preparation. At the same time, it could be said that the issues that early childhood is grappling with, such as differentiated staffing and articulation, are issues that other areas of education will confront as well. In some ways, early childhood education seems to be going back to the future. Whatever path it takes, the road will be clearer if more and better research is available to guide the way.

References

American Public Health Association and American Academy of Pediatrics. (1992). *Caring for our children. National health and safety performance standards: Guidelines for out-of-home child care programs.* Washington, DC: American Public Health Association.

Aotaki-Phenice, L., & Kostelnik, M. (1983). Attitudes of early childhood educators on multicultural/multiethnic education. *Journal of Multilingual and Multicultural Development, 4*(1), 41–46.

Arnett, J. (1989). Caregivers in day-care centers: Does training matter? *Journal of Applied Developmental Psychology, 10*(4), 541–552.

Association of Teacher Educators & National Association for the Education of Young Children (ATE & NAEYC). (1991). Early childhood teacher certification. A position statement of ATE and NAEYC. *Young Children, 47*(1), 16–21.

Association of Teacher Educators & National Association for the Education of Young Children (ATE & NAEYC). Early childhood teacher certification. A position statement of ATE and NAEYC. *Action in Teacher Education, 14*(1), 62–69.

Barona, M. S., & Barona, A. (1991). The assessment of culturally and linguistically different preschoolers. *Early Childhood Research Quarterly, 6*(3), 363–376.

Battistich, V., Solomon, D., Watson, M., Solomon, J., & Schaps, E. (1989). Effects of an elementary school program to enhance prosocial behavior on children's cognitive-social problem-solving skills and strategies. *Journal of Applied Developmental Psychology, 10*(2), 147–169.

Benham, N., Miller, T., & Kontos, S. (1988). Pinpointing staff training needs in child care centers. *Young Children, 43*(4), 9–16.

Bereiter, C. (1986). Does direct instruction cause delinquency? *Early Childhood Research Quarterly, 1*(3), 289–292.

Bergen, J. R., Sladeczek, I. E., Schwarz, R. D., & Smith, A. N. (1991). Effects of a measurement and planning system on kindergarteners' cognitive development and educational programming. *American Educational Research Journal, 28*(3), 683–714.

Berrueta-Clement, J. R., Schweinhart, L. J., Barnett, W. S., Epstein, A. S., & Weikart, D. P. (1984). *Changed lives: The effects of the Perry Preschool Program on youths through age 19*. Ypsilanti, MI: High/Scope Press.

Beyerbach, B. A., Smith, J., & Swift, P. R. (1989, March). *Exploring preservice and practicing teachers' thinking about children and teaching*. Paper presented at the annual meeting of the American Educational Research Association, San Francisco. (ERIC Document Reproduction Service No. 306 213)

Bloom, P. J., & Sheerer, M. (1992). The effect of leadership training on child care program quality. *Early Childhood Research Quarterly, 7*(4), 579–594.

Bondy, E. (1990). Seeing it their way: What children's definitions of reading tell us about improving teacher education. *Journal of Teacher Education, 41*(5), 33–45.

Boyer, E. L. (1991). *Ready to learn: A mandate for the nation*. Princeton, NJ: The Carnegie Foundation.

Bredekamp, S. (Ed.). (1987). *Developmentally appropriate practice in early childhood programs serving children from birth through age eight*. Washington, DC: National Association for the Education of Young Children.

Bredekamp, S. (1990). Setting and maintaining professional standards. In B. Spodek & O. N. Saracho (Eds.), *Yearbook in early childhood education, Vol. 1: Early childhood teacher preparation* (pp. 138–152). New York: Teachers College Press.

Bredekamp, S., & Willer, B. (1992). Of ladders and lattices, cores and cones: Conceptualizing an early childhood professional development system. *Young Children, 47*(3), 47–50.

Bryant, D. M., Clifford, R. M., & Peisner, E. S. (1991). Best practices for beginners: Developmental appropriateness in kindergarten. *American Educational Research Journal, 28*(4), 783–803.

Burton, C. B., Hains, A. H., Hanline, M. F., McLean, M., & McCormick, K. (1992). Early childhood intervention and education: The urgency for professional unification. *Topics in Early Childhood Special Education, 11*(4), 53–69.

Burts, D. C., Charlesworth, R., & Fleege, P. (1991, April). *Achievement of kindergarten children in developmentally appropriate and developmentally inappropriate classrooms*. Paper presented at the biennial meeting of the Society for Research in Child Development, Seattle. (ERIC Document Reproduction Service No. 342 506)

Burts, D. C., Hart, C. H., Charlesworth, R., Fleege, P. O., Mosley, J., & Thomasson, R. H. (1992). Observed activities and stress behaviors of children in developmentally appropriate and inappropriate kindergarten classrooms. *Early Childhood Research Quarterly, 7*(2), 297–318.

Burts, D. C., Hart, C. H., Charlesworth, R., & Kirk, L. (1990). A comparison of frequencies of stress behaviors observed in kindergarten children in classrooms with developmentally appropriate versus developmentally inappropriate instructional practices. *Early Childhood Research Quarterly, 5*(3), 407–423.

Cannella, G. (1986). Praise and concrete rewards: Concerns for childhood education. *Childhood Education, 62*(4), 297–301.

Carpenter, T. P., Fennema, E., Peterson, P. L., Chiang, C., & Loef, M. (1989). Using knowledge of children's mathematics thinking in classroom teaching: An experimental study. *American Educational Research Journal, 26*(4), 499–531.

Charlesworth, R., Burts, D. C., & Hart, C. H. (1994). The effectiveness of developmentally appropriate compared with developmentally inappropriate practices: Implications for teacher preparation. *Journal of Early Childhood Teacher Education, 15*(1), 8–12.

Charlesworth, R., Hart, C. H., Burts, D. C., & De Wolf, M. (1993). The LSU studies: Building a research base for developmentally appropriate practice. In S. Reifel (Ed.), *Advances in early education and day care* (pp. 3–28). Greenwich, CT: JAI Press.

Charlesworth, R., Hart, C. H., Burts, D. C., Thomasson, R. H., Mosley, J., & Fleege, P. O. (1993). Measuring the developmental appropriateness of kindergarten teachers' beliefs and practices. *Early Childhood Research Quarterly, 8*(3), 255–276.

Christie, J. F., & Wardle, F. (1992). How much time is needed for play? *Young Children, 47*(3), 28–32.

Clarke-Stewart, K. A. (1987). Predicting child development from child care forms and features: The Chicago study. In D. A. Phillips (Ed.), *Quality in child care: What does research tell us?* (pp. 21–41). Washington, DC: National Association for the Education of Young Children.

Committee for Economic Development. (1991). *The unfinished agenda: A new vision for child development and education*. New York: Author.

Committee for Economic Development. (1993). *Why child care matters: Preparing young children for a more productive America*. New York: Author.

Copple, C. E., Cline, M. G., & Smith, A. N. (1987). *Path to the future: Long-term effects of Head Start in the Philadelphia school district*. Washington, DC: U.S. Department of Health and Human Services.

DeVries, R., Haney, J. P., & Zan, B. (1991). Sociomoral atmosphere in direct-instruction, eclectic, and constructivist kindergartens: A study of teachers' enacted interpersonal understanding. *Early Childhood Research Quarterly, 6*(4), 449–471.

DeVries, R., Reese-Learned, H., & Morgan, P. (1991). Sociomoral development in direct instruction, eclectic, and constructivist kindergartens: A study of children's enacted interpersonal understanding. *Early Childhood Research Quarterly, 6*(4), 473–517.

Dickerscheid, J. D., Briggs, B. A., & Gnezda, M. T. (1983). Teacher selection and placement in early childhood education. *Home Economics Research Journal, 12*(1), 42–48.

Dunn, L. (1993). Proximal and distal features of day care quality and children's development. *Early Childhood Research Quarterly, 8*(2), 167–192.

Durkin, D. (1987). A classroom-observation study of reading instruction in kindergarten. *Early Childhood Research Quarterly, 2*(3), 275–300.

Durkin, D. (1990). Reading instruction in kindergarten: A look at some issues through the lens of new basal reader materials. *Early Childhood Research Quarterly, 5*(3), 299–316.

Edwards, C., Gandini, L., & Forman, G. (Eds.). (1993). *The hundred languages of children: The Reggio Emilia approach to early childhood education*. Norwood, NJ: Ablex.

Elliot, J. (1993). Are performance indicators educational quality indicators? In J. Elliott (Ed.), *Reconstructing teacher education: Teacher development* (pp. 51–64). Washington, DC: The Falmer Press.

Epstein, A. S. (1993). *Training for quality: Improving early childhood programs through systematic inservice training.* Ypsilanti, MI: High/Scope Press.

Feeney, S., & Chun, R. (1985). Effective teachers of young children. *Young Children, 41*(1), 47–52.

Fennema, E., Franke, M. L., Carpenter, T. P., & Carey, D. A. (1993). Using children's mathematical knowledge in instruction. *American Educational Research Journal, 30*(3), 555–583.

Field, T., Masi, W., Goldstein, S., Perry, S., & Parl, S. (1988). Infant day care facilitates preschool social behavior. *Early Childhood Research Quarterly, 3*(4), 341–359.

Fillmore, L. W. (1991). When learning a second language means losing the first. *Early Childhood Research Quarterly, 6*(3), 323–346.

Foster, J. E., & Loven, R. G. (1992). The need and directions for parent involvement in the 90's: Undergraduate perspectives and expectations. *Action in Teacher Education, 14*(3), 13–18.

Fox, L., & Hanline, M. F. (1993). A preliminary evaluation of learning within developmentally appropriate early childhood settings. *Topics in Early Childhood Special Education, 13*(3), 308–327.

Frede, E., & Barnett, W. S. (1992). Developmentally appropriate public school preschool: A study of implementation of the High/Scope curriculum and its effects on disadvantaged children's skills at first grade. *Early Childhood Research Quarterly, 7*(4), 483–499.

Fromberg, D. (1992). Play. In C. Seefeldt (Ed.), *The early childhood curriculum: A review of current research* (2nd ed., pp. 35–74). New York: Teachers College Press.

Gallegos, M. (1983, January). *Learning academic skills through play.* Paper presented at the annual meeting of the Southwest Educational Research Association, Houston. (ERIC Document Reproduction Service No. 225 690)

Gersten, R. (1986). Response to "consequences of three preschool curriculum models through age 15." *Early Childhood Research Quarterly, 1*(3), 293–302.

Goffin, S. G. (1989). Developing a research agenda for early childhood education: What can be learned from the research on teaching? *Early Childhood Research Quarterly, 4*(2), 187–204.

Guralnick, M. J. (1993). Developmentally appropriate practice in the assessment and intervention of children's peer relations. *Topics in Early Childhood Special Education, 13*(3), 344–371.

Hartup, W. W., & Moore, S. G. (1990). Early peer relations: Developmental significance and prognostic implications. *Early Childhood Research Quarterly, 5*(1), 1–17.

Hatch, J. A., & Freeman, E. B. (1988). Kindergarten philosophies and practices: Perspectives of teachers, principals, and supervisors. *Early Childhood Research Quarterly, 3*(2), 151–166.

Haugland, S. W. (1992). The effect of computer software on preschool children's developmental gains. *Journal of Computing in Childhood Education, 3*(1), 15–30.

Heidelbach, R. (1984). *A longitudinal study of teacher education curriculum: A first year report using quantitative and qualitative methods.* Paper presented at the annual meeting of the American Educational Research Association, New Orleans. (ERIC Document Reproduction Service No. ED 243 847)

Hewes, D. W. (1990). Historical foundations of early childhood teacher training: The evolution of kindergarten teacher preparation. In B. Spodek & O. Saracho (Eds.), *Early childhood teacher preparation, Vol. 1* (pp. 1–22). New York: Teachers College Press.

Hiebert, E. H., & Papierz, J. M. (1990). The emergent literacy construct and kindergarten and readiness books of basal reading series. *Early Childhood Research Quarterly, 5*(3), 317–334.

Holloway, S. D., & Reichhart-Erickson, M. (1988). The relationship of day care quality to children's free-play behavior and social problem-solving skills. *Early Childhood Research Quarterly, 3*(1), 39–53.

Howes, C. (1983). Caregiver behavior in center and family day care. *Journal of Applied Developmental Psychology, 4*(1), 99–107.

Howes, C. (1987). Quality indicators in infant and toddler child care: The Los Angeles study. In D. A. Phillips (Ed.), *Quality in child care: What does research tell us?* (pp. 81–88). Washington, DC: National Association for the Education of Young Children.

Howes, C. (1988). Relations between early child care and schooling. *Developmental Psychology, 24*(1), 53–57.

Howes, C., Phillips, D. A., & Whitebook, M. (1992). Thresholds of quality: Implications for the social development of children in center-based child care. *Child Development, 63*(2), 449–460.

Hundert, J., Mahoney, W. J., & Hopkins, B. (1993). The relationship between the peer interaction of children with disabilities in integrated preschools and resource and classroom teacher behaviors. *Topics in Early Childhood Special Education, 13*(3), 328–343.

Hyson, M. C., Hirsh-Pasek, K., & Rescoria, L. (1990). The classroom practices inventory: An observation instrument based on NAEYC's guidelines for developmentally appropriate practices for 4- and 5-year-old children. *Early Childhood Research Quarterly, 5*(4), 475–494.

Inagaki, K. (1992). Piagetian and post-Piagetian conceptions of development and their implications for science education in early childhood. *Early Childhood Research Quarterly, 7*(1), 115–133.

Innocenti, M. S., Stowitschek, J. J., Rule, S., Killoran, J., Striefel, S., & Boswell, C. (1986). A naturalistic study of the relation between preschool setting events and peer interaction in four activity contexts. *Early Childhood Research Quarterly, 1*(2), 141–153.

Jipson, J. (1991). Developmentally appropriate practice: Culture, curriculum, connections. *Early Education and Development, 2*(2), 120–136.

Johnston, J. (1984a). Perceived problems of day care/prekindergarten administrators. *Child Care Quarterly, 13*(4), 291–297.

Johnston, J. (1984b). Problems of prekindergarten teachers: A basis for reexamining teacher education practices. *Journal of Teacher Education, 35*(2), 33–37.

Katz, L. G., & McClellan, D. E. (1991). *The teacher's role in the social development of young children.* Urbana, IL: ERIC Clearinghouse on Elementary and Early Childhood Education.

Kim, Y., & Stevens, J. H., Jr. (1987). The socialization of prosocial behavior in children. *Childhood Education, 63*(3), 200–206.

Kisker, E. E., Hofferth, S. L., Phillips, D. A., & Farquhar, E. (1991). *A profile of child care settings: Early education and care in 1990, Vol. 1.* Princeton, NJ: Mathematical Policy Research.

Larsen, J. M., & Robinson, C. C. (1989). Later effects of preschool on low-risk children. *Early Childhood Research Quarterly, 4*(1), 133–144.

Layzer, J. I., Goodson, B. D., & Moss, M. (1993). *Life in preschool: Volume one of an observational study of early childhood programs for disadvantaged four-year-olds.* Cambridge, MA: Abt Associates.

Lazar, I., & Darlington, R. (1982). Lasting effects of early education: A report from the consortium for longitudinal studies. *Monographs of the Society for Research in Child Development, 47*(2–3, Serial No. 195).

Lee, V. E., Brooks-Gunn, J., & Schnur, E. (1988). Does Head Start work? A 1-year follow-up comparison of disadvantaged children attending Head Start, no preschool, and other preschool programs. *Developmental Psychology, 24*(2), 210–222.

Levin, J. (1992). *Expanding prospective teacher's beliefs about the reading process to enable changes in classroom practice through the use of whole language.* New York: NOVA University. (ERIC Document Reproduction Service No. 347 506)

Levy, A. K., Schaefer, L., & Phelps, P. C. (1986). Increasing preschool effectiveness: Enhancing the language abilities of 3- and 4-year-old children through planned sociodramatic play. *Early Childhood Research Quarterly, 1*(2), 133–140.

Levy, A. K., Wolfgang, C. H., & Koorland, M. A. (1992). Sociodramatic play as a method for enhancing the language performance of kindergarten age students. *Early Childhood Research Quarterly, 7*(2), 245–262.

Love, J. M., Logue, M. E., Trudeau, J. V., & Thayer, K. (1992). *Transitions to kindergarten in American schools.* Portsmouth, NH: RMC Research Corporation.

Mallory, B. L., & New, R. S. (Eds.). (1994). *Diversity and developmentally appropriate practices: Challenges for early childhood education.* New York: Teachers College Press.

Manning, M., Manning, G., & Long, R. (1990, November). *Writing development of inner city primary students: Comparative effects of a whole language and a skills-oriented program.* Paper presented at the annual meeting of the Mid-South Educational Research Association, New Orleans. (ERIC Document Reproduction Service No. 336 745)

Marcon, R. A. (1990). *Early learning and early identification: Final report of the three year longitudinal study.* Washington, DC: District of Columbia Public Schools.

Marcon, R. A. (1992). Differential effects of three preschool models on inner-city 4-year-olds. *Early Childhood Research Quarterly, 7*(4), 517–530.

McBride, B. A. (1991). Preservice teachers' attitudes toward parental involvement. *Teacher Education Quarterly, 18*(4), 57–67.

McCarthy, J. (1988). *State certification of early childhood teachers: An analysis of the 50 states and the District of Columbia.* Washington, DC: National Association for the Education of Young Children.

McCarthy, J. (1990). The content of early childhood teacher education programs: Pedagogy. In B. Spodek & O. N. Saracho (Eds.), *Early childhood teacher preparation, Vol. 1* (pp. 82–101). New York: Teachers College Press.

McCartney, K. (1984). Effects of quality of day care environment on children's language development. *Developmental Psychology, 20*(2), 244–260.

McCollum, J. A. (1987). Early interventionists in infant and early childhood programs: A comparison of preservice training needs. *Topics in Early Childhood Special Education, 7*(3), 24–35.

McKey, R. H., Condelli, L., Ganson, H., Barrett, B. J., McConkey, C., & Plantz, M. C. (1985). *The impact of Head Start on children, families and communities: Final report of the Head Start evaluation, synthesis, and utilization project.* (DHHS Publication No. OHDS 90-31193). Washington, DC: U.S. Government Printing Office.

Meisels, S. J. (1993). Remaking classroom assessment with the work sampling system. *Young Children, 48*(5), 34–40.

Miller, L. B., & Bizzell, R. P. (1984). Long-term effects of four preschool programs: Ninth- and tenth-grade results. *Child Development, 55*(4), 1570–1587.

Miller, P. S. (1992). Segregated programs of teacher education in early childhood: Immoral and inefficient practice. *Topics in Early Childhood Special Education, 11*(4), 39–52.

Mitchell, A., Seligson, M., & Marx, F. (1989). *Early childhood programs and the public schools.* Dover, MA: Auburn House.

Mitchell, C., & Maar, J. (1986). *Elementary school certification practices: Is it time for a change?* Murfreesboro: Middle Tennessee State University. (ERIC Document Reproduction Service No. ED 276 713)

Morgan, G., Azer, S. L., Costley, J. B., Genser, A., Goodman, I. F., Lombardi, J., & McGimsey, B. (1993). *Making a career of it.* Boston, MA: The Center for Career Development in Early Care and Education at Wheelock College.

Morrow, L. M. (1990). Preparing the classroom environment to promote literacy during play. *Early Childhood Research Quarterly, 5*(4), 537–554.

Moxley, R. A., Kenny, K. A., & Hunt, M. K. (1990). Improving the instruction of young children with self-recording and discussion. *Early Childhood Research Quarterly, 5*(2), 233–249.

National Association for the Education of Young Children (NAEYC). (1991a). *Accreditation criteria and procedures of the National Academy of Early Childhood Programs* (rev. ed.). Washington, DC: Author.

National Association for the Education of Young Children (NAEYC). (1991b). *Early childhood teacher education guidelines: Basic and advanced.* Washington, DC: Author.

National Association for the Education of Young Children (NAEYC) and National Association of Early Childhood Specialists in State Departments of Education. (1992). Guidelines for appropriate curriculum content and assessment in programs serving children ages 3 through 8. In S. Bredekamp & T. Rosegrant (Eds.), *Reaching potentials: Appropriate curriculum and assessment for young children. Volume 1* (pp. 9–27). Washington, DC: National Association for the Education of Young Children.

National Association of Early Childhood Teacher Educators (NAECTE). (1993). Early childhood baccalaureate teacher certification standards. *The Journal of Early Childhood Teacher Education, 14*(1), 13–16.

National Association of Elementary School Principals. (1990). *Standards for quality programs for young children: Early childhood education and the elementary school principal.* Alexandria, VA: Author.

National Association of State Boards of Education. (1988). *Right from the start.* Alexandria, VA: Author.

National Association of State Boards of Education. (1991). *Caring communities: Supporting young children and families.* Alexandria, VA: Author.

National Black Child Development Institute. (1993). *Paths to African American leadership positions in early childhood education: Constraints and opportunities.* Washington, DC: Author.

National Center for Education Statistics (NCES). (1993). *The condition of education, 1993.* Washington, DC: U.S. Department of Education.

National Commission on Children. (1991). *Beyond rhetoric: A new American agenda for children and families: Final report of the national commission on children.* Washington, DC: Author.

National Commission on Children. (1993). *Just the facts: A summary of recent information on American children and their families.* Washington, DC: Author.

National Education Goals Panel (NEGP). (1991). *National education goals report: Building a nation of learners.* Washington, DC: Author.

Oakes, P. B., & Caruso, D. A. (1990). Kindergarten teachers' use of developmentally appropriate practices and attitudes about authority. *Early Education and Development, 1*(6), 445–457.

Odom, S. L. (1987). The role of theory in the preparation of professionals in early childhood special education. *Topics in Early Childhood Special Education, 7*(3), 1–11.

Odom, S. L., & McEvoy, M. A. (1990). Mainstreaming at the preschool level: Potential barriers and tasks for the field. *Topics in Early Childhood Special Education, 10*(2), 48–61.

Ott, D. J., Zeichner, K. M., & Price, G. G. (1990). Research horizons and the quest for a knowledge base in early childhood teacher education. In B. Spodek & O. N. Saracho (Eds.), *Early childhood teacher education, Vol. 1* (pp. 118–137). New York: Teachers College Press.

Parker, J. G., & Asher, S. R. (1987). Peer relations and later personal adjustment: Are low-accepted children at risk? *Psychological Bulletin, 102*(3), 357–389.

Pease-Alvarez, L., Garcia, E. E., & Espinosa, P. (1991). Effective instruction for language minority students: An early childhood case study. *Early Childhood Research Quarterly, 6*(3), 347–361.

Peters, D. L., & Klinzing, D. G. (1990). The content of early childhood teacher education programs: Child development. In B. Spodek & O. N. Saracho (Eds.), *Early childhood teacher preparation, Vol. 1* (pp. 67–81). New York: Teachers College Press.

Phillips, D. A., McCartney, K., & Scarr, S. (1987). Child care quality and children's social development. *Developmental Psychology, 23*(4), 537–543.

Phillips, D. A., Scarr, S., & McCartney, K. (1987). Dimensions and effects of child care quality: The Bermuda study. In D. A. Phillips (Ed.), *Quality in child care: What does research tell us?* (pp. 43–56). Washington, DC: National Association for the Education of Young Children.

Piaget, J. (1970). *The science of education and the psychology of the child* (Rev. ed.). New York: Orion Press.

Powell, D. R. (1986). Effects of program models and teaching practices. *Young Children, 41*(6), 60–67.

Powell, D. R. (1989). *Families and early childhood programs.* Washington, DC: National Association for the Education of Young Children.

Powell, D. R., & Dunn, L. (1990). Non-baccalaureate teacher education in early childhood education. In B. Spodek, & O. N. Saracho (Eds.), *Early childhood teacher preparation* (pp. 45–66). New York: Teachers College Press.

Powell, D. R., & Stremmel, A. J. (1989). The relation of early childhood training and experience to the professional development of child care workers. *Early Childhood Research Quarterly, 4*(3), 339–355.

Pramling, I. (1991). Learning about "the shop": An approach to learning in preschool. *Early Childhood Research Quarterly, 6*(2), 151–166.

Public Law 99-457, Education of the Handicapped Act Amendments of 1986. (22 September 1986). *Congressional Record, 132*(125), H 7893–7912.

Public Law 101-336, Americans with Disabilities Act of 1990. (26 July 1990). *U.S. Statutes at Large, 104* (Title 42 USC 12101), 327–378.

Reiff, J. C., & Cannella, G. S. (1992, February). *Multicultural beliefs and conceptual level of early childhood preservice teachers.* Paper presented at the annual meeting of the Association of Teacher Educators, Orlando, FL. (ERIC Document Reproduction Service No. ED 344 882)

Reynolds, A. J. (1991). Early schooling of children at risk. *American Educational Research Journal, 28*(2), 392–422.

Roberts, R. B. (1991, November). *Writing abilities of first graders: Whole language and skills-based classrooms.* Paper presented at the annual meeting of the Mid-South Educational Research Association, Lexington, KY. (ERIC Document Reproduction Service No. ED 341 981)

Robinson, B. (1990). *An examination of training issues for caregivers of toddlers.* Rochester, MI: Oakland University. (ERIC Document Reproduction Service No. ED 327 279)

Rogoff, B., Mistry, J., Goncu, A., & Mosier, C. (1993). Guided participation in cultural activity by toddlers and caregivers. *Monographs of the Society for Research in Child Development, 58*(8) (Serial No. 236).

Saracho, O. N. (1984). Perception of the teaching process in early childhood education through role analysis. *Journal of the Association for the Study of Perception International, 19*(1), 26–39.

Saracho, O. N. (1987). An instructional evaluation study in early childhood education. *Studies in Educational Evaluation, 13*(2), 163–174.

Saracho, O. N. (1988a). A study of the roles of early childhood teachers. *Early Child Development and Care, 38,* 43–56.

Saracho, O. N. (1988b). An evaluation of an early childhood teacher education curriculum for preservice teachers. *Early Child Development and Care, 38,* 81–101.

Saracho, O. N. (1993). Preparing teachers for early childhood programs in the United States. In B. Spodek (Ed.), *Handbook of research on the education of young children* (pp. 412–426). New York: Macmillan.

Schrader, C. T. (1989). Written language use within the context of young children's symbolic play. *Early Childhood Research Quarterly, 4*(2), 225–244.

Schrader, C. T. (1990). Symbolic play as a curricular tool for early literacy development. *Early Childhood Research Quarterly, 5*(1), 79–103.

Schweinhart, L. J. (1993). Observing young children in action: The key to early childhood assessment. *Young Children, 48*(5), 29–33.

Schweinhart, L. J., Barnes, H. V., & Weikart, D. P. (1993). *Significant benefits: The High/Scope Perry Preschool study through age 27* (Monographs of the High/Scope Educational Research Foundation, No. 10). Ypsilanti, MI: High/Scope Press.

Schweinhart, L. J., & Weikart, D. P. (1988). Education for young children living in poverty: Child-initiated learning or teacher-directed instruction? *The Elementary School Journal, 89*(2), 213–226.

Schweinhart, L. J., Weikart, D. P., & Larner, M. B. (1986a). Child-initiated activities in early childhood programs may help prevent delinquency. *Early Childhood Research Quarterly, 1*(3), 303–312.

Schweinhart, L. J., Weikart, D. P., & Larner, M. B. (1986b). Consequences of three preschool curriculum models through age 15. *Early Childhood Research Quarterly, 1*(1), 15–45.

Scott-Little, M. C., & Holloway, S. D. (1992). Child care providers' reasoning about misbehaviors: Relation to classroom control strategies and professional training. *Early Childhood Research Quarterly, 7*(4), 595–606.

Seefeldt, C. (Ed.). (1992). *The early childhood curriculum: A review of current research* (2nd ed.). New York: Teachers College Press.

Seppanen, P. S., Godin, K., Metzger, J., Bronson, M., & Cichon, D. (1993). *Observational study of early childhood programs. Final report, Volume II: Chapter 1-funded early childhood programs.* Dover, NH: Development Assistance Corporation.

Seppanen, P. S., Kaplan de Vries, D., & Seligson, M. (1993). *National study of before and after school programs.* Portsmouth, NH: RMC Research Corporation.

Shin, E., & Spodek, B. (1991, April). *The relationship between children's play patterns and types of teacher intervention.* Paper presented at the annual meeting of the American Educational Research Association, Chicago. (ERIC Document Reproduction Service No. ED 332 803)

Silvestri, G. T. (1993). Occupational employment: Wide variations in growth. *Monthly Labor Review, 116*(11), 58–86.

Slavin, R. E., Karweit, N. L., & Madden, N. A. (Eds.). (1989). *Effective programs for students at risk.* Boston: Allyn & Bacon.

Slavin, R. E., Madden, N. A., Karweit, N. L., Livermon, B. J., & Dolan, L. (1990). Success for all: First-year outcomes of a comprehensive plan for reforming urban education. *American Educational Research Journal, 27*(2), 255–278.

Snider, M. H., & Fu, V. R. (1990). The effects of specialized education and job experience on early childhood teachers' knowledge of developmentally appropriate practice. *Early Childhood Research Quarterly, 5*(1), 69–78.

Solomon, D., Watson, M. S., Delucchi, K. L., Schaps, E., & Battistich, V. (1988). Enhancing children's prosocial behavior in the classroom. *American Educational Research Journal, 25*(4), 527–554.

Spodek, B. (Ed.). (1993). *Handbook of research on the education of young children.* New York: Macmillan.

Spodek, B., & Saracho, O. (Eds.). (1990). *Early childhood teacher preparation.* New York: Teachers College Press.

Stallings, J., & Stipek, D. (1986). Research on early childhood and elementary teaching programs. In M. Wittrock (Ed.), *Handbook of research on teaching* (3rd ed., pp. 727–753). New York: Macmillan.

Stayton, V. D., & Miller, P. S. (1993). Combining general and special early childhood education standards in personnel preparation programs: Experiences from two states. *Topics in Early Childhood Special Education, 13*(3), 372–387.

Stice, C. F., & Bertrand, N. P. (1990). *Whole language and the emergent literacy of at-risk children: A two year comparative study.* Nashville: Tennessee State University, Center of Excellence: Basic Skills. (ERIC Document Reproduction Service No. ED 324 636)

Stice, C. F., Thompson, D. L., & Bertrand, J. E. (1991). *Literacy development in two contrasting classrooms: Building models of practice toward a theory of practice.* Nashville: Tennessee State University,

Center of Excellence, Basic Skills. (ERIC Document Reproduction Service No. ED 340 004)

Stipek, D. J., & Daniels, D. H. (1988). Declining perceptions of competence: A consequence of changes in the child or in the educational environment? *Journal of Educational Psychology, 80*(3), 352–356.

Stipek, D., Daniels, D., Galluzzo, D., & Milburn, S. (1992). Characterizing early childhood education programs for poor and middle-class children. *Early Childhood Research Quarterly, 7*(1), 1–19.

Stremmel, A. J. (1993). Implications of Vygotsky's sociocultural theory for child and youth care practice. *Child and Youth Care Forum, 22*(5), 333–336.

Stremmel, A. J., & Fu, V. R. (1993). Teaching in the zone of proximal development: Implications for responsive teaching practice. *Child and Youth Care Forum, 22*(5), 337–350.

Swick, K. J., & McKnight, S. (1989). Characteristics of kindergarten teacher who promote parent involvement. *Early Childhood Research Quarterly, 4*(1), 19–29.

Vandell, D. L., & Corasanti, M. A. (1990). Variations in early child care: Do they predict subsequent social, emotional, and cognitive differences? *Early Childhood Research Quarterly, 5*(4), 555–572.

Vandell, D. L., Henderson, V. K., & Wilson, K. S. (1988). A longitudinal study of chidren with day-care experiences of varying quality. *Child Development, 59*(5), 1286–1292.

Vandell, D. L., & Powers, C. D. (1983). Day care quality and children's free play activities. *American Journal of Orthopsychiatry, 53*(4), 493–500.

Vygotsky, L. (1978). *Mind in society: The development of higher psychological processes.* Cambridge, MA: Harvard University Press.

Vygotsky, L. (1992). *Thought and language.* Cambridge, MA: The MIT Press.

Whitebook, M., Howes, C., & Phillips, D. (1989). *Who cares? Child care teachers and the quality of care in America.* Final Report of the National Child Care Staffing Study. Oakland, CA: Child Care Employee Project.

Whitebook, M., Phillips, D., & Howes, C. (1993). *Four years in the life of center-based child care.* Report of the National Child Care Staffing Study Revisited. Oakland, CA: Child Care Employee Project.

Willer, B., Hofferth, S. L., Kisker, E. E., Divine-Hawkins, P., Farquhar, E., & Glantz, F. B. (1991). *The demand and supply of child care in 1990.* Washington, DC: NAEYC.

Williams, L. R., & Fromberg, D. P. (Eds.). (1992). *Encyclopedia of early childhood education.* New York: Garland.

Wink, J., & Garcia, H. S. (1992, April). *The emergence of the framework for intervention in bilingual education.* Paper presented at the annual meeting of the American Educational Research Association, San Francisco. (ERIC Document Reproduction Service No. ED 349 839)

Wise, A. E., & Leibbrand, J. (1993). Accreditation and the creation of a profession of teaching. *Phi Delta Kappan, 75*(2), 133–136, 154–157.

·17·

ELEMENTARY EDUCATION

Richard E. Ishler
UNIVERSITY OF SOUTH CAROLINA

Kellah M. Edens
UNIVERSITY OF SOUTH CAROLINA

Barnett W. Berry
UNIVERSITY OF SOUTH CAROLINA

The preparation of elementary school teachers is intricately intertwined with public schools in terms of purposes, content, processes, and organization. This chapter focuses on the preparation of teachers for the elementary school. It reviews traditional curricular themes; synthesizes prevailing recommendations of educators, institutions, and agencies engaged in contemporary educational reform efforts; and describes projects and programs that illustrate innovative and exemplary curricular practices. Based on past and present curricular themes, conclusions about a curriculum that empowers preservice teachers to promote learning and understanding in elementary students and that equips future teachers with the skills and competencies required for the complex elementary school classroom of the 1990s and beyond are drawn.

The curriculum for the preservice preparation of elementary school teachers was not a separate topic in the first edition of the *Handbook of Research on Teacher Education* (Houston, Haberman, & Sikula, 1990), and the *Handbook of Research on Curriculum* (Jackson, 1992a) does not specifically target early childhood, elementary, or secondary teacher preparation programs as curricular categories. Although the most recent edition of the *Handbook of Research on Teaching* (Wittrock, 1986) included a chapter on curriculum programs in early childhood and elementary schools (see Stallings & Stipek, 1986), the curriculum used to prepare elementary teachers was not delineated.

Indeed, comprehensive and in-depth descriptions of curriculum content, process, and evaluation are sparse (Howey & Zimpher, 1989).

Of course, quantitative facts and figures about preservice education programs such as the required number of credit hours and graduation and certification requirements are available from state and federal regulatory and accrediting agencies. The data, however, only provide surface information about specific courses and programs and fail to adequately characterize the complexity and interrelatedness of curricular offerings of particular elementary teacher preparation programs. These programs are far more than an accumulation of courses and experiences that candidates fulfill to be recommended for initial certification. Moreover, this type of information tends to create an illusion of similitude among teacher preparation programs, which in practice differ drastically due to divergent conceptual orientations and/or implementation of coursework. The knowledge base that provides the underpinning for the design of program curricula spawns programs that possess unique attributes and thereby produce graduates with distinctive skills, competencies, and characteristics (Galluzzo & Pankratz, 1990). Therefore, it is important to examine the curriculum of elementary education teacher preparation programs from a broader and more comprehensive perspective by focusing on traditional themes and on recommendations of contemporary educational reformers.

The authors thank their chapter reviewers for their helpful input: Richard K. Jantz (University of Maryland) and Jack V. Powell (University of Georgia).

Viewed with the legacy of reform of the education of educators, current recommendations and practice provide the foundation for conditions for a model elementary teacher curriculum. To achieve this purpose, it is necessary to define the use of the term *curriculum* in this chapter; to differentiate early childhood and middle level education from the traditional conception of elementary school education; and to delineate relationships among content, process, and evaluation of teacher education curriculum and elementary school curriculum.

Definition of Curriculum

Curriculum has been defined in a myriad of ways, ranging from narrow, specific definitions to global and dynamic definitions (Jackson, 1992b). Curriculum has been viewed narrowly as a series of courses to be offered and taken, a definition derived from its Latin root origin of "racecourse" (Connelly & Lantz, 1991), or as documents that are developed to be implemented by teachers. In contrast to this limited interpretation, curriculum also is described as the ongoing experience of students. For example, curriculum has been defined as the means to obtain the ends or objectives of an educational program, and "essentially, learning takes place through the experiences that the learner has; that is, through the reactions he makes to the environment in which he is placed" (Tyler, 1949, p. 63). A concept of curriculum that "stresses purposes, content, organization, relationships, and outcomes for students" (Cuban, 1992, p. 221) promotes a view of curriculum as "a series of planned events intended for students to learn particular knowledge, skills, and values" (Cuban, 1992, p. 221).

Goodlad, Klein, and Tye (1979) contend that the broader view of curriculum contains several levels, emanating from the ideal curriculum (a theoretical model) to the formal curriculum (the courses officially adopted and offered). The layers of curriculum extend to the perceived curriculum (the interpretation of the formal curriculum by faculty), to the operational curriculum (the actual teaching, instruction, and experiences), and, finally, to the experiential curriculum (the learning experiences that are meaningful to the students). In this chapter, to encompass the interrelated and multifaceted nature of the broad view, curriculum is defined as all of the opportunities a preservice elementary education student has to learn how to teach elementary school students.

Modifications to the Traditional Conception of Elementary School Education

Traditionally, elementary teacher education programs have prepared students for teaching grades one through six. The organizational pattern of elementary schools, however, has been modified in recent years with the inclusion of kindergarten programs and the removal of grade six to the middle school. The growth of early childhood education as a distinct field addressing developmentally appropriate education of children from birth to age eight is attributed to changes in society at large, the shift of kindergartens as separate educational institutions to public elementary schools, and concern about "pushed-down" curriculum—the trend toward early academics (National Association

for the Education of Young Children (NAEYC), 1992; Spodek & Saracho, 1990). Although early childhood teachers in nonpublic childcare programs are not required to be licensed or to complete teacher training, kindergarten teachers in public elementary schools are required to be graduates of teacher preparation programs with at least a bachelor's degree and to possess a state teacher certification. In the elementary school, early childhood education spans kindergarten through grade two. The curriculum for the preparation of early childhood practitioners is described in Chapter 16 of this handbook.

The second change to the traditional conception of elementary school is the shifting of grade six to the middle school to join grades seven and eight, while grade nine merges with the high school. The middle school movement has been precipitated by research findings concerning developmental characteristics of fifth through ninth graders and the increasing focus of high schools on accreditation and college preparation programs, which is inappropriate for the middle level student. Supporting the middle school initiative, the report "Turning Points" (Carnegie Council on Adolescent Development, 1989) advocated that the curriculum be modified from the inappropriate junior high organization to accommodate better the emotional and interpersonal needs of young adolescents. The curriculum for the preparation of middle level educators is addressed in Chapter 18 of this handbook.

A considerable overlap thus exists between elementary teacher education and early childhood and middle level teacher education programs because of diversity among school districts regarding school organization. Some school districts still subscribe to the elementary (K–6), junior high, and senior high school configuration, whereas other districts reflect a shift to the elementary (K–5), middle level (grades 6–8), and high school (9–12) organization. Teachers for elementary schools, therefore, must possess the knowledge and skills essential to teach a broad age range of students and to meet the distinctive needs of early childhood and upper elementary children (grades 3–5) as well as early middle level students. In this chapter, the elementary teacher education curriculum is viewed as preparing teachers for grades 1–6. Developmentally appropriate practice for early childhood programs and middle level programs are addressed but not emphasized in minute detail as the curricula for these programs are included in Chapters 16 and 18, as previously mentioned.

The Relationship Between Elementary Schools and the Preparation of Elementary Teachers

What factors shape the curriculum of teacher preparation programs and elementary schools? Unquestionably, curriculum decisionmakers in both teacher education programs and elementary schools are pressured by societal, political, and cultural forces to adapt to change and diversity and to be responsive to other initiatives. The curriculum "is the outcome of a complex interplay of competing values and traditions as signified by different interest groups and . . . in part, reflecting the meanings they attribute to social, political, and economic conditions" (Kliebard, 1992, p. 157). Moreover, the relationship between a society and its curriculum is reciprocal for "just as the curriculum is affected by social values and perceptions of social conditions, so too the curriculum can help reshape or preserve those values and conditions" (Kliebard, 1992, p. 158).

State guidelines, accreditation agencies, and professional associations wield substantial amounts of influence, if not control, on both teacher education programs and elementary school curricula. Mandates from state legislation, state departments of education, boards, and agencies shape curricular practice in colleges and elementary schools, which, in turn, shape curriculum policy, which is indicative of a reciprocal relationship between curriculum policy and practice (Elmore & Sykes, 1992).

Although reciprocity allegedly exists between curriculum policy and practice and between curriculum and society at large, a noteworthy issue relates to the degree to which teacher education programs and elementary school curriculum in actuality inform or influence each other. Does one (teacher education programs vs. elementary schools) drive the other in terms of curricular content, process, and evaluation, or does reciprocity concerning curricular issues between the two entities truly occur? Do teacher education programs and elementary schools respond simultaneously to changing roles and responsibilities with a shared vision? The genuine relationship among content, process, and evaluation of teacher education curriculum and elementary school curriculum is indeed enigmatic and sometimes controversial.

Teacher educators encounter pressure regarding the content and structure of the curriculum from the university where they work and from the schools that will be the future employers of their graduates (Anderson, 1993). The pressures exerted by these two forces are based on divergent perspectives. According to Morine-Dershimer and Leightfield (cited in Anderson, 1993, p. 53), the university tends to push "for more subject matter content and more research-based pedagogical content," whereas school systems accentuate the need for "more practice-oriented courses and more practical experiences in classrooms." The two cultures, campus-based university/college culture and the public school culture, "experience and value different curricula . . . and provide contrasting views of the theoretical and the practical necessary to understand the present state of the curriculum" (Edmundson, 1989, p. 5). Morine-Dershimer and Leightfield (cited in Anderson, 1993) assert that the amount of emphasis placed "on field experiences in any teacher education program is determined by which of these two pressures is strongest in the given setting" (p. 53). The tension that exists between the two forces or cultures thus does not necessarily culminate in a model teacher education curriculum. Moreover, research on learning has intensified a tension between the dominant views of how elementary school children learn, as expressed by constructivists, and the implementation of the curriculum in many elementary classrooms in which recitation of facts and evaluation of students by traditional paper-and-pencil tests are stressed.

Raths noted that the tension between teacher preparation programs and elementary schools is exacerbated by the fact that evaluation in teacher education has traditionally been linked to accreditation and other forms of summative evaluation (Anderson, 1993) rather than provide evidence and formative information on which curricular decisions can be based. In addition to a deficiency in the evaluation of the curriculum, an examina-tion of a national sample of the National Council for Accreditation of Teacher Education (NCATE) elementary education clinical summative forms revealed the nonexistence of a systematic evaluation of preservice elementary teachers (Reyes & Isele, 1990). The lack of evaluation in teacher education has resulted in curricula based on "tradition, faddish popularity, or reasonable ideas offered by important and influential people" (Anderson, 1993, p. 58), a condition undoubtedly noted by practitioners in elementary schools. Whereas "practice makes policy, even as policy shapes practice" (Elmore & Sykes, 1992, p. 186) on a theoretical level, the widespread attainment of reciprocity between teacher preparation programs and elementary schools regarding curricular content, process, and evaluation is doubtful.

It is mutually advantageous, however, that university classrooms that prepare elementary school teachers and elementary schools that provide field experiences avoid contradictions in content, process, and evaluation. Goodlad (1990b) emphasizes the importance of the teacher education's programmatic and structural relationships to schools and practitioners, asserting that education of educators should be based on a distinct conception of "the educating we expect our schools to do." A more ambitious perspective of teaching and learning that emphasizes the active and meaningful construction of knowledge and authentic assessments of that knowledge, therefore, should first be modeled in the teacher education curriculum and utilized extensively in elementary schools. School sites that provide field experiences for preservice teachers then should model the teaching and learning strategies to illustrate and reinforce knowledge about teaching and learning. An alignment of curriculum goals, instructional experiences, and assessment whereby curriculum goals are translated into instructional experiences assessed by alternative assessment approaches should occur in both the university and elementary classrooms (Smith, Kuhs, & Ryan, 1993). The resulting relationship between teacher preparation curriculum and elementary school curriculum concerning content, process, and evaluation thus functions in a dynamically reciprocal and symbiotic manner. Clearly, what is called for is the simultaneous reform of elementary schools and the renewal of teacher preparation programs.

This chapter first provides a historical overview of the preparation of elementary school teachers and introduces traditional curricular themes. The second major section provides a compilation and synthesis of how groups, boards, institutions, associations, and agencies engaged in reform efforts address the traditional curricular themes along with recently emerging themes. Recommendations are presented on *the way the curriculum should look* and *what it should do,* as determined by the following:

- National Council for Accreditation of Teacher Education (NCATE)
- National Association of State Directors of Teacher Education and Certification (NASDTEC)
- National Association for the Education of Young Children (NAEYC)
- The Renaissance Group
- Project 30 institutions

- The National Network for Educational Renewal (Goodlad Consortium)
- The Holmes Group
- Carnegie Forum on Education and the Economy
- National Board for Professional Teaching Standards (NBPTS)
- Interstate New Teacher Assessment and Support Consortium (INTASC)

The next section describes programs and projects under way in specific colleges and universities. Finally, conclusions about the status of elementary teacher preparation relative to traditional and contemporary concerns and current programs are presented.

TRADITIONAL CURRICULAR THEMES IN ELEMENTARY SCHOOL EDUCATION

Brief Historical Overview

Teachers had no formal education in preparation for teaching children during the United States's first 200 years. Even in the nineteenth century, most elementary teachers were not prepared in the least for their positions, having at most completed a course of study at the elementary level with no specific instructions about teaching. By as late as 1914, it was possible to obtain a teaching certificate by passing a test and answering a few easy questions related to pedagogy (Tyack, 1967). In 1931, only about 10% of all elementary teachers had a bachelor's degree. As recent as 1946, Stinnet found that only 20 states enforced a minimum requirement of a bachelor's degree for an elementary teaching certificate, in contrast to 40 states that required a bachelor's degree for a secondary teaching certificate (cited in Kerr, 1983), and in 1952, the majority of elementary teachers still had not graduated from college (Tyack, 1967). Since the early 1970s, however, all states have required the bachelor's degree as a minimum requirement for certification in elementary education.

Evolution from the Normal School Tradition

The academic preparation of elementary school teachers evolved from the normal school tradition with coursework on subject matter and on techniques to manage a class (Feiman-Nemser, 1990). "Pedagogy—the study of the art and science of teaching—emerged as a distinct and specialized field of study in the early nineteenth century" (Borrowman, 1965, p. 1) and a highly technical curriculum was implemented in normal schools, ranging from 2 weeks to 2 years and focusing on practical aspects of teaching performance. Feiman-Nemser (1990) notes that the conception that normal schools were narrowly focused "ignores the historic context in which they evolved and their hard-won gains in differentiating professional from liberal arts education" (p. 213). Furthermore, "unlike modern-day schools of education, with their fragmented mission and defensive posture, normal schools knew that their major purpose was to serve the profession by educating prac-

titioners" (p. 214). In state normal schools, the late nineteenth century marked a shift in emphasis from training teachers for elementary classrooms to the preparation of specialized subject-matter teachers, administrators, and research specialists in educational psychology and administration. Many normal schools subsequently became 4-year teachers' colleges and the majority of universities formed schools of education. The curriculum of teacher education during this period included educational psychology, child psychology, educational measurement, special methods, history and philosophy of education, curriculum development, subject area coursework, and practice teaching.

Herbst (1989a) notes that with this change, "female elementary classroom teachers received the short end of the stick" (p. 8) as energies and appropriations were bestowed on the training of teachers for high schools and special subjects. County and city normal schools then were responsible for training elementary teachers who were viewed as requiring less training than high school teachers. Training elementary teachers was "the unfashionable cause," and male students were encouraged to make elementary teaching "a steppingstone toward high-school teaching, teaching and supervision of special subjects, and school administration" (Herbst, 1989b, p. 232). At the end of the century, America's normal schools had neglected the training of the elementary school teacher (Herbst, 1989b) and failed to create a professional corps of teachers to teach in elementary schools. Moreover, "the forgotten person . . . in the onward march of professionalization in American public education has been the American elementary school teacher" (Herbst, 1989a, p. 190).

Profile of the Elementary Teacher

Unlike the European view of school teaching as a lifetime career that appealed to a large number of males, normal schools promulgated a view of elementary teaching as temporary employment or as a gateway to future employment. Undereducated, single young women taught for a few years prior to marriage, and teaching was viewed as a low status position with a low salary (Lortie, 1975). By 1860, in Massachusetts nearly four out of five teachers were female and teaching children "was a female occupation par excellence" (Herbst, 1989a, p. 27). The feminization of the elementary classroom had begun, a trend that continues into the 1990s, for "the occupation of teaching is still women's work . . . and still offers low pay and low status relative to other occupations that involve similar preparation and responsibilities" (Cohn & Kottkamp, 1993, p. 20). Women continue to predominate elementary education classes, constituting about 90% of all preservice teachers. Ninety-five percent of the 90% female student population are white and 3% are black. Less than 3% of the students are Hispanic, Asian/Pacific Islander, or American Indian/Alaskan Native (American Association of Colleges for Teacher Education [AACTE], 1989) and students are essentially monolingual. Data obtained from 90 randomly sampled AACTE-member institutions (AACTE, 1989) in the Research About Teacher Education Project (RATE III) indicate that the typical elementary education preservice teacher is a female caucasian, approximately 25 years of age who is attending a college or university moderately close to home with the goal of teaching near home after graduation.

Less than one third of students are married, with the largest group of married students attending institutions offering baccalaureate, master's, sixth-year, and doctoral degree programs in education (AACTE, 1989).

Several misconceptions about the mid-1990s elementary education programs exist, conceptions based on the stereotypical view that many elementary education programs are less rigorous than other programs of academic study, thus attracting modestly qualified females. The view that elementary education majors are modestly able is perpetuated by college board reports that indicate that "those that would consider careers in education" score at the bottom of the distribution of the Scholastic Aptitude Test (SAT) and rank at the bottom of their high school graduating classes (AACTE, 1989). Those interested in elementary education programs are viewed as avoiding intellectually stimulating coursework while pursuing a safe, predictable career. To substantiate this stereotypical view, Lortie (1975) reported that the high availability of teacher preparation programs and low admissions standards make entry into the profession a relatively uncomplicated process. Lortie (1975) also found that teachers are attracted to teaching because they want to have a schedule with time flexibility, the opportunity to work with children, perform a service, remain in school, and acquire material benefits.

The RATE III investigation (AACTE, 1989), however, has found contradictory evidence regarding these stereotypes. For example, the RATE III study (AACTE, 1989) reported that the typical preservice teacher in elementary education averaged a combined SAT score of 898 (the national average for all entering college freshmen is 906) and graduated in the top third of his or her high school class. Almost 95% of the students indicated that they were "very positive" or "positive" about teaching as a career, and 93% indicated that they intended to teach after graduation, whereas the majority of the remaining 7% responded that they planned to go to graduate school or to work in a field related to education. The majority of the students indicated they would consider as an educational career option the role of cooperating teacher, team leader, mentor to beginning teacher, department head, school board member, and supervisor, with administrative roles (principal, superintendent) viewed as less appealing (AACTE, 1989). Combined with the growing professionalization of teaching in general, when contrasted with the historical profile of elementary teachers of the past and the more recent misconceptions based on stereotypes, well-qualified students who view teaching as a long-term career have chosen elementary education as their profession.

Many elementary teacher educators are intensely scrutinizing the curricular content of elementary education programs with the goal of designing a curriculum that is as demanding as other academic majors and secondary education programs. The perception of elementary education coursework is changing and is viewed more frequently as providing challenging and intellectually stimulating opportunities and as gaining professional sanctions from the educational community and society at large. Data indicate that the majority of both faculty and students perceive their elementary education programs as "above average" or "excellent" (AACTE, 1989). In addition, the majority of both faculty and students rated elementary education courses "as rigorous" or "more rigorous" than noneduca-

tion courses. When compared with the most advanced courses in English, history, foreign languages, science, and mathematics, elementary courses in the professional sequence were viewed by a majority of students and faculty "as rigorous" or "more rigorous," with the exception of foreign languages (AACTE, 1989).

Comparing the responses about perceptions of preparation of elementary school teachers with their responses when they were student teachers (based on the RATE III research design and instrumentation), Houston and Williamson (1992–1993) found that students reported the curriculum provided the knowledge base to teach effectively, increased their sensitivity to the moral and ethical aspects of teaching, and increased their knowledge of a variety of ways of teaching. As student teachers, the highest rated concepts were "working effectively with other teachers," "evaluating student learning," and "teaching methods," and the lowest rated area was "teaching with computers." Their attitudes changed over time, however, for their ratings at the conclusion of their first year as teachers on the same dimensions of the curriculum were consistently lower, with 10 of the 16 areas rated significantly lower as teachers than as student teachers. After a year of teaching, while their enthusiasm about teaching in general had lessened, they had a greater appreciation for their academic courses than at the end of student teaching. The majority of beginning teachers reported more positive feelings about their preparation program than they reported as student teachers. They considered methods courses and field-based experiences as strengths and noted the importance of educational theory and knowledge. Frequently cited as weaknesses were "insufficient preparation in classroom management and behavior problems" and other general comments about courses "that included busy work, were repetitious and redundant, required too much time, and inadequately involved students" (Houston & Williamson, 1992–1993, p. 39). Other weaknesses were too much theory, not enough practical useful items, and the need for more hands-on training.

Traditional Curricular Themes

Curricular reform is not an endeavor unique to the 1990s. There are numerous illustrations of reform efforts as long ago as the 1700s when the emergence of a less restrictive purpose of education prompted leaders to suggest that free public schools were necessary to support a popular government. Historically, reformers have struggled to direct educational ideology, policy, and curriculum, yet few lessons have been learned as the result of their endeavors due to "historical amnesia" (Zeichner & Liston, 1990, p. 3). Johnson's (1989) summary of the evolution of teacher preparation curriculum provides an admonition that contemporary curricular reformers should heed.

The experience in education is better described as a series of local uprisings, each decade or so, which have had little enduring impact except, perhaps to clutter the curricular landscape with dead or wounded programs and theories. Nevertheless, it is still to the university school of education that many look today to improve the research base on which teacher training ought to rest. (p. 245)

An examination of curricular recommendations during the twentieth century suggests that several themes specific to elementary education are grounded in the legacy of early teacher preparation for public schools. The first of these curricular themes is the tension between proponents of a liberal arts education versus proponents of professional preparation and relates to the debate about the knowledge base and the competencies needed to teach and the debate about the duration of the program of study. Other themes relate to the tradition of teaching diverse students at many grade levels and the generalist tradition—the tradition of teaching numerous subjects. A final tradition involves the notion of "learning by doing" or recognition of the value of apprenticeships by observation and participation.

The Traditional Debate About How Teachers Should Be Educated

What Knowledge Is Essential to Prepare Teachers? The legacy of teacher education includes a longstanding debate about how teachers should be educated, that is, what kinds of knowledge are relevant to teaching and how this knowledge is enhanced and promoted. A model of knowledge pertaining to teacher preparation (i.e., "a view of what knowledge is, how it is acquired, and how it is used" [National Center for Research on Teacher Learning (NCRTL), 1991a, p. 6]) provides a framework for the design of curriculum. Findings from the Teacher Education and Learning to Teach Study (NCRTL, 1991a) proposes three models of knowledge: (1) the liberal arts model (knowledge is "enriching" and exposure to the knowledge of different disciplines can expand the individual's intellectual powers), (2) the scientific model (knowledge consists of theory and empirical research findings that can be disseminated to students through formal courses and applied to practice), and (3) the skill or craft model (knowledge of teaching is craft/skill and is acquired through experience or through guidance from peers). The NCRTL study found "differences in the kind of knowledge that programs deemed central to teaching . . . [with] no consensus about what it means to 'prepare' someone for teaching" (NCRTL, 1991a, p. 65).

Although there are a variety of ways to view knowledge and its transmission, the curriculum of teacher preparation programs tends to consist of components somewhat analogous to the three models found in the Teacher Education and Learning to Teach Study. The first two models are the liberal arts tradition (i.e., the liberal arts model) and professional education preparation (i.e., an amalgam of the skill or craft model and the scientific model). The third component consists of subject-matter concentration (i.e., content). Reynolds (1992) provides an analogy to describe the interdependent relationship among these three components.

General subject/liberal arts might be thought of as a table top, indicating breadth of understanding, while content acts as the pedestal, or depth of understanding. General principles of teaching and learning refer to pedagogy that crosses many, if not all, subject areas and grade levels but does not require knowledge of a specific subject matter. (p. 5)

The relative emphasis on these components influences the model of knowledge endorsed by a teacher preparation program and reflects views concerning the relationship between pedagogy and subject matter. Views about the relationship between pedagogy and subject matter usually fall on a continuum between the generic view, that pedagogical skills are the same across subjects, and the perspective that pedagogy differs across subjects, contingent on the particular subject (NCRTL, 1991a). Reynolds (1992) further notes that "Of all the domains of teacher understandings, content-specific pedagogy is both the most elusive and the most discussed" (p. 5). Again, the perspective and orientation of a teacher preparation program concerning the relationship between pedagogy and subject matter determines the emphasis on subject-matter concentration.

Historical Views of Essential Knowledge for Teaching The tensions between those emphasizing liberal arts versus professional preparation is steeped in history. Contemporary proponents of the liberal arts tradition echo Horace Mann who suggested in 1838 that "Each teacher ought to know vastly more than he [or she] is required to teach" (cited in Emans, Lee, Monroe, & Monroe, 1989, p. 9) and David Page in 1847 who argued that "To be a teacher, one must first of all be a scholar. So much stress is now placed on method, and on the theory of teaching, that there is great danger of forgetting the supreme importance of scholarship and culture" (cited in Tyack, 1967, p. 412). In fact, a liberal arts education, accompanied by field-based apprenticeship, was commensurate to being prepared to teach (Borrowman, 1965). Others, such as Dewey and his followers, however, believed that the liberal arts curriculum lacked relevance and failed to adapt to social changes. In addressing the question about what a teacher needs to know, Tyack (1967) notes that

Fierce battles have been waged over the answer to this apparently innocent question, struggles which all too often have resembled the battles of the ancient Chinese warlords, who summoned their troops to an imaginary line, hurled insults at each other, and departed, leaving tempers riled but bodies intact and the landscape unchanged. (p. 412)

The commonplace strands of general education, subject-matter concentration, and professional coursework in teacher education curriculum of the 1990s thus were in place during the nineteenth century, even then arousing much debate among teacher educators concerning the amount of emphasis placed on each strand. The continuing tension between those who argue that preparation should offer specific practical solutions to practical problems and those educators who conclude that teachers should be provided primarily with the knowledge to use to solve problems on their own clearly can be traced back to these early beginnings of teacher preparation. With regard to this tradition, the curriculum pendulum has oscillated from providing teachers with a liberal arts background, to more subject-matter coursework, to courses that instruct how to teach, and back again. The pendulum continues to undulate as teacher educators debate the relative merits of emphasis on each component to ensure better the preparation of good teachers.

That teachers should have a broad general education is a belief held by many educators; it is important for a teacher to possess a broad range of knowledge that can be used to enhance the teaching process. Furthermore, teachers are responsible for the formal general education of youth and are expected to serve as models of scholars and subject-matter specialists. In particular, elementary school teachers should be more broadly and liberally educated than other college graduates because in addition to being responsible for teaching the entire elementary school curriculum, "other than a student's parents, no other person has the opportunity to influence, to motivate, to inspire a child to value the intellectual life. In fact, it may well be that the opportunity to offer role models may be the single most significant aspect of the teaching profession" (Ishler, 1987, p. 14). Historically, however, elementary school teachers have been viewed as needing less academic training; therefore, the number of general education requirements necessary to produce a critically thinking, broadly knowledgeable elementary school teacher continually has been questioned. All too often general education programs for elementary education majors are diluted because of the dual purpose of the programs: liberal education and content for subjects being taught (Ishler, 1987). Elementary education students rarely complete full academic majors, taking twice as many education courses as secondary majors (excluding many liberal arts colleges and California institutions) (Zeichner & Liston, 1990).

Recommendations based on the results of several reports compiled during the 1930s and 1940s serve as illustrations of a sense of déjà vu of current educational debate, as the pendulum continues to swing between the common strands, targeting elementary teachers in particular. For example, in 1933, the U.S. Office of Education conducted a nationwide survey on the inadequate schooling of teachers and their lack of professional training of teacher education institutions (Lazerson, 1987), an issue that recently has been underscored (e.g., Carnegie Forum on Education and the Economy, 1986; Goodlad, 1990a, 1990b; Holmes Group, 1986, 1990). Recommendations suggested that teachers in elementary and rural schools should have requirements equal to or exceeding the minimum standards of 2 years of college work. The data relating to the amount of educational preparation of elementary school teachers contributed to

a realization that the situation is unsatisfactory and the determination that something should be done to better it . . . the proposed changes would be initiated, organized, and controlled by the regularly constituted educational authorities and that the necessary modifications would be made by each State. (Lazerson, 1987, p. 105)

Therefore, current efforts to establish national professional teaching standards and state guidelines concerning teacher preparation have a familiar ring. During the 1940s, the American Council on Education's Commission on Teacher Education (cited in Borrowman, 1965) suggested that three eighths of the college experience should consist of general education coursework. Concerning advanced subject-matter preparation, the commission found "a high degree of scholarly competence is essential in a teacher; such competence requires not only knowledge and personal skill but also the ability to use both effectively in the teaching relationship" (p. 233).

Support for the liberal arts tradition also was evident in the 1950s and 1960s when the Ford Foundation and its Fund for the Advancement of Education supported efforts to strengthen the liberal arts orientation through fifth-year programs (Zeichner & Liston, 1990). In the late 1960s and early 1970s,

elementary education programs also reflected a commitment to a general education that provides a firm liberal education foundation upon which to develop the more specialized content, process, and skills of a professional training program. The curricular innovation, Competency/Performance Based Teacher Education (C/PBTE), which had its origin in the Comprehensive Elementary Teacher Education Models (CETEM), is based on the notion of isolating the skills and competencies associated with instruction. C/PBTE is grounded in the model of knowledge as a science perspective and is akin to what Zeichner and Liston (1990) term *the Social Efficiency Tradition* in education. C/PBTE has been described as "the single most influential and controversial trend in U.S. teacher education in this century" (Zeichner & Liston, 1990, p. 9). Yet, C/PBTE only slightly influenced actual practice in teacher education programs.

An important part of C/PBTE is the concept of teachers working together cooperatively in a teaching unit. The concepts of team teaching and interdisciplinary education also were present in local multiunit schools as part of the individually guided education (IGE) instructional approach. C/PBTE, however, did not prove to be the panacea to the problems of teacher education, for, in a sense, the program was preparing teachers for schools that did not yet exist. Influences of C/PBTE remain, however, because in addition to exerting much influence on preservice curriculum development, C/PBTE also served as a stimulus for the teacher competency testing movement.

In 1963, Conant was critical of both the academic and professional training offered by teacher preparation programs and suggested that the fragmented foundations of education should be eliminated. Conant (1963) refers to special methods courses, which are offered to guarantee that preservice teachers know the elementary school curriculum and how best to teach it, as "those terrible methods courses which waste students' time" (p. 137). Johnson (1989) argues that although Conant's list of 27 recommendations, which included the elimination of all state-mandated requirements concerning the number of courses or credits in education be dropped, "left the impression that a solid groundwork for the reform of teacher training had been laid" (p. 240).

In 1970, Silberman emphasized the importance of the liberal education of teachers that enables teachers to ask probing questions about how and what they teach. Silberman (1970) noted that "the central task of teacher education is to provide teachers with a sense of purpose, . . . with a philosophy of education" (p. 472) and argued that teachers "need knowledge about knowledge, about the ramifications of the subject or subjects they teach, about how those subjects relate to other subjects and to knowledge—and life—in general" (p. 489).

Thus recommendations about the appropriate curriculum for preservice elementary education teachers have reverberated during this century and curricular innovation is not a novel idea. Historically, however, recommendations have not guaranteed nor prompted change, a point that should be heeded by contemporary reformers.

Divergent Views on Liberal Arts Education, Professional Preparation, and Subject-Matter Concentration There are diverse and sometimes contradictory viewpoints about the liberal arts component, professional preparation, and subject-matter concentration. For example, according to Zeichner and Liston (1990), there are three challenges to the liberal education and subject-matter knowledge of teachers. First, according to Martin, the feminist perspective is critical of liberal arts Platonic dichotomies (e.g., "mind not head, thought not action, production not reproduction, and reason not emotion" (cited in Zeichner & Liston, 1990, p. 5) that ignore social and emotional complexities. Second, recent research on pedagogical content knowledge, "How teachers' understanding of subject matter knowledge interacts with other kinds of knowledge" (p. 6), has suggested a new, broader knowledge base as requisite for teaching. A third challenge relates to the noticeable absence of non-Western and culturally diverse viewpoints from liberal arts coursework. The emphasis on Western, white, middle-class values thus does not adequately prepare teachers for culturally and economically diverse students and schools (Zeichner & Liston, 1990).

The question of the appropriate liberal arts education and subject-matter concentration is particularly problematic for elementary teachers who should be prepared in all disciplines for the elementary classroom. Proponents of the liberal arts legacy posit that the challenging curriculum of a liberal arts program will provide "a dimension of scholarship, dignity, and respect to the profession of elementary teaching and, thereby, increase the number of capable people attracted to the profession" (Emans et al., 1989, p. 8). Opponents of this position suggest that liberal arts courses are fragmented, lack a sense of purpose, and are not connected with the application to teaching and are primarily concerned about the sequence of professional education coursework that provides specific instruction for how to teach.

Professional education courses portend to provide the specialized body of knowledge and skills necessary to the teaching profession, including methods courses and field-based experiences. The professional education coursework assumes that the knowledge and skills required to be an effective teacher have been identified. Cruikshank (1985), however, argues that "the most serious obstacle preventing teaching from having true professional status is the lack of consensus among educators regarding what constitutes the requisite specialized body of knowledge and skills for effective teaching" (p. 14), in contrast to professions such as medicine and law that have concurrence concerning a professional culture. Although the need for the professional component is not disputed, many teacher educators do not desire the addition of professional education courses at the expense of the general education and subject-matter concentration requirements. Thus, whereas teacher educators have reached consensus that the three components are essential for preparing elementary school teachers, the debate is centered around the relative distribution of credits in each of these areas.

Emphasizing the need to connect meaningfully the liberal arts component, professional coursework, and subject-matter content, the American Association of Colleges for Teacher Education's Bicentennial Commission on Education report, *Educating a Profession* (Howsam, Corrigan, Denemark, & Nash, 1976), found that many preservice teachers consider foundations courses unconnected and cannot relate the knowledge to their experience as students or as future teachers. The report pushed the teaching profession to establish consensus on the professional culture required to begin the practice of teaching. Teacher educators who reflect the beliefs of both traditions, liberal arts and professional orientations, agree that teachers need to be professionally educated to learn how to educate others formally, but the professional orientation should be defined and described.

Although the precise coursework requisite to produce an effective teacher is not delineated, several associations have described essential functions of teaching that should serve as the foundation for the design, development, and implementation of college programs preparing teachers. For example, the National Education Association (1982, cited in Cruikshank, 1985) described these functions as facilitating learning, managing the classroom, and making professional decisions. Making recommendations somewhat more specific, another AACTE publication, *Educating a Profession: Profile of a Beginning Teacher* (Scannell et al., 1983), advocates that preservice curriculum should be organized into four components: general education, preprofessional study in disciplines that support pedagogy, academic specialization, and professional study. The general education component of the curriculum should foster proficiency in the art of communication and an understanding of groups, institutions, society, work, new technologies, principles of physical and mental health, values and beliefs, and the fine arts. The preprofessional study in supportive disciplines should enable students to understand principles and methods of inquiry related to education and teaching and to have an understanding of the fundamental disciplines from which teachers draw experiences and knowledge. Professional studies or pedagogy consist of foundations of education, generic teaching knowledge and skills, specialized pedagogical knowledge and skills, and field and clinical laboratory experience.

The provision for the general education and professional components has the endorsement of teacher accreditation and program approval agencies such as NCATE and NASDTEC and state departments of education. All teacher education institutions require one third or more of the curriculum to be in general education, which provides the foundation for more specialized subject-matter concentration. AACTE has issued a position statement advocating the general education component. Fidelity to the position by teacher education institutions, however, is variable as some educators and students have shifted emphasis to the practical and technical training that lead directly into the teaching profession. Moreover, there is much diversity concerning what constitutes the general education component because the guidelines allow latitude in interpretation and implementation.

A Cursory Inspection of the Nature of Elementary Education Curriculum Given that differing philosophical orientations concerning general education, subject-matter concentration, and professional preparation requirements exist, what is the status of coursework required of preservice elementary teachers? Furthermore, what are the dominant conceptualizations and orientations of programs? Comprehensive evidence about the curriculum of preservice elementary school teachers is limited, although quantitative data are available (Howey & Zimpher, 1989). For example, based on a random, stratified sample of AACTE-member institutions, the RATE Project (AACTE, 1989) found that "the typical elementary education program consisted of approximately 132 semester hours. The aggregate profile of the elementary education program consisted of general studies (58 credits), professional studies (42 credits), an area of concentration (20 credits), and student teaching (12 credits)" (AACTE, 1989, p. 14). More specifically, 18 of the 67 institutions responding to the question concerning the nature of their elementary education program require an academic major averaging 32 credits; 11 institutions require an academic minor averaging 20 credits; 26 schools require a concentration of about 20 credits; 11 require two concentrations totaling 42 credits; and three institutions require three concentrations totaling about 66 credits. The professional coursework includes 6 hours in methods courses for teaching reading, and about 3 hours each in methods courses for teaching social studies, math, science, and language arts. The student teaching experience is usually completed at one school site and lasts for approximately 12 weeks, although at a minority of the institutions, student teachers are placed at two different school sites for 7 weeks at each site. Although there is a trend to reconsider certification areas (e.g., early childhood/primary education, intermediate grades, middle grades), of the responding institutions, 31% of the elementary education programs lead to state certification for the traditional elementary school (kindergarten through grade 6), whereas 26% lead to certification for kindergarten through eighth grade (AACTE, 1989, p. 14).

To provide an added dimension to the superficial data about number of credits, faculty and students also were asked to evaluate the characterization of their programs as one of five dominant conceptualizations: (1) development of a well-rounded, liberally educated person; (2) skill or competency oriented; (3) clinical or problem solving; (4) inquiring and reflective; and (5) humanistic and person oriented. Fifty-seven percent of the faculty and 65% of the students reported that their programs were based on one of these conceptions of teaching. Fifty-two percent of faculty at those institutions that offer only the baccalaureate degree (classified as stratum 1 institutions) perceived the liberal arts orientation as dominant compared to 10% of the institutions that, in addition to the baccalaureate degree, offer master's, specialist, and doctoral degrees (classified as stratum 2 and stratum 3 institutions). In contrast to the perceptions of faculty, the majority of students from all institutions reported the liberal arts orientation as dominant. Faculty respondents from major research universities (stratum 3 institutions) reported their programs as framed in the humanistic perspective followed by the skill or competency perspective. In addition, approximately 14% of the stratum 2 and stratum 3 institutions reported a cognitive or clinical perspective as compared to less than 4% of stratum 1 institutions (AACTE, 1989). Thus, among AACTE institutions, there is great diversity concerning conceptual orientation of teacher preparation programs.

Another frequently debated topic concerning the nature of programs relates to the merits of two different categories of teacher preparation—integrated and postbaccalaureate (Woolfolk, 1989). The postbaccalaureate category moves initial certification to the graduate level, whereas the student may be eligible for initial certification at the undergraduate level in the integrated program. Although there are variations, preparation in integrated programs starts gradually in undergraduate coursework with several education courses and experiences in the field but with the majority of coursework devoted to academic disciplines and a major. Students concentrate on professional education coursework during the fourth year or in a fifth year, which may include student teaching or an internship. The 5-year integrated program may conclude with the granting of a master's degree or only with eligibility for certification (Woolfolk, 1989).

The postbaccalaureate category of programs consolidates all professional preparation at the graduate level. Students who are admitted have already received a bachelor's degree and spend a year or more engaged in professional and field-based coursework toward a master's degree or eligibility for certification. A caveat exists, however, for "You can't judge a program by its structure" (NCRTL, 1991a, p. 64). Numerous student transferrals result in a small percentage of students actually experiencing a 5-year coordinated sequence at a single institution and "that in some fundamental ways, alternative route programs are not so different from conventional preservice programs" (NCRTL, 1991a, p. 65).

The notion of extended preparation at the graduate level for elementary teachers was tendered as early as 1934 prior to the requirement by all states of a 4-year degree and was advanced by the requirement of a minimum of 5 years of teacher preparation for elementary teachers by the passage of the Fisher Bill in California (Zeichner, 1989). There were numerous discussions and arguments for the establishment of graduate teacher education as the norm for preservice education in the 1950s and 1960s, and the Ford Foundation sponsored several graduate programs (Zeichner & Liston, 1990).

A major recommendation by contemporary reformers is that the undergraduate education major be eliminated, thus moving teacher preparation for initial certification to the graduate level (The Holmes Group, 1986, 1990; Howsam et al., 1976). This recommendation is viewed as an essential element in the professionalization of teaching, which should lead to greater funding and increased status. Those opposed to the elimination of undergraduate programs are not "against the development of graduate level programs . . . most, if not all, of the opposition is toward the idea of establishing graduate or 'extended' preparation as the *only* option" (Zeichner, 1989, p. 12). Other advocates of extended preparation are Smith, Silverman, Borg, and Fry (cited in Cruikshank, 1985) who argue that as teacher education moved from normal schools and teachers' colleges to university campuses, academic knowledge was emphasized at the expense of pedagogy. To address pedagogical deficiencies, new schools of pedagogy should be created and the 4-year undergraduate curriculum leading to a bachelor's degree should be followed by 2 years in a school of pedagogy leading to a master of pedagogy degree (Cruikshank, 1985).

In an effort to address the information deficit about the education of teachers (i.e., to render a detailed drawing about *what* is to facilitate the design of a curriculum as *it should be*), Howey and Zimpher (1989) conducted a research study of six institutions that prepare elementary teachers. The comparative case studies involved outstanding elementary education programs in diverse higher education settings ranging from a small liberal arts college to major research-oriented universities. The study included Luther College, Ball State University, University of Toledo, University of Wisconsin–Eau Claire, Indiana University, and Michigan State University. The qualitative depictions of these institutions provided an extension to the objective and quantitative design of the AACTE (1989) RATE (Research About Teacher Education) Project on elementary education.

Questions regarding curricula posed by Howey and Zimpher (1989) related to: (1) the scope and sequence of courses across different elementary programs; (2) the conception(s) of teaching, learning, and schooling apparent in the curricular design of the programs; (3) the extent of usage of simulations, microteaching, and/or peer teaching opportunities; (4) the opportunities to utilize instructional approaches at school sites congruent with the goals of the program; (5) the expectations and intellectual challenges of the curriculum; and (6) the type or level of research and evaluation of the elementary teacher education program.

The findings that emerged from across institutional analysis of the in-depth studies about the nature of preservice teacher education programs indicated the presence of an "articulated and integrated curriculum" (Howey & Zimpher, 1989, p. 212) as evidenced by the utilization of themes across programs at Michigan State University and the development of program modules that articulate clearly specified objectives and coursework continuity at the University of Toledo. In addition, the spiral nature of curriculum that resulted in continuity between and among courses at Luther College, Ball State University, and the University of Wisconsin–Eau Claire was depicted. The developmental character of the curricula was observed in the six institutions as shifting from structured observations to more intensive and prolonged interaction and teaching and from a technical approach to teaching to an approach that emphasizes complexity, interrelatedness, and the value of reflectivity. A sense of "shared ordeal" (p. 213) among students also enhanced the developmental nature of the curriculum. For example, student cohorts completing "blocks" at the University of Wisconsin–Eau Claire and the University of Toledo, Experimental Elementary Education (EXCEL) at Ball State University, and Paideia requirements at Luther College benefited by collectively experiencing certain "rituals" associated with learning to teach.

Inquiry into consensus-driven curricula, that is, curricula based on acknowledged and concurring ideas of teaching and schooling, yielded differing views of teaching across institutions. For example, the University of Wisconsin–Eau Claire and Ball State University perceived their roles as "providing the basics" by promoting the "characterization of a teacher as disciplined, well-organized, and well planned" (p. 216). At Ball State University, emphasis is placed on hands-on experiences, whereas faculty at Indiana University discussed the importance of encouraging reflection among students. Luther College, with a classical conception of the educated teacher, and the University of Toledo focus on basic communication and human relation skills including "clarity of presentation, organization, and individualized instruction" (p. 216). Whereas both schools emphasize skill attainment, the modular competency-based teacher education program at the University of Toledo grounded in a behavioral psychology framework contrasts with Luther College's liberal arts orientation. Michigan State University programs also show diversity of conceptions of teaching and learning by focusing on "learning in academic disciplines, personal responsibility and social community, and appreciation for diverse learners that exist in a diverse society" (p. 216). The in-depth portrayal of six outstanding teacher education programs provides information that should assist curricular reform because the data extend beyond superficial evidence (e.g., "course title and number of credit hours").

The Tradition of Teaching Diverse Students

The elementary school teaching profession should be well seasoned in the notion of teaching diverse students at many grade levels. After all, elementary teachers initially taught students at all levels and then students in the graded elementary school, grades 1 through 6, a configuration recommended by the Committee of Ten in 1893. A question is raised, however, concerning the present-day turf of elementary school teachers as early childhood programs and middle school programs concentrate on grades previously considered the sole domain of elementary teachers. Given that early childhood majors specialize in teaching children in prekindergarten, kindergarten, and grades 1, 2, and 3 (NAEYC, 1992), and those teachers specializing in middle school focus on grade 6 through 8, only grades 4 and 5 remain uniquely as elementary grades. Will the tradition of elementary education majors being qualified to teach children of diverse ages become a relic of the past? Will elementary education as it is now known become compressed as it is absorbed into early childhood and middle school preparation programs?

Because different grade level configurations continue in many school districts and a variety of early childhood, elementary, and middle school certification requirements exist in the states, teacher preparation programs continue to churn out teachers as generalists to be elementary school teachers. The curriculum for these teachers should emphasize developmental differences in learning and focus on teaching practices that support these differences. The underpinnings of both the NAEYC (1992) and the middle school initiative (Carnegie Council on Adolescent Development, 1989) are grounded in the recognition and thorough understanding of the developmental characteristics of very young children and older children. Elementary teacher programs, therefore, should provide preservice teachers with a comprehensive and in-depth understanding of the physical, cognitive, language, and social-emotional development of school-age children. Such a depth and breadth of understanding of developmentally appropriate practices across a broad span of grade levels enhances an understanding of what is appropriate for individual children within the classroom. The elementary education major immersed in developmentally appropriate practice should fully understand how the continuum of development is reflected through individual differences, thus specializing in *all* students, not a narrow range of grade levels.

Although efforts to prepare preservice teachers for working with diverse students have been put forth, many teachers and schools fail to meet the needs of poor children, children from specific racial and ethnic backgrounds, and children with exceptionalities. That elementary teachers are somewhat inundated by their responsibilities for addressing differences in students can be traced to the latter part of the nineteenth century and early twentieth century when "A poorly prepared and largely unqualified teaching force" (Snyder, Bolin & Zumwalt, 1992, p. 403) was overwhelmed by the deluge of children who complied with compulsory education laws.

Yet concern that teachers understand student diversity has been expressed since the mid-twentieth century. Reminiscent of the current emphasis on understanding diverse students from multicultural backgrounds, the American Council on Education's Commission on Teacher Education noted in 1946 that the development of "a special understanding of the children with whom they work and also of the society for and in which they work" was important to the professional preparation of teachers (cited in Borrowman, 1965, p. 235). Interest in multicultural pluralism in the 1960s and 1970s also had an influence on teacher education and is later reflected in National Council for Accreditation of Teacher Education (NCATE) standards (1992), which require teacher preparation institutions to provide for multicultural education in curricula, including both the general and professional studies.

Criticisms, however, abound that teachers are ill prepared to work in economically depressed and culturally diverse inner cities. Attempts to incorporate multicultural perspectives into the curricula of teacher education programs, therefore, have gained momentum in the last decade as reformers urge teachers not only to be prepared to teach for understanding, but also to "hold these ambitious learning goals for everybody's children" (The Holmes Group, 1986, 1990). Teachers are in classrooms filled with students who, traditionally, have been the most difficult to teach, that is, racially and culturally diverse students of low socioeconomic status who may speak English as a second language. Although elementary schools historically have served diverse groups of students, they have not managed "to serve them all equally well" (NCRTL, 1991b, p. 5), partially due to the traditional profile of the elementary school teacher (i.e., white and female) and to the failure of teacher preparation programs to provide opportunities that promote an understanding of student diversity. Teacher preparation programs should recruit a socially, ethnically, and racially diverse student body and faculty and then provide a curriculum that enables students to work with and to develop an understanding of children of a different class, ethnic group, and race than their own.

Mainstreaming also has illuminated inadequacies of teacher preparation, as many elementary school teachers are not equipped to meet the needs of children with disabilities. Before the 1970s, children with disabilities were isolated from "regular" students and were either educated in separate programs and institutions or were excluded from school entirely. Federal legislation in 1975, The Education for All Handicapped Children Act (PL 94-142), guaranteed that children with disabilities, regardless of the severity or type of disability, must receive a free, appropriate education in the least restrictive environment (LRE). Now referred to as the Individuals with Disabilities Education Act (IDEA) (PL 101-476), Part B requires that "separate classes, separate schooling, or other removal of children with disabilities from the regular environment occurs only when the nature of severity of the disability is such that education in regular classrooms cannot be attained satisfactorily" (Sec. 612 [5] [B]) (Eric Clearinghouse on Disabilities and Gifted Education, 1993,

p. 66). Elementary teachers, however, were not trained to provide support for the academic and behavioral needs of children with disabilities.

The availability of appropriate public education for students with disabilities has not necessarily resulted in good educational outcomes and led to reform efforts by the U.S. Office of Education in 1986. The Regular Education Initiative (REI) was a strategy for unifying regular and special education, and its supporters intended the REI to strengthen regular classrooms' teaching and learning processes by an infusion of special education resources. Historically, however, special education has been viewed as a separate educational entity; therefore, general education did not embrace the REI (Fuchs & Fuchs, 1994). General education and special education currently are in the process of redefining their relationship. The term *inclusion* is now used to describe efforts to integrate children with disabilities into regular classrooms. Although inclusion is interpreted in a variety of ways (Fuchs & Fuchs, 1994), ranging from "a new term for mainstreaming" to "the elimination of special education," the general definition of inclusion is that children with disabilities are included in the classroom to the extent appropriate to the needs of the child. Their inclusion should be viewed by all educators as a shared responsibility and privilege. The resources provided by special education are still an important component. It is imperative that general education adapt and modify the curriculum and instructional programs to accommodate the needs of all students. It is equally important for teacher preparation programs to address the identical issue relating to adaptation and modification of curricula to accommodate the needs of all future teachers. The curricula should promote the development of positive attitudes and beliefs about the potential for success of students with disabilities. In addition, it should provide opportunities to acquire knowledge about children with exceptionalities and to learn appropriate skills for co-teaching, team teaching, and serving as part of an instructional and planning team.

The Generalist Tradition: Teaching All Subjects

The elementary school curriculum is the basis for the prospective elementary teacher's area of specialty or concentration and covers subject areas such as art, health, mathematics, music, physical education, science, and social studies. Unlike secondary teachers, elementary teachers teach all the common branches. Elementary teachers have been charged with teaching "reading, writing, spelling, and arithmetic" as early as the 1600s and 1700s, a charge that later was expanded to include grammar, composition, history, geography, drawing, music, agriculture, art, civics, drama, domestic science, manual training, nature study, and other subjects. Curricular developments in elementary schools during the 1920s, however, included the consolidation of the approximately 20 discrete subjects to the broad areas of language arts, social studies, science, and so forth. A survey of elementary schools in 1926 indicated that teachers were allowed ample leeway in implementing curriculum, which essentially was the textbook used in a school (Snyder et al., 1992).

The curriculum pendulum has continued to swing in elementary schools as national curriculum projects and emphasis on the affective domain and self-concept have been popular and then fallen in disfavor. Currently, there are simultaneous calls to "return to the basics" and to "develop higher order thinking skills, problem-solving, and creativity." Furthermore, the explosion of the general knowledge base and technological advancements have made increased demands on elementary teachers. Amidst this diversity of curricular issues in elementary schools, however, are remarkable similarities. Cuban (1992) attributes the resemblance in curriculum across about 15,000 school districts to the shared goals and functions of schooling. The public's explicitly stated expectations of schools include to promote mastery of basic skills and to provide general knowledge in various subjects (Cuban, 1992).

Critics, however, maintain that elementary students are not receiving an acceptable foundation in most subject areas and are not developing an ability to reason, analyze, and understand important concepts. The general education component should provide the prospective elementary teacher with the knowledge base to encompass the content of the elementary curriculum. Yet this is not always the case as some universities may not provide courses that are supportive of the content needs of the elementary teacher. Moreover, heavy reliance on lecture with superficial discussion promotes memorization of isolated facts that lack purpose or meaning for students and are unconnected to the experience of teaching. Given the information explosion, elementary teachers should possess deeper and broader conceptual knowledge, problem-solving ability, and capacity to reason rather than an accumulation of facts, which can be accessed through information systems (NCRTL, 1991b). Teacher education students should use interactive learning technologies and media, with the use of media modeled by faculty (NCATE, 1992). Emphasis on the use of instructional and interactive media requires a thorough understanding of the study of teaching and the design of instruction, including a comprehension of the basic educational research underlying its selection and use (NCATE, 1992). In addition, preservice elementary teachers should experience interdisciplinary coursework to gain an understanding of how knowledge is interrelated, rather than fragmented into discrete courses and subjects. Again, the curriculum to prepare elementary teachers should reflect the teaching expected of elementary teachers.

At the same time, it is important to note how much of the secondary reforms of the mid-1990s, such as the middle school reforms posited by the report "Turning Points" (Carnegie Council on Adolescent Development, 1989), call for teachers to possess many of the same dispositions, skills, and knowledge suggested by the elementary teacher education curriculum. Increasingly, it is being recognized by policymakers and practitioners alike that what makes for a good elementary school teacher makes for a good secondary school teacher. There are several possible explanations for a push for preparing more teachers as generalists.

First, secondary school teachers, now more than ever, should be able to make connections among subject-matter areas as they work with increasingly diverse groups of students. Problems that both children and adults must face are increasingly multifaceted, complex, and ill-structured. Thus, plausible solutions should emerge from a variety of fields of knowledge. In addition, there is a growing body of evidence that the academic abilities of students are not fixed and that effective teachers of either children, adolescents, or adults should understand a student's cognitive development and their particular type of intelligence(s) in order to teach and guide them effectively.

Second, there is growing recognition that for school reform, in general, to succeed, teachers should be better equipped to focus primarily on the students they teach rather than on the subject matter in which they specialize. Unfortunately, most teachers are ill prepared to meet the demands of today's students and today's society. Highly transient students, increasing poverty, single-family homes, parents working two or more jobs, new immigration patterns bringing more students whose primary language is not English, and multiculturism all contribute to the complexity and unpredictability of change forces from within and without the schools. These demands require that teachers, first and foremost, become generalists who can adapt to ever-changing teaching and learning situations.

Finally, the explosion of information and the availability of technological tools contribute to the need for more "jack-of-all-trades" teachers. Indeed, the current tidal wave of new technologies, creating what Perelman (1992) calls hyperlearning, "refers not merely to the extraordinary speed and scope of new information technology but to an unprecedented degree of connectedness of knowledge, experience, media, and brains" (p. 23). Hyperlearning cannot be managed by a so-called expert doling out increasingly archaic knowledge but by networking information bases that cut across diverse fields of knowledge as well as ways of knowing.

Tradition of "Learning by Doing": Recognition of the Value of Apprenticeship by Observation and Participation

The value of experience in the classroom, observing or participating, has long been extolled, and student teaching is "the one indisputable essential element in professional education" (Conant, 1963, p. 142). "Learning by doing" provided the sole education of early teachers in many cases. In the eighteenth century, a master teacher advertised for an apprentice with the promise that "he would teach the art and mysteries of his craft" (Tyack, 1967, p. 413), and in the nineteenth century, schools that demonstrated a more practical model of teacher training utilized the apprenticeship concept (Johnson, 1989). Several large-scale apprenticeship schools, Boston Normal School, Cook County Normal School, and the New York College for the Training of Teachers (Horace Mann Practice School), successfully subordinated theory and academic instruction to practice. Yet formalized apprenticeship arrangements did not continue, not because of a revolution in pedagogical theory, but as the result of economics (Johnson, 1989). The view that "Children should be experienced, not just be studied about" (Borrowman, 1965, p. 240) and "Students should be worked with and not on" (p. 243), however, has persisted, and teacher educators tend to support John Dewey's conviction that the main purpose of experiential learning is to make the preservice teacher a true student of teaching rather than an apprentice seeking to imitate a master. Most field experiences, however, still reflect the apprenticeship model. Students are placed in a classroom with a cooperating teacher, conforming to the classroom routines and emulating the teacher's behavior. Reflective inquiry about the student teaching experience frequently is not supported.

Field-based experiences, which include observations, part-time participation, practica, and student teaching, provide direct experiences with the reality of the school classroom and they are viewed as important by educators. Unfortunately, field experiences are derived from tradition and are not based on empirical evidence. Although student teaching is seen as a critical aspect of teacher preparation, its influence on the novice teacher ranges from narrow in scope to negative. Research suggests that the actual outcomes of student teaching are primarily related to socialization into the professional culture of teaching and to development of technical competence and classroom management. The low degree of selectivity and lack of supervisory training of cooperating teachers and university supervisors also contribute to the bleak depiction of many field-based experiences. While providing authentic experiences, field-based experiences tend to maintain the status quo because of the university's dependence on local school districts for placement sites, which in many cases contradict the university's definition of good practice. The typical student teaching experience places emphasis "upon imitation of and subservience to the supervising teacher, not upon investigation, reflection, and solving novel problems" (The Holmes Group, 1986, p. 62). Problems also relate to the sequencing of the experiences and how they relate to each other and the coursework. The influence of teacher education programs on the ways prospective teachers work with students, therefore, is slight, because students tend to teach the way they were taught as students and to rely on conventional approaches observed around them in the school culture. Programs "do not challenge the 'apprenticeship of observation'—the years of teacher-watching that shape prospective teachers' views of teaching. As a result, teachers often leave preservice preparation with their initial views intact" (NCRTL, 1991a, p. 67).

Teacher preparation programs should be sufficiently forceful to influence students' beliefs and practices. An elementary teacher preparation curriculum should encourage reflective analysis and self-direction in preservice teachers at a field site that does not contradict coursework. It is imperative that prospective teachers learn in their field experiences not only to solve immediate problems, but also to inquire and reflect about classroom activities as well as short-term and long-term goals. Unquestionably, field experiences should foster processes that promote self-direction.

CONTEMPORARY REFORMISTS' PERSPECTIVE ON THE ELEMENTARY EDUCATION CURRICULUM

How do contemporary reformers address traditional curricular themes related to the preparation of elementary education teachers? Few reform reports of the last decade specify an explicit direction for the elementary education curriculum. The contents of these reports, however, have much to say about balancing tensions among (1) liberal arts and professional prep-

aration, (2) teaching a multitude of different subject matter to diverse students, and (3) theoretical and practical training.

Recently, the call has escalated for elementary school teachers to possess not only a liberal education parallel to other well-educated community members but also to understand a range of subject matters in order to teach with an interdisciplinary perspective (AACTE, cited in Emans et al., 1989). Indeed, elementary education teachers have been expected to teach a diversity of subjects and students. Recent reforms have emphasized the fundamental relationship between subject matter and pedagogy and have specified that teachers should have an in-depth knowledge of the subjects they teach. Given the current elementary education curriculum and the mid-1990s national curriculum standards movement, these cognitive requirements (in math, science, social studies, language arts, reading, etc.) present a daunting challenge to teacher educators who are preparing elementary school teachers. Yet, Petrie asserts that even though there is incredible press for elementary school teachers to know more subject matter, there is little evidence of a strong relationship between a teachers' content knowledge and better student performance (cited in Emans et al., 1989). Some researchers have argued that this contradiction emerges because the current arts and sciences coursework that is taken by prospective elementary school teachers (and other majors as well) does not provide appropriate teaching models or fundamental content for learning subject matter for public school teaching (McDiarmid, 1992). The conundrum of time for more coursework and the quality of learning experiences for prospective elementary school teachers are at the heart of this curricular issue, which is addressed in this section by reviewing the kinds of teaching required for the public schools of today and tomorrow and by summarizing relevant teacher education reform recommendation.

Teaching for the Public Schools of Today and Tomorrow

In large measure, the teaching required for the schools of the twenty-first century suggests strongly that "the teacher's job is no longer to 'cover the curriculum' but to enable diverse learners to construct their own knowledge and to develop their own talents in effective and powerful ways" (Darling-Hammond, 1993, p. 754). This conceptualization of teaching, commonly called "teaching for understanding (TFU)," defines knowledge as being constructed and therefore situated in prior experiences and existing conceptions (and misconceptions) of learners. TFU requires that the teacher become a facilitator and a co-constructor of knowledge with students. In doing so, classrooms emerge as a community of learners that supports risk taking and making mistakes and that sustains efforts in serious learning. TFU requires teachers who (1) have an intimate knowledge of student development; (2) use a variety of teacher strategies that build on students' preconceived notions, culture, interests, motivations, and learning styles; (3) diversify classroom practices with a variety of learning activities and new assessments; and (4) possess more than minimal knowledge of subject matter by knowing how to select, represent, and organize information, concepts, and procedures so that subject matter can be transformed for student understanding and application (Darling-Hammond & Berry, in press).

To teach for understanding, teachers should have an appreciation for and deep understanding of human motivation, multiple intelligences, and diverse modes of performance. Such a view should ultimately require that teachers have rigorous grounding in the following:

- Cognitive psychology, so that they understand how people learn
- Developmental psychology, so that they understand when children are ready to learn particular things in particular ways
- Learning theory and pedagogy, so that they can teach in developmentally and cognitively appropriate ways
- Professional ethics, so that they can manage schools' competing agendas in ways that keep the best interests of students at the forefront of their actions (Darling-Hammond & Berry, in press)

Teaching for understanding will require substantially more knowledge and radically different skills for teachers. Teachers should be able to make complex decisions based on growing knowledge about child development and learning theory as well as their own working knowledge garnered through countless encounters with young people. The kind of teaching required to meet these demands for more thoughtful learning cannot be produced through teacher-proof materials or regulated curriculum. Teachers should be deeply imbued with understandings of learning, cognition, child development, and pedagogy, as well as the structures of subject areas (Darling-Hammond, 1990; Shulman, 1986). Such understandings can be widely acquired throughout the teaching force by major reforms of teacher preparation and major restructuring of the systems by which states and school districts license, hire, induct, support, and provide for the continual learning of teachers (Wise, Darling-Hammond, with Berry & Klein, 1987). Indeed, this new mission for schooling and the requisite professional knowledge and skills of elementary school teachers may not be easily learned in the traditional coursework patterns described previously.

TFU requires, more than anything else, new modes of teacher development, both preservice and in-service. In fact, recent research on teachers' professional development in a "climate of educational reform" (Little, 1993) sheds considerable light on the context of preservice preparation, especially considering the growing awareness of the need to attend to teacher education as a lifelong continuum (Goodlad, 1990a; The Holmes Group, 1986, 1990).

The literature on teacher change suggests strongly that individual growth toward teaching for understanding should be viewed within the context of teachers, administrators, and students (Richardson, 1990). Similarly, Talbert and McLaughlin's research (1993) suggests that the teaching cultures in which teachers work vary widely, even inside of schools. Some teachers are able to work in each others' classes and others are not, depending on the learning community (or cohesiveness) represented within a particular school, a particular department (e.g., math, English), or a particular grade level. Thus, in large measure, the degree to which teachers learn new practices depends on who socializes with whom (e.g., the extent to which there is a learning community) and what they do together (e.g., the content of their social interactions and how it affects learning to teach). In fact, Little's (1993) design principles for professional development befitting teachers' opportunity to learn include:

- Offering meaningful intellectual, social, and emotional engagement with ideas, materials, and colleagues both in and out of teaching
- Taking into explicit account the contexts of teaching and experience of teachers (thus, "one size does *not* fit all")
- Offering support for informed dissent among colleagues and "opportunities for critiquing underlying assumptions and philosophies and alternative courses of action" (p. 138)
- Placing professional development in the larger contexts of school practice and the educational careers of students
- Preparing teachers to be inquirers and critics of "the institutional patterns of practice" (p. 139)
- Striking a balance between the interests of both individuals and institutions as well as mitigating bureaucratic constraints

Few schools maintain such optimal conditions for teacher learning, but these are indeed the conditions required for teachers' professional development to be supportive of learning to teach challenging new content and engage diverse students with it. Substantiating this claim, McCarthy and Peterson (1993) recently investigated how two elementary school teachers (one math, one language arts) created new practices that supported teaching for understanding in a professional development school. A multitude of complex organizational variables came into play. These variables included:

- The opportunity for teachers to teach the same students for a number of years
- Team-teaching arrangements that provide a referent group and act as a sounding board for new practice
- Joint planning periods for teachers during the course of a regular teaching day
- Demonstration lessons along with regular visits and observations of other classrooms both within and outside one's own school
- An on-site coach available on a regular basis in both formal and informal settings
- A professional library and journal articles readily available
- Systemic participatory management within the school
- State and district curriculum policy that does not directly or indirectly bind teachers' teaching
- Explicit supports for teacher-designed and initiated on-site professional development
- Formal and informal connections with others involved in restructuring efforts
- District officials, principal, and teachers who share a common vision of teaching for understanding

In this chapter, it is argued that the elementary education curriculum (and teacher education generally) should reflect a rather explicit notion; that is, teachers' learning experiences (both preservice and in-service) should be framed by the same assumptions and strategies used in teaching students for understanding.

Summary of Relevant Reform Recommendations

A review of issues addressed by contemporary reformists focuses on those aspects of the recommendations that shed light on preparing a new generation of elementary school teachers. First, the elementary education guidelines offered by the NCATE as well as those proposed by NASDTEC through its outcome-based standards are presented. Next, the recommendations of NAEYC are assessed for their relevance in establishing the elementary education curriculum. Then, the works of the Renaissance Group, Project 30, the National Network for Educational Renewal, the Holmes Group, and the Carnegie Forum on Education and the Economy are summarized. Since the mid-1980s, these five teacher reform groups have had considerable visibility both in terms of an action agenda as well as rhetorical influence. Finally, this review includes the tenets of the NBPTS and INTASC, both of which portend forthcoming standards and assessments that could leverage major changes in teacher (and elementary) education.

The National Council for Accreditation of Teacher Education NCATE provides for a voluntary system of accreditation for professional schools of education. Only 500 of the nation's 1,300 colleges and universities that prepare teachers subscribe to the standards; however, at the time of this writing, it is estimated that approximately 80% of all new teachers graduate from NCATE-accredited institutions. In recent years, NCATE has drawn on national specialty associations to revise and implement a more rigorous accreditation system. Until recently, NCATE unit standards related to the knowledge base, relationships to the world of practice, students, faculty, and governance/resources. Recent revisions to the unit standards (now 20) now include somewhat different categories, with a greater emphasis on more highly trained reviewers using professional judgment in assessing institutional quality. The new unit standards that have been created portend an emphasis on (1) greater attention to assessment of individuals (e.g., portfolios, interviews, videotaped performances); (2) integrative studies for initial teacher preparation; (3) use of technology (e.g., related to assessment); (4) enhanced opportunities to work in diverse, multicultural classrooms; and (5) developing a more inclusive professional community (NCATE, 1992).

As part of the folio review process, basic programs for the preparation of elementary education teachers are expected to prepare teacher candidates who can influence and improve the education of elementary students (NCATE, 1992). NCATE has developed a model framework that provides for

- The integration of supervised field experiences and input from practitioners throughout the professional studies sequence
- Understanding the multiple responsibilities of teachers for student socialization, adjustment to school environment, and academic instruction

- A breadth of study in all subjects taught including fine arts, social studies, science, math, health, physical education, reading, writing, and oral language
- A comprehensive general education and a command of the subjects prospective teachers will teach as well as a strong grounding in academic discipline, basic understanding of child growth and development, and a demonstrated ability to help students construct their own knowledge and skills
- The integration of pedagogy with content in a majority of the program courses
- Interdisciplinary preparation in both content and process
- An understanding of learning characteristics and learning needs/capacities related to age, cultural/linguistic background, and exceptionalities
- Development of curriculum and instructional strategies to meet student differences
- Multicultural perspectives that will promote democracy (NCATE, 1992)

The National Association of State Directors of Teacher Education and Certification NASDTEC is an organization that frames much of the teacher education and certification decisions emanating from state departments of education. In a recent report, NASDTEC (1992) proposes a major policy shift from the current efforts of many state departments of education (i.e., focusing state program approval on authentic outcomes rather than highly specific process indicators), calling for government agencies and professional associations to provide leadership in outcome-based education. NASDTEC has developed a report that invites a focus on customer needs and expectations, authentic assessment through portfolios and performance, and outcomes as demonstrations of learning in assessing the quality of teacher education programs. Generally, the report calls for teacher candidate demonstrations to include research, video illustrations, sample lessons and management plan, sample assessments, and resources used, all related to the specified outcome. With regard to elementary education outcomes-based standards, NASDTEC has proposed the conceptualization of the teacher as a facilitator of learning. Specifically, the elementary education major, as a candidate for state licensure, should be able to

- Translate and align classroom expectations, climate, and instructional practices with children's individual stages of readiness and developmental characteristics
- Consider, accommodate, and integrate the physical, social, emotional, cognitive, and linguistic developmental characteristics of students
- Analyze and organize curriculum into teaching units (short term and long term)
- Teach developmentally appropriate, culturally sensitive, challenging, integrated subject matter in all areas
- Assess the school curriculum and its standards of performance
- Identify, interpret, generate, and measure group and individual readiness for school and use data in school improvement initiatives
- Plan and contribute to parental support as well as nurture family involvement at home and in school

- Correlate, integrate, and apply computer-supported learning in teaching
- Recognize the needs and refer students and/or families to available district or community support service agencies
- Establish networks of people, tasks, and resources and calculate costs of time, effort, and materials to help build a cost-effective system

The National Association for the Education of Young Children NAEYC, which defines early childhood as the years between birth and 8 years of age, has developed a set of positions on developmentally appropriate practice in the primary grades. The NAEYC report (NAEYC, 1992) reflecting the most current knowledge of teaching and learning has implications for how elementary educators are prepared. For example, the NAEYC has recommended that teachers of young children "must always be cognizant of the whole child" and that "education throughout the primary grades should be integrated" (NAEYC, 1992, p. 63). Schools that serve these young children should utilize flexible grouping patterns and should recognize the enormous variance among these students in the "timing" of their physical, cognitive, and social-moral development. In addition, planned physical activities are critical to an effective curriculum as is the principle of engaging young children in active rather than passive activities. Because young children need "concrete reference points," some curricular content may be beyond their cognitive capacity. Yet, certain practices, such as engaging young children in conversation, enhance their capacity to reason and to develop other cognitive skills. Pushing young children beyond their capacities may damage their academic self-esteem and thus lessen the prospects for future school success. Children learn at a very early age whether or not they can achieve success at a particular task or activity or in a specific subject area. Concomitantly, young children's understanding of their academic worth can influence life decisions. Elementary schools that inappropriately rely on comparisons and competitions among young children may lessen their "optimism about their own abilities and school in general, and stifle motivation to learn" (p. 66). Developmentally appropriate practice for young children includes opportunities for small group, cooperative projects, peer tutoring as well as individual pacing, and the promotion of independence and responsibility. Assessments should reflect the progress of young children, recognizing that traditional grades and testing and grouping practices indeed may be harmful.

The Renaissance Group The Renaissance Group has emphasized a university-wide commitment to multicultural teacher preparation. In part, this emphasis has emerged because of the increasing need to serve a new generation of students who bring complex challenges to the public schools. The Renaissance Group has cited evidence that 25% of all 5-year-old children live below the federal poverty line, 10% of children entering first grade have physical or emotional problems, and almost half of all students will spend time in a single-parent home before they reach age 18. Teachers for these students should have an in-depth knowledge of subject matter and be able to link it to the students' knowledge base and experiences as well as know how to manage classrooms and sequence learning

experiences that reflect the students' needs and prior knowledge. To do so, teachers should understand the structure of knowledge and the interrelationship of various disciplines. More so, however, teachers should be problem solvers and understand the cultural diversity of students and the social system that links the school to the community (Renaissance Group, 1992). Member institutions of the Renaissance Group have reported the establishment of multidisciplinary approaches to multiculturalism in teacher preparation courses and the use of culturally and linguistically diverse schools as clinical sites for practica, internships, and student teaching (The Renaissance Group, 1992).

Project 30 Project 30, sponsored by the Carnegie Corporation of New York, is a collaborative effort to redesign teacher education. This reform effort of 30 or more representative institutions of higher education is most unique in that it directly involves arts and sciences faculty with education faculty in joint action for fundamental reform of teacher education. Project 30 focuses on five themes that have been identified as those that are important to clarifying the intellectual underpinnings of teacher education and the development of the teaching profession. The themes are (1) subject matter understanding; (2) general and liberal education; (3) pedagogical content knowledge; (4) international, cultural, and other human perspectives; and (5) increasing representation of underrepresented groups in teaching (Project 30, 1991).

The National Network for Educational Renewal (or the Goodlad Consortium) The Goodlad Consortium, which is a set of school–university partnerships in a number of states led by the research and development of John Goodlad and his associates (see Goodlad, 1990a), has laid forth four broad categories of expectations for teachers: (1) understanding our government as a democracy and the purpose of schools to prepare citizens for that democracy; (2) being able to participate in the human conversation and prepare students to do the same; (3) possessing a range of pedagogical knowledge and skills; and (4) understanding the structures, organizations, goals, clients, curriculum, and instruction of schools. These broad categories reflect a mission for teacher education that includes at its nub a "moral dimension" (see Soder, 1993). This moral dimension considers the teacher education curriculum a source for inculcating a set of values, knowledge, and skills among teachers who, in turn, will prepare all students to be active participants in our democratic society.

Edmundson (1989) has argued that the teacher education curriculum should prepare teachers to be educated people willing and able to participate in "the human conversation." To be an "educated person" teachers must have an integrated, interrelated, interactive view of knowledge and must be socialized as continuous learners and prepared as thoughtful decisionmakers and reflective inquirers. A commitment to teaching as a moral enterprise obligates teachers to ensure that all students have access to and engagement with learning. Finally, the teacher education curriculum should prepare teachers to participate in ongoing school renewal.

Unfortunately, as the Goodlad (1990a) research agenda has revealed, most teacher education curriculum would not meet these criteria specifically, nor support this vision generally. Edmundson (1989) reported that the first 2 years of teacher preparation are a series of unrelated courses with no linkage to becoming a teacher. She noted that many professors of education do not perceive the need for the vision, nor do they (and their arts and sciences counterparts) have high academic expectations for their students. Most teacher education faculty and programs do not take moral positions on educational issues; being "neutral" seems to be more important. The emphasis of teacher education programs is centered on fostering the development of technical skills; therefore, many teachers enter schools thinking that teaching is merely a set of technical skills. Edmundson (1989) also reported that professors do not frequently answer student questions with reference to philosophy, theory, or research as a basis for their answer; they most commonly use personal experience as a basis for answers. Moreover, few cooperating teachers are chosen because they are model teachers.

Specifically, the Goodlad Consortium is using 19 postulates (Goodlad, 1990b) to frame their teacher education reform efforts. Briefly, these include:

1. A university-wide valuing of and support for the education of educators
2. Teacher education programs having parity with other university programs
3. Teacher education programs having autonomy and a constancy of budget and personnel
4. A clearly identifiable group of academic and clinical faculty for whom teacher education is a top priority
5. A clearly articulated mission and commitment to it
6. Limiting student enrollment and employing selection criteria that emphasize moral, ethical, and cultural commitments to teaching
7. Having all teacher education candidates acquire a high level of literacy and critical thinking skills
8. Producing teachers who are continuous learners and who constantly seek to improve their pedagogy
9. Instilling in teacher education students the "culture of teaching"
10. Modeling all conditions for learning that teachers will be expected to establish in their schools
11. Promoting inquiry into the nature of teaching and schooling
12. Involving future teachers in the broader issues of public education
13. Instilling in candidates the moral obligation to equal access and education for *all* children
14. Preparing teachers to be change agents and to be able to create alternate visions for schools and education
15. Offering a wide array of field experiences
16. Helping teacher education students recognize the differences between accepted practice and research theory supporting other options
17. Easing the transition into teaching by creating linkages with graduates
18. Relying only on "enlightened, professionally driven requirements for accreditation"
19. Providing quality control for all teachers, including the protection of students from the "vagaries of state policies" that allow unqualified teachers to teach

The Holmes Group The Holmes Group, which comprises 100 major research universities committed to reforming teacher education and the teaching profession, has issued two reports, with a third in 1995. The first report of the Holmes Group (1986), *Tomorrow's Teachers,* called for extended programs of teacher education, whereby teachers would be professionally educated in 2-year graduate programs following a 4-year baccalaureate. This report also called for a three-tiered teaching career in which more experienced and able teachers would lead and induct novices into the profession. These proposals became part of an agenda to fabricate "more intellectually sound" teacher education programs; acknowledge differences in teachers' knowledge, practice, and dispositions; create more demanding standards for entry into the profession; connect universities and schools; and leverage better working conditions for teachers (Sedlak, 1987).

These conceptualizations led to a second report of the Holmes Group (1990), *Tomorrow's Schools: Principles for the Design of Professional Development Schools,* which laid out principles for professional development schools (PDSs). PDSs would be part of the reinvention of public schooling and higher education designed to highly focus on professional preparation, school-based research melding both theory and practice, and the improvement of teaching. In doing so, PDSs would focus on creating learning *communities* for students as well as for teachers, administrators, and teacher educators and ensuring that *all* students are taught and are expected to learn for understanding (The Holmes Group, 1990).

In developing its agenda, the Holmes Group has articulated what future educators need to know, when during their preparation they need to know it, and how such experiences might best be structured (Sykes, 1992). For example, with regard to knowledge about diversity, the Holmes Group has taken a rather explicit stand—simply providing information about cultural and other characteristics of students evidently is ineffective as a means of influencing practice; therefore, teacher education should provide a framework for educators to understand how social, economic, and language difficulties cause problems for minority children (Sykes, 1992). These tenets have further implications for teacher education, including expanding the role of educators to working in and learning about communities and in reforming school practices that lead to academic failure. In addition, language should be studied as both a tool through which school subjects are taught and through which connections are made with the home and community (Sykes, 1992). With regard to subject matter, the Holmes Group has argued for the interconnectedness between subject-matter knowledge and knowledge of learners, claiming that "the division of university courses into subjects and methods is a flawed sequence. . . . Students cannot be merely *told* to teach for conceptual understanding. They should learn subjects conceptually and should encounter teaching for understanding throughout their own educational careers" (Sykes, 1992, pp. 24–25).

In addition, given the complex demands and expanding discipline-based and pedagogical knowledge, the Holmes Group has argued for protracted preparation. Considering the work of Berliner (1988) and conceptualizing learning to teach as a process involving stages (novice, advanced beginner, competent, proficient, and expert), both schools and universities should forge new collaborative learning opportunities for teachers (new and otherwise). The university's involvement in 4 years of general education, subject-matter major, limited methods, and clinical experiences, and the school district's involvement in workshops, staff development courses, and so forth, are viewed as fundamentally flawed. Sykes (1992) has suggested collaborative efforts that directly support beginning teachers via networking, seminars, and other follow-up activities and assessment. Challenges coming from cognitive psychology, classroom research, and case knowledge portend new delivery systems. For the Holmes Group, the PDS, analogous to the teaching hospital in many ways (Murray, 1990), offers much promise.

The Holmes Group has developed its third major report, *Tomorrow's Schools of Education,* whereby major and controversial recommendations are advocated for schools of education. These proposals suggest major departures in terms of the education school's mission, curriculum, structure, students and faculty, assessment, and inquiry, as well as their PDSs (The Holmes Group, 1992, 1995). For example, each of tomorrow's schools of education are encouraged to create a substantial number of PDSs that meet rigorous standards and that institutionalized procedures sustain the long-term collaboration between schools and universities.

The Carnegie Forum on Education and the Economy

The Carnegie Forum on Education and the Economy (1986) and its report, *A Nation Prepared: Teachers for the Twenty-First Century,* focused on expanding the teacher candidate pool (especially minorities for a growing proportion of minority students) and regulating teacher education with a renewed emphasis on subject matter and clinical preparation. This report emphasized the need to improve education by improving the status and power of teachers and by professionalizing the occupation of teaching. In policy terms, the Carnegie report suggested greater regulation of teachers, that is, ensuring their competence through more rigorous preparation, certification, and selection, in exchange for the deregulation of teaching, which includes fewer rules and prescribing what is to be taught, when, and how (Darling-Hammond & Berry, 1988).

With regard to teacher education, the Carnegie Forum on Education and the Economy (1986) noted that elementary teachers have little exposure to the subject matter they will be expected to teach, whereas secondary teachers have very little exposure to the act of teaching. The report's authors claimed that "teachers need a command of the subjects they teach, a sound grasp of the techniques of teaching those subjects, information about research on teaching, and an understanding of children's growth and development and of their different needs and learning styles" (p. 71). Four years of college does not provide sufficient time to master both needed subject matter and skills to teach them. Undergraduate teacher preparation should focus on a broad liberal education (e.g., with core courses in history, government, science, literature, and the arts to develop essential skills of comprehension, computation, writing, speaking, and clear thinking) and a grounding in the subjects that the future teacher will teach. Professional education should be at the graduate level. The Carnegie Forum (1986)

report noted that elementary school teachers require the same kind of rigorous undergraduate preparation as secondary teachers in *each* of the subjects they will teach. Thus, the report suggested a restructuring of elementary school organization so that teachers are expected to teach fewer subjects.

The Carnegie Forum (1986) recommended a bachelor's degree as a prerequisite to teaching, an enhanced M.A.T. program, and teachers' salaries that are competitive with other professions, as well as general school restructuring that draws on the leadership potential of classroom teachers. In addition, the report also called for creating professional working environments for teachers as well as establishing lead teachers who forge the necessary redesign of schools and assist their peers in enforcing high standards for teaching practice and student learning. Lead teachers would be a "new" category of professional educators, providing a structure to utilize better the nation's best teachers as well as incentives to keep them teaching students (Carnegie Forum on Education and the Economy, 1986). Importantly, the Carnegie Forum's report also calls for creating the NBPTS, an initiative fully underway, with grand implications for the preservice education. The NBPTS, as a reformist's perspective, is reviewed next.

The National Board for Professional Teaching Standards

NBPTS, now in operation for several years, has set out a course for identifying highly accomplished teachers through a series of assessments that promise to respect the complex demands of teaching as well as its intellectual quality. The board's examinations will be the first teacher examinations in the United States developed and controlled by members of the profession rather than by governmental agencies. The field testing of NBPTS assessments for several subject areas or student developmental levels began in the 1993–1994 school year. Ultimately, the board intends to have more than 30 certification area assessments fully operational that could leverage major changes in teacher preparation (both preservice and in-service), evaluation, reward, and retention.

All work of the national board is based on five principles related to what teachers should know and be able to do (National Board for Professional Teaching Standards [NBPTS], 1989). First, teachers are committed to students and their learning, which includes an unyielding belief that all students can learn, and teachers should have the willingness and ability to adjust practice to meet individual student needs and characteristics. This principle also focuses on teachers fostering students' self-esteem, motivation, character, and civic responsibility, as well as their own respect for individual, cultural, religious, and racial differences. Second, teachers should know the subjects they teach and how to teach those subjects to students. Briefly, this principle means that highly accomplished teachers are able to create multiple paths to the subjects they teach. Third, teachers are responsible for managing and monitoring student learning, which means that they command a range of instructional techniques and can implement them as needed. Highly accomplished teachers ensure a disciplined learning environment, organize instruction accordingly, understand how to motivate and engage students, and assess the progress of individual students and the class as a whole. Fourth, nationally certified teachers should be able to reflect and to think systematically about their teaching as well as model curiosity, tolerance, honesty, fairness, respect for diversity, and appreciation for cultural differences. Their students need to be able to "see" their teachers reason and be creative. This principle reflects the need for nationally board certified teachers to be risk takers and problem solvers. Fifth, highly accomplished teachers are members of learning communities; they work collaboratively on instructional policy, curriculum development, and staff development. They also work collaboratively with parents, involve parents in the work of the school, and take advantage of community resources (Darling-Hammond & Berry, in press).

Of significance in the National Board's propositions, and in its standards and assessments, is the extent to which the highly accomplished teachers who comprise the board have clearly broken with previous conceptions of teaching as formulaic and routine. They have rejected a view of teaching as resting on the implementation of a few basic behaviors rather than the acquisition of a broad base of knowledge to be used strategically. In articulating standards that rest on the appropriate use of knowledge and techniques in a variety of ways on behalf of diverse student needs, the board has begun to capture the complex, contingent nature of teaching and to confront the challenge of assessing such knowledge and skills in an appropriate way (Darling-Hammond & Berry, in press). Importantly, the work of the National Board has drawn heavily upon Shulman's (1986) "knowledge growth in teaching" agenda that suggests a complex interplay between specific subject matter and pedagogy and their influence on teacher effectiveness.

The National Board's assessments, based on evidence from the field test protocols developed to date, indicate an invigorating approach to examining teaching. For example, in several of the initial certification area assessments, teachers will have to prepare a portfolio that includes a "student learning exercise" in which they demonstrate how they monitor students as they learn to write, a "postreading interpretative discussion" in which they demonstrate how they conduct a class discussion about a literature selection, and a "planning and teaching exercise" in which they demonstrate how they conduct instruction over a 3-week period. In addition, these teachers, at an on-site assessment center, engage in a variety of simulated teaching or professional events, including a written essay exam, an analysis of another teacher's instruction, and a cooperative group discussion regarding the selection and use of curricular materials (NBPTS, 1993).

With regard to elementary school teachers, the board's standards are rather explicit in what is expected in accomplished teaching. Although the standards for the Middle Childhood/ Generalist are only in draft form at the time of this writing, and, indeed, they represent expectations for highly accomplished, *experienced* teachers, they are clearly instructive for those considering elementary education curriculum reforms. Given the charge of such reformist groups as the Holmes Group and research findings (e.g., Berliner, 1988), it is critically important to begin casting teacher learning in developmental terms and as a seamless web of preservice/in-service experiences. The NBPTS committee charged with framing the Middle Childhood/ Generalist requirements has recommended certification to be organized into 11 standards. Highly accomplished middle childhood teachers

- Draw on their knowledge of child development and their relationships with students to understand their students' abilities, interests, aspirations, and values
- Draw on their knowledge of subject matter and curriculum to make sound decisions about what students should know and be able to do
- Establish a caring, safe, and democratic community where risk taking is valued and students can work both cooperatively and individually
- Help students learn to respect and value diversity
- Create, select, and adapt a rich set of materials to support student learning
- Help students understand how subjects they study can be used to delve into real-world issues
- Provide students with "multiple paths" to learn
- Base their instructional strategies on multiple forms of assessment, including student self-evaluation
- Draw upon a wide variety of strategies to inform and work with parents and families
- Regularly reflect upon, assess, and improve their practice
- Work with their colleagues to advance knowledge within the field and improve practice for their class, school, and professional community (NBPTS, in press)

Although the middle childhood standards have yet to be translated into assessments and used in both policy and practice, the standards have great potential and power. The board's articulations of accomplished practice through standards and assessments and the subsequent influences on teacher learning might influence teacher education in several ways. The board's influence on teacher education could be manifested by (1) the eventual widespread participation in board certification by teachers, much in the way that board certification of physicians has gradually become the norm rather than the exception; (2) adoption or translation of the board's standards into *state licensing and teacher education standards;* and (3) translation of the board's approaches to assessment into state licensing examinations and teacher evaluation practices (Darling-Hammond & Berry, in press).

The Interstate New Teacher Assessment and Support Consortium INTASC of the Council of Chief State School Officers, drawing on the initial work of the National Board, has drafted initial teacher licensure standards that will be compatible with the advanced standards articulated by the NBPTS. INTASC's 10 standards incorporate the types of knowledge, dispositions, and performances that beginning teachers need to practice responsibly to prepare them for their development as board-certified, highly accomplished teachers (Interstate New Teacher Assessment and Support Consortium [INTASC], 1992). Currently, INTASC is developing the details of the assessment system that dovetails from the National Board assessments and could be used by states in reforming their licensure systems.

INTASC efforts are now being fashioned to determine the best cluster of assessment exercises, the succession of tasks, and the time frame necessary to determine whether or not a novice has met the standards and is "safe to practice" (Darling-

Hammond, 1993). The work of INTASC reflects a paradigm shift of sorts; that is, the report reflects the need to move away from a concept of preparing teachers for schools that just "offer education" to a concept of preparing teachers for schools that ensure that all students learn and perform at high levels. INTASC standards for beginning teachers reflect the much suggested switch from teachers "covering the curriculum" to finding ways to connect with the needs of all learners. In particular, INTASC standards specify that the teacher

- Understands the central concepts, tools, and methods of inquiry related to discipline and how to create learning experiences that make these aspects of subject matter meaningful for students
- Understands how children learn and develop and can provide learning opportunities that support their intellectual, social, and personal development
- Understands how students differ in their approaches to learning and creates instructional opportunities that are adapted to diverse learners
- Understands and uses a variety of instructional strategies to encourage students' development of critical thinking and problem solving
- Uses an understanding of individual and group motivation and behavior to create a learning environment that encourages positive social interaction, active engagement in learning, and self-motivation
- Uses knowledge of effective verbal, nonverbal, and media communication techniques to foster active inquiry, collaboration, and supportive interaction in the classroom
- Plans instruction based on knowledge of subject matter, students, community, and curriculum goals
- Understands and uses formal and informal assessment strategies to evaluate and ensure continuous intellectual, social, and physical development of the learner
- Is a reflective practitioner who continually evaluates the effects of his or her choices and actions on others (students, parents, and other professionals in the learning community) and who actively seeks out opportunities to grow professionally
- Fosters relationships with school colleagues, parents, and agencies in the larger community to support student's learning and well being

As an indicator of INTASC's potential, these standards were incorporated recently into the NCATE newly adopted conceptual framework standard.

Insight into the Elementary Education Curriculum

Relative to the traditional curricular themes, the reformists' perspectives offer considerable insight. To some extent, the documents reviewed herein imply reform redux. Indeed, much of what is offered about what elementary education students need to know and be able to do has roots in Dewey's turn-of-the-century progressive education, as well as the 1960s open education movement (which later included reform efforts such as the

Competency-Based Teacher Education). Given the profound challenges that elementary teachers confront every day in classrooms (the knowledge explosion, new technologies, poverty, cultural diversity, broken homes, etc.), their learning experiences (both preservice and in-service) should be framed by the same assumptions and strategies used in teaching students for understanding. The reform of the elementary education curriculum has as much to do with reframing the work of the teacher education faculty as it does with reframing the work of the arts and sciences faculty.

First, the reformists' perspective reveals the need to resolve the longstanding *tension between liberal arts and professional preparation.* No longer can the preparation of elementary teachers be viewed as a zero-sum game between general and subject-matter knowledge expertise and pedagogy. As noted earlier, Shulman's (1986) work in defining subject-specific pedagogy (and its use in developing the standards of the National Board and INTASC) should ultimately make the liberal arts professional preparation conundrum a moot point. The explosion of content-based knowledge and increasing use of interdisciplinary problem solving (from biomechanics to biogenetics) suggests that elementary education majors should focus on learning how to learn and to connect knowledge in the best interest of all students.

Second, the reformists' perspective reveals the need to create new structures that will support *the tradition of teaching diverse students and subjects.* It is impossible (not to mention a cruel hoax) to suggest that the elementary teacher be an expert in all subjects. The reform documents imply a return to "team play" among a group of elementary teachers, each of whom has particular strengths to bring to bear on group planning, instruction, assessment, and leadership. In addition, teaching diverse students requires respect for and knowledge of cultural differences and a wide repertoire of methods to translate these understandings into practice (Villegas, 1991). Thus, as American classrooms become more diverse, it is essential for teachers, especially elementary teachers, to use multiple methods and insights from a multidisciplinary perspective.

Third, the reformists' perspective reveals the need to move beyond the false dichotomy of theory and practice. Anderson (1993) calls for the development of theories of practice that will integrate the two. To do so requires a much more protracted period of induction and socialization into teaching, one that is predominated by the development of professional ethics and values as opposed to just survival. Perhaps Little's (1993) suggestion of in-service teacher education as "informed dissent" provides an apt anchor to consider for shattering the disjuncture between theory and practice. In fact, the reformists' perspective on creating continuum of preservice and in-service education may very well be a linchpin for joining the work of those who practice teaching with those who study it.

EXEMPLARY MODELS IN ELEMENTARY EDUCATION CURRICULUM

Reformists have proposed innovative ways to prepare elementary teachers and have described the knowledge and skills elementary teachers should possess to teach diverse students and subjects effectively. Are those educators engaged in teacher preparation programs in concurrence with ideas set forth by reformists and heeding their recommendations? Exactly what is the status of elementary education curriculum? What information is available about curriculum programs for the education of elementary teachers?

Gaps in the Research Base

An in-depth look at the data available regarding the curriculum of elementary teacher education programs in the 1990s reveals enormous shortcomings. Although curricula of teacher education programs have been briefly described in education journals, in-depth narratives and data that comprehensively describe curricula of teacher education programs are scant (Howey & Zimpher, 1989). Journal publications; local, state, and national reports; and other limited resources are the primary sources of evidence regarding the state-of-the-art of elementary teacher preparation curriculum.

Lanier and Little (1986) note in the *Handbook of Research on Teaching* that inferences about changes in curriculum frequently are based on requirements from sources such as state departments of education and accrediting bodies that mandate an increase in the required number of hours in a particular area, frequently at the expense of another area. For example, increasing the requirement for field experiences may result in a reduction in opportunity for liberal arts coursework, which leads to the inference that the overall thrust of the curriculum has shifted from content to professional preparation. In fact, however, the reverse is often true.

Based on extant data on teacher education curricula, Lanier and Little (1986) report an appearance of standardization of curriculum of teacher education in 4-year colleges and universities in the nation with coursework organized under the umbrella of general education, subject-matter concentrations, and pedagogical study. Liberal arts courses include a core knowledge component in substantive areas as well as the foundations of education and fundamental pedagogical principles and practices. They warn, however, that beneath the veneer of standardization and similarity,

there is limited common substance to the teacher education curriculum. The course content that prospective and practicing teachers have an opportunity to learn is highly unstable and individualistic. The variation among and within courses and workshops at different institutions, as well as in the same institutions over brief periods of time, achieves almost infinite variety. (p. 546)

The extent to which current elementary teacher preparation programs conform to the criteria for a model curriculum based on the prevailing recommendations of reformers, therefore, is difficult, if not impossible, to ascertain. The testimony that follows concerning the current status of curriculum is, therefore, inconclusive with regard to degree of conformity to the criteria. Portrayals of examples of specific programs and projects, however, provide vivid images of the curriculum of elementary teacher education programs that strongly reflect congruence with the criteria. The portraits of elementary teacher preparation curricula that are presented range from general impressions to

distinct sketches to detailed drawings. Assuming an optimistic viewpoint, these vivid images (images of reformers' recommendations in action), which are depicted in the following section, are flourishing in many elementary teacher preparation programs throughout the country.

Overview of Elementary Teacher Preparation Curriculum

Historically, higher education institutions have prepared teachers for schools that do not exist. As alluded to earlier, prior to the nation-at-risk crisis, when little school reform was occurring, elementary teacher education programs prepared their students for "innovative" classrooms where team teaching, individually guided education, reflective teaching, and other modern practices were used. Yet, once employed, these new teachers found few schools where they could apply their newly acquired skills. Instead, what the first-year teachers found were self-contained classrooms where traditional teaching practices were used extensively. Thus, the teachers soon became socialized into the traditional school culture and quickly forgot their innovative approaches to the teaching-learning process. Teacher education was ahead of its time, preparing teachers for schools that did not exist; however, in a few cases, higher education institutions preparing teachers are working simultaneously with public schools to reform P–12 education and, at the same time, reform teacher preparation.

Since the nation-at-risk crisis, major restructuring of the nation's elementary schools has occurred and there are more good schools today than at any time in the past. If, as some believe, there are also more bad schools, it is due to the fact that more schools are attempting to educate *all* children, many of whom would not have remained in school in the past (Schlechty, 1991). Teacher education has, for the most part, been ignored in the school reform movement (Goodlad, 1990a, 1990b). As a result, many elementary schools are now employing innovative practices while most teacher education institutions have "traditional" programs. Thus, higher education institutions continue to prepare teachers for schools that do not exist, a practice that should lessen if reformists' recommendations are heeded.

Examples of Innovative Programs

The reform of schools and the reform of teacher education have rarely been connected. What follows are specific examples of initiatives designed to reform schools and to restructure teacher education simultaneously. The goal is to make certain that teachers are prepared for schools that do exist. Until there are better teachers, there cannot be better schools. As the following models suggest, better teachers are not possible without strong collaborative programs designed to bring the two institutions together.

University of Delaware At the University of Delaware, the Project 30 team that comprises education and arts and sciences faculty decided that something needed to be done to ensure better that future elementary school teachers would have a reliable understanding of the curriculum they would be teaching. The newly designed elementary teacher education program includes an interdisciplinary major that compromises reworked minors in six areas—mathematics, foreign language, social science, language arts, natural science, and fine arts. Included in each area are courses tailored to the needs of the elementary school teacher. The Project 30 team considered several ways in which the six separate minors could be reshaped to provide the best academic preparation for elementary teachers. Five themes were considered for each minor. They include: (1) philosophy of subject matter whereby students would learn the essential and fundamental aspects of the structure of the discipline; (2) text approach, which entails reading the seminal texts in each discipline coupled with an examination of school textbooks for the assumptions each makes about the particular discipline; (3) genetic epistemology, which entails the study of the developmental psychological literature from the perspective of the concepts that make up the curriculum; (4) cognitive psychology in which students would make the workings of the mind their specializations; and (5) pedagogical content knowledge, which would prepare students to transform what they know into teachable subjects.

Concurrent with the Project 30 program, the University of Delaware also developed a plan for the restructuring of the professional education component of the elementary teacher education program that reflects the Holmes Group agenda. Students pursuing careers as elementary school teachers under the restructured program earn a baccalaureate degree with approximately 130 credit hours or they can pursue the new option for a master's/undergraduate program of about 150 credit hours. This option includes a bachelor's degree with an interdisciplinary academic major and a master's degree in pedagogy (Project 30, 1991). The field experiences required for this program are conducted in professional development schools, that is, public schools engaged in restructuring.

Knox College At Knox College in Illinois, a new vision of professionalism that recognizes the centrality of moral commitment and discourse in teaching undergirds the elementary teacher education program. A commitment to providing a liberal education to students from working class families has been a central feature since its establishment 150 years ago. The firm resolve to work toward racial equality and diversity resulted in a commitment to social justice as central to the teacher preparation program. The teacher education program includes the following principles: (1) commitment to developing courses, experiences, and programs for students that integrate the study of education and preparation for teaching with liberal education; (2) commitment to the importance of diversity in American society, especially in regard to educational institutions; (3) emphasis on the fact that educational issues and practices unavoidably contain moral, political, and social questions that make an isolated, technical analysis of educational phenomena impossible; (4) commitment to the view that critical inquiry is an essential aspect of all courses and programs and that effective teaching must involve reflection, analysis, and debate, as well as opportunities for engaged practice (i.e., judgment, reflection, and personal responsibility and action are essential elements of the teacher's role); (5) focus on the fusion of theory and practice as the hallmark of programs and courses designed to help prospective teachers to improve current realities; and (6) emphasis on the involvement of students as classroom participants, researchers, and practitioners. At Knox College, future teachers have opportunities to engage in contextual, critical reflection in a way that rekindles the idea that teaching is a field of moral action and students develop moral commitments as a key part of what it means to teach (Beyer, 1991).

Brigham Young University's Partnership Schools Project
Brigham Young University (BYU) has employed the Professional Development School (PDS) model as the means to reforming its teacher education programs. These partner schools are places where university and public school educators collaborate to provide (1) preservice education for new teachers, (2) in-service education for practicing teachers, (3) curriculum development to improve the learning experiences of pupils, and (4) research and evaluation (Harris & Harris, 1992–1993).

The BYU partner schools are distinguished by four characteristics. These are: (1) the common goal of simultaneous renewal of schools and the education of educators; (2) both university and school educators are represented and actively share expertise in all organizational facets; (3) university and school educators engage in dialogue in which they build on each other's expertise, focus on insights from research and experience, acknowledge legitimacy of different perception, and avoid paternalistic attitudes; and (4) partners seek to improve their own stewardship roles for the mutual benefit of all (Harris & Harris, 1992–1993, p. 2).

A new view of teacher education is emerging at BYU as university and school educators combine their insights and expertise. They believe that excellent teacher education is more likely to occur when the university and schools collaborate to provide opportunities for students to see the relationship between theory and practice. When school-based educators join with university faculty in supervising, mentoring, evaluating, and recommending new teachers, their living laboratories become exemplary sites for excellence in teaching and learning (Harris & Harris, 1992–1993).

University of Cincinnati The impetus for restructuring the elementary teacher education program at the University of Cincinnati is its involvement in the Holmes Group. The program reflects the following features: (1) joint enrollment in the College of Arts and Sciences and the College of Education; (2) general education and a disciplinary major leading to a bachelor's degree in Arts and Sciences; (3) educational studies and professional studies leading to a bachelor's degree in the College of Education, teacher certification, and 15 hours of graduate credit; and (4) integrated clinical and field experiences culminating in fifth-year paid teaching internships in professional development schools. The expected benefits of this extended program include the following:

Benefits for students:

- Gives those going into teaching the opportunity for a more solid general and liberal education
- Ensures that each student will have studied an area in depth

- Offers career flexibility
- Integrates professional studies and practical experience through extensive field and clinical components

Benefits for the College of Education:

- Broadens the general and liberal education of its students
- Deepens the student's subject-matter knowledge in the disciplines and provides a solid foundation for pedagogical content knowledge
- Encourages faculty to interact with students throughout their undergraduate experience
- Provides for a reanalysis and restructuring of professional education coursework and experiences
- Suggests means to strengthen clinical and field experiences
- Provides more rigorous and higher quality teacher education programs

Benefits for the College of Arts and Sciences:

- Strengthens and enhances the collaborative relationship for the preparation of teachers
- Provides opportunities to increase the number of qualified adults in classrooms for little or no increased costs
- Focuses efforts to meet a variety of professional development and training needs through professional development schools
- Provides a means for addressing career ladder and other job differentiation proposals through master teacher and school-based faculty roles
- Allows a better integration of preservice instruction within the demands of practice

The University of Cincinnati elementary teacher education program regards the role of the teacher as facilitator, instructor, and fellow inquirer. The teacher is responsive to learners, is challenged through questioning rather than telling, and is knowledgeable so that the information and experiences available are as valuable as possible. Prospective teachers learn to facilitate the learning of elementary school-age children and to understand unique learning styles and differences in learners (Fowler, Smith, & Sterling, 1991). As a result of these partnerships, educational programs are enhanced for the students who attend these schools.

University of Washington In the fall of 1993, the University of Washington implemented its new elementary teacher education program, which was developed by an interdisciplinary team composed of higher education faculty, professional staff, students, and K–12 professionals. The program is based on the following principles: (1) all teachers need a firm understanding of subject matter, pedagogy, pedagogical content knowledge, and the social contexts of teaching; (2) literacy and mathematics, the foundations of early learning, are emphasized; (3) issues of classroom management, assessment, technology, motivation, and planning are best taught within the context of subject-matter instruction and field experiences; (4) multicultural issues and an understanding of the needs of all elementary-age stu-

dents will be addressed through the content blocks, field experiences, and reflective seminars; (5) teachers should be reflective practitioners and should engage in problem solving and professional exploration as they continually refine their abilities as educators; (6) coursework and reflective seminars should provide an environment that encourages teacher interns to integrate what they read, hear, and observe; (7) there should be coordination and coherence across course blocks and between coursework and field experiences; (8) collaboration is an essential component of an effective program and a characteristic of an effective professional; (9) teacher interns should be placed in exemplary sites where educators are interested in professional development and mentoring prospective teachers; (10) teacher interns need experiences working with diverse students and working in different school contexts; (11) supervision of teacher interns in the field should be a shared responsibility of university faculty and school-based educators; and (12) evaluation of interns also should be a shared responsibility and should be consistent with coursework and best practice.

The program is designed around five strands. The Social Contexts of Teaching strand allows interns to discuss their future role as educational professionals, including strategies for forming committees with other professionals, keeping current, working for change, educational policy, and school finances. In the Meeting the Needs of Diverse Elementary Students strand, topics include social, emotional, and cognitive development; cultural, gender, and individual differences; structuring effective instructional environments, including classroom management; abuse and health issues; and working with interdisciplinary professional teams, families, and communities.

The Teaching and Learning in Core Areas strand includes literacy, numeracy, science, social studies, and the arts. Learning acquired in all these areas in the block courses is applied in a culminating project—the construction of an integrated unit to be taught during student teaching.

The Integrating Field Experiences and Coursework strand operates throughout the program. Teacher interns have directed field experiences with all coursework beginning with the very first professional education course. They are required to gain experience in primary and intermediate grades and in urban and suburban settings. These field experiences take place in professional development schools or in other partner school sites.

In the Reflective Seminars strand, interns are combined from several sites and structured time is provided to reflect on classroom management, instruction, subject-matter knowledge, working with other professionals, and tensions between theory and practice. The seminars are conducted by university supervisors and site supervisors (University of Washington, 1993).

University of South Carolina At the University of South Carolina, the only avenue to the preparation of elementary school teachers is the Master of Arts in Teaching (MAT) program. Students proceed through the 15-month-long program in cohorts of 30–35 after completion of a baccalaureate degree in a content area or in an interdisciplinary major. The program begins during the summer on the campus and continues the next academic year in professional development schools where the students are placed as interns.

A foundation of constructivist learning theory and the integration of theory, practice, and research on practice are the program's distinguishinig characteristics. The program also is marked by its high intensity, student autonomy, and a break with students' conventional visions of teaching. The constructivist learning theory is the means for faculty to achieve basic philosophical agreement and for MAT students to experience conceptual coherence. For these prospective teachers, this means continually integrating their theory and methods coursework with teaching experience and classroom research they conduct during their internships.

Separate methods courses have been integrated into interdisciplinary blocks where learning experiences and internship requirements emphasize the connections among mathematics, language arts, reading, science, and social studies. Experiences within the block highlight the National Council of Teachers of Mathematics principles, cooperative learning, whole language, science experimentation, and ethnographic episodes of practicing in classrooms what they have been taught on campus. The MAT instructional team and the professional development school faculty collaborative plan and supervise the internship experience and teachers reflect with interns on their inquiry projects. These projects are designed to develop interns' understandings of the interdependence of theory, practice, and research. The research assignments help to teach interns that teacher research is a way to make good decisions about curriculum and instruction. The interns have opportunities to conduct inquiry projects in each of the major disciplines taught in the elementary school (Flake, Kuhs, Donnelly, & Ebert, 1995).

The constructivist approach used in the program is intended to influence prospective teachers in the direction of autonomy rather than obedience. Throughout the program, students make choices about such things as the type of field-based projects they complete, the amount and kind of peer or expert assistance they need, and the academic areas where they should concentrate their efforts in order to acquire new knowledge. At the conclusion of the 15-month program, students present a professional portfolio developed throughout the program, write a synthesis paper reflecting upon their coursework and internship, and complete an oral comprehensive examination in order to earn their MAT degree (The Holmes Group, 1993).

University of Connecticut It took the University of Connecticut 6 years to redesign its elementary teacher preparation program. The redesigned program is an integrated bachelor's/master's program organized around four strands: Core, Clinic, Seminar, and Subject-Specific Pedagogy. A subject-matter major in the arts and sciences is required for all students.

The Core strand focuses on the education content that has been collaboratively determined to be essential for all students regardless of certification area. The Clinic strand refers to the carefully designed and sequenced set of field experiences in which all students in the elementary teacher preparation program participate. It involves student placement in a variety of different kinds of educational settings and includes a required placement in urban schools and work with students who have disabilities.

The Seminar strand helps link Core material with Clinic experiences and promotes reflective practice. In the Subject-Specific Pedagogy strand, courses provide students with the necessary specialized preparation for subjects taught in the elementary school.

One of the key elements of the redesigned program was the development of partnerships with selected schools throughout Connecticut. The partnerships were deliberately designed to represent a variety of different kinds of schools to enable students to have experiences in urban, suburban, and rural settings. Moreover, these schools have large numbers of "at-risk" students and are characterized by ethnic, racial, and linguistic diversity. The University of Connecticut sought, through these partnerships, to transform university faculty and students by working together with public school educators and students in their schools. A clear goal from the beginning was the simultaneous renewal of schools and teacher education. The belief that teachers prepared in this program will have both the skill and fortitude to change schooling is at the heart of the program to prepare elementary teachers at the University of Connecticut (Case, Norlander, & Reagan, 1993).

Baruch College In December of 1989, the faculty of Baruch College approved an interdisciplinary elementary teacher education program leading to the Bachelor of Arts degree. Unique to the program is its emphasis not only on a combination of liberal studies and professional courses, but also on joint administration of all aspects of the program by faculty in education and in the arts and sciences. One of the important factors that had to be considered was the ethnic diversity of both the college's and the city's student populations and how the teacher education curriculum could respond to and reflect this diversity.

A highlight of the program is the capstone course that incorporates culminating experiences in a liberal studies discipline and methods of teaching that discipline. Capstone courses are available in the humanities and in the social sciences. For example, the capstone course in humanities is designed to provide elementary methods instruction within the context of an advanced interdisciplinary humanities curriculum. Implicit in every aspect of the course is a recognition of the multicultural nature of the New York City school system. Students are required to develop an interdisciplinary unit and then teach the unit in an elementary school, demonstrating the multicultural, humanistic approach (Block & McGarraghy, 1992).

Florida State Department of Education In 1990, the Florida Education Standards Commission released a report on the preparation of elementary teachers for Florida's schools. The report, based in part on perceptions of elementary school principals, included five specific recommendations: (1) the level for initial certification in elementary education should be K–6; (2) initial certification of elementary teachers in Florida and from other states for grades K–6 should be granted on the basis of graduation from a state-approved elementary education program; (3) state-developed preservice elementary guidelines and indicators should serve as the criteria for state approval of elementary education programs for teachers preparing to work with children in grades K–6; (4) an alternate teacher preparation program should be established and guidelines should be developed for these programs; and (5) a strong collaboration between the colleges of education, colleges of arts and sciences, community colleges, private institutions, the Florida Department of Education, and school districts is essential.

The commission worked on the premise that merely modifying current programs, processes, and practices for the initial certification of elementary school teachers was not the answer for producing more effective teachers. It also advocated moving away from basing initial certification on numbers of hours or credits obtained by an individual. Thus, the recommendations include guidelines and indicators for approving programs in elementary education that are believed to be necessary to facilitate the acquisition of competencies needed for effective teachers. The institutions preparing elementary teachers should be accountable for determining their individual elementary education programs and implementing the components necessary to produce these competencies for initial certification.

The recommendations of the commission are based on four assumptions that form a pattern and provide a strong framework for the preservice preparation of elementary school teachers. The assumptions are (1) the preservice preparation of elementary teachers should be a partnership among an array of institutions, that is, all institutions that can benefit from or contribute to the preparation program; (2) the preservice preparation program should be based on the linkage of appropriate research to the best known practice; (3) the guidelines should establish directions and goals rather than a specific list of prescribed courses; and (4) the focus of the recommendations should be based on the needs of children (Florida Education Standards Commission, 1990).

The programs described for the preparation of elementary school teachers provide specific examples of comprehensive efforts to improve teacher education. These examples demonstrate that strong linkages with the arts and sciences and with the public schools are necessary to strengthen programs that prepare elementary school teachers. Programs based on the premise of simultaneous renewal of schools and teacher education appear to hold the most promise for ensuring that teachers will be adequately prepared for twenty-first century schools.

CONCLUSIONS REGARDING THE ELEMENTARY EDUCATION CURRICULUM

The analysis of traditional curricular themes, prevailing reform recommendations, and illustrative exemplary practices reveals the continuing struggle to ease the tensions between liberal arts and professional preparation, the tradition and complexity of teaching diverse students and subjects, and the conflict between theory and practice. The demands for elementary teachers to have more content knowledge and a firmer grounding in the liberal arts, thus preparing teachers to make judicious, informed pedagogical decisions for "everybody's children" and to become lifelong learners, are escalating. Grounded in both the past and present, this chapter concludes by framing five, interrelated conditions and conceptions of elementary education curriculum that should vastly influence teacher education as a whole.

First, the elementary teacher education curriculum should be conceived as a fluid continuum of professional development, developed collaboratively by both public school and university

professionals. This continuum of preservice and in-service would be framed by a developmental and inquiry approach to teaching middle childhood students (Black & Ammon, 1992). The heart of this continuum should conceivably be the professional development school, that is, if current efforts can be enhanced and institutionalized. In her recent book, which assesses a number of diverse PDS efforts across the United States, Darling-Hammond (1994) describes that

Perhaps one of the most promising aspects of the schools described in this volume is that they emphasize collaborative planning, teaching, and decision making within and across institutions in such a variety of ways that they begin to redefine both the act of teaching and the nature of their home institutions. Virtually all of these PDSs have introduced or strengthened existing arrangements for team teaching at the school sites and frequently, for teacher education courses as well. Teacher educators learn more about teaching as they teach collaboratively with veteran teachers . . . . Teachers comment at the extent to which they find themselves learning from interns or student teachers as well as from each other and from their experiences as mentors. (p. 12)

Indeed, elementary schools and faculties, with a more focused student-centered perspective (compared to their secondary counterparts), can become more likely vehicles to educate not only children but also adults. Although the barriers that exist between K–12 schools and universities are profound, an increasing focus by government and foundations on interinstitutional collaboration provides considerable hope.

Second, the elementary teacher education curriculum should be interdisciplinary, integrated, problem oriented, socially constructed, and student centered. A core of integrated studies, cutting across traditional fields of specialization, may ease the urgency for elementary education teachers to be adroit in all subject-matter disciplines. Emphasizing subject-matter specialization sends the elementary education curriculum deeper into the black hole of the exploding knowledge bases of individual subject-matter disciplines. Subject-major specialization should emerge only at the advanced levels, with the expectation that novice elementary education teachers are "teamed" with other colleagues and mentors who should compensate for any current subject-matter weaknesses. Subject-matter understanding is critical, but it is not necessarily secured by accruing more course credits. As discussed earlier, the McCarthy and Peterson (1993) study revealed how two elementary school teachers learned to teacher for understanding because of collaborative and experiential learning opportunities rather than just exposure to more content knowledge.

Integrated studies should also focus on work with the community; first, in terms of additional social services to children, and second, in terms of the teachers' broader professional community and networks that should support them in learning to teach for understanding and to lead school reform. The complexity of teaching and learning today requires (almost mandates) greater collaboration among different educator roles (e.g., administrators, teachers, social service providers). In this regard, learning to work as a team is both a means and an end in the elementary education curriculum. For the elementary education curriculum, this means a focus on preparing prospective teachers in cohorts and connecting their preparation with those of other educators (including administrators and social service providers). In turn, elementary education students should be prepared to critique their own practices as well as those of their peers; therefore, they will be socialized and prepared for membership in schools that emerge as learning organizations.

Whereas several reports criticize the elementary education curriculum because of its weak focus on developing subject-matter expertise (e.g., Carnegie Foundation), others recognize the danger in creating subject-matter specialists, namely, losing a focus on teaching children (as opposed to subjects) and on developing individuals to the best of their abilities. A common core curriculum for elementary education teachers should focus on children's needs and the preservice teacher's potential. To maintain a focus on children without diluting content-area knowledge, the elementary education curriculum should be case based. According to Merseth (1990), the use of case studies in teacher education provides models of exemplary practice, demonstrates how to frame educational problems, fosters contextual awareness, and promotes analysis grounded in content knowledge. Melding the liberal arts with professional preparation in this way should enable future elementary teachers to see connections between subject matter; to learn to grapple with the "big questions" of human life and civilization; and to transform their grounded knowledge, as a collective community of learners, into informed decision making for middle childhood students. If elementary education students are taught in college through interdisciplinary, integrated, problem-oriented, socially constructed, and student-centered approaches, then chances are quite high they will teach through interdisciplinary, integrated, problem-oriented, socially constructed, and student-centered approaches as teachers in elementary schools.

Third, an integrated curriculum may be most suited for preparing elementary school teachers to teach a multitude of different subject matter to diverse students. The growing need for teachers to reach diverse students better places even more strains on the demands of subject-specific disciplinary knowledge. As Zeichner (1991) has noted, the teacher education curriculum should go beyond cultural sensitivity to develop teachers' expectations that all students can learn and to provide opportunities for them to learn strategies that build bridges between cultures. Thus, the core of the curriculum is the inculcation of values, attitudes, and behaviors that enable beginning teachers to make appropriate decisions about diverse students. To infuse multiculturalism with the teacher education curriculum does not mean simply presenting cultural information without verification of its significance. Villegas (1991) has asserted that in order to teach in a culturally responsive way, teachers "need an attitude of respect for cultural differences, procedures for getting to know the cultural resources of their students, ability to translate this knowledge into effective instruction, and skills in interactive decision making" (p. 9). In fact, research (NCRTL, 1992) has revealed that the sole presentation of information about different cultural groups may unintentionally deepen, rather than diminish, hidden prejudices that teachers may have.

On the one hand, elementary education students should be selected because of diversity and socialized to respect diversity. On the other hand, the elementary education curriculum should include opportunities for students to earn a major in interdisci-

plinary studies, with opportunities to hone in on a range of disciplinary strands and teaching problems bound by a variety of cultural contexts. Indeed, an integrative curriculum is about employing multiple perspectives and viewing the world through a variety of lenses and truths, which are critical to understanding and teaching diverse students. In particular, the elementary education curriculum would draw upon ethnographic studies that enable prospective teachers to understand their students' cognitive development as well as cultures and how to better represent subject matter(s) for them. Practica and internships should be multiple and established for a range of settings serving diverse students, including students with exceptionalities.

Preservice teachers should experience the activities and support systems of schools where successful inclusion of students with disabilities has occurred because inclusive schools provide more flexible learning environments and curricula, utilize instruction that is accessible to all, and implement many strategies that benefit everyone, that is, *all* students (not just those students with disabilities) as well as staff (Schrag & Burnette, 1994). By experiencing multiple settings, future educators should have opportunities for study and reflection about cultural capital and its educative uses and opportunities to focus on the philosophy that all students can learn and can learn at higher levels.

Fourth, the elementary teacher education curriculum should draw upon an integrated studies approach in order to narrow the conceptual and practical gaps between theoretical and practical training as well as between administrators and teachers. For the most part in teacher education, theory has been undervalued and practice has been overvalued (Anderson, 1993). This problem has been especially acute in the preparation of elementary school teachers because of the tainted history of the normal school (see Herbst, 1989b). Even today, administrators and researchers learn about organizational theory, change, and leadership, whereas teachers, especially elementary school ones, learn only about their subjects and how specifically to teach them to students. In some ways, the theory-practice gap in the preparation of elementary school teachers is rooted in the feminization of the occupation and the fact that the teaching of younger children has not been viewed by the profession and the public as an intellectual pursuit (Lortie, 1975). In other ways, the theory-practice gap is a manifestation of the lack of rigorous induction for new teachers that portends a "sink-or-swim" process (Wise, Darling-Hammond, & Berry, 1987). The current process of learning to teach socializes teachers to the norm of practicality, where survival concerns rule. The longstanding (and to some extent, artificial) separation of theory and practice have repudiated efforts to have education students systematically inquire into the relationship between what works and why. Again, this problem has been exacerbated for elementary school teachers because of their long history of isolationism in terms of professional community and research-based practice (Lortie, 1975).

Integrated studies can begin to ameliorate the disjunctures created by the common fragmented strands of general education, subject-matter concentration(s), and professional coursework, which artificially bifurcate theory and practice. Integrated studies, by their very nature, should enhance communication between the world of ideas (university-based theories) and the world of action (school-based practice) among those who conduct research (university faculty), those who manage and lead schools (administrators), and those who serve children directly (elementary school teachers). Integrated studies that also prepare elementary school teachers for leadership roles and organizational change agentry can provide much needed status to the preparation of elementary school teachers, putting them on par with other professionals in their field.

Fifth, the elementary teacher education curriculum should provide opportunities to develop technological competence, which can serve as a learning bridge for students from diverse cultures and for those who possess differing learning styles and for teachers who must assess students in multiple ways. The capacity of computers and interactive media to be used as a communication and information-seeking tool as well as a way to store and manipulate information should be emphasized. Preservice teachers should fully utilize computer applications and the wide array of innovative software to promote problem-solving skills and to foster conceptual understanding. Indeed, interactive media invite new ways of thinking and acquiring knowledge. Students are able to explore topics meaningful to them and to follow the path of their natural curiosity and desire to discover, thus networking information bases that cut across diverse fields of knowledge and ways of knowing (Perelman, 1992). In the past, students' sense of discovery has been somewhat stifled by rigid adherence to the linear instruction associated with textbooks, which is diametrically opposed to Perelman's (1992) concept of hyperlearning. Students find computers inherently motivating, and their involvement with technology/ interactive media enables them to have ready access to realistic visual, auditory, and verbal information and to engage actively in the construction of their own knowledge. In addition, students have the capacity to communicate and exchange ideals with peers.

Clearly, elementary teachers should be able to analyze, select, and utilize appropriate technological applications to promote problem solving and to enhance learning in their classrooms. At the same time, new technologies can assist teachers, who have been historically underprepared in the areas of educational measurement, to learn how to access and employ a variety of assessment methodologies. Assessing teaching and learning for diverse students requires the use of journals, portfolios, performance tasks, demonstrations, exhibitions, and videotapes, as well as traditional paper-and-pencil and multiple-choice tests. New technologies can provide a powerful means for not only teaching prospective teachers about assessment concepts and strategies but also allowing them the opportunity to use them to better judge the performance of their soon-to-be elementary school students.

In closing, it would appear that the standards of the National Board, combined with the influence of INTASC (and other critically connected reform efforts such as NCATE), may create powerful opportunities for a seamless, carefully articulated, long-term program of professional development for teachers. Indeed, other professions, such as medicine and now nursing, have used advanced certification, state licensing processes, and professional accreditation to transform professional development and practice. Teaching, including elementary school teaching, can do the same.

This type of professional development curriculum should start with interdisciplinary coursework and experiences to guide talented and committed novices toward a level of expertise required for autonomous practice as a beginning teacher, defined by INTASC standards, and continue with guiding more experienced teachers toward high levels of professional accomplishment as defined by National Board standards.

However, several caveats exist. For example, Zeichner (1991) argues reformers should use the knowledge gained from the failures of competency-based (or performance-based) teacher education (C/PBTE) 20 years ago. The new goals for teacher education in general should not degenerate into a "laundry list" of competencies that teachers should master. Not only is this laundry list approach expensive, but it is also impossible to implement, and over the long term it can encourage mediocrity. The standards cannot be viewed in a narrow way trying to blanket every discreet task a teacher should be able to know or do.

In addition, standards explicit in both INTASC and the National Board require in-depth examination of teaching practice over a protracted period of time. In the case of the INTASC, whereby prospective teachers are expected to demonstrate knowledge, skills, and performances suggesting that they are "safe-to-practice," the assessments should be embedded in a range of coursework and learning experiences. The INTASC standards in particular suggest that prospective teachers cannot demonstrate their ability in the absence of classroom and community contexts. If teacher learning is to be experiential, then the assessment must be performance based, leaving room for self-assessment and for publicly demonstrated outcomes. These assessments cannot be one shot; they must be cumulative, practiced, and performed in multiple situations.

Thus, in terms of the preparation of elementary teachers, no longer will limited practica and student teaching suffice. Instead, intensive internships in diverse settings will be required to determine if, indeed, the novice teachers meet the standards. Anything less will transform the INTASC and National Board assessments into a "laundry list" evaluation and return the elementary education curriculum to the muddle created by C/PBTE of the 1960s and 1970s. Much like the vision articulated by the National Board and INTASC, the elementary education standards must be continuously debated, refined, and enacted in the spirit of teaching's intellectual qualities.

Finally, efforts to reform the elementary education curriculum should be considered in light of the fact that both preservice and in-service teacher education remain critically underfunded (Anderson, 1993; Ebmeier, Twombly, & Teeter, 1991). In addition, investments in teacher knowledge are sorely lacking. The prospects for providing highly knowledgeable and committed teachers who have the capacity to examine critically the relationship between theory and practice are still far from being realized. Lanier and Little (1986) have noted that the average direct cost of instruction per year for preparing an undergraduate teacher education student was only 65% as much as for a public school student and only 50% as much as the average cost per undergraduate student in all university disciplines.

Programs for the preparation of elementary teachers that are based on the recommendations of reformers and are similar to the examples provided will indeed be more costly. Such programs call for extensive clinical and field-based experiences, as well as team planning and teaching, and will take longer to deliver. In addition, the development of more extensive collaborative relationships with arts and sciences faculty and with public school personnel will require additional resources.

Thus, the delivery of professional programs for the preparation of elementary teachers who have the appropriate skills to teach in tomorrow's schools will cost more than current funding levels provide in most institutions of higher education today. Yet, the elementary students of the twenty-first century deserve no less.

References

American Association of Colleges for Teacher Education (AACTE). (1989). *Research about teacher education project III.* Washington, DC: Author.

Anderson, L. W. (1993). Recurrent problems in teacher education. In T. A. Simpson (Ed.), *Teacher educators annual handbook* 1993 (pp. 50–61). Red Hill, Australia: Queensland University of Technology.

Berliner, D. (1988). *The development of expertise in pedagogy.* Washington, DC: American Association of Colleges for Teacher Education.

Beyer, L. E. (1991). Schooling, moral commitment, and preparation of teachers. *Journal of Teacher Education, 42*(3), 205–215.

Black, A., & Ammon, P. (1992). A developmental-constructivist approach to teacher education. *Journal of Teacher Education, 43*(5), 323–335.

Block, D. P., & McGarraghy, J. (1992, February). *Making it work: The first year's implementation of an interdisciplinary teacher education program.* Paper presented at the annual meeting of the American Association of Colleges for Teacher Education, San Antonio, TX. (ERIC Document Reproduction Service No. ED 346 053)

Borrowman, M. L. (1965). *Teacher education in America: A documentary history.* New York: Teachers College Press.

Carnegie Council on Adolescent Development. (1989). *Turning points: Preparing American youth for the 21st century.* Washington, DC: Author.

Carnegie Forum on Education and the Economy. (1986). *A nation prepared: Teachers for the 21st century.* New York: Author.

Case, C. W., Norlander, K. A., & Reagan, T. G. (1993). Spotlight on sites: University of Connecticut. *Center Correspondent, 5,* 2–3, 25–31.

Cohn, M. M., & Kottkamp, R. B. (1993). *Teachers: The missing voice in education.* Albany: State University of New York Press.

Conant, J. B. (1963). *The education of American teachers.* New York: McGraw-Hill.

Connelly, F. M., & Lantz, O. C. (1991). Introduction: Definitions of curriculum. In A. Lewy (Ed.), *The international encyclopedia of curriculum* (pp. 15–18). New York: Pergamon Press.

Cruikshank, D. R. (1985). *Models for the preparation of America's teachers.* Bloomington, IN: Phi Delta Kappa Educational Foundation.

Cuban, L. (1992). Curriculum stability and change. In P. W. Jackson (Ed.), *Handbook of research on curriculum* (pp. 216–247). New York: Macmillan.

Darling-Hammond, L. (1990). Teacher professionalism: Why and how? In A. Lieberman (Ed.), *Schools as collaborative cultures* (pp. 25–50). New York: Falmer Press.

Darling-Hammond, L. (1993). Reframing the school reform agenda. *Phi Delta Kappan, 74*(10), 753–761.

Darling-Hammond, L. (Ed.). (1994). *Professional development schools: Schools for a developing profession.* New York: Teachers College Press.

Darling-Hammond, L., & Berry, B. (1988). *The evolution of teacher policy.* Santa Monica: RAND Corporation (JRE-01).

Darling-Hammond, L., & Berry, B. (1995). Teacher professionalism and the commission reports: The prospects for creating a learner-centered profession of teaching. In R. Ginsberg & D. Plank (Eds.), *Commissions, reports, reforms, and educational policy.* Westport, CT: Praeger.

Ebmeier, H., Twombly, S., & Teeter, D. J. (1991). The comparability and adequacy of financial support for schools of education. *Journal of Teacher Education, 42*(3), 226–235.

Edmundson, P. J. (1989). *The curriculum in teacher education* (Tech. Rep. No. 6). Seattle: University of Washington, Center for Educational Renewal.

Elmore, R., & Sykes, G. (1992). Curriculum policy. In P. W. Jackson (Ed.), *Handbook of research on curriculum* (pp. 185–215). New York: Macmillan.

Emans, R. L., Lee, S., Monroe, H. V., & Monroe, J. D. (1989). The debate over the liberal education of elementary school teachers. *Action in Teacher Education, 11*(2), 8–17.

Eric Clearinghouse on Disabilities and Gifted Education. (1993). Including students with disabilities in general education classrooms. *Teaching Exceptional Children, 26*(1), 66–67.

Feiman-Nemser, S. (1990). Teacher preparation: Structural and conceptual alternatives. In W. R. Houston, M. Haberman, & J. Sikula (Eds.), *Handbook of research on teacher education* (pp. 212–233). New York: Macmillan.

Flake, C. L., Kuhs, T., Donnelly, A., & Ebert, C. (1995). Reinventing the role of teacher: Teacher as researcher. *Phi Delta Kappan, 76*(5), 405–407.

Florida Education Standards Commission. (1990). *Preparing elementary teachers for Florida's classrooms.* Washington, DC: U.S. Department of Education, Office of Educational Research and Improvement. (ERIC Document Reproduction Service No. ED 319 734)

Fowler, T. W., Smith, B. D., & Sterling, R. E. (1991, February). *The Cincinnati initiative: Restructuring teacher education—process, conflict, resolution.* Paper presented at the annual meeting of the Association of Teacher Educators, New Orleans. (ERIC Document Reproduction Service No. ED 337 423)

Fuchs, D., & Fuchs, L. (1994). Inclusive schools movement and the radicalization of special education reform. *Exceptional Children, 60*(4), 294–309.

Galluzzo, G. R., & Pankratz, R. S. (1990). Five attributes of a teacher education program knowledge base. *Journal of Teacher Education, 41*(4), 7–14.

Goodlad, J. (1990a). Better teachers for our nation's schools. *Phi Delta Kappan, 72*(3), 184–194.

Goodlad, J. (1990b). *Teachers for our nation's schools.* San Francisco: Jossey-Bass.

Goodlad, J., Klein, M., & Tye, K. (1979). The domains of curriculum and their study. In J. Goodlad (Ed.), *Curriculum inquiry* (pp. 43–76). New York: McGraw-Hill.

Harris, R. C., & Harris, M. F. (1992–1993). Partner schools: Places to solve teacher education problems. *Action in Teacher Education, 14*(4), 1–8.

Herbst, J. (1989a). *And sadly teach.* Madison: The University of Wisconsin Press.

Herbst, J. (1989b). Teacher preparation in the nineteenth century: Institutions and purposes. In D. Warren (Ed.), *American teachers: History of a profession at work* (pp. 213–236). New York: Macmillan.

The Holmes Group. (1986). *Tomorrow's teachers.* East Lansing, MI: Author.

The Holmes Group. (1990). *Tomorrow's schools: Principals for the design of professional development schools.* East Lansing, MI: Author.

The Holmes Group. (1992). Tomorrow's school of education: New mission? New structures? *Holmes Group Forum, 6*(3), 1, 4.

The Holmes Group. (1993). Innovations at Holmes Campuses emphasize constructivism, technology in teacher education. *Holmes Group Forum, 7*(3), 8–9.

The Holmes Group. (1995). *Tomorrow's school of education.* East Lansing, MI: Author.

Houston, W. R., Haberman, M., & Sikula, J. (Eds.). (1990). *Handbook of research on teacher education.* New York: Macmillan.

Houston, W. R., & Williamson, J. L. (1992–1993). Perceptions of their preparation by 42 Texas elementary school teachers compared with their responses as student teachers. *Teacher Education and Practice, 8*(2), 27–42.

Howey, K. R., & Zimpher, N. L. (1989). *Profiles of preservice teacher education: Inquiry into the nature of programs.* Albany: State University of New York Press.

Howsam, R. B., Corrigan, D., Denemark, G., & Nash, R. (1976). *Educating a profession.* Washington, DC: AACTE.

Interstate New Teacher Assessment and Support Consortium (INTASC). (1992). *Model standards for beginning teacher licensing and development: A resource for state dialogue.* Washington, DC: Council for Chief State School Officers.

Ishler, R. E. (1987). An approach to the liberal education of elementary school teachers. *Capstone Journal of Education, 7*(2), 14–18.

Jackson, P. W. (Ed.). (1992a). *Handbook of research on curriculum.* New York: Macmillan.

Jackson, P. W. (1992b). Conceptions of curriculum and curriculum specialists. In P. W. Jackson (Ed.), *Handbook of research on curriculum* (pp. 3–40). New York: Macmillan.

Johnson, W. R. (1989). Teachers and teacher training in the twentieth century. In D. Warren (Ed.), *American teachers: History of a profession at work* (pp. 237–256). New York: Macmillan.

Kerr, D. K. (1983). Teaching competence and teacher education in the United States. In L. S. Shulman & G. Sykes (Eds.), *Handbook of teaching and policy* (pp. 126–149). New York: Longman.

Kliebard, H. M. (1992). Constructing a history of the America curriculum. In P. W. Jackson (Ed.), *Handbook of research on curriculum* (pp. 157–184). New York: Macmillan.

Lanier, J., & Little, J. (1986). Research on teacher education. In W. C. Wittrock (Ed.), *Handbook of research on teaching* (pp. 527–569). New York: Macmillan.

Lazerson, M. (1987). *American education in the twentieth century: A documentary history.* New York: Teachers College Press.

Little, J. W. (1993). Teachers' professional development in a climate of educational reform. *Educational Evaluation and Policy Analysis, 15*(2), 129–151.

Lortie, D. C. (1975). *Schoolteacher: A sociological study.* Chicago: The University of Chicago Press.

McCarthy, S., & Peterson, P. (1993). Creating classroom practice within the context of a restructured professional development school. In D. Cohen, M. McLaughlin, & J. Talbert (Eds.), *Teaching for understanding: Challenges for both policy and practice* (pp. 130–163). San Francisco: Jossey-Bass.

McDiarmid, G. W. (1992). *The arts and sciences as preparation for teaching.* East Lansing, MI: National Center for Research on Teacher Learning.

Merseth, K. (1990). *The case for cases in teacher education.* Washington, DC: American Association for Higher Education.

Murray, F. (1990, April). *The components of the knowledge base of teacher education: Questions teachers have to answer.* Paper presented at the annual meeting of the American Educational Research Association, Boston. (ERIC Document Reproduction Service No. ED 319 716)

National Association for the Education of Young Children (NAEYC). (1992). *Developmentally appropriate practice in early childhood programs serving children from birth through age 8.* S. Bredekamp (Ed.). Washington, DC: Author.

National Association of State Directors of Teacher Education and Certification (NASDTEC). (1992). *Promoting systemic change in teacher education and certification: NASDTEC outcome-based standards and portfolio assessment.* Seattle: NASDTEC Joint Workforce 2000.

National Board for Professional Teaching Standards (NBPTS). (1989). *Toward high and rigorous standards for the teaching profession.* Detroit: Author.

National Board for Professional Teaching Standards (NBPTS). (1993). *School site portfolio.* Detroit: Author.

National Board for Professional Teaching Standards (NBPTS). (in press).

National Center for Research on Teacher Learning (NCRTL). (1991a). *Findings from the teacher education and learning to teach study: Final report.* Special Report 6/91. East Lansing, MI: Author.

National Center for Research on Teacher Learning (NCRTL). (1991b). *NCRTL special report: An agenda for research on teacher learning.* East Lansing, MI: Author.

National Center for Research on Teacher Learning (NCRTL). (1992). *Findings on learning to teach.* East Lansing, MI: Author.

National Council for Accreditation of Teacher Education (NCATE). (1992). *NCATE approved curriculum guidelines.* Washington, DC: Author.

Perelman, L. J. (1992). *School's out: Hyperlearning, the new technology, and the end of education.* New York: Wm. Morrow.

Project 30. (1991). *Year two report: Institutional accomplishments.* Newark, DE: Author.

Public Law 94-142, Education for All Handicapped Children Act of 1975. (23 August 1977). 20 U.S.C. 1401 et. seq: *Federal Register, 42*(163), 42474–42518.

Public Law 101-476, Individuals with Disabilities Education Act of 1990. (30 October 1990). *U.S. Statutes at Large, 104* (Title 20 U.S.C. 1400), 1103–1151.

The Renaissance Group. (1992). *Teachers for the new world: A statement of principles.* Cedar Falls: University of Northern Iowa.

Reyes, D. J., & Isele, F. (1990). What do we expect from elementary student teachers? A national analysis of rating forms. *Action in Teacher Education, 12*(2), 8–13.

Reynolds, A. (1992). What is competent beginning teaching? A review of the literature. *Review of Educational Research, 62*(1), 1–35.

Richardson, V. (1990). Significant and worthwhile change in teaching practice. *Educational Researcher, 19*(7), 10–18.

Scannell, D. P., Corrigan, D. C., Denemark, G., Dieterle, L., Egbert, R., & Nielsen, R. (1983). *Educating a profession: Profile of a beginning teacher.* Washington, DC: AACTE.

Schlechty, P. C. (1991). *Schools for the 21st century: Leadership imperatives for educational reform.* San Francisco: Jossey-Bass.

Schrag, J., & Burnette, J. (1994). Inclusive schools. *Teaching Exceptional Children, 26*(3), 64–68.

Sedlak, M. (1987). Tomorrow's teachers: The essential arguments of the Holmes group report. In J. F. Solitis (Ed.), *Reforming teacher education: The impact of the Holmes group report.* New York: Teachers College Press.

Shulman, L. S. (1986). Those who understand: Knowledge growth in teaching. *Educational Researcher, 15*(2), 4–14.

Silberman, C. E. (1970). *Crisis in the classroom: The remaking of American education.* New York: Random House.

Smith, L. M., Kuhs, T. M., & Ryan, J. M. (1993). *Assessment of student learning in mathematics.* Columbia: South Carolina Center for Excellence in the Assessment of Student Learning.

Snyder, J., Bolin, F., & Zumwalt, K. (1992). In P. W. Jackson (Ed.),

Handbook of research on curriculum (pp. 402–435). New York: Macmillan.

Soder, R. (1993). *On one of the fundamental relationships between the arts and sciences and the education of educators*. Seattle: University of Washington, Center for Educational Renewal.

Spodek, B., & Saracho, O. N. (1990). Introduction. In B. Spodek & O. N. Saracho (Eds.). *Yearbook in early childhood education: Vol. 1. Early childhood teacher preparation* (pp. vii–x). New York: Teachers College Press.

Stallings, J. A., & Stipek, D. (1986). Research on early childhood and elementary school teaching programs. In M. C. Wittrock (Ed.), *Handbook of research on teaching* (pp. 727–753). New York: Macmillan.

Sykes, G. (1992). *The needs of children and the education of educators*. East Lansing, MI: The Holmes Group.

Talbert, J. E., & McLaughlin, M. W. (1993). Understanding teaching in context. In D. Cohen, M. McLaughlin, & J. Talbert (Eds.), *Teaching for understanding: Challenges for both policy and practice* (pp. 167–206). San Francisco: Jossey-Bass.

Tyack, D. B. (Ed.). (1967). *Turning points in American educational history*. Waltham, MA: Blaisdell.

Tyler, R. W. (1949). *Basic principles of curriculum and instruction*. Chicago: The University of Chicago Press.

University of Washington. (1993). *Report of the elementary curriculum development team: Executive summary*. Seattle: University of Washington, College of Education.

Villegas, A. M. (1991). *Culturally responsive teaching* (The Praxis Series: Professional Assessments for Beginning Teachers Foundations for Tomorrow's Teachers—No. 1). Princeton, NJ: Educational Testing Service.

Wise, A. E., Darling-Hammond, L., & Berry, B., with Berliner, D., Haller, E., Praskac, A., & Schlechty, P. (1987). *Effective teacher selection: From recruitment to retention*. Santa Monica: The RAND Corporation.

Wise, A. E., Darling-Hammond, L., with Berry, B., & Klein, S. (1987). *Licensing teachers: Design for a teaching profession*. Santa Monica: The RAND Corporation.

Wittrock, M. C. (Ed.). (1986). *Handbook of research on teaching*. New York: Macmillan.

Woolfolk, A. E. (1989). Graduate preparation of teachers: The debate and beyond. In A. E. Woolfolk (Ed.), *Research perspectives on the graduate preparation of teachers* (pp. 1–11). Englewood Cliffs, NJ: Prentice Hall.

Zeichner, K. M. (1989). Learning from experience in graduate teacher education. In A. E. Woolfolk (Ed.), *Research perspectives on the graduate preparation of teachers* (pp. 12–29). Englewood Cliffs, NJ: Prentice Hall.

Zeichner, K. M. (1991). Contradictions and tensions in the professionalization of teaching and the democratization of schools. *Teachers College Record, 92*(3), 363–379.

Zeichner, K. M., & Liston, D. P. (1990). Traditions of reform in U.S. teacher education. *Journal of Teacher Education, 41*(2), 3–20.

·18·

MIDDLE LEVEL EDUCATION

Ronald D. Williamson

EASTERN MICHIGAN UNIVERSITY

One of the most rewarding opportunities in education is working with young adolescents. They are at once sophisticated young adults in search of solutions to the world's greatest social problems and at the same time children searching for their favorite toy or personal belonging. They are an amalgam distinguished by a vast array of developmental characteristics.

Such a range of development can afford the teacher opportunity for immense curricular and instructional flexibility, or it can be seen as a daily obstacle to planning and preparation for teaching. Precisely because of this mix of student characteristics, the role of the middle level teacher is perhaps one of the most vital in the educational continuum.

This chapter discusses education in the middle—between elementary and high school. It provides a brief look at the origins of the movement, discusses early adolescent learners and those who are most successful at teaching them, and offers some insights and perspectives into the preparation of middle level teachers.

THE ORIGINS OF MIDDLE LEVEL EDUCATION

The modern middle level school has its origins in the American junior high school first discussed in the early twentieth century. The junior high school concept arose because of dissatisfaction with the then predominant two level (8 years/4 years) grade organization. The first junior high schools were established in Columbus, Ohio and Berkeley, California in 1909 (Lounsbury, 1992). The idea of a separate program for students between the elementary and high school years became widespread. Its acceptance was influenced by the issuance of reports that recommended the establishment of a school to "bridge the gap" between elementary school and high school (Lounsbury, 1992).

By the late 1950s and early 1960s concern arose that the junior high school had in fact not become a distinct educational program designed for students in the middle. In many cases the junior high school was nothing more than a "junior" version of the senior high school program. Frequently, classes were organized into similar content-specific departments, students were assigned to classes in similar ways, and many of the curricular and cocurricular offerings were identical to those offered in the comprehensive high school.

From dissatisfaction with this model arose new perspectives on the education for students in the middle. Donald Eichhorn (1966) and William Alexander et al. (1969) wrote cogently of the new "middle school." Alexander stated the purpose of the middle school: "In the first place, the youth served are in the 'middle,' between childhood and adolescence. In the second place, the schools serving them should be in the 'middle,' between schools for childhood and for adolescent education" (Alexander et al., 1969, p. 5).

What followed was astounding. Based on the work of Eichhorn and Alexander, writers and researchers such as John Lounsbury, Gordon Vars, Conrad Toepfer, and others studied, researched, and wrote about the young adolescent students and the nature of the schools that serve them.

Dissatisfaction with the junior high school arose not because of the concept, a school between elementary and high, but because of the school it became, a smaller version of the high school. This dissatisfaction was one of several factors that precipitated the acceptance of the middle school. Other factors included "the Sputnik-induced obsession with academic mastery, particularly in mathematics and sciences; and . . . the recognition that young people were indeed maturing physically earlier" (Lounsbury, 1992, p. 10).

The junior high school movement, for the most part, failed to result in the establishment of developmentally responsive schools for young adolescents. Tension arose as to the most appropriate organization for the school in the middle—the junior high or the middle school. To neutralize some of the tension and to focus the work of educators on strategies for serving youth rather than grade configuration, George Melton, Deputy Executive Director of the National Association of Secondary School Principals (NASSP), coined the term *middle level education,* referring to those schools in the middle regardless of grade configuration or name. In 1982, the NASSP Committee on Junior High and Middle School Education changed its name to the Committee on Middle Level Education to reflect the changing terminology.

Background

During the past two decades there has been a significant shift in the grade structure of middle level schools (Alexander & McEwin, 1989; Valentine, Clark, Irvin, Keefe, & Melton, 1993). This change in grade organization has also been accompanied by a major shift in the way middle level schools are organized and provide services to students (Alexander & McEwin, 1989; Valentine et al., 1993); however, grade organization alone is not the primary indicator of an appropriate middle level program (Epstein, 1990).

Middle level education is "firmly anchored in the realities of human growth and development" (Lounsbury, 1991, p. 68). It focuses on young adolescence as a unique period in the development of the individual and as such requires a unique response from the educators who work with any individual. There is a growing understanding of the early adolescent years. The writings of Joan Lipsitz (1984), John Lounsbury (1984), and others have provided insight into the characteristics of this age group.

Beyond an understanding of the middle school student the information base regarding the organization and practices of the middle level school has grown significantly (Alexander & McEwin, 1989; Eichhorn, 1966; Epstein & Mac Iver, 1990; George & Alexander, 1993; Johnston & Markle, 1986; Lounsbury, 1984). Today, middle level educators have access to an abundant knowledge base regarding effective educational practices.

The combination of greater understanding of young adolescents along with a more complete knowledge of effective practices for teaching and working with these students was the driving force for the reexamination of the practices used by middle level schools throughout the nation.

FOCUS ON THE EARLY ADOLESCENT STUDENT

An understanding of young adolescents is essential to any significant discussion of middle level schooling. Early adolescence is a time of immense developmental change. It is easy for educators to observe the dramatic physical changes in youngsters and assume that each area of development is changing in equally dramatic ways. This is most often not the case. Middle level students are very diverse. This diversity is at once a blessing and a hurdle for the middle level educator.

Developmental Changes

Dramatic physical change and development are certainly the most visible of many changes that take place during the middle grades (Milgram, 1992; Scales, 1991). This physical change is often characterized by the term *growth spurt*. Height, weight, and physical appearance change. This changed appearance

often prompts middle level students to question who they are and how they relate to both peers and adults.

Although physical growth and maturation are the most obvious of the developmental changes, there are other developmental issues for the middle level student. The area perhaps most confounding to parents and to school staff are changes in social and emotional development. During the middle grades students increasingly seek independence from adults and increasing conformity to peers. This normal and healthy developmental behavior often raises serious concerns for parents (Scales, 1991).

Adolescence is also a time when youngsters are seeking to establish themselves in a new environment as well as a new looking body. Because the youngster is neither a child nor an adult, behaviors can be characterized as widely fluctuating. During this time of change, adolescents require the experience of frequent success. They strive for independence yet need and seek guidance. They need personal attention from adults and yet seek conformity to their peer group (Clark & Clark, 1994).

Middle level students are often overly concerned about the way they are perceived by others, particularly peers. At this age, youngsters experience the feelings of an "imaginary audience." They believe that others are constantly looking at and noting their behaviors. Therefore, in a quest to achieve acceptance, the young adolescent often overcompensates and seeks conformity in dress, hair style, music, and other indicators of the peer culture (Milgram, 1992).

While adolescents strive for increasing independence, most adolescents report positive relationships with their parents. Scales (1991) speaks to the "positive possibilities" (p. 7) of early adolescence. "Roughly one quarter of the 28 million 10–17-year-olds in the United States are at high risk of failing at school, abusing drugs, becoming delinquent, or becoming an adolescent parent. Yet 80% of young people are happy with their family lives, 70% of 15-year-olds have not had sexual intercourse, 80% of young people under 17 do not have a drinking problem, and 80% are not regular smokers" (p. 7).

Just as adolescents experience profound physical, social, and emotional changes, they undergo significant cognitive change as well (Nielsen, 1991). Although the changes in the intellectual realm are less visible than the rapid physical growth, they, too, affect both social and emotional development.

In early adolescence, youngsters begin to move away from the almost complete reliance on their own concrete experiences and toward the ability to consider alternatives (Milgram, 1992; Nielsen, 1991). The ability to develop hypotheses, to consider "what ifs," to think reflectively, and to reason abstractly characterize this period. As in the other areas of development, the changes do not take place in a linear progression but often surface in fits and starts. One day a youngster can deal with complex abstract concepts and the next day will once again require instruction in the most concrete manner (Clark & Clark, 1994).

The dilemma for the middle level teacher is that every middle level student is experiencing this cognitive change and every student's experience is unique. The challenge for the teacher is to be able to adjust the instructional program to take into account the vast daily differences in cognitive development.

Other changes in the cognitive area also occur during adolescence. In addition to great variety in learning styles and thinking ability, the interests of early adolescents change frequently. They are very exploratory and are interested in trying many different activities. This change in interests also affects the instructional program and the structure of lessons taught to the middle level student.

In addition, due to a combination of factors such as peer pressure and self-esteem, some early adolescents voluntarily suppress their own academic achievement. Some students at the middle level, quite capable of high academic achievement, choose to perform at a lower level (Clark & Clark, 1994).

The range of development ensures that every middle grades classroom includes students at various stages of physical, social-emotional, and cognitive development. This milieu provides the teacher with a wonderful mixture of interests, abilities, and attitudes. Building on this diverse base the middle level teacher is afforded the opportunity to be immensely creative and flexible in teaching practices.

Changing Societal Context

Students in today's middle level schools live in a society that is ever-changing and yet frightening in the complexity of the issues. The demographics of American society are rapidly changing and reflect a greater diversity than at any other time in our history. At the same time, the structure of the American economy has changed. The skills needed to be successful in the workplace of the 1990s are dramatically different from the skills required just a few decades ago.

American youth live in a society that is older, more ethnically and culturally diverse, and poorer. The following statistics reflect this change.

1. The percentage of the population over age 65 is expected to increase steadily in coming years (U.S. Department of Education, 1990).
2. By the year 2000, 34% of the nation's children will be African American, Latino, and Asian (Scales, 1991).
3. By 1990 the percentage of foreign-born residents increased to 7.9% from 6.2% a decade earlier (Albert, 1993).
4. Unmarried women account for an increasing number of births, rising from 18.4% of births in 1980 to 28% in 1990 (Albert, 1993).
5. The U.S. child poverty rate rose during the 1980s to 19.6% in 1989 (Children's Defense Fund, 1991).

Early adolescents are confronted by a series of social ills that both test their will and stretch their ability to cope. Recent data showed an alarming increase in crime among juveniles. Statistics show increases in nearly every category ("Crime Among Juveniles," 1993). The number of firearm-related deaths among youth ages 5–19 years nearly doubled between 1985 and 1990 ("Number of Firearm," 1993).

Such trends demand the attention of middle level educators. In the 1990s and beyond it is imperative that schools be attentive to the needs of early adolescents and the issues they confront in their daily lives. Attention to providing for the typical adolescent's need for understanding, respect, and acceptance is critical.

The challenge is enormous. "Caring is crucial to the development of young adolescents into healthy adults" (Carnegie Council on Adolescent Development, 1989, p. 33). Middle level educators must accept this challenge and care for the students they serve more than ever before.

PROGRAMS THAT SERVE EARLY ADOLESCENTS

There has been renewed interest in the education of students in the middle level in recent years. Numerous researchers (Alexander & McEwin, 1989; Epstein & Mac Iver, 1990; George & Alexander, 1993) have studied schools in the middle and have reported their findings. In addition, professional organizations such as the National Association of Secondary School Principals (NASSP) (Valentine et al., 1993) and the Association for Supervision and Curriculum Development (ASCD) (Cawelti, 1988) funded studies and reported their findings.

In 1989 the Carnegie Council on Adolescent Development issued a report on the status of education in the middle grades. *Turning Points: Preparing American Youth for the 21st Century* (1989) identified eight areas (Table 18.1) that could transform middle level education. Each of the eight areas included numerous specific recommendations as well as examples of programs that address the issue.

TABLE 18.1. Recommendations of Carnegie Council on Adolescent Development

1. *Create small communities for learning* where stable, close, mutually respectful relationships with adults and peers are considered fundamental for intellectual development and personal growth.
2. *Teach a core academic program* that results in students who are literate, including the sciences, and who know how to think critically, lead a healthy life, behave ethically, and assume the responsibilities of citizenship in a pluralistic society.
3. *Ensure success for all students* through elimination of tracking by achievement level and promotion of cooperative learning, flexibility in arranging instructional time, and adequate resources for teachers.
4. *Empower teachers and administrators to make decisions about the experiences of middle grade students* through creative control by teachers over the instructional program.
5. *Staff middle grade schools with teachers who are expert at teaching young adolescents* and who have been specially prepared for assignment to the middle grades.
6. *Improve academic performance through fostering the health and fitness of* young adolescents.
7. *Reengage families in the education of young adolescents* by giving families meaningful roles in school governance, communicating with families about the school program and student progress, and offering families opportunities to support the learning process at home and at school.
8. *Connect schools with communities,* which together share responsibility for each middle grade student's success.

Source: From *Turning Points: Preparing American Youth for the 21st Century* (pp. 9–10). A report prepared by Carnegie Council on Adolescent Development; a program of Carnegie Corporation of New York, 1989.

TABLE 18.2. Essential Elements of a "True" Middle School

1. Educators knowledgeable about and committed to transescents
2. A balanced curriculum based on transescent needs
3. A range of organizational arrangements
4. Varied instructional strategies
5. A full exploratory program
6. Comprehensive advising and counseling
7. Continuous progress for students
8. Evaluation procedures compatible with nature of transescents
9. Cooperative planning
10. Positive school climate

Source: From *This We Believe* by the National Middle School Association, 1994, Columbus, OH: Author.

Turning Points built on the prior work of several national professional organizations. *This We Believe* (National Middle School Association [NMSA], 1982) and *An Agenda for Excellence at the Middle Level* (Johnston, Arth, Lounsbury, & Toepfer, 1985) also identified elements of an appropriate middle level program.

This We Believe described the essential elements of a "true" middle school. "The middle school stands for clear educational concepts which evolve from a melding of the nature of the age group, the nature of learning, and the expectations of society" (NMSA, 1982, p. 10). Table 18.2 details the 10 components of the middle school model described by the National Middle School Association.

In 1985, the Middle Level Council of the National Association of Secondary School Principals issued *An Agenda for Excellence at the Middle Level* (Johnston et al., 1985). It detailed 11 elements (Table 18.3) of schooling that should be of highest priority to middle level schools. Each of the 11 elements offers specific suggestions for implementation. The council stated that "the commitment to excellence in education begins with an understanding of the mission of each school" (p. 1) and that middle level schools "have special missions that require cultivation and serious attention if they are to help young adolescents reach their potential" (p. 1).

This We Believe and *An Agenda for Excellence at the Middle Level* serve as the primary statements of vision for middle level

TABLE 18.3. Elements of Middle Level Schooling

1. Core values
2. Culture and climate
3. Student development
4. Curriculum
5. Learning and instruction
6. School organization
7. Technology
8. Teachers
9. Transition
10. Principals
11. Connections

Source: Adapted from *An Agenda for Excellence at the Middle Level* by J. H. Johnston, A. Arth, J. Lounsbury, and C. Toepfer, 1985, Reston, VA: National Association of Secondary School Principals.

education. In conjunction with *Turning Points: Preparing American Youth for the 21st Century*, they provide a foundation for examining and modifying educational practices in the middle grades.

Large numbers of middle level schools had implemented or were already moving toward the middle school concept when the Carnegie report was issued. *Turning Points* helped to draw attention to these efforts, provided support for the initiatives, and reinforced the steps already taken for some middle grades schools to align more closely with the developmental needs of early adolescents. Although some schools have moved to implement the Carnegie recommendations and to address implications at the school site, room remains for further progress. The challenge of implementing the Carnegie recommendations continues at the middle level.

Some researchers identified practices that align with developmental characteristics of early adolescents and provide for student achievement. Each of the practices, when strongly implemented, "yields benefits which are educationally significant" (Mac Iver, 1990, p. 464). For example, the implementation of interdisciplinary teams was found to "increase the effectiveness of instruction, to provide teachers with a much-needed support system, to help [e]nsure that students' problems will be recognized and solved, to improve students' work and attitudes, and to have a positive impact on the school's overall program" (Mac Iver, 1990, p. 464). Similar positive benefits were identified for other recommended practices.

The recommendations fall into three general categories patterned after the recommendations of the Carnegie Council: creating small communities for learning, teaching a core of common knowledge, and ensuring success for all students.

Create Small Communities for Learning The first of the areas deals with the organization of the middle level school and the relationship of children to adults. This recommendation may be implemented in a variety of ways, but the components noted most frequently in the literature include:

1. Organize instruction around interdisciplinary teams of teachers (Carnegie Council on Adolescent Development, 1989; Cawelti, 1988; Epstein & Mac Iver, 1990; George & Alexander, 1993; George & Oldaker, 1985; Johnston et al., 1985).
2. Assign an adult advisor for each student (Carnegie Council on Adolescent Development, 1989; Cawelti, 1988; Epstein & Mac Iver, 1990; George & Alexander, 1993; George & Oldaker, 1985; Johnston et al., 1985; NMSA, 1982).
3. Provide teaching teams with common planning time (Cawelti, 1988; Epstein & Mac Iver, 1990; George & Oldaker, 1985; NMSA, 1982).
4. Modify scheduling to include flexible blocks of time for teaching teams (Cawelti, 1988; Epstein & Mac Iver, 1990; George & Alexander, 1993; George & Oldaker, 1985; Johnston et al., 1985; NMSA, 1982).

Teach a Core of Common Knowledge In addition to modifying the organization and structure of the middle level school, a series of recommendations emerged that support modified curricular and instructional practices. These recommendations include:

1. Integrate subject matter across content lines (Beane, 1993; Carnegie Council on Adolescent Development, 1989; Garvin, 1986; NMSA, 1982).
2. Design and offer a full exploratory program (Carnegie Council on Adolescent Development, 1989; Cawelti, 1988; George & Alexander, 1993; Johnston et al., 1985; NMSA, 1982).
3. Offer a challenging curriculum for each student (Carnegie Council on Adolescent Development, 1989; Johnston et al., 1985).
4. Equip students with skills for lifelong learning, including the ability to think critically (Carnegie Council on Adolescent Development, 1989; Cawelti, 1988; Johnston & Markle, 1986; Johnston et al., 1985).
5. Provide opportunities for students to be active citizens (Carnegie Council on Adolescent Development, 1989; Johnston et al., 1985).

Ensure Success for All Students The third component of a sound middle level program addresses instructional issues. It is focused around teaching in ways that ensure the success of each student. The recommendations include:

1. Modify instructional practices to include mastery learning and the increased use of technology (Carnegie Council on Adolescent Development, 1989; Cawelti, 1988; George & Oldaker, 1985; Johnston et al., 1985).
2. Utilize cooperative learning strategies (Carnegie Council on Adolescent Development, 1989; Cawelti, 1988; George & Alexander, 1993; Johnston & Markle, 1986; Johnston et al., 1985).
3. Implement ability grouping only when it is temporary and flexible (Carnegie Council on Adolescent Development, 1989; Cawelti, 1988; George, 1988; George & Alexander, 1993; Oakes, 1985).

This list of suggested characteristics of the middle level school is not exhaustive. The literature is replete with numerous suggestions for specific organizational, curricular, and instructional strategies for working with the early adolescent student. The hallmark of the middle level school is its emphasis on aligning these practices with the characteristics and needs of the middle level students. The very best middle level schools are those that are attentive to student needs and respond with understanding and flexibility.

Implementation of Recommended Practices

These practices are, in fact, being implemented in middle level schools. Valentine et al. (1993) conducted a study for the NASSP and looked at a sample of 570 middle level schools. Alexander and McEwin (1989) surveyed 670 middle level schools of various grade configurations to ascertain the characteristics of their educational program. Epstein and Mac Iver (1990) sampled 1,753 public schools containing a seventh grade. Cawelti (1988) gathered data from 672 schools nationwide who served students ages 10–14 years old. McEwin, Dickinson, and Jenkins (in press) conducted a study of programs and practices in 1,798 middle level schools in 1993.

In each case, the study revealed an increasing prevalence of educational practices identified as appropriate for the middle level school. The results of these studies demonstrated use of such practices as interdisciplinary teaming, advisory programs, heterogeneous grouping practices, and flexible scheduling.

For example, the NASSP study found that 57% of the schools in their sample had some form of interdisciplinary teaming (Valentine et al., 1993). Epstein and Mac Iver (1990) had previously found that 37% of the schools in their study had interdisciplinary teaming programs. Alexander and McEwin (1989) had found 33% of their sample, and Cawelti (1988) found 16% of his sample had teaming. The number of grades 6–8 middle schools implementing teaming had increased rather significantly by the 1992–1993 school year. For example, 59% of schools utilized teaming in language arts at the sixth-grade level (McEwin, Dickinson, & Jenkins, in press).

Similar growth in the number of schools implementing teacher-based advisory programs was noted. Epstein and Mac Iver (1990) found that about "two thirds of schools that include grade seven have one homeroom or group advisory period" (p. 23). Alexander and McEwin (1989) found 39% of the schools in their sample had an advisory program, and Cawelti (1988) identified 29% of his sample had such a program. By 1993, this number had increased to 53% (McEwin, Dickinson, & Jenkins, in press).

Although homogeneous grouping continues to be utilized in many middle grades schools, efforts are underway to implement alternative practices that reduce ability grouping (Epstein & Mac Iver, 1990). The NASSP survey (Valentine et al., 1993) found that between 1981 and 1992 there was a slight reduction in the use of ability grouping by grade organization from 88% of middle level schools to 82%.

Flexibility in scheduling instructional periods is another of the consistent recommendations for modifying middle level schools. Alexander and McEwin (1989) compared the results of their 1988 survey with an earlier survey conducted in 1968. They found that a school day of uniform length class periods continues to be the prevalent practice. They found that flexible scheduling within blocks of time for interdisciplinary teams was more common at the sixth grade than at other grades, and that it was used from 20% (eighth grade) to 31% (sixth grade) of the time.

Several studies have also found a relationship between the grade configuration of the middle level school and the degree to which the school implemented characteristics of the middle school. Schools housing grades 6 through 8 are more likely than other grade configurations to implement such programs (Alexander & McEwin, 1989; Cawelti, 1988; Epstein & Mac Iver, 1990; Valentine et al., 1993).

In 1985, George and Oldaker studied "exemplary" middle level schools to determine the extent to which middle schools identified as exemplary contain program components that align with the recommendations from the literature on middle school education. The schools were identified by "1) the 1982 Study of Well-Disciplined Schools sponsored by Phi Delta Kappa, 2) the 1983 United States Department of Education National Secondary School Recognition program, 3) a panel of ten persons recognized as experts in middle school education, and

4) several lists of exemplary schools identified in recent books on middle level education" (p. 17).

Staff members from 130 schools responded. The study found that of the 130 "exemplary middle schools," 90% utilized interdisciplinary team organization. The study also found that 93% of those schools included a home-base or advisor-advisee program for each child (George & Oldaker, 1985, p. 19).

Middle level schools, in greater numbers, are implementing programs recommended to align more closely with the developmental needs of early adolescents (Alexander & McEwin, 1989; Epstein & Mac Iver, 1990; Valentine et al., 1993). The challenge educators face is the preparation of teachers to work successfully in such "developmentally responsive" schools.

Changing Relationships

A major emphasis of the middle level school is creating the potential to enhance the relationship between students and teachers. This potential is unleashed in an environment where there are "opportunities for teachers to develop sustained personal relationships with students, essential to teaching them well, and to provide guidance during the at-times turbulent period of early adolescence" (Carnegie Council on Adolescent Development, 1989, p. 37).

The Carnegie Council made three recommendations to address this issue: (1) create smaller learning environments, (2) form teams of teachers and students, and (3) assign an adult advisor for every student. "Creating a small community within the school enables teachers to develop trusting relationships with students. This encourages the kinds of risk taking needed for learning to occur. It also enables teachers to make the kinds of links between what the student already knows and new knowledge" (Arhar, 1992).

Interdisciplinary Teams Organizing middle level schools into interdisciplinary teaching teams has become a prevalent education practice. As shown in Table 18.4 studies in recent years show increasing use of interdisciplinary teams as an instructional practice (Alexander & McEwin, 1989; Cawelti, 1988; Epstein & Mac Iver, 1990; McEwin et al., in press; Valentine et al., 1993).

An interdisciplinary team is an organizational model defined by several characteristics. These include two or more teachers who share a common group of students, a common planning period, and ideally have adjacent classroom space (George & Oldaker, 1985). Within these parameters, teams vary widely. Many middle level schools have varied team structures, using different team sizes or subject combinations. For example, a school might have self-contained classrooms at the sixth grade and use interdisciplinary teams for grades 7 or 8. Yet, the school might utilize two teacher teams in grade 6, four or five teacher teams in grade 7, and a departmentalized structure for grade 8. Regardless of the teaming model, the basic goal of interdisciplinary teaming is to promote teacher collegiality, which not only benefits teachers personally, but empowers them to improve instruction for students (Arhar, Johnston, & Markle, 1989).

Several advantages of interdisciplinary team organization have been cited. The areas include academic achievement (George & Oldaker, 1985), improved attitude and motivation toward school (Mac Iver, 1990), curricular changes (Epstein & Mac Iver, 1990), student–teacher relationships (Lipsitz, 1984), improved discipline (George & Oldaker, 1985), improved staff morale (Arhar, Johnston, & Markle, 1988), and instructional responsiveness (Arhar et al., 1988).

Additional benefits of teaming have been identified. Improved discipline (George & Oldaker, 1985); greater enthusiasm for school and their teachers in school (Arhar et al., 1989); and the potential for teachers to create linkages between curricular areas, to coordinate learning skills, and to modify instructional practices in order to respond to student needs (Lake, 1989a).

A caution is in order. Although there are many identified benefits from interdisciplinary teaming, teaming in and of itself does not have an impact on the education of young adolescents. "Teaming is an organizational change that may affect the way instruction is delivered in the school. It is also a way of restructuring human interaction among teachers, and possibly among students, so that the school can become a collection of smaller, relatively cohesive groups. In other words, teaming creates an opportunity for things to be done differently in the school; it does not assure that they will be" (Arhar et al., 1989, p. 24).

Teacher-Based Advisory Programs Another recommendation for changed teacher–student relationships in the middle level

TABLE 18.4. Studies Showing Implementation of Teaming and Advisory Programs

Study	Sample	Percent with Teaming	Percent with Advisory
Cawelti (1988) Association for Supervision and Curriculum Development	Stratified sample of 2,290 schools nationwide serving students ages 10–14 with a return of 672 (34%).	16	29
Alexander & McEwin (1989)	Surveys mailed to 1,200 schools of varied grade configurations between grades 5 and 9 with a return of 670 (56%).	33	39
Epstein & Mac Iver (1990) Center for Research on Elementary and Middle Schools	Sample of 2,400 principals of schools that regularly serve seventh graders sent surveys with 1,753 returned (73%).	37	66
Valentine et al. (1993) National Association of Secondary School Principals	A stratified sample of 2,000 middle level schools was selected with 570 responses (29%).	57	N/A

school is the implementation of a teacher-based advisory program. Advisory programs are recommended as a way to develop more responsive support systems for students. Such programs are "designed to provide guidance and to monitor the academic, social and emotional welfare of individual students" (Mac Iver, 1990, p. 458).

Teacher-based advisory programs assign a small group of students to a teacher, administrator, or other staff member. This staff person meets with the students on a regularly scheduled (often daily) basis to discuss topics of importance to students. The program ensures that all students will have at least one adult who knows them well and will belong to a small, interactive group (Arnold, 1991). "In a well developed advisory concept, the advisor is the best adult school friend" (Bergmann & Baxter, 1983, p. 50).

Varied activities take place during advisory period. Some of the tasks are mechanical (e.g., taking attendance, distributing notices, making announcements, orienting students to rules and regulations); however, the advisory time is often used for social and academic support activities. This may include discussing problems with individual students; giving career guidance and information; developing student self-confidence and leadership; or discussing academic issues, social relationships, peer groups, and intergroup relations (Arnold, 1991).

Positive benefits of advisory programs have been identified. They include a reduction in the drop-out rate (Mac Iver & Epstein, 1991); reduced discipline problems; and a feeling of belonging, personal recognition, being cared for, and understanding of themselves and others (Lake, 1989b).

By assuming a role in the guidance of students, teachers are likely to gain an enhanced view of themselves as teachers. Gaining greater insights into students aids in diagnosing and responding instructionally. This more personal relationship with students provides an opportunity for teachers to make a significant contribution to the lives of middle level students (George & Alexander, 1993).

MIDDLE LEVEL TEACHER PREPARATION

Working with middle level students requires knowledge and skill that are uniquely different from those required of educators who work at other levels. The uniqueness of early adolescent development and the need to be responsive to the immense changes during this age require that educational practices be changed dramatically. An essential element of such change is the need for preservice training that appropriately prepares teachers to work in this setting and with this age group.

The Effective Middle Level Teacher

Those who work with students at the middle must possess special characteristics. McEwin and Thomason (1989) looked at competencies that promote effective instruction at the middle level and identified characteristics of effective middle grades teachers. They explicitly linked the competencies with the developmental characteristics of early adolescent learners. McEwin and Thomason stated that "to a considerable degree,

effective middle grades practitioners have two strengths in tandem. First, they have a thorough knowledge of the developmental nature of early adolescents. Second, they have subject matter and instructional expertise" (McEwin & Thomason, 1989, p. 10).

A NASSP survey (Valentine et al., 1993) of middle level principals, assistant principals, and other school leadership team members regarding the skills and characteristics of excellent middle level teachers found marked uniformity in the responses. All three groups ranked "competence in adjusting instruction to the varying skills of the students" as of greatest importance. The second ranked response from all three groups was "competence in developing positive relationship with students in the classroom." The other top five qualities were not ranked in the same order by each subgroup but were all included among items three, four, and five. They include "competence in use of varied developmentally appropriate methods of instruction," "competence in promoting student self-concept," and "competence in subject matter knowledge" (Valentine et al., 1993).

The National Middle School Association (NMSA) (1986) identified six personal qualities required for effective teaching at the middle level. "Effective teaching at the middle grades level requires to a high degree the personal qualities long associated with successful teaching at any level, including energy, enthusiasm, sensitivity, fairness, sense of humor" (p. 10). Furthermore, the characteristics and needs of the adolescent give heightened importance to a positive view of self; flexibility and openness to change; respect for the dignity and worth of each individual; willingness to cooperate with other staff members, parents, students, and others to achieve common goals; commitment to transescents; and a commitment to education.

Johnston and Markle (1986) described 18 "indicators of competency" in the behavior of middle level teachers in *What Research Says to the Middle Level Practitioner*. Based on extensive review of the literature, Johnston and Markle found that effective middle level teachers "have a positive self concept, demonstrate warmth, are optimistic, are enthusiastic, are flexible, are spontaneous, accept students, demonstrate awareness of developmental levels, demonstrate knowledge of subject matter, use a variety of instructional activities and materials, structure instruction, monitor learning, use concrete materials and focused learning strategies, ask varied questions, incorporate indirectness in teaching, incorporate 'success-building' behavior in teaching, diagnose individual learning needs, prescribe individual instruction, and listen" (pp. 16–18).

These qualities are particularly important at the middle level when students exhibit a broad range of development. Middle level teachers must possess a depth of understanding of adolescent development and develop competency in adapting the instructional program to respond to student needs.

Teacher Preparation Programs

Recognition of the need to provide an educational program that addresses the unique nature of middle level students prompted interest in the training and preparation of those who work at the middle. This recognition challenged a long-standing paradigm regarding the division of the K–12 educational program into elementary and secondary components. It challenged one of the most serious issues confronting middle level education—the need to make middle schools developmentally responsive for young adolescents. Colleges and universities traditionally have organized their programs into elementary and secondary divisions. The lack of programs specializing in the preparation of teachers for the middle level has been notable.

Professional organizations such as the NASSP and NMSA took the lead in advocating teacher preparation programs specializing on the middle level. NASSP's Council on Middle Level Education called for teachers "who understand the subjects they teach and the development of early adolescents" (Johnston et al., 1985, p. 13). The council further called for middle level teacher preparation to include training in specific areas: "adolescent development, skill in diagnosis and evaluation, advising, consultation, and problem solving, the application of technology to education, human relations, planning, classroom management, personal research and inquiry in the classroom, and, in many cases, a foreign language appropriate to the community in which the teacher will work" (Johnston et al., 1985, p. 13).

The NMSA has been a persistent advocate for the special preparation of middle level teachers. In 1980, the association adopted a position paper recognizing the importance of the preparation of middle grades teachers (NMSA, 1986). This position paper identified six personal qualities that have a heightened importance in the middle grades: (1) positive view of self; (2) flexibility and openness to change; (3) respect for the dignity and worth of each individual; (4) willingness to cooperate with other staff members, parents, students, and others to achieve common goals; (5) commitment to the young adolescent; and (6) commitment to education (NMSA, 1986).

In 1986, the NMSA produced a more comprehensive statement of beliefs, *Professional Certification and Preparation for the Middle Level*. This report stated the case for specific middle level preparation and middle level certification standards by distinguishing the preservice preparation of middle level teachers from that required for elementary or high school teaching. NMSA recommended four elements to the preservice preparation program.

1. Depth in one or two teaching fields
2. Examination of the history, philosophy, and curriculum of the middle grades
3. Special attention to
   a. The characteristics and needs of the transescent
   b. The development of the skills of continued learning in and through instruction in such courses as reading, English, social studies, science, mathematics, foreign language, home economics, and so forth
   c. The guidance/advisory role of the teacher during transescence
4. Methods and materials especially appropriate for middle grade students (NMSA, 1986, p. 11)

Alexander and McEwin (1988) identified the components of appropriate middle level teacher education programs in *Preparing to Teach at the Middle Level*. The essential elements include:

1. Thorough study of the nature and needs of early adolescents

2. Middle level curriculum and instruction
3. Broad academic background, including concentrations in at least two academic areas at the undergraduate level
4. Specialized methods and reading courses
5. Early and continuing field experiences in good middle level schools (Alexander & McEwin, 1988, p. 48)

Current Status

Growth in the number of middle level schools would logically be accompanied by growth of programs to prepare teachers to work in middle schools; however, this has not been the case. Alexander and McEwin (1988) found that only 33% of the responding institutions offered programs in middle level teacher education. They identified the requirement for middle level teacher certification as perhaps the key variable in rallying teacher training institutions to develop and implement specialized middle level teacher training programs. They identified 28 states in 1968 as having special middle level teacher certification or endorsement for teachers. Valentine and Mogar (1992) conducted an additional study of middle level teacher certification requirements and found that 33 states had some degree of middle level certification requirement, but only 11 indicated that middle level certification is mandatory. Clearly there is room for improvement. The connection between certification requirements and the availabilty of middle level preparation programs is strong.

The NMSA through its Professional Preparation and Certification Committee developed a comprehensive set of curriculum guidelines for the preparation of middle grades teachers at both the undergraduate and graduate levels (NMSA, 1991). These guidelines have been approved by the National Council for Accreditation of Teacher Education (NCATE) and serve as the official NMSA/NCATE position on middle level teacher education. Colleges and universities seeking NCATE accreditation for the middle level teacher preparation programs must submit curriculum folios to National Middle School Association's Folio Review Board for review. Therefore, these guidelines clearly have greater influence on teacher training than previous recommendations.

The National Board for Professional Teaching Standards (NBPTS) is working toward the identification of the knowledge—content and pedagogy—appropriate for teachers. One of the first areas to be developed is the Early Adolescent/Generalist. Subsequent areas will include Early Adolescent/English Language Arts, Mathematics, Science, and Social Studies/History. The NBPTS standards, which include an assessment component and an opportunity for voluntary certification, provide one option for middle level teachers to demonstrate competency to teach at that level.

The DeWitt Wallace-Reader's Digest Fund provided funding to the Center for Early Adolescence to study the effectiveness of middle grades teacher training programs. The results of that study, which asked teachers to rate their preparation, were reported in *Windows of Opportunity: Improving Middle Grades Teacher Preparation* (Scales, 1992). Teachers rated their preparation in specific areas as inadequate or poor. For example, 65% of the respondents felt that their teacher education poorly prepared them for cultural and/or language diversity, 54% felt poorly prepared for teacher-based guidance and interdisciplinary curriculum and/or teaming, and 53% felt poorly prepared for cooperative learning/grouping.

Scales also asked teachers to identify the elements that they believed most critical to middle grades teaching. Some 93% believed a knowledge of early adolescent development was essential, and 91% indicated that social relationships and self-awareness were critical.

This same study asked teachers for recommendations to improve the preparation of middle level teachers. The most frequently identified improvements included:

1. Improvement in field experiences and student teaching
2. More instruction in a greater variety of developmentally responsive teaching and assessment techniques
3. Deeper coverage of classroom management techniques
4. More comprehensive coverage of academic content areas
5. Greater understanding of early adolescent development, particularly social relationships and self awareness (Scales, 1992, p. 68)

Scales (1992) made several recommendations based on his findings. They included improving teacher education curriculum and field-based experiences by focusing on "the social and emotional needs of young adolescents and on a professional development school approach" (p. 106). In addition, he recommended that teacher training include components that provide opportunities for teachers to sharpen their advocacy skills for young adolescents. This includes an understanding of and advocacy for programs that address the needs of the "whole" young adolescent. This includes such programs as advisor-advisee, "health and life skills education, music, art, and intramural programs" (p. 133).

A further recommendation was that preservice training include the development of skills for greater teacher participation in school decision making. The very nature of the middle level school, teaming, interdisciplinary curriculum, common planning, teacher-based guidance, requires that teachers have skills at cooperation, collaboration, and decision making. Schools responsive to adolescent needs require that middle level teachers have the "ability to play key roles in site-based management" (Scales, 1992, p. 136).

The Center for Early Adolescence conducted a follow-up study in 1992 (Scales & McEwin, 1994) that asked respondents to rank the recommendations from Scales's *Windows of Opportunity* (1992) report on a five-point scale. Two elements were ranked: "(1) The degree to which the individual personally agreed with the recommendation; and (2) How important the individual believed the recommendation to be in strengthening middle-grades teacher preparation" (Scales & McEwin, 1994, p. 8). The rankings of the three most important items are detailed in Table 18.5.

Scales and McEwin (1994) studied the impact of "high quality" middle grades teacher preparation programs. The study received responses from 2,139 middle school teachers limited to teachers of English/language arts, mathematics, sciences, and social studies. Respondents were asked a series of questions about their teacher preparation programs. The study found that "the more courses preservice teachers take devoted to the

TABLE 18.5. Recommendations for Strengthening Middle Grades Teacher Preparation

Rank	Recommendation
1	Greater understanding of early adolescent development with special attention to young adolescents' social relationships and self-awareness, greater emphasis on responding to cultural and language diversity, more coverage of teacher-based guidance, and more coverage of how to involve parents/family members and community resources in young adolescents' schooling
2	Greater variety of developmentally responsive teaching and assessment techniques, especially cooperative learning, interdisciplinary curriculum and team teaching, student exhibitions, and portfolios
3	Middle grades teacher education should expose first and second year preservice middle grades teachers to extensive experiences in effective and successful middle grades schools with a diversity of young adolescents

Source: Adapted from *Growing Pains: The Making of America's Middle School Teachers* by P. Scales and C. K. McEwin, 1994, Columbus, OH: National Middle School Association and the Center for Early Adolescence.

middle level, the more likely they are to report their program was highly comprehensive. Moreover, the greater the number of courses devoted to the middle level, the more favorably respondents rated their middle level preparation programs" (p. 32).

Scales and McEwin used the results of their study (1994), as well as other studies from the Center for Early Adolescence (Scales, 1992), to draw a series of recommendations for middle grades teacher education programs. The recommendations are detailed in Table 18.6.

The trend toward greater appreciation for the uniqueness of the middle level for students and for teacher training promoted greater study of the elements of appropriate teacher training programs. The challenge during the coming years is to ensure that states, through certification requirements, recognize the value of such training, and that higher education develops and implements programs to provide the needed teacher training.

ISSUES AND TRENDS

Although there has emerged a greater understanding of the school in the middle and the needs for distinct preparation for those who teach at that level, other issues also must be addressed. This section discusses several of the issues. It is by no means inclusive of all of the areas in which improvements must be made in middle level teacher preparation.

Pedagogy

Generalist versus Specialist The role of the middle level teacher necessitates a shift in thinking for many teachers, particularly those who have been extensively prepared in secondary education. A focus on the whole student, on interdisciplinary

TABLE 18.6. Recommendations for Improved Middle Grades Teacher Education Programs

1. Be conducted at the school site as much as possible and involve considerable collaboration between middle schools and universities (with teachers providing continuing education for college faculty, with codesigned and cotaught courses) and within universities (across schools and departments)
2. Be staffed with faculty who model the techniques they expect preservice teachers to learn, especially interdisciplinary/integrative curriculum, cooperative learning, teacher-based guidance/advisor-advisee, and portfolio/exhibition assessment approaches
3. Provide resources for ongoing faculty development, including regular contact with and teaching young adolescents
4. Enable their students to engage in fieldwork in the first and second years of an undergraduate program
5. Ensure that students' fieldwork includes a variety of community settings young adolescents use in addition to middle schools
6. Maintain a core library of resources teacher educators considered essential for middle grades teacher preparation
7. Provide faculty and students with experiences of systems responding to young adolescents' characteristics, both communities/neighborhoods and restructuring schools
8. Provide extensive student experiences in how to involve families and community resources with middle schools
9. Include extensive opportunities to learn about being an advisor in a teacher-based guidance program, interdisciplinary teaming, and responding to students' cultural and language diversity
10. Ensure students acquire a comprehensive understanding of young adolescent social relationships and self-awareness concerns, especially health and sexuality

Source: From *Growing Pains: The Making of America's Middle School Teachers* by P. Scales and C. K. McEwin, 1994, Columbus, OH: National Middle School Association and the Center for Early Adolescence.

curriculum, and on the developmental needs of the student requires that teachers make a shift from seeing themselves as content specialists, interested solely in one particular subject, to that of curriculum generalists, with a strong background in one content area and on understanding of more than one field of teaching. Teachers must be generalists who understand the interrelationships between and among many curricula.

The middle level teacher is neither elementary nor high school. Therein lies the challenge. Teachers must be prepared to be knowledgeable both about children (Alexander & McEwin, 1988; McEwin & Thomason, 1989) and knowledgeable about content (Johnston et al., 1985; NMSA, 1986). The balance of the two, complemented by an understanding of the best instructional practice, ensures that the middle level teacher is both a generalist and a specialist.

Grouping Practices One of the most persistent issues in middle level education is that of grouping students for instruction. On the surface, grouping students seems to align itself with the essence of middle level education—a focus on the student's developmental needs. The range of developmental differences among middle level students seems to demand some method of sorting students to ensure appropriate instruction. Between class ability grouping, commonly called "tracking," is prevalent

in middle level schools. NASSP's recent study found that 69% of middle level schools group students into specific classes by academic ability (Valentine et al., 1993). Proponents of tracking cite the benefits to students and teachers of such an organization.

Yet, the benefits of tracking are often not those stated by its proponents. Oakes (1985) described problems with tracking systems. The problems include the overreliance on test scores to distinguish differences between students and the fact that poor and minority students are too often overrepresented in the lowest tracks.

In a study of more than 150 of "reputedly some of the nation's best middle schools" George (1988) found that nearly all of the respondents organized their schools into "heterogeneously-grouped interdisciplinary teams" and each of the teams then reflected the heterogeneity of the school in terms of gender, ethnicity, socioeconomic status, and ability. Within the teams teachers then were able to group and regroup students for specific instruction when appropriate. This reduced one of the impacts of a tracking system, sorting students into groups that remain together for the majority of the school day.

A second finding of the study was that one third of the schools reject tracking except for certain students with identified needs (e.g., gifted, special education). Among the other two thirds of the schools, the practice was to group students within the team, most often for reading and mathematics (George, 1988).

As middle level educators struggle with the appropriate approach to the grouping question, it becomes increasingly clear that opportunities for continued professional growth, for sharing of best practices and experiences, and for the opportunity to rethink current practice are essential.

Curriculum Development Significant questions regarding the middle level curriculum continue to be raised. Beane (1993) stated that "the dominant version of the middle school has two major features, the separate subject approach and separate programs for different purposes" (p. 12). He accurately described that organizing into interdisciplinary teams by itself does not ensure an interdisciplinary curriculum. Erb (1991) stated that "the preparation of new middle grades teachers to understand their role in the development and execution of middle grades curriculum must be part of the solution to this lingering problem" (p. 25).

The integration of learning is a key emphasis at the middle level. "Curriculum should not be developed solely to increase student intelligence" (Toepfer et al., 1993, p. 8). Naturally, high academic standards are critical to the success of any middle level curriculum; however, the curriculum serves other important functions. It should be exploratory and help early adolescents study and understand current living and learning needs and have an impact on future learning decisions. It should also provide opportunities for social interaction, provide differentiation based on student needs, help students to "learn how to learn," and provide critical links with the elementary and high school programs (Toepfer et al., 1993).

Beane proposed a model to reconceptualize the middle level curriculum through a blending of concern for adolescent development with current issues and topics of interest to the early adolescent. Students become active participants in determining the course of their learning by identifying the themes that permeate their lives. This focus is critical because "if the curriculum is to be authentically engaging, then the actual themes used in any particular school must reflect as closely as possible the concerns of early adolescents in that school" (Beane, 1993, p. 87).

The curriculum questions lie at the heart of the middle level school. The espoused theory for the middle level school is built on its responsiveness to early adolescent development. If this is the case then the curriculum as one of the most powerful components of the school setting must also be reformulated to take into account early adolescent development.

Multicultural Education A major issue in education is the trend toward the inclusiveness of ethnic and cultural minorities in the curriculum of the schools; however, this trend has been accompanied by concern from traditionalists who fear the dilution of Western educational standards. James Banks (1993) suggested that such stress will continue as long as several misconceptions regarding multicultural education remain. These myths include the belief that "multicultural education is for the others," the minorities, the poor, and the victimized. Multicultural education must be seen not as the study of others, but as the study of us.

A second myth that must be set aside is that "multicultural education is opposed to the Western tradition." "Multicultural education is not opposed to the West, its advocates do demand that the truth about the West be told, that its debt to people of color and women be recognized and included in the curriculum, and that the discrepancies between the ideals of freedom and equality and the realities of racism and sexism be taught to students" (Banks, 1993, p. 24). Multicultural education promotes greater understanding and promotes study of the "relationship between human values, knowledge, and action" (Banks, 1993, p. 24).

Another of the myths to be addressed is that "multicultural education will divide the nation." The traditional role of schools in the assimilation of ethnic and cultural minorities is being redefined. Multicultural education is not about division but about greater appreciation for diversity within the whole. Diversity in background, thinking, and approach builds strength. The value of greater inclusiveness should be seen as a natural extension of the traditions of American society.

American education is being reshaped by forces beyond the walls of the school. Students are increasingly diverse and the role of all schools is to accept those students, to work with them and their families in order to address their needs, and to ensure that all students are provided with the knowledge and skills to be successful contributing members of society. Multicultural education is an essential component of the education response.

RELATIONSHIPS WITH FAMILIES AND THE COMMUNITY

As noted earlier, the demographics of American society are changing significantly. The composition and size of the household have changed. In fact, the definition of a family is a topic of debate in some quarters of society.

For schools, the family, whatever the definition, is a critical link in the education of children. A continuing issue for the middle level teacher is developing an understanding of American families and designing specific strategies to engage families in the educational process.

The Carnegie Council on Adolescent Development (1989) affirmed the importance of families when it recommended that one of the essential elements of transforming the middle level schools was to "reengage families in the education of young adolescents" (p. 9). Carnegie recommended that families be provided meaningful roles in school governance, that communication with families be enhanced, and that families be provided opportunities to "support the learning process at home and at school" (p. 9).

Developing and implementing strategies to actively engage families in schooling is essential. Johnston (1990) suggested that schools must first raise their awareness of "the incredible diversity that exists in family composition in the school and the effects that standard school practices might have on those nontraditional families" (p. 25). This awareness serves as a precursor to examining every school policy and practice as to its impact on families.

Further recommendations include rethinking the role of school. Such an examination focused on providing services to "customers" provides structure for the analysis of traditional programs and practices. The role of good communication is essential in successfully engaging families. Myers and Monson (1992) offered several practical communication strategies, including the use of multiple forms of communication, conducting events throughout the year and at times convenient to families, and encouraging personal notes and telephone calls. Parents value information about their children. School communication must clearly show how the information affects their children and must reflect a balanced perspective. "Teachers and school officials must be willing to look for praiseworthy behavior and take the time to share it with parents" (Johnston, 1990, p. 30).

The parents' role in school governance is of equal importance. Through the use of school advisory groups or school-based management committees, it is possible for parents to have a more active role in the life of the school. Middle level teachers should welcome such involvement because it will strengthen the bond between the family and the school and provide potential for a more focused agenda for the early adolescent.

Understanding and working with families is critical for middle level teachers. Teachers must be open to the diversity in family composition and creative in the strategies used to engage all parents in the education of their children.

PROFESSIONAL DEVELOPMENT OF TEACHERS

Recruitment of Teachers

Education must recruit and retain the best and the brightest. Although this goal is often stated, it is countered by actions that denigrate the role of the teacher and reinforce the notion that those with the most talent do something other than teach.

It is critical that colleges and universities take proactive steps to ensure that they recruit students to their education programs just as they recruit students for other university activities. Education students must be supported by the staff, facilities, books, and equipment that ensure that they receive training and preparation comparable to other programs.

Essential to this effort are initiatives to recruit and retain students who reflect the ethnic and cultural diversity of our nation. The changing demography of the nation's schools cries out for greater representation among the teaching staff from diverse populations. Greater inclusiveness among the teaching staff has benefits for students and other staff. The power of role models is well documented; however, the impact of role models is equally important on other teaching staff. The value of diverse perspectives regarding students and their learning, the knowledge that can be gained from diversity, and the modeling of democratic principles is essential to the functioning of an American school. It is imperative that greater attention be paid to the recruitment and retention of teachers, especially those of diverse backgrounds.

Induction and Socialization of New Teachers

Equally important to the ongoing health of a school is concern for the way in which new teachers are socialized into a school. Too often the new teacher receives subtle or sometimes not so subtle messages that they should not "change the way we do things around here."

Attention must be given to the school as a social system or culture. The ways in which individuals interact and relate to one another have powerful impacts on their achievement. The culture of the school—the norms, beliefs, and patterns of behavior—influences the behavior of those who work in the school (Johnston, 1987). "Values are the bedrock of any institution. They articulate the essence of the organization's philosophy about how it goes about achieving success. They provide sense of common direction and guidelines for everyday behavior. Most importantly, values tell what your organization stands for . . . what it thinks is important" (p. 81).

Particular attention should be paid to the induction and socialization of new teachers. Schools should establish and nurture efforts to support new teachers both in implementing all that they have learned and in challenging some of the accepted practices. Opportunities should be provided for new teachers to meet and discuss their practices, to engage in collegial discussion regarding teaching strategies and procedures, and to reflect on their own professional growth. The spirit of collaboration, of collegial support, is essential. New teachers must not be isolated to find their own way.

New teachers should also be encouraged to take risks on behalf of student achievement and should be supported in these efforts. Schools should create heroes out of those who ask critical questions, challenge the norms, and trample some of the established practices and procedures.

Schools should also talk about success in terms of learning, growing, and modifying past practice. Such efforts should become accepted, valued, and prized because of the positive potential to have an impact on students. The talk of the school must be innovation and change, not the status quo.

Above all, the middle level school should be a caring environment not only for students but for the adults as well. The emphasis on teaming and collaborative efforts should be supported and carry over into the interpersonal relationships among the staff. New teachers should be supported and their efforts valued. Risk taking should be encouraged. Compassion and caring should be prized. Above all, concern for students and their growth and learning should become the accepted indicator of excellence.

There is no greater endeavor than that of challenging the status quo on behalf of improved education for students. New teachers must be encouraged to engage in this effort and assured of some support as they embark on the venture.

Continuing Professional Development

The lack of certification requirements complemented by the lack of middle level teacher preparation programs has resulted in middle level schools staffed primarily by teachers prepared to teach at either the elementary or the high school. NASSP found that only 11% of the teachers in their sampled schools held middle level certification (Valentine et al., 1993). Epstein and Mac Iver (1990) found that "middle schools tend to have a more 'balanced portfolio' of teachers—some elementary (44%) and some secondary (53%)" (p. 59). Alexander and McEwin (1989) found that more than 61% of the sampled schools reported that less than 25% of the staff had specific middle level preparation.

Therein lies a major problem in middle level education— the need for the continuing professional growth of teachers. Individual schools and districts are struggling to develop strategies for providing their staff with the knowledge and skills necessary to support a reformed middle grades program. The strategies vary. Valentine et al. found that the most frequently reported program for preparing teachers at middle level schools was in-service programs. More than 73% of the schools reported use of this option (Valentine et al., 1993). More than 40% reported that the staff had no special preparation to teach at the middle level. Other reported procedures included participation in university courses and personal study.

It is imperative that schools develop strategies for the continuing professional growth of all staff. Responsiveness requires ongoing training. Even with an increasing number of staff trained and certified for the middle level, it will be essential to provide opportunities for continued growth.

EXTERNAL INFLUENCES

Conflicting State Initiatives

Across the nation, governors, state departments of education, and superintendents of public instruction are proposing initiatives designed to improve the quality of education and to increase accountability of educators. Often the proposals conflict not only with the stated goals of individual schools but also too often with each other. Two examples illustrate the dilemma.

In some states teachers are required to pass either the National Teacher Exam or some other measure of teacher competence to be certified. Success on such tests requires years of professional preparation in both the pedagogy of teaching and the content of the area of expertise. At the same time, state leaders may suggest procedures to provide alternative certification to those who have no formal training in the field of education. This conflict between the espoused goal of high standards for teacher preparation and easier certification for those without the pedagogical background creates a dilemma for schools. This is no more apparent than at the middle level where it is critical to have an understanding of early adolescent development and a repertoire of instructional skills suited to the early adolescent, in addition to knowledge and background in an academic discipline.

Another example centers on the development of state-defined core curriculum standards. Many who cry out for heightened "academic" standards reject the notion of standards that address critical developmental issues involving decision making, problem solving, and self-concept. Often these same people decry the poor choices that young people make regarding substance abuse, use of weapons, and problem-solving techniques. On the one hand they demand action to address critical issues, and on the other hand they systematically limit the initiatives that schools may use to educate and address the concerns.

Such conflicts between state initiatives place schools and teachers in the awkward position of either using tools that may not be appropriate or of having tools denied that might be useful. The political agenda that arises from conflicting state initiatives will continue to be a hurdle that especially middle level educators will need to overcome.

CONCLUSION

The middle level student has personal and educational needs that are distinct from those of students at either elementary or high school. These unique needs require a unique response from educators. Therein lies the power of the middle level school—a school focused on serving the distinctive needs of students in the middle. The school in the middle must assume the dual role of accepting adolescents for whom they are and, at the same time, creating a structure and climate that ensures that they may become all that they can be.

Around the nation the call continues for greater accountability from the schools and those who work in them. Greater accountability is essential, that is, accountability to the students. At no level of the educational continuum is this of greater importance than at the middle level. It is critical that every constituent group—teachers, schools, districts, states, and colleges and universities—examine both the role of the teacher and the ongoing training and preparation of that teacher.

Accountability to students for their academic achievement, for their sense of belonging and self-esteem, for their acceptance as valued members of the community, and for their ability to live and work in an ever-changing society is essential. The middle level school is well positioned to accept this high level of accountability. It is critical that an investment be made in the preparation of those educators who will serve such a vital role.

References

Albert, J. L. (1993, June 24). USA's changing households. *USA Today*, p. 3A.

Alexander, W., & McEwin, C. K. (1988). *Preparing to teach at the middle level*. Columbus, OH: National Middle School Association.

Alexander, W., & McEwin, C. K. (1989). *Schools in the middle: Status and progress*. Columbus, OH: National Middle School Association.

Alexander, W., Williams, E., Compton, M., Hines, V., Prescott, D., & Kealy, R. (1969). *The emergent middle school*. New York: Holt, Rinehart and Winston.

Arhar, J. (1992). Enhancing students' feelings of school membership: What principals can do. *Schools in the Middle*, *1*(3), 12–16.

Arhar, J., Johnston, J. H., & Markle, G. (1988). The effects of teaming and other collaborative arrangements. *Middle School Journal*, *19*(4), 22–25.

Arhar, J., Johnston, J. H., & Markle, G. (1989). The effects of teaming on students. *Middle School Journal*, *20*(3), 24–27.

Arnold, J. (1991). The revolution in middle school organization. *Momentum*, *22*(2), 20–24.

Banks, J. (1993). Multicultural education: Development, dimensions, and challenges. *Phi Delta Kappan*, *75*(1), 22–28.

Beane, J. (1993). *A middle school curriculum: From rhetoric to reality* (2nd ed.). Columbus, OH: National Middle School Association.

Bergmann, S., & Baxter, J. (1983). Building a guidance program and advisory concept for early adolescents. *NASSP Bulletin*, *67*(463), 49–55.

Carnegie Council on Adolescent Development. (1989). *Turning points: Preparing American youth for the 21st century*. New York: Author.

Cawelti, G. (1988). Middle schools a better match with early adolescent needs, ASCD survey finds. *ASCD Curriculum Update*, November, 1–12.

Children's Defense Fund. (1991). *The state of America's children*. Washington, DC: Author.

Clark, S., & Clark, D. (1994). *Restructuring the middle level school: Implications for school leaders*. Albany: State University of New York Press.

Crime among juveniles a growing problem. (1993, October 29). *USA Today*, p. 6A.

Eichhorn, D. (1966). *The middle school*. New York: Center for Applied Research in Education.

Epstein, J. (1990). What matters in the middle grades—Grade span or practices? *Phi Delta Kappan*, *71*(6), 438–444.

Epstein, J., & Mac Iver, D. (1990). *Education in the middle grades: Overview of national practices and trends*. Columbus, OH: National Middle School Association.

Erb, T. (1991). Preparing prospective middle grades teachers to understand the curriculum. *Middle School Journal*, *23*(3), 24–28.

Garvin, J. (1986, March). Common denominators in effective middle schools. *Schools in the Middle*, 1–8.

George, P. (1988). Tracking and ability grouping: Which way for the middle school? *Middle School Journal*, *20*(1), 21–28.

George, P., & Alexander, W. (1993). *The exemplary middle school* (2nd ed.). Orlando, FL: Harcourt, Brace, Jovanovich.

George, P., & Oldaker, L. (1985). *Evidence for the middle school*. Columbus, OH: National Middle School Association.

Johnston, J. H. (1987). Values, culture, and the effective school. *NASSP Bulletin, 71*(497), 79–88.

Johnston, J. H.. (1990). *The new American family and the school.* Columbus, OH: National Middle School Association.

Johnston, J. H., Arth, A., Lounsbury, J., & Toepfer, C. (1985). *An agenda for excellence at the middle level.* Reston, VA: National Association of Secondary School Principals.

Johnston, J. H., & Markle, G. (1986). *What research says to the middle level practitioner.* Columbus, OH: National Middle School Association.

Lake, S. (1989a). *Interdisciplinary team organization in the middle level school.* Sacramento: California League of Middle Schools.

Lake, S. (1989b). *Supporting middle level students through counseling and teacher advisor programs.* Sacramento: California League of Middle Schools.

Lipsitz, J. (1984). *Successful schools for young adolescents.* New Brunswick, NJ: Transaction Books.

Lounsbury, J. (1984). *Middle school education: As I see it.* Columbus, OH: National Middle School Association.

Lounsbury, J. (1991). *As I see it.* Columbus, OH: National Middle School Association.

Lounsbury, J. (1992). Perspectives on the middle school movement. In J. Irvin (Ed.), *Transforming schools for middle level students: Perspectives and possibilities* (pp. 3–15). Needham Heights, MA: Allyn & Bacon.

Mac Iver, D. (1990). Meeting the needs of young adolescents: Advisory groups, interdisciplinary teams and school transition programs. *Phi Delta Kappan, 71*(6), 458–464.

Mac Iver, D., & Epstein, J. (1991). Responsive practices in the middle grades: Teacher teams, advisory groups, remedial instruction, and school transition programs. *American Journal of Education, 99*(4), 587–622.

McEwin, C. K., Dickinson, T. S., & Jenkins, D. M. (in press). *America's middle schools: Programs and practices—A 25 year perspective.* Columbus, OH: National Middle School Association.

McEwin, C. K., & Thomason, J. (1989). *Who they are, how they teach: Early adolescents & their teachers.* Columbus, OH: National Middle School Association.

Milgram, J. (1992). A portrait of diversity: The middle level student. In J. Irvin (Ed.), *Transforming schools for middle level students: Perspectives and possibilities* (pp. 16–27). Needham Heights, MA: Allyn & Bacon.

Myers, J., & Monson, L. (1992). *Involving families.* Columbus, OH: National Middle School Association.

National Middle School Association (NMSA). (1982). *This we believe.* Columbus, OH: Author.

National Middle School Association (NMSA). (1986). *Professional certification and preparation for the middle level: A position paper of National Middle School Association.* Columbus, OH: Author.

National Middle School Association (NMSA). (1991). *NMSA curriculum guidelines.* Columbus, OH: Author.

Nielsen, L. (1991). *Adolescence—A contemporary view.* Orlando, FL: Harcourt, Brace, Jovanovich.

Number of firearm and firearm related deaths. (1993, June 3). *USA Today,* p. 3A.

Oakes, J. (1985). *Keeping track: How schools structure inequality.* New Haven, CT: Yale University Press.

Scales, P. (1991). *A portrait of young adolescents in the 1990s: Implications for promoting healthy growth and development.* Carrboro, NC: Center for Early Adolescence.

Scales, P. (1992). *Windows of opportunity: Improving middle grades teacher preparation.* Carrboro, NC: Center for Early Adolescence.

Scales, P., & McEwin, C. K. (1994). *Growing pains: The making of America's middle school teachers.* Columbus, OH: National Middle School Association and the Center for Early Adolescence.

Toepfer, C., Arth, A., Bergmann, S., Brough, J., Clark, D., Johnston, J., & Kanthak, L. (1993). *Achieving excellence through the middle level curriculum.* Reston, VA: National Association of Secondary School Principals.

U.S. Department of Education. (1990). *A profile of the American eighth grader.* Washington, DC: Author.

Valentine, J. W., Clark, D. C., Irvin, J. L., Keefe, J. W., & Melton, G. (1993). *Leadership in middle level education: A national survey of middle level leaders and schools* (Vol. 1). Reston, VA: National Association of Secondary School Principals.

Valentine, J., & Mogar, D. (1992). Middle level certification—An encouraging evolution. *Middle School Journal, 24*(2), 36–43.

·19·

SECONDARY EDUCATION

Vito Perrone

HARVARD GRADUATE SCHOOL OF EDUCATION

Rob Traver

HARVARD GRADUATE SCHOOL OF EDUCATION

This chapter expresses a point of view about the secondary teacher education material that was reviewed. As a result, it goes beyond the usual gathering, sorting, and summarizing of relevant research to make an argument about how research on secondary teacher education relates to the school reform movement that is at work throughout the United States.

There are several reasons why the review appears in this particular expository form. First, presenting the work in such a manner makes more explicit the bias brought to the kinds of reviews that are assembled. Some materials were chosen for review, but certainly not all that were possible. In the process of making choices, the authors acknowledge that others might have made different selections. Second, it appears to the authors that many secondary teacher education experiences do not prepare secondary teacher education candidates to think about and contribute to the school reform movement that is at work in one way or another in most places where they will teach. This concern so permeated this examination of recent research that it was decided to let this concern motivate the chapter. Third, by purposefully adopting such a form for the chapter, the authors thought it might help signal the reader to their basic stance about the nature of relevant research.

WHAT COUNTS AS RESEARCH?

This chapter takes a broad view of the meaning of research. It goes beyond traditional empirical studies, whether qualitative or quantitative. Rigorous thinking of all kinds, some more speculative, some more idiosyncratic, has contributed a great deal to what is known and needs to be known, essentially taken

account of, for teaching effectively at the secondary level. For example, a secondary student teacher's journal, a cooperating teacher's evaluation, and a state-level administrator's report can and do make valuable statements about secondary teacher education. In addition, there are many ongoing educational projects that are not the subject of rigorous evaluation or scholarly analysis but, nonetheless, contribute significantly to the discourse underlying the central question that guides this review.

CENTRAL QUESTION

What needs to be taken account of in the preparation of teachers for secondary schools as these schools are currently evolving? What kinds of attitudes, knowledge, and skills must be formed and mastered to contribute successfully to contemporary American high school reform? Many of the chapters in this handbook touch upon a number of germane, even closely related issues and problems, particularly those relating to various subject fields, classroom management, diversity, and equity. They are obviously complementary. It is the purpose of this chapter to make explicit the *need* to link directly secondary teacher education and high school reform. In some respects, of course, this is a long-standing Deweyan notion of the need to prepare teachers for schools as they *could* be and not for what they necessarily are or have been. The largest possibilities that can be imagined must, within this formulation, be put forward.

John Goodlad, writing in *Educational Leadership* (1991), posed as a central question: "What about new teachers? Are they coming out of enlightened teacher education programs with the skills to manage classrooms as well as the ability to

The authors wish to acknowledge the research assistance of Anne L. Saks and the manuscript preparation assistance of Helen L. Spencer.

address the total array of problems and issues they will likely face in school renewal?" He continued, "As a matter of strange and puzzling fact, educators throughout this century have failed to join the reform of schools" (p. 4). Goodlad's challenge is critical to the improvement of schools and of teacher education programs as well.

In regard to the foregoing, Robert A. Levin (1990) described the teacher education curriculum as fragmented and lacking in continuity. Essentially, he noted in his research that students simply do not leave teacher education programs able to see clearly enough the big picture of schools as social institutions with various forces and factors constantly affecting their capacity to function and govern. Teaching, he suggested, is understood simply as something done with subject matter to kids in classrooms. Teaching must obviously be more than this. Second, he noted, the certification specialization process leads students and faculty to offer and follow programs of study that leave little time for collaboration across subject fields and no time to compare possibilities for constructing the best schools possible. A collaborative climate in schools is clearly critical. Gaining related experience in preservice teacher education would surely be helpful.

In relation to high school reform, several questions need to be posed. A critical first question might be: What is a high school? Any teacher education program designed to prepare secondary teachers must address this question and several related ones. What is the purpose of a high school? How did it come to look the way it does? How well does it work? What are the opportunities for and barriers to improvement? These kinds of questions suggest, of course, the need for those preparing for teaching to have a reasonable grasp of the history of secondary schooling, how definitions of purpose have evolved, what earlier reform agendas have been and what motivated them, how the current curriculum formulations were developed, and the like (Kliebard, 1989; Lazerson et al., 1985; Perrone, 1991a).

Secondary schools are, for example, relatively recent in their development. Moreover, their purposes in the twentieth century have been quite different from those of the nineteenth century (Cremin, 1961; Krug, 1964). As a result, formulations about what constitutes a good high school have changed over the past 100 years, even over the past decade. It is interesting to note, in this regard, how fully the large comprehensive high school that James Conant (1959) extolled in the 1950s became over several subsequent decades *the* model of what high schools at their best are supposed to be like. It even became the conventional wisdom to view a school with 300 courses as necessarily better than a school with 30 courses. Ted Sizer (1984, 1992), who was a researcher for Conant, now praises in contrast, and with growing support, the virtues of small schools with few courses and with teachers who view themselves first as generalists and who seek most of all to help young people use their minds well. Central Park East Secondary School, the most celebrated of Sizer's Coalition of Essential Schools, for example, has no interest in being comprehensive or larger than 75 students per grade level. Its curriculum is essentially two interdisciplinary courses that all the students take (Meier, 1987).

There are, in addition, other reform directions involving increased performance requirements for graduation, commu-

nity service, apprenticeship, specialized high schools, inclusion of all students (special and regular), multiculturalism, and schools of choice. Most have pedagogical and curricular implications that relate in one way or another to teacher education preparation.

As noted, this chapter begins with a view that secondary schools are undergoing changes. These various changes in purpose, structures, academic content, and relationships to the world surrounding them reflect larger societal issues, such as a civic culture in need of higher levels of informed participation; a burgeoning service economy with its demand for a technologically skilled and problem-solving work force; a more pluralistic student population linguistically, racially, and culturally; and a growing belief that we are losing our sense of community and basic civility. They also reflect changing views about the nature of the various disciplines and of knowledge itself. In addition, of course, the belief that secondary schools are struggling as educational institutions keeps the pressure for change omnipresent. Students preparing for teaching must take these various factors motivating change into account.

RESPONSES TO THE CENTRAL QUESTION

There are several issues and problems that arise within the American high school as it undergoes change that influences practice. The foremost include the following:

1. What dominates the lives and contexts of adolescent learners?
2. What should students be learning?
3. How should students be learning?
4. How should students be evaluated?
5. What is the context and community of schools?
6. How do new teachers grow professionally?

This review is organized around the secondary teacher education response to these questions.

The Lives and Contexts of Adolescent Learners

There are differences and similarities throughout the world. The extraordinary changing demographics of school populations, mostly the result of unprecedented levels of immigration from Haiti, Central America, Mexico, and Southeast Asia, make this abundantly clear. Students of color now comprise close to 30% of the school population, and this percentage is expected to grow substantially over the next several decades. During the 1980s, half the nation's population growth took place in the states of California, Texas, and Florida. Hawaii, New Mexico, California, and the District of Columbia are now made up of more than 50% traditional minority groups. Texas, Mississippi, Louisiana, and Arizona are above 40% (Hodgkinson & Outtz, 1992). Teachers will inevitably face these demographic changes and must embrace them if they are to remain true to the fundamental challenge of American schools: to provide a high quality education for all students that can ensure personal and community well being, ongoing opportunities for learning, economic stability, and growth in democracy.

The major response to these demographic changes has been multiculturalism, that is, support for curriculum inclusion, efforts to incorporate diverse cultural experiences into schools and classrooms, and increasing the diversity of the teaching profession, among others. The desire to make the necessary reforms is apparent in the redesign of many teacher education programs and in the plethora of professional development workshops and course offerings. Unfortunately, the practice in the schools has been less constructive than desired (Banks, 1991; Banks & Banks, 1993), indicating the great difficulty faced by teacher educators hoping to make easy inroads. An example from Los Angeles is instructive in this regard. One hundred and ten teacher education students in the Los Angeles Unified School District (McDiarmid, 1992) experienced a 15-session Multicultural Week training program. A series of questionnaires were administered at various points and a more in-depth follow-up was made of 12 participants. The results revealed well a central conundrum of multiculturalism. For example, the point of the program was to help teachers see students as individuals; yet, the instruction and discussions tended to focus on membership in one or another group—African Americans, Asians, Hispanics, and so forth. Another major result was that the teachers in training (and this would probably be the case with most other people for that matter) often followed their training by replacing a description of a behavior (e.g., he is acting shyly) with a label for that person (e.g., he is shy). Race was played out similarly. Such experiences are fairly typical.

It is increasingly common for teacher education candidates to take a required course in multicultural education. Although taking a course or two is a reasonable thing to do, it clearly is not sufficient. One wonders whether any short-term *classroom* experience, however intense, does more than just sensitize teachers to the "proper" way to talk about multiculturalism.

Cochran-Smith and Lytle (1992, 1993) prescribed, in addition to courses, action research to engage preservice teachers in the problematics of cultural diversity. Such a direction seems useful as it pushes teachers toward an understanding of diversity in practice. Those entering teaching should learn various procedures for gaining information about those cultural and racial communities represented in their classes, such as home visits, conferring with community members, talking with parents, consulting with various minority teachers, and observing students in and out of school.

Villegas (1991) noted, in this regard, "It seems clear from the research that unless teachers learn to integrate the cultural patterns of minority communities into their teaching, the failure of schools to educate students from those communities will continue" (p. 32). Those who promote this idea of culturally responsive pedagogy, an idea that goes beyond multiculturalism as sensitivity, accept the belief that system inequalities exist in the schools and need to be actively addressed. Such a view has considerable support (Delpit, 1988; Levin, 1987; Oakes, 1985; Stage, 1989; Villegas & Watts, 1991).

In relation to the growing diversity of students within the schools and the need to promote an antiracism ethic, Banks's (1991) framework that is constructed around needed attitudes, skills, and behaviors is helpful. Among the *skills* those preparing for teaching need, he noted, are ways of dealing with complex social interactions, social inequities, and collaboration. In rela-

tion to attitudes, he stressed that new teachers need to understand their own prejudices and begin to develop strategies for dealing with them. Among the behaviors are a consciousness about becoming responsible role models and agents of resocialization. Approaching preparation for multiculturalism in these terms does not suggest a single course but consciousness about multiculturalism in all courses. This infusion approach is attractive but difficult to sustain.

Nordhoff and Kleinfeld (1993) offered an infusion model that is promising. They reported on their research on the Teachers for Alaska Program, which focuses prospective secondary teachers on the following: (1) attending to multicultural classrooms and community contexts; (2) designing instruction to make connections between academic content matters and diverse students' backgrounds; and (3) learning how to learn from students, communities, and practical experience. In a sense, this parallels the work of Cochran-Smith and Lytle (1990). Nordhoff and Kleinfeld argued that this more integrated departure from what is typically offered to preservice secondary teachers is desirable and effective in preparing teachers for multicultural classrooms.

Matters of diversity also show up as a major concern in various state reform efforts. Georgia's Quality Basic Education Act (Wohlstetter, 1994), for example, requires a K–12 values education curriculum that focuses on citizenship, respect for others, altruism, integrity, and respect for self. Alongside such requirements, the Professional Standards Commission was made responsible for determining ways of working these requirements into teacher certification. California has taken the national lead in responding to demographic changes by developing more inclusive curricula through its curriculum frameworks and its textbook selection process. Although not built into teacher credentialing, teacher education programs in California are expected to take into account the changing demographic conditions and the state's more inclusive view of curriculum. Furthermore, the public policy concern in California is for increasing the number of teachers representative of the new populations. This effort has been hampered, however, by the fact that the pass rates for Asians, African Americans, and Hispanics are below Caucasian rates on the California Basic Education Skills Test (Guthrie et al., 1991). Means other than basic skills tests need to be developed if the diversification of the teacher population is to reach desired levels (Madaus, 1980).

A second major category for diversity is special education. Like so many educational reforms, economic belt tightening as well as changing views about what constitutes democratic practice are forcing states and school districts to reconsider the means for achieving the goals of special education (PL 94-142, 1975). Inclusion, or SPED inclusion as it is often called, readmits many special education students to regular education classrooms. This change highlights a number of instructional issues, such as how best to treat mixed ability/motivated students and how to work best with a second teaching professional in the classroom or in some form of consulting relationship. In Massachusetts, this concern has led to specific special education requirements for secondary teacher education programs, including some clinical responsibilities in relation to special education students (Massachusetts Department of Education, 1993). Such requirements are becoming more common, but the design of appropriate programs continues to be problematic. The most common efforts respond to matters of literacy, such as helping students enter a text, working with new words, and cooperative learning around language. Miller (1991) provided an example of an effort to merge special education and English education as a means of helping preservice teachers of English learn to implement English instruction with students with *and* without disabilities. Miller's research, as expected, indicated that students who participated in the integrated project improved their special education and English teaching skills.

As implied, special education inclusion is also related to growing interest in heterogeneous classrooms and the deliberate move away from the tracking that has come to pervade American secondary schools. The belief has been that separating students by skill, intelligence, interest, and gift, and moving toward greater classroom homogeneity, makes teaching easier and learning more productive. Even as most secondary schools track in some form, tracking has come under serious attack as it is increasingly being seen as inequitable, leaving most students with a limited education (Oakes, 1985; Wheelock, 1992). Current research has moved the concern about tracking to a concern about "the distribution of learning opportunities and students' day to day school experiences" (Oakes, 1992, p. 12). Those who argue for small schools, for example, do so with the understanding that pressures for separating students decline. More research on how to overcome the various barriers to detracking is still necessary. Without greater understanding here the broad agenda around school reform will be difficult to sustain.

The Coalition of Essential Schools addresses concerns about heterogeneity through a particular orientation toward student individuality (Sizer, 1989). Put simply, a school's goals are expected to apply to all students, although the path to the goals are understood to vary as the students themselves vary. The implication is that school practice should be tailored to meet the needs of every student, group, or class of adolescents. As a way of providing the personalization the foregoing suggests, Sizer has established the goal that no teacher have direct responsibility for more than 80 students (Coalition of Essential Schools, 1984). To capitalize on personalization, decisions about the course of study, the use of time, and the choice of teaching materials and specific pedagogies are also unreservedly placed in the hands of the principal and staff of a school. Although not all schools are following the coalition's lead, interest in school-site decision making, especially about matters of curriculum, teaching, and learning is growing rapidly.

Another contextual issue that needs to be accounted for is the difficulty of growing up in this society. Those in the schools argue that many circumstances are now more complex. They are likely correct. Many of the social support systems for young people have deteriorated and the effects of drugs, alcohol, teen pregnancy, and violence have grown large. Growing up has always had its complexities, but it may be a far more difficult period of passage today. Not to be closer to the circumstances of young people's lives is detrimental to teachers.

In this regard, Kagan and Tippins (1991) noted that secondary teacher education candidates approach student teaching with many faulty assumptions about the students. They concluded that this stems in large measure from limited prestudent teaching clinical experiences. This research also indicates that preservice teachers are too far removed from the contexts of their students' lives, making, as a result, too many questionable generalizations. Their need for more focused observations, in and out of classrooms, the reading and preparation of more intense descriptions of individual students, and more intense personal interactions seems great. Research (Perrone & Jacobs, 1993) in the Harvard master's level preservice Teacher Education Programs, which have extensive prestudent teaching experiences, found that preservice students who are directed to study individual students and community contexts and carefully describe their observations through systematic journal writing make sophisticated analyses of students and their learning. Bullough (1993) gave added credence to this understanding, reaching similar results. Drawing on insights from the use of journals and portfolios from 20 preservice secondary teachers, he noted that students learned from their reflections and also used their writing to bring greater coherence to their preservice programs.

Knowles, Cole, and Presswood (1994) contributed to this finding by publishing student teachers' narratives of their classroom experience. They note that these narratives are "far more than simply stories or vignettes of experience" (p. viii). For example, a preservice teacher in their study noted, "The ongoing process of analyzing and rethinking my observations has emphasized the importance of reflecting [on my work] as a teacher" (p. 47). The power of journal writing around questions relating to multiculturalism, social context, individual students, and matters of teaching and learning can be extremely powerful.

What Should Students Be Learning?

What kinds of academic base do those preparing to teach need? There has been a long-standing belief that secondary teachers need the equivalent of an academic major in the fields they plan to teach (Cruikshank, 1984; The Holmes Group, 1986). Even with the emerging generalist view being supported by the Coalition of Essential Schools, the belief that those who teach need a solid academic background, to include some special depth of knowledge, remains strong. Even more than coursework, however, those preparing to teach are expected to possess an *understanding* of their academic fields and be able to select from them what is most critical to teach, seeing the relationships between central elements within them and other fields of inquiry and between those central elements and the world. It is expected as well that they will possess the critical habits of mind that characterize their academic fields. This level of understanding undergirds, in part, what Shulman (1986, 1987) has characterized as pedagogical content knowledge.

The other basis of pedagogical content knowledge, of course, is the capacity to transform academic content for purposes of ongoing classroom instruction and curriculum. It is at this level, as well, that a clear understanding of the context in which the teaching-learning exchange occurs is critical. In the end, teachers need to find ways of connecting academic content to the experience and prior understandings of their many students (Kennedy, 1989; McEwan & Bull, 1991; Shulman, 1991; Wilson, Shulman, & Richert, 1987).

Grossman (1989) outlined, as one more example, the importance of content understandings for English teachers. The larger their content background, she noted from her research, the more likely they are to make connections in their teaching to history and the arts and to foster among students richer understandings. Given this larger background, they are not as dependent on textbook questions and illustrations.

Relatively inexperienced prestudent teaching preservice undergraduates notice the same thing. The following journal entry is a good example (Schreiber, 1994).

Ms. Jorsling, for instance, has two entirely different approaches to the subjects of math and science. This is partly a byproduct of her preference for teaching the former subject, a preference made clear by her tendency to spend two consecutive periods on a math lesson although the second period is officially designated as a science class. (Of course, given the difficulty in completing a lesson in forty-five minutes, I'm sure any teacher with the same group of students two periods in a row would be tempted to use them both for the same subject.) Ms. Jorsling teaches science directly out of the textbook, asking students to take turns reading each chapter aloud, and then requiring them to answer the chapter review questions and define the chapter's vocabulary terms. She clearly is unsatisfied with this approach (as are the students, who demonstrate no engaging interest in the subject), and she would love to take the students to the lab for experiments. But she is unsure if she could obtain materials like hydrochloric acid for an experiment on acids and bases, and she worries that when the class ended she would have to run to her between-periods post in the hallway outside her classroom, with no time to clean the lab.

With her math students, on the other hand, Ms. Jorsling is much more creative and confident. Nearly every lesson is a game or a project designed to expose students in a creative way to the course material (currently fractions, percentages, and probability). While most science assignments require quiet individual work, the math activities involve small groups of children busily investigating. While most science assignments are presented in terms of questions with correct or incorrect answers, the math activities are much more conducive to exploration and open-ended inquiry. For instance, one day Ms. Jorsling gave each group of three or four students some beans, tape, scissors and paper, and asked them to design a game. They created various game pieces and invented rules, usually involving flipping a coin or spinning a spinner constructed of paper and pinto beans. At the end of the class, each group explained its game, and students joined Ms. Jorsling in asking questions like "How many tries do you get?" and "How many points do you need to win?" Ms. Jorsling also asked more directed questions, like "How often do you think you'll win? Oh, so it's a 50-50 chance?" "No," the student answered in this instance, "75-25."

In considering what teachers need to know about their subject matters, Wilson and colleagues (1987) made clear from their research on novice teachers that specialized knowledge, that is, having working analogies, illustrations, and metaphors, is necessary for fostering understanding. In this regard, teaching demands knowing the content better than would be required for most other purposes.

The implication is that those preparing for teaching need not only considerable coursework in the various teaching areas, but also to possess a strong epistemic view of subject matter, with a strong knowledge of the philosophy, the limits, characteristic questions, competing theories, and so forth (The Holmes

Group, 1986; Perkins & Simmons, 1988; Scheffler, 1991). It is out of this base that strong connections can be made to other fields of inquiry (The Holmes Group, 1986).

Another element of this view of knowledge is that students preparing to teach in various fields will be in ongoing conversation, learning in the process more about possible connecting points. Goodlad (1990) and his research team, however, found in the 29 public and private universities and liberal arts colleges they studied in eight census regions throughout the United States considerable fragmentation within teacher education programs so that there was little interaction among students preparing to teach in diverse fields or among faculty in various areas. As they noted, "programs tended to comprise collections of courses, various field experiences, and student teaching—each separated from the other, each part frequently taught by different people with little or no communication among the key actors . . . . Even in places where all of the pieces appeared to be efficiently organized and under the careful coordination of one administrator, the hoped-for philosophical cohesion and continuing dialogue among a responsible faculty group were almost consistently missing" (p. 31).

Goodlad (1990) also noted that the highly visible research programs around the pedagogical content knowledge of various disciplines has made little headway in teacher education programs. He notes that some lip service is paid, but for the most part, he suggested, "This valuable and practical research is not utilized" (p. 32).

Both the Holmes Group (1986) and Project 30 (1989) have offered critiques of the subject-matter knowledge of secondary teachers. The Holmes Group challenged secondary teachers for not having a deep enough grasp of their subjects, leading them to focus on facts and fairly low level information. Project 30 brought forward four themes that it believed are critical to the preparation of teachers: understanding, which involves thorough knowledge of the disciplines teachers are licensed to teach; general and liberal education leading to the habits of mind associated with a liberal education; pedagogical content knowledge (essentially Shulman's formulation); and multicultural and international understandings. How this larger knowledge base might be acquired, however, is not dealt with thoroughly by either the Holmes Group or Project 30. An issue that remains complex is related to differences in subject matters. Is the study of one discipline like the study of another? Gardner (1991) noted differences and also suggested that those differences matter in teaching. Shuell (1992) investigated his longstanding observation that prospective teachers majoring in the sciences (physics, chemistry, biology) and math exhibit a "world view" very different from students majoring in English, literature, and history. He suggested that this difference could have an effect on a person's student teaching experience and the teaching style this person ultimately developed as a professional teacher. Thinking about various fields of inquiry in relation to habits of mind, inquiry and the meaning of expertness might help to illuminate the logic and psychology at work in these observations.

The Association of American Colleges (AAC) (1985) in its report on the Integrity of the Academic Major provided a reasonable working definition of a larger knowledge base that might be useful to teacher educators.

Study in depth requires multiple dimension; it cannot be reached merely by cumulative exposure to more and more of a specified subject matter. For instance, the study of literature is not requisitely deep if at the end the student has merely taken six or eight or ten courses in a literature department; there is not depth if the students have not brought into focus and appreciated in the interrelations a refined degree of literacy, an understanding of literature as cultural history, and knowledge of the theory of how language and literature create meaning, and of the problems of reaching aesthetic judgments. (p. 29)

This definition also gets close to what teachers in the schools should want for secondary school students who go through their various courses. It relates closely to the definitions of understanding discussed later in this chapter.

State teacher education reform efforts have also begun to address subject-matter competency in many instances. The Professional Standards Commission in Georgia (Wohlstetter, 1994), which regulates licensing and training, has raised expectations for subject-matter preparation even as it gives to the teacher preparation institutions authority for assessing competence, experience, and academic background. In California, where state reform has had little influence on teacher education reform, it was noted that a "core of teachers willing and able to undertake long-term training in single disciplines" would be required to carry out the curriculum mandates (Kirst & Yee, 1994). Massachusetts, also responding to growing demands for a more challenging academic curriculum in the schools, is requiring an academic major in the field of certification (Massachusetts Department of Education, 1993).

According to the Coalition of Essential Schools (Sizer, 1989), however, questions about the teacher's academic background are rooted in larger concerns about purpose, not just coursework. Such a view grows from the coalition's view of the school curriculum. The coalition believes, for example, that a school's goals should be simpler than much of what states recommend for reform, namely that students master a limited number of essential skills and areas of knowledge. Whereas these skills and areas may, to varying degrees, reflect the traditional academic disciplines, the coalition suggests that a program's design should be shaped by the intellectual and imaginative powers and competencies that students need, rather than by "subjects" as conventionally defined. The aphorism "less is more" aptly describes this view. "Covering material" is seen, in these terms, as the enemy of thorough student mastery and high levels of achievement. To achieve such directions, administrators and teachers in coalition schools are expected to view themselves as generalists first (teacher and scholars in general education) and specialists second (experts in one particular discipline). Moreover, they are expected to assume multiple obligations (teacher-counselor-manager) and demonstrate a sense of commitment to the entire school, essentially a commitment to active collaboration. The foregoing implies a much more enriched academic and experiential background for teachers than is common.

Relatedly, the locus of curriculum development has moved from individual classrooms and schools to specialists beyond schools and back again to individual classrooms and schools (Cuban, 1990, 1991). In many respects, the changing patterns of curriculum development have followed the political swings between interests in decentralization and centralization. As we move toward the end of the twentieth century, decentralizing tendencies are resurfacing. Whereas states are being encouraged to establish general content standards and various professional associations (e.g., National Council of Teachers of Mathematics) are producing curriculum standards, the expectation remains that teachers in individual schools and classrooms will still be critical curriculum makers. Although there is acknowledgment that there may be contradictions in the adoption of curriculum standards and the related rhetoric about teachers in individual schools being the persons who must shape the day-to-day curriculum, both general experience and research results speak repeatedly to the importance of teacher involvement, enthusiasm, understanding, and commitment in the curriculum-making process (Bird & Little, 1986; Comer, 1980; Edmonds, 1979; The Holmes Group, 1986; McDiarmid, Ball, & Anderson, 1989; Newman, 1993; Perrone, 1989; Shulman, 1986, 1991; Sizer, 1984, 1992). Such responsibility raises in a large way the following questions for teachers: What shall we teach? Why? For what purposes? Teacher education programs need to help prospective teachers develop authoritative responses to such questions.

Over the years, these kinds of questions have been guided by a number of different philosophical stances. The more integrated holistic directions have been guided by John Dewey, Jean Piaget, and Jerome Bruner. Edward Thorndike and Franklin Bobbitt, in contrast, provided an undergirding for a narrower, more reductionist content-oriented direction. For the most part, however, especially in this latter half of the twentieth century, schools have struck a middle course. At times, in relation to these philosophical perspectives, educators have viewed their challenge to be teaching for understanding. At other times the challenge has been basic skills and higher levels of information transfer. They are set apart here even as it is recognized that in practice the demarcations are not so sharp. Concerns about understanding, however, are on the increase, especially in light of beliefs that students need to be able to use knowledge in more powerful ways (Gardner, 1991; The Holmes Group, 1991).

In the face of the "back to basics" movement's documented shortcomings, the numerous criticisms of students' academic understanding found in a decade-long flurry of national reports, and the supposed higher levels of learner achievement and understanding produced by several other industrialized countries, a number of educators are again working toward models of education that draw students closer to genuine understanding of the subject matters. In this regard, the question must inevitably be, "What, if anything, might make the challenge more tractable now?"

One encouraging direction is that teacher education programs are beginning to make connections with the need for change in the schools (Goodlad, 1990). Teacher education programs are also drawing on a renewed sense of idealism among young people and are beneficiaries of a mid-career movement toward teaching by many successful individuals who believe they can contribute something important to young people in the schools (Perrone, 1991b). A belief that schools can be different than they are is growing among those going into teaching.

How Should Students Be Learning?

Virtually all secondary teacher education programs embrace a theory of teaching and learning and require students to engage in one or more clinical teaching practices. This can be inferred from the relatively widespread presence of NCATE and its requirements that teacher education programs have a coherent philosophical stance about matters of teaching and learning (Cruickshank, 1984) and from the pervasive belief among teacher educators that teaching is learned by doinig. Nonetheless, the content, duration, and quality of this overall preparation varies widely (Goodlad, Soder, & Sirotnik, 1990).

The Coalition of Essential Schools has a particular formula for how students should learn that is proving useful to many teacher education programs as it matches so much of the cognitive science findings of recent decades. Rather than focusing on technique or approach or style, it simply states that teachers should focus on helping adolescents learn to use their minds well. Schools, the coalition argues, should not attempt to be "comprehensive" if such a claim is made at the expense of the school's central intellectual purpose (Sizer, 1989). The governing practical metaphor of a coalition school is student-as-worker, rather than the more familiar metaphor of teacher-as-deliverer-of-instructional-services. A prominent pedagogy in support of such a formulation is coaching, a means of provoking students to learn how to learn and thus to teach themselves.

The coalition orientation to teaching and learning has strong roots in Deweyan philosophy. It assumes classrooms in which active learning prevails, projects are a basis for engaging students intensively, and in-depth learning of a few topics is seen as preferable to the more commonplace coverage of material. This more adventurous approach to teaching and learning, to use Cohen's (1988) formulation, is not, however, dominant in most schools in which new teachers engage in their clinical experiences. Cohen (1988, 1991) argued that such learning is also not part of the academic experience of those preparing to teach. The challenge for teacher education programs that believe in the coalition's formulations, which view reform in secondary schools in such terms, is to make the experience of preservice teachers more consonant with those directions while providing clinical sites in which teachers model this more adventurous approach to teaching and learning. The current interest in professional development schools is related to the foregoing (The Holmes Group, 1991).

The remarkable evolution of cognitive science over the past two decades, since the heyday of Bruner and his contemporaries, has begun to influence greatly the rhetoric surrounding school practice and the ways programs in teacher education view curriculum, teaching, and learning. Teaching for understanding, as a result, is gaining considerable support. A number of advances in the understanding of human development and learning make more approachable the goal of a pedagogy of understanding.

To cite one factor, research over the past several years has mapped in some detail adolescents' grasp of important concepts in science and mathematics and has documented a number of prevalent "misconceptions" not normally touched by conventional instruction (e.g., Apelman, Hawkins, & Morrison, 1985; Chi, Glaser, & Rees, 1982; DiSessa, 1982; Duckworth, 1986, 1987; Gardner, 1991; Glaser, Pellegrino, & Lesgold, 1978; Schoenfeld, 1988; Wiser & Carey, 1983). Linked to this research is the emerging concept of a "mental model," which has given cognitive psychology a relatively systematic way of talking about what understanding of a particular topic is and how understandings are attained (Gentner & Stevens, 1983; Johnson-Laird, 1983; Mayer, 1989; Perkins & Simmons, 1988; Perkins & Unger, 1989).

In addition, under the label "situated learning," a number of cognitive scientists and educators have begun to investigate the rich supportive conditions in which effective learning occurs outside of academic institutions, as in apprenticeship situations, for example. They contrast such conditions with the typical classroom, urging that sustained and effective learning cannot be expected unless classrooms incorporate some of the texture of curiosity, motivation, and contextual support characteristic of situated learning (Brown, Collins, & Duguid, 1989; Cole & Means, 1981; Greeno, 1988; Lave, 1988; Resnick, 1987; Rogoff & Lave, 1984). In some respects, this view, too, is a longstanding Deweyan perspective. In *The School and Society* (1915), for example, Dewey wrote about the schools' isolation from life. He noted that "when the child gets into the classroom he has to put out of his mind a large part of the ideas, interests and activities that predominate in his home and neighborhood" (p. 75).

Besides these advances concerning development and learning, the past decade has seen considerable progress in conceptions of the nature of intelligence and the cultivation of good thinking. Gardner's theory of "multiple intelligences" has provided, in this regard, a framework relating intelligence more closely to work in particular subject matters (Gardner, 1983). Furthermore, during the mid-1970s, teaching thinking skills, independent of any particular subject matter, was seen in the schools to be an attractive instructional agenda. More recent research and theorizing, however, have coupled more firmly the nature of thinking and subject-matter mastery (Perkins & Salomon, 1988). Moreover, it has been argued that subject matters are almost entirely isolated from one another, with slim prospects for transfer of learning. Contemporary research and theorizing on transfer, however, has begun to disclose promising prospects for transfer of learning across disciplines under appropriate conditions (Salomon & Perkins, 1988). Such findings encourage and inform the current work around a pedagogy of understanding in the schools and in teacher education programs.

Furthermore, there is a belief that teachers have been relative-ly successful in schools with students who come from middle-class families and have access to books and a variety of out-of-school educational opportunities (Graham, 1992). But what about the rest? Considerable research is being devoted to finding ways to ensure significant academic learning for *all* students, in particular those who have traditionally been less well served in the schools (i.e., the poor, African Americans, Native Americans, and Hispanics) (Quality Education for Minorities Project, 1990). Teaching for understanding is seen in these terms as being a means to reach all students more successfully.

The growing belief that teaching should be directed toward student understanding, however, goes beyond the recent work of cognitive science. It has worked its way into the growing concern about equity—the belief that all students need access to an empowering education that assumes greater equality of opportunity and full participation in the civic culture.

Research around teaching for understanding has grown, principally through support of the Spencer Foundation. The major current work is centered at Stanford (Shulman, McLaughlin), Harvard (Duckworth, Gardner, Perkins, Perrone), Michigan State (Ball, Stock), Wisconsin (Grossman), and Michigan (Lampert, Cohen). The Harvard formulation, outlined later in this section, encompasses most of the critical threads of this pedagogical-curriculum direction. Certainly teaching for understanding should be more basic to the preparation of teachers.

The assumption is that teachers want students to understand what is being taught. In general, however, students tend to understand far less than is desired. Systematic logic and algebraic formulas are often confusing, especially if any part of the context is altered; poetry is typically obscure; and students have trouble writing essays that bring forward the complexities of topics they are writing about, and they see too few connections between what they are learning in school and the world beyond school.

Do students, for example, understand the Civil War because they are able on an exam to provide the five causes listed in the textbook? Also, what if they can list the number of atoms contained in iron, or repeat the formula for determining the length of a hypotenuse of a right triangle? What if they can provide the names of the planets in the solar system including the largest and the smallest? Before conferring on these students a stamp of understanding, more would certainly be required.

Yet, what if students could describe the U.S. Declaration of Independence in terms of the tie of the language used to ideas from two or three enlightenment political philosophers such as Locke and Rousseau, put into their own words critical elements of the petitions of complaint against King George, role play what King George's response might have been, and describe the role the Declaration has played in American life, even in the present? Would this indicate understanding of the Declaration and some of the issues surrounding it? Also, if they could describe the history of the Pythagorean Theorem, demonstrate its many proofs and discuss their strengths and weaknesses, and show its uses in construction, surveying, measuring, and so forth, do they understand that as well? What if they can not only name the planets but draw them in relation to one another, provide their sizes in reasonable scale, discuss their individual characteristics, and relate their names to their mythic characters, does this too begin to approach understanding? We would argue that they are getting closer.

Understanding then is something internalized, that students can hold on to, make into a metaphor, possibly draw pictures of, use productively again and again in new settings as well as familiar settings beyond the test, the end-of-the-unit exam, and the school itself. Understanding is about making connections among and between things and not things in isolation, about deep and not surface knowledge, about greater complexity and not simpleness. The context for pursuing understanding in these terms is the belief that all students need an empowering education that goes beyond the classroom and into the world. They need to be able to *use* knowledge, not just know about a large number of things (Gardner, Perkins, & Perrone, 1993). Such a goal is grand; it raises greatly the stakes in the schools. It clearly demands more of teachers and students (Duckworth, 1991).

Duckworth (1991) noted in this regard that "our challenge as curriculum developers is to find the ways to engage learners, young and old, in the complexities of the areas we think it is important for them to know about" (p. 23). Teaching for understanding is about the recognition of complexity.

The Harvard Teaching for Understanding Framework (Gardner & Boix-Mansilla, 1994; Perkins & Blythe, 1994) is built around four conceptions that can be used for planning curriculum at the macro and micro levels. It is a framework that is central to Harvard's work with preservice and in-service teachers.

The first question posed is: What is to be taught? This is essentially a consideration of Generative Topics, those ideas, topics, events, themes, issues, objects, and questions that provide enough depth and variety of perspectives to help students develop significant understandings. Implicit is a belief that some ideas have more possibilities of engaging students than others and that some questions are richer in potential than others for helping students begin to see more complexity in the world or make connections to a wide array of issues and subject matters. The most generative topics are central to a field of inquiry, accessible to students at many different levels, and rich in implications and connections. Immigration in American history, evolution in biology, functions in mathematics, or harmony in music are generative topics. In addition, issues of perennial concern, such as justice, or objects of enduring fascination, such as the pyramids or the sun, are generative. Slavery has more potential than the military events of the Civil War period because its effects are still present. Technologies such as computers, telephones, and television are generative because they connect to so many aspects of the culture. Most of these topics have wonderful interdisciplinary possibilities, another fact that makes them generative.

The second key idea is called Understanding Goals, which represents what teachers want students to understand. Understanding goals answers the question: What do I want my students to understand about the topic under study? With the topic of immigration, for instance, what would teachers most want students to understand? Would it be that there are large numbers of immigrants, that immigration has had a continuing quality, that leaving one's country and family roots is difficult, that great hardship accompanies immigration, or that immigrants from some areas have faced extreme forms of discrimination? Or would teachers want students to understand the contributions of immigrants to American life, the life stories of immigrants, immigrants' roles in building the infrastructure of the U.S. economy, the ties between immigration from a foreign country and immigration within the United States, or what it is like to move? The list could go on, but the point is that teachers should actively determine what they want students to think about.

The third key idea is called Performances of Understanding. These are classroom activities that encourage students to demonstrate their progress toward understanding goals. What would indicate that students are understanding the goals teachers have in mind or those the students defined for immigration? The important thing is that understanding means doing something, explaining something, arguing on behalf of something, or constructing something.

The fourth key idea is Ongoing Assessment. This asks teachers as well as the students to evaluate frequently the various performances of understanding as they develop over time. At its best, ongoing assessment has a cumulative quality; it is never one final product. To speak of ongoing assessment is, of course, to make use of many of the performance assessment ideas that are beginning to be discussed widely.

Another development in schools that needs to be accounted for is the shift in thinking about vocation (Rosenstock, 1991). Academic and vocational education have long been seen as separate areas of study, generally serving different students and having divergent purposes. Increasingly, however, they are being seen as necessarily connected, and apprenticeships are understood to be useful for all students, regardless of their postsecondary plans. Integrating academic and vocational education, however, is a challenge. Addressing it at the preservice level, that is, understanding its value, would be useful.

One last comment here seems warranted. The shift in curriculum decision making to individual schools and classrooms places increased pressure on teachers. How do they create all the curriculum they need? Ben-Peretz (1990) proposed nurturing a kind of curriculum connoisseurship in teachers, that is, helping create an eye toward seeing possibilities in the work of colleagues or in descriptions written by classroom teachers for publication, because it *is* difficult for teachers to write full curriculum themselves. This seems appropriate. The best teacher education programs need to build upon such an understanding.

How Should Students Be Evaluated?

Assessment is clearly connected to work on curriculum and to decisions about the content to be taught. At its best, assessment relates to content that matters or that is critical to ongoing learning and understanding. It discerns what students really know and can do; much that is assessed in classrooms and schools is not worth the time and effort to measure and report.

Newmann and Archibald (1992) suggested that teachers should be teaching toward the curriculum goals, in this sense, "teaching to the test." Simmons and Resnick (1993) offered a similar view, noting the importance of having students perform some task that is central to curriculum goals that are highly valued. The Office of Technology Assessment (1992) outlined performance tasks on a continuum from the simplest to the most complex, believing that the upper end should be the focus. These tasks are constructed response essays, oral discourse, exhibitions, and portfolios.

As it turns out, portfolio assessment (keeping track of student learning on an ongoing basis; seeing projects and performance activities as central to student learning and a base for greater self-evaluation; and assuming an oppositional stance to standardized, externally generated assessment) is taking hold in many schools while being talked and written about extensively. It needs to be studied in teacher preparation programs and made more central to assessment practices that exist at that level.

What makes portfolio assessment so powerful is its contribution to change in schools. For example, portfolio assessment is altering many of the relationships between teachers and students. In settings where portfolio assessment is being embraced, teachers are becoming coaches with students much more engaged in the learning process as "workers," to use Sizer's formulation (Seidel, 1992; Wasley, 1991a, 1993; Wiggins, 1993). Portfolio assessment is also changing the ways teachers think about curriculum. Teaching for understanding assumes greater importance along with an understanding that students need time to acquire greater expertness. In addition, because interdisciplinary work is shown to enhance understanding, it is also given more attention (Darling-Hammond, 1992; Jervis, 1994).

Seidel (1991) described five phases in the implementation of portfolio assessment for classroom teachers: seeking help, experimentation, learning the language of portfolio assessment, development of clinical judgment skills, and development of the ability to take a classroom view for instruction and a schoolwide view for accountability. He noted further that as teachers incorporate the foregoing into their practice, a different kind of pedagogy follows.

Nathan (1994) concluded, in relation to Seidel's work, that teachers engaged in portfolio assessment consistently refer to learning about their students and their practice in new ways. Wasley (1991a), in studies of coalition teachers, noted that when teachers shifted away from a coverage model to in-depth studies, they sought interdisciplinary connections. Relatedly, Zessoules and Gardner (1991) wrote that

Authentic assessment involves complicated reevaluation of classroom activities and responsibilities, transforming the classroom among many dimensions: changing the kinds of activities students engage in on a daily basis, altering the responsibilities of students and teachers in increasingly sophisticated ways. (p. 63)

Nathan (1994) suggested further that "portfolio assessment has changed pedagogy because teachers become more reflective and more engaged in self evaluation" (p. 43). This occurs, in part, because teachers see student work and expertise grow over time.

Wolf, LeMahiew, and Eresh (1992) also showed that these new forms of assessment create the conditions for fundamental change in schools, that is, in school structure, schedules, grading, communication with parents, and curriculum. One related area that is growing in interest is completing graduation requirements by portfolios and exhibition. Darling-Hammond (1992) documented carefully the successful practice at Central Park East Secondary School. She quoted a teacher as saying, "The idea is that your work is a window into the habits of mind. What's important are the habits of mind, habits of heart, and habits of work . . . you want to ask the student, 'why did you pick these pieces?' You want to know if kids have a sense that the portfolio reflects them" (p. 70). Experience with portfolios and exhibitions for purposes of graduation would be helpful to those preparing to teach.

In schools that have gone this route, the diploma is awarded in response to exhibitions, a series of successful final demonstrations of mastery for graduation. These exhibitions by students of their grasp of the central skills and knowledge of the school's programs are often jointly reviewed by the faculty and higher education authorities. The diploma is awarded when appropriate performance levels are demonstrated. The result is that the school's program proceeds with no strict age grading and with no system of credits collected in terms of time spent in class. Schools moving in this direction try to set a tone stressing values of unanxious expectation ("I won't threaten you, but I expect much of you"); of trust ("until abused"); and of decency (the values of fairness, generosity, and tolerance). Incentives appropriate to the school's particular students and teacher are emphasized, and parents are treated as essential collaborators. Criteria or rubrics and standards for this movement toward portfolio assessment and exhibitions remain difficult, but those preparing for teaching could certainly make inroads here.

What Is the Context and Community of Schools?

In relation to the contexts for educational change, the innovation of the 1960s sounded the warning that effective innovation must pay thorough attention to the contexts of educational change, that is, the teachers, the institutions, and the social milieu. One corollary especially worth mentioning is that the 1960s emphasis on wholesale curriculum revision must, in retrospect, be seen as misplaced. For a number of economic and institutional reasons, replacement of a standing curriculum by another radically different in its philosophy encounters barriers exceedingly difficult to surmount on a wide scale (Schaffarzick & Sykes, 1979). Schools and programs in teacher education are struggling with these learnings. On the one hand, the belief that curriculum is best developed within individual schools where the context can be addressed most fully and teacher commitment can be mobilized is growing. On the other hand, at the more state and national levels, interest in national standards and more commonality of curriculum is also growing. The tensions that exist are currently large. Such a backdrop must be kept in view, even as research around context is discussed.

In attending to schools and teachers, contemporary investigators have not neglected the learners and their milieu. Attention to the social settings of education has made it increasingly apparent that conventional instruction often proceeds in ways disconnected from children's and parents' linguistic and cultural backgrounds. It is hardly surprising under such circumstances that much of conventional education seems unmotivating to many learners at the same time that many educational innovations smack of ivory tower idealism to parents worried about whether their children will achieve even baseline competencies. Unless the cultures of the classroom, the backgrounds and attitudes of teachers, the administrative structure and support system in the school, the myths and rituals of the school community, the family milieu, the neighborhood, and the wider society are taken seriously into account, even the best-intentioned efforts at reform are likely to fail (Bacharach, Bauer, & Shedd, 1986; Bird & Little, 1986; Edmonds, 1979; Heath, 1983; Jencks, 1983; Leichter, 1974; McNeil, 1986; Sarason, 1971, 1983).

As these problems have been recognized, exploratory steps have been taken to reconfigure education to speak to them, including, for example, decentralized curricula; more flexible time schedules; schools-within-schools; the involvement of parents in the planning of education; and collaborations of schools, universities, and businesses (Cazden, 1988; Cummins, 1986; Powell, Ferrar, & Cohen, 1985; Rose, 1989; Sizer, 1984). Increased attention is also being paid to norms of civility, norms of instruction, and norms of improvement (Bird & Little, 1986).

Throughout this new movement, which has been termed the *third wave* of educational reform, Dewey's dictum that education needs to connect to the lives of the learners resounds clearly.

With the increased attention to school contexts has come, as noted earlier, the increasing recognition that accountability structures, configured around standardized tests, influence to a remarkable extent what is taught and what is learned. Innovative approaches to education that highlight understanding, for example, cannot expect to thrive within a system where the only sanctioned means of testing highlight rote knowledge and the execution of algorithms. Accordingly, the development of means of assessment that reflect students' understanding and other nonrote achievements such as thinking skills has emerged as an important priority, a crucial element in remaking education to be more congenial to a pedagogy of understanding (Wiggins, 1989, 1993; Wolf, 1987/1988).

Those preparing to teach should have an understanding of this historical and contextual base surrounding the foregoing. It is the kind of understanding that is critical to the professionalization seen as important for teachers. In addition, educators need the means to reach into their context and understand it more fully. Classroom research, that process of examining closely the local context, beginning with the classroom, is a valuable process for this purpose. Although a major activity for professional development, it is discussed here as a means of getting closer to learners and their needs.

Classroom/teacher research, as it is now described, had its origins in the latter part of the nineteenth century in relation to the Child Study Movement (Cremin, 1961). It was a popular element of early progressivism but lost its vibrancy as schools of education assumed greater control of the research agendas regarding classroom practice and curriculum (Perrone, 1989). Classroom/teacher research had a revival in the 1960s "in the context of school initiated change" (Elliot, 1991, p. ix). Lawrence Stenhouse, at the University of East Anglia in the United Kingdom, as much as anyone else, gave the revival enormous intellectual leadership, working almost exclusively at the secondary school level (Rudduck & Hopkins, 1985).

Zeichner (1993) described classroom research as "systematic inquiry by practitioners about their practice." This is an appropriate definition, which recognizes that for teachers who are involved, there results a more informed practice and enlarged sense of professionalism, as well as a basis for entry into the larger discussion about classroom practice and school reform.

What seems clear about classroom research is that it alters the ways teachers see themselves and their professional roles. Cochran-Smith and Lytle (1992) suggested that instructional patterns change substantially as teachers engage in classroom research. They noted that teachers

redefine their own relationships to knowledge about teaching and learning, reconstruct their classrooms and begin to offer different invitations to their students to learn and know. (p. 318)

Several journals feature teacher research: *Teacher Research: The Journal of Classroom Inquiry* (published at the University of Maine); *Educational Action Research,* an international journal of classroom research (published at the University of East

Anglia); *Teacher's Journal* (published at Brown University); and *Insights* (published at the University of North Dakota). Such periodicals provide an outlet for teachers' writing about their classroom research, even though publication is not the principal reason for engaging in such work.

Journal writing, a major vehicle for reflection, is a good base for classroom research. A venerable means of extending thought and understanding in various subject matters, it has become increasingly a centerpiece of preservice teacher education. In the Harvard program, much of the preservice program is built around students' focused journal accounts and students leave with excellent reflective skills (Perrone & Jacobs, 1993). Knowles, Cole, and Presswood (1994) provided a strong case for the power of journal writing, rooted in their work as teacher educators. They set the following questions to student teachers:

1. Who am I as a teacher? What does it mean to be a teacher? What are the roles of teachers?
2. What are schools and classrooms like? Who works in schools and why? What goes on in schools and why?
3. How do I forge relationships with individuals in learning communities? How do I develop relationships with the various groups of people who comprise a learning community?
4. Who are the students? What are their needs as learners? What do they already know? How do I come to know them as persons and as learners?
5. How do I focus my teaching? How do I think about teaching?
6. How do I teach? What teaching methods are most appropriate?
7. How can I forge my professional development as a new teacher? (p. 67)

In relation to the what and how of teaching, Knowles et al. (1994) said:

One of the greatest learning experiences I ever had was in a nontraditional teaching context. I was fortunate that the school district [in which I was a student] strongly believed in providing opportunities for outdoor education experiences . . . . [This] residential outdoor education experience brought the world into perspective. Suddenly, the various topics I had spent so much time studying became real. They were not just in textbooks and tests. These experiences began my understanding of what learning and school was all about. (p. 70)

On the need to think about diversity, a student wrote:

Over the course of the semester I wrestled with the issues of race and diversity, and with my role as a white male in the changing society. I worked in an ethnically diverse school. We, as educators, need to be more explicit in stating curriculum objectives that encourage students to become aware of the diversity of their school, community, nation, and world. I am very aware of the need for this. By the end of the twentieth century—only a few years away—fewer than half of the people in the United States will be European-Americans. A majority of the population will be minorities. What will be my role as a white male teacher or administrator in relation to these demographic changes? This is one question with which I will continually wrestle. (p. 144)

Beginning with reflective journals at the preservice level is a good beginning for teachers to maintain themselves as learn-

ers (the students of teaching the schools need), especially if the schools are to be settings where all students learn.

The importance of gaining insights into students' perspectives about their school experience is also emerging in the research. Educational change will likely fail without greater student involvement and research from the students' point of view. ,

In "They're Talking But Who's Listening" (Carini, 1988), a paper that resulted from a longitudinal study involving 16- and 17-year-olds, Patricia Carini raised questions about how well teachers know the students they teach. She noted that

Undeniably, these young people were eager to talk . . . Listening to these young adults we were often moved by their bravery . . . . Inescapably, we were also compelled to consider what a rare privilege it was and how little known most of these youngsters—and many others—tend to be within schools. In some instances we knew from our conversations that we had knowledge of a youngster [who] was educationally important but probably not available to those responsible for [his] education. (p. 6)

Sonia Nieto (1992) engaged in several youth studies that underscore Carini's view about students' interest in sharing their perspectives about their school experience, the richness of the data from focused conversations, and the need for teachers to engage in more critical dialogue with students. She, too, makes clear how little known the students are. Following similar directions, Capella-Noya (1993) brought forward in her research based on extended work with high school students the importance of honesty in student–teacher relationships and young people's need to express themselves. Students used the conception of teacher-friend to describe the kind of relationship that built for them strong commitments to learning. Those preparing for teaching need to have occasion to get closer to students and their intentions and to understand that teaching students well also means knowing students well. Teaching in these terms suggests more reciprocity.

How Do New Teachers Grow Professionally?

What is most clear about the various standards-setting directions involving teachers (the National Board for Professional Teaching Standards [NBPTS], the Interstate New Teachers Assessment and Support Consortium [INTASC] [of the Council of Chief State School Officers], and NCATE) is that they envision "thinking teachers" (Darling-Hammond, 1994). Such a view recognizes what is most consistent about research on teaching and learning, namely that "teaching is complex, contingent on teaching goals and contexts, reciprocal and interactive with students, based on understanding learners and learning, addressing multiple styles and needs, not routine, and differentiated by the needs that students present, including the multiple cultures that are present in almost all communities" (Darling-Hammond, 1994).

Although there was much denigration of teachers and teaching in the early part of the 1980s, the public perception of teaching and of teachers is changing. Teaching is understood to be enormously complex. To deal with this complexity, teachers need to be students of teaching, persons who, as Dewey (1915) noted in his early writing about education, are not dependent on decisions made externally by persons far removed from the reality of a particular setting. To be a student of teaching in Dewey's terms is to establish a reflective capacity and to become clear and articulate about one's intentions. Such a formulation is basic to teacher professionalism and needs to be a major disposition among those who are preparing to teach. Moreover, according to Berliner (1987), teachers who become experts at their craft have learned how to reflect systematically and develop strategies for learning from their experience. Years of experience alone, his research suggests, do not make very much difference.

The challenge to teacher education, not just in colleges and universities but in school districts and state departments of education as well, is how to encourage and sustain reflective practice among those who go into teaching (Yonemura, 1982).

A rarely heeded viewpoint that could help bring about this necessary support comes from teachers themselves. Lytle and Cochran-Smith (1990) argued persuasively that teacher knowledge about teaching, especially about the teaching of the less motivated, needs to be more central to the conversation and the related policy formulations. Those preparing for teaching need to possess the kind of reflective, classroom research skills that will enable them to be more significant contributors to the ongoing discussion about teaching and learning in the schools. More importantly, however, it will enable them to make their own classrooms more responsive to *all* students through ongoing inquiries and continual reconstruction. Clark and Lampert (1986), writing in support of such a position, suggested that teaching is too complex for research-based prescriptions, and that those in classrooms can get beneath the complexity "to stimulate thought in support of self directed developments" (p. 30).

The importance of professional communities of teachers has been found to be central to schools that work well on behalf of students and in which teacher satisfaction is high (McLaughlin & Talbert, 1993). How to build and participate in such communities should be part of the education of those who complete teacher preparation programs. Efforts to demonstrate the power of collective thought at this level about matters of teaching and learning can make a difference.

Relatedly, seeing teaching as complex and filled with dilemmas is an important opening to such collaboration. Cuban (1992) defined teaching as choices, that is, responses to educational dilemmas that add up to an ongoing quest for understanding. Places where educational dilemmas abound include cultural blind spots, second language learning, diverse cultural backgrounds, selecting what is to be taught, and so forth. Moreover, dilemmas are present everywhere within the decision making that extends beyond the classroom. How, for example, are teachers to gain a more significant voice in such matters as tracking, mainstreaming, national standards, testing, and the chartering of schools (Ben-Peretz & Kremer-Hagan, 1990; Floden & Clark, 1988)?

Young teachers are often surprised by the school as a workplace. It is more isolating than they imagined and more bureaucratic than they anticipated. Moreover, adolescents often appear more complex in the school setting than the teachers expected; they are more difficult to get to know well, less motivated, and less committed to the goals of the school. Envisioning the setting in ways more conducive to teaching and learning (e.g., more collegial, more school based with regard to decision making and curriculum development, more empowering for students) is important. Otherwise, discouragement, even cynicism, can result.

Research on the school as a workplace, principally the province of sociologists, anthropologists, and historians, has become more common. Cusick's early work (1973) and his later studies (1983) are useful ethnographies that depict both student and teacher perspectives on the institutional character of the school. Lawrence-Lightfoot's (1983) research on high schools stands out for its understanding of the complexities of the school environment, socially and academically. Perrone (1985) provided portraits of several different kinds of high schools in many diverse settings. These descriptions suggest that American high schools are more mosaic than monolith with some parts working better than others. Susan Moore Johnson (1990) set forth the conditions in schools that good teachers find either encouraging or constraining, that give them hope of doing their best work or causing them to consider leaving teaching.

Lieberman and Miller (1992) addressed many of the institutional issues affecting schools, including the nature of bureaucracy, adolescence, and faculty culture. They argued that teachers must learn not to be overwhelmed or immobilized by them, otherwise it becomes impossible to negotiate change.

With regard to adolescence, Chang (1992) studied the life of adolescents through their own stories. These stories richly portray the day-to-day rhythms that students experience. Eckert (1989) also examined youth cultures in high schools with an eye toward the values and pressures teenagers face day in and day out and that influence their receptivity to what teachers offer. With regard to faculty culture, McLaughlin and Talbert (1993) researched the conditions that support high quality teaching and learning in schools. They found that in settings in which teachers become active communicators, in a community of learners, there were many positive changes in curriculum, content, and the teaching-learning exchange. Kallick (1989) had similar findings. Schools in which teachers form communities for thinking about teaching experience considerable transformation. The Coalition of Essential Schools applies these insights. In its efforts to ensure professional support, it recommends that the ultimate administrative and budget decision making take place at the school level, that the total student loads be reduced to 80 or fewer pupils per teacher, and that there be substantial collective planning time for all teachers (Sizer, 1989).

Unfortunately, much of this is more easily said than done. Kilbourn and Roberts (1991) found that a support culture is limited in schools. For example, finding a mentor who can listen, observe, offer praise, and occasionally intervene during the critical first year of teaching is rare. Peer support at other levels is no more common.

What, then, should secondary teacher education do? Those preparing for teaching need to have a road map of the obstacles, a basis for understanding why change can be difficult, if not impossible. In this regard, the Harvard experience in implementing a Teaching for Understanding Framework can be instructive.

What is seen as a fairly straightforward set of ideas is difficult to put into practice. The reasons for this are not difficult to see. *Putting understanding up front,* that is, selecting the topic around a different set of questions, making performances central, and seeing assessment as ongoing rather than a final exercise, *is a larger change than apparent on the surface.* This demands a different teacher role, assumes a high level of student responsibility, implicitly redirects the allocation of time, asks for an entirely different framing of classroom discourse, and calls for many new instructional materials. In relation to these changes, teachers have said (Gardner, Perkins, & Perrone, 1993)

- My students don't know how to read primary documents. I can't afford the time it would take to teach them how to do it successfully.

- My students are not used to writing in math class. It would be disruptive.

- My students expect me to be an authority. It would be very difficult to move so much responsibility for the content to them.

- I am expected to *cover* (a particular subject matter). If I followed the teaching for understanding format, I would only be able to cover part of it. I don't think I can do this.

- I could do one or two short units around the framework, but that would be the limit.

- I have tried using performances before—students actually doing something. They take a lot of time and the quality is mixed.

- The students are comfortable having a textbook and knowing precisely what they are to do. The teaching for understanding process keeps things too uncertain. There are too many interpretations, too many diverse activities, not enough closure.

- This would be easier if my class met for a longer time each day. Forty-two minutes doesn't leave much time to do interpretive work, organize complex projects, and engage in active learning.

- Our system wants students to have a lot of information about American history. I can't meet that responsibility and also do the kind of in-depth study the teaching for understanding framework demands.

- Where will I get all the materials needed for teaching for understanding?

- How can I be the only teacher doing this?

- I have 140 students each day to deal with. Teaching for understanding calls upon me to organize many new materials, keep track of a wider range of activities, and get students more involved in writing and presenting. I can't read carefully what students are beginning to produce.

- I have been a successful teacher doing what I have been doing. I haven't used large numbers of primary documents before. I don't really know how to use cooperative groups very well. Inquiry makes me feel less competent. I don't want to risk failure.

These concerns are understandable; they are, in the current circumstances of schools, significant constraints. Even where the Harvard research group found that teachers can easily select a topic for a short "Teaching for Understanding" unit, planning and implementing a particularly long unit of 5–8 weeks or an entire course seems quite different. The difficulty is the struggle between long-standing habits of thought and practice and the distinctly different thinking and practices required by the teaching for understanding directions. For example, most of the overall selection of content is predetermined by the textbooks in use. Teachers are not prepared to assume the important selection role when they are not used to being the principal determiners of the curriculum.

Moreover, the Harvard Teaching for Understanding Project utilizes the "less is more" premise, that is, the idea of depth, of working with ideas in diverse ways, bringing greater interpretation to what is being studied. This seems at odds with most teachers' experience and the kinds of pressures they have long felt. "More is more" has been the dominant theme of schools for at least the last two decades. What, then, is, as one teacher suggested, "all the push for additional course requirements, AP courses and more testing about?"

It also takes a while to make the required shift in the meaning and practice of setting teaching and learning goals. For a long time, goals have meant objectives, specific behaviors, or tasks. Now, *understanding goals* is tied to *understanding performances.* This is more than a shift in language or new terms for old ideas. The conception ties student understanding to being able to do something, extend learning in many different directions, use what is being learned in diverse settings, connect it to other fields of inquiry, make analyses around it, construct a model of it, describe what it is not, and so forth. Perhaps the most radical departure is that students take more responsibility for selecting the questions they pursue, for constructing and interpreting knowledge, and for exhibiting their understandings.

In addition, teaching for understanding is a more concrete, messy, materials-oriented, less linear process characterized by many opportunities for unexpected and puzzling results. It does not lend itself easily to short units of study. It does not fit well the rhythm of the typical 40–45 minute periods that dominate the schools. Furthermore, assessment as a test, as a single product, gives way in the teaching for understanding framework to a collection of performances, to final products being pieces of earlier products, and to criteria that allow students to play a role in developing and applying.

Teaching for understanding runs against much more than might be imagined. "I would enjoy teaching a seven-day teaching for understanding unit," several teachers have suggested, "but I couldn't do this kind of teaching all year." Given current school conditions, they are likely right. They do not have readily available all the materials that such a direction calls for; there are too few primary documents, too few books, and too little access to resources beyond the school. Moreover, they have too little class time, too many preparations, and virtually no planning time.

To speak of Teaching for Understanding calls for many important changes. Without more shifts in direction in the schools, teaching for understanding will remain something to try on occasion, but it will not dominate practice.

It might be useful to discuss further the structural and climate issues that affect Teaching for Understanding. One obvious question is: Must secondary schools be organized around 42–50 minute periods? Obviously not; however, that has been the pattern most secondary schools have followed for much of the twentieth century. In relation to such a schedule, it is often said that it matches well the "distributive learning" theory—learning in the various subject areas is enhanced with some focused attention on a daily basis. The reality, though, at least in the school context as opposed to a learning laboratory, is that students stop and start over six or seven times a day around an equal number of subject matters. They are asked to interact with six or seven different adults, which translates into many separate levels of negotiation. In most schools, they must continuously adapt, moving, for example, from exact, precise, short information laden answers in one class to wide ranging explorations showing originality of thought in the next. One teacher may insist on memorization and mastery of the textbook; the next may encourage open-ended discussion and independent decision making. In one class students may be expected to write every day, with expression of their ideas being most important; whereas in another class, writing may be viewed as less important, and details of grammar and spelling take priority over originality of ideas. As Deborah Meier of Central Park East Secondary School often says, "Where else but a school would we ask anyone to do such a thing?" It is a system that works against a focus on Teaching for Understanding.

In the 1960s, although there were earlier historical precedents, several educators suggested that secondary schools consider what educational advantage might be gained by allotting different subject matters, depending on their instructional purposes, variable time periods. Out of this grew what was called modular scheduling, with some courses, those thought to demand active learning arrangements, scheduled to meet in 2–3 hour blocks several days a week and other courses meeting for shorter periods on a daily basis. The logic was apparent; different subjects require different kinds of time periods to complete purposeful instruction. Yet, what was not addressed in these arrangements was the simultaneous demand that students continue taking six to seven courses at the same time. By the end of the 1970s, modular scheduling had virtually disappeared; it was seen as too complicated and too demanding on teachers. About all that survives of this innovation is the rotating schedule, which ensures that a particular course is not *always* the first, second, or last period of the day.

There were also schools in the 1960s that did everythinig thematically. Teams of teachers who comprised the four basic academic areas worked exclusively with one group of students through an entire day all year or through some part of a year, possibly in 6–12 week blocks. Many small alternative schools still maintain such a pattern. In addition, some larger urban schools have developed clusters of this sort for ninth graders as a transition into the high school. Yet, attractive as this direction is, and as accommodating as it is for teaching for understanding, it has not taken hold in very many schools.

Currently, the Coalition of Essential Schools has encouraged using larger blocks of time around a smaller number of courses, partly for simplicity and the principle of "less is more." The Central Park East Secondary School, a coalition member, for example, organizes around two integrated courses a day— Humanities and Math/Science. Each meets for 2 hours. In addition, there is a 40-minute advisory that meets 4 days a week. Beyond the structure, but also important, teachers in this school

of 500 students share a common set of beliefs about teaching-learning practice. Inquiry with a focus on understanding is a collective process.

Closely aligned to some of the organizing principles of the coalition, the Copernican Plan, developed by Joseph Carroll, former Superintendent of Schools in Topsfield, Massachusetts, is beginning to take hold in a number of large secondary schools across the country. Essentially the plan calls for schools to organize around two to three courses a day, each meeting for 100–120 minutes during a 12-week period or trimester. The argument is that students will complete six to nine courses each over the duration of a year, but they will be focusing on a small number at any one time (Carroll, 1994).

Manipulating the schedule around fewer periods each day has another important effect that is supportive of teaching for understanding, namely, fewer students for teachers to work with at any given time. In most coalition schools, the numbers have fallen well below 80, primarily because they have been offering fewer courses. At Central Park East, for example, teachers work with 40 students each day. In many Copernican schools, the numbers range from 35 to 45.

The longer periods and the small numbers of students enable teachers to diversify more easily their instruction and move more responsibility to students; in this regard, it adopts more naturally Theodore Sizer's notions of the "student as worker" and the "teacher as coach." Teachers are also able to assign and respond to more writing and more complex inquiry-oriented tasks (Taylor, 1991). The longer periods have also made more clear the need for teachers to begin to talk and plan together. This important change helps teachers break through much of the isolation that has existed. There is more sharing of ideas and materials leading to a more favorable condition for considering Teaching for Understanding (Wasley, 1993, 1991b). As an example, teachers at Central Park East have 4 hours a week of in-school time for curriculum planning. A four-person humanities team will discuss a unit they are working on, exchange ideas and materials, and determine how to extend a particular student's learning.

Stigler and Stevenson (1991), in their work on Asian teachers "polishing" their lessons, noted, for example, how much more time Asian teachers have for planning than do their American counterparts. Educators do not acknowledge this fact sufficiently. Also revealing in the Stigler and Stevenson work is their observation that "in the United States, the purpose of a good question is to get an answer. In Japan teachers pose questions to stimulate thought" (p. 12). Interpretation, full discussion, and performance are more the norm in the Asian settings Stevenson and Stigler examined. This ethic is not yet common in American schools, but it needs to be.

Wagner (1992), in his research on three schools in the process of change (via the coalition's principles), shared some of the common features, that is, things that enable teachers and administrators to work through the many barriers. He cited the following: a leadership of vision (not managerial leadership) from teachers *and* administrators; teachers in collaboration; times for people to meet; opportunities for learning new skills; autonomy and a manageable size; a strong focus; and a centrality of purposes. He noted further that school-site management was not the vehicle of change in any of the schools, even though it existed. The large scale discussions of change, new directions, large hopes, and possibilities, he notes, fueled and sustained reform.

This discussion shows that systemic factors in the school are important in determining the level of success of a pedagogy for teaching for understanding. Although this conclusion is not surprising, it helps to place the teaching for understanding research and other such efforts toward change in the appropriate context.

CONCLUSION

As those *in* schools assume greater responsibility for defining the purposes, structures, and academic/vocational programs for *their* schools, a governance direction becoming more common, they are asking certain questions more regularly. What do we most want for those who go through our schools? What kinds of skills, dispositions, and habits of mind are desired? What do we want them to understand and be able to do? Their answers, which account for *their* students, *their* particular circumstances and geographic settings, and *their* understandings of larger societal imperatives, are giving shape to a variety of changing patterns.

The major point here is that those preparing to teach in the secondary schools need to understand that change is occurring and that they will be asked to contribute to the nature of that change. Questions of purpose, structure, and curriculum need to be central to their preparation as teachers.

References

Apelman, M., Hawkins, D., & Morrison, P. (1985). *Critical barriers phenomenon in science.* Grand Forks: The North Dakota Study Group on Evaluation.

Association of American Colleges (AAC). (1985). *Report of the Project on Redefining the Purpose of Baccalaureate Degrees: Integrity in the college curriculum.* Washington, DC: Author.

Bacharach, S. B., Bauer, S. C., & Shedd, J. (1986). The work environment and school reform. *Teachers College Record, 88*(2), 241–256.

Banks, J. (1991). *Teaching strategies for ethnic studies.* Boston: Allyn & Bacon.

Banks, J., & Banks, C. M. (1993). *Multicultural education: Issues & perspectives.* Boston: Allyn & Bacon.

Ben-Peretz, M. (1990). *The teacher-curriculum encounter: Freeing teachers from the tyranny of texts.* Albany: SUNY Press.

Ben-Peretz, M., & Kremer-Hagan, T. (1990). The content and context of professional dilemmas encountered by novice and senior teachers. *Educational Review, 42*(1), 31–40.

Berliner, D. (1987). Ways of thinking about students and classrooms by more and less experienced teachers. In J. Calderhead (Ed.), *Exploring teachers' thinking* (pp. 60–83). London: Carrel Ed. Limited.

Bird, T., & Little, J. W. (1986). How schools organize the teaching occupation. *The Elementary School Journal, 86*(4), 493–511.

Brown, J. S., Collins, A., & Duguid, P. (1989). Situated cognition and the culture of learning. *Educational Researcher, 18*(1), 32–42.

Bullough, R. V., Jr. (1993). Case records as personal teaching texts for study in pre-service teacher education. *Teaching and Teacher Education, 9*(4), 385–396.

Capella-Noya, G. (1993). *Young people's perceptions of teachers' influence on their shared school experience: A dialogue.* Qualifying Paper, Harvard University Graduate School of Education.

Carini, P. (1988). *They're talking but who's listening.* North Bennington, VT: Prospect Center.

Carroll, J. (1994). *The Copernican Plan evaluated: The evolution of a revolution.* Topsfield, MA: Copernican Associates.

Cazden, C. (1988). *Classroom discourse: The language of teaching and learning.* Portsmouth, NH: Heinemann.

Chang, H. (1992). *Adolescent life and ethos: An ethnography of a U.S. high school.* Washington, DC: Falmer Press.

Chi, M. T. H., Glaser, R., & Rees, E. (1982). Expertise in problem-solving. In R. Steinberg (Ed.), *Advances in the psychology of human intelligence* (Vol. 1, pp. 7–75). Hillsdale, NJ: Lawrence Erlbaum Associates.

Clark, C., & Lampert, M. (1986). The study of teacher thinking: Implications for teacher education. *Journal of Teacher Education, 37*(5), 27–31.

Coalition for Essential Schools. (1984). *Principles of the Coalition for Essential Schools.* Providence, RI: Author.

Cochran-Smith, M., & Lytle, S. (1990). Research on teaching and teacher research: The issues that divide. *Educational Researcher, 19*(2), 2–11.

Cochran-Smith, M., & Lytle, S. (1992). Communities for teacher research: Fringe or forefront? *American Journal of Education, 100*(3), 298–324.

Cochran-Smith, M., & Lytle, S. (1993). Interrogating cultural diversity: Inquiry and action. *Journal of Teacher Education, 43,* 104–115.

Cohen, D. (1988). *Teaching practice: Plus Que Ca change.* East Lansing, MI: National Center for Research on Teacher Education.

Cohen, D. (1991). Revolution in one classroom (or, then again, was it?). *American Educator, 15*(2), 16–23.

Cole, M., & Means, B. (1981). *Comparative studies of how people think: An introduction.* Cambridge: Harvard University.

Comer, J. P. (1980). *School power: Implications of an intervention project.* New York: The Free Press.

Conant, J. (1959). *The American high school today: A first report to interested citizens.* New York: McGraw-Hill.

Cremin, L. (1961). *The transformation of the school.* New York: Vintage Books.

Cruickshank, D. R. (1984). *Models for the preparation of America's teachers.* Bloomington, IN: Phi Delta Kappan.

Cuban, L. (1990). Reforming again, again and again. *Educational Researcher, 19*(1), 3–13.

Cuban, L. (1991). *How teachers taught: Constancy and change in American classrooms, 1890–1990.* New York: Teachers College Press.

Cuban, L. (1992). Managing dilemmas while building professional communities. *Educational Researcher, 21,* 4–11.

Cummins, J. (1986). Empowering minority students: A framework for intervention. *Harvard Educational Review, 56*(1), 18–36.

Cusick, P. (1973). *Inside high school.* New York: Holt, Rinehart and Winston.

Cusick, P. (1983). *The egalitarian ideal and the American high school: Studies of three schools.* New York: Longman.

Darling-Hammond, L. (1992). *Graduation by portfolio at Central Park East.* New York: National Center for Restructuring Education Schools and Teaching, Teachers College, Columbia.

Darling-Hammond, L. (1994). Standards. *Quality Teaching, 3*(2), 7.

Delpit, L. D. (1988). The silenced dialogue: Power and pedagogy in educating other people's children. *Harvard Educational Review, 58*(3), 280–298.

Dewey, J. (1915). *The school and society*. Chicago: The University of Chicago Press.

DiSessa, A. (1982). Unlearning Aristotelian physics: A study of knowledge-based learning. *Cognitive Science, 6*(1), 37–75.

Duckworth, E. (1986). *Inventing density*. Grand Forks: The North Dakota Study Group on Evaluation.

Duckworth, E. (1987). *The having of wonderful ideas and other essays*. New York: Teachers College Press.

Duckworth, E. (1991). Twenty-four, forty-two and I love you: Keeping it complex. *Harvard Education Review, 61*(1), 1–24.

Eckert, P. (1989). *Jocks and burnouts*. New York: Holt, Rinehart and Winston.

Edmonds, R. (1979). Effective schools for the urban poor. *Educational Leadership, 37*(1), 15–23.

Elliot, J. (1991). *Action research for educational change*. London: Open University Press.

Floden, R., & Clark, C. (1988). Preparing teachers for uncertainty. *Teachers College Record, 89*(4), 506–524.

Gardner, H. (1983). *Frames of mind: The theory of multiple intelligences*. New York: Basic Books.

Gardner, H. (1991). *The unschooled mind*. New York: Basic Books.

Gardner, H., & Boix-Mansilla, V. (1994). Teaching for understanding—Within and across the disciplines. *Educational Leadership, 51*(5), 14–18.

Gardner, H., Perkins, D., & Perrone, V. (1993). *Annual report to the Spencer Foundation*. Cambridge: Harvard Graduate School of Education.

Gentner, D., & Stevens, A. L. (Eds.). (1983). *Mental models*. Hillsdale, NJ: Lawrence Erlbaum Associates.

Glaser, R., Pellegrino, J. W., & Lesgold, A. M. (1978). Some directions for a cognitive psychology of instruction. In A. M. Lesgold, J. A. Pellegrino, S. D. Fokkema, & R. Glaser (Eds.), *Cognitive psychology and instruction* (pp. 495–518). New York: Plenum.

Goodlad, J. (1990). *Teachers for our nation's schools*. San Francisco: Jossey-Bass.

Goodlad, J. (1991). Why we need a complete redesign of teacher education. *Educational Leadership, 49*(3), 4–6, 8–10.

Goodlad, J., Soder, R., & Sirotnik, K. A. (Eds.). (1990). *Places where teachers are taught*. San Francisco: Jossey-Bass.

Graham, P. (1992). *S.O.S.: Sustain our schools*. New York: Hill & Wang.

Greeno, J. (1988). Situations, mental models, and generative knowledge. *IRL Report No. 5*. Palo Alto, CA: Institute for Research in Learning.

Grossman, P. (1989). A study in contrast: Sources of pedagogical content knowledge for English teachers. *Journal of Teacher Education, 40*(5), 24–31.

Guthrie, J. W., Kirst, M., Haywood, G. C., Odden, R., Koppitch, J. E., Haywood, G. R., Adams, J., Geeping, G., & Webb, F. R. (1991). *Conditions of education in California, 1990*. Policy Paper #PP91-4-1. Berkeley: Policy Analysis for California Education.

Heath, S. B. (1983). *Ways with words: Language, life, and work in communities and classrooms*. New York: Cambridge University.

Hodgkinson, H., & Outtz, J. H. (1992). *The nation and the states: A profile data book of America's diversity*. Washington, DC: Center for Demographic Policy.

The Holmes Group. (1986). *Tomorrow's teachers: A report of the Holmes Group*. East Lansing, MI: Author.

The Holmes Group. (1991). *Tomorrow's schools: Principles for the design of professional development schools*. East Lansing, MI: Author.

Jencks, C. (1983). *Inequality: A reassessment of the effect of family and schooling in America*. New York: Cambridge University Press.

Jervis, K. (1994). *Eyes on the child: Three portfolio stories*. New York: NCREST.

Johnson, S. M. (1990). *Teachers at work: Achieving success in our schools*. New York: Basic Books.

Johnson-Laird, P. N. (1983). *Mental models: Toward a cognitive science of language, inference and consciousness*. Cambridge: Harvard University Press.

Kagan, D. M., & Tippins, D. J. (1991). How student teachers describe their pupils. *Teaching and Teacher Education, 7*(5/6), 455–466.

Kallick, B. (1989). *Changing schools into communities for thinking*. Grand Forks: North Dakota Study Group on Evaluation.

Kennedy, M. (1989). *Competing visions of teacher knowledge: Proceedings from NCRTE seminar for educational policy makers Vol. I, Academic subjects*. East Lansing, MI: National Center for Research on Teacher Education.

Kilbourn, B., & Roberts, G. (1991). May's first year: Conversations with a mentor. *Teachers College Record, 93*(2), 252–264.

Kirst, M., & Yee, G. (1994). Examination of the evolution of California state educational reform, 1983–1993. In D. Massell & S. Fuhrman (Eds.), *Ten years of state education reform* (pp. 69–103). Consortium for Policy Research in Education. Research Series RR-028. New Brunswick: Rutgers University.

Kliebard, H. (1989). *Success and failure in educational reform: Are there historical lessons?* Occasional Paper. East Lansing, MI: The Holmes Group.

Knowles, J. G., Cole, A. L., & Presswood, C. S. (1994). *Through preservice teachers' eyes: Exploring field experiences through narrative and inquiry*. New York: Merrill.

Krug, E. (1964). *The shaping of the American high school*. Madison: University of Wisconsin Press.

Lave, J. (1988). *Cognition in practice: Mind, mathematics, and culture in everyday life*. New York: Cambridge University Press.

Lawrence-Lightfoot, S. (1983). *The good high school: Portraits of character and culture*. New York: Basic Books.

Lazerson, M., McLaughlin, J. B., McPherson, B., & Bailey, S. K. (1985). *An education of value: The purposes and practices of schools*. New York: Cambridge University Press.

Leichter, H. J. (Ed.). (1974). *The family as educator*. New York: Teachers College Press.

Levin, H. (1987). Accelerated schools for disadvantaged students. *Educational Leadership, 44*(6), 19–21.

Levin, R. (1990). In J. I. Goodlad, R. Soder, & K. Sirotnik (Eds.), *Places where teachers are taught*. San Francisco: Jossey-Bass.

Lieberman, A., & Miller, L. (1992). *Teachers, their world and their work: Implications for school improvement*. New York: Teachers College Press.

Lytle, S., & Cochran-Smith, M. (1990). Learning from teacher research: A working typology. *Teachers College Record, 92*(1), 83–103.

Madaus, G. (1980). *School effectiveness: A reassessment of the evidence*. New York: McGraw-Hill.

Massachusetts Department of Education. (1993). *Teacher education regulations*. Malden, MA: Author.

Mayer, R. E. (1989). Models for understanding. *Review of Educational Research, 59*(1), 43–64.

McDiarmid, G. W. (1992). What to do about differences? A study of multicultural education for teacher trainees in Los Angeles Unified School District. *Journal of Teacher Education, 43*(2), 83–93.

McDiarmid, G. W., Ball, D. L., & Anderson, C. W. (1989). *Why staying one chapter ahead doesn't really work: Subject-specific pedagogy*. East Lansing, MI: The National Center for Research on Teacher Education.

McEwan, H., & Bull, B. (1991). The pedagogic nature of subject matter knowledge. *American Education Research Journal, 28*(2), 316–334.

McLaughlin, M., & Talbert, J. (1993). *Contexts that matter for teaching and learning*. Stanford, CA: Center for Research on the Context of Secondary School Teaching.

McNeil, L. (1986). *The contradictions of control: School structure and school knowledge*. New York: Routledge & Kegan Paul.

Meier, D. (1987). Central Park East: An alternative story. *Phi Delta Kappan, 66*(10), 753–757.

Miller, D. E. (1991). Merging regular and special education teacher preparation programs: The integrated special education-English project (ISEP). *Teaching and Teacher Education, 7*(1), 19–23.

Nathan, L. (1994). *Portfolio assessment and teacher change.* Unpublished qualifying paper. Cambridge, MA: Harvard Graduate School of Education.

Newmann, F. (1993). Beyond common sense in educational restructuring: The issues of content and linkage. *Educational Researcher, 22*(2), 4–13.

Newmann, F., & Archibald, D. (1992). The nature of authentic academic achievement. In H. Berlak, F. M. Newmann, E. Adams, D. A. Archibald, T. Burgess, J. Raven, & T. Romberg (Eds.), *Toward a new science of educational testing and assessment* (pp. 71–87). Albany: SUNY Press.

Nieto, S. (1992). *Affirming diversity: The sociopolitical context of multicultural education.* New York: Longman.

Nordhoff, K., & Kleinfeld, J. (1993). Preparing teachers for multicultural classrooms. *Teaching and Teacher Education, 9*(1), 27–39.

Oakes, J. (1985). *Keeping track: How schools structure inequality.* New Haven, CT: Yale University Press.

Oakes, J. (1992). Can tracking research inform practice? Technical, normative and political considerations. *Educational Researcher, 21*(4), 12–20.

Office of Technology Assessment, Congress of the United States. (1992). *Testing in American schools: Asking the right questions.* Washington, DC: Author.

Perkins, D., & Blythe, T. (1994). Putting understanding up front. *Educational Leadership, 51*(5), 4–8.

Perkins, D., & Salomon, G. (1988). Teaching for transfer. *Educational Leadership, 46*(1), 22–32.

Perkins, D., & Simmons, R. (1988). Patterns of misunderstandings: An integrative model for science, math, and programming. *Review of Educational Research, 58*(3), 303–326.

Perkins, D., & Unger, C. (1989). *The new look in representations for mathematics and science learning.* Paper presented at the social science research council's seminar on computers and learning, Tortola, British Virgin Islands.

Perrone, V. (1985). *Portraits of high schools.* Princeton, NJ: Carnegie Foundation.

Perrone, V. (1989). *Working papers: Reflections of teachers, schools and communities.* New York: Teachers College Press.

Perrone, V. (Ed.). (1991a). *Expanding student assessment.* Alexandria, VA: ASCD.

Perrone, V. (1991b). *Letters to teachers.* San Francisco: Jossey-Bass.

Perrone, V., & Jacobs, V. (1993). *Tracking the philosophical development of teacher education programs' candidates.* Unpublished manuscript. Harvard University Graduate School of Education.

Powell, A., Ferrar, E., & Cohen, D. (1985). *The shopping mall high school: Winners and losers in the educational marketplace.* Boston: Houghton Mifflin.

Project 30. (1989). *The reform of teacher education in the 21st century.* Washington, DC: The American Association of Colleges for Teacher Education and The Council of Colleges of Arts and Sciences.

Public Law 94-142, Education for All Handicapped Children Act of 1975. (23 August 1977). 20 U.S.C. 1401 et. seq: *Federal Register, 42*(163), 42474–42518.

Quality Education for Minorities Project. (1990). *Education that works: An action plan for the education of minorities.* Washington, DC: Author.

Resnick, L. B. (1987). Learning in school and out. *Educational Researcher, 16*(10), 13–20.

Rogoff, B., & Lave, J. (Eds.). (1984). *Everyday cognition: Its development in social context.* Cambridge: Harvard University Press.

Rose, M. (1989). *Lives on the boundary: The struggles and achievements of America's underprepared.* New York: The Free Press.

Rosenstock, L. (1991). The walls come down: The overdue reunification of vocational and academic education. *Phi Delta Kappan, 72*(6), 434–437.

Rudduck, J., & Hopkins, D. (1985). *Research as a basis for teaching: Readings from the works of Lawrence Stenhouse.* London: Heinemann Educational Books.

Salomon, G., & Perkins, D. (1989). Rocky roads to transfer: Rethinking mechanisms of a neglected phenomenon. *Educational Psychologist, 24*(2), 113–142.

Sarason, S. (1971). *The culture of schools and the problem of change.* Boston: Allyn & Bacon.

Sarason, S. (1983). *Schooling in America: Scapegoat and salvation.* New York: The Free Press.

Schaffarzick, J., & Sykes, G. (1979). *Value conflicts and curriculum issues.* Berkeley, CA: McCutchan.

Scheffler, I. (1991). *In praise of cognitive emotions.* New York: Routledge.

Schoenfeld, A. (1988). Mathematics, technology, and higher order thinking. In R. Nickerson & P. Zodhiates (Eds.), *Technology in education: Looking toward 2020.* Hillsdale, NJ: Lawrence Erlbaum Associates.

Schreiber, J. (1994). *Middle school portrait.* Spring Seminar, T-400. Unpublished manuscript. Cambridge, MA: Harvard University.

Seidel, S. (1991). *Five phases in the implementation of portfolio assessment in classrooms, schools and school districts.* Unpublished manuscript. Cambridge, MA: Project Zero, Harvard University Graduate School of Education.

Seidel, S. (1992). *Looking carefully together: A comparative analysis of four models of teachers' collaborative investigation of children's work.* Qualifying paper. Cambridge, MA: Harvard University Graduate School of Education.

Shuell, T. J. (1992). The two cultures of teaching and teacher preparation. *Teaching and Teacher Education, 8*(1), 83–90.

Shulman, L. (1986). Those who understand: Knowledge and growth in teaching. *Educational Researcher, 15*(2), 4–14.

Shulman, L. (1987). Knowledge and teaching: Foundations of the new reform. *Harvard Education Review, 57*(1), 1–22.

Shulman, L. (1991). *Aristotle had it right: On knowledge and pedagogy.* Occasional paper #4. East Lansing, MI: The Holmes Group.

Simmons, W., & Resnick, L. (1993). Assessment as the catalyst of school reform. *Educational Leadership, 50*(5), 11–15.

Sizer, T. (1984). *Horace's compromise: The dilemma of the American school.* Boston: Houghton Mifflin.

Sizer, T. (1989). Diverse practice, shared idea: The essential school. In H. Walberg & J. Lane (Eds.), *Organizing for learning: Toward the 21st century* (pp. 1–8). Reston, Va: The National Association of Secondary School Principals.

Sizer, T. (1992). *Horace's school: Redesigning the American high school.* New York: Houghton Mifflin.

Stage, E. (1989). *Strategies and materials for meeting the needs of all students in math, science, technology and health.* Sacramento: California Commission on Curriculum.

Stigler, J., & Stevenson, H. (1991). How Asian teachers polish each lesson to perfection. *American Educator, 15*(4), 12–20, 43–47.

Taylor, D. (1991). *Learning denial.* Portsmouth, NH: Heinemann Educational Books.

Villegas, A. M. (1991). *Culturally responsive pedagogy for the 1990s and beyond.* Princeton, NJ: Educational Testing Service.

Villegas, A. M., & Watts, S. (1991). *Life in the classroom: The influence of class placement and student race, ethnicity.* Paper presented at the annual meeting of the American Educational Research Association, Chicago.

Wagner, H. (1992). *Portraits of changing schools.* Unpublished doctoral thesis, Harvard University Graduate School of Education, Cambridge, MA.

Wasley, P. (1991a). From quarterback to coach, from action to direction. *Educational Leadership, 48*(8), 35–40.

Wasley, P. (1991b). *Teachers who lead: The rhetoric of reform and the realities of practice*. New York: Teachers College Press.

Wasley, P. (1993). *Teacher change studies, Coalition of Essential Schools*. Providence, RI: Brown University.

Wheelock, A. (1992). *Crossing the tracks: How "untracking" can save America's schools*. New York: The New Press.

Wiggins, G. (1989). A true test: Toward more authentic and equitable assessment. *Phi Delta Kappan, 70*(9), 703–713.

Wiggins, G. (1993). *Assessing student performance: Exploring the purpose and limits of testing*. San Francisco: Jossey-Bass.

Wilson, S., Shulman, L., & Richert, A. (1987). 150 different ways of knowing: Representations of knowledge in teaching. In J. Calderhead (Ed.), *Exploring teachers' thinking*. London: Carroll Education Limited Publisher.

Wiser, M., & Carey, S. (1983). When heat and temperature were one. In D. Gentner & A. Stevens (Eds.), *Mental models*. Hillsdale, NJ: Lawrence Erlbaum Associates.

Wohlstetter, P. (1994). Georgia reform at the crossroads. In D. Massell & S. Fuhrman (Eds.), *Ten years of state education reform* (pp. 69–103). Consortium for Policy Research in Education. Research Series RR-028. New Brunswick: Rutgers University

Wolf, D. (December 1987/January 1988). Opening up assessment: Ideas from the arts. *Educational Leadership, 45*(4), 24–29.

Wolf, D., LeMahiew, P., & Eresh, L. (1992). Good measure: Assessment as a tool for educational reform. *Educational Leadership, 49*(8), 8–13.

Yonemura, M. (1982). Teacher conversations: A potential source of their own professional growth. *Curriculum Inquiry, 12*(3), 239–256.

Zeichner, K. (1993). Action research: Personal research and social reconstruction. *Educational Action Research, 1*(2), 199–220.

Zessoules, R., & Gardner, H. (1991). Authentic assessment: Beyond the buzzwords and into the classroom. In V. Perrone (Ed.), *Expanding student assessment* (pp. 47–71). Washington, DC: ASCD.

·20·

TEACHER EDUCATION RESEARCH IN THE ENGLISH LANGUAGE ARTS AND READING

Carol J. Fisher
THE UNIVERSITY OF GEORGIA

Dana L. Fox
THE UNIVERSITY OF ARIZONA

Emilie Paille
GEORGIA STATE UNIVERSITY

This chapter focuses on a review of research concerning teacher education in English language arts and reading. Section one provides an overview of the goals of teacher education and the political influences on teacher education reform. In addition, the authors address current trends and approaches in teacher education, including theme cycles and whole language, literature-based curricula, reading-to-learn and writing-to-learn in the content areas, teacher thinking and reflective practice, and multicultural issues in teacher education. Section two provides a framework for the "knowledge base" for teaching English language arts and reading, including a discussion of what it means "to know," as well as a review of research concerning subject-matter knowledge in oral language, reading, literature, and composition. In the second section, the authors also address the importance of preservice teachers' personal histories and beliefs and review studies concerning the relationship between teachers' beliefs and their classroom practices. Section three provides an overview of subject-specific pedagogy, including studies concerning pedagogical approaches such as reading and/or writing workshops, Reading Recovery and other intervention programs, portfolio and process assessment, and instructional planning. Section four surveys research

in teacher education programs and looks carefully at a variety of recent research on professional education coursework and field experience programs. Finally, several promising directions for inquiry in English language arts and reading teacher education are discussed.

INTRODUCTION: GOALS AND TRENDS IN THE CURRICULUM

In a working introduction to the Holmes Group's "Tomorrow's Schools of Education," Sykes (1992) provides a discussion of a state-of-the-art professional curriculum for future teachers in America's elementary and secondary schools. Whereas other recent reports concerning the curricular design of teacher education programs continue to list "basic competencies and skills" for beginning teachers (e.g., Duke, 1992), Sykes contends that teacher educators must examine themselves and their programs first, and they must place the changing needs of children at the core of the learning that teachers need. In response to the question "What must future educators have the opportunity to learn if they are to respond to the needs of all the nation's

The authors wish to acknowledge the helpful suggestions from their reviewers: Patricia Anderson, Eastern Carolina University; Pose Lamb, Purdue University; and Don Zancanella, New Mexico University.

children?," Sykes discusses certain knowledge and dispositions that educators must learn, including a discussion of diversity, subject matter, repertoire, and inquiry. In addition, he points to the importance of the sequencing of such learning both at the beginning of an educator's career as well as throughout the phases of a professional teaching career, the importance of the institutional frameworks in which such learning takes place, and the importance of building communities to nourish such learning.

The Goals of Teacher Education and the Political Influences on Reform

Sykes's ideas concerning certain knowledge and dispositions for all educators may be summarized as follows. First, educators must develop knowledge, capacities, and dispositions to respond wisely and sensitively to diverse learners. Rather than merely providing a "smattering of knowledge" about certain cultural groups that could lead to stereotyping, teacher education programs should "convey a set of orienting principles and assumptions about diversity" and should "provide rich examples . . . and methods, models, and encouragement for ongoing learning about students" (Sykes, 1992, p. 15). To help students appreciate and understand cultural differences, most teacher education programs, Sykes contends, do little more than simply provide information about characteristics of a variety of students. The ultimate aim should be to enable preservice teachers to become lifelong learners, "to help beginners acquire and use knowledge of their own students that will promote their learning and development" (p. 15). This includes understanding the difficulties that complicate schooling for many minority children, understanding the importance of language as "the medium and the tool through which school subjects are taught and learned and through which connections are made to home-based ways of talking and reasoning" (p. 16), and learning to care for the growing number of children who are labeled "at risk" in schools. Finally, he urges teacher educators to begin to attract more teacher candidates who are willing and able to work with all children.

Second, educators must acquire knowledge of the subjects they teach together with knowledge of how to teach subjects to diverse learners. Sykes suggests that the division between university subject-matter courses (e.g., "The Tragedies of Shakespeare") and methods courses (e.g. "The Teaching of Literature") is a "flawed sequence": "Subject matter knowledge must be more thoroughly integrated with learning how to teach it, and the pedagogy employed by both liberal arts and education faculty must itself contribute to rich learning and to models of good teaching" (Sykes, 1992, pp. 24–25). Furthermore, Sykes contends that teacher educators have begun to embrace constructivist principles and that current trends in teacher education courses include opportunities for students to explore their own conceptions of teaching and learning, their knowledge and understanding of subject matter, and their understanding of students' learning. "The pedagogy of teacher education," Sykes reports, "is undergoing a gradual transformation itself" (p. 32). Although the outcomes of such courses are often mixed and somewhat contradictory, Sykes reminds us that the process

enables teacher educators to examine their own teaching continually, providing a model for novices.

Third, educators must acquire knowledge and skills for organizing instruction in school and classrooms and for managing crucial problems that arise, and they must develop a critical appreciation for the strengths and weaknesses of a variety of techniques and approaches to work in schools. Sykes believes that teacher educators must strike a careful balance between skills training based on modeling, coaching, and guided practice and practical reasoning about complex situations in classrooms in order to rethink known skills or techniques and to move toward inventing alternative approaches. Learning about technology in teacher education, for example, must go beyond "the typical 'one-shot' course on computers and audio-visual techniques"; for example, teacher educators might explore ways to use technology to promote reflection, self-evaluation, rich discussion of simulated teaching cases, and other visual displays.

Finally, Sykes believes that educators must cultivate the capacity and the disposition to engage in critical, reflective inquiry and dialogue about their own beliefs and practices, about children's learning and development, and about a range of social, institutional, and political issues bearing on education. Building on Gore and Zeichner's (1991) suggestions, Sykes (1992) suggests that prospective teachers should engage in critical, reflective inquiry and dialogue on five key topics or issues.

1. The representation of subject matter to promote understanding among diverse learners
2. The thoughtful application of particular teaching strategies and principles derived from research on teaching
3. The interests, thinking, and development of students as a basis for sensitive, responsive teaching
4. The critical scrutiny of the social and political context of schooling and the assessment of school and classroom processes from the perspectives of equity, social justice, and humanity
5. Self-knowledge and reflection on one's own beliefs and assumptions about the first four topics

A Shift in Focus in Research on Teachers' Knowledge and the Process of Learning to Teach

Learning to teach is clearly a complex and problematic endeavor. Unraveling and understanding this complexity provides a difficult challenge for teacher educators in their daily work with prospective teachers and in their research on teaching and teacher education. For decades, teacher education has focused on the "training of future teachers, often without much attention to these individuals' conceptions of teaching and schooling or their beliefs about subject matter. Moreover, we have paid little attention to the sources of their knowledge for teaching. Society at large has tended to overlook the complex intellectual processes involved in pedagogical reasoning" (Feiman-Nemser, 1983, p. 150). Indeed, these suggestions seem particularly relevant today.

1. Formal arrangements for teaching teachers and helping them to improve do not fit with what is known about how teachers learn to teach and get better at teaching over time.
2. Informal influences are far more salient in learning to teach, but often have miseducative effects.
3. Creating appropriate arrangements to support teachers' learning involves changing not only what educators do, but also how they think about learning to teach throughout the teacher's career.

Past research on learning to teach and on program design of undergraduate/postbaccalaureate education has focused on behaviors and skills rather than on the actual learning processes of beginning teachers. As Applebee (1988) suggests, much of the research in teacher education has been framed in a behaviorist tradition and has ignored powerful models of learning.

We need the kind of shift in our thinking that we made in our understanding of reading and writing processes during the past two decades: from a focus on the skills that [teacher education] students need to a focus on the general process of making meaning, from *what* to *why*. (p. 211)

More recent studies on learning to teach have begun to focus on the experience of the beginning teacher who is "no longer quietly tucked away in tables of aggregated data" (Carter, 1990, p. 293). Such investigations focus on the characteristics of teacher knowledge, how that knowledge is obtained, and how that knowledge develops through action and reflection. Through detailed case analyses, researchers have begun to provide an insider's perspective—descriptive accounts of the metamorphosis young women and men undergo as they prepare and begin to teach.

Biographies of teacher candidates, which describe their developing attitudes, concerns, and professional orientations, comprise much of the current body of research on learning to teach. This movement to develop the "missing paradigm" in research on teaching seems productive and shows great promise; however, this particular field of inquiry remains young and incomplete (Carter, 1990; Shulman, 1986a). As Carter (1990, 1992) suggests, recent investigations reveal that teachers' knowledge is not "highly abstract" nor can it be "formalized into a set of specific skills"; rather, teaching is "experiential, procedural, situational, and particularistic" (1990, p. 307).

Current Trends and Approaches in Teacher Education

Some of the trends or approaches currently being studied and promoted are specific to the field of the English language arts and reading; others are more widely applied. Three approaches that are primarily associated with the English language arts are the integration of the curriculum through theme cycles or whole language, the increase of literature-based curricula where literature serves as the organizing base for the study of a topic, and the use of reading and language arts to learn material in other content areas (reading and writing across the curriculum). The other trends or approaches are more widely utilized but have specific functions within the arena of the language arts. These approaches to practice involve inquiry and the reflective practitioner in planning and teaching, the teacher as researcher, and concerns about preparing teachers to work with students from many different cultures and abilities.

Whole Language or Themes: Integration of the Curriculum Whole language is thought to have its roots in the progressive curriculum reforms of the 1930s, particularly in John Dewey's writings and publications, such as *Experience and Education* (1938), that emphasized preparing students for life and developed thematic literary units. Elements of whole language are also seen in the unit teaching of the early 1960s and the publications that followed the Dartmouth Conference emphasizing personal growth, as well as in the British Primary School classrooms of the 1970s. Today it is perhaps the most widely discussed movement in elementary education and to some degree in secondary education. A range of materials and practices are labeled "whole language," although they may not fit the characteristics generally accepted as defining whole language.

Lipson, Valencia, Wixson, and Peters (1993) characterize whole language as providing authentic learning experiences, generative as it encourages students to construct meaning, integrative in promoting higher order thinking and concept transfer across disciplines, and iterative as it evolves into cyclical learning processes. A theme approach to integrating the curriculum is frequently recommended for transforming fragmented, departmentalized, isolated instruction into more meaningful learning opportunities for students where they can discover connections among content. In fact, Lipson et al. (1993) point out that a thematic approach should make the connections between *content* and *process* clearer as students acquire knowledge about processes to learn specific content. They also suggest two kinds of themes as organizing forces: intradisciplinary themes that have a strong content focus and integrate reading and writing processes with concepts across several content disciplines and literary themes that cluster selections of literature that share a theme (e.g., "People rarely appreciate what is before their eyes"). However themes are developed, the authors point out that the themes must be more than a collection of related activities; they should provide genuine coherence around important concepts and also address significant aspects of an agreed-upon curriculum.

Whole language teaching may also be organized around an inquiry curriculum as well as an integrated curriculum. Harste explains the inquiry curriculum in an interview with Monson and Monson (1994) by saying that in an inquiry curriculum questions come from living and the disciplines are used to gain a perspective on them. In such a curriculum children are allowed to inquire and to go off in directions that may not be predetermined. "All curriculum, in terms of both literacy and content learning, needs to be developed through research rather than through the memory of what it is we think we know" (p. 521).

Whole language represents change coming from the ground up, from teachers, rather than from the principal's office or the board room, according to Goodman (1992). He highlights the political impact of the whole language movement and points out the impact of whole language on the publishing industry, in both textbooks and trade books. This impact extends to the research community and to the testing community. The whole language movement has been discovered by parents and the popular press who praise it and by the far right who have made it a central target of opposition. According to Goodman, whole language builds on constructivist views of learning to read and write as students construct meaning from the base of experience they bring to the text. This evolves from Louise Rosenblatt's work in response to literature (1983) and Jean Piaget's work with Inhelder on constructivism (1969). It is built on the social learning theories of Lev Vygotsky (1978) that place learning in a social context and suggest how teachers can mediate learning. Goodman (1992) also emphasizes the impact of whole language on teachers contending they accept responsibility for their decisions and actions within the framework of their authority. In this way teachers claim power as individuals and as faculties and create a variety of new roles for themselves.

In this holistic approach, learning is connected to real experiences and the children become a community of learners with their teacher. In addition to the interrelationships among the teacher, the students, and the curriculum, Shockley (1993) added the parents so that they might witness and participate in their first-grade children's literate journey. There were three main ways parents participated: (1) in the first week of school parents were invited to talk about their children; (2) each night students brought home a book and a spiral notebook, and the child or parent was to read the story and write about it in a home response journal to which the teacher also responded; and (3) each family was asked to write a family story to include in a class book. Shockley concludes that these provided meaningful literacy experiences for the children and opportunities for their parents to play an important role in the children's education.

The role of literature in whole language was explored by Cullinan (1992), particularly its ties with reading instruction. She bases the importance of literature on research on the connections between a rich literature program and the quality of language in children's writing, the power of narrative as organizing schema for thinking, the influence of literature when students approach writing as authors do, and the gains in reading achievement by students who do a good amount of independent reading. Cullinan also discusses the debate about the importance of phonics and the role of basal readers in whole language. She reports many important signs that indicate the increasing role of literature in schools, including the number of states reporting whole language initiatives or literature-based language arts programs as well as states that reported local districts using literature and whole language; the growth in sales of children's books, the increase in the number of children's bookstores, the funding of the American Association of Publishers Reading Initiative designed to get tradebooks into classrooms, and the reports of individual teachers who are succeeding in improving children's reading through literature-based/whole language programs.

Ruddell (1992) contends that there is confusion about whole language, about what whole language means because it is used to label programs ranging from a basal reading structure applied to full-length literature selections to classrooms where students are "turned loose" to read books without any instructional component. He contends that whole language is a philosophy,

not a methodology, based on having meaning making at the center, involving literature in the context of meaning making, and with the teacher as the critical facilitator in the whole language environment. He proposes two sets of ideas that support whole language: (1) five principles of language development, and (2) seven conditions for language acquisition that can be applied to classrooms. Ruddell then examines the role of literature in reader motivation and suggests six types of motivations critical in developing internal motivation and identification with a literary work: problem resolution, prestige, aesthetic, escape, intellectual curiosity, and understanding of self. He concludes by describing the influential teacher as sensitive to student needs, motivations, and aptitudes; strategy-oriented to create an instructional flow; and someone who holds high expectations for students.

A similar concern about what is and is not whole language instruction is the focus of Pace (1991), who points out that whole language is more than using real literature, complete texts, and integrating reading, writing, speaking, and listening. She identifies key premises from whole language theory that relate to language and language acquisition: language is meaning driven; language learners must invent and try out the rules of language for themselves; language is whole; and what is true about oral language acquisition is also true of written language acquisition, that is, written language is language. The key premises from reading and writing processes are that reading and writing are learned through authentic reading and writing experiences, and readers construct meaning as they read and writers construct meaning during the act of writing. The premises relevant to a view of teaching and learning are that the teacher is a co-learner and an active participant in the learning endeavor; whole language is learner centered and the goal is empowerment through personal ownership, choice, and control; and whole language theorists view the learner as profoundly social. In the area of curriculum, a whole language curriculum features integration of language processes and integration across content areas; authentic experiences are a hallmark of whole language; and the goal is individual growth rather than achieving a particular level. These premises are explored through descriptions of classroom events and a discussion of how each event relates to the key premises of whole language.

Yetta Goodman (1989) explores the foundations of the whole language movement, placing it within the context of humanism in the respect for all learners regardless of their age, abilities, or backgrounds, and within the context of science as it borrows from discoveries in psychology, linguistics, psycholinguistics, and sociolinguistics. Those involved in whole language programs have a greater respect for the power of language and of the importance of children being actively involved in their own learning.

According to Watson (1994), teachers may approach the change into a whole language philosophy through practice (using an element often used in whole language), through theory (perhaps from the teacher training program), or through belief (based on reflection and inquiry into teaching).

Sumara and Walker (1991) report a study that was designed to articulate a more precise description of the role of two teachers in whole language classrooms. Because there is such flexibility in the whole language agenda in its stage of development as a reform movement, many very different programs and practices use the name without being based on a real understanding of its principles. Both teachers in this study defined themselves as whole language teachers creating learning environments, and each was observed for about 70 hours during a 4-month period. Specifically, the research attempted to situate the ideas of empowerment, control, predictability, and authenticity and how these concepts operated within their classrooms.

Whole language for secondary English teachers is the focus of Foster's book (1994), which includes an overview of whole language in secondary schools, changes in literacy that have fostered a whole language model, and "stories" of several teachers and their classrooms that illustrate whole language teaching. Foster points out that the focus of whole language is different in secondary classrooms with the major changes in the roles of the teacher and students. The changes in teaching composition in secondary school have promoted the writing workshops that fit so well with whole language concepts. Whole language theory also fits with the interest in reader response coming from Louise Rosenblatt's theories (1938, 1978), which emphasize the readers' interaction with the text to create meaning. There are now many exciting new books of high literary quality for adolescents dealing with modern themes and current issues to serve as a major resource for whole language teachers. The issue in secondary schools is the place of the classics, the canon, not that of skills and phonics found in elementary whole language debates. Foster sets the forces leading to a change to a whole language approach within the massive literary and cultural changes of the past 35 years. Changes of this magnitude in practice require commensurate changes in teacher preparation and, therefore, in research on teacher education.

Literature-Based Curricula Although literature is often an integral part of whole language and central to theme cycles, it is also independent of such programs or philosophies. The power of literature may come from its ability to stir the imagination, according to Brooks (1992). He contends that reading is a creative act of the individual imagination. He also contends that the imagination wants challenge, and that the books that we remember years later are those that contain some insoluble bit of mystery or ambiguity that still intrigues us because we cannot completely understand it. Books that are too simplified, that publishers have removed all but the "limited collection of Key Names and Dates and Places we carry around like some kind of restricted code" (Brooks, 1992, pp. 83–84), limit the reader's imagination. The power of literature exists because readers create experience from what they read, but only when the imagination is challenged by that which is yet to be known.

The role of literature in literacy is explored by Huck (1992), who points out that the most significant factor for children who achieved real literacy was the rich literacy environment of their childhood where books were loved and often shared. She cites two major studies to support this contention: Shirley Brice Heath's *Ways with Words* (1983) and Gordon Wells's *The Meaning Makers* (1986). The value of reading aloud to young children comes from the association they make between reading and pleasure or love, the development of narrative as a universal way of thinking, the development of vocabulary and sensitivity

to language, the sense of story or schema for how stories work, and an understanding of concepts of print. Reading aloud to children in school and rereading stories develop these same values, as does independent reading. Huck also suggests that literature-based programs can be divided into three main types: literature-based readers that include selections from real literature, the basalization of literature in which literature is treated as material for worksheets and isolated skill instruction, and comprehensive literature programs in which literature is read and responded to with the goal of producing readers.

This concern with how literature may be used (or misused) in reading programs is examined through a case study of a teacher in the process of changing from a traditional basal reading program to a literature-based approach reported by Scharer and Detwiler (1992). Their study suggests that however willing the teacher, making such a change is not simple. Detwiler's experience suggests that the following are important in supporting teacher changes: realistic time frames for change; different materials for students and professional materials for teachers; support staff (especially librarians); staff development in children's literature, reading process, classroom organization, informal assessment, and opportunities for collegial interaction; help with informal assessment tools and reconciling such assessment with traditional grading and reporting practices.

For secondary students, Langer (1990) contends that the reform within English language arts instruction has been primarily on writing instruction with virtually no research on the teaching of literature. This has led to process approaches in writing and text-based approaches in literature. Langer reports on her research on a process view of reading that suggests reading involves envisionment building, that is, the understanding a reader has about a text. She suggests four stances that a reader might adopt toward a text and gives examples of each: Being Out and Stepping In, Being In and Moving Through, Being In and Stepping Out, and Stepping Out and Objectifying the Experience. Langer contrasts reading literary and informative pieces and how the stances operate in informative works. She also suggests some possibilities for instruction, particularly areas of questioning that explore literary understanding, including questions about initial understandings, developing interpretations, reflecting on personal experiences, and elaborating and extending. The focus of instruction is on extending students' understandings of the text, not the teacher's perception of the right response.

Close's (1990) follow-up study involved teacher-researchers in implementing the process-oriented literature approach described by Langer (1990). Two concepts that Close saw operating in her class changed her teaching. First, envisionment is not a sequential process, but rather a recursive one. Second, instructional scaffolding must aid the students' thinking and then be removed as students internalize the structure. She gives many examples of specific ways she used to implement such a process in a seventh-grade classroom.

The role that one part of the content, literature, plays in a discussion of content knowledge is explored further by Grossman (1991b). She explores three of the most common orientations toward literature in the high school: (1) a reader orientation in which the interaction between the reader and the text is the focus, (2) a text orientation rooted in New Criticism in which the text serves as the source of evidence for correct interpretation, and (3) a context orientation in which the reader's interpretation is mediated by theoretical frameworks and analytical tools for other disciplines such as psychology or history. She illustrates these orientations through two case studies of beginning English teachers. For data, she conducted multiple interviews of the two teachers about their backgrounds, beliefs, knowledge of literature and writing, and their conceptions of teaching. She also observed them teach, interviewing them before about plans and objectives and afterwards about the experience. She found that the teachers' frameworks for reading literature became frameworks for teaching literature. The study suggests that the construct of content knowledge is complex and the stance toward literature is crucial in how a teacher presents literature to students.

The increased role of literature in the other language arts, in reading, writing, and literature study, has been one of the important trends as educators move toward a more process-oriented approach to literature and reading. Literature often provides the content for the other areas of the language arts.

Reading and Writing to Learn in Other Content Areas Writing to learn is a relatively new facet of composition that developed along with the interest in process-oriented writing, but reading in the content areas has been of interest throughout this century. These somewhat specialized areas of reading and writing form part of the teacher preparation curriculum in most teacher education programs, and research on their content and use is growing. Moore, Readence, and Rickelman (1983) give a very comprehensive picture of the history of content area reading in which the primary mission is to develop students' reading-to-learn strategies. They also identify five recurring issues confronting reading educators: the locus of instruction, the reading demands of various subjects, improving students' ability to study, appropriate reading materials, and the appropriate age for such instruction.

Reading in the content areas has been traditionally related only to middle school and high school learners who are applying the reading skills learned in elementary schools. More recently, teachers of much younger children have found such reading to be an integral part of their literature-based or whole language programs. Short and Armstrong (1993) report a classroom study in which literature was an integral part of the second-grade children's learning of science content, concepts, and processes. Literature was a part of the inquiry process, not just a way to develop interest in the topic and information about the content. It also supported inquiry by integrating affective and cognitive ways of knowing. The authors adapted an inquiry cycle that involved three main areas: (1) developing perspectives and focusing questions through exploration; (2) collecting, collaborating, and revising through inquiry; and (3) presenting, reflecting, and offering invitations for inquiry. Within the inquiry frame, literary experiences were not undermined, but became another way for children to explore their questions and ideas as they made sense of their world.

The research base of studies dealing with students in grades 7–12 for content area reading strategies as presented in content reading methods textbooks was examined by Alvermann and Swafford (1989). They did a content analysis of six textbooks judged representative of those with an integrated approach. They found that textbook authors cited 54 different comprehension and vocabulary strategies, such as graphic organizers, structured overview, and imaging. The research base of more than 100 studies that reported findings for 13 strategies was examined for the effectiveness of each, the grade level and ability of readers, and the type of text studied. The overall findings are that there is a broad array of content reading strategies and some of the most frequently recommended are widely researched and used; there is a very uneven research base for these practices; and strategies vary in their effectiveness by grade and topic.

Writing to learn as differentiated from writing to show learning is a relatively new purpose for writing. Once the only purpose for writing was communication; now communication is only one of several equally strong reasons for writing, such as remembering, dealing with emotions, creating something interesting, or learning. Gere (1992) sets up the premise for her text in the first two chapters: "Writing to Learn" and "Writing to Show Learning." The strategies of each are developed and demonstrated throughout the chapters in part two of her book dealing with recounting events, supporting assertions, analyzing information, explaining causes and effects, supporting proposals, and later in doing research. Writing to learn works because as we write, we discover ideas and the relationships among ideas. Writing to learn is used in this text for a range of activities, including what is sometimes called pre-writing and also clustering, listing, freewriting, creating dramatic cycles, keeping journals of different kinds, reading actively, and assembling portfolios. By contrast, writing to show learning asks the writer to reconsider the assignment, consider the audience, identify the thesis, check the organization and work by revising early drafts, and editing the final draft. The attempt to put ideas on paper forces the writer to clarify, perhaps reorganize his or her ideas; the process of doing this often leads to generating new ideas and certainly to making the things one writes about unique.

Inquiry and the Reflective Practitioner Research on teacher thought processes attempts to understand how and why the process of teaching looks and works as it does. Research on teacher thinking complements the larger body of research on teacher effectiveness (Clark & Peterson, 1986). This research does not seek to inform teacher educators about what knowledge teachers should have; rather, it informs about the kinds of knowledge teachers can use. The knowledge that teachers use is not fixed or permanent. It is, instead, tentative, that is, subject to change and transient. Research on teachers' thinking is valuable in that it provides a broader understanding of teaching as a profession.

Metaphors used by teachers when they talk about their professional work are the vehicles that Munby (1987) analyzed to provide information about how teachers think. Using examples from interviews, he describes the major metaphorical references and the similarity between the metaphors. The study suggests that the concept "metaphor" is useful in learning about teachers' practical knowledge.

Calderhead (1987) investigated how teachers learn to teach. In a study that explores teachers' interpretive frameworks, he examined student teachers in their first field-based experience. Calderhead describes the conceptions and experiences these student teachers had. Based on this study he observes that students view the field experience as an assessment hurdle, that the teacher and the college supervisor often do not continue to engage in debate with the student about teaching after the student has exhibited competence, and that the school often conceptualizes teaching as a matter of picking up practical tips rather than as a complex process that can be developed. He recommends that the "driving test" conception of the student teacher's role might be alleviated by a reorganization of the experience into two blocks. In one, the student would demonstrate basic competence, and in the second the student would evaluate and analyze his or her own teaching.

Dyson (1986) voices a concern that is similar to the "driving test" described by Calderhead (1987). A student's comments made Dyson realize that classroom activities described by the student could become the focus of teaching instead of the focus being on children. She describes the interaction between teacher and child as being dynamic and interactive so that together they work to reach goals. Dyson (1986) contends that the "reduction of curricula and teaching to activities poses clear challenges to those involved in teacher education" (p. 136). Teacher educators must convey both what is to be done and the theory that guides decision making so that teachers can both make the decisions based on theory and teach the children.

Two college professors (Christensen & Walker, 1992) collaborated in a reading course to ask questions about their own teaching and its influence on preservice teachers' thinking. This naturalistic study led them to restructure courses and created more questions for future research. At the same time, it modeled for their students both a process of considering their practice and of decision making.

The concept of reflection in teacher education draws on the work of Dewey (1933) and refers to active, persistent consideration of beliefs or knowledge based on what supports that belief or knowledge and on the consequences that follow. Orientations toward openmindedness, wholeheartedness, and responsibility, and skills of observation and analysis define reflective action.

Another view of reflection is that presented by Giroux and McLaren (1986) and by Zeichner (1983) that accepts Dewey's (1933) premises but goes beyond them. Reconceptualizing teaching and public schooling is necessary to revive the value of democratic citizenship and social justice. They suggest a teacher education curriculum that links the study of power, language, culture, and history to the practice of critical pedagogy that truly values student experience and student voice.

In the late 1980s, there was a surge of interest in reflective practice in teacher education. Three possible interpretations of this interest, according to Tom (1992), include fad, the failure of teachers to identify educational and political commitments that stand behind proposals, and the fact that teacher education is in the midst of a change of perspectives of how teaching is actually viewed. Valli (1992) describes several additional factors, such as the increase of interest in the cognitive aspects of teachers' planning and decision making, interest in moral bases of education, movement toward teacher empowerment, and a greater acceptance of ethnographic inquiry and action research.

There are few examples of teacher education programs where sustained inquiry has been part of a program-wide approach to reflective teacher education (Applegate & Shaklee, 1992; Ciriello, Valli, & Taylor, 1992; Clift, Houston, & McCarthy, 1992; McCaleb, Borko, & Arends, 1992; Oja, Diller, Corcoran, & Andrew, 1992; Putnam & Grant, 1992; Ross, Johnson, & Smith, 1992). These programs do not claim to be ideal ways to prepare teachers. Some continue to be under revision in response to conflicts that arose because of varying definitions of reflection, methods of implementation, time involved, and faculty autonomy and responsibility. These programs differ from each other in regard to the nature of the reflective process, what it is teachers reflect about, and how student teachers might become reflective. Yet, they are similar in that they struggle in their attempts to change radically the nature of teacher preparation and its impact on student teachers (Calderhead, 1992).

Questions have been raised about the extent to which these programs conceptualize a developmental process of learning to teach, how they allow for individual differences in teachers' learning styles, how they deal with the varying backgrounds that student teachers bring to teacher education programs, and whether it is reasonable to expect such reflection from preservice teachers. Major impediments for teacher education programs are lack of knowledge about student teachers' professional growth and institutions where accepted practices do not support the role of facilitator of reflective practice (Calderhead, 1992). In fact, a conventional apprenticeship model, in which student teachers learn pedagogical skills and techniques from existing knowledge, can inhibit self-directed growth of student teachers (Zeichner & Liston, 1987). The impact of the reflective programs is minimized somewhat because they are often limited to the professional education component of teacher education programs, and there has been little integration of the concepts into specialty area components (Valli, 1992).

The inclusion of reflective practice in an individual course is described by Dias (1989). Student teachers often align themselves with the supervising teacher, redefining theory previously learned by the student teachers in terms of what works in one classroom. In order to circumvent this, Dias had preservice teachers participate in a writing class with high school students. Dias taught the class, and the prospective teachers and students worked in writing groups as peers. This allowed the preservice teachers to experience the learning from the learner's perspective. Thus, they were able to understand how teaching is received by students.

In a study of preservice teachers in a reading clinic, Myers (1993) describes the diagnostic narratives that the students kept, providing useful insights for the teachers. The diagnostic narratives comprised both observations and reflections.

Roskelly (1987) reported on a new prepracticum course that developed following needs expressed when the existing program was allowing students to enter the profession without knowing the theory that would inform their teaching and without clearly understanding their own literacy. Changes were made to accommodate more active learning and more facilitative teaching. Course design was changed and teacher specialists were included as teaching resources. Incentives were offered to cooperating teachers who became a part of the university program, and selected teachers were graduates of the Boston Writing Project. In the course, connections between reading and writing are kept fluid and talk is a vital part of the program as discussions are held. Reading, writing, and research are integrated elements in the course.

Reflection on teaching, on the effectiveness of both materials and teaching methods, shows promise in improving instruction. Examining what we do and how students respond seems critical to growth.

Teachers as Researchers A trend in education that has an impact on language arts teacher education is the trend toward research conducted by teachers in their own classrooms. Cochran-Smith and Lytle (1990) define teacher research as systematic, intentional study conducted in the classroom or the school. Although this trend is described as powerful (Allen, Combs, Hendricks, Nash, & Wilson, 1988), others question whether classroom research can be conducted by the teacher. Applebee (1987) calls for separation between teaching and research because of the difference in skills and training in the two roles. Queenan (1988) also asks whether teachers are capable of conducting research in their own classrooms.

Teacher research is described as an endeavor that serves as an agency for change (Atwell, 1987; Goswami & Stillman, 1987). Lytle and Cochran-Smith (1992) argue that teacher researchers are knowers, and as such they generate knowledge for themselves and others. They assert that the many ways teachers know their practice, including subjective means such as journals and essays, should be included in the conception of teacher research. A study in which teachers did this through a school and university collaboration is reported by Allen et al. (1988). The need for this research grew from the changes already being experienced by the teachers who initiated the explorations. Through the processes involved in active recursive inquiry, these teacher researchers evolved in their teaching and researching abilities.

Myers (1985) calls for teacher education to incorporate teacher-researcher courses into existing programs. Kutz (1992) reports that the research practice of creating ethnographies in an English course moved preservice teachers from "unconfident answer knowers to more confident question-askers who come to integrate both informal and formal strategies of data-gathering and hypotheses-testing into a way of knowing" (p. 69). The concept of teacher-as-researcher was central to the design of the course. Kutz argues that teacher research provides an important model and offers opportunity for shifting perspectives, which support teachers' theory making. Cochran-Smith and Lytle (1992) cast teachers in the role of researchers by making the assumed problematic, thus opening the teachers' belief systems to allow for shifting perspectives. As teachers raised questions and attempted to answer them, they developed specific plans of action.

Kutz (1992) insists that personal theories of teaching and learning emerge from teacher research and inform practice. She also asserts that such knowledge best supports beginning teachers as they encounter new contexts in their teaching. Given this, the suggestion by Myers (1985) that teacher education programs include an introduction to teacher research becomes vital.

Multicultural Concerns A review of the literature that addresses the preparation of teachers to work with students different from themselves reveals an underlying focus on educating all students in all settings. This view of educating all students is broader than the view sometimes portrayed by the term multicultural education. There are several concurrent themes. Multicultural education must include teacher educators as well as in-service and prospective teachers; learning experiences must be real rather than vague textbook discussions of others' experiences; and the knowledge and awareness that results from the inclusion of people and experience will produce individual change and, thus, commitment.

A review of the literature on multicultural education in the United States was conducted by Sleeter and Grant (1987) and found that much of the literature at that time addressed only limited aspects of multiculturalism. They present a taxonomy to examine the term and how it is used. This involves considering the goals, language/bilingual, culture, social stratification, gender, social class, handicap, history, policy/legal issues, instructional models, curriculum, instruction, teaching guides, and project description. They suggest the framework may be helpful for educators who are concerned with articulating issues of multicultural education.

In a study of teachers' views of stereotyping and teaching culturally diverse children, McDiarmid (1992) examined a program for teacher trainees in a large school system. Following their first year of teaching, teacher trainees took part in "Multicultural Week." This consisted of a series of presentations on a variety of topics that they were to summarize and a written synthesis paper demonstrating what they had learned. McDiarmid analyzed data that included content of the presentations and interviews with teachers prior to and following the presentations. He found that trainees appeared no more likely to reject stereotypes than they had been before the sessions, nor did the teachers change in their awareness of the effects of assigning different tasks to different students. Change did not occur through this effort based on the commonly used transmission mode of multicultural awareness.

Two research initiatives, Project START and PhilWP (Cochran-Smith & Lytle, 1992), designed to provide opportunities for teachers to examine race, gender, class, and ethnicity as they relate to teaching, offer more promise. Project START (Student Teachers as Researching Teachers) and PhilWP (The Philadelphia Writing Project) encourage preservice and in-service teachers to raise their own questions about diversity, thus making cultural diversity, knowledge, and reform problematic. This forces professionals to reconsider what is taken for granted, what is known, and what is silenced. Inquiry into diversity permeated the program, including such modes as critical discussions and writing; descriptions of a child and of a child's work; structured inquiries; collaborative analyses; and questions based on classroom data, common readings, cross-grade, cross-school, cross-subject matter, and cross-school system observations. Teachers struggled to reconsider their own unexamined assumptions in many contexts. Inquiry and questioning led to commitment to individual and collaborative action for reform, a promising possibility for real change.

Noordhoff and Kleinfeld (1993) describe a program focusing on multicultural education in Alaska. This holistic program for the preparation of teachers integrated practical experience, research, and theory. Integrated units were planned and carried out in culturally diverse classrooms and were organized around the tasks, problems, and dilemmas of teaching language arts in mainstream multicultural and minority cultural settings. Students were expected to connect subject matter to the students' background experiences and frames of reference. Teacher candidates were also involved in their students' communities outside of the classroom. The researchers reported dramatic shifts in attitude and thinking as measured by a study of student teachers in this program.

The challenge that teachers experience when the demographic profile of the school where one teaches is different from one's own was examined through case studies of six preservice teachers (Ross & Smith, 1992). Through data from several sources, including interviews, written work, and observation notes, these students' perspectives were drawn. Based on these data, the researchers described changes in attitude in the six case studies, concluding that teacher education programs, even monocultural ones, may be able to assist with the knowledge and attitudes future teachers of diverse populations need.

A study of textbooks intended for future reading teachers was conducted by Edwards and Tate (1992). This study focused on African-American children, the legal mandates of the Equal Opportunity Act of 1974, and current reading methodology textbooks. Three questions were asked in relation to the texts examined. What is being done to provide prospective teachers with an understanding of the rules and consistencies of nonstandard English? How do African-American children use nonstandard English? How do you deal with problems associated with African-American children's use of nonstandard English and learning to read? Regarding the proportion of text, 1.167%, 90 out of 7,710 pages, dealt with the reading needs of African-American children. Of the 14 texts that were analyzed, five addressed all three questions, two dealt with the third question only, and seven texts did not address any of the questions posed in the study.

Edwards and Tate (1992) call for teacher education programs to implement courses immediately to inform prospective teachers "how to take advantage of the language spoken by a majority of African-American children to create an enriched learning environment" (p. 282). The authors call also for an understanding of the child's language structure that will lead to better understanding of the child's culture, and for urban field experiences to transmit skills for teaching the urban child in all areas of the curriculum.

Delpit (1988, 1992) calls on teachers to acknowledge and validate the home language of minority students, but to do so without allowing that language to limit the students' potential. She asserts that by acquiring a secondary discourse and by learning the "rules of power" established through language use, students can be successful in mainstream schools while maintaining respect for their own culture.

A question in multicultural education is, "Who is able to teach multicultural education?" Can a teacher teach children who are different from herself or himself? Although many would give an affirmative answer to this question, Haberman (1991) and Ross and Smith (1992) both argue that this is difficult.

Haberman stresses that older adults who are developmentally able to focus on those outside their own ethnic groups might be more successful than younger teachers. He further contends that young teachers cannot readily change their perceptions, nor can they teach others to do so. Haberman also suggests that university professors are not the best advocates or models for multicultural education due to their own lack of experiences teaching in multicultural settings. He calls for multicultural teacher education classes to be taught by seasoned classroom teachers.

Yet, Martin (1991) supports the ability of the college teacher education program to prepare teachers with theoretical background and expertise to go into multicultural settings, examine and evaluate that field, and successfully create an environment conducive for positive multicultural education.

A study promising to teacher education is a case study of two fifth-grade teachers who teach Latino students (Moll, 1988). Contrary to research that indicates that limited English speaking students are often assigned to rote work as are minority and poor students, this study describes two classrooms where Latino students unexpectedly excel on standardized tests. The case studies reveal that these teachers, who teach differently from each other, still exhibit similar characteristics. They focus on meaning rather than on rote learning of lower order skills, assume their students can and will learn, provide classrooms where students have the greatest possible range of oral and written language uses to obtain and communicate knowledge, and use personal experience to make sense of the classroom. Also common to these teachers is that they demand and receive political support from their administrators, which they are able to do because of their personal grounding in theory. These teachers also relied on support from peers and from the academic community. This underlines the significant role that teacher education programs can play.

Garcia and Pugh (1992) contend that even after more than a decade of rhetoric and official declarations, there has been little or no impact on the curricula of preservice teachers. They suggest that because of the mismatch between the composition of society and that of teacher education, multicultural education is viewed as "special" and a somewhat exotic phenomenon. In addition, many white faculty members have difficulty understanding and accepting the concept of cultural pluralism. While pointing out many of the issues and problems associated with multicultural education, they also suggest ways to redress the problems through clarifying the goals of teacher education and changing the knowledge base for all teachers.

The focus on educating all students in all settings must permeate teacher education programs. Research is needed to determine in what ways teacher education can best communicate the broad view of equity for all students.

THE KNOWLEDGE BASE FOR TEACHING THE ENGLISH LANGUAGE ARTS: WHAT DOES IT MEAN "TO KNOW"?

The term *knowledge base* has recently become an extremely popular concept in teacher education. According to Gideonse (1989), however, "controversy exists respecting even the concept of knowledge bases," and "the commitment to knowledge is an invitation to internal debate, to continuous change, and to the risks and opportunities of the exercise of judgment" (pp. 5, 17). Clearly, the quest for a knowledge base for teaching and teacher education in English language arts and reading represents one of the most controversial and critical issues in education today, as seen in the current discussions concerning the New Standards for English Language Arts and Reading through committees in both International Reading Association (IRA) and the National Council of Teachers of English (NCTE).

Research-Based Models of Teacher Knowledge

Research has generated a number of models of teacher knowledge. Elbaz (1983) lists five categories of knowledge that make up the "practical knowledge" a teacher uses when making instructional decisions: knowledge of self, knowledge of the milieu of teaching, knowledge of subject matter, knowledge of curriculum development, and knowledge of instruction. Grossman's (1990) research with beginning secondary English teachers focuses on four categories of teacher knowledge: general pedagogical principles, subject-matter knowledge, pedagogical content knowledge, and knowledge of context. McDiarmid, Ball, and Anderson (1989) believe teachers must develop a "flexible" understanding of subject matter in order to choose appropriate "instructional representations" and to have knowledge of learners and the learning process.

Perhaps the most often cited in the teacher education literature are Shulman's (1987) categories of the knowledge base for teaching; however, they have also provoked the most controversy (e.g., Sockett, 1987; Valli & Tom, 1988). To organize teacher knowledge in a systematic way, Shulman (1987) lists the following as category headings for this knowledge base:

• Content knowledge
• General pedagogical knowledge
• Curriculum knowledge
• Pedagogical content knowledge
• Knowledge of learners and their characteristics
• Knowledge of educational contexts
• Knowledge of educational ends, purposes, and values

Shulman's research focuses on the sources for this knowledge as well as the complex process of pedagogical thinking. He has identified four sources for the knowledge base of teaching: scholarship in content areas, educational materials and settings, research on various aspects of schooling, and the wisdom of practice. An examination of how these sources influence beginning teacher knowledge growth continues to be an important part of Shulman's research. In addition, pedagogical reasoning continues to be one of the most exciting aspects of Shulman's "knowledge growth" projects. "Pedagogical content knowledge" represents a blending or melding of content and pedagogy that is "uniquely the province of teachers, their own special form of professional understanding" (Shulman, 1987, p. 8). Shulman's model for pedagogical reasoning and action involves a cycle or a set of six recursive stages: comprehension, transfor-

mation, instruction, evaluation, reflection, and new comprehensions. Whereas new teachers must first comprehend and understand their subject matter, a transformation of this subject matter involves complex reasoning. "To reason one's way through an act of teaching is to think one's way from the subject matter as understood by the teacher into the minds and motivations of learners" (Shulman, 1987, p. 16).

This transformation involves preparing and interpreting materials, identifying alternative ways of representing ideas to students, selecting instructional methods, and adapting and tailoring the methods to fit students' needs. Pedagogical reasoning involves all of these processes of transformation and occurs both in planning lessons and conducting them.

Shulman believes that his conception of the knowledge base for teaching differs from other knowledge bases that currently exist in the literature. First, because of the importance of the relationship between subject-matter knowledge and pedagogical knowledge, Shulman believes that teacher education must become the responsibility of the entire university. In addition, he feels that an emphasis on pedagogical reasoning suggests that teaching is clearly a complex, intellectual enterprise. Finally, Shulman maintains that teacher education programs should not focus on content-free domains of pedagogy and supervision, but should emphasize pedagogical content knowledge (1987).

Shulman investigated the role that subject-matter knowledge (or lack of subject-matter knowledge) played in the planning and instruction of beginning secondary school teachers. In fact, Shulman's work has been focused on the ways in which teachers learn to "transform" their understandings of subject matter into forms that make sense to students (see Grossman, Wilson, & Shulman, 1989; Shulman, 1986b). He and his research team identified 20 prospective secondary school teachers in the fields of English, social studies, and science, all of whom were in their last stages of teacher education certification. Interviews were conducted with faculty from the teacher training institutions, and documents were collected. Many instruments were used for data collection during a 2-year period, including interviews and structured tasks. Twelve of the teachers were observed in their classrooms and interviewed during the second year of the study. Based on all the data, case studies were written and compared. The cases included intellectual biographies, descriptions of professional preparation, descriptions of teaching contexts, and descriptions of instruction (e.g., see Grossman, 1990).

As a result of the massive *Knowledge Growth in a Profession Project* investigation, Grossman, Wilson, and Shulman (1989) suggest four dimensions of subject-matter knowledge for teaching that influence the growth and development of prospective teachers: content knowledge, substantive knowledge, syntactic knowledge, and beliefs about subject matter.

Content Knowledge Content knowledge was defined as the "'stuff' of a discipline: factual information, organization principles, [or] central concepts" (Grossman, Wilson, & Shulman, 1989, p. 27). Prospective teachers should know these principles and concepts; however, "many beginning teachers will need to acquire new content knowledge as they learn to teach" (p. 28). Content knowledge (or lack of it) can affect teachers' approaches to textbooks, course organization and content, and instruction.

Substantive Knowledge This concept is related to Schwab's (1978) belief that the substantive structures in a particular discipline include the frameworks or paradigms that guide inquiry in the discipline. For example, in a literature class, both a New Critical approach and a Reader-Response approach provide frameworks or structures that guide the critic. Even though undergraduate English majors may not directly discuss these approaches in their arts and science courses, the authors contend that students would benefit from such discussion (Grossman, Wilson, & Shulman, 1989).

Syntactic Knowledge Again citing Schwab (1978), Grossman, Wilson, and Shulman (1989) believe that syntactic structures in a discipline are "the means by which new knowledge is introduced and accepted into that community" (p. 29). Without syntactic knowledge, novice teachers' abilities to learn new information are limited. The new English teachers who participated in the study believed this knowledge to be of great value: "If I hadn't had the background in literature, I probably would feel overwhelmed and discouraged even by having to familiarize myself with books I've never read before." And another novice continued: "[In teaching unfamiliar works] I'll be relying on just reading it myself, picking out what I think are important themes, just because I'm experienced at doing that kind of thing in college" (p. 30). It is worth noting that the authors believe most students currently have greater chances to acquire substantive and syntactic knowledge in advanced undergraduate and graduate coursework. They believe that discussions of frameworks should be integrated in education courses and courses in the major field throughout the program.

Beliefs about Subject Matter Preservice teachers' beliefs about teaching and their subjects play an important role in pedagogical reasoning. Prior beliefs are a persistent and powerful force that will be discussed later in this review.

Overall, Shulman and his colleagues have paid particular attention to the complex process of learning to teach. Through their detailed case studies of both beginning and experienced teachers, they have determined (1) that the depth of teachers' subject-matter knowledge affects both the content and processes of instruction, influencing both *what* teachers teach and *how* they teach it; and (2) subject-matter knowledge undergoes a transformation as teachers prepare and begin to teach. For example, Grossman's (1987b) case study of one beginning English teacher (Colleen) indicates a powerful relationship between knowledge of subject and styles of instruction. When Colleen taught a piece of literature, her teaching styles were student centered, discussion based, and interactive; however, when she felt less confident about the subject matter, such as the teaching of grammar, Colleen's teaching became more didactic. Several other case studies in the *Knowledge Growth in a Profession Project* focused on the importance of subject-matter knowledge of beginning English teachers (e.g., Grossman, 1987a, 1987b, 1987c, 1990; Grossman & Gudmundsdottir, 1987; Reynolds, 1987a, 1987b).

Codifying the Knowledge Base for Teaching

Perhaps part of the problem in establishing a clearly defined knowledge base for teaching English language arts and reading is the very definition of "knowing." To define what it means "to know," Gideonse (1989) suggests coming to an understanding of knowing as a dynamic, reflective process, an understanding that acknowledges the social nature of knowledge. He suggests that many of the metaphors used to talk about knowledge convey images that are static rather than dynamic: base, foundations, impact, solid, body, substantial, and so forth. Knowledge needs to be perceived as a dynamic, active, tentative, and expanding force. Shulman (1990) proposes a new metaphor for this foundation. The old metaphor comes from construction and suggests that the bigger the building one wants to build, the firmer and more solid the foundation one must provide. However, architects in the late 1800s designed a system that Shulman says remains in use today. They created skyscrapers that were supported by steel skeletons, scaffolding that was integral to the structure of the skyscrapers. This internal scaffolding weaves itself through the structure and becomes a part of the very structure it supports. In a sense, Shulman suggests comparing educators' understanding of knowledge for teaching to this scaffolding as interconnected scaffolding of foundations as a framework for pedagogy.

A final aspect of what it means "to know," suggests Gideonse (1989), must result in the individual's knowing beyond the known. "Knowing is important, not just because of the authority of the knowledge we have at hand, but because of the capacity knowing provides to find or approach what is not at hand" (p. 13). One can assume, given the various studies that this review examines, that knowledge about teaching English language arts and reading is at best tentative and will never be absolute or complete. To claim a codified knowledge base for teacher education programs in English language arts and reading, Griffin's (1989) 10 features of the knowledge-based school must be heeded

1. Knowledge about teaching is mutable and always under consideration for modification.
2. Teaching is complex, often ambiguous, and frequently non-linear.
3. Learning to teach is additive, ongoing, and unending.
4. Teaching and schooling are examined in light of current and historical context conditions.
5. Both pedagogical knowledge and subject-matter knowledge are valued.
6. Knowledge is actively constructed by students, with considerable participation by teachers.
7. Teachers are curriculum workers.
8. Curriculum and instruction are coherent and systematic over time and across grades and subjects.
9. Theories, research, and practical wisdom influence school programs, pedagogy, and the ways the school accomplishes its tasks.
10. Teachers demonstrate the hallmarks of professional behavior.

It is understood that total and absolute consensus on a knowledge base for teaching is highly unlikely and probably limiting, even paralyzing. In the Preface to *Knowledge Base for the Beginning Teacher* (Reynolds, 1989), the writer describes the mutable, ever-growing nature of teacher knowledge.

[Knowledge about teaching] will grow and change as it maintains contingent relations with changing contexts and as inquiry about teaching continues and improves. Thus, one can speak only of the current and existing knowledge base . . . and of plans to make continued revisions of statements of a cumulative and self-correcting nature in the future. An extremely important collateral principle is that teachers should be prepared for a career in which they are continuously involved in critical appraisal of emerging knowledge and in making adaptations in their work in accord with the changing knowledge base and their own teaching situations.

Indeed, a commitment to knowledge bases will certainly provoke discussion, debate, argument, and struggle. These authors believe this discussion will be healthy for teacher education in English language arts and reading. Gideonse (1989) provides a useful metaphor for thinking about this diversity of knowledge bases. His analogy helps to see the value in differences and helps to celebrate uniqueness and variation in the scholarship, research, and wisdom of practice that constitutes the knowledge bases for the profession.

The experience of watching a group of neighborhood children playing "cat's cradle" with a closed loop of string suggested to me . . . that the seamless web of knowledge pertinent to professional practice and preparation bears the same relationship to possible configurations (for example, "broomstick," "Jacob's ladder," or "mouse whiskers") that children learn to construct with that loop. The form of the knowledge base remains the same but its orderly manifestations can vary enormously. (p. 65)

Subject-Matter Knowledge

Teaching the English language arts and reading involves both the subject-matter knowledge and knowledge about teachers as learners. Whereas the teacher in the classroom uses knowledge of several content areas within a single day or period, often integrated with each other, this examination of the content and its unique pedagogy is divided into three traditional parts: oral language, literature and reading, and composition. There is information about the various areas of language arts essential for teaching. This section explores key studies or theoretical pieces that highlight such information.

Oral Language

LISTENING. Often called the most neglected of the language arts, listening has become less neglected after listening and speaking were added to the Federal Title II as needed competencies. Coakley and Wolvin (1990) recount the evidence for developing listening skills and describe how educators have responded through the creation of courses and materials and in the development of curricula that include goals or objectives of listening. The business community has spurred the work in listening; its importance to them reflected in the fact that more than half of the Fortune 500 companies responding to a 1989 survey reported providing listening training to their employees.

The authors describe how pedagogy in listening has developed following the 1979 founding of the International Listening Association. Groups that have supported listening skills are foreign language educators and the Speech Communication Association, as well as the International Reading Association (IRA) and the National Council of Teachers of English (NCTE). The article concludes with a list of continuing concerns that will need to be addressed.

A study to investigate current policies and programs in teacher training institutions is reported by Hoag and Wood (1990). The report includes a survey of 99 language arts professors' attitudes toward teaching listening. The study found that listening is being taught in 89% of the responding institutions, and more than 95% of the respondents provided the instruction in the teacher education department. Even though listening received less attention than the other language arts, 91% of the preservice teachers reported that they had opportunities to acquire listening knowledge.

Listening assessment was the focus of Rhodes, Watson, and Barker (1990) who point out that many lists of listening skills have little research base and are more apt to reflect subjective reviews of the listening and reading literature. The article describes both the similarities and the differences between listening and reading as decoding skills. The authors discuss three types of definitions of listening: (1) those that include responding, (2) those that emphasize the reality of the construct of listening, and (3) definitions based on some type of data collection. They present criteria for assessment and describe assessment techniques, both formal listening tests and informal techniques such as charting, using diaries or logs, or teacher observation checklists.

Effective classroom strategies are the focus of Brent and Anderson (1993) who begin by contrasting two listening situations, one that is effective and one that is not. They show how these skills can be developed within the framework of a whole language classroom through teachers' modeling attentive listening behavior, attending to the ideas and plans generated in class discussions, and in one-on-one conferences. Listening is also developed by providing specific listening instruction, such as focusing to block distractions, visualizing, or predicting and reviewing strategies and assisting students to select the most appropriate strategy. The third main aspect of developing listening skill is to provide opportunities to practice effective listening, such as during Author's Chair (when students read their writing to peers) read-aloud experiences, writing workshop, cooperative groups, readers' theater, and story retelling. Application within meaningful settings is reported as the key to effective practice.

SHARING AND DISCUSSING. Some new research on sharing time by Michaels and Foster (1985) suggests that elementary teachers need to reexamine this traditional activity and consider modifying it so that students are in charge. Their research indicates that in student-led groups children develop effective styles to hold the floor. They found two distinctive styles: the lecture demonstration and the performed narrative. Each of these is described with examples. The authors also contrast student-led discussions with teacher-led discussion, which indicate how powerful the child-led discussions are in promoting learning.

The power of children's own questions is the focus of Whitmore and Crowell's (1994) research as they explored and analyzed third-graders' discussions about books in a classroom. When the Gulf War broke out, the students had many questions and so their teacher initiated a literature study group on the subject of war and peace as an option, which was selected by eight children. They asked many questions about history, trying to tie information in the books to the event they were hearing about on the news, and some of their questions extended over the time of the study. An analysis of the data collected showed that the children's questions, not the teacher's, drove the topics of conversation as about 24% of the total turns were questions. The children talked two thirds of the time when the teacher was present in addition to meeting without her. The teacher's role in discussions is the mediator who asks for further explanation or clarification. They suggest that the power to question leads to more sophisticated opportunities for young children to construct socially a high quality process for thinking and learning.

King (1994) also found that children's questions were extremely important in learning. She examined three question-generating strategies following science lessons in fourth and fifth grades. Groups were given prompt cards with skeleton questions to prompt them to ask each other questions focused on different aspects of the lesson. In one group questions were focused on promoting connections among ideas within a lesson (How are _____ and _____ similar or different? How does _____ affect _____?). In the second group, questions were focused on promoting connections between prior experience and knowledge and the lesson (How could _____ be used to _____? What would happen if _____? How does _____ tie in with _____ that we learned before?). The control group used unguided questioning (Discuss the lesson with each other. Ask each other questions. Answer each other's questions giving explanations.).

Results of this study indicate that when children use questions that guide them to connect ideas within a lesson together or connect the lesson to their prior knowledge, they engage in complex knowledge construction which, in turn, enhances learning; and these learning effects are stronger for questions that connect to prior knowledge. (King, 1994, p. 361)

An excellent source of information and research on oral discourse is Cazden's (1988) *Classroom Discourse*. The first section of this book describes talk with the teacher, from sharing time to lessons and classroom discourse. The second section is on talk with peers, and it examines cognitive processes involved as well as contextual influences. The third section explores the teacher-talk register and the student-talk register. Three questions permeate the book: (1) how patterns of language use affect what counts as "knowledge," (2) how the patterns affect the equality or inequality of educational opportunity; and (3) what communicative competence the patterns presume and/or foster.

DRAMA AND THEATER Drama and theater programs are one of the primary curricular areas in oral language development. Salisbury-Wills (1992) suggests that some of the optimism about the arts comes from the reaction to the fact that nowhere in

America 2000: An Educational Strategy, the political directive for education (Bush, 1991), was there mention of the arts. Citizens in many communities responded by insisting that education plans include the arts, and the National Educational Goals Panel (NEGP) responded by adding to Goal 3 that a full appreciation of the fine arts and mastery of one or more foreign languages are examples of additional competencies that schools must foster. Some states have also adopted statements relative to the arts. Curriculum reform, as it involves the arts, is explored as a crossroad where educational change is being discussed.

One of the most important figures in drama in education is Dorothy Heathcote; she works with a concept of sign. "Social encounters need sign. The sign of the person, in action, using all objects, significant space, pause, silences, and vocal power to make the meaning available to others in the encounter" (Heathcote, 1984, p. 162). Heathcote explains the importance of sign in drama as

The heart of communication in social situations is the sign. All teachers need to study how to exploit it as the first basis of their work. The theatre is the art form which is totally based in sign and the drama additive to learning gives the urgency possible through using now/ imminent time. This is why we lobby for better schools when we ask that teachers wake up to the possibilities of the power of resonances in classrooms instead of verbal statements. (p. 169)

Educational drama is the focus of Grady (1992) who describes Dorothy Heathcote's work and the assumptions that inform it. It is first of all focused on the process, not on presenting a play, but discovering meaning in drama. It is improvisational and puts students in a "mess" and then helps them to find a solution, primarily through questioning or playing a role that presents new aspects with which to be dealt. Educational drama also contrasts with American creative drama, which involves theater games, pantomime, light improvisation, or enacting children's stories. Grady questions some of the assumptions underlying Heathcote's work, particularly the emphasis on finding the universals in a situation. She suggests that this may lead to cultural or social misinformation because the participants are not dealing with sufficiently contextualized experience.

Drama at the high school typically means performance or theater. Waack (1988) presents ideas for retaining theater programs in small high schools. He first states a foundation for theater as an academic discipline as well as a performing art. He recommends that if there is not a separate course in theater, there are other options such as units within the language arts. These units might focus on a Shakespearean play, the art of writing dialogue, or oral interpretation of poetry. He also suggests mini-courses or independent learning packets, artist-in-residence programs, and community theater. To produce a play, he suggests adapting classical plays, developing staged readings—readers theater or chamber theater performances— of nondramatic literature, or producing an original play.

Literature and Reading In the past in elementary classrooms, literature was not considered a part of the curriculum, although teachers often read to students especially in the primary grades, and children read library books when they had finished other work. Reading meant working with basal readers, and language arts meant English grammar/usage exercises, spelling, and handwriting. More recently reading instruction has come to include everything from increased experiences reading actual books along with the basal reading program to literature as the base of reading and the foundation and integrating factor in curriculum planning. Most research in the area of literature for elementary students reported in the past 10 years has been focused on how to use literature and involve students in literature. This may be the first step needed before examining how to instruct teachers in using literature to advantage.

Two interesting studies are examples of research in literature for children that may serve as a basis for training teachers in literature-related pedagogy. Ohlhausen and Jepsen (1992) report a study of a strategy for children to select their own books—the Goldilocks Strategy. The children learn how to decide if a book they might read is too hard, too easy, or just right, although each has a place in an individual's reading program. The description of its implementation and use should help inform practice. The other study by Nikola-Lisa (1992) examines the range of responses to literature made by young children, particularly those involving play. Two distinct categories of play emerged: language play (phonological or sound play, syntactic or pattern play, and semantic or meaning play) and dramatic play with an emphasis on pretend behavior. He concludes that the children's responses are strongly wedded to the world of play, suggesting the importance of providing ample classroom activities that encourage a range of language expression.

Andrews, Moss, and Stansell (1985) examined the effects of reading children's literature aloud to undergraduate reading methods classes. They observed that the college students being read to were more inclined to use children's literature in reading to children, creating lessons and games, and developing teaching units featuring books; they began to appreciate how literature reflects human interests; and they began to appreciate the enjoyment literature can bring. The study compared their students' insights about literature with those of students who had not been read to on a 12-item survey using a five-point Likert scale. Although the difference between means was slight, the authors say it is worth noting that for 11 of the 12 items, students who were read to showed stronger agreement than those who were not. Modeling by college instructors and familiarity with literature appropriate to be used with children seem to be important aspects of the study.

In a related study that examined the college student as a reader, Manna and Misheff (1987) report an analysis of 50 randomly selected undergraduate and graduate students' autobiographies of their reading. In the autobiography, students were asked to give general information about what influenced them as readers, specific classroom and home experiences, their interests and self-assessment, and their perceptions of themselves as teachers of reading. Analyses of the autobiographies indicate two types of readers: the "reduced" reader who never experienced reading as a pleasurable activity and the "transactional" reader for whom reading is an integral part of life.

A more recent study by Jipson and Paley (1992) also studied both undergraduate and graduate narrative descriptions of their development of reading activity during and since their university experience, descriptions of favorite readings, and how read-

ings influenced their thinking. They also found two distinct patterns, and these corresponded with the undergraduate and graduate populations. The undergraduates reported narrow interests, a limited personal reading environment oriented to popular culture, and a lack of connections made between personal habits and the models they might present to their students. The graduates, however, reported pleasure in reading and real engagement in it. Most of them valued reading and found it important in their lives.

To examine the effects of different stances toward reading, Wiseman and Many (1992) studied 52 undergraduate elementary education majors in two sections of children's literature. One section received an efferent teaching approach that focused on literary elements and illustrations and the determination of genres; the other had an aesthetic approach focused on thoughts, feelings, and emotions experienced and possible connections with their own experiences. The two contrasting approaches were used for four literary works in different genres presented throughout the semester to examine how responses differed, what effects the approaches had on students' ratings of the literary works, and what the effects were of the approach on their response to a subsequent work. The study illustrates the effects of various teaching approaches; the efferent teaching approach encouraged students to examine the literature in terms of the shared significance of the work to their literary community, whereas the aesthetic approach fostered the development of the work's personal significance. The authors suggest that using both approaches can ensure that students gain a knowledge base of the use of literary elements while allowing them to truly live the literary experience.

The orientation toward literature was a significant factor in the Grossman (1987c) study of two teachers and how their orientation toward teaching served to "mediate their experiences in teacher education and color their goals for and conduct of teaching" (p. 1). One student's orientation toward English centered around the text; she chose to teach because she loved English. Her focus was on the words and images of the text, and she believed the text of the work was the locus for interpretation. The other student's orientation was on the human aspect of literature; she chose to teach after an internship in a local school where she discovered she loved working with lower track students. Her focus was on what one can learn about oneself and others; for her the reader was the focus for interpretation. Their orientation toward literature influenced their choice of content, processes, and goals for teaching.

In addition to some rather significant changes in the role literature plays in the reading program, there has been a great deal of controversy about the place of phonics instruction in the teaching of reading. Pearson (1993), in summarizing research on teaching reading, contends that there is general agreement on the critical role that phonemic awareness plays in early reading success; the disagreement is primarily about whether or not phonemic awareness should be taught directly. The question is whether phonics knowledge and phonemic awareness are the consequence or the cause of success in authentic reading experiences. Pearson also suggests that invented spellings may be the medium through which both phonemic awareness and phonics knowledge develop. Sweet (1993), in her report on the state of the art in reading, says

Effective beginning reading instruction is that which contains a balance of activities designed to improve word recognition, including phonics instruction and reading meaningful text. Writing and spelling activities are also part of effective reading instruction because they affect overall reading ability in a positive way. . . . Effective teachers interweave these activities within their instruction and, above all, ensure that phonics teaching is not done apart from connected, informative, engaging text. (p. 5)

In the area of reading comprehension, Pearson (1993) states that the dominant view in the field of reading is that ultimately readers and writers have to build satisfying and complete models of meaning for every text they create. Context is dominant in explaining both the processes and instructional practices in reading. Instruction in comprehension has been widely recognized as a critical skill. Wendler, Samuels, and Moore (1989) examined the time spent on direct comprehension instruction by three groups of teachers: teachers who had received awards for excellence, teachers with master's degrees, and a control group of classroom teachers. The sample comprehension strategies examined were making inferences; making predictions; summarizing; and creating mental images along with prereading activities, such as building background knowledge, preteaching vocabulary, and text structure. They found no significant differences between the three groups of teachers in the amount of time allocated to prereading or direct comprehension instruction, although award-winning teachers spent more time on assignments and individual assistance. They suggest that neither more years of experience nor a greater number of graduate courses in reading appeared to result in greater use of effective comprehension instruction.

Mosenthal, Schwartz, and MacIsaac (1992) reported their case study of attempts to implement extended strategy instruction with undergraduate preservice teachers. They chose to work through one strategy in depth rather than "mentioning" many different strategies and to have their college students work with material that would present a challenge to comprehend. Reciprocal teaching was the strategy selected; it involves the students acting as teachers in generating questions, summarizing, monitoring their understanding, and making predictions for a section of text. The students' journal entries showed a generally positive experience as well as reflecting some of the difficulties in learning a new strategy. They conclude that this type of instruction requires experience learning and using strategies and is not enhanced by instruction in which such strategies are merely mentioned.

Reading in the content areas is often the focus of reading instruction in secondary schools. Farrell and Cirrincione (1986) analyzed the content and texts used for introductory courses for content area teachers. The 59 college instructors responding were asked to provide a syllabus for their course and list the five most important topics covered, indicate the text used, and describe the composition of the class. These data were used in the analysis.

Stewart and O'Brien (1989) examined the attitudes, beliefs, and knowledge that content area preservice teachers have toward teaching reading in an attempt to understand their resistance to incorporating reading instruction in the content areas. Students' answers to why they thought the state department required such a course and what they expected to learn were

analyzed, and four categories emerged: (1) personal remediation (to guarantee beginning teachers had good skills) accounted for 39% of the responses, (2) skill in diagnosing and remediating students' skills accounted for 34% of the response, (3) "right-on-target" accounted for 23% of the responses and (4) 4% of the students had no idea.

Hollingsworth and Teel (1991) examined the impact of a secondary reading course in a study of two preservice math and science teachers to investigate why secondary teachers are not teaching literacy. Although both students understood the instruction in the course, there was little evidence of implementation in the classroom. The authors point out that they had little actual practice, little guidance in their initial attempts to apply what they were learning, and a lack of models from cooperating teachers. These findings corroborate other studies of instruction, such as the one by Mosenthal, Schwartz, and MacIsaac (1992) previously discussed.

A similar study of the effectiveness of content area teachers was conducted by Patberg, Dewitz, and Henning (1984) for inservice teachers. By contrast, they found in their observations of the vocational education teachers following instruction that reading strategies were implemented for the most part in the context of a directed reading assignment and included prereading, reading, and postreading activities. They also found that teacher attitudes were a better predictor of what teachers will do than are their planning protocols.

These studies highlight the difficulties of preparing students to become teachers who use strategies that were not used when they were younger or that are not often used by the teachers in whose classrooms they participate. The most effective implementation came from in-service teachers as follow up for a class they had taken.

Composition Research in the writing process and in the use of writing to learn has continued to be a major focus of research in composition. Graves (1989), in discussing children's responses to fiction, sees it related to their development of writing fiction. He found that students' development of writing fiction could be traced through their development of characters. At first characters are either other children they know or generic good guys, bad guys, or television or comic book characters who serve to further the plot. Later characters show behaviors that are a consequence of their personality and that reflect on the events that occur. Characters also become more distinctive as children increase their understanding of the fiction they read; they gradually focus on character motives and the plot becomes less important. Then they come to discuss interrelationships of characters and later the relationships of the characters to characters in other books or to their own lives.

Students' writing and their discussions of their writing can give a good idea of the processes they use. A number of studies of writing, as well as other process-oriented areas of research, have used "think-aloud" protocols. Afflerbach et al. (1988) used this procedure to capture their own writing processes. They did so in an attempt to understand their own writing processes and the contexts in which the processes occur as well as to examine the dynamics of the group writing conferences. They hoped this would help them anticipate instructional challenges in elementary writing programs. They concluded that the think-aloud protocols both provided a record of their processes and enabled them to reflect and discuss them. The use of think-aloud protocols allowed them to observe, question, and learn about the writing process.

A case study by Florio-Ruane and Lensmire (1990) also sought to examine the process of transforming future teachers' ideas about writing instruction. They studied intensively six juniors beginning the language arts/reading/literature sequence, as well as data from all students in the course. Although the students had used a process approach themselves, the course challenged some of their assumptions in three important ways: (1) a change from reliance on genre to define text to an examination of function of the text, (2) a change in the set-up of a writing classroom and role of the teacher from traditional rows of desks with the teacher explaining at the front of the room to a workshop with the teacher as coach and assistant, and (3) a change from the view of the child learning to write from the teacher's explanations and examples to the children learning by actively manipulating the system. The authors concluded that some beginning conceptions were difficult to give up, particularly when the preservice teachers' views of school roles and curriculum changed their role in maintaining control. Other ideas such as seeing children making sense of writing on their own were easily embraced; the prospective teachers viewed the children's "mistakes" as opportunities for the teacher to plan for response and future instruction.

Shrofel's (1991) study of future secondary teachers also found that students come to the composition methods class with preexisting ideas about writing that need reshaping rather than creative molding. The first attempt to change these ideas involved presenting current information supplemented with a creative writing component, but students did not implement process writing in their field experience. The second attempt involved modeling with experiences in using the writing process in writing workshops and conferences, but the future teachers did not implement this either, blaming the cooperating teacher, the students, or the situation. She concluded that the students had not confronted themselves as learners, as writers, or as teachers. The third approach involved having each preservice teacher tutor a university-level student who was having difficulty writing in addition to a weekly seminar to discuss the tutees' progress, what was learned about writing, teaching writing, and the tutor as a writer. During a later field experience, the tutor used practices consistent with their development as teachers and writers; most of them had abandoned practices that they knew to be ineffective before they went to the field. The tutorial component shows that preservice teachers can change their teaching practices, that writing and teaching practices are closely linked, and that confrontation was the center of what happened in the program—confronting oneself as a teacher, learner, writer, and person.

Changes in prospective teachers' beliefs about the knowledge needed to teach and the ways learners from different races or social classes benefit from different curriculum and instruction are the focus of Gomez (1990). She reports a study of 31 teacher candidates in a master's level certification program in Florida. The group's beliefs regarding learners, learning, subject matter, and teaching changed in two ways over the year. First, the focus of their concerns moved from subject-matter deficits to worries about discipline and classroom management. Second, their beliefs about different learners moved from the idea that all students can benefit from a process writing approach to confusion regarding the benefits of varied curriculum and instruction for different tracks of learners, particularly grouping by tracks. She suggests that the changes are a result of some interrelated features of the school context, of the teacher education program, and of state policies.

The Teacher as Learner

Although the process of learning to teach is generally regarded as a longitudinal enterprise, many researchers have studied various phases or parts of the process. Feiman-Nemser (1983) offers a systematic framework or comprehensive view of the process of "learning to teach." She divides the process into four phases (pretraining, preservice, induction, and inservice) and argues that both formal and informal experiences connected with each phase influence teachers' continual learning. The following sections of this review deal with personal history, teacher beliefs, and the influence of beliefs on classroom practices; and teacher educators' perceptions about preservice teachers.

Personal History, Teacher Beliefs, and the Influence of Beliefs on Classroom Practices According to Feiman-Nemser (1983), students have "considerable informal preparation for teaching" long before they enter teacher education programs (p. 152). In fact, Britzman (1986) says

Prospective teachers bring to their teacher education more than their desire to teach. They bring their implicit institutional biographies—the cumulative experience of school lives—which, in turn, inform their knowledge of the student's world, of school structure, and of curriculum. All this contributes to well-worn and commonsensical images of the teacher's work. (p. 443)

Recent investigations have explored novice teachers' beliefs about teaching, their developing professional orientations, and their developing knowledge for teaching from an interpretive, critical stance (Britzman, 1986, 1991; Ritchie & Wilson, 1993). Detailed case analyses and biographies that highlight the voices of teacher candidates, student teachers, and first-year teachers comprise much of the current body of research on learning to teach (e.g., Bullough, 1989; Bullough, Knowles, & Crowe, 1991; Grossman, 1990; Stark, 1991). Much of this research describes the experience of learning to teach as "a social process of negotiation rather than an individual problem of behavior," a process that is often situated in "a largely inherited and constraining context" (Britzman, 1991, pp. 8, 14). As Bullough, Knowles, and Crowe (1991) suggest, "Becoming a teacher is an idiosyncratic process reflecting not only differences in biography, personality, and in conceptions of teaching and how well or poorly they are developed, but also in school and school-community contexts" (p. 187). Britzman (1991) believes that learning to teach is, indeed, a lifelong process in which one considers preconceptions of teaching and continually rethinks and perhaps even overcomes such images.

Learning to teach is not a mere matter of applying decontextualized skills or of mirroring predetermined images; it is a time when one's past, present, and future are set in dynamic tension. Learning to teach—like teaching itself—is always the process of becoming: a time of formation and transformation, of scrutiny into what one is doing, and who one can become. (p. 8)

It is known that many early influences affect students' views of teaching and learning, including family, former teachers, and school experiences. Lortie (1975) explores the profound influences of merely being a student or moving through what he calls an "apprenticeship of observation." After years of observing teachers in action, Lortie writes that students have developed their own clear perspectives of what teaching and learning ought to be. Through interviews with teachers, Lortie discovered that many pointed to the influence of former teachers. He found that formal teacher training rarely altered their perceptions of these individuals, and often their own teaching reflected an imitation of their past teachers. Because of this strong influence, Lortie believes that preservice teachers should be encouraged to examine their prior beliefs about teaching and schooling.

In their review of "Teachers' Thought Processes," Clark and Peterson (1986) list three types of teacher thinking: teacher planning, teachers' interactive thoughts and decisions, and teachers' theories and beliefs. Studies that concern teachers' theories and beliefs about both teaching and their subject matter have demonstrated that teachers' personal histories and personal intentions profoundly affect both their conceptions of the role of the teacher and their professional orientations and classroom practices (Grossman, 1990; Nespor, 1987; Richardson, Anders, Tidwell, & Lloyd, 1991; Weinstein, 1990; Zancanella, 1991).

Although some investigations have simply employed a series of presurveys and postsurveys, questionnaires, or attitude measures (Cline & Fixer, 1985), current studies generally consist of in-depth case study analyses, that is, descriptions of teachers' beliefs and their actions in classrooms based primarily on in-depth interviews and observations. Clandinin and Connelly (1987) have attempted to provide a framework for this type of research ("studies of the personal"), and they list various methodologies for such narrative inquiry: field notes, journal records, interviews, storytelling, letter writing, autobiographical and biographical writing, and other written documents. Witherall and Noddings (1991) suggest similar approaches to autobiographical and narrative inquiry in their *Stories Lives Tell*.

A study by Amarel and Feiman-Nemser (1988) is indicative of the recent work on prospective teachers' beliefs about teaching. Using interviews and questionnaires with preservice elementary and secondary teachers, they focused on two questions. What do students entering preservice programs think they need to know before they can begin to teach? Where and how do they expect to learn the essentials of teaching? During the interviews, the researchers probed for information on three categories of knowledge essential for teaching: knowledge of subject matter, learners, and classroom management. Although the teaching candidates believed they needed more teaching experience and management skills, they rarely mentioned subject-matter knowledge. They saw "teaching as telling," say Amarel and Feiman-Nemser, and valued the procedural and practical knowledge they felt they would gain only through experience. Most of the respondents favored a rather conventional view of their subject matter; for example, prospective secondary English teachers thought a knowledge of grammar to be "more important than having language to describe the writing process" (p. 10). Through a more detailed comparison of two contrasting elementary teacher candidates, they found that students' past histories in school had profound impacts on the way they conceived the role of the teacher. "The curriculum in teacher education pays little heed to what teachers-to-be already know and believe" (p. 3). Amarel and Feiman-Nemser's (1988) conclusions raise important concerns for teacher educators.

Students are undiscerning about what they need to know, and have considerable skepticism about the value of formal study in learning to teach . . . . Students have neither the conceptual frames nor the motivation to think analytically about teaching, and are not privy to any but the performance aspects of instruction—the complexities of teaching are largely unmasked for them. (p. 20)

Amarel and Feiman-Nemser believe teacher educators must design programs that will help preservice teachers come to terms with their prior beliefs through elaborating and transforming these conceptions.

Several teacher educators have explored preservice teachers' prior beliefs about teaching and learning (e.g., Holt-Reynolds, 1992; Knowles, 1992; Knowles & Holt-Reynolds, 1991; Moss, 1992). Other studies have delineated the importance of teachers' beliefs about teaching and about subject matter and of the nature of this influence on their teaching practices (e.g., Grossman, 1987a, 1987b, 1987c; Zancanella, 1991). Gomez (1988) studied individual perspectives toward the teaching of writing. Working with 90 students enrolled in their first professional education course, Gomez asked the participants to respond in writing to several questions concerning their own personal backgrounds in learning to write. Her findings reveal that most of the students did not feel that their college coursework was beneficial in developing their writing abilities and that their comments on whom they considered to be writers were based on questionable criteria. She maintains that prospective teachers have a limited knowledge of the definition of "good writing." When she interviewed another group of preservice teachers and asked for responses to a sample of student writing, Gomez found they focused mostly on surface features in the text.

The work of Knowles and Holt-Reynolds (1991) illustrates how teacher education programs can indeed help novices directly confront and perhaps even overcome their preconceived notions about teaching and learning. Using autobiographical writings such as personal histories, interactive journals, and reflective papers, Knowles and Holt-Reynolds invite their students to articulate and rethink their beliefs. Autobiographical inquiry (1) helps preservice teachers keep written records of their personal histories related to education; (2) serves as a vehicle for learning, especially in journal writing; (3) serves others as a window into personal perspectives and needs, often alerting others to difficulties or problems; (4) improves the quality of preservice teachers' writing; (5) has value for research; (6) facilitates interactive dialogue with others; and (7) helps develop trust between teacher candidates and teacher educators as well as among teacher candidates and thus fosters a sense of camaraderie among all participants (pp. 106–107).

Using retrospective interviews and classroom observations, Elbaz (1983) examined the ways in which one secondary English teacher in Canada developed a practical knowledge base for teaching. From her work with a teacher called Sarah, Elbaz identified a theoretical framework that serves to define and organize practical knowledge for teaching. She reports that whereas teacher education courses had little influence on Sarah's development of practical knowledge, her experiences with particular classroom situations were important. "The teacher's feelings, values, needs, and beliefs combine as she forms images of how teaching should be, and marshals experience, theoretical knowledge, and school folklore to give substance to these images" (1983, p. 134).

Like Elbaz, Nespor (1987) suggests teachers' beliefs play an important role in the complexity of teaching. Interviewing and observing eight junior high teachers to describe their belief systems, Nespor found that beliefs define teachers' work, and in order "to understand teaching from teachers' perspectives" we must uncover those beliefs (p. 323). Nespor identified three areas of beliefs that affect teaching: (1) beliefs derived from career influences, (2) beliefs derived from experience, and (3) beliefs about subject matter. Nespor points particularly to the influence of beliefs about teaching on subject-matter orientation. "Teachers' beliefs about teaching may shape the particular manner in which the content is ultimately presented" (p. 161).

In a similar fashion, the studies from the *Knowledge Growth in a Profession Project* suggest that "prospective teachers' beliefs about subject matter are as powerful as their beliefs about teaching and learning" (Grossman, Wilson, & Shulman, 1989, p. 32). Beliefs about subject matter influence what is taught and how curricula are organized. An orientation toward subject matter influences goals for teaching and choices of activities and assignments.

Zancanella (1991) also discovered important relationships between teachers' personal approaches to literature and their teaching of literature, noticing conflicts between a "school version of literature" and the teachers' "out-of-school literary lives" (pp. 26–27). Zancanella's study employed in-depth interviews and classroom observations. His case studies of five junior high school teachers of English revealed that "institutional constraints and the teachers' lack of a theoretical framework for literary studies" prevent their "pedagogically useful knowledge" from being utilized (p. 5). In particular, the less-experienced teachers in Zancanella's study (including a first-year teacher) were most influenced by the "school approach to literature" (p. 28).

Fox (1993) found that student teachers draw upon a number of sources of knowledge in learning to teach, and they participate as members of many different communities, that is, cultures that may exist in harmony with one another or may clash and cause tension. As they attempted to reconcile the differences between their own conceptions of the secondary English curriculum and their initial classroom practices, the beginning teachers in her study found themselves situated among a number of cultures: the academic community of the university English department, the English education community (including the

student teaching seminar), cooperating teachers and other local school colleagues, and the adolescent community. Often, these sources, as well as other pressures such as prescribed curricula and state-mandated achievement tests, provided them with conflicting views of English, teaching, and schooling. This conflict contributed to the discord in their induction into teaching.

Many studies concerning preservice teachers' beliefs deal with their resistance to what they encounter in teacher education program curricula (Bird, Anderson, Sullivan, & Swidler, 1993; O'Brien & Stewart, 1990). For example, O'Brien and Stewart found that preservice teachers' resistance to principles espoused in their content area reading course stemmed from "deeply rooted . . . beliefs and traditions of school life relating to teachers' roles and allegiance to content disciplines" (p. 101). Working with 250 participants representing 12 different content disciplines, O'Brien and Stewart collected data through precourse statements, learning logs, group discussions, course evaluations, and structured interviews in order to address the question: What is the nature of resistance to content reading instruction expressed by preservice teachers representing a wide variety of teaching endorsement area? Three major findings were generated through their data analysis: (1) prospective teachers perceive content area reading to be incompatible with the organization and traditions of secondary schools; (2) resistance to content area reading is based, in part, on simple misconceptions about reading; and (3) some of what appears to be resistance to content area reading is actually one facet of a broader complex of preservice teachers' assumptions about learning and teaching. O'Brien and Stewart conclude with a list of three topics that they believe should be discussed in teacher education courses "either concurrently with simple misconceptions or as a prelude to exploring misconceptions about, and practical applications of, content reading instruction" (p. 125). These are (1) the predominant organizational structure of secondary schools; (2) curricular fragmentation and tracking, and (3) explicit and implicit curricula.

How might teacher educators enable novices to unpack, examine, and perhaps even overcome their conventional beliefs and assumptions about teaching and learning? Several alternative ideas are addressed later in the section concerning research on teacher education program curricula. Newman (1987) proposes the use of discussion in teacher education courses of critical incidents to uncover current beliefs and assumptions that influence classroom practices. She suggests the discussion and sharing of stories that contribute to teachers' understandings of language and literacy learning and to their conceptions of the teacher's role in the language arts and reading classroom. She reports that beliefs about teaching and learning are "largely tacit," and that educators usually teach intuitively without "actively reflecting on what our intentions might be and what our actions could be saying to students" (p. 727). Newman maintains that "changing what we do in the classroom in any meaningful way involves changing attitudes and beliefs." However, she continues, "before we can change our attitudes and beliefs, we have to know what they are" (p. 736). Ritchie and Wilson (1993) echo Newman's suggestions.

We must provide our students with opportunities to reflect critically on their experiences in both traditional and constructivist classrooms, to delve into the assumptions on which those classrooms are based, to set those assumptions in dialogue, and to listen for the dissonances. By reclaiming and reflecting on their own histories as readers and writers, and then extending that reflection outward, our students might become participant observers of language and learning around them, and so go on to confront reductionist views of education and provoke questions for themselves that clarify their own purposes for education. (p. 82)

Interestingly, Bird et al. (1993) report that in their attempt to influence students' conventional views of teaching and learning in a preservice course, they discovered that such a process is "fraught with problems" (p. 265). Bird and his colleagues suggest that teacher educators constantly must strike a balance between establishing themselves as knowledgeable and helpful teachers and encouraging preservice teachers to take risks and to think for themselves. They are caught "between cultivating familiar ideas and promoting unfamiliar ones; between helping students think and taking over the direction of their thinking" (p. 265). Indeed, this can be a precarious position for the teacher educator.

Teacher Educators' Perceptions about Preservice Teachers

The work of Wyatt and Pickle (1993) reveals that teacher educators' beliefs are as persistent and hardy as those of their students. In their work with eight content area reading instructors, they found that these educators held to their personal beliefs even across a wide variety of circumstances. "The objectives they choose to pursue tend to fall in line with their beliefs; the setting or goals of the courses they taught held less influence over them" (p. 342). Finally, their beliefs about teaching ranged on a continuum from a transmission of knowledge model to a more interpretive, interactive model. "Most of the instructors," Wyatt and Pickle observe, "expressed philosophies that fell between those two views, but several expressed beliefs closer to the extremes" (p. 342).

Recent studies concerning teacher educators' perceptions about preservice teachers suggest that "content area methods professors may be in part responsible for the negative attitudes of preservice teachers toward a content area reading course" (Daisey & Shroyer, 1993). Daisey and Shroyer interviewed 40 content area professors, asking specifically why their students might exhibit negative attitudes about required content area reading courses. The instructors responded with the following seven explanations: (1) students do not see the rationale, (2) instructors do not communicate, (3) students are not readers/writers themselves, (4) student focus is on content, (5) students perceive the course as remedial, (6) students have heard rumors about the course, and (7) students perceive a conflict in learning styles. Daisey and Shroyer conclude by stating they saw "no evidence of negative attitudes toward reading or a content area reading course" (p. 629), and they suggest that other content area reading instructors should take time to hold conversations with content area professors.

SUBJECT-SPECIFIC PEDAGOGY

In addition to the subject-matter knowledge that is a part of the English language arts and reading, there is pedagogical knowledge that is particular to the field. Some of the subject-specific pedagogy relates to instructional or intervention programs; some to assessment and instructional planning.

Instruction

A review of the literature that describes current research in teacher education and language arts related pedagogical approaches reveals that the content of what is taught follows holistic practices in learning language. That is, as writing and reading education continue to move from a traditional paradigm of transmission to interactive and transactive models of literacy (Harste, 1985), the content of methods courses follows this move. Yet, teacher education programs typically follow the traditional paradigm, which is a transmission model of learning. Teacher education programs have typically shifted only in content, not in process. Short and Burke (1989) contend that teacher education programs must reflect holistic perspectives on language and literacy. This modeling is necessary to "change the current course of teacher education or of education in elementary and secondary schools" (p. 193). Teacher educators must begin to accept the challenge of using the same theories and research that inform the interactive and transactive model of literacy as a base for exploring how to create supportive and generative social contexts for learning in the college classroom. They poignantly write, "Although teacher educators argue that children are already readers and writers when they come to school, they do not consider undergraduates members of the teaching profession. They have moved away from concepts of reading readiness but retained a belief in teaching readiness" (p. 199).

Viewing the learner as inquirer is a stance that facilitates the creation of structures in teacher education courses or programs that are conducive to the concept of the active learner. Some changes in teacher education programs reflect this. These may include the use of journals or learning logs, formal writing taken from rough draft form through response procedures prior to final drafts, options in textbooks, and creation of communities of learners that include university faculty.

Practices in individual classes and in entire programs in teacher education illustrate this focus. Franklin (1992) describes the requirement for a paper being changed so that the preservice teachers followed a process in producing the paper that was not unlike the processes being taught to these students as content. A writer's workshop format in which college students conducted oral histories with self-described reluctant readers and wrote narratives based on interviews was studied and reported by Phillips (1992). Both of these studies describe the student teachers as having more confidence in the resulting papers and in themselves as teachers of writing following the required experiences. A strategy involving letter writing between university students and elementary classes (Burk, 1989; Crowhurst, 1992) enable teacher candidates to experience content firsthand with children's writing while being actively involved in the process.

Blanton and Moorman (1993) describe the use of a diary as a tool that teachers use as a vehicle for relating research-based instruction strategies to their practice. Because these diaries are accessible for thinking, planning, and implementing instruction, as well as for directing professional discussion, they have many implications for use in preservice and in-service teacher education.

New teacher education programs are also being implemented. The Elementary Programs in Integrated Classrooms (EPIC) at Ohio State University provide instruction with a focus on integrating across the methods courses. Consistent university faculty and selected classrooms that use integrated curricula and literature-based approaches are the key features of this program (Short & Burke, 1989).

Impediments in pedagogical change can occur when placement in a particular classroom prevents student teachers from attempting any practice that differs from that which already occurs in a classroom. This prohibits even the best teacher education programs from creating change in literacy programs. Harris and Harris (1992) involved university and school personnel in a collaboration that resulted in improving literacy teaching and learning. In a program that involves university collaboration with partner schools, the functions that previously were all determined by the university faculty are now shared. Planning, teaching, and curriculum are structured by the collaboration. Teachers, principals, and professors pursue research that follows inquiry into questions that are jointly framed.

Sometimes change does not occur even when it is the in-service teacher who is attempting change. Ray, Lee, and Stansell (1986) studied a teacher who asked for help while beginning to incorporate writing workshops into her classroom. Through discussions, interviews, and classroom observations it became clear that although this teacher was attempting new methods, she was trying to incorporate these new methods into her existing theories about writing and the amount of control she needed to exert as the teacher.

Support for complex change is also demonstrated in a study of reading teachers through a staff development project that provided an environment of support (Roehler & Putnam, 1986). Three sets of factors were found to be requisite: ownership, ability to compare old and new concepts, and ability to recognize new student behaviors.

The significance of subject-specific coursework in the development of pedagogical content knowledge is demonstrated in a contrast of the case studies of six students, three English majors and three English Education majors. Grossman's (1989a) descriptive results indicate that subject-specific coursework is significant in the student teacher's conception of the purpose for teaching English, in ideas about what to teach, and in knowledge of student understandings. Wedman and Robinson (1988) found that preservice teachers change in their abilities to analyze reading instruction problems and to prescribe instructional alternatives following reading methods coursework.

Subject-specific coursework is also shown to be of specific importance in studies of questioning and discussion in elementary grades. Matthews and Paille (1993) found that asking questions to set a purpose for reading a specific book was not prerequisite for group discussion nor for ability to answer questions about the book; however, the role of the teacher did have significant impact. Therefore, specific instruction for leading group discussions is important content for preservice teachers. In programs designed to train teachers to question, other researchers (Johnson & Evans, 1992; Wedman & Moutray, 1991) report teachers' use of higher level questions following specific instruction.

Two methods of delivering direct instruction in reading to preservice teachers were investigated in another study (Klesius, Sears, & Zielonka, 1990). This study compared students' retention and knowledge of a directed reading activity after two modes of instruction. Students who learned with videotape and related practice retained and used the knowledge for a longer time than did students who learned from lecture and discussion.

An overview of the research in pedagogy in reading/language arts indicates heavy emphasis on programs and courses that reflect current holistic practice; however, in any program there are many components. Zeichner (1993) suggests that there are four traditions in elementary teacher education based on traditions of both historical and current practice. He describes a conceptual framework for looking at the ideas and traditions and argues that to understand any approach, it is necessary to look at the content of the curriculum and at the pedagogy and social relations in the program. According to Zeichner, a single program does not represent one tradition; rather, within one program, there may be representations from any combination of the others.

Intervention Programs

Chapter I, the federal program for providing supplementary reading instruction for children, is the focus of a study by Hiebert, Colt, Catto, and Gury (1992). Although the focus of the study is on improved reading for children, it is quite relevant in a discussion of teacher education. A restructured Chapter I program, through university and school-based collaboration, resulted in positive change for students in Chapter I. This collaboration was formed when two teachers, a literacy professor, and two doctoral students began to talk about the questions the teachers initiated. After several months of study and discussion, a pilot study was conducted. Upon its demonstration of growth of participating children in the program, a project was defined and begun. The basic structure of the program was developed by the university and district team members, and the program was further defined and refined by Chapter I teachers. Many changes were made as a result of teachers' questions and suggestions. There were weekly visits to teachers' classes and feedback sessions, teaching exchanges and observations, and regular meetings of all project participants. Children's progress was discussed and problems and solutions were brainstormed. In short, there was ongoing support, opportunity for input, and feedback about instruction through extensive interaction.

Several programs focus on children during their first years in school because of the importance of these first years to later success in school. A number of programs have been implemented to attempt to correct reading problems, but the success of such programs has varied. Early attention to the problems that interfere with a child's ability to read has become a focus because of the argument that first grade is a critical year for later success (Clay, 1979). Several intervention programs are discussed from the perspective of the ways in which teachers are trained for these programs; however, no attempt is made to assess the relative success of these programs.

Reading Recovery, a preventive tutoring program based on the concept of reading as a psycholinguistic process, was developed by Clay (1985). Reading Recovery provides one-to-one tutoring to first graders who score in the lowest 20% of their classes. Thirty-minute sessions are held daily for a maximum of 60 lessons. Only certified and specifically trained teachers are Reading Recovery teachers. The intensive training includes 1½ hours of training every week for an academic year with follow-up support in subsequent years (Pinnell, 1987). Primary processes involved in developing Reading Recovery teachers include observation, practice, and feedback. During the weekly seminars, teachers conduct tutoring sessions that are observed by other teachers in the seminar and discussed by all.

Success for All (Slavin, Madden, Karweit, Dolan, & Wasik, 1992) is based on research that indicates that students need both meaningful contexts and systematic presentation of word-attack skills. It involves tutoring by special reading teachers within first-, second-, and third-grade classrooms. Success for All trains certified teachers for an initial 2 days on the basic program and 4 additional days on specific training in assessment and tutoring (Wasik & Slavin, 1993). Tutors are observed weekly and are given direct feedback. The tutoring is completely integrated with the reading program experienced in the classroom.

In the Programmed Tutorial Reading program (Wasik & Slavin, 1993), children are tutored for 15 minutes per day, supplementing classroom instruction. Tutors are trained to know strategies to teach, reinforce, and lead students through training materials based on their responses.

Wasik and Slavin (1993) discuss two other intervention programs: the Prevention of Learning Disabilities and the Wallach and Wallach program. Prevention of Learning Disabilities serves children in the first and second grade using instructional interventions they term *TEACH*. These interventions, based on a physiological view of learning, are designed to build perceptual skills. Tutoring sessions are conducted by certified teachers for three to five 30-minute sessions each week. Sessions may be either one-on-one or small group. The Wallach and Wallach program is a skills-based program that begins as a completely separate tutoring program that is later integrated with classroom instruction (Wasik & Slavin, 1993). Interventions begin with recognition of letters and phonemes for the first 10 weeks; subsequently, the next 2–3 weeks children sound out and blend easy words, then for the rest of the year they learn to apply these skills in their classroom reading materials. The Wallach program uses paraprofessionals as tutors.

Portfolio and Process Assessment

Much assessment is done by teachers in classrooms. Teacher education programs expect students to know how to assess children's performance on individual lessons and on units of instruction. In classrooms, teachers are responsible for assessment that informs their teaching and that informs the feedback they give children and parents in conferences and on children's report cards.

Research indicates that teachers receive very little training in this important area. Jett and Schafer (1992) present data based on 538 surveys of high school English teachers that demonstrate that one in five teachers had no training in classroom assess-

ment, and two and a half in five either had no training or training from one source. The preparation of teachers for assessment is limited, according to analyses of textbooks, in-service programs, and class content (Schafer & Lissitz, 1987). In addition, there is little or no research that attempts to determine what is successful in preparing preservice teachers or in-service teachers for assessment. There is interest in assessment that is considered authentic. One type of assessment that has received attention is portfolio assessment. A number of teacher education programs are attempting to use portfolios for preservice teachers as part of individual classes or blocks of classes or are requiring that portfolios of individual children be collected as part of the field-based part of the program. A survey of educators determining knowledge and use of portfolio assessment (Johns & Van Leirsburg, 1992) indicates that respondents of the survey are aware of portfolio assessment; agree with the principles that guide assessment; prefer student input into portfolios; and consider planning, managing, and organizing the portfolios as practical concerns.

Through questionnaires and interviews, Lamme and Hysmith (1991) assessed needs of teachers for in-service education about the use of portfolios. From the assessment, a scale emerged that describes the stages of teachers' involvement with portfolio assessment at one elementary school. Teachers' responses to what was easy or difficult appeared related to their own professional philosophies and theories. The researchers suggest that in-service efforts to move toward authentic assessment must first assess the extent to which authentic instruction is in place in the school.

In another school-based study of portfolio assessment, three researchers (Gomez, Graue, & Bloch, 1991) document what they call ''teachers' struggles'' with portfolio assessment. They argue that the enthusiasm currently exhibited in discussions about portfolios and other authentic assessments may be overlooking the reality of their impact on teaching and learning, student motivation, and teachers' work. In their case study description of one fifth-grade teacher, they document the tensions between the positive (collaborative power, common frameworks for discussing learning, connections between instruction and assessment) and the negative, which is that making this ''restructured assessment work falls squarely on the shoulders of already burdened teachers'' (p. 628).

Instructional Planning

Based on a case study of teacher planning, Cain (1989) describes two models of planning. The traditional rational means-end planning model stems from the scientific management era and provides a four-step procedure including formulating behavioral objectives, choosing appropriate activities, organizing activities into sensible order, and selecting evaluation procedures to assess whether or not the students have met the objectives. The creative planning model encourages recursive thinking as it considers many education design variables that affect student learning.

The behaviors of the student who planned according to the rational means-end planning model are characterized by simple definitions, implicit rationales about what students were expected to master, global assertions with little naturalistic data for support, insights aroused only by seminar requirements, unplanned interactive decisions, and a learning situation driven by desire to help students meet the stated objective. The behaviors that characterize the student who planned according to the creative planning model include more thoughtful planning, greater sensitivity to a range of educational variables, inclusion of process approaches into unit design, varied insights, prior preparation for management strategies and instructional procedures, and a learning environment that became a community of learners. Because the two students in the study were very similar in age, gender, background, completed coursework, achievement, and attitude, the differences were attributed to the creative model for planning that led to broader thinking and planning (Cain, 1989).

TEACHER EDUCATION PROGRAM CURRICULA

It is known that professional teacher education coursework has the potential to provide an occasion for prospective teachers to make the transition to pedagogical thinking, especially when preconceptions about teaching, learning, and subject matter are examined during these courses (Feiman-Nemser & Buchmann, 1985a; Grossman, 1991b). Student teaching has been cited as perhaps the most powerful aspect of preservice education; however, student teachers are "marginally situated in two worlds," part student and part teacher (Britzman, 1991, p. 13). As they struggle for their own individual voices, student teachers must often negotiate among many contradictory realities and conflicting discourses of teaching and schooling. This section of the chapter describes research concerning professional coursework and field experiences and other professional development experiences and programs.

Professional Coursework

Writing about the necessary reconceptualization of teacher education, Fosnot (1989) suggests, "If change is to occur in teacher education, the new models advanced must be based on what we know about teaching and learning, and they must aim at producing teachers who are decision makers, researchers, and articulate change agents" (p. xiii). To foster such a reflective frame of mind in novices, teacher educators have begun to redesign professional education coursework, inviting prospective teachers to participate in experiences of inquiry and reflection that support continual, lifelong, self-regulated learning (e.g., Comeaux & Gomez, 1991; Gomez, 1991; Holt-Reynolds, 1992). In addition, teacher educators have begun to rethink their own roles as teachers and learners (Wilson, 1992). Well-designed coursework has the potential to enable future teachers (as well as teacher educators) to grapple with their beliefs about teaching and learning, to explore their knowledge and conceptions of subject matter, to provide an occasion for transition to pedagogical thinking, and to engender a reflective attitude toward teaching (Grossman, 1991a, 1992b). In such professional education experiences, teacher candidates have opportunities to become confident question-askers rather than unconfident answer-knowers (Kutz, 1992). Finally, teacher edu-

cators have reported that effecting changes in teachers' beliefs through course experiences may be a slow and difficult process (see, e.g., Bird et al., 1993; Herrmann & Sarracino, 1993; Wilson, 1992).

Attending to the importance of preservice teachers' belief exploration and change in courses and other experiences, teacher educators have begun to investigate the effects of their own teaching and programs. For example, through questionnaires, Lonberger (1992) found that her course on reading methods influenced preservice teachers' belief systems as well as their instructional choices. In addition, dialogue journals and autobiographical inquiry have been utilized as modes of reflection and research in a variety of teacher education courses (see, e.g., Hennings, 1992; Richards, Gipe, Levitov, & Speaker, 1989). Wallhausen's (1990) study is indicative of much of the research on the effects of teacher education coursework. In an investigation that examined a sequence of courses' effect of students' perceptions of the reading process, Wallhausen found that students master the basic content of reading theory and methodology more rapidly than they change their conventional beliefs; their abilities to change their beliefs and preconceptions and to accommodate new models are tied to their level of cognitive development and their motivation to change; students who are motivated to change are more apt to do so if they have the opportunity to observe more than one active model of instruction; and those not adequately prepared to implement an unfamiliar strategy will resist and fall back on old models.

Tomkiewicz (1991) conducted a study to determine whether the experiences of writing to learn and reflective teaching within an interdisciplinary elementary methods course would offer undergraduates the opportunity to change their perspective from student to teacher. Data were collected through students' writing, videotaped classes, small group discussions, and researcher's field notes. Tomkiewicz believes that when students are asked to consider themselves as scientists, readers, and writers, they are able to reconceptualize all three fields and to consider how they could be taught under a new paradigm. Another major aspect of this study concerns the importance of written reflection in learning to teach.

In another study concerning the experience of writing in a preservice methods course, Lee (1987) found that whereas some of her students began the course with high levels of writing apprehension, they exited the course feeling that they would be effective writers and teachers of writing. Her pedagogical strategies required students to be active participants in process writing throughout the semester.

Feiman-Nemser and Buchmann (1985b) utilize two contrasting case studies based on an analysis of eight interviews across the first year of teacher preparation to discover how students make the transition to pedagogical thinking. The two students were enrolled in contrasting programs. Janice's academic learning program emphasized theoretical and subject-matter knowledge with limited field experiences, whereas Sarah's decision-making program stressed teaching methods and reflection in action. This study focuses on the influences of both "personal history and formal preparation in helping or hindering the transition to pedagogical thinking" (p. 252). To this end, Sarah made more progress than Janice. Janice viewed "patience" as important in teaching, saying that the university had prepared her by giving her plenty of opportunities to stand in line. She dwelt on memories and exhibited a "know-it-all" attitude that shielded her from growth and change. Janice reported that she felt she would get her answers from student teaching and from on-the-job training. In contrast, Sarah was able to think strategically and to plan globally. When she tried alternatives in teaching, she was able to reflect on her failures and to begin to learn from them. She began to make connections with her past history and the program in which she was enrolled. Teaching for Sarah seemed to be a more complicated, problematic enterprise. Feiman-Nemser and Buchmann cite the importance of both the examination of prior beliefs and university coursework.

The transition to pedagogical thinking in teaching marks a divide—a move in which future teachers learn to look beyond the familiar worlds of teaching and learning. The pull of prior beliefs is strong, however, not the least because of the long apprenticeship of observation that distinguishes teachers from other professionals . . . . In becoming a teacher, very little normatively correct learning can be trusted to come about without instruction that takes the preconceptions of future teachers into account . . . . Neither firsthand experience nor university instruction can be left to work themselves out by themselves. Without help in examining current beliefs and assumptions, teacher candidates are likely to maintain conventional beliefs and incorporate new information or puzzling experiences into old frameworks. (p. 255)

One of the most important findings of Grossman's research (1989a, 1989b, 1990, 1991a) also challenges the literature on the effects of teacher education coursework. Through contrasting case studies of six beginning English teachers, only three of whom graduated from teacher education programs, Grossman found that "subject-specific course work can be a powerful influence on how teachers think about and teach their subjects" (1989b, p. 31). Through interviews and observations, Grossman determined that subject-specific courses in English helped teachers transform their subject-matter knowledge by providing frameworks for thinking about teaching and putting the ideas into practice. Without professional coursework, teachers were unable to overcome their "apprenticeships of observation" and rethink their subject matter for teaching (Grossman, 1991a).

In Shrofel's (1991) study, one learns that the use of a tutorial component in a course on the teaching of writing allows preservice teachers to rethink their "beliefs about, attitudes toward, and experiences as writers and writing teachers" (p. 176). As they participate in tutorials, new teachers are confronted with the "gaps" in their knowledge and must focus their attention on the needs of their tutees; they must, Shrofel says, "reflect on the relationships between teaching and learning" (p. 176). Finally, Shrofel maintains that all teacher educators should confront themselves as teachers and should examine their own assumptions about teaching and the results of their practices.

A recent development in teacher education coursework and program curricula concerns the use of case methodologies to foster problem-formation and problem-solving approaches in preservice teacher thinking. Thoughtfully written or carefully produced cases hold great promise for developing and elevating the pedagogical thinking and reasoning abilities of novice teachers. For example, Risko, Yount, and McAllister (1992) have investigated the promise of video-based cases, "which represent complex teaching situations and contain multiple sources of embedded information" (p. 38). Twelve preservice teachers and their instructor participated in a discussion of three video-based cases concerning authentic situations in Chapter I classrooms. A discourse analysis of this discussion revealed four patterns of discourse within video-based case methodology: (1) active engagement and generative learning for all participants, (2) mediated learning with multiple textures, (3) rich contexts that invite in-depth analysis of information and higher-order thinking, and (4) sequenced instruction replaced by learning that is situated in rich, complex contexts. Risko and her colleagues believe that learning through case discussions "may help preservice teachers acquire mental models of authentic classes, enabling them to think flexibly and to understand the meaning of classroom events" (p. 48). Through their experiences with cases, new teachers may be better prepared to make the decisions they will need to make in their own classrooms.

Field Experiences and Professional Development

Although professional coursework may provide an important influence on novice teachers, many researchers report and generally agree that student teaching is the most beneficial and perhaps the most powerful aspect of preservice teacher education. Many researchers have begun to focus on the socialization and enculturation of the student teacher in English language arts and reading. As an example of such inquiry, Calderhead's (1987, 1991) work traces the development of teachers' professional knowledge, focusing on how students learn to teach, what they learn, and how that knowledge affects their classroom practices. Calderhead is concerned with student teachers' "interpretive frameworks" about classroom practices and how these frameworks are influenced by their professional training and their supervisors.

In one study, Calderhead followed primary-level student teachers through their major field experience in a 1-year postgraduate course using semistructured interviews and classroom observations. His findings are familiar to all teacher educators. During the first 2 weeks, student teachers reported high anxiety associated with their jobs, the university's assessment of their teaching, and their shock in discovering the reality of classroom life. All but one eventually complied with school expectations, rejecting their own "identities" as teachers. They began to model their cooperating teachers' routines, even when they disapproved of the routines. In fact, cooperating teachers "were regarded as most salient source[s] of knowledge about real teaching" (Calderhead, 1987, pp. 4–5), and notions from professional coursework were dismissed. Despite some bright moments of experimentation with new lessons, Calderhead was discouraged by the student teachers' lack of reflection and simplistic views. As a result of his study, he lists three recommendations for the design of preservice teacher education.

(1) In order to minimize anxiety and promote reflection-in-action, the field experience should be split into two blocks, the first assessed in terms of basic competence and the second on the extent to which the students were able to analyze and evaluate their own teaching.
(2) Some thought should be given to how to improve students' abilities to analyze and reflect upon their own teaching and that of teachers they observe.

(3) Teaching is not merely a matter of picking up practical tips. Learning to teach is a complex process involving interactions and changes in cognition, affect, and performance. Teacher educators must develop a greater sensitivity to the complexity of professional learning. (1987, p. 8)

Calderhead's research is reminiscent of what Feiman-Nemser and Buchmann (1985a) call the two-worlds pitfall. "The two-worlds pitfall arises from the fact that teacher education goes on in two distinct settings and from the fallacious assumption that making connections between these two worlds is straight-forward and can be left to the novice" (p. 63).

Likewise, Tighe's use of her "Attitude Scale for English Teachers" (1991) underscores the differences that novices perceive between university and local school settings. On the one hand, the interns in Tighe's study recall their positive experiences in teacher education classes; however, on the other hand, as they begin their internships in local schools, they are swayed by the demands of what Tighe calls a "real classroom" (p. 233). "In too many cases," Tighe writes, "the interns spend ten weeks teaching according to what they believe to be educationally unsound practices" (pp. 233-234). In another study concerning the perspectives of intern teachers, Kleinsasser (1989) suggests that interns believe (1) an internship is too short to develop the interpersonal relationships identified as critical to teaching, and (2) too long to be in another person's classroom.

Several recent studies attempt to counter the two-worlds pitfall by suggesting school–university collaboration in teacher education (see, e.g., Howell, 1986). One such study (Athanases, Caret, Canales, & Meyer, 1992) involves a "conversation" about teaching among several players in a teacher education program—a university professor, students in a teacher education program, a high school English teacher, and an intern teacher. Athanases and his colleagues suggest several ways to link the worlds of teaching and teacher education. They believe, for example, that the dichotomy may be collapsed as students observe models of good practice and reflect on their observations. In addition, they see a need for practicing teachers to be invited to serve as guests on campus, providing instruction and validating the practice of teaching. They urge new teachers to develop portfolios to document their planning and instruction. Finally, they suggest that school–university collaboration should be "genuinely practiced," and that both schools and universities should plan creatively and aggressively for funding of these projects (p. 49).

In another "conversation," Cadenhead and Garner (1990) discuss their contrasting experiences with a preservice course in elementary language arts. The course required that the student (Garner) teach a lesson in an elementary setting that would be supervised by their university professor (Cadenhead). In their discussion, both the student and professor reveal their assumptions about one another, about teaching language arts, and about the purposes of the educational field experience. Although they did not agree totally in the end, both Cadenhead and Garner maintain that the process of writing about the experience was worthwhile. Both agreed on revisions of the preservice course.

Fishman and Raver (1989) allow educators to participate in their shared experience with a dialogue journal, suggesting that their dialogue journal brought "insight, complexity, and stability to what could have been a superficial, one-dimensional, mechanistic relationship" (p. 92). Through their work together, Raver (a student teacher) and Fishman (her cooperating teacher) show us that "teaching is not a matter of monologue, but of dialogue, not a soliloquy, but a conversation" (p. 109). Their journal served three functions: (1) discovering, creating, and reinforcing knowledge; (2) initiating Raver into the professional community; and (3) empowering both teachers, allowing for an understanding and shaping of experience. Whereas some studies point primarily to dissonance between cooperating teachers and interns (e.g., Kleinsasser, 1989), Fishman and Raver allow educators to envision possibilities for truly collaborative relationships between experienced and inexperienced teachers.

Rorschach and Whitney (1986) provide another alternative to the two-worlds pitfall. By serving as peer observers in each other's writing courses and by meeting regularly to discuss their observations, they learned that such collaboratively designed research projects can be a means of professional development for teachers. Rorschach and Whitney believe that a primary benefit of such research is a "heightened awareness" of one's own teaching, an "expanded ability to step back and analyze" work through the process of peer observation and discussion. Finally, they contend that the gap between theory and practice may stem from teacher isolation and "limited or non-existent opportunities for on-going collaborative inquiry" (p. 171).

Gomez and Comeaux (1990) believe that educational researchers often fail to acknowledge the connection between the idiosyncratic problems and challenges novice teachers face and the purposes of induction programs for new teachers. They criticize national trends in induction programs that tend to assume that all beginning teachers are alike and will experience the same kinds of problems. Based on their work with eight student teachers in two markedly different teacher education programs, Gomez and Comeaux recommend that teacher educators look first at what novices bring with them to their classrooms and "only then create a program that will support and nurture these beginners" (p. 19). Similarly, based on their interviews and observation narratives with 39 teachers of reading, Richardson, Anders, Tidwell, and Lloyd (1991) argue that to promote worthwhile inquiry and genuine changes, staff development programs should interweave three forms of knowledge. "Teachers' background theories, beliefs, and understandings of the reading process; theoretical frameworks and empirical premises as derived from current research; and alternative practices that instantiate both teachers' beliefs and research knowledge" (p. 579).

Many teacher educators have begun to invite their students to participate in research studies as a part of their teacher education program. Kutz and Roskelly (1991), Cochran-Smith and Lytle (1993), and Zeichner and Liston (1987) maintain the importance of formal inquiries that enable teachers and teacher candidates to create their own pedagogical theories. "What is missing from the knowledge base of teaching," Cochran-Smith and Lytle (1990) write, "are *the voices of the teachers themselves* [italics added], the questions teachers ask, the ways teachers use writing and intentional talk in their work lives, and the interpretive frames teachers use to understand and improve their own classroom practices" (p. 2). Lytle and Cochran Smith (1990) have expanded definitions of teacher research to include teachers' journals and personal essays as well as more formal classroom ethnographies or case studies of individual students. Teacher research, Cochran-Smith and Lytle (1993) argue, may be defined as "systematic, intentional inquiry by teachers about their own school and classroom work" (pp. 23–24).

In addition to participating in research, Cochran-Smith (1991) proposes that prospective teachers should become both "educators and activists" and should "regard themselves as agents for change," regarding school reform as an "integral part of the social, intellectual, ethical, and political activity of teaching" (p. 279). She believes that new teachers should learn to "teach against the grain" as they work alongside experienced teachers and teacher educators who are themselves struggling to be reformers. Cochran-Smith suggests that teacher educators, experienced teachers, and student teachers engage in conversations of "collaborative resonance." Such collaborative resonance will not be possible, Cochran-Smith concludes, without the combination of several social and program/organizational structures (university-site monthly seminars, publications featuring the work of the participants, dissemination and discussion of common readings, co-planning by teacher educators and school-based teachers of seminar topics and assignments for student teachers, and participation in national networks of teacher researchers).

NEW DIRECTIONS IN THE ENGLISH LANGUAGE ARTS

Predicting future directions presents many of the same problems as predicting the weather; there are many wind shifts and new fronts that come in unexpectedly. Educational predictions present one additional problem—seeing what we want to see. The new directions presented here are not very futuristic; they are more a sense of which of the newer aspects of the field educators believe will flourish.

Research in Teacher Education

As these authors scanned the major journals in the field published during the past 10 years, they found comparatively little research in teacher education. Much of the research that does exist is concentrated in the more general aspects of teaching— field experiences and student teaching, teacher beliefs, mentoring, and so forth. What is really lacking is research in teaching prospective teachers subject-matter knowledge and content-specific methods. There are many articles on whole language, literature-based curricula, and reading/writing to learn in content areas, but almost no research in preparing teachers to implement such ideas.

Much of the research in teacher education seems to be done in dissertations. These authors have not cited these studies in the body of this chapter because they may vary significantly in quality and have not been submitted to the kind of peer review that published journal articles receive.

Reform in teacher education is a major facet of colleges of education today, and this should lead inevitably toward an increase in research in the area. Dissertations as a predictor of future areas of research also suggest that this will be the case.

Case Study Methodology

Case studies, which have been widely used in law, medicine, and business, are currently being used in education. Most of the articles on the use of case studies and most of the published case study materials have been published since 1988. Sykes and Bird (1992) review the use of cases in teacher education. They point out that there are different kinds of case studies, such as subject-specific cases, context-specific cases, cases that represent instances of theory, and cases that present problematic situations. J. Shulman (1992) states in the introduction to *Case Methods in Teacher Education* that they may be effective because they represent situated knowledge, and because reflection and substantive conversation among teachers are important ingredients in improving schools. In fact, she contends that "case methods are the most exciting potential source of improvement for the contemporary pedagogy of teacher education" (p. xvii).

Two chapters from J. Shulman's book are of particular interest in examining the future of case study methodology, one by Grossman on "Teaching and Learning with Cases" (1992a) and the chapter by Lee Shulman entitled "Toward a Pedagogy of Cases." In the latter, Shulman (1992) discusses the role of commentaries and suggests that they may add complexity and richness to case studies. He explores the purposes for case study, the pedagogy of cases, defines what a case is and what is in it, and discusses why it should work along with its disadvantages. Grossman (1992a) begins by defining a case as consisting of narrative text, but points out that it could consist of videotapes, teachers' journals or lesson plans, examples of student work, and fictional or philosophical texts. Her chapter explores the nature of learning from cases and the nature of teaching from cases. She concludes that the value of cases lies in their representation of the world of practice and their ability to stimulate problem solving. She cautions that the development of case methods must be accompanied with a research agenda to learn what prospective teachers learn and do not learn from these materials and methods.

Story as a Central Element in Teacher Education

The importance of story, even the meaning of story, has changed in a variety of ways recently. Much of the research in the language arts has been qualitative, descriptive research that tells its story in a very special manner. Case study methodology is narrative or story used in a particular fashion. Carter (1993) points out that in addition to these uses of story, educators must consider story as a way of knowing. It is uniquely suited to knowledge that comes from action. It is especially useful in dealing with situations that encompass conflict, differing motivations, causality, conflict, and it allows one to connect and interpret events. Story is central to the organization of knowledge and to the processes of comprehension and thinking. Story can operate as a way to inform the work of teaching and teacher education.

Technology in Teacher Education

Although many English language arts educators love the feel of crisp, new pages in a book; cannot imagine composing on anything other than a long, yellow lined pad; and are somewhat suspicious of all machinery, they will not prevail. New teacher educators want powerful new computers or powerbooks to take with them; they work on multimedia materials and look for projection equipment to use in class instead of their computer screens. They prepare materials using hypertext or digital media to bring a range of materials and choices to the learner— text, video, music, definitions, and related materials. Classroom teachers in the future will also prepare materials for their students using this technology. The world of distance learning is opening as the new satellites add channels for educational programming.

Reading materials for students using HyperCard (Apple computer) are being developed in an ElectroText project at the University of Oregon (Anderson-Inman, Horney, Chen, & Lewin, 1994). Students using the materials can do many things such as highlight a word they do not understand and get the definition, use questions that will search for foreshadowing or for facts, or record observations about predictive details in the margin notes option. In other programs, Hypertext enables students to touch a passage and get relevant passages from other sources, find the meaning of unfamiliar words or allusions, touch a line and receive a selection of other mentions of the same idea or image, or get various interpretations or critical evaluations of the piece read. Hypertext emphasizes connections and relationships; it has the potential to change the way one reads texts and to change the roles of author and reader.

Tierney, Stowell, Desai, and Kieffer (1993) describe a high school classroom using Hypercard stack technology set up on a network fileserver so that students can access it from any of the computers in the classroom. The teacher's focus is on civil disobedience and includes materials from Shakespeare, Thoreau, Martin Luther King, Jr., and Gandhi. There are texts, news clips, and films related to the topic in the stack. Students form groups to work on different aspects of the topic and plan ways to share their findings with the entire group. As a final culminating experience, the teacher plans a dinner party where part of the class will dress and assume the role of the fictional and nonfictional people from the study, and the rest of the class will attend the dinner and discuss the issues with the honored guests. This dinner is a kind of "virtual reality" that may someday be available technologically and allow students to enter Gandhi's era, march alongside King in Montgomery, or make a few suggestions to Jefferson as he works on the Declaration of Independence.

Materials for preparing teachers are also being developed using Hypertext; these will allow for analysis of various classroom situations and provide a new level of "observation" for preservice teachers. Using the computer, the learner can select from different options, perhaps looking at other classrooms with similar situations or checking or analyzing interaction patterns. They may shift to text elements discussing various disciplinary strategies and then look at examples of each in action. Developing these new materials and using them for maximum effect will be a challenge for college faculty.

Rose and Meyer (1994) point out that "Digital media are precipitating a revolution in communication and instruction at least as significant as that caused by print" (p. 291). Speech can be recorded without being put in print form; drawings can be digitized via a scanner and displayed on the computer screen; music from a tape, CD, or a live performance can be digitized and displayed on the computer screen; and any text can be read aloud using synthetic speech. It is easily edited, copied, changed to other formats, or restored to its original form.

As schools get more equipment and teachers become more skilled, there are sure to be important changes in the way teacher training programs operate. Teacher educators will be challenged to master the new technology and to use it to break new ground.

> We see technology as serving to complement and aid the teaching of literature at the same time as it offers the possibilities of new genres of text—that is, dynamic and multilayered texts interfaced with image, sound, and other sensations. These new genres have a potential to afford our students new vehicles for exploring and sharing ideas in ways our rather linear, print-based, and bound books have not. (Tierney et al., 1993, p. 190)

New Forms of Evaluation

These authors expect that there will be many more varied forms and formats for evaluation in the next decade or so. . The relatively quick acceptance of portfolio assessment points toward a willingness to consider something other than the traditional letter grades. In a shift away from being totally focused on "standard performance," perhaps because *standard* has become much harder to define, educators are becoming more concerned with alternative values. As they shift toward a more multicultural society, they must refocus how they evaluate students.

As one example of this new evaluation, Donmoyer (1993) proposes that educators consider adapting a four-step process of art criticism: description, analysis, interpretation, and judgment for use in evaluating compositions. Donmoyer gives examples of this process in examining art and then in examining a student's writing portfolio. He concludes that although such an approach does not serve all purposes for evaluation, "the approach . . . represents a useful supplement to more traditional evaluation methods, a supplement that can focus on phenomena and address important questions ignored by more traditional evaluation designs" (p. 259).

Teale (1988) points out that assessment methods for very young children should reflect a theoretically accurate picture of the skills and knowledge they are developing. They must be sensitive to the characteristics of young children that relate to testing. "Generally speaking, teachers will find that performance samples and observational methods tell them the most about a young child's reading and writing knowledge and skills" (p. 174).

Other nontraditional evaluation formats should help educators look more insightfully into the complex interactions involved in both teaching and learning. Particularly if educators think of evaluation as an aid to planning instruction, standard performance is less helpful than the more specific sense of what has been learned and what has not been learned that is the province of the newer evaluation schemes.

Extended Commitments to Schools and Teachers

Teacher preparation institutions have been quite well contained within the college setting, except for short excursions into schools to supervise student teachers or to conduct research. Now both supervision activities and research activities have increased the time spent in schools. Teacher educators have become involved in school partnerships and co-reform and have shifted to more ethnographically oriented research in schools.

Hollingsworth (1992) reports on a longitudinal research project involving beginning teachers who had met monthly for more than 3 years for collaborative conversations with a focus on learning to teach and more particularly on learning to teach literacy. Over the time of the study, four foci of discussion emerged in the following order: issues of classroom relationships; issues of diversity in personal, school, and community values; issues of power and professional voice; and issues of literacy instruction. The author points out the following features that supported teachers' learning: a commitment to a relational process, focusing learning on common practice-based concerns, valuing their experiences and emotions as knowledge, valuing biographical differences, developing a supported critical perspective, reinforcing learning to teach as a process, and articulating a feminist voice in narrative form. She concludes, "It may be time for entertaining different conversations about supporting learning to teach" (p. 402). The sense of growth, validation, and support that comes from such continuing conversations with graduates may suggest that more extended contacts should be a high priority in preparing teachers.

The final outcome of Goodlad's (1990b) study of the education of educators, *Teachers for Our Nation's Schools,* is summarized in a *Phi Delta Kappan* (1990a) article. "Our goal is to have in place by the year 2000 a group of exemplary settings joined in a coalition and productively engaged in renewing teacher education through programs that join schools and universities" (p. 193). He also points out, however, that simply increasing the amount of time future teachers spend in schools is not reform; in fact, that would almost guarantee that the status quo would be continued. Goodlad (1990a) outlines 19 postulates needed to move into new designs for teacher preparation.

Cochran-Smith (1991) examines the possibilities for teachers to learn to be both educators and activists who regard reform as an integral part of the social, intellectual, ethical, and political activity of teaching. She demonstrates that one way for student teachers to learn to reform teaching is to work with experienced teachers who are committed to reform. Working "within and around the culture of teaching and the politics of schooling is a significant feature of 'teaching against the grain'" (p. 22).

The Focus of Change in the Language Arts

Most of the new trends in the English language arts and reading are focused on processes as opposed to products. Most of the research studies are qualitative descriptions of the process of learning rather than traditional examinations of the products of learning. Case study methodology tends to reveal processes of learning more often and more easily than experimental studies, and story as an element of teaching and learning reveals much about how one comes to know. Technology, from word processing programs on computers to Hypertext and digital media, will offer new ways of learning and of exploring ideas and sharing them. The new evaluation procedures are also focused on process; they examine *how* students learn rather than *what* they learn. The overall trend in language arts and reading is on thinking and critical thinking processes that will enable students to communicate and create in situations that do not yet exist.

References

Afflerbach, P., Bass, L., Hoo, D., Smith, S., Weiss, L., & Williams, L. (1988). Preservice teachers use think-aloud protocols to study writing. *Language Arts, 65*(7), 693–701.

Allen, J., Combs, J., Hendricks, M., Nash, P., & Wilson, S. (1988). Studying change: Teachers who become researchers. *Language Arts, 65*(4), 379–387.

Alvermann, D. E., & Swafford, J. (1989). Do content area strategies have a research base? *Journal of Reading, 32*(5), 388–394.

Amarel, M., & Feiman-Nemser, S. (1988, April). *Prospective teachers' views of teaching and learning to teach.* Paper presented at the meeting of the American Educational Research Association, New Orleans.

Anderson-Inman, L., Horney, M. A., Chen, D., & Lewin, L. (1994). Hypertext literacy: Observations from the ElectroText project. *Language Arts, 71*(4), 279–287.

Andrews, N. C., Moss, R. K., & Stansell, J. C. (1985). Reading (aloud, that is) to undergraduate reading methods classes. *Journal of Reading, 28*(4), 315–320.

Applebee, A. N. (1987). Musings . . . teachers and the process of research. *Research in the Teaching of English, 21*(1), 5–7.

Applebee, A. (1988). The enterprise we are part of: Learning to teach. In M. Lightfoot & N. Martin (Eds.), *The word for teaching is learn-ing: Essays for James Britton* (pp. 206–216). Portsmouth, NH: Heinemann.

Applegate, J., & Shaklee, B. (1992). Stimulating reflection while learning to teach: The ATTEP at Kent State University. In L. Valli (Ed.), *Reflective teacher education: Cases and critiques* (pp. 65–81). Albany: State University of New York Press.

Athanases, S. Z., Caret, E., Canales, J., & Meyer, T. (1992). Four against "The Two-Worlds Pitfall": University-schools collaboration in teacher education. *English Education, 24*(1), 34–51.

Atwell, N. (1987). Class-based writing research: Teachers learning from students. In D. Goswami & P. Stillman (Eds.), *Reclaiming the classroom: Teacher research as an agency for change* (pp. 87–93). Upper Montclair, NJ: Boynton/Cook.

Bird, T., Anderson, L. M., Sullivan, B. A., & Swidler, S. A. (1993). Pedagogical balancing acts: Attempts to influence prospective teachers' beliefs. *Teaching and Teacher Education, 9*(3), 253–267.

Blanton, W. E., & Moorman, G. B. (1993). A diary as a tool for mediating reading teacher activity. *Reading Research and Instruction, 32*(4), 76–89.

Brent, R., & Anderson, P. (1993). Developing children's classroom listening strategies. *The Reading Teacher, 47*(2), 122–126.

Britzman, D. P. (1986). Cultural myths in the making of a teacher: Biography and social structure in teacher education. *Harvard Educational Review, 56*(4), 442–456.

Britzman, D. P. (1991). *Practice makes practice: A critical study of learning to teach.* Albany: State University of New York Press.

Brooks, B. (1992). Imagination, the source of reading. *The New Advocate, 5*(2), 79–85.

Bullough, R. V. (1989). *First-year teacher: A case study.* New York: Teachers College Press.

Bullough, R. V., Knowles, J. G., & Crowe, N. A. (1991). *Emerging as a teacher.* London: Routledge.

Burk, J. (1989). *Pen pals: A beneficial partnership.* Paper presented at the annual meeting of the National Reading Conference, Austin, TX.

Bush, G. (1991). *America 2000: An education strategy.* Washington, DC: U.S. Department of Education.

Cadenhead, K., & Garner, J. L., Jr. (1990). Learning about teaching: A shared experience. *English Education, 22*(2), 125–133.

Cain, B. N. (1989). With worldmaking, planning models matter. *English Education, 21*(1), 5–29.

Calderhead, J. (1987, April). *Cognition and metacognition in teachers' professional development.* Paper presented at the meeting of the American Educational Research Association, Washington, DC. (ERIC Document Reproduction Service No. ED 282 844)

Calderhead, J. (1991). The nature and growth of knowledge in student teaching. *Teaching and Teacher Education, 7*(5/6), 531–535.

Calderhead, J. (1992). The role of reflection in learning to teach. In L. Valli (Ed.), *Reflective teacher education: Cases and critiques* (pp. 139–146). Albany: State University of New York Press.

Carter, K. (1990). Teachers' knowledge and learning to teach. In W. R. Houston (Ed.), *Handbook of research on teacher education* (pp. 291–310). New York: Macmillan.

Carter, K. (1992). Creating cases for the development of teacher knowledge. In T. Russell & H. Munby (Eds.), *Teachers and teaching: From classroom to reflection* (pp. 109–123). London: Falmer.

Carter, K. (1993). The place of story in the study of teaching and teacher education. *Educational Researcher, 22*(1), 5–12, 18.

Cazden, C. B. (1988). *Classroom discourse: The language of teaching and learning.* Portsmouth, NH: Heinemann.

Christensen, L., & Walker, B. J. (1992). Researching one's own teaching in a reading education course. *Literacy research and practice: Foundations for the year 2000.* Kent, OH: Kent State University.

Ciriello, M. J., Valli, L., & Taylor, N. E. (1992). Problem solving is not enough: Reflective teacher education at the Catholic University of America. In L. Valli (Ed.), *Reflective teacher education: Cases and critiques* (pp. 99–116). Albany: State University of New York Press.

Clandinin, D. J., & Connelly, F.M. (1987). Teachers' personal knowledge: What counts as "personal" in studies of the personal. *Journal of Curriculum Studies, 19*(6), 2–14.

Clark, C. M., & Peterson, P. L. (1986). Teachers' thought processes. In M. C. Wittrock (Ed.), *Handbook of research on teaching* (3rd ed.). New York: Macmillan.

Clay, M. (1979). *Reading: The patterning of complex behavior.* Portsmouth, NH: Heinemann.

Clay, M. (1985). *The early detection of reading difficulties.* Exeter, NH: Heinemann.

Clift, R. T., Houston, W. R., & McCarthy, J. (1992). Getting it RITE: A case of negotiated curriculum in teacher preparation at the University of Houston. In L. Valli (Ed.), *Reflective teacher education: Cases and critiques* (pp. 116–138). Albany: State University of New York Press.

Cline, R. K. J., & Fixer, R. J. (1985). Survey of attitudes toward language arts for prospective elementary teachers. *English Education, 17*(2), 69–78.

Close, E. E. (1990). Seventh graders sharing literature: How did we get here? *Language Arts, 67*(8), 817–823.

Coakley, C. G., & Wolvin, A. D. (1990). Listening pedagogy and andragogy: The state of the art. *Journal of the International Listening Association, 4,* 33–61.

Cochran-Smith, M. (1991). Learning to teach against the grain. *Harvard Educational Review, 61*(3), 17–48.

Cochran-Smith, M., & Lytle, S. L. (1990). Research on teaching and teacher research: The issues that divide. *Educational Researcher, 19*(2), 2–11.

Cochran-Smith, M., & Lytle, S. L. (1992). Interrogating cultural diversity: Inquiry and action. *Journal of Teacher Education, 43*(2), 104–115.

Cochran-Smith, M., & Lytle, S. (1993). *Inside/outside: Teacher research and knowledge.* New York: Teachers College Press.

Comeaux, M. A., & Gomez, M. L. (1991, April). *Explicating the text of teacher education: An examination of the role of the special methods course in teacher preparation.* Paper presented at the annual meeting of the American Educational Research Association, Chicago.

Crowhurst, M. (1992). Some effects of corresponding with an older audience. *Language Arts, 69*(4), 268–273.

Cullinan, B. E. (1992, October). Whole language and children's literature. *Language Arts, 69*(6), 426–430.

Daisey, P., & Shroyer, M. G. (1993). Perceptions and attitudes of content and methods instructors toward a required reading course. *Journal of Reading, 36*(8), 624–629.

Delpit, L. D. (1988). The silenced dialogue: Power and pedagogy in educating other people's children. *Harvard Educational Review, 58*(3), 280–298.

Delpit, L. D. (1992). Acquisition of literate discourse: Bowing before the master? *Theory into Practice, 31*(4), 296–302.

Dewey, J. (1933). *How we think, a restatement of the relation of reflective thinking to the evaluative process, by John Dewey.* Boston: Heath.

Dewey, J. (1938). *Experience and education.* New York: Macmillan.

Dias, P. (1989). Becoming students to learn about teaching. *English Education, 21*(4), 196–210.

Donmoyer, R. (1993). Art criticism as a guide to student evaluation. *Theory Into Practice, 32*(4), 252–259.

Duke, C. R. (1992). Commission report: The transition to teaching. *English Education, 24*(3), 147–167.

Dyson, A. H. (1986). Staying free to dance with the children: The dangers of sanctifying activities in the language arts curriculum. *English Education, 18*(3), 135–146.

Edwards, P., & Tate, D. (1992). Addressing the reading needs of culturally and linguistically diverse children. In M. J. O'Hair & S. J. Odell (Eds.), *Diversity and teaching* (pp. 269–284). New York: Harcourt Brace Jovanovich.

Elbaz, F. (1983). *Teacher thinking: A study of practical knowledge.* New York: Nichols.

Farrell, R. A., & Cirrincione, J. M. (1986). The introductory developmental reading course for content area teachers: A state of the art survey. *Journal of Reading, 29*(8), 717–723.

Feiman-Nemser, S. (1983). Learning to teach. In L. S. Shulman & G. Sykes (Eds.), *Handbook of teaching and policy* (pp. 150–170). New York: Longman.

Feiman-Nemser, S., & Buchmann, M. (1985a). Pitfalls of experience in teacher preparation. *Teachers College Record, 87*(1), 53–65.

Feiman-Nemser, S., & Buchmann, M. (1985b). The first year of teacher preparation: Transition to pedagogical thinking? *Journal of Curriculum Studies, 18,* 239–256.

Fishman, A. R., & Raver, E. J. (1989). "Maybe I'm just NOT teacher material": Dialogue journals in the student teaching experience. *English Education, 21*(2), 92–109.

Florio-Ruane, S., & Lensmire, T. (1990). Transforming future teachers' ideas about writing instruction. *Journal of Curriculum Studies, 22*(3), 277–289.

Fosnot, C. T. (1989). *Enquiring teachers, enquiring learners: A constructivist approach for teaching.* New York: Teachers College Press.

Foster, H. M. (1994). *Crossing over: Whole language for secondary English teachers*. Fort Worth: Harcourt Brace Jovanovich.

Fox, D. L. (1993). The influence of context, community, and culture: Contrasting cases of teacher knowledge development. In C. K. Kinzer & D. J. Leu (Eds.), *The forty-second yearbook of the National Reading Conference* (pp. 345–351). Chicago: National Reading Conference.

Franklin, M. R. (1992). Learning the writing process in teacher education classes. *Action in Teacher Education, 14*(20), 60–66.

Garcia, J., & Pugh, S. L. (1992). Multicultural education in teacher preparation programs: A political or an educational concept? *Phi Delta Kappan, 74*(3), 214–220.

Gere, A. R. (1992). *Writing and learning* (3rd ed.). New York: Macmillan.

Gideonse, H. D. (1989). *Relating knowledge to teacher education: Responding to NCATE's knowledge base and related standards*. Washington, DC: AACTE.

Giroux, H. A., & McLaren, P. (1986). Teacher education and the politics of engagement: The case for democratic schooling. *Harvard Educational Review, 56*(3), 213–238.

Gomez, M. L. (1988, April). Prospective teachers' beliefs about good writing: What do they bring with them to teacher education? Paper presented at the annual meeting of the American Educational Research Association, New Orleans.

Gomez, M. L. (1990). Learning to teach writing: Untangling the tensions between theory and practice (Research Report 89-7). East Lansing, MI: National Center for Research on Teacher Education.

Gomez, M. L. (1991). Teaching a language of opportunity in a language arts methods class. In B. R. Tabachnick & K. Zeichner (Eds.), *Issues and practices in inquiry-oriented teacher education* (pp. 91–112). Philadelphia: Falmer.

Gomez, M. L., & Comeaux, M. A. (1990, April). Start with the stone, not with the hole: Matching novices' needs with appropriate programs of induction. Paper presented at the annual meeting of the American Educational Research Association, Boston.

Gomez, M. L., Graue, M. E., & Bloch, M. N. (1991, December). Reassessing portfolio assessment: Rhetoric and reality. *Language Arts, 68*, 620–628.

Goodlad, J. I. (1990a). Better teachers for our nation's schools. *Phi Delta Kappan, 72*(3), 184–195.

Goodlad, J. I. (1990b). *Teachers for our nation's schools*. San Francisco: Jossey-Bass.

Goodman, K. S. (1992). Why whole language is today's agenda in education. *Language Arts, 69*(5), 354–363.

Goodman, Y. M. (1989). Roots of the whole-language movement. *The Elementary School Journal, 90*(2), 113–127.

Gore, J., & Zeichner, K. (1991). Action research and reflective teaching in preservice teacher education: A case study from the United States. *Teaching and Teacher Education, 7*(2), 119–136.

Goswami, D., & Stillman, P. (1987). *Reclaiming the classroom: Teacher research as an agency for change*. Upper Montclair, NJ: Boynton/Cook.

Grady, S. (1992). A postmodern challenge: Universal truths need not apply. *Theater, 23*(2), 15–19.

Graves, D. H. (1989). Research currents: When children respond to fiction. *Language Arts, 66*(7), 776–784.

Griffin, G. A. (1989). Coda: The knowledge-driven school. In M. Reynolds (Ed.), *Knowledge base for the beginning teacher* (pp. 277–286). Elmsford, NY: Pergamon.

Grossman, P. L. (1987a). *Conviction—that granite base: A case study of Martha, a beginning English teacher*. Knowledge Growth in a Profession Publication Series. Stanford, CA: Stanford University, School of Education.

Grossman, P. L. (1987b). *A passion for language: A case study of Colleen, a beginning English teacher*. Knowledge Growth in a Profession Publication Series. Stanford, CA: Stanford University, School of Education.

Grossman, P. L. (1987c). *A tale of two teachers: The role of subject matter orientation in teaching*. Knowledge Growth in a Profession Publication Series. Stanford, CA: Stanford University, School of Education.

Grossman, P. L. (1989a). Learning to teach without teacher education. *Teachers College Record, 91*(2), 191–208.

Grossman, P. L. (1989b). A study in contrast: Sources of pedagogical content knowledge for secondary English. *Journal of Teacher Education, 40*(5), 24–31.

Grossman, P. L. (1990). *The making of a teacher: Teacher knowledge and teacher education*. New York: Teachers College Press.

Grossman, P. L. (1991a). Overcoming the apprenticeship of observation in teacher education coursework. *Teaching and Teacher Education, 7*(4), 345–357.

Grossman, P. L. (1991b). What are we talking about anyway? Subject-matter knowledge of secondary English teachers. In J. Brophy (Ed.), *Advances in research on teaching* (vol. 2, pp. 245–264). Greenwich, CT: JAI Press.

Grossman, P. L. (1992a). Teaching and learning with cases. In J. Shulman (Ed.), *Case methods in teacher education* (pp. 227–239). New York: Teachers College Press.

Grossman, P. L. (1992b). Why models matter: An alternate view on professional growth in teaching. *Review of Educational Research, 62*(2), 171–179.

Grossman, P. L., & Gudmundsdottir, S. (1987). *Teachers and texts: An expert/novice study in English*. Knowledge Growth in a Profession Publication Series. Stanford, CA: Stanford University, School of Education.

Grossman, P. L., Wilson, S., & Shulman, L. S. (1989). Teachers of substance: Subject matter knowledge for teaching. In M. Reynolds (Ed.), *Knowledge base for the beginning teacher* (pp. 23–36). Elmsford, NY: Pergamon.

Haberman, M. (1991). The rationale for training adults as teachers. In C. E. Sleeter (Ed.), *Empowerment through multicultural education* (pp. 275–286). Albany: State University of New York Press.

Harris, R. C., & Harris, M. F. (1992). Preparing teachers for literacy education: University/school collaboration. *Journal of Reading, 35*(7), 572–579.

Harste, J. (1985). Portrait of a new paradigm. In A. Crismore (Ed.), *Landscapes: A state-of-the-art assessment of reading comprehension research, 1974–1984* (pp. 1–24). Bloomington: Indiana University Press.

Heath, S. B. (1983). *Ways with words*. Cambridge, MA: Cambridge University Press.

Heathcote, D. (1984). *Dorothy Heathcote: Collected writings on education and drama*. London: Hutchinson.

Hennings, D. G. (1992). Students' perceptions of dialogue journals used in college methods courses in language arts and reading. *Reading Research and Instruction, 31*(3), 15–31.

Herrmann, B. A., & Sarracino, J. (1993). Restructuring a preservice literacy methods course: Dilemmas and lessons learned. *Journal of Teacher Education, 44*(2), 96–106.

Hiebert, E. H., Colt, J. M., Catto, S. L., & Gury, E. C. (1992). Reading and writing of first-grade students in a restructured chapter 1 program. *American Educational Research Journal, 29*(3), 545–572.

Hoag, C. L., & Wood, R. W. (1990). *Elementary language arts professors teaching practices for and attitudes about listening in select teacher-training institutions*. Washington, DC: ERIC. (ERIC Reproduction Service No. 236 50)

Hollingsworth, S. (1992). Learning to teach through collaborative conversation: A feminist approach. *American Educational Research Journal, 29*(2), 373–404.

Hollingsworth, S., & Teel, K. (1991). Learning to teach reading in secondary math and science. *Journal of Reading, 35*(3), 190–194.

Holt-Reynolds, D. (1992). Personal history-based beliefs as relevant prior knowledge in course work. *American Educational Research Journal, 29*(2), 325–349.

Howell, K.M. (1986). Mentors in teachers' learning. *Language Arts, 63*(2), 160–167.

Huck, C. S. (1992). Literacy and literature. *Language Arts, 69*(7), 520–525.

Jett, D. L., & Schafer, W. D. (1992, April). *Classroom teachers move to center stage in the assessment area—ready or not!* Paper presented at the annual meeting of the American Research Association, San Francisco.

Jipson, J. A., & Paley, N. (1992). Is there a base to today's literature-based reading programs? *English Education, 24*(2), 77–90.

Johns, J. L., & Van Leirsburg, P. V. (1992). How professionals view portfolio assessment. *Reading Research and Instruction, 32*(1), 1–10.

Johnson, C. S., & Evans, A. D. (1992). Improving teacher questioning: A study of a training program. In N. Padak, T. Rasinski, & J. Logan (Eds.), *Literacy research and practice: Foundations for the year 2000* (pp. 65–70). Pittsburg, KS: College Reading Association.

King, A. (1994). Guiding knowledge construction in the classroom: Effects of teaching children how to question and how to explain. *American Educational Research Journal, 31*(2), 338–368.

Kleinsasser, A. M. (1989, March). *"In medias res": Good for Greek drama but not necessarily good for pre-service language arts interns.* Paper presented at the annual meeting of the American Educational Research Association, San Francisco.

Klesius, J. P., Sears, E. F., & Zielonka, P. (1990). A comparison of two methods of direct instruction of preservice teachers. *Journal of Teacher Education, 41*(4), 34–44.

Knowles, G. (1992). Models for understanding preservice and beginning teachers' biographies: Illustrations from case studies. In I. F. Goodson (Ed.), *Studying teachers' lives* (pp. 99–152). New York: Teachers College Press.

Knowles, G., & Holt-Reynolds, D. (1991). Shaping pedagogies through personal histories in preservice teacher education. *Teachers College Record, 93*(1), 87–113.

Kutz, E. (1992). Preservice teachers as researchers: Developing practice and creating theory in the English classroom. *English Education, 24*(2), 67–76.

Kutz, E., & Roskelly, H. (1991). *An unquiet pedagogy: Transforming practice in the English classroom.* Portsmouth, NH: Boynton/Cook.

Lamme, L. L., & Hysmith, C. (1991). One school's adventure into portfolio assessment. *Language Arts, 68*(8), 629–640.

Langer, J. A. (1990). Understanding literature. *Language Arts, 67*(8), 812–816.

Lee, S. (1987, March). *Reflections from a language arts methods class: The experience of process writing and writing apprehension.* Paper presented at the National Council of Teachers of English Spring Conference, Louisville.

Lipson, M. Y., Valencia, S. W., Wixson, K. K., & Peters, C. W. (1993). Integration and thematic teaching: Integration to improve teaching and learning. *Language Arts, 70*(4), 252–263.

Lonberger, R. M. (1992). The belief systems and instructional choices of preservice teachers. In N. Padak, T. Rasinsky, & J. Logan (Eds.), *Literacy research and practice: Foundations for the year 2000* (pp. 71–78). Pittsburg, KS: College Reading Association.

Lortie, D. C. (1975). *Schoolteacher: A sociological study.* Chicago: The University of Chicago Press.

Lytle, S., & Cochran-Smith, M. (1990). Learning from teacher research: A working typology. *Teachers College Record, 92*(1), 83–103.

Lytle, S., & Cochran-Smith, M. (1992). Teacher research as a way of knowing. *Harvard Educational Review, 62*(4), 447–474.

Manna, A. L., & Misheff, S. (1987). What teachers say about their own reading development. *Journal of Reading, 31*(2), 160–168.

Martin, R. J. (1991). The power to empower: Multicultural education for student-teachers. In C. E. Sleeter (Ed.), *Empowerment through multicultural education* (pp. 287–297). Albany: State University of New York Press.

Matthews, M. W., & Paille, E. W. (1993). Impact of purpose-setting questions on children's book discussions. In T. V. Rasinski & N. D. Padak (Eds.), *Inquiries in literacy learning and instruction* (pp. 89–95). Pittsburg, KS: College Reading Association.

McCaleb, J., Borko, H., & Arends, R. (1992). Reflection, research, and repertoire in the Masters Certification Program at the University of Maryland. In L. Valli (Ed.), *Reflective teacher education: Cases and critiques* (pp. 40–64). Albany: State University of New York Press.

McDiarmid, G. W. (1992). What to do about differences? A study of multicultural education for teacher trainees in the Los Angeles Unified School District. *Journal of Teacher Education, 43*(2), 83–93.

McDiarmid, G. W., Ball, D. L., & Anderson, C. W. (1989). Why staying one chapter ahead doesn't really work: Subject-specific pedagogy. In M. C. Reynolds (Ed.), *Knowledge base for the beginning teacher* (pp. 193–205). Oxford: Pergamon.

Michaels, S., & Foster, M. (1985). Peer-peer learning: Evidence from a student-run sharing time. In A. Jaggar & M. T. Smith-Burke (Eds.), *Observing the language learner* (pp. 143–158). Urbana, IL: National Council of Teachers of English.

Moll, L. C. (1988). Some key issues in teaching Latino students. *Language Arts, 65*(5), 465–472.

Monson, R. J., & Monson, M. P. (1994). Literacy as inquiry: An interview with Jerome C. Harste. *The Reading Teacher, 47*(7), 518–521.

Moore, D. W., Readence, J. E., & Rickelman, R. J. (1983). An historical exploration of content area reading instruction. *Reading Research Quarterly, 18*(4), 419–436.

Mosenthal, J. H., Schwartz, R. M., & MacIsaac, D. (1992). Comprehension instruction and teacher training: More than mentioning. *Journal of Reading, 36*(3), 198–207.

Moss, B. (1992). Preservice teachers' reminiscences of positive and negative reading experiences: A qualitative study. In N. Padak, T. Rasinsky, & J. Logan (Eds.), *Literacy research and practice: Foundations for the year 2000* (pp. 29–35). Pittsburg, KS: College Reading Association.

Munby, H. (1987). Metaphor and teachers' knowledge. *Research in the Teaching of English, 21*(4), 377–398.

Myers, M. (1985). *The teacher-researcher: How to study writing in the classroom.* Urbana, IL: National Council of Teachers of English.

Myers, S. S. (1993). Reflective teaching in a reading instruction teacher training program. *Journal of Reading Education, 18*(2), 35–49.

Nespor, J. K. (1987). The role of beliefs in the practice of teaching. *Journal of Curriculum Studies, 19*(4), 317–328.

Newman, J. M. (1987). Learning to teach by uncovering our assumptions. *Language Arts, 64*(7), 727–737.

Nikola-Lisa, W. (1992). Read aloud, play a lot: Children's spontaneous responses to literature. *The New Advocate, 5*(3), 199–213.

Noordhoff, K., & Kleinfeld, J. (1993). Preparing teachers for multicultural classrooms. *Teaching and Teacher Education, 9*(1), 27–39.

O'Brien, D. G., & Stewart, R. A. (1990). Preservice teachers' perspectives on why every teacher is not a teacher of reading: A qualitative analysis. *Journal of Reading Behavior, 22*(2), 101–129.

Ohlhausen, M. M., & Jepsen, M. (1992). Lessons from Goldilocks: "Somebody's been choosing my books but I can make my own choices now!" *The New Advocate, 5*(1), 31–46.

Oja, S. N., Diller, A., Corcoran, E., & Andrew, M. (1992). Communities of inquiry, communities of support: The five year teacher education program at the University of New Hampshire. In L. Valli (Ed.), *Reflective teacher education: Cases and critiques* (pp. 3–23). Albany: State University of New York Press.

Pace, G. (1991). When teachers use literature for literacy instruction: Ways that constrain, ways that free. *Language Arts, 68*(1), 12–25.

Patberg, J. P., Dewitz, P., & Henning, M. J. (1984). The impact of content area reading instruction on secondary teachers. *Journal of Reading, 27*(6), 500–507.

Pearson, P. D. (1993). Teaching and learning reading: A research perspective. *Language Arts, 70*(6), 502–511.

Phillips, J. (1992, April). *Implementing control theory: One point of light.* Paper presented at the spring conference of the American Association of Colleges for Teacher Education/Association of Teacher Educators, Little Rock, AR.

Piaget, J., & Inhelder, B. (1969). *The psychology of the child.* New York: Basic Books.

Pinnell, G. S. (1987). Helping teachers see how readers read: Staff development through observation. *Theory Into Practice, 26*(1), 51–58.

Putnam, J., & Grant, S. G. (1992). Reflective practice in the Multiple Perspectives Program at Michigan State University. In L. Valli (Ed.), *Reflective teacher education: Cases and critiques* (pp. 82–98). Albany: State University of New York Press.

Queenan, M. (1988). Impertinent questions about teacher research: A review. *English Journal, 77*(2), 41–46.

Ray, K. J., Lee, S. C., & Stansell, J. C. (1986). New methods, old theories, and teacher education: Some observations of writing in a third-grade classroom. In J. A. Niles & R. V. Lalik (Eds.), *Solving problems in literacy: Learners, teachers, and researchers* (pp. 152–159). Rochester, NY: National Reading Conference.

Reynolds, J. A. (1987a). *Everyone's invited to the party: A case study of Catherine, a beginning English teacher.* Knowledge Growth in a Profession Publication Series. Stanford, CA: Stanford University, School of Education.

Reynolds, J. A. (1987b). *Learning by doing: A case study of Yvonne, a beginning English teacher.* Knowledge Growth in a Profession Publication Series. Stanford, CA: Stanford University, School of Education.

Reynolds, M. C. (Ed.). (1989). *Knowledge base for the beginning teacher.* Oxford: Pergamon.

Rhodes, S. C. , Watson, K. W., & Barker, L. I. (1990). Listening assessment: Trends and influencing factors in the 1980's. *Journal of the International Listening Association, 4,* 62–82.

Richards, J. C., Gipe, J. P., Levitov, J., & Speaker, R. (1989, March). *Psychological and personal dimensions of prospective teachers' reflective abilities.* Paper presented at the annual meeting of the American Educational Research Association, San Francisco.

Richardson, V., Anders, P., Tidwell, D., & Lloyd, C. (1991). The relationship between teachers' beliefs and practices in reading comprehension instruction. *American Educational Research Journal, 28*(3), 559–586.

Risko, V. J., Yount, D., & McAllister, D. (1992). Preparing preservice teachers for remedial instruction: Teaching problem solving and use of content and pedagogical knowledge. In N. Padak, T. Rasinsky, & J. Logan (Eds.), *Literacy research and practice: Foundations for the year 2000* (pp. 37–50). Pittsburg, KS: College Reading Association.

Ritchie, J. S., & Wilson, D. E. (1993). Dual apprenticeships: Subverting and supporting critical teaching. *English Education, 25*(2), 67–83.

Roehler, L. A., & Putnam, J. (1986). Factors which enhance or inhibit complex teacher change. In J. A. Niles & R. V. Lalik (Eds.), *Solving problems in literacy: Learners, teachers, and researchers* (pp. 160–164). Rochester, NY: National Reading Conference.

Rorschach, E., & Whitney, R. (1986). Relearning to teach: Peer observation as a means of professional development for teachers. *English Education, 18*(3), 159–172.

Rose, D. H., & Meyer, A. (1994). Focus on research: The role of technology in language arts instruction. *Language Arts, 71*(4), 290–294.

Rosenblatt, L. M. (1938, 1983), *Literature as exploration.* New York: The Modern Language Association.

Rosenblatt, L. M. (1978). *The reader, the text, the poem: The transactional theory of the literary work.* Carbondale, Southern Illinois University Press.

Roskelly, H. (1987). Active learning to active teaching: A new direction in teacher preparation. *English Education, 20*(3), 172–183.

Ross, D. D., Johnson, M., & Smith, W. (1992). Developing a PROfessional TEACHer at the University of Florida. In L. Valli (Ed.), *Reflective teacher education: Cases and critiques* (pp. 24–39). Albany: State University of New York Press.

Ross, D. R., & Smith, W. (1992). Understanding preservice teachers' perspectives on diversity. *Journal of Teacher Education, 43*(2), 94–103.

Ruddell, R. B. (1992). A whole language and literature perspective: Creating a meaning-making instructional environment. *Language Arts, 69*(8) , 612–619.

Salisbury-Wills, B. (1992). Arts education shaken up. *Theater, 23*(2), 30–34.

Schafer, W. D., & Lissitz, R. W. (1987). Measurement training for school personnel: Recommendations and reality. *Journal of Teacher Education, 38*(3), 57–63.

Scharer, P. L., & Detwiler, D. B. (1992). Changing as teachers: Perils and possibilities of literature-based language arts instruction. *Language Arts, 69*(3), 186–192.

Schwab, J. J. (1978). Education and the structure of the disciplines. In I. Westbury & N. J. Wilkof (Eds.), *Science, curriculum, and liberal education* (pp. 229–272). Chicago: The University of Chicago Press.

Shockley, B. (1993). Extending the literate community: Reading and writing with parents. *The New Advocate, 6*(1), 11–23.

Short, K. G., & Armstrong, J. (1993). Moving toward inquiry: Integrating literature into the science curriculum. *The New Advocate, 6*(3), 183–199.

Short, K. G., & Burke, C. L. (1989). New potentials for teacher education: Teaching and learning as inquiry. *Elementary School Journal, 90*(2), 193–206.

Shrofel, S. (1991). Developing writing teachers. *English Education, 23*(3), 160–177.

Shulman, J. H. (Ed.). (1992). *Case methods in teacher education.* New York: Teachers College Press.

Shulman, L. S. (1986a). Those who understand: Knowledge growth in teaching. *Educational Researcher, 15*(2), 4–14.

Shulman, L. S. (1986b). Paradigms and research programs in the study of teaching: A contemporary perspective. In M. C. Wittrock (Ed.), *Handbook of research on teaching* (3rd ed., pp. 3–36). New York: Macmillan.

Shulman, L. S. (1987). Knowledge and teaching: Foundations of the new reform. *Harvard Educational Review, 57*(1), 1–22.

Shulman, L. S. (1990). Reconnecting foundations to the substance of teacher education. *Teachers College Record, 91*(3), 300–310.

Shulman, L. (1992). Toward a pedagogy of cases. In J. Shulman (Ed.), *Case methods in teacher education* (pp. 1–30). New York: Teachers College Press.

Slavin, R. E., Madden, N. A., Karweit, N. L., Dolan, L. J., & Wasik, B. A. (1992). *Success for all: A relentless approach to prevention and early intervention in elementary schools.* Arlington, VA: Educational Research Service.

Sleeter, C. E. & Grant, C. A. (1987). An analysis of multicultural education in the United States. *Harvard Educational Review, 57*(4), 421–444.

Sockett, H. T. (1987). Has Shulman got the strategy right? *Harvard Educational Review, 57*(2), 208–219.

Stark, S. (1991). Toward an understanding of the beginning-teacher experience: Curricular insights for teacher education. *Journal of Curriculum and Supervision, 6*(4), 294–311.

Stewart, R. A., & O'Brien, D. G. (1989). Resistance to content area reading: A focus on preservice teachers. *Journal of Reading, 32*(5), 396–401.

Sumara, D., & Walker, L. (1991). The teacher's role in whole language. *Language Arts, 68*(4), 276–285.

Sweet, A. P. (1993). *State of the art: Transforming ideas for teaching and learning to read*. Washington, DC: U.S. Department of Education.

Sykes, G. (1992, January). The needs of children and the education of educators: Social responsibility in the learning society. Holmes Group Working Paper. Dallas: The Holmes Group.

Sykes, G., & Bird, T. (1992). Teacher education and the case idea. *Review of Research in Education, 18,* 457–521.

Teale, W. H. (1988). Developmentally appropriate assessment of reading and writing in the early childhood classroom. *The Elementary School Journal, 89*(2), 172–183.

Tierney, R. J., Stowell, L., Desai, L., & Kieffer, R. (1993). New possibilities for literature teaching and technology. In G. E. Newell & R. K. Durst (Eds.), *Exploring texts: The role of discussion and writing in the teaching and learning of literature* (pp. 175–190). Norwood, MA: Christopher-Gordon.

Tighe, M. A. (1991). Influencing student teacher attitudes: Who, what, and how. *English Education, 23*(4), 225–242.

Tom, A. R. (1992). Foreword. In L. Valli (Ed.), *Reflective teacher education: Cases and critiques* (pp. vii–x). Albany: State University of New York Press.

Tomkiewicz, W. C. (1991, April). *Reflective teaching and conceptual change in an interdisciplinary elementary methods course*. Paper presented at the annual conference of the National Association of Research in Science Teaching, Fontana, WI.

Valli, L. (Ed.). (1992). *Reflective teacher education: Cases and critiques*. Albany: State University of New York Press.

Valli, L., & Tom, A. R. (1988). How adequate are the knowledge base frameworks in teacher education? *Journal of Teacher Education, 39*(5), 5–12.

Vygotsky, L. (1978). *Mind in society: The development of higher psychological processes*. Cambridge, MA: Harvard University Press.

Waack, W. L. (1988). Theater programs in the small high school: Creation, maintenance, enrichment. *NASSP Bulletin, 72*(504), 111–117.

Wallhausen, H. A. (1990). *The effect of first teacher education courses on students' perception of the reading process*. (ERIC Document Reproduction Service No. ED 322 490)

Wasik, B. A., & Slavin, R. E. (1993). Preventing early reading failure with one-to-one tutoring: A review of five programs. *Reading Research Quarterly, 28*(2), 179–200.

Watson, D. J. (1994). Whole language: Why bother? *The Reading Teacher, 47*(8), 600–607.

Wedman, J. M., & Moutray, C. (1991). The effect of training on the questions preservice teachers ask during literature discussions. *Reading Research and Instruction, 30*(2), 62–70.

Wedman, J. M., & Robinson, R. (1988). Effects of a decision-making model on preservice teachers' decision-making practices and materials use. *Reading Improvement, 25*(2), 110–116 .

Weinstein, C. S. (1990). Prospective elementary teachers' beliefs about teaching: Implications for teacher education. *Teaching and Teacher Education, 6*(3), 279–290.

Wells, G. (1986). *The meaning makers*. Portsmouth, NH: Heinemann.

Wendler, D., Samuels, S. J., & Moore, V. K. (1989). The comprehension instruction of award-winning teachers, teachers with master's degrees, and other teachers. *Reading Research Quarterly, 24*(4), 382–401.

Whitmore, K. F., & Crowell, C. G. (1994). What makes a good question is . . . *The New Advocate, 7*(1), 45–57.

Wilson, S. (1992). A case concerning content: Using case studies to teach about subject matter. In J. H. Shulman (Ed.), *Case methods in teacher education* (pp. 64–89). New York: Teachers College Press.

Wiseman, D. L., & Many, J. E. (1992). The effects of aesthetic and efferent teaching approaches on undergraduate students' responses to literature. *Reading Research and Instruction, 31*(2), 66–83.

Witherall, C., & Noddings, N. (Eds.). (1991). *Stories lives tell: Narrative and dialogue in education*. New York: Teachers College Press.

Wyatt, M., & Pickle, M. (1993). Good teaching is good teaching: Basic beliefs of college reading instructors. *Journal of Reading, 36*(5), 340–348.

Zancanella, D. (1991). Teachers reading/readers teaching: Five teachers' personal approaches to literature and their teaching of literature. *Research in the Teaching of English, 25*(1), 5–32.

Zeichner, K. M. (1983). Alternative paradigms of teacher education. *Journal of Teacher Education, 34*(3), 3–9.

Zeichner, K. M. (1993). Traditions of practice in U.S. preservice teacher education programs. *Teaching and Teacher Education, 9*(1), 1–13.

Zeichner, K. M., & Liston, D. (1987). Teaching student teachers to reflect. *Harvard Educational Review, 57*(1), 23–48.

MATHEMATICS TEACHER EDUCATION

Douglas A. Grouws
UNIVERSITY OF IOWA

Karen A. Schultz
GEORGIA STATE UNIVERSITY

Teacher education is a large, complex endeavor oriented toward preparing professionals to teach effectively in elementary and secondary school classrooms. This chapter focuses on teacher education in mathematics, which involves preparing and assisting teachers to facilitate successfully student learning of mathematics. The process of becoming a teacher is viewed as a continuum spanning preservice, induction, and in-service experiences (Brown & Borko, 1992). Themes that cut across these three temporal levels of experiences having significant implications for developing and studying teacher education programs are examined. The chapter begins with a brief retrospective summary of teacher education during the past few decades and then examines the three themes of teacher pedagogical content knowledge, systemic initiatives and collaboratives, and theory building in teacher education.

LOOKING BACK

In the 1960s, the primary emphasis in teacher education was on increasing the mathematical content knowledge of teachers. Much of this professional development work with practicing teachers was conducted through summer institutes funded by the National Science Foundation (NSF). Little evidence emerged, however, to suggest a relationship between the amount of mathematics studied by a teacher and student learning. Pedagogy was at best a secondary consideration in the national initiatives of this period (Brown, Cooney, & Jones,

1990). The closest work to developing teachers' pedagogical knowledge was the emerging influence of Piaget's research on cognitive stages of development. Although school curricula were revised to include the "new math," there was neither sufficient conviction nor sustained increases in student achievement to support a strong continuation of reform.

In the 1980s the *Agenda for Action* (National Council of Teachers of Mathematics [NCTM], 1980) was published putting in motion a concerted effort to include mathematical problem solving in the curriculum and in daily school mathematics instruction. Along with problem solving came other initiatives, such as the renewed interest in the use of manipulatives, reform in teacher education, and an emphasis on technology, especially the use of calculators and computers. The agenda was present but the action was experimental. The agenda led to an appreciation of new kinds of research questions that needed to be answered. Instead of asking, "Does method A produce higher achievement than method B?", researchers started to ask, "How would you characterize the learning process when _____ is implemented?" These questions led to related questions concerning teachers' pedagogical knowledge. This shift in research questions promoted a movement toward research paradigms that include more qualitative methodology. This shift also resulted in more action research with teacher partners, a greater response to the natural learning processes, and a more reflective account of the construction of knowledge. Teachers were asked to participate in meaningful ways to inform researchers about how they teach and how children learn

We wish to express our appreciation to Judith Sowder, Doug Jones, and Joan Ferrini-Mundy for their helpful comments at various stages in the development of this chapter. We also want to thank our graduate students, Patricia Daniel, Carol Howald, Joan Jones, and Patricia Trafton, who helped us in numerous ways.

mathematics. Reflective research practices elucidated interpretation of children's idiosyncratic mathematical meanings. The 1980s witnessed spread of reflective teaching practices and laid the ground work for coreform as an outgrowth of the research partnership in education.

The 1980s marked the transition from identifying the problems of mathematics education to a focus on reform. The need for reform in mathematics education was carefully delineated in *Everybody Counts* (National Research Council, 1989), and mathematics content standards were clearly outlined in the *Curriculum and Evaluation Standards for School Mathematics* (NCTM, 1989). Standards for teaching practice soon followed with the *Professional Standards for Teaching Mathematics* (NCTM, 1991).

A Perspective for the 1990s

There is a noticeable lack of empirical research on mathematics teacher education. Studies that examine a substantial part of the learning-to-teach curriculum are indeed rare, although there have been some recent exceptions that take account of the fact that becoming a teacher is a lengthy process within a complex environment. In mathematics, a notable example is the Borko et al. (1990) study where the preservice and induction experiences of a cluster of students involved in becoming mathematics teachers were examined using multiple research perspectives. Although these investigations address a significant portion of the teacher education experience, they do not provide needed information about the long-term effects of teacher education experiences. In other words, the links between early teacher education experiences (i.e., preservice and induction experiences) and teaching practice in schools several years later are seldom explored. Thus, information about what experiences have important and lasting impact is missing. No doubt part of the reason for the dearth of such studies is the length of time it takes to conduct them, but the lack of grant support for long-term studies is also a factor.

Two previous examinations of research on mathematics teacher education have handled the scarcity of research within the field of mathematics in different ways. Brown et al. (1990) in their chapter chose not to do a traditional literature review but instead focused attention on philosophical issues in research on mathematics teacher education. In contrast, Brown and Borko (1992) in their chapter in the *Handbook of Research on Mathematics Teaching and Learning* took a more conventional approach and carefully analyzed the existing research base. They did not, however, limit their literature survey to mathematics, but rather examined the full spectrum of studies on becoming a teacher, giving special attention to studies that informed work in mathematics teacher education.

In this chapter the research literature shortfall is handled in yet another way. The approach is based on the existence of two current conditions. First, the major expansion of research in mathematics education that began in the early 1970s (Kilpatrick, 1992) is continuing. Unfortunately, as previously mentioned, too little of this research is directly focused on teacher education. Second, a major reform movement is underway in mathematics education. The reform is continuously stimulated by new reports and articles detailing the shortcomings of student

learning in mathematics. The direction taken by this reform is guided by the National Council of Teachers of Mathematics' (NCTM) *Curriculum and Evaluation Standards for School Mathematics* (NCTM, 1989), *Professional Standards for Teaching Mathematics* (NCTM, 1991), and *Assessment Standards for School Mathematics: Working Draft* (NCTM, 1993). These standards, grounded in more universal ownership than reform movements of the past, although apparently influential, are yet to have an impact on formal mathematics teacher education programs. Together these two conditions of increased research and attention to standards have resulted in a number of research studies and teacher development projects in which enhancing student learning involves, directly or indirectly, changing traditional teacher practice. These teacher-change studies and projects provide a basis for gaining insight into the process of teacher change, the factors associated with such change, and the processes for facilitating these changes. They provide a major focus for this literature review. These authors wish to acknowledge at this point their review of teacher education studies focused primarily on the American literature. There were several reasons for this decision. First, much of the international literature is not in English, and this was a problem. Second, much of the international work on teacher education is based on postbaccalaureate programs, and such programs are not common on the American scene, California being a notable exception.

Along with changing teacher practice, these studies often deal with other changes advocated for the mathematics classroom. These include technology, discourse, writing across the curriculum, alternative assessment, and equity. They are important because emphasis on, for example, calculators and computers or on social discourse as mainstays of the teaching/learning process have strong implications for in-service and preservice teacher education. The study of these factors has uncovered evidence of students' mathematical ways of knowing that gives indicators of teaching effectiveness through content-specific pedagogy.

Writing in mathematics has found meaning in teaching and learning. It is becoming a natural vehicle for monitoring mathematical understandings and misunderstandings. This monitoring marks the reflective practices that are seen more in the development of pedagogical content knowledge. However, because all these issues relate to the three themes of pedagogical content knowledge, systemic initiatives and collaboratives, and theoretical development, they are not discussed separately.

In subsequent sections, projects and studies that exist under the rubric of *pedagogical content knowledge,* then efforts that can be labeled *systemic initiatives and collaboratives,* and finally recent efforts toward *theoretical models and future research* in mathematics teacher education are examined.

PEDAGOGICAL CONTENT KNOWLEDGE

Central to this chapter is research and thinking about teacher knowledge. Shulman (1986) revived interest in teacher knowledge in his 1985 AERA Presidential Address when he delineated a type of content knowledge that he termed *pedagogical content knowledge,* describing it as "the ways of representing and formulating the subject that make it comprehensible to others" (p. 9). Pedagogical content knowledge is thus content knowledge that is useful for teaching.

In mathematics, pedagogical content knowledge includes, but is not limited to, useful representations, unifying ideas, clarifying examples and counterexamples, helpful analogies, important relationships, and connections among ideas. Thus pedagogical content knowledge is a subset of content knowledge that has particular utility for planning and conducting lessons that facilitate student learning.

Lampert (1990) indicates there also is an important difference between knowledge in the discipline and school mathematics. "The issue of intellectual authority is central to this comparison between how mathematics is known in school and how it is known in the discipline" (p. 32).

Attention to pedagogical content knowledge in research studies has provided new insights into the professional development of teachers. These insights deepen one's understanding of becoming a good teacher and suggest ideas for improving teacher education at both the preservice and in-service levels. These research projects have demonstrated, for example, that providing teachers with certain types of pedagogical content knowledge results in teachers changing their classroom practice in ways that result in increased student learning. The teaching changes are in directions advocated by the *Professional Standards for Teaching Mathematics* (NCTM, 1991), and the student achievement increases are in areas identified as important in the *Curriculum and Evaluation Standards for School Mathematics* (NCTM, 1989).

To make the point about pedagogical content knowledge clear, the following is an account of where this knowledge was absent in one teacher's personal reformation. Cohen (1990), in "A Revolution in One Classroom: The Case of Mrs. Oublier," sends a message to everyone involved in teacher education. Cohen's article reported on a study of the relationship between instructional policy and teaching practice in the mid-1980s in California, where state officials initiated reform in mathematics education. He claims that although "policy has affected practice in this case, . . . practice has had an even greater effect on policy" (p. 311).

Mrs. Oublier, Cohen reports, took a workshop where she discovered how to focus on student mathematical understandings by relating to their knowledge and experience. She taught under modest conditions in southern California. Her classroom was a portable, prefab unit in the back of the schoolyard to accommodate growing enrollments of city migrants. After being inspired by the "innovative curriculum guide," *Math Their Way* (Baratta-Lorton, 1976), she claimed that her teaching revolution wound up where the California framework (California State Department of Education, 1985), intended to be. Surprisingly, however, to Cohen, her classes were "an extraordinary melange of traditional and novel approaches to math instruction" (p. 312). What happened was that Mrs. Oublier conducted lessons from the new curriculum materials, but in a thoroughly traditional way. She "conveyed a sense of mathematics as a fixed body of right answers, rather than as a field of inquiry in which people figure out quantitative relations" (p. 313). Her didactic approach kept the students from mathematical discourse where they would explore their ideas. "There was teach-ing for mathematical understanding here, but it was blended with other elements of instruction that seemed likely to inhibit understanding" (p. 313).

Baratta-Lorton's book models that the natural way for kids to learn mathematics is through concrete materials. Neither the nature of mathematical knowledge nor the explanation of mathematical ideas is addressed. Hands-on activities are viewed as sufficient. The book provides a wealth of information about materials, activities, and lesson format. Mrs. Oublier was convinced that implementation of this resource explained de facto how children come to understand mathematics. Mrs. Oublier saw no need to do more than to teach this way.

In what sense was Mrs. O teaching for understanding? The question opens up a great puzzle. Her classes exuded traditional conceptions of mathematical knowledge, and were organized as though explanation and discussion were irrelevant to mathematics. Yet she had changed her math teaching quite dramatically. She now used a new curriculum specially designed to promote students' understanding of mathematics. And her students' lessons were very different than they had been. They worked with materials that represented mathematical relationship in the concrete ways that the framework and many other authorities endorse. Mrs. O thought the change had been decisive: She now teaches for understanding. She reported that her students now understood arithmetic, whereas previously they had simply memorized it. (Cohen, 1990, p. 318)

Mrs. Oublier did not teach in a manner that invited or allowed open-ended participation in mathematical discourse. "There were few opportunities for students to initiate discussion, explore ideas, or even ask questions" (p. 322). Mrs. Oublier did not have a strong mathematics background, which appeared to prevent her from learning from her efforts to "teach for understanding." This phenomenon has been labeled "conservative progressivism" (Cuban cited in Cohen, 1990, p. 323).

Mrs. Oublier, who "revolutionized" her mathematics teaching, implemented conventional teacher-centered classroom practices. Where Cohen thought she might be near the beginning of growth toward revolutionizing her mathematics teaching, Mrs. Oublier saw herself as having made the transition, as having mastered a new practice.

It seems that the story of Mrs. Oublier sends a chilling message to mathematics teacher educators. It is possible to graduate teachers who have mastered the use of manipulatives, board buddies, cooperative group learning, technology, and "good" educational resources, but who still do not appreciate how children come to know mathematics and how guided flexible discourse invites mathematical thinking. The teacher must be informed of this thinking so that his or her teaching can be based on existing mathematical conceptions and preconceptions of the students. This is what enables children to develop a mathematical identity of their own and mathematical knowledge based on logical reasoning.

The following section highlights several projects and studies that address mathematics teacher education. The projects and programs are considered representative of those available.

Cognitively Guided Instruction

The Cognitively Guided Instruction (CGI) research program at the University of Wisconsin has shown that providing teachers with knowledge of how students think and develop strategies in specific content domains influences their teaching practices and, in turn, student learning. First- and second-grade teachers who participated in a CGI research study that provided them with knowledge about student thinking and strategy development in the domain of addition and subtraction subsequently spent more time teaching problem solving in their mathematics lessons and more time assessing student thinking as part of their instruction than did control teachers who were given an equivalent amount of in-service training. Students in CGI classes demonstrated increased learning, particularly in problem solving, when compared to students in control classes. There were no performance differences between the two groups on computational tasks (Carpenter, Fennema, Peterson, Chiang, & Loef, 1989).

The success of the CGI model in enhancing the professional development of practicing teachers led to investigations of using the CGI concepts and methods in the preparation of preservice teachers. Phillip, Armstrong, and Bezuk (1993) implemented CGI principles in a mathematics methods course for preservice elementary school teachers and then conducted a case study of a student teacher who had participated in the methods course. They specifically investigated the extent to which this teacher utilized research information received in the methods course about how children think in the lessons she taught as a student teacher. That is, they examined whether the CGI methods course influenced her practice, and if so, in what specific ways her teaching was affected and what factors mediated the use of the new knowledge that the teacher had acquired in the methods course.

Based on classroom observations, interviews, and rating scales where the teacher conveyed information about her practice and beliefs, Phillip, Armstrong, and Bezuk (1993) concluded that "a preservice teacher can utilize pedagogical content knowledge about how children think in such a way that it influences her practice" (p. 165).

Interestingly, the authors also point out that there were many occasions when their teacher's knowledge of student thinking did not translate into instructional decisions. After concluding the case study, the researchers identified five potential reasons why a teacher's knowledge of students' mathematical understanding might not be accessed and used when making instructional decisions. Briefly, these reasons were: (1) the teachers' knowledge of mathematics might not be sufficiently structured to allow him or her to fit observations of his or her students' understanding into a coherent mathematical picture, (2) the teacher might view the curriculum as given and thus might not be open to change, (3) the teacher might not possess a map of the curriculum that includes a sense of what important mathematical ideas should be included, (4) a teacher's knowledge of students' thinking may not fit into a larger conceptual framework, and (5) teachers may be constrained by their view of how children develop understanding and underestimate the time required for students to develop it.

In the Phillip et al. (1993) case study, the authors conclude that the student teacher they studied was constrained primarily by the third and fifth reasons listed. That is, the teacher did not have a sufficiently clear picture of the important mathematical ideas to be developed and did not adequately take into account

the amount of time it takes for students to develop mathematics concepts. Of course, for other teachers, other reasons or other combinations of reasons may surface. Phillip and colleagues are conducting follow-up research with other preservice teachers to shed light on this issue. Whether there is a differential impact of the five reasons in the new case studies will be of interest, but regardless of these findings, the reasons for lack of influence on teaching practice hypothesized in this work does provide a basis for additional research and worthwhile standards to consider when changes in preservice teacher education programs are being examined.

Problem-Centered Mathematics Project

The Problem-Centered Mathematics Project (PCMP) at Purdue University is another example of research that focused primarily on student learning during its first year. In subsequent years it quickly expanded to include study of the teacher and the teaching context to make sense of the complex nature of student learning in classroom settings. This project is particularly noteworthy because classroom situations were analyzed from two perspectives and because the situations studied spanned several contexts. Both psychological and sociological analyses were employed and the contexts considered included the individual student, students working in small groups, whole class interactions, and the larger context of the mathematics program in the school and community settings.

In the second year of the project a teaching experiment was conducted in a second-grade classroom of 20 students with a teacher who had taught mathematics "straight by the book" for 15 years. Cognitively based instructional activities were developed by the project staff and were used in the classroom during the school year as part of the teaching experiment. The project also attempted to facilitate the teacher's development of classroom practice (Cobb, Yackel, & Wood, 1991).

The activities that were developed, along with the general instructional approach adopted, differed radically from those found in most elementary school classrooms in the United States. There was, for example, no individual paper-and-pencil seatwork or grading of written work. Instead, the children first attempted to complete the instructional activities with a partner and then participated in a teacher-orchestrated discussion of their mathematical problems, interpretations, and solutions. (Cobb, Wood, Yackel, & Wheatley, 1993, p. 3)

The activities and the instructional strategies developed during this teaching experiment were based on a constructive, problem-solving view of mathematics learning where student experience, activity, and communication were essential components. For a full discussion of the findings of this study in each of the contexts previously mentioned, see Wood, Cobb, Yackel, and Dillon (1993). The results of the teaching experiment were informative and promising to the extent that a comparative study was initiated the following school year.

Other project work (Cobb, Wood, et al., 1991) involved 10 volunteer second-grade teachers and their students. At the end of the year-long study, results from these classrooms were compared with results from eight nonproject classrooms from the same school district. Analyses of student standardized achievement test scores showed no significant difference between project and nonproject students on the computation subtest, but a significant difference in favor of the project students on the concepts and applications subtest. Data from the *Project Arithmetic Test* developed by the research team supported the preceding findings and also suggested that there were qualitative differences in the arithmetical algorithms used by the students in the two groups. Differences in student questionnaire responses indicated that project students held stronger beliefs than nonproject students about the importance of understanding and collaborating in mathematics.

Important for teacher education considerations were teacher responses to a beliefs questionnaire that measured teacher orientation toward behaviorist or socioconstructivist perspectives. Project teacher beliefs were significantly more compatible with a socioconstructivist perspective than were those of their nonproject colleagues. There are two significant caveats to this important finding. First, the data from two specially designed items on the beliefs instrument showed that an inclination toward a socioconstructivist perspective may not be differentiated from a perspective that "children's problem-solving methods develop freely and, presumably the teacher's role is limited to providing nutrients for this natural growth of knowledge" (Cobb, Wood, et al., 1991, p. 24). Thus, project teachers that were more oriented toward the socioconstructivist position may actually be more inclined toward a position that attributes little importance to the teacher's role in facilitating student learning in the classroom.

Second, teacher beliefs were not measured at the beginning of the year; therefore, the differences found at the end of the school year could be artifacts of initial differences in beliefs, especially because nonproject teachers were those who did not volunteer for the project in-service training and subsequent active involvement in the project. The doubts cast by the preceding caveats are somewhat mitigated by the informal observations of project teachers over the entire school year by the researchers. These observations suggested substantive changes were occurring in both the project teachers' beliefs and actions. (See Wood, Cobb, and Yackel [1991] for a case study of changes in one of the project teacher's briefs and practices.)

Students in the PCMP showed important growth in mathematical thinking and skills as well as the establishment of beliefs that are valued in the mathematics reform movement. Similarly, project teachers seemed to have changed their beliefs and practices in desirable directions. Thus, it is worthwhile to examine the structure and nature of the training program employed in this project. The project teachers participated in a 1-week in-service training course prior to the beginning of the project. A focus on this course was to help the teachers come to realize that certain aspects of their current teaching practice were problematic (Cobb, Wood, et al., 1991). This was accomplished by showing project teachers videorecorded interviews of children completing place value tasks. The tasks illustrated what students learned in the course of traditional textbook instruction, the separation students typically make between school mathematics and solving everyday problems using mathematics, and the distinction that can exist between correct procedures and conceptual understanding. In addition, teachers viewed videotapes of small group work and whole class interactions. Furthermore,

the teachers solved problems in small groups, familiarized themselves with the instructional activities, and visited a simulation of the project classroom.

Finally, the project staff as part of the teacher in-service did give specific answers to the teachers' pragmatic questions and "were relatively directive when discussing their [the teacher's] role in initiating and guiding the development of social norms in their classrooms" (Cobb, Wood, et al., 1991, pp. 13–14). The purpose of providing this direction was to establish an appropriate learning environment in the classrooms as quickly as possible. The providing of some direction for teaching practice is a contrast to the CGI project discussed previously where they made a point of not providing any direction for project teachers. Support for project teachers was provided in their classrooms by the research team throughout the school year, initially once a week and later every 2 weeks. Also, four 2-hour workshops that focused on children's arithmetic problem-solving methods were provided during the school year.

The extensive development component of this project has not been formally studied with preservice teachers. One difficulty with implementing this component in a teacher education program is that preservice teachers have very little sense of classroom practice, particularly classroom practice of their own. Consequently, it is more difficult to have them come to realize the shortcoming of traditional classroom practice than it is to establish this fact with experienced teachers, as was done in the Cobb research. Nevertheless, given the results of this work it seems appropriate to develop ways to implement the ideas in its teacher development component in both in-service and preservice teacher development programs and to study carefully effects on teachers and students in classroom settings.

The Atlanta Math Project

The Atlanta Math Project (AMP) at Georgia State University was one of several initiatives funded in 1990 with the goal of facilitating mathematics teachers in implementing the NCTM standards through in-service. AMP's second goal of studying in-service teacher change over time made it one of the first significant efforts in this direction. Implementation of the essentials of AMP's reflective teaching model (Hart, Schultz, Najee-ullah, & Nash, 1992) includes monthly planning of at least one mathematics lesson with an AMP partner who then observes a live or videotaped lesson and follows up with a nonevaluative reflective debriefing. This year-long site-based practice occurs after a research and theory-based in-service for all participants on mathematics pedagogy and its association with the NCTM standards. Implementing these essentials is resulting in increased teacher use of questioning versus direct instruction techniques, manipulatives versus symbolic abstractions, cooperative groups instead of whole class instruction, spontaneous innovations versus predictable teaching practices, and sharing of authority with learners (Schultz, Hart, Najee-ullah, Nash, & Jones, 1993; Wagner, 1994). These research findings show that the sharing of authority, where the teacher relinquishes strong control of the evolution of mathematics concepts and procedures in children, appears to trigger other changes in teacher behaviors. Subsequently, acceptance of more than one way of problem interpretation, of finding a solution and representing solutions, was observed. Use of manipulatives, group processing, classroom mobility, board buddies, and think-pair-share tended to become the norm for the classroom.

Reflective teaching partnerships help teachers construct pedagogical content knowledge, develop mathematics content knowledge, improve their pedagogy (Brown & Borko, 1992; Schultz & Hart, 1988), and experiment with alternative assessment (Nash, 1993). Furthermore, reflective processes seem to motivate professional collegiality among teachers. It has also been found that for mathematics teachers to shift from predominantly direct instructional practices to those practices that support the standards, a trust relationship between reflective partners is needed (Daniel, 1994). AMP's essentials, a manageable approach to "implementing the Standards," self-review of one's videotaped lessons, written logs, oral debriefings with a partner, being observed by a partner, and observing others teach lead to successful learning outcomes (Hart et al., 1992). Preliminary evaluation of student performance in AMP teacher classrooms is showing greater gains in achievement levels than by students in non-AMP classrooms and increased confidence in mathematical ability (Thomas, 1993).

The indicators of success for teacher enhancement projects such as AMP are signals to teacher education programs to examine courses, programs, and the teacher educator practices in coursework, fieldwork, and service. The value of teacher partnerships for the preservice and induction phases of professional development of teachers is supported by AMP. During their earliest classroom experiences with children, preservice teachers learn to value the benefits of professional collegiality when they are assigned a peer partner to facilitate their planning, teaching experiences, and debriefings within a structured format. Second, the idea of modeling is important in AMP's Reflective Teaching Model. Teacher educators who model reflective practices for preservice teachers also model professional behaviors that otherwise are often not present in any other place in the teacher development programs. The image (and practice), however, of even the "best" university professors does not typically include seeing them reflect aloud on their teaching in a frank and open way in front of preservice teachers. This, however, is essential for progressive teacher education programs. Specifically, it is a productive practice for teacher educators to plan with a partner colleague, teach, then debrief with their partner. These events are modeled to the preservice teacher as a participant/observer either in the college classroom or at a school.

A characteristic of AMP that has implications for teacher education programs is revealed in AMP's evaluation model. Ostensibly, AMP was to study teacher change over time; however, AMP's research team also assumed responsibility for evaluating students, mathematics school system supervisors, and the AMP leadership (same as research team) as well, viewing these combinations of parties as an ecosystem. From the very beginning of AMP all these groups were challenged to make a shift that would be expressed in every domain of mathematics education. When students at first appeared stiff and unattached in group problem solving, for example, that indicated the need for an adjustment period for the students as they adapted to the new classroom environment. The AMP leadership was committed to model teaching in the classroom of each AMP teacher

and to model the kind of classroom environment they were promoting. They modeled the kind of empowering practices with the teachers that was being promoted in the teachers' classrooms. The mathematics supervisors, who worked closely with the AMP leadership in many cases, assumed the same modeling practices as the AMP leadership.

Parallel modeling in teacher education programs is implied. The mathematics professor and the preservice teachers at the teacher education institution and the students and classroom cooperating teacher at the school constitute a similar network of people in the mathematics education domain. All parties are to respond to the reform movement and professional development (or in the case of the children, mathematical development). The infrastructure that can create a mutually supportive environment is the professional development school (Woloszyk & Davis, 1993), where the notion of coreform prevails; that is, both institutions collaborate on their respective efforts to improve and change. The school facilitates the teacher education institution's thinking toward improved teacher education programs and the institution facilitates the school's thinking toward improved teaching practices. School teachers do research-driven teaching and teacher education institutions do teaching-driven research. Research partnerships are encouraged in such arrangements.

Elementary Mathematics Project

Other projects that offer a great deal to the thinking of teacher preparation and in-service professional development include the program at Michigan State University (MSU). There, MSU researchers are questioning commonly held beliefs underlying the teaching and learning of mathematics.

Cultural assumptions about the ways mathematics becomes known are also being challenged. Most often children associate mathematics with certainty, knowing it, and with being able to get the right answer quickly. Doing mathematics is associated with following teachers' rules. Knowing mathematics means remembering and applying the correct rule and having the answer ratified by the teacher. These beliefs are acquired by students through years of watching, listening, and practicing (Lampert, 1990).

In the classroom, the teacher and the textbook are the authorities, and mathematics is not a subject to be created or explored. In school, the truth is given in the teachers' explanations and the answer book; there is no zig-zag between conjectures and arguments for their validity, and one could hardly imagine hearing the words *maybe* or *perhaps* in a lesson. Knowing mathematics in school therefore comes to mean having a set of unexamined beliefs. (p. 32)

Few teachers encourage students to verbally analyze the assumptions they make in finding answers, and it is unlikely that they model this process for students. Students believe that the teacher knows the correct answers, and teachers believe that if one follows the rules in books, one will do well. "That teachers and students think this way about mathematical knowledge and how it is acquired is both a cause and a logical consequence of the ways in which knowledge is regarded in school mathematics lessons" (Lampert, 1990, p. 32).

The Elementary Mathematics Project at Michigan State University challenged these cultural assumptions about knowing mathematics and attempted to change prospective elementary teachers' knowledge and beliefs during a 2-year intervention. From 1987 to 1989, Wilcox, Schram, Lappan, and Lanier (1991) designed and implemented three nontraditional mathematics courses, a mathematics methods course, and a seminar on curriculum. The mathematics courses consisted of an exploration of numbers and number theory, geometry, and probability and statistics. The methods courses and seminar addressed the content courses in relation to field experiences engaging preservice teachers in rethinking their beliefs about mathematics education.

Content for the mathematics courses was selected by considering these questions: "What does knowing this idea enable a student to do? To what other mathematical ideas is it connected? Does it require students to engage in *doing* mathematics—analyzing, abstracting, generalizing, inventing, proving, and applying?" (Wilcox et al., 1991, pp. 5–6). In addition, the courses were designed to require students to communicate their thinking in more than one way, such as in discourse with other students, with teachers using natural and symbolic language, and writing about teaching and learning mathematics. Finally, a stable cohort of students who would engage in common study for the duration of their program was viewed as a community of learning, which was the major focus of the seminar. The vision for the project was a classroom where students and professor together engaged in mathematical study. "In this community, developing ways of knowing was a fundamental mathematical goal" (p. 6).

One of the most significant developments observed among the participating students was a shift away from the instructor as the sole source of authority for knowing. The prospective teachers changed their behavior as learners of mathematics; their self-reliance increased as their ability to decide if a mathematical problem had been resolved improved. They began relying on their group members more and the teacher less. They realized the value of group work for their own learning of mathematics.

These prospective teachers had difficulty, however, translating the vision of a community of learners to their own classrooms when they started teaching. This suggested to Wilcox et al. (1991) that beginning teachers who desire to teach for understanding in their own classrooms need continued support during the induction years of teaching. These results emphasize that the development of a community of mathematics learners is not a trivial task; nor is it a simple matter for prospective or new teachers to understand what it means to come to know mathematics (Ball, 1988).

Ball (1989) in discussing her conceptualization of a methods course indicates that teacher education courses include too much theoretical material on cognitive science research, which does not influence how prospective teachers act when they are teaching. Instead, teacher educators should focus on the beliefs and knowledge that prospective teachers have when they enter teacher education programs. She says that methods courses have inherent tensions that are not in other types of courses. Prospective teachers need to learn about mathematics as well as about how mathematics is learned and taught. Students in a methods course are expected to learn mathematics while at the same time learning to teach mathematics. Many have expectations of learning to teach mathematics in one 10-week course. Ball's goal for students in a methods course is for them to continue to learn on their own, as mathematics teachers.

Teacher Education and Learning to Teach Study

The Teacher Education and Learning to Teach study at Michigan State University was a longitudinal study that examined what teachers are taught and what they learn in 11 diverse preservice, induction, in-service, and alternative route programs across the country (Ball & Wilson, 1990). Ball (1990) identified three common assumptions about learning to teach elementary or secondary school mathematics that teacher educators should challenge: (1) traditional school mathematics content is not difficult, (2) precollege education provides teachers with much of what they need to know about mathematics, and (3) majoring in mathematics ensures subject-matter knowledge. She states that these assumptions underlie current teacher education practices as well as new proposals to reform the preparation of teachers.

In examining these hypotheses, prospective teachers' knowledge and beliefs about mathematics were evaluated in the following areas: (1) the relationship between perimeter and area, (2) insufficiency of proof by example, (3) ability to explain division by zero, and (4) ability to generate an appropriate representation of the meaning of division of fractions with a story problem.

Ball and Wilson tested the assumptions that liberal arts majors understand their subjects better than education majors, and that if preservice teachers have the necessary content knowledge, their experience in schools can teach them everything else they need to know (Ball & Wilson, 1990). The researchers found that both assumptions were false for both traditional and alternate route teacher education students. The prospective teachers' knowledge of mathematics lacked understanding of the underlying relationships in mathematics. "Less than half of our novice mathematics teachers—in teacher education programs or alternate routes—could critically examine the problems presented to them and convincingly answer questions concerning the mathematics represented in those problems" (Ball & Wilson, 1990, p. 5).

The prospective teachers also had difficulty with pedagogical content knowledge. For example, more than 59% of informants could not generate a real-world example of division of fractions. In addition, many could not explain why division by zero is undefined. "Our analyses suggest that neither group is prepared to teach mathematics for understanding nor to teach mathematics in a way that differs from the traditional pedagogy of telling and drilling algorithms into students" (Ball & Wilson, 1990, p. 10).

The results of the Teacher Education and Learning to Teach study dispel the belief that teacher candidates with liberal arts backgrounds and a major in mathematics have greater understanding of mathematics. Neither the elementary education majors nor the mathematics majors showed conceptual understanding of elementary mathematics. Also distressing, most of these students' understandings did not change during their teacher education program. "In fact, over half of those who entered the programs unable to generate an appropriate representation for division of fractions or unconcerned with issues of mathematical proof left the programs still lacking these understandings" (Ball & Wilson, 1990, p. 10).

Teacher educators must overcome their students' lifetime of experience in traditional classrooms in a culture that holds as valid a number of assumptions about mathematics and mathematics teaching. These assumptions are that doing mathematics means following the rules laid down by the teacher; knowing mathematics means remembering and applying the correct rule when the teacher asks a question; mathematical truth is determined when the answer is ratified by the teacher; traditional school mathematics content is not difficult; precollege education provides teachers with much of what they need to know about mathematics; and majoring in mathematics ensures subject-matter knowledge. Unless teacher educators realize that making an impact on prospective teachers requires powerful interventions, it is unlikely that teacher educators will be able to alter the continuity of traditional mathematical teaching and learning.

Quantitative Understanding: Amplifying Student Achievement and Reasoning Project

The goal of the Quantitative Understanding: Amplifying Student Achievement and Reasoning (QUASAR) Project at the University of Pittsburgh is to implement instructional programs fostering acquisition of mathematical thinking and reasoning skills by students attending middle school in economically disadvantaged communities (Silver, 1993). Teachers at the selected schools are trying to incorporate the NCTM standards into their teaching practice in ways appropriate for diverse student populations in urban schools that have little financial or community support (Silver, 1994).

Teachers in these schools are supported by QUASAR resource partners who are faculty members at local universities. The resource partners work with teachers and administrators who have competed to have their school site chosen as a QUASAR site. The school sites have built collaborative communities of learners—teachers learning new ways to teach and students learning new ways to do mathematics. These communities were formed during the 5 years of the project.

Resource partners from local universities provided a broad range of support or assistance activities. Traditional university-based support activities were summer workshops, in-service during the school year, and college coursework. Resource partners tailored workshops and coursework to meet needs specified by the classroom teachers at their QUASAR site. The content of workshops at each site varied by the site's expressed needs. The resource partners also entered the teachers' classrooms, sharing the daily experience of the classroom teacher. The partners' activities included collaborative planning, model teaching, reflecting, and observing the classroom teacher for reflection purposes.

Teachers were provided with opportunities to reflect, alone and/or with partners, about their teaching practice. Teachers were given opportunities to work as school teams developing curriculum, instructional strategies, and assessment models.

Teachers participated in national and local conferences, both attending and presenting (Brown & Smith, 1994).

Data gathered from the project indicate that for classroom teachers the meaningfulness of different support activities varied according to the amount of experience the teacher had in the project. Beginning teachers, located both at the temporal beginnings of the project and as new initiates to QUASAR, found the traditional opportunities to learn about the new curriculum beneficial. As the teachers and the project matured, time spent on community activities became more meaningful for the teachers, whereas time spent in activities planned by the resource partners as teacher enhancement activities became less meaningful (Stein, Silver, & Smith, 1994).

A framework of "communities of practice" as proposed by Lave and Wenger was used by QUASAR researchers to analyze the phenomena of teacher learning (Stein et al., 1994). This framework looks at the community of learners as the unit to be studied, rather than individual teachers as the unit of study.

QUASAR researchers studied how teachers became leaders in the collaborative community. Teachers moved from peripheral roles to central roles as they became comfortable with the risks of teaching in a new style and as they became vested in the community's vision. Newly initiated teachers listened to veteran project teachers tell stories about their own experiences learning to teach in the new way. Teachers moved from newly initiated to project veteran as they: a) participated in all forms of practice provided through the project; b) experienced multiple types of learning opportunities in school-based collaborations—workshops, classroom partnerships, and reflection; c) listened to and told stories about the community's experience, both privately in the community and to the public through presentations; d) developed identity as a community member; and e) learned useful skills for teaching a standards-based curriculum (Stein et al., 1994).

The teachers at the QUASAR sites are creating new teaching practices that are unique to each teacher and each site. These practices represent that teacher's and that community's unique interpretation of the ideas expressed in the NCTM standards (Silver, 1994).

A fundamental element of teacher learning has been the school community. The community, including teachers at the site, administrators, and resource partners, has forged an ongoing dialogue where teachers can construct their own meanings about good teaching and learning (Silver, 1994). This collaborative community is the heart of the QUASAR method of in-service teacher education with strong implications for preservice teacher education.

SummerMath for Teachers

The SummerMath for Teachers Program at Mt. Holyoke College has been in existence since 1983. It was designed to introduce teachers to a constructivist perspective in mathematics education and to respond to the following concern:

The instructional paradigm championed by influential sectors of the current reform movement presupposes teachers able to navigate fluently the mathematics they are charged with teaching. Yet many teachers have only a tenuous understanding of how mathematical meaning is made. Only as such teachers can be induced, in in-service activities, to engage in explorations of number and space will they begin to infuse content into the symbols and procedures they have known since childhood. And only then will they come to know the importance of working through problems on their own and the sense of enhanced intellectual autonomy that they can bring. (Schifter & Fosnot, 1993, p. 81)

Four principles guide the work of SummerMath.

1. The approach to learning and teaching mathematics presented in the in-service translates to learning and teaching in general. Teacher education should be based on the same pedagogical principles as mathematics instruction.
2. If teachers are expected to teach mathematics for understanding, they must become mathematics learners.
3. Regular classroom consultation provides support for continued reflection as changes are introduced into the classroom, sustaining teachers' learning in the context that matters most.
4. Collaboration among teachers is essential to reform (Schifter & Fosnot, 1993).

Many teachers beginning the program were not proficient in mathematics even at the elementary level. They expressed feelings of anxiety and incompetence. They held the common belief that mathematics is an inert body of knowledge consisting of facts and rules to be memorized and passed from the expert to the student. The teachers felt their job was to tell these facts and rules to students. The SummerMath experience challenged their assumptions about the nature of mathematics and how children learn mathematics.

The SummerMath program runs in 2-year cycles consisting of 2-week summer in-service and continues with weekly clinical supervision during the school year. Teachers spend this time in three distinct activities. They learn mathematical concepts and problem solving in a classroom where construction of meaning is valued, encouraged, and planned for; they participate in a logo and computer class; and they participate in jazz dance and tennis instruction for the purpose of relaxation and reflecting on themselves as learners in these recreational instructional formats (Simon & Schifter, 1991). Opportunities for reflection, focused both on what mathematics is and what good mathematics instruction could be, are provided in small group discussion, in large group discussion, and individually through journal writing.

Participants expressed high levels of disequilibrium during the course. They discovered new ways to define mathematics and mathematical activity that were in conflict with their existing knowledge structure. They experienced learning mathematics in ways very different from the ways they had learned and the ways they taught. For many teachers the process of recognizing alternative modes of thought about instruction was challenging and painful. The new ideas conflicted with their prior practice, which they had considered successful and appropriate classroom practice (Schifter & Fosnot, 1993). By experiencing learning in a collaborative, constructive environment, the teachers began to realize how students construct meaning for mathematics and began to build empathy for student misconceptions about mathematics.

The experience of learning in a new and different way was a catalyst for many teachers to try changing their own practice the following school year. Some of the practices encouraged were (a) using nonroutine problems; (b) exploring alternative solutions; (c) asking nonleading questions; (d) using manipulatives, diagrams, and alternative representations; (e) having students work in groups and pairs; (f) pursuing thought processes on both "right" and "wrong" answers; (g) working with Logo; (h) employing wait time; and (i) encouraging student paraphrase of ideas expressed in class (Simon & Schifter, 1991).

Observation of teachers' practices produced two taxonomies of change (Schifter & Fosnot, 1993). The first is called the Level of Use (LoU) rating. This scale rates use of the instructional strategies modeled during the in-service. Teachers begin at level I, "orientation," and level II, "preparation." They progress to greater degrees of sophistication in levels III "mechanical use," IVA "routine use," and IVB "refinement," where teachers can adapt the innovation to meet student needs.

The second scale is the Assessment of Constructivism in Mathematics Instruction (ACMI).

1. Constructivism is a belief that conceptual understanding in mathematics must be constructed by the learner. Teachers' conceptualizations cannot be given directly to students.
2. Teachers strive to maximize opportunities for students to construct concepts. Teachers give fewer explanations and expect less memorization and imitation. This suggests not only a perspective on how concepts are learned, but also a valuing of conceptual understanding. (Simon & Schifter, 1991)

Similar to the LoU, the ACMI involved an interview and ascribing of the rating. At level 0, the teacher does not have or use a constructivist epistemology. Levels I and II, like the LoU scale, refer to becoming familiar with an innovation and getting ready to use it. In level III, teachers demonstrate rudimentary understanding of constructivism, but this does not show up in practice. At level IVA, teachers demonstrate an increase in student activity with less teacher telling. At level IVB, teachers are spontaneous at concentrating on student learning; that is, they are less preoccupied with their own actions. At level IVB teaching is guided by student learning.

In the school year following the summer in-service, teachers were intensively supervised. A project staff member visited the classroom once each week. The supervision included model teaching by the staff member, lesson planning, and reflection on lessons by the teacher and staff member. Project participants progressed through changes in strategy and constructivist epistemology at very different rates. Some were quick to change their classroom practice; some slowly changed over the course of several years. Some teachers became leaders in their schools, helping to bring about change in their home schools and systems. These teachers think of their work as reinventing mathematics education (Schifter & Fosnot, 1993).

The new paradigm for mathematics instruction can be enacted only when teachers themselves grasp the big ideas, internalize the models, and then put them into play. For example, as teachers come to understand the big ideas that underlie the mathematics they teach, they also realize that they cannot simply "transmit" these ideas to their students. Instead, they must provide opportunities for their students to explore and to wrestle with concepts as they arise. Such a practice cannot rely on predetermined scripts but depends on one's capacity to respond spontaneously to students' questions and discoveries.

As the locus of pedagogical authority shifts from experts and administrators to classroom teachers, those teachers must become more dependent on one another. With greater autonomy comes greater responsibility for structuring the learning process. Teachers will need opportunities for collective reflection in order to make considered and effective instructional decisions. (Schifter & Fosnot, 1993, pp. 197–198)

The SummerMath program provides opportunities for teachers to experience mathematics instruction of the type it is hoped they will provide for their students. They are supported as they learn about mathematics and as they change their teaching practice.

Teachers Improving Mathematics Education

Project TIME (Teachers Improving Mathematics Education) at the Center for Education Change in Mathematics and Science, University of California, Santa Barbara, was designed during a 2-year period from 1983 to 1985 and was in operation for 4 years from 1986 to 1990 (Mumme & Weissglass, 1991). The purpose of Project TIME was to improve mathematics education in schools by

1. developing teacher leadership for school-based change in mathematics instruction
2. assisting teachers to bring their instructional practices more in accord with the constructivist* epistemology
3. increasing teachers' knowledge about mathematics and changing their attitudes about mathematics and mathematics teaching
4. improving collegiality among teachers
5. raising educators' awareness of equity issues and changing teachers' practices with regard to race and gender equity
6. changing assessment practices so that they reflect instructional goals

Project TIME assumed a view of mathematics as a creative human endeavor that is both a way of knowing and a way of thinking about the world. Math consists of concepts and procedures constructed from "exploring, investigating, conjecturing, evaluating, communicating, specializing, generalizing, abstracting, and justifying" (Mumme & Weissglass, 1991, p. 5). Respect for thinking and feelings is taken seriously in an environment that encourages questioning.

Project TIME activities directly involved four groups: teaching specialists, teachers, principals, and parents as integral to the teaching process. A model of educational change gave importance to four components. First, the project was designed to provide teachers with opportunities to obtain more information about mathematics, teaching strategies, the learning pro-

cess, and current issues in mathematics education. Second, the project emphasized the need for teachers to reflect and plan. Teachers had opportunities to think, discuss, and write about their beliefs and classroom practices. Third, the project assumed responsibility to help teachers with their feelings about participating in a reform movement. TIME played a major role in facilitating development of emotionally supportive relationships through teacher support groups, discussion groups, one-to-one support, and dyads. Finally, acting was seen as trying new things, such as small cooperative groups, using manipulatives, encouraging mathematical investigations, team teaching, and Family Math evenings for parents.

Project outcomes were monitored by surveys, written opinions, and interviews. Change occurred in classroom practices, teacher attitudes, communication, and district practices. In the classroom, the amount of time per week of actual mathematics instruction increased 20% from 4.2 to 5.1 hours. The percent of class time students used manipulatives increased from 28% to 35%, and the percent of teacher use of calculators increased from 23% to 74%. Other observable changes were improved student attitudes toward mathematics, improved student attendance, and changing evaluation practices.

Teacher attitudes were found in improved self-confidence and increased awareness of significant issues in mathematics education. Teachers reported that their increased confidence encouraged them to use more mathematics in all subject areas with students. Finally, teachers talked more to one another and established more productive collegial working environments in their schools. Even though the support groups were not always easy to implement and were disliked by some of the teachers, the teaching specialists and principals reported an increase in collegiality and morale.

The implications for teacher education, these authors believe, have to do with the culture of the schools and the school environment as the primary place for teacher development to occur. There is often interference when a new graduate from a teacher education program arrives on the job to teach mathematics using innovative, constructivist, hands-on, technological progressive, and problem-solving oriented strategies. He or she is frustrated in trying to implement a manner of teaching that supports the beliefs and skills they bring to the school; moreover, there is little opportunity to talk out their frustrations or their concerns about why they have to cater to the culture rather than to their convictions and beliefs about how mathematics should be taught. Weissglass (1992) wrote,

One advantage of situating change efforts in a cultural context is that it enables educators to address the complex psychological and political reality of schools and classrooms, rather than focus on more technical issues (new methods of assessment, curricular or achievement standards, and technology, for example). (p. 196)

The potential for mathematics teacher education to contribute to the reform movement in mathematics is to build learning environments and experiences in the culture of the school

---

* Constructivism assumes that learning is the result of learners constructing their understanding through interaction with the environment (Mumme & Weissglass, 1991).

contexts themselves. It is Weissglass's (1993) belief that the continuing lack of success in educational reform efforts is due in large part to not providing structures to support the personal and social transformations necessary to change patterns of behavior. He says that the social and psychological dimensions of changing educational practices are extremely complex and that "any reform effort that does not provide methods for people to systematically and profoundly address their feelings, emotions and values related to the reforms will be inadequate" (p. 3). In this context, issues between trust and distrust, confidence and lack of confidence, activity and passivity, reality and pretense, acceptance and denial of emotions, and equity and inequity can be properly addressed. All this serves to encourage mathematics teacher education to build field experiences that deal head on with the sociopolitical culture of the school. As discussed in the concluding remarks in the section "Problem-Centered Mathematics Project," however, a difficulty with this might be that preservice teachers do not have enough prior experience to appreciate the relationship between the school culture and classroom practice. It appears that if in-service and preservice teachers joined in support groups for conversation on the larger issues surrounding lesson planning and the executing of it, educational reform would be encouraged. (See Weissglass [1990, 1994a, 1994b] for more background, guidelines, and descriptions of a model for educational change support.)

COLLABORATIVES AND SYSTEMIC INITIATIVES

Educational reformers are suggesting very different sets of assumptions about what mathematical knowledge is and how it might be acquired (Griffin, 1990; National Research Council, 1989; NCTM, 1989; Yinger & Hendricks, 1990). The Holmes Group, working with the intent to improve teacher education, is trying to have an impact on the thinking of teacher education and the development of knowledge in children in mathematics and all subject areas. To pursue improvement in teacher education, faculty in colleges of education are making new connections with faculty in arts and sciences. There are teacher and school collaborations, professional development schools, and so forth. In many places the focus of university–school linkages include practice-sensitive researchers at the university and researcher-sensitive teachers in schools (Yinger & Hendricks, 1990), where the study of how to improve the teaching and learning of mathematics pervades the work of the collaborative.

Coreform and Urban Collaboratives

Coreform collaboratives are a connection to other stakeholders in teacher education, such as faculty from colleges of education, faculty from arts and sciences, and teachers and school administrators collaborating with one another to redesign teacher education (Yinger & Hendricks, 1990). Major mathematics and science coreform efforts are currently underway through the National Science Foundation.

Coreform is recursive because in-service teachers, preservice teachers, and professional teacher educators facilitate one another's reform efforts. Professors and teachers facilitate each other's personal reform of their respective teaching practices. Both district-wide policy change and university teacher education program restructuring and teaching practices are affected. With the emphasis put on teacher empowerment, much reform is grounded in teacher- or school-focused professional development.

The importance placed on teacher effectiveness motivates mathematics teacher education programs to work toward a better grounding in developing teachers who themselves construct their own mathematical ways of knowing. Also, because mathematical ways of knowing are not easily measured by traditional means, professional standards have stimulated interesting research on teacher behaviors and student learning in relation to these teacher behaviors that accommodate reform in mathematics teacher education. Consequently, some teacher education faculty are reconsidering their own professional practices. Coreform collaboratives expect that universities will revise the reward structures for faculty so that even mathematics faculty will be rewarded through tenure and promotion for participating in pedagogical research and development as they have been rewarded for pure research in the past. Another practice that must be recognized in this new culture is participation in school–college linkages, especially, formally, through professional development schools (PDS) (Woloszyk & Davis, 1993). "The PDS will not serve as merely a bridge between the school and university; it is, instead a new institution composed of a community of professionals committed to fundamental change which will make education more effective and efficient in producing new learning for all children, youth, and adults" (p. 6).

Coreform collaborative projects funded by the National Science Foundation require intrainstitutional and interinstitutional collaboration, thus offering a fresh perspective on research in mathematics and science education. Interinstitutional collaboration requires teacher education programs across institutions to solve the problems of education through partnerships instead of in competition with one another. Teacher preparation benefits because teacher development can occur in more diverse school cultures, in the most innovative technological environments, with the strongest faculty and professional development school linkages, and with an eye to meeting the needs of society.

Intrainstitutional collaboration requires mathematics and science education faculty of colleges of education and mathematics, science, and engineering faculty of schools of arts and sciences to collaborate. Historically, in the United States this has not been common practice. Mathematics education and mathematics faculty co-planning their respective required courses in a teacher preparation program with follow-through to student teaching is breaking new ground. The press to model exemplary teaching to future teachers in these courses cannot be ignored.

Since NSF funded the first three state teacher collaboratives in 1992–1993, mathematics and science teacher education research has expanded to new dimensions and now calls for a paradigm of collaboration in educational research. Tracking the research and development that occurs in these funded teacher collaboratives will be imperative for improving teacher education research and future teacher education programs.

The goal of urban collaboratives is to improve the quality of mathematics education in urban schools by enhancing the professional lives of teachers in those schools. Beginning in 1985, the Ford Foundation has provided financial support for the development of 16 such collaboratives through its Urban Mathematics Collaboratives (UMC) project. In a study of these sites, Heck, Webb, and Martin (1994) found varying degrees of success among the sites with little self-evaluation data available in most sites. Whereas two of the sites have become non-functional, others have demonstrated the important effects that collaboration can have. One of the key findings from this study is that participating teachers' goals and practices change as a result of opportunities to interact with other teachers in the collaborative. "In particular, as specific innovations demonstrate their effectiveness in the classrooms of colleagues, improvements in teacher practices tend to have broad impacts on the teachers at any given collaborative site" (p. 6). For example, in one site the success of one teacher in using a variety of materials instead of a textbook resulted in other teachers emulating this practice. These teachers now "rely, instead, on supplementary materials and software, or on the ideas, conjectures, and conclusions that students derive when they are directed by their teachers" (p. 21). In another site some of the collaborative teachers demonstrated the usefulness of calculators as a teaching tool, and subsequently a significant number of their colleagues began experimenting with uses for calculators in their teaching.

This study lends support to the premise that collaboration can play a significant role in changing teachers' objectives and teaching practices. There is an important message here for teacher education, namely, that facilitating collaboration among preservice and in-service teachers may be a powerful means to assist teachers in examining their beliefs and actions. Furthermore, it seems clear that such collaboration also has the potential for enhancing the likelihood that changes in instructional goals get translated into changes in teaching methods. However, the study does not indicate a particular way to organize or foster such collaboration. Indeed, it indicates contrarily that there are a variety of ways to organize successfully such collaboration, and it may be that encouraging teachers to implement their own preferences with respect to collaboration is the best way to proceed.

Systemic Initiatives

Multimillion dollar Statewide Systemic Initiative (SSI) grants and Urban Systemic Initiative (USI) grants have been funded by the National Science Foundation for the purpose of creating comprehensive reform in mathematics and science education. These initiatives have focused primarily on improving curriculum and instruction in the schools with systemic planning, wide participation, and evaluation by stakeholders. The SSI program, begun in 1991, provided up to $10 million of federal money for each cooperative agreement for 5-year periods of time to state partnerships of education agencies, higher education, and reform-minded groups. Measurable progress toward reform is expected in return. The USI program is awarding up to $15 million to each of 25 of the nation's largest urban public school systems and their partnerships to assist them in reforming mathematics and science education during a 5-year effort.

Two million dollars per year for statewide reform and $5 million per year for urban school system reform is a fraction of what is needed to create and sustain significant change in the way mathematics and science are taught and learned in schools. Among the systemic initiatives' valued outcomes may be a determination as to whether new teachers from teacher education institutions are suitably prepared for new classroom environments created by these initiatives.

THEORETICAL MODELS AND FUTURE RESEARCH

In previous sections of this chapter, the authors highlight successful aspects of teacher change and coreform projects that have implications for reforming teacher education in mathematics. These project-specific suggestions provide stepping stones that are helpful in bridging the gap between current experiences associated with becoming a teacher that reflect traditional views of learning and knowledge and new experiences that are more in harmony with recent advances in the knowledge of student learning and that reflect a more contemporary view of knowledge, namely, constructivism. As useful as these results are in teacher education reform, it is clear from a practical as well as an academic perspective that an encompassing theory that meaningfully ties together these findings is needed.

The fact that useful recommendations and research questions in mathematics teacher education presently stem primarily from individual studies and projects rather than a unifying theory, or unifying theories, attests to the primitive state of teacher education and research on teacher education. Teacher education is primitive not in the sense of the amount of work that has been done or its value, but rather in the sense of the limited extent of the current understanding and the amount of work that remains to be done. Although there are no well-developed theories to help understand mathematics teacher education, there are implications from recent work that have promise for contributing to the development of useful theories; some of this work is characterized in the following sections.

Teacher Education as a Process

Teacher education must be viewed by researchers as a process rather than an event if the professional development of mathematics teachers is going to be positively influenced by research. For too long and in too many studies the focus has been on a narrow band of experiences and how these experiences influence and affect the participants. Sometimes these experiences have involved a college methods course or a program of study, and at other times they have involved a summer institute or a series of workshops with a variety of follow-up mechanisms. Frequently in these situations the experience provided for the teachers or prospective teachers has been of short duration, especially short when viewed from the perspective of teacher development as a career-long endeavor. In addition to the duration problem, the factors considered to influence teacher development in these studies have been unnecessarily narrow. That is, too often researchers, while focusing on a central concern such as developmental stages of teachers, have ignored or disregarded other crucial factors such as socialization and context issues.

Fortunately, there are recent research and scholarly efforts that have addressed the preceding problems and these provide guidance for subsequent investigations and theory development. In their synthesis of the teacher education literature, for example, Brown and Borko (1992) are explicit about the importance of viewing teacher education broadly by indicating that it is "a life-long process" and that teachers begin to learn about teaching long before their formal teacher education begins, and they continue to learn and change throughout their careers (p. 210). The work of Borko et al. (1990) is an example of a mathematics teacher education research effort that warrants careful study because its design takes account of some of the shortcoming of previous investigations. In the Learning to Teach project they addressed the problem of studies of short duration by studying in depth four middle grade teachers during a 2-year period. During the first year they gathered data from eight teachers completing their final year of a university preservice teacher preparation program. This included a mathematics methods course and a student teaching experience. During the second year of the study, data were collected on four of these eight teachers as they progressed through their first year of teaching. During the entire study there was a concerted effort to examine the influence of a broad range of factors and circumstances, thus operationalizing the researcher's position that becoming a teacher is a complex process. Data were gathered on participants' beliefs, their classroom teaching and learning experiences, their university experiences, their personal history, and the influence of being a part of the research project. Individual interviews, classroom observations, and survey instruments were used to gather data, thus enabling the researchers to capture a comprehensive picture of the learning-to-teach process.

Findings from the Borko et al. (1990) research show that the complexities of learning to teach mathematics manifest themselves in a variety of ways. In this study, for example, the complexity of the process was evident during the last year of the university teacher education program. The participants during this year were involved simultaneously in a mathematics methods course and student teaching experiences. In the schools the students were confronted with implementing their own conception of what is important in teaching and the realities of fulfilling the time-consuming responsibilities of daily teaching. Furthermore, there were substantial responsibilities and demands associated with their mathematics methods course. Borko and colleagues found that not only were these multiple demands very time consuming, but also they were often in conflict with one another. On one hand, they found that the prospective teachers felt strongly that they should teach mathematics in a conceptual manner, make mathematics fun, and exercise firm classroom control. Thus, they were urgently seeking specific suggestions and activities to implement in the classroom. However, their methods course had a conceptual orientation to prepare them to deal effectively with the wide variety of topics and contexts they would have to accommodate during their teaching career. Thus, there was a focus on meaning and understanding and general guidelines and principles.

The conflict that arose was one of immediate needs versus preparation to deal independently with a wide range of teaching situations in the future. This disparity created a difficult tension for the prospective teachers that influenced directly and indirectly their learning and teaching behavior.

Although the results of this study are interesting and valuable, the study's long-term contribution may be its message to theory builders; that is, that the development of theoretical frameworks for teacher education must take account of the complexity of becoming a teacher, in particular theories must embody not only the complexity of the process but also the fact that it is a continuous process of lengthy duration. Thus, theoretical models must consider experiences prior to formal entry into a teacher education program, the teacher education program with its many components, the induction year of teaching, and subsequent teaching years. The relationships within and among these components must be detailed in the theory with participants' points of view and actions accounted for. The beliefs and dispositions of prospective teachers can interact with such things as course goals to have a significant impact on the development of teachers. Examples for other instances of the importance of interactions among other components are not difficult to generate. This emphasizes the importance of a comprehensive model for mathematics teacher education.

Although the preceding argues for a global and comprehensive theoretical base for mathematics teacher education, it is likely that progress toward this end will involve researchers and research groups developing local theories that inform the field about specific situation, factors, variables, and so forth, and that these local theories in turn will become part of a more comprehensive theory. Progress is needed in the theory building endeavor, and, fortunately, there seem to be an increasing number of researchers interested in this activity. This section of the chapter closes by examining some examples of the kinds of work that are moving the field forward in this area.

Learning Cycles Model

Using a constructivist perspective on knowledge, Simon (1994) has proposed a framework for thinking about mathematics teacher education. Adapting earlier work by Karplus et al. (1977), Simon shows how a learning cycle composed of an exploration stage, a concept identification stage, and an application stage that triggers a new exploration stage can be used to generate a model for mathematics teacher education. His Learning Cycles Model, composed of six related cycles, employs teachers' personal learning of mathematics to facilitate their learning about mathematics learning; this in turn is used to develop their learning about mathematics teaching. The cycles are interconnected and recursive with the first cycle associated with a teacher's own mathematical experiences, the second cycle with learning about the nature of mathematics, the third with developing a general theory of mathematics learning, the fourth with understanding students' learning of specific mathematics content, the fifth with planning mathematics instruction, and the sixth cycle with aspects of teaching that involve interacting with students.

The first three cycles of this model have been useful in conceptualizing two teacher development projects. The Educational Leaders in Mathematics Project involved in-service teachers in a summer program with academic year follow-up, and the Construction of Elementary Mathematics project (Simon & Blume, 1994a, 1994b) involved preservice elementary teachers. The model also appears to have potential for providing a perspective on other teacher development research. For instance, the Cognitively Guided Instruction project and the Problem-Centered Mathematics project discussed earlier seem to be closely related to cycle four, understanding student learning in specific mathematical contexts, and cycle six, interacting with students.

In the constructivist tradition, Simon, in discussing his model, indicated that it is not an attempt to represent reality, because there is no direct access to reality, but rather an attempt to create a framework that is useful and generative in thinking about teacher education. The model accomplishes that purpose and is a good example of the current work mentioned earlier that will contribute to a deeper and more comprehensive understanding of mathematics teacher education.

Cognitive Conflict Model

Another study by Movshovitz-Hadar and Hadass (1990) investigated a phenomenon called cognitive conflict, which is likened to a mathematical paradox. "A cognitive conflict is strongly related to paradoxes. A *paradox* is created when two (or more) contradicting statements seem as if both are logically provable" (Movshovitz-Hadar & Hadass, 1990, pp. 265–266). Movshovitz-Hadar and Hadass's study investigated the potential of dealing with paradoxes for the purpose of preparing student teachers for their future professional life as mathematics educators.

The example given by the authors shows that 2 is irrational by assuming that $2 = \sqrt{4}$ is rational (i.e., that $2 = a/b$). Then there exist two integers p and q, relatively prime, such that $p/q = \sqrt{4}$.

$$p/q = \sqrt{4}$$
$$p^2/q^2 = 4$$
$$4q^2 = p^2$$
$$p^2/4 \Rightarrow p/4 \ (*)$$
$\Rightarrow$ There exists an integer n such that $p = 4n$, hence
$$4q^2 = 16n^2$$
$$\Rightarrow q^2 = 4n^2$$
$$\Rightarrow q^2/4 \Rightarrow q/4 \ (*)$$
(*) These were false assumptions.

Therefore p and q have a common divisor greater than 1, and so they are *not* relatively prime. This makes the assumption false. So, $\sqrt{4}$, which is 2, is *not* a rational number.

The worksheet given to students included a detailed proof without supporting arguments that $\sqrt{2}$ is irrational. Then the proof for $\sqrt{3}$ is outlined and blanks are provided. Finally, the "proof" for $\sqrt{4}$ only shows the starting assumption ("Assume, by negation, that $\sqrt{4}$ is irrational, therefore _____") and the last statement ("It follows, therefore, that $\sqrt{4}$ is _____").

After the worksheet, reflective discussion covered the following:

- Resolution of the paradox
- Discussion of the problem-solving strategies applied by individual students to resolve the paradox
- Discussion of the educational merits of the particular paradox
- Reflection on the cognitive roots of the paradox and on the psychological aspects of being in a state of a cognitive conflict (Movshovitz-Hadar & Hadass, 1990, p. 270)

The following summarizes the work of Movshovitz-Hadar and Hadass:

1. They propose a mathematical paradox model that provides a convenient ground for a nonroutine review and polish of high school mathematics, as well as an introduction to the history of mathematics.
2. A paradox based on high school mathematics can put an adult student, whose background includes some university-level mathematics (prospective teacher), in a perplexing situation, which they call a cognitive conflict.
3. The impulse to resolve the paradox is a powerful motivator for change of what it means to come to know mathematics.
4. Working on resolving a paradox can sharpen student teachers' sensitivity to mathematical loopholes, mistakes, inaccuracies, and so forth, and to the crucial role of recovering from making an error.
5. The challenge inherent in a paradox can improve students' awareness of problem-solving heuristics and metacognitive strategies.
6. Mathematical readiness is an important factor in using paradoxes in teacher education.
7. The teaching method adopted in this research is not necessarily a good practice to be imitated in school, but might be most effective in a teacher education program.

This mathematical paradox model provides the kind of mathematical experiences that positions prospective teachers to view their mathematical understandings with a more reflective stance (somewhat like the way the SummerMath jazz dance and tennis lessons engaged those teachers to reflect on what it meant to learn in those recreational contexts).

Teaching and Planning Model

Burns and Lash (1988) studied the constraints teachers have to deal with in implementing the curriculum, making it necessary to compromise instruction. Some of these constraints are internal and others are external to the teacher. A major constraint, or "frame factor," internal to the teacher and related to teacher planning is teacher knowledge consisting of subject-matter knowledge and pedagogical knowledge. Subject-matter knowledge is further delineated into content knowledge, pedagogical content knowledge, and curriculum knowledge. Organizing teacher knowledge this way is helpful and necessary in teacher development. It appears even clearer to consider all pedagogical knowledge as subject-matter specific.

It is necessary, therefore to distinguish between different pedagogical knowledges, each specific to a subject matter, and then to speak about pedagogical content knowledge, as Shulman suggests, as knowledge about how to teach topics within a particular subject. (Burns & Lash, 1988, p. 370)

Burns and Lash examined how 7th-grade teachers' conceptions about teaching mathematics influence the manner in which they plan instruction in mathematical problem solving. Problem solving was selected for the study because it requires distinctly different teaching strategies than basic skills topics. Mathematics, in general, tends to draw the "standard" teaching techniques of showing students how to work problems and then assigning practice problems of the same type. How to teach problem-solving strategies is less clear to most teachers. Another reason problem solving was selected for the study is that as the problem-solving material increases in difficulty, the teachers' need to teach the material that causes the least trouble for students increases.

Planning for the problem-solving unit revealed that teachers had a limited knowledge of teaching techniques and that they focused more on materials and problems than on how their students would come to know how to do problem solving. They did not know specific techniques for teaching problem solving, but it was expected that they would use techniques that were familiar to them from other topics in mathematics. Teaching students to identify key words and to solve problems was a logical transfer from the way teachers taught basic computation skills. It was a concrete approach that teachers could present to students, and it could be taught through drill and practice. Burns and Lash agreed, however, that using key words was not the best approach to teaching problem solving.

Understanding why and how the teachers resorted to traditional basic skills instructional techniques for teaching problem solving requires looking into the various types of teacher knowledge available to them. Burns and Lash (1988) present the Model of Teacher Knowledge and Planning in which a "critical feature of the model is the distinction between delivery systems conceptualized as part of pedagogical knowledge, and teaching techniques, conceptualized as part of pedagogical content knowledge" (p. 381). This, Burns and Lash believe, is at the heart of explaining how the seventh-grade teachers in their study planned their problem-solving units.

Delivery systems (e.g., lectures, discussions, demonstrations, videotapes) present content to students, but the form of delivery is independent of the actual content. (Delivery systems and the method of grouping students, however, are not independent. The grouping arrangements place constraints on selecting the method to deliver the content.) Burns and Lash conceptualize delivery systems and the grouping arrangements as pedagogical knowledge.

Unlike delivery systems, teaching techniques relate to specific subject matter. Teaching techniques are found in abundance in teachers' editions of textbooks and subject matter professional literature (practitioners' journals).

Conceptually, teaching techniques are pedagogical content knowledge. However, since teaching techniques often concern what subject matter might be included in a lesson or how it should be organized and sequenced for presentation, teaching techniques are also closely related

to content and curricular knowledge, and the conceptual distinction between the three types of subject matter knowledge sometimes becomes blurred. (Burns & Lash, 1988, p. 382)

The implications for teacher education are important. Teaching teachers how to plan for instruction needs to include this distinction. Planning can involve pedagogical content knowledge when choosing the use of a particular teaching technique or it can mean reverting to the teaching techniques associated with delivery systems. New research is needed to study the processes and outcomes of learning and practicing this distinction in teacher education programs.

CONCLUSION

It is said that every 4 months computer and related technologies advance a year. Whether it is mathematics teacher education or medicine, the role of technology is propelling society into the future long before many appropriate research questions can be answered. Distance learning, teleconferencing, or multimedia interactive CD roms can now bring innovative dimensions to the university teacher education classroom. Teacher formation programs can offer frequent school "visits," giving a new definition to the term *field-based coursework*. These innovations, however, should not change the fundamental concerns about educating future teachers.

Mathematics teacher education programs need to develop conceptual understandings of mathematics content, provide information about the latest research, and develop pedagogical content knowledge. Planning for instruction is where this knowledge converges as one focuses on increasing the mathematical understanding of children. Teachers need to learn to reflect more often on their teaching to ensure that better lessons are taught each day. Reflecting on pedagogical delivery systems, such as cooperative group learning, peer tutoring, or manipulatives is insufficient. Planning must focus on subject matter as it relates to three important factors: (1) the content itself—the discipline of mathematics and pedagogical content knowledge; (2) knowledge of how one promotes conceptual and operational understanding in students; and (3) curriculum knowledge—the framework of mathematical structures at different developmental stages. The most difficult of these to manage for beginning teachers is pedagogical content knowledge because it is in this domain that one cannot be satisfied with teachers planning and teaching like traditional teachers. It is also in this domain that the greatest demand for future research exists.

In conclusion, just as the relationship between mathematics teacher and student demands research attention, so does the relationship between the mathematics teacher educator and the mathematics teacher. This decade, moreover, requires a broader coordination of educational research faculty in teacher education programs. Research is needed on reform and coreform, on systemicness and collaboration, and on how it relates to science education, because mathematics is the language of science. There is much to be done, but there are some promising ideas and results to build upon.

References

Ball, D. L. (1988). *Unlearning to teach mathematics* (Issue Paper 88-1). East Lansing: National Center for Research on Teacher Learning, Michigan State University.

Ball, D. L. (1989). *Breaking with experience in learning to teach mathematics: The role of a preservice methods course* (Issue Paper 89-10). East Lansing: National Center for Research on Teacher Learning, Michigan State University.

Ball, D. L. (1990). Prospective elementary and secondary teachers' understanding of division. *Journal for Research in Mathematics Education, 21*(2), 132–144.

Ball, D. L., & Wilson, S. M. (1990). *Knowing the subject and learning to teach it: Examining assumptions about becoming a mathematics teacher* (Research Report 90-7). East Lansing: National Center for Research on Teacher Learning, Michigan State University.

Baratta-Lorton, M. (1976). *Math their way*. Boston: Addison-Wesley.

Borko, H., Brown, C. R., Underhill, R. G., Eisenhart, M., Jones, D., & Agard, P. C. (1990). Learning to teach mathematics (Year 2 Progress Report submitted to the National Science Foundation). Blacksburg: Virginia Polytechnic Institute and State University.

Brown, C. A., & Borko, H. (1992). Becoming a mathematics teacher. In D. A. Grouws (Ed.), *Handbook of research on mathematics teaching and learning* (pp. 209–239). New York: Macmillan.

Brown, C. A., & Smith, M. S. (1994, April). Building capacity for mathematics instructional innovation in urban middle schools: Assisting the development of teachers' capacity. In E. A. Silver (Chair), *Mathematics instruction innovation in urban schools: Implementation and impact in the QUASAR Project, 1990–1993*. Symposium conducted at the annual meeting of the American Educational Research Association, New Orleans.

Brown, S. I., Cooney, T. J., & Jones, D. (1990). Mathematics teacher education. In R. Houston (Ed.), *Handbook of research on teacher education* (pp. 639–656). New York: Macmillan.

Burns, R. B., & Lash, A. A. (1988). Nine seventh grade teachers' knowledge and planning of problem-solving instruction. *The Elementary School Journal, 88*(4), 369–386.

California State Department of Education. (1985). *Mathematics framework for California public schools, kindergarten through grade twelve*. Sacramento, CA: Author.

Carpenter, T. P., & Fennema, E., Peterson, P. L., Chiang, C., & Loef, M. (1989). Using knowledge of children's mathematics thinking in classroom teaching: An experimental study. *American Educational Research Journal, 26*(4), 499–531.

Cobb, P., Wood, T., Yackel, E., Nicholls, J., Wheatley, G., Trigatti, B., & Perlwitz, M. (1991). Assessment of a problem-centered second-grade mathematics project. *Journal for Research in Mathematics Education, 22*(1), 3–29.

Cobb, P., Wood, T., Yackel, E., Wheatley, G. (1993). Introduction: Background to the study. In T. Wood, P. Cobb, E. Yackel, & D. Dillon (Eds.), *Rethinking elementary school mathematics: Insights and Issues* (pp. 1–4). *Journal for Research in Mathematics Education Monographs, 6*. Reston, VA: National Council of Teachers of Mathematics.

Cobb, P., Yackel, E., & Wood, T. (1991). Curriculum and teacher development: Psychological and anthropological perspectives. In E. Fennema, T. P. Carpenter, & S. J. Lamon (Eds.), *Integrating research on teaching and learning mathematics* (pp. 83–119). Albany: State University of New York Press.

Cohen, D. K. (1990). A revolution in one classroom: The case of Mrs. Oublier. *Educational Evaluation and Policy Analysis, 12*(3), 311–329.

Daniel, P. (1994, January). *Teacher change through conversation: Providing effective support for classroom teachers in times of change*. Paper presented at the 1994 Conference on Qualitative Research in Education, Athens, GA.

Griffin, G. A. (1990). Curriculum decision making for teacher education. *Theory into Practice, 29*(1), 36–41.

Hart, L. C., Schultz, K., Najee-ullah, D., & Nash, L. (1992). Implementing the professional standards for teaching mathematics: The role of reflection in teaching. *Arithmetic Teacher, 40*(1), 40–42.

Heck, D., Webb, N. L., & Martin, S. (1994, April). *Case studies of United States innovations in mathematics and science and technology education in an international context: Case study of urban mathematics collaboratives*. Madison: Wisconsin Center for Educational Research.

Karplus, R., Lawson, A., Wollman, W., Apple, M., Bernoff, R., Howe, A., Rusch, J., & Sullivan, F. (1977). *Science teaching and the development of reasoning*. Berkeley: University of California.

Kilpatrick, J. (1992). A history of research in mathematics education. In D. M. Grouws (Ed.), *Handbook of research on mathematics teaching and learning* (pp. 3–38). New York: Macmillan.

Lampert, M. (1990). When the problem is not the question and the solution is not the answer: Mathematical knowing and teaching. *American Educational Research Journal, 27*(1), 29–64.

Movshovitz-Hadar, N., & Hadass, R. (1990). Preservice education of math teachers using paradoxes. *Educational Studies in Mathematics, 21*(3), 265–287.

Mumme, J., & Weissglass, J. (1991). Improving mathematics education through school-based change. In N. D. Fisher, H. B. Keynes & P. D. Wayreich (Eds.), *Mathematicians and education reform 1989–1990, Conference Board of the Mathematical Sciences: Issues in mathematics education* (Vol. 2). Providence, RI: American Mathematical Society.

Nash, L. E. (1993). What they know vs. what they show: An investigation of teachers' practices and perceptions regarding student assessment. *Dissertation Abstracts International, 54*(7), 2498A. (University Microfilms No. AAC93-35068)

National Council of Teachers of Mathematics (NCTM). (1980). *Agenda for action*. Reston, VA: Author.

National Council of Teachers of Mathematics (NCTM). (1989). *Curriculum and evaluation standards for school mathematics*. Reston, VA: Author.

National Council of Teachers of Mathematics (NCTM). (1991). *Professional standards for teaching mathematics*. Reston, VA: Author.

National Council of Teachers of Mathematics (NCTM). (1993). *Assessment standards for school mathematics: Working draft*. Reston, VA: Author.

National Research Council. (1989). *Everybody counts: A report to the nation on the future of mathematics education*. Washington, DC: National Academy Press.

Phillip, R. A., Armstrong, B. E., & Bezuk, N. S. (1993). A preservice teacher learning to teach mathematics in a cognitively guided manner. In J. R. Becker & B. J. Pence (Eds.), *Proceedings of the fifteenth annual meeting of PME-NA* (Vol. 2, pp. 159–165). Pacific Grove, CA: San Jose State University.

Schifter, D., & Fosnot, C. T. (1993). *Reconstructing mathematics education: Stories of teachers meeting the challenge of reform*. New York: Teachers College Press.

Schultz, K., & Hart, L. (1988, April). *An experiential teacher educating model for reflective teaching.* Paper presented at the annual meeting of the National Council of Teachers of Mathematics, Chicago.

Schultz, K. A., Hart, L. C., Najee-ullah, D., Nash, L., & Jones, J. (1993, April). *Categories of change: A study on implementing the NCTM Standards.* Paper presented at the annual meeting of the American Educational Research Association, Atlanta.

Shulman, L. S. (1986). Those who understand: Knowledge growth in teaching. *Educational Researcher, 15*(2), 4–14.

Silver, E. (1993). *Quantitative understanding: Amplifying student achievement and reasoning.* Unpublished manuscript, University of Pittsburgh, Learning Research and Development Center, Pittsburgh.

Silver, E. (1994). *Building capacity for mathematics instructional reform in urban middle schools: Contexts and challenges in the QUASAR project.* Paper presented to the annual meeting of the American Educational Research Association, New Orleans.

Simon, M. A. (1994). Learning mathematics and learning to teach: Learning cycles in mathematics teacher education. *Educational Studies in Mathematics, 26,* 71–94.

Simon, M., & Blume, G. (1994a). Building and understanding multiplicative relationships: A study of prospective elementary teachers. *Journal for Research in Mathematics Educating, 25,* 472–494.

Simon, M., & Blume, G. (1994b). Mathematical modeling as a component of understanding ratio-as-measure: A study of prospective elementary teachers. *Journal of Mathematical Behavior, 13,* 183–187.

Simon, M. A., & Schifter, D. (1991). Towards a constructivist perspective: An intervention study of mathematics teacher development. *Educational Studies in Mathematics, 22*(4), 309–331.

Stein, M. D., Silver, E., & Smith, M. S. (1994). *Mathematics reform and teacher development: A community of practice perspective.* Issue paper. Pittsburgh: University of Pittsburgh, Learning Research and Development Center.

Thomas, C. D. (1993). *Constructivism and African-American students' confidence in mathematics.* Unpublished doctoral dissertation, Georgia State University, Atlanta.

Wagner, D. (1994). *A comparative study of Atlanta Math Project and future Atlanta Math Project teachers' questioning and interactive decision-making strategies.* Unpublished doctoral dissertation, Georgia State University, Atlanta.

Weissglass, J. (1990). Constructivist listening for empowerment and change. *The Educational Forum, 54*(4), 351–370.

Weissglass, J. (1992). Changing the culture of mathematics instruction. *Journal of Mathematical Behavior, 11,* 195–203.

Weissglass, J. (1993). The social and psychological dimensions of educational change. Santa Barbara: University of California, Center for Educational Change in Mathematics and Science.

Weissglass, J. (1994a). *Changing mathematics teaching means changing ourselves: Implications for professional development.* 1994 National Council of Teachers of Mathematics Yearbook. Reston, VA: National Council of Teachers of Mathematics.

Weissglass, J. (1994b). Reflections of educational change support groups. *People and Education, 2*(2), 225–248.

Wilcox, S. K., Schram, P., Lappan, G., & Lanier, P. (1991). *The role of a learning community in changing preservice teachers' knowledge and beliefs about mathematics education.* Paper presented at the annual meeting of the American Educational Research Association, Boston.

Woloszyk, C. A., & Davis, S. (1993, February). *Restructuring a teacher preparation program using the professional development school concept.* Paper presented at the annual meeting of the Association of Teacher Educators, Los Angeles.

Wood, T., Cobb, P., & Yackel, E. (1991). Change in teaching mathematics: A case study. *American Educational Research Journal, 28*(3), 587–616.

Wood, T., Cobb, P., Yackel, E., & Dillon, D. (1993). Rethinking elementary school mathematics: Insights and issues. *Journal for Research in Mathematics Education Monographs,* 6.

Yinger, R. J., & Hendricks, M. S. (1990). An overview of reform in Holmes Group institutions. *Journal of Teacher Education, 41*(2), 21–26.

·22·

SCIENCE EDUCATION

Charles R. Coble
EAST CAROLINA UNIVERSITY

Thomas R. Koballa, Jr.
UNIVERSITY OF GEORGIA

Why is educating the youth of America in science important? Two main purposes of education are often articulated; one is specific to the individual, and the other is related to the society in which we exist. Education contributes to the social, emotional, and intellectual development of the individual, while at the same time serving to develop citizens that can contribute to the society in productive and responsible ways. When these purposes are applied to science education, they suggest general learner outcomes. Students should come to understand the tentative nature of science and be able to judge the assertions made by both scientists and nonscientists. Students should understand the concepts, principles, and theories central to the disciplines of physics, chemistry, biology, and earth sciences. In addition, students should come to view science not as magical or mysterious, but as a powerful and productive means of answering questions about the world and themselves. A person possessing these understandings should be able to think scientifically and apply the knowledge and skills of science when confronting both individual and societal problems.

Yet, at a time when science and technology permeate daily life, too many students are not receiving a scientific education that will enable them to achieve these goals. The majority of students are not benefiting from the science education offered in schools today. This is particularly true for students from populations who have traditionally opted out of science as early as possible, such as students from low-income families, women, African Americans, Hispanic Americans, and Native Americans. Even college-bound students, for whom school science has been traditionally targeted, have not fared well. They graduate from high school knowing science facts without understanding the evolution of science ideas and how science affects and is affected by world cultures and societies.

During the last decade, reform has been a major part of science education. Whereas rhetoric suggests that reform is about improving students' academic performance in order to increase the nation's economic competitiveness, the primary focus of the reform movement also has focused on reshaping the vision for science education. This new vision provides all students, especially those students from populations traditionally underrepresented in science, with opportunities to participate in a fulfilling science experience. Science experience should extend learning beyond the confines of the classroom and the period of formal schooling. A critical aspect of this new vision is the learning opportunities developed and fostered by teachers that beckon students to explore the world in which they live.

REFORM IN SCIENCE EDUCATION

The first wave of reform in science education following the release of *A Nation at Risk* (National Commisssion on Excellence in Education, 1983) called for an increase in the number and rigor of science courses for students. Science courses bored students and did not motivate them to learn or to achieve in science. What was needed was a new conception of science instruction (College Entrance Examination Board [CEEB], 1990, p. 2).

As noted by the authors of the College Entrance Examination Board (1990) *Educational Equality Project,* two myths have contributed to the poor condition of science achievement by students in the United States as compared to other industrialized nations. "The first is the widespread belief that the ability to learn science is possessed by only a select few. The second myth is that studying science primarily involves memorizing facts found in textbooks and that performing experiments is simply an exercise in verifying known phenomena" (p. 1).

459

Fortunately, a growing body of research-based knowledge helps to both reshape our understanding and to conceptualize a new science of science instruction. This new knowledge base serves as the rationale for the curriculum, teaching, and assessment strategies suggested in the American Association for the Advancement of Science, Project 2061 and the National Science Teachers Associations' (NSTAs) Scope, Sequence and Coordination Project. These science reform initiatives and others are attempting to change *what* science content is taught, the *way* science is taught, and *how* students' learning is assessed (Fisher, 1991).

Project 2061

In 1985, the year of the most recent transit of Halley's Comet, the American Association for the Advancement of Science (AAAS) initiated Project 2061 (the year of the next near-earth passage of Halley's Comet). Project 2061 is a long-term transformation of K–12 science, mathematics, and technology education. The primary goal is to ensure science literacy for all high school graduates (Rutherford & Ahlgren, 1989).

Project 2061 has three phases. Phase 1 developed a conceptual base for reform by defining the science knowledge, skills, values, and attitudes that all students should acquire as a result of their total school experience by graduation from high school. The AAAS's publication of *Science for All Americans* (1989) was the culmination of phase 1, and it included a set of recommendations by the National Council on Science and Technology Education (NCSTE) on what habits of mind are essential for all citizens in a scientifically literate society (AAAS, 1989, p. 3).

Science for All Americans defined the scientifically literate person as "one who is aware that science, mathematics, and technology are interdependent human enterprises with strengths and limitations; understands key concepts and principles of science; is familiar with the natural world and recognizes both its diversity and unity; and uses scientific knowledge and scientific ways of thinking for individuals and social purposes" (AAAS, 1989, p. 4).

Phase 2 of Project 2061 is an extension of the first phase. Its main purposes are the following:

1. To produce a diverse array of curriculum models for kindergarten through high school based on the recommendations of the report
2. To create a set of blueprints for reforming the other components of education that complement curriculum reform
3. To increase the pool of educators and scientists able to serve as experts in school curriculum reform
4. To foster public awareness of the need for reform in science, mathematics, and technology education, and to promote reform efforts among teachers, administrators and education policy makers (AAAS, 1989, p. 161).

Developing "reform tools" has the highest current priority in phase 2 of Project 2061. Four types of tools are completed or are under development.

1. Benchmarks for Science Literacy
2. Alternative Curriculum Models
3. Resource Database
4. Blueprints for Reform

The AAAS Benchmarks for Science Literacy (1993) provides guidelines for what students should know and be able to achieve in science, mathematics, and technology education by the end of grades 2, 5, 8, and 12. Project 2061 staff envision the Benchmarks as reasonable checkpoints to determine students' progress toward meeting the goals of scientific literacy recommended in *Science for All Americans.*

The Alternative Curriculum Models and the Resource Database are useful for science teachers and other educators to develop specific curriculum matched to local conditions but keyed to the goals of *Science for All Americans.* The data base is accessed electronically and makes available not only curriculum models but also resources for teacher training and for school and university consultants who understand the 2061 approach (AAAS, 1992, p. 2023).

Project 2061 is taking a systemic approach to reform. The Blueprints for Reform focus on 11 key elements of the education system that must be aligned to support science literacy for all students. The 11 blueprint elements are teacher education, assessment, materials and technology, curriculum connection, school organization, parents and the community, higher education, business and industry, educational research, finance, and equity and educational policy (AAAS, 1992, pp. 24–25).

Phase 3 of Project 2061 is a widespread collaborative effort, that will last a decade or longer, in which many groups active in educational reform will use the resources of phases 1 and 2 to move the nation toward science literacy. This phase, if successful, will ultimately transform the teaching and learning of science, mathematics, and technology (AAAS, 1992).

The Scope, Sequence, and Coordination of Secondary School Science Project

The project on Scope, Sequence, and Coordination of Secondary School Science (SS&C) was conceived by Bill Aldridge, Executive Director of the National Science Teachers Association (Aldridge, 1989). SS&C seeks to stimulate a major reform in the content, organization, instruction, and assessment of science. Funded by both the National Science Foundation and the U.S. Department of Education (DOE), SS&C projects are underway in California, North Carolina, Iowa, Puerto Rico, Texas, and more recently in Alaska (Aldridge, 1992).

The SS&C philosophy supports two tenets of Project 2061: (1) *all* students can and should learn science, and (2) less emphasis should be placed on teaching facts and more on understanding a few key concepts (i.e., less is more). SS&C is also attempting to break down the "layer cake" approach to science that characterizes American secondary science. In the United States, science is typically taught in 1-year separate courses of biology, chemistry, and physics, taken by 95%, 45%, and 20% of high school students, respectively (National Committee on Science Education Standards and Assessment [NCSESA], 1993).

SS&C promotes the teaching of every science, including earth and space science, every year, to all students spaced over time. The project also calls for the teaching of science through direct experience followed by introduction of terminology at successively higher levels of abstraction and taking into account students' conception. SS&C also strongly encourages learning in mixed ability groups (Aldridge, 1992; Fisher, 1991).

Two documents have guided and supported the SS&C project: *SS&C: The Content Core* (National Science Teaching Association [NSTA], 1992a) and *SS&C: Relevant Research* (NSTA, 1992b). *The Content Core* presents the principle implementation strategies and the proposed content for each science discipline grades 6–12. *SS&C: Relevant Research* is a compilation of research studies that support the SS&C tenets of spacing, all students learning science, mixed ability classes, students' conceptions, and constructivisim.

Each of the funded SS&C projects has applied the SS&C tenets, the content core, and relevant research to teacher development and curriculum construction in different ways. California, for example, is characterized by a great deal of teacher participation in school decision making. By 1992, high schools and 45 feeder schools were implementing the basic premises of SS&C, consistent with the *California Science Framework.* Regional and "hub" meetings have provided opportunities for teacher in-service education and teacher "support" for SS&C (Boyd, Montgomery, Upton, & Weiss, 1993).

Baylor College of Medicine in Houston, Texas has led the SS&C initiative in the Houston Independent School District (the fifth largest in the country) and in a suburban school district. Much of the effort of the staff has been on developing seventh- and eighth-grade instructional "blocks." Classroom teachers provided input and revisions of the materials based on teacher feedback (Boyd et al., 1993, p. 18).

The Iowa SS&C project has been guided by two factors. First is the strong commitment by project staff at the University of Iowa to the Science, Technology, and Society (STS) approach to science education. Second is a commitment to teacher ownership. Teachers are the primary designers of SS&C courses with support of the project staff (Boyd et al., 1993, p. 20).

The North Carolina SS&C project is a cooperative effort between East Carolina University and the Department of Public Instruction in North Carolina. Teachers in seven pilot and 15 field-test sites have worked closely with project staff to create integrated and coordinated instructional modules for grades 6, 7, and 8, organized around key questions (Coble, Parke, & Auito, 1993).

The Puerto Rico SS&C project is unique in many ways. It is the only SS&C site that fully integrates mathematics with science and where all materials are written in Spanish. The University of Puerto Rico staff has worked diligently with teachers in 6-week summer institutes and academic year in-service to help ensure effective implementation of the 7th- and 8th-grade curriculum blocks (Boyd et al., 1993).

The Alaska site was funded recently; therefore, no results are yet reported. However, it is clear that all SS&C sites are attempting to design instructional materials and teaching strategies that challenge students to address three fundamental questions: What do we mean? How do we know? Why do we believe? (Boyd et al., 1993).

Project 2061 and SS&C are but two of the many reform initiatives underway in the United States. In 1985, the National Academy of Sciences and the Smithsonian Institution established the National Science Resources Center (NSRC), which develops and distributes materials and trains teachers for hands-on science in the elementary school (Lapp, 1991). The National Center for Science Teaching and Learning was established at The Ohio State University in 1990 "to support research in science education for grades K–12" (White & Klapper, 1991). The National Science Center for Improving Science Education, located in Washington, D.C., was established in 1989. The purpose of this center is to promote change in state and local policies and practices in science curriculum, teaching, and assessment (NCISE, n.d.). The Education Development Center (EDC) in Newton, Massachusetts; the Biological Sciences Curriculum Study (BSCS) in Boulder, Colorado; the Lawrence Hall of Science near San Francisco; and other science-related organizations continue their productive efforts. These and other initiatives, such as the DOE-funded 10 Regional Consortia for Mathematics and Science Education, the National Clearinghouse for Mathematics and Science Education, and State Curriculum Frameworks, all funded initially in 1992, plus the NSF-funded Statewide Systemic Initiatives (SSI) and many other government, foundation, and private industry initiatives are providing an unprecedented momentum and consensus for major reform of all aspects of science education in the United States (Moore, 1993).

National Sciences Standards

In 1991, the president of the NSTA, with unanimous NSTA Board approval, requested through Dr. Frank Press, Chairman of the National Research Council (NRC), that the NRC coordinate a process that would produce a set of national science education standards for K–12. The NRC eventually agreed to take the lead with initial funding provided by the U.S. Secretary of Education to support start-up activities. An 89-member National Committee on Science Education Standards and Assessment (NCSESA), chaired by Dr. James Ebert, Vice President of the National Academy of Sciences, organized into working groups to define science content standards, teaching standards, assessment standards, and program and policy standards. These standards

1. Define the understanding of science that all students, without regard to background, future aspirations, or prior interest in science, should develop
2. Present criteria for judging science education content and programs at the K–4, 5–8, and 9–12 levels, including learning goals, design features, instructional approaches, and assessment characteristics
3. Include all natural sciences and their interrelationships, as well as the natural science connections with mathematics, technology, social science, and history
4. Include standards for the preparation and continuing professional development of teachers, including resources needed to enable teachers to meet the learning goals
5. Propose a long-term vision for science education, some elements of which can be incorporated almost immediately in most places, others of which will require substantial changes in the structure, roles, organization, and context of school learning before they can be implemented

6. Provide criteria for judging models, benchmarks, curricula, and learning experiences developed under the guidelines of ongoing national projects; state frameworks; or local district, school, or teacher designed initiatives
7. Provide criteria for judging teaching, the provision of opportunities to learn valued science (including such resources as instructional materials and assessment methods), and science education programs at all levels (NCSESA, 1993).

The NCSESA explicated a set of principles that underlie their work. They are

1. All students, regardless of gender, cultural or ethnic background, physical or learning disabilities, future aspirations, or interest and motivation in science should have the opportunity to attain high levels of scientific literacy.
2. The science that all students are expected to learn is defined so that students have sufficient time to develop a deep understanding of essential scientific ideas rather than superficial acquaintance with many isolated facts. All students can attain science knowledge with understanding.
3. Learning science is an active process in which all students engage. In science, students ask questions, construct explanations of natural phenomena, test those explanations in many different ways, and communicate their ideas to others.
4. Science in school will reflect the intellectual tradition, modes of inquiry, rules of evidence, and ways of formulating questions that characterize the practice of contemporary science.
5. Science education reform is a systemic process in which all persons have roles and the responsibility to change. (NCSESA, 1994)

The guiding principles articulated by the NCSESA group are consistent with those articulated by Project 2061, SS&C, and other reform initiatives. This provides reasonable assurance that the science standards published in 1994 will be acceptable and supported by most science educators and others in the future.

The National Science Education Standards are organized into five categories.

1. *Science System Standards* specify the support systems and resources needed to provide all students with the opportunity to learn science. They include the criteria that each component and/or level of the education system as well as the whole system must meet, and they define how systems function to support the vision of science education presented in the *National Science Education Standards*.
2. *Science Program Standards* specify the nature, design, and consistency of the school and district science program that affects students learning science.
3. *Science Teaching and Professional Development Standards* specify the criteria for the exemplary practice of science teaching. Such teaching provides students with experiences that enable them to achieve the understanding and ability of the Science Content Standards. Teaching standards also describe the knowledge and skills that are the foundation of such practice and the professional development of science teachers.
4. *Science Assessment Standards* specify criteria for assessing and analyzing students' attainments in science and the op-

portunities to learn which school science programs afford students.
5. *Science Content Standards* specify expectations for the development of proficiency in conducting inquiry, including the use of scientific modes of reasoning, and the ability to apply and to communicate scientific knowledge; scientific understanding of concepts, laws, theories, and models; understanding of the interdependent relationship of science and technology; and understanding of the influence of science on societal issues, both contemporary and historical. (NCSESA, 1994)

The National Science Standards are envisioned, currently, as voluntary standards; however, with the support they are enjoying from so many areas of the science-related community and Washington policymakers, the standards will likely become general expectations over time.

A new conception of teaching is critical to realizing a new vision of science education. Consistent with the new vision, the teacher must assist students to construct new knowledge. The teacher can no longer be the giver of factual information; rather the teacher must be "a facilitator and role model who gently guides students through the adventure of learning, encouraging them with questions and feedback and sharing their curiosities and excitement" (Kober, 1993, p. 63). The teacher must operate as part of a learning community where questions about the natural world or human problems spur investigation and where the ideas generated from investigation are communicated and acted upon.

This new vision of science education also demands that changes occur in the culture in which science teaching and learning take place. Change must be sweeping and systemic. School administrators, parents, scientists, university educators, and people from business, industry, and state and federal agencies must all be involved in the change process. Nevertheless, most strategies proposed for implementing this new vision of science education begin with teachers. This is so because teachers are directly responsible for implementing the changes associated with this new vision of science education in the classrooms. However, what is known about the attitudes, beliefs, and actions of science teachers suggests that they are not adequately prepared to enact the changes that accompany this new vision of science education. For this reason, science teacher education is of critical importance (Bruner, 1992).

Science teacher education consists of the "conscious attempts to help teachers or prospective teachers learn what they need to know" to teach science (Loucks-Horsley et al., 1989, p. 19). Ideally, it is a continuous sequence that begins when a person first voices an interest in becoming a science teacher and ends with retirement. In practice, however, science teacher education occurs in two distinct phases—preservice education and in-service education. The preservice phase, traditionally associated with the requirement of a baccalaureate degree, includes coursework in science and professional education and field experiences. The in-service phase focuses on enhancing the knowledge and skills of teachers through their participation in workshops, summer institutes, and so forth. Presently, "no one institution or formal collection of institutions [is] responsible for ensuring that teachers have the science and science teaching knowledge they need" (Loucks-Horsley et al., 1989, p. 19).

TEACHER KNOWLEDGE

The questions of what teachers of science should know and be able to do to meet the instructional challenges that accompany the reform have become extremely important. Several recent reports have contributed to the discussion about the knowledge base of science teachers. Among them are Project 2061's *Science for All Americans* (Rutherford & Ahlgren, 1989); NSTA's *Scope, Sequence, and Coordination of Secondary Schools: The Content Core* (NSTA, 1992); booklets on elementary, middle, and secondary teacher development and support by The National Center for Improving Science Education (1991, 1992; Bybee et al., 1989); and *Fulfilling the Promise: Biology Education in the Nation's Schools* (National Research Council [NRC], 1990). The understandings considered important for teachers mirror those considered important for the students they teach. Much consistency is found among the major elements that constitute the common core of teacher knowledge described in each report.

Science Content Knowledge

Several reports offer recommendations about the science knowledge that a scientifically literate person should possess, but none are more explicit than Project 2061's *Science for All Americans* (Rutherford & Ahlgren, 1989). While not speaking directly to teacher education, *Science for All Americans* explicates several "big ideas" of science that concern the physical setting, the living environment, the human organism, and the technological world. These "big ideas" should form the core of the science content knowledge of all teachers, with depth of understanding reflected in the teacher's chosen level of teaching. According to NCSESA (1993), a measure of sufficient depth for secondary teachers is their ability to guide inquiries based on students' questions. At the elementary level, breadth is required. The depth of the middle level teacher's science content knowledge falls between that of the elementary and secondary teacher, with greater emphasis on breadth of science knowledge to meet the demands of the interdisciplinary curriculum.

Science Concepts

With regard to the *physical setting* in which humans exist, teachers should be knowledgeable of the "structure of the universe and the major processes that have shaped the planet earth, and the concepts with which science descibes the physical world in general—organized for convenience under the headings of matter, energy, motion, and forces" (Rutherford & Ahlgren, 1989, p. 47). A basic knowledge of the *living* world should include understandings about the "diversity of life . . . ; the transfer of heritable characteristics from one generation to the next; the structure and function of cells . . . ; the interdependence of all organisms and their environment; the flow of matter and energy through the grand-scale cycles of life; and

how biological evolution explains the similarity and diversity of life" (Rutherfor & Ahlgren, 1989, p. 59). Extending the basic knowledge to the human organism and world altered by humans through technology, teachers should possess basic understandings about the human life cycle, basic body functions, physical health, and the effect of human uses of technology on such areas as agriculture, manufacturing, energy sources and use, health technology, and information processing (Rutherford & Ahlgren, 1989).

Scientific Enterprise

All teachers, regardless of level, need to understand science as a human endeavor and something about how the history of science has contributed to the current understanding of the universe. Three principle subjects that characterize the scientific endeavor are scientific world view, scientific inquiry, and scientific enterprise (Rutherford & Ahlgren, 1989). From a scientific world view, scientific knowledge is durable, yet subject to change; there are some questions of interest to humans that cannot be answered by science; and the universe is understandable by applying knowledge gained in one context to others. Scientific inquiry is a process that can be used to explain and predict. It involves logical reasoning, imagination, objectivity, and a willingness to accept new ideas based on evidence. The scientific enterprise is a complex activity that influences and is influenced by the context in which it occurs, an activity that is organized into various fields and disciplines to facilitate research and the communication of research findings, and one in which participants usually conduct themselves within the boundaries of ethical norms (Rutherford & Ahlgren, 1989).

History of Science

History brings context to an understanding of the scientific enterprise. Teachers must be acquainted with this history for two reasons (Rutherford & Ahlgren, 1989, p. 111). First, knowledge of the history of science enables a teacher to provide illustrations of the culture in which scientific ideas were conceived and what led to their acceptance or rejection by the scientific community. Second, knowledge of history also provides insight into how science affects culture. For example, turning points in Western civilization are linked with Darwin's writings on evolution of species and Pasteur's discovery of the relationship between infectious diseases and microscopic organisms. Historical accounts of scientific discoveries and progress of Western culture with which teachers should have some familiarity include "the planetary earth, universal gravitation, relativity, geologic time, plate tectonics, the conservation of matter, radioactivity and nuclear fission, the evolution of species, the nature of disease, and the Industrial Revolution" (Rutherford & Ahlgren, 1989, p. 111).

Thematic Ideas

Teachers of science also need to recognize the thematic ideas that transcend the boundaries of the sciences, technology, and other school subjects. Those identified by Project 2061 are systems, models, stability, patterns of change, evolution, and scale. The National Center for Improving Science Education (NCISE) (Bybee et al., 1989) adds organization, cause and effect, structure and function, variations, and diversity; whereas in *The Liberal Art of Science* (AAAS, 1990), four major integrative concepts of science are identified: causality and consequence, scale and proportion, dynamic equilibrium, and change and evolution. A somewhat different set of organizing themes resulted from the NSTA's Project Synthesis (Harms & Yager, 1981). They are academic preparation, personal needs, societal issues, and career awareness. All the thematic ideas appear repeatedly no matter what science is studied. For example, the thematic idea "systems" pervades the investigation of simple machines, energy flow in an ecosystem, a school's transportation system, and the feedback system of a room thermostat. These thematic or organizing ideas function as "powerful explanatory concepts" (Bybee et al., 1989). They should be a part of the thinking and explanations of all teachers. Knowledge of these themes has lasting value for teachers and the students they teach.

Scientific Attitudes

Attitudes are "disposition[s] to behave in certain ways and habits of mind that may result in predictable actions" (Bybee et al., 1989, p. 50). Because teachers of science are responsible for the attitudinal development of their students, they must be knowledgeable about the types of attitudes they are expected to promote. First, teachers must come to appreciate the power of "verifiable data, testable hypotheses, and predictability in science" (Rutherford & Ahlgren, 1989, p. 134). Second, they must engender the scientific attitudes (or attributes) commonly associated with scientists, including relying on data, a willingness to modify explanations, respecting reason, and cooperation. Project 2061 identifies "curiosity, openness to new ideas, and skepticism" as especially important attributes (Rutherford & Ahlgren, 1989, p. 134). In addition, teachers must recognize the strengths and weaknesses of science and maintain a positive outlook toward learning science and toward themselves.

There is some concern over whether these attributes associated with the scientific enterprise should be called attitudes because they do not express likes or dislikes, which is the central feature of the attitude concept (Shrigley, Koballa, & Simpson, 1988). This is not a problem with the attitudes toward science or self identified as important outcomes of science education by Bybee et al. (1989), which are true expressions of likes or dislikes.

Science Skills

Finally, teachers must be able to utilize the skills associated with science learning in order to help their students acquire these skills. Bybee and his colleagues (1989) described three levels of organization for skill development: information gathering, problem solving, and decision making. Information-gathering skills, also called process skills, and problem-solving skills are necessary for addressing scientific questions and resolving technological problems. Observing, classifying, measuring, predicting, inferring, communicating, controlling variables, designing experiments, and formulating models are among the information gathering skills that teachers should be able to practice. The skills required for problem solving include those needed for information gathering plus the ability to state questions, identify problems, and interpret data. The ability to identify alternative solutions and assess the cost, risks, and benefits of solutions are additional skills needed when dealing with issues of technology (Bybee et al., 1989). Decision making in science utilizes critical thinking and analytic skills. After considering alternative solutions, decision making involves choosing the best option and then deciding how to operationalize the option while considering safety, available resources, and the required standards. The final stage of decision making often involves communication and critical responses to science-related and technologically related assertions and arguments (AAAS, 1989).

The knowledge necessary to be a competent and confident teacher of science is more inclusive than science content. A strong science background is essential (Yeany, 1991), but so is knowledge of the learner, general pedagogy, and curriculum materials. Yeany stated that pedagogical content knowledge represents the interface between teaching and learning.

Knowledge of the Learner

A different view of learning has emerged in recent years that teachers of science must understand. This emerging perspective of learning has its foundations in constructivism, a theory about how people learn. To aid in explaining constructivism, it is often contrasted with objectivism. From an objectivist perspective, knowledge is something that is found in books and is separate from the person. Thus, learning is viewed as the transfer of knowledge from the teacher to the students. In contrast, constructivism implies that knowledge is within the individual and an image of the world is built by acquiring information through the senses (von Glasersfeld, 1992). When constructivism is used as a referent, the learner is not passive, but actively constructs meaning from personal experiences. Knowledge, from a constructivist view, consists of conceptual structures that are viable in terms of the learner's present range of experience (von Glasersfeld, 1992).

Questions about how a constructivist view of knowledge can be fostered in instruction were raised by Bybee and his colleagues (1989). These questions center on the importance of students' prior knowledge, learning style, and depth versus breadth of understanding. All of these have implications for what teachers should know about designing science learning experiences to accommodate a constructivist perspective.

Prior Knowledge

Students' prior knowledge about scientific phenomena has grown in importance in light of recent research findings. Research has shown that students come to science class with preexisting conceptions about science topics that differ markedly from a scientific perspective (Baxter, 1989; Tamir, Gal-Choppin, & Nussinovitz, 1981). These preexisting conceptions are based on past experiences. Students continue to develop knowledge by drawing inferences from observations that seem to be related to their past experiences.

Students' personal conceptions about the world are considered when constructivism serves as a referent for science education (Lorsbach & Tobin, 1992). Research indicates that students' conceptions about natural phenomena are held tenaciously and are difficult to change when standard methods of instruction are used. For example, Osborne and Wittrock (1983) found that science instruction that fails to address students' prior knowledge often leaves unchanged many of their science misconceptions. Research by Murnane and Raizen (1988) indicated that children do not discard their initial conceptions unless the beliefs are directly challenged to do so in science lessons. Summarizing the research in this area, Kyle, Abell, and Shymansky (1992) pointed out that "If we wish to improve students' conceptions we must acknowledge that: (a) students come to science class with ideas, (b) students' ideas are often different from scientists', (c) students' preconceptions are strongly held, (d) traditional instruction will not lead to substantial conceptual change, and (e) effective instructional strategies enable teachers to teach for conceptual change and understanding" (p. 33).

Science teachers must understand the need for restructuring students' existing knowledge if the goal of science education for *all* is to be realized. It is imperative for teachers to learn as much as they can about students' prior experiences and what they have learned from these experiences. The design of instruction should be based on an awareness of students' prior knowledge according to Minstrell (1992). A teacher's understanding of students' initial beliefs can serve as a beginning point for helping students reorganize their science knowledge.

Learning Styles

Teachers of science must also be aware of students' learning styles. Conventional wisdom concerning learning styles reflects the need to present scientific information in a manner that addresses the preferences of learners. For example, Kuerbis (n.d.) offered a model devised that includes both processing and perceiving continua. When combined, the two continua result in four learning types: concrete experience, reflective observation, abstract conceptualization, and active experimentation. However, the application of knowledge about learning styles must go beyond the design of instruction based on such models. A new and exciting focus on learning styles is provided by a constructivist perspective in which learning styles relate to the meaning students construct from their prior experiences. A study of Kagan and Tippins (1991), for example, revealed the need for greater sensitivity on the part of teachers to the diversity of student learning styles. In their study, they show that a teacher who valued active student involvement was critical of an "A" student because of the student's preference for abstracting and imagining over active involvement.

The cultural diversity of society also has implications for science teachers' understanding of student learning styles. To be effective, science teachers need to have a "multicultural viewpoint" (Atwater, 1989). The multiple perspectives that students of different cultures bring to science classrooms affect the ways in which they make sense of science learning experiences

(Oakes, 1990). Science teachers must value the diversity of their students and provide them with opportunities in science classes to develop conceptual understandings (Atwater, 1993). Conceptual understanding comes about when students are encouraged to use their own "cultural tools," according to Gallard (1992). "These tools include language, cognitive referents which include myths—personal beliefs and metaphors, images, preferred learning styles, and the time and space to apply extant knowledge to problem-solving situations" (Gallard, 1992, p. 86). Meaningful science learning for students whose first language is not English begins with hands-on experience followed by discussion of the experience in the students' native language. Sense making in the native language first has been shown to enhance learning of both subject matter and English (Pugh, 1990).

Research also indicates that science teaching does not always benefit men and woman equally (Rosser, 1990). Kahle (1992) identified gender bias teaching behaviors and strategies that contribute to women receiving a significantly poorer science education than males. Characteristics for the nonbiased science classroom have also been elucidated through research. Teachers need to be familiar with these characteristics to ensure that their teaching encourages both males and females to continue in science courses and careers. Scantlebury and Baker's (1992) review offered guidance about how to promote gender equity in science classrooms.

1. Avoid calling on males more than females, ask both male and female students the same types of questions, and include both male and female nouns and pronouns when teaching.
2. When using cooperative learning groups, do not allow females to be passive group members or to assume stereotypic roles such as group recorder. If possible, assign females to all-female groups.
3. Promote cooperative classroom climate rather than a competitive one and deemphasize the difficulty of science.
4. Encourage females to manipulate science equipment, celebrate the scientific contributions of women, and teach in a way that illustrates the relationships between science and people.
5. Use assessment strategies that mix extended written and short-answer questions with multiple choice questions and quantitative problems; assess often; and avoid application questions that require knowledge of male experiences, such as football and auto repair.

Teaching Knowledge

The science teacher's role is a very complex one because the act of teaching science is so complex. This is particularly true if a constructivist approach to teaching is used. When teacher's actions are guided by constructivism, they shift from teacher-dominated activities where their function is mainly that of information disseminator to student-centered learning. The teacher becomes the facilitator of science learning whose job is determining if students are making sense of the learning experiences provided (Tobin & Tippins, 1993).

Learning Facilitator

As a facilitator of science learning, a teacher must present students with experiences designed to challenge their existing conceptions. For this strategy to be successful, a teacher needs to know how students construct knowledge (as previously described) and the science misconceptions students are likely to hold at a given age. Research shows that students come to school with incomplete or faulty conceptions about light (Anderson & Karrqvist, 1983), water (Osborne & Cosgrove, 1983), evaporation (Russell, Harlen, & Watt, 1989), the earth (Nussbaum & Sharoni-Dagan, 1983), and many other science topics. Students are especially likely to maintain their faulty or commonsense conceptions when what is being taught cannot be directly observed. Such is the case with photosynthesis, where the idea that plants obtain their food from the soil interferes with students' understanding that plants make their own food through the process of photosynthesis (Roth, 1985). In addition, a teacher should learn how to execute cooperative learning and problem-solving strategies that provide meaningful context for students to connect new experiences to prior knowledge. The construction of meaning can be facilitated through the opportunities for dialogue found in cooperative learning environments.

Studies of cooperative learning reported by Manning and Lucking (1992) indicate that group dialogue permits students to present their notions about the world and have them challenged. The challenges can lead to cognitive development as individuals realign their thinking as a result of having participated in the dialogue. Cooperative group work also serves to build peer realtionships that foster science learning (Kutnick, 1990).

Students' construction of meaning can be advanced through inquiry-based problem solving. Teachers can structure demonstrations and laboratory investigations to challenge students' ideas about a science phenomenon or to encourage students to look for unexpected solutions. To facilitate student inquiry, the teacher must ask probing questions and arrange simulated and real experiences that allow students to identify and solve problems. An example of a simulated arrangement to promote problem solving was described by Simmons (1991). Using the computer software *Catlab,* high school students crossed two white cats that they assumed were "pure" bred for color. When the computer generated cross showed offspring of different colors, the students first had to reconstruct their conceptions of inheritance pattern of the coat color of cats before going on to predict the results of other crosses.

Two well-researched science teaching models that utilize science problem solving and cooperative learning to facilitate the learner's construction of meaning are the Learning Cycle, first described by Karplus and Thier (1967), and Osborne and Wittrock's (1983) Generative Learning Model. The Learning Cycle is an inquiry-based instructional strategy that has three phases: exploration, conceptual invention, and application (Karplus & Thier, 1967). The exploration phase typically involves the learners in laboratory experiences, whereas the conceptual development phase has them trying to make sense of their laboratory experiences, often through class discussion. During the application phase, learners are challenged to apply what they have learned in a different context. The focus of the Generative Learning Model is teaching for conceptual change (Osborne & Wittrock, 1983). It "promotes a learning environment that engages students in an active construction of new knowledge" (Kyle et al., 1992, p. 33) through a four-phase process. In the preliminary phase, learners are questioned about their ideas about science concepts prior to instruction. Learners explore a concept in a motivating context during the focus phase, which often involves manipulation of materials. The challenge phase, intended to cause students to reconsider the ideas with which they feel comfortable, gives learners time to discuss their views and may involve the instructor presenting new evidence via a discrepant event. The application phase, similar to that of the Learning Cycle, completes the sequence.

The inductive approach to teaching and learning advocated in the Learning Cycle and the Generative Learning Model are very effective in bringing about conceptual change (Kyle et al., 1992), teaching reasoning and scientific processes (Lawson & Lawson, 1980), and improving attitudes (Abraham & Renner, 1986). Both teaching models encourage students to question their naive conceptions, to recognize them as flawed, and then to reconstruct their own understandings by framing their naive conceptions in meaningful contexts.

Assessor of Learning

Assessment in science has received much attention in recent years due to an emphasis on accountability and the poor match observed between what is taught and what is assessed. Raizen et al. (1989) advocated assessment that addresses three areas of science learning: (1) factual and conceptual science knowledge; (2) skills in the use of apparatus and equipment necessary to do science, including hands-on performance and the science thinking skills and general thinking skills used in reasoning and problem solving in science; and (3) the disposition to apply science knowledge and science-based skills outside the classroom.

They concede, however, that skill assessment is difficult due to "problems of exercise design and performance interpretation" (p. 21) and the techniques used to assess dispositions that require more work before they can be used with any degree of confidence.

Despite methodological shortcomings linked to the various assessment techniques, a teacher who is able to assess students' knowledge, skills, and dispositions in a variety of ways can better understand what students know, not just what they do not know. From a constructivist perspective, assessment provides the teacher with a glimpse of how students organize their science knowledge and information about students' progress and motivation.

Several assessment practices that have been used in science classes were described by Lawrenz (1992), including portfolios, observations and interviews, projects, and essay tests. Research has shown that teachers' use of portfolios to make judgments about student learning in science actually changes how they teach science (Jorgensen, 1993). Other types of assessment discussed by Lawrenz (1992) that require a few words of explanation are practical assessment and dynamic assessment. Practical assessment may involve students actually measuring a substance with a balance or conducting an investigation to solve a problem, whereas dynamic assessment focuses on the way in which students solve problems rather than on the problem's solution.

Reflective Practitioner

Teachers of science must be reflective practitioners; that is, they should be able to ask questions about the science learning they facilitate and seek answers for those questions in a systematic way (Raizen & Michelsohn, 1994). Reflection is most effective when its target is not well-defined problems but rather situations and events that are out of the ordinary. When ill-defined problems are encountered, teachers who can reframe the problem in a context that makes sense and are able to make tacit knowledge explicit will be able to use reflection as a vehicle for improving their science teaching (Roychoudhury, Roth, & Ebbing, 1993). Learning to be a reflective practitioner takes time, but it is important that science teachers develop the ability to reflect about the practice of teaching because the teacher "is in total control of deciding whether to reflect, and as a result, whether and how to change his or her practice" (Kottkamp, 1990, p. 199).

Curriculum Knowledge

Teachers need to be acquainted with science curriculum materials appropriate for the level and area they teach. The "alphabet soup" science curricula developed during the 1960s and 1970s offer teachers numerous units and lessons that can be used as is or adapted to meet their own instructional needs. Among the best known and widely adopted alphabet soup curricula are Elementary Science Study (ESS), Science Curriculum Improvement Study (SCIS) (Carin & Sund, 1985), and Science-A Process Approach (SAPA) at the elementary level (Carin & Sund, 1985); Earth Science Curriculum Project (ESCP) and Introductory Physical Science (IPS) at the middle level (Simpson & Anderson, 1981); and the three versions of Biological Sciences Curriculum Study (BSCS), Chemical Education Materials Study (CHEM Study), and Harvard Project Physics (HPP) at the secondary level (Simpson & Anderson, 1981). Research has shown that the students in classes using the alphabet soup curricula learn more (Shymansky et al., 1990) and hold more positive attitudes toward science than most students in traditional science courses (Kyle, Bonnsetter, & Gladsen, 1988). More recently developed curriculum materials that show promise include *Activities that Integrate Mathematics and Science* by the AIMS Educational Foundation (Gega, 1986), the Biological Sciences Curriculum Study's *Science for Life and Living* (Neyman, 1993), the Lawrence Hall of Science's Full Option Science System (Gega, 1986), and *ChemCom* developed by the American Chemical Society (1988). Knowledge of curriculum materials developed during the 1960s and 1970s as well as those developed in more recent times provides teachers with access to exciting lessons and units.

Curriculum knowledge is not limited to the materials and programs from which teachers choose when deciding what to teach, but also includes technology, especially computers and new alternatives to assessing students' understandings of sci-

ence. Ellis's (1992) study identified six categories of competencies needed by science teachers to use microcomputers effectively.

1. Computer awareness—how to operate a microcomputer, how it affects education and other fields
2. Applications in science teaching—how the microcomputer is used to enhance learning and teaching
3. Implementation of educational computing—how to overcome barriers to integrating the microcomputer into science teaching
4. Evaluation of software—how to identify, evaluate, and adopt materials for educational computing in science teaching
5. Resources—how to identify, evaluate, and use a variety of sources of information regarding computer uses in science education
6. Attitudes—the development of positive attitudes, values, beliefs, and efficacy about the use of educational computing in science teaching (Ellis, 1992).

Using a microcomputer as a computer-based laboratory may be added to this list of competencies. A microcomputer-based laboratory (MBL) is a microcomputer and attached probes that can be used to collect and record data in real time. When MBL is used in science classes, learning is enhanced in the areas of science process skills, science content, graphing skills, and problem solving (Krajcik & Layman, 1992). These improvements, according to Krajcik and Layman (1992), are attributable to the interactive nature of the MBL that enables students to ask and answer their own "what if " questions.

Less Is More

Traditional curricula design has been to emphasize coverage of many topics in a superficial fashion, resulting in students' completing years of science courses with a memory of isolated science facts but little understanding of complex science concepts. Factors such as state curricular guidelines and positive reinforcement from influential stakeholders to "cover the book" aggravate the problem. An overcrowded curriculum mitigates against teaching and learning guided by a constructivist perspective. In a constructivist classroom, students have time to address their misconceptions and to construct personal meaning from the learning experience. Curriculum is no longer viewed as that communicated by programs, texts, or computer software, but as what a teacher does with students affected by the teacher's imagination and background as well as the available teaching materials.

Research on students' understanding of science affirms the need to pursue fewer concepts in greater depth (Resnick, 1987). "Less is more" implies that students will learn more when less content is covered in a given period of time. "If students learn a few concepts in depth, then they can apply them to new situations or problems," according to leaders of the Scope, Sequence and Coordination of Secondary School Science project (NSTA, 1992a, p. 2). This message is articulated by the frameworks for science teaching and learning recently developed by the AAAS (1989) and by the NCISE elementary, middle, and secondary levels (Bybee et al., 1989; NCISE, 1991, 1992).

A consensus of sorts seems to be building in support of "less is more" within the science education community as teachers are being urged to make decisions about what science should and should not be taught.

Pedagogical Content Knowledge

Pedagogical content knowledge is the combination of pedagogical knowledge, knowledge of students, content knowledge, and knowledge of the curriculum (Shulman, 1987). It is the "knowledge that makes science teachers teachers rather than scientists" (Cochran, 1992, p. 4). Studies of novice science teachers and experienced science teachers, when questioned outside their primary teaching fields, reveal that "pedagogical content knowledge is highly specific to the concepts being taught, is more than just subject matter knowledge alone, and develops over time as a result of teaching experience" (Cochran, 1992, p. 7). A teacher's pedagogical content knowledge is continually restructured through reflection and involves identifying new ways to represent information, adapting instructional materials, and tailoring materials to the specific needs of students (Cochran, 1992). Pedagogical content knowledge is reflected in a teacher's understanding of what concepts are difficult for students to learn, the selection of appropriate instuctional materials, and the use of metaphors and analogies to help students make sense of a learning experience. Pedagogical content knowledge is important because "Much of science teaching involves predicting which concepts students will find difficult, assessing any misconceptions students have about the concepts taught, knowing particular sets of science activities that might help students learn certain concepts, and anticipating which concepts to avoid with students of a certain age" (Raizen & Michelson, 1994, p. 82).

Emerging Consensus

Kober (1993) presented a picture of an emerging consensus based on research and policy about the knowledge and skills that teachers of science should possess. To be successful at enacting a constructivist approach that reflects the reform movement, teachers should know and be able to do the following:

1. Understand the key concepts of science, how they developed through history, and how they relate to each other.
2. Devise incisive questions.
3. Choose materials and activities that are likely to lead to new discoveries and information.
4. Model qualities that they would like their students to have, such as curiosity and enthusiasm.
5. Skillfully observe students' learning processes.
6. Lead provocative and substantive discussions without lecturing.
7. Be able to informally assess the development of understanding. (pp. 63–64)

In addition to these understandings and skills, Kober identified four attributes that are possessed by most effective teachers of science.

1. They are learners themselves and are committed to improving their knowledge about science and science teaching throughout their careers.
2. They are willing to learn from other teachers and resource people in their school.
3. They have a vision for how they want to change their classrooms.
4. They spend time reflecting on their own teaching practices (p. 63).

Kober made the point that a "substantial and renewed commitment" to the education of prospective and in-service teachers is essential if this new vision of the teacher is to become a reality (p. 64).

Increasing the standards, expectations, and incentives for teachers to continue to improve is part of the desired outcomes of the National Board for Professional Teaching Standards (NBPTS). The mission of the NBPTS is "to establish high and rigorous standards for what teachers should know and be able to do, to certify teachers who meet those standards, and to advance related education reforms for the purpose of improving student learning in America" (NBPTS, 1993, p. 2).

The NBPTS seeks to identify and to certify nationally highly accomplished teachers who demonstrate the knowledge, skills, dispositions, and commitments reflected in the following core propositions:

1. Teachers are committed to students and their learning. They
   a. Recognize individual differences in their students and adjust their practice accordingly
   b. Understand how students develop and learn, and treat students equitably
2. Teachers know the subjects they teach and how to teach those subjects to students. They
   a. Appreciate how knowledge in their subjects is created, organized, and linked to other disciplines
   b. Command specialized knowledge of how to convey a subject to students
   c. Generate multiple paths to knowledge
3. Teachers are responsible for managing and monitoring student learning. They
   a. Call on multiple methods to meet their goals
   b. Orchestrate learning in group settings
   c. Place a premium on student engagement
   d. Regularly assess student progress
   e. Are mindful of their principal objectives
4. Teachers think systematically about their practices and learn from experience. They
   a. Continually make different choices that test their judgment
   b. Seek the advice of others and draw on education research and scholarship to improve their practice
5. Teachers are members of learning communities. They
   a. Contribute to school effectiveness by collaborating with other professionals
   b. Work collaboratively with parents
   c. Take advantage of community resources (NBPTS, 1993)

The National Board will issue three science certificates: Middle Childhood (ages 7–12), Early Adolescence (ages 11–15), and Adolescence and Young Adulthood (ages 14–18+). Standards for each of these three areas are being developed by different but coordinated science committees (NBPTS, 1993).

It is the stated intention of the NBPTS that National Board certification will place attention on the need to improve both preservice teacher education and the continuing professional development of teachers (NBPTS, 1991). An essential part of the national strategy to improve preservice education in science is to improve the content and pedagogy of science courses in higher education. The Committee on Education and Human Resources of the Federal Coordinating Council for Science, Engineering, and technology (FCCSET) recommended undergraduate science curriculum reform, support for science faculty preparation and enhancement in effective pedagogical techniques, and a closer working relationship with schools of education to integrate better science research and teaching (FCCSET, 1992).

One of the larger NSF-supported projects directed at reform in undergraduate science is Project Kaleidoscope. Project Kaleidoscope seeks to serve as a catalyst for action that will encourage reform in undergraduate science and mathematics in the United States, especially among liberal arts colleges and other predominantly undergraduate institutions. The project has produced *Volume I: What Works: Building National Science Communities* (Narum, 1991) and *Volume II: What Works: Resources for Reform* (Narum, 1992). Both are useful documents to science faculty in higher education who are interested in substantive program reform and designing a research agenda to evaluate the effects of changes on students' knowledge and understanding.

Because teacher education programs function as the primary point of contact for persons entering the science teaching profession, they shoulder the major responsibility for ensuring that teachers enter the profession with the knowledge, skills, and attitudes needed to be successful in a student-centered classroom. In "Revitalizing Teacher Preparation in Science," Glass, Aiuto, and Anderson (1993) acknowledged the responsibility that colleges and universities have for science teacher education and present six guiding principles for the preparation of teachers of science for the next century. They recommended that

1. Every elementary, middle, and secondary science education preservice student should experience the investigative nature of science.
2. Every elementary, middle, and secondary science education preservice student should have classroom and laboratory experiences in biology, chemistry, Earth/space science, and physics.
3. All elementary, middle, and secondary science education preservice students should understand the interrelatedness of science disciplines and the connections between science and other areas of knowledge.
4. All elementary, middle, and secondary science education preservice students should learn scientific content and thinking processes in the context of contemporary, relevant, personal, and societal issues and problems.
5. All elementary, middle, and secondary science education preservice students must have a sound understanding of the

nature of learning and how it can be applied to the learning of science.
6. All elementary, middle, and secondary science education preservice teachers should have several intense and extended clinical teaching experiences at a variety of grade levels in diverse socioeconomic and cultural settings.

Policy and research provide insight regarding what teachers of science need to know and be able to do. The science knowledge that teachers must possess is vast and, in order to be useful in an instructional context, must be accompanied by knowledge of pedagogy, the curriculum, and the learner. Lederman, Gess-Newsome, and Zeidler (1993) pointed out that the creation of policy that lacks a research base is easily discredited. It is important to reiterate two points made by Yeany (1991) about the knowledge base for teaching. The knowledge base for teaching is always in flux, and teacher development is not about training teachers to perform without thinking but "should educate teachers to reason and make decisions regarding teaching as well as to perform skillfully" (Yeany, 1991, p. 2). These two points support the idea that no teacher is ever fully competent in any of the knowledge bases and that what will be learned shifts with the teacher's needs and concerns. As suggested by Fuller's (1969) *Concerns Based Adoption Model,* the concerns of a teacher change from personal concerns to concerns for students as an innovation becomes more familiar. It is important to keep this in mind when thinking about what teachers of science should know and be able to do. A preservice teacher does not have the same concerns as the veteran teacher, and thus what each needs to know and chooses to learn will be different.

PRESERVICE SCIENCE EDUCATION

Science teacher education programs have traditionally prepared teachers of science for either the elementary or secondary level. With the recent emergence of the middle school as a distinct educational unit, programs have begun to appear that prepare teachers of science for the middle grades. In this section, the status of preservice science teacher education at each level is addressed followed by a discussion of the prevailing and emerging practices of science teacher education related to science content, pedagogy, and professional field experiences, including student teaching and induction activities.

Status of Science Teacher Education

Generalists with a wealth of experience in pedagogy have traditionally been the products of elementary teacher education programs. These mostly undergraduate programs typically consist of an academic core that includes courses in humanities, fine arts, mathematics, and the natural and social sciences, as well as courses related to the major in elementary education. Requirements specific to a major in elementary education include such courses as methods of teaching science, classroom management, and student teaching.

Several studies assessed the status of elementary science teacher education programs. Tolman and Campbell (1991) surveyed public and private institutions that graduate at least 75 elementary education majors per year. Yager (1991) surveyed 76 small 4-year colleges. Barrow (1991) compared the programs offered by 132 institutions in the Midwest states with 87 in New England. All reported that the majority of institutions from which data were collected failed to meet the NSTA's standards for content preparation. Less than one third of the institutions that graduate at least 75 students per year comply with the standard for 12 semester hours of science courses. For institutions in the Midwest states and those in New England, compliance on this standard is 30% and 10%, respectively. Whereas nearly 45% of the Midwest institutions offer science courses that are specifically designed to meet the needs of prospective elementary school teachers as the NSTA recommends, nationwide only about 20% do so. At 4-year colleges, students take an average of 8.5 semester hours of science. Yager (1991) contended that the science courses offered at 4-year colleges may better address the needs of prospective elementary teachers because of their applied and "citizen-oriented" nature. Most of the programs offer a separate science methods course that averages 3 semester or 5 quarter hours, although many programs at 4-year colleges and at institutions in New England provide instruction in science teaching methods as part of a generic methods course. History and philosophy of science courses are typically not a part of elementary teacher preparation programs.

Work by Barrow (1987, 1992) provides information about the instructors of elementary science methods courses. In general, the instructors are males with teaching experience at both the elementary and college levels. Many are generalists, lacking substantive coursework in science and science education. The instructors believe that more high school and college science courses should be taken by prospective elementary teachers, and they tend to stress investigative (process) skills, inquiry teaching, models of science instruction based on the work of Piaget, and questioning strategies in the methods courses they teach.

The middle level is a period of transition for students as they move from the elementary school to high school. Teacher education at this level should address the unique intellectual, physical, social, and emotional needs of early adolescents; however, the preparation of prospective teachers for the middle grades (which includes both middle and junior high schools) is not based on a consistent philosophy (National Research Council, 1990). At institutions such as the University of Texas at Austin and the University of Virginia, students intent on teaching in the middle grades must enroll in a secondary science teacher education program. In Georgia, Iowa, North Carolina, and other states where commitment to the middle school concept is strong, separate programs for the preparation of middle grades science teachers exist. McEwin and Alexander (1987) reported that only about one third of teacher education institutions have middle school programs.

Insitution type and affiliation influence the science education of preservice secondary teachers more so than their elementary and middle level counterparts (National Research Council, 1990). Many programs for educating teachers of science at institutions with schools or colleges of education include a science major and education coursework. In others, students major in education but take the same science courses required of the science major. Both program types can be completed in 4 years, with a graduate receiving a bachelor's degree and being eligible for teacher certification. Another model is favored by universities that are Holmes Group members. At the University of Virginia, for example, a science major is coupled with a fifth year of pedagogical and practical experiences. The graduate finishes the program with both bachelor's and master's degrees and eligibility for teacher certification. In California schools, 5-year programs lead to a bachelor's degree and teaching certification.

Studies that assessed the status of secondary science teacher education programs include those by Barrow (1987, 1988) and Gilbert (1992). Barrow collected information about the secondary science preparation programs offered by institutions in New England and the faculty who teach in the programs. On average, the programs require 34 semster hours of science, with two fifths requiring less than 32 semester hours. The programs stress science content and process over science teaching skills. The most common single field science specialization is biology. Barrow concluded that regardless of science specialization, graduates tend to be inadequately prepared to teach about science, technology, and society issues. About three quarters of the programs require a secondary science methods course and a practicum before student teaching. The length of student teaching is typically a full semester. In general, the science methods faculty who teach in these programs are male; have taught secondary school science; and emphasize inquiry teaching, the nature of science, classroom management, and laboratory instruction and safety in their teaching.

The findings of Gilbert's (1992) survey provide additional information about secondary science methods courses and the instructors who teach them. Methods courses offered at the institutions in Ohio, Indiana, and Illinois average 2.6 semester hours and emphasize inquiry lessons, discussions and demonstrations, lesson planning, science safety and liability, and planning laboratory activities. More than three quarters of the instructors are male and represent three distinct groups: practicing teachers, college science faculty, and education or science education faculty. The groups differ considerably in their secondary teaching experience and professional activity, with practicing teachers having the most experience, averaging just more than 17 years, and the college science faculty having little, if any, secondary teaching experience. Education faculty were more involved professionally, attending science education conferences and regularly reading science education journals. Methods courses offered at smaller institutions are more likely to be taught by a teacher or science faculty members than an education faculty member.

In response to concerns about shortages of qualified science teachers, several school districts and universities have initiated nontraditional teacher preparation programs. A study by Darling-Hammond, Hudson, and Kirby (1989) pointed out both strengths and limitations of these programs. A strength of nontraditional programs is their efforts to "reduce or overcome some of the potential barriers to entry into teaching" (p. viii), such as cost and time required to complete the program, and making it easier for former teachers, midcareer transferees, and retirees to become science teachers. The authors believed that the programs were most vulnerable, however, because they were truncated and thus unable to provide recruits with the necessary pedagogical coursework before entering the classroom. Also, the programs often are supported by outside funds and tended to focus their efforts on a target pool that may not find science teaching particularly attractive once they learn about teaching's relatively low salary level or experience precollege science teaching first hand. Making some programs less vulnerable has been their affiliation with a university's science teacher certification or master's degree program. The fact that nontraditional teacher certification programs may supply nearly 10% of new science teachers in some locales (Darling-Hammond et al., 1989) warrants further study of the effects of these programs on science teaching practice and student learning.

A concern across all levels of science teacher preparation is students' understanding of the nature of science that can be obtained by learning about the history and philosophy of science. It is important that the nature of science be addressed in preservice programs because teachers' decisions about how and what to teach are affected by their understanding about the nature of science (Brickhouse, 1990). Studies by Loving (1989), Yager (1991), and Bybee et al. (1989) indicated that little attention, if any, is given to the history and philosophy of science in science methods courses. Loving's findings led her to recommend that science teacher preparation programs include a course on the philosophy of science.

Practices of Preservice Science Teacher Education

Loucks-Horsley and colleagues (1989) described two phases of preservice science teacher education. In the first phase, students enrolled in university teacher preparation programs take courses in science while fulfilling liberal arts requirements. In the second phase, students learn about science teaching within the context of one or more science methods courses and field experiences. The relationships envisioned among the courses by the program designers are often not shared with the learners. The length of field experiences vary, usually beginning and ending during the student's final year in the program. Recently, courses specific to classroom management and the effective use of computers in teaching science have been added to many programs. With some variation, this two-phase sequence holds true for elementary, middle, and secondary level programs.

Science Content

Science content is the centerpiece of science teacher preparation at all levels. Some programs have specially designed science courses for preservice elementary and middle level teachers, but the science courses required as part of teacher preparation are usually the same liberal education courses taken by other nonscience majors. A fundamental purpose of the college science coursework taken by prospective teachers is to develop a firm knowledge base that can be used to develop instruction. Unfortunately, few of the science courses provide prospective teachers the appropriate opportunities to use the knowledge. In general, these survey courses focus on the major achievements of a science area (Arons, 1980). In addition, prospective secondary science teachers take courses required of

students pursuing a science-related profession or graduate degree in science (National Research Council, 1990). Most of these college science courses consist of a large lecture section where concepts are conveyed verbally by an instructor. The lecture is accompanied by structured laboratory activities where students follow experimental procedures in "cookbook" fashion. In these courses, science is presented as a body of facts to be learned, with little emphasis given to science as a process of inquiry.

These science courses have been criticized for several reasons. Too much information is presented in too brief a time for students to understand science concepts, principles, and theories (Arons, 1989). Arons found fault with the verbal presentations, saying that the courses consist of no more than verbal indoctrination that "leaves virtually nothing permanent or significant in the student mind" (1980, p. 82). Lemke (1989) was critical of college science teaching because of its failure to acknowledge the humanness of science. Rosser (1990) pointed out how stereotypic and sexist language serves to dehumanize science for women. Carter, Heppner, Saigo, Twitty, and Walker (1990) affirmed the finding that college science courses teach isolated concepts and rote problem solving, while neglecting critical thinking, collaboration, and open-ended laboratory investigation. The courses also serve to perpetuate inferior models of teaching (Carter et al., 1990). Requiring education majors to take more science courses will not result in better prepared teachers according to Arons (1989).

In addition to this fairly standard type of science course, Michelsohn and Hawkins (1994) identified three other approaches to teaching science content that are used primarily in elementary and middle grade programs. In the first approach, preservice teachers are taught science using tried-and-true school science activities. Activities from elementary science programs such as Science Curriculum Improvement Study (SCIS) and Elementary Science Study (ESS) may constitute the bulk of the science course curriculum. These courses "reflect the philosophy that the science content that prospective elementary school teachers should study ought to focus primarily on the subject matter they will be expected to teach" (p. 5). The second approach differs from the first in that the focus is geared to the interests of adults rather than children, but the audience is still preservice teachers. Course themes may range from historical aspects of science to individual investigative skills to pollution and recycling. General scientific literacy is the goal of these courses, with the assumption being that the broad perspectives of science learned can be utilized when developing science learning experiences for children. The third approach, described by Michelsohn and Hawkins (1994), involves teaching science content and science methods courses in tandem or combining the content and methods into a single course. The arrangement is intended to strengthen the relationship between science content and science learning experiences appropriate for children.

Many criticisms leveled at the standard approach to teaching science content could also be leveled at each of these three alternative approaches. No matter what approach is used, student learning will be stifled if the content course is fast paced and communicates conflicting purposes (e.g., introduction to science area, weed out poor students, preparation for science career), lecture is used as the only means to introduce new information, exams stress memorization and rote learning, and classes are large (Tobias, 1992). In contrast to these, Tobias (1992) identified elements of successful science learning experiences that point to a change in the cultural values within the higher education institution. The change is from a world of individual competition and isolationism to one of learning community. The characteristics she found in successful science education programs include real laboratory problems, attention to the process of teaching and learning, group work, faculty functioning as managers of change, and convenient access to computers and laboratories.

Science learning experiences that display the characteristics identified by Tobias include those described by Lawson, Rissing, and Faeth (1990), Stefanich and Kelsey (1989), and Roychoudhury and Roth (1992). Lawson et al. (1990) developed an introductory biology course that uses the learning cycle method of instruction. In the course, science laboratory exploration of biological phenomena precede lecture and discussion, and lectures incorporate a historical perspective. Students complete the course with an enhanced understanding of the nature of science inquiry and improved reasoning abilities. Another learning cycle method is the success-oriented content course constructed by Stefanich and Kelsey (1989) for elementary education majors. The course addresses both biological and physical concepts and hands-on teaching strategies and is taken in addition to two general education science courses and a science methods course. Students who completed the course held more positive attitudes toward science and science teaching and manipulating science equipment than did students who had not taken the course. Also, Roychoudhury and Roth (1992) devised a physical science laboratory experience that utilized collaborative grouping. They reported that the experience led to subject matter mastery, decreased science anxiety, and improved interactions among elementary education majors.

A convincing picture of the effects of changing the science curriculum and the culture of an institution may be found in the Florida State University's project to reform the teaching and learning of science by preservice elementary teachers (Barrow & Tobin, 1992). The project called for the development and implementation of integrated science courses in physical, earth, and biological sciences by the end of 3 years. Reform started with beliefs held by the professors who would teach the courses and involved each course instructor working as part of a 10-member development team. In addition to the course's instructor, each development team included other scientists, science historians and philosophers, science educators, teaching assistants, and preservice teachers as members of a course development team. Starting with the professors' beliefs was considered essential due to the strength of the culture in which the professors operate, a culture that perpetuates teaching that relies almost exclusively on lecture and the use of textbooks. Changes observed in the courses and the professors' views of teaching and learning college science are described as "adaptive rather than revolutionary" by Barrow and Tobin (1992); adaptive because change came about gradually as a result of the professors' teaching the new courses, viewing videotapes of course sessions, reflecting about their teaching, and "negotiating with others within the cultural context, about

what has happened, what appears to succeed, and what does not appear to succeed" (p. 119).

Reflected in the science courses developed at Florida State University and new science courses developed at other institutions are elements that make them different from the more standard science courses. Rather than teaching students about the "scientific method," these new science courses introduce students to a variety of methods used by scientists to understand the physical and natural world. Features common to the different scientific methods include: (1) coming up with a question, (2) developing procedures to answer the question, (3) operationalizing the procedures, (4) formulating and assessing outcomes, and (5) communicating the outcomes (Raizen & Michelsohn, 1994). When learning about how scientists work, touching on the human aspects of science is unavoidable. Considerations of the ethics of some types of scientific research often lead to discussions of scientific attitudes, those attributes associated with the work of scientists such as accepting ambiguity, exhibiting healthy skepticism, collaborating, and being willing to modify judgments and explanations. These new courses also teach students how to educate themselves. Learners are provided with a framework for understanding the world and assimilating new knowledge when they come to understand science in terms of a small number of integrative concepts or "Big Ideas" of science such as cause and effect, systems and interaction, structure and function, and probability and prediction. These big ideas are not the focus of instruction, per se, but are used as curriculum organizers. Because these big ideas overstep the boundaries of the science disciplines and will not change with the passing of time, they are useful to the learner at a time when the facts, concepts, and theories proffered in a science course are long forgotten.

Another feature common to many of these new courses is an inquiry-based, constructivist approach. In the introductory biology course developed by Lawson et al. (1990) at Arizona State University, instruction often begins in the laboratory where learners gain first-hand experience with a science concept. Opportunities for learners to make sense of what they experienced occur through a process of social negotiation, where learners' science understanding is questioned, misconceptions are unveiled, and understanding is reconstructed. Finally, the learners are challenged to apply what they have learned, often in a different context. This type of teaching has been shown to be very effective in bringing about conceptual change (Kyle, Abell, & Shymansky, 1992), teaching reasoning and scientific processes (Lawson & Lawson, 1980), and improving attitudes (Abraham & Renner, 1986).

Science Pedagogy

Teachers of science, regardless of level, need more than a good foundation in science to create a quality science learning environment for students. Few would argue the point that knowing science and knowing how to teach science are very different. Thus, an important mission of all teacher preparation programs is to help preservice teachers construct the understandings they need to be successful teachers of science. Science methods courses traditionally have shouldered this responsibility, but other courses, including science courses, seminars, and practica that make up preservice programs have also shared in this responsibility. The question, then, is which learning experiences addressed in teacher preparation programs help foster the understandings needed to help preservice teachers become successful teachers of science.

According to Raizen and Michelsohn (1994) from NCISE, preservice teachers need to be provided with learning experiences that

1. Are designed to help preservice teachers "construct" their own knowledge about learning and teaching
2. Provide multiple structured opportunities for interaction and communication among preservice students
3. Model multiple paths for learning
4. Unfold over time
5. Provide opportunities to create and synthesize
6. Include opportunities for reflection and self-correction
7. Incorporate opportunities to practice the craft of teaching in real and simulated situations
8. Reflect the values of patience, diversity, honesty, skepticism, and risk taking

Taken as a whole, Shymansky et al. (1990) argued that these characteristics of effective preservice teacher learning experiences carry the inquiry-based, constructivist approach to teaching and learning into the realm of science teacher education. Central to these characteristics is the position that preservice teachers, not unlike the students they will some day teach, are theory builders, rely on physical knowledge when learning something new, and are social beings who need encouragement and support in order to develop.

Major support for the inquiry-based, constructivist approach to science teacher education advocated by these characteristics comes from the writings of von Glasersfeld (1992) who claims that learners do not acquire knowledge from a book or teacher but construct knowledge through their own intellectual activities. Research carried out mostly in science methods courses indicates that the Learning Cycle and Generative Learning Model described earlier are quite effective in helping preservice teachers construct their own knowledge (Kyle, Abell, & Shymansky, 1989; Rubba, 1992). An important ingredient of both the Learning Cycle and the Generative Learning Model is the social context in which knowledge is constructed. Social interaction is necessary if learners are to be exposed to new ideas about science teaching and learning and to coordinate their own ideas with the ideas of others.

Cooperative learning is one instructional strategy that promotes student interaction and communication. Three cooperative learning models have been used in elementary science methods classes by Jones (1989). The first, "Inquiry Task Groups," involves group members in specific jobs as they work together to investigate a science phenomenon. The "Two Level Content Study Groups" is based on Jigsaw II developed by Slavin (Slavin & Karweit, 1981), but differs in that it allows for variable group size, and the functions of the two group levels have been formalized as "home team" and "expert group" (Jones, 1989, p. 1). The third model is "Test Review Teams" that presents a pattern for students to work together in preparing for tests. Study of the three models indicates that working in cooperative groups promotes the construction of knowledge in a social context and has positively affected students' attitudes toward science and test performance, particularly among weaker students (Jones, 1989).

In addition, engagement in "open discussion, argument, explanation, and elaboration" was shown to help preservice elementary teachers at the University of West Florida grow in their understanding of science teaching (Briscoe, Peters, & O'Brien, 1993, p. 13). At the same time, the types of interaction and communication expected of preservice teachers were also modeled by university instructors. Collaboration among the education and science faculties at the University of West Florida served to facilitate problem solving about programmatic concerns and led to the development of a systematic approach to elementary teacher education in science. Overall, the research suggests that preservice teachers' learning is enhanced when the learning experiences in which they engage encourage interaction and cooperation.

During the dialogue promoted by cooperative learning, preservice teachers make statements about science phenomena and about teaching and learning that represent syntheses of their own experiences. According to Flick (1991), these statements "are analogical or metaphorical in nature because comparisons are made either explicitly or implicitly to previous experiences" (p. 61). Thus, when preservice teachers use analogies and metaphors to express their thinking, they are synthesizing information by transferring attributes and relationships between objects in a well-developed knowledge base to one not so well developed. For example, preservice teachers' knowledge of the particle nature of sugar cubes can be used to help them develop an understanding of the states of water (Flick, 1991). Concept mapping also helps preservice teachers to synthesize their thoughts about science concepts and teaching and learning (Davis, 1990). In addition, analogies, metaphors, and concept mapping encourage the preservice teachers to express their thoughts about new phenomena.

Planned opportunities for reflection increasingly are becoming a part of the pedagogical experiences of preservice science teachers. Preservice teachers are encouraged and assisted to develop the habits of self-questioning that enable them to inquire into their teaching. Baird, Fensham, Gunstone, and White (1989) studied preservice teachers who participated in a yearlong seminar that emphasized reflection on practice, whereas Trumbull and Slack (1991) looked into preservice teachers' reflection resulting from their participation in structured interviewing assignments. Changes in the preservice teachers' self-confidence and beliefs about the nature of teaching science were noted by Baird and his associates. Trumbull and Slack found that preservice teachers grew in their awareness of the weak content background of peers, of the difficulties associated with asking authentic questions, and of the poor relationship between the science knowledge used daily and that taught in school. The results of a study by Mason (1992) indicate that concept mapping is an effective tool to help preservice teachers reflect on science teaching and learning. Besides reflecting at a "technical level" that tends to focus on what works in the classroom, Raizen and Michelsohn (1994) recommended that preservice teachers also be guided to reflect at a "critical level," where questions of caring, fairness, honesty, ethics, and democratic values are addressed. Collectively, the research suggests that significant and lasting change in both the cognitive and affective realms can be brought about by reflection.

Teachers of science should develop a thorough understanding of concepts such as constructivism, multiculturalism, and cooperative learning. An understanding of any complex concept cannot be expected by the end of a couple of lessons or by the end of a single science methods course, so years may be required to develop such concepts fully. For this reason, preservice teachers need to be provided with multiple opportunities to revisit important concepts many times during their preservice program, according to Raizen and her colleagues. Research in psychology (Dempster, 1992) suggests that spacing instruction over time helps "students in integrating knowledge and in constructing abstract concepts" (Pearsall, 1992, p. 23). Soon, results of tests of the "spacing effect" at school sites implementing curricula based on the Scope, Sequence and Coordination Project's Content Core should provide recommendations applicable to preservice science teacher education.

Field Experiences

Opportunities for students to observe science classes and to interact with students individually or in small groups is a component of most science teacher preparation programs. These experiences often occur as part of or in conjunction with a science methods course and contribute to preservice teachers' understanding of the science teaching and learning milieu; however, it is during student teaching that preservice teachers are most able to operationalize what they have learned in science and science methods courses and receive feedback on matters of science teaching and learning. Student teaching has been described by Head (1992) as the "liminal phase of an educational rite of passage"; liminal because student teachers are no longer students yet not fully teachers.

A microteaching course is one means typically used to help preservice teachers' transition from methods course to student teaching. Studies by Lederman and Gess-Newsome (1989, 1991) indicate that while a microteaching course does help preservice teachers develop concerns for their students, it does not function as a true simulation for student teaching. Preservice teachers only became concerned about actual students and their learning problems and about the paperwork and time constraints imposed by teaching near the beginning of student teaching. The concern about instructional planning initially expressed by students during the microteaching course persisted through student teaching. Rather than focusing on development and the rehearsal of plans, as during microteaching, the student teachers' concerns centered on "finding those easily implemented 'teaching tricks' or 'neat' demonstrations which effectively convey subject matter and maintain student attention" (p. 453). To curb this undesirable shift, the researchers recommended that student teaching should be a gradual assumption of responsibilities rather than a "sudden immersion" into the culture of science teaching.

Very much in line with this recommendation are the features described by Loucks-Horsley et al. (1989) that make for a successful student teaching experience: "the gradual assumption of increasingly more classroom responsibilities, with intense

coaching; and a placement where exemplary practice is continually modeled and discussed" (p. 37). Unfortunately, given current practices, these two features are not a part of all science student teaching experiences. Head (1992) reported that cooperating teachers perpetuate the myth that the public school culture is separate from that of the university and do not always view themselves as mentors who have the responsibility of helping student teachers develop professionally. Such actions and beliefs may be a result of the lack of guidance given cooperating teachers about how to assist student teachers in their professional development. Providing cooperating teaching with training in peer coaching may help prepare them to work effectively with student teachers (Koballa et al., 1992). In addition, time must be allowed for the preservice teacher to experiment and reflect if student teaching is to be a beneficial experience (Roychoudhury, Roth, & Ebbing, 1993), often accomplished through weekly seminars.

Completion of student teaching does not signal a readiness to take on all the responsibilities of science teaching without assistance. Nevertheless, beginning teachers are all too often left to their own devices to learn the accepted practices of the teaching profession. Induction programs are needed to extend and support the professional development of beginning teachers. Loucks-Horsley et al. (1989) described the attributes of a quality induction program.

1. Well chosen, well trained mentor teachers who are both models of good teaching and supportive adults . . . They help orient new teachers to the norms of the school.
2. Support structures that allow time for working together and getting into each others' classrooms. It is also important for new teachers to observe their mentors and for their mentors to observe them. And time for processing the observations, articulating concerns and engaging in mutual problem solving must be a legitimate part of both teachers' work.
3. Assignments for beginning teachers that are not the most difficult nor the most complex . . . . A good induction program recognizes the need for a new teacher to master teaching during the first year or two, a task that is difficult with even the least taxing assignment. (p. 39)

A science teacher induction program that incorporates a number of these attributes is the Teacher Support Team (TST) model (Nichols, French, Wiggins, & Calvert, 1993). The TST was designed to support beginning middle and secondary science teachers and was field tested in Northeast Georgia during the 1992–1993 school year. The model pairs a beginning science teacher with an internal mentor and an external mentor. An experienced science teacher from the beginning teacher's school served as the internal mentor, and a university science educator functioned as the external mentor. Similar teaching assignments were an important criterion used to match the beginning science teachers with an internal mentor. The model also included seminars that were held throughout the year.

Study of the TST (Nichols et al., 1993) revealed the benefits of both the internal and external mentors to the beginning teachers. "The internal mentors were valued for their school-related tasks and also their everyday presence," whereas external mentors were valued for the distant perspective brought to the beginning teachers' problems and concerns (Nichols et al.,

1993, p. 20). The seminars were viewed by the beginning teachers as a time to learn about the classroom experience of other novices and to reflect on their own teaching.

Model Science Teacher Preparation Programs

A science teacher preparation program is the combination of science courses, pedagogy courses, and field experiences. An improved program is the result when these parts are well coordinated and incorporate cutting-edge thinking and practices. The Iowa-UPSTEP secondary science teacher preparation program (Yager, 1991) demonstrates this assertion. The program is credited with developing within preservice teachers the characteristics of exemplary teachers (Krajcik & Penick, 1989). Students who completed the program and exemplary teachers were found to be similar in several ways, including teaching strategies used, course objectives, and uses of science equipment and materials. Unique features of the Iowa UPSTEP program include three semesters of methods coursework, four field experiences, 15 taped critique sessions, and courses in the history and philosophy of science.

Other model science teacher education programs are those that prepare elementary teachers at the University of West Florida and the University of Michigan. At the University of West Florida a constructivist framework is applied to a four semester sequence of experiences designed to develop students' pedagogical content knowledge in science (Briscoe et al., 1993). Courses and field experiences combine science content and pedagogical learning and address the needs of science by multicultural and female learners. Students who completed the program report they are prepared to teach science to young children (Briscoe et al., 1993). The focus of the University of Michigan program is on the preparation of new teachers who understand physical science and are able to develop meaningful learning experiences in physical science for upper elementary level students (Krajcik et al., 1993). Defining elements of the program include integrated coursework in science and pedagogy, an early teaching apprenticeship where groups of students develop lessons keyed to pertinent planning and teaching issues, and use of technology to enhance student interest and communication about science topics. These model programs clearly show the benefits of comprehensive efforts to improve the science teacher education program.

IN-SERVICE/PROFESSIONAL STAFF DEVELOPMENT

The purpose of the development of teachers after they begin to teach is improvement of practice; however, the results are often less than desirable. What is generally missing in the literature are studies of comprehensive programs for continuous teacher development and support over time. Loucks-Horsley and colleagues (1989) characterized the typical teacher renewal opportunity as short, one-shot in-service workshops or decontextualized university coursework. The authors believed that neither of these approaches were optimal for learning and using new content or professional knowledge.

Just as important may be failing to appreciate both the natural resistance to change and the complexity of school change. As Tobin (1990) noted from his work with science teachers, changes that require major reconstruction of classroom teaching might take 1 or 2 years for veteran teachers to accomplish.

Loucks-Horsley and her associates (1987) summarized what they viewed as 10 characteristics of successful teacher development. They are

1. Collegiality and collaboration
2. Experimentation and risk taking
3. Incorporation of available knowledge bases
4. Appropriate participant involvement in goal setting, implementation, evaluation, and decision making
5. Time to work on staff development and to assimilate new learnings
6. Leadership and sustained administrative support
7. Appropriate incentives and rewards
8. Designs built on principles of adult learning and the change process
9. Integration of individual goals with school and district goals
10. Formal placement of the program within the philosophy and organizational structure of the school and district

The NCISE (1992) listed five principles for teacher development and support, all of which must be in place to ensure success in middle school science. They apply to other levels of education as well. In summary, they are

Principle 1. Science teachers for young adolescents need special knowledge, skills, and attitudes. These are knowledge of students in the middle grades; knowledge of science and technology content and skills in "doing" science; knowledge and skills in science pedagogy, general pedagogy, and classroom management; knowledge of the middle school concept; and professional attitudes and commitment.

Principle 2. Staff development opportunities for middle level science teachers should reflect the constructivist perspective (i.e., they should provide opportunities for teachers to make sense of their experiences, construct meaning from new information, and form theories to explain the worlds of teaching and learning, as well as science and technology).

Principle 3. Staff development for middle level science teachers should be continuous and ongoing; encourage choices that match teachers' interests, stages of development, and competence; encourage collaboration and experimentation; and use formats in addition to traditional workshops (e.g., peer coaching, institutes, action research).

Principle 4. Schools must become settings that encourage continuous learning on the part of their staffs, collaboration, and experimentation. They must provide teachers with adequate and accessible resources, time for planning and reflection, and opportunities to take part in decision making that affects their students.

Principle 5. District and school leadership must take responsibility for establishing school settings where good science instruction can thrive. This includes providing clear direction and vision, instructional leadership, strong communication networks, and moral and material support for teachers.

A study and recommendation of ways to promote effective staff development by Arends, Hersh, and Turner (1980) is still applicable in today's climate of reform in science education. Remembering that teachers are adults with knowledge, skills, beliefs, attitudes, and personal motivations formed over time must be taken into account in considering staff development. Who they are, what they want, what they believe, what they know, what they can do, and what they do now are all factors that must become a part of any staff development effort. The development of in-service teachers must proceed as an extension of who they are as humans and what they already know, rather than a need to "fix" some deficiency. They must also be involved in helping design the in-service activities to match their needs in their school over time.

Constable and Long (1991) conducted a 2-year study of a short course on teaching science for in-service teachers. They concluded that teachers' existing knowledge was an important factor in obtaining a critical grasp of constructivism and its application to practice. They concluded that demonstrations of constructivism in action were necessary to obtain the fidelity between philosophy and action desired. O'Brien's (1992) summary of the research on in-service education revealed that there must be (1) a diagnostic/prescriptive phase to build awareness within teachers of the need for change, (2) a presentation and discussion of theory/concept to provide the background and understanding on what it is teachers are to learn and why, (3) skill instruction modeling techniques and behaviors to be acquired, and (4) practice as needed under simulated conditions with feedback such as microteaching and role playing. Joyce and Showers (1983) provided a convincing argument that follow-up and coaching in the schools with teachers helping teachers using peer feedback, support, and modeling are essential to making changes in instructional behavior.

A positive trend in the professional development of science teachers is teachers teaching other teachers. In a thorough study of ways to improve high school science (NCISE, 1991), the authors concluded that "Teaching knowledge can be learned best from colleagues. Teachers should have opportunities to share, discuss, and critique the activities they have taught, the resources they have used, and the handout materials they have produced" (p. 94). Lawrenz and McCreath's (1988) study of two 3-week in-service programs supported by NSF provided evidence that master teachers, when trained in methods and content and then supported to develop their own course outlines to in-service their peers, can make a qualitative difference. A study by Ross (1990) on the use of key teachers to deliver in-service as compared to delivery of in-service to all teachers showed that key teachers can faithfully convey the knowledge and skills obtained in a science in-service to other teachers. Rowland and Stuessy (1990) reported on a model for teachers teaching the basic process skills to other elementary teachers. Pretest and posttest comparisons of teachers' ability to identify all process skills taught and their ability to observe and classify were statistically significant.

One area of needed study is on ways to utilize better science reading materials, especially textbooks. The overreliance on textbooks that stress facts and present science as a completed body of knowledge is a long-standing criticism of science teaching in the United States (Yager, 1983). Benson's (1989) case

study of three secondary biology teachers' epistemological beliefs and how they taught showed a discrepancy between their belief that students should learn concepts and the teachers' practice of teaching detailed information. The constructivist perspective of students' learning gave way to verifying knowledge. The author argued that teachers will have to genuinely change their views of knowledge, learning, teaching, and curriculum before classroom practice will change. A large survey by Shymansky, Yore, and Good (1991) found that elementary teachers, similar to secondary school science teachers, idealize hands-on activity but continued to place a high priority on content coverage and preparation for the next grade. Given the persistence of textbooks as a major curriculum source, Chiappetta, Fillman, and Sethna (1991) sought to develop a method for identifying themes of scientific literacy consistent with Project 2061 and other sources. They suggested that identifying literacy themes may be useful to teachers in selecting future texts.

Yore's (1991) study of secondary science teachers and science textbooks shows that whereas science teachers in British Columbia do reject the text-driven model of reading, they lack alternate models. When selecting learning activities, the teachers evidenced an appreciation for accessing students' prior knowledge and establishing conceptual schema before reading; however, few science teachers utilized focus questions, establishing purposes, or other effective reading strategies prior to assigning text reading. These and other studies show a continuing need to provide professional development opportunities for teachers in making effective use of science reading materials and how to use textbooks as just one of the tools, and not the dominant tool, for teaching science.

One of the most prevalent complaints of teachers is that they need more time to prepare for and teach science, especially where teachers are not relying on a "read about science" approach to teaching but are designing hands-on science instruction. Wier (1988) conducted a study of the effect of a 4-week institute on minimizing the obstacles to science teaching among primary grade teachers. The summer experience of learning science content and writing a complete unit of instruction resulted in an improvement in science teaching during the academic year, as reported by institute participants.

A central criticism in science education is that teachers do not know enough science content to teach it effectively. The study by Trumbull and Kerr (1989) generated some evidence that the way secondary teachers have been taught science has a major influence on their development. Their interviews with university teaching assistants and scientists revealed that they had no goals beyond content coverage and had no theories about teaching, learning, evaluation, or the effects of testing on some students. They also had no planned methods for demonstrating how scientists make knowledge claims or utilize their knowledge. Carlsen's (1988) doctoral dissertation explored the effects of science teachers' subject-matter knowledge on teacher questioning and classroom discourse. Four beginning biology teachers were subjects for the study. The teachers with limited knowledge of a particular topic were prone to discourage student discourse and also discouraged student questioning; however, the frequency of teacher questioning increased on topics about which they had little knowledge. Moore (1990) conducted a study to determine if elementary teachers' self-efficacy and teaching of science improved if their content knowledge and science-related beliefs improved. An intensive in-service program resulted in the subjects significantly increasing self-efficacy, teaching more science, using better methods, and being more active than two control groups in sharing science information with their colleagues. Butts (1990), in a summary of 36 research studies, concluded that "what teachers know influences what they do; what teachers do influences the success of their students; and, when students experience success, teachers feel good about it" (p. 280).

SUPPORT FOR SCIENCE EDUCATION

It is generally accepted that high-quality science and mathematics require significant financial support. In the past, however, it has been difficult to identify the level or source of support for quality information. Recognizing the problem, the National Research Council (NRC) established the Committee on Indicators of Pre-college Science and Mathematics Education, which identified "indicators of financial and leadership support" as one of a set of indicators to measure progress in science and mathematics education (Murnane & Raizen, 1988).

A supplementary indicator of the committee was a recommendation to construct a reliable data base on the level of federal financial support for science and mathematics education. A second supplementary indicator was for measures of budgetary data of scientific bodies and information on staff time and volunteer time devoted to the improvement of science and mathematics education in the schools (Murnane & Raizen, 1988).

The purpose for developing indicators of federal and scientific organizational support was to provide evidence of the social commitment to science and mathematics education. Federal resources, in particular, are one way to put into effect the intent of public policy. Certainly it is not sufficient to create policies that simply declare that "by the year 2000, U.S. students will be first in the world in science and mathematics achievement" (National Goals Panel Report, 1991). The policymakers, the president, and Congress must ensure that financial resources are available and are aligned with policy.

The NRC committee recognized that collecting information on the level of federal funding of science and mathematics is not straightforward. It is even less obvious how much or even who is providing support for preservice and in-service teacher development. Science teacher development does not always (or even usually) appear as a separate line item in agency or society budgets. The committee did determine that where data were available, they found macrolevel agency budgets and appropriations and microlevel projects and activities (Murnane & Raizen, 1988, pp. 145–147).

At the macro level, the National Science Foundation (NSF) is the most recognized source of support for advancing science education in general and science teacher enhancement in particular. Under NSF's current organization, the Directorate for Education and Human Resources (EHR) is responsible, among other things, for furthering the health of science education nationally. EHR's Division of Elementary, Secondary and Infor-

mal Education administers a variety of programs to improve science instruction. The Teacher Enhancement Program provides, through competitive grants, support for developing effective approaches and creative materials for the continuing education of elementary, middle, and secondary science and mathematics teachers (NSF, 1993).

The Teacher Enhancement program and its antecedent organizations within NSF have been the primary source of continuing professional development of science teachers for about three decades. Much of the research on the in-service development of science teachers has been conducted from studies focused on NSF-supported teacher enhancement projects.

Other NSF-supported programs such as Instructional Materials Development, Informal Science Education, and the Presidential Awards for Excellence in Science and Mathematics Teaching provide opportunities for developing the knowledge and skills of in-service teachers. The recently initiated SSI program is a major effort by NSF to encourage improvement in science and mathematics education that has an impact on both in-service and preservice teacher preparation (NSF, 1993).

The 1994 NSF budget of $3 billion included almost $570 million for science and mathematics education. These numbers are up dramatically from $251 million for science and mathematics education in 1991. The increased NSF funding makes funds available for several new programs in science education. One or more Institutes for Sciences Education will be funded at about $2 million a year for 5 years. The purpose of the institutes is to give more research-based direction in science and mathematics education, particularly in the area of reform, student assessment, national delivery systems, teacher education, and other areas (Moore, 1993).

Another new program is the Infrastructure for Education Networking, an $8.7 million joint program between the EHR and NSF's Computer and Information Science and Engineering Directorate. Three to five awards a year will go to consortia to develop models and prototypes of effective uses of advanced technologies in science education (Moore, 1993).

As mentioned earlier, one of the critical needs for reform in science education relates to college and university undergraduate education in science. As some writers and researchers have observed, it is important that the federal government in general and NSF in particular overcome its reluctance to consider a K–16 continuum in attempting to reform science education (Raizen, 1992). NSF's Division of Undergraduate Education within EHR has followed closely recommendations in two National Science Board reports, *Undergraduate Science and Mathematics* and *Engineering Education 1 and 2* in developing and supporting programs in the division. Collaborative for Excellence in Teacher Preparation is a major program in NSF's undergraduate division. College and universities that have the capacity to prepare significant numbers of teachers are eligible to submit proposals (NSF, 1993).

NSF's Division of Human Resource Development (HRD) is broadly responsible for broadening the participation of underrepresented groups in science and engineering. Programs within the division are designed to support the identification, preparation, and retention of minorities, women, and people with disabilities in science-related careers (NSF, 1993, pp.

19–23). Involvement of science teachers in HRD programs enhances their development to meet these critical needs.

The Division of Research, Evaluation, and Dissemination within NSF has provided financial support for a host of individuals, institutions, agencies, and studies, and reports on policy and indicators of success and research on teaching and learning school science and mathematics. The *State Indicators of Science and Mathematics Education, 1993* by the Council of Chief State School Officers (CCSSO, 1993) and *The Scope, Sequence, and Coordination of Secondary School Science, Volume II: Relevant Research* (NSTA, 1992) are two of many published works supported by NSF, U.S. Department of Education.

As significant as NSF has been to the advancement of science education in the United States, it is not the only source of support. Recently, the Department of Education, whose $8 billion K–12 budget dwarfs that of the NSF, has become a major player in strengthening science education, primarily through the professional development of practicing science teachers.

The re-authorization of the Elementary and Secondary Education Act (ESEA) in 1988 created the Dwight D. Eisenhower Mathematics and Science Education Program. Initially funded at $130.5 million in 1989, it grew to $246 million by 1993. The Eisenhower Program goal is "To strengthen the economic competitiveness of the United States by improving the skills of teachers and the quality of instruction in mathematics and science in the nation's . . . schools through assistance to state educational agencies, local education agencies, and institutions of higher education" (D'Agostino & Simpson, 1992, p. 33).

In 1991, SRI International and Policy Studies Associates released a national study of the Eisenhower program. Four themes summarized their findings (Knapp, Zucker, Adelman, & St. John, 1991).

1. The program occupies an otherwise unfilled niche among reform initiatives. Through its intensive small grants program, more than 93% of the school systems nationally (in 1989) receive Eisenhower funds.
2. The program expands the array of professional development opportunities. An estimated one third of all teachers of mathematics and science in the nation (in 1989) have taken part in program activities. (Note: Conversations with program officials in late 1993 indicate that much higher numbers of teachers have been involved.)
3. The program supports leadership but does not create it. (Note: More recent DOE initiatives targeted specifically to develop teacher leadership made this theme obsolete in 1994.)
4. The program provides necessary but not sufficient resources for promoting change in teacher practice. The program has been successful at rejuvenating large numbers of teachers and taking a much smaller number of teachers farther along the road to reform. (Note: Recent funding of NSTA's Scope, Sequence, and Coordination of Secondary School Science Projects in Alaska and Houston are indicators of the department's interest in funding long-term systemic reforms [Aldridge, 1992].)

President Clinton's proposed reauthorization of ESEA entitled "Improving America's School Act of 1993" expanded the Eisenhower program to be the Dwight D. Eisenhower Professional Development Program (1993). Embodied within the legislation is the following rationale:

A crucial component of the strategy for achieving [National Education Goals Three and Four] is ensuring, through sustained and intensive high quality professional development, that all teachers can provide challenging learning experiences in the core academic subjects for their students . . . . The Federal Government has a vital role in helping to make sustained and intensive high quality professional development in the core academic subjects become an integral part of the elementary and secondary education system. (H.B. 3130, Sec. 2101)

The president's expanded plan for the Eisenhower program is at odds with a national study of the program by the SRI and the Policy Studies Association. The concluding recommendation of the joint study was that "one of the most powerful features of the current program structure is the fact that it targets resources exclusively on mathematics and science education" (DOE, 1991, p. 38). The President's reauthorization plan does have a provision that virtually guarantees $250 million annually (minimally) for science and mathematics education. Thus, the Department of Education will remain a key player in the professional development of science and mathematics teachers.

In terms of dollars invested, NSF and DOE are the key agents for advancing science and mathematics education in the United States; however, some 14 other federal agencies contribute through microlevel projects and activities, including the Departments of Energy, Defense, Health and Human Services, Labor, and Agriculture, the National Aeronautics and Space Administration, and the Environmental Protection Agency. They each provide unique opportunities for the professional development of science teachers and students.

All of the federal agencies listed in the previous paragraph are part of the FCCSET Committee on Education and Human Resources (CEHR). The committee's priority is "to enhance the skills and enthusiasm of teachers by having them participate in cutting-edge science in the 750-plus federally operated or financed research laboratories" (FCCSET, 1992, p. 7). A study of the DOE's Teacher Research Associates program involving more than 400 science teachers who participated at 21 laboratory sites showed significant gains in teacher knowledge, interest, leadership, and professional renewal (Vivio & Stevenson, 1992).

Future Trends in Funding for Science Education

In 1991, the Carnegie Commission on Science, Technology, and Government issued a report entitled *In the National Interest: The Federal Government in the Reform of K–12 Math and Science Education*. This important report noted that NSF and DOE account for 86% of the federal investment in precollege math and science improvement (including funded support for preservice and in-service teacher preparation). All of the other agencies combine for only 14% of the total federal investment. Thus, the commission felt it was particularly important for NSF and DOE to create a closer collaboration and that all other FCCSET agencies should devote some percentage of their research and development funds to math and science education (Carnegie Commission, 1991).

The Carnegie Commission report quoted NSF Director Walter Massey as saying "Separating science from science education is wrong, but separating science education from education is wrong, too" (Carnegie Commission, 1991, p. 56). To help ensure greater collaboration in the future, the commission proposed an NSF/DOE Joint Office for K–12 Math and Science Improvement. The mission of the proposed joint office would be to ensure coordination of policy, programs, and communication between the two agencies (Carnegie Commission, 1991).

Funding for science educators is likely to increase in the near future with a great mix of federal, state, and local support, as well as increased business, industry, and private foundation support. Business investment and support for reform, particularly in science and mathematics, derive from concern for national competitiveness in a global economy. The embodiment of that concern was stated, quite bluntly, in *A Nation at Risk*.

Our Nation is at risk. Our once unchallenged preeminence in commerce, industry, science, and technological innovation is being overtaken by competitors throughout the world . . . . The educational foundations of our society are presently being eroded by a rising tide of mediocrity that threatens our very future as a nation and a people. (National Commission on Excellence in Education, 1983, p. 5)

American business and others have largely moved beyond school and teacher "bashing" as an initial reaction to *A Nation at Risk* and have begun to work with educators, policymakers, and elected officials to create solutions. The Council on Research and Technology (CORETECH), a cross section of corporations, universities, research institutes, and associations supporting science and economic development, has developed recommendations for both industry and government to improve science education. In summary, they are

1. Reinforce K–12 teacher's knowledge of science with summer internships or employment with industry scientists.
2. Expand corporate scholarships to university students in science-related fields and help academic university research facilities.
3. Hire more minorities and women and support their advanced education in the sciences.
4. Provide industry support of continuing education programs for employees through university links.
5. Expand communication and collaboration among government, industry, and education partners (Hanson, 1989).

One area in which greater business/industry cooperation and support for improved science (and mathematics) education is clear and compelling is in the area of technology. This assertion is based on the premise that technological progress is more important to an industrialized country's growth than the size of the labor force or investments in new factories (Collens, 1993).

At a historic meeting in Boulder, Colorado in 1991, three national organizations, representing more than 60 technology-based corporations, assembled to develop action plans to help bring about systemic change in schools nationwide. Developing alliances among schools, business, government, and higher education was seen as a key ingredient to systemic change. In 1991, more than 600 business-education alliances were known to exist across the nation (Triangle Coalition for Science and Technology Education, 1991).

Business and education alliances range from local adopt-a-school programs to system-wide and even regional agreements. Business support may vary from donation of equipment, scientist-on-loan, and teacher work-learn programs to more complex, broad-based systemic initiatives. The Triangle Coalition for Science and Technology Education (1991) compiled a helpful guide for building alliances that describe examples and outline the steps necessary for building successful alliances to promote reform.

Alliances such as those proposed by The Triangle Coalition are aligned with the recommendations in the Secretary's Commission on Achieving Necessary Skills (1991) report *What Work Requires of School: A SCANS Report for America 2000*. The report identified thinking skills, problem solving, understanding systems, and computational skills as among those intellectual abilities that must be developed by all students if the nation's schools are to be transformed into high-performance organizations that safeguard our individual and the nation's economic future. It seems clear that mobilizing American industry is an important, even necessary, source of support for the continuing improvement and reform of science education.

CONCLUSION

The emerging consensus of what successful teachers of science need to know and be able to do is extensive. Given all that teachers should know and be able to do, what can be expected of all teachers, novice and veteran? How can beginning teachers be assisted to acquire the pedagogical content knowledge and reflective skills possessed by veteran teachers? How can the enthusiasm of novice teachers be sustained in veteran teachers?

The reform initiatives affect all of science education. How can these initatives be consolidated to present a single unified voice for what needs to happen in K–16 science education?

It is well documented that science courses do not provide prospective teachers with an accurate picture of science. What can be done to improve the science courses taken by prospective teachers? What kinds of in-service teacher education are appropriate for college science teachers? How can the "less is more" idea be operationalized in science courses?

Constructivism serves as the basis for restructuring how science is taught and learned. Constructivism also seems to be the viable epistemology for science teacher education. What can be done to help science teacher educators adopt a constructivist perspective in their teaching?

Science teacher education programs that combine courses in science, pedagogy, and field experience help teacher candidates to construct the pedagogical content knowledge (PCK) needed by novice teachers. Several different arrangements of varying lengths have been tried. More needs to be known about the nature of the courses and field experiences. Should science content and method courses be taught concurrently? What kind of field experiences should come before science methods courses and student teaching? Are teachers of broad field science better able to meet the demands of middle grades and high school teaching than teachers prepared in one science discipline?

Alternative certification programs for teachers of science, particularly at the secondary level, were tried in recent years. The short-term effect has been preparation of teachers for schools in need of science specialists. What are the long-term effects of alternative science certification programs? How do the graduates of these programs compare with graduates of traditional programs?

Induction programs recently have been proposed as a way to make science teacher education a seamless process of professional growth. More needs to be known about the role of induction programs in science teacher education. Specific questions include: Who should serve as science teacher mentors? What special training should be provided to science teacher mentors? Should new teachers and mentors be matched by content expertise and/or class assignments? Are two or more mentors required for an effective experience? How can induction programs facilitate interactions between new teachers?

New standards for science teaching and learning are being developed with implications for the certification and continued development of science teachers. What new structures or realignments of old structures need to occur if prospective teachers are to be introduced to the new vision of science education and if in-service teachers are to maintain currency in the knowledge and pedagogy of science?

Funding for the professional development of science teachers in the elementary, middle, and secondary schools has waxed and waned over the years. What can be done to de-politicize and stabilize funding to ensure long-term teacher and program development in science?

The National Science Foundation, U.S. Department of Education, and many other federal agencies provide support for the development of teachers, but with little coordination of the various funding sources. In what ways can federal support for improvement in science education be better coordinated? Should it be?

The literature documents the need for a more wholistic look at science reform. The unit of reform needs to be the school, not just individual teachers. How can we structure professional development programs in science that enfranchise and affect the entire school?

The reform of science education in the United States has largely proceeded with minimal involvement of other discipline areas, even mathematics; however, the world does not work along discipline lines. In what ways can science reforms be more inclusive of other academic disciplines and other learning specialists and better match an interdisciplinary world?

One of the major concerns fueling the concerns for improved science education is the nation's economic competitiveness in the global economy. Our schools have largely separated science from vocational applications. In what ways can or should we science teacher educators more closely link the academic study of science to practical vocational applications? If so, at what levels of schooling should that occur?

References

Abraham, M. R., & Renner, J. W. (1986). The sequencing of learning cycle activities in high school chemistry. *Journal of Research in Science Teaching, 23*(2), 121–143.

Aldridge, B. G. (1989, January/February). Essential changes in secondary school science: Scope, sequence, and coordination. *NSTA Reports,* pp. 4–5.

Aldridge, B. G. (1992). Project on scope, sequence, and coordination: A new synthesis for improving science education. *Journal of Science Education and Technology, 1*(1), 13–21.

American Association for the Advancement of Science (AAAS). (1990). *The liberal art of science: Agenda for action.* Washington, DC: Author.

American Association for the Advancement of Science (AAAS). (1992). *Update Project 2061: Education for a changing future.* Washington, DC: Author.

American Association for the Advancement of Science (AAAS). (1993). *Benchmarks for science literacy.* New York: Oxford University Press.

American Chemical Society. (1988). *ChemCom: Chemistry in the community.* Dubuque, LA: Kendall-Hunt Publishing.

Anderson, B., & Karrqvist, C. (1983). How Swedish pupils, aged 12–15 years, understand light and its properties. *European Journal of Science Education, 5*(4), 387–402.

Arends, R., Hersh, R., & Turner, J. Jr. (1980). *Conditions for promoting effective staff development.* Washington, DC: ERIC Clearinghouse in Teacher Education. (ERIC Document Reproduction Service No. ED 183 506)

Arons, A. B. (1980, November). Using the substance of science to the purpose of liberal learning. *Journal of College Science Teaching,* 81–87.

Arons, A. B. (1989). What science should we teach? In *Curriculum development for the year 2000* (A BSCS Thirteenth Anniversary Symposium, pp. 13–20). Colorado Springs: Biological Sciences Curriculum Study.

Atwater, M. M. (1989). Including multicultural education in science education: Definitions, competencies, and activities. *Journal of Science Teacher Education, 1*(1), 17–20.

Atwater, M. M. (1993). Multicultural science education. *The Science Teacher, 60*(3), 32–37.

Baird, J. R., Fensham, P., Gunstone, R., & White, R. (1989, March 30–April 1). *A study of the importance of reflection for improving science teaching and learning.* Paper presented at the annual meeting of the National Association for Research in Science Teaching, San Francisco. (ERIC Document Reproduction Service No. ED 307 151)

Barrow, D., & Tobin, K. (1992). Reflections on the role of teacher education in science curriculum reform. In P. Rubba, L. Campbell, & T. Dana (Eds.), *Excellence in educating teachers of science.* Auburn, AL: Association for the Education of Teachers of Science.

Barrow, L. H. (1987). Demographic survey of New England's preservice secondary science teacher education program. *Science Education, 71*(5), 713–720.

Barrow, L. H. (1988). Professional preparation, course content, and responsibilities of New England's secondary science methods faculty. *Science Education, 72*(5), 585–595.

Barrow, L. H. (1991). Status of preservice elementary science education in the big eight states: A comparison with New England. *Journal of Elementary Science Education, 3*(2), 14–25.

Barrow, L. H. (1992). Professional preparation, course content, and responsibilities of big eight elementary science methods faculty. *Journal of Elementary Science Education, 4*(2), 23–34.

Baxter, J. (1989). Children's understanding of familiar astronomical events. *International Journal of Science Education, 11*(5), 503–514.

Benson, G. (1989). Epistemology and science curriculum. *Journal of Curriculum Studies, 21*(4), 329–344.

Boyd, S. E., Montgomery, D. L., Upton, J. B., & Weiss, I. R. (1993). *National Science Teachers Association scope, sequence, and coordination project cross-site analysis.* Chapel Hill, NC: Horizons Research, Inc.

Brickhouse, N. W. (1990). Teachers' beliefs about the nature of science and their relationship to classroom practice. *Journal of Teacher Education, 41*(3), 53–62.

Briscoe, C., Peters, J. M., & O'Brien, G. E. (1993). An elementary science program emphasizing teacher's pedagogical content knowledge within a constructivist epistemological rubric. In P. Rubba, L. Campbell, & T. Dana (Eds.), *Excellence in educating teachers of science.* Auburn, AL: Association for the Education of Teachers in Science.

Bruner, J. (1992). Science education and teachers: A Karplus lecture. *Journal of Science Education and Technology, 1*(1), 6.

Butts, D. P. (1990). Invited commentary. *Science Education, 74*(3), 280–283.

Bybee, R. W., Buchwald, C. E., Crissman, S., Heil, D. R., Kuerbis, P. J., Matsumoto, C., & McInerney, J. D. (1989). *Science and technology education for the elementary years: Frameworks for curriculum and instruction.* Washington, DC: National Center for Improving Science Education.

Carin, A. A., & Sund, R. B. (1985). *Teaching science through discovery* (5th ed.). Columbus, OH: Merrill.

Carlsen, W. S. (1988). The effects of science teacher subject-matter knowledge on teacher questioning and classroom discourse (Doctoral dissertation, Stanford University). *Dissertation Abstracts International, 49*(2), 1, 94-A.

Carnegie Commission on Science, Technology, and Government. (1991). *In the national interest: The federal government in the reform of K–12 math and science education.* New York: Author.

Carter, J. L., Heppner, F., Saigo, R. H., Twitty, G., & Walker, D. (1990). The state of the biology major. *Bioscience, 40*(a), 678–683.

Chiappetta, E. L., Fillman, D. A., & Sethna, G. H. (1991). A method to quantify major themes of scientific literacy in science textbooks. *Journal of Research in Science Teaching, 28*(8), 713–725.

Coble, C. R., Parke, H., & Auito, R. (1993). The scope, sequence, and coordination of secondary school (SS&C) in North Carolina. *Journal of Geological Education, 41*, 315–317.

Cochran, K. F. (1992). Pedagogical content knowledge: Teachers' transformations of subject matter. In F. Lawrenz, K. Cochran, J. Krajcik, & P. Simpson (Eds.), *Research matters . . . to the science teacher* (p. 4). Manhattan, KS: National Association for Research in Science Teaching.

College Entrance Examination Board (CEEB). (1990). *Academic preparation in science (2nd ed.): Teaching for transition from high school to college.* New York: Author.

Collens, L. (1993). The futures of engineering and science education. *Vital Speeches of the Day, 59*(12), 370.

Constable, H., & Long, A. (1991). Changing science teaching: Lessons for a long-term evaluation of a short in-service course. *International Journal of Science Education, 13*(4), 405–420.

Council of Chief State School Officers. (1993). *State indicators of science and mathematics education, 1993.* Washington, DC: Author.

D'Agostino, J. S., & Simpson, R. E. (1992). *The Eisenhower program: History and promise.* Washington, DC: U.S. Department of Education.

Darling-Hammond, L., Hudson, L., & Kirby, S. N. (1989). *Redesigning teacher education: Opening the door to new recruits to science and mathematics teaching.* Santa Monica, CA: RAND Publications.

Davis, N. T. (1990). Using concept mapping to assist prospective elementary teachers in making meaning. *Journal of Science Teacher Education, 1*(4), 66–69.

Dempster, F. N. (1992). The spacing effect. In M. K. Pearsall (Ed.), *Scope, sequence, and coordination of secondary school science, Vol. II: Relevant research.* Washington, DC: National Science Teachers Association.

Eisenhower Professional Development Program. (October 12, 1993). *Improving America's School Act of 1993: HR 3130, Sec. 2101.* Washington, DC: U.S. Department of Education.

Ellis, J. (1992). Integrating educational computing into science instruction. In F. Lawrenz, K. Cochran, J. Krajcik, & P. Simpson (Eds.), *Research matters . . . to the science teacher.* Manhattan, KS: National Association for Research in Science Teaching.

Federal Coordinating Council for Science, Engineering and Technology (FCCSET). (1992). *By the year 2000: First in the world.* Report of the FCCSET Committee on Education and Human Resources. Washington, DC: Office of Science and Technology Policy.

Fisher, A. (1991). Mathematicians set the pace. *Mosaic, 22*(4), 38–44.

Flick, L. (1991). Analogy and metaphor: Tools for understanding inquiry science methods. *Journal of Science Teacher Education, 2*(3), 61–66.

Fuller, F. (1969). Concerns of teachers: A developmental conceptualization. *American Educational Research Journal, 6*(2), 207–226.

Gallard, A. J. (1992). Creating a multicultural learning environment in science classrooms. In F. Lawrenz, K. Cochran, J. Krajcik, & P. Simpson (Eds.), *Research matters . . . to the science teacher.* Manhattan, KS: National Association for Research in Science Teaching.

Gega, P. C. (1986). Science in elementary education, (6th ed.). New York: Macmillan Publishing.

Gilbert, S. W. (1992). A survey of science methods courses and instructors in Illinois, Ohio, and Indiana. *Journal of Science Teacher Education, 3*(2), 33–39.

Glass, L., Aiuto, R., & Anderson, H. (1993). *Revitalizing teacher preparation in science: An agenda for action.* Washington, DC: National Science Teachers Association.

Hanson, D. (1989). Corporate, federal cooperation to improve science education urged. *Chemical and Engineering News, 67*(19), 22–23.

Harms, N. C., & Yager, R. E. (Eds.). (1981). *What research says to the science teacher* (Vol. 3). Washington, DC: National Science Teachers Association.

Head, F. A. (1992). Student teaching as initiation into the teaching profession. *Anthropology and Education Quarterly, 23*(2), 89–107.

Jones, R. M. (1989). Cooperative learning in the elementary science methods course. *Journal of Science Teacher Education, 1*(1), 1–3.

Jorgensen, M. (1993, April). *Authentic assessment for multiple users.* Paper presented at the annual meeting of the National Association for Research in Science Teaching, Atlanta.

Joyce, B., & Showers, B. (1983). *Power in staff development through research or training.* Alexandria, VA: Association for Supervision and Curriculum Development.

Kagan, D., & Tippins, D. (1991). Helping student teachers attend to student cues. *Elementary School Journal, 91*(4), 343–356.

Kahle, J. B. (1992). Why girls don't know. In M. Pearsall (Ed.), *Scope, sequence, and coordination of secondary school science, Vol. II: Relevant research.* Washington, DC: National Science Teachers Association.

Karplus, R., & Thier, H. D. (1967). *A new look at elementary school science.* Chicago: Rand McNally.

Knapp, M. S., Zucker, A. A., Adelman, N. E., & St. John, M. (1991). *The Eisenhower mathematics and science education program: An enabling resource for reform, summary report.* Washington, DC: U.S. Department of Education, Office of Planning, Budget and Evaluation.

Koballa, T. R., Eidson, S. D., Finco-Kent, D., Grimes, S., Kight, C., & Sambs, H. (1992). Peer coaching: Capitalizing on constructive criticism. *The Science Teacher, 59*(6), 42–45.

Kober, N. (1993). *What we know about science teaching and learning.* Washington, DC: Council for Educational Development and Research.

Kottkamp, R. B. (1990). Means for facilitating reflection. *Education and Urban Society, 22*(2), 182–203.

Krajcik, J., Blumenfeld, P., Starr, M. L., Palincsar, A., Coppola, B., & Soloway, E. (1993). Integrating knowledge bases: An upper-elementary teacher preparation program emphasizing the teaching of science. In P. Rubba, L. Campbell, & T. Dana (Eds.), *Excellence in educating teachers of science.* Auburn, AL: Association for the Education of Teachers in Science.

Krajcik, J. S., & Layman, J. W. (1992). Microcomputer-based laboratories in the science classroom. In F. Lawrenz, K. Cochran, J. Krajcik, & P. Simpson (Eds.), *Research matters . . . to the science teacher.* Manhattan, KS: National Association for Research in Science Teaching.

Krajcik, J. S., & Penick, J. E. (1989). Evaluation of a model science teacher education program. *Journal of Research in Science Teaching, 26*(a), 795–810.

Kuerbis, P. J. (n.d.). *Research matters . . . to the science teacher: Learning styles and science teaching.* Manhattan, KS: National Association for Research in Science Teaching.

Kutnick, P. (1990). A social critique of cognitively based science curricula. *Science Education, 74,* 87–94.

Kyle, W. C., Abell, S. K., & Shymansky, J. A. (1989). Enhancing prospective teachers' conceptions of teaching and science. *Journal of Science Teacher Education, 1*(1), 10–13.

Kyle, W. C., Abell, S. K., & Shymansky, J. A. (1992). Conceptual change teaching and science learning. In F. Lawrenz, K. Cochran, J. Krajcik, & P. Simpson (Eds.), *Research matters . . . to the science teacher* (p. 33). Manhattan, KS: National Association for Research in Science Teaching.

Kyle, W. C., Bonnsetter, R., & Gladsen, T. (1988). An implementation study: An analysis of elementary students' and teachers' attitudes toward science in process-approach vs. traditional science classes. *Journal of Research in Science Teaching, 25*(2), 103–120.

Lapp, D. M. (1991). Science: Resource for hands-on science. *Educational Leadership, 48*(5), 95.

Lawrenz, F. (1992). Authentic assessment. In F. Lawrenz, K. Cochran, J. Krajcik, & P. Simpson (Eds.), *Research matters . . . to the science teacher.* Manhattan, KS: National Association for Research in Science Teaching.

Lawrenz, F., & McCreath, H. (1988). Integrating quantitative and qualitative evaluation methods to compare two teachers inservice training programs. *Journal of Research in Science Teaching, 25*(5), 397–407.

Lawson, A. E., & Lawson, C. A. (1980). A theory of teaching for conceptual understanding, rational thinking, and creativity. In A. E. Lawson (Ed.), *The psychology of teaching for thinking and creativity: 1980 AETS yearbook* (pp. 104–149). Columbus: ERIC, Ohio State University.

Lawson, A., Rissing, S. W., & Faeth, S. H. (1990). An inquiry approach to nonmajors biology. *Journal of College Science Teaching, 19*(b), 340–346.

Lederman, N. G., & Gess-Newsome, J. (1989, March 30–April 1). *A qualitative analysis of the effects of a microteaching course on preservice science teachers' instructional decisions and beliefs about teaching.* Paper presented at the annual meeting of the National Association for Research in Science Teaching, San Francisco. (ERIC Document Reproduction Service No. ED 305 254)

Lederman, N. G., & Gess-Newsome, J. (1991). Metamorphosis, adaptation, or evolution?: Preservice science teachers' concerns and perceptions of teaching and planning. *Science Education, 75*(4), 443–456.

Lederman, N. G., Gess-Newsome, J., & Zeidler, D. L. (1993). Summary of research in science education 1991. *Science Education, 77*(5), 465–559.

Lemke, J. L. (1989). The language of science teaching. In C. Emihovich (Ed.), *Locating learning: Ethnographic perspectives on classroom research* (pp. 216–239). Norwood, NJ: Ablex.

Lorsbach, A., & Tobin, K. (1992). Constructivism as a referent for science teaching. In F. Lawrenz, K. Cochran, J. Krajcik, & P. Simpson (Eds.), *Research matters . . . to the science teacher.* Manhattan, KS: National Association for Research in Science Teaching.

Loucks-Horsley, S., Carlson, M. O., Brink, L. H., Horwitz, P., March, D. D., Pratt, H., Roy, K. R., & Worth, K. (1989). *Developing and supporting teachers for elementary school science education in the middle years.* Washington, DC: The National Center for Improving Science Education.

Loucks-Horsley, S., Harding, C., Arbuckle, M. A., Murray, L. B., Dubea, C., & Williams, M. K. (1987). *Continuing to learn: A guidebook for teacher development.* Andover, MA: The Regional Laboratory for Educational Improvement of the Northeast and Islands and National Staff Development Council.

Loving, C. (1989). *Current models in philosophy of science: Their place in science teacher education.* Paper presented at the annual meeting of the National Association for Research in Science Teaching, San Francisco. (ERIC Document Reproduction Service No. ED 307 143)

Manning, M. L., & Lucking, R. (1992). The what, why, and how of cooperative learning. In M. K. Pearsall (Ed.), *Scope, sequence, and coordination of secondary school science, Vol II: Relevant research.* Washington, DC: National Science Teachers Association.

Mason, C. L. (1992). Concept mapping: A tool to develop reflective science instruction. *Science Education, 76*(1), 51–64.

McEwin, C. K., & Alexander, W. (1987). *Preparing to teach at the middle level.* Columbus, OH: National Middle School Association.

Michelsohn, A. M., & Hawkins, S. (1994). Current practices in science education of prospective elementary school teachers, summary. In S. A. Raizen & A. M. Michelsohn (Eds.), *The future of science in elementary school: Educating prospective teachers.* San Francisco: Jossey-Bass.

Minstrell, J. (1992). Teaching science for understanding. In M. K. Pearsall (Ed.), *Scope, sequence, and coordination, Vol. II: Relevant research.* Washington, DC: National Science Teachers Association.

Moore, P. A. (1990). The effects of science in-service programs on the self efficacy belief of elementary school teachers (Doctoral dissertation, University of San Diego). *Dissertation Abstracts International, 51*(3), 823-A.

Moore, P. (1993). New briefing: NSF increase speeds new education grants. *Federal Grants and Contracts Weekly, 17*(43), 8.

Murnane, R., & Raizen, S. A. (Eds.). (1988). *Improving indicators of the quality of science and mathematics education in grades K–12.* Washington, DC: National Academy Press.

Narum, J. (Eds.). (1991, June). *Vol. I. What works: Building national science communities.* Washington, DC: Project Kaleidoscope, Independent College Office.

Narum, J. (Ed.). (1992, January). *Vol. II. What works: Resources for reform.* Washington, DC: Project Kaleidoscope, Independent College Office.

National Board for Professional Teaching Standards (NBPTS). (1991). *Toward high and rigorous standards for the teaching profession* (2nd ed.). Detroit, MI: Author.

National Board for Professional Teaching Standards (NBPTS). (1993). *Preparing for our future: 1992 annual report.* Detroit, MI: Author.

National Center for Improving Science Education (NCISE). (1991). *The high stakes of high school science.* Washington, DC: Author.

National Center for Improving Science Education (NCISE). (1992). *Building scientific literacy: A blueprint for science in the middle grades.* Washington, DC: Author.

National Center for Improving Science Education (NCISE). (n.d.). *About the National Center for Improving Science Education.* Andover, MA: The Network, Inc.

The National Center for Science Teaching and Learning. (1993). CSERP: The first year and beyond. *COGNOSOS, 2*(1), 2.

National Commission on Excellence in Education. (1983). *A nation at risk: The imperative for educational reform.* Washington, DC: U.S. Government Printing Office.

National Committee on Science Education Standards and Assessment (NCSESA). (1993). *National science education standards: An enhanced sampler.* Washington, DC: National Research Council.

National Committee on Science Education Standards and Assessment, (NCSESA). (July 1, 1994). *National science education standards: Discussion summary.* Washington, DC: National Research Council.

National Goals Panel Report. (1991). *Building a nation of learners.* Washington, DC: Author.

National Research Council (NRC). (1990). *Fulfilling the promise: Biology education in the nation's schools.* Washington, DC: National Academy Press.

National Science Foundation. (1993). *Guide to programs.* Washington, DC: Author.

National Science Teaching Association (NSTA). (1992a). *The scope, sequence, and coordination of secondary school science, Vol. I: The content core.* Washington, DC: Author.

National Science Teaching Association (NSTA). (1992b). *The scope, sequence, and coordination of secondary school science, Vol. II: Relevant research.* Washington, DC: Author.

Nichols, B. K., French, D., Wiggins, J. R., & Calvert, R. B. (1993). The teacher support team approach to induction. In A. Gallard (Ed.), *Abstracts of papers presented at the NARST annual meeting* (p. 20). Manhattan, KS: National Association for Research in Science Teaching.

Neuman, D. B. (1993). *Experiencing elementary science.* Belmont, CA: Wadsworth Publishing.

Nussbaum, J., & Sharoni-Dagan, N. (1983). Changes in second grade children's preconceptions about the earth as a cosmic body resulting from a short series of audio-tutorial lessons. *Science Education, 67*(1), 99–114.

Oakes, J. (1990). *Lost talent: The underparticipation of women, minorities, and disabled persons in science.* Santa Monica, CA: Rand Corporation.

O'Brien, T. (1992). Science inservice workshops that work for elementary teachers. *School Science and Mathematics, 92*(8), 422–426.

Osborne, R. Y., & Cosgrove, M. M. (1983). Children's conceptions of the changes of state of water. *Journal of Research in Science Teaching, 20*(9), 825–838.

Osborne, R., & Wittrock, M. C. (1983). Learning science: A generative process. *Science Education, 67,* 489–508.

Pearsall, M. K. (1992). *Scope, sequence and coordination of secondary school science, Vol. II: Relevant research.* Washington, DC: National Science Teachers Association.

Pugh, S. (1990). Introducing multicultural science teaching to a secondary school. *Secondary Science Review, 71*(256), 131–135.

Raizen, S. A. (1992). Larger U.S. role in math, science. In *Forum for applied research and public policy: Math and science education* (pp. 5–14). Knoxville: The University of Tennessee.

Raizen, S. A., Baron, J. B., Champagne, A. B., Haertel, Emullis, I., & Oakes, J. (1989). *Assessment in elementary school science education.* Washington, DC: National Center for the Improvement of Science Education.

Raizen, S. A., & Michelsohn, A. M. (Eds.). (1994). *The future of science in elementary schools: Educating prospective teachers.* San Francisco: Jossey-Bass.

Resnick, L. (1987). *Education and learning to think.* Washington, DC: National Academy Press.

Ross, J. A. (1990). Student achievement effects of the key teacher method of delivering in-service. *Science Education, 74*(5), 507–516.

Rosser, S. (1990). *Female-friendly science.* New York: Pergamon Press.

Roth, K. (1985). *Food for plants: Teacher's guide.* East Lansing: Michigan State University. (ERIC Document Reproduction Service No. ED 256 624)

Rowland, P., & Stuessy, C. L. (1990, March). The effectiveness of mentor teachers providing basic science process skills in-service workshops. *School Science and Mathematics, 90*(3), 223–231.

Roychoudhury, A., & Roth, W. (1992). Student involvement in learning: Collaboration in science for preservice elementary teachers. *Journal of Science Teacher Education, 3*(2), 47–52.

Roychoudhury, A., Roth, W., & Ebbing, J. (1993). Becoming a reflective science teacher: An exemplary endeavor by a preservice elementary teacher. In P. Rubba, L. Campbell, & T. Dana (Eds.), *Excellence in educating teachers of science.* Auburn, AL: Association for the Education of Teachers in Science.

Rubba, P. (1992). The learning cycle as a model for the design of science teacher preservice and inservice education. *Journal of Science Teacher Education, 3*(4), 97–101.

Russell, T., Harlen, W., & Watt, D. (1989). Children's ideas, about evaporation. *International Journal of Science Education, 11*(5), 568–578.

Rutherford, J. F., & Ahlgren, A. (1989). *Science for all Americans.* Washington, DC: American Association for the Advancement of Science.

Scantlebury, K., & Baker, D. (1992). *Achieving a gender equitable classroom.* In F. Lawrenz, K. Cochran, J. Krajcik, & P. Simpson (Eds.), *Research matters . . . to the science teacher.* Manhattan, KS: National Association for Research in Science Teaching.

The Secretary's Commission on Achieving Necessary Skills. (1991). *What work requires of school: A SCANS report for America 2000.* Washington, DC: U.S. Department of Labor.

Shrigley, R. L., Koballa, T. R., & Simpson, R. D. (1988). Defining attitude for science educators. *Journal of Research in Science Teaching, 25*(8), 659–678.

Shulman, L. S. (1987). Knowledge and teaching: Foundations of the new reform. *Harvard Educational Review, 57*(1), 1–22.

Shymansky, J. A., Hedges, L. V., & Woodworth, G. (1990). A reassessment of the effects of inquiry-based science curricula of the 60's on student performance. *Journal of Research in Science Teaching, 27*(2), 124–144.

Shymansky, J. A., Yore, L. D., & Good, R. (1991). Elementary school teachers belief about and perceptions of elementary school science reading, science textbooks, and supportive instructional factors. *Journal of Research in Science Teaching, 28*(5), 437–454.

Simmons, P. (1991). Learning science in software microworlds. In S. Glynn, R. Yeany, & B. Britton (Eds.), *Psychology of learning science.* Hillsdale, NJ: Lawrence Erlbaum Associates.

Simpson, R. D., & Anderson, N. D. (1981). *Science, students, and school: A guide for the middle and secondary school teacher.* New York: John Wiley & Sons.

Slavin, R. E., & Karweit, N. L. (1981). Cognitive and affective outcomes of an intensive student team learning experience. *Journal of Experimental Education, 50*(1), 29–35.

Stefanich, G. P., & Kelsey, K. W. (1989). Improving science attitudes of preservice elementary teachers. *Science Education, 73,* 187–194.

Tamir, P., Gal-Choppin, R., & Nussinovitz, R. (1981). How do intermediate and junior high school students conceptualize living and nonliving? *Journal of Research in Science Teaching, 18*(3), 241–248.

Tobias, S. (1992). *Revitalizing undergraduate science: Why some things work and most things don't.* Tucson, AZ: Research Corporation.

Tobin, K. (1990). *Metaphors and images in teaching: What research says to the science and mathematics teacher.* (Number 5). Perth, Australia: Curtin University of Technology.

Tobin, K., & Tippins, D. (1993). Constructivism as a referent for teaching and learning. In K. Tobin (Ed.), *The practice of constructivism in science education.* Washington, DC: AAAS.

Tolman, M. N., & Campbell, M. K. (1991). Science preparation requirements of elementary school teachers in the United States. *Journal of Science Teacher Education, 2*(3), 72–76.

Triangle Coalition for Science and Technology Education. (1991). *A guide for building an alliance for science, mathematics and technology education.* College Park, MD: Author.

Trumbull, D. J., & Kerr, P. (1989, March 30–April 1). *University researchers inchoate critique of science teaching: A case for the study of education.* Paper presented at the annual meeting of the National Association for Research in Science Teaching. San Francisco. (ERIC Document Reproduction Service No. ED 306117)

Trumbull, D. J., & Slack, M. J. (1991). Learning to ask, listen, and analyze: Using structured interviewing assignments to develop reflection in preservice science teachers. *International Journal of Science Education, 13*(2), 129–142.

Vivio, F. M., & Stevenson, W. L. (1992). *U.S. Department of Energy teacher research associates program: Profile and survey of 1990–1991 participants.* Oak Ridge, TN: Oak Ridge Institute for Science and Education.

von Glasersfeld, E. (1992). Questions and answers about radical constructivism. In M. Pearsall (Ed.), *Scope, sequence, and coordination of secondary school science, Vol. II: Relevant research.* Washington, DC: National Science Teachers Association.

White, A., & Klapper, M. (1991). Greetings from the directors. *Cognosos 1*(1), 1.

Wier, E. A. (April, 1988). *Breaking down barriers to teaching primary science: Did a summer science institute help?* Paper presented at the annual meeting of the National Association for Research in Science Teaching, Lake of the Ozarks, MO. (ERIC Document Reproduction Service No. ED 292 619)

Yager, R. E. (1983). The importance of terminology in teaching K–12 science. *Journal of Research in Science Teaching, 20*(6), 577–588.

Yager, R. E. (1991). Science teacher education in four-year colleges 1960–1985. *Journal of Science Teacher Education, 2*(1), 9–15.

Yeany, R. H. (1991). Teacher knowledge bases: What are they? How do we affect them? In P. Prather (Ed.), *Effective interaction of science teachers, researchers, and teacher educators* (p. 2). Charlottesville, VA: Southeastern Association for the Education of Teachers in Science.

Yore, L. D. (1991). Secondary science teachers' attitudes toward and beliefs about science reading and science textbooks. *Journal of Research in Science Teaching, 28*(1), 55–72.

·23·

THE PROFESSIONAL DEVELOPMENT OF SOCIAL STUDIES EDUCATORS

Beverly J. Armento

GEORGIA STATE UNIVERSITY

"All of schooling is actually 'teacher education,' a paideia socializing teachers in how to teach and what to learn" (Shor, 1986, p. 416).

Just how is it that social studies teachers are "socialized" over the lifetime of their school careers and over the lifetime of their professional careers to know *what and how to learn* and *what and how to teach?* How is one's precollege social studies experience translated into belief and behavior systems that define one's social studies classroom? If the dominant view of precollege social studies (Armento, 1986, 1993; Brophy, 1993) is correct, and if most students see social studies as factual, unidimensional, boring, and unimportant, then is that also the message believed by prospective social studies teachers? If so, what are the effects of teacher education programs on beliefs, knowledge, and pedagogy?

What is the status of current teacher education efforts in social studies? What is the status of *research* on the education of social studies teachers? What insights might be drawn from the research in the field to inform program improvement and future inquiry? The overall aim of this chapter is to provide a synthesis of the theoretical and empirical work in this domain since the mid-1980s and to propose tentative answers to such questions.

This task, however, is complicated by at least three major factors: (1) a lack of consensus and clarity about the goals of social studies and, thus, by implication, the goals for teacher preparation in social studies; (2) a general level of discontent with the status quo of social studies education at precollege levels as well as in teacher preparation programs; and (3) serious weaknesses in the empirical and conceptual base underlying the professional education of social studies teachers. A brief discussion of these three factors provides some of the necessary context for this chapter.

Any critique of the research or the practice of a field should be grounded in a conception of the "subject's proper aims" (Thornton, 1994, p. 223). Throughout the history of social studies education, though, conflict has characterized discussions of these aims (Armento, 1993; Fullinwider, 1991; Hertzberg, 1981; Thornton, 1994); even today, with the talk of reform and the publication of numerous national reports, the social studies professional community has yet to rally around a consensus view of the field. Beyond the general agreement that social studies aims to nurture citizens for a democratic society (Barr, Barth, & Shermis, 1978; Engle & Ochoa, 1988), educators disagree on the particular ways in which this might happen, on the definition of citizenship, and even on whether the notion of citizenship ought to guide the field (Leming, 1991, 1992; Marker & Mehlinger, 1992). For example, some argue (Marker & Mehlinger, 1992) that because citizenship defines the broad goal of all schooling, it is difficult to distinguish the particular contribution and responsibility of the social studies curriculum.

Some of the disagreement in the field is reflected in recent national reports on social studies. The Bradley Commission on

The author wishes to thank Dr. Lee Ehman, Indiana University, and Dr. Jean Luckowski, The University of Montana, for their insightful comments and critique.

485

History in the Schools (1989) proposed that history should be the conceptual center of the social studies curriculum; *Charting a Course,* the report of the Curriculum Task Force of the National Commission on Social Studies in Schools (1989) emphasized that the disciplines of history and geography should be at the heart of school studies; and the National Education Goals Panel (1991; adapted in 1994) specified in the Educate America Act, Goal Three, that "By the year 2000, United States students will leave grades 4, 8, and 12 having demonstrated competency over challenging subject matter including . . . civics and government, economics, . . . history, and geography." National curriculum standards are currently being completed for each of these four disciplinary areas as well as for social studies; whether these five independently developed sets of standards will add clarity to the field is yet to be seen.

Some social studies educators, though, argue that the lack of consensus reflects the dynamic and controversial nature of the knowledge that constitutes the field. For example, constructivist and interpretive views of history and the social sciences promote the notion of multiple perspectives and ongoing inquiry rather than a static, factual version of the past. Others respond that philosophical positions on the nature of knowledge are exactly the sort of principles that should constitute a statement of the nature and goals of the field.

If there were more consensus on social studies goals, it would be appropriate to assess teacher preparation programs on their ability to develop educators who could facilitate the attainment of such aims. Also, it would be appropriate to critique research on teacher preparation programs on its ability to address the critical goals of the field. For the purposes of this chapter, however, the confusion and discord over goals becomes an important element of the context in which the research is examined.

There is a long history of discontent with the quality and power of social studies programs in schools (Adler, 1991; Armento, 1986, 1991, 1993; Marker & Mehlinger, 1992; Stodolsky, Salk, & Glaessner, 1991; Thornton, 1994) and with the ability of formal social studies teacher preparation programs to influence meaningful change in teachers, schools, and the social studies curriculum (Adler, 1991; Banks & Parker, 1990). Such discontent, couched in an era of teacher education reform (Goodlad, 1990; Goodlad, Soder, & Sirotnik, 1990; Russell & Morrow, 1986), might predict a tendency toward greater attention to research on teacher preparation programs and more efforts toward "research as praxis" (Lather, 1986) as social studies researchers collaborate with precollege educators to improve teaching and learning at all levels. To investigate the parameters and possible trends of current research, the author searched major social studies and educational research publications, including journals, books, and dissertations published mainly since the mid-1980s.

The two most comprehensive and current syntheses of the research on the education of social studies teachers are those by Banks and Parker (1990) in the *Handbook of Research on Teacher Education* and by Adler (1991) in the *Handbook of Research on Social Studies Teaching and Learning.* Adler (1991) found it difficult to generalize about effective practices in the preparation of social studies teachers given the noncumulative and particularistic nature of the research she reviewed.

She found much of the work to be descriptive or quasiexperimental, with insufficient attention paid to the complexities of teacher preparation. Banks and Parker (1990) also found a paucity of research on the education of social studies teachers and concluded that most of the work reflected an emphasis on pedagogy rather than on content or other aspects of curriculum and instruction. In addition, Banks and Parker suggested that the research questions asked often reflected an attitude that teachers should learn the knowledge, skills, values, and perspectives needed to survive in schools as they are currently structured. That is, the research reflected status quo values rather than critical perspectives necessary to reform schools and social studies education. In other words, a critical vision of social studies teacher education was missing from the research Banks and Parker reviewed.

It is interesting to note that out of Adler's (1991) 92 references and Banks and Parker's (1990) 116 references, only 18 citations are common to both chapters, even though these were written in the same general time period and each search extended over the previous decade (see Table 23.1). Of the 18 common citations, six of these are research studies and another six are summaries of research. Comparing the Adler (1991) and the Banks and Parker (1990) chapters and this chapter, only six references were cited by all the chapter authors. The caution for the reader is that even handbook writers apply subjective judgment to the commissions and omissions of data selection as well as to the interpretation of what they have chosen to examine. Although many of the conclusions may be common across these three chapters, the data examined differ, and undoubtedly the criteria for selection of the data differ.

Following an extensive search for the theoretical and empirical work conducted mainly within the last decade on social studies teacher education, the following six major categories emerged.

1. What is known about social studies teacher educators, prospective social studies teachers, and social studies teacher education programs?
2. What is known about prospective teachers' *beliefs* about social studies education? What effects do teacher education programs have on beliefs?
3. What is known about prospective social studies teachers' content knowledge? What effects do teacher preparation programs have on *content knowledge?*

TABLE 23.1. Frequency of References Cited in Three Chapters on Social Studies Teacher Preparation

Author(s)	Total References	References in Common	
		Armento	Banks and Parker
Adler (1991)	92	8	18
Armento (1996)	129	—	—
Banks and Parker (1990)	116	13	—
Adler/Banks and Parker	—	6[a]	—

[a] Six common citations included five empirical studies (Adler, 1984; Goodman & Adler, 1985; Kickbusch, 1987; Parker, 1987; Shermis & Washburn, 1986) and one research synthesis (Lanier & Little, 1986).

4. What is known about prospective social studies teachers' dispositions toward *reflection and thoughtfulness?* What effects do teacher education programs have on such dispositions?
5. What is known about prospective social studies teachers' knowledge and beliefs on *cultural diversity?* What effects do teacher education programs have on such knowledge and beliefs?
6. What is know about the social studies student teaching experience?

This chapter (1) synthesizes the research that addresses the six questions listed earlier and provides specific recommendations for each category of research, (2) proposes a comprehensive conceptual model representing key variables in the professional development of social studies educators, and (3) proposes central issues and needed research in the development of social studies educators.

RESEARCH ON SOCIAL STUDIES PREPARATION PROGRAMS AND ON PROSPECTIVE SOCIAL STUDIES TEACHERS

What do we know about social studies preparation programs? What is known about the demographic, attitudinal, and life history characteristics of social studies teacher educators and prospective social studies teachers? Leming (1992) believes that an "ideological chasm" (p. 293) separates social studies teacher educators and classroom teachers of social studies, with the college professors holding more "leftist" political orientations and greater allegiance to "citizenship" goals than the general population of social studies classroom teachers. Classroom social studies teachers tend to respond to ideological questions in a moderate (57%) to conservative (28%) manner, more like the majority of classroom teachers than like social studies teacher educators at colleges and universities who tend to be more liberal and who often hold critical or radical reform agendas (Leming, 1991).

Leming's surveys of teacher educators drew on members of the major professional association, the National Council for the Social Studies; however, in Stepanske's (1987) study, the majority of those who identified themselves as social studies teacher educators did not belong to the National Council for the Social Studies. In addition, in Shermis and Washburn's (1986) survey of 25 social studies college professors, most had no or little graduate work in the social sciences, even though all taught social studies methods classes and identified themselves as social studies educators. These teacher educators' perceptions of their students (prospective social studies teachers) were that they tend to be "mediocre, somewhat deficient, and rather ordinary" (Shermis & Washburn, 1986, p. 336); however, the college professors had more positive words for classroom teachers, claiming that social studies textbooks were the "major culprit" (p. 336) behind weak social studies instruction. Although Shermis and Washburn categorized the professors in their sample as "somewhat liberal, egalitarian, and committed to values of cultural pluralism," they also described these teacher educa-

tors as "white, male, Christian, middle-aged, mid-western" and not apt to critically question institutional structures or to raise social issues.

A more positive picture of both social studies teacher educators and classroom teachers emerges from the Brophy, Prawat, and McMahon (1991) intensive qualitative study of three nationally recognized social studies teacher educators and three outstanding elementary social studies classroom teachers. Brophy et al. found many areas of agreement on the goals and nature of social studies education among the six social studies educators in this study. The disagreements reflected minor points. In general, the classroom teachers tended to be more student oriented and more focused on learning activities, and the professors were more subject-matter oriented and more critical of social studies textbooks and curriculum than were the classroom teachers. The authors suggested that the goals of social studies would be served better if both sides developed more empathy for the concerns of the other.

A great deal of the social studies literature stresses the lack of apparent consensus on the goals of the field; however, Martorella's (1991) study of 11 social studies teacher educators points up the value of using Delphi techniques to achieve agreement on goals and major problems in the field. Martorella found that the teacher educators in his sample agreed that the goals of social studies are to develop citizens who can participate in a democratic political system; foster knowledge of facts, concepts, and generalizations from the social sciences and history; promote critical thinking and problem-solving skills; foster attitudes that are open-minded, objective, and nondogmatic; teach students to function efficaciously in the political, economic, and social environment; promote democratic beliefs and values; and provide students with a sense of orientation toward the future. The teacher educators in this study also thought that two of the major problems facing the field were the need to improve the ways teachers teach and to improve teacher education.

Just what content and experiences are included in social studies teacher education programs? How are social studies methods courses taught? What are the expectations for student teaching? What types of university–school collaborations exist for teacher education programs in social studies? Scant evidence exists to answer any of these questions.

Although some social studies educators (Bruce, Podenski, & Anderson, 1991; Butts, 1993; Gilliom & Hart, 1990; Kickbusch, 1987) urge that civic and global perspectives be integrated throughout entire teacher education programs, the only major, systematic, and coherent studies describing exemplary teacher education programs committed to global education are those conducted by Merryfield (1991, 1992). Using a reputational survey to identify teacher education programs that prepare secondary social studies teachers to teach with a global perspective, Merryfield identified 88 programs. She described 32 programs in some detail, and six exemplary teacher education programs were eventually identified for in-depth examination. Merryfield (1992) found consensus across these six programs on their goals—teachers must have knowledge and appreciation of cultural differences and similarities within the United States and around the world; knowledge of the world as an interdependent system; and understanding of contemporary global issues, conflicts, and change.

In addition, the six exemplary programs are sophisticated, well articulated, and well networked with local schools, state departments of education, and professional associations. All have extensive preservice as well as in-service programs, and most have external as well as internal funding. Merryfield identified four factors associated with the perceived effectiveness of these programs: (1) scope of program offerings and ongoing support to graduates is extensive and reliable; (2) collaboration and communication with other organizations and institutions is ongoing and leads to program change; (3) program leadership is stable, creative, enthusiastic, and committed; and (4) opportunities exist for professional growth and leadership for teachers and school administrators.

From the larger sample of global awareness teacher education programs, Merryfield (1991) suggested areas that need strengthening. Among these is the fact that little attention is given to the integration of global knowledge into required high school courses, such as U.S. and world history classes. Thus, prospective teachers are challenged to apply their content knowledge to new, broader contexts, left unpracticed in the teacher preparation program. In addition, the ongoing professional development of social studies teachers is often "stopgap" at best, consisting of short workshops on selected global topics. Such an approach usually highlights "hot" topics or areas of the world in the news, but falls short of addressing a comprehensive approach to global education.

Aside from Merryfield's descriptive research on social studies teacher preparation programs devoted to global education, very little is known about the goals, nature, and form of social studies teacher preparation programs. In virtually every state, a social studies methods course, student teaching, and content courses in history/social sciences are required for secondary school certification; beyond that, teacher education programs vary in the extent and nature of coursework and teaching internships required. Very little is known about these essential program components: What is taught? by whom? in what manner? toward what goals? in collaboration with whom? Furthermore, What is learned by prospective social studies seachers? What exactly do secondary, middle, and elementary school social studies teachers "get" in their history/social science classes or in their methods classes?

What is needed is a more comprehensive examination of the "status quo" in teacher education programs in social studies. Just what is happening within these programs? What conceptions of social studies are dominant, and how are social studies teachers being prepared? Descriptive studies and intensive case studies on social studies teacher preparation programs, on the social studies methods class, and on university–school collaboration would help to address the gaps in current knowledge and bring to light a deeper, richer understanding of the nature and quality of current social studies teacher education programs. In addition, greater insight on social studies teacher educators would be helpful. Baseline demographic data, beliefs about social studies and teacher preparation, and basic knowledge of the field could be obtained from surveys sent to a random sample of social studies teacher educators at large and small colleges, public and private institutions, and urban and suburban campuses. At present, very little is known about who is preparing social studies teachers, and even less is known about the substance and form of preparation programs.

Research on Prospective Social Studies Teachers' Beliefs

What beliefs, conceptions, misconceptions, and expectations do prospective and novice teachers have about social studies education? What do they think the goals of social studies are and ought to be? How are these beliefs changed during and after the teacher preparation program?

"Social studies researchers give an inordinate amount of attention to the purpose of social studies" (Marker & Mehlinger, 1992, p. 845). Indeed, this is one of the most heavily researched areas in social studies teacher education: "What do people believe social studies is?" Some researchers (Malone, 1991) have developed courses to influence prospective teachers' beliefs about social studies. Others (Brousseau, Book, & Byers, 1988; Brown, 1988; Cornett, 1987, 1990; Johnston, 1990; Kagan, 1992a; McCutcheon, 1981; Nelson & Drake, 1994; Parker, 1984, 1986, 1987; Parker & Gehrke, 1986; Passe, 1988; Ross, 1987; Sanders & McCutcheon, 1986; Smith, 1983) have examined the influence of school culture on prospective teachers' beliefs and on their curricular decisions in social studies. Still others (Adler, 1984; Angell, 1991; Bennett & Spalding, 1992; Goodman & Adler, 1985; Kickbusch, 1985; Powell, 1991) have examined the substance of prospective teachers' beliefs about the goals of social studies and the meanings they attach to social studies education.

Most of the contemporary research on teacher beliefs about social studies are qualitative studies of a small number of prospective teachers, and in some cases, the study extends over a substantial period of time. For example, Goodman and Adler (1985) followed 16 elementary prospective social studies teachers, observing and interviewing them over the entire year. Powell's (1991) examination of the beliefs and knowledge acquisition schemata of 16 graduate level initial certification teachers was illuminated by having the prospective teachers develop concept maps of their belief/knowledge changes over the course of the 12-month program. In addition, videotapes of lessons and other artifacts were analyzed for changes in vocabulary, concepts, and conceptions of teaching. Bennett and Spalding's (1992) studies of preservice teachers (68 in entire sample; intensive case studies on 7) also used a range of qualitative techniques: autobiographic interviews, concept mapping, stimulated recall interviews, classroom observations, and follow-up interviews to capture preservice teachers' perspectives on teaching and on social studies.

Interestingly, most of these researchers reported that teachers' beliefs and perspectives on social studies, and on teaching in general, remain relatively stable over time, demonstrating little change over the course of the entire teacher preparation program. The range of perspectives about social studies is broad and includes ideas such as social studies as a nonsubject, as citizenship indoctrination, as school knowledge, and as education for social action (Goodman & Adler, 1985). Some of these patterns are reminiscent of Barr, Barth, and Shermis's (1978) classic definition of the field as citizenship transmission, social science education, or reflective inquiry. Goodman and Adler (1985) suggested that such belief systems are a function of the prospective teachers' childhood conceptions of social studies, the influence of significant individuals such as cooperating teachers and university faculty, and institutional expectations found in the practicum sites as well as social forces outside the classroom such as the demand for higher reading performance. Bennett and Spalding (1992) proposed that teachers' perspectives serve as filters, screening incoming information and selecting ideas that harmonize with prior thoughts; therefore, any attempt to change teachers' perspectives must be "nurtured with negotiation and dialogue" (p. 265).

Angell's (1991) intensive examination of three preservice teachers' beliefs about social studies went a much needed step beyond most of the work on teacher perspectives by hypothesizing an explanatory way of conceptualizing changes in belief structures. Drawing on the theoretical work of von Glaserfeld (1987) and Vosniadou and Brewer (1987), Angell posited a controlled receptivity model of equilibration, suggesting that an individual's belief system has barriers that selectively interpret incoming stimuli for their relevance and compatibility. Information that fits these criteria is easily assimilated; however, if the incoming stimuli are thought to be irrelevant or incompatible with prior beliefs, the information is disregarded, unless it carries the force of *overlap* or *intensity*. Intense information may result in cognitive dissonance, precipitating accommodation, reorganization, or revision of the belief system. One's degree of "willingness to change" acts as a conscious determinant of receptivity and mediates the belief restructuring process.

Such theorizing adds a central and pivotal component to the research on teacher beliefs. Angell's research is an important example of how the level of sophistication can be enhanced in this line of inquiry, of how theoretical constructs can be applied to patterns observable in qualitative inquiry, and of how teacher educators might structure experiences aimed at influencing teacher beliefs about social studies. After all, the teacher preparation program is a "treatment" of sorts, the effects of which can be measured. How might the program be structured to influence maximally prospective teachers' beliefs about social studies and teaching and learning? Angell's work provides some of the necessary clues. It would be helpful for some researchers with "highly successful" programs to investigate the effects on prospective teachers' beliefs over time. In addition, larger samples would add to the reliability and credibility of research on teacher beliefs.

The research on teachers' beliefs about social studies could be advanced even further by greater attention to the social and psychological processes (Kagan, 1992a) that mediate change in conceptual and value structures and by research that explores attempts actually to restructure teacher beliefs. However, such experimental work can only proceed if there is a clear vision of what teachers ought to believe about social studies and about teaching and learning social studies. Without such a vision guiding social studies teacher education programs, prospective teachers will simply create their own versions of the field.

Research on Prospective Social Studies Teachers' Content Knowledge

What content knowledge (and pedagogical content knowledge) of the social studies curriculum do prospective teachers have? How is this knowledge organized, and what beliefs about the nature of knowledge do they hold? How do the content knowledge and the accompanying beliefs change as a function of the social studies preparation program?

Most of the contemporary research addressing these questions employs Shulman's (1987) construct of pedagogical content knowledge or that special blend of methodology with domain-specific knowledge. Most of this research is qualitative, and the focus is usually on small numbers of prospective or novice teachers. In addition, most of the research has been conducted on secondary school teachers' knowledge of history (Brophy, 1992, 1993; Downey & Levstik, 1988; Evans, 1988; Grossman, Wilson, & Shulman, 1989; Gudmundsdottir, 1990, 1991a, 1991b; McEwan & Bull, 1991; Thornton, 1988, 1991; Wilson, 1991; Wilson & Wineberg, 1988, 1993; Wineberg & Wilson, 1991). The current research emphasis has been to obtain a qualitative "deep look" at the nature of teachers' domain-specific knowledge in social studies. There is very little experimental research in which an effort is made to influence teacher knowledge or beliefs about knowledge. Even in the studies where the teacher education program is clearly "an intervention," very little attention is given to possible influences of the program on teacher content knowledge.

There is little doubt that one's conception about knowledge and the actual domain-specific knowledge (both substantive and syntactic) that one possesses is important. Teachers' conceptions of history influence their plans for teaching (Wilson & Wineberg, 1988), and a good deal of congruence exists between one's classroom instruction and one's orientation to the subject matter (Gudmundsdottir, 1991b). One's orientation to and knowledge of the subject matter influences one's choice of pedagogy as well as one's perceptions of students' instructional needs (Gudmundsdottir, 1991a). In addition, if teaching is to be more than the now-dominant lecture mode, secondary social studies teachers must be able to create learning situations in which students actively construct ideas (Armento, 1986; Torney-Purta, 1991; Wittrock, 1986), build concepts, see relationships, get excited about social ideas and issues (Tobias, 1994), and understand how historical and social science knowledge are created.

To do that, teachers must understand the relevant knowledge well enough (Alexander & Judy, 1988) to flexibly create multiple representations of ideas that bridge the gap between what students know and what is to be learned (Wilson, Shulman, & Richert, 1987; Wilson & Wineberg, 1993); this process includes creating examples, visual organizers, and mental schemata. In addition, content knowledge allows teachers to generate the questions and tasks necessary to illuminate major ideas, points, and issues (McDiarmid, Ball, & Anderson, 1989). It is interesting to note, though, that in a survey of 138 secondary social studies teachers and 96 secondary principals, Russell and Morrow (1986) found that "knowledge of subject matter" ranked last out of a listing of the 10 most common instructional problems for teachers. Teachers in this study said their most pressing concerns were student motivation, providing for individual differences, classroom discipline, and evaluation of students.

Research on social science problem-solving skills (Voss, Greene, Post, & Penner, 1984; Voss, Tyler, & Yengo, 1983) illuminates the critical role of domain-specific knowledge in higher order thinking. Those who know more, who have better organized categories of knowledge, who are able to see relationships between and among ideas, who understand the causal-relational-hierarchical patterns among ideas, who understand how knowledge is created, and who are able to generate viable alternatives and identify subproblems are better able to address social science problems and issues thoughtfully.

Prospective social studies teachers appear to vary widely in their perceptions of historical knowledge, in their actual content knowledge of history, and in their ability to generate instructional representations of subject matter. For example, prospective teacher Fred thinks that "history is the basic facts of what happened" (Grossman, Wilson, & Shulman, 1989); David sees his history text as a dictionary; and Harry sees the textbook as "bad history" (Gudmundsdottir, 1991a).

The four prospective secondary social studies teachers studied by Wilson and Wineberg (1988) differed along dimensions important to the teaching of history: the role of factual knowledge, the place and meaning of interpretation, the significance of chronology and continuity, and the meaning of causation. Evans (1988) found distinct differences in three prospective secondary U.S. history teachers. Not only did each prospective teacher have a different valuation of history, but they almost became "preachers" in the classroom, each "pushing" a particular point of view (p. 210). David and Harry (Gudmundsdottir, 1991a) illustrate the idea that what a teacher selects to stress, omit, or include is really a matter of the values and beliefs the teacher holds about what is important. What the teacher believes serves as a screen to filter curricular choices and instructional actions.

Of course one of the critical issues in this line of inquiry is the accurate and meaningful assessment of teacher knowledge. The difficulties and ethical dilemmas raised are illuminated in recent efforts to create performance-based assessments for mature teachers (Wilson & Wineberg, 1993). Through the Stanford University Teacher Assessment Project, secondary U.S. history teachers were asked to evaluate student essays, analyze a textbook selection, and plan for the use of documentary materials in an instructional activity. Two of the participating teachers demonstrated different subject-matter knowledge, different conceptions of their roles and responsibilities, and different views of student ability and motivation. The dilemma, once again, is which of these competing views is "better"? This question pertains to the study of preservice teachers' perceptions of knowledge and their ways of representing knowledge. Social studies teacher educators and researchers must "take a stand" or at least must clarify what it is that novice teachers need to know about the subject matter in the field if inquiry and teacher education practice are to progress.

Wilson (1991) proposed that because future social studies teachers have few models of good history teaching throughout their high school and college careers, that historians and social studies teacher educators must work together to strengthen the intellectual content and coursework for prospective teachers. Wilson called for an end to the unproductive arguments in the field regarding the role of knowledge in social studies education, suggesting that educators agree at least that an image of good teaching is grounded in subject matter and that effective teachers use knowledge of history to further other goals, such as critical thinking and perspective-taking dispositions and skills.

Many questions remain on the issue of teachers' awareness and understanding of social studies content knowledge and pedagogy. There is very little inquiry into elementary/middle school teachers' knowledge of content, very little work outside of teachers' understanding of historical knowledge, and very little work that goes beyond Shulman's concept of content knowledge. Sockett (1987) argued that Shulman's concept of pedagogical content knowledge tends to ignore the broader social context in which knowledge is generated and the socio-moral context in which teaching and learning knowledge are created. This is a particularly relevant concern for social knowledge, which is constructive, interpretive, multidimensional, and embedded with ethical issues, and it has the capacity to enlighten and empower learners. Little is known about how "expert" social studies teacher educators represent social knowledge and how effective prospective teachers make sense of and represent domain-specific knowledge in different school settings.

The research on teacher knowledge provides little insight into teacher preparation programs or on any of the program elements, such as the social studies methods class, arts and sciences course, and the teaching practicum in which one's pedagogical content knowledge may be influenced, developed, and altered. How do effective teacher preparation programs create teaching-learning situations for prospective teachers in which they come to better understand the nature of knowing social knowledge? There are very important research questions that demand investigation and attention. Collaborative research projects linking history, geography, political science, and social studies researchers could develop powerful courses for prospective teachers and examine the effects on content knowledge and epistemological beliefs.

Research on Prospective Social Studies Teachers' Dispositions Toward Reflection and Thoughtfulness

What inquiry dispositions (thoughtfulness, reflection, criticism, openness to new ideas, and so forth) do prospective social studies teachers profess and practice? How are these dispositions applied to one's own learning and to the work one does in the teacher preparation program? How are these dispositions refined and altered throughout the program? How do prospective and novice social studies teachers apply dispositions of thoughtfulness in their teaching with children?

The four prospective social studies teachers in Adler's (1984) study "talked one story and acted another" when it came to their beliefs and actions toward thinking skills, inquiry, and decision making in the classroom. Perhaps a little insight into this phenomena can be drawn from the rather extensive surveys Jantz, Weaver, Cirrincione, and Farrell

(1985), and Weaver, Jantz, Farrell, and Cirrincione (1985) conducted with more than 400 classroom teachers and 197 college and university members of the National Council for the Social Studies on the issue of inquiry in social studies classrooms. Most of the classroom teachers in the survey were secondary educators (60%), 20% were middle school teachers, and 4% taught in elementary schools; the rest were secondary department chairs. Most of the respondents (college and classroom teachers) said that inquiry was not widely implemented by the general population of social studies teachers and, in part, blamed this on the "back-to-basics" movement. Both groups claimed that appropriate instructional materials were limited, and they were concerned about the ability and preparation of children to use inquiry techniques and skills. The classroom teachers claimed that their teacher preparation programs failed to teach them how to use inquiry techniques and that their methods' professors were more theoretical than practical in their attention to inquiry.

Conceptual work on teacher competence (Stanley, 1991) and the theoretical and empirical work on teacher and student thoughtfulness (King, 1991; Newmann, 1990, 1991, 1992; Onosko, 1991) provide frameworks for goal setting for social studies programs and for future research on teachers' development of thoughtfulness dispositions. Going beyond the teacher effectiveness and pedagogical content knowledge views of competence, Stanley (1991) proposed "critical thinking and critical pedagogy" as views of competence or teaching for critical thought and action. In other words, the competent teacher should demonstrate the capacity to think critically and have the ability to help students acquire this competence. In addition, the competent teacher would employ empowering pedagogy that enables students to question critically social reality.

Newmann (1991) proposed that social studies (and, by implication, social studies teacher preparation programs) should be grounded in a conception of higher order thinking or in the expanded use of one's mind. This occurs as a person interprets, analyzes, or manipulates information to answer a question or solve a problem that cannot be answered through routine application of previously learned knowledge. Teacher educators and researchers could benefit from the application of Newmann's indicators of classroom thoughtfulness and his characteristics of a thoughtful teacher and student to aid in their reflection on the goals of teacher education programs and the foci of research on prospective teachers' beliefs, knowledge, and skills. Among other things, the thoughtful social studies teacher asks challenging questions, carefully considers explanations and reasons, encourages students to generate original explanations and solutions, understands the nature and sources of knowledge, incorporates students' personal experiences into lessons, employs Socratic techniques, and is a model of thoughtfulness (Newmann, 1990).

How do these dispositions interact with a prospective teacher's content knowledge? Are social studies methods classes examples of reflection and thoughtfulness? How can these dispositions be nurtured in teacher educators and in prospective social studies teachers? All of these are important research questions waiting for examination.

Research on Prospective Social Studies Teachers in School Settings

Are prospective teachers aware of their students' conceptions of social studies? Stodolsky, Salk, and Glaessner (1991) interviewed 60 fifth-grade students from 11 classrooms about their attitudes toward math and social studies. Students tended to discuss social studies in the context of its being "interesting or boring" (not difficult, not challenging). Students think of social studies as a "horizontal arrangement of various topics, many of which are approached in a similar fashion" (Stodolsky et al., 1991, p. 110). The fifth graders in this sample generally were not concerned about their performance in social studies, for they thought of it as an "enrichment" subject, carrying less importance than other subjects such as math (see also Shaughnessy & Haldyne, 1985).

How do prospective teachers learn about such student attitudes toward social studies and how do they use this knowledge? The literature on social studies teacher education does not give much information on these questions; however, as Evans (1988, 1990) noted, students often can discern the dispositions of their teachers. In Evans's study of three prospective secondary social studies teachers, the students in the three respective classes were able to identify their student teacher's conception of history. In addition, the students tended to share the conception of the practicing teacher, thus raising questions about the nature of the teaching–learning interactions during student teaching.

Many questions can be raised about the knowledge, attitudes, and beliefs prospective social studies teachers have toward and about their prospective students; however, very few of these questions have been investigated in the context of social studies teacher preparation.

Research on Prospective Social Studies Teachers' Knowledge and Beliefs on Cultural Diversity

What beliefs, knowledge, and expectations do prospective and novice social studies teachers have for student achievement, ability, motivation, and learning capacity? Do these beliefs differ by student ethnicity, gender, and socioeconomic class? How do prospective teachers' beliefs and knowledge about students change throughout teacher preparation programs and over the course of professional development? Although a great deal of theoretical and empirical work is currently being conducted in teacher education on these questions, there is not a substantial amount of attention in the social studies teacher education research literature given to these important questions.

Given the vast diversity of the student population in this country; the growth of the mainly white and middle-class teacher population; the persistence of equity issues surrounding schools (especially urban schools) and children (Montero-Sieburth, 1989; Zeichner, 1993); the salience of curricular issues, especially in social studies, about the inclusion of all peoples and the role of multiple perspectives; and ongoing questions about "historical honesty" in the social studies curriculum, it is clear that the social studies teacher preparation research agenda should be very full and focused on a range of diversity-related issues.

Garcia (1984) surveyed 57% of all the social studies teacher educators in California and Texas to determine their agreement with and ranking of five basic tenets of multiculturalism. The ranked list represents a priority listing of the reasons for a multicultural curriculum: attaining positive self-identity, interacting effectively, understanding cultural differences, fostering cultural pluralism, and promoting equity. Not explored in the Garcia study, but important to know, is the way these, and other, basic beliefs about diversity influence social studies teacher education programs. To what extent are diversity and equity issues addressed in social studies teacher preparation programs? How are historical content issues examined? What knowledge and skills are novice teachers learning in order to critique and improve unbalanced curriculum? Few answers to such questions can be found in the current social studies literature.

Ross and Smith (1992) attempted to assess prospective social studies teachers' perspectives on their commitment to teach diverse learners and their beliefs about student failure. Over the course of the year, the orientations of the six preservice teachers in the study became increasingly more complex. Of particular note in this study is the description of the coordinated set of learning activities designed to influence prospective teachers' knowledge and beliefs; these included a personal theory paper, a child-study project, and reaction/reflection papers on the course experiences.

Avery and Walker's (1993) study of 152 preservice teachers (65% elementary; 10% secondary social studies; the rest, other secondary majors) is an important examination of prospective teachers' perceptions of ethnic and gender differences in children's academic achievement. The researchers designed two open-ended problems—one focusing on gender, the other on ethnicity—and respondents had 40 minutes to write an essay explaining reasons for differences in academic performance. These essays were then coded for the types and complexity of explanations given.

In general, most prospective teachers in this study wrote rather simplistic explanations of student performance. Gender differences in achievement were attributed generally to societal factors whereas ethnic differences were attributed to reasons having to do with culture and family values. In addition, the prospective secondary teachers were more likely to locate their explanations for academic differences in the wider society and to display more complex understanding of achievement issues than were the elementary teachers (Avery & Walker, 1993).

Bennett, Niggle, and Stage (1990) have been conducting research over the last several years on the multicultural teacher education program at Indiana University and, in particular, on the effects of a particular multicultural course. Although social studies education majors are not the only students in this program, it is important to note this research for its grounding in theories of adult development, for its longitudinal aspect, and for the ways that program development, teaching, and research are integrally interrelated. This multicultural program and course are based on four interactive goals: (1) development of historical perspectives and cultural consciousness; (2) development of intercultural competence; (3) eradication of racism, prejudice, and discrimination; and (4) successful teaching of multicultural students (Bennett et al., 1990). The particular program experiences were developed with attention to adult devel-

opment, especially to prospective teachers' degree of openness, prior knowledge about diversity, and other attitudes.

In general, Bennett et al. (1990) have found that the more open the prospective teacher is, the more knowledge about diversity the person has at the beginning and at the end of the program. Social distance from persons different from oneself is inversely related to one's degree of openness. In addition, there is probably a ceiling effect on attitude change for those students who are most open at the beginning of the teacher education program.

How do social studies teachers learn how to be successful teachers in cross-cultural classrooms (Zeichner, 1993) and how do they learn to create and teach effectively a more honest, complete, and balanced social studies curriculum? How can theoretical work on cognitive restructuring and on adult learning provide ideas for social studies teacher education experiences? How shall the effects of these experiences be measured over the short and long term?

If good social studies teachers must be "culturally sensitive and sensible" (Montero-Sieburth, 1989), how can teacher development programs contribute to this goal? If good teachers must be able to teach difficult topics and issues, such as slavery, the Holocaust, and civil rights, how can teacher education programs contribute to this goal? These questions demand serious attention by the social studies research and teacher education communities. Research on teacher beliefs and on culturally responsive pedagogy and theoretical work on content issues in the social studies curriculum demand the attention of the best scholars.

Research on Prospective Social Studies Teachers, Students, and Social Studies During Student Teaching

Teaching social studies has to do with one's beliefs, content knowledge, and much more. It has to do with one's understanding of children, with understanding the multiple ways they learn; it has to do with the joy and power of learning and with all the ways teachers can integrate their knowledge, skills, and dispositions to create learning environments that help children create meaning in their lives. Prospective teachers try to synthesize their knowledge, beliefs, values, and skills as they interact with children during teaching internships and student teaching. Yet, during their student teaching, the seven prospective social studies teachers in Kickbusch's (1987) study were unable to generate pedagogical skills that went beyond minimal content coverage in their middle and high school classrooms. Social studies instruction was focused mainly on transmission of factual content, with no attention given to social issues or multiple interpretations of events or topics. The gap between the content of the social studies methods class and the prospective teacher's ability to teach was once again very evident.

Much of the general research on the student teaching practicum (Kagan, 1992b; Zeichner, 1992) documents the problems prospective teachers have in conceptualizing, developing, and implementing sound, creative, and thoughtful instruction. Britzman's (1985) explanation for this phenomena is that prospective social studies teachers were themselves once highly socialized students, and their entrance into familiar school territory encourages an evocation of their own student biographies or scripts that inform their pedagogical decisions. Because young teachers lack the critical understanding needed to analyze school culture and their roles within it, they have little choice but to resort to their prior knowledge of school life.

Onosko (1991) identified school barriers that tend to block higher order thinking; perhaps these are some of the same factors that inhibit student teachers' attempts to promote thoughtfulness. These barriers include teachers' views that instruction is knowledge transmission and that curriculum has to do with content coverage, teachers' low expectations for students, the lack of teacher planning time, the large number of students per teacher, and the prevalence of personal and intellectual isolation for teachers in their school lives.

The well-documented gaps between prospective teachers' ideals and the realities of student teaching (Cochran-Smith, 1991; Cole & Knowles, 1993a; Feiman-Nemser & Buchmann, 1986; Lanier & Little, 1986; Zeichner, 1986, 1992) can be attributed to issues of school culture or issues in the prospective teachers' own biographies and beliefs or to the inability of teacher preparation programs to develop truly effective novice teachers who are able to operate within schools to implement sound and important social studies teaching and learning.

In a study of 57 teacher educators and 896 entry level teacher candidates, Brousseau and Freemann (1988) found that teacher educators tend to reinforce (rather than challenge) prevailing and inappropriate educational beliefs and fail to encourage prospective teachers to form their own opinions on open-ended issues. Without a commitment by social studies teacher educators to examine critically their own beliefs and to challenge prospective teachers to do the same, and to build the teaching knowledge, skills, and affect necessary to match beliefs, then social studies teacher education programs will have minimal impact on the nature and quality of the next generation of social studies educators. These are both development and research issues, and, again, they demand the attention of serious social studies scholars.

CONCEPTUAL MODEL FOR THE PROFESSIONAL DEVELOPMENT OF SOCIAL STUDIES EDUCATORS

Research in social studies education has long been criticized for being atheoretical, noncumulative, and particularistic (Armento, 1986); research on the preparation of social studies educators suffers from some of the same criticisms (Adler, 1991; Banks & Parker, 1990). New, more holistic and comprehensive ways of conceptualizing the field and its issues are needed. Such conceptual models could illuminate relevant factors in the development of social studies educators, could serve as a rubric for synthesizing prior theoretical and empirical work, and could aid in the identification of future research questions. One such model is proposed here.

The professional development of social studies educators can be thought of as lifelong growth resulting from learning that occurs from interactions taking place in a variety of venues each situated in and influenced by its own relevant contextual factors. Three major dimensions underlie the proposed conceptual model: (1) *four aspects of professional growth*—the initial preparation of social studies teachers, the development from novice to expert teacher, the development of leaders in social studies, and the preparation of social studies teacher educators; (2) *the relevant social-political-cultural-economic contextual factors* that define, constrain, influence, or mediate in some way the beliefs, knowledge, actions, and interactions occurring in the various venues across the aspects of professional development; and (3) the interactions that take place in the various contextualized venues, most particularly *those relationships and interactions between and among teachers, students, and the social studies curriculum itself.*

The conceptual model being proposed here can be visually represented as a pyramid on a square base. The four triangular sides represent the aspects of professional development; the base represents the contextual factors that influence professional development; and the three points of each triangle represent the three major interacting elements, that is, the *subject matter* (social studies curriculum, social studies teacher education programs) and the persons playing the roles of *teachers* and *learners* within each aspect of professional development. Utilizing this model, one can identify the range of research questions relevant to the professional development of social studies educators, and thus use these questions as a framework for examination of the literature in the field and for the generation of new hypotheses. In this section of the chapter, the three dimensions of the conceptual model are discussed and possible research questions are identified.

Four Aspects of Professional Development of Social Studies Educators

Who are social studies educators and what are the aspects of their professional development? Looking within the profession at any given time, one would see educators at various stages of professional maturity. For example, some are just completing their teacher preparation programs and are in social studies methods classes; some have taught for several years and are becoming more thoughtful and skillful; some are in leadership training programs, actively involved in professional associations, and conducting staff development programs; and others are in doctoral social studies programs and will soon become college professors and, thus, teacher educators. Each of these professional transition points is critical, although the literature is most abundant at the early career stages and very sparse at the latter stages.

The preparation of secondary school social studies teachers is the most focused, coherent, and distinct aspect of social studies teacher education and also the most researched. Secondary teachers select either content specialization or more general, integrated studies routes to licensure as social studies teachers. Content specialists most often major in history, but may also concentrate in one of the social sciences. Integrated, interdisciplinary, or broad field options are also possible for secondary social studies majors, with these students taking a number of history and social science courses to fulfill the content requirements of their teacher education programs. In recent years, many teacher education programs have required a liberal arts degree in the content field, with the social studies teacher education preparation courses and experiences being considered a program option leading to licensure.

Middle or junior high school social studies teachers may develop either a major or minor content concentration in history or social sciences during their general teacher preparation programs; elementary school teachers who teach social studies are usually prepared as generalists who vary widely in their background knowledge and skill in teaching social studies.

What is known about the learning processes of these social studies teachers across the lifetime of their professional careers? How do the beliefs, knowledge, and teaching competence of social studies educators change over time? In addition, what is it about teacher education programs, life experiences, or other events that prompt or hinder professional development?

The initial preparation of social studies teachers most likely is set in a college or university venue but interfaces with precollege schools, especially through student teaching and other practica. The novice stage of teacher education occurs in the context of school–university collaboration as the prospective teacher "practices" teaching social studies. Throughout one's teaching career, in the venue of one's classroom and school, teachers experience professional growth, in part, as they actively "keep up" with their field of specialization, as they reflect on their educational beliefs and their instructional actions, and as they conduct action research in their social studies classrooms.

Leadership development may be prompted as educators interact with one another, reflecting over and seeking better answers to common problems (Cole & Knowles, 1993b; Hargreaves, 1994; Tetenbaum & Mulkeen, 1986), learning in any of a wide variety of professional networks and arenas available to social studies teachers. These networks include staff development classes, colleagues with whom one team teaches, professional associations such as the National Council for the Social Studies, graduate programs, computer bulletin boards, and research collaborators. Depending on the situation, the teacher may serve the roles of mentor, teacher, or learner as he or she interacts to become a more expert, knowledgeable, and powerful social studies leader. What are the qualities of social studies leaders? What personal and professional experiences have the greatest impact on the growth of social studies leaders? These and other important questions have received little attention by the social studies research community.

Some social studies educators continue their professional development by becoming social studies teacher educators themselves. This occurs mainly, but not exclusively, through university doctoral programs in social studies education. What doctoral program courses and experiences constitute "training" for the preparation of teacher educators? Is any explicit attention given to the education of social studies teacher educators? If so, what is the nature of these experiences and how do prospective social studies teacher educators change as a function of them? Research on these questions and on this very important aspect of the professional development of social studies educators is almost nonexistent.

The Contexts of Professional Development

"Context" has to do with the various factors of the environment that influence each of the four aspects of social studies teacher development. There is no "predetermined set of contextual factors" (Cornbleth, 1991, p. 269), but those relevant to any particular social studies teaching-learning setting are of a "multifaceted, nested and fluid nature" (Cornbleth, 1991, p. 269).

Relevant contextual factors might include: (1) moral/ethical beliefs about what ought to be (Fenstermacher, 1990; Liston & Zeichner, 1987, 1990) . . . in terms of such things as the outcomes of social studies education or the nature of the relationships between teachers and students (Noddings, 1992; Zeichner, 1993); (2) the sociocultural-economic milieu within which the teacher preparation and professional development occur; (3) legislative/moral-suasive guidelines, rules, and standards for professional competence, such as state licensure regulations; (4) political/historical factors of the macro society (Giroux, 1983) that frame and constrain/or define teacher development; (5) intellectual advances and perspectives of the academic fields that contribute to social studies education and teacher education, including the various social sciences and history as well as perspectives on effective teaching, meaningful learning, advances in technology, and so forth; and (6) the cultural/structural context of schooling, school practices, and curriculum that establish and frame roles, procedures, and relationships.

Teaching (and professional development) are grounded in the fundamental moral principles of justice, freedom, democracy, and human caring (Sirotnik, 1990). Good teaching is more than knowing the "knowledge base"; it has to do with "enlightenment of the young, the emancipation of the mind and soul, and the development of human virtue" (Fenstermacher, 1990). Teachers who can inspire and empower students must first hold egalitarian attitudes and then be able to create classrooms where equality permeates highly participatory, student-centered interactions (Shor, 1986). Such ethical principles and moral practices apply to the teaching-learning context of teacher preparation programs and to precollege settings as well as to the professional development of social studies leaders and teacher educators. Teacher education programs, as gatekeepers to the profession, have a particular responsibility to make explicit the hidden questions about schooling, to promote a critical and reflective attitude about teaching and learning, to nurture a probing sense of inquiry, and to stimulate a commitment to and caring for children among prospective teachers.

Within each of the four aspects of teacher development, the societal structures within which students and teachers live and work must be considered educationally relevant, as must the cultural, religious, ethnic, economic, language, and gender diversity of students, teachers, and the community. Teachers must be aware of and knowledgeable about these factors and be able to ask and reflect upon critical questions about the "social realities of schooling" (Liston & Zeichner, 1990, p. 610) and about issues of equity, justice, and freedom in children's lives.

Conceptual notions of competence (Reynolds, 1992; Stanley, 1991) serve to guide practice, as well as the rules of licensure and professional association standards. In general, state standards for licensure in secondary social studies call for more and earlier school-based experiences; more work in history and the social science disciplines and less in the behavioral sciences; more technology skills; and more work with exceptional students (Dumas, Weible, & Evans, 1990).

The major social studies professional association, the National Council for the Social Studies (NCSS), develops standards that also form part of the normative context for teacher preparation and development. NCSS's guidelines for multicultural education (1992) imply that teachers should recognize and respect ethnic and cultural diversity and be able to create classroom environments consistent with democratic ideals and cultural diversity. NCSS's standards for powerful teaching and learning in social studies (1993) propose that teaching be active, challenging, value based, integrative, and meaningful. NCSS's standards for social studies teacher preparation (1988) propose that prospective secondary teachers take 40%, prospective middle school social studies teachers take 30%, and elementary and early childhood teachers take 15% of their college coursework in history and social sciences. These standards also propose that prospective social studies teachers have experiences using a range of instructional approaches in a variety of settings with diverse student populations.

Teachers' perceptions of and knowledge about relevant contextual factors shape their choices and actions in the classroom and their relationships with colleagues and children. How do teachers learn about relevant contextual factors throughout their careers? What roles do initial teacher preparation programs play to help prospective teachers raise critical questions about the social milieu in which they teach and work? How does the relevant context influence the research questions asked and the interpretation of data?

Interactions Between and Among Teachers, Students, and Social Studies

Hawkins (1974) proposed that teaching–learning relationships are different from other adult–child relationships in that the participants are mutually involved with something outside of themselves. For the purposes of this chapter, that "something" is the social studies curriculum or the social studies teacher education program, or the "IT" in Hawkins's "I-THOU-IT" triangle used to represent teaching-learning situations. For Hawkins, the "I" represents the teacher, "THOU" the learner, and "IT" the subject matter.

Applying the I-THOU-IT model to the initial teacher education phase of professional development, social studies teacher educators serve as the *teachers,* the prospective social studies teachers are the *students,* and the total social studies teacher education program, including courses and experiences, becomes the *curriculum* or the content over which teachers and students interact. (See Figure 23.1.)

Initial preparation is inextricably linked with schools and children as the prospective teacher becomes a novice teacher during student teaching. Thus, another set of relationships becomes relevant, that is, the relationships that exist between prospective teachers, children, and the school social studies curriculum during teaching internships and student teaching. (See Figure 23.2.)

Figures 23.1 and 23.2 represent two sides of a four-sided pyramid, illustrating the initial and novice-to-expert phases of the professional development of social studies educators. The interactions between these two phases of professional develop-

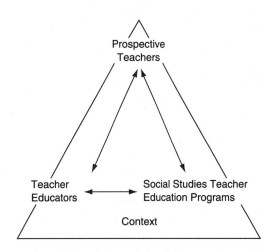

FIGURE 23.1. The professional development of social studies educators: Initial preparation.

ment are represented in Figure 23.3. Here, the college-based preparation of prospective teachers is intimately related to schools through the student teaching process. Thus, prospective teachers are not only playing the role of learner, but also of teacher as they implement social studies instruction to children in precollege contexts. University teacher educators relate to the prospective teacher as both student and colleague as they move from the university to school settings to mentor and coach the novice in the skills and knowledge of the profession.

Similar figures could be drawn to represent the two remaining phases of professional development proposed in this chapter, the leadership phase and the development of teacher educators phase. For example, during the leadership phase, social studies educators play the role of learners, interacting with other colleagues through professional organizations, staff development, and self-study programs as they refine the knowledge and skill of the field. The focus of their learning is on social studies education. During the development of teacher educators phase, the prospective teacher educator becomes primarily a

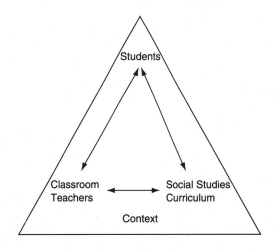

FIGURE 23.2. The professional development of social studies educators: Novice-to-expert stage.

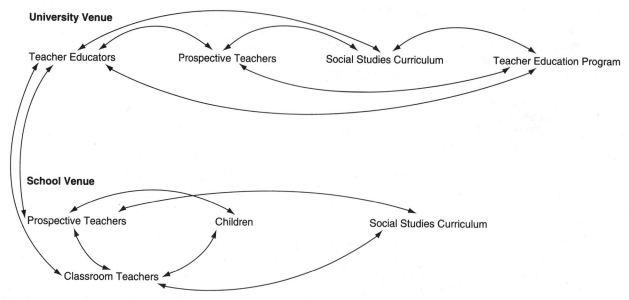

FIGURE 23.3. Interactions between and among the initial preparation and novice-to-expert phases of professional development.

TABLE 23.2. Research Questions Derived from the Conceptual Model

Relationships Between Teacher (Educators) and Students (Prospective Teachers)

- What is known about the demographic, attitudinal, and life history characteristics of both social studies teacher educators and prospective social studies teachers?
- What beliefs and expectations do teacher educators and prospective teachers have for themselves and one another?
- What knowledge do teacher educators and prospective teachers have about the relevant social-economic-cultural factors influencing their own and one another's lives?
- What beliefs and knowledge do teacher educators have about how adults learn and become teachers, and how is this understanding translated to the teaching-learning settings with prospective teachers?

Relationships Between Teacher (Educators) and the Social Studies Program (and Social Studies as a School Subject)

- What background and prior knowledge and training do social studies teacher educators have about the field, about the history and goals of social studies, about the content areas of history and the social sciences, about the nature and issues of school social studies curricula, about alternative approaches to social studies, and about philosophical and psychological issues in the teaching and learning of social studies?
- What do social studies teacher preparation programs look like? What knowledge, skills, experiences, and goals guide the range of programs? What beliefs about social studies education dominate teacher education programs? What collaborative relationships exist with pre-college schools, and what efforts at coreform, collaborative research, collaborative teaching, and mentoring of prospective teachers exist?
- What do social studies teacher educators believe about the goals and means of social studies, and how are these understandings translated into teacher education programs?
- How do social studies teacher educators define their own professional development, and what plans and actions do they take to ensure their own growth?

Relationships Between Students (Prospective Teachers) and the Social Studies Teacher Education Program (and Social Studies as a School Subject)

- What life experiences and formal training do prospective social studies teachers have learning social studies?
- What beliefs, conceptions, misconceptions, and expectations do prospective teachers have about their teacher preparation program and about social studies at precollege levels? What do prospective teachers think the goals of social studies are and ought to be? How are these beliefs changed during and after the teacher preparation program?
- What content knowledge of the social studies curriculum do prospective teachers have? How is this knowledge organized, and what beliefs about the nature of knowledge do prospective teachers hold? How do the content knowledge and the accompanying beliefs change as a function of the social studies teacher preparation programs?
- What pedagogical knowledge and skill do prospective teachers have and how well are they able to create meaningful, important, and powerful teaching-learning environments?
- What inquiry dispositions (thoughtfulness, reflection, openness to new ideas, ability to discern validity and reliability of data, etc.) do prospective social studies teachers profess and practice? How are these dispositions applied to one's own learning and to the work one does in the teacher preparation program? How are inquiry dispositions altered and refined through the course of the teacher preparation program?

(continued)

TABLE 23.2. Research Questions Derived from the Conceptual Model (*continued*)

Relationships Among Teacher (Educators), Students (Prospective Teachers), and the Social Studies Teacher Education Program

- How do all these beliefs, attitudes, prior and current knowledge, skills, and emotions come together to create such events as the social studies methods class and other teacher preparation program interactions? How do the various persons and the social studies curriculum relate to each other? How do teacher educators model effective social studies education? What relationships, roles, and critique occur in the methods class and the practica? Over what issues? For what purposes? Toward what ends?
- What expectations do teacher educators have for their students' performance, for their attitudes and beliefs, for their knowledge, and for their commitment to education and to social studies? How are these expectations manifested in the teacher preparation program?

Relationships Between (Prospective) Teachers and Children/Students

- What knowledge and beliefs do (prospective) teachers have about the social/cultural/economic lives of their students and of the issues they face? How does this knowledge mediate teaching and learning choices and actions?
- What beliefs and expectations do (prospective) teachers have for student achievement, ability, motivation, and learning capacities? Do these beliefs differ by student ethnicity, gender, and socioeconomic status? What types of experiences and knowledge influence teacher beliefs and their expectations for children?
- What beliefs and knowledge do (prospective) teachers have about how students learn and the roles knowledge, skill, attitudes, and motivation have in the lives of children?
- What do (prospective) teachers know about student interest in and knowledge of social studies related topics?

Relationships Between Children and the Social Studies Curriculum

- How do children perceive the social studies curriculum? What beliefs, knowledge, and attitudes do they have about this aspect of schooling? What relevance do they see for their lives?
- How do the social/political realities of children's lives influence their attitudes toward schooling and toward the social studies curriculum?
- What about the social world is of interest to children? How do children explore and learn about such topics?

Relationships Between and Among (Prospective and Novice) Teachers, Children, and the Social Studies Curriculum

- How do prospective and novice teachers create, implement, evaluate, and reflect upon social studies teaching and learning?
- What is the quality, extent, and nature of critique given novice teachers for their social studies teaching by children, classroom teacher mentors, and college teacher educators? How is this critique received and used?
- What structural and contextual factors influence novice teacher beliefs and behavior and attitudes about teaching and learning social studies?

---

learner in the context of a university doctoral program; the teachers in this setting are typically the current university professors of social studies, and the focus of learning is the content of the social studies doctoral program. Thus, a four-sided pyramid could be visualized to represent the range of the development of social studies educators, from the prospective teacher to the teacher educator.

The I-THOU-IT triangle and the multi-dimensional model proposed here enable us to identify pairs of relationships (McDiarmid, 1991) that occur within and between each aspect of professional development. For example, the paired relationships include teachers and students with one another, students with the curriculum and teachers with the curriculum. Each of these relationships is influenced by relevant contextual factors. The paired relationships offer a focus for framing research questions within each phase of professional development. The following research questions focus primarily on the initial and novice phases of professional development. Similar questions could be derived for the leadership and teacher educator phases. (See Table 23.2.)

CONCLUSION

If prospective educators are to create meaningful, powerful, coherent, and thoughtful social studies instruction for their students, they must first experience this type of learning in their own lives. They must not only experience this, but they must also critically reflect on their learning and on the social/political context in which it occurs as well as on the context in which they themselves will create meaningful learning situations for others.

Social studies teacher preparation programs have a special responsibility to model and nurture exemplary social studies teaching, learning, and inquiry; to collaborate with schools to create supportive and professional relationships and experiences for novice social studies teachers; to build ongoing and stimulating collaborative linkages among social studies educators at various stages of professional development to promote the growth of all (including the teacher educators); and to take seriously their professional obligation to provide only outstanding social studies teachers for the nation's children.

The research on social studies teacher preparation does not really indicate if any of this is indeed happening. Rather, glimpses are provided into aspects of the minds and behavior of prospective social studies teachers and, occasionally, into the social studies teacher preparation programs through which these students are traveling.

The body of literature reviewed for this chapter is rich, particularly for its insights into prospective teachers' beliefs about social studies and prospective teachers' historical content knowledge. This work provides an interesting and sometimes insightful view of the meanings and reasons social studies teachers build on their journey into the profession. Much of the current research, however, derives from an interpretive paradigm that seeks deeper understanding rather than conclusions and generalizations. Thus, this synthesis of the research since the mid-1980s cannot conclude with a list of "What we now know" about the research on social studies teacher education. Interpretive research is very important for obtaining a deeper understanding of the dynamics of teachers' minds, actions, and lives; however, the current literature gives a limited, narrow, and perhaps distorted view of the reality of social studies teacher education because of its dependence on the qualitative examination of very small numbers of prospective or novice teachers.

Although there are perhaps hundreds of social studies teacher preparation programs in the country, relatively little research describes, assesses, or critiques these programs or provides a critical examination of the teaching–learning interactions taking place in the methods classes, the practicum, or in the "content" classes. More social studies teacher educators need to believe that research on their own practice is an integral part of their own professional growth. In addition, such modeling, especially if it includes collaborative relationships with social studies teachers and with prospective teachers, would provide important lessons for the professional development of all the partners.

Missing from the social studies teacher education literature is also a sense of urgency and concern about the quality and impact of teacher preparation programs and about the quality of research on lifelong professional development. Explanations by researchers for problems faced by prospective teachers or for their simplistic beliefs and inadequate knowledge are often grounded in attributions to the culture of schools or to the personal biographies of the prospective teachers. That is, researchers tend to ignore the fact that their subjects are actively involved in a teacher preparation program that might, could, or should have an effect on the prospective teachers' beliefs or content knowledge. Are social studies teacher education programs not influencing beliefs, knowledge, and commitment to teaching social studies? If not, why not? If so, what factors are critical to the professional development process? How can teacher educators and researchers utilize psychological knowledge about cognitive restructuring and schema theory, for example, to develop preparation programs that empower future social studies educators? How can the effects of such programs be examined over the short and long term? How can teacher educators better communicate development and research ideas to one another and collaborate to build a more coherent research base?

Research (Cochran-Smith & Lytle, 1993; Lytle & Cochran-Smith, 1990) on social studies teacher education and the recreation and reform of social studies teacher professional development programs should inform one another, with research insights leading to program improvement as well as to contributions to the field's general knowledge about teacher empowerment. Future research on social studies teacher preparation can be strengthened by greater attention to conceptual and methodological concerns.

Conceptual Recommendations

Research on social studies professional development could be enhanced if researchers were guided by questions that gave greater attention to the social context and to the dynamics of prospective teachers' growth and learning. In addition, researchers should remember that the teacher preparation program itself is a "treatment," not merely the invisible context within which prospective teachers build ideas, knowledge, and skills. The conceptual model and the research questions proposed in this chapter are a starting point for articulating a research agenda for social studies teacher education. In addition, both teacher educators and researchers should consider the following fundamental conceptual questions.

What view of social studies education guides the teacher preparation program? How clearly articulated is this view throughout the entire program, and how closely is it held by faculty and students? How common are these guiding principles across programs? We need an "authentic conversation within the social studies community . . . in order to build consensus and focus in the field and to consider rationales presently held to justify curricular and pedagogical choices" (VanSledright & Grant, 1991, p. 286). Until this conversation occurs, the field would benefit from clarity on the questions posed here.

What views of teaching and learning permeate the program? Are these views grounded in theory (Leinhardt, 1992; Vosniadou & Brewer, 1987), and are prospective teachers viewed as learners, actively constructing new ideas and reorganizing and restructuring old and less useful ideas? What purposeful attention is given by teacher educators and later by prospective teachers to prompt knowledge and belief system restructuring? How are restructuring processes conceptualized and what techniques, such as Socratic dialogue (Vosniadou & Brewer, 1987), are employed to actively prompt radical restructuring of knowledge and beliefs about the social world?

What views of teachers and of professional development are stressed throughout the program? How do teacher educators model, reinforce, and apply these beliefs in their own teaching, collaborating, and research? How are the voices of teachers (Lytle & Cochran-Smith, 1990) and prospective teachers brought into the dialogue, and what messages about the profession are developed? What attitudes about teacher inquiry, teacher empowerment, and the ethics of teaching and of professional growth are stimulated in the program?

Research Paradigm Recommendations

Empirical-analytic, interpretive, and critical research orientations should each be employed to address the many serious questions and issues facing the professional development of social studies educators. Quantitative studies are needed to describe the important dimensions and characteristics of current programs and to examine formally the effects of particular programs and program elements. The research in social studies education has finally taken a much-needed turn toward interpretive inquiry; however, experimental research is now almost nonexistent in the current literature. Surely, "treatments" occur, and their quality, nature, and effects are important to know and to share. Viewing teacher education programs as "treatments," examining their effects, and critically assessing the construction and delivery of teacher preparation programs would bring a needed level of openness to the field.

In addition, knowing more about the demographic characteristics of teacher educators and prospective teachers as well as the description of program elements would contribute to a better grasp of just what is happening in the field.

Interpretive research contributes the critical "deep understanding" of what is "really happening" in one's mind and in one's actions and interactions. The interpretive paradigm now appears to be a dominant approach in the research on social studies teacher education; however, the work could make more important contributions if researchers gave more attention to the following critical next steps.

- A broader view is needed of entire social studies teacher education program(s) with in-depth case studies of particular program elements, such as the social studies methods class. What is happening in methods classes? How are knowledge, skills, and dispositions represented in the class? What modeling of thought processes occurs? How is the social studies curriculum represented to and with prospective teachers? How do prospective teachers process the program? What restructuring of their ideas and knowledge occurs?

- An examination is needed of prospective teacher beliefs and attitudes (about children, social studies, teaching and learning, etc.), couched in the context of the teacher education program or in the culture of the school. What are the program qualities that aim to influence teacher beliefs? How do prospective teachers internalize these elements?

- Case studies are needed of successful school–university collaboratives for social studies teacher development and for collaborative work with teacher educators, children, and teachers.

- Case studies are needed of programs attempting to influence prospective teachers about diversity and to develop balanced social studies curricular approaches.

- Case studies are needed of outstanding novice teachers (during school practicum).

- A closer look at how programs, and then prospective teachers, blend beliefs, knowledge, and other factors to create powerful learning situations for social studies is needed.

Critical questions should be raised not only about programs themselves but also should be reflected in research on teacher education. Issues of power, justice, and fairness permeate the lives of social studies teachers, especially through the curriculum they teach. Do teacher education programs and teacher educators nurture the raising of and reflecting on central issues in the lives of children and teachers? Do teacher educators critically reflect on their own beliefs and actions? How are ethical and moral issues examined? How are prospective teachers challenged to address equity issues? What experiences in the schools or community are specifically designed to uncover critical issues? What is the nature of the dialogue that surrounds these issues?

The "learning model we set for schools is the model that socializes future teachers in how to teach" (Shor, 1986, p. 416). The time is now for social studies professional development programs to creatively, coherently, collaboratively, and critically ask how to focus programs and research to better prepare social studies educators for today's children.

References

Adler, S. (1984). A field study of selected student teacher perspectives toward social studies. *Theory and Research in Social Education, 12,* 13–30.

Adler, S. (1991). The education of social studies teachers. In J. Shaver (Ed.), *Handbook of research on social studies teaching and learning* (pp. 210–221). New York: Macmillan.

Alexander, P. A., & Judy, J. E. (1988). The interaction of domain specific and strategic knowledge in academic performance. *Review of Educational Research, 58,* 375–404.

Angell, A. V. (1991). *Social studies methods, student teaching, and the restructuring of preservice teacher beliefs: A case study.* Unpublished doctoral dissertation, Emory University, Atlanta.

Armento, B. J. (1986). Research on teaching social studies. In M. C. Wittrock (Ed.), *Handbook of research on teaching* (3rd ed., pp. 942–951). New York: Macmillan.

Armento, B. J. (1991). Changing conceptions of research on the teaching of social studies. In J. P. Shaver (Ed.), *Handbook of research on social studies teaching and learning* (pp. 185–196). New York: Macmillan.

Armento, B. J. (1993). Reform revisited: The story of elementary social studies at the crest of the 21st century. In W. Wilson, J. Litle, & G. Wilson (Eds.), *Teaching social studies: Handbook of trends, issues, and implications for the future* (pp. 25–44). Westport, CT: Greenwood Publishing Company.

Avery, P. G., & Walker, C. (1993). Prospective teachers' perceptions of ethnic and gender differences in academic achievement. *Journal of Teacher Education, 44,* 27–37.

Banks, J. A., & Parker, W. C. (1990). Social studies teacher education. In W. R. Houston, M. Haberman, & J. Sikula (Eds.), *Handbook of research on teacher education* (pp. 674–686). New York: Macmillan.

Barr, R. D., Barth, J. L., & Shermis, S. S. (1978). *The nature of the social studies.* Palm Springs, CA: ETC Publications.

Bennett, C., Niggle, T., & Stage, F. (1990). Preservice multicultural teacher education: Predictions of student readiness. *Teaching and Teacher Education, 6,* 243–254.

Bennett, C., & Spalding, E. (1992). Teaching the social studies: Multiple approaches for multiple perspectives. *Theory and Research in Social Education, 20,* 263–292.

Black, A., & Ammon, P. (1992). A developmental-constructivist approach to teacher education. *Journal of Teacher Education, 43,* 323–335.

Bradley Commission on History in Schools. (1989). Building a history curriculum: Guidelines for teaching history in schools. In P. Gagnon & the Bradley Commission (Eds.), *Historical literacy: The case for history in American education* (pp. 16–47). Boston: Houghton Mifflin.

Britzman, D. P. (1985). *Reality and ritual: An ethnographic study of student teachers.* Unpublished doctoral dissertation, University of Massachusetts, Cambridge.

Brophy, J. (1992). Fifth-grade U.S. history: How one teacher arranged to focus on key ideas in depth. *Theory and Research in Social Education, 20,* 141–155.

Brophy, J. (Ed.). (1993). *Advances in research on teaching: Case studies of teaching and learning in social studies.* Greenwich, CT: JAI Press.

Brophy, J., Prawat, R., & McMahon, S. (1991). Social education professors and elementary teachers: Two purviews on elementary social studies. *Theory and Research in Social Education, 19,* 173–188.

Brousseau, B. A., Book, C., & Byers, J. L. (1988). Teacher beliefs and the cultures of teaching. *Journal of Teacher Education, 39,* 33–39.

Brousseau, B. A., & Freemann, D. J. (1988). How do teacher education faculty members define desirable teacher beliefs? *Teaching and Teacher Education, 4,* 267–273.

Brown, D. S. (1988). Twelve middle school teachers' planning. *Elementary School Journal, 89,* 69–87.

Bruce, M. G., Podenski, R. S., & Anderson, C. M. (1991). Developing a global perspective: Strategies for teacher education programs. *Journal of Teacher Education, 42,* 21–27.

Butts, R. F. (1993). The time is now: To frame the civic foundations of teacher education. *Journal of Teacher Education, 44,* 326–334.

Cochran-Smith, M. (1991). Reinventing student teaching. *Journal of Teacher Education, 42,* 104–118.

Cochran-Smith, M., & Lytle, S. L. (Eds.). (1993). *Inside/outside: Teacher research and knowledge.* New York: Teachers College Press.

Cole, A. L., & Knowles, J. G. (1993, April). *Shattered images: Understanding expectations and realities of field experiences.* Paper presented at the annual meeting of the American Educational Research Association, Atlanta.

Cole, A. L., & Knowles, J. G. (1993b). Teacher development partnership research: A focus on methods and issues. *American Educational Research Journal, 30,* 473–495.

Cornbleth, C. (1991). Research on context, research in context. In Shaver, J. P. (Ed.), *Handbook of research on social studies teaching and learning* (pp. 265–275). New York: Macmillan.

Cornett, J. W. (1987). *Teacher personal practical theories and their influences upon teacher curricular and instructional actions: A case study of a secondary social studies teacher.* Unpublished doctoral dissertation, Ohio State University.

Cornett, J. W. (1990). Teacher thinking about curriculum and instruction: A case study of a secondary social studies teacher. *Theory and Research in Social Education, 18,* 248–273.

Downey, M. T., & Levstik, L. S. (1988). Teaching and learning history: The research base. *Social Education, 52,* 336–342.

Dumas, W., Weible, T., & Evans, S. (1990). State standards for the licensure of secondary social studies teachers. *Theory and Research in Social Education, 18,* 27–36.

Engle, S. H., & Ochoa, A. S. (1988). *Education for democratic citizenship: Decision making in the social studies.* New York: Teachers College Press.

Evans, R. W. (1988). Lessons from history: Teacher and student conceptions of the meaning of history. *Theory and Research in Social Education, 16,* 203–225.

Evans, R. W. (1990). Teacher conceptions of history revisited: Ideology, curriculum, and student belief. *Theory and Research in Social Education, 18,* 101–138.

Feiman-Nemser, S., & Buchmann, M. (1986). Pitfalls of experience in teacher preparation. In J. D. Raths & L. G. Katz (Eds.), *Advances in teacher education* (Vol. 2, pp. 61–73). Norwood, NJ: Ablex.

Fenstermacher, G. (1990). Some moral considerations on teaching as a profession. In J. Goodlad, R. Soder, & K. Sirotnik (Eds.), *The moral dimensions of teaching* (pp. 130–151). San Francisco: Jossey-Bass.

Fullinwider, R. K. (1991). Philosophical inquiry and social studies. In J. P. Shaver (Ed.), *Handbook of research on social studies teaching and learning* (pp. 16–26). New York: Macmillan.

Garcia, M. J. (1984). *Acceptance by social studies teacher educators of the basic tenets of multicultural education.* Unpublished doctoral dissertation, University of Michigan.

Gilliom, M. E., & Hart, J. E. (1990). *Introducing an international dimension into the social studies methods courses.* Bloomington, IN: ERIC Clearinghouse for Social Studies/Social Science Education.

Giroux, H. A. (1983). *Theories and resistance in education.* South Hadley, MA: Bergin and Garvey.

Goodlad, J. I. (1990). *Teachers for our nation's schools.* San Francisco: Jossey-Bass.

Goodlad, J. I., Soder, R., & Sirotnik, K. A. (Eds.). (1990). *Places where teachers are taught.* San Francisco: Jossey-Bass.

Goodman, J., & Adler, S. (1985). Becoming an elementary social studies teacher: A study of perspectives. *Theory and Research in Social Education, 13,* 1–20.

Grossman, P. L., Wilson, S. M., & Shulman, L. S. (1989). Teachers of substance: Subject matter knowledge for teaching. In M. C. Reynolds (Ed.), *Knowledge base for the beginning teacher* (pp. 23–36). New York: Pergamon Press.

Gudmundsdottir, S. (1990, April). *Story makers, story tellers: Narrative structures in curriculum.* Paper presented at the annual meeting of the American Educational Research Association, Boston.

Gudmundsdottir, S. (1991a). Pedagogical models of subject matter. In J. Brophy (Ed.), *Advances in research on teaching* (Vol. 3, pp. 265–304). Greenwich, CT: JAI Press.

Gudmundsdottir, S. (1991b). Values in pedagogical content knowledge. *Journal of Teacher Education, 41,* 44–52.

Hargreaves, A. (1994, April). *Development and desire: A postmodern perspective.* Paper presented at the annual meeting of the American Educational Research Association, New Orleans.

Hawkins, D. (1974). *The informed vision: Essays on learning and human nature.* New York: Agathon Press.

Hertzberg, H. W. (1981). *Social studies reform, 1880–1980.* Boulder, CO: Social Science Education Consortium.

Jantz, R. K., Weaver, V. P., Cirrincione, J. M., & Farrell, R. T. (1985). Inquiry and curriculum change: Perceptions of school and college university faculty. *Theory and Research in Social Education, 13,* 61–72.

Johnston, M. (1990). Teachers' backgrounds and beliefs: Influences and learning to teach in the social studies. *Theory and Research in Social Education, 18,* 207–233.

Kagan, D. M. (1992a). Implications of research on teacher belief. *Educational Psychologist, 27,* 65–90.

Kagan, D. M. (1992b). Professional growth among preservice and beginning teachers. *Review of Educational Research, 62,* 129–169.

Kickbusch, K. W. (1985). Ideological innocence and dialogue: A critical perspective on disclosure in the social studies. *Theory and Research in Social Education, 13,* 45–56.

Kickbusch, K. W. (1987). Civic education and preservice educators: Extending the boundaries of discourse. *Theory and Research in Social Education, 15,* 173–188.

King, M. B. (1991). Leadership efforts that facilitate classroom thoughtfulness in social studies. *Theory and Research in Social Education, 19,* 367–390.

Lanier, J. E., & Little, J. W. (1986). Research on teacher education. In M. C. Wittrock (Ed.), *Handbook of research on teaching* (3rd ed., pp. 527–569). New York: Macmillan.

Lather, P. (1986). Research as praxis. *Harvard Educational Review, 56,* 257–277.

Leinhardt, G. (1992). What research on learning tells us about teaching. *Educational Leadership, 49,* 20–25.

Leming, J. S. (1991). Teacher characteristics and social studies education. In J. P. Shaver (Ed.), *Handbook of research on social studies teaching and learning* (pp. 222–236). New York: Macmillan.

Leming, J. S. (1992). Ideological perspectives within the social studies profession: An empirical examination of the "two cultures" thesis. *Theory and Research in Social Education, 20,* 293–312.

Liston, D. P., & Zeichner, K. M. (1987). Critical pedagogy and teacher education. *Journal of Education, 169,* 117–137.

Liston, D. P., & Zeichner, K. M. (1990). Teacher education and the social context of schooling: Issues for curriculum development. *American Educational Research Journal, 27,* 610–636.

Lytle, S. L., & Cochran-Smith, M. (1990). Learning from teacher research: A working typology. *Teachers College Record, 92,* 83–103.

Malone, P. M. (1991). *Liberal and post-liberal rationales for citizenship education and the preparation of preservice social studies teachers.* Unpublished dissertation, University of Lowell, Lowell, MA.

Marker, G., & Mehlinger, H. (1992). Social studies. In P. W. Jackson (Ed.), *Handbook of research on curriculum* (pp. 830–851). New York: Macmillan.

Martorella, P. H. (1991). Consensus building among social educators: A Delphi study. *Theory and Research in Social Education, 19,* 83–94.

McCutcheon, G. (1981). Elementary school teachers' planning for social studies and other subjects. *Theory and Research in Social Education, 9,* 45–66.

McDiarmid, G. W. (1991). What teachers need to know about cultural diversity: Restoring subject matter to the picture. In M. M. Kennedy (Ed.), *Teaching academic subjects to diverse learners* (pp. 257–270). New York: Teachers College Press.

McDiarmid, G. W., Ball, D. L., & Anderson, C. W. (1989). Why staying one chapter ahead doesn't really work: Subject-specific pedagogy. In M. C. Reynolds (Ed.), *Knowledge base for the beginning teacher* (pp. 193–205). New York: Pergamon Press.

McEwan, H., & Bull, B. (1991). The pedagogic nature of subject matter knowledge. *American Educational Research Journal, 28,* 316–334.

Merryfield, M. M. (1991). Preparing American secondary social studies teachers to teach with a global perspective: A status report. *Journal of Teacher Education, 42,* 11–20.

Merryfield, M. M. (1992). Preparing social studies teachers for the twenty-first century: Perspectives on program effectiveness from a study of six exemplary teacher education programs in global education. *Theory and Research in Social Education, 20,* 17–46.

Montero-Sieburth, M. (1989). Restructuring teachers' knowledge for urban settings. *Journal of Negro Education, 58,* 332–344.

National Commission on Social Studies in Schools. (1989). *Charting a course: Social studies curriculum for the 21st century. A report of the Curriculum Task Force.* Washington, DC: Author.

National Council for the Social Studies (NCSS). (1988). Standards for the preparation of social studies teachers. *Social Education, 52,* 10–12.

National Council for the Social Studies (NCSS). (1993). A vision of powerful teaching and learning in the social studies: Building social understanding and civic efficiency. *Social Education, 57,* 213–223.

National Council for the Social Studies (NCSS), Task Force on Ethnic Studies Curriculum Guidelines. (1992). Curriculum guidelines for multicultural education. *Social Education, 56,* 274–294.

National Education Goals Panel. (1991). The national education goals report: Building a nation of learners. Washington, DC: Author.

Nelson, L. R., & Drake, F. D. (1994). Secondary teachers' reactions to the new social studies. *Theory and Research in Social Education, 22,* 44–73.

Newmann, F. M. (1990). Higher order thinking in teaching social studies: A rationale for the assessment of classroom thoughtfulness. *Journal of Curriculum Studies, 22,* 41–56.

Newmann, F. M. (Ed.). (1991). Promoting higher order thinking in social studies: Overview of a study of 16 high school departments. *Theory and Research in Social Education, 19,* 324–340.

Newmann, F. M. (Ed.). (1992). *Student engagement and achievement in American secondary schools.* New York: Teachers College Press.

Noddings, N. (1992). *The challenge to care in schools.* New York: Teachers College Press.

Onosko, J. J. (1991). Barriers to the promotion of higher-order thinking in social studies. *Theory and Research in Social Education, 19,* 341–366.

Parker, W. C. (1984). Developing teachers' decision-making. *Journal of Experimental Education, 52,* 220–226.

Parker, W. C. (1986). Dorothy's and Mary's mediation of a curriculum intervention. *Phenomenology and Pedagogy, 4,* 20–31.

Parker, W. C. (1987). Teachers' mediation in social studies. *Theory and Research in Social Education, 15,* 1–22.

Parker, W. C., & Gehrke, N. J. (1986). Learning activities and teachers' decision-making: Some grounded hypotheses. *American Educational Research Journal, 23,* 227–242.

Passe, J. (1988). The role of internal factors in the teaching of current events. *Theory and Research in Social Education, 6,* 83–89.

Powell, R. R. (1991). Acquisition and use of pedagogical knowledge among career change preservice teachers. *Action in Teacher Education, 13,* 17–23.

Reynolds, A. (1992). What is a competent beginning teaching? A review of the literature. *Review of Educational Research, 62,* 1–35.

Ross, D. D., & Smith, W. (1992). Understanding preservice teachers' perspectives on diversity. *Journal of Teacher Education, 43,* 94–103.

Ross, E. W. (1987). Teacher perspective development: A study of preservice social studies teachers. *Theory and Research in Social Education, 15,* 225–243.

Russell, T. E., & Morrow, J. E. (1986). Reform in teacher education: Perceptions of secondary social studies teachers. *Theory and Research in Social Education, 14,* 325–330.

Sanders, D. P., & McCutcheon, G. (1986). The development of practical theories of teaching. *Journal of Curriculum and Supervision, 2,* 50–67.

Shaughnessy, J. M., & Haldyne, T. M. (1985). Research on student attitude toward social studies. *Social Education, 49,* 692–695.

Shermis, S. S., & Washburn, P. C. (1986). Social studies educators and their beliefs: Preliminary data from Indiana colleges and universities. *Theory and Research in Social Education, 14,* 331–340.

Shor, I. (1986). Equality is excellence: Transforming teacher education and the learning process. *Harvard Educational Review, 56,* 406–426.

Shulman, L. S. (1987). Knowledge and teaching: Foundations of the new reform. *Harvard Educational Review, 57*(1), 1–22.

Sirotnik, L. A. (1990). Society, schooling, teaching, and preparing to teach. In J. I. Goodlad, R. Soder, & K. A. Sirotnik (Eds.), *The moral dimensions of teaching* (pp. 296–327). San Francisco: Jossey-Bass.

Smith, B. D. (1983). Instructional planning: Attitudes, decisions, and preparation time among secondary social studies teachers. *Journal of Social Studies Research, 7*(1), 1–22.

Sockett, H. T. (1987). Has Shulman got the strategy right? *Harvard Educatonal Review, 57,* 208–219.

Stanley, W. B. (1991). Teacher competence for social studies. In J. P. Shaver (Ed.), *Handbook of research on social studies teaching and learning* (pp. 249–262). New York: Macmillan.

Stepanske, J. E. (1987). *An analysis of the elementary social studies methods courses in colleges and universities of Tennessee and selected institutions outside of Tennessee.* Unpublished doctoral dissertation, The University of Tennessee, Knoxville.

Stodolsky, S. S., Salk, S., & Glaessner, B. (1991). Student views about learning math and social studies. *American Educational Research Journal, 28,* 89–116.

Tetenbaum, T. J., & Mulkeen, T. A. (1986). Designing teacher education for the twenty first century. *Journal of Higher Education, 57,* 621–636.

Thornton, S. J. (1988). Curriculum consonance in U.S. history classrooms. *Journal of Curriculum and Supervision, 3,* 308–320.

Thornton, S. J. (1991). Teacher as curricular-instructional gatekeeper in social studies. In J. P. Shaver (Ed.), *Handbook of research on social studies teaching and learning* (pp. 237–248). New York: Macmillan.

Thornton, S. J. (1994). The social studies near century's end: Reconsidering patterns of curriculum and instruction. In L. Darling-Hammond (Ed.), *Review of research in education, 20,* 223–254.

Tobias, S. (1994). Interest, prior knowledge, and learning. *Review of Educational Research, 64,* 37–54.

Torney-Purta, J. (1991). Schema theory and cognitive psychology: Implications for social studies. *Theory and Research in Social Education, 19,* 189–210.

VanSledright, B. A., & Grant, S. G. (1991). Surviving its own rhetoric: Building a conversational community within the social studies. *Theory and Research in Social Education, 19,* 283–304.

von Glaserfeld, E. (1987). *The construction of knowledge.* Seaside, CA: The Systems Inquiry Series, Intersystems Publication.

Vosniadou, S., & Brewer, W. F. (1987). Theories of knowledge restructuring in development. *Review of Educational Research, 57,* 51–67.

Voss, J. F., Greene, T. R., Post, T. A., & Penner, B. C. (1984). Problem-solving skill in the social sciences. In G. Bower (Ed.), *The psychology of learning motivation: Advances in research theory* (pp. 165–213). New York: Academic Press.

Voss, J. F., Tyler, S. W., & Yengo, L. A. (1983). Individual differences in the solving of social science problems. In R. F. Dillon & R. R. Schmeck (Eds.), *Individual differences in cognition* (pp. 205–232). New York: Academic Press.

Weaver, V., Jantz, R., Farrell, R., & Cirrincione, J. (1985). A case study in curriculum innovation: Whatever happened to inquiry? *The Social Studies,* 160–164.

Wilson, S. M. (1991). Parades of facts, stories of the past: What do novice history teachers need to know? In M. M. Kennedy (Ed.), *Teaching academic subjects to diverse learners* (pp. 99–116). New York: Teachers College Press.

Wilson, S. M., Shulman, L. S., & Richert, A. E. (1987). 150 different ways of knowing: Representations of knowledge in teaching. In J. Calderhead (Ed.), *Exploring teachers' thinking* (pp. 104–124). London: Cassell Education.

Wilson, S. M., & Wineberg, S. S. (1988). Peering at history through different lenses: The role of disciplinary perspectives in teaching history. *Teachers College Record, 89,* 525–539.

Wilson, S. M., & Wineberg, S. S. (1993). Wrinkles in time and place: Using performance assessments to understand the knowledge of history teachers. *American Educational Research Journal, 30,* 729–769.

Wineberg, S. S., & Wilson, S. M. (1991). Subject matter knowledge in the teaching of history. In J. E. Brophy (Ed.), *Advances in research on teaching.* Greenwich, CT: JAI Press.

Wittrock, M. C. (1986). Students' thought processes. In M. C. Wittrock (Ed.), *Handbook of research and teaching* (3rd ed., pp. 297–314). New York: Macmillan.

Zeichner, K. M. (1986). Individual and institutional influences on the development of teacher perspectives. In J. D. Raths & L. G. Katz (Eds.), *Advances in teacher education* (Vol. 2, pp. 135–163). Norwood, NJ: Ablex.

Zeichner, K. M. (1992). Rethinking the practicum in the professional development school partnership. *Journal of Teacher Education, 43,* 296–307.

Zeichner, K. M. (1993). *Educating teachers for cultural diversity: Special report.* East Lansing, MI: National Center for Research on Teacher Learning.

·24·

CLASSROOM MANAGEMENT

Vern Jones

LEWIS AND CLARK COLLEGE

Managing classrooms in the 1990s and beyond will be a demanding task. Problems with school funding have, in many states, brought about increased class sizes. At the same time, teachers are being asked to include a wider range of students in their classrooms. This includes not only students with special needs previously served in "pull-out" programs, but an increasing number of students who come to school with personal, social, and emotional needs that have a negative impact on their ability to benefit from the learning environment. At the extreme are fetal alcohol syndrome and "crack" babies. Many more students, however, are suffering less obvious but significant emotional problems stemming from poverty, parent divorce or separation, and adult neglect and abuse. These changes come at a time when the public is increasingly concerned about the quality of public school education and when teachers are confronted with major changes in curriculum, instruction, and school organization. This chapter attempts to examine the role effective classroom management plays in assisting teachers in dealing with these demands.

This chapter is more than a compilation of current research on classroom management. It is also an examination of the role classroom management plays in the lives of teachers and students and the connection between classroom management and the goals of public education in this country. It is important to keep in mind that most classroom management research has involved elementary and junior high school classrooms (Evertson & Harris, 1992) and whole-class instruction and seatwork within traditional instructional formats (Brophy, 1988). This chapter moves beyond examining classroom management as it relates to traditional instruction in elementary classrooms, a task that has been effectively accomplished by others (Brophy, 1983a, 1988; Doyle, 1986; Duke, 1979). Whereas references are made to these works, this chapter attempts to develop a conceptualization of management that will assist teachers in responding to the complex demands described. In addition, little research has involved inner-city high school classrooms where management problems may be the most serious. This

chapter reviews research that has implications for the effective management of disruptive high school classrooms as well as the increasing demands of working with younger students who display serious disruptive behavior.

McCaslin and Good (1992) provided insight into the direction management must take when they wrote that "Classroom management can and should do more than elicit predictable obedience; indeed, it can and should be one vehicle for the enhancement of student self-understanding, self-evaluation, and the internalization of self-control" (p. 8). At its best, classroom management is not only a means to effective instruction, it also becomes a vehicle for providing students with a sense of community and with increased skills in interpersonal communication, conflict management, and self-control. McCaslin and Good (1992) stated

> We believe that the intended modern school curriculum, which is designed to produce self-motivated, active learners, is seriously undermined by classroom management policies that encourage, if not demand, simple obedience. We advocate that a curriculum that seeks to promote problem solving and meaningful learning must be aligned with an authoritative management system that increasingly allows students to operate as self-regulated and risk-taking learners. (p. 4)

THE IMPORTANCE OF CLASSROOM MANAGEMENT

Numerous reports and studies suggest that classroom management is a major factor influencing teachers' effectiveness and mental health. A recent meta-analysis of factors influencing student learning identified classroom management as being the most important factor (Wang, Haertel, & Walberg, 1993). In March, 1984, a 10-member panel on the Preparation of Beginning Teachers, chaired by Ernest Boyer, President of the Carnegie Foundation for the Advancement of Teaching, issued a report listing three major areas of expertise needed by beginning teachers: (1) knowledge of how to manage a classroom, (2) knowledge of subject matter, and (3) understanding of their students' sociological backgrounds (Boyer, 1984).

A publication from the Association for Supervision and Curriculum Development entitled *Effective Schools and Classrooms: A Research-Based Perspective* (Squires, Huitt, & Segars, 1983) stated that effective teachers, those whose students demonstrate consistently high levels of achievement, possess skills in: "1. planning, or getting ready for classroom activities; 2. management, which has to do with controlling students' behavior; and 3. instruction, which concerns providing for or guiding students' learning" (p. 10). In his chapter on classroom management in the *Handbook of Research on Teaching* (3rd ed.), Walter Doyle (1986) stated that the classroom teachers' role involves the two major functions of establishing order and facilitating learning. In a study of teacher efficacy factors, Emmer and Hickman (1991) reported that classroom management and/or discipline is a separate category from other types of teacher efficacy.

Teacher and community concerns regarding student behavior problems support this contention that classroom management skills are an essential ingredient to effective teaching. In 1991, 44% of teachers in a nationwide sample reported that student misbehavior interfered substantially with their teaching (Mansfield, Alexander, & Ferris, 1991). In this study, 19% of teachers reported being verbally abused by a student during the previous 4 weeks and 28% viewed physical conflicts among students as a serious or moderate problem in their school. In his review of beginning teacher studies throughout the world, Veenman (1984) concluded that "classroom discipline was the most seriously perceived problem area for beginning teachers" (p. 153). Similar findings regarding student teachers' concerns about discipline have been reported by other writers (Abernathy, Manera, & Wright, 1985; Thompson & Ellis, 1984). Veeman's analysis also indicated that principals viewed classroom discipline as being the most serious problem for beginning teachers.

Reporting on a large sample of elementary and secondary teachers, Blase (1986) concluded that teachers perceive as most stressful student behavior that is aggressive and that interrupts classroom events. In a 1987 study conducted for the Center for Educational Statistics, teachers estimated that 7% of their students had habitual behavior problems; 44% of public school teachers reported more disruptive classroom behavior in their schools than 5 years earlier; and 29% of public school teachers stated that they had seriously considered leaving teaching because of student misbehavior. In a study on teacher stress, Feitler and Tokar (1992) reported that 58% of the 3,300 K–12 public school teachers in their sample "ranked 'individual pupils who continually misbehave' as the number one cause of job-related stress" (pp. 456, 457). Emmer (1994) also reported that many of the events that evoke negative teacher emotions are related either directly or indirectly to issues of student behavior.

The public echoes teachers' concerns. During its first 16 years, the annual Gallup Poll of the Public's Attitudes Toward the Public Schools showed school discipline as the biggest problem facing public schools. From 1986 to 1991, discipline ranked second only to drug use. In 1992 and 1993, concerns regarding student behavior ranked behind school funding and drug use as the public's main concerns.

Although studies about classroom management issues certainly point to the centrality of this topic in teacher education, studies on academic time-on-task present further concern. In a study of 132 teachers in six elementary schools, Rich and McNelis (1988) reported that students were on-task in academic learning during only 32.2% of the school day. While many events such as recess and lunch reduce academic engagement time, issues of classroom management are central to effective engagement. Gump (1967) reported that approximately half of teachers' actions involved such management functions as organizing and arranging students for instruction (23%), dealing with misbehavior (14%), and handling individual student problems (12%). Similar data have been reported in British schools (Wragg, 1984).

The Changing Student Population

One cannot work with veteran teachers without hearing how dramatically students and their behavior have changed since the mid-1980s. Whereas only 11% of children born in the 1950s experienced their parents being separated or divorced, nearly 55% of students born in the 1990s will experience this phenomenon (Whitehead, 1993). In addition, one in every four children growing up in the 1990s will live in a step-family, and it appears that, by their teens, nearly half of these children will experience a second divorce as their step-family breaks up. The out-of-wedlock birth rate jumped from only 5% in 1960 to 27% in 1990. The United States has the highest reported rate of teenage pregnancy among industrialized nations (Reynolds, 1989). Reporting on a study from the Children's Defense Fund, Haycock (1990) indicates that 12 million children (more than 20%) live in poverty and have no health insurance. Families with children constitute the fastest growing group of homeless people in this country. The Child Welfare League of America reports more than 2 1/4 million abused or neglected children, and at least one out of every six students lives in a home affected by drug or alcohol abuse (Wenger, 1985). Students spend more time watching television than attending school (Singer & Singer, 1990). In addition, while attending school, the average high school student works more than 20 hours per week (Freiberg, 1991).

Stress within homes clearly has an impact on students' ability to function effectively in school. Based on the National Longitudinal Study of 1988, in which a cohort of 25,000 eighth graders from across the nation was followed through 1990, the data from the National Center for Education Statistics showed that

Students . . . who were from single-parent families, or who had frequently changed schools were more likely than other students to have low basic skills in mathematics and reading and were more likely to drop out regardless of their sex, race-ethnicity, or SES. (Kaufman, Bradby, & Owings, 1992, pp. 15, 16)

For many students, stress and violence within the home are matched by similar problems in the community. In a study of southside Chicago elementary children, 26% reported having seen someone shot, whereas 29% had observed a stabbing (O'Neil, 1991).

The importance of creating positive, well-managed classrooms that facilitate learning for all students has implications far beyond school walls. In her book, *Adolescents at Risk: Prevalence and Prevention,* Joy Dryfoos (1990) examined current research on the causes, possible prevention, and response to such serious problems as drug use, early pregnancy, school failure, and delinquency. She summed up the important role school personnel play when she wrote that

Many of the interventions in the other fields incorporated educational enhancement as the major program component. In fact, the prevention of delinquency appears to be embedded in the prevention of school failure. Whether delinquency prevention is actually a field in itself or whether it should be subsumed under the rubric of educational remediation is an unresolved issue. To a great degree, this may be true of prevention of substance abuse and teen pregnancy as well. The acquisition of basic skills at appropriate ages appears to be a primary component of all prevention. (pp. 235, 236)

UNDERSTANDING EFFECTIVE CLASSROOM MANAGEMENT

If teachers are to respond effectively to the increasing demands described, it seems obvious that they must be provided with effective training in a range of management techniques. Before examining these methods, however, it is essential to consider several key issues and to develop a working definition of classroom management.

The Issue of Power, Control, and Caring

In his book, *Constructive School Discipline,* Smith (1936) wrote

It must be admitted, however, that the failure of the old disciplinary regime, not inaptly styled 'beneficent tyranny,' has left the situation somewhat chaotic. Many have discarded the authoritative type of control without developing any adequate system to take its place. . . . Discipline under the new regime cannot be made easier, but it may be made a more vital element in moral education than it ever could under any system of autocratic domination. (pp. 8, 9)

Anyone who has recently been involved in in-service teacher training knows that Smith's 60-year-old commentary is as relevant today as it was then. Despite such student-centered additions to curriculum and instruction as whole language, community-based learning, self-regulated learning, and cooperative learning, student discipline is still viewed largely as providing rewards and consequences to students (McCaslin & Good, 1992; Short & Noblit, 1985).

When dealing with the issue of control and authority in the classroom, teachers are clearly not faced with an either-or situation. All teachers care about students, and all teachers need to work with students to develop a safe and orderly classroom climate. Nevertheless, a central issue in defining classroom management will always be the manner in which the teacher chooses to develop safety and order.

Although many teachers chose to enter the teaching profession because they cared about students (McLaughlin, 1991), research indicates that beginning teachers display a strong tendency to become increasingly controlling of their students (Moser, 1982; Silvernail & Costello, 1983; Tabachnick & Zeichner, 1984; Zeichner & Gore, 1990). As teachers move from the idealism of helping young people learn to the reality of maintaining an orderly learning environment in a classroom of 30 students, it is essential that they develop a philosophy and supporting strategies related to classroom management. Curwin and Mendler (1988) suggest that teachers must decide whether to use the obedience model or the responsibility model of authority. In the early 1970s, John Holt noted that teachers had to choose whether they would use natural authority or arbitrary, role-bound authority. Recently, H. James McLaughlin wrote

A teacher's *legitimate* authority has four characteristics: it derives from personal and positional relationships with students; it is both assumed and conferred; it is constrained or enabled by school and societal contexts; and it is predicated on the transformation of control by caring. (1992, p. 4)

Bowers and Flinders (1990) have suggested that "control and caring are not opposing terms; but the form of control is transformed by the presence of caring" (p. 15).

As teachers face increasing numbers of students who desperately need models of caring adults who can simultaneously provide a sense of order and safety in their lives, it becomes increasingly necessary to blend caring and controlling in the classroom. In addition, as more students enter the classroom feeling disempowered and confused, the decisions teachers make in selecting approaches to curriculum, instruction, and classroom management become increasingly important in teaching caring, communication skills, and democratic principles.

Issues of control are related to student motivation and achievement as well as to student behavior and mental health. Ames (1992) wrote

A positive relationship between the autonomy orientation of the classroom environment and students' intrinsic motivation has been supported across numerous studies . . . . The perception of control appears to be a significant factor affecting children's engagement in learning and quality of learning. (p. 266)

An Historical Perspective

Jones (1989) suggests that since the 1960s, approaches to dealing with student behavior problems have included three major trends. During the 1960s and 1970s, the emphasis in the area of student management was on what to do when students misbehaved. Because education in the late 1960s and 1970s was heavily influenced by humanistic psychology, a major emphasis was placed on enhancing students' self-esteem and using counseling methods to assist students who were behaving inappropriately. Writers such as LaBenne and Green (1969) and Purkey (1970, 1978) emphasized the relationship between students' self-esteem and student behavior and learning. This work was expanded into methods for dealing with student behavior by such works as Dreikurs, Grunwald, and Pepper's (1971) *Maintaining Sanity in the Classroom;* Dreikurs and Cassel's (1972) *Discipline Without Tears;* Gordon's (1974) *Teacher Effectiveness Training;* and Glasser's (1965, 1969) *Reality Therapy* and *Schools Without Failure.* Although these methods have been centerpieces for staff development (Charles, 1992; Duke & Meckel, 1984), research provides only limited support for these approaches (Emmer & Aussiker, 1990; Hyman & Lally, 1982).

With increasing social uneasiness regarding youth and the greater emphasis on serving a wider range of children in American public schools, educators began to consider how to implement behavioral methods into the classroom. This phase of classroom discipline generated such works as O'Leary and O'Leary's (1972) *Classroom Management: The Successful Use of Behavior Modification;* Becker, Englemann, and Thomas's (1975) *Teaching I: Classroom Management;* Sloane, Buckholdt, Jenson, and Crandall's (1979) *Structured Teaching: A Design for Classroom Management and Instruction;* and Walker's (1979) *The Acting-Out Child: Coping with Classroom Disruption.* This phase of classroom management was perhaps best characterized by Canter and Canter's (1976) *Assertive Discipline.* Research on both earlier and subsequent forms of behavior modification has consistently supported their effectiveness in bringing about changes in students' behaviors (Carpenter & Apter, 1988; Stoner, Shinn, & Walker, 1991). Research has, however, failed to support the benefits of behavioral principles when applied in such "canned" classroom-level programs as assertive discipline (Emmer & Aussiker, 1990; Hyman & Lally, 1982).

During the late 1970s and early 1980s the emphasis began to change from how to respond to behavior problems to how to prevent or reduce unproductive student behavior. This work was initially stimulated by Jacob Kounin's (1970) benchmark study and by the Texas Teacher Effectiveness Study (Brophy & Evertson, 1976). This research was supported and expanded by the Beginning School Year Studies by Emmer and Evertson (Emmer, Evertson, & Anderson, 1980; Evertson & Emmer, 1982). Emmer and Evertson developed training manuals based on their research and, in the best tradition of educational research, studied the impact instruction in these methods had on teachers' and students' classroom behaviors (Evertson, 1985, 1989; Evertson, Emmer, Sanford, & Clements, 1983).

Since the mid-1980s, all of these trends have been both expanded and increasingly integrated. The humanistic and counseling tradition has been continued by Glasser in his books, *Control Theory* (1985) and *The Quality School* (1990). Curwin and Mendler's *Discipline with Dignity* (1988) and Mendler's (1992) *What Do I Do When . . . ?: How to Achieve Discipline with Dignity in the Classroom* have expanded the focus on students' needs and problem solving as key aspects of effective student management. Training programs such as Jim Fey's "Discipline with Love and Logic" have combined with continued training in Glasser's reality therapy to provide educators with training options in this tradition. James McLaughlin's (1991, 1992) work on caring and control and the importance of mutual respect and dialogue in the classroom has been an important addition to this approach. Recently, Forrest Gathercoal's (1993) *Judicious Discipline* has provided teachers with a theoretical

framework and practical methods for developing democratic classrooms at all age levels.

The behavioral tradition has also been characterized by change and the integration of concepts from other models. Lee Canter has expanded his initial focus on controlling student behavior by adding materials on beginning the school year, working with parents, and helping students with homework. While Jones (1987a) continued the behavior control paradigm with his emphasis on teacher control through the use of nonverbal cues and a system of reinforcements, he supplemented this with his book on effective instruction. In addition, the classical behaviorism of the early 1970s, with its emphasis on reinforcers and consequences, has given way to cognitive behaviorism with its focus on self-management and social skills training (Carpenter & Apter, 1988).

In their books, *Classroom Management for Elementary Teachers* (Evertson, Emmer, Clements, & Worsham, 1994) and *Classroom Management for Secondary Teachers* (Emmer, Evertson, Clements, & Worsham, 1994), Evertson and Emmer have continued their focus on beginning the school year by effectively organizing the classroom and developing rules and routines. They have also included chapters on "Communication Skills for Teachers" and "Managing Problem Behaviors." Another book in this vein is Weinstein and Mignano's (1993) *Elementary Classroom Management: Lessons from Research and Practice.* These authors use a case approach emphasizing how skilled teachers organize the classroom environment, develop rules and procedures, and manage various types of instructional activities. They too include chapters from the relationship ("Working with Families") and behavioral ("Helping Children with Special Needs") approaches. In their book, *Comprehensive Classroom Management,* Jones and Jones (1995) provide a balanced approach that incorporates all three major paradigms.

A Working Definition of Classroom Management

Before exploring specific classroom management strategies that have stemmed from the research paradigms described, it is important to develop a working definition of classroom management. Numerous writers have presented ideas on the meaning of classroom management. Doyle (1990b) wrote

To say a classroom is orderly, then, means that students are *cooperating in the program of action defined by the activity a teacher is attempting to use.* Misbehavior, in turn, is any action by students that threatens to disrupt the activity flow or pull the class toward an alternative program of action. (p. 115)

Doyle (1990b) suggests that the probability of students cooperating in the program of action is influenced by three factors: (1) the types of activities in which students are involved, (2) the physical characteristics of the classroom, and (3) the type of work students are assigned.

Brophy (1988) provided a thoughtful, thorough definition when he wrote

Good classroom management implies not only that the teacher has elicited the cooperation of the students in minimizing misconduct and can intervene effectively when misconduct occurs, but also that worthwhile academic activities are occurring more or less continuously and that the classroom management system as a whole (which includes, but is not limited to, the teacher's disciplinary interventions) is designed to maximize student engagement in those activities, not merely to minimize misconduct. (p. 3)

Jones and Jones (1986) describe five teacher skills and general functions that serve as the basis for what they term *comprehensive classroom management*. These authors note that effective management is based on

1. An understanding of current research and theory in classroom management and students' psychological and learning needs
2. The creation of positive teacher–student and peer relationships
3. The use of instructional methods that facilitate optimal learning by responding to the academic needs of individual students and the classroom group
4. The use of organizational and group management methods that maximize on-task behavior
5. The ability to use a range of counseling and behavioral methods to assist students who demonstrate persistent and/or serious behavior problems

These five methods parallel Brophy's (1988) statement that the major teaching functions needed to establish an effectively managed classroom include "instruction, classroom management, student socialization, and disciplinary intervention" (p. 2). In this chapter, current "best accepted practice" in classroom management is examined using the categories described by the Joneses and Brophy.

CLASSROOM MANAGEMENT AND THE SCHOOL AND CLASSROOM CONTEXT

Before continuing with a review of practices supported by research, it is important to highlight the concept that context variables must be considered when making classroom management decisions. Numerous writers have discussed the importance of examining such context variables as instructional goals and methods, students' ages, socioeconomic level, cultural norms, and cognitive skills (Ballenger, 1992; Brophy & Evertson, 1978; Cohen, Intili, & Robbins, 1979; Darling-Hammond, Wise, & Pease, 1983; Diaz-Rico, 1993; Doyle, 1979b; Kuykendall, 1992; Soar, 1983; Zumwalt, 1982).

Students' Characteristics and Needs

Ballenger (1992) provides an engaging description of an American teacher's discovery that the perspective from which she viewed behavior control and her use of language needed to be altered if she were to effectively manage young Haitian children. Macias (1987) reported similar findings in her study of Papago preschoolers (members of a Native-American group in Arizona). In an ethnographic study of five student teachers placed in schools with students from cultural backgrounds dramatically different from their own, Dana (1992) found that students reported major problems with classroom management. Her findings suggest that the student teachers attributed their difficulties to their students' backgrounds and found their efforts to implement the prepackaged technique of assertive discipline to be ineffective and frustrating. In her book, *From Rage to Hope: Strategies for Reclaiming Black and Hispanic Students,* Crystal Kuykendall (1992) argues for considering students' cultural needs when developing instructional and management methods. Recent data on school suspensions reported by the U.S. Department of Education's Office for Civil Rights (1993) indicate that 54% of suspended students were white, 32% were black, and 12% were Hispanic. These data suggest a disproportionate suspension rate for students of color and raise a serious question of whether school environments are biased against the learning and social-emotional needs of these students.

Studies also suggest that girls may respond to different instructional and management methods than boys, and that boys and girls may receive different responses from teachers. For example, in his study on the effects expectations and task value have on students' intention to continue taking mathematics courses, Ethington (1991) found significant differences in factors influencing motivation for boys and girls. In its 1992 report, *How Schools Shortchange Girls,* The American Association of University Women reviewed extensive research indicating that girls have different learning needs than boys and that schools too often support the needs and learning preferences of boys (AAUW, 1992). Similarly, in her study of classroom discipline in Australia, Robinson (1992) found major differences between teachers' responses to boys and girls. Jones and Wheatley (1990) studied teacher–student dyadic interactions in 30 physical science and 30 chemistry classes and reported that boys had both more positive and negative interactions with their teachers. Torrance (1986) reported that teachers were three times as likely to reward creative behavior in boys than girls. It is also true, however, that boys are disproportionately served in special education programs for students with learning disabilities and with serious emotional and behavioral problems (U.S. Department of Education [DOE], 1992) and are more often suspended from school (Haynes, 1986; McFadden, Marsh, Price, & Hwang, 1992; Morgan, 1991).

In a similar vein, writers have examined specific management skills that may be most effective with students with special needs. This has included talented and gifted students (Jones, 1983), and students with behavioral disorders (Gable, Hendrickson, Young, & Shokoohi-Yekta, 1992; Jones, 1992, in press; Stoner, Shinn, & Walker, 1991), attention-deficit disorders (Burcham, Carlson, & Milich, 1993; Fiore, Becker, & Nero, 1993; Friedman & Doyal, 1992; Shaywitz & Shaywitz, 1992), and mild retardation (Brigham, Bakken, Scruggs, & Mastropieri, 1992).

As was mentioned earlier, virtually all classroom management research has been conducted in elementary and junior high classrooms. Brophy and Evertson (1978) noted that teachers' approaches to management should be influenced by their students' intellectual and social development. It appears likely that older students will be more overtly sensitive to issues of control and empowerment. Glasser (1988) noted that approximately 80% of student misbehavior is related to students' attempts to empower themselves in a rather controlling environment. Jones (1980) has described the importance of attending to students' key developmental needs as a central factor influencing the effectiveness of management methods with adolescents. Kohn (1993) presents a powerful argument for increasing students' experiences with choice and negotiation. Curwin and Mendler's (1988) book, *Discipline with Dignity,* emphasizes the importance of treating students respectfully. While it seems unlikely that classroom instructional and management methods that fail to empower students will be effective with many of today's adolescents, it appears certain that they will be highly ineffective with youth who enter school feeling alienated and disenfranchised.

Instructional Tasks

There is increased awareness that management methods may be most effective when they are tailored to the teachers' instructional methods. Several writers have highlighted the fact that as teachers move away from teacher-directed presentation and recitation, classroom management methods become more complex (Cohen, Intili, & Robbins, 1979; Doyle, 1979b; Doyle & Carter, 1984; McCaslin & Good, 1992). Educators have begun to explore the types of classroom management methods that facilitate such varied instructional methods as whole language instruction (Baumann, 1992) and cooperative learning (Anderson & Pigford, 1988; Ward, 1987). The use of these instructional methods will require teachers to instruct students in specific procedures in areas such as working effectively in groups and providing editorial assistance to peers.

The School Context

It is impossible to separate management from such issues as school climate, structure, decision making, and the type of professional support that is provided within the building. Numerous writers have described the central impact school variables have on student behavior and learning (Aleem & Moles, 1993; Bickel & Qualls, 1980; Cohen, 1983; Cusick, 1983; Duke, 1990; Duke & Meckel, 1980; Goodlad, 1983; Gottfredson & Gottfredson, 1985; Lightfoot, 1983; Lipsitz, 1984; Moles, 1990; Mortimore & Sammons, 1987; Rutter, Maughan, Mortimore, Ouston, & Smith, 1979; Sizer, 1984, 1992; Villa Thousand, Stainback, & Stainback, 1992; Wayson & Pinnell, 1982; Wehlage & Rutter, 1986; Wehlage, Rutter, Smith, Lesko, & Fernandez, 1989; Weishew & Peng, 1993). Schools in which staff have developed a unified sense of mission and where they work collaboratively to support one another in reaching clear goals are characterized by fewer student behavior problems. Likewise, behavior is more positive in schools where students experience a sense of belonging and support and in which instructional activities engage them in meaningful ways connected to their own lives and cultures. To establish learning environments in which students feel less alienated and isolated, an increasing number of secondary school staff are examining ways to structure the school day so students have longer class periods or blocked classes. This allows students to work for extended periods of time with one adult and one group of peers. The focus on student and teacher

empowerment and quality of life within schools will be an essential component in educators' ongoing efforts to create safer, more productive learning environments.

Researchers at the Center for Research on the Context of Secondary School Teaching (CRC) at Stanford University are currently studying factors in high schools that support learning (Phelan, Davidson, & Cao, 1992). Their studies focus on determining students' perceptions regarding the school community. In examining the impact of social versus school factors, Phelan et al. (1992) note

Of most importance to practitioners and policy makers is the fact that many of the forces students mention are not objective constraints but factors under the control of teachers and principals. Furthermore, these young people present a view of themselves that may be surprising to those who are convinced that the plethora of social problems precludes effective responses through school improvement efforts. We find that, despite negative outside influences, students from all achievement levels and sociocultural backgrounds want to succeed and want to be in an environment in which it is possible to do so. (p. 696)

Although the next section examines a wide variety of specific methods researchers have found to be effective in creating positive, well-managed classrooms, it is important to keep in mind that, as suggested, no one strategy or set of strategies can be given to teachers as a panacea. Teachers must examine this research in light of such contextual variables as their students' cultural values, developmental and cognitive levels, the teacher's instructional goals and methods, and the teacher's own personal style.

The real issue is whether teachers can use this information to become informed decision makers and reflective practitioners. In speaking about the translation of educational research into practice, Eisner (1984) noted that responsible use of research requires that educators should "have examined a body of research studies, extracted generalizations, determined that the theory is supported by the evidence, and then used the theory as a tool for shaping decisions" (p. 448). The next section examines the existing research in the key areas outlined by Jones and Jones (1986) and Brophy (1988). The final section considers how teacher educators can most effectively assist students in completing the tasks outlined by Eisner.

KEY SKILLS IN EFFECTIVE CLASSROOM MANAGEMENT

This section examines the four areas of student socialization, instruction, classroom management, and disciplinary interventions. Key research findings are described and each section concludes with a statement regarding needs and directions for further research.

Socialization: Creating Positive Teacher–Student and Peer Relationships

As mentioned earlier, the changing environments in which today's students are socialized have created a situation in which more students enter school with major personal needs not hav-

CLASSROOM MANAGEMENT • 509

ing been met. In discussing students who are at risk for school failure, Morse (1985), an expert on children with emotional and behavioral disorders, wrote

We have observed that increasing numbers of children are coming to school at risk because their self-development remains immature. School is a place designed for children who have absorbed the lessons from an effective primary group. . . .

But the child who comes without these accomplishments will be compelled to work on them even though the school is a secondary group, rather than a family group. (p. 27)

The extent to which students will have their personal needs met is strongly influenced by the quality of both teacher–student and peer relationships that exist within the classroom.

Teacher-Student Relationships A considerable body of research conducted during the 1960s and 1970s suggests that the academic behavior of students is influenced by the quality of teacher–student relationships. Studies report that students who perceive their teachers as caring and supportive are more positive about school (Aspy & Roebuck, 1977) and have higher academic achievement (Davidson & Lang, 1960; Kleinfeld, 1975; Morrison & McIntyre, 1969; Truax & Tatum, 1966).

More recent studies in middle schools and high schools support these findings. In reviewing the results of their study at the Center for Research on the Context of Secondary School Teaching at Stanford University, the researchers state

A recurring theme in students' comments is the tremendous value they place on having teachers who care. . . .

In fact, the number of student references to "wanting caring teachers" is so great that we believe it speaks to the quiet desperation and loneliness of many adolescents in today's society. (Phelan, Davidson, & Cao, 1992, p. 698)

In their extensive study of school environments that meet the needs of adolescents at risk for school failure, Wehlage and his colleagues (1989) report that students at risk need a more personal and supportive relationship with adults than schools typically provide. The authors note that

In addition, there are four teacher beliefs and/or values, accompanied by corresponding sets of behaviors, that together constitute a positive teacher culture facilitating membership and engagement for students. These beliefs are: teachers accept personal *accountability* for student success; they believe in practicing an *extended teacher role*; they accept the need to be *persistent* with students who are not ideal pupils; they *express a sense of optimism* that all students can learn if one builds upon their strengths rather than their weaknesses. (p. 135)

Lipsitz (1984) reported similar findings in her study of effective middle schools. In describing these schools, Lipsitz remarked that they provided a warm, personal environment, a factor she reported as particularly important for early adolescents. Story (1985) found that teachers who used both physical touch and verbal interactions characterized by humor, warmth, and encouragement were more effective in facilitating the learning of talented and gifted students. In her review of research on competent beginning teaching, Reynolds (1992) indicates

that certain personality characteristics are needed for teachers to competently perform their teaching tasks.

In addition to the general positive quality of teacher–student relationships, there are additional, more specific teacher–student relationship factors associated with positive student behavior. Among the best researched of these factors are teacher expectations and the provision of feedback to students. Numerous studies report the effect teacher expectations have on student achievement (Brophy, 1983b; Cooper & Good, 1983; Dusek, 1985). Brophy (1983b) notes that "these effects make only a 5–10 percent difference, on the average. . . . These conclusions clearly imply that even ideal teacher education related to the topic of teacher expectations will not work miracles in our schools" (p. 635). He further notes, however, that these findings are based on averages and that teacher expectations can have a dramatic impact in some classrooms and with some students. Clearly, teachers' understanding of these effects and an ability to implement this knowledge so as to minimize the negative effects of teacher expectations are important aspects of teacher training in classroom management.

A third area that has received attention is teacher feedback to students (Brophy, 1981; Kahle, 1990; Sadker & Sadker, 1985). Studies suggest that feedback is most effective when it is clear and specific (Kulhavy & Stock, 1989), immediate (Kulik & Kulik, 1988), and when it focuses on students' specific performance and effort (Clifford, 1990). Studies also suggest that students perform better in settings in which teachers emphasize student effort and achievement gains rather than comparisons with other students (Maher, 1987; McColskey & Leary, 1985; Slavin, 1980).

Although earlier studies of teacher–student relationships argued for teachers who were warm and supportive, newer studies are needed to examine how these factors interact with such factors as how classroom rules and procedures are established, the manner in which instruction is organized, and the way teachers respond to incidents of disruptive student behavior. It appears likely that there are patterns of teacher behaviors across these classroom management factors that help to establish classrooms in which students have the sense of safety, security, empowerment, and support that facilitate learning positive social and academic skills.

Peer Relationships This is perhaps the least emphasized area related to classroom management. Only one of the leading classroom management textbooks written in the 1990s includes a chapter on establishing positive peer relationships. This seems shortsighted in light of research on the importance of these relationships and the increased use of methods, such as peer tutoring and cooperative learning, that depend on positive student interaction as a prerequisite to learning.

Lewis and St. John (1974) studied the factors that influenced the achievement of black students in classrooms in which the majority of students were white. Their results indicated that the presence of high-achieving white students was not sufficient to enhance academic achievement among the black students. Achievement was, however, increased when the black students felt accepted by their white classmates. Additional studies support the finding that student attendance and achievement are enhanced by the creation of classroom norms characterized by diverse, positive peer relationships (Reynolds, 1977; Schmuck, 1966; Walberg & Anderson, 1968). Studies suggest that peers can be important partners in enhancing learning (Barrell, 1991; Dyson, 1987) and that students prefer classrooms that include cooperative learning activities (Allen, 1986). A good summary of research and theory on peer relationships in the classroom can be found in Schmuck and Schmuck's (1992) *Group Processes in the Classroom.*

Whereas the development of cohesive group norms and diverse liking patterns received considerable attention during the 1970s, cooperative learning was the major focus of classroom group processes in the 1980s. Good and Brophy (1991) summarized the effects associated with cooperative learning.

Effects on outcomes other than achievement are even more impressive. Cooperative learning arrangements promote friendship choices and prosocial patterns of interaction among students who differ in achievement, sex, race or ethnicity, and they promote the acceptance of mainstreamed handicapped students by their nonhandicapped classmates. Cooperative methods also frequently have positive effects, and rarely have negative effects, on affective outcomes such as self-esteem, academic self-confidence, liking for the class, liking and feeling liked by classmates, and various measures of empathy and social cooperation. (p. 416)

Given the considerable body of knowledge supporting the benefits of classrooms characterized by diverse liking patterns and cooperative group structures, it is surprising that current materials used to train teachers in classroom management place almost no focus on establishing positive peer relationships. One can only surmise that this is in part due to the perception that classroom management is intended to serve the end of increasing time-on-task, that the important tasks of the classroom are mastery of academic content, and that time spent developing a cohesive group might detract from this end.

In this light, it is interesting to note that in its 1983 report, *Basic Skills in the U.S. Workforce,* the Center for Public Resources stated that, based on a nationwide survey of businesses, labor unions, and educational institutions, 90% of people fired from their jobs were dismissed not for lack of technical skills, but for problems associated with interpersonal relationships and behaviors. Similarly, in the 1988 report, *Workplace Basics: The Skills Employers Want,* the American Society for Training and Development and the U.S. Department of Labor, Employment and Training Administration listed the following four of the seven categories of skills most wanted by employers: (1) group effectiveness: interpersonal skills, negotiation, and teamwork; (2) listening and oral communication; (3) personal management: self-esteem, goal setting/motivation; and (4) organizational effectiveness and leadership. In their examination of national and regional studies on educational requirements needed for the job market, researchers from the Sandia National Laboratories (1993) wrote, "According to business leaders polled, the most important workplace 'skills' for future employees were not academic skills. Rather, behavioral 'skills' . . . were all listed in the 'highly critical' categories" (p. 295). It would seem that using classroom management methods that focus on teaching students to interact and collaborate more effectively may not only enhance classroom behavior but also may help students develop important life skills.

In the future, additional research needs to be conducted to determine the impact positive peer relationships and cooperative work have on such variables as student attendance, on-task behavior, and achievement based on a broad range of outcome variables.

Instruction

The relationship between classroom management and instruction has been argued effectively by several leaders in the field (Brophy, 1988; Doyle, 1983, 1990a; McCaslin & Good, 1992). Clearly, when students are actively engaged in interesting work at which they can be successful, problems of student misbehavior are minimized. Unfortunately, there are almost no controlled studies that examine the relationship between instructional strategies and student behavior.

Studies suggest that student motivation and behavior may be influenced by the fact that many students spend a large portion of the school day engaged in activities that require only lower level cognitive tasks and for which the students cannot clearly articulate the meaning (Anderson, 1984; Brophy, 1986; Brophy, Rohrkemper, Rashid, & Goldberger, 1983; Goodlad, 1983; Hansen, 1989). Research (Doyle, 1983; Doyle & Carter, 1984; Hansen, 1989) also indicates that, when faced with what they perceived to be difficult academic tasks, students asked questions and used other stalling techniques to postpone work demands.

Evidence is beginning to accumulate that student engagement can be enhanced by implementing instructional methods that more actively and personally engage students in the learning process (Ames, 1990; Blumenfeld et al., 1991; Jervis, 1986; Maehr & Midgley, 1991; Rothenberg, 1989; Slavin, 1990). Maher (1987) found that when behavior problem students with a history of school failure were involved in discussing instructional plans and goals with teachers, their behavior and academic performance improved dramatically. Jervis (1986) reported how a teacher obtained similar results in a fourth-grade classroom.

Research suggests that students are more motivated by instructional strategies focusing on progress, effort, and goal attainment than on comparison to others (Ames, 1992; Ames & Archer, 1988; Dweck, 1986; Krampen, 1987; Locke & Latham, 1990; Marshall, 1990; McGowen, Sutton, & Smith, 1990; Mitman & Lash, 1988; Pressley, Johnson, Symons, McGoldrick, & Kurita, 1989). Fuchs et al. (1990) suggest that a combination of goal setting and self-monitoring can assist students with patterns of school failure to improve their behavior and reduce the need for referral to special education. DeCharms's (1984) work with inner-city elementary students found that student attendance and achievement can be increased by teaching students to establish objectives and determine strategies for meeting these objectives. Students with a history of school failure appear to benefit from programs that combine attribution retraining with training in strategies for reaching their goals (Ames, 1987; VanOverwalle, Segebarth, & Goldschstein, 1989). Because an overemphasis on reinforcing effort may reduce students' sense of their own abilities, it is important to assist students in attributing success to their abilities as well as to effort and the use of newly developed strategies.

Teachers may increasingly need to view misbehavior as students' failure to develop effective learning strategies (Weinstein & Mayer, 1986) and to make meaning of their work (Newby, 1991). In an interesting study of one teacher struggling with classroom management problems, Diaz-Rico (1993) reported that the teacher successfully responded to these problems by developing improved skills in implementing curriculum and instructional methods that responded to the students' cultural context and approaches to learning. This concept of connecting content to students' cultural context has been examined by others (Alton-Lee, Nuthall, & Patrick, 1993; Banks, 1991; Butler, 1993; Tetreault, 1993).

Greater research emphasis needs to be placed on examining the curriculum and instructional methods associated with such outcomes as student achievement, on-task behavior, and positive student attitudes about school. It is interesting that a method as widespread as Lee Canter's "assertive discipline" has placed absolutely no emphasis on examining classroom curriculum and instruction as a factor influencing student behavior.

Classroom Management

A study of teacher training in classroom management would not be complete without a brief discussion of research on organizing the classroom and maintaining student attention. No area of classroom management has been studied as thoroughly as methods for beginning the school year and maintaining on-task behavior (see Doyle, 1986).

Beginning the School Year Some of the best research in classroom management examines methods for establishing desirable student behavior at the beginning of the school year. The initial studies involved observations in 27 elementary classrooms (Emmer, Evertson & Anderson, 1980) and 51 junior high school teachers (Evertson & Emmer, 1982). Results of these studies indicated that teachers whose students made higher achievement gains and demonstrated higher rates of on-task behavior effectively taught students clear rules and procedures, carefully monitored behavior, and responded when students failed to follow the prescribed behaviors. The researchers then took the step of developing a manual to train teachers in implementing these methods and conducted research comparing behaviors in classrooms in which teachers had been trained in these methods to behavior of students taught by a control group (Evertson, Emmer, Sanford, & Clements, 1983; Evertson, 1985, 1989). These studies consistently found that teachers provided with this training were more successful at increasing student task engagement and reducing inappropriate student behavior.

Prescriptions stemming from this series of studies have been incorporated into virtually all approaches to teacher training in classroom management. During the early 1990s, Lee Canter modified his "assertive discipline" to include training in developing rules and procedures. Classroom training sponsored by Madeline Hunter has incorporated these methods, and virtually every leading textbook on classroom management includes at least one chapter based on Evertson and Emmer's work. Evertson and Emmer have expanded their manual into textbooks with a major focus on these findings and those described in the following section.

Gathercoal (1993) developed a model for placing the development of classroom rules within the context of students' rights. Gathercoal's approach involves students in realizing that in order for their constitutional rights to be upheld, it is imperative (and legally mandated) that the rights of others (termed *compelling state interests*) be upheld. Whereas controlled studies need to be conducted to ascertain the benefits of this program, materials have been developed (McEwan, 1991) and the approach has been field tested at virtually every grade level.

Freiberg (Freiberg, 1993; Freiberg, Huang, Stein, & Waxman, 1994; Freiberg, Prokosch, Treister, & Stein, 1990) has presented exciting data indicating that his consistency management program is associated with improved achievement and behavior in inner-city elementary classrooms. The program emphasizes providing students with opportunities to be responsible for meaningful organizational tasks within the classroom and throughout the school. Rather than the teacher developing the classroom rules, teachers are encouraged to have students create their own set of behavioral expectations. The program also involves incentives for student achievement and community and school service.

Maintaining High Rates of On-Task Behavior Prior to the work by Emmer and Evertson, Kounin (1970) had examined the classroom behavior of teachers who were more successful at obtaining high rates of on-task student behavior. Kounin discovered that although student involvement in class activities was not closely related to teacher desistances or corrections, involvement was related to a series of proactive teacher behaviors. These behaviors include "withitness," overlapping, smooth transitions, and variety and accountability in seatwork. Subsequent studies (Brophy & Evertson, 1976; Emmer, Evertson, & Anderson, 1980) confirmed the benefits of these behaviors. This work has provided teacher educators with a solid basis for providing prospective teachers with classroom management training. Many leading textbooks on classroom management either integrate this material into their work or provide one or more chapters dealing with methods stemming from Kounin's work and related findings.

These principles of classroom management are based on studies in classrooms in which the transmission mode of teaching was dominant. Although they are very likely to apply to classrooms in which the constructivist approach is emphasized, these methods need to be viewed as general principles rather than rigid management guidelines. Teachers will be most effective in applying these principles if they realize that their management system should be designed to support their instructional system. Having first determined the instructional objectives, a teacher selects instructional methods to reach these goals. These methods in turn suggest certain student roles and behaviors. Teachers need to use effective instructional strategies to teach students many of these behaviors. Finally, the manner in which a teacher responds to students' failure to utilize these skills will be most effective if it is congruent with the learning goals and instructional process. If the teacher's instructional goals include students working collaboratively to solve real-world problems, it would seem appropriate that some form of conflict resolution would be used to assist students in bringing their behavior in line with agreed-upon standards. Therefore, instructional goals and methods become the foundation for classroom management decisions.

Responding to Inappropriate Student Behavior Teachers who effectively attend to the socializing function, develop interesting and meaningful lessons, work with their students to develop rules and procedures, and implement "withitness" and other effective management methods unquestionably have significantly fewer disruptions and less inattentive student behavior than teachers who fail to implement these methods. Teachers are, however, asked to educate an increasing number of students who are experiencing serious emotional problems; therefore, even teachers who implement "state of the art" proactive teaching and classroom management methods will be confronted with unproductive student behavior that requires further interventions.

As suggested earlier, teachers rank individual students who have serious and/or persistent behavior problems as their number one cause of stress (Feitler & Tokar, 1992). Many teachers question whether they have the skills necessary to work effectively with students with special needs (Semmel, Abernathy, Butera, & Lesar, 1991). Leyser and Abrams (1986) report that both regular and special education student teachers rate classroom management as an area in which they need additional training in order to work effectively with mainstream students. Studies of teachers' interactions with special needs students suggest that teachers have not acquired the skills necessary to work effectively with them (Leyser, 1988; Thompson, White, & Morgan, 1982). Based on a large survey conducted in Washington, Haring and his colleagues (Haring, Jewell, Lehning, Williams, & White, 1987) reported that almost half of all regular classroom teachers surveyed felt they were not receiving adequate assistance from special education personnel for dealing with students experiencing serious behavior problems. These same teachers listed "behavior management strategies" as their most significant in-service need. In a review of their Classroom Strategy Study involving 98 experienced teachers' strategies for coping with 12 types of problem students, Brophy and McCaslin (1992) reported

> Still, it seems clear that elementary teachers could benefit from systematic instruction in diagnosing and responding to chronic behavior problems. This would make their responses more "planful" and systematic, and it would arm them with additional concepts and strategies that they are unlikely to develop on their own. (p. 58)

In the future, to be successful classroom managers, teachers will need skills in implementing a range of proven strategies for responding to disruptive student behavior. These strategies can be categorized into the general areas of: (1) problem solving, (2) social skill training, (3) self-monitoring and self-instruction, and (4) contracting (Jones, in press; Jones & Jones, 1995). Teachers will also need the assistance of support staff to develop and implement these strategies and of administrators who may use sanctions such as suspensions to ensure a safe and productive learning environment.

Problem Solving and Conflict Resolution As was suggested earlier, the problem-solving approach has been utilized for many years. Classroom management texts that provide an overview of various discipline theories offer summaries of the works of Dreikurs (Dreikurs & Cassel, 1972; Dreikurs, Grunwald, & Pepper, 1971), Glasser (1965), and Gordon (1974). Many school staffs have implemented programs in conflict resolution (Cahoon, 1988; Carlsson-Paige & Levin, 1992; Roderick, 1988). Although these programs appear to provide an important social skill for students, and many articles outline methods and present testimonials, there are currently no experimental studies demonstrating the effect these programs have on specific student outcomes.

Whereas teachers require support in implementing these methods within the fast, complex flow of classroom events, most educators would argue that teachers need skills in solving problems with students and resolving conflicts between students. Indeed, in their extensive review of classroom discipline methods, Emmer and Aussiker (1990) found support for these methods.

Social Skill Training In their landmark work on serving students with serious behavior problems, Knitzer, Steinberg, and Fleisch (1990) noted that most programs focus on behavior control rather than on helping students learn important behaviors that would help them be successful in the school setting. Whether students are simply taking "time-out" in the back of the room, have been sent to the principal's office, or have been assigned an in-building or at-home suspension, it is almost always the case that the student had some problem in dealing with others and expressing emotions in a satisfactory manner. This suggests that these students will need assistance in developing a new repertoire of skills to enable them to successfully cope with the social interaction demands of the school setting.

Social skill training is one approach to providing these strategies. In its most basic form, this occurs when teachers effectively begin the school year by teaching students key classroom and common area procedures. For some students, however, more detailed training in appropriate behavior may be necessary. Materials such as Goldstein, Sprafkin, Gershaw, and Klein's (1980) *Skillstreaming the Adolescent;* McGinnis's (1990) *Skillstreaming in Early Childhood;* Walker's (1987) *ACCESS Program;* and King and Kirschenbaum's (1992) *Helping Young Children Develop Social Skills* present key components in effective social skill development. Research indicates that these methods can be effective in altering a range of student behaviors (Sabornie, 1991; Zaragoza, Vaughn, & McIntosh, 1991). Although these skills will often be taught by someone other than the classroom teacher, it is important that teachers work collaboratively with support staff to ensure the integration of these skills into the classroom setting.

Self-Monitoring and Self-Instruction Self-monitoring involves assisting a student or group of students in establishing a system for monitoring and recording individual behavior. This method has been found effective in changing a range of specific unproductive behaviors with a diverse population of students (Carr & Punzo, 1993; Cole, 1992; Prater, Joy, Chilman, Temple, & Miller, 1991). Although self-monitoring can provide excellent results by itself, it is often combined with strategies for self-instruction, self-evaluation, and self-reinforcement (Cole, 1992; DiGangi &

Maag, 1992; Lloyd, Landrum, & Hallahan, 1991; Mace, Brown, & West, 1987; Skinner & Smith, 1992).

Developing Contracts with Students. Contracts are a classic form of contingency management. During the early phase of behavior modification, contracts were a popular form of bringing the principles of reinforcement and punishment to bear in the classroom (Blackham & Silberman, 1975; Walker, 1979). Although some work suggests that, particularly in elementary classrooms, a token economy or group contract can be developed to obtain the benefits of contracting with the entire class (Brigham et al., 1992; Gallagher, 1988; Myles, Moran, Ormsbee, & Downing, 1992), in most cases contracts will be developed with individual students functioning at lower levels of cognitive development and requiring clear structure to alter their behavior (Jones, 1980; Jones & Jones, 1981, 1995).

The Use of Punishment and Sanctions Against Students When students are involved in serious misbehavior or when teachers' efforts have failed to bring about an adequate reduction in the rate of less severe behaviors, administrators may be asked to provide sanctions in the form of corporal punishment, suspensions, and expulsions. Corporal punishment has been banned by 19 states and a prohibition is currently under consideration in four states. Even in those states in which corporal punishment is allowed, many major school districts have abolished the practice (Yell, 1990).

Suspension from school is used to deal with a variety of misbehaviors. During the 1990–1991 school year, 1 million students were suspended from school and 1.4 million students were given some form of in-school suspension. Virtually no research exists that examines the effects of suspension or compares various types of suspension. For example, although some schools have adopted policies that involve alternatives to suspension or the combination of suspension and conflict resolution, the literature does not include well-designed studies examining the effects of these alternatives.

Helping Teachers Develop Comprehensive Plans Given the demands placed on teachers by difficult-to-manage students and the extent and sophistication of strategies available to assist these students, it is imperative that teachers learn how to utilize assistance in developing special classroom interventions for students with serious and/or persistent behavior problems. Numerous writers have presented models and data to support the development of collaborative consultation between classroom teachers and other educational resource staff (Chalfant & Pysh, 1989; Chaffant, Pysh, & Moultrie, 1979; Curtis, Zins, & Graden, 1987; Fuchs, 1991; Fuchs et al., 1990; Graden, Casey, & Bonstrom, 1985; Graden, Casey, & Christenson, 1985; Hayek, 1987; Jones, in press; McEvoy, Davis, & Reichle, 1993; Nelson, Smith, Taylor, Dodd, & Reavis, 1992). During both preservice and inservice training, teachers will benefit from developing skills for working in such collaborative prereferral intervention teams.

TEACHER EDUCATION IN CLASSROOM MANAGEMENT

A number of studies report that preservice teachers feel poorly prepared in the area of classroom management (Goodlad, 1990;

Reed, 1989; Rickman & Hollowell, 1981; Wesley & Vocke, 1992). In describing the classroom management and discipline curriculum in teacher education, Perry and Taylor (1982) stated that, "A majority of colleges of education or teacher training institutions subordinate or include discipline as a *minor* subject area in courses such as educational psychology and curriculum" (p. 417). Goodlad (1990) suggested that this topic is presented as, "bits and pieces of good counsel . . . received in methods classes" (p. 248). In their study of teacher education programs in 111 colleges and universities, Wesley and Vocke (1992) reported that 36.9% of programs offered separate courses in discipline or classroom management. In their detailed examination of 27 secondary programs in Maryland, Washington, DC, and Delaware, Wesley and Vocke found that only 3 of 18 programs offered a separate course on classroom management, and that when management was offered within another course it was allocated approximately 13% of a semester course. They also reported that only 2 of the 21 institutions they studied planned to increase their offerings in this area.

Although the data are somewhat limited, it does appear that preservice teacher education in classroom management is quite limited and is generally infused throughout a teachers' preservice preparation program. No specific research is available to indicate whether teachers are better prepared by more intense, focused, and coordinated instruction in this area.

Brophy (1988) suggested that to manage classrooms effectively, teachers need to have knowledge of principles stemming from research on classroom management, information on how to implement these in the classroom, and an understanding of when and why methods should be used. He also notes that this material must be related to the context in which the teacher will be working so that issues of content and instruction can be interwoven with classroom management knowledge.

Doyle (1985, 1990b) postulated that teacher education in classroom management has overemphasized instruction in specific methods. He states that teachers must have a solid understanding of the relationship between management decisions and decisions related to curriculum and instruction. Doyle argues that teachers should be provided with assistance in interpreting events and making decisions within the highly complex and rapidly paced classroom setting. He notes that, "Management must be presented in an intellectual framework for understanding classroom events and consequences rather than simply as a collection of tricks and specific reactions to behavior" (1985, p. 33). Similarly, Jones (1982) criticized the patchwork, compartmentalized approach to training in classroom management.

Research by Stoiber (1991) supported these writers' concerns. Stoiber conducted a study comparing technical and reflective preservice instruction in classroom management. Her findings suggest that teachers trained using a reflective-constructive approach develop more positive perceptions of themselves as problem solvers within the classroom, are able to generate more solutions to classroom management problems, take more responsibility for classroom events, and report more concern about students' feelings and attitudes than teachers provided with technical training based on the beginning school year studies.

In a similar vein, Carter (1992) argued for a reflective, constructive view of classroom management instruction. She suggests that teachers develop organizing concepts and related principles regarding classroom management and that developing one's own classroom management approach involves examining these underlying constructs and exploring optional views and methods. Carter (Carter & Gonzales, 1993) noted the critical nature of relating teachers' developing knowledge to their experiences in the classroom. She suggests that providing novice teachers with access to expert teachers' thinking about classroom events and decisions followed by dialogue about these decisions is an important component of assisting novices in examining and restructuring their own concepts and skills.

Many other writers suggest that for experience to lead to meaningful and productive change, it must be accompanied by reflection (Anning, 1988; Schon, 1987; Shulman, 1986). The importance of integrating the knowledge-based and reflective, constructivist approach to teaching classroom management has been supported by Winitzky's (1992) finding of a positive correlation between the complexity of teachers' knowledge structure and their ability to thoughtfully reflect on classroom practice. Given the fact that the school milieu may not facilitate thoughtful reflection (Little, 1987; Rosenholtz, Bassler, & Hoover-Dempsey, 1986), it seems imperative that teacher education programs structure this reflection. Richardson (1990) summarized this concern as follows:

Taking control of one's justifications involves reflection on practices, that is on activities and their theoretical frameworks, and an ability to articulate them to others in a meaningful way . . . .

Research then, should provide practitioners not just with findings in the form of activities or behaviors that work, but ways of thinking and empirical premises related to teaching and learning . . . .

Without an understanding of the theoretical framework and the opportunity to talk about how the premises in the theory agree or disagree with the teachers' own premises, teachers may accept or reject practices on the basis of whether they meet the personality needs of the teacher and other more ecologically created concerns such as classroom management . . . and content coverage. (p. 16)

Richardson's last point is particularly critical. Classroom management decisions occur in a complex, fast-paced setting. In addition, student misbehavior generates strong emotions in teachers (Blase, 1986; Cambone, 1990; Emmer, 1994) and is related to such central personal issues as authority, power, and stress. These factors increase the likelihood that classroom management decisions will more likely be intuitive rather than reflective (Calderhead, 1987). Therefore, it is critical that when developing their classroom management philosophy, teachers be assisted in developing a clear theoretical position that is congruent with their instructional goals and their students' personal and developmental needs.

A number of researchers have also highlighted the important role teachers' preconceptions play in teacher decision making (Anderson, 1989; Brickhouse & Bodner, 1992; Hollingsworth, 1989; Kaplan, 1992; Richardson-Koehler & Fenstermacher, 1988). Clandinin and Connelly (1986) suggest that teachers develop practical strategies by integrating their preconceptions (personal biographies) with their interpretations of classroom situations. Studies report significant relationships between teacher personality factors and their orientation to classroom management (Halpin, Halpin, & Harris, 1982; Lunenburg & O'Reilly, 1974; Victor, 1976; Wakefield, Cunningham, & Edwards, 1975). In a study of 156 preservice teachers, Kaplan (1992) found that "teachers' disciplinary experiences in their families of origin are predictive of the strategies they select for classroom management" (p. 263). Therefore, when educating teachers about classroom management, it seems likely that meaningful behavior change will be enhanced by including discussions about underlying beliefs related to issues of power, control, and authority and about teachers' instructional and management goals and the congruence between these and their management strategies.

Given the complexities of classroom life, the increasing needs of diverse and often needy students, the expanding body of knowledge in classroom management, the highly personal nature of classroom management, and the importance of reflection on practice, it seems obvious that teacher education programs must consider expanding and improving classroom management training (Reed, 1989; Wright, O'Hair, & Alley, 1988). No longer can one consider a course in "assertive discipline" or a text describing the leading models as an effective approach to providing teachers with skills in classroom management. Teacher educators need to consider carefully how best to provide students with an overview of research and associated practice, ways to help them reflect on their own beliefs about children and learning, and approaches for using this knowledge to reflect on their observations and experiences in classrooms.

At a minimum, this would appear to require a course in which students carefully examine the research described in this and other reviews of classroom management (Doyle, 1986; Duke, 1979) and in which they discuss the relationship between their own beliefs and instructional goals and this research. In addition, this must be supported by giving beginning teachers opportunities to observe veteran teachers and to discuss with both these teachers and university faculty the decision making they observe regarding classroom management. Finally, beginning teachers will need to participate in a similar process as they take responsibility for a classroom. This reflection of their own practice may involve dialogue with their mentor teacher and careful examination of observation notes and videotapes with their college supervisor and fellow interns or student teachers. This entire process must be centered around the teachers' academic goals and efforts to respond to students' personal and social skill development.

DIRECTIONS FOR FUTURE RESEARCH

Classroom management has too often focused on mechanical methods rather than on viewing the classroom environment as a complex, interactive system of personal, social, and cognitive demands. Considerable research exists concerning classroom management methods that enhance on-task behavior in traditional elementary school classrooms (Doyle, 1986). Few studies examine the management of classrooms with older, diverse student populations or in which varied instructional strategies are being implemented. For example, whereas considerable research exists concerning school climate factors influencing student behavior (Duke, 1990), almost no classroom management work has focused on social factors within the classroom. Likewise, almost no research examines the relationship between classroom management decisions and such important variables as students' cultural values and developmental tasks or teachers' instructional goals and methods.

For example, in secondary classrooms where peer relationships and questions of authority are major issues related to students' developmental tasks, it seems logical that effective classroom management would be enhanced by developing rules using the methods outlined in Forest Gathercoal's *Judicious Discipline* (1993). Likewise, secondary classrooms would appear to benefit from such methods as teaching students procedures for working effectively in cooperative groups; utilizing goal setting and self-recording; implementing thematic, project-based units; and responding to inappropriate behaviors using problem-solving and conflict management approaches. Classroom management research has not, however, examined the impact systematic use of such developmentally appropriate practices has on student learning and behavior.

Similarly, little research exists concerning the relationship between instructional strategies and classroom management methods. For example, it would seem congruent that an elementary classroom utilizing a whole language approach with an emphasis on peer editing groups would teach extensive classroom procedures related to these skills and would use a combination of self-monitoring, problem solving, conflict negotiation, and social skill training as methods for responding to problem behavior.

An example of the type of research needed was conducted by Hawkins and his colleagues (Hawkins, Doueck, & Lishner, 1988) at the University of Washington, who examined the effects of providing teachers with an in-service training package involving proactive classroom management methods, interactive teaching strategies, and cooperative learning. The research explored the behavior, attitudes, and achievement of low-achieving seventh-grade students at risk for serious and extended behavior problems. The results indicated that low-achieving, at-risk students in the experimental classrooms had more positive attitudes toward the subject matter, felt more involved in school, had greater expectations for continued school success, and had less serious misbehavior than did students taught by teachers in the control group. There were no significant differences between the student groups on standardized achievement tests or rates of delinquency or drug use. In this experimental study, the instructional and classroom management approaches were selected in light of both the students' developmental tasks and specific behavioral goals based on the target students' academic and behavioral histories. Outcome data focused on each of the variables considered when developing the intervention program. Similarly, H. Jerome Freiberg's work (Freiberg, 1993; Freiberg, Huang, Stein, & Waxman, 1994; Freiberg, Prokosch, Treister, & Stein, 1990) has examined school improvement and teacher training in classroom management that is associated with significant gains in student behavior and achievement in inner-city elementary schools.

Finally, although beginning teachers list difficulties with classroom management as a major factor influencing their effectiveness and enjoyment of teaching, little work has been done to determine the most effective methods of educating teachers in classroom management. Studies are needed to examine various approaches to educating teachers in classroom management and the long-term impact these have on student behavior and learning and teachers' perceptions regarding their ability to motivate and manage students effectively.

References

AAUW report: How schools shortchange girls. (1992). Washington, DC: National Education Association.

Abernathy, S., Manera, E., & Wright, R. (1985). What stresses student teachers most? *The Clearing House, 58*(8), 361–362.

Aleem, D., & Moles, O. (1993). *Review of research on ways to attain goal six: Creating safe, disciplined, and drug-free schools.* Washington, DC: OERI.

Allen, J. (1986). Classroom management: Students' perspectives, goals, and strategies. *American Educational Research Journal, 23*(3), 437–459.

Alton-Lee, A., Nuthall, G., & Patrick, J. (1993). Reframing classroom research: A lesson from the private world of children. *Harvard Educational Review, 63*(1), 50–84.

American Society for Training and Development & the U.S. Department of Labor, Employment and Training Administration. (1988). *Workplace basics: The skills employers want.* Washington, DC: Author.

Ames, C. (1987). The enhancement of student motivation. In M. Maehr & D. Kleiber (Eds.), *Advances in motivation and achievement. Vol. 5: Enhancing motivation* (pp. 123–148). Greenwich, CT: JAI Press.

Ames, C. (1990). Motivation: What teachers need to know. *Teachers College Record, 91*(3), 409–421.

Ames, C. (1992). Classrooms: Goals, structures, and student motivation. *Journal of Educational Psychology, 84*(3), 261–271.

Ames, C., & Archer, J. (1988). Achievement goals in the classroom: Students' learning strategies and motivation processes. *Journal of Educational Psychology, 80*(3), 260–267.

Anderson, L. (1984). The environment of instruction: The function of seatwork in a commercially developed curriculum. In G. G. Duffy, L. R. Roehler, & J. Mason (Eds.), *Comprehension instruction: Perspectives and suggestions* (pp. 93–103). New York: Longman.

Anderson, L. (1989). Learners and learning. In M. C. Reynolds (Ed.), *Knowledge base for the beginning teacher* (pp. 85–99). New York: Pergamon.

Anderson, L., & Pigford, A. (1988). Teaching within-classroom groups: Examining the role of the teacher. *Journal of Classroom Interaction, 23*(2), 8–13.

Anning, A. (1988). Teachers' theories about children's learning. In J. Calderhead (Ed.), *Teachers' professional learning* (pp. 128–145). New York: Falmer.

Aspy, D., & Roebuck, F. (1977). *Kids don't learn from people they don't like.* Amherst, MA: Human Resource Development Press.

Ballenger, C. (1992). Because you like us: The language of control. *Harvard Educational Review, 62*(2), 199–208.

Banks, J. (1991). *Teaching strategies for ethnic studies* (5th ed.). Boston: Allyn & Bacon.

Barrell, J. (1991). *Teaching for thoughtfulness.* New York: Longman.

Baumann, J. (1992). Organizing and managing a whole language classroom. *Reading Research and Instruction, 31*(3), 1–14.

Becker, W., Englemann, S., & Thomas, D. (1975). *Teaching I: Classroom management*. Champaign, IL: Research Press.

Bickel, F., & Qualls, R. (1980). The impact of school climate on suspension rates in Jefferson County public schools. *The Urban Review, 12*(2), 79–86.

Blackham, G., & Silberman, A. (1975). *Modification of child and adolescent behavior*. Belmont, CA: Wadsworth.

Blase, J. (1986). A qualitative analysis of sources of teacher stress. *American Educational Research, 23*(1), 13–40.

Blumenfeld, P., Soloway, E., Marx, R., Krajcik, J., Guzdial, M., & Palincsar, A. (1991). Motivating project-based learning: Sustaining the doing, supporting the learning. *Educational Psychologist, 26*(3), 369–398.

Bowers, C., & Flinders, D. (1990). *Responsive teaching*. New York: Teachers College Press.

Boyer, E. (1984). *Report of a panel on preparation of beginning teachers*. The Carnegie Foundation for the Advancement of Teaching. Princeton, NJ: Henry Chauncey Center.

Brickhouse, N., & Bodner, G. (1992). The beginning science teacher: Classroom narratives of convictions and constraints. *Journal of Research in Science Teaching, 29*(5), 471–485.

Brigham, F., Bakken, J., Scruggs, T., & Mastropieri, M. (1992). Cooperative behavior management: Strategies for promoting a positive classroom environment. *Education and Training in Mental Retardation, 27*(1), 3–12.

Brophy, J. (1981). Teacher praise: A functional analysis. *Review of Educational Research, 51*(1), 5–32.

Brophy, J. (1983a). Classroom organization and management. *The Elementary School Journal, 83*(4), 265–285.

Brophy, J. (1983b). Research on the self-fulfilling prophecy and teacher expectations. *Journal of Educational Psychology, 75*(5), 631–661.

Brophy, J. (1986, April). *Socializing students motivation to learn*. Paper presented at the annual meeting of the American Educational Research Association, San Francisco.

Brophy, J. (1988). Educating teachers about managing classrooms and students. *Teaching and Teacher Education, 4*(1), 1–18.

Brophy, J., & Evertson, C. (1976). *Learning from teaching: A developmental perspective*. Boston: Allyn & Bacon.

Brophy, J., & Evertson, C. (1978). Context variables in teaching. *Educational Psychologist, 12*(3), 310–316.

Brophy, J., & McCaslin, M. (1992). Teachers' reports of how they perceive and cope with problem students. *Elementary School Journal, 93*(1), 3–68.

Brophy, J., Rohrkemper, M., Rashid, H., & Goldberger, M. (1983). Relationships between teachers' presentations of classroom tasks and students' engagement in those tasks. *Journal of Educational Psychology, 75*(4), 544–552.

Burcham, B., Carlson, L., & Milich, R. (1993). Promising school-based practices for students with attention deficit disorder. *Exceptional Children, 60*(2), 174–180.

Butler, J. (1993). Transforming the curriculum: Teaching about women of color. In J. A. Banks & C. A. McGee Banks (Eds.), *Multicultural education* (pp. 149–167). Boston: Allyn & Bacon.

Cahoon, P. (1988). Mediator magic. *Educational Leadership, 45*(4), 93–94.

Calderhead, J. (1987). Exploring teachers' thinking. London: Cassell.

Cambone, J. (1990). Tipping the balance. *Harvard Educational Review, 60*(2), 217–236.

Canter, L., & Canter, M. (1976). *Assertive discipline*. Los Angeles: Lee Canter Associates.

Carlsson-Paige, N., & Levin, D. (1992). Making peace in violent times: A constructivist approach to conflict resolution. *Young Children, 48*(1), 4–13.

Carpenter, R., & Apter, S. (1988). Research integration of cognitive-emotional interventions for behaviorally disordered children and youth. In M. Wang, M. Reynolds, & H. Walberg (Eds.), *Handbook of special education: Research and practice* (Vol. 2, pp. 155–169). New York: Pergamon Press.

Carr, S., & Punzo, R. (1993). The effects of self-monitoring of academic accuracy and productivity on the performance of students with behavioral disorders. *Behavioral Disorders, 18*(4), 241–250.

Carter, K. (1992). Toward a cognitive conception of classroom management: A case of teacher comprehension. In J. Shulman (Ed.), *Case methods in teacher education* (pp. 111–130). New York: Teachers College Press.

Carter, K., & Gonzalez, L. (1993). Beginning teachers' knowledge of classroom events. *Journal of Teacher Education, 44*(3), 223–232.

Center for Educational Statistics. (1987). *Public school teacher perspectives on school discipline*. Washington, DC: OERI Bulletin, Center for Educational Statistics.

Center for Public Resources. (1983). *Basic skills in the U.S. workplace*. New York: Author.

Chalfant, J. & Pysh, M. (1989). Teacher assistance teams: Five descriptive studies on 96 teams. *Remedial and Special Educator, 10*(6), 49–58.

Chalfant, J., Pysh, M., & Moultrie, R. (1979). Teacher assistance teams: A model for within-building problem solving. *Learning Disability Quarterly, 2*(3), 85–96.

Charles, C. (1992). *Building classroom discipline*. White Plains, NY: Longman.

Clandinin, D., & Connelly, E. (1986). Rhythms in teaching: The narrative study of teachers' personal practical knowledge of classrooms. *Teaching and Teacher Education, 2*(4), 377–387.

Clifford, M. (1990). Students need challenges not easy success. *Educational Leadership, 48*(1), 22–26.

Cohen, E., Intili, J., & Robbins, S. (1979). Task and authority: A sociological view of classroom managment. In D. Duke (Ed.), *Classroom management* (78th yearbook of the National Society for the Study of Education, Part 2) (pp. 116–143). Chicago: The University of Chicago Press.

Cohen, M. (1983). Instructional management and social considerations in effective schools. In A. Odden & L. D. Webb (Eds.), *School finance and improvement: Linkage for the 1980s* (Fourth Annual Yearbook) (pp. 17–50). Cambridge, MA: American Education Finance Association.

Cole, C. (1992). Self-management interventions in the schools. *School Psychology Review, 21*(2), 188–192.

Cooper, H., & Good, T. (1983). *Pygmalion grows up: Studies in the expectation communication*. New York: Longman.

Curtis, M., Zins, J., & Graden, J. (1987). Prereferral intervention programs: Enhancing student performance in regular education settings. In C. Maher & J. Zins (Eds.), *Psychoeducational interventions in schools: Methods and procedures for enhancing student competence* (pp. 7–25). Elmsford, NY: Pergamon.

Curwin, R., & Mendler, A. (1988). *Discipline with dignity*. Alexandria, VA: Association for Supervision and Curriculum Development.

Cusick, P. (1983). *The egalitarian ideal and the American high school*. New York: Longman.

Dana, N. (1992, February). *Towards preparing the monocultural teacher for the muticultural classroom*. Paper presented at the 72nd annual meeting of the Association of Teacher Educators, Orlando. (ERIC Document Reproduction Service No. ED 350 272)

Darling-Hammond, L., Wise, A., & Pease, S. (1983). Teacher evaluation in the organizational context: A review of the literature. *Review of Educational Research, 53*(3), 285–328.

Davidson, H., & Lang, G. (1960). Children's perceptions of their teachers' feelings toward them. *Journal of Experimental Education, 29*(2), 109–118.

DeCharms, R. (1984). Motivation enhancement in educational settings. In R. Ames & C. Ames (Eds.), *Research on motivation in education, Vol. 1: Student motivation* (pp. 275–310). New York: Academic Press.

Diaz-Rico, L. (1993). From monocultural to multicultural teaching in an inner-city middle school. In A. Woolfolk (Ed.), *Readings in applied educational psychology* (pp. 272–279). Boston: Allyn & Bacon.

DiGangi, S., & Maag, J. (1992). A component analysis of self-management training with behaviorally disordered youth. *Behavioral Disorders, 17*(4), 281–290.

Doyle, W. (1979a). Classroom tasks and students' abilities. In P. L. Peterson & H. J. Walberg (Eds.), *Research on teaching: Concepts, findings, and implications* (pp. 183–209). Berkeley, CA: McCutchan.

Doyle, W. (1979b). Making managerial decisions in classrooms. In D. L. Duke (Ed.), *Classroom management* (78th yearbook of the National Society for the Study of Education, Part 2) (pp. 42–74). Chicago: The University of Chicago Press.

Doyle, W. (1983). Academic work. *Review of Educational Research, 53*(2), 159–199.

Doyle, W. (1985). Recent research on classroom management: Implications for teacher preparation. *Journal of Teacher Education, 36*(3), 31–35.

Doyle, W. (1986). Classroom organization and management. In M. C. Wittrock (Ed.), *Handbook of research on teaching* (3rd ed.) (pp. 392–431). New York: Macmillan.

Doyle, W. (1990a). Classroom knowledge as a foundation for teaching. *Teachers College Record, 91*(3), 347–360.

Doyle, W. (1990b). Classroom management techniques. In O. C. Moles (Ed.), *Student discipline strategies: Research and practice* (pp. 113–127). Albany: State University of New York Press.

Doyle, W., & Carter, K. (1984). Academic tasks in the classroom. *Curriculum Inquiry, 14*(2), 129–149.

Dreikurs, R., & Cassel, P. (1972). *Discipline without tears: What to do when children misbehave.* New York: Hawthorn.

Dreikurs, R., Grunwald, B., & Pepper, F. (1971). *Maintaining sanity in the classroom.* New York: Harper & Row.

Dryfoos, J. (1990). *Adolescents at risk: Prevalence and prevention.* New York: Oxford University Press.

Duke, D. (Ed.). (1979). *Classroom management* (78th yearbook of the National Society for the Study of Education, Part 2). Chicago: The University of Chicago Press.

Duke, D. (1990). School organization, leadership, and student behavior. In O. C. Moles (Ed.), *Student discipline strategies: Research and practice* (pp. 19–46). Albany: State University of New York Press.

Duke, D., & Meckel, A. (1980). Student attendance problems and school organization: A case study. *Urban Education, 15*(3), 325–358.

Duke, D., & Meckel, A. (1984). *Teacher's guide to classroom management.* New York: Random House.

Dusek, J. (Ed.). (1985). *Teacher expectations.* Hillsdale, NJ: Lawrence Erlbaum Associates.

Dweck, C. (1986). Motivational processes affecting learning. *American Psychologist, 41*(10), 1040–1048.

Dyson, A. (1987). The value of "time off task": Young children's spontaneous talk and deliberate text. *Harvard Educational Review, 57*(4), 396–419.

Eisner, E. (1984). Can educational research inform educational practice? *Phi Delta Kappan, 65*(7), 447–452.

Emmer, E. (1994, April). *Teacher emotions and classroom management.* Paper presented at the annual meeting of the American Educational Research Association, New Orleans.

Emmer, E., & Aussiker, A. (1990). School and classroom discipline programs: How well do they work? In O. C. Moles (Ed.), *Student discipline strategies: Research and practice* (pp. 129–165). Albany: State University of New York Press.

Emmer, E., Evertson, C., & Anderson, L. (1980). Effective classroom management at the beginning of the school year. *Elementary School Journal, 80*(5), 219–231.

Emmer, E., Evertson, C., Clements, B., & Worsham, M. (1994). *Classroom management for secondary teachers* (3rd ed.). Boston: Allyn & Bacon.

Emmer, E., & Hickman, J. (1991). Teacher efficacy in classroom management and discipline. *Educational and psychological measurement, 51*(3), 755–765.

Ethington, C. (1991). A test of a model of achievement behaviors. *American Educational Research Journal, 28*(1), 155–172.

Evertson, C. (1985). Training teachers in classroom management: An experimental study in secondary school classrooms. *Journal of Educational Research, 79*(1), 51–57.

Evertson, C. (1989). Improving elementary classroom management: A school-based training program for beginning the year. *Journal of Educational Research, 83*(2), 82–90.

Evertson, C., & Emmer, E. (1982). Effective management at the beginning of the school year in junior high classes. *Journal of Educational Psychology, 74*(4), 485–498.

Evertson, C., Emmer, E., Clements, B., & Worsham, M. (1994). *Classroom management for elementary teachers.* Boston: Allyn & Bacon.

Evertson, C., Emmer, E., Sanford, J., & Clements, B. (1983). Improving classroom management: An experiment in elementary school classrooms. *Elementary School Journal, 84*(2), 173–188.

Evertson, C., & Harris, A. (1992). What we know about managing classrooms. *Educational Leadership, 49*(7), 74–78.

Feitler, F., & Tokar, E. (1992). Getting a handle on teacher stress: How bad is the problem? *Educational Leadership, 49*(6), 456–458.

Fiore, T., Becker, E., & Nero, R. (1993). Educational interventions for students with attention deficit disorder. *Exceptional Children, 60*(2), 163–173.

Freiberg, H. (1993). A school that fosters resilience in inner-city youth. *Journal of Negro Education, 62*(3), 364–376.

Freiberg, H., Huang, S., Stein, T., & Waxman, H. (1994, April). *The effects of classroom management on student learning in inner city elementary schools.* Paper presented at the annual meeting of the American Educational Research Association, New Orleans.

Freiberg, H., Prokosch, N., Treister, E., & Stein, T. (1990). Turning around five at-risk elementary schools. *School Effectiveness and School Improvement, 1*(1), 5–25.

Freiberg, P. (1991, June). Teens' long work hours detrimental, study says. *APA Monitor, 22,* 19–20.

Friedman, R., & Doyal, G. (1992). *Management of children and adolescents with attention deficit-hyperactivity disorder* (3rd ed.). Austin, TX: PRO-ED.

Fuchs, D. (1991). Mainstreaming assistance teams: A prereferral intervention system for difficult-to-teach students. In G. Stoner, M. S. Shinn, & H. M. Walker (Eds.), *Interventions for achievement and behavior problems* (pp. 241–267). Silver Spring, MD: National Association of School Psychologists.

Fuchs, D., Fuchs, L., Gilman, S., Reeder, P., Bahr, M., Fernstrom, P., & Roberts, H. (1990). Prereferral intervention through teacher consultation: Mainstream assistance teams. *Academic Therapy, 25*(3), 263–276.

Gable, R., Hendrickson, J., Young, C., & Shokoohi-Yekta, M. (1992). Preservice preparation and classroom practices of teachers of students with emotional/behavioral disorders. *Behavioral Disorders, 17*(6), 126–134.

Gallagher, P. (1988). *Teaching students with behavior disorders: Techniques and activities for classroom instruction.* Denver, CO: Love Publishing Co.

Gathercoal, F. (1993). *Judicious discipline* (3rd ed.). San Francisco: Caddo Gap Press.

Glasser, W. (1965). *Reality therapy: A new approach to psychiatry*. New York: Harper & Row.

Glasser, W. (1969). *Schools without failure*. New York: Harper & Row.

Glasser, W. (1985). *Control theory in the classroom*. New York: Harper & Row.

Glasser, W. (1988). On students' needs and team learning: A conversation with William Glasser. *Educational Leadership, 45*(6), 38–45.

Glasser, W. (1990). *The quality school: Managing students without coercion*. New York: Harper & Row.

Goldstein, A., Sprafkin, R., Gershaw, N., & Klein, P. (1980). *Skillstreaming the adolescent*. Champaign, IL: Research Press.

Good, T., & Brophy, J. (1991). *Looking in classrooms* (5th ed.). New York: Harper & Row.

Goodlad, J. (1983). A study of schooling: Some findings and hypotheses. *Phi Delta Kappan, 64*(7), 465–470.

Goodlad, J. (1990). *Teachers for our nation's schools*. San Francisco: Jossey-Bass.

Gordon, T. (1974). *T.E.T.: Teacher effectiveness training*. New York: Peter H. Wyden.

Gottfredson, G., & Gottfredson, D. (1985). *Victimization in schools*. New York: Plenum.

Graden, J., Casey, A., & Bonstrom, O. (1985). Implementing a prereferral intervention system: Part II, The data. *Exceptional Children, 51*(6), 487–496.

Graden, J., Casey, A., & Christenson, S. (1985). Implementing a prereferral intervention system: Part I, The model. *Exceptional Children, 51*(5), 377–384.

Gump, P. (1967). *The classroom behavior setting: Its nature and relations to student behavior* (final report). Washington, DC: U.S. Office of Education, Bureau of Research. (ERIC Document Reproduction Service No. ED 015 515)

Halpin, G., Halpin, G., & Harris, K. (1982). Personality characteristics and self-concept of preservice teachers related to their pupil control orientation. *Journal of Experimental Education, 50*(4), 195–199.

Hansen, D. (1989). Lesson evading and lesson dissembling: Ego strategies in the classroom. *American Journal of Education, 97*(2), 184–208.

Haring, N., Jewell, J., Lehning, T., Williams, G., & White, O. (1987). Research on severe behavior disorders: A study of statewide identification and service delivery to children and youth. In N. G. Haring (Ed.), *Assessing and managing behavior disabilities* (pp. 39–174). Seattle: University of Washington Press.

Hawkins, D., Doueck, H., & Lishner, D. (1988). Changing teaching practices in mainstream classrooms to improve bonding and behavior of low achievers. *American Educational Research Journal, 25*(1), 31–50.

Haycock, K. (1990, June). *Closing remarks*. Presentation at the AAHE/College Board Conference on Mainstreaming University/School Partnerships, Chicago.

Hayek, R. (1987). The teacher assistance team: A pre-referral support system. *Focus on Exceptional Children, 20*(1), 1–7.

Haynes, D. (1986). *Statistics on students leaving the Seattle public schools, 1981–85*. Seattle: Seattle Public Schools Department of Management Information Services. (ERIC Document Reproduction Service No. ED 274 732)

Hollingsworth, S. (1989). Prior beliefs and cognitive change in learning to teach. *American Educational Research Journal, 26*(2), 160–189.

Hyman, I., & Lally, D. (1982). A study of staff development programs for improving school discipline. *The Urban Review, 14*(3), 181–196.

Jervis, K. (1986). A teacher's quest for a child's questions. *Harvard Educational Review, 56*(2), 133–149.

Jones, F. (1987a). *Positive classroom discipline*. New York: McGraw-Hill.

Jones, F. (1987b). *Positive classroom instruction*. New York: McGraw-Hill.

Jones, M., & Wheatley, J. (1990). Gender differences in student–teacher interactions. *Journal of Research in Science Teaching, 27*(9), 861–874.

Jones, V. (1980). *Adolescents with behavior problems: Strategies for teaching, counseling and parent involvement*. Boston: Allyn & Bacon.

Jones, V. (1982). Training teachers to be effective classroom managers. In D. L. Duke (Ed.), *Helping teachers manage classrooms* (pp. 52–68). Alexandria, VA: Association for Supervision and Curriculum Development.

Jones, V. (1983). Current trends in classroom management: Implications for gifted students. *Roeper Review, 6*(1), 26–30.

Jones, V. (1989). Classroom management: Clarifying theory and improving practice. *Education, 109*(3), 330–339.

Jones, V. (1992). Integrating behavioral and insight-oriented treatment in school-based programs for seriously emotionally disturbed students. *Behavioral Disorders, 17*(3), 225–236.

Jones, V. (in press). Developing a comprehensive treatment plan for students with emotional and/or behavioral disorders. *Teaching Exceptional Children*.

Jones, V., & Jones, L. (1981). *Responsible classroom discipline*. Boston: Allyn & Bacon.

Jones, V., & Jones, L. (1986). *Comprehensive classroom management* (2nd ed.). Boston: Allyn & Bacon.

Jones, V., & Jones, L. (1995). *Comprehensive classroom management* (4th ed.). Boston: Allyn & Bacon.

Kahle, J. (1990). Why girls don't know. In M. Rowe (Ed.), *What research says to the science teacher: The process of knowing* (pp. 55–67). Washington, DC: National Science Testing Association.

Kaplan, C. (1992). Teachers' punishment histories and their selection of disciplinary strategies. *Contemporary Psychology, 17*(3), 258–265.

Kaufman, P., Bradby, D., & Owings, J. (1992). *National longitudinal study of 1988: Characteristics of at-risk students in NELS: 88*. Washington, DC: U.S. Office of Education, Office of Educational Research and Improvement.

King, C., & Kirschenbaum, D. (1992). *Helping young children develop social skills: The social growth program*. New York: Brooks-Cole.

Kleinfeld, J. (1975). Effective teachers of Indian and Eskimo students. *School Review, 83*(2), 301–344.

Knitzer, J., Steinberg, Z., & Fleisch, B. (1990). *At the schoolhouse door: An examination of programs and policies for children with behavioral and emotional problems*. New York: Bank Street College of Education.

Kohn, A. (1993). Choices for children: Why and how to let students decide. *Phi Delta Kappan, 75*(1), 8–20.

Kounin, J. (1970). *Discipline and group management in classrooms*. New York: Holt, Rinehart and Winston.

Krampen, G. (1987). Differential effects of teacher comments. *Journal of Educational Psychology, 79*(2), 137–146.

Kulhavy, R., & Stock, W. (1989). Feedback in written instruction: The place of response certitude. *Educational Psychology Review, 1*(1), 279–308.

Kulik, J., & Kulik, C. (1988). Timing of feedback and verbal learning. *Review of Educational Research, 21*(1), 79–97.

Kuykendall, C. (1992). *From rage to hope: Strategies for reclaiming Black and Hispanic students*. Bloomington, IN: National Educational Service.

LaBenne, W., & Green, B. (1969). *Educational implications of self-concept theory*. Pacific Palisades, CA: Goodyear.

Lewis, R., & St. John, N. (1974). Contribution of cross-racial friendship to minority group achievement in desegregated classrooms. *Sociometry, 37*(1), 79–91.

Leyser, Y. (1988). Pupil behavior and student management styles in mainstream classrooms. *Reading Improvement, 25*(2), 152–158.

Leyser, Y., & Abrams, P. (1986). Perceived training needs of regular and special education student teachers in the area of mainstreaming. *The Exceptional Child, 33*(3), 173–180.

Lightfoot, S. L. (1983). *The good high school.* New York: Basic Books.

Lipsitz, J. (1984). *Successful schools for young adolescents.* New Brunswick, NJ: Transaction Books.

Little, J. (1987). Teachers as colleagues. In V. Richardson-Koehler (Ed.), *Educators' handbook: A research perspective* (pp. 491–518). New York: Longman.

Lloyd, J., Landrum, T., & Hallahan, D. (1991). Self-monitoring applications for classroom intervention. In G. Stoner, M. R. Shinn, & H. M. Walker (Eds.), *Interventions for achievement and behavior problems* (pp. 201–213). Silver Spring, MD: National Association of School Psychologists.

Locke, E., & Latham, G. (1990). *A theory of goal setting and task performance.* Englewood Cliffs, NJ: Prentice Hall.

Lunenburg, F., & O'Reilly, R. (1974). Personal and organizational influence on pupil control ideology. *The Journal of Experimental Education, 42*(3), 31–35.

Mace, F., Brown, D., & West, B. (1987). Behavioral self-management in education. In C. Maher & J. Zins (Eds.), *Psychoeducational interventions in the schools* (pp. 160–176). New York: Pergamon.

Macias, J. (1987). The hidden curriculum of Papago teachers: American Indian strategies for mitigating cultural discontinuity in early school. In G. Sprindler & L. Spindler (Eds.), *Interpretive ethnography of education: At home and abroad* (pp. 363–380). Hillsdale, NJ: Lawrence Erlbaum Associates.

Maehr, M., & Midgley, C. (1991). Enhancing student motivation: A schoolwide approach. *Educational Psychologist, 26*(3, 4), 399–427.

Maher, C. (1987). Involving behaviorally disordered adolescents in instructional planning: Effectiveness of the GOAL procedures. *Journal of Child and Adolescent Psychotherapy, 4*(3), 204–210.

Mansfield, W., Alexander, D., & Ferris, E. (1991). *Teacher survey on safe, disciplined, and drug-free schools.* Washington, DC: U.S. Department of Education, National Center for Educational Statistics.

Marshall, H. (1990). Beyond the workplace metaphor: The classroom as a learning setting. *Theory into Practice, 29*(2), 94–101.

McCaslin, M., & Good, T. (1992). Compliant cognition: The misalliance of management and instructional goals in current school reform. *Educational Researcher, 21*(3), 4–17.

McColskey, W., & Leary, M. (1985). Differential effects of norm-referenced and self-referenced feedback on performance expectancies, attributions, and motivation. *Contemporary Educational Psychology, 10*(3), 275–284.

McEvoy, M., Davis, C., & Reichle, J. (1993). Districtwide technical assistance teams: Designing intervention strategies for young children with challenging behaviors. *Behavioral Disorders, 19*(1), 27–33.

McEwan, B. (1991). *Practicing judicious discipline: An educator's guide to a democratic classroom.* Davis, CA: Caddo Gap Press.

McFadden, A., Marsh, G., Price, B., & Hwang, Y. (1992). A study of race and gender bias in the punishment of school children. *Education and Treatment of Children, 15*(2), 140–146.

McGinnis, E. (1990). *Skillstreaming in early childhood: Teaching prosocial skills to the preschool and kindergarten child.* Champaign, IL: Research Press.

McGowen, T., Sutton, A., & Smith, P. (1990). Instructional elements influencing elementary student attitudes toward social studies. *Theory and Research in Social Education, 18*(1), 37–52.

McLaughlin, H. (1991). Reconciling care and control: Authority in classroom relationships. *Journal of Teacher Education, 42*(3), 182–195.

McLaughlin, H. J. (April, 1992). *Seeking solidarity and responsibility: The classroom contexts of control and negotiation.* Paper presented at the annual meeting of the American Educational Research Association, San Francisco. (ERIC Document Reproduction Service No. ED 349 644)

Mendler, A. (1992). *What do I do when . . .?: How to achieve discipline with dignity in the classroom.* Bloomington, IN: National Educational Service.

Mitman, A., & Lash, A. (1988). Students' perceptions of their academic standing and classroom behavior. *Elementary School Journal, 89*(1), 55–68.

Moles, O. (Ed.). (1990). *Student discipline strategies.* New York: State University of New York Press.

Morgan, H. (1991, April). *Race and gender issues: In school suspension.* Paper presented at the annual conference of the American Educational Research Association, Chicago. (ERIC Document Reproduction Service No. ED 351 416)

Morrison, A., & McIntyre, D. (1969). *Teachers and teaching.* Baltimore: Penguin.

Morse, W. (1985). *The education and treatment of socio-emotionally impaired children and youth.* Syracuse, NY: Syracuse University Press.

Mortimore, P., & Sammons, P. (1987). New evidence on effective elementary schools. *Educational Leadership, 45*(1), 4–8.

Moser, C. (1982). Changing attitudes of student teachers on classroom discipline. *The Teacher Educator, 18*(1), 10–15.

Myles, B., Moran, M., Ormsbee, C., & Downing, J. (1992). Guidelines for establishing and maintaining token economies. *Intervention in School and Clinic, 27*(3), 164–169.

Nelson, R., Smith, D., Taylor, L., Dodd, J., & Reavis, K. (1992). A statewide survey of special education administrators regarding mandated perreferral interventions. *Remedial and Special Education, 13*(4), 34–39.

Newby, T. (1991). Classroom motivation: Strategies for first-year teachers. *Journal of Educational Psychology, 83*(2), 195–200.

Office for Civil Rights, Department of Education. (1993, February). *Fall 1990 elementary and secondary school civil rights survey: Revised national statistical estimates.* Washington, DC: Author.

O'Leary, K. D., & O'Leary, S. (1972). *Classroom management: The successful use of behavior modification.* New York: Pergamon.

O'Neil, J. (1991). A generation adrift? *Educational Leadership, 49*(1), 4–10.

Perry, F., & Taylor, H. (1982). Needed: A methods course in discipline for preservice teachers. *Education: A Complete Index, 102*(4), 416–419.

Phelan, P., Davidson, A., & Cao, H. (1992). Speaking up: Students perspectives on school. *Phi Delta Kappan, 73*(9), 695–704.

Prater, M., Joy, R., Chilman, B., Temple, J., & Miller, S. (1991). Self-monitoring of on-task behavior by adolescents with learning disabilities. *Learning Disability Quarterly, 14*(3), 164–177.

Pressley, M., Johnson, C., Symons, S., McGoldrick, J., & Kurita, J. (1989). Strategies that improve children's memory and comprehension of text. *Elementary School Journal, 90*(1), 3–32.

Purkey, W. (1970). *Self-concept and school achievement.* Englewood Cliffs, NJ: Prentice Hall.

Purkey, W. (1978). *Inviting school success: A self-concept approach to teaching and learning.* Belmont, CA: Wadsworth.

Reed, D. (1989). Student teacher problems with classroom discipline: Implications for program development. *Action in Education, 11*(3), 59–65.

Reynolds, A. (1992). What is competent beginning teaching? A review of the literature. *Review of Educational Research, 62*(1), 1–35.

Reynolds, C. (1977). Buddy system improves attendance. *Elementary School Guidance and Counseling, 11*(2), 305–336.

Reynolds, M. (1989). Students with special needs. In M. Reynolds (Ed.), *Knowledge base for the beginning teacher* (pp. 129–142). Oxford, England: Pergamon Press.

Rich, L., & McNelis, M. (1988). A study of academic time-on-task in the elementary school. *Educational Research Quarterly, 12*(1), 37–46.

Richardson, V. (1990). Significant and worthwhile change in teaching practice. *Educational Researcher, 19*(7), 10–18.

Richardson-Koehler, V., & Fenstermacher, G. (1988, February). *The use of practical arguments in staff development*. Paper presented at the annual meeting of the American Association of Colleges of Teacher Education, New Orleans. (ERIC Document Reproduction Service No. Sp 030 047)

Rickman, L., & Hollowell, J. (1981). Some causes of student teacher failure. *Improving College and University Teaching, 29*(4), 176–179.

Robinson, K. (1992). Class-room discipline: Power, resistance and gender. A look at teacher perspectives. *Gender & Education, 4*(3), 273–287.

Roderick, T. (1988). Johnny can learn to negotiate. *Educational Leadership, 45*(4), 86–90.

Rosenholtz, S., Bassler, O., & Hoover-Dempsey, K. (1986). Organizational conditions of teacher learning. *Teaching and Teacher Education, 2*(2), 91–104.

Rothenberg, J. (1989). The open classroom reconsidered. *Elementary School Journal, 90*(1), 69–86.

Rutter, M., Maughan, B., Mortimore, P., Ouston, J., & Smith, A. (1979). *Fifteen thousand hours: Secondary schools and their effects on children*. Cambridge, MA: Harvard University Press.

Sabornie, E. (1991). Measuring and teaching social skills in the mainstream. In G. Stoner, M. R. Shinn, & H. M. Walker (Eds.), *Interventions for achievement and behavior problems* (pp. 161–177). Silver Spring, MD: National Association of School Psychologists.

Sadker, D., & Sadker, M. (1985). Is the o.k. classroom o.k.? *Phi Delta Kappan, 66*(5), 358–361.

Sandia National Laboratories. (1993). Future requirements: Workforce skills. *Journal of Educational Research, 86*(5), 293–297.

Schmuck, R. (1966). Some aspects of classroom social climate. *Psychology in the Schools, 3*(1), 59–65.

Schmuck, R., & Schmuck, P. (1992). *Group processes in the classroom* (6th ed.). Dubuque, IA: Wm. C. Brown.

Schon, D. (1987). *Educating the reflective practitioner: Toward a new design for teaching and learning in the professions*. San Francisco: Jossey-Bass.

Semmel, M., Abernathy, T., Butera, G., & Lesar, S. (1991). Teacher perceptions of the regular education initiative. *Exceptional Children, 58*(1), 9–24.

Shaywitz, S., & Shaywitz, B. (1992). *Attention deficit disorder comes of age: Toward the twenty-first century*. Austin, TX: PRO-ED.

Short, P., & Noblit, G. (1985). Missing the mark in in-school suspension: An explanation and proposal. *NASSP Bulletin, 69*(484), 112–116.

Shulman, L. (1986). Those who understand: Knowledge growth in teaching. *Educational Researcher, 15*(2), 4–21.

Silvernail, D., & Costello, M. (1983). The impact of student teaching and internship programs on preservice teachers' pupil control perspectives, anxiety levels, and teaching concerns. *Journal of Teacher Education, 34*(4), 32–36.

Singer, D., & Singer, J. (1990). *The house of make-believe: Children's play and the developing imagination*. Cambridge, MA: Harvard University.

Sizer, T. (1984). *Horace's compromise: The dilemma of the American high school*. Boston: Houghton Mifflin.

Sizer, T. (1992). *Horace's school: Redesigning the American high school*. Boston: Houghton Mifflin.

Skinner, C., & Smith, E. (1992). Issues surrounding the use of self-management interventions for increasing academic performance. *School Psychology Review, 21*(2), 202–210.

Slavin, R. (1980). Cooperative learning. *Review of Educational Research, 50*(2), 315–342.

Slavin, R. (1990). *Cooperative learning: Theory, research, and practice*. Englewood Cliffs, NJ: Prentice Hall.

Sloane, H., Buckholdt, D., Jenson, W., & Crandall, J. (1979). *Structured teaching: A design for classroom management and instruction*. Champaign, IL: Research Press.

Smith, W. (1936). *Constructive school discipline*. New York: American Book Company.

Soar, R., (1983, March). *Impact of context variables on teacher and learner behavior*. Paper presented at the annual meeting of the American Association of Colleges for Teacher Education, Detroit.

Squires, D., Huitt, W., & Segars, J. (1983). *Effective schools and classrooms: A research-based perspective*. Alexandria, VA: Association for Supervision and Curriculum Development.

Stoiber, K. (1991). The effect of technical and reflective preservice instruction on pedagogical reasoning and problem solving. *Journal of Teacher Education, 42*(2), 131–139.

Stoner, G., Shinn, M., & Walker, H. (Eds.). (1991). *Interventions for achievement and behavior problems*. Silver Spring, MD: National Association of School Psychologists.

Story, C. (1985). Facilitator of learning: A micro-ethnographic study of the teacher of the gifted. *Gifted Child Quarterly, 29*(4), 155–158.

Tabachnick, B., & Zeichner, K. (1984). The impact of the student teaching experience on the development of teacher perspectives. *Journal of Teacher Education, 35*(6), 28–36.

Tetreault, M. (1993). Classrooms for diversity: Rethinking curriculum and pedagogy. In J. A. Banks & C. McGee Banks (Eds.), *Multicultural education* (pp. 129–148). Boston: Allyn & Bacon.

Thompson, M., & Ellis, J. (1984). Identifying and comparing anxieties experienced by male and female secondary student teachers. *College Student Journal, 18*(3), 289–295.

Thompson, R., White, K., & Morgan, D. (1982). Teacher-student interaction patterns in classrooms with mainstreamed mildly handicapped students. *American Educational Research Journal, 19*(2), 220–236.

Torrance, E. (1986). Teaching creative and gifted learners. In M. C. Wittrock (Ed.), *Handbook of research on teaching* (3rd ed., pp. 630–647). New York: Macmillan.

Truax, C., & Tatum, C. (1966). An extension from the effective psychotherapeutic model to constructive personality change in preschool children. *Childhood Education, 42*(6), 456–462.

U.S. Department of Education. (1992). *Fourteenth annual report to Congress on the implementation of the Education of the Handicapped Act*. Washington, DC: U.S. Government Printing Office.

VanOverwalle, F., Segebarth, K., & Goldschstein, M. (1989). Improving performance of freshmen through attributional testimonies from fellow students. *British Journal of Educational Psychology, 59*(1), 79–85.

Veenman, S. (1984). Perceived problems of beginning teachers. *Review of Educational Research, 54*(2), 143–178.

Victor, J. (1976). Relations between teacher belief and teacher personality in four samples of teacher trainees. *The Journal of Experimental Education, 45*(1), 4–9.

Villa, R., Thousand, J., Stainback, W., & Stainback, S. (1992). *Restructuring for caring and effective education: An administrative guide to creating heterogeneous schools*. Baltimore: Paul H. Brookes Publishing Co.

Wakefield, J., Cunningham, C., & Edwards, D. (1975). Teacher attitudes and personality. *Psychology in the Schools, 12*(3), 345–347.

Walberg, H., & Anderson, G. (1968). The achievement-creativity dimension and classroom climate. *Journal of Creative Behavior, 2*(4), 281–292.

Walker, H. (1979). *The acting-out child: Coping with classroom disruption*. Boston: Allyn & Bacon.

Walker, H. (1987). *The ACCESS Program (Adolescent Curriculum for Communication and Effective Social Skills)*. Austin, TX: PRO-ED.

Wang, M., Haertel, G., & Walberg, H. (1993). Toward a knowledge base for school learning. *Review of Educational Research, 63*(3), 249–294.

Ward, B. (1987). *Instructional grouping in the classroom. School improvement research series close-up No. 2.* Portland, OR: Northwest Regional Educational Lab. (ERIC Document Reproduction Service No. ED 291 147)

Wayson, W., & Pinnell, G. (1982). Creating a living curriculum for teaching self-discipline. In D. L. Duke (Ed.), *Helping teachers manage classrooms* (pp. 115–139). Alexandria, VA: Association for Supervision and Curriculum Development.

Wehlage, G., & Rutter, R. (1986). Dropping out: How much do schools contribute to the problem? *Teachers College Record, 87*(3), 374–392.

Wehlage, G., Rutter, R., Smith, G., Lesko, N., & Fernandez, R. (1989). *Reducing the risk: Schools as communities of support.* London: Falmer Press.

Weinstein, C., & Mayer, R. (1986). The teaching of learning strategies. In M. C. Wittrock (Ed.), *Handbook of research on teaching* (3rd ed., pp. 315–327). New York: Macmillan.

Weinstein, C., & Mignano, A. (1993). *Elementary classroom management: Lessons from research and practice.* New York: McGraw-Hill.

Weishew, N., & Peng, S. (1993). Variables predicting students' problem behaviors. *Journal of Educational Research, 87*(1), 5–17.

Wenger, S. (1985, May 2). Prepared statement before the Select Committee on Children, Youth, and Families, House of Representatives. Washington, DC: U.S. Government Printing Office.

Wesley, D., & Vocke, D. (1992, February). *Classroom discipline and teacher education.* Paper presented at the annual meeting of the Association of Teacher Educators, Orlando. (Eric Document Reproduction Service No. ED 341 690)

Whitehead, B. (1993, April). Dan Quayle was right. *The Atlantic Monthly,* 47–84.

Winitzky, N. (1992). Structure and process in thinking about classroom management: An exploratory study of prospective teachers. *Teaching & Teacher Education, 8*(1), 1–14.

Wragg, E. (Ed.). (1984). *Classroom teaching skills.* New York: Nichols.

Wright, R., O'Hair, M., & Alley, R. (1988). Student teachers examine and rate classroom discipline factors: Help for the supervisor. *Action in Teacher Education, 10*(2), 85–91.

Yell, M. (1990). The use of corporal punishment, suspension, expulsion, and timeout with behaviorally disordered students in public schools: Legal considerations. *Behavioral Disorders, 15*(2), 100–109.

Zaragoza, N., Vaughn, S., & McIntosh, R. (1991). Social skills interventions and children with behavior problems: A review. *Behavioral Disorders, 16*(4), 260–275.

Zeichner, K., & Gore, J. (1990). Teacher socialization. In W. R. Houston, M. Haberman, & J. Sikula (Eds.), *Handbook of research on teacher education* (pp. 329–348). New York: Macmillan.

Zumwalt, K. (1982). Research on teaching: Policy implications for teacher education. In A. Lieberman & M. McLaughlin (Eds.), *Policy making in education* (81st yearbook of the National Society for the Study of Education) (pp. 215–248). Chicago: National Society for the Study of Education.

Part

·V·

CONTINUING PROFESSIONAL GROWTH, DEVELOPMENT, AND ASSESSMENT

·25·

TEACHER SOCIALIZATION
FOR CULTURAL DIVERSITY

Kenneth M. Zeichner
UNIVERSITY OF WISCONSIN–MADISON

Karen Hoeft
UNIVERSITY OF WISCONSIN–MADISON

This chapter addresses several aspects of one of the major policy issues in U.S. teacher education for the foreseeable future: the need to help all teachers acquire the attitudes, knowledge, skills, and dispositions needed to work effectively with a culturally diverse student population. In the coming years, American students will be increasingly different in background from one another and from their teachers, and many will be poor (Gomez, 1994; Zimpher & Ashburn, 1992). Because the demographic composition of the teaching force is unlikely to change significantly, even under the most optimistic scenario for the success of efforts to increase the percentage of teachers of color (Banks, 1991), the task of educating teachers for cultural diversity, in many instances, will continue to be one of educating white, monolingual teacher education students to teach an increasingly diverse student body composed of many poor students of color.

Although these demographic characteristics lead to a focus in the literature on the preparation of white teachers to teach poor students of color, it cannot be assumed that teachers of color are culturally affiliated with their students (Gay, 1993b) or that they can necessarily translate their cultural knowledge into culturally relevant pedagogy and success for pupils (Montecinos, 1994). The focus in socializing teachers for cultural diversity must remain on the preparation of all teachers to teach a culturally diverse student body.

If one adopts a pragmatic and contextualized definition of culture, taking into account each individual's membership in multiple and overlapping microcultural groups (e.g., according to race, gender, social class, primary language, religion, age), then, by definition, all individuals are intercultural beings and all teachers have to be concerned with the challenge of intercultural communication regardless of their particular cultural identity and the demographic composition of their students (Gollnick, 1992; Villegas, 1991). Although an adequate definition of cultural diversity needs to be broad and inclusive, the use of the terms cultural diversity and diverse learners in this chapter is concerned primarily with differences related to race, ethnicity, social class, and language.

This chapter examines the research literature related to the socialization of teachers to teach culturally diverse students. The task of teacher socialization for cultural diversity is one that has three dimensions: (1) the problem of selection into teacher education programs, (2) the problem of teacher education through curriculum and instruction, and (3) the problem of institutional change. These aspects of teacher education for diversity are examined in relation to both preservice and in-

This research was funded by the National Center for Research for Teacher Learning, which is in turn funded by the Office of Educational Research and Improvement, U.S. Department of Education. The opinions expressed in this paper do not necessarily reflect the position, policy, or endorsement of the Office, Department, or Center.

The authors thank Gloria Ladson-Billings and Ana Marie Villegas for their fine job of critiquing chapter drafts.

service teacher education. The focus is on reviewing the strategies for selection, curriculum and instruction, and institutional change that have been used in U.S. teacher education programs and on the evidence regarding the success of these different strategies in preparing teachers for cultural diversity.

This chapter also briefly examines the strategies used in other fields to prepare workers for "cross-cultural" work. The authors discuss some of the strategies used by educators in preparing counselors, social workers, lawyers, and nurses, and some examples of the insights that can be gained by teacher educators through examining these literatures.

HISTORICAL CONTEXT

The task of preparing all teachers to teach a diverse student body is not a new concern in U.S. teacher education. For example, in 1969, the widely publicized task force report of the National Institute for Advanced Study in Teaching Disadvantaged Youth, *Teachers for the Real World* (Smith, 1969), clearly identified the failure of teacher education programs to prepare teachers to teach diverse students. This report identified three problems in preparing teachers to teach the poor: (1) teachers were unfamiliar with the backgrounds of poor students and the communities where they live, (2) teacher education programs have ordinarily done little to sensitize teachers to their own prejudices and values, and (3) teachers lack preparation in the skills needed to perform effectively in the classroom. In concluding that most teacher education programs prepared students to teach children much like themselves, instead of children of any racial and social origin, this report called for a major overhaul of teacher education programs in terms of their approaches to diversity and equity.

Racial, class, and ethnic bias can be found in every aspect of current teacher education programs. The selection processes militate against the poor and minorities. The program content reflects current prejudices; the methods of instruction coincide with learning styles of the dominant group. Subtle inequalities are reinforced in institutions of higher learning. Unless there is scrupulous self-appraisal, unless every aspect of teacher training is carefully reviewed, the changes initiated in teacher preparation as a result of the current crisis will be, like so many changes which have gone before, merely differences which make no difference. (Smith, 1969, pp. 2–3)

Eddy (1969) also charged that teacher education programs failed to prepare teachers for working with students from backgrounds different than their own. She argued that prospective teachers entered their teacher education programs with little significant intercultural experience and that their programs left them encapsulated within their own sociocultural backgrounds. It often was argued that teacher education programs were doing an outstanding job of educating teachers to teach middle-class white students, but that they were failing miserably when it came to preparing teachers to work with poor children of color (O'Brian, 1969).

Although most teacher education programs acknowledge in principle the importance of preparing teachers for cultural diversity, evidence suggests that the situation has not changed very much in the 27 years since Smith and Eddy delivered their condemnations of American teacher education. For example, despite the progress indicated by the existence of program accreditation standards related to multicultural education, Gollnick (1992) found that of the first 59 teacher education institutions that sought accreditation under the 1987 NCATE standards, only eight (13.6%) were in full compliance with the minimum multicultural education standards for teacher education programs.

Although most institutions included references to multicultural education in the unit's objectives or mission statement, NCATE evaluators were often unable to detect where they were implemented in the curriculum. (p. 236)

Several other recent analyses of U.S. teacher education have confirmed that many teacher education programs continue to represent a monocultural approach and that teacher education students generally seek to avoid teaching in urban schools and other schools serving the poor where the need is the greatest and the work is the most demanding (Goodlad, 1990; Grant, 1993; Haberman, 1988; Trent, 1990).

Schools and colleges of teacher education are turning out class after class of young, white, female teachers who would rather work in white, middle class suburbs. Unfortunately, their services are most needed in low-income schools, whose students come from races, cultures, and language groups for whom these new teachers feel unprepared. (Ladson-Billings, 1990, p. 25)

PRESERVICE TEACHER EDUCATION FOR CULTURAL DIVERSITY

This chapter first examines the socialization of teachers at the preservice level for teaching in a culturally diverse society. First, the authors will examine four dimensions along which preservice programs vary with regard to diversity. It is argued that all preservice teacher education programs can be described according to the positions they take with regard to these four dimensions. Following this general look at stances toward diversity in preservice teacher education, the authors examine the backgrounds and beliefs of preservice teacher education students in the United States and the ways in which the characteristics of teacher education students place limits on the socialization of teachers that can occur within preservice teacher education programs. Finally, the authors examine various strategies that have been employed within preservice teacher education programs together with the strength of the empirical evidence supporting the use of particular strategies.

Dimensions of Variation

Despite the marginalization of teacher education for cultural diversity by the teacher education research community (Grant & Secada, 1990), a number of different strategies have been employed in U.S. teacher education programs in an attempt to better prepare teachers to teach all students to high academic standards. These strategies are generally organized in one of two ways: (1) through the *infusion* approach, which integrates attention to cultural diversity throughout a program's courses and field experiences; or (2) through the *segregated* approach, which treats cultural diversity as the focus of a single course or as a topic in a few courses whereas other components of the program remained untouched by this concern.

Despite a clear preference for the infusion approach to teacher education for diversity by scholars who have assessed the work of teacher education programs (e.g., AACTE Commission on Multicultural Education, 1973; Gay, 1986), the segregated approach is clearly the dominant model in use (Garibaldi, 1992; Grant & Sleeter, 1985; Ladson-Billings, in press). It is very common for any coursework related to cultural diversity to be optional rather than compulsory beyond a basic introductory course (Gay, 1986). The concern for the integration of issues related to cultural diversity throughout the entire curriculum of a teacher education program is a specific case of the more general position that curriculum designs in teacher education should represent an outgrowth of shared conceptions of teaching, learning, and schooling among faculty who offer programs (Barnes, 1987).

Issues related to cultural diversity, similar to many other aspects of the teacher education curriculum, have suffered from the fragmentation and lack of curricular cohesiveness that has historically plagued teacher education in colleges and universities in the United States. With regard to multicultural teacher education, this lack of curricular cohesiveness is a reflection of various structural barriers to infusion such as the absence of incentives and rewards for curriculum development work and the lack of expertise about diversity among teacher education faculty (Clifford & Guthrie, 1988; Liston & Zeichner, 1991; Nolan, 1985).

Very few teacher education programs of a permanent nature have integrated attention to diversity throughout the curriculum. Many of the programs in which an integrated or infusion approach has been used were externally funded programs of limited life that ended once the funding expired (e.g., Grant, Zeichner, & Gillette, 1988; Weiner, 1993). Both of the major federal efforts to inject a concern for diversity into the fabric of teacher education institutions, The National Teacher Corps and the Trainers of Teacher Trainers (TTT) program, remained marginal to teacher education institutions and had little impact on changing the institutional context for teacher education over the long run (Weiner, 1993).

There is good reason for the preference for an integrated approach to issues of cultural diversity. Although there is little empirical evidence demonstrating the superiority of an infusion model, research studies have clearly shown the very limited long-term impact of a segregated approach to teacher education for diversity on the attitudes, beliefs, and practices of teachers (e.g., Bennett, Okinaka, & Xio-Yang, 1988; Grant & Koskella, 1986; McDiarmid & Price, 1990b; Reed, 1993). Sleeter (1988) concluded the following from her analysis of coursework in multicultural education in Wisconsin teacher education institutions:

Including a relatively small amount of multicultural education training in students' preservice programs does not have much impact on what

they do. It may give them a greater repertoire of teaching strategies to use with culturally diverse students, and it may alert them to the importance of maintaining high expectations. For significant reform of teaching to occur however, this intervention alone is insufficient. (p. 29)

A second dimension along which preservice teacher education for diversity efforts vary is with regard to the attention they give to *culture-specific* or *culture-general* socialization strategies. In a culture-specific approach, the emphasis is on preparing teachers to teach particular students in specific contexts such as urban Puerto Rican students. In a culture-general approach the concern is to prepare teachers to be successful in any context that involves cross-cultural interactions with a focus on developing teaching competence with a variety of different cultural groups. This latter approach also focuses on identifying and understanding general cognitive processes that mediate cross-cultural interactions and emphasize experiences that people are likely to have during cross-cultural encounters. According to Kushner and Brislin (1986), teachers who experience a culture-general emphasis in their preparation programs:

would be expected to be more knowledgeable about factors that contribute to cross-cultural misunderstanding, be sensitive to such factors when interacting with students and parents and be able to approach potentially conflicting situations with an awareness and ability to ask questions in such a way that takes culturally determined factors into account. (p. 54)

An example of a culture-specific approach that seeks to prepare teachers to be culturally sensitive and interculturally competent with regard to specific groups of students is the community-specific and community-controlled approach advocated by a U.S. Department of Education commission on teacher education in 1976 (Study Commission, 1976). In this approach, specific communities of people develop teacher education experiences designed specifically for their own schools and communities. Other examples of a culture-specific emphasis are the alternative route programs run by school districts preparing teachers specifically for particular schools in those districts (e.g., Stoddart & Floden, in press) and special university-based programs, such as Indiana University's American Indian Project and Teachers for Alaska, which focus on the preparation of teachers for particular communities. Although culture-specific preparation for teaching particular groups of students in specific contexts (e.g., Navajos) may help develop sensitivities and capabilities among teachers that are useful in other cross-cultural contexts (Willison, 1994), the emphasis is on the particular contexts into which teachers are being inducted.

Another dimension along which teacher education for diversity efforts vary is the degree to which they emphasize *interacting with cultures* as opposed to *studying about cultures*. Although all programs that seek to prepare teachers to teach diverse students probably include at least some direct field experience in diverse schools and communities, programs vary as to how much they put their students into contact with pupils and adults from different backgrounds. On the one hand, some programs are mostly college and university based and include only the minimally required number of hours in school placements or only placements in schools serving students and families with backgrounds similar to those of student teachers. On the other hand, those are programs that require extensive school and community experiences with students and families with backgrounds different from those of the student teachers. In some cases (e.g., Noordhoff & Kleinfeld, 1993), student teachers are required to live in the "culturally different" communities in which they are teaching and to do substantial community work as part of their student teaching (Mahan, Fortney, & Garcia, 1983).

A fourth dimension along which teacher education for diversity efforts vary is the degree to which the teacher education program itself is a model of the cultural inclusiveness and cultural responsiveness so often advocated by teacher educators for K–12 schools. On the one hand, truly multicultural teacher education efforts are responsive to and build upon the diverse backgrounds, life experiences, learning style preferences, and teaching conceptions brought to the program by prospective teachers. Student teachers are actively engaged in constructing their own education for teaching, and the program responds to varied student needs. On the other hand, multicultural education is transmitted to prospective teachers in an additive manner with little regard for their backgrounds and experiences. Teacher education students are put in the position of passive recipients of knowledge *about* a culturally responsive approach to teaching, but they do not get to experience it in their education for teaching.

For example, programs that require keeping journals as the only means to structure teacher reflection, with no room for options, or programs that present multicultural material to student teachers as the enlightened viewpoint with little support for the discussion of different perspectives, sometimes cause student teacher resentment and resistance (e.g., Friesen-Poirier, 1992; Sheppard, 1992). Teacher education programs that focus only on educating prospective white teachers about pupils of color, but that ignore the task of educating their students of color about themselves as cultural beings and for greater intercultural competence, is another example of teacher education programs that are multicultural in rhetoric but not in practice (Montecinos, 1994, in press).

The Problem of Selection

Much has been written in recent years about the growing disparity in backgrounds and life experiences between prospective teachers and teachers on the one hand and public school students on the other hand. For example, there is little doubt that the student population in public schools has become increasingly diverse and that it will continue to do so for the foreseeable future. Predictions are that about 40% of the nation's school-age youth will be students of color by the year 2020 (Pallas, Natriello, & McDill, 1989). Already, students of color comprise about 30% of public school students in the United States, are the majority in 25 of the nation's 50 largest school districts (Banks, 1991), and are the majority in a few states such as New Mexico, Texas, and California (Quality Education for Minorities Project, 1990). In the 20 largest school districts, students of color comprise more than 70% of the total school enrollment (Center for Education Statistics, 1987).

These students of color are more likely to be poor, hungry, in poor health, and to drop out of school than their white counterparts (Children's Defense Fund, 1991). The failure of American public schools to enable all children to receive a high-quality education regardless of their race, ethnic, and social class and background represents a major crisis in U.S. education and is clearly in conflict with the purposes of education in a democratic society (Bastian, Fruchter, Gittel, Greer, & Haskins, 1985; Committee on Policy for Racial Justice, 1989; Quality Education for Minorities Project, 1990).

The composition of the teacher education student group is in sharp contrast to that of public school pupils. Several recent studies have shown that teacher education students are overwhelmingly white, monolingual, from a rural (small town) or suburban community, and come to their teacher education programs with very little direct intercultural experience (American Association of Colleges for Teacher Education [AACTE], 1987, 1989; Gomez, 1994; Irvine, 1989; LaFontaine, 1988), even in states such as California with much cultural diversity (Ahlquist, 1991). Teacher education students often feel uncomfortable about personal contact with ethnic and language minority parents (Larke, 1990), a very serious problem given the importance of having community conscious teachers and noncondescending parent involvement in the education of ethnic and language minority students (Delgado-Gaitan, 1991; Edwards, 1992; Fruchter, Gallenta, & White, 1992).

According to recent AACTE (1987, 1989) data on teacher education students across the country, few teacher education students come from urban areas, and only 15% would like to teach in urban areas. This is not surprising given the historical concentration of teacher education institutions outside of urban areas (Haberman, 1988). Some evidence shows that prospective teachers from historically black teacher education institutions enter teaching in urban schools at a higher rate than the general population of teacher education students (Reed & Simon, 1991), but this is not enough to deal with serious teacher shortages in many urban school districts.

Zimpher (1989) in her analysis of some of the AACTE data concluded with the observation that there appears to be a general affinity among preservice teacher education students to teach students who are like themselves in communities that are familiar to them (also see Mahan & Boyle, 1981). Two thirds of the white teacher education students surveyed in the AACTE/Metropolitan Life survey of teacher education students across the United States (AACTE, 1990) indicated that they would not like to teach in a situation with limited English proficient students. According to Howey (1992), the majority of teacher education students nationally report that they are neither well prepared nor disposed to teach ethnic and language minority children.

Recent research has shown that many teacher education students come to their preparation programs viewing student diversity as a problem rather than as a resource, that their conceptions of diversity are highly individualistic (e.g., focusing on personality factors such as motivation and ignoring contextual factors such as ethnicity), and that their ability to talk about student differences in thoughtful and comprehensive ways is very limited (Birrell, 1993; Paine, 1989). These students generally have very little knowledge about different cultural groups in the United States and their cultures, histories, and participation in and contributions to life in the United States

(Lauderdale & Deaton, 1993; Wahab, 1989; Wayson, 1988), and often they have negative attitudes about cultural groups other than their own (Law & Lane, 1987; Valli, 1994).

Although it may be possible for these and other similar factors to be remedied to some extent by preservice teacher education programs, the likelihood is that they are not adequately addressed by most teacher education programs as they are currently organized. Although research on teacher learning has demonstrated that teacher education programs, under certain conditions, are able to have an impact on certain aspects of teacher development (e.g., Grossman & Richert, 1988), the empirical evidence overwhelmingly supports a view of preservice teacher education as a weak intervention (Zeichner & Gore, 1990).

Some teacher educators, such as Haberman (1991, 1993), have argued that typical teacher education students who are young, inexperienced, and culturally encapsulated are not developmentally ready to make the kinds of adjustments needed for successful cross-cultural teaching. Haberman and others are pessimistic about the likelihood that preservice teacher education can become a powerful enough intervention to change the attitudes and dispositions developed over a lifetime that teacher education students bring to teacher education programs. This argument seems especially strong in relation to the 1-year alternative route teacher education programs that have become increasingly common. It also seems strong in relation to the scope of the task of teacher education for diversity. For as Nieto (1992) argued, becoming a multicultural teacher entails becoming a multicultural person. This process of becoming a multicultural person needs to involve, according to some, the abandonment of racism and the development of nonracist identities (Tatum, 1992). Given the cultural encapsulation that characterizes the majority of teacher education students across the United States, it seems unreasonable to expect teacher education programs as they are now constructed with their fragmented curricula and low status in the institutions that house them (Liston & Zeichner, 1991) to overcome the cultural limitations posed by the anticipatory socialization of prospective teachers.

It is becoming increasingly clear that some selection procedures, such as the interviews developed by Haberman (1987) to screen candidates for teaching in urban schools, must also be used to determine potential abilities to become successful teachers in cross-cultural situations. Haberman (1991) identified factors such as organizational ability and physical and emotional stamina that he thinks predicts who will be successful teachers in diverse urban schools. The research evidence on the socializing impact of preservice teacher education programs supports the view that instead of relying solely on grade point averages, test scores, and the glowing testimony of young college students wanting to be teachers because they love kids, teacher educators have to find ways, as Haberman (1991) has argued, to focus more on picking the right people rather than on trying to change the wrong ones through teacher education.

Strategies of Curriculum and Instruction

There are several specific strategies that have been employed within teacher education programs in an attempt to prepare teachers for cultural diversity. These are building high expectations among prospective teachers for the learning of all students; increasing the knowledge of prospective teachers about themselves and their place in a multicultural society; providing prospective teachers with cultural knowledge about the experiences, lifestyles, and contributions of various groups in society; and providing teachers with opportunities to develop competence in building relationships and in teaching strategies that will help them to succeed in schools serving children and families with backgrounds different than their own. Some of these strategies, such as case-based teaching, involve work mainly in college or university-based courses, whereas others involve experiences in schools and communities.

Building High Expectations One of the most common elements addressed in teacher education for diversity is the expectations that teacher education students hold for pupils. Goodlad (1990) found in his national study of teacher education that most of the teacher education students interviewed held low expectations for the learning of some students.

The idea of moral imperatives for teachers was virtually foreign in concept and strange in language for most of the future teachers we interviewed. Many were less than convinced that all students can learn; they voiced the view that they should be kind and considerate to all, but they accepted as fact the theory that some simply cannot learn. (p. 264)

Hilliard (1974) argued that the educational failure of ethnic and language minority students is less a matter of the failure of teachers to use particular teaching strategies than it is of teachers' fundamentally negative feelings toward and low expectations for the learning of these students. Given the widespread problem of low teacher expectations for the learning of ethnic and language minority students, it is reasonable to conclude that instruction in culturally relevant teaching strategies by itself is an inadequate response to preparing teachers to teach all students to high academic standards. Ways must be found to help prospective teachers reexamine and reconsider the negative assumptions about students and their families that many prospective teachers bring to their teacher education programs.

The most pedagogically advanced strategies are sure to be ineffective in the hands of educators who implicitly or explicitly subscribe to a belief system that renders ethnic, racial, and linguistic minority students at best culturally disadvantaged and in need of fixing. (Bartolome, 1994)

One strategy used by teacher educators to counter the low expectations that prospective teachers hold for some students is to expose them either through readings or by direct contact to successful teaching of ethnic and language minority students who are often the targets of teachers' low expectations. This attention to cases of success is often supplemented by helping prospective teachers examine ways in which schools help structure inequality through various practices in curriculum, instruction, grouping, and assessment.

An example of this strategy is elementary PROTEACH at the University of Florida where teacher education students are required to read specific books and articles describing the successful teaching of students who often do not succeed in school (Ross, Johnson, & Smith, 1991). The kinds of readings used in this strategy include Lucas, Henze, and Donato's (1990) rich descriptions of several successful California high schools serving Latino students, Ladson-Billings' (1990, 1991a, 1994) studies of successful teachers of African-American students, Moll's (1988, 1992) studies of successful teaching of Latino students, and accounts of the numerous examples throughout the country of specific schools that have succeeded in educating poor ethnic minority students whereas most schools in similar contexts have failed (e.g., Collins & Tamarkin, 1990; Cummins, 1989; First & Gray, 1991).

Despite the existence of several discussions in the literature of efforts to counter the low expectations of teacher education students, there is little empirical evidence regarding the success of these efforts in influencing the beliefs and practices of prospective teachers. Recent research on teacher learning, although not explicitly addressing the problem of the negative attitudes of prospective teachers toward ethnic and language minority students, has supported an approach to teacher education that begins with surfacing and challenging the beliefs and assumptions prospective teachers bring to teacher education (e.g., Wubbels, 1992).

Another way in which teacher educators have attempted to counter low expectations for student learning and to give prospective teachers a framework for organizing classroom learning environments is to give attention in the teacher education curriculum to sociocultural research on the relationships among language, culture, and learning, including research about language acquisition and second language learning. This body of research has convincingly demonstrated the superiority of a situational, as opposed to a stable trait, view of intelligence and competence, which sees behavior as a function of the context of which it is a part (Cazden & Mehan, 1990). This research also has provided numerous examples of how learning environments created in schools and classrooms have facilitated the success of students who in many cases have not been successful in school (e.g., Tharp & Gallimore, 1988). Examples of this strategy are the recent requirements in some states, such as California, that all prospective teachers receive instruction in research related to language acquisition and in required courses focusing on issues of language, culture, and learning. The incorporation of a sociocultural knowledge base into teacher preparation programs has been advocated for many years, first in relation to preparing teachers for urban schools (e.g., Clothier & Hudgins, 1971) and then as a more general recommendation for all teachers as the demographics in the United States have moved cultural diversity beyond urban schools (e.g., Gay, 1993a; Leighton, Hightower, Wingley, Paton, Pechman, & McCollum, 1994; Mehan & Trujillo, 1989).

The literature is clear about the importance of creating a classroom context in which all students feel valued and capable of academic success (Cummins, 1986; Olsen & Mullen, 1990). According to Ladson-Billings (1990), a personal bond needs to be created between the teacher and his or her pupils. The teacher then ceases seeing his or her students as "the other" and addresses students' psychological and social development along with their academic development. According to Comer (1988), no matter how good the administrators, teachers, curric-

ulum, or equipment; no matter how long the school day or year; and no matter how much homework is given, if the students do not attach and bond to the people and program of the school, less adequate learning will take place.

If teachers treated the fates of all of their students as they treat those of their own children, according to Grumet (1988), we would come closer to realizing the purposes of education in a democratic society. Few teachers would excuse their own children from their futures in the way that they sometimes do other people's children.

If ethics and the common culture could gather together the concern and attention that we devote to our own children and extend this nurture to other people's children, then we might find in the school the model for a just society. (p. 164)

One example of a teacher education program that has sought to create the kind of personal bonding between prospective teachers and ethnic and language minority students believed to be so important for successful intercultural teaching is the Minority Mentorship Project at Texas A&M University (Larke, Wiseman, & Bradley, 1990). In this program, 24 prospective elementary teachers mentored an African-American or Mexican-American elementary student during a 3-year period while completing a course on multicultural education for 1 credit hour each semester. The multicultural class included discussions of the ongoing mentoring relationships and focused on issues of curriculum, instruction, and cultural awareness. The mentoring relationships included tutoring and a variety of social and cultural activities in the school, in homes, and in the community. These cross-cultural mentoring experiences resulted in a change in the attitudes of the preservice teachers toward African-American and Mexican-American students, moving them from a focus on pity and apathy toward an emphasis on students' strengths. It is unknown, however, if these mentoring experiences affected the prospective teachers' attitudes and beliefs over time or their teaching practices.

Valli's (1994) study of six student teachers underlines the importance of the establishment of trusting interpersonal relations between prospective teachers and their pupils in overcoming negative attitudes and low expectations for ethnic and language minority students. Valli demonstrates that through such practices as risking personal revelations, evoking student voice, and directly handling racial confrontations in their classrooms, student teachers were able to establish strong personal bonds with their pupils that enabled them to implement successful teaching strategies. Valli (1994) argued on the basis of her study that

Prospective teachers will not be able to scaffold, communicate high expectations, or develop culturally responsive teaching strategies unless they first establish personal relations with their culturally diverse students. (p. 2)

Increasing Self-Knowledge One of the places that teacher education for diversity often begins is with helping teacher education students better understand their own cultural experience and develop more clarified ethnic and cultural identities, that is, to see themselves as cultural beings in a culturally diverse society. Spindler and Spindler (1993) referred to this process of helping teachers to see themselves as cultural agents as "cultural therapy."

For teachers, cultural therapy can be used to increase awareness of the cultural assumptions they bring to the classroom that affect their behavior and their interactions with students—particularly students of color. For teachers, cultural therapy is an intervention that can be used as a first step to impact behaviors, attitudes, and assumptions that are biased (and often discriminatory) and thus detrimental to students whose cultural backgrounds are different from their own. Our use of cultural therapy has been directed at helping teachers and other adults to understand their own cultural positions and to reflect and analyze the reasons why they might find the behavior of a culturally different person objectionable, shocking, or irritating. (p. 29)

There is a consensus in the literature that the development of one's own cultural identity is a necessary precursor to cross-cultural understanding (Banks, 1991; Hidalgo, 1993; Quintanar-Sarellana, 1991). The recognition of the degree to which we are culture bound facilitates the leap into the cultural perspectives of others (Mahan & Rains, 1990).

Examples of this approach of helping teacher education students locate themselves within this culturally diverse society include the work of King and Ladson-Billings (1990) at the University of Santa Clara; the work of Hollins (1990) at California State University, Hayward; and the work of Gomez and Tabachnick (1991) at the University of Wisconsin–Madison. All of these examples involve an autobiographical component in which students learn to recognize and appreciate their own cultural heritage as present and worthwhile.

Part of the teacher education curriculum should be aimed at resocializing preservice teachers in ways that help them view themselves within a culturally diverse society. This could entail restructuring self-perceptions and world views. Part of designing appropriate experiences for preservice teachers is making meaningful connections between the students' personal/family history and the social context of life as experienced by different groups within a culturally diverse society. (Hollins, 1990, pp. 202–203)

A next step, according to some teacher educators, is to help prospective teachers learn more about and then to reexamine the attitudes and values they hold toward ethnic and racial groups other than their own. As Banks (1991) argued,

Helping students understand their own cultural experience and to develop more clarified cultural and ethnic identifications is only the first step in helping them to better understand and relate to other ethnic and racial groups. They also need experiences that will enable them to learn about the values and attitudes they hold toward other ethnic and cultural groups, to clarify and analyze those values, to reflect upon the consequences of their values and attitudes, to consider alternative attitudes and values, and to personally confront some of their latent values and attitudes toward other races. (p. 141)

Some teacher educators who have written about their efforts to help their students reexamine their attitudes and beliefs about various ethnic and racial groups have stressed the importance of both intellectual challenge and social support that comes from being in a group of teacher education students (e.g., Gomez & Tabachnick, 1991; King & Ladson-Billings, 1990;

Young, 1993). A cohesive cohort group in which students stay in close contact with each other and a given group of faculty over a period of time often is cited as a critical element of attitude change (e.g., Grant, Zeichner, & Gillette, 1988; Nelson-Barber & Mitchell, 1992). Even with the existence of these collaborative learning environments, however, the process of helping prospective teachers confront their often negative attitudes toward other groups is often a very difficult one in which teacher education students sometimes resist the efforts of teacher educators to have them examine their attitudes (Ahlquist, 1991; McCormick, 1993). There is substantial evidence that more than conventional university classes are needed to foster self-examination and to avoid simply reinforcing the prejudices and misconceptions that students bring to their teacher education programs (e.g., Cross, 1993; Mortenson & Netusil, 1976).

Gomez (1991) helps her language arts methods students at the University of Wisconsin–Madison reexamine their attitudes toward people of color by having them read various accounts of what it is like to live and be educated in the United States for many minorities. Her teacher education students read such works as Richard Rodriguez's (1982) autobiographical account of his schooling, *Hunger of Memory,* and Taylor and Dorsey-Gaines' (1988) stories of the lives of poor African-American families, *Growing Up Literate.* Through these and other class assignments implemented in a concurrent practicum experience (e.g., observations of children), students become more sensitive to the cultures and lives of their own pupils and learn effective strategies for teaching literacy skills to all of the diverse learners in their classrooms.

Providing Cultural Knowledge Another strategy used by teacher educators is to try to overcome the lack of knowledge among many teacher education students about the histories of different cultural groups and their participation in and contribution to the making of this nation. Ellwood (1990) argued that an ethnic studies component in a teacher education program can potentially do much to prevent mistakes by teachers that are rooted in cultural ignorance.

If student teachers studied linguistics long enough to understand that, say, an African-American dialect is as rulebound and linguistically sophisticated as the dialect which has gained prominence as "standard American English," they may be less inclined to judge their students as unintelligent simply because they speak a different dialect. If they also studied Afro-American history and literature, gaining an appreciation for the immense love of language running through African-American culture, they might be able to recognize in their own Black students, skills and linguistic strengths that could be built upon in the classroom. Similarly, if they gained an appreciation for the tenacious struggles minority people have waged historically in this country around education, it might be a little bit harder to jump to the immensely unlikely conclusion that "those parents" do not care about the education of their children. (p. 3)

Ladson-Billings's (1991b) work at the University of Santa Clara shows that exposing students to seriously neglected aspects of American history appears to cause many students to question their own education and to ask why they were not given access to certain points of view. For example, two of

Ladson-Billings's (1991b) former students remarked in their journals after viewing "Eyes on the Prize," an award winning civil rights documentary,

This [video] made me so angry because of how little I know about the Civil Rights movement. I'm 21 years old and almost all of this is completely new to me (white female liberal arts major).

I had no idea of the riots and marches and violence that went on for civil rights. Why wasn't I taught this? (white male communications major). (p. 13)

Another part of this strategy is to provide students with information about some of the unique characteristics and learning styles of students from different ethnic groups; however, because these are general characteristics not limited to specific cultural groups or necessarily applicable to individual learners in specific classrooms, many have argued that it is necessary to be careful to avoid stereotyped responses to students as members of groups that ignore individual characteristics (McDiarmid & Price, 1990a). A necessary supplement to providing information about general group characteristics is teaching to learn about and then incorporate into their instruction information about students, their families, and communities. This involves an examination of the cultures of the home and community and an assessment of the congruence between these, as well as the culture of the classroom and school. Teachers must learn how to incorporate home and community culture into their classrooms as the starting point for curriculum and instruction (Villegas, 1991).

The baseline for the curriculum should be the local cultural community, with everything else being built up around and grounded in that reality. Whatever piece of the curriculum you are responsible for, imbed it first in the world with which the students are familiar and work outward from there . . . . Wherever possible, make use of the local community to bring real world significance to that which you are teaching. (Barnhardt, 1992, pp. 4–5)

Garcia (1993) identified three different ways in which successful teachers of culturally and linguistically diverse students have accomplished this task: (1) by using cultural referents in both verbal and nonverbal forms to communicate instructional and institutional demands, (2) by organizing instruction to build on rules of discourse from the home and community cultures, and (3) by respecting equally the values and norms of the home and community cultures and the school culture.

An important supplement to teachers' examination of the cultural traditions and resources brought to school by their students is study of the culture of their classrooms. Teachers must be taught how to examine the particular traditions and rules that govern life and define success in their classrooms, such as the implicit rules that govern classroom discourse and participation in various classroom activities (Cazden, 1986). This aspect of providing culturally relevant instruction has received far less attention in the literature than efforts to teach prospective teachers to study home and community cultures.

The literature on culture and learning discusses cognitive and learning styles of specific ethnic and language groups (e.g., Anderson, 1988; Gilbert & Gay, 1985; Huber & Pewewardy, 1990; Little Soldier, 1989; Shade, 1982, 1994; Swisher & Deyhle,

1987). On the one hand, this literature identifies certain characteristics of the cognitive and learning styles of specific ethnic and language minority groups (e.g., relational and field dependent learning styles) and argues that specific groups of students will learn best under particular kinds of conditions, such as in cooperative groups (e.g., Strickland & Ascher, 1992). On the other hand, this literature also cautions about the dangers of generalizing about learning and cognitive styles when formulating teaching plans. Gilbert and Gay (1985) warned, for example, about the variation within groups and argue that teachers should use a variety of teaching styles and learning environments that will address the diverse needs within every group of students.

McDiarmid and Price (1990a) described how providing information about general group characteristics of particular ethnic and language minority group populations can have a negative effect on the socialization of prospective teachers. After evaluating the impact of a 3-day intensive training workshop emphasizing cultural diversity on the attitudes and beliefs of prospective teachers from various institutions in Michigan, they concluded the following:

The presentation of information on ethnic and religious groups may actually encourage prospective teachers to generalize and, eventually, to prejudge pupils in their classrooms. More commonly, teacher education students may become unsure about how to think about culturally different children. On the one hand, they are taught to be suspicious of any generalization about a group of people; on the other, they encounter materials and presentations that, in fact, make generalizations about normative values, attitudes, and behaviors among different groups. (p. 15)

It has been argued that those entering teaching should be expected to know various procedures by which they can gain cultural information about the various communities represented in their classrooms, to see themselves as cultural researchers (Pytowska, 1990). These include, according to Villegas (1993), "making home visits, conferring with community members, talking with parents, consulting with minority teachers, and observing children in and out of school" (p. 7).

One example of a teacher education program that attempts to teach prospective teachers to learn about their students, their families, and their communities is the Teachers for Alaska (TFA) program, the secondary teacher education program at the University of Alaska–Fairbanks. This program supplements the giving of cultural information about specific groups of people with a focus on developing prospective teachers' dispositions to find out about the context in which they are teaching, helping them learn experientially about their own students, and then helping them learn how to use that information to tailor their instruction to particular cultural contexts. One way in which TFA faculty help prospective teachers learn how to tailor their instruction to particular contexts is by providing them with examples of such adaptations that have been preserved in case studies written by local teachers (Kleinfeld, 1992).

Another example of a teacher education program in which prospective teachers are encouraged to learn about the cultural norms in the communities in which they teach is Indiana University's American Indian Project (Mahan, 1982a; Mahan, Fortney, & Garcia, 1983). Here student teachers live and work on American Indian reservations in the southwest for a semester and engage in various community experiences outside of the school as part of their student teaching. Student teachers submit detailed reports to program staff about what they are learning about community values and beliefs and their implications for their classroom practice. Native American dormitory aides with whom the student teachers live help the prospective teachers make friends in the community and facilitate their participation in community activities, such as chapter house meetings, pow-wows, rodeos, and so forth (Willison, 1994).

In another program at Portland State University (Narode, Rennie-Hill, & Peterson, 1994), student teachers receive training in ethnographic-like research methods and are sent into inner-city communities for a minimum of 30 hours in a semester to interview people about their views on education and to observe community activities. Student teachers who have participated in these community study experiences report that they have become more positive about parents and the communities in general and that the field experiences helped generate a commitment to combat racism in their teaching (Narode et al., 1994).

There is much discussion in the literature on teacher education about how teachers can take the knowledge they gain about the students they are teaching and about different groups in this multicultural society and make use of it in developing multicultural curriculum materials and culturally relevant instructional strategies and classroom organizational structures. Much of this work focuses on the integration of a multicultural perspective into all that a teacher does in the classroom (e.g., Bennett, 1990). With regard to curriculum, the emphasis often is on two things: (1) developing skills in analyzing existing curriculum materials for bias and adapting them to correct for these biases, and (2) developing teachers' capabilities in developing multicultural curriculum materials on their own (e.g., Sleeter & Grant, 1988; Tiedt & Tiedt, 1990). With regard to instruction, prospective teachers often are taught various instructional strategies and classroom organization schemes that are sensitive to cultural and linguistic variations and that enable them to build upon the cultural resources that students bring to school (Au & Kawakami, 1994). Prospective teachers also are taught about a variety of curriculum-based and potentially culturally sensitive methods of student assessment, such as portfolio development (Beckum, 1992; Garcia & Pearson, 1994).

Case-Based Teaching

Another instructional strategy used to prepare teachers for cultural diversity is case-based teaching, which is the reading and writing of cases by prospective teachers. In the Teachers for Alaska program at the University of Alaska–Fairbanks (Kleinfeld, 1989, 1991, 1992), in the "Case Methods in Multicultural Education Project" in California (Gallagher, 1993; Shulman, 1992; Shulman & Mesa-Bains, 1990), and at the University of Washington (Banks, 1991), teacher educators use case studies to illustrate the challenges of teaching diverse students and to prepare more culturally sensitive and interculturally competent teachers.

Teacher educators have argued that cases are uniquely suited to the analysis of the complex and often emotionally charged issues of teaching in culturally unfamiliar contexts. They believe that cases can help prospective teachers develop a social map of a cultural terrain and to interpret the social meaning of unfamiliar cultural events.

Case discussions, rich with contextualized detail and verisimilitude about the challenges of teaching diverse students, can provide a context for teachers to confront their own assumptions and feelings about teaching diverse students. If teachers are given the opportunity to explore collaboratively and debate critical moments in the cases, they can develop the analytical skills to reframe problems from different perspectives and to expand their repertoire of instructional practices tailored to the needs of their students. They also can test their generalized knowledge about different cultural groups with the specific situations in the cases while simultaneously becoming more skillful in adapting their interactional and instructional practices to the needs of their own diverse learners. (Kleinfeld, 1989, p. 2)

The literature on case-based teaching in teacher education has provided some evidence that the use of cases has developed greater cultural sensitivity among prospective teachers. For example, in the Teachers for Alaska program, student papers written about cases depicting aspects of the Yupik social world revealed a developing understanding of that world (Kleinfeld, 1989). Student teachers writing cases about their student teaching experiences in remote Alaskan communities helped move them to more complex ways of viewing the world.

The structure of students' thinking changed as they reflected upon their experience and wrote a case about it. Student teachers typically began with a map of the world that was rigid, simplistic, and implicit. They ended the case with a map of the world that was much more complex, conditional, contextual, and explicit. (Kleinfeld, 1991, p. 2)

Also, Shulman (1992) provided some evidence that the use of cases concerned with issues of diversity can influence teachers' awareness and sensitivity to cultural diversity. Several beginning teachers who participated in a special 10-week, case-based teacher education seminar reported that this seminar gave them a greater understanding of their own students and of their own cultural biases and limitations. Other seminar participants reported that the seminar helped them to realize the importance of going beyond the classroom and reaching out to students, that it helped them listen more to the concerns of their students, and that it helped change their communication patterns with their students and their parents. Only 2 of the 15 teachers in the seminar, however, reported that the case-based seminar led to changes in their instructional strategies. Shulman (1992) cautioned that the use of cases by themselves to prepare teachers for cultural diversity does not lead to greater cultural sensitivity and intercultural competence. She argued that the cultural sensitivity of the teacher educators who engage in case-based teaching is critical.

Cases, even with commentaries, do not teach themselves. Discussion leaders must not only be sensitive to the issues represented in the cases but also acutely aware of their own biases and intercultural blindness. They must understand the problems portrayed from multiple perspectives. And they must be able to anticipate in detail the variety of responses each case evokes, both emotionally and intellectually. (pp. 21–22)

Given the limited intercultural teaching experience of most teacher educators (Haberman, 1988), the use of cases to prepare teachers for cultural diversity, without efforts to increase the cultural competence of the existing group of teacher educators or to bring more culturally competent individuals into the community of teacher educators, is problematic.

School and Community Field Experiences

Perhaps the most common strategy advocated in the literature for preparing teachers for cultural diversity is field experiences that put teacher education students in direct contact with pupils and adults with cultural backgrounds different from their own. These experiences range from relatively brief experiences and guided reflection activities associated with particular courses (e.g., Tran, Young, & DiLella, 1994) to full-scale community immersion experiences where prospective teachers live and teach over an extended period of time in culturally different communities. There has also been the use of various kinds of simulation experiences, such as "Ba Fa Ba Fa" and the "Inner City Simulation" to promote greater intercultural competence (Cruickshank, 1971). Teacher educators agree that coursework and academic analysis alone are insufficient for encouraging the kind of affective and emotional response by prospective teachers needed to develop greater intercultural competence.

If teachers are to work successfully with students from cultures different from their own, it is imperative that the training program provide far more than intellectualization about cross-cultural issues. Teacher growth in this area is possible only to the extent that the teacher's own behavior in a cross-cultural setting is the subject of examination and experimentation. (Hilliard, 1974, pp. 49–50; see also, Goodwin, 1990)

One example of a relatively brief field experience is the human service project option in the required School and Society course at Knox College. The purpose of this option, according to Beyer (1991), is to help prospective teachers, many with lives distant from poverty, to come to grips with social inequality in a direct way. In addition to reading about poverty in the class, students who elect the field option work in various social service agencies or in some more informal socially or economically disadvantaged setting such as a home (see also, Gonzalez & Picciano, 1993).

Other direct experiences include the required completion of a number of practicum and student teaching experiences in schools serving ethnic and language minority students (Bowen & Salsman, 1979; Cooper, Beare, & Thorman, 1990; Ross, Johnson, & Smith, 1991). Some states, such as California, have recently required that all teacher education students experience a variety of culturally different schools prior to certification (California Commission on Teacher Credentialing, 1988). Some scholars such as Ford (1991) have stressed that placements in culturally diverse schools should be in situations where teachers are succeeding in educating ethnic and language minority students, a requirement that seems difficult to fulfill given the large failure rate for schools that work with ethnic and language minority students. Because there are currently too few examples of schools that are successfully educating ethnic and language minority students, Cochran-Smith (1991a) and Pugach and Pasch (1994) have argued that field placements in culturally diverse schools should be in those schools or with

those teachers who are working to change the conditions of practice that have led to failure for ethnic and language minority students.

Another type of cross-cultural field experience is the overseas student teaching experience in which U.S. teacher education students complete a portion or all of their student teaching in another country. These experiences vary greatly as to the amount of cultural immersion they actually provide (e.g., some student teachers live in dormitories and teach in American schools), but it has been argued that overseas student teaching under certain conditions enhances cultural sensitivity and cross-cultural teaching capabilities (e.g., Mahan & Stachowski, 1985).

Completing practicum experiences and student teaching in schools serving pupils with cultural backgrounds different from that of prospective teachers is, to many educators, an inadequate preparation for cross-cultural teaching unless these experiences extend out into the community. Many have argued over the years that the center of gravity of teacher education programs should be shifted to the community, including extending field experiences beyond the boundaries of the school (e.g., Blair & Erickson, 1964; Cuban, 1969; Flowers, 1948; Hayes, 1980; Hodgdon & Saunders, 1951). There have been many examples of field experience programs that brought prospective teachers out of schools and into the community, including the National Teacher Corps where interns spent about 20% of their internships working in communities (also see Clothier & Hudgins, 1971; Kapel & Kapel, 1982; Kohut, 1980; Mungo, 1980, 1982; Smith, 1980).

Some field experiences that extend into the community precede the time that prospective teachers have substantial teaching responsibilities in schools (Mungo, 1980). An example of this is the 1-week immersion experience in the Teachers for Alaska program in which prospective secondary teachers spend 1 week living and working with students in an Athabascan community. During this experience, student teachers are encouraged to

Put themselves in roles outside of the classrooms (e.g., community basketball, skin sewing or beading groups, church attendance) and to spend time in such places as the store and post office where people are likely to congregate or share news. We advise our students to seek out the expertise of teacher's aides who live in the community and to make home visits. (Noordhoff & Kleinfeld, 1993, p. 34)

The purpose of these visits in the Teachers for Alaska program is to help student teachers learn how to tailor instruction to the particular cultural context in which they are working as well as sensitizing them to different cultural realities. How student teachers use the information they gain about their students and the students' communities in their classrooms is of central concern.

Another kind of community experience in teacher education occurs in conjunction with the students' student teaching experience. For many years, Jim Mahan at Indiana University has coordinated American Indian and Latino cultural immersion programs in which student teachers have lived and worked either on Indian reservations or in Latino communities in the southwest (Mahan, 1982a, 1982b, 1993; Mahan, Fortney, & Garcia, 1983; Willison, 1989). In these programs, student teachers complete a year-long cultural preparation in which they study about the specific culture in which they will work. During the time that student teachers are working in these communities, they complete several community service experiences and engage in an activity such as sheepherding, identify what they have learned about the culture through that activity, and discuss the implications of these cultural learnings for their teaching. This information is then communicated back to program staff through a series of cultural reports. One important aspect of these experiences is the use of community people of color, usually without professional education backgrounds, as teacher educators both during the preparation for the experience and during the experience (Mahan, 1993).

Often school and community experiences in schools that provide cross-cultural encounters for prospective teachers are coupled with seminars that provide structured and guided reflection about the field experiences. For example, Gomez and Tabachnick (1992), operating out of a tradition of narrative inquiry, have their students in an experimental program at the University of Wisconsin–Madison tell stories about their teaching in culturally diverse schools in their weekly seminars. Gomez and Tabachnick (1991) presented convincing evidence that the telling of stories about teaching in a collaborative context that is intellectually challenging and socially supportive helps student teachers reexamine the "scripts" that guide their teaching. The literature on clinical teacher education and teacher development clearly supports the view that this kind of guided reflection about teaching during practica and student teaching under conditions of support and challenge is critical to determining the educational value of a field experience (e.g., Farber & Armaline, 1994), and that teaching experience without such guided reflection is often miseducative (Baty, 1972; Zeichner, 1990).

Under some conditions, however, cross-cultural school and community experiences serve to strengthen and legitimate the very prejudices and stereotypes they were designed to correct (e.g., Haberman, 1991; Haberman & Post, 1992). Certain conditions appear to be necessary in these experiences to avoid these negative consequences. These include careful preparation of students for the field experiences, as in the year-long cultural training experienced by participants in the American Indian and Latino projects at Indiana University, and careful monitoring of the experiences while students are in the field, such as in student teaching seminars (Goodwin, 1990). Carter and Larke (in press) argue that the people who supervise cross-cultural field experiences should have successful teaching experience in the kinds of communities in which the student teachers are working.

Much work going on currently throughout the United States is aimed at situating teacher education field experiences within new institutional partnerships created in schools that have adopted teacher education as a central part of their missions— professional development schools, professional practice schools, or partnership schools (e.g., Darling-Hammond, 1993; Levine, 1992). Situating teacher education field experiences in professional development schools or in subcultures within schools where a special commitment has been made to teacher development (Cochran-Smith, 1991b) has come to be seen as a desirable direction for clinical teacher education. Very little evidence, however, indicates that shifting student teaching and

practicum experiences to professional development schools necessarily does a better job of preparing teachers to teach all students to high academic standards. For example, studies have shown that even in professional development schools discussion among student teachers of controversial issues such as racism is rare (Gillette, 1990). The placement of student teachers on teams or in multiple classroom placements, a common feature in professional development schools, also does not necessarily overcome the narrowness of field experiences and their lack of attention to community contexts. The professional development school literature rarely discusses efforts to help student teachers become knowledgeable about the communities served by their schools and how to use this knowledge in their teaching (Zeichner, in press).

The Effectiveness of Different Instructional Strategies

In general, empirical evidence regarding the success of these different instructional strategies of teacher education for diversity is very weak. On the one hand is a series of studies that have underlined the impotency of preservice teacher education in overcoming the anticipatory socialization of culturally encapsulated prospective teachers. These studies show that in some cases teacher education programs actually strengthen and reinforce the very attitudes and beliefs they were attempting to change. For example, Haberman and Post (1992) provided a summer multicultural field experience together with related seminars and courses for teacher education students in Wisconsin. Haberman and Post (1991) detailed the failure of this experience to change student teachers' values and level of cultural awareness and concluded that

Indeed, many of our students became more insensitive and hardened in their positions by attributing more negative values to school children, their parents, and their neighborhoods. After 120 hours of direct experience in schools serving a multicultural population, these preservice students became better at supporting their original predispositions. . . . Rather than the cure-all assumed by teacher educators, direct experience in these culturally diverse situations merely served to enhance and strengthen the social values with which our students began. (p. 29)

On the other hand, some research contradicts studies that show the negative or negligible impact of teacher education. Teacher educators such as Beyer (1991), Gomez and Tabachnick (1991), and Ladson-Billings (1991b) have presented the stories and journal writings of their students that demonstrate a powerful impact of teacher education experiences on prospective teachers, at least in the short run. One of Ladson-Billings's (1991b) students commented on the impact of a community field experience involving volunteering in a soup kitchen and homeless shelter.

This experience affected me in a very powerful way. Being a part of this atmosphere, brief as it was, taught me a few things about our society. It showed me a completely new perspective on life that I had never before been exposed to. I learned quite a bit about the differences and similarities between my life and their lives. . . . Talking to Elvin (a boy in the shelter) showed me how very similar he is to me. It was apparent to me that his life could have taken a very different path, and that likewise, that my life could have taken a very different path. The realization was very sobering to me and taught me to empathize with his situation. On the other hand, the world of Julian Street is so very different from my world on campus. I noticed how easy it is to become narrow minded when my perspectives are constantly being influenced by the same atmosphere. (pp. 15–16).

Beyer (1991) presented some of the journal writings of Heidi, one of his students, which discuss the impact of viewing the film "The Women of Summer" in an educational foundations course. This film is a documentary about a reunion of students from Bryn Mawr College's summer school program for women workers in the 1920s and 1930s.

Saw Women of Summer and I couldn't believe it. The entire time I was in complete awe. . . . These women did things because they felt it, not because it was the proper or socially acceptable thing to do. . . . I sat through the movie with my textbooks and notepads, wearing nice clothes and feeling relatively secure in my life. All the time I'm wondering what does this all mean? Everything I have and all my material possessions don't add up to much when compared to the actions that these women took. (p. 124)

Finally, Hollins (1990) shared a journal entry by one of her students in her educational foundations course at California State University, Hayward that demonstrates the impact of class activities that were designed to help students develop a greater sense of their own ethnocultural identities.

I got a renewed sense of my identity and I focused on the idea that I too belong to an ethnic group. With this realization came a renewed sense of pride in my ethnic origins. I have begun to understand the pride that the other ethnic groups feel and the damage that our society causes by stigmatizing people who are different. (pp. 206–207)

Some studies also exist that go beyond documenting a personal impact on prospective teachers and show that teachers think that particular experiences in their teacher education programs greatly influenced how they approach their teaching. For example, a recent graduate of Indiana University's American Indian Project reflected on the impact of the community experiences that were part of her teacher education program.

Getting to know the families changed how I taught things. I think that's how it should be everywhere. The more you learn about the family and the way things are done at home, the easier it is for you to do things and teach the students the way they're used to being taught. For example, I never knew that some of the kids in my kindergarten class only spoke Navajo at home. It was real hard for them to come in the morning and have to go from Navajo to English and back and forth. So I would try to do as much as I could in Navajo and English, even if it was just the days of the week and months of the year.

I also visited their homes. The school bus driver took us around to each of the kids' houses. I saw how many kids there were around the house, how much of the extended family was living with the kids. Back in the classroom, rather than saying, "Did Mom help you with this," or "Did Dad say you could do that?" I could say, "Oh, your Uncle Joe was there; did he talk with you about this at all? Did you ask him about this kind of thing?" and they'd know that I was making the effort. . . . Most of the parents were really receptive. The kids would introduce me and each kid would have something they'd want to show us at home. . . . We had made a big project out of it, writing and

picture drawing and everything. We had them draw maps of how to get to their houses.

Where I live, the kids go to a soccer game or go out with their parents to a movie, but these kids don't do these kinds of things. Some of them are home alone all weekend, some of them have to go straight home from school and herd their sheep, some of them are involved in dance competitions with their pow wows, and every weekend they travel for that kind of thing. Some of them are real talented artists. So we did a lot of writing and group books. We created some materials for the library. I had kindergarten and first grade, so they weren't really professionally done materials, but they were things that they'd do at their homes, following traditions that their families have. We tried to cover that a lot.

The more I got involved in the community, the more it made me realize that these kids bring so much to the classroom already. . . . It really helps me to be a more effective teacher I think, when I can relate things to what I knew the kids were thinking.

I think it's done wonders. It's made me see things through other people's eyes a lot more. I take more time to sit and say, "Why are they doing it this way, or why are they thinking this way?" It made me much more patient, because I had to do a lot more waiting, listening, and learning, rather than the "go get 'em" thing that I'm used to doing. And I think that's real helpful too. There's times when I'd just have to sit back and watch, and let the kids do their thing. It made me more educated. I know so much more about not only a specific culture but likenesses and differences just with anybody. I really am learning.

I think it's too bad that most teachers don't get to do what I've gotten to do. I have had a lot of diverse experiences that have made me ready for anything. (Zeichner & Melnick, 1995)

Whether or not these and other similar changes in the perspectives of prospective teachers are associated with long-lasting impact on their world views, values, dispositions, and practices is still an open question. Very little evidence exists in the literature that the changes documented by teacher educators are long lasting (see Bennett et al., 1988, for a rare example of a 1-year follow-up study) or that they actually influence the way prospective teachers teach and how successful they are with ethnic and language minority students. Generally very little is known about the development of teacher education students' cognitions, beliefs, and skills with respect to the teaching of diverse learners (Grant & Secada, 1990; Grant & Sleeter, 1985) and about what makes the difference between experiences that reinforce stereotypes and the ones in which stereotypes and prejudices are questioned.

One issue that needs to be addressed in studies of teacher education for cultural diversity is the varying impact that particular strategies might have on different students. For example, as Montecinos (1994, in press) points out, few studies have identified the racial and ethnic backgrounds of prospective teachers when reporting data related to the impact of particular teacher education strategies. It seems reasonable to expect that teacher education strategies (e.g., immersion experiences in particular ethnic and language minority communities) will have different effects on prospective white teachers than they will on prospective teachers of color given the different circumstances faced by whites and people of color in a society where racism is an enduring characteristic (Sleeter, 1994). There is some evidence that the perspectives and needs of prospective teachers of color are being ignored in preservice teacher education programs (e.g., Hood & Parker, 1994) and that multicultural teacher education is being focused primarily on the numerically dominant group of white students. Although the same strategies (e.g., case studies, immersion experiences) might be useful in developing cultural sensitivity and intercultural teaching competence among all teachers, it is necessary to learn more about how to modify and adapt these general strategies to meet the needs of different teacher education students.

THE INSTITUTIONAL ENVIRONMENT OF TEACHER EDUCATION

The preceding discussion of socialization strategies through curriculum and instruction indicates some possibilities for developing greater cultural sensitivity and intercultural competence among prospective teachers despite the lack of empirical evidence of long-term impact on teachers and their practices. A fundamental problem, however, is that in using these potentially effective socialization strategies, teacher educators often define the task of teacher education for diversity as only a problem of curriculum and instruction and ignore both the issue of selection into teacher education programs and the institutional environment in which teacher education exists. The institutional environment in which a teacher education program is embedded is critical in determining the success of curriculum and instructional strategies designed to promote greater intercultural teaching competence.

One aspect of the problem with regard to the institutional environment for teacher education is a cultural insularity in the education professoriate, similar to that among teacher education students. Recent studies of U.S. teacher education have clearly shown that both within and outside of schools and colleges of education is an absence of significant numbers of faculty of color (Ducharme & Agne, 1989; Howey & Zimpher, 1990). According to some, this lack of faculty of color, together with the absence of students of color in teacher education programs, makes the task of educating teachers for cultural diversity especially difficult because of the importance of a culturally diverse learning community to the development of intercultural teaching competence.

If we are going to promote an appreciation for diversity and equity in the organization and content of our programs, it must be simultaneously reflected in the make-up of our programs, both among students and faculty. Prospective teachers will be better prepared to help students appreciate cultural diversity if they have learned through experience to appreciate it as a reality and not as an academic exercise, a reality they experience through interactions with a diverse faculty and student body. (Hixson, 1991; p. 18)

In addition to limitations posed by the cultural insularity of the teacher education faculty, there is often also a general lack of a broad institutional commitment to diversity in the college and university environments that offer teacher education programs (Grant, 1993). Such things as an institutions' hiring practices, student recruitment and admissions policies, and curricular programs are evidence of the degree of institutional commitment. Making issues of diversity central to the intellectual life of a college or university community legitimizes efforts within programs to educate teachers for diversity.

The success of any teacher education program in restructuring for diversity is largely influenced by the norms and processes of the host institution. Teacher education programs found in institutions actively committed to the inclusion of people from diverse backgrounds are more likely to succeed in addressing issues of diversity than those located in institutions that are insensitive to or silent on matters of cultural inclusion. (Villegas, 1993, p. 3)

At least four different approaches have been used in trying to strengthen the institutional context of teacher education for diversity. The first is the active recruitment of faculty of color through the establishment of programs with creative incentives for diversifying teacher education faculties.

A second approach is the creation of a consortium, where a group of institutions combine their resources to hire staff with expertise in teacher education for diversity to provide part of the teacher education program, usually field experiences and a few courses and seminars related to teaching for cultural diversity. The Urban Education Program of the Associated Colleges of the Midwest in Chicago, for example, employs a staff of four people not directly associated with the colleges whose expertise is in teacher education for diversity. This program, which has existed since the fall of 1963, has provided courses in multicultural education and instruction for limited English proficient students and school and community field experiences for hundreds of prospective teachers from small liberal arts colleges (Melnick & Zeichner, 1994).

Other examples of consortia that have emphasized the preparation of teachers for cultural diversity include the Cooperative Urban Teacher Education program (CUTE) and the urban education semester of the Venture Consortium (Levine & Pignattelli, 1994). The CUTE program, begun in 1967 and based on an earlier program at Central Missouri State College (McCormick, 1990; Soptick & Clothier, 1974), currently involves more than 20 colleges and universities in six states. This program has graduated more than 2,000 teachers to date and, at one point during the 1970s, was adopted by institutions across the country. The Urban Education semester of the Venture Consortium in New York City coordinated by Bank Street College is an experience for college juniors who have not necessarily made a commitment to a career in teaching. This program involves interdisciplinary coursework at Bank Street and field experiences in East Harlem schools.

All three of these consortia, the Urban Education program of the Associated Colleges of the Midwest, the CUTE program, and the Urban Education semester of the Venture Consortium, have provided preparation for teaching in urban schools for students from colleges that are without the resources or expertise to implement an intensive cross-cultural teacher education program themselves.

Although there is a lack of empirical data about the long-term impact of these programs, some evidence from the CUTE program shows that its graduates choose to teach in greater proportions than non-CUTE graduates in inner-city urban schools and that they have consistently been ranked higher in teaching competence than CUTE graduates in the eyes of administrators (Soptick & Clothier, 1974).

A third approach to strengthening the institutional context for teacher education for diversity involves the provision of systematic staff development for teacher education faculty on various aspects of teacher education for diversity and how to incorporate it into their institutions and programs. For example, the Multicultural Education Infusion Center at San Diego State University, with funding from the U.S. Office of Bilingual Education and Minority Affairs, provided teams of faculty from 15 teacher education institutions with 2-week intensive institutes in June 1993, and a follow-up network experience that was designed to prepare teachers for work with diverse students.

Also, the Association of Teacher Educators and George Mason University, with funding from the U.S. Office of Bilingual Education and Minority Language Affairs, have been offering a series of 3-day institutes around the country for school and university teacher educators. These institutes, "Educating Language Minority Students," are designed to encourage teacher educators to give more explicit attention to language-related issues in the preparation of all teachers. To date, no evidence has been presented in the literature related to the effects of these institutes on teacher education faculty and programs.

A fourth approach to the institutional aspects of teacher education for diversity is partnership agreements between predominately white teacher education institutions and colleges and universities with significant numbers of faculty and students of color or schools and school districts in areas with large numbers of ethnic and language minority students. An example of this approach was the agreement involving both faculty and students from Louisiana Tech, a formerly white segregated institution, and Grambling State University, a historically black institution (Mills, 1984). Another form of partnership to enhance the capacity of a teacher education program to prepare teachers to teach diverse students involves teacher education programs located in predominately white areas and K–12 schools and school districts that provide teacher education students with field placements in schools serving students of color. The American Indian and Latino Cultural Immersion projects at Indiana University (Mahan, 1982a) and the partnership between Moorhead University in Minnesota and the San Juan–Alamo School District in South Texas (Cooper, Beare, & Thorman, 1990) are examples of these school and university partnerships.

IN-SERVICE TEACHER EDUCATION FOR CULTURAL DIVERSITY

Most scholars who have examined the literature on in-service teacher education for insights about how to prepare teachers better for cultural diversity have concluded that little attention is given to issues of diversity. The literature on staff development discusses the different purposes for staff development and effective practices of staff development for the achievement of these various purposes. Staff development for the development of specific teaching skills has also received much attention (e.g., Joyce & Showers, 1988). The literature includes such recommendations as involving teachers as planners of staff development activities, placing an emphasis on self-instruction with differentiated activities, emphasizing demonstration, providing supervised trials, giving ongoing feedback and support, and linking staff development to schoolwide improvement efforts (Sparks & Loucks-Horsley, 1990).

Because of the complex and demanding nature of the personal and professional changes needed to enable teachers to become more capable intercultural teachers (e.g., changes in attitudes toward race), these recommendations about staff development for skill training are insufficient by themselves for guiding staff development for cultural diversity. Haberman (1991) identified five levels of change that can serve as standards for assessing the effectiveness of staff development for diversity. These levels begin with the recognition of differences and tolerance of diversity and end with active efforts to combat racism and discrimination (see also, Grant & Melnick, 1976).

A few programs are discussed in the literature that seek to have an impact on teachers that goes beyond Haberman's beginning surface levels of influence. These programs often involve a substantial cultural immersion experience in which teachers live and work in a minority community. One program is a 6–8-week summer experience for teachers on the Navajo reservation in the southwest (Mahan & Rains, 1990), and a second program is a 1-week intensive immersion experience in a remote fishing village for teachers new to Alaska (Pfisterer & Barnhardt, 1992). Both programs are carefully structured and monitored and are closely connected to graduate university coursework. Here, as in many of the preservice field experiences, noncertified ethnic and language minority adults play key roles as teacher educators.

Another staff development program for teachers reported in the literature that aims for a deeper level of influence on teachers is an antiracist course for teachers taught by Julie Kailin in Wisconsin school districts (Kailin, 1994). This course offers teachers a critique of multicultural education as merely a "celebration of diversity" and aims to sensitize them to the racist constructions of reality in their attitudes and behavior, in their curriculum, and in the institutions in which they work. The course also seeks to mobilize teachers to act against these racist ideas and practices.

To date, very little empirical evidence has been reported in the literature related to the ability of these kinds of staff development programs to facilitate greater intercultural sensitivity and intercultural teaching competence. Although there is some evidence that suggests that staff development programs can be designed in ways that have an immediate impact on some aspects of teachers' beliefs, attitudes, and ideas (e.g., Baty, 1972), there is little evidence available concerning the impact of staff development programs focusing on issues of cultural diversity on teaching practice in the short or long run. The kind of evidence that is available related to changes in teaching practice is typically self-reports by teachers, without information about the quality of implementation or about how these activities affected the academic success of students.

For example, Mahan and Rains (1990) indicated that teachers who participated in their 6–8-week summer cultural immersion field experience program on American Indian reservations in the southwest reported that they experienced both changes in self and changes in professional practice. With regard to personal changes, the teachers reported that they now listened much more, thought much more before speaking, and had become more modest and nonaggressive. In terms of professional changes, the teachers reported that they went back to their schools and created new courses or modified existing courses that incorporated content about Native Americans and Native American perspectives into the curriculum.

Teachers who participated in staff development workshops in multicultural education at the University of Wisconsin–Parkside gave increased attention to African-American males in their classrooms and demonstrated a greater use of cooperative learning strategies after the sessions; yet, according to Sleeter (1992) who actually observed teachers in their classrooms before and after the staff development program, few teachers experienced a transformation in thought or practice. It was much more common according to Sleeter (1992) for teacher initial perspectives to be strengthened and reinforced.

If teachers' initial perspective about low income people and/or people of color was a deficiency perspective, they added more data to it rather than questioning it. If their mode of relating to students' homes and neighborhoods was to send messages home, they added more such messages. (p. 168)

Given the paucity of evidence regarding the success of staff development for cultural diversity, it does not seem possible at this point in time to articulate a set of design principles for these programs that are analogous to Little's (1993) principles for the design of staff development activities in general. Little (1993) proposed six principles for the design of staff development programs that she thinks measure up to the complexity of reforms now being undertaken in schools, including those reforms aimed at promoting greater equity among a culturally diverse student population. These principles include:

Professional development offers meaningful intellectual, social and emotional engagement with ideas, with materials, and with colleagues in and out of teaching . . . professional development takes explicit account of the contexts of teaching and the experience of teachers . . . professional development prepares teachers (as well as students and their parents) to employ the techniques and perspectives of inquiry. (pp. 138–139)

This vision of staff development proposed by Little is far different than the shallow, fragmented, and standardized content and passive roles for teachers that are common in many staff development programs (Fenstermacher & Berliner, 1985). Little's proposals for staff development acknowledge and encourage the revolution in staff development practice that is occurring in many parts of the United States where teachers are assuming much more active and collaborative roles in their own professional development and where reliance on external "experts" is diminishing. The recent explosion of interest across the country in teacher research and other forms of "ground-up" staff development for teachers (e.g., Cochran-Smith & Lytle, 1993; Hollingsworth & Sockett, 1994) is an example of how the character and quality of in-service teacher education programs is undergoing a fundamental reconstruction. "Delivery" modes of staff development are slowly beginning to give way to a form of in-service education where external expertise, where it is used at all, is fed into the ongoing inquiries of teachers into their own practices.

One example of staff development for diversity where teachers have worked cooperatively with external advisors is an innovative project conducted by Moll and several colleagues in an urban Arizona school district (Moll, 1992; Moll & Greenberg, 1992; Moll, Velez-Ibanez, & Greenberg, 1988). In this project, teachers working with teacher educators and anthropologists spend time in the Latino community and in the homes of their students gathering information about "funds of knowledge" in the community that can be incorporated into classroom lessons (e.g., by inviting parents and community members to make substantitive contributions to lessons). These funds of knowledge in the community are diverse and abundant and include such things as knowledge about folk remedies, animal husbandry, and carpentry. The teachers learn ethnographic research methods from the anthropologists, go into the community to learn about its funds of knowledge, and then meet with the university advisors in regular study groups to analyze and reflect about the possible classroom implications of their community observations. Many examples are cited in the writings of Moll and his colleagues of culturally relevant instruction by teachers that resulted from observations that documented funds of knowledge in the Latino community in this Arizona school district (e.g., see Moll, 1992). Moll (1992) argued that the key to successful staff development is the creation of settings that facilitate long-term collaborative work between teachers and researchers and among teachers. The expertise of the university researchers and teacher educators is utilized but in a manner very different from the hierarchial relationship patterns that are common in skill training workshops.

Although there is generally a lack of empirical evidence regarding the success of different approaches to multicultural staff development for teachers, it seems reasonable to conclude that the kinds of personal transformations that are discussed as necessary in the multicultural teacher education literature, such as the elimination of racist attitudes and practices and the changing of culturally encapsulated people into multicultural people, can only be accomplished by an approach to staff development that goes beyond the skill training and informational or curriculum package delivery workshops that have dominated practice to date. Although skill training staff development has, under certain conditions (e.g., adequate classroom follow up), proven itself able to develop particular technical skills among teachers, this development of technical skills alone does not address the personal changes in teachers that are needed; nor does merely providing teachers with information about different cultural groups address these personal changes. As was argued earlier, no teaching methods used by teachers who hold deficit views about ethnic and language minority students will enable those students to be successfully educated (Bartolome, 1994).

Guskey (1986) argued, contrary to this conclusion and to the shift in focus in the teacher learning literature from changes in teachers' behaviors to changes in teachers' practical knowledge and cognitions (Richardson, 1990), that enduring changes in teachers' attitudes and beliefs will follow changes in teachers' practices and in the learning outcomes for their students. His position suggests that staff development for cultural diversity should focus initially on getting teachers to use classroom practices that will lead to an improvement in student outcomes, regardless of the teachers' attitudes and beliefs. This approach would mean, for example, that once teachers saw that their students were capable of achieving at high standards, their beliefs about the inability of students to learn or about the deficits in students' home cultures would change.

Most discussions of multicultural staff development for teachers focus either on the personal transformation of teachers' attitudes and beliefs (e.g., Mahan & Rains, 1990) or on a combination of attitude change and skill development (e.g., Sleeter, 1992). More research is needed to test out the relevance of Guskey's (1986) claims for staff development that is aimed at fostering greater intercultural sensitivity and intercultural teaching competence.

Whether the initial emphasis is on personal transformation, on skill development, or on both, it is clear as Guskey (1986) pointed out, that teacher change is a gradual and long-term process and not an event that takes place at a single point in time. It is also clear as Sleeter (1992) pointed out, that changes brought about by staff development structured around a model of individual teacher development will be limited in how much it can accomplish, no matter which specific instructional strategies are used. Sleeter (1992) argued, consistent with this chapter's earlier recommendations regarding preservice teacher education for diversity, that efforts to foster institutional change must accompany those to promote individual development (see also, Sparks, 1992). When the development of teaching skills or competence with particular curriculum approaches is at issue, the guidance given in the general staff development literature such as providing ongoing support and feedback (Sparks & Loucks-Horsley, 1990) and creating institutional structures that promote collegiality (McLaughlin, 1991) seem useful. When there is a need for personal and institutional transformation that goes beyond this, the creation of settings that enable the kind of long-term joint productive activity among teachers and between teachers and external advisors discussed by Little (1993) and Moll (1992) becomes critical.

A NOTE ON OCCUPATIONAL SOCIALIZATION FOR CULTURAL DIVERSITY

One very noticeable characteristic of the teacher education literature that is concerned with issues of cultural diversity is the lack of acknowledgment, with few exceptions (e.g., Kushner & Brislin, 1986), of the work going on in other fields to develop greater cultural awareness and sensitivity and greater intercultural professional competence. This section briefly discusses some of the work in the fields of social work, counseling psychology, nursing, and law with regard to issues of occupational preparation and cultural diversity. There is also a very large literature in intercultural education that is beyond the scope of this chapter (e.g., Batchelder & Warner, 1977; Landis & Brislin, 1983). The purpose of this very brief look at a very large and rapidly growing body of literature is to suggest to those involved in teacher education that there is potential to gain a great deal from a more thorough mining of these inquiries outside of teacher education and from ongoing interactions with researchers from these other fields of study.

There has been much concern in several areas of occupational preparation for doing a better job of educating human services workers for cultural diversity and an acknowledgement of the failure to date to have provided adequate services to meet the needs of many ethnic and language minority clients/patients (e.g., Casas, Ponterrotto, & Gutierrez, 1986; Chau, 1992; Ponterotto & Casas, 1987; Steiner & Devore, 1983; Sue et al., 1982). Similar to the increasing emphasis in teacher education on developing competence in culturally relevant forms of instruction (e.g., Ladson-Billings, 1994), other fields also have begun to stress cultural competence and cultural congruence in the provision of care and services. The concern for the preparation of culturally skilled counseling psychologists (Pederson, 1985; Sue et al., 1982), culturally competent and ethnic-sensitive social workers (Chau, 1990, 1992; Haynes & Singh, 1992), and for culturally relevant and competent care by nurses (Lynam, 1992; Millon-Underwood, 1992; Thobaken & Mattingly, 1993) are examples of this trend.

There are many similarities between the preparation for cultural diversity literatures inside and outside teacher education. For example, just as is the case in teacher education, other human services worker educators draw a distinction between the development of cultural sensitivity and the development of cultural competence and argue that cultural sensitivity is inadequate by itself as a goal for occupational preparation. It has been argued in the human services preparation literature that individuals need to learn how to translate their cultural sensitivity and cultural knowledge into culturally competent practice in specific situations (e.g., Lynam, 1992). Several specific intercultural training approaches (e.g., "the culture assimilator") have been criticized for their overemphasis on developing awareness of cultural differences and for their lack of attention to the development of cross-cultural expertise (Johnson, 1987).

As is the case in the teacher education literature, substantial agreement exists in the human services literature about the inadequacy of cognitive and didactic approaches alone in developing cultural awareness/sensitivity and intercultural professional competence. Throughout this literature is an emphasis on combining cognitive activities such as reading and discussing with experiential learning. The experiential component that is advocated in the preparation of human services workers includes cross-cultural field and immersion experiences, role playing, simulations, case studies, and structured self-reflection (e.g., Barton & Brown, 1992; Chau, 1990, 1992; Christensen, 1992; Gunter, 1988; Hing, 1993; Wuest, 1992). Just as in teacher education, some of these experiential components involve immersion experiences in other countries that include living with families and structured study of the languages and cultures in those countries (e.g., Bond & Jones, 1993); an emphasis on the importance of carefully structuring these experiential components of training programs and providing regular times for systematic reflection about the experiences (e.g., see Barton & Brown, 1992); and discussion of the importance of using representatives from various cultural groups as cultural experts in the training process (Hing, 1993; Johnson, 1987).

The quality of evidence in these studies about the impact of training experiences on cultural awareness/sensitivity and intercultural competence is very similar to that which exists in teacher education. Most of the evidence is concerned with the effects of particular training approaches and experiences on the ideas, attitudes, and beliefs of prospective human services workers. Although much of the work involves the description of programs and practices without any investigation of their impact, there are numerous reports in the literature of how particular methods and approaches affected the knowledge levels, attitudes, and beliefs of prospective human services workers. For example, Katz and Ivey (1977) reported that a specific approach to racism awareness training that they used in a Dynamics of Racism course resulted in more positive attitudes toward African Americans. Beale (1986) reported that the use of a specific training technique, the "cross-cultural dyadic encounter," resulted in a greater respect for cultural differences among the student counselors who experienced it. Here, as in the teacher education literature, are also self-reports by students about the impact of particular training experiences on them as persons and as professionals. Thobaken and Mattingly's (1993) citations from the journal of a student nurse who completed a practicum on an American Indian reservation is an example of this student self-report data and is very similar to the kind of data cited earlier from students in teacher education programs.

Looking back now, I see that my aspirations were innocently naive to the complexities that exist when working in a transcultural setting. I, like many of the people had a very ethnocentric view of what Native Americans need and want in terms of outside assistance to cope with their problems. My thoughts and my ideas about what they wanted or needed were based on my own culturally rooted ideas of what I would want if I was in their situation . . . . What I found to be effective in transcending our cultural differences is what Dobson terms transcultural reciprocity. That is to develop a collaborative relationship where a client and nurse participate on equal terms . . . . I found that by offering instead of telling and by listening, learning, and watching, I was eventually able to gain a sense of trust from the Hoopa people. (pp. 61–63)

A general problem in the human services literature similar to that in the teacher education literature is a lack of empirical evidence regarding the impact of particular training experiences on the practices of students in occupational preparation programs, either in the short and long term and on the quality of their work with clients of different backgrounds. Although much can be learned from the human services literature about training practices that foster cultural knowledge and sensitivity, very little can be learned from this literature at this point in time about practices that foster intercultural competence in the work setting.

Much research in the human services literature is about the use of particular intercultural training methods that focus on building cultural awareness and the development of greater cultural sensitivity. A number of clearly identifiable strategies used in human services preparation programs could potentially inform work in teacher education (e.g., Shechtman & Or, 1994). Research about the character and quality of experiential training components can be useful to the work of teacher educators. Mio's (1989) study, which examined the effects on student counselors of two different ways of organizing cross-cultural encounters, is an example of this research. Mio investigated the relative impact of a more intensive relationship with a single member of a different ethnic group and a variety of short experiences with different members of a single group and concluded that the depth of experience that was possible in the long-term

relationship with a single individual was a key factor in the development of cross-cultural sensitivity. Mio's findings are very similar to those discussed earlier from an evaluation of a mentorship program in which prospective teachers developed long-term relationships with individual ethnic and language minority students (Larke, Wiseman, & Bradley, 1990).

Despite the limitations that exist in the occupational socialization for diversity literature with regard to evidence about the efficacy of particular practices, it is important for teacher education researchers whose work is concerned with issues of cultural diversity to begin to pay attention to the research going on in these other areas. The almost total isolation from each other of research efforts in different fields all concerned with the same general issues makes little sense. The field of teacher education can only gain from efforts to learn more about how human services workers in other fields are prepared for cultural diversity.

CONCLUSION

This chapter examined the issue of teacher socialization for cultural diversity by reviewing research literature in preservice teacher education related to issues of selection, socialization within programs, and institutional change. It also examined studies related to in-service teacher education for diversity and research on the preparation for diversity in occupational education programs outside of teacher education.

This review identified four dimensions along which all teacher education programs for diversity vary and a number of specific strategies such as case studies, cultural therapy, and community field experiences that seem to offer some promise in developing greater cultural knowledge, cultural sensitivity, and intercultural teaching competence among teachers in the United States. It also identified four strategies that are being used in the United States to create a more favorable institutional context in colleges and universities for teacher education for cultural diversity.

Although there is much evidence in extant research with regard to practices that facilitate a greater knowledge level about cultural diversity and greater intercultural sensitivity, there is very little evidence either in the teacher education or occupational socialization literatures about practices and strategies that enable the development of greater intercultural competence in the workplace. A priority in research on teacher education for cultural diversity should be to investigate how particular kinds of experiences for teachers at the preservice or in-service levels are connected to the character and quality of their teaching. Have any of the specific programs and practices described in this chapter made a lasting difference in the education experienced by ethnic and language minority students? Does the teaching of people who have completed particular kinds of experiences in teacher education programs look any different than the teaching of those who have not done so? At this point, there is little research that addresses these kinds of questions.

Another limitation in conducting the analyses for this chapter was the rather vague and incomplete descriptions of programs and strategies that exist in the literature. More elaborate and detailed descriptions available of courses and programs both as they are planned and as they are implemented are needed to understand the relationships between experiences in teacher education and personal and professional changes in teachers. Detailed case studies of the use of particular practices and of programs would be valuable additions to the literature on teacher education for cultural diversity.

Much of the work that goes on in teacher education never reaches the research literature, in part because of the labor-intensive nature of teacher education and the lack of time and resources available to many teacher educators to write about their practice (Schneider, 1987). If the kinds of case studies proposed here are going to make a significant contribution to practice in the field, educators need to find ways to tap into the wealth of expertise that exists in the practices of teacher educators who do not write about their own work, but whose work is exemplary with regard to the preparation of teachers for cultural diversity. One alternative is to provide more incentives and support for teacher educators to document their own practices. Another is to encourage those researchers who do have the resources to locate and study these programs. Whichever path is taken, the focus in studies of teacher education for cultural diversity must extend beyond those teacher education programs in the relatively few institutions that have the faculty

and resources to carry out research programs. Much of the exciting work with regard to cultural diversity is going on outside of these institutions and needs to be understood (e.g., see Melnick & Zeichner, 1994).

Finally, as is the case in many areas of teacher education research, efforts in the United States to prepare teachers for cultural diversity would benefit from an examination of research on similar efforts in other countries. Teacher socialization for cultural diversity is an international issue and research exists in several countries that addresses the same kinds of issues that were discussed in this chapter (e.g., see Verma, 1993). Although particular social and political contexts are very different in different countries, many countries are currently experiencing increased cultural diversity in their populations and the challenge of educating teachers to provide a high quality education to a broader range of students. Here again, U.S. teacher education can only gain by developing a greater awareness of and interaction with non-American research on educating teachers for cultural diversity. Hopefully, in the next *Handbook of Research on Teacher Education,* the chapter that examines the education of teachers for cultural diversity can offer a much more interdisciplinary and international perspective on research in this area than is currently possible.

References

AACTE Commission on Multicultural Education. (1973). No one model American. *Journal of Teacher Education, 24*(4), 264–265.

Ahlquist, R. (1991). Position and imposition: Power relations in a multicultural foundations class. *Journal of Negro Education, 60*(2), 158–169.

American Association of Colleges for Teacher Education (AACTE). (1987). *Teaching teachers: Facts and figures. Research about teacher education project.* Washington, DC: Author.

American Association of Colleges for Teacher Education (AACTE). (1989). *Rate III— Teaching teachers: Facts and figures.* Washington, DC: Author.

American Association of Colleges for Teacher Education (AACTE). (1990). *AACTE/Metropolitan Life survey of teacher education students.* Washington, DC: Author.

Anderson, J. (1988). Cognitive styles and multicultural populations. *Journal of Teacher Education, 39*(1), 2–9.

Au, K., & Kawakami, A. (1994). Cultural congruence in instruction. In E. Hollins, J. King, & W. Hayman (Eds.), *Teaching diverse populations* (pp. 5–24). Albany: State University of New York Press.

Banks, J. (1991). Teaching multicultural literacy to teachers. *Teaching Education, 4*(1), 135–144.

Barnes, H. (1987). The conceptual basis for thematic teacher education programs. *Journal of Teacher Education, 38*(4), 13–18.

Barnhardt, R. (1992). *Teaching/learning across cultures: Strategies for success.* Fairbanks, AK: College of Rural Alaska, University of Alaska–Fairbanks.

Bartolome, L. (1994). Beyond the methods fetish. Toward a humanizing pedagogy. *Harvard Educational Review, 64*(2), 173–194.

Barton, J., & Brown, N. (1992). Evaluation study of a transcultural discovery learning model. *Public Health Nursing, 9*(4), 234–241.

Bastian, A., Fruchter, N., Gittel, M., Greer, C., & Haskins, K. (1985). *Choosing equality: The case for democratic schooling.* Philadelphia: Temple University Press.

Batchelder, D., & Warner, E. (1977). *Beyond experience.* Battleboro, VT: Experimental Press.

Baty, R. (1972). *Reeducating teachers for cultural awareness.* New York: Praeger.

Beale, A. (1986). A cross-cultural dyadic encounter. *Journal of Multicultural Counseling & Development, 14*(2), 72–76.

Beckum, L. (1992). Diversifying assessment: A key factor in the reform equation. In M. Dillworth (Ed.), *Diversity in teacher education* (pp. 215–228). San Francisco: Jossey-Bass.

Bennett, C. (1990). *Comprehensive multicultural education: Theory and practice.* Boston: Allyn & Bacon.

Bennett, C., Okinaka, B., & Xio-Yang, W. (1988, April). *The effects of a multicultural education course on preservice teachers: Attitudes, knowledge and behavior.* Paper presented at the annual meeting of the American Educational Research Association, New Orleans.

Beyer, L. (1991). Teacher education, reflective inquiry and moral action. In B. R. Tabachnick & K. Zeichner (Eds.), *Issues and practices in inquiry-oriented teacher education* (pp. 113–129). Bristol, PA: Falmer Press.

Birrell, J. (1993). *A case study of the influences of ethnic encapsulation on a beginning secondary teacher.* Paper presented at the annual meeting of the Association of Teacher Educators, Los Angeles.

Blair, L., & Erickson, P. (1964). *The student teacher's experiences in the community.* Reston, VA: Association of Teacher Educators.

Bond, M., & Jones, M. (1993). Cultural immersion: Student experiences in Mexico. *Imprint, 40*(3), 65–68.

Bowen, E., & Salsman, F. (1979). Integrating multiculturalism into a teacher training program. *Journal of Negro Education, 48*(3), 390–395.

California Commission on Teacher Credentialing. (1988). *Adopted standards of program evaluation and effectiveness.* Sacramento: Author.

Carter, N., & Larke, P. (in press). Preparing the urban teacher: Reconceptualizing the experience. In M. O'Hair & S. O'Dell (Eds.), *Educating teachers for leadership and change.* Thousand Oaks, CA: Corwin Press.

Casas, J. M., Ponterrotto, J. G., & Gutierrez, J. M. (1986). An ethical indictment of counseling research and training: The cross-cultural perspective. *Journal of Counseling Development, 64*(5), 347–349.

Cazden, C. (1986). Classroom discourse. In M. Wittrock (Ed.), *Handbook of research on teaching* (3rd ed., pp. 432–463). New York: Macmillan.

Cazden, C., & Mehan, H. (1990). Principles from sociology and anthropology: Context, code, classroom, and culture. In M. Reynolds (Ed.), *Knowledge base for the beginning teacher* (pp. 47–57). Washington, DC: American Association of Colleges for Teacher Education.

Center for Education Statistics. (1987). *The condition of education*. Washington, DC: U.S. Government Printing Office.

Chau, K. (1990). A model for teaching cross-cultural practice in social work. *Journal of Social Work Education, 26*(2), 24–33.

Chau, K. (1992). Educating for effective group work practice in multicultural environments of the 1990s. *Journal of Multicultural Social Work, 1*(4), 1–15.

Children's Defense Fund. (1991). *The state of America's children*. Washington, DC: Author.

Christensen, C. (1992). Training for cross-cultural social work with immigrants, refugees, and minorities. *Journal of Multicultural Social Work, 2*(1), 79–97.

Clifford, G. J., & Guthrie, J. W. (1988). *Ed school: A brief for professional education*. Chicago: The University of Chicago Press.

Clothier, G., & Hudgins, B. (1971). *Unique challenges of preparing teachers for inner-city schools*. Kansas City, MO: Mid-Continent Regional Educational Laboratory. (ERIC Document Reproduction Service No. ED 056 971)

Cochran-Smith, M. (1991a). Learning to teach against the grain. *Harvard Educational Review, 61*(3), 279–310.

Cochran-Smith, M. (1991b). Reinventing student teaching. *Journal of Teacher Education, 42*(2), 104–119.

Cochran-Smith, M., & Lytle, S. (1993). *Inside-out: Teacher research and knowledge*. New York: Teachers College Press.

Collins, M., & Tamarkin, C. (1990). *Marva Collins way*. Los Angeles: Jeremy P. Tarcher.

Comer, J. (1988). Educating poor minority children. *Scientific American, 259*(5), 42–48.

Committee on Policy for Racial Justice. (1989). *Visions of a better way: A black appraisal of public schooling*. Washington, DC: Joint Center for Political Studies Press.

Cooper, A., Beare, P., & Thorman, J. (1990). Preparing teachers for diversity: A comparison of student teaching experiences in Minnesota and South Texas. *Action in Teacher Education, 12*(3), 1–4.

Cross, B. (1993). How do we prepare teachers to improve race relations? *Educational Leadership, 50*(8), 64–65.

Cruickshank, D. (1971). *Simulation as an instructional alternative in teacher preparation*. Reston, VA: Association of Teacher Educators.

Cuban, L. (1969). Teacher and community. *Harvard Educational Review, 39*(2), 253–272.

Cummins, J. (1986). Empowering minority students: A framework for interventions. *Harvard Educational Review, 56*(1), 18–36.

Cummins, J. (1989). *Empowering minority students*. Sacramento: California Association for Bilingual Education.

Darling-Hammond, L. (Ed.). (1993). *Professional development schools*. New York: Teachers College Press.

Delgado-Gaitan, C. (1991). Involving parents in the schools: A process of empowerment. *American Journal of Education, 100*(1), 20–46.

Ducharme, E., & Agne, R. (1989). Professors of education: Uneasy residents of academe. In R. Wisniewski & E. Ducharme (Eds.), *The professors of teaching: An inquiry* (pp. 67–86). Albany: State University of New York Press.

Eddy, E. (1969). *Becoming a teacher: The passage to professional status*. New York: Teachers College Press.

Edwards, P. (1992). Involving parents in building reading instruction for African-American children. *Theory Into Practice, 31*(4), 350–359.

Ellwood, C. (1990). The moral imperative of ethnic studies in urban teacher education programs. In M. Diez (Ed.), *Proceedings of the fourth national forum of the Association of Independent Liberal Arts Colleges for Teacher Education* (pp. 1–6). Milwaukee: Alverno College.

Farber, K., & Armaline, W. (1994). Examining cultural conflict in urban field experiences through the use of reflective thinking. *Teacher Education Quarterly, 21*(2), 59–76.

Fenstermacher, G., & Berliner, D. (1985). Determining the value of staff development. *Elementary School Journal, 85*, 281–314.

First, J., & Gray, R., Jr. (1991). *The good common school: Making the vision work for all children*. Boston: National Coalition of Advocates for Students.

Flowers, J. G. (1948). *School and community laboratory experiences in teacher education*. Oneonta, New York: American Association of Teachers Colleges.

Ford, B. (1991). Developing teachers with a multicultural perspective: A challenge and a mission. In C. Grant (Ed.), *Toward education that is multicultural: Proceedings from the first annual meeting of the National Association for Multicultural Education* (pp. 132–139). Morristown, NJ: Silver Burdette.

Friesen-Poirier, C. (1992). A student teacher's voice: Reflections on power. *Journal of Education for Teaching, 18*(1), 85–92.

Fruchter, N., Galletta, A., & White, J. L. (1992). *New directions in parent involvement*. Washington, DC: Academy for Educational Development.

Gallagher, P. (1993, April). *Teacher's cultural assumptions: A hidden dimension of school teaching*. Paper presented at the annual meeting of the American Educational Research Association, Atlanta.

Garcia, E. (1993). Language, culture, and education. In L. Darling-Hammond (Ed.), *Review of research in education, 19* (pp. 51–100). Washington, DC: American Educational Research Association.

Garcia, G., & Pearson, D. (1994). Assessment and diversity. In L. Darling-Hammond (Ed.), *Review of research in education, 20* (pp. 337–391). Washington, DC: American Educational Research Association.

Garibaldi, A. M. (1992). Preparing teachers for culturally diverse classrooms. In M. Dillworth (Ed.), *Diversity in teacher education* (pp. 23–39). San Francisco: Jossey-Bass.

Gay, G. (1986). Multicultural teacher education. In J. Banks & J. Lynch (Eds.), *Multicultural education in western societies* (pp. 154–177). New York: Praeger.

Gay, G. (1993a). Building cultural bridges: A bold proposal for teacher education. *Education & Urban Society, 25*(3), 285–299.

Gay, G. (1993b, April). *Effective strategies for multicultural professional development*. Paper presented at the annual meeting of the American Educational Research Association, Atlanta.

Gilbert, S., & Gay, G. (1985). Improving the success in school of poor black children. *Phi Delta Kappan, 67*(2), 133–137.

Gillette, M. (1990). *Making them multicultural: A case study of the clinical teacher-supervisor in preservice teacher education*. Unpublished doctoral dissertation, University of Wisconsin–Madison.

Gollnick, D. (1992). Multicultural education: Policies and practices in teacher education. In C. Grant (Ed.), *Research and multicultural education* (pp. 218–239). London: Falmer Press.

Gomez, M. L. (1991). Teaching a language of opportunity in a language arts methods class: Teaching for David, Albert & Darlene. In B. R. Tabachnick & K. Zeichner (Eds.), *Issues and practices in inquiry-oriented teacher education* (pp. 91–112). Bristol, PA: Falmer Press.

Gomez, M. L. (1994). Teacher education reform and prospective teachers' perspectives on teaching other people's children. *Teaching & Teacher Education, 10*(3), 319–334.

Gomez, M., & Tabachnick, B. R. (1991, April). *Preparing preservice teachers to teach diverse learners*. Paper presented at the annual meeting of the American Educational Research Association, Chicago.

Gomez, M., & Tabachnick, B. R. (1992). Telling teaching stories. *Teaching Education, 4*(2), 129–138.

Gonzalez, G., & Picciano, A. (1993). QUEST: Developing competence, commitment, and an understanding of community in a field-based, urban teacher education program. *Equity & Choice, 9*(2), 38–43.

Goodlad, J. (1990). *Teachers for our nation's schools.* San Francisco: Jossey-Bass.

Goodwin, A. L. (1990). *Fostering diversity in the teaching profession through multicultural field experiences.* Paper presented at the AACTE National Symposium on Diversity, Tampa.

Grant, C. (1993). The multicultural preparation of U.S. teachers: Some hard truths. In G. Verma (Ed.), *Inequality and teacher education* (pp. 41–57). London: Falmer Press.

Grant, C., & Koskella, R. (1986). Education that is multicultural and the relationship between preservice campus learning and field experiences. *Journal of Educational Research, 79*(4), 197–204.

Grant, C., & Melnick, S. (1976, November). *Developing and implementing multicultural inservice teacher education.* Paper presented at the annual meeting of the National Council of States on Inservice Education, New Orleans.

Grant, C., & Secada, W. (1990). Preparing teachers for diversity. In W. R. Houston, M. Haberman, & J. Sikula (Eds.), *Handbook of research on teacher education* (pp. 403–422). New York: Macmillan.

Grant, C., & Sleeter, C. (1985). The literature on multicultural education: Review and analysis. *Harvard Educational Review, 37*(2), 97–118.

Grant, C., Zeichner, K., & Gillette, M. (1988). *Preparing students to work effectively with diverse students in multicultural settings, final report.* Madison: Wisconsin Center for Education Research.

Grossman, P., & Richert, A. (1988). Unacknowledged knowledge growth: A reexamination of the effects of teacher education. *Teaching & Teacher Education, 1*(1), 53–62.

Grumet, M. (1988). *Bitter milk: Women and teaching.* Amherst: University of Massachusetts Press.

Gunter, L. M. (1988). Notes on a method for teaching transcultural nursing. *Recent Advances in Nursing, 20,* 122–136.

Guskey, T. (1986). Staff development and the process of teacher change. *Educational Researcher, 15*(5), 5–12.

Haberman, M. (1987). *Recruiting and selecting teachers for urban schools.* New York: ERIC Clearing House on Urban Education, Institute for Urban & Minority Education.

Haberman, M. (1988). *Preparing teachers for urban schools.* Fastback #267. Bloomington, IN: Phi Delta Kappa Educational Foundation.

Haberman, M. (1991). The rationale for training adults as teachers. In C. Sleeter (Ed.), *Empowerment through multicultural education* (pp. 275–286). Albany: State University of New York Press.

Haberman, M. (1993). Teaching in multicultural schools: Implications for teacher selection and training. In L. Kremer-Hayon, H. Vonk, & R. Fessler (Eds.), *Teacher professional development* (pp. 267–294). Amsterdam: Swets & Zeitlinger B. V.

Haberman, M., & Post, L. (1992). Does direct experience change preservice students perceptions of low-income minority children? *Midwestern Educational Researcher, 5*(2), 29–31.

Hayes, S. (1980). The community and teacher education. In H. P. Baptiste, Jr., M. Baptiste, & D. Gollnick (Eds.), *Multicultural teacher education: Preparing educators to provide educational equity* (pp. 94–108). Washington, DC: American Association of Colleges for Teacher Education.

Haynes, A., & Singh, R. (1992). Ethnic-sensitive social work practice: An integrated, ecological, and psychodynamic approach. *Journal of Multicultural Social Work, 2*(2), 43–52.

Hidalgo, N. (1993). Multicultural introspection. In T. Perry & J. Fraser (Eds.), *Freedom's plow* (pp. 99–106). New York: Routledge.

Hilliard, A. (1974). Restructuring teacher education for multicultural imperatives. In W. A. Hunter (Ed.), *Multicultural education through competency-based teacher education* (pp. 40–55). Washington, DC: AACTE.

Hing, B. (1993). Raising personal identification issues of class, race, ethnicity, gender, sexual orientation, physical disability, and age in lawyering courses. *Stanford Law Review, 45,* 1807–1833.

Hixson, J. (1991, April). *Multicultural issues in teacher education: Meeting the challenge of student diversity.* Paper presented at the annual meeting of the American Educational Research Association, Chicago.

Hodgdon, E. R., & Saunders, R. (1951). Using the community in teacher education. *Journal of Teacher Education, 2*(3), 216–218.

Hollingsworth, S., & Sockett, H. (1994). *Teacher research and educational reform.* Chicago: The University of Chicago Press.

Hollins, E. (1990). Debunking the myth of a monolithic white American culture; Or, moving toward cultural inclusion. *American Behavioral Scientist, 34*(2), 201–209.

Hood, S., & Parker, L. (1994). Minority students informing the faculty: Implications for racial diversity and the future of teacher education. *Journal of Teacher Education, 45*(3), 164–171.

Howey, K. (1992). Teacher education in the U.S.: Trends and issues. *Teacher Educator, 27*(4), 3–11.

Howey, K., & Zimpher, N. (1990). Professors and deans of education. In W. R. Houston, M. Haberman, & J. Sikula (Eds.), *Handbook of research on teacher education* (pp. 349–370). New York: Macmillan.

Huber, T., & Pewewardy, C. (1990). *Maximizing learning for all students: A review of the literature on learning modalities, cognitive styles and approaches to meeting the needs of diverse learners.* Washington, DC: ERIC Clearinghouse on Teacher Education. (ERIC Document Reproduction Service No. ED 324–289)

Irvine, J. J. (1989, December). *Cultural responsiveness in teacher education: Strategies to prepare majority teachers for successful instruction of minority students.* Paper presented at the annual meeting of Project 30, Monterey, CA.

Johnson, S. (1987). Knowing that versus knowing how: Toward achieving expertise through multicultural training for counseling. *The Counseling Psychologist, 15*(2), 320–331.

Joyce, B., & Showers, B. (1988). *Student achievement through staff development.* New York: Longman.

Kailin, J. (1994). Anti-racist staff development for teachers: Considerations of race, class, and gender. *Teaching & Teacher Education, 10*(2), 169–184.

Kapel, D., & Kapel, M. (1982). *The preparation of teachers for urban schools: The state of the art in preservice and in-service education.* New York: Columbia University Institute for Urban & Minority Education. (ERIC Document Reproduction Service No. ED 219 482)

Katz, J., & Ivey, A. (1977). White awareness: The frontier of racism awareness training. *Personal & Guidance Journal, 55,* 485–489.

King, J., & Ladson-Billings, G. (1990). The teacher education challenge in elite university settings: Developing critical perspectives for teaching in a democratic and multicultural society. *European Journal of Intercultural Studies, 1*(2), 15–30.

Kleinfeld, J. (1989, March). *Teaching taboo-topics: The special virtues of the case method.* Fairbanks: College of Rural Alaska.

Kleinfeld, J. (1991, April). Wrestling with the angel: What student teachers learn from writing cases. Paper presented at the annual meeting of the American Educational Research Association, Chicago.

Kleinfeld, J. (1992). Learning to think like a teacher: The study of cases. In J. Shulman (Ed.), *Case methods in teacher education* (pp. 33–49). New York: Teachers College Press.

Kohut, S. (1980). Field experiences in preservice professional studies. In H. P. Baptiste, M. Baptiste, & D. Gollnick (Eds.), *Multicultural teacher education* (pp. 73–93). Washington, DC: AACTE.

Kushner, K., & Brislin, R. (1986). Bridging gaps: Cross-cultural training in teacher education. *Journal of Teacher Education, 37*(6), 51–54.

Ladson-Billings, G. (1990). Culturally relevant teaching. *The College Board Review, 155,* 20–25.

Ladson-Billings, G. (1991a). Like lightning in a bottle: Attempting to capture the pedagogical excellence of successful teachers of black students. *International Journal of Qualitative Studies in Education, 3*, 335–344.

Ladson-Billings, G. (1991b, April). *When difference means disaster: Reflections on a teacher education strategy for countering student resistance to diversity.* Paper presented at the annual meeting of the American Educational Research Association, Chicago.

Ladson-Billings, G. (1994). *The dream keepers.* San Francisco: Jossey-Bass.

Ladson-Billings, G. (in press). Multicultural teacher education: Research, policy and practice. In J. Banks (Ed.), *Handbook of research on multicultural education.* New York: Macmillan.

LaFontaine, H. (1988). Educational challenges and opportunities in serving limited-English-proficient students. In Council of Chief State School Officers, *School success for students at risk* (pp. 120–153). Orlando, FL: Harcourt Brace Jovanovich.

Landis, D., & Brislin, R. (Eds.). (1983). *Handbook of intercultural training.* New York: Pergamon.

Larke, P. (1990, April). *Cultural awareness inventory: Assessing the sensitivity of preservice teachers.* Paper presented at the annual meeting of the American Educational Research Association, Boston.

Larke, P., Wiseman, D., & Bradley, C. (1990). The minority mentorship project: Changing attitudes of preservice teachers for diverse classrooms. *Action in Teacher Education, 12*(3), 5–11.

Lauderdale, W. B., & Deaton, W. L. (1993). Future teachers react to past racism. *The Educational Forum, 57*(3), 266–276.

Law, S. G., & Lane, D. S. (1987). Multicultural acceptance by teacher education students. *Journal of Instructional Psychology, 14*(1), 3–9.

Leighton, M., Hightower, A., Wingley, K., Paton, K., Pechman, E., & McCollum, H. (1994, April). *Developing an effective instructional workforce for students with limited English proficiency.* Paper presented at the annual meeting of the American Educational Research Association, New Orleans.

Levine, M. (Ed.). (1992). *Professional practice schools: Linking teacher education and school reform.* New York: Teachers College Press.

Levine, L., & Pignatelli, F. (1994). *Imagining change through ethnographic inquiry.* Paper presented at the annual meeting of the American Educational Research Association, New Orleans.

Liston, D., & Zeichner, K. (1991). *Teacher education and the social conditions of schooling.* New York: Routledge.

Little, J. W. (1993). Teacher's professional development in a climate of educational reform. *Educational Evaluation & Policy Analysis, 15*(2), 129–151.

Little Soldier, L. (1989). Language learning of Native American students. *Educational Leadership, 46*(5), 74–75.

Lucas, T., Henze, R., & Donato, R. (1990). Promoting the success of Latino language-minority students: An exploratory study of six high schools. *Harvard Educational Review, 60*(3), 315–340.

Lynam, M. J. (1992). Towards the goal of providing culturally sensitive care. *Journal of Advanced Nursing, 17*(2), 149–157.

Mahan, J. (1982a). Community involvement components in culturally oriented teacher preparation. *Education, 102*(2), 163–172.

Mahan, J. (1982b). Native Americans as teacher trainers: Anatomy and outcomes of a cultural immersion project. *Journal of Educational Equity & Leadership, 2*(2), 100–109.

Mahan, J. (1984). *Cultural immersion for inservice teachers: A model and some outcomes.* (ERIC Document Reproduction Service No. ED 254 923)

Mahan, J. (1993, February). *Native Americans as non-traditional, usually unrecognized, influential teacher educators.* Paper presented at the annual meeting of the Association of Teacher Educators, Los Angeles.

Mahan, J., & Boyle, V. (1981). Multicultural teacher preparation: An attitudinal survey. *Educational Research Quarterly, 6*(3), 97–103.

Mahan, J., Fortney, M., & Garcia, J. (1983). Linking the community to teacher education: Toward a more analytical approach. *Action in Teacher Education, 5*(1–2), 1–10.

Mahan, J., & Rains, F. (1990). Inservice teachers expand their cultural knowledge and approaches through practica in American Indian communities. *Journal of American Indian Education, 29*(2), 11–24.

Mahan, J., & Stachowski, L. (1985). Overseas student teaching: A model, important outcomes, recommendations. *International Education, 15,* 9–28.

McCormick, T. (1990). Collaboration works: Preparing teachers for urban realities. *Contemporary Education, 61*(3), 129–134.

McCormick, T. (1993, April). *Teaching a course on multicultural non-sexist education to a predominately white female population of future teachers.* Paper presented at the annual meeting of the American Educational Research Association, Atlanta.

McDiarmid, G. W., & Price, J. (1990a). *Prospective teachers' views of diverse learners: A study of the participants in the ABCD project.* East Lansing, MI: National Center for Research on Teacher Education.

McDiarmid, G. W., & Price, J. (1990b). *What to do about differences? A study of multicultural education for teacher trainees in the Los Angeles Unified School District.* East Lansing, MI: National Center for Research on Teacher Learning.

McLaughlin, M. W. (1991). Enabling professional development: What have we learned? In A. Lieberman & L. Miller (Eds.), *Staff development for education in the 90's* (pp. 61–82). New York: Teachers College Press.

Mehan, H., & Trujillo, T. (1989). *Teacher education issues.* Santa Barbara: University of California, Linguistic Minority Research Project.

Melnick, S., & Zeichner, K. (1994, February). *Teacher education for cultural diversity: Enhancing the capacity of teacher education institutions to address diversity issues.* Paper presented at the annual meeting of the American Association of Colleges for Teacher Education, Chicago.

Millon-Underwood, S. (1992). Educating for sensitivity to cultural diversity. *Nurse Educator, 17*(3), 7.

Mills, J. (1984). Addressing the separate but equal predicament in teacher preparation. *Journal of Teacher Education, 35*(6), 18–23.

Mio, J. S. (1989). Experiential involvement as an adjunct to teaching cultural sensitivity. *Journal of Multicultural Counseling & Development, 17*(1), 38–46.

Moll, L. (1988). Some key issues in teaching Latino students. *Language Arts, 65*(5), 465–472.

Moll, L. (1992). Literacy research in community and classrooms: A sociocultural approach. In R. Beach, J. L. Green, M. L. Kamil, & T. Shanalas (Eds.), *Multidisciplinary perspectives on literacy research* (pp. 211–244). Urbana, IL: National Council of Teachers of English.

Moll, L., & Greenberg, T. (1992). Creating zones of possibilities: Combining social context for literacy instruction. In L. Moll (Ed.), *Vygotsky and education* (pp. 319–348). Cambridge, UK: Cambridge University Press.

Moll, L., Velez-Ibanez, C., & Greenberg, J. (1988). *Project implementation plan. Community knowledge and classroom practice: Combining resources for literacy instruction.* Tucson: University of Arizona School of Education and Bureau of Applied Anthropology.

Montecinos, C. (1994, February). *The legacy of the common culture: Displacing teachers of color in multicultural teacher education.* Paper presented at the annual meeting of the American Association of Colleges for Teacher Education, Chicago.

Montecinos, C. (in press). Multicultural teacher education for a culturally diverse teaching force. In R. Martin (Ed.), *Practicing what we preach: Confronting diversity in teacher education.* Albany: State University of New York Press.

Mortenson, W. P., & Netusil, A. J. (1976). *Attitudes of prospective teachers toward the culturally different.* (ERIC Document Reproduction Service No. ED 113 614)

Mungo, S. (1980). *Experiential cross-cultural approaches in multicultural early field experiences in the small community.* (ERIC Document Reproduction Service No. ED 240 120)

Mungo, S. (1982). *Mental health and the intern. A teacher training model.* (ERIC Document Reproduction Service No. ED 240 121)

Narode, R., Rennie-Hill, L., & Peterson, K. (1994). Urban community study by prospective teachers. *Urban Education, 29*(1), 5–21.

Nelson-Barber, S., & Mitchell, J. (1992). Contributions of research on teacher assessment to culturally appropriate teacher education. In M. Dillworth (Ed.), *Diversity in teacher education* (pp. 229–262). San Francisco: Jossey-Bass.

Nieto, S. (1992). *Affirming diversity: The sociopolitical context of multicultural education.* New York: Longman.

Nolan, J. (1985). Potential obstacles to internal reform in teacher education: Findings from a case study. *Journal of Teacher Education, 36*(4), 12–16.

Noordhoff, K., & Kleinfeld, J. (1993). Preparing teachers for multicultural classrooms. *Teaching and Teacher Education, 9*(1) 27–39.

O'Brian, J. (1969). A master's degree program for the preparation of teachers of disadvantaged youth. In B. Tuckman & J. O'Brian (Eds.), *Preparing to teach the disadvantaged: Approaches to teacher education* (pp. 167–242). New York: The Free Press.

Olsen, L., & Mullen, N. (1990). *Embracing diversity: Teachers voices from California's classrooms.* San Francisco: California Tomorrow Project.

Paine, L. (1989). *Orientation towards diversity: What do prospective teachers bring?* Research report 89-9. East Lansing, MI: National Center for Research on Teacher Learning.

Pallas, A., Natriello, G., & McDill, E. (1989). The changing nature of the disadvantaged population: Current dimensions and future trends. *Educational Researcher, 18*(5), 16–22.

Pederson, P. (1985). *Handbook of cross-cultural counseling and therapy.* Westport, CT: Greenwood.

Pfisterer, B., & Barnhardt, R. (1992, Spring/Summer). Cross-cultural orientation at Old Minto camp. *College of Rural Alaska Newsletter.*

Ponterotto, J., & Casas, J. M. (1987). In search of multicultural competence within counselor education programs. *Journal of Counseling & Development, 65*(8), 430–434.

Pugach, M., & Pasch, S. (1994). The challenge of creating urban professional development schools. In R. Yinger & K. Borman (Eds.), Restructuring education: Issues and strategies for schools, communities and universities (pp. 129–156). Norwood, NJ: Ablex.

Pytowska, E. (1990). The teacher as cultural researcher. *Momentum, 21*(4), 40–42.

Quality Education for Minorities Project. (1990). *Education that works: An action plan for the education of minorities.* Cambridge, MA: Author.

Quintanar-Sarellana, R. (1991, April). *Training teachers for a multicultural society.* Paper presented at the annual meeting of the American Educational Research Association, Chicago.

Reed, D. (1993). Multicultural education for prospective teachers. *Action in Teacher Education, 15*(3), 27–34.

Reed, D., & Simon, D. (1991). Preparing teachers for urban schools: Suggestions from historically black institutions. *Action in Teacher Education, 13*(2), 30–35.

Richardson, V. (1990). Significant and worthwhile change in teaching practice. *Educational Researcher, 19*(7), 10–18.

Rodriguez, R. (1982). *Hunger of memory: An autobiography, the education of Richard Rodriguez.* Toronto: Bantam Books.

Ross, D., Johnson, M., & Smith, W. (1991, April). *Helping preservice teachers confront issues related to educational equity: Assessing revisions in coursework and fieldwork.* Paper presented at the annual meeting of the American Educational Research Assocation, Chicago.

Schneider, B. (1987). Tracing the provenance of teacher education. In T. Popkewitz (Ed.), *Critical studies in teacher education* (pp. 211–241). New York: Falmer Press.

Shade, B. (1982). Afro-American cognitive style: A variable in school success. *Review of Educational Research, 52*(2), 219–244.

Shade, B. (1994). Understanding the African-American learner. In E. Hollins, J. King, & W. Hayman (Eds.), *Teaching diverse populations* (pp. 175–190). Albany: State University of New York Press.

Shechtman, Z., & Or, A. (1994, April). *Applying counseling methods to challenge teacher beliefs with regard to classroom diversity & mainstreaming.* Paper presented at the annual meeting of the American Educational Research Association, New Orleans.

Sheppard, S. (1992, February). *The research says: Moving away from theory-based teacher education towards a constructive action research approach.* Paper presented at the annual meeting of the Western Canadian Association for Student Teaching, Edmonton.

Shulman, J. (1992, April). *Tender feelings, hidden thoughts: Confronting bias, innocence, and racism through case discussions.* Paper presented at the annual meeting of the American Educational Research Association, San Francisco.

Shulman, J., & Mesa-Bains, A. (1990). *Teaching diverse students: Cases and commentaries.* San Francisco: Far West Laboratory for Educational Research and Development.

Sleeter, C. (1988). *Preservice coursework and field experiences in multicultural education: Impact on teacher behavior.* Kenosha, WI: University of Wisconsin–Parkside, School of Education.

Sleeter, C. (1992). *Keepers of the American dream: A study of staff development and multicultural education.* London: Falmer Press.

Sleeter, C. (1994, April). *Multicultural education, social positionality, and whiteness.* Paper presented at the annual meeting of the American Educational Research Association, New Orleans.

Sleeter, C., & Grant, C. (1988). *Making choices for multicultural education.* Columbus, OH: Merrill.

Smith, B. O. (1969). *Teachers for the real world.* Washington, DC: American Association of Colleges for Teacher Education.

Smith, W. (1980). The American Teacher Corps Programme. In E. Hoyle & J. Megarry (Eds.), *World year book of education: Professional development of teachers* (pp. 204–218). New York: Nichols.

Soptick, J., & Clothier, G. (1974). *CUTE installation and diffusion project* (second phase). Kansas City, MO: Midcontinent Regional Educational Laboratory. (ERIC Document Reproduction Service No. ED 095 171)

Sparks, D. (1992). Staff development for diversity: An interview with Carl Grant and Christine Sleeter. *Journal of Staff Development, 13*(2), 12–15.

Sparks, D., & Loucks-Horsley, S. (1990). Models of staff development. In W. R. Houston, M. Haberman, & J. Sikula (Eds.), *Handbook of research on teacher education* (pp. 234–250). New York: Macmillan.

Spindler, G., & Spindler, L. (1993). The process of culture and person: Cultural therapy and culturally diverse schools. In P. Phelan & A. Locke Davidson (Eds.), *Renegotiating cultural diversity in American schools* (pp. 27–51). New York: Teachers College Press.

Steiner, J., & Devore, W. (1983). Increasing descriptive and prescriptive theoretical skills to promote ethnic-sensitive practice. *Journal of Education for Social Work, 19*(2), 63–70.

Stoddart, T., & Floden, R. E. (in press). Traditional and alternative routes to teacher certification: Issues, assumptions, and misconceptions. In K. Zeichner, S. Melnick, & M. L. Gomez (Eds.), *Complexities of reform in U.S. teacher education.* New York: Teachers College Press.

Strickland, D., & Ascher, C. (1992). Low income African-American children and public schooling. In P. Jackson (Ed.), *Handbook of research on curriculum* (pp. 609–625). Washington, DC: AERA.

Study Commission on Undergraduate Education and the Education of Teachers. (1976). *Teacher education in the United States: The responsibility gap.* Lincoln: University of Nebraska Press.

Sue, D. W., Bernier, J. E., Durran, A., Feinberg, L., Pedersen, P., Smith, E., & Vasquez-Nuttall, E. (1982). Position paper: Cross-cultural counseling competencies. *The Counseling Psychologist, 10*(2), 45–52.

Swisher, K., & Deyhle, D. (1987). Styles of learning and learning of styles: Educational conflicts for American Indian/Alaskan native youth. *Journal of Multilingual and Multicultural Development, 8*(4), 345–360.

Tatum, B. D. (1992). Talking about race, learning about racism: The application of racial identity theory to the classroom. *Harvard Education Review, 62*(1), 1–24.

Taylor, D., & Dorsey-Gaines, C. (1988). *Growing up literate: Learning from inner-city families.* Portsmouth, NH: Heinemann.

Tharp, R., & Gallimore, R. (1988). *Rousing minds to life: Teaching, learning and schooling in social context.* New York: Cambridge University Press.

Thobaken, M., & Mattingly, H. J. (1993). Cultural sensitivity. *Home Healthcare Nurse, 11,* 61–63.

Tiedt, P., & Tiedt, I. (1990). *Multicultural teaching: A handbook of activities, information and resources.* Boston: Allyn & Bacon.

Tran, M. T., Young, R., & DiLella, J. (1994). Multicultural education courses and the student teacher: Eliminating stereotypical attitudes in our ethnically diverse classroom. *Journal of Teacher Education, 45*(3), 183–189.

Trent, W. (1990). Race and ethnicity in the teacher education curriculum. *Teachers College Record, 91,* 361–369.

Valli, L. (1994, April). *Learning to teach in cross-cultural settings: The significance of personal relations.* Paper presented at the annual meeting of the American Educational Research Association, New Orleans.

Verma, G. K. (1993). *Inequality and teacher education: An international perspective.* London: Falmer Press.

Villegas, A. M. (1991). *Culturally responsive pedagogy for the 1990's and beyond.* Princeton, NJ: Educational Testing Service.

Villegas, A. M. (1993, April). *Restructuring teacher education for diversity: The innovative curriculum.* Paper presented at the annual meeting of the American Educational Research Association, Atlanta.

Wahab, Z. (1989). *The melting pot revisited.* Paper presented at the annual conference of the Oregon Multicultural Association, Salem, OR.

Wayson, W. (1988, April). *Multicultural education among seniors in the College of Education at Ohio State University.* Paper presented at the annual meeting of the American Educational Research Association, New Orleans.

Weiner, L. (1993). *Preparing teachers for urban schools.* New York: Teachers College Press.

Willison, S. (1989). *Cultural immersion of student teachers on an American Indian reservation.* Unpublished doctoral dissertation, Indiana University.

Willison, S. (1994). Community field experiences in the American Indian Project. In K. Zeichner & S. Melnick (Eds.), *The role of community field experiences in preparing teachers for cultural diversity.* East Lansing, MI: National Center for Research on Teacher Learning.

Wubbels, T. (1992). Taking account of student teachers' preconceptions. *Teaching and Teacher Education, 8*(2), 137–149.

Wuest, J. (1992). Joining together: Students and faculty learn about transcultural nursing. *Journal of Nursing Education, 31*(2), 90–92.

Young, L. (1993, February). *Learning about me, learning about them: Pluralism in a preservice education classroom.* Paper presented at the annual meeting of the Association of Teacher Educators, Los Angeles.

Zeichner, K. (1990). Chaning directions in the practicum: Looking ahead to the 1990s. *Journal of Education for Teaching, 16*(2), 105–132.

Zeichner, K. (in press). Designing educative practicum experiences for prospective teachers. In K. Zeichner, S. Melnick, & M. L. Gomez (Eds.), *Complexities of reform in teacher education.* New York: Teachers College Press.

Zeichner, K., & Gore, J. (1990). Teacher socialization. In W. R. Houston, M. Haberman, & J. Sikula (Eds.), *Handbook of research on teacher education* (pp. 329–348). New York: Macmillan.

Zeichner, K., & Melnick, S. (1995). *The role of community field experience in preparing teachers for cross-cultural teaching.* Paper presented at the annual meeting of the Association of Teacher Educators, Detroit.

Zimpher, N. (1989). The RATE project: A profile of teacher education students. *Journal of Teacher Education, 40*(6), 27–30.

Zimpher, N., & Ashburn, E. (1992). Countering parochialism among teacher candidates. In M. Dillworth (Ed.), *Diversity in teacher education* (pp. 40–62). San Francisco: Jossey-Bass.

·26·

BEGINNING TEACHER SUPPORT

ATTRITION, MENTORING, AND INDUCTION

Yvonne Gold

CALIFORNIA STATE UNIVERSITY, LONG BEACH

The concept of support is the central theme of this chapter. The purpose of induction programs, mentoring, and related components is to provide assistance to beginning teachers. They are the means of operationalizing support. Effective support is multidimensional, addressing the variety of developmental needs of teachers in this phase of their careers, including areas such as pedagogical, curricular, psychological, logistical, and classroom management. These various needs have interactive effects as well. Teachers cannot create a learning environment without classroom management skills, cannot teach without instructional skills, and cannot use their instructional or management skills unless psychological needs are met (Gold & Roth, 1993). Thus support must be comprehensive in nature and varied in type.

Few experiences in life have such a tremendous impact on the personal and professional life of a teacher as does the first year of teaching. The initial experiences are imprinted, embedding perceptions and behaviors regarding teaching, students, the school environment, and their role as teacher. This phenomenon of imprinting etches impressions and feelings during a critical period of the teacher's life. When encountering similar experiences throughout their career, these feelings and impressions are elicited. Thus, a teacher's instructional and teaching-related behaviors are influenced significantly by initial imprinting.

Hess defined imprinting as "a type of process in which there is an extremely rapid attachment, during a specific critical period, of an innate pattern to specific objects which thereafter become important elicitors of that behavior" (Hess & Petrovich, 1977, p. 2). Janov (1983) included three critical factors involved in the imprinting process that he defined as "input (or quantity), response (or quality) and timing" (p. 228).

How this imprinting process relates to beginning teachers can be observed as they make attachments during the critical period of their first year. These attachments are made to specific individuals and to significant experiences related to the school environment and to teaching. When the initial experiences are pleasurable, the imprinting is mainly positive and the transference is positive; however, when the first experiences are negative, paired with feelings of discouragement and discomfort, the imprinting is negative, and these feelings and behaviors are elicited in similar circumstances in the future. In many instances, continued reinforcement of unpleasant experiences may result in a decision to end a teaching career.

The fundamental role of imprinting during the initial enculturation period strongly emphasizes the importance of offering support to new teachers so that the imprinting takes place in a manner that is as pleasurable and as successful as possible. Because support can direct the imprinting process, the purpose of this chapter is to review the nature of support being offered to new teachers and to analyze related critical issues.

The chapter begins with a review of the rationale and impetus for new teacher support and focuses on the attrition rates and burnout statistics of new teachers. The loss of significant numbers of capable new teachers provides a foundation for the necessity of building strong support programs to assist them. Attention then turns to the nature and elements of support as well as clarifying various types of support now offered to new

The author expresses appreciation to Peggy Ishler (University of Northern Iowa), Leslie Huling-Austin (Southwest Texas State University), and editors John Sikula and Edith Guyton for their reviews and feedback.

teachers. Particular notice in this analysis is given to the need for offering various levels of support, both personally and professionally, to all beginning teachers so that the imprinting process can be established in the most positive way. The next section reviews support programs and focuses on a need for comprehensive and thorough conceptual or theoretical frameworks for teacher support programs. The fourth section of the chapter provides a review of support providers with special emphasis on mentor teachers. Analysis of the literature reveals a shift away from the concept of a mentor teacher, who is considered to be the expert training a novice, to that of a support provider who offers assistance to a respected new professional colleague. The chapter concludes with a review of the critical issues and persistent concerns regarding teacher induction today and focuses on some of the emerging conceptions and promising practices that may provide direction for the nature of beginning teacher support and support programs in the future.

RATIONALE AND IMPETUS FOR BEGINNING TEACHER SUPPORT

There are a variety of factors that provided the impetus for beginning teacher support. These include issues such as retention, performance, and professional well-being. One of the more salient of these is retention, which is an issue of increasing concern in education. High rates of attrition among beginning teachers have been well documented in the literature (Harris and associates, 1992, 1993; Schlechty & Vance, 1981, 1983). Recent developments in organizational theory suggest a broadened definition of retention; one which encompasses not only teachers' decisions to leave teaching or to stay but also the concept of engagement or involvement in teaching. This definition suggests a corresponding commitment to teaching that needs to be a focus of retention, not simply retaining all teachers on the job. This section of the chapter reviews research that reports attrition rates and burnout statistics along with career satisfaction and retention and rapid changes in the workplace. However, rather than simply describing the literature and research studies, the intent also is to examine causes and concerns that contribute to new teacher attrition. The importance of the critical period of imprinting for appropriate enculturation of the new teacher to prevent attrition also is analyzed.

Attrition Rates and Burnout Statistics

Concern regarding the attrition of beginning teachers is growing as studies continue to document statistics on those who choose to leave the profession (Heyns, 1988; Schlechty & Vance, 1981, 1983). At the same time, few of the induction programs have systematically collected or reported data regarding retention. As pointed out by Huling-Austin (1989a), "this clearly is an area in need of additional investigation" (p. 21). It is necessary to know how many leave the profession; and it is essential to learn why teachers are choosing to leave a profession so early in their careers after they have spent 4 or more years preparing for it.

A review of the literature on attrition/retention shows that a small number of research studies have addressed the numer-

ous and essential factors associated with teacher retention and have done so in mainly an anecdotal manner. Some findings are inconsistent and even contradictory. These inconsistencies may be found in the various constructs identified for investigation, in the range of instrumentation used, and in both the sizes and types of samples selected.

Until recently, few models or theories have provided explanations for teachers' decisions to remain in or leave teaching (Chapman, 1983). Several models have been offered to explain teachers' career satisfaction and/or psychological burnout related to attrition; yet, most fall short of modeling the influences on attrition itself.

There are a number of concerns in evaluating the attrition studies of beginning teachers. A few of these are: (1) the majority of the studies do not use a national sample to estimate attrition rates, rather many small and regional teacher samples are used; (2) generalizations are often made to populations other than the one sampled; (3) data on teachers and their attrition rates are sometimes inaccurate and unreliable; (4) many research studies have been characterized by inconsistencies and even contradictions; and (5) definitional problems and a lack of important variables exist in teacher attrition research.

Although the research is limited, there are a few informative studies that shed some light on the problem of teacher retention. Several of these studies are reviewed and analyzed.

Another area of importance in reviewing beginning teacher attrition is that of teacher burnout. It has been documented that those who work directly and continuously with people who need their services are particularly susceptible to a condition known as burnout. Because teachers are helping professionals, it is of utmost importance that this phenomenon of burnout be investigated as to how it contributes to attrition.

In the first section, teacher attrition studies are examined concentrating on the more recent and larger studies related to teacher retention and attrition. The next section reviews the research on teacher burnout, and the final section concludes with a discussion of the major causes and concerns related to beginning teacher attrition.

Attrition Studies and Outcomes

In reviewing studies of teacher attrition, several trends emerge. First, the public schools and teachers have long been the target of considerable criticism in the media leading to a diminishing respect in the eyes of the public. As a result, many teachers report that they no longer receive the nonmonetary rewards of teaching that they expected when they first began their careers. When dissatisfaction leads to prolonged disillusionment, burnout occurs and teachers often choose to leave the profession (Gold & Roth, 1993). Second, it has been estimated, with some samples, that 25% of beginning teachers do not teach more than 2 years and that nearly 40% leave the profession within their first 5 years of teaching (Harris, 1992, 1993; Heyns, 1988; Schlechty & Vance, 1981, 1983). Third, there is evidence from the studies reported that the academically talented leave the profession early in their career (Heyns, 1988; Schlechty & Vance, 1981, 1983). These statistics are of grave concern to educators who then question whether the quality of education also will diminish. Fourth, factors that influence career satisfaction suggest that teacher retention is a function of: (1) meeting teachers' unmet psychological needs (Gold, 1990; Gold & Roth, 1993); (2) amount of education (Bloland & Selby, 1980); (3) initial commitment to teaching (Chapman & Hutcheson, 1982); (4) adequacy of teacher preparation programs and student teaching (Zeichner, 1980), or early teaching experience (Elliott & Steinkellner, 1979); (5) professional and social integration into teaching (Chapman & Hutcheson, 1982); and (6) the role of the administrator (Berry, Noblit, & Hare, 1985). These six factors relate to teachers' decisions to remain in or leave teaching.

Rapid changes in the conditions that describe a teacher's workplace have contributed to teachers' discontent and decision to leave. Many teachers entered teaching with the belief that they would be allowed considerable career mobility only to discover that they no longer have the mobility they initially believed was available to them. Currently, teachers report that they have little if any lateral mobility and even less upward mobility than do individuals in most other careers (Farber, 1991). This dissatisfaction and discouragement can lead to burnout and attrition and needs to be researched using samples of beginning teachers. Workplace factors other than mobility to be considered here are financial rewards, lack of parents' interest and support, and discipline problems.

These trends focus on the major concerns of educators and reflect some of the leading factors associated with teacher attrition. Given these alarming reports, it is essential that existing studies be reviewed and analyzed. These studies are discussed under each of the trends described.

Erosion of Respect for Teachers: The Effects of Public Criticism

Issues of public support and respect are of utmost concern for teachers as was noted in The Metropolitan Life Survey of the American Teacher that began in 1984 and the Gallup Poll of the public's attitudes regarding public schools beginning in 1969. The results of these surveys pointed out a number of critical areas regarding teachers and the public and their views toward each other. First, negative attitudes of the public toward education grew between 1974 and 1983, according to the Gallup Poll. Even allowing for some sampling error, the figures represented a negative change of opinions on the part of 25–30 million people, which Elam (1984) stated was "a significant change indeed" (p. 3). This change is demonstrated through the percentage of people rating their local school A or B (i.e., excellent or good), which dropped from 48% to 31%. There was also an increase in the lower ratings, which reported that 11% and 20% of those surveyed rated their local schools D or F in 1974 and 1983, respectively. Second, the public judged teachers as having a low status in comparison to other occupational groups in the 1981 Gallup Poll, ranking them third in their contributions to the general good of society (after clergymen and physicians), second in terms of the amount of stress or pressure they encounter (after physicians), and eighth in terms of prestige or status (after physicians, judges, clergymen, bankers, lawyers, business executives, and public school principals). Thus, the public's respect for teachers is not consistent with

their understanding of the contributions teachers make or the amount of pressure they encounter (Elam, 1984). Third, 20% to 35% of the parents in the Metropolitan Life survey (Harris and Associates, 1987) did not hold in high esteem teachers or the job they were doing. This group of parents reported that teachers were doing only a "fair" or even "poor" job in terms of how much they seemed to care about their students. They regarded the competence and qualifications of teachers in their own child's school as either fair or poor and believed that the overall education their child was receiving was only fair or poor. It may well be that these minority yet strong opinions have a significant influence on the feelings and self-regard of individual teachers and have an impact on beginning teachers who are highly vulnerable to public opinion.

Harris and Associates (1987), authors of the Metropolitan Life survey, stated that "this critical minority provides a strong consistency for reform and change" (p. 18). Apparently, this critical group acts as a force to undermine teachers' efforts and their morale. These data can suggest two major characteristics regarding the lack of public respect for teachers: (1) lack of respect coming from a significant and anonymous segment of the general public often mirrored in media interpretations of teachers; and (2) the lack of respect that originates from a small, yet highly influential, minority of parents who are familiar with community schools and speak out against them.

Along with the lack of respect for teachers is the absence of appreciation for their efforts. In the 1992 Metropolitan Life Survey of the American Teacher, the reason most often cited as a major factor for leaving teaching was "lack of support or help for students from their parents" (Harris and Associates, 1992, p. 15). Forty percent of the teachers who intended to leave their profession named this reason as a major factor in their decision. Lack of parental support and cooperation was an area of major dissatisfaction and discouragement for new teachers. Teachers seldom are praised for their successes in educating and socializing the millions of children in the United States. Instead, they usually are blamed for their failures and sometimes the failures of society regarding students. This criticism comes not only from society but also from the students, parents, and administrators.

The degenerating morale of teachers is reflected in reports that describe the profession as being in a crisis. Wendt (1980) stated that education is in "a sense of crisis," and Farber (1991) called it *Crisis in Education: Stress and Burnout in the American Teacher*. The Association for Supervision and Curriculum Development (ASCD) conducted a study of its membership to determine critical issues for 1990–1992. The study reported that the status of teaching and, as a result, morale remains at an all-time low (Hodges, 1990). Other studies of teacher dissatisfaction include the NEA 1980 (35% dissatisfied/very dissatisfied), the Harris Poll 1988 (13% dissatisfied), and the Carnegie Foundation 1988 (23% dissatisfied).

Along with these surveys and reports, the 1990 Carnegie Report also indicated that "nearly 40 percent of the teachers reported that if they had it to do over, they would not become a public school teacher." "Sixty-one percent of the teachers say morale at their school is only 'fair' or 'poor'", and fifty-six percent say political interference in education has increased since 1983, and 60 percent report more state regulation" (Carnegie Foundation, 1990, pp. 3–5).

The 1993 Gallup Poll (Elam, Rose, & Gallup, 1993), however, reported the largest 1-year improvement in the grades given by the public to their own local public schools since the question was first asked in 1974. Of those who responded, the percent of As or Bs jumped from 40% in 1992 to 47% in 1993, after nearly a decade of relative stability. The nation's schools came off a poor second to the local schools. Only 19% awarded an A or B to schools of the nation as a whole, whereas 47% of the public thought their own schools merited either an A or a B. Whereas discipline, drugs, and finances had been the uppermost problems in the minds of respondents in former surveys, the 1993 poll reported a lack of proper financial support as clearly the number one public school problem. Twenty-one percent of poll respondents named financial support as the number one problem, whereas 16% named drug abuse and 15% cited lack of discipline. Concern over financial support was considerably greater in the West (30%) and the Midwest (29%) than in the South (13%) and East (15%) (p. 139). A large majority of citizens (81%) reported concern about inner-city schools and viewed it as "very important" to improve these schools, whereas 15% responded as it being "fairly important." These alarming problems have an impact on new teachers as they are forming their perceptions of teaching and are learning to adjust to their role as teacher. Public perceptions regarding the desirability of teaching as a career have fluctuated over the years of the Gallup Poll surveys. The high was recorded in 1969 when 75% of the respondents said they would like their child to become a teacher; the low came in 1983, which was reported at only 45%. The 1993 poll reported 67% responding to the question in the affirmative (Elam et al., 1993).

This slow wearing away of the morale of teachers also has its effect on teachers just entering the profession. New teachers usually demonstrate an idealism and excitement about teaching. When confronted with public criticism, low morale in their school, and little administrative support, many of these new teachers become disillusioned and begin to withdraw from others, which can result in leaving the profession (Gold & Roth, 1993).

In summary, criticism has a way of wearing individuals down so that their morale and self-esteem are greatly damaged. In fact, teachers are affected in a number of ways. Many feel forced to do low-quality teaching as a result of the psychological pressures. Added stress often affects them physically (illness, etc.). Other teachers choose to try and keep high standards in their teaching, which often leads to physical and psychological distress that has an effect on them and also on their families. For some teachers, the choice is to leave the profession. Research is greatly needed to understand better the effects of criticism on new teachers and how this relates to attrition.

Loss of Teachers Early in Their Careers: Fact or Fiction

A great deal of evidence suggests that beginning teachers leave teaching early in their career. Based on their sample of North Carolina beginning teachers, Schlechty and Vance (1983) re-

ported that "it seemed reasonable to estimate that from 40% to 50% of first-year teachers this year (1983) will not be teaching seven years from now. Furthermore, two-thirds to three-fourths of those who leave will do so in the first four years of teaching" (p. 176). Their best estimate was that first-year teachers leave at an annual rate of 15% and at a rate of 10% for second-year teachers.

Using a sample of 50–55 public school systems of the five counties in the Missouri portion of the St. Louis metropolitan area during the period from 1969 to 1982, Mark and Anderson (1985) reported rapid rates of dropout in early years of teaching with declining percentages of teachers dropping out in later years. They also found that 29.5% of the teachers who started teaching in 1969 did not survive to the second year of teaching. It took from the second to the seventh year for another 30% to drop out, and only 11.5% left teaching from the seventh to the fourteenth year. It was clear in their study that the number of new teachers was still declining each year.

Rand analyzed computerized personnel data on approximately 35,000 teachers from four states—Illinois, Michigan, New York, and Utah—since 1970. Annual attrition rates in the early years of teaching were almost 15%, dropping to around 10% for those between 25 and 34 years of age, and dropping still further to 3% for those between 35 and 54 years of age (Grissmer & Kirby, 1987).

Heyns (1988) used the National Longitudinal Study-72 (NLS-72) of the 1972 high school class's fifth wave survey for her analysis of attrition. She concluded that teacher turnover, where teachers return later, is higher than the low levels of attrition suggest, and that the patterns of attrition were high, particularly in the first 3 or 4 years of teaching. She reported that former teachers are more likely to have left the good schools rather than the problem schools. She also found that 18% of experienced teachers reentered at some point in their career, and that men were slightly more likely to leave than women. Heyns's analyses were not multivariate, however, and did not include the influence of family formation, major field, or wage variables.

Hafner and Owings (1991) also reviewed the NLS-72 study and reported that 37% of the teacher cohorts left within the first 5 years (1977–1981); however, many individuals moved in and out and back into teaching. Although the average attrition rate during a 10-year period was 7%, the average annual net increase for any starters or leavers for the period was 1.6%. Much mobility was evident in these teachers' careers, and the percentage of the teachers leaving the field did not seem to be increasing; over time attrition seemed to be very low or nonexistent.

The Metropolitan Life 1992 Survey of "The Second Year" (Harris & Associates, 1992) stated that nearly "one fifth (19%) of teachers who began their teaching career two years ago say it is 'very' (6%) or 'fairly' (13%) likely that they will leave the teaching profession to go into some different occupation within the next five years" (p. 3). The report also stated that this "sign of extreme discouragement with the teaching profession was particularly common among new teachers teaching high school (27%) in inner city or urban settings (24%), and in schools having large numbers of minority (23%) and lower income (21%) students" (p. 15). These statistics were similar to the California report by Smith-Davis (1991) who found approximately 50% of new teachers are leaving the classroom by their fifth year.

Based on these studies, the attrition rate for new teachers is high. Follow-up studies regarding the return rate of these teachers in contrast to their permanently leaving the profession are necessary for a more accurate evaluation.

Academically Talented Teachers Who Leave the Profession Early in Their Career

Although there is strong evidence that the most able students do not choose teaching as their career and that many of the most able teachers choose to leave teaching, it is important to look at specific research studies regarding this third trend. Recent research has indicated specifically that (1) the academically talented high school graduates tended not to choose teaching as a career (Vance & Schlechty, 1982); (2) of those high school graduates who do enter teacher training, the academically more able students are more likely to change to another career; in fact, the higher a teacher's NTE score, the shorter the predicted duration in teaching (Murnane & Olsen, 1990; Schlechty & Vance, 1981); and (3) approximately one out of every four students who does complete a teacher training program never enters a teaching career or leaves teaching within the first 5 years (Chapman & Hutcheson, 1982).

Taking a different research approach than Schlechty and Vance (1981), who used a statistical analysis of existing data bases, such as the analysis of the National Longitudinal Study, Berry, Noblit, and Hare (1985) conducted qualitative studies of the teacher labor market. They used a case study methodology to understand the situational context of the teachers' labor market in the Southeast. Six universities and six school systems were involved. They found that school system officials reported that they were not necessarily interested in prospective teachers with the "best academic qualities" (p. 105). What they did want were those with "a certain amount of intelligence"; however, what was more important to them was that the teacher was able to "relate to children and parents," "organize," "disclose," "withstand pressure," and be active in extracurricular activities (p. 105). They also reported that the "very bright" were not necessarily what the system officials needed or wanted (p. 105). The rural administrators reported that they were seeking nonacademic characteristics in teachers for their areas. Thus, academically highly qualified teachers were in less demand in both urban and rural areas because different contexts required different teaching roles. In rural systems, teachers had to fit into the community. The reviewers believed that their qualitative research reveals the social context and salient characteristics from the perspective of insiders and thus is necessary for policy implementation.

Using a new longitudinal data set providing information on the career histories of 13,890 North Carolina teachers, Murnane and Olsen (1990) argued that "teachers with high opportunity costs, as measured by test scores and subject specialities, stay in teaching less long than other teachers do, and that salaries influence duration less for teachers with high test scores than for teachers with lower scores" (p. 106).

The 1991 Analysis Report on the National Longitudinal Studies of the High School Class of 1972 (Hafner & Owings, 1991) reported that more than 1,000 individuals responded to the follow-up survey that included detailed information. Those still teaching were clearly different on several variables compared to former teachers and those who never taught. They found, in contrast to Chapman and Green's (1986) results, that academic aptitude and achievement were related to career patterns. This study reported that "individuals no longer teaching and those who never taught had higher academic aptitude scores than those still teaching, whereas individuals who never taught had the highest aptitude scores" (p. 29). Results suggest that it is premature to assume that attrition "necessarily depletes" the teaching profession of its most talented teachers. In fact, the report noted that "if the most talented teachers are more likely to leave, they are also more likely to re-enter" (p. 30) and their returning tended to raise the averages for current teachers.

Although these studies are informative, it is apparent that the variables affecting teacher retention are highly complex and indeed far more subtle than many researchers and analysts initially believed.

Career Satisfaction and Retention

Career satisfaction, the fourth major trend, covers a number of areas: (1) meeting teachers' unmet psychological needs, (2) amount of education, (3) new teachers' initial commitment to teaching, (4) teacher preparation programs, (5) professional and social integration into teaching, and (6) the role of the administrator in teacher retention. Attempts to address the first area have been categorized under the heading of emotional support in which mentors or support individuals are encouraged to "offer support by listening empathically and sharing experiences" (Odell, 1989, p. 31) or provide personal support such as "emotional support, befriendment, and encouragement" (Enz, 1992, p. 74) and "emotional support and encouragement" (Wolfe, 1992, p. 106). Although listening and offering support are important and need to be continued and reinforced, they are only one part of meeting teachers' personal and psychological needs. It is essential that beginning teachers' psychological needs are identified and addressed. In fact, at the closing session of the ATE Advanced National Academy on Induction and Mentoring, Peggy Ishler (1990) reviewed the major issues related to needs for helping beginning teachers. Psychological support was cited as one of the most critical needs identified at the conference. To address these needs, a comprehensive program of psychological support was proposed by Gold (1990, 1992) and by Gold and Roth (1993) that addresses teachers' needs in three areas: emotional-physical, psychosocial, and personal-intellectual. Using inventories to assess each of these areas, teachers identify their needs and then work on a planned program to meet them. They also learn new coping skills to behave more successfully in stressful situations, such as discipline cases, difficult parents, and administrators who are not supportive. Learning to identify and meet personal and psychological needs is critical for beginning teachers. It has been documented (Ward, 1987) that when teachers are personally insecure, lack confidence, or have a sense of not being in control of themselves or their environment, it is not likely they can be successful at teaching, regardless of how strong the technical preparation has been. As described by Ward (1987), no matter how well trained, individuals suffer "reality shock" when placed in classrooms as the sole person responsible for the education of some 30 students. Incorrectly handled, the impact of this experience may wash out any skills and knowledge prospective teachers learn in formal college training.

The second area focuses on the "amount of education." Traditionally, new college graduates have been the primary source of additional teachers. The Survey of 1985–1986 Recent College Graduates conducted by NCES (Choy et al., 1993) included a number of specific questions asked about 1985–1986 college graduates' training and experience in teaching. Among the approximately 933,000 bachelor's degree recipients in 1985–1986, 12% were newly qualified teachers. The percentage of graduates who were newly qualified teachers varied according to the field of study in which the graduates majored. After education majors, 76% of whom were newly qualified teachers, graduates who majored in the humanities were the second most likely group to be newly qualified teachers. Of all recent bachelor's degree recipients, 10% were employed as teachers, 75% were employed in other occupations, and 15% were not employed.

One question related to increasing the pool of teacher candidates is why some newly qualified teachers do not seek teaching positions. In their survey, NCES reported that 28% of newly qualified teachers did not apply for teaching jobs, and a number of newly qualified teachers expressed more or less negative attitudes toward teaching (Choy et al., 1993).

The research on teacher change shows no relationship between educational attainment and occupational mobility of teachers. Although the relationship of increased education to career mobility has been widely discussed in the literature, there appears to be little agreement on its importance for teachers. Career patterns do not appear to be related to either teachers' academic achievement or respondents' ratings of the successfulness of their teacher education programs. In addition, many women who have selected teaching have reported that they do not really plan to teach. They believe that teaching provides a back-up to a more desired career or marital possibility.

To meet teacher shortages, individuals who have not completed their training are often hired. In these situations follow-up studies are needed to assess the attrition rate of these individuals. A study of attrition in Wisconsin (Bogenschild, Lauritzen, & Metzke, 1988) surveyed a sample of 400 teachers (100 special education teachers and 100 general education teachers who had remained in teaching, and 100 special education and 100 general education teachers who had left teaching). A completed survey instrument was returned by 61% of the sample (including 100% of the special education teachers who were still teaching). Significant differences in attrition rates were found for fully certified and provisionally certified (not yet certified) special education teachers and general and special education teachers. Teachers with provisional certification were more likely to leave teaching than were fully certified teachers during the first 2 years of study. It would seem that even though provisional certification may be used in an emergency situation, it does not offer a long-term solution to the problem of the teacher shortage in Wisconsin. This phenomenon was especially true for special education teachers; nearly one fifth of these teachers left teaching during the first 3 years of study.

The New Jersey State Board of Education in 1984 adopted revised regulations for teaching certification that permitted provisional certificates to be issued to applicants who did not complete an approved teacher preparation program. Since 1985, more than 2,200 beginning teachers had been hired with provisional certification. Of those who completed the program requirements, 98% were recommended for standard teaching certificates. Attrition rates of first-year teachers trained in the Provisional Teacher Program were consistently and significantly lower than attrition rates of traditionally prepared beginning teachers. On the average, 18% of new teachers prepared in traditional collegiate programs leave their classrooms at some point during the first year of teaching. Provisionally certified teachers, however, demonstrated an average 5% rate of attrition during the first year on the job. They attribute this success to an induction program with support and supervision for these teachers provided by the members of their professional support teams (Ellis, Klagholz, Schechter, & Newman, 1991).

Other studies of alternative route candidates reported that the performance was much more uneven than that of trained teachers, with a much greater proportion of them, from 2 to 16 times as many, likely to be rated "poor" on each of the teaching factors evaluated (Gomez & Grobe, 1990). Also, alternative route teachers from short-term programs often experienced less job satisfaction than did the fully certified beginning teachers (Lutz & Hutton, 1989), and they reported less satisfaction with their preparation and less commitment to remaining in teaching than other recruits (Darling-Hammond, Hudson, & Kirby, 1989).

It is apparent that a number of factors must be considered in evaluating the amount and quality of education teachers receive. Also, many variables enter into a teacher's decision to stay in or to leave teaching.

The third area under career satisfaction and retention is related to the new teacher's initial commitment to teaching. Initial commitment to teaching is a highly important and sensitive variable to measure and has been researched by a number of individuals with varying results. Chapman (1984) reported from his research with 1,282 University of Michigan certificate recipients that the strongest predictor of retention was initial commitment to teaching. Extended studies of University of Michigan teaching recipients who graduated in 1963, 1967, and 1971 (Chapman & Green, 1986) concluded that the "roots of attrition reach back to differences in initial career commitment and early work experiences" (p. 277). Thus, the initial imprinting of new teachers must be a central focus for principals and administrators. Chapman and Green believe that a model that incorporates early attitudes and work experiences to explain subsequent career decisions is important to a more complete understanding of teacher attrition. In a study using a small sample of beginning teachers (160) from New Mexico the data were consistent with the Chapman and Green (1986) model that had identified the quality of the first teaching experience to be the most heavily weighted factor influencing teacher retention (Odell & Ferraro, 1992). This has importance in studying new teacher induction programs and support.

Using a qualitative approach, Berry, Noblit, and Hare (1985) found that teachers stayed in teaching because of a commitment to teaching, a love of children or adolescents, an unwillingness to move into business or industry, and a commitment to preserving a lifestyle. It would seem, then, that this area is one where preservice experiences and student teaching training could make a major contribution toward reducing new teacher attrition by assisting individuals in identifying and clarifying their desires and goals for choosing teaching as their profession and to recognize the rewards for them in teaching.

The 1992 Metropolitan Life Survey (Harris & Associates, 1992) reported nearly one fifth of the teachers polled stating that it was likely they would leave teaching in the next 5 years. The new teachers in the 1992 survey cited their reasons for leaving teaching as being the lack of parental help, low pay, lack of support from school administrators, and the impact of serious social problems on students that makes teaching difficult. With these types of pressures on teachers, initial commitment to teaching for some may be lost when the pressures become so great and discouragement sets in.

In the Metropolitan Life Survey, nearly half of the teacher sample rated their school excellent on the qualifications of its teachers and the level to which teachers care about their students. About 70% said working with their students had been a very satisfying experience during their 2 years of teaching and that they made a difference in their students' lives (Harris & Associates, 1992). It would be helpful to learn the difference in initial commitment to teaching in each of these two groups.

Lortie (1986) asserted that to retain able and experienced teachers, new ways must be found to sustain their commitment to working in schools. He continued by saying that it is not enough to think only about those individuals now entering the field; we must also attend to the circumstances that experienced teachers face, especially if teacher attrition is to be minimized for all teachers.

These findings regarding the importance of the initial teaching experience support the premise presented at the beginning of this chapter describing the significance of imprinting on new teachers during these first months of teaching.

The fourth area under career satisfaction and retention considered is preparation as a factor in attrition, that is, teacher preparation programs, student teaching, and early teaching experience. Zeichner (1980) argued that student teaching can be miseducation, whereas Chapman and Green (1986) reported that career patterns for teachers do not appear to be related to either teachers' academic achievement or respondents' ratings of the adequacy of their teacher education programs. Therefore, in contrast to Zeichner, Chapman and Green believed it was unlikely that attrition was related to program inadequacies.

A number of studies have described the first year of teaching as a time of discouragement and disillusionment for the new teacher. This early discrepancy of what teachers believed teaching to be and what it was in reality has been reported as contributing greatly to early attrition. A study of 1,282 randomly selected teaching certificate recipients who graduated from the University of Michigan (Chapman, 1984) between 1946 and 1978 found that among those who entered teaching, the quality of the first teaching experience was more strongly related to subsequent attrition than was either their academic perfor-

mance or the perceived adequacy of their education program. Findings from this study have indicated that the actual classroom experience provided these teachers important information for career decision making not contained in academic training. In fact, in the Chapman and Green (1986) research, which extended the previous research of Chapman (1984), the quality of the first teaching experience was the most heavily weighted factor influencing teacher retention. Thus, the impact of the initial imprinting stage on teacher attrition is most evident here and the need for both instructional and psychological support is essential.

It appears that this early imprinting has enormous consequences for new teachers. Studies by Chapman and Green (1986) suggest that a successful first teaching assignment could be positively related to retention, and the rewards and successes to be experienced during this time need to be strongly considered in working with student teachers and new teachers.

The fifth area for consideration is professional and social integration into teaching. Chapman (1983) provided a general conceptual model of the influences associated with teacher retention/attrition. The model is grounded in social learning theory and the belief that psychological functioning can be explained in terms of the interaction of personal characteristics, environmental determinants, and previous behavior (e.g., learning). His model presents a longitudinal approach, and a suggested number of factors needed to be taken into consideration to understand a teacher's decision to stay in or to leave teaching.

When testing the model, Chapman (1984) included data on 1,282 individuals who fit the grouping criteria; discriminant analysis was used. One unexpected result in this study was the relatively small contribution of professional integration variables such as values, skills, and achievements to the discriminant functions, especially given the importance of some of these variables in their previous studies. In analyzing the possibilities for the findings, there were differences in this study in that the subjects were more homogeneous than subjects in their earlier studies, leaving the researchers to recommend that future research include more objective indicators of the facets of professional integration.

In a further examination of Chapman's model, Chapman and Green (1986) concluded that the results suggested that the attention of administrators to ensuring the quality of professional life of new teachers can have a long-term impact on the career development of these teachers. Thus, the need for support during this critical time is obvious.

Additional research regarding professional and social integration into teaching is essential to assist new teachers in these areas. A variety of research models and studies would give new information that is needed.

A sixth and final area for review is the role of the administrator in teacher retention. Findings from Chapman's (1984) study reported that variables related to voluntary attrition were not easily influenced by an administrator. In fact, there was little evidence of a direct relationship between administrator behavior and attrition. However, Chapman did believe that an administrator may be able to shape the tone and quality of a new teacher's first teaching experience, which may influence the desire to stay in the profession. A substantial contribution that an administrator can make toward teacher retention may be to assist beginning teachers during their stages of imprinting.

In surveying former public school teachers, Bobbitt, Faupel, and Burns (1991) reported "dissatisfaction with teaching as a career" (p. iii) as one of their main reasons for leaving the profession, and 7.3% cited "poor salary" as their main area of dissatisfaction, along with 26.4% who cited "inadequate support from the administration" as their main area of dissatisfaction. Although these factors relate to attrition of teachers at various levels of experience, their particular relevance to new teachers warrants further investigation.

New teachers in the Metropolitan 1992 Survey stated that their experience with school administrators had been disappointing. Specifically, of the 1,000 teachers surveyed, just under half (48%) reported their experience with their principal as being very satisfying, yet only 32% gave similar rating to the experience with other administrators (Harris & Associates, 1992, p. 12). Teachers in inner city or urban locations cited the lack of support from school administrators as a major factor in their decision to leave teaching. In fact, when asked which was the "most important factor" in their decision to change professions, the greatest percentage (18%) cited lack of support from parents and school administrators.

The role of the administrator is a vital one according to many new teachers and certainly has important implications for the imprinting of new teachers. Further attention to this area may lend insight into the influence an administrator can have regarding new teachers and their decisions to stay in or leave teaching.

Rapid Changes in the Workplace

Most teachers enter teaching with a certain amount of idealism. They have high expectations regarding teaching students as they look forward to using the new approaches brought forth from their teacher preparation. Providing their students with encouragement and opportunities for involvement are major incentives for their selecting teaching as a profession. New teachers also are eager to be a part of the teaching profession and to share with other colleagues. These expectations often prove to be unrealistic because new teachers are usually assigned to some of the most difficult classrooms. As they begin to interact with students, other teachers, administrators, and parents, their optimism often turns to disappointment, discouragement, and disillusionment. What they too often find are bureaucratic impediments, administrative indifference, apathy from colleagues, and students who are disruptive and disrespectful. The workplace often is not what they experienced during teacher training. With rapid changes in many of the nation's schools, new teachers find themselves ill equipped to handle the pressures. Lack of teacher mobility, financial rewards, parents' interest and support, along with discipline problems are a few of the other major concerns under the heading of workplace that have been discussed in the literature. They are reviewed here.

A first area to be reviewed is teacher mobility. Berry et al. (1985) found little mobility among rural teachers because, in large part, they chose to teach in the communities from which they came. Teachers stayed in teaching because of a commitment to teaching, a love of children or adolescents, an unwilling-

ness to move into business or industry, and a commitment to preserving a lifestyle. The investigators believed that if career ladders were to have a positive impact on the teacher labor market, local systems and state education agencies need to address the divergent mobility patterns between urban and rural teachers.

Choy et al. (1993) stated that teachers were most likely to report that their primary reason for leaving teaching was a family or personal move (38%). Yet, many left for reasons that suggest a dissatisfaction with teaching—14% of 1987–1988 teachers left the profession because they wanted to pursue career opportunities outside of education, 8% because they were dissatisfied with teaching, and 6% because they wanted to improve their salaries or benefits. Almost one third of the teachers in this sample who left for jobs outside of education became managers or professionals. Public school teachers who were male or who had earned a bachelor's degree or less were about as likely to become salespersons as they were to become managers or professionals. Among all teachers who left, 18% became salespersons, 13% became administrative support personnel or supervisors, 10% became clerical workers, 9% became postsecondary school teachers, 8% entered other occupations, 7% became service workers, 3% became engineers or scientists, and 2% became technicians.

Heyns (1988) discussed career mobility of the National Longitudinal Study-1972 (NLS-72) teachers and found that the portrait differed from conventional views of attrition because it demonstrated quite dramatically the numbers of late entrants and reëntrants to teaching from this group. The figures suggested high rates of turnover among teachers, along with the well-documented high rate of attrition in early years. She found that former teachers were more likely to leave the profession if they were single and unencumbered by children.

Financial rewards is a second area for consideration. A number of studies have addressed the issue of teachers leaving the profession for positions that offer higher monetary rewards. As reported in the Teacher Followup Survey of 1988–1989 (Bobbitt et al., 1991), about two thirds of the public and private school teachers who stayed in the same school between school years 1987–1988 and 1988–1989 felt that "providing higher salaries or better fringe benefits" is the most effective step that schools might take to encourage teachers to remain in teaching (p. iii). However, among the former public school teachers who cited "dissatisfaction with teaching as a career" as one of their main reasons for leaving the profession, 7.3% cited "poor salary" as their main area of dissatisfaction, whereas 26.4% cited "inadequate support from the administration" as their main area of dissatisfaction. The attrition rate from the teaching profession for this group of teachers was 5.6% in public schools and 12.7% in private schools. The sample included a total size of 7,172 teachers, 2,987 leavers and 4,185 stayers and movers. All public schools were stratified by the 50 states and the District of Columbia and then by three grade levels.

In the Second Gallup Phi Delta Kappa Poll of Teachers' Attitudes Toward The Public Schools (Elam, 1989), lack of proper financial support was the second most frequently mentioned problem; "an overwhelming 82% of all teachers believed that they are underpaid, whereas only 37% of the general public believe that teachers are underpaid" (p. 785). Many teachers recognized how closely the lack of financial support was related to other school problems. The most frequently mentioned reason given by teachers as to why people leave the profession was low salaries, which was chosen by 77% of respondents in 1989. Significantly, "lack of public financial support for education" was selected much more frequently in 1989 than in 1984, 69% versus 26%. There were 830 individuals who responded to the survey of teachers from all 50 states and the District of Columbia.

Almost 3 in 10 second-year teachers (Harris & Associates, 1992) cited financial reasons—needing or wanting to earn more money (29%)—as a major factor in considering giving up teaching. Murnane and Olsen's research (1990), based on a new longitudinal data set providing information on the career histories of 13,890 North Carolina teachers, provided information showing that salaries have a marked impact on the length of time teachers stay in teaching. They stated that "beginning teachers who are paid more stay longer" (p. 107).

A different study (Chapman & Green, 1986) reported that teachers who left teaching showed a lower mean income than those who continued to teach. People who changed careers tended to fall behind both those who taught continuously and those who never began teaching in their reward attainment. The reviewers believed that this finding challenged the widespread belief that teachers leave teaching to earn more money in other careers.

Berry et al. (1985) stated that teacher pay needs to be increased. "However, this is not because of its potential effect on the labor market. Rather, it is a direct expression of how society values education and teaching" (p. 109).

"Lack of parents' interest and support" is a third area for review. The most frequently mentioned problem in the Second Gallup Poll (Elam, 1989) was parents' lack of interest and support. A variety of responses were given: "no backing from parents on discipline," "parents don't help students realize the importance of preparing for the future," "parent apathy," and "parents lack faith in the school system." Elementary teachers were somewhat more likely than secondary teachers (39% to 25%) to mention lack of parental interest and support (p. 786). The Metropolitan Life Survey on The Second Year (Harris & Associates, 1992) found that new teachers who are likely to leave the teaching profession in the next 5 years most often cite lack of parental support as a major factor in their decision (40%). This was a major area of dissatisfaction and discouragement for these new teachers.

The fourth and final area to be considered is the discipline problem. In the Second Gallup Poll (Elam, 1989), about half of all teacher respondents viewed discipline as either a very serious or a fairly serious problem. In the qualitative studies of the teacher labor market, Berry et al. (1985) concluded that if teachers left teaching because of dissatisfactions, it was usually because they "can't handle disadvantaged kids" or they were "frustrated with the lack of disciplinary action taken by administrators" (p. 106).

In summary, professional working conditions are widely viewed as the single most important reason for high rates of teacher attrition (Heyns, 1988). Where schools are improved,

teacher professional status is increased, and parental support is more positive, there may be increases in retention rates.

Teacher Burnout: Attrition's Elusive Partner

Many of the studies reviewed in the literature indicated that the greatest problems encountered by beginning teachers were overwhelming feelings of disillusionment and believing that they were unable to cope with the multitude of pressures encountered each day. These are manifestations of various stages of burnout. These factors, along with the stresses experienced, have resulted in poor levels of performance and dropout. As the levels of burnout among beginning teachers increase, understanding basic tenets of burnout and its influences on beginning teachers is essential when designing programs of support. The term *burnout* is a familiar one to most teachers. Originally the concept of burnout was conceived by Freudenberger (1973) who stated that burnout occurs in highly motivated individuals who react to stress by overworking until they collapse. Subsequent definitions have attributed burnout to: (1) an individual's response to chronic, everyday stress rather than to occasional crises (Maslach, 1981); (2) a mismatch between what workers feel they are getting in return from their work and what they feel they are giving to others (Cherniss, 1980); (3) a work-related syndrome that stems from an individual's perception of a significant discrepancy between effort and reward (Farber, 1991); and (4) a syndrome that emanates from an individual's perceptions of unmet needs and unfulfilled expectations (Gold & Roth, 1993).

To have a greater understanding of burnout, a review of definitions within the literature is presented here. Essentially, each of the researchers of burnout took a somewhat different approach in examining the phenomenon. Freudenberger (1973) took a clinical approach and placed the entire phenomenon of burnout within a specific social context where individuals paid a "high cost" for "high achievement." Maslach (1982) presented a social-psychological approach, with a picture of the burned-out individual as having "nothing left to give" and not caring any more. Cherniss (1980) posited in three sources of burnout at the individual, organizational, and societal levels, an organizational perspective. He examined the individual's expectations and goals, the institutional constraints, and the public's perceptions of the nature of work. Farber (1991) mainly saw burnout as related to the individual's perceptions of a discrepancy between input and output, being influenced by individual, organizational, and social factors. Gold and Roth (1993) described their psychotherapeutic model, which presents burnout as "emanating from an individual's perceptions of unmet needs and unfulfilled expectations. It is characterized by progressive disillusionment, with related psychological and physical symptoms which diminish one's self-esteem. It develops gradually over a period of time" (p. 41).

All of these definitions have in common that the individual has feelings of inconsequentiality—feelings that their efforts to serve others have not been effective, that the work is endless, and that the payoffs for them personally are negative in terms of recognition, appreciation, accomplishment, and advancement. Thus, a slow process of disillusionment sets in until the individuals have nothing left to give; they are burned out.

Early Research on Teacher Burnout

With the many pressures felt by teachers over the past few years, burnout has become a problem of increasing professional concern. Many teachers in the United States report feelings of irritability, fatigue, frustration, and disillusionment. These symptoms are associated with the phenomenon commonly called *burnout* (Gold, 1985). Until the 1980s, little had been researched in the area of teacher burnout. Early studies (Anderson, 1981; Gold, 1984, 1985; Iwanicki & Schwab, 1981; Schwab & Iwanicki, 1982a, 1982b) that contributed to a foundation of research in the area of teacher burnout have been built upon the exploratory work of Maslach and her colleagues' research in the helping professions. The self-report Maslach Burnout Inventory (MBI) was used initially to assess the perceived level of burnout among individuals in the helping professions and was later used in the studies cited to measure perceived level of burnout among teachers. The MBI consists of three subscales or components of burnout (emotional exhaustion, depersonalization, and personal accomplishment) (Maslach & Jackson, 1981). On the basis of the results obtained with a sample of 469 Massachusetts teachers (Iwanicki & Schwab, 1981) and in another empirical study of 462 elementary, junior high, and high school teachers in Southern California (Gold, 1984), it was reported that the MBI measures the same basic constructs or factors as those identified in investigations in which individuals in the helping professions have been tested, namely, emotional exhaustion, depersonalization, and personal accomplishment.

Since the early 1980s, there has been considerable research on teacher burnout using the MBI. A compilation of the findings of this research report: (1) female teachers in comparison with male teachers tend to register perceptions of a slightly lower level of depersonalization and of a marginally lower level of personal accomplishment (Gold, 1985; Schwab & Iwanicki, 1982b); (2) in comparison with older teachers, younger ones are inclined to express perceptions indicating both greater amounts of emotional exhaustion and higher degrees of depersonalization but a stronger sense of personal accomplishment (Banks & Necco, 1990; Byrne, 1991); (3) teachers who are single may encounter a slightly greater risk of burnout than those who are or have been married (Gold, 1985; Mo, 1991); (4) the total number of years of instructional experience at the same school can be expected to exhibit little if any relationship to the three constructs of burnout (Gold, 1985); (5) teachers who teach at higher grade levels (4–12) can be anticipated to demonstrate perceptions of slightly greater emotional exhaustion and somewhat higher degrees of depersonalization than those teachers providing instruction at lower levels below fourth grade (Gold, 1985; Schwab & Iwanicki, 1982b); (6) teachers who perceive student control as having become more difficult are likely to report perceptions of slightly greater depersonalization and a somewhat lower sense of personal accomplishment than those teachers who perceive difficulty of control as remaining about the same or as having become easier (Byrne, 1991; Hock, 1988); (7) early childhood teachers working in child care centers in large metropolitan areas who had negative parent relations demonstrated higher levels of perceived burnout (Townley, Thornburg, & Crompton, 1991); (8) school culture variables,

such as lack of trust in teachers' professional adequacy, circumscribing school culture, and disagreeable physical environment, contributed to teacher burnout (Friedman, 1991); (9) personality characteristics such as anomie (characterized by a sense of meaninglessness and alienation), personality type A or B, and empathic self-concept were significant predictors of teacher burnout (Mazur & Lynch, 1989); and (10) a study in Israel found that environmental factors are the principle agents in burnout (Kremer-Hayon & Kurtz, 1985).

Cherniss's (1980) model regarding organizational burnout shows that certain types of work-setting characteristics interact with individuals who enter the job with particular career orientations, with extra work demands and different types of support. These factors result in particular sources of stress being experienced to varying degrees by job incumbents. Individuals cope with these stressors in different ways. Cherniss believes that burnout occurs over time, is a process, and represents one way of adapting to or coping with particular sources of stress. His model has been used to measure burnout in the teaching profession and has received considerable empirical support. Burke and Greenglass (1989) reported from their research, using Cherniss's model, that it "is quite appropriate now to think about reducing professional burnout through intervention in the workplace" (p. 272).

In another research study involving a secondary analysis of longitudinal data collected from 245 school-based educators, Wolpin, Burke, and Greenglass (1991) argued that negative work-setting characteristics and marital dissatisfaction were associated with greater work stressors, which in turn were associated with increased burnout that resulted in decreased job satisfaction.

Furthermore, Russell, Altmaier, and Van Velzen (1987) examined the effects of job-related stressful events and social support on burnout among 316 teachers in Iowa. Their conclusions were consistent with findings in previous research, in that teacher characteristics such as age, sex, and grade level taught were predictive of burnout. Also, teachers who reported that they had supportive supervisors and indicated that they received positive feedback concerning their skills and abilities from others were less vulnerable to burnout.

Since the mid-1980s, the understanding of teacher burnout has become much clearer and more carefully defined as a result of the research regarding this phenomenon. There is substantial evidence that burnout is associated with (1) poor physical health; (2) emotional symptoms, such as depression, which are most consistently linked to burnout; (3) behavioral symptoms that have been most clearly related to burnout through unproductive work behaviors and even turnover; and (4) negative interpersonal relations with students, other teachers, and parents.

Sources of Teacher Burnout

In analyzing teacher retention and attrition, it is essential that the sources derived from research that contribute to teacher burnout be investigated. The sources most related to burnout as reported in research are: (1) negative work-related factors (Wolpin et al., 1991); (2) student violence and discipline problems (Banks & Necco, 1990); (3) insensitivity of the administration (Friesen, Prokop, & Sarros, 1988); (4) parents who are both unreasonable and/or unconcerned (Townley et al., 1991); (5) criticism from the public (Friesen et al., 1988); (6) excessive paperwork and demanding work load (Friesen et al., 1988; Mazur & Lynch, 1989); (7) lack of promotional opportunities (Vavrus, 1987); (8) a negative workplace environment (Burke & Greenglass, 1989); (9) role conflict and role ambiguity (Schwab & Iwanicki, 1982a); (10) marriage and family relationships (Schwab & Iwanicki, 1982b); (11) teachers who are single and have fewer years of teaching experience, especially less than 5 years (Gold, 1985; Russell et al., 1987); and (12) personality characteristics (Mazur & Lynch, 1989).

Loss of a Dream

Specifically for teachers, a sense of inconsequentiality is found in their working with students who are not responsive. This leaves many teachers feeling a lack of personal accomplishment along with feeling little or no appreciation from others. When parents are not supportive and society is quick to criticize, many teachers feel there is little recognition for their efforts, which often leaves them feeling hurt and angry. To alleviate these negative conditions, teachers often explore some avenue of change or path of mobility. When these options are closed to them, discouragement and even despair result. Personal needs to feel helpful, useful, accomplished, and successful are not being met and many teachers in these types of situations are deprived of the opportunities to realize their personal gratifications and meet their goals. The end results often produce teachers who suffer from a loss of self-esteem, forgotten ideals, and little or no rewards. Under these conditions they give up caring.

Beginning Teacher Burnout

One greatly negelected area in the research is that of beginning teacher burnout. However, a few research studies assist in understanding burnout with this population.

Schonfeld (1992) conducted a longitudinal study involving 255 newly appointed female teachers. He reported that women who worked in the most adverse school environments showed the most depressive symptoms, even though there were no preemployment differences on the depression scale. By contrast, women who obtained jobs in the "best" schools tended to show the fewest symptoms. He also found that the effect of school conditions on symptoms was quite sizable when other risk factors were controlled.

The link between adverse school conditions and depressive symptoms is not surprising because many beginning teachers' work may be characterized by danger, crime, lack of discipline, lack of parental support, and in many cases lack of administrative support. Therefore, their imprinting of negative feelings and attitudes affects their ability to cope.

To measure teacher burnout, a modified version of the MBI for teachers, named the Educators Survey (Maslach, Jackson, & Schwab, 1986), was developed. The inventory was designed to assess teacher burnout in each of three scales representing constructs of emotional exhaustion, depersonalization, and personal accomplishment. In a study by Gold, Roth, Wright, Michael, and Chen (1992), with a sample of 133 elementary and secondary school beginning teachers, it was concluded that this multidimensional instrument provided a promising level of construct validity for assessing teacher burnout.

One major criticism in measuring burnout for teachers was the fact that the MBI was not originally written for teachers. With the modified version of the MBI now available for educators, Gold, Roth, Wright, and Michael (1991) used the Educators Survey (ES) for a sample of 132 beginning teachers and investigated the relationship of three teaching-related variables identified as (1) the extent to which the teacher perceived teacher training courses prepared him or her for the first years of teaching; (2) the level of workload experienced during the first 3 years of teaching; and (3) if an individual were to begin his or her career again, would he or she select teaching as the first career choice. Results suggested that younger male teachers may be more susceptible to stress factors underlying burnout. Teachers who experienced higher rather than lower levels of emotional exhaustion tended to perceive less than adequate preparation in their teacher training courses. They reported heavier workloads than had been anticipated, and were less inclined to choose teaching again as a career. Teachers in the higher grades compared to those in lower grades tended to experience more frequent job-related feelings classified as depersonalization and a lower sense of personal accomplishment.

From the research studies reported, it is evident that adverse school environments for female beginning teachers, younger male teachers, teachers who report emotional exhaustion, heavy workloads, and teachers who teach students in higher grade levels (middle school and high school) need to be especially supported during their first few years of teaching to prevent early signs of burnout. Additional research on beginning teacher burnout is greatly needed to better understand the role of burnout with these teachers.

Programs to Reduce Beginning Teacher Attrition and Prevent Burnout

Attempts to reduce teacher attrition rates have been evident through the development of a few programs that offer support to teachers who are attempting to handle stress and prevent burnout (Bertoch, Nielsen, Curley, & Borg, 1989; Esteve & Fracchia, 1986; Gold, 1989; Gold & Roth, 1993). A number of stress prevention programs have been successful in training and supporting teachers as they try to handle the many daily stressors they encounter. Too often teachers are required to make adaptations without receiving adequate preparation for how they are to make necessary changes. These changes can be of a personal type, such as learning how to handle angry parents or violent students. This type of training is not offered in their professional preparation programs. In fact, the harsh realities of the classroom too often leave young teachers with feelings of inadequacy and insecurity as they try to adjust to their first teaching assignment. This crisis of professional identity has been well documented in studies of beginning teachers (Veenman, 1984; Vonk, 1983).

To assist teachers in handling the many pressures they encounter, Stress Inoculation Training (SIT) was developed and used by Esteve and Fracchia (1986). In their program, the training through stress induction is carried out in three stages: modeling phase, learning trial, and generalized applications. In the modeling phase the aim is to acquire competencies that help to serve as resources in situations that may prove to be difficult. The trial learning involves role playing and videotaping to record teacher behavior. During the generalized applications the video is played back to teachers where there is a constant emphasis on resources and skills.

One of the goals of the program is to reduce unwanted emotions and to reinforce adaptive behaviors. In the final evaluation, 44% of the students emphasized the practical value of the training in reinforcing their self-confidence as first-year teachers. Follow-up studies to measure longer term retention of the skills would be most useful for this type of program.

In another study using both pretreatment and post-treatment, a group of 30 in-service teachers who were selected for high stress levels participated in a program that was developed to reduce significantly symptoms of stress. The processes used during the treatment phase were lecture-discussion, small-group sharing of progress and problems, audiovisual presentations, written test evaluations, and homework. Content for the sessions included the concept of stress, task-based and role-conflict stress, assertiveness lifestyle, relaxation and breathing, meditation, nutrition, exercise, holistic living, coping with disappointment and chemical stressors, support systems, understanding situations, and letting go of resentments. Results indicated that the experimental group demonstrated substantially lower stress levels than control group members after the treatment (Bertoch et al., 1989). Future research to investigate which of the variables covered in the treatment contribute most to stress reduction, and treatment strategies that determine how to maximize stress reduction within the teacher population will be important areas for assisting future program development.

Gold (1989) developed a program that addresses both stress and burnout through induction years. Some of the key factors in this program are: (1) identification of stress levels using a variety of stress instruments, (2) identification of perceived levels of burnout using the Maslach Burnout Inventory for Educators, (3) development of individual stress reduction plans that deal with stress and burnout through specific coping strategies, and (4) establishment of support systems to assist the beginning teachers during these transition years as they learn new coping strategies for personal and instructional areas of need. The program has been in existence since 1987 with a low attrition rate for the teachers who have been involved.

Gold and Roth (1993) developed a psychotherapeutic model to assist teachers with their stress and burnout as a means of improving their personal and professional life. The program focuses on: (1) identifying psychological needs through specific inventories; (2) learning how to meet emotional, social, physical, and intellectual needs; (3) identifying stress levels through specific instruments and helping individuals in developing necessary coping strategies to handle pressures and minimize stress; (4) identifying burnout levels through burnout inventories and learning strategies to alleviate burnout; (5) learning relaxation techniques, monitoring eating and sleeping habits, and concentrating on getting enough physical exercise; (6) gaining individual insights to make necessary changes

for personal growth; (7) using guided group processes to problem solve specific issues related to their personal and professional life; (8) developing a life plan that will assist after leaving the training; and (9) establishing support groups to guide and assist individuals as they develop new coping skills during and after the program.

Teacher stress and burnout are not just fads that will evaporate given time, but are profound problems that must be addressed if the retention of teachers is to improve. The increased turbulence in society that affects school environments is being manifested by many teachers through burnout (disillusionment) and/or teacher militancy (anger); however, these negative forces can be reduced if the root causes are recognized and remediation takes place. In most cases, teachers tend to support and empower one another and are strongly committed to education and its goals. By encouraging this unity and sense of pride in self and profession, what can be realized is their own potential to influence the teaching profession and thus society.

Evidence has been presented that programs planned to meet teachers' psychological needs along with their professional needs clearly can lead to greater satisfaction, productivity, and lower attrition rates.

The flames of stress and burnout are spreading as many teachers describe symptoms of fatigue, worry, alienation, cynicism, griping, anger, and a desire to "get away from it all." Central to the matter is the realization that program efforts must be linked with the individual needs of teachers. Attention must be given to their personal and professional growth and development, which in turn will contribute to efficient performance and improved welfare for them and their students.

Causes and Concerns

Extensive research data to support the fact that beginning teacher attrition and burnout are serious and must be addressed have been presented. The variables affecting teacher attrition are highly complex and involve many factors. Both quantitative and qualitative studies have been reviewed that contribute to a greater understanding of teacher attrition.

To add to the knowledge of attrition, current models on teacher retention have been developed and some have been presented in this analysis. The major ones are: (1) Chapman's (1983) model of the influences on teacher retention, which is grounded in both social learning theory and Holland's theory of career choice (Holland, 1985); (2) Murnane and Olsen's (1990) recently developed teacher attrition model that is based on an economic cost-benefit analysis framework and uses human capital theory; and (3) a model presented by the National Center for Educational Statistics (Hafner & Owings, 1991) that draws from both social learning theory and human capital theory.

These models have contributed a great deal to the knowledge and understanding of attrition. Research reported the following important findings: (1) satisfaction with pay was a significant predictor of retention (Hafner & Owings, 1991); (2) social and environmental variables found to be important in predicting retention were parental education, number of children, teaching in a public school, and satisfaction with job (Chapman & Green, 1986); (3) environmental work conditions such as full-time teaching, student ability level, and percent of minority students within the student body were not significant predictors of retention (Chapman & Green, 1986); (4) family formation factors such as having no children or few children were found to relate to retention (Chapman & Green, 1986); (5) wages, opportunity costs, and other economic incentives were stronger influences than family formation on duration of teaching (Hafner & Alsalam, 1989); and (6) women teachers with preschool children had longer first teaching spells than others (Hafner & Alsalam, 1989).

A major problem with the current attrition research, as presented by Grissmer and Kirby (1987), is its failure to categorize and measure important subgroups of teachers who terminate their employment. These data are vital for obtaining better subgroup estimates to identify and evaluate policies and conditions effective in attracting and retaining teachers. These reviewers also concluded that the current forecasts of attrition are weak and the data on teachers and their attrition rates are often unreliable and inaccurate (Grissmer & Kirby, 1987). They believed that what is needed is a national information system that tracks teachers longitudinally. In addition, there has been little information available on the career patterns of teachers and on attrition from teaching (Sweet & Jacobsen, 1983).

Data on teacher attrition are important; however, understanding attrition decisions is a vital part of this process. Reliable, consistent attrition data and better understanding of teacher attrition and mobility are essential to address beginning teacher dropout and plan programs of support. Necessary issues to consider are: (1) identify and evaluate policies and conditions that are effective in both attracting and retaining better teachers; (2) review what factors affect teacher attrition rates; (3) know how much mobility and attrition rates vary across states and districts; (4) decide how new teachers should be selected to decrease early attrition among new, better quality teachers; (5) learn how the structure of the salary and promotion system contribute to teacher attrition patterns; (6) develop a number of dynamic models that include as variables potential teachers, the responses of teachers, school districts, and states to changing labor and market conditions; (7) identify the policy flexibility of states and districts needed to increase the supply of teachers through enhanced recruiting efforts and scholarships; (8) collect reliable data on teacher attrition at the national level; (9) follow longitudinally a national sample of teachers who do not leave teaching; (10) identify what teacher characteristics are actually desirous and needed by various regions of the country; (11) collect data on retention rates of teachers who receive training and assistance with meeting their personal and professional needs; and (12) explore what types of support are necessary during stressful times in teachers' careers.

Rationale for Burnout Remediation

What has been evident in the teacher attrition studies is a gradual loss of commitment to teaching and, therefore, a condition defined as disillusionment or burnout. It has also been reported that many professionals develop a gradual loss of caring about their students; over a period of time they are not able to sustain the commitment they once had. They report a state of physical, emotional, and mental exhaustion characterized by physical

depletion, feelings of hopelessness and helplessness, emotional drain, and the development of negative attitudes toward their work, life, and other people.

To combat burnout, stress reduction and burnout prevention programs have been used successfully with groups of teachers. These programs report that it has been possible to alter the burnout process by instructing educators in how to identify and meet their psychological needs, reduce stress, and develop new and effective coping skills. This type of research must be encouraged and carried out throughout the country so that determinations can be made regarding regional differences in burnout statistics. Teachers must be alerted to the destructive and powerful forces that take place during the process of burnout. The relationship of burnout to the factors associated with attrition would be of considerable assistance in helping teachers.

A major challenge to educators today is one of offering the right type of support to new teachers during the transition period so that they may be encouraged to keep the flame of commitment and the excitement for teaching burning brightly throughout their careers. The following section focuses on the nature of support for new teachers, as well as types of support offered through induction programs.

NATURE AND ELEMENTS OF SUPPORT

One of the major reasons for developing support for new teachers has been concern regarding attrition. A question that must be raised is what can be learned from the studies of attrition, particularly the causes, that can be used in designing support programs and in determining the nature of support that is needed for beginning teachers. Even though the relationships are not very direct, there is enough information within the studies to provide guidance.

The need for support for beginning teachers has been well documented throughout the literature on teacher attrition. Many believe that some type of assistance must be offered to prevent the loss of talented, intelligent teachers early in their career. As noted by Willis Hawley of Vanderbilt University (Lieb, 1992), "Colleges of teacher education can train people to do anything. However, when teachers enter the schools they do not do those things. . . . Even in the most powerful programs, the slippage, the fadeout is pretty high. When teachers enter their classrooms, much of what they have learned dissipates" (p. 13). A program of support that will assist them in making the transition from university to the classroom is vital in order to sustain and expand upon what is learned in preservice teacher education.

Interest in providing support for beginning teachers has been increasing steadily since the mid-1980s and has been carefully reviewed in the induction literature (Anderson & Shannon, 1988; Gehrke & Kay, 1984; Healy & Welchert, 1990). Educators have become so concerned regarding this issue that numerous support programs have been organized throughout the country. Research reporting different types of support and support programs is still evolving, and there is an urgent need for data regarding the effectiveness of different types and sources of support for new teachers.

Therefore, providing personal and professional support has become a key issue regarding the retention of dedicated and talented new professionals. Offering quality support is critical because the professional literature addresses the fact that lack of professional support is one of the most frequently cited reasons for why teachers leave teaching (Billingsley & Cross, 1991; Darling-Hammond, 1984; Gold & Roth, 1993; Lawrenson & McKinnon, 1982).

It is critical that there be an investigation of the types of support offered and the success rate of existing support programs. This section of the chapter concentrates on the following areas: (1) concepts of support, (2) instructional support, (3) need for and application of psychological support, (4) individual and group support, and (5) computer networks as a means of support.

Concepts of Support

Although the literature on support for beginning teachers is expanding, the need remains for a more complete understanding of this phenomenon as applied to education. Specifically, an exploration of the types and sources of support that can be made available to novice teachers and their impact on retention could be of benefit to future research and to existing and future support programs. Because support is the critical component, exploring the concept of support will be undertaken.

Various types of support are available that can be helpful for novice teachers. These come under two major headings: (1) instructional-related support that includes assisting the novice with the knowledge, skills, and strategies necessary to be successful in the classroom and school; and (2) psychological support for which the purpose is to build the protege's sense of self through confidence building, developing feelings of effectiveness, encouraging positive self-esteem, enhancing self-reliance, and learning to handle stress that is a large part of the transition period.

People who have a strong support system are both psychologically and physiologically healthier and less prone to stress and burnout than are those who lack support. For instance, studies have shown the positive influences of support in people's professional lives (Maslach, 1982; Paine, 1982).

Specifically in education, teachers who have supportive supervisors and colleagues are less vulnerable to negative stress and to burnout (Russell et al., 1987). Whatever the nature of the support, investigators conclude that when it incorporates some form of positive communication that includes trust, respect, and liking by significant others, there is a noticeable impact in the recipient's life. To better understand this type of social support, House (1981) gave one of the most inclusive and exhaustive definitions. He stated that social support is an interpersonal transaction involving one or more of the following: (1) emotional concern (liking, love, empathy); (2) instrumental aid (goods or services); (3) information (about the environment); or (4) appraisal (information relevant to self-evaluation). House's definition provided four separate and distinct types of social support that can be beneficial for educators. These are emotional, instrumental, informational, and appraisal. Another means of broadly classifying beginning teachers' needs is through the categories of personal and instructional. The

personal needs are encompassed by the psychological domain that includes House's categories of emotional and appraisal. The instructional-pedagogical domain includes House's instrumental, informational, and appraisal categories.

The need for providing support for novice teachers has been well established. The essential issue here lies in the importance of developing support systems that are positive, meaningful, and that include different types of support to meet the varying needs of beginning teachers. Two major types of support, instructional and psychological, are examined.

Instructional Support

To identify the areas where instructional support will be most helpful for beginning teachers, it is important to incorporate the knowledge of researchers and practitioners who have studied the needs and concerns of new teachers within the context of the profession. Veenman (1984), in an extensive review of the literature on beginning teachers, identified the perceived needs of teachers where no assistance was given. He analyzed descriptive interview and questionnaire studies of teachers during their first year of teaching. It was reported, in rank order, that these teachers needed assistance in disciplining students, motivating them, dealing with individual differences of their students, assessing students' work, relating to parents, organizing class work, and obtaining materials and supplies.

As can be seen, problems classified as management or discipline related were the most pressing problems of beginning teachers in Veenman's review and have been widely discussed by others (Huffman & Leak, 1986; Murphy, Merseth, & Morey, 1990; Zimpher & Rieger, 1988). As a result of Veenman's study regarding the needs of beginning teachers, many educators advocated instructional support as being most important and they began some type of support or support program to offer assistance of this type (Huling-Austin, 1989b; Ishler & Edelfelt, 1989). Yet, Feiman-Nemser (1992) believed that these types of management and discipline problems frequently arise because teachers are unclear about their purposes, have chosen inappropriate tasks, or have not given students adequate direction. Therefore, she felt that management or discipline problems were more strongly connected with curriculum and instruction issues for these teachers. Teachers, therefore, need assistance in these areas.

Taking another approach, Lee Shulman (1986) expressed strong opinions regarding the knowledge base of teachers. He stated that in the emergent research base on teaching and teaching effectiveness, researchers ignored one central aspect of classroom life—subject matter. He believed that the omission of the subject matter was characteristic of most research paradigms in the study of teaching. No one focused on the subject matter itself. Also, no one asked how subject matter was transformed from the knowledge of the teacher into the content of instruction. The importance of content, according to Shulman, has been forgotten, and the content of instruction is being treated as though it were "relatively unimportant" (p. 6).

This absence of focus on subject matter among the various research paradigms for the study of teaching is referred to as the "missing paradigm" (Shulman, 1986). In a similar vein, it is a central issue that needs to be addressed in detail within the induction research and literature. The research on teaching emphasizes how teachers manage their classrooms, organize activities, allocate time and turns, structure assignments, plan lessons, formulate the different levels of questions, and assess general student understanding (Shulman, 1986). An additional focus ought to be, according to Shulman, on the study of content. Constructing this paradigm in the literature and research on beginning teacher support would add a significant dimension.

Many induction programs may well be giving support mainly in the process of teaching rather than focusing on the more essential need, which is helping beginning teachers with the content of the lessons taught, with explanations they are offering, and with the types of questions they are asking. Essential issues to consider in helping beginning teachers are related to how efficiently the beginning teacher transforms their expertise in the subject matter into a form that their students can comprehend and how they draw on expertise in the subject matter in the process of teaching.

Therefore, there are four central areas to be considered when giving instructional support. First, does the beginning teacher understand the structure of knowledge and how it is transformed into content knowledge? Are they prepared to go beyond just the knowledge of the facts or concepts of a domain? Do they understand the structures of the subject matter (Shulman, 1986)? Second, have beginning teachers been trained in process or pedagogical content knowledge that includes the most useful forms of representation of ideas, illustrations, examples, analogies, explanations, and demonstrations? Are they able to represent and formulate the subject matter so that it is comprehensible to their students (Shulman, 1986)? Third, are beginning teachers prepared to teach a particular subject and specific topics at a given level and to use a variety of instructional materials (Shulman, 1986)? Fourth, are beginning teachers thinking reflectively and critically about practice? Do they "possess the skill and understanding needed to acquire the continually expanding knowledge base about teaching and the academic content they impart to students" (Fenstermacher, 1990, p. 169)?

Instructional support must deal with these four major areas in preservice education, induction, and in-service education. Too often instructional support deals primarily, if not exclusively, with the processes of pedagogy. When this type of support does deal with curricular knowledge, it often presents it as content to be delivered to students rather than academic content to be built upon continually.

Beginning teachers need to develop the skill and understanding needed to acquire and to deliberate on their continually expanding knowledge base, to think critically and reflectively about their own practice, and to analyze how they impart the academic content to their students. They also must be assisted with evaluating their actions through the use of sound theory and research, developing the capacity to be reflective, evaluating themselves based on objective understanding, and learning how to handle the consequences of their actions. In return, the profession will, over time, gain well-prepared teachers who are better able to assist their students. This type of instructional support must be planned around the needs of the beginning teacher and support offered in a sequence that they are able to handle.

The first few years of teaching are of great importance in assisting teachers as they develop their first impressions regarding "what teachers should be on their own" and "what type of teacher do I want to be." In the first few months many will be attempting to "put it all together" for themselves as they try to understand the dynamics of a classroom when they are the only teacher in the classroom. They are also trying to understand the complexities of their school and their place in the profession as they attempt to handle their personal life outside of school.

With all of these pressures, most beginning teachers are struggling to survive and during this transition must have some survival skills. It is essential to offer them the instructional support they need so they can survive; however, this support must not be limited just to training in classroom discipline and management and the instructional needs expressed in Veenman's (1984) study. To limit the majority of the instructional support to these needs fails to provide the beginning teacher with an understanding of the more complex nature of the structure of knowledge and the process of acquiring pedagogical content knowledge that is needed.

Psychological Support: The Critical Factor in Assisting New Teachers

The first year of teaching has for a number of years been the focus of widespread concern with little debate that it is a traumatic experience for many and a considerable shock for most. The major personal problems mentioned by a large number of beginning teachers were physical fatigue, stress, financial worries, loneliness, isolation, and disillusionment (Bolam, 1987; Gold & Roth, 1993).

The beginning teacher's transition from student to teacher often involves a great deal of stress. Lack of self-confidence, conflicts between personal life and professional requirements, and inability to handle stress have undermined many otherwise promising teachers. When teachers are personally insecure, lack confidence, or have a sense of not being in control of themselves or their environment, it is not likely that they can be successful at teaching regardless of how strong the instructional preparation has been.

The inability to handle the pressures of the profession is a major factor in both unsuccessful teaching as well as in decisions to drop out from the profession. To learn how to handle pressures and to manage stress, new teachers must be given the knowledge, skills, and support from others that will assist them through this difficult phase of teaching. They need what is referred to as psychological support.

Psychological support has been defined in a number of ways by various individuals (Gold, 1992; Thies-Sprinthall, 1984; Thies-Sprinthall & Gerler, 1990). It has been described as emotional support, positive regard, accurate empathy, empathic listening, and meeting psychological needs. Educators also have stated that psychological support includes an array of skills and strategies including confidence building, reinforcing a positive self-esteem, guidance in developing a sense of effectiveness, instilling a sense of self-reliance, learning how to handle stress, and psychological assistance.

Where instructional support is based primarily at an informational level, psychological support is essentially a form of therapeutic guidance. It includes various forms of assessing individual psychological needs, setting up a personal plan to assist the new teacher in meeting his or her needs, learning how to overcome stressors and to manage stress, acquiring new coping strategies to handle problems, utilizing communication skills to enhance personal growth, and attention to burnout prevention techniques. To assist new teachers in the area of psychological support, many educators suggest that induction programs include the promotion of growth and development, not simply survival skills (Bolam, 1987; Gold, 1987; Thies-Sprinthall & Gerler, 1990).

As early as preservice training Thies-Sprinthall (1984) reported that "the student teachers complete their experiences at lower stages of psychological development than at the outset" (p. 53). Her research study used a cognitive-developmental theory to promote psychological growth. She indicated that it may be possible to "create educationally meaningful programs to affect the level of psychological stage development" (p. 58). Thies-Sprinthall also argued that the current school climate and organization may drive out the more psychologically mature teachers.

Featherstone (1992) also believed that self-knowledge is a "major fruit" of the early teaching experience and that those who are the most strict in their discipline may be struggling to manage their students' behavior due to their own struggle to understand and change themselves. She continued with the idea that "teaching calls for different spiritual, social, emotional and intellectual qualities than 'studenting,' and so the attempt to teach shows us ourselves in a somewhat new light" (p. 7).

Meeting the psychological needs of teachers is an important and vital dimension of any professional preparation program. The need has always been there and the necessity to address it is increasing at a rapid rate. Unfortunately, it is not fully recognized as an essential part of the preparation and professional development curriculum. This phenomenon may be due to the fact the educators are not specifically trained in psychology, as are therapists and psychologists, and thus may view psychological support mainly as giving emotional support through empathic listening and attention giving rather than a more in-depth support to assess and meet individual psychological needs.

Giving support is essential because it has been reported that there is positive value in the life of the individual, particularly in the work setting, when people receive some type of social support (Maslach, 1982; Paine, 1982). The major issue then is the type of support and the value of that support to the welfare of the new teacher.

Another area of concern is the fact that many needy people do not seek help even when it is readily accessible. In fact, individuals are often willing to refuse help even when the alternatives of tolerating problems or putting forth additional efforts are costly (Gross & McMullen, 1983). Therefore, because the most important personal cost related to help seeking is the damage to self-esteem that can take place when an individual seeks assistance, it is essential that programs of psychological help are initiated and carried out in a way that protects the individuals involved. Programs must have a strong ethical code

of confidentiality and need to encourage individuals to take responsibility for finding solutions to their problems rather than evaluating, judging, or criticizing others. Because negative feelings associated with seeking help usually occur when people feel threatened with loss of self-esteem, interpret their help seeking as a sign of inadequacy, or feel indebted in some way, it is understandable why many teachers, both new and experienced, could demonstrate negative reactions to receiving help when they have prior experience with social support that has not been positive. Both personal costs (self-esteem and self-concept) and social costs (interpersonal relationships and perceptions of others) must be considered.

For these reasons, it is essential that a program of psychological support include the following areas: (1) awareness of individual needs, (2) knowledge of how to meet these needs, (3) learning specific strategies to change negative thinking and behavior, (4) a personalized plan for change, (5) trained support individuals to guide and assist throughout the learning process, and (6) commitment to the process of change (Gold & Roth, 1993). This review regarding the two major types of support offered to beginning teachers leads to a consideration of the types of support being offered to individuals and groups.

Individual and Group Support

Investigators report that limited opportunities for professional exchange and lack of professional support are two of the most frequently cited reasons for teachers leaving the profession (Billingsley & Cross, 1991; Darling-Hammond, 1984; Lawrenson & McKinnon, 1982). Yet, the need for support is only part of the issue. Additional considerations are stated by Thoits (1982), who argued that the types of support, sources of support, and amount of support are all important. Types of support include emotional concern (often operationalized as listening, concern, and trust), instrumental aid (time), information (advice/information), and appraisal (feedback). Sources of support include individuals such as friends in and out of school, family, teachers, principals, and mentors or others who perform a similar function. Length of time for support varies from a single meeting to a year or more depending on the needs of individuals involved.

Glidewell, Tucker, Todt, and Cox (1983) discussed social support and reported that support needs to include a great deal more than just exchanging advice. They believed that it included interdependency, shared concerns, a sense of common fate, and a feeling that others "stand by" when an individual is under stress. It is also important for giving suggestions, advice, recommendations, explanations, direct aid, and assistance.

In light of the necessity for support, individual and group support are the two most commonly used types in induction programs. Individual support has been provided through a number of sources, such as support provider, professional associate, and even buddy. The most widely used has been a mentor teacher, which is discussed in detail in the next major section of this chapter.

Individual support is of great importance to a new teacher when it includes the development of mutual trust, understanding, appreciation of one's uniqueness and abilities, and encouragement to work through problems and weaknesses. At the same time, the protégé needs to develop respect and appreciation regarding the insights and viewpoints of the support person. A mutual respect needs to be established. Because the support person brings knowledge, wisdom, and experience to the relationship, the new teacher has an opportunity to develop an attitude of respect and confidence over a period of time as the relationship develops. As new teachers learn to feel safe with the support person, they are more able to open up to more in-depth analysis of their personal and professional needs (Fox & Singletary, 1986; Huffman & Leak, 1986). This does not happen automatically; rather, it is developed over time.

Support individuals have been found to be of greatest benefit when they assist the new teacher in both the personal and professional life dimensions (Gold & Roth, 1993; Hardcastle, 1988). This dual support is especially important because instructional support is necessary, and yet it is hardly sufficient when attempting to handle personal problems such as feelings of isolation, insecurity, and loneliness. Support persons must be trained to provide assistance with both personal and professional high-stress situations through problem-solving strategies, stress reduction techniques, and knowledge regarding psychological needs of new teachers. Individual support is a vital component of induction and is examined in greater depth in the section on mentoring.

Most beginning teachers gain from the assistance received from the one-on-one of interpersonal support, and at the same time group support can be an essential complement to individualized assistance. In her work with student teachers, Fuller (1969) outlined the positive aspects of support groups when they were led by professionals with counseling and group facilitation skills. The group leaders gave assistance in stress reduction as well as providing the challenge required to foster professional growth. Over time the student teachers demonstrated less anxiety, became less egocentric, and were more able to focus on the initial tasks required of them in teaching.

The importance of support programs utilizing the knowledge and strategies learned from psychology and especially counseling have proven to be effective with new teachers. Thies-Sprinthall and Gerler (1990) used counselor-led support groups as a means of complementing the supervision process with beginning teachers. Their purpose was to provide relaxed reflection regarding the professional demands experienced by new teachers. They described the structure for the small groups, presented guidelines to be used, and reported results from implementing counselor-led groups. One of the outcomes for new teachers who were involved in small-group counseling was for them to be able to face themselves and to refocus their personal concerns from self to the teaching process and, subsequently, to their students. This was consistent with an earlier finding in Paisley's (1987) research where two samples of beginning teachers, one rural and one urban, had positive trends in movement through the phases of concern using small-group support.

Use of experts from the helping professions, such as counselors, has been found to be most beneficial for new teachers. This has been emphasized by a psychotherapist who reported that when support groups were led by individuals who are trained to use guided group interaction strategies, interpersonal support strategies, and individual insight strategies, new teachers moved from self-absorption and reacting to stress, from negative thinking and negative behavior patterns, to focusing on problem-solving solutions where they were then able to handle the complexities of the teaching tasks (Gold & Roth, 1993). Leadership that encourages self-disclosure, recognition of commonalities, appreciation of differences, and opportunities to risk assisted new teachers in developing positive self-esteem and the sense of personal competence. In an atmosphere free of evaluation, new teachers can learn to identify their own needs and to make independent, professional judgments.

The importance of both group and individual support has been recognized as new teachers express positive feelings about themselves and about their teaching. The intensity of new teacher training and assistance is related to new teachers' perceptions of themselves and their teaching. For teachers who were provided support, their perceptions of teaching as a career were more positive than were new teachers in similar schools who were not receiving support (Colbert & Wolff, 1992).

It has been clearly documented that providing support does enable new teachers to survive their first year; however, issues that still need considerable study are those that relate to the type and quality of the support provided, long-term effects on new teachers who have received various types of support and training such as instructional and psychological support, and the different types of training offered to support providers. Rigorous studies in both quantitative and qualitative research along with longitudinal studies could provide much assistance in evaluating the existing support programs and in planning new ones that are research based.

Support Through Computer Networks

With the necessity for support during the first year of teaching being well established in the attrition research, it is essential that a variety of methods be explored to provide both instructional and emotional support to new teachers. To meet the need of providing a more continuous type of support, a relatively new type of contact is being offered to beginning teachers through computer interaction at the Harvard Graduate School of Education. A Beginning Teacher Computer Network (BTCN) offers support and direction to novice teachers during their first year (Merseth, 1989, 1990). The exclusive purpose of this university-based network is the support of beginning teachers. A new cohort of first-year teachers uses the system each year.

New teachers use the network to transfer electronically text messages from one person to another or to a group of individuals. They may exchange information and messages of support to one another on computer screens. Individuals who use personal computers linked through modems and telephone lines to a host computer have the opportunity to exchange messages throughout the day or evening rather than having to wait until a scheduled meeting to get or give support. Frequent support can be a tremendous advantage to those who need more continuous contact with others.

There are various types of networks available other than the Beginning Teacher Computer Network (BTCN). There are systems such as BITNET, INTERNET, and USENET that are supported by large university mainframe computers that provide for members of many universities throughout the world to communicate with one another. Some types of networks only have the capacity to send and receive confidential and private messages. These types of systems are called e-mail, whereas other networks offer "bulletin boards" or "forums" where individuals may read and send messages to other users. All messages, whether public or private, identify the sender, the date sent, and a referent line provided by the sender that indicates the content of the message.

Although research in this area is in its infancy, Merseth (1991) conducted a study of 39 first-year teachers who were graduates of three different teacher education programs at Harvard University. These teachers taught in middle and high schools across the United States. Using their personal computers at their schools and homes to communicate with one another in public and private messages and in both individual and group discussions on topics related to their teaching experiences, they were all able to take part in this study. Data were collected through mail surveys of which 79% responded. The host computer provided information regarding the frequency and variation in use throughout the academic year, and 10 of the participants completed individual structured follow-up interviews. Results of the study indicated that for this sample the network was most effective in providing participants with moral support. It was also indicated that "keeping in touch with friends received a significantly higher mean rating than the objective of lesson and curricular planning" (p. 144). The outcome of the personal interviews, where a small sample was used, was that the network reduced participants' feelings of isolation and offered them privacy or confidentiality. This finding was also reported by Casey and Roth (1991–1992) who used a sample of student teachers and found that they no longer felt isolated when they established support systems through computer networking.

Even though the sample was small in Merseth's study and there are limitations to electronic networking, the findings are important in light of the research on psychological support. It may well be that when left to their own choices and where confidentiality is guaranteed, new teachers will seek emotional support over instructional support. It may also need to be considered that support teachers are more comfortable and experienced with giving instructional support and tend to offer it over emotional support for which they have little or no training. Thus, new teachers when interacting personally with a support teacher do not initiate help at their greatest area of need—emotional support. These elements need further research and evaluation.

With the availability of computer networks at a few other universities, such as the University of Virginia (Bull, Harris, Lloyd, & Short, 1989) and the University of Michigan (Stanzler, 1994), faculty and school site practitioners can interact to enhance the emotional support and education of new teachers. As the availability to carry out this type of support increases, continued research with large samples of beginning teachers across the nation can add to the effectiveness of giving increased emotional and instructional support to new teachers.

SUPPORT PROGRAMS: NEW TEACHER INDUCTION

The number of teacher induction programs has grown tremendously over the past few years to assist new teachers and to reduce attrition (Huling-Austin, 1990b); however, there are criticisms that suggest that few programs include a comprehensive and thorough conceptual or theoretical framework and that rhetoric and fast-paced implementation of programs have outpaced conceptual development in teacher induction (Huffman & Leak, 1986; Schaffer, Stringfield, & Wolfe, 1992).

To understand the types of support programs and their effectiveness, it is essential that existing programs be reviewed. To describe current induction programs, it would be informative to: (1) develop a framework that includes specific components with which to review, compare, and analyze various programs, (2) use the framework to characterize the status of state programs, and (3) provide some program descriptions.

Framework

The NASDTEC manual (Mastain, 1991) provides a framework with which to review, compare, and analyze programs. The framework includes the following components: (1) the beginning teacher support system (btss) includes some beginning teachers, but not necessarily only beginning teachers; (2) the btss includes a mentor teacher or support system of educators to work with the beginning teacher throughout the school year; (3) the btss includes a training component for the mentor teacher or support team to assist them in becoming increasingly more effective in supporting the beginning teacher; (4) an inservice program is provided for the beginning teacher that is based on needs determined by the beginning teacher and the mentor teacher; (5) a btss includes additional funding from the state, or the employing school district, or both, which is specifically earmarked for the support of the new teacher; (6) a btss includes a process to assess the new teacher as a beginning teacher, rather than the process used for teachers not in the beginning teacher support system; and (7) a btss includes a process to evaluate the effectiveness of the support system and to determine needed changes (p. 1).

Status of State Programs

In 1991, 31 states reported having a beginning teacher support system that complied with the NASDTEC definition in their framework (Mastain, 1991). Twenty-two of the states had implemented a btss with state funding, whereas six states implemented a btss without state funding. Three of the 31 states were still in the initial stages. Only 18 of the 28 states that had implemented a btss included 100% of the beginning teachers. The remaining states had varying conditions ranging from 6.2% of all beginning teachers in the state to 80% of all beginning teachers participating.

The criteria and process of selection of beginning teachers varied. Seventeen of the states included all beginning teachers as required by the state licensing agency. In five states the criteria and processes selected by the local district determined the participation; three states had voluntary participation for the district and the teacher; one state included all beginning teachers, although it was voluntary for both beginning teachers and the districts; one state had mandatory teacher participation for the districts, who had volunteered to participate; and one state required that all participants in the alternate certification project were automatically selected for the btss.

Regarding support systems, 27 of the 28 implemented programs included a support system, and 21 of the 28 implemented btss programs included training for the support team. In-service was provided for beginning teachers in 19 of the 28 implemented btss programs.

In analyzing criteria and processes for the selection of mentors or support teams, eight of the states selected support members based on criteria and processes established by the state licensing agency; 10 states used criteria and processes determined by the local school district or consortium; three states based their criteria on the process established by the state and local school district or consortium of districts; one state selected the mentor through the school principal and the beginning teacher; and another state had the mentor teacher selected by local administrators. One state required that the mentor teacher hold a teacher support specialist certificate, and another state required a teacher certificate for their mentor teachers. It was also reported by NASDTEC that one state was basically evaluative, rather than supportive, so the criteria were not applicable to them.

Evaluation of beginning teachers varied. Fourteen states reported the evaluation was part of the btss and carried out by either the mentor teacher, the principal, or a member of the support team. Evaluation of beginning teachers in 14 states followed the same pattern as was used for other staff members. Some states prohibited evaluation as part of their btss.

Amounts and sources of the funds allocated specifically for the btss were different among the states. Nineteen states of the 28 provide some state funds specifically for the support of beginning teachers or for the evaluation of them. State funds allocated specifically for the beginning teacher support system ranged from $20,000 to more than $1 million, and the annual stipend paid to mentors ranged from $500 to $1,200 in different states. At the same time, one state funded its mentor program other than through the btss sources where mentor teachers were paid a stipend of $4,000 per year and the duties extended beyond support of the beginning teacher. Some other states were funded with local district monies, local funds in addition to state funds, and one state had the funding come from the beginning teacher in the then alternate certification program.

A number of the states made specific demands on the employer as to the assignment of the beginning teacher; however, no state made any demands other than those described in the btss program. Some states would do one or more of the following: "limit the number of students assigned to the beginning teacher; limit the number of behavior problems that could be assigned the beginning teacher; decrease the number of different subjects the beginning teacher would be required to prepare for; require a certain amount of release time for observation or inservice education; or, in some other way recognize the importance and difficulty of the beginning years of teaching" (Mastain, 1991, p. 5).

The success rate, the attrition rate, and the job satisfaction of beginning teachers during their first 1–5 years were reported. Seventeen of the states did keep data on the success rate and/or the attrition rate and/or the job satisfaction of the beginning teacher. Four states kept data on success rate, attrition rate, and

job satisfaction of all beginning teachers in their btss programs. One state kept track of the success rate, attrition rate, and job satisfaction on all beginning teachers; eight states kept data on the success rate and attrition rate of beginning teachers in their btss program; one state kept success rate and attrition rate data on all beginning teachers; 10 states kept data on success rate; and one state kept attrition rate data.

Nineteen of the 28 implemented btss programs included an evaluation of the program according to the NASDTEC report (Mastain, 1991). Findings from the NASDTEC report suggest that there is a range of differences among the 31 states responding to their questionnaire. Important findings are that btss programs in this sample are similar in placing a priority in the following areas: (1) implementing a support system for all beginning teachers, (2) including support persons/teams, (3) supplying training for the support team, (4) including in-service for beginning teachers, (5) providing additional funding from the state and/or local districts and/or foundation, (6) reporting evaluation of the beginning teacher as a part of the btss, and (7) including evaluation of the btss.

In the 1994–1995 NASDTEC manual (Andrews, 1994), 28 states responded to a questionnaire that contained 10 questions based on the NASDTEC framework regarding support systems for beginning teachers. Of the states that complied with the NASDTEC framework, 16 of the 28 states had implemented a btss that included 100% of the beginning teachers. Five states reported that the btss is voluntary for beginning teachers, and 16 states reported they did not have voluntary participation of the beginning teachers.

Regarding support systems, 25 of the 28 btss programs included a support system. Fifteen states included an evaluation of the beginning teachers. Additional funding was provided in 17 of the 26 states. Twenty states included training for the support teams, 17 states included an in-service program for the beginning teachers, and 16 states included an evaluation of the btss. It was also stated that some states did not respond to each question, resulting in incomplete information.

The 1991 NASDTEC manual (Mastain, 1991), which collected information on support systems for beginning teachers, reported that in 1984 eight states had initiated support programs. By 1991, 31 states had launched beginning teacher programs, and 22 of these had received state funding. The 1994–1995 NASDTEC manual (Andrews, 1994), reported that 25 of the 28 states responding to the questionnaire stated that they had a support system. Of the 27 states that responded to the question "What are the amounts and sources (1993–1994) of the funds allocated specifically for the beginning teacher support system," 15 states replied that they received some type of state support. It is clear from these reports that impetus for educational policy changes and programs mainly came from state leadership rather than from local or national government; however, the number of states receiving state support declined from 1991 to 1994, according to the questionnaire respondents.

Beginning teacher performance evaluation programs highly influence the career of the new teacher. The type of evaluation has an effect on their teaching styles and their perceptions of teaching. The nature of evaluation and how it is interpreted by the beginning teacher can influence both their commitment to teaching and their decision to continue in or leave the profession. Understanding these conditions and how beginning teachers are affected by them is crucial.

State departments of education have only been involved in the past decade in designing and implementing programs concerning the evaluation of beginning teachers; however, the pace of change has been rapid. The first of the recent state initiatives for beginning teacher induction was in 1980. By 1984, eight states had enacted policies, and by 1988, 12 states required some specified supervision and/or evaluation procedures. At the start of 1990, 18 states were implementing beginning teacher supervision/evaluation programs, whereas another 30 had proposals under consideration. Today, 45 states and the District of Columbia have enacted beginning teacher evaluation programs or requirements (Sclan & Darling-Hammond, 1992).

A more recent approach to beginning teacher performance evaluation recognizes the importance of relying on a broader base of knowledge to provide a foundation for teacher's judgments and reflections on their teaching. Many of these new approaches take the form of internship programs such as in California, Massachusetts, Minnesota, New York, and Vermont.

These programs concentrate on the complex and unpredictable nature of teaching and acknowledge that the teacher's reflectiveness and forethought are vital parts of their work. The newer programs concentrate on evaluation as being more successful when teachers and evaluators collaborate in determining goals, processes, outcomes, and when the process provides for context-specific assistance.

Another internship program, Minnesota, is based on the belief that teachers use a set of principles and strategies derived from an informal personal philosophy of education, that they reflect on their own teaching and its effects on learners, and that they engage in critical and divergent thinking and problem solving with students. This proposed Minnesota internship experience differs from the beginning teacher programs in most other states. It is not merely a set of evaluations to which beginners are introduced during their first year. They teach partial loads under careful supervision while assuming greater responsibility over time. The program is structured so that interns gain experience in applying their knowledge to major tasks of teaching, analyzing and using research, and reflecting on their own and others' teaching experiences.

New program approaches are based on the premise that judging teachers on the capacity for reflective action is more likely to engender teacher approaches, which incorporate a range of teaching techniques and increased responsiveness to students. A "collaborative growth oriented environment is created to instill an active style of teaching with an ever-expanding range of strategies" (Sclan & Darling-Hammond, 1992).

Some important issues that warrant further investigation include: (1) What types of support are being offered to new teachers? (2) Specifically, how do support providers and new teachers interact? (3) What is the impact of support on the new teacher's perceptions of teaching? (4) Does additional educational training improve teacher performance? and (5) What types of assessment procedures are being used? Specifically, what are the outcomes of the assessments in assisting the new teacher?

Specific Programs: Program Descriptions

Programs may be established for different purposes, depending on local needs and the political context. A synthesis of the research on teacher induction programs was conducted by Huling-Austin (1989a) who identified the following five goals that she believed to be common to most induction programs: (1) improve teacher performance, (2) increase retention of promising beginning teachers during the induction years, (3) promote the personal and professional well-being of beginning teachers, (4) satisfy mandated requirements, and (5) transmit the culture of the system. These goals provide a framework for understanding program characteristics.

Program evaluations and case studies are beginning to present more detailed accounts of the actual interactions of mentors or support providers with beginning teachers, as well as more detailed information on individual programs. Because there are a great number of support programs, only a few are reviewed here using the NASDTEC framework previously presented. These programs either have been prevalent in the literature, provide variety to the program descriptions, offer alternative structures, include different program components (e.g., integration of support and assessment), or include program evaluation data.

The California New Teacher Project According to a study by Policy Analysis for California Education [PACE], it was estimated that "simply to keep pace with enrollment growth, the state will need to hire, by 1994–1995, 75,000 new teachers (Policy Analysis for California Education (PACE), 1991, p. 50). To upgrade the preparation, support, and credentialing programs for new teachers, the state legislature authorized the creation of the California New Teacher Project (CNTP). The CNTP began in 1988 as a pilot program jointly administered by the Commission on Teacher Credentialing (CTC) and the California Department of Education (CDE).

The CNTP had three components. First, support; the project provided funds for local pilot projects to enable first- and second-year teachers to receive assistance from more experienced teachers and/or to attend innovative training sessions, seminars, peer discussion groups, and other professional development sessions. Second, evaluation; this component examined the impact of cost-effective support on the performance, retention, and satisfaction of CNTP's beginning teachers. Third, assessment; this component involved developing, pilot testing, and analyzing innovative forms of new teacher assessment to identify ways to create an assessment package that fully informed the credentialing process and enhanced the quality of teaching.

The CNTP is an example of a "second generation" of performance assessment that recognizes a broader knowledge base as a foundation for teachers' judgments and reflection. The teachers' role is viewed as decision maker rather than technician (Sclan & Darling-Hammond, 1992).

An independent evaluation of the support component was completed by the Southwest Regional Educational Laboratory (SWRL) from 1988–1989 through 1990–1991. SWRL examined the effects of the support projects and identified the most important features of effective projects. The following elements were identified as most important to the effective delivery of support services to new teachers by the evaluators (Pearson & Honig, 1992): (1) involving experienced teachers, carefully selected and specially trained, in guiding and assisting new teachers; (2) providing scheduled, structured time for experienced and beginning teachers to work together; (3) providing instruction to groups of new teachers—training that is directly related to their immediate needs and their current stage of professional development; and (4) individual follow up by experienced educators so new teachers learn to use new skills effectively in their own classrooms.

When support services were well designed and effectively delivered, SWRL reported the following findings:

1. The support projects reduced the overall attrition of new teachers by more than two thirds, virtually eliminating the problem of beginning teachers quitting due to isolation, frustration, or burnout. The local pilot projects achieved high retention rates among minority teachers and teachers serving in hard-to-staff urban and rural schools.
2. When compared with other new teachers, beginning teachers in the pilot projects more consistently (a) used instructional practices that improve student achievement; (b) used more complex, challenging instructional activities that enabled students to learn advanced thinking skills and cooperative work habits; (c) did long-term planning of curriculum and instruction, ensuring that students were taught the entire set of skills and knowledge to be learned during the year; (d) motivated diverse students to engage in productive learning activities; and (e) gave the same complex, challenging assignments to classes of diverse pupils as they did to classes that were ethnically and culturally homogeneous.
3. Experienced teachers who served as support providers for beginning teachers also learned new methods of instruction. Both beginning and veteran teachers became more reflective about their practices and more enthusiastic about their careers in teaching. Ninety-six percent of school principals in the CNTP said that the pilot projects also had positive effects on communications among the new and experienced teachers in the schools (Commission on Teacher Credentialing, 1993a).

The report also indicated that in the most successful CNTP projects, most support activities occurred in the new teachers' own classrooms and schools. Projects that served large numbers of districts and geographical areas were most effective when districts were similar in size, location, and need. Support produced the most positive gains for new teachers in urban and rural settings.

The evaluation also reported that the intensity (i.e., the scope, timeliness, relevance, and frequency) of the support and instruction given to beginning teachers did differ across projects and had an impact on new teachers' perceptions of teaching and their performance in the classroom. The projects that offered the most intense support and instruction were the most effective in improving new teachers' performance. New teachers perceived these projects as having significant effects on their success in the classroom (Commission on Teacher Credentialing, 1993b, pp. 3, 4).

California: The Beginning Teacher Support and Assessment Program The Beginning Teacher Support and Assessment (BTSA) program was established by the legislature and Governor Wilson as a consequence of the CNTP pilot study by the CTC and the CDE. During its "peak year," the CNTP included 37 local pilot programs that served approximately 1,700 beginning teachers. During 4 years, more than 3,000 beginning teachers and more than 1,500 experienced teachers participated in the CNTP. Significant findings reported by the CNTP (Pearson & Honig, 1992) were that intensive support, continued training, and informative assessments of teachers in their first professional years result in higher beginning teacher retention rates and significantly better instruction for students.

The CTC and the CDE provided two significant policy recommendations:

1. A need to redesign efforts to provide for a better transition from student of teaching to the role of teacher and to establish an integrated system of new teacher support and assessment, beginning with university preparation and continuing through induction into teaching.
2. Sufficient state and local resources, including new funds as they become available, must be committed to the success of beginning teachers. (Pearson & Honig, 1992, pp. 2, 3)

In response to these recommendations, a state budget of almost $4.9 million for grants to local education agencies was established by Governor Wilson for 1992–1993. Eight statutory purposes were established for the BTSA programs. These included: (1) to provide an effective transition into the teaching career for first- and second-year teachers; (2) to improve educational performance through improved training, information, and assistance; (3) to enable effectiveness in teaching students who are culturally, linguistically, and academically diverse; (4) to ensure professional success and retention of new teachers who show promise; (5) to identify teaching novices who need additional assistance; (6) to improve the rigor and consistency of individual teacher performance assessments; (7) to establish an effective, coherent system of performance assessments based on skills, abilities, and knowledge needed; and (8) to examine alternative ways to ensure the general public and the education profession that new teachers who remain have attained acceptable levels of professional competence. Universities, colleges, school districts, county offices, and professional organizations were encouraged to collaborate. Fifteen local BTSA programs were funded to serve approximately 1,100 first-year and second-year teachers.

Because BTSA programs are no longer "pilot" programs, they are beginning to implement and be guided by a set of standards of program quality derived from the findings of the CNTP. These standards established a common set of expectations for new teacher induction programs. The standards are still in draft form and will be refined and tested in the BTSA program.

Novice teachers have not been given a coherent set of expectations regarding their knowledge, skills, and abilities as beginning professionals in teaching. *A Framework of Knowledge, Skills and Abilities for Beginning Teachers* is under development by the CTC and the CDE. Advocates project that when this framework is completed, it will articulate for new teachers a strong, clear image of their stage of professional development in their early years of teaching.

The CNTP demonstrated the need for better assessment of teacher performance that could help to shape the directions of support services and individualize the training and mentoring of each teacher. Several new features were built into the BTSA programs to achieve the important purpose of individualizing induction services for these adult learners.

One important feature included in all newly funded BTSA programs was the use of valid, reliable assessments that move beyond pencil-and-paper testing to an actual, "authentic" measure or measures of teaching performance.

Newly funded BTSA programs are using one or more assessment approaches to inform, guide, shape, and individualize the support provided to new teachers. The Individualized Induction Plan (IIP) is the vehicle for planning this integration of support and assessment for each teacher. Information about the teacher's professional growth will be gathered. This information will be used to select and propose growth activities.

Florida The Florida legislature passed the Florida Beginning Teacher Program (BTP) in 1982, funded by the state and revised in 1990. The purpose of the BTP is to "increase student learning by providing a set of supervised support services for teachers in the first year(s) of teaching in Florida to assist them in their continuing development" (Rule 6A-r.75[2Z]FC) (Stakenas, 1989, p. 33).

At the present time the program is called the Professional Orientation Program (POP) for beginning teachers. All beginning teachers participate in the POP. Local districts develop their own POP and must meet the legal requirements, be approved annually by the Commissioner of Education, and be reviewed by the Department of Education. Each beginning teacher has a support staff assigned to them. The support staff is made up of a principal, a peer teacher, and another professional educator. The staff observes the beginning teacher at least five times. The observations include: (a) one diagnostic/screening observation, (b) three formative observations, and (c) one summative observation. Clinical activities are conducted to assist beginning teachers in refining their teaching competencies and to provide induction into the profession. The Florida Performance Measurement System (FPMS), a formative and summative instrument, is used by most of the districts.

A Professional Development Plan (PDP) assists each beginning teacher to improve and demonstrate performance on the minimum essential competencies. The PDP includes criteria by which successful performance will be assessed. Provision for review and modification of the plan at stated intervals during the year are included. The PDP is developed by the support staff with the knowledge and participation of the beginning teacher. Three formative evaluation conferences are included.

Portfolios are included in the PDP, as is any formative evaluation for the beginning teacher. Exhibits of successful performance during participation in the Florida Beginning Teacher Program may also be included.

Formative evaluation includes the ongoing process of observing, providing feedback, and helping the beginning teacher improve teaching performance. Summative evaluation is used to determine the successful demonstration of the minimum

essential competencies of the beginning teacher and includes observation instruments and evaluation procedures. Once the summative evaluation process is concluded, the building-level administrator transmits the results with a recommendation to the district superintendent who makes the final determination and verification to the Department of Education regarding successful or unsuccessful completion of the BTP by a specific teacher.

The BTP has been implemented in all 67 public school districts since the 1982–1983 school year. In the 1987–1988 school year, among public school beginning teachers, 72% completed the program, 22% were carried over to the next year, nearly 1% were unsuccessful in completing the program, and another 5% dropped out due to resignation or other reasons.

The BTP has had ongoing evaluation studies since its inception in 1982–1983. Early studies reported that the BTP participants perceived the BTP as an effective program and wanted to see it continue with minor modifications (Stakenas, 1989).

Data provided by the Bureau of Teacher Education reported that the BTP "failure" rate is very low (i.e., approximately 1%). Various reasons for the low failure rate were given. Forty percent of the BTP coordinators believed that the failure rate was so low because nearly all beginning teachers are capable due to their prior preparation. Two percent reported that the failure rate was so low because the standards for judging competency were set too low. Another 13% gave a variety of other reasons. Finally, the most surprising finding was that 48% of the BTP coordinators believed that administrators were reluctant to fail a beginning teacher even when existing standards were not really met (Stakenas, 1989); however, in many cases these same administrators did not rehire them. Unfortunately when this happens, the weak candidate obtains a teaching certificate and is then able to seek employment elsewhere. Two of the reasons why administrators may be reluctant to exercise their function of "gate keeping" were: (1) to avoid an unpleasant situation in which the new teacher would have to be told that he or she had failed, and (2) a lack of willingness to fail a beginning teacher because an appeal and possible litigation may result.

North Carolina Initial Certification Program The North Carolina Quality Assurance Program originated in recognition of the need to improve teaching effectiveness by extending the preparation of teachers through their first 2 years and by changing the certification procedures (North Carolina Initial Certification Program, 1990, p. 1). In fact, North Carolina was among the first states to institute a formal induction program for beginning teachers. The North Carolina Initial Certification Program (ICP) began in 1985–1986. Prior to this, during the 1982–1983 academic year, steps toward full-scale implementation of the program were taken. Newly authorized funds supported 13 pilot projects in public and private institutions across the state. Results of the project were utilized in the formulation of related administrative procedures for consideration and adoption by the State Board of Education. After considerable work on testing requirements and new standards for the approval of teacher education programs, in 1984 the State Board of Education established the Initial Certificate to be awarded to all prospective teachers completing institution of higher education teacher education programs after January 1985 and called for demonstrated performance prior to the award of a continuing certificate. The extension of the professional education preparation of teachers includes an Initial Certification Program (ICP). At the end of the 2-year period, a decision must be made to grant or deny continuing certification for an employee.

A comprehensive plan to ensure the establishment of a support and performance review system for initially certified personnel must be developed in collaboration with each local education agency and a neighboring institution of higher education. The ICP offers support for an individual's professional growth during the first 2 years of employment. A support team or mentor team documents performance with periodic assessment of skills, satisfactory evaluation of performance, and completion of a professional development plan.

The 2-year process for initially certified personnel begins with a system-wide orientation. A mentor team or support team for each initially certified person is assigned. The support team should be from the same school and teaching/subject area whenever possible, and the mentor/support team members are required to have specific training.

The Effective Teaching Training Program for new teachers is based on 10 3-hour sessions that are designed to prepare educators to recognize and apply the effective teaching practices identified over the last few years in numerous research studies. The Performance Appraisal Training Program is interrelated with the Effective Teaching Training Program. The training includes eight 3-hour sessions divided into four modules. The sessions include data collection on teaching, analyzing and synthesizing classroom data, and translating classroom data. Portfolios are required and include a copy of the PDP, identified strengths and areas for development, a summative data report, and evidence of completion of strategies on the PDP.

The local education agency, institution of higher education, and the State Department of Public Instruction evaluate the ICP. The evaluation is based on the desired outcomes of the program. An ongoing evaluation of the instruments and practices associated with the assessment of performance is also conducted.

The program has been evaluated periodically. In 1989, the evaluation report by an independent evaluator concluded that: (1) there had been a high degree of program implementation even with limited resources, (2) participants believe in the need for the program and view it positively, (3) institutions of higher education (IHEs) had not been well integrated into the ICP, (4) there was extreme variation in how the program had been implemented across the state, (5) participants were frustrated by the lack of resources available to support the program, (6) the program was far from achieving its full potential, and (7) program implementation will likely diminish without sustained and increased support (North Carolina Initial Certification Program, 1990).

In 1990, an independent agent conducted a fiscal impact study of the ICP. He reported that: (1) few IHEs are financially capable of providing intensive ICP support to Local Education Agencies (LEAs), (2) current ICP expenditures vary from LEA to LEA, (3) current state allotment of $100 per ICT per year had little if any impact on the current expenditures incurred by LEAs, and (4) LEAs reported that their implementation of the ICP at the local level was not complete (North Carolina Initial Certification Program, 1990).

Along with the preceding reports, the Commission used an opinionnaire to solicit opinions and suggestions from North Carolina educators about the ICP. The most serious problem addressed regarding the implementation of the ICP was the lack of time for proper mentoring.

The studies revealed the following points: (1) the ICP is very valuable, (2) the ICP is not realizing its full potential, and (3) additional resources must be provided to support the ICP (North Carolina Initial Certification Program, 1990). It could be stated that there is a disparity between the intent of the ICP and the operation of the ICP in some schools and some districts.

One of the needs is for additional research studies, which would include the following:

1. More accurate data on the attrition rate of new teachers, and, specifically, it is important to know why these teachers leave the profession.
2. More accurate data on the extent to which LEAs are complying with state ICP regulations. Also, the extent to which LEAs and ICPs are actively assisting Initially Certified Teachers (ICTs).
3. Determining whether or not the evaluative component of the ICP, especially the use of the Teacher Performance Appraisal Instrument (TPAI), is sufficiently rigorous and realistic. For the state to create and enforce policy, the information indicated must be provided and reported with sufficient rigor.

Oklahoma The Oklahoma Entry-Year Assistance Program has been adopted as a model by a number of other states. It was implemented in 1981 as a result of House Bill 1706. The intent of the legislation was to establish qualifications of teachers in the accredited schools of the state of Oklahoma through licensing and certification requirements (Garrett, 1994). The licensed teacher is required to participate in the Entry-Year Assistance Program during the initial year of teaching in an accredited school under the guidance of an entry-year assistance committee to qualify for an Oklahoma teaching certificate. The term *entry-year teacher* is defined as any licensed teacher who is employed in an accredited school to serve as a teacher under the guidance and assistance of a teacher consultant and an entry-year assistance committee.

The Entry-Year Assistance Committee is a committee composed of a teacher consultant–classroom teacher, a principal, assistant principal or administrator designated by the local board, a teacher educator in a college or school of education of an (Oklahoma) institution of higher learning, or an educator in a department or school outside the institution's college of education, as well as a chairperson who shall be chosen by each committee. The entry-year assistance committee works with the entry-year teacher to assist in all areas concerning classroom management and in-service training for the new teacher.

The teacher consultant in the Oklahoma project is defined as any teacher holding a standard certificate who is employed in a school district as a teacher. The teacher consultant is appointed to provide guidance and assistance to the entry-year teacher and must be a classroom teacher with a minimum of

2 years of classroom teaching experience as a certified teacher. Teacher consultants are selected by the principal from a list submitted by the bargaining unit. The requirements for teacher consultants include the requisite knowledge and skills for assisting the beginning teacher, a standard certificate in the same area as the beginning teacher, and current status teaching in the same area as the new teacher (Garrett, 1994). The teacher consultant spends 72 hours per year in consultation with and observation of the first-year teacher and receives a stipend of $500.

A standard observation instrument is used by each entry-year assistance committee to evaluate an entry-year teacher for certification purposes only. The committee utilizes the following criteria: (1) uses meaningful parental input as one criterion in evaluating the entry-year teacher's performance, (2) meets with the entry-year teacher a minimum of three times per year for evaluation review and recommendations, (3) observes the entry-year teacher a minimum of three times per year, (4) reviews progress with the entry-year teacher and formulates recommendations concerning teaching performance, and (5) makes a recommendation concerning certification (Garrett, 1994).

Numerous studies on the Oklahoma Entry-Year Assistance Program have been completed during the 12 years since the program has been implemented; however, an extensive statewide data base has not existed for doing longitudinal effectiveness studies or valid comparative analysis. The Oklahoma Commission on Educational Planning and Assessment reported on the Entry-Year Assistance Program by 1985. Findings from a survey for the report indicated that 92% of the 527 respondents indicated that the Entry-Year Assistance Committees are an effective way to provide guidance and assistance to first-year teachers. The report also stated that 85% of all respondents agreed that the Entry-Year Assistance Program contributed to the success of the first-year teacher (Garrett, 1993).

The Oklahoma Legislature appointed a special task force in 1987 to study the effects of the program in the Teacher Reform Act of 1980. The recommendations included: (1) use reduced-size classes for first-year teachers, (2) exempt them from additional or extra duties, (3) give them release time for training opportunities, and (4) the state board should consider increasing the teacher consultant stipend. The recommendations, however, were never implemented (Garrett, 1993).

The value of the Oklahoma Entry-Year Assistance Program was recognized by the legislature when the development of a 3-year mentor program for the beginning teacher was requested in House Bill 2246 (Garrett, 1993).

The success rate of the Oklahoma program was evident when it was reported that of the 15,464 first-year teachers who had participated in the 1991–1992 school year, 14,862 had successfully completed the program and were recommended for certification. A second year in the program was recommended for 264 of the new teachers and 111 successfully completed the additional year and were recommended for certification in Oklahoma. There were 602 new teachers who did not complete the program (Garrett, 1993).

Three concerns were summarized regarding the program: (1) the program funding had not been commensurate with the increased responsibilities of higher education institutions that had resulted from House Bill 1017 legislation; (2) the program is not being systematically evaluated using formal scientific procedures for gathering data that would allow for a continuing comprehensive assessment of program effectiveness statewide as determined by well-defined program objectives and expected outcomes and of the means and methodologies by which these might be achieved; and (3) the program has no formal system-wide training program for ensuring that all participants have a common understanding of program objectives and expected outcomes and of the means and methodologies by which they may be achieved (Garrett, 1993).

Induction Program For Beginning Teachers: Texas Working in conjunction with the Texas Higher Education Coordinating Board, Senate Bill 994 directed the State Board of Education (Anderson, 1991) to develop a comprehensive induction program for beginning teachers. Effective with school year 1991–1992, all beginning teachers with zero years of creditable experience were assigned a mentor teacher. Beginning teachers were required to participate in specialized induction program activities that were approved by the district.

In 1991, there were three funded projects for the induction of beginning teachers piloted by the Texas Education Agency. Training of trainers and resource materials were made available to districts through regional education service centers that were available during the school year 1991–1992.

Workshops were designed to give assistance to school districts as they initiated programs for beginning teachers through the assignment of mentor teachers for support and assistance. Specialized training for mentor teachers and beginning teachers was encouraged, although it is not required in the absence of state funding support.

The Texas Education Code 13.038: Teacher Induction states that "(a) The State Board of Education and the Coordinating Board, Texas College and University system, should develop a comprehensive teaching induction program for the probationary period; and (b) the induction program shall include a one-year period of teaching cooperatively supervised by experienced teachers, school administrators, and faculty of institutions of higher education" (Anderson, 1991, p. 1).

The goals for beginning teacher induction programs include the following: (1) to ensure quality instruction for students of induction year teachers, (2) to provide quality mentor and administrator training, (3) to increase retention of promising induction-year teachers, (4) to promote the professional and personal well-being of induction year teachers, and (5) to evaluate and improve the program (Holden, 1993). The effectiveness of this program has yet to be documented.

The importance of support programs to assist new teachers and to reduce the attrition rate is apparent. What is essential at this time is more rigorous attention to (1) collection of sufficient data to document unsatisfactory performance, including attempts to remediate ineffective teaching behavior; (2) administrators and support providers who are willing to exercise professional judgment and prohibit persons who have not been able to perform the minimum essential teaching competencies from gaining continuing membership in the teaching profession; (3) the types of support being offered to new teachers and the effectiveness of the support; (4) continued research to identify the most important factors associated with new teacher retention; (5) identification of the causes of capable new teachers leaving the profession and comparing the information gathered with what has already been learned regarding attrition rates; (6) the development of conceptual frameworks that describe how the program is organized to achieve the desired outcomes; and (7) determining the influence of policy, such as mandates that dictate program elements.

SUPPORT PROVIDERS: MENTORS

The concept of mentoring is a significant element of support. It has been defined and operationalized in various ways, and it is perhaps the most common means found in providing support. Mentors are a critical component in both formal induction programs, as well as in less-organized programs of support. In many situations, the mentor is viewed as the primary provider of support and guidance for the novice teacher; therefore, it is of importance to analyze the nature of mentoring by reviewing the definitions, roles, responsibilities, selection, and training of mentors.

Much has been written regarding the roles of mentors and their functions (Galvez-Hjornevik, 1986; Gray & Gray, 1985; Kram, 1983, 1985; Little, 1990; Merriam, 1983; Wildman, Magliaro, Niles, & Niles, 1992). In these reports, several attempts have been made to describe "what a mentor does." In fact, a number of authors have presented a range of attributes that they feel teachers need if they are to be considered for this role. Some of the distinctions reported are: (1) a trusted guide and counselor or teacher-guardian (Galvez-Hjornevik, 1986); (2) a teacher, confidant, role model, sponsor, and protector (Gehrke & Kay, 1984); (3) change-facilitators who are responders, managers, and initiators (Huling-Austin, 1990a); (4) clinical support teachers (Odell, 1989); (5) teacher, sponsor, encourager, counselor, and befriender (Anderson & Shannon, 1988); and (6) a professional health provider (Gold & Roth, 1993).

An earlier appraisal by Schein (1978) argued that the term *mentor* had been loosely used to mean teacher, coach, trainer, positive role model, developer of talent, protector, opener of doors, sponsor, and successful leader. Schein also believed that the term mentor ought to apply only to those individuals who play several of these roles.

Consensual agreement on the defined roles of a mentor has not been accomplished in the mentoring literature. There are those who argue that the continued application of mentoring in teaching depends on better definitions (Healy & Welchert, 1990).

To date, there have been few research studies published that focus specifically on teacher–teacher relationships and the phenomenon of mentoring in elementary and secondary schools (Fagan & Walter, 1982; Gehrke & Kay, 1984). In one such study (Gehrke & Kay, 1984), 188 teachers from 12 schools responded to a questionnaire concerning their careers in teaching. Forty-one of the teachers in the sample were selected to be interviewed. From their research, the investigators stated that teachers do have relationships that fit the mentor–protege description and that they occur during the training and induction periods of teaching. The investigators also reported that the

descriptions of these relationships were found to be "strikingly similar" to the descriptions found in business and management, and most of the relationships seemed to be likely to continue; however, if they chose to end the relationship it was without negative feelings. From this study, descriptions of the mentor's role rather than definitions of mentoring were provided.

In viewing mentoring roles and activities, a critical observation by Wildman et al. (1992) was that programs that have been implemented have done so with too little conceptual understanding of mentoring and have had unrealistic expectations and poorly thought-out implementation strategies. Elmore (1989) argued that rhetoric and action had outpaced both conceptual development and empirical warrant. In fact, he believed that there was a certain "manic optimism" that prevailed.

With such diversity in the literature regarding mentoring, the purpose of this section is to examine: (1) the origin of mentoring, (2) definitions of mentoring, (3) the value of mentoring, (4) selection criteria for mentors, (5) preparation of mentors, and (6) mentors' perceptions of their role.

Origin of Mentoring

The term *mentor* has its origin in the poem by Homer titled *The Odyssey* (Dimock, 1989). In this classical tale, Odysseus entrusts the care of his son Telemachus to an old man named Mentor who is to educate and nurture him while Odysseus is away fighting the Trojan War. Mentor's responsibility, as a loyal and trusted friend of Odysseus, was to demonstrate integrity, wisdom, and personal involvement with Telemachus, who as protégé, was to demonstrate respect for Mentor. This relationship was to be mutually respectful and highly personal as well as demanding and rewarding. From this relationship comes the sense of mentoring as being an emotional interaction between a younger person and an older one in which the mentor's responsibility is to help shape the growth and development of his or her protégé. This concept of mature individuals sharing their wisdom with future generations began in the 1970s as many governmental agencies and corporations launched mentoring programs. In the 1980s, colleges, universities, and school districts also adopted the concept believing that because mentoring had value in business, government, and other fields, it would also have value in education, especially for helping new teachers. Thus, teacher mentoring programs were developed with the idea that those who assume the role of mentor take on the responsibilities as being trusted guides, teacher guardians, role models, and protectors.

Galvez-Hjornevik (1986), in reviewing its historical connotation, argued that the use of the term mentor for teachers in induction programs is probably incorrect or at least not totally accurate. She stated that "the term mentor historically denoted a trusted guide and counselor and the relationship as a deep and meaningful association" (p. 6), which she felt may not apply to teaching.

Other individuals have reviewed mentoring in education over the past few years and have voiced strong concern that (1) "studies from educational settings reveal no clear notion of how a mentor is different from an influential teacher, and if they can be differentiated" (Merriam, 1983, p. 169); (2) "mentoring in some cases has proven to be a less than ideal reform tactic, especially when programs have been implemented with too little conceptual understanding of mentoring, unrealistic expectations, and poorly thought out implementation strategies" (Wildman et al., 1992, p. 205); and (3) there is a "certain skepticism that mentor relationships at their richest could be achieved by formal arrangement" (Little, 1990).

These concerns and criticisms must be addressed and careful consideration given to the evolving role of the support person or mentor. One of the questions to consider is in regard to whether or not it is necessary to have close relationships that have deep meaning in which the mentor is the older, wiser person. Or do we need to reexamine the role of mentoring that is appropriate for the type of setting that education demands? For these reasons, definitions of mentoring that have been discussed in the literature are highlighted in the next section.

Definitions of Mentoring

An analysis of the literature reveals that a universal definition of mentoring is lacking even though the spread of mentoring programs became a national phenomenon by the end of the 1980s. In fact, many educators believe that better definitions of mentoring are essential if the efforts toward teacher development are to continue with their application of mentoring.

Gehrke and Kay (1984) used cautiously the terms *mentor* and *protégé* to describe relationships that were healthy and positive. They distinguished the term mentor from the often used label *sponsor* and took the position that "mentor–protégé relationships are good for both persons and ought to be fostered, just as good parent–child relationships should be fostered" (p. 24). They also believed that this relationship serves a purpose in socializing the young and that all who wish to mentor and all who wish to be a protégé should have the opportunity to do so. This description of the mentor role is fairly consistent with the concept of mentor from Homer's poem in that the mentor is the older and wiser person who is responsible to nurture and educate the young.

Another interpretation, based on evaluation of an advisory program, examined the classroom interactions of advisors with beginning and experienced teachers (Little, Galagaran, & O'Neal, 1984). (Advisors were teachers on special assignment, released full-time from the classroom and paid according to the established teacher's pay scale). The research from this Teacher Advisor Project in California revealed that the advisor was more interested in assisting rather than taking charge of a teacher. They reported that "Advisor and teachers alike are attracted by the idea of leadership roles for teachers. By their language, however, both convey the impression that facilitating teachers is more acceptable than leading them; facilitation is more respectful of colleagues as persons and professionals, more gentle toward their humanity and work" (p. 19). From this description, the support role is more of assisting protégés to fulfill their own potential as separate and unique individuals who are already professionals with contributions to make to teaching, rather than being viewed as young and needing an older wiser person to train them, such as an apprentice.

In addition to these operational definitions of mentoring, Kay (1990) proposed a definition that states, "Mentoring is a comprehensive effort directed toward helping a protégé develop the attitudes, and behaviors (skills) of self-reliance and accountability within a defined environment" (p. 27). Kay's work on self-reliance and accountability are reflected here as fundamental aspects of mentoring. He identified important environmental considerations such as cooperation and unselfishness on the part of the mentor. This definition places the mentor in a role in which he or she is "helping" the protégé develop skills and attitudes, and it implies that the mentor is in a position of being the wiser and more knowledgeable guide.

Another viewpoint on defining mentoring was used by Hardcastle (1988) who described a more abstract, interpersonal, life-changing mentoring relationship in comparison to other more limiting ones and suggests that a mentor be considered as a "significant mentor." Hardcastle believed that protégés were attracted to mentors who were wise, caring, committed to their profession, and who demonstrated integrity, and that protégés desired mentors who were able to point out their particular strengths, to motivate them to grow professionally, and to show them "new ways to be." In addition to these more personal qualities, it was important that mentors have the ability to act as a catalyst, to possess high expectations, and demonstrate a sense of humor. These descriptions were all thought to be important mentor characteristics.

Parkay (1988) defined mentoring from his own personal university experience with a mentor. He believed it was important to share a similar style of thinking between the mentor and the protégé, that modeling by the mentor of a commitment to a professional way of life was important, and that encouraging the protégé to determine the direction and mode of learning was also essential.

According to the view of Healy and Welchert (1990), no widely accepted definition of mentoring has been articulated. They believe that "without such definitional consensus, efforts to develop a knowledge base relevant to mentorships in education have been haphazard" (p. 17). To advance a knowledge base for future research, they offer a definition of mentoring grounded in contextual-developmental theory and consistent with the findings of past investigators. They consider mentoring to be "a dynamic, reciprocal relationship in a work environment between an advanced career incumbent (mentor) and a beginner (protégé) aimed at promoting the career development of both" (p. 17). They see the protégé moving from an understudy to one of self-directing colleague, and for the mentor, the relationship is a vehicle for achieving midlife *generativity* (using Erikson's term).

Various challenges have been raised regarding who should define mentoring. One such challenge is made by Wildman et al. (1992). In concluding their research study with approximately 150 mentor-beginner dyads, they stated that mentoring programs should not attempt to specify rigidly mentoring roles. They believed that with support, "experienced teachers can provide assistance tailored to the circumstances of beginning teachers in individual schools" (p. 205). The investigators go on to say that "it is a mistake to develop any external definition or conception of mentoring and impose it by means of political pressure or high powered staff development activity. Mentoring, like good teaching, should be defined by those who will carry it out" (p. 213).

In summary, the phenomenon of mentoring is not clearly conceptualized nor is a universal definition available. In fact, some even believe that a universal definition is unnecessary and would be limiting, and that mentor roles are largely incompatible with prevailing values, norms, and structures of teaching. Others believe strongly in the role of the mentor and in specific guidelines for their selection and training. These conflicting perspectives point to the necessity of reexamining the role of support in education. Specifically, is the definition of a mentor as borrowed from Homer's poem, which so many have adopted, appropriate for education? If the purpose of support for new teachers is not consistent with the role of a mentor, then the need to reconceptualize both the role and the training of support providers is essential. It may be that the definition of support for new teachers will be defined somewhere in between what now exists in the literature and what is still being learned regarding this function.

The Value of Mentoring

Studies in several contexts have illustrated a value of mentoring. In her research with using mentors in business, Kram (1983) reported that the relationship of a mentor to the individual in early adulthood and also in the midcareer can significantly enhance development. She studied 18 developmental relationships in business and reported how a mentor relationship moves through the phases of initiation, cultivation, separation, and redefinition. She believed that a mentor relationship can enhance both individuals' development; however, Kram also reported that, under certain circumstances, the relationship became destructive for one or both individuals. Thus, in business, mentoring can be both positive and negative depending on the individuals and the types of relationships that develop.

The literature pertaining to mentoring adults in higher educational settings has been growing since borrowing the concept from business. Bova and Phillips (1984) reported on protégés in university settings and concluded from their research that mentoring relationships were critical for developing professionals in higher education. The protégés in this study learned risk-taking behaviors, communication skills, political skills, and skills related to their professions. Thus, they regarded mentoring as being quite positive. Since mentoring was found to be of value at this level, it would be helpful if the qualities of the mentors and the protégés were identified and interactions of each were researched to assist in defining more specifically the significance of mentoring at this level.

The Houston Mathematics and Science Improvement Consortium also produced evidence of the value of mentoring (Miller, Thomson, & Roush, 1989). The National Science Foundation sponsored the program, which was coordinated by the Baylor College of Medicine. Practicing scientists and mathematicians were mentors for secondary science and math teachers for improving their teaching skills. They also helped teachers to increase their self-respect and to renew their enthusiasm for teaching. Many of the teachers in the project expressed a renewed sense of professionalism as a result of their participation in the project. Most mentors spoke of the "great respect" that they had gained for teachers by working with them. Another important outcome was that the network of teachers and men-

tors continued to exist beyond the life of the project. The value of mentoring in this study was clear and can be useful for future research in studying the dynamics of these types of relationships. Huffman and Leak (1986) made two important observations from their study of mentors.

1. It was highly desirable to use mentors who teach the same grade level or subject matter to provide a full range of assistance. They addressed issues such as classroom management and instructional methodology as well as content, knowledge, and experience in a similar discipline or grade level.
2. A primary factor in addressing the needs of the beginning teachers was that of providing adequate time for informal and formal conferencing, planning, and conversation between the mentor and the beginning teacher.

The use of mentors in business and in education has been valuable in most instances as reported throughout the literature. If mentoring is of value, then one of the most important considerations in successful outcomes of the mentor–protégé relationship is the selection and preparation of mentors.

Selection Criteria for Support Providers

Because the purpose of mentoring is to assist novice teachers and to foster their success during the first years of teaching, it is essential that the selection procedures be given careful attention. Unfortunately, this area has not been rigorously researched; however, there are many perspectives presented in the literature that do lend insights. The most important attributes that many believe need to be considered first as essential elements in the selection of support providers are: (1) mentor teachers viewed as experts by their peers (Bird, 1986; Galvez-Hjornevik, 1986; Ward, 1987); (2) the demonstrated ability for the mentor teacher to be reflective and analytical regarding teaching (Borko, 1986); (3) a keen desire to be a mentor and to work with a new teacher (Varah, Theune, & Parker, 1986); and (4) an uncommon commitment to their role of leadership (Howey & Zimpher, 1986). Other factors considered to be of importance in the selection of support providers include the following: (1) age and gender, (2) grade level and content area, (3) teaching style and ideology, and (4) physical proximity (Odell, 1990).

In selecting support providers there are others who believe that the individual should be an older experienced teacher who is willing to act as a confidante and guide throughout the protégé's first year of teaching (Ryan, 1986). In the New York City project, Ryan discussed the use of retired teachers who were used as mentors. At the same time he acknowledged that those mentors who were close in age to new teachers may demonstrate more empathy for what is happening to a new teacher. Other than age, there are some who felt that expertise in terms of how many years they have taught needed to be considered in the selection process. Varah et al. (1986) believed that a minimum of 3–5 years was necessary. It also has been suggested by some that many complexities may occur when there are male–female mentoring relationships. Others support mixed gender matching (Hunt & Michael, 1983). Another more intangible variable that has been suggested is one where the support provider demonstrates respect for the protégé (Varah et al., 1986). Being able to show respect for self and others seems to be an area that is more difficult to describe, yet is essential for a successful relationship.

Gold and Roth (1993) presented other attributes considered critical in the selection process of support providers when they described the beginning teachers' emotional, physical, social, and intellectual needs. They recommended selection of support individuals who are both qualified and desire to provide this type of professional health training and support.

All of the attributes presented point toward the necessity for establishing specific criteria that assist in selecting support providers. These criteria are: (1) a definition of teacher expertise that includes competence in the classroom and number of years of experience; (2) a record of improving their own teaching through analysis and reflection; (3) commitment to the role of providing support through previous experience in using these skills and by demonstrating a willingness for preparation and service; (4) experience with other professionals that demonstrates an ability to model empathy, integrity, and a genuine concern for the growth of others; (5) ability to identify beginning teachers' emotional, social, and intellectual needs and training in how to assist them in handling stress and preventing burnout; and (6) demonstration of leadership abilities in professional activities.

Along with the attributes described, it also is necessary that support providers continue to improve both their instructional skills and their personal skills. Familiarity with educational literature regarding effective schooling, classroom discipline, management skill, and current issues in curriculum development are all vitally important in assisting new teachers. Also, consideration must be given to the psychological welfare of new teachers. Being able to assist in areas of emotional welfare along with demonstrating personal problem-solving techniques are essential if the new teacher is going to be successful in handling the stress that comes with the many adjustments being made during the first years.

In the California mentor initiative, which included five districts, selection criteria, processes, and outcomes were three of the eight criteria that Ruskus (1988) suggested teachers and mentors use in judging the overall effectiveness of their program. The perceived validity of selection "was the most important determinant of perceived program effectiveness" (p. 199) across districts. The district with the highest rating on selection (and also the highest program effectiveness rating) employed a two-stage selection process where extensive paper screening and principals' ratings were followed by interviews and observations of the highest ranking candidates. One third of the applicants were selected based on an objective rating form that included stated criteria. In contrast, a district that had consistently low ratings on selection (and the lowest rating on effectiveness) employed a more cursory review procedure and conducted interviews with all candidates, but no observations were included. The reviewers were also criticized by some teachers as relying on "subjective feelings" rather than "real evidence" (pp. 202–203).

Another important issue in selecting mentors is the one that questions the extent to which formal selection processes (which may include formal applications, interviews, peer and supervi-

sor recommendations, portfolios, simulations, or observations) reflect teachers' expectations of a mentor's role. To investigate this, case study accounts that recorded teachers' complaints anecdotally suggested that a selection process that centered on a small sample of a potential mentor's work may prove to be inadequate to ensure the breadth and depth of a candidate's experience and knowledge that may be essential prerequisites to mentoring. Also, Peterson (1984) believed that available case studies provided few examples of the selection process in which multiple lines of evidence are assembled persuasively. Teachers in one case study proposed that selection criteria balancing their classroom expertise along with their ability to work with colleagues would "be more in keeping with the meaning of a 'mentor'" (Shulman, Hanson, & King, 1985, p. 14).

A more critical approach regarding the selection of mentors has been taken by Little (1988) who believed that "the most volatile issue in formal teacher leadership initiatives has been teacher selection. . . . The selection of leaders has been cast both as a technical problem (what are the acceptable criteria for performance?) and as a political problem (who will teachers accept as leaders, if anyone?)" (pp. 100–101). More currently, Little (1990) expressed the selection problem as being "an artifact of isolated work in schools, a problem that achieves its present magnitude only because many teachers have no sensible grounds on which to grant or deny someone the right to lead them" (p. 305).

In summary, it appears that selection criteria alone do not completely cover the demands on mentors' expertise, which are frequently far greater than a prospective mentor may anticipate. With these types of weighty concerns, it is of utmost importance that selection criteria and evaluation procedures for support providers be evaluated. Also, studies of the effectiveness of selection procedures along with the long-term influences of mentoring will contribute much to assisting those involved in the selection of mentors and in the eventual success of their programs.

Preparation of Support Providers

Throughout the literature on teacher induction there has been widespread disagreement regarding the need for organized training for support providers. Opponents have voiced a concern that "experienced teachers possess an extensive repertoire of helping strategies and that, with opportunities for collaboration, teachers can develop and shape complex mentoring roles that meet beginning teachers' needs" (Wildman et al., 1992, p. 205). Hardcastle (1988) believed that mentors who are appreciated by their protégés for their high personal values and character traits may be the key, rather than any programs that assign mentors to protégés. Advocates of training, however, discuss the demands of giving support and believe that preparation for teaching provided little or no preparation for giving support (Bey, 1990; Brooks, 1987; Huling-Austin, 1990a; Thies-Sprinthall & Sprinthall, 1987a).

Concern for mentor teachers' performance has led several states and districts to offer mentors skill training (Bird & Little, 1985; Kent, 1985; King, 1988). Through this type of training, mentors are helped to make use of their own knowledge of curriculum, instruction, and classroom management. In addition, these mentors are also expected in many instances to adopt terminology and concepts derived from classroom research (Kent, 1985) and from local and state teacher evaluation guidelines (Huffman & Leak, 1986). A large number of these training agendas have been concerned with consultation strategies, communication skills, and classroom observation techniques (Little & Nelson, 1988; State of Connecticut Department of Education, 1988). An investigation of these training activities illustrates an emphasis on promoting smooth interpersonal relations between mentors and protégés.

Training of support providers at the school level has been more successful when teachers and administrators have been able to define clearly the support provider's role and the school-level goals; however, where there are clearly defined policies and purposes regarding the role of the support provider and the availability of training, there are also barriers that dictate the content of the training.

Structured training and support were included in the Los Angeles Unified School District's assignment of mentors to new teachers, in Connecticut's use of mentors for teacher certification, and in Toledo's involvement of experienced teachers in the evaluation and tenure of new teachers (Little & Nelson, 1988). It appears then that structured training and support are more likely to be offered where mentoring is linked to policies or to district goals.

In contrast, California's state-supported programs during the first 2 years reported that nearly 40% of participating districts allocated no resources for postselection support of support providers. This situation was in contrast to many other programs that depended on occasional workshops that were sponsored by county offices of education or on other out-of-district opportunities (Bird & Alspaugh, 1986).

Of those who do believe that training of support providers is necessary, it is generally recommended that the selection take place and then a training component be provided (Heller & Sindelar, 1991). Too often, though, teachers assumed their new leadership role without the benefit of some type of training or support. In these instances, the roles remain less clearly related to the priorities of specific programs or institutions.

Another concern in the selection of those to be trained revolves around the need for assessing a prospective support provider's skills and abilities to work well with others, to be a leader in professional practice, and to share expertise and materials with others (Smylie, 1989).

In respect to whether or not support providers should be selected before or after training, it is unfortunate that there is an absence of studies that trace the contributions made by postselection training to the subsequent performance of the support provider. Nor are there studies to measure their successes in relationships with teachers or administrators. There is also an absence of studies comparing support providers who do receive training with those who are without such training. In addition, as Little (1990) so aptly pointed out, "there have not been any attempts to assess the relative leverage to be gained by investing institutional resources in postselection training versus various forms of preselection preparation of individuals, groups, or organizations" (p. 309).

Because research reports information about teaching that can then be passed on to beginning teachers, it is believed by many of the supporters of training that support providers need preparation in ways to help new teachers handle instructional problems such as "classroom management, basic lesson designs and delivery, and evaluating student progress" (Little & Nelson, 1990, p. 2). Some educators and psychotherapists believe that support providers need training in developing strategies to help new teachers with their emotional and psychological needs. These needs are grouped into categories of emotional-physical needs related to stress and burnout, psychosocial needs regarding personal problems and issues with people both in their personal and professional interactions, and personal-intellectual needs of intellectual fulfillment due to the lack of this type of stimulation while trying to keep up with the daily paperwork during the first years (Gold & Roth, 1993).

Various programs have been developed to assist in the training of support providers. For instructional support, Little and Nelson (1990) prepared a *Mentor Teacher: A Leader's Guide to Mentor Training* to assist in the training of mentors. The preparation included: orientation to the mentor role; assisting the beginning teacher; classroom organization and management for new teachers; classroom consultation, observation, and coaching; mentor as staff developer; and cooperation between the administration and mentor. Each section is divided into specific training segments with activities, handouts, and directions for how teachers can practice particular skills in their school. This type of training promotes a perspective of mentoring as a technical activity that applies specific strategies and techniques.

Criticism of the program states that the training favors the procedural knowledge derived from research and minimizes the mentors' experiences and the wisdom and expertise they have acquired in their career (Feiman-Nemser, Parker, & Zeichner, 1992). These critics also stated that using the *Mentor Teacher* gives one little sense of teaching as an intellectual or moral activity and "pays little attention to the mentor's own ideas about teaching and learning to teach" (p. 6).

Others believe training programs for support providers should be multifaceted and go well beyond the important areas of traditional teacher education and staff development programs that focus on the acquisition of and analysis of teaching skills (Howey & Gardner, 1983; Wolfe, 1992). As Wolfe (1992) pointed out, the following components should be examined in conjunction with specific purposes of the mentor program and considered for inclusion in the training: adult development, interpersonal skills, coaching and modeling, nonevaluative styles of supervision, needs of beginning teachers, and the mentoring process. Wolfe also stated that mentors "should be prepared for their complex roles and functions of mentoring through a well-designed, multi-faceted, and ongoing training program" (p. 108). She also emphasized the importance of training programs that allow mentors the opportunity to direct their own learning to fulfill the need for autonomy. In addition to this type of training, the inclusion of a psychological support program that offers explanation and assistance with teacher stress and burnout as related to beginning teacher needs is an essential component in the training of support providers if they are to help beginning teachers as they adjust to their first years of teaching (Gold & Roth, 1993).

The use of case studies to help prepare support providers to work with beginning teachers has been included in only a few of the training programs. Carter (1988) proposed that the use of case studies is a helpful way for support providers to assist beginning teachers in the process of solving many of the complex teaching problems they encounter. They are also helpful in modeling step by step how experts solve problems. Although Carter (1988) did give a word of caution in stating that "Asking mentor teachers to embark on this task (developing case studies) as an 'add on' without supporting their work either through monetary rewards or release time will doom the effort to failure" (p. 221).

Wildman et al. (1992) took a different perspective when they suggested that experienced teachers already possess an extensive repertoire of helping strategies and that, with opportunities for collaboration, teachers can develop and shape complex mentoring roles that meet beginning teachers' needs. They reported that "mentoring programs should not attempt to rigidly specify mentoring roles. With support, experienced teachers can provide assistance tailored to the circumstances of beginning teachers in individual schools" (p. 205). Their study included seven ways of providing assistance to beginning teachers. Of the seven categories, five centered on providing professional assistance with varying degrees of directness; however, most reported a more indirect role where they modeled a reflective posture while analyzing a situation or solving a problem with the protégé. Category 6 placed an emphasis on a combination of professional and personal support, whereas categories 7 and 8 included ways of providing indirect personal/professional assistance. In fact, the actions extended beyond the dyad in which the mentor acted as a mediator or a broker. In other words, the mentors sent their protégés to other teachers and administrators in their schools and tried to connect them to important personnel and resources outside the school and school system. They believed that mentors should not be burdened with more responsibilities than they can carry and that their primary responsibility is to meet early career teachers' needs, whatever they may be. Mentoring, they stated, "is not a substitute for staff development programs, nor should mentoring programs be conceived primarily to provide career incentives to experienced teachers" (p. 212).

As seen throughout the literature, the training of support providers has received much attention. It is strongly supported by many that additional attention be given to specific ways in which support providers are prepared for their role. As Little (1990) stated, this must take place along with making the reality of mentoring more in tune with the rhetoric of mentoring.

Perceptions of Support Providers

Giving support to others provides many benefits for the individual who offers the assistance. Some of these benefits are related to the status associated with the title, compensation, sharing knowledge and insights with someone new to the profession, and in some cases the resources provided. As support providers share what they know with others, their own performance and learning can expand and mentoring can be quite rewarding. As opportunities for professional development increase, they usually find these to be personally and professionally gratifying

as well as intellectually stimulating. Some of these benefits were expressed by a support provider in the Houston-area project (Miller et al., 1989) who stated, "My respect for teachers has gone up by a factor of 100. They are really incredibly talented people who, with a little bit of direction, can do so much more" (p. 467).

The promises of offering support can also bring the possibility of career advancement for those who are looking for this type of incentive (Ruskus, 1988). In fact, by granting experienced teachers the status of mentorship, they often experience a renewal and empowerment that brings excitement and enthusiasm into their own teaching, which in turn is passed on to other teachers. The benefits to the district can be a lowering of the attrition rate for gifted and experienced teachers.

Another perception was expressed by an individual who was one of eight support teachers in the Graduate Intern/Teacher Induction Program, a joint venture of the University of New Mexico and the Albuquerque Public Schools. He believed that, "Being a support teacher means helping people grow and become good teachers. It's a combination of basing teaching techniques on what we are like as people, our personalities, interests, inclinations" (Feiman-Nemser, 1992, p. 8).

In contrast, some support providers have negative perceptions of mentoring regarding the difficulties they have with making and finding time to work with their protégés. Parker (1990) reported that some of the mentors even plan to discontinue the job because of time pressures. One mentor reflected these criticisms when she commented on the pressures of not having enough time.

To actually observe (beginning teachers) a little bit more and . . . be available to help when they needed help. But they [the persons directing the mentor programs] don't want us to get away from the classroom situation so that we don't lose our ideas teaching kids. Therefore I only have a limited amount of time which means I don't see and observe Chris as often as I would like. . . . I thought I was going to have time to help anyone who needs it and I don't have that much time. I will observe the teachers that I feel need my help more. (p. 13)

What often begins as a positive incentive for many teachers can sometimes end in discontent and disharmony. In fact, the selection criteria of support providers along with what takes place during the mentoring process comprise much of many teachers' overall perceptions regarding mentor programs and their judgments about what seems to go wrong. Data gathered from interview procedures from teachers in one career ladder site reported, "discontent and eroded commitment to the district emerged . . . when teachers questioned the quality of selection and discrimination associated with the new roles" (Hart & Murphy, 1990, p. 240).

Perceptions of the role and the functions of support providers are too often ambiguous. The literature has documented uncertainties of mentors, teachers, and administrators regarding the central purpose of mentoring, specific behaviors that mentors might engage in, and assessment procedures they should or could use. This ambiguity and conflict that accompany role definition are greatest where norms are unfavorable to professional growth or career mobility, where the roles of support providers remain unlinked to any real perspective, and where teachers needed to "figure out what they want to do and how to go about it" (Hart, 1990, p. 519). In one situation a teacher stated, "We need to know what we should do" (Hart, 1990, p. 524). This reflected their confusion and uncertainty. This criticism regarding teachers' ambiguity and conflict when they were left to invent their own roles as they went along is in opposition to Wildman et al. (1992) who found that experienced teachers already possessed an extensive repertoire of helping strategies and that they can develop and shape complex mentoring roles.

Smylie and Denny (1990) recorded other negative perceptions regarding their role as support provider. Their 13 teacher leaders showed their concerns regarding other teachers when they stated that "they were much less certain about whether their fellow teachers understood their leadership roles and what those teachers and their principals expected of them in those roles" (p. 8). In a study of 24 mentor teachers, Ganser (1993) reported that they emphasized the curriculum and instructional needs of beginning teachers while "their focus on these topics was largely to the exclusion of other broader topics, both personal and professional" (p. 8). Ganser stated that the mentors in this study had a somewhat limited vision of their roles and functions and that their impression of mentoring was "an unclearly defined and poorly supported professional development activity" (p. 9). It was evident that those mentors saw their role as being more of a coach rather than as a role model for the beginning teacher. It is easily seen that ambiguity and conflict accompany role definition and have an effect on teachers' perceptions of mentoring. This is especially true throughout the case literature where support providers are so fearful of collegial criticism that they often are too humble in regard to their own expertise.

In each of these cases, clearly defined characteristics of "experienced teachers" must be researched and information made available if future selection of support providers who meet these selected criteria for mentoring is to be successful. Otherwise there exists a system that continues to perpetuate inconsistent guidelines. Those who are qualified to mentor often become frustrated and discouraged with the restrictions placed on them, and those who do not feel they are qualified usually become frustrated and choose to quit due to lack of training and support for their new role.

The new teacher and support provider relationship can be a most rewarding one when experienced teachers are carefully selected, rewarded, and encouraged to use their level of expertise and wisdom to guide and inspire new teachers who are beginning their careers. It also is essential for new teachers who need encouragement, guidance, and support through their most impressionable months of beginning their careers to feel free to discuss their needs with a support person if they are to continue in the profession. Because they are beginning, the imprinting process that will define for them their role and commitment to teaching the first few months is critical. Perhaps what is needed is to reexamine the entire concept of mentoring that has been in operation for the past few years. To explore bold new alternatives for offering support to new teachers may prove to extract the best from what has been learned and may lead to a more successful and meaningful induction of new teachers into the profession.

CRITICAL ISSUES AND PERSISTENT CONCERNS

The first year of teaching places many demands on new teachers and has been documented as a critical time. Despite the contributions of preservice training, it has been well established that most new teachers need some type of support if they are to survive the first years.

Support programs have sprung up across the nation to assist new teachers in making necessary adjustments through their initial years of teaching; however, current issues that persist are in large part unresolved as a consequence of opposing philosophies, a lack of financial support, and a paucity of research and evaluation studies. Many proponents of support programs are strongly functional in their thinking. These individuals propose programs that focus on instructional strategies and organizational concerns where effectiveness and competence are viewed mainly in performance terms. As a result, the support programs often embody ideology, logic, and protocols closely associated with training regimens. Support here seems to be something that is done to new teachers; therefore, programs of this type operate as though thinking and behavior can be imposed on teachers.

Others are mainly concerned with philosophical and conceptual issues and view teaching as an intellectual, political, psychological, and moral endeavor. For this concept of support, differences among teachers must be welcomed, and teachers are united during their induction by the moral, intellectual, psychological, and political commitments that they share. Therefore, recognizing individual differences of teachers is of great importance. Addressing teachers' individual and professional needs is emphasized. Support is believed to be experienced by new teachers, rather than being done to them. Thus, support should concentrate on the unique qualities of teachers and focus on developing teachers' identities and their competence as individuals who are also teachers.

Because there are opposing philosophies, which can be challenging and growth producing, it has been suggested that it is useful to consider different "ecologies of induction" (Lawson, 1992). In the following review, critical issues and persistent concerns are identified and opposing views are considered.

Context as a Force in Shaping Practice

From the perceptions of new teachers, the beginning months of teaching are crucial in their decision to make a commitment to teaching and to remain in the profession. One of their major goals for this first stage of teaching is to be in an assignment that is congruent with how they perceive themselves and the teaching role. If the situation is too challenging, they feel overwhelmed. If it is too lacking in opportunities for growth and development, they tend to be disappointed and discouraged. The context, therefore, into which the new teacher is placed is of utmost importance for the new teacher's success. A definition of context is viewed broadly by Vaughan (1979). He defined it as "the interaction of the knowledge, skills, attitudes, and behaviors of educational personnel, students and others with factors and conditions such as type of training activities, physical setting, role-expectations, socialization processes and stages of adult development and is not seen simply as structural or organizational conditions although these certainly are viewed as one part of context" (p. 70). In reviewing the literature, four major context dimensions are dominant: (1) assignment, (2) principal, (3) curriculum and learning, and (4) socialization.

The assignment of the new teacher sets the stage for a successful beginning experience, a mediocre beginning, or even a disastrous start that may end in attrition. In many instances new teachers are assigned to the least desirable schools and classrooms. In fact, they often are given those students or assignments with which experienced teachers do not wish to deal. Instead of giving new teachers a nurturing environment, they are often thrown into a negative setting where the demands are more than they can handle and the attrition rates are excessively high. The new teachers often question their own competence in teaching, their ability to meet the needs of their students, and their own desire to remain in teaching. The conditions under which they carry out the first year of teaching have a strong influence on the level of effectiveness that they are able to achieve and sustain over the years. The attitudes that govern their behavior and the decision whether or not to continue in the profession are mostly imprinted during the first year. In fact, for some new teachers, these attitudes and decisions are imprinted during the first few months of teaching.

It is therefore of utmost importance that new teachers are placed in assignments where they have opportunities to use the training they have acquired and receive encouragement to build on past experiences. They need an environment where they are supported and permitted to exercise good judgment in meeting the needs of their students. An atmosphere that guides and encourages them as they develop their perceptions of their role as a teacher is an essential step in the imprinting process.

Not all programs offer a nurturing environment. Borko (1986) criticized state-mandated beginning teacher programs, stating that the primary function of state programs is gatekeeping or screening. Fox and Singletary (1986) also argued that few beginning teacher programs focus on providing the novice with the necessary assistance required to ease the critical transition from student to teacher. Thus, many of the beginning teacher programs have not made an impact on providing a supportive initial assignment for new teachers, primarily because this is a local district prerogative.

If teaching is to attract and retain talented new teachers, it is essential that they be given every opportunity to begin their careers in assignments that are supportive and that offer them assistance in making the transition from novice to professional.

A second major dimension to evaluate is that of the principal who plays a key role in the career of the new teacher. The principal assigns new teachers, assists or fails to assist them with disruptive students, can act as a buffer for difficult parents, support or refuse to give support, assist or fail to assist with curriculum needs, and, if interested, can have much to do with their professional growth (Wildman, Niles, Magliaro, & McLaughlin, 1989). The types of support offered by the principal are vital for the well-being of the new teacher. The relationship with a principal is essential in the imprinting of new teachers. It is in the development of this initial relationship that many new

teachers make the decision to continue or to leave teaching, according to the teacher attrition studies. The role that the principal projects helps to set the type of context to which the teachers will respond. This can be either supportive, aloof, or, in some cases, even destructive.

The third essential dimension related to context is that of curriculum and learning. New teachers, in most cases, have learned from experience that teaching is complex and demanding. They must take the curriculum and transform it and adapt it as they plan to meet the needs of their students. Through their decisions their lessons are paced, sequenced, and emphasized. They must plan for every area of their program. This type of planning is often a solitary activity that receives little or no institutional support, even though it is central to their professional success. The decisions they must make are situation specific. They must take into account the immediate situation and the many aspects involved. The context helps to shape the teacher's thinking and allows the teacher to make sense of the knowledge brought to teaching. It is essential that new teachers receive nurturing and encouraging during their initial years as they make the transition from student to professional and learn to transform the curriculum that is known to them into meaningful lessons for their students. They must also incorporate what they know about pedagogical strategies to challenge their students' thinking and develop higher level thinking skills. At the same time, they struggle with developing classroom discipline techniques.

New teachers must be given assistance in learning how to invest their actions on the spot and how to draw from the knowledge bank they already have. Clandinin (1985) described how teachers conceive of their environment as a dynamic image, a thought structure derived from the experiences they have working in the context as they adjust to make changes in that context.

Helping new teachers become self-directed professionals where teaching is rewarding must be a goal of all support programs. Encouraging them to think about and to organize the subject matter they teach deserves critical attention. Particular answers or solutions are not provided for in research on teacher thinking; however, this area is a major one to which educators need to focus their attention and creative endeavors if new teachers are to be guided during this critical period.

The final dimension of context is one of teacher socialization. An individual's socialization into teaching is often complex. New teachers enter teaching with different beliefs and expectations about teaching and with a wide variety of preparedness for the work. The major determinants in the socialization of teachers reported in the literature are students, parents, and colleagues. These factors are interrelated with a beginning teacher's beliefs and expectations. They also affect new teachers in a number of ways that they may not understand or be able to control (Wildman et al., 1989). The three determinants are discussed separately.

Beginning teachers enter the profession with beliefs and expectations regarding their students. They have certain expectations for student performance and behavior that they have developed over the years from their own schooling and also during their teacher preparation. As they become enculturated the first weeks and months, their feelings, attitudes, and levels of competence are shaped depending on how their prior expectations are being met. When the students are receptive and cooperative and when they respond to the new teacher consistently with the beliefs and expectations of the new teacher, the induction process is usually a positive one. In contrast, new teachers who have difficulties with students whose attitudes, values, and behaviors are very different from their own usually perceive the situation as threatening or undesirable for them personally. When they receive little or no support with these difficulties, they usually over a period of time become less effective and may choose to leave teaching.

The parents of their students are another important factor in the socialization of the beginning teacher. In many instances it has been found that new teachers receive little or no training in dealing with parents. When the new teacher has supportive parents, his or her feelings of competence are enhanced. In contrast, negative parents usually contribute to feelings of discouragement and disillusionment and the results are feelings of incompetence that diminish confidence as an effective teacher. Giving new teachers support and training in how to deal with difficult parents is critical in helping them concentrate on learning to teach and subsequently to gain confidence.

New teachers enter their first teaching assignment with memories of college friends and other teachers in training. In most cases they have given and received support from other student teachers and received support and encouragement from supervising teachers and from their college advisors. They look forward to their new professional role and want to be accepted and become part of a faculty. Some of their expectations are to meet other teachers with whom they can share ideas and give and receive support. Some new teachers seek assistance with their planning and curriculum areas. Colleagues can play a critical role in assisting new teachers during the initial adjustment period. To know that someone cares about them and will offer them empathy for what they are experiencing is essential.

When new teachers feel isolated and separated from other teachers on their faculty, loneliness and discouragement develop, which often lead to burnout (Gold, 1985). Assistance from colleagues is an essential part of their socialization process; however, the socialization process cannot be hurried. The data in this area reveal that it takes well into the third year of teaching before the major learning/socialization events occur (Wildman & Niles, 1987). For these reasons, support from colleagues needs to take place throughout the first few years, even though the first few months are essential.

When teaching assignments are too difficult, new teachers are so preoccupied with trying to survive that they are unable to focus on their teaching. As negative student behavior and disruptive students occupy a new teacher's energies and thoughts, there is little motivation to put toward teaching and learning to teach. Assigning new teachers to difficult schools with disruptive students can force new teachers to compromise their beliefs and modify their behaviors to an extent that they feel they no longer want to teach. Administrators and experienced teachers must take the responsibility to ensure that new teachers will have assignments that are rewarding enough so they have a chance to succeed.

A final point is that new teachers also need colleagues who want to understand them and who desire to offer encouragement and support. In environments where they feel secure and successful, new teachers will have an opportunity to teach and apply the knowledge they have learned as they develop necessary skills in learning to teach. An environment where they can grow and develop from a novice to a successful professional is an essential part of their first year of teaching.

The Role of the University in Induction Programs

With a great deal of emphasis regarding the crisis in education and concern for the future teacher shortages, universities and school district educators are increasingly recognizing the need for cooperation in the effective preparation of teachers. No longer are university programs thought of as being separate from school districts' needs. The emphasis in the literature continues to argue a need for continuous and relevant instruction that begins in the undergraduate programs and extends into the beginning years (Johnston & Kay, 1987; Roth, 1990).

To meet these needs, universities have begun to provide on-site beginning teacher support and professional development. The major purposes of these programs are to assist new teachers in making the transition from student to student teacher to professional teacher. Programs are concentrating on the professional skills such as integration of content knowledge and instructional strategies. Personal skills, which include communication and psychological support, are also being emphasized in some programs.

Many universities are concentrating on beginning teacher programs to increase the retention rates of new teachers, to improve their effectiveness in the classroom, and to provide personal support throughout the induction years. One catalyst for this activity has been the NCATE standard that requires teacher education programs to provide support for beginning teachers. Crosser, Griggs, and Haynes (1994) surveyed 219 institutions regarding the extent to which they provided assistance to graduates who are first-year teachers and/or beginning professionals as specified in NCATE accreditation guidelines, Standard II.B criterion 35 (National Council for Accreditation of Teacher Education [NCATE], 1992, p. 50). They received 123 responses resulting in a 55% return rate. The findings reported that 67% of the responding institutions had established formal plans to assist beginning teachers and 95% of those had implemented their plans. However, they also found that 36% of the institutions provided assistance through beginning teacher programs that indicated they had not yet evaluated their model.

Mentoring and providing workshops or seminars appeared to be the two most frequently offered support services for first-year teachers. Mentoring was provided in a variety of ways: (1) mentoring by university faculty either as assigned faculty load or on a volunteer basis, (2) university training of teacher mentors to provide peer assistance to beginning teachers, and training principals to act as mentors, and (3) matching recent graduates with alumni mentors. Fifth-year program internships included formal, and perhaps the most intensive, assistance programs. Other support services offered were telephone hotlines, newsletters, social meetings, support groups, monthly inservice meetings with an advisory council, videotaping services, on-site visits by teams of faculty, computerized bulletin board services, and providing modems to first-year teachers linking them to campus by computers and telephone lines.

The survey reported types of support in six categories. Examples of findings from each category are as follows: (1) on-site assistance from university faculty; (2) mentoring by practicing professionals; (3) on-campus seminars/workshops; (4) communication models; (5) miscellaneous, which included a variety of services such as a course for beginning teachers taught on campus by master teachers or requiring mentors to enroll in coursework in principles of mentoring; and (6) curricular support models (Crosser et al., 1994). Another finding was that funding for beginning teacher support services came from a variety of sources such as state departments of education, private and federal grants, and in some cases the universities or colleges absorbed the costs of the programs.

In a similar study, Ishler and Selke (1994) examined education institutions' involvement in induction in relation to criterion 35. Institutional reports and Board of Examiners' summary reports prepared for NCATE accreditation review were examined. The sample consisted of institutions of higher education that had completed NCATE reports processed during 1991 and 1992. Of the 87 institutions meeting criteria for inclusion in the sample, 49 were public and 38 were private. Sixty-one of the 87 institutions reviewed by the NCATE Board of Examiners' teams in 1991–1992 were recognized by NCATE for having implemented programs of beginning teacher assistance.

The most frequently mentioned forms of support included faculty conferring with graduates on an informal basis, formal mentors from colleges or universities working with beginning teachers, and formal mentors provided by the school districts in which beginners work. The authors felt that "it was apparent that many NCATE colleges and universities are taking an active role in the teacher induction process" (p. 16).

From the findings of these studies, institutions of higher education are demonstrating a growing willingness to provide services. Also, educators in universities and colleges can play an important role in providing support to beginning teachers. The major questions that need investigation are: (1) What types of support are being offered to new teachers? (2) What are the short and long-term results of the support? and (3) What is the role of higher education institutions in beginning teacher support programs?

Collaboration between universities and school districts has helped the universities to be involved in follow-up programs where observing the performance of their graduates assists them in enhancing their preservice programs. Thus, universities are better able to assist teachers during their training with the strategies that apply more directly to the classroom. Therefore, new teachers are learning not just the knowledge to be applied to the classroom, but also they are learning how to teach. Not only will new teachers benefit from collaboration efforts, but so will the experienced teachers. As Haberman (1985) stated, "What is needed is a resource system or resource network, possible through one of the numerous 'inter-institutional arrangements' now sprouting up nearly everywhere" (p. 261). He believed that these informal links already exist between individual teachers, schools, and resource centers within and outside the university community. If these links are reinforced,

a professional development mechanism is available that may be more effective than many of the ones now being used.

Institutions of higher education (IHEs) are beginning to look more closely at their roles in the professional induction of new teachers. As they consider their roles, setting specific goals is a necessary first step in determining how IHEs can contribute to the teacher induction process. Johnston and Kay (1987) proposed five broad goals of teacher induction programs that they recommend for IHEs. These include: (1) orientation, (2) psychological support, (3) acquisition and refinement of teaching skills, (4) retention, and (5) assessment and evaluation. Although these goals are not inclusive, they do give some direction for IHEs in beginning their programs.

Universities traditionally have been known for their advancement of knowledge and the dissemination of research findings to others in the field. Education faculty have contributed other forms of scholarship, such as publications, presentations, consultations, and, in many instances, research. They often assist public school personnel with the integration of new knowledge with practice. Developing, piloting, and evaluating new teaching programs and models are many of the ways the IHE can assist.

Literature documents that new teachers have critical needs for specific types of information, for assistance with learning how to teach, and for specific kinds of strategies to assist them (Barnes, 1989; Grossman, Wilson, & Shulman, 1989; Shulman, 1987). Also included is the most pronounced need of new teachers, the need for personal support, as they shift from the role of student to that of the teacher who is solely responsible for a class of students (Gold & Roth, 1993; Thies-Sprinthall & Gerler, 1990).

Universities can have a unique role in assisting beginning teacher programs. They can offer their services through the development of intensive and comprehensive programs where IHE and local school districts collaborate to meet the needs of new teachers. In addition, and more important, universities can offer assistance in areas that in-service programs are not designed to address. Universities and colleges are intended and designed for reflection and contemplation. As Fenstermacher (1990) argued

In a professional school or college, this reflective and contemplative attitude is connected to practice in ways that permit a back-and-forth between thought and action, theory and practice, research and decision making. With this dynamic relationship between reflective consideration and considered action, the higher education setting is without peer (provided of course, that it has not lost its own way). (p. 181)

The critical role that the university can play is that of assisting new and future teachers in acquiring the training to analyze their teaching, to evaluate their work with students, to anticipate the needs of their students, and to provide a variety of ways of meeting students' needs. Universities can assist teachers in incorporating new research and theory into their teaching, to conduct their own research, and to learn to meet their personal and professional needs. This type of assistance is in contrast to many in-service programs that "typically have low immediate payoff, moderate-to-low craft legitimacy or local adaptiveness, dismal accessibility, and virtually no continuity" (Haberman, 1985, p. 261).

Universities have an important role in leading teacher education for both preservice preparation and beginning teacher induction. A critical factor in exercising this leadership is in developing productive working relationships with local schools. Strengthening university–school collaboration is emerging as a major movement through professional development schools, clinical schools, and to some extent beginning teacher induction programs. Higher education has a responsibility to guide these programs and ensure professional preparation and to avoid the tendency toward apprentice models such as those encouraged by many of the alternative teacher training programs.

The Assessment versus Evaluation Paradox

The importance and necessity of evaluating the beginning teacher has gained momentum in recent years; however, a confounding factor is the distinction between *assessment* and *evaluation*. Little has been done in the induction literature to clearly point out the distinction between the two. In fact, the two terms have often been used synonymously, which has confused the purposes and roles of evaluation and assessment.

At the outset, these terms need to be clearly defined. For the purpose of this review, evaluation will be distinguished from assessment. Evaluation suggests that a judgment must be made regarding what constitutes worth or value. Thus, the term *evaluation* typically is associated with how effective or ineffective, how adequate or inadequate, how valuable or invaluable, and how appropriate or inappropriate a given action, process, or product is. Assessment, however, is for feedback; it is formative in nature to guide professional growth. It provides information to teachers so they are able to make appropriate adjustments in their teaching or program.

One of the needs in the evaluation and assessment-assistance literature regarding new teachers is related to defining and clarifying the purposes of each. This clarification will then help in determining what data are examined for each, which processes are used for gathering and sharing the information, who will be responsible for the collection and interpretation of the data, and how the data will be used.

Within the induction literature some educators support assessment of performance of new teachers by the support provider at regular intervals for the purpose of assisting the new teacher's growth and development. In this instance, the information is used for diagnostic purposes. It is believed that trust can be developed between the new teacher and the support provider in such a way that this type of assessment does not need to be threatening. Opposing forces state that support providers should not be involved in the assessment process. These individuals believe that it will hinder the development of trust and new teachers will refrain from confiding in support persons. This implies the role of evaluation.

These functions, assessment and evaluation, need to be carefully defined to guide the role of the support provider and the types of support to be offered to the new teacher. It is important to consider that assessment is diagnostic and need not be threatening to the new teacher and contaminate the support component. To enhance the process of assessment, the following principles should be considered and clearly stated:

1. The purpose for which it is being used
2. The manner in which it is conducted by the support provider
3. The setting in which it takes place and the nature of interpretation
4. The training of the support provider in conducting the process and in interpreting the findings to the new teacher
5. How often it will occur
6. The perceptions of the new teacher being observed regarding the process and its purposes
7. How well prepared the new teacher is for the process
8. The degree of security the new teacher feels in the process
9. The degree of trust that has been established prior to and during the process

A number of efforts are underway to assist new teachers with their growth and development. California is identifying alternative methods of teacher assessment to ascertain whether and how such assessment should be used (potentially in tandem with a beginning teacher support program) in the process of credentialing of future teachers. To achieve these goals, 15 projects providing support to new teachers (first and second year) were funded. Teachers involved in these support projects agreed to participate in the pilot tests of teacher assessments. With these specifications (among others), the California New Teacher Project included the support component, the assessment component, and an evaluation component to determine the efficacy of differing methods of new teacher support. In developing and/or testing a broad variety of new teacher assessments, information was used to assemble a package of assessments.

The new assessments were to serve both a formative and summative purpose. The findings suggested that teachers were very interested in receiving information from the assessments that would enable them to know their strengths and weaknesses. Both teachers and assessors supported the formative purpose of the assessments; however, consideration was given to the fact that if certification depended on the summative evaluations, teachers may not be inclined to reveal their areas of uncertainty or weakness during an interview. Yet, "they may reveal these areas to obtain support and assistance if the assessment is to serve a formative purpose" (Estes, Stansbury, & Long, 1990, p. 104).

Findings from the pilot projects were incorporated into the current California Beginning Teacher Support and Assessment (BTSA) program. Each BTSA program includes an assessment component locally designed to meet local needs. The most significant requirement was that the local assessment process functions as an integrated component of the support program for participating teachers who participate voluntarily in the program. The RFP stated that

During the induction period, new teachers should be supported and assessed in ways that recognize the complexity of teaching and the variety of approaches that contribute to teaching success. . . . Each new teacher will work with a cooperating experienced colleague to design an individualized induction plan. Each new teacher's induction plan should include participation in an ongoing formative assessment . . . to identify the teacher's strengths and areas that need improvement. (Commission on Teacher Credentialing, 1993b, p. 12)

Thus, California has provided assessment of new teachers by trained teachers who in some projects were their support providers. The evaluation of programs was provided through an outside agency, the Far West Laboratory for Educational Research and Development. There were two types of evaluation—new teacher and program.

Induction programs need to include careful attention to defining the role of assessment and evaluation in their programs, as well as identifying who will perform each of these. Separating assessment from evaluation, as in the California program, and clarifying the purposes and goals of each would help to eliminate much of the current confusion regarding the assessment versus assistance controversy that exists today.

Failure to appropriately assess new teachers, to ignore systematic sharing of results with them, and to refrain from offering support and encouragement in how to improve needed areas are all injustices to new professionals. New teachers need clear, definite information regarding their strengths and weaknesses in an environment where they do not feel threatened by job loss or loss of personal integrity. They also need assurance that they too are professionals who can grow and develop into professional teachers. To do less for new teachers is to rob them of personal satisfaction and of opportunities to grow professionally. In separating the assessment component from the evaluation component, California is providing an opportunity to both assess and support new teachers.

The Impact of Policy on Induction Programs

Since the mid-1970s, both legislative and judicial policies in education have been directed toward guaranteeing the rights of individual children. As a result, teacher recruitment, training, employment, and supervision in the schools have been given some emphasis with state-funded new teacher support programs.

In 1986, a survey was conducted to determine the status of new teacher induction programs in the 50 states and the District of Columbia (Hawk & Robards, 1987). Among the findings were that 19 had no statewide teacher induction program (STIP) and had no plans for initiating any. Fifteen states at the beginning of 1986 had teacher induction programs in the planning stage, six states were piloting their programs, and the District of Columbia and 10 states had statewide implementation.

Funding for planning, developing, and piloting induction programs had been made available by all states who had STIPs; however, only two of the STIPs appeared to receive financial aid for implementation and continued operation at the level of funding projected from the piloting data. States having support teams as part of their assistance component reported higher estimated costs per beginning teacher than those states with only a staff development component. Most of the respondents to the questionnaire believed that the major road block to implementation of their STIP was inadequate funding. Teacher supply and demand vary considerably from state to state, even district to district, and the needs of new teachers do not hold the same degree of interest for each state. With a declining economy over the past few years, education has faced fierce competition for scarce dollars leaving teacher support programs as a lesser priority for policymakers who must decide which problems

must be addressed. Yet, a few states have continued to make new teacher programs a priority. The state-supported California New Teacher Project and the Inner City New Teacher Retention Project were among the more imaginative and far-reaching of the new school support policies (Mitchell & Hough, 1990).

Because policymakers must decide which problems should be addressed and how much money, programmatic support, or regulatory attention should be allocated to ameliorating them, the California projects were funded based on the following rationale:

1. Teacher shortages and rapid turnover in staff are affecting the quality of instruction for many school children and fiscal incentives can significantly reduce the shortage of teachers. California will need between 15,000 and 17,000 teachers each year through the 1990s, whereas the number of new teachers being trained in colleges and universities is on the decline. Fiscally as well as nonfiscally, incentives for eligible teacher candidates need to be significantly raised (Mitchell & Hough, 1990).

2. Professors in schools of education in California have moved to collaborate their programs more fully with educators in the public schools. The Comprehensive Teacher Education Institute, a state-funded initiative, seeks to involve public schools more with teacher training programs. Increasing in popularity among policymakers is the offsetting of teacher training costs through shared personnel and increased investment in teacher preparation programs.

3. Fiscal policies needed to make the induction of new teachers successful center around direct funding to create and sustain various support services. The direct funding provided in the California projects for new teachers enables state policymakers to define the nature and extent of the support provided.

4. Fiscal policies aimed at professional development for successful teachers include funding for merit-based career ladder programs and broad-based support for professionalism among teachers as means to retain highly qualified teachers who too often leave the profession. In California's newly funded Beginning Teacher Support and Assessment (BTSA) program, which was a consequence of their pilot study, one of the major purposes was to ensure the professional success and retention of new teachers who show promise of becoming highly effective professionals. Also, support providers (experienced teachers) are included in the programs to work with new teachers, thus providing incentives.

5. Policymakers also pay careful attention to whether or not new teachers are best served by enhancing pedagogical and subject-matter knowledge and skills. In their final CNTP report to the state legislature, the Commission on Teacher Credentialing (CTC) and the California Department of Education (CDE) recommended that a "state framework must be developed that will outline the knowledge, skills and abilities expected of beginning teachers, and will serve as the basis for accurate information about their performance" (Pearson & Honig, 1992, p. 4). The legislature responded to this recommendation by passing SB 1422, which contains provisions for new teacher support programs. It required a broad framework including professional skills, abilities, and knowl-

edge needed by new teachers to improve teacher preparation and support programs.

California is one of the states that has received funding for a pilot program and also a BTSA program. There is a tremendous need in the induction research and literature for an overview of state-funded programs and the characteristics and accomplishments of each.

Because policies represent moral and political imperatives, those who make policy and those who carry it out must have the welfare of the new teacher as a central focus. Policies must be adopted that bring about programs that meet both the personal and professional needs of new teachers during the most critical time of their career if the attrition rate is to decline. Also, if new teachers are to be given an opportunity to develop professionally and to use the knowledge and training they bring with them, they must receive support as they are initiated into the profession. The question of what are educators' responsibilities toward new teachers must be considered in greater depth than has been in the past.

Methodological, Theoretical, and Conceptual Limitations: Research Issues and Concerns

During the 1980s and into the 1990s, support for new teachers gained momentum as the spread of mentoring programs became a national phenomenon by the end of the decade (Hawk & Robards, 1987; Huling-Austin, 1990b). Even though the interest in these programs has remained strong, a certain degree of concern has emerged. In fact, some educators criticize support programs by saying that they have been implemented with too little conceptual understanding of mentoring, with unrealistic expectations, and with poorly thought-out implementation strategies (Little, 1990). Others argue that programs have not offered a rigorous theoretical basis for advocating the mentor's role. These critics continue to voice their concerns that the mentor's role has been largely based on the cultural legacy of the mentor–protégé relationship and its potential for providing support for beginning teachers. Instead, they believe the need for support providers has presented a new professional responsibility for experienced teachers (Wildman et al., 1992).

Looking at the problems regarding teacher retention, Chapman (1983) proposed that little research has addressed, other than in an anecdotal way, the important factors associated with teacher retention; therefore, much of the research that is conducted is not cumulative in its impact.

Murnane, Singer, and Willett (1988) reported other concerns for teacher supply and methodological implications for research. They believed that "a promising research approach is to examine how policies influence teachers' careers" (p. 29) and to examine the mechanisms through which policies may have their impact. To achieve this, the researchers proposed what they call a "new and powerful methodology, proportional hazards modeling" (p. 29), and recommended its use in isolating the influences of a particular policy, such as a mentoring program, on duration in teaching from the many other factors that influence duration.

These concerns, along with others, have led some in the field of teacher education to develop programs that are based on conceptual frameworks with strong research bases. A few of those more clearly described in the literature are presented.

Barnes (1987) took a strong stand regarding the conceptual basis for programs with thematic teacher education programs as her focus. She maintained that the cornerstone of a thematic program is its conceptual framework, and she described a framework that presents the program's assumptions, philosophy, and research base and that outlines the implications of that knowledge for teaching. The conceptual framework described how the program is organized to achieve the desired outcomes. She believed that the important factor is not what the theme is, per se, but that the theme provides a clear and distinctive conception of teaching and is firmly grounded in research and understanding of effective teaching practice. Barnes also recommended that more research studies are needed that focus directly on the impact of thematic programs or the development of the schemata of teacher candidates. Barnes defined schemata to mean "complex cognitive structures that include both theoretical and practical knowledge and an understanding of the interrelatedness of these knowledge sources for informing judgement and action" (1987, p. 17). Adopting thematic programs for the preservice and in-service training of teachers could be most helpful in improving the assistance components of new teacher programs.

In reviewing mentoring programs, Little (1990) argued that "rhetoric and action have nonetheless outpaced both conceptual development and empirical warrant" (p. 297). She also reported that many of the available studies of mentoring are based on a small number of sites and concluded that there is limited evidence of systematic variation in the contextual features that most possibly will affect the outcomes of the programs.

One of the major concerns in the literature regarding mentoring programs is that no structural studies compare formal mentor arrangements with the conditions, contexts, dynamics, and consequences of mentor relations that naturally occur. Most of the studies focus on the early stages of implementation of programs and role development. Longitudinal designs that clearly distinguish between short-term and long-term effects on both the individual and the institutions are needed. Gathering data on systematic examinations of the actual practices and circumstances of mentoring would greatly enhance the understanding of the role of the support provider for existing and future programs. Observations of the work of mentors are infrequent in study designs and even more lacking in published reports; however, Little stated that "The sheer scale of practical experimentation with mentor roles suggests that methodological remedies, like theoretical sophistication, are well within reach" (1990, p. 344).

A review of the literature also reveals that several investigators have hypothesized that an individual's support system helps to moderate or buffer the effects of stress on one's psychological state and physical well-being (Bertoch et al., 1989; Esteve & Fracchia, 1986; Gold & Roth, 1993). To meet these needs, support programs have rapidly developed across the country with the purpose of assisting new teachers in making adjustments from student to teacher and in handling the stress that is so great during the initial imprinting stage.

Although there is evidence that assistance through support providers, such as mentors, can buffer the psychological and physical impacts of the first years of teaching, the evidence needs to be examined from a more detailed theoretical framework. The conceptualizations and operationalizations of support need to be defined and more thoroughly researched to provide new information as programs are improved and new programs are developed.

Research and development in new teacher support will require significant money from society. The outcomes in terms of training new teachers, rewarding and inspiring experienced teachers, and benefiting youth are well worth the time and investment.

EMERGING CONCEPTIONS AND PROMISING PRACTICES

Assisting beginning teachers in their development toward becoming competent professionals is critically important and includes the expertise of many disciplines. The new teacher's developmental growth, attitudes, feelings, expectations, style of teaching, and ability to adjust to the school environment as a professional must all be taken into consideration. Two disciplines that provide assistance in these areas are sociology and psychology.

Links to Sociological and Psychological Foundations

Lacey (1977) and Lortie (1975), in their research on teacher socialization, showed that becoming a teacher is not a simple transition from one role to another. What they did find was that this transition is a social process that involves complex interactions between and among new teachers and experienced teachers and their social situations. Zeichner and Gore (1990) characterized teacher socialization as "contradictory and dialectical" and "situated within the broader context of institutions, society, culture, and history" (p. 343). As this complex view of socialization has developed within the induction literature, the original conception of induction has broadened and grown.

More research is needed regarding how teachers are socialized at various points in their careers. This is especially true where there is increasing agreement regarding the highly interactive nature of the socialization process and about the constant interplay between constraint and choice in the process of learning to teach (Zeichner & Gore, 1990).

As the term *socialization* is redefined through continued research and findings from these studies are applied to future induction programs, new teachers' lives will benefit as will the lives of their students. A number of essential dimensions must be recognized in assisting new teachers, with some being more evident than others. For example, pedagogical, curricular, intercultural, and logistical areas are all important dimensions where new teachers have need of assistance and are easily identified.

Yet, one dimension, psychological, has not been identified for what it is; rather, it has been used synonymously with emotional support and thus has not been correctly defined or utilized. Emotional support has been defined throughout the literature as "empathic listening" or "giving encouragement."

It is necessary to offer empathy through listening and to reflect on the new teacher's feelings; however, identifying new teachers' psychological needs through assessment instruments and planning an individualized program to meet these needs (Gold & Roth, 1993) is very different from just offering empathic listening and giving encouragement. It is essential that induction programs clarify the difference between emotional support and psychological support and include specific training in giving psychological support to new teachers.

Many beginning teachers identify psychological support as their greatest area of need (Murphy, Merseth, & Morey, 1990) and express their desire for help with their own inability to handle the psychological pressures of their first years of teaching.

A number of professionals have recognized the necessity for offering psychological support. Roth (1990) placed the psychological needs of teachers as the highest need in his conceptual model of induction years. Theis-Sprinthall and Gerler (1990) worked with preservice teachers to prepare more psychologically mature teachers, and Gold and Roth (1993) proposed training in psychological support for mentor teachers. The essential area of psychological support clearly needs to have a prominent place in induction programs.

Case Studies

The use of case studies in teacher induction programs is in its infancy; however, proposals for the use of cases in educating teachers has its roots as far back as 1933. Interest in cases has been renewed, yet the "case literature" in teaching is still limited.

There are those who believe that the use of case studies for mentor teachers as they engage beginning teachers in the process of solving complex teaching problems is an effective method (Carter, 1988; Shulman & Colbert, 1987). The positive aspects of case studies include: (1) the cases could become a permanent professional school library for teachers, (2) they could be a valuable part of teacher induction programs, (3) teachers could use the case studies to improve their teaching, (4) they serve as useful tools to engage new teachers in analyzing situations and gaining insight, and (5) they can promote the professional growth of new teachers and experienced teachers. In support of case knowledge Sykes and Bird (1992) stated that "the most effective way to represent knowledge in teaching is through cases that capture both the routines and the problematic, unique situations that call for reflection, analysis, and continued inquiry" (p. 44).

Future development of professional case literature could give teachers insight as they learn from one another throughout the country. It can also act as a catalyst for discussion and change. A form of educational discourse that focuses on experiences and reflections of thinking and learning could assist teacher development in numerous ways. For more about cases in teacher education, readers are referred to Chapter 31 of this handbook by Merseth (1996).

Learning-to-Mentor Studies

Mentor programs have spread rapidly since the mid-1980s. With the pressure to move quickly following policy making, little or nothing was gained by haste in implementing many of the mentor programs. Too often the time left by the state for planning and implementation of the mentor program was limited. As a result of the many pressures, Little (1990) concluded that "the problem is exacerbated when the pace of implementation outstrips the human and material resources available to manage the change" (p. 305).

With concern regarding the effectiveness of a mentor's performance, along with selection procedures for mentors, many states and districts have begun to provide mentors with skill training. Through this training, mentors sometimes are helped to make accessible their own knowledge of curriculum, instruction, and classroom management. A large share of most training programs includes communication skills, consultation strategies, and classroom observation techniques (Little & Nelson, 1988). In fact, specialized training for mentors has become an increasingly common and prominent component of role development (Thies-Sprinthall, 1986).

As early programs got under way, there were widespread disputes regarding the need for organized training and support; however, structured training and support appeared more likely where mentoring was linked to a district goal or to a state policy. Only rarely was a mentor required to have experience in mentor-like capacities prior to selection in most programs. Few if any criteria for selection were used. In reviewing the literature, "there are virtually no studies that trace the contributions made by postselection training to the subsequent performance of the mentor, or to their success in relationships with teachers or administrators. No studies compare mentors who receive training with those who are left to their own resources" (Little, 1990, p. 309).

There also is a lack of research regarding the specialized training of mentors in giving psychological support to new teachers. There are also no studies in offering psychological support to mentors as part of their own well-being. There is mention of offering emotional support, even though this is a small percentage of officially recorded support activities.

The present inadequacies of teacher induction have forced mentoring to develop. Problems in selection and training of mentors have increased. What is greatly needed in the research are studies that are designed to examine mentoring and the degree to which it is congruent with other forms of support in assisting beginning teachers. Because mentoring in education has originated from inadequacies in the induction of teachers, the rationales must be tested. The outcomes would provide education with a profile of those teachers whose professional record is highly regarded and who have the acceptance and respect from other teachers. The major gains for the profession would be career retention and enhanced commitment and concomitant long-term benefits of contributions to the profession.

The Growing Knowledge Base for Beginning Teachers

While teacher induction programs are beginning to look more carefully at what beginning teachers need, one critical area is a structured knowledge base for new teachers. Educators hold different views regarding what should be included at different points in a teacher's formal education; however, the successful completion of a college program is not sufficient evidence of an individual's knowledge nor of his or her ability to practice what is learned.

Questions arise in the induction literature regarding a new teacher's understandings of teaching, subject matter, learning, and learners, as well as how these are applied during the teaching-learning process. As new teachers begin to use the knowledge they have acquired, they often voice their concerns regarding how students think and understand the content. What they are expressing is a need to know how to represent or present specific content to specific students. To meet this need, teachers must have another kind of subject-specific knowledge. They need a special blend of content and pedagogy, what Shulman (1987) referred to as "pedagogical content knowledge." It includes useful ways to conceptualize and represent commonly taught topics in a given subject. To do this, new teachers need to be able to (1) store information, (2) use information as a format into which they can place new information so that it can be comprehended, (3) apply this as they direct their thinking and teaching, and (4) fill in the missing parts of their knowledge bank. Thus, they need to be able to observe what is happening, interpret situations, consider alternatives, and build elaborate schemata to connect the theoretical and practical knowledge into their teaching.

To assist beginning teachers in this process, educators are beginning to recognize the need to select more carefully the knowledge and experiences they include in their initial teacher preparation programs (Barnes, 1987). Some of the major questions that must be considered by educators center around what knowledge and experiences should be included in preparation programs that will enhance the training of teachers and will have long-term effects.

These are complex issues to be decided; however, "the task must be undertaken if teacher educators hope to increase the power of their interventions. If the goal is to help teachers develop meaningful frameworks for teaching, then how teacher educators think about and draw from relevant domains of knowledge makes a difference" (Barnes, 1989, p. 20).

Some argue that the research on teachers' pedagogical thoughts, judgments, decisions, and behavior are neglected aspects of teacher education and induction (Lawson, 1992). Others state that the subject-matter issue is critically important for many beginning teachers who lack preparation in this area and that those who do have some expertise in the content they teach may not be proficient in transforming it in ways their students can comprehend (Huling-Austin, 1992).

Induction programs cannot and will not create a knowledge base for beginning teachers by themselves. Universities and the schools will need to work together in teacher preparation and in-service programs to meet the challenges facing beginning teachers in transforming their knowledge of the subject matter into a form of knowledge that is appropriate for their students and for the specific task of teaching. New teachers will also need to gain knowledge of learners and learning, of curriculum and context, of goals and objectives, and of pedagogy.

CONCLUSION

Embedded in each of the topics of attrition, mentoring, induction, and support are a number of issues that form complex webs in terms of both depth and breadth of interaction. This makes formulating conclusions particularly problematic.

This chapter began with a review of the disconcerting statistics indicating that many new teachers leave early in their careers. These data are essential in understanding attrition decisions to address beginning teacher dropout and to plan programs of support. Many significant issues are identified for further study. The relationship of burnout to the factors associated with attrition is also in need of further investigation and application of findings to new teacher support.

An area that particularly needs attention is the nature of support for new teachers. Much of the research on support programs has taken the form of policy studies or program evaluation that may or may not assist new teachers in areas where they need the most help. It is essential that the more focused questions regarding in-depth studies on the context, content, process, and consequences of providing support be addressed if the support components of programs are to be effective. In addition, it is necessary to learn why experienced teachers choose mentoring positions, what rewards they find in the role both short term and over time, and how they can significantly influence the profession in this role.

Understanding how support providers assist new teachers, as well as analyzing the personal interactions between the two, would provide essential data for future program planning. The characteristics of support providers who are sought out by new teachers also need investigation. Clarifying the characteristics of teachers that prompt new teachers to ask them for help would add greatly to assisting in the selection and training of support providers.

Examination of different approaches to support could add significantly in offering help to new teachers. Two related approaches are suggested. The first is the personalized approach where new teachers are encouraged to develop self-efficacy and to come to terms with their own personal and professional needs as well as learning ways of meeting them. They also acquire meaning related to their teaching and develop their own style of teaching. Processes for creating a supportive learning environment to promote growth are encouraged, and psychological maturity as well as pedagogical expertise are emphasized.

The second approach is the technical and experiential, which focuses on the technical skills of teaching and relies heavily on apprenticeship where the mentor is a key figure. An emphasis here is given to knowledge in the core disciplines, selective training, and rigorous standards.

How each approach perceives its primary function will dictate its focus. Whether the primary function is perceived to be giving instructional support to new teachers or offering personal and professional support will dictate the direction and the consequences. Studies conducted on each approach could lead to a blending of the strengths of each whereby they mutually enhance the total development of the new teacher instead of separating the professional from the personal. Either approach alone is an imperfect model; both are needed in enhancing the

development of new professionals and helping to improve the profession. Therefore, researching the strengths and weaknesses of each approach, as well as their combined effects, would assist in developing new support programs and revitalizing existing ones.

Along with conducting research on these two major approaches, relationships between support providers and new teachers must be given careful study. Social support and psychological support need to be separately defined and evaluated along with studying the effects of each on a new teacher's thinking and teaching performance. At the same time, policy and programs in and of themselves must not remain the primary concerns of induction as they often are now. The new teacher must remain the central focus, not just in thought but in practice. An important question to pursue is how policy can help to create the future of the profession through the vehicle of initiating competent individuals into the profession.

From a different perspective, the entire process of imprinting that takes place in the life of the new teacher has been neglected in the literature. Three types of imprinting are noted here that describe how teachers learn how to teach and assume the responsibilities of teaching. The first of these is described by Lortie (1975) who argued the position on teacher socialization that occurs through the internalization (largely unconscious) of teaching models during thousands of hours spent as students in close contact with teachers. He believed the latent culture acquired, or as Zeichner and Gore (1990) stated, "the students' predispositions" (p. 332), is the major influence in shaping the new teacher's conceptions of the teaching role and role performance.

In the 1980s, Tabechnick and Zeichner (1984) reported that student teachers in their study were encouraged to clarify their perspectives toward teaching and to develop in a direction that was consistent with their own perspectives that they brought to student teaching. At the same time it was reported that there were underlying and contradictory messages that urged the students to conform and to adapt as smoothly as possible to the practices carried out in the schools. For some student teachers in their sample, it was reported that they generally acted in ways required of them in their teaching situation while they maintained strong private reservations about needing to do so. At the end of the student teaching assignment, their perspectives remained at essentially the same place as they had been at the beginning. Their findings generally supported the position of Lortie (1986) who argued that student teaching plays little part in altering the course set by anticipatory socialization.

A second type of imprinting, in contrast to Lortie's beliefs, takes place during the teacher preparation socialization period. This position maintains that teacher preparation at the university level does have considerable impact on the attitudes and practices of beginning teachers. This is a fundamental premise of teacher preparation programs. In a review of empirical research on the process of teacher socialization of elementary and secondary school teachers throughout the preservice and inservice phases, Staton and Hunt (1992) concluded that the prior experience (or imprinting) prospective teachers bring to the preservice setting initially influences their teaching. As these teachers continue through their preservice and in-service teaching, they communicate continuously with others and make changes (affective, cognitive, and behavioral) as a routine part of the socialization process. The authors (Staton & Hunt, 1992) believed that the changes during this socialization process occur "through an interplay among internally held beliefs, the forces of the context as communicated through agents, and the actions one takes in consideration of these forces" (p. 131). This suggests that imprinting does take place through socialization during the teacher preparation process.

Although changes are being made in areas such as attitudes, beliefs, and behavior, the conditions under which this may be perceived as "imprinting" need further clarification. As noted earlier, imprinting occurs during a "specific critical period" (Hess & Petrovich, 1977, p. 2). When one enters a new environment, culture, or ecosystem, for example, this is a specific critical period. Teacher education students entering full-time teaching are encountering a new environment and role relationship and are passing through a specific critical period often characterized by reality shock. They also are making changes through socialization, just as they did in preservice preparation, as noted by Staton and Hunt. The perceptions, beliefs, behaviors, and attitudes acquired are internalized as innate patterns. Thus the imprinting phenomenon is evident in the lives of new teachers.

The nature of the initial experiences in teaching and the potential influence on these through viable support are therefore of considerable importance. Being able to assess beginning teachers' initial impressions of their instructional and interpersonal approaches and guiding them through the socialization process will play an important part in their career. The need for the right types of support during these critical periods is essential to the new teacher's personal and professional growth.

Lastly, the imprinting that takes place in the first months of the first year of teaching anchors the feelings and perceptions of new teachers in powerful ways. When the majority of the experiences with principals, other teachers, and students are disappointing and, in some cases, overwhelming, the negative feelings and experiences can be so intense that previous training and experiences are blocked out and strong negative feelings become dominant. This is very similar to the pain-pleasure principle in which pain cancels feelings of pleasure. When these types of situations occur, most beginning teachers struggle just to survive the situation. If the negative experiences and feelings continue, many new teachers leave teaching in order to survive. The depth of research on attrition may well be attesting to this fact. Because new teachers are often placed in assignments that are less than desirable, the right type of support is essential if they are to learn how to adjust to these challenging types of situations. Gathering information on how mentors can make a difference in the imprinting process of new teachers will be extremely helpful.

Although intuitively and experientially supported, there is little empirical evidence found in the literature on the impact of the beginning years regarding teacher's perceptions and conceptions of the role of teaching. In fact, there has been considerable misconception regarding how these teachers are internalizing the act of teaching when they perceive the situation to be threatening and unfulfilling. Learning the perceptions that new teachers have regarding their role as teacher and understanding how they perceive the totality of the experience is essential.

Receiving support in difficult situations can help new teachers to identify negative feelings and cope with the psychological trauma they are experiencing. With the right kinds of support to help them understand the imprinting process they are going through and with clarification of how they can apply the teaching techniques they have already learned, new teachers will be better equipped to handle the pressures and to develop their own style of teaching. Research on how the new teacher imprints needs greater attention, and the findings should be used by educators to clarify for new teachers the process they are involved in and how they can interpret and handle their initial perceptions of teaching and the teaching environment.

In recent years there has been much written regarding beginning teacher support. The majority of this literature has emphasized instructional support and has guided the direction of many of the support programs now in existence. Many new teachers have received assistance from this type of support and it has been helpful to some extent. At the same time, the area of personal-psychological support has been neglected. The major thesis of this chapter is that attention to meeting both the instructional and the psychological needs of teachers must be addressed both in research and in practice. Because educators tend to focus mainly on the instructional aspects of teaching, it would be beneficial to collaborate with researchers and members of the counseling and psychology communities to redesign research and programs that focus on the personal and psychological needs of new teachers as well.

Because concepts of support are diverse and are often conflicting, more rigorous research is needed to validate and clarify contributions of each. These types of investigations need to focus on providing greater understanding of new teachers' personal and professional needs. To accomplish this, a critical issue needing attention is the role of induction in relation to precedent and antecedent events. Focus on the antecedent factors should include such considerations as the role of induction in assisting the new teacher in processes such as becoming a self-learner, engaging in analysis of one's own instruction, and directing one's own personal and professional development. The function thus is to develop attitudes and strategies to guide professional development throughout a career.

If support is operating out of a deficit model, then it is assumed that the training would include the types of basic teaching skills new teachers did not receive in the preservice period. This makes it necessary to incorporate techniques and concepts needed for survival, and the teacher would be viewed as a technician. Yet, if the induction period is built out of a professional continuum, then the skills learned during the preservice training would be enhanced and the teacher's needs and potential for professional growth would be emphasized during this time. The induction period would include an individualized form of support where the new teacher is offered opportunities for personal and professional growth. Early experiences that had stored up countless impressions of teaching and the role of the teacher would be clarified, analyzed, and improved upon. With the right types of support, new teachers would develop new impressions that go far beyond survival techniques. They would be given opportunities to learn more effective and enduring teaching practices, as well as be encouraged and guided to develop into mature professionals. The conceptual models that emerge from such inquiry can guide decisions regarding the types of support programs to be developed and the types of support to be offered to new teachers.

Finally, where do we as a profession go from here? One means of providing guidance is to create a vision of the future that captures the nature of programs that are hoped for and needed. An element of that vision is beginning teacher support that provides assistance for developing psychological maturity for new teachers. The vision proposed throughout this chapter promotes programs that are committed to assessing psychological and instructional needs of new teachers and to offering assistance in developing potential in both of these areas. New support programs will be actively engaged in inquiry and will be guided by a knowledge base derived from research in the areas of psychology, sociology, teacher development, teacher effectiveness, content pedagogy, induction, and attrition. The vision includes educators who welcome change as both a chal-

lenge and an opportunity to develop more effective practices for new teachers and an environment where change is considered, encouraged, and expertly carried out.

Perhaps the most critical element in this vision is one of perspective that embodies the principle of "totality of experience." This principle recognizes that beginning teachers are affected by the impact of all of the elements in their environment during these impressionable years. Furthermore, these factors interact in a myriad of ways to create a total experience. To focus on one or only a few of these is insufficient. The entire life space of the teacher must be considered. In essence, the focus is on what the individual experiences in the physical, pedagogical, sociological, and psychological domains.

As we educators discover the constructs, empower the system, and assist the beginning teacher toward becoming more emotionally and professionally adept, we also build the profession.

References

Anderson, E. M., & Shannon, A. L. (1988). Toward a conceptualization of mentoring. *Journal of Teacher Education, 39*(1), 38–42.

Anderson, M. B. G. (1981). A study of the differences among perceived need deficiencies, perceived burnout, and select background variables for classroom teachers. (Doctoral dissertation, University of Connecticut, 1980). *Dissertation Abstracts International, 41*(10), 4218A.

Anderson, T. E., Jr. (1991). *Induction program for beginning teachers.* Austin, TX: State Board of Education.

Andrews, T. E. (Ed.). (1994). *The NASDTEC manual 1994–1995.* Dubuque, IA: Kendall/Hunt.

Banks, S. R., & Necco, E. G. (1990). The effects of special education category and type of training on job burnout in special education teachers. *Teacher Education and Special Education, 13*(3–4), 187–191.

Barnes, H. L. (1987). The conceptual basis for thematic teacher education programs. *Journal of Teacher Education, 38*(4), 13–18.

Barnes, H. L. (1989). Structuring knowledge for beginning teaching. In M. C. Reynolds (Ed.), *Knowledge base for the beginning teacher* (pp. 13–22). New York: Pergamon Press.

Berry, B., Noblit, G. W., & Hare, R. D. (1985). A qualitative critique of teacher labor market studies. *The Urban Review, 17*(2), 98–110.

Bertoch, M. R., Nielsen, E. C., Curley, J. R., & Borg, W. R. (1989). Reducing teacher stress. *The Journal of Experimental Education, 57*(2), 117–128.

Bey, T. M. (1990). A new knowledge base for an old practice. In T. M. Bey & C. T. Holmes (Eds.), *Mentoring: Developing successful new teachers* (pp. 51–73). Reston, VA: Association of Teacher Educators.

Billingsley, B. W., & Cross, L. H. (1991). Teacher's decisions to transfer from special to general education. *The Journal of Special Education, 24*(4), 496–511.

Bird, T. (1986). *The mentors' dilemma.* San Francisco: Far West Laboratory for Educational Research and Development.

Bird, T., & Alspaugh, D. (1986). *1985 survey of district coordinators for the California Mentor Teacher Program.* San Francisco: Far West Laboratory for Educational Research and Development.

Bird, T., & Little, J. W. (1985). *From teacher to leader.* San Francisco: Far West Laboratory for Educational Research and Development.

Bloland, P. A., & Selby, T. J. (1980). Factors associated with career change among secondary school teachers: A review of the literature. *Educational Research Quarterly, 5*(3), 13–24.

Bobbitt, S. A., Faupel, E., & Burns, S. (1991). *Characteristics of stayers, movers, and leavers: Results from the Teacher Followup Survey, 1988–89.* Washington, DC: Office of Educational Research and Improvement.

Bogenschild, E. G., Lauritzen, P., & Metzke, L. (1988). *A study of teacher attrition.* Reston, VA: National Clearinghouse for Professionals in Special Education.

Bolam, R. (1987). Induction of beginning teachers. In M. J. Dunkin (Ed.), *The international encyclopedia of teaching and teacher education* (pp. 745–757). Oxford: Pergamon.

Borko, H. (1986). Clinical teacher education: The induction years. In J. V. Hoffman & S. A. Edwards (Eds.), *Reality and reform in clinical teacher education* (pp. 45–63). New York: Random House.

Bova, B. M., & Phillips, R. R. (1984). Mentoring as a learning experience for adults. *Journal of Teacher Education, 35*(3), 16–20.

Brooks, D. M. (Ed.). (1987). *Teacher induction: A new beginning.* Reston, VA: Association of Teacher Educators.

Bull, G., Harris, J., Lloyd, J., & Short, J. (1989). The electronic academical village. *Journal of Teacher Education, 40*(4), 27–31.

Burke, R. J., & Greenglass, E. R. (1989). Psychological burnout among men and women in teaching: An examination of the Cherniss Model. *Human Relations, 42*(3), 261–273.

Byrne, B. M. (1991). Burnout: Investigating the impact of background variables for elementary, intermediate, secondary, and university educators. *Teaching and Teacher Education, 7*(2), 197–209.

Carnegie Foundation for the Advancement of Teaching. (1988). *The condition of teaching: A state-by-state analysis.* Princeton, NJ: Author.

Carnegie Foundation for the Advancement of Teaching. (1990). *The condition of teaching: A state-by-state analysis.* Princeton, NJ: Author.

Carter, K. (1988). Using cases to frame mentor-novice conversations about teaching. *Theory Into Practice, 27*(3), 214–222.

Casey, J. M., & Roth, R. A. (1991–1992). An impact analysis of technology-based support in student teaching. *Teacher Education and Practice, 7*(2), 23–30.

Chapman, D. W. (1983). A model of the influences on teacher retention. *Journal of Teacher Education, 34*(5), 43–49.

Chapman, D. W. (1984). Teacher retention: The test of a model. *American Educational Research Journal, 21*(3), 645–658.

Chapman, D. W., & Green, M. S. (1986). Teacher retention: A further examination. *Journal of Educational Research, 79*(5), 273–279.

Chapman, D. W., & Hutcheson, S. M. (1982). Attrition from teaching careers: A discriminant analysis. *American Educational Research Journal, 19*(1), 93–105.

Cherniss, C. (1980). *Professional burnout in human service organizations*. New York: Praeger.

Choy, S. P., Bobbitt, S. A., Henke, R. R., Medrich, E. R., Horn, L. J., & Lieberman, J. (1993). *America's teachers: Profile of a profession* (pp. 23–46). Washington, DC: U.S. Department of Education.

Clandinin, D. J. (1985). Personal practical knowledge: A study of teachers' classroom images. *Curriculum Inquiry, 15*(4), 361–385.

Colbert, J. A., & Wolff, D. E. (1992). Surviving in urban schools: A collaborative model for a beginning teacher support system. *Journal of Teacher Education, 43*(3), 193–199.

Commission on Teacher Credentialing. (1993a). *Beginning teacher support and assessment program descriptions: Year one*. Sacramento: California Department of Education.

Commission on Teacher Credentialing. (1993b). *Beginning teacher support and assessment program: Local programs of beginning teacher support and assessment-purposes and accomplishments*. Sacramento: California Department of Education.

Crosser, S., Griggs, I. L., & Haynes, M. (1994, February). *Status of beginning teacher support programs in NCATE accredited institutions*. Paper presented at the annual meeting of the American Association of Colleges for Teacher Education, Chicago.

Darling-Hammond, L. (1984). *Beyond the commission reports: The coming crisis in teaching*. Santa Monica: Rand Corporation.

Darling-Hammond, L., Hudson, L., & Kirby, S. N. (1989). *Redesigning teacher education: Opening the door for new recruits to science and mathematics teaching*. (Report No. ISBN-0-8330-0957-5) Santa Monica: Rand Corporation. (ERIC Document Reproduction Service No. ED 309 144)

Dimock, G. E. (1989). *The unity of the Odyssey*. Amherst: The University of Massachusetts Press.

Elam, S. M. (1984). *The Phi Delta Kappan Gallup Polls of attitudes toward education 1969–1984: A topical summary*. (Report No. ISBN-0-87367-792-7) Bloomington, IN: Phi Delta Kappa. (ERIC Document Reproduction Service No. ED 252 573)

Elam, S. M. (1989). The second Gallup/Phi Delta Kappa poll of teachers' attitudes toward the public schools. *Phi Delta Kappan, 70*(10), 785–798.

Elam, S. M., Rose, L. C., & Gallup, A. M. (1993). The 25th annual Phi Delta Kappa/Gallup poll of the public's attitudes toward the public schools. *Phi Delta Kappan, 75*(2), 137–152.

Elliott, P., & Steinkellner, L. (1979). Weaknesses in in-service and pre-service teacher training. *The Clearing House, 52*(9), 421–423.

Ellis, J., Klagholz, L., Schechter, E., & Newman, J. (1991). *Provisional teacher program implementation guidelines*. Trenton, NJ: State Department of Education.

Elmore, R. (1989, March). *Issues of policy and practice in mentor programs*. Paper presented at the annual meeting of the American Educational Research Association, San Francisco.

Enz, B. J. (1992). Guidelines for selecting mentors and creating an environment for mentoring. In T. M. Bey & C. T. Holmes (Eds.), *Mentoring: Contemporary principles and issues* (pp. 65–78). Reston, VA: Association of Teacher Educators.

Estes, G. D., Stansbury, K., & Long, C. (1990). Beginning teacher assessment activities and developments in California. In A. I. Morey & D. S. Murphy (Eds.), *Designing programs for new teachers: The California experience* (pp. 97–106). San Francisco: Far West Laboratory for Educational Research and Development.

Esteve, J. M., & Fracchia, A. F. B. (1986). Inoculation against stress: A technique for beginning teachers. *European Journal of Teacher Education, 9*(3), 261–269.

Fagan, M. M., & Walter, G. (1982). Mentoring among teachers. *Journal of Educational Research, 76*(2), 113–118.

Farber, B. A. (1991). *Crisis in education: Stress and burnout in the American teacher*. San Francisco: Jossey-Bass.

Featherstone, H. (1992). *Learning from the first years of classroom teaching: The journey in, the journey out*. East Lansing: Michigan State University, National Center for Research on Teacher Learning.

Feiman-Nemser, S. (1992). *Helping novices learn to teach: Lessons from an experienced support teacher* (Report No. 91-6). East Lansing: Michigan State University, National Center for Research on Teacher Learning.

Feiman-Nemser, S., Parker, M. B., & Zeichner, K. (1992). *Are mentor teachers teacher educators?* (Report No. 92-11). East Lansing: Michigan State University, The National Center for Research on Teacher Learning.

Fenstermacher, G. D. (1990). The place of alternative certification education of teachers. *Peabody Journal of Education, 67*(3), 155–185.

Fox, S. M., & Singletary, T. J. (1986). Deductions about supportive induction. *Journal of Teacher Education, 37*(1), 12–15.

Freudenberger, H. J. (1973). The psychologist in a free clinic setting: An alternative model in health care. *Psychotherapy: Theory, Research, and Practice, 10*(1), 52–61.

Friedman, I. A. (1991). High- and low-burnout schools: School culture aspects of teacher burnout. *Journal of Educational Research, 84*(6), 325–333.

Friesen, D., Prokop, C. M., & Sarros, J. C. (1988). Why teachers burn out. *Educational Research Quarterly, 12*(3), 9–19.

Fuller, F. F. (1969). Concerns of teachers: A developmental conceptualization. *American Educational Research Journal, 6*(2), 207–226.

Galvez-Hjornevik, C. (1986). Mentoring among teachers: A review of the literature. *Journal of Teacher Education, 37*(1), 6–11.

Ganser, T. (1993, February). *How mentors describe and categorized their ideas about mentoring roles, benefits of mentoring, and obstacles to mentoring*. Paper presented at the annual meeting of the Association of Teacher Educators, Los Angeles.

Garrett, S. (1993). *Entry-year assistance program*. Oklahoma City: Oklahoma State Department of Education.

Garrett, S. (1994). *Entry-year assistance program packet 1994–95*. Oklahoma City: Oklahoma State Department of Education.

Gehrke, N. J., & Kay, R. S. (1984). The socialization of beginning teachers through mentor-protege relationships. *Journal of Teacher Education, 35*(3), 21–24.

Glidewell, J. C., Tucker, S., Todt, M., & Cox, S. (1983). Professional support systems: The teaching profession. In A. Nadler, J. D. Fisher, & B. M. Depaulo (Eds.), *New directions in helping: Vol. 3. Applied perspectives on help-seeking and receiving* (pp. 189–212). New York: Academic Press.

Gold, Y. (1984). The factorial validity of the Maslach Burnout Inventory in a sample of California elementary and junior high school classroom teachers. *Educational and Psychological Measurement, 44*(4), 1009–1016.

Gold, Y. (1985). The relationship of six personal and life history variables to standing on three dimensions of the Maslach Burnout Inventory in a sample of elementary and junior high school teachers. *Educational and Psychological Measurement, 45*(2), 377–387.

Gold, Y. (1987). Stress reduction programs to prevent teacher burnout. *Education, 107*(3), 338–340.

Gold, Y. (1989). Reducing stress and burnout through induction programs. *Action in Teacher Education, 11*(3), 66–70.

Gold, Y. (1990, June). *Treatment of stress and prevention of burnout through psychological support for beginning teachers*. Keynote address at an advanced leadership academy on planning and implementing induction, internships, mentoring and beginning teacher programs. Sponsored by the Association of Teacher Educators &

National Academy for Leadership in Teacher Education, Anaheim, CA.

Gold, Y. (1992). Psychological support for mentors and beginning teachers: A critical dimension. In T. M. Bey & C. T. Holmes (Eds.), *Mentoring: Contemporary principles and issues* (pp. 25–34). Reston, VA: Association of Teacher Educators.

Gold, Y., & Roth, R. A. (1993). *Teachers managing stress and preventing burnout: The professional health solution.* London: Falmer Press.

Gold, Y., Roth, R. A., Wright, C. R., & Michael, W. B. (1991). The relationship of scores of the educators survey, a modified version of the Maslach Burnout Inventory, to three teaching-related variables for a sample of 133 beginning teachers. *Educational and Psychological Measurement, 51*(2), 429–438.

Gold, Y., Roth, R. A., Wright, C. R., Michael, W. B., & Chen, C. Y. (1992). The factorial validity of a teacher burnout measure (educators survey) administered to a sample of beginning teachers in elementary and secondary schools in California. *Educational and Psychological Measurement, 52*(3), 761–768.

Gomez, D. L., & Grobe, R. P. (1990, April). *Three years of alternative certification in Dallas: Where are we?* Paper presented at the annual meeting of the American Educational Research Association, Boston.

Gray, W. A., & Gray, M. M. (1985). Synthesis of research on mentoring beginning teachers. *Educational Leadership, 43*(3), 37–43.

Grissmer, D. W., & Kirby, S. N. (1987). *Teacher attrition: The uphill climb to staff the nation's schools* (Report No. ISBN-0-8330-0869-2). Santa Monica, CA: Rand Corporation. (ERIC Document Reproduction Service No. ED 291 735)

Gross, A. E., & McMullen, P. A. (1983). Models of the help-seeking process. In A. Nadler, J. D. Fisher, & B. M. Depaulo (Eds.), *New directions in helping: Vol. 2. Helping-seeking* (pp. 45–70). New York: Academic Press.

Grossman, P. L., Wilson, S. M., & Shulman, L. S. (1989). Teachers of substance: Subject matter knowledge for teaching. In M. C. Reynolds (Ed.), *Knowledge base for the beginning teacher* (pp. 23–36). New York: Pergamon.

Haberman, M. (1985). What knowledge is of most worth to teachers? A knowledge-use perspective. *Teaching and Teacher Education, 1*(3), 251–262.

Hafner, A. L., & Alsalam, N. (1989, March). *An event analysis of entry, and re-entry into the teaching profession: Evidence from the high school class of 1972.* Paper presented at the annual meeting of the American Educational Research Association, San Francisco.

Hafner, A., & Owings, J. (1991). *Analysis report of careers in teaching: Following members of the high school class of 1972 in and out of teaching.* Washington, DC: U.S. Department of Education, Office of Educational Research and Improvement. (Preport No. NCES 91-470)

Hardcastle, B. (1988). Spiritual connections: Proteges' reflections on significant mentorships. *Theory Into Practice, 27*(3), 201–208.

Harris, L., and Associates. (1987). *The Metropolitan Life Survey of the American Teacher: Strengthening links between home and school.* New York: Metropolitan Life Insurance.

Harris, L., and Associates. (1988). *The Metropolitan Life Survey of the American Teacher: Strengthening the relationship between teachers and students.* New York: Metropolitan Life Insurance.

Harris, L., and Associates. (1992). *The Metropolitan Life Survey of the American Teacher. The second year: New teachers' expectations and ideals.* New York: Metropolitan Life Insurance.

Harris, L., and Associates. (1993). *The Metropolitan Life Survey of the American Teacher: Violence in America's public schools.* New York: Metropolitan Life Insurance.

Hart, A. W. (1990). Impacts of the school social unit on teacher authority during work redesign. *American Educational Reseach Journal, 27*(3), 503–532.

Hart, A. W., & Murphy, M. J. (1990). New teachers react to redesigned teacher work. *American Journal of Education, 98*(3), 224–250.

Hawk, P., & Robards, S. (1987). Statewide teacher induction programs. In D. M. Brooks (Ed.), *Teacher induction: A new beginning* (pp. 33–43). Reston, VA: Association of Teacher Educators.

Healy, C. C., & Welchert, A. J. (1990). Mentoring relations: A definition to advance research and practice. *Educational Research, 19*(9), 17–21.

Heller, M. P., & Sindelar, N. W. (1991). *Developing an effective teacher mentor program.* Bloomington, IN: Phi Delta Kappa Educational Foundation.

Hess, E. H., & Petrovich, S. B. (1977). *Imprinting.* Stroudsburg, PA: Dowden, Hutchinson & Ross.

Heyns, B. (1988). Educational defectors: A first look at teacher attrition in the NLS-72. *Educational Researcher, 17*(3), 24–32.

Hock, R. R. (1988). Professional burnout among public school teachers. *Public Personnel Management, 17*(2), 167–189.

Hodges, H. (1990). *ASCD's international polling panel: 1990–92, resolutions survey: Executive summary.* Alexandria, VA: Association for Supervision and Curriculum Development.

Holden, J. (1993). *Mentoring frameworks for Texas teachers.* Austin: Texas Education Agency.

Holland, J. L. (1985). *Making vocational choices: A theory of vocational personalities and work environments.* Englewood Cliffs, NJ: Prentice Hall.

House, J. S. (1981). *Work stress and social support.* Reading, MA: Addison-Wesley.

Howey, K. R., & Gardner, W. E. (1983). *The education of teachers: A look ahead.* New York: Longman.

Howey, K. R., & Zimpher, N. L. (1986). *Requisites for the teacher-mentor: Uncommon commitment and commonplace knowledge.* Unpublished manuscript, Ohio State University, Columbus.

Huffman, G., & Leak, S. (1986). Beginning teachers' perceptions of mentors. *Journal of Teacher Education, 37*(1), 22–25.

Huling-Austin, L. (1989a). A synthesis of research on teacher induction programs and practices. In J. Reinhartz (Ed.), *Teacher induction* (pp. 13–33). Washington, DC: National Education Association.

Huling-Austin, L. (1989b). Beginning teacher assistance programs: An overview. In L. Huling-Austin, S. J. Odell, P. Ishler, R. S. Kay, & R. A. Edelfelt (Eds.), *Assisting the beginning teacher* (pp. 5–18). Reston, VA: Association of Teacher Educators.

Huling-Austin, L. (1990a). Mentoring is squishy business. In T. M. Bey & C. T. Holmes (Eds.), *Mentoring: Developing successful new teachers* (pp. 39–50). Reston, VA: Association of Teacher Educators.

Huling-Austin, L. (1990b). Teacher induction programs and internships. In W. R. Houston, M. Haberman, & J. Sikula (Eds.), *Handbook of research on teacher education* (pp. 535–548). New York: Macmillan.

Huling-Austin, L. (1992). Research on learning to teach: Implications for teacher induction and mentoring programs. *Journal of Teacher Education, 43*(3), 173–180.

Hunt, D. M., & Michael, C. (1983). Mentorship: A career training and development tool. *Academy of Management Review, 8*(3), 475–485.

Ishler, P. (1990, May 31–June 3). *An advanced leadership academy on planning and implementing induction, internships, mentoring and beginning teacher programs.* Summary of conference sponsored by the Association of Teacher Educators and National Academy for Leadership in Teacher Education, Anaheim, CA.

Ishler, P., & Edelfelt, R. A. (1989). Impact of beginning teacher assistance programs. In L. Huling-Austin, S. J. Odell, P. Ishler, R. S. Kay, & R. A. Edelfelt (Eds.), *Assisting the beginning teacher* (pp. 57–78). Reston, VA: Association of Teacher Educators.

Ishler, P., & Selke, M. J. (1994). *A study of the involvement of NCATE institutions in the support of beginning teachers.* Unpublished manuscript, University of Northern Iowa.

Iwanicki, E. F., & Schwab, R. L. (1981). A cross validation study of the Maslach Burnout Inventory. *Educational and Psychological Measurement, 41*(4), 1167–1174.

Janov, A. (1983). *Imprints: The lifelong effects of the birth experience.* New York: Coward-McCann.

Johnston, J. M., & Kay, R. (1987). The role of institutions of higher education in professional teacher induction. In D. M. Brooks (Ed.), *Teacher induction—A new beginning* (pp. 45–60). Reston, VA: Association of Teacher Educators.

Kay, R. W. (1990). A definition for developing self-reliance. In T. M. Bey & C. T. Holmes (Eds.), *Mentoring: Developing successful new teachers* (pp. 25–38). Reston, VA: Association of Teacher Educators.

Kent, K. M. (1985). A successful program of teachers assisting teachers. *Educational Leadership, 43*(3), 30–33.

King, R. M. (1988). *A study of shared instructional leadership by mentor teachers in southern California.* Unpublished doctoral dissertation, University of San Diego.

Kram, K. E. (1983). Phases of the mentor relationship. *Academy of Management Journal, 26*(4), 608–625.

Kram, K. E. (1985). Improving the mentoring process. *Training and Development Journal, 39*(4), 40–43.

Kremer-Hayon, L., & Kurtz, H. (1985). The relationship of personal and environmental variables to teacher burnout. *Teaching and Teacher Education, 1*(3), 243–249.

Lacey, C. (1977). *The socialization of teachers.* London: Methuen.

Lawrenson, G. M., & McKinnon, A. J. (1982). A survey of classroom teachers of the emotionally disturbed: Attrition and burnout factors. *Behavior Disorders, 8*(1), 41–49.

Lawson, H. A. (1992). Beyond the new conception of teacher induction. *Journal of Teacher Education, 43*(3), 163–172.

Lieb, B. (1992). *Proceedings of the OERI study group on educating teachers for world class standards: The challenge for educating teachers.* Washington, DC: U.S. Department of Education.

Little, J. W. (1988). Assessing the prospects for teacher leadership. In A. Lieberman (Ed.), *Building a professional culture in schools* (pp. 78–106). New York: Teachers College Press.

Little, J. W. (1990). The mentor phenomenon and the social organization of teaching. In C. B. Courtney (Ed.), *Review of research in education: Vol. 16* (pp. 297–351). Washington, DC: American Educational Research Association.

Little, J. W., Galagaran, P., & O'Neal, R. (1984). *Professional development roles and relationships: Principles and skills of "advising."* San Francisco: Far West Laboratory for Educational Research and Development. (ERIC Document Reproduction Service No. ED 267 515)

Little, J. W., & Nelson, L. (Eds.). (1988). *Preparing mentors for work with beginning teachers: A leader's guide to mentor training.* San Francisco: Far West Laboratory for Educational Research and Development.

Little, J. W., & Nelson, L. (1990). *Mentor teacher: A leader's guide to mentor training* (Report No. ISBN-0-86552-099-2). Eugene, OR: ERIC Clearinghouse on Educational Management.

Lortie, D. C. (1975). *Schoolteacher: A sociological study.* Chicago: The University of Chicago Press.

Lortie, D. C. (1986). Teacher status in Dade County: A case of structural strain? *Phi Delta Kappan, 67*(8), 568–575.

Lutz, F. W., & Hutton, J. B. (1989). Alternative teacher certification: Its policy implications for classroom and personnel practice. *Educational Evaluation and Policy Analysis, 11*(3), 237–254.

Mark, J. H., & Anderson, B. D. (1985). Teacher survival rates in St. Louis, 1969–1982. *American Educational Research Journal, 22*(3), 413–421.

Maslach, C. (1981). Burnout: A social psychological analysis. In J. W. Jones (Ed.), *The burnout syndrome: Current research, theory, interventions* (pp. 30–53). Park Ridge, IL: London House Press.

Maslach, C. (1982). *Burnout: The cost of caring.* Englewood Cliffs, NJ: Prentice Hall.

Maslach, C., & Jackson, S. (1981). *Human services survey.* Palo Alto, CA: Consulting Psychologists Press.

Maslach, C., Jackson, S. E., & Schwab, R. L. (1986). *Educators survey.* Palo Alto, CA: Consulting Psychologists Press.

Mastain, R. K. (Ed.). (1991). *The NASDTEC manual.* Dubuque, IA: Kendall/Hunt.

Mazur, P. J., & Lynch, M. D. (1989). Differential impact of administrative, organizational, and personality factors on teacher burnout. *Teaching and Teacher Education, 5*(4), 337–353.

Merriam, S. (1983). Mentors and proteges: A critical review of the literature. *Adult Education Quarterly, 33*(3), 161–173.

Merseth, K. K. (1989). Computer networks for new teachers. *Harvard Education Letter, 5*(4), 7–8.

Merseth, K. K. (1990). *Beginning teachers and computer networks: A new form of induction support* (Research No. 90-9). East Lansing: Michigan State University, National Center for Research on Teacher Education.

Merseth, K. K. (1991). Supporting beginning teachers with computer networks. *Journal of Teacher Education, 42*(2), 140–147.

Miller, L. M., Thomson, W. A., & Roush, R. E. (1989). Mentorships and the perceived educational payoffs. *Phi Delta Kappan, 70*(6), 465–467.

Mitchell, D. E., & Hough, D. (1990). A policy framework for new teacher support. In A. I. Morey & D. S. Murphy (Eds.), *Designing programs for new teachers: The California experience* (pp. 85–96). San Francisco: Far West Laboratory for Educational Research and Development.

Mo, K. W. (1991). Teacher burnout: Relations with stress, personality, and social support. *CUHK Educational Journal, 19*(1), 3–11.

Murnane, R. J., & Olsen, R. J. (1990). The effects of salaries and opportunity costs on length of stay in teaching—evidence from North Carolina. *The Journal of Human Resources, 25*(1), 106–124.

Murnane, R. J., Singer, J. D., & Willett, J. B. (1988). The career paths of teachers: Implications for teacher supply and methodological lessons for research. *Educational Researcher, 17*(6), 22–30.

Murphy, D. S., Merseth, K. K., & Morey, A. I. (1990). Content and strategies for assisting new teachers. In A. I. Morey & D. S. Murphy (Eds.), *Designing programs for new teachers: The California experience* (pp. 26–39). San Francisco: Far West Laboratory for Educational Research and Development.

National Council for Accreditation of Teacher Education (NCATE). (1992). *Standards, procedures, and policies for the accreditation of professional education units.* Washington, DC: Author.

National Education Association (NEA). (1980). *Nationwide teacher opinion poll.* Washington, DC: Author.

North Carolina Initial Certification Program. (1990). *Guidelines and procedures manual.* Raleigh, NC: Department of Education, Division of Teacher Education Services, Teacher Education Section.

Odell, S. J. (1989). Developing support programs for beginning teachers. In L. Huling-Austin, S. J. Odell, P. Ishler, R. S. Kay, & R. A. Edelfelt (Eds.), *Assisting the beginning teacher* (pp. 19–38). Reston, VA: Association of Teacher Educators.

Odell, S. J. (1990). *Mentor teacher programs.* Washington, DC: National Education Association.

Odell, S. J., & Ferraro, D. P. (1992). Teacher mentoring and teacher retention. *Journal of Teacher Education, 43*(3), 200–204.

Paine, W. S. (Ed.). (1982). *Job stress and burnout: Research, theory, and intervention perspectives.* Beverly Hills, CA: Sage.

Paisley, P. O. (1987). *The developmental effects of a staff development program for beginning teachers.* Unpublished doctoral dissertation, North Carolina State University.

Parkay, F. W. (1988). Reflections of a protege. *Theory Into Practice, 27*(3), 195–200.

Parker, M. B. (1990). *Adolescent dancing and the mentoring of beginning teachers* (Report No. 90-13). East Lansing: Michigan State University, National Center for Research on Teacher Learning.

Pearson, M. J. T., & Honig, B. (1992). *Success for beginning teachers: The California New Teacher Project.* Sacramento: Commission on Teacher Credentialing.

Peterson, K. (1984). Methodological problems in teacher evaluation. *Journal of Research and Development in Education, 17*(4), 62–70.

Policy Analysis for California Education (PACE). (1991). *Conditions of education in California 1990* (Policy Paper No. PP91-4-1). Berkeley: Author.

Roth, R. A. (1990). Bridging the gap: Preservice through induction. *Newsletter of the California New Teacher Project, 3*(1), 1–9.

Ruskus, J. A. (1988). *A multi-site evaluation of the California Mentor Teacher Program.* Unpublished doctoral dissertation, University of California, Los Angeles.

Russell, D. W., Altmaier, E., & Van Velzen, D. (1987). Job-related stress, social support, and burnout among classroom teachers. *Journal of Applied Psychology, 72*(2), 269–274.

Ryan, K. (1986). *The induction of new teachers: Fastback No. 237* (Report No. ISBN-0-87367-237-2). Bloomington, IN: Phi Delta Kappa Educational Foundation. (ERIC Document Reproduction Service No. ED 268 117)

Schaffer, E., Stringfield, S., & Wolfe, D. (1992). An innovative beginning teacher induction program: A two-year analysis of classroom interactions. *Journal of Teacher Education, 43*(3), 181–192.

Schein, E. H. (1978). *Career dynamics: Matching individual and organizational needs.* Reading, MA: Addison-Wesley.

Schlechty, P. C., & Vance, V. S. (1981). Do academically able teachers leave education? The North Carolina case. *Phi Delta Kappan, 63*(2), 106–112.

Schlechty, P. C., & Vance, V. S. (1983). Recruitment, selection and retention: The shape of the teaching force. *Elementary School Journal, 83*(4), 469–487.

Schonfeld, I. S. (1992). A longitudinal study of occupational stressors and depressive symptoms in first-year female teachers. *Teaching and Teacher Education, 8*(2), 151–158.

Schwab, R. L., & Iwanicki, E. F. (1982a). Perceived role conflict, role ambiguity, and teacher burnout. *Educational Administrative Quarterly, 18*(1), 60–74.

Schwab, R. L., & Iwanicki, E. F. (1982b). Who are our burned out teachers? *Educational Research Quarterly, 7*(2), 5–16.

Sclan, E., & Darling-Hammond, L. (1992). *Beginning teacher performance evaluation: An overview of state policies* (Paper No. 7). Washington, DC: ERIC Clearinghouse on Teacher Education.

Shulman, J. H., & Colbert, J. A. (Eds.). (1987). *The mentor teacher casebook.* San Francisco: Far West Laboratory for Educational Research and Development.

Shulman, J. H., Hanson, S., & King, R. (1985). *California Mentor Teacher Program case study: Implementation in the Waverly Unified School District, 1984–1985.* San Francisco: Far West Laboratory for Educational Research and Development.

Shulman, L. S. (1986). Those who understand: Knowledge growth in teaching. *Educational Researcher, 15*(2), 4–14.

Shulman, L. S. (1987). Knowledge and teaching: Foundations of the new reform. *Harvard Educational Review, 57*(1), 1–22.

Smith-Davis, J. (1991). *Percentage change-teachers by state to 1992.* SpecialNet, Supply Demand Bulletin Board (Msg: FGJB-4583-8108).

Smylie, K. E. (1989, March). *Teachers' collegial learning: Social and psychological dimensions of helping relationships.* Paper presented at the annual meeting of the American Educational Research Association, San Francisco.

Smylie, M. A., & Denny, J. W. (1990). Teacher leadership: Tensions and ambiguities in organizational perspective. *Educational Administration Quarterly, 26 (3), 235–259.*

Stakenas, R. G. (1989). *Evaluation of components of the RAISE and reform legislation, Vol. III: Beginning teacher program.* Tallahassee: Florida State University, Center for Needs Assessment and Planning, Learning Systems Institute.

Stanzler, J. (1994). *Interactive communications and simulations.* Ann Arbor: University of Michigan.

State of Connecticut Department of Education. (1988). *A core training manual for the preparation of cooperating teachers and mentor teachers.* Hartford: Author.

Staton, A. Q., & Hunt, S. L. (1992). Teacher socialization: Review and conceptualization. *Communication Education, 41*(2), 109–137.

Sweet, J. A., & Jacobsen, L. A. (1983). Demographic aspects of the supply and demand for teachers. In L. S. Shulman & G. Sykes (Eds.), *Handbook of teaching and policy* (pp. 192–213). New York: Longman.

Sykes, G., & Bird, T. (1992). *Teacher education and the case idea.* East Lansing: Michigan State University, National Center for Research on Teacher Learning.

Tabachnick, B. R., & Zeichner, K. (1984). The impact of the student teaching experience on the development of teacher perspectives. *Journal of Teacher Education, 35*(6), 28–36.

Thies-Sprinthall, L. M. (1984). Promoting the developmental growth of supervising teachers: Theory, research programs, and implications. *Journal of Teacher Education, 35*(3), 53–60.

Thies-Sprinthall, L. M. (1986). A collaborative approach for mentor training: A working model. *Journal of Teacher Education, 37*(6), 13–20.

Thies-Sprinthall, L. M., & Gerler, E. R., Jr. (1990). Support groups for novice teachers. *Journal of Staff Development, 11*(4), 18–22.

Thies-Sprinthall, L. M., & Sprinthall, N. A. (1987a). Experienced teachers: Agents for revitalization and renewal as mentors and teacher educators. *Journal of Education, 169*(1), 65–79.

Thoits, P. A. (1982). Conceptual, methodological and theoretical problems in studying social support as a buffer against life stress. *Journal of Health and Social Behavior, 23*(2), 145–158.

Townley, K. F., Thornburg, K. R., & Crompton, D. (1991). Burnout in teachers of young children. *Early Education and Development, 2*(3), 197–204.

Vance, V. S., & Schlechty, P. C. (1982). The distribution of academic ability in the teaching force: Policy implications. *Phi Delta Kappan, 64*(1), 22–27.

Varah, L. J., Theune, W. S., & Parker, L. (1986). Beginning teachers: Sink or swim? *Journal of Teacher Education, 35*(1), 30–34.

Vaughan, J. (1979). The interaction of context with teachers, and teacher education: An emphasis on the beginning years. In K. R. Howey & R. H. Bents (Eds.), *Toward meeting the needs of the beginning teacher* (pp. 67–84). Minneapolis: Midwest Teacher Corps Network and University of Minnesota/St. Paul Schools Teacher Corps Project.

Vavrus, M. (1987). Reconsidering teacher alienation: A critique of teacher burnout in the public schools. *The Urban Review, 19*(3), 179–188.

Veenman, S. (1984). Perceived problems of beginning teacher. *Review of Educational Research, 54*(2), 143–178.

Vonk, J. H. C. (1983). Problems of the beginning teacher. *European Journal of Teacher Education, 6*(2), 133–150.

Ward, B. A. (1987). State and district structures to support initial year of teaching programs. In G. A. Griffin & S. Millies (Eds.), *The first years of teaching: Background papers and a proposal* (pp. 35–64). Chicago: University of Illinois State Board of Education.

Wendt, J. C. (1980). *Coping skills: A goal of professional preparation* (Report No. SP 019 605). Houston, TX: University of Houston, Department of Health, Physical Education and Recreation. (ERIC Document Reproduction Service No. ED 212 604)

Wildman, T. M., Magliaro, S. G., Niles, R. A., & Niles, J. A. (1992). Teacher mentoring: An analysis of roles, activities, and conditions. *Journal of Teacher Education, 43*(3), 205–213.

Wildman, T. M., & Niles, J. A. (1987). Essentials of professional growth. *Educational Leadership, 44*(5), 4–10.

Wildman, T. M., Niles, J. A., Magliaro, S. G., & McLaughlin, R. A. (1989). Teaching and learning to teach: The two roles of beginning teachers. *Elementary School Journal, 89*(4), 471–493.

Wolfe, D. M. (1992). Designing training and selecting incentives for mentor programs. In T. M. Bey & C. T. Holmes (Eds.), *Mentoring: Contemporary principles and issues* (pp. 103–109). Reston, VA: Association of Teacher Educators.

Wolpin, J., Burke, R. J., & Greenglass, E. R. (1991). Is job satisfaction can antecedent or a consequence of psychological burnout? *Human Relations, 44*(2), 193–209.

Zeichner, K. M. (1980). Myths and realities: Field-based experiences in preservice teacher education. *Journal of Teacher Education, 31*(6), 45–55.

Zeichner, K. M., & Gore, J. M. (1990). Teacher socialization. In W. R. Houston, M. Haberman, & J. Sikula (Eds.), *Handbook of research on teacher education* (pp. 329–348). New York: Macmillan.

Zimpher, N. L., & Rieger, S. R. (1988). Mentoring teachers: What are the issues? *Theory Into Practice, 27*(3), 175–181.

·27·

TEACHER EMPOWERMENT AND
SITE-BASED MANAGEMENT

Richard W. Clark
UNIVERSITY OF WASHINGTON

Laraine K. Hong
UNIVERSITY OF COLORADO, DENVER

Michael R. Schoeppach
BELLEVUE EDUCATION ASSOCIATION

In the 1990s, teacher empowerment and site-based management are popular elements of many plans to restructure schools throughout the United States. Unless there is a major change in direction, teachers entering the profession in this decade can expect to work within federal, state, and local guidelines designed to increase their power and to focus management of their work at the school level.

Notions of individual empowerment and localization of the management of local schools represent one end of a political and philosophical continuum that has deep roots in the United States. In one sense, the questions debated in the *Federalist Papers,* argued in the hot summer of the framing of the Constitution, fought over in the Civil War, and constantly tested in the courts and legislatures of the country, are variations of the same themes—to what extent are individuals to be empowered and to what extent is authority to be centralized?

Although other countries that are seeking universal schooling have done so through national ministries, the United States has persisted with a system featuring thousands of local school districts operating within charters provided by separate states rather than by the federal government. Indeed, *loose coupling* has been a term frequently used to define the governance structure of education. In part, this localization of control has reflected America's emphasis on individual rights.

Still, in contrast to the democratic and populist notions that are evident in considering the structure of U.S. education, the America of the twentieth century has been a democracy preoccupied with management of its institutions in ways that are neither democratic nor empowering for individuals. Scientifically managed factories featuring assembly lines, time-and-motion studies imposed on office workers, hierarchical organizations in which "chain of command" and "span of control" become bywords, represent efforts to increase productivity that have migrated from the nation's businesses to its educational institutions.

As the twentieth century comes to a close, advocates of reform in the schools seem to be suggesting solutions to perceived shortcomings in schools that simultaneously increase the centralization and decentralization of control in schooling. On the one hand, educators face legislated and professional pushes for the development of national standards. Apparently dissatisfied with the consequences of leaving outcomes to local school boards, Congress, two consecutive presidents (Bush and Clinton), and major professional organizations in fields as varied as mathematics, history, and the visual arts have pushed hard for the establishment of national goals. At the same time, privately funded initiatives such as the National Standards Board seek to create common professional standards for teachers throughout the United States. While these initiatives are being promoted (and often by the same people), school-based management and empowerment of individual teachers are being put forward as replacements for control by local school boards and state educational agencies. It is the latter populist notions to which we turn our attention in this chapter. However, it is important to remember that as popular as they have become, populist notions are in some ways antithetical to the centralist concepts of standards for students and teachers that are evolving along with them.

Industrial unions emerged during the twentieth century as a force in our society to counter the depersonalization and exploitation of workers in industrial organizations. Following World War II, government workers, including those in schools, turned to unionization as a way of overcoming many of the same complaints that had led to the creation of unions in business. Today, unions represent a centralizing force along with school districts. The traditional ways of both entities are challenged by proposals to empower teachers and to concentrate decision making at the school level. Parents and other community members also find their traditional ways of relating to schools challenged by such changes in the roles of professionals.

Teacher empowerment and site-based management evolved as specific strategies out of the political and philosophical traditions of our nation. They also have roots in traditions of research in the social sciences. Students of management and human relations have long advocated many of the concepts represented by such proposals for changes in the culture of our school systems. As we review the research related to these changes, we are repeatedly struck by the lack of consensus concerning the meaning of widely used terms. Repeatedly, we are forced to comment that differences in terminology restrict conclusions about the constructs.

With regard to teacher empowerment, one may be dragged quickly into examinations of formal power or influence, political or professional questions, personal or professional questions, questions of self-esteem and productivity, collective or individual power, and power in relation to a number of specific kinds of educational decisions, as well as power in relation to vertical relations within the hierarchy.

With regard to site-based management, widely different practices parade under the same banner. School-based management sometimes is closely linked with teacher empowerment as professionals gain the dominant role in decision making. In other instances, such as in the Chicago school system, parents are being empowered and are dominating the structures of the local school governance mechanisms (Bryk, Easton, Kerbow, Rollow, & Sebring, 1993). In still other situations, such as in Edmonton, Alberta, the principal is empowered and the image of the powerful, positional leader as the key instrument in creating effective schools (Brown, 1987) plays itself out.

One chapter cannot do justice to all the issues surrounding these topics. Therefore, beyond these introductory comments, this chapter generally provides minimal attention to the historical and philosophical issues associated with the movements. However, these issues are important to a full understanding of both topics. This chapter concentrates its examination on the research in the social sciences that helps us understand the

efficacy of the widely promoted notion that empowering the individuals closest to the students to make the essential decisions needed to implement sound educational programs will indeed lead to greater satisfaction for those employees and, ultimately, to better education for the students. The final section of the chapter discusses the implications of these studies and writings for those charged with educating educators and comments on questions that need further inquiry.

TEACHER EMPOWERMENT

Background and Context

Juxtaposing empowerment with site-based management suggests a direct relationship between the two concepts and further implies the existence of straightforward definitions. Unfortunately, the notion of teacher empowerment represents a formidable complex of shifting interpretations, historical antecedents, philosophies, purposes, and practical translations (Ashcroft, 1987; Bolin, 1989; Clift, 1991; Henderson, 1992; Kreisberg, 1992; Maeroff, 1988; Prawat, 1991; Sprague, 1992; Yonemura, 1986). This indeterminate nature of empowerment is not surprising given its relatively brief history as a specifically identified issue in the education literature. Efforts to define empowerment are small when considered against the backdrop of centuries-long ruminations over its parent concept, power.

As a reflection of human behavior and human relationships, power historically has served as a compelling topic for a diverse collection of historians, social scientists, philosophers, and other thinkers, each contributing to a large body of contrasting theories and ideas. A complete review of this work clearly would exceed the scope of this chapter; however, acknowledging the link between power and empowerment requires some discussion.

With Thomas Hobbes, Bertrand Russell, and Max Weber providing the foundational notions of power, Kreisberg (1992) concluded that subsequent theories and research on power as emanating from the social sciences, tend to agree "as to the fundamental underlying nature and definition of power" (p. 35). He suggested that although most prominent contemporary theories and definitions of power may vary in emphases, implications, and application, they appear to

. . . share a common conception of power as a *relationship of domination*, as *power over*. Dominating relationships are characterized by inequality; situations in which one individual or group of individuals, in order to fulfill their own desires, have the ability to control the behavior, thoughts, and/or values of another individual or group of individuals. (p. 36, original emphasis)

Power in this sense of "power over" is a natural corollary to hierarchical structures, in which competition spurs achievement and control is the prize. Relationships are structured with deliberate levels of subordination and rely on externally imposed tactics to influence decision making.

This form of power can be readily associated with the modern age, dating at least from the mid-nineteenth century to post–World War II, which Hargreaves (1994) characterized as rest[ing] upon Enlightenment beliefs that nature can be transformed and social progress achieved by the systematic development of scientific and technological understanding, and by its rational application to social and economic life. (p. 25)

These beliefs were conspicuously manifested in the rise of the modern factory system, outsized organizational bureaucracies, and centralized control. The effects of such efforts to achieve the utmost in wide-scale efficiency, Hargreaves (1994) pointed out, were not confined to economic organizations but reached deeply into our politics, institutions, and individual selves and identities. For schools, the story is familiar. Early in the twentieth century, pressed to educate the greatest number of students possible while committing minimal resources, time, and personnel, schools became similar to factories, adopting standardized curricula, specialized departments, teacher-centered instruction, age-based grouping, and bureaucratic hierarchies to control work and the workers. In this context, power is palpable. The organizational chart depicts the flow of power, from school boards to school districts and superintendents, through all the successive layers of bureaucracy, down to principals, and then to teachers and students.

The majority of school systems in the United States exhibit this kind of power relationship. This power of imposition, one entity's will over that of another, thus continues as a topic of study and is manifested, for example, in examinations of the teacher's power or authority to influence or control events and learning within the classroom (O'Hair & Blase, 1992; Richmond & McCroskey, 1992). The focus also can analyze more broadly power relationships among teachers, students, and the larger bureaucratic, policy-making structures (Blase, 1991; Dippo, Gelb, Turner, & Turner, 1991; McNeil, 1986) and various ideological or political interests within society (Burbules, 1986).

In contrast, as directly addressed in the next section, the concept of *empowerment* represents a significant shift away from these more traditional interpretations of power. However, with ideas still evolving and without a fully circumscribed, agreed-upon definition for empowerment, educational theorists, policymakers, researchers, and practitioners have been advancing their own interpretations since the mid-1980s to accommodate their various priorities. Discussions of empowerment thus have focused not only on teachers but also on parents and community (Hess, 1992; Moore, 1992; Zeichner, 1989, 1991), students (Delpit, 1988; Nel, 1992; Simon, 1987; Smith & Johnson, 1993), or the entire school entity (Lightfoot, 1986). Clift (1991) added another facet in her contention that a major impediment to the empowerment of teachers has been the lack of empowerment among teacher educators. In a related vein, Labaree (1992) discusses the relationship between teacher professionalization and the professional status of teacher educators.

However, the intent of this section is to provide an overview of perspectives on *teacher empowerment,* acknowledging the overlaps with other facets of empowerment in education and then moving from the overview to focus on aspects of teacher empowerment that most directly support or are relevant to site-based management and the ultimate goal of school reform. In addition, each interpretation of empowerment holds direct and indirect implications for teacher education. Although explaining these implications obviously is a major goal of this chapter, the immediate need for a coherent theory and sound body of research in this area is apparent. So, heavily laden with philosophical and political shadings, teacher empowerment is still more of an abstract concept than a readily identified set of behaviors, skills, or attitudes that can hold still long enough to be fostered, shaped, or measured. We begin with a consideration of personal and professional empowerment and move to the constructs of collective empowerment and the dependency of all forms of empowerment on the setting in which work is performed.

From Power to Empowerment—Personal, Professional, and Knowledge-Based

Such phrases as "balance of power," "power grabbing," and "stripped of power" imply finite amounts of power to be variously distributed within a given hierarchy, usually with most of it accumulated at the upper echelons. This easily results in individuals or groups either having or lacking power. The powerless, as well as those dissatisfied with their own particular allotments of power, seek empowerment by acquiring or increasing the power they have. Such an interpretation of empowerment keeps it in the traditional domain of *power over,* that is, power deriving from an ability or authority to control others, a social/political (more than personal) construct.

As interpretations have progressed over the years, however, empowerment has acquired some contrasting connotations and possibilities. In a comprehensive effort to distinguish empowerment from power per se, Ashcroft (1987) argues for a more individual–personal approach. Eschewing power as something that can be bestowed, Ashcroft views power as "personal in origin and intention" and cites Dewey's (1916) idea that "power" refers to an individual's inherent abilities or capabilities: "The adult uses his powers to transform his environment, thereby occasioning new stimuli which redirect his powers and keep them developing" (p. 50). Ashcroft concludes that "an empowered person . . . would be someone who believed in his or her ability/capability to act, and this belief would be accompanied by able/capable action" (p. 143). In this sense, empowerment is not defined in terms of the acquisition of external political or social power but suggests individual funds of power that may be personally identified and developed. In a positive sense, it suggests that an empowered person's final satisfaction is in their condition.

Placing such a personal foundation under empowerment is not a completely recent or new suggestion. Immediate precursors to this effort may be found in theories from humanistic psychology. Rogers (1971), for example, describes the notion of "becoming a person," asserting that "the goal the individual most wishes to achieve, the end which he knowingly and unknowingly pursues, is to become himself" (p. 70). That achievement, he adds, leads to an enhanced sense of personal control, in which one moves from dependence on the approval of others toward asking, "Am I living in a way which is deeply *satisfying* to me, and which truly expresses me?" (p. 70, emphasis added). The goal is a renewed sense of self accompanied by a belief in one's own standards of evaluation and an ability to assume responsibility for decisions and choices.

When applied to teachers, Fuller (1971) translated this as "the developing capacity to cope" (p. 3). Effecting changes in teaching behaviors, she asserts, requires changes within individual teachers, "in how they think, feel, and respond, as well as in what they know" (p. 3). She suggests using psychological assessment techniques to learn more about prospective teachers and to establish counseling-oriented seminars to help facilitate personal growth. Her eventual goal is to help these student teachers develop "coping behaviors" as they confront the various challenges and problems of their initial extended teaching experiences.

Combs, Blume, Newman, and Wass (1974) took a similar "humanistic" approach in their own discussion of teacher education. They made extended suggestions, which sounded notes of relevance for current movements to improve teacher education programs. For example, they suggested that instead of trying to help students simply model the teaching of the master teachers, supervisors should be helping them to find their own "best ways of teaching." Instead of being preoccupied by the acts or results of teaching, supervisors should "learn to concentrate on how student teachers feel, think, believe—about themselves, their students, their purposes, and the subject matter they are charged with teaching" (p. 127). The authors envisioned a program in which the student assumes more responsibility for his or her own learning and growth:

Responsibility, however, is learned from being given responsibility. It is never learned by having it withheld. A program of professional education must treat its students as responsible people and encourage the growth of responsibility through independent action on the part of the students. (Combs et al., 1974, p. 145)

This humanistic view of teacher education stood as distinct counterpoint to the then-prevailing emphasis on prescriptive views of teaching with teachers more as technicians than professionals. As late as the 1970s and for a good part of the 1980s, most persons conceptualized teaching as a vocation requiring close adherence to externally determined step-by-step procedures, manuals, and formulas. The effective schools movement promoted the principal as "instructional leader," and early reform reports directed attention primarily toward broad accountability and policy issues.

Ashton and Webb (1986) conducted a study and interpreted the problem of school improvement as a problem of "teacher motivation" and self-esteem, which they translated into the concept of sense of efficacy to refer to the belief that teaching can influence student learning. David Berliner, in the introduction to Ashton and Webb's book, comments, "Self-efficacy begins by making people feel that they have the power to change their own world" (p. vii).

As a result of their study of selected middle and high school teachers, Ashton and Webb (1986) concluded that sense of efficacy has specific links to student achievement but is itself "susceptible to many interactive influences" within the school context. The corollary, they proposed, is that a teacher candidate's sense of efficacy will be similarly tied to specific educational experiences in a teacher preparation program. They suggested applying this knowledge in developing successful teacher education experiences and also monitoring factors in-

fluencing the novice teacher's sense of efficacy in the first year of teaching to help manage difficult or discouraging situations.

One interesting attempt to define aspects of personal growth and professional empowerment even more narrowly came from Meyer, Linville, and Rees (1993). Their premise was that the development of a positive self-concept leads to increased self-esteem, which in turn allows for more assertive behavior. Assertiveness, they said, might allow a teacher to "assume a greater role in policy-making and the development of curricula in the teacher's own school, one of the goals of the movement for empowerment of teachers" (p. 34).

Studying a group of 97 students in their first year of teacher education, the researchers divided them into a control group and three experimental groups. Each experimental group received assertiveness training for a different period of time—3 hours, 6 hours, and 9 hours. Training consisted of lectures, demonstrations, class exercises, journal writing, and films. Self-esteem was measured before and after training, using the Berger Self-Acceptance Scale and the Tennessee Self-Concept Scale. The results showed a significant increase in self-concept and self-acceptance following the assertiveness training, with length of training having an augmenting effect. The researchers concluded that the assertiveness training used in their study did have a substantive effect on the self-acceptance and self-concept of their subjects. This kind of training program, they suggested, "could represent a major step in preparing teachers for the increasing power that may soon be theirs" (p. 34).

Because few of the efforts in the early 1980s showed significant improvements within the school systems, the second wave of school reform evolved with a different perspective. The 1986 reports from the Holmes Group and the Carnegie Task Force and the trilogy of study reports emanating from the Study of the Education of Educators (Goodlad, 1990; Goodlad, Soder, & Sirotnik, 1990a, 1990b), specifically addressed teacher preparation, teachers' working climate and conditions, and the quality of teachers as fundamental to the improvement of schools. "The Holmes and Carnegie reports took the position that the 'professionalism' of the teaching force and the creation of a 'collegial' working environment are necessary for true educational excellence" (Wirsig, 1987, p. 41).

Directly linking school reform with the status and preparation of teachers, the roles they assume, and the conditions under which they work greatly expands the ways in which teacher empowerment can be interpreted and applied—from the political power of teacher unions to school governance and participation in curriculum decisions. The reports coming from the Study of the Education of Educators expanded the standard boundaries of the teacher's role even more as they talked about teachers' moral and political responsibilities as educators for advancing the agenda for education in a democracy. Although definition struggles continue, perhaps more strenuously than ever, the notion of teacher empowerment has become firmly attached to the larger debates about and studies of teacher professionalism and its impact on the improvement of schools.

Among other things, the second wave of school reform sought to involve teachers in shaping and setting the direction for their own professional lives. Qualitative researchers writing about this wave provided us with additional ways of thinking about teacher empowerment. Maeroff (1988) suggested that empowerment is "somewhat synonymous" with professionalization, in the sense of having "the power to exercise one's craft with confidence and to help shape the way that the job is to be done" (p. 4) or "working in an environment in which a teacher acts as a professional and is treated as a professional" (p. 6). Maeroff also interpreted empowerment as an issue of status; he suggested that the way to enhance that status is to improve teachers' images of themselves and of their colleagues, to add to their academic and pedagogical knowledge, and to provide opportunities to work on an equal footing with both principals and fellow teachers. Lieberman (Brandt, 1989) viewed the expanded role of teachers as "empowering (them) to participate in group decisions: to have real decision-making roles in the school community" (p. 25). Similarly, Bolin (1989) offered a broad definition, in which teacher empowerment "requires investing in teachers the right to participate in the determination of school goals and policies and the right to exercise professional judgment about the content of the curriculum and means of instruction" (p. 82).

Views such as these, acting as mandates as well as premises for research, in turn engender different practical approaches to the empowerment of teachers. With its early antecedents in organizational theory and the distribution of power, discussions of teacher empowerment include a particular focus on teachers' participation in school decision making. The result has been broad restructuring efforts at state and local levels to develop site-based management arrangements that would involve teachers directly affecting the quality of instruction.

This chapter reviews the research on teacher empowerment and site-based management. Focusing on empowerment only as related to site-based management, however, could yield a narrow, rusty interpretation of empowerment simply as acquisition of political/social power. Although this may be a particular outcome of teacher participation in governance and curriculum decision making, it is important to bear in mind that a major impetus for such an expanded role is a desire for enhanced professionalism. Such professionalism is based on more than a few added responsibilities. As Talbert and McLaughlin (1994) summarize,

Primary among the conditions that distinguish a "profession" from other occupations are a specialized knowledge base and shared standards of practice, a strong service ethic, or commitment to meeting clients' needs, strong personal identity with, and commitment to, the occupation, and collegial versus bureaucratic control over entry, performance evaluations, and retention in the profession. (p. 126)

Such conditions imply something deeper than perfunctory participation in bureaucratic decision making. With such influences as earlier humanistic psychology, feminist theory, and constructivist ideas, empowerment through professionalism also appears to depend on a strong sense of individual autonomy, enhanced self-image, increased knowledge, and personal growth.

Zehm and Kottler (1993) said that to "retain their sense of potency" and to be effective in the classroom, teachers need to become "reasonably well-adjusted human beings" (p. 15):

Teachers who are ineffectual, wimpy, whiney, who are perceived as weak and ineffective in their basic style of interaction, earn little respect from students or their peers. Likewise, those teachers . . . who appear in charge of their own lives, who radiate power, tranquility, and grace in their actions, are going to command attention and respect. People will follow them anywhere. (p. 15)

In this case, the authors suggest that personal growth and increased self-confidence lead to greater control over external issues and elements within the educational context. They warn beginning teachers of the serious challenges facing today's schools—the lack of resources and funding, pressures and impediments from top-down bureaucracies, the low public regard for teachers, and the extraordinary problems that many students bring with them into the classroom.

Lichtenstein, McLaughlin, and Knudsen (1991) seem to support this idea, suggesting that decentralization of decision making involving greater teacher participation may not, in itself, automatically lead to teacher empowerment. After surveying a sample of California schools and school districts identifying themselves with restructuring efforts and after searching the literature for examples of "new institutional arrangements and empowered teachers," the researchers reported that there is little evidence systematically tying teacher empowerment to institutional decentralization. (See more on this topic in the following section.) Given these findings, they decided to examine what they call knowledge-based reforms—reform efforts based on teachers' capabilities and professionally relevant knowledge.

The writers conducted interviews with 30 secondary school teachers participating in the Urban Mathematics Collaborative (UMC), a project that began in 1985 in Los Angeles and San Francisco "to empower teachers by developing teacher networks that include professionals in industry and academia" (p. 5). Although they admit that their sample of teachers may be "particular" to the enhanced interest of those teachers in improving instruction and being involved in the project, Liechtenstein et al. (1991) argued that these are "typical" teachers in terms of the diversity of motivations, capacities, and points of view. The writers asserted their own belief that these teachers' experiences can be generalized to develop a broad model of teacher empowerment.

The results of the interviews suggested three areas of professional knowledge—knowledge of professional community, education policy, and subject areas—that can significantly enhance teachers' sense of efficacy and competence, which they equate with the professional empowerment of teachers. Knowledge of professional community involves leaving one's classroom and actively communicating with one's colleagues, acknowledging one's own expertise. Knowledge of education policy means that teachers become more intimately aware of the larger policy debates potentially affecting their schools. Increased knowledge in this area leads to greater sense of personal authority and confidence in actually affecting policy decisions. Knowledge of subject areas, the researchers assert, is the basis for individual sense of authority, professionalism, and involvement in the professional community and in policy decisions.

Basically arguing that empowerment comes from a sense of authority that begins within the individual teacher rather than as something bestowed by the organizational system, Lichtenstein et al. (1991) conclude that "without such knowledge and capacity, institutional strategies dependent primarily on changes in authority and participation to empower teachers—new roles and responsibilities—may comprise an empty warrant" (p. 20).

Cornett (1991) similarly asserts that teachers' extended participation in school decision making will have little impact unless teachers simultaneously engage in developing their own professional knowledge. "By continuing to grow and mature as a professional," he says, "the teacher increasingly earns trust and respect and warranted status as an educational decision maker" (p. 73).

Empowerment Through Knowledge, Inquiry, and Reflection

The issue of how both practicing and preservice teachers acquire the necessary knowledge and self-awareness to support professional empowerment obviously can be answered in several ways. One of the more frequently offered responses, however, has come through a now substantial literature on teacher reflection or reflective inquiry. Although the idea of reflective thinking can be traced back to Dewey (1933), most of the current interest appears to stem from Schön's (1983) writing on teachers' reflective practices. Reacting to the view that teaching is based on essentially technocratic, rational practices, considerable discussion emerged to follow Schön's lead and consider the variable, indeterminate character of teachers' knowledge (O'Loughlin & Campbell, 1988; Rubin, 1989; Smyth, 1989). These discussions suggested that teachers must engage in an ongoing process of praxis, "exploration, action, and reflection" (O'Loughlin & Campbell, 1988) in order to understand and creatively manage the intricate mix of factors that determine whether and how students will learn.

Some general agreement seems to exist that reflection, in giving teachers a means by which to develop and shape their own ideas and ways of thinking, can be a major factor in teacher empowerment. Colton and Sparks-Langer (1993) write that, "many of tomorrow's schools will be restructured communities requiring empowered, reflective, decision-makers" (p. 45). O'Loughlin and Campbell (1988) say:

It seems to us axiomatic that if teachers are to have input into pedagogical management . . . teachers-to-be should experience reflective inquiry in teacher preparation programs. It is in this reflection that the beginnings of teacher empowerment lie. (p. 44)

At the same time, however, complete agreement is lacking regarding the actual meaning and application of reflective thinking.

Especially active in studying the role of reflective thinking in teacher education, Colton and Sparks-Langer (1993) (see also Sparks-Langer & Colton, 1991) developed a "conceptual framework" that includes three major strands of theory. They cite theories of motivation and caring that include concepts of self-efficacy and risk taking. They agree that cognitive psychology contributes a constructivist view of learning, in which the learner (teacher) uses prior experiences and learnings as the basis for making sense of immediate events and information.

Finally, Colton and Sparks-Langer say that critical reflection emphasizes consideration of "multiple perspectives or viewpoints and weighing the long-term social and moral consequences of decisions" (p. 46).

In an earlier discussion of reflective thinking, Sparks-Langer and Colton (1991) identified teacher narratives as a significant element in the process. They suggest that reflective journals containing such narratives can be used effectively in teacher education programs to help provide a deeper and richer context for teachers' perceptions and understandings. This suggestion adds another facet to the literature on reflective activity. Colton and Sparks-Langer (1993) make it clear that they do not expect students' journal entries to be the result of reflection limited by external standards of objectivity and rational modes of thinking as characteristic of positivist doctrine (O'Loughlin, 1992). Instead, as some feminist theorists have argued, students' construction of knowledge requires that they have direct access to and broad latitude for applying their own individual experiences and personal histories (Belenky, Clinchy, Goldberger, & Tarule, 1986; Cornett, 1991; Miller, 1990; O'Loughlin, 1992). Ellsworth (1989) also argues that critical pedagogy and other conventional approaches to the construction of knowledge historically have inadequately considered the particular frameworks that students carry with them, such as ethnic, gender, political, ideological, racial, and cultural backgrounds, even including additional personal references such as obesity.

Empowerment as Collective Autonomy—Power With Rather Than Power Over

Self-knowledge and related practices such as inquiry and reflection support the individual's sense of autonomy and personal responsibility. More recent discussions, however, have identified another facet of teacher empowerment. Given the increasing emphasis on teaming, collaboration, and teacher collegiality, it may be inevitable that empowerment can also be viewed as a result of a form of collective autonomy. O'Loughlin's (1992) study set out to help practicing teachers engage in "emancipatory knowledge construction" through individual study, but an apparently unexpected finding was that however inspired teachers were to return to their respective schools to institute change, they were frustrated in their attempts to apply or extend their learning beyond their own classrooms. O'Loughlin concluded that if teachers are to be engaged in "emancipatory knowledge construction," the institutional power structures of schools need to be changed in order to provide the climate and opportunity for radically reconstructing classroom practices. His comments suggest that individual teacher knowledge, sense of professional competence, and self-awareness are insufficient catalysts to major school change. O'Loughlin noted that he and some teachers from the Hofstra Institute intended to form a "network of activist teachers." This response in turn reflects the collective side of teacher empowerment, which we treat in more detail when discussing site-based management.

Over recent years the concept of teacher empowerment has evolved from conventional notions of "power over" to what Kreisberg (1992) distilled from various sociological and political interpretations as "power with," a concept of power different from those premised on systems of hierarchical control. Ashcroft (1987) similarly summarized views of several theorists and made a distinction between competitive power and cooperative power, with the latter including components of "belief, capability, and effective action." The role of teachers as shaped by this view is consistent with recommendations emerging from second-wave reform discussions.

In her review of research on teacher participation in school decision making, Conley (1991) observes that most of the discussion focused on teacher involvement in issues associated with the "vertical," or higher levels, of organization. She notes that teacher decision making can also be "lateral," with teachers at the same organizational level making decisions as peers and colleagues. Noting the traditional isolation of teachers from one another, Conley points out that "research suggests that the need for greater collegial interaction, and information exchange constitutes another benefit of enhanced teacher participation" (p. 243).

In a comprehensive effort to examine the relationship between collegial interactions and teacher professionalism, Talbert and McLaughlin (1994) analyze data collected from surveys of some 800 teachers in 16 diverse secondary schools. For this study "professionalism" was defined according to three criteria: (1) technical culture (shared knowledge and standards), (2) service ethic (a sense of responsibility and caring for students), and (3) professional commitment (to teaching, subject matter, and professional growth). Correlational results suggested that strong teacher communities (based in departments, entire schools, districts, or collaborative networks) bear a positive relationship with the development of teacher professionalism, at least in terms of technical culture and professional commitment. However, the researchers noted the lack of comparable correlation with a service ethic. They suggested that although strong teacher communities promote a technical culture and professional commitment, those very cultures and norms may "vary significantly in ways that matter for students' learning opportunities and educational equity" (p. 140). The caveat in this research may be that because professionalism—and empowerment—can be defined so variously, positive indicators in any given situation should not immediately be generalized to include improved student behavior or attitudes. Research on the effects of enhanced professionalism and empowerment on student behaviors and performance require exceptionally clear definitions and identification of variables. However, the compelling possibility still remains that teachers' sense of personal and professional authority are significantly linked to the genuine collegial, collaborative opportunities available to them.

Thus, power is not simply an issue of control of one group over another, but, reconceived as *empowerment,* it means being able to act *together* for the purpose of solving significant problems. In the case of teachers, these problems center around their ability to make a difference for their students, their ability to do what they set out to do when they became teachers. In a 2-year study of 85 teachers in 5 northern California school districts, each differing in size and socioeconomic makeup, McLaughlin and Yee (1988) reported that these teachers expressed little interest in power achieved through climbing some hierarchical organizational ladder. Rather, they indicated a desire to stay in their classrooms, concentrating their efforts on improving instruction for their students and engaging in collaborative activities with their colleagues for this purpose.

The irony, of course, is that although teachers may be "central figures of authority and control in the classroom, in the larger hierarchy of the educational bureaucracy they are remarkably isolated and often strikingly powerless" (Kreisberg, 1992, p. 9). Another, and even less pleasant, thought is that teachers are the end of a string of abusive power relationships, the classroom being the setting in which they exercise power in a negative way on the children they have been entrusted to teach (Sarason, 1990). One issue, then, becomes how teachers, as colleagues, can participate more substantively in organizational, policy, and instructional decisions that directly affect their ability to be fully successful teachers on their own terms. Two related subissues appear to be in any response: (1) the specific areas over which teachers would have decision-making authority, and (2) how that authority would be defined, established, applied, and sustained.

In this regard, Conley (1991) made a distinction between traditional and "new forms of participation." Commenting on the efficacy of each, Conley concluded that:

A critical issue is the degree [both of these] forms of participation provide teachers with an advisory or consultative role (influence) or with final decision-making power (authority). Research is not clear on this question [p. 245]. . . . In some cases, new forms of participation appear to offer advantages over traditional systems; in other cases, the advantages are unclear. (p. 253)

Specific efforts to study the advantages of "new forms of participation" point to some especially appropriate areas, such as site-based management, curriculum design, research and inquiry, and staff development.

The research, however, has tended to be primarily descriptive in a broad effort to define the different facets of teacher participation, the variables affecting the effectiveness and degree of participation, and how these areas can be variously approached through teacher education. Consider the following examples.

Teacher involvement in curriculum decision making may be of particular current interest, but it is not a new notion (e.g., Harnack, 1968). Farris and Hancock (1989) posit that the empowerment of teachers includes a greater role in curriculum decisions. The authors' approach to exploring this issue as related to preservice and inservice teachers was to focus on language arts instruction and to exchange their own teaching situations. The college faculty member spent a year as a consultant and observing language arts instruction in 40 elementary classrooms in six schools, while the regular elementary teacher assumed responsibility for teaching an undergraduate language arts methods course. They based their conclusions about their respective experiences primarily on self-reports, anecdotals, and observation records.

In teaching the college methods course, the classroom teacher found her students especially lacking in self-confidence and needing substantial concrete experience in connecting theory and practice. For the college teacher, the challenge was to move the classroom teachers from everyday "survival" concerns toward thinking about and trying different ways of teaching. Through a combination of demonstration lessons, workshops, informal conversations, and hand-outs relating research to practical classroom suggestions, the authors reported a noticeable increase in self-confidence and willingness to apply new ideas among some of the teachers. Positive comments from parents were construed as indicators of enhanced status for these teachers. The authors also reported that even though the teachers tended to work cooperatively rather than competitively, it was difficult for them to collaborate because of the organizational structure of their buildings and districts. The alternative, they suggested, is assistance from an outside party, such as a curriculum specialist or university faculty member.

Monson and Monson (1993) commented that structural reforms, such as site-based management, tend to involve curricular reform efforts (a point of view that, we note later, is not universally held) and assume that with involvement teachers acquire "new authority." In their report of how teachers in Westwood, Massachusetts, worked to implement whole language in all of their elementary classrooms, Monson and Monson gave a general overview of how this process was conducted within a framework of collective decision making. They noted that staff development helped develop the appropriate knowledge base as well as skills for making informed individual decisions.

Empowerment as Research and Inquiry

Collectively, teachers may assume greater responsibility for curricular and instructional decisions, but will they assume the additional role of engaging in the research and inquiry to inform these decisions properly? To maintain a disjuncture between these two functions would be to perpetuate what Houser (1990) described as an historical gap, where university-based researchers manage and control studies and curriculum specialists develop plans, while teachers are left with implementation. In many cases, too, teachers simply have not been interested in such research, believing that it has no immediate classroom application. In contrast, Houser argued that teachers should be more directly involved in all phases of research, allowing more immediate connections between theory and practice, enhancing their professional knowledge and sense of efficacy. In this way, Houser says, "teachers may begin to perceive themselves as the experts—intellectuals capable of shaping their professional lives and the profession itself. This is empowerment" (p. 59).

Although Cochran-Smith and Lytle (1990) agree that teacher research could play a significant role in the professionalization (empowerment) of teaching, they emphasize that such research should not be expected to follow the traditional model of university-based research. Instead, teachers' own unique perspectives, questions, ways of working, and access to the classroom environment mean that teacher research will necessarily be realized in other ways. They also assert that, although different in approach, methodology, and application of results, teacher research should be accepted as no less valuable than conventional research.

Empowerment Through Collaborative Inquiry

While advocating teacher research as a significant vehicle for improving teacher knowledge, professionalism, and, eventually, it may be hoped, schools themselves, Cochran-Smith and Lytle (1992) also acknowledge the fundamental lack of supportive conditions within the existing educational structure. To counter "obstacles" such as teacher isolation and a somewhat self-protective historical image of teachers as all-knowing and independent, they suggest that teacher research efforts can become viable when pursued as collaboration. In this regard, they link inquiry with the concept of collective autonomy. They cite a decade of "innovative arrangements (that) include in-school and school-university structures such as cross-visitation, teacher study groups, schools within schools, writing projects, student teacher-cooperating teacher discussion groups, and on-site courses and seminars that focus on teacher inquiry" (p. 305).

In her overview of several projects involving teacher research, Lieberman (1986) also focuses on the collaborative aspect of such efforts. She points out that teachers working together provide greater opportunities for reflection and collegial interaction. A proponent of active involvement of teachers in many phases of research, Lieberman emphasizes their access to the most immediate issues of the classroom and a realistic appreciation of its nuances and complexities (see also Smyth, 1991). Lieberman summarizes several benefits of teacher collaboration teams, including a greater sense of empowerment through new roles and opportunities for leadership.

Gove and Kennedy-Calloway (1992) reported on a 5-year staff development project in an urban district in Ohio, that demonstrates how collaborative action research can help teachers simultaneously improve instruction and achieve a greater sense of empowerment. Teams of teachers investigated different strategies to improve reading and writing instruction with at-risk students. They developed their own hypotheses, planned and implemented procedures, and analyzed their data. A series of interviews with the 20 participants led to three generalizations: (1) increased enthusiasm for teaching, (2) closer collegial interactions, and (3) "focused, data-based feedback about teaching performance." Gove and Kennedy-Calloway noted that new insights and knowledge about teaching influenced teachers' perceptions of their ability to improve students' learning, which the authors identify with Ashton and Webb's (1986) concept of "teacher efficacy." We examine the implications of some of these studies later. Next, we turn to ways in which the research on empowerment has merged with inquiry about school leadership.

Empowerment Through Participation and Teacher Leadership

Basing the empowerment of teachers to a great extent on authentic participation in pivotal areas such as curriculum, research, staffing, and supervision necessarily leads teachers into new roles within the larger educational structure. Embodied in this premise is a reversal of the practice common for most of the twentieth century of teachers confined to narrow decision making within their own classrooms and effectively divorced from the larger policy-making and goal-setting processes of their own school settings and districts. This separation has been detrimental to teacher job satisfaction. In her careful and extensive study of 78 elementary schools, Rosenholtz (1989) reported a direct relationship between teachers' professional satisfaction and the social organization of schools. In what she calls "low consensus" schools, teachers functioned on their own, detached from any extended community. Lacking a sense of common purpose and opportunities for shared governance, these teachers tended to express frustration and discouragement, which were manifested in their attitudes toward their students.

In contrast, "high consensus" schools were characterized by principal–teacher agreement on goals and relevant instruction and by enthusiastic, committed collaboration among teachers. Rosenholtz (1989) submitted that their genuine sense of community led to constructive action, most especially concentrating on and improving classroom instruction. A prevailing theme in her discussion was the power of collaboration and cooperation, supported by the social organization of schools, to influence a teacher's commitment, openness to change, and belief in possibilities. Rogus (1988), in his review of effective schools research, confirmed this view with his conclusion that, "An effective school ethos is characterized by faculty collegiality, collaboration, and sense of community" (p. 46). At the same time, however, it seems obvious that such an environment does not happen spontaneously, that the factors engendering such internal cohesion are, of course, several, complex, and intertwined.

Lieberman (1988) characterizes this as building a professional culture in the schools, as part of the comprehensive restructuring suggested by the second wave of reform efforts. She writes:

Involved in that restructuring is the building of a new set of relationships between and among all members of the school community, including an enlargement of the leadership team in schools, new roles for teachers and administrators, changed organizational arrangements, and even a rethinking of the substance of what is to be taught. (p. vii)

In this context, the challenge to schools is to reshape traditional roles and relationships while changing organizational structures both to accommodate and facilitate the revised shifts in authority and responsibility. In practice, this has tended to take the form of teacher leadership and site-based management.

If there is any concept immediately signaling teacher empowerment, it is that of teacher leadership. The Carnegie Report's (1986) recommendations for the professionalization of teachers included the idea of "Lead Teachers" in each school, recognized by their colleagues for exceptional expertise and teaching skill. Their roles would be interpreted in various ways, depending on the organization and priorities of the school, the needs and expertise of the teachers. The Carnegie Task Force reasoned that if a school could trust its own staff's judgments in making decisions supportive of instructional and organizational goals, the result would be greater professional autonomy and closer collegial relations. This concept, in fact, has expanded and emerged in recent years as offering particular potential for better understanding the extended role of the teacher in school restructuring efforts, especially as tied to improvement of instruction.

The notion of teacher leadership as a manifestation of teacher independence and effectiveness also appears to have acquired enough legitimacy to become incorporated in some teacher-preparation and in-service efforts. The Coalition of Essential Schools, for example, conducted staff development in its expanding network of schools by placing experienced Coalition teachers into schools new to the network who acted as consultants and resource persons (Cushman, 1990). A drastically revised teacher-preparation program at the University of Colorado at Denver includes "leadership areas" that allow new teachers to develop a specialization area (e.g., math, science, integrated curriculum) that can help them eventually assume leadership roles in their careers.

Despite such practical recognition of teacher leadership, this area continues to beg study and discussion. Some of the difficulty lies in that, as with empowerment itself, there is no clear definition of teacher leadership or how it actually should be put into practice. Wasley's (1991) case studies of several identified "teacher leaders" demonstrate not only the wide variability in roles but also the impediments to definition because "it has not been perceived as important in any aspect of teacher preparation or continuing education" (1991, p. 147). Wasley also noted that discussion of this issue among teachers themselves has been inhibited by a strong egalitarian tradition, reinforced by union perspectives and collective bargaining positions.

However, Little's (1988) definition seems sufficiently broad to provide a working framework: "Teachers who lead leave their mark on teaching. By their presence and their performance, they change how other teachers think about, plan for, and conduct their work with students" (p. 84).

Referring to Devaney's (1987) six "arenas" for leadership, Little notes that they offer "a balance between leadership that advances a school program . . . and leadership that moves people" (p. 85), which may be a helpful initial approach to identifying different facets of teacher leadership. Teacher leaders have been observed, for example, modeling effective teaching practices and conducting courses (Smylie, 1992b; Wasley, 1991), managing teacher centers and working with staff (Lieberman, Saxl, & Miles, 1988; Mertens & Yarger, 1988), assuming governance roles to support school programs (Fay, 1992), and conducting research and inquiry for dissemination to other teachers (Miller, 1992). Of course, the actual range of such roles is arguably limitless, especially as Barth (1990) conceptualizes the school as being potentially a "community of leaders," where leadership is freed from "administration" and tied to the shared goal of transforming schools to improve students' learning and teachers' own professional satisfaction.

Not surprisingly, such leadership appears to require some specific traits and skills. In a long-term study of 17 teacher leaders, Lieberman, et al. (1988) identified a cluster of recurring characteristics, including teaching mastery, an understanding of the school culture, effective use of resources, management and coordination skills, and the ability to build collegiality in a school. The latter itself subsumes skills such as working through conflict and establishing trust and rapport. Placing teacher leadership in the general context of leadership and organizations, Rogus (1988) distilled out similar and related behaviors, such as having a vision, being self-directed learners, being oriented toward the larger organizational culture, and building trust through collegial interaction. (See also Bolin, 1989; Livingston, 1992; Wasley, 1991.)

Empowerment and the Creation of Empowering Contexts

The institutionalization of teacher leadership roles remains problematic in many respects, such as time, training, incentives, resources, relationships with colleagues and with administrators, teachers' own uncertainties and reluctance. At the same time, this manifestation of teacher empowerment persists as a viable concept that has potential for influencing the professional status of teachers, allowing them to assume a central role in school reform in order to improve instruction for students. Accepting this premise, the question becomes how best to prepare teachers to assume various leadership roles and how to support and assist them in fulfilling those roles in the schools. As Mertens and Yarger (1988) asserted, "Involvement of teachers simply does not occur in the absence of formalities for ensuring that it does" (p. 35). In other words, teacher leadership evolves only when the right context for it has been created. There is no denying that schools are complex workplaces. Any change, no matter how ostensibly innocuous, has potential for provoking anxiety, confusion, and conflict. Initiatives related to teacher leadership and empowerment can then be especially prickly and problematic. Significant changes in the traditional role of teachers necessarily lead to repercussions throughout the organizational structure and within the social dynamics of the school.

Clift, Johnson, Holland, and Veal (1992) examined role relationships among teachers, administrators, and university personnel during a 3-year project in which a university team worked with five schools to develop "action plans" to identify and meet specific needs. In one instance, for example, a team of teachers worked out a plan for using resources from the project to free teachers to meet and identify ways of assisting novice teachers. The results of the Clift et al. (1992) study demonstrated both the complexity and long-term nature of applying shared leadership to schoolwide initiatives and confirmed the importance of the larger school and district context:

If concepts such as shared leadership and teacher direction are to become a reality, policy must support new conceptions of practice. . . . the espoused theory of teacher leadership will be undermined if theories in action stress teacher compliance as opposed to creative risk-taking [p. 906]. . . . In other words, role change is at once a function of an environment that encourages change and individuals who are willing to take advantage of the environment. (p. 907)

Lieberman et al. (1988) suggested that these new leadership roles imply different ways of structuring schools and working with both teachers and the rest of the school community. They wrote that "a combination of these new roles and structures (appear) necessary to professionalize the school culture and . . . bring a measure of recognition and respect to teachers" (p. 166).

In her model for "empowering leadership," Bolin (1989) also emphasized that "empowerment of teachers will not be at the expense of students, community, principal, or other school staff" (p. 86). Empowering leadership, she added, is based on authority derived from cooperation, genuine sharing of responsibility for school decisions, and continued dialogue and discussion. The criteria for decisions are determined by the needs of those directly involved rather than by external, objective authority.

Lightfoot (1986) linked empowerment with the opportunities a person has for "autonomy, responsibility, choice, and authority" and said that such opportunities should be available within all levels of a school—students, teachers, administrators. Referring to her own study of six high schools that exhibited characteristics of empowerment, Lightfoot noted that although the teachers held the central role in the "chain of empowerment" that the culture of a school must effectively nurture and support, teachers must also contribute to the broader school community interests.

The discussions on teacher leadership and, indirectly, empowerment, suggest that teachers' roles within each school are defined by a complex of factors embedded within the entire school community, especially and specifically in the nature of the organizational structure and in the decision-making processes used within that structure.

In the next section, we turn to further consideration of the way in which contexts may empower involved people (professionals, students, parents) as we examine the literature on site-based management.

RESEARCH RELATED TO SITE-BASED MANAGEMENT

Site-based management has recently been one of the most touted strategies for improving the nations' public schools (e.g., David, 1989; Hill & Bonan, 1991; Mauriel & Lindquist, 1989; National Education Association, 1991). The strategy also appears to have spread rather widely in public school systems. According to a survey conducted by the National Education Association (1991), 30% of the nearly 6,000 local associations responding indicated some form of site-based management project operating in their school districts. Yet, although much has been written about the subject from the perspective of what can be termed "opinion," much less is available in the form of critical inquiry from a research standpoint.

This section explores several issues related to site-based management in public schools. First, we examine the strategy in relationship to past efforts in the business and public education sectors. Then, we discuss available research on recent implementation attempts. Next, we describe current research related to links between site-based management and participant satisfaction. This discussion returns directly to issues raised by empowerment. Finally, we discuss research that examines relationships between improved student performance and site-based management. Again, there is a link with the earlier discussion of empowerment: the notion that high-performing students would be "empowered." Prior to beginning these efforts, however, we describe more explicitly the definitions of site-based management used by the various authors.

Authors reporting research about what we generically term site-based management utilize definitions that differ significantly. For example, Brown (1987), examining processes in operation in the Edmonton Public Schools in Alberta, Canada, described school-based management as "the delegation of authority *to make some of the budgetary decisions from the central office to the school*" (p. 5, emphasis added).

Chapman and Boyd (1986), in describing "decentralization" and "devolution" wrote of the experience in Australia that "*it seeks school improvement* through democratic, school-based management, *with extensive community and staff involvement,* which necessitates a revised management role for principals" (p. 28). The authors continued, "Administrative Committees were established to offer *advice* to the principal on the implementation of the Industrial Agreement (union contract) and on general school operation" (p. 35, emphasis added).

Differing definitions are not confined to authors writing about efforts in countries other than the United States. As Hill and Bonan (1991) explained in reporting about efforts in the United States:

According to the premise underlying site-based management (SBM), *individual schools that take responsibility for devising their own educational programs* will serve students better than schools that deliver standard services mandated from above. Thus, SBM places institutional decisions in the hands of *teachers and principals,* the people with the closest day-to-day contact with students. (p. 1, emphasis added)

Similarly Weiss (1993) wrote:

Structures for shared decision making *give teachers a voice* in what had largely been principal-made decisions. . . . Shared decision making, as we use the term, is *a formal system for the representation of teachers in a decision-making body.* (p. 69, emphasis added)

Finally, Smylie (1992a) explained:

They [opportunities to participate in decision making] have also come from establishing or reconstituting governing bodies and advisory groups to *involve teachers with administrators and perhaps parents in decision-making processes.* (p. 53, emphasis added)

Does site-based management mean only making budgetary decisions at the school level that used to be made at the central office? Is the strategy limited to giving to principals "advice" that they need not follow? Are school principals and their teaching staff members the only people who get to be involved in decision making? Even more fundamental, what should we call the strategy? Site-based management? School-based management? Devolution? School-centered decision making? Shared decision making? A sampling of the research provides no commonly accepted answer to such questions.

We now report on research associated with efforts to decentralize decision-making processes in public school systems to the school level. We examine processes where stakeholders other than the building administrator were expected to make actual decisions and other processes where stakeholders were expected only to advise the administrator.

Groundings in Earlier Efforts

Decentralizing decision making to improve the quality of the work accomplished by an organization is not a strategy unique to education. At the outset, we commented on how this issue is linked to the fundamental issues associated with the governance of the United States. A number of authors also have suggested recently that site-based management in school systems derives from private-sector business experience (e.g., David, 1989; Hill & Bonan, 1991; National Education Association, 1990).

Some form of decentralized decision making in the private sector are evident throughout our history. Relevant examples may be found at the turn of the century and continue intermittently through World War II (National Education Association, 1990). Rather recently, such strategies have become widely encouraged and practiced.

Faced with increased competition from foreign companies, corporate America began to see their profits slip away by the early to mid-1970s (Bluestone & Bluestone, 1992; National Education Association, 1990; Reich, 1992). In response to this new reality, business leaders searched for strategies to recover their earlier advantage. One of these was to decentralize decision making and to increase employee involvement in decisions associated with industrial production. By the early 1980s, authors such as Drucker (1980), and Ouchi (1981) were encouraging business leaders to simplify their organizations by reducing bureaucracy and decentralizing decision making to take better advantage of the skills of their employees.

To what extent have efforts to decentralize decision making in the private sector been successful in improving the quality of products and the profitability of the businesses employing such a strategy? Examples cited by the early authors seem relevant (Ouchi, 1981), and authors writing more recently continue to cite specific examples claiming success (Peters, 1988; Senge, 1990; Waterman, 1987). Specific research also is cited that suggests that employee involvement in decision making in private industry broadens skill development, increases information flow, and improves the implementation of technology, organizational processes and procedures, and employee relations (Eaton & Voos, 1991). Similar research reports that worker production is increased, as is product quality, and that there is a reduction in scrappage and waste (Cooke, 1990). Reich (1992) linked this research with education, suggesting that,

Pushing responsibility for what is taught and how it is taught down to teachers and parents, and away from educational bureaucracies, is one such step (analogous to the shift in responsibility within the corporation from high-volume hierarchies to high-value webs). (p. 255)

Some forms of decentralized decision making were practiced in public education in the 1960s and 1970s. Although they were grounded in populist notions similar to those encouraging current activities, these efforts were directed primarily at improving administrative efficiency, giving more political authority to communities, or addressing state authority (David, 1989). In the 1980s, however, decentralized decision making in education was being advocated for reasons not dissimilar to those advanced in the private sector. Improving the quality of education in the face of failures in the public education system became a reason for focusing at the school level (e.g., Goodlad, 1984), just as improving the quality of products to achieve profitability was the motivation in the private sector. As Bryk et al. (1993) explained: "More specifically, reform [site-based management] would help engage all participants in the school's mission and would provide substantial support for significant changes in classroom instruction and, ultimately, in student learning" (p. 2).

To be successful, the strategy would have to be implemented effectively. To what extent has that occurred? In those places where it has been or is being implemented, is there a link between the strategy and teacher satisfaction? Finally, is there a link between site-based management and improved student learning?

Formative Studies—Attempts to Determine Extent of Implementation

Much of the research addressing the degree to which site-based management has been successfully implemented provides similar reports. Chapman and Boyd (1986) report that the Australian effort in the state of Victoria involving the giving of advice to principals by committees of teachers and parents had not developed into "a fully collaborative decision-making model" (p. 51). Malen and Ogawa (1988) in their study of eight schools using school councils that include administrators, teachers, and parents in Salt Lake City, Utah, did not confirm changes in school and district decision making. Similarly, Weiss (1993) in a longitudinal study of 12 high schools in 11 states involving principals and teachers in the decision-making processes concluded that, "Over the period of fieldwork, we did not see linear progression in the efficacy of SDM [Shared Decision Making] in any of the schools" (p. 85). Malen (1992), also reporting on one school district's effort to implement the strategy where school councils of teachers, parents, principals, and, at the middle and high school levels, students were responsible for making decisions, concluded that, "Although some groups appear to be operating effectively, others, at least on the global indicators used in this report, are not yet functioning as strong problem-solving collectives" (p. 42). Hill and Bonan (1991), in their five school district study of teacher and principal decision making, reported that decentralization has progressed slowly and with difficulty. Finally, Bryk et al. (1993) reported on the Chicago experience at the elementary school level where parents, teachers, and the principal had been given broad decision-making powers:

We estimate conservatively that of the schools most in need of change, where student assessment reports are significantly below national norms, one third have developed strong democratic participation within their school community that is now focused on a systemic approach to whole school improvement. In addition, perhaps another third of the schools share some of these characteristics but are not as far along in the organizational change process. (p. 37)

These results seem consistent with the experiences of others (e.g., Etheridge, Hall, Brown, & Lucas, 1990; Mauriel & Lindquist, 1989; Smylie, 1992a).

A few studies are more positive. Brown (1987), reporting on the decentralization of budget authority in two school systems in Canada said that, "The two school districts studied appear to be considerably decentralized, judging from the method of lump-sum allocations to schools and the large proportion of dollars which is given to schools" (p. 32). However, he qualified the success by explaining that,

the decentralization observed is organizational and not political, which means that it exists at the pleasure of the boards and schools are accountable to the boards. There are no parent advisory committees which act as neighborhood school boards and make school personnel decisions. (p. 32)

White (1992) noted a high degree of decentralized authority in the three school districts she studied where teachers and principals were responsible for decision making. However, his findings are also qualified:

Even from the teacher's standpoint, decentralization in these districts is not without its blemishes. Financial constraints restrict the amount of training offered on shared decision making and limit teacher flexibility regarding input on the budget and curriculum. Reluctance on the part of administrators to allocate authority and encourage teacher input sets limits on teacher participation. (p. 81)

The research suggests that implementation of site-based management has not been complete in the systems studied. As the National Education Association (1991) reported in its census of local associations concerning site-based management, *"The majority of the projects reported on in this publication do not meet the criteria set forth above and would not be judged acceptable if these criteria were strictly applied"* (p. 4, emphasis in original). The National Education Association's criteria are certainly restrictive, yet the conclusion is consistent with that of other reports. Unlike what David (1989) called the "conceptual arguments, how-to guides, and testimonials from practitioners" (p. 45), the research studies appear to reveal no totally successful efforts.

In many cases, the research reviewed contains suggestions as to why implementation of site-based management has not been completely successful in those cases examined. One of the primary issues identified is the prevailing patterns of influence that traditionally exist in schools. Malen and Ogawa (1988) in the Utah experience reported that no significant change was found in the pattern of relationships whereby the school principal controls building policy and procedure considerations, teachers control the classroom component, and parents assume a supportive role. The work done by Smylie (1992a) concurred. He concluded:

Teachers appear substantially more willing to participate in all areas of decision making if they perceive their relationships with their principals as more open, collaborative, facilitative, and supportive. They are much less willing to participate in any area of decision making if they characterize their relationships with principals as closed, exclusionary, and controlling. (p. 63)

This analysis is consistent with other findings (e.g., Bryk et al., 1993; Chapman & Boyd, 1986; Etheridge et al., 1990; National Education Association, 1991).

In addition to the principal–teacher relationship issue, Smylie (1992a) reported that the willingness of teachers to participate in making decisions concerning staff development, curriculum, instruction, and personnel is influenced by "the norm of professional privacy" (p. 64). Like the principal–teacher relationship, this issue is a part of the traditional pattern of influence found in schools. It is, however, related to "teachers' opposition to peer judgment—one of the pivotal norms defining their relationships with other teachers" (p. 64). He reported that although this norm is less significant than the principal–teacher relationship in the willingness of teachers to participate in making decisions concerning these subjects, it plays a role.

Besides the barriers presented by existing system norms, several other issues are identified in the research as potential impediments to successful implementation. Several authors (e.g., Etheridge et al., 1990; Mauriel & Lindquist, 1989; White, 1992) cited the lack of training for participants as a problem. Researchers also mentioned that the lack of time for participation in decision-making processes has a negative impact on success (Bryk et al., 1993; DeLacy, 1990; Malen, 1992; Mauriel & Lindquist, 1989). Finally, they pointed out that the lack of clarity concerning the appropriate boundaries for the decision-making process resulted in a perception by decision-making participants that the scope of influence they had was severely limited (Malen, 1992; Malen & Ogawa, 1988).

In sum, these reports suggest that simply establishing the intention to engage teachers and others in decision-making processes at the school level is not enough to ensure success. Factors such as existing system norms, the lack of training and time for decision making, and the ambiguity of provisions governing the processes appear to have an impact on successful implementation of site-based management systems. As a result, the research reports generally conclude that full implementation of site-based management has been elusive.

As Conley (1991) explains, "schools are complex organizational settings, requiring both vertical and horizontal coordination and subject to important constraining forms of external authority (e.g., school boards, departments of education, accreditation agencies)" (p. 257). She suggests that the unresolved problem is how to implement true participation systems that establish teacher decision making beyond the scope of the classroom, without threatening the traditional authority structures of schools and school districts. The problems related to the implementation of current site-based management systems as reported in the research may well be a manifestation of the issue presented by Conley and the supporting systems associated with staff development, time allocation, and the definition of who has authority to make decisions that those traditional authority structures have created. In any event, any judgments made about the results obtained from efforts at achieving school-based management must be considered in light of this evidence of weak implementation.

Site-Based Management and Participant Satisfaction

One of the claims made by advocates for site-based management is that, "It signals to teachers, parents, and the community that teachers, as professionals, are worthy of regard and respect. It heightens their [teachers] sense of vocation and improves their morale" (Weiss, 1993, p. 70). In short, it "empowers" teachers in several of the ways suggested in the first part of this chapter. Although research reports conclude that full implementation of site-based management has not been achieved, does research suggest that the strategy, regardless of the stage of implementation achieved, can have some impact on participant satisfaction? First, we turn our attention to satisfaction level of teacher participants.

In 1985 the National Education Association conducted a national research survey concerning the working conditions faced by teachers in the United States (National Education Association, 1988). Approximately 1,800 randomly selected teachers participated in this survey. One series of questions addressed the area of teacher involvement in decision making. Bacharach, Bauer, and Shedd (1986) discussed these findings:

Very few teachers feel that they have more than an occasional chance to participate in decisions on organizational policies. At least 75 percent of the respondents feel that they have little chance to participate in decisions in all five areas [Organizational policies, Student–teacher interface, Teacher development and evaluation, Work allocation, and Teaching process]; as many as 94 percent feel this way in regard to staff-hiring decisions. (p. 21)

Furthermore, the authors' analysis of the survey data showed that 63% of responding teachers wanted more involvement in decisions in shaping organizational policies, 84% wanted more influence over standardized testing policies, 73% desired more involvement in expenditure priorities, 70% wanted more participation related to budget development, 65% desired more involvement on designing and planning the use of facilities, and 63% wanted more influence on staff hiring. The data showed that few teachers desired less involvement in decisions concerning these issues. The authors concluded:

In sum, the decisional deprivation results demonstrate convincingly that teachers feel that they should have considerably more of a chance to be involved in decision making. Substantially fewer teachers find their current opportunities to be involved in decision making appropriate, and relatively insignificant percentages of teachers feel saturated with opportunities to get involved. (p. 24)

Presumably, site-based management enhances opportunities for teachers to be involved in decision making and, thereby, increase their job satisfaction. However, research results related to this increased involvement and satisfaction are not consistent.

A number of researchers reported that the implementation of the site-based management systems they studied resulted in little increase in decision making by teachers over significant issues. Malen and Ogawa (1988) in the Salt Lake City, Utah, analysis indicated that principals dominated the decision-making processes over teachers and parents, that decisions actually made by the participants were routine and peripheral in nature and that little evidence existed that teachers (or parents) had significant influence over important matters in those systems.

Likewise, Mauriel and Lindquist (1989), in describing their analysis of two school districts implementing site-based management, questioned how long these site councils "will remain satisfied making small decisions" (p. 20).

In her study of a broadly representative sample of 115 teachers from a wide range of school districts and economic areas, Johnson (1990) also found that the majority did not exert their influence through any systematic or formal procedures. Even as many said that they had held a variety of governance positions (e.g., committees, councils, unions), they usually indicated having had little influence of consequence. One English teacher expressed "a deep feeling of powerlessness to affect any policy." The majority of teachers surveyed had no authentic opportunities to participate in schoolwide governance, and they generally felt their views were discounted in any policy discussions and decisions, even those directly affecting teachers' work and students' learning. Johnson described proposals for school-site management as including teacher involvement and sharing of formal authority with administrators. She noted at the same time, however, that teachers in her study emphasized that they themselves had to be willing to participate and commit the time and energy required to exert more professional influence in education.

Also, Weiss (1993) in her analysis of six high schools implementing site-based management and six high schools organized in the traditional fashion, found little difference between teacher involvement in decision making in the two types of systems over issues such as curriculum. Where substantive decisions were made, they were initiated by the principal in both types of systems. In brief, the lack of good implementation noted previously negatively affects teacher satisfaction.

However, other studies suggest that participants in site-based management systems are involved in making decisions about significant issues. For example, the National Education Association (1991) stated that of the more than 1,600 districts responding to their census, 84% said that curriculum was a subject addressed in site-based management projects, 79% indicated that staff development was covered, 71% answered that program evaluation was discussed, 65% responded that instructional materials were covered, 53% included student assessment, and 49% reported that school budget and student grouping were addressed.

Here, research on teacher empowerment through development of new leadership roles overlaps with research on site-based management. Not only do operational decisions become the province of individual schools rather than district offices, but site-based management can also "provide a context for fully empowering and involving teachers in professional matters that concern them" (Mertens & Yarger, 1988). Mertens and Yarger argued that even though site-based management is commonly connected to more bureaucratic arenas, it can offer teachers a forum for applying their own expertise and experience to educational problem solving. They concluded that efforts to reform the professionalization of teaching should be premised on the structural and organizational reform of schools.

White (1992) conducted more than 100 interviews with teachers and administrators to study the impact of school decentralization on issues of teacher empowerment. In decentralized schools, she found that authority is more evenly distributed with teachers more involved in decisions and assuming diverse roles. "Overall," White observed, "the decentralized schools were run democratically, rather than by a few administrators who controlled all important decisions" (p. 75). She reported minimal change actually engendered by decentralization, but she noted a direct relationship between teachers' participation in decision making and how they perceive their work and themselves. White concluded that for most teachers increased decision-making authority enhanced teachers' interest in their work, reduced isolation, and enhanced self-esteem. Such changes, she suggested, bear strong potential for improving the instructional environment for students.

White (1992) also stressed that teachers in the three districts where she conducted interviews responded that they were involved in decisions associated with school budget, curriculum, and staffing. For example, 71 of the 90 teachers interviewed, "reported that the involvement [in budget decisions] gave them a feeling of importance and of being in charge" (p. 73). In addition, "all 90 of the teachers in the three districts indicated that they were satisfied with the authority they had over school budget decisions" (p. 73). With respect to curriculum, "90 percent of the teachers reported that they were involved personally in making curriculum decision" (p. 73), and, "37 percent of the teachers indicated that they had served on panels to hire teachers" (p. 74). White explained that this last percentage was smaller than in the preceding examples, because two of the three districts studied were experiencing small growth rates that reduced the potential for teacher involvement in personnel selection.

A similar, positive report from Chicago is provided by Bryk et al. (1993). Teachers generally indicated that they had been involved in developing their SIP (School Improvement Plan) and that this was a positive experience. Several teachers said that involvement in planning the SIP was instrumental in empowering teachers and the community:

A key indication of teachers' sense of personal well being is how they feel about their jobs. When asked what it's like to teach in their school, they spoke in glowing terms about their work, their colleagues and their children. (p. 33)

Finally, DeLacy (1990), in the first year of a longitudinal study of the Bellevue, Washington, school district's school renewal efforts, which include a site-based management system, also highlighted a more positive outcome of the process. The site-based management process studied includes administrators, classified and certificated staff, and parent and student representatives on school councils who make decisions at the school level. DeLacy reported that nearly 80% of the teachers "agreed more than disagreed" that serving on a site council was a worthwhile use of their time. More than 68% of teachers "agreed more than disagreed" that their site council handled agenda items in depth, rather than giving them superficial attention. More than 57% of the teachers "agreed more than disagreed" that they had sufficient influence over school decisions that affect their jobs. More than 53% of the teachers "agreed more than not" that they had sufficient influence over budget decisions at their school. Only about 25% of the teachers responded that they just wanted to do their job and would live with the decisions others made.

The Bellevue Education Association, which represents certificated employees in the Bellevue, Washington, district, conducted surveys of teachers and certificated support staff at the elementary level in 1992 and at the secondary level (middle and high schools) in 1993, yielding data supporting the DeLacy findings (Bellevue Education Association, 1992, 1993a, 1993b). These data indicate that 69%, almost 78%, and nearly 67% of the elementary, middle school, and high school staff members, respectively, disagreed that their principals exert undue influence over decisions at their schools. Furthermore, 71%, 78%, and more than 71% of the elementary, middle, and high school staff members, respectively, agreed that the increased involvement of parents in decision making had been positive at their building. In addition, 74%, more than 72%, and more than 74% of elementary, middle, and high school staffs, respectively, agreed that they had been given ample opportunity to make recommendations to improve education in their schools. Concerning the principal–teacher relationship, 71%, almost 78%, and 59% of elementary, middle, and high school staff members, respectively, felt comfortable expressing their concerns to their principal, even when an individual staff member's opinion differed from the administrator's. Finally, 77%, 75%, and almost 70% of the elementary, middle, and high school staff members, respectively, agreed that they were allowed to be as authentically involved in decision making at their school as they should be.

Information from the National Education Association (1991) census, White (1992), Bryk et al. (1993), DeLacy (1990), and the Bellevue Education Association (1992, 1993a, 1993b) appear to contrast with the reports of Malen and Ogawa (1988), Mauriel and Lindquist (1989), and Weiss (1993). Furthermore, the data from White (1992), DeLacy (1990), and the Bellevue Education Association (1992, 1993a, 1993b) contrast significantly with the National Education Association survey data (Bacharach et al., 1986). Employees in the systems studied by White and DeLacy that employ forms of site-based management appear considerably more involved in decision making than their colleagues in the National Education Association random sample.

One potential variable that has been suggested by some as influencing the satisfaction of participants in site-based management efforts and even the viability or significant, positive impact of the strategy where attempted is the degree of involvement of the employee organization in the implementation effort (National Education Association, 1991).

Data from the National Education Association (1991) census was interpreted by its authors to suggest that, "Local associations play a critical role in site-based decisionmaking projects" (p. 1). They assert that where local association involvement exists, a wide range of educational issues are more likely to be discussed by site councils than when the local association is not involved, and that participation by parents, students, and support personnel is higher when the local association is involved than when it is not. Finally, the authors suggest that where some form of agreement, whether informal, a letter of agreement, or a collective bargaining provision exists between the employee organization and the district that governs the site-based management process, "A much higher proportion of projects jointly managed by the association and district address job satisfaction (78% vs. 54%) and the decisionmaking role of the education employees (86% vs. 57%) than projects with no association involvement" (p. 9).

Although it may be possible that formal involvement by an employee organization in establishing provisions that govern site-based management processes has a positive effect on implementation, the reports of other researchers call that motion into question. Clark (1993), for example, suggested that the attitude and approach of the employee organization in the setting he examined had another impact. According to him,

the PFT (Philadelphia Federation of Teachers) is very concerned that decisions not be delegated to the schools which would lessen in any way protection they perceive they have won for teachers. Therefore, there is no willingness to have decision making groups in schools with significant say over hiring or other personnel decisions or over roles of employees once hired. (p. 18)

Finally, one might surmise that the involvement of an employee organization in the establishment of provisions governing site-based management processes might assist in addressing the ambiguity reported by some researchers concerning the authority of the participants to make decisions (e.g., Malen, 1992; Malen & Ogawa, 1988). However, that remains an open question. The National Education Association (1991) data suggest that it may, but information from Malen (1992) calls that into question.

Clearly, the current research does not suggest a consistent conclusion regarding whether the current degree of implementation of site-based management in a school district results in involvement of teachers in decision making concerning issues of significance or in improved teacher satisfaction. It appears that in at least some school districts such is not the case, whereas in others it may well be. The research does suggest that the results of site-based management are mixed, and the ability of the strategy to engender satisfaction may be impacted by a number of factors.

An answer of more certainty appears to be available from the research concerning the extent to which building principals are satisfied with site-based management systems. Where this question is addressed, many principals reported feeling disaffected. Chapman and Boyd (1986), describing the Australian efforts at implementing a site-based management system that involved other participants in advising the principal who still made the decision, reported:

He or she is no longer able to see him or herself as the authority figure, "the organization man" supported and at times protected by Departmental rules and regulations. Instead, he or she must be a coordinator of a number of people representing different interest groups among the school community, who together will determine the direction the school is to follow. In the words of the past president of the Victorian Primary School Principals Association, Vern Wilkinson, "The principal now becomes relocated from the apex of the pyramid to the center of the network of human relationships and functions as a change agent and a resource" (p. 55)

The relocation described is neither met with enthusiasm nor seen as positive by all principals. Chapman and Boyd illustrated these points quoting a teacher interviewee as contending that, "the principal is now just a facade, the Department has taken all his power" (p. 36). They quoted a high school principal who explained, "The principal's power is zilch" (p. 36). Another principal offered, "This is creating a situation in which teachers think they are more qualified than experienced administrators to make administrative decisions" (p. 37).

Principal concern or outright resistance to the strategy are not limited to Australia. In their analysis of the Salt Lake City, Utah, processes, Malen and Ogawa (1988) reported that teachers and parents only had influence when the principal permitted. They found that principals controlled council agendas and processes. Principals allegedly saw the councils as a means to obtain support for their ideas, provide information, and manage criticism. Principals did not use site-based management as an opportunity to share decision-making authority or modify roles. Instead, they continued to protect their traditional role and control over issues for which they perceived they should be responsible. Thus, their satisfaction appeared to be limited to the extent to which they could retain control of the process.

Weiss (1993) in her study of high schools reported similar results. She reported that most of the changes that took place in the schools studied resulted from principal-initiated efforts and that teachers continued to be conservative because, "if they spoke up too much, they could expect retribution, especially if they opposed the principal's ideas or challenged his or her prestige in public" (p. 83). She concluded:

Still, it is hard to avoid the sense that in most of the SDM [Shared Decision Making] schools we studied, teachers are being co-opted. They are given a limited role in decision making, and the extent of their authority is ambiguous. Whatever authority they have can be withdrawn. . . . Canny administrators, therefore, can manipulate the SDM process with small cues about where the zone of acceptability ends. Should teachers actually propose an action that meets administrative resistance, everybody knows who will win. (p. 89)

Again, administrators' satisfaction with site-based management seems tied directly to their ability to maintain control of the decisions.

DeLacy (1990), examining the Bellevue, Washington, efforts, indicated a similar conflict: "It [site-based management] was not accepted with open arms, especially by administrators who were caught off guard" (p. 2). And, although she wrote that progress is being made in this regard among principals, conflict still remains.

Malen (1992) also investigated the Bellevue experience. When the site-based management process was first implemented in 1986, responses from principals, although varied, still illustrate the disaffection:

They saw it as a major shift in power relations that simultaneously stripped them of positional authority and strapped them with greater accountability. Crisply put, "Principals felt like the district had rolled over to the association and left them with the responsibility for making their cave-in work out. (pp. 22–23)

This tension has not completely disappeared. DeLacy (1992) reported this recent interview response from one principal in Bellevue: "There is a lack of group accountability. The principal is accountable for group decisions. We've gone too far!" (p. 21).

Other authors provided similar, though less explicit, comments (Bryk et al., 1993; Etheridge et al., 1990; Mauriel & Lindquist, 1989). Consequently, although the research is not consistent concerning whether teachers experience increased satisfaction from systems implementing site-based management, a thread runs through the research suggesting that principals are more consistently disquieted where the strategy is being attempted.

Danzberger (1994) reported findings that may help explain principals' views. A 1991–1992 study of six urban districts conducted by the Institute for Educational Leadership in Washington, DC, revealed that the majority of school board members in these districts who had stated their intentions to devolve authority on individual schools were "unsure about how (or unwilling to try)" to move more authority to the schools (p. 370). It may be that principals are attuned simply to the wishes of the governing body or that principals and board members share the same misgivings about empowering others at school sites. In any event, the research does reveal that at least a number of principals in systems implementing site-based management express resistance.

Links of Site-Based Management to Student Performance

An even more explicit conclusion from the research is evident with respect to whether implementation of site-based management systems results in improved student performance. As Weiss (1993) suggested, advocates for site-based management contend that:

Given the areas of teacher expertise, decisions under SDM [Shared Decision Making] will focus on teaching, learning, and student issues. Unlike administrators, who devote serious time to bureaucratic concerns, paperwork, and managerial routines, teachers can be expected to point the decision-making apparatus at things that matter to student performance. (pp. 69–70)

Does the research support the assertion that under site-based management student performance will improve? Weiss (1993) found that their "data do not suggest that greater teacher control over school decisions focuses more attention on curriculum, let alone on a reorientation of curriculum to emphasize understanding and application" (p. 87). She concluded, "So far it [site-based management] looks like an OK deal for teachers, but perhaps not a great one for students" (p. 90). This view is echoed by numerous other researchers (e.g., Chapman & Boyd, 1986; David, 1989; Malen, 1992; Malen & Ogawa, 1988). Even researchers providing more positive data about authentic employee involvement through site-based management share a similar perspective. Bryk et al. (1993) explained, "Finally, as noted earlier, short term trends in student achievement are not very informative at this point" (p. 36). They report that principals believe that student achievement is improving, but no data are provided to support the claim. Similarly, DeLacy (1990) expressed the concern in the system she studied about "the apparent lack of connection between the renewal initiatives [including site-based management] and student progress" (p. 5). White (1992) did suggest that student performance improved in the systems she studied. Her conclusions, however, appeared to be based only on teacher perceptions and not substantive data directly related to student performance improvements. Some reports on broad restructuring initiatives that include site-based management as one component of change have identified student gains. For example, Clark (1993) mentions increased attendance, higher grades, improved promotion rates, and fewer discipline cares for students in restructuring high schools in Philadelphia. In that setting, site-based management/shared decision making was identified as one of six major elements of change.

Overall, in spite of some positive observations, the research reviewed generally provided little data supporting the claim that implementation of site-based management in a school system by itself improved student performance.

Significantly, no studies reviewed provided a design that allowed for the analysis of the discrete impact of implementing site-based management on student performance. Thus, we are left without answers to the key question about its effect on school productivity. Sarason (1990) contended that "it would be egregiously wrong to justify the proposal on the grounds that it will improve educational scores, decrease dropout rates, and transform uninteresting classrooms into interesting ones" (p. 63). He advocates the adoption of the initiatives "based upon the belief that when a process makes people feel that they have a voice in matters that affect them, they will have greater responsibility for what happens to the enterprise" (p. 61). Still, it is, of course, the effects on productivity that have contributed to the popularity of decentralization efforts in the private sector and to recommendations from that part of our society for implementing site-based management in school districts.

Summary

An examination of the recent research on site-based management leads us to several conclusions. Researchers do not use the same terms to describe similar processes that have significantly differing components. No common definition of the strategy is used by those studying the subject concerning who is involved in the decision-making processes; the subject matter that is the focus of the decision making; or whether participants give advice to the principal who actually makes the decisions, as opposed to participants actually making the decisions in collaboration with the principal.

Current research does suggest that site-based management has not been completely implemented in any school system studied. Even those reports of the most promising nature temper their optimism with caveats about the lack of time for decision making or training for participants in the necessary processes.

The current research varies with respect to whether significant decisions concerning substantive issues are the focus of site-based management processes. Some researchers report that such is rarely the case, whereas others maintain that substantive issues are being addressed. Likewise, some researchers maintain that teachers really are provided little decision-making authority over significant matters, while others suggest that the contrary is true.

Recent research does consistently concur on two conclusions. First, the principal is an important participant in processes associated with the strategy and may frequently be disaffected by implementation attempts. It seems that principals see the strategy as merely undermining their traditional authority, rather than enhancing their ability to accomplish what traditional structures prevented. Second, no research reviewed provided specific data establishing a causal link between site-based management as a single strategy and improved student achievement. The research regarding site-based management we examined did not tend to conclude, as did the research on teacher empowerment described at the outset of this chapter, that "empowerment" leads to better instruction or is a critical ingredient in "effective schools" where students perform better.

Finally, as a result of our review of the research associated with site-based management, we pose several questions. Is it possible that the successful implementation of a site-based management system is impeded by the failure of those attempting such implementation to understand, acknowledge, and accommodate in their efforts the organizational complexity of school systems as described by Conley (1991) and Malen and Ogawa (1988)? Sarason (1990) asserted with respect to why attempts at school reform, including involvement of employees in decision making, fail; that is,

like almost all other complex traditional social organizations, the schools will accommodate in ways that require little or no change. This is not to say that the accommodation is insincere or deliberately cosmetic but rather that the strength of the status quo—its underlying axioms, its pattern of power relationships, its sense of tradition and therefore what seems right, natural, and proper—almost automatically rules out options for change in that status quo. (p. 35)

Is Sarason correct? Does involvement of an employee organization in the establishment of provisions governing site-based arrangement processes have an impact on successful implementation? Is it also possible that the often-reported disaffection of the building principal is associated with a significant role shift that is necessary for successful implementation of the strategy, but not explicitly addressed as part of implementation? Finally, is the lack of evidence for improved student achievement as a result of implementing site-based management due to a failure of the strategy itself, by inadequate research designs, or a failure to modify the fundamental organizational structure of the school system by utilizing just one school restructuring strategy? This last question seems particularly important in light of David's (1994) findings regarding the need for changes in roles of school board members, superintendents, and district personnel (p. 712). These questions may guide future research.

LESSONS AND IMPLICATIONS OF RESEARCH FOR TEACHER EDUCATORS

As noted, teachers entering the profession during the last part of the twentieth century are very likely to work in an environment that identifies empowerment of professionals (and others) in the school setting as a goal. Frequently, they will be in settings that practice some form of site-based management as a vehicle to achieve that empowerment.

As they come into the schools, new teachers will discover that people are unsure of their roles. Principals may also feel disaffected. Experienced teachers are likely to be unclear regarding the extent to which they have final authority, unsure of which decisions are theirs to make. The role of parents (and other community members) will vary considerably depending on the particular approach to empowerment/site-based management adopted by the school district or imposed by the state in which the new teacher begins work.

The research we have reviewed suggests that teachers today are much less likely to experience a career in which they work as isolates, as has been the case during most of the twentieth century. They will be expected, in some manner or another, to participate in decisions concerning the broader school community of which they are a part. They are likely to be faced with conflict in these relationships, which will require them to work collaboratively in tense situations marked by sharp differences in values. This situation suggests that they will need to know how to resolve interpersonal conflicts. Moreover, it suggests they will need to be clear on their values and the purposes of schooling in a democratic society. Without being well grounded in such matters, it will be difficult for them to function in the emerging environment.

New teachers need to be prepared to participate in systems that will continue to embody the tension between national goals and priorities and empowerment of local schools and teachers. It is unlikely that those responsible for preparing teachers will be able to teach their charges how to behave in a specific decision-making model. It is more likely that they will need to provide the new teachers with the values and the skills in group problem solving, communications, and conflict resolution necessary for negotiating successfully new systems in the settings where they are employed. Certainly, researchers have suggested, teachers will need a strong sense of self-efficacy. As noted, Meyer et al.'s (1993) work suggests that assertiveness training may become a necessary part of preparing teachers for these new expectations. One of the most obvious implications of the need for such education is that field experiences (student teaching, internships) will have to be designed to develop these understandings and skills as well as to develop proficiency in classroom performance.

An especially crucial element in these efforts, given an interpretation of empowerment as a collective concept, would be to provide teachers with opportunities for working together and engaging in specific processes such as reflection, problem solving, and decision making. The professionalization of teaching, Darling-Hammond (1985) argued, requires major changes in teacher education to support the development of standards of practice. Her suggestions reflect a significant emphasis on teacher collaboration. Induction of teachers, for example, would require more than perfunctory evaluations; it would involve frequent and continuous consultation, assistance, and feedback from expert teachers in the intern's own teaching area over an extended period. Classroom teachers would have opportunities for "discourse and inquiry . . . about real, immediate problems of practice." Acknowledging the debilitating effects of teacher isolation on professional growth and knowledge, Darling-Hammond wrote:

Teachers need opportunities to observe and be observed by their colleagues, to jointly diagnose school problems and invent new approaches, to share teaching ideas, to develop programs and curricula,

to assess the progress of their school and the students, and to learn from each other. (1985, p. 214)

Implicit in all of these suggested paths to teacher empowerment is a major transformation of the teacher's role, which necessarily invokes significant rethinking and revision of teacher education. In the several years after Darling-Hammond made these particular recommendations, Goodlad (1991) continued to stress the need for "a complete redesign of teacher education" based on his own extensive study of teacher education in the United States. He emphasized that simultaneous renewal of the education of educators (preservice and staff development programs) and of schooling is essential to the larger mission of providing the education needed by children in this democracy. This changed, professionalized role of the teacher as an empowered educator is one of the critical elements of the reforms Goodlad (1990) did not see in the approaches being taken by the institutions that prepare teachers in the United States.

Troen and Boles (1988) described a school–university partnership, which they believe could have a simultaneous impact on both practicing and preservice teachers. Their project subsequently became part of a school–university partnership linked with Goodlad's efforts through Wheelock College. As the elementary public school teachers directing the partnership, Troen and Boles focused on developing alternative teacher roles, such as researcher, trainer, or curriculum writer. In addition to the university partnership arrangement, crucial elements were team teaching to promote collaboration and collegial interaction, the participation of experienced teachers in training and supervising interns, and conducting college seminars. As common with projects of this nature, the results were limited to and by general observations and self-reports. The purpose of the Troen and Boles project was to ensure "the continuous renewal of teachers by restructuring their worklife" (p. 692). Results were reported basically as a single statement that central administration's "consciousness . . . has been raised concerning teachers' need for reflective time and possible alternative roles" (p. 692). Such efforts are reported widely in recent descriptions of Professional Development Schools (Darling-Hammond, 1994) and are part of the work of the National Network for Educational Renewal and of the Holmes Group.

There are additional implications of this review of research for teacher educators. Our inquiry concerning site-based management suggests that, when working with prospective teachers, teacher educators must be particularly careful not to impose views concerning site-based management that fail to take into account the limited and occassionally contradictory evidence about these subjects provided by research. For example, research does appear to be fairly conclusive that site-based management has not been implemented as intended. Therefore, to conclude as some authors have that it does (or does not) work is clearly unfounded.

Research provides some rather direct suggestions for teacher education regarding empowering teachers through their engagement in reflective professional thought. Reagan (1993) argued that while reflective practices in a teacher preparation program can and should be incorporated throughout the curriculum, courses in "philosophy of education, in particular, can be especially effective in preparing reflective practitioners" (p. 192). Pultorak (1993) reviewed the research on specific training methods (e.g., conferences, journal writing, seminars, action-oriented research) for developing reflective thinking in novice teachers, which also serves as significant evidence of the acceptance of this concept as a critical element in teacher preparation. Although this type of research focuses on specific methods for instilling reflective practices in preservice teachers (e.g., Hermann & Sarracino, 1993; Kennedy, 1991; Wedman & Martin, 1991), others are interested in the possibilities for practicing teachers.

Anders and Richardson (1991) and O'Loughlin (1992) reported on projects designed to lead teachers through an extended process of reflection and dialogue with the ultimate goal of improving classroom practice. Anders and Richardson conducted an ethnographic staff development project at two elementary schools that focused on teachers' beliefs and practices in teaching reading comprehension. The O'Loughlin project was a summer institute at Hofstra University for elementary and secondary teachers. Whereas the earlier project focused on a specific curricular area (reading instruction), the Hofstra project had a broader orientation:

This intensive institute is designed to provide an opportunity for elementary and secondary teachers to gain a sense of renewal and professional growth by coming together to reflect on their teaching in a collaborative and supportive environment. (p. 339)

Although these studies differ in their formats, they are comparable in their general approach and openness to personal, creative (constructivist) reflective activity. Both projects mention enhanced teacher awareness and understanding of the beliefs and knowledge shaping classroom practice. On the basis of their results, Anders and Richardson recommend similar staff development activities for cohorts of teachers, who can then engage in and become "skilled in the art of practical arguments and reflection and using that process to study their own teaching" (p. 321).

Miller (1992) engaged five teachers, formerly students in her seminar, in 3 years of "collaborative teacher-research" using discussions, readings, questioning, and shared experiences, to explore individual issues of classroom practice. Beyond this focus, however, the project sought to use collaboration and its process of teacher-centered inquiry to reveal "forms of oppression and imposition within school settings" (p. 154). In other words, Miller suggested that preservice and in-service teacher education can establish a context in which teachers create their own questions and frameworks for collaborative inquiry rather than having to be pressed into a "predetermined agenda" set by various institutional orders.

Brown (1992) reported on three ethnographic studies concerned with clarifying curriculum needs in mathematics and science for students in rural areas. One of these studies involved intensive reflection, discussion, and problem solving among a Georgia team of administrators and teachers representing a rural primary and secondary constituency. Brown points out that "the process rather than the product seemed to be of most value" (p. 45). After confirming that rural students need the same science and math concepts and skills as do students in other areas, the Georgia teachers then determined that instructional strategies did need to be adapted to their particular population of rural students. Brown suggested that reflective inquiry allowed these rural teachers to augment their own professional knowledge, empowering them then to become directly involved in defining curricular needs for their students and designing the appropriate instruction.

Working with preservice education, Colton and Sparks-Langer (1993) offered an especially comprehensive model designed to prepare novice teachers, through reflective activity, to assume central responsibility for setting goals, developing plans, making appropriate evaluations, and reflecting on their own professional thinking. They implemented this model in the form of three pilot teacher-education programs conducted over a 6-year period, which included both a teacher-induction and student-teaching program. These programs were characterized by significant reliance on experienced teachers as mentors, extensive training in various reflective activities, interpersonal skills, collaborative problem solving, and coaching techniques. Each phase of each program involved numerous opportunities for reflective activity, including journals, action research projects, written self-analyses, and development of a "growth plan." Although the writers indicated "promising" initial reactions from teachers and teacher educators, their report did not include evidence of other systematic, formal evaluation supporting the effectiveness of their programs.

CONCLUSION

There appears to be some broad agreement as to the potential influence of empowering teachers to engage in more active and informed decision making. However, substantive research is still needed to determine the relative effects of various reflective activities and styles of promoting these activities, what should be the content of such activity, and how these activities directly relate to specific practices, both those in the classroom as well as practices related to broader professional responsibilities of teachers. The literature on teacher reflection is also heavily weighted in descriptive and theoretical discussions rather than in well-defined, systematic research. If teacher reflection is to be readily accepted as a valid prerequisite to or concomitant factor in developing the knowledge, behaviors, and attitudes necessary for fully empowered teacher participation in all aspects of education, scholars need to generate a more substantial body of rigorous research, both qualitative and quantitative, that is grounded in a framework of coherent theory. This theory should somehow make possible the seemingly impossible and sensibly reconcile the various strands of related interests—constructivist theories, critical and feminist pedagogues, self-actualization, personal professionalism of teachers, collective autonomy, power and organizations, and site-based management. The considerations of teachers engaged in collaborative inquiry must address systemically the effects of the settings in which this inquiry takes place.

Even though they are far from conclusive, studies examined in this chapter suggest that preservice and in-service programs should be helping teachers acquire the knowledge, strategies, habits, and attitudes to enable them to make curricular decisions as well as to engage in the research and inquiry to support such decisions (see Sprague, 1992, for a critical perspective). Conventional methods courses generally do not have such a focus (Goodlad, 1990). Teachers need much more, including familiarity with curriculum models and theory, a solid grounding in the various disciplines, and a clear understanding of the principles of learning. Beyond the usual tests and measurements course, teachers should be exposed to standard research practices, both quantitative and qualitative, and engage in their own action research projects.

Our studies indicate that, whatever the findings of research about the efficacy of empowerment and site-based management, these practices are finding increasingly broad support within the policy community of the United States. New teachers will have to contend with them, for better or worse. Just as the philosophical disputes about individual versus state rights persist within the nation, questions continue about organizational, professional, and personal decision-making roles at schools.

References

Anders, P. L., & Richardson, V. (1991). Staff development that empowers teachers' reflection and enhances instruction. *Language Arts, 68,* 316–321.

Ashcroft, L. (1987). Defusing "empowering": The what and the why. *Language Arts, 64*(2), 142–156.

Ashton, P. T., & Webb, R. B. (1986). *Making a difference: Teachers' sense of efficacy and student achievement.* New York: Longman.

Bacharach, S. B., Bauer, S. C., & Shedd, J. B. (1986, April). The learning workplace: The conditions and resources of teaching. In *Conditions and resources of teaching.* Washington, DC: National Education Association.

Barth, R. S. (1990). *Improving schools from within.* San Francisco: Jossey-Bass.

Belenky, M. F., Clinchy, B. M., Goldberger, N. R. & Tarule, J. M. (1986). *Women's ways of knowing: The development of self, voice, and mind.* New York: Basic Books.

Bellevue Education Association. (1992). *1992 elementary survey aggregate data display.* Bellevue, WA: Author.

Bellevue Education Association. (1993a). *1993 survey perceptions of high school employees aggregate data display.* Bellevue, WA: Author.

Bellevue Education Association. (1993b). *1993 survey perceptions of middle school employees aggregate data display.* Bellevue, WA: Author.

Blase, J. (1991). *The politics of life in schools: Power, conflict, and cooperation.* Newbury Park, CA: Sage.

Bluestone, B., & Bluestone, I. (1992). *Negotiating the future: A labor perspective on American business.* New York: Basic Books.

Bolin, F. S. (1989). Empowering leadership. *Teachers College Record, 91*(1), 81–96.

Brandt, R. (1989). On teacher empowerment: A conversation with Ann Lieberman. *Educational Leadership, 46*(8), 23–26.

Brown, D. J. (1987). *A preliminary inquiry into school-based management.* Ottawa, Canada: Social Sciences and Humanities Research Council.

Brown, M. M. (1992). Rural science and mathematics education: Empowerment through self-reflection and expanding curricular alternatives. In G. A. Hess, Jr. (Ed.), *Empowering teachers and parents* (pp. 29–46). Westport, CT: Bergin & Garvey.

Bryk, A. S., Easton, J. Q., Kerbow, D., Rollow, S. G., & Sebring, P. A. (1993). *A view from the elementary schools: The state of reform in Chicago.* Chicago: The Consortium on Chicago School Research.

Burbules, N. C. (1986). A theory of power in education. *Educational Theory, 36,* 95–114.

Carnegie Forum on Education and the Economy. (1986). *A nation prepared: Teachers for the 21st century.* New York: Carnegie Corporation.

Chapman, J., & Boyd, W. L. (1986). Decentralization, devolution, and the school principal: Australian lessons on statewide educational reform. *Educational Administration Quarterly, 22*(4), 28–58.

Christenson, L. M. (1992). *Empowerment of preservice educators through effective mentoring.* University of Alabama. (ERIC Document Reproduction Service No. ED 338 614)

Clark, R. W. (1993, July 9). *Annual report: Philadelphia school restructuring.* Seattle: Institute for Educational Inquiry.

Clift, R. T. (1991). Teacher education and teaching empowerment for whom? when? *Teacher-Educator, 27*(1), 14–23.

Clift, R. T., Johnson, M., Holland, P., & Veal, M. L. (1992). Developing the potential for collaborative school leadership. *American Educational Research Journal, 29*(4), 877–908.

Cochran-Smith, M., & Lytle, S. L. (1990). Research on teaching and teacher research: The issues that divide. *Educational Researcher, 19*(2), 2–11.

Cochran-Smith, M., & Lytle, S. L. (1992). Communities for teacher research: Fringe or forefront? *American Journal of Education, 100*(3), 298–324.

Colton, A. B., & Sparks-Langer, G. M. (1993). A conceptual framework to guide the development of teacher reflection and decision making. *Journal of Teacher Education, 44*(1), 45–54.

Combs, A. W., Blume, R. A., Newman, A. J., & Wass, H. L. (1974). *The professional education of teachers: A humanistic approach to teacher preparation.* Boston: Allyn & Bacon.

Conley, S. (1991). Review of research on teacher participation in school decision making. *Review of Research in Education, 17,* 225–266.

Cooke, W. N. (1990). *Labor management cooperation.* Kalamazoo, MI: Upjohn Institute.

Cornett, J. W. (1991). Earned powerment not empowerment of teachers: The role of teachers' systematic reflection in restructuring schools. *Social Science Record, 28*(1), 71–77.

Cushman, K. (1990). Practice into theory: Teachers coaching teachers. *Horace, 7*(2), 1–8.

Danzberger, J. P. (1994). Governing the nation's schools: The case for restructuring local school boards. *Phi Delta Kappan, 75*(5), 367–373.

Darling-Hammond, L. (1985). Valuing teachers: The making of a profession. *Teachers College Record, 87*(2), 209–218.

Darling-Hammond, L. (Ed.). (1994). *Professional development schools.* New York: Teachers College Press.

David, J. L. (1989). Synthesis of research on school-based management. *Educational Leadership, 46*(8), 45–53.

David, J. L. (1994). School-based decision making: Kentucky's test of decentralization. *Phi Delta Kappan, 75*(9), 706–712.

DeLacy, J. (1990). *The Bellevue evaluation study: Studying the effects of school renewal.* Bellevue: Institute for the Study of Educational Policy, University of Washington and the Bellevue School District.

DeLacy, J. (1992). *The Bellevue evaluation study (second report): Studying the effects of school renewal.* Bellevue: Institute for the Study of Educational Policy, University of Washington and the Bellevue School District.

Delpit, L. D. (1988). The silenced dialogue: Power and pedagogy in educating other people's children. *Harvard Educational Review, 58*(3), 280–298.

Devaney, K. (1987). *The lead teacher: Ways to begin.* Paper prepared for the Task Force on Teaching as a Profession, Carnegie Forum on Education and the Economy, New York.

Dewey, J. (1916). *Democracy and education.* New York: The Free Press.

Dewey, J. (1933). *How we think: A restatement of the relation of reflective thinking to the educative process.* Chicago: D.C. Heath.

Dippo, D., Gelb, S. A., Turner, I., & Turner, T. (1991). Making the political personal: Problems of privilege and power in postsecondary teaching. *Journal of Education, 173*(3), 81–95.

Drucker, P. F. (1980). *Managing in turbulent times.* New York: Harper & Row.

Eaton, A. E., & Voos, P. B. (1991). *Unions and contemporary innovations in work organizations, compensations, and employee participation.* Cited in Bluestone, B., & Bluestone, I. (1992). *Negotiating the future: A labor perspective on American business.* New York: Basic Books.

Ellsworth, E. (1989). Why doesn't this feel empowering? Working through the repressive myths of critical pedagogy. *Harvard Educational Review, 59*(3), 297–324.

Etheridge, C. P., Hall, M. L., Brown, N., & Lucas, S. (1990). *Establishing school based decision making in seven urban schools in Memphis, Tennessee: The first year.* Memphis: Center for Research in Educational Policy, College of Education, Memphis State University.

Farris, P. J., & Hancock, M. R. (1989). To and from the ivory tower: Theory, practice, and empowerment. *Teacher Educator, 24*(4), 8–14.

Fay, C. (1992). Empowerment through leadership: In the teachers' voice. In C. Livingston (Ed.), *Teachers as leaders: Evolving roles* (pp. 57–90). Washington, DC: National Education Association Professional Library.

Fuller, F. F. (1971). Intensive individualization of teacher preparation. In L. F. Natalicio & C. F. Hereford (Eds.), *The teacher as a person* (pp. 1–26). Dubuque, IA: Wm. C. Brown.

Goodlad, J. I. (1984). *A place called school.* New York: McGraw-Hill.

Goodlad, J. I. (1990). *Teachers for our nation's schools.* San Francisco: Jossey-Bass.

Goodlad, J. I. (1991). Why we need a complete redesign of teacher education. *Educational Leadership, 49*(3), 4–6, 8–10.

Goodlad, J. I., Soder, R., & Sirotnik, K. A. (Eds.). (1990a). *The moral dimensions of teaching.* San Francisco: Jossey-Bass.

Goodlad, J. I., Soder, R., & Sirotnik, K. A. (Eds.). (1990b). *Places where teachers are taught.* San Francisco: Jossey-Bass.

Gove, M. K., & Kennedy-Calloway, C. (1992). Action research: Empowering teachers to work with at-risk students. *Journal of Reading, 35*(7), 526–534.

Hargreaves, A. (1994). *Changing teachers, changing times.* New York: Teachers College Press.

Harnack, R. S. (1968). *The teacher: Decision maker and curriculum planner.* Scranton, PA: International Textbook Co.

Henderson, J. G. (1992). Curriculum discourse and the question of empowerment. *Theory into Practice, 31*(3), 204–209.

Hermann, B. A., & Sarracino, J. (1993). Restructuring a preservice literacy methods course: Dilemmas and lessons learned. *Journal of Teacher Education, 44*(2), 96–106.

Hess, G. A. (Ed.). (1992). *Empowering teachers and parents: School restructuring through the eyes of anthropologists.* Westport, CT: Bergin & Garvey.

Hill, P. T., & Bonan, J. (1991). *Decentralization and accountability in public education.* Santa Monica, CA: RAND.

Holmes Group. (1986). *Tomorrow's teachers: A report of the Holmes Group.* East Lansing, MI: Author.

Houser, N. O. (1990). Teacher-researcher: The synthesis of roles for teacher empowerment. *Action in Teacher Education, 12*(2), 55–60.

Johnson, S. M. (1990). *Teachers at work.* New York: Basic Books.

Kennedy, M. M. (1991). Some surprising findings on how teachers learn to teach. *Educational Leadership, 49*(3), 14–17.

Kreisberg, S. (1992). *Transforming power: Domination, empowerment, and education.* Albany: State University of New York Press.

Labaree, D. (1992). Power, knowledge, and the rationalization of teaching: A genealogy of the movement to professionalize teaching. *Harvard Educational Review, 62*(2), 123–154.

Lichtenstein, G., McLaughlin, M., & Knudsen, J. (1991). Teacher empowerment and professional knowledge. Rutgers, NY: Consortium for Policy Research in Education.

Lieberman, A. (1986). Collaborative research: Working with, not working on. . . . *Educational Leadership, 43*(5), 28–32.

Lieberman, A. (Ed.). (1988). *Building a professional culture in schools.* New York: Teachers College Press.

Lieberman, A., Saxl, E. R., & Miles, M. B. (1988). Teacher leadership: Ideology and practice. In A. Lieberman (Ed.), *Building a professional culture in schools* (pp. 148–166). New York: Teachers College Press.

Lightfoot, S. (1986). On goodness in schools: Themes of empowerment. *Peabody Journal of Education, 63*(3), 9–28.

Little, J. W. (1988). Assessing the prospects for teacher leadership. In A. Lieberman (Ed.), *Building a professional culture in schools* (pp. 78–106). New York: Teachers College Press.

Livingston, C. (Ed.). (1992). *Teachers as leaders: Evolving roles.* Washington, DC: National Education Association Professional Library.

Maeroff, G. I. (1988). *The empowerment of teachers.* New York: Teachers College Press.

Malen, B. (1992). Bellevue: Renewal and school decision making. Claremont, CA: The Claremont Graduate School.

Malen, B., & Ogawa, R. T. (1988). Professional-patron influence on site-based governance councils: A confounding case study. *Educational Evaluation and Policy Analysis, 10*(4), 251–270.

Mauriel, J. J., & Lindquist, K. M. (1989). *School-based management: Doomed to failure?* San Francisco: American Educational Research Association.

McLaughlin, M. W., & Yee, S. M. (1988). School as a place to have a career. In A. Lieberman (Ed.), *Building a professional culture in schools* (pp. 23–44). New York: Teachers College Press.

Mertens, S., & Yarger, S. J. (1988). Teaching as a profession: Leadership, empowerment, and involvement. *Journal of Teacher Education, 39*(1), 32–37.

Meyer, M. M., Linville, M. E., & Rees, G. (1993). The development of a positive self-concept in preservice teachers. *Action in Teacher Education, 15*(1), 30–35.

Miller, J. (1990). *Creating spaces and finding voices.* Albany: State University of New York Press.

Miller, L. (1992). Teacher leadership in a renewing school. In C. Livingston (Ed.), *Teachers as leaders: Evolving roles* (pp. 115–130). Washington, DC: National Education Association Professional Library.

Monson, M. P., & Monson, R. J. (1993). Who creates curriculum? New roles for teachers. *Educational Leadership, 51*(2), 19–21.

Moore, D. R. (1992). The case for parent and community involvement. In G. A. Hess Jr. (Ed.), *Empowering teachers and parents* (pp. 131–156). Westport, CT: Bergin & Garvey.

National Education Association. (1988). *Conditions and resources of teaching.* West Haven, CT: Author.

National Education Association. (1990). *Business and the reshaping of public education.* Washington, DC: Author.

National Education Association. (1991). *Studies in collective bargaining site-based decisionmaking: The 1990 NEA census of local associations.* West Haven, CT: Author.

Nel, J. (1992). The empowerment of minority students: Implications of Cummins' model for teacher education. *Action in Teacher Education, 14*(3), 38–45.

O'Hair, M., & Blase, J. (1992). Power and politics in the classroom: Implications for teacher education. *Action in Teacher Education, 14*(1), 10–17.

O'Loughlin, M. (1992). Empowering teachers in emancipatory knowledge construction. *Journal of Teacher Education, 43*(5), 336–346.

O'Loughlin, M., & Campbell, M. B. (1988). Teacher preparation, teacher empowerment, and reflective inquiry: A critical perspective. *Teacher Education Quarterly, 15*(4), 25–53.

Ouchi, W. (1981). *Theory Z: How American business can meet the Japanese challenge.* Reading, MA: Addison-Wesley.

Peters, T. (1988). *Thriving on chaos.* New York: Knopf.

Prawat, R. (1991). Conversations with self and settings: A framework for thinking about teacher empowerment. *American Educational Research Journal, 28*(4), 737–757.

Pultorak, E. G. (1993). Facilitating reflective thought in novice teachers. *Journal of Teacher Education, 44*(4), 288–295.

Reagan, T. (1993). Educating the "reflective practitioner": The contribution of philosophy of education. *Journal of Research and Development in Education, 26*(4), 189–196.

Reich, R. (1992). *The work of nations: Preparing ourselves for the 21st century.* New York: Knopf.

Richmond, V. P., & McCroskey, J. C. (Eds.). (1992). *Power in the classroom: Communication, control, and concern.* Hillsdale, NJ: Lawrence Erlbaum Associates.

Rogers, C. R. (1971). What it means to become a person. In L. F. S. Natalicio & C. F. Hereford (Eds.), *The teacher as a person* (pp. 59–74). Dubuque, IA: Wm. C. Brown.

Rogus, J. F. (1988). Teacher leader programming: Theoretical underpinnings. *Journal of Teacher Education, 39*(1), 46–52.

Rosenholtz, S. J. (1989). *Teachers workplace: The social organization of schools.* New York: Longman.

Rubin, L. (1989). The thinking teacher: Cultivating pedagogical intelligence. *Journal of Teacher Education, 40*(6), 31–34.

Sarason, S. (1990). *The predictable failure of educational reform.* San Francisco: Jossey-Bass.

Schön, D. (1983). *The reflective practitioner: How professionals think in action.* New York: Basic Books.

Senge, P. M. (1990). *The fifth discipline: The art and practice of the learning organization.* New York: Doubleday.

Simon, R. (1987). Empowerment as a pedagogy of possibility. *Language Arts, 64*(4), 370–382.

Smith, J. L., & Johnson, H. A. 1993. Control in the classroom: Listening to adolescent voices. *Language Arts, 70*(1), 18–29.

Smylie, M. A. (1992a). Teacher participation in school decision making: Assessing willingness to participate. *Educational Evaluation and Policy Analysis, 14*(1), 53–67.

Smylie, M. A. (1992b). Teachers' reports of their interactions with teacher leaders concerning classroom instruction. *Elementary School Journal, 93*(1), 85–98.

Smyth, J. (1989). Developing and sustaining initial reflection in teacher education. *Journal of Teacher Education, 40*(2), 2–9.

Smyth, J. (1991). *Teachers as collaborative learners: Challenging dominant forms of supervision.* Philadelphia: Open University Press.

Sparks-Langer, G., & Colton, A. (1991). Synthesis of research on teachers reflective thinking. *Educational Leadership, 48*(6), 37–44.

Sprague, J. (1992). Critical perspectives on teacher empowerment. *Communication Education, 41*(2), 181–203.

Talbert, J. E., & McLaughlin, M. W. (1994). Teacher professionalism in local school contexts. *American Journal of Education, 102*(2), 123–153.

Troen, V., & Boles, K. (1988). The teaching project: A model for teacher empowerment. *Language Arts, 65*(7), 688–692.

Wasley, P. (1991). *Teachers who lead: The rhetoric of reform and the realities of practice.* New York: Teachers College Press.

Waterman, R. H. (1987). *The renewal factor.* New York: Bantam Books.

Wedman, J. M., & Martin, M. W. (1991). The influence of a reflective student teaching program: An evaluation study. *Journal of Research and Development in Education, 24*(2), 33–41.

Weiss, C. H. (1993). Shared decision-making about what? A comparison of schools with and without teacher participation. *Teachers College Record, 95*(1), 68–92.

White, P. A. (1992). Teacher empowerment under "ideal" school-site autonomy. *Educational Evaluation and Policy Analysis, 14*(1), 69–82.

Wirsig, M. E. (1987). Holmes and Carnegie: The myth of bold new reform. *Teacher Education Quarterly, 14*(1), 40–51.

Yonemura, M. (1986). Reflections on teacher empowerment and teacher education. *Harvard Educational Review, 56*(4), 473–480.

Zehm, S. J., & Kottler, J. A. (1993). *On being a teacher.* Newbury Park, CA: Corwin Press.

Zeichner, K. M. (1989). Preparing teachers for democratic schools. *Action in Teacher Education, 11*(1), 5–9.

Zeichner, K. M. (1991). Contradiction and tensions in the professionalization of teaching and the democratization of schools. *Teachers College Record, 92*(3), 363–379.

TEACHING EFFECTS AND TEACHER EVALUATION

Thomas L. Good

UNIVERSITY OF ARIZONA

This chapter summarizes not only what is known about effective teaching, but also how such knowledge informs teacher evaluation practices. Summarizing the history, traditions, and knowledge in these two areas is a formidable task.

Many authoritative articles, chapters, and books have been written on teacher evaluation and teacher effectiveness, and interest in this topic continues. Indeed, Haney, Madaus, and Kreitzer (1987) have noted that issues of society's concern for evaluating teaching can be traced back to colonial times. Similar to other important, controversial subjects, research on teaching and teacher evaluation has received attention for reasons both positive and negative.

CHAPTER ORGANIZATION

Given the abundance of relevant publications available, it seems inappropriate simply to review extant literature in this chapter. However, I would be remiss not to discuss major topics and resources for graduate students and other readers who are approaching the issues of teacher evaluation and effectiveness for the first time. This chapter emphasizes that teacher evaluation is a complex activity that has technical requirements as well as academic, political, and social consequences. Teaching is a complex and demanding task that can be viewed from various theoretical orientations; multiple dimensions of teaching call for integrative analysis and evaluation. In this chapter the argument is made that appropriate evaluation necessitates that one understand and use the knowledge and concepts that have been produced by various research traditions. However, such knowledge must also be integrated with other types of knowledge, including that derived from practice.

Social and Political Contexts

In this chapter stress is placed on the strong social context of teaching, in which citizens have firmly held views of what constitutes appropriate outcomes of teaching and schooling. The chapter argues that societal expectations, although strongly socialized, are, to some extent, contrary to modern theoretical perspectives on the promotion of classroom learning. Citizens are more likely to understand the need to change the conditions of schooling if educators focus on both the social needs of students and broader conceptualizations of curriculum and learning. In fact, parents and educators probably agree more on many social issues (e.g., safety, personal responsibility) than they do on what constitutes academic excellence and progress (e.g., to what extent should student work be knowledge-driven or problem-solving oriented). This is partly why citizens routinely rate the local school more favorably than schools in general (more on this later).

After discussing the social context of education, the chapter addresses the political context in which education is debated and viewed by society. I argue that the restrictive conceptualization of successful education as high scores on standardized tests is antiquated and unproductive. Achievement tests, particularly standardized achievement tests, are political symbols as much as assessment devices. Educators must demand that broader and more appropriate visions of schooling and related outcome measures be included in the debate. At a minimum, standardized tests must undergo significant modification in form and function.

Review of Research: Teacher Effectiveness and Evaluation

Having established that teacher evaluation (and most certainly resources for teacher evaluation and development) is heavily

The author acknowledges the helpful comments provided by Tom Buttery, Lyn Corno, Pat Hinchey, Gail Hinkel, Terry Mason, Mary McCaslin, John Mergendoller, and John Sikula. I also want to thank Jo Ann Santoro for typing multiple copies of this chapter.

linked to societal and political forces, the chapter discusses the literature on effective teachers and schools. Logically, one important source for building useful teacher evaluation programs is the knowledge base from research: What is known about teachers' experience, thinking, instructional behavior, and so on, and how do these dimensions relate to how students think, what they know, and how they feel. The chapter briefly describes several research programs and traditions that have been used to explore questions of effectiveness since 1960. As will be argued later, the field is characterized by isolated research traditions whose focus is constantly shifting. However, much progress has occurred in research, and I argue the need for integrating concepts and insights and discuss the need for more inclusive and integrating paradigms. One such possibility, the teaching for student understanding perspective, is addressed.

Although several research traditions are identified and analyzed, a brief critique focuses on two research perspectives: process-product and constructivist/teaching-for-understanding. The chapter contends that research provides language and concepts that help us think more carefully and productively about teaching and its evaluation. However, both the conduct and interpretation of research are affected by political and social factors, and educators need to consider research in the context of the particular school or class, as well as local values, resources, and so on (Good & Brophy, 1994). Many critical questions related to teacher evaluation have never been explored systematically. Moreover, some research has yielded equivocal or inconsistent findings. Some questions, for example, on teacher responsibility and moral conduct, are inherently difficult to research in any systematic fashion (Mohatt, 1994; Oser, Dick, & Patry, 1992).

After clarifying the research on effective teachers and schools, the chapter turns to teacher evaluation, a topic that has been written about extensively and researched occasionally. Although I identify sources of useful analytical constructs, empirical data, and descriptions of ethical and moral considerations, as with research on teaching, evaluation and its logical consequences must be debated and calibrated in a local context. Performance evaluation is productive when (1) values and goals are articulated, (2) all participants understand the framework for evaluation (perceive it to be fair and equitable), (3) evaluation is implemented as intended (i.e., goals, processes, and rewards are congruent, and all participants understand the ideology that undergirds the evaluation system), and (4) the system is reexamined and modified periodically, both in terms of new knowledge about the process per se and in relation to emerging goals for new ways of thinking about individual and community performance.

The Need to Increase Research and Development

Having acknowledged some of the benefits from research and scholarship in the area, I argue that increased funding for research and development might make classroom evaluation much more helpful to educators as they implement (and recalibrate) curriculum and instructional theory. With a better research and development base and better performance appraisal systems, American schools could be improved in important ways. Current conceptions of teachers, students, curriculum, and instruction have moved beyond the format of traditional tests. That is, current models of instruction focus on active learners who define and solve problems as opposed to learners who memorize disconnected facts. Thus, we need not only research and development to further our knowledge of student learning in schools but also research to identify better assessment procedures.

Although there is much creative development under way, it is beyond the scope of this chapter to describe and comment on the various large-scale teacher assessment initiatives that are under way. However, it is useful to mention that several major efforts are in progress (National Board of Professional Teaching Standards, New Standards Project, Interstate New Teachers Assessment and Support Consortium, etc.) and to acknowledge that some states (e.g., California, Connecticut, Kentucky, Vermont, etc.) are making major efforts to improve assessment systems. These projects may have a strong impact on the field in the future; however, at this point they are best seen as work in progress. Similarly, it also is beyond the scope of this chapter to explore international work that addresses issues of authentic assessment, national assessment, and related issues (e.g., Torrance, 1993).

Modern constructions of learning and instruction have had fewer effects on practice than many believe. There have been some changes in the curriculum, but the gap between the recommendations of professional groups (e.g., National Council of Teachers of Mathematics [NCTM], National Council of Teachers of English [NCTE], etc.) for reform and the typical eighth-grade class is often considerable (Good, 1991; Hinchey, 1994). As is argued later in the chapter, new information is not well assimilated in the field because there are too few resources invested in building an *infrastructure* that helps teachers adaptively integrate new ideas and concepts into their teaching. For example, teachers need more than software and computers; they also need training in how to adapt software to their instructional needs. Teachers benefit immensely from organizations such as the Bay Area Writing Project, a free-standing organization that works collaboratively with teachers to help them learn about and implement process writing approaches in their classrooms. Thus, we need to encourage the development of new models of dissemination and extended forms of professional support if modern conceptions of teaching are to be implemented widely.

However, if the field narrowed the gap between normative professional beliefs and classroom practices, such progress might be reflected in lower scores on conventional standardized tests unless these tests were altered in important ways. Successful teaching for student understanding and integrating across concepts may well result in lower scores when such conventional tests mainly stress memorization of isolated facts or principles. Clearly, there is a need simultaneously to develop congruent conceptions of testing and learning, to help citizens understand the need for new approaches, and to free teachers from the constraint that the only formula for successful teaching is high scores on standardized tests.

Enhanced Communication and Political Socialization

The chapter then asserts that political attitudes directly influence academic research and development. Hence, educators need to do a better job of communication with the public. As a starting point, researchers and educators must change the language of assessing schools and how they describe successful education.

Standardized tests are part of the social and political fabric of our society. They are assumed to measure important school outcomes, based on the belief that these scores are a proxy for what ultimately counts in society. Educators need to confront this mistaken belief directly. To change the debate over important outcomes in American schools, educators must change the language and broaden the vision of what constitutes success for schools and students. New dependent measures must be argued for, and we must widen the conception of students to recognize them as social beings who are more than simply learners of subject matter (McCaslin & Good, in press a, in press b).

Of pressing importance is the development of sophisticated and useful models of student and teaching performance assessment that are related to current conceptions of instruction. Furthermore, the diversity of successful practice needs to be recognized as teachers must be able to use various instructional models—and valid performance measures—if they are to be successful with a diverse population of students. Financial resources from government and commitment from educators will be required to develop and socially validate new measures. As these models are developed and refined, political socialization to persuade policymakers and citizens that emerging systems merit support will also be necessary. Also important, policymakers need to understand that a call for new measures is insufficient; needed resources must be provided to develop sophisticated and workable measures. The same forces that encouraged the public to accept standardized achievement test scores as a proxy for student progress (in schools preparing students for a factory-model society) can, at least theoretically, be used to illustrate that current standardized achievement tests are inadequate for an "information society."

In developing the argument for new methods of instruction and assessment, the chapter focuses on two of many relevant and exciting new possibilities, the use of portfolios and small-group instructional models. The importance of evaluating these new assessment methods based on the *quality* of their implementation is stressed. Renewed research and development in these areas hold great potential. If the study of teaching is to be improved in ways that lead to enhanced student performance on measures that matter, researchers must coordinate social and political support in building a better infrastructure for research and development.

THE SOCIAL CONTEXT OF EVALUATION

Standardized achievement tests in their present form should play only a limited role in assessing student progress, even though tests are the accepted scoring system for the nation's schools. I want to challenge the validity of the scoring system in our nation's schools.

At the 1994 Olympics, there was a large outcry in the American media concerning who should have won the women's Olympic skating title. Most public attention focused on the judges and reliability; few, if any, questioned the validity of the

scoring system. Evaluation surrounds and embraces contemporary society. We attempt to differentiate athletic capability (as in the Olympics) by using scoring systems that often lead to hotly debated outcomes, even though criteria for performance are well known. Although evaluation has a long history (e.g., the Olympics), the emphasis on evaluation seems especially acute and ever present. We have known some forms of evaluation for some time: (1) All-star basketball and Little League teams are selected, and (2) parents worry about whether their son or daughter is in the second- or the fourth-highest reading group. The courts judge parents' care-giving abilities even to the point that a custody decision sometimes rests on how well a parent can play patty cake (other fields also have problems in utilizing appropriate dependent measures!). Citizens are involved more actively in evaluating judges (a recent development). As institutions are downsized (or rightsized, depending on one's political point of view), there is more evaluation of job performance—on the line, in the office, and in executive headquarters. Universities are consumed with internal evaluation that requires much time and money and, some would argue, yields little of practical import.

Although readers may challenge my observation that evaluation is more prevalent now than ever before, most readers would agree that we live in a society in which evaluation is ever present. Youths compare their tennis shoes, and middle-age Americans compare their homes, their children, and other indices of wealth and status. Evaluation is so constant that we often tend not to think about it at all and to accept it as a given.

A special problem for teachers is that most people consider themselves experts on classroom teaching, a fact that has important consequences. We have all been in classrooms (being stimulated in many and being bored or belittled in a few). If citizens believe evaluation is simple and straightforward ("I can tell you who my favorite teachers were and *why*"), then they do not see a need to invest in professional development in order to train principals or teachers to become better evaluators (or stimulators, or facilitators) of teachers. Thus, teacher evaluation is often taken for granted. Berliner (1986) noted that although considerable money is spent on training judges for horse, cattle, or dog shows, little is allocated to improve judgments of effective or outstanding teaching. Evaluation of teaching often involves little conceptual planning or research review. It frequently is ineffective and sometimes unfair or biased. Indeed, too often teacher evaluation systems erode rather than boost teacher morale, which is one of their putative purposes.

There is currently a great deal of excitement and controversy surrounding the issue of testing, of teachers as well as of students. Testing is a frequent topic in newspapers and at professional meetings. The following are titles of only a few of the numerous sessions involving testing that were presented at the 1994 meeting of the American Educational Research Association: How Teachers View the Classroom Assessment Process; Understanding State Efforts to Reform Teaching and Learning; The Social Construction of Assessment; Revision of Standards for Educational and Psychological Testing; Using Evaluation in the Service of Student Learning; Revision of Standards for Educational and Psychological Testing—Advice from the Membership; Using the New Program Evaluation Standards; Alternative Assessment in Higher Education—Putting the Spotlight on

Student Experiences; Performance-Based Assessment; Issues of Equity and Fairness; Educational Assessment—Are the Politicians Winning Two Years Later?; Alternative Assessment—Escalating Revolutionary Change or Leading to a Revolving Door?; two sessions on Computer-Based Performance Assessment; A Measurement-Driven Instruction versus Instruction-Driven Measurement Debate—Who Should Be Behind the Wheel? Multiple papers were presented at each session.

Later it is argued that perhaps educators and policymakers can use the public's interest in testing to gain support for generating new norms for conceptualizing and assessing school performance. My guarded optimism resides in the fact that professional interest in the topic is matched by citizens' interest.

THE POLITICAL CONTEXT OF EVALUATION

The public attention focused on school accountability and teacher evaluation is considerable. It is also a political issue. Editorials, front-page newspaper stories, and general news, both in print and in the visual media, focus heavily on schools. Unfortunately, the image of schooling presented by contemporary media is largely pejorative. Society willingly spends one half a billion dollars to implement standardized testing programs each year (Paris, Lawton, Turner, & Roth, 1991). This is a conservative spending estimate, because it does not include the vast human resources necessary to prepare for achievement testing, the time spent interpreting scores, or consideration of how students and teachers might better spend class time that is currently allocated to preparing for tests.

Furthermore, it is clear that the movement toward more performance-based assessment will increase testing costs substantially. For example, McDonnell (1994) notes that the cost of national testing varies widely, with some estimates suggesting that the bill for national testing using performance-based models would increase substantially.

Obviously, testing is big business and, like any business, many persons stand ready to protect their investment. Mehrens and Lehmann (1987) noted that about 200 million achievement tests are given in the United States annually. Further, Haney, Madaus, and Lyons (1993) report that use of such tests continues to increase. The business started and maintains itself, however, because of explicit needs. For certain groups the achievement test is a powerful tool that helps maintain privilege (e.g., the opportunity to win scholarships on the basis of ability, only certain students get in algebra in the seventh grade, etc.).

To take advantage of public and professional interest in evaluation, educators and researchers must understand the political context in which they operate. Court decisions, public opinion, and specific votes will become salient factors affecting whether funds are increased for school districts with poor financial resources. For example, Ivor Peterson (1994) reported that a special commission appointed by the New Jersey governor has proposed that all schools in the state (except for those in the poorest districts) assume considerably more of the cost of running school districts. This proposal, if enacted, would transfer costs for teacher retirement from the state to local taxpayers.

It is important to ask why a public that is so interested in holding educators accountable is becoming more unwilling to

fund education and support teachers (especially in inner-city or rural schools). Not only are public policymakers becoming more resistant to paying for public schools, but they also are becoming more vocal in seeking alternatives (e.g., vouchers). The effect is to undermine public schooling. I submit that policymakers have created the perception that educators could take control—could improve schools—but choose not to do so. Policymakers thus argue that if funds currently invested in schools are poorly used, educators should not be given more money. Moreover, what better way to prove that schools are doing a poor job than to use measures of schooling outcomes that are inconsistent with many educators' views of the way school success should be measured (memorization versus understanding).

However, in fairness, it should be noted that standardized tests in some situations have been improved. In California, much work has been done on testing formats using enhanced multiple-choice items. See, for example, the sample items in Figure 28.1. Furthermore, Scriven (1993) has described a machine-scorable approach that requires students to exercise judgment. I stress that my argument against the excessive use of multiple-choice tests is aimed at their present level of conceptualization. Perhaps, as Scriven argues, more viable forms can be developed.

In some cases, such political views are based on the belief that schools are indeed poor investments, but in other cases it appears that the political motivation is to be certain that some students have more advantages than others. However, no matter what the reason, the argument that resources are unrelated to student growth and that schools are categorically a poor investment is fallacious. Hedges, Laine, and Greenwald (1994a, 1994b) reanalyzed studies of the relation between resource inputs and school outcomes. Their results provide strong empirical support that increased resources improve student performance, especially for global resource variables and teacher experience:

Even if the conclusions drawn from the studies analyzed in this paper are correct, we would not argue that "throwing money at schools" is the most efficient method of increasing educational achievement. It almost surely is not. However, the question of whether more resources are needed to produce real improvement in our nation's schools can no longer be ignored. Relying on the data most often used to deny that resources are related to achievement, we find that money *does* matter after all. (Hedges et al., 1994a, p. 13)

One contribution of educational researchers is to illustrate the value of economic and research investment in schooling. It might also be prudent for educators or researchers occasionally to help the public become more aware of the costs of *not* investing in education. We know that students who drop out of school are less likely to be employed and that citizens who lack meaningful employment are more likely to commit crimes—and often go to jail. As Rosenbaum (1994) noted, the biggest tax increase (about 96%) from 1985 to 1991 was at the county level. County taxes have increased largely because of the need for the construction and maintenance of more jails.

Valid reasons must be given for increasing educational funding at a time when many Americans find their incomes "pinched." As Beatty (1994) argued:

Sample Test Form—Grade 10

A person breathes 20 times a minute at sea level and takes one additional breath per minute for each increase of 1,500 feet in altitude. How high, in feet above sea level, is the person if he breathes 24 times a minute?

A. 1,500 feet
B. 3,000 feet
C. 4,500 feet
D. 6,000 feet

(Scratch work)

Square tiles are laid out in a continuous pattern, a part of which is shown below. Which one of the following numbers will **not** appear at a corner?

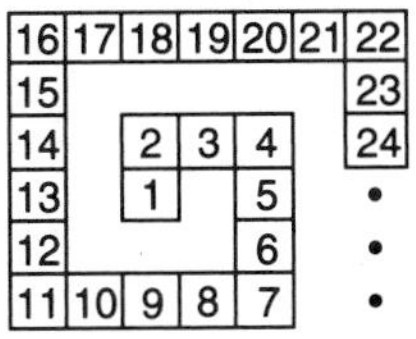

A. 29
B. 37
C. 45
D. 56

(Scratch work)

FIGURE 28.1. Examples of Enhanced Multiple-Choice Items. (*Source*: California Department of Education, *Examples of Enhanced Multiple Choice Items* (Sample test forms, grades 10, 11. Addendum, Preliminary Edition. 1993. Reprinted with permission.)

The crisis of the middle class feeds the property-tax revolt that in many school districts has forced cutbacks in school budgets, just as competition from abroad is requiring dramatic improvement in education. People cannot be expected to pay more taxes if their incomes are declining or their jobs are threatened. (p. 70)

There is a profound catch-22 for educators; many of us, including myself, believe that standardized tests, in their traditional form, play only a limited role in helping us understand student learning. Many educators believe that if teachers encourage students to think, reflect, and challenge ideas, achievement test scores may even go down. If the public perceives a decline in test scores (which is equated with student learning), their support for education will erode further. Needed especially are more data on attitudes of older Americans, who are becoming both a larger and more active component of the American electorate and who appear to have a lessening commitment to finance schooling. Educators who are interested in developing modern assessment systems that are matched to emerging theories of instruction must deal with public attitudes and political expectations as well as develop new and workable models for assessment.

THE SEARCH FOR EFFECTIVE TEACHING: A HISTORY

It is beyond the purpose in this chapter to present a comprehensive review of modern observational and interview research in classrooms. I present a brief historical sketch in outline form to illustrate how rapidly interest in classroom teaching and learning has expanded since 1960. The field has become much

Sandra wants to have a "4" as her winning number. Which spinner should she choose?

A.

B.

C.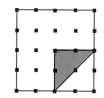

D.

Scratch work

Atish shaded a small part of his large square as shown above. What fractional part of the large square is shaded?

A. $\frac{1}{2}$ B. $\frac{1}{3}$ C. $\frac{1}{4}$ D. $\frac{1}{8}$

Scratch work

FIGURE 28.1. (continued)

more complicated with the explosion of knowledge. However, more recent research studies and programs are not necessarily more *complex* than earlier research, because current research programs are typically episodic and relatively insulated. They are not integrative. Nevertheless, the research area per se has become much more complicated in terms of the range of hypotheses and factors that it now subsumes.

Organizing an historical account is difficult even for professional historians (see Tuchman, 1978). Organizing a recent history of research on teaching is especially difficult because the period that is characterized is relatively brief and because so many developments have overlapped in time. For example, when one program of research is at its apogee, another is just beginning, and yet another is beginning to decline. Moreover, although most research in a particular category (e.g., student mediation) has tended to ignore teacher behavior and expectations, some studies of student mediation have explored teacher behaviors as well (e.g., Rohrkemper, 1981). Furthermore, a single study may include interviews with teachers and students as well as the collection of data describing classroom interactions. Thus, the categories in the outline that follows are best seen as heuristics that divide the field into analytical areas so that research contributions can be explored in an orderly fashion. Although some of the classifications are somewhat arbitrary, I believe that the outline helps illustrate that research on teaching has not been cumulative. The field moves from interest to interest and in some ways is *circular* rather than spiral. That is, new questions do not build on prior knowledge. They are simply new. Many insights gained by research in a particular family are unfortunately lost in new research programs that stress newness, not integration. Finally, numerous researchers could be associated with particular categories of research. The outline only identifies a few of the major contributors and exemplars of research in each tradition.

Observational and Interview Research Classrooms: 1960–1995

1. Teacher Personality
   a. General teacher characteristics (Getzels & Jackson, 1963; Ryans, 1960)
   b. Classroom interaction and climate (Amidon & Flanders, 1961; Flanders, 1965)
2. Program Implementation (Gallagher, 1970; Taba, Levine, & Elzey, 1964)
3. Classroom Ecology and Classroom Teaching
   a. Teacher expectations (Brophy & Good, 1970, 1974; Rosenthal & Jacobson, 1968)
   b. Teachers and classroom cultures (Barker, 1968; Dreeben, 1973; Jackson, 1968; Philips, 1983; Smith & Geoffrey, 1968)
4. Teacher Behavior
   a. Specific behaviors, such as clarity, enthusiasm, questioning, and so on (Gage, 1965; Rosenshine & Furst, 1971; Wright & Nuthall, 1970)
   b. Management behavior toward the whole class (Gump, 1969; Kounin, 1970)
   c. Wait time (Rowe, 1969)
   d. Process-product, naturalistic (Brophy, 1973; Gage, 1972)
   e. Time and academic learning time research (Berliner, 1979; Bloom, 1980; Carroll, 1963, 1993)
   f. Process-product, experimental (Clark et al., 1979; Evertson, Anderson, Anderson, & Brophy, 1980)
   g. Instructional pace content coverage (Barr & Dreeben, 1983; Freeman & Porter, 1989; Lundgren, 1972)
5. Teacher Cognition Research
   a. Teacher expectations (Good & Brophy, 1974)
   b. Teacher decision making, planning (Borko, Cone, Russo, & Shavelson, 1979; Borko & Shavelson, 1983; Clark & Peterson, 1986; Shavelson, 1976, 1983)
   c. Teaching as task engineering (Doyle, 1979, 1983)
   d. Student grouping as task engineering (Slavin, 1980)
   e. Teachers' conceptions of lessons (Leinhardt & Putnam, 1987)
   f. Teacher conceptions of subject matter (Shulman, 1986b, 1987)
   g. Teacher progress: Novices to expert (Berliner, 1992)

   h. Teacher responsibility, morality, ethics (Jackson, Boostrom, & Hansen, 1993; Noddings, 1984; Oser, 1994; Philips, 1983; Shulman, 1992; Tom, 1984)
6. Student Mediation
   a. Student social cognition (Blumenfeld, Hamilton, Bossert, Wessels, & Meece, 1983; Marx, 1983; Rohrkemper & Corno, 1988; Rosenholtz & Simpson, 1984; Weinstein, 1983)
   b. Student learning in small groups (Cohen, 1994; Webb, 1983)
   c. Student task literature (Alton-Lee, Nuthall, & Patrick, 1993; Anderson, 1981; Blumenfeld, 1992; Leinhardt & Putnam, 1987; Mergendoller, Marchman, Mitman, & Packer, 1988; Winne & Marx, 1982)
   d. Student passivity (Good, Slavings, Harel, & Emerson, 1987; Goodlad, 1984; Newman & Goldin, 1990; Sizer, 1984)
   e. Students' self-regulated learning (Corno & Mandinach, 1983; Pressley & Levine, 1983; Zimmerman & Schunck, 1989)
   f. Teaching for understanding (Blumenfeld, 1992; Newmann, 1992)
   g. Student volition (Corno, 1992, 1993; Snow, Corno, & Jackson, in press)
   h. Goal co-regulation (McCaslin & Good, in press a, in press b)
7. An Emerging Paradigm: Teaching for Student Understanding

Systematic Use of Observational Research: Traditions of Research

Observation has long been a part of educational research (it is possible to find observational studies at the turn of the century); however, for the first 50 to 60 years of the twentieth century most instructional process research was relatively isolated and not an integral part of research on teaching.

Teacher Personality The precursor to intensive observation of instructional behavior was research on teachers' personalities and teachers who showed certain personality characteristics were predicted to do well in the classroom. By the mid-1960s leading educational researchers were beginning to debunk the myth that there was a "personality for teaching" or at least one that was easy to define and identify (Getzels & Jackson, 1963). In the 1960s, some work continued on teacher personality issues and the classroom climate teachers created. For example, Ned Flanders and colleagues explored the relation between the variables of teacher warmth and indirectness and students' classroom responding.

Teacher-Proof Curriculum Some of the first systematic use of observation in research occurred in the mid-1960s and early 1970s as investigators attempted to develop teacher-proof curricula. Research on curriculum implementation had often showed that there was as much variation within a program as among programs (Gallagher, 1970). With the knowledge that teachers' use of curriculum mediated the intentions of designers, investigators became more interested in the role of teachers, especially teachers' instructional behaviors.

Interest in Naturalistic Settings In 1968 two significant books, reflecting the field's emerging interest to leave the armchair and/or the laboratory to explore classrooms, were published (*Life in Classrooms* and *Pygmalion in the Classroom*). In the latter book, Rosenthal and Jacobson focused on teachers' expectations for student performance, the possible influence of expectations on classroom processes, and, ultimately, on student achievement. Jackson (1968) was more interested in identifying enduring classroom structures. In the late 1960s some research also was beginning to focus on the culture of the school or classroom (e.g., Smith & Geoffrey, 1968). By the mid-1980s this work became even more explicit and more frequent (e.g., Philips, 1983). Interest in culture continues in the 1990s (e.g., Jackson et al., 1993).

Ironically, at a time when educators were becoming more convinced of the importance of teachers in implementing curricula and influencing students' attitudes and achievements, several reports by sociologists challenged the assumption that teachers and/or schools could make any important difference in students' learning (Coleman et al., 1966; Jencks et al., 1972). These reports by sociologists led to a flurry of activity among educators, especially psychologists, and stimulated much process-product research motivated to show that teachers did indeed affect students' learning.

Teacher Behavior One major goal of educational researchers was to demonstrate that variation in teacher behavior and in schooling more in general could be related to variation in student learning. The category of research in the outline called "teacher behavior" subsumes hundreds of studies with different intentions, research methods, and findings. In the past few years much of the research in this category has been incorrectly categorized as "process-product research." (More on process-product research appears later.)

Within the major category of teacher behavior there is considerable variation in approaches taken to research classrooms. For example, the work of Mary Budd Rowe (1969) stimulated a great deal of research on the relation between teachers' willingness to wait for individual students to think and respond and students' subsequent performance (indeed 25 years later work in this tradition continues [Duell, 1994]). Like many other investigators in the teacher behavior tradition, Rowe's research made the teacher salient in the learning process. Through their instructional behavior, teachers were seen as fundamental sources of influence on student performance. In contrast, Kounin's (1970) management research deemphasized teacher personality and characterized the teacher as one part of the classroom ecology and the signal system that it provided for students.

Teacher Behavior and Time Allocations Another program of research within the teacher behavior tradition examined how teachers utilized classroom time. Perhaps the one seminal work in this area was Carroll's model (1963). Important modifications in the measurement and use of time have been made by other researchers (Berliner, 1979). Research on academic learning time (ALT) became especially popular in the 1970s. According to Berliner (1979), ALT added a new dimension to process-product studies:

In this conception of research on teaching, the content area the student is working on must be specified precisely, the past engagement of the student must be judged, the level of the difficulty of the task must be rated, and time must be measured. The constructed variable of ALT, then, stands between measures of teaching and measures of student achievement. (p. 125)

Shulman (1986a) noted that although ALT emphasized student mediation of teaching (how students think about what teachers have done), the model was conceptually similar to process-product orientations and, thus, characterized by the same strengths and weaknesses. In particular, students' thinking was inferred but not measured.

Although researchers in general have tended to move to other issues, time allocation issues remain a pressing agenda in current schools (e.g., given recent claims about the decline of students' writing ability, how much time should be spent in learning to write persuasive essays?).

As a case in point, Mitman, Mergendoller, Marchman, and Parker (1987) discuss the marked variation in how much time teachers allocate to different conceptions of "scientific literacy" and note that different allocations of time influence how students think about what it means to study science. Carroll (1993), in a provocative article, argues that as we move into the twenty first century, one of the challenges that still confronts educators is how to accommodate differences in students' learning rates, issues that he raised and eloquently addressed in the 1960s.

Following the focus on patterns of teacher behavior and its relationship to student achievement came an interest in curriculum and individual pace. Although work on instructional decision making and pace had been raised earlier (e.g., Lundgren, 1972), interest in questions of curriculum selection (e.g., difficulty of concepts) and pace became more evident in the 1980s (Barr & Dreeben, 1983; Freeman & Porter, 1989). In part, this interest was because there were many "competing hypotheses" about how classroom process might have an impact on student outcomes. Many researchers wanted to broaden conceptions of teaching beyond that of "performance behavior." Ironically, this interest in the teacher as allocator of time for particular subject-matter concepts did not build on the wait-time or expectation literature that could have integrated variations at the class level (how much time does teacher A in comparison to teacher B spend on drill versus concepts versus problem solving?) with variation at the individual student level. These movements within the teacher behavior tradition tended to move from question to question without much integrative effort.

Finally, within the teacher behavior tradition some process-product researchers conducted both naturalistic and field experiments to see whether teaching behaviors could be related more directly to student outcomes. (More on this later in the chapter.)

Teacher Cognition The fifth tradition of research is listed in the outline that centers on studies of teacher cognition. The first program of research listed under this tradition examined teachers' expectations—a category that was also included within the teachers and classrooms tradition. As noted, it is difficult to fit a research program neatly into one tradition, and this was especially the case for research on teachers' expectations. This area is elusive because, although the primary motivation of most researchers was to examine differential teacher behavior, research in this area also involved teachers' thinking (the formation of expectations), the recognition that teachers form their expectations on the basis of cues from students (e.g., physical characteristics, etc.), and the acknowledgment, at least at an inferential level, that student mediation was important (students exhibit the expectation effect). Researchers argued that teachers engaged in differential instructional behavior because of differential interpretations of student behavior (Good & Brophy, 1974).

As with the tradition of research on teacher behavior, research programs subsumed in the teacher cognition tradition also showed great variation. Among the first topics studied in this tradition were *teachers' decision making* and *planning* (Clark & Peterson, 1986; Shavelson, 1976) and *teaching as task engineering* (Doyle, 1979). Persons working in the area of teacher cognition emphasized that teachers were thoughtful, that they made decisions, and that they interpreted classroom events. Many educators criticized studies of teaching behavior (of both teacher effectiveness and teacher expectations) because it was believed to be mechanistic and argued for research on teachers' planning and decision making. However, initial studies of teachers' thinking about classrooms examined teachers' views of whole classes. Thus, just as researchers who had studied teacher behavior began by focusing on how the teachers treated entire classes (and painfully and slowly moved to the examination of how teachers interacted differently with students as a function of ability, ethnicity, etc.), the teacher planning literature also started at the global, main-effect level. Thus, despite the rich data base showing dramatic differences in contact between teachers and certain types of students, researchers of teacher thinking and decision making largely ignored how teachers viewed the instructional needs of different types of students (Good & Brophy, 1974). Many interesting questions bridging these two research perspectives could have been raised but basically went unasked: For example, do teachers think that they can narrow the gap between high- and low-achieving students as the year progresses? Do subject-matter concepts need to be presented differently for high- and low-achieving students? What strategies do they use to accomplish such goals? Do teachers think a lesson is good for all students, or only for some?

The teaching-as-task-engineering perspective suggested that how teachers thought about tasks and how they defined accountability and work for students determined students' cognitive engagement (Doyle, 1979). From Doyle's perspective, tasks, not teacher instructional behaviors, taught students. Thus, in many ways Doyle's analysis and his focus on accountability and work are similar to the teacher-proof curriculum research conducted in the early 1960s. If teachers were smarter about designing tasks, student involvement could be more successfully engineered.

Studies of classroom activity structures and academic work tasks have yielded new dimensions of classrooms that should be examined. This research perspective criticized the focus of previous research on teachers' thoughts and behavior and emphasized the need to consider how task requirements affect student performance. This work, similar to previous research areas, yielded important concepts, and especially notable in this tradition was the clear indication that too much time was spent in American classrooms on low-level tasks.

This literature, however, developed relatively independently of findings from teacher effectiveness research, expectations research, and teacher planning research. Although the paradigm argued that students interpret teacher behavior in classroom tasks, little attention was paid to individual students' conceptions of tasks. Of many exciting, bridging questions that could be raised, the following are examples: Do students who fail frequently see memory tasks as riskier than process questions? Do students who have trouble with classroom recitations view open-ended questions or assignments as less threatening than questions that have a single correct answer? When students work in small groups, how does the task demand (e.g., degree of risk or ambiguity) influence student performance? Can students tolerate more ambiguity in a group than they can as individuals?

Again, we see the limitations of "main-effects" thinking. Given the absence of previous research on classroom tasks, the importance of classroom tasks became overreified and many simple arguments followed (e.g., all students find ambiguous tasks threatening). We now have empirical research to indicate that the original views of task research were too simplistic. Fields (1990) has illustrated that many students like ambiguous tasks because accountability is less, not more, stringent!

Other studies and research traditions raised issues about the students' role in learning. Early work in this tradition (Slavin, 1980) called for students to work in small groups. This work, in many aspects, was similar to teacher behavior in making a direct mechanistic claim. Whereas earlier research suggested that you look at teacher behavior to understand classrooms, this tradition claimed that you focus on students' behavior to understand classrooms. However, this work appears to be more closely aligned with the task-engineering perspective. Student process was not observed, and it was assumed that if teachers engineered and thought about small-group learning in a particular way, productive learning would follow.

More recent studies in this tradition describe teachers' progress in moving from novices to experts (Berliner, 1992). Researchers have made important distinctions between expert and novice teachers' cognitive orientations and subsequent performance. However, studies on novice/expert teachers are based primarily on a transmission and additive model that argues that dimensions of successful teaching can be isolated and presented to teachers in educational programs (much like the process-product tradition). However, research in this area has yielded rich concepts for thinking about what it means to be an expert or an expert teacher (Berliner, 1992; Ericsson & Charles, 1994).

Another more recent area of research within the teacher cognition tradition focuses on teachers' conceptions of subject matter. Shulman (1986b) has argued persuasively that how teachers develop examples and models affects how students understand subject matter. Although many considered research on teachers' pedagogical subject-matter knowledge to be a new 1980s concept, there are examples of related interests in earlier times. For example, in 1965 Gage was arguing that teachers' problem-solving capacities were an important element of teaching. In particular he highlighted the work of researchers at Indiana University, Dick Turner and Nick Fattu, who were studying teachers' ability to recognize the importance and meaning of various students' subject-matter mistakes and the misconceptions associated with those mistakes.

In the 1980s many researchers began to focus on teachers' knowledge of subject matter. Some of the impetus for the initial movement into this area was growing dissatisfaction with the relative nondynamic studies of teacher planning and decision making, awareness that teachers must think about different aspects of the lesson, and awareness that students also mediate lesson structure. Leinhardt and Putnam (1987) argued that the lesson had primarily been examined from the perspective of the instructor. They articulated a framework for examining how a successful student comes to conceptualize the intended content of the lesson. In their work they provide the caveat that their model of a student learning is descriptive of a student who is willing and motivated to learn and who is actually involved in attempting to learn the new material (conditions that unfortunately do not always pertain). Thus, work by Leinhardt and Putnam suggested the need to pay more attention to the bridge between lesson content and lesson organization and contributed to the growing interest in conceptualizing subject-matter variables. The studies also stimulated concern for student mediation, and they provide another example of work that crosses the boundaries of research traditions.

Furthermore, studies in this tradition, following Shulman, emphasized how teachers could transform their own knowledge of subject matter in ways that would promote their students' understanding. As Fenstermacher (1994) noted, Lee Shulman (1987, 1992) touched off a productive cottage industry of research in this area. This work has produced some important conceptualizations in various subject areas.

This work is exciting; however, it is also characterized by the narrowness of previous research. For example, teachers' views of subject matter and how it should be presented to more and less capable students have largely been ignored. Moreover, although students' misconceptions vary widely even in a single classroom, many researchers view misconceptions as a class-level variable rather than an individual-student variable. Perhaps most disappointing is that studies of subject-matter variables and how teachers' and students' roles in teaching for understanding differ from their roles in transmission and lecture models have not helped us much in understanding students as students, including the emotions, attitudes, beliefs, and preferences that students bring to the classroom generally and to learning a particular subject.

This is a notable shortcoming because persons have criticized students for their lack of commitment, poor work habits, and so on (Tomlinson, 1993), rather than attempting to understand how difficult it is for some students to maintain volition (Snow et al., in press) and to handle the multiple tasks that they must coordinate simultaneously if they are to be "successful" classroom learners (McCaslin & Good, in press a). As the case literature on teachers and, to some extent, teaching expands (Shulman, 1992), students' learning has largely been ignored. There has been, however, some continuing interest in student variables (Corno, 1993). As a case in point, some researchers have attempted to identify students' perspectives and the conflicting messages students must integrate from school, community, and home (McCaslin & Murdock, 1991). As argued earlier, researchers need to explore subject matter, teaching, and stu-

dents in the same ecological system to take a more holistic viewpoint that builds on and integrates prior research knowledge.

Much important research is examining what subject-matter knowledge and pedagogical-content knowledge teachers need to enhance student learning. However, it seems likely that teachers' beliefs about subject-matter knowledge and pedagogical strategies for helping students to understand subject matter are probably tied to other important beliefs. In many ways, I suspect that other teacher beliefs control how teachers will use their subject-matter knowledge. For example, teachers' beliefs about equal opportunities for students to respond, their expectation for students' general performance, and their views of how students learn may be as important as their pedagogical-content knowledge. Others agree. Presently there is considerable interest in exploring the role of teachers' beliefs about responsibility, morality, and other ethical considerations that might affect subject-matter teaching.

Ironically, in teacher cognition research, the teacher has become more salient over time. Previous research acknowledged that teachers and students and tasks reciprocally influence one another; classroom life is codetermined. It is ironic that the conception of multiple, reciprocal causes has disappeared, with more recent research on teachers' conceptions of subject matter and teacher responsibility and morality. The teacher is the causal agent in the class. Criticisms of the "mechanistic" teacher behavior research wherein teachers were believed too omnipotent seem equally valid, but, thus far, they remain unstated in this literature.

Student Mediation The sixth research tradition in the outline is student mediation. Students' social cognition, including their conceptions of teachers, classroom management, and equity has received much attention, as has student mediation of classroom learning. Many well-known scholars focused their work on student thinking, including Linda Anderson (Anderson, Brubaker, Alleman-Brooks, & Duffy, 1985), Phyllis Blumenfeld (Blumenfeld et al., 1983), Lyn Corno (Corno & Mandinach, 1983), Ron Marx (Winne & Marx, 1982), Mary Rohrkemper (Rohrkemper, 1981, 1984), Rhona Weinstein (Weinstein, 1982), and Phil Winne (Winne & Marx, 1982).

Webb's (1983) work on student behavior in small groups provided an important bridge to new conceptions. Although her work did not call for interviewing students, the focus on classroom process focused attention on the impact of group configuration (e.g., match or mismatch of achievement levels of group members) and illustrated that the task was more complex than the classroom task-engineering approach suggested and the recommendations of earlier researchers who studied cooperative learning. Still, student intent was inferred, not directly studied. Subsequently, some workers in the small-group tradition have considered more active models (e.g., Cohn, 1994).

As this area matured, many studies began to include interviews with students to explore with them their thinking about teachers, instructional behavior, and classroom tasks. This perspective yielded rich data to illustrate that students mediate events (i.e., the same instructional behavior is interpreted in different ways).

Studies clearly show that students interpret and mediate classroom events in important ways (Rohrkemper & Corno, 1988). For example, Weinstein (1983) found that students are aware not only of differential teacher behavior afforded to students who vary in academic ability, but also that students make inferences about teachers' intentions and so on. The student mediation literature, in contrast with the teaching-as-task-engineering perspective, focuses more dynamically on students' views of curriculum and assigned work. Whereas the earlier tradition (Doyle, 1979) emphasized the teacher's role in designing tasks, more recent work in this area has examined student mediation (Blumenfeld, 1992; Mergendoller et al., 1988; Winne & Marx, 1982). Doyle's early work did express concern for student mediation, but the mediation *assumed* was at a main effect level: Student processing was predictable and mechanical if you knew what tasks students were working on. More recent work in this area has productively (1) moved to explore how students may react differently to the same task, (2) recognized that ambiguity for some students may be stimulating, and (3) explored how social aspects of the task setting are as important as the academic aspects.

However, all research paradigms have limitations. I believe that researchers who studied mediation paid too little attention to teachers' views of student thinking and to how variation in teachers' views was related to differences in instruction. Others criticized this research because too little attention was paid to the academic tasks students were assigned (Shulman, 1986a).

It is significant that although Shulman devoted many pages to research on student mediation in his 1986 review, he did not even mention it in his 1992 review chapter. Shulman's more recent review has moved from process-product research, to teacher thinking, to collaboration and research on teaching, to context and culture, to teacher knowledge, to effective, responsible teaching.

His apparent abandonment of the student paradigm was both premature and unfortunate. We cannot understand classroom learning without analyzing students' thinking and behavior. Students are also more than their achievement: most parents are as interested in students' social and affective responses as they are in academic performance.

The student self-regulated learning research programs primarily drew on lines of research that were only indirectly represented in previous traditions of research on teaching. In particular, one line of influence ultimately leading to work on students' self-regulated learning was personality and motivational theory. Here, traditionally, psychological researchers had been interested in dispositional versus situational influences on performance. The other line of research that was drawn upon to form this new research direction was research on learning and thinking—within the information-processing tradition (e.g., elaboration of Simon, 1969). Thus, students' self-regulated learning became the fusion of motivation and strategic thinking, often referred to as the integration of will with skill. That is, if students do not have enabling learning strategies, their goals are irrelevant, and if students have well-defined learning strategies but lack goals, the value of student learning and work (particularly from an intrinsic motivation perspective) becomes problematic. Although researchers were influenced by various

research programs and theoretical perspectives, perhaps the largest source of influence in this type of research came from the work of Bandura (1989) in fusing interest in thought, expectancy, and behavior. In particular, his work on personal agency became translated as the nonability determinant of personal competence.

Again, as in all traditions, there are important and healthy arguments going on within the group of researchers who address students' self-regulation. Two of the newer developments within this area are volitional conceptions (e.g., Snow et al., in press) and goal coordination work (McCaslin & Good, in press a, in press b). These two theoretical orientations emphasize different aspects of student learning and coping, but both are essentially complementary.

Volitional research and conceptualization place more emphasis on helping students maintain their intentions to complete goals. Goal coordination and coregulation theory emphasizes the need for students to coordinate among multiple goals, to reevaluate periodically their commitment to particular goals, and to alter or delete them as appropriate. Furthermore, a coregulation perspective stresses that the student is not in it alone—relationships with teachers, parents, and society provide important structural supports and resources as well.

Process-Product Research

Having framed the field as a whole it is useful to examine two lines of research more closely to explore possible relationships between research and practice—especially evaluation. First, the evaluation of process-product research is explored. Then newer research in the teaching for understanding tradition is examined.

As noted, some educators in the late 1960s strongly contended that teachers and schools were not differentially effective (Coleman et al., 1966; Stephens, 1967). As a result of such arguments, much research was conducted to explore effective teaching and effective schooling. Until 1970 the literature concerning whether teaching in schools did make a difference in student achievement was equivocal, primarily because of inadequate research designs, including the failure to observe classroom processes and, hence, to differentiate quantity from quality of instruction (Campbell & Stanley, 1963; Dunkin & Biddle, 1974; Good, Biddle, & Brophy, 1975).

Although critics could fault the literature on teaching and school effectiveness on various dimensions, the quantity of studies was not one of them! Gage (1960) noted that more than 10,000 studies had examined teacher effectiveness, that the literature was overwhelming, and that even bibliographies had become unmanageable. According to Gage, most studies were poorly designed and reported only weak relationships. Moreover, the evidence was contradictory. The committee on teacher effectiveness of the American Educational Research Association (AERA) (1953) aptly summarized the situation:

The simple fact of the matter is that, after forty years of research on teacher effectiveness during which a vast number of studies have been carried out, no one can point to a few outcomes that a superintendent of schools can safely employ in hiring the teacher or granting him [sic] tenure, that an agency can employ in certifying teachers, or that a teacher-education faculty can employ in planning or improving teacher-education programs. (p. 65)

Twenty-two years after the AERA committee report, however, Good et al. (1975) reevaluated this literature in a more positive light: "We suspect that the reason for lack of success in early teacher effectiveness research was poor design features rather than any inherent ineffectiveness of the teaching process. However, this is our opinion, not fact" (p. 14).

Do Teachers Influence Student Achievement? Dunkin and Biddle (1974) identified several important weaknesses of teacher effectiveness research, including a lack of theory and observation and an abundance of "dust-bowl empiricism." Dunkin and Biddle noted the peculiar and inadequate criteria often used to assess effectiveness. Furthermore, they began the discussion of contextual effectiveness and noted that effectiveness may vary by grade level, by subject, and so on. Perhaps the most important contribution of the Dunkin and Biddle book, *The Study of Teaching,* was to begin to sensitize researchers to the importance of context.

Because of the pioneering work of scholars like Nate Gage, Bruce Biddle, and Mick Dunkin, many educational scholars were encouraged to frame and to reframe issues related to the process of schooling and student outcomes. Duncan and Biddle hypothesized various knowledge relationships in the classroom; however, the assertion that captured most research attention was their sixth claim. Duncan and Biddle (1974) stated:

The sixth and last class of knowledge concerns relationships between the processes and products of teaching. Surely this class requires the least justification of any we have discussed. If we are to be successful teachers, we must not only maintain a bright and cheerful atmosphere, a schedule, a disciplined and orderly environment, but we also must *teach.* Thus, we should also seek to discover teaching strategies that will maximize pupil growth. Our sixth task then is to discover how the processes of teaching affect the growth and development of pupils. (p. 50)

Unfortunately, this chapter cannot review all of this literature, which is both enormous and complex (for detailed reviews, see *Looking in Classrooms,* Good & Brophy, 1994; *Handbook of Research on Curriculum,* Jackson, 1992; and *Handbook on Research on Teaching,* Wittrock, 1986).

However, I do wish to mention some of the most significant patterns of findings that resulted from this research. These findings can be grouped under the following broad headings: teacher expectations/role definitions/sense of efficacy; student opportunity to learn; classroom management and organization; curriculum pacing; providing opportunities for students' practice and application; and a supportive learning environment (see Good & Brophy, 1994, for details). These are important elements that provide part of a foundation for exploring the evaluation of classroom settings.

Effective Schools Efforts to find effective teachers were soon matched by process-product efforts to find effective schools. Among the many findings of the school-effects literature, the following variables are associated with increased student achievement: (1) strong academic leadership and goal commit-

ment, (2) a safe, orderly school climate, (3) appropriate teacher expectations toward students, (4) an emphasis on instruction (not just filling time or engaging frequently in nonacademic activities) and on classroom assignments, (5) careful monitoring of progress toward goals through student testing and appropriate staff evaluation programs, (6) strong parent involvement programs, and (7) consistent emphasis on the importance of academic achievement (public recognition). The reader interested in additional details can see Freiberg, Prokosch, Treister, and Stein (1990) and Teddlie, Kirby, and Stringfield (1989). These data are also relevant to issues of school and teacher evaluation, but they are far from complete. In particular, these findings discuss variations in existing schools, not what might be possible with new conceptualization and additional resources.

Chrispeels (1992) illustrated that school factors such as leadership, academic focus, high expectations, recognition, and a shared mission continue to be relevant to school functioning. Smylie (1994) concurred that school effectiveness research has yielded important knowledge about the relation between school organizational factors and student achievement. However, Smylie also cautioned that researchers have not systematically examined how and why certain school-level variables are associated with improvements in school organization or student learning:

Good and Weinstein (1986) raised similar concerns: It is now time for the development of expanded models of effective schools—models built on and tested by new types of research. Increased funding will be necessary for conducting this research. Further, we hope that in the future, research by a wider range of social scientists will complement the efforts of the relatively small number of scholars who currently explore school environments. If public education is to be understood and improved, it must be studied using diverse theoretical frameworks. We need studies that examine extant practice, but we also need researchers who build new models of what schools can be and who are willing to help implement these strategies in the complex social settings in which schools operate. (pp. 1096–1097)

Policy Issues These early teaching effects and school-effects studies were significant because they provided prima facie evidence that variation in teachers and schools could be related to achievement. However, because these studies were conducted at a time when many educators and policymakers questioned whether teachers and schools could make a difference in the intellectual progress of American youth, educators and policymakers were excited (probably too excited) about data suggesting that investments in teachers and schools (both in preservice and in-service programs) might notably improve student learning.

I believe that most process-product research was not designed to produce a program or perspective on *how* to teach; rather it was designed to test the hypothesis that teachers make a difference in students' achievement. Secondarily, researchers became interested in generating implications for teachers. The models of teaching that emanated from process-product research (e.g., Good & Grouws, 1979) consisted of viable practices, many of which are still relevant today in particular contexts (e.g., teaching intellectual skills). As critics have commented, however, policymakers overresponded to findings of these studies, and in many school districts overly narrow and rigid definitions of teaching practice are still followed.

When there is relatively little knowledge (in this case, linking instruction and achievement), it tends to become too precious and to be overapplied as dissemination moves further from the original source and as practitioners make increasing extrapolations. Perhaps the best way to guard against the overreliance on a single or set of research findings or perspectives of research is to have an array—many research and development programs under way and a rich supply of alternative models that teachers can consider.

Many educators failed to recognize that different learning objectives (mastering well-defined knowledge or skills versus applying them to complex problem solving or using them creatively) require different instructional procedures and learning environments. Moreover, other schooling outcomes (the social development of students) also require unique instructional models. Thus, despite the initial importance of teaching-effects research, it became apparent in the following years that the resultant model was vulnerable on several grounds. Although important research in this tradition still continues, many researchers have moved from the process-product perspective in order to examine new models (for a comprehensive critique of this research, see Shulman, 1986a).

Teaching for Understanding

Currently, the most powerful integrative tradition for influencing classroom practice, in my opinion, is the teaching-for-understanding perspective. Although it has been influenced to some extent by recent work on conceptions of subject matter and earlier work on process-product studies of teaching, I believe that the teaching-for-understanding framework fundamentally evolved from the student mediation perspective.

However, it should be noted that the teacher cognition tradition has also had an important influence on the teacher education community. Bringing subject matter more centrally to the research on classrooms was a needed and helpful contribution. In particular, the teacher's conception of subject-matter perspective has had a powerful impact by stressing the need for a better conceptual understanding of subject matter and better ways to represent that subject matter. Ironically, the current direction in the teacher cognition tradition is to discuss what teachers (and to some extent students) do in the class, and most often emphasis is placed on teachers' justification for the particular lesson (subject-matter variables) and actions. Rarely do we have data or stories to explain or to describe how such particularized lessons influence students' subsequent learning.

In contrast, the teaching-for-understanding paradigm uses the student mediation perspective extensively and, thus, deals more systematically with student learning and outcomes (e.g., the issue of how teachers scaffold knowledge in ways that help students both understand concepts and progressively assume more responsibility for directing their learning over time). However, as noted, researchers in the teacher cognition and student mediation paradigms often switch boundaries in complex ways. Still the distinctions here are useful for examining the evaluation of ideas and for exploring conceptions of a modern, instructional perspective. One of the current unique tensions within the student mediation perspective that is now beginning to be argued actually is that students are not only learners of subject matter but also social learners. Thus, as researchers in the 1980s were concerned about teachers' adequate representation of subject matter, many educators working in the teaching for understanding paradigm worry in the 1990s that some teachers have an *inadequate conception of the student*. This aspect of student mediation work is now beginning to influence work on teaching for understanding.

Changes in Approach to Research Both the teacher cognition tradition and the teaching-for-understanding tradition have had impact on how classroom research is conducted. For example, recent research on subject-matter teaching has involved exemplary teachers who know their subjects well and who attempt to develop student understanding. There are many excellent examples of studies that have focused on subject-matter learning and teaching for understanding. Among this rich literature, one can see examples in mathematics (Ball, 1993; Cobb, 1986; Hiebert & Wearne, 1992; Lampert, 1989); social studies (Fraenkel, 1992; Newmann, 1992); science (Blumenfeld, 1992; Eaton, Anderson, & Smith, 1984); writing (Florio-Ruane & Lensmire, 1989); and reading (Anderson, Hiebert, Scott, & Wilkinson, 1985; Duffy, 1993).

Researchers focus on certain curriculum units or lessons, consider teachers' instructional goals, and record detailed information about classroom processes. Furthermore, this research also attempted to assess students' learning, both in the classroom and in other settings, and used evaluation measures aligned with instructional goals. Assessment often includes detailed interviews or portfolios of student work, in addition to or instead of more conventional objective tests. Unfortunately, there is seldom any comparison group, so it is not possible to determine if student performance is due to novelty effects or altered conditions of learning.

What It Means to Teach for Understanding Research focused on subject-matter learning has had an impact on the work of researchers exploring what it means to teach for understanding. Although teaching for understanding is conceived in a variety of ways, several conceptions recognize that (1) knowledge is constructed, (2) knowledge networks are structured around powerful ideas, (3) prior knowledge influences how students integrate new knowledge, (4) knowledge restructuring and conceptual change are important, (5) knowledge is socially constructed, (6) learning needs to be tied to authentic tasks, and (7) teachers progressively should transfer the responsibility for managing learning from themselves to learners (Blumenfeld & Marx, in preparation; Good & Brophy, 1994). In brief, in the 1980s and 1990s, researchers have become interested in constructivist perspectives and in more detailed accounts of how students integrate and understand content. Invited addresses at the American Educational Research Association by Phyllis Blumenfeld (1993) and Gary Griffin (1993) helped illustrate how curriculum and instructional considerations are beginning to overlap in the teaching-for-understanding paradigm. Table 28.1 contrasts some of the emerging views of instruction with views that were dominant from the 1950s through the late 1970s.

The teaching-for-understanding/constructivist perspective has been successful in many respects. Similar to other research paradigms or theoretical perspectives, it focuses more on some issues than on others. (For examples of this work, see Ball, 1993; Blumenfeld, Krajcik, Marx, & Soloway, 1994; Krajcik, Blumenfeld, Marx, & Soloway, 1994; Marx et al., 1994; Newmann, 1992.) These works provide exciting examples of how teachers are learning to construct new classroom environments and to implement instructional programs that emphasize students' understanding of significant subject matter.

However, although this paradigm has emphasized the role of student mediation, it has largely ignored (in terms of research) the social lives of students and students' understanding of the informal curriculum (e.g., fairness). Furthermore, the approach is basically *cold cognition*—little attention is placed on students' affect or emotions. This is indeed unfortunate from a Vygotskyian perspective as students' affect (e.g., their knowledge of the feeling of outrage when promises are broken) may be an important bridge to understanding concepts such as contracts or constitutions.

Teaching for Student Understanding

Although I have been critical of all paradigms, I believe that all modern paradigms of teaching have yielded rich data and concepts that help us better understand teaching and that have potential value for teacher evaluation. Perhaps it is time for one or more new, more integrative paradigms that integrate past insights and research knowledge into more inclusive but focused models. One such emerging research focus could be called the teaching-for-student-understanding perspective. This tradition could take from the teacher cognition tradition the need to consider subject-matter variables seriously and draw from the teaching-for-understanding perspective the need to include a focus on instructional variables, task, and student mediation. Furthermore, it could draw from goal coordination work to recognize more fully the social aspects of the student (e.g., the need for acceptance, affiliation, and achievement) and potential conflicts among goals. A teaching-for-student-understanding perspective would require that attention be placed on developing new measures for assessing student performance broadly.

Whatever the new paradigm is called requires us to attend to student displays of integrative knowledge in a problem-solving context and to students' abilities to grow as responsive and productive social beings. The new paradigm has a rich base and several distinct research traditions to draw upon, as well as the challenging opportunity to merge modern conceptions of teachers, students, and instruction with new approaches to measurement.

APPLYING THE KNOWLEDGE BASE

As this review indicates, much has happened in research on teaching since 1960. Making inferences about the relation between instructional practices and student achievement is a complex and difficult task. However, educational research has yielded concepts and insights that can be useful in developing professional evaluation plans at the local school level.

The argument here is that each research tradition (student mediation, teacher behavior) has yielded significant ideas that are relevant to the design of evaluation systems that not only are sufficient accountability devices (e.g., satisfy the public and

TABLE 28.1. Teaching and Learning as Transmission of Information versus as Social Construction of Knowledge

Transmission View	Social Construction View
Knowledge as fixed body of information transmitted from teacher or text to students	Knowledge as developing interpretations constructed through discussion
Texts, teacher as authoritative sources of expert knowledge to which students defer	Authority for constructed knowledge resides in the arguments and evidence cited in its support by students as well as by texts or teacher; everyone has expertise to contribute
Teacher is responsible for managing students' learning by providing information and leading students through activities and assignments	Teacher and students share responsibility for initiating and guiding learning efforts
Teacher explains, checks for understanding, and judges correctness of students' responses	Teacher acts as discussion leader who poses questions, seeks clarifications, promotes dialogue, helps group recognize areas of consensus and of continuing disagreement
Students memorize or replicate what has been explained or modeled	Students strive to make sense of new input by relating it to their prior knowledge and by collaborating in dialogue with others to construct shared understandings
Discourse emphasizes drill and recitation in response to convergent questions; focus is on eliciting correct answers	Discourse emphasizes reflective discussion of networks of connected knowledge; questions are more divergent but designed to develop understanding of the powerful ideas that anchor these networks; focus is on eliciting students' thinking
Activities emphasize replication of models or applications that require following step-by-step algorithms	Activities emphasize applications to authentic issues and problems that require higher-order thinking
Students work mostly alone, practicing what has been transmitted to them in order to prepare themselves to compete for rewards by reproducing it on demand	Students collaborate by acting as a learning community that constructs shared understandings through sustained dialogue

Source: Thomas L. Good, & Jere Brophy (1994). *Looking in classrooms* (p. 420). New York: HarperCollins. Reprinted by permission of HarperCollins College Publishers.

legislators that funds are well spent) but also, more important, offer exciting opportunities for teachers' professional growth (Rosenholtz, 1989). Teachers and policymakers need to understand the complex relationship between research and practice and especially to recognize both the value and limitations of research. There are competing views as to the research base and its putative value for practice. Although some writers hold that only certain types of research are useful, I believe that most researchers and educators view research as only one of *many* sources of knowledge that can inform evaluation policy.

Are Teaching Behaviors and Instructional Research Invalid Measures?

For example, Lee Shulman, one of the leaders in articulating a modern conception of the teacher and research on teaching, has recently argued that teaching behavior research is harmful. Shulman (1992) writes: "Meanwhile, unfortunately and dangerously, educational policymakers remain most heavily influenced by the older work on teacher behavior" (p. 26). Unfortunately, Shulman uses no evidence to support his conclusion. First, inappropriate implementation of research is not confined to work on teacher behavior. I suspect that too many school districts *do* use antiquated models of direct teaching and use them too narrowly. However, I suspect that too many principals also overvalue laboratory or small-group work as they insist on active learning environments. As we will see later, active classrooms are not always thoughtful classrooms.

Second, research on teacher behavior, old or new, does not seem particularly well represented in educational policy. Perhaps the most important policy initiative presently under way in the United States is the Goals 2000 legislation (see, for example, National Education Goals Panel, 1993a, 1993b). This initiative does not focus on teacher behavior—indeed, the legislation suffers because there is not enough attention paid to current instructional theory and its implication for performance assessment (more on this later in the chapter). Recent directives from a Florida school district that teachers should teach the moral superiority of the American culture seem to flow not from research on teacher behavior but from curricular or moral considerations. One wonders what policies (if any) research on teacher behavior is informing.

Third, maybe policy related to teacher behavior would not be all that detrimental. According to Shulman (1992), "In part, the influence of process-product research is stronger because its findings are older and more easily translated into prescriptions for policy. Unlike most research on teaching, it ties the acts of teaching directly to socially valued student outcomes" (p. 26). I fail to find this a compelling indictment of process-product research. The conceptualization and implementation of research that explore socially valued outcomes seem to represent a fundamental potential source for informing schooling. Indeed, perhaps one of the problems of new teacher research is that although it provides a more comprehensive and richer image of institutional variations, it often fails to provide evidence that students' short- or long-term problem-solving capabilities (academic or social) are enhanced.

Fourth, research-based initiatives are not necessarily antithetical to practitioner goals. Shulman (1992) continues, "Perhaps most significantly, this work is also most readily compatible with a top-down view of educational reform and policymaking, in which the best approaches are determined at the top and teachers are then trained, advised, and mandated to behave accordingly" (p. 26). Oddly, Shulman seems to argue that teachers are not concerned with students' progress on socially valued outcomes and that certain concepts and findings from process-product research are attractive only to administrators. Smylie (1994), who studies teachers' professionalization, reached a different conclusion. He recently completed a comprehensive review of the area and identified the concept of a professional community of teacher scholars who voluntarily work together because they value collegiality. The *integrating principle* around which their efforts are directed is students' growth on socially valued outcomes. (More on this later in the chapter.)

Fifth, it seems reasonable to predict meaningful student growth in socially valued outcomes when teachers and administrators share goals, beliefs, and knowledge. Earlier, in his chapter in the *Handbook for Research on Teaching*, Shulman (1986a) described the impact of process-product research this way:

Within the limits of whatever activities standardized achievement tests were measuring, the program was palpably successful. Not only were the proposed interventions effective, they were typically acceptable and credible to experienced teachers. . . . the program produced scientific support for approaches to instruction with which the majority of teachers, administrators, and parents felt intuitively and professionally comfortable. (p. 11)

I hesitate to use this dated reference, because my own views have changed significantly since 1986; however, the reference seems appropriate given Shulman's writings in 1992 on the dangers of process-product research. Shulman (1992) attempts to equate support for process-product research with administrative dictates; however, he (1986a) describes this same research base as one "with which the majority of teachers, administrators, and parents felt intuitively and professionally comfortable" (p. 11).

Apparently, some concepts and findings from process-product research have been, and continue to be, attractive to teachers. I am *not* defending process-product thinking but, rather, suggesting that teachers can benefit from research findings, concepts, and theories whether those are derived from quantitative or qualitative research. The *shoulds* of research that Shulman advocates seem to me unacceptable: His position is hard to assess empirically or to understand theoretically. Shulman (1992) writes, "To be properly comprehensive, we will need to forego our traditional training of a social *science* of education. We will instead move toward a more local, case-based, narrative field of study, as exemplified in Lampert's research" (p. 26). I agree that Lampert's research is useful for those with her experience, but I find experiments exploring social injustice—and what can be done to alleviate structural conditions of poverty—to be much more compelling, informative, and inclusive (e.g., Kaufman & Rosenbaum, 1992). In addition, large-scale policy studies exploring the relation between funding and educational progress are significant (e.g., Hedges et al., 1994a). Sometimes "local" is only idiosyncratic.

In quarrelling with Shulman's conclusions, I am arguing that research needs to be integrative and that educators and researchers can learn from different perspectives. The work of Thorndike, Jackson, Dewey, Gage, Carroll, Biddle, Duncan, Blumenfeld, Mergendoller, Corno, McCaslin, Rosenshine, Schaub, Berliner, Brophy, Shulman, Snow, Slavin, and others is relevant to the design of evaluation plans.

As educators and researchers design modern classrooms, they must stop thinking in terms of winners and losers and ask how they can use the best ideas from various theoretical perspectives and empirical work to implement effective, socially relevant, and contextually sensitive educational environments.

Teaching Behaviors Are Important Aspects of Evaluation

Although some educators have found fault with behavioral measures of teaching (and I share their views when measures focus on discrete behaviors and when no attention is paid to context, goals, or values), this criticism has become so extreme as to be counterproductive. I believe that some of the strongest messages teachers communicate to students are expressed through *classroom behavior*. Teachers can model fairness, honesty, and respect through their behavior. Important equity, gender, and ethnic issues may be directly and fairly assessed by attention to teachers' classroom behavior. Teachers who call on girls less frequently or ask them only low-level questions in math and science classes sustain the myth that science-related careers are not feasible or appropriate for females. Teachers may have the best intentions in the world, but if they behave inequitably, real damage occurs.

As an example of damaging differential teacher behavior, Damico and Scott (1988) note that teachers were more likely to encourage and support the academic behavior of white females but pay more attention to and provide support for the social behavior of African-American females. Some teachers were more likely to call on African-American females to help peers with nonacademic tasks and to ask white females to help peers with academic tasks. In part, such differences appear to be related to differential expectations—some teachers may perceive African-American females to be socially, but not cognitively, mature.

Walker (1992) notes that African-American females are likely to be perceived as responding inappropriately to teachers and are sometimes perceived by teachers as being "overactive." Walker, on the basis of her observations in classrooms, reports that she sees young women who are actively attempting to participate in the class but do not understand teachers' rules for turn taking. Clearly, to be effective in the classroom teachers must respect and understand cultural differences in students. They also need to *monitor* their own behavior to avoid unintended communication. Otherwise, the classroom behaviors of teachers can provide students with prima facie evidence that they are not understood or valued.

Teaching Behaviors Can Be Misused

As Good and Mulryan (1990) noted, most early research focused on evaluating teachers (usually for administrative purposes), and few attempts were made to develop methods that would help teachers analyze and improve their instruction. Since the mid-1970s, rating systems for assessing teachers on general dimensions were replaced with observational instruments that provided detailed information about specific aspects of classroom teaching. The new instruments indicated that certain teacher behaviors (clarity of communication; classroom management principles) were associated with improved student classroom performance. Attempts to apply this knowledge in practice have been largely unsuccessful, however, because knowledge about instructional behaviors was overgeneralized (used without regard to context) and equated with effective teaching per se. Simply doing a behavior (quantity) was seen as appropriate, regardless of how well the behavior was performed or when it occurred (quality). Good and Mulryan (1990) described the problem as follows:

Overgeneralizing the utility of knowledge from process-product research on teaching is similar to equating a good physician with the ability to interpret an x-ray correctly, defining a successful mechanic as one who can tune a car, or reducing a competent basketball player to one who can hit a 15-foot jump shot. The skills and knowledge required to be successful in any vocation are numerous and diverse (a good physician must understand cell structure, bone structure, as well as principles of physiology and pharmacology, to name but a few; a good mechanic must know about carburetors, fuel-injection systems, principles of suspension, and how to identify the cause of engine malfunctions; or a basketball player must have skills of defense, rebounding, running the court, and passing, as well as court presence). (pp. 206–207)

Similar caveats could be written for different research areas.

To reiterate, teaching for understanding involves more than teaching students subject matter. It is also vital that students learn skills such as self-evaluation and social skills that can enhance cooperative problem solving.

Failure to Integrate

However, as new research questions and paradigms have been initiated, researchers have tended to emphasize the newness of their findings and to suggest, yet again, sweeping reform for schooling practice. In this process, researchers and educators often ignore useful information yielded by previous research rather than attempt to consolidate what is known with emerging knowledge. Indeed, Vockell, Asher, Dinuzzo, and Bartok (1994) illustrate that researchers tend primarily to cite recent sources. One important aspect of building an appropriate teacher evaluation system is to clarify and integrate what research and theory are available and the relationship between such knowledge and local values or purposes. Unfortunately, education has always been noted for fadism and radical transformations rather than the systematic synthesis of knowledge. For example, in the current push for performance-based assessment (a movement that I support theoretically), teachers are urged to implement new types of measurement techniques. However, no substantial knowledge base is available for conceptualizing, implementing, or evaluating performance assessments (i.e., at particular grade levels for specific "new" subject content and for various types of learners). I will return to this issue later in the chapter.

Understanding the Role of Research

As anyone who has studied the literature on teaching knows, I have only briefly summarized research on teacher effectiveness, a literature that is complex to the point of being exhausting to examine. How, then, can research findings be used to develop teacher evaluation programs? One way to begin is to recognize the complexity and multidimensionality of teaching, to understand the role of research in evaluation, and to recognize the need for quality and balance in evaluation programs.

The role of research is not to provide simple solutions for educators, although one important task of research is to evaluate the effectiveness of various instructional models for improving students' thinking, learning, and motivation. It should be apparent that some models will work for particular learners under certain conditions and others will not (Cronbach & Snow, 1977). Reformers often miss the point that extant systems of curriculum and instruction may be most useful for some learning goals or for some types of students. For this reason professional recommendations tend to go from one extreme to another (individual learning format to whole class, from teacher control to student control, from principal as leader to site-based management, etc.). For example, students who come from homes where control is direct may benefit—even need—active teaching and structure more often and in more situations than other students. These students may end public school with as much capacity for self-direction as other students, but only if they get active teaching in elementary and middle schools.

A case in point illustrating the critical tension that teachers often deal with is the unfortunate condition of schooling in which sometimes school success is constructed as an immoral contract in which minority youth are asked to assimilate and join a society that discriminates against them as it requires them to give up their ethnic identity (see, e.g., Secada & Lightfoot, 1993). Finding a balanced, adaptive approach in this area is difficult in helping students develop real talents. Delpit (1992) contends that she has met many progressive and sympathetic literacy teachers who have a strong need to empower and politicize their students. She contends that, unfortunately, sometimes teachers define empowerment as refusing to teach grammar, form, or strategies for communicating in the dominant discourse. Delpit strongly argues that learning to utilize the dominant discourse to express oneself does not mean that one necessarily must reject one's home identity and values. She contends, "Teachers must acknowledge and validate students' home language without using it to limit students' potential" (p. 301).

Delpit suggests that just as one can be oppressive by forcing students to abandon local culture and language, it is possible to be equally insensitive to real needs by denying students the chance to develop academic skills and insights. Indeed, there is a shared perception among some authors that many African-

American students especially value teachers who are directive and authoritative in the classroom. Independent of intentions, certain teacher behaviors—refusing to answer questions completely or not explaining material clearly—are seen as unhelpful by these students, and they may resent such behaviors (Walker, 1992). Research cannot yield simple answers such as how much active teaching certain types of students need and for how long. However, research is critically important in illustrating the need for multiple models because students' needs do vary.

The more teachers know about models and their limits, the more flexibility they will have for meeting the needs of individual learners. The task of research is to broaden, not to narrow, teachers' conceptions of practice (Biddle & Anderson, 1991). In this sense, research yields theories for framing problems and planning possible actions, for broadening the range of student outcomes possible, and for building the technical skills and vocabulary necessary for teachers to discuss schooling with one another. Research also provides practical information about the effects of instructional strategies implemented under well-specified conditions.

The Complexity of Teaching

Teachers fulfill many roles. Raths (1971) argued that teaching involves at least the following functions:

1. Explaining, informing, showing how
2. Initiating, directing, administering
3. Unifying the group
4. Giving security
5. Clarifying attitudes, beliefs, and problems
6. Identifying learning problems
7. Making curriculum materials
8. Evaluating, recording, and reporting
9. Enriching community activities
10. Organizing and arranging classrooms
11. Participating in school activities
12. Participating in professional and civic life

Shulman (1992) noted that broad conceptions of teaching are certainly not new. According to him, as early as 1885, Page had presented a broad and inclusive view of teaching, as reflected by the chapter titles of his textbook: The Spirit of the Teacher; The Responsibility of the Teacher; Habits of the Teacher; Literary Qualifications; Right Views of Education; Right Modes of Teaching; Conducting Recitations; Exciting Interest; School Government; School Arrangement; Relating to Parents; Teacher's Care of His Health; Teacher's Relations to His Profession; and Rewards of Teaching.

Although these teacher duties and responsibilities vastly exceed those examined in the extant research base, they *underestimate* the vastness of the teacher role. For example, Rohrkemper and Corno (1988) stressed that teachers also need to understand issues of "informative student failure" and "mindless success." Modern conceptions of classrooms also show that teachers need to construct environments that allow students to develop both "volitional dispositions" (Snow et al., in press) and the capacity for goal coordination, including the ability to change goals and to create new goal structures (McCaslin & Good, in press a).

Teaching must also be viewed from multiple perspectives—teachers' thinking, values, and behavior and their combined effects on students' thinking, values, and behavior must be considered when teaching is evaluated. For example, teachers should help students develop more capacity for self-evaluation. Thus, even in a given classroom, "good teaching" is not static; it varies with student growth (e.g., capacity for independent learning and with lesson purposes, etc.). Lessons with similar purposes can be taught in alternate ways.

Instructional Quality

Proponents of reform often forget about instructional quality. Hence, they go from issue to issue as though (magically!) a single strategy epitomizes effective teaching. This search is, of course, illusionary and, as I noted some time ago (Good, 1983), researchers need to become more integrative in thinking about what constitutes appropriate, *high-quality* instruction and learning. Altogether too much time and energy have been spent examining the form of learning—its cosmetic aspects. The issue is not whole-class or small-group format or teacher- or student-centered accountability, the issue is what constitutes a high-quality learning environment and how that varies over time and with the type of student and instructional intent.

Instructional Balance

Reformers often tell educators that they need a new approach, that the old story—the old method—is completely wrong. For example, recently the lecture method of instruction has been criticized frequently, and some critics have even argued that the radical decline in performance of American students is simple to explain: too much teacher lecture. This analysis obscures the fact that when American students were world-class students in mathematics and science, the primary instructional mode in secondary schools and colleges was the lecture method! What is needed, however, is more balance, and more variety, in the instructional approaches teachers use. However, rather than adapt a plausible goal (both in terms of instructional soundness and the realities of reform) such as reduce lectures by 30%, reformers advocate the elimination of lecture and direct instruction. The rhetoric of all enthusiasm for other models is not matched by compelling data.

GENERAL PRINCIPLES OF EVALUATION

Evaluation can be conducted from many perspectives and for many purposes. How can teachers be helped to reach personal goals? Is the school as a system healthy? How can citizens be assured that schools use resources well and have desirable influences on students? Are the goals achieved by the school consistent with those desired by citizens? In this section of the chapter, the focus is on the evaluation of teachers rather than on system issues or the view of institutions and evaluation as political symbols.

Although there is healthy debate among researchers, scholars, and teacher educators who write on the topic of teaching effectiveness and evaluation, educators agree for the most part about relevant, desirable approaches to evaluation in several areas. However, the extent to which research guides these practices is questionable because in some areas the results are equivocal.

Still, most practices are supported by research and scholarship and are consistent with resource books on teacher evaluation. The reader is encouraged to consult sources such as the following for more detail: *Handbook of Educational Psychology,* Berliner and Calfee (in press); *Handbook of Research Synthesis,* Cooper and Hedges (1994); *The International Encyclopedia of Teaching and Teacher Education,* Dunkin (1987); *Handbook of Research on Teaching,* Gage (1963); Travers (1973); Wittrock (1986); *Cognitive Approaches to Assessment,* Gifford and O'Conner (1992); *Handbook of Testing,* Haney and Madaus (1988); *New Directions in Educational Evaluation,* House (1986a, 1986b); *Handbook of Research on Teacher Education,* Houston (1990); *Handbook of Research on Curriculum,* Jackson (1992); *The New Handbook of Teacher Evaluation: Assessing Elementary and Secondary School Teachers,* Millman and Darling-Hammond (1990); *Knowledge Base for the Beginning Teacher,* Reynolds (1989); and *Handbook of Teaching and Policy,* Shulman and Sykes (1983).

The New Handbook of Teacher Evaluation, edited by Millman and Darling-Hammond (1990), includes an extensive discussion of issues related to teacher evaluation, including chapters on these topics: Licensure and Certification; Teacher Selection; Assistance and Assessment for Beginning Teachers; Beyond Minimum Competence; Evaluation for Professional Development; Evaluating Teachers for Career Awards and Merit Pay; Evaluations for Tenure and Dismissal; Teacher Evaluation for School Improvement; Classroom Observation; Teacher Ratings; Self-Assessment Using Students' Scores to Evaluate Teachers; and Setting Standards on Teacher Certification Tests.

Readers are encouraged to examine this voluminous and rich literature. The chapter provides an introduction to this literature and summarizes what I believe are widely held beliefs about teacher evaluation.

Important District-Level Variables

Clarity of Purpose Virtually anyone writing on evaluation of teachers would agree that evaluation systems have multiple purposes. Furthermore, a district needs to be clear about the goals of assessment if good measurement is to occur (Wise, Darling-Hammond, McLaughlin, & Bernstein, 1985).

Goals can conflict because evaluation systems can be in place to (1) help beginning teachers grow, (2) identify beginning teachers who need to be dismissed from the profession, (3) identify veteran teachers who need either remediation or dismissal, (4) provide professional growth and development for inexperienced teachers, and (5) offer professional growth and development for more experienced and more capable teachers. Within these broad categories, further distinctions can be made. For example, professional growth and development programs for experienced teachers could focus on individual or group development.

The district purpose for staff development and evaluation should be very explicit. Philosophical approaches to evaluation can vary from school district to school district; however, the following goal elements would seem to be important principles and should be considered in building an evaluation system: (1) developing an environment of respect and trust, (2) promoting cooperation and collegial sharing of knowledge, (3) developing the full potential of teachers by providing important continuing opportunities for continuous learning, (4) promoting staff empowerment and involvement, (5) achieving excellence in individual teacher performance and performance across the school; (6) developing leadership capabilities of all teachers, and (7) communicating effectively with parents and the broader community.

Aligning District Philosophical Orientations and District Evaluation Instruments Any measuring device is more sensitive to certain factors than to others, and, indeed, certain instruments are orthogonal to and/or negatively related to certain goals. For example, if a district values small-group instruction but does not measure the quantity and quality of such instruction, the evaluation system is inconsistent with the philosophical direction of the district. Reactivity of measurement is a long-understood principle suggesting that those things actually measured reflect what a district most values, and practices that are measured tend to be reified and supported by the district. Although this point appears obvious, many districts employ evaluation systems and philosophical orientations that are incompatible (Wise et al., 1985). For example, it is not uncommon to find districts in which the curriculum emphasizes reflective problem solving, but the approach to classroom management demands that students comply blindly with school rules (McCaslin & Good, 1993). Similar disparities in expectations and evaluation systems for teachers are common. The need for the integration of philosophy and shared discourse into the evaluative process is becoming more salient (see, e.g., Delandshere & Petrosky, 1994).

The Need for Multiple Systems There is growing recognition that because any evaluation system has limitations, a district should use multiple systems. It has become popular, for example, to differentiate between the needs of beginning teachers (both in terms of teacher professional growth and district accountability to the public) and evaluation that focuses on more experienced teachers' growth and development (McLaughlin & Pfeifer, 1988; Wise et al., 1985). Teachers, especially experienced teachers, view evaluation systems designed only to identify incompetence (or minimum competence) as punitive, limiting, and inconsistent with teacher improvement. A good evaluation system should help all teachers to reflect on their practice and to grow professionally.

Differentiating Accountability and Professional Growth

A district's use of separate evaluation systems for beginning and experienced teachers does not ensure that the focus of the evaluation changes as teachers gain experience. To many educators and citizens, the term *evaluation* suggests accountability, which they view as the identification of incompetent teachers and demands that minimal classroom performance standards be met. Some districts that use two systems of teacher evaluation focus on accountability (defined narrowly), even for experienced teachers, and devote few resources to helping teachers grow.

However, accountability also means paying attention to excellent performance. McLaughlin and Pfeifer (1988) suggested that when teachers reflect on their practice, self-improvement often follows. They noted that individual teachers' plans for evaluation and improvement may be combined with district plans so that the entire school benefits. Peterson and Comeaux (1990) found that teachers' ratings of evaluation systems were related to their conceptions of effective teaching. Hence, although districts may want beginning teachers to demonstrate the ability to implement certain instructional models, there is evidence to suggest that, as teachers gain experience, they should have more say in defining their work environment.

Traditional systems of evaluation have often prevented administrators and teachers from focusing on classroom instruction and on how to improve it. Ironically, new incentive plans or professional growth programs may exaggerate this problem by encouraging work on activities other than classroom teaching (Henson & Hall, 1993).

Targeting Areas of Development

McLaughlin and Pfeifer (1988) conducted case studies of four school districts that had made significant progress in implementing a stronger teacher evaluation program. As they noted, experienced teachers are expected to continue to grow and to move beyond minimal competence. According to these authors, teacher development will necessarily vary from district to district. The following list presents 14 competency objectives for more experienced teachers developed by the Charlotte-Mecklenburg School District (McLaughlin & Pfeifer, 1988):

1. To maintain mastery of the subject matter he or she is assigned to teach and to maintain technical expertise in his or her assigned area(s) of responsibility
2. To assess and to monitor student performance in a manner consistent with the best available knowledge in the field of evaluation
3. To provide effective management and instruction consistent with the best available knowledge in the field of teaching and learning
4. To provide students with maximum access to resources in the school system and in the community
5. To recognize and to respond positively, appropriately, and with concern to the needs of all students, including students from diverse cultural and ethnic backgrounds, the handicapped, and the gifted
6. To establish high expectations for students' performance and to provide motivation, management, instruction, guidance, and support to ensure that students meet these expectations

7. To communicate effectively with staff, parents, and students about his or her area of expertise or job assignment
8. To participate in planning, implementing, and evaluating school programs
9. To participate in and to support activities designed to enhance the school and to achieve its goals
10. To serve as a role model for other teachers
11. To participate in research and development activities to improve instruction, such as the creation and testing of alternative curriculum materials and strategies
12. To engage in continuous self-evaluation and to alter his or her performance in response
13. To participate in the evaluation process to determine if he or she is meeting the requirements for Career Level I status
14. To maintain an awareness of trends and issues addressed by professional organizations and to become involved, when appropriate, in addressing those issues (McLaughlin & Pfeifer, 1988).*

In contrast, in the Mountain View–Los Altos system one of the primary aspects of teacher evaluation is a student survey. The instrument was developed by teachers and administrators, and it calls for the students to rate their teachers from weak to very strong on 40 dimensions of teaching that are subdivided within the following 10 categories:

1. Teacher preparation
2. Student–teacher relationship
3. Individual needs of students
4. Teaching methods
5. Clarity of communication
6. Control of class
7. Classroom atmosphere
8. Class procedures
9. Ideas and skills to be learned
10. Value of skills taught (McLaughlin & Pfeifer, 1988)*

In the Santa Clara Unified School District, the following dimensions are utilized in the teacher evaluation process:

1. Teacher as assessor of student needs
2. Teacher as planner of instruction
3. Teacher as presenter of instruction
4. Teacher as controller
5. Teacher as evaluator of student progress and instructional purposes
6. Teacher as communicator of the educational process
7. Teacher as professional

As McLaughlin and Pfeifer (1988) note, the dimensions focused on in this evaluation are similar to those used in many school districts. However, what distinguishes the Santa Clara evaluation plan is the fact that staff development is intimately related to teacher evaluation and there is an explicit, formal remediation process in the district. The list of 10 standards for beginning teachers that follows presents yet another framework for thinking about standards for teaching. This outline comes from the Interstate New Teacher Assessment and Support Consortium. The argument I make here is that although the dimensions of teaching focused on are important, the ways (and quality) in which these dimensions are explored is the critical factor:

Principle 1: The teacher understands the central concepts, tools of inquiry, and structures of the discipline(s) he or she teaches and can create learning experiences that make these aspects of subject matter meaningful for students.
Principle 2: The teacher understands how children learn and develop and can provide learning opportunities that support their intellectual, social, and personal development.
Principle 3: The teacher understands how students differ in their approaches to learning and creates instructional opportunities that are adapted to diverse learners.
Principle 4: The teacher understands and uses a variety of instructional strategies to encourage students' development of critical thinking, problem solving, and performance skills.
Principle 5: The teacher uses an understanding of individual and group motivation and behavior to create an environment that encourages positive social interaction, active engagement in learning, and self-motivation.
Principle 6: The teacher uses knowledge of effective verbal, nonverbal, and media communication techniques to foster active inquiry, collaboration, and supportive interaction in the classroom.
Principle 7: The teacher plans instruction based upon knowledge of subject matter, students, the community, and curriculum goals.
Principle 8: The teacher understands and uses formal and informal assessment strategies to evaluate and ensure the continuous intellectual, social, and physical development of the learner.
Principle 9: The teacher is a reflective practitioner who continually evaluates the effects of his or her choices and actions on others (students, parents, and other professionals in the learning community) and who actively seeks out opportunities to grow professionally.
Principle 10: The teacher fosters relationships with school colleagues, parents, and agencies in the larger community to support students' learning and well-being.

Linking Professional Rewards and Evaluation Systems

Bacharach, Conley, and Shedd (1990) noted that merit pay plans can decrease rather than increase constructive discussion of teaching; that is, teachers cannot be expected to volunteer information that might keep them from getting a merit increase. Furthermore, some career ladder plans, which have often been heralded as a way to promote teacher professionalism, tend to

---

* From McLaughlin, M., & Pfeifer, R. (1988). *Teacher evaluation: Improvement, accountability, and effective learning.* New York: Teachers College Press. Reprinted by permission.

reinforce the myth that classroom teaching is less of a profession than educational administration (Bacharach et al., 1990) and suggest that out-of-class teacher activity is more important than teachers' classroom contributions (Henson & Hall, 1993). Many states have quotas at each step in the career ladder, so that the claim that career advancement depends solely on an individual teacher's qualifications is suspect.

According to Bacharach et al. (1990), fundamental questions must be raised in building compensation systems: For example, "Are we trying to purge low performers from the system, or are we trying to reward excellent performers, or are we trying to improve performance of *all* system members?" (p. 136).

Implementing Evaluation Systems: Clarification and Consensus

McLaughlin and Pfeifer (1988) pointed out that teacher evaluation often creates a dilemma: On the one hand, the public wants high-quality schools; on the other hand, teacher evaluation may work against this objective by decreasing teachers' professional time, flexibility, and responsibility. Research has shown that policymakers demand more accountability for better classroom teaching, whereas teachers push for increased professional autonomy. Unfortunately, in many districts evaluation is conceptualized as a no-win activity for everybody and therefore becomes just an annoying irritation rather than a central dimension of the school system (McLaughlin & Pfeifer, 1988).

Teachers and administrators need to have open discussions about the purposes of evaluation, explore alternative systems for collecting data (Evertson & Green, 1986; Good & Brophy, 1994; Stodolsky, 1990), and reach consensus on the objectives for using each system. Without such clarification and consensus, evaluation will be a fruitless activity no matter how carefully administrators and teachers perform their leadership roles.

Characteristics of Good Systems

Reliability and Validity McLaughlin and Pfeifer (1988) contend that every district with successful evaluation practices emphasizes reliability and validity. They maintain that flexibility and consistency must coexist:

While the value of flexible instruments lies in the ability of evaluators to tailor their comments to a particular teacher and a particular classroom, evaluation outcomes that appear to covary with the identity of the evaluator quickly lose credibility, rendering evaluative feedback useless. (p. 55)

Obviously, one of the purposes of evaluation is to identify problems that need to be addressed. However, resources must be provided to help teachers correct problems and develop skills in new areas.

Sense of Fairness Teachers must perceive an evaluation system as fair, as recognizing that all teachers have bad days and that one poor performance will not unnecessarily influence the outcome of evaluation. Teachers must also perceive that administrators are committed to the fair and accurate assessment of performance. According to McLaughlin and Pfeifer (1988):

Checks and balances, in short, play a number of important functions. They diffuse the "gotcha" quality possible in an evaluation and increase teachers' comfort and thus their openness about their performance. In this way, a system of checks and balances extends and reinforces the trust and confidence necessary to get started with teacher evaluation. (p. 44)

The principle of checks and balances can be implemented in many ways (e.g., teachers have a voice in what will be evaluated, teachers can request a second opinion, etc.).

Developing Evaluation Skills Many teachers complain that principals are poor evaluators—that they do not provide direct and honest feedback to teachers about their deficiencies. Bridges (1986, 1990) and others have argued that principals, similar to many people, have difficulty delivering bad news. Also, in some cases principals may not have adequate subject-matter knowledge (especially in secondary schools) and may have to delegate responsibly some of their evaluative role to department heads.

One way that mutual respect and evaluation skills can be developed is to train administrators and teachers jointly so that both are videotaped discussing and learning an evaluation system in which both groups will participate. Shared language can foster collegiality among participants and allows evaluators to provide feedback that is relevant to specific and shared conceptions of effective teaching (Rosenholtz, 1989).

System Renewal Every level of the evaluation process needs to be examined for ways in which it can be improved. Although teachers and administrators may agree on the philosophical orientation of an evaluation system and on how it should be implemented, once a system is implemented, it might not work as originally conceptualized. That is, after principals and others have been trained to observe and provide feedback, the quality of their reports should be examined (this is another form of checks and balances). Otherwise, quantity may take precedence over quality. As new findings from research on teaching and learning emerge, their implications for changes in evaluation should be considered. For example, recent theory and research on teaching for understanding should be a part of any teacher evaluation system, although their emphasis will vary by district. At the same time, established research knowledge (process product, academic learning time, student mediation, teacher decision making and planning, etc.) should continue to provide a basis for evaluation plans.

Ownership According to Peterson and Comeaux (1990), in addition to teachers' traditional views of evaluation (i.e., as an opportunity for professional growth versus a nuisance), in many instances evaluation may be irrelevant. That is, teachers may use the type of teaching required by the evaluation system only when they are being observed, even though the model of teaching encouraged by the district (e.g., small-group) may be altogether appropriate in some contexts. To gather evidence for public accountability, a district may believe that it is important that a teacher be able to use several instructional models: (1) organize students for an active discourse (Ball, 1993), (2) engage students in appropriate small-group instruction (Cohen, 1994), and (3) lead demonstration/discussion (Good & Brophy, 1994).

At the same time, the district might also assert that teachers should decide when to use a certain instructional model or organizational format. What is counterproductive and disingenuous, however, is to evaluate teachers on the implementation of only one model—a model chosen by the administration with little or no input from teachers. It seems essential that teachers begin to "own" evaluation systems by being able to assert their own preferences (for areas of professional growth), assuming that those preferences are consonant with effective teaching strategies and informed theories of teaching.

Perhaps one of the best ways in which to encourage teacher ownership of the system is to enable tenured teachers to define both the content and the procedures of evaluation systems. For example, Peterson and Comeaux (1990) extol the virtues of an evaluation system that allows the evaluator to stop a tape of classroom teaching and to ask the teacher to explain the classroom event (e.g., why the teacher ended small-group work at that particular moment). In my opinion, a better procedure would be to allow experienced teachers to stop the tape when in their professional opinion an important event had occurred (or was about to occur). Teachers should be able to identify and explain critical instances, not just answer the evaluator's questions. This area begs for empirical research and conceptualization to guide the field as it attempts to provide procedures that are rigorous and fair and constitute significant forms of communication that stimulate professional growth. As a case in point, Sommers, Muller, Saba, Draisin, and Shore (in press) describe research on "reflection on videotape" procedure used with medical resident students. Sommers et al. (in press) have not only generated new knowledge about the one-on-one process of clinical teaching, but also they have provided a provocative setting for medical residents to examine and reflect on their own behaviors and beliefs. This procedure is a nice example of how researchers could integrate research on teaching, teacher evaluation, and opportunities for professional growth.

Even at a time when participant management strategies are popular, many teachers still do not believe that they are active partners in evaluation. A poll conducted by the Carnegie Foundation for the Advancement of Teaching (1988) indicated that only 10% of teachers felt that they had any say in teacher evaluation. This percentage appears to have increased in the past few years thanks to the movement to redesign the work conditions of teaching in order to make it more of a profession (Smylie, 1994).

Teacher evaluations occur frequently in American schools. For example, according to a report released by the National Center for Education Statistics (1994), 98% of elementary teachers reported that they had been evaluated at least once in the school in which they were currently teaching. Indeed, 42% indicated that they had been evaluated 6 to 14 times in their current schools, and 29% reported that they had been evaluated more than 15 times. Furthermore, teachers reported general satisfaction with the evaluation process. However, the report found that:

A majority of teachers reported four aspects of teaching that had been considered only to *a small extent or not at all* when they were last evaluated. These were test construction skills (cited by 68 percent), grading methods (61 percent), neighborhood or school problems affecting one's teaching (60 percent), and involving parents in the learning process (57 percent). (p. 9)

Ironically, at a time when the nation is engaging in a serious discussion of performance assessment, it appears that school districts are giving scant formal attention to issues of teacher knowledge and competence in assessing student learning. This area merits additional research, because increased teacher control of evaluation broadens the models of teaching that are evaluated and makes evaluation seem fairer and more of an integral part of the educational system. However, as Smylie (1994) notes, research linking teachers' professional opportunities and students' learning is needed.

Staff Development

Many researchers have called for staff development independent of teacher evaluation systems. Since the 1970s, in our book *Looking in Classrooms,* Jere Brophy and I have been encouraging the role of teachers as professional colleagues who can benefit from self-study and reflection in a collegial environment (Good & Brophy, 1973, 1994). We originally thought that teachers would benefit from observing one another and providing feedback about curriculum and instruction. We continue to believe in the usefulness of peer observation, and in the past 20 years many other forms of collaboration have been articulated. Among these are the call for discussion (Glatthorn, 1987), curriculum development (Glatthorn, 1987), peer coaching (Joyce, 1981; Showers, 1984), and action research (Lieberman, 1986). (For a review of all these techniques, see Good & Brophy, 1994.) There also is considerable valuable information about master teacher programs, mentoring and other teacher leadership programs (Griffin, 1985; Smylie, 1992), and staff development for beginning teachers (Huffman & Leak, 1986; Wildman, Niles, Magliaro, & McLaughlin, 1989; Zeichner & Tabachnick, 1985).

Smylie (1994) noted that since the mid-1980s school improvement efforts have focused on teachers and the organization of their work. Many initiatives have attempted to make teaching more satisfying and more of a profession. Among the options explored have been school-based management, participative decision making, teacher leadership programs, mentor programs, and career ladder plans. The redesign of teachers' work, however, often creates tasks for teachers that are peripheral to and may even compete with classroom instruction (Eisner, 1992; Henson & Hall, 1993; Smylie, 1994). A central issue in redesigning teachers' work is to ask how altered responsibilities for teachers outside the classroom inform and promote change within the classroom (Smylie, 1994). Despite an abundance of programs, Smylie (1994) cautions that there are few data linking work redesign to student achievement.

Despite the limited and equivocal nature of the findings, this literature yields two tentative conclusions (Smylie, 1994). First, when classroom outcomes have been shown to exist, they are more likely to be demonstrated by teachers who directly assume redesigned roles than by teachers who are assumed to benefit from other teachers' assumption of these roles. Second, work redesign initiatives that involve collective, collaborative activities and professional orientations toward teachers' work and change are more likely to be associated with changes in classroom performance than initiatives based on individualistic, bureaucratic, or hierarchical orientations. These conclusions appear similar to those reached by other investigators (Richardson, 1990).

In his review, Smylie (1994) also identifies the concept of "professional community" as one promising development that merits attention:

Teacher professional learning and development is an integral component of the community. Collective as opposed to individual professional autonomy, responsibility, and accountability for student success are guiding forces. Teachers openly discuss problems—their students' and their own—and mutually develop strategies for dealing with them. In many ways, these communities demonstrate the effective exercise of the control, motivation, and learning mechanisms analyzed in this review. Their approach to change is collective rather than individualistic. While these communities show a distinct direction for the redesign of teachers' work, it is not clear how such communities come to be or how they may be created and sustained through programs and policies. (pp. 164–165)

Adapting Existing Evaluation Systems

It is beyond my purpose here to provide extensive recommendations for designing teacher evaluation and staff development programs. Clearly, school districts are at different points in terms of developing effective evaluation and staff development programs. For example, some school districts have not involved teachers centrally in defining and implementing the process, and, hence, those school districts must focus attention on those foundational aspects. In contrast, other school districts have important processes in place and their attention should be focused on issues of fine-tuning and expanding the scope of information exchange. As noted earlier, there is a striking discrepancy between the focus on the teacher as an evaluator of student growth and the current national interest on how we might assess student learning more appropriately.

However, it is useful to discuss briefly some factors that should be considered in helping teachers to reflect on their attempts to teach for understanding. This area is chosen because it is a powerful integrating theme and an area that I believe is important to consider in district evaluation plans.

Blumenfeld (1992) developed case studies of fifth- and sixth-grade science teachers to identify classroom practices that promoted student thoughtfulness. Her findings could assist a district that wanted to evaluate science teachers in this area if the research (data-collection methods, etc.) were congruent with district goals. Good and Brophy (1994) summarized Blumenfeld's findings:

Opportunities: Topic coverage focuses on a few key ideas developed in-depth: learning activities relate to these main ideas, focus on application rather than mere verification, and involve engagement in meaningful problems relating to children's experience or to real events; the products produced through these activities also relate to the main ideas and require processing at higher cognitive levels.

Instruction: Clear presentations highlight main points and critical information, take into account students' prior knowledge, and use examples, analogies, and metaphors; these presentations build connections by linking with prior knowledge, making relationships among new ideas evident, focusing on similarities and differences among ideas, and showing their application; they include scaffolding in the form of modeling of learning and of metacognitive and problem solving strategies.

Press (use of questions and feedback): Questions focus attention on main ideas; teacher checks understanding by asking comprehension questions, asking for summarization, asking for application, focusing on content rather than procedures, adding higher-level questions to worksheets, and asking for alternative representations of content; teacher draws out student reasoning by probing, asking for justification or clarification, and elaborating on student responses; teacher uses errors to diagnose and clear up misunderstandings; teacher encourages making of connections by asking about relationships of key ideas to prior knowledge, relationships among new ideas, how an activity's procedures related to its content, and how the results of the activity illustrate main ideas; teacher ensures widespread responding by calling on many students, using debate, and using voting or asking who agrees or disagrees with a statement.

Support: Teacher helps students to accomplish tasks by breaking down problems, simplifying procedures, modeling procedures, or providing models and examples; teacher promotes independence, self-regulation, and co-operation by encouraging students to work together, providing time for planning, asking about students' individual contributions to group work, and asking students whether they agree or disagree with their group's conclusions.

Evaluation: Teacher holds students accountable for understanding by adding questions to worksheets that focus on the meanings of key ideas; evaluation focuses on learning rather than performance, features recognition of individual contributions and improvement, and de-emphasizes grades and correct answers. (pp. 442–443).

After examining the research base, teachers and administrators next would clarify how their context differs from that in Blumenfeld's research and discuss the many activities and tasks teachers could use to promote understanding in science classrooms, including lectures, demonstrations, laboratory work, computer simulation, small-group discussions, and teacher-led class discussions. The district should emphasize quality of instruction and the integration of instructional approaches rather than a single format or activity.

Next administrators and teachers can discuss which rating forms and narrative data-collection procedures are appropriate. Figures 28.2 and 28.3 present two forms that a district might consider.

The figures depict only two of many measurement forms, and the type(s) of methodology that measurement used (narrative record, rating scale, notes, teacher and student diaries and portfolios, etc.) should be based on research (which is often uneven, particularly in new areas), professional guidelines (e.g., from groups such as the National Council of Teachers of Mathematics, etc.), and district guidelines and philosophy. Measurement should emerge from discussion among teachers and administrators about how they can develop an evaluation sys-

PURPOSE: To assess the degree to which the teacher teaches content not just for memory but for understanding and application.

USE: When you have detailed information about the curriculum, instruction, and evaluation enacted during a content unit or strand.

Enter a checkmark for each of the following features that was included effectively in the content unit or strand, and a zero for each feature that was omitted or handled ineffectively. Then add detailed comments on a separate sheet, emphasizing constructive suggestions for improvement.

Checklist

_____ 1. *Goals* were expressed in terms of long-term student outcomes (acquisition of knowledge, skills, values, or dispositions to be applied to life outside of school), not just in terms of short-term content mastery.

_____ 2. Limited content was taught in sufficient *depth* to allow for development of understanding.

_____ 3. The *knowledge* content was represented as *networks* of related information structured around powerful key ideas.

_____ 4. In presenting and leading discussions of the content, the teacher helped students to recognize the centrality of key ideas and to use them as bases around which to structure larger content networks.

_____ 5. In addition to providing explicit explanations, the teacher asked questions and engaged students in activities that required them to process the information actively, test and if necessary repair their understanding of it, and communicate about it.

_____ 6. *Skills* (procedural knowledge) were taught and used in the process of applying information (propositional knowledge) content rather than being taught as a separate curriculum.

_____ 7. Most skills practice was embedded within inquiry, problem solving, decision making, or other whole-task application contexts rather than being limited to isolated practice of part skills.

_____ 8. If skills needed to be taught, they were taught with emphasis on modeling their strategic use for accomplishing particular purposes, as well as explaining when and why the skills would be used.

_____ 9. Content-based *discourse* emphasized sustained and thoughtful discussion featuring critical or creative thinking about key ideas, not just fast-moving recitation over specifics.

_____ 10. *Activities and assignments* called for students to integrate or apply key ideas and engage in critical and creative thinking, problem solving, inquiry, decision making, or other higher-order applications, not just to demonstrate recall of facts and definitions.

_____ 11. In *assessing* student learning, the teacher focused on understanding and application goals, not just low-level factual memory or skills mastery goals.

FIGURE 28.2. Teaching Content for Understanding and Application. (*Source: Looking in classrooms,* 6th ed. Thomas L. Good and Jere Brophy [1994] p. 456. New York: HarperCollins. Reprinted by permission of HarperCollins College Publishers.)

tem that allows teachers to gather relevant information and reflect on it in order to design more effective learning environments.

A comprehensive plan for teacher evaluation and development in the district would require various types of data. First, information about how teachers and administrators conceptualize teaching and evidence about how teachers actually implement their vision of effective instruction are needed. Furthermore, it is important to know how teachers attempt to validate and to gather evidence that helps them change instructional

USE: When a teacher engages students in reflective discussion designed to stimulate construction of knowledge.

PURPOSE: To assess the degree to which the discussion includes features that support social construction of knowledge.

Check each feature that was included in the discussion:

A. Poses a well-chosen problem
_____ 1. Problem is appropriate in familiarity, difficulty: Students have enough prior knowledge to allow them to discuss it intelligibly, but they also must engage in reasoning and higher-order thinking
_____ 2. Problem is authentic, significant to the students
_____ 3. Teacher requires them to predict, explain, develop justified problem-solving or decision-making strategies that call for applying the powerful ideas being developed

B. Elicits suggestions and related justifications
_____ 1. Students act as learning community, teacher facilitates
_____ 2. Poses problem, calls for ideas about how to approach it
_____ 3. Lists suggestions on board or overhead
_____ 4. Doesn't judge but calls for clarification, elaboration, justification

C. Elicits assessments and discussion
_____ 1. Invites students to critique by offering justified arguments for or against contributed ideas
_____ 2. Invites contributors to revise their thinking if they wish
_____ 3. Encourages student–student interaction and debate
_____ 4. If necessary, scaffolds by breaking question into separate issues or substeps, asking about a neglected aspect, listing what is given or has been agreed upon separately from what still is at issue

D. As issues get clarified, moves students toward resolution(s)
_____ 1. Tests for consensus when it appears to have developed; if disagreement still exists, asks about unresolved issue(s)
_____ 2. If necessary, asks questions to focus attention on unwarranted assumptions, misconceptions, or complications that have not yet been recognized
_____ 3. If necessary, temporarily interrupts discussion to allow students time to get more information or interact more intensively in subgroups
_____ 4. When consensus is finally achieved, asks questions to help students reformulate what they have discovered about this particular case into more general principles

E. Constructs summary of main ideas and their connections
_____ 1. Invites students to summarize what has been learned
_____ 2. If necessary, asks clarification and elaboration questions to make sure that the summary includes all main points and connections between them that need to be emphasized
_____ 3. Follows up by having students work individually or in small groups to reconstruct the new knowledge (by writing in journals or composing reports, etc.) and perhaps to apply it to new cases

FIGURE 28.3. Social Construction of Knowledge. (*Source*: Thomas L. Good and Jere Brophy [1994], *Looking in classrooms*. New York: HarperCollins, p. 456. Reprinted by permission of HarperCollins College Publishers.)

methods and procedures as necessary. In particular, it is instructive to know not only what kinds of evidence teachers collect for making judgments about possible modification in the instructional program but also how they attempt to develop students' conception of subject matter and progress over time.

Hence, in addition to the types of observational data suggested in Figures 28.2 and 28.3, it is likely that teachers' logs and students' diaries and work samples (e.g., video segments, term papers, etc.) would be necessary elements of an evaluation plan. As we move into a new paradigm, teaching for student understanding (as argued for in this paper), it will be important to place more emphasis on teachers' ability to evaluate student outcomes and performances more broadly than has been the case historically.

Stages of Development and Evaluation

If a school district is to be fair and to develop talent productively, it must provide an integrative development plan for teachers that explicitly communicates what aspects of professional development are emphasized at a particular point in time. Although it is true that a teacher has to engage in virtually all functions of teaching immediately, it does not follow that teachers necessarily have to be experts in all functions at the same time. In fact, to expect too much too soon from a teacher or any beginning professional may be unrealistic and dysfunctional. Figure 28.4 illustrates one hypothetical approach that a district could take in providing a stage approach to evaluation.

Early in the process teachers have to demonstrate, at a high performance level, an ability that they can be fair, personable, and equitable in their dealings with students. Later, we might expect more mature dispositions, such as not only acknowledging and accepting diversity but also valuing it. It is reasonable to expect that teachers can immediately construct productive management systems and productive learning systems. Thus, as suggested in Figure 28.4, teachers should have well-conceived and thoughtful goals about how to implement a system of instructional communication that represents a coherent and organized set of beliefs and principles. However, independent of the clarity and rigor of a teacher's motivational framework, the teacher's *behavior* in implementing the system is important. A poorly implemented philosophy is not very helpful.

Teachers need to understand the complexity of classroom behavior and to realize that students may interpret classroom management systems in different ways; for example, some students may see alerting behaviors as teacher behaviors that announce what students will be held accountable for as helpful clues, whereas other students may see alerting behaviors as an expression of low expectations. Teachers should be capable of gathering evidence to find out how the students have *mediated* (understood and interpreted) the management system and to be able to use that information in making instructional decisions for the next day, next week, and next year (e.g., how to introduce a laboratory procedure more adequately).

Teachers' ability to reflect on data and experience to plan new events is an important characteristic of adaptive potential for decision making and growth. Thus, a teacher who has a good motivational system, average management skills as reflected in observed behavior, but good plans for change might be rated more highly than a teacher who manages reasonably well but has no plans for improvement.

In some schools, there might be an active interest in teachers' illustrating their ability to construct small-group learning environments or good ability to communicate with parents during the first year of teaching; whereas in other school districts these expectations might be expected for the second year. The essential issue is that teachers know the areas of expertise that they are expected to develop most quickly in their teaching context.

Similarly, in the first year of teaching it would be expected that teachers could communicate and implement a grading policy that students can understand and generally accept as fair and legitimate. Although one might hope that beginning teachers can also make major inroads in helping students to become better at tasks of self-evaluation and self-identification of learning goals, it is reasonable that formal evaluation of these abilities might be delayed until the second or third year of teaching (reasoning that it takes time to develop refined dispositions and capacities). Classroom tests might be an issue for year 1; whereas the focus moves to more complicated performance measures in year 2. Similarly, it might be unreasonable to expect teachers to serve as leaders (presenting research and development ideas to other teachers in peer workshops as they enter the profession). Indeed, it might be better for teachers to avoid such experiences early in their careers so that they can spend more time learning how to work productively with students. However, by year 3 teachers should be able to function as valuable colleagues and leaders.

After they are granted tenure and perhaps the most pressing accountability issue for the district is resolved, teachers could progressively have more opportunity and responsibility for self-directing their professional growth (both planning and documenting). As noted, the form of such staff development could allow for both individual and cooperative plans and could focus on a wide range of topics and formats.

The hypothetical stages presented in Figure 28.4 suggest that teachers should elaborate on knowledge over time and that teachers should grow as professionals. The staff development and evaluation plan should promise evidence that teachers are adaptive and that teachers can work well with students, parents, and peers. In essence, the teacher should be a professional who continues to grow. Susan Rosenholtz (1989) expressed the issue succinctly by noting that some teachers that have 10 years of experience simply have the same experience 10 times. Teachers who are "stuck" should be encouraged to seek other careers. Thus, districts have the need to provide an environment that encourages teachers' growth over time, and teachers need to demonstrate an expanding understanding of students, subject matter, and classroom processes.

THE ROLE OF STANDARDIZED TESTS IN EVALUATING SCHOOL SUCCESS

We must become clearer about what constitutes successful schooling in the twenty-first century. Citizens' conceptions of successful schooling need to be obtained as well as those of theorists and researchers. Furthermore, in addition to new definitions we need new measures for assessing school success.

Criticisms

Educators' conceptualization and defense of standardized tests are inconsistent and conflicting and, hence, confusing to the public. Educators have become increasingly critical of standardized tests. Haertel and Calfee (1983) contend, however, that despite much criticism, standardized tests were accepted as

Year 1

Teacher as manager → Goals → Classroom behavior → Student beliefs → Reflective revision

Teacher as presenter → Goals → Classroom behavior → Student beliefs → Reflective revision

Teacher as discussion leader → Goals → Classroom behavior → Student beliefs → Reflective revision

Teacher as grader → Goals → Classroom behavior → Student beliefs → Reflective revision

Year 2

Teacher as designer of small-group tasks → Goals → Classroom behavior → Student beliefs → Reflective revision

Teacher as designer/stimulator of independent study options → Goals → Classroom behavior → Student beliefs → Reflective revision

Teacher as communicator with parents → Goals → Classroom behavior → Student beliefs → Reflective revision

Teacher as facilitator of students' affective and social growth → Goals → Classroom behavior → Student beliefs → Reflective revision

Year 3

Teacher as colleague → Goals → Classroom behavior → Student beliefs → Reflective revision

Teacher as co-constructor of knowledge → Goals → Classroom behavior → Student beliefs → Reflective revision

Teacher as leader → Goals → Classroom behavior → Student beliefs → Reflective revision

Teacher as stimulator of students' capacity for self-reflection → Goals → Classroom behavior → Student beliefs → Reflective revision

FIGURE 28.4. Hypothetical Illustration of Differential Evaluation Tasks.

significant indicators of success for pupils, teachers, and school districts and were playing a greater role in program evaluation, in management of instruction, and in public debates on educational policy and funding. According to them, however, "Few existing tests provide the kinds of diagnostic information that can reveal whether real-world competence in a curriculum area has been obtained" (p. 130). They describe the limitations of tests and how they can be improved:

For the time being, test experts and test users in the schools can strive to become more aware of the limitations of objectives stated in behavioral terms, can scrutinize more closely the processes and knowledge provided by tests, and can work to create a stronger demand for better measures of achievement. Construction of the next generation of achievement tests will require new skills and new lines of communication between educational psychologists, subject-matter specialists, and psychometricians. Achieving this goal will not be a simple matter, but the outcome will permit assessment that is one notch closer to the goals of instructional validity and diagnostic utility that were so clearly expressed at the beginning of the century. (p. 130)

Tests and the Curriculum

The rise in the use and costs of tests in education (and elsewhere) is aptly summarized by Haney, Madaus, and Lyons (1993). They clearly illustrate that despite stated concerns about the usefulness of standardized tests, their use increases.

There is a growing gap between the theoretical (normative) and the actual curriculum and test content. As can be seen in Figure 28.5, I hypothesize that the match between school curriculum and standardized achievement tests has diminished in the 50-year period from 1945 to 1995.

The hypothetical figure makes the argument that the normative curriculum was broader (included more school-related expectations) than the actual (i.e., implemented) curriculum in 1945. Although the match (extent to which test items are part of the curriculum) between the actual curriculum and achievement tests was far from complete in 1945, it was reasonably good. As the figure also shows, we do more testing now than in 1945, but we obtain less data about curriculum effects. The figure does not include the relation between standardized tests and the normative curriculum. However, in both comparisons the match between the actual curriculum and achievement tests was probably better than the match between the tests and the normative curriculum.

The normative curriculum in 1995 includes many more expectations than it did in 1945. Figure 28.5 illustrates that the actual curriculum in 1995 has expanded considerably. Teachers are engaging in more activities than in 1945 (e.g., more use of cooperative groups, somewhat more attention to problem solving than work on isolated concepts, etc.).

More problematic in my own estimation is the extent to which the actual curriculum in 1945 is closer to the normative curriculum than is the actual curriculum in 1995. I am assuming that the distance between the normative and actual curriculum, although roughly equivalent, has widened somewhat. What is critical in my comparison (and begs for theory and research) is that the standardized achievement test is much less adequate now as a proxy for both the normative curriculum and the

implemented curriculum than it was 50 years ago. Thus, achievement tests need to be aligned more closely to modern conceptions of instruction, and new measures of schooling outcomes need to be developed (i.e., many important aspects of the modern curriculum are not presently addressed).

Complexity of Developing New Measures

We have known for some time that developing and refining measurement devices were complex and labor-intensive tasks. For example, as early as 1918 Thorndike wrote:

One who is eager to find imperfections can find many in present measurements of educational products. Nor is it a hard task to make constructive suggestions for improvement. An intelligent student of education could probably in a single day note a score of sure ways of improving the scales and tests which we now use. That is really child's play. The hard thing is the actual expert work of remedying the imperfection, for this involves hundreds of hours of detailed expert planning, experimenting and computing. (p. 158)

Thorndike (1918) was right—developing tests that measure complex understanding is not easy. Haertel and Calfee (1983) correctly noted that standardized achievement tests were beginning to diverge from measuring important instructional objectives (see also Haertel, 1991). I restate and expand their arguments here and emphasize even more strongly that new methods of assessing students' performance are badly needed. These methods must stem from new theories of school success.

PERFORMANCE TESTING: A NEW WINDOW INTO SCHOOLING FOR THE PUBLIC?

If the contention that standardized achievement tests are no longer a good proxy for either the intended or actual curriculum were shown to be valid, two major questions follow. First, what types of assessment measures are reasonable proxies for the curriculum? And second, will educators see these measures as representative of the normative curriculum, and will citizens and policymakers view the measures as consistent with their beliefs about what constitutes *success* in American schools?

New Measures and Societal Expectations

It is hard to overrepresent the role of standardized achievement tests in American society. For example, it is not uncommon for real estate agents to sell prospective buyers a home in a particular neighborhood because of how a nearby school performs on standardized achievement tests. School quality is also a major consideration when businesses decide to locate a new firm or plant in a city. Despite the popular cry, "We want to be sure that management can find productive workers," the decision is likely to be more personal: "How good will these schools be for my daughter and son?"

Others, too, have also questioned the relation between "new measurement" methods and societal expectations. Linn (1994) described the problem:

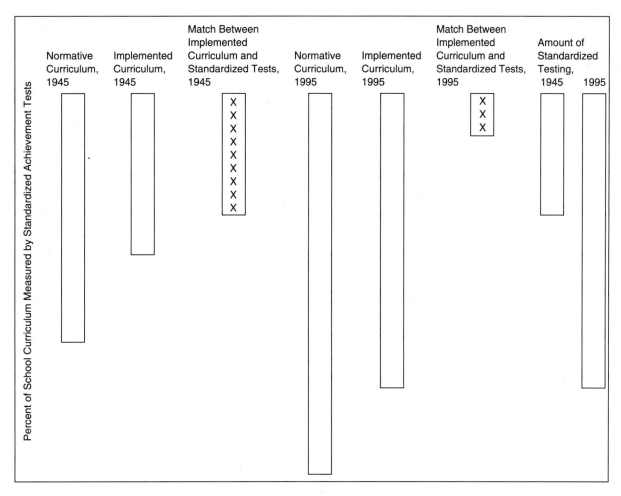

FIGURE 28.5. Hypothesized Match Between the Curriculum and Achievement Tests and the Amount of Testing, 1945 and 1995.

One of the clear claims for performance-based assessment and standards-based reporting being introduced by states and encouraged by the *Goals 2000* legislation is that the assessments will contribute to improved student achievement. Hence, the evaluation of consequences, both intended and unintended, takes on greater priority. The content standards are expected to define what students should know and be able to do and the assessments are expected to determine whether students know and are able to do what the content and performance standards specify. Thus, evidence that the assessments measure the reasoning, communicating, and problem solving skills and the knowledge of major concepts and ideas defined by content standards clearly needs to have high priority. (p. 18)

New Measures and Curriculum

Linn (1994) also anticipated enormous conflict within the profession in defining the bridge between "new measurement" and the "new normative curriculum." He cites intense political pressure involved in articulating educational standards even in negotiation among professional groups (AERA, APA, NCME), to say nothing of the negotiation required between government officials, citizens, and so on. Others have also discussed political compromise and the complexity involved in achieving consensus across diverse perspectives (e.g., Haney & Madaus, 1988).

In fact, rhetoric has far outpaced change. For example, Barton and Coley (1994) indicated that the multiple-choice format continues to account for 70% of tests given in statewide programs (in 1992–1993), despite the growing argument for a variety of performance assessments. The solution is much more complicated and complex than simply changing the format of tests for a population of students. Different types of tests are needed for students in grades 6–7 from those for grades 11–12. Also, new tests must be more inclusive and relevant to a variety of student groups (Carter & Goodwin, 1994; García & Pearson, 1994). Linn (1994) alluded to the problem of inclusiveness of new performance measures in terms of LEPs (students with limited English proficiency) and IEPs (students with individualized education plan). Educators, researchers, and policymakers must determine what performance measures are appropriate for these students.

New Measurement: Conceptual and Technical Issues

Why will educators have trouble reaching consensus about the direction of new tests? The good news is that most individuals agree that *validity* is the cornerstone on which new measurement should rest. However, some individuals, such as Moss (1994), argue that validity might be established better through critical dialogue and confrontation rather than only by using concepts of high agreement (see also Delandshere & Petrosky, 1994). Other educators believe that some consistency is critical, for both determining whether students can perform a task (internal considerations) and illustrating to citizens and policymakers that student learning has indeed occurred and that such learning is important or valuable (external reasons).

There is also the question of where to begin efforts to achieve validity. School districts that are implementing performance assessments in classrooms face a great challenge. Whatever funds and other resources they have are largely allocated to in-service training programs that enable teachers to develop explicit criteria for judging writing and problem solving. However, a district could begin the quest for validity in many other ways. Shavelson, Baxter, and Gao (1993) found that the measurement error due to *task* is likely to be much greater than the measurement error due to raters. Nevertheless, few, if any, school districts have thought seriously about task selection and its implications for student performance. One important component of task selection is choice. It seems useful (in terms of fairness and public relations) for teachers to allow students to pick the topics of important writing assignments that go into their portfolios or their cumulative files that go to "next year's teacher." However, Wainer and Thissen (1994) pointed out how difficult it is to build examinee choice into a test or measurement procedure such as portfolio analysis.

Perhaps one of the most positive aspects of performance assessment is the chance for teachers (1) to consider and discuss what constitutes appropriate school performance and to learn from one another, and (2) to include parents in the dialogue by examining student performance rather than describing performance using symbols that no one fully understands (i.e., grades). However, many administrators who are excessively concerned about traditional reliability (or time and money) might consider engaging teachers in such ways as wasteful. Linn (1994) described the problem this way:

The process of working together with other teachers on achieving a shared understanding of assessment criteria can be valuable staff development. On the other hand, bureaucratic demands and mistrust of teachers are apt to lead to a greater emphasis on top-down quality control whether through the use of a reference exam or external audits and rescoring of samples of locally scored portfolios. (p. 36)

Debate among educators will also be hampered by fadism and professional politics. Education's historical disinterest in integrative solutions (e.g., combining multiple-choice exams and performance assessment) will likely continue. The search for simple solutions and dichotomous thinking needs to end. Scriven (1993) has nicely summarized the case against fadism and simple solutions. He has argued that approaches to authentic assessment (e.g., portfolios, group work, embedded testing) have been disappointing and do not represent feasible replacement for multiple-choice items (MCIs). He states:

Alone or in combination, these are largely romantic ideals, conceived without attention to the economic realities of testing, i.e., without serious evaluation of testing. While their advocates are right to reject an all-MCI diet, they jump us straight out of the frying pan of oversimplified testing into the fires of overcomplicated scoring and administration, and dubious validity. (pp. 1–2)

Vu and Barrows (1994) reviewed research on the use of standardized patient technology in medicine and concluded that such usage is feasible, valid, and at least moderately reliable, although it is more costly than other forms of assessment (multiple-choice test, etc.). Performance assessment in medicine, architecture, and law has become popular as the perception that an objective test is not the ideal way to assess whether competence has grown (Vu & Barrows, 1994). According to these authors, "Since the main objective of the training of physicians is to ensure that they will deliver competent, quality care when encountering various patient problems, different formats of performance assessment have been developed to evaluate clinical competence" (p. 23). Much performance assessment in medicine focuses on physicians' clinical skills (e.g., interviewing patients), use of medical procedures, and their ability to communicate with and educate patients. This is in direct opposition to what many teacher educators advocate: the need to assess teachers' knowledge instead of their classroom performance. Indeed, some teacher educators are even leery of teacher knowledge assessment and want only to assess teacher beliefs. What better evidence do we need of political and social effects? Medicine relies on medical school to teach knowledge and currently assesses the ability to communicate in field settings; however, some teacher educators are leery of measuring teachers' communicative ability in the field. Furthermore, it seems that some educators do not trust teacher education programs to measure teachers' conceptions of subject matter.

Again, these choices do not have to be dichotomous. For example, Corno (1994) illustrated how data on student self-regulated classroom learning can be used to integrate information about student performance and teachers' thinking about that performance. This integration is helpful in developing construct validity that embodies multimethod assessment, multitrait sampling, and, eventually, reasonably comprehensive measures.

Citizens' Reactions to Performance Measures

Standardized achievement tests do not always reflect the normative and actual curriculum; however, improving these tests and/or altering them substantially will be a complex, substantial task involving both internal and external difficulties. Furthermore, it should be clear that simply teaching for understanding and using new performance measures will not translate into automatic classroom gains. Shepard et al. (1994) explored the effects of introducing classroom performance assessments on students' learning. They conclude that it is possible to be both pessimistic and optimistic given the findings of the study. In the area of reading, there were no changes due to the project as third graders in the participating schools did roughly the same as third graders had done the previous year and did not outperform control schools. However, in the area of mathematics, there was a small gain that could be attributed to the performance assessment. The authors reached the conclusion that those interested in reform need to understand the importance of providing for sustained professional development if teachers are to implement a thinking curriculum. These views are similar to those expressed previously by Good (1991) and Hinchey (1994).

DEVELOPING NEW INSTRUCTIONAL MODELS AND NEW APPROACHES TO ASSESSMENT

In this section of the chapter, two areas of reform are discussed that will help to make some general issues more concrete and will illustrate the negative effects on practice of the limited investment in educational research and development. The chapter first looks at one mechanism for conducting student performance assessments, the portfolio. As will be seen, the rhetoric advocating performance assessment is persuasive; however, data illustrating its value (for students, teachers, parents, and policymakers) are sparse.

As a primary example of *not* learning from the past, the recent research on portfolio assessment is largely devoid of observation (i.e., how do teachers and students actually interact with regard to planning or discussing a portfolio task?). Previous research has shown repeatedly that normative principles of what constitutes appropriate instruction and actual instruction are not similar. Early work on teacher effectiveness and the broader study of teaching demonstrated the need to include process measures if researchers are to understand the effects of instruction. If it is not possible to specify what occurs in the classroom, even in some rough form, it is difficult to draw any lessons for reflection.

In the second part of this section of the chapter, the potential use of small-group methods for assisting educators in teaching for understanding is discussed. Given many educators' belief that students should actively construct knowledge, it is important to learn whether and how grouping can help students to be more active and successful learners. Grouping is only one of many strategies for pursuing the goal of teaching for understanding (Ball, 1993), and there is a need for more research and development on all of these strategies if educators are to understand the complexities involved in teaching for understanding.

Increasing the Use of Portfolio Assessment

Content As Valencia (1990) and other educators have discussed, the *content* of a portfolio necessarily varies depending on curriculum goals and students. Conceptually, what a portfolio represents varies widely from author to author. Some contend, for example, that portfolios should represent the classroom processes and products to which students are exposed. However, other educators argue that portfolios should only include a student's best work. Sometimes the portfolios are produced independently by the student; in other cases, the portfolio is simply illustrating a student's ability to carry out directions.

Self-Assessment Some arguments for portfolios are compelling. Some are interested in this assessment method because in many classrooms teachers do most of the thinking and reflecting and students have little opportunity to organize and analyze content or their growth in understanding. Numerous claims have been made concerning the influence of portfolio work on students' understanding. For example, Wolf (1989) maintains that when students develop portfolios, they are able to assess better their own progress as learners. However, few systematic data are available for assessing such hypotheses. As a case in point, Mergendoller et al. (1988) found that science tasks in American classrooms emphasize following procedural directions and memorizing. In contrast, the use of portfolios could promote other types of learning that involve analysis, synthesis, problem solving, and so on (Mitchell, 1992; Wiggins, 1993).

Communication Flood and Lapp (1989) noted that portfolios can be useful means for communication between teachers and parents. According to them, parents are almost lulled to sleep by report cards that indicate, for example, that a student is getting a "C" in math the first term, the second term, and the third term. Some parents have difficulty interpreting such grades and assume that their children are not learning and progressing. In contrast, portfolios can provide parents with a variety of performance measures of their children's work: students' self-assessment, writing samples, and scores on norm- and criterion-referenced measures (Flood & Lapp, 1989). Still, teachers who must explain new performance standards to parents often tell me that parents have trouble distinguishing between a "3" and a "4" on some scoring rubric and that many parents say, "I know what an 'A' is." Some parents lament the lack of an honor roll and other traditional indices of achievement. A frequent problem with scoring rubrics used to evaluate portfolio assignments is an overreliance on rating scales rather than descriptions of specific performance. Increased use of rating scales as reporting devices may not improve communication. Unfortunately, we have a paucity of data to describe how the use of particular portfolios in specific contexts influence parent–teacher communication.

Wolf (1989) identified other problems with using portfolios:

Portfolios are messy. They demand intimate and often frighteningly subjective talk with students. Portfolios are work. Teachers are asking students to read their own progress in the "footprints" of their work, have to coax and bicker with individuals who are used to being assessed. Half-way through the semester, at least half a dozen recalcitrants will lose every paper or sketch or tape they have ever owned. More important, teachers have to struggle to read and make sense of whole works and patterns of growth. (p. 37)

Need for Theory Perhaps the greatest problem for those who advocate portfolios is theoretical and conceptual. Too often, the answer to the question, "What does a portfolio represent?" is a long series of possibilities or an "It can be anything." It seems to me, however, that the answer must have construct validity that is based on the knowledge, dispositions, and competencies that we want students to acquire. For example, portfolios should enable students to think critically about important, identifiable content and/or to develop discernible dispositions such as the willingness to engage in critical self-evaluation. Portfolios should also help teachers, students, parents, and citizens understand what students have learned. Hence, school districts using portfolios must develop a theory of portfolio and build an appropriate measurement system (see also, Delandshere & Petrosky, 1994).

Need for Research The school district's or state agency's ability to develop a theory could be sharpened by research and development addressing issues such as the following: Given developmental differences among students, what portfolio tasks would be appropriate in grades 1, 5, and 9? How can portfolio work be designed to provide relevant feedback that a student values? Should portfolios exhibit student performance to parents or increase the exchange of information between parents and teachers? Do differing conceptions of portfolios as a school–home link influence the content and procedures associated with portfolio work? To what extent do different school–home models of portfolios actually work? Do they improve parents' conceptions of schooling? How could we find out?

Countless other questions could be raised. Should students work alone or in groups on portfolios? When and why? How do variables such as gender, subject matter, student developmental level, language ability, and so on influence the usefulness of portfolios? Do portfolios reflect student progress in the normative and actual curriculum better than do standardized tests or teacher-constructed tests? Is this question of match answered differently by teacher educators, educational researchers, policymakers, parents, and citizens?

Of course, some research is under way on performance assessment. For example, Athanases (1994) noted that teachers' attention to working with students as they developed literacy portfolios had positive effects on teachers' assessment practices. For example, use of student portfolios led teachers to obtain more varied and detailed records of students' literacy development. Furthermore, many teachers became more attentive to students' individual progress over time.

As a result of their study of the Vermont assessment program, Koretz, Stecher, Klein, and McCaffrey (1994) wrote:

Although the Vermont program has shown promising effects on instruction and modest improvement in measurement quality of mathematics, the basic lesson to be drawn from its experience is the need for modest expectations, patience, and ongoing evaluation in our national experimentation with innovative, large-scale performance assessments as a tool of educational reform. (p. 32)

The stance of Koretz et al. (1994) seems reasonable. How quickly new types of assessment can be implemented will depend on the amount and quality of conceptualization, research, and development that precede implementation.

Need for Infrastructure Building an infrastructure that helps teachers to move from the vision to informal practice (e.g., dealing with the problems alluded to by Wolf, Bixby, Glenn, & Gardner [1991]) is something that educators tend not to do. Wolf et al. (1991) argue that the field needs to develop a culture of assessment such that teachers (and students) would develop through discussion and reflection better understanding about what constitutes good work, appropriate rules of evidence, and so on. Although generally supporting the NCTM's guidelines for effective instruction in mathematics, I have noted that the inability to build an adequate infrastructure will impede the use of the standards in actual practice (Good, 1991). Hinchey (1994) has reached similar conclusions about reform in English education, and as noted, Shepard et al. (1994) reached the same conclusions in trying to shift to a "thinking" curriculum.

Need for Balance The use of new performance measures, including portfolios, seems promising, but they must not be viewed as a new *answer* to educational problems, especially when there are so few studies addressing questions of theory and implementation. Teachers and researchers need to experiment with progressive ideas. As Dewey (1902) noted long ago, it is a responsibility of a teacher to explore and to experiment with new ideas. However, teachers should ask more focused and more context-based questions, such as what types of assessments, for what audience, and for what purpose would be most amenable to portfolio development? In what ways can portfolios enhance standardized achievement measures? It is probably better to have one or two high-quality assignments using one or two performance assessment methods than to shift frequently from one measurement approach to another. Moreover, given the multiple responsibilities teachers face (e.g., dealing with resistance from parents, communicating with the teacher at the next grade level, devising new scoring systems to assess student performance), teachers might be better off phasing in new assessment-related activities; that is, perhaps move 10% to 25% of the curriculum to performance assessment in a given year. Scholars who have written on the more general topic of change processes have reached similar conclusions (e.g., Sarason, 1982, 1993).

It seems to be a better idea to argue for funding, to support exploratory research and development concerning how students use portfolios and how teachers, policymakers, and citizens react to such models before advocating that teachers use portfolios extensively. At a minimum, teacher educators should probably use portfolios in their own classrooms and help preservice teachers reflect on the strengths and weaknesses of the method for particular contexts and tasks before urging adoption.

Others, too, have argued against dichotomous thinking and have noted trade-offs between structured and open-ended assessments. Messick (1994) discussed this issue:

To begin with, it must be recognized that the contrast between multiple-choice items and open-ended performance tasks is not a dichotomy, but a continuum representing different degrees of response structure. This continuum is variously described as ranging from multiple-choice to student-constructed products or presentations (Bennett, Ward, Rock, & LaHart, 1990), for example, or from multiple-choice to demonstrations and portfolios. (Snow, 1993, p. 15)

Social and Political Context As Moss (1994) noted, it is ironic that some educators (e.g., Resnick & Resnick, 1992) have urged that teachers' judgments not be used for accountability purposes. Other educators (e.g., Darling-Hammond & Snyder, 1992) emphasize that if teachers' voices are not included in accountability assessments, then the assessments are suspect because the people who understand the local context are excluded from making judgments. According to Moss (1994):

There is a crisis mentality accompanied by a flurry of activity to design assessment and accountability systems that both document and promote desired educational change. Current conceptions of reliability and validity in educational measurement constrain the kinds of assessment practices that are likely to find favor, and these in turn constrain educational opportunity for teachers and students. (p. 10)

New Conceptualizations of Assessment I agree with Moss that as researchers move forward they should experiment with new ways of conceptualizing and exploring topics such as reliability and validity. As an example of a more holistic or hermeneutic approach to assessment, Moss described several types of high-stakes assessments that are not standardized. For instance, when faculty members make decisions about hiring colleagues, not every aspect of the candidate's background is assessed independently by each faculty member. Rather, every faculty member on the committee searches all of the relevant information and reaches an integrative judgment about the qualification of the candidate. However, these judgments may be unreliable or invalid on a number of grounds. Some candidates spend a great deal of time preparing transparencies, slides, handouts, and so on, and other candidates simply present their papers.

Part of the problem with evaluating portfolios that candidates might present is that no one understands the selection procedure or, typically, is in a position to verify it. If a candidate presents five or six student comments as typical, how does one know whether these are the five best teaching ratings the candidate has received in the last 10 years or if they are truly representative? Thus, open-ended approaches to reliability have many of the same problems as independent consensus approaches.

Learning From Practice Moss (1994) noted that in some school districts (e.g., Pittsburgh, PA) committees of teachers who are developing districtwide portfolio assessment systems have had the freedom to bring in educators from outside the district to evaluate (audit) the portfolio system. Other districts (e.g., at the Brooklyn, NY, New School) have attempted to include students and families in educational decisions and to involve outside researchers to ensure that accountability is measured adequately. The field should encourage funding of case study and comparative research so that educators can learn more about the types of measurement and accountability for which portfolios are best suited.

Increasing the Use of Small-Group Models

One major deficiency of research on small-group learning has been researchers' failure to observe what actually occurs during instruction. Given the method's promise for involving students more actively in discussing and debating significant content, many researchers have encouraged more studies of group processes (Bossert, 1988–1989; Good & Biddle, 1988; Good, Mulryan, & McCaslin, 1992). As McCaslin and Good (1992) argued, educational policymakers move quickly from reform to reform with little interest in obtaining research-derived knowledge on which to base change.

With few data (at least of the sort to guide massive implementation), however, policymakers and reformers continue to offer simplistic strategies (e.g., more grouping) for solving students'

learning problems. For example, Bill Honig, former California Superintendent of Public Instruction, was quoted in a *Newsweek* article (see Kantrowitz & Wingert, 1991) as saying: "It's like we have a cure for polio, but we're not giving the inoculation" (pp. 64–65). The research evidence suggests that small-group learning may benefit some types of learners in some situations, but it is far from a cure for major learning problems. Indeed, in some cases group learning may cause problems rather than solve them.

Good, McCaslin, and Reys (1992) found that students' reports of satisfaction with group work may mask problems (e.g., high-achievers' domination) in group functioning. Thus, both teachers and researchers need to develop strategies for collecting accurate group process data. Researchers who have observed group processes extensively have identified many problems in group functioning (Good & Brophy, 1994; McCaslin & Good, in press a, in press b; Webb, 1983).

Gains in Student Understanding Are Not Automatic Student work groups do not automatically result in increased student understanding of content. Even if appropriate academic tasks are assigned to students, much remains to be learned about how a task is mediated by a group of learners (Good, McCaslin, & Reys, 1992). For example, in some work groups members' subject-matter knowledge is increased. Some educators argue that when students work together in math, for instance, it is more likely that someone will know how to begin the problem-solving process or will recognize or construct a key formula that applies to the process. The knowledge of mathematical or scientific processes and content that the group possesses is almost always greater than the knowledge of any individual student. Thus, with the combined knowledge of group members, problem-solving strategies are more varied and more powerful.

However, Good, McCaslin, and Reys (1992) cautioned that students' misconceptions can also be reinforced in work group settings. Students often have misconceptions about academic content that are difficult to change, even with direct, explicit instruction. These misconceptions may simply be reinforced during small-group interactions if other group members also hold common misconceptions (Eaton et al., 1984).

Countless questions about grouping merit investigation. Some students might, for example, become more active and independent when they work in small groups. Conversely, a shift in dependency from teacher to peers could also occur. The fact that the teacher is not an active participant may mean that certain students assume the role of authority figures. Hence, the shift from whole-class to small-group instruction may be superficial or cosmetic rather than structural.

Blumenfeld (1992) and her colleagues studied the influence of classroom tasks on the motivation and cognitive engagement of 275 fifth and sixth graders from 10 classes. She found that although cooperative small-group work was more motivating, students' active learning declined in such settings. This finding supports a conclusion matching those that colleagues and I reached (Good, Reys, Grouws, & Mulryan, 1989–1990) that when small-group tasks are poorly designed, students are "swamped" by procedural problems (they spend more time carrying out superficial procedures than thinking about the meaning of tasks).

Curriculum Tasks and Small Groups Despite a growing consensus that school assignments should stress students' understanding and in-depth coverage of fewer topics (rather than superficial coverage of numerous topics), studies of the structure of school tasks indicate that teachers tend to assign isolated, discrete concepts that encourage students' memorization rather than understanding or application (Blumenfeld, 1992; Fisher & Hiebert, 1990; Mergendoller et al., 1988; Porter, 1989). Thus, some have argued that the shift from whole-class work to small-group work might improve the quality of assigned tasks.

Blumenfeld (1992) found that simply assigning more complex and challenging tasks does not lead automatically to more student thinking. Considering that few teachers have been trained to teach for understanding and that most teachers are incredibly busy, how will teachers who want to use small-group methods find time to explore new instructional models, build curriculum units, and develop new ways to assess student performance? It is also important to ask whether teachers will be motivated to transform the curriculum when successful schooling is defined narrowly in terms of performance on standardized tests (i.e., teaching for understanding may not be the best way to optimize students' scores on traditional achievement tests).

New Content To complicate matters further, the mathematical content (e.g., geometry and statistics) currently emphasized by professional groups such as the NCTM for inclusion in the elementary school curriculum is largely absent from the current curriculum. Moreover, the type of student learning (problem solving) that is needed is not measured on achievement tests used in most state assessment programs (however, some states, such as Connecticut, have begun to address this issue). Thus, supporting reforms in math education involves risk for administrators because they are accountable to local citizens who may favor increasing students' standardized test scores. Helping teachers to be more adept and knowledgeable in understanding geometry and estimation may not lead to enhanced student performance (i.e., this content is not heavily sampled by the standardized test).

Resisting Fadism The problems with students' weak mathematics performance are diverse and complex. For example, if in 1960 U.S. students led the world in mathematics achievement (as many contend) while being taught with the recitation model, then the current reliance on this model cannot be the sole reason for declining student performance (again, such simple and wrong fadism must be difficult for astute citizens to understand). The recitation/discussion model can do some things (teach concepts, intellectual skills, dispositions about mathematics), but it is unlikely to foster adequately outcomes such as inquiry, discovery, and experimentation. The argument here is not intended to defend a recitation/discussion model (although it is a viable model under some circumstances), because I believe that teachers need to emphasize problem solving and inquiry more. The argument is to suggest that the current NCTM *Standards* can be interpreted too narrowly and too simply.

In efforts to reform mathematics classrooms, educators must recognize that no single instructional format is an answer per se and that quality and connectedness of learning are the critical issues (Good, 1983). There are always trade-offs with the use of any method. Interestingly, as small-group formats are becoming more attractive to U.S. educators, in Russia concerns are being raised about the long-term effects of small-group learning on individual initiative, responsibility, and creativity (Tudge, 1991). In the past many Russian educators argued that individuals' initiative only emerges through the dialogue of the collective. Their beliefs are now being reexamined. It is important now that researchers integrate developmental and social considerations into the task literature and into the broader discussion of teaching for understanding and of what subject matter is most worth having students actively construct. Hence, again the issue of balance needs examination to determine when and how small-group models should be used.

Need for Research and Development Although the literature illustrates that under certain circumstances small-group instruction leads to increased student achievement (e.g., Cohen, 1994), research yields more questions than answers. Teachers' implementing this model would benefit from a rich research and development effort. In this section discussion focuses on three research topics, group stability, developmental variables, and the student–teacher relationship, that could improve the relation between theory and the implementation of grouping (for more examples, see Good, Mulryan, & McCaslin, 1992).

One might ask, for example, how many models of small-group instruction should be presented? Does the presentation of models encourage teacher experimentation and flexibility or premature commitment to a particular teaching style? Do different instructional models (e.g., teacher-directed, recursive, student-directed) interact with different types of task structures?

There are advantages and disadvantages in having students work together in the same group for a relatively long period (e.g., 2 weeks). Group stability allows students to become familiar with the work styles, competencies, and personal characteristics of other group members and allows group norms for student behavior to develop. Moreover, students who work in relatively permanent groups might be more likely to work out their differences than students in groups whose membership changes frequently. In contrast, changing group membership after one or two class periods may benefit some students by allowing them to work with a wider range of students and perhaps to avoid the personal conflicts and disagreements that might characterize more stable groups. Clearly, tasks are mediated by the social and intellectual characteristics of the students in a group, and the history of a group is likely to influence its cohesiveness, the willingness of its members to take risks, and so on.

Teachers need to assign cooperative group tasks that are appropriate for students at different ages or grades. Thus, researchers need to study whether students in the primary grades work cooperatively on mathematics tasks (or social studies tasks) to the same degree and in the same way as students in intermediate grades. Another topic that merits research attention is what cooperation means to students of various ages and the implications of these differences for planning, implementing, and evaluating cooperative group methods.

The student–teacher relationship also needs to be examined, especially from a developmental perspective. For example, first-grade teachers would likely have difficulty explaining to students the differences between the teacher's role during small-group versus whole-class instruction. Because first graders have learned that the teacher dominates during whole-class instruction, they might not understand that they are to learn from peers as well as from the teacher during group work. In contrast, the issue of teacher authority would pose relatively few problems in fifth-grade classrooms. Because fifth graders are preoccupied by questions such as who they are and how they relate to their peers, they enjoy exchanging ideas with peers and would be less concerned about attempting to please the teacher.

These are only a few of the numerous research topics that merit investigation. Given a more generous budget for research and development, we could increase our knowledge about small-group learning considerably. In addition to research exploring the integration of student, subject-matter, and teaching variables, attention must focus on new means of assessing learning as well. Finally, if administrators are recommending the use of small-group teaching, how can we assess teachers' effectiveness in designing and implementing this strategy? This is another area that calls for rich research and development.

The Need to Integrate Research Areas

The two current examples I have chosen to discuss (performance assessment and cooperative group learning) illustrate nicely the *isolated* ways in which research traditions operate in education. Oddly, the argument for performance assessment continues with little apparent interest in cooperative learning or group performance. Although it is possible to find some mention of cooperative group performance, advocates of performance assessment primarily argue for the assessment of individuals.

This isolated development is also reflected in the literature on cooperative grouping. Although there is some focus on problem solving and the need for active exchange among students, there is little advocacy for the type of public performance that Sizer (1984) called for in his book, *Horace's Compromise* (and which spurred renewed interest in creating a more active student role). To reiterate, educational reform suffers from an inadequate research and development base and from the advocacy of one-dimensional changes instead of programs based on a synthesis of ideas.

MOVING FORWARD

Some believe that citizens' support for public education is eroding. It is beyond my purpose in this chapter to develop and defend this assertion; however, I suggest that the daily barrage of newspaper and magazine articles and other media reports contains numerous assertions, both explicit and implicit, that public schools are failing and need major reform. Perhaps a constructive place for moving forward is to understand if and why this occurs, whether such allegations are fair, and if not, how a more supportive view of schooling might be created.

Others, too, have noted the tendency of the American press to be overly critical of schooling. In her editorial, "Shame on the Press," in the January 1994 issue of *Phi Delta Kappan*,

Pauline Gough noted that American newspapers responded with negative headlines and stories that implicitly indicted schools when the Department of Education released the dismal results of a study entitled "Adult Literacy in America." After analyzing the ways in which newspapers had misrepresented findings in the report, she concluded her analysis by condemning the negative journalism:

So a report that should have reinforced the public's view of the value of education was instead allowed—by the nation's press—to demoralize teachers and administrators and to reaffirm the widely-held (but erroneous) view that public education is failing to educate. Shame on the press for its widespread failure to set the study's findings fully in context. American education deserves better. (p. 355)

Citizens' Beliefs About School Effectiveness

Despite such negative characterizations, most citizens (particularly parents) report that their neighborhood schools are doing a reasonably good job of educating students. Gallup (1986) notes in his 1986 survey that public schools are perceived favorably with 41% of Americans rating the public schools locally (in this particular community) as either A or B. Gallup notes that the closer the contact between rater and schools, the higher the rating:

Public school parents grade the public schools in their own community substantially higher than the public schools nationally, and they rate the public schools their own children attend even higher than the local schools. In the current survey, only 28% of parents give the public schools, nationally, an A or B; nearly twice as many (55%) give the local schools an A or B, and almost 2/3 (65%) give the school their children attend one of the top two grades. (p. 46)

Elam, Rose, and Gallup (1994) note that these general trends continue. They noted that about 44% of Americans give the public schools in their area an A or B. Citizens who have children rate public schools higher: 57% of public school parents give public schools a grade of A or B.

In the past most citizens believed in schools (although teachers and schools have always been criticized at some level), but currently schools appear to have declining public support. Although citizens support the local school, there is a marked reluctance to believe in schools more in general. Attacks on public schools seem to have advanced successfully the belief that schools generally are marginal or poor investments.

Unfortunately, few researchers have examined how teachers, parents, and other citizens view schools with regard to *specific* teaching models and learning outcomes. This is an interesting area of research as schools that espouse a particular learning approach might have distinguishable outcomes, but they also could create a distinct identity with favorable or unfavorable long-term consequences. Occasionally, researchers have measured parents' or citizens' beliefs about standardized achievement tests and their utility relative to new performance measures, but respondents were not asked about specific performance measures or what might be missing in the new measurement methods. Rather, citizens are seen as relatively passive validators or critics of school.

As an exception to my argument that we have no knowledge of parent beliefs about testing, Shepard and Bliem (1993) asked parents in three California schools about their preferences for obtaining information on the basis of standardized achievement tests or from more open-ended questions used in performance assessments. Figure 28.6 illustrates the type of questions that were asked in the area of reading and math. Interestingly, parents reported liking both formats; however, performance assessments had higher approval ratings than did standardized tests—especially when parents were using the "strongly approve" category. The preference for performance assessment information was stronger in reading (58% favored performance assessment; 21% preferred standardized tests) than was the case in mathematics (44% favored performance assessment; 31% favored standardized tests). Similarly, more data on formats for reporting student progress would be helpful. As a case in point Elam et al. (1994) noted that parents reported preferring written descriptions of student progress over traditional A-to-F reports. More research on parents' and citizens' beliefs about assessment and the reporting of progress would be helpful. An especially valuable area for research would be parents' reactions to *classroom process* (e.g., videotapes of small-group work, video teacher reports, etc.).

Limited Policy Role for Parents and Citizens

Educators' interests in parents as resources have varied. Historically, parents appeared to have been seen by professional educators as a necessary evil (we know what to do—do not interfere). As parents became more active politically, they gained rights and access (especially parents of special education students). More recently educators have courted parents (invitations to visit and tutor regularly, etc.) and have viewed parents as educational partners. Indeed, some policymakers are now taking the role of parent as educator so seriously that parents are blamed when students do not perform! Within this evolving relationship between home and school there has been, and continues to be, a marked reservation on educators' part for

allowing parents a policy role. (Clearly, there have been some notable exceptions, such as in the Chicago public schools.) Although school boards have elected members, such boards are hardly representative of the school constituency, and there is scant evidence to support that citizen board members actively solicit input from other citizens. Indeed, it is clear that some citizens' groups have organized politically to ensure that board policy is dominated by a narrow, specific view (the religious right has been notorious in this regard). The argument here is that there has been little attempt (by school officials or by parent board members) to assess public opinion about schools (e.g., what constitutes success) and to create forums for discussion. Attempts to communicate are more likely to center on how to convince parents that this is a good program.

Policymakers' Role in School Reform

McDonnell (1994) contended as interest in "Goals 2000" has developed, Congress has been in a reactive position (with Bush originally taking the initiative and later informing Republican Congress members and Clinton subsequently providing leadership for the ideas and then negotiating with Democratic members of Congress). She writes:

Not only has Congress been in a reactive position, but only a few members of both houses and their staffs are interested in standards and assessment, well-informed about the issues, and actively engaged in the policy process. Similarly, those states that have chosen to move ahead on alternative assessment have largely done so at the initiative of their executive branch, either through the governor or the chief state school officer. In most cases, state legislatures have entered the process much later, in their role as funds appropriator. (p. 31)

Although executive energy and commitment seem notable, one might ask in what, if any, ways the interests of citizens have been considered in the development of goals and assessment methods that define success in American schools. Thus, it appears that congressional policymakers have been responding primarily to presidential initiatives, and it appears that citizens have had little role in emerging legislation.

Standardized Test Questions	Performance Assessment Problems
How much change will you get if you have $6.55 and spend $4.32? ( ) $2.23 ( ) $2.43 ( ) $3.23 ( ) $10.87	Suppose you couldn't remember what 8 x 7 is. How could you figure it out?
A good title for this story would be: ( ) The Pet Store ( ) A Strange Occupation ( ) Going on a Trip ( ) Danny's Pet Snake	At the end of the story, the little old man and the little old woman go on living in the little old house. Do you think this is a good ending? Tell why or why not.

FIGURE 28.6. Parent Reactions to Standardized Tests and Performance Assessments.

Influences of Teacher Education on Reform

Educators' conceptions of teaching effects have changed rapidly and radically since the 1960s, and it would not be a leap of faith to suggest that they may change again in the next few years. In 1970 many educators argued that teachers did not make a difference in students' achievement. By the 1980s many writers blamed teachers when students did not learn. In the 1990s teachers became the solution to problems of schooling. Some educators currently blame students' failure to learn on inadequate home environments, parents' shortcomings, and students' unwillingness to work (Tomlinson, 1993). Such shifts in the field's thinking may be difficult for the average citizen to follow.

Some scholars have claimed that new teachers in the 1980s were less talented (in terms of aptitude) than those in the 1960s and 1970s. If this is true, then teacher education programs have improved dramatically (given that teachers today are more of a solution and teachers a decade ago were more of a problem!). I'm not sure that many educators would want to make this claim. Here I am obviously being polemical to make the point that perhaps citizens have difficulty understanding educators' pleas for more resources when views of teachers' importance have fluctuated so dramatically over short periods. Undoubtedly, many citizens are puzzled when teacher educators argue that schools are morally deficient (Oser, 1994) and on the decline, while they hold that more preservice teacher education should take place in schools rather than college classrooms! Because educators often present their case poorly to the public, teacher educators are open to radical—and often persuasive and successful—attacks that may be unfair and unjust. Such publications keep citizens (already skeptical of educational funding) from becoming any more enthusiastic about paying for preservice and in-service teacher education programs. As educators communicate with the public, we need to be clearer with the public about student outcomes that teachers can and cannot influence (McCaslin & Good, 1992) and about resources that teacher educators need in order to be successful (e.g., to help teachers in training to develop appropriate understanding of performance testing). Obviously, many teacher educators are articulate forces for reasonable, responsible, and successful reform; however, we can do more. The point here is that in the zest for meaningful change teacher educators must become more effective in communicating with the public the rationale for change and a better understanding of what the requirements are for change (time, money, etc.).

What Is the Nature of the Problem and Who Owns It?

Although I am aware of many problems of public schools, it is difficult to separate these problems from the broader communities that surround a school. Scores on standardized achievement tests reflect much more than students' and teachers' classroom experiences: They are also affected by families, neighborhoods, and investments in education (Berliner, 1993; McCaslin & Good, 1992).

Political Influences How can educators improve the public's perceptions and obtain more support from citizens? First, we need to recognize that many individuals, institutions, and organizations are working hard to disseminate a negative view of school effectiveness. Although some groups use arguments based on data, others have drawn premature conclusions and disseminate information in selective and polemical ways for relatively narrow purposes (see, e.g., Berliner & Biddle, 1995). Even government agencies are not neutral in their attempts to interpret and implement policy; rather, at times, they exert political influence in striking ways. For example, recently government agencies have presented many comparisons, often in tabular form, of the problems of teachers in the 1940s, 1980s, and 1990s. These lists suggest that running in the halls, chewing gum, and getting out of line were critical school discipline problems in the 1940s. In the 1980s teachers identified problems such as drug and alcohol abuse, pregnancy, and suicide. Today extortion, gun toting, arson, and assault are leading school problems.

According to O'Neill (1994), such comparisons are a bit too tidy. When he was in school, he worried more about boys stealing his lunch or starting fist fights. He notes that results of a 1984 Gallup poll indicated that teachers thought the biggest school problems were parent apathy and a lack of financial support. (Drugs appeared near the bottom of their list.) In 1991 the National Center for Education Statistics conducted a survey about safety issues and found that tardiness, absenteeism, and fighting were top complaints; drugs fell near the bottom (O'Neill, 1994).

O'Neill (1994) contends that such lists of school problems teachers describe actually reflect characteristics of society rather than of schools per se. He discusses *the role of politicians* in disseminating the perspective of moral decline for political reasons and ends his analysis this way:

The lists are not facts, but a fundamental expression of attitudes and emotions. They overlook the successes of American public education, its great expansion since 1940, and its high quality despite taxpayer resistance. The lists' broad sweep ignores that some public schools are devastated by violence and substance abuse, and others hardly touched at all. They should not guide our choices on education policy. (p. 49)

What is the political motivation for socializing the view that schools are morally deficient places where little of value is learned? I suspect that multiple factors were at work, but I believe that one motivation was that many conservative members of Congress and conservative members of state legislatures in power did not want to spend money on education, they wanted to invest resources in other areas. One strategy for limiting potential outcries over reduced educational funding is simply to show that although American youth deserve better schools, schools are misusing money. Until schools prove their commitment and seriousness of purpose, they should not receive additional funds—they will only waste the money.

Economic Politics Many people want schools to fail for other *social* or *economic reasons*. If one owns land outside a suburban setting, it seems only reasonable to conclude that if there is growing concern about the quality of the local school, those with sufficient economic resources may move a few miles outside the city and build their own school. There are economic consequences associated with rapid turnover in property whether it be due to white flight, African-American flight, or Hispanic flight. Those who prefer a more homogeneous student population may well want schools that emphasize diversity to fail.

Other groups also use influence to manipulate the curriculum for political or religious reasons. McCarthy (1993) notes that conservative citizen groups have organized and engaged in various forms of political ideas. She notes that various conservative groups have combined to discourage secular humanism and writes, "Materials that encourage students to think critically, to examine alternatives, or to clarify values—in other words, to become active learners—are alleged to represent this antitheistic belief" (p. 55).

Clearly, there are many honest critics of public schooling who are deeply concerned about the quality of schools. Much of the controversy is real in the sense that people believe there are inadequacies and they want to document them as a first step in improving schools. However, to gain support for public education and to counter the many groups disseminating negative views of schools, educators must increase dialogue with citizens. In the process, citizens need information, including data that help them understand the consequences of inadequate funding and the need for both more and more focused resources.

Challenging Myths About Unsuccessful Schooling

Berliner (1993) illustrated that many arguments against American schooling are myths, not reality. In particular, he debunked the myth that, compared to students of the past, today's youth cannot think as well, are not as smart, and perform inadequately on standardized achievement tests. Berliner also contended that spending on schooling can be associated with student performance. His data indicated that the more talented teachers are (higher aptitude, more graduate courses, etc.), the better their students do on academic achievement tests. He also found that factors such as class size are related to student achievement. As mentioned, other studies also show a positive relation between school resources and student achievement (Hedges et al., 1994a).

Berliner's arguments are especially important because, even though standardized achievement tests are poor proxies for students' success in contemporary schools, they are still the scoring system for the nation. As we call for broader and more integrative measures of student performance, we must do so from a strong position. An argument for change is stronger when it asserts that American students continue to do well on conventional achievement measures, despite the growing diversity of the student population and declining financial support. The evidence seems to support the fact that schools are doing better than the image conveyed in the popular press (see, e.g., Berliner & Biddle, 1995).

Need for Funding

Pat Graham (1993) in her presidential comments in the annual report for the Spencer Foundation aptly summarized the decline in support for educational research:

Some of the most vociferous voices in the debate of the last decade have come from those in the federal government, the sponsor of *A Nation at Risk*. What they have not called for in the face of the apparent illness of the school system is research. In fact, the federal government, which historically has been the principal funder of educational research, has dramatically cut its expenditure for educational research during this period. A National Academy of Sciences report in 1992 estimated that twenty years ago the entire federal government spent $1.1 billion (in 1990 constant dollars) on educational research and development while in 1991, it spent less than one-third that amount. At the Office of Educational Research and Improvement (OERI) only 2 percent of its funds support individual researchers who propose the topics they wish to study. The comparable percentages for this kind of research at the National Institutes of Health is 56 percent and at the National Science Foundation, 94 percent. OERI now spends only 5.5 percent of its budget on basic research while the percentages for basic research of the National Institutes of Health and the National Science Foundation research and development budgets are 60 percent and 94 percent, respectively. (p. 5)

Clearly, some policymakers do not see a clear need for investments in research. Perhaps it is time to argue for the value of research more convincingly.

Communicating with the Public

As I have argued, it is vital that the normative curriculum and normative view of instruction (e.g., teaching for student understanding, NCTM *Standards,* etc.) be more sharply defined and better communicated to citizens. New theories of measurement and new models for evaluating and representing progress need to be developed. If educators believe that standardized achievement tests are inadequate means of assessing student progress, they need to make citizens and policymakers aware of this. Furthermore, citizens' views about "what counts" in schools need to be better understood.

Gallup (1986) has also collected information from citizens about the goals of education. In the response to the question, "People have different reasons why they want their children to get an education. What are the chief reasons that come to your mind?," It was clear that for many Americans financial and job-related opportunities are important. In the survey, 34% cited job opportunities, 8% reported the need for getting a better paying job, and 9% reported the goal was to help children achieve financial security. In addition, 28% of citizens mentioned general preparation for life, whereas only 10% indicated the importance of acquiring knowledge per se. Given that citizens are concerned about preparing students for jobs, it is instructive to note that Berliner (1992) has argued that the primary reason workers are fired is because of poor interpersonal skills and the failure to take personal responsibility—not because of poor skills in algebra!

STUDENTS AS SOCIAL BEINGS

Researchers and teachers need to understand students as learners and as members of their classroom community, as well as in the broader social community in which they reside. Educators must communicate their awareness to the public that students are more than their academic performances and standardized test scores. As McCaslin and Good argued in *Listening in Class-*

rooms (in press b), students are more than persons who attend school and are engaged in a curriculum. Gender, age, race, and ethnicity are critical aspects of anyone's identity, but students are considerably more than this. Most students have political beliefs and career aspirations, and all students have status, affiliation, and safety needs. Students live in families that vary considerably in membership, structure, beliefs about children and schooling, and social and economic resources. Students have friends and enemies. They endure and sometimes benefit from sibling relationships, as well as relationships with employers. Thus, countless factors from society, home, neighborhood, and school help define who a student is and what—who she or he aspires to become (McCaslin & Good, in press b).

Soltis (1994), when describing the characteristics of the new teacher, mentions social-ethical sensitivity and political awareness as needed characteristics:

The new teacher sees his or her practice embedded in a larger social context where power, dominance, and social injustices exist. The school as a social institution serves social purposes whose worth and moral goodness need to be consciously and conscientiously appraised. School practices and pedagogical actions may carry with them the unintended consequences of reproducing undesirable and unjust social prejudices and arrangements. The new teacher must cultivate a nose for unintentional curriculum and a sense of moral obligation to right its wrongs in a way consonant with fundamental democratic values of equality and justice, and human values of nurturance and love. (pp. 248–249)

Need to Supplement a Subject-Matter Perspective

The subject-matter perspective must therefore be supplemented with focus on students as *social beings* who are learning more than (and perhaps at the expense of) the formal curriculum. Students not only construct personal knowledge of subject matter, but also they continually estimate the importance of schoolwork and its implications for themselves and their social world, both in the present and the future. I believe that the average citizen is as concerned about students' ability to self-evaluate and to work cooperatively as he or she is about students' knowledge of differential equations. The School to Work Opportunities Act would appear to provide testimony to the perceived importance of students' being able to work together, define and complete independent tasks, show up on time, respect diversity, and so on. Indeed, some citizens are more concerned about students' dispositions than their mastery of subject matter per se. Thus, teachers should be encouraged to develop strategies for engaging students in conversation and interviewing them to learn more about how students understand subject matter and how they think and feel about social issues in society, including what occurs in classrooms. We also need to develop ways of assessing teachers' competence in these areas.

To reiterate, in the United States we spend up to one half billion dollars a year on testing students (Paris et al., 1991), and we may see this figure increase substantially in the near future (McDonnell, 1994). Enormous personal and economic resources are utilized to find out what students can remember or perform. However, we invest few resources in asking students what they think or what they feel about things that matter—to us and/or to them (McCaslin & Good, in press b).

Developing Realistic Expectations for Schooling

The legislative act, "Goals 2000, Educate America Act," recommends academic standards for students in fourth, eighth, and eleventh grades. Although the goals are relatively vague and participation is voluntary, the act is significant because it creates a federal stake over what transpires in classrooms. Historically, the federal government's role in public schools has focused on disabled children and civil rights protection (Celis, 1994).

As I mentioned at the beginning of the chapter, there is reason for guarded optimism that some reform might occur simply because controversy about testing in American schools is so salient. This controversy has even brought renewed interest, and indeed some commitment, from the federal government to the improvement of American schools. If, however, these new opportunities for dialogue are to be utilized effectively, educators must not overpromise, and we must effectively argue how difficult it is to design new measurement systems. In particular, it is important that school success be defined in terms of students' affective and social development as well as of their subject-matter knowledge. Students need advanced integrated knowledge, but they also need to develop appropriate dispositions and goal-coordination strategies if they are to be successful and if they are to use the knowledge in socially constructive ways.

McDonnell (1994) notes that although policymakers realize that new assessment will cost more than traditional multiple-choice tests, many of them still see assessment as the least expensive strategy for reforming schools. She writes, "A Congressional staffer expressed this sentiment, 'People settle on assessment as a cheap way to fix problems. One of the most prominent governors sees assessment as an important lever to change American education. . . . It's a lever for change without having to spend a lot of money'" (p. 23).

According to McDonnell (1994), policymakers hold varied and sometimes conflicting views about the central purpose of assessment. Assessment purposes ranged from providing data about the general status of the educational system to assistance in making decisions about individual students, to holding individual schools and individual students accountable for their performance. Between these two extremes are those who believe that assessment can be used to achieve greater curriculum coherence, to motivate students to perform better, and to serve as an impetus for change in curriculum and instruction and to promote teachers' self-reflection and professional development (McDonnell, 1994).

It seems that citizens and educators need to convince policymakers that reform involves more than testing and that new instructional formats will be expensive. Schools need to develop sophisticated models for supporting student growth and measuring performance for both important subject-matter and social understanding.

EXPANDING RESEARCH AND DEVELOPMENT

The chapter has already provided examples of practical areas of schooling where research and development are woefully inadequate (e.g., performance assessment and small-group instruction). Additional funds would help to provide a more focused knowledge base and would allow teachers to reflect more on research findings. Research and development would also lead to rich concepts and alternative practices that teachers could consider. Finally, research and development should involve a variety of topics, theoretical positions, and research methods. To make the argument more concrete, two other areas where research would likely yield substantial dividends are examined. Finally, the chapter again stresses the need for building an infrastructure.

Curriculum

With the increasing interest in subject-matter variables in classrooms, research and development involving the identification of key concepts in academic subjects will be necessary. Considering the change from a focus on content coverage to content understanding, many more decisions will have to be made about key curriculum concepts that should be taught at various grades. Members of the academic community should be involved in setting content standards. Such involvement (in addition to the clear benefit of experts' participation in the dialogue) would likely make the public more aware of how complex and important these decisions are and might increase citizens' support for educational research and public schools.

Much has been written about the need for teachers to focus more on problem solving and on the application of knowledge to personal and social issues, but the problems that students are to explore have not been carefully conceptualized. In what ways should problems or social issues that third and sixth graders study differ? What concepts should be taught in fourth- and eleventh-grade science, mathematics, and history classrooms? What strategies are best for teaching particular concepts to certain types of students? How can researchers identify, extend, and validate pedagogical content knowledge across student developmental levels? If the knowledge of teaching subject matter in certain settings (e.g., science and social studies concepts in fourth, fifth, and sixth grades) becomes more advanced, how might the considerable time previously used in grade 6 to reteach, review, and correct students' misconceptions be reallocated so that students could explore science and social studies in novel ways?

The notion of differentiating and specifying the tasks, concepts, and problems taught at different grade levels are goals of the new California state curriculum framework. It is unfortunate that there is no rich data base to enhance this effort.

Student Mediation

There is a paucity of information about which assignments and teacher behaviors are most likely to engage student thinking. It is popular to assume that when students "do" they are more likely to think, although there is little evidence on this topic. It should be clear that "hands-on" does not necessarily mean "minds-on." Activity in classrooms is in many respects similar to activity elsewhere. One would not argue that U.S. automobile factory workers on an assembly line engage in much systematic job-related thinking. Similarly, activities that involve students in applied work may not stimulate their thinking, particularly

if students engage in them frequently. For example, many students will "tune out" if they frequently work in groups. If teachers lecture for long periods, students' attention may begin to wander, although certain types of teacher talk may stimulate active thinking. Researchers need to describe various types of classroom presentations and activities and explore whether, for what duration, and in what combinations these promote student thinking and covert reaction.

It is clear that students think and that their thinking mediates teacher behavior and class assignments. (The same assignment will mean different things to different students.) However, researchers need to identify teacher statements and classroom activities that lead to higher-order thinking, especially on the part of students who have been passive learners for several years. It is vital to integrate theories of learning and development, such as the role of social language in facilitating learning (McCaslin & Rohrkemper, 1989), with theories of classroom context. (For extended discussion of related issues, see McCaslin & Good, in press b).

However, to reiterate, students think about many things other than subject matter (e.g., how to improve relations with peers). Students even consider teachers and what constitutes ethical practice in classrooms. Although educators have written lengthy essays about student thought, little knowledge exists about how students view responsible teachers.

On the basis of interviews with 98 students in grades 1–6, Fulk and Smith (in press) found that first-, fifth-, and sixth-grade students generally favored teachers' use of academic and behavioral adaptations (for students with behavior or learning problems) when needed. However, students were generally opposed to some students' getting more difficult work. Given that the student population is becoming more diverse, teachers will probably have to employ more varied teaching strategies and curriculum than they have in the past. However, as Fulk and Smith noted, teachers' beliefs about equity and whether to differentiate instruction are important, and many regular classroom teachers wonder whether it is fair to accommodate to the needs of a few students. Vaughn, Schumm, Niarhos, and Gordon (1993) found that although teachers were generally in favor of adaptations, they clearly saw some as more important and feasible than others. In this study teachers gave low ratings to adapting curriculum materials and using alternative sources, both in terms of feasibility and importance.

Building an Infrastructure

To develop outcome measures consistent with new theories of teaching and learning (e.g., teaching for student understanding) requires a vast investment of funds in building the infrastructure. It seems ironic that policymakers would accept the fact that a major airline company (with all its resources as well as federal funds) took a decade to design a new plane but would expect educators to revise a performance assessment system completely in half of that time and with virtually no resources.

Winfield and Woodward (1994) have reached similar conclusions:

Changes in national standards and assessments are not the necessary conditions for improving student and school achievement. Policy and practices that directly assess conditions of current inequities in opportunites to learn at the school, district, and state levels have a greater probability of improving school learning and achievement. Such policies include equitable school financing, funding curriculum development, increasing training and staff development for teachers and administrators in content area assessments, and improving assessment course content and requirements in universities. These policies which affect teaching and learning are more closely related to practices in schools and classrooms. Additionally, investments in local research and development units to expand types of tests used, and collaborative ventures between schools and industry and between schools and research and development centers are viable alternatives to improve assessment practices in use in the nation's schools. (pp. 22–23)

Winfield and Woodward (1994) argued that national standards and assessments are policies that will serve only symbolic and political functions unless a strong and serious commitment to measuring opportunities to learn develops.

Good theoretical conceptualization is critical, but it only goes so far. As I have argued elsewhere (Good, 1991), the NCTM *Standards* placed too much of the blame and too much responsibility for the solution of problems with mathematics curriculum and instruction on classroom teachers. Reform will require more than efforts of individual teachers, and we must find ways to change schools and school systems, as well as individual classrooms, if the standards are to enrich classroom instruction. Without an infrastructure, the best ideas will not be communicated and classrooms will remain largely unaffected, except for some of the rhetoric used to describe them.

Messick (1994) noted that there may be unintended consequences (e.g., based on gender and/or racial and ethnic groups) associated with performance assessment. He puts the argument this way:

It is not just that some aspects of multiple-choice testing may have adverse consequences for teaching and learning, but that some aspects of all testing, even performance testing, may have adverse as well as beneficial educational consequences. And if both positive and negative aspects, whether intended or unintended, are not meaningfully addressed in the validation process, then the concept of validity loses its force as a social value. (p. 22)

Ironically, although many individuals have written recently on the moral dimensions of teaching, few have addressed the consequences of moral requirements for allowing teachers to do appropriate work. Do teachers, for example, have appropriate time lines for engaging students in intellectual tasks? Do teachers have the necessary knowledge to design and evaluate new performance tests? Are teachers' space and resources sufficient (e.g., as required by performance activities)? Do teachers' resources vary as a function of teaching in schools? with high or low socioeconomic status (SES)? The issue of providing needed resources must be addressed, and in this sense, perhaps political activism (where necessary and appropriate) on the part of teachers is appropriate professional behavior (see also, Sikula, 1996).

It seems to me an inescapable obligation of teacher education programs to model alternative approaches to assessment and to provide careful technical information, philosophical information, and general awareness of the trade-offs associated with different approaches to measurement. Ironically, many teacher education programs (often in response to political at-tacks on teacher education programs) have recently eliminated or cut back substantially the amount of information they provide to preservice teachers about general issues of assessment. Whereas measurement topics used to be addressed in a central fashion, now they are often relegated to a small part of a methods course. How can we, on moral grounds, place teachers in the classrooms when they do not have the technical and philosophical skills necessary for dealing with performance assessment? How can we, as a field, eloquently plea for teachers to use performance assessments when we do not use those assessments in teacher education? How can we expect teachers with no philosophical or technical training in performance assessment to communicate eloquently, articulately, and productively with parents and citizens about the potential of performance evaluation? How can we passively stand by and read the many statements written suggesting that pursuing the goals for the year 2000 agenda will result in an important new way of measuring and evaluating student and teacher performance in American schools? It seems to me that the resources that are being offered for this daunting task (both conceptually and technically) are so meager that change cannot be supported by an informative knowledge base. Why is it that we understand that for Boeing or any other airline company to produce a new prototype plane it may take 10 years of research and development for a relatively simple and straightforward engineering task? Why is it that less funds and imagination are being spent on designing an evaluation system for the entire nation than the cast for producing one or two planes and that we do not protest? Why is it that the complexities of teaching receive so little public funding and sustained interest?

DEVELOPING APPROPRIATE EXPECTATIONS AND AVOIDING THOUGHTLESS POLICY

Unfortunately, too many policymakers are unwilling to invest in serious research and development and in a systematic effort to improve schools. Rather, as noted, many policymakers want only the symbol of change and want to invest but minimally in education (new testing is a good solution because it is relatively cheap).

Is More Time Needed for Basic Subjects?

At the time I was writing this chapter yet a new policy direction for American education was announced. The National Education Commission on Time and Learning (1994) noted that American high school students are estimated to spend only 1,460 hours on basic math, science, and history. In contrast, high school students elsewhere spend considerably more time studying basic subject-matter content: Japan, 3,170; France, 3,280; and Germany, 3,528 hours. The commission concluded that this is alarming and urged a longer school day and school year. Although these differences may be of some concern, I find myself drawing a somewhat different conclusion than did members of the Commission. American students appear to be doing incredibly well given the limited amount of time they invest in study!

What are the implications of these findings? Should time allocations be shifted radically in the American high school in order, for example, to allow more study of history? If so, which schools, urban, suburban, affluent, poor? Many editors appear to think this is a good idea. For example, an editorial, "Wasted Days," that appeared in the *Arizona Daily Star* (1994, May 7) enthusiastically endorsed the Commission's report. The editorial included the following quote from the report, "The traditional school day must now fit in a whole set of requirements for what has been called the 'new work of the schools'—education about personal safety, consumer affairs, AIDS, conservation and energy, family life and driver's training" (p. 18A).

Here, again, we see a runaway "fad train" carrying an indiscriminate problem statement and a woefully simplistic solution for a complex but undefined problem. Why is this report shallow? To begin with, the argument that schools try to do too much is not new (see Chapter 5 in Good, Biddle, & Brophy [1975]). If the curriculum includes some study of family life, it is because some political constituency and citizens thought this content would improve the curriculum. Perhaps educators and citizens were concerned because children were having children and children were killing children. They may have thought that information about family life and personal safety might allow sixth graders to make it to high school so that they could receive extra instruction in history. Were these citizens and policymakers wrong? Do the arguments that led them to add these curriculum units no longer pertain? Unfortunately, the report ignores important substantive issues such as these. The real issue about allocating curriculum time is what should be taught given a limited amount of time. For example, although I believe that driver's training is not a primary function of schooling, I would *not* substitute more memorization of historical facts (masquerading as more history) for less instruction about AIDS, conservation, and family life.

Inequality of Resources Is the Critical Issue

However, my major disappointment with the Commission's report is related to my belief that the real problem of schooling is not insufficient time. The problem is *unequal resources* among American schools and the issue of community poverty. It seems to me that less use of crack cocaine and other substances would have more effect on learning than increased time for instruction in history or other subject-matter content. In addition to societal threats to personal safety (drugs, gangs, etc.) that many American youth confront daily, there is also the issue of impoverished schools. Unfortunately, these two variables are highly correlated. The youth whose personal safety is threatened daily as they maneuver dangerous streets are the same students who arrive at school only to find impoverished labs and a scarcity of books and other supplies.

Given extant data describing the deplorable conditions in many American schools (e.g., Kozol's *Savage Inequalities*, 1991), it is baffling that anyone could argue that a longer school day in and of itself would significantly improve student learning in all schools. Schools that are impoverished will not benefit from a longer school day. Unfortunately, resources allocated to lengthen the school day almost guarantee that poor schools do not get the increased funding they deserve.

Structural Support

Mary McCaslin and I have argued the need for structural support for students if learning is to be enhanced (McCaslin & Good, 1992). Others, too, are for increased resources for schools. Berliner (1993) put his argument this way:

Let me be clear. We have failing schools in this nation. But where they fail we see poverty, inadequate health care, dysfunctional families, and dysfunctional neighborhoods. Where our public schools succeed—in Princeton, NJ; in Grosse Pointe, MI; in Manhasset, NY—we see well-paying jobs, good health care, functional families, and functional neighborhoods. Families that can live in dignity send the schools children who have hope. Those children we can educate quite well. Families that have lost their dignity function poorly. They send us children with no hope for the future. Those children we cannot easily educate. (p. 640)

Quality of Time Increased time for learning might improve performance in some schools (e.g., those serving middle-class and affluent communities). However, even in these schools the real issue is quality of time (and quality of time is heavily related to structural supports, such as time for teacher planning and reflection as well as modern materials). Students in middle-class schools who use computers to learn mathematical facts will not learn to become world-class mathematicians simply because they drill for 2 hours a day instead of 1. Indeed, 2 hours of drill may even make it more likely that they will not become world-class mathematicians! Furthermore, students will not learn more because the ratio of computers to students in the classroom is reduced from 1 to 10 to 1 to 5. However, increasing the availability of technology *and* providing increased time for teachers to plan (e.g., designing meaningful curriculum tasks) may enhance learning. Issues of equity also must be dealt with. It is not fair to have schools that have vastly more resources (e.g., technology) and a supporting infrastructure (e.g., meaningful and continuing educational support for infusing technology into the curriculum).

International Comparisons International comparisons with education in other countries suggest that there are various hypotheses that merit investigation. One of the more intriguing examples of qualitative as opposed to cosmetic reform involves time for thinking. Stevenson and Stigler (1992), for example, argue that Japanese teachers have more time for thoughtful planning and exchange with peer teachers and spend less time with students than do American teachers. Similarly, Japanese students have more physical activity and more breaks in school than do American students. Furthermore, Japanese students appear to study fewer topics more deeply than do their American counterparts. Importantly, Japanese students are full-time students and do not deal with time conflicts between school and part-time jobs as do American students. Clearly, there is more structural support for schooling than is the case for American schools.

These same tired ideas were reported in *A Nation at Risk* (National Commission for Excellence in Education, 1983) merely a decade ago (e.g., longer school day, etc.). Have we learned nothing about the futility of making simple cosmetic changes in schooling while we ignore deep structural problems? If more time was not an answer then, it is an even less compelling argument now—given the increasingly diverse student population, the fragmented curriculum, and the decay and deterioration of school buildings in inner-city and rural settings.

It may appear to some readers that I have drifted from my topic; however, I believe that I speak directly to the heart of the issue. Again we see results from an assessment (comparing a homogeneous population of students in Japan, Germany, and France to a diverse group of American students) used in an attempt to create school policies. This trivializes the complexity of curriculum and classroom instruction. Until we recognize the need to invest in an infrastructure (including money for research and development to better understand how to use time productively, rather than to simply spend it in the economic sense), and funds to provide impoverished schools with computers, rich curriculum materials, and well-prepared teachers, we will continue this cycle of alarm and crisis without improvement.

CONCLUSION

In this chapter I have argued that the study of teaching and learning in classrooms has rich implications for improving student learning, teacher growth, and teacher evaluation systems. However, teaching effectiveness research, no matter how well conceived and how abundant, will always have to be interpreted in relation to the context and values of local situations. Research yields perspectives and new questions, not answers (Anderson & Biddle, 1991). Accordingly, school districts will have to identify appropriate research and scholarship; share it with teachers; discuss values and philosophy; develop observational procedures; clarify and implement procedures for collecting, sharing, and using evaluation data; and redesign the system periodically in the light of new data and evolving conceptions of what constitutes successful schooling in the district. Furthermore, it will be useful to involve parents in meaningful dialogue about what constitutes appropriate performance in schools.

It is my argument that extant school evaluation plans are less complete and helpful than they could be, in large measure because these plans, like research on teaching, move from fad to fad. It is necesssary to recognize not only that multiple teaching and evaluation models can be useful but also that teachers moving through a professional career will benefit from flexibility in evaluation procedures and from more input into the design of teaching evaluation plans.

I have pointed out that standardized tests and the normative curriculum proposed by professional groups have moved so far apart such that current standardized tests are no longer adequate proxies for successful schooling as they may have been in the 1940s and 1950s. Because I believe strongly in accountability of the educational system, I do not think that the gap between modern instructional theory and current tests should sound the death knell for these tests. However, this gap calls for rigorous, new conceptualizations and for research and

development to create, evaluate, and demonstrate new evaluation models (see also, Scriven, 1993).

On one level, I am optimistic, because there is clear interest on the part of both the general public and the federal government in new approaches to conceptualizing and measuring school success. However, if we are truly to build a better measurement system, the research and development costs will be enormous. Furthermore, as I have noted, the infrastructure for developing and implementing new models is weak in teacher education programs (where students in some cases do not receive meaningful coursework in performance assessment), as it is in schools.

As important as it is to improve performance assessment, I believe it even more important, indeed imperative, to broaden the scope of how we define success in American schools. Some of this work is underway in Connecticut (see, e.g., Mason et al., 1994). Teacher educators, researchers, teachers, and administrators must work in concert to help policymakers and citizens understand that students are more than learners of subject matter, that students must be seen as needing to learn self-evaluation, goal coordination, and social responsibility. There are various voices arguing that students must be seen as social beings and future responsible citizens, not just learners of subject matter (McCaslin & Good, in press b).

I am not proposing a new paradigm of exclusion. Rather, what I advocate is a paradigm of inclusion, teaching for student understanding, that supports and extends the constructivist teaching-for-understanding perspective but with an expanding emphasis on students as social beings and future citizens as well as subject-matter learners and future professionals and workers. The politics of inclusion argued here also calls for more involvement of citizens, academics from various disciplines, and members of the public sector and policymakers in the design, funding, and implementation of meaningful and successful educational programs in American schools. If schools are to be improved in important ways, vast structural changes (e.g., the way schools are funded) are required and require the contributions and support of all Americans. Citizens need to join educators and policymakers in the design and funding of schools that serve students well. Ironically, the most recent zeitgeist of school reform to sweep the country, school-based management, has largely failed to examine whether student performance has been enhanced by various reform or innovations (U.S. General Accounting Office, 1994). To some advocates, change per se is so consuming that often reformers ignore the question, "Is the change in instructional process or school management system worth it in terms of increased students' understanding or performance?"

Perhaps it is time to realize that improving schools is a complex task and to learn from past school reform efforts that simple and inexpensive reforms are not likely to have much impact. What is needed is greater clarity about what constitutes success in American schools, extensive research and development that focuses on operationalizing, at some level, indicators of success, and extensive research and development in school settings to understand how school curriculum and learning activities can be most appropriately designed, and how time can be allocated in ways that enhance progress toward important goals.

In my opinion, given current levels of funding and the immense societal problems that youth face, schools are doing a reasonable job on traditional measures (e.g., student performance on standardized tests). Generally, as has been argued in the paper, when we have poor-quality schools, we see impoverished schools that are placed in the midst of an impoverished community. Furthermore, there are some data to indicate that when resource allocations change (both in the school and in the community setting), student achievement can be enhanced in positive ways (Kaufman & Rosenbaum, 1992). To expect more of schools is to expect more of society. If schools are to improve, teacher education programs need to improve (e.g., it is unreasonable to expect that teachers can design and/or utilize new performance measures when they have not received appropriate experiences in the teacher education program) and research and development efforts must be enhanced. In turn, to improve, research and development will require more funding and, hence, a greater commitment from the government and citizens for improving education. Although there are exceptions, I believe that most teachers are working very hard under difficult circumstances. If we are to expect teachers to continue extraordinary efforts and to improve the extant curriculum, it is necessary to provide the incentives and structural supports that professional teachers need to be successful. To reiterate, using conventional measures, schools seem to be doing reasonably well. However, in terms of new performance standards (whatever those standards turn out to be) and in terms of new performance measures, it seems to me that the only answer to the question, "How do schools measure up on new performance measures?" is that it is problematic—no one knows. To the extent that we want radically to transform schools and to include more active strategies for involving students in learning (and in evaluating their own learning), it seems to me that the instruction and measurement task is an exceedingly large one that will call for larger commitment from society in terms of resources.

References

Alton-Lee, A., Nuthall, G., & Patrick, J. (1993). Reframing classroom research: A lesson from the private world of children. *Harvard Educational Review, 63,* 50–84.

American Educational Research Association. (1953). Second report of committee on the criteria of teacher effectiveness. *Journal of Educational Research, 46,* 641–658.

Amidon, E., & Flanders, N. (1961). The effects of direct and indirect teacher influence on dependent-prone students learning geometry. *Journal of Educational Psychology, 52,* 286–291.

Anderson, D., & Biddle, B. (1991). *Knowledge for policy.* London: Falmer.

Anderson, L. (1981). Short-term student responses to classroom instruction. *Elementary School Journal, 82,* 97–108.

Anderson, L., Brubaker, N., Alleman-Brooks. J., & Duffy, G. (1985). A qualitative study of seat work in first-grade classrooms. *Elementary School Journal, 86,* 123–140.

Anderson, R., Hiebert, E., Scott, J., & Wilkinson, I. (1985). *Becoming a nation of readers: A report of the Commission on Reading.* Washington, DC: National Institute of Education.

Athanases, S. (1994). Teachers' reports of the effects of preparing portfolios of literacy instruction. *Elementary School Journal, 94,* 421–439.

Bacharach, S., Conley, S., & Shedd, J. (1990). Evaluating teachers for career awards and merit pay. In J. Millman & L. Darling-Hammond (Eds.), *The new handbook of teacher evaluation: Assessing elementary and secondary school teachers* (pp. 133–146). Newbury Park, CA: Sage.

Ball, D. (1993). With an eye on the mathematical horizon: Dilemmas of teaching elementary school mathematics. *Elementary School Journal, 93,* 373–398.

Bandura, A. (1989). Human agency in social cognitive theory. *American Psychologist, 44,* 1175–1184.

Barker, R. (1968). *Ecological psychology.* Stanford, CA: Stanford University Press.

Barr, R., & Dreeben, R. (1983). *How schools work.* Chicago: University of Chicago Press.

Barton, P., & Coley, R. (1994). *Testing in America's schools.* Princeton, NJ: Educational Testing Service, Policy Information Center.

Beatty, J. (1994, May). Who speaks for the middle class? *The Atlantic Monthly, 273,* 65.

Bennett, R., Ward, W., Rock, D., & LaHart, C. (1990). *Toward a framework for constructed-response items* (ETS RR 90-7). Princeton, NJ: Educational Testing Service.

Berliner, D. (1979). Tempus educare. In P. Peterson & H. Walberg (Eds.), *Research on teaching* (pp. 120–135). Berkeley, CA: McCutchan.

Berliner, D. (1986). In pursuit of the expert pedagogue. *Educational Researcher, 16,* 5–13.

Berliner, D. (1992, February). *Educational reform in an era of disinformation.* Paper presented at the annual meeting of the American Association of Colleges for Teacher Education, San Antonio, TX.

Berliner, D. (1993). Mythology and the American system of education. *Phi Delta Kappan, 74,* 632–640.

Berliner, D., & Biddle, B. (1995). *The manufactured crisis.* White Plains, NY: Longman.

Berliner, D., & Calfee, R. (Eds.). (in press). *The handbook of educational psychology.* New York: Macmillan.

Biddle, B., & Anderson, D. (1991). Social research in educational change. In D. Anderson & B. Biddle (Eds.), *Knowledge for policy: Improving education through research* (pp. 1–20). London: Falmer.

Bloom, D. (1980). *All our children learning.* Hightstown, NJ: McGraw-Hill.

Blumenfeld, P. (1992). The task and the teacher: Enhancing student thoughtfulness in science. In J. Brophy (Ed.), *Advances in research on teaching* (Vol. 3, pp. 81–114). Greenwich, CT: JAI Press.

Blumenfeld, P. (1992, April). *Teaching for understanding in the classroom: What does it mean? What does it take?* An invited address presented at the AERA annual meeting, Atlanta, GA.

Blumenfeld, P., Hamilton, V., Bossert, S., Wessels, K., & Meece, J. (1983). Teacher talk and student thought: Socialization into the student role. In J. Levine & M. Wang (Eds.), *Teacher and student perceptions: Implications for learning* (pp. 143–192). Hillsdale, NJ: Lawrence Erlbaum Associates.

Blumenfeld, P., Krajcik, J., Marx, R., & Soloway, E. (1994). Lessons learned: How collaboration helped middle-grade science teachers learn project-based instruction. *Elementary School Journal, 94,* 539–551.

Blumenfeld, P., & Marx, R. (in preparation). Teaching for understanding. In B. Biddle, T. Good, & I. Goodson (Eds.), *The international handbook of research on teaching.* Norwell, MA: Kluwer.

Borko, H., Cone, R., Russo, N., & Shavelson, R. (1979). Teachers' decision making. In P. Peterson & H. Walberg (Eds.), *Research on teaching: Concepts, findings and implications* (pp. 136–160). Berkeley, CA: McCutchan.

Borko, H., & Shavelson, R. (1983). Speculations on teacher education: Implications of research on teachers' cognitions. *Journal of Education for Teaching, 9,* 210–224.

Bossert, S. (1988–1989). Cooperative activities in the classroom. In E. Rothkopf (Ed.), *Review of research in education* (Vol. 15, pp. 225–250). Washington, DC: American Educational Research Association.

Bridges, E. (1986). *The incompetent teacher.* Philadelphia: Falmer.

Bridges, E. (1990). Evaluation for tenure and dismissal. In J. Millman & L. Darling-Hammond (Eds.), *The new handbook of teacher evaluation: Assessing elementary and secondary school teachers* (pp. 147–157). Newbury Park, CA: Sage.

Brophy, J. (1973). Stability of teacher effectiveness. *American Educational Research Journal, 10,* 245–252.

Brophy, J., & Good, T. (1970). Teachers' communication of differential expectations for children's classroom performance: Some behavioral data. *Journal of Educational Psychology, 61,* 365–374.

Brophy, J., & Good, T. (1974). *Teacher–student relationships: Causes and consequences.* New York: Holt, Rinehart and Winston.

Campbell, D., & Stanley, J. (1963). Experimental and quasi-experimental designs for research on teaching. In N. Gage (Ed.), *Handbook of research on teaching.* Chicago: Rand McNally.

Carnegie Foundation for the Advancement of Teaching. (1988). *Condition of teaching: A state-by-state analysis.* Princeton, NJ: Princeton University Press.

Carroll, J. (1963). A model of school learning. *Teachers College Record, 64,* 723–733.

Carroll, J. (1993). Educational psychology in the 21st century. *Educational Psychologist, 28,* 89–95.

Carter, R., & Goodwin, A. (1994). Racial identity and education. In L. Darling-Hammond (Ed.), *Review of research in education* (Vol. 20, pp. 291–336). Washington, DC: American Educational Research Association.

Celis, W., III. (1994, March 30). New education legislation defines Federal role in nation's classrooms. *The New York Times,* p. B7.

Chrispeels, J. (1992). *Purposeful restructuring: Creating a culture for learning and achievement in elementary schools.* New York: Falmer.

Clark, C., Gage, N., Marx, R., Peterson, P., Stayrook, N., & Winne, P. (1979). A factorial experiment on teacher structuring, soliciting, and reacting. *Journal of Educational Psychology, 71,* 534–552.

Clark, C., & Peterson, P. (1986). Teachers' thought processes. In M. Wittrock (Ed.), *Handbook of research on teaching* (3rd ed., pp. 255–296). New York: Macmillan.

Cobb, P. (1986). Making mathematics: Children's learning and the constructivist tradition. *Harvard Educational Review, 56,* 301–306.

Cohen, E. (1994). Restructuring the classroom: Conditions for productive small groups. *Review of Educational Research, 64,* 1–35.

Coleman, J., Campbell, E., Hobson, C., McPartland, J., Mood, A., Weinfeld, F., & York, R. (1966). *Equality of educational opportunity.* Washington, DC: U.S. Department of Health, Education, and Welfare, Office of Education.

Cooper, H., & Hedges, L. (Eds.). (1994). *The handbook of research synthesis.* New York: Russell Sage Foundation.

Corno, L. (1992). Encouraging students to take responsibility for learning and performance. *Elementary School Journal, 93,* 69–84.

Corno, L. (1993). The best-laid plans: Modern conceptions of volition in educational research. *Educational Researcher, 22,* 14–22.

Corno, L. (1994, April). *Implicit teachings and self-regulated learning.* An invited address (Division K and C) at the 1994 meeting of the American Education Research Association, New Orleans.

Corno, L., & Mandinach, E. (1983). The role of cognitive engagement in classroom learning and motivation. *Educational Psychologist, 18,* 88–108.

Cronbach, L., & Snow, R. (1977). *Aptitudes and instructional methods.* New York: Irvington.

Damico, S., & Scott, E. (1988). Behavior differences between black and white females in desegregated schools. *Equity and Excellence, 23,* 63–66.

Darling-Hammond, L., & Snyder, J. (1992). Reframing accountability: Creating learner-centered schools. In A. Lieberman (Ed.), *The changing context of teaching* (91st yearbook of the National Society for the Study of Education). Chicago: University of Chicago Press.

Delandshere, G., & Petrosky, A. (1994). Capturing teachers' knowledge: Performance assessment. *Educational Researcher, 23*(5), 11–18.

Delpit, L. (1992). Acquisition of literate discourse: Bowing before the master? *Theory into Practice, 31,* 296–302.

Dewey, J. (1902). *The school and society.* Chicago: University of Chicago Press.

Doyle, W. (1979). Classroom tasks and student abilities. In P. Peterson & H. Wahlberg (Eds.), *Research on teaching: Concepts, findings, and implications* (pp. 183–209). Berkeley, CA: McCutchan.

Doyle, W. (1983). Academic work. *Review of Educational Research, 53,* 155–199.

Dreeben, R. (1973). The school as a workplace. In R. Travers (Ed.), *Second handbook of research on teaching.* Chicago: Rand McNally.

Duell, O. (1994). Extended wait time and university student achievement. *American Educational Research Journal, 31,* 397–414.

Duffy, G. (1993). Rethinking strategy instruction: Four teachers' development and their low achievers' understandings. *Elementary School Journal, 93,* 231–247.

Dunkin, M. (Ed.). (1987). *The international encyclopedia of teaching and teacher education.* New York: Pergamon Press.

Dunkin, M., & Biddle, B. (1974). *The study of teaching.* New York: Holt, Rinehart and Winston.

Eaton, J., Anderson, C., & Smith, E. (1984). Students' misconceptions interfere with science learning: Case studies of fifth-grade students. *Elementary School Journal, 84,* 365–379.

Eisner, E. (1992). Educational reform and the ecology of schooling. *Teachers College Record, 93,* 610–627.

Elam, S., Rose, L., & Gallup, A. (1994). The 26th annual Phi Delta Kappa/Gallup poll of the public's attitudes toward the public school. *Phi Delta Kappan, 76,* 41–56.

Ericsson, K., & Charles, N. (1994). Expert performance: Its structure and acquisition. *American Psychologist, 49,* 725–747.

Evertson, C., Anderson, C., Anderson, L., & Brophy, J. (1980). Relationships between classroom behaviors and student outcomes in junior high mathematics and English classes. *American Educational Research Journal, 17,* 43–60.

Evertson, C., & Green, J. (1986). Observation as inquiry and method. In M. Wittrock (Ed.), *Handbook of research on teaching* (3rd ed., pp. 162–213). New York: Macmillan.

Fenstermacher, G. (1994). The knower and the known: The nature of knowledge and research on teaching. In L. Darling-Hammond (Ed.), *Review of research in education* (Vol. 20, pp. 3–56). Washington, DC: American Educational Research Association.

Fields, R. (1990). *Classroom tasks, children's control perceptions, and their relation to inner speech.* Unpublished dissertation, Bryn Mawr College, Bryn Mawr, PA.

Fisher, C., & Hiebert, E. (1990). Characteristics of task in two approaches to literacy instruction. *Elementary School Journal, 91,* 3–17.

Flanders, N. (1965). *Teacher influence, pupil attitudes, and achievement* (Cooperative Research Monograph No. 12). Washington, DC: U.S. Office of Education.

Flood, J., & Lapp, D. (1989). Reporting reading progress: A comparison portfolio for parents. *The Reading Teacher, 42,* 508–514.

Florio-Ruane, S., & Lensmire, T. (1989). The role of instruction in learning to write. In J. Brophy (Ed.), *Advances in research on teaching. Vol. 1: Teaching for meaningful understanding and self-regulated learning*. Greenwich, CT: JAI Press.

Fraenkel, J. (1992, November). *A comparison of elite and nonelite social studies classrooms*. Paper presented at the annual meeting of the National Council for the Social Studies, Detroit.

Freeman, D., & Porter, A. (1989). Do textbooks dictate the content of mathematics instruction in elementary schools? *American Educational Research Journal, 26,* 403–421.

Freiberg, H., Prokosch, N., Treister, E., & Stein, T. (1990). Turning around five at-risk elementary schools. *School Effectiveness and School Improvement, 1,* 5–25.

Fulk, C., & Smith, P. (in press). Students' perceptions of teachers' use of instructional and management adaptations. *Elementary School Journal.*

Gage, N. (1960). Address appearing in "Proceedings," *Research Resumé,* 16. Burlingame: California Teachers Association.

Gage, N. (1963). Paradigms on research on teaching. In N. Gage (Ed.), *Handbook of research on teaching* (pp. 91–141). Chicago: Rand McNally.

Gage, N. (1965). Desirable behaviors of teachers. *Urban Education, 1,* 85–95.

Gage, N. (1972). *Teacher effectiveness and teacher education: A search for a scientific basis.* Palo Alto, CA: Pacific Books.

Gallagher, J. (1970). Three studies of the classroom. In J. Gallagher, G. Nuthall, & B. Rosenshine (Eds.), *Classroom observation.* American Educational Research Association Monography Series on Curriculum Evaluation, Monograph No. 6. Chicago: Rand McNally.

Gallup, A. (1986). The 18th annual Gallup poll of the public's attitudes toward the public schools. *Phi Delta Kappan, 68,* 41–58.

García, G., & Pearson, P. (1994). Assessment and diversity. In L. Darling-Hammond (Ed.), *Review of research in education* (Vol. 20, pp. 337–392). Washington, DC: American Educational Research Association.

Getzels, J., & Jackson, P. (1963). The teacher's personality and characteristics. In N. Gage (Ed.), *Handbook of research on teaching* (pp. 506–582). Chicago: Rand McNally.

Gifford, B., & O'Conner, M. (Eds.). (1992). *Cognitive approaches to assessment.* Boston: Kluwer-Nijhoff.

Glatthorn, A. (1987). Cooperative professional development: Peer-centered options for teacher growth. *Educational Leadership, 45,* 31–35.

Good, T. (1983). Classroom research: A decade of progess. *Educational Psychologist, 18,* 127–144.

Good, T. (1991, April). *Reflection on NCTM's professional standards for teaching mathematics.* A paper presented at the National Council of Teachers of Mathematics, New Orleans.

Good, T., & Biddle, B. (1988). Research and the improvement of mathematics instruction: The need for observational resources. In D. Grouws & T. Conney (Eds.), *Perspectives on research on effective mathematics teaching* (Vol. 1, pp. 112–114). Hillsdale, NJ: Lawrence Erlbaum Associates.

Good, T., Biddle, B., & Brophy, J. (1975). *Teachers make a difference.* New York: Holt, Rinehart and Winston.

Good, T., & Brophy, J. (1973). *Looking in classrooms* (1st ed.). New York: Harper & Row.

Good, T., & Brophy, J. (1974). Changing teacher and student behavior: An empirical investigation. *Journal of Educational Psychology, 66,* 390–405.

Good, T., & Brophy, J. (1994). *Looking in classrooms* (6th ed.). New York: HarperCollins.

Good, T., & Grouws, D. (1979). The Missouri mathematics effectiveness project: An experimental study of fourth-grade classrooms. *Journal of Education Psychology, 71,* 355–362.

Good, T., McCaslin, M., & Reys, B. (1992). Investigating work groups to promote problem solving in mathematics. In J. Brophy (Ed.), *Advances in research on teaching. Vol. 3. Planning and managing learning tasks and activities* (pp. 115–160). Greenwich, CT: JAI Press.

Good, T., & Mulryan, C. (1990). Teacher ratings: A call for teacher control and self-evaluation. In J. Millman & L. Darling-Hammond (Eds.), *The new handbook of teacher evaluation: Assessing elementary and secondary school teachers* (pp. 191–215). Newbury Park, CA: Sage.

Good, T., Mulryan, C., & McCaslin, M. (1992). Grouping for instruction in mathematics: A call for programmatic research on small-group processes. In D. Grouws (Ed.), *Handbook of research on mathematics teaching and learning* (pp. 165–196). New York: Macmillan.

Good, T., Reys, B., Grouws, D., & Mulryan, C. (1989–1990). Using work groups in mathematics instruction. *Educational Leadership, 47,* 56–62.

Good, T., Slavings, R., Harel, K., & Emerson, H. (1987). Student passivity: A study of student question-asking in K–12 classrooms. *Sociology of Education, 60,* 181–199.

Good, T., & Weinstein, R. (1986). Schools make a difference: Evidence, criticisms, and new directions. *American Psychologist, 41,* 1090–1097.

Goodlad, J. (1984). *A place called school: Prospects for the future.* New York: McGraw-Hill.

Gough, P. (1994). Shame on the press. *Phi Delta Kappan, 75,* 355.

Graham, P. (1993, March 31). The president's comments. *The Spencer Foundation Annual Report 1993* (pp. 5–8). Chicago: The Spencer Foundation.

Griffin, G. (1985). The school as a workplace and the master teacher concept. *Elementary School Journal, 86,* 1–16.

Griffin, G. (1993, April). *Slicing through the system: Necessary conditions for understanding.* An invited address presented at the AERA annual meeting, Atlanta, GA.

Gump, P. (1960). Intra-setting analysis: The third-grade classroom as a special but instructive case. In E. Willems & H. Raush (Eds.), *Naturalistic viewpoints in psychological research* (pp. 200–220). New York: Holt, Rinehart and Winston.

Haertel, E. (1991). New forms of teacher assessment. In G. Grant (Ed.), *Review of Research in Education, 17,* 3–30. Washington, DC: American Educational Research Association.

Haertel, E., & Calfee, R. (1983). School achievement: Thinking about what to test. *Journal of Educational Measurement, 20,* 119–132.

Haney, W., & Madaus, G. (1988). *Handbook of testing.* Amsterdam: North-Holland.

Haney, W., Madaus, G., & Kreitzer, A. (1987). Charms talismatic: Testing teachers for the improvement of American education. *Review of Research in Education, 14,* 169–238.

Haney, W., Madaus, G., & Lyons, R. (1993). *The fractured marketplace for standardized testing.* Boston: Kluwer.

Hedges, L., Laine, R., & Greenwald, R. (1994a). Does money matter? A meta-analysis of studies of the effects of differential school inputs on student outcomes. *Educational Researcher, 23,* 5–14.

Hedges, L., Laine, R., & Greenwald, R. (1994b). Money does matter somewhere: A reply to Hanushek. *Educational Researcher, 23,* 9–10.

Henson, B., & Hall, P. (1993). Linking performance evaluation and career ladder programs: Reactions of teachers and principals in one district. *Elementary School Journal, 93,* 323–353.

Hiebert, J., & Wearne, D. (1992). Links between teaching and learning place value with understanding in first grade. *Journal for Research in Mathematics Education, 23,* 98–122.

Hinchey, P. (1994). Lost in translation: Perils on the uncertain route from reform theory to practice. *Council Chronicle, 3,* 20, 6, 7.

House, E. (1986a). How we think about evaluation. In E. House (Ed.), *New directions in educational evaluation* (pp. 30–50). London: Falmer.

House, E. (Ed.). (1986b). *New directions in educational evaluation*. London: Falmer.

Houston, W. (Ed.). (1990). *Handbook of research on teacher education*. New York: Macmillan.

Huffman, G., & Leak, F. (1986). Beginning teachers' perceptions of mentors. *Journal of Teacher Education, 37,* 22–25.

Jackson, P. (1968). *Life in classrooms*. New York: Holt, Rinehart and Winston.

Jackson, P. (1992). *The handbook of research on curriculum*. New York: Macmillan.

Jackson, P., Boostrom, R., & Hansen, D. (1993). *The moral life of schools*. San Franscisco: Jossey-Bass.

Jencks, C., Smith, M., Acland, H., Bane, M., Cohen, D., Gintis, H., Heyns, B., & Michelson, S. (1972). *Inequality: A reassessment of the effect of family and schooling in America*. New York: Basic Books.

Joyce, B. (1981). A memorandum for the future. In B. Dillon-Peterson (Ed.), *Staff development/organization development*. Alexandria, VA: Association for Supervision and Curriculum Development.

Kantrowitz, B., & Wingert, P. (1991, June 17). A dismal report card: Rich and poor, north and south, black, brown, and white, eighth graders flunk the national math test. What can be done about this scandal? *Newsweek,* pp. 64–67.

Kaufman, J., & Rosenbaum, J. (1992). The education and employment of low-income black youth in white suburbs. *Educational Evaluation Policy and Analysis, 14,* 229–240.

Koretz, D., Stecher, B., Klein, S., & McCaffrey, D. (1994). The Vermont portfolio assessment program: Findings and implications. *Educational Measurement: Issues and Practices, 13*(3), 5–16.

Kounin, J. (1970). *Discipline and group management in classrooms*. New York: Holt, Rinehart and Winston.

Kozol, J. (1991). *Savage inequalities: Children in America's schools*. New York: Crown.

Krajcik, J., Blumenfeld, P., Marx, R., & Soloway, E. (1994). A collaborative model for helping middle-grade science teachers learn project-based instruction. *Elementary School Journal, 94,* 483–497.

Lampert, M. (1989). Choosing and using mathematical tools in classroom discourse. In J. Brophy (Ed.), *Advances in research on teaching. Vol. 1: Teaching for meaningful understanding and self-regulated learning* (pp. 223–264). Greenwich, CT: JAI Press.

Leinhardt, G., & Putnam, R. (1987). The skill of learning from classroom lessons. *American Educational Research Journal, 24,* 557–587.

Lieberman, A. (1986). Collaborative research: Working with, not working on. . . . *Educational Leadership, 43,* 28–33.

Linn, R. (1994, April). *Performance assessment: Policy promises and technical measurement standards.* An invited address (Division D) presented at the annual meeting of the American Educational Research Association, New Orleans.

Lundgren, U. (1972). *Frame factors in the teaching process*. Stockholm: Almquist & Wiksell.

Marx, R. (1983). Student perception in classrooms. *Educational Psychologist, 18,* 145–165.

Marx, R., Blumenfeld, P., Krajcik, J., Blunk, M., Crawford, B., Kelly, B., & Meyer, K. (1994). Enacting project-based science: Experience of four middle-school grade teachers. *Elementary School Journal, 94,* 517–538.

Mason, T., Rigazio-Digilio, A., Stansbury, K., Lemma, P., Adams, M., Pearson, D., Leone, L., & Barton, K. (1994). *Toward a vision of elementary teaching and learning*. Draft monograph prepared for the Connecticut Elementary Educator Assessment Project, Connecticut State Department of Education.

McCarthy, M. (1993). Challenges to the public school curriculum: New targets and strategies. *Phi Delta Kappan, 75*(1), 55–60.

McCaslin, M., & Good, T. (1993). Classroom management and motivated student learning. In T. M. Tomlinson (Ed.), *Motivating students to learn: Overcoming barriers to high achievement* (pp. 245–261). Berkeley, CA: McCutchan.

McCaslin, M., & Good, T. (1992). Compliant cognition: The misalliance of management and instructional goals in current school reform. *Educational Researcher, 21,* 4–17.

McCaslin, M., & Good, T. (in press, a). The informal curriculum. In D. Berliner and R. Calfee (Eds.), *The handbook of educational psychology*. New York: Macmillan.

McCaslin, M., & Good, T. (in press, b). *Listening in classrooms*. New York: HarperCollins.

McCaslin, M., & Murdock, T. (1991). The emergent interaction of home and school in the development of students' adaptive learning. In M. Maehr & P. Pintrich (Eds.), *Advances in motivation and achievement* (Vol. 7, pp. 213–259). Greenwich, CT: JAI Press.

McCaslin, M., & Rohrkemper, M. (1989). Self-regulated learning and academic achievement: A Vygotskian view. In B. Zimmerman & D. Schunk (Eds.), *Self-regulated learning and academic achievement* (pp. 143–168). New York: Springer-Verlag.

McDonnell, L. (1994). *Policymakers' views of student assessment*. Santa Monica, CA: The Rand Corp.

McLaughlin, M., & Pfeifer, R. (1988). *Teacher evaluation: Improvement, accountability and effective learning*. New York: Teachers College Press.

Mehrens, W., & Lehmann, I. (1987). *Using standardized tests in education* (4th ed.). New York: Longman.

Mergendoller, J., Marchman, V., Mitman, A., & Packer, M. (1988). Task demands and accountability in middle-grade science classes. *Elementary School Journal, 88,* 251–265.

Messick, S. (1994). The interplay of evidence and consequences in the validation of performance assessments. *Educational Researcher, 23,* 13–23.

Millman, J., & Darling-Hammond, L. (Eds.). (1990). *The new handbook of teacher evaluation: Assessing elementary and secondary school teachers*. Newbury Park, CA: Sage.

Mitchell, R. (1992). *Testing for learning: How new approaches to evaluation can improve American schools*. New York: Free Press.

Mitman, L., Mergendoller, J., Marchman, V., & Packer, M. (1987). Instruction addressing the components of scientific literacy and its relation to student outcomes. *American Educational Research Journal, 24,* 611–633.

Mohatt, G. (1994). Cultural negotiation and schooling: New idea or new clothing for an old idea? *Peabody Journal of Education, 69,* 172–185.

Moss, P. (1994). Can there be validity without realiability? *Educational Researcher, 23,* 5–12.

National Center for Education Statistics. (1994, March). *Public elementary teachers' views on teacher performance evaluations*. (Statistical Analysis Report NCES 94-097). Washington, DC: U.S. Department of Education, Office of Educational Research and Improvement.

National Commission for Excellence in Education. (1983, April). *A nation at risk: The imperatives for educational reform*. Washington, DC: U.S. Department of Education, National Commission for Excellence in Education.

National Education Commission on Time and Learning. (1994, April). *Prisoners of time*. Washington, DC: U.S. Government Printing Office.

National Education Goals Panel. (1993a). *The National Education Goals Report: Building a nation of learners. National report* (Vol. 1). Washington, DC: U.S. Government Printing Office.

National Education Goals Panel. (1993b). *The National Education Goals Report: Building a nation of learners. State reports* (Vol. 2). Washington, DC: U.S. Government Printing Office.

Newman, R., & Goldin, L. (1990). Children's reluctance to seek help with schoolwork. *Journal of Educational Psychology, 82,* 92–100.

Newmann, F. (Ed.). (1992). *Student engagement and achievement in American secondary schools*. New York: Teachers College Press.

Noddings, N. (1984). *Caring: A feminine approach to ethics and moral education*. Berkeley: University of California Press.

O'Neill, B. (1994, March 6). The history of a hoax. *The New York Times Magazine*, section 6, 46–49.

Oser, F. (1994). Moral perspectives on teaching. In L. Darling-Hammond (Ed.), *Review of research in education* (Vol. 20, pp. 57–128). Washington, DC: American Educational Research Association.

Oser, F., Dick, A., & Patry, J. (Eds.). (1992). *Effective and responsible teaching*. San Francisco: Jossey-Bass.

Paris, S., Lawton, T., Turner, J., & Roth, J. (1991). A developmental perspective on standardized achievement testing. *Educational Researcher, 20,* 12–20, 40.

Peterson, I. (1994, April 8). Plan asks all the poor schools to pay more. *The New York Times*, p. A9.

Peterson, P., & Comeaux, M. (1990). Evaluating the systems: Teachers' perspectives on teacher evaluation. *Educational Evaluation and Policy Analysis, 12,* 3–24.

Philips, S. (1983). *The invisible culture: Communication in classroom and community on the Warm Springs Indian Reservation*. New York: Longman.

Porter, A. (1989). A curriculum out of balance: The case of elementary school mathematics. *Educational Researcher, 18,* 9–15.

Pressley, M., & Levine, J. (Eds.). (1983). *Cognitive strategy research: Educational applications*. New York: Springer-Verlag.

Raths, L. (1971). What is a good teacher? In J. Raths, J. Pancella, & J. Van Ness (Eds.), *Studying teaching* (2nd ed., pp. 3–9). Englewood Cliffs, NJ: Prentice Hall.

Resnick, L., & Resnick, D. (1992). Assessing the thinking curriculum: New tools for educational reform. In B. Gifford & M. O'Conner (Eds.), *Cognitive approaches to assessment*. Boston: Kluwer-Nijhoff.

Reynolds, M. (Ed.). (1989). *Knowledge base for the beginning teacher*. Oxford, England: Pergamon Press.

Richardson, V. (1990). Significant and worthwhile change in teaching practice. *Educational Researcher, 19,* 10–18.

Rohrkemper, M. (1981). *Classroom perspectives study: An investigation of differential perceptions of classroom events*. Unpublished doctoral dissertation, Michigan State University, East Lansing.

Rohrkemper, M. (1984). The influence of teacher socialization style on students' social cognitions and reported interpersonal classroom behavior. *Elementary School Journal, 85,* 245–275.

Rohrkemper, M., & Corno, L. (1988). Success and failure on classroom tasks: Adaptive learning and classroom teaching. *Elementary School Journal, 88,* 297–312.

Rosenbaum, D. (1994, April 10). This much is clear: Taxes just aren't what they seem. *New York Times*, section 4, p. 1.

Rosenholtz, S. (1989). *Teachers' workplace: The social organization of schools*. New York: Longman.

Rosenholtz, S., & Simpson, C. (1984). The formation of ability conceptions: Developmental trend or social construction? *Review of Educational Research, 54,* 31–63.

Rosenshine, B., & Furst, N. (1971). Research on teacher performance criteria. In B. Smith (Ed.), *Research in teacher education: A symposium*. Englewood Cliffs, NJ: Prentice-Hall.

Rosenthal, R., & Jacobson, L. (1968). *Pygmalion in the classroom: Teacher expectations and pupils' intellectual development*. New York: Holt.

Rowe, M. (1969). Science, silence, and sanctions. *Science and Children, 6,* 11–13.

Ryans, D. (1960). *Characteristics of teachers*. Washington, DC: American Council on Education.

Sarason, S. (1982). *The culture of the school and the problem of change* (2nd ed.). Boston: Allyn & Bacon.

Sarason, S. (1993). *Schooling in America: Scapegoat and salvation*. New York: Free Press.

Scriven, M. (1993, September 30). *Multiple-rating items: The "Third Way."* A paper presented at the Beryl Buck Institute for Education, Novato, CA.

Secada, W., & Lightfoot, T. (1993). Symbols and the political context of bilingual education in the United States. In *Bilingual education: Politics, practice, and research* (pp. 36–64). Chicago: University of Chicago Press.

Shavelson, R. (1976). Teachers' decision making. In N. Gage (Ed.), *The psychology of teaching methods,* 75th yearbook of the National Society for the Study of Education (Part I). Chicago: University of Chicago Press.

Shavelson, R. (1983). Review of research on teachers' pedagogical judgements, plans, and decisions. *Elementary School Journal, 83,* 392–413.

Shavelson, R., Baxter, G., & Gao, X. (1993). Sampling variability in performance assessments. *Journal of Educational Measurement, 30,* 215–232.

Shepard, L., & Bliem, C. (1993, October). *Parent opinions about standardized tests, teacher's information and performance assessments* (CSE Technical Report 367). Los Angeles: National Center for Research on Evaluation, Standards, and Students Testing (CRESST).

Shepard, L., Flexer, R., Hiebert, E., Marion, S., Mayfield, V., & Weston, T. (1994, April). *Effects of introducing classroom performance assessments on student learning*. Paper presented at the annual meeting of the American Educational Research Association and the National Council on Measurement in Education, New Orleans.

Showers, B. (1984). *Peer coaching: A strategy for facilitating transfer of training*. Eugene: University of Oregon, Center for Educational Policy and Management.

Shulman, L. (1986a). Paradigms and research programs in the study of teaching: A contemporary perspective. in M. Wittrock (Ed.), *Handbook of research on teaching* (3rd ed., pp. 3–36). New York: Macmillan.

Shulman, L. (1986b). Those who understand: Knowledge growth in teaching. *Educational Researcher, 15,* 4–14.

Shulman, L. (1987). Knowledge and teaching: Foundations of the new reform. *Harvard Educational Review, 57,* 1–22.

Shulman, L. (1992). Research on teaching: A historical and personal perspective. In F. Oser, A. Dick, & J. Patry (Eds.), *Effective and responsible teaching* (pp. 14–29). San Francisco: Jossey-Bass.

Shulman, L., & Sykes, G. (1983). *Handbook of teaching and policy*. New York: Longman.

Simon, H. (1969). *The sciences of the artificial*. Cambridge, MA: MIT Press.

Sizer, T. (1984). *Horace's compromise: The dilemma of the American high school*. Boston: Houghton Mifflin.

Slavin, R. (1980). Cooperative learning. *Review of Educational Research, 50,* 315–342.

Smith, L., & Geoffrey, W. (1968). *The complexities of an urban classroom*. New York: Holt, Rinehart and Winston.

Smylie, M. (1992). Teachers' reports of their interactions with teacher leaders concerning classroom instruction. *Elementary School Journal, 93,* 85–98.

Smylie, M. (1994). Redesigning teachers' work: Connections to the classroom. In L. Darling-Hammond (Ed.), *Review of research in education* (Vol. 20, pp. 129–178). Washington, DC: American Educational Research Association.

Snow, R. (1993). Construct validity and constructed response test. In R. Bennett & W. Ward, Jr. (Eds.), *Construction versus choice in cognitive measurement: Issues in constructive response performance testing, and portfolio assessment* (pp. 45–60). Hillsdale, NJ: Lawrence Erlbaum Associates.

Snow, R., Corno, L., & Jackson, D. (in press). Individual differences in conative and affective functioning in educational psychology. In D. Berliner & R. Calfee (Eds.), *The handbook of educational psychology*. New York: Macmillan.

Soltis, J. (1994). The new teacher. In S. Hollingsworth & H. Sockett (Eds.), *Teacher research and educational reform. Ninety-third yearbook of the National Society for the Study of Education,* (Part 1, pp. 245–260). Chicago: University of Chicago Press.

Sommers, P., Muller, J., Saba, G., Draisin, J., & Shore, W. (in press). Reflections-on-action: Medical students' accounts of their implicit beliefs and strategies in the context of one-to-one clinical teaching. *Academic Medicine*.

Stephens, J. (1967). *The process of schooling*. New York: Holt, Rinehart and Winston.

Stevenson, H., & Stigler, J. (1992). *The learning gap.* New York: Summit.

Stodolsky, S. (1990). Classroom observation. In J. Millman & L. Darling-Hammond (Eds.), *The new handbook of teacher evaluation: Assessing elementary and secondary school teachers* (pp. 175–190). Newbury Park, CA: Sage.

Taba, H., Levine, S., & Elzey, F. (1964). *Thinking in elementary school children* (USOE Cooperative Research Project, No. 1574). San Francisco: San Francisco State College.

Teddlie, C., Kirby, P., & Stringfield, S. (1989). Effective versus ineffective schools: Observable differences in the classroom. *American Journal of Education, 97,* 221–236.

Thorndike, E. (1918). Specific uses of measurement in the solution of school programs. In G. Whipple (Ed.), *The 17th yearbook of the National Society for the Study of Education, Part II: The measurement of educational products.* Bloomington, IL: Public School Publishing.

Tom, A. (1984). *Teaching as a moral craft.* White Plains, NY: Longman.

Tomlinson, T. (1993). Educational reform: The ups and downs of good in good intentions. In T. Tomlinson (Ed.), *Motivating students to learn: Overcoming barriers to high achievement* (pp. 3–20). Berkeley, CA: McCutchan.

Torrance, H. (1993). Combining measurement-driven instruction with authentic assessment: Some initial observations of national assessment in England and Wales. *Educational Evaluation and Policy Analysis, 15*(1), 81–90.

Travers, R. (Ed.). (1973). Second handbook of research on teaching. Chicago: Rand McNally.

Tuchman, B. (1978). *A distant mirror. The calamitous 14th century.* New York: Ballantine.

Tudge, J. (1991). Education of young children in the Soviet Union: Current practice in historical perspective. *Elementary School Journal, 92,* 121–133.

U.S. General Accounting Office. (1994, August). *Education reform. School-based management results in changes in instruction and budgeting* (Publication No. GAO/HEHS-94-135). Washington, DC: U.S. General Accounting Office/Health, Education, and Human Services Division.

Valencia, S. (1990). A portfolio approach to classroom reading assessment: The whys, whats, and hows. *The Reading Teacher, 43,* 338–340.

Vaughn, S., Schumm, J., Niarhos, F., & Gordon, J. (1993). Students' perceptions of two hypothetical teachers' instructional adaptations for low achievers. *Elementary School Journal, 94,* 87–102.

Vockell, E., Asher, W., Dinuzzo, N., & Bartok, M. (1994). Information sources in research literature. *Journal of Experimental Education, 62*(2), 169–174.

Vu, N., & Barrows, H. (1994). Use of standardized patients in clinical assessments: Recent development and measurement findings. *Educational Researcher, 23,* 23–30.

Wainer, H., & Thissen, D. (1994). On examinee choice in educational testing. *Review of Educational Research, 64,* 159–195.

Walker, E. (1992). Falling asleep and failure among African-American students: Rethinking assumptions about process teaching. *Theory into Practice, 31,* 321–327.

Wasted days. (1994, May 7). *Arizona Daily Star,* p. 18A.

Webb, N. (1983). Predicting learning from student interaction: Defining the interaction variable. *Educational Psychologist, 18,* 33–41.

Weinstein, R. (1982, May). Students in classrooms [Special Issue]. *Elementary School Journal, 82,* 397–398.

Weinstein, R. (1983). Student perceptions of schooling. *Elementary School Journal, 83,* 287–312.

Wiggins, G. (1993). *Assessing student performance: Exploring the purpose and limits of testing.* San Francisco: Jossey-Bass.

Wildman, T., Niles, J., Magliaro, S., & McLaughlin, R. (1989). Teaching and learning to teach: The two roles of beginning teachers. *Elementary School Journal, 89,* 471–494.

Winfield, L., & Woodward, M. (1994, February). *Assessment, equity, and diversity in reforming America's schools* (CSE Technical Report 372). Los Angeles: National Center for Research on Evaluation, Standards and Student Testing (CRESST).

Winne, P., & Marx, R. (1982). Students' and teachers' views of thinking processes for classroom learning. *Elementary School Journal, 82,* 493–518.

Wise, E., Darling-Hammond, L., McLaughlin, M., & Bernstein, H. (1985). Teacher evaluation: A study of effective practices. *Elementary School Journal, 86,* 61–121.

Wittrock, M. (Ed.). (1986). *Handbook of research on teaching* (3rd ed.). New York: Macmillan.

Wolf, D. (1989). Portfolio assessment: Sampling student work. *Educational Leadership, 46,* 35–39.

Wolf, D., Bixby, J., Glenn, J., III, & Gardner, H. (1991). To use their minds well: Investigating new forms of student assessment. *Review of Research in Education, 17,* 31–74.

Wright, C., & Nuthall, G. (1970). Relationships between teacher behaviors and pupil achievement in three experimental elementary science lessons. *American Educational Research Journal, 7,* 477–491.

Zeichner, K., & Tabachnick, R. (1985). The development of teacher perspectives: Social strategies and institutional control in the socialization of beginning teachers. *Journal of Educational Psychology, 7,* 1–25.

Zimmerman, B., & Schunck, D. (1989). *Self-regulated learning in academic achievement: Theory, research, and practice.* New York: Springer-Verlag.

·29·

TEACHER PROFESSIONAL DEVELOPMENT

Norman A. Sprinthall
NORTH CAROLINA STATE UNIVERSITY

Alan J. Reiman
NORTH CAROLINA STATE UNIVERSITY

Lois Thies-Sprinthall
NORTH CAROLINA STATE UNIVERSITY

Teacher development has become an increasingly important focus for the process of school reform and educational excellence. Certainly the addition to Goals 2000 of a national goal for teacher professional development is a case in point. It is clearly a truism in education to note that there is no such thing as a teacher-proof curriculum. The massive failures of national curriculum projects of the 1960s stand as testimony to such a legacy, a national landscape strewn with failed ideas, unused curriculum guides, and tarnished hopes. Of course this could have been predicted. Horace Mann long ago made two important points: as is the teacher so is the school, and we cannot teach for democracy by the methods of slavery. By implication then, teacher characteristics, attitudes, conceptions of self, and intellectual and interpersonal dispositions in large measure determine both the explicit and the so-called hidden agenda of the classroom. The formal curriculum is represented by the materials, lesson plan, and objectives, but the informal agenda is the atmosphere, or climate, in the classroom, as indicated by important teacher characteristics.

OVERVIEW OF RESEARCH

Prior Models for Teacher Development

Not until relatively recently has the importance of the teacher in the process of education received adequate theoretical and research attention. There were prior attempts, but the paradigms were insufficiently robust to provide adequate understanding for program development. For example, the trait and factor model led to an enormous number of studies of fixed personality characteristics, yet it produced almost no firm basis for either teacher selection or teacher education (Shulman, 1986). Assessing apparently permanent personality traits did not produce a cumulative research and theory base. Perhaps as a reaction to such rigid conceptions of teachers, the dynamic model from the psychoanalytic tradition (Jersild, 1955) was developed. Unfortunately, such a global psychoanalytic conception of human development with current behavior as an overdetermined function of very early experience was intriguing but clearly flawed as a directing construct for teacher growth.

Although not advertised as a third force between narrow and numerous personality tracts and global psychoanalytic concepts, the emergence of the so-called process-product model can be conceptualized as a reaction to the failures of earlier models. In that model, specific teacher behaviors were identified as training objectives. The skills were shaped through behavior modification and the teachers were expected to then incorporate such individual behaviors (a process) to promote student learning (a product). As Shulman (1986) has pointed out, the teaching learning process is not a one-way street, nor can we view it one variable at a time. The road is more like a busy intersection at five o'clock. Interactions of consonance and

The authors thank editors John Sikula and Tom Buttery. Preparation of the chapter was supported in part by the College of Education and Psychology, North Carolina State University, and the Model Clinical Teaching Program, University of North Carolina System.

dissonance of teacher–pupil, pupil–teacher, and pupil–pupil effects were far too complex for such a model.

The Emergence of New Models

Given the inadequacies of these prior paradigms, the current period in teacher development research can be considered as a time of transition. The old models have literally burst. In their place a series of new initiatives have been appearing since the mid-1980s. The goals are broad, namely, to create a firm basis in theory and research for the practice of professional teacher development.

It may be premature, however, to suggest anything more than the possibility of a growing consensus. Can an emergent developmental paradigm accommodate quantitative and qualitative research models? Can stage conceptions of growth with group data be extended to explain idiographic and individual differences? Certainly the dilemma of the broad gauge versus the narrow gauge theory always create difficulties. Katz and Raths (1985) have stated the problem clearly and cleverly with their "Goldilocks Principle." Some theory for teacher development is extremely broad and abstract, creating a theoretical bed that is too big for the actual process of teacher development. Certainly some of the psychoanalytic and humanistic theories stand as good examples of such excessively broad propositions. Yet, Katz and Raths also note the other side of the problem. Theory and research can be so focused on specifics that the framework becomes too narrow. The process-product behavioristic approach represents just such an instance of reducing human complexity to a few simple-minded propositions. Thus the behavioristic model creates a theoretical bed that is far too small. Goldilocks as a metaphor for teacher development then wanders from place to place seeking a better fit as the field itself tries to build theory, research, and practice. Without a careful integration of the three components Goldilocks will continue to traverse from fad to fad—perhaps blissfully unaware of the distinctions between the cosmic and the trivial.

Elements for Effective Teacher Development

The overall problem, then, is difficult. There is no neat linear equation from theory to practice nor the other way from practice to theory. Is theory embedded in practice and is practice visible in theory? The lines are different sides of the same coin yet absolutely essential to the process of teacher development. Gary Griffin (1987) underscores the importance of this interaction. Grounded in careful quantitative and qualitative inquiry, the research includes a number of prominent teacher educators: Virginia Richardson, Willis Copeland, Hilda Borko, Beatrice Ward, and Kenneth Zeichner. The central theme of their work is that clinical teacher education is one of the most promising trends for teacher professional development, yet is seldom and poorly practiced. In fact, a number of central assumptions about teacher education are seriously compromised once initially prepared teachers enter the classroom. Learning to teach is developmental, yet beginning teachers are expected to manage full assignments. Observation and feedback are acknowledged as crucial, yet there is a paucity of school settings in which such

practices are the norm. Clinical differentiated supervision is recognized as an important tool, yet rarely are teachers able to employ the skills with adequate depth and versatility. Background knowledge of relevant theory and research is vital, yet most cooperating teachers and many teacher educators have a very limited background. Faced with these contradictions, a research program (Research in Teacher Education—RITE) was created at the Research and Development Center for Teacher Education at the University of Texas at Austin. Supported by the National Institute of Education, the research team conducted three major studies:

1. A large-scale multimethod, multisite descriptive study of student teaching
2. An experimental study of in-service teacher education
3. An analytic study of formal state-mandated teacher induction programs (Griffin, 1986, p. 3)

Although the results were voluminous, analysis of the separate studies led to the identification of elements of an effective teacher education program across the cover span. "The program must be embedded in a school context (defining property), and be (1) context-sensitive, (2) purposeful and articulated, (3) participatory and collaborative, (4) knowledge-based, (5) ongoing, (6) developmental, and (7) analytic and reflective" (Griffin, 1986, p. 7). Using these features, effective teacher education programs are based on a conception of teacher growth and development; acknowledge the complexities of classroom, school, and community; are grounded in a substantial and verifiable knowledge base; and are sensitive to the ways teachers think, feel, and make meaning from their experiences. Keeping these elements of effective teacher development in mind, we now turn to the parameters for the review of research.

Parameters for the Review of Research

With these considerations in mind, the chapter covers both theoretical considerations and practical applications. In both cases, however, the presentations will go beyond a descriptive account. The material in both areas is analyzed from the standpoints of adequacy. How broad is the evidence base for specific claims as generalized explanations of teacher growth? In this instance the question is focused on variables that may predict behavior, such as stage, age, or phase as an independent variable. Do any of those variables actually relate to performance? Certainly theory no matter how carefully stated will have little utility for teacher development if the connections to performance cannot be determined.

The second major section reverses the question. Rather than viewing theories of teacher growth as predictors, it focuses on practice. Programs for teacher development are examined with teacher outcomes viewed as a dependent variable. What is the evidence to support claims of program effectiveness? How do such intervention activities as workshops, extended training programs, and new role-taking opportunities actually affect teachers? Do they perform differently and more effectively after such training, or is such in-service just another time-wasting endeavor?

The second set of questions is clearly more complex and more difficult. Years ago Jerome Bruner (1966) described these issues insightfully. Research in the first area, namely, to uncover theoretical relationships between stage/phase and behavior, is basic. Theoretical propositions emerge that describe causal links and form an overall picture of teacher development. Such a basic model is also heuristic and open-ended. Piagetian work with children is often cited as the best example of such basic research, including his insistence that the work remain far removed from practice.

The problem, of course, is obvious—what about practice? Bruner suggests the need for a different epistemology. Instead of basic research and further theoretical elaborations describing what development is, there is the need for a theory of instruction. The difference is between describing and prescribing. In the latter case the issue is programmatic and educative. How to arrange formal and informal educational experiences that produce growth involves an entirely different set of questions. The philosopher Gilbert Ryle (1984) provided a succinct differentiation between knowledge about (theory-description) and knowledge how-to (program-prescription). He, like Bruner, sees the rationale for both types of knowledge but also the requirement to carefully distinguish between these two modes. As a result, then, I attend to both questions and analyze and evaluate a variety of current approaches to theory and to practice through critical analysis. In the first major section, then, basic research is examined to outline the knowledge base about teacher development, that is, Ryles's knowing about. In the second major section, the knowledge how to, or application, is analyzed. At the conclusion of this examination of both strands, a summary and synthesis is presented. The goal will be to center an emergent framework for teacher development at a point of parsimony between the overly abstract and the narrowly reductionistic.

THEORIES FOR THE TEACHER AS AN ADULT LEARNER

This section reviews major theories that focus on the teacher as a developing adult, and a variety of models are presented along with an analysis of the research base. The adequacy of each model is assessed on the basis of intellectual coherence, the relationship to prior work, and the extensiveness of the research evidence. In short, the current state of the art in theory for teacher development is represented in this part of the review as a contemporary indicator of the knowledge base about the teacher as an adult learner.

Age and Phase Theories

When developmental psychology gradually shifted its focus from childhood and adolescence to adults, it was Erik Erikson who became the major theorist in such a change. His case studies of adults (Martin Luther, Mahatma Gandhi), his observations of native American tribes (the Sioux and Yurok), and his insights from the psychoanalytic treatment of adults became the basis for extending the epigenetic principle of development throughout the life cycle (Erikson, 1963, 1975). His perspective was extremely broad and essentially described three very comprehensive psychosocial tasks for adults: early adulthood as intimacy versus isolation, adulthood as generativity versus stagnation, and old age as integrity versus despair. These bipolar tasks followed the same format as those for children and adolescents. More recently, Erikson (1982) revised his scheme somewhat by outlining conceptualization of how the bipolar tasks can be resolved whether successfully or unsuccessfully depending on the current interaction with the environment and also on how the prior stages were resolved.

Each adult stage may be resolved with a basic strength, *Love, Care, Wisdom* or a basic antipathy, *Exclusivity, Rejectivity,* or *Disdain.* Also it is clear that Erikson's main focus of the scheme is now toward adulthood itself and the question of generativity versus stagnation. He views that stage as the generational link between the young and the old. There is an urgency to this stage as the very spirit of adulthood or what, "Hindus call 'the maintenance of the world'" (1982, p. 66). The virtue is a commitment to *care* as the most appropriate integration of the polarities. Care is defined broadly as a responsibility for other persons, products, and ideas and is illustrated by the story of an elderly dying man. During his last moments, his spouse carefully names every member of the family who is there to wish him shalom. "And who, he suddenly asks, sitting up abruptly, who is minding the store?" (1982, p. 66).

Erikson stresses that such care is not limited to one's own circle but rather to a universal focus, the qualitative improvement of life for all, a new sense of communitarianism. He also is careful to point out that the generative stage is still in a sequence that depends on an adequate resolution of the early adult stage of intimacy versus isolation. During that period, Erikson views the problem of adult affiliation and connectedness as integrated in the virtue of *Love* versus the antipathy of *Exclusivity;* a mature "I"–"You" experience or an "Isolation à deux" as protecting both partners from the next stage (1982, p. 71). He then discusses how the early adulthood period relates to perhaps his best-known stage of identity formation during late adolescence.

As noted, the theory has been created largely on the basis of philosophical construct validity, cross-cultural observations, and his encounters with clinical patients. This means that the work rests on subjective and qualitative analysis. Its appeal and justification clearly derive from the power of his rhetoric including his revised and expanded psychoanalytic interpretations. Although a strength, this is also considered as a weakness since most of the usual canons of research, particularly more objective empirical cross-validation, is missing. Such is not the case with his stage of adolescent development, identity. In fact, both Waterman (1984) and Marcia (1976) have created an impressive body of research that has advanced our knowledge of that stage. Also that research has demonstrated clear connections between Erikson identity statuses and other measures of cognitive development such as Kohlberg's stages of moral development and Loevinger's stages of ego development (Waterman, 1992). This indicates that there is now a growing empirical base to support a stage and structure theory for identity formation during late adolescence and early adulthood. In the view of Snarey, Kohlberg, and Noam (1983) the addition of the virtues to each bipolar task may make the connection more theoretically understandable as well. Certainly the identity achievement stage connects very clearly to the initial phase of teacher development as the large sample research of Walters and Stivers (1977) demonstrated. Their research with a large sample of novice teachers documented a relationship between ineffective teacher behavior and Erikson's stage of ego identity diffusion.

As to implications for teacher development beyond the initial stage of identity achievement, however, the current empirical research on statuses raises some intriguing questions about young adulthood and adulthood itself. Waterman and Archer (1990) have found in cross-sectional and longitudinal studies that adulthood in general is a period of relative stability in identity formation. Yet two findings raise some important issues. One study indicated that a majority of adult females were classified as "Foreclosed" in identity, which is the earliest phase in the sequence. A second study of adult women demonstrated that specific life circumstances can trigger the process of identity formation. Archer (1990) found that divorce often generated a movement by adult women out of foreclosure and toward identity achievement. Married women with no history of divorce are not as likely to engage in such identity exploration (p. 97).

These findings from empirical research then create something of an anomaly. The Erikson scheme suggests turning points during early adulthood and adulthood, yet the research seems to indicate a relative high frequency of identity foreclosure by adults. This, of course, can raise doubts concerning development as an invariant sequence. Another possibility may be that the rating scheme for identity status may overrate college students and underrate adults. In fact Waterman and Archer (1990) noted that the same interview statements by a college student, classed as "achieved identity," would be considered naive if voiced by an adult. Thus, either the theory must change or the classified system needs revision to account for these findings.

On the other hand, if new research continues to indicate that during adulthood a foreclosed identity does indeed occur frequently, then experienced school teachers may be quite far removed from the tasks of generativity and comprehensive care. The implications for practice would be substantial, suggesting that classroom contexts in general may be prematurely arresting the process of adult growth. In such a case, an important research base is clearly needed to substantiate such a level of development.

Other adult theorists such as Levinson (1978) and Vaillant (1977) can be considered as variations on the Erikson model. The theories are largely descriptive, interview based, and seek to sketch phases of the life cycle and an age–stage relationship. The research is either cross-sectional or, when longitudinal, the research sample is so narrowly focused (e.g., Harvard College graduates) that generalizations are risky. The research also seems somewhat confusing. The concepts of stage, gender, context, phase, task, and age are all mingled. Finally, in addition to the confusion over life cycle tasks there has been no experimental investigation focused on a most important question: how, in fact, does such growth occur? Or is the life cycle process just that, a process through which all adults pass, but with varying degrees of impact? It certainly appears as if these life cycle theorists and theories may have peaked as an influence for new theory and practice. Admittedly these are formidable, even daunting theoretical and empirical problems. It does seem that attempting to build theory almost exclusively on narrative will always confound individual differences, cultural imperatives, functional roles, cognitive developmental structures, and subjective (albeit clinical) judgment. It would certainly help the understanding of the significance of the life cycle phases if researchers could identify (perhaps following the lead of the identity status researchers) different levels or statuses within the age phase framework and systematically test out these as potential paths of growth.

It is well to note Lawrence's (1992) observations concerning theories of adulthood phases based largely on intuition and subjective impressions. This may be an important first step in theory building, but it is clearly not yet comprehensive. She notes that the refinement of description is important but that a substantial gap remains between such description and explanation. "What it does not yet explain is how it works" (p. 248).

As a result, the compatibility of the life span and the cognitive structuralist approaches remains theoretically ambivalent. The life span view emphasizes the importance of societal, cultural, and professional conditions as such events impact the individual during the process of adult aging. That view then places a heavy emphasis on the external determinants of a person's development. The structuralists, however, emphasize how each individual interprets the meaning of those events according to the complexity of one's cognition. As Noam, Powers, Kilkenny, and Beedy (1990) point out, a 13-year-old, a 30-year-old, and even a 70-year-old may all structure the experience of interpersonal relationships in terms of social perspective at the same stage of development in spite of contextual differences. These authors note a similar position with regard to cognition involving stages of Piagetian formal operations. Some adults never achieve such a stage and remain at the same level as an early adolescent. Thus the theoretical problem is how to synthesize the impact of sociological life span forces with the cognitive structural stage considerations into a meaningful theory for adult development.

Concerns-Based Adoption Model

Research on teacher concerns was inaugurated by Frances Fuller in the late 1960s. Working with undergraduate teacher education majors, Fuller initiated a series of clinical studies to examine student teachers' motivations, perceptions, problems, and attitudes toward teaching.

Emerging from the field trials was Fuller's seminal "Concerns of teachers: A developmental conceptualization" (1969). In this article, Fuller proposed that student teacher "concerns" could be categorized and that the categories appeared to represent a set of relationships between the amount of teaching experience and the category of concerns expressed (pre-teaching phase, no concerns; early-teaching phase, concern with self; and late-teaching phase, concerns for students/impact).

In 1970 as a consequence of the research, Fuller proposed a model of "personalized" teacher education. In this model education curriculum and field experiences would be structured so that they match the current development of preservice students at each phase of concern.

Extending the work of Fuller, a number of her colleagues at the Research and Development Center for Teacher Education applied concerns theory to teachers across the career span. In particular, this new line of research explored the concerns of teachers who were engaged in adapting educational innovations. Called the Concerns Based Adoption Model (CBAM), a paper-and-pencil questionnaire was designed to assess concerns of educators. Early work addressed reliability and validity issues, and only later was the questionnaire applied in cross-sectional and longitudinal studies (Burden, 1990).

Recently Hall and Rutherford (1990) revisited the theory and conducted a review of studies that employed the Stages of Concern questionnaire. Although not exhaustive, their review summarizes, reviews, and critiques a 20-year history of research and development on Stages of Concern about innovations.

Drawing on studies from Australia, Belgium, the Netherlands, and North America with a variety of different user contexts, the studies are, in most cases, supportive of the original concepts and hypotheses developed first by Fuller. The Stages of Concern appears a reliable assessment of teachers and teacher educators involved in the change process. Nonetheless there are a number of methodological problems in Stages of Concern research that have not been resolved. As Hall and Rutherford (1990) acknowledge, "Most data collections have been one time occurrences. In only one study is there a control group, and when multiple data assessments of Stages of Concern have been made, the time interval has not been very long" (p. 11).

An additional concern about the CBAM is that it "fakes high." Because it is a recognition questionnaire, respondents may identify all concerns as being very important. Nonetheless, the general dynamics of concerns across studies tend to be consistent.

It is interesting to note that recently an adaption of the Stages of Concern has been created for assessing the phases of concern of change facilitators. The questionnaire has proven effective when working with principals, staff developers, and lead teachers who have a role in facilitating implementation and use of innovations.

Career Development Phases

While the Erikson (1975) approach has been to chart a relationship between the psychological aspects of development and chronological aging, and the CBAM model assesses concerns and attitudes toward educational innovations, career development theory has focused on ages and phases of occupational progression. In a sense the shift is from the teacher as a developing person to the work environment. The rationale appears to be borrowed from an industrial or a corporate model through a specification of a stepwise promotion sequence, but in this case applied to the career pathways for teachers.

Teacher career development addresses changes in teachers' professional experiences throughout their careers. In general, the theory and limited research on teacher career development describe and report some changes in career experiences and knowledge, as well as changes in a teacher's attitudes toward

teaching, commitment to teaching, and career satisfaction. Career events, such as preparation, entry into, and retirement from teaching are central to the theories on career cycles.

The works of Burden (1980), Fessler and Christensen (1992), and Huberman (1993) are fairly representative of the research that has been conducted in teacher career development. Burden (1980) in a qualitative study of elementary teachers' perceptions about their entire careers, reported three career cycles. The *survival cycle* is the first year of teaching. Teachers reported limited knowledge of instruction and of the school setting, lack of professional insight, and a desire to conform to preconceived images of teaching. In the *adjustment cycle,* which occurred for the teachers in the second through fourth years of teaching, teachers enlarged their instructional repertoire, increased their curriculum knowledge, and gained confidence in a personal style of teaching. The building of competencies is a central theme of the cycle. In the *mature cycle,* which comprised the fifth and subsequent years of teaching, the teachers reported professional insight and a greater student-centered focus. In addition, the teachers reported high professional enthusiasm.

A major limitation of this study is the sample. Teachers who dropped out of teaching were not included in the study. If their perspectives had been included, a richer career cycle pattern would have emerged. Two additional limitations of the study are that the data were self-selected by teachers as they recounted their careers and the sample only included elementary suburban teachers.

Perhaps the most thorough description of teacher career cycles is offered by Fessler and Christensen (1992). Their model extensively draws from the germinal research of Frances Fuller (1969) and is based on interviews with 160 teachers across the career span. The framework includes eight levels; among them are: preservice, induction, competency building, enthusiastic and growing, career frustration, stable and stagnant career, wind-down, and career exit. The framework also acknowledges that a teacher's career cycle is influenced by personal experiences such as family and crises, as well as organizational influences such as management styles and societal expectations. The career cycle is not unidirectional. Instead, it represents an ebb and flow with teachers moving in and out of positions in the cycle in response to professional experiences, as well as personal and organizational influences. Each position on the career cycle represents a distinct set of experiences and attitudes. The first four career positions (preservice, induction, competency building, and enthusiastic and growing) in general are characterized by high motivation, high task accomplishment, teacher identity formation, and particularly during the enthusiastic and growing position, a time of generativity—giving back to the profession.

The remaining four career positions represent the other half of the career coin, so to speak. Each position signifies a diffusion of expectations about teaching and a waning of career satisfactions. For example, the career frustration position is characterized by feelings of frustration and disillusionment with teaching. This waning of job satisfaction typically occurs at the midpoint of the career. And the teacher is frequently questioning self-worth and the worth of teaching. As mentioned, the career cycle is not unidirectional. Therefore, if a teacher at the career frustration position became involved in professional development that was revitalizing, the teacher could return to the enthusiastic and growing position in the career cycle.

The revisions of Fessler and Christensen acknowledge developmental stage theory and research, particularly the work of Loevinger (1976) and Hunt (1976). Furthermore, Fessler and Christensen have begun to address how new roles such as becoming a mentor teacher or school-based teacher educator can revitalize teacher careers. They miss, however, the essential connections between stage growth and new role-taking experiences and leave unanswered the crucial interplay between conceptual and ego stages and career development. Perhaps as they further refine their model greater integration of cognitive-developmental theory can be reached.

Huberman (1993) offers yet another iteration of teachers' career trajectories that is influenced by the work of Erikson (1963). The study describes how teachers' lives are ameliorated or constrained by the passage of time and the normal crises that are part of the social and cultural milieu. Huberman's model of career trajectories also has much in common with the work of Fessler and Christensen. The work is based on in-depth case studies of 160 teachers. Each career period is defined by the number of years of teacher experience and global attitudes at each career phase.

Arguing against prediction and invariance, Huberman submits that career trajectories cannot be fully explained by the cognitive-structural approach (e.g., everyone passes through stages in the same hierarchical order independent of the conditions in one's life work). This position, however, is a misrepresentation of cognitive development and it is a misrepresentation of Huberman's own work, which, on closer analysis, confirms much of what has been learned from the cognitive-developmental field. Teacher career trajectories do have a logical linear progression where each subsequent new phase represents a qualitative change that is unique and more complex than the former.

The study confirms that even when one looks across teachers' careers in a variety of contexts, there are remarkable consistencies in career socialization. It appears that the research of Huberman has reasserted Lewin's famous insight that what it means to be human is influenced by both social influences and maturational factors. However, this being said, the methodological decision to employ lengthy interviews of 160 teachers has revealed more of the social influence. To Huberman's credit, the research is rigorous and the data voluminous. It adds to our understanding of how teachers resolve individual challenges and social and cultural crises.

Future directions in the study of teacher career cycles are numerous. Research must integrate investigations of the person's cognitive growth with investigations of cultural and situational conditions. Attention to both psychological and nonpsychological phenomena will yield a richer understanding. In addition, greater attention needs to be given to teachers at all ages, cognitive-developmental stages, and cultures. Perhaps Erikson's construct of identity could unify life and career cycle literature. Vondracek (1992) submits that Erikson's construct of identity could frame a dynamic developmental conceptualization of the construct of career identity. All of Erikson's levels have implications for teacher career development, and Erikson

(1982) often described the central importance he assigned to the individual's ability to work.

Perhaps the most visible example of career cycles theory has been the implementation of career ladders. In effect, the programs attempted to reward teachers as they moved up the professional ladder. Career ladders are now described.

Career Ladders and Merit Pay Plans

Career ladders and merit pay plans appeared in the 1980s in the midst of a national debate over how to promote school improvement. The debate turned on a number of beliefs that gave momentum to the career ladders movement. Most prominent among the concerns/beliefs was an assumption that money incentives will motivate highly qualified persons to select teaching and encourage them to stay in the profession. A related belief was that the teaching profession cannot retain exemplary teachers because it lacks a performance-based financial incentive plan. A final belief shared by many policymakers was that merit pay must be connected to national and state efforts to upgrade education. Implicit was an assumption that merit pay will promote quality that may not exist in schools. Where political figures talked of "turning the tide" in the 1980s, now they talk of "world-class schools," a not-so-veiled desire to be superior in the global economy.

Perhaps the most contentious issue for teacher unions and organizations, school boards, and administrators was the choice between raising base salaries for all teachers or creating a differentiated salary. Many teacher unions persuasively argued that base salaries must be raised for all teachers before a differentiated pay plan would be initiated. State policymakers and school boards countered that tight fiscal resources as well as a reluctance to reward mediocre teachers favored merit pay plans. There was little disagreement that merit pay and career ladder plans would not be able to offer financial incentives comparable to those in accounting, law, and business. The question was whether merit pay and career ladder plans can help, in a minor way, to encourage new teachers to join the profession and to retain experienced teachers.

Typically, the career ladder plans specified three or four levels in the teaching career. The first level for probationary teachers usually included all teachers that had not attained tenure. The second level was the career teacher. Once tenure had been attained, progressing to the third and fourth levels depended on teacher initiative. These steps were often referred to as associate teacher and master teacher.

Regardless of one's philosophical position, history offers some important lessons. Merit pay has been tried repeatedly, and since its inception in Newton, Massachusetts, in 1908, the concept has ridden a rollercoaster, undulating between periods of boom and bust in popularity. Between 1938 and 1958, more than 170 school districts tried to implement merit pay plans, and by 1968, 11% of all districts with 6,000 or more students indicated they had merit pay (ASCD, 1985). However, most of these initiatives have been abandoned because of administrative constraints, the lack of a fail-safe and objective evaluation system, teacher morale problems, and shifting political agendas. Thus, merit pay as an incentive for professional development has an abysmal record of failure.

Career ladders have experienced a similar history. While merit pay plans used evaluated performance as a basis for differentiated financial rewards, career ladders used variable levels of responsibility and length of the work year to justify variable salaries. Most differentiated staffing plans have been discontinued because of a host of problems, including hasty implementation, lack of federal and state support, and top-down implementation.

In 1986 the Southern Regional Education Board's (SREB) Career Ladder Clearing House (Cornett, 1986) reported that teacher incentive programs were "spreading like wildfire," either as pilot projects or as full-scale statewide programs. More than 29 states were implementing or had mandates to develop career ladder or teacher merit pay plans. In SREB's annual update (Cornett & Gaines, 1993), only Arizona appeared to have a career ladder program that had held firm to its original intent to link teacher advancement to student performance. Most other states have tended to move away from funding career ladders. Instead, the new trend is to offer "whole school incentives." "Other states with similar mandates in their early legislation have tended to downplay or move away from an emphasis on performance pay" (p. 7). Nonetheless, a few states like Tennessee and Texas continue to promote career ladder plans.

Perhaps the most compelling aspect of career ladders is the implicit assumption that professional teachers, as they become more experienced with greater new expertise through staff development, will be highly valued in the school system. Promoting greater diversity in teachers' roles contributes to the educational community by breaking down the traditional role structures where the only option for teachers is to become a counselor or a principal. Certainly the roles of mentor teacher, lead teacher, instructional resource teacher, and school-based management team leaders represent just a few of the potentially significant new roles that teachers could embrace. Perhaps the challenge in the future is how to select, prepare, and reward teachers who have assumed complex new helping roles within their schools and within the larger educational arena. In the future, as staff development is seen as a lifelong need, teachers with particular expertise can be called upon to serve as school-based teacher educators in this selected area of expertise (Sparks, 1987). The career ladder career development model, however, does need a broader theoretical base or it will surely degenerate to a seniority system based on years of service rather than effectiveness of performance.

The career ladder approach does not address the question of teacher cognition as a significant variable. Kagan (1990) has pointed out that credible research on teacher growth must include concepts of cognition as well as appropriate assessment techniques. As a result, the current review switches focus at this point to research and theory on teacher cognition as a basic variable in the current knowledge base about teacher growth. This includes information processing and stages of cognition in relationship to adult behavior in general and teacher behavior specifically.

Information Processing

In the Information Processing model either child or adult cognition is conceptualized as representing a linear continuum from the less complex to greater amounts of cognitive complexity. It is important to note that such a model does not connote a stage conceptualization or that such conceptual development goes through an invariant sequence of cognitive transformations. Instead the model focuses more attention on specific cognitive processes such as how an individual inputs, stores, and retrieves information. In a manner similar to computer modeling and artificial intelligence, then, the cognitions are charted along a series of dimensions such as short- and long-term memory according to "chunking," cue association, mnemonics, and other methods (Anderson, 1990).

Although by far most of the work in the model has focused on the process of student learning (Pintrich, Marx, & Boyle, 1993), it can be applied to adults in general and specifically to the development of cognitions in adult teachers. The goal of this model is to outline a system of cognitive learning that will lead to conceptual mastery by any group of humans. Prior research has shown quite clearly that teachers, like adults in general, either distort or ignore information that is in conflict to their current cognitions. The classic research by Nisbett and Ross (1980) provided multiple examples of such failures in syllogistic reasoning and inadequacy of adult judgment in general. The need and rationale for improving cognitive process is clearly compelling.

Thus far the major effort in this area has focused on cognitive information processing and teacher planning (Clark & Yinger, 1987). This approach, which derives from the teacher as decision maker, has charted the actual planning systems employed by teachers with different amounts of experience. Thus far there are some differences between the novice and the expert planner in terms of metacognition (Royer, Cisero, & Carlo, 1993). An earlier review also has shown some specific differences in domain knowledge, organization of information (branching, etc.) and tacit knowledge (Carter, 1990).

The current state of the art in this area is both promising and problematic. The promise is that the framework will help untangle the problem of how teachers may learn and reach higher levels of complexity as decision makers. However, the assessment problems in this area are substantial. In a massive review Royer et al. (1993) focused specifically on the instructional question. How reliable and valid are the measures employed to assess the acquisition of cognitive change? In teacher development terms, can the measurement of improved cognitive planning and other aspects of metacognitives be considered an adequate basis for intervention programs? The answer appears to be a strong negative. Royer, Cisero, and Carlo (1993) found that, "In all of the research that [they] read, there was not a single report of a reliability index for an assessment procedure, and indices of validity were available only as inferences of the form" (p. 235). As a result, their conclusion was that very significant research on so-called authentic assessment is a necessary prior step to any procedures designed to promote the acquisition of metacognitive skills in either students or adults. Certainly the theory has many potential benefits as causal explanations of the critical link between teacher cognition and effective classroom performance, but this framework remains to be validated before programs can emerge.

An alternate possibility could be to work on both issues simultaneously, through programs that promote more efficient cognitive problem solving by teachers and through authentic assessment in order to judge the effectiveness of the interventions. Such an effort could become a basis for teacher development, particularly as it relates to the model of the teacher as decision maker. In a sense this situation is almost prototypical of the tension between basic research and practice. The basic researchers issue a careful plea denoting the gaps in this knowledge base. Program developers, however, are attracted to the concept of cognitive information processing and seek immediate translations into practice. It will be interesting to see how the tension may be resolved over the next 5 to 10 years as to the emergence of an adequate theoretical base for practice. Otherwise the teacher as decision maker may become just another failed fad.

An exception to this view of the state of the art may be the work of Peterson and her colleagues, more fully explained in a later section (Peterson, Fennema, Carpenter, & Loef, 1989). Their work on assessment, however, does connect directly to the position noted by Royer et al. (1973). The Peterson group is in the process of creating assessment procedures, though admittedly cumbersome in the extreme, that give evidence that teacher cognition can be examined and classified with respectable levels of measurement reliability and validity. This could point the way to a broad method of assessment and perhaps even to intervention strategies.

The National Center for Research on Teacher Learning issued a special report that does add an important note of urgency to the information process model (Kennedy, 1991). The researchers found clear connections between the teacher's level of cognitive process and student outcome. Teachers who comprehended the importance of focusing on improving student ideation did, "in fact produce students with far more problem-solving ability than other teachers" (p. 8). The problem then becomes how to expand the information-processing ability of teachers given that the vast majority continue to believe in an inadequate set of conceptions about teaching and students. Teachers resiliently continue "to believe that teaching entails little more than telling students what they need to know and measuring their ability to recite it back" (p. 8). As a result, then, levels of teacher cognition represent a framework from less to greater complexity. Such a continuum may not be clearly hierarchical, but it does suggest a similarity to the stage and sequence framework of the structuralistic cognitive-developmental view that we now consider.

Cognitive-Developmental Approaches

There have been substantial gains at both the theoretical and empirical levels in the constructivist framework with implication for adults in general and for teachers as adult learners. The major theoretical assumptions are that all humans may progress through stages of cognition as they construct meaning from experience. The sequence of stages is both hierarchical and invariant. Thus, the more complex stages are conceptualized as more adequate in the use of problem-solving strategies, more flexible in modes of thought and action, and more morally efficient in understanding and applying democratic principles for conflict resolution.

It also should be noted that stages of development are conceptualized as representing cognitions and behavior in a variety of domains of growth. Each domain is seen as an important, focused sector of human development. For example, conceptual development is viewed as encompassing the domain of rational process and thinking skills originally researched by Piaget (1973). Self awareness or ego development represent a parallel domain that is almost Socratic in conceptualization as self-knowledge. Jane Loevinger's (1976) research has been the primary focus of knowledge in this area. Moral and ethical judgment represents a third domain with a focus on how humans in a democratic society view questions of social justice and fairness based mostly on Kohlberg's original contribution (1969).

Other domains may have significance for the process of adult growth, such as Selman's (1980) work on interpersonal relationship stages, Gardner's (1993) work on stages of aesthetic development, and Damon's (1988) work on social development. These theorists, however, have concentrated on children and adolescents, so implications for adult growth have yet to be outlined. Table 29.1 outlines the major contemporary theorists in the three domains of adult development. The cognitive complexity cluster includes Piaget (1973), Perry (1970), Hunt (1974), Arlin (1984), and King and Kitchener (1994). The domain of self-knowledge or ego includes Erikson (1963) and Loevinger (1966). The area of moral/ethical reasoning includes the work of Kohlberg (1969), Rest (1986), and Snarey (1985).

The Research Evidence: Ego and Moral Development Originally cognitive-developmental stages were held as relevant only to children, adolescents, and young adults (Kohlberg & Kramer, 1969). More recent longitudinal studies of moral and ego development (Lee & Snarey, 1988) and conceptual development (King & Kitchener, 1994) have required a major alteration. Stage growth does not halt suddenly at some point between adolescence and early adulthood. Rather the process of growth through stages may continue throughout the life span.

Certainly the most crucial piece of evidence in this regard comes from a longitudinal study of Lee and Snarey (1988). With a sample of more than 600 adults, they examined stage growth in two domains, ego or self development based on Loevinger's theory (1976) and moral judgment based on Kohlberg's theory (1969). Adults demonstrated a pattern of slow growth in both domains, yet with important differences in the sequence. During early adulthood (ages 19–29) ego development with its emphasis on self-knowledge and interpersonal relations was found to be in advance of moral development. In other words, the test scores of the same subjects demonstrated a higher level of ego stage than moral stage. The cross-tabulation method, however, revealed that during middle adulthood (ages 30–49) the scores were equal in stage level (e.g., ego and moral level were equivalent). For the older group (ages 50–80) there was yet another shift whereby moral judgment stage was higher than ego stage. Theoretically, these findings outline important changes that adults may use as they construct meaning from experience. Questions of self and self-in-relationships appear to have greater salience in the first phase, whereas questions of social justice, fairness, and integrity become more salient in the last phase of adulthood. Lee and Snarey (1988) interpret

TABLE 29.1. The Teacher as an Adult Learner: Cognitive Developmental Domains

	Cognitive Complexity	Ego/Self Development	Moral/Ethical Development
Major Theorists	Piaget (1973) Perry (1970) Hunt (1974) Arlin (1984) King & Kitchener (1994)	Erikson (1963) Loevinger (1966)	Kohlberg (1969) Rest (1986) Snarey (1985)
Stage and Sequence	Concrete; dualism Early formal operations Formal operations Postformal operations; wisdom	External focus; social acceptability; identity foreclosure Moratorium and achievement Autonomy and responsibility Interdependence generativity/care	Social conformity Law and duty orientation Principled concepts of justice Universalistic perspective
Domains	Ego / Conceptual / Moral (cube diagram)		
Combined			

these results in a number of interesting ways. First, that cognitive stages should be conceptualized as representing a series of interrelated domains such as ego, moral, conceptual, and so on. Adults do exhibit both the potential for growth and, though modest, actual growth through stages. Such growth, however, varies by age and phase with ego as preeminent during early adulthood and moral judgment as preeminent much later. Finally, they suggest that these findings may provide empirical support for many of Erik Erikson's contentions already noted. Clearly ego issues of identity and relationship parallel Erikson's focus during late adolescence and early adulthood just as clearly as Lee and Snarey's midpoint relates to Erikson's ideas of generativity and care. The final phase with the emphasis on social justice coincides with Erikson's view of wisdom and integrity. If such an interpretation is valid, it may provide concurrent validity to connect the cognitive-developmental stage theory to Erikson's psychosocial framework and vice versa.

The Lee and Snarey findings also complement the longitudinal studies by Kohlberg (1984) from his original all-male sample. Kohlberg reported that his subjects ($N = 59$) always progressed (slowly) through the sequence in an invariant order, without regressions or skipping. The subjects were retested every 4 years over a 20-year span and their pattern of a gradual increase in moral reasoning can be viewed as strong research validation of the stage and sequence model. The method of assessment, the moral judgment interview (MJI) reported reliability coefficients in excess of +.95 for interrater and test–retest situations. Another longitudinal study (Rest & Narvez, 1994) of high school, college, and graduate students also clearly shows the same trends from less complex to more complex judgment in the domain of moral analysis. Rest's research, in addition, indicates highly similar stages of growth through 40 cross-cultural comparisons including Western, non-Western, industrialized, and nonindustrialized countries. Such findings are highly congruent with Kohlberg's cross-cultural studies (Snarey, 1985) in some 50 countries throughout the world and with more recent studies reported by Gielen (1991). The highest levels on the Kohlberg system were found to be similar structurally to Hindu metaphysics, Confucianism ethics, and socialist ideals for an egalitarian society (Gielen, 1991, p. 46), as well as the Jewish prophets and Siddhartha (the Buddha). All this would indicate a strong research base for the claims of stage and sequence for adult moral development.

Further confirmation of the relationship between Loevinger ego stage and teaching was reported by Cummings and Murray (1989). A study of 58 experienced teachers in Canada showed a strong relationship between ego level and the teachers' conceptions of the instructional role. At ego stage I-3 (conformist), the role was as a presenter of information; at I-4 (autonomous) the role included modeling, concerns for students, and a mastery of teaching skills. At the highest level I-4/5 and 5 (interdependent), the role included challenge, concern for the whole child, and teaching/learning as a search. Quite important, they found that the concept of caring for students also had different meanings according to ego level. At the lowest level the teacher, "likes children." At the autonomous level the teacher "is empathic and understands the needs of the child." At the highest level the teacher is "a model, a catalyst and a facilitator of growth." Each conception clearly represents a qualitatively different meaning for the teacher as a caring person. They also reported an indirect effect between ego level and performance through path analysis. A major difficulty was the narrow dependent variable, grades and instructor ratings. In an overall sense, however, the study adds to the validity and the importance of cognitive stage variables such as ego development and teaching not only for experienced teachers but also for student teachers.

They comment that student teachers at I-3 (conformist) simply copy the teaching style of their instructors, thus behaving in accord with their developmental level (Cummings & Murray, 1989, p. 31).

The work of Glickman, Hayes, and Hensley (1992), which has recently shifted from supervision into a broader context, school improvement, adds further theoretical rationale for the stage model. Based on extensive observations of programs designed to empower teachers, they now posit a tri-stage framework for teacher performance and conceptions about teaching. Their descriptions are elaborations and a synthesis of perspectives on empowerment that connote different levels of complexity, much in the manner of Cummings and Murray (1989). For example, Glickman cites different levels of caring, such as to be cared for, to be cared about, and to care for and about, as representing the different perceptions. There are similar descriptions for other dimensions of school change such as communication, outcome, community, and so on. Although formal research is still in the offing, their scheme is compatible with other developmental frameworks.

The Research Evidence: Conceptual Development In the domain of conceptual development there were suggestions by Piaget (1972) that adults might manifest growth in formal operations. More recently Arlin (1984) has created a theoretical framework for such a possibility with her conceptualization of a fifth stage in the Piagetian sequence. In neither case, however, has there been validating cross-sectional or longitudinal research. David Hunt's (1974) cross-sectional research on the other hand clearly demonstrates adult differences in the ability to conceptualize between concrete versus abstract thinking. He also has provided substantial research on the predictive validity of his conceptual level (CL) stages and behavior (outlined in the following section). The longitudinal framework, however, has yet to be researched as a means of documenting the stage and sequence pathway. Similarly, William Perry's (1970) research on stages or "positions" of conceptual development has been enormously influential as a basis for understanding college student growth but has not focused on adult research samples.

By far the most significant research on cognitive-developmental growth with adults is the work of Patricia King and Karen Kitchener (1994). In the 1970s they thought of extending and transforming Perry's stages of conceptual dualism, relativism, and committed relativism into a framework denoted as stages of reflective judgment. They also created a method of assessment through problem-solving scenarios in which subjects talked out loud in their solutions to questions of inquiry, evidence, and awareness of alternative solutions. In a generic sense they were interested in finding how often students and adults actually employed scientific problem solving in reaching conclusions to questions such as how to figure out which theory may be more accurate in how, for example, the pyramids were built, or a problem involving an ecological disaster. The assessment method involved the ratings of interviews according to levels of Reflective Judgment Index (RJI) with correlation coefficients in the +.90 level for interrater and test–retest reliability. Their longitudinal sample was composed of 80 subjects retested over a 10-year period. In addition they collected cross-sectional data on almost 1,000 subjects.

The results indicated that adults do exhibit stage and sequence growth in reflective judgment from authority-based concrete thought, to quasi–self-reflective abstract, and then to "true" reflective judgment. This highest stage is similar to Dewey's original conception of scientific problem solving and to the highest level of conceptual development in the David Hunt scheme. As was the case with Kohlberg's longitudinal research, King and Kitchener found the process of adult growth to be slow; yet there were no regressions, no one skipped a stage, the problems themselves were context resistant. Their research, then, lends substantial credibility to the earlier theoretical propositions that a stage framework can be applied to the process of conceptual growth of adults. There is, however, one other very significant finding. Age by itself does not predict growth in reflective judgment. Stage growth was most apparent for adults who continued the informal education and professional development. This is an important reminder of a central cognitive development axiom, stage growth does not unilaterally unfold but requires a stimulating and supportive environment. This issue is described more fully in the section on practical applications, but it is well to note here that growth requires appropriate interaction.

The Gender Question

Ever since Carol Gilligan's (1982) remarkable book there has been a challenge to stage theory as biased against women. Somewhat ironically there have been very few studies and even fewer research studies to support her claims. Her research samples were small and local (e.g., 25 Harvard college students in one of her classes, a follow-up study of 29 women having abortions in the Boston area, and a cross-sectional study of 36 male and female subjects between the ages of 6 to 60 [Loevinger, 1987]). Nonetheless her view has become almost a standard criticism of stage theory as male oriented on one hand and bereft of empathy and caring on the other.

A careful review of research by both male and feminist scholars, however, reveals quite a different finding. Male researchers such as Rest (1986) and Walker (1986, 1991) have summarized studies of from 6,000 to 10,000 subjects and consistently report either no gender differences or slight trends in favor of females. Female scholars such as Brabeck (1982), King and Kitchener (1994), Mednick (1989), and Scott-Jones (1991) also report no significant gender differences in stage scores. The longitudinal study already noted by Lee and Snarey (1988) was composed of 400 females and 225 males, with no gender differences on either ego or moral stage. Finally, Lind (1993) reported no gender differences in a large-scale ($N = 4,000$), cross-cultural study in Europe.

These findings are highly congruent with gender findings in more general areas. For example, Case (1992) has found no gender differences in children and adolescents across six comparisons on Piaget tasks. Hyde and Linn (1988) in a meta-analysis of some 1.5 million subjects, found no gender differences by verbal ability. These same researchers (Linn & Hyde, 1989) in another metaanalysis, had shown only one difference by gender in mathematical and scientific abilities across 18 comparisons.

Thus the general summary indicates that earlier research reports and case studies suggesting gender differences are not valid. In fact Linn and Hyde (1989) suggest that the only bias may have been from male editors rejecting articles showing no differences and publishing articles that emphasized gender differences.

Stage and Behavior

Even though the recent research does support the assumptions of the stage and sequence framework for adults from a construct and concurrent validity standpoint, perhaps the most significant question concerns predictive validity. What is the relationship between the level of cognitive developmental stage and behavior? Does how a person constructs experience predict how such a person may behave? The short version of the question asks simply is higher better? Before examining recent research on the issue, it is necessary to point out a singularly important question, the task at hand. Higher stages of cognitive development must always be viewed from the standpoint of the problem situation. For example, an important study of brain activity (the amount of glucose burned during problem solving) indicated two important outcomes. Subjects assessed at higher stages of cognition on Piagetian formal operations were more efficient (burned less glucose) when the task required more complex problem solving. The subjects were asked to solve increasingly more difficult abstract patterns on Raven's Progressive Matrices. The reverse was also true. When the task was simple, rotelike, and boring, requiring visual vigilance, the abstract thinkers were less efficient than the concrete thinkers (Hostetler, 1988). Thus when it comes to predicting behavior from cognitive stage, one must always examine the complexity of the task requirements.

From such a perspective there is now a large body of research evidence that consistently indicates that various domains of cognitive-developmental stage do predict behavior in complex situations. Bielke (1979) found that higher stages on Loevinger's ego development predicted effective parenting behavior assessed by reliable observation scales over a 6- and 12-month interval with a sample of more than 200 young mothers. Blasi's (1980) metaanalysis indicated that in 59 of 74 studies there were positive correlations between moral stage and moral behavior. In dramatic studies of adult obedience under duress, such as the Milgram research or a study by McNamee, more than 75% of the subjects assessed at principled stages on Kohlberg resisted the authoritarian commands versus less than one-third of the subjects at lower stages (summarized in Sprinthall, Sprinthall, & Oja, 1994).

A recent study by MacCallum (1993) examined teacher moral judgment in the Kohlberg system and approaches to student discipline. Teachers at higher stages exhibited more complex perspective taking, were more sensitive to students' rights, and employed rules to promote student understanding. Their cohorts at lower levels of moral judgment were primarily concerned with maintaining order. There were no gender differences in moral judgment. Female teachers, however, demonstrated a greater ability to coordinate a variety of perspectives in different discipline issues. They could more easily identify the needs of the different stakeholders when the content of the controversies varied between moral and nonmoral issues.

It is noteworthy that there is an increasing body of contemporary research documenting the relationship between moral cognition and ethical behavior for adults in a variety of professions. Rest and Narvez (1994) report studies indicating that professional accountants at higher stages of reasoning are far more likely to detect fraudulent practice than those at lower stages. Similar findings are reported for groups of dentists, nurses, and veterinarians. These outcomes are highly consistent with earlier research but also add new insights. For example, in the large sample study of accountants, age and experience was not related either to stage score or to fraud detection. In fact, the senior officials reasoned at lower levels and were less likely to discover unethical practice. Thus there is substantial evidence to support the generalization of higher stage as a predictor of democratic principled action as well as the reverse.

What about research focused on teachers and counselors? Similar outcomes have been reported in extensive studies of teachers summarized in a meta-analysis by Miller (1981). After analyzing some 60 studies that employed the Hunt Conceptual Systems Test (CST) as a measure of cognitive stage complexity, he concluded that persons functioning at higher stages on the CST exhibited behaviors such as (1) a reduction in prejudice, (2) greater empathic communication, (3) greater focus on internal control, (4) longer decision latencies, (5) more flexible teaching methods, (6) more autonomy and more interdependence, and (7) superior communication and information processing. Hunt (1976) noted that higher CST scores for teachers allowed for "reading and flexing" in the classroom, which meant the ability to change the learning environment in accord with pupil needs.

A similar set of findings were reported by Thies-Sprinthall (1980) with an added dimension of significance for teacher supervision. She found that higher cognitive level (CL) supervising teachers were more accurate in their evaluations of student teachers, as all of Miller's meta-analysis would suggest. She also found what can be termed a disordinal interaction between the stage of the supervision and the stage of the student teacher. The disordinal match was noticeable in one set of dyads focused on the supervising teachers at lower CL stages than their student teachers. In that quadrant (High CL student teacher and Low CL cooperating teacher) the evaluations were both inaccurate and negative. The Low CL cooperating teachers were excessively judgmental and perceived the flexible teaching methods of the student teachers as inadequate. Such a study should serve as reminder of the downside of cognitive-developmental findings.

A study of McKibbin and Joyce (1981), also rarely reported, revealed a similar set of positive and negative findings concerning developmental stage and teaching performance. They provided teachers with a series of workshops on innovative strategies for the classroom and returned 1 year later to assess generalization in actual practice. With a measure of psychological development assessed at pretest, they found a direct relationship between higher-stage teachers and employment of innovative methods from the workshops. They also found the opposite. The lower-stage teachers resisted and virtually failed to employ any but the most simple and concrete methods. These findings then serve as a reminder of both aspects of the developmental question. Higher is more adequate and lower is less adequate. The McKibbin-Joyce study also explains the truism that new curricular guides are not teacher proof and the fact that so many of those guides end up gathering dust in the bottom drawers of teachers' desks.

A study by Newmann (1993) examined student teachers' ability to represent real-life teaching problems. Using Case's (1992) neo-Piagetian conceptual framework, Newmann investigated a nonrandom sample of 39 intermediate student teachers. Faculty supervisors also completed rating forms and observations of the student teachers. Results indicated that student teachers grew in complexity of problem representation during the practicum. Newmann pointed to the role-taking experience and reflection on the experience as the major contributors to student teacher development. Furthermore, she found that student teachers at more complex levels could coordinate more student differences.

The research literature in counseling and counselor education focusing on the relation between stage and behavior reveals a set of findings highly congruent with the teaching research. These findings provide further research validation of the claims of the stage and behavior relationship. For example, Holloway and Wampold (1986) reported a meta-analysis from 69 studies. With both analog and actual counseling skills as dependent variables, the conceptual stage of the counselor predicted counseling behavior. Higher-stage counselors were more accurate in empathic responding, more complex in diagnostic assessment, and more flexible in their choice of counseling procedures. A specific example of this research is a study of Strommer, Biggs, Haase, and Purcell (1983). They examined the nonverbal behavior of counselors when meeting a client with a physical disability. This is particularly important because an oft-cited criticism of developmental assessments is their heavy reliance on verbal assessment. The study, however, revealed that even a verbal measure of developmental stage was an accurate predictor of nonverbal behavior. The high-stage counselors maintained appropriate eye contact, minimal body posture anxiety, voice tone variation, and breath control. The lower-stage counselors did not and instead exhibited what might be termed nonfacilitative, nonverbal behavior such as body posture anxiety, avoidance of eye contact, gasps in breathing, and so on.

In a sense the findings on the behavior stage relationship can be construed as supporting the concept of Attribute Treatment Interaction (ATI). In this case the attribute is the developmental stage of the adult professional as he or she interacts with pupils, curriculum materials, or beginning professionals in supervision. As a result, the current research base provides strong support identifying the relationship between stage and complex behavioral task requirements. That relationship clearly indicates two sets of findings. In problem-solving situations requiring complex and humane response, adults in general and teachers specifically who process experience at higher stages of development are more competent, effective, and efficient. Adults in general or teachers specifically who process at lower stages of development perform at increasing levels of incompetence when faced with complex tasks.

The next question, however, may be even more important. Can the stage of development, here viewed as a predictor or independent variable, become a dependent variable? Can stage level be modified and improved? That question is addressed in the later section of this review when the focus is on systematic teacher development programs.

TEACHER DEVELOPMENT: APPROACHES AND PROGRAMS

In this section the focus shifts to the second part of the Gilbert Ryle framework from knowledge about to knowledge how-to. First, how are the current models for program development or teacher education interventions linked to theory? Second, what are the quantitative and qualitative findings that support the claims of effect? In this manner judgments can be derived as to the adequacy of theory and research in practice and the visibility of practice in research and theory.

The Craft Model

In this model for practice the assumptions are direct. A body of knowledge exists in the hearts and minds of experienced teachers that should form either an exclusive or at least a major basis for teacher development. Grimmett and MacKinnon (1992) have provided an elaborated and stirring defense of the craft model as not only an alternate model but also one that they implicitly believe is superior to any of the variations of the applied science paradigm. They denote a new concept, pedagogical learner knowledge based on the dailiness of experience from the classroom. Such classroom savvy also referred to as "crafty" knowledge (not a pejorative) represents the accumulated wisdom from teachers and/or practice-oriented researchers.

Grimmett and MacKinnon also reject most of the procedures that the applied science model employs to validate views. In fact, the major thrust of the argument is humanistic, subjective, and intuitive. Throughout their presentation there is reference to poetic expression, intuition, feelings, and personal authenticity reminiscent of the romantic educational views of the 1960s, as exemplified by writers such as Silvia Ashton-Warner (1963) and George Leonard (1968). To substantiate their view they rely heavily on case study excerpts, narratives, and examples from teachers' lives over time. Whether such examples are the exception rather than the rule is irrelevant. They see such material as a rich source of information that will transform the lives of both preservice and in-service teachers by convincing them of the power of craft knowledge as revealed through the *voices of practitioners*.

Examples of the craft knowledge base then are cited in various forms. In the first instance a dialog is presented between a supervisor and a student teacher (Grimmett & MacKinnon, 1992, p. 397) to illustrate how the former has recognized an error in teaching and helps the beginner develop deeper understanding in practice. A second basis for such craft knowledge can be derived from popular narratives in recent movies such as *Stand and Deliver, Dead Poet's Society,* and *Madame Sousatzka.* Grimmett and MacKinnon point out that such teacher "heroes" succeed in exemplifying uniquely innovative pedagogical moves, yet also reflect the difficulties of social context experienced particularly by school teachers.

At the same time the authors are somewhat cognizant of the Achilles' heel of the craft model, the problem of reflection. As Dewey (1933) made it so abundantly obvious many years ago, experience can be educative or miseducative. There is no guarantee that any human, teacher or not, will necessarily learn anything at all from experience. In fact, almost in spite of all of the recent writings on reflection, there is very little actual creation of programs geared to reflection-in-action. This is not to say that there are not a plethora of calls for reflection, but as Richardson (1994) has pointed out, little of this framework is evident in practice. Clearly the craft model stands or falls on the concept of learing how to extract new meaning from the "rich" lode of experience. The authors do make a few suggestions on activities that may help develop a reflective capacity, but these suggestions seem conventional at best and more likely appear as a major letdown to a teacher educator looking for ways to achieve the craft model goals. The ideas of case studies, developing one's own credo, the use of guided fantasy, photos, and on-site teaming in classrooms appear as somewhat lightweight translations of the craft model, leaving aside the obvious set of research questions vis-à-vis the relative potency of different methods. In this sense, then, the craft model may be begging the question. How do, or even can, practitioners by themselves draw new and innovative meaning from experiences as a means of creating a body of knowledge or teaching lore? Clearly one of the main philosophical criticisms of the experiential model is that it may only succeed in passing down a conservative and perhaps jejune repetition of past practice. Indeed a critic like Paulo Friere (1983) would be even more polemical in pointing out how past practice in teaching is necrophilic at best. Dewey's question then remains, is it 10 years of teaching or 1 year 10 times over?

In fact, the research evidence is not sanguine concerning the quality of teaching by experienced teachers. Nate Gage some years ago found that experience by itself bore almost no relationship to either teaching effectiveness or student achievement (1978). More recently, the National Center for Research on Teacher Education (NCRTE, 1991) study reached the same conclusion. There were no significant differences between beginner and experienced (10 years) teachers in elementary schools, and the experienced secondary school teachers were "somewhat better" (p. 31). That study assessed attitudes, conceptual skills, and classroom practice in a longitudinal sample of 700 participants. The school subjects included math and writing, and the attitudes included how the teachers viewed student diversity. Probably most disconcerting was the overall finding supporting the importance and centrality of experience as the most highly valued teaching asset at all career phases. Even though the research indicated a highly traditional pattern of teaching in the classrooms, stereotyped views of student diversity, and an inability to explain the conceptual basis for instruction in math and writing, the teachers at all levels ranked learning from experts lowest. The vast majority (75%) agreed that, "You have to find what works for you" (p. 71). Certainly, the recent theory and research of Gardner (1993) in the Harvard Project Zero offers an exclamation point to our argument. Using the lens of multiple intelligences and development, a host of

concerns can be raised about the ultimate ineffectiveness of teaching that relies on simply craft knowledge. Gardner's work is a clarion call for careful examination of new ways to help teachers teach for understanding, an occurrence found too little of in his research efforts.

The second difficulty concerns the issue raised at the outset, exactly who does remain in teaching after the first 5- to 7-year phase (Colbert & Wolff, 1992; Huling-Austin, 1990; Schlechty, 1985; Schlechty & Vance, 1981). If, as the figures show, such a large number of cohorts leave during the survival phase, is there a feeling of confidence that only those who were incompetent shifted fields? Certainly the national survey by Vance and Schlechty (1982) would give pause to the notion that the best and the brightest stay in the classrooms. Thus, the craft model may face, in research terms, a major mortality problem with the loss of significant numbers of practitioners who move from the school to other professions or to the university classrooms. In fact, Grimmett and MacKinnon (1992) at least obliquely acknowledged this issue when they pointed out in an extensive footnote that they excluded exemplary teacher educators (e.g., Maxine Greene, Alan Tom, Lee Shulman, Vito Perrone, Eleanor Duckworth, David Hawkins, William Ayers, and Esteele Fuchs) because not one, "is a recognized school teacher" (p. 443). Research would show, however, that such exemplars did have classroom teaching experience. Apparently, if such experience is not contemporary, the insights are no longer valid.

To further their point, they cite an interesting case study about an intuitive sea captain with no formal training who successfully guided his ship through dangerous passages. After the state discovered he was unlicensed, he dutifully enrolled and passed a certification program in scientific navigation. When queried as to the impact of his new skills when confronted with untoward circumstances at sea, he replied, "I went up on the deck, listened to the wind in the rigging, got the drift of the sea, gazed at a star, and corrected my computations" (Grimmett & McKinnon, 1992, p. 388). This, of course, was the system he employed prior to formal scientific training.

The moral of the story becomes obvious. An intuitively gifted person needs no scientific information and in fact such data are nearly useless. Unfortunately for the craft model, however, such a method of problem solving has been investigated very carefully and found wanting. In a classic study by the Minnesota psychologist Paul Meehl (1956), such subjective/intuitive clinical prediction was compared to scientific prediction. In every case the scientific method outperformed the clinical in assessment of diagnostic accuracy. Such an outcome is particularly understandable in light of George Miller's basic research on cognitive processing. That research indicated quite clearly that humans can retain only five to seven pieces of information at any one time for clinical analysis (Miller, 1969). Statistical computations, of course, can accommodate a far greater number. Or another way to put it in the metaphor of our sea captain, what might happen on a stormy night with no stars and the inability to understand an electronic guidance system for ships?

The craft model clearly relies heavily on the Rousseauist view of individual dignity and development unfettered by the intervention of experts similar to our intuitive navigator. The same view is often held concerning other performing arts. In sports, particularly baseball, commentators refer to a "natural." In this regard Ted Williams, the last .400 hitter, is usually described as the ultimate example of such self-development, referring to the hundreds of hours he spent alone as a 12-year-old swinging at imaginary baseballs in his small backyard. Careful inspection of his history, however, yields a different and more complex picture. He did develop a natural swing, but not content with such intuition, he also generalized some scientific lessons learned as a naval aviator. He was intrigued with the theory of wind resistance and lift. He soon realized that bat speed, not weight, was a critical element by applying Daniel Bernoulli's principles to the art of home run hitting, not just to the theory of wing lift in airplanes (Linn, 1993, p. 185).

Perhaps the clearest current example of the craft model can be found in the program at the University of Dayton, "Capturing and Releasing Teacher Thought" (Rowley & Hart, 1993). The program received the Distinguished Research Award for that year from the Association of Teacher Educators. Using scenarios and vignettes depicting the common problems faced by beginning teachers, a focus group of veteran teachers discussed their problem-solving strategies on videotape. The eight case studies were then presented to the beginners for dialog and discussion, with the findings indicating an improvement in a clinical attitude, thinking skills on the presented cases, and knowledge retention when compared to those preservice cohorts in the regular program. The expert knowledge, then, is transmitted to the beginner through the dialog method. Whether such a procedure has any effect on actual teacher performance would be the next step in the assessment of effectiveness, as well as the question of possible impact on other veteran but perhaps not exemplary teachers.

A general way to view the craft model is at an affective level. Overall humans are more comfortable with the ideas of subjectivity, intuition, and the dignity of each person. Theory and science (basic or applied) is usually viewed as cold and impersonal, reducing the human condition to a machine. Existential philosophers speak of the tree of life as green and growing, whereas theory is gray. Rogerian psychologists praise individualism and personal authenticity as fundamental to the human condition (Rogers, 1961). Quite naturally humans cheer for the underdog, the amateur, and the free-lancer and company to come up with new insights and new practice. It reaffirms our own sense of humanness and individuality. Compare that view at an affective level to the ideas of an applied science working slowly and ploddingly through successive approximations, which at times, may seem like the speed of a glacier. The first reaffirms spirit, optimism, and positive feelings. The latter seems tiresome and boring.

Career development of teachers in the craft model can be summed up succinctly, encourage and support teachers in their classroom tinkering. Grimmett and MacKinnon quote extensively from a life cycle study of teachers reported by Huberman (1991) to the effect that teachers denoted as positive focusers stayed within the boundaries of their own classrooms and tinkered (note that such teachers did not "experiment") and avoided all of the schoolwide innovations. "Tending one's private garden, pedagogically speaking, seems to have more payoff in the long haul than land reform" (Huberman, 1991, p. 183).

Variations of the Craft Model

In this section some of the recent attempts to create a quasi-craft model are outlined. In these examples there is usually an attempt to overcome the complete separation of university and/or applied science information for the continuous professional development of teachers.

Essential Schools Although Grimmett and MacKinnon provide a detailed account of Sizer's model, "The Coalition of Effective Schools," it does seem as if that model does not stand or fall as an exemplar of craft. Clearly Sizer himself as a former teacher, dean, and headmaster does not expect the teachers to discover or reinvent his principles (Sizer, 1992). In fact the opposite is the case. The teachers and districts who may be interested in the model carefully implement the basic tenets and must agree in advance to support those principles that represent a distillation of educational theory for school practice. At that point, however, the model shifts in focus. Teachers from school districts seeking to join the coalition often meet with their counterparts from participating schools to discuss procedures such as handling the expanded time periods, the portfolio assessment methods, and gaining community support. Thus the model really combines expert knowledge under Sizer's almost indefatigable energy and the wisdom of practice from the experienced teachers already involved in one of the network schools. As yet there is modest success in the ability of these schools to achieve their goals with estimates of about 20% to 25% of the schools that enter the coalition remaining as exemplars of the model. Given the scope of the enterprise, however, such an outcome may be understandable. Certainly there are very few, if any, examples of successful reform at the secondary level. To combine that effort with the equally important task of in-service teacher education is obviously an extremely complex problem. A careful examination will be needed in the near future to analyze the array of conditions that facilitate the implementation of the coalition model versus the opposite. Such an analysis might also reveal how in-service programs may be improved as well.

Autobiographical Case Study Another variation of the craft model is the case study approach to professional development. This is particularly true when cases are autobiographical, designed to organize and capture significant reflections of preservice or in-service teachers. Such an approach stands in contrast to those designed to compare and contrast lived experience with general principles, research findings, and theories that originate at the university. Sykes and Bird (1992) describe narrative knowing as a unique type of case that heavily relies on the notion of craft knowledge. Whereas some cases promote "strategic understanding" (Shulman, 1986), the wise application of specific principles and theories to the world of practice, "the narrative mode deals in good stories, stirring drama, and richly portrayed historical accounts" (Sykes & Bird, 1992, p. 473). To date, too little systematic study has explored narrative cases and their role in professional development. A brief review has been done by Connelly and Clandinin (1990), and Carter (1990), in a provocative chapter on teacher knowledge, examines narrative as a form of personal practical knowledge. But much work still needs to be done. This may be why Sykes and Bird (1992) direct a significant amount of their review of the case method to approaches that rely less on the narrative approach and more on the blending of theory, research, and practice. Their exploration of the case approach rests against a backdrop of the challenges facing teacher educators and staff developers hoping to employ the approach. For example,

Much evidence amply documents that novice teachers have faulty, incomplete, biased, or limited knowledge about the subjects they will teach, the pedagogies involved, the nature of knowledge and of learning, the nature of teaching as role and activity, and the nature of the learners they will encounter. (Sykes & Bird, 1992, pp. 490–491)

Sykes and Bird conclude that the narrative case approach will have few implications for teacher education and teacher professional development if the tacit knowledge cannot be made explicit and/or tested for validity and applicability. Kathy Carter (1993) completes the brushstroke by cautioning teacher educators and teachers that, in the extreme, teachers' voice in their narratives is given an authenticity that is simply unwarranted. Because teachers are not privileged authors with direct access to truth, making such a claim of teachers' personal knowledge invites confusion.

Although not limited exclusively to the autobiographical/qualitative approach, the work of Goodson (1992) represents a clear example of this framework for teacher development. The Goodson view is strongly embedded in the craft model. In particular, there is constant and almost vituperative criticism of the academy, the university, and behavioral science research. All such theoretical and research efforts are characterized by Goodson as superficial and worthless. "Researchers even when they had stopped treating the teacher as a numerical aggregate, historical footnote or unproblematic role incumbent still treated teachers as interchangeable types unchanged by circumstance or time" (p. 4). Goodson proposes what has now become almost a cliché, to focus on the existential self of teachers and to help them tell their "stories" through interviews. Subjectivity and context become the relevant foci. The researcher is to become a catalyst and listener to elicit the voice of a teacher in constructing a collaborative autobiography because any other approach only serves the interests of the academy and demeans the teacher. "The goal is to know, to listen to, and to speak with the teacher" (p. 234).

The Goodson model is based on phenomenology and is remarkably similar to the early work in humanistic psychology (Rogers, 1961) as a philosophical system. As such, it also shares the same weaknesses of attempting to replace an extensive knowledge base in both theory and practice of teacher development stages, phases, and levels of cognitive complexity with a celebration of individual dignity, subjectivity, and authenticity. The difficulty is stark. Abandon any and all means of quantitative assessment. Join with teachers in an existential moment and become a therapeutic agent to free them from the constraints imposed by the educational establishment. How this is to come about is somewhat obscure, but how we are to know the effects is nearly impossible to discern, unless we simply accept such stories on face value. As a result, the movement appears as an educational ideology and clearly suffers from all the shortcomings of such a framework. While the humanistic/existential

model for counseling gradually eroded in the face of substantial behavioral science research, the same fate may befall the current efforts to rely exclusively on subjectivity, phenomenology, and qualitative accounts.

A less strident qualitative approach can be found in the work of Bullough and Stokes (1994). Their work in fact may be the next step in the life history model. They reported the results from an analysis of personal teaching metaphors employed by a small sample of secondary education students. The goal of the study was to focus on teacher beliefs and self-development through narrative. By listening to teacher voice through metaphors, the approach would then identify common group themes and those that were idiosyncratic. The themes of change, loss of innocence, and rhythm represented the major categories from the life histories. From a development standpoint, however, the authors reported four subsamples in cognitive ability to understand and employ personal metaphors in reference to teaching: (1) Never got it ($N = 3$); (2) got it, but did not like it ($N = 3$); (3) went along, but did not work up a sweat ($N = 7$); and (4) got it and used it ($N = 9$). Although there was no formal assessment of cognitive complexity, it does seem reasonable to view the taxonomy from a cognitive complexity framework. The teacher voice through metaphor then actually may become an index of differentiation. Some secondary education students may benefit substantially from such discussions and reflection. Others apparently either miss the point or become uncomfortable with such a level of personal abstraction. The study appears to be the first of the new wave of qualitative investigations that goes beyond an elaboration of individual themes. The authors not only listened to their subjects but also stepped back and in a grass-roots sense clustered the themes according to levels of complexity. This also may be a first step in suggesting a differential use for personal history and metaphor as an educational strategy.

School-Based Management Teams Yet another exemplar of the craft model draws from the emergence of school-based management teams. Proposals for the restructuring of schools were initiated when various state legislatures found that their teacher performance appraisal programs were not changing teachers or student outcomes. On its heels, legislatures decided to shift from mandating careful expectations about teacher performance to, at least at first glance, "mandating" greater teacher control over how the school is to be managed. Newmann (1993) argues that this movement to restructure education through initiatives like school-based governance and management largely rests on a foundation of common sense and wisdom of experience. Why should school-based governance and management be expected to promote professional development or improve education for students? The movement rests on an implicit assumption that this type of staff development and professional reorganization will "increase either the commitment or the competence of teachers and students" (Newmann, 1993, p. 4). Unfortunately, new structures like school-based management teams without purpose and applied theory run the risk of wandering between the cosmic and the trivial without understanding the difference. Restructuring initiatives like school-based management and governance are a necessary but not sufficient condition for lasting teacher professional development. This point is underscored in a study of restructuring and school-based decision making in 12 schools conducted by Lieberman, Darling-Hammond, and Zuckerman (1991). The study illustrates the persistence of conflict, the difficulties of changing teachers' roles, and the necessity of integrating content with process.

School-based management and governance draw from three beliefs: (1) individual schools should have autonomy from district and state regulations in basic decisions on curriculum, hiring, and budget; (2) teachers, administrators, and parents should share decision-making authority and governance; and (3) there should be more opportunity for teachers to plan and work together. A common approach to this form of professional development is to create a smaller leadership team made up of experienced teachers, administrators, support staff, and, in selected cases, parents, to guide the direction of the school. The assumption is that the school-based management structure will utilize the accumulated wisdom and craft knowledge of the team to guide the school. Newmann argues, however, that such decentralization efforts should not be expected to enhance teacher commitment (Newmann, 1993).

What is needed for this particular form of teacher professional development is the acquisition of a particular domain of competencies and a shared set of commitments to guide practice (Newmann, 1993). Relying on the wisdom of experience and/or changed structures will only lead to disillusionment and cynicism. Instead, Newmann suggests that such professional development efforts, if they are to be successful, must employ substantive curriculum and instruction aimed more toward depth of understanding; promote success for all students; initiate complex new roles for teachers with concomitant extended preparation that substantially departs from the familiar role of pedagogue within a self-contained classroom; and a renewed commitment to promoting schools and staff development that engenders caring, empathy, and more principled behavior.

The Teacher Center A final example of the craft model is the teacher center, and perhaps the best recent summary of teacher centers has been constructed by Yarger (1990). What tied the Teacher Centers Program to the craft model was its chief principle of being responsive to teachers' self-determined needs. Federal legislation in 1976 supported the creation of 90 teacher centers throughout the United States. Each center was managed by a policy board and practicing elementary, secondary, and special education teachers constituted a majority of each policy board. These teachers were selected by popular vote or by bargaining agent, and they had supervisory powers over the teacher center projects. These policy boards, although they worked well as managers of the centers, probably did not produce any qualitatively new in-service patterns. To support this point, Yarger compared the teacher center programs with other federally sponsored in-service and professional development programs. In particular, a comparison was made with the Rand Change Agent Study (Berman & McLaughlin, 1976). In general Yarger found congruence on all 13 dimensions of in-service education, such as in-service activities directed at teacher-identified needs, small-group programming, use of teachers as in-service agents, voluntary involvement, and emphasis on local materials development.

The teacher centers were notable for a number of reasons. On the whole they offered highly focused, brief in-service, typically lasting a day or less. Another characteristic of the teacher centers was their ability to serve individual as well as group needs. According to Yarger, a typical center served slightly more than 1,700 teachers in small group activities and nearly 2,300 teachers per year individually. Teacher centers also provided materials and resources such as professional release time so that teachers could participate in in-service during the school day. In his summary, Yarger submits that

Perhaps the most distinctive contribution is the cadre of staff development professionals that developed over the three-year life of the program. As a group they were clearly different, being dedicated almost completely to the betterment of teaching through sensitive support of their colleagues. (p. 112)

Teacher centers are reemerging. New York, for example, has funded 75 teacher centers through the state (Wenz, 1987). Other states and local school districts have begun to follow suit. For example, the Schenley High School Teacher Center in Pittsburgh, Pennsylvania, has developed a structure for housing a teacher center as a comprehensive high school. Teachers come in groups of 48 for 8 weeks at a time. These "visiting" teachers have fully certified replacement teachers that cover home-school classrooms. The goals of the 8-week residency are to:

(a) refine and expand instructional skills; (b) increase sensitivity to adolescents and the culture of youth; (c) update knowledge in specific content areas; (d) disseminate knowledge about district-wide educational improvement initiatives; (e) provide opportunities for personal and professional enrichment; and (f) encourage the development of individualized follow-through plans for continued professional growth. (Bickel et al., 1987, pp. 9–10)

To facilitate these goals the center was "overstaffed" by 20%. This additional staffing permitted 24 resident faculty to be designated as clinical teachers (CRTs) who teach three 45-minute periods per day as compared to the norm of five periods. The remainder of their day is dedicated to collegial planning, demonstration teaching, observations, and feedback conferences. Clinical teachers receive special preparation during the summer. In addition, they receive 12 hours of in-service per semester. The program has conducted sustained evaluation through classroom observations, interviews, and questionnaires. In general it finds that visiting teachers (VTs) implement new skills and value the collegial process. In addition, the CRTs improve their teaching and feel revitalized by their new role. Perhaps the major limitation of the model is the difficulty with follow-up. The program's structure does not provide a way for CRTs to support VTs in their home schools to ensure that new skills have transferred. Later we elaborate on new ways that teachers are being prepared for work as school-based teacher educators.

Teacher Renewal Recently, the regional teacher center emerged (Oldendorf, 1992). The North Carolina Center for the Advancement of Teaching (NCCAT) is the first statewide program of its kind in the nation. The center offers residential weeklong seminars for career teachers that are interdisciplinary and emphasize creativity and intellectual stimulation. The seminars are conducted by experts in a given field and tend to focus on aesthetic and sensory expression for teacher renewal. A sampling of topics includes Appalachian Spring; Founding Documents; Carl Sandburg's America; Living and Singing the Blues; Artistry in Literature and Film; The Child as Hero; and India: Contemporary Conflict in an Ancient Setting.

Perhaps as important, teachers are given the "royal" treatment while they are in residence. Private fully furnished rooms are provided; travel expenses and seminar expenses are paid; and the cost of having a substitute teacher is paid for participants. Like teacher centers, NCCAT offers seminars that are brief and episodic. However, a clear strand in all the weeklong seminars is discourse about the moral and ethical dimensions of teachers' work. A testimony to the center's popularity is its spread to other states. Both Florida and Minnesota plan to develop a residential center for teacher renewal very similar to NCCAT.

Program evaluation is nascent at best. An external alumni survey was conducted by the Educational Research and Development Center at the University of West Florida (1992). More than 3,480 NCCAT alumni were sent surveys. Of the surveys mailed, 2,011 (57.8%) were returned. In general, teachers responded that NCCAT renewed their interest and commitment to teaching (87.3%) and strengthened or enriched subject matter in the classroom (81.74%).

Such survey research, however, can only be considered as a positive trend. If such experiences are not directly connected to career performance and follow-up, it is doubtful that more competent performance will ensue. The renewal programs as currently structured apparently ignore nearly all of the staff development tenets as outlined by Griffin in the introduction, and certainly more careful research is needed.

The Expert Model

In this section varieties on the use of expert teacher trainers are reviewed. The variations all share a similar set of assumptions. There is a core of information and skills that expert and professional teacher educators have developed. This knowledge base forms the framework for in-service programs within a variable time frame, such as short- or long-term workshops. There is also variation in the nature of the skills and processes to be acquired from a single discrete concrete activity such as a 5-second pause in questioning, to a comprehensive model for classroom management. In spite of such differences, however, the overall framework is that experienced teachers like beginners and/or student teachers need expert advice to improve practice.

Expert Knowledge: The Liberal Arts Model Almost at the opposite end of the continuum from the craft model based exclusively on teacher experience is the expert liberal arts framework. In this case the assumption is as direct as the craft model but from the other extreme. True education is liberal education, and it is assumed (actually in spite of the evidence to the contrary) that most teachers have only a superficial understanding of the liberal arts. Thus expert academicians without any

necessary experience or exposure to the professional aspects of teaching offer exposure to the older traditions to teachers in the form of short courses, summer workshops, or through a lecture series. Whether these activities may be delivered in a patronizing mode is not the real issue. Instead the idea is to develop an inquiring mind-set by the participants through academic expert knowledge. As one critic put it some years ago, it may be seen as a kind of crash course in civilization for the benefit of "nouveau arrivé."

A prime example of the model was described recently in an article in *The Key Reporter* (Five chapters sponsor, 1993). A number of local Phi Beta Kappa chapters sponsored weeklong workshops for area public school teachers. The Society's committee selected a number of prominent professors as presenters and the theme itself, "Chaos in Contemporary Thought and Letters." This included presentations in Western thought, mathematics, art, international relations, and on the future of chaos theory. The enterprise was described as a method of underscoring "The society's appreciation of instructional excellence at all levels of the national educational system" (Five chapters sponsor, 1993, p. 1).

At the highest level of abstraction, of course, the model assumes substantial gaps in a teacher's knowledge base and that the expert professor selects the area for educational growth. Also the aim is intellectual growth rather than any immediate connection to professional and/or career development. In fact, the liberal arts tradition if it assumes anything at all attempts to steer clear of anything that resembles vocationalism. Certainly Schön's critique (1983) argues that contemporary universities give privileged status to the tradition of expert knowledge. Also, as might be expected, there is very little in the way of assessment of impact beyond the usual subjective course evaluation at the end of the workshop or seminar. The liberal arts tradition does eschew the empirical, preferring to rely more on the global assumptions of intellectual inquiry through challenge, controversy, and an exposure to leading academic minds. These assumptions, of course, also may represent the major shortcomings of the model. The level of abstraction and the implicit assumptions (knowledge for knowledge's sake) may be so far removed from the teacher's activity that it may be another version of ships passing in the night.

An interesting new theory in any particular discipline may be quite esoteric to the teacher. Thus, the ideational base may be obscure. The instructional system, as well, might seem a mystery. The experts would have no particular insights on how to teach children and/or adolescents unless such professors attempted to generalize from their own college classrooms. However, this model is probably well entrenched in the minds of the academic professoriate in spite of the apparent weaknesses of the model. It represents a vivid example of the continued bifurcation between practice and reflection. Unfortunately, as we have come to see with growing clarity since the mid-1970s, the complexities and problems of real-world practice do not present themselves as neat and tidy reformulations of the humanities. Rather, the challenges are complex and ill-defined and require the teacher to construct meaning from a large melange of personal, school, and community factors.

The Process-Product Model This model, which reached its zenith in the 1970s and early 1980s, was best exemplified by the work of Good and Brophy (1984) and Good (1979). On an overall basis, a list of strategies has been developed by an expert. Usually such strategies are highly explicit, for example, how to greet students, how to praise, how to scan the room, how to move at a brisk and businesslike pace, how to review homework, how to state goals in behavioral terms, how to ask higher level questions, to name but a few of the most common. The trainer then sets up a variety of workshops to transmit the skill or skills to the selected experienced teachers. The information comes from outside the classroom and the rationale is simply that research has shown positive effects on student achievement from employing one or more of such strategies (Rosenshine, 1987, p. 90).

An important line of research in the process-product model was conducted by Gliessman, Pugh, Dowden, and Hutchins (1988). They conducted a metaanalysis of variables influencing the acquisition of explicit and generic teaching skills, in particular questioning skills. The variables identified through an analysis of 26 studies were classified under three general categories: (1) method of training, (2) characteristics of trainees, and (3) characteristics of the training setting. Methods of training included instruction and instruction/practice. Instruction-based approaches involved comprehension, demonstration, and analysis of the targeted skill, in this case questioning. Instruction/practice included opportunities for practice with feedback for the targeted skill. Trainee variables included the amount of academic background and of experience. Setting variables were identified as simplified (i.e., teaching a single topic within a limited time frame to a small group of students) versus unsimplified (i.e., conventional subject matter in a typical classroom setting).

With these variables in mind a number of hypotheses were formed. Among them were: (1) training based on instruction and practice results in significantly greater use of questioning skills than does training based on instruction alone, (2) more extended training time results in significantly greater use of the targeted skill, and (3) trainees who practice in simplified settings exhibit a significantly greater use of questioning skills than do trainees who practice in less simplified settings.

The results of this meta-analysis were somewhat of a surprise. Foremost and expected, the trained groups demonstrated a significant mean effect of 0.82. Thus, the major hypothesis that training results in a significant difference between the means of experimental and control groups was supported.

The hypothesis that training incorporating both instructional and practice methods (i.e., instruction/practice) results in a significantly greater mean effect size than training based on instructional methods alone (i.e., instruction) was not supported. Also the hypothesis concerning temporal variables, that more extended general and specific training times result in a significantly greater mean effect size, was not supported. A general training period of longer than 3 school weeks did not result in a significantly greater effect size (0.90) than the mean (0.75) for a period of 3 school weeks or less.

Several limitations suggest caution in the implications that might be drawn. The meta-analysis was restricted to (1) generic skills that are (2) assessed immediately or shortly following the training. Furthermore, the skills did not involve great complexity. Nonetheless,

It is worth noting that in the studies reviewed the median specific training time in instruction studies was only two hours, whereas the median general training was less than a day. In instruction/practice/ studies, in contrast, training consumed more than four times as many hours in specific training time (a median of eight and one half hours) and extended over many more times the number of days in general training time (a median of 20 school days) for no greater gain in skill. The least defensible procedure in terms of both effectiveness and efficiency may be extensive practice without instruction. (Gliessman et al., 1988, p. 40)

Because the programs are so explicit, the goals appear most likely as a type of fine-tuning of rudimentary skills. Because most of the process-product model is drawn from behavioral psychology, there is little consideration, if any, to a change in teacher cognitions or the cognitive developmental dispositions of the teachers in training. This is certainly true of the meta-analysis that was just reviewed. Instead, the assumption is linear and quantitative. Teach the skill as effectively as possible and the teacher will use the method. Certainly short-term research has shown that student achievement does improve, as Walberg's (1986) meta-analysis has documented. However, the long-term results are less sanguine. Richardson and Anders (1994) note that there is a real paucity of research on the follow-up effects of the process-product training. Certainly the best-known process-product model has been the Madeline Hunter approach, which includes a series of highly explicit steps in the classroom. Even though the training was comprehensive, expensive, and focused on a relatively small number of teachers, the results suggested extremely modest outcomes on student achievement. Even more of a concern, however, was the gradual erosion of the model in practice (Stallings & Krasavage, 1986). As a result there appears to be much less current interest in the process-product approach for teacher development. The model may be too singular in the materials and skills selected and perhaps too prescriptive, at least as transmitted by the trainers. Hunter has always maintained the need for teacher flexibility in how the methods are applied in the classroom, yet the training itself may not nurture nor encourage such teacher flexibility.

Expanding the Repertoire

This view of professional development has garnered much attention during the 1980s and is best exemplified by the work of Joyce and Showers (1988). In general the focus is less on highly explicit and discrete instructional strategies and more on the acquisition of comprehensive instructional models of teaching, like direct instruction (knowledge transmitter model), inductive inquiry, and interpersonal approaches to learning. A teaching model is a group of strategies that is logically consistent with a set of assumptions about how students learn best. In addition, most models include a rationale and in some, but not all, cases, a tested and defendable theory about how persons learn, grow, and develop. A number of programs incorporate this approach to training and perhaps the best exemplar is peer coaching.

Generally speaking, "fine-tuning" existing approaches to instruction is much different than learning or mastering alternative curriculum or new models of teaching. Joyce and Showers (1980) acknowledge that when fine-tuning is the goal, instruction with demonstration probably is sufficient. However, when complex models of teaching are being introduced, the Joyce and Showers (1980) analysis of more than 200 studies indicated that instruction, demonstration, practice with feedback, and coaching (in-class follow-up by a supportive adviser who helps a teacher correctly apply novel skills, curriculum, or models of teaching) are crucial.

In 1980 Joyce and Showers submitted five working hypotheses for teacher education and school-based staff development. The five hypotheses were framed as components for the effective acquisition of teaching models and included the following: (1) presentation of theory or description of the new strategy, (2) modeling or demonstration of skills or models of teaching, (3) practice in simulated and classroom settings, (4) structured and open-ended feedback, and (5) coaching for application (hands-on, in class assistance with the transfer of skills and strategies to the classroom). These components have been introduced to school systems via peer coaching and, in a few cases, have been empirically tested. In a peer-coaching program teachers are introduced to several new models of teaching. The format follows. Teachers are introduced to a new model like cooperative learning. Relevant research and theory are shared and demonstrations of the model are provided. In addition, teachers are provided with opportunities to practice the new strategy or model with feedback offered by facilitators. The coaching component is then initiated by having teams of two to four teachers who visit and observe their colleagues as they attempt to implement the new model. According to Joyce and Showers (1988), this final step is most important. Table 29.2 describes the effect of each of the components on knowledge, skill acquisition, and transfer to the classroom.

A number of important findings can be gleaned from the table. First, the gradual addition of training elements does not appear to impact transfer noticeably. However, a large effect size (1.68) occurs when in-class coaching is added to the initial training experience. If the transfer of significant new skills and/or models of teaching is the goal of professional development, training will need to be more extensive and in-class coaching will be needed (Joyce & Showers, 1995).

A limited number of studies have been conducted to test peer coaching empirically as well as the hypotheses generated by Joyce and Showers in their original work (1980). Sparks (1986) compared three groups who participated in different sets of training activities. Group I participated only in workshops. Group II participated in workshops and received the results of two classroom observations by a peer. Group III participated in the workshops and received two in-class coaching sessions from the trainer. Employing the Stallings Secondary Observation Instrument (SSOI) to measure teaching behavior, each teacher was observed three times to assess implementation of the effective use of time. Only Group II, which received the results of classroom observations from a peer, showed significant change. Because the peer observers were involved in the analysis and coding of teacher and student behavior, the experience may have helped them to analyze their own teaching more accurately and make more significant changes in their own teaching. Although tentative, the results of the study indicated that peer observation may be a more powerful training activity than trainer-provided coaching.

In Frieberg, Waxman, and Houston (1987) the results of different types of feedback were compared. Employing multiple measures of student teacher classroom performance, the study analyzed student teacher performances. The control group received the usual feedback from the cooperating teacher and university supervisor. Group II received the usual feedback as well as written behavioral data from three observations. The data were explained in a 1-hour seminar, but no additional training or coaching was given on how to transfer the data back into the classrooms. The experimental group (Group III) attended a series of three 2-hour seminars. In the seminars the behavioral data were shared, potential follow-up strategies were discussed, and there was peer discussion. Although there were no significant findings, the student teachers in the experimental group did improve their teaching in desired directions, whereas the feedback and control student teachers did not change their behaviors. Other studies of coaching principles include Buttery (1988) and Anderson and Roit (1993). Both studies employed quasi-experimental designs, and in both cases, the experimental group that received peer coaching and feedback showed significant gains in use of the predetermined innovation.

Other studies are available, but most rely on anecdotal information as the major form of assessment. Clearly there are a limited number of studies with methodologically strong designs.

TABLE 29.2. Effect Sizes for Training Outcomes by Training Component

Training Components and Combinations	Knowledge	Skill	Transfer of Training
Information	0.63	0.35	0.00
Theory	0.15	0.50	0.00
Demonstration	1.65	0.26	0.00
Theory/demonstration	0.66	0.86	0.00
Theory/demonstration/practice		0.72	0.00
Theory/demonstration/ practice/feedback	1.31	1.18	0.39
All of the above and coaching	2.71	1.25	1.68

Source: Student achievement through staff development by Bruce Joyce and Beverly Showers. Copyright © 1988 by Longman Publishers USA. White Plains, NY: Longman (p. 81).

And too few of the studies examine all levels of impact for individuals in a peer-coaching program. Continued research needs to be conducted to address systematically how the peer-coaching model affects the transfer of learning. Nonetheless, there is a growing consensus that coaching makes a difference in acquisition of complex models of instruction. Two examples of researched models of instruction follow.

Higher-Order Thinking Perhaps no topic in professional development literature has garnered more recent attention than higher-order thinking. Since the 1980s research on teaching gradually has shifted from instruction of basic skills toward teaching for higher-order thinking (Bereiter & Scardamalia, 1987; Newmann, 1993). Further, the Association of Supervision and Curriculum Development (ASCD) has dedicated itself to supporting curriculum development and staff development on higher-order thinking. *Developing Minds: A Resource Book for Teaching Thinking* (Costa, 1991) is the culmination of this organization's work on the topic. Unfortunately, to the extent that teaching for higher-order thinking is manifest, evidence suggests that it occurs more often in high-track classes (Page, 1990).

Researchers have continued to search for better understandings of the conditions that promote higher-order thinking. Two recent studies, using different research designs with preservice and in-service teachers, exemplify current attempts better to understand the conditions that foster higher-order thinking. Raudenbush, Rowan, and Cheong (1993) observed variations among teachers' emphases on higher-order thinking. Their study relied on self-reports of emphasis on teaching for higher-order goals. The sample included 303 teachers in 16 diverse school settings. Subject-matter emphases included mathematics, science, social studies, writing, and literature. Probably the most prominent result of the study was the link between track and emphasis on higher-order objectives. This link was highly significant statistically across all the disciplines.

Although there is plenty of evidence for rejecting the contention that higher-order objectives are less appropriate for low-track classes, the self-report study offered evidence that teachers disagree.

If promoting higher-order thinking is a priority for all students, teacher educators, staff development specialists, school-based teacher leaders, and policymakers must recognize the formidable institutional obstacles that confront them. Because the results showed large between-teacher and between-school variation in English and social studies, the investigators call for "better theories and measures to understand how teacher and school differences influence the pursuit of teaching for higher-order thinking" (Raudenbush et al., 1995, p. 550).

A provocative study by Fennema, Franke, Carpenter, and Carey (1993) described how one teacher used knowledge of childrens' thinking in instructional decision making. The teacher selected for the case study, when compared with other teachers who were involved in formal observations, listened more to the children as they reported their thinking, ranked high in questioning children about their thinking, offered multiple complex explanations for instructional decisions that were based on student thinking, and expected multiple solution strategies at a higher level than most of the other teachers observed by the investigators.

The study, situated in the Cognitively Guided Instruction (CGI) line of inquiry, describes the teacher's mathematics curriculum, the expectations the teacher had for the children, and the way the classroom was structured to assist the teacher in assessment of the first-grade students' thinking and knowledge. An ambitious data collection occurred over 4 years. During the first year, general information was obtained, a structured interview was conducted to ascertain knowledge of childrens' knowledge, a semi-structured interview was initiated to ascertain beliefs related to the teacher's cognitive perspective, and the CGI belief instrument was employed. During the second year, the teacher participated in an experimental study that included more than 20 classroom observations. In the third year (the case study year), the teacher participated in group discussions, numerous individual interviews, and more than 60 classroom observations. In the fourth year, the teacher participated in numerous interviews throughout the year and was formally assessed.

Two significant themes emerged from the study. Foremost was the observation that research-based knowledge about childrens' thinking was important to the teacher. It enabled the teacher to structure teaching so that children could learn more than any group of children the teacher had taught previously. The CGI knowledge enabled the teacher to understand the complexity of thinking of the students, which in turn, led to more student thinking and learning. The authors point out that teacher adoption of curriculum and instruction innovations does not depend on student outcomes; rather, it is interactive with student outcomes. When teacher use of an innovation leads to more student learning, the teacher will enlarge the use of the innovation. For this reason, the theory and understanding of the Concerns Based Adoption Model may need to look more carefully at intervention research that encourages shifts in concerns from self and task to student. Obviously teachers involved with an intervention like CGI need to be student focused if they are going to be successful with the innovation.

The second important theme of the study relates to the teacher. The CGI curriculum is organized in well-defined levels of difficulty so that students can be matched and mismatched accordingly. The assumption is that the teacher chooses a problem at a slightly more complex level when the student is ready, thereby moving the student through the levels of the mathematics curriculum in small steps. The teacher was able effectively to pose problems and assess the childrens' abilities, and the teacher was able to employ the research-based knowledge in a less hierarchical and more expansive fashion than was anticipated by the investigators. Rather than use the framework as a strict template for instructional decisions, the teacher used the framework flexibly and more intensively, ultimately raising her own expectations of what the students could do and solve. The researchers acknowledge that the characteristics of the teacher were quite unique and similar to descriptions of conceptual complexity identified by Miller (1981). Most important, the study expands our understanding of the crucial relationship between teacher characteristics and student higher-order thinking and problem solving.

Two leading exponents of higher-order thinking are Costa (1991) and Marzano (1992). Through the sponsorship of the Association for Supervision and Curriculum Development, both authors have prepared resources and conducted workshops for teachers, principals, teacher educators, and staff development specialists interested in teaching higher-order thinking as an integrated component of instruction. In fact, Costa has edited an eclectic volume called *Developing Minds: A Resource Book for Teaching Thinking* (1991). The resource book offers multiple perspectives and multiple curricula purported to develop students' thinking abilities and to enhance teachers' instructional strategies. Readers or workshop participants are encouraged to use or adapt the ideas, to gather additional resources, and to see the curricula as incomplete and successive approximations.

The curricula draw on an extraordinarily diverse array of educators that includes linguists, curriculum specialists, cognitive psychologists, and philosophers. Each contributor offers his or her own spin to the need to address higher-order thinking, and no less than 29 programs are described in *Developing Minds: Programs for Teaching Thinking* (Costa, 1991). Examples include Guilford and Meeker's Structure of Intellect (SOI) model, Marzano's Tactics for Thinking, Sternberg's Triarchic Program for Training Intellectual Skills, Lipman's Philosophy for Children, and Parnes's Creative Problem Solving. In each case the volume overviews the model, identifies the audience for whom the program is intended, addresses the theoretical and/or philosophical assumptions on which the model is based, provides any research or evidence of the program's success in achieving its goals, and identifies contacts for further information. Preparation to use the varied frameworks varies from a few hours to 2 to 3 hours per week over a 2- to 3-year period with in-class coaching. But perhaps the most important critique is that most of the programs have not been carefully evaluated and most of the programs lack consistent research data about the outcomes for preservice teachers and in-service teachers and the students.

A second model of instruction that has garnered attention is called Cognitively Guided Instruction and is now described.

Cognitively Guided Instruction (CGI) The recent work of Penelope Peterson and her colleagues at both Wisconsin and Michigan State represents a further departure from the process-product approach to teacher development through expert training. Their research findings while still emergent suggest some valuable and perhaps even provocative directions for teacher development. Two studies are particularly representative of their current positions.

In Peterson et al. (1989) the results compared teaching performance student achievement in mathematics between two groups of experienced first-grade teachers. Employing an elaborate set of multiple measures of teacher beliefs (interviews, questionnaires, content knowledge), they could classify the teachers' cognitive/conceptual complexity into two general modes, less cognitively based (LCB) and more cognitively based (CB). The actual teaching performance of the two groups was substantially different. The CB group employed higher-order teaching skills, such as problem posing, active listening, ongoing assessment, and continuous adaptation. The LCB group exhibited an opposite set of rigid, fact-based, rote approaches to instruction. The results for student achievement cut two ways. Both sets of students in LCB and CB classrooms did equally well on number facts achievement tests, but the students in the

CB classes also did much better on problem-solving tests. These findings, although they come from only one study, are in fact remarkably consistent with the huge number of research studies in the 1960s and 1970s employing the Hunt Conceptual System Test and both teaching performance and student achievement. Miller's (1981) metaanalysis indicated quite clearly that teachers rated as more cognitively (high CL) complex performed in a manner similar to the first-grade teachers classified as CB. Also the description of CB teachers reported by the Peterson study is similar to Hunt's earlier descriptions of teachers who "reach and flex" in their instruction (Hunt, 1974). This indicates that the Peterson study can be considered as having greater implications than would ordinarily be the case from one study. Essentially this work indicates the importance of teacher cognitive complexity as an important construct in teacher performance.

The second study (Knapp & Peterson, 1991) provides further insight as to teacher cognitions. Whereas the first study noted was a standard comparison study between two groups of teachers (LCBs and CBs), the second study was a longitudinal (4-year) investigation of a teacher training program in CGI. In short, if the level of cognition, low versus high, makes a difference in classroom learning, can the independent variable (CB) become the object of an intervention program, that is, the dependent variable? With a group of 20 elementary teachers, the researchers created an intervention sequence designed to promote the use of CGI in first-grade mathematics through a month-long summer school workshop. Assessments were conducted 3 years later and focused on the teachers' beliefs and classroom performance. Employing a combination of qualitative and quantitative indices, the 20 teachers were classified into three groups. Group 1 ($N = 8$) continued to understand and employ CGI as intended; Groups 2 and 3 ($N = 4$ and 6, respectively), however, failed to implement the program either completely or in significant aspects (2 of the 20 teachers could not be accurately classified). The researchers also found that the teachers in Group 1 were affected by the CBI process. Their teaching became more interactive, "As teachers began using some of CGI ideas in their teaching, they saw their students solve complex problems and listened to them using sophisticated mathematical thinking. This, in turn, encouraged them to give their students more opportunities" (Knapp & Peterson, 1991, p. 11). Although their conclusions are appropriately and carefully drawn, the results do suggest that whether or not CGI works depends on the cognitive complexity of the teacher. Finally, they also consider the problem of in-service teacher education most broadly. Would extended coaching or other forms of follow-up instruction have helped the teachers in Groups 2 and 3 to adapt more successfully? Or would a higher structure and greater prescriptiveness in the program itself have made the instruction more effective for those teachers? Again Hunt (1974) had found the importance of high structure for students at low levels of cognitive complexity and Thies-Sprinthall (1980) found the same outcome for in-service teachers. Similarly, McKibbin and Joyce (1981) in a study much like the Knapp and Peterson (1991) research, investigated the ability of elementary school teachers to employ innovative workshop techniques in their own classes 1 year after the intervention. The results are remarkably similar. The teachers assessed at higher levels of cognitive complexity (Maslow's index) were the only ones who genuinely continued to employ the innovations. Their "low group" had characteristics that paralleled the LCB or Group 3 teachers in the Knapp and Peterson review.

A third finding of interest is the effects of CGI on the CB teachers. As noted, Frances Fuller's research had shown a pattern of concerns that she applied to student teachers but that Gene Hall and colleagues (1990) have shown can be applied to any educational innovation. Knapp and Peterson presented an innovation to experienced teachers. The CB teachers at least implicitly (an inference drawn from their statements) were able to "travel" through all the phases includinig the highest level of adapting and refocusing. There is some other research evidence (Herring, 1989; Paisley, 1990) that preservice and in-service teachers/counselors assessed at more complex levels of cognitive complexity move further on the CBAM scale than their less complex cohorts. Thus, another important question arises as to the relation between CBAM concerns as factors affecting the ability to adopt and adapt innovations and the level of the teachers.

CGI then can be considered as an early point of development with implications for teacher development programs. Important basic research has started, although it is focused mostly in one content area and covers a narrow range of grade levels. However, it clearly suggests that teacher cognitions are very important as regulators of the ability to use innovations. The research also has at least very significant indirect connections to a large body of early research focused on cognitive complexity and research on the phases of concern. Now it is clearly time to experiment with a variety of in-service approaches designed to promote the cognitive base that teachers employ not only in daily decision making but also in how they adapt instruction to the needs of the pupils. A final point on this research is in order. Gage (1978) has suggested that general indirect teaching strategies were mostly effective in secondary schools. As a partial result of that finding and the results from the process-product research on direct instruction, there has been an implicit view that a high-structure, teach-the-facts approach is the model for early grades. The research of Peterson and her colleagues, however, raises serious questions about that view, even in the case of first-grade students learning how to add. This also is a reminder of how interactive the entire enterprise really is among teaching, learning, and teacher education. These themes will be picked up again in the section on the cognitive developmental model for teacher education.

THE INTERACTIVE MODELS

This section reviews the interactive models for teacher development. The assumptions are drawn from the basic cognitive and cognitive developmental research from children, adolescents, college students, and now applied to adults. Learning that impacts cognitive structure and promotes more complex cognitions requires the active participation of the learner (Anderson, 1990; Piaget, 1972; Vygotsky, 1978). The interactive models all seek to engage the teacher as an active participant in the learning process.

The Practical Argument Staff Development

Virginia Richardson (1994) has created a format for interactive or collaborative teacher development in her somewhat oddly titled practical argument staff development (PASD) program. There is a heavy emphasis on discourse analysis between her corps of staff developers and the experienced teachers in the project. The goals of the project were also broad, including a change in teacher *beliefs* about reading instruction, a change in *instructional* strategies, and a change in the level of *discourse* from both the teachers and the staff developers. The teachers were in grades 4–6, and the staff included Richardson and her colleague Patricia Anders from the University of Arizona. The major problem to overcome in this model is the built-in barrier to equality of participation, colleagueship, co-investigation, and the teacher–learner principle. Richardson (1994) found that there were two dimensions of difficulty, the difficulty that any teacher has in seeing him- or herself on equal footing with a professor and a broader problem in the school context, that is, how the program participants were viewed by the rest of the school staff.

These questions were of great significance as the project goal was to consolidate a developer–teacher coequal status. As a result, the developer had to walk a very fine line to stay away from the teachers' initial desire to receive expert advice. As a result, they employed a low-key, "self-effacing" strategy from Paulo Freire (1983) to break the set and slowly to rebuild the ratio of their teacher-to-teacher talk to greater equality. In another sense this group's leadership style seems close to a Rogerian approach (teacher centered) with strong overtones of a Brunerian inductive discussion strategy. There is an imbalance in the procedure, since only the teachers presented their videotapes for discourse. A dilemma here is clearly obvious. Should not all undergo the same analysis of practice if we are all teacher-learners? However, might such an activity simply reinforce the difference between university experts and teachers because the developers wanted to avoid any connotation of imparting new practice? The asymmetrical relationship is certainly a major difficulty endemic with such a collaborative model. It also was clear on the basis of an analysis of the pretest beliefs and teaching performance that many of the teachers were far from ideal in either area. Thus, equality was not and could not be the starting point for shared professional competence.

The results of the PASD study were presented in somewhat nontraditional terms given the format of the program. The developer and teacher observed a video, and then the developer would ask for reasons with the teacher then providing a "practical argument" as a rationale. These "arguments" would be explored by the developer in the role of a "critical friend." Thus, one outcome was to assess the change in complexity of the teacher's reasons from such extended discourse. One main result was a shift toward more child-centered beliefs versus the skills/word model of reading instruction. A second result was a parallel behavior change in general methods to include prereading, the use of literature, and dynamic assessment versus reliance on the basal reader. Finally, there was qualitative evidence of an increase in teachers' feelings of empowerment. This latter finding might be attributable to the discourse analysis, which showed a marked shift in "talk" between developer and teacher during the framing, reframing, and second episodes of practical arguments. This could indicate that the developers were successful in eluding the expert expectation assumptions through skillful questioning.

Although no formal control was used and the teachers were volunteers, a subset comparison was made to validate one of the major assumptions, the relation between teacher belief and instructional strategies. In the Reading Instructional Study (RIS) the results indicated some differences in reading achievement (locally measured) in favor of the PASD teachers versus teachers in a comparison school.

Probably the most important conclusion from this one rather small-size but intensive study was (1) the significance of teacher beliefs and classroom performance, and (2) the critical nature of setting up and carrying out of a collaborative model. However, there is certainly a huge literature that already documents the first assumption (Miller, 1981), but how to create the second is more problematic. Richardson mentions over and again how difficult it was to overcome the initial differences in viewpoints. It obviously requires very substantial tact to create a working relationship that moves toward collaboration.

The Teacher in Residence Partnership Program

Originated by Buttery, Henson, Ingram, and Smith (1985), the Teacher in Residence (TIR) program was created as another means of collaboration between the university and local school districts for teacher education. Outstanding elementary school teachers were selected on the basis of experience with an advanced degree, tenure, and enthusiasm. Two-year appointments were entitled TIR Fellows, with responsibilities similar to those of an adjunct or visiting professor. This means that such experienced school teachers would have direct instructional responsibility for undergraduate teacher education. The overall purpose was to infuse the undergraduate program with significant practitioner input and to offer experienced teachers a new role as a teacher educator. Subjective comments indicated support for both these goals.

A more extensive qualitative account of program effects are reported by Kagan, Dennis, Igon, Moore, and Sparks (1993) and Kagan, Freeman, Horton, and Roundtree (1993). Rather than attempt a formal evaluation, the program effects are reported as selected excerpts of dialog by the participants. The interview data indicated to the first author (Kagan) that the TIR experience was positive in clarifying what, "Seasoned practitioners had always known and believed about their craft" (Kagan, Dennis, et al., 1993, p. 439). Her notes indicated that the teachers were affected subtly, learned about the university culture, clarified their professional identities, and expanded their role repertoire in the classroom. Also noteworthy was the effect of the program on the university faculty, described vividly, as shown by the folllowing:

Dona suddenly realized how sensitive and private the material was and how fully Charlotte [the TIR] was trusting her to help her express it in a constructive way. . . . Dona and Barbara had apparently touched lives in ways they had never intended. They wonder if every school-university partnership has the potential to affect teachers' lives so profoundly, and they find the possibility intimidating. (Kagan, Freeman, et al., 1993, p. 508)

Reading such a narrative does suggest a model quite similar to a system of ego counseling proposed some years ago by Mosher and Purpel (1972). The focus of that model was heavily inductive and experiential, toward the person as well as the professional role. Kagan's use of the interview, narrative, and discussions with the TIRs is certainly a parallel in terms of intensity. At the same time the Kagan method does seem to beg one very obvious question, the assumption that experienced teachers are in fact ready to assume university roles as teachers and supervisors. Actually, because the TIRs for the most part had advanced degrees the teaching competence question might be moot, but the supervision question certainly remains, particularly in light of Kagan's (1988) review. At that time she called for the creation of a systematic and collaborative research initiative for supervision and suggested that such an effort at least start by building on the extensive knowledge base from counselors-in-training. That research, as well as early research by Thies-Sprinthall (1980), suggests quite clearly that the cognitive developmental level or the level of social cognition of the supervisor is a major consideration in supervisor behavior. Thus, a program for teacher development that includes the new role of supervisor would seem an ideal place for systematic instruction and research in the supervision process. A broader evaluative framework beyond the selective teacher narratives will also be requisite to establish the validity of the TIR model; otherwise it may remain an interesting, yet highly idiosyncratic, method of teacher development.

Teacher as Reflective Practitioner

Another attempt at interactive teacher professional development comes from the "reflection movement." Teacher educators have been caught up in what Smyth (1992) calls an "inexplicable wave of enthusiasm" (p. 268) for reflective approaches. Fifty years after Dewey's seminal differentiation between "routine action" (action that takes the definition of social reality for granted) and "reflective action" ("active, persistent and careful consideration of any belief or supposed form of knowledge in light of the grounds that support it and the further consequences to which it leads" [Dewey, 1933, p. 9]), the preservice and in-service teacher education literature abounds with descriptions of reflective thinking as a crucial process for teacher professional growth. The resurgence of interest can be linked to three bodies of inquiry that have emerged in the late 1970s and throughout the 1980s.

The first comes from the work of Schön. Most would agree that Schön's two books *The Reflective Practitioner* (1983) and *Educating the Reflective Practitioner* (1987) had a significant effect on mainstream educator thinking about reflection. As it turns out, both volumes are an outgrowth of Schön's doctoral dissertation on John Dewey's theory of inquiry. In his first book Schön argues for a new epistemology of practice where professional growth, competence, and artistry are framed by an individual's ability to reflect-in-action (thinking what they are doing while they are doing it), a contemporary version of Dewey's reflective action. But the question of how to promote this new kind of epistemology of practice was left unanswered until the second volume. Looking at professional schools such as architecture, music, and counseling institutions, he explored how "coaching" or guided reflection is the mainstay of these professional programs. The dialog between the coach and the student in a reflective practicum is, he argues, a needed exemplar for a new epistemology of practice. Yet, few studies exist in the Schön genre. Only MacKinnon (1987), working with preservice teachers, developed a set of criteria for detecting Schön's reflection-in-action during student teachers' supervisory conferences.

The second important line of inquiry that has contributed to interest in teacher thinking and reflection has been the work of cognitive developmentalists. They have carefully worked in field settings to describe how human beings construct meaning from experience across a series of interdependent domains (i.e., conceptual, ego, epistemological, moral/ethical, and reflective judgment). Theorists such as Erikson (1982), Hunt (1974), King and Kitchener (1994), Loevinger (1976), Perry (1975), and Piaget (1972) describe the fundamental cognitive and affective processes that children, adolescents, and adults employ as they construct meaning from experience.

Three central components of the developmental perspective are particularly relevant to the reflection literature. First, Piaget's concept of equilibration has great explanatory potential for the reflection process. How persons accommodate to new perspectives and/or assimilate unfamiliar or indeterminate ideas and experiences circumscribes what Schön calls reflection-in-action. Second, young adults have qualitatively different capacities for reflection depending on their "current" stage of development. Third, reflection is most crucial when it occurs in the crucible of action (Friere, 1983; Mead, 1934; Reiman & Parramore, 1993; Sprinthall, Reiman, & Thies-Sprinthall, 1993).

Most studies in this genre support the general finding that human beings have an intrinsic need to be professionally and personally competent, and that competence will grow through qualitatively distinct stages when there is positive interaction in a supportive environment (White, 1959). The studies also show, and this point is an important one, that prospective teachers as well as experienced teachers will vary in their capacity and "willingness" to engage in reflection. Concrete teachers at conformity levels will, in all likelihood, be opposed to any "coaching" or "guided reflection" that encourages them to link theory with practice. An abstract teacher at the autonomous level will be open to Schön's "indeterminate zones of practice" (Schön, 1987, p. 6). The ability or inability to engage in reflection is not, however, a permanent classification for teachers. Rather it is their current preferred system of solving complex human helping problems. How to promote growth to more complex stages is addressed shortly.

The third body of literature comes from the information-processing line of inquiry. Cognitive theorists, using the computer as their basic model and E. C. Tolman as their ancestral hero, have developed a theory of learning and memory called information processing. They have addressed such issues as the organization of thinking, the role of meaning in learn-

ing, and cognitive strategies in problem solving. A torrent of studies from laboratory research have firmly established the information-processing model. The linkage to reflection is fairly direct. For example, a number of educational psychologists such as Berliner (1986) have begun to examine differences in how beginning teachers and experienced teachers practice their profession. Their work draws heavily on information processing, describing how the cumulative experiences of teaching allow expert teachers to cluster understandings of the teaching/learning process and to retrieve information more quickly. In this model Dewey's reflective action might be defined as one's ability to retrieve information quickly and relate it to new knowledge. And studies have proven that retrieval can be facilitated by the following: (1) overlearning, (2) understanding new information, (3) building an organized knowledge base, (4) relating new material to the existing knowledge base, (5) using cue associations, and (6) using mnemonics (Sprinthall et al., 1994).

Influenced by these three lines of inquiry, a number of teacher educators have written extensively on the topic. Clift, Houston, and Pugach (1990) have summarized a number of teacher education programs that feature reflection. Zeichner (1987) has overviewed instructional strategies that can be employed in preservice teacher education for preparing reflective teachers. Among the strategies are action research, ethnography, writing, supervisory approaches, curriculum analysis and development, and Cruickshank's (1987) reflective teaching procedure. Tom (1985) has mapped out some of the crucial parameters of an inquiry-oriented approach to teacher education, and Calderhead (1989) has examined the varied definitions of reflective teaching and argues that teachers' development, teachers' knowledge, and the context of teachers' learning have great potential in extending our understanding of the role of reflection in teacher education. Likewise, Korthagen (1988), drawing on the developmental model, suggests that student teachers differ in their learning orientation. Some with an internal orientation view learning and reflection as an exciting and self-guided process. They readily examine their own practice. Others with external orientations require high structure from instructors and conform to peers' views of teaching.

Nolan and Huber (1989) have reviewed the literature of instructional supervision as it relates to reflection. Their review positions itself within the Schön genre and highlights the aims of supervision, which are "(1) engaging the teacher in the process of reflective behavior while (2) fostering critical inquiry into the process of teaching and learning, thereby (3) increasing the teachers' understanding of teacher practice and (4) broadening and deepening the repertoire of images and metaphors the teacher can call on to deal with problems" (p. 129).

Perhaps one of the most interesting theories for preparing reflective teachers is described by Ross (1988). Linked to the developmental genre, Ross submits that theory is essential to a definition of reflection. Her program defines reflection in terms of progressive developmental stages of competence in making reflective judgments (King & Kitchener, 1994). Longitudinal research on reflective judgment shows that college students become increasingly complex over their 4 years, passing through seven stages that vary on such criteria as one's view of the nature of knowledge, one's view of the nature and use of convincing evidence, one's willingness to accept responsibility for one's decisions, and one's openness to new evidence once a decision has been made. The levels of reflective judgment increase with both age and education (Schmidt, 1985; Welfel & Davidson, 1986). Thus, the good news is that education contributes to more complex reflective judgment. The bad news is that few college seniors move beyond moderate levels of reflective judgment (e.g., in stage 4 whim is used as often as logic in making decisions). For Ross the central question for teacher educators is to examine how our own programs contribute to more mature reflective judgment. It is therefore crucial to move beyond the debate about the merits of reflection to intervention programs that are intentionally designed to develop more psychologically mature teachers. This issue is addressed shortly.

Educational Policy and Teacher Development

Little (1992) and Cohen and Ball (1990) have explored how organization, policy, and occupational conditions affect teachers' opportunities and motivations to learn and grow. Both works examine policies and programs in California. Little relies on data from a 1-year study of staff development in 30 school districts, and Cohen and Ball explore how five teachers accommodate to mandated curriculum reforms in mathematics. Both studies lead to a number of conclusions. First, educational policy attempts to force teachers to change their instructional behaviors. Second, policies live or die in the hands of teachers. Third, school districts have designed staff development programs to implement new policy, and these programs, at first glance, incorporate coaching principles. However, when the programs are analyzed more carefully, it becomes clear that coaching principles are rarely employed in practice. Fourth, some teachers are far more willing to embrace innovations whereas other teachers are predisposed not to employ innovations or to use innovations in a concrete fashion. And last, that current monetary expenditures encourage a skill-dominated conception of teaching, that has "taken the form of 'service delivery' fed by a nearly inexhaustible market-place of packaged programmes and sophisticated presenters" (Little, 1992, p. 175). One cannot help but be struck by these prevailing patterns as educational policy confronts the classroom.

Perhaps the most helpful note in the studies is the observation that teacher enthusiasm for professional development is greatest in schools that made both formal and informal learning an integral part of the teachers' work. Furthermore, teacher-to-teacher consultation and classroom observation was "systematically carved out of otherwise crowded days" (Little, 1992, p. 181).

The studies highlight the sometimes unbridgeable gap between policy and practice. Fullan and Hargreaves (1992) confirm the existence of the gap, and they point out how the successful innovations usually worked in the narrow sense, that is, a single innovation was implemented. Schools are not in the business of implementing single innovations one at a time; rather, they are in the business of implementing multiple innovations. What is needed is a more meaningful and comprehensive framework that systematically attends to the interface between developing policy, school context, and the teacher as

person (Fullan & Hargreaves, 1992). A recent study by Hopkins (1990) may be instructive in this regard.

Hopkins (1990) hoped to extend the ideas and findings of McKibbin and Joyce (1981). In their study McKibbin and Joyce concluded: "The general milieu of the school and the social movements of the times interact powerfully with the personalities of the teachers to create personal orientations which greatly influence how teachers view the world (and themselves in it), and those views largely control what the individual can see as possibilities for personal and professional growth and the kind of options to which they can relate" (p. 254). Hopkins's study introduced school climate as an additional variable. In particular, he and his colleague were interested in the link between the psychological state of the individual teacher and the process of using educational ideas in the classroom.

The study involved 30 teachers from six primary schools. It focused on teachers' use of ideas that were introduced in an in-service aesthetics course. The course extended over a calendar year. Participants had frequent opportunities to discuss the ideas and how they could be implemented in their respective school settings. On completion of the course, participants independently attempted to develop and implement the strategies learned in the course over a 5-month period. At this point, the researchers spent another 6 months collecting data on participant use of the innovations. Data collection consisted of interviews, questionnaires, and participant observation. Information was gathered on school climate, psychological state of the teacher, and the level of use of the educational ideas.

The major conclusion of the study was that the more abstract and cognitively complex the teacher, the greater the use of the educational ideas. In fact, they found that the teachers at higher psychological levels used the educational ideas at a rate that was four times greater than their counterparts at concrete and less complex psychological states. In addition, they found that the more open democratic school climates facilitated the use of educational ideas. In particular, it appeared that the disposition of the principal as well as the opportunity for schoolwide consensus on significant school goals contributed to higher implementation of educational ideas. Their analysis supported the conclusion that a school's climate, as well as the psychological state of the teachers, influences the implementation of new staff development innovations. In their concluding remarks, they state that "change in teacher behaviour is the result of a dialectic between specific and general motivation, between individual motivation and school climate" (Hopkins, 1990, p. 62). Although the study was of a small scale, it largely replicates the work of McKibbin and Joyce (1981) and supports the need to integrate teacher development with school improvement.

Teacher Induction Programs

Starting in the 1980s, mentoring programs in education have abounded, with many states having some type of program of support for beginning teachers (Huling-Austin, Odell, Ishler, Kay, & Edelfelt, 1989). The aims of the formal teacher induction programs are to improve learning and teaching for students; to retain and induct novice teachers; to reward and revitalize experienced teachers in mentor roles; and to increase professional efficacy. These goals are laudable. However, although there is an extensive body of knowledge on the teaching/learning process that is guided by theory and research, our understanding of teacher induction is, at best, emergent.

Contrast the state of the art in teaching with teacher induction. Are there promising theories and/or conceptual frameworks for teacher induction? Quite the opposite is the case. Little (1990) has reviewed mentoring and teacher induction in the United States and provides convincing evidence that theoretical and conceptual frameworks are absent and research is minimal. Perhaps the only well-documented research describes the difficulties of beginning teachers (i.e., Veenman, 1984). Granted, initiatives like ATE's National Commission on the Role and Preparation of Mentor Teachers are laudable. They have begun the painstaking work of explicating relevant theory, research, and principles for mentoring. But again it may be a case of ships passing in the night. Both Little's (1990) and Huling-Austin's (1990) reports of a majority of formal teacher induction programs reveal a ubiquitous trend. Decisions about the content and character of teacher induction programs are most often based on political and legislative mandate rather than sound educational planning. The result is near unilateral implementation of mentoring as defined by state policymakers with little acknowledgment of individual districts' needs or relevant theory and research. And Huling-Austin (1990, 1992) has urged more bridging of research on teaching/learning with the limited research on teacher induction. There are, however, some emerging trends that have involved full participation between teachers, administrators, university personnel, and state policymakers, and that may, with continued research, hold promise in shaping our understanding of teacher induction.

Griffin (1985) and Thies-Sprinthall (1986) describe a number of needs of new teachers that have begun to frame program design and subsequent research. These needs of new teachers include: (1) help in developing as competent persons, not screening (see Reynolds, 1989, for an in-depth description of new teacher competence); (2) mentor teachers who are on-site and skilled as collegial supervisors; (3) time for the mentor and the new teacher to work together; (4) opportunities for the new teachers to talk with one another in a setting free of evaluations; (5) orientation to the school; and (6) a realistic assignment with regard to the number of classes, type of classes, and number of extracurricular activities. Two of these needs are now related to recent professional development programs.

Participation in Support Groups Beginning teachers may learn more readily when they have opportunities to meet with their peers in a setting free of evaluation. Thies-Sprinthall and Gerler (1990) in their theoretical and program review of support groups for beginning teachers state, "It can be argued that novices in any high-stress, unfamiliar yet demanding new role may need more than individual supervision by a master teacher. Group support can be an important complement to individualized help" (p. 19). They point out that developmental theorists such as Furth (1981) and Vygotsky (1978) have recommended that a supportive atmosphere is necessary if learners are to master new and complex thought and action.

Fuller's work (1969) is a specific application of the ideas supported by Furth and Vygotsky. She demonstrates the posi-

tive effects of support groups for student teachers who are guided by professionals with the necessary individual and group facilitation skills. Student teachers in these groups, provided with time for guided reflection and discussion on the teaching/learning process, became less egocentric, less anxious, and more able to focus on the initial tasks of teaching. Thies-Sprinthall and Gerler (1990) have extended Fuller's ideas to support for beginning teachers. Two studies, one with student teachers (Herring, 1989) and one with beginning teachers (Paisley, 1990) have found positive trends in new teachers' movement through Fuller's phases of concern. Although these few studies with relatively small samples do not prove the point, they do indicate positive empirical trends.

Preparation of Mentor Teacher Colleagues The importance of the mentor teacher has recently surfaced in the literature (Huling-Austin, 1992). However, Little (1990) cautions that rhetoric, action, and optimism have "outpaced both conceptual development and empirical warrant" (p. 297). Her review deserves close examination by anyone interested in the mentoring phenomenon. Malen and Hart (1987) also caution that such initiatives are susceptible to the problem of vanishing effects. They argue that mentor initiatives constitute a substantial challenge to some of the most established norms of teaching. This problem is exacerbated when the pace of implementation outstrips the resources, both human and material, to manage the innovation.

Clearly a high level of teacher, school, and district commitment is needed if programs are to be sustained over time. Even when commitment is present, selection and preparation of mentors often ends up being a "post hoc accommodation" (Little, 1990, p. 309). Against this backdrop Reiman and Thies-Sprinthall (1993) report 10 years of research in the development of a specialized yearlong preparation program for mentor teachers. In particular, their studies have found that mentor teachers become more conceptually complex and more principled as a result of the preparation program. Their line of inquiry has explored the relationship between complex new role taking and guided reflection. In addition, Reiman and Edelfelt (1990) traced the contributions made by the preparation program to the subsequent performance of the mentors as well as the success in their relationships with the beginning teachers. Unfortunately, no studies have compared mentors with substantive preparation with mentors who are left to their own resources (Little, 1990).

Cognitive-Developmental Approaches

Theory and research on cognitive-developmental approaches have shown an increasing focus on practice that derives directly from the basic research. That research demonstrates that (1) adult learners have the potential to develop to more complex stages; (2) higher stages of development are more adequate for performance in complex human interactions; and (3) the stage framework is composed of a series of related domains of growth, particularly cognitive, ego (or personal), and moral.

Role Taking and Social Interaction The shift from theoretical description to practical prescription has its roots in two practical theorists, George Herbert Mead (1934) and Lev Vygotsky (1978). Mead outlined the particular significance of actual role taking as a mechanism for growth. In his view role taking involves the actual participation by a person of significant "real-world" activity rather than role playing and/or simulated experience. A second component of such instruction has been derived from Vygotsky. In a separation from Piaget, who conceptualized the developmental learner as a lone eagle (Lindberg, Earhart, or Robinson Crusoe), Vygotsky stresses the importance of social interaction, such as discussions and dialog in small groups, as the primary method of producing cognitive-structural growth in the learner.

Developmental theorists agree that new structural learning may begin with a "perturbation" or a knowledge disturbance. The learner is confronted with problems that the current cognitive structures cannot solve adequately. In teacher education the examples abound. As noted, Peterson's (1989) research, Thies-Sprinthall's (1984) studies, and the work of McKibbin and Joyce (1981), Hopkins, Walters, and Stivers (1977), and the Michigan State team (Kennedy, 1991) (NCRTL), among others, all describe situations in which the current system of teacher problem solving is inadequate.

The recognition of such inadequacies, complete with affective dissonance, can provide the opportunity for new learning. It is noteworthy that the important work of Frances Fuller already noted actually fits this aspect of the Vygotsky theory. Her phases of personal concern can represent the gradual recognition of the need to improve on one's ability to adopt new and more complex problem-solving strategies. Also during this phase, because of affective dissonance, there is the need for group support and what Hans Furth (1981) calls an atmosphere of relaxed reflection. These views also clearly indicate that developmental instruction for adults must include an emphasis on affect just as much as on intellectual understanding. Paulo Freire (1983) is often referred to in the teacher empowerment literature; yet his concept of the codification of emotional themes is just as often ignored. That dimension also helps illuminate the strange language of developmentalists like Piaget when he notes that the cognitive is also the affective and vice versa. That conundrum makes particular sense when the perturbation brings with it affective dissonance as well as intellectual puzzlement. Thus the current theory for developmental instruction includes an equal emphasis on the affective and the cognitive. One criticism that is often voiced by philosophers such as Peters (1978) and psychologists such as Lapsley (1991) suggests that the framework is devoid of feelings so much so that humans are composed only of "thin selves." In fact, affect does play a large part in the teacher development programs. The dissonance created by new role-taking activities must be addressed for structural change to occur.

Domains as Dependent Variables Current theory also opens up the possibility that cognitive developmental practice needs to conceptualize objectives as focused on domains of growth, rather than on one single global disposition. The basic research with teachers does indicate that domains such as cognitive development from either the Hunt (1974) Conceptual Level (CL) system or the King and Kitchener Reflective Judgment (1994) provide insight to the domain of concrete to formal operations. Theories by Loevinger (1976) and Erikson (1982) in the domain of self, ego, and identity development represent another important target for growth. And clearly the research of Kohlberg (1984), Rest (1986), and Perry (1970) with the teacher as a moral and ethical agent adds a further important domain to the development. Although it is clear that each such domain correlates modestly with other domains, each also contributes uniquely to the overall development of humans. This view also provides an answer to the "Goldilocks" problem noted earlier.

A systematic research program for cognitive developmental applications actually started in the early 1970s, but it focused on high school students (Sprinthall, 1980). As developmental theory changed to include a stage framework for adults, the teacher as an adult learner became the focus for a series of studies (Glassberg & Sprinthall, 1980; Oja & Sprinthall, 1978; Sprinthall & Bernier, 1979). These studies produced some promising trends and support for an overall theory for instruction but could not be considered highly definitive and were not as clear-cut as the findings with teenagers.

Research Findings: Teacher as Supervisor A program developed and tested by Thies-Sprinthall (1984) was a first step in refining the approach for adults. She created a method of using a training model from Weil and Joyce (1978) in concert with developmental conditions. Specific and focused skills of supervision were taught to a group of experienced teachers in a sequence of rationale, modeling, peer practice, and generalization for each component. The role-taking teacher was to become a teacher supervisor. Journals and readings were added for guided reflection. The program was the equivalent of a two-semester course to provide for continuity. In fact, one of the major goals was to help such teachers apply different models of supervision according to the developmental needs of the beginning teacher. In the David Hunt sense this meant mastering the process of systematically varying the amount of structure provided, matching and mismatching. This competence included the ability to assess the developmental level of the neophyte to "start where the learner is." The instructional process was varied in accord with the developmental stage of the teacher. Examples were concrete or abstract, reinforcement was immediate or spread out, and assignments were focused or extended. The overall atmosphere in the class meetings was framed around the necessity to discuss ideas and emotions in a relaxed mode using the Vygotsky, Furth, and Freire instructional principles.

The results demonstrated two points. It was almost impossible to provide enough structure, guided reflection, and support to help experienced teachers who initially functioned at very modest levels of development. Teachers in the low Defining Issues Test range on moral judgment and low Conceptual Level on the Hunt never seemed to really connect with the program. There was some positive change, yet not enough for confidence that a cognitive restructuring had taken place. However, for the majority of teachers, the results were quite positive. Their gains on both developmental instruments were significant. Also the narrative accounts and interviews cross-validated the empirical results (Thies-Sprinthall, 1986).

TEACHER PROFESSIONAL DEVELOPMENT • 693

Further refinements in the model are from the current work of Reimán and Thies-Sprinthall (1993). Vygotsky's work in particular suggests that the optimal focus for developmental growth is his zone of proximal growth. The zone is conceptualized as the area of problem solving and dissonance just beyond the current preferred stage. By varying assignments and role-taking instruction, the prior studies had involved adjusting the activities to the different zones in which the teachers were functioning. There was, however, only a loose connection between such zones and the reflective capacity of the teachers. Reiman created a systematic method of dialoging in journal responses that allowed the instructor to match and mismatch the writing samples. The method, following Freire, included equal attention to the thoughts and emotional themes presented in journal form. Without such systematic responses, journal entries by themselves may remain at the initial levels. Experience in general can be educative or miseducative depending in part on the learners' ability to extract meaning from experience. The Reiman system, though labor-intensive, does show how the learners' level of reflective complexity can be promoted through journal dialoging.

Recent studies by De Angelis Peace (1992) and Mann (1992) have applied the same model to a group of in-service school counselors being educated for the new role of counselor mentor and to a group of college students being prepared for the new role of tutor to high school students. The Peace study found results similar to those of Reiman and Thies-Sprinthall. The counselors developed higher-order cognitions as measured by the Hunt (CL) index and exhibited higher-order supervisor skills in practice (e.g., in both structural and behavioral change). Similarly, Mann found college tutors developing higher-order cognitions as measured by the Perry scale. Within-group analysis of the journals also revealed qualitative differences in how the tutors reflected on their experience. Tutors identified as on the "high road" to development wrote journal entries that included more perspective taking, more personal disclosure of feelings, and more effective diagnosis of tutee learning difficulties and needs. These results are consistent with work by Anson (1989) who has analyzed student writing for evidence of cognitive-developmental level.

Developmental Instructional Conditions

These studies, then, can be synthesized into a model for cognitive-developmental instruction. The elements include:

1. *Role taking* (not role playing). Selecting a more complex role for the teacher, counselor, or college student (preservice). This could include student teaching, beginning to teach, mentoring, peer coaching, supervision, action research, community action, a "teacher in residence," a teacher as building leader for mainstreaming, or a teacher-led initiative to develop a peer-mediation program. Typically, the new role would entail learning a set of new skills delivered through a sequenced curriculum.
2. *Reflection.* A sequence of readings, demonstrations, practice activities, case studies, and weekly journalizing for dialog on the meaning of the experience.

3. *A balance* of role taking (action) and discussion/analysis (reflection) that forms an interactive praxis.
4. *Continuity.* Because structural growth is slow, often painful, programs usually require 9 months or so of weekly seminars and application to bring about generalizations in the new role.
5. *Support and challenge.* The challenge is usually built in from the new role requirements as student teaching, beginning to teach, supervisor, mentor, or peer coach. The support in the Vygotsky/Furth sense is requisite for the teachers to move "up" on the Fuller (1969) CBAM scale and to adopt more complex behaviors. Henry David Thoreau (1966) captured the difficulty of giving up one way of life in order to be renewed when he commented on his decision to leave the solitary life at Walden Pond. "I left the woods," he wrote, "for as good a reason as I went there . . . it seemed to me that I had several more lives to lead, and could not spare any more time for that one. It is remarkable how easily and insensibly we fall into a particular route, and make a beaten track for ourselves" (p. 213).

This last point is probably the least understood by nondevelopmentalists. Progressing to higher-order cognitions is not an affectively neutral process. Restructuring means giving up one's current system and often entails strong feelings of fear and sometimes (even) antagonism. Perry (1975) often asked the rhetorical question, "If development is so good, why doesn't everyone just grow?" The barrier to growth is viewed as one's own comfort level with our current "tried-and-true" methods. Variously described as a loss of innocence or even a coming of age, the main point is that affective apprehension goes hand in hand with the gradual recognition of the need to adopt new and seemingly precarious ways of knowing. The journals contain many statements to such feelings. A parallel set of qualitative commentary is also evident in some of the recent interactive work of Richardson (1994) and Kagan (1993), as noted. In fact, of all the developmental conditions, the ability to balance support and challenge is probably the most difficult and the most necessary.

Certainly David Hunt's (1987) most recent views on the importance of experiential and affective reflection as the starting point for teacher development coincide with the action-reflection model. He is highly critical of the traditional top-down, or outside-in, method of professional education. Instead, he seeks a reciprocity model that is neither top-down nor bottom-up and results in mutual adaptation. He also stresses the importance of concrete experience in practice as the bridge between the teacher and the "resident-visitor" (e.g., trainer). Because he now eschews empirical assessments of outcomes of his workshop model, the results can only be judged from his qualitative accounts and appear as very positive. One of the intriguing questions, however, is the consistent reference to metaphorical thinking throughout his examples of staff development. If concrete experience through careful reflection does lead to an increase in metaphorical and abstract reasoning, then the theory from practice component of development may become a critical element in the growth process. His central point is that staff developers must remember that teachers are persons, too, and that all of us can become our own best theorists (Hunt, 1987, p. 133).

Role Taking for Teachers and Teacher Education

The research base for the elements continues to expand and indicates that role-taking experience without reflection does *not* promote growth. The opposite is also true. Reflection without role taking does not work (e.g., simply reviewing all the research on academic coursework). Short-term workshops versus continuity over time indicates that the former does not produce growth. Atmospheres that are either exclusively supportive in a Rogerian sense or exclusively challenging do not produce growth (Sprinthall, Reiman, & Thies-Sprinthall, 1993).

The research results and follow-up studies indicate that experienced school teachers can perform the functions of a new role as supervisor with a high degree of competence. Even more important may be the findings that indicate very clearly that such experienced teachers can also become school-based teacher educators, that is, a cadre of "clinical" faculty. For example, in a select group of North Carolina public schools there is now a network of some 40 two-person teams of school-based teacher educators in 12 school systems who instruct their colleagues in yearlong courses in supervision and coaching. The overall network now consists of 1,500 teachers educated in the new role of mentors and school-based teacher educators with full instructional responsibility. The network was started some 10 years ago with one university faculty member and 12 experienced teachers from one school system. The program can be conceptualized as an operational example of Don Davies triple "T" framework (Provus, 1975), university faculty as the third "T," experienced school-based teacher educators as the second "T," and mentor teachers as the first "T." The mentors then serve to induct both preservice and beginning teachers in their initial assignments. Such a model of staff development then involves a series of interacting components. The new teachers gain from careful mentoring. The mentors improve their own teaching skills as models for the beginners. The school-based teacher educators improve their supervision skills as models for the mentors, and the university faculty improve their instructional skills as models for the school-based teacher educators.

Teacher as Instructional Peer Coach

Glickman (1990) encourages a developmental view of supervision. He maintains that knowledge of how teachers grow and develop must serve as a guiding principle for supervisors. The understanding of how teachers can become more empathic, more caring, and more flexible in instruction provides a necessary backdrop for successful work in supervision. His own research on developmental stages of supervising teachers has provided a crucial lens for viewing the teacher change process. And he has begun to explore, along with his associates, possible interventions to assist teachers to move to more complex stages of conceptual and moral reasoning.

Phillips and Glickman (1991) have begun work designed to engage teachers as peer coaches while stimulating their cognitive development. In the Phillips and Glickman model, teachers were placed in the new role of peer coach. Over a 7-month period the teachers were introduced to supervisory strategies that they learned to employ with their colleagues. While the sample size was small (22) and depended on volunteers, Phillips and Glickman found that their developmentally based peer-coaching program raised teachers' conceptual levels, helped reduce teacher isolation, and developed more positive teacher attitudes toward their own growth experiences. As Phillips and Glickman conclude, "The peer coaching program gave teachers the opportunity to come together in collegial groups, assume more complex roles, reflect together in their work, and take an important step toward lasting professional growth" (p. 25).

Teacher as Action Researcher

Action research, a term first used by Kurt Lewin in the 1940s, refers to the application of social science methods to practical problems with the goals of contributing to theory and knowledge in education and improving teaching practice. Lewin (1948), a prominent social psychologist, wanted to unite experimental research with programs of social action. He believed, much like Mead, that social problems should propel inquiry. Much of Lewin's early work modeled this belief. He focused on helping minorities address psychological and social problems caused by prejudice.

More recently, educators have framed action research as inquiry done by practitioners with the help of a consultant—the interactionist perspective. They attribute four characteristics to action research: (1) It is collaborative, (2) it addresses practical classroom problems, (3) it bolsters professional development, and (4) it requires a specialized structure to ensure both time and support for the research initiative.

As just mentioned, an expected outcome of action research is professional development. Oja and Smulyan (1989) have examined action research as a new role undertaken by teachers. Using a cognitive-developmental framework, they are interested in how action research projects can transform teacher thinking, empathy, and perspective taking. Their Action Research on Change in Schools project (ARCS) is an extensive multicase study that analyzes key elements of effective collaborative action research. It focuses in particular on the collaborative processes that interact with action research. Oja and Smulyan use theory in group dynamics and adult development to explain how individual teacher researchers and groups develop.

Their findings "suggest that the type and quality of collaborative action research are dependent on the developmental stages of the teachers involved" (Oja & Smulyan, 1989, p. 136). Transcripts of action research meetings over the 2 years of the ARCS project allowed description of five individual teacher behaviors over time. The investigators found that a teachers' cognitive-developmental stage perspective defines a meaning system through which the teacher interprets and acts on issues related to teaching and action research. In particular, at the conformist stage of ego/self-development (Loevinger, 1976) they have documented a teacher researcher's tendency to conform to external rather than self-evaluated standards with little appreciation of multiple possibilities in problem-solving situations. At the conscientious ego/self-stage, the teacher researcher shifted toward more self-evaluated standards and demonstrated a fuller recognition of individual differences in attitudes. Finally, at the transition between individualistic and autonomous stage of ego development, the teacher researcher assumed multiple perspectives, utilized a wider variety of coping behaviors in response to school and research team pressures, employed a larger repertoire of group process and change strategies, and was very self-reflective and highly effective in collaborative action research (Oja & Smulyan, 1989, p. 138). The Oja and Smulyan ARCS project is yet another study that examines how a teacher's stage of development may influence his or her personal and professional development.

The Discourse Method

Some work by Oser (1991) complements some of these cognitive-developmental findings. Working in a German school system with some 84 (K–12) teachers, he actually employed two related methods for in-service teacher education. One system involved 30 hours of training in what he termed the Discourse II method. The content and process included dilemma discussions focused on issues of justice, care, and teaching effectiveness. The overall theoretical objectives were to promote higher-order moral reasoning and higher-order teaching skills. The so-called "Discourse II" produced a reduced security orientation, less single-handed conflict management, and more interactive teaching methods. He employed a broad set of outcome measures, questionnaires, interviews, video lessons, student evaluations, and moral judgment indices. A second intervention involved a much broader scope, the "Just Community" model. Based on Kohlberg's work in the United States, Oser created a school community of teachers and pupils involving all the elements of the Just Community. Town meetings led by the students discussed and voted on discipline methods as well as school policy and methods. The use of teacher–learner dialogs and similar aspects of a democratic school method were incorporated. After 2 years of study, Oser (1991) commented, "The most astonishing effect is not on the side of the students. The teachers developed in a most dramatic way" (p. 225). They behaved as "Discourse II" teachers. As a result he said the teachers reached an equilibrium across all three domains of justice, care, and truthfulness. His final point was to underscore that the teachers themselves were not extraordinary educators to begin with, nor were they much above average in the levels of moral judgment. Oser's most recent review (1994) of research in this genre extends our understanding of teaching responsibility and the deep knowledge that must inform moral teaching.

Rulon (1992) has reported similar outcomes in her staff development work with a Just Community high school in this country. In such a setting, the teachers need to become comfortable and skillful in a version of Oser's Discourse II method. The dialog approach is highly interactive and inductive. Rulon found that participation in the Just Community "Town Meetings" did promote developmental growth among the teachers over the 2-year period of the project. A comparison group of teachers showed no change on either the quantitative or qualitative assessments. Of particular significance was the complete absence of Stage 2 reasoning in the experimental group at posttest and the continued use of that level of preconventional judgment by the teachers in the comparison group. Both groups were equivalent at pretest.

It is important to remember that the Just Community approach was a daily experience over extensive periods. Such an intensive model for teacher growth does produce positive results on teacher cognition and behavior.

EMERGING ISSUES

This section focuses on some of the most recent issues that confront the area of teacher development. Included is a discussion of the problem of faculty development in higher education settings and the overall criticism of the teacher education enterprise from the deconstructionist viewpoint. This is followed by a summary that seeks to integrate the massive amount of material covered in this review and point out profitable new directions for continued research, theory, and practice.

College Teacher Education Faculty Development: Goodlad's Findings

In order to understand the context of teacher development from the perspective of higher education it is important to consider the results of a 5-year national survey of administrators and faculty conducted by John Goodlad (1990) and his investigative team. The overall rationale is clear and succinct. "The renewal of schools, teachers and the programs that educate teachers must proceed simultaneously" (p. 4). The research scope was substantial, including 29 institutions of higher education (IHEs) representing different categories from public "flagships" to small private liberal arts colleges. Interviews included faculty, administrators, and students. Observations included classes and field sites. Documents included nine survey questionnaires and reviews of each institution's catalogs and mission statements. The overall results when added together represent a disciplined and scholarly indictment of the present enterprise. The results that focused only on college faculty are examined here.

In the main Goodlad reported that faculty associated at either end of the continuum appeared to be productive and relatively well regarded by their peers, that is, those in flagship public universities and those in small private liberal arts colleges. The expectations for professional development of faculty, however, was extremely different between these sets of institutions. The flagship faculty were essentially required to emulate the published inquiry traditions of the academy, and the small private college faculty focused on undergraduate instruction. There was also some difference in resource allocation with small-college faculty apparently receiving substantial resources. From a faculty view, however, it was in the large public regional universities where the differences were most pronounced. Goodlad referred to the problem as one of a dislocated and muddled mission for this group of IHEs. It is also important to note that these institutions as a whole produce by far the greatest number of teachers for the nation's schools. Such institutions historically were transformed normal schools. Most important, the transformation has included a shift in emphasis from teacher preparation to scholarly productivity. Goodlad's team found that this dislocation created pain, bitterness, and low morale, especially among the senior faculty. They felt trapped and betrayed, associate professors with virtually no chance of promotion, full professors facing a continued decline in status, while being shunned by young and "productive" assistant professors. Such an environment created an atmosphere of low self-esteem with an estimate of professional melancholia as high as 20% (p. 159).

However, there is a deep irony in the Goodlad report. With the single exception of the small private institutions, he sees the entire IHE enterprise as valuing the flagship model of published inquiry first. One level of irony is that in spite of such striving, schools of education exist only at the periphery of most universities. "Prestige deprivation" (p. 167) is his phrase. One has only to read Derek Bok's (1987) account of schools of education as (in his metaphor) pinballs bouncing from pole to pole to capture the emotional effect of such a phrase.

The second irony is that Goodlad is convinced that such an overall shift will not improve either the quality of teacher education or the quality of schooling. In fact the not-so-hidden message in this report is clearly that continuing to emulate the arts and science model for a faculty of a professional school will only make the current problem worse. In a real sense, then, Goodlad would view programs for faculty development in the current IHE framework as a dilemma at best and a contradiction at worst. Instead, what he proposes is to restructure the IHE format more along the lines of professional schools in general, or at least to create Centers of Pedagogy as a means of revising the mission and the reward structure. Certainly the idea of faculty development in higher education would be vastly different in a professional school context more akin to medicine, law, and business than to the present model of a school controlled by the arts and sciences academy model.

A related investigation lends support to Goodlad's conclusions. A special report by the Carnegie Foundation for the Advancement of Teaching entitled Scholarship Reconsidered: Priorities of the Professoriate (Boyer, 1990) examined what it means to be a scholar. In this national survey of 5,450 faculty from 34 institutions, Boyer reported a growing schism between teaching, research, and service. Increasingly, comprehensive, doctorate-granting, and research universities favor research and publication to teaching and service. The imbalance constricts potential for creative faculty professional development. "Such a suffocatingly restricted view of scholarship leads frequently to burnout or plateaus of performance as faculty are expected to do essentially the same things, year after year" (p. 43). The irony of this study was that although research and publication was perceived as increasingly important, 70% of today's professors identified teaching as their primary interest. This figure was lower for research institutions with one-third of the faculty identifying teaching as their primary interest.

From Goodlad's perspective, however, restructuring priorities from an arts and science model would not yield an appropriate context for teacher education. The academy by definition will always designate professional education as inferior. Teacher education will be seen in a manner similar to what critics of the time said of the Monroe Doctrine. Without a real navy at the time our country was viewed as a "cork boat in the wake of a British Man-of-War."

The Deconstructionist Critique

There have been and continue to be criticisms and revisions focused on teacher education and development. However, the deconstructionist view is undoubtedly the clearest and most direct. Under the rubric of critical pedagogy, this model for teacher development requires teachers to become revolutionary in outlook and in behaviors. The assumption is that a democratic, capitalist, consumer-driven society is fundamentally flawed. To work in the current enterprise in any form is equated with a bourgeois mentality, being a lackey for the white male, sexist, racist, exploitative society and the dehumanizing military-industrial complex. In fact this language does not do justice to the deconstructionists' critique. Speaking of our society as only a version of neocolonialization and a white settler mentality, "Teachers and students are currently menaced by the views of corporate citizenship that assume we possess self-authenticating, self-regarding, homogenous, seamless and coherent identities. . . . Our identities are structured in material relations of power and privilege. . . . We are historicized, bounded subjects" (Estrada & McLaren, 1993, p. 29).

The model for teacher development, then, is to be focused not only on the political, social, and economic causes of injustice but also on enacting new practice that will overturn the capitalist system and seek new forms of social life. In a sense, then, the educational deconstructionists see teacher education as a potential training ground to produce a revolutionary cadre to overturn the current tyranny. The deconstructionist view, then, actually resides almost entirely as a basic critique of a capitalist democracy with teacher development as training for the requisite revolution. This view is reminiscent of an earlier 1970 criticism of, say, an Ivan Illich and the need to burn the schools down before constructive change might be possible. The deconstructionists add in the capitalist society to the Illich fire (1971). While such criticism may be extreme and based almost exclusively on political/philosophical issues, it does serve as a valuable reminder of the need to maintain vigilence in the slow evolution of the democratic ethic in a capitalist society.

CONCLUSION

In one sense, the concept and process of teacher development can be viewed as a field in disarray given the widely divergent theoretical view and diverse research models described in this review. Quite a different view emerges, however, if the historical context is considered. The most common models for theory and research until recently were clearly inadequate. The long history of fixed traits, psychoanalytic concepts, and process-product behaviorism did not move the field forward but sideways at best. Also prior to the recent developments of meta- and path analysis, the research enterprise largely represented an impassable barrier. Each study could be examined according to the tenets of either Campbell and Stanley (1963) or Underwood (1957), and if one single condition was not met for a truly experimental design, the results were dismissed. Thus, the dual barriers of inadequate theory and a research agenda that only uncovered flaws created a long vacuum concerning the issues of teacher development.

Intellectual history does show that during periods of transition, from the frozen period toward a new model, there is often a time of wide exploration and experimentation (Kuhn, 1970). The removal of the old hindrances from narrow empirical research and/or from the need to jam the human development of adults into the straitjackets of trusts, unconscious motives, or behavior modification means that the field itself is a point of innovation rather than of a new consensus.

This new spirit brings with it both positive and negative components. The positives are important. New ideas are emerging. It is clear that staff development cannot be imposed from the outside or top-down. It is also clear that teacher development will not occur unilaterally. Collaboration then is requisite, yet it is extraordinarily difficult. Reading the work of Virginia Richardson (1994), Dona Kagan (1993), Carl Glickman (1990), Ann Lieberman (1992), and the efforts of the current authors, among others, reveals just how complex the process of collaboration is. Theoretically, the dilemma is stark—how to balance different sets of knowledge that reflect different levels of experience and epistemology. Yet, this also indicates that the problem itself is being addressed, rather than avoided, and that a series of pathways may yield a succession of positive effects.

On the positive side, it is also clear that the conception of the teacher as an adult learner is in the process of replacing prior views. The theoretical work, while arguably incomplete, is grappling with the Goldilocks problem. A theoretical meandering is waning, and direct constructs are emerging. The age, stage and sequence, and phase theories provide insights about the process of adult development. If education seriously takes the dictum, "Start where the learner is," then these frameworks may become the means of shifting the John Dewey question from children to adults. If we know what adult development *is,* then we also will know what adult teacher education *ought* to be. That framework, however, cannot be either too broad or too narrow. The early works in formulating a cognitive or a cognitive-developmental conception are good examples of an overly broad scheme.

Teacher cognitions, under the general rubric of disposition of thoughtfulness or cognitive-developmental stage theory as encompassing a single generic domain, such as generativity, did not rest on sufficient theoretical rigor. That work has now progressed. The stage theorists are now outlining important domains of adult growth (conceptual, ego, and moral) that are adequately described independent varibles in relation to effective performance in complex humane endeavors. This means that the debate over the relationship between cognitive-developmental stage and performance in complex human interaction tasks has been largely resolved. There is ample research evidence to document the "higher is better" assertion. It also is now clear that the conditions needed for teacher development are essentially the same ones that enable students to learn as well. This point is made abundantly clear by Lieberman (1992).

Similarly, though not yet as comprehensive, the works in cognitive development and information processing are providing an emergent research base. The more cognitively complex teachers appear as more adequate in adapting learning environments that induce pupil exploration. Both the cognitive approach and the cognitive developmental approach share two major similarities and one major difference. The similarities are the concept of cognitive structure, the schema from which each person makes meaning from experience, and that there are distinctively different levels of such cognitive complexity. The major difference is that stage theorists conceptualize levels as a series of transformations, whereas the cognitive theorists view the process as a gradual linear process from the less to the more complex. Both view cognitive capacity as a major determinant of behavior, and the research does validate this claim. It is pointless to omit the cognitions of teachers from teacher development programs.

A second major area of positive change is toward the creation of theoretically linked applied programs, the other half of the Dewey question. The linkage varies between knowing "about" and knowing "how to," but programs are grappling with the issue. The Lewin dictum remains as a guiding reminder that theory is practical and practice is theoretical. Constructing an effective theory of developmental instruction, however, is fraught with difficulties. In fact, one negative trend noted is a continued separation of research agendas (e.g., basic research to identify and possibly even "reidentify" the problem versus programmatic research designed to promote teacher growth. In fact, in the future, teacher research ought to be interactive rather than allow a continued separation between basic descriptions and applied interventions. For example, the Michigan State research (Kennedy, 1991) provides an up-to-date, but hardly new, description of the problem. Further fine-grained examinations of the modest levels of teacher cognitions and teacher performance are not needed. Instead, it is possible to learn more about such basic information while trying out programs designed to promote greater complexity in thought, feeling, and action. McClelland (1985) has always maintained that the best way to understand any human phenomenon is to try to change it. Interactive research and development appear as a most promising alternative to the present separate approach, the current federal model to the contrary not withstanding.

There are fewer examples of theory, research, and practice for teacher development, but there are some very positive trends. Field-based programs focus on teacher classroom performance, action research, and supervision for effective mentoring, for example. As university-based professors collaborate with classroom teachers and focus on practice for longer time periods than the usual workshop, new research issues appear. Peterson and her group came to ask the important question of how to improve the levels of cognition. After viewing the different levels of performance and the cognitive base, they are now designing interventions toward the goal of increased complexity. These same themes are also apparent in the Richardson and Kagan programs. Thies-Sprinthall and Reiman realize the importance of guided reflection through journalizing as they examine the effectiveness of each of the five conditions for growth. A similar theme was noted in the work of Oser and his European colleagues as they moved from describing teachers' levels of development to programs oriented toward greater complexity in three domains of growth. While Glickman and his colleagues have moved to an even broader framework, school change, the program goals clearly involve methods designed to nuture empowered development by school personnel. The revised focus by Joyce and Showers to embed skill acquisition within a framework of teacher growth also represents a further example. There are other researchers committed to the approach of collaborative programs and interactive research (Odell & O'Hair, 1993; Oja & Smulyan, 1989; Phillips & Glickman, 1991). These directions, however, are only in a beginning phase. For example much of the research already cited, of Peterson, Richardson, Kagan, and Oser, has focused on elementary teachers. The research of Thies-Sprinthall and Reiman does include K–12 teachers, but it has yet to establish a direct link between supervision and actual teaching performance of beginning teachers. Glickman's research with developmental supervision is provocative, yet it is limited to small samples.

Even the research on peer coaching is limited to a small number of studies with small samples. Granted, the theoretical model is based on more than 200 studies, but research on the application of the model is still needed. And Howey (1993) points out that too few studies have examined the multiple effects of teachers in new or expanded roles. Nonetheless, the collaborative model does now appear as a major framework for teacher development in a new mode, housed in a new location, and encompassing cycles of formative research.

There are other frameworks on the contemporary scene. Certainly both the craft model and the expert model continue to appear in the literature. The craft approach seems to assume that the widespread failure of prior models suggests that a major separation is in order. Omit formal or interactive school university programs and let each teacher learn from experience with intuition as the guiding principle. The expert model conversely suggests that teachers need greater immersion in the liberal arts tradition. The antipathy is obvious, experience versus intellectual exposition. Although the models are in opposition, they share a similar view that such claims are validated exclusively on a subjective basis. This, of course, makes it extremely difficult to judge the effectiveness of either approach. In fact, most of the research conducted on these questions raises serious doubts concerning such claims. Philosophers and behavioral scientists have shown the weaknesses of experiential learning, as well as the limits of academic programs built on actual behavior in complex tasks.

Two major issues arise from the current review: (1) the need for a broad conception of research; and (2) the need for greater coordination of program efforts. There appears to be a major disagreement as to research method, the quantitative/qualitative debate that affects teacher education research. The empirical tradition blinds us from the subjective and experiential. As a result, there are new forms of narrative, subjective "voice," literature, and even the suggestion that an individually crafted novel can form a new research base. More traditionally trained researchers, however, are quick to point out the severe difficulties with the qualitative position. Paul Meehl (1956) sitting with a twentieth-century version of Occam's razor noted the deficiency of clinical judgment. And narrative is after all the basis for a well-known but now discarded theory of psychoanalysis. Finally, developmentalists can show just how much difference there is in narrative accounts according to the stage of the person, indicating that qualitatively different levels of cognitions produce qualitatively different narratives. Thus, the weaknesses of prior empirical approaches should not become justifications for singular qualitative methods. To replace one defective method with a new method just as defective does not represent a process of successive approximations.

Instead, it may be possible and certainly would be desirable to merge the qualitative and the quantitative. Of course from a quantitative standpoint changes would be required. The idea that only random assignment and true experimental designs are worthwhile actually can be discarded. The evidence through metaanalysis indicates that quasi-designs are just as robust, and as long as caution is followed in claiming generalizations, volunteer subjects are valid (Gage, 1978). There is also no major obstacle to including narrative accounts such as journal entries, participant observations, and interview material along with quantitative assessment measured. In fact the idea of multimodal assessment can easily accommodate both the qualitative and the quantitative. Both modes can enhance the understanding of the program effects. Each can serve as a check and balance to the other (Sprinthall, 1975). It is not necessary to toss out the baby with the empirical bath water nor leave it toweled only in subjectivity. Gage (1985) has always maintained that we can achieve "hard gains in soft sciences," but only if we avoid narrow scientism and global subjectivism.

The second major change that is needed and apparent from the review is the lack of coordination and perhaps even an ignorance of current research. The positive side of the current paradigm shift is the creation of new approaches. The negative is the isolation and somewhat narrow scope of the efforts. Examples are numerous. Kennedy (1991) in her summary of the Michigan State research after 3 years of study with in-service and preservice teachers reported a remarkable stability of their conceptions as to the nature of teaching and learning. In general, neither preservice nor in-service education seemed to have any significant impact on teacher views. Even more important, however, was the finding on the nature of these views. From interviews and questionnaires she reported,

We found that many teachers perceive school subjects not as bodies of knowledge that might be uncertain or worthy of debate nor as relating to every day life. Instead, many teachers perceive the live subjects we studied, mathematics and writing, as collections of fixed rules and procedures. (Kennedy, 1991, p. 7)

From a developmental standpoint these descriptions are strikingly similar to the research of William Perry (1970). His description of one of the early positions, referred to as "dualism" in cognition, is almost exactly parallel to Kennedy's descriptions. A dualist views the world of teaching and learning, which Perry called the student's epistemology, as a series of absolute facts to be memorized, accepted without question, and then handed back to the instructor. Knowledge is fixed like a revealed truth or tablet in the sky. There is little room for uncertainty, debate, or different points of view. From this cognitive frame of reference, the individual learner constructs meaning in a factual and linear mode (Perry, 1970, p. 72). These same themes have been researched on a broader sample by King and Kitchener (1994), as noted. Their early stages of cognition (Stages 1 & 2) cross-validate Perry's "dualism" and Kennedy's description of the modes of thought by the national sample of preservice and in-service teachers. If one reads Peterson's description of a less cognitively complex teacher and Richardson's description of some of the early cognitions of some of her teachers, it is remarkably similar to the material researched by Cummings and Murray (1989) in Canada and low ego stage, the non "Discourse Two" teachers of Oser. The less conceptually complex teachers of Hunt (1974) and supervisors of Thies-Sprinthall (1980), and the early stages of Glickman et al.'s (1992) waiting to be empowered teacher are further examples. The problem succinctly put is that almost none of these researchers (mea culpa included) are particularly aware of anyone else's work. Independence and autonomy are important, but the lack of collaboration, especially and perhaps ironically on school university collaborative research, severely restricts the ability to build a tolerable consensus for research theory and practice in teacher development.

The same separation in basic research is also apparent in program research. Many of these same researchers are creating programs designed to stimulate the structural growth of the participants. Reading descriptions of these efforts indicates how little, if any, recognize other programs. This is even more unfortunate in this instance. Field-based interactive teacher education is about as difficult a problem to solve as exists. How to create the balance between affective support and relaxed reflection and methods for effective challenge is at the heart of the dilemma. Too much support is as ineffective as too much challenge. This is also where cognitive and cognitive development theories run directly into the problem of individual differences. More coordinated research from the program developers could illuminate which procedures not only work well in accord with general stage differences but also vary within stages and across domains. This is obviously a special case of the attribute treatment interaction question applied to adult development. Progress on this knotty question will be very slow indeed if the research programs continue in the current fragmented way.

Without belaboring the obvious, the importance of teacher education research and development is compelling. Teachers face two particularly urgent demands: cultural diversity and a predicted huge increase in children with special needs (Reynolds, 1989). These factors will increase the range of individual differences in the classrooms. At the same time there are rising expectations for teachers to perform and with greater competency. The hope is that these dual demands will not outrun our ability to build the requisite programs. The continued isolation and separation of research efforts will undercut needed solutions. Coordination of efforts to build on the current base may be slow, but it must not be circular.

The great French patriot Georges Clemenceau made the classic comment, "War is too important to be left to the Generals." Teacher education is too important to be left either to the university or to the school. Alone both fail. Together both may grow.

References

Anderson, J. R. (1990). *The adaptive character of thought*. Hillsdale, NJ: Lawrence Erlbaum Associates.

Anderson, V., & Roit, M. (1993). Planning and implementing collaborative strategy instruction for delayed readers in grades 6–10. *The Elementary School Journal, 94*(2), 121–137.

Anson, C. (1989). Response styles and ways of knowing. In C. Anson (Ed.), *Writing & response* (pp. 332–366). Washington, DC: National Council of Teachers of English.

Archer, S. L. (1990). Females at risk: Identity issues for adolescents and divorced women. In C. Vandenplas-Holper & B. Campos (Eds.), *Interpersonal and identity development* (pp. 87–102). Porto: University of Porto, Portugal.

Arlin, P. K. (1984). Adolescent and adult thought: A structural interpretation. In C. Armon, M. Commons, & F. Richards (Eds.), *Beyond formal operations: Late adolescent and adult cognitive development* (pp. 258–271). New York: Praeger.

ASCD Task Force on Merit Pay and Career Ladder. (1985). *Incentives for excellence in America's schools*. Washington, DC: Association of Supervision and Curriculum Development.

Ashton-Warner, S. (1963). *Teacher*. New York: Simon & Schuster.

Bereiter, C., & Scardamalia, M. (1987). An attainable version of high literacy: Approaches to teaching higher-order skills in reading and writing. *Curriculum Inquiry, 17*(1), 9–29.

Berliner, D. (1986). In pursuit of the expert pedagogue. *Educational Researcher, 15*(7), 5–13.

Berman, R., & McLaughlin, M. (1976). Implementation of educational innovation. *Educational Forum, 60*(3), 347–370.

Bickel, W., Denton, S., Johnston, J., LeMahieu, P., Saltrick, D., & Young, J. (1987). Clinical teachers at the Schenley Teacher Center: Teacher professionalism and education reform. *Journal of Staff Development, 8*(2), 9–14.

Bielke, P. W. (1979). *The relationship of maternal ego development to parenting behavior and attitudes*. Unpublished doctoral dissertation, University of Minnesota, Minneapolis, MN.

Blasi, A. G. (1980). Bridging moral cognition and moral action: A critical review of the literature. *Psychological Bulletin, 88*(1), 1–45.

Bok, D. M. (1987). *The president's report, 1985–86*. Cambridge, MA: Harvard University.

Boyer, E. (1990). *Scholarship reconsidered: Priorities for the professoriate*. Princeton, NJ: The Carnegie Foundation for the Advancement of Teaching.

Brabeck, M. (1982). Moral judgment: Theory and research on differences between males and females. *Developmental Review, 3*(3), 274–291.

Bruner, J. S. (1966). *Toward a theory of instruction*. New York: Norton.

Bullough, R., & Stokes, D. (1994). Analyzing personal teaching metaphors in preservice teacher education as a means for encouraging professional development. *American Educational Research Journal, 31*(1), 197–224.

Burden, P. W. (1980). *Teachers' perceptions of the characteristics and influences on their personal and professional development*. Manhattan, KS: Author. (ERIC Document Reproduction Service No. ED 198 087)

Burden, P. W. (1990). Teacher development. In R. Houston (Ed.), *Handbook of research on teacher education* (pp. 311–328). New York: Macmillan.

Buttery, T. (1988). Group clinical supervision as a feedback process. *Journal of Research and Development in Education, 26*(4), 5–12.

Buttery, T., Henson, K., Ingram, T., & Smith, C. (1985). The teacher in residence partnership program. *Action in Teacher Education, 7*(4), 63–66.

Calderhead, T. (1989). Reflective teaching and teacher education. *Teaching and Teacher Education, 5*(1), 43–51.

Campbell, D. T., & Stanley, J. C. (1963). *Experimental and quasi-experimental designs for research.* Chicago: Rand McNally.

Carter, K. (1990). Teachers' knowledge and learning to teach. In R. Houston (Ed.), *Handbook of research on teacher education* (pp. 291–310). New York: Macmillan.

Carter, K. (1993). The place of story in the study of teaching and teacher education. *Education Researcher, 22*(1), 5–12.

Case, R. (1992). *The mind's staircase.* Hillsdale, NJ: Lawrence Erlbaum Associates.

Clark, C. M., & Yinger, R. K. (1987). Teacher planning in D.C. In D. Berliner & B. V. Rosenshine (Eds.), *Talks to teachers* (pp. 342–365). New York: Random House.

Clift, R., Houston, R., & Pugach, M. (Eds.). (1990). *Encouraging reflective practice in education: An analysis of issues and programs.* New York: Teachers College Press.

Cohen, D., & Ball, D. (1990). Policy and practice: An overview. *Educational Evaluation and Policy Analysis, 12*(3), 233–239.

Colbert, N., & Wolff, D. (1992). Surviving in urban schools: A collaborative model for a beginning teacher support system. *Journal of Teacher Education, 43*(3), 193–199.

Connelly, F. M., & Clandinin, J. (1990). Stories of experience and narrative inquiry. *Educational Researcher, 19*(5), 2–14.

Cornett, L. (1986). Incentive programs for teachers and administrators: How are they doing? In *Career Ladder Clearinghouse.* Atlanta: Southern Regional Education Board.

Cornett, L., & Gaines, G. (1993). *Incentive programs: A focus on program evaluation.* Atlanta: Southern Regional Education Board.

Costa, A. L. (Ed.). (1991). *Developing minds: A resource book for teaching thinking.* Alexandria, VA: Association for Supervision and Curriculum Development.

Cruickshank, D. (1987). *Reflective teaching.* Reston, VA: Association of Teacher Educators.

Cummings, A., & Murray, H. (1989). Ego development and its relation to teacher education. *Teaching and Teacher Education, 5*(1), 21–32.

Damon, W. (1988). *The moral child.* New York: Free Press.

Dewey, J. (1993). *How we think: A restatement of the relation of reflective thinking to the educative process.* Chicago: Henry Regnery.

Educational Research and Development Center. (1992). *An evaluation of the North Carolina Center for the Advancement of Teaching.* Pensacola, FL: The University of West Florida.

Erikson, E. H. (1963). *Childhood and society.* New York: Norton.

Erikson, E. H. (1975). *Life history and the historical moment.* New York: Norton.

Erikson, E. H. (1982). *The life cycle completed.* New York: Norton.

Estrada, K., & McLaren, P. (1993). A dialogue on multiculturalism and democratic culture. *Educational Researcher, 22*(3), 27–33.

Fennema, E., Franke, M., Carpenter, T., & Carey, D. (1993). Using children's mathematical knowledge in instruction. *American Educational Research Journal, 30*(3), 555–584.

Fessler, R., & Christensen, J. (1992). *The teacher career cycle: Understanding and guiding the professional development of teachers.* Boston: Allyn & Bacon.

Five chapters sponsor teacher workshops in Washington Area. (1993). *The Key Reporter, 58*(4), 1–4.

Frieberg, H. J., Waxman, H., & Houston, R. (1987). Enriching feedback to student teachers through small group discussion. *Teacher Education Quarterly, 14*(3), 71–82.

Friere, P. (1983). *Pedagogy of the oppressed.* New York: The Seaburg Press.

Fullan, M., & Hargreaves, A. (1992). Teacher development and educational change. In M. Fullan & A. Hargreaves (Eds.), *Teacher development and educational change* (pp. 1–9). Bristol, PA: The Falmer Press.

Fuller, F. (1969). Concerns of teachers: A developmental conceptualization. *American Educational Research Journal, 6*(2), 207–226.

Furth, H. (1981). *Piaget and knowledge.* Chicago: University of Chicago Press.

Gage, N. L. (1978). *The scientific basis for the art of teaching.* New York: Teachers College Press.

Gage, N. L. (1985). *Hard gains in soft sciences.* Bloomington, IN: Phi Delta Kappa.

Gardner, H. (1993). *Multiple intelligences: The theory in practice.* New York: Basic Books.

Gielen, V. (1991). Research on moral reasoning. In L. Kuhmerker (Ed.), *The Kohlberg legacy* (pp. 18–38). Birmingham, AL: REP.

Gilligan, C. (1982). *In a different voice.* Cambridge, MA: Harvard University Press.

Glassberg, S., & Sprinthall, N. A. (1980). Student teaching: A developmental approach. *Journal of Teacher Education, 31*(2), 31–35.

Glickman, C. (1990). *Supervision of instruction: A developmental approach.* Boston: Allyn & Bacon.

Glickman, C., Hayes, R., & Hensley, F. (1992). Facilitation of school empowerment: Complexities and dilemmas. *Journal of Staff Development, 13*(2), 22–27.

Gliessman, D., Pugh, R., Dowden, D., & Hutchins, T. (1988). Variables influencing the acquisition of a generic teaching skill. *Review of Educational Research, 58*(1), 25–46.

Good, T. (1979). Teacher effectiveness in the elementary school: What we know about it now. *Journal of Teacher Education, 30*(2), 52–64.

Good, T., & Brophy, J. (1984). *Looking in classrooms* (3rd ed.). New York: Harper & Row.

Goodlad, J. I. (1990). *Teachers for our nation's schools.* San Francisco: Jossey-Bass.

Goodson, I. (1992). *Studying teachers' lives.* New York: Teachers College Press.

Griffin, G. (1985). Teacher induction: Research issues. *Journal of Teacher Education, 36*(1), 42–46.

Griffin, G. (1986). Clinical teacher education. In J. Hoffman & S. Edwards (Eds.), *Reality and reform in clinical teacher education* (pp. 1–24). New York: Random House.

Griffin, G. (1987). Clinical teacher education. *Journal of Curriculum and Supervision, 2*(3), 248–274.

Grimmett, P., & MacKinnon, A. (1992). Craft knowledge and the education of teachers. In G. Grant (Ed.), *Review of Research in Education, 18* (pp. 385–456). Washington, DC: American Educational Research Association.

Hall, G., & Rutherford. (1990). *A preliminary review of research related to stages of concern.* Paper presented at the annual meeting of the American Educational Research Association, Boston.

Herring, R. (1989). *Psychological maturity and teacher education: A comparison of intervention models for preservice teachers.* Doctoral dissertation, North Carolina State University, Raleigh.

Holloway, E., & Wampold, B. (1986). Relation between conceptual level and counseling related tasks. *Journal of Counseling Psychology, 33*(3), 310–319.

Hopkins, D. (1990). Integrating staff development and school improvement: A study of personality and school climate. In B. Joyce (Ed.), *ASCD yearbook: Changing school culture through staff development* (pp. 41–67). Alexandria, VA: Association for Supervision and Curriculum Development.

Hostetler, A. (1988). Smart brains work better not harder. *APA Monitor, 19*(5), 15.

Houston, R. (Ed.). (1990). *Handbook of research on teacher education.* New York: Macmillan.

Howey, K. (1993). Altered roles and expanded responsibilities for teachers. *Teaching and Teacher Education, 9*(3), 327–332.

Huberman, M. (1991). Teacher development and instructional mastery. In M. Hargraves & M. Fullan (Eds.), *Understanding teacher development* (pp. 171–195). London: Cassells.

Huberman, M. (1993). *The lives of teachers*. New York: Teachers College Press.

Huling-Austin, L. (1990). Teacher induction programs and internships. In R. Houston (Ed.), *Handbook of research on teacher education* (pp. 535–548). New York: Macmillan.

Huling-Austin, L. (1992). Research on learning to teach: Implications for teacher induction and mentoring programs. *Journal of Teacher Education, 43*(3), 173–180.

Huling-Austin, L., Odell, S., Ishler, P., Kay, R., & Edelfelt, R. (1989). *Assisting the beginning teacher*. Reston, VA: Association of Teacher Educators.

Hunt, D. E. (1974). *Matching models in education*. Toronto, Canada: Ontario Institute for Studies in Education.

Hunt, D. E. (1976). Teachers' adaptation: "Reading and flexing" to students. *Journal of Teacher Education, 27*(3), 268–275.

Hunt, D. E. (1987). *Beginning with ourselves*. Cambridge, MA: Brookline Books.

Hyde, J., & Linn, M. (1988). Gender differences in verbal ability: A meta-analysis. *Psychological Bulletin, 104*(4), 53–69.

Illich, I. (1971). *Deschooling society*. New York: Harper & Row.

Jersild, A. (1955). *When teachers face themselves*. New York: Teachers College.

Joyce, B. R., & Showers, B. (1980). Improving inservice training: The messages of research. *Educational Leadership, 37*(5), 379–385.

Joyce, B. R., & Showers, B. (1988). *Student achievement through staff development*. White Plains, NY: Longman.

Joyce, B. R., & Showers, B. (1995). *Student achievement through staff development*. 2nd ed. White Plains, NY: Longman.

Kagan, D. (1988). Research on the supervision of counselors- and teacher-in-training: Linking two bodies of literature. *Review of Educational Research, 58*(1), 1–24.

Kagan, D. (1990). Ways of evaluating teacher cognition: Inferences concerning the Goldilocks principle. *Review of Educational Research, 60*(3), 419–469.

Kagan, D., Dennis, M., Igou, M., Moore, P., & Sparks, K. (1993). The experience of being a teacher in residence. *American Educational Research Journal, 30*(2), 426–443.

Kagan, D., Freeman, L., Horton, C., & Roundtree, B. (1993). Personal perspectives on a school-university partnership. *Teaching & Teacher Education, 9*(5), 499–509.

Katz, L., & Raths, J. (1985). Dispositions as goals for teacher education. *Teaching and Teacher Education, 1*(4), 301–307.

Kennedy, M. (1991). *An agenda for research on teacher learning* (technical report). East Lansing, MI: Michigan State University.

King, P. M., & Kitchener, K. S. (1994). *Developing reflective judgment: Understanding and promoting intellectual growth and critical thinking in adolescents and adults*. San Francisco: Jossey-Bass.

Knapp, N., & Peterson, P. (1991, April). *What does CGI mean to you? Teachers' ideas of a research-based intervention four years later*. Paper presented at the annual meeting of the American Educational Research Association, Chicago.

Kohlberg, L. (1969). Stage and sequence: The cognitive-developmental approach to socialization. In D. Goslin (Ed.), *Handbook of socialization theory and research* (pp. 347–480). New York: Rand McNally.

Kohlberg, L. (1984). *Essays on moral development* (vol. II). New York: Harper & Row.

Kohlberg, L., & Kramer, R. (1969). Continuities and discontinuities in children and adult moral development. *Human Development, 12*(1), 93–120.

Korthagen, F. (1988). The influence of learning-orientations on the development of reflective teaching. In J. Calderhead (Ed.), *Teachers' professional learning*. London: Palmer.

Kuhn, T. (1970). *The structure of scientific revolutions*. Chicago: The University of Chicago Press.

Lapsley, D. (1991, November). *Moral psychology in the post-Kohlbergian era*. Paper presented at the annual meeting of the Association for Moral Education, Athens, GA.

Lawrence, J. (1992). What if the how is why? In J. Ascendorpf & J. Valsiner (Eds.), *Stability and change in development* (pp. 240–248). London: Sage.

Lee, L., & Snarey, J. (1988). The relationship between ego and moral development. In D. Lapsley & C. Power (Eds.), *Self, ego and identity* (pp. 151–178). New York: Springer-Verlag.

Leonard, G. (1968). *Education and ecstasy*. New York: Delacorte.

Levinson, D. (1978). *The seasons of a man's life*. New York: Ballantine.

Lewin, K. (1948). *Resolving social conflicts*. New York: Harper.

Lieberman, A. (1992). Introduction: The changing context of education. In A. Lieberman (Ed.), *The changing contexts of teaching. Ninety-first yearbook of the National Society for the Study of Education* (pp. 1–10). Chicago: The University of Chicago Press.

Lieberman, A., Darling-Hammond, L., & Zuckerman, D. (1991). *Early lessons in restructuring schools*. New York: Teachers College, Columbia University.

Lind, G. (1993). *Moral und Bildung*. Heidelberg: Roland Asanger Verlag.

Linn, E. (1993). *Hitter: The life and turmoils of Ted Williams*. New York: Harcourt Brace.

Linn, M., & Hyde, J. (1989). Gender, math and science. *Educational Researcher, 18*(8), 17–27.

Little, J. (1990). The mentor phenomenon and the social organization of teaching. In B. Cazden (Ed.), *Review of Research in Education* (Vol. 16, pp. 297–351). Washington, DC: American Educational Research Association.

Little, J. (1992). Teacher development and educational policy. In M. Fullan & A. Hargreaves (Eds.), *Teacher development and educational change* (pp. 170–193). Bristol, PA: Falmer.

Loevinger, J. (1966). The meaning and measurement of ego development. *American Psychologist, 21*(3), 195–206.

Loevinger, J. (1976). *Ego development*. San Francisco: Jossey-Bass.

Loevinger, J. (1987). *Paradigms of personality*. New York: Freeman.

MacCallum, J. (1993). Teacher reasoning and moral judgment in the context of student discipline situations. *Journal of Moral Education, 22*(1), 3–18.

MacKinnon, A. M. (1987). Detecting reflection-in-action in preservice elementary science teachers. *Teaching and Teacher Education, 3*(2), 135–145.

Malen, B., & Hart, A. (1987). Career ladder reform: A multi-level analysis of initial efforts. *Educational Evaluation and Policy Analysis, 9*(1), 9–23.

Mann, A. (1992). *A quantitative and qualitative evaluation of a peer tutor-training course: A cognitive-developmental model*. Unpublished doctoral dissertation, North Carolina State University, Raleigh.

Marcia, J. (1976). Identity six years after: A follow-up study. *Journal of Youth and Adolescence, 5*(2), 145–160.

Marzano, R. (1992). *A different kind of classroom: Teaching with dimensions of learning*. Washington, DC: Association for Supervision and Curriculum Development.

McCelland, D. (1985). *Human motivation*. New York: Scott Foresman.

McKibbin, M., & Joyce, B. R. (1981). Psychological states. *Theory into Practice, 19*(4), 248–255.

Mead, G. H. (1934). *Mind, self, and society*. Chicago: The University of Chicago Press.

Mednick, M. (1989). On the politics of psychological constructs: Stop the bandwagon, I want to get off. *American Psychologist, 44*(8), 1118–1123.

Meehl, P. (1956). The tie that binds. *Journal of Counseling Psychology, 3*(3), 163–164.

Miller, A. (1981). Conceptual matching models and interactional research in education. *Review of Educational Research, 51*(1), 33–84.

Miller, G. (1969). *The psychology of communication.* Baltimore: Penguin.

Mosher, R. L., & Purpel, D. M. (1972). *Supervision: The reluctant profession.* Boston: Houghton Mifflin.

National Center for Research on Teacher Education. (1991). *Final report.* East Lansing: Michigan State University.

Newmann, F. M. (1993). Beyond common sense in educational restructuring. The issues of content and linkage. *Educational Researcher, 22*(2), 4–13.

Nisbett, R., & Ross, L. (1980). *Human inference: Strategies and shortcomings of human judgment.* Englewood Cliffs, NJ: Prentice Hall.

Noam, G., Powers, S., Kilkenny, R., & Beedy, J. (1990). The interpersonal self in life-span developmental perspective: Theory, measurement, and longitudinal case analyses. In P. Baltes, D. Featherman, & R. Lerner (Eds.), *Life-span development and behavior* (vol. 10, pp. 60–104). Hillsdale, NJ: Lawrence Erlbaum Associates.

Nolan, T., & Huber, T. (1989). Nurturing the reflective practitioner through instructional supervision: A review of the literature. *Journal of Curriculum and Supervision, 4*(2), 126–145.

Odell, S., & O'Hair, M. J. (Eds.). (1993). *Diversity and teaching: Teacher education yearbook I.* New York: Harcourt Brace Jovanovich.

Oja, S. N., & Smulyan, L. (1989). *Collaborative action reseach: A developmental approach.* London: Falmer.

Oja, S. N., & Sprinthall, N. A. (1978). Psychological and moral development for teachers. In N. A. Sprinthall & R. L. Mosher (Eds.), *Value development as the aim of education* (pp. 117–134). Schenectady, NY: Character Research Press.

Oja, S. N., & Reiman, A. J. (1996). Developmental supervision across the career span. In G. R. Firth & E. F. Pajak (Eds.), *Handbook of research on school supervision.* New York: Macmillan.

Oldendorf, W. (1992). Adventures for the intellect. In A. G. Rud & W. Oldendorf (Eds.), *A place for teacher renewal.* New York: Teachers College Press.

Oser, F. (1991). Professional morality: A discourse approach. In W. Kurtines & J. Gewirtz (Eds.), *Handbook of moral behavior and development* (vol. 2, pp. 191–228). Hillsdale, NJ: Lawrence Erlbaum Associates.

Oser, F. (1994). Moral perspectives on teaching. In L. Darling-Hammond (Ed.), *Review of research in eduction* (pp. 57–128). Washington, DC: American Educational Research Association.

Page, R. (1990). Games of chance. *Curriculum Inquiry, 20*(3), 250–281.

Paisley, P. O. (1990). Counselor involvement in promoting the developmental growth of beginning teachers. *Journal of Humanistic Education and Development, 29*(1), 20–31.

Peace, S. D. (1992). *A study of school counselor induction: A cognitive developmental mentor supervisor training program.* Unpublished doctoral dissertation. North Carolina State University, Raleigh.

Perry, W. G. (1970). *Forms of intellectual and ethical development.* New York: Holt, Rinehart & Winston.

Perry, W. G. (1975). Sharing in the costs of growth. In C. Parker (Ed.), *Encouraging development in college student* (pp. 267–276). Minneapolis: University of Minnesota Press.

Peters, R. (1978). The place of Kohlberg's theory in moral education. *Journal of Moral Education, 7*(3), 147–157.

Peterson, P., Fennema, E., Carpenter, T., & Loef, M. (1989). Teachers' pedagogical content beliefs in mathematics. *Cognition & Instruction, 6*(1), 1–40.

Phillips, M., & Glickman, C. (1991). Peer coaching: Developmental approach to enhancing teacher thinking. *Journal of Staff Development, 12*(2), 20–25.

Piaget, J. (1972). Intellectual evolution from adolescence to adulthood. *Human Development, 15*(1), 1–12.

Piaget, J. (1973). *The child and reality.* New York: Penguin.

Pintrich, P., Marx, R., & Boyle, R. (1993). Beyond cold conceptual change: The role of motivational beliefs and classroom contextual factors in the process of conceptual change. *Review of Educational Research, 63*(2), 167–199.

Provus, M. M. (1975). *The grand experiment: The life and death of the TTT program as seen through the eyes of its evaluators.* Berkeley, CA: McCutchan.

Raudenbush, S., Rowan, B., & Cheong, Y. F. (1993). Higher-order instructional goals in secondary schools: Class, teacher, and school influences. *American Educational Research Journal, 30*(3), 523–554.

Reiman, A. R., & Edelfelt, R. (1990). *School-based mentoring programs: Untangling the tensions between theory and practice.* Research Report No. 90-7. Raleigh: North Carolina State University.

Reiman, A. R., & Parramore, B. M. (1993). Promoting preservice teacher development through extended field experience. In M. O'Hair & S. Odell (Eds.), *Teacher education yearbook I: Diversity and teaching* (pp. 111–121). Fort Worth: Harcourt Brace Jovanovich.

Reiman, A. R., & Thies-Sprinthall, L. (1993). Promoting the development of mentor teachers: Theory and research programs using guided reflection. *Journal of Research and Development, 26*(3), 179–185.

Rest, J. R. (1986). *Moral development: Advances in research and theory.* New York: Praeger.

Rest, J. R., & Narvez, D. (1994). *Moral development in the professions: Psychology and applied ethics.* Hillsdale, NJ: Lawrence Erlbaum Associates.

Reynolds, A. (1992). What is competent beginning teaching? A review of the literature. *Review of Educational Research, 62*(1), 1–34.

Reynolds, M. C. (1989). *Knowledge base for the beginning teachers.* Oxford: Pergamon.

Richardson, V. (1994). *Teacher change and the staff development process: A case of reading instruction.* New York: Teacher College Press.

Richardson, V., & Anders, P. (1994). Staff development and the study of teacher change. In V. Richardson (Ed.), *A theory of teacher change and the practices of staff development.* New York: Teachers College Press.

Rogers, C. R. (1961). *On becoming a person.* Boston: Houghton Mifflin.

Rosenshine, B. (1987). Explicit teaching. In D. C. Berliner & B. V. Rosenshine (Eds.), *Talks to teachers* (pp. 75–92). New York: Random House.

Ross, D. (1988). Reflective teaching: Meaning and implication for preservice teacher educators. In H. Waxman, H. J. Freiberg, J. Vaugham, & M. Weil (Eds.), *Images of reflection in teacher education.* Reston, VA: Association of Teacher Educators.

Rowley, J., & Hart, P. (1993). Catching and releasing expert teacher thought. In M. O'Hair & S. Odell (Eds.), *Diversity and teaching: Teacher education yearbook I* (pp. 122–137). Fort Worth: Harcourt Brace Jovanovich.

Royer, J., Cisero, C., & Carlo, M. (1993). Techniques and procedures for assessing cognitive skills. *Review of Educational Research, 63*(2), 201–243.

Rulon, D. (1992). The just community: A method for staff development. *Journal of Moral Education, 21*(3), 217–224.

Ryle, G. (1984). *The concept of mind.* Chicago: The University of Chicago Press.

Schlechty, P. (1985). A framework for evaluation induction into teaching. *Journal of Teacher Education, 36*(1), 37–41.

Schlechty, P., & Vance, V. (1981). Do academically able teachers leave education? The North Carolina case. *Phi Delta Kappan, 63*(2), 106–112.

Schmidt, J. A. (1985). Older and wiser? A longitudinal study of the impact of college on intellectual development. *Journal of College Student Personnel, 26*(5), 388–394.

Schön, D. (1983). *The reflective practitioner.* New York: Basic Books.

Schön, D. (1987). *Educating the reflective practitioner.* San Francisco: Jossey-Bass.

Scott-Jones, D. (1991). From 'voice' to 'fugue' in females' development. *Educational Researcher* (2), 31–32.

Selman, R. L. (1980). *The growth of interpersonal understanding*. New York: Academic Press.

Shulman, L. (1986). Paradigms and research programs in the study of teaching: A contemporary perspective. In M. Wittrock (Ed.), *Handbook of research on teaching* (pp. 3–36). New York: Macmillan.

Sizer, T. R. (1992). *Horace's compromise: The dilemma of the American high school*. Boston: Houghton Mifflin.

Smyth, J. (1992). Teachers' work and the politics of reflection. *American Educational Research Journal, 29*(2), 267–300.

Snarey, J. (1985). Cross cultural universality of socio-moral development. *Psychological Bulletin, 97*(2), 202–232.

Snarey, J., Kohlberg, L. M., & Noam, G. (1983). Ego development in perspective: Structural stage, functional phase, & cultural age-periods models. *Developmental Review, 3*(3), 303–338.

Sparks, G. (1986). The effectiveness of alternative training activities in changing teaching practices. *American Educational Research Journal, 23*(3), 217–225.

Sparks, G. (1987). Promoting the professional development of teachers in career ladders. In P. Burden (Ed.), *Establishing career ladders in teaching: A guide for policy makers* (pp. 5–27). Springfield, IL: Charles C Thomas.

Sprinthall, N. A. (1975). Fantasy and reality in research: How to move beyond the unproductive paradox. *Counselor Education & Supervision, 14*(4), 310–322.

Sprinthall, N. A. (1980). Psychology for secondary schools: The saber tooth tiger revisited? *American Psychologist, 35*(4), 336–347.

Sprinthall, N. A., & Bernier, J. W. (1979). Moral and cognitive development for teachers: A neglected arena. In T. C. Hennessy (Ed.), *Value moral education: The schools and the teachers* (pp. 119–144). New York: Paulus Press.

Sprinthall, N. A., Reiman, A. J., & Thies-Sprinthall, L. (1993). Roletaking and reflection: Promoting the conceptual and moral development of teachers. *Learning and Individual Differences, 5*(4), 283–299.

Sprinthall, N. A., Sprinthall, R. C., & Oja, S. N. (1994). *Educational psychology: A developmental approach* (6th ed.). New York: McGraw-Hill.

Stallings, J., & Krasavage, E. (1986). Program implementation and student achievement in a four-year Madeline Hunter follow-through project. *Elementary School Journal, 87*(2), 117–138.

Strommer, D., Biggs, D., Haase, R., & Purcell, M. (1983). Training counselors to work with disabled clients: Cognitive and affective components. *Counselor Education and Supervision, 23*(2), 132–141.

Sykes, G., & Bird, T. (1992). Teacher education and the case idea. In G. Grant (Ed.), *Review of research in education* (vol. 18, pp. 457–521). Washington, DC: American Education Research Association.

Thies-Sprinthall, L. (1980). Supervision: An educative or miseducative process? *Journal of Teacher Education, 31*, 17–30.

Thies-Sprinthall, L. (1984). Promoting the developmental growth of supervising teachers: Theory, research programs, and implications. *Journal of Teacher Education, 35*(3), 53–60.

Thies-Sprinthall, L. (1986). A collaborative approach for mentor training: A working model. *Journal of Teacher Education, 37*(6), 13–20.

Thies-Sprinthall, L., & Gerler, E. R. (1990). Support groups for novice teachers. *Journal of Staff Development, 11*(4), 18–23.

Thoreau, J. (1966). *Walden*. Princeton, NJ: Princeton University Press.

Tom, A. (1985). Inquiring into inquiry-oriented teacher education. *Journal of Teacher Education, 36*(5), 35–44.

Underwood, B. J. (1957). *Psychological research*. New York: Appleton Century Crofts.

Vaillant, G. (1977). *Adaptation to life*. Boston: Little, Brown.

Vance, V., & Schlechty, P. (1982). The distribution of academic ability teaching force. *Phi Delta Kappan, 64*(1), 22–27.

Veenman, S. (1984). Perceived problems of beginning teachers. *Review of Educational Research, 54*(2), 143–178.

Vondracek, F. (1992). The construct of identity and its use in career theory and research. *The Career Development Quarterly, 41*(2), 130–141.

Vygotsky, L. (1978). *Mind in society: The development of higher psychological processes*. Cambridge, MA: Harvard University Press.

Walberg, H. J. (1986). Synthesis of research on teaching. In M. Wittrock (Ed.), *Handbook of research on teaching* (3rd ed., pp. 214–229). New York: Macmillan.

Walker, L. K. (1986). Sex differences in the development of moral reasoning. *Chlid Development, 57*(2), 522–526.

Walker, L. K. (1991). Sex differences in moral reasoning. In W. Kurtines & J. Gewirtz (Eds.), *Handbook of moral behavior and development* (vol. 2, pp. 333–364). Hillsdale, NJ: Lawrence Erlbaum Associates.

Walters, S., & Stivers, E. (1977). The relation of student teacher's classroom behavior and Eriksonian ego identity. *Journal of Teacher Education, 31*(6), 47–50.

Waterman, A. S. (1984). Identity formation: Discovery or creation? *Journal of Early Adolescence, 4*(4), 329–341.

Waterman, A. S. (1992). Identity as an aspect of optimal psychological functioning. In G. R. Adams, T. P. Gullotta, & R. Montemayor (Eds.), *Adolescent identity formation* (pp. 50–72). Newbury Park, CA: Sage.

Waterman, A. S., & Archer, S. L. (1990). A life-span perspective on identity formation: Developments in form, function, and process. In P. Baltes, D. Featherman, & R. Lerner (Eds.), *Life span development and behavior* (vol. 10, pp. 30–59). Hillsdale, NJ: Lawrence Erlbaum Associates.

Weil, M., & Joyce, B. R. (1978). *Social models of teaching: Expanding your teaching repertoire*. Englewood Cliffs, NJ: Prentice Hall.

Welfel, E. R., & Davidson, M. (1986). The development of reflective judgment during the college years: A four year longitudinal study. *Journal of College Student Personnel, 27*(3), 209–216.

Wenz, A. (1987). Teacher centers: The New York State experience. *Journal of Staff Development, 8*(2), 4–10.

White, R. W. (1959). Motivation reconsidered. The concept of competence. *Psychological Review, 66*(5), 297–333.

Yarger, S. (1990). The legacy of the teacher center. In B. R. Joyce (Ed.), *Changing school culture through staff development* (pp. 104–116). Alexandria, VA: Association for Supervision and Curriculum Development.

Zeichner, K. (1987). Preparing reflective teachers: An overview of instructional strategies which have been employed in preservice teacher education. *International Journal of Educational Research, 11*(5), 565–575.

· 30 ·

AUTHENTIC ASSESSMENT

Kip Tellez

UNIVERSITY OF HOUSTON

Tests tell us who we are when we are not quite sure.
—Hanson, *Testing Testing*

Educational connoisseurs recognize the signature that individual teachers give to their work. . . . We need to recognize the pervasive qualities of teaching as they are displayed in some form and a judgment—one that is difficult to ask—of how teaching might be enhanced.

—Eisner, *The Enlightened Eye*

The changing contexts of education, schooling, and teaching and the emphasis on reflective practice in progressive, innovative teaching pose special problems for the assessment of teaching. Few would argue that what is considered "excellent" teaching has remained a singular and static construct. Fewer still would argue that contemporary assessments of teaching that are traditional in perspective are adequate to capture the subtleties of innovative instructional practice (Grover, 1991; Smith, 1990). Those who find traditional measures lacking are searching for more contextually and personally sensitive ways to assess the complex professional practices of teachers. The purpose of this chapter is to honor the spirit of this search by examining theoretical and practical perspectives on authentic teacher assessment.

When teachers and teacher educators understand their work, they understand their role as members of a complex profession, which, in turn, promotes an examination of the deeper meanings of practice and the assumptions behind those practices. The term *authentic assessment* denotes those assessments of practice that emerge from context-sensitive understandings of pedagogical and personal principles that underpin the work of

teaching. Centrally, the proponents of authentic assessment want to engage teachers in thoughtful, self-conscious, and ongoing examinations of the important problems of their work in the situations where they work. Such examinations rest on teachers' descriptions of their own practices. Asking the question, "What am I doing?" provides the context and perhaps the motivation needed for teachers to stand back and examine their practices. If teachers can describe what it is that they do in a day or over time—independently or with the assistance of others—they may be better positioned to think about central questions that define their work. The ebb and flow of professional life occasions the opportunity to think about another central question, "How am I doing?"

ASSESSING TEACHING

Provided that teachers have sufficient information about the "what" and "how" of their practice, they may be compelled to ask a third, equally important, question, "How can I do better?

I thank Tom Bird (Michigan State University), Ardra Coles (Ontario Institute of Studies in Education), Pat Holland (University of Houston), and Carol Mullen (Ontario Institute of Studies in Education) for their formative reviews of this chapter. A special thanks goes to J. Gary Knowles (University of Michigan) who provided assistance in earlier drafts of this chapter. I am, however, solely responsible for any inaccuracies or shortcomings.

or "How can I enhance my practice?" Teacher educators, those who promote professional practice in education, are fundamentally concerned with the processes by which emerging professionals ask and answer these questions. From the perspective of a teacher educator, these central questions can be examined this way: The job of professional preparation is to facilitate (1) the degree and intensity with which emerging teachers ask "what" and "how" they are doing, and (2) the insights and enhanced views of practice that come from internal assessments of "how" they can do better. University teacher educators and school administrators responsible for teacher evaluation face similar predicaments in their external assessments of teachers. As a teacher educator working in a program of initial teacher preparation, the author has sought to make assessment more authentic within a program designed to prepare teachers for urban schools and acknowledges that even his most concerted efforts still fall short of the ideal. However, as an emerging discipline, authentic assessment of teaching will require a level of indeterminacy and vagary as it comes into its own.

To clarify the use of terms in this chapter, *emerging teacher* encompasses both preservice teachers who are seeking teaching certification and beginning teachers, although it is acknowledged that many experienced teachers may consider themselves as emerging, as lifelong learners, much like emerging teachers. The term *student* is reserved for pre–K–12 children and youth. *Teacher* is used as a general term for both in-service and preservice teachers.

Recently, much emphasis in the professional literature has been placed on teachers' interest in and concern with asking about how they are doing. In a broad sense, this focus is central to the work of reflective practice. The opposite of the reflective teacher is one who rarely or never considers in depth the "what" or "hows" of practice. Such a teacher functions uncritically, even within ever more complex contemporary educational, social, and political landscapes.

The assessment of teaching is problematic, riddled with tensions and challenges. On the one hand, the centrality of reflective practice in innovative teaching is more suitable to inquiry and dialog rather than to formal assessments and evaluations. On the other hand, professional practice itself is in need of reassessment, as are theories about, and stances on, assessment. In other words, one cannot be exclusively concerned with the promotion of particular professional practices for and by teachers. This chapter's focus is on assessment from the perspective of "productive diversity rather than standard uniformity" (Eisner, 1991, p. 79) within the multiple, overlapping landscapes of teachers' work and individual/personal signatures; innovative and sensitive methods/modes of practice; and documentation of the increasingly varied/complex topography of assessment in research-based theory and technique.

Even a representation of teacher assessment is itself problematic. For example, this chapter often relies on a language borrowed from a heritage of teacher evaluation that might be considered "inauthentic," primarily because the language of authentic assessment is emerging. This dilemma draws attention to the minimal work pursued, as evidenced in the educational literature, on what has recently been called authentic forms of assessment. The author proceeds with full recognition that there exists a rich foundation of professionally enhancing teacher assessment, but the focus of this chapter (on the advice of the editors) is on the recent literature in the area. Therefore, the chapter grew into less of a formal review of literature and more of an exploration of possibilities.

The unevenness in the assessment literature draws attention to a distinction between what is relatively easy to measure but not very interesting and what is extraordinarily difficult to understand and document but highly important. Schön (1987) points out this tension in *Educating the Reflective Practitioner:*

In the varied topography of professional practice, there is a high hard ground overlooking a swamp. On the high ground, manageable problems lend themselves to solution through the application of research-based theory and technique. In the swampy lowland, messy confusing problems defy technical solution. The irony of this situation is that the problems of the high ground tend to be relatively unimportant to individuals or society at large, however great their technical interest may be, while in the swamp lie the problems of greatest human interest. (p. 3)

Schön's description, as a suggestive analogy, portrays the current state of research in teacher assessment. The high ground in traditional teacher evaluation is represented by lesson-length observations in which the evaluator arrives at the classroom with a checklist of "teaching behaviors" to be found. Although sometimes useful, such an evaluation obscures the day-to-day, encompassing, and behind-the-scenes work of a teacher and says little about his or her influence. For instance, typical and traditional assessments rarely explore and document the extent to which a teacher has created a democratic classroom where issues are raised about race, class, and gender. How many traditional assessments of teaching strive to capture the finely textured meanings and patterns of practice? Rarely does a checklist examine the educational experience of students, for example, or how teachers' core assumptions about practice are evidenced in actions, activities, and resources.

Gitlin and Smyth (1989) can be turned to for their distinction between "educative" and "dominant" views of teacher evaluation. The dominant view, they argue, serves to perpetuate the notion of teaching as a semi-profession. They cite Gitlin and Goldstein (1987) to support this stance:

These abrupt observation visits are initiated with little sense of the classroom's history and upon completion are not integrated into its ongoing history. In making these judgments, the administrator is usually armed with a summative rating scale which lists any number of desirable teaching outcomes. . . . The evaluator acts as an expert who knows the script and score and has in mind how it can be best realized. The teacher satisfies or does not satisfy the expert in varying degree. . . . The activity is essentially monologic, essentially a process of communiqués, of one way declarations about the state of things. (p. 7)

It is not a question about whether traditional, dominant constructs are theoretically sound but, rather, about the sensitivity with which educational professionals and their practices, contexts, and situations are understood. Traditional assessment works well if the teaching practices are themselves traditional. In a classroom and student context, for example, if a teacher's instruction is designed so that students remember the date of the signing of the Declaration of Independence, then traditional multiple-choice type tests serve a useful purpose; however, if a teacher hopes for students to understand deeply the concept of democracy and how this peculiar system of government is realized in modern cultures, then most traditional assessments are likely to fail. Similarly, if a teacher educator facilitates and encourages emerging teachers' practices to exhibit use of anticipatory sets in setting up a lesson, then traditional teacher assessments may be potentially very useful; however, if the instructional goal is more slippery and elusive and focuses on such concepts as "reflective teaching" or culturally sensitive teaching, teacher behavior checklists are undeniably inadequate.

However, the difficulty in assessing teaching should not prevent teacher educators from attempting to uncover the critical issues in teaching practice. Just as the direction of instructional assessment of students has recently loosened the bonds that held it closely to multiple-choice, true-false, and other "objective" measures, so, too, assessment connected to teacher education must continue to explore and formalize authentic ways to assess teaching.

Some readers may be disappointed to discover that this chapter does not review the salient literature in the field and present the "best form" or forms of authentic assessment. Even if the literature on authentic assessment were large enough to provide a more substantial, analytical review, authentic assessment of teaching is a constantly emerging concept. As an evolving concept, authentic assessment is, perhaps most appropriately, configured as both an ideal to which teacher educators aspire and an attitude or way of thinking about professional practice rather than a "measure" of teaching performance. This review discusses some of the ways in which people are using the term *authentic assessment,* some of the ideas on which authentic assessment is based, and some of the things people are doing under the heading of authentic assessment. Readers should also note that because teacher evaluation is a value-laden activity, one cannot entirely eliminate individual bias.

Teacher Assessment in the 1980s and 1990s

The "crisis" reports on education in the early 1980s motivated changes in teacher preparation and assessments of the teaching profession (Sikula, 1990). The interest in teacher preparation and development led to increased attention to teacher assessment from professional bodies: existing teacher education–related organizations and at least two significant organizations whose aims included enhancing teaching professionalism. Well-known is the energetic effort of the Educational Testing Service (ETS) in developing statewide certification tests for both preservice and in-service teachers (Dwyer, 1993). For instance, the Praxis Series for beginning teacher assessment measures academic skills, subject-matter knowledge, and classroom performance (Educational Testing Service, 1992). With the addition of the classroom performance assessment portion of the series, it seems that ETS is poised to provide teacher evaluation services to schools.

Perhaps the most visible of the newly formed groups is the National Board for Professional Teaching Standards (NBPTS). The NBPTS's own standards, reported in the document, *Toward High and Rigorous Standards for the Teaching Profession,* were published along with the Board's perspectives about the assessment of teachers (National Board for Professional Teaching Standards, 1986). Their perspectives on assessment, perhaps better interpreted as expectations, represent the position that the assessment procedures, encompassing a variety of methods, have an effect on the teacher's role, on student learning, and on the public's perception of schools and education more in general. The model proposed by the NBPTS suggests that the assessment of teachers involves two modules (Baratz-Snowden, 1993). The first centers on data collected from an actual teaching setting such as videotapes of classroom instruction and student artifacts (such as projects, student portfolios, and essays). The activities of the second module take place in an "assessment center" where teachers engage in interviews, simulations, and written tests designed to corroborate evidence gained at the school site. Exactly who would evaluate the evidence created in both modules is not specified.

Although the efforts of the NBPTS might be considered a substantial innovation in teacher assessment, they do not, in the author's view, reflect authentic assessment procedures. Both the model proposed by the NBPTS and the language used, even in the context of this representation, are reminiscent of common traditional methods and philosophies. The NBPTS's standards and certification procedures may be useful in many ways but this work does not reflect authentic assessment. However, it must be recognized that the work of the NBPTS is clearly difficult and may reflect the conceptual tension that arises when traditional perspectives on assessment are used to capture new and progressive practices. The NBPTS standards are but one example of recent attempts to renew the debate on teacher assessment. As other professional groups and practitioners explore new methods of teacher assessment, the issue of authentic assessment will receive additional attention.

The Call for Renewed Assessment in Teacher Education

Highly visible and diverse organizations, such as the NBPTS and the ETS, are currently exploring new forms of teacher assessment and evaluation. The vigorous funding and support of such groups and their efforts imply, among other things, a dissatisfaction with the ways in which teachers are presently assessed.

The call for renewed forms of teacher assessment turns on the distinction between "bureaucratic" and "professional" teacher evaluation (Darling-Hammond, 1986). As the descriptor suggests, a bureaucratic view of teacher assessment assumes that the teacher's work is highly rule-governed and prescribed and is tantamount to ensuring that personnel (i.e., teachers) perform tasks supported by the larger organizational structure. However, a professional view of teacher evaluation suggests that teachers are thoughtful about their practices and that the contours of their profession necessitate that they frequently modify those practices. It also assumes that teachers engage in professional practice in spite of the bureaucratic routinization and constraints of their work.

Murnane and colleagues (Murnane, Singer, Willet, Kemple, & Olsen, 1991) have broadened the audience of those interested in teacher preparation and assessment, especially in the area of certification and licensing. As a policy analyst, Murnane has argued that traditional tests of licensure such as the National Teacher Exam (NTE), with its core battery and professional knowledge sections, fails to discriminate between levels of teaching skill and eliminates a disproportionate number of minority prospective teachers from the pool. He also argued that performance-based licensing should supplant traditional licensing examinations.

For many years, teacher educators have acknowledged that standardized tests or traditional assessments of teachers have little content validity with respect to actual teaching practice (Grover, 1991). Therefore, what is surprising for some is not the call for reform of teacher assessments but the intensity of involvement of the manifold policy groups in asserting their interests. Recall that Murnane is not a teacher educator but a policy analyst. The licensure and maintenance of licensure of teachers impacts a wide range of professional and policy groups that have vested political, membership, and financial interests. Attention paid since the mid-1980s to teacher evaluation appears more vigorous than in earlier years.

Also critical in the renewed attention for teacher evaluation is who is participating in the reform agenda. For instance, to what extent have teacher associations become involved in the process? This feature is critical at least for in-service teacher evaluation in strongly unionized states. Peterson and Chenowith (1992) have demonstrated that teachers must have some control over the evaluation development and process if they are to consider an assessment system both valid and useful and, more important, meaningful and valuable.

Defining "Authentic"

Although the term *authentic assessment* is emerging in the educational literature and in the field, not all who use the term agree on its meaning, nor do those who agree on its meaning necessarily practice a similar form of authentic assessment. The strength of authentic assessment is revealed in situations involving sensitivity to complex contexts. Another strength rests in its potential for acknowledging and exploring relational qualities. The very lack of consensus of meanings attributed by professionals may, in fact, provide evidence of a contextual responsiveness at work. In spite of the confusion surrounding the term, teacher educators and others seem to be in agreement that if the type of assessments typically in use are not authentic, then new ones are required.

It is important to point out that providing definitions of *authentic* is not the primary purpose of this chapter. However, in order to discuss what teacher educators and others are calling authentic, a common but provisional understanding must be created. What might authentic mean with respect to assessment and evaluation? Authenticity implies that an assessment is "genuine," "real," "uncompromised," "natural," or "meaningful." Although these descriptors clearly outrun common dictionary definitions of authentic, they are appropriate when referring to this alternative form of assessment.

Assessments are authentic according to the degree to which they are meaningful to and helpful for teachers in the exploration of their practices. The role of the individual teacher involves negotiation of desirable methods of assessment, it is not to satisfy others involved in the assessment processes. Rather,

entering into dialogues about alternatives to existing practice gets at the heart of authentic assessment processes. Authenticity turns on teachers and their classroom practices—and the histories of those practices—as well as their own perceptions of roles, experiences, and work more in general. However, it is important to point out that authentic assessment practices should not be associated with benevolence toward the learner or, in this case, teacher. Authentic assessments may indeed be better received by teachers than less authentic forms of assessment, but that charge is not being extolled here. Teachers, for instance, may claim that authentic assessments divert their attention from matters that more directly impact students. In the next section authentic assessment in the context of teacher evaluation is more fully described.

Separating "Authentic," "Alternative," and "Traditional"

Two emerging terms represent the new category of assessment used in many educational settings: a distinction may be drawn between "authentic" and "alternative" forms of assessment and "traditional" assessments. Again, the point here is not to provide specific definitions of terms but to explore the potential use of the terms *authentic* and *alternative*. Of course, as emphasized earlier, not all educators would agree with this usage, nor would the author expect such agreement. The discussion, therefore, is to illustrate, not to define.

Authentic assessment in the context of teacher evaluation may include variations on alternative assessments that meet two criteria: (1) that teachers have a voice in how they are assessed and in creating the climate that is conducive to assessment, and (2) that the assessment is embedded in the specific contexts of teachers' work, including their perceptions of roles, experiences, and practices. As the teacher education community dialogs about the place of "authentic assessment" in theory and in practice, changes in meanings of the term will occur. The following examples further describe the use of these terms.

Alternative assessments represent any evaluative process that varies significantly from traditional forms of assessment. Alternative assessments, then, deviate from traditional assessments such as "objective" evaluations and checklists of teaching behaviors. For instance, the state of Texas, like nearly all others, requires all those seeking state certification or specialist endorsements to pass professional development tests. This battery of tests is known as the Examination for the Certification of Teachers in Texas. Before 1993 all tests were in a multiple-choice format, measuring discrete learning outcomes, representing traditional assessment forms, and a number of the tests still represent this view. The following example is taken from the Professional Development Test study guide for the reading specialist endorsement:

Which of the following factors is considered most important in top-down reading models?
a. decoding
b. textual input
c. syntax
d. prior knowledge (Study Guide 45, Reading, National Evaluation Systems, 1990, p. 23)

The form of this assessment is traditional and is also inauthentic for several reasons. It follows the common form of a multiple-choice item, measures a discrete and disintegrated learning skill, requires no experiential basis in order to answer, and has one and only one correct answer. Although not authentic as defined in this chapter, this test question and others like it may serve a useful purpose. Certainly, the multiple-choice format continues to be widely used in every type of educational setting.

The current elementary comprehensive test, however, is moving toward an alternative assessment and requires emerging teachers to read a series of cases and to respond to several questions regarding teacher thinking. Fifteen "competencies" frame these dimensions and the test items correspond to each. The following item is taken from the study guide.

Each student in Ms. Burgess's third-grade class has been working on writing a story for the past week. Ms. Burgess observes that several of her students are spending their daily writing period adding on to their stories, making them longer but not necessarily better, and doing no revision except occasional corrections of misspelled words. She wants to encourage these students to take a broader, more exploratory approach to revision—to review and evaluate their work and then reshape it according to their new insight. Which of the following teaching strategies would be most effective in achieving this goal?
(a) asking students to think about what parts of their story are most important and whether they have described these parts clearly and effectively.
(b) encouraging each student to place an appropriate limit on the length of his or her story based on the number of characters and events the student intends to include.
(c) having students brainstorm words related to the subject of the stories they are writing and decide which words might be incorporated in their work.
(d) suggesting that students begin each writing period by drawing an illustration that depicts the main story idea they wish to convey that day and then resume work on their writing. (National Evaluation Systems, 1993, p. 41)

The new form of the ExCET tests might be considered an alternative to the traditional assessment. The latter example is not "traditional" in that it attempts to test teacher knowledge in a more integrated way, but because it remains insensitive to (1) emerging teachers' prior individualized knowledge, (2) the context of preparation to teach and work, and (3) the resolution of lived problems, it is regarded as less than authentic. Its authenticity is questioned not only because it uses a multiple-choice (one correct answer) format but also because it does not consider the implicit theories held by teachers in relation to their practices. Again, this type of assessment may be useful in a certain context. The purpose of the ExCET is to screen thousands of potential teachers, making more context-sensitive assessments prohibitively expensive.

The two previous questions provided examples of assessments divorced from the actual context of the classroom. How might assessments conducted in the classroom be categorized? Sikorski, Niemiec, and Walberg (1994) provided an example of a traditional performance-based assessment: a checklist of teaching behaviors based on what the authors maintain are the best teaching practices. The instrument is divided into five sections, including "Presenting the Lesson" and "Student Participation." The observer is asked to respond "yes," "no," or "not observed" to approximately seven statements in each of the five categories, yielding a total of 39 items. An example taken from the lesson presentation section requires the observer to ascribe a "yes," "no," or "not observed" to the statement, "Asks higher-order questions." This teaching checklist clearly represents a traditional and inauthentic assessment of teaching. The teacher being observed was not invited to participate in either the formation of the categories or the items themselves. The context is perhaps authentic, but the method of data collection discourages any kind of personal exploration. Calling this assessment "traditional" may imply that all other teacher evaluation programs before today have been equally inauthentic. This implication is not intended. Indeed, the use of a behavior checklist in the classroom could engage both the observer and the teacher in a discussion of the merits of the checklist itself. Teaching checklists have also been used as a starting point for discussing what happened in a lesson. However, claiming to have discovered best practices in teaching and vesting their qualities in a checklist seems both inauthentic and unlikely.

In summary, the changing grounds on which the various definitions of assessment rest must be emphasized. Many authors make no fundamental distinction between the concepts of alternative and authentic assessments, for example, and the resulting lack of clarity provides readers and reviewers of research reports with considerable challenges.

Recent Descriptions of Authentic Assessment

Authentic assessments represent those measures that ring as being true to the learner. Herman, Aschbacher, and Winters (1992) suggested that authentic assessment (although they used the term alternative), "requires [learners or teachers] to actively accomplish complex and significant tasks, while bringing to bear prior knowledge, recent learning, and relevant skills to solve realistic or authentic problems" (p. 2). Using this definition, which is not without its problems, it is evident that the old form of the ExCET is clearly inauthentic and the new form troublesome as well.

Zessoules and Gardner (1991) suggested that authentic assessment meets four criteria not typically associated with other assessments: (1) nurtures complex understandings, (2) develops reflection as a habit of the mind, (3) documents learners' (teachers') evolving understandings, and (4) uses assessment opportunities as a moment of learning. All of these features can be understood as representing growth in learning, a central element of and in the authentic assessment of teaching. Growth in learning and self-growth together loosely provide the conditions for educative experiences (Dewey, 1938) as those that promote both growth in general and the conditions for further growth. The metaphor of "growth as education and education as growth" might serve as the epistemological basis of authentic assessment processes. In addition, with respect to the final criteria, as noted by Zessoules and Gardner, the opportunity for teacher assessments is not often conceptualized as an occasion when teachers learn more about prospective practice in what might be described as a "teachable moment." In a similar vein, Marzano and Kendall (1991), drawing on their explorations of the scant literature on authentic assessment, noted several features of authentic assessment, one being the notion of personal relevance as related to personal professional goals. Returning to the earlier example, and using these definitions, the Professional Development ExCET tests and checklists of teaching behaviors are determined as being inauthentic.

The Continuum of Assessment

The temptation to view assessment as a dualism may divert attention away from the fundamental issues in the evaluation of teaching. Because there are no well-accepted definitions for authentic assessment, teacher educators may be inclined to accept that some assessments are authentic simply because their form is different from traditional assessments. For instance, the use of portfolios has emerged as a form of authentic assessment, but simply using portfolios in no way promises that the assessment is authentic. Documents in individual portfolio files prepared by teachers (in this case) represent and articulate, through various meaningful media, crucial elements of their work. Portfolios, whose writers help shape the foci, therefore, are compilations of documentary evidence that illustrate teachers' practices and work activities in their complexities and in their contexts. Similarly, portfolio assessments of students' work potentially give both teachers and students control over the representation of students' learning and performance. As a worst-case scenario, it is easy to imagine a teacher's so-called portfolio containing nothing more than a series of external lesson-length observations by an observer unfamiliar with either the teacher, the classroom, or the students. The focus should not be on the labels for evaluation styles but rather on the substance of what is being evaluated. This task, however, may prove difficult to accomplish.

Humankind's penchant for thinking in dualisms has been well documented by Dewey (1938) and others. Dualisms often make discussions lively and concepts easier to reckon, but they often hide critical issues embedded in the dualism itself. As the educational research community has debated the lines between and the assumptions behind qualitative and quantitative research methodologies (Howe, 1992), new lines are being established in the debate over authentic and traditional assessments (Cizek, 1991, 1993; Shepard, 1993; Wiggins, 1991). With respect to the debate about quantitative and qualitative research, Eisner (1991) argued that the "line" between them is not unambiguous: some forms of qualitative research involve quantification, whereas some forms of quantitative inquiry make use of qualities. Perhaps it is possible that the major issues in qualitative inquiry—"generalization, objectivity, ethics, the preparation of qualitative researchers, validity, and so forth" (p. 7)—are no less shared in quantitative inquiry. Issues of assessment, then, are illuminated by the expansiveness of lines and divisions, not by the steadfastness of dualisms. Just as an educational inquiry process in and of itself is neither valid nor invalid, the success of an assessment process is determined by a number of dimensions, including the potential for improvement of practice through reflectivity; the potential for dialog (involving facilitation, negotiation, and decision-making processes) among participating parties;

and the forms of representation within the assessment climate and the assessment literature itself.

This author takes the view that external assessments are less likely to be authentic, especially when the teacher is left out of the design and implementation of the "instrument" or when the teacher does not know of or agree with evaluator's version of good teaching. Even internal assessments or some forms of self-evaluation might be inauthentic under certain circumstances. More strongly put, self-deception is recognized as an epistemological orientation to both experiencing and reconstructing the self (Crites, 1979). We can all become convinced that we are doing poorly or well in spite of evidence to the contrary. The challenge for the teacher education community is to avoid the generalizing dualisms and to appeal to the aims of the particular assessment process. An assessment process in and of itself is neither "good" nor "bad," valid or invalid. Rather, an assessment's worth and merit is ultimately determined by its actual use and by the subsequent claims made.

Thus far, a substantial discussion has not occurred about the assumptions underlying both authentic and traditional assessment processes. In effect, the teacher education community is in the process of determining whether different kinds of assessment are even possible given constraints imposed by institutional structures, systems, and processes. Whereas it is not advisable to organize the discussion within the context of the dualism between authentic/traditional or even between authentic/alternative, disagreements about whether assessments are authentic or inauthentic are not wholly undesirable. Discussions of the underlying perspectives may in fact provide opportunities for redefining terms.

Teacher evaluation at the in-service level has clearly become a political instrument at times, yet the discussion has not centered on the level of authenticity suggested by the various forms of assessment. Rather, teachers and policymakers have argued about the qualifications and credentials of the assessor, the frequency of assessments, and their stated purpose and intended use.

The Concern Over Validity

Consider several of the features Poster and Poster (1991), whose work in Great Britain represents a shift away from traditional teacher assessment, suggest are present in a well-run appraisal system:

- Integrates the individual and the organization.
- Provides the opportunity to initiate problem-solving and counseling interviews.
- Encourages self-development.
- Provides the basis for an institutional audit.
- Provides for the dissemination of career development advice.
- Gives individuals greater clarity of purpose through the provision of clear objectives, while allowing for autonomy of method.
- Helps build collective morale.
- Encourages and inspires individuals and enhances their self-esteem and self-confidence.

- Reduces alienation and removes resentment.
- Facilitates the identification of potential talent.
- Enhances the communication of organizational aims to all staff and facilitates the coordination of effort.
- Channels individual effort into organizational goals.
- Provides a mechanism whereby individual effort can be recognized even if no financial rewards can be offered.
- Provides a mechanism whereby individuals can influence the organization.

Poster and Poster admit that few appraisal systems can achieve all of these goals; however, many practicing educators typically find that the assessment and evaluation of their teaching meet few of these goals.

Authentic assessment focuses attention on the value of the experience for participants (as evidenced in the central questions that opened the chapter) and on the interpretations of practice as gathered from teachers' experiences. The questions of what constitutes the "data," who uses them, and how are of primary importance. Validity, within an authentic assessment climate, is associated with the thoughtful consideration of teachers' needs and the value, held for those involved, of processes (including decision making), documentation, and representation. Validity, within a traditional assessment context, is commonly understood in terms of whether or not the process measures what it claims to measure. However, by focusing only on the assessment itself, many educators miss an important feature of validity. As Cronbach (1971) noted, "One validates not a test, but an interpretation of data arising from a specified procedure" (p. 447). The ritual and ceremony in social sciences include techniques designed to substantiate the validity of "tests" of teaching. These procedures may establish that an assessment achieves a level of criterion validity and performs well on tests of reliability among experts, but they may not appeal to Cronbach's standard. Validity is established both in the interpretation and use of the data produced by an assessment technique. For instance, a classroom observation instrument may yield data that appear on the surface to "measure" what it claims to "measure," but validity may be compromised if the data are then used to rank teachers for the purpose of merit pay.

Authentic assessment focuses attention on the use and interpretation of information. It articulates teachers' understandings about the contexts of their experiences as well as understandings of those experiences. Again, the questions of who uses these interpretations, why, and how are of primary importance. Generally, alternative assessments have not contributed to the understandings and development of those being assessed. Just as in the public school context traditional forms of assessment have focused on ranking, sorting, and grading students rather than on explicitly promoting their development as learners, so it is in the context of teacher education and evaluation. Traditional forms of teacher evaluation likewise are less concerned with teacher development per se and more focused on ranking, sorting, and grading teachers according to reward or merit structures.

As the educational community has grown in its interest in authentic assessments for student evaluation, validation experts have rushed to caution educators on the widespread use of

such assessments (Messick, 1994). Others have claimed that gauging the validity of authentic assessments can follow validation patterns similar to those used in traditional types of assessments, although a marked interpretive stance must also be taken (Moss et al., 1992).

FOUNDATIONS OF AUTHENTIC ASSESSMENT PERSPECTIVES

Reappraising Phenomenology

Like education in general, teacher education since the 1970s has undergone a transformation. That transformation could be described as a movement away from behaviorism, with its emphasis on external evidence of learning and observable learning "objectives," to constructivism or cognitivism. Constructivism, for example, emphasizes the learner's prior knowledge as critical to the learning process, something which behaviorism ignored or downplayed considerably. More broadly, constructivism assumes that learning is private and that the evidence of learning is often hidden from the view of the onlooker.

In teacher education one might recognize this shift as one that began with competency-based teacher education (Houston & Howsam, 1972) in which the objectives for teaching were clearly defined and measurable, to a "reflective" (Zeichner & Liston, 1987) or "contructivist" (Fosnot, 1989) teacher education that suggests that teachers are responsible for building meaning into their own pedagogies. However, these shorthand descriptions represent a larger philosophical movement that anticipated and, to some extent, defined these shifts.

In the most general terms, education has moved "indoors" to where individuals' experiences are viewed as central to understanding learning and teaching. This change in educational discourse may be considered the result of the attack on positivism brought on by phenomenology, one of several schools of thought questioning the claims of the logical positivists. Phenomenology, as articulated by Husserl (1962), maintains that each individual's experience is crucial to understanding the nature of reality, crucial to understanding consciousness, and therefore central to understanding learning. Phenomenology owes much to Socrates' disillusion with the methods of science, which led him to study not the physical realities of the world but, instead, the mind and the products of the mind. Edie (1987) describes the phenomenological experience this way:

Concepts are not things or substances or forces at all; they are rather meaning or structures forged by the mind in its experience of things. "In itself" the world is neither true nor false, nor is it meaningful or valuable, it takes on meaning only in relation to a mind which orders and relates its parts, which thus institutes objects of thought and, by thinking the world, introduces into it the relationship of knowledge, of possible truth and falsity. What the mind creates is a tissue of possibilities. (p. 4)

In contrast to a strictly positivistic view of reality, phenomenologists assert that the subjective is vitally important (Husserl, 1962; Merleau-Ponty, 1962). This stance places value squarely on the self; however, it must undergo a modification or extension within the context of teaching. Teaching is about persons-in-relation, primarily the relation between teachers and students. The professional development of teachers places weight on a much broader range of possibilities with respect to self and others. What Husserl and other phenomenologists make clear is that so-called subjective experiences are central to understanding, whether those experiences are derived alone or with others.

Grumet (1992) recognizes the value of contextual understandings, the "impact of milieu," for and on the self: "autobiographical methods are rooted in context" (p. 40). Context, in this view, is embedded in "metatheory" that honors interpretations of human experience and educational (research) endeavors. For teachers, the path of inquiry extends inward and outward, in lived practices and in implicit and explicit theories.

Because authentic assessment seeks to throw teachers back on to themselves, teacher educators with a desire to help teachers think more clearly about their world may begin with a dialog. Rather than meeting a particular teaching competency, as judged by an outside observer who, by implication, represents a world independent of a teacher's consciousness, questions can shift to the teacher. "What happened?" comes out of the central question that heads this chapter: "What am I doing?" As another example, the question, "Did you feel that you met the intents of the 'lesson'?" asked of a teacher might come out of a second and third fundamental question, "How am I doing?" and "How can I do better?" or "How can I enhance my practice?" Such questions may provide direction for dialog between teachers and observers and for teachers in their more private moments. For the phenomenologist, the question, "What am I doing?" is of central importance.

Phenomenology plays a central role for those interested in authentic assessment. Authentic assessment seeks to help "the learner" become more aware of the learning process; therefore, the phenomenological perspective emerges as genuine. Because authentic assessment seeks to involve the teacher-as-learner in the assessment process and in a control role, the process is a phenomenological one. A low-inference teaching evaluation instrument (such as a teaching "checklist") as a tool to gauge the quality of a teacher's lesson that further represents the sum of his or her teaching fails to consider the perceptions of the teacher during the observed lesson. For instance, teachers are centrally concerned with the welfare of children and youth, and, from the phenomenological outlook, such concerns must be taken into account. Indeed, the private experiences of the teacher are what have the greatest validity or, more appropriately, most value. Therefore, the process of evaluating teaching becomes one of individual exploration, but as embodied in action and in sensitivity to context. Grumet (1992) made the argument that a

phenomenology of educational experience examines the impact of acculturation on the shaping of one's cognitive lens. Existentialism recognizes culture as the given situation . . . through which the individual expresses his [sic] subjectivity, embodied in acts in the world. Awareness of self develops not in hermetic introspection, but in the response of subjectivity to objectivity. (p. 40)

Barber (1990), for example, points out the value of self-evaluation and suggests that self-assessment when used in a

threatening environment can greatly enhance professional development. Elliot (1989) recognizes the phenomenological in teacher assessment, suggesting that when teaching is considered a reflective practice within the boundaries of a professional ethic, "it constitutes a form of moral science in which teachers' self-evaluations play a central role in the development of professional knowledge" (p. 256).

Other researchers also point out indirectly that teachers' perceptions are crucial in their own evaluations of their work. In a study that directly examined teachers' perspectives on their own evaluations, Peterson and Comeaux (1990) found that an alternative evaluation procedure, in which teachers watched a videotape of their lessons and were asked to respond to series of questions about their lessons, was rated highest among several other evaluation systems (such as teacher behavior checklist) by both experienced and emerging teachers working in Florida and Wisconsin. McLaughlin and Pfeifer's (1988) statement that, "Any teacher evaluation system depends finally on the responses of those being evaluated, the teachers" (p. 4), suggests that teachers must value and respect the evaluation process and product if the assessment is to be effective. Although reliance on such evidence is not unproblematic, the essential point is that teachers must not only have a central role in the assessment of their own teaching but also must see it as a valuable and valid process.

The focus on the phenomenological perspective taken here should not suggest that all those working in the authentic assessment of teaching agree with the assumptions of phenomenology. The recent attention to poststructuralism in education may also offer a vehicle for advancing authentic teacher assessments. For instance, Delandshere and Petrosky (1994) argue that the interpretive narratives written by teachers may play an important role in the assessment of teaching. Within a poststructuralist framework, teacher narratives become stories that can then be interpreted much like works of fiction. Such a reading, they argue, allows teacher educators, for example, to read emerging teachers' personal narratives by using codes and systems of text interpretation. The poststructuralist view of teacher narratives also suggests that teachers create new knowledge (not simply describe their experiences) as they construct a narrative. These features are honored within the phenomenological perspective as well.

In addition, educators working toward authentic assessment may also base their work in cognitive science, particularly those studies focused on the nature of consciousness (Dennett, 1991). If authentic assessment is based on teachers' views of their own experience, then the study of what we know (consciousness) takes its rightful place in the discipline of teacher assessment. However, whether the study of consciousness is the domain strictly of philosophy or of science is a matter of great dispute.

Teacher educators working toward authentic assessment of teaching may rely on a range of theoretical and epistemological perspectives as they approach their work. Clearly, the innovations under way in the authentic assessment of teaching have had little time to become firmly rooted in any one theoretical viewpoint and are unlikely to do so. Phenomenology may not emerge as the primary philosophical perspective of authentic assessment, and this chapter makes no such prediction. However, phenomenology might be considered as the philosophy at the heart of many recent theories of learning and teaching that focus on the experiences of learners (e.g., constructivism).

Also important are the types of "data" that teachers may use in creating a picture of their teaching. What evidence might a teacher or teacher educator use in assessing teaching? And how might these data be considered authentic? These questions are examined in following sections.

ROLES IN AND APPROACHES TO AUTHENTIC ASSESSMENT

Roles of the Self

Internal Information Gathering: Autobiographical Writing and Other Forms of Self-Assessment The authentic assessment of the self in professional school settings can involve autobiographical writings and explorations that place the individuals and their experiences at the center. The primary value of autobiographical writing within teacher education is "rooted in the process of coming to terms with oneself" (Knowles & Holt-Reynolds, 1991, p. 106).

Conceptualization of the autobiographical method as a vehicle for reflecting on and assessing practice in teacher education rests on the creation and development of texts about such practice. Personal or life history accounts; journals of various kinds; explorations of personal metaphors; reflective accounts of practice; professional development summaries (representing many such reflective accounts); and other formal and informal records and writings provide the basis (Holly, 1989; Knowles & Cole, in press).

These multiple text approaches to self-reflexivity aim to enhance emerging teachers' self-understandings, as well as their thinking about teaching and learning. Personal history accounts enable writers to understand their present inclinations to practice in light of meanings associated with earlier experiences. For example, such accounts may include elements of artistic expressions of various kinds that focus on the primacy of stories about early learning experiences in educational settings. These accounts are also likely to focus on and illuminate the implicit theories, values, and beliefs that underpin emerging teachers' orientations to becoming education professionals and the subsequent development of their practices. Within such mental landscapes of emerging ideas about practice the notion of authenticity can be established because such personal documents contain representations of formative experiences in relation to more immediate "professional" thinking.

Autobiographical writers generate stories of experience and accounts of practice that, in turn, can become the basis for continuing conversations with others about the process of becoming a teacher (Clandinin, Davies, Hogan, & Kennard, 1993; Knowles, 1993). Sensitive teacher educators can, moreover, facilitate emerging teachers' reflexivity through engaging in ongoing conversations and writing about their practices. This kind of personal exploration in relation with others is the hallmark of the principles of experiential education (Dewey, 1938). Such explorations into the inquiring self do not have to take place in isolation.

One of the roles of university-based teacher educators, for example, may be to facilitate the professional development of preservice teachers by facilitating collaboration with their peers. Among the many ways in which preservice teachers might work together is sharing autobiographical writing and developing collective accounts that arise about early experiences in schools, teaching together, or out of other joint or group work associated with being teachers in preparation. Emerging teachers' "horizontal evaluations" (Gitlin & Smyth, 1989) of each other's teaching practices, for example, could take place within several contexts and could encourage collegial collaboration (Knowles & Cole, with Presswood, 1994).

In keeping with the proposed definition of authentic, forms of self-assessment are not viewed as unproblematic, perhaps partly because of the freedom of writers to construct less accurate and trustworthy, and even reliable, accounts of their thinking and life. Crites (1979) reminded us that "experience is an imaginative construction" and that "in our experiencing we employ the same imaginative forms that appear, highly refined, in artistic expression" (p. 107). Assuming that the constructive process is integral in experiencing, it follows, Crites claims, that self-delusion is rooted in this very process. However, goals for critical self-inquiry are not intended to be clearly defined and "measurable," nor is a single version of pedagogy to be encouraged (Eisner, 1991). From this perspective, individuals' interpretations of experience are considered central to authentic assessments. It is the autobiographical presence itself in writing that is at the heart of authenticity, the search for justification, and the assessment of teaching practices. Some authors (Connelly & Clandinin, 1991; Eisner, 1991; Geertz, 1988) consider the question of signature as a significant criterion of authenticity in a writer's identity. As Eisner (1991) writes:

each person's history, and hence world, is unlike anyone else's. This means that the way in which we see and respond to a situation, and how we interpret what we see, will bear our own signature. This unique signature is not a liability but a way of providing individual insight into a situation. (p. 34)

When teachers ask "what" and "how" questions about their practice, they might desire to know more about how they can personally go about both engaging and constructing versions of their own pedagogies and professional development. At such points they are at the doors of self-inquiry, constructivism, and phenomenological reflexivity. Their signatures and voices must be validated in order for the process of authentic teacher assessment to be handled sensitively, ethically, and meaningfully. In a broader sense, even this criterion of authentic assessment must be continually reviewed and revisited by preservice teachers and teacher educators alike. Authentic assessments, then, could be considered as those that emerging teachers experience as genuine and that actually rescript their thinking about practice.

In the process of assessing their practices, emerging teachers might also learn more about the theoretical views of experience. Such perspectives may validate the efforts of inquiring selves to make sense of experiences. University teacher educators might also benefit from engaging emerging teachers' narratives; the narratives can provide a window into the context of preservice teacher education itself and its relevance for personal inquiry and formal research (Knowles, 1993; Knowles & Cole, with Presswood, 1994). Finally, emerging teachers might also learn more about the primacy of stories as a vehicle for both understanding and constructing authentic practice.

External Information Gathering

Persons associated with teaching and learning as an inquiry-based phenomenon gather external information to inform their thinking about contexts and practices. This process is implemented in various educational environments and by various professionals. Observations, interviews, and artifacts are examples of external information-gathering techniques that typically provide opportunities for the development of sensitivities to classroom environments and understandings about teaching practices. Like internal forms of information gathering or assessment, external approaches to exploring teaching can promote personal and professional understanding of the central questions, "What am I doing?," "How am I doing?," and "How can I do better?"

External forms of information gathering and assessment, like internal forms of assessment, involve a similar set of processes. Whether information is being generated or collected about the environment; its contexts, processes, events, and people; or about the self, both demand a sensitivity to how moments, events, and circumstances can be heard and seen, documented and understood, and then finally visited and revisited. Some qualitative researchers, for example, struggle with the distinction between the "internal" and the "external" as sources of experience and information. Traditional practices of doing ethnographies promote distance, models, fixed and stable realities, and detachable conclusions (Rose, 1990), but for teachers involved in both the internal and external representation of practices, this difficulty may be less evident.

Alternative ways of assessing teaching must be rendered credible through increasingly introspective methods of engagement and analysis. Like ethnographers, reflexive teachers struggle to bring the self and the environment into intelligible relationships. Geertz (1988), for example, recommended journal writing as a channel for ensuring that ethnographic accounts are both reliable and personal. Rose (1990), another ethnographer, experimented "until [he] . . . broke with the old categories and inaugurated a new narrative responsiveness to changing world cultural relations" (p. 15). Such progressive forms of ethnography can be appreciated in relation to work being produced within the teacher education community. Contributors to this autoethnographic approach include Diamond (1992), Middleton (1993), and Mullen (1994). To continue this tradition into the arena of classroom work is not altogether a new suggestion. For example, Gitlin et al. (1992) suggested that explorations of both personal and institutional histories are prerequisites for "educational research" activities, the bases for initiating enhanced practices in schools.

The internal and external modes of practice that allow teachers to construe understandings of their work as a basis for assessing teaching have been highlighted. Potentially meaningful information-gathering approaches, such as participant observation, interviewing, or collecting documents or artifacts, and analytical practices such as ethnography, are at the heart of authentic documentation of teachers' work and inquiries. The value of these information-gathering and -documenting processes is rooted in their sensitivity to the central questions of assessment that arise out of inquiry into educational contexts.

Changes in Participants' Roles

The incorporation of alternative assessments in preservice teacher education will no doubt change the way in which the various participants carry out their respective roles. For instance, the questions posed at the beginning of this chapter must become a habit to teachers thinking about their practice. These same questions presume that teacher educators facilitate the development of reflective inquiry-oriented teachers with habits, attitudes, and practices of self-assessment and development. Authentic assessments take into account information about the teacher in relation to students, colleagues, school- and university-based teacher educators, and others. In inquiry-oriented preservice teacher education (see, e.g., Clandinin et al., 1993; Knowles & Cole, in press; Knowles & Cole, with Presswood, 1994; Zeichner & Liston, 1987), preservice teachers learn to engage in inquiry into and to assess the multiplicities of roles, contexts, and relationships that define their emerging practice. As an example, portfolio assessment of preservice teachers may invite school-based teacher educators to become the preservice teachers' advocates. A teacher educator who assists in the development of an emerging teacher's portfolio functions to best represent abilities and achievements of the new teacher. Instead of the gatekeeper function typically held, the school-based teacher educator emerges as a portfolio advisor. Such school-based teacher educators prepared for such activity would likely see their role differently. But, even more so, portfolio development places greater responsibility in the hands of emerging teachers who have to make difficult decisions about the form and focus of their public representations.

The Role of University-Based Teacher Educators

The authentic assessment of emerging teachers suggests new roles for university-based teacher educators. Quite possibly their most important function is to work toward understanding field experiences from the perspectives of preservice teachers. Much understanding can come about from engaging with written and spoken narrative accounts of preservice teachers' experiences (Clandinin et al., 1993; Knowles & Cole, with Presswood, 1994). The writing on autobiographical and other forms of self-assessment advocated in this chapter reflect such a perspective.

A final issue of competing importance is the evidence that university-based teacher educators are inquiring into and formalizing their own developing perspectives as teachers/researchers (e.g., Cole & Knowles, in press; Diamond, 1992; Hunt, 1987; Knowles, 1992; Middleton, 1993). For example, as an experienced outdoors educator Knowles (1992) wrote about a peak teaching experience involving students from a New Zealand high school. After canoeing to a glow worm grotto that inspired students to marvel at the "power of beauty and

. . . the organization and design of Nature's panoramic night display" (p. 7), Knowles was silent during his "greatest teaching moment," one that offered an opportunity for personal assessment and professional writing embedded in the site of a special event. Bullough (1994) provided another example. As a teacher educator grappling with aspects of curriculum development and his own pedagogy, he explores the meanings of particular teaching experiences through the exploration of aspects of his personal history. Similarly, Rafferty (1994) traces the development of her particular approach to portfolio development in teacher education.

The Role of the School-Based Teacher Educators

Processes associated with the authentic assessment of emerging teachers suggest a new role for cooperating teachers and other school-based teacher educators. In considering teacher involvement in authentic assessment, Herman et al. (1992) suggest that new instructional and other roles for both teacher educators and emerging teachers need to be discovered. In the typical student teaching arrangement, for example, school-based teacher educators serve an important evaluative role, although several studies show that college supervisors provide emerging teachers with more substantial evaluative feedback (Guyton & McIntyre, 1990). However, emerging teachers tend to place more value on their cooperating teachers' evaluations than on those of their college supervisors (Yates, 1981). Typically, school-based teacher educators are asked to provide one or two formal evaluations of the emerging teacher. The format of these evaluations is generally provided and is sometimes prescribed by the teacher preparation institution; however, the many informal but formative evaluations of emerging teachers by the school-based teacher educators are intended to improve practice. Authentic assessment strategies may serve to capture the subtleties of these ongoing "suggestions" for improved teaching because of the expanded range of legitimate information about practice that can be potentially drawn.

Authentic assessment may also change the role of school-based teacher educators. One example of the changing role of school-based teacher educators is provided by the University of Houston's Pedagogy for Urban and Multicultural Action (PUMA) program. Student teaching "interns" present their exit portfolios to a group of educators and peers in the professional development school where their teaching experience took place. In this reflective conversation, school-based teacher educators are asked to report in what area they provided the greatest assistance. In addition, each member of the portfolio review committee reports what he or she learned from the student intern, thus blurring the lines between teacher and student. The focus of the portfolio presentation in the PUMA program is on the emerging teacher's experience; the committee offers additions and reinterpretations of the emerging teacher's thoughts.

In portfolio assessment stakeholders in the evaluation process (such as university faculty and a school district) can often shift their role from "gatekeeper" to advocate for those being evaluated. The role of advocate may be a proper fit for the school-based teacher educator. Instead of assisting in the gatekeeping function of evaluation, school-based teacher educators help emerging teachers develop substantial portfolios that represent their own professional development. As school districts in Pittsburgh, Houston, and Tucson, for instance, experiment with and refine their own evaluation procedures, many are making use of portfolio assessment in a variety of contexts.

The Role of Peers

Working in isolation has been a norm of school culture and of teachers' work (Hargreaves, 1990; Johnson, 1990; Rosenholtz, 1989). Increasingly, however, widespread efforts are being made to challenge the isolationist mode of teaching and working in schools by encouraging teachers to engage in collaborative or joint work. Like their experienced counterparts, preservice teachers also have traditionally been very much alone in their work:

Student teaching can be characterized somewhat as the teaching profession has been—as a lonely profession. In the same way that practicing teachers tend to be isolated from their colleagues by the organization of schools and by the ways in which schools are designed, the student teacher–cooperating teacher dyad appears to be isolated from other dyads and, indeed, from other cooperating teachers and student teachers. (Griffin, 1989, p. 362)

Preservice teacher education programs typically do little to change this pattern. Placing preservice teachers in individual classrooms and keeping their attention focused within the confines of that classroom and on the more technical aspects of teaching (on which they are typically evaluated) foster the perpetuation of norms of isolation and a relatively narrow conception of teachers' work.

If teachers are expected to change the way they think about and carry out their work and to learn from collaborative assessment of their practices, the experience of isolation and its subsequent focus on individual development within teacher preparation programs must change. Preservice programs hold particular promise for challenging traditional norms because old socialization patterns stand the chance of being interrupted by a new generation of teachers who conceptualize and carry out their work in more collaborative ways. Authentic assessment opportunities in which preservice teachers work with their peers are likely to enhance and encourage collaborative practices and careerlong professional development. Examples of collaborative self-assessment practices include developing collaboratively constructed group and individual portfolios; sharing autobiographical writing; group activities and discussions; and peer observations of practice.

The Role of Students

Whereas the teacher's self-evaluation is critical in the implementation of authentic assessment, all thoughtful teachers, at some point, turn their attention to the students' experiences in their classrooms. Some teachers may even invite students to provide their own views of the educative experience the teacher has provided. The question to be raised is, "What role does student assessment of teaching play in the authentic assessment of teaching?"

Students in colleges and universities are regularly invited to provide their own assessment of the teacher's instruction. Although the assessment of teaching in higher education is slow at moving toward alternatives, let alone authentic assessments, student evaluations of teaching may hold a promise of authenticity. However, as they are currently designed, most course and instructor evaluations resemble the teaching checklists that have been demonstrated to be quite inauthentic, in addition to other fundamental flaws. In spite of the obvious shortcomings of teaching evaluations in higher education, the results of such evaluations are often used in high stakes decisions (e.g., tenure) (Marsh, 1987). In order to create more authentic student assessments of teaching, teachers themselves must have a voice in the type of evaluation methods and materials used. For instance, typical assessments of teaching in higher education are predetermined forms that may or may not reflect the goals of an individual instructor. It seems, too, that the students providing the ratings must be given the opportunity to respond to more authentic questions about their teacher's work.

Student evaluations have been generally ignored by K–12 teachers primarily because of the perceived unreliability of students' observations of teachers and the propensity of younger children to acquiesce to those in leadership roles. Nevertheless, student evaluations of teaching effectiveness may be considered as an alternative element to traditional assessments of teaching, especially if such assessments can be integrated into a broader self-reflective evaluation scheme in which teachers view the students' assessments as a form of "internal" data.

The important issue is whether student evaluations can be considered a form of authentic assessment of teachers' work. Young children are less likely to provide "reliable" assessments of their teachers' professional work. This criticism is worthy only if we assume that student assessments remain inauthentic themselves. Typical student evaluations at the university level do not represent authentic assessments of their instructors. Students are given many opportunities over the course of a school year to critique their teachers' work in relatively free form. Such input might become well suited to improve teaching. Shor (1987) suggested that students provide teachers with critiques of provided educative experiences in a forum of open and honest communications. The blurring of the teacher/student distinction, Shor claims, is demonstrated by student critiques, essential for liberatory teaching. To include student evaluations as elements within authentic assessments of teaching is appropriate when the form of such contributions is less confining, less "traditional," and more authentic.

The Role of School Administrators

School administrators play a major role in teacher evaluation. Hickox and Musella (1992) outlined the typical performance evaluation conducted by school principals—a ritual familiar to most practicing teachers. But perhaps the greatest impact of principals' performance appraisals is felt during the first few years of teachers' careers. Typical beginning teacher evaluation procedures illustrate the critical role of school administrators (Peterson, 1990).

The practices of many emerging teachers are closely scrutinized. The average of three formal evaluations that administra-

tors—usually the school principal or assistant principal—impose on emerging teachers is stressful. By treating the assessment of emerging teachers in a sensitive manner, administrators can have a great influence on how these teachers perceive their professional selves. Thus, the organizational demands that require more intensive evaluation of emerging teachers can either enhance or disrupt initial socialization into the profession; new teachers may fear and even resent administrators' obligatory evaluations or may instead view them as an opportunity for professional growth.

Those who evaluate emerging teachers are often bound by standards imposed by school districts and state bureaucracies. A highly structured assessment system, based on bureaucratic scrutiny designed to remove incompetent teachers, can actually work against an institution's best interests. The application of "minimum" teaching standards can frustrate good teachers to the point of quitting (McLaughlin & Pfeifer, 1988). Nearly all emerging teachers believe they will be treated as professionals, yet when administrators impose strict minimum competencies, many may feel apprehensive about inquiries into their practices and official perceptions of them. The implied denial of professional status that results from imposed assessments of practice may account for why many teachers leave teaching soon after they begin (Schlechty & Vance, 1983).

EXAMPLES OF EFFORTS IN AUTHENTIC TEACHER ASSESSMENT

Self-Assessment as Narrative

Personal Knowledge in Teaching Personal knowledge is a critical component of teacher assessment. It is a powerful vehicle for enhancing learning and approaching writing as a problem-solving or thinking-through process (Knowles & Cole, with Presswood, 1994). Personal knowledge can be constructed through life history accounts and other forms of autobiographical writing. Such accounts are intended to bring forward stories of experience of learning in formal and informal settings and the meanings attributed to those experiences. Personal history accounts, for example, provide a medium for preservice teachers to access their private mental worlds and to assist their professional development.

The self, if approached as an invaluable research "instrument" (Glesne & Peshkin, 1992), is central to genuine teacher assessment. Personal history accounts, for example, sometimes draw attention to preconceptions of teaching, implicit beliefs about good teachers, appropriate learning contexts, family values, sources of inspiration that influenced the decision to teach, and more (Knowles, 1993). Such topics can be pursued as chapters in more fully developed narrative accounts of personal and professional practice.

The notion of assessment does not sit easily within formal educational studies of personal knowledge. Indeed, the concept of "authentic assessment" would probably be viewed as somehow out of whack by those whose exclusive focus is on the development of personal knowledge. The impetus for personal knowers is to address issues and phenomena of greatest human concern, not of technical interest and accuracy. Having acknowledged this divergence, it is also important to clarify that positions on "assessment" do exist in the literature on personal knowledge. As indicated in the section on "Internal Information Gathering," the issue of narrative criteria is rooted in a researcher's autobiographical presence. In other words, the more visible the writer and his or her self, the more reliable the basis for assessing the research. As Connelly and Clandinin (1994) write, "a text written as if the researcher had no autobiographical presence would constitute a deception about the epistemological status of the research. Such a study lacks validity" (p. 11).

Conceptions of autobiographical presence, together with signature and voice, underscore issues of integrity *and* rigor. Efforts to develop authentic assessments strive to address these overlapping dimensions. Integrity can be thought of as that which involves the "personal participation of the knower in the knowledge he [sic] believes himself to possess," that which "takes place within a flow of passion" (Polanyi, 1962, p. 300). Like integrity, rigor can be understood as inextricably linked to one's convictions and deepest passions. Another dimension of rigor draws attention to the criteria that guide the text and by which it may be read and assessed.

Teachers as researchers of their own practices strive to clarify such matters while also liberating themselves from "objective" measures of knowledge. This intellectual tension is at the heart of the issue of narrative assessment for qualitative researchers. The process of authentic assessment for researchers can therefore be mapped according to a cyclical movement: the realization is that "we can voice our ultimate convictions only from within our convictions." The vision is to "aim at discovering what [we] truly believe in and at formulating the convictions which [we] find [ourselves] holding" (Polanyi, 1962, p. 267).

As preservice teachers prepare themselves to begin the "real" work of teaching in schools, they assert that context for learning about teaching is the classroom itself. This section was created with the intention of honoring this conviction. It was also created with the intention of honoring an authentic approach to assessment. This approach empowers teachers and researchers alike to become engaged in reflection on their own practices and narratives of observation. In turn, they can equip themselves more fully to respond to pressing concerns that grow out of the core questions, "How am I doing?" and "How can I do better?"

Portfolio Assessment

The popularity of implementing portfolio assessment in both in-service and preservice education contexts is growing, but there are very few noteworthy examples in the available research literature. Although this lack of documentation is of concern, it may simply represent the lag between design and implementation of practice and lacked opportunities for researching and research reporting (Bird, 1990).

Collins (1991) outlined the use of portfolios among experienced secondary biology teachers. This portfolio assessment, Biology Teacher Assessment Project (BioTAP), calls on teachers to document their instruction in several broad areas. In one element of the portfolio teachers were asked to provide background information, including a professional biography and a profile of the school and community setting and the internal school environment, to provide a context for the remainder of the portfolio. Collins reports that teachers regarded this work and the portfolio content as being relatively unimportant, perhaps because those who participated in this pilot project already knew one another.

In a second element of the portfolio teachers were asked to show evidence of their planning and preparation by developing a unit of instruction. The teachers were asked to document the activities of the unit, to complete a daily lesson log, and to reflect on the implementation of the unit in specific ways. A third element invited teachers to submit evidence, including a videotape of a lesson that used either alternate materials or an innovative laboratory activity. A fourth element, designed to document teachers' assessment skills, asked that they maintain a 6-week-long journal of their responses to the various forms of evaluation. A fifth element asked teachers to submit evidence of their work in the larger educational community, recognizing that professional teachers, besides practicing in classrooms, also engage in interchanges with local school and community leaders. This element was less well received by the teachers primarily because they believed that their primary responsibility was teaching students subject matter, not serving on committees or local professional organizations, for instance. A sixth element, an "open" category, invited teachers to submit any other evidence they deemed valuable.

The elements of the BioTAP assessment that received the most positive ratings from the teachers were highly student-centered. Notwithstanding the incongruity between the research methodology and the intention of the assessment process in postproject interviews, the teachers indicated that the experience embedded in the portfolio process, although not enjoyable, was valuable for three reasons: (1) the devoted interest and concern toward their profession from "outsiders"; (2) the "face validity" of the portfolio (it looked like their teaching); and (3) the fact that the portfolio development process "impelled them to clarify their intentions and beliefs about students, about biology, and about teaching" (Collins, 1991, p. 164). The teachers reported that they would not engage in portfolio development if rewards were not forthcoming.

Miller and Tellez (1993) outlined the use of teaching portfolios for emerging teachers working in a professional development school. In such school contexts, they argued, portfolio assessment can reach its full potential. For example, at the completion of the student teaching period, emerging teachers "present" their portfolio to university- and school-based faculty members, some of whom have observed emerging teachers' practices. A peer of the emerging teacher also participates with faculty in the evaluation process. The contents of the portfolio are similar to those used in the BioTAP example. What seems most powerful in this model is the presentation of the portfolio to a committee of experts. The portfolio presentation serves both as a professional growth activity (for both preservice and in-service teachers) and as an entree into the profession. In interviews regarding the portfolio process, the emerging teachers initially regarded the process as a program requirement but partway through the process felt ownership in what they were doing, viewing the portfolio as theirs.

Bird (1990) articulated both the problems and possibilities of using portfolios of teaching. He argues for their use but notes that research evidence of their value does not yet exist. By outlining a typology for the contents of a teacher's portfolio, Bird suggests that the contents be defined by the participants (e.g., the teacher alone, the teacher in concert with other educators, or someone outside the classroom) and by the degree of formality required of the documents (e.g., ranging from notes from a parent to diploma and licenses).

Bird's primary emphasis was on the potential collaboration with other educators, which portfolio assessment may encourage. As an assessment issue, collaboration deserves considerable attention as a vehicle for improving teacher assessment and evaluation processes generally. Bird (1990) claimed that,

Schoolteachers would spend considerable time working with their portfolios and with their colleagues to examine, refine, and share a growing stock of strategies, practices, plans, activities, and materials—a body of increasingly refined solutions to the concrete problems of school teaching. (p. 254)

King (1991) reported on portfolio assessment use in the Teacher Assessment Program (TAP) at Stanford University, as did Wolf (1991) who described the use of portfolio assessments. After considering the issues associated with their use, Wolf concludes that the primary benefit of teaching portfolios is their contextual sensitivity to teaching and consideration of the personal histories of teachers.

Many teacher educators advocate teaching portfolios for the purpose of assessment. Portfolios are accepted by both teacher education faculty and emerging teachers. But there remains an important distinction between the creation of portfolios and their evaluation. Furthermore, there is the issue that the contents of portfolios need to articulate the spirit and work of teachers' practices. Teacher educators need to be thoughtful about the essential difference between the creation of teaching portfolios themselves and related assessment issues. Few may argue about the value of a teaching portfolio as a tool for self-improvement, but when the portfolio is tied to an evaluation system used to determine certification, potential consequences may then carry high stakes.

Performance-Based Assessment

Assessment in teacher education is typically performance-based, but the implementation and articulation of performance assessment are typically very specific and highly selective. Rarely does a teacher evaluation system not rely on some form of classroom performance criteria embedded in university classrooms and courses or in field experience classrooms and schools. In their review of research on the assessment of teaching, Andrews and Barnes (1990) described six teacher programs in detail, and all but one use performance-based assessment. Over half of these evaluation programs were developed in state departments of education for use in the assessment of experienced teachers. Many university preservice programs emulate the evaluation design of local school districts or the state, aware that their students will soon be measured by such systems.

It is important to point out that performance-based assessment of teaching is not necessarily new (this point is discussed later in this section) and that its implementation in no way guarantees authenticity. The studies explored here may indeed remind one of the distinction between alternative and authentic assessment made earlier in this chapter. Readers may discover that recent investigations into performance-based assessments reflect the alternative assessment perspective but fall short of authenticity.

Performance-based assessments may invite teachers into "assessment centers," sites removed from their own classrooms. The sites presume that the conditions under which assessment take place can be better controlled in a center. The best-known assessment center was developed at Stanford University in association with the TAP whose primary mission was the development of assessments for potential use by the NBPTS. One recent research example of performance assessment developed at the TAP, and which purported to be authentic, invited two secondary history teachers—one an experienced man, the other a beginning woman—to demonstrate their practice in three exercises: (1) evaluation of student papers, (2) use of documentary materials, and (3) textbook analysis (Wilson & Wineburg, 1993). As might be expected, the two teachers' performances differed substantially. For example, when asked to assess the "historical soundness of the text, particularly as it applied to the history of women and minorities" (p. 750), the veteran teacher claimed the sample text to be sound because it devoted attention to women and minorities. However, the younger teacher reported dissatisfaction with the sample text because it neglected important historical references to women and minorities. Wilson and Wineburg avoided comparing the teachers' performance but admitted that the younger teacher's responses fell more in line with their views on teaching and learning. Even with respect to the divergent views on the treatment of women and minorities, Wilson and Wineburg pointed out that the experienced teacher's thoughtful but not radical views are to be valued as those of a generalist. They also noted that the youthful idealism and critical orientation of the younger teacher has "showed little staying power" in schools, perhaps best predicting burnout and early exit from the profession. Are those evaluating teachers any closer to understanding and assessing teachers' complex work? The answer to this question depends largely on who is asking the question. The basis for questioning the authentic nature of this performance assessment lies in the less-than-comprehensive approach to understanding practice.

Haertel outlined a performance test that is completed outside the teachers' classrooms in a "quasi-laboratory" environment. Noting the lack of any systematic research into teacher performance/assessment activities completed outside classrooms, Haertel outlines several prototype exercises developed by the TAP (Shulman, Haertel, & Bird, 1988). Again, such assessments may reflect alternatives to typical classroom performance assessments, but do they reflect the authentic perspective?

Linn, Baker, and Dunbar (1991) noted that the call for authentic assessment is not new, pointing out that Linquist (1991) made explicit the tasks of achievement test authors: "to make the elements of his test series as nearly equivalent to, or as much like, the elements of the criterion series as consequences of efficiency, comparability, economy, and expediency will permit" (p. 52). Linquist's recommendations, made over four decades ago, suggest that in the clamor to develop achievement tests, the educational community somehow took a wrong turn. The majority of achievement tests, including those designed to assess knowledge of teaching, bear little resemblance to the elements of the established criteria. The current attention to authentic assessment, then, can be conceived not as an entirely new direction but, rather, as the rediscovery of a once-illuminated path.

In keeping with the spirit of Linquist's work, Linn et al. (1991) suggested that to achieve adequate levels of validity (their term) authentic assessments must meet several criteria. Authentic assessments must include evidence "regarding the intended and unintended consequences, the degree to which performance on specific assessment task transfers, and the fairness of the assessments" (p. 20). They must also be explicit about the cognitive complexity required to "solve" problems posed. The meaningfulness of such assessments for teachers (and students) must be addressed. Required also is an appropriate basis for judging the content quality and comprehensives.

CONCLUSION

It is one matter to conclude that it is of fundamental importance that assessment methods and procedures be reconstrued, but it is quite another to implement authentic forms of assessment in institutional contexts. The difficulty of using such forms rests in the possibility that they may be viewed as exceedingly complex, unfeasible, unmanageable, or all three. However, a focus on the nonmeasurable, nonquantifiable aspects of teaching gives importance to the subjective and idiosyncratic elements of practice that are usually lost in institutional and bureaucratic environments. As Eisner (1991) wrote: "The cultivation of productive idiosyncrasy in the art of teaching is as important as in the art of painting" (p 79).

This chapter argues the need for and the place of authentic assessment of teachers' practices in classrooms and in schools. Although the focus of this chapter has been on emerging teachers with respect to the value of their assessments of teaching, teachers at more advanced stages in their careers benefit from authentic explorations of their practices. Because the innovations are both promising and necessary, authentic teacher assessment has a place in the reinvention of teacher education. It is critical that the educational community think about how further research on authentic forms of assessment can be carried out in preservice teacher preparation programs in universities, schools, and classrooms. Research-based theory and technique need to become more culturally and contextually sensitive than previously conceptualized. One struggle encountered in writing this chapter grows out of the deep entrenchment of traditional concepts of assessment within discussions of authentic and alternative assessments. Nonetheless, researchers and practitioners must be sensitive to the understandings that configure integrated interpretations of teachers' work. Consequently, it is hoped that this chapter promotes conversations in the education community.

In the third edition of the *Handbook of Research on Teaching*, Shavelson, Webb, and Burstein (1986) aligned the measurement of teaching to applications of generalizability theory, the view that sources of error in measurement can be reduced by explicitly assessing each source of error and reducing its contribution to overall error in the measurement. One of the studies on which they drew to discuss generalizability theory assessed the effect of error introduced by different observers, occasions, and books used in a teacher's lesson. The different aspects of this study are too numerous to describe here. However, the lesson on which teachers were observed in collecting the data is illustrative. In that study the teachers were observed teaching lessons from "Books A, B, and C of the Distar Language I program" (p. 67). The measurement of teaching was whether or not the "teacher followed the Distar format in group activities and individual activities" (p. 67). After assessing teachers' instruction using this lesson format, the researchers were unable to reduce a significant portion of the error in these assessments from overall error present in assessing teaching. They concluded that more research must be conducted to improve the applications of generalizability theory to the assessment of teaching.

The intent here is not to be critical of earlier work in teacher assessment. On the contrary, all research is conducted in its own time and sensitive to existing constraints and opportunities. The type of research just described likely led to improved pedagogical skills, and whether such assessments have a role in contemporary teacher evaluation is yet undecided. The author recognizes—and hopes—that the current emphasis on authentic assessment will give way to more comprehensive assessments in the future. However, the preceding example alone illustrates the need for more authentic ways of assessing teachers. If psychometricians have been unable to measure teachers' ability to instruct using a preprogrammed, highly behavioral-based educational model such as Distar, how can teacher educators maintain that the traditional measurement methods will work when a teacher uses indeterminate instructional strategies such as reader-response instruction or readers' workshop approaches (e.g., Graves, 1983)? The pedagogical evaluation of current innovations does not respond to traditional measures—for either students or their teachers. The assessment of teaching must recognize the phenomenological nature of educational life while recognizing earlier efforts to assess the complex act known simply as teaching.

Much as Schön (1987) described the way in which easy problems can be solved using research-based theories and techniques, those aspects of teaching that can be evaluated using traditional approaches tend not to be highly important to the work of teachers. As the analogy of the swamp captures the complexities of teaching practices, so too does its richness offer opportunities for authentic assessments of teaching practices.

Far from reviewing a large corpus of research in authentic teacher assessment, this chapter examines a small but growing number of studies in teacher education. It is difficult to avoid relying on the common (and annoying) habit among social scientists: suggestions that further research must be conducted before much conclusive can be said about the phenomena under investigation. However, in this case, there may be more justification than is normally encountered.

Future work in the area of authentic assessment should engage in efforts to transform monologic, unidimensional rating scales, measurement, and teaching outcomes. In developing a coherent, internally consistent vision of authentic assessment—an aesthetic of assessment—researchers and practitioners will need to acknowledge, describe, record, and utilize the tensions that exist between the "high ground" of theory and the "low ground" of practice, between critical, theoretical spaces and those that are contextually sensitive and relational.

REMAINING QUESTIONS

Because the innovations are promising and because I believe that authentic teacher assessment has a place in the reinvention of teacher education, I offer, for consideration, several questions about authentic assessment. Some of these questions represent suggestions for future research; others encourage critical involvement in practice:

- What are the multiple ways in which authentic assessment is cast by teacher education practitioners?
- If authentic assessment of teachers is an answer, what is the question? On what epistemological and moral ship does one embark on the authentic assessment journey?
- What are the questions that might best steer improvements in the assessment of practice?

- What are the influences of authentic teacher assessment on emerging teachers? On experienced in-service teachers? On school and university teacher educators? On school administrators? On emerging and beginning teacher peers? On others?
- Can authentic assessment processes be encouraged and developed in climates of accountability?
- How can current research methodologies (both qualitative and quantitative) help in studying the authentic assessment of teaching? Does the teacher education community need an altogether novel approach to study authentic teacher assessment?
- Can the authentic assessment of teaching realistically be fostered in highly politicized, interest group–driven, educational climates? What influences might shape the development of authentic assessment in ways other than those offered in this chapter?
- What are the ethical dimensions of authentic assessment? Who is responsible for ensuring ethical practices?
- To what extent are the underlying assumptions of authentic assessment incompatible with the structures and perspectives underlying traditionally oriented schools and classrooms? What might be the status of these competing but evolving perspectives in the future?

Addressing such questions constitutes the future of authentic assessment.

References

Andrews, T. E., & Barnes, S. (1990). Assessment of teaching. In W. R. Houston (Ed.), *The handbook of research on teacher education* (pp. 569–598). New York: Macmillan.

Baratz-Snowden, J. (1993). Assessment of teachers: A view from the national board for professional teaching standards. *Theory Into Practice, 32*(2), 82–85.

Barber, L. W. (1990). Self-assessment. In J. Millman & L. Darling-Hammond (Eds.), *The new handbook of teacher evaluation* (pp. 216–228). Newbury Park, CA: Sage.

Bird, T. (1990). The schoolteacher's portfolio. In J. Millman & L. Darling-Hammond (Eds.), *The new handbook of teacher evaluation* (pp. 241–256). Newbury Park, CA: Sage.

Bullough, R. V. (1994). Personal history and teaching metaphors. A self-study of teaching as conversation. *Teacher Education Quarterly, 21*(1), 107–120.

Cizek, G. J. (1991). Innovation or enervation?: Performance assessment in perspective. *Phi Delta Kappan, 72*(9), 695–699.

Clandinin, D. J., Davies, A., Hogan, P., & Kennard, B. (1993). *Learning to teach, teaching to learn.* New York: Teachers College Press.

Collins, A. (1991). Portfolios for biology teacher assessment. *Journal of Personnel Evaluation in Education, 5*(2), 147–168.

Connelly, F. M., & Clandinin, D. J. (1994). Narrative inquiry. In T. Husen & T. N. Postlethwaite (Eds.), *The international encyclopedia of education* (2nd ed.). Oxford: Pergamon Press.

Crites, S. (1979). The aesthetics of self-deception. *Sounding, 62,* 107–129.

Cronbach, L. J. (1971). Test validation. In R. L. Thorndike (Ed.), *Educational measurement* (pp. 443–507). Washington, DC: American Council on Measurement.

Darling-Hammond, L. (1986). A proposal for evaluation in the teaching profession. *Elementary School Journal, 86*(4), 531–551.

Delandshere, G., & Petrosky, A. R. (1994). Capturing teachers' knowledge: Performance assessment a) and post-structuralist epistemology, b) from a post-structuralist perspective, c) and post-structuralism, d) none of the above. *Educational Researcher, 23*(5), 11–18.

Dennett, D. (1991). *Consciousness explained.* Boston: Little, Brown.

Dewey, J. (1938). *Experience and education.* New York: Macmillan.

Diamond, C. T. P. (1992). Accounting for our accounts: Autoethnographic approaches to teacher voice and vision. *Curriculum Inquiry, 22*(1), 67–81.

Dwyer, C. A. (1993). Teaching and diversity: Meeting the challenges for innovative teacher assessments. *Journal of Teacher Education, 44*(2), 119–129.

Edie, J. M. (1987). *Edmund Husserl's phenomenology.* Bloomington: Indiana University Press.

Educational Testing Service. (1992). *The Praxis series: Professional assessments for beginning teachers.* Princeton, NJ: Author.

Eisner, E. W. (1991). *The enlightened eye: Qualitative inquiry and the enhancement of educational practice.* New York: Macmillan.

Elliot, J. (1989). Teacher evaluation and teaching as a moral science. In M. L. Holly & C. S. Mcloughlin (Eds.), *Perspectives on teacher professional development* (pp. 239–258). London: Falmer.

Fosnot, C. T. (1989). *Enquiring teachers, enquiring learners: A constructivist approach for teaching.* New York: Teachers College Press.

Geertz, C. (1988). *Works and lives: The anthropologist as author.* Stanford, CA: Stanford University Press.

Gitlin, A., Bringhurst, K., Burns, M., Cooley, V., Myers, B., Price, K., Russell, R., & Tiess, P. (1992). *Teachers' voices for school change: An introduction to educative research.* New York: Teachers College Press.

Gitlin, A., & Goldstein, S. (1987). A dialogical approach to understanding: Horizontal evaluation. *Educational Theory, 37*(1), 17–27.

Gitlin, A., & Smyth, J. (1989). *Teacher evaluation: Educative alternatives*. New York: Falmer.

Glesne, C., & Peshkin, A. (1992). *Becoming qualitative researchers: An introduction*. White Plains, NY: Longman.

Graves, D. (1983). *Writing: Teachers and children at work*. Portsmouth, NH: Heinemann.

Griffin, G. (1989). A descriptive study of student teaching. *The Elementary School Journal, 89*(3), 343–364.

Grover, B. W. (1991). The teacher assessment dilemma: What is versus what ought to be! *Journal of Personnel Evaluation in Education, 5*(2), 103–119.

Grumet, M. R. (1992). Existential and phenomenological foundations of autobiographical methods. In W. S. Pinar & W. M. Reynolds (Eds.), *Understanding curriculum as phenomenological and deconstructed text* (pp. 28–43). New York: Teachers College Press.

Guyton, E., & McIntyre, D. J. (1990). Student teaching and school experiences. In W. R. Houston (Ed.), *The handbook of research on teacher education* (pp. 514–534). New York: Macmillan.

Hanson, F. A. (1993). *Testing testing*. Berkeley: University of California Press.

Hargreaves, A. (1990). Cultures of teaching. In I. Goodson & S. Ball (Eds.), *Teachers' lives*. New York: Routledge.

Herman, J. L., Aschbacher, P. R., & Winters, L. (1992). *A practical guide to alternative assessment*. Alexandria, VA: Association for Supervision and Curriculum Development.

Hickox, E. S., & Musella, D. F. (1992). Teacher performance appraisal and staff development. In M. Fullan & A. Hargreaves (Eds.), *Teacher development and educational change* (pp. 156–169). London: Falmer.

Holly, M. L. (1989). *Writing to grow: Keeping a personal professional journal*. Portsmouth, NH: Heinemann.

Houston, W. R., & Howsam, R. B. (1972). *Competency-based teacher education: Progress, problems, and prospects*. Chicago: Science Research Associates.

Howe, K. R. (1992). Getting over the qualitative-qualitative debate. *American Journal of Education, 100*(2), 236–256.

Hunt, D. (1987). *Beginning with ourselves: In theory, practice and human affairs*. Cambridge, MA: Brookline Books/OISE Press.

Husserl, E. (1962). *Ideas: General introduction to pure phenomenology*. Translated by W. R. Boyce Gibson. New York: Collier.

Johnson, S. M. (1990). *Teachers at work: Achieving success in our schools*. New York: Basic Books/HarperCollins Publishers.

Kerchner, C. K., & Mitchell, D. (1983). Unionization and the shaping of teachers' work. *Teacher Education Quarterly, 10*(4), 71–88.

King, B. (1991). Thinking about linking portfolios with assessment center exercises: Exercises from the Teacher Assessment Project. *Teacher Education Quarterly, 18*(3), 31–48.

Knowles, J. G. (1992). Geopiety, the concept of sacred place: Reflections on an outdoor education experience. *Journal of Experiential Education, 15*(1), 6–12.

Knowles, J. G. (1993). Life history accounts as mirrors: A practical avenue for the conceptualization of reflection in teacher education. In J. Calderhead & P. Gates (Eds.), *Conceptualizing reflection in teacher development* (pp. 70–92). London: Falmer.

Knowles, J. G., & Cole, A. L. (In Press). Developing practice through field experience. In *A knowledge base for teacher educators*. San Francisco, CA: Jossey-Bass, Committee on the Professional Knowledge Base, American Association of Colleges for Teacher Education.

Knowles, J. G., & Cole, A. L., with Presswood, C. S. (1994). *Through preservice teachers' eyes: Exploring field experiences through narrative and inquiry*. New York: Merrill.

Knowles, J. G., & Holt-Reynolds, D. (1991). Shaping pedagogies through personal histories in preservice teacher education. *Teachers College Record, 93*(1), 89–113.

Lindquist, E. F. (1991). Preliminary considerations in objective test construction. In E. F. Lindquist (Ed.), *Educational measurement* (pp. 119–184). Washington, DC: American Council on Education.

Linn, R. L., Baker, E. L., & Dunbar, S. B. (1991). Complex, performance-based assessment: Expectations and validation criteria. *Educational Researcher, 20*(8), 15–21.

Marsh, H. W. (1987). Students' evaluations of university teaching: Research findings, methodological issues, and directions for future research. *International Journal of Educational Research, 11*(3), 253–388.

Marzano, R. J., & Kendall, J. S. (1991). *A model continuum of authentic tasks and their assessment*. Aurora, CO: Mid-continent Regional Educational Laboratory.

McLaughlin, M. W., & Pfeifer, R. S. (1988). *Teacher evaluation: Improvement, accountability, and effective learning*. New York: Teachers College Press.

Merleau-Ponty, M. (1962). *Phenomenology of perception*. New York: Humanities Press.

Messick, S. (1994). The interplay of evidence and consequences in the validation of performance assessments. *Educational Researcher, 23*(2), 13–23.

Middleton, S. (1993). *Educating feminists: Life histories and pedagogy*. New York: Teachers College Press.

Miller, A., & Tellez, K. (1993). *Innovative use of teaching portfolios in a professional development school*. Paper presented at the annual meeting of the Association for Teacher Educators, Los Angeles.

Miller, M. D., & Legg, S. M. (1993). Alternative assessment in high stakes environment. *Educational Measurement: Issues and Practice, 12*(2), 9–15.

Moss, P. A., Beck, J. S., Ebbs, C., Matson, B., Muchmore, J., Steele, D., Taylor, C., & Herter, R. (1992). Portfolios, accountability, and an interpretive approach to validity. *Educational Measurement: Issues and Practice, 11*(3), 12–21.

Mullen, C. (1994). *Imprisoned selves: A narrative inquiry into incarceration and education*. Unpublished doctoral dissertation, University of Toronto, Canada.

Murnane, R. J., Singer, J., Willet, J., Kemple, J., & Olsen, R. (1991). *Who will teach? Policies that matter*. Cambridge: Harvard University Press.

National Board for Professional Teaching Standards. (1986). *Toward high and rigorous standards for the teaching profession*. Detroit, MI: Author.

National Evaluation Systems. (1990). *Study guide: Reading test*. Amherst, MA: Author.

National Evaluation Systems. (1993) . *Preparation manual: Elementary comprehensive test*. Amherst, MA: Author.

Peterson, K. D. (1990). Assistance and assessment for beginning teachers. In J. Millman & L. Darling-Hammond (Eds.), *The new handbook of teacher evaluation* (pp. 104–115). Newbury Park, CA: Sage.

Peterson, K. D., & Chenowith, T. (1992). School teachers' control and involvement in their own evaluation. *Journal of Personnel Evaluation in Education, 6*(2), 177–190.

Peterson, P. L., & Comeaux, M. A. (1990). Evaluating the systems: Teacher's perspectives on teacher evaluation. *Educational Evaluation and Policy Analysis, 12*(1), 3–24.

Polanyi, M. (1962). *Personal knowledge: Towards a post-critical philosophy*. Chicago: The University of Chicago Press.

Poster, C., & Poster, D. (1991). *Teacher appraisal: A guide to training*. London: Routledge.

Rafferty, C. D. (1994, February). *Portfolio assessment and secondary methods classes: What happens when the twain meet?* Paper presented at the annual meeting of the Association of Teacher Educators, Atlanta.

Rose, D. (1990). *Living the ethnographic life*. Newbury Park, CA: Sage.

Rosenholtz, S. J. (1989). *Teachers' workplace: The social organization of schools*. White Plains, NY: Longman.

Schlechty, P., & Vance, V. (1983). Recruitment, selection, and retention: The shape of the teaching force. *The Elementary School Journal, 83*(4), 469–487.

Schön, D. (1987). *Educating the reflective practitioner*. San Francisco: Jossey-Bass.

Shavelson, R. J., Webb, N. M., & Burstein, L. (1986). Measurement of teaching. In M. C. Wittrock (Ed.), *Handbook of research on teaching* (3rd ed., pp. 50–91). New York: Macmillan.

Shepard, L. A. (1993). The place of testing reform in educational reform: A reply to Cizek. *Educational Researcher, 22*(4), 4–9.

Shor, I. (1987). *Critical teaching and everyday life*. Chicago: The University of Chicago Press.

Shulman, L. S., Haertel, E. H., & Bird, T. (1988). *Toward alternative assessment for teachers: A report on a work in progress*. Stanford: Teacher Assessment Project, Stanford University.

Sikorski, M. F., Niemiec, R. P., & Walberg, H. J. (1994). Best teaching practices: A checklist for observations. *NASSP Bulletin, 78*(561), 50–54.

Sikula, J. (1990). National commission reports of the 1980s. In W. R. Houston (Ed.), *The handbook of research on teacher education* (pp. 72–82). New York: Macmillan.

Smith, K. E. (1990). Developmentally appropriate education or the Hunter teachers assessment model: Mutually incompatible alternatives. *Young Children, 45*(2), 12–13.

Wilson, S. M., & Wineburg, S. S. (1993). Wrinkles in time and place: Using performance assessments to understand the knowledge of teachers. *American Education Research Journal, 30*(4), 729–770.

Wiggins, G. (1991). A response to Cizek. *Phi Delta Kappan, 72*(9), 700–703.

Wolf, K. (1991). The schoolteacher's portfolio: Issues in design, implementation, and evaluation. *Phi Delta Kappan, 73*(2), 129–136.

Yates, J. W. (1981). Student teaching in England: Results of a recent survey. *Journal of Teacher Education, 32*(5), 44–46.

Zeichner, K., & Liston, D. P. (1987). Teaching student teachers to reflect. *Harvard Educational Review, 57*(1), 23–48.

Zessoules, R., & Gardner, H. (1991). Authentic assessment: Beyond the buzzword and into the classroom. In V. Perrone (Ed.), *Expanding student assessment* (pp. 47–71). Alexandria, VA: ASCD.

·31·

CASES AND CASE METHODS IN
TEACHER EDUCATION

Katherine K. Merseth

HARVARD UNIVERSITY

Cases and case methods offer a particularly promising possibility for teacher educators, teacher education programs, and those who wish to understand more deeply the human endeavor called teaching. Although a number of researchers have provided extensive commentary on the promise of cases and case-based instruction (Doyle, 1990; Hutchings, 1993; Kagan, 1993; Merseth, 1991a; Sykes & Bird, 1992), this chapter documents the growing interest in cases, examines the developing lines of research related to case use, and offers suggestions for future investigation and activities related to cases in teacher education.

Although many chapters in this handbook present the results of long-standing traditions of empirical research, such a focus for this chapter proves more challenging. Cases and case methods, as described in this chapter, are relatively new phenomena in teacher education programs and have been growing in popularity since the mid-1980s. Only recently have teacher educators turned their attention to the myriad empirical questions that relate to case materials and approaches. This situation puts the topic of cases and case methods in a curious position: At this point, the collective voice of its proponents far outweighs the power of existing empirical work. However, this imbalance also defines a time of great opportunity and excitement for teacher educators who wish to explore this emerging pedagogy in order to understand more deeply the processes by which people learn to teach.

This chapter begins by examining the developing interest and state of play of cases and case methods in teacher education. Although cases have been used sporadically in teacher

education programs as far back as the 1860s, it is only since the mid-1980s that a distinctive, identifiable conversation has emerged among teacher educators about case-based instruction. Thus, this chapter considers the questions, "Why cases, and why now?" To shed light on these questions, the chapter briefly discusses current developments in the field of teacher education that encourage enthusiasm for cases and case methods. These developments include the ongoing conversations about and interest in teacher knowledge and cognition, the calls for reform in teacher education, and the experience with this pedagogy of other professional fields.

To orient the reader to the current status of cases and case methods in teacher education, this chapter describes the range of definitions, purposes, and uses for cases. These issues vary considerably in the literature, often confusing the dialog when terms such as *cases* or *case methods* are used with different meaning and intent. In order to explore the various purposes and uses of cases, the chapter introduces a typology of case use that seeks to guide the reader through the large, sometimes diffuse, descriptive literature.

Utilizing this typology of case use, the chapter next turns to the claims being made for the use of cases and case methods in teacher education and summarizes the available empirical research that addresses these claims. The chapter explores assertions that relate to *what* teachers think, *how* they think, and the *contextual factors* that influence the impact of cases and case methods on learners. Because of the relative paucity of empirical work in the United States, the chapter briefly considers scholarship from other countries on cases and case methods for additional insights.

The author wishes to express her gratitude to Rita Silverman and Audrey Kleinsasser for their reactions to an early draft of the manuscript and to Mark Cosdon and Mary Askew for their care and dedication in the preparation of the manuscript.

The final section of the chapter explores the future of cases and case methods in teacher education. Will cases and case methods assume a dominant role in teacher education programs in the twenty-first century? Will teacher educators witness continued growth for cases? In order to answer these questions, the chapter argues that more work is required to develop additional materials and methods while undertaking an ambitious research agenda. As some have suggested, cases may play a transformative role in the reform of teacher education. Because the path to success is neither easy nor certain, this chapter sketches one possible path for future research and development.

WHY CASES AND WHY NOW?

In his 1985 presidential address to the American Educational Research Association (AERA), Lee Shulman delivered a wake-up call to teacher educators to use cases and case methods in teacher education (L. Shulman, 1986). Outlining a new understanding of teacher knowledge and its representation, Shulman urged educators to look seriously at propositional knowledge. He suggested three fundamental types of propositional knowledge, each corresponding to the sources of knowledge about teaching. These included empirical inquiry, practical experience, and moral or ethical reasoning. In his speech, he observed that propositional knowledge can be limited in its ability to guide practitioners in action. He introduced the notion of "case knowledge," which is "knowledge of specific, well-documented, and richly described events" (L. Shulman, 1986, p. 11). The "case idea," as Sykes and Bird (1992) refer to it, was in the air.

Shortly after this address, the Carnegie Forum on Education and the Economy issued a report of the Task Force on Teaching as a Profession. Acknowledging the need for high standards in the preparation and performance of teachers and the necessity of teacher education reform to achieve this objective, this group of scholars and practitioners made a number of recommendations. In particular, the report called for the introduction of a new master of teaching degree. The curriculum of such a program would include the use of the case method:

The second approach to instruction that should be incorporated into the design of the post-graduate programs is the case method, well-developed in law and business, but almost unknown in teaching instruction. Teaching "cases" illustrating a great variety of teaching problems should be developed as a major focus of instruction. (Carnegie Forum on Education and the Economy, 1986, p. 76)

At about the same time, a number of professional organizations initiated activities focused on case-based instruction. For example, the Carnegie Foundation funded the American Association for Higher Education (AAHE) to create the Presidents' Forum on Teaching as a Profession. This effort, designed to engage college and university presidents in discussions about the nature of teaching and teacher education on their campuses, uncovered a developing fascination with cases and case methods on some campuses. Similarly, Judith Shulman and Joel Colbert of the Far West Regional Laboratory for Educational Research and Development discovered strong interest within the in-service education community for case-based instruction (Shulman & Colbert, 1987, 1988). As a result, in 1989 the AAHE and the Far West Regional Laboratory convened a working conference to explore the potential of this pedagogy. An outgrowth of the conference was a small, yet active, network of teacher educators interested in the use of cases and case methods at the undergraduate and graduate level.

Soon, other professional educational organizations, such as the American Association of Colleges for Teacher Education (AACTE) and the AERA, began to encourage the examination of this pedagogy. For example, the AACTE offered a preconference workshop on "Applying the Case Method to Teacher Education" at its national meeting in 1990, and the AERA listed "case methods" for the first time in the program index of its 1989 annual meeting. Special journal issues focusing on the topic of case methods in teacher education began to appear (Ashton, 1991; Green, Grant, & Shulman, 1990). Books of cases (Kleinfeld, 1988; Kowalski, Weaver, & Henson, 1990; Silverman, Welty, & Lyon, 1992) and books about cases and case methods (J. Shulman, 1992; Wasserman, 1993) also became available.

Today, interest in this pedagogy appears to be increasing, supported by a continually expanding cadre of individuals and organizations. Workshops are offered, subgroups of professional organizations are formed, e-mail user groups are established, and membership, both nationally and internationally, grows in specialized professional organizations such as the World Association for Case Method Research and Application (WACRA), based at Bentley College in Waltham, Massachusetts. All are engaged in the development of knowledge and inquiry about cases and case-based instruction. Many share the hope that Lee Shulman articulated about cases and case methods in 1992:

I envision case methods as a strategy for overcoming many of the most serious deficiencies in the education of teachers. Because they are contextual, local, and situated—as are all narratives—cases integrate what otherwise remains separated. . . . Complex cases will communicate to both future teachers and laypersons that teaching is a complex domain demanding subtle judgments and agonizing decisions.

Interest in Cases and Case Methods

Three factors have both stimulated and accelerated the interest in cases as a pedagogy for teacher education. The first factor is the recent and active consideration by teacher educators of the nature of teacher knowledge. Current work in constructivist teacher education, teacher cognition, teacher knowledge, and the nature of teaching provides a hospitable environment for considering cases and case methods. Second, some researchers recently have pointed out that the use of cases in education is not a concept entirely new to the field (Doyle, 1990; Kagan, 1993; McAninch, 1991; Sykes & Bird, 1992). These individuals have identified a small number of case materials from earlier teacher education programs. Finally, the current conversations in the United States regarding school reform and the reform of teacher education (Holmes Group, 1990) also support a closer examination of alternative methods of instruction in teacher education programs. The following sections briefly consider each of these factors.

Nature of Teacher Knowledge There is a growing debate in teacher education circles about the nature of teacher knowledge and the nature of teaching: Is it situation-specific and context-dependent, or is it generic and propositional? For example Dona Kagan (1993) stated:

[I]t may not be coincidental that one finds classroom cases used in these different contexts today, for their somewhat contradictory epistemological foundations appear to reflect a growing ambivalence in our perception of teaching: namely, whether and to what degree it may be idiosyncratic rather than generic, a self-expressive art rather than an applied science. (p. 704)

This tension is evident in the different responses to the question of what is teacher knowledge. On the one hand, some researchers have argued that teacher knowledge can be codified, captured, and delivered to teachers (Brophy & Good, 1986; Gage, 1978). Teachers can derive the "right answers" through the application of the appropriate principles and theories. In this characterization, the task for the teacher is to determine and apply a suitable theory or principle to a given situation. In other words, the teacher utilizes theory to determine action.

On the other hand, a different appraisal of teacher knowledge suggests that skillful teachers do not operate from a set of principles or theories but rather build, through experience in contextualized situations, multiple strategies for practice. Recent research on teacher thinking has broadened the conceptualization of the teacher from one who operates with a narrow set of prescribed theories or propositions to one who defines his or her knowledge as situation-specific, context-dependent, and ever emerging (Calderhead, 1987; Clark & Peterson, 1986; Clark & Yinger, 1977). According to this latter understanding, knowledge is context-specific, nonfixed, and continually evolving (Clark & Lampert, 1986; Lampert, 1985). Teacher action derives from induction from multiple experiences, not deduction from theoretical principles.

It may be more realistic to believe that skillful teachers ground their practice in a mixture of theory and praxis—a fertile middle ground between these two extreme interpretations of the knowledge base of teaching. Certain principles in teaching do exist and are relevant to the teachers' task. However, they do not ground every teaching action. Reviewing poor conceptions of teacher knowledge, Lee Shulman (1992) noted:

Apparently, learning is much more situation-specific than heretofore imagined. . . . Thus, the specificity and localism of cases as instructional materials may not be problematic for learning; indeed, they may be far more appropriate media for learning than the abstract and decontextualized lists of propositions or expositions of facts, concepts, and principles. (p. 24)

Like Shulman, Doyle (1990) also observed that the increased interest in cases and case knowledge is a direct result of a "fundamental shift that is taking place in teaching and teacher education, a shift from a preoccupation with behavior and skills to a concern for the complex cognitive processes that underlie successful performance in classroom settings" (p. 8).

These developments in the field of teacher cognition appear to encourage the consideration of cases and case methods. The apparent ability of cases and case-based instruction to present theoretical knowledge as well as to provide an opportunity to exercise judgment and to develop analytical skills matches well with the current views of teacher knowledge and what teachers need. Hutchings (1993) notes this ability of cases to span the vast middle ground:

A powerful argument for cases is, then, their ability to situate the conversation about teaching on this middle ground between process and content (or technique and substance) where a particular teacher, with particular goals, teaches a particular piece of literature (in this instance) to a particular student. (p. 10)

Historical Roots in Professional Fields A number of researchers have observed that the use of cases in education is not an entirely new phenomenon (Doyle, 1990; Kagan, 1993; McAninch, 1991; Sykes & Bird, 1992). In fact, Doyle (1990) identifies case materials from 1864, and Sperle (1933) describes case material used at the New Jersey State Teachers College in Montclair during the late 1920s. As early as 1924, the method was a topic of discussion at the Harvard Graduate School of Education. Observing the apparent success of the use of cases at the neighboring schools of business and law, the dean of the Graduate School of Education, Henry W. Holmes, tried to interest his faculty in adopting the method. In a letter to the dean of the Harvard Business School in 1924, Holmes stated:

I very much hope that you can give a similar talk before our faculty. It may be the beginning of an attempt to do for Education at Harvard what has been done in the Law and Business. Our problem is different from the problem in your School or the problem in the Law School, but the same general principles can be applied. (Dean Henry W. Holmes, letter to Dean Wallace B. Donham, 22 December, 1924, Harvard Business School Archives)

Holmes had noticed the apparent success of cases in the fields of law, business, and medicine. Case teaching first emerged in law in the 1870s at the Harvard Law School under the guidance of Dean Christopher Columbus Langdell. The law faculty emphasized the analysis and discussion of individual cases by students (Carter & Unklesbay, 1989). By 1915, many law schools around the country employed the case method. Shortly after the emergence of cases in legal education, the method spread to medicine and then to business.

In 1919, with the appointment of Wallace B. Donham (a Harvard-trained lawyer) as dean of the Harvard Business School, the case method of instruction inherited a strong supporter in the field of business administration. The method spread to the teaching of public administration during the 1930s and 1940s (cf. Stein, 1952) and enjoyed prominence in educational administration training in the 1950s (cf. Sargent & Belisle, 1955). A number of scholars offer more complete reviews of the development of cases and case methods (Bok, 1979; Christensen & Hansen, 1987; Culbertson, Jacobson, & Reller, 1960; McNair, 1954; Merseth, 1991a).

Teacher educators interested in the use of cases and case methods are turning to the literature detailing the use of cases in other professional fields to draw parallels for teacher education (McAninch, 1993; Merseth, 1991b; Wasserman, 1993). In part, their interest may stem from the belief, suggested by Kennedy in 1990, that there is a common tension in the design of professional education that cases may address. A professional education curriculum both seeks to deliver a codified, theoretically based knowledge base and intends to teach reasoning skills and strategies for analyzing and acting professionally. Such a curriculum is grounded in the obligation of professional education to prepare practitioners for uncertain practice. Kennedy (1990) observed that professional educators have done both:

Professional educators have devised two general strategies for responding to this problem. One is to develop, codify, and give to students as much knowledge as possible—knowledge about every conceivable situation they might ever encounter. . . . The other strategy is to prepare students to think on their feet, giving them both reasoning skills and strategies for analyzing and interpreting new situations. (p. 813)

School Reform and the Reform of Teacher Education Since the release of the *A Nation at Risk* report in 1983 and the 1986 Carnegie report, *A Nation Prepared,* conversations in state legislatures, school board rooms, teachers' rooms, and living rooms have focused on the reform of teacher education. Although it is not the purpose of this chapter to review these recommendations, it is important to observe that these conversations, interests, and policies expressed by various stakeholders in the educational process have created a positive environment to explore the materials and methods by which teachers are educated.

Teacher educators have embraced the challenge to reconsider the design and delivery of teacher education. Professional organizations such as the Holmes Group (1990), AACTE (1993), and the Association of Teacher Educators (1991) have issued influential reports and recommendations for the improvement of teacher education. These considerations focus not only on the structure of the programs, including the merits of undergraduate or fifth-year programs and undergraduate majors, but also on the source and quality of students and the curricula and methods used in the programs. For example, such sacred cows as traditional foundations courses that emphasize theoretical and scientific knowledge over practical, situated knowledge have come under attack (Tozer, Anderson, & Armbruster, 1990). Sykes and Bird (1992), commenting on these particular conversations, noted:

In their rethinking of foundational studies, they appear to be moving from a conception of the psychology, history, sociology, and philosophy of education as bases and sources for practice to a conception of those subdisciplines as resources for dealing with practice or useful ways to talk about practice. (p. 468)

The exhortations about the importance of education and school reform coming from elected officials, policymakers, and parents have given energy to the reform of teacher education. This energy has encouraged teacher educators to study and to change their teacher education programs. It is this environment that is motivating the consideration of alternative pedagogies, including cases and case methods, in teacher education.

However fervent the hopes of teacher educators for the success of cases in teacher education, their actual use depends on their form, content, and stated purposes. Thus, the next section of this chapter reviews the definitions of cases currently employed in the literature and offers a typology of the various purposes and uses of cases found in teacher education today. Doyle (1990) stressed the importance of the connection between how a case is defined and how it is used: "What a case is and how it is used depends, that is, upon fundamental understandings of what teachers do and how they acquire the ability to carry out their work successfully" (p. 8). Although cases appear to offer a means by which the field can integrate competing conceptions about learning to teach, the next section illustrates that they actually reflect distinct and sometimes different epistemological traditions and foundations.

DEFINITIONS, PURPOSES, AND CONCEPTUAL FRAMEWORK

The literature on cases in teacher education abounds with multiple definitions and related terminologies. This situation exists not because the field is confused but also because of the more active and extensive use of the materials. Teacher educators have not had ample time to come to an agreement on terms, nor should they. Many would argue that definitions and terminologies, while clearly in need of articulation, should be fluid and open at this early stage of development in order not to foreclose potentially productive options and designs.

Beyond multiple definitions, the literature in the field also demonstrates a variety of intended purposes and uses of cases and case methods. For some teacher educators, the most effective use of cases is to explore the complex and messy problems of practice for which explicit theories do not exist. In this instance, the purpose is to educate students in skills of analysis, decision making, and problem solving in the classroom (Merseth, 1991a, 1992a; Silverman et al., 1992). Others use cases as examples, as precepts to establish demonstrations of theoretical principles, and to illustrate exemplary practice (Broudy, 1990; Doyle, 1990; L. Shulman, 1986). A further extension of case use is to stimulate personal reflection in order to develop habits of reflection and skills of self-analysis (Richert, 1991a, 1991b, 1992). Thus, to examine cases and case methods more closely and to build a foundation for the review of related empirical work, the chapter now turns to a consideration of definitions, purposes, and conceptual framework.

Definitions

The field of teacher education utilizes many terms that relate to case-based instruction or pedagogy. The most important terms to examine include *cases* and *case methods* because of their centrality to this pedagogical approach and because of their diverse definitions.

Cases Many case developers in education appear to build directly on the definition of cases that is used in business education (Culbertson et al., 1960; Greenwood & Parkay, 1989; Kowalski et al., 1990; Merseth, 1990b; Risko, 1992; Shulman & Colbert, 1987, 1988; Silverman et al., 1992; Wasserman, 1993). Christensen and Hansen (1987) offer one of the clearest articulations of this business perspective:

A case is a partial, historical, clinical study of a situation which has confronted a practicing administrator or managerial group. Presented in narrative form to encourage student involvement, it provides data—substantive and process—essential to an analysis of a specific situation, for the framing of alternative action programs, and for their implementation recognizing the complexity and ambiguity of the practical world. (p. 27)

For the teacher educators who rely on this business perspective of cases, a case is a descriptive research document based on a real-life situation or event. It attempts to convey a balanced, multidimensional representation of the context, participants, and reality of the situation. It is created explicitly for discussion and seeks to include sufficient detail and information to elicit active analysis and interpretation by users. This definition reaffirms three essential elements of cases: They are real; they rely on careful research and study; and they provide data for consideration and discussion by users. The emphasis on reality-based cases is important for these teacher educators. They do not develop materials that are fictionalized or designed primarily for purposes other than discussion.

In addition to representing reality, these cases are designed to stimulate thought and debate. Hansen (1987), for example, suggested that a case should include "enough intriguing decision points and provocative undercurrents to make a discussion group want to think and argue about them" (p. 265). Finally, cases are created as teaching instruments, developed for study, examination, and discussion. For this reason, excerpts from popular cinema, novels, or research studies, though often interesting and sometimes stimulating, are not considered as cases in this review.

The emphasis on reality also specifically excludes other pedagogical activities sometimes found in teacher education. For example, simulations, critical incidents, and protocols sometimes are called cases by teacher educators (Kagan, 1993). Such pedagogical approaches in teacher education often seek to isolate skills and attempt to provide learning experiences that can be controlled and replicated (Merseth, 1994). In describing simulations, Copeland (1982) observed:

If all characteristics of the real world were contained in the activity, that activity would not be a simulation but a slice of reality. [In simulations,] situational characteristics may be omitted because they are considered unimportant . . . or because their inclusion would pose a danger to the trainee or lend an excess of unpredictability to the activity. (p. 1014)

These activities are in contrast to the cases just defined. They do not seek to bring a "chunk of reality" into the classroom (Lawrence, 1953), nor do they emphasize the unpredictability of a situation (Christensen, 1981).

The distinction between cases that encourage and utilize the messiness of reality and those that control reality helps explain the "amnesia" that Kagan (1993) ascribes to teacher educators who describe cases as "a relatively new phenomenon in teacher education" (Silverman et al., 1992, p. xv). Kagan views simulations, protocols, and critical incidents as cases and therefore argues that cases are not new to teacher education. Such activities, she accurately observes, have been present for some time in teacher education. The "amnesia" that Kagan refers to results not from forgetfulness but, rather, from the fact that these are different definitions of the term *case*.

Collections of cases are now appearing in teacher education casebooks, which also include discussion or study questions and instructor or discussion leader notes. Some are generically organized, covering many aspects of instruction (Kowalski et al., 1990; Silverman et al., 1992), while others target specific audiences, such as intern or mentor teachers (Shulman & Colbert, 1987, 1988) or high school students (Bickerton et al., 1991). Some individuals have developed collections of cases focused on specific themes, such as multicultural education (Kleinfeld, 1988; J. Shulman & Mesa-Bains, 1990) or assessment (Silverman, Welty, & Lyon, 1994).

Nonnarrative Cases The vast majority of the cases in use in teacher education today are in narrative form, and thus they are the primary focus of this review. However, it is important to acknowledge that many recent and promising innovations in case design utilize other media, including videos, computers, and videodiscs. Such technologically enhanced environments allow case developers to present case material through hypermedia, a variety of media (multimedia) linked in innovative (hyper) ways (Ball, Lampert, & Rosenberg, 1991; Bransford et al., 1986; Goldman, Barron, & Witherspoon, 1991; Risko, 1992). Currently, groups of teacher education researchers (Ball et al., 1991; Goldman et al., 1991; Risko, 1992) offer ongoing projects and prototype materials of hypermedia case environments based on real events. Although not yet widespread and somewhat expensive to develop, these emerging technological tools, including interactive videodisc technology and computer programming, are particularly exciting (Merseth & Lacey, 1993).

Case Methods Closely related to the definition of cases are the many ways that cases are used in teacher education programs. Case methods are employed, for instance, to frame conversations between mentors and novices (Carter, 1989), as stimulants to reflection (Richert, 1991a, 1991b), as techniques to enrich field experiences (Florio-Ruane & Clark, 1990), or to orient novices to particular ways of thinking (Greenwood & Parkay, 1989; Kleinfeld, 1992b; Shulman & Colbert, 1988). Case methods may include large- and small-group discussion of cases, role playing suggested by cases, or the writing of cases.

Case may be used as exemplars to be studied, or they may be occasions for the active development and exchange of perspectives regarding hypothetical action plans. Although cases may initiate self-reflection and individual study, they are more commonly discussed with groups of students.

The forms of these case discussions often vary, although they usually include individual responses to questions from the instructor and other participants that seek to build a deeper understanding of the case. Through the utilization of multiple perspectives and comments, individual case instructors encourage case participants to become active contributors and astute listeners during these exchanges.

To structure these discussions, some instructors (cf. Christensen, 1981; Sykes, 1989; Wasserman, 1994; Welty, 1989) suggest that case participants first study the assigned case individually, reviewing important data and answering study questions provided with the case by the instructor. These questions focus the student's individual preparation toward important aspects of the case. Sometimes students also form "study groups," smaller groups of four or five, that gather prior to the meeting of the larger seminar or class to discuss the case. The purpose of these study groups is to share insights and opinions and to allow for close analysis and questioning by peers of positions and interpretations. The goal of these small groups is not consensus but, rather, to help students advance their individual understanding of the case. Next, the larger seminar group comes together for a significant period of time, sometimes 60 to 90 minutes, to discuss the case.

In the large-group case discussion, the discussion leader plays a very important role—guiding, probing, directing, giving feedback, or sometimes simply observing the exchanges and contributions among the class members. As in the smaller study groups, consensus is not typically sought but, rather, the development of a deeper understanding by the participants of the material in order to learn about teaching.

Cases and case discussion methods must be considered together, not separately. The synergy of the two is much too powerful to ignore. To focus on discussion-based instruction or other methods without reference to the cases or material being discussed is analogous to considering teaching without reference to the learner or to the content being imparted. It matters both *what* is discussed and *how* it is discussed. Hansen offered a powerful analogy in her essay on case discussions: "Just as a piece of music exists only partially when it isn't being sung or played, a case comes fully to life only when it's being discussed" (Hansen, 1987, p. 265). This duality is one of the reasons why case-based instruction is so challenging, a topic this chapter addresses in a later section.

The use of casebooks in teacher education classes, whether they are in foundations, methods, or student teaching seminars, can vary significantly. Some instructors use casebooks as texts, discussing many of the cases in the volume. Others employ the casebook selectively, choosing specific cases to match the content of the course (Sudzina & Kilbane, 1992). A number of publishers offer customized casebooks that allow instructors to select a small number of cases from a large inventory to produce a customized collection of cases.

The wide variety of cases and case methods in teacher education programs today calls into question the presumed purposes that cases serve. The chapter considers this topic next.

Purposes

The purpose of cases and case-based instruction in any professional field relates directly to the nature of the body of knowledge that exists in that field (Kennedy, 1992; Merseth, 1991b; Merseth & Lacey, 1993). For example, Sykes and Bird (1992) stress the interdependence of knowledge in the field and cases: "Case development depends on the context of use and on the part cases will play in the knowledge of the field" (p. 479). Case purpose will help define the field at the same time that the field will help define the purpose of cases.

A number of teacher educators have offered valuable examinations of case purpose and use (Doyle, 1990; L. Shulman, 1986, 1992; Sykes & Bird, 1992). A brief review of this work provides a valuable background for further consideration of the purpose and use of cases.

Doyle (1990) began his discussion of the purpose and use of cases with the following sentence: "Any teacher education strategy is built upon presuppositions about teaching and the learning-to-teach process" (p. 8). He then articulated two ways in which cases can serve as a foundation for the way teachers are prepared. He identified the first, most common purpose of cases as "precept and practice" (p. 9). Precepts include propositions, theories and "maxims, aphorisms, and tips" derived from practical experience. Cases are used as examples or exemplars inserted into text or lecture to identify theories and generalize actions. In this instance, Doyle (1990) asserted that "The purpose [of these cases] . . . is to make a principle or a practice concrete rather than stimulate deliberation and problem-solving" (p. 9).

The second purpose Doyle identified focused on "problem-solving and decision-making" (p. 10). Here, the emphasis is on the development of a way of thinking—a heuristic of problem solving to accomplish its purpose—that emphasizes the messy, complex nature of teaching. Cases are used "as pedagogical tools for helping teachers practice the basic professional processes of analysis, problem solving, and decision making" (p. 10).

Doyle also notes that cases can advance "knowledge and understanding." This purpose reflects the view that teachers possess propositional knowledge organized according to tasks or events where cases serve as prototypes that "instantiate theoretical knowledge about teaching" (p. 13) in a fully elaborated context. These cases supply teachers with a foundation for developing necessary knowledge structures. Elaborating, he stated: "The student's task in studying prototypes is not to find the right answer but to interpret the situation and understand the theoretical issues involved" (p. 13). Cases are used as examples, as objects of study, as in the use of cases in his first framework.

Doyle (1990) summarized the purpose and use of cases in the following way:

Within a cognitive framework, cases can be used in two ways. First, they can serve as precedents to provide occasions to practice analysis, interpretation, and problem solving. Second, they can be used as prototypes to develop essential knowledge about teaching events. In this second use, the study of cases focuses on understanding the situation and the actions taken by teachers and students. (pp. 13–14)

Sykes and Bird (1992) provide a second examination of case use in their extensive review of "the case idea" in the *Review of Research in Education*. These authors describe four "communities of practice" in which cases are found. The first two communities parallel those described by Doyle (1990). In the first, cases appear as "instances of theory"; in the second, cases are used as "problems for deliberate and reflective action" (p. 466).

The third and fourth communities that Sykes and Bird identify relate more directly to the form and internal logic of cases rather than to the purpose they serve or the knowledge base they reflect. The third community relies on narrative forms of knowing, including personal stories, reflections, and writings of individual community members, and the fourth describes the mode of reasoning—"casuistry"—with cases that does not rely on theory but rather on internal logic developed through the consideration of multiple cases.

Other researchers shed light on the case idea by detailing schemes similar to those of Doyle and Sykes and Bird. For example, Lee Shulman (1986) asserted that there are three types of knowledge: propositional knowledge, case knowledge, and strategic knowledge, with propositional knowledge including philosophical inquiry, practical experience, and moral reasoning. Case knowledge is "knowledge of specific, well-documented, and richly described events" (p. 11). Reflecting Doyle and Sykes and Bird, he suggested that "cases may be examples of specific instances of practice—detailed descriptions of how an instructional event occurred . . . [or] they may be exemplars of principles, exemplifying in their detail a more abstract proposition or theoretical claim" (p. 11). More recently, Shulman (1992) has elaborated on his view of the purpose of cases, suggesting that they can represent a strategy for "transforming more propositional forms of knowing into narratives that motivate and educate" (p. 17). Commenting on this elaboration, Fenstermacher (1994) observed that Shulman is now asserting that propositional knowledge can be transformed into practical knowledge through the use of cases and that these descriptions may be less of a *type* of knowledge than a *way* to describe how this knowledge is held.

Conceptual Framework

To guide the reader through the diverse literature and empirical work on cases and case methods, this chapter now offers a simple conceptual framework as an organizing scheme. The framework is built on the work of Doyle (1990), Lee Shulman (1986, 1992), and Sykes and Bird (1992) and divides case purpose and use into three categories: cases as exemplars, cases as opportunities to practice analysis and contemplate action, and cases as stimulants to personal reflection.

Cases as Exemplars As noted, the literature frequently mentions the use of cases as examples. In this instance, the emphasis of these cases is on the theoretical, the prescriptive, the model. Their purpose is to develop a knowledge of theory or to build new theories; their function is "to exemplify the desired principle, theory or instructional technique" (Sykes & Bird, 1992, p. 480). These cases give priority to general, propositional knowledge (Doyle, 1990).

Broudy (1990) placed great faith in this type of case, which he called "paradigm cases of professional practice" (p. 454). He suggested that "the key to the improvement of teacher education lies in the identification of a set of problems that legitimately can claim to be so generic and so important that all who teach will be familiar with them" (p. 453). Broudy saw these cases as exemplars, as generic examples of practice, that all teachers should know and understand. Kagan (1993) also discussed the generic nature of cases.

Broudy was concerned about the legitimacy of generic cases, mirroring the thinking of other early proponents of case education. For example, in 1926, when the case method was being discussed for use at the Harvard Graduate School of Education, Harvard President A. Lawrence Lowell opined in a personal letter to Education Dean Henry W. Holmes:

I doubt whether much can be gained by the collecting of a large number of cases. They would have to be almost infinite, and far more accurate than is possible, in order to draw conclusions from them by a process of induction; and an attempt to collect merely instances without a preconceived theory that they are to prove or disprove will not, I fear, lead anywhere. (President A. Lawrence Lowell, letter to Dean Henry W. Holmes, 12 April 1926, Harvard University Archives)

Some collections of cases, such as *The Intern Teacher Casebook* (Shulman & Colbert, 1988) or *Teaching Cases in Cross Cultural Education* (Kleinfeld, 1988), seek to provide a collection of exemplars. For example, Shulman and Colbert (1988) stated:

Cases may also be exemplars of principles, describing by their detail a general pattern of practice. All the narratives . . . included in this casebook meet this criterion. They have been selected, because they are representative of a larger class of experiences. (p. ix)

Using cases as exemplars also can be used to honor "best practice" or to make effective teaching more public. Ingvarson and Fineberg (1992) collected a number of cases in Australia that seek to capture (in the Broudy sense) exemplary practice. These researchers use these materials in in-service education programs across Australia. Exemplar cases can also serve to make teaching more public and more available for discussion and review. Hutchings (1993), describing cases about higher education teaching, noted that "cases make teaching public" because they offer a legitimate vehicle for opening "windows on practice" (p. 11). Such windows seem quite rare in elementary, secondary, and higher education.

Cases as Opportunities to Practice Analysis and Contemplate Action Some case developers embrace a second purpose for cases, namely, as opportunities to practice decision making and problem solving. Here, case materials are used to help teachers "think like a teacher" (Doyle, 1990; Kagan, 1993; Kleinfeld, 1990; Merseth, 1991b; L. Shulman, 1992; Wasserman, 1994). In this conception, cases are not used explicitly to exemplify theory but rather to present situations from which theory emerges. This use of cases works well with the conception of teaching as a complex, messy, context-specific activity. The cases present problematic situations that require analysis, problem solving, decision making, and action definition. With such cases, students can, within the confines and safety of a teacher education classroom, "practice such professional skills as interpreting situations, framing problems, generating various solutions to the problems posed and choosing among them" (Sykes & Bird, 1992, p. 482).

Cases that focus on problem solving and decision making typically are based on a real situation where "an actual instance of practice is presented in much of its complexity rather than an episode constructed to illustrate a point" (Doyle, 1990, p. 10). This approach:

doesn't presuppose any tidy correspondence between theory and cases, but aims to cultivate analytic skills in the application of ideas and to convey theoretical knowledge in a form useful to the interpretation of situations, the making of decisions, the choice of actions, and the formation of plans and designs. (Sykes & Bird, 1992, p. 469)

Others have commented on this use of cases. For example, Wasserman (1994) argued that "cases promote students' ability to discern the essential elements in a situation, to analyze and interpret data, and to use data to inform action" (p. 606). Barnes (1989) also observed that teachers must "untangle situations that are complex and undefined and impose a coherence of their own making" (p. 17), and Merseth (1990b, 1991a, 1992a) suggested that cases be used as opportunities to practice action. These individuals argue that the challenge of complex practice requires that aspiring teachers have opportunities to practice the skills of disentanglement. Rather than being presented with codified and theoretically specified examples of practice, the case reader must analyze and respond as a professional.

These comments about problem-solving and decision-making cases often find support in the experience of case use in professional business schools. For example, C. Roland Christensen of the Harvard Business School and the Harvard Graduate School of Education states: "The minimum end product of a case discussion is an understanding of what needs to be done and how it can be accomplished" (Christensen & Hansen, 1987, p. 30).

Cases as Stimulants to Personal Reflection The third purpose of cases is to stimulate personal reflection. In this instance, the emphasis is on personal professional knowledge and the individual (Richert, 1991a, 1991b; Zeichner & Liston, 1987). It responds to the exhortations in the teacher education literature for the development of reflective teachers (Grimmett, 1988; Grimmett & Erickson, 1988) and takes its intellectual roots from Dewey (1933), Schön (1983, 1987, 1991), and Zeichner (1986). Reflection derives from a directly or vicariously experienced situation that puzzles or surprises:

[It] begins with observations made by oneself or others . . . [which] in turn suggest possible courses of action. Together data (observations) and ideas (suggested courses of actions) constitute "two indispensable and correlative factors" (Dewey, 1933, p. 104) of reflection. (Grimmett, 1988, p. 6)

Given this description, the increasing excitement about the contribution of cases to the development of reflection is quite understandable. Cases represent "the data," and the discussion of the cases articulates the possible "courses of action." As Richert (1991b) stated, "Cases provide the potential for connecting the act of teaching with the cognitions and feelings that motivate and explain that act. They offer a vehicle for making the tacit explicit" (p. 117).

A number of scholars advocate case discussion to foster reflection. For example, Richert (1991b) claims that "cases require teachers to reflect on practice" (p. 122), and Kleinfeld (1992b) suggests that cases can stimulate "the habit of reflective inquiry" (p. 47). Others proclaim the power of cases to enhance reflection, but they limit their case sources to those written as self-reports of individual experience (Shulman & Colbert, 1989; Shulman, Colbert, Kemper, & Dmytriw, 1990). This use stresses the internal process of writing cases rather than the external process of discussing them (J. Shulman, 1991). This emphasis on construction pays less attention to Dewey's second "indispensable" factor for reflection, developing courses of action. Instead, it is the casewriting process itself, with intense coaching from researchers and editors, that is claimed to induce reflection.

Richert (1991a) also has explored the use of teacher-constructed cases along with other sources of cases for reflection. She used cases written previously by researchers, teacher educators, or students as well as cases written by current students in her teacher education classes. With regard to the construction of self-reported cases, she observed that "preparing cases involves developing skills central to reflective practice" (p. 139). Choosing what to write, the particular focus or frame, developing a story, and learning what to accentuate are all components of reflection, according to Richert: "Learning to listen and to focus, then, are two outcomes of constructing cases according to my students" (1991a, p. 139).

Those who write about case use and reflection in teacher education seem to agree on at least one thing: Cases appear to foster learning from experience, whether it is from their own experience or the experience of others. The next section examines the empirical evidence that supports this and other arguments for cases in teacher education.

RESEARCH CLAIMS AND EMPIRICAL EVIDENCE

The extent to which individual writers assert the benefits of cases and case methods far outweighs the actual empirical work that confirms these benefits. Although this is particularly true in teacher education, where the use of cases and case methods, as defined in this chapter, is relatively new, it is not a phenomenon unique to the education profession. Notably, the fields of business and law also offer few empirical studies about the use of cases in the training of managers and lawyers (Masoner, 1988).

Given the large number of asserted benefits of cases and case-based instruction, one way to examine the existing empirical research is to explore the assertions and research according to three categories of claims: (1) research about the influence of cases on *what* teachers think about, including multicultural issues, student motivation, classroom management, pedagogical content knowledge, and personal authority; (2) research on the influence of cases on *how* teachers think—the processes of teacher thinking, including how case users frame problems, perceive multiple perspectives, generate plausible action plans, and reflect on their personal experience; and (3) research on the claims about the *context* in which individuals consider cases. This last category includes a small but growing body of literature about the method itself, exploring, for example, the role of the instructor and of the learning community and the influence of various factors, such as experience, age, or gender, on the experience of case users.

Ideally, one would like to read research that links classroom effectiveness to study and work with cases. However, there is only limited research on the influence of case-based instruction on classroom performance. Instead, researchers appear to emphasize teacher thinking rather than teacher action in their work. This emphasis implicitly suggests that cognitive abilities of teachers, including flexibility, are a proxy for classroom performance. Appropriately, many teacher educators question this leap of faith. Indeed, it is possible that students who study cases only learn to articulate what could or should be and do not, in any appreciable way, perform more effectively in the classroom.

Nonetheless, cognitive flexibility is a particularly attractive area of inquiry because of its congruence with the uncertain, "ill-structured" nature of teaching. Recent advances in cognitive psychology have lent credence to the importance of cognitive flexibility in ill-structured domains. Perhaps the most popular cognitive scientists quoted by those advocating case use in teacher education are Rand Spiro and his colleagues, who discussed the acquisition of advanced knowledge in particularly complex, ill-structured domains such as teaching (Spiro, Coulson, Feltovich, & Anderson, 1988; Spiro, Vispoel, Schmitz, Samarapungavan, & Boerger, 1987). These researchers have argued that complex knowledge is best conveyed by the representation of that knowledge in multiple, context-dependent situations. In order to achieve cognitive flexibility in knowledge representation, they suggested the application of several cases to a particular domain, where each case presents an opportunity to explore the content domain from different vantage points and perspectives. They believed that this educational method best approximates the way individuals access and use knowledge:

The best way to learn and instruct in order to attain the goal of cognitive flexibility in knowledge representation for future applications is by a method of case-based presentations which treats a content domain as a landscape that is explored by "criss-crossing" it in many directions, by re-examining each case "site" in the varying contexts of different neighboring cases, and by using a variety of abstract dimensions for comparing cases. (Spiro et al., 1987, p. 178)

With this brief explanation of cognitive flexibility theory serving as background, the following sections explore the empirical evidence about cases and their ability to influence how and under what conditions they influence teacher thinking.

The Influence of Cases on What Preservice and In-Service Teachers Think

Research in teacher education classrooms has produced a number of early findings about the influence of cases on what teachers think. For example, researchers have discussed case use to develop multicultural perspectives (Noordhoff & Kleinfeld, 1991), knowledge about motivation (Richardson, 1993), formal authority (Barnett & Tyson, 1993a, 1994), and management (Stoiber, 1991). In addition, some research has focused on how cases can foster deeper understandings of theories and the relationship between theory and practice (McAninch, 1993). Finally, important work has examined the ability of cases to develop pedagogical content knowledge (Barnett, 1991a, 1991b; Ingvarson & Fineberg, 1992; Kleinfeld, 1992a; Wilson, 1992). A brief review follows for each of these areas of research.

Multicultural Perspectives Some teacher educators have developed cases designed to enhance the development of multicultural perspectives. The declared purpose of these cases is to help novices "develop a social map of unfamiliar cultural terrain" (Kleinfeld, 1990, p. 44) so that they will be able to operate more effectively in settings culturally different from

their own. Kleinfeld (1990) claimed that "the case method . . . is uniquely suited to the analysis of the complex and emotionally charged issues of teaching in culturally unfamiliar contexts" (p. 44). Materials that are designed for this purpose include the series *Teaching Cases in Cross Cultural Education*, by Kleinfeld (1988) and *Diversity in the Classroom: A Casebook for Teachers and Teacher Educators*, edited by Shulman and Mesa-Bains (1990). These cases appear either as exemplars to illustrate the actions of model teachers or as opportunities to practice culturally appropriate responses.

Early, but limited, research regarding these assertions suggests some success in achieving these goals. The work of Kleinfeld and her colleagues in a specialized teacher education program in Alaska dominates the field. Employing qualitative methods to analyze pre– and post–student teaching videotapes and written papers before and after case discussions, these researchers have documented gains in the ability of students to understand and respond to cultural diversity (Kleinfeld, 1990; Noordhoff & Kleinfeld, 1991).

Theoretical Perspectives Although the development of multicultural perspectives is achieved by using two types of cases, exemplars and opportunities to practice action, the development of theoretical understandings of concepts in teacher education is primarily achieved by using cases as models or examples. In building a case-based curriculum, Shulman suggested that one must first identify the theoretical principle to be taught and then search for or create cases that exemplify the theories. He observed that "Cases are occasions for offering theories to explain why certain actions are appropriate. . . . Cases thus come to exemplify or to test principles" (L. Shulman, 1992, p. 3).

In her book *Teacher Thinking and the Case Method* (1993), another teacher educator, McAninch, suggested that one of the contributions that cases can make to teacher education "is related to teaching theory" (p. 90). She worked with the early typology of teacher knowledge presented by Lee Shulman (1986), positing a case construction process wherein students first study a general topic or concept from a theoretical perspective and then move to construct a narrative in order to develop a case about the theory. Following the construction of a narrative, a competing theory might be considered and the narrative reinterpreted. The expected outcome of this process is that teacher education students would develop a solid grasp of theory and would develop the ability to frame concrete experiences in theoretical terms.

Although there is no empirical evidence to determine the success of McAninch's particular case methodology, it is important to note that this construction of and use of cases is the reverse of that suggested by other case proponents. Many case developers in teacher education (Greenwood & Parkay, 1989; Kowalski et al., 1990; Shulman & Colbert, 1987, 1988; Silverman et al., 1992, 1994; Wasserman, 1993) begin with practical problems and then apply theories to these problems. McAninch's emphasis on the theoretical may stem, in part, from her lack of experience at the K–12 level.

Richardson suggested a different approach to the development of theoretical perspectives; her work examines how cases can be used to develop a deeper understanding of methods to motivate students. She based her work on the belief that even though students are exposed to theories of motivation in their teacher education programs, they do not seem able to apply this knowledge in actual classroom teaching experiences. She looked for a way to "effectively immerse preservice students in issues, problems, and solutions of student motivation" and decided that one possible method is "through the use of cases" (Richardson, 1993, p. 57). In her research to determine whether cases would be effective in this regard, she analyzed the content of eight case studies that offered a variety of methods to motivate children and were rich in examples of successful and unsuccessful motivational techniques. One important finding from her research was that studying cases without the benefit of a class discussion and leadership by a teacher educator may diminish potential learning. Richardson observed that students could be asked to read these cases without discussing them, but her work suggested that learning outcomes would be restricted and possibly harmful. She stated:

[M]y sense is that the impact of such reading would be slight as compared to asking students to read the cases and discuss and summarize them for themselves. . . . These potential problems [of misinterpretation and discouragement] call for active involvement of a teacher educator in guiding students through the interpretations of the cases (p. 59)

Pedagogical Content Knowledge and Authority A number of scholars have explored how cases might be used to extend the development of pedagogical content knowledge (Barnett, 1991a, 1991b; Barnett & Cwirko-Godycki, 1988; Barnett & Tyson, 1993b, 1994; Ingvarson & Fineberg, 1992; Kleinfeld, 1992a; Wilson, 1992). These proponents see cases as tools to help "illuminate the critical processes new teachers undergo in trying to translate their disciplinary knowledge into classroom curricula" (Carter, 1989, p. 215). In describing her efforts to impart both subject-matter knowledge and pedagogical content knowledge through case use in her teacher education classes, Wilson (1992) stated:

The subject-matter knowledge required for accomplished teaching requires that we develop new methods and new content for teacher preparation. . . . While the creation of new courses is one promising area of development, another is the development of instructional materials and methods that can be used in preexisting teacher education courses. . . . One such method worth exploring involves using cases. (p. 65)

Barnett and her colleagues at the Far West Regional Laboratory also see the value of cases in enhancing pedagogical content knowledge and have developed cases in mathematics for use with novices and experienced teachers. Three years into the effort, Barnett (1991a) declared that "by prompting mathematics teachers to frame problems, analyze situations, and argue the benefits and drawbacks of various alternatives, cases can play a critical role in expanding and deepening pedagogical content knowledge" (p. 263). This view has stimulated similar case development projects in mathematics at the secondary level (Merseth, 1992c).

Barnett and her colleagues have conducted extensive research to determine the effectiveness of cases in expanding pedagogical content knowledge (Barnett, 1991a; Barnett & Cwirko-Godycki, 1988; Barnett & Tyson, 1993a, 1993b). Initially, this research considered ways in which novice and veteran teachers responded to cases on mathematical topics, such as rational numbers. They found that novices reacted to the cases differently from the experienced teachers, with novices typically emphasizing pedagogy less than content. Still, the researchers declared that "case discussions are nevertheless helping them construct pedagogical content knowledge" (Barnett & Cwirko-Godycki, 1988, pp. 29–30). More recently, the work of these scholars has focused on the development of internal feelings of autonomy in addition to a deepening of content knowledge (Barnett & Tyson, 1993a, 1993b, 1994). The topic of autonomy is explored in a following section.

Another experienced case developer and researcher, Judith Kleinfeld (1992a), explored the use of cases to develop pedagogical content knowledge in the field of language arts. In this work, Kleinfeld developed a case about teaching *Hamlet* to diverse students as an exemplar for teacher education students to study how an expert teacher works with this particular content. In order to assess what students learned from this case, Kleinfeld asked them to respond to a series of questions related to content and pedagogy both before and after the case discussion. She analyzed these papers using quantitative data-analysis techniques that consider, for example, the number of problems and methods that students identified in helping students understand *Hamlet*.

Kleinfeld (1992a) found that the case she was researching "succeeded in increasing students' understanding of a sound rationale for selecting literature, their ability to anticipate students' problems and perspectives, their repertoire of pedagogical methods and curriculum alternatives, and their general understanding of fundamental purposes in the teaching of literature" (p. 16). She also found that students' prior content knowledge significantly influenced what they learned from the case. Other researchers who have examined the use of cases to develop pedagogical content knowledge include Wilson (1992) in language arts and Goldman and Barron in elementary mathematics (1990).

The Influence of Cases on How Teachers Think

The literature identifies at least four aspects of cases that influence how teachers think. These include the ability of cases to help develop problem-solving and decision-making skills, the ability of cases to increase awareness of multiple perspectives and other educational settings, the ability of cases to enhance beliefs about personal authority and efficacy, and the ability of cases to develop habits of reflection.

Problem-Solving and Decision-Making Skills One widely acclaimed advantage of case-based pedagogy, in education as well as in other professional fields, is its effectiveness in helping students develop skills of critical analysis, problem solving, and strategic thinking (Christensen & Hansen, 1987; Greenwood & Parkay, 1989; Hunt, 1951; Kowalski et al., 1990; McNair, 1954; Merseth, 1991b; Silverman et al., 1994; Wasserman, 1994). Hunt (1951), for example, discussing the case method in the early 1950s, offered a listing of specific problem-solving characteristics:

the power to analyze and to master a tangled circumstance by selecting the important factors. . . . [T]he ability to utilize ideas, to test them against the facts of the problem, to throw both ideas and facts into fresh combination . . . for the solution of the problem. . . . [T]he ability to recognize a need for new factual material or the need to apply technical skills. . . . [T]he ability to use the later experiences as a test of the validity of the ideas already obtained. (p. 178)

This conceptualization, reflecting what other researchers say about what it means to think like a teacher (Feiman-Nemser, 1980; Grossman, 1990), goes beyond specific skills and knowledge—the *what* that teachers think about—and extends to include the *how*. Kleinfeld, for example, observed that to think like a teacher means that one is able to "formulate educational problems, design strategies that fit specific children, and reflect on the ethical and policy issues as well as on the pedagogical issues embedded in everyday instructional decisions" (Kleinfeld, 1992b, p. 34).

In teacher education, titles of recent casebooks make clear their intent to promote problem solving and to influence how teachers think: *Case Studies for Teacher Problem Solving* (Silverman et al., 1992); *Classroom Assessment Cases for Teacher Problem Solving* (Silverman et al., 1994); *Case Studies for Teacher Decision Making* (Greenwood & Parkay, 1989); and *Cases for Decisions in Teacher Education* (Merseth, in press—a). Primarily utilizing dilemma-ridden, action-forcing cases as described in the preceding section, these authors believe that case users acquire important thinking skills by wrestling with cases of complex, situation-dependent dilemmas.

Very few researchers have explored the veracity of these claims. Kleinfeld (1991a) studied 54 students to determine whether case methods "could develop students' skills in spotting the issues in an ill-structured domain, framing the problems in productive ways, understanding the conflicts from the perspectives of different actors, and developing problem-solving alternatives" (p. 4). Focusing on two classes, one taught with cases and another taught through discussions of readings and practical examples, she studied mid-term examinations that included cases to analyze, classroom observations, an attitudinal survey, and the standard university evaluation process. Based on an analysis of these data, she determined that "students taught by the case method approach showed significantly greater ability to analyze an educational problem" than those in the control group (p. 10).

Kleinfeld (1991a) further asserted that the students in the case section were able to spot issues in problematic situations and to identify possible alternatives for action. Although the students in the experimental section found the cases interesting, they did not rate the case methods class more favorably than the conventional discussion or control classes. Even though it seemed clear to Kleinfeld that students in the case class gained greater analytic skills in analyzing cases, she acknowledged that this result tells us nothing about their ability to use these skills in actual classroom settings.

Increased Awareness of Other Educational Settings and the Generation of Multiple Perspectives

A second claim regarding the influence of cases on how teachers think suggests that cases can help teachers become aware of unfamiliar settings and that cases can help students of teaching appreciate perspectives other than their own (Noordhoff & Kleinfeld, 1991; Shulman & Colbert, 1987, 1988; Shulman & Mesa-Bains, 1990). In this instance, cases are used to provide students with vicarious experiences. Merseth (1991b), for instance, observed:

Good cases and skillful instruction work as an antidote to oversimplification, moving students toward greater sensitivity to context and uniqueness. This technique exposes learners to differing interpretations of complex situations and provides them an opportunity to examine and to rehearse the skills required of effective teachers. (p. 17)

Although cases can portray settings, locations, or cultures unfamiliar to students, they also can exemplify "taboo" topics seldom explored in teacher education programs, such as the emotional demands on teachers or sexual harassment of young student teachers. In describing her Teachers for Alaska Program, Kleinfeld (1992b) noted that:

One of the important contributions of a case literature is to give students emotional preparation for dealing with an unjust world. Cases—due to their very particularity—create opportunities to talk about those injustices that are taboo topics if raised as general problems. (p. 44)

Research related to this ability to develop greater awareness and multiple perspectives is scant. Florio-Ruane and Clark (1990) provide some insights on this topic through their study of case use in three teacher education courses at Michigan State University. They argued that cases help students observe more acutely in the field: "Currently, our case studies of the teaching and learning of writing are being used to work with students to develop new ways of seeing and understanding the practice of teaching" (p. 21). The analytical activities related to case work aim to:

engender in the beginning teachers a sense of the possibilities as well as a sense of what is; an awareness of the multiple realities present in classroom, [sic] not as 'given' but as 'made'; and a valuing of observant participation in the field experiences and ultimately in their own classrooms. (p. 22)

Welty, Silverman, and Lyon (1991) conducted a small study to examine the ability of cases to help students appreciate a broader range of perspectives in certain educational dilemmas. Using pre- and post-analyses of writing about problematic situations portrayed in a case, these researchers examined the students' use of the conditional tense. They asserted that the greater use of phrases such as "could," "might have," and "perhaps," as well as the acknowledgment of more than one or two perspectives on a particular issue, could indicate broadened awareness. The researchers offered their methodological approach as experimental; the results from this work were inconclusive.

Beliefs About Authority and Personal Efficacy

Barnett and Tyson (1993a, 1993b) have extended their research on math cases to consider how case discussions prompt informed strategic inquiry and beliefs about authority and efficacy. They found that casework leads to changes in teachers' conceptions and beliefs about teaching. Cases do this, they posited, by involving teachers in a critical analysis of teaching as they discuss the cases. Through the collaborative process presented and modeled in the case discussions, and the fact that teachers involved in the discussions began to see themselves as "change agents" (Barnett & Tyson, 1993b), these researchers suggested that case use fostered the development of strategic knowledge.

In a related work, Barnett and Tyson (1993a) noted that the use of math cases in professional development programs seemed to shift teachers' perceptions of authority from formal, external sources to internal, collective sources. Using an extensive data-collection system that included videotapes of case discussions with 20 teachers over a 2-year period, pre- and post-assessments of their mathematical knowledge about rational numbers, structured oral interviews, and observation notes from the case discussions, the researchers found that "teachers developed an increasing predilection to offer critical analysis of the case, of each other's comments, and of their own teaching" (p. 9). Furthermore, they found that through each successive discussion, "their understanding of rational numbers becomes deeper and more refined" (p. 10). Certainly, with such extensive data, one can expect to understand a great deal more about the use of cases and the development of pedagogical content knowledge and other influences, such as increased sense of self-capability and wisdom in the group.

The Ability of Cases to Develop Habits of Reflection Empirical work to support the assertion that cases help develop habits of reflection is also scant. One researcher who has explored this topic is Richert (1991b, 1992). She examined the experiences of small numbers of teacher education students (17 and 11 students, respectively) with cases in her teacher education courses. These are largely descriptive works, capturing the feelings and reactions of the students to the use of cases. Students in general found the experience "stimulating, intellectually challenging, rewarding" (1992, p. 172), although no control group or any comparison to other methods were offered. Teachers studying cases "mentioned frequently" (1991b, p. 123) that cases helped them focus their thinking and enabled them to become more precise in their thinking, allowing the students to "zero-in" on educational dilemmas. Such self-reports led Richert to declare that "cases capture the wisdom of practice and allow teachers to examine that practice (and that wisdom) analytically and systematically as well as intuitively" (1991b, p. 126).

The work of J. Shulman and her colleagues (J. Shulman, 1991, 1992; Shulman & Colbert, 1989; Shulman et al., 1990) also represents a more descriptive and less empirical exploration of the use of cases to develop reflective thinking in teachers. Shulman and her colleagues at the Far West Regional Laboratory describe a case writing process to transform a teacher's self-report into a more theoretically based case. In describing this work, J. Shulman (1991) stated: "Our final role as researchers during this stage was to work with an editor to fine-tune the teacher's writing to make the final case an interesting and compelling narrative that incorporated all the components of a teaching case" (p. 259). Shulman's process takes the self-report of a teacher and turns it into a teaching case.

Some may question whether this transformation process deviates from the criterion that case represent actual experience and are based in reality. With such an active role for the editors and researchers, it is possible that the case writer may end up changing the story, possibly in ways that do not represent the actual reality of the situation but rather reflect the interpretation of an outside reviewer or editor. Commenting on this, J. Shulman noted, "We have learned that these reviewers often provide important *new* information or perspectives that lead authors to revise sections of their cases" (1991, p. 258, emphasis added).

The role of the editor in this case-development process is important—perhaps more important than that of the case writer. J. Shulman (1991) observed:

Without such editorial activity and support, teacher-written cases and commentaries are unlikely to achieve the clarity and power they deserve and their audience requires. (p. 260)

This editorial process addresses the difficulty that practitioners sometimes have when writing teaching cases about personal experiences that accurately represent multiple perspectives and opinions (including those of others) about the incident. Clearly, it is difficult to write a case about a deep personal experience without bias. However, as the original case material gets altered, sometimes significantly, it becomes a less accurate reflection of reality.

Nevertheless, it is important to note that special benefits seem to accrue to case writers no matter what method is used. On this topic L. Shulman (1992) observed that, "Case *writing* may well bring special benefits to those who write them, prompting them to reflect on their practice and to become more analytic about their work" (p. 9, emphasis in original). It seems self-evident that writing about personal experience can enhance personal reflection.

Perhaps it is unrealistic to expect self-reflective writing to meet the strict criteria of a teaching case. In general, case developers know that self-reports do not become effective teaching cases without additional research to include other perspectives and multiple points of view. However, sometimes the event or the experience is not amenable to additional inquiry and data gathering.

J. Shulman also adds commentary to cases "so that the cases become part of the community of practitioners and scholars and are tools that can inform and educate new and experienced teachers" (1991, p. 259). However, it is not clear that commentary causes cases to become part of the community of practitioners, nor is it clear that commentary is necessary to add "complexity and richness," as L. Shulman has suggested (1992, p. 12). If a case is well researched and well documented, it should be, by definition, rich and complex.

In fact, many case developers and researchers (Kleinfeld, 1990; Kowalski et al., 1990; Merseth, 1992a; Silverman et al., 1992; Wasserman, 1993) do not include written commentary at the end of their cases because they feel that commentary has the potential to reduce, rather than increase, the complexity of the cases. Furthermore, commentary may introduce aspects that are not supported by the reality of the original case. Perhaps the greatest objection to commentary is that its inclusion may inhibit the construction of knowledge by novices. When novices read what "experts" have said about a case, they may tend to abandon or suspend their own beliefs in favor of the "delivered wisdom." Empirical research on the influence of commentary on teacher thinking would help clarify this conversation.

Other researchers emphasize how students learn to reflect about teaching by developing case writing skills (Florio-Ruane, 1990; Florio-Ruane & Clark, 1990; Kleinfeld, 1991b; LaBoskey, 1992). Florio-Ruane (1990) and Florio-Ruane and Clark (1990) suggested that learning *about* the methods of case writing, whether they actually use the methods or not, offers a powerful technique to enhance the ability of novices to "see" more clearly in their field experiences. LaBoskey (1992) perceived case writing or "case investigations" as a research methodology that is important for novices to learn. She included this case investigation technique in the Stanford University Teacher Education Program, suggesting that "the purpose of case investigations is to help students learn how to think reflectively and to develop a long-term inquiry orientation toward teaching" (p. 178). Her descriptive piece does not, however, provide any empirical data to determine whether this actually occurred.

The Influence of Context on What and How Teachers Learn Through Cases

The third set of claims and research about cases and case methods centers on the influence of contextual factors on teacher learning through cases. Whether teachers are learning substance or process skills, it seems obvious that the context—the participants, the way the cases are integrated with other teaching materials, and the role of discussion leader—will have a strong influence on what is learned. The next sections consider research about the influence of context in case-based instruction.

The Construction of Knowledge in Learning Communities Teacher educators face the challenge of urging their students to construct knowledge rather than receive it passively from so-called experts, be they university faculty, supervisors, commentators, or textbook authors. Students need opportunities to develop the type of knowledge teachers use, a "case" type of knowledge (Doyle, 1986; L. Shulman, 1986) that is constantly being formed and reformed with each day's experience.

Proponents of case methods in teacher education often argue that cases and case discussion can create an environment wherein students of teaching have an opportunity not only to see alternative conceptions of teaching but also to build their own understandings as they interact with these cases and their colleagues (Barnett & Tyson, 1993a; Harrington, 1994; Harrington & Garrison, 1992; Lacey & Merseth, 1993; Merseth & Lacey, 1993). These authors argue that it is important for novice teachers to come to know themselves as persons who create knowledge and who hold important, often implicit, views as they prepare for professional life. Implicit in this advocacy for case use is the acknowledgment of the pitfalls of prior experience and the need for teacher education curricula directly to confront these prior experiences and knowledge (Feiman-Nemser & Buchmann, 1985; Hollingsworth, 1989). Without aggressive intervention, students may well replicate past practice rather than transform it in their new role as teachers. Furthermore, these case advocates suggest that cases foster the creation of productive learning communities and can develop expectations among

teachers that encourage sharing in discussions about teaching. Such should be the norm, not an exception (Holmes Group, 1990).

The discussion of constructivist learning through cases includes the use of cases in written form (Barnett & Tyson, 1993a; Levin, 1993; Richert, 1991b) and in electronic form, such as with video and hypermedia (Bransford et al., 1986; Goldman & Barron, 1990; Richardson & Kile, 1992; Risko, 1992) or computer networks (Cutler, 1992; Lacey & Merseth, 1993; Merseth, 1990a, 1992b). Descriptions of these constructivist environments almost always refer to the increasing ability of students or novice teachers to access, connect, and interact with an ever-growing variety of ideas, perspectives, and data. For example, Richert (1991b) observed:

In addition to understanding particular teaching situations and thus learning about teaching by reflectively examining cases of practice, teachers construct knowledge as they create and analyze cases. . . . As teachers write and talk about their work, they come to know what they know. The process is dialectical. (p. 125)

An electronic example of the construction of knowledge through case discussion is available from research about interactive computer networks used to connect beginning teachers. In this work, beginners present a dilemma or "case" for others to comment on and offer strategies for action (Cutler, 1992). Research showed that initial responses to the "case" were often specific to the context of the commentator, but as the conversation developed and more perspectives were added, the nature of the subsequent contributions frequently moved to broader, more philosophical, and sometimes theoretical conceptualizations of the case. Merseth (1990a) described the impact of these electronic case discussions:

Engaging in conversations and discussions on the network about teaching had the dual effect of making them keenly aware of their own particular teaching experience as well as inducing a broader perspective of education. The give and take of the exchanges, the multiple perspectives of the individuals, and the wide range of experiences helped the beginners conceptualize the meaning of his or her situation. . . . It stimulated debate, discussion, and reflection. (p. 20)

Barnett and Tyson (1993a) identified a similar "development of a critical stance" by teacher participants in the use of written cases about mathematics with experienced teachers. In this research, it is clear that the construction of knowledge is influenced by the environment in which it occurs. Levin (1993) concurred, commenting that the "[S]ocial construction of knowledge in a setting like a case discussion has implications for teachers' individual construction of knowledge" (p. 210).

The Role of Discussions in Case Learning Many researchers (Barnett & Tyson, 1993a, 1994; Bransford et al., 1986; Goldman & Barron, 1990; Harrington, 1994; Harrington & Garrison, 1992; Richardson, 1993; Silverman, 1994; Silverman et al., 1992; Wasserman, 1993; Welty, 1989) place great emphasis on the discussion of views and perspectives as a key element in the construction of knowledge about teaching through cases. These researchers suggest that it is the *discussion* of the case that promotes the construction of knowledge about teaching; cases are incomplete without some form of discussion or shared inquiry. For example, Harrington and Garrison (1992) argued that cases can initiate shared inquiry. According to these researchers, the purpose of a case is to stimulate a public exchange and construction of knowledge and a public articulation of beliefs. They viewed cases as "problems that initiate shared inquiry" (p. 719) and argued that cases establish a dialogic model of connecting theory and practice through the case-based method of teaching.

Barnett (1991a) also asserted that teachers learn more through case discussions than by reading alone. For example, she stated that "The Tolley case does, however, show that when teachers engage in group deliberation, they can construct ideas that might not have occurred to them through personal reflection about their own teaching" (p. 270). She observed that during case discussions, "a mutual educational process takes place" (p. 270). However, not all researchers place such an emphasis on the importance of case discussions. L. Shulman (1992), for example, offered a contrary opinion on the importance of discussions. He observed that "there is no *necessary* relationship between cases and discussion" (p. 13, emphasis in original).

One empirical study sheds light on this difference of opinion. In her doctoral dissertation (1993), Levin examined the effect of case discussion on teachers' thinking about teaching practice. Using control and experimental groups, she found that reading and writing cases without discussion provided little stimulus for teachers to elaborate on their understanding or to construct new knowledge. She found that discussion was an important aspect in the development of teacher thinking and knowledge because it "appears to affect teachers' thinking in ways that seem likely to promote teacher development about teaching and learning issues" (p. 210). Levin believed that the "social interactions" that occurred during the discussions created disequilibria for the participants that led to "both assimilations and accommodations" in their thinking (p. 205). Furthermore, she documented the different effects of case discussions on student teachers, novices, and experienced teachers.

Case discussions appear to have the power to create opportunities for collaborative inquiry by teachers because such discussions occur in a professional community, thus taking advantage of the power of shared professional inquiry (Cochran-Smith & Lytle, 1990). The discussion of cases, whether in narrative, hypermedia, or electronic form, may offer an opportunity for teacher educators to model collective inquiry for their students. As Lacey and Merseth (1993) noted:

As students and teachers work together to plumb and expand multiple ways of viewing and transforming different situations of teaching, they become fellow inquirers, emulating in preservice education the broader professional search to improve practice. . . . Through its medium, new teachers and teacher-educators exercise the habits of collegial study. (pp. 548–549)

Many see this ability to create active learning communities as one of the distinctive contributions of case discussions (Barnett & Tyson, 1993a; Richert, 1991a, 1991b; Wasserman, 1993).

The Role of the Discussion Leader The role of the case discussion leader undergirds the use of cases and their ability to foster the construction of knowledge and communities of learners. A number of writers in many professional fields have discussed the challenges for effective discussion leaders (Christensen & Hansen, 1987; Frederick, 1981; McAninch, 1993; Wasserman, 1993, 1994; Welty, 1989). One widely read author on this topic is C. Roland Christensen of the Harvard Business School and the Harvard Graduate School of Education. He has written extensively and has offered seminars about the role of the facilitator since the early 1970s (Christensen, 1981; Christensen & Hansen, 1987). His work explores topics such as establishing instructor–student learning contracts, gaining student respect, leading versus controlling a discussion, and designing course curricula. Without a doubt, anyone who has considered case-based teaching carefully will attest to its challenges, its rewards, and its difficulty (Sykes, 1989; Wasserman, 1993; Welty, 1989).

Summarizing these challenges, Merseth (1991b) noted that "effective case-method instruction requires extensive, specialized skill on the part of faculty who use the pedagogy" (p. 20). These skills include a change in many of the traditional assumptions about the role of faculty and students in higher education. In case-based instruction, instructors must prepare not only the content of the case but also the process of teaching the case. Furthermore, students must assume greater responsibility for their learning. They must be active, not passive, and they must construct their own knowledge with this pedagogy. Discussing the changes required by case use in higher education, Goldman and Barron (1995) commented:

We continue to be amused by the tenacity of the "culture" of higher education. The professor is "supposed" to lecture, and the students are "supposed" to take notes. . . . We believe that hypermedia technology has the potential for creating a new type of teacher education program—one that moves traditional college and university courses away from a teacher-directed lecture format and into a problem-solving/analytical mode. (p. 29)

Wasserman (1994) offered a helpful review of various elements that she has found useful in case discussion classrooms, including the use of small groups, study questions, and follow-up techniques. She observed that case discussions often require a new role for the instructor, one that "removes the professor from the center stage and into a position of partnership with students in examining issues of substance" (p. 611).

One area of research related to the case discussion leader is the influence of the instructor's goals and purposes for using cases. How a case discussion leader chooses to use a case directly influences the outcome of the discussion. For example, Saunders (1992) explored the discussion processes and comments of 38 undergraduates stimulated by the use of video cases in an introductory course about teaching. Although one of the intentions of the creators of the video case was that it would give students practice in problem solving and decision making, the case instructor did not use the case in this way. Instead, it was her intention to use the case to explore the students' motives for teaching. Writing about this conflict between the original case writer's purpose and the instructor's goals, Saunders concluded her study with a very important point: "Clearly, any case's success in encouraging specific behaviors in prospective teachers is dependent on the degree to which the case's goals are congruent with the instructor's goals and behaviors" (1992, pp. 22–23). The discussion leader must consider the goals of the instructor and the appropriateness of the materials used to achieve those goals.

A limited number of studies exist about the role of the facilitator in case discussions. Three important contributions to this literature include the recent work of Barnett and Tyson (1994), Levin (1993), and Morine-Dershimer (1993). Utilizing discourse analysis, Levin analyzed her own role as a case facilitator. She found that the pattern of interaction between herself and her students differed from the typical discourse pattern, where an instructor *initiates* a sequence, to which a *response* is given by a student, which is then followed by an *evaluative* comment by the teacher. This is the familiar initiation, response, and evaluation (IRE) pattern. Furthermore, in most classroom situations, comments from the instructor typically account for nearly two-thirds of the utterances. In Levin's case discussions, the interaction frequently followed an IRRRRR-IRRRR-IRRRRRR pattern, which is markedly different from the familiar IRE pattern. She also noted that the instructor spoke less than 20% of the time.

Morine-Dershimer (1993) also explored the actions of the case facilitator and their influence on what is learned by case users. She studied three teacher educators who used the same cases in four sections of a generic methods course in a 5-year teacher education course and in a 2-year postgraduate program. Data collected on the discussions of the same case in each of the four sections included videotapes of the case discussion, as well as written information from the participants indicating the "key idea" of the case analysis discussion. Morine-Dershimer analyzed these data for the degree of teacher direction in the discussion, the typical emphasis, and the apparent key events (as indicated by the students) of the discussion. She found that case discussions with a greater degree of student structuring of the discussion (i.e., less faculty direction and talking) exhibited "more active student involvement, more sustained student attention, and more complex processing of information by students" (1993, p. 33). Class size and the program area of students also seemed to influence learning. In larger classes where a conscious decision was made to break the class into smaller discussion groups, and with secondary education students, as opposed to elementary education students, there was greater student structuring and involvement in the discussion.

Barnett and Tyson (1994) conducted research on the facilitator's role in case discussions about mathematics teaching and learning. Using videotapes, transcripts of case discussions, written personal retrospective reflections, and interviews of eight classroom teachers who participated in a series of class discussions, they focused on the ability of the facilitator to capitalize on learning opportunities, to promote consideration of diverse perspectives, and to build shared vocabulary and experiences with the discussion group. The researchers found that the facilitator was able to guide the discussion toward specific and deeper mathematical and pedagogical content understanding by phrasing questions carefully (so that she did not put any words into the discussants' mouths), by slowing and focusing the discussion by writing examples on the chalkboard, and by pushing case participants to clarify

statements and provide examples. They also found that the facilitator played a key role in creating a learning community that both articulated and supported a diversity of beliefs about teaching.

The Role of Age, Gender, and Experience Recently, a number of researchers have begun to explore the influence of gender, age, and experience on learning stimulated by case discussions (Kleinfeld, 1991a; Levin, 1993; Lundeberg & Fawver, 1993). This research reveals some interesting trends as well as areas of disagreement. For example, in a study of 70 preservice students, Lundeberg and Fawver (1993) set out to measure the degree to which case studies affected the "reflective cognitive growth" of students in an educational psychology course. Specifically considering flexibility, perspective taking, and connectedness of the students' statements about the cases, they determined that women generated significantly more decisions and identified more issues than did men. They also found that older students (they do not say how much older) generated more than twice the number of issues and decisions as did younger students. These results contradict those of Kleinfeld (1991a), who found no differences between traditional- and non–traditional-age students, and of Richardson and Kile (1992), who found greater benefits for traditional-age students. Clearly, this area is rich with additional research possibilities to gain a deeper understanding about the effects of gender and age on case learning. McAninch (1993), for example, posited a central question about gender when she declared:

It is unclear, however . . . how readily a form of pedagogy developed for the graduate education of elite men [at Harvard Business School] can serve as a model for teacher education. The special challenges of promoting intellectual growth among primarily non-elite undergraduates, the majority of whom are women, have yet to be criteria for examining case methods in other fields. (p. 62)

Another context issue relates to the influence of previous professional experience on case users. Many case teachers in other professional fields, such as business, have suggested informally that case methods are more successful with practitioners who have had previous professional experience. Exploring this topic in education, Levin examined the differences elicited by case discussions in the thinking of eight student teachers, eight first-year teachers, and eight experienced teachers. She found that less experienced teachers exhibited thinking that was more declarative, critical, and less complex than the more experienced teachers:

For very experienced teachers, discussion of the case seemed to be a catalyst for reflection and promoted metacognitive understandings of important issues in teaching and learning. For the less experienced teachers in this study the case discussion appeared to allow these teachers to clarify and/or elaborate their thinking about particular issues in the case. (Levin, 1993, p. 204)

Additional research will help the field of teacher education examine the influence of prior professional experience (whether in the same field or for those making a career change) on case learning. Such investigations will be particularly important for those who wish to use cases in professional development programs.

Case Type Very little research exists on the compelling question of case form and type. It seems reasonable to expect that students will learn different things in different ways, depending on whether the case is an exemplar intended to demonstrate successful practice with no action formulation required or whether the case is oriented toward problem solving and decision making. Although not directly related to case-based instruction, Stoiber (1991) conducted an interesting study of different instructional techniques by using cases with 67 preservice students in a teacher education program. One approach (for the control group) emphasized technical skills and principles through a lecture-student participation mode using cases as exemplars, faculty lectures about specific skills, and role plays by the students. The second approach emphasized reflective and constructive processes. Here, students were encouraged to "think reflectively and solve classroom problems rather than simply accept principles without evaluating their rationale. To achieve this goal, the treatment was based on the analysis of classroom cases" (Stoiber, 1991, p. 133).

Using a video-stimulated interview method, Stoiber and her colleagues assessed the pedagogical reasoning and problem-solving ability of the students in both groups. She asserted that those students who experienced the reflective-constructive environment exhibited higher pedagogical reasoning and a greater sense of responsibility toward students and the learning environment. Perhaps Stoiber's most important finding for this review focused on the different results that appear to stem from different uses of cases. Both approaches, the technical and the reflective-constructive, used cases. However, the ways in which cases were used differed markedly. Stoiber (1991) explained:

In the technical approach, cases were used to teach prescriptive techniques used by exemplary teachers. This approach emphasizes learning through accepting, acquiring, and conforming to illustrated techniques. In contrast, in the reflective condition the cases were used to enable preservice teachers to construct useful conceptions and strategies of classroom management. (p. 136)

These results suggest that preservice teachers are capable of constructing concepts and learning problem-solving skills through cases that require active construction and articulation of teaching strategies. However, Stoiber also observed that her study does not tell us what these preservice teachers will do in their classrooms; it only reports what they expect to do. It would be necessary to extend the study in order to determine the effect these different uses would have on the classroom performance of the teachers.

Exploring the impact of cases and case methods on the performance of teachers in classrooms, Goldman and Barron (1990) conducted an important study on the actual classroom performance of novice teachers who were trained with cases. Using videodisc materials in their mathematics methods classes, they explored the students' reaction to this form of case material, and whether the use of video case materials makes a difference in student performance on traditional test items and in the way the students taught in their practicum or student-teaching placements. Utilizing questionnaires, interviews, and observa-

tions in the students' classrooms, the researchers determined that "when video illustrations are used in the methods class to provide context for the topics studied and to demonstrate effective teaching techniques, students tend to incorporate these techniques into their own lessons" (p. 28). This represents a crucial area of inquiry, because the ultimate goal of implementing a new or different pedagogy in teacher education must be to enhance the teacher's classroom performance. Unfortunately, available research on this crucial question of the impact of cases and case methods on teacher performance in classrooms is extremely limited.

Case Method Use and Research in Other Countries

Examples of case method use in professional education in other countries, though limited, is informative. Much of this work (e.g., in Canada, Europe, Scandinavia, and the United Kingdom) refers to business or public policy education (Klein, 1992; Myrman & Kjellen, 1993; Stuhler & Ó Súilleabháin, 1990). More specific consideration of teacher and administrator education utilizing cases and case methods is available in Canada, Australia, and Japan. Selected education faculty in these three countries have written about cases and case methods. For example, at the University of Ottawa's School of Education, Faculté d'éducation de l'Université d'Ottawa, Michel Saint-Germain teaches students of educational administration. His use of cases involves students both in writing and in discussing cases. Initially, he tried using cases developed for the anglophone culture but decided that francophone cases were required.

Saint-Germain (1993) designed a process to have his students write and interpret francophone cases. In this process, he asked students to draft a case and then reexamine the case in light of educational theory. The theory, he claimed, helped illuminate the events and reframe the naive language and concepts encountered in the initial phases. Finally, he asked students to rewrite the case using their newfound understandings. Noting the particular requirements of case teaching, Saint-Germain (1993) pointed out that teaching by the case method demands mastery over the material and requires the teacher to be "un gymnaste conceptuel" (p. 9).

Manabu Sato (1991a, 1991b, 1992) of the University of Tokyo also has worked with cases developed by practitioners. Sato informs his readers that the case method is not new to Japan. Over 100 years ago, casebooks were being used in a "theory *into* practice approach" (p. 5). In the 1920s, as a result of the progressive movement in American education, a "theory *through* practice approach" was used with cases. This process was called the "practice-critique-development approach" (p. 9). After a short hiatus following World War II, when a national curriculum was imposed, the case method drawing on the theory *through* practice approach was reintroduced into teacher education and teacher development in Japan.

The cases that Sato described all include videotapes and commentary written by teachers, researchers, and experts that cross various disciplinary lines. He writes that "describing cases with language only is limited" (p. 14) and therefore is a strong advocate for videotapes to accompany written narratives. He sees cases as records of teachers' practical wisdom rather than as exemplars of practice, although he clearly values the perspectives of veteran teachers, researchers, and experts from other fields. His use of cases stresses the examination of practice as "pedagogical puzzles." He has produced two books of cases, videotapes, and commentary (1991a, 1991b).

Work by Lawrence Ingvarson and Warren Fineberg (1992) at Monash University in Clayton, Australia, takes a third, slightly different, approach. These researchers undertook a project to enhance the professional development of teachers through the collection of cases that document "the wisdom of practice" (p. 1). The purpose of this case collection was to gather examples of successful teaching practice in Australia for study and modeling by science teachers across the country. For these researchers, cases are exemplars—evidence of best practice—in science teaching.

Besides using cases as exemplars to enhance practice, Ingvarson and Fineberg (1992) also acknowledged several other purposes for their project. In particular, they suggested that collecting such cases could become a way of lifting the status of teachers' professional knowledge. They also consider cases as a way of documenting teachers' work for the purposes of professional evaluation and promotion and, finally, as vehicles in professional development for clarifying what "counts."

The cases developed by these researchers are not puzzles to be worked out, as in Japan, Canada, and in some instances in the United States but, rather, examples to teach, to demonstrate, to exemplify. Ingvarson and Fineberg (1992), noted:

Whereas many case studies are designed to foster discussion and deepen understanding about familiar classroom situations, such as classroom management or socio-cultural issues, our case studies aim to provide the essential information that will enable another teacher to use the case with as full an understanding of the pedagogical reasoning behind it as possible. (p. 9)

The actual method of developing a case is a long and involved process through which a "project team" identifies content, approaches used by the teacher, theories that underlie the teacher's actions, suggestions for further extension of the lesson, and significant moments in the lesson. Finally, the cases are used by the teachers themselves. "[T]he major benefits," the authors wrote, "come through situations where groups of teachers are using the cases and reflecting upon them" (p. 22).

As in the United States, researchers in other countries seem to be examining many of the same questions of purpose, use, and construction of cases in teacher education. As research on cases and case methods moves forward in these countries, it will be important for teacher educators in the United States to maintain close contact with their international colleagues.

THE FUTURE OF CASES AND CASE METHODS

The myriad claims for the use of cases and case methods far exceed the volume and quality of research specific to cases and case methods in teacher education. In fact, the imbalance between promise and empirical data legitimately may allow one to question why a chapter on case use in teacher education is included in a handbook dedicated to the review of research. Will cases and case methods become the new standard peda-

gogy in teacher education for the twenty-first century? At the present time, the answer is unclear because the understanding of cases and case methods is incomplete. Where should teacher educators go to find the answer? What research topics and developmental activities will build an adequate understanding of this approach to serve teachers and teacher educators best in the future?

To advance the understanding of cases and case methods, the teacher education community may find it productive to engage in both empirical research and the development of cases and case methods while attending to the ever-expanding knowledge base about teaching. To explore cases and case methods more deeply, it will be important to attend to the familiar interaction of material, teacher and student, invoking the familiar "I–Thou–It," or curriculum–student–teacher triangle of instruction (Hawkins, 1974). For case-based instruction, this interaction presents teacher educators with a bit of a dilemma: In order to explore the use of cases in teacher education, the field must have an adequately developed collection of cases. However, in order to justify the investment of significant time, money, and effort to develop cases, the field must be convinced that this is a worthwhile investment. Sykes and Bird (1992), in their comprehensive review of the "case idea," suggested this conundrum and observed:

The future of the case idea, we suspect, rests more on development than research, or perhaps on research in the context of development. We mean that the central task ahead is to create and use rich and interesting case materials in a variety of settings for a variety of purposes, while simultaneously studying those uses. (p. 509)

Thus, the final task of this chapter is to explore these two areas of concern: potential lines of research and inquiry about cases and case methods in teacher education and the necessary development of viable case materials and pedagogies.

Paths of Research

Sykes and Bird (1992) offered an excellent articulation of the range of research on cases and case methods that awaits teacher educators. Although the literature reviewed earlier in this chapter indicates the existence of important work that *describes* the use of cases, the task before teacher educators now is to *assess* more fully the use of cases and to develop research on the effects of variations in use. As this chapter has illustrated, work in this area has only begun, signaling the need for increased activity.

To begin this work, Sykes and Bird suggested that teacher educators compare the use of cases and case-based instruction with other instructional materials and techniques in teacher education. This charge is an ambitious one because the successful comparison of cases and case methods with other instructional materials and approaches requires a clear understanding of the variety of purposes and uses of the pedagogy. In addition, methodological challenges and potential pitfalls may add to this challenge. Teacher educators will need to work toward an understanding of the nature of case practice before they can compare this practice with other instructional approaches.

What, then, should be done to understand more fully the nature of case practice in teacher education?

First of all, researchers should be clear about the intended outcomes of case use. Are they looking for effects on teacher cognition, on teacher behavior in classrooms, or on personal beliefs and feelings? As noted, some researchers (Fenstermacher, 1994; Kagan, 1993; Merseth & Lacey, 1993) have suggested that the relationship between the purpose, use, and outcome of case work varies widely and often is neither clearly stated nor well defined by teacher educators. Although initial research has explored the cognitive and personal outcomes of case use, virtually no one, with the notable exception of Goldman and Barron (1990), has tackled the most important question of the influence of case study on teacher and student performance in classrooms.

A particular challenge for this research is the interactive influences of material, instructor, and student. As Cronbach (1975) observed in discussing the search for empirical generalizations between specific teaching treatments and student outcomes, "Once we attend to interactions, we enter a hall of mirrors that extends to infinity" (p. 119). Thus, a prudent first step before engaging in the interactions may be to step back and build a deeper understanding of cases and case methods through an exploration of the materials and the methods independently.

Research on Case Materials The research on case materials reported in this chapter explored the range of different materials explicitly designed as teaching cases. However, what about cases that are not developed in this way? How will cases that are simply artifacts, such as grade books, student materials, or school district financial data influence student learning? As one researcher stated, "[A]ll of these artifacts are potentially cases" (McAninch, 1993, p. 97). How does learning from the discussion of a paragraph in Vivian Paley's *White Teacher* (1979) differ from the discussion of a case crafted explicitly for class discussion? What difference will it make in student learning if the material that is used as a "case" was originally intended and/or created for a different purpose and use? One study might compare teachers' thinking as they read, write, and discuss an article in expository form with their thinking about a case, based on identical sources, in narrative prose. Furthermore, what do we know about the influence of the protagonist, the setting, and the length of cases? Will student teachers learn more from a case that describes another student teacher or from a case that describes a 20-year veteran? Will students learn more from settings more similar to than different from that of their experience? Certainly, the work of colleagues in the cognitive science field will be important to teacher educators as they pursue many of these questions.

Other questions regarding the content of cases in teacher education classrooms exist. For instance, what differences in teacher learning will result from the recent development of cases focusing on content knowledge (Barnett, 1991a, 1991b; Hutchings, 1993; Kleinfeld, 1992a; Merseth, 1992b)? Will these cases stimulate greater cognitive gains than will cases focusing on such topics as multicultural education (Noordhoff & Kleinfeld, 1991; Shulman & Mesa-Bains, 1990)? One might speculate that the effects of content-based cases would be easier to assess because they often are written with greater clarity of purpose and objectivity.

Another area in which more research is necessary focuses on the medium of cases. What is known about the difference between video, written, and a combination of video and written cases in hypermedia format? Early research has helped teacher educators develop a deeper understanding of each of these media individually, but no empirical studies have compared these approaches. Furthermore, educators could explore whether video cases intensify or lessen personal involvement. It seems reasonable to expect that the medium in which cases are presented would result in different outcomes depending on the experience, age, and prior knowledge of the students.

Case materials also may vary according to their context or supporting material. For example, questions focusing on whether, how, and when commentary is included have yet to be explored. Teacher educators need empirical data to determine the influence of commentary. And if it is used, then what is known about its use? Does its introduction before, during, or after the discussion of the case produce different outcomes? Another element of supporting materials involves different types of "study questions" offered at the end of a case. How do variations in cognitive level, specificity, or theory dependence influence student learning? Furthermore, consideration might be given to the relationship of cases to other materials in courses (Sykes, 1989). One study by Sudzina and Kilbane (1992) explored the benefits of integrating cases with a theory-based textbook in a teacher education course. What materials best accompany cases in teacher education?

Research on Case Methods A second line of research about the use of cases in teacher education should explore variations in method. Basically, this work would investigate how, where, when, and by whom cases are used. One category of questions in this realm takes up the curriculum of teacher education programs and examines the variable aspects of organization, sequence, and assessment. For example, issues related to the organization of curricula surface when one considers teacher education program content or specific courses (Merseth & Lacey, 1993). The fundamental question is what content is presented most effectively through case-based instruction? How would teachers who experience an entirely case-based teacher education program differ from those who have only a few or no case-based courses? As one case researcher noted, only half in jest, "Would students studying a curriculum that was 50% case-based learn only 50% as much as students studying a curriculum that was 100% case-based?"

Furthermore, one could explore questions about sequence, both within programs and within courses. Although Barnett and her colleagues have begun this work by considering the influence of multiple cases on teacher learning about rational numbers within a professional development program (Barnett & Tyson, 1993a), a deeper understanding of case sequencing within a program awaits investigation. Another question concerns the sequence of cases within courses. Is it more productive to consider five cases set in the same context about five different topics or five cases about the same topic in five different settings? And what are the most appropriate forms of assessment? Should students who study cases be evaluated with cases or with other instruments? What should teacher educators expect if portfolios or National Teachers Exam scores are used as measures of cognitive development in case-based curricula?

Myriad questions regarding methods also exist about the physical arrangements of case-based instruction. Is there an optimal class size or an ideal seating arrangement? Should students be asked to meet in small groups before a larger seminar discussion? Should students be given advance notice when they are asked to present a case, or are "cold calls" more effective? Other questions about physical space move the research toward the role of the instructor. Should the instructor stand, sit, or move around the classroom? And what about the use of the blackboard and wait time? There are few limits to the number of questions of this type. Clearly, these questions also pertain to any instructional approach, not just to cases and case methods.

The earlier discussion of research in this chapter touched on the importance of the instructor (Levin, 1993; Morine-Dershimer, 1993). Fascinating questions build on this work. For example, is a more active, participatory discussion leader likely to elicit greater learning than a passive leader? What is the nature of interaction between certain types of cases—exemplars, decision making, or reflection—and the discussion style of the case facilitator? It seems reasonable to expect that certain types of cases would work better for some instructors than for others. How is learning affected if cases are discussed without a formal leader? Would differences vary depending on the type of case? Once again, the number and range of questions regarding case methods seem limitless.

Research on the Characteristics of Learners Although some initial research has been conducted on the influence of student characteristics on case learning (Levin, 1993), this represents an area where additional research is important. Questions about the interaction of learner characteristics and the form and use of cases abound. For example, is there a measurable threshold of prior understanding or familiarity with the situation presented in the case in order for optimal learning to occur? Is it reasonable to expect student teachers' learning to be enhanced more by studying cases about student teachers than about experienced teachers? How will the learning of student teachers, novice teachers, and experienced teachers differ? How will these groups react to different materials and different instructional techniques? Further consideration must also be given to prior teaching experience, particularly if cases and case methods are used in in-service teacher education programs.

Other areas of research might focus on gender differences in learning from cases. If cases are used in learning communities that seek collectively to support the learning of all members of the environment, will women or men feel more comfortable and learn more? Similar explorations might investigate the possible influence of cultural beliefs and perspectives on case learning.

Implicit in this discussion of possible research is the assumption that the field has access to appropriate methodological techniques to assess the influence of cases on teacher learning and knowledge acquisition. However, this may not be the case. In informal conversations, L. Shulman and Sykes have suggested that new methodologies are needed to develop a fuller understanding of cases and case methods.

These opportunities for an active research agenda about cases and their use in teacher education are exciting yet daunting. However, if teacher educators pursue their work with the objective of first understanding more completely the elements of case-based pedagogy—namely, the materials, the methods, and the students—and then engage in more complicated research that explores the interaction of these elements, significant contributions may be realized.

Paths for Development

Sykes and Bird (1992) also noted that efforts to develop a rich body of cases will be as important and necessary to the field as empirical research. Cases and case methods rely not only on creative empirical research but also on the active development of case materials and methodologies. Without a sustained development of materials and pedagogical techniques, the field will have little to study. A number of issues surface for teacher educators as they consider the development of case materials and case-based pedagogies.

Development of Case Materials Since the mid-1980s, more cases have been written for use in teacher education classrooms than ever before. Interest in the topic is growing. This interest has stimulated the creation of a number of centers for case development, including the Far West Regional Laboratory (Judith Shulman, director); Judith Kleinfeld's Center for Cross-Cultural Education in Alaska; the Roderick MacDougall Center for Case Development at Harvard University (Katherine Merseth, director); the Pace University Center for Case Development (Rita Silverman and Bill Welty, directors); and the University of Virginia Commonwealth Center (Robert McNergney, director). These centers are each developing cases with a particular style or "signature" that, in some instances, differ significantly.

These differences offer one reason why the development of a centralized source or clearinghouse for case materials may be problematic at this time. A move to standardize the variety of purpose, design, and use assumes that the field of teacher educators is clear about the most desirable form and use of cases and case methods. Creating a clearinghouse, along with a peer-review board to ensure that high-quality materials are available, suggests that teacher educators have solid empirical research on which to make judgments and recommendations. This does not appear to be the current situation.

A second reason why it may be difficult to develop a centralized collection of case materials rests on the lack of clear incentives for faculty both to write and to teach with cases. Unlike other professional fields, such as business and law, few in the education profession are willing to consider the development of a case equivalent to a publishable article in a refereed journal. Even though experienced case writers know that the development of a good teaching case requires careful data collection, a thorough review and understanding of the related literature, and considerable writing skill, the rewards for this work are not yet commensurate with other, more traditional forms of publication.

Furthermore, the issue of distribution of materials is not easily separated from teaching methodologies. Cases are not the same as articles; they include clearly intended teaching actions. Therefore, implementing case-based instruction fundamentally is more complicated than simply creating a case literature.

Development of Case Methods Many educators who teach with cases comment on the challenges of using cases effectively in teacher education classrooms (Christensen & Hansen, 1987; Sykes, 1989; Wasserman, 1994; Welty, 1989). In response to this challenge, a number of case centers, including those at the Far West Regional Laboratories, Harvard, Pace, and Virginia, now offer professional development opportunities for teacher educators. The purpose of these institutes and workshops is to assist educators who wish to enhance and expand their case teaching and writing skills. Another example of support in the field is the Teaching Initiative sponsored by the AAHE (Hutchings, 1993). This project has grown out of a concern about the relative paucity of serious professional discourse on college campuses about teaching. Although not limited to teacher educators or to case-based instruction, the project has already made a significant contribution to the professional development of college faculty.

Finally, a number of activities can be undertaken at the local campus level to enhance the development of case-teaching skills (Merseth, 1991b). Faculty seminars to discuss methods, teaching group meetings among faculty using the same cases, peer observation, and the assignment of mentors to less experienced colleagues are valuable strategies.

Leaders in the field of teacher education should encourage multiple case development efforts, seeking creative and diverse interpretations of the genre. Just as the field needs to cast a wide net of empirical research to intensify its understanding of case-based instruction, it also needs to find ways to encourage, stimulate, and disseminate alternative case materials.

CONCLUSION

Cases and case methods of instruction offer a promising opportunity for teacher educators to explore new methods, content, and pedagogies for teacher education programs. The growing interest in cases, the early results of empirical research about the materials and the methods, and the opportunities for further research all suggest that this topic offers great opportunities to those who wish to use it to pursue a deeper understanding of the process of learning to teach.

References

American Association of Colleges for Teacher Education. (1993). *Setting standards and educating teachers.* Washington, DC: Author.

Ashton, P. T. (Ed.). (1991). Case methods [special issue]. *Journal of Teacher Education, 42*(4).

Association of Teacher Educators. (1991). *Restructuring the education of teachers.* Reston, VA: Author.

Ball, D. L., Lampert, M., & Rosenberg, M. L. (1991). *Using hypermedia to investigate and construct knowledge about mathematics teaching and learning.* Paper presented at the annual meeting of the American Educational Research Association, Chicago.

Barnes, H. (1989). Structuring knowledge for beginning teaching. In M. C. Reynolds (Ed.), *Knowledge base for the beginning teacher* (pp. 13–22). Oxford: Pergamon Press.

Barnett, C. S. (1991a). Building a case-based curriculum to enhance the pedagogical content knowledge of mathematics teachers. *Journal of Teacher Education, 42*(4), 263–272.

Barnett, C. S. (1991b). *Case methods: A promising vehicle for expanding the pedagogical knowledge base in mathematics.* Paper presented at the annual meeting of the American Educational Research Association, Chicago.

Barnett, C. S., & Cwirko-Godycki, J. (1988). *Learning to teach problematic instructional material: Cases from "experienced" and "novice" teachers.* Paper presented at the annual meeting of the American Educational Research Association, New Orleans.

Barnett, C. S., & Tyson, P. A. (1993a). *Case methods and teacher change: Shifting authority to build autonomy.* Paper presented at the annual meeting of the American Educational Research Association, Atlanta.

Barnett, C. S., & Tyson, P. A. (1993b). *Mathematics teaching cases as a catalyst for informed strategic inquiry.* Paper presented at the annual meeting of the American Educational Research Association, Atlanta.

Barnett, C. S., & Tyson, P. A. (1994). *Facilitating mathematics case discussions while preserving shared authority.* Paper presented at the annual meeting of the American Educational Research Association, New Orleans.

Bickerton, L., Chambers, R., Dart, G., Fukui, S., Gluska, J., McNeil, B., Odermatt, P., & Wassermann, S. (1991). *Cases for teaching in the secondary school.* Coquitlam, Canada: Case Works.

Bok, D. C. (1979). *The president's report, 1977–1978.* Cambridge: Office of the President, Harvard University.

Bransford, J. D., Goin, L. I., Hasselbring, T. S., Kinzer, C. K., Sherwood, R. D., & Williams, S. M. (1986). Learning with technology: Theoretical and empirical perspectives. *Peabody Journal of Education, 64*(1), 5–26.

Brophy, J. E., & Good, T. L. (1986). Teacher behavior and student achievement. In M. C. Wittrock (Ed.), *Handbook of research on teaching* (3rd ed., pp. 328–375). New York: Macmillan.

Broudy, H. S. (1990). Case studies—why and how. *Teachers College Record, 91*(3), 449–459.

Calderhead, J. (Ed.). (1987). *Exploring teachers' thinking.* London: Cassel Educational Limited.

Carnegie Forum on Education and the Economy. (1986). *A nation prepared: Teachers for the 21st century* (Report of the Task Force on Teaching as a Profession). Hyattsville, MD: Author.

Carter, K. (1989). Using cases to frame mentor-novice conversations about teaching. *Theory Into Practice, 27*(3), 214–222.

Carter, K., & Unklesbay, R. (1989). Cases in teaching and law. *Journal of Curriculum Studies, 21*(6), 527–536.

Christensen, C. R. (1981). *Teaching by the case method.* Boston: Harvard Business School Case Services, Harvard Business School.

Christensen, C. R., & Hansen, A. J. (1987). *Teaching and the case method.* Boston: Harvard Business School Press.

Clark, C. M., & Lampert, M. (1986). The study of teacher thinking: Implications for teacher education. *Journal of Teacher Education, 37*(5), 27–31.

Clark, C. M., & Peterson, P. (1986). Teachers' thought processes. In M. C. Wittrock (Ed.), *Handbook of research on teaching* (3rd ed., pp. 255–296). New York: Macmillan.

Clark, C. M., & Yinger, R. J. (1977). Research on teacher thinking. *Curriculum Inquiry, 7*(4), 279–304.

Cochran-Smith, M., & Lytle, S. L. (1990). Research on teaching and teacher research: The issues that divide. *Educational Researcher, 19*(2), 2–11.

Copeland, W. L. (1982). Laboratory experiences in teacher education. In H. E. Mitzel (Ed.), *Encyclopedia of educational research* (Vol. 2, pp. 1008–1019). New York: The Free Press.

Cronbach, L. J. (1975). Beyond the two disciplines of scientific psychology. *American Psychologist, 30*(2), 116–127.

Culbertson, J. A., Jacobson, P. B., & Reller, T. L. (1960). *Administrative relationships*. Englewood Cliffs, NJ: Prentice Hall.

Cutler, A. (1992). *A network of novices: Exploring the first year of teaching*. Unpublished doctoral dissertation, Harvard University, Cambridge, MA.

Dewey, J. (1933). *How we think*. Boston: D. C. Heath.

Doyle, W. (1986). Content representation in teachers' definitions of academic work. *Journal of Curriculum Studies, 18*(4), 365–380.

Doyle, W. (1990). Case methods in the education of teachers. *Teacher Education Quarterly, 17*(1), 7–16.

Feiman-Nemser, S. (1980). Learning to teach. In L. S. Shulman & G. Sykes (Eds.), *Handbook of teaching and policy* (pp. 150–170). New York: Longman.

Feiman-Nemser, S., & Buchmann, M. (1985). Pitfalls of experience in teacher preparation. *Teachers College Record, 87*(1), 53–66.

Fenstermacher, G. D. (1994). The knower and the known: The nature of knowledge in research on teaching. In L. D. Hammond (Ed.), *Review of research in education* (Vol. 20, pp. 3–56). Washington, DC: American Educational Research Association.

Florio-Ruane, S. (1990). Creating your own case studies: A guide for early field experience. *Teacher Educational Quarterly, 17*(1), 29–42.

Florio-Ruane, S., & Clark, C. M. (1990). Using case studies to enrich field experiences. *Teacher Education Quarterly, 17*(1), 17–28.

Frederick, P. (1981). The dreaded discussion: Ten ways to start. *Improving College and University Teaching, 29*(3), 109–114.

Gage, N. L. (1978). *The scientific basis of the art of teaching*. New York: Teachers College Press.

Goldman, E., & Barron, L. (1990). Using hypermedia to improve the preparation of elementary teachers. *Journal of Teacher Education, 41*(3), 21–31.

Goldman, E., Barron, L., & Witherspoon, M. L. (1991). Hypermedia cases in teacher education: A context for understanding of research on the teaching and learning of mathematics. *Action in Teacher Education, 13*(1), 28–36.

Green, D., Grant, G., & Shulman, J. (Eds.). (1990). Case methodology in the study and practice of teacher education [special issue]. *Teacher Education Quarterly, 17*(1).

Greenwood, G. E., & Parkay, F. W. (1989). *Case studies for teacher decision making*. New York: Random House.

Grimmett, P. P. (1988). The nature of reflection and Schön's conception in perspective. In P. P. Grimmett & G. L. Erickson (Eds.), *Reflection in teacher education* (pp. 5–16). New York: Teachers College Press.

Grimmett, P. P., & G. L. Erickson (Eds.). (1988). *Reflection in teacher education*. New York: Teachers College Press.

Grossman, P. L. (1990). *The making of a teacher: Teacher knowledge and teacher education*. New York: Teachers College Press.

Hansen, A. J. (1987). Reflections of a casewriter: Writing teaching cases. In C. R. Christensen & A. J. Hansen (Eds.), *Teaching and the case method* (pp. 264–270). Boston: Harvard Business School Press.

Harrington, H. L. (1994). Perspective on cases. *Qualitative Studies in Education, 7*(2), 117–133.

Harrington, H. L., & Garrison, J. (1992). Cases as shared inquiry: A dialogical model of teacher preparation. *American Educational Research Journal, 29*(4), 715–736.

Hawkins, D. (1974). *The informed vision: Essays on learning and human nature*. New York: Agathon Press.

Hollingsworth, S. J. (1989). Prior beliefs and cognitive change in learning to teach. *American Educational Research Journal, 26*(2), 160–189.

Holmes Group. (1990). *Tomorrow's schools: Principles for the design of professional development schools*. East Lansing: Michigan State University College of Education.

Hunt, P. (1951). The case method of instruction. *Harvard Educational Review, 21*(3), 175–192.

Hutchings, P. (1993). *Using cases to improve college teaching: A guide to more reflective practice*. Washington, DC: American Association for Higher Education.

Ingvarson, L., & Fineberg, W. (1992). *Developing and using cases of pedagogical content knowledge in the professional development of science teachers*. Paper presented at the annual meeting of the American Educational Research Association, San Francisco.

Kagan, D. (1993). Contexts for the use of classroom cases. *American Educational Research Journal, 30*(4), 117–129.

Kennedy, M. M. (1990). Choosing a goal for professional education. In W. R. Houston (Ed.), *Handbook of research on teacher education* (pp. 813–825). New York: Macmillan.

Kennedy, M. M. (1992). Establishing professional schools for teachers. In M. Levine (Ed.), *Professional practice schools: Linking teacher education and school reform* (pp. 63–80). New York: Teachers College Press.

Klein, H. E. (Ed.). (1992). *Forging new partnerships with cases, simulations, games, and other interactive methods*. Boston: World Association for Case Method Research and Application.

Kleinfeld, J. (Ed.). (1988). *Teaching cases in cross cultural education*. Fairbanks, AK: College of Education.

Kleinfeld, J. (1990). The special virtues of the case method in preparing teachers for minority schools. *Teacher Education Quarterly, 17*(1), 43–52.

Kleinfeld, J. (1991a). *Changes in problem solving abilities of students taught through case methods*. Paper presented at the annual meeting of the American Educational Research Association, Chicago.

Kleinfeld, J. (1991b). *Wrestling with the angel: What student teachers learn from writing cases*. Paper presented at the annual meeting of the American Educational Research Association, Chicago.

Kleinfeld, J. (1992a). *Can cases carry pedagogical content knowledge? Yes, but we've got signs of a "Matthew Effect."* Paper presented at the annual meeting of the American Educational Research Association, San Francisco.

Kleinfeld, J. (1992b). Learning to think like a teacher: The study of cases. In J. H. Shulman (Ed.), *Case methods in teacher education* (pp. 33–49). New York: Teachers College Press.

Kowalski, T. J., Weaver, R. A., & Henson, K. T. (1990). *Case studies on teaching*. New York: Longman.

LaBoskey, V. K. (1992). Case investigation: Preservice teacher research as an aid to reflection. In J. H. Shulman (Ed.), *Case methods in teacher education* (pp. 175–193). New York: Teachers College Press.

Lacey, C. A., & Merseth, K. K. (1993). Cases, hypermedia and computer networks: Three curricular innovations for teacher education. *Journal of Curriculum Studies, 25*(6), 543–552.

Lampert, M. (1985). How do teachers manage to teach? *Harvard Educational Review, 55*(2), 178–194.

Lawrence, P. R. (1953). The preparation of case material. In K. R. Andrews (Ed.), *The case method of teaching human relations and administration: An interim statement* (pp. 215–224). Cambridge: Harvard University Press.

Levin, B. B. (1993). *Using the case method in teacher education: The role of discussion and experience in teachers' thinking about cases*. Unpublished doctoral dissertation, University of California, Berkeley.

Lundeberg, M. A., & Fawver, J. E. (1993). *Cognitive growth in case analysis.* Paper presented at the annual meeting of the American Educational Research Association, Atlanta.

Masoner, M. (1988). *An audit of the case study method.* New York: Praeger.

McAninch, A. R. (1991). Casebooks for teacher education: The latest fad or lasting contribution? *Journal of Curriculum Studies, 23*(4), 345–356.

McAninch, A. R. (1993). *Teacher thinking and the case method.* New York: Teachers College Press.

McNair, M. P. (Ed.). (1954). *The case method at the Harvard Business School.* New York: McGraw-Hill.

Merseth, K. K. (1990a). *Beginning teachers and computer networks: A new form of induction support.* East Lansing, MI: National Center for Research on Teacher Education.

Merseth, K. K. (1990b). Case studies and teacher education. *Teacher Educational Quarterly, 17*(1), 53–62.

Merseth, K. K. (1991a). *The case for cases in teacher education.* Washington, DC: American Association of Colleges for Teacher Education.

Merseth, K. K. (1991b). The early history of case-based instruction: Insights for teacher education today. *Journal of Teacher Education, 42*(4), 243–249.

Merseth, K. K. (1992a). Cases for decision making in teacher education. In J. H. Shulman (Ed.), *Case methods in teacher education* (pp. 50–63). New York: Teachers College Press.

Merseth, K. K. (1992b). First aid for first-year teachers. *Phi Delta Kappan, 73*(9), 678–683.

Merseth, K. K. (1992c). *Mathematics case development project: Converting barriers to bridges.* A proposal to the National Science Foundation, Harvard Graduate School of Education, Cambridge.

Merseth, K. K. (Ed.). (In press—a). *Cases for decisions in teacher education.* New York: HarperCollins.

Merseth, K. K. (1994). Instructional methods and conceptual orientations in the design of teacher education programs: The example of simulations, hypermedia, and cases. In K. R. Howey (Ed.), *The professional development of teacher educators* (pp. 139–174). Cincinnati, OH: Ablex Publishing Corporation.

Merseth, K. K., & Lacey, C. A. (1993). Weaving stronger fabric: The pedagogical promise of hypermedia and case methods in teacher education. *Teaching & Teacher Education, 9*(3), 283–300.

Morine-Dershimer, G. (1993). *What's in a case—and what comes out?* Paper presented at the annual meeting of the American Educational Research Association, Atlanta.

Myrman, Y., & Kjellen, B. (1993). *Case method teaching in a Swedish context.* Paper presented at World Association for Case Method Research and Application, Bratislava, Vienna.

Noordhoff, K., & Kleinfeld, J. (1991). *Preparing teachers for multicultural classrooms: A case study in rural Alaska.* Paper presented at the annual meeting of the American Educational Research Association, Chicago.

Paley, V. G. (1979). *White teacher.* Cambridge: Harvard University Press.

Richardson, V. (1993). Use of cases in considering methods for motivating students. In H. Harrington & M. Thompson (Eds.), *Student motivation and case study manual* (pp. 57–60). Boone, NC: Appalachian State University.

Richardson, V., & Kile, S. (1992). *The use of videocases in teacher education.* Paper presented at the annual meeting of the American Educational Research Association, San Francisco.

Richert, A. E. (1991a). Case methods and teacher education: Using cases to teach teacher reflection. In B. R. Tabachnik & K. Zeichner (Eds.), *Issues and practices in inquiry-oriented teacher education* (pp. 130–150). London: Falmer.

Richert, A. E. (1991b). Using teacher cases for reflection and enhanced understanding. In A. Lieberman & L. Miller (Eds.), *Staff development for education in the 90's* (pp. 113–132). New York: Teachers College Press.

Richert, A. E. (1992). Writing cases: A vehicle for inquiry into the teaching process. In J. H. Shulman (Ed.), *Case methods in teacher education* (pp. 155–174). New York: Teachers College Press.

Risko, V. J. (1992). Videodisc-based case methodology: A design for enhancing preservice teachers' problem-solving abilities. In B. Hayes & K. Camperell (Eds.), *Literacy: International, national, state, and local* (Vol. 11, pp. 121–136). Logan: Utah State University, American Reading Forum.

Saint-Germain, M. (1993). *L'Ecriture de cas.* Rimouski: ACFAS.

Sargent, C. G., & Belisle, E. L. (1955). *Educational administration: Cases and concepts.* Boston: Houghton Mifflin.

Sato, M. (1991a). *Case method in Japanese teacher education: Traditions and our experiments.* Paper presented at the annual meeting of the Japan/U.S. Teacher Education Consortium, Stanford.

Sato, M. (1991b). *Cases and commentaries: Practical discourse of teachers, personal lesson of editing three types of casebooks.* Paper presented at the working conference on the role of the case in teacher education, San Francisco.

Sato, M. (1992). "Japan." In H. B. Leavitt (Ed.), *Issues and problems in teacher education* (pp. 155–168). New York: Greenwood.

Saunders, S. (1992). *The nature of preservice teachers' comments in discussing a videotaped teaching case.* Paper presented at the annual meeting of the American Educational Research Association, San Francisco.

Schön, D. A. (1983). *The reflective practitioner: How professionals think in action.* New York: Basic Books.

Schön, D. A. (1987). *Educating the reflective practitioner: Toward a new design for teaching and learning in the professions.* San Francisco: Jossey-Bass.

Schön, D. A. (Ed.). (1991). *The reflective turn: Case studies in and on educational practice.* New York: Teachers College Press.

Shulman, J. H. (1991). Revealing the mysteries of teacher-written cases: Opening the black box. *Journal of Teacher Education, 42*(4), 250–262.

Shulman, J. H. (Ed.). (1992). *Case methods in teacher education.* New York: Teachers College Press.

Shulman, J. H., & Colbert, J. A. (Eds.). (1987). *The mentor teacher casebook.* Eugene, OR: ERIC Clearinghouse on Educational Management, Educational Research, and Development. Washington, DC: ERIC Clearinghouse on Teacher Education.

Shulman, J. H., & Colbert, J. A. (Eds.). (1988). *The intern teacher casebook.* Eugene, OR: ERIC Clearinghouse on Educational Management, Educational Research, and Development. Washington, DC: ERIC Clearinghouse on Teacher Education.

Shulman, J. H., & Colbert, J. A. (1989). Cases as catalysts for cases: Inducing reflection in teacher education. *Action in teacher education, 11*(1), 44–52.

Shulman, J. H., Colbert, J. A., Kemper, D., & Dmytriw, L. (1990). Case writing as a site for collaboration. *Teacher Education Quarterly, 17*(1), 63–78.

Shulman, J. H., & Mesa-Bains, A. (Eds.). (1990). *Diversity in the classroom: A casebook for teachers and teacher educators.* San Francisco: Research for Better Schools.

Shulman, L. S. (1986). Those who understand: Knowledge growth in teaching. *Educational Researcher, 15*(2), 4–14.

Shulman, L. S. (1992). Toward a pedagogy of cases. In J. Shulman (Ed.), *Case methods in teacher education* (p. 1–30). New York: Teachers College Press.

Silverman, R. (1994). *Case facilitation as a changing role.* Paper presented at the annual meeting of the American Educational Research Association, New Orleans.

Silverman, R., Welty, W. M., & Lyon, S. (1992). *Case studies for teacher problem solving.* New York: McGraw-Hill.

Silverman, R., Welty, W. M., & Lyon, S. (1994). *Classroom assessment cases for teacher problem solving*. New York: McGraw-Hill.

Sperle, D. H. (1933). *The case method technique in professional training*. New York: Teachers College Press.

Spiro, R. J., Coulson, R. L., Feltovich, P. J., & Anderson, D. K. (1988). Cognitive flexibility theory: Advanced knowledge acquisition in ill-structured domains. In *Tenth annual conference of the cognitive science society* (pp. 377–383). Hillsdale, NJ: Lawrence Erlbaum Associates.

Spiro, R. J., Vispoel, W. L., Schmitz, J. G., Samarapungavan, A., & Boerger, A. E. (1987). Knowledge acquisition for application: Cognitive flexibility and transfer in complex content domains. In B. K. Britton & S. M. Glynn (Eds.), *Executive control processes in reading* (pp. 177–199). Hillsdale, NJ: Lawrence Erlbaum Associates.

Stein, H. (Ed.). (1952). *Public administration and policy development*. New York: Harcourt, Brace.

Stoiber, K. C. (1991). The effect of technical and reflective preservice instruction on pedagogical reasoning and problem solving. *Journal of Teacher Education, 42*(2), 131–139.

Stuhler, E., & Ó Súilleabháin, M. (Eds.). (1990). *Research on the case method in a non-case environment*. Köln, Germany: Bohlau.

Sudzina, M. R., & Kilbane, C. R. (1992). Applications of a case study text to undergraduate teacher preparation. In H. E. Klein (Ed.), *Forging new partnerships with cases, simulations, games, and other interactive methods* (pp. 149–158). Boston: World Association for Case Method Research and Application.

Sykes, G. (1989). Learning to teach with cases. *Colloquy, 2*(2), 7–13.

Sykes, G., & Bird, T. (1992). Teacher education and the case idea. In G. Grant (Ed.), *Review of research in education* (Vol. 18, pp. 457–521). Washington, DC: American Educational Research Association.

Tozer, S., Anderson, T. H., & Armbruster, B. B. (1990). Psychological and social foundations in teacher education: A thematic introduction. *Teachers College Record, 91*(3), 293–299.

Wasserman, S. (1993). *Getting down to cases: Learning to teach with case studies*. New York: Teachers College Press.

Wasserman, S. (1994). Using cases to study teaching. *Phi Delta Kappan, 75*(8), 602–611.

Welty, W. M. (1989). Discussion method teaching: How to make it work. *Change, 21*(4), 40–49.

Welty, W. M., Silverman, R., & Lyon, S. (1991). *Student outcomes from teaching with cases*. Paper presented at the annual meeting of the American Educational Research Association, Chicago.

Wilson, S. (1992). A case concerning content: Using case studies to teach subject matter. In J. H. Shulman (Ed.), *Case methods in teacher education* (pp. 64–89). New York: Teachers College Press.

Zeichner, K. M. (1986). Preparing reflective teachers: An overview of instructional strategies which have been employed in preservice teacher education. *International Journal of Educational Research, 11*(5), 565–575.

Zeichner, K. M., & Liston, D. (1987). Teaching student teachers to reflect. *Harvard Educational Review, 57*(1), 23–48.

Part

·VI·

DIVERSITY AND EQUITY ISSUES

SELECTING AND PREPARING CULTURALLY COMPETENT TEACHERS FOR URBAN SCHOOLS

Martin Haberman

UNIVERSITY OF WISCONSIN–MILWAUKEE

Reviewers synthesizing what is known about educating teachers for urban and culturally diverse schools find a lack of consistency in the use of terms (King, 1993). *Urban* is commonly used as a catchall category and euphemism for denoting conditions perceived as undesirable, such as violence, poverty, drug use, crime, dysfunctional families, inadequate housing, and poor schools. Similarly, "cultural diversity" is a catchall phrase denoting groups that may differ on the basis of race, religion, ethnicity, language, gender, sexual preference, age, class, disabling conditions, or combinations of these differences. Some even use characteristics such as life-style (e.g., single parent), occupation (e.g., migrant worker), or life experience (e.g., ex-convict) as criteria for designating people as members of a particular "culturally diverse" group. Given this range of meaning attributed to "cultural diversity" in the literature, it is likely that the use of the term in this chapter represents all the common confusions in the citations summarized and unlikely that in discussing preparing teachers for urban schools serving children in poverty from diverse cultural backgrounds, a common set of referents is definitively identified.

This lack of agreement of common meanings for terms used in the professional literature is no minor matter. Not only is discourse made difficult, but also reviewers of written contributions find the meaning of research findings confounded by the multiple meanings attributed to terms and the continual introduction of new terms. Those who argue that urban education is not a legitimate field of study point to this confusion of terminology as evidence that almost any issue may be studied and labeled "urban." They also contend that urban issues are essentially a set of problems found in but not limited to urban schools. They argue that since every urban problem (e.g., school violence, dropouts, racial integration, dysfunctional families, low achievement, and the need for greater multicultural curriculum and teaching) is also found in suburban and small-

town schools, "urban education" is a spurious distinction of no analytical or scholarly value. They argue that no new insights, hypotheses, or fruitful lines of analyses will result from making this artificial and arbitrary distinction. Differences in degree (i.e., higher rates of problems in urban schools) are not accepted as constituting differences in the kind of know-how required of the new teacher. This universal approach to teacher education assumes that when present constituencies of teacher candidates are prepared to deal with one or two *individual* children who are abused, in gangs, on drugs, living in violent neighborhoods, and in dysfunctional families, they are learning the same knowledge base and the same effective behaviors as teachers prepared to teach total *groups* of children in poverty making normal responses to their living conditions. Those who make this argument maintain that the theories and principles commonly used in professional education are universal in nature and are not contextual; that is, the principles of child and adolescent development, effective teaching, and meaningful learning apply to all children and are not different for urban children or those from a particular culture group. In the vernacular the universal argument contends that "kids are kids," "teaching is teaching," and "learning is learning."

UNIVERSAL VERSUS CONTEXTUAL TEACHER EDUCATION

The universal approach to teacher education has been 170 years in the making. Reverend Hall established the first Normal School in Concord, Vermont, in 1823 (Meyer, 1957). American teacher education has since developed in direct response to the organizational needs of elementary and secondary schools for teachers. As the public schools organized themselves by age, subjects to be taught, and children with special needs, the states generated licensure requirements and the schools of education followed by offering preparation programs based on these same three organizational characteristics. It is not an accident that teachers are prepared and licensed as elementary (common branches) or secondary teachers of a particular subject and that when a critical mass of schools developed junior high and later middle schools, that the public school's need for teachers was also reflected in state licenses and school of education preparation programs.

The schools and colleges of education found these organizational and political needs compatible with the knowledge bases developing in the university. These knowledge bases dealt with the nature of the learner and learning, the subject matters to be taught, and the presence of children with disabling conditions. The universal approach to teacher education recognizes only these three distinctions (i.e., the age of the child, subject matter to be taught, and children with special needs) and challenges urbanists with questions such as the following: Are 5-year-olds' basic needs different because they live in a city (age)? Does 2 + 2 = 5 in "urban" math (content)? Does a child with brain damage require a different kind of special education teacher in a big city school (handicapping conditions)? All the requirements in teacher education programs as well as their undergirding knowledge bases can be slotted into these three realms. General liberal studies focus on the content to be taught and learned. Education psychology deals with the nature of the learner and learning. Methods courses focus on both normal children and those with special needs. Finally, student teaching integrates principles and practice from all three areas and enables the teacher candidate to demonstrate competence in actual schools with real children.

Psychology and its offspring, educational psychology, is the dominant discipline in the knowledge base of teacher education (Haberman, 1982). Beginning with the nature of the learner and learning, educational psychology now commonly includes studies in preschool through adolescent development, abnormal development, testing, research, counseling, and school learning. This hegemony of educational psychology over the entire teacher education curriculum is not apparent by simply looking at whether all the requirements in a program are labeled educational psychology, considering that different colleges organize themselves into different departmental structures. The issue is best understood by examining the theoretical constructs and ways of knowing that dominate teacher education courses and experiences. For example, concepts such as motivation, reward and punishment, readiness, retardation, giftedness, self-esteem, self-concept, and the lexicon of terms related to norm-referenced testing (e.g., bottom half) are now an integral part of the syllabi of all courses in teacher education regardless of whether the particular course is labeled educational psychology or not. Typically, future teachers do not learn alternative theoretic constructs to concepts such as motivation or self-concept as ways of explaining children's behavior. Future teachers do not routinely learn alternative explanations of human behavior in which the unit of analysis is not the individual. Rarely, if ever, are they presented with ways of explaining human behavior in which individual personality constructs are not assumed to be the primary causes of children's behavior.

Foundational studies of education (e.g., history, philosophy, economics, and sociology of education) that focus on societal and ideational influences as ways of explaining human behavior have always occupied a minor and, more recently, a shrinking role in the knowledge base of teacher education (Borman, 1990). It is now common for future teachers to take one foundations course in their preparation (many programs require none) and to evaluate "theory" as largely irrelevant to their needs as beginning teachers (Feiman-Nemser & Buchmann, 1983). Preservice students accept this emphasis in their preparation programs for explaining human behavior by understanding the individual personalities involved. The constant and strong criticism made by graduates of their preparation is not that they were given limited or insufficient paradigms, theoretic constructs, and ways of understanding children and their behavior, but that the knowledge base they were offered was not sufficiently and adequately extended into practice. Graduates do not question the efficacy or relevance of the reward–punishment paradigm as the basic discipline strategy, whether concepts such as self-concept, motivation, or readiness are the best explanations of students' behavior, or whether there are not more powerful theories; they simply complain that student teaching was not long enough to give them sufficient time to practice with different children in different classrooms.

A final but critical point is necessary for understanding this traditionally universal approach to teacher education. The university provides a particular context for offering teacher education (Corrigan & Haberman, 1990). The preparation of those who complete doctorates in educational specializations and who become teacher educators in universities is based on slotting new faculty into existing university specializations (Howey & Zimpher, 1990). This structure of school of education departments taking in new assistant professors with particular doctoral specializations was developed to support existing university organizational structures and offerings. The programs are universalistic in nature and account for all the courses offered on the basis of the three distinctions noted earlier: the nature of the learner and learning; the nature of the content and teaching that content; and the nature of youngsters with special needs. The expertise that teacher educators develop in their doctoral programs as well as the bases on which they are hired and tenured into universities is represented by these same assumptions regarding the knowledge base needed for future teachers. New bases for organizing university preparation programs that would require new forms of faculty expertise not now held by education faculty or that fundamentally contradict present ways of organizing faculty expertise are likely to be perceived by many teacher educators as threatening. As a result, the pattern whereby faculty with particular specializations hire new faculty with similar specializations not only supports existing organizational structures but also limits teacher education programs to only the traditional ways of knowing. These realities in no way vitiate the quality of the arguments raised against urban education; they simply provide background and a more complete analysis of the source of the arguments made by education faculty against a form of teacher education that would make "urbanness" or "cultural diversity" as important a knowledge base as the learner's developmental level, the content to be taught, or the nature of handicapping conditions.

Those who argue that urban teaching is sufficiently distinctive to require different forms of teacher preparation or that socialization into a particular culture group is as great a determinant of human behavior as dimensions of personality raise questions that in effect threaten both the completeness and validity of the knowledge bases that currently characterize teacher education. Their argument leads them to emphasize the importance of contextual distinctions in the ways children develop, the ways they learn, and the nature of the content they learn. These advocates argue for a form of cultural determinism in understanding the processes of human development and schooling in our society. In effect, they contend that "kids are not kids," "teaching is not teaching," and "learning is not learning."

Some researchers argue that central tendencies characterize the learning styles of children from various culture groups but that all good teachers are sensitive to these differences and use effective strategies that successfully account for all differences among their children (Hilliard, 1974). In effect, they contend that the styles of learning are different but the teaching should be just the same (Swisher & Deyhle, 1989). Other researchers disagree and contend that children of color hold differing worldviews and develop learning styles that distinguish them from Euro-American children (Anderson, 1988; Irvine, 1990; Shade, 1982). For example, it is asserted that the components of an African-American worldview emphasize cooperation, collective responsibility, and interdependence rather than competition, individual rights, separateness, and independence, which are associated with a Euro-American worldview. This literature also suggests that African-American teachers may be more able to involve African-American children and youth in wanting to achieve academically (Foster, 1990).

THE DEBATE

The debate about whether factors such as urban poverty, race, or membership in a particular culture group demand new forms of teacher preparation and practice is not likely to be resolved readily. Both sides undergird their research with ideological commitments that make purely objective analyses difficult. This may be quite appropriate as definitions of good teaching practice and even more, disagreements regarding the purposes of good teaching, are as much a normative perception of the analyst as they are a dispassionate, scientific judgment. Not surprisingly, those whose expertise involves viewing human development in terms of universal stages that they believe apply across all cultures and who explain human behavior primarily as reflections of personality attributes, perceive that the way to make schools more effective and less violent is for every *individual* involved in schools to learn to work with and respect every other *individual*. If they think about it at all, those committed to a psychological way of knowing think of culture as merely an accumulation of individual personalities. Accepting this approach, many teacher education graduates are taught to believe that making generalizations about groups of people is a process of stereotyping individuals and should be avoided. Conversely, it should not be surprising that those who believe pedagogy should be derived from knowledge of how diverse culture groups socialize and control children's behavior, including knowledge of how some culture groups have devalued and dehumanized other culture groups in American society, advocate a form of pedagogy and teacher preparation that they believe would lead to more culturally competent teachers.

There is a second, fundamental difference between these positions. Those who support traditional teacher certification programs differentiate only on the basis of learners' age, the content to be taught, and handicapping conditions. They reject using urban poverty or cultural diversity as an additional basis of teacher preparation and defend their position by viewing teaching and learning in ideal terms. They justify current teacher education programs as preparing teachers who *should* teach in the best ways. Those in favor of training for specifically urban schools and for children in poverty from diverse backgrounds couch their arguments in terms of how ineffective schools and teachers now miseducate approximately 12,000,000 children and youth in the largest 120 school districts. When this latter group produces status studies of high teacher turnover, high student dropout rates, low student achievement, and high incidence of school violence, the former group points out that this does not reflect inadequacies in the way the teachers are prepared but horrific social conditions that impinge on schooling and interfere with best practice. When educators focused on urban poverty and the need for more culturally competent teachers spell out proposed "new" methodologies (e.g., more hands-on activity, more cooperative learning, more verbal interaction, more direct experience, and greater relevance to students' lives), those in favor of current programs indicate first, that these methodologies are already in teacher preparation programs, and second, that these methodologies would be equally appropriate for teaching suburban, affluent, and Euro-American children. There is no actual dialog between the two positions because advocates of traditional teacher education justify their preparation programs in terms of how graduates *should* practice if (1) they learned everything they were taught, and (2) they were permitted to implement these ideals in bad urban schools. Advocates of new forms of teacher education seek to hold teacher education programs, not only public schools, responsible for the *actual* performance of ineffective teachers. In effect, this is a nondialog between those claiming to prepare ideal teachers capable of best practice anywhere and those who attribute a major portion of urban school ineffectiveness to narrowly prepared teachers miseducated by only one way of knowing and studying human behavior. Traditional teacher educators demand differences in *ideal* teacher practice as prerequisite to their recognizing differences in the *real* world. Their standard for accepting that the cultural diversity in real urban schools demands new forms of pedagogy and new forms of teacher education is that these new forms have never been thought of or advocated; they will not accept the argument that these forms of pedagogy are new because they have never been widely practiced in urban schools. Conversely, those in favor of more urban and culturally competent teachers charge that the problems of real teachers in real schools with real children are overwhelming and that there is sufficient evidence of a teacher education that is fundamentally misconceived and undertheorized regarding all the ways of explaining human behavior.

Both sides can present a case that their advocacy is prevailing. Traditional teacher education remains universal in nature at institutions granting graduates licenses to teach in all 50 states with all children in all types of schools. There are no license restrictions related to not being prepared to teach children in poverty or children from diverse cultural backgrounds. Traditional programs have absorbed and withstood the criticism that they are not responsive by adding courses in "Urban Education" or "Multicultural Education" to their regular programs. In many universities students are also given the option of student-teaching in a poverty school serving diverse students. The thrust of this preparation is based on the theoretic position that there are many types of children with "special" needs. And just as future teachers are prepared to mainstream children with handicapping conditions, they are also prepared to teach children who must grow up in violent neighborhoods in dysfunctional families, in poverty, and from "different" cultural backgrounds. This approach supports the knowledge base that individual personality constructs account for and predict human behavior and that it is the work of the teacher to understand, relate to, and help each child.

Political, publicly funded institutions, schools, and colleges of education have withstood the charge that they are unresponsive to the needs of the urban poor and the culturally "different" by initiating pilot and special programs. Almost every major university's school of education has a special urban or multicultural program (involving usually less than 30 students) preparing teachers for schools serving children in poverty. These programs are frequently funded by special temporary state funds or private "soft" funds. Many of the nondoctoral institutions (which certify 80% of the nation's teachers) have also initiated such special or pilot programs. This strategy is an effective means whereby institutions may claim that they are being responsive to "urban and cultural problems" without having to change their regular programs (which may be preparing several thousand students to teach), "limit" their preparation solely to urban poverty schools, or become "limited" to educating all future teachers for culturally diverse groups.

A major distinction between the two positions involves the definition of normal. Those supporting traditional programs regard factors such as "urban," "poverty," or "cultural diversity," as causing individual children to develop special needs. The psychological paradigm for children growing up in urban poverty and violence is that they suffer the same range of ailments and emotional impediments to normal development as children who grow up in a war zone (Garbarino, Dudrow, Kostelny, & Pardo, 1992). This conceptual stance relegates all the distinctions made about children's cultural backgrounds and societal influences as simply other forms of exceptionality, conceptually akin to any other handicapping condition. This explains why many Euro-American teachers and teacher educators continue to use terms such as "minority" even when most of the children or youth in a given school district are a statistical majority. "Minority" becomes merely another euphemism for an adverse condition that intrudes on an *individual's* development and learning. Pre- and in-service teachers have not been taught to define normal as typical. This would have led them to see that those who grow up in violence or poverty are making perfectly normal responses to undesirable social conditions. Instead,

teachers and teacher educators typically make normal synonymous with healthy and desirable. Therefore, if children grow up in adverse conditions they cannot be conceived of as developing normally or making normal responses or even being normal because, obviously, they are learning bad things and behavior perceived as undesirable and cannot possibly be defined as normal. When this limited way of perceiving growth and development is overlaid by factors of cultural diversity, the result is frequently insensitivity and nascent racism. "Minority" cannot be perceived as being a normal condition if the perceiver regards it as less than desirable. In this way, even when there is the statistical reality of a new majority, the perceiver holds on to the conception of minority in order to signal that there are serious problems with even a majority of *individual* children.

CONSEQUENCES

What specifically have these differences in conceptual meaning led to in this debate? Supporters of traditional forms of teacher education prepare future teachers to deal with all forms of individual abnormality (undesirable things that should not have happened to the individual child) on an individual basis. Regardless of how many individuals "suffer" from poverty or are children of color, even if they were to total 100%, they would be conceived of and taught as children with "special needs" because that is the paradigm on which traditional teacher education is conceptualized. This usage is also common among the large number of in-service teachers in the major urban school districts who seriously and honestly believe that most (all in some cases) of their students should not be in their classrooms because they need special help; are not achieving on their normal grade levels; are abnormal in their interests, attention, and behavior; are emotionally not suited to school; and are in need of alternative schools, special classes, or teachers trained to work with exceptional individuals. In some urban areas and in some schools within those districts, many teachers perceive over 90% of their students as people who they should not have to teach because they are not "normal" (Payne, 1984).

A similar perception exists among a majority of newly certified teachers in many states. In Minnesota, 58% of those certified do not take jobs; in Wisconsin, it is 70% (Haberman, 1989). While there are many reasons for this, the fact that the available jobs are in urban areas teaching "minority" children with "special" needs must be considered as a possible explanation.

Those arguing in favor of a teacher preparation more sensitive to children in urban poverty from diverse backgrounds claim that the current approach to universal licensure is wrong because those presently being certified cannot effectively teach in all schools serving all children. They argue that if the fundamental error of universal licensure is to be continued, all future teachers should be prepared to teach in the most challenging situations. They contend that neophytes who can effectively teach in urban poverty schools serving children from all culture groups will also be effective should they teach in schools with smaller classes, more materials, and more affluent children—but the reverse is not true. Other experts have identified multicultural goals for all children and youth and determined how schools might implement them (Banks, 1993). The debate is played out on this final point. Traditional teacher educators define cultural diversity or poverty as other forms of specialness requiring that a course in multicultural education be added to the regular program to prepare future teachers to teach such *individuals*. Those advocating for more culturally competent teachers argue that if universal licensure continues, all teachers must be prepared with new training paradigms for the most difficult situations. The major implication of this difference is that the pattern whereby schools and colleges of education have special, small programs directed at urban teaching while the mass of students are universally prepared would be discontinued. If traditional teacher educators were to accept this argument, all students would be required to prepare for teaching in the most diverse, most difficult urban schools. Even more radical, the knowledge base in teacher education would have to change to reflect more than psychological explanations of human behavior. Given the nature of faculty training and university culture, such changes are highly problematic.

At the same time, advocates of preparing teachers for urban poverty and cultural diversity can point to changes that indicate that they are prevailing in the conceptual as well as in the political battle for new forms of teacher education. Forty-one states and the District of Columbia now have alternative certification. Fifty thousand teachers have been licensed since 1986, half in the last 2 years, most of whom work in urban poverty schools serving diverse culture groups. There are approximately 68 alternative licensing programs supported by states, with 38 created since 1990 (Feistritzer & Chester, 1991). Although such programs vary widely in quality and purpose, they permit school districts and new forms of university–school alliances to prepare teachers in the real world for the real world. Almost every major urban area and large numbers of smaller urban school districts now recruit and train adult college graduates from fields other than teacher education to teach diverse groups of poverty children as their "normal" workload. Those who are hired and trained to teach in these schools are typically educated to believe that the children or youth they teach represent the diverse culture groups of the urban area and are not "special," "minority," or somehow different from the "regular" children they should be teaching. The realities of urban living, including some strong parent groups and the very active cultural and community groups, exert real influence over these schools on a daily basis. There is no way new teachers can be trained under the aegis of an urban school system and remain unresponsive to such formidable constituencies. In effect, the evolution of teacher education is occurring largely outside of schools and colleges of education in the training programs offered by the urban school districts themselves or through collaboratives.

This is a marked departure from past efforts to educate teachers for urban poverty schools. The National Teacher Corps, initiated more than 30 years ago and based on the Milwaukee Intern Program, was intended to be a universal improvement to teacher education. Testimony before the U.S. Senate Subcommittee on Education stated that older students committed to social service would be a viable constituency of urban teachers; however, representatives from the Wisconsin Improvement Program testified that this approach of learning to teach by teaching would also be the best way to prepare all teachers and that the Wisconsin Improvement Program model was already

proving itself to be effective in small towns and suburbs as well as in urban areas (Higher Education Act, 1965). The National Teacher Corps remained in effect for over a decade preparing over 10,000 teachers, most of whom worked in urban poverty schools. The most exhaustive analysis of this effort raised serious questions about the "federal government's capacity to lead social reforms and, indeed, about whether it is possible to make marked improvements solely by working from within established institutions" (Corwin, 1973, p. 394). Other analysts placed greater responsibility for the demise of the National Teacher Corps on (1) the resistance of schools of education to accepting "urban" as a distinctive set of problems, and (2) their unwillingness to become jointly accountable with school districts for resolving problems in urban schools (Haberman, 1971).

CONSTITUENCIES RECRUITED

In the 1980s most studies of entry-level students who reported that they always wanted to teach support the stereotypes: 94% are white; 74% are female; two-thirds of the males express preference for high school teaching; two-thirds of females express a preference for elementary schools; and 12% of both sexes prefer middle school teaching (Book, Byers, & Freeman, 1983).

These students were overwhelmingly from rural and suburban areas. Few of them have had all their previous schooling in urban areas, and fewer still express a desire to teach in urban schools. Only 57% indicated they plan to remain in teaching for more than 10 years. About half who plan to leave the profession indicated advanced training and career change as their reason; the other half plan to raise a family.

Almost 80% of future teachers report that they were "leaders" in high school (and earlier), took mostly academic or advanced courses, and had little or no involvement in vocational education. The majority of these students attended school in the same community, kindergarten through grade 12. They were successful and enjoyed school. Many decided on a teaching career by observing their own teachers. About 80% indicate they had been camp counselors, aides, or Sunday School teachers.

The overriding perception of most of these students was that "teaching is an extended form of parenting about which there is little to learn other than through instinct and one's own experiences as a child" (Book et al., 1983, p. 10). About one quarter expressed a high degree of confidence and another two thirds a moderately strong degree of confidence they could begin teaching immediately without any teacher training. (One of the unstudied reasons why traditional teacher training may have such minimal impact on teacher education students is that students do not *expect* to learn much in these programs.) The two functions preservice students expressed the least confidence about performing immediately after they take their first teaching jobs were relating to pupils with special needs and managing discipline problems. These fears may be interrelated because "relating to" children with special needs is likely to also involve the fear of not being able to manage and discipline children. These two areas of perceived inadequacy are especially interesting because they are clearly related to candidates' perceptions of urban teaching. If urban schools are surrounded by violent communities and diverse culture groups that teacher training has defined as composed of children with "special needs," it may be that participating in a teacher education program will itself feed students' fear of relating to "such" children and being able to manage them (Haberman, 1988b).

The nature of teachers' backgrounds remained constant when assessed in 1993: Recruits are a predominantly white, female, monolingual constituency who attend college and seek employment as teachers relatively close to where they are raised (Zimpher & Ashburn, 1992). These parochial characteristics seem constant for both preservice and practicing teachers.

Recruiting and attracting new populations and constituencies into teaching has been a continuing problem. Edelfelt (1986) suggested 16 new constituencies who might be tapped. The basic difference between traditional programs of teacher education and those focused on preparing culturally competent teachers for urban schools comes down to a critical issue of self-perception. Individuals who can perceive themselves as *students* (i.e., at the undergraduate, post–baccalaureate certification, or master's level) are willing to enter programs of teacher education offered by schools, colleges, and departments of education. Other constituencies, including a majority of those interested in teaching in urban and cultural diverse situations are willing and able to conceive of themselves as *teachers* but not necessarily as *students*. Some of the reasons for this self-perception are not known; others might relate to the fact that these urban constituencies lock in on real teaching once they make their commitment and do not see the need or value (for a variety of reasons) for becoming students in a university teacher education program. A second explanation is that these constituencies are older and have more urgent needs for getting into classrooms—also for a variety of reasons. The net result is that those who are or who can be comfortable with the role of university student are unlikely to seek urban teaching jobs, whereas those who seek urban teaching jobs are predisposed to perceive of themselves as teachers but reject the status and role of university student—even graduate student. For these reasons, urban programs conducted by universities and school districts, as well as alternative certification programs of every variety, have seemed naturally to attract more culturally diverse and older constituencies into urban teaching. A substantial case can be that older candidates are the most appropriate for becoming culturally competent teachers in urban poverty schools. This argument is based on the fact that such teachers stay longer and teach more effectively because they are at a more appropriate life stage for such service than typical undergraduate teacher education students (Haberman, 1990).

SELECTION

The foregoing debate has obvious implications for selection. If the only sources of new teachers for urban schools were the traditional routes through colleges and universities, there would be few teachers of color (approximately 8%; NEA, 1991). Although this figure represents a small increase over previous years, it merely returns to the level of 1971. If the sources of new teachers were alternative certification programs, the

numbers of new teachers of color are markedly higher: 33% in Los Angeles (Stoddard, 1990) and 47% in Houston Independent School District (HISD, 1989).

The fact that most new teachers will continue to come through traditional rather than alternative routes focuses the problem of educating teachers for cultural diversity primarily in the university. This issue will continue to be one of educating primarily white, monolingual, female teacher education students in undergraduate, preservice teacher education programs to teach in culturally diverse urban settings. Of even greater importance is that a majority of this population is under 25 years of age and did not have the experience of graduating from urban high schools. This last point has some importance considering that the major influence on the behavior of beginning teachers is their own school experience and the press of the school situations in which they begin (Zeichner & Tabachnick, 1981). An unexplored but fruitful hypothesis may well be that a primary means for gaining more culturally sensitive teachers is to recruit and select from populations who have themselves had *successful* experiences in urban high schools. The argument here is that this population will have had the experience of attending a larger, impersonal, highly bureaucratic school system and will not go into culture shock when faced with the debilitating mindlessness of the Chicago Public Schools or any other great city school system (Payne, 1984). The typical culture shock discussed in the literature focuses on divergent culture groups and the rival expectations between teachers and students. But the experience of teaching in large urban school systems must also include the impact on beginners of factors such as isolation, burnout, impersonal relationships, endless paperwork, nonteaching duties, school violence, teacher safety, annual threats of no-raise or teacher strike, high turnover of colleagues, particularly new teachers, over 100 classroom interruptions per week, and self-defeating policies that impede everything from taking field trips to making a modest purchase of supplies. The typical urban teacher still has no access to a telephone in his or her classroom. The impact of this counterproductive bureaucracy is approximately 1½ years of lowered achievement (Chubb & Moe, 1989). Were teachers recruited who were themselves successful graduates of urban high schools, a natural increase in the number of candidates of color would occur because African Americans, Hispanics, Asians, and many other culture groups reside in cities and attend urban high schools. They also serve as models of academic success from urban high schools.

The more typical argument for recruiting more teachers of color emphasizes historical patterns, particularly among African Americans, for educating leaders and for holding them accountable and responsible for the educational achievement of children (Franklin, 1990). There is also an impressive literature of case studies and biography about African Americans who have succeeded despite poverty, racial discrimination, and numerous other obstacles, with the help of committed teachers and parents (Haynes & Comer, 1990). In response to a majority community that is perceived as limiting its objectives for children of color to "get a job and stay out of jail," there is an emphasis on education that contributes to "achieving pride, equity, power, wealth, and cultural continuity" (Lee, Lomotey, & Shujaa, 1990). A growing literature, summarized by Sabrina Hope King (1993) includes the positive influences of teachers of color on children and youth in their personal development and in their achievement. This argument does not negate the potential of Euro-American teachers to teach effectively children of color. It does, however, point to factors in the selection and training of Euro-American teachers that are not now present in traditional teacher education programs.

CRITERIA FOR SELECTION

Various institutions attach different weights to each criterion. Traditional university programs of teacher education use the following criteria:

1. *Completion of specific courses.* In those institutions in which students are admitted as freshmen these are minimal and typically include a few basic courses in math, English, or speech. In universities where admission is delayed until the junior year, this criterion involves a distribution of required courses sufficient to achieve junior status.
2. *GPA.* In some institutions this level is set at the GPA needed for graduation or higher if there are enrollment caps. In other institutions seeking higher enrollments, this level may be set at a lower level for initial entry.
3. *References.* It is still common for students to be asked to have faculty complete references attesting to their academic potential and their fitness for teaching.
4. *Written statements.* Many institutions have developed essay-type questions intended to assess students' philosophies, reasons for wanting to teach, and beliefs regarding children, schools, or teachers. These essays are typically read by faculty committees, who then grade them and use them as part of students' ranking as potential candidates for admission.
5. *State tests of basic skills.* Several states require students to pass standardized tests of basic skills as part of the admission requirements to a teacher certification program.
6. *Fieldwork.* Many institutions now typically require candidates to complete a given number of hours or a course involving direct experiences with children or youth as a prerequisite for admission into the teacher education program.
7. *Competency in Standard English.* Typically this is accomplished as part of the candidate's distributive requirements and involves either a course(s) in writing and/or a written exam graded by the faculty in the English department. In some cases this might be an exam administered by Education faculty.

In addition to these criteria there is typically a certain number of admission places reserved for "minorities" who may have lower scores or evaluations on one or more of these criteria. It is not unusual for programs to set aside 10% to 15% of their admissions in this manner and still not find a sufficient number of "minority" applicants who even apply.

These criteria have not changed in any important ways since the author surveyed 386 schools, colleges, and departments of education (SCDEs) in 1972 and found the following criteria being used (Table 32.1).

Several critical points are necessary to understand this process more fully in terms of how "the system" actually works in practice. First, there is no admission rule in any university bulletin for which an exception cannot be made. Second, there is no decision regarding any university admission that cannot be appealed, reconsidered, and reversed on some grounds. The difference between many applicants actually admitted to education and applicants denied admission is that some applicants naively believe what they read in catalogs and are told, whereas other applicants do not and follow up on one or both of the two principles stated. The third critical point to understand regarding these admission criteria is that they are derived from university traditions and faculty expertise. They represent what experts believe are criteria for selecting, not those who will be effective teachers in practice, but those who will be successful in completing the remainder of their university and licensure requirements. The number of institutions whose selection criteria are derived from research evidence regarding what makes their graduates effective in subsequent teaching practice is close to zero. The concept that selection criteria *should* be derived from teaching practice and used to predict the graduates' subsequent effectiveness is regarded as a debatable issue and is not likely to be agreed on by faculty in schools and departments of education. In any event, the point is moot, because traditional criteria are directed at and are highly successful in predicting who will complete the required coursework in education but nothing more, not even who will seek a job.

The fourth critical point is that the admission criteria frequently are embedded in a philosophical explanation of the particular institution's reasons for using them. For example, it is common for a school or college of education to state something like "Admission to the teacher education program is a continuing process. Students may be counseled with to determine their appropriateness for continuing at any point in the program." In actual practice, it is common for very few students to be counseled out. The relatively few who leave are likely

TABLE 32.1. Criteria Used by 386 Colleges and Universities for Selecting Students Into Teacher Education Programs

Rank	Criteria	Frequency
1	College grades	344
2	English proficiency	238
3	Speech proficiency	237
4	Academic references	205
5	Direct experiences with children/youth	172
6	References	164
7	Direct interview	161
8	Physical examinations	158
9	"Why I Want to Teach" statements	128
10	Varied personality examinations/attitude tests	84
11	High school grades	59
12	Police record	31
13	Loyalty oath	16

Source: Haberman, 1972.

to self-select out. It is also typical for students to complain about the lateness of student teaching in their programs considering that this is the primary basis they use for self-selecting out.

The fifth point is the most critical for understanding how selecting criteria are typically used in most SCDEs. GPA is the dominant criterion. This is true for two reasons: (1) Faculty and admissions officers are chary of lawsuits and even time-consuming and embarrassing appeals. They seek the security of having an objective criterion to support a difficult decision, and (2) very few institutions have ever been able to answer the question, "What would keep a student with a high GPA from entering your program?" This question raises an extremely critical issue because there is no research connection between high GPA and teacher effectiveness and most faculty know this. This widespread practice of keeping GPA as the dominant criterion supports the contention that the selection criteria in traditional programs of teacher education are used to select successful university students, not effective teachers, and to avoid the hassle of too many appeals and lawsuits.

The sixth and final point to consider for understanding the criteria used by traditional programs of teacher education is that the programs must scrupulously avoid the charge that they are based on an ideology or set of beliefs that may be controversial. (This is not necessarily true in universities and colleges with religious affiliations.) In public universities and colleges faculty would be uneasy in using students' ideology as a basis for admission or exclusion. The traditions of academic freedom, even in the current age of political correctness, mitigate digging into the belief systems of applicants as bases for admitting them. In the current situation it is possible for an applicant to write a letter stating the following: "I don't believe girls have the potential to learn math and science as well as boys" or "I believe there is solid research evidence to support inherent differences in native ability between Asians, whites, and African Americans, and I plan to teach students based on their higher or lower inherent potential." If such a letter were mailed to the admissions office of a SCDE in a public institution, or even to a state bureau of licensure in any of the 50 states, it could *not* be used as a basis for denying an individual admission to a teacher education program or licensure at the completion of one. In this regard education is different from other professions. If an applicant to a law school wrote a letter stating he or she did not *believe* in habeas corpus or an applicant to a medical school wrote a letter stating he or she *believed* some patients should be helped to die, these *beliefs* could and would be used as a basis for denying admission to training and/or licensure. In practice, admission to teacher training is treated as a student right, not a privilege. The burden of proof for denying admission is on the SCDE rejecting the admission of an applicant.

Programs focusing on urban poverty for culturally diverse children and youth exemplify a wider variation in how admission and selection are accomplished. In urban programs still under the aegis of the university there is a similarity to the admission process used in traditional teacher education. The most common exception is GPA because the applicants are frequently on the post-baccalaureate level and are older or "nontraditional" students. In this case undergraduate GPAs, especially if they are more than 10 years old, are frequently treated with discretion and

are not necessarily the dominant criterion. In programs under the aegis of public schools the selection of interns becomes similar to the hiring procedures of any beginning teacher. Here, personnel officers feel free to ask many questions related to applicants' beliefs and commitments and to make frequent global, and/or subjective judgments. Applicants may be turned down on the basis of appearance, physical conditions or mannerisms, accents, or any number of criteria that interviewing personnel may regard as important.

This is not to contend that school districts do not also use objective standards. They frequently use scores on tests of basic skills or on the National Teacher Examination. Urban school districts typically check arrest records, histories of mental or emotional treatment, place of residence, financial records, family status, and other items that may or may not be legally probed by federal or state statutes against discrimination (e.g., "Are you married?" "Do you have children?").

SELECTION INTERVIEWS

Several standard interview systems claim to be able to predict success in all schools or in schools serving children in poverty from diverse cultural backgrounds. Some of these interview procedures are sold by private companies, other have been developed by academics and are generally available. Almost all of the 120 largest school districts who participate in some form of teacher training utilize some form of systematically developed instrument. The characteristic these interviews share is that they claim to be derived from the best practice of classroom teachers and to be able to predict the success of applicants in their subsequent classroom teaching. In contrast to the criteria used by university faculty that predict success in the university, these instruments are sold or distributed on the basis of their claims that attributes assessed in interviews correlate with subsequent teacher effectiveness. In many states there are also requirements that candidates pass a nationally standardized examination of teachers in (1) subject-matter knowledge, and (2) knowledge of professional methods of teaching.

The attributes assessed by personnel officers in selecting urban teachers vary depending on the particular instruments utilized. These tests are copyrighted and carefully protected so that applicants cannot know in advance how they will be assessed and be able to prepare for being interviewed. The interviews are also kept secret in order to not permit entrepreneurs or college faculty from training whole classes on how to do well on a particular interview. In the interests of not revealing these instruments' content but to give the reader some understanding of what they seek to assess, examples are limited here to the author's own instrument, which is used by many alternative certification programs as well as in the hiring of first-year teachers in urban school districts (Haberman, 1987). It assesses seven teacher functions that separate the behavior of star urban teachers from those of failures and quitters. The research on which it is based also includes six additional functions that also separate the behavior of stars from quitters and failures in urban schools, but for which no interview questions have ever been developed. These functions are presented for the reader's background and are not stated in a form that will enable the reader to use them in an interview or for a candidate to prepare for an interview.

Part I. Functions on the Urban Teacher Selection Interview

1. *Persistence.* The predisposition to pursue activities at which children or youth will succeed and to resolve problems that intrude on learning
2. *Response to authority.* The predisposition to protect children or youth experiencing success in learning against bureaucratic constraints
3. *Application of generalizations.* The ability to relate theory to practice and vice versa
4. *Approach to at-risk students.* The propensity of the teacher to take responsibility for children's learning
5. *Professional versus personal orientation.* The expectation of and need for rapport with children and youth
6. *Causes and preventions of burnout.* The perception of teachers to the problems of working in bureaucracies
7. *Fallibility.* The expectation and orientation of teachers to their own errors

Part II. Additional Distinctions Between Stars and Quitter/Failures not on the Urban Teacher Selection Interview

1. *Organizational ability.* The predisposition to engage in planning and gathering of materials
2. *Physical-emotional stamina.* The ability to persist in situations characterized by violence, death, and other crises facing children or youth
3. *Teaching style.* The predisposition to engage in coaching rather than directive teaching
4. *Explanations of success.* The predisposition to emphasize effort rather than ability
5. *Basis of rapport.* The approach to student involvement. Whose classroom is it? Whose work is to be protected?
6. *Readiness.* Who should be in this classroom? The teacher's approach to children's prerequisite knowledge. Teacher versus sorter

THE MEANING OF BEST AND BRIGHTEST FOR URBAN SCHOOLS

Using these criteria, the best and the brightest teachers are not 25-year-old white females from small towns or suburbs with high GPAs who "always wanted to teach." The profile of the best and the brightest for culturally diverse children in urban poverty is as follows:

- Did not decide to teach until after graduation from college.
- Tried (and succeeded) at several jobs or careers.
- Is between 30 and 50 years of age.
- Attended an urban high school.
- Has raised several children, is a parent, or has had close, in-depth meaningful relations with children and youth.
- Currently lives in the city and plans to continue to do so.
- Is seeking and preparing for a teaching position in only an urban school system.

- Doesn't believe that "teaching is teaching" or "kids are kids."
- Has had personal and continuing experiences with violence and with living "normally" in a violent community and city.
- Has majored in anything in the university.
- May or may not have an above-average GPA.
- Expects to visit the homes of the children she or he teaches.
- Is to some degree aware of, or has had personal contact with, a range of health and human services available in the urban area.
- Expects that school bureaucracy will be irrational and intrusive on the teachers' work.
- Is likely not to be of Euro-American background.
- Is likely to be sensitive to, aware of, and working on his or her own racism, sexism, classism, or other prejudices.

These are merely some of the attributes that, taken together, provide a thumbnail sketch. Taken singly, each has no predictive validity. Taken together they characterize but do not explain teaching success. They are cited here merely to provide a real-world alternative to the best and the brightest stereotype that emanates from blue ribbon committees, national reports, foundation monographs, and professional organizations and that still connects high GPA and undergraduate youth with high potential for teaching in poverty schools.

The best and brightest teachers for urban schools tend to be individuals who share most, if not all, of the attributes cited. Many also share the experience of living in poverty themselves. Indeed, many of them are currently living in poverty and need not recollect former periods of their lives. In a very real sense these new teachers are "at risk" themselves because of their income levels. Typical experiences of the best and brightest for urban schools include the following:

- Death of a child, immediate family member, or death of the teacher him- or herself
- Critical, life-threatening injuries to a member of the teachers' immediate family
- Violence at home, either abuse from a spouse or child abuse
- Bankruptcy
- Forced moving (i.e., the need to find a new residence for the family)
- Inability to secure affordable home or car insurance
- Serious illnesses requiring unforeseen surgery or rehabilitation
- Chemical or drug dependency
- Serious and continuing transportation problems
- Marital problems of all types and severity
- Child custody problems
- Law suits related to a variety of out-of-school issues for which the teacher could not afford counsel
- Poor nutrition, exercise, and sleep habits
- No preventive medicine for themselves or their families
- Mental and emotional problems, treated and untreated (Haberman, 1991)

The ability of these beginning teachers to weather these storms at the same time they learn to be satisfactory, superior, or star teachers in extremely demanding urban schools is a remarkable challenge.

The implication of these data is that carefully selected best and brightest *urban* teachers are college graduates who are themselves in poverty, close to poverty, or recently in poverty, will require new forms of selection and preparation. For example, these individuals know what it means for a child to sneak to school early so that she or he does not get beaten up by gangs and why it is important for schools to have *un*locked doors and serve breakfast. They show great understanding not only for the children but also for the parents. They demonstrate tough love. They follow through and insist on parents performing their responsibilities (just as they do themselves) at the same time they demonstrate empathy for life conditions they can appreciate and well understand.

They are also interprofessional practitioners. Teachers cannot themselves perform the range of health and human services their students need, but they can learn to identify conditions (e.g., abuse) and even more, expect and anticipate the needs of their students for such services. Teachers can be taught to help their students' families to make the connections they will need to get services they do not know they need, do not know are available, or do not know how to access. Teachers with such prior or current life experiences are frequently among the best and brightest.

Many in teacher education still advocate simplistic racial or ethnic matching as a way to get diverse urban children the teachers they need. Finding and selecting future teachers who have also shared the urban poverty experience may enhance the potential for selecting effective teachers, those who can connect their students' life experiences to school curricula. These individuals have been successful in similar contexts facing similar life challenges and opportunities. None of these programs or studies indicate that there are no middle-class whites who can become culturally competent teachers of children in poverty. They strongly support the likelihood that other constituencies than those typically found in traditional programs of teacher education should become the primary pool for selecting and preparing culturally competent teachers.

PROGRAMS FOR CULTURAL DIVERSITY

After summarizing the literature on educating teachers for cultural diversity, Zeichner (1993) concludes that teachers are not now being prepared by SCDEs for cultural diversity. He proposes 15 key elements for making traditional teacher education more effective at preparing teachers for diversity.

1. Screen candidates on their sensitivity to why many poor students of color do not succeed in school.
2. Help candidates develop their own cultural identities.
3. Have candidates examine their attitudes toward other ethnocultural groups.
4. Teach dynamics of prejudice in the classroom and how to deal with it.

5. Teach candidates about social oppression and economic inequities.
6. Address the contributions of various ethnocultural groups.
7. Teach candidates about learning styles of various groups and the limitations of this information.
8. Provide knowledge about the relationship of language, culture, and learning. Teach procedures for studying their own classrooms.
9. See relationships between learning at home and at school.
10. Teach candidates to adapt instruction and assessment to students' backgrounds.
11. Expose candidates to examples of successful teaching of diverse students.
12. Give candidates community experiences with various culture groups.
13. Have students practice-teach in schools serving diverse groups.
14. Have students live and teach in a "minority" community.
15. Embed teacher education that has both intellectual challenge and social support. (p. 71)

While these concepts and advocacies are identified as still to be achieved by traditional programs of teacher education, they are common fare in programs that define themselves as urban and are directed at serving culturally diverse constituencies in urban poverty schools. If one does not make the error of assuming that culturally competent teachers must be prepared by SCDEs in universities but are more typically prepared by certification programs offered by urban school districts or by cooperative efforts between urban schools and consortia of local universities, then there is a range of promising models.

EIGHT DISTINCTIVE MODELS OF URBAN TEACHER EDUCATION

Following are the most promising models of urban teacher education for cultural diversity. The first is a statewide effort that sought to involve all the institutions involved with teacher preparation at any level. The second is a most complete undergraduate preservice program. The third is a post-baccalaureate certification program offered cooperatively by two universities and a public school system. The fourth model is a collaborative in one of the great cities. The program leads to certification and a master's degree. The fifth model is an alternative certification program dealing with two special cohorts: military retirees and Teach for America Corps members. The sixth model is a consortium model that includes both an undergraduate preservice track and a post-baccalaureate certification program. Seventh is a model of a career ladder for teacher aides. The eighth model is the largest alternative certification program in America.

Statewide Program

A few states have zeroed in on urban teacher education and have supported efforts to make the entire state's teacher preparation more urban and more responsive to cultural diversity. A most notable effort occurred in Pennsylvania where for 6 years

(1986–1992) approximately $500,000 of regular state funding was directed at this effort.

The Pennsylvania Academy for the Profession of Teaching, an initiative of the State System of Higher Education, was a unique venture in collaborative reform. Supported by a line item in the state system budget, its services were open to all entities throughout the Commonwealth of Pennsylvania. In its 6 years of existence it supported 10 major initiatives, each with its own projects and activities. It started and sustained the first Governor's School for Teaching, a Summer Academy for the Advancement of College Teaching, an Alliance for Early Childhood Education, and a Society of Urban Scholars. Through a system of grants and technical assistance, it provided for the support of major reform efforts on all levels involving 146 school districts; 52 community colleges and universities; 26 intermediate units; and 104 community and other organizations.

More information regarding this truly unique statewide initiative can be obtained from the Academy's last Director, Dr. Susan Arisman, Dean of Education, Cheyney University of Pennsylvania.

Undergraduate Preservice Program

A most thorough undergraduate preservice program for preparing urban teachers is offered by Alverno College (Diez & Murrell, 1991). The emphasis is on the integration of knowledge and action. This program is not an add-on (i.e., not simply another required course in multicultural education) but a "total development of the prospective candidate" (p. 6). By "ability to perform," the faculty at Alverno mean "an integration of knowledge, professional skill, and professional predispositions that define what a practitioner knows and is able to do" (p. 7). The program has other notable features, including its emphasis on future teachers working with the children's parents and other professionals, reconceptualized fieldwork and student teaching, and a thoroughly individualized assessment program. This holistic approach, in effect, led to the development of a knowledge base for urban teacher education.

Post-Baccalaureate Program

The Memphis State University offers a program for DeWitt Wallace-Reader's Digest Fellows. This urban teacher education program collaborative involves Memphis State University, Le Moyne-Owen College, and the Memphis City Schools. The program is underwritten for a 4-year period, 1993 through 1996. This program involves interns actually performing in the role of teachers, with the aid of mentors, while they complete required coursework. One of the distinctive features of this program is the role of and the training offered to the classroom teachers serving as mentors. Upon completion of the program (1 year), interns are recommended for licensure by the university *and* the employing district (Chance, 1993).

Master's Level Program–Great Cities Collaborative

Teachers for Chicago is a collaborative effort of the Chicago Public Schools, the Chicago Teachers Union, the Golden Apple Foundation, and the Council of Chicago Area Deans of Education, to attract college graduate, mid-career people to the teaching profession in the Chicago Public Schools.

The program extends over a three-summer, 2-year period. The intern starts immediately in the classroom under the supervision of a mentor, who is freed from the classroom and is responsible for four interns.

The intern must submit to a selection process and be accepted into a master's program by one of nine participating universities. Upon completion of the program the intern with a master's degree must commit to and is guaranteed a position for at least 2 years in Chicago. The intern receives a modest salary, medical benefits, and paid tuition to the university (Knauth, 1993).

Special Cohorts: Retired Military and Teach for America

This program is sponsored by the Baltimore public schools and is operated under state guidelines for alternative certification. It is a post-baccalaureate program focused on two cohorts: military retirees and other career changers, and a group of corps members from Teach for America. One summer of work precedes service as a teacher. Mentors from the school system and faculty from a cooperating university serve as staff. This is an example of an alternative certification model focusing on particular cohort groups. Dr. Rochelle Clemson of the Maryland Department of Education is the source for more complete information.

The Northwest Indiana Consortium

This consortium is distinctive for a variety of reasons. Most notable is that it includes three separate school districts, represented by both the school superintendents *and* the heads of the local teachers' unions. The seventh member of the consortium is the local university. This may be the only teacher education program in which parents are represented in policy development and have an equal policy-level vote with district and university representatives. The three school districts and unions are Gary, East Chicago, and Hammond. The university is Indiana University Northwest. Funded initially by the Lilly Foundation, the program is also supported by in-kind and matched contributions of the university and local school districts. This effort is notable for the professional development centers (elementary, middle, and high school) that it coordinates among the three districts. The contact is Dr. Charlotte Reed, Director, Urban Teacher Education Program, Indiana University Northwest.

Career Ladder for Teacher Aides

This program is a post-baccalaureate certification program offered by the Milwaukee Teachers Education Association (the local teachers' union), the Milwaukee Public Schools, and the School of Education of the University of Wisconsin-Milwaukee. It is distinctive because resident teachers earn 37 university credits while working as full-time, employed teachers. Residents complete these credits in alternative ways and not by taking traditional college classes. Candidates for admission to the program must be college graduates and currently employed as teacher aides or paraprofessionals in the Milwaukee Public Schools. Each resident teacher works full-time as a classroom teacher and has a mentor who is an outstanding classroom teacher released from working with children to coach. They also receive instruction from Milwaukee school supervisors, teachers, principals, community resource people, and university faculty. The ratio of full-time mentors to resident teachers is 4 to 1. The resident teachers are guaranteed teaching contracts in the Milwaukee schools upon completion of the program. The behavioral performance required of resident teachers demands that they demonstrate the following in urban, poverty schools:

1. Can orchestrate a learning environment
2. Have a strong belief in students' abilities to learn
3. Can assume another person's perspective
4. Can function within the purposes and intent of public education
5. Show a high regard for the opinions and experiences and responsibilities of others
6. Have knowledge of the support structures available to protect teachers' rights
7. Are willing and able to discover and gather useful resources
8. Can expand others' awareness of the world
9. Can build a positive support system for the benefit of children and youth
10. Are open to and accepting of the thoughts and suggestions of others
11. Are thoughtful, accurate appraisers of their own strengths and weaknesses (Haberman, 1988a)

Alternative Certification

Started in 1984, the Houston Independent School District is the largest producer of first-year teachers employed in Texas schools. In total, approximately 3,000 teachers have been trained and certified in this model. This is a complex program, including every level of teaching specialty, including all areas of special education. The workshops offered teachers by the school district, the coaching and mentoring, and the initial process of selection all focus on recruiting and preparing teachers for children in poverty from diverse culture groups. The percentage of African-American and Hispanic teachers in this program has been over 50% in some years.

The program is funded by the local school district by deducting a $2,500 laboratory fee from interns' first-year teaching salaries to pay for workshops, mentoring, and other district costs. This program has been a rich source of data for answering questions of how well alternatively prepared teachers specifically trained to function in urban schools compare with traditionally trained teachers prepared to teach with universal principles. Using criteria such as length of teacher service, children's achievement, and principals' ratings, such contextual preparation has clearly been effective. The contact person for further information is Director, Alternative Certification, Houston Independent School District.

FACULTY DEVELOPMENT MODELS

Proponents of traditional teacher education approaches and those seeking to shift to the special focus of urban, culturally diverse contexts inevitably disagree on defining faculty and the nature of faculty expertise. The former group naturally focuses on existing faculty expertise and the development of new forms of knowledge among regularly appointed, doctoral-level faculty. Classroom teachers are frequently added in adjunct, clinical, or other subordinate roles. It must be emphasized here that the guidelines for a SCDE being nationally accredited preclude them from relying too heavily on part-time faculty or those not "regularly" appointed as career faculty at the university. This ensures that in order to prove that they have high-quality faculty SCDEs will never be able to utilize master urban classroom teachers currently working with children and youth as anything other than second-class citizens in their teacher education programs. The need for national accreditation is not the only obstacle to recognizing practitioners. The university requirement of the doctoral degree as a base requirement for faculty appointment as an assistant professor also mitigates against infusing the practical knowledge of urban classroom teachers into traditional teacher education programs. As a result, the theoretical emphasis of educational psychology will inevitably continue to dominate and carry greater prestige than other theoretical approaches or the practical, craft emphasis. Also, because the "how-to-do-it" skills are delivered primarily by classroom teachers, universities (assuming that they continue to uphold their faculty culture and to seek national accreditation) will inevitably make subordinates and junior partners of classroom teachers who cooperate in their programs.

Those creating new forms of urban teacher education tend to move in the opposite direction. The craft knowledge of outstanding urban teachers is the basis of their programs. Those who actually can demonstrate teaching and cultural competence with urban children or youth in poverty schools serving diverse constituencies are the most highly respected experts. University faculty are generally regarded as irrelevant; the few university faculty who cooperate in these field-based programs represent a range of academic fields other than educational psychology and serve in subordinate and supporting roles to the practitioners. Despite differences within the two groups that represent these types of programs, the generalizations that distinguish them are as follows. Much initial study of theoretical constructs from educational psychology and some subsequent practice characterize the forms of teacher education that are based on the traditional or universal approach to teacher education. Much in-depth practice, first supported by interdisciplinary theory, later tend to characterize those forms of teacher education that claim that the preparation of urban teachers is essentially contextual.

The most complete effort for reconceptualizing teacher education for teachers in urban settings is a consortium effort. It is a 3-year program involving Simon Fraser University, Ohio State, Teachers College, Columbia, the University of Connecticut, the University of Miami, and the University of Tennessee. The project directly involves the dean, two faculty, and a local classroom teacher from each institution and numerous others in each locality through these leadership teams. The program seeks to develop several "strands": leadership, organization, and change; leadership for the improvement of teaching and learning; leadership development for program design and assessment; and the development of clinical faculty as a contribution to both preservice teacher preparation and urban renewal. These leadership development programs seek to change the knowledge bases as well as the practice of those who would function as urban teacher educators (Howey, 1993).

CURRENT STATUS

In 1969 B. O. Smith concluded that there needed to be a major overhaul of teacher education before teachers would be adequately prepared to work with children of any social origin:

Racial, class and ethnic bias can be found in every aspect of current teacher preparation programs. The selection processes militate against the poor and minorities. The program content reflects current prejudices; the methods of instruction coincide with learning styles of the dominant group. Subtle inequalities are reinforced in institutions of higher learning. Unless there is scrupulous appraisal, unless every aspect of teacher training is carefully reviewed, the changes initiated in teacher preparation as a result of the current crisis will be, like so many changes which have gone before, merely differences which make no difference. (pp. 2–3)

Twenty-four years later a remarkably thorough summary of the teacher education literature seeking evidence of how teachers are being prepared for cultural diversity demonstrated that little has changed. Even searching for reports and documents that were not research or published documents generated an exceedingly small "literature" of even fugitive material. Zeichner (1993) concludes that in regard to educating teachers for cultural diversity:

There is a lot of evidence that the situation hasn't changed much in the 24 years since Smith delivered this condemnation of teacher education. . . . If teacher education programs were successful in educating teachers for diversity, we might not have today such a massive reluctance by beginning teachers to work in urban schools and in other schools serving poor and ethnic- and linguistic-minority students. Just educating teachers who are *willing* to teach in these schools however, only begins to address the problem of preparing teachers who will *successfully* educate the students who attend these schools. Educating teachers for diversity must include attention to the quality of instruction that will be offered by these teachers. More of the same kind of teaching, which has largely failed to provide a minimally adequate education to poor and ethnic- and linguistic-minority students, does not improve the situation. (pp. 4–6)

A review of the literature for preparing teachers for children in poverty from diverse culture groups leads to the conclusion that there is a lot less going on than meets the eye. Universities remain committed to the age of the learner, the content to be taught, and handicapping conditions as the bases of their programs. They operationally define poverty, urbanness, or cultural diversity as special conditions and prepare teachers for it in the same conceptual way they prepare teachers for teaching other individuals with handicapping conditions (by adding a course in urban or multicultural education). The knowledge base of traditional teacher education continues to be universal rather than contextual (e.g., all normal children develop in the same way and pass throughout the same developmental stages) and focuses on the individual rather than the culture group that socializes the individual as the unit of analysis. The concepts of educational psychology continue to dominate, narrow, and limit teacher preparation to basically one knowledge base rather than the multiple bases it needs.

In a 30-year (1960–1990) review of the literature undergirding traditional teacher education, Weiner (1991) concluded that not only is the urban knowledge base missing but that faculty also refuse to acknowledge that they "lack this understanding—and need to acquire it" (p. 168).

At the same time, the growing number of special, small programs in universities, the accelerated growth of alternative certification programs controlled by the great cities' school districts, and the growing number of urban school district and university collaboratives, are developing a whole new form of contextual urban teacher education. These programs focus on particular ethnic groups in particular school systems, with particular needs, problems, and aspirations. In these emerging forms of teacher education the knowledge bases for teachers do not emanate from one limited scholarly discipline (e.g., psychology) or universal questions (e.g., "How do children learn?"). These new forms of teacher education begin with specific practical questions (e.g., "How can violence be reduced in this school in St. Louis?") and bring interdisciplinary approaches to bear on the search for solutions. In the future, the preparation of urban teachers will be even much broader than interdisciplinary approaches. They will be *interprofessional* and *interdisciplinary*. To meet the needs of real children and youth in the real world, future teachers will be prepared to access the services of the full range of human service professionals: nurses, physicians, dentists, and all forms of social and human service personnel. There are already models of such programs being offered that prepare culturally competent teachers who can respond to the needs of urban children and their families. The best source of these programs and literature is the Association of Teacher Educators' Commission on Interprofessional-Human Services. Initiated by former President Leonard Kaplan, it is chaired by Dean C. Corrigan of Texas A&M (Kaplan, 1992). (See Chapter 41 by Corrigan and Udas in this handbook.) At present, this literature demonstrates more and greater initiatives by those preparing medical health and human service professionals who seek to work with schools and teachers than vice versa. In the future, teachers of children and youth in urban poverty will need to be interdisciplinary practitioners. As always, the question will be whether traditional programs of teacher education will be able to repond to all of America's children in any serious, major way or whether they will continue to make cosmetic changes in order to maintain existing programs. It is likely that both poverty and cultural diversity will continue to increase. As a result, school districts serving the poor and the culturally diverse will also continue to grow and need teachers. It is reasonable to expect that they will continue to expand their own alternative teacher education programs in order to provide themselves with culturally competent teachers.

References

Anderson, J. A. (1988). Cognitive styles and multicultural populations. *Journal of Teacher Education, 39*(1), 2–9.

Banks, J. (1993). Multicultural education: Development, dimensions and challenges. *Phi Delta Kappan, 75*(1), 22–28.

Book, C., Byers, J., & Freeman, D. D. (1983). Student expectations and teacher education traditions with which we cannot live. *Journal of Teacher Education, 34*(1), 9–13.

Borman, K. M. (1990). Foundations of education in teacher education. In W. R. Houston (Ed.), *Handbook of research on teacher education* (pp. 393–402). New York: Macmillan.

Chance, L. H. (1993). *Pathways to teaching program.* Memphis: School of Education, Memphis State University.

Chubb, J. E., & Moe, T. M. (1989). *Educational choice: Answers to the most frequently asked questions about mediocrity in American education and what can be done about it.* Milwaukee: Wisconsin Policy Research Institute.

Corrigan, D. C., & Haberman, M. (1990). The context of teacher education. In W. R. Houston (Ed.), *Handbook of research on teacher education* (pp. 195–211). New York: Macmillan.

Corwin, R. G. (1973). *Reform and organizational survival: The Teacher Corps as an instrument of educational change.* New York: Wiley.

Diez, M. R., & Murrell, P. J. (1991). *Assessing abilities in expert teaching practice in diverse classrooms.* Paper presented at the fourth annual conference on Racial and Ethnic Relations in American Higher Education, Washington, DC.

Edelfelt, R. A. (1986). Managing teacher supply and demand. *Action in Teacher Education, 8*(2), 31–36.

Feiman-Nemser, S., & Buchmann, M. H. (1983). Pitfalls of experience in teacher education: A curricular case study. In P. Tamir, A. Hofstein, & M. Ben-Peretz (Eds.), *Preservice and inservice education of science teachers* (pp. 197–206). Philadelphia: Balaban International Science Services.

Feistritzer, C. E., & Chester, D. J. (1991). *Alternative teacher certification: A state by state analysis.* Washington, DC: National Center for Education Information.

Foster, M. (1990). The politics of race: Through the eyes of African American teachers. *Journal of Education, 172*(3), 123–141.

Franklin, V. P. (1990). They rose and fell together: African-American educators and community leadership. *Journal of Education, 172*(3), 39–64.

Garbarino, J., Dudrow, N., Kostelny, K., & Pardo, C. (1992). *Children in danger.* San Francisco: Jossey-Bass.

Haberman, M. (1971). Twenty-three reasons universities can't educate teachers. *Journal of Teacher Education, 22*(2), 133–140.

Haberman, M. (1972). *Guidelines for the selection of students into programs of teacher education.* Washington, DC: Association of Teacher Educators and ERIC Clearinghouse on Teacher Education.

Haberman, M. (1982, February). The legacy of teacher education: 1800–2000. *The Hunt Lecture.* Houston: American Association of Colleges for Teacher Education.

Haberman, M. (1987). *The urban teacher selection interview.* Milwaukee: School of Education, University of Wisconsin–Milwaukee.

Haberman, M. (1988a). *The metropolitan multicultural teacher education program.* Milwaukee: School of Education, University of Wisconsin–Milwaukee.

Haberman, M. (1988b). *Preparing teachers for urban schools.* Bloomington: Phi Delta Kappan Educational Foundation.

Haberman, M. (1989). More minority teachers. *Phi Delta Kappan, 70*(10), 771–776.

Haberman, M. (1990). The rationale for training adults as teachers. In C. Sleeter (Ed.), *Empowerment through multicultural education* (pp. 27–42). Albany: State University of New York Press.

Haberman, M. (1994, January 24–February 6). Redefining "best and brightest." *In These Times,* 26–27.

Haynes, N. M., & Comer, J. A. (1990). Helping black children succeed. In K. Lomotey (Ed.), *Going to school: The African American experience* (pp. 103–113). Albany: State University of New York Press.

Higher Education Act. (1965). *Hearings before the Senate Subcommittee on Education, 89th Congress* (Bill S600, Part II) (pp. v and 1437). Washington, DC: U.S. Government Printing Office.

Hilliard, A. G. (1974). Restructuring teacher education for multicultural imperatives. In W. A. Hunter (Ed.), *Multicultural education through competency based teacher education* (pp. 40–55). Washington, DC: American Association of Colleges for Teacher Education.

Houston Independent School District. (1989). *An evaluation of HISD's alternative certification program.* Houston: Author.

Howey, K. R. (1993). *An addendum to reforming teacher education for teachers in urban settings.* Columbus: College of Education, Ohio State University.

Howey, K. R., & Zimpher, N. L. (1990). Professors and deans of education. In W. R. Houston (Ed.), *Handbook of research on teacher education* (pp. 349–370). New York: Macmillan.

Irvine, J. J. (1990). *Black students and school failure—Policies, practices and prescriptions.* New York: Greenwood.

Kaplan, L. (Ed.). (1992). *Education and the family.* Boston: Allyn & Bacon.

King, S. H. (1993). The limited presence of African American teachers. *Review of Educational Research, 63*(2), 116–124.

Knauth, S. M. (1993). *Teachers for Chicago: First year evaluation report.* Chicago: Golden Apple Foundation.

Lee, C. D., Lomotey, K., & Shujaa, M. (1990). How shall we sing our sacred song in a strange land? *Journal of Education, 172*(2), 45–61.

Meyer, A. E. (1957). *An educational history of the American people.* New York: McGraw-Hill.

National Education Association. (1991). *Status of the American public school teacher, 1990–1991.* Washington, DC: Author.

Payne, C. M. (1984). *Getting what we ask for: The ambiguity of success and failure in urban education.* Westport, CT: Greenwood.

Shade, B. S. (1982). African-American cognitive style. A variable in school success. *Review of Educational Research, 52*(2), 219–244.

Smith, B. O. (1969). *Teachers for the real world.* Washington, DC: American Association of Colleges for Teacher Education.

Stoddard, T. (1990). Los Angeles Unified School District (LAUSD) Intern Program: Recruiting and preparing teachers for an urban center. *Peabody Journal of Education, 67*(3), 102–105.

Swisher, K., & Deyhle, D. (1989, August). The styles of learning are different but the teaching is just the same: Suggestions for teachers of American Indian youth. *Journal of American Indian Education* (special issue), 1–14.

Weiner, L. L. (1991). *Perspectives on preparing teachers of at-risk students in urban schools, 1960–1990.* Unpublished doctoral dissertation, Harvard University.

Zeichner, K. (1993). *Educating teachers for cultural diversity.* East Lansing, MI: National Center for Research for Teacher Learning.

Zeichner, K., & Tabachnick, B. R. (1981). Are the effects of university teacher education washed out by school experience? *Journal of Teacher Education, 32*(3), 7–11.

Zimpher, N. L., & Ashburn, E. (1992). Countering parochialism among teacher candidates. In M. Dilworth (Ed.), *Diversity in teacher education* (pp. 40–62). San Francisco: Jossey-Bass.

·33·

MULTICULTURAL EDUCATION

LANDSCAPE FOR REFORM IN THE TWENTY-FIRST CENTURY

Francisco Hidalgo
TEXAS A&M UNIVERSITY–KINGSVILLE

Rudolfo Chávez-Chávez
NEW MEXICO STATE UNIVERSITY

Jean C. Ramage
UNIVERSITY OF NEBRASKA, KEARNEY

This chapter surveys the intellectual evolution of multicultural education and analyzes it within a naturalistic framework for understanding the cultural differences and the dynamics of culture contact in an increasingly diverse society. It covers the intellectual terrain, historical roots, and societal contexts and gives special attention to applications in teacher education.

SCHOLARLY DIRECTION AND POLITICAL CONTROVERSY

Multicultural education, with its foundation in pluralism and diversity, is grounded in the principles of democracy, equity, and justice. It demands a holistic grasp of the interactive politics involved in the creation and understanding of knowledge, learning, and the dynamics of education (Banks, 1991, 1993a, 1993b, 1993c; Banks & Banks, 1993; Gollnick, 1992; Grant, 1992; Nieto, 1992, 1994). Nieto (1994) suggests that criticism originates from across the ideological and political landscape. Cummins (1992) addresses the controversy along an ideological spectrum from right to left. Western traditionalists believe that the multicultural movement undermines the canon (i.e., estab-

lished truth [Bloom, 1987; D'Souza, 1992; Hirsch, 1987; Ravitch, 1990; Schlesinger, 1992]). These Western traditionalists defend the established curriculum that is dominated by Euro-American male writers (Banks, 1993b). Their critique originates from an epistemological framework that negates multiplicity and difference. In their paradigm, truth is sought through the positivist approach. Critical theorists, however, argue that the movement is anemic for restructuring education and society.

The controversy centers on how multicultural education will be defined. Nieto (1994) asserts that teaching and learning must challenge racism, sexism, and other forms of social domination and intolerance. Thus, curriculum making should incorporate the sociocultural contexts of subject matter. This leads to the realization that multiple perspectives on truth exist and to competition for ideological hegemony. Although multicultural education theoretically encompasses inclusiveness and social critique, few examples have surfaced that challenge racism and sexism within systematic multicultural curricula. Instead, curricula continue to focus on heroes, holidays, and discrete cultural elements (Banks, 1994; Nieto, 1994). Suzuki (1980) called this superficial approach to multicultural education "simply celebrating ethnicity by highlighting ethnic foods, holidays, and costumes" (p. 1).

In keeping with this mandate for inclusiveness and social critique, transformational scholars and critical theorists argue that knowledge is not neutral but is influenced by human interests. Curricula do reflect the power and social relationships within a society, and an important purpose of knowledge construction is to help people improve society (Code, 1991; Harding, 1991; hooks & West, 1991; King & Mitchell, 1990; Minnich, 1990). Thus, racism, sexism, and other practices of domination are brought to the banquet of engagement for transformational curricular design.

Curricula that reflect postmodern assumptions and goals challenge some key assumptions about mainstream academic knowledge (Rosenau, 1992). A benchmark of this perspective is to enable students to understand "concepts, issues, themes, and problems" (Banks, 1994, p. 26) from different perspectives and viewpoints. Knowledge is considered a social construction that needs to be questioned and challenged. The *social action level* builds on the transformative curriculum by enabling students to pursue goals and actions that make personal, social, and civic sense. Teachers who are critical and transformative develop a pedagogy of social action and advocacy that "celebrates diversity" (Ayers, 1988), not just selected holidays, isolated cultural artifacts, festivals, and food.

Despite the struggle to develop this new field, there are vigorous indications of the formalization of multicultural education. There has been a proliferation of articles, both popular and academic, textbooks, and scholarly books in this maturing field. Authors from a variety of disciplines and perspectives have begun to formulate the philosophical and theoretical underpinnings of multicultural education (Banks, 1994; Bennett, 1990; Colangelo, Dustin, & Foxley, 1985; Gollnick & Chinn, 1986; Grant, 1992; Grant & Sleeter, 1988a, 1988b; Lynch, 1989; Nieto, 1992; Tiedt & Tiedt, 1976). Most teacher education programs now have the rudiments of multicultural education incorporated in their curriculum.

The movement toward multicultural education has been supported by the National Council for Accreditation of Teacher Education's (NCATE, 1982) multicultural requirement. Since 1979 NCATE standards have required that teacher education programs incorporate multicultural perspectives and cultural diversity. NCATE's definition of multicultural education includes a focus on ethnicity, gender, race, religion, class, and exceptionality—aspects of culture discussed in the literature on multicultural education (Gollnick, 1992).

The focal point of multicultural education is the learning process. The goal is to consider the range of beliefs and attitudes of individuals and groups whose cultural membership is integral to the learning process (Davidman & Davidman, 1994). Teaching from a multicultural perspective involves compiling, interpreting, and making institutional and management decisions that incorporate sociocultural considerations, often leading to different conclusions from those that are accepted traditionally.

Multicultural education entails creating equitable educational opportunities within environments that promote critique, social justice, and pluralism (Banks, 1991; Banks & Banks, 1989; Giroux, 1983; Sleeter & Grant, 1987; Sleeter & McLaren, in press). The student in a multicultural setting is assisted in learning and evaluating different types of knowledge.

The validity of the curriculum content is a central theme in multicultural education. For example, Kohl (1993) criticized the characterization of Rosa Parks in social studies textbooks as a tired, poor seamstress. In fact, Parks was also the Executive Secretary of the Montgomery NAACP at the time. Her actions were consonant with the awakening civil rights movement.

The multicultural education movement is developing a stronger theoretical framework on which to continue building advocacy positions. This framework lies in socially constructed theories that fundamentally challenge the positivist treatment and Eurocentric account of the knowledge base.

What is emerging is a transformational mode of teaching and learning. For example, Lynch (1986) described three ideological orientations: (1) economic efficiency, (2) democracy and equality of educational opportunity, and (3) interdependence and partnership with an emphasis on negotiation and social discourse. In each of these orientations, values, knowledge structures, and social controls are treated differently.

Another way of viewing these orientations is to define inequality within ideological frameworks, such as economic, political, or sociocultural. Within the economic ideological framework, reward is used as an incentive and poverty is offset by the gains of the rich. From the political ideological framework, inequality is viewed as the denial of fundamental rights (e.g., voting, right to seek political office, or equal treatment by the courts). From the sociocultural standpoint, inequality would be reflected by a society that ignores a group's history, taboos, obligations, or aspirations (Ray, 1992).

The essence of the multicultural education movement lies in socially constructed theories. The traditional, established knowledge base reflects mainstream precepts, ideas, and findings that have supported one main point of view. The major challenge is to the racism, sexism, and classism of the Eurocentric orientation (Banks, 1993).

In an early challenge to the Eurocentric perspective, Suzuki (1977) contradicted the notion that Asian Americans had reached middle-class status by being assimilated into the American mainstream. His historical approach explained behavioral patterns of Asian Americans in terms of their cultural values and norms within the context of the larger society. He presented the factors within a multicultural framework, challenging the *model minority* theory for Asian Americans.

More recently, Nieto (1994) introduced the concept of a moral center. She argued that this moral center can be irresponsibly sacrificed in the interest of indiscriminate inclusiveness. Nieto asserted that

[to] make every "perspective" of equal validity . . . we would be hard pressed to deny curriculum inclusion to those who claim that the Holocaust never happened, to those who insist that creationism is a science, and so forth . . . an uncritical multiplicity of perspectives might very well result in our students believing that there is neither truth nor ethics, except on a personal or purely relative level. (p. 266)

The moral center recognizes that cultural values and norms are transmitted through our schools. John Dewey (1966) wrote that if education is to become a meaningful social process, then the vision of an achievable society must be defined; that is, the values and norms need to be explicitly declared. Multicultural education defines this process with a dialectic of values and norms that are not neutral. Bull, Fruehling, and Chattergy (1992) addressed two general approaches to values in the midst of conflict: consequentialism and nonconsequentialism. Consequentialism "holds that alternative actions or policies should be judged according to their outcomes" (p. 14). Nonconsequentialism "or deontological ethics, holds that different actions or policies should be judged according to whether they are inherently right rather than according to their consequences" (p. 14).

These difficult axiological considerations are at the core of multicultural education's social controversy. The conflicts would be contentious enough if there was a common understanding of the meaning of multicultural education. However, when even the definitions show a lack of consensus, intellectual disagreements about social policy and educational practice degenerate into an untenable impasse over the need for multicultural education.

Today, the theoretical framework appears somewhat disjointed as the multiple voices are heard. The common strands in multicultural education build on challenging the mainstream precepts that are grounded in racist, sexist, and classist Eurocentric tradition (Banks, 1993c). However, until a strong conceptual framework is reached, the actual application, and more critically, the interpretation of multicultural education, is too often left to the teacher in the classroom (Perry & Fraser, 1993).

EVOLVING CONCEPTIONS OF MULTICULTURAL EDUCATION

As the thinking, the conversation, and the practice in multicultural education advance past descriptive and polemical stages and into an intellectually coherent stage, the field of vision widens and application diversifies. Key authors are deriving critical elements and are formulating emerging taxonomies. A growing number of writers from education, anthropology, history, philosophy, and other fields are participating intellectually and professionally in this ongoing conceptual discovery. They do so as they also clarify the evolution from early culture contact origins through political definition in the civil rights era and into evolving applications in education and society.

Elements and Levels of Multicultural Education

The definition of multicultural education conceptualized here emerges in part from its political roots in the United States, its models of application in a variety of societies, and from the emerging consensus about the critical components of multicultural education (Gay, 1994). Definitions range in scope from the narrow to the global, from curricular to contextual, from ethnic-specific to socially inclusive, and from socially neutral to politically prescriptive.

The following primary points of agreement emerge from Gay's (1994) synthesis:

1. *Diversity-centered and historically based curriculum.* Cultural diversity, history, and contextual conditions are critical curriculum components in this type of definition of multicultural education.

2. *Reform-oriented philosophy.* Multicultural education provides a philosophical foundation for promoting educational reform.

3. *Diversity-directed instruction.* Cultural diversity provides the direction for multicultural instruction and for selected policy reforms.

4. *Context-dependent curricula.* Individual definitions will be tailored to individual conditions and applied in accordance with the particular setting.

5. *Permeative.* Multicultural education penetrates all contexts and is widely applicable.

6. *Comprehensive.* Multicultural education must encompass all levels of schooling.

Gay (1994) suggested that a constructed definition of multicultural education is appropriate. The points of agreement constitute the acceptable general boundaries for this customized understanding of multicultural education. The user's perspective and operational context provide the freedom for this process. These contexts are predominantly curricular in their focus. Even its reform statement is confined to educational policy and practice. Gay's (1994) synthesis suggests a politicized social justice version of multicultural education. Gay indirectly alludes to the social and political dimensions of the educational reform caused by multicultural education.

Nieto (1992) offers a definition that more directly addresses these contextual issues:

> Multicultural education is a process of comprehensive and basic education for all students. It challenges and rejects racism and other forms of discrimination in schools and society, and accepts and affirms pluralism . . . that students, their communities, and teachers represent. Multicultural education permeates the curriculum, the instructional strategies used in schools, interactions between teachers, children, and parents, and the very way that schools conceptualize the nature of teaching and learning. (p. xxiii)

Nieto's (1992) definition more clearly explicates the social justice and antiracist mandates of multicultural education because it uses critical pedagogy as its underlying philosophy and focuses on knowledge, reflection, and action (praxis) as the basis for social change. Multicultural education, as expressed in this format, furthers democratic principles of social justice.

Nieto's "additive" and critical model of multicultural education is reflected in a "variety of levels of attitudes and behaviors" (Nieto, 1992, p. 276). Beyond its monocultural counterpart, its levels range from mere tolerance, to acceptance, to respect, and at the epitome, to affirmation, solidarity, and critique. At its most sophisticated level, multicultural education not only deromanticizes culture in general but also accommodates and even welcomes the conflict of values and behaviors inherent in culture contact. The affirmation of differences and an attitude of inclusion about cultural realities are fundamental to multicultural education. Teachers exercise the emancipatory imperative by participating as advocates of social justice and managers of critical learning in intercultural encounters (Nieto, 1994).

Banks (1994) in his multicultural education explanation proposes a "multifactor, holistic theory of multicultural education" (p. 102). He applies Kuhn's (1970) concept of paradigm hesitantly because of "the paucity of universal laws, principles, and theories in social science and because social science is characterized by many competing systems of explanations" (p. 103). He surveys the 10 multicultural education paradigms critically along the ethnic revitalization continuum. He discusses earlier typologies of ethnic diversity theory, and in doing so, dismisses the cultural pluralist and cultural assimilationist duality as inadequate for framing the cultural realities of complex societies. The pluralist's exaggeration of the individual's ethnic loyalties and the assimilationist's ethnocentric and wishful view of a universal national culture are critiqued as unrealistic portrayals in a complex world of intercultural interdependence.

Seeking an appropriate model for intercultural effectiveness in a modern society, Banks (1994) promotes a "multicultural ideology" (p. 128) as a more realistic approach to sustaining social cohesion while allowing freedom of cultural expression. Yet, he concedes that even this more suitable approach fails to propose viable solutions to the conflicts that inevitably arise in a culturally open society.

The same cultural relativism that naive multiculturalists promote as essential to valuing diversity was presented by Bull et al. (1992) as an inadequate strategy when cultural differences are not distinct and when the cultural contact is ongoing and inevitable among groups. Cultural differences may lead to conflicts in ethics and values, some of which are irreconcilable. The educator must decide whether to seek conflict resolution or merely to appreciate the conflicts and their cultural genesis (Bull et al., 1992). They offer a model for applying three perspectives on political morality to situations but leave the final decision to the reader.

Banks (1994) and Bull et al. (1992) raise difficult questions about how to achieve social consensus on widely diverse cultural practices in a society of intensifying and unprecedented levels of intercultural contact. The established multicultural education literature emphasizes the importance of peaceful intercultural coexistence in reaction to the assimilationist pressures of social policymakers, educators, and the general community. As pluralistic practices increasingly are prescribed in schools, universities, and service agencies, individual practitioners look to multiculturalists for answers to a new generation of questions. As racial intermarriage, desegregated housing, integrated workplaces, and international business encounters bring diverse people together in greater numbers and in equal relationships, policy issues are shifting from the need for democratic social practices to understanding the facts of culture-specific behaviors and values and making social decisions about those behaviors and values that are socially viable.

Davidman and Davidman (1994) developed a "synthesis conception of multicultural education" that they call *Multicultural Education Plus*. They provide educators with a practical guide for implementing multicultural lessons and teaching in a multicultural instructional format. Their premise is that equity is essential to educational excellence. They join several others (Brown, 1992; Lynch, 1989; Ramsey, Vold, & Williams, 1989) who reviewed the evolution of multicultural education from its civil rights origins through its current state.

Ramsey et al. (1989) traced the twentieth-century evolution of multicultural education and cited and annotated literature that defined multicultural education at various stages in its development through the late 1980s, especially as it was translated from a vision of a pluralist society to educational practice in K–12 schools and higher education. Their distinctions of multicultural education from multiethnic education and intercultural education are useful for educators who use these terms interchangeably and too freely.

Ramsey et al. (1989) summarize the debate about multicultural education's purpose (political agenda of social action or disguised strategy for maintaining white Anglo-Saxon control). They advocate its social action agenda and support Grant's belief in deghettoizing the concept by favoring its configuration as education that is multicultural. Their book is a valuable historical reference that guides the reader to key literature in multicultural education through 1989. Its sociopolitical perspective makes it particularly valuable by underlining multicultural education's historical social justice agenda.

The evolution of multicultural education has also been analyzed in global dimensions. Lynch (1989), in *Multicultural Education in a Global Society*, describes multicultural education in terms of phases of sophistication. The "additive phase" (p. 36) parallels the ethnic studies approach by adding culturally specific content. In this phase children from the majority culture are often excluded from participating in the appended curricula. An equally serious problem with this phase is that the main curriculum still fails to emphasize common elements in the minority and majority curricula.

In Lynch's (1989) next phase, folkloric multicultural education, customs, dress, and festivals are introduced into the mainstream curriculum, again emphasizing the differences, not the commonalities. This oversimplified and celebratory view of culture also renders it safe to teach as a foreign and quaint set of ethnic manifestations. Teachers could experience the culture of the Chicano, for example, through intensive cultural immersions and then return to serve as cultural brokers of ethnically segregated schools. Target cultures could be studied as separate objects of inquiry, with selected elements of cultural behavior incorporated for strategic curricular use, and yet fail to lead to mutual accommodation. At this level, cultural knowledge remains a tool for more effective cultural assimilation in much the same way that the content of foreign service training is a tool for diplomatic and strategic interaction, not a vehicle for genuine reciprocal learning between equals. The folkloric stage fails to offer teachers a framework for addressing the more profound and persistent social justice issues.

Lynch (1989) describes the permeative phase as the introduction of culturally appropriate content, teaching materials, and methods across the curriculum. An attempt is made to strike an equilibrium between cultural distinctions and cultural commonalities. Still, this more authentic infusion effort lacks the activist impetus of the subsequent antiracist, intergroup, and prejudice reduction phases that explicitly confront the more delicate systemic issues of established policy and practice.

Lynch's (1989) analysis of multicultural education in the global arena identified four common characteristics:

1. Creative attention to issues of cultural diversity
2. Consensus through discourse
3. Emphasis on human justice through a commitment to equitable and antidiscriminatory practices

4. Policy of inclusion in the civic infrastructure of a pluralist democratic society

These concepts flow directly from the three major aims of multicultural education: "creative development of cultural diversity, the maintenance of social cohesion, and the achievement of human justice" (Lynch, 1989, p. xiv).

Lynch (1989) relates multicultural education to human rights education and peace education in a global context. He further espouses the global multicultural education curricular applications that relate to social justice issues. Social justice maintains the balance between the other two aims: cultural diversity and social cohesion. Social justice is presented not only as a noble goal to be pursued by educators and policymakers but also as a moral compass as they struggle with the dilemma that faces democratic societies. How does a demographically plural and systemically complex society promote political unity and simultaneously celebrate the social diversity that challenges that unity?

In one of the most insightful accounts and analyses of multicultural education's evolution, Weiner (1993) traced multicultural education development in its political, historical, and intellectual contexts. The title, *Preparing Teachers for Urban Schools: Lessons from Thirty Years of School Reform*, clearly represents the urban education focus of the book and implies the teacher's central role in urban school reform. That role has floated from the service provider needing basic preparation or staff development in discreet competencies to the emerging professional seeking empowerment within the educational system to the partner in a systemic network of societal attention to reform. Weiner's book illustrated that as the discussion about multicultural education evolves in search of solutions to social inequalities, academic disparities, and intercultural discontinuity, the scholarly discourse is shifting from a dispute over causative linkages (environment versus heredity, students versus parents versus teachers) to a more holistic consideration of contextual factors.

Concurrently, multicultural education is transforming from a set of curricular solutions to deficits and problems to a theoretical framework for (1) valuing demographic diversity as an enriching social context; (2) promoting a multicultural curriculum as a whole-school knowledge base; (3) promoting instructional strategies that structure heterogeneous, learner-centered, and critical processes; (4) promoting collaborative and unifying relationships among all the participants, not necessarily as service providers and clients, in the education enterprise; and (5) demanding personal commitments to these principles.

Personal Investment in Multicultural Education

As the definition of multicultural education advances toward confronting contextual and political issues, it also demands a greater level of engagement from its advocates. The proponent is challenged to extend his or her interest in multicultural education beyond understanding and into personal internalization.

In a summary of a 2-year, school-based staff development project in multicultural education, Sleeter (1992) extended the social justice agenda of multicultural education from its impact on personal attitudes and behaviors toward students in diverse settings to its responsibility for systemic reform. Her brief definition revealed her belief in the whole-school process of reform: "multicultural education can be defined broadly as any set of processes by which schools work with rather than against oppressed groups" (p. 1).

Sleeter's (1991) view of multicultural education as a process of systemic reform was espoused from a more personal approach in her trialog with two white colleagues. In that discussion, she challenges fellow white academicians to translate their proficient discourse on racism into action. Sleeter boldly espouses personal responsibility for reducing racism and white hegemony because of one's membership in a racial group. Sleeter (1991) suggests that collective action by the dominant group to share their ascribed power is an expression of personal commitment to systemic reform. Sleeter's position was part of a contentious discourse in which the relevance of the discourse itself was seriously questioned. This debate reflects a general disagreement about the oppressor's personal and professional responsibility for conditions of inequality that have deep historical roots. The debate remains unsettled in both the popular and the professional arenas, but Sleeter's message in her study on staff development reinforced the teacher's responsibility as a potential change agent to combat the organizational obstacles to implementing multicultural education (Sleeter, 1992). She cites Nieto (1992) in pointing to the school's structural features as regenerators of inequality and calls upon teachers and administrators to internalize the concepts of multicultural education as a framework for coherent curricular reform. The school then becomes the conduit for the individual's commitment to multicultural education as systemic reform.

Brown (1992) outlines the legislative initiatives and the historical education movements that set the political framework for the diversity-related restructuring of education. He notes, with disappointment, the lack of reform in K–12 and teacher education despite (1) claims by school administrators about accomplishments in multicultural education, and (2) accreditation mandates in teacher education that produce teachers who are technically prepared for the challenges of teaching in culturally diverse settings.

Brown (1992) concedes that the structural changes appearing in the schools are perhaps facilitating a climate of freedom, rising expectations, a sense of professional community, and egalitarianism. Outcome-based education, teacher empowerment, and heterogeneous grouping are significant examples of the curricular and administrative reforms that contribute to a diversity-friendly atmosphere in the schools. Brown's (1992) reluctant hopefulness in restructuring as a partner to diversity differs only in degree from Nieto's own view of the school's structural features as obstructions to equality.

In a 1990 issue of *Education and Urban Society on Cultural Diversity and American Education: Visions of the Future*, Arvizu and Saravia-Shore (1990), in concert with fellow anthropologists who reacted to Hirsch's (1987) and Bloom's (1987) momentous and controversial books, make a case for cross-cultural literacy. From this cross-cultural perspective, phenomena in their cultural contexts should be studied in systematic and scientific ways in order for teachers to use methods and tools to learn cultural competencies. Such competencies consist in "becoming aware of, observing, eliciting, and understanding the values and expectations of parents and students, as well as the resulting cultural patterns of interaction between adults and children, particularly between teachers and students" (Arvizu & Saravia-Shore, 1990, p. 372). However, even though they extend the multicultural education discourse to encompass the same critical issues discussed by Nieto (1992) and Sleeter and Grant (1987), they stop short of explicitly declaring the individual educator's personal responsibility to serve as warriors of social justice.

Ogbu (1990), critiquing his anthropologist colleagues' reactions to Bloom (1987) and Hirsch (1987) within the same issue of *Education and Urban Society* (1990), also proposes an extension of the educator's responsibilities in cultural diversity beyond acquiring and applying the cultural knowledge and languages of their students. However, the extension is not of the educator's responsibility but of the ownership of that responsibility. The goal in this approach is to achieve cultural diversity that allows for maximum school success for all populations in the school—majority or minority. In turn, students commit to learning and using the language and culture of the schools. Thus, Ogbu (1990) introduces the reciprocal nature of cross-cultural learning. The responsibility for cultural borrowing and accommodation is shared between teachers and students.

Multicultural education demands not only the individual practitioner's understanding and adoption of multicultural education as a framework for curricular improvement but also his or her commitment to challenging (1) the business-as-usual approach to teaching, (2) the organizational obstacles that peripheralize non-Anglo ethnicity and non-English languages, and (3) the profession's ideological neutrality or passivity to equity-oriented social action.

ESTABLISHING THE MULTICULTURAL EDUCATION TERRAIN

Multicultural education as an idea and emerging practice began with the civil rights movement and for many years stayed on the educational horizon. After decades of curricular experimentation with multicultural education, the education community has seen multicultural education gradually migrate from the margins and secure its place in the mainstream. In the process, the movement has involved considerable debate. Multicultural education has come to mean different things to different people (Gay, 1994, p. 1). Gay argues that depending on how long one has been in the field, one will have a different conceptual understanding of its profundity and its application to schooling. Similarly, different academic lenses such as sociology, psychology, and economics will cast their own perspectives on the multicultural education panorama. Moreover, depending on the values and interests of those seeking to influence it, multicultural education has become an *esprit de force,* whether positive or negative, that is sweeping it through a whirlwind of passionate debate in both the popular and academic press (Asante, 1990; Asante & Ravitch, 1991; Banks, 1993a; Bloom, 1987; Cornbleth & Waugh, 1993; Hirsch, 1987; Ravitch, 1990, 1991–1992; Schlesinger, 1991; Simonson & Walker, 1988).

Competition for the Canon

Banks (1993a) noted that at least three different groups are participating in the canon debate on multicultural education:

the Western traditionalists, the multiculturalists, and the Afrocentrists. In addition, political interests on this debate have skewed the multicultural education playing field within the United States (Cornbleth & Waugh, 1993; Estrada & McLaren, 1993; Giroux, 1992). Those seeing multicultural education as constricting the democratic principles by which the United States was founded (i.e., Western traditionalists) argue that it is radical and divisive (Broudy, 1975; Hirsch, 1987). In like manner, the conservative restoration of the late 1970s, the 1980s, and now the 1990s, has ascribed to a multicultural education that is neonativist in practice. Critical theorists and neo-Marxists would argue that multicultural education through the lenses of a neonativist would be more reproductionist and would continue to deliver the status quo (Apple, 1990; Estrada & McLaren, 1993; Giroux, 1992).

Similarly, neonativists, according to Cornbleth and Waugh (1993), "would contain diversity and individualism by a standardized education—by national standards in core subjects, national assessment, and a *de facto* national curriculum" (p. 32). Cornbleth and Waugh maintained that the neonativist agenda has set the tone and terms of the [canon] debate to influence the course of school curricula into the twenty-first century. The focus of the neonativists' concerns, however, has been on the growing interests by multiculturalists and Afrocentrists to bring educational equity into all facets of the educational enterprise.

The California Case California is generally perceived as a trendsetter in the public and private sectors. It also became a prime target of the neonativists who attacked the California History-Social Science Framework report. The original draft of the framework was created by committee, rewritten by Charlotte Crabtree and Diane Ravitch, and adopted by the California State Board of Education in 1990 (Cornbleth & Waugh, 1993). The revision simply solidified the one-dimensional, uncritical, traditional view of history that has promoted a Eurocentric perspective (Hilliard, 1991–1992; Reed, 1993). According to the writers, however, the new framework emphasized a national identity and common values (California Department of Public Instruction, 1988). This is reminiscent of the New York City schools in the 1850s where (Apple, 1990):

[e]ducation was the way in which the community life, values, norms, and economic advantages of the powerful were to be protected. Schools could be the great engines of a moral crusade to make the children of the immigrants and the Blacks like "us." (p. 66)

In the tradition of Western traditionalism, early school leaders, and social engineers who molded schools to the present and persisting form, cultural differences were perceived and treated as illegitimate and problematic elements. They insisted on perpetuating a curricular order based on democratic foundations considered fundamental to Western democracy as reasoned through their ontological lenses (Ravitch, 1990; Ravitch & Finn, 1987; Schlesinger, 1991). Apple (1990), however, clearly asserted that curriculum manifests itself differentially depending on the student population, even within the same "curricular order":

If a set of students is seen as being prospective members of a professional and managerial class of people, then their schools and curriculum seem to be organized around flexibility, choice, inquiry, etc. If, on the other hand, students' probable destinations are seen as that of semiskilled or unskilled workers, the school experience tends to stress punctuality, neatness, habit formation, and so on. (p. 65)

These differences were the "tip of an iceberg made up of waters containing mostly impurities and immorality" (Apple, 1990, p. 66). Western traditionalists' present rationale stratifies, mismeasures, and tracks students, especially those who come from ethnically, radically, and linguistically distinct groups (Gamoran, 1990; Gamoran & Berends, 1987; Gould, 1981; Oakes, 1985, 1990).

The New York Case In 1987, the New York State Education Department was in the process of constructing its own social studies curriculum. The New York experience greatly differed, if not in results, at least in process. The task force's first report, *A Curriculum for Inclusion,* was met with a critical fury of reaction to its alleged inflammatory language and its limited inclusion of whites (one) and historians in the original task force. It was ridiculed for antagonizing the major ethnic groups (Cornbleth & Waugh, 1993).

The final report, *One Nation, Many Peoples: A Declaration of Cultural Interdependence* (New York State Department of Education, 1991), recognized the social diversity within the United States. Its authors acknowledged the importance of civic-mindedness and the centrality of "developing awareness and knowledge of America as a multicultural society, and of a multicultural world, past and present; engendering civic responsibility within this context; and helping develop the tools necessary for critical thinking, reflective reading, deliberate writing, and social action" (p. 7).

The seven guiding principles embraced by the committee are democracy, diversity, economic and social justice, globalism, ecological balance, ethics and values, and the individual and society. Cornbleth and Waugh (1993) acknowledged that the document recognized inequities in U.S. society. In wanting to provide a balanced view of the document Cornbleth and Waugh (1993) admitted that "[i]t is not a radical document—but it can be seen as undermining the conventional 'heroes and contributions' approach to school history, and as a challenge to California's grand immigrant narrative" (p. 35).

As multicultural education has moved from the bungalows to the main building, its new presence has fomented an upsurge of debate. Banks (1993c) represents a concern for a multicultural curriculum and summarizes this stance, stating, "the curriculum should be reformed so that it will more accurately reflect the histories and cultures of ethnic groups and women" (p. 4). In contrast, the Afrocentrists "maintain that African culture and history should be placed at the center of the curriculum to motivate African American students to learn and to help all students to understand the important role that Africa has played in the development of Western civilization" (Banks, 1993c, p.4).

Multicultural Education as Nonneutral and Polemical

At stake in the deliberations within our educational community is the notion of truth. The education enterprise is not neutral (Apple, 1986). Thus, in this case, multicultural education creates a duality of sorts, a centric force that simultaneously creates detachment, energy, resistance and coercion, and repercussions based on how reality is apprehended and what and whose knowledge will be valued. Will reality be gauged as one that is single, tangible, and fragmented, or will it be gauged as multiple, constructed, and holistic (Lincoln & Guba, 1985)? In addition, will knowledge value be based on hegemonic power reached through coercive consensus (Apple, 1986), or will it be based on unfolding democratic principles that mirror the diverse and pluralistic society we now experience?

Given that educational systems now accept the interdependence of everyday reality and the valuing of knowledge, one point becomes clear in the multicultural education discourse—a holistic approach is needed. Further knowledge construction must impact ontological and epistemological hypotheses that mirror the diverse and pluralistic communities that schools serve. Holism "implies that a phenomenon cannot be understood by reducing it to smaller units; it can be appreciated only by viewing it as a nonlinear process, an integrated whole" (Kincheloe & Steinberg, 1993, p. 313). We will ground our presuppositions by way of a critical constructivist perspective (Guba, 1992; Kincheloe & Steinberg, 1993; Lincoln & Guba, 1985; O'Loughlin, 1992). Having declared this perspective as our own focus (and as authority laden as it may be), this chapter simultaneously faces our positivist selves, an identity that is integral to our schooling and deeply embedded in the English language (Reddy, 1979).

Guba (1992) states that the postpositivist paradigm enjoys hegemony. This chapter disputes this claim. An inspection of our fragmented school structures and of how teachers and students think, as manifested in the metaphor of the factory school, bears this out (Sizer, 1984, 1992). There are educational oases that exude goodness, responsibility, and caring as well as academic standards for all students that far exceed the norms of everyday schooling (Lightfoot, 1983; Meier, 1987). However, in the common school culture, the modernist, positivist paradigm continues to maintain its hegemony. Educators, in response to the reproductive and segmented constructs of modernism, are rethinking and reconstructing their teaching realities by demanding of themselves a new language requiring more appropriate metaphors that apply a critical, constructivist stance. Many educators, however, find it difficult to wean themselves from their own modernist schooling (Gardner, 1991). Others have made a decisive leap that has brought hope and possibility to the educational enterprise (Apple, 1990; Cornbleth, 1990; Macedo, 1993). Nonetheless, it may be a mistake totally to reject modernism, because its roots contain progressive and democratic features (Giroux, 1991; Kincheloe & Steinberg, 1993) on which postmodernity must build. Multicultural education that draws on the postmodern provides insights into "the failure of reason, the tyranny of grand narratives, the limitations of science, and the repositioning of relationships between dominant and subordinate cultural groups" (Kincheloe & Steinberg, 1993, p. 296).

Consensus Building and the Constructing of Truth

The following section assembles important presuppositions in the multicultural education landscape as configured by Christine Sleeter (1989) and Sonia Nieto (1994), two important writers in the field of multicultural education. Their works illustrate many of the issues that have evolved as multicultural education has become part of the educational terrain and will be used to propel considerations of consensus building and truth constructing. These issues have catapulted multicultural education into multilayered paradigmatic structures that may assist in the reform of education in the 1990s and well into the first decade of the 2000s.

Sleeter (1989) argues that multicultural education serves as a form of resistance to oppression. Although she expected little support from the conservative right, she was not expecting to encounter "dismissal by many radical educators" (p. 51) of multicultural education as radical educators have joined in mounting a "challenge to oppression in society and schooling" (p. 51). Sleeter contends that (1) radical theorists have failed to take multicultural education seriously, and (2) multicultural education has been misrepresented as a field that has come into its own right and requires continuing clarification as it develops. As Sleeter reviewed the critique that targeted multicultural educators in the U.S. during the mid to late 1980s, she found two overarching concerns: (1) that multicultural education proponents sidestep the real issues multicultural education should endeavor to address (i.e., racism), and (2) that the structure of multicultural education is serving as a vehicle for "social control rather than for social change" (p. 53). Sleeter (1989) argues that such disagreements have oversimplified the field of multicultural education, creating caricatures of misdirection, and that it would be more "productive to identify ways in which the field works to challenge oppression, and to amplify and develop those dimensions of thought and practice" (p. 53).

Multicultural education is not intellectually stagnant. On the contrary, it is subject to ensuing internal debates. Sleeter (1989) invited radical educators to work with, rather than against, the multicultural education advocates.

Five areas of complexity make multicultural education unique in the United States. First, its genesis in the United States is unique when compared to multicultural education in Britain, Australia, or Canada. Second, based on her earlier work coauthored with Carl Grant (Grant & Sleeter, 1988a), Sleeter (1989) distinguishes among five different multicultural education approaches: (1) teaching the culturally different, (2) human relations, (3) single-group studies, (4) American multicultural education, and (5) multicultural education and social reconstructionism. Each approach has a unique theoretical and philosophical orientation, yet qualifies under the umbrella of multicultural education. Third, critics and educators from all levels must carefully differentiate between the deep theoretical constructs and the surface, often haphazard, application of those constructs. Fourth, several classifications of culture were made when advocating a multicultural perspective (i.e., "race and ethnicity; race, ethnicity, and gender; race, ethnicity, and language; and multiple forms of diversity" [Sleeter, 1989, p. 56]). Fifth, Sleeter argued strongly that multicultural education using the human relations approach may create the inroads to genuine school reform all multicultural education educators seek, especially as so many white educators (the majority of the teaching force) provide the schooling experiences for majority and minority students. Sleeter (1989) stated:

While no Human Relations educator in Wisconsin or Minnesota would argue that this work sufficiently resolves institutional discrimination in either state's education system—indeed it only begins to address it— the requirement has created considerable space in teacher education programs for addressing oppression and institutional racism. And this has been accomplished by appealing to white educators and legislators in language they would listen to. Had this requirement been articulated within the language of antiracist education, it probably would not have become institutionalized. Paradoxically, while terms such as "Human Relations" can be criticized for depoliticizing race relations, use of such terms can be politically quite effective. (p. 57)

In Sleeter's (1989) holistic view, multicultural education is a form of "resistance to oppressive social relationships. It represents resistance by educators to white dominance over racial minority groups through education, and (to many) to male dominance" (p. 59). She affirms that the field "needs to speak to oppression and struggle today much more explicitly than it did in its inception" (p. 59). Notwithstanding, the common interpretation of multicultural education has lagged behind the changes in the political context. What changed was how multicultural education is delivered to teachers: from an angry polemic about historically rooted racism to a more practice-oriented approach. Teachers are now asked to examine their own ethnic cultures as part of their orientation. "The assumption is that white teachers will see that the needs, feelings, and experiences of racial minority groups are not so very different from their own" (Sleeter, 1989, p. 62). Reflecting on multicultural education in the 1990s, Sleeter (1989) advises:

the field must develop in ways that are consonant with its original mission: to challenge oppression, and to use schooling as much as possible to help shape a future America that is more equal, democratic, and just, and that does not demand conformity to one cultural norm. And it must reaffirm its radical and political nature. (p. 63)

Sleeter (1989) suggested five tasks germane to this review that further demarcate multicultural education's theoretical grounding. The first calls for multicultural education theorists, "to articulate more clearly what social changes are desired, and to clarify the relative importance of addressing individual prejudice and stereotyping versus inequality among groups" (p. 63). The second task consists in "delineating exactly who is struggling against whom over what, and developing strategies to promote solidarity and a clear sense of an agenda for social action" (p. 65). The third task emphasizes creating organizational structures to promote multicultural education, such as the creation of the National Association for Multicultural Education (NAME), as well as the incorporation of multicultural education principles into working documents used for accreditation of teacher education programs (i.e., NCATE Standards and Indicators, state curriculum frameworks) and into mission and goal statements of professional organizations. The fourth task asks readers to confront the politics of social change and in turn, create related practices for the classroom. The final task stresses the need to incorporate multicultural education into all facets of the educational enterprise.

Nieto (1994) expresses the bewilderment now apparent in the field of multicultural education: "From classrooms to state boards of education, from national news rooms to the sanctuaries of intellectual discourse, the dilemmas, and pitfalls of multicultural education are everywhere discussed" (p. 1). Nieto summarized the criticisms multicultural education has received since the mid- to late 1980s by both the political left and the political right. The former has ridiculed the movement for its romantic optimism "in the face of persistent structural inequalities" (p. 1); the latter has criticized the movement for derailing the Western traditionalists' canon from its absolute dominance. Nieto (1994) considered the most prevalent criticisms, embarked on explaining them from different ideological perspectives, and ended by reframing multicultural education as a concept into a more critical and comprehensive one that captures and responds to the several critiques. In revisiting the assaults laid on multicultural education from critics on the right, Nieto revealed that those critics have substantially ignored the array of writings in multicultural education and have instead focused their criticism on explosive examples of what is popularly perceived as multiculturalism rather than on the multicultural education of the everyday that manifests itself in a variety of classrooms. Nieto (1994) argued that what is at stake are epistemological frameworks that seem to approach truth.

The critics from the left argue that multicultural education has developed a discourse of pluralism that has allowed general meritocracy to exist. The left, therefore, questions "the superficiality and criticizes it for not taking responsibility for exploring the political dimensions of education" (Nieto, 1994, p. 5). Of vast importance here, and what Nieto skillfully decenters, is the traditional epistemology (i.e., knowledge that is valued by the dominant perspective). This epistemology traditionally has supported meritocracy and in turn, has been critically analyzed by the left who argue that such knowledge has been from a single-minded perspective that greatly delimits the possibilities of multicultural education that embody difference as well as other truths.

Schooling, Truth, and Multicultural Education

Following Foucault's (1979) insights, McLaren (1989) describes truth, whether it is educational, scientific, religious, or legal, as not a set of discovered laws but that which must be understood within the realms of power and knowledge relations and which somehow correspond with the real. Truth cannot be known except through its effects. Truth, argued McLaren (1989), is relational and depends on history, cultural context, and relations of power operative in a given society, discipline, and institution. Truth and knowledge within a learning and teaching context become inextricably bonded where knowledge should be analyzed to determine whether it is oppressive or exploitive, not whether it is true or false (Maxcy, 1992). Popkewitz (1990) argued that:

Learning and teaching, as well, have social implications that are more than the measurement of achievement or the mastery of concepts. Schooling is an institution whose pedagogy and patterns of conduct are continually related to larger issues of social production and reproduction. In this context, pedagogical practice is a form of social regulation in which particular social knowledge is selected and cast for children to guide their everyday lives; yet the social differentiations in the larger society make school knowledge not equally accessible or equally available for all who come to school. (pp. 48–49)

Truth, then, is socially constructed and largely based by those in power who initiate an ontology and epistemology judged necessary and important to the survival and establishment of the group. Moreover, depending on class and ethnic differentiations that are socially constructed by those in power, cultural capital that allows for economic advancement is controlled (Giroux, 1983). "Control is exercised as well through the forms of meaning the school distributes. That is, the 'formal corpus of school knowledge' can become a form of social and economic control" (Apple, 1990, p. 63). Schools, then, not only control people but also, in effect, control, maintain, and legitimate epistemological contexts—"The knowledge that 'we all must have,' schools confer cultural legitimacy on the knowledge of specific groups" (Apple, 1990, p. 64). Truth within the teaching and learning context of schools emerges not as one objective view "but rather as the composite picture of how people think about the institution and each other" (Bogdan & Taylor, 1975, p. 11). Drawing on a qualitative research stance, Bogdan and Taylor (1975) maintain that truth is comprised of several perspectives from administrators, faculty, support staff, outsiders, volunteers, custodial staff, the larger community, and family.

A multicultural education curriculum based on truth, argues Hilliard (1991–1992), would be a pluralistic curriculum where:

The primary goal of a pluralistic curriculum process is to present a truthful and meaningful rendition of the whole human experience. This is not a matter of ethnic quotas in the curriculum for 'balance;' it is purely and simply a question of validity. Ultimately, if the curriculum is centered in truth, it will be pluralistic, for the simple fact is that human culture is the product of the struggles of all humanity, not the possession of a single racial or ethnic group. (p. 13)

Without addressing multicultural education per se, Hilliard (1991–1992) argues for curriculum equity. He supports multicultural education by addressing curriculum that must be equitably distributed, with high-quality instruction, and comes to the realization that academic content is not neutral, "nor is the specific cultural content of any ethnic group universal in and of itself" (p. 13). In contrast, Bullard (1991–1992) perceives a lack of tolerance among some multiculturalists, a need to transcend moral relativism that distorts basic issues of fairness and common sense, the need for cultural differences to be expressed "within the context of a nation with laws" (p. 6), and a real danger of stereotyping inherent to a multicultural perspective. Such generalizations may breed race-based expectations that model prejudice and intolerance.

These disparate recent developments illustrate the forces that will infuse multicultural education into all facets of the educational enterprise. The following developments indicate the direction of multicultural education.

Multicultural Education and the Social Construction of the Everyday

Utmost to the evolution of the multicultural education is that it is bound to the social reality that is part of institutions within the state (Apple, 1986). This situation has led to the canon debate—the latest controversy in multicultural education. That is, within the field there is an ideological battle over which canon will reign. Apple (1986) addressed the shortcomings of overusing the concept of hegemony to explain cultural and economic reproduction. This view does not, however, preclude its use as we begin to understand its implications in multicultural education. Depending on who delivers the message, multicultural education becomes political (i.e., hegemony is not free-floating). Apple argued that hegemony is not an accomplished social fact but rather a process where a dominant group and/or class manages to "win the active consensus over whom they rule" (p. 29). Overwhelmingly, the institutions within the state (i.e., schools) are the sites of racial group, gender, and class interaction and conflict, where those in power must either force or cajole many contending groups. In this manner, an institution maintains its own legitimacy but not without integrating "many of the interests of allied and even opposing groups under its banner" (Apple, 1986, pp. 29–30). In turn, the whole process involves compromise, conflict, and active struggle to maintain hegemony.

Multicultural education represents a significant challenge and threat to the established hegemony proposed by Western traditionalists. Many authors in the field are addressing the pervasive dominant hegemony fostered and maintained by institutions and schools where learners from diverse backgrounds function on a daily basis. All writers in multicultural education (and to a lesser degree, the Western traditionalists) are establishing their work within the reality of a diverse and pluralistic society.

The diversity and the pluralism encountered in the everyday serve as the temporal structures that determine how multicultural education will be constructed in the world of everyday life in the 1990s and well into the twenty-first century (Berger & Luckmann, 1967). They argue that:

To exaggerate the importance of theoretical thought in society and history is a natural failing of theorizers. It is then all the more necessary to correct this intellectualistic misapprehension. The theoretical formulations of reality, whether they be scientific or philosophical or even mythological, do not exhaust what is "real" for the members of a society. Since this is so, the sociology of knowledge must first of all concern itself with what people "know" as "reality" in their everyday, non- or pre-theoretical lives. In other words, common sense "knowledge" rather than "ideas" must be the central focus for the sociology of knowledge. It is precisely this "knowledge" that constitutes the fabric of meanings without which no society could exist. (p. 15)

Berger and Luckmann's (1967) concept of the "common sense knowledge" of "everyday life" (p. 15) refers to multicultural authors who belong to the postwar generation and started working as professionals in the 1950s and who continue active professional involvement through the present. This era is "*located* within a much more comprehensive history and this 'location' decisively shapes [the social context]" (Berger & Luckmann, 1967, p. 28) and, in turn, the polemics of multicultural education.

Daily life imposes not only prearranged sequences on the agenda of any single day but also itself on reality as a whole. Berger and Luckmann (1967) insist that everyday life retains its accent of reality only within a temporal structure. Discussing, researching, and writing about and for multicultural education are encounters with the everyday social context of which each of us, including the children we serve in our schools, is a part. Hence, as we reveal the multicultural education literature we are, in essence, reentering the reality of everyday life (Berger & Luckmann, 1967) with all its complexity and its very real diversity and plurality.

UNFOLDING THE EMERGING PRINCIPLES OF NATURALIST MULTICULTURAL EDUCATION

Multicultural education is a complex phenomenon that requires educators to apprehend the ontological and epistemological complexities of diverse and pluralistic contexts. An inquiry perspective is needed to provide the lenses and resulting foci to comprehend fully multicultural education and all its manifestations. The naturalist paradigm (Lincoln & Guba, 1985) can serve as a relevant and useful guide for the student of culture and cultural dynamics, the teacher of students in a multicultural education course, and the teacher educator responsible for the supply and quality of future teachers. The naturalist axioms purported by Lincoln and Guba (1985) address reality, truth, and their relation to the knower. They provide a framework for (1) gaining realistic perspectives on cultural groups and their social contexts, (2) understanding our own impact on the contexts we encounter and investigate, (3) formulating informed and viable options and alternatives about the many ethnic and cultural groups that populate our society, and (4) respecting the histories, perceptions, and practices of these groups. This framework may guide us in viewing differences and commonalities as well as specifics and generalities not only among cultural groups but also regarding our understanding of individuals and their uniqueness.

Table 33.1 illustrates five guiding positions for the naturalist axioms as elaborated by Lincoln and Guba (1985, p. 37) that guide our framework. Table 33.1 portrays the five axioms as guided by the positions. Lincoln and Guba remind us that "[a]xioms may be defined as a set of undemonstrated (and indemonstrable) 'basic beliefs' accepted by convention or established by practice as the building blocks of some conceptual or theoretical structure or system" (p. 33). They provide the example of Euclidean geometry. Euclid formalized the *rules of thumb* used by the land surveyors. These rules were not proven, yet they were known by and were valid for all.

These authors have applied the naturalist paradigm to a multicultural education framework (see column three of Table 33.1), creating a naturalist approach to address the multicultural education literature. Guba (1990) commented that "[t]he term 'naturalistic' inquiry [was] often used in the past to denote what . . . is called 'constructivist' inquiry" (p. 22). The concept naturalistic is identified by Guba with a paradigm while the term natural is identified with methodology (i.e., the doing part of a paradigm). The authors consider it consistent with our method of inquiry. In addition, democracy and social action are also part of the multicultural education conceptual terrain that takes seriously "quality, justice, freedom, and difference" (Giroux, 1992, p. 154). Giroux believes in reclaiming the progressive notions of the "'public' in public schooling so that education can become a real public service" (p. 155). In addition to democracy, some basic beliefs in multicultural education have placed

TABLE 33.1. Multicultural Education Applications of the Naturalist Paradigm

Axioms	Naturalist Paradigm	Multicultural Education Applications
Nature of reality	Realities as multiple, constructed, and holistic	Cultural pluralism as societal goal; teachers as guides to valuing multiple sources and interpretations of knowledge; teacher racism, expectations of student achievement; nonreductionist; cultural pluralism not merely a pedagogical mechanism for assimilation
Knower and the known	Knower and known are interactive and inseparable	Teachers' backgrounds affect the curriculum; the canon wars; students' backgrounds/beliefs affect the curriculum; multiple voices are valued; learning styles, cultural styles
Possibility of generalization	Idiographic, not nomothetic—only time- and context-bound working hypotheses are possible	Understanding other cultures as complex, dynamic; using case studies, personalized approaches; process of continuous learning; interactive approaches; cultural generalizations filtered through personal interpretations
Possibility of causal linkages	All entities are in state of mutual simultaneous shaping; impossible to distinguish causes from effects	Multiple explanations for events, for at-risk status; minimize blaming; seek multiple factors; process management
Role of values	Inquiry as value bound	"Policy option"; reflective practice by teachers regarding their own beliefs, backgrounds, and their explicit impact on learners; guide the learner in understanding biases of sources, including those of teachers; question the knowledge filters; value the multiple literacies; inductive approaches

Source: Adapted from Lincoln & Guba, 1985.

it in the forefront of many educational discourses, causing the entire educational enterprise to take notice. The mainstream reform literature was quick to incorporate concepts and practices from the multicultural education literature. However, these were used to redefine learning and teaching issues without addressing multicultural education explicitly.

The reader must realize that when Lincoln and Guba (1985) spoke to each of the five axioms, they contrasted the naturalist paradigm to the positivist paradigm. It is beyond the scope of this chapter to describe the positivist paradigm. This chapter presumes that positivism and multicultural education are on opposite sides of the ideological and theoretical continuums. This section addresses each axiom and its implications and applications to multicultural education.

Axiom 1: The Nature of Reality (Ontology)

Multiple constructed realities can be studied only holistically; inquiry into these multiple realities inevitably will diverge (each inquiry raises more questions than it answers) so that prediction and control are unlikely outcomes although some level of understanding can be achieved (Lincoln & Guba, 1985, p. 37).

The multicultural education literature assumes that our society is comprised of many cultural and ethnic and racial groups, gender groups and preferences, class differentiations, age groups, exceptionalities, and religions. These factors were assessed and integrated into the educational arena through multicultural education literature. For example, the Sadker and Sadker (1993) research on gender bias provided an integral perspective to addressing gender stereotypes and discrimina-

tion, ability grouping practices in the math and science classrooms, class, cultural issues, and the implications of gender classifications. It provided insights into how daily learning and teaching may be improved. On a different magnitude, Bull et al. (1992) asserted that the various groups within our national borders are variant and dynamic. Such cultural expressions are to be understood, not reduced, to cultural characteristics, at best, or to stereotypes, at worst. In the same vein, intercultural exploration is valued without the compelling need for firm answers about cultural characteristics. On the one hand, multiculturalists stipulate that the discovery of cultural expressions and preferences are valued; and, on the other hand, prediction and external control of cultural destinies are not options for consideration. Moreover, cultural differences often lead to conflict over ethics and values, some of which are often irreconcilable. When educators are faced with such dilemmas they must decide whether to seek conflict resolution or merely to appreciate the conflicts and their cultural genesis (Bull et al., 1992).

Multicultural theorists often speak to these encounters and the necessity for all educators to make sense of them. Examples of constructed realities that are central to and sometimes peripheral to the multicultural education literature are cultural stereotypes, teacher expectations, student self-concept, gender, ability groupings, schooling and institutional structures, equality and inequality, sociocultural contexts, socioeconomic contexts, racism, lingualism, ageism, and homophobia (Aboud, 1987; Allington, 1991; Banks, 1993b; Cárdenas & First, 1985; Comer, 1989; Díaz, Moll, & Mehan, 1986; Erickson, 1987; Fine, 1991; Grant & Secada, 1990; Grant & Sleeter, 1988b; Hilliard, 1990; Kozol, 1991; Ladson-Billings, 1992; Nieto, 1992; Oakes, 1986a,

1986b; Oakes & Lipton, 1990; Ogbu, 1987; Trueba, 1989; Walsh, 1987).

Axiom 2: The Relationship of Knower to Known (Epistemology)

"The inquirer and the 'object' of inquiry interact to influence one another; knower and known are inseparable" (Lincoln & Guba, 1985, p. 37). To comprehend fully the discourse of multicultural education, it is impossible not to consider the various implicit and explicit interactions that result because of all the individuals grounded in the social context of the everyday. Mainstream educators and educational researchers traditionally have broken down and dichotomized many of the multicultural issues (e.g., race, class, gender, exceptionalities, and age) into distinct categories of inquiry. Generally, their approach is psychometric and does not consider the importance of cumulative interactions of class, race, and gender. In actuality it

has involved a powerful consolidation and naturalization of methods of quantification and measurement, the predominance of positivistic empiricist approaches to the analysis of educational and social phenomena, and the steady incorporation of mainstream research into establishment policies and agendas. Mainstream research has too often chosen a recourse to a genetic epistemology, grounding its hypotheses and findings ultimately in biology and "science." Its theories have usually cast the individual learner as the object of scientific/psychological inquiry. (McCarthy & Apple, 1988b, pp. 11–12)

The inquirer and the object of inquiry have been studied as distinct entities, as if such interactions do not influence one another.

Multicultural education, on the other hand, stipulates the mutual interaction and learning among members of different groups (Nieto, 1992, 1994; Rivera & Poplin, in press; Sleeter & McLaren, in press). Members of the studied culture change and at the same time create a new mainstream. They also change the inquirer. This phenomenon emphasizes the importance of introspection for researchers and theorists, as their perceptions of their own culture and identity affect conclusions about the culture and identity of the participants.

The separation of the knower from the known can also be found in the discourse of white racism. Scheurich (1993) argued that whites apply an individualized perspective to racism and deny their own racism based on the absence of overtly racist behavior. They deny that metaphorically and psychologically racism may be part of their everyday life.

Axiom 3: The Possibility of Generalization

"The aim of inquiry is to develop an idiographic body of knowledge in the form of 'working hypotheses' that describe the individual case" (Lincoln & Guba, 1985, p. 38). This axiom applies to both the cultural mainstream and cultures of the other. Ethnographies, case studies, and other qualitative approaches engender a more accurate understanding of the educational enterprise. Working hypotheses presume the interactive and dynamic evolution of all cultures (Trueba, Rodriguez, Zou, &

Cintrón, 1993). In turn, conclusions about the dynamics of the teaching and learning processes are reached through inductive and contextual investigations. These approaches may be more accurate and useful than ones emerging from a priori premises about teachers and learners within the context of schooling. This axiom avoids stagnant characterizations of a culture and the unrealistic romanticizing of its history. Rather, it stresses the need to accept cultural change and adaptation as necessary for that culture to continue.

Axiom 4: The Possibility of Causal Linkages

"All entities are in a state of mutual simultaneous shaping so that it is impossible to distinguish causes from effects" (Lincoln & Guba, 1985, p. 38). The complex nature of diversity in a pluralistic society necessitates rethinking and reformulating the different realities (Macedo, 1993) that include dominant and subservient structures, the perceptions of the native versus the perceptions of the immigrant, and the everyday happenings of a majority group compared to the everyday happenings of a minority group. These interactions mutually contaminate and enrich, and thus lead to new intricate and unpredictable experiences. The false assumption regarding the effective delivery model in the school reform movement of the late 1980s is an example. Such an assumption often ignores the social contexts of student learning as a factor (Fine, cited in Weiner, 1993, p. 86). Fine states, "The first part emphasizes the ways in which schools may perpetuate inequalities directly, in that messages distributed through schools are linked to student background characteristics" (in McCarthy & Apple, 1988, pp. 1–2).

Nieto (1992) provides a compelling argument for the "state of mutual simultaneous shaping." She posits that in ethnically distinct students, "underachievement is caused by school structures because they reproduce a system that is racist and classist and/or by cultural incompatibilities between the home and the school" (p. 192). Such thinking, Nieto (1992) believes:

provide[d] a more cogent analysis of academic failure by placing schools in a political and social context. However, these analyses, too, are not wholly satisfactory because they can fall into mechanistic explanations of dynamic factors. Such theories fail to explain why some ethnic groups have generally succeeded in school in spite of striking cultural incompatibilities or why some schools in poor communities are extraordinarily successful in spite of tremendous odds. (p. 192)

Mutual simultaneous shaping is also apparent in how ethics unfold within a multicultural education environment. Bull et al. (1992) brought to the multicultural education discourse ethics and its impact on diversity. They discussed the correctness of ethical decisions based on acceptable and tolerable values coupled with practices that surface from cultural contact and conflict within a multicultural society. All these point to the complexity and the mutual simultaneous shaping that will undoubtedly occur and that are part of the multicultural education terrain.

Axiom 5: The Role of Values in Inquiry (Axiology)

Inquiry is value-bound in at least five ways, captured in the corollaries that follow (Lincoln & Guba, 1985):

Corollary 1: Inquiries are influenced by inquirer values as expressed in the choice of a problem, evaluation, or policy option and in the framing, bounding, and focusing of that problem, evaluation, or policy option.

Corollary 2: Inquiry is influenced by the choice of the paradigm that guides the investigation into the problem.

Corollary 3: Inquiry is influenced by the choice of the substantive theory utilized to guide the collection and analysis of data and in the interpretation of findings.

Corollary 4: Inquiry is influenced by values inherent in the context.

Corollary 5: With respect to Corollaries 1 through 4, inquiry is either value resonant (reinforcing or congruent) or value dissonant (conflicting). Problem, evaluation, or policy option, paradigm, theory, and context must exhibit congruence (value resonance) if the inquiry is to produce meaningful results.

Wong (1994) states that:

[e]ducational inequality remains a major challenge to policymakers as our nation prepares to enter the twenty-first century. As social institutions, public schools are shaped by the deleterious effects of poverty, family disorganizations, and racial and cultural isolation. Inequality in the life chances of children growing up in different socioeconomic environments is clearly evident in the schools they attend. . . . Inequity in education resources has been perpetuated by the design and practice of our governing system. (p. 257)

Furthermore, two particularly pervasive causes of this inequity are (1) the functional fragmentations of the three levels of government, and (2) the high degree of jurisdictional fragmentation at the local level. Wong (1994) concludes that:

federal goals in social redistribution can be frustrated by local educational agencies. . . . The educational needs of the disadvantaged are not likely to be given high local priority; many districts continue to assign the least experienced teachers to remedial programs, distribute outdated curricula to poor schools, and maintain substandard equipment in the lower tracks . . . states' territorial equity policies can be tempered by the widening taxing capability between rich and poor districts. Enjoying their fiscal autonomy, rich districts have increased their school spending even when the state economy is in recession. As big-city systems turn into predominantly low-income, minority institutions, middle-class suburban districts quickly organize themselves to ensure that the state-aid allocation formula does not undermine their interests. The politics of fragmentation . . . tend to disburse state funds widely and have produced very limited success in reducing spending disparity among districts in industrialized states with a strong minority presence. (pp. 282–283)

Transparent in this quote is the dominance of privilege. Wong enriches the discussion by systematically illustrating the economic means of control and power in the distributions of school finances. However, he leaves the reader stranded by not firmly articulating that policies are created by fallible human agents. Central to the corollaries is the notion that policy based on scientific or nonscientific grounding for planning and reform is always contextually and culturally dependent. It may also be extended to the dynamics of class, race, and gender. Cultural membership of the policymakers has implications and the hu-

man agents' perspective will be shrouded in the paradigmatic complexities of class, race, and gender. Considering the philosophical controversy and the profound public policy implications surrounding the collection, allocation, distribution, and use of public funds, the axiological posture must include an ethical stance, that "contests racism, sexism, class exploitation, and other dehumanizing and exploitive social relations as ideologies and social practices that disrupt and devalue public life" (Giroux, 1983, p. 101). Furthermore, ethics become a continued engagement in which the "social practices of everyday life are interrogated in relation to the principles of individual autonomy and democratic public life—not as a matter received as truth but as a constant engagement" (Giroux, 1983, p. 102). Thus, the concept of value-laden personal commitment becomes integral to this axiom. Given the perspectives of Arvizu and Saravia-Shore (1990), Brown (1992), Nieto (1992), Ogbu (1990), and Sleeter (1992), clearly the agents for multicultural education must consider all the participants in the educational enterprise ranging from students to policymakers.

MULTICULTURAL ISSUES IN THE TEACHER EDUCATION CURRICULUM

In struggling to surpass the basic issues of definition, description, and direction, the research literature seeks meaning for multicultural education through attention to issues of personal engagement and curricular application. Educators and teacher educators increasingly are taking responsibility for the management of student and community diversity. This trend is expected as teacher demographics and student demographics move in opposite directions. Hidalgo and Huling-Austin (1993) discuss these quantitative discrepancies as part of the backdrop for teacher education's responsibility to provide a diversity-friendly curriculum for the preparation of interculturally competent teachers for Latino students in the Southwest. Hidalgo and Huling-Austin propose that qualitative issues also relate to the equitable supply of Latino teachers. They further warned that inappropriate assessments and curricula will undermine the noblest of minority teachers' outreach efforts. The personal responsibilities of K–12 teachers to provide an equitable classroom environment and a multiculturally literate curriculum cannot be divorced from teacher education's responsibility to attend to the quantitative and qualitative issues surrounding the *who* of teaching.

Zimpher and Ashburn (1992) approach the issue of the teacher education curriculum for a diverse society by focusing on (1) teacher parochialism and global interdependence, and (2) infusion versus add-on approaches to curricular diversification. Although not directly addressing the demographic discrepancy between teachers and students, they promote several beliefs to be embedded in the teacher education curriculum as a strategy for neutralizing the parochialism that emerges from teacher homogeneity.

The authors propose three beliefs to be infused in any teacher education program: (1) belief in the appreciation of diversity, (2) belief in the value of cooperation, and (3) belief in the importance of a caring community. As difficult as these affective qualities may be to assess in individuals, Zimpher and Ashburn (1992) compound the collective responsibility by emphasizing the importance of modeling these beliefs within our teacher education programs if we expect our prospective teachers to apply these successfully. "More specifically, we propose that teacher educators must first examine their own thinking for its parochial nature" (Zimpher & Ashburn, 1992, pp. 40–41).

The matter of personal investment in multicultural education extends across the ranks of professional educators at all levels of instruction. Teacher educators often have taken the lead in advocating school reform and increased teacher engagement in the public schools. While the call for reform and personal commitment has been extended to higher education, the struggles to incorporate multicultural education at that level has its own set of institutional complications.

Infusion Versus Add-On Approaches to Multicultural Teaching

The discussion over the specific content of a multicultural teacher education curriculum is active and diverse within the profession. Recent conference programs of the annual meetings of the Association of Teacher Educators and the American Association of Colleges for Teacher Education are replete with examples of multicultural curricula that claim to incorporate the ethnic, gender, and class diversity differences of their clientele's clientele. Banks (1994), Davidman and Davidman (1994), Gollnick and Chinn (1994), and Tiedt and Tiedt (1994) offer textbooks to guide the teacher educator in planning not only the content for diversity teaching but also the conceptual framework for implementing it with professional sincerity. Garibaldi (1992) outlines a series of general skills that prospective teachers should internalize during their preparation:

Thus, the teachers of today's culturally diverse classrooms must understand that there are differences between the sociological dimensions of 'culture' and 'class' as they prepare to teach; know how to plan and organize effective instructional situations, how to motivate students and manage their classrooms . . . in addition to being competent in the assessment of the academic strengths and weaknesses of all children; and learn how to encourage the cooperation of their students' families and communities in the conduct of their daily responsibilities. (p. 25)

Even among teacher educators who promote a context-sensitive multicultural curriculum for their students, there is an ongoing debate over the manner in which such a curriculum should be formatted. Zimpher and Ashburn (1992) criticize the traditional "add-on" treatment that diversity teaching receives in universities (p. 52). They promote, instead, an infusion approach that leads to true valuing of diversity implied in "an understanding of the broad array of differences among people and how these differences interact with subject matter and with teaching" (p. 52). They further admonish us that the continued peripheralization of this content "leads to social alienation and perpetuation of the existing parochialism" (p. 53).

Modeling an introspective approach to multicultural teaching will continue to challenge teacher educators regardless of the format used to incorporate it into the curriculum. Some

faculties prefer an add-on format because it concentrates the multicultural content in one or more courses to which specially prepared faculty members can be assigned. This format is especially useful in cases where a stable faculty group intends to protect a core curriculum composed of generic content. In cases in which institutional growth cannot match community demographic transformations, a stable faculty is unable to conduct a radical modification of its curriculum without jeopardizing their own positions or imposing drastic retooling demands on themselves. However, schools normally have the flexibility to add one or two specialized faculty members to teach diversity-related courses. This format allows the faculty to delegate multicultural education to these selected instructors and its content to a controlled set of competencies, whether integral or supplemental. In this model, multicultural education is treated as a subject area for which there is a discreet course and set of field experiences. Accreditation agencies can easily locate the competencies, experiences, and activities that are designated to multicultural education.

In the add-on approach, however, faculty in the core curriculum remain poised further to entrench their own content without significant multicultural adjustments. Assuming these faculty members continuously update their course materials to adapt to developments in their own fields, for them, developments in multicultural education remain material for the designated faculty to incorporate. Critics of this add-on approach consider it a segregation of subject matter from issues of cultural, linguistic, and contextual diversity. Prospective teachers perceive that institutional commitment to cultural pluralism is limited to its advocacy in one or two selected courses. Local school administrators observe the hypocrisy in an approach that seems to endorse the curricular ghettoization that their own schools are attempting to dismantle through heterogeneous groupings and school desegregation. If junior or part-time faculty are assigned to teach these special courses, a further level of subtle devaluing occurs. When selected instructors are identified with these courses, the assignment may become personalized and the offering may become subject to personnel availability, or worse yet, to faculty misassignment. Finally, in such a model, multicultural education is perceived primarily as discreet content that can be learned without necessarily internalizing a commitment to valuing the principles of multicultural education. Although the individual instructor may model an introspective approach to multicultural teaching, this format condones the continued peripheralization of multicultural education and creates a cynicism toward any introspection that prospective teachers may have experienced toward personal commitments to diversity-appropriate professional behavior.

Faculty seeking to model a genuine integration of diversity-appropriate teaching have a more formidable organizational challenge before them. Universitywide commitment to teacher education and multicultural education is the ideal context in which to infuse multicultural education across the curriculum. Within teacher education, this approach requires additional faculty members whose degrees and professional experiences prepare them for the special demands of diversity-appropriate teaching and curriculum development. However, it also requires a commitment by the established faculty to professional development in multicultural education. Contrary to the fears of some teacher educators, the commitment is to the integration of existing knowledge bases to the contexts of diversity and the principles of cultural pluralism. Faculty are not asked to replace their subject areas or their pedagogical areas with multicultural education. This would not only be unrealistic but inappropriate. All K–12 students need to learn reading, math, science, social studies, and physical education. Teachers should continue to learn these subjects and their related pedagogies. Faculty searches, professional development, and curricular integration should continue in these subjects. They should continue to be taught to promote critical thinking and subject mastery. Cooperative learning and experiential strategies should not be interrupted in the name of multicultural education. Quite appropriately, these goals and strategies are consistent with pedagogies that are egalitarian and emancipatory. Faculty who build multicultural education principles on their own knowledge bases will consider multicultural education not as retooling, but as enrichment. Successful curricular integration between subject areas and multicultural education will spread the responsibility for both across a team of faculty. This form of institutional commitment to multicultural education and professional development will communicate an important message of consensus about goals and values to prospective teachers.

Toward a Transformational Curriculum

Schoem, Frankel, Zuniga, and Lewis (1993) refer to higher education's struggle with the "linkages between knowledge and behavior, between understanding and action" (p. 8). They apply this discrepancy to higher education in general by eliciting a sense of "intellectual and personal responsibilities" (p. 8) for the multicultural learning that is achieved. In their own chapter, *The Meaning of Multicultural Teaching: An Introduction,* they present their book as "part of an ongoing process among university faculty to enhance teaching and learning in an increasingly interconnected multicultural society" (p. 1). They refer to the "three interconnected dimensions of multicultural teaching: content, process and discourse, and diversity of faculty and students" (p. 1). The implicit issues of power, conflict, and change communicate to the reader that the treatment of multicultural education extends well beyond the curricular and into the social contexts in which teaching and learning occur in higher education. Perhaps in anticipation of faculty apprehension about their designs for Western civilization, they feel compelled to reassure the reader that their "spirit of inclusiveness" (p. 2) encompasses a legitimate role for Western civilization within a diversified curriculum. Nonetheless, Schoem et al. (1993) assert their belief in an interconnected and transformational approach to multicultural teaching. They present a variety of inclusion patterns in their book as a framework for understanding the levels of curricular infusion. These stages of cultural transformation, reinforced by fellow scholars McIntosh (1991) and Schuster and Van Dyne (1985) range from information about ghettoization at the first stage to the fourth stage in which "there is a synergy of the course content, classroom process, and diversity among faculty and students that elevates understanding to a new level of depth and complexity" (p. 3).

The team work, the professional development, and the institutional commitment invested in the name of multicultural teacher education, educational counseling, special education, and school administration may easily be extended to other cross-curricular values and practices. When an institution and a faculty's mission articulate a commitment to a set of principles, whether to multicultural education or otherwise, the clientele is more confidently poised to internalize them as practices that carry personal meaning that can lead to the social impact that emancipatory multicultural education intends.

References

Aboud, F. E. (1987). The development of ethnic self-identification and attitudes. In J. S. Phinney & M. J. Rotheram (Eds.), *Children's ethnic socialization: Pluralism and development* (pp. 29–51). Newbury Park, CA: Sage.

Allington, R. L. (1991). Effective literacy instruction for at-risk children. In M. S. Knapp & P. M. Shields (Eds.), *Better schooling for the children of poverty* (pp. 9–30). Berkeley, CA: McCutchan.

Apple, M. W. (1986). *Teachers & texts: A political economy of class & gender relations in education.* New York: Routledge & Kegan Paul.

Apple, M. W. (1990). *Ideology and curriculum.* (2nd ed.). New York: Routledge.

Arvizu, S. F., & Saravia-Shore, M. (1990, August). Cross-cultural literacy: An anthropological approach to dealing with diversity. *Education and Urban Society, 22*(4), 364–376.

Asante, M. K. (1990). *Kemet, Afrocentricity, and knowledge.* Trenton, NJ: Africa World Press.

Asante, M. K., & Ravitch, D. (1991). Multiculturalism: An exchange. *The American Scholar,* 267–275.

Ayers, W. (1988). Young children and the problem of the color line. *Democracy and Education, 3*(1), 20–26.

Banks, J. A. (1991). Multicultural literacy and curriculum reform. *Educational Horizons, 69*(3), 136–140.

Banks, J. A. (1993a). The canon debate, knowledge construction and multicultural education. *Educational Researcher, 22*(5), 4–14.

Banks, J. A. (1993b). The culture wars, race and education. *National Forum, 73*(4), 39–41.

Banks, J. A. (1993c). Multicultural education: Historical development, dimensions, and practice. In L. Darling-Hammond (Ed.), *Review of research in education* (Vol. 19, pp. 3–50). Washington, DC: American Educational Research Association.

Banks, J. A. (1994). *An introduction to multicultural education.* Boston: Allyn & Bacon.

Banks, J. A., & Banks, C. A. (1989). *Multicultural education: Issues and perspective.* Boston: Allyn & Bacon.

Banks, J. A., & Banks, C. A. (1993). *Multicultural education: Issues and perspective* (2nd ed.). Boston: Allyn & Bacon.

Bennett, C. I. (1990). *Comprehensive multicultural education: Theory and practice.* Boston: Allyn & Bacon.

Berger, B. L., & Luckmann, T. (1967). *The social construction of reality: A treatise in the sociology of knowledge.* New York: Anchor.

Bloom, A. (1987). *The closing of the American mind: How higher education has failed democracy and impoverished the souls of today's students.* New York: Simon & Schuster.

Bogdan, R., & Taylor, S. J. (1975). *Introduction to qualitative research methods.* New York: Wiley.

Broudy, H. S. (1975). Cultural pluralism: New wine in old bottles. *Educational Leadership, 33,* 173–175.

Brown, C. E. (1992). Restructuring for a new America. In M. E. Dilworth (Ed.), *Diversity in teacher education* (pp. 1–22). San Francisco: Jossey-Bass.

Bull, B. L., Fruehling, R. T., & Chattergy, V. (1992). *The ethics of multicultural and bilingual education.* New York: Teachers College Press.

Bullard, S. (1991–1992). Sorting through the multicultural rhetoric. *Educational Leadership, 49*(4), 4–7.

California Department of Public Instruction. (1988). *History-social science curriculum framework.* History-Social Science Curriculum Framework and Criteria Committee.

Cárdenas, J. A., & First, J. M. (1985). Children at risk. *Educational Leadership, 43*(1), 5–8.

Code, L. (1991). *What can she know? Feminist theory and the construction of knowledge.* Ithaca, NY: Cornell University Press.

Colangelo, N., Dustin, D. L., & Foxley, C. H. (1985). *Multicultural nonsexist education: A human relations approach.* Dubuque, IA: Kendall/Hunt.

Comer, J. P. (1989). Racism and the education of young children. *Teachers College Record, 90,* 352–361.

Cornbleth, C. (1990). *Curriculum in context.* New York: Falmer Press.

Cornbleth, C., & Waugh, D. (1993, October). The great speckled bird: Education policy-in-the-making. *Educational Researcher, 22*(7), 31–37.

Cummins, J. (1992). Language proficiency bilingualism and academic achievement. In P. A. Richard-Amato & M. A. Snow (Eds.), *The multicultural classroom: Reading for content area teachers.* White Plains, NY: Longman.

Davidman, L., & Davidman, P. T. (1994). *Teaching with a multicultural perspective: A practical guide.* White Plains, NY: Longman.

Dewey, J. (1966). *Democracy and education.* New York: Free Press.

Díaz, S., Moll, L. C., & Mehan, H. B. (1986). Sociocultural resouces in instruction: A context specific approach. In California State Department of Education (Ed.), *Beyond language: Social and cultural factors in schooling language minority children* (pp. 187–230). Los Angeles: Evaluation, Dissemination and Assessment Center, California State University.

D'Souza, D. (1992). *Illiberal education: The politics of race and sex on campus.* New York: Vintage.

Erickson, F. (1987). Transformation and school success: The politics and culture of educational achievement. *Anthropology and Education Quarterly, 18*(4), 335–356.

Estrada, K., & McLaren, P. L. (1993). A dialogue on multiculturalism and democratic culture. *Educational Researcher, 22*(3), 27–33.

Fine, M. (1991). *Framing dropouts: Notes on the politics of an urban public high school.* Albany: State University of New York Press.

Foucault, M. (1979). Power and knowledge: Selected interviews and other writing, 1972–1977. In C. Gordon (Ed.), *Discipline and punish: The birth of the prison* (A. Sheridan [Trans.]). New York: Pantheon.

Gamoran, A. (1990). Instructional organizational practices that affect equity. In H. P. Baptiste, H. C. Waxman, J. Walker de Felix, & J. E. Anderson (Eds.), *Leadership, equity, and school effectiveness.* Newbury Park, CA: Sage.

Gamoran, A., & Berends, M. (1987). The effects of stratification in secondary schools: Synthesis of survey and ethnographic research. *Review of Educational Research, 57,* 415–435.

Gardner, H. (1991). *The unschooled mind: How children think and how schools should teach.* New York: Basic Books.

Garibaldi, A. M. (1992). Diversity in teacher education: New expectations. In M. E. Dilworth (Ed.), *Preparing teachers for culturally diverse classrooms.* San Francisco: Jossey-Bass.

Gay, G. (1994). A synthesis of scholarship in multicultural education. (Urban Monograph Series). Oakbrook, IL: North Central Regional Educational Laboratory.

Giroux, H. A. (1983). *Theory and resistance in education: A pedagogy for the opposition.* New York: Bergin & Garvey.

Giroux, H. A. (Ed.). (1991). *Postmodernism, feminism, and cultural politics: Redrawing educational boundaries.* Albany: State University of New York Press.

Giroux, H. A. (Ed.). (1992). *Border crossings: Cultural workers and the politics of education.* New York: Routledge.

Gollnick, D. M. (1992). Multicultural education: Policies and practices in teacher education. In C. A. Grant (Ed.), *Research and multicultural education: From the margins to the mainstream.* Washington, DC: Falmer.

Gollnick, D. M., & Chinn, P. C. (1986). *Multicultural education in a pluralistic society* (2nd ed.). Columbus: Merrill.

Gollnick, D. M., & Chinn, P. C. (1994). *Multicultural education in a pluralistic society* (4th ed.). Columbus: Merrill.

Gould, S. J. (1981). *The mismeasure of man.* New York: Norton.

Grant, C. A. (1992). *Research and multicultural education: From the margins to the mainstream.* Washington, DC: Falmer Press.

Grant, C. A., & Secada, W. G. (1990). Preparing teachers for diversity. In W. R. Houston (Ed.), *Handbook of research on teacher education* (pp. 403–422). New York: Macmillan.

Grant, C. A., & Sleeter, C. E. (1988a). *Making choices for multicultural education: Five approaches to race, class, and gender.* New York: Macmillan.

Grant, C. A., & Sleeter, C. E. (1988b). Race, class, and gender and abandoned dreams. *Teachers College Record, 90,* 19–40.

Guba, E. G. (1990). *The paradigm dialogue.* Newbury Park, CA: Sage.

Guba, E. G. (1992). Relativism. *Curriculum Inquiry, 22*(1), 17–23.

Harding, S. (1991). *Whose science? Whose knowledge? Thinking from women's lives.* Ithaca, NY: Cornell University Press.

Hidalgo, F., & Huling-Austin, L. (1993). Alternate teacher candidates: A rich source for Latino teachers in the future. *Reshaping teacher education in the Southwest: A response to the needs of Latino students and teachers.* Claremont, CA: Tomas Rivera Center.

Hilliard, A. G., III. (1990). Misunderstanding and testing intelligence. In J. I. Goodlad & P. Keating (Eds.), *Access to knowledge* (pp. 145–158). New York: College Entrance Examination Board.

Hilliard, A. G., III. (1991–1992). Why we must pluralize the curriculum. *Educational Leadership, 49*(4), 12–16.

Hirsch, E. D. (1987). *Cultural literacy: What every American needs to know.* Boston: Houghton Mifflin.

hooks, B., & West, C. (1991). *Breaking bread: Insurgent black intellectual life.* Boston: South End Press.

Kincheloe, J. L., & Steinberg, S. R. (1993). A tentative description of post-formal thinking: The critical confrontation with cognitive theory. *Harvard Educational Review, 63*(3), 296–320.

King, J. E., & Mitchell, C. A. (1990). *Black mothers to sons: Juxtaposing African American literature with social practice.* New York: Lang.

Kohl, H. (1993). The myth of "Rosa Parks, the tired." *Multicultural Education, 1*(2), 6–10.

Kozol, J. (1991). *Savage inequalities: Children in American schools.* New York: Crown.

Kuhn, T. S. (1970). *The structure of scientific revolutions* (2nd ed.). Chicago: The University of Chicago Press.

Ladson-Billings, G. (1992). Culturally relevant teaching: The key to making multicultural education work. In C. A. Grant (Ed.), *Research and multicultural education* (pp. 106–121). London: Falmer Press.

Lightfoot, S. L. (1983). *The good high school: Portraits of character and culture.* New York: Basic Books.

Lincoln, Y. S., & Guba, E. G. (1985). *Naturalistic inquiry.* Newbury Park, CA: Sage.

Lynch, J. (1986). *Multicultural education: Principles and practice.* London: Routledge & Kegan Paul.

Lynch, J. (1989). *Multicultural education in a global society.* New York: Falmer Press.

Macedo, D. P. (1993). Literacy for stupidification: The pedagogy of big lies. *Harvard Educational Review, 63*(2), 183–206.

Maxcy, S. J. (1992). *Educational leadership: A critical pragmatic perspective.* New York: Bergin & Garvey.

McCarthy, C., & Apple, M. W. (1988). Race, class, and gender in American educational research: Toward a nonsynchronous parallelism position. In L. Weis (Ed.), *Class, race, and gender in American education.* Albany: State University of New York Press.

McIntosh, P. (1991). Interactive phases of curricular and personal revision with regard to race. In J. Butler & J. Walter (Eds.), *Transforming the curriculum: Ethnic studies and women's studies.* Albany: State University of New York Press.

McLaren, P. (1989). *Life in schools.* New York: Longman.

Meier, D. (1987). Central park east: An alternative story. *Phi Delta Kappan, 88*(10), 753–757.

Minnich, E. K. (1990). *Transforming knowledge.* Philadelphia: Temple University Press.

National Council for Accreditation of Teacher Education (NCATE). (1982). *Standards for accreditation of teacher education.* Washington, DC: Author.

New York State Department of Education. (1991, June). *One nation, many peoples: A declaration of cultural interdependence.* Albany: Author.

Nieto, S. (1992). *Affirming diversity: The sociopolitical context of multicultural education.* White Plains, NY: Longman.

Nieto, S. (1994). From brown heroes and holidays to assimilationists' agendas: Reconsidering the critiques of multicultural education. In C. E. Sleeter & P. McLaren (Eds.), *Multicultural education, critical pedagogy and the politics of difference.* Albany: State University of New York Press.

Oakes, J. (1985). *Keeping track: How schools structure inequality* (4th ed.). Boston: Yale University Press.

Oakes, J. (1986a). Tracking and ability grouping: A structural barrier to access and achievement. In J. I. Goodlad & P. Keeting (Eds.), *Access to knowledge* (pp. 187–204). New York: College Board.

Oakes, J. (1986b). Tracking, inequality, and the rhetoric of reform: Why schools don't change. *Journal of Education, 168*(1), 60–80.

Oakes, J. (1990). *Multiplying inequalities: The effects of race, social class, and tracking on opportunities to learn mathematics and science.* Santa Monica, CA: Rand Corporation.

Oakes, J., & Lipton, M. (1990). Tracking and ability grouping: A structural barrier to access and achievement. In J. I. Goodlad & P. Keeting (Eds.), *Access to knowledge* (pp. 187–204). New York: College Board.

Ogbu, J. U. (1987). Variability in minority school performance: A problem in search of an explanation. *Anthropology and Education Quarterly, 18,* 312–334.

Ogbu, J. U. (1990, August). Understanding diversity: Summary comments. *Education and Urban Society, 22*(4), 425–429.

O'Loughlin, M. (1992, September). *Appropriate for whom? A critique of the culture and class bias underlying developmentally appropriate practice in early childhood education.* Paper presented to conference on Reconceptualizing Early Childhood Education: Research, Theory, and Practice, Chicago.

Perry, T., & Fraser, J. W. (1993). *Freedom's plow.* New York: Routledge.

Popkewitz, T. S. (1990). Whose future? Whose past?: Notes on critical theory and methodology. In E. G. Guba (Ed.), *The paradigm dialogue.* Newbury Park, CA: Sage.

Ramsey, P. G., Vold, E. B., & Williams, L. R. (1989). *Multicultural education: A source book.* New York: Garland.

Ravitch, D. (1990, September). The troubled road to California's history textbooks. *Los Angeles Times,* M5.

Ravitch, D. (1991–1992). A culture in common. *Educational Leadership, 49*(4), 8–11.

Ravitch, D., & Finn, C. E., Jr. (1987). *What do our 17-year-olds know?* New York: Harper & Row.

Ray, D. (1992). Modern inequality and the role of education. In D. Ray & D. H. Poonwassie (Eds.), *Education and cultural differences.* New York: Garland.

Reddy, M. J. (1979). The conduit metaphor—A case of frame conflict in our language about language. In A. Ortony (Ed.), *Metaphor and thought* (pp. 184–324). London: Cambridge University Press.

Reed, J. (1993). Choice, race, and truthful curriculum: An interview with Asa G. Hillard. *Multicultural Education, 1*(3), 12–14.

Rivera, J. A., & Poplin, M. (In press). Multicultural, critical, feminine, and constructive pedagogies seen through the lives of youth: A call for the revisioning of these and beyond: Toward a pedagogy for the next century. In C. E. Sleeter & P. McLaren (Eds.), *Multicultural education, critical pedagogy, and the politics of difference.* Albany: State University of New York Press.

Rosenau, P. M. (1992). *Post-modernism and the social sciences: Insights, inroads, and intrusions.* Princeton, NJ: Princeton University Press.

Sadker, M., & Sadker, D. (1993). *Failing at fairness.* New York: Scribner's.

Scheurich, J. J. (1993). Toward a white discourse on white racism. *Educational Researcher, 22*(8), 5–10.

Schlesinger, A. M. (1991). *The disuniting of America.* Monograph. Knoxville, TN: Whittle.

Schoem, D., Frankel, L., Zuniga, W., & Lewis, E. (1993). The meaning of multicultural teaching: An introduction. In D. Schoem, L. Zuniga, & E. Lewis (Eds.), *Multicultural teaching in the university.* Westport, CT: Praeger.

Schuster, M. R., & Van Dyne, S. R. (1985). Stages for curriculum transformation. In M. R. Schuster & S. R. VanDyne (Eds.), *Women's place in the academy: Transforming the liberal arts curriculum.* Totowa, NJ: Rowman and Allanheld.

Simonson, R., & Walker, S. (Eds.). (1988). *The graywolf annual five: Multicultural literacy.* Saint Paul, MN: Gray Wolf Press.

Sizer, T. R. (1984). *Horace's compromise: The dilemma of the American high school.* Boston: Houghton Mifflin.

Sizer, T. R. (1992). *Horace's school: Redesigning the American high school.* New York: Houghton Mifflin.

Sleeter, C. E. (1989). Multicultural education as a form of resistance to oppression. *Journal of Education, 171*(3), 51–71.

Sleeter, C. E. (Ed.). (1991). *Empowerment through multicultural education.* Albany: State University of New York Press.

Sleeter, C. E. (1992). Restructuring schools for multicultural education. *Journal of Teacher Education, 43*(2), 141–148.

Sleeter, C. E., & Grant, C. A. (1987). An analysis of multicultural education in the United States. *Harvard Educational Review, 57*(4), 421–444.

Sleeter, C. E., & McLaren, P. (in press). Introduction: Exploring connections to building a critical multiculturalism. In C. Sleeter & P. McLaren (Eds.), *Multicultural, critical pedagogy, and the politics of difference.* Albany: State University of New York Press.

Suzuki, B. H. (1977). Education and the socialization of Asian Americans: A revisionist analysis of the "model minority" thesis. *Amerasia Journal, 4*(2), 23–51.

Suzuki, B. H. (1980, April). *An Asian-American perspective on multicultural education: Implications for practice and policy.* Paper presented at the second annual conference of the National Association for Asian and Pacific American Education, Washington, DC.

Tiedt, P. L., & Tiedt, I. M. (1976). *Multicultural teaching: A handbook of activities, information and resources* (1st ed.). Boston: Allyn & Bacon.

Tiedt, P. L., & Tiedt, I. M. (1994). *Multicultural teaching: A handbook of activities, information and resources* (3rd ed.). Boston: Allyn & Bacon.

Trueba, H. T. (1989). *Raising silent voices: Educating the linguistic minorities for the 21st century.* New York: Newbury House.

Trueba, J. T., Rodriguez, C., Zou, Y., & Cintrón, J. (1993). *Healing multicultural America: Mexican immigrants rise to power in rural California*. Washington, DC: Falmer Press.

Walsh, C. (1987). Schooling and the civic exclusion of Latinos: Toward a discord of dissonance. *Journal of Education, 169,* 115–131.

Weiner, L. (1993). *Preparing teachers for urban schools: Lessons from thirty years of school reform*. New York: Teachers College Press.

Wong, K. K. (1994). Governance structure, resource allocation, and equity policy. In L. Darling-Hammond (Ed.), *Review of research in education* (pp. 157–289). Washington, DC: American Educational Research Association.

Zimpher, N. L., & Ashburn, E. A. (1992). Countering parochialism in teacher candidates. In M. E. Dilworth (Ed.), *Diversity in teacher education: New expectations* (pp. 40–41). San Francisco: Jossey-Bass.

·34·

THE CRISIS IN TEACHER EDUCATION

IN AMERICA

ISSUES OF RECRUITMENT AND RETENTION OF CULTURALLY DIFFERENT (MINORITY) TEACHERS

James B. Boyer
KANSAS STATE UNIVERSITY

H. Prentice Baptiste, Jr.
KANSAS STATE UNIVERSITY

Research in teacher education since the mid-1970s has focused on teachers' specific behaviors, on the knowledge base of traditional instructional practice, and on components of traditional basic "methods" of teaching the traditional subjects found in the elementary curriculum. At the same time, demographic pictures of American student populations are changing so rapidly that few agencies have been able to upgrade themselves at the same pace, including those preparing teachers, colleges, and universities. Although there is so much yet to be researched within teacher education, the priorities must now be shifted to deal with some of the more urgent factors of appropriately serving America's diverse pupil population during their first 18 years of life, from preschool through high school.

The world we live in today is extremely diverse. The world population is 56% Asian; 21% European; 9% African; 8% South American; and 6% North American. The religions of the world are diverse with 30% Christian; 19.5% Moslem; 13.8% Hindu; 8.5% Buddhist; 5.7% Animist; and 22.5% no affiliation or atheist (Gomillion, 1991; Hodgekinson, 1985; Jackson, 1988; Johnson & Packard, 1987).

The United States has been seen as a leader in diversity issues because of the many diverse groups living in our country (Baptiste & Hughes, 1993). However, the past practice of valuing diversity in the United States has not been successful. Assimilation, the primary strategy used to manage diversity, values sameness, not diversity. It promotes the values and causes of the dominant group as the right way and as being relevant to all. It has not created a climate of acceptance for diversity; instead, it creates pressure to conform, role confusion, exclusion, isolation, and ethnic and class tension that frequently lead to violent outcomes. Perhaps Sills and Merton (1991) state it best:

The notion that the intense and unprecedented mixture of ethnic and religious groups in American life was soon to blend into a homogenous end product has outlived its usefulness, and also its credibility. . . . The point about the melting pot . . . is that it did not happen. (p. 79)

As Ravitch (1990) states, "Paradoxical though it may seem, the United States has a common culture that is multicultural" (p. 3). By the twenty-first century it is predicted that people of color will outnumber whites in this country for the first time. The "browning of America" will alter everything in society from politics and education to industry, values, and cultures.

Throughout the 1990s demographics project that people of color, white women, and immigrants will account for 85% of the net growth in our nation's labor force. By the year 2010, white men will account for less than 40% of the total American labor force. By the year 2005, the U.S. population is expected to grow by 42 million. Hispanics will account for 47% of this growth; African-Americans 22%; and Asians and other people of color will make up 18%. In contrast, an increase of 13% is projected for whites (Johnston & Packard, 1987).

As we look at these statistics, the words of John F. Kennedy are recalled: "Let us not be blind to our differences, but let us direct our attention to our common interest and to the means by which those differences can be resolved. And if we cannot end now our differences, at least we can make the world safe for democracy and for diversity." These words are as meaningful today as they were when he first stated them. American society is currently preparing for these changes and ensuring that the culture of the systems must change, not the culture of the people. The United States is not a melting pot but, instead, a great mosaic or a kaleidoscope (Fuchs, 1990).

As history has shown, when Americans face a crisis they look to their educational systems, the schools, to solve the problem. Student populations in schools across the United States are becoming increasingly diverse. Most students will be from various minority groups; more students will come from families in which English is not the first or primary language; and more students will live in poverty or even in the streets. The schools must be restructured to serve these students (Hodgekinson, 1991).

Change has been slow, but many educational institutions now include diversity issues in their mission statements. Curriculum committees are looking at cultural issues when selecting and purchasing textbooks and when implementing the curriculum. Teacher education programs now include cultural sensitivity, interpersonal relations training, multicultural courses, and field experiences with culturally diverse groups in their degree requirements. However, as we will later point out in this chapter, this is not enough.

Those offering professional instructional services to schools in America represent one profile of Americans, but many of the students will represent another profile. Stated differently, there are Caucasian teachers and multiethnic/multiracial student populations in many American classrooms. According to the American Association of Colleges for Teacher Education (AACTE, 1987), the teacher education professoriate is about 93% white, nearly 3% African American, and 3% Hispanic; and American Indians, including Alaskan natives and other people of color, constitute a total of only 1%. Few studies have been conducted on this reality and on its implications for recruitment, retention, and restructuring. This chapter makes the broad assumption that the major crisis is in teacher education (rather than a crisis in recruitment). Second, it assumes that research perspectives have been too narrow in terms of the total instructional environment and in terms of the impact of total instructional interaction (teaching).

As Edmund Gordon, Fayneese Muller, and David Rollock discuss in a 1990 issue of *Educational Researcher,* bias can enter research questions and contaminate the findings not only via the type of questions being examined but also via the researcher posing the question.

Finally, the concept of research may have been defined too narrowly within teacher education to address adequately elements of diversity now being discussed in professional literature. These are all critical factors, in addition to the historical realities of the past two or three decades, such as increased occupational opportunities for persons of color that were not available in earlier times. The civil rights era has provided professional opportunities for persons of color that did not exist before, and many culturally different college graduates have chosen careers other than teaching, because they appeared to offer better beginning salaries than did the teaching profession and because corporate America was often more flexible in its recruitment and interviewing processes.

The recruitment of culturally different teachers will continue to reflect something of a crisis until teacher education begins to address societal issues, racial issues, gender issues, economic issues, issues of negotiation, and classroom power sharing.

TOTAL INSTRUCTIONAL ENVIRONMENT

Total instructional environment refers to the settings in which teaching and learning occur, including the subject matter of classrooms, laboratories, athletic facilities, learning centers, and other places where instruction is delivered. Furthermore, instructional environments are defined as the total ecological structure created by those who are credentialed and contracted for offering teaching services. Instructional environments have been studied primarily in terms of what the teacher does in "management" of the classroom. From Madeline Hunter to scores of others, the almost scientific declaration of the instructional center is well known. That environment now must be researched in terms of the indirect learning that occurs.

Issue 1: Total Instructional Interaction

Total instructional interaction refers to the verbal behavior of both the teacher and the learner in any setting in which formal teaching and learning are under way. Such interactions include the nature of the teacher's organizational guidelines when he or she talks to establish the focus of a lesson and the verbal or nonverbal responses of those who are present as clients, or students. Useful questions are: What is the meaning of verbal cues by both teachers and students? Of the nonverbal clues? These are important because language patterns, both oral and written, and communication symbols all work to create an emotional atmosphere in which schooling occurs.

The National Study of School Evaluation published *Evaluation Guidelines for Multicultural/Multiracial Education* (1973) and included racial differences in its Student Opinionnaire as a factor in assessing instructional interaction and instructional environment. Since that time, few publications have addressed race or ethnicity as research factors in evaluation, instruction, or teacher education.

The Mosaic of the Teaching Force Of the more than 1,200 teacher preparation institutions in the United States, some 90% tend to follow the traditional teacher preparation pattern of 60 plus credits of the liberal arts courses and 30 to 45 credit hours in professional courses, including the "methods" of teaching various subjects, foundational work, and student teaching. This kind of program has been attractive for Caucasian, middle-income persons who have been socialized to performing well on "paper-and-pencil" tests assumed to denote competency. Culturally different persons have not found such programs particularly attractive as they have not addressed issues of significance to diverse populations. The present teaching force is overwhelmingly Caucasian, female, English-speaking, and from rural and suburban backgrounds. Even though this profile corresponds to that of teachers populating classrooms in thousands of communities and is considered adequate for the goals of traditional schooling, the reality is that the student population is changing drastically, with implications for student–teacher "instructional connectedness."

The icon of higher education as the stronghold of middle- and upper-class white Americans has been shattered by the reality of increasing cultural, racial, and ethnic diversity in academia. Future projections on the size and composition of the U.S. population indicates an accelerated increase of diverse populations participating in higher education (Hsia, 1988).

The ethnic socialization of teacher education has resulted in an assumption that "any teacher can teach anything to any student" in any kind of classroom. What teachers need is "ethnic socialization," an understanding of how an individual processes his or her total identity as part of the learning setting—with due regard for race, gender, first language, and economic status.

Vaz (1987) eloquently supports this position:

Black students differ from white students in their demographic characteristics, developmental tasks and their opportunities for professional growth. Demographically, many parents of black students are urban dwellers, have lower status jobs and earn less than whites. Black students tend to have been more exposed to racially different groups than white students. They may also differ in their expectations of college. Black students may expect college to be liberal on political and social issues. They expect that the university promotes a respect for cultural diversity, while maintaining the ability to treat all students equally. This view is not infrequently held by Black students with limited interracial exposure. (p. 23)

African-American students, for example, enter a transitional developmental phase as they progress from secondary to postsecondary education. The growth challenges confronting all students at this stage include the nurturing of good study habits, adjusting to college life, deciding vocational and educational choices, the enhancement of a positive self-concept, and the inauguration of career and personal aspirations. The meeting of these developmental tasks depends on the student's characteristics and financial resources, along with the support systems provided by the university (Carter & Sedlacek, 1984).

Many people believe that the concept of the United States of America implies that little (if any) reference should be made to the *profile of the teacher* in either teacher preparation or in instructional delivery. Today, much of what is known from the fields of child development, industrial psychology, social psychology, learning theory, and instructional design help us make inferences and draw implications for improving the education of the American teacher.

Issue 2: Recruitment in Teacher Education of the Culturally Different Teacher

Programs in teacher education have a history, a tradition, and an image. Many practitioners in the field would prefer to keep that tradition and image intact out of a sense of allegiance because they are products of that programmatic design. Even though a strong commitment to the tradition of public education is notable, the times and profiles of prospective teachers, along with expectations of the consumers (students) are demanding a serious confrontation with aspects of that heritage and tradition. Historically, students of color, in adjusting to college life, must learn how to maneuver the bureaucracy of university culture. Historically teacher education programs have preserved the need for the culturally different student to learn how to play the student's role (i.e., appropriate mainstream dress and dialect, "right" cultural references to literature, music, and the arts, and involvement in campus activities). African-American students and other students of color, as such, who need only the encouragement from professors by way of direct academic and cultural involvement, other than classes, to develop fully as students are grossly neglected (Vaz, 1987). Unfortunately many students of color attending professional programs in white institutions are not privy to the informal mentoring and university cultural support systems to which white students have access. The informal lunches, meetings, and invitations to attend regional and national conferences are significant learning occasions not usually accessible to many students of color.

The general absence of positive faculty–student exchanges and professional opportunities forces students of color to provide their own cultural support systems and networks. Universities that have provided specific courses and programs such as Hispanic, Native-American, and African-American studies have enabled students of color to develop a shared sense of community and supportive friendship networks. As an example, Hispanic student networks include Hispanic faculty and white faculty members, Hispanic staff members, and Hispanic graduate and undergraduate students. These networks provide students of color with counseling and mediational services with the wider campus (Vaz, 1987). These friend–kin networks provide a sense of "groupness" that enables students of color to enhance their self-concept.

Several educators (Garcia & Baptiste, 1990–1991; Nicklos & Brown, 1989; Vaz, 1987) argue the need for special retention systems for students of color in predominantly white institutions. These support systems must include, but not be limited to, financial support, mentor relationships with university faculty, student interaction with positive cultural learning experiences, academic and financial counseling with culturally sensitive faculty, special seminars designed for professional orientation to teaching as a discipline, and networking with honor students with high academic expectations. It is our experience that retention systems have direct implications for facilitating the adjustment of students of color to postsecondary life as well as increasing the probability of their success.

Hodgekinson (1988) conducted studies on the demographics in American schooling. He indicates that the Class of 2000 (which was the first-grade class of 1988) has the following characteristics: (1) 24% were born in poverty (according to federal government standards or declarations of impoverished families), (2) 14% were born handicapped or exceptional by some definition of PL 94-142 (Education of All Handicapped Children Act), (3) 40% were classified as culturally different (meaning

(meaning learners other than Caucasian Americans of European descent who have English as a first language).

One profile of students virtually ignored in cultural literature and teacher education and school curriculum is the biracial population. These children, born either to white fathers and black mothers, or black fathers and white mothers, Mexican-American fathers and Native-American mothers, Puerto Rican fathers and Asian-American mothers make up the full range of cultural-ethnic-racial mixes.

This pupil profile is quite diverse, but the teaching population is becoming increasingly monoracial, monocultural, and monolingual, predominantly Caucasian education students coming from middle- to upper middle-income backgrounds. Teacher education can no longer ignore these realities. These data are further confirmed in the U.S. Census data, especially 1990.

The issue involves the dimension of teacher–learner similarity in learning style, image of authority, and clear instructional communication. Who teaches whom? Who learns best from whom? How significant is the profile of teachers and learners in the educative process? To what extent is the teacher's profile reflected in the teacher's level of believability and receptivity in the eyes of culturally different learners? If teacher education is committed to "anyone can teach anything to any learner," then its research and development efforts will continue to de-emphasize racial, ethnic, and gender profiles in recruiting and retention.

Several decades ago (1965) W. E. B. Du Bois, a preeminent African-American scholar, wrote about the inappropriate treatment of African Americans in the social sciences and education:

It is a peculiar sensation, this double consciousness, this sense of always looking at one's self through the eyes of others, of measuring one's soul by the tape of the world that looks on in amused contempt and pity. One even feels his twoness, an American, a Negro; two souls, two thoughts, two unreconciled strivings; two warring ideals in one dark body, whose dogged strength alone keeps it from being torn asunder. (p. 215)

His elegant statement from the *Souls of Black Folk* is still very valid today to characterize the plight of African Americans.

Gordon, Miller, and Rollock (1990) further support the general prejudicial bias of social science and educational research regarding African Americans in the following quote:

Examination of the social and educational research knowledge bases relative to Afro-Americans indicated that these sciences have tradition-ally attempted to understand the life experiences of Afro-Americans from a narrow cultrocentric perspective and against equally narrow cultrocentric standards. Diversity has been viewed as deviance and differences have been viewed as deficits. Thus, the issue of cultural and ethnic diversity has been completely or inadequately assessed, and has insufficiently influenced knowledge production. These problems are compounded when we recognize that the traditionally dominant, communicentric bias not only frames the conceptual paradigms we use to study social phenomena, but also frames the methodological paradigms as well. We tend to forget that many of the core propositions upon which the sciences rest, such as objectivity, positivism, and empiri-cism, are cultural products and thus may be culture-bound. These hallmarks of science may be more limited in their explanatory useful-ness than is generally presumed. (p. 15)

It is our contention that communicentric bias is true not only of social science and educational research regarding African Americans but also of the research conducted in the entire western arena about other groups of color, especially for Hispanics and Native Americans. Therefore, academic socialization levels of academic comfort should be part of the decision to pursue a teaching career.

Unresearched Issues Does the issue of "indirect learning" warrant academic attention? In other words, what does a student learn from an adult teacher that is not part of the traditional lesson plan? How comfortable is a learner who is racially differ-ent from the teacher? If these issues are considered insignificant, then the crisis in teacher education will continue for some time, and recruitment issues will not subside.

Issue 3: The Need for Persons With Cross-Racial, Cross-Ethnic Skills

Culturally different populations will make up a large percentage of the American work force by the year 2000. Teachers in America will need to understand the issues involved in cross-racial and cross-ethnic teaching and learning because the over-whelming majority of all new teachers entering the profession have the typical Caucasian, English-speaking, suburban, or rural profile. Although the student populations are becoming more diverse, the teaching population is becoming less diverse.

In the field of teacher education, little attention has been given to the dynamics of cross-racial, cross-ethnic teaching and learning. More attention has been given to issues of exceptional-ity and gender than to the other areas. Competency may be defined in traditional terms, but today's pluralistic society de-mands much more than we have generally expected from the instructional role. Historically, instructional competency rested solely on a student's ability to pass paper-and-pencil tests and to conform to mass-produced systems of public education. The reality is that America's educational enterprise is much too diverse to continue to expect both such conformity and limited strategies for determining competency. Those being served to-day are multicultural, multilingual, multiethnic, and multiracial. What has been traditionally used as recruitment assumptions must now be revised to consider the highest levels of diversity. Can any teacher education program be excellent if it is not diverse? Can any teacher education program be of high quality if it does not reflect the kinds of training and experiences that develop skills in cross-racial and cross-ethnic teaching?

Issue 4: Research on Specific Populations Using Authentic Researchers

Boyer (1986) identifies a distinction between authentic re-searchers and basic researchers with implications for teacher education. A *basic research* team is one that does not include a person about whom the research is being conducted. In other words, if an African-American research team with no Caucasian persons on it attempts to conduct a study on Caucasian learners, this would be basic research.

Authentic research occurs only when the research team or principal investigator represents the profile of those being used as subjects in the research design. When Native Americans study Native-American students and their learning styles, such research can then be considered authentic. The Native-American principal investigator brings not only the professional research skills to the project but also a lifetime of experience from that population to the research endeavor.

Teacher education has assumed that such factors are insignificant. The position taken here is that America is too diverse to have such factors continually ignored. To those who suggest that the presence of a Native American on a research team or as the principal investigator "contaminates" the quest for objectivity in research, the premise of this chapter is that the absence of that voice and perspective is a greater "contaminating" factor. Perspective in research is extremely important. Authentic perspective is essential.

How does this connect with recruitment of culturally different teachers? People are becoming quite sensitive to negative descriptors in research findings. Although it is true that many culturally different people are accurately reflected in negative statistics, teacher education and teacher recruitment must begin to find the "positive" elements as part of the motivation for culturally different persons to pursue teaching as a lifetime endeavor. Also, what are the chances of being nurtured and mentored while one pursues teacher preparation? Kevin Simms (1990) studied African-American males in colleges using only the authentic voices. One of his findings was that many felt that they could not be really mentored by faculty persons who were not also African-American males. If this is a reality-based perception of these students, then it must be considered in both recruitment into teacher preparation programs and in priorities for practice within the teaching profession.

Issue 5: Various Images of Concern

The *Miami Herald,* one of the nation's largest newspapers, now has an Hispanic edition with a circulation of 88,100 on weekdays and 102,000 on Sundays. Does that tell us anything about linguistic and language diversity? We now are seeing the Native-American community insist upon a Native-American Museum to become part of the Smithsonian Institution in Washington, DC. Given the fact that many secondary teachers become coaches of athletic teams bearing Indian names, the issues of academic appropriateness, cultural validity, and professional respect all become part of the image of the institutions wanting the services of bright, intellectually capable persons of color to join the ranks of those who teach.

Further, what is the image of culturally different people in college-level textbooks? How many courses are complimentary to the heritage, history, and image of Hispanic women? of African-American males? of Asian-American people? of Native-American customs? These are serious issues related to the attractiveness of teaching to and teacher education by people of color.

Many colleges that prepare teachers are still debating whether they should close school or cancel classes on the third Monday in January (Martin Luther King, Jr., Holiday). Some teacher educators are suggesting that it is a "Black Holiday" and should not be observed by non-black people or programs.

Nothing could be further from the truth. It is a national holiday and should be so recognized as are other national holidays. The fact that Martin Luther King was an African-American male has little to do with the fact that his ideas, his work, and his life represented the most influential vision of the past 100 years. His vision led us to understanding that America was not living up to its promises of fairness and "liberty and justice for all." When a recruiting school district or teacher education program attempts to invite persons of color into service with them, these are some of the policy images and program indexes that are considered.

Issue 6: Issues of Research Topics, Research Design, and Required Courses

Teacher education is broad and multifaceted. Every teaching certificate usually will require between 125 and 140 or more semester credits. (In the quarter system, that is increased by one third.) Teacher education has been woefully traditional and almost 100% Eurocentric. The assumptions of most coursework is that the student will be Caucasian, middle-income, and economically stable. The courses, the experiences, the readings, and the laboratory assignments have been primarily without context and devoid of the richness of cultural/racial/ethnic diversity. Consequently, new teachers enter public education with little or no historical, sociological, or psychological competency regarding the culturally different. American public education took its cue from the Boston Latin Grammar School, which dates back to 1635, and the university took its curriculum cue from Harvard University, which was founded in 1636. Both of these assumed at that time that audiences would be males who were Caucasians, of European descent, with English as a first language, and who were from well-to-do families with no handicapping conditions. Such basic assumptions are no longer appropriate, and teacher education programs cannot assume that such policies are the norm. For example, recently a graduate student in an education program wanted to conduct research using African-American males as his only population. Having no African-American males on the faculty in the program being pursued, his supervisory team was composed of non-Black persons. He was denied the privilege of using that population as his sole pool of subjects because the advisor felt that his findings "would not be generalizable." This kind of fallacious adisement is another barrier to the recruitment of culturally different people into teacher education.

In another state university, a young Hispanic woman requested permission to take a three-credit course on Women's History and have it count toward graduation in a program requiring some 12 credits in history. She was denied the privilege. Given the fact that she was in a teacher education program of some 130 credits, it would seem that three credits could be devoted to the contributions and legacy of women in America. This kind of limited perspective and "academic gatekeeping" account for much of the apprehension of culturally different people to pursue teaching and teacher education. This is a serious barrier to recruitment. Research activity is a major part of all professions, including teaching. The diversity of that research production and of the research topics will become major factors in the decades to come.

Rozzelle (1990) studied African-American males between grades five and eight in an urban setting. Part of her findings included a major concern with the absence of respect for profiles of students and the "communicated" value placed on the lives of Black males. The implications for teacher education recruitment are numerous. One concern is the fact that African-American males provide many of the negative statistics in our society. It is too often the case that these students' difficulty within the educational settings start with female teachers who react to the natural behaviors of males and define them as disruptive and nonconforming. The expectation that all populations will conform to the *same style* of learning, behaving, and perceiving as the female Caucasian teacher may be the most damaging expectation. The implication for recruitment and retention is that persons of color are not likely to be attracted to fields where the basic expectation is not liberatory and empowering for groups traditionally disenfranchised. One should not be expected to *duplicate* the style, content, perspective, and behaviors of those already in positions of power.

Butler (1990) studied the inclusion of African-American females in much of the published research consumed by those in the social sciences, education, and similar human services. By examining the profile of subjects used to reach major conclusions about adolescence, she found very few instances in which African-American females were included in the subjects or samples of the research. There was, however, no hesitancy to assume that such research findings could be *generalized to culturally diverse populations*. It is believed that these are powerful considerations for the crisis in teacher education related to issues of diversity in recruitment and retention of personnel.

Issue 7: Issues of Historical Reality: Why Few Persons of Color Choose Teaching

Historically, in America, persons of color chose teaching as one of a very few careers in which they felt welcome and one in which they believed they could make a difference in the lives of children. In addition, schools (under the separate but equal, segregated society) had to be staffed, so the perception of possible career placements (jobs) was always one of "possibility." Shortly after 1954 (*Brown vs. Board of Topeka*) and subsequently after the 1964 Civil Rights Act, legal mandates for school desegregation became intensified. Over the following 15 years, more than 30,000 African-American teachers and administrators were displaced from their instructional and administrative roles (Moore, 1974). Schools were combined in many districts, and the very schools where African-American teachers were employed were dissolved or closed as attendance centers. During this time, there were almost no African-American, Hispanic or Native-American school board members in America. Policies and procedures employed by school districts were, in many instances, *not* reflective of an honorable, integrity-based perspective. In other words, as persons who were reluctant to embrace a desegregated society sought to impede the progress, they also embraced negative attitudes about those fighting for social justice and equity in school matters. This historical reality

is not easily forgotten by people of color, and it has an impact on career decisions.

The Children of Displaced Educators The children of displaced educators not only were discouraged from pursuing a teaching career, but also they saw the frustrations of their parents in seeking justice. In addition, they heard their parents talk about separate pay or salary schedules based solely on race and sometimes on gender. Some school boards published schedules in which Caucasian teachers were to be paid more than teachers of color in the same school districts teaching the same subjects at the same grade levels. The children of these educators were not impressed with teaching and teacher education. They are still not being attracted to the profession.

Then where are the children of these educators? Many are pursuing careers in business, engineering, architecture, medicine, and other areas often closed to their parents at earlier times. Corporate America did not welcome people of color in earlier times. The children of displaced educators are now pursuing careers in politics, management, and areas that appear to be more open than teaching.

Traditional forms of recruitment for this population will never be adequate. There is a major historical disillusionment with our profession, although everyone recognizes that no society can exist without those who teach. New approaches to recruitment must be embraced in order to begin to tap that resource for possible participation in teaching careers.

The Testing/Competency Issue Across America, certification offices, state school boards, and teacher preparation institutions embrace a "higher standards" mentality for teachers. Translated, this means requiring a higher test score for entry into teacher education programs. A higher test score does not necessarily mean a more knowledgeable or competent person working with multiethnic populations in a teaching and learning setting. Some persons of color have attempted to enter professional studies and have fallen short of the entry-level score by one or two points. Denied entry, they pursued careers in other areas with a higher entry-level salary than teaching. For example, one program requires 172 on a test (where the highest possible score is 192) and a person of color made 171. Can one say with assurance that the person with 172 is a significantly better teacher than the person making 171? Of course not! These are arbitrary decisions about "cut-off" scores and have little to do with real competency.

With very few exceptions, teacher education has not created "test-taking clinics" designed to assist these persons in such cases. It is assumed, however, that their presence in the ranks of teachers will become more critically urgent. To be defined solely by a paper-and-pencil test score is much too limiting to define the total behavioral output of professional educators. A test-taking clinic would work to improve the chances of culturally different applicants to "duplicate" the same scores made by others. Until America comes to terms with these policy procedure perspectives, persons of color will continue to migrate to fields other than teaching.

Priorities Within Teacher Recruitment People of color who are now in teaching roles are generally experienced educators who passed all the tests, endured all the negative policy decisions, and chose to remain in the profession. The next generation of persons are less willing to endure those discrepancies and injustices. Although not focused directly on teaching and teacher education, Cox (1993) in *Cultural Diversity in Organizations: Theory, Research and Practice,* documents case after case in which organizations have either created policies of questionable integrity or who failed to follow policies of promoting, encouraging, or retaining persons of color. Until the management of teacher education becomes committed to diversity, little change will occur in the crisis. Even though it is true that the American school is the gateway to effective living in a democracy, that gateway will become increasingly closed to many unless its gatekeepers embrace diversity in programming, personnel, and evaluation. Race and ethnic relations are at an all-time low within the context of a desegregated society. This climate is mirrored in public school and university settings, as reflected by intense debates over issues of equity and social justice. For instance, affirmative action policies and multicultural curriculum proposals are now challenged by fundamentalist groups as being evidence of reverse discrimination. Although proponents of such arguments offer little documentation, the arguments are waved as a banner by those opposing equity issues. Some suggest that racial desegregation in America has been a failure because of the numerous avenues through which racial discrimination can occur. Institutionalized racism and institutionalized sexism are alive and well in the 1990s–2000 and beyond. Given this reality, teacher education must assume more responsibility for improving race and ethnic relations through its programming.

Cross (1993) documented that teachers' values, beliefs, attitudes, and prejudices affect their teaching. She further noted that many teacher education specialists (professorial colleagues) are ambivalent about a commitment to improving race relations. In summary, Cross concluded that we cannot think of education apart from its connection to improving race relations. The preparation of the American teacher (both Caucasian teachers and prospective teachers of color) must include numerous opportunities to develop a friendly confrontation with their own racial history and racial/ethnic socialization.

Nel (1992) made a strong case for the empowerment of minority students by citing demographic changes and the school's failure to serve minority students adequately as evidence of the need for visionary leadership within teacher education. Probably the most critical issue in recruitment and retention of culturally different persons into teacher education is the absence of visionary leadership within the ranks of teacher educators. Even the persons now charged with individually contacting teachers of color were professionally prepared in teacher education programs. Consequently, our leadership must become accountable for the problems associated with the absence of cultural diversity within the ranks of teachers and other school personnel.

Issue 8: Related Problematic Issues in the Recruitment and Retention of Educators of Color

Because the numerical concept of minority is an inaccurate description, culturally different teachers and prospective teachers now prefer to be described as *people of color* or *culturally/ethnically different educators.* The following issues might need to be explored, researched, discussed, analyzed, and included within teacher education in order to transform recruitment and retention of "different educators" within our ranks.

Point 1: Curriculum Bias and Instructional Discrimination Curriculum bias means inherent favoritism toward one racial or ethnic group over another in the content and perspectives used in curriculum delivery in most schools. This bias is reflected in the materials, textbooks, standardized tests, and various artifacts making up the school center. If you create a curriculum that lauds the achievements of one group and omits and distorts the achievements of another, it has a negative effect. Instructional discrimination occurs when pedagogical acts, practices, or behaviors result in unfair and inappropriate responses to the varied learning styles that learners bring to the school. Culturally influenced learning styles have not generally been part of teacher education in America, and the incidence of instructional discrimination is increasing. Improving this situation involves recognizing that curriculum bias exists within the content of teacher education courses, experiences, assignments, and research. Second, it involves radical changes to transform instructional delivery to eliminate instructional discrimination.

Point 2: Prospective Teachers' Experiences in the Age of Diversity Historically, those experiences required of persons who choose teaching as a career have been inadequately planned, executed, or evaluated with respect to issues of diversity. As a result, people of color are rarely excited about participating in programs that psychologically exclude them, their priorities, and their styles of learning and perceiving. In the future, more and more preservice experiences (and staff development experiences) must deal with the following four areas:

1. *Recognizing the racial history of educators, both in public schools and in institutions of teacher education.* What has been the nature of the professor's experiences with culturally different people in the first 18 years of his or her life? How does that history interface with the values around which an equitable program is built? What behaviors do we require in teacher education? How has it impacted our "gatekeeping" policies and procedures?
2. *Embracing options and alternatives for all people in academic pursuits.* A mentality that says that *"one size fits all"* is not an appropriate framework within which to recruit, teach, learn, or evaluate. To expect people of color to duplicate everything Caucasian teachers do and embrace is a grave error in the quest for diversity.
3. *Studying culturally influenced learning styles.* Little research and emphasis have been placed on such influence. How does the Mexican-American learner approach learning tasks at his or her most comfortable level? What is different about Puerto Rican learners and the way they choose to learn new data? To what extent has Janice Hale's work (1982) on African-American learners been explored? Barbara Shade's work (1989) ought to be required knowledge base in this area.

4. *Developing skills for cross-racial, cross-ethnic parent conferencing.* An increasing incidence of communication distortion is occurring within this framework, and little effort is made to decrease its impact.

Point 3: Decreasing Instructional Violence and Understanding the Role of Instructional Modeling and Mentoring
"Instructional violence" occurs when educators engage in any behaviors viewed as unfair, disproportionate, negative, or inappropriate when the learner has no recourse in a given situation. This involves sharing the power of instructional decision making and modeling the collaborative ideology of teaching. When the teacher makes all the decisions, it is equivalent to becoming prosecutor, jury, judge, and warden in all situations of possible conflict. Is this appropriate for a democracy? Modeling and mentoring are new competencies needed by those who offer their services as school employees. This includes administrators, counselors, secretaries, food service workers, librarians, and all others who earn their living working with learners in a multiethnic setting.

Teacher education has a major responsibility to admit the existence of academic violence, to confront its practice, and to design preparation programs reflecting nonviolence in all its aspects. To what extent do we prepare teachers to share classroom power? Although some would say that children have no capacity to help make classroom decisions, today's children are quite different from those in the 1970s. People of color interested in teacher education are keenly aware of the arbitrary decisions made about students, their learning style, their intellectual capacity or potential, which, in their judgment, represent major crimes of instructional violence.

Point 4: Recognizing Academic Racism and Working Toward Its Reduction Academic racism exists when the practices associated with teaching and learning assume that intellectual inferiority or superiority of a student, faculty member, or staff member is based primarily on his or her race or ethnic identity. It reflects an imbalance based on instructional preference that results in extremely limited learnings about racially and ethnically different persons, ideas, heritages, and events.

It is understood that many in teacher education and in full-time recruitment are quite uncomfortable with terms like academic racism. However, reluctance to deal openly with our problems may be a major element in the lack of success with recruiting and retaining diverse teachers—and with educators of color choosing a teaching career.

A More Comprehensive View of Recruitment/Retention
Although America is become more racially and ethnically diverse, the major academic institutions of our society have given limited attention to the impact of changing demographics on race and ethnic relations. Deliberate attention must now be given to the skills, concepts, and perspectives associated therewith. A racially desegregated society can never emerge into a racially integrated society until different parties begin to think of each other as social equals. This means that when programs of education upgrade to accommodate diversity, they will not view the action as "lowering their standards" or decreasing their commitment to quality.

Recruitment within teacher education is much more than finding a bag of tricks to yield more people of color into the ranks of American teachers. It will require a total transformation of the way recruiters think, as well as the way they pursue their craft. It will require a transformation in the way teacher educators think, as well as the way they create academic policy, design teacher education curriculum, and evaluate prospective teachers' efforts and profiles. Commitment precedes everything. When the commitment is there, programs begin to reflect that commitment—and change occurs.

It should be recognized that many teacher educators are quite happy with all Caucasian teachers and numerous students of color. The teacher in any given situation is a major symbol of power, especially intellectual power. Caucasian intellect is almost always a given assumption within schooling. The crisis in recruitment and retention, then, must involve confrontation with that set of assumptions. This will be difficult because it requires new analyses. Difficult tasks, however, are not impossible tasks.

In programs of recruitment, the most obvious responsibility will include high priorities on diversity and its value to the academic enterprise. Following are some suggested priorities for the recruitment of people of color as well as males into elementary programs and classrooms (not necessarily listed in order of importance).

PRIORITIES OF RECRUITMENT

Item 1: Policy on Diversity as a Top Priority

Every teacher education program that lacks a diverse application pool should make it a top priority to recruit culturally diverse individuals, starting with a written policy. The traditional channels of affirmative action and goal setting have been useful, but they have *not* resulted in the level of diversity needed in teacher education or in the public school classrooms of America. Again, this may be difficult if policymakers, administrators, and teacher educators do not see the value of such priority. Diversity is a strength, not a liability. A policy reflects philosophy, and when a policy is created on diversity, it sends a philosophical message to all parties and participants. Although the policy will not preclude the presence of Caucasian teacher with pupils of color, it will invite the presence of persons of color in instructional roles and other academic roles within the schooling enterprise. Until a policy is created and disseminated, high levels of ambivalence will prevail.

Item 2: Consider Creative Staffing in Classrooms

Creative staffing involves seeking *males* from other roles and from other programs who may serve as teacher assistants, teacher aids, or instructional associates, especially in elementary schools. In an age of growing consciousness about the way females in our society have been short-changed in many ways, this may be met with major opposition. However, if 16 million children do not live with their fathers, the presence of adult males in classrooms may be one of the most empowering priorities that could be initiated. The crisis involves the recognition of the significance of modeling within the classroom. The absence of males in elementary classrooms is equivalent to the devaluing of the academic experience for all males. This is also related to the disproportionate presence of males in prisons in our society. There is some level of instructional distortion under way in elementary classrooms that results in males being punished more, reprimanded more, having their names placed on the chalkboard more, and so on. Messages of "psychological exclusion" are delivered in these situations. The only adult in such environments is usually a female educator. *Creative staffing* means increasing the number of responsible adults in classrooms.

Although many would refer to this idea as an inefficient use of taxpayers' money, we have had an academic bargain for many years in our system of employing only one teacher/adult to serve some 25 or 30 learners over an academic year. However, bargain basement finds are rarely adequate over a long term, and the cost of providing an adequate, diverse education will be greater than in the past.

Item 3: Recruiting from Community College Athletes

Hundreds of 2-year and 4-year colleges across the country have been successful in recruiting males for their athletic programs. Such recruitment is accompanied by resources (financial and personal) to make their athletic experiences palatable and sustaining. Teacher education recruitment might take cues from such efforts. Mentoring must become a higher priority in such recruitment/retention efforts. As these athletes complete the first 60 credits of a program, they might represent a pool of possible instructional talent to staff schools. This process will also require options and alternatives because this population is influenced by the attractiveness of careers outside of teaching and our creative energies must be poured into such activity.

Item 4: Developing Minority Male Teacher Academies

Leading the list of almost all negative statistics in America is the minority male profile, particularly the African-American male. Programs that are serious about diversity regarding this group will begin to establish teacher education sequences especially targeting this population. Some school districts have employed the Black Male Teacher Academy for learners in an effort to decrease the social crises impacting this group (Baltimore, Milwaukee, Detroit). The idea here is for teacher education (colleges and universities) to adopt the Black Male Teacher Academy and focus on the preparation of this population for roles in schools. One such program is now under way in Livingston College in North Carolina.

Item 5: Visitations to Possible Places of Employment

The opportunity to visit a site where employment might become a reality has always been a powerful motivational factor. The suggestion here is for school districts to bring in prospective teachers to observe the strengths of a school's program with the intention of influencing their decisions. Corporate America has long engaged in this kind of recruiting. It could work for people of color in places where the culturally different population is extremely low. Needless to say this approach would involve budgetary priorities and the use of persons of color who may already be employed in the school district. The same idea should be employed by teacher education programs that have historically not recruited because thousands of Caucasian females apply daily for programs to prepare classroom teachers. Consequently, there has been no effort to recruit culturally different teacher education candidates. Again, this is tragic. If schools are becoming more diverse, so must the pool of candidates for providing instruction in those schools.

Item 6: Recruiting for Possible Job Sharing

The task of teaching in a "mass-production format" (one teacher per 30 learners) may be less attractive to persons of color than we think. As we move to a 24-hour society, schools and other traditional agencies must begin to think of job sharing, part-time roles, and collaborative teaching. Recruitment may consider attracting persons engaged in nonteaching careers to become part-timers in the education of America's children. Again, this will mean that some persons now engaged in full-time teaching could become involved in other related careers sharing the instructional responsibilities with professionals from other fields. The idea is to increase diversity within schools and classrooms. Such diversity is not proposed just so that learners of color can have persons of their identity involved in their educative process. Indeed, Caucasian learners need the experience and exposure of being taught and guided by persons unlike themselves.

Item 7: Understanding the Economic Dimension of Diversity

One of the first lessons learned in the study of economics and economic conditions is that "when an item is in short supply, its cost increases." In the 1940s and 1950s, some states paid males more for teaching than they did females. Although we do not advocate such imbalance, successful recruitment of people of color and males for elementary classrooms will require economic incentives. Such incentives may include benefits not now in place. Further, they may include quests for alternative certification, for alternative classroom designs, and for diversity in teacher-to-pupil ratios. Again, America has used the mass-produced system at nominal costs for educating the masses. This system is on its deathbed, and additional resources are now required. There seems to be no hesitancy to place security guards in schools, to erect high fences, to build more prisons, or to install metal detectors. Cost is almost always approved by those who hold such action as high priority. Once we hold diversity at the same level, some of these ideas will be activated. Schools will be different, and the teaching force of America will become diverse.

CHALLENGE AND CONCLUSION

This chapter has focused on elements of teacher education, on the perspectives of those who make policy, implement curriculum, and evaluate programs and personnel. Some items not fully discussed include the absence of postbaccalaureate programs for teacher certification in many institutions; the reluctance to engage in alternative certification; the absence of major test-taking clinics; the absence of advocacy for the minority presence in schools; and policy gatekeeping in teacher education.

Several alternative teacher preparation programs have been developed to meet the challenge of teacher shortages, especially teachers of color in urban school districts. These range from the well-known Teach for America to school district teacher preparation programs such as the Dallas Independent School District Alternative Teacher Preparation Program. These alternative programs have proven that nontraditional models can prepare teachers who can be effective instructors in urban school settings. Most important, many of the recruits are people of color with bachelor degrees in other areas who are attracted to these programs because of the early immersion in public classrooms and the shorter time to initial certification. Unfortunately, many teacher preparation programs in colleges and universities are too tradition bound to change and to investigate other models for preparing teachers.

Simply to restate the problem is no longer adequate. Ideas included here are designed to be explored and adopted. Traditional programs and endorsement of teacher candidates will soon become outdated.

All persons who offer instructional services must possess different skills, concepts, knowledges, and behaviors adequately to meet the needs of the current clientele. Among the most urgent skills and studies useful for educators of the future are the following:

1. *Studies on culturally influenced learning styles.* Since the mid-1970s, the field of teacher education has embarked on a major task of exploring preferred learning styles of elementary learners as well as secondary learners. The idea was to prepare teachers to provide instruction more aligned with the learning styles of those being taught. On further examination, almost none of this work focused on cultural and/or racial differences. Our position is that both those institutions that claim a primary research function and those that pride themselves on practical pedagogy must explore approaches to learning characterized by race, ethnicity, economic class, and, in some instances, gender. For example, in what physical arrangements do many Mexican-American learners prefer to engage in the learning activity? Most schools still use classrooms organized in rows with all students facing the teacher. Is this their preferred arrangement? Is it most appropriate? Much research needs to be done on factors such as these and on the best way to prepare teachers for such culturally sensitive instructional response.

2. *Studies on academic racism and institutional racism.* Many researchers on teacher education deny that academic racism exists. Academic racism exists when the practices associated with teaching and learning assume that the traditional intellectual inferiority or superiority of a student, faculty member, or staff member is based primarily on his or her race or ethnic identity. Racism reflects an imbalance based on instructional preference that results in extremely limited learnings about racially and ethnically different persons, ideas, heritages, and events. Few studies have been conducted on such factors because they engage the philosophical basis of what teaching and learning must embrace. (It gets down to the worldview of those that teach and their understanding of the social ills of our society.) Institutional racism is the creation, implementation, and enforcement of a policy or program that, on initial examination, appears to be fair and equitable, but that categorically and adversely affects large groups of clients supposedly being served by that institution. The American school is one such institution that, although not intended to be racist in its policies, often produces that result. Major research needs to be done in this area.

3. *Studies on human sexuality and its expressions.* Because the American school is a composite of the larger society, it can no longer assume that its program and operation will occur in a vacuum. Human sexuality is a part of each human being's existence. However, many communities and many teacher preparation programs do not address this as a factor in their clients. A clearer understanding of its many manifestations and their implications must become a stronger part of the research within teacher education. With the attention given to sexual harassment in today's schools and the early onset of sexual activity by students, teachers must be prepared better to address each issue. Little is presently being done in research or in instruction in this respect.

4. *Studies on African-American, Asian-American, Hispanic-American, and Native-American History, Literature, and Music.* If demographic projections hold, the American pupil population will continue to become more diverse. Culturally different students are already claiming major irrelevance of the curriculum to their lives, their world, and their cultural orientation. At the same time, most teachers entering the profession do not come from these groups but will be teaching persons from these highly visible groups. An increased level of literacy on the history, literature, music, and art of these groups will address the issue of cultural accommodation. Research studies must be done on teacher education programs and how they should embrace such literacy.

5. *Studies on nonviolent conflict resolution (negotiation skills, classroom power sharing, etc.).* Anyone who reads the papers, listens to the news, or works in an academic institution is well aware of the increase in violent behavior emerging primarily from unresolved conflict between human beings. What skills are being given in teacher education programs that address such issues? We need a major focus on research, instruction, and service that will prepare teachers to respond to a mentality of violence. Many culturally different teachers are needed for areas such as these. We need skills of negotiation, on how to share classroom power, and on how to respect a "minority opinion" on an issue. In most

classrooms, the teacher holds all the power of decision making and never shares it.

6. *Studies on biracial learners.* Except for two or three researchers, the teacher education literature has failed to explore the dynamics of teaching and learning with biracial learners. For many years, America was in denial that biracial learners existed. Today, the increased numbers and the open dialog on such profiles demand that teacher education begin exploratory research and instruction on how best to serve that population. It cannot occur, however, without the teacher's exploration of his or her personal beliefs about such profiles. In addition, the socialization of such learners must become part of the teacher's understanding of the most appropriate instruction.

7. *Studies on academic sexism and institutional sexism.* Academic sexism occurs when instruction, curriculum, policies, programs, and practices assume that boys and girls will behave and respond in exactly the same ways. When this does not happen, one or the other is quietly but consistently penalized in the academic arena. While the American Association of University Women has published reports on how girls are shortchanged in the American classroom, little has been done to restructure teacher education so that new practitioners provide a more balanced program of instruction. Our contention is that males are significantly shortchanged in the American classroom and that the absence of male teachers throughout the primary grades is a major barrier to the elimination of academic sexism. Research must be undertaken on the impact of such realities and then teacher preparation instruction must be upgraded based on the findings of such research.

8. *Studies on the racial history of teachers, gender history of teachers, and related issues.* Little research has been done on the personal experiences of those who apply to join the ranks of American educators. Each person has a racial history that impacts the way in which they view race and all of its implications. This is more than a generic study of prejudice and discrimination. This is an analysis of the origins of one's personal values and the biographical impact of how one makes decisions and delivers instruction when the student population may be racially different from the instructor. Whatever parents and significant others told teachers during their growing years about racially different people as well as themselves could have a major impact on the way one delivers instruction. Few people study their racial history, and almost none of this aspect has been part of teacher education research—particularly its impacts on teaching philosophy.

9. *Studies on the impact of poverty.* Two decades ago, there were many studies on poverty and its reflections in the workplace and the school place. When the face of poverty changed to encompass more young families and senior citizens, few studies emerged. Our position is that poor people who turn to the schools for the education of their children are looking for a more appropriate curriculum and a more sensitive level of instruction that respect impoverished families. Few studies are devoted to the economic status of families with children in schools. Such studies are sorely needed—not just to describe poverty but to analyze its implications for teaching and learning.

10. *Studies on visual literacy and the impact of images on learners.* Visual literacy involves learning from sight, with or without sound. It embraces "one picture is worth a thousand words." Diagrams and photographs have been used for generations in instruction, and we are now proposing that research be conducted on the powerful impact of greater utilization of sight for instructional purposes. This is tied to cultural orientation of the students who come for instruction.

11. *Studies on cross-racial, cross-ethnic parent conferencing.* Most teacher education programs have embraced parent conferencing as a major aspect of the teacher's professional responsibility. In cases where the teacher represents one race and the parent represents another, major difficulties have occurred during parent–teacher communication. The basic assumption is that parents and teachers are partners in the education of children. In many communities, there is an adversarial relationship between parents and teachers, especially when there is cross-racial or cross-ethnic conferencing. Research studies are needed to determine how teacher education can embrace the skills of nonadversarial teacher–parent conferencing.

12. *Studies on gender equity (male and female).* Women's Studies (as a discipline) may be finding a place in the academic mainstream, but gender equity is much more than pointing out discrepancy in pay in the workplace or how the school executes its various "reward systems." Our position is that gender equity studies should embrace higher levels of male–female communication and should include work on how teachers could reduce the confusion growing out of male–female behaviors within an academic environment.

13. *Studies on cross-racial, cross-ethnic teaching and learning (instructional dynamics, therapeutic instructional ideas).* For years, there was an assumption that any teacher could teach any learner anything so long as the teacher knew the content. We now know that this is an erroneous assumption. Instructional delivery is now much more personalized whenever it is offered in a context to which all learners can relate. For instance, even though girls might have difficulty believing they could be like Einstein, might not they envision themselves as scientists if they see pictures of prominent female scientists along with that of Einstein? The same applies with students of color. In electronic instruction, communication needs are slightly different. But whenever the instructor works in close proximity to learners (as in a classroom), the opportunity for "instructional distortion" is critically increased when teacher and learner come from different racial or ethnic groups. The instructional dynamics of this reality are rarely studied. Our call is for major studies on instructional dynamics and on therapeutic instruction for the teacher education profession.

14. *Psychological accommodation of diverse population.* Psychological accommodation involves an instructional relationship, a strong invitation to learn, and symbols that suggest that the learners are not just tolerated but also celebrated. The psychological accommodation of learners

across racial and ethnic lines will rest, in part, on the psychological health of both the teacher and the learner. They will engage in productive behaviors that will be perceived to be mutually desirable and beneficial to all participants. Gender will also be an issue in the complexity of such accommodation. Race and gender are such powerful variables that all relationships are conditioned thereby. Teacher education assumed that the legal initiatives of school desegregation would take care of all such concerns. Now, we are suggesting that we need new channels of assessing the level of psychological accommodation felt by the learner. The psychological reference to instruction is, in part, a function of how the "instructor *feels* about those being instructed. Are they worthy of being taught? How important does this set of learners appear to be to the future of America? Does the instructor feel that the learners are capable of engaging in the academic enterprise? We now need research and development on the psychological accommodation of diverse student populations in the American

school. These will start with the preparation of teachers and administrators.

15. *Studies on the nature of research production and policy formation.* There are several critical dimensions of multicultural education that the research community must embrace in order to upgrade itself for the level of diversity in America. Decisions about research topics, questioning the fallibility of research designs and reaching conclusions about findings when the research team is not diverse are all major considerations for upgrading what teacher education uses as data for program substance and decisions. Educational research must now ask new questions about the "approved" topics for a thesis, a dissertation, or a funded research project from a foundation or governmental agency. Who is conducting the research? What traditional limitations are placed on it? Why do we hold to such traditions that were established centuries ago? Are they infallible? These are not comfortable questions. Boyer (1992) raised questions of multicultural concerns in educational research. We continue to raise some of the same questions.

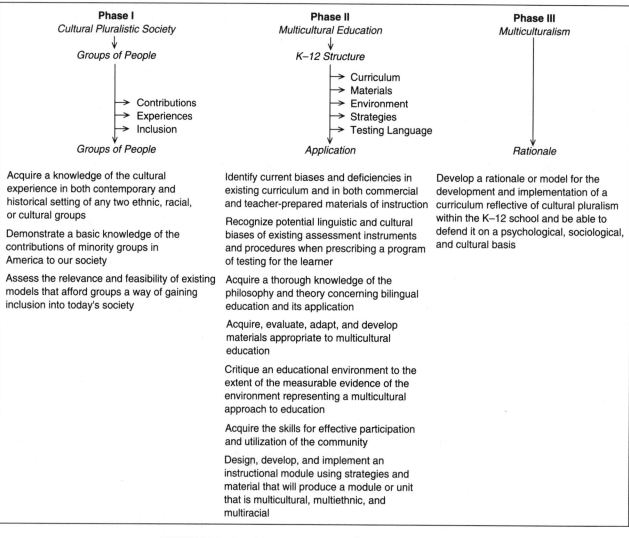

FIGURE 34.1. Cognitive Competencies for Acquiring Multiculturalism. (*Source*: Baptiste, 1980.)

Baptiste (1977), H. Baptiste and M. Baptiste (1979), M. Baptiste and H. Baptiste (1980), and Boyer (1985, 1989) cited competencies (see Figures 34.1 and 34.2) that should be part of teacher preparation programs and that address the behaviors and more appropriate parameters of collegiate instruction to avoid instructional discrimination. Baptiste, through his research, has identified 11 cognitive and 8 affective competencies that teacher educational candidates should be required to acquire before exiting any teacher preparation program. Most important is the premise that any teacher preparation program that includes these competencies will be characterized by a "cultural demeanor" that will make it more attractive and amenable to teacher candidates of color. These ideas are to be explored as part of a commitment to diversity, as well as for the expansion of recruitment of diverse populations to the teaching force.

The restructuring of recruitment and retention strategies in teacher education will require a major commitment to diversity. Until America comes to terms with such a commitment, the crisis in teacher education will continue (Gose, 1994). A major step toward this commitment by teacher educators is the multiculturalization of teacher preparation programs, as described by the typologies of Baptiste (1986), Baptiste & Archer (1994),

Banks (1993), and Sleeter and Grant (1988). We utilize Baptiste's typology here to illustrate the extent of commitment necessary for teacher preparation programs.

If teacher educators are serious about recruiting students of color, then they must be committed to restructuring teacher preparation programs qualitatively and quantitatively for cultural diversity. In other words, the internalization of the previously suggested competencies in teacher education programs will require radical restructuring of teacher preparation programs. As outlined in this typology, teacher preparation programs must undergo an evolutionary qualitative and quantitative change if colleges of education are serious about the *recruitment* and *retention* of students of color as teacher candidates. As Geneva Gay (1994) pointed out so eloquently in her book, *At the Essence of Learning: Multicultural Education:*

the position of this book is that "national identity and cultural pluralism, general education and multicultural education, *pluribus* and *unum* are not inherently contradictory and reciprocal. These relationships can be discerned by analyzing the major social values and related principles fundamental to the goals, programs, and practices of the educational process. (p. 2)

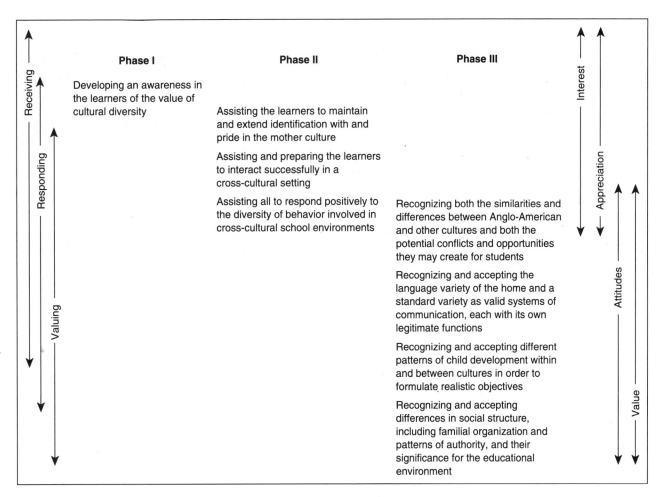

FIGURE 34.2. Affective Competencies for Acquiring Multiculturalism. (*Source*: Baptiste, 1980.)

We agree with this position. Further, Garcia (1993) stated that intellectual diversity should guide recruitment. Both positions require a qualitative, or philosophical, change in teacher preparation programs. Baptiste's (1986, 1994) typology of multiculturalism is based on the idea that educational entities, including teacher preparation programs, manifest three distinct levels of multiculturalism and that each level differs qualitatively regarding emphasis on product, process, and philosophy. This typology is primarily concerned with the qualitative aspect, because it is from a qualitative perspective that multiculturalism is internalized (see Figure 34.3).

A moral commitment and visionary perspective toward recruitment and retention of people of color in teacher preparation programs will require teacher preparation programs to perform at Level III of this typology. Unfortunately no research has reported any teacher preparation programs functioning at the top level of Baptiste's, Banks's (1993), or Sleeter and Grant's (1988) topology.

Achievement of Level III is accomplished only after successfully completing Level II. Level III represents a highly sophisticated internalization of the process of multiculturalism and the added dimension of a philosophical orientation that permeates the educational environment. This pervasive quality causes the teacher preparation program to respond to its mission and goals in a manner consistent with the conceptualized principles and goals of multiculturalism (see Gay [1994], Chapter 2). Subse-

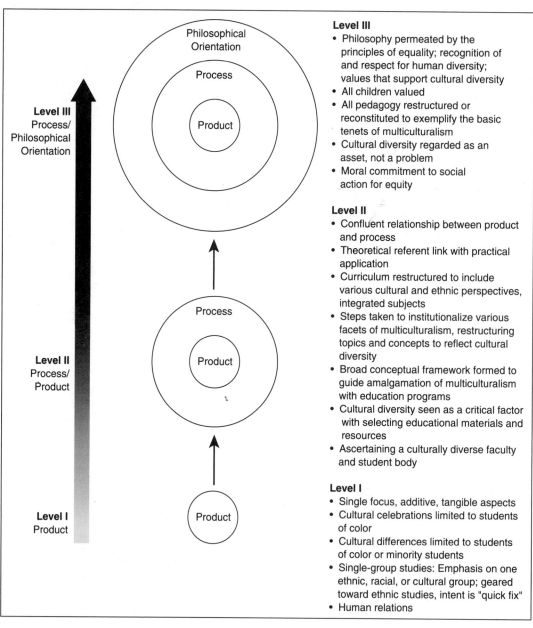

FIGURE 34.3. Typology of Multiculturalizing Teacher Preparation Programs. (*Source*: Adapted from Baptiste, 1994.)

quently, mission statements supporting multiculturalism, programmatic goals, objectives, and competencies, and programmatic delivery systems purporting to be multicultural will be transformed into the reality of a cultural diverse philosophy of experiences for the teacher candidates. Furthermore, at this level, cultural diversity is essential for *intellectual honesty* and is also regarded as an asset, not as a problem. Teacher preparation programs at this level have a sense of *moral commitment* to the philosophy of multiculturalism (Suzuki, 1979) and thus the legitimacy of multiculturalism is no longer a question, although debatable issues do exist. Finally, teacher educators operating at this level have internalized the basic tenets of a philosophy of multiculturalism that provides them with an agenda and a commitment to action. They are social activists, that is, multiculturalists. A multiculturalist leader in a school of education will not be afraid to have his or her school assume a major leadership role in the recruitment of people of color in their university. Also schools of education functioning at Level III will not be recalcitrant about establishing relationships with urban school districts to try to increase the academic achievement of all students, thereby addressing the more fundamental problem—the lack of students of color in higher education (Garcia, 1993). Increasing the achievement level of all students in secondary schools will lead to a higher graduation rate for all students, including students of color. Therefore, a greater number of students of color will enter institutions of higher learning and thus be available for teacher preparation programs. This could also ensure that a larger number of students of color with bachelor's degrees are available for master's level and doctoral studies. However, as Garcia (1993) pointed out, the most salient solution to our recruitment and retention problem must be to address the problem at a more general and systematic level. Thus, we must increase the culturally diverse pool of graduates from our secondary schools. This means that schools and colleges of education must forsake their traditional ivy tower attitude and become morally committed to a philosophy of *grassroots* education.

Finally, the retention of persons of color in teaching and teacher education will depend heavily on the *psychological accommodation* of the workplace and the school place. How "welcome" are people of color in American classrooms not staffed by people of color? The environmental factors of verbal and nonverbal behaviors will continue to increase in significance. Those teacher understandings and teacher behaviors that would more effectively serve teacher education are not yet utilized extensively or institutionalized in most programs (Boyer, 1990). Research, development, instruction, curriculum, and assessment must now become part of the recruitment and retention focus, and that focus must become high priority for teacher education if people of color are to be influenced to participate in academic enterprises.

References

American Association of Colleges for Teacher Education (AACTE). (1987). *Teaching teachers: Facts and figures.* Washington, DC: Author.

Banks, J. A. (1993). *Approaches to multicultural curriculum reform in multicultural education: Issues and perspectives.* Boston: Allyn & Bacon.

Baptiste, H. P., Jr. (1977). Multicultural education evolvement at the University of Houston: A case study. In *Pluralism and the American teacher: Issues and case studies* (pp. 171–184). Washington, DC: American Association of Colleges for Teacher Education.

Baptiste, H. P., Jr. (1986). Multicultural education and urban schools from a socio-historical perspective: Internalizing multiculturalism. *Journal of Educational Equity and Leadership,* Winter, 295–312.

Baptiste, H. P., Jr. (1994). The multicultural environment of schools: Implications to leaders. In L. W. Hughes (Ed.), *The principal as leader* (pp. 89–109). New York: Macmillan.

Baptiste, H. P., Jr., & Archer, C. (1994). A comprehensive multicultural teacher education program: An idea whose time has come. In M. M. Atwater, K. Radzik-Marsh, M. Strutchens (Eds.), *Multicultural education: Inclusion of all* (pp. 65–90). Athens: University of Georgia.

Baptiste, H. P., Jr., & Baptiste, M. L. (1979). *Developing the multicultural process in classroom instruction: Competencies for teachers.* Washington, DC: University Press of America.

Baptiste, H. P., Jr., & Hughes, K. (1993, September). *Education in a multicultural society.* Paper presented at the fourth International School Year 2020 conference, Bogensee, Germany.

Baptiste, M., Jr., & Baptiste, H. P., Jr. (1980). *Competencies toward multiculturalism in multicultural teacher education: Preparing educators to provide educational equity (Vol. 1).* Washington, DC: American Association of Colleges for Teacher Education.

Boyer, J. B. (1985). *Multicultural education: Product or process.* New York: ERIC Center on Urban Education, Teachers' College, Columbia University (now available through the College of Education, Kansas State University).

Boyer, J. B. (1986). Developing a mentality of equity: Expanding academic and corporate leadership challenges. *Journal of Educational Equity and Leadership, 6*(2), 139–151.

Boyer, J. B. (1989). *Collegiate instructional discrimination index (multiethnic, multilingual, cross-racial, non-sexist).* Manhattan: Kansas State University, College of Education.

Boyer, J. B. (1990). Teacher education to enhance equity. In H. Prentice Baptiste, H. C. Waxman, J. W. deFelix, & J. E. Anderson (Eds.), *Leadership, equity and school effectiveness.* Newbury Park, CA: Sage.

Boyer, J. B. (1992). Multicultural concerns in educational research. *Midwest Educational Researcher, 5*(2), 7–8.

Butler, A. (1990). *A content analysis of education and social science research related to young African-American females, K–12.* Doctoral dissertation, Kansas State University, Manhattan.

Carter, R., & Sedlacek, W. (1984). *Interracial contact, background and attitudes: Implications for campus programs* (Report No. 13-84). College Park: University of Maryland Counseling Center. (ERIC Document Reproduction Service No. 268-422)

Cox, T., Jr. (1993). *Cultural diversity in organizations: Theory, research & practice.* San Francisco: Berrett-Moehler.

Cross, B. (1993). How do we prepare teachers to improve race relations? *Educational Leadership, 50*(8), 64–65.

Du Bois, W. E. B. (1965). *The souls of black folk.* New York: Fawcett.

Fuchs, L. (1990). *The American kaleidoscope: Race, ethnicity, and the civic culture.* London: Wesleyan University Press.

Garcia, J. (1993). A commentary on increasing minority faculty representation in school of education. *The Educational Forum, 57*(4), 420–429.

Garcia, R., & Baptiste, H. P., Jr. (1990–1991). Minority recruitment and retention in teacher education. *The Journal of the Texas Association of Colleges for Teacher Education, 6*(2), 13–22.

Gay, G. (1994). *At the essence of learning: Multicultural education*. West Lafayette: Kappa Delta Pi.

Gomillion, M. M. (1991). Strange new world. 3.5 *Plus, 1*(4), 14–24.

Gordon, E., Miller, F., & Rollock, D. (1990). Coping with communicentric bias in knowledge production in the social sciences. *Educational Researcher, 19*(3), 14–19.

Gose, B. (1994, July 13). Tripling black enrollment in a single year. *The Chronicle of Higher Education, 45,* A31–A32.

Hale, J. E. (1982). *Black children: Their roots, culture, and learning styles*. Provo, UT: Brigham Young University Press.

Hodgekinson, H. (1985). *All one system*. Washington, DC: The Institute for Educational Leadership.

Hodgekinson, H. (1988, June). Lecture at the University of Oklahoma, National Conference on Race and Ethnic Relations in Higher Education, Norman.

Hodgekinson, H. (1991, September). Reform versus reality. *Phi Delta Kappan, 73*(1), 8–16.

Hsia, J. (1988). *Asian Americans in higher education and at work*. Hillsdale, NJ: Lawrence Erlbaum Associates.

Jackson, J. (1988). *Common ground*. Speech to the 1988 Democratic Convention in Atlanta, Georgia.

Johnson, W., & Packard, A. (1987). *Workplace 2000*. Indianapolis: Hudson Institute.

Moore, A. (1974). *A descriptive study of the effects of school desegregation on black principals in Alabama—1967–1973*. Doctoral dissertation, Kansas State University, Manhattan.

National Study of School Evaluation. (1973). *Evaluation guidelines for multicultural/multiracial education*. Arlington, VA: Author.

Nel, J. (1992). The empowerment of minority students: Implication of Cummins' Model for teacher education. *Action in Teacher Education, 14*(3), 38–45.

Nicklos, L. B., & Brown, W. S. (1989). Recruiting minorities into the teaching profession: An educational imperative. *Educational Horizons, 67*, 145–149.

Ravitch, D. (1990). Multiculturalism-plunibish plunes. *Amene Scholar, 59,* 3.

Rozzelle, N. (1990). *Case studies of African American males: Grades 5–8 in communication within cross-racial teaching and learning*. Doctoral dissertation, Kansas State University, Manhattan.

Shade, B. J. (Ed.). (1989). *Culture, style, and the educative process*. Springfield, IL: Charles C Thomas.

Sills, D., & Merton, R. (Eds.). (1991). *International encyclopedia of social sciences*. New York: Macmillan.

Simms, K. (1990). *An investigation of enhancement factors impacting the collegiate academic participation and completion by African American males*. Doctoral dissertation, Kansas State University, Manhattan.

Sleeter, C., & Grant, C. (1988). *Making choices for multicultural education: Five approaches to race, class and gender*. Columbus: Merrill.

Suzuki, B. H. (1979). Multicultural education: What's it all about? *Integrated Education, 17*(1–2), 43–49.

Vaz, K. (1987). Building retention systems for talented minority students attending white universities. *The Negro Educational Review, 38,* 23.

35

TEACHER PREPARATION PROGRAMS AT HISTORICALLY BLACK COLLEGES AND UNIVERSITIES

Rose M. Duhon-Sells
McNEESE STATE UNIVERSITY

VerJanis A. Peoples
SOUTHERN UNIVERSITY

William E. Moore
SOUTHERN UNIVERSITY

Alma Thornton Page
SOUTHERN UNIVERSITY

During the late nineteenth century when the majority of African Americans were freed slaves, teacher education programs at black colleges in the southern and border states were established to provide for the basic educational needs of emancipated slaves. Newly freed slaves eagerly sought and embraced opportunities to acquire an education. Enthusiastic for learning, the number of black children in the elementary schools increased, creating a need for more elementary teachers. As early as 1866, the Freedmen's Bureau's general superintendent for education reported a need for 20,000 teachers and urged the establishment of normal schools to train black teachers (Kujovich, 1993–1994). Missionary groups and religious organizations were the first to respond by funding private black institutions. As colleges and universities emerged throughout the South, they began providing for the educational needs of free African Americans.

The major assets of teacher education programs today in historically black institutions are the quality of instruction, culturally sensitive education environments, innovative approaches to implementing educational strategies and techniques, and pedagogically sound approaches to teaching, along with commitment, dedication, and determination to enhance the quality of life for African Americans.

Teacher education programs at the 117 historically black colleges and universities (HBCUs) tend to differ in many respects. Philosophically, a few subscribe to the Holmes Model, but others tend to be more traditional in professional and liberal arts requirements. Other HBCUs rely on portions of the National Teacher Examinations (NTEs) as entrance and exit requirements or use preprofessional skills tests and state-mandated guidelines for entry and certification. Differences can also be found in public and

This chapter was especially commissioned by the senior editor, John Sikula, upon the advice of the Editorial Advisory Council. The current president of the ATE was asked to be senior author of the chapter. This is an emerging and important area of future research in teacher education. Currently, the research base is very small, accounting in large part for the shortness of this chapter. It is hoped that this groundbreaking chapter will stimulate additional needed research.

private institutions in the HBCU community. These variations underscore the absence of distinct parameters to describe teacher education at HBCUs. Despite these differences, most HBCUs share the goal of addressing the vast underrepresentation of African Americans in the teaching profession. All believe that ways must be found to attract the best and brightest to the teaching profession; and the great majority embrace the philosophy that average students can become excellent teachers if they are prepared in a nurturing environment where expectations are high and serious attention is directed to addressing deficiencies.

HISTORICAL PERSPECTIVE ON TEACHER EDUCATION PROGRAMS AT HISTORICALLY BLACK COLLEGES AND UNIVERSITIES

Teacher training is one of the core academic components at HBCUs. As a result of rapid population growth and the barring of blacks from other professions, a need for black educators developed. To meet these demands, normal schools were organized to train black teachers and offered 2-year programs that certified graduates to teach in elementary schools. These early normal schools were named after the French *écoles normales* and were expected to provide teachers with an established norm or accepted standard of teaching. They provided for the development of teacher training programs in HBCUs across the country. For many years, private black institutions produced the majority of black college graduates. The demand of the black population for education and the need for teachers to satisfy that demand led to some state funding of black normal schools shortly after the Civil War.

In the context of a general hostility toward and fear of black education, state support for the training of black teachers was usually given, if at all, only as an unpleasant alternative to the presence of northern white teachers in black elementary schools. Many blacks favored staffing their schools with black teachers because they served as a source of racial pride and status and ensured that black youth would not be instructed by teachers hostile to their education. Despite many obstacles, black educators and community leaders found ways to provide for the educational needs of African Americans.

In the years following the Civil War, numerous public and private institutions for blacks were established. After the war, the Freedmen's Bureau, supported by federal funds, helped establish more than 4,000 schools for blacks in the South. Various missionary societies joined in the effort. Many schools for blacks grew out of the determined efforts of a remarkable bank of hardy ex-slaves who saw in education the prime hope for the rise of their people.

A majority of HBCUs were founded as state colleges, and many had significant black leadership. For example, Elizabeth City State University was created in 1891 by a bill introduced into the North Carolina legislature by Hugh Cale, a black legislator from Pasquotank County. In 1871 Alcorn A&M College, formerly Oakland College, a school for white males, was officially opened for Mississippi's black citizens. Hiram R. Revels, the first black elected to the U.S. Senate, resigned his seat to become the first president.

Initially, 13 HBCUs were organized under private auspices, generally with gifts from both black and white individuals and groups. The soldiers and officers of the 62nd U.S. Colored Infantry gave $5,000 to provide funds for Lincoln University's incorporation in Missouri and are credited with the college's funding and eventual financing. Fort Valley State College was established in 1895 by leading local white and black citizens and was generously supported by gifts from Miss Anna T. Jones of Philadelphia. Albany State College in Georgia was begun as the Albany Bible and Manual Training Institute, receiving financial support from the Hazard family of Newport, Rhode Island, as well as from concerned local philanthropists. Financial problems led some colleges to seek state support, and some became public institutions (Deyoung, 1972).

As HBCUs were established, education programs prepared classroom teachers to function in many capacities. The teachers served as role models for students and citizens in the community. They were expected to dress as professionals and to have a positive impact on community life. Many black schools had inadequate buildings, insufficient school supplies, and outdated classroom equipment, but teachers were expected to teach with maximum effectiveness.

In 1964 more than 51% of all blacks in college were still enrolled in the HBCUs. However, since that time, the percentage of students enrolled in HBCUs has significantly decreased. By 1970 the proportion was 28% and by fall 1978, 16.5%. In contrast, as recently as 1977, 38% of all blacks receiving baccalaureate degrees earned them at an HBCU. In the 4-year college sector, excluding universities, the proportion of blacks at HBCUs was 32.8%. In addition to increasing blacks enrolled during the latter part of the 1970s, many HBCUs have experienced increased enrollment of white students.

Teacher preparation programs at HBCUs have survived many adversities. Yet the ills of society continue to challenge the structure of HBCUs. The number of candidates for teacher preparation programs has dwindled. In 1963 Florida A&M University, the state of Florida's largest producer of black teachers, graduated more than 300 teachers each year, but in 1985, it graduated fewer than 100.

Until 1927 the black land-grant colleges in Georgia received an annual appropriation of only $2,000. In Florida, the average state appropriation was approximately $7,600 per year until the early 1920s; in Louisiana, the state constitution limited black land-grant appropriations to an annual sum of $10,000 until 1919. The shortage of resources for equipment, buildings, and other capital improvements was acute, resulting in a convention of land-grant colleges and universities. Although HBCUs received disproportionate funding, teacher training programs developed nonetheless.

ISSUES FOR HISTORICALLY BLACK COLLEGES AND UNIVERSITIES

Studies of teacher education programs in black colleges have revealed that they have done a commendable job in the areas of individualizing instruction, evaluating students on performance, and field experiences programs in the community. Complex and interrelated factors that impinge on opportunities for entry into teaching and survival on the job for African American teachers include: (1) racism in the regulation of teacher selection and evaluation processes; (2) invalidity of standardized testing; (3) culturally limited curricula of teacher education programs; (4) narrow range of undergraduate majors for prospective black teachers; (5) white seniority in education employment in black communities; (6) limited black research agenda in HBCUs; (7) lack of successful black teachers; and (8) instructional racism and structural barriers limiting vertical occupational mobility. Black teachers are less likely to hold principalships or other school administrative positions and are more likely to be forced to teach in poor school districts or placed with little or no support.

These factors have led to a survival imperative for the black educators. Some of the reasons for the declining enrollment of minorities in teacher education programs are: (1) the transfer of block grant programs to state control thereby losing a national focus; (2) a dearth of minority teacher role models; (3) reliance on the preprofessional skills tests and the NTEs for which minority students are poorly prepared; (4) ineffective recruitment techniques in postsecondary education; and (5) low entry-level salaries.

HBCUs remain committed to training new generations of classroom teachers and administrators. Of the 900 instructional programs offered by historically black land-grant campuses leading to bachelor's degrees, about 300 education programs make up the largest single block of courses and degree programs offered collectively by these institutions. These institutions offer a wide range of teacher education programs at the graduate level. Of the 226 instructional programs leading to master's degrees at these campuses, 125 programs, or 55%, are in teacher education. And, of the 342 teacher education programs provided at these colleges and universities, 125 programs, or 37%, are courses of study leading to master's degrees in teacher education. Of the 10 doctoral programs offered at these schools, 5 programs are in teacher education.

HBCUs have a strong tradition of providing a nourishing, caring, and understanding academic environment for all students—particularly minorities, the poor, and marginal students. Black institutions deserve to be given credit for what has been done without monetary resources. They have done so much, for so many, with so little.

The programs in HBCUs are designed to help students conceptualize the teaching profession as an opportunity to serve in a helping capacity. The teaching role is veiwed as one that not only disseminates a body of knowledge but also nurtures the total developmental process of the students.

The primary purpose of teacher education programs is to prepare instructional personnel. However, in many instances HBCUs have been given the added role of serving as change agents for social reform. Historically in HBCUs teaching was viewed as a vehicle for upward mobility in the professional arena. However, in the 1980s, teacher education has been viewed negatively, a situation that has caused great concerns for educators. Johnnie R. Mills indicated (1980) that we no longer appear to be working diligently for curriculum innovations, race desegregation, student retention, discipline strategies, sex discrimination, or even refinement of pedagogy of teaching. These problems, though virtually unsolved, have had

to be tucked away for later. In their stead have loomed problems much larger and much more demanding than ever before; an increasing teacher shortage; devastating attacks on the competency of teachers and teacher educators; the dismantling of teacher training institutions; a syphoning of teacher talent by other professions; demands to turn over the training of teachers to public schools; alternative certification schemes; and teacher tests that are fast bringing black teachers and historically black institutions to the brink of extinction. This new array of problems has forced the administrators and faculties to review, revise, and restructure the total curricula for teacher preparation programs, to address societal ills, and to best prepare teachers to be capable of effectively meeting the academic needs of the students they will teach.

B. O. Smith (1980) stated:

The failure of colleges to address public dissatisfaction with schools and teachers has created a vacuum into which state and federal governments have moved. Governmental actions are splintering the process of pedagogical education, some of it drifting into teacher centers, some into state departments of education, some into Teacher Corps projects. More and more the tendency is for state and federal legislators with little or no knowledge of a real current classroom setting to lay down directions, policies, programs, and even curricula content, which in turn are interpreted and transformed into regulations by bureaucratic agencies staffed with persons who know little about pedagogical education. (p. 64)

Mandated testing programs and required passing scores on the NTEs have prompted concerns for the survival of these programs, as well as a decline in the number of teacher education candidates. Although blacks never have been in charge of their own education, nevertheless, they have had to bear the blame for its alleged poorer quality and inferiority.

Aspects of stereotypes are still prevalent in our society. These cause some people to view white teachers as being better educated than black teachers. In the 1990s many new inexperienced teachers are placed in predominantly black schools in order to learn through trial and error at the expense of poor black children. The policy appears to be that the novice teachers are placed in those schools for a few years and when they have achieved some success in teaching, they are transferred to other schools.

G. Pritchy Smith (1992), considered by many to be one of the nation's leading authorities on the effect of teacher testing on minorities, concluded that based on the available data and if present trends continue, the minority representation in the nation's teaching force could fall to 5% by the year 2000. This fact indicates that the ability of predominantly black institutions to attract black students to the teaching profession is decreasing (Antonelli, 1985). Black students need black role models to encourage them to achieve and to consider teaching as a career possibility.

Through the late 1970s the majority of blacks and Hispanics in college chose education as a major. Presently, however, the choices of majors for these groups closely mirror those of white students. Those studying the phenomenon of the vanishing minority teacher agree almost unanimously on this point. The broadening practice of competency testing for teachers, prospective teachers, and graduates seeking certification has been likened by some as "an academic electric chair." If the policy-makers for HBCUs are not willing to change the status quo and to look realistically at valid means of attracting more black students in teacher education, they will become an "endangered species" within the next few years. Historically black institutions need to reconceptualize recruitment and retention strategies to increase the pool of black teachers as the year 2000 approaches. To achieve this will be almost impossible without appropriate funding. The J. K. Hayes Foundation is seeking support of a two-phase plan for increasing the supply and employment of black teachers in Louisiana. Phase One will focus on the development of programs for increasing the availability of certified, competent, and effective black teachers. Phase Two will address problems related to the employment of more black teachers in various school systems in the state.

Mills (1980) stated that the decline in our black teaching force may be attributed to competency testing and that blacks are indeed the casualties of tests, either admission tests for entering teaching training programs or exiting tests for entering the profession. Other factors that may lead to this decline are increased career options; low pay scales; increased accountability standards; problems in schools; parental influence; influence of other teachers; teacher selection processes; and various types of evaluation. The National Center for Education Statistics has indicated that only 12% of the national teaching force is comprised of minority teachers; the number of black teachers is estimated at 8.6%. Considering that historically black institutions contribute the greater percentage of minority teachers, efforts to keep these programs functioning effectively is of utmost importance.

ADDRESSING THE PROBLEMS

In an effort to promote changes and improvements in teacher education programs, HBCUs are involved in collaborative efforts with public schools and other universities. Curriculum innovations have been in a process of continuous change. Clark (1986) argued that HBCUs have developed significant educational changes and procedures, many of which have already been implemented. One example is a change in admission requirements.

In reference to admission, Clark reported that in most instances, students at HBCUs complete 2 years of general education requirements before declaring a major. As students apply to the schools, colleges, and departments of education (SCDEs), the application process generally includes several activities. First, a basic skills evaluation is followed by an evaluation of written and oral communication skills. In states where successful performance on the NTE Pre-Professional Skills Test is a criterion for admission to the teacher education program for teacher certification, that test, or a portion of it, is usually the instrument used to assess basic skills. Some HBCUs also administer institutionally developed basic skills tests in addition to their own tests of academic knowledge in professional education. It is recognized that these tests do not capture the full range of growth the students are expected to develop during their undergraduate preparation.

Other changes have been implemented at Coppin State University, where the admissions function is conducted by the Teacher Education Student Review Committee. This committee, chaired by the education dean, is composed of faculty from teacher education, art and sciences, and personnel from the Maryland State Department of Education. This broad input is a positive factor in student selection and in securing community advocacy for the activities in teacher education. Another activity of the admissions process involves individual student advisement based on the results of the basic skills and the communication skills tests and on professional knowledge test. Advisement proceeds along one of four avenues: (1) admission to a teacher education major, (2) probationary admission to a teacher education major, (3) admission to a nonteaching major within the teacher education unit, or (4) counseling and advisement into a degree program outside the unit. For those students admitted to one of the degree programs, data forms, which provide detailed strengths and weaknesses, must be completed.

Some HBCUs have complemented the traditional teacher education curricula with a selection of nonteaching options for those students who will not or cannot enter the traditional teacher education degree programs. Nonteaching curricula such as sports management, counseling special needs students, educational journalism, educational programming for the visual media, and day care management have been developed and implemented.

The following strategies are employed by various HBCUs to strengthen their teacher education programs: (1) increased entry requirements; (2) concentration on developing test-taking awareness skills in teacher education majors; (3) revising the teacher education curricula to ensure compatibility with the expectations of the profession, the revelations of recent research, the concerns of various accreditation and credentialing agencies, and standardized academic knowledge tests; (4) providing on-the-job assistance to graduates; (5) developing closer relationships with public schools to identify high-ability students early (9th/10th grade), taking care to nurture their career choices to include education; (6) assigning special faculty to selected students; (7) conducting faculty development activities in test construction, testing, and test-taking skills; (8) participating in groups designed to improve teacher education and general education curricula; (9) establishing performance criteria for all curricular areas; (10) reassessing institutional expectations for all faculty; (11) clarifying institutional expectations of all students; (12) conducting extensive intrainstitutional test development and student testing with feedback to faculty for input into the curriculum development process; (13) improving the delivery of student advisement and counseling; and (14) initiating structural changes and capital improvements, particularly those that affect the "academic climate."

Black colleges and universities also are recognizing the benefits of warranting their graduates via the "fifth-year" contact. Antonelli (1985) indicated that the University of Arkansas at Pine Bluff, Coppin, Grambling, and others are maintaining "fifth-year" contact with program graduates. On-the-job training and technical assistance are provided to graduates making the transition from student to classroom teacher. This fifth-year contact is a cooperative working relationship involving the graduate, the teacher education unit, and the employing school system. The goals are to ensure the success of the newly employed teacher at a minimum of expense and effort to the school system and to collect data on the strength and needs of these fifth-year teachers so that the college can evaluate its programs better. Each graduate is visited at least twice monthly for 2 to 3 years.

The School of Education and the College of Arts and Sciences at North Carolina Agricultural and Technical State University, according to Barnett and Taylor (1986), have always had a close working relationship in the development of teachers. This is due, in part, to the fact that the general education curriculum (English, history, mathematics, biology, and the arts), which is the foundation for both the personal and professional development of students, is housed in the College of Arts and Sciences. This collaborative tradition has intensified since the mid-1980s because of: (1) public criticism of the quality of teacher performance; (2) state mandates for increasing the general competence of students; (3) national studies that emphasized the need for a better public educational system; and (4) increased societal realization of the importance of the optimal utilization of human services.

COURSEWORK

In general, upon completion of course requirements in teacher education, majors are asked to select an art and sciences minor or a minor in education. Colleges of Education have designed specific core courses to reflect the major of the student. Repeated testing, computerized achievement monitoring procedures, and academic knowledge mastery of its majors are common at HBCUs (Clark, 1986).

Clark cited other activities that occur during coursework at HBCUs. These affect the students and/or the curriculum.

1. Monitoring GPAs
2. Requiring essay items on all midterm and final exams, which are constructed in part using a multiple-choice format
3. Providing peer review of midterm and final exams
4. Utilizing collegewide writing standards documented in all classes
5. Developing an introductory methods and curriculum development course for all education majors that ensures that students receive a common foundation
6. Building method courses from introductory courses
7. Requiring a course seminar or some formal experience that sharpens test-taking skills

Teacher education majors at Southern University (1993) register for the following courses the first semester of matriculation prior to taking any part of the NTE: (1) introduction to education, (2) critical thinking, and (3) education psychology. The professors teaching the courses develop a team that meets monthly to plan and evaluate students' progress. The course syllabus for introduction to education indicates the following requirements:

1. Students must successfully complete 32 hours in the laboratories with a "satisfactory assessment" awarded by the laboratory director before a grade will be received in the introduction course.
2. Students with an "unsatisfactory assessment" will be required to request an "I" grade for the semester.

The laboratories provide activities/materials related to the three courses. They are in charge of keeping records of the laboratory experiences of each student. In addition, students are required to have passed two of the four parts of the NTE before enrolling in 300-level courses. In order to enroll in student teaching, the student must have taken all four parts of the NTE. Activities that occur during the coursework and practical experience include NTE workshops, monitoring of GPA, organization of course syllabi, and taking courses to reflect the competencies and test skills needed to pass the NTE, plus engaging in computerized practice sessions and a practice test.

According to Joiner (1986) at Grambling State University, by the end of the sophomore year, students must have a 2.5 GPA; pass the institutional tests in reading, math, and English; complete a minimum of 20 hours in observation and participation; and meet the designated cutoff scores on the departmental academic knowledge test(s) and the NTE Communication Skills and General Knowledge tests. By the first semester of the senior year, students complete all professional coursework, pass the NTE Professional Knowlege Test, the departmental subject area test(s), and apply for student teaching.

It is well-known among those familiar with the literature that where entrance and certification testing occur, a disproportionate number of minority candidates are excluded from the profession (Smith, 1980). In more than 40 states where legislation has passed requiring prospective teachers to pass tests to enter teacher education programs and to be certified to practice their profession, the impact on the minority teaching force has been devastating. Mary Futrell, past National Education Association (NEA) president, contended that the challenge of improving minority test scores cannot be met without vast improvement in public education and seeing to it that underrepresented students get to college earlier (Futrell & Robinson, 1986). Ivie (1982) and Slaughter (1986) both reported negative trends for HBCUs. However, HBCUs are implementing strategies that are reversing the negative trends and data-based projections that were reported by these researchers. Two contributing factors in the decreasing college attendance on the part of minority students are: (1) the pressure to raise admission standards; and (2) the use of the NTEs to determine whether a teacher education graduate will be certified. One possible means to address this problem involves encouraging active involvement of minority alumni groups.

There is an expanding, although still incomplete, body of empirical and theoretical literature dealing with what HBCUs are doing in the teacher preparation programs. In brief, this literature confirms that HBCUs are developing and refining programs designed to make a positive impact on the academic growth of minority students.

FUTURE TRENDS

HBCUs have taken the lead in advocating the implementation of multicultural education in the school curriculum to improve the quality of the teaching and learning process. Multicultural education is an essential tool for uniting all Americans regardless of their background, gender, or race. Multiculturalism focuses on having people learn each other's uniqueness without prejudging one's character based on appearances such as gender and skin color. The first step in this process is for individuals, particularly teachers, to learn about the value adopted by other cultural groups.

John Dewey made the following statement in 1916:

No matter how loudly anyone proclaims his Americanism, if he assumes that any one racial strain, any one component of the culture, no matter how early settled it was in our territory, or how effective it has proven in its own land, is to furnish a pattern to which all other strains and cultures are to conform, he is a traitor to an American nationalism.

Hodgkinson (1985) noted the implications of the changing demographics for curriculum in the American school. For example, most Americans will not have grandparents who came to America from Europe. Grandparents will have been born either in the United States, South or Central America, Asia, Africa, or the Middle East. This change of origins raises some questions about curriculum. Historically, the school curriculum was founded largely on the background of the Western traditions. This Eurocentric curriculum will no longer be the case if we are to reflect accurately the heritage of all Americans.

Authorities (Clark, 1986; Glazer, 1988; Haberman, 1987; Hodgkinson, 1985) have presented profiles of the changes in America. We know that in the year 2000, 50% of all urban school children will be from nonwhite ethnic and racial groups. By the year 2000, 53 major American cities are predicted to enroll a majority of minority children. Presently, of the 15,438 school districts in the United States, 350 of those districts enroll 75% of all African American children (Smith, 1992).

The growing culturally diverse population of the United States is standing firm and steadfast in its demand for recognition and acknowledgment of its contributions to the making of America. Professional organizations and efforts by others to unify people of this country need to view diversity as a positive force to improve the quality of life of all Americans. The teacher education curriculum of the future must thus address the needs of all students, recognizing the demographic shifts taking place.

Increasingly, HBCUs also are considering the role that technology can play in preparing competent teachers who might have entered college underprepared. Modern technology is synonymous with increased access to information. Whether that information is provided via satellite, video conferencing, nationwide computer networks, a videocassette recorder, or a personal computer, it has the potential for revolutionizing the way in which we prepare teachers. Hence, all HBCUs envision the use of some form of technology as a means of facilitating the preparation of African American teachers.

Technology in a teacher education program is not limited to improving the academic skills of prospective teachers. It must be imparted as a tool that teachers will take to the classroom itself. Much of the school reform that is sweeping the country today is technology centered. We know more about how students learn than at any time in prior history. The teacher of the twenty-first century must be equipped with sufficient background in technology to help students learn. The HBCU faces the challenge of preparing teachers who will understand the value of multimedia technology in teaching and who will have the desire to develop multimedia courseware and applications.

A few HBCUs are increasingly considering the role that consortia can play in addressing the problem of underrepresentation of minority teachers. In many cases, the effectiveness of these consortia will be determined by the degree to which the consortia incorporate modern technology and use networking.

CONCLUSION

This chapter attempts to describe teacher education programs at HBCUs. Teacher education programs on these campuses will face the turbulence and the promise of continuing to prepare teachers for the diverse classrooms as traditional structural barriers to teacher education programs are dismantled. Educators in higher education will be required to respond to the changes and challenges that teacher education programs are facing with increasing understanding, sensitivity, courage, creativity, and competence. The fiber that is so deeply rooted in the past of these institutions must be maintained to provide the strength to continue into the future. Historically black colleges and universities are vital to the presence of black public school teachers in the profession. These institutions sponsor the largest number of undergraduate teacher education programs in which minority students enroll. Therefore, the sincere commitment to maintain viable teacher education programs in HBCUs must be as strong today as ever.

References

Antonelli, G. A. (1985). The reconceptualization of teacher education in Arkansas. *Education Week, 36.*

Barnett, D. R., & Taylor, E. F. (1986). *Education and the liberal arts: The A&T connection.* Paper presented at the annual conference on the Preparation and Survival of Black Public School Teachers, Norfolk, VA.

Clark, V. L. (1986). *Enhancing teacher education at Coppin State College.* Presentation at the Educational Testing Service Historically Black Institutions Collaboration Project Workshops, Princeton, NJ.

Dewey, J. (1916). Nationalizing education. In J. A. Boydston (Ed.), *John Dewey: The middle works, 1899–1924.* Carbondale: Southern Illinois University Press.

Deyoung, C. A. (1972). *American education.* New York: McGraw-Hill.

Futrell, M. H., & Robinson, S. P. (1986). Testing teachers: An overview of NEA's position, policy, and involvement. *NEA Today, 55,* 397–404.

Glazer, N. (1988). Education for American citizenship in the twenty-first century. *Education and Society, 12,* 5–10.

Haberman, M. (1987). *Recruiting and selecting teachers for urban schools.* New York: ERIC Clearinghouse on Urban Education.

Hodgkinson, H. L. (1985). *All one system: Demographics of education: Kindergarten through graduate school*. Washington, DC: Institute for Educational Leadership.

Ivie, S. D. (1982, February). Why black students score poorly on the NTE. *High School Journal*, 165–175.

Joiner, B. (1986). *Improving teacher education at Grambling State University*. Presentation at the Educational Testing Service Historically Black Institutions Collaboration Project Workshops. Princeton, NJ.

Kujovich, T. (1993–1994, Winter). Long history of unequal funding. *Journal of Blacks in Higher Education*, 23–28.

Mills, J. R. (1980). *Improving teacher education: A conscious choice*. Dubuque, IA: Kendall/Hunt.

Slaughter, B. A. (1986, October). *Achievement tests and black teacher education students: Hearing and responding to the message*. Presentation at the seventh annual National Conference on the Preparation and Survival of Black Public School Teachers, Norfolk, VA.

Smith, B. O. (1980). *A design for a school of pedagogy*. In collaboration with Silverman, S. H., Borg, J. M., & Fry, B. V. Washington, DC: U.S. Department of Education.

Smith, G. P. (1992). *Multicultural education: Implications for the culturally responsive teaching of all our children*. Proceedings of the second annual conference of the National Association for Multicultural Education, Orlando.

Southern University. (1993). *General catalog, 1992–93*. Baton Rouge: Author.

36

PREPARING INSTRUCTIONAL PROFESSIONALS FOR LINGUISTICALLY AND CULTURALLY DIVERSE STUDENTS

Eugene E. Garcia
OFFICE OF BILINGUAL EDUCATION AND MINORITY LANGUAGE AFFAIRS

Recent data indicate that one seventh of all U.S. school-age children speak a language other than English at home and that most of them enter school with limited English proficiency. While proficiency in their home language supports membership in the family and community and constitutes a long-run economic asset, acquiring English proficiency along with content mastery is essential for success in school and participation in civic life. Since the mid-1980s, the population of students who enter public schools needing to learn English has grown by about 70%. Estimates of the total number vary from 3.5 to 5.5 million, depending on the process used for identification. About three quarters of these students speak Spanish, and many of the others speak Vietnamese, Hmong, Cantonese, Cambodian, or Korean. Demographic projections indicate that this diversity will continue. Moreover, distinctive settlement patterns cause the proportion of students in particular language groups to vary widely within and among districts. For example, three quarters of those enrolled in California's programs for limited English proficient (LEP) students are Spanish-speaking, but some California schools serve as many as 22 different language minority groups, a situation replicated many times over in other regions across the country. This makes the challenge of teaching particularly complex.

The increase in numbers of LEP students who would benefit from specialized programs outstrips the increase in numbers of teachers with skills necessary to serve them. A 1991 report by the U.S. Department of Education's Office of Bilingual Education and Minority Languages Affairs (OBEMLA) concluded that schools need an additional 175,000 trained and certified teachers to serve LEP students adequately.

This concern to train and credential teachers to be effective instructors is not new. From the earliest days of education program evaluation, the quality of the instructional staff has been considered a significant feature (Heath, 1982). For teachers serving language minority students, the evaluation of "effectiveness" has been consumed by an empirical concern regarding the significance of the use or nonuse of the students' native language and the academic development of the English language (August & Garcia, 1988). Very little attention is given to the attributes of the professional and paraprofessional staff who implement the myriad of models and program types omnipresent in the service of language minority students. Typically, attention to the characteristics of such a staff is restricted only to the years of service and the extent of formal educational training received (Olsen, 1988). Yet, most educational researchers will grant that the quality of that intervention's implementation is directly related to the expertise of the instructor(s).

Attention to "exemplary" teachers comes from the great dissatisfaction language minority educators feel about the limited conclusions and unproductive debates regarding the relative effectiveness of bilingual education (Hakuta, 1985; Hakuta & Garcia, 1989). This field has been continually subjected to national evaluations; the most recent is the Ramirez, Yuen, Ramey, and Pasta (1991) study, which attempts to assess the academic effects of various bilingual, English as a second language (ESL), and other approaches. Such studies are continually criticized for their methodological flaws and have little effect on what teachers do in the classrooms (August & Garcia, 1988). Beginning with Tikunoff (1983), more in-depth studies of "effective" language minority schools and classrooms addressed the specific organizational and instructional characteristics in programs that were "working" for language minority students. Such an emphasis suggests that there is much to learn from programs that are serving language minority students well. Instead of searching for the "best" program by doing large-scale comparative studies, all of which are likely to be methodologically flawed, this new line of inquiry suggests that we search out effective programs and carefully document the attributes that make them effective. From such data, other programs seeking to serve language minority students better could at least compare themselves to these "exemplary and effective" organizational features, instructional practices, and teacher attributes (Carter & Chatfield, 1986; Garcia, 1988; Pease-Alvarez, Espinosa, & Garcia, 1991). More important, perhaps, are the educational systems responsible for setting the guidelines to prepare and credential educators to use this knowledge base to improve the education delivered to their LEP students. The present chapter offers but one facet of this most diverse issue, and it attempts specifically to advance our understanding of what makes "effective" language minority teachers. It is not the purpose of this discussion to suggest that all "effective" language minority teachers need to be like the ones receiving attention here. The chapter is an occasion to review the major studies that have contributed to the field and to describe the professional development mechanisms, assessments, and certifications that would better serve the growing number of LEP students.

THEORETICAL/CONCEPTUAL FRAMEWORKS

Before addressing the previous questions directly, it seems appropriate to frame this discussion in a broad educationally relevant theoretical continuum. At one end of this continuum, it is argued that addressing culturally diverse populations calls for a deeper understanding of the interaction of a students' culture and the prevailing school culture (Tharp, 1989). This position on cultural significance is supported by a rich research contribution that suggests that the educational failure of "diverse" student populations is related to this culture clash between home and school. Evidence for such a position comes from Boykin (1986) for African American students; Heath (1983) for poor white students; Wiesner, Gallimore, and Jordan (1988) for Hawaiian students; Vogt, Jordan, and Tharp (1987) for Navaho students; Garcia (1988, 1991) for Mexican-American students; and Rodriguez (1989) for Puerto Rican students. In essence, these researchers have suggested that without attending to the distinctiveness of the contribution of culture, educational endeavors for these cultural distinct students is likely to fail. Theoretically, students do not succeed because the difference between school culture and home culture leads to an educationally harmful dissonance—*a home-to-school "mismatch."* Sue and Padilla (1986) directly enunciating this position argue: "The challenge for educators is to identify critical differences between and within ethnic minority groups and to incorporate this information into classroom practice" (p. 62).

At the other extreme of this theoretical continuum lies the position that instructional programs must ensure the implementation of appropriate *general principles of teaching and learning.* The academic failure of any student rests on the failure of instructional personnel to implement what we know "works." Using the now-common educational analytical tool known as meta-analysis, Walberg (1986) suggests that educational re-

search synthesis has identified robust indicators of instructional conditions that have academically significant effects across various conditions and student groups. Other reviews (Baden & Maehr, 1986; Bloom, 1984; Slavin, 1989) have articulated this same position. In this vein, a number of specific instructional strategies, including direct instruction (Rosenshine, 1986), tutoring (Bloom, 1984), frequent evaluation of academic progress (Slavin, Karweit, & Madden, 1989), and cooperative learning (Slavin, 1989), have been particular candidates for the "what works with everyone" category. Expectations play an important role in other formulations of this underachievement dilemma. Levin (1988) has suggested that students, teachers, and school professionals in general have low academic expectations for culturally and linguistically diverse students. The more popular dramatization of high school math instructor Jaime Escalante in the film, *Stand and Deliver,* exemplifies this position. Raising student motivation in conjunction with enhancing academic expectations with a challenging curriculum is a prescribed solution. Implied in this "general principle" position is that the educational failure of "diverse" populations can be eradicated by the systemic and effective implementation of these understood general principles of instruction that work with "all" students.

Interspersed within this continuum are other significant conceptual contributions that attempt to explain the academic underachievement of culturally and linguistically diverse students. Paulo Fiere (1970) has argued that educational initiatives cannot expect academic or intellectual success under social circumstances that are oppressive. He and others (Cummins, 1986; Pearl, 1991) suggest that such oppression taints any curriculum or pedagogy and that only a pedagogy of empowerment can fulfill the lofty goals of educational equity and achievement. Similarly, Bernstein (1971), Laosa (1982), and Wilson (1987) point to socioeconomic factors that influence the organization of schools and instruction. Extensive exposure over generations to poverty and related to disparaging socioeconomic conditions significantly influence the teaching and learning process at home, in the community, and in schools. The result is disastrous, long-term educational failure and social disruption of family and community. Ogbu and Matute-Bianchi (1986) offer an alternative, macrosociological perspective on the academic failure of culturally and linguistically diverse students. Such a conceptualization interprets this country's present social approach to several immigrant and minority populations as "castelike." In this theoretical attempt to explain underachievement, theorists argue that these populations form a layer of our society that are not expected to excel academically or economically and are therefore treated as a "castelike population." These expectations are transformed into parallel self-perceptions by these populations with academic underachievement and social withdrawal as the result.

Clearly, the conceptualizations are not presented here in any comprehensive manner. The "cultural match/mismatch" of the "general principles" continuum needs not to be interpreted as a set of incompatible approaches in the attempt to understand the educational circumstances of culturally diverse students. Instead, this short introduction should make evident that a wide variety of scholars have seriously dealt with this topic of attempting to understand why so many culturally and linguistically diverse students are not well served by today's educational institutions. These conceptual contributions have not espoused multicultural education principles or educational equity policies. Instead they have attempted to address the issues surrounding the educational issues of educating a culturally diverse population by searching for explanations for those conditions.

These contributions take into consideration the work of Fiere (1970), Bernstein (1971), Cummins (1979, 1986), Heath (1986), Ogbu (1986), Trueba (1987), Levin (1988), and Tharp and Gallimore (1989). All suggest that the schooling vulnerability of culturally diverse students must be understood within the broader contexts of life circumstances in this society, for students in and out of schools. No quick fix is likely under social and schooling conditions that mark the student for special treatment of his or her cultural difference without considering psychological and social circumstances. This approach warns us against the isolation of any single attribute (poverty, language difference, learning potential, etc.) as the only variable of importance. This more comprehensive view of the schooling process includes an understanding of the relationship between home and school, the psycho-socio-cultural incongruities between the two, and the resulting effects on learning and achievement (Tharp & Gallimore, 1989).

Embedded in this perspective is the understanding that language, culture, and their accompanying values are acquired in the home and community environment (Cummins, 1986; Goldman & Trueba, 1987; Heath, 1981), that children come to school with some knowledge about what language is, how it works, and what it is used for (Goodman, 1980; Hall, 1987; Smith, 1971), that children learn higher level cognitive and communicative skills as they engage in socially meaningful activities (Duran, 1986), and that children's development and learning is best understood as the interaction of linguistic, sociocultural, and cognitive knowledge and experiences (Trueba, 1988). A more appropriate perspective of learning, then, is one that recognizes that learning is enhanced when it occurs in contexts that are both socioculturally and linguistically meaningful for the learner (Diaz, Moll, & Mehan, 1986; Heath, 1986; Scribner & Cole, 1981; Wertsch, 1985).

Such meaningful events, however, are not generally accessible to culturally diverse children. Schooling practices that contribute to the academic vulnerability of this student population and that tend to dramatize the lack of fit between the student and the school experience are reflected in the monolithic culture transmitted by the schools in the forms of pedagogy, curricula, instruction, classroom configuration, and language (Walker, 1987). Such practices include the systematic exclusion of the students' histories, language, experience, and values from classroom curricula and activities (Giroux & McLaren, 1986; Ogbu, 1982). These practices also include "tracking," which limits access to academic courses and learning environments, does not foster academic development and socialization (Duran, 1986; Eder, 1982; Oakes, 1990) or a perception of self as a competent learner and language user, and offers limited opportunities to engage in developmentally and culturally appropriate learning (i.e., not restricted to teacher-led instruction) (Garcia, 1988).

The implication of this rethinking has profound effects for the teaching and learning for culturally diverse students (Garcia,

1991). This new pedagogy envisions the classroom as a community of learners in which speakers, readers, and writers come together to define and redefine the meaning of the academic experience. It might be described by some as a pedagogy of empowerment (Cummins, 1986), by others as cultural learning (Heath, 1986; Trueba, 1987), and by others as a cultural view of providing instructional assistance or guidance (Tharp & Gallimore, 1989). In any case, it argues for the respect and integration of the students' values, beliefs, histories, and experiences and recognizes the active role that students must play in the learning process. However, this responsive pedagogy expands students' knowledge beyond their own immediate experiences while using those experiences as a sound foundation for appropriating new knowledge. For many minority students, this includes the utilization of the native language and/or of bilingual abilities that are a substantive part of a well-functioning social network in which knowledge is embedded.

Furthermore, a responsive pedagogy for academic learning requires a redefinition of the instructor's role. Instructors must become familiar with the cognitive, social, and cultural dimensions of learning. They need to recognize the ways in which diversity of instruction, assessment, and evaluation affect learning. They should become more aware of the classroom curriculum, its purpose, and the degree to which it is implemented. Of significance are the configuration of the classroom environment and the nature of student–teacher and student–student interactions. Furthermore, instructors must also recognize that the acquisition of academic content also requires helping students display their knowledge in ways that suggest their competence as learners and language users. Analyzing these dimensions may help equip the classroom for the particularly sensitive task of ensuring success for culturally diverse students.

Finally, teachers must destroy preconceived myths about learning processes and the potentially underprepared student, in particular myths about those who come from lower socioeconomic households and/or from homes in which English is not the primary language. For those embracing this new concept of responsive pedagogy, new educational horizons for themselves and their students are not only possible but also inevitable.

CHARACTERISTICS OF EFFECTIVE TEACHERS FOR LANGUAGE MINORITY STUDENTS

Tikunoff (1983) in his report of the Significant Bilingual Instructional Features (SBIF) study, reports commonalities in the teacher's response to the organization and instruction of classrooms. The 58 teachers observed in this study worked at six sites with students who spoke a variety of non-English languages. All classes were considered "effective" based on two criteria: First, teachers were deemed by members of four constituencies—teachers, other school personnel, students, and parents—as being effective. Second, teaching behaviors produced rates of "academic learning time" (a measure of student engagement in academic tasks) as high as or higher than reported in other effective teaching research.

An initial set of instructional features identified for the effective teachers pertains to the delivery and organization of instruction:

1. Successful teachers of LEP students specify task outcomes and what students must do to accomplish tasks. In addition, teachers communicate high expectations for LEP students in terms of learning and a sense of efficacy in terms of their own ability to teach.
2. Successful teachers of LEP students, not unlike effective teachers in general, exhibit the use of "active teaching" behaviors found to be related to increased student performance on academic tests of achievement in reading and mathematics including:
   a. Communicating clearly when giving directions, specifying tasks, and presenting new information
   b. Obtaining and maintaining students' engagement in instructional tasks by pacing instruction appropriately, promoting involvement, and communicating their expectations for students' success in completing instructional tasks
   c. Monitoring students' progress
   d. Providing immediate feedback on students' success whenever required
3. Successful teachers of LEP students mediated instruction for LEP students by using the students' native language and English for instruction, alternating between the two languages whenever necessary to ensure clarity of instruction. Although this type of language switching occurred, teachers did not translate directly from one language to another.

The SBIF study also reports that the teacher made use of information from the LEP students' home culture so as to promote engagement in instructional tasks and to contribute to a feeling of trust between children and their teachers. The SBIF researchers found three ways in which home and community culture was incorporated into classroom life: (1) cultural referents in both verbal and nonverbal forms were used to communicate instructional and institutional demands, (2) instruction was organized to build on rules of discourse from the primary language culture; and (3) values and norms of the primary language culture were respected equally with those of the school.

In more recent research that focused on Mexican-American elementary school children, Garcia (1988) reported several strategies related to instruction utilized in "effective" schools. These schools were nominated by language minority colleagues and had students scoring at or above the national average on Spanish and/or English standardized measures of academic achievement. Garcia's research characterized instruction in the effective classrooms as follows:

1. Students were instructed primarily in small groups, and academic-related discourse was encouraged between students throughout the day. Teachers rarely utilized large-group instruction or more individualized (mimeographed worksheets) instructional activities. The most common activity across classes involved small groups of students working on assigned academic tasks with intermittent assistance by the teacher.
2. The teacher tended to provide an instructional initiation (often reported in the literature—e.g., Mehan, 1979; Morine-Dershimer, 1985). Teachers elicited student responses but

did so at relatively non–higher order cognitive and linguistic levels.
3. Once a lesson elicitation occurred, teachers encouraged students to take control of the discourse by inviting fellow student interaction, usually at higher order cognitive and linguistic levels.

Teachers in the Garcia study fulfilled general expectations reported by Mehan (1979) for regular classroom teachers and by Ramirez (1985) for language minority teachers. Teachers did not invite instructional interaction in other than the most communicatively simple mode (factual and truncated "answer giving"). This type of elicitation style may be particularly problematic for Hispanic language minority students in that these students may not be challenged by this style of instructional discourse to utilize either their native or second language to express complex language functions that reflect higher order cognitive processes.

However, teachers were clearly allowing student-to-student interaction in the student reply component of the instructional discourse segment. Teachers encouraged and engineered general student participation once the instructional peer interaction was set in motion. This finding is particularly significant. Garcia (1983) suggests that such student-to-student interaction discourse strategies are important to enhanced linguistic development. Wong-Fillmore and Valadez (1986) report that peer interaction was particularly significant for enhancing second language oral acquisition in Hispanic children. Moreover, Kagan (1986) has suggested that schooling practices that focus on collaborative child–child instructional strategies are in line with developed social motives in Mexican-American families. The interactional style documented in this study seems to be attuned to what is most beneficial, both linguistically and culturally, to Mexican-American students.

Garcia (1992) reports a descriptive study focused on three Spanish/English bilingual teachers, a first-grade, third-grade, and fifth-grade teacher. These teachers were consistently identified at the school site level and at the district level as "effective" teachers. The findings of this study with regard to teacher attributes were divided into four distinct but interlocking themes: (1) knowledge, (2) skills, (3) dispositions, and (4) affect.

Knowledge

These teachers were all bilingual and biliterate in English and Spanish. They had the prerequisite state teacher credentials and had graduated from specific bilingual, teacher-training programs. They had an average of 7.1 years' experience as bilingual teachers. Therefore, these were not novice teachers with little general teaching or language minority teaching experience. In addition, they reported that they routinely participated in staff development efforts, either taking courses or attending workshops on techniques that they want to implement in their classrooms. These teachers also participated in courses that they sought out and financed on their own, some related to Spanish language development and others related to pedagogy, at the same time attending mandatory workshops sponsored by the school district.

These teachers were quite knowledgeable and articulate about the instructional philosophies that guided them. They communicated these quite coherently in their interviews. They never hesitated in addressing "why" they were using specific instructional techniques and usually couched these explanations in terms of a theoretical position regarding teaching and student learning. Principles and parents also commented on these teachers' ability to communicate effectively the rationales for their instructional techniques.

Skills

Despite their differing perspectives, the teachers demonstrated specific instructional skills. They used English and Spanish in highly communicative ways, speaking to students with varying degrees of Spanish and English proficiency in a communicative style requiring significant language switching. Direct translation from one language to another was a rarity, but language switching in appropriate contexts was common.

Variations existed among these exemplary teachers. However, each had developed a particular set of instructional skills that led to individual effectiveness and had adopted an experiential stance toward instruction. Along with many of their colleagues, these exemplary teachers had abandoned a strictly skills-oriented approach to instruction. To varying degrees they organized instruction in their classes so that children first focus on what is meaningful to them. Early-grade teachers used an approach to reading instruction that treats specific skills in the context of extended pieces of text (e.g., an entire book, passage, or paragraph). They initiated shared reading experiences by reading to and with children from an enlarged book, pointing to each word as they read. Because most of these books rely on a recurring pattern (e. g., a repeating syntactical construction, rhyming words, repetitions), children who cannot read words in isolation are able to predict words and entire construction when participating in choral reading activities. With time the teacher encouraged students to focus on individual words, sound–letter correspondences, and syntactic constructions. The teacher also encouraged children to rely on other cueing systems as they predict and confirm what they have read in a group or individually.

These teachers also utilized a thematic curriculum. Science and social studies themes are often integrated across a variety of subject areas. Once a theme was decided on, usually in consultation with students, the teacher planned instruction around a series of activities that focus on that theme. For example, a unit on dinosaurs included reading books about dinosaurs, categorizing and graphing different kinds of dinosaurs, a trip to a museum featuring dinosaur exhibits, writing stories or poems about a favorite dinosaur, and speculating on the events that led to their disappearance. In the third-grade classroom, a student suggested that the theme address "the stuff in the field that makes my little brother sick: pesticides." The teacher developed a 4-week theme that engaged students in understanding the particular circumstances with regard to pesticide use.

Despite the use of instructional strategies that depart from traditional skills-based approaches to curriculum and instruction, these teachers did sometimes structure learning around individual skills or discrete components. For example, they devoted a week or two to preparing students for standardized tests. During this time they taught skills that would be tested and they administered practice tests: "I don't like testing. But we have to do it. I teach my kids to mark the bubbles and I make sure that they take their time. We practice test taking, but we don't take it seriously."

Teachers provide opportunities for active learning by organizing a good portion of class time around a series of learning activities that children pursue either independently or with others. During science and math, children work in small groups doing a variety of hands-on activities designed to support their understanding of a particular concept (e.g., classification, estimation, place value) or subject area (e.g., oceanography, dinosaurs).

Each teacher's commitment to active learning was revealed in commitment to a studio or workshop format for literacy instruction. Instead of teaching students about reading and writing, teachers organize their program so that students actively read and write. Real reading and writing takes place in the context of a literature-based reading program and during regularly scheduled times when students write in their journals on topics of their own choosing and teachers respond to their entries. There is also time for students to engage in a writer's workshop. During this time students generate their own topics, write, revise, edit, and publish their finished writings for a larger audience. Like adult published authors, they share their writing with others and often receive input that helps them revise and improve on what they have written. For example, one teacher commented, "These kids produce their own reading material and they take it home to share it with their parents. It's real good stuff. I help a little, but it's the kids that help each other the most."

Teachers encourage collaborative/cooperative interactions among students by organizing instruction so that students spend time working together on a wide range of instructional activities. The two primary-grade teachers in the study structure their day so that students work on group and individual activities (e.g., graphing, journal writing, science projects) in small heterogeneously organized groups. Students worked in small groups on their own art project, journal, or experiment and did not necessarily interact with other members of their group. Teachers explained that students, particularly those who do not share the same dominant language, often ignore one another during these kinds of group activities. They felt that cross-cultural interactions are much more likely to take place when students are obliged to work together to complete a single task.

Dispositions

The following descriptions of teacher attributes were considered "dispositions." They are individual characteristics and are likely to be relevant to their success more as professionals than as teachers. For instance, these teachers were highly dedicated. They reported working very hard, getting to school first and being the last to leave, working weekends, and sometimes feeling completely overworked. They reported spending close to $2,000 of their own resources in modifying their room and obtaining the materials their students needed. They indicated that they saw themselves as "creative," "resourceful," "committed," "energetic," "persistent," and "collaborative." They sought out assistance from their colleagues and were ready to provide as much assistance as they received.

Although these teachers feel that they were effective, they were not complacent. They continued to change their instructional practices and in some cases their philosophies over the years. They reported experiencing great change in their approach to learning and instruction, having shifted "paradigms." These teachers, who once advocated skills-based and authoritarian modes of instruction such as "DISTAR," were now considering and experimenting with child-centered approaches. Moving away from authoritarian modes in the classroom, teachers felt that they enjoyed a certain degree of autonomy in their school. They feel that they were free to implement the changes. In short, these teachers had been involved in individual and group efforts to improve the quality of education at the school and were highly committed to improving themselves personally as well as the education profession and the service to students in general. Above all, they were highly confident about their teaching abilities.

Affect

These teachers felt strongly that classroom practices that reflect the cultural and linguistic background of minority students are important ways of enhancing student self-esteem and that part of their job was to provide the kind of cultural and linguistic validation that is missing in a community known for deprecating the Latino culture and Spanish language. According to them, learning Spanish and learning about Latino culture benefits Anglo students as well as Latino students. In their eyes, people who learn a second language tend to be more sensitive to other cultures. Like other teachers, they feel that being bilingual and bicultural will enrich their students' lives.

Latino culture is reflected in the content of the curriculum in various ways. The two primary-grade teachers, who organized their curriculum around a variety of student-generated themes, addressed, the cultural experiences of Latino students within the themes. For example, in a unit on monsters they might highlight Mexican legends and folktales that deal with the supernatural. In addition, these teachers emphasized the importance of reading and making available literature that reflects the culture of their Latino students. They also encourage students to share favorite stories, poems, and sayings that they have learned at home.

The teachers had high expectations for all their students. In many respects, they portrayed themselves as quite demanding, taking no excuses from students for not accomplishing assigned work and willing to be "tough" on those students who were "messing around." However, each teacher spoke of the importance of strong and caring relationships among class members and particularly between the teacher and the students. They feel that such an approach provides students with a safe environment that is conducive to learning.

INSTRUCTIONAL PROFESSIONALS

In line with new conceptions of K–12 schooling, educators have invested in new designs for teacher education that ensure adequate expertise in the disciplines that candidates will teach, in the developmental characteristics that affect students' learning, and in the knowledge and skills pedagogy. The National Board for Professional Teaching Standards (1991) characterizes highly effective professional teachers as those who demonstrate: (1) commitment to students and their learning, (2) knowledge of the subjects they teach and the best methods of teaching them, (3) skill in managing and monitoring student learning, (4) ability to reflect systematically on their practice and to learn from experience, and (5) active participation in professional learning communities. Effective teacher preparation programs promote this complex vision of professional life and help candidates move toward competence along these dimensions.

Like specialists in other fields, members of the National Association for Bilingual Education (NABE) and of the Teachers of English for Speakers of Others Languages (TESOL) have developed standards for preservice education programs for candidates who aim to work with LEP students. These students build on general program standards, such as those advocated by the NBPTS and the National Council for Accreditation of Teacher Education, adding requirements related to their special work. Because language minority students may enter the professional pipeline suffering the ill effects of poor early educational opportunities, NABE's program standards (1992) call for remediation and enrichment to strengthen candidates' abilities so they may meet reasonable admission standards. The standards require program personnel to be familiar with the particular obstacles to success faced by language minority students and to provide candidates with ongoing assessments at designated checkpoints to ensure timely identification and resolution of problems. Prospective bilingual teachers must complete advanced coursework in both languages of instruction and demonstrate high levels of proficiency in both, a requirement also often made of ESL teachers, to ensure their familiarity with issues of second-language acquisition and to expand their language repertoire.

In some states where the large size and wide dispersion of the LEP population make it inevitable that most teachers will be called upon to show competence in meeting the needs of LEP students, preservice education programs for all prospective teachers are adding coursework in language development and second-language acquisition. Experienced teachers facing this particular challenge for the first time may learn the principles of language development as well as other content that help them adjust their practice in continuing education programs.

Continuing education programs, including school- and district-based learning, college courses, and other experiences, help regularly certified teachers acquire the skills they need to serve LEP students. The evidence suggests that effective instruction for LEP students features heavy use of minority languages to maintain students' progress in overall language development, promotes mastery of core subjects, and creates a strong and broad foundation for learning English (Garcia, 1994; General Accounting Office [GAO], 1987; Lessow-Hurley, 1991; Nieto, 1992; Ramirez et al., 1991). However, even in states committed to using minority languages as much as possible, the increase in the LEP population's size and diversity and the limited number of qualified bilingual teachers preclude implementing bilingual programs for all LEP students. Because of these and other factors, districts choose a variety of approaches to serve LEP students, and each approach depends to some extent on different teacher competencies. In addition to the areas of professional strength required of all teachers, four special types of expertise are frequently cited about effective teachers of LEP students (see, e.g., National Clearinghouse for Bilingual Education, 1985):

1. They facilitate students' comprehension, using many strategies to help students understand the content of a lesson. They know what is familiar to students and help them bridge to the unfamiliar. Their knowledge of the content of students' cultures opens avenues for communication and analysis.
2. They promote active use of language, involving students extensively in language production and responding to the content of students' communications rather than form, for the most part. In their classes, as early and as often as possible, students use, manipulate, and explore the content of lessons, apply the content to new situations, and develop associated vocabulary.
3. They encourage the use of students' primary languages to promote elaboration of new information and ideas, critical thinking, and concept attainment. Bilingual teachers model appropriate standard forms of primary languages. If teachers cannot speak the students' languages, they invite teaching assistants, volunteers, and other students to do so whenever it will facilitate content learning and general language development.
4. They integrate academics and language development. Whether or not they are working in formal language programs or teaching language arts, teachers incorporate language development as a regular element in all lessons involving LEP students.

Zeichner (1992) has summarized the extensive literature that describes successful teaching approaches for diverse populations. From his review, he distilled several "key elements for effectively teaching ethnic and language minority students":

• Teachers have a clear sense of their own ethnic and cultural identities.
• High expectations for the success of all students and a belief that all students can succeed are communicated to students.
• Teachers are personally committed to achieving equity for all students and believe that they are capable of making a difference in their students' learning.
• Teachers have developed a bond with their students and cease seeing their students as "the other."
• Students are provided with an academically challenging curriculum that includes attention to the development of higher level cognitive skills.
• Instruction focuses on students' creation of meaning about content in an interactive and collaborative learning environment.
• Students see learning tasks as meaningful.
• The curriculum includes the contributions and perceptions of the different ethnocultural groups that compose the society.

• Teachers provide a "scaffolding" that links the academically challenging curriculum to the cultural resources that students bring to school.
• Teachers explicitly teach students the culture of the school and seek to maintain students' sense of ethnocultural pride and identity.
• Community members and parents or guardians are encouraged to become involved in students' education and are given a significant voice in making important school decisions related to program (i.e., about resources and staffing).
• Teachers are involved in political struggles outside the classroom that are aimed at achieving a more just and humane society.

How can these general concerns and previously discussed issues be transformed into clear teacher training activities and related credentials? California has been struggling with this question since the 1970s. The next section provides a recent answer.

CALIFORNIA REFORMS IN THE PREPARATION AND CREDENTIALING OF TEACHERS FOR A LINGUISTICALLY AND CULTURALLY DIVERSE STUDENT POPULATION

Since 1990 the Commission on Teacher Credentialing, with guidance from its Bilingual Cross-cultural Advisory Panel (BCAP), has been developing a new system for the preparation and credentialing of teachers for LEP students. The new system includes reforms in teacher preparation programs and coursework, in teacher credentialing examinations, and in the credentials or certificates that authorize the teaching of LEP students. This initiative by the Commission is based on the assumption that teachers of LEP students need specialized skills and knowledge. The increasing number and diversity of LEP students in California and the limitations in the earlier policies related to the preparation and credentialing of teachers for LEP students created the need for reform. In 1987 the Commission appointed an 18-member panel to advise the Commission on all matters related to the preparation and credentialing of teachers and other professionals who provided services to LEP students. Members of the BCAP were selected from nominations submitted by school districts, county office of education, institutions of higher education, professional organizations, the California Department of Education, and the California Legislature.

From 1987 through 1989, the BCAP converted the compliance guidelines for bilingual credential programs into quality-oriented standards. By 1990, however, the limitations of the procedures existing at that time for the preparation and credentialing of teachers for LEP students had become clear to the BCAP.

In 1990, the Commission staff and the BCAP brought these concerns to the Commission with a recommendation that the existing system be replaced. The Commission directed the panel to begin the difficult task of designing a new system. In the initial stages of its work the panel consulted with a number of social scientists who were involved in research about the education of LEP students in California and in the United States. Panelists also heard expert testimony in the areas of language development, bilingual education, and culture and cultural diversity.

The BCAP identified a number of goals that a new system of preparation and credentialing should address. These included the following:

- The new system of teacher preparation and credentialing should serve equally the needs of students from all language groups.
- The new system should be demographically responsive, that is, it should be able to react quickly and efficiently when changing demographics require modifications.
- The new system should alleviate, rather than exacerbate, the shortage of teachers trained and certified to teach LEP students.
- The new system should be clear, equitable, and internally consistent, allowing candidates access to credentials through a variety of comparable routes and providing school personnel with clear information about the authorizations associated with each credential
- The new system should recognize and incorporate the common core of knowledge and skills needed by all teachers of LEP students.
- The new system should incorporate knowledge and skills in the various methodologies used with LEP students (English-language development, specially designated content instruction delivered in English, and primary-language instruction) and a general understanding of culture and cultural diversity.
- The new system should encompass both (1) teacher training programs for preservice teachers, and (2) examinations for already credentialed teachers. Because both routes lead to the same authorizations, the scope and content of the programs should be as congruent as possible with the scope and content of the exams.

With these goals in mind, the BCAP conceptualized the new system for the preparation and credentialing of teachers for LEP students. In the spring of 1991 the panel presented a design for the new system to the Commission and the Commission adopted it. The new system includes the following elements:

- The Cross-cultural, Language and Academic Development (CLAD)/Bilingual, Cross-cultural, Language and Academic Development (BCLAD) Emphasis Credential
- The CLAD Specialized Authorization
- The CLAD/BCLAD Examinations
- The CLAD/BCLAD Specialist Credential

The CLAD and BCLAD components attempt to incorporate language and pedagogy foundations for LEP teachers, including the following domains:

- *Domain 1: Language structure and first- and second-language development.* Domain 1 includes two primary areas. The first is language structure and use, including universals and differences among languages and the structure of English. The second area includes theories and models of language development as well as psychological, sociocultural, politi-

cal, and pedagogical factors affecting first- and second-language development.

- *Domain 2: Methodology of bilingual English-language development and content instruction.* Three areas are included in Domain 2. The first covers theories and models of bilingual education at a level needed by all teachers of LEP students (not just teachers whose primary instructional responsibility is LEP students). This area includes the foundations of bilingual education, organizational models, and instructional strategies. The second area covers theories and methods for instruction in and through English, including approaches with a focus on English-language development, on content area, instruction, and work with paraprofessionals. The third area consists of the knowledge and skills needed to assess students' language abilities and subject-matter achievement appropriately.
- *Domain 3: Culture and cultural diversity.* Domain 3 includes the nature and aspects of the students' culture that teachers should learn about, ways in which teachers can learn about their students' cultures and use cultural knowledge, issues and concepts related to cultural contact, and the nature of cultural diversity in California and the United States, including demographic and immigration patterns and effects. It does not focus on any specific cultural group but on culture in general and its impact on education.
- *Domain 4: Methodology for primary-language instruction.* Domain 4 includes the characteristics of bilingual programs, instructional delivery in bilingual classrooms (which includes organizational strategies, the use of English and of the primary language, and working with paraprofessionals), and factors to consider in the selection and use of primary-language materials.
- *Domain 5: The culture of emphasis.* Domain 5 consists of the knowledge and skills related to the culture associated with a bilingual teacher's language of emphasis. It includes the origins and characteristics of the culture of emphasis and the major historical periods and events, demography, migration and immigration, and contributions of the culture of emphasis in California and in the United States.
- *Domain 6: The language of emphasis.* Domain 6 includes proficiency in the language in which the teacher wishes to be authorized to provide primary-language instruction. Language proficiency will be required in the areas of speaking, listening, reading, and writing.

These six domains of knowledge and skill are the heart of the new CLAD/BCLAD system. The requirements for each of the credentials or authorization in the system are based on these domains. They reflect our present knowledge base and serve as an excellent guide. However, several remaining issues require our attention.

REMAINING ISSUES

Strengthening Early Professional Education

Once candidates have made a commitment to become bilingual educators, their progress toward professional competence depends on the adequacy of their preparation program. According to research on learning to teach and recommendations of professional groups, several program features may be critically important. Some of these features deal with logistics, others with the foundations of learning, and others with the content of professional education. Projects serving teacher candidates use these factors to promote success:

- *Coordinating the support for and demands on teacher candidates.* Many teacher candidates have multiple adult roles: teacher aide, student, and family member, to name a few. Reducing unnecessary role conflicts, coordinating work and course schedules, and dovetailing resources can make an enormous contribution to success.

- *Providing academic enrichment and/or remediation.* Some candidates need help to reach program admission standards, pass tests in their second language, or maintain steady progress. Offering extra tutoring, workshops, and other experiences that build competence facilitates later success while supporting appropriate standards for professional performance.

- *Promoting the attainment of high standards of skill and knowledge in content area and pedagogy.* To meet the demands of new K–3 curricula, teachers must learn more than ever before about the core disciplines. Shallow coverage of math, science, social studies, and literature does not provide the basis for good lessons. Furthermore, the fluid, on-the-spot instructional decision making and peer leadership expected in restructured schools requires sophisticated pedagogical training. Sound preparation programs lay strong foundations for professional practice.

- *Promoting the attainment of high standards in first- and second-language proficiency.* Facility in using standard language forms is essential for communicating clearly in the wider society, in English and other languages. Teachers must be able to model how to speak, write, and read appropriately in any language targeted for student proficiency.

- *Extending and monitoring field experiences to strengthen theory and practice.* An important part of learning a profession is to apply its principles to real settings. Because teaching language minority students presents a special set of circumstances, candidates may need more than the customary amount of field experiences to learn the expanded repertoire on which they will depend. These experiences should provide models of good practice for candidates to emulate, and supervision should address the conceptual as well as the practical lessons.

- *Cultivating a professional attitude toward career development.* The way in which candidates learn about teaching must prepare them for lifelong learning. As the role of teacher expands to include more responsibilities and as expectations of schooling grow to include high achievement for all students, continuous professional improvement will be an essential part of teachers' work.

- *Expanding the competence of career professionals.* Stimulating and supporting the growth of LEP students while adding English to their language repertoire require special instructional skills. Experienced teachers serving LEP students for the first time may need to acquire these skills to create the kind of learning environment necessary for students' success. The application of these skills varies according to the particular circumstances of projects, but, in general, teachers use five strategies to boost professional competence:

1. *Building teachers' capacity to provide comprehensible inputs.* When students do not understand the language of instruction, teachers must use pictures, demonstrations, experiences, and other strategies to promote concept development and skill mastery, which can then provide a foundation for language learning.

2. *Building teachers' capacity to elicit students' active, confident use of target language.* While language production may normally lag behind comprehension, until students begin using the language, instruction teachers will find it difficult to assess their mastery of content. Framing lessons that stimulate conversations among second-language learners will pose new challenges for teachers.

3. *Cultivating teachers' respect for and use of students' primary languages.* Language development in the primary language supports students' overall cognitive growth, connections with intimate community, and self-esteem. It appears to provide a strong foundation for second-language acquisition. In multilingual classrooms or where the teacher does not know the students' primary language, using it as a resource presents a pedagogical challenge.

4. *Developing teachers' ability to apply principles of language development and acquisition to content-area instruction.* People learn new languages more readily when they are motivated to communicate; content-based language lessons offer the grounds for conversation.

5. *Cultivating critical reflection.* Managing the challenges and opportunities presented by a multilingual class requires the disposition and the analytic skill to learn from experience. No book of how-to's can cover every circumstance. Effective teachers must know how to find and weigh evidence about their performance and use available resources to improve their practical skills.

District-Level Credentialing

If the connoisseur model is not possible on a grand scale, it may not be impossible to do well on a smaller scale. Recognizing that the university programs were not, in the short term, able to meet the growing demand for linguistic minority teachers, extensive in-service training initiatives have become the typical vehicle for meeting these growing professional needs. Since 1974 federal resources have been dedicated to the in-service enterprise. Bilingual education service centers conducted needs assessments on a regional basis and implemented regular in-service training activities from 1975 through 1982. In the late 1980s a smaller federally funded effort located in regional multifunctional resource centers continued this activity. In addition, state offices of education in states highly affected by linguistic minority students have developed their own resources for in-service training programs.

Significantly, local school districts have implemented extensive in-service programs to meet their particular needs in substantively increasing the linguistic minority expertise of their teaching personnel. One such program in Denver, Colorado, exemplifies this in-service training activity. This urban district, highly affected by linguistic minority students, determined that its needs could be partially met by the professional development of its existent teaching staff. Several training presuppositions guided the development and implementation of the in-service training: (1) Teachers needed theoretical grounding and practical application of instruction reflecting that theory, (2) external consultants with linguistic minority expertise should work collaboratively over an extended time (4–6 years) with a cadre of local teachers, (3) a local teacher group demonstrating enhanced expertise should provide mentor support to their district colleagues, and (4) development of new mentor groups at individual school sites would ensure the systematic increase of linguistic minority experts throughout the district. The district also developed its own "credentialing" requirements, feeling that the state requirements were considerably too generous and left significant holes. A recent analysis of this in-service strategy indicates that over 500 district teachers participated in this training from the mid-1980s to the late 1980s. Significant gains in service delivery to Denver's growing population of linguistic minority students have been documented. A corps of 100 linguistic minority mentors now exists in support of the over 500 linguistic minority teachers. This mentor corps continues to provide formal training experiences, classroom demonstrations, local site networking, and curricular leadership. These experts or connoisseurs also serve to evaluate new teaching professionals.

What was born out of great necessity in Denver, Colorado, may serve to instruct us regarding the development of language minority teaching professionals and how to evaluate them. First, professional training takes on a localized characteristic. Such a local emphasis recognizes the diversity of students and programs in the local district. Over time, a corps of connoisseurs is developed locally, and these connoisseurs serve in an evaluative capacity. Therefore, highly relevent local knowledge of language minority education needs is transformed into locally developed experts who in turn evaluate, using local norms, the professional expertise of their colleagues. This is the connoisseur model at its best considering the innovative and complex nature of language minority education.

This alternative form of teacher training and district-level "credentialing" was born of immediate needs that could not be met through normal teacher training or state-level credentialing standards. It demonstrates a useful and highly responsive solution to a problem many school districts face with linguistic minority populations. This alternative form of local training and "credentialing" training could be appropriate for enhancing the effectiveness of most educational professionals, but it is worthy of particular mention in the field of language minority education.

CONCLUSION

It seems clear that language minority students can be served effectively by schools and educational professionals. They can be served by schools organized to develop educational structures and processes that take into consideration both the broader attributes of effective schooling practices and specific attributes relevant to language minority teachers (Carter & Chatfield, 1986; Garcia, 1988, 1991; Tikunoff, 1983).

Although the training of language minority education teachers is in a developmental period and in need of further clarifying research, it is clearly not in its infancy. A serious body of literature addressing instructional practices, organization, and their effects is emerging. The training of professional innovators is a challenge for university and federal, state, and local educational agencies. The needs are great, and the production of competent professionals has lagged. However, professional organizations, credentialing bodies, and universities have responded with competencies, guidelines, and professional evaluation tools. These evaluation tools' reliability and validity are problematic. The most often utilized professional evaluation model is the "connoisseur" model. At the state level, this model is problematic. However, local school districts have had to engage in substantial training endeavors, and they have or can develop professional evaluation models, locally derived credentials, with locally developed connoisseurs. This alternative, district-level credentialing process is worthy of serious consideration. The challenge for all those engaged in such an enterprise is to consider the rapidly expanding literature regarding linguistic minority teachers, to evaluate its implications critically, to apply it to local language minority education contexts, and to depend on locally developed connoisseurs.

References

August, D., & Garcia, E. E. (1988). *Language minority education in the United States.* Springfield, IL: Charles C Thomas.

Baden, B., & Maehr, M. (1986). Conforming culture with culture: A perspective for designing schools for children of diverse sociocultural backgrounds. In R. Feldman (Ed.), *The social psychology of education* (pp. 189–309). Cambridge: Harvard University Press.

Bernstein, B. (1971). A sociolinguistic approach to socialization with some reference to educability. In B. Bernstein (Ed.), *Class, codes and control: Theoretical studies towards a sociology of language* (pp. 146–171). London: Routledge and Kegan Paul.

Bloom, B. (1984). The search for methods of group instruction as effective as one-to-one tutoring. *Educational Leadership, 41*(8), 4–17.

Boykin, A. (1986). The triple quandary and the schooling of Afro-American children. In U. Neisser (Ed.), *The school achievement of minority children* (pp. 57–92). New York: New Perspectives.

Carter, T. P., & Chatfield, M. L. (1986). Effective bilingual schools: Implications for policy and practice. *American Journal of Education, 95*(1), 200–234.

Cummins, J. (1979). Linguistic interdependence and the educational development of bilingual children. *Review of Educational Research, 19,* 222–251.

Cummins, J. (1986). Empowering minority students: A framework for intervention. *Harvard Educational Review, 56*(1), 18–36.

Diaz, R. M., Moll, L. C., & Mehan, H. (1986). Sociocultural resources in instruction: A context-specific approach. In *Beyond language: Social and cultural factors in schooling language minority students* (pp. 197–230). Los Angeles: Evaluation, Dissemination and Assessment Center, California State University.

Duran, R. (1986). *Improving Hispanics' educational outcomes: Learning and instruction*. Unpublished manuscript, Graduate School of Education, University of California, Santa Barbara.

Eder, D. (1982). Difference in communication styles across ability groups. In L. C. Wilkinson (Ed.), *Communicating in the classroom* (pp. 245–263). New York: Academic Press.

Fiere, P. (1970). *Pedagogy of the oppressed*. New York: Seabury Press.

Garcia, E. E. (1983). *Bilingualism in early childhood*. Albuquerque: University of New Mexico Press.

Garcia, E. E. (1988). Effective schooling for Hispanics. *Urban Education Review, 67*(2), 462–473.

Garcia, E. E. (1991). Bilingualism, second language acquisition in academic contexts. In A. Ambert (Ed.), *Bilingual education and English-as-a-second-language: A research annual* (pp. 181–217). New York: Garland.

Garcia, E. E. (1992). Effective instruction for language minority students: The teacher. *Journal of Education, 173,* 130–141.

Garcia, E. E. (1994). *Understanding and meeting the challenge of student cultural diversity*. Boston: Houghton Mifflin.

General Accounting Office. (1987). *Research evidence on bilingual education* (GAO/PEMD-87-12BR). Washington, DC: Author.

Giroux, H. A., & McLaren, P. (1986). Teacher education and the politics of engagement: The case for democratic schooling. *Harvard Review, 56,* 213–238.

Goldman, S., & Trueba, H. (Eds.). (1987). *Becoming literate in English as a second language: Advances in research and theory*. Norwood, NJ: Ablex.

Goodman, Y. (1990). The roots of literacy. In M. P. Douglass (Ed.), *Reading: A humanizing experience* (pp. 286–301). Claremont, CA: Claremont Graduate School.

Hakuta, K. (1985). *Mirror of language: The debate on bilingualism*. New York: Basic Books.

Hakuta, K., & Garcia, E. (1989). Bilingualism and education. *American Psychologist, 44*(2), 374–379.

Hall, N. (1987). *The emergence of literacy*. Portsmouth, NJ: Heinemann.

Heath, S. B. (1981). Towards an ethnohistory of writing in American education. In M. Farr-Whitman (Ed.), *Variation in writing: Functional and linguistic-cultural differences. Vol. 1. Writing: The nature, development and teaching of written communication* (pp. 225–246). Hillsdale, NJ: Lawrence Erlbaum Associates.

Heath, S. B. (1982). Ethnography in education: Defining the essentials. In P. Gilmore & A. A. Glatthorn (Eds.), *Children in and out of school*. Washington, DC: Center for Applied Linguistics.

Heath, S. B. (1983). *Ways with words*. Cambridge, England: Cambridge University Press.

Heath, S. B. (1986). Sociocultural contexts of language development. In California State Dept. of Ed., Bilingual Ed. Office (Ed.), *Beyond language: Social and cultural factors in schooling language minority students* (pp. 143–186). Los Angeles: Evaluation, Dissemination and Assessment Center, California State University.

Kagan, S. (1986). Cooperative learning and sociocultural factors in schooling. In California State Dept. of Ed., Bilingual Ed. Office (Ed.), *Beyond language: Social and cultural factors in schooling language minority students* (pp. 231–298). Los Angeles: Evaluation, Dissemination, and Assessment Center, California State University.

Laosa, L. M. (1982). School, occupation, culture and family: The impact of parental schooling on the parent–child relationship. *Journal of Educational Psychology, 274.*

Lessow-Hurley, J. (1991). *The foundations of dual language instruction*. White Plains, NY: Longman.

Levin, I. (1988). *Accelerated schools for at-risk students*. (CPRE Research Report Series RR-010). New Brunswick, NJ: Rutgers University Center for Policy Research in Education.

Mehan, H. (1979). *Learning lessons*. Cambridge: Harvard University Press.

Morine-Dershimer, G. (1985). *Talking, listening and learning in elementary classrooms*. New York: Longman.

National Association for Bilingual Education. (1992). *Professional standards for the preparation of bilingual/multicultural teachers*. Washington, DC: Author.

National Board of Professional Teaching Standards. (1991). *What makes a good teacher?* Washington, DC: Author.

National Clearinghouse for Bilingual Education. (1985). *Annual conference jounal*. Washington, DC: Author.

Nieto, S. (1992). *Affirming diversity: The sociopolitical context of multicultural education*. White Plains, NY: Longman.

Oakes, J. (1990). *Multiplying inequalities: The effects of race, social class, and tracking on opportunities to learn mathematics and science*. Santa Monica, CA: Rand.

Ogbu, J. U. (1982). Socialization: A cultural ecological approach. In K. M. Borman (Ed.), *The social life of children in a changing society* (pp. 253–267). Hillsdale, NJ: Lawrence Erlbaum Associates.

Ogbu, J. U. (1986). The consequences of the American caste system. In U. Neisser (Ed.), *The school achievement of minority children: New perspectives* (pp. 19–56). Hillsdale, NJ: Lawrence Erlbaum Associates.

Ogbu, J. U., & Matute-Bianchi, M. E. (1986). Understanding sociocultural factors: Knowledge, identity and school adjustment. In California State Dept. of Ed., Bilingual Ed. Office (Ed.), *Beyond language: Social and cultural factors in schooling language minority students* (pp. 73–142). Los Angeles: Evaluation, Dissemination and Assessment Center, California State University.

Olsen, L. (1988). *Crossing the schoolhouse border: Immigrant students and the California public schools*. San Francisco: California Tomorrow Policy Research Report.

Pearl, A. (1991). Democratic education: Myth or reality. In R. Valencia (Ed.), *Chicano school failure and success* (pp. 101–118). New York: Falmer.

Pease-Alvarez, C., Espinosa, P., & Garcia, E. (1991). Effective instruction for language minority students: An early childhood case study. *Early Childhood Research Quarterly, 6*(3), 347–363.

Ramirez, A. (1985). *Bilingualism through schooling*. Albany: State University of New York Press.

Ramirez, J. D., Yuen, S. D., Ramey, D. R., & Pasta, D. J. (1991). *Final report: Longitudinal study of immersion strategy, early-exit and late-exit transitional bilingual education programs for language-minority children*. San Mateo, CA: Aguirre International.

Rodriguez, C. E. (1989). *Puerto Ricans born in the U.S.A.* Winchester, MA: Unwin Hyman.

Rosenshine, B. (1986). Synthesis of research on explicit teaching. *Educational Leadership, 43*(3), 60–69.

Scribner, S., & Cole, M. (1981). *The psychology of literacy*. Cambridge, MA: Harvard University Press.

Slavin, R. E. (1989). The pit and the pendulum. Fadism in education and how to stop it. *Phi Delta Kappan, 70.*

Slavin, R., Karweit, N., & Madden, N. (1989). *Effective programs for students at risk*. Needham Heights, MA: Allyn & Bacon.

Smith, F. (1971). *Understanding reading*. New York: Holt, Rinehart and Winston.

Sue, S., & Padilla, A. (1986). Ethnic minority issues in the United States: Challenges for the educational system. In California State Dept. of Ed., Bilingual Ed. Office (Ed.), *Beyond language: Social and cultural factors in schooling language minority students* (pp. 35–72). Los Angeles: Evaluation, Dissemination and Assessment Center, California State University.

Tharp, R. G. (1989). Psycholocultural variables and K constants: Effects on teaching and learning in schools. *American Psychologist, 44,* 349–359.

Tharp, R. G., & Gallimore, R. (1989). *Challenging cultural minds*. London: Cambridge University Press.

Tikunoff, W. J. (1983). *Compatibility of the SBIF features with other research instruction of LEP students* (SBIF-83-4.8/10). San Francisco: Far West Laboratory.

Trueba, H. T. (1987). Success or failure? *Learning and the language minority student*. Scranton, PA: Harper & Row.

Trueba, H. T. (1988). *Rethinking learning disabilities: Cultural knowledge in literacy acquisition*. Unpublished manuscript, Office for Research on Educational Equity, Graduate School of Education, University of California, Santa Barbara.

U.S. Department of Education. (1991). *The condition of bilingual education in the nation: A report to congress and the president*. Washington, DC: Author.

Vogt, L., Jordan, C., & Tharp, R. (1987). Explaining school failure, producing school success: Two cases. *Anthropology and Education Quarterly, 18*(4), 276–286.

Walberg, H. (1986). What works in a nation still at risk? *Educational Leadership, 44*(1), 7–11.

Walker, C. L. (1987). Hispanic achievements: Old views and new perpectives. In H. Trueba (Ed.), *Success or failure? Learning and the language minority student* (pp. 15–32). Cambridge, MA: Newbury House.

Wertsch, J. V. (1985). *Vygotsky and the social formation of mind*. Cambridge: Harvard University Press.

Wiesner, T. S., Gallimore, R., & Jordan, C. (1988). Unpackaging cultural effects on classroom learning. Native Hawaiian peer assistance and child-generated activity. *Anthropology and Education Quarterly, 19*(4), 327–353.

Wilson, W. J. (1987). *The truly disadvantaged: The inner city, the underclass, and public policy*. Chicago: The University of Chicago Press.

Wong-Fillmore, L., & Valadez, C. (1986). Teaching bilingual learners. In M. S. Wittrock (Ed.), *Handbook on research on teaching* (pp. 648–684). Washington, DC: American Educational Research Association.

Zeichner, K. (1992). *Educating teachers for cultural diversity*. East Lansing, MI: National Center for Research on Teacher Learning.

37

FAMILY, COMMUNITY, AND SCHOOL COLLABORATION

Steven F. Arvizu

CALIFORNIA STATE UNIVERSITY, MONTEREY BAY

Voluntarism is an invaluable resource for schools of the future facing reform and the challenges of diversity. Schools and programs seeking greater effectiveness must build bridges between the school and community and strengthen home–school linkages. As demonstrated by many studies as well as experience with program directors, evaluators, and researchers, parent participation is an important variable in the success of innovative programs and projects. Studies on the relationship between parent involvement and student achievement conclude that the evidence is beyond dispute: Parent involvement improves student achievement. When parents are involved, children do better in school, and they go to better schools. Lindner (1987), however, raises the issue of diversity in parent participation by reporting that to involve parents programs must take into account the diversity of families, schools, and communities and their varying needs. Different types of schools, families, and communities require different strategies for involving parents. Cross-cultural strategies for achieving parent participation have not explicitly been explored in the research literature, but there is some implicit evidence from innovative program and project efforts to suggest that bilingual and cross-cultural strategies do work in some diverse environments.

In order to establish an overall conceptual framework for exploring family, community, and school collaboration this chapter discusses: (1) some of the relevant literature from bilingual, migrant, early childhood and parenting education; (2) a cross-cultural philosophy of parent participation; (3) conceptual and theoretical models; (4) major areas and roles; and (5) questions and challenges for the future.

CROSS-CULTURAL PHILOSOPHY

The author, former director of the Cross Cultural Resource Center (CCRC) at California State University, Sacramento, adopts here an anthropological approach to problem solving based on that discipline's traditions of cultural knowledge, comparison, holism, and field techniques. Such a cross-cultural and comparative perspective is a necessary philosophical and pedagogical base for success in bilingual and other education programs. It fosters an understanding of people, problems, solutions, and issues from various cultural orientations, as well as respect for the human rights and ways of life of individuals and groups. It makes possible a connection among each individual and groups and transcends specific cultures in both study and action. For example, a social studies teacher employing a cross-cultural perspective is able to teach a global perspective through presenting materials on the cultural background of not only students in the classroom but also other people of the world and relate them to general American cultural customs.

Although schools and communities must be recognized as major arenas for cultural transmission and interaction, it is also important that the people belonging to them maintain a balance between the positive aspects of pride in, understanding of, and respect for their own way of life, as well as an understanding of and a respect for the ways of life of others. A cross-cultural perspective goes beyond a belief in cultural nationalism (i.e., commitment to the interests and independence of one cultural group above others), or even biculturalism (commitment to or

A special thank you is expressed to John Sikula, dean of the College of Education at California State University, Long Beach, who was given free reign in putting this chapter in appropriate form.

competencies into cultural systems or groups), or multiculturalism (commitment to or competencies in many cultural systems or groups). It necessarily approaches phenomena in their cultural context(s), treating them in a systematic and scientific manner. The insight made possible through such systematic comparison helps clarify the cultural complexities within and between groups. It is not an easy matter to develop a cross-cultural perspective and related skills among students, parents, and school personnel. However, it is possible to do so through the use of the more successful social science tools and techniques used to train such personnel as anthropological fieldworkers, Peace Corps volunteers, and diplomats in their respective fields.

Since 1966 this author has advocated cross-cultural training for personnel in bilingual education. It is important that programs attempt to institute anthropological concepts and techniques to develop a cross-cultural and comparative perspective in dealing with the cultural aspects of teaching and learning. Conceptual tools and methodologies from anthropology may also be useful in developing conceptual clarity about home–school linkages and parent participation and in investigating these relationships empirically. Additional conceptual tools can be derived from important relevant bodies of theory and various case studies and models of parent participation (Arvizu & Snyder, with Espinosa, 1978).

BACKGROUND LITERATURE

Of the many resources available to bilingual, cross-cultural programs, the parent community probably has the most potential for contributing to their success. Title VII and many other federally and state-supported programs mandate parent participation as one of the activities required for the development and implementation of programs. Discretionary and formula-funded projects often experiment with features and activities involving parents, the results of which are seldom reported through the research literature. The following are some examples of citations from reports, unpublished theses, articles, and conference presentations that illustrate the value of home–school linkages.

Matute-Bianchi's (1979) analysis of bureaucratic conditions argued for more meaningful parent–community involvement in bilingual programs to achieve more ideal results. Arvizu and Alonzo (1969) studied successful bilingual programs and found parental involvement to be an important innovative feature of programs, especially in achieving cultural relevance in instruction plans. McConnell (1977) reported that active parental participation in bilingual program management decisions, hiring of teaching staff, and program evaluation resulted in meeting or exceeding program achievement goals. Carrasquillo and Carrasquillo (1979) described how bilingual parents can help teachers reinforce learning through culturally relevant learning activities and through supporting learning in different language settings. Berry-Caban (1983) described the positive impact of training for Hispanic parents and bilingual programs in Milwaukee, Wisconsin. Goldenberg's (1987) case studies indicate Hispanic parents' ability to transcend low-income conditions in facilitating achievement of their children's language skill development. Bermudez and Padron (1987) found that successful programs train teachers in improving home–school partnerships through curriculum development relevant to minority community issues. In addition, Arvizu et al. (1982) found by contrasting two exemplary programs that successful bilingual programs fully utilize parent, community, and cultural resources and that less successful programs underutilize parents.

Early childhood and family projects have similarly expressed the importance of parent participation in programs in minority environments (see Chapter 16 by Bredenkamp in this Volume). Buriel's (1980) study of locus of control revealed parent and teacher contributions to child socialization and learning. Parental involvement in migrant bilingual/bicultural day care also resulted in positive program impact (DeAvila, 1976). Successful Head Start projects have used bilingual parent education and training to support parents as the primary educators of their children and to increase parent involvement in program activities (Hutchison, 1986). Laosa's (1980) study of Latino mothers teaching their own 5-year-old children revealed that teaching strategies in the home influence the development of cognitive styles of learning. Amodeo et al. (1982) found that parents can have a strategic influence on the evaluation and assessment of giftedness as well as in programming through direct participation in the classroom or by indirectly interacting with the school and teachers.

CONCEPTUAL MODELS

Various conceptual models can be applied when analyzing family, community, and school collaboration. Families or communities can be examined and compared in a cross-cultural context. Cultural beliefs, values, customs, practices, and institutions can be reviewed across major ethnic groups or countries. And social class differences are frequently examined, as are ethnic idiosyncrasies in building different types of community support.

Collaboration involves building bridges and increasing consultation and participation. This chapter reviews three basic conceptual models for building collaboration and parent involvement, with examples from the practitioners' world. By examining conceptual or theoretical models one can come to appreciate and evaluate practices and see whether they are clear and consistent with stated missions, philosophy, or goals.

The literature concerning parent participation provides examples of many different approaches that vary according to the ways in which home–school relations are conceptualized, structured, and practiced in different communities. The following three theoretical frameworks of equilibrium, conflict, and eclecticism each has its own respective assumptions and relative strengths and weaknesses for analyzing different models of parental involvement. The basic ideas involving equilibrium and conflict theories have been presented by many social scientists, but Roland G. Paulston, in his book *Conflicting Theories of Social and Education Change* (1976), presents a comprehensive and contrastive explanation, some of which is used here. Eclecticism comes from a tradition in anthropology of drawing on many disciplines. As used here, it is consistent with the CCRC's ideas of constructive marginality, cultural brokerage, and "code switching."

Equilibrium Approach

An equilibrium theoretical framework values consensus and the maintenance of balance among opposing or divergent influences or elements. Such a framework assumes that, although it needs some reforms, the existing system is basically worth preserving. It also gives primary concern to harmonious relations among various parts of the system (Paulston, 1976). Reform and incremental adjustments within the existing system are mediated in an orderly and systematic manner, and changes are smooth and cumulative.

An approach to parent participation based on the equilibrium theory will attempt to build harmony and order between the school and the home in the processes and methods employed. Arrangements will routinely and methodically regulate the interactions and contributions of different groups to program goals and activities. The strength of this approach is that it does not require major structural changes in relationships. Thus, it is less threatening to the established order. Its major weaknesses are that only changes that can be integrated within the existing system are allowed, and that changes occur slowly, over a long time.

Example: The PLACER System The PLACER System (Krear, 1979) uses a modified Delphi technique for systematically obtaining input and participation from a wide variety of opposing groups in order to arrive at a consensus for decision making. It was developed and tested with the parent participation component of the Valley Intercultural Program, a bilingual consortium project operating within seven different school districts and various communities in the greater Sacramento area. The system uses interrelated processes to facilitate the collection and comparison of quantified, documented information from community, educators, and decision makers. The enumeration and order of educational and life goals elicited from many different segments of a community are compared through Venn diagramming (a way of identifying mutually accepted areas of overlap) to arrive at an orderly consensus of goals, objectives, and policy decisions. The first part of the technique integrates community contributions by systematically eliciting educational data. The second part systematically translates educational data into methods. The third part involves evaluating and weighing goals. In using this technique, the bilingual staff maximizes harmony and support for the reconciled goals, objectives, and policies as realized in the operations of the bilingual program. Ideally, then, the community, the school personnel, and the policy-making board are orchestrated into a position supportive of the program.

Conflict Approach

A conflict theoretical framework places emphasis on struggle for change, especially as applied by the less powerful, in the relationships between opposing or divergent influences or elements. This approach emphasizes the inherent instability of social systems and views conflict as a commonly occurring consequence of interaction. Change is assumed to be a natural result of contact and conflict. Another assumption on which

this framework is based is that the existing system basically does not work and that large-scale and/or radical changes leading to major restructuring are needed. Attention is devoted to the development of alternative systems. The goal of the conflict approach is major and rapid change. Nonconformity, diversity of ideas, and dialog are considered important to the struggle for rearrangement of relations.

An approach to parent participation based on conflict theory attempts to stimulate both contact between home and school and change in the processes and methods employed by the system. The interactions and inputs of different groups into program goals and activities are mediated in such a manner as to foment contrast and to highlight needed changes.

Example: The United Bronx Parents The United Bronx Parents was a group organized in New York City to protect the participants' children from the harmful effects of the school system. A major overall strategy of the group was to organize so as to acquire greater power in dealing with schools that were dysfunctional and hostile to these children. The issue that brought the parents together convinced them that the schools were organized to serve the school system, not their children. They assumed that the schools required major changes. Their strategy for participating in achieving such changes included learning how to fight the system. In her book *How to Change the Schools,* Ellen Lurie described (1970), in case-study detail, how this group worked. The United Bronx Parents' strategies included the following areas of concentration, each with action checklists:

1. How to make a school visit
2. Reviewing the curriculum
3. Staffing (hiring, supervising, firing)
4. Reporting (parent–teacher conferences)
5. Cumulative record cards
6. Student suspension and rights
7. Public hearings
8. Parents' rights
9. Organizing against the system

Eclectic Approach

An eclectic theoretical framework emphasizes choice and selection of what seems best from varied sources. A basic assumption of this approach is that flexibility in implementing alternative strategies is pragmatically useful for realizing goals. An eclectic approach to parent participation sometimes prescribes an attempt to function harmoniously within the existing system; at other times, an attempt to change the system through organized conflict. In this approach, the parental community typically makes a choice among various and diverse options.

Two examples of eclectic models for parent participation follow. The first describes the role played by parents in the St. Lambert experiment in Montreal, Canada; the second, parents' roles in Crystal City, Texas.

Example: The St. Lambert Experiment The St. Lambert experiment was an effort toward bilingual education made in Quebec,

Canada, initiated by a parents' group. The English-speaking parents involved were "agents of change" within the public school system. They were able to introduce, and gain acceptance of, an innovative change in their children's school—a bilingual program that emphasized second language immersion, in French. The methods they used to create change and to realize success were quite eclectic, reflecting both conflict and cooperation with the status quo (school board members, administrators, and teachers).

The parents laid their groundwork by organizing, requesting a program from the school board, building a mass-media campaign, and exercising pressure through local political action to get an experimental class accepted. The parents' follow-up work included playing a supportive role by forming a study group as a watchdog. The group's final strategy was to help institutionalize the program. They accomplished this by electing members to the school board, and by becoming organizers and advocates of bilingual education in other communities. The parents participated in affecting the school program by combining support and cooperation with critical scrutiny and political action. From 1963 to the present they have, after careful consideration, selected those strategies most appropriate for accomplishing their particular goals at particular times.

Example: Crystal City, Texas Crystal City is a rural town in south Texas, historically controlled by a minority of Anglos. However, it has undergone marked transformation as the result of an organized takeover of city government and schools by Chicanos, who make up approximately 85% of the population (Shockley, 1973). The interesting aspect of the "Chicano Revolution" in Crystal City is that issues involving school problems accelerated change—first through a conflict approach, later through an equilibrium approach. Although there were preconditions that stimulated the Chicanos to organize, it was a walkout by students protesting school inequities that mobilized parents to organize and confront the existing system. Working within the electoral system, the Chicanos elected a majority of their representatives to the City Council and the School Board. Once control was achieved, this group created major and radical changes in the schools, such as banning testing, forcing a large turnover in school personnel, and lowering the median age of teachers by approximately 10 years (Melendez, 1971). After major changes were accomplished, it was considered important to minimize disorientation and to reassemble in an orderly manner the operation of schools.

Before the takeover, Crystal City had a dropout rate of 80%. Subsequently, the proportion of Mexican Americans on the faculty and in administration increased, and the dropout rate for Chicano children declined. In order to eliminate discrimination and to pursue goals of self-determination, the Chicano voters eventually created an alternative system, *La Raza Unida Party,* rather than working through the existing two political parties. This new political party was constructed on family and friendship networks and manifested confidence, pride, and a feeling of community. The contact between Anglos and Chicanos in Crystal City had to involve conflict initially, in order for Chicanos to eliminate their political and cultural subordination. After restructuring and change, the Chicanos could afford to employ a strategy that reestablished equilibrium.

MAJOR AREAS AND ROLES FOR PARENTS IN BUILDING HOME-SCHOOL INTERACTION

The literature concerning parent participation ranges considerably in the topics and issues addressed and varies in quality of treatment. Bibliographies, some of which are annotated, do exist, and are available through the usual library, National Network, and National Clearinghouse sources. For listings of centers and for information from the clearinghouse the reader can call the toll-free number 1-800-336-4560. The major areas usually addressed are: (1) basic information; (2) parents as teachers in the home and community; (3) parents as helpers/teachers in schools; (4) parents and advisory committees; (5) parents and monitoring, evaluation, and research; and (6) parents as cultural political brokers.

Basic Information

Information is essential for effective parent participation. Parents who are somewhat active, but not informed, are vulnerable to manipulation or misdirection in thier efforts. Parents who are well informed tend to be more active, as well as more effective, in their activities. Information confers considerable power, as is evident in the efforts of those in power to control access to it, as well as the success of parents seeking change who have utilized to organize themselves. By becoming personally informed about their children's school, parents may gain an insider's view of these institutions, and how they operate. Ellen Lurie's book, *How to Change the Schools* (1976), is one guide to becoming informed. At the very least, parents should have access to documents and information concerning: (1) children's and parents' rights; (2) an educational rationale for parental involvement; (3) pertinent laws, guidelines, and district policies as a complement to the specifics of program proposals, budgets, and evaluation reports; and (4) information on particular issues. Some of the materials provided in training legislation contain such information, such as Title VII, ESEA, guidelines and state legislation, as well as resources available through state education departments, parent advocacy groups, and professional associations such as the National Association for Bilingual Education.

Teachers in the Home

Parents in all cultures are transmitters of knowledge and, as a natural consequence of child rearing, are teachers and facilitators of learning. Prior to entering the public school setting, the basic interaction between the children and their environment is mediated by their parents, other adults, and other children. Anthropologists refer to this process of teaching the young what they need to survive in their family and cultural community as "enculturation." In most cases, the parents of students are the "original" teachers and remain a knowledgeable source of insights into the children's particular learning styles, motivations, and attributes. Some writers are beginning to describe how teachers can use parents as a resource for out-of-school follow-ups of school activities. Although helping their children with homework is an important function, one hopes that parents will be seen in the future as guides to learning in deeper and more comprehensive ways.

Helpers/Teachers in the School

Much of literature concerning parent participation deals with parents' assistance in schools as volunteers and community aides. The CCRC sequence on culture suggests specific techniques enabling parents to pursue "teaching" roles in schools, such as providing "insider" information on culture and on life history technique. The series of monographs is available from the Cross Cultural Resource Center, California State University, Sacramento, 6000 Jay Street, Sacramento, CA 95819. The relationship between school and home must be mediated by personnel who are able to facilitate the participation of parents as helpers and teachers in school, as well as the complementary participation of teachers as helpers in the community.

Advisory Committees

Advisory committees are a critical area of involvement, because they serve as a clue to the structure of home–school relations. A number of theses and dissertations have focused on parent advisory committees and their effectiveness (e.g., Reyes, 1972). Various districts and agencies have created manuals for the operation of such groups. However, the literature in this area addresses more than the mechanics of constructing and operating a committee; it also gives attention to policy, decision making, representation, and evaluation. The composition of an advisory committee and its operation relative to parental input as it influences a program reveal the depth of its commitment to parent participation. Its participants should have a sense of how their committee functions in comparison to advisory committees in other settings.

Monitoring, Evaluation, and Research

Although some literature (that of the Latino-Institute in Chicago, for example) gives attention to parents as participants in program monitoring and evaluation, attention is seldom given to the possibility of including parents as participants in the research process. Some programs do attempt to develop research and inquiry skills among parents, allowing them to critique research done on themselves and other parents and children, and enabling them to create research priorities for their respective programs. But not enough is known about the significance of particular kinds of parent participation in the learning of children. Parents are not generally informed on the inadequacies and limitations of testing instruments or on their rights in protecting their children from abuse as human subjects involved in research. A well-informed and active person interested in parent participation will not neglect this vital area.

Cultural and Political Brokers

This area addresses innovation, power, and change in schools and communities. Parents and teachers are not only transmitters of cultural knowledge but also active political beings who can innovate, mediate, and solve cultural problems. A broker is a go-between, a person who links different entities, or mediates opposing forces. Accepting such a role implies that a person has reflected on what exists and what should be and is committed to bringing the two into relationship. For parents and teachers to become effective cultural and political brokers, it is imperative that they become proficient at building linkages and bridges between the home and school. The role, or roles, that a parent or teacher assumes should be informed by a comparative understanding of the various roles that are possible and a careful consideration of strategy and impact. Good training does not leave the formulation of such strategies to chance but attempts to develop various alternatives from which the participant can choose. Ultimate *choice* and *action* are the responsibility of individuals and their respective groups and communities.

CONCLUSION

Parent participation may affect major changes in the relationship between the school and the home community and the impact of this relationship on students. It also runs the risk of becoming routinized and institutionalized into traditional insignificant forms. The degree of impact that parent participation will make on education depends greatly on the quantity of resources and the quality of effort devoted to it. This author's position is that high minimum standards must be set for implementing parent involvement and that critical thinking and conceptual clarity must be brought to bear on the creation of a strong parental component. It is suggested that integration of the cultural domain of teaching and learning with those components of programs involving parents and community would work to strengthen each other. It is difficult to implement adequate cross-cultural instruction without an adequate plan for parent participation. Where a program has developed such home–school linkages, it is probable that cultural resources from the surrounding community are being utilized. It is also suggested that parent participation should not be treated merely as that which is permitted by narrow interpretations of what presently exists. For bilingual education and all of schooling to succeed as an innovative experimental movement, it is important that its clients (i.e., students and parents) participate actively with school personnel in creating and testing innovative approaches.

This chapter by exploring comparative models has focused on the kinds of training that may be needed for effective parental involvement to occur. The task of making schools more responsive to various language and cultural groups requires a wide repertoire of strategies, skills, and approaches, as well as the conceptual and theoretical tools necessary for developing clarity of direction and for minimizing contradiction and waste of resources. The literature concerning parent participation examined here does not yet point clearly to any one direction or plan of action. But perhaps continuing to ask basic questions can challenge each of us to strive for excellence in parent participation as we strive for excellence in other aspects of the teaching and learning process. Acting on the assumption that asking the right questions is a key to arriving at adequate solutions, the following questions are offered for consideration:

1. What training is necessary for school personnel to understand the world of the home and to help them become effective cultural brokers in home–school relations?
2. What kind of training is important for parents to understand the world of the school and to help them be effective cultural brokers in home–school relations?
3. How can we develop quality and clarity of direction in parent participation components?
4. What does "parent participation" mean in different communities?
5. How is parent participation related to student learning?
6. What rules or codes of conduct at work in the various communities served by the school does one need to know in order to build home–school linkages?
7. Do certain approaches to parent participation work better than others?
8. What are the responsibilities of parents? teachers? administrators? students?
9. What are the various roles in building home–school linkages? for oneself? for others?
10. What are the ideals for home–school linkages and parent participation in bilingual education programs?
11. What is the reality with regard to parent participation in bilingual programs? Are there disparities between the ideals and realities?

Finding answers to these and other similar questions will help shape the future potential of bilingual and cross-cultural education and other innovative pedagogical movements.

Finally, further research is needed to advance knowledge about family, community, and school collaboration. A sampling of questions in need of further study follows:

1. How can school change be best promoted during an era of economic retrenchment?
2. What types of staff development are needed in schools to allow appropriate changes to be made?
3. How do changing demographics in local schools and communities affect the nature and rate of educational and personnel changes needed?

Finding workable answers to these questions will go a long way in addressing the current crisis in American schooling.

References

Amodeo, L., et al. (1982, October). *Parental involvement in the identification of gifted Mexican American children*. Paper presented at the Council for Exceptional Children national conference, Phoenix, AZ.

Arvizu, S., et al. (1982). *Bilingual education community study project. Final report*. Washington, DC: National Institute of Education.

Arvizu, S. F., & Alonzo, M. (1969). *A procedural manual for implementing successful bilingual programs*. Sacramento: California State University.

Arvizu, S. F., & Snyder, W., with Espinosa, F. T. (1978). *Conceptual and theoretical tools for demystifying culture*. Sacramento: Cross Cultural Resource Center.

Bermudez, A., & Padron, Y. (1987). Integrating parental education into teacher training programs: A workable model for minority parents. *Journal Educational Equity and Leadership, 7*(3), 235–244.

Berry-Caban, C. (1983). Parent–community involvement: The effects of training in a public school bilingual education program. *Small Group Behavior, 14*(3), 359–368.

Buriel, R. (1980, May). *The relation of Anglo and Mexican American children's locus of control beliefs to parents' and teachers' socialization practices*. Paper presented at the Western Psychological Association, Honolulu, HI.

Carrasquillo, A., & Carrasquillo, C. (1979, Winter). Bilingual parents can help you teach reading and language arts in English. *Journal for the National Association for Bilingual Education*, 83–91.

DeAvila, M. F. (1976). *A model parental involvement program for bilingual/bicultural development day care*. Unpublished master's thesis, Washington State University, Pullman.

Goldenberg, C. (1987). Low-income, Hispanic parents' contributions to their first-grade children's word-recognition skills. *Anthropology and Education Quarterly, 18*(3), 149–179.

Hutchison, M. A. (1986). *Strengthening Head Start families: Reducing high risk through mental health prevention intervention*. Final report. San Fernando, CA: Latin American Civic Association Head Start.

Krear, M. L. (1979). *The PLACER system: A three part accountability model*. Auburn, CA: Placer County, Office of Education.

Laosa, L. (1980). Maternal teaching strategies and cognitive styles in Chicano families. *Journal of Educational Psychology, 72*(1), 45–54.

Lindner, B. (1987, November). *Parental involvement in education: The ECS survey of state initiatives for youth at risk*. Denver: Education Commission of the States.

Lurie, E. (1970). *How to change the schools*. New York: Random House.

Matute-Bianchi, M. E. (1979, June). *The federal mandate for bilingual education: Some implications for parent and community participation*. Paper presented at the Ethnoperspectives Forum on Bilingual Education, Ypsilanti, MI.

McConnell, B. (1977). *Bilingual mini schools tutoring project. Final evaluation report*. Wenatchee: Washington Intermediate School District, 171.

Melendez, A. (1971). *Crystal City: A case study in educational innovation*. Unpublished masters thesis, California State University, Sacramento.

Paulston, R. G. (1976). *Conflicting theories of social and educational change: A typological review*. Pittsburgh: University of Pittsburgh.

Reyes, R. (1972). *The role of school district advisory committees in the educational decision making process of ESEA Title I programs for disadvantaged children in California*. Unpublished dissertation, Michigan State University, East Lansing.

Shockley, J. (1973). Crystal City: Los cinco Mexicanos. In *Chicano: The evolution of people*. Minneapolis: Winston Press.

·38·

SPECIAL EDUCATION AND INCLUSION

Jennifer Lowell York

UNIVERSITY OF MINNESOTA

Maynard C. Reynolds

UNIVERSITY OF MINNESOTA

Special education operates at the tough, moving edge of schools that are expected, indeed mandated, to serve literally all children, and to do so without segregating against or isolating any children. The challenge of achieving universal and inclusive education is increasing because of the growing diversity of children to be served. Changes associated with globalization of the economy have left backwater regions of disinvestment in the inner cities and some rural areas, in which the lives of many families and their children have fallen into disorder and neglect. Increasing numbers of children and their families are poor and many of them live in unsafe, unhealthy, and decaying communities. Students exhibiting all forms of social morbidity are entering the schools, where they need to be understood and helped to learn. Placements of children with severe disabilities in residential institutions have dropped to near zero rates and have increased in local schools (Bruninks & Lakin, 1985). A Rand report tells that the numbers of migrant children entering the schools in the 1980s was larger than in any other decade in U.S. history (McDonnell & Hill, 1993). Large numbers of poorly educated immigrant children enter schools, especially the already overburdened schools of the large cities.

Education for students who are exceptional calls for engagement with special educators and kindred workers, such as school psychologists, social workers, and general education teachers, and work with parents. In increasing numbers of communities, new linkages are being established among schools, social and health agencies, and corrections authorities in order to add coherence to the broad patterns of service required by some students and their families. Special educators are often the pioneers in seeking broadly framed, collaborative relationships among schools, families, and community agencies.

In 1975, the year of passage of the Education for All Handicapped Children Act (PL 94-142), there were approximately 51 million children in schools of the United States, a figure projected to drop to 44 million a decade later (U.S. Bureau of the Census, 1983). The decline in enrollment reduced general demands for school funds and lowered needs for new teachers (actually many teachers lost jobs in that period), but this came exactly in a time of rapidly growing special education programs that took up some of the developing slack in teacher employment. In Minnesota, for example, the number of special education teachers for students with disabilities increased by 95% from 1974 through 1983; in the same period the number of regular secondary and elementary teachers in the state decreased by 25% and 9.5%, respectively (*Newsletter,* 1984). Significant numbers of teachers released from general education positions took training to qualify for openings in special education and other categorical programs.

In 1985, a small increase in the school-age population was observed nationally and predictions suggested a trend moving the K–12 enrollment count back to about 50 million by the year 2000. This puts us now (in the 1990s) in a period of general expansion of school enrollments, but with the recently developed categorical programs now competitive with general education for funds and for teachers.

Special education is expensive. Rising costs for special programs in the 1950s, 1960s, and early 1970s were affordable because of the expanding national economy. Slowed economic development in the mid-1970s occurred at a time of decline in the general child population, which enabled the continuing relatively high per-pupil support of schools. But now that situation has reversed; there is high demand but very tight resources. The public debt is enormous, and resistance to tax increases is high.

A situation in New York City illustrates the current troublesome economic scene. At a time when the city was required to cut its school budget by more than $500 million, it was noted that 25% of the total school expenditures were tied to special education (Berger, 1991). Governmental rules and regulations put the special education funds largely beyond control of the school authorities. Clearly, special education in the 1990s exists in a cash-short and highly competitive economic environment.

MOVEMENT TOWARD INCLUSION

Another feature of the present context is a marked turn against practices that label some children in potentially demeaning ways and set them aside in separate places for their education. For most of its history, and in an effort to meet individual instructional needs, special education turned in what must be judged now as the wrong direction—toward isolation. *Inclusion* is now emerging as a dominant principle in student placements and programs. Pressures to be inclusive within the regular schools of the community extend even to the students who show the most severe and profound disabilities. The *inclusive* trend involves renegotiation of relations not only between special education and general education but also among all forms of categorical programs.

A major question emerges in that busy context, "What should be the design characteristics of an inclusive school system?" Clearly, it is not a sufficient strategy simply to return students with disabilities to unchanged mainstream programs. The need is for re-created regular school programs that can meet more effectively the diverse and individual needs of all students with good results. One of the greatest challenges is to create educational programs that meet individual needs in an increasingly diverse general education, community, and social context. Students who have special education needs are only some of the many students who require carefully designed interventions and support to enhance their learning and life situation.

At least since the early 1960s the idea of a continuum of administrative arrangements has been prominent in special education policies and practices (Reynolds, 1962). The continuum includes placement possibilities for special education students ranging from regular day school classes to specialized part-time resource rooms and on to special classes and special schools. The policy associated with the continuum idea suggested that exceptional students should remain in regular classes and schools whenever this was feasible and be separated only for compelling reasons and always at a minimum level. This is the "least restrictive environment" policy, as now specified by federal law. The following list presents excerpts from federal statutes related to the presumption of inclusive educational services for students with disabilities:

- Unless a handicapped child's individualized education program requires some other arrangement, the child is educated in the school which he or she would attend if not handicapped. (34 CFR 300.552)
- School districts which receive Federal funds . . . "shall educate, or shall provide for the education of, each qualified handicapped person in its jurisdiction with persons who are not handicapped to the maximum extent appropriate to the needs of the handicapped person. A recipient [of Federal funds] shall place a handicapped person in the regular educational environment operated by the recipient unless it is demonstrated by the recipient that the education of the person in the regular environment with the use of supplementary aids and services cannot be achieved satisfactorily. Whenever a recipient places a person in a setting other than the regular educational environment . . . it shall take into account the proximity of the alternate setting to the person's home. (34 CFR 104.34)

Today, there is much disagreement about the continuum model (Laski, 1991; Nevin, Villa, & Thousand. 1992; Taylor, 1988). On one side, Lou Brown, a leading advocate for programs that include all students, even those with severe and profound disabilities, speaks decisively of "continuum tolerators" (Brown, 1991). He argues for total inclusion of students with disabilities in general education schools, classrooms, and community environments, along with the provision of necessary services and supports. Taylor (1988) raises concern that a continuum model erroneously asserts that amount of service and location of service are covariates, that in order to get service and support, students must go to a more restrictive (segregated) environment. Nevin et al. (1992) suggest a change in paradigm from a *continuum* to an *array* of services, with unique learner challenges addressed first by the primary instructional resource for all students, the members of a collaborative team. Effective collaborative approaches, they argue, can result in creative solutions and expanded local capacity to address instructional and organizational challenges. Similarly, Skrtic (1991) proposes fundamental changes, including a turn to "adhocracies" to replace the ineffective professional and bureaucratic structures currently in place in schools.

However, in his widely read column in *The New York Times*, Albert Shanker (1993), President of the American Federation of Teachers, takes quite a different view:

No other country in the world has total inclusion. Its rapid spread constitutes a decision, based on ideology, to experiment on 40 million children—the disabled and the rest. . . . The people who advocate this brand of inclusion are likely to fail when taxpayers, disgusted with the further deterioration of the public schools, turn to vouchers and private schools, and disabled children are left behind in the public schools. (p. E4)

Also voicing opposition to the inclusion movement are some advocates in the area of hearing impairments. Moores (1987) contends that individuals who are deaf face a complex situation and often learn best in a deaf culture where their communication and the other unique needs specific to their disability are accommodated.

Despite sometimes strong opposing perspectives, undoubtedly the strong trend in educational placements is toward inclusion, and it has important implications for the learning of all students and for the functioning of all educators. Inclusion requires integrated operations of the bureaucracies, funding systems, professional organizations, institutions of higher education, and advocacy groups. It requires corresponding changes—toward inclusiveness—in teacher education programs. Achieving changes across these side elements of the "system" may be the most difficult part of implementing an inclusion policy because it involves diverse values, putting money into different channels, and other changes requiring political negotiations. Organizations that were effective in causing the development of special education in its present model may find it difficult to support a different course.

PERSONNEL SUPPLY AND DEMAND

Table 38.1 summarizes current facts of supply, demand, and training resources relating to special education teachers. About 297,000 special education teachers are employed in the nation in the early 1990s. Nearly 10% of that number were estimated to be "needed," defined to include vacancies and positions filled by noncertified personnel. Unfortunately, the attrition rate for special education teachers (estimated at 7.3% per year) tends to be higher than for general educators (5.6%) (Hoover & Bowen, 1993).

A turnover or attrition rate of 7.3% applied to the total number of teachers employed ($N = 296,862$ in 1990–1991) suggests a need for 21,670 new teachers annually just to replace those who leave the field of special education. The number of teaching positions has been increasing, which also needs to be taken into account in calculating needs for new special education teachers. For example, the increase in numbers of teachers in the 1-year period between 1988–1989 and 1989–1990 was 1.4%. Combining attrition and growth data, one might estimate for recent years a need annually for new teachers at about 8.7% of the total employed. This yields the number 25,827, a figure distinctly higher than the total number of degrees being offered in the field by institutions of higher education (see Table 38.2).

The interpretation of data on new trainees is complicated by a number of factors. As reported in Table 38.2, the colleges and universities of the nation awarded 15,871 degrees in special education in the academic year 1989–1990. Most of the degrees (except at the doctoral level) undoubtedly were focused in teacher preparation. A report on "newly qualified teachers" (NQT) for the year 1991 showed that 76.2% of the NQT in

TABLE 38.1. Special Education Teacher Supply, Needs, and Attrition

	Numbers
Special education teachers employed in K–12 programs in United States and insular areas in the 1990–1991 school year (U.S. Department of Education, 1992)	296,862
Special education teachers "needed" in these same areas in 1990–1991 (U.S. Department of Education, 1992)—includes vacancies and positions filled by noncertified persons	26,934
	Percentages
Attrition rate per year (National Center for Educational Statistics, 1991)	
Special education teachers	7.3
Total teachers	5.6
Teachers of students with mental retardation	12.6
Teachers of students with learning disabilities	4.3
"Other" special education teachers	8.4

TABLE 38.2. Summary Data on Trainees and Programs of Teacher Education in Special Education

Degree[1]	Number		
Bachelor's	6,625		
Master's	9,033		
Doctorate	213		
All degrees	15,871[2]		

Degree/Level[3]	Public	Private	Total
Bachelor's degree and post-bachelor's	326	160	396
Master's degree and post-master's	312	133	445
Doctoral degree	45	11	56

[1]Special education professionals obtaining degrees in 1989–1990 (Broyles & Morgan, 1992).

[2]This represents a steadily declining number since 1977–1978 when the number of special education degrees was 20,703. About 90% of all special education degree recipients in 1989–1990 were women.

[3]Number of higher education institutions (public and private) offering special education programs in the United States during 1989–1990 (Broyles & Morgan, 1992).

special education were actually teaching one year later. Of those teaching, only 60.1% reported that they felt prepared to teach (U.S. Department of Education, National Center for Education Statistics, 1993).

Data on teacher education graduates are ambiguous for some purposes, because qualification for special education teaching does not always involve a college degree. Teachers who already hold general teaching credentials are known frequently to take the necessary courses, but not a new degree, to qualify for certification in the field of special education teaching. Table 38.2 shows that about 396 institutions of higher education offered preparation at the bachelor's level and 445 at the master's and post–master's degree levels in special education.

An interesting and significant study by Singer (1993) tells of another complication in considering needs for new teachers. She gathered longitudinal data on all special education teachers employed in the State of Michigan between 1972 and 1985. Of the 2,700 who left the field, 34% reentered the classroom within 5 years. She concluded that "a return to teaching after a brief interruption may be a common career path" (p. 58) for special education teachers. This indicates that most calculations, usually based on short-term studies, probably yield too high an estimate of needs for new teachers and that former teachers comprise a significant reserve pool for new hires in special education and in other fields as well. In a study conducted on teachers in the State of Virginia, Cross and Billingsley (1994) concluded that school districts "can modify the work-related variables that influenced job satisfaction, which in turn may influence intent to stay" (p. 419). Clearly, a concern for teacher supply requires attention to complex topics besides simple rates on those leaving and on new entrants.

Studies in which attempts are made to estimate so-called "burnout" rates of special educators continue to vary in conclusions; and it is not clear that burnout correlates highly with attrition. A study by Frank and McKenzie (1993) showed that measured stress increased over a 5-year period for beginning teachers; their data also confirmed the oft-cited observation that burnout is particularly frequent and severe for teachers of students showing behavior problems.

A particularly challenging problem in teacher supply concerns instruction for students who are disabled and who have other special needs as well, for example, newly immigrant children who show low English proficiency plus a disabling condition. In major cites, such as Los Angeles, there are substantial needs for special education teachers who are also bilingual or able to offer credible instruction in English as a second language (ESL). Qualifications for multiple teacher certification are expensive in both time and money and often the rewards do not compensate fully. This is an area requiring extraordinary attention and creativity.

TEACHING STUDENTS WITH DISABILITIES IN INCLUSIVE SETTINGS: A REVIEW OF LITERATURE

In the late 1970s and the early to mid-1980s a substantial mainstreaming literature emerged from educational programs designed for students (predominantly those with mild disabilities) who were mainstreamed into general education classes. Much of that literature was summarized in the 1990 *Handbook of Research on Teacher Education* (Reynolds, 1990).

Quite early in the history of the so-called regular education initiative (REI) (Lloyd, Singh, & Repp, 1991), a movement proposing that increased efforts were required by general educators to accommodate students with disabilities, a number of research efforts were reported that used a scale produced by Walker and Rankin (1983). The scale was used with teachers to reflect standards held in their classes for learning and behavior. For example, a teacher might indicate that certain behaviors would be tolerated in his or her class (e.g., drooling, hyperactivity), other behaviors would be acceptable only if technical assistance were provided (e.g., low self-help), and still other behaviors would be unacceptable (e.g., incontinence). The idea was that "simply placing a student with a disability in a regular education environment can be an extremely punishing, frustrating, and negative experience if . . . the student is unprepared to deal with the minimal demands and performance requirements of the setting" (Walker & Bullis, 1991, p. 75). But the argument might be advanced that the preparation of the teacher is equally relevant with that of the student, as is the presence of appropriate services and support. In that sense, the studies conducted using the Walker-Rankin and other similar scales are helpful in revealing domains of importance in teacher preparation (Gersten, Walker, & Darch, 1988; Safron & Safron, 1984).

To move beyond this early literature, the search made in preparation of this chapter began with publications since 1987 in which the language of integration or inclusion is gaining preference over mainstreaming. This review focuses on teacher education research related to educating students with the full range of disabilities in inclusive settings and on implications for both general education and special education teachers.

A search was made through the ERIC system using the key words of mainstreaming (inclusion is not recognized by ERIC as a key word), regular educators (general educators is not recognized by ERIC), special educators, preservice, and in-

service. The key word mainstreaming alone yielded approximately 5,000 resources. When crossed with the additional descriptors, 178 entries were located. Of this set, 32 were deleted because they addressed practices in countries that follow policies distinctly different from those in North America or practices related to unique applications (e.g., vocational schools). The remaining 146 articles were reviewed for this chapter. In addition, selected books and education journals were used to supplement this review.

In this section, we attempt to report an objective review of literature allowing the themes to emerge from the sources. A Q-sort of individual references was conducted to determine categories for reporting the findings from the literature. The review is organized into two parts in accord with a distinction between declarative and procedural knowledge. Declarative knowledge, that is, what teachers should know, is the major corpus of knowledge and encompasses scientific knowledge, maxims, beliefs, values, behaviors (competencies), and other factors that have credibility for their influence on teaching and learning. Declarative knowledge can tend to be abstract in the sense that it does not suggest *how* it can be or should be attained; and it does not encompass elements of context that are always encountered in practice. A knowledgeable teacher will know, for example, that encouraging students to be self-managing or metacognitive in learning is important, but there surely are innumerable ways to learn about this topic and still more matters to consider in the context of real-life teaching. Procedural knowledge concerns *how* to ensure learning in particular knowledge domains. Issues of declarative and procedural knowledge are reflective in the following questions that frame this literature review: (1) What is the well-confirmed knowledge relating to the educational needs of students with disabilities when served in inclusive settings? (2) How might this knowledge be acquired?

Declarative Knowledge for Teacher Education Related to Students with Disabilities: What Should Teachers Know?

In considering declarative knowledge, a first concern is to delineate the domains to be encompassed. Our review revealed three relatively distinct areas, each of them presenting a delineation of knowledge domains of importance. One addresses what might be valuable for special educators to know, even though it is not specifically focused on the inclusion topic. A second area suggests what general education teachers might profit from in knowing how to support students with disabilities in mainstreamed classes. Striking in this literature was a distinct absence of presumption that mainstreamed teachers would receive support by special educators in their classrooms. The third area focuses on what is known about effective teaching and learning, regardless of professional roles. This third area indicates a common base or core of knowledge for all educators.

Knowledge for Special Educators   The literature relating to special education teachers has been dominated by topically organized lists of competencies they "should have," largely generated by consensus of professional opinion (Blanton, 1992). The

Council for Exceptional Children, for example, delineates eight categories of essential knowledge and skill:

1. Philosophical, historical, and legal foundations of special education
2. Characteristics of learners
3. Assessment, diagnosis, and evaluation
4. Instructional content and practice
5. Planning and managing the teaching and learning environment
6. Managing student behavior and social interaction skills
7. Communication and collaborative partnerships
8. Professionalism and ethical practices (Swan & Sirvis, 1992)

These statements are principled in the perspective of embracing individual differences rooted in the Council for Exceptional Children's Code of Ethics.

In a synthesis of literature in the first edition of *Handbook of Research on Teacher Education,* Reynolds (1990) described a knowledge base for teachers in special education as encompassing:

1. Legal and ethical principles
2. Curriculum
3. Educational (primarily instructional) theories and systems
4. Classroom management
5. Basic literacy skills
6. Self-regulation and strategic behavior
7. Assessment
8. Technology
9. Positive interdependence among students with disabilities and their nonhandicapped peers
10. Communication and consultation
11. Working with parents
12. Interactive teaching for cognitive change

It was interesting to note that these competency areas are remarkably similar to the listing of capability clusters offered by Lakin and Reynolds (1983) almost a decade earlier, not long after passage of the Federal Education for All Handicapped Children Act of 1975. Reynolds suggested that these domains of knowledge are important for all teachers, but especially so for special education teachers who offer support services for students with unique needs.

The knowledge domains just delineated would need to be extended when considering the unique needs of students who are hearing or visually impaired, or who have other low-incidence disabling conditions. Knowledge and skills in the areas of medical/health challenges, community-based instruction, and transdisciplinary teamwork would be added related to students with severe and multiple disabilities (Falvey, 1989; Fox & Williams, 1992; Orelove & Sobsey, 1991; Rainforth, York, & Macdonald, 1992; Thousand, Nevin-Parta, & Fox, 1987).

Close inspection of specific competencies identified in the literature revealed varying degrees of depth and breadth across knowledge areas. Greatest specificity was provided in areas related to instructional methods and technology. With only a few exceptions, much less depth and specificity were evidenced

concerning collaboration or special education services than support functions in general education contexts. Notable exceptions are reflected in the work of Dettmer, Thurston, and Dyck (1993); Idol, Paolucci-Whitcomb, and Nevin (1986); Thousand and Villa (1992); and West and Cannon (1988). These authors identified critical competencies related to collaboration for both general and special educators: consultation theory/models; research on consultation theory, training, and practice; personal characteristics; interactive communication; collaborative problem solving; systems change; equity issues; and values/belief systems.

Knowledge for General Educators In a review and synthesis of literature, Adams (1987) identified general education teacher functions (and related competencies) considered essential for effective mainstreaming:

1. Prepare class for mainstreaming
2. Assess the needs of students and set goals
3. Evaluate learning
4. Understand curriculum
5. Establish effective parent–teacher relationships
6. Teach fundamental skills
7. Understand exceptional conditions
8. Conduct professional consultations
9. Understand the nature of mainstreaming
10. Foster student–student relationships
11. Be aware of attitudes
12. Be knowledgeable about resource and support systems
13. Manage the learning environment
14. Demonstrate competent interpersonal communication
15. Teach communication skills
16. Supervise aides and volunteers
17. Individualize teaching
18. Manage the class
19. Use appropriate teaching techniques
20. Understand legal issues
21. Carry out behavior modification appropriately
22. Be able to analyze tasks
23. Teach social skills

In separate reports, Cannon, Idol, and West (1992) and Landers and Weaver (1991) identified similar competencies required for mainstream teachers, most of which they also indicated as essential for both general and special educators.

Textbooks written for use in preservice general education teacher training tend to be organized by categorical or by separate disability areas (see Gearheart, Weishahn, & Gearheart, 1992; Heward & Orlansky, 1992). Some also provide information and strategies for making curricular and instructional accommodations within specific content areas (Chaote, 1993; Schulz, Carpenter, & Turnbull, 1990). It is interesting to note that mainstreaming textbooks are intended primarily for a general education audience—perhaps indicating an assumption that methods for special educators to support students with disabilities in general education contexts would be covered in special education methods texts and courses.

Knowledge for Educators, Regardless of Role Blanton (1992) points out that, historically, the most common means of determining teacher competencies has been expert opinion and validation. "Experts" may be expected to consider research findings, but Blanton reports a lack of reliance on research—specifically research on learning and teaching in the 1980s. Clearly evident in our search were research and discussion supporting a *common* knowledge base for general and special educators. This knowledge base includes findings from the more traditional process-product research, plus a broadened perspective provided by social constructivist theory and research (Englert, Tarrant, & Mariage, 1992).

An important resource for this component of our review was the Spring 1992 issue of *Teacher Education and Special Education*. The focus of this special issue was on developing effective special education teachers (Westling, 1992). Three articles in particular were useful in showing how knowledge about effective teaching and learning has evolved and why we are at a complex but encouraging point in the evolution of this knowledge (see Blanton, 1992; Englert et al., 1992; Lessen & Frankiewicz, 1992). The quite remarkable article by Englert et al. (1992) provides a set of rating scales encompassing a wide range of teacher behavior covering both process-product and social constructivist research.

From the beginning of this century until the late 1960s, effective teaching research focused on high inference variables, such as teacher personality, background, and life perspectives (Buck, Morsink, Griffin, Hines, & Lenk, 1992; Lessen & Frankiewicz, 1992). Results of this early research were disappointing, suggesting a need for new approaches. The 1970s gave rise to process-product research to identify what are considered low inference variables for effective teaching, that is, specific teacher behaviors (processes) that correlate highly with specific student achievement outcomes (products) (Blanton, 1992; Englert et al., 1992; Lessen & Frankiewicz, 1992). Findings indicate that specific teacher behaviors related to classroom management, organization and management of instructional time, lesson presentation, and seatwork correlate highly with student achievement (Englert et al., 1992).

In 1990 Wang, Haertel, and Walberg (1990) conducted a massive metareview of research on "what influences learning." A complete report was published in the Fall, 1993, issue of the *Review of Educational Research,* along with eight critiques of the study. The study has been the focus of some controversy. The review utilized three methods—content analysis, expert ratings, and metaanalyses of results—to quantify the importance and consistency of variables that influence learning. Literature in both general and special education were reviewed. Data were recorded on more than 11,000 relationships between various factors and learning outcomes; these were summarized in 228 categories.

In a follow-up study to the Wang et al. (1990) review, various groups of educators were asked to rate the importance of each of the 228 variables (Reynolds, Wang, & Walberg, 1992). Average ratings by special education teachers and general education teachers of the various factors were nearly identical ($r = .95$), leading Reynolds et al. to conclude that "much can be done in common in colleges and university in the preparation of special education and classroom teachers . . . with emphasis on shared or common principles of pedagogy" (p. 10). These were a few of the top-rated variables by both groups of teachers: (1) time on task (student time engaged actively in learning); (2) time spent in direct instruction on basic skills in reading; (3) time spent in direct instruction on basic skills in mathematics; (4) providing frequent feedback to students about their performance; (5) comprehension monitoring by the teacher; and (6) explicitly promoting self-responsibility and effective metacognitive learning strategies.

Recently, a broadened knowledge base grounded in teaching and learning has emerged, referred to as *social constructivist* literature. This emergence is due, in part, to criticism of a dominant focus on process-product research (Blanton, 1992; Buck et al., 1992). Using this framework, researchers have attempted to expand the understanding of variables affecting teaching and learning beyond specific teacher competencies and behaviors. Englert and colleagues (1992) identify four principles of instruction that have emerged from this research: (1) embedding instruction in meaningful activities; (2) promoting classroom dialog for self-regulated learning; (3) demonstrating instructional responsiveness to individual learner needs and realities; and (4) establishing learning communities in classrooms.

In the Englert et al. (1992) review, findings from the effective teaching and learning literature were compared with instructional conditions in many special education resource rooms. Resource room practice was found frequently to violate principles derived from both the process-product and social constructivist literature. For example, findings from the process-product literature indicate that seatwork is effective when students understand the purposes and strategies for their seatwork, when responding is active rather than passive, when high rates of accuracy are assured, and when work is closely monitored. Common resource room practice includes heavy reliance on seatwork, but often low levels of accuracy are evidenced by students (Reith & Evertson, 1988). Other studies have shown that direct, active instruction may be no greater in many resource rooms than in general education classrooms (Allington & McGill-Franzen, 1989). From a *social constructivist* framework, resource room practice often violates learning principles related to the importance of context and student learning to be self-managing in broad, insightful ways.

Scardamalia and Bereiter (1989) describe situations in which teaching is very complex and in which teachers settle for a "well-managed" class rather than advancing student achievements. They call this a "problem-minimizing" approach, one in which content that students find difficult is eliminated. Avoiding referrals to the principal's office becomes a primary concern. Some special education classes appear to be well-managed in this limited sense.

Underlying assumptions of the process-product and the social constructivist effective teaching and learning literature are different, but they are not incompatible. Blanton (1992) suggests that by combining the knowledge generated from both approaches, there is promise for answering perhaps the most important of all questions about effective learning and teaching—under what conditions (conditional knowledge considering individuals and contexts) are specific instructional approaches (declarative and procedural knowledge) most effective? That is, beyond an understanding of what teachers need to do is the need to understand how and when to do it (Kennedy, 1989).

One final area of emerging literature in teacher education that relates to students with disabilities elevates the role of teachers as value-driven change agents (Fullan, 1993; Goodlad, 1990b). Fox and Williams (1992) emphasize the importance of value-based decision making, especially related to individuals who have the most severe disabilities and who are, therefore, most likely to be segregated and denied equal opportunities. In two recent studies, strong personal values of equity, combined with an holistic view of children with disabilities as individuals with unique capacities, were found to be common characteristics among general and special educators involved in inclusive schooling efforts (York, Schultz, Kronberg, Doyle, & Crossett, in review). In these studies, as well as in a study conducted by Giangreco, Dennis, Cloninger, Edelman, and Schattman (1993), personal involvement and a sense of self-efficacy were significant influences on general educators developing a positive perspective on students with disabilities being included in their classrooms. Assuming a perspective that inclusion involves a degree of social change, it is relevant to add that some researchers view positive socialization and induction of new teachers as offering hope for both education and social reform (Pugach, 1992). The work of Rosenholtz (1989) offers promise in identifying the conditions in schools that promote a culture of professional growth so that beginning and more experienced teachers remain creative and positive in their role as educators of today's children and youth.

Knowledge for Educators of Students with Disabilities: One Conclusion In sum, there is a substantial body of literature focused on competencies for effective teaching of students with disabilities. For special educators, competencies to promote collaboration and inclusive service delivery were emerging, but not central aspects of knowledge and skill development. For general educators, the competencies for effective mainstreaming did not reflect an assumption that special educators would join in the support of students with disabilities in general education contexts. These findings may indicate that research has not caught up with current and emerging practices in the field related to more collaborative and inclusive approaches. For educators in general, the literature focus is toward expansion of the knowledge base of effective teaching and learning by examining contextual circumstances and individual variations. This literature does not focus on distinctions between the professional roles of general and special educators. Instead, the focus is on conditions that promote learning, and the result is support for the view that there is a common knowledge base for educators, regardless of "general" or "special" professional role.

Procedural Knowledge for Teacher Education Related to Students with Disabilities: How Should Teachers Be Taught?

This component of the literature review is organized in two sections. First, literature is summarized related to how and how well general educators are prepared to teach students with disabilities. Second, special education teacher education literature is presented. Only some of this relates to the changing role of special educators given the inclusion initiative. Changes are occurring in special education teacher education, but some see the changes quite conservatively, assuming that special education will continue as a separate system. Others envision more radical changes and suggest a comprehensive merging of general and special education teacher preparation.

Preparation of General Educators Research indicates that general educators are not adequately prepared to meet the needs of students with disabilities. Practicing teachers have indicated that they need and want training related to Individualized Education Plans (IEPs), classroom management, and adapting curriculum (Askamit, 1990; Askamit & Alcorn, 1988). Most preservice programs require little or no special education coursework or experience (Schlosser & Millar, 1991). When courses are required, the content focus tends to be categorical and descriptive with little, if any, information on inclusive interventions or on support and consultation functions (Reiff, Evans, & Cass, 1991). A categorical focus can have negative effects by increasing stereotypic attitudes (Dove Jones & Messenheimer-Young, 1989). Kearney and Durand (1992) found that less than one third of teacher preparation institutions in New York offered coursework on collaboration and that only 14% provided preservice special education teachers-in-training with information about how to consult in mainstream environments. Berra (1989) reports inadequate training of Canadian general educators for mainstreaming and proposed that either special education courses be required or that general and special education teacher preparation be merged.

It is commonly assumed that special education coursework, and related fieldwork, will be useful as the means of preparing general educators to meet the needs of students with disabilities. The literature offers mixed support for this assumption. In two studies, studies and performance of general education teachers did not change after practicum or other field-based experience with students having disabilities (Hoover, 1984; Sanche & Smith, 1990). Hanrahan and Rapagna (1987) found that of academic background in special education and special education teaching experience, only the variable of academic background correlated with willingness of teachers (K–2) to integrate students with mental handicaps. A follow-up study of graduated preservice teachers conducted by Williams (1990) indicated that those who had taken a special education course during preservice training felt that the topics covered in the course were important and felt fairly competent for dealing with special education students in their mainstreamed classes. Stone and Brown (1987) reported improvement in attitudes toward children with special needs and in understanding classroom management after a mainstreaming course during preservice preparation. Ayres and Meyer (1992) and Janney and Meyer (1990) asserted that coursework in any form would be inadequate and that site-based consultation and technical assistance for general educators is needed in schools and classrooms. Representing a more diverse perspective, Korinek (1987) suggested that special coursework is not needed given the common knowledge base for teaching and learning across general and special education.

In considering how practicing general educators might be prepared to support students with disabilities in their classes, numerous approaches to in-service professional development have been tried. Some involve training organized in course, workshop, or seminar formats. Other programs were more specifically site-based and focused on professional development of teams of general and special educators.

Brady, Swank, Taylor, and Freiberg (1988, 1992) reported that a six-session teaching effectiveness training program with 40 volunteer social studies teachers and again with 18 middle school social studies and science teachers resulted in significant positive changes in both teacher and student behavior. Reetz and Hoover (1989) developed curriculum modules for preservice or in-service training of secondary general educators to support students with learning disabilities. The focus of the modules was on methods and interventions and included a bank of curriculum modifications. Malouf and Pilato (1991) created the Special Needs Adaptation Program (SNAP) system for in-service general educators, consisting of three modules, each with a different topic focus: (1) background on special education, mainstreaming, and team member roles; (2) improving academics; and (3) behavior management. The system was designed to assist teachers in identifying their own training needs and having these needs met through individual access to more than 175 learning and behavior strategies. Heller, Spooner, Spooner, and Algozzine (1992a, 1992b) offered a summer school program for general education teacher education students focused on strategies for accommodating students with disabilities in general education classes. The results indicated positive response, especially related to understanding of individual student needs.

Six examples of site-based, or at least field-based, approaches to in-service development were located. Showers (1990) presented a comprehensive staff development model for in-service general educators designed on the principles of adult learning and sensitive to the conditions of practice for teachers. Strategies included multiple demonstrations of innovations, opportunities for practice in a training setting, and coaching to facilitate transfer in actual settings. These strategies were employed in low-income, low-achievement schools with good results reported. Also designed to provide direct support focused on interventions was the in-service program developed by Thousand et al. (1987) in Vermont. This model employed on-site methods of modeling, coaching, and feedback about collaboration and other competencies for supporting students with severe disabilities in inclusive settings.

Focusing most specifically on collaborative consultation, Rule, Fodor-Davis, Morgan, Salzberg, and Chen (1990) developed an in-service program for teams of educators that stressed collegial (as opposed to hierarchical) relationships among educators, provided forums for sharing classroom problems and generating possible solutions, and promoted the development of technical skills for designing instructional programs for students. Meyers, Gelzheiser, and Yelich (1991) found that when special educators supported students in general education classrooms (referred to as a "pull-in" approach, as opposed to a "pull-out" approach to service provision), there were more frequent collaborative meetings between the special and general education teachers, greater focus on instructional issues, including more exchange of interventions. They stated, "the most important finding of this study is that pull-in approaches foster collaboration focused on instructional planning . . . pull-in programs served as vehicles for staff development for both

classroom teachers and specialist teachers" (Meyers et al., 1991, p. 13).

Another site-based collaborative approach was reported by Bailey (1991). His *Together Schools* in-service program was designed to bring together elementary teachers, special educators, and administrators to address attitudes toward integration, communication between general and special educators, skills for classroom teachers, and strategies for maintaining collaboration within the building. The program involved 25 participants and occurred over two weekends. Results indicated an increased willingness to work together. Supports for in-building collaboration included administrative support, teacher release time, recognition for participation, and prereferral or intervention assistance. Finally, Stewart (1988) reported on the development of a professional elementary school that included a merger of general and special education so that all general educators develop the skills and confidence necessary to teach intellectually and culturally heterogenous groups of students.

The literature on general education preparation for meeting the needs of students with disabilities indicates a preservice focus on categories and handicapping conditions. The in-service education focuses on interventions, accommodations, and collaboration.

Preparation of Special Educators Within the special education teacher education literature, three clusters of information emerged related to *how* teachers are, or should be, prepared. First, there continues to be research and discussion related to how much "categorical-ness" is necessary, valid, or appropriate in special education. This discussion focuses on the high incidence of mild disabilities. The trend away from discrete categories toward more generic approaches, including teacher certification in mild disabilities, is clear.

Second, stemming in part from the "categorical-ness" debate, there is considerable discussion of new approaches to special education teacher preparation. Two of the frequent redesign elements are: (1) organization of program by chronological age as opposed to disability area; and (2) increased collaboration among faculty in institutions of higher education and practicing professionals in public schools.

Third, there is growing support for merging general and special education teacher education programs. The "merger" approaches usually combine initial training for all educators, followed by specialized advanced training. Each of the three themes of the special education teacher education literature are discussed: (1) the "categorical-ness" debate, (2) program redesign with special education, and (3) merged general and special education teacher education. The first theme that emerged was the "categorical-ness" debate. The categorical versus cross-categorical versus noncategorical discussion has an enduring history, beginning most notably with the Dunn (1968) article with contributions since then by teacher educators such as Blackhurst (1981); Burello, Tracy, and Schultz (1973); Deno (1970); Lilly (1971, 1989); McKenzie, Egner, Knight, Perelman, Schneider, and Gavin (1970); and Reynolds (1979, 1990). The discussion pertains mainly to students with mild disabilities, those traditionally labeled as educable mentally disabled, learning disabled, and emotionally/behaviorally disabled. The lack of research to support distinct and valid interventions for each of the several categories is often cited as a basis for undoing the classification procedures.

Clearly the trend since the mid-1970s has been an increase in the number of cross-categorical and noncategorical special education teacher education programs and a corresponding trend in state certification systems. In a recent national survey of state education agency officials, 33% of the states offered categorical certification only (Cranston-Gingras & Mauser, 1992). In 1985, 51% of the states offered categorical only (Chapey, Pyszkowski, & Trimarco, 1985), and in 1979, 80% of the states were cited as categorical (Belch, 1979). Cranston-Gingras and Mauser (1992) indicated that the primary criticism of cross- or noncategorical programs occurs only when extended beyond the mild disability area to include students with moderate, severe, and multiple disabilities and those with low-incidence disabilities.

Cobb, Elliott, Powers, and Voltz (1989) surveyed teachers of students with mild disabilities 5 years after certification and also surveyed their respective superintendents and special education coordinators. There was agreement that "cross-handicap" certification was attractive at the undergraduate level with a major rationale being more flexible use of generically certified special educators. The same respondents, however, also indicated a desire for more categorically focused coursework within the generic certification program. More recently in a national opinion survey of state directors of special education and of special educators, Elliott, Cobb, Powers, and Voltz (1991) found general support for generic/noncategorical teacher preparation programs, but again a desire for categorical courses within such programs.

In a survey of national certification requirements for teachers of students with mild handicaps, Putnam and Vanselow Habanek (1993) found tremendous variation across states and proposed five questions that need to be addressed: (1) Are differing grade levels (of certification) necessary?; (2) Does current thinking necessitate specific categories?; (3) Do current certification requirements restrict teacher mobility (across states)?; (4) Are services for students with mild disabilities hampered by certification inconsistencies?; and (5) Do we need common language for national certification? Also raising questions in regard to certification, Bondurant-Utz, Gorbett, and Quinby (1992) asserted that "the relevant question should be whether teachers from a categorical or a non-categorical teacher preparation program are better prepared to teach children and why" (p. 16). Lilly (1992) adds another perspective:

it could be argued, of course, that recent developments in general and special education have rendered much of the discussion of noncategorical licensure "old hat." . . . Paradigm shifts are afoot that will change the very definition of special education. (p. 157)

Simpson, Whelan, and Zabel (1993) identify a range of specific influences creating a need for substantial change in the role and function of special educators. Included were the need to increase the supply of qualified direct service and leadership personnel, increasing pressures to promote cost-effective services, expanding partnerships, addressing the needs of at-risk students, and supporting students with disabilities in general education programs. To prepare special educators for the twenty-first century, they recommend a heightened focus on collaborative consultation, increased IHE/LEA partnerships (in the form of Professional Development Schools), processes of pedagogy, interagency collaboration, and use of technology. In the Outcome-Based Teacher Education model they propose, a key assumption is that necessary competencies must be modeled by teacher education faculty.

The second emergent theme in the literature was program redesign with special education. Turning now to changes in special education teacher education programs, the most common redesign feature proposed in recent literature is the organization of special educator preparation by chronological age of students, as opposed to the more traditional organization by disability or handicapping condition. Cranston-Gingras and Mauser (1992) proposed a pre-kindergarten, elementary, and secondary program breakdown. Keeping with a similar chronological age orientation, Sindelar, Davis McGray, and Westling (1992), added separate foci on mild disabilities and on severe disabilities within each age division.

Sindelar et al. (1992) suggested that for preschool-age children, prime attention should be on ameliorating developmental disabilities and increasing students' abilities to benefit from interactions in the environment. At the elementary level, there should be greater attention on supporting academic growth and functional skills. At the secondary level, attention should shift to preparation for postsecondary life—work, community, or further education. Content areas for teachers preparing for work with students with mild disabilities would focus on: academics; diagnostic-prescriptive assessment; curricular and instructional adaptations; behavior management; and collaboration with general education classroom teachers. Within the severe disabilities focus, a functional and age-appropriate orientation to curriculum, teaching in natural settings, and addressing the needs of students with multiple handicapping conditions are suggested as areas of emphasis.

Another prominent design change in special education teacher education centers on increased and improved collaborative partnerships between institutions of higher education and local education agencies. These collaborative efforts often take the form of on-site program development as well as teacher preparation. A comprehensive description of this type of collaborative was provided by Paul, Duchnowski, and Danforth (1993) of the University of Southern Florida, recognizing that "The restructuring movement in general education and the inclusion movement in special education affect every aspect of education and schooling, including teacher education" (p. 95).

An increased focus on the field-based aspects of teacher education was also evidenced in studies of on-the-job training, mentoring, and coaching models (Buck et al., 1992). Peer coaching at the preservice level was found to increase effective teaching behaviors (Morgan, Gustafson, Hudson, & Salzberg, 1992). In this study, peers served as coaches to promote feedback. However, considerable faculty/staff time was required to train the coaches. An intensive apprenticeship model for supporting the development of consulting teachers resulted in significantly better outcomes than standard training (i.e., teachers not mentored or provided with an apprenticeship) (Gersten, Darch, Davis, & George, 1991). Alternative route training is growing in consideration, in part because of the need to accommodate students with liberal arts degrees and shortages in specific areas—especially the critical problem of underrepresentations of educators of varied ethnic and cultural backgrounds (Sindelar & Marks, 1992). A university–public school collaborative in Polk County, Florida, prepares paraprofessionals to become special educators (Epanchin & Wooley-Brown, 1992). This program developed to respond to critical shortages of special education teachers.

Finally, the literature review emerged a third personnel development theme focused on the merger of general and special education teacher education. Within the special education teacher education ranks are individuals advocating for very substantial changes. Nevin (1992) asserts that "The categorical-cross categorical-noncategorical question may be a distraction from focusing on more comprehensive political and sociological issues that plague the education community" (p. 14). Peck, Richarz, Peterson, Hayden, Mineur, and Wandscheider (1989) make a similar point:

Segregated special education programs were not invented nor have they ever been justified, as a pedagogically superior arrangement for meeting the needs of children. Rather, they have historically represented a socially and politically acceptable response to pressure from parents and other advocates seeking access to service for a traditionally disenfranchised group of children. (p. 296)

Bondurant-Utz et al. (1992) support noncategorical teacher preparation and certification at the bachelor's level, along with a strong move to merge general and special education certification. The rationale for their recommendation is that enrollment in general education classes "isn't regular anymore." They suggest a bachelor's level focus "on how children learn best and on what are the best teaching practices in an ecologically sound learning environment" (p. 17). They indicated that all teachers require knowledge about the processes of child and youth development, conditions for learning, how to provide for these conditions in a school environment, and how to examine and address specific needs of individual learners. Graduate programs should offer more advanced and specific focus on these same learning challenges.

Bunsen (1990) stated that the reform in American schools requires simultaneous reform of teacher education—specifically, a greater partnership between general and special education. He discusses two approaches: (1) infusion of content into each respective program; and (2) merger of general and special education. Given the resistance to infusion models, he proposes a teacher education program that merges general education and low-incidence disabilities.

Lilly (1989), writing about the impact of inclusive schooling on teacher education, offers recommendations along a similar path:

The new system of teacher preparation will be built on a basis of initial preparation of teachers for early education, elementary education, and secondary education. . . . This program will include a strong general education, expanded subject area preparation, professional education (including historical, philosophical, social, and psychological foundations and other general and subject-specific pedagogy), and substantial clinical experience, including a supervised internship in the school at least one semester in duration. Beginning teachers will be provided

induction experiences and supervision by mentor teachers who will help them bridge the gap between their preparation experiences and their assumption of full teaching duties [p. 146]. . . . [Another] explicit assumption of this model is that separate, heavily regulated systems of special education are dysfunctional and must be replaced with coordinated systems of support. (p. 149)

In support of the merged model of education, Lilly (1989) articulated problems with the current system of special education:

(a) the referral to placement process is complex, costly, and of questionable validity; (b) pull-out is disruptive to general class routines and may impede the ability of students to meet classroom teacher expectations; (c) the many pull-out programs exist alongside one another and are not coordinated; (d) diagnostic and placement procedures are time consuming and delay attention to instructional problems in the classroom; (e) rules governing special education discourage the provision of direct help to classroom teachers and typically prevent special education teachers from working with groups of children experiencing common challenges; (f) labels often are inaccurate and invite overgeneralization; and (g) special education encourages teachers to see themselves as incapable of teaching certain students. (pp. 149–150)

Bickel and Bickel (1986) lend support to the merged general and special education teacher education proposals by indicating that:

there is a growing knowledge base about how to organize schools and instruction that is relevant to both special and regular educators and that there is a growing rationale for special and regular educational programming to become more integrated at the school level. . . . Special and regular educators have much to learn from each other. (p. 497)

An example of a combined general and special education teacher education program is provided by the Integrated Elementary and Special Education Program at Syracuse University (Meyer & Biklen, 1992). This program replaced five undergraduate programs and qualifies graduates for the New York provisional licensure in elementary education (K–6) and special education (K–12). The program features include: (1) shared values of inclusion and equity; (2) teacher as decision maker; (3) recognition of multiculturalism in education; (4) the necessity for innovations in education; and (5) emphasis on field-based experiences. Extensive fieldwork requirements begin in the sophomore year and include considerable amounts of time with families, including those who have children with disabilities.

Preparation of Educators of Students with Disabilities: One Conclusion In summary, it appears to us that something near consensus has been achieved in the mild disability area, to the extent that distinct categorical teacher preparation in special education is not advised. We concur with Lilly's (1992) contention that there is no compelling reason for general and special education to remain separate, at least in the initial levels of teacher education. From a broad and general perspective, Goodlad (1990a) puts it this way:

Suffice it to say that *all* children must be prepared for responsible participation as citizens and for critical dialogue in the human conversation, and that the pedagogy and stewardship of teachers must embrace *all* children and young people and the whole of the schools' moral functioning in a social and political democracy. (p. 186)

We agree with Goodlad (1990a) that "The necessary conditions for effective teacher education are not in place" (p. 186) and that radical reform is in order.

A LOOK TO THE FUTURE

This final section offers some personal speculations about the future of special education and of teacher preparation in the field. It is probably the most arguable section of the paper. As in all preceding sections, the theme of inclusiveness is a primary concern. The presentation is in the form of several scenarios for the future. The scenarios are not clear predictions. They represent an attempt to pull together the findings of research, the mandates of public policy, and the major tenets and values of a democratic society. They are presented in an experimental mode, or as hypotheses, as "good ideas," yet certainly in need of careful evaluation.

Before presenting the scenarios, we suggest here that any future schooling system consider the following questions:

1. Is it totally inclusive, yet attentive to varying individual needs of students (suspension and expulsions are at zero level)?
2. Is it managed and operated so as to enhance the learning and development of all students (this requires extraordinary flexibility and variability in curriculum and modes of instruction)?
3. Does it encourage mutual understanding, interdependence, and appreciation among all students and staff and across all racial, ethnic, gender, and ability classes (isolation, alienation, and racism are at a minimum)?
4. Does it develop and offer a learning and social climate that is demanding, yet pleasurable and rewarding for all participants?
5. Does it promote continuing evaluation of all programs with a clear focus on progress and successful outcomes for *every* student (it demonstrates readiness and capacity to make programmatic changes whenever data show poor progress in existing programs; data are collected on *literally* all students and programs)?
6. Do parents, students, and all other stakeholders understand and support the programs and have a voice in policy developments that affect the school?

Futures Scenarios

Futures Scenario 1: Mini-Schools The concept of "mini-schools" has evolved in an attempt to create a structure that promotes innovation by decreasing the size and complexity of the unit of educational and organizational change. In a mini-school a small cluster of teachers works as a team to serve a relatively small cluster of students. Students and teachers stay together for a longer time than is common in school today. Opportunities to develop genuinely caring relationships or to

reduce student alienation are enhanced. The research evidence concerning mini-schools is positive, especially so when teachers are given freedom, encouragement, and responsibility to make major changes in the school program and schedule, when students are given choices at the maximal level, and when the program expresses genuine and pervasive "caring" for each student (Raywid, 1984, 1989). The mini-school is considered here as one way of expressing principles emerging from the "resilience" research (Masten, 1989). As described in the mini-schools future scenario, the learning and development facilitator would have a background in many of the same areas as general education teachers and additional knowledge and skills to serve in an essential support role, particularly related to strategies for addressing unique and complex instructional needs of students and for creating and maintaining high degrees of collaboration among team members:

The school (800 students) is divided into eight mini-schools (or "houses" or charters"), each with about 100 students and 5 teachers, one of them a learning and development facilitator, and two paraprofessionals. Units are deliberately heterogeneous in both student and staff characteristics and capacities. Central to the design of the mini-schools is the need to promote a sense of community and positive interdependence among members. Students and staff of each mini-school stay together for a minimum of three years.

An extremely high degree of autonomy is given to each mini-school to organize the curriculum and schedule (perhaps not the calendar) of the school program. While strong school–community partnerships exist that support implementation of an innovative curriculum, the total curriculum is managed by the five teachers. Occasionally, a specialist joins the group to expand the staff capacity to meet unique student needs and potential. Students with extraordinary needs and capacity may access opportunities off school grounds. For example, a student with interpersonal talents may pursue independent study in a neighborhood-based conflict resolution, mediation center; an exceptional violin player participates in the citywide junior symphony orchestra; a student who is blind attends an intensive 2-week intersession workshop focused on access in complex urban settings and at the same time learns about the most innovative means of communication via telecommunications. Students and their parents are given a wide array of choices about the mini-school they wish to enter and about aspects of the program.

The learning and development facilitator on the staff team for each mini-school provides numerous essential functions, for students previously considered to have special education or other easily identified needs and also for students with no formally identified needs. An important orientation of this person is the search for and development of capacities in students, as opposed to the more traditional search for and remediation of deficits. The facilitator is a resource for the teams in many ways: (a) manages a great deal of the assessments for the entire program of the mini-school; (b) offers intensive instruction to individual students and to small groups who show limited progress in learning or who have particular needs; (c) handles many of the contacts with parents; (d) coordinates the work of specialists (such as school psychologists, social workers, braille teachers, counselors, speech pathologists, etc.) who support the program so that all students can remain full members of the learning community; (e) collaborates in the design of individualized program adaptations to accommodate varying learning styles and rates; (f) handles much of contact required with community agencies, such as in corrections or mental health; (g) teaches in some special areas (such as social skills) as may be necessary, while also working broadly with classroom teachers on the curriculum; (h) oversees compliance with special legislation, rules, and court orders, etc. (such as preparation of IEPs); and (i) serves as team leader (among the teachers) in "case study" activities concerning exceptional pupils in the group, as well as in other areas of staff development and renewal.

Zetlin, Valdez, and Ramos (1994) have advanced a schematic representation of the scenario (Figure 38.1). Represented on the left end of the schematic, classroom teachers can act almost totally and directly on matters of instruction for many students. In moving to the right, the figure suggests that there are students who require more varied forms and levels of support. At the far right, students require intensive supports in order to participate in the school program. The learning and development facilitator as described in this first scenario takes primary responsibility for operations of the support system. All staff members, however, continue to share responsibility with all students and with one another in working cooperatively to create adaptations and support so that each student learns. There are no impermeable boundaries between the instructional and support systems. Indeed, the school as a whole has open boundaries, indicating the increasing trend toward collaboration among educators and staff and other community agencies. The mini-schools scenario is compelling not only in its potential better to meet the increasingly complex needs of today's children and youth, but also in its potential to create a collaborative culture necessary in a self-renewing school.

Futures Scenario 2: Services in Rural Areas Every disabled child in the United States has a legal right to appropriate education. But delivery of appropriate education is particularly difficult in sparsely populated areas, partly because students having "special" needs are so widely scattered and few colleges in rural regions can justify offering specialized teacher preparation. There is a broad north–south region of the nation extending westward from a line described by Federal Interstate highway I-35 (from Minneapolis southward through Des Moines, Kansas City, Oklahoma City, and Dallas) to the Rocky Mountains in which the population is widely scattered and problems with finding specialized staff are very difficult. Problems exist also in other parts of the nation, as in far northeastern sections of New England. The Southern Regional Educational Board has helped to solve staffing problems in a multi-state southeastern section of the nation, but problems persist in most rural areas. We propose one scenario that might help solve this problem of teacher education and supply, as follows:

Ms. Jane Doe, a highly regarded third-grade teacher in Appletown, Montana, has been awarded a special 1-year fellowship that will enable her to study at California State University, Los Angeles (or another highly specialized teacher preparation center). Her studies will prepare her for teaching and consultation concerning education for students who are visually impaired. Upon completion of her preparation, she will return to Appletown to work in special education programs in a broad rural region. It is known that seven students of the region are blind and in need of special education. Ms. Doe will have records of these seven students with her as she pursues her studies.

The local school board recommended Ms. Doe to the State Department of Education for the fellowship. The fellowship is at a dollar level of two-thirds of her regular salary as a teacher plus tuition and travel costs. An additional one-third of her salary will be paid by the Appletown School Board, contingent on Ms. Doe's commitment to return to the special teaching position in this region after completing her training. The state has been enabled to operate this unique fellowship program through funds from the federal government. The program represents a broadly coordinated effort by federal, state and local authorities to provide high quality and appropriate education for all disabled children—including children who live in sparsely populated areas and who wish to remain with their families and in local schools.

In this scenario it is proposed that the best of teacher preparation resources, wherever located, be made available to sparsely populated areas. The key element in the proposal is the selection of people for training who have already made a commitment to live and work in rural areas of the nation. The proposal is similar to one used in the Commonwealth of Nations, headed in Great Britain. There it has been common for teachers to come from many distant parts of the world to prepare for teaching deaf students (as at the University of Manchester) and in other special areas.

There are, of course, other scenarios that one can imagine to meet the problems of distribution of specialized teachers, but we have yet to solve problems of providing truly excellent specialized "low-incidence" teachers to sparsely populated regions. The most specialized programs of teacher preparation tend to be offered by colleges in large metropolitan settings, but currently such programs do not succeed well in distributing trainees to rural areas. Innovations are needed.

Futures Scenario 3: Teacher Education

The College of Education has merged its programs in general and special education. All students take the full general program in teacher education, differentiated only by level (early education, elementary, secondary). Candidates for learning and development facilitation (special education) take additional preparation to prepare themselves for managing support systems and intensive forms of instruction. Areas of emphasis would include, for example, individual assessment of challenges and capacities, family studies, counseling and consultation, social skills training, remedial and compensatory teaching in basic literacy skills, in addition to a series of courses and experience focused on adult learning and collaboration. In practica, the special education trainees work in a common setting with general educators but are given extensive experience in one-on-one and small group teaching.

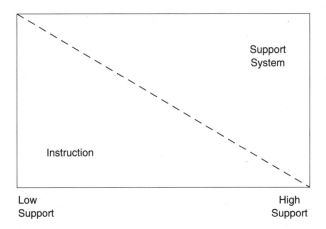

FIGURE 38.1. Zetlin's Conceptual Model of Varying Degrees of Support Needs

Teacher candidates to support the unique learning needs of students who are visually impaired, hearing impaired, physically or medically challenged would follow somewhat different programs, emphasizing specific skills and accommodations for maximizing learning potential given obvious physical challenges. For example, braille and mobility without sight would be essential knowledge and skill domains for teachers supporting students with visual impairments; communication without hearing would be the focus related to students with hearing impairments; communication and effective use of body movement would be essential in the support of students with physical challenges.

A key feature of Scenario 3 is that students go together to a common set of professional development schools for their practica in which they work together in inclusive arrangements. The practicum setting represents a fully inclusive form of school organization, including all forms of the current categorical programs, and high degrees of collaboration among educators. In addition to a practicum in school situations, learning and development facilitator trainees do an early part of their practicum in clinical and community agency settings where they have opportunities to work with social workers, psychologists, physicians, and parents. This beyond-school experience is essential to develop an understanding of the roles, functions, and supports available through community partnerships. This community agency aspect of the development process is intended to help prepare learning and development facilitators for their support role in the schools, including leadership in collaboration with community agencies beyond the schools. This feature of teacher education also serves to challenge colleges to bring together representatives of multiple disciplines and professions (education, psychology, social work, medicine, nursing, family studies, law) for conducting coordinated teacher education programs.

SYSTEMWIDE IMPLICATIONS

To achieve fully inclusive education for all students and to create a correspondingly inclusive teacher education program it will be necessary, of course, to achieve broad systemic change. Laws, rules, regulations, and funding systems will need to be changed, perhaps by waiver procedures at first (Lilly, 1992). This process will be difficult, both conceptually and practically. Many people are well rewarded for leaving more segregated and disjointed systems in place. Nevertheless, it appears to us that changes are under way, taking the schools toward more inclusive arrangements.

In Figure 38.2 we represent a view or model for how schools can be linked to teacher preparation, to professional organizations, and to research operations; the model is adapted from a proposal by Havelock (1969). There are several key features of the model:

1. The model proposes continuous two-way linkages between researchers (often located in universities), professional associations, and the schools; these may be thought of as *diffusion* and *needs transmissions* (see two-way arrows in figure).
2. Preservice teacher education departments in Institutions of Higher Education (IHEs) would engage in continuous two-way communications with the central, or "inner core," disciplinary structures of the university.

3. The teacher education staff would inform the disciplinary units concerning needs it discovers in practice and in consumer systems and would help screen for relevant basic knowledge. They would serve also to draw talents from the total university structure to concerns, needs, and developments in community settings. They would also scan and search beyond their own universities for relevant knowledge and systems for influencing practice.
4. The teacher education faculties would also design their activities (training, research, and service) in concert with agents of the practice and consumer system.
5. In a similar fashion, agencies representing practice or professional systems (such as teacher associations or unions) would be linked two ways: (1) to the teacher educators in IHEs for partnership in continuing education and professional development and (2) to the consumer system (e.g., local school districts) for organizations of in-service education activities and for general operations in accordance with high standards expression of need and interest.

It is important to see this model not simply as a Research → Development → Diffusion Model or as a way of making Institutions of Higher Education (IHEs) into mere subcontractors to Local Education Agencies (LEAs), State Education Agencies (SEAs), or teacher associations. The model proposes more than a system for soft interactions and mutual stimulation and consultation at points of shared interests. Instead, it proposes a strong partnership in which needs assessments, resource analyses, and planning are cooperative efforts with inputs from and major effects for all concerned. Problems are identified cooperatively, alternatives are generated and evaluated, and decisions are made accordingly. The summative result is a new paradigm for education of exceptional and other students and for their teachers.

In the framework proposed here, the IHE is seen as the lead organization in the creation of training systems, rather than as the operator of a relatively stable set of programs. It is prepared to help design retraining programs for teachers, principals, parents, school boards, superintendents, and others, and it does so in the context of varieties of other activities, including evaluation, research, writing of technical reports, and the like. The work of the college or department concerned with teacher preparation is coordinated in broader ways as well, with the medical school, the department of family studies, the school of social work, the department of psychology, and so on. In this mode of operation the IHE does not give up its desire to create generalizable knowledge; that desire and drive are as strong as ever. What is new is the interaction of the teacher education unit with other units within the University, as well as within the P–12 schools, recognizing all of their realities and encumbrances in community situations.

It is not enough to prepare and deploy teachers in inclusive schools. In Figure 38.3, we represent the several levels of relationship required. At Level I we see clusters of teachers and students. Ultimately, that is the essential level for the teaching and learning of students and for testing the total system. Level II shows a necessary support system. Here is where specialists who support the school operation and who work generally for school and community betterment are deployed. Large school

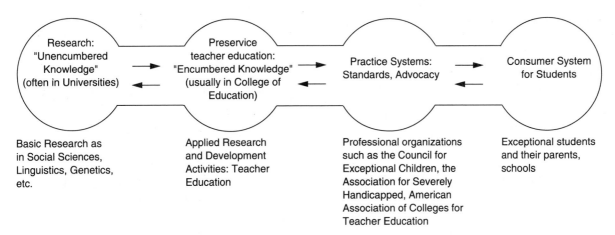

FIGURE 38.2. A Macrosystem Model

systems will often employ substantial numbers of Level II staff. Only occasionally will they be special education teachers. More often they will be experts on teaching reading, classroom management, school psychology, or in other areas that are useful in supporting inclusive schools. Some of the specialists will be working in non-school community agencies, such as mental health clinics or court services, and will come to school settings for part of their work. At Level III the figure shows the important role of colleges and universities in preparing staff for both Levels I and II and for conducting research. Staff at Levels II and III will often be interchangeable; that is, a Level II specialist on a subject such as mobility for the blind might also serve as

an instructor in college preparatory programs. Figure 38.3 is intended to show that "inclusion and integration are for more than students." Inclusion is for all elements of a revised system.

Collaborative problem solving across all levels of services to children and in support structures presents an opportunity for exciting and important work by educators at all levels. This kind of framework is needed for public appreciation and support of teacher education and the schools in the years ahead. There are very few, if any, rewards for school and community arrangements that involve separations, disjointedness, inefficiency, and demeaning labels. The time is here for inclusion—at all levels.

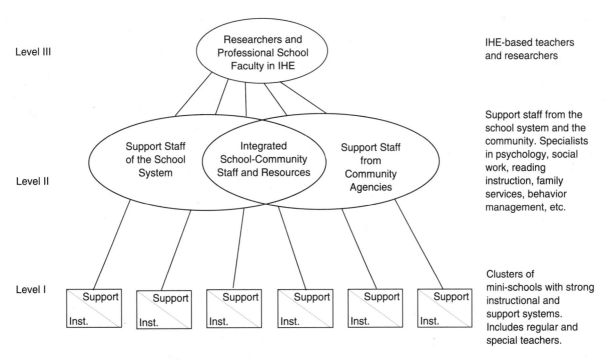

FIGURE 38.3. Systemic Interagency Organization for Education and Related Services

References

Adams, P. R. (1987). *A review and synthesis of teacher competencies necessary for effective mainstreaming*. Final report. Washington, DC: U.S. Department of Education.

Allington, R. L., & McGill-Franzen, A. (1989). School response to reading failure: Instruction for Chapter 1 and special education students in grades two, four, and eight. *Elementary School Journal, 89,* 529–542.

Askamit, D. L. (1990). Practicing teacher perceptions of their preservice preparation for mainstreaming. *Teacher Education and Special Education, 13*(1), 21–29.

Askamit, D. L., & Alcorn, D. A. (1988). Preservice mainstream curriculum infusion model: Student teachers' perceptions of program effectiveness. *Teacher Education and Special Education, 11*(2), 52–58.

Ayres, B., & Meyer, L. H. (1992). Helping teachers manage the inclusive classroom. *School Administrator, 49*(2), 30–31, 33, 35, 37.

Bailey, C. R., Jr. (1991, April). *Together schools—Training regular and special educators to share responsibility for teaching all students*. Paper presented at the annual convention of the Council for Exceptional Children, Atlanta.

Belch, P. J. (1979). Toward noncategorical teacher certification in special education—Myth or reality? *Exceptional Children, 46,* 129–131.

Berger, J. (1991, April 30). Costly special classes serve many with minimal needs. *The New York Times,* R12.

Berra, M. (1989). Integration and its implications for teacher preparation. *British Columbia Journal of Special Education, 13*(1), 55–65.

Bickel, W. E., & Bickel, D. D. (1986). Effective schools, classrooms, and instruction: Implications for special education. *Exceptional Children, 52,* 489–500.

Blackhurst, A. E. (1981). Noncategorical teacher preparation: Problems and promises. *Exceptional Children, 48,* 197–205.

Blanton, L. P. (1992). Preservice education: Essential knowledge for the effective special education teacher. *Teacher Education and Special Education, 15*(2), 87–95.

Bondurant-Utz, J. A., Gorbett, K. T., & Quinby, S. S. (1992). Do we have to choose categorical versus noncategorical? *Remedial and Special Education, 14*(3), 15–17.

Brady, M. P., Swank, P. R., Taylor, R. D., & Freiberg, J. (1988). Teacher-student interactions in middle school mainstreamed classes: Differences with special and regular education students. *Journal of Education Research, 81*(6), 332–340.

Brady, M. P., Swank, P. R., Taylor, R. D., & Freiberg, J. (1992). Teacher interactions in mainstreamed social studies and science classes. *Exceptional Children, 58*(6), 530–540.

Brown, L. (1991). Introduction: Who are they and what do they want? An essay on TASH. In L. H. Meyer, C. A. Peak, & L. Brown (Eds.), *Critical issues in the lives of people with severe disabilities* (pp. 25–27). Baltimore: Paul H. Brookes Publishing Co.

Broyles, S., & Morgan, F. (1992). *National trends, education degrees conferred*. Washington, DC: U.S. Department of Education, National Center for Education Statistics.

Bruninks, R. H., & Lakin, K. C. (Eds.). (1985). *Living and learning in the least restrictive environment*. Baltimore: Paul H. Brookes Publishing Co.

Buck, G., Morsink, C., Griffin, C., Hines, T., & Lenk, L. (1992). Preservice training: The role of field-based experiences in the preparation of effective special educators. *Teacher Education and Special Education, 15*(2), 108–123.

Bunsen, T. D. (1990). *Restructuring teacher education: The integration of undergraduate curriculum*. (ERIC Reproduction Service No. ED 343 335)

Burello, L., Tracy, M., & Schultz, E. (1973). Special education as experimental education: A new conceptualization. *Exceptional Children, 40,* 29–34.

Cannon, G. S., Idol, L., & West, J. F. (1992). Education of students with mild handicaps in general classrooms: Essential teacher practices for general and special education. *Journal of Learning Disabilities, 25*(5), 300–317.

Chaote, J. S. (1993). *Successful mainstreaming: Proven ways to detect and correct special needs*. Boston: Allyn & Bacon.

Chapey, G., Pyszkowski, I., & Trimarco, T. (1985). National trends for certification and training of special education teachers. *Teacher Education and Special Education, 8,* 203–208.

Cobb, H. B., Elliott, R., Powers, A. R., & Voltz, D. (1989). General vs. categorical special education teacher preparation. *Teacher Education and Special Education, 12,* 19–26.

Cranston-Gingras, A., & Mauser, A. J. (1992). Categorical and noncategorical teacher certification: How wide is the gap? *Remedial and Special Education, 14*(3), 6–9.

Cross, L. H., & Billingsley, B. S. (1994). Testing a model of special educators' intent to stay in teaching. *Exceptional Children, 60*(5), 411–421.

Deno, E. (1970). Special education as developmental capital. *Exceptional Children, 40,* 29–34.

Dettmer, P., Thurston, L. P., & Dyck, N. (1993). *Consultation, collaboration and teamwork for students with special needs*. Boston: Allyn & Bacon.

Dove Jones, S., & Messenheimer-Young, R. (1989). Content of special education courses for preservice regular education teachers. *Teacher Education and Special Education, 12*(4), 154–159.

Dunn, L. (1968). Special education for the mildly handicapped: Is much of it justifiable? *Exceptional Children, 35,* 5–22.

Elliott, R., Cobb, H., Powers, A., & Voltz, D. (1991). Generic teacher preparation: Has the issue been resourced? *Teacher Education and Special Education, 14,* 140–143.

Englert, C. S., Tarrant, K. L., & Mariage, T. V. (1992). Defining and redefining instructional practice in special education: Perspectives on good teaching. *Teacher Education and Special Education, 15*(2), 62–85.

Epanchin, B. C., & Wooley-Brown, C. (1992). A university–school district collaborative project for preparing paraprofessionals to become special educators. *Teacher Education and Special Education, 16*(2), 110–123.

Falvey, M. A. (1989). *Community-based instruction: Instructional strategies for students with severe handicaps*. Baltimore: Paul H. Brookes Publishing Co.

Fox, L., & Williams, D. G. (1992). Preparing teachers of students with severe disabilities. *Teacher Education and Special Education, 15*(2), 97–107.

Frank, A. R., & McKenzie, R. (1993). The development of burnout among special educators. *Teacher Education and Special Education, 16*(2), 161–170.

Fullan, M. G. (1993). Why teachers must become change agents. *Educational Leadership, 50*(6), 12–17.

Gearheart, B. R., Weishahn, M. W., & Gearheart, C. J. (1992). *The exceptional student in the regular classroom* (2nd ed.). New York: Macmillan.

Gersten, R., Darch, C., Davis, G., & George, N. (1991). Apprenticeship and intensive training of consulting teachers: A naturalistic study. *Exceptional Children, 57*(3), 226–236.

Gersten, R., Walker, H., & Darch, C. (1988). Relationships between teachers' effectiveness and their tolerance for handicapped students. *Exceptional Children, 54*(5), 433–438.

Giangreco, M. F., Dennis, R., Cloninger, C., Edelman, S., & Schattman, R. (1993). "I've counted Jon": Transformational experiences of teachers educating students with disabilities. *Exceptional Children, 59*(4), 359–372.

Goodlad, J. I. (1990a). Better teachers for our nation's schools. *Phi Delta Kappan, 72*(3), 185–194.

Goodlad, J. I. (1990b). *Teachers for our nation's schools*. San Francisco: Jossey-Bass.

Hanrahan, J., & Rapagna, C. (1987). The effects of information and exposure variables on teachers' willingness to mainstream mentally handicapped children into their classrooms. *The Mental Retardation and Learning Disabilities Bulletin, 15*(1), 1–6.

Havelock, R. G. (1969). *Planning for innovation through dissemination and utilization of knowledge*. Ann Arbor: Institute for Research, University of Michigan.

Heller, H. W., Spooner, M., Spooner, F., & Algozzine, B. (1992a). Helping general educators accommodate students with disabilities. *Remedial and Special Education, 15*(4), 269–274.

Heller, H. W., Spooner, M., Spooner, F., & Algozzine, B. (1992b). Meeting the needs of students with handicaps: Helping regular teachers meet the challenge. *Action in Teacher Education, 13*(4), 44–54.

Heward, W. L., & Orlansky, M. D. (1992). *Exceptional children* (4th ed.). New York: Macmillan.

Hoover, J. J. (1984). Effects of special education classroom experiences of preservice elementary teachers on ability to work with the handicapped. *Education, 105*(1), 58–62.

Hoover, J., & Bowen, M. (Guest Eds.). (1993). *Teacher Education and Special Education, 16*(3), 203–293.

Idol, L., Paolucci-Whitcomb, P., & Nevin, A. (1986). *Collaborative consultation*. Salem, MA: Aspen.

Janney, R. E., & Meyer, L. H. (1990). A consultation model to support integrated educational services for students with severe disabilities and challenging behaviors. *Journal of The Association for Persons with Severe Handicaps, 15*(3), 186–199.

Jones, S. D. (1989). Content of special education courses for preservice regular education teachers. *Teacher Education and Special Education, 12*(4), 154–159.

Kearney, C. A., & Durand, V. M. (1992). How prepared are our teachers for mainstreamed classroom settings? A survey of postsecondary schools of education in New York State. *Exceptional Children, 59*(1), 6–11.

Kennedy, M. M. (1989). Knowledge base for the beginning teacher. Two views—Mary Kennedy's perspective. *Journal of Teacher Education, 40,* 53–57.

Korinek, L. (1987). Questioning strategies in special education: Links to teacher efficacy research in general education. *Journal of Research and Development in Education, 21,* 16–22.

Lakin, K. C., & Reynolds, M. C. (1983). Curricular implications of Public Law 94-142 for teacher education. *Journal of Teacher Education, 34*(12), 13–17.

Landers, M. F., & Weaver, R. (1991, April). *Teaching competencies identified by mainstream teachers: Implications for teacher training*. Paper presented at the annual conference of the Council for Exceptional Children, Atlanta.

Laski, F. J. (1991). Achieving integration during the second revolution. In L. H. Meyer, L. A. Peck, & L. Brown (Eds.), *Critical issues in the lives of people with severe disabilities* (pp. 407–421). Baltimore: Paul H. Brookes Publishing Co.

Lessen, E., & Frankiewicz, L. E. (1992). Personal attributes and characteristics of effective special education teachers: Consideration for teacher educators. *Teacher Education and Special Education, 15*(2), 124–131.

Lilly, M. S. (1971). A training-based model for special education. *Exceptional Children, 37,* 741–749.

Lilly, M. S. (1986). The regular education initiative: A force for change in general and special education. *Education and Treatment of Mental Retardation, 23,* 253–260.

Lilly, M. S. (1989). Teacher preparation. In D. Kerzner Lipsky & A. Gardner (Eds.), *Beyond separate education: Quality education for all* (pp. 143–158). Baltimore: Paul H. Brookes Publishing Co.

Lilly, M. S. (1992). Research on teacher licensure and state approval of teacher education programs. *Teacher Education and Special Educations, 15*(2), 148–160.

Lloyd, J. W., Singh, N. N., & Repp, A. C. (Eds.) (1991). *The regular education initiative: Alternative perspectives, concepts, issues and models*. Sycamore, IL: Sycamore Publishing.

Malouf, D. B., & Pilato, V. H. (1991). *The SNAP system for inservice training of regular educators. Final project report*. (Contract No. G008730016). Washington, DC: U.S. Department of Education.

Masten, A. S. (1989). Resilience in development: Implications of the study of successful adaptation for developmental psychotherapy. In D. Cicchetti (Ed.), *The emergence of a discipline: Rochester Symposium on Developmental Psychopathology* (Vol. 1, pp. 261–294). Hillsdale, NJ: Lawrence Erlbaum Associates.

McDonnell, L. M., & Hill, P. T. (1993). *Newcomers in American schools*. Santa Monica, CA: Rand.

McKenzie, H., Egner, A., Knight, M., Perelman, P., Schneider, B., & Gavin, J. (1970). Training consulting teachers to assist elementary teachers in the management and education of handicapped children. *Exceptional Children, 37,* 137–143.

Meyer, L., & Biklen, D. (1992). *Inclusive elementary and special education teacher preparation program*. Syracuse: Syracuse University, Division for the Study of Teaching and Division of Special Education and Rehabilitation.

Meyers, J., Gelzheiser, L. M., & Yelich, G. (1991). Do pull-in programs foster teacher collaboration? *Remedial and Special Education, 12*(2), 7–15.

Moores, D. F. (1987). *Educating the deaf: Psychology, principles, and practices* (3rd ed.). Boston: Houghton Mifflin.

Morgan, R. L., Gustafson, K. J., Hudson, P. J., & Salzberg, C. L. (1992). Peer coaching in a preservice special education program. *Remedial and Special Education, 15*(4), 249–258.

National Center for Education Statistics. (1991). *Digest of education statistics: Schools and staffing survey (for 1987–88)*. Washington, DC: U.S. Government Printing Office.

Nevin, A. (1992). Categorical vs. noncategorical vs. cross categorical teacher certification in special education: None of the above. *Remedial and Special Education, 13*(4), 13–15.

Nevin, A., Villa, R., & Thousand, J. (1992). An invitation to invent the extraordinary: Response to Morsink and Lenk. *Remedial and Special Education, 13*(6), 44–46.

Newsletter. (1984). Minneapolis: Education Student Affairs Office, College of Education, University of Minnesota.

Orelove, F. P., & Sobsey, D. (1991). *Educating children with multiple disabilities: A transdisciplinary approach* (2nd ed.). Baltimore: Paul H. Brookes Publishing Co.

Paul, J. L., Duchnowski, A. J., & Danforth, S. (1993). Changing the way we do our business: One department's story of collaboration with public schools. *Teacher Education and Special Education, 16*(2), 95–109.

Peck, C. A., Richarz, S., Peterson, K., Hayden, L., Mineur, L., & Wandschneider, M. (1989). An ecological process model for implementing the least restrictive environment mandate in early childhood programs. In R. Gaylord-Ross (Ed.), *Integration strategies for students with severe handicaps* (pp. 281–298). Baltimore: Paul H. Brookes Publishing Co.

Pugach, M. (1992). Uncharted territory: Research on the socialization of special education teachers. *Teacher Education and Special Education, 15*(2), 133–147.

Putnam, M. S., & Vanselow Habanek, D. (1993). A national survey of certification requirements for teachers of students with mild handicaps: States of confusion. *Teacher Education and Special Education, 16*(2), 155–160.

Rainforth, B., York, J., & Macdonald, C. (1992). *Collaborative teams for students with severe disabilities: Integrating therapy and education.* Baltimore: Paul H. Brookes Publishing Co.

Raywid, M. A. (1984). Synthesis of research on schools of choice. *Educational Leadership, 41*(7), 70–78.

Raywid, M. A. (1989). The mounting case for schools of choice. In J. Nathan (Ed.), *Public schools by choice.* Minneapolis: Free Spirit Press.

Reetz, L. J., & Hoover, J. H. (1989). *Learning disability curriculum models: Instructional module. An instructional module for preservice or inservice training of regular secondary educators.* Vermillion: University of South Dakota.

Reiff, H. B., Evans, E. D., & Cass, M. (1991). Special education requirements for general education certification: A national survey of current practices. *Remedial and Special Education, 12*(5), 56–60.

Reith, H. B., & Evertson, C. (1988). Variables related to the effective instruction of difficult-to-teach children. *Focus on Exceptional Children, 20*(5), 1–8.

Reynolds, M. C. (1962). A framework for considering some issues in special education. *Exceptional Children, 28,* 367–370.

Reynolds, M. C. (1979). Categorical vs. non-categorical teacher training. *Teacher Education and Special Education, 2*(3), 5–8.

Reynolds, M. C. (1990). Educating teachers for special education students. In W. R. Houston (Ed.), *Handbook of research on teacher education* (pp. 423–436). New York: Macmillan.

Reynolds, M. C., Wang, M. C., & Walberg, H. J. (1992). The knowledge bases for special and general education. *Remedial and Special Education, 13*(5), 6–10.

Rosenholtz, S. J. (1989). *Teachers workplace.* New York: Longman.

Rule, S., Fodor-Davis, J., Morgan, R., Salzberg, C. L., & Chen, J. (1990). An inservice training model to encourage collaborative consultation. *Teacher Education and Special Education, 13*(3–4), 225–227.

Safron, S., & Safron, J. (1984). Elementary teachers' tolerance of problem behaviors. *Elementary School Journal, 85,* 247–253.

Sanche, R. P., & Smith, D. J. (1990). Preservice teacher attitudes toward mainstreaming before and after internship. *British Columbia Journal of Special Education, 14*(3), 233–240.

Scardamalia, S., & Bereiter, L. (1989). Conceptions of teaching and approaches to core problems. In M. C. Reynolds (Ed.), *Knowledge base for the beginning teacher* (pp. 37–46). Oxford: Pergamon Press.

Schlosser, G., & Millar, G. (1991). *Special education professional development and training in Alberta: A status report.* Edmonton, Alberta: Alberta Department of Education.

Schulz, J. B., Carpenter, C. D., & Turnbull, A. P. (1990). *Mainstreaming exceptional students: A guide for classroom teachers* (3rd Ed.). Boston: Allyn & Bacon.

Shanker, A. (1993, September 19). A rush to inclusion. *New York Times,* E9.

Showers, B. (1990). Aiming for superior classroom instruction for all children: A comprehensive staff development model. [Special issue]. *Remedial and Special Education, 11*(3), 35–39.

Simpson, R. L., Whelan, R. J., & Zabel, R. H. (1993). Special education personnel in the 21st century: Issues and strategies. *Remedial and Special Education, 14*(2), 7–22.

Sindelar, P. T., & Marks, L. J. (1992). Alternative route training: Implications for elementary education and special education. *Teacher Education and Special Education, 16*(2), 146–154.

Sindelar, P. T., Davis McGray, A., & Westling, D. L. (1992). A proposed certification model for special education. *Remedial and Special Education, 13*(4), 10–13.

Singer, J. D. (1993). Once is not enough: Former special educators who return to teaching. *Exceptional Children, 60*(1), 58–72.

Skrtic, T. (1991). *Behind special education: A critical analysis of professional culture and school organization.* Denver: Love.

Stewart, D. A. (1988). A model professional development school: Merging special education and general education in the work place. *British Columbia Journal of Special Education, 12*(3), 215–226.

Stone, B., & Brown, R. (1987). Preparing teachers for mainstreaming: Some critical variables for effective preservice programs. *Education Research Quarterly, 11*(2), 7–10.

Swan, W. W., & Sirvis, B. (1992). The CEC common core of knowledge and skills essential for all beginning special education teachers. *Teaching Exceptional Children, 25*(1), 16–20.

Taylor, S. J. (1988). Caught in the continuum: A critical analysis of the principle of least restrictive environment. *Journal of The Association for Persons with Severe Handicaps, 13*(1), 41–53.

Thousand, J., & Villa, R. (1992). Collaborative teams: A powerful tool for school restructuring. In R. Villa, J. S. Thousand, W. Stainback, & S. Stainback (Eds.), *Restructuring for caring and effective education: An administrative guide to creating heterogenous schools* (pp. 73–108). Baltimore: Paul H. Brookes Publishing Co.

Thousand, J., Nevin-Parta, A., & Fox, W. L. (1987). Inservice training to support the education of learners with severe handicaps in their local public schools. *Teacher Education and Special Education, 10*(1), 4–13.

U.S. Bureau of the Census. (1983). *Projections of the populations of the United States: 1982 to 2050.* Current Population Reports (Series P25, No. 922). Washington, DC: Author.

U.S. Department of Education. (1992). *Fourteenth annual report to Congress on the implementation of the Individuals with Disabilities Act.* Washington, DC: Author.

U.S. Department of Education, National Center for Education Statistics. (1993). *New teachers in the job market, 1991 update* (pp. 93–392). Washington, DC: Author. (Table B-17, p. B-18)

Walker, H., & Bullis, M. (1991). Behavior disorders and the social context of regular classes. In J. W. Lloyd, N. N. Singh, & A. C. Repp (Eds.), *The regular education initiative* (pp. 75–93). Sycamore, IL: Sycamore Publishing.

Walker, H., & Rankin, R. (1983). Assessing the behavior expectations and demands of less restrictive settings. *School Psychology Review, 12,* 274–284.

Wang, M. C., Haertel, G. D., & Walberg, H. J. (1990). What influences learning? A content analysis of review literature. *Journal of Educational Research, 84*(1), 30–43.

West, J. F., & Cannon, G. S. (1988). Essential collaborative consultation competencies for regular and special educators. *Journal of Learning Disabilities, 21*(1), 56–63.

Westling, D. L. (Ed.) (1992). Overview: Effective special education teachers. *Teacher Education and Special Education, 15*(2), 59–61.

Williams, D. (1990). Listening to today's teachers: They can tell us what tomorrow's teachers should know. *Teacher Education and Special Education, 13*(3–4), 149–153.

York, J., Schultz, T., Doyle, M. E., Kronberg, R., & Crossett, S. (in review). *Inclusive schooling in the Community Schools: Understanding the process and people of change.*

Zetlin, A., Valdez, A., & Ramos, C. (1994). *What collaboration means in a school-based integrated services center.* Unpublished manuscript.

·39·

EQUITY CHALLENGES

Patrice LeBlanc Kohl

BARRY UNIVERSITY

Elaine P. Witty

NORFOLK STATE UNIVERSITY

EQUITY

Definition

What is equity? Equity addresses the primary goal of education in the United States—educating all children. Equity should not be confused with equality. Equality calls for all children to be treated equally. State equalization formulas for distribution of finances are an example; all children receive equal amounts of funding for schooling. However, equity focuses on the redistribution of funds to those who need it most. Here disadvantaged children receive more funding for education to decrease the gap between where they are and where average U.S. students are. A more specific example is special education funding, where the cost of educating special children over the past 20 years has been twice the cost of children receiving regular education (Chaikind, Danielson, & Brauen, 1993).

The premise for equity is that the funding should go to those in greatest need to ensure that all children are educated. Hence emerge conflicts that cause confrontations over the funding for equity programs. Competition for scarce dollars coupled with interest groups that promote values other than equity exert influence on the political process, thus creating variations in both the actual funding and the implementation of equity programs.

Historically, federal intervention to promote equity began after the 1954 *Brown v. Board of Education* decision, but most notably with the passage of the Civil Rights Act and with the approval of the Elementary and Secondary Education Act (ESEA) in the mid-1960s. In particular, the needs of disadvantaged students were recognized and financially addressed through categorical funding in ESEA (Gorton & Thierbach-Schneider, 1991).

The plethora of categorical programs continued, along with federal funding, until the 1980s when federal education dollars began to decline. In 1981 Terrel Bell, head of the U.S. Department of Education, formed the National Commission on Excellence in Education, which issued the famous report *A Nation at Risk* (Gardner) in 1983. At that time the Republican Administration was committed to reducing involvement in education and in abolishing the Department of Education (Bell, 1993). *A Nation at Risk,* however, succeeded in bringing education to the attention of the public, where it has remained for an unprecedented length of time. With that attention, and subsequent federal administrations, the country has seen waves of reports, state legislation, and reform.

Equity as One of the Four Values of Education

Analysis of equity as one of the four basic values that drive education—quality, efficiency, equity, and choice—provides a basis for exploring the current status of equity in education. Marshall, Mitchell, and Wirt (1989) advanced the notion that these four values are subsumed in all school policy. The premise proposed here is that they are not only subsumed in school policy but also actually drive the political culture responsible for the decision making of school policy at the federal, state, and local levels. In the subsequent paragraphs these values are defined (Wirt & Kirst, 1992), and then school policy decision making is explored.

Quality is an end goal for all educational endeavors and focuses on substantial improvement for those affected by policy. The value of quality is actualized in policies such as state teacher certification requirements, district use of instructional resources, and local and state testing programs. *Efficiency* looks at the economy of educational efforts to achieve goals—

837

minimizing costs, controlling of power, monitoring and assuming accountability. Actualization of efficiency can be seen in district budgetary processes, local student teacher ratios, and state accountability legislation. The value of *equity* maintains that the education of all children is the primary goal and therefore focuses on the redistribution of resources based on children's needs. Federal and state laws for special education and desegregation orders are examples of equity policies in action. *Choice* focuses on the public's participation in decision making in key areas such as policy making. Voucher plans are the most controversial form of choice, but local parent advisory boards and school board elections are also examples of the value of choice impacting school policy.

Equity and the Issue Attention Cycle

As discussed, the public's attention to education in the United States has been maintained for an exceptional length of time. This issue-attention cycle can be explained with dissatisfaction theory. Lutz and Merz (1992) maintained that policy is made that reflects community values. If those values shift, for example because of demographic or economic changes, policy dissatisfaction occurs. This results in an increase in political activity, ranging from voting in school board elections to filing court cases, until policy then changes. This cycle is evidenced by briefly examining some of the history of federal equity interventions.

Federal intervention increased beginning with the *Brown* court decision (equity). The passage of the Civil Rights Act (equity) came about through public political activity. The Elementary and Secondary Education Act evolved from the movement to educate all children (equity) and from the scientific and economic challenges introduced with the Cold War (quality and efficiency). The 1970s saw legislation for equity, examples being gender equity with Title IX and special education with PL 94-142. The waves of reform from *A Nation at Risk* (Gardner, 1983) were based on a public outcry for excellence in education (quality). Subsequent efforts by governors and state legislatures initially focused on school improvement (quality), but more recently they have focused on accountability (efficiency). Looking at this history in terms of the issue-attention cycle, the value decisions that have emerged since the 1960s can be traced. In identifying those values it is easy to see the shift from equity as the predominant value in the 1960s and 1970s to quality in the 1980s and, most recently, efficiency in the 1990s.

So, where educational equity stands today is a direct result of the political process. The values of quality, efficiency, equity, and choice provide the foundation for the political decisions that are made. Which value is promoted in the issue-attention cycle dictates the changes in education. It is therefore up to educators and other citizens who believe in equity to push this value into the public's issue-attention cycle in order to maintain progress toward true equity.

The Challenge Of Equity to Teachers and Teacher Educators

Keeping the value of equity in the eye of the public is in itself a challenge, but what is even more challenging is keeping up with the political and legal processes, educational research, and the impact of these areas on current practice. The purpose of this chapter is to review these areas and to analyze them in light of the previously defined political framework—values and the issue-attention cycle. This conceptual understanding can enable teachers and teacher educators better to rise to the equity challenges they are faced with daily.

Questions for Examining Equity

In order to achieve the goal of equity in education, teachers must be prepared to reach beyond their own existential worlds and develop frames of reference and points of view similar to their students who come from diverse backgrounds (Gay, 1993). Study of the following questions can help teachers use the rich body of literature on educational equity in shaping their instructional attitudes and skills:

- What has been the impact of policymakers' decisions based on the values of quality, efficiency, and choice on educational equity? How is educational equity promoted and/or protected today?
- In what ways do school policies and practices reflect society's concern or lack of concern for equity and quality?
- What are the most appropriate and effective approaches to providing educational programs for children and youth who have disabilities?
- How have legal actions impacted the opportunities to learn that children from ethnic/racial groups face today?
- How does schooling enhance or limit the educational opportunities of girls and women? Why?
- In what ways do special programs enable or hamper the educational achievements of children from low-income families?

EQUITY GROUPS

Selection of Equity Groups

In originally determining the content of this chapter, the authors considered the inclusion of many equity groups—culture, disabilities, ethnicity/race, gender, language, religion, sexual preference, and socioeconomic status. However, the quantity of writing and research for each equity group is vast. In order to treat each group thoroughly, it would be necessary to write an entire book. Therefore, the focus of this chapter is on four equity areas: disabilities, ethnicity/race, socioeconomic status, and gender. The selection was not meant to slight any other equity group; it was a decision based on the authors' areas of expertise and the reality of space constraints.

Organization of Equity Group Discussion

To begin the discussion of equity groups, this chapter defines each of the four equity groups. Then the authors discuss the legal issues and related theory. A summary of research trends for each of the four equity areas follows. Next, the chapter discusses interpretations of the research trends and themes as they impact practice, with recommendations for teachers and teacher educators for working through equity challenges. Integration of the political framework occurs throughout the chapter, serving as a guide for interpreting the literature and research in the equity areas explored.

DISABILITIES

Definition

The term *disability* has become the preferred term for describing people who experience some impairment or handicap that prevents them from reaching their full capacity without special accommodations. It implies that problems impair a person's ability to function when he or she interacts with the environment. The term disability is thought to be less demeaning than terms previously used to describe this population (Blackhurst & Burdine, 1993).

People who are disabled, "the largest minority group in the United States" (Kohl & Greenlaw, 1992, p. 214), are provided federal protection for their civil rights. This protection has been guaranteed through a combination of court decisions and laws, defined in greater detail in the next section of this chapter. It is important to note here one piece of critical legislation, PL 94-142. It serves the national interest by providing disabled youngsters and adults with equal protection under the law (Blackhurst & Burdine, 1993) and by ensuring that they receive an education that enables them "to become contributing and self-sufficient members of society" (*121 Congressional Record,* 1975, 23703). Programs for the disabled have grown since this federal legislation, and the related field of special education has grown with it.

Special education, individualized educational instruction geared to the needs of disabled or exceptional persons (Blackhurst & Burdine, 1993), is a curriculum in itself because exceptional people cannot have their needs met through the standard curriculum. In fact, what has evolved is a "second system" of categorical programs for children and young adults with learning difficulties (Jenkins, Pious, & Jewell, 1990). This "second system" meets the needs of exceptional people through specialized curricula and teaching methodologies. Questions arose in recent years as to the justifiability of such a second system. Subsequent amendments to PL 94-142 and the Americans with Disabilities Act (ADA) of 1990 have all supported the notion of provision of the least restrictive environment—that people with disabilities be educated, live, and work as much as possible with those who do not have disabilities (Bishop & Jones, 1993; Shelton, 1993). Today's focus in special education placement centers around the debate of the "second system"—to what extent should the least restrictive environment occur? The names for the placement initiatives in this debate are: mainstreaming, inclusion, and the regular education initiative. These placement initiatives are discussed in detail later in this chapter.

Even more important than the debate over where disabled people will receive educational services is who will receive those services. Assessment is the name for the process that identifies persons with disabilities. It involves the use of tests and other instruments to ascertain the functioning levels of a student's performance and behavior (Venn, 1994). The data that assessment provides enable educators to determine who will receive services.

Assessment procedures for placement of students in special education programs are under critical review. An example of the rationale for such criticism is the overrepresentation of ethnic minority students in programs for the mentally disabled because "indiscriminate use of psychological tests combined with the linguistic and cultural orientation of school programs" (Cummins, 1984, p. 1). Inappropriate use of assessment led to multiple court cases, with decisions that uphold the rights of the student and mandate assessment with appropriate instruments (Salvia & Yesseldyke, 1991).

The major criticism of assessment is the use of specific tests and processes that center on middle-class, monocultural values and evaluate based on deviance from these values—a deficit model motivated by sociopolitical values (Cummins, 1984). Based on the use of the medical diagnostic-prescriptive technique mandated by law, this model views people with disabilities as "deficit." There is currently a call for educators to broaden their views of assessment to include the functional model—assessing behavior that reflects students' adaptation to the environment (Venn, 1994)—and the behavioral model—"assessing the performance of students over time" (Venn, 1994, p. 11). In essence, there is a call for a shift in paradigm in special education, from a purely objectivist model to a multiparadigmatic, proactive paradigm (Skrtic, 1986). The notion is that by shifting the paradigm, with its inherent values, the assessment of students with disabilities will be more equitable. It then follows that various special education and least restrictive environment placements in turn would be more equitable, because the values and philosophy guiding placements would not be middle-class and monocultural.

Legal Issues: Court Decisions

The first two court cases that clearly defined the education rights of disabled citizens were *Pennsylvania Association for Retarded Citizens (PARC) v. The Commonwealth of Pennsylvania* (1972) and *Mills v. Board of Education in the District of Columbia* (1972). The remedy for the first court case mandated the provision of an appropriate public education for the mentally disabled from the ages of 6 to 21. Included as part of the remedy were set procedures for due process, placement, and reevaluation. The second court case reaffirmed the remedies from the *PARC* case and added that lack of funds could not be used as an excuse for not providing education to disabled students (Blackhurst & Burdine, 1993).

Three other court cases from the early 1970s are related to the issues discussed in this chapter. These three cases further defined and broadened the parameters of special education services. *Diana v. the State Board of Education in California* (1970) found that placements of Mexican-American children in classes for the mentally disabled was inappropriate. Intelligence quotient (IQ) tests were the basis of the *Larry P. v. Riles* (1972) court case. Here the court decided that African-American students could not be placed in classes for the mentally disabled on the basis of IQ tests alone. The third important case, *Lau v. Nichols* (1974), was the beginning of formal bilingual special education. The court decision was that bilingual special education services must be provided for non–English-speaking students.

Legal Issues: Court Decisions and Theory

These five cases are important because they relate to the establishment of the "second system" of categorical programs for the disabled, and they evidence the emergence of the issues of assessment and placement.

The cases described, along with others decided during the same time frame, reflected active participation of parents and citizens in forwarding educational equity for the disabled. The decisions from these cases created and maintained the impetus for some of the major legislation addressing education for the disabled. They were part of the political activity that sparked the issue-attention cycle that, in turn, resulted in new public policy promoting equity. From the late 1970s onward court decisions for educational equity for the disabled were not so favorable (Blackhurst & Burdine, 1993). The political framework traced in the earlier section of this chapter explains this fact. The public attention, which became focused on other educational values, coupled with a conservative political climate, affected the course of these decisions.

Legal Issues: Legislation

The piece of legislation most frequently seen as the cornerstone of special education is Section 504 of the Vocational Rehabilitation Act of 1973. This law guaranteed the civil rights of the disabled. Although the regulations took 4 years to develop, their implementation provided the following protections for disabled persons: equal job opportunities, access to public facilities, a free appropriate public education, and prohibition of discrimination in institutions of higher education and in social service programs (Blackhurst & Burdine, 1993).

The next important piece of legislation related to disabilities was the 1974 Family Rights and Privacy Act (PL 93-380). This law guaranteed parents and students over 18 "the opportunity to inspect, challenge and correct" (Salvia & Yesseldyke, 1991, p. 55) educational records. The law also guaranteed nondiscriminatory testing, due process for determining educational placements, and confidentiality of student records.

The passage in 1975 of The Education for All Handicapped Children Act (PL 94-142) expanded on the promise of a free appropriate public education for children of school age and due process rights, holding state and local systems responsible regardless of finances. In 1983 and again in 1986 amendments were added to PL 94-142 to include services from birth through to postsecondary programs for disabled children and young adults. The 1986 revision changed the title of the original legislation to the Individuals with Disabilities Education Act (IDEA), thus updating the term *handicap* to the more socially acceptable term of *disability*. The amendment in 1990 increased the list of disabilities and required the development of an individualized educational plan (IEP) that addresses transition services for

students when they reach the age of 16. The goal of the latter addition is to prepare disabled students for the world of work better, thus further advancing the initial intent of PL 94-142 to educate students to be productive citizens who contribute to society.

The Americans with Disabilities Act of 1990 defined disabilities broadly in a fashion similar to the 1973 Rehabilitation Act's definition. This broad definition covers an estimated 58 million Americans (Kohl & Greenlaw, 1992). The ADA relates to education in that the law requires that reasonable accommodations must be made to enable access for the disabled to public services and accommodations. Thus, the legislation applies to those employed by the schools as well as to those served by the schools. Examples of areas of implementation include reasonable accommodations for the disabled; nondiscriminatory policies, practices, and regulations; provisions for vision- or hearing-impaired individuals; and removal of physical barriers (Shelton, 1993).

Vocational education for students with low socioeconomic levels and/or with disabilities came through the Vocational Education Amendments of 1968 (PL 90-576) and 1976 (PL 94-482). Vocational education broadened with the Carl D. Perkins Vocational and Technical Education Act (PL 98-524). That legislation encouraged mainstreamed vocational placements and definition of vocational placements in students' IEPs. The 1990 amendments to this legislation built on the previous legislation. The name of the law was revised to the Carl D. Perkins Vocational and Applied Technology Education Act, and it provided for the increase of vocational programs to a variety of equity groups including exceptional students and low-socioeconomic-status students. An additional piece of legislation also affected the vocational/technological education of the disabled. The Technology-Related Assistance for Individuals with Disabilities Act of 1988 (PL 100-407) allowed the disabled to benefit from assistive and adaptive technologies (Blackhurst & Burdine, 1993).

Legal Issues: Legislation and Theory

The laws outlined here show clear intent for providing appropriate services for the disabled. Their rights are guaranteed, and funding to ensure equity is recommended. In addition, the laws fully define the parameters of acceptable assessment and placement.

Although new gains for educational equity have recently been somewhat limited in the courts, the legislature has continued to support the notion at the federal level through legislation. Interestingly, since the legislation for special education began, the momentum has held steady. New legislation has occurred as well as amendments to some of the foundation laws that have sought to improve the quality of special education services. These federal categorical programs, once established, have been able to maintain a share of the funding to education. ADA also attests to society's concern with the civil rights for the disabled.

Such sustained momentum shows the power of keeping the equity value in the issue-attention cycle. However, there is a gap between the intent of the legislation and current trends in special education for assessment and placement. This gap is discussed in the following sections of this chapter.

Research Trends

Two areas are currently major issues in the research on special education. The first is assessment for determination of disability for subsequent placement, and the second is placement itself.

Assessment Assessment of students for special education placement takes two forms: standardized, also referred to as formal assessment, and alternative, also known as informal assessment. Areas assessed to determine if a student has a disability may include: intelligence, achievement, adaptive behavior, developmental skills, and actual classroom behavior (Venn, 1994). Each of these areas, when taken in isolation, reflects a particular model for assessment. The models include: (1) the medical model, also known as the deficit model, which uses the diagnostic-prescriptive technique to assess intelligence and achievement; (2) the functional model, which examines adaptive behavior; (3) the developmental model, which explores mastery and skill attainment in relation to developmental or curriculum standards; and (4) the behavioral model, which uses direct observation to ascertain students' daily performance.

It should be noted here that the traditional definition of developmental assessment is limited to preschool-age children, where assessment through formal and informal means are used to determine if a child follows the normal sequence of development (Venn, 1994). For the purposes of this chapter the developmental model includes developmental and curriculum assessment. Developmental standards reflect what content can be taught at various ages based on cognitive, affective, and psychomotor development. Because these standards create the basis for curriculum, it is appropriate to group the two forms of assessment.

As discussed, a blend of assessment from all of these models rather than reliance solely on the medical/deficit model is what is needed to bring about true equity in assessment. Rather than defining disabilities by deficits from the middle-class monocultural norm that is the existing special education paradigm, assessment needs to be multiparadigmatic (Skrtic, 1986) using multiple models. The multiparadigmatic view provides a broader range of information that allows educators to view the total student. Multiple comparisons can then be made that provide a clearer picture of the student's possible disabilities. The information culled from this broader assessment also provides more appropriate information for potential placements.

The resulting shift to a multiparadigmatic view would bring additional benefits. It would allow the field of special education to be more proactive. The result would be a pluralistic standing, where multicultural viewpoints are honored.

Assessment: Standardized or Formal Standardized or formal assessment comprises the traditional model for determining the abilities and achievement of children. The typical instruments used in this form of assessment are standardized published tests, which are frequently norm-referenced and checked for reliability and validity. However, there are several major criticisms of these standardized instruments.

The first criticism of standardized tests has to do with the groups used for norm referencing. The normative group may not have the same experiential background as the students taking the test. For example, the normative group might be from a white, middle-class suburban school while the students taking the test may be African American or bilingual students from a low socio-economic urban school. Clearly the experiential background of the normative group and the examinees in this example differ. Since norm referencing compares the examinee's performance with that of his or her peers—those with similar experiential backgrounds—the normative group that is the basis for comparison is of critical importance for making valid comparisons. Salvia and Yesseldyke (1991) in their text on assessment noted that:

Unfortunately, many psychologists, counselors, remedial specialists, and others who select tests to be administered to students often do so with little regard to the characteristics of the students who constitute the normative samples. Many school administrators routinely purchase tests with more concern for price than for the technical adequacy and appropriateness of those tests. (p. 18)

Other criticisms of standardized assessment are the use of one test to dictate placement and the comparison of test results from one test to another without equating test scoring systems. It is critical therefore that the person who gives the test be skilled at test administration. The examiner must keep in mind such factors as bias and random error and ensure that adequate information is collected to observe present behavior in order to make predictions about future behavior (Salvia & Yesseldyke, 1991). Surprisingly, these criticisms continue to be valid today, despite court decisions and laws mandating appropriate use of testing.

Assessment: Alternative or Informal Alternative or informal assessment refers to a growing movement toward broadening the assessment instruments used. These trends in assessment require a shift in thinking about assessment. This new line of thought views assessment data as indicators of learning on which a judgment is made, not as an evaluation in itself (Chittenden, 1991). The distinction is important because it reflects the notion of assessment as a process rather than as an end in itself. In addition, alternative assessment allows inclusion of three models of assessment: functional, developmental, and behavioral. Thus, it reflects the beginnings of a paradigm shift in educational assessment.

The recent trend toward exploring alternative forms of assessment also indicates a shift in thinking in several foundation beliefs about learning. These beliefs include a viewpoint that moves from outcomes to process, from passive learning to active learning, and from specific isolated skills and facts to integrated application of learning (Herman, Aschbacher, & Winters, 1992). This shift in beliefs about practice requires practitioners to be knowledgeable about new developments in the field and to apply those developments. Under alternative assessment, practitioners cannot rely solely on standardized tests for assessment or teach facts in isolation in a passive learning environment. Rather, practitioners are required to implement new techniques for both learning and assessment, showing their abilities to analyze and synthesize data that will eventually lead to judgments about student performance and, in turn, possible modifications in the teaching process.

The forms that alternative assessment can take include a wide range of techniques. A few of these are: interviews; observations; journals and logs; behavioral checklists; and scoring criteria for student essays, projects, experiments, and artwork (Herman et al., 1992). In addition, part of the assessment may include a student's work in a group. Teaching of interdependence, accountability, and collaborative social skills occurs through well-structured cooperative learning groups (Male, Johnson, Johnson, & Anderson, 1986, cited in Male, 1994). Assessment of these skills needed for productive living is again evidence of the broad scope of alternative assessment.

Samples of student work, using some of the techniques described, frequently make up what is known as a portfolio. This portfolio is composed of student work samples over a period of time (Herman et al., 1992). As a result, rather than providing a snapshot of performance, as formal assessment devices do, the portfolio is able to provide a broader view of student performance over a longer period.

Another form of assessment that can be termed alternative is often referred to as curriculum-based assessment. Part of the developmental model as defined in this chapter, curriculum-based assessment attempts to determine the student's achievement in relation to the curriculum being taught. For example, criterion-referenced tests determine a student's level of mastery for particular developmental skills (Salvia & Yesseldyke, 1991). These tests are frequently developed within classrooms by teachers, thus allowing assessment of ongoing learning.

Currently, as part of the accountability movement in education, states are developing and administering basic competency tests that are designed to assess students' knowledge of areas presumed to be key concepts in the curriculum at specific grade levels. These criterion-referenced tests are used to draw comparisons among schools throughout a state. Scores may also be used within a school to determine the success of teaching. These uses, however, are considered formal assessment.

Placement Special education students must be placed in appropriate educational settings, in the least restrictive environment. This means that students must be educated, as much as possible, with their nondisabled peers (Salend, 1994). Three types of placements are currently being used to provide the least restrictive environment to students. They are mainstreaming, inclusion, and the regular education initiative. Rogers (1993) defined these three terms, also making a distinction between two types of Inclusion. These definitions are summarized next.

Mainstreaming refers to special education students placed in the regular classroom only for specific classes. The notion is that students attend classes in the regular classroom for areas in which they can succeed at the same level as peers. Students receive other educational services through a pull-out program, where they obtain specialized instruction. *Inclusion* refers to educating the special needs youngster within the regular classroom and sending the support services into the classroom for that child. The notion behind this placement is that the child may experience some benefit from the regular classroom, not

necessarily that the child must "keep up" with all of the regular expectations and work. Rogers (1993) described full inclusion as placement of the special education student within the regular classroom, but in lieu of providing additional practitioners that enter the classroom to assist the special needs student, the existing regular education teacher is trained to provide those services. Finally, the regular education initiative (REI) refers to the merger of governance and/or funding structures for both regular and special education. It focuses on the administrative aspect of programs, not on the actual delivery of services.

Although Rogers (1993) identified clear and precise definitions of these terms, an examination of the literature reveals that the terms are not always so clearly defined, as is particularly the case with the REI (Muir & Hutton, 1989). These terms are also frequently used synonymously.

Many articles criticize regular classroom placements without some type of special education services for the disabled. Lerner (1987) acknowledged the reluctance on the part of regular educators to meet special education students' needs and suggested that only through training and changes in practice will this condition improve. She suggested that the learning disabled may experience school failure with REI and noted that regular classroom placements are inappropriate for the severely learning disabled. She recommended "more robust data and evidence of effectiveness" (Lerner, 1987, p. 6) before changing the current system. Wagner's (1990) study of learning disabled high school students confirmed Lerner's fears. The study found that, regardless of student ability, IQ, or demographic variables, grade failure and subsequent dropping out were positively correlated with the lack of tutoring assistance. Apparent to many educators is the fact that the special characteristics of the learning disabled population will require continued special services (Bryan, Bay, & Donahue, 1988). For the mentally disabled, it has been suggested that regular classroom placement is not always preferable to the self-contained placement (Gottlieb, 1990). A plethora of articles support special education services for all types of disabilities. Even the results of some surveys of teacher attitudes favor pull-out programs (Semmel, Abernathy, Butera, & Lesar, 1991).

However, much literature favors regular classroom placements. The meta-analysis of Wang, Anderson, and Bram (Salend, 1994) supported the successful effects of full-time regular classroom placements. The analysis found that students performed better both academically and socially, regardless of their disability type, than full-time special education students or partially mainstreamed students. Surveys of teachers also support regular classroom placements. However, when teachers show a willingness to accept disabled students, qualifications usually exist. For example, Myles and Simpson's (1992) survey found teachers willing to accept learning disabled and behavior disordered students with the appropriate type and quality of support personnel to assist them. Davis and Maheady (1991) had similar survey findings, but teachers and administrators suggested that pragmatic factors such as planning time and funding pose barriers to successful implementation. Parent surveys have also indicated support for regular classroom placement with modifications for the students (Myles & Simpson, 1990).

Successful regular classroom placement—regardless of whether it is called mainstreaming, inclusion, or REI—appears to be contingent on a series of factors. First, administrative and family support are important (Buswell & Schaffner, 1990; Roller, Rodriquez, Warner, & Lindahl, 1992; Villa & Thousand, 1990). Another factor is support personnel. An integration specialist (Hanline, 1990) or a learning specialist (Margolis & McCabe, 1989) ease adjustments to the regular classroom for special education students. And, most important, fundamental changes in the process of instruction are needed (Baker & Zigmond, 1990). Diagnosing teachers' competencies (Maheady & Algozzine, 1991) and providing appropriate staff development for teachers are critical first steps. Educating teachers to use successful practices must be part of this staff development. Successful practices include: cooperative teaching or a team approach between regular educators and special education teachers (Friend & Cook, 1992; Jenkins & Pious, 1991; Thousand & Villa, 1991); use of specific learning strategies such as peer tutoring and cooperative learning (Vergason & Anderegg, 1991); and modifications in assessment such as curriculum-based assessment (Vergason & Anderegg, 1991) and oral testing (Vallies, Sullivan, & McLaughlin, 1992).

For further discussion of issues raised in this chapter section, readers are referred to Chapter 38 by York and Reynolds in this handbook.

ETHNICITY/RACE

Definition

Ethnicity/race as an equity group refers to children from African-American, Hispanic, Asian, Pacific Islander, Native-American, and other minority group families. Children from ethnic/racial minority groups constitute 31.5% of the school population according to reports from the National Center for Education Statistics (U.S. Department of Education, 1994).

Membership in an ethnic or racial minority group in American schools places children at risk of inequitable access to effective instruction, adequate resources, equal opportunity, and equal outcomes. The National Assessment of Educational Progress (NAEP) Reports on academic achievement reveal substantial inequities in the accomplishments and representations of racial and ethnic groups (Mullis & Jenkins, 1988; Mullis, Owen, & Phillips, 1990). Because school populations are becoming more ethnically and racially diverse, schools and teachers must respond to a wide variety of needs and strengths brought by the children they intend to educate.

Children from ethnic and racial minority groups are more likely to be isolated and excluded from extracurricular activities that expand the formal curriculum. Further, ethnic and racial minority children are more likely than their peers to be tracked into low-challenging programs (Oakes, 1990), placed in special education groups, expelled from school, and to drop out of school (U.S. Department of Education, National Center for Education Statistics, 1993b).

Children from Hispanic, African-American, Asian or Pacific Islander, and Native-American families face a lack of proportional representation of their backgrounds and culture on the teaching and administrative staff of the schools. Even though about a third of the children in public schools are from ethnic or racial minority groups, only 13% of the teachers represent these groups (U.S. Department of Education, National Center for Education Statistics, 1993b). This mismatch is critical because a monocultural teaching and administrative staff is less likely to be able to use the values, cultural backgrounds, family experiences, and community strengths of these children in the instructional activities and curriculum.

The student population in schools, like that of society in general, is rapidly becoming more racially and ethnically diverse. In 1990, the U.S. population was 12.1% African American, 9% Hispanic, 2.9% Asian or Pacific Islander, 4.7% other races, and 71.3% non-Hispanic white (U.S. Department of Commerce, Bureau of the Census, 1993). These demographics are reflected in the school population. In 1991 African-American children made up 16.4%, Hispanic children made up 11.8%, Asian or Pacific Islander children made up 3.4%, and Native-American children made up 1% of the school population. White children made up 67.4% (U.S. Department of Education, Office of Educational Research and Improvement, 1993b). African-American and Hispanic students have constituted a majority of the public school students in central cities since 1980 (U.S. Department of Education, National Center for Education Statistics, 1993a). It is projected that by the year 2000, one out of every three students will be Hispanic, African American, or Asian.

In addition to challenges presented by ethnic and racial identifications, children from these groups are more likely than their peers to experience the negative impact of low socioeconomic status. Even though the majority of the poor children are white, ethnic and racial minority children are much more likely to live in a poor family. About 44% of all African-American children and more than 37% of Hispanic children are poor, compared to 15% of the white children (U.S. Department of Commerce, Bureau of the Census, 1992).

Children from ethnic and racial minorities have experienced entrenched institutional inequities in their quest for education. Responses to the need to provide equity in educating ethnic/racial minority children will require attention to quality, efficiency, and choice as values in education. America cannot have a high-quality educational system as long as increasing numbers of the school population are underserved and fail to achieve at optimal levels. A really integrated democracy is also impossible without educating all of the citizens so that they contribute to the production of goods and services. School policies that lead to the undereducation of large portions of the population are inherently inefficient. Remediation is costly. Subsidized lives of school dropouts and nonproductive school graduates drain the national coffers. It is more efficient to provide the education that is needed in early childhood and other school programs than to try to remediate learning inadequacies in later years. (See Chapter 41 by Corrigan and Udas in this handbook.) Efforts to correct the inequities have been promoted through legal action.

Legal Issues: Court Decisions

The courts have been used to help fight for equity in education through challenges to such problems as desegregation, busing, bilingual education, school finance, and educational rights of children with disabilities. Table 39-1 summarizes the major court findings.

One of the major issues related to equity for racial and ethnic groups is desegregation of public schools. The Equal Protection Clause of the Fourteenth Amendment to the U.S. Constitution requires that public schools not be operated by the states on a racially segregated basis. Although this clause prohibits state-fostered discrimination, racial or ethnic segregation resulting from the influence of social forces outside of government sponsorship is not prohibited. In the 1954 landmark decision, the Supreme Court struck down state laws that required public schools to be racially segregated (*Brown v. Board of Education*, 1954).

A major method used by school districts to eliminate segregation is busing students from their communities to schools in other communities. Courts have generally upheld desegregation plans that included busing and have even required some school districts to develop a plan for busing students (*Columbus Board of Education v. Pencik*, 1979). However, a Detroit multi-district, areawide busing plan was rejected (*Milliken v. Bradley*, 1974).

Legal responses to desegregation and busing have led to mixed results. Dissatisfaction with mandatory cross-town busing can lead to "white flight." In Norfolk, Virginia, large numbers of white parents sent their children to private white academies or moved to the suburbs rather than permit them to be bused. The U.S. Supreme Court of Appeals, Fourth Circuit, held that preventing white flight was a valid school board objective and that the neighborhood school assignment plan was a reasonable attempt to keep white students in the public school system (*Riddick v. School Board of Norfolk*, 1986).Under the Norfolk plan, some elementary schools became as much as 100% black and some as little as 16% black.

A similar school board initiative was disapproved by the U.S. Court of Appeals, Tenth Circuit, in which the court ruled that the inquiry was not whether the school board intended to reestablish segregation, but whether stopping busing would create racial imbalance (*Board of Education of Oklahoma City Public Schools v. Dowell*, 1986).

Legal Issues: Court Decisions and Theory

Court decisions on desegregation of schools, like decisions on other equity issues, reflect the political activity of parents and community leaders. Values held by policymakers are reflected in the responses to legal challenges. Participation of educational researchers in forcing attention to equity has kept the issue of educational achievement of minority children on the agenda of professional and community organizations. The recent report by Orfield (1993) on school integation and the reports by Bartz and Gordon (1994) and the Network of Regional Desegregation Assistance Centers (1989) highlight the continuing need for school districts to be pushed on equity matters.

Orfield's study of school integration in the 1990s indicated that segregation remains high in big cities and that it is serious in midsize cities. The study revealed that resegregation in southern cities grew significantly from 1988 to 1991.

Legal Issues: Legislation

Legislation has been an important part of the struggle for equity in education. The Civil Rights Act of 1964 was passed by Congress to speed up the desegregation of public schools. The Act provided for the withholding of federal funding to schools still practicing racial discrimination. The Civil Rights Act of 1964 (Section 402) also authorized the Commissioner of Education to conduct a survey to determine the lack of availability of equal educational opportunities in public schools for individuals because of race, color, religion, or national origin. The survey was conducted by Coleman and associates and published in a comprehensive report *Equality of Educational Opportunity* (Coleman et al., 1966). Findings from this survey were used to support the development of a variety of programs for disadvantaged children.

A second important piece of legislation was the Elementary and Secondary School Act of 1965 (PL 89-10). This act provided large sums of federal dollars for the improvement of schooling for children from low socioeconomic backgrounds. Most of these children were minorities.

Legal Issues: Legislation and Theory

Policymakers and educators used research findings from the Coleman Report (Coleman et al., 1966) to develop programs designed to improve the education of minority children. The findings led to an interpretation of a theory of cultural deprivation of poor families (Bennett & LeCompte, 1990). This theory justified the compensatory education programs that were funded by the Elementary and Secondary Education Act of 1965. The success of these programs in providing equity in education has been mixed and limited. Parents, community activists, and policymakers have rejected the cultural deprivation theory on which these programs are based. Evaluation of the Chapter 1 programs, which are revisions of the older ESEA programs, show that new strategies are needed. The report, *Reinventing Chapter 1,* sponsored by the U.S. Department of Education, shows that these programs have not improved the performance of students in programs for which they were intended (U.S. Department of Education, Office of Educational Research and Improvement, 1993c).

Research Trends: Theoretical Frameworks

Several theoretical frameworks may be identified as the basis for research designed to address equity issues relating to ethnicity and race. Early research on academic achievement of African-American students was framed from a genetic deficit theory (Jackson, 1993).

National attention focused on the achievement gap between poor and ethnic minority youth and their advantaged and white counterparts in the 1960s. At that time, the cultural deprivation theory replaced the genetic deficit theory and emerged as the dominant paradigm to explain the differences in the educational performance of minority and majority group students (Bloom, Davis, & Hess, 1965; Reissman, 1962). Researchers who supported the cultural deprivation concept maintained that low-

TABLE 39.1. Major Court Findings for Equity

Equity Group	Issue	Date	Case	Finding
Ethnicity/race	Desegregation	1954	Brown v. Board of Education (Supreme Court)	Struck down state laws that required public schools to be racially segregated; decided that the concept of "separate but equal" schools was unconstitutional and guaranteed all children equal opportunity for education.
Ethnicity/race	Language needs	1969	Hobsen v. Smuck (DC Circuit)	Ruled to outlaw tests that were proven to be unfair.
Ethnicity/race	Desegregation	1969	Board of Public Instruction of Taylor County v. Finch (5th Circuit)	Promoted desegregation by providing for expenses incurred in desegregation efforts and authoring federal agency regulations and supervisions of desegregation plans.
Disabilities and ethnicity/race	Placement	1970	Diana v. the State Board of Education in California	Determined that California schools could not place students in special education on the bases of culturally biased tests or tests not in the child's primary language.
Ethnicity/race	Desegregation	1971	Swann v. Charlotte-Mecklenburg Board of Education	Held that district courts may fashion remedies to eliminate segregation in schools where the school authorities fail to provide remedies.
Disabilities	Educational rights of disabled citizens	1972	Mills v. the Board of Education in the District of Columbia	Mandated the provision of the appropriate public education for the mentally retarded person from ages 6 to 21; set procedures for due process placement and re-evaluation; determined that lack of funds could not be used as an excuse for not providing education to disabled students.
Ethnicity/race	Language needs	1972	Cisneros v. Corpus Christi Independent School District	Ruled that language needs traceable to de jure segregation were remediable as a part of a desegration order.
Ethnicity/race and disabilities	Assessment of placement	1972	Larry P. v. Riles	Determined that African-American children could not be placed in classes for the retarded based on IQ tests alone.
Socioeconomic	School finance inequities	1973	San Antonio Independent School District v. Rodriguez (U.S. Supreme Court)	Ruled that the Texas school finance system, which included wide interdistrict revenue disparities created by dependence on local property taxes, did not violate the equal protection clause of the Fourteenth Amendment; declared that education is not a fundamental right guaranteed by the U.S. Constitution.
Ethnicity/race	Busing	1974	Milliken v. Bradley	Rejected multidistrict areawide busing plan.
Ethnicity/race	Bilingual education	1974	Lau v. Nichols (Supreme Court)	Determined that bilingual special education services must be provided for non–English-speaking students.
Ethnicity/race	Language needs	1978	Guadulupe Organization, Inc. v. Tempe Elementary School District (9th Circuit)	Denied claims of constitutional right to bilingual education.
Ethnicity/race	Desegregation	1974–1975	Lee v. Autanga County Board of Education (5th District)	Prohibited school boards from creating racially identifiable schools in the guise of fixing school locations or drawing attendance boundaries.
Ethnicity/race	Busing	1979	Columbus Board of Education v. Penick (U.S. Court)	Upheld desegregation plan that included busing.
Ethnicity/race	Busing	1986	Riddick v. School Board of Norfolk (4th Circuit) Court of Appeals	Held that white flight prevention was a valid school board objective and that the neighborhood school assignment plan was a reasonable attempt to keep white students in the public school system.
Ethnicity/race	Busing	1986	Board of Education of Oklahoma City Public Schools v. Dowell (10th Circuit)	Rejected a school board initiative to end busing because of white flight; ruled that the question was whether stopping busing would create racial imbalance in the school district rather than whether the board intended to reestablish segregation.

Source: Data from 1988 Deskbook Encyclopedia of American Law. (1988). Rosemount, MN: Data Research, Inc., and Valente, W. D. (1989). Laws in Schools (2nd ed.). Columbus, OH: Merrill. Used with permission.

income and minority students were not achieving well in school because of the culture of poverty in which they were socialized. Programs supported by the cultural deprivation theory were compensatory and remedial (Gordon & Wilkerson, 1966). The Head Start program is an example of a compensatory program. Title I, and its successor, Chapter I, are examples of remedial programs that reflect the cultural deprivation theory.

Rejection of the assimilation feature of the cultural deprivation theory led some researchers to propose the cultural difference theory (Stent, Hazard, & Rivilin, 1973). According to this view, ethnic minority children are culturally rich rather than culturally deprived. It was suggested that school problems for these children resulted from the lack of value placed on this richness by the school. The cultural difference theory holds that ethnic and racial minority students therefore achieve less in school because the school culture favors the culture of white mainstream students and places students from other backgrounds and cultures at a serious disadvantage (Hale, 1986). Programs based on the cultural difference theory include the early ethnic studies and cultural pluralism programs. Cultural difference theorists also view languages spoken by students as strengths rather than problems (Ovando & Collier, 1985).

A more encompassing theory is the multicultural theory. This theory also views ethnic/racial minority culture as different from mainstream white culture. Unlike the cultural difference theory, however, the multicultural theory focuses more on ways to provide equity in education than on explanations of the causes for inequality in schooling. It is recognized that various cultural groups exist in different social and cultural environments, and as a result they differ in both structure and ways of functioning. Multicultural theorists maintain that the schools should acknowledge the differences and incorporate them into the instructional program (Banks, 1994a; Gollnick & Chinn, 1994; Hernandez, 1989).

The multicultural education concept has encompassed a variety of approaches. As an umbrella concept, it relates to culture, race, language, socioeconomic class, gender, and disability. Sleeter and Grant (1994) constructed the typology of five approaches to multicultural education: (1) Teaching the exceptional and the culturally different, which focuses on adopting instruction to student differences to help these students succeed in the mainstream; (2) human relations approach, which focuses on respect for differences and more effective communication to bring people who differ closer together; (3) single-group studies, an approach that focuses on ethnic studies and women's studies to raise consciousness regarding oppression and to mobilize for social action; (4) multicultural education approach, which focuses on celebrating human diversity and equal opportunity; and (5) education that is multicultural and social reconstructionist, which focuses on not only celebrating human diversity and equal opportunity but also fighting oppression and challenging social stratification.

J. A. Banks (1993) described multicultural education as a complex, multidimensional concept with five major components. These components are: (1) content integration, (2) the knowledge construction process, (3) prejudice reduction, (4) an equity pedagogy, and (5) an empowering school culture and social structure.

Content integration deals with the extent to which teachers use examples, data, and information from a variety of cultures and groups to illustrate the key concepts, principles, generalizations, and theories in their subject area or discipline. The knowledge construction process encompasses the ways teachers help students understand how knowledge is created and how it is influenced by factors of race, ethnicity, gender, and social class.

The prejudice reduction component focuses on the characteristics of children's racial differences. It also focuses on strategies that can be used to help students develop more positive racial and ethnic attitudes.

An equity pedagogy involves using techniques that promote the learning and cultural styles of diverse groups. Teaching methods that facilitate the academic achievement of students from all racial and ethnic groups and from all social classes are also included in this component.

An empowering school culture and social structure involves making structural changes within the school environment. It includes focusing on culturally responsive teaching, using fair assessment techniques, and conducting educational programs based on the belief that all children can learn.

Another theory that addresses the equity issues was proposed by Cummins (1986). He suggested that the disempowerment of minority students and the empowerment of majority group students result from the resistance on the part of schools to (1) incorporate students' language and culture into school programs, (2) encourage minority community to participate in children's education, (3) promote intrinsic motivation on the part of students to use language actively in order to generate their own knowledge, and (4) involve professionals as advocates for minority students during assessments.

Cummins's theoretical framework involves three sets of relationships: (1) majority/minority societal group relations, (2) school/minority community relations, and (3) educator/minority student relations. According to Cummins, the educational failure of minority students must be analyzed as a function of the extent to which schools reflect or counteract the power relations that exist within the broader society. Cummins concluded that:

Specifically, language minority students' educational progress is strongly influenced by the extent to which advocates for the promotion of students' linguistic talents, actively encourage community participation in developing students' academic and cultural resources, and implement pedagogical approaches that succeed in liberating students from instructional dependence. (p. 32)

In describing educator role definitions, Cummins considered the level of incorporation of minority students' language and culture along a continuum from "additive" to "subtractive." In interaction with community participation, the educator is viewed on a continuum from "collaborative" to "exclusionary." The educator's instructional procedures are viewed on a continuum from "reciprocal interaction oriented" to "transition oriented." Assessment is viewed on an "advocacy-oriented" to "legitimization-oriented" continuum. Programs that illustrate the Cummins framework include the Carpinteria Program (Cummins, 1986) and the Kamehameha Program (Tharp and Gallimore, 1988).

The cultural mismatch theory attributes poor academic performance of minority students to the cultural disjunctures between home and school (Villegas, 1988). Researchers have examined differences in dialects, cognitive style, and language. Advocates of the cultural mismatch theory argue that a better understanding of the use of language across the home and school setting will enable educators to develop culturally sensitive solutions that will remedy the communication problems and improve the academic performance of minority students. After reviewing the literature on the cultural mismatch theory, Villegas (1988) concluded that this theory "diverts attention away from the social inequalities that sustain the widespread academic failure of minority students" (p. 254).

Another theory on inequalities based on ethnicity and race in the educational system is Ogbu's theory on the labor market perspective for involuntary minorities. Ogbu argued that inequity in access to employment over many generations has made members of some minority groups cynical about their life chances in American society. This cynicism is communicated to the children and causes them to respond in ways that hamper school success (Ogbu, 1987). Children of involuntary minority groups are convinced that school success will not help them break out of a cycle of poverty that they perceive as evidence of racism in society. Ogbu maintained that the poor school performance of castelike minority students is an adaptive response to a history of limited opportunities in society at large. Ogbu contended that core curriculum and multicultural advocates do not yet understand and take into account the fact that the crucial issue in cultural diversity and learning is the relationship between minority cultures and the American mainstream culture. When children's cultural frame of reference is "oppositional" to American mainstream culture, they have greater difficulty crossing cultural barriers at school to learn. Ogbu's theory is supported by Matute-Biainchi (1986) and Saurez-Orozco (1987).

Research Trends: Synthesis

Since the 1960s, a wide range of research activities have been conducted to explore problems, issues, and programs related to equity in education for ethnic and racial minorities. Themes that emerge in this body of research include: (1) documentation and exploration of inequities, (2) curriculum reform, (3) improvements in pedagogical practice, (4) underrepresentation of ethnic and racial minorities in the teaching profession, and (5) teachers' attitudes and preparation for teaching ethnic and racial minority students.

Documentation and Exploration of Inequities Five major reports illustrate research that documents and explores inequitable educational experiences and outcomes: the Coleman Report (Coleman et al., 1966), *Savage Inequalities* (Kozol, 1991), the National Assessment of Educational Progress reports (Mullis & Jenkins, 1988; Mullis, Owen, & Phillips, 1990), *Multiplying Inequalities* (Oakes, 1990), and *Education That Works* (Quality Education for Minorities Network [QEM], 1990).

The Coleman Report was the result of an extensive study commissioned by Congress to explore conditions in the nation's schools and the extent of educational inequality. The study suggested that school achievement depended more on students' social class and family background than on school facilities and curricula (Coleman et al., 1966). The report concluded that the achievement gap between minority and majority group students continued to widen through the elementary grades.

Kozol (1991) not only identified the inequities in schools but also presented them in a way that removed the mask and revealed the remarkable degree of racial segregation that persisted throughout the nation. Through intensive school observations and interviews in 30 neighborhoods throughout the nation, Kozol documented the disparity between schools serving minority children in inner cities and schools serving majority group children in suburban America.

Reports of the National Assessment of Educational Progress (NAEP) serve as the nation's report card on academic achievement. Starting in 1969, periodical assessments have been conducted on students' achievement in reading, mathematics, science, writing, history/geography, and other fields. Performance comparisons by race and ethnicity have documented inequitable educational outcomes at each level and in each field tested (Dossey, Mullis, Lindquist, & Chambers, 1988; Hammack et al., 1990; Mullis & Jenkins, 1988). A summary of findings from 20 years of NAEP reports showed that despite the fact that achievement of minority students has improved across time compared to that of white students, significant disparities were evident (Mullis et al., 1990).

Concern over the absence of minorities in careers based on mathematics and science led to considerable research documenting the inequalities in educational opportunities for minorities in the K–12 educational system. The National Science Foundation supported a Rand Corporation study on the extent to which uneven distribution of opportunities to learn science and mathematics might be contributing to unequal outcomes in science and mathematics. The study, conducted by Oakes (1990), concluded that:

During the elementary grades, the science and mathematics experiences of children from low-income families, African American and Hispanic children, children who attend school in central cities, and children who have been clustered in "low-ability" classes differ in small but important ways from those of their more advantaged and white peers. By the time the students reach secondary school, their science and mathematics experiences are strikingly different. (p. 3)

Oakes found inequalities in relation to the distribution of judgments about ability, access to science and mathematics programs, access to qualified teachers, access to resources, and classroom opportunities.

The Quality Education for Minorities Network (1990) conducted a "comprehensive examination of the educational status, needs, and possibilities of minority children, youth, and adults" (p. v). The report documented the minority experience in education and explored the myths and obstacles to quality education for Alaskan Natives, American Indians, Black Americans, Mexican Americans, and Puerto Ricans. School obstacles identified were low expectations, tracking, inadequate school financing, too few minority teachers, overreliance on testing, poorly prepared teachers, and disregard of language and cultural diversity. Other school obstacles identified were poverty and hopelessness, absence of educational legacy, and negative peer pressure.

Curriculum Reform Multicultural education emerges as the major curriculum reform movement related to equity for ethnic and racial minority children. Advocates of multicultural education point out that the many different racial, ethnic, religious, and cultural groups are given scant attention in many school curricula, textbooks, and other teaching materials. Most curricula in schools today focus on white Anglo-Saxon Protestants, the dominant cultural group in the United States. Such curricula are one of the major ways in which racism and ethnocentrism are reinforced and perpetuated in the schools and in society. J. A. Banks (1993) represents the view of many multicultural education researchers in maintaining that curriculum reform is needed. The mainstream-centric curriculum: (1) reinforces the false sense of superiority of mainstream students, gives them a misleading conception of their relationship with other racial and ethnic groups, and denies them the opportunity to benefit from the knowledge, perspectives, and frames of reference that can be gained from studying and experiencing other cultures and groups; (2) denies mainstream students the opportunity to view their culture from the perspective of other cultures and groups; and (3) marginalizes the experiences and cultures of minorities and does not reflect the dreams, hopes, and perspectives of students of color.

Multicultural education theorists believe that many school practices related to race and ethnicity are harmful to students and reinforce many ethnic stereotypes and discriminatory practices in Western societies (Banks, 1994a). Gollnick and Chinn (1994) point out that a major rationale for multicultural education is to understand and utilize students' cultural backgrounds in developing educational programs.

Moving the multicultural education concept toward inclusion of social justice issues and empowering young people to make social changes, Sleeter and Grant (1994) suggested focusing on education that is multicultural and social reconstructionist. According to Sleeter and Grant (1994), multicultural education involves complete reform of the entire education process to reflect and support diversity, addressing dimensions of schooling such as curriculum, but also including a focus on tracking and grouping, staffing the school, and testing. After reviewing more than 200 articles and 60 books on multicultural education, Sleeter and Grant (1994) proposed an approach that deals more directly with oppression and social structural inequality based on racism, social class, gender, and disability.

Banks maintained that there is a need for a holistic theory of multicultural education that can be used to guide educational practice and research (1994b). He described 10 major concepts and paradigms that have been used to explain the low academic achievement of ethnic racial and low-income students and analyzes the values and assumptions of the educational programs and practices that exemplify each paradigm. Based on this review of the historical development and impact of multicultural education, Banks (1994b) presented 23 curriculum guidelines for multicultural education and a comprehensive Multicultural Education Program Evaluation Checklist.

The Role of the Teacher and Pedagogical Practices Even in the face of pervasive institutional barriers and inequities, it is possible for teachers to reduce the inequities in educational opportunities for ethnic and racial minority children by changing instructional practices and teacher attitudes.

A growing body of research shows that culturally responsive teaching improves the academic achievements of diverse groups of students (Locke, 1988). More than any other discipline, pedagogical practices in science and mathematics instruction for ethnic and racial minority students and female students have been widely studied (Beane, 1988; National Science Board, 1987; Oakes, 1990). Analyses of access to science and mathematics curricula, resources, and instructional activities reveal clear and consistent patterns of unequal opportunities to learn mathematics and science. Low-income, minority, and low-ability students have considerably less access to science and mathematics knowledge, fewer material resources available to help them learn these subjects, less engaging learning activities, and less qualified teachers (Oakes, 1990).

Equity issues related to bilingual education and reading and language development also have received considerable study. Children for whom English is a second language face inequities in education related to instruction and to assessment. These children comprise approximately 5% of the school population and their numbers are growing (National Education Association [NEA], n.d.–a) even in states not previously noted for large populations of families for whom English is a second language. For example, in Virginia there were 9,102 students with limited English proficiency (LEP) enrolled in English as a Second Language (ESL) classes in 1985. In 1991 there were 15,150 students enrolled in those classes (Governor's Commission on Educational Opportunity for All Virginians, 1991).

Instructional approaches used with LEP students include bilingual approaches and immersion or submersion approaches. Since the 1968 Bilingual Education Act (Title VII of the Elementary and Secondary Education Act) and the subsequent amendments, research issues have focused primarily around effective instruction for language minority students through bilingual or immersion/submersion approaches (Hakuta & Gould, 1987; Willig, 1985). A more promising approach to bilingual studies advocated by Moll (1992), Pease-Alvarez and Hakuta (1992), and Snow (1992) supports the use of a sociocultural perspective that takes into account the community and family resources available to children.

Other research issues related to equity for children for whom English is a second language include the need for more teachers who are trained in languages and in instructional effectiveness, more research on the psychosocial aspects of second-language acquisition and use, better evaluation and assessment, and more research on parental and community involvement.

Assessment Ethnic/racial minority group children experience double jeopardy in assessment. Not only do they perform less well on formal standardized tests than their majority group peers (Dossey et al., 1988; Hammack et al., 1990; Mullis & Jenkins, 1988), but their teachers are more likely to rely on data from commercial tests to develop curriculum plans and deliver instruction in a less enriching way. Thus, equitable access to good teaching is limited for ethnic minority children, partly because of the manner in which they are assessed (Hilliard, 1991). When income levels and proficiency in standard English are taken into account, the performance gap is lowered, but not eliminated. Asian Americans who tend to score higher on mathematics tests, score lower on formal tests that regard verbal abilities as standard English and/or knowledge of the majority group culture (College Entrance Examination Board, 1993).

Although the tests themselves have been debated, the issues related to assessment of ethnic minority children run much deeper than the tests. The validity of the tests, the results of the tests, and, beyond these issues, the use of the tests and their results remain in serious question.

Research trends on assessment have centered on: (1) what the tests tell us about student mastery versus students' rank by test results; (2) multiple forms of intelligence that are not tapped by traditional assessment measures; (3) consequences for students based on test results and use of results to limit students' access to good teaching and rich curricula; (4) use of tests to mask deficiencies in teaching or to mask the absence of quality teaching; (5) overreliance on testing; and (6) development and implementation of policies that permit educators to make decisions about students' educational futures based on suspect measures alone. These issues are addressed in earlier pages of this chapter.

Underrepresentation of Ethnic and Racial Minorities in the Teaching Profession Failure of the schools to provide a teaching and administrative staff that is representative of the students' ethnic and racial backgrounds contributes to the inequities students experience. The need to increase the number of ethnic and racial minorities in the teaching profession has been reported on by numerous researchers (American Association of Colleges for Teacher Education, 1987; Carnegie Forum on Education and the Economy, 1986; Education Commission of the States, 1990; Fielder, 1993; Garibaldi, 1989; King, 1993; Witty, 1982, 1989). (See Chapter 34 by Boyer and Baptiste and Chapter 35 by Duhon-Sells in this handbook.)

Minorities represent less than 13% of the teaching corps (U.S. Department of Education, National Center for Education Statistics, 1993a). Minority children represent about 30% of the student population. This imbalance is critical because teachers filter the curriculum and learning opportunities through their own experiences and backgrounds. Valverde (1993) maintains that "Teachers with different life-styles, different cultures, and different attitudes will not fully understand the life experiences of their students, their students' family circumstances, and their students' points of view about what is possible for them" (p. 228). This reduces the possibilities that teachers have to relate the learning experiences to meaningful connections for many students. A proportional number of teachers who represent the backgrounds of the students increases the opportunities that all children have to learn.

Research on recruitment and retention of ethnic and racial minority teachers is limited. Reports on special efforts to increase the number of minority students in teacher preparation program suffer from weak evaluation components. Although numerous reports are available on programs designed to attract minorities into teaching (Garibaldi, 1989; Greer & Husk, 1989; James, 1991; Pasch, Krakow, Johnson, Slocum, & Stapleton, 1990; Recruiting New Teachers, 1993), few provide evidence on their effectiveness. To what extent did the projects actually increase the number of minorities entering the profession? Research is needed to provide the answer to this question.

Teachers' Attitudes and Preparation for Teaching Ethnic and Racial Minority Students Even if schools provide equity in resources, curriculum, and program, ethnic and racial minority children may experience inequitable opportunities to learn if teachers are unprepared to teach them. Because many teachers live in different existential worlds and do not have frames of reference and points of view similar to their ethnically and racially different students (Gay, 1993), careful attention must be given to the preparation and in-service education they receive. Gay (1993) maintains that no one should be allowed to graduate from a teacher certification program or be licensed to teach without being well grounded in how the dynamics of cultural conditioning operate in teaching and learning. Four challenges for teacher preparation were identified by Gay: Teachers should be able to (1) identify stress-provoking factors in cross-cultural instructional interaction and how to alleviate them, (2) determine the strengths and cultural competencies different students bring to the classroom and design learning experiences to capitalize on them, (3) understand the concept of learned helpfulness in schools and develop attitudes and behaviors to avoid its perpetuation, and (4) practice cultural context teaching, placing the mechanics and technical components of teaching and learning into the cultural frameworks of various ethnic, racial, and social groups.

King (1991) maintained that prospective teachers need both an intellectual understanding of schooling and inequity and self-reflective, transformative emotional growth experiences. Such experiences should be provided by teacher education programs. King's research explores that effectiveness of a Foundations of Education course through which students are helped to analyze dysconscious racism.

Research on teacher education programs that prepare teachers to provide more equitable instruction has been done by numerous researchers (Ahlquist, 1991; Martin & Koppelman, 1991; Nel, 1992; Reed & Simon, 1991; Sherritt, 1990; Zeichner, 1992). Central to this research is the concept stated by Nel (1992) that "teachers' thinking, knowledge, perceptions and beliefs could be a major contributing factor in the empowerment or the disabling of minority students" (p. 13). The way teacher educators teach multicultural education to preservice teachers may be a crucial factor in determining the ultimate success or failure of minority students in schools.

SOCIOECONOMIC STATUS

Definition

Inequities in the distribution of wealth in American society impact negatively on individual children, schools, and school districts. Studies by numerous researchers have documented the relationship between socioeconomic level and academic success (College Entrance Examination Board, 1993; Darling-Hammond, 1985; U.S. Department of Education, Office of Educational Research and Improvement, 1993c). The assumption that poverty and educational achievement are significantly related formed the basis for the federal government's funding formula for Title I of the Elementary and Secondary Education Act and its successor program, Chapter I.

The effect of socioeconomic status on school achievement is entangled with the effect of race on achievement. However, children from low-income families are more likely to achieve less well in school than their peers (Cook & Brown, 1993; Virginia Department of Education, 1992). Schools in suburban communities are more likely to have adequate resources and programs than schools in inner-city and rural areas. For example, in 1990 the number of academic courses offered in high schools in Virginia ranged from 39 in one school division to 164 in another school division. The per pupil expenditures varied from about $3,300 to $7,800 (Governor's Commission on Educational Opportunity for All Virginians, 1991). For many children, equity in opportunity and outcomes is denied because of their family's socioeconomic status.

The primary determinants of socioeconomic status are occupation, educational attainment, and income. The *High School and Beyond* study (U.S. Department of Education, Office of Educational Research and Improvement, 1984) used a composite of the five equally weighted, standardized components: father's education, mother's education, family income, father's occupation, and household items to determine socioeconomic status index. Based on a combination of these variables, social stratification in society places families in low, middle, and high ranks. Children from families in the low socioeconomic rank who live in poverty and children who attend schools with high concentrations of children in poverty are disadvantaged in American schools as they are currently designed (Orland, 1990).

As a group denied equity in schools, children from low-income families make up a large proportion of the classes teachers should be prepared to teach. Census data revealed that in Hispanic families, 37.7% of the children under 18 years live below the poverty level and that in Hispanic families headed by females, 68.4% of the children under 18 years live below the poverty level. In white families, 15.1% of all children under 18 years, but 45.9% of children in families headed by females, lived in poverty (U.S. Department of Education, Office of Research and Improvement, Center for Education Statistics, 1992).

Legal Issues: Court Decisions

One of the major sources of inequities in schools is the disparity in educational funding within states and districts. Because school financing is tied to the wealth of the state, district, and community, children in the poorest communities tend to receive fewer educational opportunities and children in the wealthiest communities tend to receive more educational opportunities. Equalization of educational funding continues to be a challenge and appears to be even more out of reach today than it was in the 1970s.

The inequality of incomes in the United States is more pronounced today than it has been for many years (Phillips, 1991). In 1988 the population in the lowest quintile had 4.6% of the income as compared to 44 percent of the income controlled by the population in the highest quintile. In *State of the World*,

Durning's (1990) study of economic inequality and social immobility among American people, it was revealed that in 1979 the equity of income distribution in the United States began to deteriorate rapidly; by 1986 disparities in earnings were the worst on record. Durning found that the United States ranks 15th out of 16 countries compared on economic inequality.

Schools reflect the economic situation in society. The deterioration in the relative position of the poor is complicated by the increased fiscal burden mounted on the public schools due to the demand to serve an increasingly diverse population. Social and economic fragmentation of society creates higher operational costs for the public schools. Families in poorer economic circumstances have children with greater and more complex educational problems, the redress of which requires, a far greater outlay of school financial resources (Alexander, 1992).

The decline in the federal government's contribution to education placed a greater burden on the states. Many poor local school districts receive less money per pupil merely because they have low fiscal capacity. State governments have failed to correct these inequities (Alexander, 1992). Consequently, the standard of quality continues to decline in poor school districts relative to more affluent school districts.

In order to rectify the inequalities, legal questions have been raised. Should the quality of a child's education be determined by place of birth? Why should children in poor school districts receive an education that costs half as much as children in the wealthier school districts? These questions were first addressed by several lower courts in the early and mid-1970s following the first calls for school finance reform (Wise & Gendler, 1989). To date, many decisions have been rendered and several are pending. The plaintiffs in these cases simply maintain that state constitutional provisions are violated when state legislatures give more funds per pupil to school districts that have greater property wealth, greater family income, and higher adult educational attainment, while giving less to school districts that are poorer in property wealth, income, and have lower adult educational attainment. The plaintiffs argue that the state cannot justify giving more to the less needy and less to the more needy (Alexander, 1992).

Plaintiffs have been hampered, however, by the U.S. Supreme Court's decision in *San Antonio v. Rodriguez* (1973) that held that education is not a fundamental right under the Equal Protection Clause of the Fourteenth Amendment. Some states have departed from the precedent and held that education is a fundamental right under their respective state constitutions. These states are Connecticut, Washington, West Virginia, Kentucky, California, Texas, Tennessee, and Wyoming. States that have cited *Rodriguez* in maintaining that education is not a fundamental right are Maryland, Colorado, Oklahoma, Georgia, New York, Ohio, Idaho, Michigan, Pennsylvania, North Carolina, and Louisiana (Alexander, 1992).

Three arguments are used to oppose school finance reform. First, in states where there is no explicit educational clause, it is argued that education is not a fundamental right and is therefore not subject to the close scrutiny implied by the Equal Protection Clause. Second, in states that accept education as a fundamental right, it is argued that local control outweighs the rights of districts to equal funding. The third argument is that financial input has no effect on the quality of the education a district is able to offer. (For further discussion of related issues see Chapter 12 by Monk and O'Brent in this handbook.)

In response to the issue of local control, proponents of school finance reform argue that local control of education does not hold when states use standardized tests, statewide curricula, uniform textbooks, and standard teacher evaluations. These state actions have been taken in the pursuit of excellence in which many states have moved to improve and control local schools through regulation.

The third argument against school finance reform builds on Coleman's Equality of Educational Opportunity Report's conclusion that "schools bring little influence to bear on a child's achievement that is independent of his background and general social contact" (Coleman et al., 1966, p. 325). Although there is no body of research yet available to refute this claim, it is commonly accepted that resources do affect educational quality. Districts that spend more money provide more educational opportunities.

Wise and Gendler (1989) pointed out that school quality is more related to low-cost administrative and attitudinal changes than to financial input. Finance reform proponents maintain that even if schools could overcome the handicaps caused by inequities in financial support by improving administrative leadership, school climate, high expectations, and other instructional changes, financial inequities are not justified.

Legal Issues and Theory

Children who attend well-financed schools are more likely to come from high-income families than are children who attend poorly financed schools. Inequities may be created by the public school system where efficiency as a value carries more influence than equity as a value.

The courts may be used to support a guarantee of constitutional rights. Implementing programs to provide these rights are the responsibility of the legislative process. Political activity should be used to influence state legislatures shape educational policy. Wise and Gendler (1989) pointed out that when a state legislature regulates outputs, it may create an obsessive concern with test score performance as a measure of quality. When a state regulates process, it may entangle local boards and teachers in minutiae. However, if a state regulates input, it satisfies its constitutional command will encouraging local initiative. By regulating inputs, state legislatures can ensure that educational opportunity is independent of the level of income of the families and communities.

Research Trends: Theoretical Frameworks

Conflicting theories have been advanced to explain the inequities in educational outcomes for children from low socioeconomic backgrounds. Because ethnic and minority groups tend to be overrepresented in the low-socioeconomic status, it is difficult to isolate inequities related solely to socioeconomic factors. The theories discussed here focus primarily on socioeconomic status although other factors, including race and gender, are acknowledged.

The structuralist theory holds that schools actively prepare students for unequal futures. Theorists who support this view examine the ways in which schools perpetuate inequities through such measures as their organization and procedures (Bowles & Gintis, 1976), hidden curriculum, ability grouping, and tracking systems (Oakes, 1985, 1990).

The culturalists theorize that differences in student outcomes result from students' responses to school structures and students' own construction of cultures in the schools. They examine the ways in which students respond to the maintenance of structural inequities thereby contributing to their own lessvalued positions in society (Weis, 1988).

Willis (1977) formulated the cultural reproduction and resistance theory with a British study adopted by American researchers. The resistance theory holds that working-class youth consciously or unconsciously reject the meaning and knowledge taught by the schools and turn to working-class adults or to street people as a source of materials for resistance and exclusion. These students repudiate the schools by forming countercultures that eventually impede their school success and employability in the more desirable sector of mainstream economy (Willis, 1977).

Why do they reject school knowledge and meanings? Working-class and minority students reject school knowledge and meanings because they seem to understand that the kind of education they are receiving cannot solve their collective problems of subordination (Ogbu, 1987).

Recent theorists have proposed the opportunity to learn concept as another way of understanding the disparate achievement levels of various groups of children. In 1983, the National Science Foundation set a goal "to provide high standards of excellence for all students wherever they live, whatever their race, gender, or economic status, whatever their immigration status or whatever language is spoken at home by their parents, and whatever their career goals" (Oakes, p. iii). In seeking to realize this goal, the National Science Foundation raised the question of whether an uneven distribution of opportunities to learn science and mathematics might be contributing to unequal outcomes (Oakes, 1990).

Inequalities in opportunities to learn assist some children in achieving academically while limiting the achievement of other groups of students, thereby perpetuating disparities in achievement. The opportunity to learn conceptual framework encompasses four variables that have a powerful influence on teacher instructional practices and student learning (Stevens, 1993). The variables are content coverage, content exposure, content emphasis, and quality of instructional delivery. Content coverage variables measure whether or not students cover the core curriculum for a particular grade level or subject area. Content exposure variables take into consideration the time allowed for and devoted to instruction (time-on task) and the depth of the teaching provided. Content emphasis variables influence which topics within the curriculum are selected for emphasis and which students are selected to receive instruction emphasizing lower order skills or higher order skills. Quality of instructional delivery variables reveal how classroom teaching practices affect students' academic achievement.

Research Trends: Synthesis

Research trends in research on equity related to ethnicity/race and to socioeconomic status reflect movements from main-effect analyses to transactional analyses; from between-groups studies to within-group studies; and from quantitative analyses to more qualitative analyses. These trends are evident in studies related to ethnicity and race and to socioeconomic status.

Rather than attempting to identify one variable responsible for educational outcomes, contemporary researchers examine multiple and interrelated effects of numerous variables from the micro to the macro levels (Banks, 1994b; Comer, 1990; Ogbu, 1992).

Research that explores the fact that some children within the various minority groups experience positive school outcomes while others do not is an emerging interest. Most research in the 1960s and 1970s was based on a view of low-economic-status minority children as a homogeneous group at risk for low IQ and school performance. Researchers are now examining the variability within groups.

In an effort to address generalizations about ethnic and racial minority group children, more qualitative studies are emerging. These studies make a significant contribution to the knowledge base by capturing the rich and unique underpinning of low-socioeconomic and minority children that are often overlooked in large sample quantitative studies.

Since the publication of *Equality of Educational Opportunity* (The Coleman Report) in 1966 (Coleman et al., 1966), considerable research on inequality and equity related to socioeconomic status of students has been reported. Researchers have reported that however socioeconomic or social class is measured, it is found to be related to how well students do in school (Bennett & LeCompte, 1990).

Several themes run through the research on social class and equity in education. Because ethnic and racial minority children compose a disproportionate number of the children in the low-socioeconomic status, most research includes attention to both concerns. However, several themes focusing on socioeconomic status and equity are identified. Why do students from higher socioeconomic backgrounds tend to get better grades and stay in school longer than do students from lower-class backgrounds? Does the structure of schooling in the United States promote unequal educational results? Do the beliefs held by educators result in instructional and interactional patterns that deny equal educational opportunities? Does the curriculum in schools limit opportunities to learn for low-socioeconomic students?

Structure of Schooling Educational opportunities for children may be determined by whether they attend urban, rural, or suburban schools in America. Opportunities to learn may also be determined by whether children attend public or private schools. A major focus of research in this area is on inequities in school finance. While many states are involved in legal actions to resolve questions on funding formula, children from higher socioeconomic backgrounds continue to have better schools than children from low-income backgrounds (Hollifield, 1990; Kearney, Philip, & Chen, 1990; Wise, 1993).

A related concern is equity in access to computer technology. Computers in schools have been identified as a new source of inequity (Kirby, Oescher, Wilson, & Smith-Gratto, 1990). Becker (1985) used data from a national survey of microcomputer uses in schools to study the differences in access to and uses of computers by students. Students in higher socioeconomic levels have more access and a higher order of computer use than children from low economic levels. Kirby et al.'s (1990) study confirmed that student access to computers is directly related to students' ability classification and socioeconomic status. Sutton's (1991) review of a decade of research revealed that the use of computers has maintained and exaggerated inequities with poor, minority, and female students having less access to computers at home as well as at school.

School Choice The debate over school choice reflects another student equity concern. Although not a new concern, school choice on today's research agenda reflects an economic value in school reform (Chubb & Moe, 1988). School choice plans provide parents with the opportunity to select the school in the district that they want their children to attend. In some plans, parents may choose public or private schools. Choice plans may also provide some financial assistance to parents in the way of vouchers and tuition tax credits.

In some school districts, school choice through magnet schools is used as a means for promoting stable integration of schools. In others, school choice has been used as a means for escaping racial integration of schools. Vocational/technical schools, designed to promote school-to-work transitions, tend to have higher proportions of minority students than assigned schools. These schools are also choice plans that constitute a more segregated school environment for minorities (Plank, Schiller, Schneider, & Coleman, 1992).

Federal interest in policy related to choice was noted in America 2000 (U.S. Department of Education, 1991). By 1992 at least 13 states had instituted some type of choice plan (NEA, n.d.–b). Local school districts across the nation have also taken steps to introduce some type of choice plans. Milwaukee provides an example of a voucher plan that permits disadvantaged students to use public dollars to attend private school.

Proponents of choice argue that parental choice and open enrollment plans will improve education by weeding out the least successful schools. They also argue that choice will increase equity and opportunities for students who presently receive an inadequate education in their community schools, including ethnic minorities and the poor (Chubb & Moe, 1988). Opponents of school choice plans argue that such plans will undermine the commitment to improving all schools, that elitism and discrimination will replace concern for equal educational opportunity in educational policy making, and that even with free public transportation, poor and minority children will continue to have limited access to good schools (Wells, 1992).

Teacher Beliefs, Attitudes and Knowledge Inequities in the educational experiences of children from low socioeconomic backgrounds may result from their interactions or lack of interactions with teachers. Many severe and systemic impediments to the delivery of effective education are beyond the direct control of individual educators, but classroom teachers do control certain aspects of their students' school experiences.

The role of teacher expectations in academic achievement of children and teacher–student interaction has received considerable study. Braun (1985) suggested that there is a clear relationship between teachers' expectations of individual students and the child's self-expectations and subsequent academic performance. Braun's research is supported by a considerable body of literature (Babad, 1990; Baron, Tom, & Cooper, 1985; Brophy, 1985; Dusek & Joseph, 1985; Ritts, Patterson, & Tubbs, 1992; Witty & Debaryshe, 1994). According to Braun, data from students' cumulative folders, gender, name, ethnic background, physical characteristics, and socioeconomic status are all factors that contribute to the development of teachers' expectations about students' academic performance. Teachers' beliefs are communicated to students through behaviors such as grouping, expectant voice prompting, quantity of interaction, and differential activities and questions. Students respond to such differential treatment by internalizing their teachers' expectations and using them as basis of their own self-evaluations. Students' self-expectations affect their motivation and behavior with the end result being a positive or negative influence on learning and academic achievement. Researchers have found that children from low socioeconomic background are systemically and disproportionately the target of negative teacher expectations (Baron et al., 1985; Dusek & Joseph, 1985).

Two types of teacher expectations have been studied. The first is the self-fulfilling prophecy effect in which teachers form expectations on the basis of erroneous data and behave in a manner that causes the expectation to become true. The second type is the sustaining expectation effect in which teachers expect students to sustain previously developed patterns and fail to see and capitalize on change in students' potential.

The potentially damaging effects of teacher expectations on children from low socioeconomic levels point to the need for continuing research in this area. Good and Brophy (1994) suggested that new directions in research on teacher expectations should address the following questions: teachers' decisions about content, teachers' knowledge of subject matter, and the effects of different teachers' expectations across consecutive years.

Tracking and Teaching Practices A growing body of research questions whether assessments of students' intellectual abilities play a major role in the differential allocation of school experiences (Gamoran, 1987; Lee & Bryk, 1988; Oakes, 1985, 1988, 1990; Slavin, 1987, 1990). Judgments about students' academic ability are often used to group students and to place them in various curriculum tracks. Different tracks provide different opportunities to learn. The pace and content of instruction in the groups differ according to the classification of the students. Instruction in problem solving and critical thinking is more likely to occur in high tracks than in low tracks (Oakes, 1985). Instruction in low tracks tends to be fragmented, emphasizing worksheets and recitation (O'Neil, 1993). In low-ability groups, more time is spent on behavior management and less time on instruction (Oakes, 1985). Students placed in low-ability classes throughout their elementary school years receive a strikingly inferior education than that received by their peers in high-ability groups. Low-ability groups tend to be composed disproportionately of children from low-income families. This research leads educators to question whether ability grouping and tracking is equitable (Gamoran, 1992; Slavin, 1987, 1990). Gamoran's (1992) synthesis of research on grouping indicates that "grouping and tracking rarely add to overall achievement in a school, but they often contribute to inequality. Typically, high-track students are gaining and low-track students are falling behind" (p. 13). Students from low socioeconomic backgrounds are more likely than students from high socioeconomic backgrounds to be placed in the low tracks.

Advocates of untracking schools are challenged by parents of gifted children and special educators who question whether it is equitable to eliminate special programs in gifted education. Specifically, will teachers be able to teach mixed-ability classes without losing the students at the upper end of the achievement continuum (O'Neil, 1993)?

Analyses of research findings on the effects of tracking are mixed partly because there is confusion over the ways in which the educators and researchers define tracking, ability grouping, untracking, and detracking. Further, factors such as where tracking is used, how it is implemented, and the skills and attitudes of the teachers add to the complexity of the research questions raised.

GENDER

Definition

To begin a discussion on gender equity, it is important to differentiate between the terms gender and sex. In most of the research, gender is the preferred term as it refers to not only the biological differences of sex but also to society's expectations and limitations placed on people because of that sex. Therefore, in this chapter, the broader term gender is used.

What makes gender an equity group? The debate on education that has sustained the public's attention since the mid-1980s has failed to explore the notion that educational experiences are different for girls and boys. The American Association of University Women (AAUW) in its report *How Schools Shortchange Girls* (1992), examined 35 reports issued from many organizations that have examined educational issues since the 1983 *A Nation at Risk* (Gardner, 1983) report. Only one report out of the 35 reviewed by AAUW directly addressed Title IX of the Education Amendments of 1972 that prohibits sex discrimination in education programs receiving federal funds. The AAUW (1992) report concluded that:

Most of the reports do not define the educational issues under review in terms of gender, nor do they include sex as a separate category in their data analyses and background information. Few of the recommendations are framed with sex or gender in mind. (p. 6)

Additional evidence that gender equity is not an important issue are the National Education Goals. The goals themselves do not address gender issues, and none of the strategies currently proposed include gender concerns (AAUW, 1992).

Differences in education for boys and girls range from academic achievement and testing, to participation patterns in classrooms, to school staffing patterns. These differences affect girls as they mature into women and assume responsibilities in society. The result is that problems are created for the larger society, particularly of an economic nature.

Women, in general, earn less money than men—54 cents on a man's dollar even when women's education level is the same as that of their male counterparts (U.S. House of Representatives, 1990). Another trend is that college-educated women's salaries decreased as their age increased compared with their male counterparts—from 66 cents on a man's dollar at ages 25–34, to 46 cents on the dollar in the 45–55 age range. This last trend is disturbing because it shows that for older women less money is available to support them and their families. These statistics on the power of earnings are particularly important given the demographic trends of families.

By 1991 women headed 33% of all family households (U.S. Department of Commerce, Bureau of Census, 1990). Recent statistics have shown that single female-headed families have high poverty rates, 47% among whites and 72% among African Americans, with that rate increasing for women without high school diplomas, 77% for whites, and 87% for African Americans (U.S. House of Representatives, 1990). The total rate of poverty for female-headed households is 56% indicating that significant numbers of children are growing up poor.

Clearly, gender equity issues must be addressed in order to maintain the value of education for all, but also because the cost of not addressing these issues is so high. Generating political activity, pushing the issue-attention cycle to focus on gender equity, is necessary to develop gender equity. It may require appealing to the value of efficiency—the financial cost of failing to address gender equity—to move forward. As noted, part of the motivation behind PL 94-142 for special education was the cost to society of failing to educate its disabled citizens. A similar tactic might be employed to promote gender equity. Also, as with special education assessment, a theoretical shift toward a pluralistic multicultural perspective promotes gender equity. This focus is discussed in further detail in the next section of this chapter. With these kinds of changes, the specific gender issues for educational equity may be addressed.

Legal Issues: Legislation

The Educational Amendments of 1972 included a section, Title IX, prohibiting gender discrimination in educational programs receiving federal funding. However, the law is enforced only through complaints. In essence, the federal government does not pursue compliance with Title IX (AAUW, 1992). Research has shown that violations still exist in schools and that "gender equity issues are still not well understood by many educators" (AAUW, 1992, p. 8). In general, "changes in sexist attitudes and behaviors have been slow in coming, and enforcement of Title IX has been spotty and ineffective" (Colangelo, Dustin, & Foxley, 1985, p. 251).

Legal Issues: Legislation and Theory

As mentioned, attainment of gender equity will take an appeal to the value of efficiency—the economic cost of failing to educate girls and women properly. Also needed is a shift in thinking about girls and women and their roles in society.

Feminist phase theory explains the development of thought about women—their history, life experiences, rituals, and traditions. Thompson Tetreault (1989) developed this theory into a five-phase model. The common phases she identified are explained in terms of what society values, and these values are then connected to educational curriculum. The values that are inherent in each of these phases are briefly described here, followed by connections to the education values that drive political theory as described previously.

The first phase is the *male-defined curriculum*. In this phase the male experience is "valued, emphasized, and viewed as the knowledge most worth having" (Thompson-Tetreault, 1989, p. 126). In the second phase, *contribution curriculum,* the male norm is still used to judge greatness. This phase considers only women who have characteristics of the male norm as noteworthy. *Bifocal curriculum* is the third phase. In this phase there is a shift toward viewing greatness from a woman's perspective. A dual or bifocal perspective is the lens for viewing life. Men's experiences continue to be evaluated in terms of the public sphere, but women's lives center on the private sphere. Scholars criticize this perspective because it tends to view women in sex role stereotypes, thus perpetuating existing inequities. *Women's curriculum,* the fourth phase, introduces the development of "women's consciousness of their own distinct role in society" (Thompson-Tetreault, 1989, p. 132). The definition of women by their own viewpoint, now seen as valuable, explores the historical-cultural perspective of women. The final phase is the *gender-balanced curriculum*. It focuses on how men and women coexist and relate to each other within everyday life. The points at which their experiences overlap are a key focus. The values inherent in this point of view support pluralism and multiculturalism.

This five-phase model is important because it clearly describes the evolution of thinking about gender. It traces the steps involved in rethinking women's roles in society, beginning with the middle-class monocultural viewpoint in male-defined curriculum and ending with a pluralistic, multicultural viewpoint in the gender-balanced curriculum phase. It is clear that society in general has not developed fully through the phases of thinking about girls and women. The lack of enforcement of Title IX is clear evidence that society's viewpoint still reflects the male-defined curriculum, the middle-class, monocultural viewpoint. As discussed, the equity value sees the education of all children as the primary goal of schooling. This value reflects the need for pluralistic and multicultural thinking as the norm, not the middle-class monocultural viewpoint. This same thinking is necessary in all equity areas for true educational equity to occur.

Research Trends

Academic Achievement and Testing There has been an extensive amount of research on gender as it relates to academic achievement and testing. In achievement of basic skills, most areas that showed gender differences previously are now more equal. For the areas of language arts and reading, in tests of verbal ability girls tended to outscore boys. However, Hyde and Linn's (1988) metaanalysis compared older research studies with current work and found that there are currently no gender differences in verbal ability according to existing measures. The AAUW report *How Schools Shortchange Girls* (1992) reviewed research on achievement in reading. Gender differences indicated that girls tended to score better than boys at an early age, but as they grow older the gender differences narrowed and boys outperformed girls. The report indicated that differences may not be real but, rather, due to testing bias. An example of testing bias is tests that may have reading passages that appeal more to boys than to girls. In the area of writing, research has found no gender differences between girls and boys (Yarbrorough & Johnson, 1989). For mathematics, recent metaanalyses have indicated that achievement differences are minimal (Friedman, 1989; Hyde, Fennema, & Lamon, 1990). Finally, in the area of science, the gender differences favor boys. In reviewing the research on science achievement, the AAUW (1992) reported that even though girls tended to receive higher grades in science than boys, boys outscored girls on standardized science tests.

Gender differences in tests continue to be evident despite the prohibition against bias by Title IX. A test is gender biased if one of the following conditions is found to be true: (1) If a male or female group's scores are consistently higher than the other gender group's scores on a consistent basis, (2) if the content of test items refers to people, characters, or objects of gender with a disproportionate number of references to one gender, (3) if references are presented in sex role stereotypes, and (4) if the test uses sexist language. Examples of continued test bias occur in both the Scholastic Achievement Test (SAT) and the Graduate Record Exam (GRE) (AAUW, 1992; Stanley, Benbow, Brody, Dauber, & Lupkowski, 1991) as they meet one or more of the defined criteria for gender bias. Of even greater concern than the gender bias of tests themselves is the fact that scholarships are awarded based on test scores, resulting in boys receiving more awards (AAUW, 1992; Sadker, Sadker, & Long, 1989).

Curriculum These same criteria for determining gender bias also apply to curriculum. Sadker, Sadker, & Long, (1989) identified forms of gender bias in the curriculum in addition to those defined earlier. These include: the omission of women's accomplishment or the treating of these accomplishments "as unique occurrences" (p. 108) or the failure to discuss controversy such as prejudice.

Interestingly, during the first wave of educational reform, 1983 to 1987, only 1% of 138 published education articles addressed gender equity. Only one article discussed differential treatment by gender in the curriculum, classroom, or athletics (Sadker, Sadker, & Steindam, 1989). Yet, examples of gender bias in the curriculum abound. Stereotypical roles have been found to be prevalent in common fairy tales (Moore, 1985), with a predominance of references to male characters over females found in award-winning elementary school story books (Engel, 1985). There is male dominance of characters in the books required for reading in high school English classes (Applebee, 1989). And the use of sexist language and sex role stereotypes is coupled with ignoring of gender equity issues

in texts widely used in teacher education programs (Sadker, Sadker, & Hicks, 1985).

Aside from the actual curriculum reflected in textbooks and materials, a hidden curriculum exists in the form of preferential treatment in classrooms. A pattern of more teacher attention to males is prevalent from the early grades onward (Jones, 1989; Vandell, 1989). Just a few of the differences documented show that boys call out answers more than girls but are not reprimanded for their behavior and girls are (Sadker & Sadker, 1985; Sadker, Sadker, & Thomas, 1981); girls received less attention than boys (Sadker & Sadker, 1985; Serbin, O'Leary, Kent, & Tonick, 1973); and feedback to boys is more precise than that given to girls (AAUW, 1992; Sadker & Sadker, 1986).

As discussed, Thompson-Tetreault's models (1989) for curriculum clearly identify the stages of development that move education toward a gender fair curriculum. Developing such a curriculum requires a shift in thinking. A change in teachers' teaching methods toward gender-fair teaching is needed as well (Chandler & Pennington, 1986; Rose & Dunne, 1989; Vandell, 1991). Changing teaching to enhance equity is discussed more fully in the next section of this chapter.

Women in Administration A third area currently under research in the area of gender equity is women in administration. Women make up approximately 84% of all elementary school teachers, but only 17% of elementary school principals; women make up 50% of all secondary school teachers, but only 4% of all secondary school principals; women make up 66% of all school personnel, but only 3% are superintendents (Shakeshaft, 1989). Shakeshaft's (1989) work, *Women in Educational Administration,* reviewed much of the recent literature on women in educational leadership positions. She cited the most common barriers to women obtaining leadership positions, which are briefly described here.

First, women's career paths in education do not support movement up the career ladder. Women tend to move up through positions as specialists, supervisors, and eventually become elementary school principals (Bagenstos, 1987; Shakeshaft, 1989). They do not move along the career path typically associated with positions of power in the school system.

Women's socialization is another barrier to women in administration. The following statistics about women reflect their socialization and its subsequent effect on women in educational administration: "The profile of the 'typical' woman administrator is of a woman who either (a) does not have children; (b) whose children are grown; or (c) who has private child care in the form of a full-time housekeeper or, more often, her own mother" (Shakeshaft, 1989, p. 112). These findings support the notion that women are socialized toward marriage and child rearing as their primary goal, not toward career options outside the private sphere. This finding also reinforces the descriptions in Thompson-Tetreault's models (1989) that showed women as being concerned with the private sphere as opposed to public life. Her models also connect with another barrier, sex role stereotyping.

Sex role stereotyping prevents women from obtaining administrative positions and causes difficulty for women when they are obtained (Marshall, 1984). For example, despite "the overwhelming amount of research that shows that women are better than men at maintaining discipline" (Shakeshaft, 1989, p. 70), women have not been selected for positions that require discipline, which are also the positions that provide a career path to higher level administrative posts. Sex role stereotyping plays into what Thompson-Tetreault (1989) identified as the male-dominated view of what is important and valued. This view, typically known as androcentrism, also plays into the structure of educational organizations (Schmuck, 1987). This poses an additional barrier to women.

The structures of educational organizations reflect male dominance and a bureaucratic, authoritarian style of leadership. An educational leadership literature synopsis by Gupton and Appelt-Slick (1993) reported that women have received higher ratings in several areas when administrators are compared by gender in terms of their effectiveness. In the area of curriculum and instruction, Andrews and Basom (1990) found that women were more likely to be seen as instructional leaders, providing material and instructional resources, being communicators and a visible presence in the school (Smith & Andrews, 1989). They have distinct strengths in developing and implementing instructional systems and in teacher performance evaluations (McGrath, 1992). Also, women evaluate student progress and model behavior that promotes learning and student achievement more often than men (Shakeshaft, 1989). In general leadership abilities women leaders are skilled in communication, problem solving, and team building (Gardenswartz & Rowe, 1987; McGrath, 1992; Shakeshaft, 1989). The collaborative work style that women use has been found to be an important factor in women being rated as effective leaders (Shakeshaft, 1989). Women establish feminine principles in leadership that move away from a bureaucratic hierarchy of power and control to a structure that is more supportive and inclusive. According to Helgesen (1990), in her book *The Female Advantage: Women's Ways of Leadership,* this structure "affirms relationships, seeks ways to strengthen human bonds, simplifies communications, and gives means an equal value with ends" (p. 52). In short, women are peopled centered. It is easy to see how the organizational structure prohibits women from advancing, as the male-centered view does not value highly the female traits described above. Interestingly enough, current trends in educational leadership are calling for the use of more facilitation, collaboration, and problem solving to create positive change in education (Leithwood, 1992). What is being called for to change education are, in fact, the very characteristics that women leaders exhibit.

RESEARCH IMPLICATIONS ON PRACTICE AND RECOMMENDATIONS

In each of the areas of equity research reviewed in this chapter, themes emerge from research trends that are discussed. Three themes have universal implications for schooling and are discussed here as they relate to the equity areas: research, education, and political activity. Their impact on practice is discussed with recommendations for activity on the part of educators to address equity issues and challenges.

Research

The review of the existing research presented in this chapter points to the need for continued research in all areas of equity. Specific examples presented here are grouped into two categories: research on the organization and structure of schooling and research on teaching.

Organization and Structure of Schooling More research is needed on the relationship between the current reforms in decentralized governance and resource allocation on equity issues and also on the effects of state aid on equity for children. In addition, a helpful suggestion made by Wong (1994) is that more research is needed on "the relationship between governance reform and instructional organization, including the use of ability grouping, the allocation of instructional time, and curricular coordination between targeted services and the mainstream setting" (p. 284).

Curriculum assessment as a form of research is needed. Evaluation of existing curriculum in schools for bias will provide empirical data to support change.

Educational researchers should expand the research on interracial schooling. More data are needed on the needs of Latino, Asian, and African-American students in interracial settings. Studies should not be limited to an emphasis on minority student gains. Data are needed on the impact of various types of desegregation plans and on the ability of white students to function effectively in interracial settings (Orfield, 1993).

Family and administrative support have been cited in the research reviewed in this chapter as important components for effective education for equity. More research is needed in the area of family involvement, particularly research that moves beyond the notion of families as deficit (Davies, 1991). The positive results of capitalizing on the existing strengths of families has been documented (Heleen, 1990) but needs to continue in order to ensure movement toward more equitable involvement of families in schooling. Administrative support has been found to be a key factor in the success of staff development (Fullan, 1990; McLaughlin & Marsh, 1990; Miles, 1986, cited in Fullan, 1990; Sparks & Loucks-Horsley, 1990), innovation and change in school culture (Goldman & O'Shea, 1990; Johnston, Bickel, & Wallace, 1990; McLaughlin & Marsh, 1990; Simpson, 1990), and parent and citizen involvement (Foster, 1984; Solomon, 1991; Williams & Chavkin, 1989). These three factors discussed here are important components in the movement of schools toward true equity for students, and research on the relationship between administrative support and implementation of equity is critical.

Current research in leadership for effective schools indicates that principals employ certain strategies and behaviors that are consistent with female approaches to administration (Shakeshaft, 1989). Research on gender differences between educational leaders needs to continue in order to advance the body of work on leadership for effective schools. In addition, research needs to continue to investigate women's career paths and the influences of the organization on women's job placements.

Teaching The dearth of teachers from ethnic/racial groups contributes to the inequitable educational opportunities children experience in schools. Research indicates that only 13% of the female teachers and 10% of the male teachers in the current teaching force are from minority groups. Because teachers filter the curriculum through their own background experiences and cultural frames of reference, the overwhelmingly white teaching force is disadvantaged in providing the type of multicultural education needed. Majority group students are also disadvantaged by a teaching force that is not representative of the society and world in which they will live and do business. Therefore, research on the effectiveness of programs designed to increase the number of minorities in teaching should be conducted and data on the successful features of those programs disseminated widely to schools, colleges, and community leaders.

Research on teacher expectations and differential treatment of students within the classroom needs to continue. Experimenter effects and reactive arrangements noted in educational research parallel what occurs in the classroom. More research is needed on teachers that relates to: (1) the Rosenthal effect (Gay, 1987) as a teacher's personal biases may affect that teacher's expectations and interactions with students, (2) the self-fulfilling prophecy, and (3) the sustaining expectation effect. In addition, specific research on the type and kind of teacher interaction in classrooms needs to continue. For example, "Research on teacher–student interactions has rarely looked at the interaction of gender with race, ethnicity, and/or social class" (AAUW, 1992, p. 70).

Additional research on effective instruction needs to be done that identifies specific equity groups in the study samples. In this way the effects of specific instructional strategies and methods can be identified for specific groups. Coupled with the research on effective instruction is a need for continued research on program placement options to determine effectiveness for various types of students.

Research and development are sorely needed in the area of alternative assessment. Assessment procedures and instruments are needed on two levels. First, alternative forms of assessment for students must be developed in order to reduce the inappropriate placement of students into special programs. These alternative forms must encompass the range of assessment models described previously in this chapter. Development of a charting system or a matrix to unify the information gathered by the various models can provide educators with an organized format that presents the broadest possible picture of a student. Second, assessment procedures and instruments used to determine teacher competency and educational needs should be examined for their effectiveness and usefulness in identifying gaps in teacher knowledge and performance skills related to equity.

Education

The need for education of educators at both preservice and inservice levels is the most obvious theme that emerged from the research trends. The authors suggest that in order for equity training to be effective, it must follow the specific sequence of steps prescribed here. First, educators must broaden their basic values, moving from a monocultural perspective to a pluralistic multicultural view. Second, school culture must be enhanced. The broadened values need to become a part of the school culture in order to operationalize an equity balance in schools. The third step in the training process is curriculum revision to address equity issues. The fourth step is to improve teaching strategies to match the pluralistic multicultural view of the school culture and the school's curriculum. The necessity of following these steps in order becomes evident in the following discussion.

Broadening the Value Base Today's schools still have the role of assimilating students into the U.S. culture (C. Banks, 1993). The schools "convey to children the knowledge, skills, language, and habits they will need to participate successfully in their own society" (Ravitch, 1992, p. 8). However, the question arises as to what values dictate the content of what is conveyed. Whose culture are students being assimilated into?

Hilliard (1992) discussed the fact that "the white European culture was considered both 'universal' and 'superior' to all other cultures" (p. 13). He maintained that this view is still held by some U.S. educators today. The medical-diagnostic model for assessment described previously in this chapter is a concrete example of what Hilliard described. This assessment model requires judgments based on a monocultural value base, the result of which is the placement of a disproportionate number of children from various equity groups into special programs.

Students in today's schools represent the ever-growing diversity of the United States. For example, migrations occurring from the 1960s to this writing have been dominated by Asian, Hispanic, and Caribbean people (National Coalition of Advocates for Students, 1988). It is projected that by the year 2020, the white population will account for only 70% of the total in the United States, moving down to 60% by 2050 (National Coalition of Advocates for Students, 1988). Therefore, the U.S. culture is no longer, and will not be a white European culture.

In light of these demographic shifts, the controversy around "whose culture" takes on an even stronger meaning. Educators maintain that sharing a common culture will allow respect for diversity (Hilliard, 1992; Hirsch, 1987; Ravitch, 1992; Thompson-Tetreault, 1989). Sharing a common culture means the search for truth, tolerance, respect for dissenting opinions, and an interplay among economic and political systems. In essence, the value base must be centered on a "holistic view of the human experience" (Thompson-Tetreault, 1989, p. 134). Such a value base then encompasses all of the citizens within the U.S. culture.

In order to move beyond the rhetoric that calls for sharing the values of a common culture, educators need to clarify their own value base first because it is impossible to move forward without knowing from where you have come. Training activities and exercises on values and educational philosophies can provide the medium for values clarification. Educators can examine the existing value base, understand how it affects their philosophy of schooling, and explore the gaps or discontinuities in their philosophies. Discussions around values and philosophies can parallel adult moral development (Oja, 1991), leading educators to examine ethical principles that apply to all. Such activities and exercises can enable educators to see how monocultural values and philosophies can promote exclusionary effects on whole segments of the school-age population. Recognition of exclusion can lead educators to the critical need to broaden their value base and philosophy to encompass pluralism and multiculturalism. In essence what will result is the shift in paradigm called for by Skrtic (1986). Values clarification therefore provides the foundation for building any training effort for equity.

Enhancing School Culture Values have a direct impact on culture, which leads to the second step in the sequence of training—enhancing school culture. Values drive the beliefs that guide daily behavior and constitute what we know as school culture (Deal, 1987; LeBlanc, 1990; Patterson, Purkey, & Parker, 1986). With a broadened values base and philosophy, the resultant new paradigm for educators can impact school culture dramatically. Because values drive the school culture, these broadened values can shift the culture away from the monocultural viewpoint still held by some educators and still used as the socializing agent to assimilate students into the U.S. culture. The new pluralistic multicultural viewpoint—the shifted paradigm that the literature reviewed in this chapter cries out for—can become the basis of school culture. Thus, enhancing school culture in this way provides a supportive framework for the changes needed to address equity challenges.

The question then arises, how is this paradigm shift for school culture accomplished? Deal (1987) identified the need for transition rituals for school culture that "transform meaning, to graft new starts onto old roots" (p. 8). Teachers and administrators can achieve this through the realization that nothing has been lost, but that new broadened values can be celebrated. Deal (1987) developed additional suggestions for enhancing the school culture by using what he terms "tangible cultural forms" (p. 6). These forms are: "values," "heroes and heroines," "rituals," "ceremonies," "stories," and the informal cultural "network of priests and priestesses, storytellers, gossips and spies" (Deal, 1990, pp. 137–139). These tangible cultural forms can support change for equity balance. Some specific examples include (1) celebrating heroes/heroines—teachers and administrators that work collaboratively, share decision making, and are successful in conducting and supporting change for equity; (2) developing rituals that support values—administrator supervision of teachers to ensure that lessons and assessment are based on pluralism and multiculturalism; and (3) enhancing the cultural network—storytelling about the successes of new models and techniques for teaching equitably. Celebrating these cultural forms clearly reinforce the elements and behaviors that have been found to sustain innovation such as collegiality, empowerment, shared decision making, and leadership (Goldman & O'Shea, 1990; Johnston, Bickel, & Wallace, 1990; Simpson, 1990). By making the broadened value base part of the school culture and reinforcing it through celebration of successful behaviors institutionalization of change will occur.

It is important to note here that schools are often criticized for not changing. Authors writing about school change have identified multiple forms of resistance to change. These include the structure of schools (Deal, 1987; Fullan, 1982), politics (Cuban, 1990; Deal, 1987), and individual resistance (Deal, 1987; Sarason, 1982). The latter is related to the fact that "change can be very deep, striking at the core of learned skills and beliefs and conceptions of education" (Fullan, 1982, p. 37). It is sug-

gested here that these resistance factors can be addressed through broadening the value base and reinforcing and celebrating the behaviors that sustain change, thus enhancing the school culture. Some of the current literature on the successes and failures of the recent waves of reform provides support for these suggestions (C. Banks, 1993; Farkas & Johnson, 1993; McCarthy, 1993; Sarason, 1990; Wagner, 1993).

Curriculum Development The third step in the sequence of education for equity is curriculum development. Researchers and writers in all of the equity areas recommend various models for curriculum development and make suggestions for the content of curriculum to promote equity. These recommendations are well documented in the literature and include notions such as "content integration" and "knowledge construction" (Banks, 1993, p. 25), and "seeing where there is a common denominator of experience" (Tetreault, 1989, p. 137).

It is suggested here that the broadened value base and a school culture that supports change are preliminary to the curriculum development process. Without these two precursory steps, efforts to implement any changed curriculum will have limited success, especially because curriculum development is not a neutral process. Choices and selections of what content is conveyed are driven by values. The whole notion of the hidden curriculum alluded to in the research reviewed in this chapter supports the contention that curriculum is value laden. Therefore, in order to revise existing curriculum successfully, an appropriate curriculum development process must be implemented that clearly articulates the broadened value base proposed in this chapter.

The curriculum development process itself is also important. First, planning must take into account for four foundation areas for curriculum: society, knowledge, human growth and development, and the learning process (Wiles & Bondi, 1993). Inherent in these four areas are society's changing demographics that affect today's U.S. culture, knowledge of equity issues, judgment of human growth and development based on multicultural norms, and the process of learning that requires a pluralistic approach. Second, the process utilized to revise the curriculum must incorporate the basics of any development cycle: needs assessment, planning, implementation, and evaluation that feeds back into needs assessment. Needs assessment for revision of curriculum to reflect equity must assess what exists and identify forms of bias using criteria informed by the research. Planning must be an open inclusive process that identifies objectives that support equity as well as nonbiased materials to accomplish instruction of those objectives. Implementation must be monitored effectively. Clinical supervision and peer coaching can be effective techniques for monitoring the implementation of a revised curriculum. Finally, evaluation of the curriculum should include an examination of the development process as well as the products of implementation. The resultant data can be used then to make additional revisions and improvements in the curriculum.

Teaching Strategies Even if schools provide equity in resources and curriculum, children with disabilities, children from ethnic/racial minority groups, children from low socioeconomic families, and girls and women may experience inequitable opportunities to learn if teachers are unprepared to teach them. Teacher's actions may empower or disable these children, depending on teachers' knowledge and beliefs. Teachers need a thorough understanding of schooling as a result of a political process and of their role in promoting and providing equity in education for all children.

Strategies that enable student learning for all equity groups must be used. These strategies must fit with the newly revised curriculum. These techniques will be used consistently and effectively if they promote cherished values and are used in a school culture that supports change.

Teaching strategies that have been documented as effective for instruction fall into one of four categories or models for learning (Joyce, Showers, & Rolheiser-Bennett, 1987). One category of strategies is personal models. These models refer to student-centered teaching that reflects a humanistic philosophy of schooling. Examples of personal models are synectics and nondirective teaching methodologies. Synectics is used to enhance creativity, quantity of idea generation, and generation of multiple solutions to complex problems. Nondirective teaching methodologies are sometimes referred to as family models, where learners are grouped into communities that enhance self-concept, social skills, and achievement.

Information-processing models are another category of effective strategies. The techniques used provide systems to organize information, enhance memory, exercise reasoning, and master concepts. Methods include such techniques as advanced organizers and mnemonics. Advanced organizers refer to the presentation of concepts or organizing ideas prior to, during, and after exposure to material presented through traditional methods. Mnemonics devices make use of linkages between the material to be learned and material that is common knowledge, such as association by words or silly sentences (Burden & Byrd, 1994).

Another category for effective teaching encompasses social models. Learning takes place in cooperative structures such as peer tutoring or one of many cooperative learning approaches that utilize small-group work (Burden & Byrd, 1994; Vergason & Anderegg, 1991). Joyce et al. (1987) identified that:

> cooperative environments . . . have substantial effects on the cooperative behavior of students, increasing feelings of empathy for others, reducing intergroup tensions and aggressive antisocial behavior, improving moral judgment, and building positive feelings toward others including those of other ethnic groups. (p. 17)

The fourth category for effective teaching is the behavioral model. Teaching strategies apply behaviorist theory through such techniques as programmed instruction and simulations. These models have been used successfully with special needs students to increase their achievement.

In addition to models for effective teaching, teacher expectations impact student achievement (Joyce et al., 1987). Teacher expectations influence teacher–student interactions and student achievement. Important to interaction is the frequency of contacts with children as well as the content of those contacts. The review of the research in this chapter indicated that teachers' expectations and interactions with students tie in with equity issues (AAUW, 1992; Baron et al., 1985; Dusek & Joseph, 1985; Jones, 1989; Sadker & Sadker, 1985, 1986; Sadker et al.,

1981; Washington, 1980, 1982). The authors recommend training around issues related to teacher expectations because such training has been found to contribute to "a more equitable classroom environment" (AAUW, 1992, p. 69). Training needs to provide teachers with the opportunity to diagnose their competencies (Maheady & Algozzine, 1991) and use observation and feedback procedures (Kerman, 1979). A training program that incorporates these opportunities, as well as those recommended in the subsequent paragraphs of this section, provides teachers with the opportunity to examine their teaching expectations and to modify them using effective teaching strategies.

In order for equity training programs to be effective, they must follow the framework that researchers have identified as key to successful staff development programs. Programs must provide opportunities for active involvement of participants through the planning, implementation, and evaluation phases of the program (Fullan, 1990; Zide, LeBlanc, McAllister, & Verge, 1987). Multiple methodologies for training are needed such as modeling, lecture, observation, and simulations (Oja, 1991; Zide et al., 1987). Of critical importance is a program structure that (1) includes multiple opportunities for participants to practice implementing new techniques and (2) provides feedback on their use (Joyce & Showers, 1988; Oja, 1991; Zide et al., 1987). Such an approach allows teachers to select strategies and methods that match their broadened value base and the newly revised curriculum for equity, thus integrating those strategies and methods into their repertoires. With widespread use and continuing administrative support successful teaching processes that enhance equity and increase student achievement can become institutionalized (Fullan, 1990).

Political Activity

The legal, theoretical, and research areas presented in this chapter were viewed as they related to the political model presented, the four values and the issue-attention cycle that drive educational decision making in the United States. In particular, the research trends reviewed point to the need for increased political activity on the part of educators. Political activity takes various forms for input into the political system.

The primary source of political input into the system is voting. Voting takes two forms: direct and indirect. Direct voting is when a citizen votes for a referendum or in a school board election. Indirect voting refers to the representative vote, as in a legislator's votes in the state's capital or in Washington. The representative vote is typically influenced by citizen's grassroots movements; professional and professionally oriented interest groups; and interest groups representing, for example, testing agencies, textbook companies, and foundations. Another source of political input is, of course, litigation. The positive effects of litigation on equity were discussed in this chapter. Through the various input forms described here educators, families, and communities clearly have the power to impact the political choices made for schooling.

An example of the impact of political activity on educational decision making is the recent effort of conservative groups such as fundamentalist Christians. These conservative groups are attempting to challenge school curriculum on the grounds that it is anti-Christian and anti-American, requesting changes in subject matter from banning specific books to the removal of the teaching of critical thinking (McCarthy, 1993). These groups have attempted input into the political system via several forms. Their use of litigation has been largely unsuccessful because the courts tend to defer to school boards (McCarthy, 1993). As a result, these groups are now affecting school policy through another input form, voting in school board elections. A case in point was the school board of Lake County, Florida, that became dominated by conservative fundamentalists. They ruled that teachers must teach that America's culture is superior to all other cultures. The teachers' union sued the school board on the grounds that the policy violated the First Amendment of the U.S. Constitution and Florida law that requires multicultural education in the public schools ("American Culture Brings Rift," 1994). This case illustrates the power of political activity on both sides of an issue.

Other groups wield political power for education as well. In a recent speech Usdan (1991) identified and discussed two important groups. These groups are (1) the business community who want more input into the education of their future employees, and (2) the growing senior population who want to keep the costs of education low. Politicians and policymakers listen to these two groups. Business involvement in education has drawn continuous attention in the media, keeping business interests prominent in the issue-attention cycle. Seniors pack power in the vote as they have a higher voting rate than other segments of the population. In addition, the American Association of Retired People (AARP) is the largest individual member organization in the United States, giving it great political power to advance the issues of its membership.

There has also been a recent shift in the political control of professional interest groups. Professional interest groups have lost their control over education decision making and policy. They are viewed as a "predictable and static force" (Kaplan & Usdan, 1992). What has emerged are new networks out of the issues-attention cycle. Public concern and a need for public responses have helped move these networks to the forefront (Kaplan & Usdan, 1992). An example is the network that established the original America 2000 goals made up of governors who drew on already existing networks and expertise with the media to push forward their recommendations to address public concern. Educators and professional groups thus fell into a reactionary role, rather than a proactive one.

Of great concern is the fact that the groups and networks who hold power are not dealing with some of the substantive issues that impact equity, such as financial disparities. No networks are championing the causes of needy children (Kaplan & Usdan, 1992). As described at the beginning of this chapter, the values that are driving education are currently focused on quality and efficiency. And again, as pointed out in this chapter, the United States cannot have a high-quality educational system as long as whole segments of the school-age population fail to achieve because of inequity in the system. In addition, we have also pointed out that policies that lead to large numbers of undereducated people are inherently inefficient. Without equity first, quality and efficiency will never be achieved. Therefore it is up to educators to become proactive politically.

One way in which educators can have a significant impact

is to become a part of the existing networks that are defining the direction of schooling (Kaplan & Usdan, 1992). Another option is to develop an umbrella network or a coalition among existing professional interest groups in order to raise equity issues into the issue-attention cycle. The option of developing an umbrella network has particular merit for two reasons. First, professional interest groups have worked collaboratively in the past on an issue-by-issue basis (Kaplan & Usdan, 1992). This history could provide linkages among organizations around equity issues. Also, relationships and behavioral norms developed during previous collaborations could feed into the creation of a supportive culture for the new umbrella network. Second, some successful umbrella organizations do exist, such as the Education Commission of the States (Kaplan & Usdan, 1992). Study of their successes and the successes of smaller individual networks can provide valuable insights for development and management of the umbrella network. For example, staff development networks have been found to be powerful in creating policy change through an indirect approach (Leiberman & McLaughlin, 1992). A new umbrella network could have the potential to redesign the interaction among professional interest groups in a way that could champion the value of equity.

Since the outcomes of politics "may be altered not only by seeking them directly but also indirectly by redesigning interaction" (Wildavsky, 1992, p. 125), what is needed is proactivity on the part of educators. Educators have the opportunity to be proactive politically through several forms: voting, litigation, and activity in professional interest groups. However, given the shifting power in politics described in this section, the most viable forms for input may now be activity in existing networks or a new umbrella network. An example of how such proactivity might be accomplished follows.

In a recent Gallup Poll (Elam, Rose, & Gallup, 1993), "the lack of proper financial support . . . (emerged as the number one public school problem" (p. 137). Because finance is an area of concern for the general public and is already in the issue-attention cycle, it may be the area on which educators can focus to address equity issues. Currently, federal funding targets social redistribution for equity such as for children with disabilities. State funding addresses interdistrict or territorial inequity in fiscal capacity due to disparities in taxable wealth. Local funding addresses distributive inequity among schools within districts and among classrooms within schools (Wong, 1994). However, the policies followed by these three levels of governance have not closed the resources gap for equity. Wong (1994) suggested that a reconceptualization of governance structure and its effects on resource allocation is needed. Included in the new governance structure should be policy coherence among the three levels of government, more effective management of the jurisdictional contention between city and suburban schools, and a new kind of statewide coalition for funding. The new governance structure should be supported by research directed at legislative politics, the implementation process, and bureaucratic rule making at each of the three levels of government. Movement toward a new governance structure could address the public's concern around the finance of public schooling while advancing the value of equity. An umbrella network could unify existing organizations providing the power needed to impact the political system. This is just one example of the myriad of opportunities that educators have to become proactive for equity in education.

CONCLUSION

This chapter provides a review of legal issues, research, and their implications on practice for four equity groups. Viewing these areas from the framework of the four values and the issue-attention cycle that drive the politics of education policy and decision making enables educators to use this rich body of literature effectively.

Schools in America can provide an equitable education for all children. A new research agenda using the recommendations posited here can provide the data for promoting equity. Although many issues require additional research, considerable research literature already exists that describes the changes needed in teacher and administrator preparation and training, curriculum and finance structures to create equitable education. Evidence is also available that defines the types of political activity educators need to support. Such activity will push equity into the issue-attention cycle, giving the momentum needed to fund and promote necessary changes. It is up to us as educators to use our knowledge effectively, to ensure that the shift in paradigm needed to educate all children via a multicultural, pluralistic view takes place.

References

Ahlquist, R. (1991). Position and imposition: Power relations in a multicultural foundations class. *Journal of Negro Education, 60*(2), 158–169.

Alexander, K. (1992). Financing the public schools of the United States: A perspective on effort, need, and equity. *Journal of Education Finance, 17*(3), 122–144.

American Association of Colleges for Teacher Education (AACTE). (1987). *Minority teacher recruitment and retention: A public policy issue.* Washington, DC: Author.

American Association of University Women. (1992). *How schools shortchange girls.* Washington, DC: Author.

American culture brings rift. (1994, May 26). *The Sun-Sentinel*, p. 21A.

Americans with Disabilities Act (ADA) of 1990 (PL 101-336), § 2, 104 Stat. 328 (1991).

Andrews, R., & Basom, M. (1990). Instructional leadership: Are women principals better? *Principal, 70*(2), 38–40.

Applebee, A. (1989). *A study of book-length works taught in high school English courses.* Albany: Center for Learning and Teaching of Literature, State University of New York School of Education.

Babad, E. (1990). Measuring and changing teachers' differential behavior as perceived by students and teachers. *Journal of Educational Psychology, 82,* 683–690.

Bagenstos, N. T. (1987). Minorities and women in educational administration. *Resources in education.* (ERIC Document Reproduction Service No. ED 319 110)

Baker, J., & Zigmond, N. (1990). Are regular education classes equipped to accommodate students with learning disabilities? *Exceptional Children, 56*(6), 515–526.

Banks, C. A. M. (1993). Restructuring schools for equity: What we have learned in two decades. *Phi Delta Kappan, 75*(1), 42–48.

Banks, J. A. (1993). Multicultural education: Development, dimensions, and challenges. *Phi Delta Kappan, 75*(1), 22–28.

Banks, J. A. (1994a). *An introduction to multicultural education.* Boston: Allyn & Bacon.

Banks, J. A. (1994b). *Multiethnic education: Theory and practice* (3rd ed.). Boston: Allyn & Bacon.

Baron, R. M., Tom, H., & Cooper, H. M. (1985). Social class, race and teacher expectations. In J. B. Dusek (Ed.), *Teacher expectancies* (pp. 251–270). Hillsdale, NJ: Lawrence Erlbaum Associates.

Bartz, D. E., & Gordon, W. M. (1994). Monitoring desegregation. *National Forum of Applied Educational Research Journal, 7*(1), 8.

Beane, D. B. (1988). *Mathematics and science: Critical filters for the future of minority students.* Washington, DC: The Mid-Atlantic Equity Center.

Becker, H. J. (1985). *The second national survey of instructional uses of school computers: A preliminary report.* Paper presented at the World Conference on Computers in Education, Norfolk, VA. (ERIC Document Reproduction Service No. ED 274 307)

Bell, T. (1993). Reflections one decade after *A Nation at Risk. Phi Delta Kappan, 74*(8), 592–597.

Bennett, K. P., & LeCompte, M. D. (1990). *The way schools work: A sociological analysis of education.* New York: Longman.

Bilingual Education Act of 1968.

Bishop, P. C., & Jones, A. J., Jr. (1993). Implementing the Americans with Disabilities Act of 1990: Assessing the variables of success. *Public Administration Review, 53*(2), 121–128.

Blackhurst, A. E., & Burdine, W. H. (Eds.). (1993). *An introduction to special education* (3rd ed.). New York: HarperCollins.

Bloom, B. S., Davis, A., & Hess, R. (1965). *Compensatory education for cultural deprivation.* New York: Holt.

Board of Education of Oklahoma City Public Schools v. Dowell, 795 F.2d 1516 (10th Cir. 1986).

Board of Public Instruction of Taylor County v. Finch, 414 F. 2d 1068 (5th Cir. 1969).

Bowles, S., & Gintis, H. (1976). *Schooling in capitalist America.* New York: Basic Books.

Braun, C. (1985). Teacher expectations and instruction. In T. Husen & T. N. Postlethwaite (Eds.), *The international encyclopedia of education* (Vol. 9, pp. 5008–5016). New York: Pergamon.

Brody, L. (1987). *Gender differences in standardized examinations used for selecting applicants to graduate and professional schools.* Paper presented at the annual meeting of the American Educational Research Association, Washington, DC.

Brophy, J. E. (1985). Teacher student interaction. In J. B. Dusek (Ed.), *Teacher expectancies* (pp. 303–328). Hillsdale, NJ: Lawrence Erlbaum Associates.

Brown v. Board of Education, 347 U.S. 483 (1954).

Bryan, T., Bay, M., & Donahue, M. (1988). Implications of the learning disabilities definition for the Regular Education Initiative. *Journal of Learning Disabilities, 21*(1), 23–28.

Burden, P. R., & Byrd, D. M. (1994). *Methods for effective teaching.* Boston: Allyn & Bacon.

Buswell, B., & Schaffner, C. (1990). Families supporting inclusive schooling. In W. Stainback & S. Stainback (Eds.), *Support networks for inclusive schooling: Independent integrated education* (pp. 219–229). Baltimore: Paul H. Brookes Publishing Co.

Carl D. Perkins Vocational and Technical Education Act. (1984) (PL 98-524).

Carnegie Forum on Education and the Economy. (1986). *A nation prepared: Teachers for the 21st century*. The report of the Task Force on Teaching as a Profession. New York: Author.

Chaikind, S., Danielson, L., & Brauen, M. (1993). What do we know about the costs of special education? A selected review. *The Journal of Special Education, 26*(4), 344–370.

Chandler, P., & Pennington, V. (1986). Sexism. *Resources in education.* (ERIC Document Reproduction Service No. ED 344 036)

Chittenden, E. (1991). Authentic assessment, evaluation, and documentation of student performance. In V. Perrone (Ed.), *Expanding student assessment* (pp. 22–31). Alexandria, VA: Association for Supervision and Curriculum Development.

Chubb, J. E., & Moe, T. M. (1988). Politics, markets, and the organization of schools. *American Political Science Review, 82*(4), 1065–1087.

Cisneros v. Corpus Christi Independent School District (1972).

Civil Rights Act of 1964, 42 U.S.C. § 2000 (1964).

Colangelo, N., Dustin, D., & Foxley, C. (1985). *Multicultural nonsexist education: A human relations approach* (2nd ed.). Dubuque, IA: Kendall/Hunt.

Coleman, J., Campbell, E. Q., Hobson, C. J., McPartland, J., Mood, A. M., Weinfeld, F. D., & York, R. L. (1966). *Equality of educational opportunity*. Washington, DC: U.S. Department of Education, Office of Education.

College Entrance Examination Board. (1993). *College bound seniors: 1993 profile of SAT and achievement test takers*. New York: Author.

Columbus Board of Education v. Penick, 443 U.S. 449 (1979).

Comer, J. P. (1990). Home, school, and academic learning. In J. Goodlad & P. Keating (Eds.), *Access to knowledge: An agenda for our nation's schools* (pp. 23–42). New York: College Board.

Cook, J. T., & Brown, J. L. (1993). *Two Americas: Racial differences in child poverty in the U.S.* Medford, MA: Center on Hunger, Poverty and Nutrition Policy.

Cuban, L. (1990). A fundamental puzzle of school reform. In A. Lieberman (Ed.), *Schools as collaborative cultures: Creating the future now* (pp. 71–77). New York: Falmer.

Cummins, J. (1984). *Bilingualism and special education: Issues in assessment and pedagogy*. San Diego: College-Hill.

Cummins, J. (1986). Empowering minority students: A framework of intervention. *Harvard Educational Review, 56*(1), 18–36.

Darling-Hammond, L. (1985). *Equality and excellence: The status of black Americans*. New York: College Entrance Examination Board.

Davies, D. (1991). Schools reaching out: Family, school, and community partnership for student success. *Phi Delta Kappan, 72*(19), 376–382.

Davis, J., & Maheady, L. (1991). The Regular Education Initiative: What do three groups of education professionals think? *Teacher Education and Special Education, 14*(4), 211–220.

Deal, T. (1987). The culture of schools. In L. Sheive & M. Schoenheit (Eds.), *Leadership: Examining the elusive* (pp. 3–15). Alexandria, VA: Association for Supervision and Curriculum Development.

Deal, T. (1990). Healing our schools: Restoring the heart. In A. Lieberman (Ed.), *Schools as collaborative cultures: Creating the future now* (pp. 127–149). New York: Falmer.

Diana v. the State Board of Education in California (1974).

Dossey, J. A., Mullis, I. S., Lindquist, M. M., & Chambers, D. L. (1988). *The mathematics report card: Are we measuring up?* Princeton, NJ: Educational Testing Service.

Durning, A. B. (1990). Ending poverty. In L. R. Brown (Ed.), *State of the world 1990* (pp. 139–153). New York: Norton.

Dusek, J. B., & Joseph, G. (1985). The bases of teacher expectancies. In J. B. Dusek (Ed.), *Teacher expectancies* (pp. 229–250). Hillsdale, NJ: Lawrence Erlbaum Associates.

Education for All Handicapped Children Act of 1975 (PL 94-142), 20 U.S.C. § 1401 (1975).

Education Amendments of 1972, Title IX, 20 U.S.C. § 1681 (1972).

Education Commission of the States. (1990). *New strategies for producing minority teachers*. Denver: Author.

Elam, S. M., Rose, L. C., & Gallup, A. M. (1993). The 25th annual Phi Delta Kappa/Gallup Poll of the public's attitudes toward the public schools. *Phi Delta Kappan, 75*(2), 137–152.

Elementary and Secondary Education Act of 1965 (PL 89-10), H. R. 2362, 89th Congress, 1st Session. Reports, Bills, Bebated, and Act.

Engel, R. (1985). Is unequal treatment of females diminishing in children's picture books? In N. Colangelo, D. Dustin, & C. Foxley (Eds.), *Multicultural nonsexist education: A human relations approach* (2nd ed., pp. 293–298). Dubuque, IA: Kendall/Hunt.

Family Rights and Privacy Act (PL 93-380) (1974).

Farkas, S., & Johnson, J. (1993). From goodwill to gridlock: The politics of education reform. *The Education Digest, 59,* 4–7.

Fielder, D. J. (1993). Wanted: Minority teachers. *The Executive Educator, 15*(5), 33–34.

Foster, K. (1984). Parent advisory councils. *Principal, 63,* 26–31.

Friedman, L. (1989). Mathematics and the gender gap: A metaanalysis of recent studies on sex differences in mathematical tasks. *Review of Educational Research, 59*(2), 185–213.

Friend, M., & Cook, L. (1992). The new mainstreaming. *Instructor, 10*(7), 30–36.

Fullan, M. (1982). *The meaning of educational change*. New York: Teachers College Press.

Fullan, M. (1990). Staff development, innovation and instructional development. In B. Joyce (Ed.), *Changing school culture through staff development* (pp. 3–25). Alexandria, VA: Association for Supervision and Curriculum Development.

Gamoran, A. (1987). The stratification of high school learning opportunities. *Sociology of Education, 60*(3), 135–155.

Gamoran, A. (1992). Is ability grouping equitable? *Educational Leadership, 50*(2), 11–17.

Gardenswartz, I., & Rowe, A. (1987, November–December). Getting to the top: The five success secrets of women who have made it. *Executive Female,* 34–38.

Gardner, D. P. (Chair). (1983). *A nation at risk: The imperative for education and reform*. National Commission on Excellence in Education. Washington, DC: U.S. Government Printing Office.

Garibaldi, A. M. (Ed.). (1989). *Teacher recruitment and retention*. Washington, DC: National Education Association.

Gay, G. (1993). Building cultural bridges: A bold proposal for teacher education. *Education and Urban Society, 25*(3), 285–299.

Gay, L. R. (1987). *Educational research competencies for analysis and application* (3rd ed.). Columbus, OH: Merrill.

Goldman, C., & O'Shea, C. (1990). A culture for change. *Educational Leadership, 47*(8), 41–43.

Gollnick, D. M., & Chinn, P. C. (1984). *Multicultural education in a pluralistic society* (4th ed.). Columbus, OH: Merrill.

Good, T. L., & Brophy, J. E. (1994). *Looking in classrooms* (2nd ed.) New York: HarperCollins.

Gordon, E. W., & Wilkerson, D. A. (1966). *Compensatory education for the disadvantaged*. New York: College Entrance Examination Board.

Gorton, R., & Thierbach-Schneider, G. (1991). *School based leadership: Challenges and opportunities* (3rd ed.). Dubuque, IA: Wm C. Brown.

Gottlieb, J. (1990). Mainstreaming and quality education. *American Journal on Mental Retardation, 95*(1), 16–17.

Governor's Commission on Educational Opportunity for All Virginians. (1991). *Final report: Governor's commission on educational opportunity for all Virginians*. Richmond: Author.

Greer, R. G., & Husk, W. L. (1989). *Recruiting minorities into teaching*. Bloomington, IN: Phi Delta Kappa Educational Foundation.

Guadulupe Organization, Inc. v. Tempe Elementary School District (1978). (9th Circ.).

Gupton, S., & Appelt-Slick, G. (1993, February). *Education's women administrators: Literature review and national survey.* Paper presented at the Association of Teacher Educators Conference, Los Angeles.

Hakuta, K., & Gould, L. J. (1987). Synthesis of research on bilingual education. *Educational Leadership, 44*(6), 38–45.

Hale-Benson, J. E. (1986). *Black children: Their roots, culture, and learning styles.* Baltimore: Johns Hopkins University Press.

Hammack, D. C., Hartoonian, M., Howe, J., Jenkins, L. B., Levstik, L. S., MacDonald, W. B., Mullis, I. V. S., & Owen, E. (1990). *The U.S. history report card.* Princeton, NJ: Educational Testing Service.

Hanline, M. (1990). A consulting model for providing integration opportunities for preschool children with disabilities. *Journal of Early Intervention, 14*(4), 360–366.

Heleen, O. (Ed.). (1990). Schools reaching out: Families and schools build new partnerships. *Equity and Choice, 6*(3).

Helgesen, S. (1990). *The female advantage: Women's ways of leadership.* New York: Doubleday.

Herman, J., Aschbacher, P., & Winters, L. (1992). *A practical guide to alternative assessment.* Alexandria, VA: Association for Supervision and Curriculum Development.

Hernandez, H. (1989). *Multicultural education: A teacher's guide to content and process.* Columbus, OH: Merrill.

Hilliard, A. G. (1991). Equity, access, and segregation. In S. L. Kagan (Ed.), *The care and education of America's young children: Obstacles and opportunities.* Ninetieth yearbook of the National Society for the Study of Education, Part I. Chicago: National Society for the Study of Education.

Hilliard, A. G. (1992). Why we must pluralize the curriculum. *Educational Leadership, 49*(4), 12–15.

Hirsch, E. D., Jr. (1987). *Cultural literacy: What every American needs to know.* Boston: Houghton Mifflin.

Hobsen V. Smuck (D. C. Circuit) (1969).

Hollifield, J. (1990). State education finance systems: Inequitable, immoral, and illegal. *R & D Review, 5*(1), 2–3.

Hyde, J., Fennema, E., & Lamon, S. (1990). Gender differences in mathematics performance: A meta-analysis. *Psychological Bulletin, 107*(2), 139–155.

Hyde, J., & Linn, M. (1988). Gender differences in verbal activity: A meta-analysis. *Psychological Bulletin, 104*(1), 53–69.

Individuals with Disabilities Education Act (PL 101-476), 20, U.S.C. § 1401 (1986).

Jackson, J. F. (1993). Human behavioral genetics, Scarr's theory, and her views on interventions: A critical review and commentary on their implications for African American children. *Child Development, 64*(5), 1318–1332.

James, J. (Ed.). (1991). *Recruiting people of color for teacher education.* Bloomington, IN: Phi Delta Kappa Educational Foundation.

Jenkins, J., & Pious, C. (1991). Full inclusion and REI: A reply to Thousand and Villa. *Exceptional Children, 57*(6), 562–564.

Jenkins, J., Pious, C., & Jewell, M. (1990). Special education and the Regular Education Initiative: Basic assumptions. *Exceptional Children, 56*(6), 479–491.

Johnston, J., Bickel, W., & Wallace, R. (1990). Building and sustaining change in the culture of secondary schools. *Educational Leadership, 47*(8), 46–48.

Jones, M. G. (1989). Gender bias in classroom interactions. *Contemporary Education, 60*(4), 218–222.

Joyce, B., & Showers, B. (1988). *Student achievement through staff development.* New York: Longman.

Joyce, B., Showers, B., & Rolheiser-Bennett, C. (1987). Staff development and student learning: A synthesis of research models on teaching. *Educational Leadership, 45*(2), 11–23.

Kaplan, G., & Usdan, M. (1992). The changing look of education's policy networks. *Phi Delta Kappan, 73*(9), 664–672.

Kearney, C. P., Philip, C., & Chen, L. (1990). Race and equality of opportunity: A school finance perspective. *Journal of Education Finance, 15*(3), 333–350.

Kerman, S. (1979). Teacher expectations and student achievement. *Phi Delta Kappan, 60,* 716–718.

King, J. E. (1991). Dysconscious racism: Ideology, identity, and the miseducation of teachers. *Journal of Negro Education, 60*(2), 133–147.

King, S. H. (1993). The limited presence of African-American teachers. *Review of Educational Research, 63*(2), 115–149.

Kirby, P. C., Oescher, J., Wilson, D., & Smith-Gratto, K. (1990). Computers in schools: A new source of inequity. *Computers in Education, 14*(6), 537–541.

Kohl, J. P., & Greenlaw, P. S. (1992). The Americans with Disabilities Act of 1990: Its impact on business and education. *Journal of Education for Business, 67*(4), 214–217.

Kozol, J. (1991). *Savage inequalities.* New York: Crown.

Larry P. v. Riles, 343 (N. D. California, 1972) F. Supp. 1306 (1972).

Lau v. Nichols, 414 U.S. 563 (1974).

LeBlanc, P. (1990). *Massachusetts school improvement councils and the local political culture.* Ann Arbor, MI: University Microfilms International. (Order Number 9024719)

Lee v. Autanga County Board of Education, 514 F.2d 646 (5th Cir. 1974).

Lee, V. E., & Bryk, A. S. (1988). Curriculum tracking as mediating the social distribution of high school achievement. *Sociology of Education, 61*(2), 78–94.

Leiberman, A., & McLaughlin, M. W. (1992). Networks for educational change: Powerful and problematic. *Phi Delta Kappan, 73*(9), 673–677.

Leithwood, K. (1992). The move toward transformational leadership. *Educational Leadership, 49*(5), 8–12.

Lerner, J. (1987). The Regular Education Initiative: Some unanswered questions. *Learning Disabilities Focus, 3*(1), 3–7.

Locke, D. C. (1988). Teaching culturally-different students: Growing pine trees or bonsai trees. *Contemporary Education, 59*(3), 130–133.

Lutz, F. W., & Merz, C. (1992). *The politics of school/community relations.* New York: Teachers College Press.

Maheady, L., & Algozzine, B. (1991). The Regular Education Initiative—Can we proceed in an orderly and scientific manner? *Teacher Education and Special Education, 14*(1), 66–73.

Male, M. (1994). *Technology for inclusion: Meeting the special needs of all students* (2nd ed.). Boston: Allyn & Bacon.

Male, M., Johnson, R., Johnson, D., & Anderson, M. (1986). *Cooperative learning and computers: An activity guide for teachers.* Santa Cruz, CA: Applecations.

Margolis, H., & McCabe, P. (1989). Easing the adjustment to mainstreaming programs. *Education Digest, 55*(4), 58–61.

Marshall, C. (1984). From culturally defined to self-defined: Career stages of women administrators. *Resources in Education.* (ERIC Document Reproduction Service No. ED 272 968)

Marshall, C., Mitchell, D., & Wirt, F. (1989). *Culture and education policy in the American states.* New York: Falmer Press.

Martin, R. J., & Koppelman, K. (1991). The impact of a human relations/multicultural education course on the attitudes of prospective teachers. *Journal of Intergroup Relations, 18*(1), 16–27.

Matute-Bianchi, M. E. (1986). Ethnic identities and patterns of school success and failure among Mexican-descent and Japanese-American students in a California high school: An ethnographic analysis. *American Journal of Education, 95,* 233–255.

McCarthy, M. M. (1993). Challenges to the public school curriculum: New targets and strategies. *Phi Delta Kappan, 75*(1), 55–60.

McGrath, S. T. (1992). Here come the women! *Educational Leadership, 49*(5), 62–65.

McLaughlin, M. W., & Marsh, D. D. (1990). Staff development and school change. In A. Lieberman (Ed.), *School as collaborative cultures: Creating the future now* (pp. 213–232). New York: Falmer Press.

Mercer, J. R. (1973). *Labeling the mentally retarded*. Los Angeles: University of California Press.

Miles, M. (1986). *Research findings on the stages of school improvement*. Ontario: Conference on Planned Change, The Ontario Institute for Studies in Education.

Milliken v. Bradley, 418 U.S. 717, 94 S. Ct. 3112 (1974).

Mills v. the Board of Education in the District of Columbia, 348 F. Supp. 866 (1972).

Moll, L. C. (1992). Bilingual classroom studies and community analysis: Some recent trends. *Educational Researcher, 21*(2), 20–24.

Moore, R. B. (1985). From rags to witches: Stereotypes, distortions and antihumanism in fairy tales. In N. Colangelo, D. Dustin, & C. Foxley (Eds.), *Multicultural nonsexist education: A human relations approach* (2nd ed., pp. 300–307). Dubuque, IA: Kendall/Hunt.

Muir, S., & Hutton, J. (1989). Regular Education Initiative: Impact on service to mildly handicapped students. *Action in Teacher Education, 23*(4), 234–239.

Mullis, I. V. S., & Jenkins, L. B. (1988). *The science report card: Elements of risk and recovery*. Princeton, NJ: Educational Testing Service.

Mullis, I. V. S., Owen, E. H., & Phillips, G. W. (1990). *Accelerating academic achievement: A summary of findings from 20 years of NAEP*. Washington, DC: Office of Educational Research and Improvement, U.S. Department of Education.

Myles, B. S., & Simpson, R. (1990). Mainstreaming modification preferences of parents of elementary-age children with learning disabilities. *Journal of Learning Disabilities, 23*(4), 234–239.

Myles, B. S., & Simpson, R. (1992). General educators' mainstreaming preferences that facilitate acceptance of students with behavioral disorders and learning disabilities. *Behavioral Disorders, 17*(4), 305–315.

National Coalition of Advocates for Students. (1988). *New voices: Immigrant students in U.S. public schools*. Boston: Author.

National Education Association. (n.d.–a). *Bilingual education: An overview*. Washington, DC: Author.

National Education Association. (n.d.–b). *School choice and equal educational opportunity*. Washington, DC: Author.

National Science Board. (1987). *Science and engineering indicators 1991* (10th ed.). Washington, DC: U.S. Government Printing Office.

Nel, J. (1992). The empowerment of minority students: Implications of Cummins' model for teacher education. *Action in Teacher Education, 14*(3), 38–45.

Network of Regional Desegregation Assistance Centers. (1989). *Resegregation of public schools: The third generation. A report on the condition of desegregation in America's public schools*. Portland, OR: Northwest Regional Educational Laboratory.

North Carolina State Board of Education v. Swann, 402 U.S. 43 (1971).

Oakes, J. (1985). *Keeping track: How schools structure inequity*. New Haven, CT: Yale University Press.

Oakes, J. (1988). Tracking in mathematics and science education: A structural contribution to unequal schooling. In L. Weis (Ed.), *Class, race, and gender in American education* (pp. 106–125). Albany: State University of New York Press.

Oakes, J. (1990). *Multiplying inequalities: The effects of race, social class, and tracking on opportunities to learn mathematics and science*. Santa Monica, CA: Rand.

Ogbu, J. U. (1987). Variability in minority school performance: A problem in search of an explanation. *Anthropology and Education Quarterly, 18*(4), 312–334.

Ogbu, J. U. (1992). Understanding cultural diversity and learning. *Educational Researcher, 21*(8), 5–14, 24.

Oja, S. N. (1991). Adult development: Insights of staff development. In A. Lieberman & L. Miller (Eds.), *Staff development for education in the 1990s* (2nd ed., pp. 37–60). New York: Teachers College Press.

O'Neil, J. (1993). Can separate be equal? Educators debate merits, pitfalls of tracking. *ASCD curriculum update*. Alexandria, VA: Association for Supervision and Curriculum Development.

Orfield, G. (1993). *The growth of segregation in American schools: Changing patterns of separation and poverty since 1968. A report of the Harvard Project on School Desegregation to the National School Boards Association*. Cambridge: The Harvard Project on School Desegregation.

Orland, M. E. (1990). Demographics of disadvantage: Intensity of childhood poverty and its relationship to educational achievement. In J. I. Goodlad & P. Keating (Eds.), *Access to knowledge* (pp. 43–58). New York: College Entrance Examination Board.

Ovando, C. J., & Collier, V. P. (1985). *Bilingual and ESL classrooms: Teaching in multicultural contexts*. New York: McGraw-Hill.

Pasch, M., Krakow, M. C., Johnson, C., Slocum, H., & Stapleton, E. M. (1990). The disappearing minority educator-no illusion: A practical solution. *Urban Education, 25*(1), 207–218.

Patterson, J., Purkey, S., Parker, J. (1986). *Productive school systems for a nonrational world*. Alexandria, VA: Association for Supervision and Curriculum Development.

Pease-Alvarez, L., & Hakuta, K. (1992). Enriching our views of bilingualism and bilingual education. *Educational Researcher, 21*(2), 4–6.

Pennsylvania Association for Retarded Citizens v. the Commonwealth of Pennsylvania, 343 F. Supp. 279 (1972).

Phillips, K. (1991). *The politics of rich and poor*. New York: Harper Perennial.

Plank, S., Schiller, K., Schneider, B., & Coleman, J. (1992, October). *Choice in education: Some effects*. Paper presented at Symposium of the Economic Policy Institute, Washington, DC.

Quality Education for Minorities Project (1990). *Education that works: An action plan for the education of minorities*. Cambridge: Quality Education for Minorities Project, Massachusetts Institute of Technology.

Ravitch, D. (1992). A common culture. *Educational Leadership, 49*(4), 8–11.

Recruiting New Teachers, Inc. (1993). *Teaching's next generation: A national study of precollegiate teacher recruitment*. Belmont, MA: Author.

Reed, D. F., & Simon, D. J. (1991). Preparing teachers for urban schools: Suggestions from historically black institutions. *Action in Teacher Education, 13*(2), 30–35.

Rehabilitation Act of 1973 (PL 93-112), § 504, 29 U.S.C. § 794 (1973).

Reissman, F. (1962). *The culturally deprived child*. New York: Harper.

Riddick v. School Board of Norfolk, 784 F.2d 521 (4th Cir. 1986).

Ritts, A., Patterson, M. L., & Tubbs, M. E. (1992). Expectations, impressions and judgments of physically attractive students: A review. *Review of Educational Research, 62*(4), 413–426.

Rogers, J. (1993). The inclusion revolution. *Research Bulletin, 11*, 1–6.

Roller, E., Rodriquez, T., Warner, J., & Lindahl, P. (1992). Integration of self-contained children with severe speech-language needs into the regular education classroom. *Language, Speech, and Hearing Services in Schools, 23*(4), 365–366.

Rose, T., & Dunne, F. (1989). Gender equity for a new generation: Teacher educators can make a difference. *Contemporary Education, 61*(1), 29–31.

Sadker, M., & Sadker, D. (1985). Is the OK classroom OK? *Phi Delta Kappan, 66*(5), 358–361.

Sadker, M., & Sadker, D. (1986). Sexism in the classroom: From grade school to graduate school. *Phi Delta Kappan, 67*(7), 512–515.

Sadker, M., Sadker, D., & Hicks, T. (1985). The one-percent solution? Sexism in teacher education texts. In N. Colangelo, D. Dustin, & C. Foxley (Eds.), *Multicultural nonsexist education: A human relations approach* (2nd ed., pp. 300–307). Dubuque, IA: Kendall/Hunt.

Sadker, M., Sadker, D., & Long, L. (1989). Gender and educational equality. In J. Banks & C. A. Banks (Eds.), *Multicultural education: Issues and perspectives* (pp. 106–123). Boston: Allyn & Bacon.

Sadker, M., Sadker, D., & Steindam, S. (1989). Gender equity and educational reform. *Educational Leadership, 46*(6), 44–47.

Sadker, M., Sadker, D., & Thomas, D. (1981). Sex equity and special education. *The Pointer, 26*(1), 33–38.

Salend, S. (1994). *Effective mainstreaming: Creating inclusive classrooms* (2nd ed.). New York: Macmillan.

Salvia, J., & Yesseldyke, J. E. (1991). *Assessment*. Boston: Houghton Mifflin.

San Antonio v. Rodriquez, 411 U.S. 1 (1973).

Sarason, S. B. (1982). *The culture of the school and the problem of change* (2nd ed.). Boston: Allyn & Bacon.

Sarason, S. B. (1990). *The predictable failure of educational reform: Can we change course before it's too late?* San Francisco: Jossey-Bass.

Schmuck, P. (1987). Gender: A relevant concept for educational leadership. *Resources in Education*. (ERIC Document Reproduction Service No. ED 286 254).

Semmel, M., Abernathy, T., Butera, G., & Lesar, S. (1991). Teacher perceptions of the Regular Education Initiative. *Exceptional Children, 58*(1), 9–24.

Serbin, L., O'Leary, K. D., Kent, R., & Tonick, I. (1973). A comparison of teacher response to the preacademic and problem behavior of boys and girls. *Child Development, 44,* 796–804.

Shakeshaft, C. (1989). *Women in educational administration*. Newbury Park, CA: Sage.

Shelton, M. (1993). Americans with Disabilities Act (ADA): What principals need to know. *Principal, 73*(2), 35–37.

Sherritt, C. (1990). Multicultural teacher preparation: A study of teacher migration patterns and certification requirements. *Teacher Educator, 25*(4), 16–21.

Simpson, G. (1990). Keeping it alive: Elements of school culture that sustain innovation. *Educational Leadership, 47*(8), 34–37.

Skrtic, T. M. (1986). The crisis in special education knowledge: A perspective on perspective. *Focus on Exceptional Children, 18*(7), 1–16.

Slavin, R. E. (1987). Ability and achievement in elementary schools: A best-evidence synthesis. *Review of Educational Research, 57*(3), 293–336.

Slavin, R. E. (1990). Achievement effects of ability grouping in secondary schools: A best-evidence synthesis. *Review of Educational Research, 60*(3), 471–499.

Sleeter, C. E., & Grant, C. A. (1994). *Making choices for multicultural education: Five approaches to race, class and gender*. New York: Macmillan.

Smith, W. F., & Andrews, R. L. (1989). *Instructional leadership: How principals make a difference*. Alexandria, VA: Association of Supervision and Curriculum Development.

Smuck v. Hobson, 132 U.S. App. D. C. 372, 408 F. 2d 175, 12 Fed. R. Serv. 2d (Callaghan) 622 (1969).

Snow, C. E. (1992). Perspectives on second-language development: Implications for bilingual education. *Educational Researcher, 21*(2), 16–19.

Solomon, Z. (1991). California's policy on parent involvement: State leadership for local initiatives. *Phi Delta Kappan, 72*(5), 359–361.

Sparks, D., & Loucks-Horsley, S. (1990). Models of staff development. In W. R. Houston (Ed.), *Handbook of research on teacher education* (pp. 234–250). New York: Macmillan.

Stainback, W., & Stainback, S. (1990). *Support networks for inclusive schooling*. Baltimore: Paul H. Brookes Publishing Co.

Stanley, J., Benbow, C., Brody, L., Dauber, S., & Lupowski, A. (1991). *Gender differences on eighty-six nationally standardized aptitude and achievement tests*. Paper presented at the Henry B. and Jocelyn Wallace National Research Symposium on Talent Development, University of Iowa, Iowa City.

Stent, M. D., Hazard, W. R., & Rivilin, H. N. (1973). *Cultural pluralism in education: A mandate for change*. New York: Appleton-Century-Crofts.

Stevens, F. (1993). *Opportunity to learn: Issues of equity for poor and minority students*. Washington, DC: National Center for Education Statistics.

Suarez-Orozco, M. M. (1987). Becoming somebody: Central American immigrants in U.S. inner city schools. *Anthropology and Education Quarterly, 18*(4), 287–299.

Sutton, R. E. (1991). Equity and computers in the school: A decade of research. *Review of Educational Research, 61*(4), 475–503.

Swann v. Charlotte-Mecklenburg Board of Education (1971).

Technology-Related Assistance for Individuals with Disabilities Act of 1988 (PL 100-407).

Tharp, R. G., & Gallimore, R. (1988). *Rousing minds to life: Teaching, learning, and schooling in social context*. Cambridge: Cambridge University Press.

Thompson-Tetreault, M. K. (1989). Integrating content about women and gender into the curriculum. In J. Banks & C. Banks (Eds.), *Multicultural education: Issues and perspectives* (pp. 124–144). Boston: Allyn & Bacon.

Thousand, J., & Villa, R. (1991). A futuristic view of the Regular Education Initiative: A response to Jenkins, Pious and Jewel. *Exceptional Children, 57*(6), 556–562.

Usdan, M. (Speaker). (1991). *The shifting politics of education* (Cassette Recording Number 612-91153). Alexandria, VA: Association for Supervision and Curriculum Development.

U.S. Department of Commerce, Bureau of Census. (1990). *Statistical abstract of the United States, 1990* (110th ed.). Washington, DC: U.S. Government Printing Office.

U.S. Department of Commerce, Bureau of Census. (1992). *Statistical abstract of the United States, 1992* (112th ed.). Washington, DC: U.S. Government Printing Office.

U.S. Department of Commerce, Bureau of Census. (1993). *Statistical abstract of the United States, 1993* (113th ed.). Washington, DC: U.S. Government Printing Office.

U.S. Department of Education, Office of Educational Research and Improvement. (1984). *High school and beyond 1980 senior cohort second follow-up 1984. Data file user's manual*. Washington, DC: Author.

U.S. Department of Education. (1991). *America 2000: An education strategy*. Washington, DC: Author.

U.S. Department of Education, Office of Educational Research and Improvement, National Center for Education Statistics. (1992). *Digest of education statistics*. Washington, DC: Author.

U.S. Department of Education, Office of Educational Research and Improvement, National Center for Education Statistics. (1993a). *The condition of education, 1993*. Washington, DC: Author.

U.S. Department of Education, Office of Educational Research and Improvement, National Center for Education Statistics (1993b). *Digest of education statistics*. Washington, DC: Author.

U.S. Department of Education, Office of Educational Research and Improvement. (1993c). *Reinventing Chapter I*. Washington, DC: Author.

U.S. Department of Education, Office of Educational Research and Improvement, National Center for Education Statistics. (1994). *Mini digest of education statistics*. Washington, DC: Author.

U.S. House of Representatives, Committee on Ways and Means. (1990). *Overview of entitlement programs: 1990 Green Book* (p. 523, Table 25). Washington, DC: U.S. Government Printing Office.

Vallies, J., Sullivan, M., & McLaughlin, T. (1992). A comparison of oral and written testing with primary aged mainstreamed learning disabled students. *Reading Improvement, 29*(3), 188–192.

Valverde, L. A. (1993). Editor's introduction. *Education and urban society, 25*(3), 227–230.

Vandell, K. (1989). *Equitable treatment of girls and boys in the classroom.* Washington, DC: American Association of University Women.

Vandell, K. (1991). *Stalled agenda: Gender equity and the training of educators.* Washington, DC: American Association of University Women.

Venn, J. (1994). *Assessment of students with special needs.* New York: Macmillan.

Vergason, G., & Anderegg, M. (1991). Beyond the Regular Education Initiative and the resource room controversy. *Focus on Exceptional Children, 23*(7), 1–7.

Villa, R., & Thousand, J. (1990). Administrative supports to promote inclusive schooling. In W. Stainback & S. Stainback (Eds.), *Support networks for inclusive schooling: Independent, integrated education* (pp. 201–218). Baltimore: Paul H. Brookes Publishing Co.

Villegas, A. M. (1988). School failure and cultural mismatch: Another view. *The Urban Review, 20*(4), 253–265.

Virginia Department of Education. (1992). *RFP #92-25: Educational attainments of students living in poverty. Final report.* Richmond, VA: Author.

Vocational Education Amendments of 1968 (PL 90-576).

Vocational Education Amendments of 1976 (PL 94-482).

Wagner, M. (1990). *The school programs and school performance of secondary students classified as learning disabled: Findings from the National Longitudinal Transition Study of Special Education Students.* Paper presented at the annual meeting of the American Research Association, Boston.

Wagner, T. (1993). Systemic change: Rethinking the purpose of school. *Educational Leadership, 51*(1), 24–28.

Wang, M., Anderson, K., & Bram, P. (1985). *Toward an empirical data base in mainstreaming: A research synthesis of program implementation and effects.* Pittsburgh, PA: Learning Research and Development Center, University of Pittsburgh.

Washington, V. (1980). Teachers in integrated classrooms: Profiles of attitudes, perceptions, and behavior. *The Elementary School Journal, 80*(4), 193.

Washington, V. (1982). Racial differences in teacher perceptions of first and fourth grade pupils on selected characteristics. *Journal of Negro Education, 51*(1), 60–72.

Weis, L. (1988). Excellence and student class, race, and gender cultures. In P. Altbach, G. P. Kelly, & L. Weis (Eds.), *Excellence in education: Perspective on policy and practice.* Buffalo, NY: Prometheus Press.

Wells, A. S. (1992, October). *The sociology of school choice: Why some win and others lose in the educational marketplace.* Paper presented at the Symposium of the Economic Policy Institute, Washington, DC.

Wildavsky, A. (1992). *Speaking truth to power: The art and craft of policy analysis.* New Brunswick, NJ: Transaction Publishers.

Wiles, J., & Bondi, J. (1993). *Curriculum development: A guide to practice.* New York: Macmillan.

Williams, D. L., & Chavkin, N. F. (1989). Essential elements of strong parent involvement programs. *Educational Leadership, 47*(2), 18–20.

Willig, A. C. (1985). A meta-analysis of selected studies on effectiveness of bilingual education. *Review of Educational Research, 55*(3), 269–317.

Willis, P. (1977). *Learning to labor: How working class kids get working class jobs.* New York: Columbia University Press.

Wirt, F. M., & Kirst, M. W. (1992). *The politics of education: Schools in conflict.* Berkeley, CA: McCutchan.

Wise, A. E. (1993). Equal opportunity for all? *Quality Teaching, 3*(1), 4–7.

Wise, A. E., & Gendler, T. (1989). Rich schools, poor schools: The persistence of unequal education. *The College Board Review, 151,* 12–17, 36–37.

Witty, E. P. (1982). *Prospects of black teachers: Preparation, certification, and employment.* Washington, DC: ERIC Clearinghouse on Teacher Education. (ERIC Document Reproduction Service No. ED 213 659).

Witty, E. P. (1989). Increasing the pool of black teachers: Plans and strategies. In A. W. Garibaldi (Ed.), *Teacher recruitment and retention* (pp. 39–44). Washington, DC: National Education Association.

Witty, E. P., & Debaryshe, B. D. (1994). Student and teacher perceptions of teachers' communication of performance expectations in the classroom. *Journal of Classroom Interaction, 29*(1), 1–8.

Wong, K. (1994). Governance structure, resource allocation, and equity policy. In L. Darling-Hammond (Ed.), *Review of research in education,* (Vol. 20, pp. 257–289). Washington, DC: American Educational Research Association.

Yarbrorough, B., & Johnson, R. (1989). Sex differences in written language among elementary pupils: A seven year longitudinal study. *Psychological Reports, 64,* 407–414.

Zeichner, K. (1992). Rethinking the practicum in the professional development school partnerships. *Journal of Teacher Education, 43*(4), 296–307.

Zide, M. M., LeBlanc, P. R., McAllister, P., & Verge, C. (1987). Five years of success: A collaborative staff model that works. *Resources in education.* (ERIC Document Reproduction Service No. ED 278 633).

·VII·

EMERGING DIRECTIONS IN TEACHER EDUCATION

·40·

THE MORAL RESPONSIBILITIES OF EDUCATORS

Kenneth A. Strike

CORNELL UNIVERSITY

This chapter develops a view of the moral concepts important for educational professionals to understand and to act upon in their professional lives, the dispositions or virtues that are necessary to sustain behavior informed by these concepts, and the form of community required to cultivate and sustain these virtues. It applies its conclusions to the preparation of professionals in education.

Consider first some ethics criteria for preservice or in-service that educational programs should meet.

1. Ethics for educators must be conceived narrowly enough so that the duty to be ethical does not become coextensive with the duty to perform responsibly the range of one's professional duties. A view of professional ethics that makes ethical teaching coextensive with good teaching is vacuous.
2. A conception of ethics for educators should be more than a generic ethic, one that governs the relationships between human beings in most contexts and social situations. It should also distinctively illuminate educational practice.
3. A conception of ethics for educators should be practicable in two different ways. First, it should generate a conception of and standards for ethics that could reasonably inform educational practice. Aspirations such as that teachers should ensure the actualization of the full potential of all their students are too utopian and vacuous to be of use. Platitudes should be eschewed. Second, a view of ethics that can illuminate preservice and in-service instruction must have goals that are appropriate to and can be achieved under the conditions likely to exist in college classrooms or other common-place instructional fora. Thus we should not expect instruction in ethics to reform morally damaged people, to cure pathologies, or to succeed on other "redemptive" tasks. Worthy as these are, they are likely beyond the power of college classrooms.
4. Although no view of ethics is likely to meet with universal agreement, a viable view of ethics for educators should be of such a nature as to receive broad public and professional support. Meeting this criterion may require that such a view: (a) not require any deeply controversial philosophical or religious justification, (b) be commensurable with basic American political, legal, and moral conceptions, and (c) be consistent with pluralism reasonably conceived.

The approach taken here is guided by these criteria, although not entailed by them. It can be described as follows: Think of teachers and administrators (as well as students and their parents) as occupying the role of citizens. They are citizens of the United States, which has a certain form of political community—it is a liberal democracy. They are citizens of a special-purpose community, the school. That they are citizens in (for the most part) public institutions means that their conduct should be informed by certain concepts and principles that regulate civic life, "a public ethic." Moreover, these concepts express a framework for thinking about civic issues, a "public reason." That this ethic and its associated way of thinking is public implies that there are ethical concepts that might be thought of as private. These are such concepts as are associated with nonpublic associations. Religious concepts are paradigmatic, but are far from exhaustive here. The public ethic requires tolerance for a diversity of nonpublic associations and conceptions.

Philosophers have devoted much energy in recent years to arguing about and trying to describe a public ethic and public reason. In recent years they have also begun to rediscover an old theme. This theme is that a society that expects to conduct its public affairs according to the requirements of a public ethic requires people who have certain virtues. A view of this sort was nearly self-evident to most of the nations' founders, and it dominated their discussions of education (see Pangle & Pangle, 1993). Yet it has not been central to the discussions of ethics and political philosophy among philosophers until recently (see Kymlicka & Norman, 1994). Arguably the idea that it is a central role of schooling to help create virtuous citizens is a theme that educators might also rediscover.

Let us suppose that this is true. Schools have among their responsibilities teaching the public ethic and creating those virtues required to sustain it in application. Teachers and administrators are custodians of such institutions. How does this help us understand their moral responsibilities?

Developing a connection between the responsibility of schools to create citizens for a liberal democratic society and the moral responsibility of educators involves several assumptions, three of which are noted here. The first is *the principle of fit,* the second is *the principle of isomorphism,* and the third is *the principle of ethical pluralism.*

The *principle of fit* holds that a sustainable moral life requires coherence between moral concepts, personal characteristics, and social forms. For example, if we believe that it is important to moral life that people seek to guide their interactions by principles that they find mutually acceptable and that they have achieved by open dialog, then it will also be important that individuals possess virtues such as reasonableness and tolerance and that social forms provide space for free and open discussion.

The *principle of isomorphism* holds that there must be a suitable degree of isomorphism between the institutional forms in which moral concepts, practices, and virtues are learned and those where they are to be practiced. For example, it seems unlikely that people can be adequately prepared to function in a democratic society in institutions that are highly authoritarian. Even if democratic concepts could be taught in an authoritarian context, the virtues that sustain democratic practice, like all virtues, are developed and sustained by participation and practice. The principle of isomorphism requires that we give due regard to the ancient conviction that the laws teach.

These two assumptions suggest that an inquiry into ethics for educational professionals needs to be approached, at least in part, as a problem of social reproduction. We need to view educational institutions as places where students acquire the concepts and virtues that sustain a morally adequate form of society. The ethical principles that guide the conduct of educational professionals are those that are necessary to create and to sustain educational communities that accomplish these ends. The principle of isomorphism informs us that those concepts and virtues that should inform social life, constitute the school as a community, and inform the practice of educational professionals are significantly, if not altogether, the same.

The *principle of moral pluralism* holds that no general moral principle can suitably account for all moral phenomena. This is not an assertion of moral ignorance. Rather, particular moral concepts are generally crafted to fit particular contexts or situations. Justice, for example, is the first virtue of social institutions (Rawls, 1971). The concept of justice, however, is crafted to characterize our duties to "generalized" others (Benhabib, 1987, 1992). It is an incomplete guide to what counts as rich personal relationships specifying, at best, their minimal conditions (see Callan, 1992, for discussion). Justice is thus not overly helpful in understanding trust, caring, love, or friendship. This is, however, a defect of a conception of justice only if one assumes that a conception of justice is supposed to play such a role or that justice is the central moral conception from which all others are derived. There is an irreducible plurality of moral conceptions, and it is a mistake to treat justice (or any of its alleged competitors) as *the* center of the moral life.

This chapter emphasizes an approach to the ethics of education that focuses on those concepts that are part of the public ethic (to which justice is central). This is not, however, a sufficient approach either to the moral life in general or to the moral responsibilities of educators. This perspective needs to be supplemented by such conceptions as trust and integrity about which communitarianism is illuminating, and caring, where feminism has much of worth to say.

Is this set of aspirations coherent? What other aspirations might there be? One supposes that if one were to ask the proverbial "person on the street" what conduct he or she expected from teachers and administrators, one might get suggestions such as that they should not molest children or steal from their employers. And without doubt ethical educators should not steal or molest children. But to emphasize this as central to our aspirations would send our inquiry off in a very different direction. What should our aspirations be?

ASPIRATIONS

Is it not evident that educational professionals ought to be ethical? Professionals have power, and they are often self-regulating and autonomous. It is especially important that educational professionals be ethical. They have power over the powerless, our children. They have the future of our nation in their hands. Thus, it seems evident that instructional programs for educational professionals should be concerned with ethics.

Fine words! But they are not self-evidently true. If preservice programs are to be concerned with ethics, we must have reasons to suppose that teaching ethics to aspirant educational professionals will make them more ethical, and we must have some idea of what this means. It is one thing to agree with abstractions about ethics. It is another to agree on a curriculum and an educational strategy. If, as Goodlad suggests (1990), agreement assumes a consensus about the public purposes of education, there are formidable obstacles to such a consensus (for discussion, see Bull, 1993). Concrete proposals are likely to attract dissent quickly. (For collections or special journal editions expressing a range of conflicting proposals, see Althof & Oser, 1993; Dill and Associates, 1990; Geiger, 1986; Goodlad, Soder, & Sirotnik, 1990; and Strike & Ternasky, 1993.) Attempts to deal with ethical issues are especially vulnerable to the charge that they involve an illicit imposition of values or that they are inconsistent with pluralism. Thus, the temptation to seek a minimal set of shared values or to speak only in platitudes is strong. Can we find a path between the Scylla of platitudinousness and the Charybdis of dissent? Is there a strategy consistent with pluralism?

Consider three possibilities as to what we might wish to accomplish in teaching ethics to educational professionals.

1. *We might wish to emphasize instruction that minimizes egregiously bad behavior.* It appears that much of the impetus for public concern about professional ethics comes from the adverse publicity that has attended some noteworthy public scandals. Watergate and the insider trading of Ivan Boesky were, perhaps, the most visible examples. Educators, too, have had their days of shame. Accusations of child abuse, drug ped-

dling, falsifying credentials, sexual misconduct with students, graft, and theft are all commonly made against teachers and administrators (for some data on teachers charged with immoral conduct in New York State together with an illuminating discussion of the legal complexities involved, see Gross, 1988, 1993). Often here we are dealing with conduct that is not only widely regarded as immoral but is also often criminal (see Fischer, Schimmel, & Kelly, 1991, for discussion).

2. *We might wish to emphasize instruction that focuses on the "public ethic"* (the arguments of Strike, 1993a, 1993b; Strike, Haller, & Soltis, 1988; and Strike & Soltis, 1992, are constructed on this assumption). Our society is committed to a set of moral principles, many of which have constitutional standing. These include free speech, press, and association; freedom of religion; privacy; democratic decision making; due process; and equal protection. These concepts clearly have relevance for educators both because they are important to educating children to be citizens of a liberal democracy and because they are part of our public notion of justice. They are central in the NEA code of ethics (Strike & Soltis, 1992). Teachers who grade need a conception of due process. Teachers who allocate their time to different students need a view of equality. Teachers who debate and reason need a view of intellectual liberty. Teachers who deal with records or confidentialities need a sense of privacy.

These concepts, for the most part, apply well beyond the sphere of educational institutions. They are generic in the sense that they are moral concepts that regulate the behavior of public officials in a wide variety of public institutions. Thus, they do not seem to flow from any particular conception of education or any view of moral duties that are distinctive to educational professionals.

This is noteworthy in that another factor that may have generated interest in ethics for educational practitioners is the recent emphasis on making teaching a profession (Darling-Hammond, 1985; Strike, 1990b). One of the things that characterizes a profession is that it and its members are self-regulating (Hoy & Miskel, 1991). Part of the idea of a self-regulating profession is that the training of professionals should be adequate, not only to make them competent but also to ensure that they are committed to an ethic guided by professional standards and by client interest. Perhaps, then, we should seek a view of ethics for educators that is internal to a vision of education in the way in which much of medical ethics is directly concerned with questions of health care.

The idea that we need to seek a view of ethics that is more intimately associated with education than is the public ethic might also be argued from the perspective that teaching itself is an inherently moral activity (Bull, 1993; Fenstermacher, 1990; Goodlad, 1990; Nord, 1990; Sockett, 1993; Tom, 1984). Whatever else this phrase means, it seems at least to mean that teaching depends not only on technical considerations about how morally neutral goals might be accomplished but also on a moral conception of the character of the activity.

This suggests a third view of ethics for educational professionals.

3. *We might wish to emphasize a conception of ethics for educational professionals that flows from a conception of the nature of a good education or from a moral conception of teaching.* However, it is not readily apparent as to what a professionalized conception of ethics might require. We might seek to discover ethical concepts that are in some fashion internal to education. Academic freedom might be an example. Or we might emphasize those moral virtues that are particularly important for teachers (Nash & Griffin, 1987; Sockett, 1993). These might include intellectual virtues such as respect for truth (Green, 1971), or relationships to students such as caring (Noddings, 1984, 1992, 1993) or trust (Sockett, 1990, 1993; Strike, 1991).

There are difficulties associated with each of these three emphases. It is unclear that the first is appropriate for or could be achieved in classroom settings. Injunctions against grossly immoral behavior may not have much intellectual content. One supposes that those who steal from their school districts or sexually abuse children do not need to be informed that these behaviors are wrong. Most people know this, and those that do not are likely to be the victims of pathologies not readily remedied in classrooms. Moreover, an emphasis on curbing egregiously bad behavior in preservice programs seems to require us to believe that classroom instruction under the circumstances likely to obtain in such programs is able to alter character significantly. It is far from obvious that a few hours of instruction in ethics can do much to make people more honest or cure their pathologies.

The idea that instruction should emphasize developing facility with the public ethic seems more reasonable. There is a recognizable set of concepts embedded in our legal and political traditions that is important to the governance of public institutions. These concepts have clear relevance to teaching and administration. Finally, teaching such concepts is a cognitive task that seems suitable for the classroom. Although it is unlikely that a curriculum emphasizing such concepts will be universally accepted, the fact that these concepts are rooted in American political traditions and law gives them some importance, and the fact that they can be pursued as a cognitive task makes them practicable for classrooms. For these reasons, instruction in the public ethic should constitute part of the curriculum for educational professionals (Howe, 1993; Strike, 1993b, 1993d).

It is also appropriate to seek a view of ethics for educational practitioners that is more strongly linked to a vision of a good education and thus is more internal to the practice of educational professionals. At the same time the pursuit of such an expanded agenda raises difficulties of an order of magnitude beyond the difficulties thus far enumerated. Americans do not agree on what counts as a good education. Moreover, insofar as we value pluralism, it is not self-evident that such an agreement ought to be pursued. Arguably, one of the commitments of a free society is that people are entitled to form and to pursue their own conception of a good life free from unwarranted governmental interference (Bull, Fruehling, & Chattergy, 1992). If so, than a conception of a good education rooted in a vision of good lives is illiberal, and even though a vision of the good life might pervade the education provided in a private or religious school (Peshkin, 1986), public schools might be expected to be neutral. Their curriculum should be rooted in a conception of the public interest, but not in some private vision (for legal background, see *Pierce v. Society of Sisters* [1925] and *Wisconsin v. Yoder* [1972]).

DIFFICULTIES

To get a more detailed sense of the difficulties involved in trying to articulate a vision of professional ethics, let us discuss a few comments made in the introduction to a section of Dill et al., *What Teachers Need to Know*, entitled "The Moral Dimensions of Teaching" (1990). The authors begin with a mention of Ernest Boyer who is represented as saying that the great teachers he knew possessed characteristics of integrity and authenticity that were essential to student trust. Boyer also is said to have claimed that "fidelity to a set of values and an uncompromising effort to relate values professed to choices made are essential characteristics of good teaching" (p. 151).

The authors then go on to define "values" as "moral or ethical principles . . . such as respect for persons, justice or truth, and as precepts regulating human conduct, such as duties and obligations" (Dill et al., 1990, p. 151). They proceed to suggest that the goals of instruction in ethics are "to develop students' capacities for moral reasoning, their abilities to decide what ought to be done in particular contexts, and their skills in resolving professional moral dilemmas or conflicts" (pp. 151–152).

Is there anything to object to here? Perhaps few readers will object to integrity and authenticity. Respect for persons, justice, and truth may also seem noncontroversial (although that, as we shall see, is incorrect). No doubt students do need to have their capacity for moral reasoning developed. What could be simpler? These views seem sensible and agreeable, if not overly informative in their detail.

But doubts begin to arise if we try to put any flesh on these bones. Reference is made to precepts that regulate human conduct. Is there agreement on what these are? How do they apply to teaching? Can they be legally enforced? What are the abilities required to decide what ought to be done in particular contexts? How do we decide when a dilemma has been decided rightly? And who gets to decide this?

In fact, it is not obvious that we can be unequivocally and without controversy committed to such values as truth and justice. Some feminist authors have argued that justice is a male construction (Noddings, 1984) and have proposed an ethic of caring and relationships (Gilligan, 1982). Is justice sexist? Truth may be a commitment that is central within the Western epistemological tradition, but recent argument has called much of this tradition into doubt (Rorty, 1979, 1982, 1989). The idea that there is a Truth to be sought is viewed by some as legitimating forms of dominance or cultural imperialism (Banks, 1993; Ellsworth, 1989; Strike, 1994). Truth can be characterized as the pursuit of what some postmodernists (Lyotard, 1984) have called grand metanarratives or totalizing discourses. These are not friendly labels. Truth, it seems. is always someone's Truth and can be an instrument of oppression.

There are other issues to be concerned about in the vocabulary that Dill et al. (1990) and Boyer use to characterize their seemingly innocent views about the moral requirements of teaching. Respect for persons and for justice are characterized as principles. Let us suppose that a principle is a kind of rule. If so, then a search for the content of the ethics of teaching might be formulated as a search for the moral rules that prescribe how teachers ought to behave. Instructing teachers might then be viewed as teaching these rules, using them to understand situations, and developing a suitable commitment to them.

Moral rules might, but need not, be specific. "Thou shalt not kill" and "Thou shalt not steal" are moral rules that forbid certain kinds of actions. However, Kant's (1956, p. 30) categorical imperative ("So act that the maxim of your will could always hold at the same time as a principle establishing universal law") governs all moral action. This is also true of the central commitment of utilitarianism (Bentham & Mill, 1961), which holds that right actions are those that produce the greatest good for the greatest number. Moral rules thus can range from rather narrowly formulated prescriptions or prohibitions to broad moral theories that can be employed to analyze moral situations of all sorts.

Are the moral responsibilities of teaching to be specified as a set of rules of either sort? If we are interested in specific rules, we might then interest ourselves in developing and teaching codes of ethics (Sockett, 1990). Or we might emphasize teaching broader moral theory. Should teacher education aim at teaching and building loyalty to either ethical codes or moral philosophies? There is a considerable literature that questions the idea of an ethic of principle, often arguing that it undercuts sensitivity to context (Benhabib, 1992; Hostetler, 1994; Noddings, 1984; Nussbaum, 1990; Sichel, 1988).

Another perspective is also suggested by Boyer's remarks. Integrity and authenticity are not described as rules, but as characteristics of people. In the language of an earlier era, these are virtues that are not reducible to the predisposition to follow moral rules. An ethical perspective that is dominated by a concern for the virtues is concerned for character, the kinds of people we are. To be concerned for the virtues is to be concerned that people be wise, honest, courageous, or just. To think of the ethics of teachers in this way is to want teachers to be people of good character. A program of teacher education that emphasized character would need to identify the virtues that teachers need to be good teachers (Sockett, 1993) and a program for selecting or producing such people. Its concerns would thus be rather different from the strongly cognitive emphasis of a moral theory that sees following moral rules as central to the moral life. An ethics of rules and an ethics of virtue need not be seen as simple competitors. It is more complicated than that. However, they are not easy bedfellows either. Historically they are personified in the very different ethical theories of Kant (1956, 1961) (rules), and Aristotle (1941a) (virtues).

Dill (Dill et al., 1990) also talks about values. Although he defines values in terms of moral principles such as justice, there are good reasons to question that move. Consider two points. First, it makes as much sense (perhaps more) to say that preferences for ice cream or olives are values as to say that justice is a value. Thus the word *value* is at least broader in scope than the idea of a moral principle. Second, and more important, the word *value* is akin to words like *preference* or *taste*. To say that one has a value, preference, or taste is to say that one has certain kinds of feelings, positive ones, likings, in the direction of the valued object. But moral principles constitute duties and obligations. They are not obviously tastes or feelings. Moral principles are objects of reason and duty, more than choice. If one has a duty to do A, then one ought to do A because there are good reasons for doing A. Thus the duty to do A is not contingent on whether one values A. To describe a moral principle such as justice as a value is to intimate that being just or not is a matter of taste, rather than liking olives or not is a matter of taste. That justice is an appropriate object of public reason and that principles of justice exact duties of us that are independent of our preferences is, at best, obscured by calling justice a value (Strike, 1993a).

To think of the ethical development of educators as having to do with values also changes our orientation as to what we want to accomplish in teacher education. Values, as we are informed by a popular educational program, are objects of clarification (Raths, Harmin, & Simon, 1966). The criteria of their choice are personal satisfaction and a kind of authenticity. Although these are standards of appraisal, they are rather different standards from the categorical imperative, respect for person, or the principle of the average utility. A teacher education program that emphasizes values is unlikely either to attempt to form character or to inform teachers as to their moral duties and obligations.

This point can be put in the more fashionable language of discourses. A discourse is a particular way of speaking that is characterized by its purposes, a distinct vocabulary, and its standards of judgment or appraisal. Moral theories that emphasize rules, character, or values involve different discourses. A discourse is formed by a history and is meaningful as a whole. Thus a discourse has assumptions that are embedded in its vocabulary and its principles of inference. Discourses that emphasize principles are different from those that emphasize virtues and those that emphasize values. One should not overstate the tension between them. However, we cannot simply and uncritically blend these discourses together in a verbal melange without sacrificing clarity and coherence. To treat moral principles or virtues as "values" is to promote confusion.

Thus these rather benign and palatable comments of Dill et al. (1990) and Boyer conceal a host of controversies. These controversies are not, of course, unique to Dill or Boyer. Such issues are likely to be raised in almost any attempt to say something of substance. But the discussion suggests more than just that people disagree about things moral. The eclecticism and vagueness of the language used to describe these various moral concerns suggest that the moral language of our culture is itself in some disarray.

One account of this is that the vagueness and eclecticism of our moral language express the dissolution of any coherent moral tradition in Western civilization. Such a claim has been made by Alastair MacIntyre (1981, 1988), who argues that the failed ethical theories of the Enlightenment have reduced our moral language to nothing but fragments of moral speech from various parts of the moral tradition.

If MacIntyre is right, any attempt to describe an ethic for professional educators awaits the achievement of a new ethic or the rediscovery of the rightness of an old one. Such an achievement does not seem to be immediately on the horizon. However, perhaps this conclusion is too pessimistic. There are intellectual resources available to us that we can employ to make progress. To avail ourselves of them will take serious intellectual effort and a willingness to look at our current position in terms of some intellectual history.

PHILOSOPHICAL BEARINGS

An Historical Sketch

Premodern (or pre-Kantian) views on ethics were often dominated by a concern for the nature of the good life and for the nature of the virtues appropriate to a community informed by a suitable conception of the good life. Aristotle's ethics (1941a) and politics (1941b) may serve as paradigm cases. Aristotle's work is dominated by a concern to articulate a vision of the good life and of a political community suitable to sustain such lives. Essential to his view is that the virtues are essential both to living a good life and to sustaining the political community in which such lives are led. Education is thought about principally in terms of developing these virtues.

It is nearly impossible to approach education in this way in the modern era. This is so for at least two reasons that feed on each other. The first is skepticism that it is possible to know that there is a single conception of a good life that is best. The second is that it seems inappropriate for one group in a society to force its view of a good life on others who do not share it (Gutmann, 1987). These are ideas that have deep and multiple roots in our society. The following characterizes some lines of argument for these views, although it cannot adequately represent the diversity of opinion required.

Skepticism about the objectivity of views of the good life has been much abetted by the development of the natural sciences and the epistemological conceptions associated with science. Aristotle's view of the good life was rooted in the idea that there was an essential human nature. The good life consisted in actualizing this nature. Aristotle's ethic is thus subordinate to his metaphysics in that it assumes a view of the universe that sees it as constructed of form (or essence) and matter. In this universe, "values" exist in nature. A thing's essence is not only that which it is but also its ideal state. In Aristotle's universe, ethics is in the nature of things.

The development of modern science made this metaphysics untenable and with it Aristotle's ethics. The world came to be seen as matter in motion. In Newton's universe, values no longer live in nature. Philosophers such as Descartes (1956) and Locke (1975) moved them into human consciousness. The universe became dualistic. Ends became subjective.

Modern forms of empiricism often capture this view. The positivism of the nineteenth and twentieth centuries, for example, insisted that the only forms of objective knowledge were mathematics and the empirical sciences. In the positivist's universe, values are noncognitive, merely matters of taste and personal preference (Ayer, 1946). They are outside the grasp of reason. If so, there is no possibility of achieving an objective view of the good life. There are only preferences and empirical knowledge about how to satisfy them.

A second development is the idea of a public ethic whose central values include a high regard for tolerance and freedom of conscience. After the Protestant Reformation, it was no longer possible for many of the nations of Europe to consider themselves moral communities united by a shared faith. In such communities, religious dissent is a form of treason. Dissent against the state religion threatens the foundations of the state. States faced with religious pluralism would seem to face a choice between unrelenting civil strife or secularization. They have generally chosen the latter.

The ideas of toleration that have among their roots doctrines of religious liberty (Locke, 1946) have been broadened by liberal philosophers into a distinction between a public and a private sphere of conduct. The public sphere is that area of life over which civil authority can be exercised. The private sphere is that over which the individual is sovereign. J. S. Mill (1956), for example, argued in "On Liberty" that governments may exercise authority over individuals only in order to prevent harm to others. Modern liberals are likely to express an analogous idea holding that governments must be neutral between competing conceptions of a good life (Ackerman, 1980; Dworkin, 1977, 1984; Rawls, 1971). So formulated, liberal views not only require the separation of church and state but also support a broad commitment to pluralism.

A third development, one significantly attributable to the influence of Hegel in the nineteenth century, but which has been underscored by the twentieth-century nonfoundationalist epistemologies of Wittgenstein (1963) and Kuhn (1970) is the historicizing of reason. The philosophical tradition has tended to see reason either as grounded in human nature or in nature itself. Despite widespread disagreement about Reason's character, philosophers assumed that an adequate characterization of Reason would tell us what Reason was always and everywhere. Hegel's (1961) work showed that the character of Reason changed from place to place and era to era. Reason had a history.

Some of Hegel's successors have used Hegel's insights to argue not only that reason has a history, but also that this history is often a history of power and domination. Marx (Marx & Engels, 1976), for example, claimed that the ruling ideas of an era are those that serve the interests of the ruling class. Postmodernists, although they have largely abandoned the economic determinism that often was associated with the Marxist critique of ideology, have nevertheless continued its critical tradition, arguing that various forms of reason and argumentation are likely to express interests and power.

The direction that this critical tradition will take seems as yet unclear. It has the potential to provide useful reminders that ways of thinking can conceal exclusion and domination. It may prove to support a means to a more robust, democratic, and egalitarian pluralism. At the same time, its pervasive relativism and cynicism and its dissociation from Marxism may prevent it from developing any sustainable and positive social program.

Ideas such as these have been formative of how we think about education. We are likely to be suspicious of and resistant to views of education rooted in someone's particular vision of a good life. We are apt to be doubtful of claims that anyone has achieved the Truth about this, and, even so, we are unlikely to see the putative Truth of some idea of a good life as a sufficient justification for the power of its holder to rule our lives. Few these days are interested in philosopher kings.

The conception of education that results is likely to emphasize the presentation and discussion of diverse views of a good life, a respect for pluralism, and a concern for the instrumental and material conditions required to sustain a wide variety of different conceptions of a good life (Ackerman, 1980; Strike, 1989).

Note how these views structure the conception of a profession of teaching. Teachers are unlikely to think of themselves as experts about what constitutes a good life (Bull, 1990). Empiricist views of what can count as knowledge do not give much entitlement to such claims of expertise, and they are illiberal in any case. However, there are no such constraints on claims about the means whereby education is accomplished. The techniques of teaching and administration may be viewed as scientific and as morally neutral. Several generations of social and behavioral scientists have been trained in the belief that the kinds of knowledge they seek to attain meet the positivist's requirements for objective knowledge and that they provided important knowledge about how to teach or administer. Educational practitioners can be professionals insofar as their practice is grounded in such scientific knowledge (Brophy & Good, 1986). Such professionals are experts in the means, not the ends, of education.

Having said this, however, we must note that the concern for efficiency of means is likely to be expressed in a way that presupposes certain moral commitments. That teachers may not impose their vision of a good life on their students presumes commitments to autonomy and tolerance. Liberal neutrality requires a certain view of equal opportunity. If the state is both to respect people equally as ends and to be neutral concerning their differing visions of a good life, it must also provide individuals a fair and equal chance to articulate and pursue their own vision of a good life (Bull et al., 1992; Howe, 1993; Kymlicka, 1989). Neutrality thus entails an affirmative duty to provide equal opportunity. Similarly, liberal educators may not unfairly disadvantage some groups against others in their attempts to realize their conception of the good. Thus they must grade fairly, use tests that are not culturally biased, and generally respect the idea of due process in their decision making. And they must both tolerate and facilitate the open discussion of different conceptions of a good life.

These reflections suggest that the ethics of teaching is, in fact, rooted in something that we might call a public ethic. The commitments just described seem to be those that are appropriate to the educational system of a liberal democracy. However, we have now begun to understand the idea of a public ethic in a way that has special salience for the ethic of a community of educational professionals. The crucial moves in connecting the public ethic and the ethic of a community of educational professionals are twofold. First, we have begun to view the public ethic in a way that goes beyond a set of rules according to which our society functions. Instead, we have begun to see the public ethic as constitutive of this form of community. We are not a society committed to certain ends, in which (incidentally) tolerance is viewed as important. Tolerance is constitutive of this form of society. Second, we have begun to note that the creation and/or reproduction of this form of society has educational conditions. If so, then the public ethic cannot be viewed as merely the background rules according to which educational institutions as well as other public institutions are run. Instead, it is the business of the schools to create citizens for a liberal democratic society and, in doing so, to produce and reproduce this society. Looked at in this way, the public ethic is also the centerpiece of the ethic of a community of professional educators.

This view might be clarified if we contrast how we might think of education if we take the question of the nature of a good life as the central concern with the picture we get if we take the reproduction of a liberal democratic society as central.

In the first case we might ask these questions:

1. What is the good life for human beings?
2. What kind of community sustains such a good life?
3. What kinds of virtues and moral commitments are required of the citizens of such a community?
4. How can we educate people such that they will have these virtues and commitments?

In the second case, we are more likely to ask these questions:

1. What is the nature of a political community that respects the equal right of individuals and communities to form and pursue a conception of their lives that they deem satisfactory? A more democratic formulation would be: What is the nature of a political community that respects the equal right of individuals and communities to participate in the formulation and pursuit of collectively chosen goods?
2. What commitments and virtues must the members of such a community possess if they are to live peaceably and justly in a society where they must cooperate with others, many of whom are unlikely to share their vision of a good life?
3. How can we educate people such that they will have these commitments and virtues?

It is this second set of questions that a society such as ours must address. And this set of questions is central to forming a professional ethic.

There is a special problem to be solved in addressing the second set of questions. The emphasis in the education of a liberal democratic society must be on producing or reproducing a public ethic. The public ethic of such a society will be described by answering question 2. However, any society committed to pluralism must also recognize that initiation into the public ethic is not sufficient. Ex hypothesi, a pluralistic society will recognize that there are diverse communities with diverse visions of a good life and that these communities will also wish and need to reproduce themselves. To put the point in a slightly different way, a pluralistic society will have numerous nonpublic communities and associations that will have their own educational agenda. The public education of such a society must facilitate, not interfere or compete with, the educational aspirations of nonpublic communities and associations so long as their agendas are consistent with justice (Rawls, 1993, Chapter 5). If it fails, at best it will erode much that is valuable in life. At worst it will be insidiously oppressive. Oppressive because it will prevent people from forming and pursuing their own vision of a good life. Insidious because it will do so in the name of liberty and justice (Strike, 1994).

Contemporary Views

If we are to work out the details of the professional ethic of the educators of such a society, we will need to look more closely at some contemporary philosophical perspectives. This section reviews several contemporary ethical theories. The discussion is arranged as a kind of argument between them, and this argument is used to glean some ideas as to how the questions expressed might be answered. By the end of this discussion, hopefully, there will emerge a picture of the moral concepts and virtues that are important to a view of the ethics of schools and pursuant to the ethics of a professional community of educators.

Utilitarianism Utilitarianism achieved its classical formulations in the nineteenth century in the work of philosophers such as Bentham and Mill (1961). Despite the fact that it has been widely criticized in the second half of the twentieth century (Smart & Williams, 1973), it continues to be influential. One reason is that it is intertwined with modern economic theory. Another is that it has some affinity with the positivism that has prevailed in the social and behavioral sciences in its reliance on instrumental empirical knowledge in determining the best action. Thus, although it is not widely ascribed to by current philosophers, it may afford the best account of much actual practice in decision making.

The central commitment of utilitarianism is to the greatest good for the greatest number. Utilitarianism, thus characterized, requires both individuals and societies to judge either acts or rules on a maximization criterion. This maximization criterion is sometimes expressed as the principle of the average utility, which can be represented as $(\text{pleasure} - \text{pain})/N$, where N equals the number of individuals in the relevant population. Typically, then, utilitarianism is consequentialist and hedonistic. Consequentialism is any ethical theory that judges the morality of an action by its consequences. Hedonism is the view that pleasure is the good.

What kinds of capacities and dispositions does utilitarianism require? Consider first the forms of reasoning that are appropriate to utilitarianism. It is important to note that utilitarianism does not provide much need to assess ends. It is a given that pleasure is good and that pain is bad. That something is pleasurable or painful is immediately given to consciousness. Although it is possible for people to be wrong about what is good in the sense that they may misjudge the consequences of some act for their overall happiness, nevertheless, utilitarians have usually held that people are the best judge of their own good (Mill, 1956). At the social level, individuals' sense of their own good, their preferences, are aggregated, but not judged. Thus the intellectual skills required by a utilitarian view concern the empirical assessment of the consequences of a given act or policy for the average welfare. Utilitarian reasoning is instrumental reasoning.

Utilitarianism requires no particular form of social organization but judges social forms by their consequences for the average utility. The tendency has been for utilitarians to be liberal and democratic because such institutions are thought to promote the average welfare. Democracy, for example, may be seen as an effective means of aggregating preferences in ways such that as many people get as much of what they want as is practicable. Equality of opportunity promotes efficient use of human resources. Free speech and a free press promote efficient decision making. Liberty allows each to be the judge of his or her best interests. At the same time, because utilitarianism may require quite sophisticated judgments about the consequences of some policies or actions, it has a tendency to promote decision making by experts and government by economists who are often seen as the keepers of the average utility.

The professionalization of teaching can be expressed within this framework. Here teachers and administrators possess various technical competencies about the nature of efficient educational practices. Given this, among the "virtues" supported by utilitarianism may be the willingness to respect and guide one's behavior by the results of empirical research. Some of the virtues of utilitarianism are those appropriate to a technocracy.

Utilitarianism may have paradoxical results concerning moral motivation (this argument relies on Williams, 1985). Suppose we ask whether utilitarians are supposed to be motivated by a concern to maximize the average utility. Neither yes nor no seems a satisfactory response. Consider that in calculating the average utility, no one person's welfare can count any more than another's (Sidgwick, 1986). If we assume that morally upright people should be motivated by a desire to achieve the average utility, such people may not prefer their own interests or projects to those of others. Indeed, given that it is almost always possible to imagine some act that one could perform that would make others better off at one's own expense, utilitarianism might seem to require a life of unremitting self-sacrifice to the average welfare. Paradoxically, because utilitarians, being hedonists, generally believe that people are motivated by their own rational self-interests, it seems that the psychology of utilitarianism precludes people from acting for the sake of the average utility. Moreover, it has been argued (Sidgwick, 1986; Williams, 1985) that a society in which people were motivated by the desire to promote that average utility and were, therefore, given to self-sacrifice on behalf of the welfare of others would fail to actually maximize the average welfare.

A rather different response to the problem of moral motivation is to hold that the rational actions of self-interested agents are conducive to the maximization of the average utility. A society of self-interested rational agents freely seeking to maximize their own welfare maximizes the average utility "as by an invisible hand" (Smith, 1985). In this case, utilitarianism generates the anomaly that the average utility is most likely to be maximized when people are not motivated by a desire to act according to it.

Given this account, utilitarianism might see little need for ethics as a distinguishable subject in educational professional training programs. What teachers need to know are the consequences of various educational strategies. Presumably these are what they are taught to judge throughout their preparation. Professional knowledge (beyond subject-matter knowledge) would be essentially technical. This is not to say that concepts such as equal opportunity or due process would disappear. However, they will be regarded as rules that inform us about policies that are seen to have good results and are trumped by persuasive evidence to the contrary. Thus they lose their distinctive moral character and are subordinated to empirical knowledge.

Perhaps the most serious criticism of utilitarianism is that it is capable of justifying practices and institutions that seem not only unjust but also reprehensible. For example, some historians of economics have argued that slavery was an efficient institution (Fogel & Engerman, 1989). Consider that the principle of the average utility requires us to believe that slavery was just *if* it were the form of economics that in its historical context maximized the average utility. This is because utilitarianism is concerned only for the average welfare, but is concerned for neither how it is produced nor the equality of the distribution of welfare (Rawls, 1971).

This, to put it mildly, is counterintuitive. And it suggests, at the very least, that any adequate moral theory must be able to distinguish between morality and social or economic efficiency and to recognize that efficient policies can, nevertheless, be unjust.

That utilitarianism has a paradoxical view of moral motivation providing little space between unremitting self-sacrifice and unqualified self-interest seems especially problematic in professional contexts. What seems required here is a motivational theory for an ethic that emphasizes a concern for professional integrity, service, and client welfare. This does not require professionals to discount their own projects (one would suppose it desirable for professional integrity and service to be a part of the projects of professionals), but neither does it permit them to be motivated entirely by their own self-interests.

This criticism suggests two features that an ethic for professional educators should have that are difficult to reconcile with utilitarianism. First, a suitable view of ethics must be able to explain when and why moral considerations overrule considerations of efficiency. Second, it must provide some understanding of the motivation for a service-oriented ethic that finds a middle ground between self-interest and self-sacrifice.

A more Kantian ethic has some potential to address at least the first of these weaknesses.

Neo-Kantianism and Deontological Liberalism Utilitarianism is one of the major ethical theories that has been produced in the modern era in response to the failure of classical conceptions. Perhaps the other most influential view has been the ethics of Kant. Both utilitarianism and Kantianism have been seen as providing the foundations of the modern liberal democratic state.

The central ideas of a Kantian outlook are these:

1. *A central commitment should be made to equal respect for persons.* As rational moral agents human beings have intrinsic worth and thus must be treated as ends in themselves.
2. *Moral claims are judged on the basis of consistency and universality, not on the basis of consequences.* Kant (1956, p. 30) provides a version of the Golden Rule that he calls the categorical imperative. It goes "So act that the maxim of your will could always hold at the same time as a principle establishing universal law." The force of the categorical imperative is to require people to judge their actions impartially; that is, they must ask whether they could be committed to the same principle or act in the same way regardless of how

they are affected. Those who steal must be willing to be stolen from. As this is unlikely, no one could consistently want stealing to be a universal rule of human conduct.

3. *Autonomy is a central commitment.* People are to be governed by neither moral convention nor self-interest, but by self-chosen moral principles. Such principles are chosen because they express the moral law. Autonomous actions are thus also acts done out of respect for the moral law.

4. *The morality of actions is not determined by their consequences for human welfare.* Thus the varieties of Kantianism are nonconsequentialist. This point is often expressed in the claim that the right (what's moral) is independent of or prior to the good (what is worthwhile).

Transformed into a political theory, Kantian ethics have often been seen as supporting what is sometimes called deontological liberalism ("deontological" is roughly equivalent to "nonconsequentialist").

Deontological liberalism sees civil society as a cooperative scheme in which all members of society are entitled to their own (just) conception of their own good. Liberal society is ruled by a conception of justice that establishes the fair basis of cooperation.

This idea of justice as fairness (Rawls, 1971) can be expressed as a view of equal opportunity. People are understood to have a right to pursue a self-chosen conception of a good life. Fairness consists in a scheme of social cooperation, grounded in a doctrine of equal rights, in which each individual has a fair chance to realize his or her conception of the good so long as it is not unjust.

These ideas are often formulated as requiring liberal society to be neutral or impartial. Bruce Ackerman (1980, 1989), for example, characterizes a liberal state as one in which claims over social resources must be justified by discussion or dialog. Liberal dialog must, however, be neutral. As a principle of liberal dialog, neutrality requires us to reject any argument in which we must assert either that one person or group is intrinsically better than another, or that one vision of a good life is better than another. To illustrate, slavery or a privileged aristocracy are examples of social institutions that violate the first part of neutrality. A society with an established religion violates the second.

The kind of society required by deontological liberalism is essentially a constitutional democratic regime in which people are guaranteed certain rights. John Rawls (1987) specifies the requirements of such a society as

first, a specification of certain basic rights, liberties and opportunities (of the kind familiar from constitutional democractic regimes); second, an assessment of a special priority to those rights, liberties and opportunities, especially with respect to the claims of the general good and of perfectionist values; and third, measures assuring to all citizens adequate all-purpose means to make effective use of their basic liberties and opportunities. (p. 18)

The educational system of such a society would emphasize the desirability of students' being able to autonomously formulate and pursue their own conception of their own good. Schools should be neutral between competing conceptions of the good, should make as wide a range of choices as is practica-

bly available to students, and should provide appropriate equal educational resources to students from different backgrounds or with differing conceptions of their lives. The liberal school, thus, might be characterized as a "just cafeteria" of cultural goods.

The capacities and virtues that liberal schools might wish to cultivate are of two general sorts. First are the capacities required to formulate and pursue a rational life plan (Rawls, 1971). These might be called the capacities of self-government and would include autonomy (the psychological capacity to make independent decisions) and the capacity to access and evaluate relevant information. Second is a sense of justice and the willingness to act justly. Among the requirements here are respect for persons, tolerance, reasonableness, and respect for public reason. Tolerance involves the obligation to respect the choices and the equal right of others to hold and to pursue their own conception of their good. Reasonableness has to do with the willingness to "propose principles and standards as fair terms of cooperation and to abide by them willingly, given assurance that others will likewise do so" (Rawls, 1993, p. 49). Reciprocity is thus central to reasonableness. Respect for public reason has to do with the willingness and capacity to discuss cooperative relationships with others by appealing to reasons that are shared and that characterize the basic commitments of a constitutional regime.

Because this perspective has been central in the deliberations of philosophers since the publication of Rawls's *Theory of Justice* (1971), it has received an immense amount of quite varied criticism. Because, to a considerable extent, this criticism has also been formative in the development of the alternative views that follow, no critique of deontological liberalism is developed at this point. However, it may be useful to note one development in the recent work of Rawls. His *Theory of Justice* (1971) is an attempt to develop the implications of a Kantian position in ethics for political philosophy. In his latter work (1985, 1987, 1993), Rawls has rejected this view in favor of one that sees liberalism as a political theory that is "free floating," in that it is not seen as the political application of any more comprehensive moral or philosophical theory. Rather, it is an "overlapping consensus" that can be held by people who ascribe to diverse comprehensive doctrines or worldviews.

Rawls's motivation for this position is the recognition that political liberalism cannot simultaneously represent itself as tolerant of a diverse range of moral outlooks and see itself as the political application of one of them. Regarding liberalism as free floating significantly reduces this tension.

Although this reinterpretation of liberalism may seem a technical matter largely of interest to philosophers, in fact, it is of the greatest importance. Some of the criticisms of liberalism carry far more force as criticism of liberalism seen as the political expression of a neo-Kantian moral theory. They carry less force against Rawls's more recent interpretation. The virtue of this is that it permits not only a defense of liberalism against its critics but also a form of liberalism that can incorporate many of the valuable insights of this criticism.

The idea that liberalism is a free-floating, overlapping consensus is also important in another context. In our society, many educators and their students consider religion to be central to their moral lives. Most religious people freely accept the religious pluralism of our society, but they are unlikely to freely accept a secular conception of justice if that secular conception is rooted in a religiously antagonistic philosophy.

Here we should remind ourselves that the theories we have thus far reviewed were often seen by those who developed them as replacements for the failed religions of the West or as putting ethics on a rational (as opposed to religious) basis. Orthodox believers cannot consistently be utilitarians or Kantians. They will rightly experience a state or a school grounded in one of these perspectives to be alien, and they will inevitably be second-class citizens in it. (This is the kernel of truth in the claim that schools promote a religion of secular humanism.)

By developing a conception of justice that is free floating, Rawls avoids creating such tensions of conscience. The view of public reason embedded in justice as fairness is thus more likely to be accepted and practiced by all equally in our society, despite deep philosophical and religious differences. The language of the public ethic can be viewed as a kind of moral pidgin (Stout, 1988)—a moral language crafted especially to permit communication and cooperation between people who disagree about fundamentals.

Communitarianism Communitarians have argued that deontological liberalism fails to recognize the importance of community in people's lives (MacIntyre, 1981; Sandel, 1982). People are not, as liberalism might seem to represent them, self-creating rational agents. They are socially constituted (Taylor, 1992) beings who understand their lives and their moral obligations as members of particular communities. These socially embedded selves make decisions and moral judgments in a way that takes their particular context and their community associations seriously. Their lives have a narrative structure. They are born into certain relationships that give structure to their decision making. In MacIntyre's (1981) words:

we all approach our own circumstances as bearers of a particular social identity. I am someone's son or daughter, someone else's cousin or uncle; I am a citizen of this or that city; I belong to this clan, that tribe, this nation. Hence what is good for me has to be the good for one who inhabits these roles. As such, I inherit from the past of my family, my city, my tribe, my nation, a variety of debts, inheritances, rightful expectation and obligations. These constitute the given of my life, my moral starting point. This is in part what gives my life its own moral particularity. (p. 205)

There are some virtues that might be held to be central to any communitarian outlook. Loyalty is perhaps one (Bull et al., 1992). However, generally, for communitarians, the virtues and capacities required can only be addressed within a particular form of community. The moral particularism that communitarians wish to substitute for liberal universalism precludes generalization. However, there are two important moral conceptions that have special saliency for educators that can be developed from a communitarianism perspective. These are trust and integrity. These, as well as the broader educational force of communitarianism, can be developed by considering a communitarian critique of a liberal conception of schooling.

Liberals are inclined to give considerable weight to the right of children to choose their own conception of their own good. Liberals, however, have also recognized that there are prerequi-

sites to competent choice. Bruce Ackerman (1980), for example, claims:

Indeed, many school buildings are nothing more than an extension of the child's primary culture, with "educators" interested only in weeding and pruning youngsters so that they will better accord to the parental design. In contrast, a liberal school has a different mission: to provide the child with access to the wide range of cultural materials that he may find useful in developing his own moral ideals and patterns of life. (pp. 155–156)

This freedom to choose that children possess is constrained by the requirement that they require a certain degree of "cultural coherence" (Ackerman, 1980, p. 141) if they are to develop into competent citizens. This gives parents some right to direct the education of young children.

Schools thus become "liberal cafeterias" offering students a free choice between the widest feasible range of educational goods. The range of choices available can be constrained by liberal principles of justice and, one assumes, practical and logistical considerations. The student's freedom of choice is constrained only by the vague, but clearly minimal, criterion of cultural coherence.

Communitarians should find this picture of choice untenable in that it ignores the extent to which the capacity for reasonable choice is formed by how children are socially constituted. This can be shown by looking at some ideas of Alastair MacIntyre. Among the objects of educational choice are the kinds of things that MacIntyre (1981) calls practices. He describes practices as

any coherent and complex form of socially established cooperative human activity through which goods internal to that form of activity are realized in the course of trying to achieve those standards of excellence which are appropriate to, and partially definitive of, that form of activity, with the result that human powers to achieve excellence, and human conceptions of the ends and goods involved, are systematically extended. (p. 175)

Consider now three claims about practices:

1. The goods internal to most complex human activities are not transparent to the uninitiated. This is so for such reasons as that learning a practice involves acquiring a new vocabulary for describing it; learning and internalizing the standards of appraisal appropriate to it; and experiencing what it is like to be a competent practitioner. Ex hypothesi none of these are fully available to the uninitiated.
2. The criteria of choice available to the uninitiated will be transformed by the process of initiation. Practices are not merely means to ends. People will be transformed by their initiation into a practice such that their ends are changed and transformed.
3. Criteria of choice between practices are embedded in: (a) the communities formed by complex human practices; and (b) the sundry moral traditions that live in different human communities.

If these claims are true, they bring Ackerman's views about choice in the liberal cafeteria of educational goods into considerable doubt. They suggest that students who enter the liberal cafeteria armed only with cultural coherence are, in fact, likely to be choosing largely on the basis of untutored desire.

A coherent view of educational choice cannot view relatively unformed children as autonomous agents picking among a selection of educational goods whose character is transparent to them. People who pursue a given practice or who are members of a given community often discover, not choose, their ends. Children can only become choosers by undergoing a dialogical process of initiation and by being embedded in some particular ethical/social environment. Children cannot be seen as motivated in this process solely by reasoned convictions that their educational activities are means to goals they currently have and interests they currently understand. Trust and bonding to the adult members of communities must play a part.

This argument suggests two things:

1. If students are to be motivated to learn what schools wish to teach, especially when what is being taught is not fully transparent to the students, they will need to be moved by confidence that the practices that the adults represent and try to communicate to them will form part of the conceptions of good lives that students will eventually experience as worthwhile. Identification with and trust of the adults are likely important to mediating this connection between students and practices.
2. This kind of trust and bonding might have three conditions:
   a. The student must feel sufficient "kinship" with the teacher for this bond to form. Seeing the teacher as in some way a member of the student's community is, no doubt, often helpful, as is a recognition by the teacher of the worth of the student's culture (see Taylor, 1992).
   b. The student must believe that the teacher is providing a faithful representation of the practice being taught. It follows that teachers must represent their subject matters with integrity to their students.
   c. Students must believe that the teacher cares for them.

The first of these conditions suggests the importance of a faculty as diverse as the students who are taught and the importance of allowing the processes of group affiliation to take place in school. The second and third suggest that integrity with respect to one's subject and caring are virtues that are central to successful teaching and thus central to the professional ethics of teachers. Integrity with respect to one's subject consists of respect for its truths, methods, and standards of judgment, and its values. Caring (as we see later) requires not only a proper concern for the welfare of one's students but also the capacity to express this in one's relations to them.

An Ethic of Care Several feminist scholars (Gilligan, 1982; Noddings, 1984, 1993) have developed a critique of liberal theories of justice that suggests that justice reasoning expresses a masculine voice and that it is an inadequate account of the ethical experience of women. In the case of Gilligan and, to a lesser extent, of Noddings, the critique is focused on the work in moral development of Lawrence Kohlberg.

Noddings (1993) summarizes the feminist critique of the tradition as follows:

Feminists . . . argue that such an ethical tradition strips human life of its humanity—its personal attachments, projects, and sense of community. Contemporary liberal theories of justice . . . call upon us to do what is "right" without regard to any particular person's whole situation . . . these ethics prepare us to deal with a "generalized" other but not with the particular, concrete others we meet in real life. (p. 44)

Noddings (1993) also provides a summary of recent analyses of caring:

1. *Caring* is used to describe both a relation that has certain characteristics and the behavior, thinking, and attitude of the carer in the relation. In the former use, it is necessary to discuss the contribution of the recipient of care (or cared-for) and the condition in which the relation is embedded.
2. A carer attends to the cared-for in a special act of receptivity (nonselective attention or engrossment). In this act, a carer hears, sees, and feels what is in the other.
3. A carer is disposed to help—often with direct involvement in the other's project, but sometimes with advice or even admonition. The carer's thinking and action are often guided by interests in the preservation, growth, and acceptability of those cared for (Mayeroff, 1971; Ruddick, 1980). Carers want to preserve the lives and well-being of cared-fors; promote their growth; and support them in acceptable behavior (all of these concepts require separate analyses, for which see Mayeroff, 1971; Noddings, 1992; Ruddick, 1980, 1989).
4. Carers are guided by a thoroughgoing consideration of care; that is, attention and the desire to help are directed not only at the particular cared-for but also outward across the entire web of relations. This is necessary because the well-being of both carers and cared-fors depends on the health of their relationships.
5. The contribution of the cared-for is vital to the relation; not only does the response of the cared-for sustain carers in their efforts but also it is the essential material by which carers monitor the quality and effects of their caring, in continuous cycles of attention and response.
6. Carers, because they care, strive for competence in whatever reactions or arenas their efforts are applied (Noddings, 1993).

In considering these views, two points shall be noted. The first relates to moral pluralism. From the perspective of moral pluralism, there is no reason to see an ethic of care as a competitor to an ethic of justice. There are no doubt instances where caring and justice compete for centrality in dealing with a specific set of circumstances. Grading is one of them (Noddings, 1984). Sorting out such cases requires judgment and wisdom, additional virtues important to teaching in a world of moral ambiguity (Bricker, 1993). However, such turf disputes do not require us to view justice and caring as competitors at the theoretical level where they are represented as comprehensive moral theories to be chosen between. Posing ethical issues in this way misrepresents the plurality of the ethical life.

Second, the position that Rawls has taken in his recent work is quite important to this understanding of the relationship between justice and caring. If justice is merely the political application of Kantian ethics and if one sees this ethic as making claims to moral sufficiency, then justice and caring are competitors. That the early work of Kohlberg (1981) seemed to take this stance does much to account for the fact that some of his feminist critics saw their views as alternatives. If, however, justice is a political view that is "free floating," the need to see justice and caring as competitors is much reduced.

Democractic Theory and Discourse Ethics Amy Gutmann (1987), in *Democratic Education* (see also Gutmann, 1993), has presented an important statement of a democratic view of education. Her view emphasizes what she calls conscious social reproduction. The basic idea of conscious social reproduction is that education should pursue goals that are chosen by means of democractic discussion. A democratic society is thus distinguishable from a communitarian society in which the central goals of education might be thought to be those ends that are constitutive of the community, but also from a liberal society where ends are largely individually self-chosen. A democratic society has no given ends; however, ends may be collectively chosen so long as they are democratically chosen.

A democratic society, however, does have certain features that are not open to democratic decision making because these features are necessary for the society to be democratic. First, whatever else the educational ends of the schools of a democratic society might be, they must include the development of what Gutmann calls democratic character. Democratic character consists in those capacities and dispositions that are necessary to enable a person to be a successful participant in the deliberations of a democratic society (for discussion, see Galston, 1991; Gross, 1992; and Kymlicka & Norman, 1994). Surprisingly, given that democratic character is the sine qua non of democratic education, Gutmann fails to provide a sustained characterization of it. Nevertheless, it involves such aspects as tolerance and openness to argument. It also involves the ability to employ reasons of a public sort—the sort that can be expressed within a secular and scientific language that Gutmann regards as the common language of a democratic society. Arguably (although Gutmann does not say so), democratic character might also involve a virtue that could be called consensuality. If a democratic education is to pursue democratically chosen goals, such a society is likely to be successful only if people are willing not only to accede to a democratic decision but also to allow a developing consensus to be a factor in their own goal formation. Groups that wish to pursue collectively chosen goals are likely to be more successful if their members find that a developing consensus provides at least a reason, if not a sufficient reason, why they should want what they perceive others are coming to want.

Second, democratic education must be conducted in ways that are consistent with those processes that govern democratic deliberations. Gutmann describes two principles that she names the *principle of nonrepression* and the *principle of nondiscrimination*. Essentially the principle of nonrepression forbids the exclusion of relevant ideas from democratic deliberations. The principle of nondiscrimination prevents the exclusion of competent speakers.

Thus, Gutmann's view of democratic education might be put as follows: The goals of the educational system of a democratic society are (1) the development of democratic character, and (2) such other goals as may be chosen by a process of demo-

cratic deliberation, provided that the principles of nonrepression and nondiscrimination are respected.

Gutmann's views can be distinguished from a more liberal outlook in several ways. First, there is more emphasis on collective decision making. Educational goals that liberals wish to leave to individual choice are likely to be treated by Gutmann as objects of collective decisions.

Second, Gutmann's views placed more emphasis on the capacities to participate in democratic processes of collective choice and less on the individual development of a rational life plan. Thus democratic character becomes central.

Finally, various liberal rights such as free speech or equal opportunity are reconceptualized by Gutmann not as means to ensure fairness in the pursuit of one's chosen view of a good life but as means to preserve the open and nondiscriminatory character of democratic deliberations.

Jürgen Habermas (1973, 1984, 1990) has developed a view of ethics that has some significant similarities to Gutmann's views. Habermas emphasizes the question of the legitimation of social norms. According to Habermas, norms are legitimated when they are (or could have been) a product of consensus in what he terms an "ideal speech community." An ideal speech community is one in which no relevant idea or argument is excluded and where no competent speaker is excluded.

Among the virtues of Habermas's view is that it resolves several tensions that have been implicit in other social philosophies. When a decision is legitimated as the result of the deliberations of an ideal speech community, social direction is achieved without the need of coercion. Habermas characterizes the processes of rational deliberation as a process of will formation. When consensus is achieved, no one is coerced, because everyone is doing what he or she wants. Similarly, decisions are legitimated both because they are reasonable and because they are freely chosen. Thus, for Habermas it is essential that people be able to participate in forms of communication that are not distorted by ideology and that are open and undominated. Virtues such as tolerance and the willingness to listen and to be persuaded would seem crucial.

Thus the views of both Gutmann and Habermas make the processes of communication and deliberation crucial, and both regard their openness to argument and their inclusion of competent speakers as the crucial features of communication. Their views make dialog central to educative communities and a pedagogy to which dialog is central and an essential part of teaching in such a community (Burbules, 1993).

Postmodernism Postmodernism might best be seen as the heir to the critical tradition that can be traced to Marx. It retains Marx's Hegelian historicization of rationality and Marxism's suspicion that views are often ideological, expressions more of the will to power than of reason, and that we thus need to critique them to discover what interests they privilege. Postmodernism, however, has abandoned the Marxist commitment to economic determinism and declines to see all injustice as an expression of class struggle. Indeed, it tends to be highly suspicious of all global visions of society referring to them as "grand Metanarratives" and "totalizing discourses" (Lyotard, 1984).

Lyotard (1984) defines postmodernism as follows:

I define postmodernism as incredulity toward metanarratives. This incredulity is undoubtedly a product of progress in the sciences . . . the society of the future falls less within the province of a Newtonian anthropology (such as structuralism or systems theory) than a pragmatics of language particulars. (p. 10)

Thus postmodern criticism tends to emphasize "difference" (Ellsworth, 1989) and to disavow attempts at grand theory as both unjustified and oppressive.

Burbules (1993) describes three central commitments of postmodernism:

First, is the centrality of an analysis of power and hierarchy as the basic dynamic of social and political organization . . . [second] is an emphasis on the irreducible plurality of cultural world views . . . [third is] the assault on what is often termed "the logic of identity"—the philosophical view that our intellectual aim is to find common underlying principles, generalizable rules, universal definitions as the sign of theoretical coherence and credibility. (pp. 2–3)

Burbules and Rice (1991) suggest that the value of postmodernism is that it challenges teachers "to consider the political consequences of the vocabulary, structures of argument, and substantive conclusions of his or her teaching and writing" and "to consider also the ways in which their statements and actions exist within a system of power and privilege" (p. 396).

At the same time Postmodernism may have two related defects. The first is its potential to have a corrosive and fragmenting effect on the ideals of public life and public reason (Aronowitz & Giroux, 1991; Beyer & Liston, 1992; Tamir, 1993). The second is that postmodernism seems to have the potential to cultivate the vice of cynicism. The point here is not that we should be willing to tolerate a little injustice, oppression, and domination for the sake of social stability but, rather, that the exposure of injustice, oppression, and dominance are valuable in the service of a vision of a just and nonoppressive society. The critique of ideology loses its value when all views are regarded as ideological and no affirmative views can survive critique. Similarly, a critique of reason loses its point if all perspectives are nothing more than expressions of the will to power of their advocates.

Nevertheless, postmodernism has this to contribute to the search for a just and stable multicultural society. The critical skills it can hone are important in avoiding those forms of exclusion and domination that inhere in ideology and language forms. Perhaps more important in the long run is postmodernism's insistence that the variety of moral voices to be heard in modern society are real and are not reducible to some underlying common denominator. Although such a view may pose the question of the basis of social stability in an unusually difficult form, it also should encourage us to learn to hear the nuances of different moral voices and to regard the capacity to do so as essential both to moral sensitivity and to good teaching.

Summary

The discussion of this section suggests the following as appropriate to the content and aspirations of a view of professional ethics for educators.

1. The central concepts of professional ethics for educators are those that form a part of public reason. These concepts are important to the ethics of educational professionals because they play an important role in the production or reproduction of a liberal democratic society.
2. These concepts are associated with certain capacities and virtues. These include the liberal virtues of self-governance and tolerance and the democratic virtues of reasonableness, consensuality, and deliberativeness. They also include the critical capacities required to expose ideology and to sensitize us to excluding and dominating language and behavior.
3. There are additional moral concepts, virtues, and capacities that are important to those who teach but that do not flow from the requirements of public reason or social reproduction. These are trustworthiness and their associated virtues of integrity and caring.
4. A fourth set of virtues are associated with ethical pluralism. Ethical pluralism teaches us that the moral universe is complex. People often must choose under circumstances where there are competing goods and principles and in the absence of any overarching moral theory that orders such tensions and delivers a clear outcome to our deliberations. In such a moral universe, educators need those skills required to balance conflicting goods. They need wisdom and judgment and perhaps, occasionally, courage and a sense of the tragic. And they need a sensitivity to diversity and the capacity to hear the differences in the moral voices around us.

PRACTICES

Given the argument to this point, the consideration of practices that will facilitate ethical competence among educational professionals needs to address three topics. The first is a discussion of classroom practices for teaching ethics; the second is the characteristics of schools as moral communities; and the third is the characteristics of an educational profession that sustains moral competence in such institutions. Because the principal concern here lies with the preparation of teachers and administrators, this section emphasizes the first topic, with only brief treatment of the second and third. What is crucial is the creation of pedagogical practices and institutions that develop competence in moral dialogue and that develop and sustain the virtues required by such dialogue.

To begin the discussion of the educational practices that should constitute the preparation of teachers and administrators, let us investigate a picture that we may have of how ethics connects to good teaching. To do this, consider the following case once used in an article on the ethics of teaching (Strike & Soltis, 1986):

The dismissal bell rang, but Maria Spencer kept the children in their seats. A girl started to sniffle, afraid she would miss her bus. Miss Spencer, a third grade teacher for six years, had never been so frustrated by a classroom situation. Someone had stolen Karl's 50-cent piece. It was the third theft this month. This time she was going to find out who did it, even if it took all afternoon and she had to drive the bus children home herself! She even thought she might have to search everyone if the guilty party didn't confess soon. There seemed no other way out. Stealing is wrong and the kids needed to learn that. (p. 38)

This case was provided in an article that had discussed another case that focused on the ethics of group punishment. In both cases, there are certain quasi judicial norms that we thought important to the case. Group punishment, for example, seems to involve the punishment of innocent people. Moreover, the discussion of that case took pains to point out that such issues were involved. In the above case, group punishment might be involved, but another issue concerns the children's privacy and the conditions under which a potentially intrusive search might be warranted.

The authors made no suggestions about how to analyze this case. However, the readers were invited to write in with their own suggestions as to how the case might be handled. A modest number of readers responded. What was noteworthy about these responses, varied as they were, was that the respondents had great difficulty in identifying the moral components of the problem, at least not in the way the authors intended. Each respondent identified some goal to achieve, usually the maintenance of classroom order and the apprehension of the guilty party, and proceeded to discuss strategies to achieve the chosen ends. Moral considerations, when they occurred at all, were introduced only as a belated constraint on means chosen for reasons of efficiency.

This instance suggests two things about teacher reasoning about ethical issues. The first is that teachers are strongly inclined to employ forms of reasoning that are instrumental in character. Even though the collection of these comments and their analysis are hardly scientific, they nevertheless support Goodlad's (1990) contention that "The idea of moral imperatives for teachers was virtually foreign in concept and strange in language for most of the future teachers we interviewed" (p. 264). The second is that these teachers may possess (at some intuitive level) a picture of the relationship between morality and instrumental reasoning that could be characterized as a four-step decision-making process.

1. Select the mix of ends to be accomplished.
2. Identify possible means and order them according to their efficiency in accomplishing this mix of ends.
3. Identify any of these ordered means that are morally objectionable and eliminate them.
4. Act on the most efficient of the remaining options.

The account given in this article of those concepts and virtues that are important for the professional life of educators is inconsistent with this picture. This picture makes morality into something that is external to good educational practice. Good practices are chosen on grounds of efficiency in relation to desired ends. Morality serves only to reject some otherwise efficient means on the grounds that they are morally unacceptable. This account, however, indicates that ethics is internal to what counts as good educational practice. This is the case, first, because the concepts of public reason are constitutive of the form of society where it is the school's responsibility to produce and reproduce and thus, given the principles of fit and isomorphism, to form schools like communities and to the practice of educational professionals. Second, this is the case because trustworthiness, caring, and integrity are internal to good teaching. If so, it follows that ethics is far more central to the education of educa-

tional professionals than current opinion and practice would suggest. Every case of teaching is also an occasion for teaching the public ethic and for practicing the virtue of trustworthiness, care, and integrity.

The key to the transformation of these views into the training of educational professionals is the principle of fit and the principle of isomorphism and the view that communities are constituted, in part, through dialogue.

The principles of fit and isomorphism require that the concepts and virtues sketched earlier are unlikely to be acquired in the robust form required to effect practice unless they are constitutive of practice and community in both schools and in the places where practitioners learn their art. The claim that communities are constituted by dialogue means that students are likely to acquire the concepts and virtues required only in communities wherein these concepts are commonly employed in discussion about practice and in which they are also reflected in the practice of learning. Coherent communities are places wherein people "talk the talk and walk the walk." People learn moral concepts, learn how to attach them to the world, and acquire the virtues required to sustain them in practice by being initiated into the practices of such communities.

Sockett (1993) illustrates what this means. He is showing how a capable teacher employs moral speech in a classroom of young children. But the point is generalizable.

"Mr. Thomas has come to paint the new door this morning," she said in a very quiet voice, "and I think we ought not to go near it until the paint's dry. Can anyone tell me why?"

One or two murmurs and then several hands were raised:

"Because we might get paint on our clothes, miss."

"That's right. Sheila, but does that matter?"

"Because it would look all messy on my skirt, and my mum would have to clean it off."

"Yes," said the teacher, "Sheila's right. Mum will have to clean your clothes if you get paint on them, won't she?"

Various voices added comments on their mothers' washing habits, and one small aspiring painter said, "The painter's clothes get very mucky."

"But they are really overalls," Mrs. Simpson immediately pointed out, "like the overalls you wear when you paint, aren't they, Wayne? Why else do you think we mustn't go near the paint?"

"Because Mrs. Higgins [the school principal] wouldn't like it," said another child.

"Because the door would get all messed up," said Yvonne, a diffident little girl standing near the teacher with her arm cocked around her ear as if to protect herself from the surprise of her interjection.

"Does that matter?" said the teacher, "It's bound to get dirty sometime."

"Oh yes," replied Yvonne, more confident now, "But the painter's work would get all spoilt."

"And Mrs. Higgins wants us to keep the hallway neat and tidy," added Kevin.

"That's right," said Mrs. Simpson, "So we want to keep clear of the door today, don't we? Or we'll get paint on our clothes and Mum will have to wash them, the painter's work will be spoilt, and the hallway will look untidy and spoilt so we won't enjoy it as much. Do you understand that, Paul? Is that right, Lesley? Does anybody not understand that?" A general murmur of acknowledgment. "Thank you, Miss Johnson," she ended as she slipped out into the corridor, leaving the space for blue lions and red Androcleses to make their way from the children's imaginations onto paper. (Sockett, 1993, pp. 2–3)

The most obvious point to make here is that moral speech is acquired in use rather than by definition and precept. No one says "Here is what respect for persons means and here are the duties that follow." No rules, moral lectures, or pieties are uttered. Children are instead taught to use the words in the context of discussing a case that they illuminate and where they are given reasons for appropriate conduct. This has three virtues. The first is that the language is firmly attached to practice. Respect for persons is not given as an empty abstraction. It has concrete attachment to something that counts as a case of respect. Children are taught concretely that mum, Mrs. Higgins, and the attractiveness of the physical environment their community occupies count as moral reasons. Second, moral speech is used in a way that evokes and expands the moral sentiments, feelings, and emotions that are appropriately felt and that are required to sustain moral practice. Children learn not only desirable moral speech but also how they are to feel and act. Respect for persons is sustained by being able to put ourselves in the other's position and to feel as the other might feel. Children engaged in this form of dialog are thus shaped in a far stronger way than is suggested by the notion that they are learning moral speech. They are rather learning moral practice for which a certain form of speech is required. Third, children are forming expectations and skills required to constitute and sustain a form of community.

This discussion suggests criteria that can be used to judge and attempt to teach ethics:

1. A set of concepts appropriate to the practice they govern must be taught.
2. If students are to learn these concepts as a language and thus be able to employ them in their analyses of moral situations, then the concepts must be taught in a way that attaches them to the world.
3. If students are to have their character formed in ways that sustain the employment of competent moral speech in practice, then moral speech must be reasonably pervasive in their lives, and it must be taught in a way that evokes and deepens the habits and moral sentiments that sustain moral behavior.
4. Contexts for learning moral speech should develop skills and expectations suitable to a dialogical and educative form of community.

The teacher must possess a set of virtues if this lesson is to succeed. Children must trust the teacher, and they must see the teacher's moral practice as something to be emulated. The bond between teacher and student must be such that the fact that the teacher behaves, talks, and feels in a certain way is taken by the children as a reason why they should behave, talk, and feel in the same way. To earn this trust, the teacher must be trustworthy and caring. The teacher must be someone with whom the children can bond. These features seem equally apt for the university classroom.

However, these features seem progressively difficult to achieve in the context of the in-service training of educational professionals. The first merely requires that a suitable inventory of moral concepts be identified and that they be taught. The second requires some connection between the language and the world, but it might be accomplished in the classroom by the use of cases. The last two require that both in-service training and schools have social forms that encourage moral language in practice and the commitment of instructors both to their students and to building a form of community. The fragmentation of the curriculum in training programs, the predominance of instrumental language in professional training, and the fact that most moral learning does not occur in classrooms are not encouraging here, although if moral conceptions were as pervasive in the speech of education classes as concern for efficiency and profit are in business classes, one supposes that much progress could be made.

Similarly, schools are not currently operated in ways that encourage moral dialogue (Burbules, 1993). Teachers are still relatively isolated in their practice (Jackson, 1968) such that they are unlikely to have much opportunity for sustained discussions about their practice with other teachers, let alone parents, students, or administrators. Moral discussions seem most likely when teachers are being called on the carpet by an administrator for some alleged indiscretion. Authority is hierarchical, not dialogical.

Although this author is not particularly optimistic that a more sustained attempt to include ethics in the preparation of practitioners is likely to be greatly successful, he does believe that there are things worth doing and trying and that there are things that ought not to be done. Let us look at these under two headings. First, look at some seriously flawed approaches for dealing with ethics in educational contexts. Second, let us discuss the use of ethics cases in teaching ethics. Third, let us review some proposals for institutionalizing ethical decision making in schools.

Classroom Approaches to Ethics

Two approaches have been developed for discussing ethical issues in public schools. These are values clarification and the practices that flow from the theories of moral development of Lawrence Kohlberg. These enterprises might be easily adapted as ways of introducing ethical issues to prospective teachers and administrators. They ought not to be.

Values Clarification Values clarification (Raths et al., 1966) provides a variety of simple techniques to enable people to discover or clarify their values. Its chief foils are imposed values and indoctrination. Almost any source of socialization is viewed as a kind of imposition. A central value of values clarification is authenticity. Values clarification assumes that what legitimates the holding of a given value is that it has been freely chosen and/or it represents the individual's true feelings about something. Its techniques often seem to suppose that in some way people "really know" what their values are but that they may be confused about them, perhaps because they have been indoctrinated by others into other, unauthentic values. If values are discovered, they are discovered within and not, say, as the result of action or experimentation, in literature or philosophical reflection.

Values clarification has several deficiencies. One is the paucity of its vocabulary (Strike, 1993a). For example, some philosophers have found it important to distinguish between the right and the good. Questions about the good have to do with the nature of worthwhile activities, objects, and, indeed, lives. Questions about the right have to do with the nature of our moral duties and obligations—with the kinds of actions that are right or wrong.

One aspect of the distinction between the right and the good is that it seems intuitively more reasonable to hold that people may freely choose their goods than it does to hold that they may freely choose their moral principles. There seems little of social interest at stake in whether one values pickles over olives. However, there is considerable social interest involved in whether people prefer dishonesty or murder. Moral principles differ from claims about the good in that the former seem more appropriately obligatory and enforceable. If my neighbor is not freely committed to the proposition that it is wrong to steal, it is nevertheless true that I have a right to expect that my neighbor not steal my property.

Values clarification fails to distinguish between the right and the good, treating both as just values. As a result, it often ends up treating moral principles as though they were goods and both as though they were a matter of taste or personal preference.

Consider the following conversation from Raths et al. (1966) between a student and a teacher:

Ginger: Does that mean we can decide for ourselves whether we should be honest on tests here?
   Teacher: No, that means that you can decide on the value. I personally value honesty, and although you may choose to be dishonest, I shall insist that we be honest on tests here. . . .
   Ginger: But then how can we decide for ourselves? Aren't you telling us what to value? . . .
   Teacher: Not exactly. I didn't mean to tell you what you should value. That's up to you. . . . All of you who choose dishonesty as a value may not practice it here, that's all I'm saying. (pp. 114–115)

Values clarification has left this teacher in an untenable position. Because he has insisted that values are up to the students, he cannot consistently hold that there are reasons why Ginger should value honesty or that Ginger is morally obligated to be honest, however she feels. He must simply claim that honesty is his value and that, because he is in power, Ginger is compelled to comply. In short, he has moved in a few sentences from moral skepticism to moral fascism. Values clarification makes all moral principles into values and values into matters of personal preference. Having done so, the enforcement of any value can only be an act of arbitrary will.

Values clarification thus has at least the following difficulties as a program in ethics for professional educators.

1. Its reduction of our moral vocabulary to talk about values leaves us with a moral vocabulary that is insufficient to sustain serious moral deliberation.
2. Its relativism and individualism make it difficult to approach ethical issues with the conviction that some ethical commitments are important and obligatory because they are right or because they sustain desirable forms of community. If one thinks of moral dialog as a process whereby ethical norms are proposed and validated through argument, then

the relativism and individualism of values clarification are antidialogical.
3. Its tendency to see authentic values as discovered by introspection may undermine "external" sources of ethical content including discussion, philosophy, literature, and religion (for further discussion of values clarification, see Lockwood, 1976, 1978; and Sockett, 1992).

Kohlberg Lawrence Kohlberg has developed another view of moral education that has been widely used in schools. Kohlberg's views are rooted, on one hand, in a developmental psychology that owes much to Jean Piaget (1965) and, on the other, in a view of ethics that owes much to Kant and to the philosophers Rawls and Jürgen Habermas. According to Kohlberg (1981), growth in moral judgment is characterized by a progression through a sequence of moral stages. Each stage can be characterized as a particular set of criteria or standards according to which moral judgments are made. These stages are progressively more mature in their moral content. Higher is better.

While people go through these stages in an invariant sequence, it is by no means inevitable that people will progress through them at any particular rate or that they will ever reach the higher stages. Generally, Kohlberg holds that there are six stages but that most people do not get above the third or fourth.

The task of moral education is conceived as moving individuals to higher stages. Because the "engine" of moral development is cognitive conflict, one way this can be accomplished is by means of moral dilemmas. These are "hard cases" that cannot be adequately dealt with at the current stage of development. In Piagetian language, the student cannot assimilate the problem in his or her current moral schema. If the dilemma is to be resolved, he or she must move to a higher stage.

Kohlberg (1971) describes stage six, the highest of his moral stages, as follows:

The universal ethical principle orientation. Right is defined by the decision of conscience in accord with self-chosen *ethical principles* appealing to logical comprehensiveness, universality, and consistency. These principles are abstract and ethical (the Golden Rule, the categorical imperative); they are not concrete moral rules like the Ten Commandments. At heart, these are universal principles of *justice,* of the *reciprocity* and *equality* of human *rights,* and of respect for the dignity of human beings as *individual persons.* (p. 165) (emphasis original)

Among the reservations one might have about Kohlberg's views are these: First, it is overly cognitive in its view of ethics. It seems to have little place for the virtues or moral sentiments. Second, Kohlberg tends to see justice as the central moral concept from which all others derive. His views are thus inconsistent with moral pluralism, and they serve to unreasonably narrow the range of moral concepts that are important to a full human life. Educationally, this philosophical narrowness may lead to a curriculum that fails to see such things as literature and stories (Coles, 1989) as important to moral education. It is unlikely to be adequately sensitive to the educative features of the kind of moral discussion exhibited by Sockett's teacher since cognitive conflict seems absent from it.

Even if Kohlberg's views on moral development are largely correct, they do not provide an adequate basis for teaching teachers about ethics. The problem is that the emphasis is on the development of abstract principles of moral reasoning instead of instruction in the more concrete ethical principles that should inform the daily activities of the practicing teacher. Perhaps it is desirable that teachers acquire sophisticated and abstract principles of moral reasoning in terms of which concrete principles that should guide their professional conduct seem reasonable. But a teacher who has a good grasp of abstract moral principles may nevertheless lack an adequate grasp of specific moral concepts, such as due process. Moreover, teachers who have not achieved the highest level of moral reasoning (which will be most of them) nevertheless must inform their conduct by reasonable moral rules.

The point may be put more generally. Even should growth in sophistication in abstract moral reasoning be a good thing, it should not be assumed to be sufficient to promote the capacity for moral reflection. This requires, in addition, a store of more specific moral principles that deal more concretely with various kinds of human activities. Such principles do not come automatically with respect for persons or with the categorical imperative. They must be specifically acquired, and people must learn how to apply them to concrete situations. However, Schrader (1993) suggests that Kohlberg was aware of this limitation and believes that it was addressed in his "just schools" proposals (Kohlberg, 1985), which seem to be more full-blooded moral communities.

To put the point in one more way, it is unclear to what extent professional ethics should be viewed as a matter of moral development (in the sense of advancing through stages) and undesirable to treat it entirely as a matter of development. This chapter has argued that what educators principally need is a set of concrete moral concepts (the public ethic) and a set of virtues, such as reasonableness, required to sustain them in practice. Perhaps there are developmental prerequisites for the public ethic. If so, then professional ethics cannot entirely ignore moral development. Even here, however, the antipathy of Kohlbergians to any notion of the virtues and the overly cognitive picture of moral growth of a Kohlbergian orientation to professional ethics makes this approach, at best, insufficient.

We should not ignore some of the strengths of Kohlberg's approach. Its concern for justice is commendable even if overly abstract. Moreover, the emphasis on discussion of cases is likely to involve dialog of the sort that is essential to moral learning, even if the theoretical point of such dialog is overly concerned for cognitive conflict. However, moral development, as Kohlberg understands it, should not be the central emphasis (Strike, 1990c) in teaching professional ethics.

The Role of Philosophy in Teaching Ethics Values clarification and Kohlbergian approaches can be used to illustrate a different point. Their views on teaching ethics seem to devolve from a deep philosophical justification of practice.

A "deep philosophical justification of practice" means that practice is viewed as justified in the context of a comprehensive ethical theory that takes a broad view of life and ethics and that is, therefore, likely to be highly controversial and unlikely to be widely shared. Suggesting that values clarification and Kohlbergian views assume a deep philosophical justification, does not mean to imply that they are philosophically articulate

or sophisticated. Although this is generally true of Kohlberg's views, values clarification is embarrassingly philosophically uninformed. But the important point here is that the practices recommended by both approaches are rooted in broad and general philosophical doctrines. Values clarification might be seen as a form of hedonism that has been influenced by existentialism and client-centered therapy. It exhibits a commitment to the centrality of personal satisfaction and authenticity in life. These commitments are sharply inconsistent, for example, with traditional religion or with Kantian forms of ethics. Kohlberg, in contrast, is committed to a form of Kantianism.

Following Rawls (1993), it can be argued that no perspective that is the expression of a "comprehensive doctrine" can achieve the status of an overlapping consensus and thus of a public ethic. Insofar as both values clarification and Kohlberg's views are expressions of comprehensive doctrines, they are unsatisfactory as the ethics for those who are to work in public institutions.

This argument, together with the discussion of Sockett's teacher, supports additional reasons for emphasizing the concrete principles of the public ethic in teaching professional ethics to educators, and they suggest a limited role for academic philosophy in professional ethics. Comprehensive philosophical doctrines such as utilitarianism or Kantianism are not required to justify the lower order principles of the public ethic such as, for example, the importance of due process in grading or personnel decisions. Indeed, part of the justification of such comprehensive theories is their ability to account for our considered moral intuitions in these more concrete cases. Nor are abstract philosophical doctrines known for their power to motivate to good behavior (for further discussion, see Bull, 1990; and Howe, 1986).

Instruction in ethics that emphasizes concrete principles applied in real life contexts is thus not essentially or necessarily a philosophical activity if by this one means an attempt to justify such principles by showing them to be instances of some background philosophical doctrines.

There may be a limited point to such philosophical reflection in professional ethics. Sometimes it is helpful in deepening our understanding of what is at stake in a concrete principle to try to see it as an expression of the average utility or of respect for persons. Philosophy, perhaps, can shed light at the margins of interpretation or on hard cases. The emphasis in teaching professional ethics, however, should be on developing a more concrete shared vocabulary. Philosophy is only of modest value here.

These comments may be bad news for unemployed philosophers, but they imply two benefits for teaching professional ethics. First, they reduce its elitism by emphasizing concepts that are widely shared and not the distinct province of philosophers or any other professional guild. Second, they permit ethics to be taught throughout the preservice curriculum. Ethics need not be confined to the philosophy class.

A Case-Oriented Approach

Strike and Soltis (1992) have developed an approach to teaching ethics to educational professionals that involves the following assumptions (for discussion, see Sykes & Bird, 1992).

1. The emphasis on teaching ethics is dialogical competence in the public language. The principal assumptions of this emphasis are:
   a. That the public moral language is central to if not sufficient for the moral lives of educational professionals in their practice.
   b. That the public moral language provides the unity among difference required for a society that wishes to be just and also to respect pluralism.
   c. That the emphasis in instruction should be on facility with this language requiring that teachers be able to "see" cases as instances falling under these concepts and that they be able to employ them competently with others to achieve satisfactory resolution of issues.
2. Instruction involves discussion of cases in conjunction with a textual discussion of a range of moral concepts that is intended: (a) to teach the content of concepts such as due process or equality of opportunity, and (b) to show how these concepts can be represented in the contexts of utilitarianism and deontological liberalism. The assumptions behind the use of cases are:
   a. That moral language is acquired in use, and that well-crafted cases can, to some degree, provide a classroom substitute for the real world.
   b. That discussion serves not only to teach specific moral concepts, but also to evoke the feelings appropriate to them, to develop the skills and virtues of a dialogical approach to ethical issues, and to begin the process of community formation (for discussion about the use of cases in teaching ethics, see Strike, 1993d; and Bull et al., 1992).
   c. That although philosophical ethics is not central in teaching professional ethics, philosophical theories can illuminate case analysis at the margins of interpretation or in hard cases.

A number of concerns and issues might be raised about the uses of cases. Consider one. In a pluralistic society, it is important to take an approach to instruction in ethics that has adequate substance to be useful, but that is not partisan. Given the rise of religious fundamentalism and the suspicion that public education is a bastion of secular humanism, it is especially important that instruction be religiously neutral and that people of diverse creeds be able to participate.

No approach easily triumphs over intolerance and dogmatism (for discussion, see Ternasky, 1993). However, let us resist the assumption that those who are strongly religiously motivated must be intolerant for that reason or that nonreligious people cannot be intolerant for reasons of their own. Moreover, the prevalence in school programs of values clarification with its relativism and its emphasis on authenticity and personal satisfaction—values that the religious rightfully find offensive when taught to their children by agents of government (see Strike, 1990a)—has done much to enhance suspicion of public efforts in moral education.

An approach that emphasizes developing dialogical competence in the public language through cases can help here for several reasons. First, teachers need not be seen as advancing a particular view. Indeed, promoting a view is often inconsistent with the openness to argument required. Second, the concepts that are central to the public ethic have been crafted in the context of a constitutional regime that has taken religious neutrality seriously. A good argument can be made that they are religiously neutral. Finally, a case approach can help to develop virtues of listening, understanding, reasonableness, and tolerance (see also Berkowitz, 1985).

Strike and Ternasky (1993) summarize six recommendations that have been offered by the contributors to their volume concerning classroom dialog (also see Bull, 1993, on the effective use of cases). These are:

1. Establish the ground rules for dialog before the conversation begins.
2. Maintain an open exchange that is not dominated by any person or group. As Ternasky suggested, although dialog permits conflict and may lead to the conclusion that someone is actually wrong, this can justifiably occur only if these criteria are satisfied.
3. Hold adamant conviction in suspense. This does not imply that persons should avoid nonnegotiable topics or seek Strike's "liberal silence." It does assert, however, that if one enters into a conversation convinced that everyone else is dreadfully wrong, and one is further prepared to inform the infidels of their error, then we might call the ensuing exchange many things, but not dialog. As Ternasky mentioned, if we are to converse in the public sphere, we must risk having our ideas altered by the thinking and experience of others, and this cannot happen unless we entertain the idea that those with whom we disagree may have something to teach us.
4. Attend to the real-life experience of participants. Hypothetical situations are valuable tools for manipulating ideas, but the resulting insights often transfer poorly to our day-to-day life.
5. Reflect on the ethical principles underlying one's own convictions before rejecting another's position or advancing one's own. In doing so, we can seek to discover both whether our convictions are justified and whether our proposed response sensibly follows from acceptable principles.
6. Anticipate insight from unexpected sources by carefully listening to the contribution of the typically silent member of the group or that of the person not intimately involved in the issue. Also, tap frequently ignored sources: original ideas embedded in, say, religious thought, history, or the literature on culture or gender bias. (p. 228)

Strike and Ternasky (1993) also suggest four crucial beliefs that underlie a dialogical approach to teaching ethics. These are: (1) that moral beliefs are objects of assessment and that such assessment is important; (2) that the central purposes of dialogical instruction are not so much to make students more moral, but to help them to see issues in new ways and to help make their intuitive moral convictions explicit; (3) to help students grasp the range of potentially relevant moral considerations; and (4) to encourage commitment to those moral and political principles that underlie tolerance (pp. 228–229).

This approach cannot be regarded as a fully satisfactory approach to teaching ethics in professional contexts for several reasons. First, it lacks an approach to teaching those virtues that are less strongly linked to the public ethic and to dialogue. It is unlikely to make teachers more trustworthy, caring, or wise. Second, it makes only a modest attempt at community building. An adequate approach here requires change in both schooling and the character of teacher education in the direction of making them more accommodating to moral dialogue. Third, it does not make use of other resources that are important to moral growth. Stories, art, and literature are not there. Hopefully, they will be elsewhere in the student's education. A liberal education has much to contribute to moral sensitivity.

Features of Schooling

Teachers and administrators are not likely to become morally competent people in the ways that have been discussed if schools fail to be places in which the various skills of moral competence are regularly employed and count for something. In short, the practices of schools must be appropriate to a "discourse ethics," and the structural features of schools must be such as to sustain these practices. A useful starting point here is provided by Oser (1991).

Discourse ethics suggests that the procedure of justification of norms and evaluation of claims does not only require the willingness to take the role of each party involved, but also the actual possibility of each party involved to make itself heard. The discourse has to be undertaken in reality, not only in the head of the individual decision maker. One of the implications is that in searching for a consensus the individual actors must presuppose that the others are equally open to practical reason; that they are equally able to decide what course of action is most justified, and to take responsibility for following it through. (p. 201)

Three features implicated in these comments seem important. First, a process of ethical decision making must emphasize achieving consensual acceptable norms through a process of reasoned discussion. Second, there must be real participation in discussion. Reflection cannot be monological, and consensus cannot be hypothetical. Third, discourses must be predicated on the assumptions that they involve reciprocal discussions between free, equal, and rational people.

The tradition of discourse ethics from the perspective of which Oser (1986, 1991) is writing (Benhabib, 1992; Habermas, 1984) provides a normative justification of these requirements. Consensual decisions that are achieved as the result of reasoned discussion between free, equal, and reasonable agents are what count as legitimate decisions. In this context, however, another kind of justification should he noted. This is that decision making of this sort is what is required in order to develop and sustain the competencies, dispositions, and virtues that are central to ethical decision making.

It is especially important here to note that discursive procedures of this sort are inconsistent with organizational structures that emphasize centralized decision making and focus on securing compliance from other members of the organization. That is, the processes of discourse ethics are at odds with bureaucratic and hierarchical decision-making procedures.

At the same time, some qualifications may need to be considered concerning this view. First, we need to note that people in schools are likely to differ quite dramatically in both their competence to engage in discursive decision making and in their willingness to do so. This is relevant both in that it constrains the forms of participation that may be desirable or possible for students and in that it suggests that the educational potential of such participation is an especially important factor to consider. Second, even though schools may be places where students learn to become participants in a democratic society, they are also places that seek to initiate students into various academic subject matters. Students are novices in such matters. Moreover, the authority structure of intellectual disciplines is characteristically and appropriately more expert-dominated than is civil authority (Strike, 1982). This may constrain the appropriateness of participatory roles for students in democratic schools. Finally, the emphasis on consensus achieved in local decision making needs to be accommodated both to the practical difficulties of achieving consensus on matters of importance and to the fact that the larger society outside of the school has a legitimate interest in what goes on in the school, which it often has expressed in law and policy. The vision of a democratic society as one in which decisions are legitimated by consensus achieved in discussion is somewhat in tension with another vision of democratic society that understands political sovereignty as vested in an elected legislature. The key to school governance is to find ways to balance these emphases (Strike, 1993c).

One should not be a purist about the notion of constituting schools as discursive democratic communities. This view does contain insights that need to be respected and balanced against other concerns. The better question is not how schools can be made into discursive communities but how they can be made more like discursive communities than they now are.

There may be structural requirements for such schools. For example, scale may be important. Power (1985, 1993), who works out of a Kohlbergian schools model (Kohlberg, 1985), has suggested that overcoming peer culture and the isolation of students from adults requires smaller schools or small self-contained units within schools (see also Thomas, 1990).

Features of Education as a Profession

The idea that teaching is a profession is ambiguous so far as the argument of this chapter is concerned (for discussion, see Burbules & Densmore, 1991; Kimball, 1988; Macmillan, 1993; Soder, 1990; Strike, 1993c). On one hand, attempts to constitute teaching as a profession are generally allied with the movement to decentralize and localize the authority structure of schooling. This seems all to the good. If schools are to be places that develop and sustain the moral competence of their members, they cannot be overly dominated by external authority. The idea that teachers should participate significantly in governing the work of education is thus a significant step in the direction of dialogical schools and discursive educational practice insofar as it tends to promote meaningful moral dialogue among teachers. Moreover, it is important to distinguish between professionalism and professionalization (Sockett, 1993). The ideas that teachers should behave professionally or that they should meet suitable professional standards seem unexceptionable and should be distinguished from the view that teaching should be organized as a profession.

There are several difficulties with the idea of organizing teaching as a profession in which teachers collectively have significant autonomy over their own work. These stem from the tendency to rest the claim to professional status on the possession of a body of esoteric knowledge and to model a profession of teaching on law and medicine. This tendency raises several concerns.

First, professionalism thus understood may give rise to forms of moral elitism inconsistent with the dialogical emphasis of this chapter. One issue concerns the scope of teachers' authority over their own work. Presumably the work of teaching includes such matters as curriculum development or textbook selection. But on what principles are such decisions to be made? Are they to be made in the light of teachers' conceptions of what constitutes a good education? Will these conceptions of a good education assume views of the nature of a good life? Can they avoid such assumptions? A conception of professionalism that puts teachers in the position of making determinations about the nature of a good life for the rest of us has begun to constitute teachers as philosopher kings and has taken a markedly illiberal and undemocratic turn (for discussion, see Bull, 1990; and Strike, 1993c). Of course teachers who assert the right to be organized as a profession have asserted no claim to the status of philosopher king. Neither have they shown great sensitivity to the potential elitism and illiberality inherent in claiming professional authority over the curriculum.

There is the danger of another form of elitism. Often professionals are people who have clients. Even, as in schools, when the relationship is not precisely one of professional to client, it is nevertheless an unequal relationship. The relationship between professionals and clients is one of inequality in which professionals are entitled to make expert judgments about their clients "treatment" and where clients' rights tend to be limited to the right to choose among professionals and informed consent. For obvious reasons, in public schools, even these "client's" rights are unlikely to have much force. It is unclear that the relationship between teachers and students or teachers and parents is properly represented as analogous to a professional–client relationship. Conceiving the relationship between teacher and student or teacher and parent as analogous to that between professional and client tends to be inconsistent with the dialogical character of schooling and thus with the establishment of the environment in which the virtues required to sustain moral competence are nurtured. The relationship between professionals and clients over professional matters is not dialogical if that means a shared and reasoned discussion among equals.

The issue can be put in a different way. Regardless of whether there is an esoteric body of knowledge about pedagogy that grounds a profession of teaching, it is reasonable to believe that many teachers are in possession of an esoteric body of knowledge in their subject matters. Physics and mathematics are esoteric bodies of knowledge. Thus the relation between teacher and student is often that of expert to novice or of mature to immature. It is a relationship of inequality. At the same time, teachers, administrators, students (at least prospectively), and parents are also citizens of a liberal democracy. In democratic societies this relationship is understood as

one of equality. In schools these different relationships are in tension. Sorting them out and achieving a coherent view of educational authority are no small or trivial tasks (Strike, 1993c). The danger of constituting teaching as a profession is that the status of students and parents as equal citizens will be overly subordinated to an expert novice conception of the relationship.

There is another sort of concern. Because the alleged knowledge base for a profession of teaching is most likely to be thought to be grounded in the behavioral sciences, professionalization of teaching is likely to abet the dominance of technical over moral considerations (for a "technical" account of the knowledge base of teaching, see Wang, Haertel, & Walberg, 1993; and for discussion of its implicit moral assumptions, see Kerdeman & Phillips, 1993).

These considerations raise concerns about the use of codes of ethics in education and the extent to which the self-regulatory character of professions is appropriate for teaching with respect to the enforcement of ethical standards. Most professions have codes of ethics. In many cases these codes are enforceable by some agency of the profession against the profession's members. Sockett (1990, 1993), who argues that an ethics code is a significant factor in developing trust for a profession of education, suggests that a code with sanctions provides the profession with two things:

(1) pressure to adhere to the code as a guide to follow, not as a set of regulations to obey, and (2) confidence that competence, standards, and results can be measured because of the opportunity for the public to seek redress. (p. 239)

Enforcement is of course a significant difficulty. One problem is that codes of ethics for teachers, personified by the NEA code (1992), are quite abstract and general. They are reasonably suited for educational or hortatory functions, but they do not have the precision required for enforcement.

If there is to be any enforcement mechanism concerning ethics, it seems reasonable that this mechanism will have to perform certain quasi-judicial tasks. The basic task to be performed is the development of a body of wisdom and precedent that will be analogous to case law. Case law normally functions to build interpretive bridges between abstract doctrine and concrete cases. It also provides for continuity in decision making both from case to case and between jurisdictions.

Two procedures for dealing with ethical issues at an institutional level can be profitably compared. Florida has created an agency, the Educational Practices Commission (EPC) that is empowered (among other things) to enforce a code of ethics that Macmillan (1993, p. 197) describes as much like the NEA code. This code has the force of law, and the EPC has the power to discipline teachers who violate its provisions.

Betty Sichel (1993) has proposed that schools create school ethics committees that are analogous to the institutional ethics committees that have been established by most health care organizations. These committees might have various functions that include education and consultation in addition to (possible) decision-making authority. Among the advantages of school ethics committees, according to Sichel, are that they are conversational fora that will serve to promote communication and dialogue. Presumably this flows from the fact that they function at the building level and involve discussion among members of the local school community.

The localism of school ethics committees may, however, lead to some weaknesses if they are to serve decision-making or policy-making functions. It would seem undesirable for different schools or different school systems to evolve significantly different enforcement environments about ethics. This is especially problematic if decisions have the force of law. In such a case, consistency between jurisdictions seems a necessary requirement not provided for by school ethics committees.

This is a difficulty that enforcement mechanisms such as Florida's are unlikely to have. However, Florida's mechanism seems likely to remove ethical reflection from the local school community. Moreover, as Macmillan notes, there is some tension between the aspirations of professionalism and the fact that Florida's ethics code and the decisions of the EPC have the force of law. The latter tends to take decision making out of the hands of members of the profession and out of the local school building.

This discussion thus suggests that there is some tension between the need to constitute schools as dialogical communities and the need for consistency in decision making between various jurisdictions. Similarly there is tension between the elitism of professionalism and the aspiration to have ethical decision making "owned" by the entire school community.

It is at least possible to imagine institutions that combine the localism of wide participation in school ethics committees with the enforcement coherence of Florida's system. In such a system moral deliberations would principally occur at the building level, and more central decision-making bodies would serve a review function. However, if such a function is not to rob locals of the possibility of meaningful moral dialogue, considerable weight must be attached to locally achieved decisions.

Given this, the relationships between professionalism, professional codes of ethics, and the desire to promote schools as moral, dialogical communities is quite unclear and is a fruitful topic of research and discussion.

CONCLUSION

There might be three sets of aspirations for instruction in ethics for educational professionals: curbing immoral behavior, transmitting a "generic" public ethic, and transmitting an ethic that is distinctive to the aspirations of educational professionals. There are reasons for emphasizing the third set of aspirations while claiming that these aspirations include the second.

The major results of our inquiry into the nature of an ethic that is distinctive to the needs of educational professionals are these:

1. Emphasis should be given to achieving dialogical competence in the public moral language. However, the concepts of this language are necessary, but not sufficient for the ethics of educational professionals. Also important are trust, caring, and integrity.
2. An adequate view of ethics for educational professionals needs to address not only the concepts that are important to it but also the competencies, capacities, and virtues that are required to sustain practices in which these concepts are competently and successfully employed.
3. Although a case approach has much to commend it, so far as teaching ethics is concerned, a fully adequate approach must seek to build communities in which competent ethical deliberations are encouraged and in which practices that develop and sustain the required competencies, capacities, and virtues are developed and sustained. Both public schools and colleges of education should seek to become such communities.
4. The key feature of such communities is that they should emphasize discursive deliberations in which the range of ethical concepts suitable to a professional ethic for educators are elicited, developed, and deepened and in which the competencies, capacities, and virtues required to sustain such deliberations are evoked and reinforced.

References

Ackerman, B. (1980). *Social justice in the liberal state*. New Haven: Yale University Press.

Ackerman, B. (1989). Why dialogue. *Journal of Philosophy, 86*(1), 5–22.

Athof, W., & Oser, F. (Eds.). (1993). Professional morality: Ethical dimensions of teaching [Special issue]. *Journal of Moral Education, 22*(3).

Aristotle. (1941a). *Nicomachean ethics*. In R. McKeon (Ed.), *The basic works of Aristotle* (pp. 935–1126). New York: Random House.

Aristotle. (1941b). *Politics*. In R. McKeon (Ed.), *The basic works of Aristotle* (pp. 1127–1324). New York: Random House.

Aronowitz, S., & Giroux, H. A. (1991). *Postmodern education: Politics, culture, and social criticism*. Minneapolis: University of Minnesota Press.

Ayer, A. J. (1946). *Language, truth and logic*. New York: Dover.

Banks, J. A. (1993). The canon debate, knowledge construction, and multicultural education. *Educational Researcher, 22*(5), 4–14.

Benhabib, S. (1987). The generalized and concrete other. In S. Benhabib & D. Cornell (Eds.), *Feminism as critique: On the politics of gender* (pp. 77–95). Minneapolis: University of Minnesota Press.

Benhabib, S. (1992). *Situating the self: Gender, community and postmodernism in contemporary ethics*. New York: Routledge.

Bentham, J., & Mill, J. S. (1961). *The utilitarians: An introduction to the principles of morals and legislation*. Garden City, NY: Doubleday.

Berkowitz, M. W. (1985). The role of discussion in moral education. In M. W. Berkowitz & F. Oser (Eds.), *Moral education: Theory and application* (pp. 197–218). Hillsdale, NJ: Lawrence Erlbaum Associates.

Beyer, L. E., & Liston, D. P. (1992). Discourse or moral action? A critique of postmodernism. *Educational Theory, 42*(4), 371–393.

Bricker, D. C. (1993). Character and moral reasoning: An Aristotelian perspective. In K. A. Strike & P. L. Ternasky (Eds.), *Ethics for professionals in education: Perspectives for preparation and practice* (pp. 13–26). New York: Teachers College Press.

Brophy, J. E., & Good, T. L. (1986). Teacher behavior and student achievement. In M. C. Wittrock (Ed.), *Handbook of research on teaching* (3rd ed., pp. 328–375). New York: Macmillan.

Bull, B. L. (1990). The limits of teacher professionalization. In J. I. Goodlad, R. Soder, & K. A. Sirotnik (Eds.), *The moral dimensions of teaching* (pp. 87–129). San Francisco: Jossey-Bass.

Bull, B. L. (1993). Ethics in the preservice curriculum. In K. A. Strike & P. L. Ternasky (Eds.), *Ethics for professionals in education: Perspec-*

tives for preparation and practice (pp. 69–83). New York: Teachers College Press.

Bull, B. L., Fruehling, R. T., & Chattergy, V. (1992). *The ethics of multicultural and bilingual education.* New York: Teachers College Press.

Burbules, N. C. (1993). *Dialogue in teaching: Theory and practice.* New York: Teachers College Press.

Burbules, N. C., & Densmore, K. (1991). The limits of making teaching a profession. *Educational Policy, 5*(1), 44–63.

Burbules, N. C., & Rice, S. (1991). Dialogue across differences: Continuing the conversation. *Harvard Educational Review, 61*(4), 393–416.

Callan, E. (1992). Finding a common voice. *Educational Theory, 42*(4), 429–441.

Coles, R. (1989). *The call of stories: Teaching and the moral imagination.* Boston: Houghton Mifflin.

Darling-Hammond, L. (1985). Valuing teachers: The making of a profession. *Teachers College Record, 87*(2), 205–218.

Descartes, R. (1956). *Discourse on method* (2nd ed., Rev. ed.). New York: Liberal Arts Press.

Dill, D. D., and Associates (Eds.). (1990). *What teachers need to know: The knowledge, skills, and values essential to good teaching* (Introduction to Part 3, *The moral dimensions of teaching*, pp. 151–156). San Francisco: Jossey-Bass.

Dworkin, R. M. (1977). *Taking rights seriously.* London: Duckworth.

Dworkin, R. M. (1984). Liberalism. In M. J. Sandel (Ed.), *Liberalism and the limits of justice* (pp. 60–79). New York: New York University Press.

Ellsworth, E. (1989). Why doesn't this feel empowering? Working through the repressive myths of critical pedagogy. *Harvard Educational Review, 59*(3), 297–324.

Fenstermacher, G. D. (1990). Some moral considerations on teaching as a profession. In J. I. Goodlad, R. Soder, & K. A. Sirotnik (Eds.), *The moral dimensions of teaching* (pp. 130–151). San Francisco: Jossey-Bass.

Fischer, L., Schimmel, D., & Kelly, C. (1991). *Teachers and the law* (3rd ed.). White Plains, NY: Longman.

Fogel, R. W., & Engerman, S. L. (1989). *Time on the cross: The economics of American Negro slavery* (Rev. ed.). New York: Norton.

Galston, W. (1991). *Liberal purposes: Goods, virtues, and diversity in the liberal state.* Cambridge, England: Cambridge University Press.

Geiger, J. O. (Assoc. Ed.). (1986). [Special issue]. *Journal of Teacher Education, 37*(3).

Gilligan, C. (1982). *In a different voice.* Cambridge: Harvard University Press.

Goodlad, J. I. (1990). *Teachers for our nation's schools.* San Francisco: Jossey-Bass.

Goodlad, J. I., Soder, R., & Sirotnik, K. A. (1990). *The moral dimensions of teaching.* San Francisco: Jossey-Bass.

Green, T. F. (1971). *The activities of teaching.* New York: McGraw-Hill.

Gross, J. A. (1993). The legal context of professional ethics: Values, standards, and justice in judging teacher conduct. In K. A. Strike & P. L. Ternasky (Eds.), *Ethics for professionals in education: Perspectives for preparation and practice* (pp. 202–216). New York: Teachers College Press.

Gross, J. A. (1988). *Teachers on trial.* Ithaca: Industrial & Labor Relations Press.

Gross, M. L. (1992). Democratic character and democratic education: A cognitive and rational reappraisal. *Educational Theory, 42*(3), 331–349.

Gutmann, A. (1987). *Democratic education.* Princeton: Princeton University Press.

Gutmann, A. (1993). The challenge of multiculturalism in political ethics. *Philosophy & Public Affairs, 22*(3), 171–206.

Habermas, J. (1973). *Legitimation crisis* (T. McCarthy, Trans.). Boston: Beacon Press. (Original work published 1973.)

Habermas, J. (1984). *The theory of communicative action.* (T. McCarthy, Trans.). Boston: Beacon Press. (Original work published 1981.)

Habermas, J. (1990). *Moral consciousness and communicative action* (C. Lenhardt & S. W. Nicholsen, Trans.). Cambridge: MIT Press. (Original work published 1983.)

Hegel, G. W. F. (1961). *The phenomenology of mind* (2nd ed., J. B. Baillie, Trans.). New York: Macmillan. (Original work published 1910.)

Hostetler, K. (1994). The priority of the particular in practical rationality. In A. Thompson (Ed.), *Philosophy of education 1993: Proceedings of the forty-ninth annual meeting of the Philosophy of Education Society* (pp. 41–49). Urbana, IL: Philosophy of Education Society.

Howe, K. R. (1986). A conceptual basis for ethics in teacher education. *Journal of Teacher Education, 37*(3), 5–12.

Howe, K. R. (1993). The liberal democratic tradition and educational ethics. In K. A. Strike & P. L. Ternasky (Eds.), *Ethics for professionals in education: Perspectives for preparation and practice* (pp. 27–42). New York: Teachers College Press.

Hoy, W. K., & Miskel, C. G. (1991). *Educational administration. Theory, research, and practice* (4th ed.). New York: McGraw-Hill.

Jackson, P. W. (1968). *Life in classrooms.* New York: Holt, Rinehart and Winston.

Kant, I. (1956). *Critique of practical reason* (L. W. Beck, Trans.). Indianapolis: Bobbs-Merrill. (Original work published 1788.)

Kant, I. (1961). *The moral law; or Kant's Groundwork of the metaphysic of morals* (H. J. Paton, Trans.). London: Hutchinson University Library. (Original work published 1794.)

Kerdeman, D., & Phillips, D. C. (1993). Empiricism and the knowledge base of educational practice. *Review of Educational Research, 63*(3), 305–313.

Kimball, B. A. (1988). The problem of teacher authority in the light of the structural analysis of professions. *Educational Theory, 38*(1), 1–9.

Kohlberg, L. (1971). From is to ought: How to commit the naturalistic fallacy and get away with it in the study of moral development. In T. Mischel (Ed.), *Cognitive development and epistemology* (pp. 151–236). New York: Academic Press.

Kohlberg, L. (1981). *The philosophy of moral development.* San Francisco: Harper & Row.

Kohlberg, L. (1985). The just community approach to moral education in theory and practice. In M. W. Berkowitz & F. Oser (Eds.), *Moral education: Theory and application* (pp. 27–87). Hillsdale, NJ: Lawrence Erlbaum Associates.

Kuhn, T. S. (1970). *The structure of scientific revolutions* (2nd ed.). Chicago: The University of Chicago Press.

Kymlicka, W. (1989). *Liberalism, community, and culture.* Oxford: Clarendon Press.

Kymlicka, W., & Norman, W. (1994). Return of the citizen: A survey of recent work on citizenship theory. *Ethics, 104*(2), 352–381.

Locke, J. (1946). *A letter concerning toleration* (W. Popple, Trans.). Oxford, England: Basil Blackwell. (Original work published 1689.)

Locke, J. (1975). *An essay concerning human understanding.* New York: Dover. (Original work published in 1690.)

Lockwood, A. (1976). A critical view of values clarification. In D. Purpel & K. Ryan (Eds.), *Moral education . . . It comes with the territory* (pp. 152–170). Berkeley: McCutchan.

Lockwood, A. (1978). The effects of values clarification and moral development curricula on school-age subjects: A critical review of recent research. *Review of Educational Research, 48*(3), 325–364.

Lyotard, J. F. (1984). *The postmodern condition: A report on knowledge: Vol. 10. Theory and history of literature* (G. Bennington & B. Massumi, Trans.). Minneapolis: University of Minnesota Press.

MacIntyre, A. (1981). *After virtue: A study in moral theory.* Notre Dame, IN: University of Notre Dame Press.

MacIntyre, A. (1988). *Whose justice? Which rationality?* Notre Dame, IN: University of Notre Dame Press.

Macmillan, C. J. B. (1993). Ethics and teacher professionalization. In K. A. Strike & P. L. Ternasky (Eds.), *Ethics for professionals in education: Perspectives for preparation and practice* (pp. 189–201). New York: Teachers College Press.

Marx, K., & Engels, F. (1976). The German ideology. In *Karl Marx, Frederick Engels: Collected works* (Vol. 5, pp. 19–539). New York: International Publishers.

Mayeroff, M. (1971). *On caring*. New York: Harper & Row.

Mill, J. S. (1956). *On Liberty* (C. V. Shields, Ed.). Indianapolis: Bobbs-Merrill.

Nash, R. J., & Griffin, R. S. (1987). Repairing the public-private split: Excellence character and civic virtue. *Teachers College Record, 88*(4), 549–566.

National Education Association (NEA). (1992). Code of ethics of the education profession. In K. A. Strike & J. F. Soltis (Eds.), *The ethics of teaching* (2nd ed., pp. ix–xi). New York: Teachers College Press.

Noddings, N. (1984). *Caring, a feminine approach to ethics and moral education*. Berkeley: University of California Press.

Noddings, N. (1992). *The challenge to care in schools: An alternative approach to education*. New York: Teachers College Press.

Noddings, N. (1993). Caring: A feminist perspective. In K. A. Strike & P. L. Ternasky (Eds.), *Ethics for professionals in education: Perspectives for preparation and practice* (pp. 43–53). New York: Teachers College Press.

Nord, W. A. (1990). Teaching and morality: The knowledge most worth having. In D. D. Dill and Associates (Eds.), *What teachers need to know: The knowledge, skills, and values essential to good teaching* (pp. 173–198). San Francisco: Jossey-Bass.

Nussbaum, M. C. (1990). *Love's knowledge: Essays on philosophy and literature*. New York: Oxford University Press.

Oser, F. K. (1986). Moral education and values education: The discourse perspective. In M. C. Wittrock (Ed.), *Handbook of research on teaching* (3rd ed., pp. 917–941). New York: Macmillan.

Oser, F. K. (1991). Professional morality: A discourse approach (The case of the teaching profession). In W. M. Kurtines & J. L. Gewirtz (Eds.), *Handbook of moral behavior and development: Volume 2. Research* (pp. 191–228). Hillsdale, NJ: Lawrence Erlbaum Associates.

Pangle, L. S., & Pangle, T. L. (1993). *The learning of liberty: The educational ideas of the American founders*. Lawrence: University Press of Kansas.

Peshkin, A. (1986). *God's choice: The total world of a fundamentalist Christian school*. Chicago: The University of Chicago Press.

Piaget, J. (1965). *The moral judgment of the child* (M. Gabain, Trans.). New York: Free Press.

Pierce v. Society of Sisters of the Holy Names of Jesus and Mary. 268 U.S. 510, 45 S.Ct. 571 (1925).

Power, C. (1985). Democratic moral education in the large public high school. In M. W. Berkowitz & F. Oser (Eds.), *Moral education: Theory and application* (pp. 219–238). Hillsdale, NJ: Lawrence Erlbaum Associates.

Power, F. C. (1993). Just schools and moral atmosphere. In K. A. Strike & P. L. Ternasky (Eds.), *Ethics for professionals in education: Perspectives for preparation and practice* (pp. 148–161). New York: Teachers College Press.

Raths, L. E., Harmin, M., & Simon, S. B. (1966). *Values and teaching: Working with values in the classroom*. Columbus: Merrill.

Rawls, J. (1971). *A theory of justice*. Cambridge: Harvard University Press.

Rawls, J. (1985). Justice as fairness: Political not metaphysical. *Philosophy and Public Affairs, 14*(3), 223–251.

Rawls, J. (1987). The idea of an overlapping consensus. *Oxford Journal of Legal Studies, 7*(1), 1–25.

Rawls, J. (1993). *Political liberalism*. New York: Columbia University Press.

Rorty, R. (1979). *Philosophy and the mirror of nature*. Princeton: Princeton University Press.

Rorty, R. (1982). *Consequences of pragmatism*. Minneapolis: University of Minnesota Press.

Rorty, R. (1989). *Contingency, irony, and solidarity*. Cambridge: Cambridge University Press.

Ruddick, S. (1980). Maternal thinking. *Feminist Studies, 6*(2), 342–367.

Ruddick, S. (1989). *Maternal thinking: Towards a politics of peace*. Boston: Beacon Press.

Sandel, M. (1982). *Liberalism and the limits of justice*. Cambridge: Cambridge University Press.

Schrader, D. E. (1993). Lawrence Kohlberg's approach and the moral education of education professionals. In K. A. Strike & P. L. Ternasky (Eds.), *Ethics for professionals in education: Perspectives for preparation and practice* (pp. 84–101). New York: Teachers College Press.

Sichel, B. A. (1988). *Moral education: Character, community, and ideals*. Philadelphia: Temple University Press.

Sichel, B. A. (1993). Ethics committees and teacher ethics. In K. A. Strike & P. L. Ternasky (Eds.), *Ethics for professionals in education: Perspectives for preparation and practice* (pp. 162–175). New York: Teachers College Press.

Sidgwick, H. (1986). *The methods of ethics*. Charlottesville, VA: Ibis Publishers.

Smart, J. J. C., & Williams, B. (1973). *Utilitarianism for and against*. Cambridge: Cambridge University Press.

Smith, A. (1985). *An inquiry into the nature and causes of the wealth of nations*. New York: Random House.

Sockett, H. (1990). Accountability, trust, and ethical codes. In J. I. Goodlad, R. Soder, & K. A. Sirotnik (Eds.), *The moral dimensions of teaching* (pp. 224–250). San Francisco: Jossey-Bass.

Sockett, H. (1992). The moral aspects of the curriculum. In P. W. Jackson (Ed.), *Handbook of research on curriculum* (pp. 543–569). New York: Macmillan.

Sockett, H. (1993). *The moral base for teacher professionalism*. New York: Teachers College Press.

Soder, R. (1990). The rhetoric of teacher professionalization. In J. I. Goodlad, R. Soder, & K. A. Sirotnik (Eds.), *The moral dimensions of teaching* (pp. 35–86). San Francisco: Jossey-Bass.

Stout, J. (1988). *Ethics after Babel: The languages of morals and their discontents*. Boston: Beacon Press.

Strike, K. A. (1982). *Liberty and learning*. Oxford: M. Robertson.

Strike, K. A. (1989). *Liberal justice and the Marxist critique of education: A study of conflicting research programs*. New York: Routledge.

Strike, K. A. (1990a). Are secular ethical languages religiously neutral? *The Journal of Law and Politics, 6*(3), 469–502.

Strike, K. A. (1990b). The ethics of educational evaluation. In J. Millman & L. Darling-Hammond (Eds.), *The new handbook of teacher evaluation: Assessing elementary and secondary school teachers* (pp. 356–373). Newbury Park, CA: Sage.

Strike, K. A. (1990c). The legal and moral responsibility of teachers. In J. I. Goodlad, R. Soder, & K. A. Sirotnik (Eds.), *The moral dimensions of teaching* (pp. 188–223). San Francisco: Jossey-Bass.

Strike, K. A. (1991). Humanizing education: Subjective and objective aspects. *Studies in Philosophy and Education, 11*(1), 17–30.

Strike, K. A. (1993a, November 16). Against "values": Reflections on moral language and moral education. *Educational Policy Analysis Archives: An Electronic Journal*, pp. 1–18.

Strike, K. A. (1993b). Ethical discourse and pluralism. In K. A. Strike & P. L. Ternasky (Eds.), *Ethics for professionals in education: Perspectives for preparation and practice* (pp. 176–188). New York: Teachers College Press.

Strike, K. A. (1993c). Professionalism, democracy, and discursive communities: Normative reflections on restructuring. *American Educational Research Journal, 30*(2), 255–275.

Strike, K. A. (1993d). Teaching ethical reasoning using cases. In K. A. Strike & P. L. Ternasky (Eds.), *Ethics for professionals in education: Perspectives for preparation and practice* (pp. 102–116). New York: Teachers College Press.

Strike, K. A. (1994). On the construction of public speech: Pluralism and public reason. *Educational Theory, 44*(1), 1–25.

Strike, K. A., Haller, E. J., & Soltis, J. F. (1988). *The ethics of school administration*. New York: Teachers College Press.

Strike, K. A., & Soltis, J. (1986). Who broke the fish tank? and other ethical dilemmas. *Instructor, 95*(5), 36–39.

Strike, K. A., & Soltis, J. F. (1992). *The ethics of teaching* (2nd ed.). New York: Teachers College Press.

Strike, K. A., & Ternasky, P. L. (Eds.). (1993). *Ethics for professionals in education: Perspectives for preparation and practice*. New York: Teachers College Press.

Sykes, G., & Bird, T. (1992). Teacher education and the case idea. In G. Grant (Ed.), *Review of research in education* (Vol. 18, pp. 457–521). Washington, DC: American Educational Research Association.

Tamir, Y. (1993). United we stand? The educational implications of the politics of difference. *Studies in philosophy and education, 12*(1), 57–70.

Taylor, C. (1992). *Multiculturalism and "the politics of recognition": An essay*. Princeton: Princeton University Press.

Ternasky, L. (1993). Coping with relativism and absolutism. In K. A. Strike & P. L. Ternasky (Eds.), *Ethics for professionals in education: Perspectives for preparation and practice* (pp. 117–134). New York: Teachers College Press.

Thomas, B. R. (1990). The school as a moral learning community. In J. I. Goodlad, R. Soder, & K. A. Sirotnik (Eds.), *The moral dimensions of teaching* (pp. 266–295). San Francisco: Jossey-Bass.

Tom, A. R. (1984). *Teaching as a moral craft*. New York: Longman.

Wang, M. C., Haertel, G. D., & Walberg, H. J. (1993). Toward a knowledge base for school learning. *Review of Educational Research, 63*(3), 249–294.

Williams, B. (1985). *Ethics and the limits of philosophy*. Cambridge: Harvard University Press.

Wisconsin v. Yoder. 406 U.S. 205 (1972).

Wittgenstein, L. (1963). *Philosophical investigations* (G. Anscombe, Trans.). Oxford, England: Blackwell. (Original work published 1958.)

41

CREATING COLLABORATIVE, CHILD- AND FAMILY-CENTERED EDUCATION, HEALTH, AND HUMAN SERVICE SYSTEMS

Dean C. Corrigan

TEXAS A&M UNIVERSITY

Ken Udas

TEXAS A&M UNIVERSITY

The concept of integrated education, health, and human services systems and the interprofessional development and research programs to support them are ideas whose time has come—again. A rereading of the American Association of Colleges for Teacher Education (AACTE) Bicentennial Commission Report, *Educating a Profession* (Howsam, Corrigan, Denemark, & Nash, 1976) shows that more than 40 pages were devoted to the notion of linking education and human services back in 1976.

In contrast, today's calls for collaboration come from a wide variety of powerful forces outside as well as inside the involved professions. A sense of urgency to reform the system is being forced by the threats facing America's children and their families. As documented in the Children's Defense Fund's Annual Report, *The State of America's Children* (1994), conditions are so bad that they can no longer be ignored. The report was released to coincide with President Clinton's State of the Union Address. America's worst nightmares are coming true, more children are living in extreme poverty today than any year since 1975, when such data were first collected. The increase in poverty in 1992 was particularly dramatic for America's youngest children. One in every four children less than 6 years of age was poor, as were 27% of all children younger than age 3. Child poverty rates compared to previous years moved higher for white, black, and Latino children. These conditions and the concomitant short- and long-term education, health, social, and economic problems they produce cry out to the policymakers and professions responsible for their services to reinvent the current system.

Until recently, the response of policymakers to each education, health, and human service crisis has been to develop a single issue or categorical program. As these concerns have expanded and become more complex, it becomes evident that many agencies are serving the same client (Hodgkinson, 1987) and that the professional responsibility for specific services is often uncoordinated and dysfunctional. State and national policymakers now recognize that new organizational relationships at the family and community levels must be developed among educational institutions, health agencies, and other human service organizations. A systemic, collaborative approach is imperative.

This chapter details the threats to America's children, reviews the policies undergirding new proposals for changing the status

The authors thank reviewers Jill Tarule (University of Vermont), Cal Sia (Hawaii Medical Association), and Roy Edelfelt (University of North Carolina–Chapel Hill). Thanks also to Constance Lehman and Bud Fredericks for sharing the annotated bibliography that they compiled with the Research Committee of the Association of Teacher Educators' *Commission on Leadership in Interprofessional Education, to Create Collaborative, Education, Health and Human Service Systems*.

quo, and reports on integrated service programs currently in operation and the design and development of interprofessional education programs to support them. Particular implications are drawn for the role that research and development must play in creating collaborative, child- and family-centered, education, health, and human services systems. Interprofessional collaboration and participatory research are the key words of the 1990s.

CONDITIONS OF CHILDREN

Policymakers and practitioners seem to agree that if new collaborative efforts must emerge from and be judged by the effect they have on improving the conditions of children and their families today they must be client-based. To begin with, then, it is essential to know what current conditions are.

Poverty

Poverty in America is ever present and on the rise. Since the mid-1980s the rich have gotten richer, and the poor have become more numerous and poorer. Children in America have fared the worst of all segments of the population. In 1989, the poverty line for a family of three was $9,890, pretax annual income. Children under 6 were more than twice as likely to be poor than adults between the ages of 18 and 64. Minority children were the hardest hit; 48% of all African-American children and 42% of all Hispanic children under 6 were poor in 1987 (National Center for Children in Poverty, 1990).

Nearly 5 million children in 1990 lived in families with incomes of less than half of the poverty level. Approximately 43% of single-parent, mother-only families are poor (National Commission on Children, 1991). Homelessness has reached epidemic proportions in this country. Families are the fastest growing segment of the homeless population. At least 100,000 children are homeless in America on any given night (Melaville, Blank, & Asayesh, 1993).

Vanishing Dreams (Children's Defense Fund, 1992) documented the worsening plight of young children in young families. A child in a family headed by a parent in 1992 who was younger than 30 was twice as likely to be poor as a comparable child in 1973; one third as likely to be living in a home owned by his or her family than a child just a decade earlier; and three times more likely to live in a family that pays more than half its income for rent than in 1974.

Families

Rapid changes have taken place in the fabric of our society. Most significant are changes in traditional family structures and roles. In 1970, 12% of all children lived with only one parent; by 1989 the figure rose to approximately 25%. The United States has the highest divorce rate in the world. In 1960, 5% of all births in the United States were to unmarried women; in 1988 more than 25% were (National Commission on Children, 1991).

An increasing percentage of children have mothers in the paid work force. In 1970, 32% of mothers with children less than the age of 6 were in the work force, while in 1990 the percentage rose to 58% (National Commission on Children, 1991). Between 1962 and 1992 the amount of time parents spent with their children had decreased by approximately one third (Hamburg, 1992). In 1987, 20% of all children under 6 lived with single mothers. The poverty rate among children living with single mothers is 61.4%. A child living with a single mother is more than five times as likely to be poor than a child living in a married-couple family (National Center for Children in Poverty, 1990).

Children living in families with better educated parents are less likely to be poor than children living in families with less educated parents. Sixty-two percent of all children in 1987 whose single parent or better educated parent had not completed high school lived in poverty, while only 4% of all children lived in poverty whose single parent or better educated parent had at least some postsecondary education (National Center for Children in Poverty, 1990). In 1985, children of single nonpoor mothers were more than twice as likely to receive support from absent fathers than children of poor mothers (National Center for Children in Poverty, 1990).

The rate of outside-of-marriage births by teenagers increased from 15% to 61% from 1960 to 1986 (National Center for Children in Poverty, 1990). Approximately 1 million teenage girls become pregnant each year. Most teenage births occur outside of marriage. Children of unmarried teenage mothers are four times more likely than children in other families to be poor, and they are more likely to remain poor for an extended time (National Commission on Children, 1991). Thirty-one percent of eighth- and tenth-grade female dropouts in 1990 did so because they were pregnant (National Education Goals Panel, 1992). The percent of all births to single teens increased by 16% from 1986 to 1991 (Center for the Study of Social Policy, 1993b). Pregnancy and childbirth accounted for 65% of all hospital discharges for women between 15 and 19 years old (U.S. Department of Health and Human Services, 1992).

Health

Poor children are at greater risk of impaired health than are other children. Health risks that are associated with poverty include low birth weight, prenatal drug exposure, AIDS, poor nutrition, lead poisoning, accidental injury, and parental lifestyles (National Center for Children in Poverty, 1990). Schools and medical facilities today must serve children they never had to deal with before. AIDS has become a serious threat to children. Teenage pregnancies are escalating, and the consequences of inappropriate care include a rise in infant mortality and morbidity rates. In 1991, 13.4 million children, representing approximately 21% of America's child population, had not seen a physician in the past year (Plante, 1993).

Twenty-five percent of American babies are born to women who receive inadequate prenatal care. These women are about three times more likely to deliver a low-birth-weight baby than women who receive adequate prenatal care (Plante, 1993). In 1992, 44.7% of all 2-year-olds had not been fully immunized against preventable childhood diseases (Children's Defense Fund, 1994). Infant mortality rates in the United States are higher than in 21 other developed nations. Nearly 40,000 American babies die within a year of birth. In 1990, approximately 32 million Americans, 8.3 million of which were children, were without health insurance (National Commission on Children, 1991).

In 1986, the incidence of child maltreatment was nearly seven times greater for children living in families with incomes less than $15,000 than for children living in families with incomes above that level. Fatal injuries were three times greater for low-income children, and serious-injury impairment was more than six times greater for low-income families (National Center for Children in Poverty, 1990).

Poor children under 6 have fewer doctor visits and less continuity of care than other children. Barriers faced by poor parents obtaining health care for their children include lack of health insurance, rising costs of job-related insurance, medical expenses for the uninsured, state restrictions on Medicaid coverage, and a growing proportion of pediatricians who limit the amount of Medicaid patients they will accept. Many health services are not available to poor families (National Center for Children in Poverty, 1990).

In 1990, 33% of all white children lacked employer-based health insurance, and 60% of all African-American and Hispanic children lacked employer-based health insurance. The breakdown of employer-based health insurance has put great stress on the Medicaid system (Rosenbaum, Hughes, Harris, & Liu, 1992).

In a 3-day search conducted by the House Committee on Government Operations (1990), more than 7,000 illegally employed minors were identified. In 1989, 22,500 child labor violations were reported by the Department of Labor. Violations included hours of work, employment of children younger than 14, and working children under the age of 18 in dangerous, prohibited occupations. The Labor Department believes that the reported violations represent a very small percent of total violations (House Committee on Government Operations, 1990). Only 2% of all Japanese students work during the school year, but approximately 65% of all American youth work during the school year (House Committee on Government Operations, 1990).

Violence

Many communities and neighborhoods no longer function as systems of support within which children can safely grow into adulthood and become self-sufficient. Violence has permeated the social environments of families at all socioeconomic levels. Communities still are split by racism, prejudice, and polarization. In far too many places, individual differences are mocked and ridiculed rather than viewed as a source of richness. Substance abuse is increasing and creates serious disruptions in the lives of children and families, as well as threats to their health and safety.

Teenage suicides and violent deaths are increasing at an unprecedented rate. It is estimated that 12% to 15% of all children suffer from mental disorders. The adolescent suicide rate increased from 3.6 per 100,000 in 1960 to 10.2 per 100,000 in 1988 (National Commission on Children, 1991). The number of reported child abuse cases increased 31% from 1985 to 1990 (U.S. Department of Health and Human Services, 1991).

The juvenile violent crime arrest rate increased 48% from 1986 to 1991 (Center for the Study of Social Policy, 1993b). The death rate due to homicide of children from ages 1 to 9 tripled from 1960 to 1988 (U.S. Department of Health and Human Services, 1991). More teenage males die of gunshot wounds than all natural causes combined. Gunshot deaths among teen males increased by 40% from 1984 to 1988 (National Commission on Children, 1991).

In 1987 the rate of arrests involving individuals of ages 14 to 17 years was 56% greater than the rate of arrests for individuals between the ages of 25 to 34 (Office of Educational Research and Improvement, 1991). In 1989 more than twice as many arrests of individuals under 18 years were made for serious crimes than for all other crimes. Examples of serious crimes included murder, forcible rape, aggravated assault, and arson; other crimes included stolen property, drunk driving, disorderly conduct, and drug abuse (Office of Educational Research and Improvement, 1991).

The National Research Council estimated that it costs between $20,000 and $30,000 per year to keep an adolescent in a penal or reform institution (Hechinger, 1992). The relationships between education and crime are striking, in that 82% of America's prisoners are high school dropouts (Texas Education Agency, 1993).

Effect of Dropping Out

Value systems are being transformed as children see materialistic rewards coming from dealing drugs and other illicit activities rather than from the kinds of jobs that they can obtain as a result of schooling. Dropping out of school is associated with later unemployment, poverty, and poor health (U.S. Department of Health and Human Services, 1992). Social and health problems associated with adolescent dropout include substance abuse, delinquency, intentional and unintentional injury, and unintended pregnancy (U.S. Department of Health and Human Services, 1992). As of 1992, 76% of all 16- to 24-year-old Americans who had graduated from high school and were not enrolled in college were employed, but only 53% of high school dropouts were employed (Lewit, 1992).

In 1986, high school graduates of high socioeconomic status were more than twice as likely to be enrolled in postsecondary education as high school graduates of low socioeconomic status (National Education Goals Panel, 1992). The percent of students graduating from high school from 1985 to 1990 decreased for whites, African Americans, and Hispanics. In 1985 the graduation rate among white students was 76.7%, 62.8% for African Americans, and 49.5% for Hispanics. In 1990, the rates were 73.4% among whites, 60.7% among African Americans, and 41.6% among Hispanics (Center for the Study of Social Policy, 1993b).

Relationships of Poverty and Access to Opportunity

Economic, health, and family conditions for all children strongly influence a child's readiness to learn. Because of the relationship between poverty and access to educational opportunity, children from poor families find themselves at the bottom of the heap. Poor children are more likely than nonpoor children to be low achievers in school, to repeat one or two grades, and to eventually drop out of school. They are more likely to engage in delinquent and criminal behavior, to become unmarried teen parents, and to be welfare dependent; they are also likely to earn less if they are employed (National Center for Children in Poverty, 1990).

A significant relationship exists between the number of years that a child spends in poverty and the likelihood that at 16 or 18 years of age he or she will be below expected grade level. Each year of poverty increases by 2% the likelihood of being below expected grade level (Orland, 1990).

Currently, education, health, and human service delivery systems are not organized in ways that are responsive to the needs of single-parent families, aggregate families, families with two working parents, and poor people. Access to adequate child care is needed to meet the enormous responsibilities involved when parents must engage in child rearing and full-time employment. Quality preschool programs can improve a child's social skills, problem-solving ability, and self-esteem. The Consortium for Longitudinal Studies found decreased rates of subsequent special education placement, decreased grade retention, and increased graduation rate to be associated with preschool program experiences (U.S. Department of Health and Human Services, 1992). Studies show that every dollar invested in preschool education services saves $4.75 that would otherwise be spent on future costs of special education, crime, and welfare (Adams & Sandfort, 1992).

Data from 1988 showed that children in families with annual incomes of $40,000 or more were far more likely than children with family incomes of less than $10,000 ever to have received child care, 70% compared to 48% (Dawson & Cain, 1990). Twenty-eight percent of eighth- and tenth-grade female dropouts in 1990 reported that they would likely reenroll if child care were available at school. Nearly half of all eighth- and tenth-grade dropouts in 1990 reported that they would likely return to school if they could attend classes at night or on weekends (National Education Goals Panel, 1992).

In 1972, it was estimated that men between the ages of 25 to 35 in 1969 who were high school dropouts would cost the nation $237 billion in income over their lifetime and would cost $71 billion in lost federal revenue, and $24 billion in lost state and local revenue. There was also an estimated additional $6 billion annual cost for welfare and crime associated with failure to complete high school (Levin & Bachman, 1972). Estimated annual costs in Texas associated with high school dropouts are $652 million in benefits such as welfare, training, crime and incarceration, unemployment, and placement. An additional sum of $16.893 billion is estimated to be lost in the form of lost wages and tax revenue, totaling an estimated cost of $17.545 billion (Robledo et al., 1986).

In the face of such evidence, society has been unwilling to support the development of its children. In 1990, half of all states spent less than $25 annually per child on the education of its youngest children. In 1990, 11 states spent at least 24 times more on corrections and prisons than was spent on care and education of preschool children. Many states only serve a small percent of the families eligible for child education. In 1990, California served only 10% to 20% of all eligible children,

while New York served about 14%. Investment for child care per child in 1990 ranged from $0.24 in Idaho to $152.04 in Massachusetts (Adams & Sandfort, 1992).

Overall, using dollars adjusted for inflation, funding for community health centers fell 38% from 1981 to 1991. The United States ranks 70th in the world for its rate of adequately immunized nonwhite infants (Liu & Rosenbaum, 1992).

In *Ready to Learn* Boyer (1991) summarized the condition of children. He believes that America is losing sight of its children. In decisions made every day, Americans place children at the very bottom of the agenda, with grave consequences for the future of the nation. Boyer warned that it is intolerable that millions of children are physically and emotionally disadvantaged in ways that restrict their capacity to learn, especially when we are aware of the terrible price that will be paid for such neglect, not just educationally, but in tragic human terms as well.

Interrelationships Across the System

What is most important to understand about these data is the reality they describe for children and families at risk and the services not rendered by education, health, and human service professionals who could provide them. Consequences can be visualized by placing children and families in the center of a comprehensive system of community services and examining the relationships of the data, the interrelatedness of entities, information flows, and activities (see Figure 41.1).

Entities in the education, health, and social service system that relate to families and children include social work, health care, housing, education, justice and law enforcement, and business and industry. These entities are represented by professions that relate with one another as well as with the families and children to which they provide services. The social system model implies that actions taken by one entity in the system influence the environment that the other entities exist in and consequently impact the behavior and products of other system components. If the output of an entity does not affect other entities, then the first entity is not in actuality part of the system.

As components of a system, entities have attributes or characteristics that help define their nature. Children and families possess attributes such as poverty level and family structure, and education has other attributes such as dropout rates, the existence or nonexistence of preschool, adequate or inadequate levels of financing, and access to or lack of access to health care and jobs. Many attributes associated with one entity are also intimately related to other entities. For example, relationships exist between the number of years children spend in poverty and their academic success (Orland, 1990). Poor children are more likely than their nonpoor counterparts to be low academic achievers, to repeat grades, and to drop out of school (National Center for Children in Poverty, 1990). Dropping out of school influences future unemployment, level of income, and health (U.S. Department of Health and Human Services, 1992). Dropouts are also 3.5 times more likely than high school graduates to get arrested and six times as likely to become unmarried parents (National Commission on Children, 1991). Furthermore, children of unmarried teenage mothers are four times more likely than children in other families to be poor, and

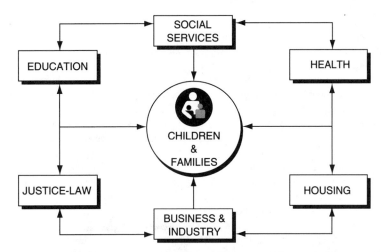

FIGURE 41.1. Comprehensive Community Services, Children, and Families System

they are likely to remain poor for an extended time (National Commission on Children, 1991). Poverty, lack of education, and teen pregnancy relate to form a self-perpetuating cycle.

The cycle is further illustrated and reinforced by the fact that 31% of eighth- and tenth-grade female dropouts in 1990 dropped out because they were pregnant, and 28% report that they would likely return to school if child care were available at school (National Education Goals Panel, 1992). Many poverty-education-work cycles exist. For instance, involvement in a quality preschool program can improve a child's social skills, problem solving, and self-esteem (U.S. Department of Human Services, 1992). By staying in school, young people can learn to identify, organize, and allocate resources; to work with others; and to understand a variety of new technologies. In addition, good schools teach the basic foundations needed by all workers and citizens: reading, writing, critical thinking, and personal qualities like self-esteem and self-responsibility (U.S. Department of Labor, 1991). Because poor children are less likely to participate in preschool programs than are non-poor children, they are less likely to have these learnings that are necessary to succeed in the workplace (National Center for Children in Poverty, 1990). Lack of educational opportunity and dropping out lock the poor into not only a cycle of poverty but also of futility; as a result, the country is denied the compentent work force it needs to compete in today's global economy.

In summary, poverty, family, health, and violence interact in every community. These conditions affect employment (Lewit, 1992), incarceration and crime (Levin & Bachman, 1972; Texas Education Agency, 1993), immunizations rates, mortality rates, suicides, drug abuse (Hamburg, 1992; National Center for Children in Poverty, 1990), enrollment in postsecondary education (National Education Goals Panel, 1992), receipt of support from absent fathers, and child abuse (National Center for Children in Poverty, 1990). The number and scope of issues that have many points in common indicate how interrelated the problems are and how important it is for education, health, and social service professionals to work together.

Another set of connecting data also must be mentioned because it involves the future of all Americans. The most rapidly growing age group in America is people over 85. Some 2.2 million people in America are over age 85; 34,000 citizens are 100 years of age or older. Twenty-four million people are over the age of 65. In 1983, the United States crossed a major watershed; for the first time, the United States had more people over age 65 than teenagers (Hodgkinson, 1987). Young families can now expect to spend as many years taking care of dependent parents as they spend taking care of dependent children.

The ratio of Americans under the age of 18 to citizens 65 and over has decreased substantially since 1960. In 1950, 16 workers contributed to social security for every retiree drawing social security benefits; in 1960 the ratio was 5 to 1; by 1990 the ratio had decreased to 3 to 1; and demographers predict that the ratio will be approximately 2.2 to 1 by 2020 (National Commission on Children, 1991).

The student dropout situation takes on a new sense of urgency when viewed beside the data on the decline in the number of youth and the increase in the elderly. With a shortage of youth and a rapidly growing senior citizen population, the future of the aging white middle class will be determined in part by the successes of young minorities in getting a sound education and a good job. If 50% of minority students continue to drop out of school before the tenth grade and stay on welfare until they are 65, no one will be able to retire. More than ever, because of demographics, all Americans are interdependent— the futures of the young and old are all inextricably interlocked.

NATIONAL AND STATE COMMITMENT TO COLLABORATION

Historical Perspective

The notion that education, social services, and health care are intimately related and linked to the families and children they support is not novel. At the turn of the century, public schools were involved with providing a wide range of health and human services to children and families (Texas Education Agency, 1993). From 1890 to World War I, social activists pushed for extensive integration of social services with public schools (Tyack, 1992). Reformers pushed for clinics, medical and dental inspections, school lunches, special classes for handicapped children, and guidance and placement counseling to address the problems of truancy, delinquency, and poor nutrition. Settlement houses provided services that went beyond education and health care to include recreation and vocational guidance counseling to children and their families (Tyack, 1992).

Other events such as high levels of foreign immigration, the decline of economic and social conditions, dissatisfaction with school outcomes, and the war on poverty resulted in the initiation of a variety of separate programs to support families and children. The uncoordinated creation of programs resulted in a complex web of services and a high degree of overlap and fragmentation that make access to appropriate services difficult (Morrill, 1992). Issues regarding the growing complexity of the human service bureaucracy, coupled with economic and social pressures, and the worsened conditions of poor children and their families have become the central motivating forces for collaboration among education, health, and social service agencies (Kagan & Rivera, 1991). Most recently, interest in collaboration has extended beyond traditional human services providers to include business and industry personnel (Committee for Economic Development, 1985; Kearns & Doyle, 1988; Larson, Gomby, Shiono, Lewit, & Behrman, 1992). Calls to put the pieces of this puzzle together come from policy analysts as well as politicians (Dunkle & Usdan, 1993; Hewlett, 1991; Kagan & Rivera, 1991; Kirst, 1991).

Commitment to the concept of collaboration also is reflected in many newly established entities such as those being supported by Ernest Boyer of the Carnegie Foundation for the Advancement of Teaching, C. Everett Koop, former Surgeon General, the National Ready to Learn Council, and the Safe for Kids Programs. Numerous collaborative programs are funded by private foundations such as the New Futures Programs of the Annie E. Casey Foundation and Hogg Foundation, and the School/University/Community Leadership Programs funded by the Danforth Foundation. The Young and Rubicam Foundation (1991) described its model for collaboration in *The One Place: A New Role for American Schools*. The Education Commission of the States (1992) highlighted the commitment of state governors in *Putting It Together: Redefining Education and Family Services for Children*.

A collaborative reform strategy is central to the directions proposed by President Clinton's education and health and human services team: former Governor Richard Riley, Secretary of Education, and Dr. Donna Shalala, Secretary of Health and Human Services. *Together We Can: A Guide for Crafting a Profamily System of Education and Human Services* (Melaville et al., 1993) was developed jointly by the U.S. Department of Education and the U.S. Department of Health and Human Services. This report recognized that the current system of programs serving children is fragmented, confusing, and inefficient.

The Integration and Continuity of Services Subcommittee (1993) of the Federal Interagency Coordinating Council has stated that one of its primary objectives is to figure out how to create responsive systems of integrated services. The subcommittee's framework includes a set of principles: (1) Services should be family centered, (2) identification of special needs should be community based and occur in accessible integrated

environments, and (3) interagency coordination of resources should result in better quality of services (e.g., greater community care) and a reduction in the cost of services (e.g., the elimination of duplicative efforts).

A clear response to the new agenda is also evident in the private sector. For example, the American Academy of Pediatrics, through its Community Access To Child Health (CATCH) program, emphasizes community-based problem-solving and systems development as the most effective method for ensuring that families receive the services they require. From these and countless other examples it is clear that the directions for changes in programs are, and will continue to be, collaborative, child and family centered, and community based.

Federal Legislation

Evidence of widespread commitment to implement the concept of collaborative service can also be seen most directly in federal and state legislation. The special education experience since the mid-1970s has probably been the earliest and most far-reaching effort to encourage cooperation between health and education professionals, and it came as part of implementing PL 94-142. This legislation ensures the provision of free and appropriate public education services to children with specific disabilities. It also outlines a process by which these children should, to the extent possible, be educated in the least restrictive environment and be provided individual educational plans to meet their learning needs. Parents must be directly involved in the process.

Because many of the children involved were medically fragile or had special health needs, health professionals became involved in designing and implementing individual education plans (IEPs) for each child. In effect, the legislation mandated cooperation between health and education professionals, and systems were put into place to streamline this service and facilitate coordination.

PL 94-142 demonstrated the need for a better way to coordinate a broad range of services for children with disabilities. Although it did not formally encourage collaboration between health and education service providers, implementors identified several issues related to service coordination that needed to be addressed in order to serve the targeted populations adequately.

The amendments to PL 99-457 continued the initiative and extended services to preschool children, toddlers, and infants. Services to school-age children remained basically unchanged, and more innovative approaches to service delivery were mandated by Part H of the law for infants and toddlers with disabilities and their families. Moreover, the legislation called for formal interagency coordination at the state level in both planning and delivery of Part H services, which include the identification of infants and toddlers with developmental delays or those who are at risk of becoming developmentally delayed. Such diagnoses became the primary responsibility of physicians, who, by extension, are needed to actively collaborate with the schools in the development of an IEP for each client and his or her family.

For the first time, the federal education legislative process challenged states to make changes in existing service systems through a coordinated, managed early intervention process. Some of the most creative examples of collaboration between education and health professionals can be found in the extensive interagency planning process that is now occurring as states create service delivery systems in local jurisdictions for infants and toddlers with disabilities and their families. Adding new elements, The Education of the Handicapped Act Reauthorization of 1993, PL 98-199, established priorities on related services and a focus on parents of children with disabilities (Nelson & Pearson, 1991).

Other federal laws contain provisions that fostered child- and family-centered community-based delivery systems. The Adoption Amendments and Child Welfare Act of 1980 (PL 96-272) established a federal priority on intensified programs to support families, as opposed to the creation of alternatives to natural living environments (Nelson & Pearson, 1991). Title V of PL 99-660, entitled State Comprehensive Mental Health Service Plans, established the mandate necessary to direct planners and policymakers toward community-based, interagency services for the individuals affected. The Family Support Act (FSA), a federal law enacted in 1988, was designed to strengthen the nation's child support enforcement system. The FSA created a federal program called JOBS (Job Opportunities and Basic Skills) designed to help recipients to become self-sufficient. The JOBS program requires states to develop welfare-to-work programs (Smith, Blank, & Collins, 1992). The Kildee Education Bill also called for an integrated services approach. The concept had the support of both political parties as well as the White House (U.S. Department of Education, 1994).

State Legislation

At least 15 states have passed legislation fostering the coordination of health, social services, and education. Probably the most comprehensive piece of state legislation is Kentucky H.B. 940. Many other states are considering variations of the Kentucky plan, and in many states education, health, and human service agencies are writing together 5-year coordinated strategic plans and are creating sites where multiple agencies are located for easy access.

Kentucky House Bill 940 created two mandates with profound implications for interagency services in Kentucky. The first mandate established Family Resource Centers, located in or near each elementary school in which at least 20% of the student population is eligible for free school meals. The Family Resource Centers are part of a plan to promote the identification and coordination of resources. The plan includes the provision of full-time preschool child care, after-school child care, summer and nonschool time child care, family training, parent and child education, support and training for day care providers, health services, and health service referral. The second mandate is the creation of Youth Service Centers. These centers are being located following the same criteria as the Family Service Centers. They will provide referral to health and social services, employment counseling, training and placement, summer and part-time job development, drug and alcohol abuse counseling, and family crisis and mental health counseling (Nelson & Pearson, 1991).

Several sections of Kentucky's House Bill 940 produced early childhood initiatives that have been integrated into the Kentucky early childhood education delivery system. The vision of

the Kentucky Education Reform Act (KERA) Preschool Programs is a comprehensive early childhood educational delivery system that provides developmentally appropriate practices to children, integrated services to families, and interdisciplinary and interagency collaboration among organizations serving young children (Kentucky Department of Education, 1991). Imperatives include the establishment of the Kentucky Early Childhood Advisory Council, provision by school districts of half-day preschool educational programs for 4-year-old children considered at risk, and the creation of preschool educational services for 3- and 4-year-old children with identified disabilities. The final imperative conforms with the federal mandate in PL 99-457 for preschool disability services (Kentucky Department of Education, 1991). KERA is being implemented over a 5-year period. The centers are to address the needs of children with emotional and behavioral disorders and their families and to function as a vehicle for interagency planning and service delivery (Nelson & Pearson, 1991).

Prior to KERA, Kentucky House Bill 838, 1990, enabled the creation of a program called Kentucky IMPACT (Interagency Mobilization for Progress in Adolescent and Children's Treatment). That legislation mandated interagency planning for community-based services to children and youth with severe emotional disorders (Nelson & Pearson, 1991).

Among the chief goals of the Kentucky JOBS program is to break the cycle of poverty that tends to be transferred from one generation to the next. Administrators of the JOBS program in Kentucky have pursued a course of collaboration with several existing programs. JOBS has coordinated its services with school reform, Head Start programs such as Operation Family and the Head Start Family Care Center, the Family Care Center in Lexington, and a state-sponsored family literacy program called Parent and Child Education (PACE) (Smith et al., 1992). This collaboration spans programs associated with education, health, and human services, and it has become a model for the rest of the country (Steffy, 1993).

California Assembly Bill number 2765 (AB 2765) of California (AB 1763, 1993), which is similar to the Kentucky plan, makes various legislative findings and declarations in regard to the need for professionals with training or experience in working in integrated children and family services (California Legislature, 1992). The bill mandates the formation of a task force on professional development for integrated children and family services. The legislation declares several items of action including: (1) collaboration with child, family, and school to assess educational, health, and social service needs, (2) development of child and service plans with a mix of educational, health, and human services, (3) development of common procedures for various services and programs, (4) development of a common data base for all participating agencies, (5) organization of a team composed of professionals from a variety of disciplines, and (6) demonstration of a commitment to collaboration.

Assembly Bill number 1741 (AB 1741) of California focuses on the need to coordinate the use and allocation of funds. The bill requires the coordinator to establish a 5-year pilot program for the blending of funds for various children's services allocated to designated participating counties (California Legislature, 1992).

Florida The Florida Full-Schools Act (Statute 402.3026) mandates that the State Board of Education and the Department of Health and Rehabilitative Services provide services to high-risk students through facilities established within the grounds of the school and that the Department of Health and Rehabilitative Services carry out specialized services as an extension of the educational environment. Such services may include unlimited nutritional services, basic medical services, aid to dependent children, parenting skills, counseling for abused children, and adult education (Kadel, 1992). In the Florida health care plan coordinators use local JOBS for outreach to families that do not know how to access health services (Smith et al., 1992).

Vermont Vermont is developing policies that ensure the preparation of all children for school. Children's welfare will be addressed from birth onward with both a focus on the child and the family. New policies also direct education and social services agencies to work jointly with families to develop individualized programs based on family need (Mitchell & The Early Education/Child Care Work Group, 1992).

Texas Texas House Bill 7, entitled Providing Client Access, calls for coordinated planning across state agencies and authorizes funding for pilot studies to enhance proximity and intercommunication across human service providers by locating them on the same site. In 1993 Senate Bill 155 created the Texas Commission on Children and Youth to recommend ways in which the education, health, juvenile justice, and families service agencies can work together more effectively.

New Mexico In New Mexico a new position titled Secretary of Children, Youth, and Family Programs has been created. The Secretary meets periodically with the heads of each of the departments of government involved with programs serving children and families to coordinate delivery of services and program funding in contrast to project funding.

Policy Reports

Another indication that the integrated services idea is high on the national agenda is the spate of national reports on this topic. A few of the most useful reports are identified here.

The Forgotten Half: Pathways to Success for America's Youth and Young Families argued that unmet needs usually exist in bundles for children and families (e.g., the same family may need day care, employment training, and substance abuse counseling). Programs to address families with multiple problems must be comprehensive. The report also provided brief descriptions of some collaborative programs. The commission recommended that states and the federal government ensure that all young people and their families have access to developmental, preventive, and remedial services by joining with public and private local efforts to develop comprehensive services and coordinated delivery systems (William T. Grant Foundation Commission on Work, Family and Citizenship, 1988).

The National Commission on Children (1991) suggested in their report *Beyond Rhetoric: A New American Agenda for Children and Families* that collaboration among human ser-

vices providers and agencies is one way of addressing many service delivery and development problems. The report gave examples of how collaboration may help and the qualities that characterize effective service systems. The Commission recommended a series of steps to (1) promote greater collaboration among children's programs, (2) prevent costly social problems through policies and programs that promote children's health and development, and (3) improve the caliber of staff programs serving children and families (National Commission on Children, 1991).

The National Center for Children in Poverty (1990) in *Five Million Children: A Statistical Profile of Our Poorest Young Citizens* recommended investment in both programs and mechanisms for service coordination. The report pointed toward integration and coordination as means to address the fragmentation problem in the social services system (National Center for Children in Poverty, 1990).

Smith et al. (1992), in a report called *Pathways to Self-Sufficiency for Two Generations: Designing Welfare-to-Work Programs That Benefit Children and Strengthen Families,* sponsored by the Foundation for Child Development, came to the conclusion that many recent state and federal initiatives now recognize the interrelatedness of the problems that children and families in poverty experience. These authors also realize the consequent value of coordinating the different forms of assistance needed to overcome these problems. Programs that are to break the poverty cycle by addressing the needs of both child and family represent a two-generation approach (Smith et al., 1992).

Nelson and Pearson (1991) in a policy guide called *Integrating Services for Children and Youth with Emotional and Behavioral Disorders,* sponsored by Special Education Programs in Washington, DC, developed a cogent rationale for integrated services. The authors traced the historical background that recognizes the need to improve delivery systems and recognizes that without interagency collaboration, individual specialists are likely to fail in providing adequate services. They also acknowledged that interagency coordination has not developed in this country, and they point to the policy barriers to collaboration. Obstacles to collaboration include an entrenched bureaucracy and legislation that has not traditionally mandated or addressed the issue of collaboration.

The Future of Children: School-Linked Services (Behrman, 1992), sponsored by the David and Lucile Packard Foundation Center for the Future of Children, presented a variety of perspectives on school-linked services. It began with an analysis of the current status of the approach. The introductory chapter defined service integration and explained the rationale for integrated services. The report presented a list of seven criteria for effective school-linked services in conjunction with a summary of six critical issues that must be addressed as school-linked services are implemented.

The report is a compilation of articles by authorities on school-linked services issues. The topics addressed include: health and social services in public schools; an overview of service delivery; a sampling of existing school-linked service efforts; an analysis of potential financing strategies; evaluation methods; strategies for developing and implementing a school-linked services approach; new roles and responsibilities for school personnel; a discussion of school-based versus community-based models; and a review of past and current federal efforts to sponsor comprehensive integrated services. These chapters are followed by a feature article on drop-out rates. Appendices include reference information regarding confidentiality, in addition to brief descriptions of 16 current school-linked service efforts and their evaluation plans.

Probably the most quoted reference in garnering political support for the integrated services approach is Schorr's and Schorr's (1989) *Within Our Reach: Breaking the Cycle of Disadvantage*. It has served as a rallying call for the education, health, and social service professions to work together in the interest of America's children. Schorr and Schorr examined factors contributing to negative outcomes for at-risk children and families in the United States. The high cost to individuals and society is presented. The authors discussed the impact of the political process on policy decisions affecting support services for the economically and socially disadvantaged. They described the problems within the system, provided supporting evidence for a number of program approaches, and emphasized preventive services while analyzing 17 effective programs in family planning, prenatal care, child health, child welfare, family support, child care, and preschool/elementary school education.

Schorr and Schorr asserted that effective approaches have been identified based on a combination of theory, quantitative data, research, and experience. Successful programs are comprehensive, intensive, employ high-quality professionals who have the time to be effective, and tailor support to the specific needs of individuals and families served. Such support is not inexpensive. When evaluating the effectiveness of programs, it is important to measure benefits in terms of both human and fiscal outcomes. The book concluded by restating the importance of overcoming the myth that nothing works. This myth allows society to proceed with what has been shown to be ineffective.

INTEGRATED SERVICE PROGRAMS AND INTERPROFESSIONAL EDUCATION

A number of integrated service programs are under way based on the premise that no single institution or human service profession can be expected to take ownership of the associated problems of poverty, dropouts, community violence, teen pregnancy, and youth unemployment. Nor can the health and social service agencies or the schools be blind to the fact that only through working together can they solve the problems of children and families today.

Poverty, emotional problems, family upheaval, drugs, AIDS, and other family concerns can place children and youth at risk of failing for reasons seemingly unrelated to academic matters but that directly affect a child's condition for intellectual/personal growth.

Integrated Services Programs

In view of these resounding calls to reform the system, it is not surprising that integrated services programs are being initiated

by each of the professions participating in new collaborative child- and family-centered systems. The programs vary in emphasis depending on the profession designing and implementing them, but all models place children and families at the center, and in doing so they have increased the need to link with others. As professional partners begin to serve families' health, social, and economic needs, they discover that they interlock with educational needs.

The following case descriptions provide examples of programs initiated by particular professions but involving collaboration with other professions. The New Futures and Total Inclusion Program were initiated by educators; the Healthy Learners Program by social workers; and the Medical Home by pediatricians.

New Futures The New Futures Initiative (Wehlage, Smith, & Lipman, 1992) was created through the Annie E. Casey Foundation as an action-oriented approach to address the serious problems faced by at-risk youth in the nation's urban areas. The foundation committed $40 million over a 5-year period for the development of programs in four medium-size cities and designated the grant funds to be used to affect human service structures and to alter significantly the life chances of at-risk youth. New Futures adopted an institutional problem-solving orientation based on two fundamental assumptions: (1) that the organizations in a community have as much to do with the failure of youth as do individual children and their families, and (2) that the solution to human service problems lies in the coordinated, collaborative efforts of local institutions. The four communities selected by the foundation were Dayton, Ohio; Little Rock, Arkansas; Pittsburgh, Pennsylvania; and Savannah, Georgia. Proposals to the foundation were developed by participants in each community based on the current adequacy of education, health, social services, employment services, and the capacity of the private sector. Each proposal included methods to address child- and youth-related problems.

The New Futures organizers believed that three program components were imperative. First, participating communities were expected: (1) to form collaborative organizations to coordinate plans and to implement programs designed to identify youth issues, and (2) to raise community awareness regarding problems in delivering services to at-risk youth and to develop strategies and goals regarding responsiveness to the needs of at-risk youth. The foundation also wanted each city to develop case management systems that provided the most vulnerable youth with a caring adult to provide support during at least the middle school years, to help provide increased access to services within the community; and to provide the collaborative with relevant and timely information on the problems of youth and institutions designed to serve them. Finally, the need for exchanging timely information for intervention, goal setting, and policy development necessitated the development of an appropriate management information system (MIS). The MIS had to be able to access demographic information on the community services provided and on the individual children and families served.

The foundation also determined that organizational restructuring, curriculum change, and new teaching strategies were essential to increase the likelihood of academic success for many youth. Five "long-term structural reforms" were identified as needed to address school-related problems. They were: (1) restructuring for increased autonomy, freeing educators from the constraints often imposed by a centralized bureaucracy; (2) providing teachers with the needed flexibility to group students, to create positive learning environments, and to develop innovative curricula; (3) restructuring to make schools more responsive to individual student needs; (4) supporting teachers who are working with at-risk youth through training and staff development; and (5) finding ways of collaborating with other internal and external organizations. The New Futures Initiative was designed to yield long-term results.

Healthy and Ready to Learn Center The Healthy and Ready to Learn Center (Sia, 1993) in Hawaii is incorporated as part of several preexisting programs including: (1) Hawaii's child abuse and neglect prevention program, Healthy Start; (2) the Medical Home and the Physician Involvement Projects, which heightened awareness among primary care physicians about the psychosocial problems of children and families as they relate to community and child health; and (3) Part H, PL 99-457, federal funds, Hawaii Zero to Three Project with early intervention services for at-risk infants and toddlers. The center is the educational component of a system of programs and services that integrates health and family support addressing the need for school readiness. A central concern of the center is to promote healthy children who are ready for school.

The Healthy and Ready to Learn Center collaborative is composed of practicing professionals from health, human services, and education. Members of the Operating Foundation, Private Social Service Agency, Tertiary Maternal and Children's Medical Center, Professional Physician Organization, and the College of Medicine at the University of Hawaii work together with practitioners to overcome barriers, solve problems, and take best advantage of available resources. Program organizers believe that interprofessional collaboration in small groups utilizing individual case scenarios will facilitate problem solving and promote a team-oriented response to meeting the needs of families and children.

The concept of organizing as a collaborative is a strong cultural force that influences decisions regarding center staffing, structure, service delivery, client identification, need identification, and goal formulation. The values held by the center collaborative drive goal identification, and the synergy created by the collaborative itself increases the likelihood of goal attainment. Some of the major goals of the center include: (1) encouraging family-centered, community-based, coordinated, and culturally competent care; (2) ensuring utilization of basic health care, social support, and education for all family members with special focus on mothers and babies; (3) promoting primary prevention and early identification of health problems; (4) fostering collaboration between the families' medical home, quality early education, and family support services; (5) encouraging new dimensions in providing health care services, professional education and training; and (6) promoting fiscally responsible programs that will endure a changing health care system. In addition to interprofessional collaboration, the center is committed to the active participation of children and families in program evaluation and problem relief. Family empowerment and the

creation of conditions that allow children and families to reduce their immediate stresses and start to positively invest in their own lives are goals of the collaborative process.

Center coordinators have recognized the need for a training and staff development function that orients the Healthy and Ready to Learn Center staff to interprofessional collaboration. The center has a 3-month in-service training program that focuses on introducing the roles of the professionals involved. Each professional learners about the role and responsibility of the other professionals and through experiential training the staff develops the interprofessional role in the center. Past training sessions sparked many questions among staff and team members. Questions have included: (1) the kinds of skills interprofessionals need, (2) how collective information is obtained and maintained without duplication, (3) how one deals with jargon unique to a particular profession, and (4) how one deals with professional cultures that clash with the values of collaboration.

Several environmental conditions existed that facilitated the development of the Healthy and Ready to Learn Center. Formal support by the Clinton and Bush administrations and the National Governors' Association Educational Goals 2000 provided the impetus. Goals one called for all children in America to start school ready to learn. Not only was this the first national educational goal, but it also was the new focus for targeted communities in the state of Hawaii. National emphasis on early education programs like Head Start and interest by the local legislature and business community in school readiness provided a favorable climate for the center in Hawaii. Growing interest in collaboration and the development of the family center concept, among some social service agencies, coupled with private financial support through the Consuelo Zobel Alger Foundation, also helped program development.

Environmental conditions proved impediments to developing the center: (1) an economic recession on the national and state levels provided increased scrutiny of new and innovative programs, (2) program coordinators found it difficult to find leaders with understanding and vision to fill key positions, and (3) there existed continued fear among ongoing institutions that they would lose resources or prestige by joining a collaborative.

Through taking advantage of pro-family legislation, multiple funding sources, and a generally favorable environment, the Healthy and Ready to Learn Center placed families in the center of the health, education, human services, and Medical Home system. The philosophy of the center and its leaders placed a priority on child health problems because of the inherent vulnerability of children and because it is in early childhood that positive and negative conditions have the greatest leverage on conditions in later life.

Total Inclusion Program The Total Inclusion Program (Cooper, 1990; Dreher, 1993; West Feliciana Parish Schools, 1992, 1993) in West Feliciana, Louisiana, originated in response to a perceived gap between the academic and life skills provided to students while in school and those needed to function effectively after they leave school. Of particular concern was that students seemed to enter special education programs and never reemerge. This observation pointed to a need for providing unsegregated social, educational, and health programming for all students and also for recognizing that the need extended beyond the classroom and the campus to broad health and societal issues in the community.

Total Inclusion Program coordinators and participants transformed identified needs into a vision and system of goals. Components of the vision included provision of integrated services to all children and the formation of collaborative service systems. Program goals in the vision included: (1) creating classroom environments most appropriate for each child's educational and emotional development, (2) becoming more sensitive to the individual differences of students, (3) making more efficient use of resources, particularly dollars, (4) improving student performance, and (5) creating school and community environments that maximize the potential benefits of education by ensuring that each child has a sound body and mind and strong family support.

Integration takes place in the program on two levels. The first level of integration directly relates to students. An effort is made to integrate all students into appropriate general education classrooms and/or community-based instructional programs. Primary reliance on special resource rooms and self-contained classrooms to meet the needs of at-risk and special needs students has been erased. The underpinning values that such integration addresses and promotes are expressed in terms relevant to each child. Preferred outcomes are that each child is valued and respected and that each child experiences optimal learning by being in a sensitive and appropriate environment. Important environmental factors include physical, functional, social, and societal programming aimed at promoting the maximum level of interaction with peers at school and in the community. Program planners at the West Feliciana Parish operate under the assumption that all children are at risk.

The second type of integration occurs at the service provision and delivery level. The act of integrating students into a common educational environment drives other needs. One of the practical consequences of total inclusion is a need for integrated services and collaboration interagency service planning and delivery. On the most elementary level, collaboration occurs in the classroom between special and regular education staff to assist in meeting needs of all students. Collaborative activity among teachers alters in fundamental ways how agencies relate while supporting activities.

In West Feliciana, governing health, education, and human services agencies have integrated the planning and delivery levels to make total inclusion a reality. The collaborative is conceived in terms of a safety net. Collaboration takes place among health and human services programs that are in turn linked to schools. Programs are organized by services and by the children linked to the programs. The structure seeks to maximize service usefulness, flexibility, and individualization.

Open communications across disciplines and agencies is essential for a collaborative program like Total Inclusion. In the West Feliciana Parish, mental health therapists, nurses, regular and special education teachers, physicians, social workers, psychologists, early childhood specialists, and case managers collaborate to provide services and to get advice from clients on program planning, design, and operation. Clients have both formal input through an advisory group, and an informal system of communication that has developed between clients and staff.

Each member of the collaborative is expected to bring some expertise in a particular domain and to have the ability to work as part of a team. Program collaborators recognize willingness to share responsibilities, to learn new terminology and professional cultures, and to value a great deal of flexibility as essential characteristics of a good collaborative partner.

In addition to collaboration among practitioners, clients, and community members, there exists a need for integration between programs and universities. Other needs are for universities to provide preservice training to teachers, educational administrators, and other human services professionals. Universities must also provide training in collaboration and how one functions as a professional in a collaborative and in integrated classrooms and multiservice schools. The West Feliciana Parish is developing relationships with the College of Education at Louisiana State University for appropriate preservice teacher training.

Interagency collaboration and the provision of integrated services tend to result in a high degree of system complexity. Managing any coordinated effort requires structures for planning, organizing, staffing, resource allocation, internal and external communication, and the accomplishment of operational tasks. The West Feliciana Parish developed their Comprehensive Assessment Model as one tool to provide structure for the program.

The Assessment Model was presented in the form of a metaphor of two locomotives. The first locomotive is called the Educational Engine. It is composed of goals' framework, outcomes, and initiatives. The second locomotive is the Assessment Engine. It was configured with indicators, input, process, and output. The metaphor explained that the model works best when the internal components of the two engines are coordinated and when the two engines are pulling in the same direction. The simplicity of the locomotive metaphor is quite superficial. Inherent in the Comprehensive Assessment Model are ways of approaching three of the most challenging issues faced by any collaborative working system: communication, control, and feedback.

Goals and broad categories were redefined into more specific categories. Examples of specific goals are: students' math and science competencies will exceed the national average, and public understanding of and participation in education will be increased. Goals set the tone of the project and serve to check and refine the vision. Because of the complexity of the Total Inclusion Program, a framework for assessment had to be developed. The framework identified three domains that were broken into several areas. One domain is the student. Areas classified under student are school achievement, comprehensive health, social skills, and job placement/continuing education. Subdividing the areas provided the level of structure and specificity needed. The model also specifies outcomes. Outcomes are stated in specifications related to stated goals. A sample outcome is: reach and maintain an attendance rate of 97% at each grade level. The outcomes are quantifiable. Finally, the Initiative Component of the model serves to identify and quantify the programs that exist in the community and those that need to be developed. In addition, once identified, the initiatives are connected to domains and areas in the framework.

The four components of the Assessment Engine are divided into two categories: (1) indicators, and (2) input, process, and output. *Indicators* are the instruments and models for data collection. The criteria for selecting indicators are definability, reliability, and validity. The *input, process,* and *output* components of the Assessment Engine are concerned with constructing the assessment infrastructure. The infrastructure includes data collection, analysis, and feedback for decision support and program assessment.

The data collected in 1992 showed encouraging trends. In addition to significant progress in targeted areas such as referrals to the principal and promotion rates, the West Feliciana Parish Schools reported increases in the percent of students scoring above the national median in the national reading and math tests between 1990 and 1992. The percentages rose from 36.3% to 45.9% in reading, and from 43.4% to 54% in math.

Program coordinators indicated that the willingness of the superintendent, supervisors, and the administrative staff in the West Feliciana Parish to make changes in the system to serve *all* children was a major positive force that facilitated the development of Total Inclusion. Other positive factors were the willingness of some teachers to take on programs, financial support, and volunteers from collaborating agencies. Impediments to program development included the conservative attitudes of some administrators and teachers and physical space.

Healthy Learners Healthy Learners (Briar, 1993; Healthy Learners, 1993a, 1993b; Yanez, 1993) is a community-based, family-centered program modeled on the school serving as hub of a *family support village*. Two overriding values of the program are community participation and empowerment. The Healthy Learners Project was initiated in March of 1991 with a grant provided by the Danforth Foundation. The program site was the Fienberg/Fisher Elementary School on Miami's South Beach in Dade County, Florida. The project was a joint effort of the Dade County Public Schools, Florida International University, and the Department of Health and Rehabilitative Services. The use of collaboratives to improve health care, social services, and educational services was a fundamental principle of the program. The collaborative approach was meant to maximize parental and community leadership to address current problems and develop new goals. The program is now being replicated at other sites.

The major goal of the program is to promote better outcomes for children, families, the school, and community. The outcomes that the program wants to promote are multidimensional and affect the capacity of the community. One of the most effective and critical components of Healthy Learners is the Referral And Information Network (RAIN). RAIN is composed of a family advocate and group of community mothers who are called RAINMAKERS. RAINMAKERS serve as family and child advocates and as resources for families, teachers, and other service providers. Although RAIN is located in the school, RAINMAKERS spend much of their time engaged in the community visiting families and children.

The RAINMAKERS serve hundreds of families each year through a system of services. Some of the services are based on immediate need, and others have been identified and developed through community meetings where all members are

encouraged to participate. This approach to problem solving and service delivery captures the meaning of family and community empowerment. Some of the services provided by RAIN-MAKERS include: (1) the absenteeism home-intervention team that contacts families when a child has missed school for 3 consecutive days (this service has sharply reduced absenteeism), (2) homework clubs to help eliminate some of the barriers to doing homework that students face, and (3) educational and health programs to address specific crises such as a recent lice epidemic. In addition, RAINMAKERS have initiated microenterprises, job clubs, housing strategies, food initiatives, a food voucher distribution system, and child care centers to address the root causes and effects of poverty, homelessness, unemployment, displacement by developers, and hunger. The RAIN-MAKERS serve as need identifiers, service providers, and change agents. Each RAINMAKER is a member of the community they serve. As a member, every success in the community strengthens the RAINMAKER, and each tragedy diminishes the RAINMAKER.

RAIN is not the only component of the Healthy Learners Program. Community members developed a Consumer Bill of Rights to delineate and specify how clients can be expected to be treated by service providers. The children involved with the program have also developed a Children's Bill of Rights. Key philosophical components of the program include defining barriers in terms of family and community empowerment issues, viewing the community as a collective, and viewing the problems and conditions that families experience as opportunities that provide expertise and knowledge to be used for problem solving.

Within the village, interprofessional collaboration has been good, but the university response to collaboration has varied. Faculty express commitment to the ideals of collaboration and the need for training professionals to function collaboratively, but current structures within the university do not readily promote co-teaching and collaboration between disciplines and departments. The training in the village has been community based and sets specific goals. Empowering families to serve themselves and each other implies a status that transcends the traditional client-server model accepted in most academic communities. This relationship places unique demands on training. In-service strategies promote empowerment, blame-free dynamics, and family-centered and culturally inclusive approaches focusing on community development. In addition, RAINMAKERS have been afforded the opportunity to receive intensive training in nutrition and labor and employment studies through the university and government agencies. The information and skills acquired through training programs are then taught by the RAINMAKERS to community members, creating a multiplier effect.

Factors that have helped promote the program include strong support by school administrators and parents. Parents trained as paraprofessionals and treated as such have shown high levels of commitment and have created an environment of personal accountability for all members of the community. Community members show a willingness to attend and to participate in consortium meetings that serve as the major action committee that provides resources and information to promote the program. Among the factors that inhibit the program is displacement of community members by developers. Evictions are primarily due to the project's being located in a prime real estate area.

Although assessment of the program is conceived in terms of community capacity and empowerment, several directly quantifiable indicators are available. Healthy Learners uses evaluation criteria such as student achievement scores, pre-post outcomes of clients, and reduction of risk factors. Positive indicators have included: (1) elimination of police sweeps, (2) elimination of graffiti on school buildings, (3) reduced school absenteeism, and (4) lower evictions in the community.

Walbridge Caring Communities The Walbridge Caring Communities (Philliber & Swift, 1991) collaborative program is located in inner-city St. Louis. The program uses a multidisciplinary staff to address the needs of children and families who face problems related to substance abuse, poverty, and alienation, among other conditions. The program's mission extends beyond delivery of services to strengthening community values. The core values of the program are expressed in seven principles associated with an African credo (called the Nguzo Saba): (1) unity, (2) self-determination, (3) collective work and responsibility, (4) cooperative economics, (5) purpose, (6) creativity, and (7) faith. The initiative has a strong and pervasive community orientation. Program activities reflect the understanding that children live in families and families live in communities; therefore, the needs of children can only be addressed through family and community.

The Nation of Tomorrow The Nation of Tomorrow (TNT) (Booth, 1991; Nucci et al., 1990) was developed in 1989 at the University of Illinois, Chicago. It was established in four Chicago communities with objectives to: (1) enhance learning opportunites for school children, (2) enable parents to contribute to all facets of their children's growth and development, (3) increase the availability of high-quality child care and youth programs, and (4) develop school-based primary health care programs. Three of the components of TNT were School Enhancement, Family Ties, and Partners in Health, all of which were developed and implemented collaboratively. One of the unique features of TNT is that the parents and youth involved with the program produce a publication called *The Journal of Ordinary Thought,* which features articles written by participants about their life experiences.

New Jersey School-Based Youth Services Program The School-Based Youth Services Program (SBYSP) (Dolan, 1992; New Jersey Department of Human Services, 1992a, 1992b) in New Jersey started in 1988. It links education, social services, employment, and health care systems together to serve teenagers at 29 sites throughout the state. Program sites are in or near middle schools, high schools, and vocational schools. The Program served over 19,000 teenagers in 1989. The program's success is critically linked with collaboration among the schools and other service providers. The absence of a state mandate for services allows for a high degree of flexibility to address the community's particular needs. The SBYSP is actively engaged in creative approaches to prevent violence, adolescent pregnancy, school dropout rates, and suspension. Problem awareness and prevention are conducted through group discussions, workshops, conferences, trips, and recreational activities.

IS 218 and the Children's Aid Society (Children's Aid Society, 1993). In 1989, the Children's Aid Society and the New York City Public Schools joined in a partnership to address the needs of children and families in the northern-Manhattan neighborhood of Washington Heights in the Bronx. In 1992, the Salome Urena Middle Academies IS 218 opened and started a new era of collaboration focused on children and families. This included a continuum of school activities and extended programs that change in a fundamental way when and how the school serves and supports the community. The Family Resource Center provides students and families with access to counseling, housing assistance, emergency food assistance, and a means to access many other educational, health, and human services. The center is located in the main entrance of the school along with a full-service medical and dental clinic that is open to all children and families in the community. Services are provided in English and Spanish. IS 218 also sponsors innovative learning activities that speak to issues of community. These include Teen Travel Camp and an Entrepreneurial Camp. These activities provide children with an opportunity to learn about the community through trips to museums, parks, and historical sites and to gain an understanding of how to build the economic infrastructure of the community.

Interprofessional Education Programs

The quality of integrated services programs will depend on the quality of the training and research programs that are developed to support them. The following case studies are examples of interprofessional education programs getting under way.

Seattle University's Community Service Learning Partnership (Anderson, 1993; Anderson & Guest, 1993). In 1990, the teacher education program at Seattle University was redesigned and became the Master in Teaching (MIT) program. The MIT program is a 4-quarter, 60-credit teaching certification program that admits two cohorts of 50 students each year. It involves integrated, team-taught courses, extensive and varied pre–student teaching field experiences, and a post–student teaching course in which students reflect on their experiences and new knowledge. The MIT students are exposed to interprofessional education and collaboration through a content-oriented course and through field experiences.

At the crux of the MIT program is the community internship (EDMT 520). The community internship is a two-term program requirement. The purpose of the internships is to extend the students' experience beyond the university classroom into the community. Prospective teachers study and experience the role of educator as a partner in developing collaborative efforts within the larger community.

The community internship has four components. First, the Community Internship Coordinator introduces students to the internship. An overview of the course, service learning, community service projects, project design, implementation, and research findings on service learning are provided. Second, the MIT student then establishes a placement site where the internship will take place. Information on prospective placement sites is available through three resources on campus. After identifying a possible placement, the MIT student submits a proposal that includes a rationale, description of activities, description of the agency, and a time schedule indicating service performance for approval. The third component is the internship. The community internship stretches over a period of 4 to 8 months and concludes with a report filed by the agency supervisor confirming completion of service hours and describing contributions made by the intern to the agency. Members of each student cohort participate in the Community Internship Conference. The conference provides a forum for MIT students to describe their internship experiences and to learn from the experiences of other students. The final component is a reflection session. During the reflection session students work through exercises and share insights regarding community service, policy issues, and procedures for creating collaborative partnerships. Community internship students produce a short written reflection paper at the conclusion of the experience.

Several general outcomes are expected of MIT students as a result of their participation in the community internship. Students must: (1) enhance and develop the knowledge, skills, and attitudes necessary for successful collaboration with individuals and organizations inside and outside of P–12 schools and meet the needs of youth and families, (2) identify a variety of human services agencies that can assist teachers in addressing student needs, (3) demonstrate a personal commitment to social responsibility, and (4) develop and enhance the attitudes and interpersonal skills needed to work effectively with culturally diverse groups of students. The synthesis of these four goals helps prepare prospective teachers to see children and families at the center of an interprofessional network of service providers.

MIT students graduating from Seattle University have worked closely with social workers, counselors, public administrators, nurses, physical and occupational therapists, psychologists, clergy, law enforcement personnel, lawyers, and doctors as part of their community internship. Providing collaborative educational environments with an extensive array of professionals requires a shared understanding of program and collaborative goals and of the roles and responsibilities of all individuals participating in the program. Developing an understanding among members of a collaborative requires clear written and oral communication and hands-on assessment of collaborative development.

Beyond the interprofessional training provided through direct contact at the program site, training is extended in a 2-day conference, which is the concluding activity of the community internship. MIT students, community agency professionals, agency clients, and practicing P–12 teachers participate in the conference. During the conference all participants share experiences, insights, and reflections regarding the internship and other important issues. The conference serves as part of the MIT students' interprofessional training as well as that of the other practitioners involved.

Although there is no formal collaboration between the MIT program and programs at other universities, within Seattle University, the MIT and the Master of Public Administration (MPA) programs join in implementing the community internship. MPA students can take courses on community learning with MIT

students. One of the chief impediments to forming collaborations between universities is the lack of time needed to initiate contacts and discuss and develop programs. Most faculty members already are overburdened with their existing commitments.

When a university interacts with nonacademic external entities, a set of expectations is assumed by both parties involved in the interaction. In the case of the MIT program, academic program members have certain expectations regarding the roles and responsibilities that various community agencies assume regarding interns. In addition, the agencies have expectations of the MIT students and faculty. Members of the MIT program expect the community agencies to: (1) work with the intern to design an internship experience that allows for direct contact with agency clients and professionals rather than exclusively conducting clerical functions, (2) provide an orientation and the training needed to help ensure a successful internship, (3) engage in analysis and reflection activities with the MIT intern, and (4) complete an evaluation from their perspective of the intern's accomplishments. In turn, the community agencies expect the program to send them qualified, enthusiastic MIT interns.

Program clients have the opportunity to influence the design and operation of the community internship program through two formal channels. They can affect the system through an advisory council and through the evaluation component of the community internship conference. The clients can also interact with MIT faculty informally.

Most of the assessment activity is directed at the MIT student. Evaluation includes official verification that the internship has been completed, that the student has made a community leadership conference presentation, and that a short reflection paper has been written by the MIT student. The MIT faculty are developing studies to determine if the community internship influences teaching practices of the MIT graduates.

Several conditions at Seattle University have facilitated the development of the MIT program and of the community internship. Seattle University's Jesuit tradition promotes the view of human beings as social beings who relate through the community. This tradition lends itself to the notion of interprofessionalism rather than reductionism. In addition, the university has an historical commitment to the development of leaders for service. The MIT faculty share this commitment. In addition to an established system of traditions and core values that are consistent with the MIT goals, the administration staff of the School of Education and of the university and the faculty have provided support that has been essential to the successful implementation of the program.

University of New Mexico Interdisciplinary Collaboration Program The Interdisciplinary Collaboration Program (Kane, 1993) at the University of New Mexico was conceptualized over a period of years by a group of individuals in the College of Education. A reorganization of the College of Education that disbanded all departments, a request for proposals from the American Association of Colleges for Teacher Education (AACTE), and a growing interest throughout the college in interprofessional education, created the environment from which the program formed.

The College of Education is now organized by programs. Among them are Community Health Education, Family Studies, and Teacher Education. The Interdisciplinary Collaboration Program (ICP) functions as a metaprogram where students from any other program can participate in collaborative field experiences and seminars, allowing the ICP to function across programs and enhancing the opportunity for exposure to collaborative studies for all students in the College of Education. Students involved in the ICP work with faculty from both programs to establish appropriate field experiences.

Faculty involved with the ICP have two major research goals. The first is to establish a project that will provide insights on how colleges of education can prepare students who are client advocates and who have the understanding and skills to work collaboratively to support and to advance the healthy development of children, youth, and family.

The second goal is to develop research that yields information relevant to colleges of education in their efforts to work collaboratively with professionals in education, health, and social services to support children, youth, and families. More specifically, the research project will develop and pilot-test community-based and school-site initiatives to inform and train preservice and practicing professionals in education, health, justice, social services, and family studies. The initiatives will train professionals to plan and work collaboratively to enhance opportunities for children and youth to develop healthy behaviors and to reach their full potential. Program goals include disseminating findings related to collaborative service and education through reports, publications, and presentations.

Practitioners and students from several professions participate in the ICP. Members of the following groups are included in the collaborative: (1) preservice elementary and middle school teacher education students, (2) preservice community health education students, (3) preservice family studies students, (4) practicing teachers and professional staff in elementary and middle schools, and (5) professionals working in community health, social service, and criminal justice agencies. Possible future participants include medical, counseling, and educational administration students.

The ICP approach to collaboration includes the notion that collaboration occurs between individuals and not between organizations. Individuals partake in collaboration while organizations tend to obstruct potential collaboration. Individuals must get to know each other and develop relationships that are based on mutual respect and trust. After establishing relationships, it is important to communicate a descriptive understanding, within the collaborative, on how each collaborator's organization works and interacts with children and families.

Collaborative efforts require a central focus occupied by families and children. In addition, it is important that all members of the collaborative employ the concept of a shared mission. Building relationships, shared understandings, and shared missions can greatly facilitate developing a group understanding of the perceptions of policies, operating procedures, and constraints under which all parties operate.

Utilizing a creative problem-solving approach to develop interactions between individuals attempting to collaborate can prove helpful. The use of case studies to work through problems forces individuals to examine their roles and relationships with their clients and other professionals. Resolution of the case-based results in learning provides collaborative members with a sense of satisfaction regarding the time and effort put into collaboration. Realistic case studies often lead to creative conflict that results from the tension between the desire to help children and the perceived constraints of the organization. Successfully addressing the conflict by working through solutions together provides for learning and growth that point toward real empowerment. The use of case-based problem solving serves as both a tool for training and an instrument for change.

Collaborative programs like ICP's tend to involve diverse participants, both individual and organizational. Participants join the collaborative with different perception of what their roles and responsibilities might be in collaborative work and what are reasonable expectations for outcomes. Members of the ICP highlight the following expectations: (1) the schools and agencies involved with the program want specific and concrete results for their kids in a short time, (2) the project staff wants to establish a mechanism from which information on how to foster collaboration can be produced, and (3) the ICP staff feels that an increased level of participation from school and community agency personnel is desirable. These three examples of expectations provide a contrast between participants who value long- and short-term program results, emphasis on outcomes versus process, and different levels of resource commitment.

The clients in the collaborative include the ICP students, practicing professionals, and the children and families served by students and professionals. The ICP students and professionals are involved with designing, operating, and evaluating the program and individual projects. Client participation extends to the design of field placement and seminars. Design and content of program activities are built on the daily interactions of students and professionals. Evaluation is an ongoing activity that provides feedback that directs project development and represents learning outcomes.

Interprofessional training is a central concern of the ICP. Training tends to be context oriented, emerging from the needs of students and professionals as they work through problems and address the needs of children, youth, and families. Interdisciplinary collaboration training occurs in several forums. Integration of cross-professional information is infused into foundations coursework of future teacher educators, community health educators, and family studies professionals. Field placements that include cross-professional experiences for preprofessional students and paid release time for cross-professional experiences for school and agency personnel are critical training components. Bimonthly meetings structured as seminars are conducted that involve students and community practitioners. The seminars take place at a local community center where participants establish working relationships with each other and approach issues associated with providing support and services to children and families. In addition, there is often a central topic of discussion and learning associated with the seminar. Finally, monthly debriefings are conducted that involve students and faculty. The meetings address successes, lessons learned, and the problems students are experiencing in their field placements. Through evaulation of experiences and needs identification, students provide feedback to the faculty from whom future learning experiences are built.

The ICP faculty subscribe to an ongoing evaluation program. Students routinely respond to evaluation questions in writing while interviews with students and professionals are conducted. In addition, seminars and debriefings are audio- or videotaped for future study. These represent some of the data-collection tools used for program feedback and evaluation.

Several factors are credited with facilitating the development of the ICP. Facilitating conditions include: (1) national initiatives and reports that emphasize the need for and promote collaborative efforts, (2) the establishment of a State Department of Children, Youth and Families that is part of a statewide attempt to serve children, youth, and families in New Mexico better, (3) a refocusing of the College of Education to be more responsive to the needs of families and children and a reorganization in the College to provide a structure to meet the new priorities, (4) the existence of talented and committed principals, teachers, and parents in local school districts where the needs of children and families are addressed, and (5) an existing professional development school program involving the College of Education and the Albuquerque public schools.

Although many internal and external factors existed that supported the development and implementation of the program, other factors served to impede its progress. Program progress was slowed by the historical and rigid structures within the College of Education, the Albuquerque School District, and community agencies and by the existence of individuals who defended content areas and inherited policies, procedures, and institutions. Within the community and the college there existed conflicting philosophical beliefs regarding education and ethics. Any policy regarding provision of educational, health, and social services is value laden and must be interpreted through a personal ethics framework.

One of the organizational factors that facilitated the development of the program also functioned as an impediment. Although the reorganization of the College of Education was generally a positive influence on the ICP, the vacuum left by disbanding departments created some difficulty in determining which groups and individuals needed to be consulted for decision making and who was responsible for approving decisions.

A second set of impediments was found within the university regarding participation in interdisciplinary study and community programs. The time required of faculty and administrators for developing new programs and structures is short. In addition, entrenched values in pedagogy and a reward system in the university that does not foster interdisciplinary program development acted as impediments. The historical perceptions of the relative importance of course *content* versus *process* associated with experiential learning works against collaborative study. The university's promotion and tenure system is such an integral part of the academy that it colors all of its activities. The types of activities recognized as scholarly and rewarded tend to be limited to quantitative research published in refereed journals. The bulk of outcomes associated with field work do not fit the definition of highly valued and rewarded academic products but instead are viewed as service activities.

California State University, Fullerton (CSUF) (Center for Collaboration for Children, 1993; School of Human Development and Community Service, 1993a, 1993b, 1993c; Topol, 1994). Primarily two forces drove the concept of offering a Master's Degree in Services Integration (MSI) at CSUF. The first factor was the existence of the Center for the Collaboration for Children, established through the efforts of faculty and administration in the School of Human Development and Community Service. The second force came from the faculty, fellows, and center director who recognized that changes in the ways education, health, and social services professionals meet the needs of children and families necessitated changes in the ways these professionals are prepared.

Although the master's program is not fully developed, the School of Human Development and Community Service offered two integrated services courses in the spring semester of 1994. One of the courses was primarily content based, and the second course was a field-based practicum.

The Center for Collaboration for Children was founded in 1991 at CSUF. It was administered and funded by the Chancellor of the California State University System for its first 3 years and subsequently became a systemwide initiative. The CSUF center promotes cross-agency, school-based, and community-based collaborative models that serve the whole child in the context of the child's family and community. The center's mission is to improve the CSU system's capacity to meet the needs of children and youth in the twenty-first century by pursuing the following goals: (1) strengthening the abilities of professionals to help clients who require multiple services, as opposed to providing isolated services through the existing fragmented system; (2) developing models of multicultural collaboration that promote inclusion of groups across racial and ethnic boundaries; (3) facilitating interagency collaboration among community organizations, schools, public agencies, and the university through workshops, planning, grant development, and technical assistance; (4) revising existing and developing new university curriculum, fieldwork experience, preservice and in-service education to support the center's goals; and (5) conducting research and data collection that enhance the goals of the center.

The CSUF center served as a prime mover in the development of the MSI program. In particular the program is the result of the fourth mission statement regarding the university and the center's goal. One of the goals established for the MSI program included providing preservice education that prepares students to work collaboratively in interdisciplinary teams, reflecting the realization that no single profession or discipline can effectively respond to the needs of a child or family alone. In addition, students should understand that value is measured in terms of outcomes not caseloads or other artificial categorical requirements.

CSUF offered a two-semester collaborative services seminar that attracted over 200 student and faculty participants from five departments. The seminar and internal discussions among fellows and center staff developed several points of consensus regarding the direction, needs, and goals of the interprofessional education program. Consensus points for the MSI program addressed issues of governance, program and curriculum development, funding, and admissions goals. Some areas of agreement included the use of individualized programs to maximize flexibility, the desire to enroll a diverse group of students with differing professional, racial and cultural backgrounds, linking with other campuses in the CSU system, seeking external funding, recognition that strong faculty involvement and staff coordination was critical to program success, and the development of a Degree Program Committee to provide oversight of the program.

The coursework offered prior to full program development demonstrates an integrative approach to curriculum development. The content-based course, *Theory and Methods of Services Integration*, is primarily a theory course with some fieldwork required. The course content includes the state of current service delivery systems, the changing environment of children and families, the nature of collaboration at the policy level, community-based services development and implementation, and outcomes-based funding and evaluation.

One objective of the course is to provide students with the knowledge and tools to exhibit an understanding of the philosophy, history, and current state of collaborative service delivery. In addition, the students should be able to explore how collaboration affects service provision and to understand the daily practice of service providers and how integrated services impact the lives of children and families. Students should also be able to analyze trends in public policy regarding service provision and be able to make critical judgments about how collaborative service systems compare with their traditional monolithic counterparts, including the likely outcomes of different approaches to service delivery. As part of the educational experience, students function as members of an interdisciplinary team for several hours of fieldwork observation, and they individually read a variety of articles, reports, and books on specific content areas. Students are expected to respond to the literature through discussion and writing. The course is offered on weekends to accommodate best the needs of students and community agents who work full-time.

The second course, *Practicum in Services Integration*, provides students with the opportunity to work in interdisciplinary teams in a setting in which integrated services are provided to families and children. They report on their experiences and findings. Through observation and participation in the field and participation in seminars, students learn to identify needs assessment and program evaluation processes most appropriate for the design and implementation of collaborative services. In addition, students become able to evaluate current service systems and design integrated service delivery systems. The practicum is designed to build from the theory course and to introduce additional theory from analysis of field experiences, readings, and group discussion.

Members of several service-providing departments participate in the program. Teams from elementary/bilingual education, nursing, child development, human services, educational administration, and criminal justice contribute to the center and the program. Successful collaboration is predicated on eliminating the deleterious effects of professional and personal ego. The ego problem has been addressed by making participation voluntary. Everybody involved in the program wants to be involved. The individuals and groups that feel as if the collaborative has nothing to offer their students are absent. The collaborative simply moves on without their input.

The MSI program design has been primarily developed by members of the faculty. It is the desire of the center and faculty to include students in future program development. Many of the students in the School of Human Development and Community Service work in the community as practicing professionals. It is hoped that they can reflect the perspectives of their clients into the design process.

Coursework and field experiences provide interprofessional training for students in the program. The center actively engages in providing interprofessional training in the field to community agents and educators. Because many of the students in the program are also professionals in the community, the formal academic education offered through the school reaches both student and practitioner populations.

The establishment of the Center for Collaboration for Children and the development of the Master's Degree in Services Integration were driven by the evident failure of human services delivery in California. Progressive legislation mandating integrated services and collaborative planning, coupled with strong support for action from the Chancellor of the California State University System, facilitated the development of programs.

Although there were few impediments associated with establishing the center, some have arisen in developing the master's program. Territorial disputes and funding issues are among the political complications that have held back program developers. The campus community has had trouble adjusting to the changing needs of the community. Because interdisciplinary endeavors are perceived as less scholarly than traditional, narrowly defined academic disciplines, some members of the faculty have shown reluctance to participate in interdepartmental programs. They also feel that projects that do not comport to the traditional model of scholarly work are less likely to be considered important by those judging qualifications for promotion, tenure, and merit pay.

The University of Houston (Tellez & Hlebowitsh, 1993). The Teacher Education Program at the University of Houston has recently added a field-based social services component. The emphasis on community participation and volunteerism derives from dissatisfaction with the way traditional program experiences prepare future teachers to work in urban environments. Program faculty found that their students could not relate to or effectively educate a population of young people from which they have been isolated. The faculty became convinced that direct contact and participation in urban social service activities was likely to be the most effective way for students to discover for themselves some of the problems faced by the people they were being trained to serve. The volunteer reports produced by students after their experience indicated that goals such as increasing awareness of urban conditions and investment in the community were being met. In addition, some students indicated that they found that teaching goes far beyond presentation of content and that social service activities extend beyond delivery of services. For some students the experience provided an understanding of the links that exist between the university, social service, schools, and children.

California State University, Fresno (CSUF) (Center for Collaboration for Children and Families, 1993; D. Smith, 1993). The development of an interprofessional academic program at CSUF is the direct result of having the Center for Collaboration for Children and Families on campus. The Option II Multiple Subjects Credential Program at CSUF prepares early childhhood students to teach in elementary schools with an emphasis on developing, working in, and problem solving in interprofessional, interdisciplinary collaboratives. Training is integrated throughout three semesters of coursework, fieldwork, and student teaching. Two interprofessional courses are required. A content course called Cultural Foundations Seminar exposes students to the terminology, principles, and public policy associated with interprofessional collaboration involving education, health, and social services. Students also design and analyze different collaborative models. Students observe children and families in natural settings, develop a case study, and design an interprofessional service plan based on their observations and understanding of interprofessional collaboration in a fieldwork course entitled Psychological Foundations Fieldwork. The classes are intended to help students develop their own philosophy of early childhood education and interprofessional collaboration.

Other Programs Several other universities have developed or are currently developing interprofessional education programs. These include Miami University of Ohio, University of Louisville, University of Oklahoma, University of Washington, George Washington University, Ohio State University, University of Alabama at Birmingham, University of Vermont, and Texas A&M University.

RESEARCH AND EVALUATION REPORTS

Integrated Services Programs

Admittedly there is not much long-term research on the effects of new integrated services and interprofessional preparation programs, but there is an impressive collection of documentation from pilot programs. The focus has been on systematic investigation by the people involved to examine what they are doing, with the purpose of using findings to improve programs. What many are engaged in is more than research, it is research and assessment that result in alterations when conclusions are not sufficiently aligned with goals. Educators and other social scientists may need to be more engaged in this kind of activity because each situation is unique and because data must be internalized by participants if real change is to result from reflective study. Therefore, this section is not a review of traditional research findings. It is more a sharing of activities under way and lessons learned from them.

Lehman and Fredericks (1993), working with the Research Committee of the Association of Teacher Educators (ATE) Commission on Leadership in Interprofessional Education, have compiled a valuable beginning annotated bibliography. Selected sources in this listing are reported here. As part of its work plan, the ATE Commission will continue to expand this bibliography as well as case studies of programs under way.

United States General Accounting Office In December 1993 the U.S. General Accounting Office (GAO) released a report responding to Senator Kennedy's request for: (1) a review of multiservice, school-linked approaches used to deliver child and family services, their relative strengths and weaknesses, and under what circumstances particular approaches are most appropriate; (2) identification of problems and barriers associated with school-linked service provision; and (3) determination of the role the federal government could take in advancing school-linked approaches to service delivery. The GAO conducted a literature review, interviewed leaders involved in school-linked programs, and reviewed 10 comprehensive school-linked programs.

The GAO reported the existence of strong connections between educational failure and level of income, lost tax revenue, and incarceration. Among school-linked models, the GAO noted community biases regarding the services offered and a high degree of diversity driven by the unique needs of students in the school community. Common characteristics of school-linked programs included: (1) strong leadership, (2) high value placed on the views of school staff, (3) use of school staff to identify at-risk youth, (4) use of interdisciplinary teams to connect students with services, and (5) follow-up with children and families to ensure that the services received were appropriate. The GAO also found that five of six programs studied had positive effects on school dropout rates, absenteeism, and academic achievement.

The GAO's suggestions and recommendations to the Secretary of Health and Human Services and the Secretary of Education included: (1) providing funding for planning and long-term program support, (2) providing technical assistance for program development and evaluation, (3) providing information to state and local agencies regarding the use of school-linked programs as a means to increase high school completion rates, and (4) developing an approach for evaluating the impact of school-linked programs. Both of the departments concurred with the recommendation, pointing to future involvement in school-linked programs by the federal government.

Community-Based Models The comprehensive overview of collaborative community-based integrated service efforts by Boyd (1992) described these programs as family-focused, community-based, single-sourced and case-managed, noncategorical and wrap around, individualized, interdisciplinary, and interagency. An extensive descriptive review of the literature regarding the values, principles, and rationales influencing integrated service systems for children and families was presented. This review included significant elements of legislation, such as Part H of the Individuals with Disabilities Education Act (IDEA) and its direct and indirect impact on integrated services efforts. Boyd summarized problems facing families and failing systems as the preface to presenting solutions to those problems.

Emerging models and their components were highlighted in a state-by-state format as well as proposed strategies for integrating systems to improve services to children and families. His recommendations fall within the categories of specific services, community initiatives, fiscal issues, and education and training. Appendices provide a variety of information including graphic representations of integrated services frameworks, an outline of components within an integrated system of care, and sample legislation to create a collaborative system of services and funding.

The New Beginnings Team Report (San Diego City Schools, 1990) described an interagency collaborative involving the City and County of San Diego, San Diego Community College District, and San Diego City Schools that was formed in 1988. The collaborative carried out an action research project to test the feasibility of a one-stop services center or other integrated services approaches to streamline and improve services to children and families and the impact of services provided by local agencies and the Hamilton Elementary School in San Diego. The report outlined the design of the study followed by the findings.

Nine key findings are stated in the following categories: (1) need for reform, (2) role of the school in collaboration, (3) need for a common philosophy, (4) priority of caseloads, (5) new roles of agency workers, (6) changes in policies and procedures, (7) respect for differing perceptions of needs, (8) increased input from families, and (9) deterrents to mobility. Recommendations are presented for the New Beginnings approach to integrated services based on these findings followed by an outline of explicit steps for implementation beginning with one school attendance area.

Crowson, Smylie, and Chou Hare (1992) described administrative issues involving a collaborative program called the Nation of Tomorrow, based at the University of Illinois, Chicago. Philosophical and organizational background was followed by an analysis of the project. The report covered many issues including (1) service coordination and the principalship, (2) perspectives and mentalities associated with service coordination, and (3) administration and coordination of service coordination. Successes and barriers associated with the Nation of Tomorrow were identified and were illustrated in the report.

The Zero to Three/National Center for Clinical Infant Programs (NCCIP) functions as a national resource center promoting the physical, emotional, cognitive, and social development of children 3 and younger, their families, and care providers. The Zero to Three NCCIP Report (1993), described how the center serves as a means to translate academic research and clinical experience to policy and practice. The center was established to stimulate policy development, to provide higher quality services, and to enhance services through training and the identification of best practices. Criteria for successful programs were identified as were lessons learned.

Burt, Resnick, and Matheson (1992) described programs targeting at-risk younger adolescents aged 10 to 15. The focus of their study was to learn more about the ability of programs to provide more comprehensive services through service integration. It examined the methods used to gather information, the barriers encountered, reviews of the literature related to risk definitions, prevalence of behaviors, strengths and weaknesses of traditional programs, a review of ways of evaluating integrated service programs, and observations made on site at nine programs.

The most striking implications of the findings is the need to conceptualize service integration more broadly. The Joint Initiative in Colorado Springs, which had the highest level of commitment from all of the partners, is highlighted. The authors found great interest in conducting research and evaluation but found limited resources to do it the way it should be done, especially when the research design must consider all program activities and participants.

Dolan (1992) examined five model integrated services programs. His analysis was supported by the Center for Research on Effective Schooling for Disadvantaged Students (CDS) whose mission is to improve educational services for disadvantaged students at each level of education. It documented some of the characteristics of effective programs and outlined potential evaluation strategies that might facilitate garnering a better understanding of client and community impact. The model programs reviewed were: (1) School-Based Health Clinics, Baltimore; (2) Success for All, at 35 sites nationally; (3) School-Based Youth Services, New Jersey; (4) The New Beginnings Program, San Diego; and (5) the Comer School Development Program, nationally represented. Seven lessons learned and several evaluation issues were discussed in the report.

State Interagency Collaboration Interagency collaboration approaches being implemented in four western states, Arizona, California, Nevada, and Utah, were described by Guthrie and Scott (1991). The introduction provided background information and the rationale for integrating services, followed by brief descriptions of six approaches to interagency collaboration implemented in nine selected programs. The programs ranged from localized efforts that concentrate social services at a single school site, to countywide coordination and management of services. In addition to location, contact person, and address, each program profiled included information about the historical development, organizational structure and goals, community description, services provided, and evidence of outcomes. Three of the programs included descriptions of evaluation activities.

In their report of a project funded by the Ford Foundation to launch a national effort to help education and human service sectors work together to aid children and families at risk, Levy and Copple (1989) summarized substantive knowledge gained from cross-sector collaboration. The authors included the results of a survey sent to all state education and human service agencies in an effort to list the current state-level examples of collaborative task forces, agreements, and initiatives. Survey results showed that a great deal of collaborative interagency planning was already under way.

Buckley and Bigelow (1992) described a Multi-Service Network program in Vancouver, British Columbia. The program is a collaboration among mental health, alcohol/drug treatment, corrections, forensic, social service, and housing agencies. The purpose of the project was to provide more effective services at less cost for multiproblem, service-resistant individuals. Three case studies and the results of two evaluative studies were summarized. The case studies presented are those identified as exemplary. Two evaluations were conducted. The first measured fiscal impacts with results showing some increases in welfare costs, together with decreases in institutional costs. The second addressed agency outcomes. Documenting information on the multiple needs of clients and the number of separate agencies serving the clients were considered the most important outcomes. The goal of reducing agency time spent with clients was not accomplished.

The final evaluation of the Communities in Schools (CIS) Program (E. Smith, 1993), conducted 5 years after the first interdependent evaluation, reported successful results as measured by student retention, lower rates of arrests of at-risk youth for serious offenses, employment, academic performance, and school attendance. Thirteen cities participated in CIS when this evaluation was conducted, and the sample included students from kindergarten through high school. The report described the history of CIS, its mission and organization, project objectives and methodology, data-collection instruments, and limitations of the study. The results indicated the success of the program in terms of outcomes for secondary school students.

Integrated Services for Special Populations Dollard, Silver, and Huz (1991) described New York State's Intensive Case Management Program (NYICM), evaluation plan, and outcome data. NYICM is a statewide intervention whose primary goal is to keep children with serious emotional disturbance (SED) in the least restrictive environment appropriate to their needs. It was introduced in 1988 to expand community-based support options and to improve care for children with SED who were unserved or underserved by the mental health system. The program model is an intensive, client-centered service provided on a 24-hour, 7-days-a-week basis. Each case manager had a caseload of 10 children. Flexible service dollars were provided to purchase services. These dollars could be accessed by all children, including those not enrolled in NYICM.

Data-collection and analysis procedures were presented. The evaluation was driven by client characteristics and outcomes, service system characteristics and outcomes, and intensive case manager characteristics and behavior domains. Preliminary outcomes were reported. At the time of the report, only 12% of children had been discharged from the program. The average stay was 10 months. The program appeared to have positive results in that the majority of children stayed in the community living situations. In addition, there was a significant reduction in admission to hospitals and in the number of inpatient days spent at the hospital post NYICM.

Nelson and Pearson (1991) provided a foundation for policy and program planners interested in developing collaborative interagency programs for children and youth with emotional and behavioral disorders (EBD). The authors presented a rationale for interagency service provision by reporting child and family demographic information, problems inherent in a fragmented system, and successful integrated service efforts. Several model programs were described, including the Alaska Youth Initiative, the Ventura Model, and the Bluegrass Interagency Mobilization for Progress in Adolescent and Children's Treatment (IMPACT). Evaluation procedures were explained and interagency resources were identified.

A comprehensive effort to redesign services to children and youth with EBD in Kentucky was studied by Phillips, Nelson, and McLaughlin (1993). Need for the program was discussed, followed by a description of three key events that produced a climate conducive to systems change. These events were the Kentucky State Board for Elementary and Secondary Education's study verifying prior underidentification of students with EBD; the Department for Mental Health and Mental Retardation Services' (DMHMRS) response to national priorities in develop-

ing a call for action for coordinated, community-based services; and the Kentucky Department of Education and DMHMRS hiring personnel with a broad-based vision and an orientation toward collaboration. The result was legislation (HB 838), passed in 1989, which directed agencies to provide community-based services to children and families. The plan is known as Kentucky IMPACT.

The authors described tangible outcomes that emerged from these efforts. The plan has led to a technical assistance manual, expanded school and community-based service delivery options, funding allocations for service coordination, mental health options, and funding allocations for service professionals and legislators. The program evaluation plan was described and includes a list of the seven major questions. The evaluation included student outcomes, nature and scope analyses of interagency collaboration, and cost-efficiency studies of service delivery. In addition, student follow-up data were collected at 3-, 6-, and 12-month intervals. The authors concluded their report with an extensive reference list of integrated programs currently being implemented across the country.

Burns and Friedman (1990) examined the research base for child mental health services and policies. They emphasized the importance of research that examined the overall community-based system of care, stressing the need to maintain a systems perspective. In addition, the authors provided an overview of the kind of studies conducted on a variety of mental health services. These services included psychiatric hospitalization, residential treatment centers and therapeutic group homes, partial hospitalization and day treatment, home-based treatment, outpatient psychotherapy, case management, and individualized service models.

Soler and Shauffer (1993) presented case studies that emphasized the need for an integrated system of service delivery to children and families. In addition, two model coordinated mental health programs, the Willie M. Program and the Ventura Model, were described. The barriers that had to be overcome in implementing the programs were demonstrated. Important to note were two key elements facilitating coordination, case management and the management information system. The description of the Ventura Model included 11 guiding principles that the authors pointed out were remarkably similar to those for the Willie M. Program. The article concluded with the presentation of current research being conducted by the Youth Law Center to determine the factors that are necessary for effective coordination of services, and to identify barriers to successful coordination. The authors identified several elements indicative of success under four categories: (1) general system values, (2) system processes, (3) ability to provide quality services, and (4) systems management.

Interprofessional Education Programs

Just as integrated services programs are developing, a number of interprofessional training programs in universities and staff development programs in schools and community agencies are emerging to support them. Commonalties exist across curricula such as seminar courses that are team facilitated, internships, and other field experiences that cross disciplines. Many of the courses and workshops emphasize interprofessional leadership training, organizational theory, service coordination, and collaboration.

Lehman and Fredericks (1993), with the Research Committee of the ATE Commission on Leadership in Interprofessional Education, have also provided a useful beginning list of sources on new interprofessional education programs. Selected references from the ATE Commission annotated bibliography are summarized here.

Interprofessional Development Components Drawing on his experience with the Commission on Interprofessional Education and Practice at Ohio State University, Casto (1987) presented a set of principles central to a program of preservice interprofessional education. These principles included courses that cover a wide range of social and professional problems, a faculty team approach, opportunities for graduate students and practicing professionals to take courses together, maintenance of a mix of professions, and use of a case-study approach. The author described courses being offered including course objectives and content. Lavern L. Cunningham, director of the Ohio State University Center and a national leader, has been a pioneer in developing interprofessional collaborative ventures for many years.

Snyder (1987) proposed a theory of interprofessional practice and education. Both dimensions were described in normative and prescriptive ways. Initially, the author presented conditions to be addressed when developing interprofessional support for patients/clients and then explained how a theory for interprofessional preparation can be developed based on the kind of collaboration specified by a parallel theory of interprofessional practice. The barriers to collaboration were discussed in addition to trends and events that are moving education, health, and human services toward more interprofessional activities.

Haberman and Delgadillo (1994) compared two groups of beginning teachers, who were themselves predominately African American and Hispanic, in their first year of teaching in urban schools serving low-income children. This experience constituted their professional training year because they were all residents in an intern teaching program. Findings and recommendations focused on: (1) the impact of training teachers about specific health and human services offered to students in their classrooms, establishing a cooperative system of sharing information among public health and human service agencies, public schools, and families; (2) identifying the essential elements in teacher–student relationships to improve student learning; (3) helping school systems provide in-service training for teachers to share information with other professionals and caregivers; and (4) preparing beginning teachers to work effectively with children in poverty.

Gallmeier and Bonner (1992) provided a description of 10 university-based interdisciplinary training programs, supported by the National Center on Child Abuse and Neglect, that deal with child maltreatment. The organizational structure, student composition, and interdepartmental academic requirements of the programs were described. One program was covered in detail to provide a model for replication. Securing adequate funding from complex interdepartmental and cross-college organizational policies and structures was stated as a crucial factor.

Second, the authors recommended that integrated service programs established in a comprehensive university system of higher education must identify a core faculty and at least one full-time faculty member to assume responsibility for coordinating the program. The authors believe that the curriculum must provide didactic and clinical components with a variety of opportunities to develop interdisciplinary skills and that supervision and teaching should be conducted by a broad range of community professionals as well as university faculty.

Interprofessional Preparation for Special Populations State policy recommendations on leadership training that resulted from a group discussion on emerging trends in special education and implications for teacher education were summarized by Lowenbraun (1990). The study concluded that the education of special educators and regular educators evolves from different origins and proceeds in different directions. It recommended that the isolation between the two be reduced by providing cooperative instruction and responsibility throughout training programs. Barriers to attaining interdisciplinary skills, knowledge, and attitudes included the lack of appropriate mentors and interprofessionally oriented role models in higher education and public education. The length and expense of preparation programs that require extensive interdisciplinary training was also stated as a significant obstacle. The study recommended changes in the nature of federal funding for leadership training programs.

Bruder and McCollum (1991) analyzed plans for special education personnel development by those states submitting applications for Part H of PL 99-457, the Education of the Handicapped Act Amendments of 1989. The eight states used a variety of approaches in addressing the law's two primary components: (1) standards for early intervention personnel, and (2) a comprehensive system of personnel development (CSPD). Included in plans were audiologists, special educators, nurses, nutritionists, occupational therapists, physical therapists, physicians, psychologists, social workers, and speech/language pathologists. The report included a table with questions to guide the development of a statewide personnel development system.

Garland and Buck (1990) described a 3-year training project to form program staff that serve children from birth to 3 years who have disabilities, are developmentally delayed, or are at risk. Twenty programs and 282 professionals in six states received training. The project coordinated training and technical assistance with the state agency responsible for overseeing the programs. The project developed and field-tested training units that addressed family systems, interagency collaboration, team building, and case management. Follow-up data showed that 85% of the programs developed plans to change what they were doing. The most frequently mentioned change areas were the development of a family focus and team functioning.

Profiling 10 programs, Fenichel and Eggbeer (1990) discussed issues and made recommendations to policymakers on the preparation of practitioners to work with infants, toddlers, and their families. Their study provided examples of promising approaches to enhancing competence through training in preservice, in-service, and continuing education. Further, the authors suggested priorities for collaborative action among policymakers, parents, educators, and professionals to improve training. A set of core concepts in nontechnical language to be used across disciplines was presented.

Ten projects to prepare personnel to provide vocational education to students with special needs were analyzed by MacArthur and Allen (1981). Each program description provided an overview of goals, effective strategies, and problems encountered. The approaches emphasized in-service training for delivering comprehensive vocational and career education services. Descriptions of interdisciplinary personnel preparation, cooperative interdisciplinary personnel development projects, and a master's degree program in vocation/special education were included.

Winton (1992) described an interdisciplinary curriculum for teaching a families course that was designed to be used by graduate students studying early intervention with families of young children with disabilities. The curriculum contact provided information on theory, research, policy, and law with direct application for working with families. Students had the opportunity to engage in interdisciplinary discussions and activities. Instructional objectives were established at the knowledge and attitude, rather than the behavioral, levels. The interdisciplinary component provided training in collaboration, communication strategies, and service coordination. There was an emphasis on including families as team members. Course and student evaluation information were included.

FUTURE CONSIDERATIONS

Analysis of the aforementioned studies of current integrated service programs and of the interprofessional training and research programs to support them provides some lessons learned that each of the professional partners may want to consider as they work together.

Barriers

Creating interprofessional collaboration among major service providers, families, children, and communities to plan and deliver services is a radical departure from the current state of the art in most systems. It should be expected that efforts to change funding, organizational structures, evaluation policies and procedures, and even the definition of who the client is, incur significant resistance. Following are some of the most often cited barriers that have been encountered by those involved in developing collaborative systems. Many of the conflicts cluster around the issues of governance, finance, information sharing, and participant alignment.

Governance and Organizational Structure When a particular agency is perceived as owning an interagency partnership, other agencies are likely to participate in name only (Gardner, 1992). In effect the partnership becomes a facade. In addition, restructuring the reporting lines and relationships among personnel to serve the collaborative best will often present difficulties.

Finance, Funding, and Other Resources If a particular agency is seen as being in charge of the collaborative it may be difficult

to attract funding from other agencies. The process of maintaining a flow of funds can be derailed if funding agencies are not involved in deciding what are desired outcomes and what evaluation tools are acceptable (Gardner, 1992). If the funding agency is not included, it may not know when the program is progressing successfully, or it may not agree with the program coordinator's progress and outcomes assessment. In addition, the uncertainty associated with temporary or undependable funding streams can make planning difficult and can cause instability in the program (Chase & Cahn, 1992; Schmid & Dawes, 1992). Funding streams to public agencies are normally categorical (Bruner, 1991), which tends to reduce agency flexibility and impose artificially narrow definitions on eligibility and use of funds (Farrow & Joe, 1992). Resources and funds must be shared within a collaborative (Melaville & Blank, 1991), and categorical funding can make resource sharing difficult. The lack of organizational and personal resources other than funding also acts as a barrier. Three resources cited as lacking in organizations that affect the development of collaboratives are time (Gardner, 1992; Schmid & Dawes, 1992), personnel (Bruner, 1991), and facilities (Gardner, 1992).

Information Sharing As noted, collaboratives require sharing of resources. Information is one of the most important resources needed to run a service organization. Although a necessity, client information confidentiality can pose a barrier to effective collaboration (Gardner, 1992). In *Confidentiality and Collaboration: Information Sharing in Interagency Efforts,* Greenberg and Levy (1992) suggested applying a *need to know* standard and a rigorous information delivery system to facilitate the exchange of confidential information. A second barrier to effective information sharing is poorly designed or obsolete information systems, both computerized and manual (Gardner, 1992).

Participant Alignment There are many barriers to participant alignment in a collaborative. Some of the barriers are: (1) not including constituents in the planning process (Gardner, 1992); (2) the fact that professionals are trained to specialize, not generalize (Farrow & Joe, 1992); (3) different foci among the professions regarding the importance of achieving near-term and long-term goals (Chase & Cahn, 1992); (4) differences in bureaucratic structures among collaborating organizations (Chase & Cahn, 1992); and (5) the fact that collaborating organizations open themselves to having their current structures, professional assumptions, and reward systems challenged (Bruner, 1991).

Meaning of Collaboration As Ladd (1969) stated years ago, each group participating in the collaborative venture means new help for achieving its objectives. It means that, in a sense, members of one group become the others' agents. For the new help that each group expects to get from the other, over and above any explicit quid pro quo, it may have to pay and it pays in several important ways. These include accepting and learning new habits, giving up old ways of doing things, and confronting differences that may cause misunderstanding or even resentment.

Collaborative ventures must accommodate a wide range of differences in customs, characteristics, and styles of operation.

Differences exist in the way policy is made; the role of the written word and means of communication; workload and scheduling; attitudes toward cooperation; expenditure of funds and budgeting patterns (merit systems, civil service, single salary schedules); research and development procedures; personnel practices; degrees of personal commitment to the goals of the organization; each particular profession's perceived relative status or self-esteem (self-image); and each partner's willingness to express education, political, and social views (Corrigan, 1992).

Perhaps the most difficult factor in developing collaborative efforts in education, health, and human services is that the most needy clients are often the poorest. The challenge is to cut across wealthy suburbs and inner cities, to get wealthy suburbanites to take seriously the problems of the city they may have fled. As Hodgkinson (1992) pointed out, it is difficult to get economic classes to work together. Places exist where whites, African Americans, Hispanics, Asians, and Native Americans live together in peace and harmony, but places where rich and poor people live together in peace and harmony are rare. Much of what appears to be a problem between races in America is actually a problem between classes (Fredericks, 1993).

Although the problems of reluctance to change the status quo, turfism, organizational restructuring, declining monetary resources, and lack of interprofessionally trained personnel are formidable barriers, probably the greatest challenge for leaders in education and health and human services is to convince this generation of Americans to accept responsibility for ensuring the human rights of others as well as their own rights—to achieve a sense of human connectedness. We must replace the politics of greed and fear with the politics of caring. In the future, *all* of the children of *all* of the people (rich and poor) must have access to the opportunity to become all they are capable of becoming. The degree to which the aforementioned factors are understood, anticipated, and planned for by leaders of new collaborative ventures will determine, in large measure, success or failure.

Research as Means Not Ends

The quality of research associated with the establishment, operation, and evaluation of community-based programs is likely to have an impact on the support of programs and to influence future public policy. Because so much is at stake, there is a great deal of debate about appropriate research designs and tools for data collection and dissemination. Perhaps most important is the debate about the purpose of research itself.

The concept of participatory research is being considered as an alternative to, or used in addition to, agency-centered research (Center for Study of Social Policy, 1993a; Levin & Greene, 1994). The Center for Study of Social Policy suggested that evaluation designs focus on the sum total of the collaborative system's efforts. The individual units should track their own performance as a subsystem to maintain accountability on that level. This arrangement requires the collaborative to identify goals and needs as well as to design a systematic process to conduct research and self-evaluation.

Levin and Greene (1994) have developed a cogent argument for the use of participatory program evaluation for integrated service and interprofessional education programs. Participatory evaluation compliments collaborative service development and delivery in both structure and philosophy. Participatory program evaluation, like interprofessional collaboration, involves a multitude of diverse program stakeholders. Participatory design allows all stakeholders to contribute to the system in a constructive, meaningful way. The information generated from research is fed back into the system for reflection and analysis. As feedback, the information is used for program improvement, not just for publication and presentation. Beyond the benefits of fostering group ownership, consensus, and responsibility regarding the system, a diverse group of stakeholders helps provide contextually rich information from multiple perspectives that will likely improve the capacity of the system and quality of decisions. In addition, participatory research or program design is consistent with democratic ideals associated with empowerment (Levin & Greene, 1994).

This approach is in sharp contrast to the way most university research is designed today. Historically, university research has been defined rather narrowly, with the subject acting primarily as a passive participant. Practitioners, families, and children are often the subjects of research on program development and evaluation, but mostly are not involved beyond that. Ironically, practitioners and clients are likely to have the most direct access to data and are often most qualified to interpret the data. Who knows more about why some kids miss school than a child who has lived in several homeless shelters? Who can better estimate the effects that alcohol and substance abuse have on employability, school attendance, and child abuse than those that live with those conditions? Who really knows why an unwanted or unexpected pregnancy occurred? Members of the service population know. It also would not be entirely unexpected to find that data contained in eviction records, medical records, and police records would provide some insights into why some children miss school. School workers such as custodians, grounds keepers, cafeteria employees, and secretaries can amass an incredible amount of knowledge regarding how things really work in the school and where potential health and safety hazards exist.

A wonderful revelation regarding the activities of clients, peers, and other practitioners is that they are conducting and creating research by just doing their jobs. Moreover, the data that they create and have access to are useful to other people in the system. Unfortunately, so long as individuals performing formal research isolate investigators engaged in *living research,* this potential for meaningful inquiry is lost. It is only when living research is considered legitimate and clients and practitioners are allowed to participate in research design, execution, and analysis that this resource can be realized.

In this scenario, research is viewed as a means, not an end. The expected end of participatory research is to create effective collaborative education, health, and human service delivery systems that produce healthy learners who possess the knowledge, skills, and values needed to get and keep a job, create healthy families, and know how to work together to create healthy human communities. Research, as well as training, are means to achieve this end. This view of research, as a means not an end, will require far-reaching changes in the prevailing attitudes and reward systems of universities, as well as in the perceptions of the public (clients) regarding the role and value of university-based research.

Focus interviews and other feedback show that clients and staff involved in integrated service programs do not trust the university. They see the university as a separate, elite culture that wants to change others while it remains the same. When professors come into the community to help, they come as experts. Or worse, they come with their predetermined frameworks that immediately put the client's problems into categories. For example, setting up programs that respond to the needs of homeless children and families who live under a bridge or in a tunnel does not fit nicely into the current infatuation with national standards and testing. Research professors sometimes cannot think outside of their own paradigms. They suffer from a hardening of the categories. They are unable to put themselves inside the skin of the people they are studying. Most of the current research paradigms do not look at the whole system, or the whole child, or the whole family, or the whole community.

Involvement in participatory research, shared community governance, and decision making presents special problems for universities. The most successful programs operate from two of the most fundamental principles of change: (1) People who are going to implement a plan must be involved in developing the plan, and (2) never do for others what they can do for themselves—people must be empowered to act on their own behalf. When community leaders and their clients jointly develop strategies based on these principles, education problems, health problems, and human service problems often become political problems that require political action. Universities have difficulty getting involved with political problems—they find it hard to be advocates for anything political or controversial that may get in the way of their own self-interest with the community or legislature.

It is not surprising that collaborative efforts that have the most successful involvement with universities seem to be in situations where the university is a partner in a community-based entity that takes the lead. Instead of the university faculty making a frontal attack as experts, they share their talents in the areas where they are asked to assist. They respond to needs identified by clients. They exert leadership by honestly participating with others in solving mutual problems facing their communities. Such a collaboratively developed community-based entity defines its own policies, roles, rewards, and expectations from a child- and family-centered perspective and assists the partners in getting their home institutions to accept those conditions as part of the contract for their institution's participation. Within this environment, university professors can act without the ritual, rules, and reward systems of the culture of the university. Clients and peers in the collaborative, community-based system, care most about one thing—do university faculty have something to offer to the goals of the program? In this context, training, research, and evaluation become instruments for improving services to clients. If someone gets an article or two out of the experience or a book, that is fine, but the primary purpose of the collaborative, interprofessionally oriented effort is to improve the quality of life of America's most needy children and families.

Participatory research grows out of practice and returns to practice to improve it. The quality of the research undertaken is judged by how much it helps solve the problems of clients, not how much it adds to the research professor's resume or how good a paper presentation or article in a refereed journal it will make. This research rationale is based on the notion that some of the most important knowledge that needs to be discovered today is how to use knowledge to improve the quality of life in America. As Boyer (1990) pointed out in *Scholarship Reconsidered,* in addition to the scholarship of discovery, the university must begin to enhance and reward the scholarship of integration, of application, and of teaching. Communities need scholars who can *act* on thinking—scholars whose espoused theory matches their *theory in use.*

Thus far, few university presidents and boards of regents have given improved service to America's most needy children and families a high priority in the current reexamination of university mission statements and faculty reward systems (promotion, tenure, and merit pay criteria). In a country where one of four children now lives in poverty, perhaps a new generation of visionary leaders will emerge. As the current debate regarding the role of the university continues, these leaders will have to convince the public and policymakers that knowledge (research) is as critical to the moral and social development of America as it is to economic development.

Simultaneous Reform

As on past occasions in the history of professional education, the policymakers have not incorporated interprofessional development in reform proposals. Even though training is the key to reforming the system, very little attention has been given to it in policy formulation. Practitioners do not change by passing laws; they only change if they have the opportunity to learn new knowledge and skills. It seems that the policymakers and the politicians need to be reminded again that the reform of professional practice and of the teaching and research arm of the participating professions must take place simultaneously. Change in one without change in the other will not work.

It must also be recognized that the kind of training needed is more complex because interprofessional education requires universitywide changes. Even though some interprofessional programs are emerging, a comprehensive view of higher education shows that there are few interactions between education, health, and human services faculty in the development and implementation of their respective professional curricula. In view of the calls for reform reported in this chapter, university faculty must confront a most vivid truth—if they do not model collaborative behavior in the training and research arm of the education, health, and human services professions, it is unlikely that future providers will understand the importance of such coordination or be prepared to function in the new unified system that is emerging. The education profession, in conjunction with the other human service professions, must identify the particular knowledge, skills, and values needed by teachers, counselors, and administrators in order to be effective collaborators with health and human services providers, and vice versa. They must ensure that the aforementioned knowledge, skills, and values become part of the curriculum in each field of specialization and that they are infused appropriately into interprofessional programs.

In addition to reforming university preparation on campus, creative ways must be developed to make appropriate knowledge and related skills a part of continuing education efforts. Because it is unlikely that there will be adequate staff in schools and health and human services agencies who are prepared to offer such training, practitioners will need to work with their respective professional associations and collaborating universities to offer staff development programs. Adjunct faculty will need to be trained so that they can serve as trainers and mentors in interprofessional development programs on community sites.

Central to the conceptualization of interprofessional education as a means for reforming education, health, and human services is a recognition of the fact that colleges of education, schools, and community agencies are interrelated and interacting components of one system. In this system schools will have to be legitimized as a locus of advocacy for all children, the poor and deprived, not just the rich and powerful. Because schools are the only community institutions that see every child every day, school leaders will need to accept the responsibility to help mobilize community resources, and colleges of education must prepare their graduates for this mission.

It is important to note that the advocacy role does not mean that all services are performed on the school site. The schools' main functions are: (1) to teach relevant knowledge—to develop the intellect so that all students can make intelligent decisions regarding the complex problems that children and their families face in today's world, (2) to connect children and their families with professional in other agencies dealing with the health and human service needs of the community, and (3) to network with others in developing a collaborative systemic strategy to develop policies and programs that increase the civic capacity to create healthy humane communities.

Lawson (1994), who journeyed throughout the United States studying full-service schools, pointed out that such schools are not just engaged in structural changes. The changes go much deeper. Purpose and substance are changed by actually developing schools as family-friendly support environments. He used Briar's (1993) pioneering work in Florida as an example that involves parents delivering social and educational services while recasting the roles of social workers, health care professionals, community developers, teachers, school psychologists, and school principals. She integrated the strategies of family empowerment and community development into a systems change agenda. The full-service concept cultivates educational communities by expanding their activities and participants during the non-school hours in school facilities. In fact, it changes these facilities too. The child- and family-centered community development approach involves nothing short of the reimagining and reinvention of schools, community agencies, and their relationships.

Dryfoos (1994) described the components of full-service schools that serve as one stop unfragmented collaborative institutions. Deriving from more modest school-based health centers, many of these schools, particularly in disadvantaged neighborhoods, provide families a range of social services from parenting education to housing and employment assistance. A look into the future indicates that many of tomorrow's schools will be the hub of a community network for facilitating access to various components of the education, health, and human services delivery system.

Interprofessional Development Schools

When full-service schools are designed and utilized as centers of inquiry for preservice and in-service training and research, as well as hubs of the network of community-based integrated service programs, they become interprofessional development schools. As seen in the case studies presented in this chapter, an increasing number of school sites have social workers, psychologists, child care workers, health clinics, tutors, mentors from business and industry, adult literacy, and parenting specialists, and so on. Now that the professional development movement is well under way, this interprofessional dimension can be added to the design of future professional development schools. In fact, interprofessional development schools may be the best setting in which to start interprofessional training and research because that is where the interface across professions is taking place and where it will take place in the future.

Conceptualizing interprofessional development schools as centers of intellectual inquiry that will lead their communities in developing a system of integrated services and that will help children and families meet the intellectual, economic, demographic, and social challenges of the twenty-first century is a significant enough purpose, with important enough consequences, to be a powerful motivator. The most severe shortcoming of past reform movements is that educators have concentrated on means rather than ends. The education profession has been so enamored with the means of education, (organizational changes [longer days, year-round schools] and technological changes [testing, computers, and television]), that it has failed to examine the fundamental purposes of American public education.

The first priority for all of the partners involved in designing interprofessional development schools and other education and human services collaborative efforts today must be the construction of purposes. So many past reform efforts have not lasted because the purposes of the reforms were not clear enough and the consequences of the reforms were not powerful enough to sustain the reforms over the long haul.

The primary strategy for change in the past was to set up model projects that lasted only as long as the government or private sector funding kept flowing. When the money ran out, or the political advocate for a particular model project died or moved on to other priorities, the reform faded into the night. It will take a big idea to match the enormity of the problems facing education and society in the twenty-first century. America must create a comprehensive collaboratively designed, community-based, family-oriented, integrated infrastructure that involves professional leaders from all of the education, health, and human service agencies in communities across the country.

CONCLUSION

Much of the groundwork has been laid to build collaborative education, health, and human services systems. The degenerating and debilitating living conditions that many children and families in America experience are clearly stated in the form of statistics and case studies. The reality that these statistics and observations convey has resulted in the identification of needs and has provided the motivation for comprehensive reform. Integrated service programs and the interprofessional education and research programs to support them are becoming a reality. The concept of integrated service systems is being endorsed by the involved professions in the form of policy statements; by government in the form of legislation; and by the research and training arm of the professions through centers for the study of collaboration and the development of interprofessional training programs. Public- and private-sector funds have been provided to an increasing number of community-based collabortives and interprofessional organizations that are willing to share lessons learned for others to examine. A number of interprofessional commission designed to study and disseminate the concept and provide information about programs and research have been established, including the Association of Teacher Educators National Commission on Leadership in Inter-professional Education to Create Collaborative, Child and Family Centered, Education, Health and Human Service Systems (Corrigan, 1994).

Because education is such an essential component of the new collaborative system, SCDEs must be in the forefront of this interprofessional education movement. America needs a new cadre of leaders in each of the involved professions who possess vision and can manage cooperation—professionals who realize that collaboration in education, health, and human services today is not an option—it is a necessity and an obligation of leadership. In order for leaders from the various professions to interact effectively, an understanding of the professional cultures of each must be acknowledged. This can only occur as dialog among groups is fostered. Only as a new generation of interprofessionally oriented leaders views today's education, health, and social problems from other perspectives, and learns to walk in other shoes, can barriers be replaced with bridges of understanding. This chapter is our contribution to that dialog.

References

Adams, G., & Sandfort, J. R. (1992). *State investments in child care and early childhood education*. Washington, DC: Children's Defense Fund. (ERIC Document Reproduction Service No. ED 353 033)

Anderson, J. (1993). *Response sheet: Program information on integrated services and interprofessional education*. Unpublished raw data, University of Seattle.

Anderson, J., & Guest, K. (1993, February). *Meeting the needs of children and youth: Seattle University's community service program for preservice teachers*. Paper presented at the meeting of the American Association of Colleges for Teacher Education, San Diego.

Behrman, R. E. (Ed.). (1992). *The future of children. 2*(1). Washington, DC: Center for the Future of Children, The David and Lucile Packard Foundation.

Booth, S. (1991). TNT building the nation of tomorrow today. *Illinois Quarterly, 3*(1), 6–10.

Boyd, L. A. (1992). *Integrating systems of care for children and families. An overview of values, methods, and characteristics of developing models, with examples and recommendations*. Tampa: University of Florida, Florida Mental Health Institute.

Boyer, E. L. (1990). *Scholarship reconsidered: Priorities of the professoriate*. Princeton: Carnegie Foundation for the Advancement of Teaching.

Boyer, E. L. (1991). *Ready to learn: A mandate for the nation*. Princeton: Carnegie Foundation for the Advancement of Teaching.

Briar, K. (1993). *Response sheet: Program information on integrated services and interprofessional education*. Unpublished raw data, Florida International University, Miami.

Bruder, M. B., & McCollum, J. (1991). *Analysis of state applications for year 4: Planning for the personnel components of Part H of IDEA*. Chapel Hill: North Carolina University, Frank Porter Graham Center. (ERIC Document Reproduction Service No. ED 340 171)

Bruner, C. (1991). *Thinking collaboratively. Ten questions and answers to help policy makers improve children's services*. Washington, DC: Education and Human Services Consortium.

Buckley, R., & Bigelow, D. A. (1992). The multi-service network: Reaching the unserved multi-problem individual. *Community Mental Health Journal, 28*(1), 43–50.

Burns, B. J., & Friedman, R. M. (1990). Examining the research base for child mental health services and policy. *The Journal of Mental Health Administration, 17*(1), 87–98.

Burt, M. R., Resnick, G., & Matheson, N. (1992). Comprehensive services integration programs for at risk youth: Final report. Washington, DC: Urban Institute.

California Legislature. Assembly bill No. 2765 (1992).

Casto, R. M. (1987). Preservice courses for interprofessional practice. *Theory into Practice: Interprofessional Education, 26*(2), 103–109.

Center for Collaboration for Children. (1993). Untitled and unpublished manuscript, California State University, Fullerton, School of Human Development and Community Service.

Center for Collaboration for Children and Families. (1993). *Interprofessional Teacher Training*. Unpublished manuscript, California State University Fresno, School of Education.

Center for the Study of Social Policy. (1993a). *Community services and supports to improve the outcomes for children*. Washington, DC: Author.

Center for the Study of Social Policy. (1993b). *Kids count data book: State profiles of child well-being*. Washington, DC: Author. (ERIC Document Reproduction Service No. ED 357 110)

Chase, Y., & Cahn, K. (1992). Schools of social work and child welfare agencies: Barriers and bridges to better collaboration. In K. Hooper Briar, V. Hooker Hansen, & N. Harris (Eds.), *New partnerships: Proceedings from the National Public Child Welfare Training Symposium* (pp. 113–125). Miami: Florida International University.

Children's Aid Society. (1993). *Building a community: A revolutionary design in public education*. New York: Author.

Children's Defense Fund. (1992). *Vanishing dreams: The economic plight of America's young families*. Washington, DC: Author.

Children's Defense Fund. (1994). *The state of America's children, yearbook 1994: Leave no child behind*. Washington, DC: Author.

Committee for Economic Development. (1985). *Investing in our children: Business and the public schools*. New York: Research and Policy Committee of the Committee for Economic Development.

Cooper, P. (1990). *West Feliciana Parish Schools Integrated Services Program: Year four*. Unpublished manuscript, West Feliciana Parish Schools, LA.

Corrigan, D. (1992). Reflections on thirty years of building collaborative efforts. *Teaching Education, 4*(2), 1–10.

Corrigan, D. (1994). Future directions of partnerships in education: Schools, universities, and human service systems. In M. J. O'Hair &

S. J. Odell (Eds.), *Partnerships in education: Teacher education yearbook II* (pp. 281–292). Fort Worth: Harcourt Brace.

Crowson, R. L., Smylie, M. A., & Chou Hare, V. (1992). *Administration in coordinated children's services: A Chicago study.* Chicago: University of Illinois.

Dawson, D. A., & Cain, V. S. (1990). *Child care arrangements: Health of our nation's children.* Hyattsville, MD: National Center for Health Statistics. (ERIC Document Reproduction Service No. ED 325 251)

Dolan, L. J. (1992). *Models for integrating human services into the school* (Report No. 30). Baltimore: Johns Hopkins University, Center for Research on Effective Schooling for Disadvantaged Students.

Dollard, N., Silver, E., & Huz, S. (1991). *Evaluation of New York State's children and youth intensive case management program.* Albany: New York State Office of Mental Health. (ERIC Document Reproduction Service No. ED 337 486)

Dreher, N. (1993). *Response sheet: Program information on integrated services and interprofessional education,* Unpublished raw data, West Feliciana Parish Schools, LA.

Dryfoos, J. G. (1994). *Full service schools. A revolution in health and social services for children, youth, and families.* San Francisco: Jossey-Bass.

Dunkle, M., & Usdan, M. D. (1993). Putting people first means connecting education to other services. *Education Week, 12*(23), 34–44.

Education Commission of the States. (1992). *Putting it together: Redefining education and family services for children.* Denver: Author.

Farrow, F., & Joe, T. (1992). Financing school-linked, integrated services. *The Future of Children, 2*(1), 56–67.

Fenichel, E. S., & Eggbeer, L. (1990). *Preparing practitioners to work with infants, toddlers and their families: Issues and recommendations for policymakers.* Washington, DC: National Center for Clinical Infant Programs, Training Approaches for Skills and Knowledge Project. (ERIC Document Reproduction Service No. ED 321 853)

Fredericks, B. (1993). *Integrated service systems for troubled youth.* Unpublished manuscript, Western Oregon State College, Teaching Research Division, Monmouth.

Gallmeier, T. M., & Bonner, B. L. (1992). University-based interdisciplinary training in child abuse and neglect. *Child Abuse and Neglect, 16*(4), 513–521.

Gardner, S. L. (1992). Key issues in developing school-linked, integrated services. *The Future of Children, 2*(1), 85–94.

Garland, C. W., & Buck, D. M. (1990). *Project trans/team inservice training project: Final report.* Lightfoot, VA: Williamsburg Area Child Development Resources, Inc. (ERIC Document Reproduction Service No. ED 344 366)

Greenberg, M., & Levy, J. (1992). *Confidentiality and collaboration: Information sharing in interagency efforts.* Denver: Education Commission of the States.

Guthrie, L. F., & Scott, B. L. (1991). *School–community linkages in the western region.* San Francisco: Far West Laboratory for Educational Research and Development, Student At Risk Programs. (ERIC Document Reproduction Service No. ED 342 136)

Haberman, M., & Delgadillo, L. (1994). *The impact of training teachers of children in poverty about the specific health and human services offered to the students in their classrooms.* Unpublished manuscript, School of Education, University of Wisconsin, Milwaukee.

Hamburg, D. A. (1992). *Children of urban poverty: Approaches to a critical American problem.* New York: Carnegie.

Healthy Learners. (1993a). *Healthy learners, healthy schools, healthy communities.* Unpublished manuscript.

Healthy Learners. (1993b). *The "Healthy Learners" Service Integration Project Feinberg/Fisher Elementary Community school.* Unpublished manuscript.

Hechinger, F. M. (1992). *Fateful choices: Healthy youth for the 21st century.* Washington, DC: Carnegie Council on Adolescent Development.

Hewlett, S. A. (1991). *When the bough breaks: The cost of neglecting our children.* New York: Basic Books.

Hodgkinson, H. L. (1987). *Higher education: Diversity is our middle name.* Washington, DC: The National Institute of Independent Colleges and Universities.

Hodgkinson, H. L. (1992). *A demographic look at tomorrow.* Washington, DC: Institute for Educational Leadership. (ERIC Document Reproduction Service No. ED 359 087)

House Committee on Government Operations. (1990). *Children at risk in the workplace: Hearings before the Employment and Housing Subcommittee of the Committee on Government Operations, House of Representatives, one hundred and first Congress, Second Session, March 16 and June 8, 1990.* Washington, DC: U.S. Congress, House Committee on Government Operations. (ERIC Document Reproduction Service No. ED 334 359)

Howsam, R. B., Corrigan, D. C., Denemark, G. W., & Nash, R. J. (1976). *Educating a profession: Relating to human services education.* Washington, DC: American Association of Colleges for Teacher Education.

Integration and Continuity of Services Subcommittee. (1993). *A proposed framework for committee functioning.* Unpublished manuscript.

Kadel, S. (1992). *Interagency collaboration: Improving the delivery of services to children and families.* Tallahassee, FL: Southeastern Regional Vision for Education. (ERIC Document Reproduction Service No. ED 349 511)

Kagan, S. L., & Rivera, A. M. (1991). Collaboration in early care and education: What can and should we expect? *Young Children, 47*(1), 51–56.

Kane, W. (1993). *Response sheet: Program information on integrated services and interprofessional education.* Unpublished raw data. Albuquerque: University of New Mexico.

Kearns, D., & Doyle, D. P. (1988). *Winning the brain race: A bold plan to make our schools competitive.* San Francisco: Institute for Contemporary Study Press.

Kentucky Department of Education. (1991). *Kentucky Education Reform Act (KERA) preschool programs, 1990–1991. Final report.* Frankfort: Kentucky State Department of Education. (ERIC Document Reproduction Service No. ED 340 478)

Kirst, M. W. (1991). Improving children's services. *Phi Delta Kappan, 72*(8), 615–618.

Ladd, E. (1969). *Sources of tension in school–university collaboration.* Atlanta: Emory University, Urban Laboratory in Education.

Larson, C. S., Gomby, D. S., Shiono, P. H., Lewit, E. M., & Behrman, R. E. (1992). Analysis. *The Future of Children, 2*(1), 6–18.

Lawson, H. A. (1994). Toward healthy learners, schools, and communities. *Journal of Teacher Education, 25*(1), 62–70.

Lehman, C., & Fredericks, B. (1993). *Annotated bibliography on integrated services.* Unpublished manuscript, Western Oregon State College, Teaching Research Division, Monmouth.

Levin, H. M., & Bachman, J. G. (1972). *The effects of dropping out. The costs to the nation of inadequate education: A report prepared for the select committee on equal educational opportunity of the United States Senate.* Washington, DC: U.S. Congress. (ERIC Document Reproduction Service No. ED 072 171)

Levin, R., & Greene, J. (1994). Evaluation of coordinated children's services: A collaborative, participatory approach. In R. Levin (Ed.), *Greater than the sum: Professionals and a comprehensive services model* (pp. 174–183). Washington, DC: AACTE.

Levy, J. E., & Copple, C. (1989). *Joining forces: A report from the first year.* Alexandria: National Association of State Boards of Education. (ERIC Document Reproduction Service No. ED 308 609)

Lewit, E. M. (1992). Dropout rates for high school students. *The future of children, 2*(1), 127–130.

Liu, J. T., & Rosenbaum, S. (1992). *Medicaid and childhood immunizations: A national study.* Washington, DC: Children's Defense Fund. (ERIC Document Reproduction Service No. ED 349 093)

Lowenbraun, S. (1990). Leadership training for teacher educators. In L. M. Bullock & R. L. Simpson (Eds.), *Critical issues in special education: Implications for personnel preparation.* Seattle: University of Washington. (ERIC Document Reproduction Service No. ED 343 337)

MacArthur, C. A., & Allen, C. (1981). *Vocational education for the handicapped: Models for preparing personnel.* Personnel Development Series: Document 1. Urbana: Illinois University, Leadership Training Institute/Vocational and Special Education. (ERIC Document Reproduction Service No. ED 211 720)

Melaville, A. I., & Blank, M. J. (1991). *What it takes: Structuring interagency partnerships to connect children and families with comprehensive services.* Washington, DC: Education and Human Services Consortium.

Melaville, A. I., Blank, & Aszyesh. (1993). *Together we can: A guide for crafting a profamily system of education and human services.* Washington, DC: Office of Educational Research and Improvement.

Mitchell, A., & The Early Education/Child Care Work Group. (1992). *Moving toward a unified system of child development and family support services in Vermont: Increasing coordination among early education, early childhood special education (birth through five), child care, Head Start and parent child centers.* Montpelier: Vermont State Department of Education. (ERIC Document Reproduction Service No. ED 350 110)

Morrill, W. A. (1992). Overview of service delivery to children. *The Future of Children, 2*(1), 32–43.

National Center for Children in Poverty. (1990). *Five million children: A statistical profile of our poorest young citizens. Data sourcebook.* New York: Columbia University.

National Commission on Children. (1991). *Beyond rhetoric: A new American agenda for children and families.* Washington, DC: Author.

National Education Goals Panel. (1992). *The national education goals report 1992: Building a nation of leaders.* Washington, DC: U.S. Government Printing Office.

Nelson, C. M., & Pearson, C. A. (1991). *Integrating services for children and youth with emotional and behavioral disorders. Current issues in special education No. 1.* Washington, DC: Special Education Programs. (ERIC Document Reproduction Service No. ED 342 147)

New Jersey Department of Human Services. (1992a). *Data collection at the New Jersey school based youth services program.* Unpublished manuscript.

New Jersey Department of Human Services. (1992b). *The establishment of New Jersey's school based youth services program.* Unpublished manuscript.

Nucci, L., Hughes, R., Jr., Todd, C. W., Gast, G. G., Smylie, M. A., & McElmurry, B. J. (1990). The "Nation of Tomorrow"—a land-grant university experiment. *Illinois Research, 32*(1, 2), 6–8.

Office of Educational Research and Improvement. (1991). *Youth indicators 1991: Trends in the well-being of American youth.* Washington, DC: Author. (ERIC Document Reproduction Service No. ED 335 363)

Orland, M. E. (1990). Demographics of disadvantage: Intensity of childhood poverty and its relationship to educational achievement. In J. I. Goodlad & P. Keating (Eds.), *Access to knowledge: An agenda for our nation's schools* (pp. 43–58). New York: College Entrance Examination Board.

Philliber, S., & Swift, J. (1991). *The caring communities programs: A preliminary evaluation of progress.* New York: Philliber Research Associates.

Phillips, V., Nelson, C. M., & McLaughlin, R. (1993). Systems change and service for students with emotional/behavioral disabilities in Kentucky. *Journal of Emotional and Behavioral Disorders, 1*(3), 155–164.

Plante, K. L. (1993, February). *The competitiveness and productivity of tomorrow's work force: Compelling reasons for investing in healthy children.* (Fact sheet prepared for participants in children as capital corporate health policy retreat). Washington, DC: American Academy of Pediatrics & Washington Business Group on Health.

Robledo, M., and others. (1986). *Texas school dropout survey project: A summary of findings.* San Antonio: Intercultural Development Resource Association. (ERIC Document Reproduction Service No. ED 279 752)

Rosenbaum, S., Hughes, D., Harris, P., & Liu, J. (1992). *Children and health insurance: Special report.* Washington, DC: Children's Defense Fund. (ERIC Document Reproduction Service No. ED 349 097)

San Diego City Schools. (1990). *New beginnings: A feasibility study of integrated services for children and families. Final report and appendices.* San Diego: Author.

Schmid, D. L., & Dawes, K. J. (1992). North Dakota model of collaboration. In K. Hooper Briar, V. Hooker Hansen, & N. Harris (Eds.), *New partnerships: Proceedings from the National Public Child Welfare Training Symposium* (pp. 101–111). Miami: Florida International University.

School of Human Development and Community Service. (1993a). *Prospectus for graduate level program in integrated services.* Unpublished manuscript, California State University, Fullerton.

School of Human Development and Community Service. (1993b). *Syllabus, HCS 500 Theory and Methods of Services Integration.* Unpublished manuscript, California State University, Fullerton.

School of Human Development and Community Service. (1993c). *Syllabus, HCS 501 Practicum in Services Integration.* Unpublished manuscript, California State University, Fullerton.

Schorr, L. B., & Schorr, D. (1989). *Within our reach: Breaking the cycle of disadvantage.* New York: Doubleday.

Sia, C. C. J. (1993). *Response sheet: Program information on integrated services and interprofessional education.* Unpublished raw data, Healthy and Ready to Learn Center, Ewa Beach, HI.

Smith, D. O. (1993). *Response sheet: Program information on integrated services and interprofessional education.* Unpublished raw data, Center for Collaboration for Children and Families, Fresno, CA.

Smith, E. G. (1993). *Communities in schools program evaluation final report prepared for: Texas Employment Commission.* Austin: Publishers Resource Group.

Smith, S., Blank, S., & Collins, R. (1992). *Pathways to self-sufficiency for two generations: Designing welfare-to-work programs that benefit children and strengthen families.* New York: Foundation for Child Development. (ERIC Document Reproduction Service No. ED 344 963)

Snyder, R. D. (1987). A societal backdrop for interprofessional education and practice. *Theory into Practice, 26*(2), 94–98.

Soler, M., & Shauffer, C. (1993). Fighting fragmentation: Coordination of services for children and families. *Education and Urban Society, 25*(2), 129–140.

Steffy, B. E. (1993). *The Kentucky education reform: Lessons for America.* Lancaster, PA: Technomic.

Tellez, K., & Hlebowitsh, P. S. (1993). Being there: Social service and teacher education at the University of Houston. *Innovative Higher Education, 18*(1), 87–94.

Texas Education Agency. (1993). *Family and community support: Coordinated education, health and human services.* Austin: Author.

Topol, K. (1994). *Response sheet: Program information on integrated services and interprofessional education.* Unpublished raw data, Center for Collaboration for Children, Fullerton, CA.

Tyack, D. (1992). Health and social services in public schools: Historical perspectives. *The Future of Children, 2*(1), 19–31.

U.S. Department of Education. (1994). *Department of education reports, 15*(4). Washington, DC: Author.

U.S. Department of Health and Human Services. (1991). *Child health USA '91.* Rockville, MD: Health Resources and Services Administration, Office for Maternal and Child Health Services. (ERIC Document Reproduction Service No. ED 345 437)

U.S. Department of Health and Human Services. (1992). *Healthy children 2000: National health promotion and disease prevention objectives related to mothers, infants, children, adolescents, and youth.* Boston: Jones and Bartlett.

U.S. Department of Labor. (1991). *What work requires of school: A SCANS report for America 2000.* Washington, DC: Author.

U.S. General Accounting Office (1993). *School-linked human services: A comprehensive strategy for aiding students at risk of school failure.* Washington, DC: Author.

Wehlage, G., Smith, G., & Lipman, P. (1992). Restructuring urban schools: The New Futures experience. *American Educational Research Journal, 29*(1), 51–93.

West Feliciana Parish Schools. (1992). *Safety net: The development of "at-risk" services for all children and youth.* Unpublished manuscript.

West Feliciana Parish Schools. (1993). *Comprehensive assessment model, engines for success: A report to the school board, September 21, 1993.* Unpublished manuscript.

William T. Grant Foundation Commission on Work, Family and Citizenship. (1988). *The forgotten half: Pathways to success for America's youth and young families.* Washington, DC: Author.

Winton, P. J. (1992). *Working with families in early intervention: An interdisciplinary preservice curriculum* (2nd ed.). Chapel Hill: University of North Carolina, Frank Porter Graham Child Development Center. (ERIC Document Reproduction Service No. ED 347 743)

Yanez, L. (1993, April 30). Gore visits school, calls it a 'model.' *Sun-Sentinel,* 3B.

Young & Rubicam Foundation. (1991). *The one place: A new role for American Schools.* New York: St. Martin's Press.

Zero to Three/National Center for Clinical Infant Programs Report. (1993). *Promoting success in Zero to Three services: A case study of six community service systems.* Arlington, VA: Author.

42

ALTERNATIVES TO PUBLIC SCHOOLING

James J. Bosco

WESTERN MICHIGAN UNIVERSITY

When the American public school was created in the nineteenth century it was widely perceived as a solution to the problem of how to educate the youth of a rapidly growing and increasingly urbanized, industrial nation. National leaders acclaimed the public school system and citizens took pride in it. Now a century and a half later, public education is considered by many to be a failure. Politicians and business leaders, as well as public school teachers and administrators have expressed the need for urgent and sweeping changes in public schooling. One cannot expect, nor will one find, unanimity of opinion on the condition of American public education. Some observers, such as Bracey (1992), Hodgkinson (1991), and Jaeger (1992), have argued that the critics of the public schools have either overstated the case about the deficiencies in the nation's public schools or overestimated how much of the problem is social rather than educational. Yet articles, reports, speeches, newspaper and magazine articles, and television programs abound contending that the public schools require extensive and fundamental change or even that the public school system as it currently exists needs to be dismantled or abandoned.

The system of American public schooling that was instituted in the nineteenth century had three critical elements. The first was tax support. Those responsible for creating the American public school system fought many difficult battles but were ultimately successful in establishing laws that guaranteed public funding for primary and secondary schooling for every American child. Even though compulsory attendance laws were still being developed at the turn of the century, and enforcement of these laws at their inception was often lax, the American people accepted the principle that the place for children from approximately age 6 until age 18 was in school and that it was a task of government to provide this schooling.

A second critical element in the American system of schooling was that it was common schooling. The great educational reforms of the nineteenth century came at a time of a major influx of immigrants to America, and there was considerable concern about the integration of large numbers of people who spoke different languages, adhered to diverse customs, and attended various churches. The need to amalgamate a people comprised of various ethnic origins and to create a common culture was not only a topic for philosophic speculation but also a highly pragmatic issue. Many feared that neither the political institutions of the Republic nor the locks on the doors of their houses might be secure enough against the growing numbers of "foreigners" who were making up a rapidly growing interclass. The American public school was created as a "melting pot" institution wherein such persons could become Americanized.

When the reformers spoke about the "common school" they were not just referring to a standard academic curriculum; the public school also was expected to equip the youth of the nation with a common set of sensibilities and dispositions essential to enable them to fit into American society. Private and parochial schools were tolerated, but there was tension between those who chose to separate themselves from the mainstream schooling in the public schools and those who saw the public school as the best means for ensuring the perpetuation of an American tradition.

Finally, public schooling was systematic. The reformers were highly critical of the various and sundry ways in which schools of their times operated. There was no regularity in regard to what the child would be taught, when they would learn it, who would teach it to them, and how it would be taught. Throughout the writings of the reformers the word "system" appears with great frequency. Their strong belief in the value of "system" was encouraged by reports written by Americans who visited European schools. There they found age-graded schools with carefully constructed curricula that had been planned in terms of scope and sequence. The schools that American visitors found in Europe during the early years of the nineteenth century were highly systematic, and the reformers believed that the solution and *the* way to create an educated citizenry had been discovered. The term *school system* often is used to indicate the political jurisdiction of particular school districts as in "the

Grand Rapids school system." The term *school system* has another important meaning that refers to the regularized and patterned procedures of the operation of schools. School systems function as bureaucratized local education authorities with rules governing the delivery of services. There is a high degree of similarity among school districts throughout the United States as "school systems" in this latter sense. Cuban (1984) has documented the stability of the processes and techniques pertaining to the delivery of instruction over the past century. Grouped instruction, teacher-centered classrooms, age grading, and curricula designated in a hierarchical fashion have proven to be a robust solution to the problem of providing mass education in state-supported and -run schools.

Proposals to improve the public schools have been a standard feature of life in America. School reform movements have occurred in the United States every couple of decades. Dissatisfaction with the public schools has been a recurring theme; many have devoted considerable energy to creating, disseminating, or implementing recommendations on how to improve the public schools. A long list of reforms has been attempted, such as progressive education, team teaching, life adjustment, back to the basics, individualized instruction, open-space classrooms, educational television, accountability, effective schools, and computers, to name but a few. Yet, the history of educational reform has been characterized as having little substantial impact on the conduct of schooling.

The beginning of the current wave of reform is often linked with the publication of *A Nation at Risk* in 1983 by the National Commission on Excellence in Education. Although this report intensified the reform movement, there was already considerable concern in many places about the condition in American schools when it was published. This reform movement is unlike those that preceded it. Since the mid-1970s the discussion about school reform moved in a direction that constitutes a significant qualitative change from the discussions of the past. The reform movement of the 1980s and 1990s has put the three critical elements (tax support, common schooling, and system) undergirding American public education on the table. Those who believe that the solution goes well beyond repairing what exists represent a large, vocal, and resourceful constituency. Popular words in this movement have been "restructuring," "reinventing," "reengineering," and "break the mold." Although the precise meaning of these words has often been obscure, it is clear that they signify the need to find new ways to disconnect schooling from the laws, policies, traditions, and practices of the past and to find new methods to school American youth.

This chapter presents a descriptive analysis of some of the efforts to respond to the call to create new and different schooling structures and practices. Some of these efforts are focused at the macro level and entail actions pertaining to the political or organizational structure of public schooling in America. Other efforts are at a micro level and entail teaching and learning transactions between students, teachers, and teaching resources. At this time, it is too soon to know how successful those promoting reforms will be in achieving the reforms or how effective the reforms will be in terms of the costs and consequences of schooling. Nevertheless, the efforts described in this chapter represent an attempt to remedy what many see as substantial failures in the capacity of the public schools to educate adequately American youth. As will be seen, the remedies challenge long-standing and fundamental elements of American education.

PRIVATIZATION

The meaning of the word *public* in the term public schools is that such schools are financed by money from the state treasury and that they are operated by employees of the state; the public schools are open and available to all. Although there is argument about how much of a tax levy there should be to support schooling, there is little organized opposition to the provision of levying taxes to support the cost of schooling of children. However, the benefits of state operation of schools has come under sharp attack, and privatization is finding an increasing number of proponents. In other words, the belief that funding from the state treasury should be used to support the schooling of children in schools other than those maintained by the local educational authority is finding more and more support.

The idea of privatization or the transfer of publicly produced goods and services to the private sector has grown in popularity in recent years. The appeal of privatization is a function of the convergence of ideological and economic considerations. Some espouse privatization because they believe in small government and/or because they expect the cost of services to be lower when provided by a private company than by a public agency.

In 1988 President Ronald Reagan established a President's Commission on Privatization. In the introduction of the report, the commission explained the reason for its formation as follows:

The interest [in privatization] has been stimulated in part by concern that the federal government has become too large, too expensive, and too intrusive in our lives. The interest also reflects a belief that new arrangements between the government and private sector might improve efficiency while offering new opportunities and greater satisfaction for the people served.

The report of the commission dealt with opportunities for privatization over a broad range of government activities such as low-income housing, housing finance, federal loan programs, air traffic control and FAA functions, postal service, military commissaries, prisons, Amtrack, naval petroleum reserves, Medicare, international development programs, urban mass transit, and, most relevant to the issues here, education. The commission's findings were in all instances favorable to increasing privatization.

The section of the commission's report dealing with education focuses on educational choice. The report begins with these words, "The recent record of educational achievement has fallen far short of the basic goals Americans set for their schools" (*Privatization: Toward More Effective Government; Report of the President's Commission on Privatization*, 1988, p. 85). The commission argues that choice would result in improvements by providing market pressures to provide better schools.

The question of what the impact of choice is in the market share of students for public and private schools is quite important. Data in the report from Gallup Polls in 1982 and 1986 (as reported in the commission report) are furnished that indicate that 45% of parents in 1982 and 49% of parents in 1986 said that they would choose private schools for their children if they had the means. It is difficult to rectify the Gallup finding with the position expressed in the ending summary of the report of the Commission on Privatization:

The nation is ill-served by a public school system whose teachers and policy makers have so little confidence that policy decisions of many prominent education organizations are dominated by a fear that students would flee if their parents had the resources. Parents are unlikely to remove their children from established institutions until clearly better alternatives are available. (p. 85)

Given the Gallup data, the fear of substantial migration from public schools seems warranted, and if the dysfunctional rigidity of the public schools is the reason for the current educational distress, as the commission believed, then it could be argued that substantial migration is not only possible but really essential.

An ambitious school reform project produced by COMMIT (a coalition formed by CEOs of major corporations in the State of Indiana) and intended for use in Indiana raised the privatization issue in a brochure that was disseminated in 1991. Under the heading, "Free the parents," the brochure stated:

You can send your child to private school. If you have the money. Or you can move to a "better" school district. If you have the money. Otherwise, you're stuck with the schools you have.

But what if you could send your child to any school you want?

It's an idea whose time has come. "Public education" should mean public funds to educate children not to support specific school systems. We need to let *all* parents decide where they send their children to school.

A radical concept? Not really. It is integral to the three ideas that precede it. It's a simple, cost effective way to assure the success of rigorous standards and competition among schools.

And it has already been adopted, or is being considered, by no fewer than 20 other states. (COMMIT, 1991, p. 11)

This statement sounds the two major themes in the argument for privatization of schooling, the first of which is parental choice and fairness, that is, that all parents should have the same opportunities that some parents have. The COMMIT statement indicates that if parents do not have the option to send their children to nonpublic schools, they are then "stuck" with one public school. Clearly, this statement is intended to appeal to those parents who feel that the public school system is inadequate or inappropriate for their children. For such parents, the issue is not merely that they are deprived of the degree of control they ought to have with regard to the education of their children but also that they are compelled, because of limited financial means, to send their children to schools that will provide an inferior education.

One of the prominent proponents of privatization is Chester Finn, Jr. Finn served in the Bush administration and worked with Secretary of Education Alexander in planning that administration's major education initiative, America 2000. In his book, *We Must Take Charge: Our Schools and Our Future,* Finn (1991) argues that the lack of competition is at the heart of the failure of the schools. Echoing the commission's report on privatiza-

tion, Finn contends that privatization would provide parents with consumer power and would generate the opportunity for educational entrepreneurs to construct schools that respond to client needs rather than schools that serve the interests of those administering and teaching in them.

The COMMIT statement also touches on the second major theme in the debate about privatization. The reference to cost-effectiveness incorporates the belief that privatized schools will lower the costs of schools because, as proponents argue, private businesses operate with tighter fiscal standards. Proponents of privatization argue that competition or private enterprise can provide services that are more economical than those that are offered by public agencies.

As Butler (1985) points out, there are two aspects to the cost reduction argument in discussions of privatization. Some argue the case for privatization as the way to improve the performance of services provided by state agencies. In essence, the belief is that competition among schools will serve as the basis for fostering improvements not only in cost but also in performance. Others support privatization as a means of eliminating particular services that have been provided at public expense. The report of the President's Commission on Privatization (1988) cites a number of illustrations of the savings resulting from privatization. The city of San Francisco franchised garbage collection in 1932. The commission's report refers to a 1975 study that showed that San Franciscans were paying $40.00 a year for private service whereas New Yorkers in comparable neighborhoods were paying $297.00 for municipal garbage service. The City of Little Rock contracted out its janitorial service for city hall in 1977 and achieved a 50% savings. Orange County, California, reduced its costs for data processing by 33% by moving services from a municipal department to a contractual arrangement with a private company.

Privatization takes on a number of forms (Clarkson, 1989), the most radical of these is the discontinuation of the service by government. This has been referred to as "service shedding." In such cases, the service may be taken over by a private provider, or it may cease to be offered. In effect, government "gets out of the business" and by doing so creates a business opportunity for the private sector, such as was mentioned earlier with various illustrations. None of the major proposals for privatizing schooling has called for the total dismantling of state-supported and state-run schools. Yet, one possible consequence of privatization, given the assumption that privatization will yield better services at lower cost, is the substantial reduction or complete termination of public schools.

The other forms of privatization that Clarkson (1989) identified are:

Contracting-out—Government contracts with a private firm (profit or nonprofit) to produce and/or to deliver a service or part of a service.

Franchise Agreements—Government grants a private organization either an exclusive or non-exclusive right to provide a particular service within a specific geographical area.

Grants/Subsidies—Government makes a financial or in-kind contribution to a private organization or individual to facilitate the private provision of a service at a reduced cost to consumers.

Vouchers—Government issues redeemable certificates to eligible citizens who exchange them for services from approved private providers. The service providers then return the vouchers to the issuing government for reimbursement.

Self-help—Individuals, neighborhood groups, or community organizations supplement or take over a service. Those providing the service are also the ones who benefit from it.

Incentives—Local government uses its regulatory and taxing powers to encourage private firms to provide public services or to encourage individuals to reduce their demand for such services.

User Fees—Consumers are charged either a flat or quality-related fee for the use of a particular service. (pp. 144–145)

In education, unlike other domains of governmental activities, privatization has a long-standing tradition. Private and parochial schools have existed from the Colonial era. There has never been any substantial effort, even during the formation of the American public school system, to eliminate such schools. No special legal authorization is required to establish a private school, but private schools operate within the framework of state laws governing schools as a franchise type of privatization. As Lieberman (1993) points out, although private schools have existed throughout American history, with the formation of the American public schools, private schools have functioned with a very significant market disadvantage in competition with public schools, that is, private schools charge a fee.

At present, vouchers represent a central focus of privatization of schooling. The first use of vouchers in a U.S. school district was in Milwaukee in 1989 when the Wisconsin Legislature adopted "the Milwaukee Plan." As enacted, the Milwaukee Plan restricted the number of vouchers that could be awarded (1% of the school enrollment of the Milwaukee schools); the pupils to whom they could be awarded (pupils from families whose family income does not exceed 175% of the poverty level); where the vouchers could be used (schools affiliated with religious denominations or profit-making schools were excluded); and a number of other conditions regulating the use of vouchers (e.g., schools that accept vouchers could not charge more for tuition than the amount of the voucher). Legislation providing for vouchers has been introduced in many state legislatures. Voters in Colorado and California defeated ballot initiatives to provide vouchers in those states.

It is clear that a voucher system challenges the conception of the American public school as a common school. Many generations of educators and public figures have held the belief that the public school was the place where young Americans should learn knowledge and skills and acquire the dispositions to make them effective citizens. The public schoolrooms of America were supposed to be the meeting ground for Americans of all social classes. Nevertheless, public policy in the United States has never restricted the option of nonpublic schools for those who favored schooling for their children along religious or social class bases, so long as those parents were prepared to pay for it. The tone of recent discussion about vouchers makes it clear that many Americans no longer believe that the public schools can or need to be the common school for all Americans. The value of commonality that was so impor-

tant to the founders of the public school has been replaced for many by the value of choice and options.

Less conspicuous in the privatization controversy than vouchers is the contracting-out form of privatization. Contracting out is occurring in different sectors of public school operations. In June 1990 Education Alternatives, Inc., was awarded a contract to manage an 800-pupil elementary school in Florida's Dade County School District (David, 1992). Dade County has the fourth largest school district in the United States. Two years later, in 1992, the same corporation entered into a contract with the Baltimore Public Schools to run eight elementary schools and one middle school. In the Baltimore project, Education Alternatives, Inc., was joined by Peat Marwick, as well as Johnson Controls World Service. The schools included in the contract were located in poor, urban communities and Education Alternatives, Inc., was to receive $5,415 (the annual per-pupil cost) for each pupil and contracted to raise student achievement scores to at least grade level in 5 years. The three companies hoped to make a profit by using the school buildings for other purposes such as day care, and any profits were to be split between the district and the three companies involved in the contract.

Dade County was involved in another "contracting-out" type of privatization that involved the formation of "satellite" schools in facilities owned by private businesses. The school district paid for the cost of teachers and instructional materials, and the business paid for the cost of space, maintenance, and facilities. For the school district this meant a savings of $50,000 per classroom. For the company the availability of a school at their site provided a benefit for their employees, which, according to employers, resulted in a substantial decline in absenteeism, tardiness, and turnover.

School districts enter into contracts with private firms for such services as accounting, lunch programs, and staff development. Yet even though all of these are examples of contracting-out privatization, they are seen in a different light from when a school district enters into a contract to provide instructional services that have been provided routinely by district personnel. An example of a for-profit firm that is contracting to provide instructional services traditionally provided by the district is Ombudsman Educational Services (David, 1992). During the 1991–1992 school year, Ombudsman Educational Services was providing dropout education for nearly 2,000 students in Arizona, Illinois, and Minnesota. Ombudsman cites a 90% retention rate accomplished at a lower per-pupil cost than the national average per-pupil cost.

The sites for Ombudsman's schools are usually in shopping centers or business and industrial parks. The program is directed to basic skill development in English, reading, and mathematics. Students are assessed before entering the program, which makes use of computer instruction for assessment. Students attend for 3 hours per day, 5 days a week. The ratio of certified teachers to students is no higher than 1 to 10.

In December of 1993 the Minneapolis School Board announced that it would contract the consulting firm of Public Strategies Group, Inc., to assume the superintendency of the school district. Public Strategies Group, Inc.'s, president, Peter Hutchinson, served as the superintendent. According to information released by Korn/Ferry International, who had run the search resulting in the contract with Public Strategies Inc., the company will not be paid unless Mr. Hutchinson achieves the goals enunciated by the Minneapolis Board of Education (Korn/Ferry International, n.d.).

The strongest opposition to privatization has come from public-sector unions (Aharoni, 1986; Clarkson, 1989), and in the case of schools, these are teachers' unions. Privatization threatens job security, so it is not surprising that public school teacher unions would resist any movement of jobs from the sector of the market that they control to the private sector. Apart from the issue of job security, one of the most dominant concerns about privatization efforts in schooling has been the fear that the children of low-income or underserved populations will be even more poorly treated.

The benefits or shortcomings of privatization are often argued in a highly charged and strongly ideological context. Starr (1988), who reviewed evidence of the impact of privatization on costs, reports that there is some evidence that suggests that private providers have lower costs. However, Starr's analysis suggests that the issue of the benefit of privatization is somewhat ambiguous:

1. There is contradictory evidence as to the cost benefit of privatization.
2. Differences between the services performed between public and private providers make simple comparisons misleading. Because public and private hospitals, social agencies, and schools draw on different clientele, per-patient, client, or student cost comparisons may not be appropriate.
3. The analyses of differences in costs generally lack any information on quality of services; thus, even if lower costs are indicated by the private or public provider, it is not possible to weigh such cost improvements in terms of the quality of services.
4. In some instances, private firms lower costs by reducing wage levels and employing more part-time workers with lower benefits.

Starr's analysis argues for caution in issuing generalizations about the benefits of privatization and indicates that the determination about either cost savings or performance improvements need to be made on a case-by-case basis. Starr's findings focused on the economic and political aspects of privatization and indicated little about the extent to which privatized schools provide a different or innovative environment for teaching and learning. Even though claims that such would occur are frequently issued by proponents of privatization, empirical evidence on this point does not exist.

The Netherlands provides an example of a long-standing system of public and private schools through a voucher system (James, 1984). The 1920 Law of Education in the Netherlands enabled groups of parents to establish schools with the revenue for the initial costs of the schools as well as the ongoing costs coming from the government. The law stipulated that a certain number of parents were required to petition for a school. One hundred and twenty-five parents were needed in a community of 100,000; 100 in a community of 50,000 to 100,000; 75 in a community of 25,000 to 50,000; and 50 in a community of less than 25,000. The law enabled parents to establish a school

based on a distinctive pedagogical or religious conviction, and most of the private schools formed were by persons of a particular religious denomination. Nearly three fourths of the primary and secondary schools are private, with nearly all of them being either Protestant or Catholic.

The Dutch system emerged in a context of a nation comprised of groups of diverse religious orientations, each of which wishing to maintain its own approach to education and none of which being strong enough to impose its own will on the others. The private schools in Holland are generally nonprofit and exist within a context of strict regulations and provisions intended to ensure equity as well as to maintain a public school system. All teachers, both public and private, are paid by the central government, and all are paid based on the same scale. The number of teachers to which a school is entitled is based on a standard teacher-to-pupil ratio. The buildings for both public and private schools are provided by the municipality. Each parent receives a voucher that can be used in either a public or private school. Private schools can charge a fee to supplement the voucher, but those fees are not to be used for basic education costs but for other auxiliary resources such as libraries or swimming pools. Fees are only a minor element in the funding of Dutch private schools.

The Dutch experience reveals the use of a voucher system without many of the problems that opponents of such a system in the United States have cited, but it does so by imposing restrictions that would be opposed by those in this country who are seeking a voucher system to break loose of governmental control. The student-to-faculty ratio, salaries, number of hours teachers are required to work, and other work conditions typically covered by master contracts in the United States are regulated by the central government. Schools are also limited with regard to their discretion in hiring and firing teachers. Those in the United States who fear that governmental funding will lead to governmental control can cite the Dutch experience to support the legitimacy of their concern.

Kolderie (1990) speaks of "withdrawing the exclusive franchise in public education" as the crucial factor in creating a new and responsive approach to schooling. He and others, such as Lieberman (1993) and Perelman (1992), see little likelihood that public school restructuring, when such refers to internal efforts to make the needed changes, will yield the magnitude of changes that are required. Kolderie (1990) contends that institutions need external pressure to change:

Restructuring does not give the school district a compelling reason to change. It continues the traditional assumption that altruism is an adequate motivational basis for change. It expects that board, superintendents and teachers will do things they find personally difficult and institutionally unnecessary because these things are important for the country and for kids. (p. 8)

Cognizant of the charge that his position may be attacked as a "silver bullet" strategy, Kolderie asserts that states should withdraw the exclusive franchise given to school districts to provide schools. He reminds us that legally schools do not exist, but rather school districts exist.

The state deals with districts, not with schools. Only districts can change the schools. Governors and legislatures can propose and promise, plead and threaten. They can give money. They can issue orders. Often the districts respond. But whether they do or not in the end is up to them. If the district does not do better the state does not send in another organization that will. It accepts the pace of improvements at which the district is able or willing to move. (Kolderie, 1990, p. 9)

For-Profit Schools: Whittle Schools

The role of proprietary schools in the United States has been largely confined to specialized training for adults ranging from business training to trade schools such as those for truck drivers, beauticians, graphic artists, and other skilled occupations. Although there are some for-profit primary and secondary schools in the United States, for the most part such schools have been operated on a nonprofit basis. One of the most comprehensive presentations of the case for for-profit schools has been developed by Lieberman (1993). Lieberman contends that a market system that places the control of the services in the hands of the consumers rather than in the hands of the producers as is now the case is essential to create a new generation of schools responsive to the needs of society. Such cannot occur unless schooling becomes a three-sector industry composed of private, public, and for-profit schools. Lieberman argues that the reasons why parents send their children to private or public schools have little to do with innovations or improvements being made in schools. The children who move from one type of school to the other may be better off, but such mobility does not impact the school that has lost the student in the same way that a business is affected when it loses a customer.

Although for-profit primary and secondary schools still are relatively few in the United States, they are sufficiently prevalent to warrant the formation of an association. The National Independent Private Schools Association, which is based in Bradenton, Florida, has 100 members in 10 states, and the president of the Association estimates that the organization represents only about 10% of all for-profit schools in the United States.

The most conspicuous activist in the for-profit schooling movement has been Christopher Whittle and his Edison Schools. Whittle became a controversial figure when he established Channel One. Channel One provides approximately $50,000 worth of television equipment such as a satellite dish, monitors, and VCRs to those schools that agree to carry his 10-minute-a-day news program with 2 minutes of commericals. School boards around the United States debated, often heatedly, the propriety of commercials being played for students during school time.

The purpose of the Edison Project when it was announced was to create a nationwide chain of schools operated on a for-profit basis. When the project was announced in 1991, the plan was to invest $2.5 billion into the development of the schools. The inventors (as the designers are called) were directed to begin with a clean slate and to define all aspects of the school, teacher and student roles, curriculum, instructional procedures, and physical environment without any preconceptions. Unlike public schools that enroll children from age 5 through 18 and from around 8:00 A.M. until 3:00 P.M., Whittle's schools are to be available to children from a few months of age to age 18, the school day will correspond to the work day, and the school will be year round. All of this is meant to adjust the scheduling of school to the life conditions of families in the twentieth century.

In 1991, when the project began, the goal was to open 200 schools by the fall of 1996 with the first students enrolled to be children of preschool age. The first high school graduation class was expected to be in 2010, and by that year the projection was that there would be two million students enrolled in Whittle schools on 1,000 campuses nationwide.

Whittle expects to make a profit through revenues generated by tuition, as well as sales of instructional materials that will be developed by the R&D operations that are a part of the enterprise. The projected rate of tuition was to be comparable to the per-pupil expenditure, which in 1991 averaged $5,208. To offset further the concern that these schools would find only a white, middle-class clientele, 20% of the students were to be enrolled on a scholarship basis. Once these schools proved effective, Whittle anticipated contracting with local school authorities to run individual schools or even entire districts (Brodinsky, 1993).

In 1994 Whittle began the financial restructuring of his holdings, which was motivated, or necessitated, by the need to raise capital for the Edison venture. In August 1994, *The New York Times* reported that he had reached an agreement to sell Channel One for $300 million ("Whittle Said . . . ," 1994). Earlier in the same month it was reported that he had canceled his Medical News Network ("Whittle Cancels . . . ," 1994). *Time* magazine carried an article titled "Entrepreneurs: The Whittling Down of Chris Whittle," in which the scaling back of the Edison Project was described. From the early, highly ambitious plans in 1991, a more limited conception emerged. By 1994 Whittle was concentrating his efforts on connecting the "for-profit" schools venture with the charter school movement (described in the following section) and with contracts to run public schools ("Entrepreneurs . . . ," 1994). Unfortunately, little attention in education literature has been devoted to the Edison Project.

The conception of primary and secondary schooling in a profit-making context seems implausible to some and inappropriate to others. The implausibility stems from the fact that Whittle is not marketing these schools to wealthy families; rather, he has indicated that these schools would serve the same clientele as is served by public schools. Yet he contends not only that he can educate the same clientele being served by the public schools with less expense but also that the Edison schools can provide a superior education. Whittle's schools represent the belief that a profit-making corporation can both provide better services than a governmental agency and make a profit.

Criticism of the Edison Project has been both strong and extensive. One of the concerns was expressed by Governor Ann Richards of Texas at a meeting in 1992 when Whittle discussed the Edison Schools with the nation's governors. She said:

You [referring to Whittle] are going to come in with your schools and strip off our African-American kids who are the smartest and the brightest. You're going to strip off the Mexican-American kids who are the role models in the public schools in South Texas, and whom we really need there. But you're not going to take our kids that are so disabled that they are literally diapered by the teachers, because by law that's whom we've got to teach. So how do I deal with my fear that the public school is going to be left with those you don't want, those who are the hardest to educate, the most expensive to educate? As a consequence, my Texas public school system is not going to look very good when it's compared with the opportunities you're going to have to reject the kids we can't reject. (Brodinsky, 1993, p. 542)

Whittle responded to this concern by saying, "We are not designing another private school system that is elitist in nature. We plan to create a school that confronts as many of the problems [as] a typical public school confronts" (Brodinsky, 1993, p. 542). Whittle's schools, he asserted, would be in inner cities and rural areas as well as suburbs and affluent communities. The central issue is not whether there is a market for private schools but rather the nature and extent of that market. Lieberman (1993) contends that the business success of Edison schools is questionable, not because it would not be possible to provide better education at a lower per-pupil cost than is provided by public education, but because the Edison school will face strong opposition from the education establishment and especially teacher unions that will put pressure on public officials to use existing statutes and regulations covering teacher certification, building codes, zoning, pupil transportation, class size, corporation taxes, and child labor laws in the most obstructive way possible to thwart efforts to create new charter schools.

The issue of the feasibility of Edison schools is connected to the issue of the ethics of the Edison schools as a for-profit venture. The Representative Assembly of the National Education Association passed a resolution to oppose for-profit schools, mentioning specifically the Whittle schools in the resolution. The resolution stated, "The emphasis of our public school system should be to provide an equal educational opportunity for our children, not to make a profit from them. If profit becomes the motive, the children will be secondary" (Rist, 1991, p. 25).

In May of 1992, Benno Schmidt, president of Yale University, resigned his position to join the Edison project. In October of 1993 the superintendent of the Detroit Public Schools, Deborah McGriff, announced that she was leaving her position to become the director of marketing for the Edison Schools. Schmidt's willingness to leave one of the most prestigious university presidencies in the United States "signified that Whittle was serious, the members of the Edison Project were serious, and the investors were serious about this project" (McLaughlin, 1992, pp. 23–24). As reported in the *Detroit News & Free Press* of October 16, 1993, McGriff's decision reflected her recognition that she could not achieve her goal of turning a big-city school system beset by crime and poverty into a positive educational agency for children, and as a consequence she decided to continue her own work in education outside of the public sector where she felt she might be more effective in achieving the goal of creating better educational opportunities for children of all social and educational backgrounds (McGriff, 1993). Thus, the Edison Project was born amidst high promise as a result of the perceived financial resources available to Whittle and the caliber of personnel who affiliated themselves with the project.

Christopher Whittle's projections of the number of private schools he expected to create did not materialize, and the Edison Project moved in a new direction in 1993. Numerous news reports carried stories about the decision of the Whittle organization to turn from building the extensive system of new for-profit schools to entering into contracts to run public schools. There were reports made of conversations with public school officials in Massachusetts, Maryland, Virginia, and Washington, DC. Some observers saw this as increasing the likelihood of success for Whittle's organization because the new strategy represents an approach less dependent on massive capital resources and a direction that will be less politically arduous.

Charter Schools

The origin of the charter schools movement dates from a 1988 report by Ray Budde who was an educational consultant for the state of Massachusetts (Budde, 1988). The conception of a charter school stems from a belief in the consequences of teacher empowerment. In conception a charter school is intended to be "designed and run by teachers; offer innovative instructional methods and programs; be free from state regulation and district management; be attended by students who choose the school; operate under contract with a public sponsor (such as a local school board); meet student performance standards specified in the contract; and be nonsectarian, nondiscriminatory, and tuition free" (Williams & Buechler, 1993). Charter schools would give teachers the opportunity to attend to the needs of students freed of the cumbersome and dysfunctional strictures of school district policies.

Minnesota was a pioneer in the development of school choice through legislation enacted in 1988. Three years later, Minnesota also pioneered in the enactment of legislation for charter schools. Charter school legislation enables an existing school to be designated as a "charter school," and as such it is granted exemptions from existing state law regulating schools, while it maintains state funding. The first charter schools in the nation were established in 1992 in Minnesota. These were a Montessori school that shifted from private school status to charter school status and a small rural school that prior to achieving charter school status was intended to be closed.

In Minnesota there were significant changes in the legislation as enacted from that which had been proposed. The Minnesota Senate passed a charter school bill that permitted an unlimited number of charter schools, nonlicensed personnel to teach in them, and also various public agencies such as universities, museums, nonprofit service agencies, and the State Board of Education to sponsor charter schools. When the bill was signed by the governor it limited the establishment of charter schools to eight for the state, required that all teachers be certified, and restricted sponsorship of charter schools to local school boards.

California passed a charter school bill in 1992 similar to the one enacted in Minnesota, allowed 100 charter schools in the state, but no more than 10 per district. As in Minnesota, the sponsorship was limited to local school boards, but in California nonlicensed personnel were eligible to teach in charter schools. Minnesota permitted private schools to become charter schools, but in such situations the private school was required to relinquish some of the prerogatives it had as a private school, such as the right to employ nonlicensed teachers and to set admission standards. In California private schools were not eligible for charter school status.

In every state that has enacted charter school legislation there has been criticism from both proponents and opponents of charter schools about the legislation. The strongest criticism has come from teacher unions that have argued that charter schools jeopardize collective bargaining and tenure (Williams & Buechler, 1993). Others objected that the charter school legislation did not go far enough and that compromises were made to ensure sufficient votes for enactment in the legislature.

Neither California nor Minnesota provided any funding for development costs in their charter school legislation. Schools get the same per-pupil funds as existing schools. There are no provisions for capital outlay or for development costs such as R&D costs. The assumption seems to be that the factors that most hinder the effectiveness of schools are the rules and regulations under which public schools must exist. Freed of these restrictions, the charter school might be able to deliver a successful program. The intent of charter schools is to create a new variety of schooling. As such, R&D becomes an important means to generate the new understandings and techniques that are required. The nature of charter schools is such that autonomy is cherished. Each individual charter school typically develops a program that they consider appropriate for their clientele. It is generally impractical for individual charter schools to maintain their own R&D enterprise, but given the intent to "break a new path," resources are required to furnish charter schools with information enabling them to assess practices and procedures and to revise and improve them.

In England "grant-maintained schools" are directly comparable to charter schools in the United States. In 1992 there were 219 such schools in England. The grant-maintained schools are established by grants from England's Department of Education and Science. Unlike the situation with charter schools in the United States, England's grant-maintained schools are able to receive funding for start-up costs. These funds are to be used to assist the school as it prepares for operation under the new arrangement. There are also grants available to enable the school to finance payments to staff who are laid off or retire when the restructuring alters existing staff positions (Wohlstetter & Anderson, 1992).

Another resource provided to grant-maintained schools to assist them during their development stage is the Grant-Maintained Schools' Center. This center provides information and consultation services to schools as they move through the transitional period. The center was provided with government funding for only a 5-year period. Its continued existence is contingent on the extent to which schools purchase its services. In addition to providing informational, consultative, and training services to the schools, the center also serves a lobbying function for the schools with the Department of Education and Science.

New American Schools

In October 1991 the New American Schools Development Corporation (NASDC) issued a call for proposals. The NASDC was one component of the Bush Administration educational reform program called AMERICA 2000. AMERICA 2000 proposed six goals for American education that defined the expected levels of performance of American schools.

AMERICA 2000 contained a number of program initiatives, one of which was the formation of the NASDC, which was established as a private corporation funded by corporations and foundations. NASDC is governed by a Board of Directors headed by David T. Kearns, the former Deputy Secretary of Education and retired Chairman and CEO of the Xerox Corporation. The 21-member Board of Directors includes chief executives of major corporations such as IBM, Boeing, Exxon, Merrill Lynch, and Eastman Kodak, among others. The 18-member advisory panel consists of educators from higher education and public and private education (New American Schools Development Corporation, 1993).

When it was founded in 1991 the target goal for fund raising was $200 million. The original plan called for creating 535 schools through NASDC, one for each Congressional District in the United States. By the time the call for proposals was issued, the goal of creating 535 schools was substantially reduced, even though the purpose of the program remained consistent with earlier formulations. As the call for proposals put it, "At the heart of AMERICA 2000 lies a bold challenge: Reinvent American education by designing new schools for a new century. This request for proposals launches that designing effort so that communities across the country can re-create their own schools" (New American Schools Development Corporation, 1991, p. 7).

NASDC received 686 proposals. According to one report 80% to 90% were poorly constructed, not innovative, and easy to reject (Mecklenburger, 1992). The intent was to fund approximately 20 to 30 contractors for the first year to do design work with between $500,000 to $3,000,000 for each design team. Upon receiving the proposed designs, a second selection process was to reduce the number of funded projects to 10 to 15, each of which would receive funding of from $2,000,000 to $15,000,000 for the development and testing phase. In actuality, only 11 awards were made in July 1992. Nine of these design teams were awarded second-year contracts. Thus, from the point of initiation of the New American Schools concept to the point of actual development of schools, the number of sites dropped from 535 to 9.

Mecklenburger (1992) reviewed all of the winning proposals and 60 of those not funded and found a number of common elements in the funded designs:

Virtually all of the NASDC's projects attend to school readiness, changing relationships between community and school, increased use of technology (although the published summaries of most of these projects don't yet reflect much sophistication about technology), altered school schedules and calendars, site-based management, various spins on performance assessment, teachers acting as "guide" and coaches," and curriculum ideas that favor the integration of subject matter. In a sense, these ideas are fast becoming the conventional wisdom about next-generation schooling and NASDC's projects promise to give the nation several variations on these themes. (Mecklenburger, 1992, p. 283)

Mecklenburger also points out the surprising emphasis on working within the public sector in the funded proposals. Although several of the design teams involved participants from the private sector, only one of them had the private sector as the leader of the design team.

Near the end of 1993, NASDC had raised $53 million, well below the goal of $200 million. In December of 1993 Walter J. Annenberg announced a gift of $500 million to public education, $50 million of which was ear-marked for NASDC. The infusion of the Annenberg funds into the NASDC project was considered to be the stimulus needed to enable NASDC to have a significant impact in education. Christopher Cross, the director of education programs at the Business Roundtable, said that as long as NASDC was "stalled at the $50 million level, its impact was questionable, but this really gives it [NASDC] the critical mass to be really influential" (Sommerfeld, 1994).

The extent to which the NASDC initiative has led to innovative school designs that yield improvements in learning is yet to be seen. Moreover, the extent to which NASDC schools have any influence beyond the scope of the nine design teams also remains to be seen. In June 1994 members of the nine design teams agreed to contract 40 school jurisdictions in urban areas that demonstrated an interest in school restructuring to explore replication of NASDC design concepts (Olson, 1994). As of this writing, it is still uncertain what will come of these discussions.

Both the New American Schools Development Corporation and the Edison Schools began with a conception of a massive national effort to reform schools. These projects attempted to move out of the mainstream and were to involve a large number of sites to demonstrate that the innovations were not so fragile as to require a protective and limited environment. As these projects developed, a considerable scaling down of scope and a movement back toward public education occurred. In the next 1 or 2 years the initial impact of both of these efforts should be known.

CONCLUSION

In the years since the publication of *A Nation at Risk* school reform has been a pervasive topic on the national agenda. Most of the state legislatures have enacted reform legislation, and local school boards, teachers, and administrators in many school districts have implemented changes. Numerous organizations and agencies, such as those described in this chapter, have set in motion programs and processes intended to create a new generation of schools. The literature on this topic is generally anecdotal or polemic. There is a lack of empirical or even careful analytical literature on the topic. Given the fact that most of the developments of alternatives to public schooling are quite new, it is not surprising that the research literature on the topic is slight.

Since *A Nation at Risk* was published, there has been no decrease in interest in creating alternatives to public schooling. In a number of states there is a significant level of activity pertaining to the function of charter schools. Home schooling and the use of information technology offer still other alternatives for those who believe that the reform of public schools has a low probability of success. Ultimately, however, the question of the impact of any of these approaches in the lives of children centers on the specifics of the experiences that are provided. To the extent that charter schools, New American Schools, and Edison schools provide similar experiences under a different aegis, there is little reason to expect different outcomes. Thus the critical, and at this point unanswered, questions are: What is the character of the programs of the "new schools"? and what outcomes in terms of the children who attend them result from these schools? Subsequent careful research needs to be devoted to addressing these and related questions.

References

Aharoni, Y. (1986). *The evolution and management of state-owned enterprises*. Cambridge, MA: Ballinger.

Bracey, G. W. (1992). The second Bracey Report on the condition of public education. *Phi Delta Kappan, 74*(2), 104–117.

Brodinsky, B. (1993). How "new" will the "new" Whittle American school be? A case study in privatization. *Phi Delta Kappan, 74*(7), 540–547.

Budde, R. (1988). *Education by charter: Restructuring school districts. Key to long-term continuing improvement in American education.* Andover, MA: Regional Laboratory for Educational Improvement of the Northeast & Islands. (ERIC Document Reproduction Service No. ED 295 298)

Butler, S. M. (1985). *Privatizing federal spending: A strategy to eliminate the deficit.* New York: Universe.

Clarkson, K. W. (1989). Privatization at the state and local level. In P. W. MacAvoy, W. Y. Standbury, G. Yarrow, & R. J. Zeckhauser (Eds.), *Privatization and state-owned enterprises: Lessons from the United States, Great Britain, and Canada* (pp. 143–194). Boston: Kluwer.

COMMIT. (1991, November). *Reaching higher.* Indianapolis: Author. (Available from COMMIT, 251 N. Illinois, Suite 1800, Indianapolis, IN 46204-1953.)

Cuban, L. (1984). *How teachers taught: Constancy and change in American classrooms, 1890–1980.* New York: Longman.

David, A. (1992). *Public-private partnerships: The private sector and innovation in education. Policy insight number 142.* Santa Monica, CA: Reason Foundation. (ERIC Document Reproduction Service No. ED 351 794)

Entrepreneurs: The Whittling Down of Chris Whittle. (1994, August). *Time,* p. 31.

Finn, D. E. (1991). *We must take charge: Our schools and our future.* New York: Maxwell Macmillan.

Hodgkinson, H. (1991). Reform versus reality. *Phi Delta Kappan, 73*(1), 8–16.

Jaeger, R. M. (1992). World class standards, choice and privatization: Weak measurement serving presumptive policy. *Phi Delta Kappan, 74*(2), 118–128.

James, E. (1984). Benefits and costs of privatized public services: Lessons from the Dutch educational system. *Comparative Education Review, 28*(4), 605–624.

Kolderie, T. (1990). *Beyond choice to new public schools: Withdrawing the exclusive franchise in public education* (Policy Report 8). Washington, DC: Progressive Policy Institute.

Korn/Ferry International. (n.d.). Minneapolis schools break the mold: Korn/Ferry International's Ira Krinsky conducts national search. *News from Korn/Ferry International.* New York: Author.

Lieberman, M. (1993). *Public education: An autopsy.* Cambridge: Harvard University Press.

McGriff, D. Detroit's schools will miss a gifted superintendent. (1993, October 16). *Detroit News and Free Press*, p. 10A.

McLaughlin, J. M. (1992). Schooling for profit: Capitalism's new frontier. *Educational Horizons, 72*(1), 23–30.

Mecklenburger, J. A. (1992). The braking of the "break-the-mold" express. *Phi Delta Kappan, 74,* 280–289.

National Commission on Excellence in Education. (1983). *A nation at risk: The imperative for educational reform.* Washington, DC: Author.

New American Schools Development Corporation. (1991). *Designs for a new generation of American schools.* Arlington, VA: Author.

New American Schools Development Corporation. (1993). *NASDC facts.* Arlington, VA: Author.

Olson, L. (1994, June 22). NASDC grantees to hammer out plan to replicate "break the mold" schools. *Education Week,* pp. 12–13.

Perelman, L. J. (1992). *School's out.* New York: Avon.

President's Commission on Privatization. (1988). *Privatization: Toward more effective government: Report of the President's Commission on Privatization.* Urbana: University of Illinois Press.

Rist, M. C. (1991). Here comes "McSchool." *The American School Board Journal, 178*(9), 30–31.

Sommerfeld, M. (1994, January 26). $50 Million shot in the arm gives NASDC new life. *Education Week,* pp. 1, 10.

Starr, P. (1988). *The limits of privatization* (Report No. ISBN-0944826-01-6). Washington, DC: Economic Policy Institute. (ERIC Document Reproduction Service No. ED 311 243)

Whittle cancels news network for doctors. (1994, August). *The New York Times,* p. D3.

Whittle said to agree to sale of school channel. (1994, August). *The New York Times,* p. D3.

Williams, S., & Buechler, M. (1993). *Charter schools. Policy bulletin* (Report No. PB-B16). Bloomington: Indiana University Education Policy Center. (ERIC Document Reproduction Service No. ED 356 540)

Wohlstetter, P., & Anderson, L. (1992). *What can U.S. charter schools learn from England's grant-maintained schools?* Washington, DC: Office of Educational Research and Improvement. (ERIC Document Reproduction Service No. ED 345 354)

·43·

ALTERNATIVE TEACHER CERTIFICATION

Vicky S. Dill
SCHREINER COLLEGE

What can be done about teacher shortages? What creative solutions might address the frequent misassignment of teachers, especially in urban areas where students are often in precarious socioeconomic and educational situations? What might make the teaching profession more demographically representative of the students taught? How can the profession better accommodate midcareer entrants? Why do education students often have lower grade point averages than students seeking other professions? Would a more "hands-on" approach better prepare new recruits for the task of teaching? When in the course of the preparation should the internship occur? Do alternative forms of teacher preparation diminish educators' sense of the knowledge base on which they build curriculum? Does alternative teacher certification deter efforts to professionalize teaching?

These questions indicate the pressures teacher educators have felt frequently since the mid-1980s, a time of reform in which a new term, *alternative certification,* entered their vocabulary along with new types of colleagues in their midst, alternative teacher certification interns, deans, and directors. By now it would appear that yet more debate is in order as many of the quandaries that inspired alternative routes to certification still go unresolved. How does the story begin? Where is it moving?

Formulating a synthetic history from the variety of alternative teacher certification initiatives that occurred around the country would, in fact, be quite difficult. States began programs; they named, renamed, defined, and redefined the programs frequently, citing a diversity of reasons why changes were made or approaches modified (Feistritzer, 1991). One state's alternative mirrors another's emergency route. Appearing around the nation often simultaneously, but without coordination, the pro-

grams and the reasons for their generation in fact defy facile synthesis. Programs and initiatives evolved from a shortage of teachers in certain areas, from political pressure, and as a direct result of pressure to reform higher education. What is clear, however, is that researchers have produced increasingly large volumes of description, commentary, analysis, and some data, usually internal and far from adequate, about the success of alternatively certified teachers. Burgeoning numbers of alternative teacher certification programs do suggest growing criticism of current traditional teacher education practices. Why is alternative teacher certification necessary? Are there ways in which traditional models of teacher education fail to provide adequately for certain populations of students, such as the urban, rural, poor, special education, and bilingual populations for which shortages are chronic? Exploration into a variety of forms of teacher education that met shortage needs subsequently expanded, resulting in programs of alternative teacher certification nationwide that answered the criticisms in a variety of ways.

THE EARLY YEARS

As early as 1982, central and critical themes in the literature of alternative teacher certification set the research agenda. In that year, the state of Virginia mandated provisional teaching certification for all teachers; individuals who did not take education courses could take the nine credit hours required during the first 2 years of teaching in lieu of student teaching. Although the legislation was originally designed to broaden the pool of secondary teachers in particular, it was expanded to include kindergarten through grade 12 areas of certification. Virginia's

The author thanks reviewers Emily Feistritzer (National Center for Education Information) and Karen Zumwalt (Teacher's College, Columbia University) for their helpful comments and suggestions of earlier drafts of this chapter. Martin Haberman (University of Wisconsin–Milwaukee) and Delia Stafford (Houston Independent School District) gave invaluable vision and expertise. Thanks to Jan Anderson (Texas Education Agency), Mark Littleton (Tarleton University), and the Schreiner College (Kerrville, TX) Library for their help finding materials.

goal was to accommodate midcareer switchers, a theme common to many alternative certification programs (Cornett, 1990, p. 62). Schlechty and Vance (1983) introduced additional major themes. These included recruitment of a demographically representative teaching force, concerns about the quality of the preparation traditional programs offered, the quality of the candidates recruited, and issues of retention on the job. Similar concerns continued to inform the discussion about the goals, appropriateness, effectiveness, and costs of teacher certification and licensure, including alternative teacher certification.

Dynamics Leading to the Reforms of the 1980s

In 1983 Schlecty and Vance divided the time prior to commencement of alternative teacher certification initiatives into two periods, 1950–1970 and 1970–1983. The authors noted that between 1950 and 1970 the number of new teachers increased from 913,671 in 1950 to approximately 2 million in 1969. This early period saw rapid influxes of teachers into the schools, accompanied by significant growth in colleges of education and lengthened certification requirements. Teacher turnover was high, with 73% of the least academically capable teachers remaining longer in the classroom. Other studies that ranked prospective teachers on ability scales determined "those with the shortest commitment to teaching as a career had the largest proportion high on the academic index" (p. 473).

The second period Schlecty and Vance examined, the 1970s, demonstrated a declining interest among high-ability individuals in the career of teaching. Data revealing escalating turnover rates led the authors to conclude, "Given the conditions outlined above and the arguments presented earlier, it seems irresponsible to dismiss the fact that education is having difficulty attracting and retaining the services of academically able college students" (p. 477). Poor conditions in the workplace, lack of career advancement opportunities, increasing numbers of viable options for those most likely to pursue teaching, and lack of a strong university commitment to the college of education were pivotal dynamics in an exacerbated teacher shortage and a sense of diminished quality in the work force.

In recommendations to remedy a growing crisis in work force quality in the schools, Schlechty and Vance provided impetus for significantly altered forms of governance characterized as "alternative teacher certification." Among other suggestions, they recommended, "Responsibility for the professional training of teaching should be divorced from institutions of higher education, and teacher education should once again be placed where it in fact occurs—in the public schools" (p. 484). Adding that site-based training would more systemically emphasize research and destigmatize teacher education by removing it from the source of the stigma, the university, the authors suggested a baccalaureate degree as the prerequisite for admission to a site-based program. This system, the authors averred, would more than double the number of potential teacher candidates than were available in 1950, would save money, improve retention, and support development of differentiated career paths for academically able teachers. Although its conclusions were considered extreme at the time, Schlecty and Vance's research was instrumental in the legislative initiatives that eventually

led to establishment of a wide variety of alternative teacher certification programs nationwide.

Financing teacher education has always been problematic in universities where large numbers of education majors provide funds often siphoned off for noneducation majors. Would alternative teacher certification solve this dilemma? In a 1983 study, Denton and Smith discussed the cost-effectiveness of alternative teacher preparation programs for secondary majors. The research reported two findings: (1) that alternative programs described were more expensive (1.67 times more) because of the lower number of students involved in the program, and (2) traditional programs yielded a 10% advantge in learner cognitive attainment. Denton and Smith concluded that extended programs do result in greater cognitive gains at somewhat higher costs, about $73 per semester per student; however, the authors noted that if costs are the primary consideration and are kept down, the cognitive gains will be proportionately abbreviated.

Who Is Competent to Teach? What Is a Professional? The Questions That Ignited a Debate

During the fall of 1984, the first of what became virtually a flurry of point/counterpoints in the alternative teacher certification discourse appeared. Hazlett (1984) noted that although "The certification process in some states has grown into a tangled thicket, "the states proposing to begin alternative certification processes have broader changes in mind" (p. 46). Of great concern to Hazlett was the part of the debate proposing to alter who teaches pedagogy to prospective students. The author warned:

Besides pointing to inadequacies in the process of certification, the alternative plans betoken, in one degree or another, an assault on education as a field of university study. In them, subject-matter competence is held in indispensable regard, but the same cannot be said for education, instruction in which is pared down, compressed, treated almost as an afterthought, and in some cases removed from the university setting. It is a painful irony that all the protestations about raising quality, attracting talent into classrooms, and increasing professional standards should be accompanied by a calculated reduction in the amount of knowledge about education to be required of teachers. (p. 46)

Hazlett asserted that thinking of teaching as best learned via an apprenticeship model implied that the pursuit is toward not a profession but a craft, and he juxtaposed craft and profession at opposing ends of a continuum. Hazlett reasoned that if an intelligent learner can rapidly master "the tricks of the trade . . . on the job," then the end product of the process is clearly a craft (p. 47). Hazlett thought of legitimate teaching, however, in quite another light:

That teaching is a complex psychological and social enterprise, that it is a problematic and contingent activity, that its operations should involve judgments based on systematic knowledge, that it could foster inquiry and the discovery of new knowledge—that it might, in a word, be a profession—are propositions that never received assent in most of the reform community—nor do they now. (p. 47)

A "tradelike conception of teaching," intensely craft-centered and easy to learn, was thereafter associated with the view of teaching inherent in the alternative teacher certification approaches. Hazlett recommended, instead of such a reconception, changing the nature of teachers' workplaces, giving them more decision-making capacity and power and increasing salaries instead of solving the problems in education with "skimpily trained functionaries and retreads from other occupations" (p. 48). "Misplaced" enthusiasm for such reforms, Hazlett concluded, will only "make matters worse" (p. 48).

While Schlecty, Vance, Hazlett, and others were attempting to frame the debate in terms of the "craft" versus "professional" nature of the competencies needed, others detailed the extent of imminent teacher shortages and worked out the implications for school districts of the new alternative teacher certification processes being discussed nationally, lamenting the decline of a profession. In November of 1984, addressing the National Council of States on Inservice Education meeting in Florida, Schussler and Testa (1984) noted the demographic trends that accelerated the hiring of teachers on emergency permits, the importing of teachers from northern and midwestern states to southern states, and trends such as the flight of teachers from urban to suburban districts.

The authors articulated two additional aspects of the alternative teacher certification question: (1) that emergency permits allowing uncredentialed individuals to teach continued to rise even as colleges of education were, in fact, decreasing in enrollment; and (2) the effects such teacher education responsibilities may have on school districts (Schussler & Testa, 1984). Noting that New Jersey's alternative teacher certification process "virtually eliminates preservice training of secondary teachers by colleges of education," the writers reasoned that the burden of the training will fall on school districts while "children will be taught by apprentices who may not possess the skills necessary to be effective in the classroom" (p. 4). The authors bemoaned the added burden on districts that certainly could not be expected to provide "full-blown teacher training programs" and that did not enjoy the collaboration of state departments, school districts, and university officials in the teacher training effort at this early date.

How Reform Dynamics Led to Alternative Certification Initiatives

As soon as the state of New Jersey unveiled its alternative teacher certification program in September 1985, controversy over the proposal was widespread (Cooperman & Klagholz, 1985). Touted as a result of "more than two years of study and discussion of teacher preparation and certification in New Jersey," the authors articulated the state's response in terms of both quality and quantity issues, promising an era "more open to change" and reform in teacher education. Noting the poor average Scholastic Aptitude Test (SAT) scores of individuals who entered or planned to enter the teaching profession as well as the ubiquitous presence of emergency-certified or "permit" teachers, the authors declared that the state's response addressed decades of teacher education critique culminating in the call of Ernest Boyer and other reformers for leadership and decision-making skills in a quality teaching force.

Initially, the New Jersey State Department of Education proposed to open seven regional training centers that would provide 200 hours of generic instruction to candidates (Cooperman & Klagholz, 1985). Candidates' qualifications included (1) a bachelor's degree; (2) passing a competency test in the subject matter to be taught; (3) 30 credit hours or equivalent work experience in the subject to be taught or, for elementary teachers, 30 credit hours in any single field; and (4) approval of the individual by district personnel according to carefully outlined criteria. A key ingredient of the highly centralized proposal was district-based supervision of all candidates. The projected benefits of the proposal included an expanded pool of qualified candidates as well as new enthusiasm and innovative methods of instruction demonstrated by individuals who knew their subject matter well. Eventually, it was the centralized and undifferentiated nature of the regional training center curriculum that gave the New Jersey program its mixed reviews (see Smith, 1991).

Reactions Early observers of emerging alternative teacher certification programs attempted to define the ubiquitous chameleon known as "alternative teacher certification." The New Jersey alternative teacher certification initiative and the later ones in Texas and California helped generate the initial definition of "alternative teacher certification," a sticking point for many voices early in the discussion. Oliver and McKibben (1985) noted:

The responsibility for the professional development of teacher trainees ultimately lies with the school district, mentor teacher, and teacher trainee. Although school districts must collaborate with institutions of higher education, they are not legally mandated to implement recommendations offered by the institutions. In this regard, institutions of higher education are seen as potential partners in the preparation of teacher trainees. The institutions of higher education are also viewed as potential providers for the range of possible services and activities (e.g., courses, seminars, curriculum materials, supervision, and diagnostic evaluation). This latter arrangement pre-empts the traditional role of institutions of higher education as providers of professional preparation programs. (pp. 20–23)

In addition to the "craft versus professional" issues, the authors discussed the pivotal role of the colleges as providers of teacher preparation. Would certification routes circumvent higher education institutions? Would proposals include a menu of possible roles for institutions of higher education? Would higher education involvement be mandatory for certification? These new questions remained a critical and occasionally contentious feature in the discussion.

Other writers cited additional ambiguities. What were the similarities and differences between "emergency" teacher certification or permits and "alternative" teacher certification as it gradually emerged? While "emergency" documents were designed as merely temporary certification, alternative routes to teacher certification led to permanent certification. Did the innovation, therefore, offer hope that alternative routes would address issues surrounding the quality and supply of mathematics and science teachers (Rumberger, 1985)? Responses to these questions and dynamics varied even as alternative certification programs emerged. The Houston Independent School District (HISD) implemented provisions of Texas's 1984 reform legislation allowing for alternative teacher certification processes in direct response to criticism that large numbers of emergency credentialed teachers lowered the quality of students' education and that alternative teacher certification could alleviate teacher shortages while maintaining educational quality (Texas Education Agency, 1993b).

The role of teacher preparation institutions remained ambiguous and led authors to additional avenues of inquiry. Evertson, Hawley, and Zlotnik's (1985) analysis of reform strategies outlined growing discussion about the relative value of teacher preparation that, the authors noted, included calls for higher standards as well as requirements for more extensive preentry coursework. In a comparison of "provisional teachers" with minimal preparation or incomplete certification with regularly certified teachers, the authors concluded that "teachers who participate in preservice teacher preparation programs are more likely to be (or to be perceived by administrators as) more effective than teachers who have little or no formal training" (p. 4). The authors concluded that competence was not possible outside of completion of certain steps: (1) completion of a liberal arts undergraduate education, (2) competence in the subject being taught as measured by the equivalence of a major, (3) completion of 8 to 10 courses plus a related practicum to be taken prior to or after graduation, (4) a yearlong internship in a "teaching school" analogous to a physician's internship, (5) a 1- or 2-year induction period with specific characteristics, and (6) ongoing individualized professional development (p. 8). The role of teacher preparation institutions as final arbiters of who is and who is not certifiable remained a critical question. If school districts or consortia instead of higher education institutions alone defined competence, what other dynamics and what other issues would emerge?

IMPLICATIONS OF REFORM INITIATIVES IN THE MID-1980S

By 1986, several issues including the roles of teacher induction, program standards, and evaluation relative to alternative teacher certification emerged in the literature.

Induction

Huling-Austin (1986) raised the issue of appropriate novice induction and observed that high-quality preparation for alternatively certified interns as well as acceptable levels of retention in the profession made induction a vital force in the future of all interns. If teachers received abbreviated training, their growth after certification would be even more critical. For these "accelerated" students of education to succeed, program directors must consider the nature of the teaching assignment, the helpfulness of the support teacher, inclusion of a flexible program designed to meet their varying needs, and the potential of the program to "arouse positive concerns that have not yet fully developed" (pp. 55–57). From the mid-1980s on researchers examined the issues related to alternative teacher certification and induction: What type of field experience is adequate preparation? Can teachers learn on the job? How does student teaching differ from an alternative certification internship? Are all types of experience created equal?

National Standards

Culver, Eicher, and Sacks (1986), noting the irony that alternative teacher certification programs proliferated simultaneously with discussions about national standards for admission to teacher education and increased course rigor, developed options that "use professional standards" (p. 23). These options included selective admission standards, American Association of Colleges for Teacher Education (AACTE)–supported curriculum, a supervised internship, and competency examinations. These components constituted a "professionally defensible" option to the alternative teacher certification routes, which the authors concluded varied widely in quality (p. 23).

Haberman (1986) further described the discrepant discussion about raising standards while generating alternative routes and gave five reasons why this discrepancy will persist: (1) public unwillingness to fund adequately a pool of well-prepared teachers, (2) public concern for quality teaching remaining relatively low compared with other public concerns such as social security, health care, etc., (3) inadequate funding of colleges of education, (4) unwillingness of prepared teachers to work in urban settings, and (5) demographics pointing to exacerbation of shortages in urban areas.

While the paradoxes inherent in the standards versus alternatives debate remained a constant, ideas to solve the teacher shortage dilemma proliferated during the mid-1980s, as if to ward off the spread of alternative teacher certification initiatives and keep standards high (Edelfelt, 1986). Differentiated staffing patterns, Peace Corps and national human services corps, partnership or job-sharing arrangements, attracting traditionally certified reentries into the profession, and assuring job security were among the 16 suggestions Edelfelt proposed for solving the supply and demand dilemma.

In yet another response to the tidal wave of reform initiatives begun in 1985, Galen and Kardon (1986) proposed a model distinct from both traditional and alternative certification paradigms. Featuring collaboration between teacher training colleges/universities, the public school system, and the government/business community, the model provided "on-site" classroom "integration of research and theory and necessitated completion of a five-year master's level program" (pp. 46–47). Culminating in a 3-year research project, the plan attempted to enhance integration of research into practice while maintaining high standards.

An Ongoing Motif: Program Evaluation and Assessment of Alternative Certification

Considerations also quickly emerged regarding how program directors, policymakers, school districts, and others should evaluate alternative teacher certification programs. Program directors designed teacher education curricula to improve the quality of the candidate pool as well as the quality of teacher preparation programs while offsetting shortages and teacher supply inequities. What criteria should determine the success of alternative routes? As experts in the field solidified what constitutes the teacher's professional knowledge base, Galluzzo and Ritter (1986) reasoned that outcome criteria would be the best guides to evaluation. The extent to which graduates of any route demonstrated these outcomes, not the extent to which new routes solved shortage, candidate quality, or delivery system dilemmas, determined the success of any reform effort. Insight from vocational teacher assessment, possibly of interest because vocational teachers frequently did not possess traditional teacher education, proved inconclusive but helpful in that it led evaluators to take into account what experience and training the individual had prior to entry into the classroom. Further, Suydam (1986) counseled that impacts on financial costs, the issue of "harm to students," as well as gains in number, quality, and retention of recruits are indeed factors critical to evaluation (unpaginated).

Adequate definitions of successful outcomes, however, proved illusory. In a research review crafted to help advise policymakers, Roth and Lutz (1986) defined alternative teacher certification as "either (a) alternative means of entering the classroom, or (b) alternative means of achieving standard teacher certification" (p. 2). The authors noted that the former path of entering the classroom is designed to be a temporary response to shortages, whereas programs of the type that achieve standard certification demonstrated some common characteristics. The operant definition of "alternative" Roth and Lutz chose provided entry to the classroom prior to or without full preparation for entry, accepted nontraditional students who already possessed a bachelor's degree or experience in lieu of traditional preparation, bypassed traditional preparation routes, and was established through state policy. Using this definition, the authors framed "the nature and length of teacher preparation" as the "major factor" that distinguished traditional from alternative teacher certification (p. 4). Concerns over teacher quality, the size of the prospective pool, and the quality of teacher education programs prompted the establishment of alternative routes, the authors said.

Making a distinction between "alternate" and "alternative," Roth and Lutz (1986) suggested that "alternate" teachers are utilized when no fully certified teacher is available; "alternatives" are hired in instances where the district is not required to document availability of a fully certified individual. Examining the concerns of teacher quality, teacher quantity, and the critique of traditional teacher education programs, they concluded that "any one or any combination of these purposes could be the motivation behind the establishment of an alternative certification program" (p. 9). Roth and Lutz surveyed the status of programs being initiated around the nation and observed that alternative certification programs experienced both opposition and support. Those who opposed it, including at the time both the AACTE and the NEA, implied that only in a profession bereft of a knowledge base would educators permit this restructuring: "In no other profession would non-trained individuals be allowed to practice" (p. 16). However, supporters of alternative certification maintained that the knowledge base was simply differently taught and that outcomes would be equivalent. Supporters soon included personnel in California, New Jersey, and the Southern Regional Education Board.

Why start an alternative program? Whereas some authors focused on outcomes, others encouraged policymakers to focus on program purpose when considering alternative teacher certification initiatives. Noting that, "Many institutions of higher education are developing experimental programs," Roth and Lutz suggested that, "When alternative programs are developed to increase the quality and/or quantity of teachers in the classroom, it is much easier to build alliances with teacher-training institutions" (p. 18). Program components should contain at least eligibility requirements, pre-classroom preparation, continued training and supervision, evaluation, and ultimately, certification. In sum, the authors intoned, "The message here is that the term alternative certification means different things to different people, and that the variety of alternative route programs requires that each be evaluated on its own merits" (p. 20). Evidently educators could not decide on what basis they should judge a certification program—a goal such as improving quality or quantity, or an outcome such as student achievement or equity.

Colleges of Education—New Roles? Noting the historical context from which the relationship between policymakers and teacher educators evolved, Parramore (1986) traced the growing tension many colleges of education felt; the university at large expected one set of behaviors to eventuate from certification programs and state education agencies expected yet another. "Schools and departments of education have not been able to take charge of their own destiny," the author observed (p. 8). Introducing the concept of "deregulation," Parramore recalled that, as early as 1964, Conant linked professional classroom teachers with universities in a "clinical teacher-professor" role (p. 9). Teacher centers later emerged to denote the "beginning of a true shift in authority for teacher education from higher education to local schools" (p. 9). Fleshing out the trend to make more accountable institutions that prepared educators, legislators also initiated teacher examinations designed to ensure quality. Differentiated roles for teachers, teacher centers, and certification examinations are all seen as signs of a maturing profession. The author listed other questions germane to the new routes. As overregulation becomes deregulation, will collaboration become possible? Will universities allow distinct colleges to be flexible enough to join partnerships? How well will individual school districts monitor their own programs for quality? How can programs both serve shortage designs and fulfill quality imperatives? Will students suffer as experimentation continues? These and other questions integral to the discussion remain to be answered, Parramore observed.

Tightly woven into the discussion about the purpose of certification and standards to be achieved was a discussion about deregulation—who should be responsible for generating and overseeing teacher certification programs? Is a market economy paradigm advisable? Roth (1986b) focused on three questionable staffing practices that could be detrimental to educators if teacher shortages were to grow. These included issuing emergency certificates, misassigning teachers, and allowing the uncontrolled expansion of alternative routes to certification. Noting the wide variety of influences, including state departments as well as local administrators, on issues of who ends up teaching what, Roth warned that misassignment of teachers is not to be dismissed lightly; it is a major policy issue with dramatic effect on the "integrity of the teaching profession" (p. 727).

Being "certified" to teach a field and being "qualified" to teach that subject are two different terms, Roth contended. The author traced the growth in use of teachers with emergency certificates as a percentage of total certificates issued and observed that bilingual, special education, computer science, vocational education, science, and mathematics students were the most likely to have uncredentialed or misassigned teachers. If alternative teacher certification was begun for the purpose of reducing those numbers of individuals who teach without adequate training, Roth suggested, the programs would have some merit. If, however, the alternative teacher certification programs were designed to bypass traditional coursework, implying that there is no vital knowledge base to be learned in that coursework, such a practice represents "a serious threat to the profession" (p. 726). Roth believed that the knowledge base could be learned best in the higher education classroom and in traditional coursework. Suggesting increased public awareness of the importance of proper credentialing, differentiated staffing arrangements, incentive programs to entice people into teaching, and increased cooperation, the author concluded that these issues deserve to be "the focus of national attention, and resolving them must become a national priority" (p. 727).

What Does "Professional" Mean? Educators further debated the definition of a "profession." Roth (1986a) reviewed various programs' directions at that time. He noted that policymakers appeared to be moving in ways that contradicted research findings, exacerbating the danger of deprofessionalizing teaching through instituting alternate routes, forgetting that vocational educators nontraditionally prepared suffered higher turnover rates than their traditionally trained counterparts, and ignoring research attesting that numbers of college credits correlated positively, not negatively, with teacher evaluations. Positive correlation of college credits to teacher evaluations indicate the need for more teacher education, not accelerated programs. Roth points out that policymakers should hasten to discontinue alternative teacher certification as soon as shortages disappear.

Continuing along the same theme, that alternative routes were potentially damaging shortcuts into the profession, Watts (1986) noted that it is large, inner-city schools that are experiencing the most severe shortages and that, "Those students who need the most capable, best trained teachers will be served by weak, poorly prepared counterfeits" (p. 29).

Making careful distinctions between types of alternative teacher certification programs, Wisniewski (1986) proposed that "Alternative preparation programs can be very positive" (p. 37). Resisting "knee-jerk reactions," Wisniewski indicated that where teacher educators developed alternatives in collaboration with school systems and the teaching profession, as "carefully designed experiments that alter and test the content and process of teacher preparation" (p. 37), they would both enhance and strengthen the profession. Wisniewski (1986) outlined the characteristics of some alternative teacher certification programs that professionalized teaching: (1) a strong commitment to academic competence and professional performance, (2) partnerships between universities and school systems, (3) collaboration on such processes as selection, preparation, and mentoring of participants, and (4) campus coursework blended with supervised internships. He acknowledged that teacher education has suffered from inertia and may benefit from such a bold dynamic. Remarking that "innovation is vital to an in-

stitution's survival," the author gave a detailed description of both a revitalized traditional and an alternative teacher preparation program, "The Lyndhurst Program," at The University of Tennessee–Knoxville. Noting that it was not yet possible to gauge the long-term effects of all the changes in the structure of teacher education that the experiments entailed, the writer affirmed the value of flexibility, responsiveness to changing times, and the vitality that innovation, properly nurtured, can bring.

Legislators Joined the Call for Alternative Programs and Ongoing Monitoring Soon legislatures were energetically studying and competing to enact alternative teacher certification initiatives. Designed largely to fill specified shortages and improve teacher quality, programs began in Arizona, Arkansas, Connecticut, and Florida (Feistritzer, 1991; McKibben, 1988a). By 1988, programs existed in 20 states (McKibben, 1988b). In almost every case, addressing shortages, recruiting high-quality candidates, creating articulation of theory and practice, supporting new teachers during induction, and eliminating misassignment of teachers were cited as reasons for building an alternative teacher certification option. McKibben also early articulated the "experiment" theory: that alternative teacher certification programs "can serve as laboratories for exploring new methods for the recruitment, selection, training, and support of teachers" (p. 35).

If outcomes were the measure of success, little guidance emerged from legislatively initiated agenda. Statewide analyses of the California program begun in 1983 and reports in 1988 (McKibben, 1988a) found "no statistically significant differences among the three groups of beginning teachers (interns, probationary teachers, and emergency teachers) on five out of six criteria. On only one criterion, "cognitive activity," interns scored significantly lower than the other two groups. Retention of interns was 80%, with 40% retention in the other two groups. Legislators in California concluded that the alternative program was at least as successful as traditional programs. Statewide analyses of the Texas program begun in 1985 (Irons & Wale, 1988) were still inconclusive, and early data from the Florida initiative indicated low numbers of applicants because of the ready availability of temporary certificates (Florida State Department of Education, 1988).

Feeling threatened, some colleges of education responded immediately to legislative agendas supporting alternative certification. Roth (1988) cited lack of resources provided to colleges of teacher education, that is, "capped" enrollments, as a source of dwindling numbers of credentialed graduates that exacerbated shortages. Further, the author noted, out-of-state individuals were discouraged from entering the California teacher pool by required testing offered at inconvenient times. Widespread debate continued to surround sweeping legislative reform measures in Texas as well, including discussion of the 18-hour limit or "cap" on professional education coursework. Alluding to (1) the growing knowledge base required of teachers seeking to fulfill the mandates of the new reform, (2) certain inability to meet guidelines established by the NCATE, and (3) the relatively high numbers of credits required of other professions, Ishler (1988) urged scrutiny of the new rules by a broad range of educators and, among other resolutions, "decried the actions of the state legislature which limit the ability of the academy and the profession to develop programs which will prepare teachers of the highest quality" (p. 49). The quiet days of conversation and compromise between various arenas of concern for teacher preparation grew more scarce.

In 1989 the AACTE issued a policy statement describing what "must constitute the core of alternative preparation programs for licensure" (p. 1). Appreciating that "teaching is more than telling," the statement supported the centrality of professional education and urged states to identify a common set of standards to be "rigorously applied to all applicants" (p. 2). Components recommended by the AACTE incorporate selective admission standards "including but not limited to: (a) a baccalaureate degree; (b) assessment of subject matter or area competency; (c) assessment of personal characteristics; and (d) assessment of communication skills" (p. 2). Other recommendations were (1) curriculum and skills reflecting the knowledge base for beginning teachers, (2) supervised internship *jointly* (emphasis theirs) developed and supervised through cooperative university–school arrangements, and (3) sophisticated assessment—beyond paper-and-pencil tests—of both the pedagogy and subject area. Recognizing the need to relieve teacher shortages, the authors of the AACTE statement supported recognizing the value of both nontraditional students' backgrounds and a single set of standards for all entering the profession. The AACTE issued similar guidelines for alternative teacher certification programs entitled *Alternatives, Yes. Lower Standards, No!* (AACTE, 1989). The guidelines defined alternative teacher certification as characterized by certain conditions. These conditions included: (1) involvement of the state legislature or state education agency in establishing "a legally sanctioned process for licensing teachers who have not had prior professional training" (p. 2), (2) empowerment of school districts to recommend candidates for certification, (3) the admission of individuals other than those prepared in regular teacher education programs, (4) the nature of the professional preparation being hands-on and supported by workshops, and (5) the school-based nature of the programs featuring optional university involvement. Multiple screening criteria, entrance tests, direct experiences with children, mentoring and support services, reduced teaching loads, temporary certification, and collaboration as well as other criteria comprised the 23 recommendations for a program the ATE defined as "appropriate" (p. 3).

Alternative teacher certification programs actually in operation varied widely in how they were managed and implemented. Some programs, such as that run by the New Jersey and Connecticut state departments of education, were highly centralized with training, monitoring, and supervision originating at the state level. Other programs such as the ones in Los Angeles and Houston made maximum use of school district expertise supplemented by local professors to introduce certification candidates to pedagogy. Training in the form of clock hours from the state department or school district trainers or in the form of semester hours of instruction from a college or university prepared individuals already possessing bachelor's degrees for entry into the classroom. Some programs required

a promise of employment after training in order to begin the alternative program. Supervision of the first year of full-time teaching was performed by site-based as well as by external mentors such as regional education consultants, college professors, school district curriculum directors, or principals in a variety of combinations.

Early Evaluations Showed Picture As the call for evaluation of alternative certification programs gained momentum, early results of the Houston program for alternative teacher certification emerged. Executive summaries (Goebel, 1986) for the 1985–1986 class presented three findings: (1) principals and administrators surveyed felt that interns' abilities were equal to those of first-year certified teachers, (2) most interns planned to return for the 1986–1987 school year, and (3) student achievement scores and teacher appraisal scores did not vary significantly between the groups of certified first-year teachers and interns. The results of the initial experiment, although clearly not flawless, warranted the continued development of the program in Houston based on its ability to fill vacancies and to prepare well-qualified teachers (Texas Education Agency, 1993a).

Hutton (1987) evaluated the district-based Dallas Independent School District alternative teacher certification program begun in the 1986–1987 school year. The researchers concluded that although it would not significantly impact the overall teacher shortage, the program had produced some qualified teachers to fill positions in shortage areas. Findings also showed that the high quality of the interns' performance was due to appropriate screening; that participation of advisors, principals and supervising teachers was critical to the program; that assignment of the intern as teacher of record (fully responsible for the class) should occur initially in the year; that alternative teacher certification programs offered teacher educators fruitful laboratories for study of the "metamorphosis of teachers"; and that mentors were critically important to the success of an alternative teacher certification program (p. 8).

In the results of a third early study in South Carolina, Million (1987) affirmed the value of "realistic classroom experiences" such as student teaching or an internship. The timing of the experience was less consequential than previously argued, though Million called for additional empirical comparisons of varying approaches to field experience timing.

Early Evaluations Fueled Further Controversy Increases in the number of alternative teacher certification programs occurred simultaneously with growing debate, criticism, and early program evaluations. Perhaps the most widely quoted of the early studies was the "Rand Study" (Darling-Hammond, Hudson, & Kirby, 1989). Reviewing 64 mathematics and science certification programs in four categories, mid-career, recent BA, alternative certification, and retraining, the authors sought to answer questions such as: (1) What are the educational and occupational backgrounds of recruits? (2) From which parts of the teacher reserve pool are recruits being drawn? (3) What attracted these recruits to mathematics and science teaching? (4) What has happened to graduates of the various programs?

(5) How do recruits' experiences differ from their expectations? (6) What plans do the recruits have? (7) For those who chose not to enter the classroom or who have left teaching, what were the reasons for doing so?

"Nontraditional recruitment programs" were those "designed to provide potential teachers from nontraditional pools with the course work and other requirements for full certification in mathematics and/or science. These programs do not require changes in state policies regarding teacher training or licensure" (p. 302). "Alternative certification programs" were defined as those "designed to increase the potential supply of teachers by preparing them to meet revised state certification requirements for entering teaching"; "retraining programs" are designed to help teachers already trained in other fields to obtain endorsement or certification in mathematics and/or science (p. 302).

The study (Darling-Hammond et al., 1989) revealed that many of the recruits (43%) had been teaching in other settings such as private school the year before entering the public school system; about half were in managerial and professional specialties prior to recruitment. Of the group not teaching the year before, three quarters had some kind of teaching experience such as being a tutor, a teaching assistant, an instructor, or a science fieldworker in private industry. Although policymakers assumed that labor market demand and job security were factors in the motivations of those already teaching but changing fields to mathematics and science, high interest in the subject-matter field was rated as "the most important reason for entering mathematics and science teaching" (p. 313). This interest in the subject matter was more intense than for traditionally trained individuals whose primary interest was to work with young people, whose secondary interest was in the value or significance of education in society, and whose third-rated motivation was interest in the subject matter. The study described other issues such as program cost, expectations, and satisfaction levels. Overall, the recruits surveyed were higher than average in representation of minority populations, were more female for populations of mathematics and science teachers, and were older than traditional teacher program recruits; nontraditional recruits resembled traditional recruits in their interest in positively affecting children's lives, in subject matter, and in their enjoyment of nonfinancial rewards.

Although many of those surveyed had taught before, the authors pointed out that their prior teaching experience does not ensure that they are "fully prepared—either in terms of pedagogical knowledge or more general expectations—for entering the K–12 classroom" (Darling-Hammond et al., 1989, p. 320). Satisfaction with their new career and retention appeared to be comparable to or better than that of traditionally trained teachers. Noting how comparable in many ways the two groups were, the authors concluded that "for all their promise, nontraditional teacher preparation programs cannot fully overcome other attributes of teaching that make recruitment and retention of teachers difficult" (p. 321). For even though these programs may ease entry, the authors concluded, they did not increase the ability of the profession to attract, through higher wages and better working conditions, individuals who will stay and succeed.

Because of low pay and because only entry into the profession, not the actual act of teaching itself, can be made substantially easier, shortages of teachers remain a constant in a continually evolving profession. Shortages in Arkansas, for example, led the Arkansas State Board to authorize alternative certification for as many as 50 teacher "trainees" a year (Bell & Roach, 1989). The "Alternative Certification Pilot Project" did not address many of the ATE's Recommended Standards, and researchers found repeated in the Arkansas experience the irony that in the same state, where all teacher preparation institutions were NCATE-accredited and thus attempting to increase standards, state-sponsored alternative teacher certification initiatives required "minimal preparation" (p. 8).

Evaluative comparisons of traditionally prepared, alternatively certified, and emergency permit teachers also emerged. In a Texas study of a university-based alternative teacher certification program published in 1989, researchers found overall grade point averages of the 63 individuals evaluated highest for alternative certification candidates who averaged an overall GPA of 3.04, lower for traditionally prepared teachers whose overall GPA was 2.79, and lowest for emergency permit teachers whose overall GPA was 2.41 (Brown, Edington, Spencer, & Tinafero, 1989). No significant differences were found, however, for GPA in teaching fields, which averaged 2.98 for traditional teachers, 3.04 for emergency-permit teachers, and 3.22 for alternatively certified teachers. Teacher performance, as measured individually by domain on the Texas Teacher Appraisal System (TTAS), was unambiguous:

The findings suggest that the academic and classroom performance of the three groups of teachers involved in the study were similar, although alternative certification program participants showed significant differences in measures of academic performance. That is, the alternative certification program paticipants earned overall GPA's, teaching field GPA's, and pre-professional skills test (P-PST) scores that were comparable to, or better than traditionally trained teachers and teachers on emergency permits. . . . It would appear that this type of teacher training provides a viable option for fulfilling the serious teacher shortages which exist in this area. (p. 23)

Another Texas study of a school district–based program in Houston Independent School District (HISD) yielded similar results. The achievement scores of students whose teachers were either experienced (EXP) teachers, alternatively certified (AC) teachers, or traditionally trained first-year (FYC) teachers analyzed for the 1988–1989 school year revealed that "the achievement of students assigned to EXP teachers and AC interns with experience is slightly greater than the achievement of students assigned to FYC teachers and AC interns with little or no experience" (Goebel & Ronacher, 1989, pp. 5–6). Researchers noted that variables including teacher groups and covariates such as ethnic and socioeconomic status (SES) variables accounted for 45% of the total variance in student achievement scores. The study included comparative demographics of alternatively certified interns, first-year certified teachers, and experienced teachers; how many vacancies were filled by alternatively certified interns; the academic achievement of students taught by alternatively certified compared to traditionally trained teachers; and the levels of support given to interns. The demographic aspect of the study revealed that about 45% of the teachers studied were black and 45% were white with a minority of positions filled by Hispanics and Asians except among first-year teachers, of whom 25% were black and 70% were white. Most elementary teachers were female. The writers indicated that significant vacancies (662 by 1988–1989) are being filled by the alternative teacher certification program. Differences between student achievement levels were significant according to teacher group; however, only 4% of the variance in student achievement as measured by the test used in HISD were attributable to teachers. Results bolstered HISD's resolve to continue its AC program.

Reform legislation in North Carolina encouraged teacher educators there to reflect on and evaluate both the need for and the effectiveness of alternative teacher certification initiatives. Allowing that the profession of education indeed has a knowledge base, that shortages of teachers guiding classes for which they are trained represent a threat to the schools and to the success of reform efforts, and that teacher education should be an effort combining the talents of colleges of education, public schools, and state departments of education, researchers prepared slowly to implement programs as late as 1989, some 4 years after major legislation had passed (Graham, 1989). First, authors noted that alternative teacher certification initiatives would not put undergraduate teacher education programs out of business. Affected by funding projections as well as fueled by shortages, alternative teacher certification programs provided at that time only 2% of the new teachers supplied, although that figure represented 15% of mathematics teachers. The research also quelled fears that individuals on accelerated or alternative programs would bring less academic talent to the classroom and that such programs would depend on retired businessmen and military personnel with dispositions unsuited to public school interaction. These fears did not materialize, Graham asserted, and she compared the program more to a 5-year program that attracts those who "desire to make a difference" than to a back-door certification process that threatens progress. Hawk and Schmidt (1989) in another North Carolina study that compared traditional and alternative (lateral entry program, LEP) approaches to teacher education concluded that, within the limitations of the small study of mathematics and science teachers, "The evaluations of the LEP participants indicated that they were competent in the school classrooms and as successful on NTE (National Teacher Examination) exams as traditionally prepared teachers" (p. 57).

Like North Carolina, Georgia also began an alternative teacher certification program, which Hassard (1989) reviewed for the 1988–1989 school year. Research on attitudes (directive as compared to student-centered) of regularly certified (RC) and AC teachers showed that, by mid-year, the attitudes of the two groups were comparable (Hassard, 1989). The importance of mentors for both RC and AC teachers was critical. On another measure, sense of efficacy, research also demonstrated the comparability of the two differently trained groups. In summarizing findings of several studies, Hassard noted, "Results of initial research studies aimed at evaluating these programs' effectiveness have been encouraging. In each case, the model of alternative certification used in these separate institutions is preparing teachers who fare as well during their first year of teaching as those beginning their careers through a traditional program. . . . The alternative certification models need to be studied, and tested" (p. 21).

As models of alternative teacher certification proliferated and as program graduates continued to enter the field, controversy mounted regarding the relative benefits of new models of teacher education. Gursky (1989) contrasted the relative success of the graduates of New Jersey's program with the overall emphasis many policymakers and reformers place on pedagogy and rigorous standards. Skeptics critical of alternative programs, Gursky added, note that graduates of alternative programs may more frequently begin in poor, inner-city school districts where the expense of adequate supervision may be more problematic. However, because alternative teacher certification programs tend to recruit more minorities than do traditional routes, these school districts may benefit most from a more demographically representative teaching force.

Lessons from the 1980s

Undoubtedly alternative teacher certification, with its focus on "hands-on" training, has accelerated researchers' opportunities to develop aspects of teacher induction and mentorships. As a growing body of induction literature would indicate, keeping a repertoire of behaviors available mentally is not the same thing as putting those repertoires into action (Huling-Austin, Odell, Ishler, Kay, & Edelfelt, 1989). Shulman's case studies (1989) verified that substantial resources and commitment are needed to induct a beginning teacher appropriately, no matter how trained. These case studies further suggested that merely assigning a mentor was inadequate to meet the needs of trainees; appropriate matches in subject area and grade level are also desirable. Finally, and clearly, assigning a new teacher to classrooms in which even veterans struggle is unwise. Most findings are meant to apply to any type of teacher education program, but the Shulman study evaluated only the Los Angeles Unified School District alternative teacher credentialing program. A similar case study of a collaborative in New Mexico, which involved the University of New Mexico in Albuquerque, the Santa Fe public schools, and several campuses of St. John's College, also found positive benefits from the careful assignment of mentors in an alternative teacher certification program and to paired, not single, internships. In such a setting two individuals taught in a vacancy, and daily reflection on practice was nurtured by a clinical, district-based supervisor (Day, 1989).

Educators also learned the value of public relations efforts on behalf of teacher education programs. Alarmed at the possibility that states' reduction of the number of education credits allowed prior to certification ("caps") might become a trend, Roth (1989) viewed the tendency to develop alternatives to traditional college-based teacher certification routes as "an image" problem. The same rationale used to "cap" the number of credits has been used to develop alternative teacher certification programs. The desire to deal with teacher shortages was exacerbated by the perception that education courses are insubstantial; further, state funding policies thwarted the mission of the college of education, perpetuating the view that colleges of education should provide funding for other colleges and for noneducation students. Of the three options for action Roth saw possible— (1) to move teacher education into the public schools, (2) to retain teacher education programs in institutions of higher education but concentrate them into shorter time periods to increase accessibility, and (3) to retain teacher education programs in higher education but significantly strengthen them, increasing credibility—he supported the last option. A comprehensive program of research on teacher education, faculty "exemplars in the instructional process," highly selective admissions policies, better funding of college of education programs, and adherence to guidelines for redesign of teacher education programs according to NCATE guidelines would include several critical changes needed to bring about program credibility. Roth suggested accompanying all efforts to improve teacher education in the colleges with sound publicity.

INTO THE 1990S: EVALUATING NEW MODELS

Even though program evaluation has been growing in quantity and quality since the mid 1980s, the body of evidence is far from conclusive. The following questions characterize much of the conference and publishing agenda for the 1990s: (1) How can the nation's institutions best be linked into collaboratives? (2) Who should do what? (3) What is the role of minority concerns in shortage-heavy urban areas? and (4) What is the nature of the nexus between politics and education?

Reforms Debated Effective Institutional Links

As the 1990–1991 school year opened, Goodlad (1990) published a summary of his massive 5-year Study of the Education of Educators. Goodlad's 19 "postulates" would be embedded in a "center of pedagogy" devoted to incarnating the goals and premises proposed. Institutional collaboration and systemwide reform would be seamless. At the same time, Goodlad denounced "the shortsighted who would remove teacher education from the knowledge-producing context of the university and, in so doing, abort the chances of teaching standing alongside our strongest profession" (p. 186).

Two published replies to Goodlad touched on the highly controversial placing of some alternative teacher education initiatives entirely within the auspices of school districts. Eubanks and Parish (1990) noted that, "teacher preparation programs and schooling might be disconnected as a way of guaranteeing that they continue to produce the same dreadful outcomes for the poor and the minorities that schooling in America has produced for 300 years" (p. 197). Eubanks and Parish envisioned the gap between the university and the public schools as a cultural breach that supported the status quo and ensured unfair treatment for minorities and poor students. Advocacy of alternative teacher certification as an equity issue is echoed in Dill's reply as well. Dill (1990) noted that the structure of higher education itself, requiring several years of full-time study and an extensive unpaid student teaching experience, is an impediment to minorities and the poor who wish to enter the teaching profession. The author reviewed research indicating that minorities in alternative routes frequently outscored minorities in traditional routes on standard certification examinations and that alternative certification routes, by recruiting and certifying

capable minority candidates, better serve to make the teaching force demographically representative.

Building Consensus for Change The National Education Association (NEA, 1990), cognizant of the 1989 AACTE and ATE statements on alternative teacher certification, issued recommendations on the subject in 1990. The statement placed alternative routes in the context of NEA's primary goal of staffing all of the nation's classrooms with fully qualified and licensed educators. The statement focused on the development of a diverse and demographically representative teaching force and on maintaining high standards while meeting shortages: "There is compelling reason to encourage and enable qualified individuals to achieve full licensure through carefully structured nontraditional route programs" (p. 2). Part of an overall restructuring program, the appropriate nontraditional teacher education program should "be conducted in conjunction with a state-approved college or university teacher education program" (p. 3). The statement further urged policymakers to avoid programs that would allow individuals to be teachers of record prior to full licensure, described the teacher candidate's relationship to the association, emphasized the importance of maintaining equivalent standards for all candidates, no matter how prepared, and outlined full guidelines for nontraditional route programs and intern/mentor programs.

Researchers discovered that traditional routes to certification were changing too slowly, as was evident in the publication of *Profile of Teachers in the U.S.—1990* by Emily Feistritzer (1990a). The study, which included 469 teachers who had participated in alternative teacher certification programs as well as 2,380 public and 352 private school teachers, found the work force becoming "older, whiter, and more female" (p. 3). In contrast to the traditional routes, alternative routes attracted high numbers of minority students. Feistritzer further found that, no matter how prepared, teachers believed that preparation should combine coursework with fieldwork and that, independent of how prepared, few felt they were adequately prepared when they first started teaching. Those interviewed also felt that however they were prepared was the best way to prepare teachers. Feistritzer found that 8 out of 10 teachers agree that "Students, regardless of their socioeconomic backgrounds, can perform at the highest levels of achievement" (p. 39), with 86% of alternative route teachers being inclined to think all students can achieve at high levels compared to 75% of traditionally prepared recruits who had not taught before. More nonwhite teachers think students are apt to feel pride in themselves only if they can see examples of success by members of their racial/ethnic/linguistic/religious group. Alternative route teachers are more in agreement that "pay based on performance, market-driven pay, career ladders and a national entrance examination for teachers would improve the teaching profession" (p. 4). Finally, more alternatively prepared teachers were willing to teach in inner cities than were traditionally prepared teachers. The Feistritzer study contributed to an increased awareness of options for ways to structure teacher preparation, options about which the public supporting reform needed to become more informed and active.

Just as state legislatures have felt, either from a concern for equity or some other agenda, a political imperative to act on the option of alternative routes to certification, so has the federal government shown interest in the topic of alternative teacher certification. President George Bush gave significant visibility to alternative teacher certification initiatives during his presidency. White House press releases highlighted alternative teacher certification in general and the Houston Independent School District program specifically as demonstrating one of several strategies to increase collaboration and reform the public education system (Texas Education Agency, 1990).

Federal Interest Attempted to Prod Reform In 1990 the Office of Educational Research and Improvement (OERI) commissioned a collection of articles on the topic of alternative teacher certification. Submitted in 1991, the series was first published in the *Peabody Journal of Education* and was reprinted as monograph No. 14 by the ERIC Clearinghouse on Teacher Education in December 1992. Edited by Willis Hawley, the early collection provided a series of articles grouped singularly around the topic of alternative teacher certification. Claiming not to reflect the viewpoint of the OERI or any organization, the volume posed new questions as well as gave articulation to a number of alternative teacher certification issues.

In the overview that opened the volume, the editor (Hawley, 1990) noted that alternative teacher certification gained large numbers of proponents from those concerned about teacher shortages. Shortages exist, the author asserted, because some view undergraduate teacher education as a barrier to the profession and others view it as a door. Barriers include the price of tuition, full-time student status, the cost of student teaching, and childcare. The "barrier" theorists buttress their argument, he postulated, by adding that traditional undergraduate courses reflected a lack of rigorous curriculum in addition to their barriers; therefore, some say, traditional routes both hampered capable applicants prior to entry and harassed them with poor courses after entry. Evidently a wide variety of responses to the shortage issue as well as the issue of the legitimacy of preservice course work are possible, Hawley noted, framing the arguments along the lines of a last-resort argument for the shortage discussion and an "art and craft" argument for the issues relating to quality of preservice programs.

Some of these tensions Hawley detailed were better understood and resolved by looking at roles and functions within the act of (a) certification, a process in which individuals take courses at an institution to receive the credential, and (b) licensure, in which alternative certification is "an act by the state to authorize individuals to teach" (p. 5). Assessment is critical, Hawley attested, whether or not alternative teacher certification lowers the numbers of emergency certified individuals. Ongoing research needs to examine, he wrote: the relationship between career knowledge in mid-career switchers and content knowledge in the classroom; attrition rates; the relative price tags of each model; the abilities to increase reflective behavior in both alternatively certified and traditionally certified candidates; what effects alternative certification may have on traditionally certified individuals; how alternative certification may improve teacher education; and how reformers might improve alternative teacher certification itself.

Although he did not comment on improvements that might be appropriate in traditional preservice programs, Hawley

(1990) asserted that alternative teacher certification could be improved by: (1) increasing the quality of mentoring alternative certification teachers receive; (2) creating richer learning opportunities, and (3) ensuring that new teachers learn "how to learn about teaching," asserting that "if experience is our only teacher, we shall be poor learners indeed" (p. 29). Noting that incorporating these suggestions would signal dramatic improvement over most present alternative teacher certification programs, Hawley concluded that the nation's willingness to make such changes may indeed indicate how willing voters are in general to invest in children's education.

Federal support for restructuring of teacher education is a mixed blessing, according to Darling-Hammond, 1990, who recalled that alternative route strategies received extensive support from the Bush presidency, which numbered the initiative among its most important education goals. Political agendas, undefended assertions, and half-truths, Darling-Hammond observed, have obscured the appropriateness of the solution of alternative teacher certification for the problems it proposed to remedy; further compounding the problem are the widely varying definitions and standards represented by the different alternative teacher certification programs nationwide, not to mention the numerous variations present in traditional teacher certification programs.

Arizona, Connecticut, and New York are, according to Darling-Hammond (1990), "high-standards" states because of the number of credits necessary and the "lengthy supervised practicum or internship in addition to subject matter preparation" candidates must acquire whereas New Jersey and Texas are "low-standards" states that limit the number of pedagogy credits required to 18. From her analysis Darling-Hammond derived two conclusions: "First, state standards for teacher preparation vary widely both within and across certification categories" (p. 126). Some states required less teacher preparation than others, alternative programs requiring even less; other states have reduced requirements for both traditional and alternative teacher certification programs, keeping the requirements of each route approximately equivalent, with New Jersey and Texas falling in this category. Other states have added requirements for certification such as a graduate-level master's degree.

"Second," Darling-Hammond observed, "just as alternate routes to certification differ dramatically across the states, so do traditional routes" (p. 127). Noting the lack of consensus among state governmental officials regarding the goal of teacher education, the author added that wide variations have reduced opportunities for reciprocity among states and have exacerbated problems of teacher mobility. Further, increased variations among state trends in teacher certification are at odds with other professional groups such as the Holmes Group, the National Council for Accreditation of Teacher Education (NCATE), and the National Board for Professional Teaching Standards, all of which are trying to gain a national consensus on certification and accreditation processes. National trends toward greater variation are in addition complicated by an increase in those empowered to certify, such as local employers who, Darling-Hammond assumed, are not "representing some broader standard of professional practice" (p. 128). Problems they encountered include the fact that employers may not be looking out for the best interest of their clients but, in fact, may be taking the "cheapest" or "most expedient" course of action. Certification programs aimed at district-specific practices may not articulate well to other settings. Darling-Hammond summed, "the concept of 'alternatives' to traditional state certification leaves a great deal of room for varied meaning" (p. 129).

Darling-Hammond (1990) then reflected on two questions to clarify thinking about the most appropriate way to educate teachers: "What kinds of knowledge and training play important roles in the development of teachers' skills and abilities? and How are these best acquired?" (p. 130). Although the author found answers to the second of these questions not yet definitively available, answers to the first would point to direct links between "fully prepared" teachers and student success. Darling–Hammond noted that recent research as well as "studies conducted during the shortage era of the 1960s and early 1970s when many teachers entered through temporary and alternate routes" all support the importance of "full preparation" (p. 130). In addition to lower general performance, lack of "full preparation" was thought to cause teachers to develop students' higher order thinking skills inadequately, to be less sensitive to students, less able to plan and redirect instruction, less able to anticipate students' knowledge and potential difficulties, and more likely to blame students if their teaching is not successful.

Darling-Hammond further reviewed studies where alternatively certified interns' knowledge was "uneven," their job satisfaction was lower, and where problems resulting from inadequate preparation may have led to early attrition. These findings led Darling-Hammond (1990) to conclude that where adequate preservice preparation is added to intensive on-the-job supervision, "cumulative power" and higher satisfaction rates may eventuate. Research demonstrated that subject matter is important "up to a point" (p. 133); that stronger relationships were demonstrated between education coursework and teacher performance than were demonstrated between subject-matter coursework and teacher effectiveness, and that, even though unsupervised on-the-job training is insufficient preparation, the mentoring literature clearly demonstrated the value of thoroughly supervised, high-quality, intensive clinical learning experiences (p. 132). She concluded that "policies providing alternate routes to teacher certification may be evaluated in terms of the extent to which they incorporate opportunities to acquire these different elements of teaching knowledge, an evaluation which will determine . . . whether states are acting responsibly on behalf of students" (p. 136).

Darling-Hammond made a distinction between "alternate" route programs (AR), which often include a master's degree and provide for mid-career entry into the profession and "alternative" certification programs (AC), which the author defined as "shorter-term" programs providing less pedagogical course work, subject-matter coursework, or extended practicum experience (Darling-Hammond, 1990). "Adequacy of program preparation" is difficult to assess, and results of initial evaluation, decidedly sketchy, "suggest that assessments of program preparation often depend on whether one wants to see the glass as half empty or half full" (p. 137).

Generally, the kind of training AR recruits receive is different from that of AC recruits; it tends to be longer, provide more

pedagogical coursework, include subject-matter coursework, focus on specific as opposed to generic skills, and include a range of methods. Pressures to shorten programs and to limit supervision of practica may be fiscal in nature or may be a result of inadequate implementation of program designs. Overall, Darling-Hammond asserted that the smaller, more selective, and more costly AR programs achieve better results because they support reflective practice, recruit high-ranking professionals instead of those in "lower-paid jobs" (p. 141), are more resistant to labor market forces, and provide teachers who, early data suggest, might stay longer in classrooms. Darling-Hammond noted that both AR and AC aim to increase both the quality and the quantity of teachers available, but that rates of hiring on emergency certificates are not decreasing. The author wondered if the new routes are accomplishing anything. Finally, framing the trends of AR and AC within normal labor market dynamics, the author concluded that if states were willing to "invest either in teachers' salaries at competitive levels or in serious preparation for those who would like to teach but cannot afford the expenses of training," the "quick fix forms" of alternative teacher certification would not be needed (p. 147). Issues of demographically and generically representative teaching forces are not directly addressed. With the simple labor market equation in mind, Darling-Hammond concluded,

In the final analysis, alternate routes to teacher certification will be deemed a policy success to the extent that they improve teacher preparation while working in concert with other state policies to expand the supply of highly qualified and committed teachers to all children and communities. Current evidence suggests that some approaches to alternatives are much more promising in this regard than others. (p. 149)

Regional Voices Described Concurrent but Uncoordinated Efforts

Cornett (1990) adopted a less sweeping perspective on the alternative teacher certification enterprise in "Alternative Certification: State Policies in the SREB States." When in 1980 the Southern Regional Education Board (SREB) issued 25 recommendations for regional education reform, half of the recommendations, Cornett noted, "were aimed at improving the quality of teachers for the region's classrooms" (p. 55). Again, overall quality of the teaching force as well as teacher shortages in mathematics and science inspired policy initiatives that soon led to all 15 states (Alabama, Arkansas, Florida, Georgia, Kentucky, Louisiana, Maryland, Mississippi, North Carolina, Oklahoma, South Carolina, Tennessee, Texas, Virginia, and West Virginia) having some form of alternative teacher certification legislation on the books.

Cornett defined alternative teacher certification as altered licensure requirements through: "(a) completing a different set of standards (i.e., limiting the number of education courses required); and (b) meeting licensure requirements by demonstrating competency (i.e., passing tests for certification, on the job evaluations, and/or completing a supervised internship)" (p. 60). Cornett examined all 15 states to discover similarities and differences in state policies, who is entering teaching via the routes, how effective the programs are, and the strengths and weaknesses of each.

Even though initial evaluations would tend to demonstrate similar results in teacher effectiveness between the two routes—traditional and alternative—thorough evaluations are uniformly in short supply in the SREB states, Cornett observed. Several conclusions could be drawn, however, from the studies: (1) More teachers are being prepared through alternative certification programs; in fact, more than twice as many were being thus prepared in 1990 as in 1988; (2) alternative teacher certification programs were attracting individuals who would otherwise not enter the profession at all; (3) even though evaluation of the effectiveness of the teachers being produced the new way is not conclusive, what is available shows them to be equally effective as those produced traditionally; and (4) higher education schools are beginning to collaborate according to state mandates that they do so. Cornett reiterated the need to track and evaluate comprehensively teachers prepared in a variety of new as well as traditional ways.

Researchers also discussed regional perspectives in states that did not have shortages of teachers. Bliss (1990) explored Connecticut's initiative, which the Department of Higher Education sponsored. Highly selective (30% of applicants accepted) and driven by quality concerns, the program attempted to educate career explorers, career changers, second-career or retired individuals, and uncertified educators, who constituted about 40% of the total group. Bliss noted that, unlike the loosely coupled courses traditional programs often offered, the residential program was organized "as a coherent, integrated curriculum—presumably a bellwether for the state's 14 college- and university-based programs" (p. 41). Although competition for jobs was keen, the alternate certification candidates were hired at a rate higher than their traditionally certified peers, and external, mentor, and supervisor review of the program rated teachers "good to excellent."

Regarding the goal of the initiative, Bliss (1990) added that the program, ". . . encouraged faculty members in some Connecticut universities to examine their curriculum and the organizational structure of course offerings" (p. 50) and that the project may have spurred the growth of postbaccalaureate programs as well as professional practice schools. Although the state's experience in alternative teacher certification was positive and valuable, the author reflected, it should not be viewed as an endorsement of alternative programs that "take a different," presumably shorter, approach (p. 52).

Noting the criticism school district–based and state-mandated alternative certification programs have received from proponents of traditional teacher education, Stoddart (1990) characterized the Los Angeles Unified School District (LAUSD) Intern Program not as a "quick fix" but as "an attempt on behalf of states and school districts to upgrade teaching standards already downgraded by teaching shortages that result in the use of emergency credentialed and misassigned teachers" (p. 84). Stoddart's contribution to the federally sponsored volume was a case study of LAUSD designed to examine four key areas: (1) ability to recruit academically able teachers to urban environments, (2) differences between alternative and traditional teacher candidates pools, (3) nature of the teacher education program offered by LAUSD, and (4) a comparison of the graduates of the LAUSD and traditional paradigms.

Recounting the situation of chronic shortages of qualified teachers for urban settings, Stoddart (1990) detailed the role of emergency certificated and misassigned teachers as it negatively impacted the students greatly in need of excellent instruction. Stoddart noted how customary shortages of qualified teachers for urban areas are compounded in southern California by high populations of students with diverse language needs. Indeed, shortages affect up to 60% of bilingual education classes that are being taught by inappropriately credentialed teachers. The writer concluded, "There is little hope of recruiting sufficient teachers to meet Southen California's need through traditional sources of teacher supply" (p. 89). In fact, traditional teacher education college programs are inadvertently compounding the problem by raising academic requirements, capping enrollments, and limiting the number of entrants into the student teaching phase.

Recalling the legislative history in California, which facilitated district-driven teacher education programs, Stoddart (1990) reported that between 1984 and 1990 some 1,100 novice teachers were recruited and trained by the LAUSD route, a sizable group from whose experience, she speculates, teacher educators could learn much. In terms of teacher recruitment, Stoddart found that LAUSD, which trains 300 interns yearly, has reduced the number of emergency credentialled teachers in the district without adversely affecting the recruitment of college-trained teachers. In particularly difficult-to-staff areas such as bilingual classrooms, findings suggested that as many as 25% of new elementary bilingual hires were LAUSD trained. Analyses of subject-matter preparation using transcript examination, GPA, and institution attended showed the subject-matter preparation of interns to be comparable to that of graduates from California institutions, with the majority of the secondary interns graduating from academically rigorous institutions. Attrition rates of interns after 3 years compared favorably to national attrition rates, possibly because of mentor support received during the first 2 years and possibly because of the fact that 2 years of experience are required in order to receive a clear credential. Typically, interns reported preference for an alternative teacher certification program over a traditional teacher certification program due to financial need, a preference for hands-on learning via practical experience, and a reluctance to take additional college coursework.

Uniformly older than traditional college of education recruits, LAUSD secondary interns did not carry as much work-related experience directly into the classroom as might be thought. Only 11% of English credentialled individuals and 22% of mathematics credentialled individuals taught in the field of their academic discipline. However, fully 44% of science majors came from environments where science was their livelihood, leading Stoddart to conclude that "Over the past 6 years LAUSD has consistently recruited small but significant numbers of qualified and experienced scientists into teaching" (p. 100). Stoddart found the LAUSD program attracted higher percentages of minorities (about 33%) than did colleges of education in California, averaging about 13%. It also recruited 60% males compared to 30% in traditional programs. Ethnic and gender advantages in the intern program made it easier for interns, who often grew up and now chose to live in the same areas from which the students are drawn, to know well and understand the student groups they chose to teach.

Stoddart further examined training and support systems for interns. District-specific training presented both advantages and disadvantages for novices. The intern program was not as academically rigorous as a typical college-based program. Although formulaic and not rigorous in theory, the training provided interns with only "one way" things are done in the district; ideally, experienced teachers branch out from there into more personally satisfying, creative, and effective models. Stoddart's research found that even though many topics covered by LAUSD interns are the same topics college candidates would cover, the LAUSD instructors focused more on practical and immediate application than on underlying principles or critical approaches. One notable exception was the multicultural education of interns, which was lengthier than that taken by traditional college students but similar in its approach. Stoddart also detailed mentoring procedures and evaluation techniques for interns in the LAUSD program.

Comparing traditional teacher education to the program at LAUSD was difficult indeed, the author observed, like comparing apples and oranges, and led the author to comment, "The findings indicate the need for caution in making generalizations about either form of teacher preparation." (p. 117). Apparently the comparisons did generate some important questions, however: (1) Should teacher preparation be context specific or context free? and (2) How might colleges actually meet the growing demands of burgeoning multicultural inner-city school students? Stoddart concluded, "Traditional programs, unless radically restructured, are unlikely to recruit sufficient teachers to meet this need. Developing alternative route programs that primarily serve to socialize teacher candidates into prevailing school practice, while providing teachers, will not help improve instruction for at-risk students" (p. 118). Universities and school districts need to work more together, the writer added, to serve better an increasingly diverse clientele. But how might these entities design a collaboration that would work to satisfy a broad band of diverse constituents? Stoddart's detailed and probing analysis of LAUSD leaves that question unanswered.

The fact that universities and public schools have not collaborated enough has been pivotal in establishing a distinctly political agenda to the alternative teacher certification conversation. Fenstermacher (1990) proposed both to elucidate and update the meaning of "alternative certification" and assess its value "relative to other forms of teacher preparation" (p. 155). Clarification of the meaning of "alternative certification" occurs through an imaginary dialog set in a graduate class of education in the year 2092. The teacher has difficulty differentiating between defining alternative certification and giving an explanation of how the phenomena came about; thus, Fenstermacher pointed to the political agenda underlying some alternative certification initiatives as well as the trend to differentiate between "certification" and "licensure." "Licensure" eventually comes to denote the "function of the state acting on its authority to protect and promote the general welfare" and "certification . . . is a function of the profession itself acting to acknowledge those who demonstrate advanced capabilities" (pp. 156–157). Suggesting "alternative certification" should actually be called "alternative licensure," in that context, the reflections included

a variety of considerations about why alternative certification came about—shortages, the low quality of available recruits, repudiation of present forms of teacher education, and more. Even in 2092, Fenstermacher conjectured, the reasons for its rise are "simply not clear—not even a century later" (p. 159). Whether prominent lawmakers supported alternative teacher certification as a result of frustration with the perceived vacuous nature of most pedagogy courses, with the lack of rigor in many students' subject concentration, or because it was politically advantageous for them to support some form of "choice," also remained unclear, and Fenstermacher concluded that "Alternative certification seems to have been an idea that was in the right place at the right time" (p. 161).

Commentary on variations in the quality of programs followed in the Fenstermacher (1990) study. The author provided some history on why associations such as NEA and AACTE demonstrated ambivalence toward or eventually granted only qualified support for alternative approaches. Citing the "locus of control" issue, the author added, "Most programs of alternative certification seemed to place initial teacher preparation in the hands of the employing school district rather than a teacher education institution. Perhaps that is part of [what] worried teacher educators and their associations" (p. 162). Projecting ahead for a synthesis of the matter and a sense of outcome, the prediction read, "Well," said Teaone (Teacher One), "the matter did not get resolved in such a way that you can say that one approach or the other prevailed" (p. 163).

Calling the state of affairs a "policy battle of some proportion," Fenstermacher then proceeded to address the relative merits of both the alternative and traditional approaches to teacher education. Noting that a variety of routes were available for individuals to enter the profession, the author showed how difficult it is to evaluate the outcomes of these routes in the relative vacuum of agreement among teacher educators on "what constitutes the proper proficiencies and abilities of a beginning teacher" (p. 164). Debates relevant to the alternative teacher certification discussion included vying ideas about where teachers should be educated, what knowledge bases should be mastered, and whether or not it is the theoretical, ideal world the process should prepare students for, or the real, present world of schools.

Allowing that if resources and time were appropriately distributed, one might say that for initial teacher entry into the classroom, either system, alternative teacher certification or traditional teacher education, might do the job. When one looks at a longer time frame, however, Fenstermacher (1990) contended that the skills of a seasoned teacher require the ability to reflect, the "freedom to place the day-to-day operating skills of teaching into a context that best accounts for the individual and collective lives of the students in the classroom, for the unique character and ability of the teacher, and for the circumstances of the particular school and classroom environment" (p. 170). Asserting that alternative teacher certification may place practical impediments to building reflective skills because it touts itself as a "quick entry" route, Fenstermacher also allowed that the closeness of the training to the actual experience "presents an enviable opportunity for the kind of interaction that grooms a person to be critically effective" (p. 171). "Structured carefully," the author continued, "programs of alternative certification might achieve many or all of valued outcomes of a fine traditional teacher education program" (p. 171).

Fenstermacher (1990) also weighed the concomitant question that can be asked of traditional preparation paradigms: "How many of the 1,000 plus traditional teacher education programs in the United States can be identified as having faculties of master teacher educators who in turn prepare their students to be reflective practitioners?" (Fenstermacher, 1990, p. 171). Because, as he noted earlier, no standards or goals are consistent across all programs, and because evaluation remains a moot point, it would appear that a variety of routes into the teacher profession will remain the norm. Analogizing the tension between traditional and alternative routes to a poker game in which a variety of outcomes is possible, the author suggested that one outcome might be that all the players "mellow" into peaceful coexistence. However, competing players could work together to strengthen their pursuit.

Introducing the idea of the "professionalization" of teaching, Fenstermacher eventually described a dichotomy in which alternative teacher certification is viewed as the "democratic," broad-based, and political end of the continuum; traditional teacher education is viewed as the "professional" end of the continuum representing a rapidly expanding body of knowledge those once totally in control of entrance to the profession felt teachers needed. From the direct clash between the "professionalization" proponents and the "democratization" proponents, Fenstermacher envisioned the possibility of "fundamental changes" emerging (p. 178). After noting the influence of the federal government in teacher preparation, which is usually left up to individual states, the author summarized:

Here, then, may be found the key differences between what we have called traditional teacher education programs and alternative certification. Carefully designed alternative certification programs offer a way to deal with teacher shortages that are superior to the granting of emergency certificates; alternative certification offers a career path into teaching for the academically qualified person who seeks a teaching position but lacks the means or opportunity for a period of sustained professional growth. Alternative certification relieves some of the political pressure built up by the demand for choice and for a deregulated economy; finally, alternative certification provides a programmatic alternative for those politicians who want to do some teacher education bashing without great fiscal consequence or much damage to their reputations. (pp. 181–182)

Noting that neither enterprise has a corner on success in teacher education, Fenstermacher concluded:

There may be value in ceasing to think of them as oppositional to one another. Perhaps the best course of action lies in blending these ideas, wherein the advantages of being close to practice are maintained, but so are the advantages of reflective and critical approaches to pedagogy. (p. 182)

Although Fenstermacher's lengthy exploration of the meaning of alternative teacher certification reflected a creative and unique approach to analyzing their dynamics, it yielded few new or startling insights.

Alternative Teacher Certification: Experiment or Solution?

It is unclear how many university presidents would have agreed with Boston University president John Silber, who, in October of 1990, admonished that official closing of the schools of education would be the "best thing that could happen to them" (Leslie & Lewis, 1990, p. 59). Public perception of deterioration in the public schools facilitated the appearances of articles in the popular press that described traditional teacher education as thoroughly bankrupt: The indictment: "the wrong people are studying the wrong things in the wrong places" (p. 58). Clearly, the article noted, politicians increasingly saw alternative teacher certification as a solution that, in the best case scenario, prompted institutions to act on their own to improve. If alternative teacher certification was high on the agenda of policymakers and legislators, it was not high on that of the general population of educators who responded to the ATE First Annual Survey of Critical Issues. That issue was among the lowest rated areas of concern (Buttery, Haberman, & Houston, 1990).

Did any type of institutional improvement occur as a result of alternatives? Some tinkering around institutional edges did occur, but most changes were cosmetic or designed to increase access for more students to enter an essentially unchanged higher education setting. As we entered into the 1990s, studies attempted to address not wholesale reform but questions about how graduates of alternative programs might differ from or be similar to graduates of traditional programs. While lamenting the deprofessionalizing effect of widespread deregulation on teacher preparation, Banks and Necco (1990) sharpened the questions that research must answer in order to be able to evaluate alternative forms of teacher preparation:

Will alternatively certified teachers demonstrate a competency level equal to the traditionally certified teachers? Will student achievement scores indicate any differences between the two routes for teacher certification? Will the time/cost factors in an alternative certification program be comparable to the regular certification program? Will the job burnout and job attrition rates be the same for the two methods of teacher certification? (p. 24)

Several studies appeared to begin addressing these questions. Knight, Owens, and Waxman (1990–1991) compared students' perceptions of their learning environments in the classes of alternatively and traditionally certified teachers and found that the traditionally certified teachers' students thought that their classroom environment promoted more higher thought processes, better pacing, and more group cohesiveness than did the alternatively certified teachers' students. The authors noted, however, that results "must be interpreted with caution since little is known about other characteristics of teachers in the study which may have contributed to differences in student perceptions" (p. 33) and that the study actually pointed to the need for more careful research.

Other research by Barnes, Salmon, and Wale (1990) found a number of strengths among the 1,215 interns studied in Texas: Programs attracted highly motivated, enthusiastic interns, higher percentages of whom passed the certification tests than did traditional education students; a feeling on the part of principals and supervising teachers that the particular intern they supervised was somehow unique; doubts expressed initially about the programs were eliminated by the end of the year based on the intern's(s') performance; colleges and universities were communicating more with school districts as a result of the alternative certification programs; larger proportions of minority candidates were certified through alternative routes than through traditional programs because the alternative route allowed continuation of income; equally high marks were generally given to college and to school district preparation units; the paid internship in the alternative program was attractive; and student achievement of alternatively certified interns compared favorably to student achievement of traditionally trained beginning teachers statewide. Similar findings of equivalent students' achievements marked programs in the Houston, Dallas, and El Paso Independent School District studies (Feistritzer, 1990b). Weaknesses cited included program administrators overwhelmed by inquiries from the public about the program; a need to start the program earlier in the year in order to have interns feeling fully composed and ready on the first day of school; and better orientation of supervising teachers (Barnes et al., 1990). Explorations into experimental forms of alternative teacher certification in Texas eventually led to legislation supporting professional development schools (Texas Education Agency, 1993b).

What is a certification program designed to do? What is the nature of the expertise it nourishes? Marchant (1990) noted that it is not usually a lack of content expertise but a lack of ability to teach the subject effectively that should be the focus of teacher education reform. The author asks, "How is expertise developed?" (p. 11). This knowledge is developed over time and through reflection. Although it has the advantage of offering extensive hands-on training, the alternative certification programs did not focus extensively on pedagogical knowledge and might not provide adequate time and supervision in the development of decision-making skills. Another study (Ball & Wilson, 1990), which compared alternatively certified and traditionally trained teachers of mathematics, concluded, "It is striking that, despite apparently dramatic structural and philosophical differences between university-based and alternate route programs, so much remains the same about these novice mathematics teachers" (p. 11). Ball and Wilson's work, in fact, indicated both routes as not capable of producing mathematically thoughtful experts capable of instructing youth in mathematics.

While scholars were debating the pros and cons of the new approach to certification, popular press releases occasionally focused on the creativity or "fresh" approaches alternatively certified interns brought to the public schools. "The grand task of cultivating a productive and creative society cannot be left to a temple of mediocrity like our current education system," alternatively certified teacher Jerry Rosiek (1990) told *The New York Times;* the only way to change school, with all its bureaucracy, the intern asserted, was to be "subversive" (p. 4). Similarly, intern Dena E. Franke (1991) told *Educational Leadership,* "teaching is my life, a love of mine" (p. 34). Patricia Hines (1992), who worked with transition into teaching programs resulting from army downsizing, told *The Wall Street Journal* that, "Considering the academic credentials of some of our current teachers and the quality of our teacher-training

programs, the U.S. is in no position to deny itself the windfall of talent preparing to leave the armed forces" (p. 8). Articles like these kept the political agenda alive while reinforcing the suggestion that institutional barriers were keeping out of the classroom individuals of great talent and expertise.

By the end of 1991, researchers completed significant national and state studies in a variety of aspects of a growing alternative teacher certification phenomenon. Propelled by the Bush administration's support for alternative certification, Baird (1991a, 1991b) in the U.S. Department of Education completed a state-by-state study of progress to date. Noting untapped talent pools and impending teacher shortages, Baird coordinated political initiatives to support alternative teacher certification throughout the Bush years as manager of the national alternative certification program initiative.

Feistritzer's (1991) state-by-state analysis, published the same year, was the first document widely disseminated that clarified definitions of various types of programs and enabled educators and voters alike to see which states provided alternative routes, however defined. Feistritzer organized state programs into classes from A through I. Class A, for example, featured "true" alternatives "designed for the explicit purpose of attracting talented individuals who already have at least a bachelor's degree in a field other than education into elementary and secondary school teaching" (p. 17). By 1991, 11 states were sponsoring "Class A" programs, defined as those that were not restricted to areas of teacher shortage and that provided teaching with a trained mentor and formal instruction in the theory and practice of teaching in a variety of times and formats. Other classifications described programs that served areas of teacher shortage (Class B), gave major responsibility for the programs to school districts (Class C), were based on transcript review followed by higher education coursework (Class D), were postbaccalaureate programs based on courses taken in institutions of higher education (Class E), were essentially emergency routes that allowed an individual to teach while taking higher education coursework (Class F), required completion of a minor number of courses to receive certification, often by reciprocity from another state (Class G), allowed eminently qualified individuals such as Nobel prize winners to teach certain subjects (Class H), or were not in 1991 implementing an alternative route but may have one under consideration (Class I).

Between 1983 and 1991, states reporting some form of alternative teacher certification route rose from 8 to 39, with all states reporting a total number of routes to certification of 91. The year 1991 saw a large rise in the number of states offering "true" alternatives from 2 in 1985 (i.e., New Jersey and Texas) to 11 states by 1991 (Feistritzer, 1991). As the definition of "alternative teacher certification" evolved, some states sought to be identified as having "true" alternatives and some wished not to be identified as having "true" alternatives; however, overall, the term became more synonymous with those "programs designed specifically to bring high quality adults who already have at least a bachelor's degree—and many who have considerable life experience—into the teaching profession" (p. 12).

Few serious educators or politicans would doubt the value of bringing academically talented individuals who wish to teach into the classroom; rather, the question often centered around the issue of whether or not more than one route to certification was desirable. Murnane, Singer, Willett, Kemple, and Olsen (1991) identified the need to facilitate the switch of "academically talented college graduates" to the classroom as a vital issue in licensing reform. Citing the New Jersey experiment, the authors concluded that at least three positive outcomes appeared: (1) Many college graduates are interested in teaching but find the structure of undergraduate programs inappropriate for them, (2) alternative programs serve well the goals of minority recruitment, and (3) attrition of alternative route individuals is lower than attrition of traditional undergraduate candidates. The authors concluded that a variety of training programs would best serve the variety of constituents who needed trained teachers and that "requiring that all candidates complete particular courses creates a captive audience for the institutions and faculty providing these courses. This significantly reduces incentives to improve instruction" (p. 101).

Reform of teacher education through alternative routes prompted the publication of a complete issue of the *Journal of Teacher Education* on alternative teacher certification (Ashton, 1991). The series of articles explored the topic from a selection of possible perspectives with the goal in mind to "stimulate research and development that enables teacher educators to confront the political threat with reasoned argument and empirical evidence of the need for coherent programs that develop teachers' professional judgment and effectiveness" (p. 82). The journal gave a broad outline of the discussions surrounding alternative teacher certification in the early 1990s.

Viewing alternative teacher certification programs as "a variety of context-specific naturally occurring experiments," Zumwalt (1991, p. 83) recounted the heated debate on both sides for and against such programs, as variously defined. After describing the Los Angeles, New Jersey, and Connecticut programs, the author compared the three programs in each of four areas: (1) policy context; (2) elements in the preparation program such as admission criteria, role of higher education, and coursework; (3) support from the school in which the program is based; and (4) steps needed to obtain certification. Noting significant differences in programs considered "alternate," Zumwalt cautioned readers to judge programs in light of their goals and contexts, in addition to their impact on students and on teaching in general. The author also probed whether, in exploring certain experimental directions, other efforts to provide equity and professionalism are being undermined. Clearly, seeing alternative teacher certification approaches as experiments in design and implementation will benefit educators more than would conceptualizing these programs as competition.

Also conceptualizing alternate routes as explorations, McDiarmid and Wilson (1991) analyzed the knowledge base of mathematics teachers in preservice, induction year, alternate route, and staff development programs of a number of different types. Expanding on ongoing studies reported in Ball and Wilson (1990), McDiarmid and Wilson were particularly concerned about findings that the eight alternate route teachers studied—none of whom had majored in mathematics—could generate appropriate stories or examples to explain mathematics concepts. Alternate route teachers tended to refer more to the need to memorize certain concepts instead of understanding why

certain concepts worked in the way that they do; traditional secondary teachers of mathematics performed better. The authors also concluded that learning mathematics while teaching was not inevitable; even though those with degrees in mathematics tended to be more successful, the question remained regarding whether or when the teachers would gain these concepts and how thorough would be the students' education in the interim.

McDiarmid and Wilson (1991) observed that the subject-matter understanding of new teachers, regardless of how they are prepared, is "sorely lacking" (p. 102) and noted that their research was most valuable for its clear questioning of assumptions often facilely made about the transferability of content knowledge and the inevitability of "hands-on learning" (p. 102). Denton and Morris (1991) completed another study of mathematics and science recruits made during the summer of 1991. It focused not on interns' ability to conceptualize but primarily on the recruitment and selection of mathematics and science interns. This research explored certain assumptions about the technical challenges of running an alternative teacher certification program, such as district hiring practices during times of economic hardship, the timing of training opportunities and district hiring practices relating to experienced, mature, young, or especially strong candidates.

A *Journal of Teacher Education* issue further detailed descriptions of two fifth-year programs designed to solve some of the same dilemmas that alternative teacher certification initiatives sought to address. Cochran-Smith (1991) outlined three "contrasting relationships" that characterized "reinvented" student teaching experiences—consonance, critical dissonance, and collaborative resonance (p. 104). Cochran-Smith's research identified "collaborative resonance" as that type of relationship that, through collaboration, brought "resonance or intensification based on the co-labor of learning communities" (p. 109). Concurring with McDiarmid and Wilson that learning by doing is not automatic, Cochran-Smith (1991) wrote that "programs based on resonance seek to develop felicitous contexts for students within a broader professional culture that supports teachers' learning. What makes this possible is the co-labor of school-based teachers, university-based educators, and student teachers" (p. 109). Essentially a postbaccalaureate preservice fifth-year program, the project on which Cochran-Smith focused, nurtured new teachers to be reformers as well as effective teachers. Evidence indicated that a program characterized by "collaborative resonance" did indeed generate effective teachers, researchers, and reformers, a combination occasionally difficult to obtain.

Bennett (1991) described other forms of teacher education reform in the fifth-year program, "The Teacher as Decision Maker Program." The program was designed for career changers who wished to add value and service to their lives. Conceptualized as a "thematic" teacher education program, the preparation sought to "enable preservice teachers to make decisions like those made by more experienced teachers" (p. 121). Three years of experience analyzing the actions and quality of the interactions of novice teachers taught the researcher the value of thematic teacher preparation for career switchers, the need to develop beyond novice teachers' naive and idealistic preconceptions of teaching, and the value of action research to provide a flexible program that takes advantage of each career switcher's unique strengths.

The Standards and Knowledge Base Debate—To Be Continued

As alternative teacher certification initiatives matured, teacher educators and researchers explored the relationship of these accelerated programs to traditional teacher certification programs that are based on standards the NCATE was in 1991 revising. Should alternative teacher certification programs be certified by NCATE? Then president of that organization, Art Wise, responded:

Obviously, if programs are university-based, then we take a look at them as we review institutions. Speaking totally personally, however, I have at this present time little interest in looking into school district–based teacher education programs because I believe they ultimately fail to provide the intellectual substance that I believe beginning teachers must have. I think it is very important that new teachers acquire the professional pedagogical knowledge base before they teach. So I draw a big distinction between legitimate university-based alternate routes to teaching and "quicky" programs that are really an excuse for letting anybody become a teacher. (Hodge, 1991, p. 10)

Seeing the alternative teacher certification controversy as a "quality control" issue, Wise asserted that the best way to provide excellence and equity in teacher education was through maintaining a "true quality control system" (p. 12). Commenting further with Darling-Hammond on alternative certification, Wise and Darling-Hammond (1991) told *Education Week,* "Alternate routes to teacher certification have spread across the country like dandelions in a suburban yard" (p. 56). "Alternatives" in fifth-year program, the authors asserted, "provide an option to the traditional undergraduate teacher-education program, which is designed primarily for 18- to 21-year-olds" (p. 56). These "alternatives" compare favorably to "alternative certification procedures" that, the authors contended, provide substantially less preparation than university-based alternatives. Analogizing alternative certification to other oxymorons such as "cruel kindness" and "military intelligence," Wise and Darling-Hammond pointed out that states seemed to be circumventing their own rules in order to solve long-term dilemmas: To address the teacher shortage, upgrade low-prestige college of education courses, attract mid-career switchers and content specialists, revamp "licensing" procedures, and raise salaries for teachers (p. 56). Citing failures in the alternative certification plan in New Jersey and successes in Connecticut after teachers' salaries were raised, the authors concluded, "There are alternatives to alternative certification that bode better for the future of our schools. We should pursue them rather than struggling to make sense of an oxymoron" (p. 46).

Replying directly to Wise and Darling-Hammond, Haberman (1991a) applauded the alternative certification movement as the grass-roots response of the American people to an education dilemma. Haberman categorized the oxymoron analogy as one that exposed special interests and self-serving systems. "Those opposed to alternative routes to teacher certification," Haberman wrote, "can stop the movement dead in its tracks. All they need do is start preparing teachers for all the children and youths of America" (p. 36). Citing statistics verifying the failure of colleges of education to prepare teachers for urban and poor students, Haberman noted that in states across America, the majority of regularly certified graduates seek positions where they are not needed (small towns and suburbs) and avoid teaching in the districts where they are needed (metropolitan districts and remote rural areas). Lacking in accountability and confused about who its clients really are, traditional colleges of education, Haberman responded, acquiesce to the agendas of their tuition-paying students; he added, "The fact that publicly supported universities can in no way be held accountable for staffing public schools is equally well known to the public" (p. 36). Citing the ability of alternative teacher certification programs to capture minority teachers, its success in urban student achievement, and its effectiveness in preparing teachers using "hands-on" approaches, Haberman concluded, "As we move into the 21st century, the nature of productive new forms of teacher education are already taking shape and being offered" (p. 29). Wise's comments, Haberman decried, reflect an attitude imprisoned by present paradigms; that a scholar would consider school districts to be inherently bereft of intellectual substance is most disconcerting considering universities often employ school district teachers with advanced degrees to teach their courses.

At the first annual conference of the National Alternative Certification Association in 1991, Haberman (1991b) further described the characteristics that mark an excellent alternative teacher certification or, for that matter, a traditional teacher education program; these "five standards of excellence" dealt with "what we should be striving for in the preparation of teachers, and not merely with the usual question of how weak does a teacher education program have to become before we close it down" (p. 1). The Haberman standards covered: (1) selection, (2) faculty, (3) content, (4) method, and (5) evaluation of the teacher preparation program.

Selection criteria included: preparation of individuals who have reached the developmental level of adulthood; the demonstrated ability to establish rapport with low-income children/youth of diverse ethnic backgrounds; teacher candidacy assessment using valid and reliable interviews to predict the candidate's success; and the recognition of practicing classroom teachers as peers. Haberman further identified experienced, currently practicing classroom teachers as the faculty, the source of "the essential expertise" for relevant teacher preparation programs (p. 9). These teacher educators derive their scholarship from an experiential knowledge base and are expert at evaluating ideas; expert teachers of low-income, minority, and culturally diverse constituencies of children/youth; capable of coaching candidates' actual teaching behavior and of modeling best practices; and knowledgeable teachers as well for the nonteaching schoolwide and community responsibilities of teachers.

Haberman (1991b) then outlined what sources of knowledge or content would contribute to an excellent program of teacher education. Sources included theory, research, common sense and folklore, expert opinion, and experience or craft knowledge. Situation- and context-specific solutions to real problems in real classrooms emerge from "the cumulative experience of effective practitioners . . . heavily influenced by the contexts in which the teaching occurs and the constraints which control best practice" (p. 13). Methods of excellent teacher preparation dictate that it occur on site, preferably in the "very schools in which teachers are being prepared" (p. 19). Functioning in the role of teacher and being held responsible for the full range of tasks and duties, teachers learn "by a process of coaching" (p. 19). Workshops and community resources enhance the site-based program; carefully selected traditional university courses are taught to novice teachers several years after they have commenced their career. Finally, Haberman enumerated the standards of evaluation that alternative teacher certification programs of excellence can employ. These included: selection of personnel based on criteria that predict subsequent effectiveness with children/youth of low-income and cultural diversity; the primary role of current teacher practitioners in the education of novices; the primacy of craft experience, supported by relevant research, theory, and expert opinion; the essential element of on-site experience and coaching by an effective classroom teacher; and evaluation of both teacher and student outcomes to include, but not be limited to, standardized test scores. Throughout the history of education, both in Europe and in the United States, university-based teacher educators have ignored the needs of the poor and culturally diverse. Haberman (1991b) observed:

It is now incredible to me and ought to be a source of concern to fair-minded people everywhere, that university-based teacher education, which has an almost perfect history of intentionally turning its back first on children of the London slums, then on the millions of European ethnics who settled in urban areas and more recently on the children of color, the poor and bilingual, now takes the role of being outraged that they are being circumvented. (p. 21)

In his list of standards, Haberman offered the First National Alternative Teacher Certification Conference attendees a compendium of "standards of excellence" that did not contradict but added a "dimension of excellence" and a voice of advocacy to the "minimum standards" proposed in 1989 by the ATE (Association of Teacher Educators, 1989).

Studies Evaluating Collaborative Initiatives

Guyton, Fox, and Sisk (1991) also examined teacher attitudes, effectiveness, and performance of alternative and traditional novices in the Georgia program, begun in 1988. The study demonstrated that "On almost all measures, the AC (alternative certification) and RC (regularly certified) teachers were similar" (p. 7). Some differences were worth noting, however. Alternatively certified individuals decided to become teachers more recently; they also reflected a less positive attitude about teaching at the end of the year, although AC and RC retention were equivalent. Guyton et al. proposed that mentor support, not provided for RC novices, may have helped "compensate for lack of earlier field experiences and more extensive pedagogical preparation" (p. 7). The authors concluded that, even though it is expensive, the program provided support for the conclusion that "condensed pedagogical preparation and a supervised internship are a reasonable alternative to traditional teacher prep-

aration programs for persons with degrees in the subject they will teach" (p. 7).

Throughout the South in the 1990s, Texas played a central role in defining and experimenting with new forms of alternative teacher certification. In addition to hosting the first National Alternative Certification Association conference on South Padre Island in April 1991, researchers were active in conceptualizing what elements of new designs best served teacher education students. Littleton, Beach, Larmer, and Calahan (1991) described a university-based effort that met the AACTE guidelines for an "alternative" program that does not bypass pedagogical preparation. The authors outlined a collaborative program that entailed rigorous screening, an intense core curriculum, use of trained mentors, field experience, collegiality, evaluation, and evolutionary design. Screening for the program was multifaceted and collaborative. The program offered intense and extensive core curricula, summer practica, script-taped and video-taped laboratory teaching, seminars throughout the internship, postinternship coursework during the summer following the internship, and induction with mentor teachers. Reflective journal keeping, induction-trained mentors, professional collegiality nurtured by the partnership between the districts and the university, and an evolutionary design that was based on evaluative data characterized the program. Principal surveys, standardized teacher competency tests, and committees functioning collaboratively evaluated the program, which was considered effective enough to be continued and to be recommended by the authors as an effective university-based model.

Alternative teacher certification programs based in universities also grew in number in California. By 1991, McKibben (1991) reported that 21 colleges sponsored alternative teacher internship programs, representing about 3% of the university's total personnel preparation. Noting that in alternative programs, interns provide professional services earlier than in traditional programs, McKibben attributed the programs' success to high entry standards, a salaried internship, a blend of theory and practice, and movement through the program in cadre formation. Los Angeles, which has a district-sponsored program, also reported the results of evaluation that compared alternatively to traditionally prepared teachers. Even though secondary school teachers, however prepared, rated themselves effective on the 12-criteria survey, high school teachers prepared by the district rated themselves higher. Junior high school teachers prepared by traditional programs tended to rate themselves higher on the 12 criteria than did district-prepared teachers, and secondary school principals generally found that teachers prepared by the district-based program were at least as effectively prepared as were those prepared by traditional teacher preparation programs. When novices rated what factors best prepared them for teaching, working with mentor teachers and student teaching were rated most highly; education methods courses and educational philosophy courses were rated least helpful.

The New Jersey's program evaluations demonstrated significant areas that need improvement, but researchers drew important lessons from the experience. Districts ill prepared for the responsibilities that the state-developed program entailed left important standards poorly enforced. Noting that school districts already financially strapped were becoming emotionally frayed as well, Smith (1991) questioned whether or not anyone cared if interns were poorly prepared. While not discrediting alternative teacher certification initiatives at large, Smith concluded that additional funding sources now sought to provide collaboration from other entities that would, it was hoped, provide the needed extra support.

Natriello and Zumwalt's (1992) in-depth study of the New Jersey program examined issues of improving the pool of qualified candidates, staffing schools experiencing shortages, professionalizing teaching, and retaining teachers. The researchers found neither the traditionally certified (TC) nor the alternatively certified (AC) students to be "consistently superior" on measures traditionally used to indicate talent. Natriello and Zumwalt found that although alternate route teachers attended more selective colleges, traditional education students were more likely to have majored in the subject they were teaching. Majoring in the subject they were teaching, however, was not reflected in higher scores on the national teacher exam. On that measure, alternate route teachers outscored traditional teachers uniformly. Alternate route teachers were more likely to want to teach in urban areas than were traditionally prepared teachers; however, by the third year of teaching the percentage of alternate route and traditionally prepared teachers teaching underprivileged and gifted students tended to even out. Although many differences in teaching placement disappear by the third year, "alternate route teachers are more likely to be teachers in low-socioeconomic-status districts and in harder-to-staff middle school grades" (p. 68). If professionalization of teaching is defined in part by the reasons why an individual chooses to become a teacher, then Natriello and Zumwalt discovered that AC and TC routes built equally professional groups. Projected retention figures favored college-prepared elementary teachers with 81.7% projecting retention, whereas only 40% of alternate route math teachers expected to remain in the public schools; many planned to move to higher education. About the differences between teachers of different subjects, the authors summed:

The alternate route mathematics teachers found more aspects of teaching worse than expected, received lower evaluations of their teaching, and were the least likely to report that they would advise a son or daughter to enter teaching. In contrast, the alternate route English teachers found more aspects of teaching better than expected, were more likely to stay in teaching than their college counterparts, were more likely to intend to remain in K–12 education than the alternate route mathematics teachers, and were the most likely of all groups to report that they would advise a son or daughter to enter teaching. (p. 73)

Lessons From the 1990s

Feistritzer (1992) also completed research on individuals seeking certification alternatively. The author found that by 1992, 40,000 individuals had been certified to teach via alternative teacher certification routes. What were these people like? Were they unemployed transients? Married with families? Attorneys? Dentists? Why did they want to teach? Because of the large numbers of individuals in the potential alternative certification pool, policymakers as well as the public had questions about what these individuals sought, what types of jobs they left to enter teaching, and what types of backgrounds they brought

into the classroom. The most ambitious study of its type to date, Feistritzer's research indicated who was seeking to teach, who was getting hired to teach, and what was the status and content of alternative routes to teacher certification in all 50 states and the District of Columbia.

Data were compared to a 1990 study of the current teacher work force or to teacher education majors in traditional programs. Survey results showed that applicants to alternative teacher certification programs were 54% male and 17% nonwhite, compared to 29% male and 9% nonwhite in the public school work force. Forty-one percent of all inquirers had taught perviously or were currently teaching. The population of individuals interested in alternative teacher certification differed from traditional teacher education majors and current work force teachers in that inquirers tended to be more reformminded than individuals currently teaching; more favored national standards, a national curriculum, and national tests; and more cited "value or significance of education in society" as the impetus to become a teacher (69% compared to 32%). Forty percent of nonwhites felt that a demographically representative teaching force could best teach students of a given race/ethnic group compared to 17% of whites who felt that a demographically representative teaching force improved instruction.

Feistritzer (1990a) and the National Center for Education Information (NCEI) found that 6% of all surveyed were unemployed at the time they inquired about alternative teacher certification. Thirty percent were employed in noneducation occupations, and that the next largest group, 24%, of those inquiring were currently employed in education but wished to teach a different field, change state, move from private to public school, or upgrade their license; 2% were just curious. Sixteen percent were in military service. The population who want to teach is a population greatly needed, the author implied. Forty-four percent interviewed were willing to teach in inner cities, compared with 4% of teacher education students who said they wanted to teach in inner cities, while 8% wanted to teach bilingual education compared to fewer than 0.5% surveyed and currently teaching.

Those currently teaching exhibited more student centeredness and flexibility than those inquiring about teaching through alternative teacher certification routes. Feistritzer also found that about one third of inquirers held master's degrees, 15% of those in business, 5% in political science, 5% in history, 4% in English/Literature, 4% in psychology, 3% each in biology/life sciences, communication, engineering, and mathematics, and 27% in some field of education. Most striking was the reason individuals wanted to enter the classroom. Feistritzer (1990a) noted:

Persons inquiring about alternative teacher certification gave dramatically different reasons for their interest in teaching than did public school teachers surveyed by NCEI in 1990. Nearly seven out of ten (69 percent) interested in alternative teacher certification gave "Value or significance of education in society," as one of the three main reasons they wanted to teach. By contrast, only 32 percent of public school teachers surveyed in 1990 cited this as a reason they entered teaching and only 38 percent as a reason they stayed in teaching. (p. 22)

With so many new teachers entering via alternative routes, associations and regional entities continued to research, ask questions, and debate gains. In updating the AACTE on alternative teacher certification, Otuya (1992) identified teacher organization of knowledge as crucial to students' conceptual connectedness and hence to academic gains. Questioning the depth of alternatively certified individuals' knowledge base, Otuya noted that lack of formal teaching training could "limit the learning horizon of the students and adversely affect the quality of the students' overall educational experiences" (unpaginated). The author added, however, that alternative certification routes add diversity to the teaching force, which, in turn, encourages student learning by drawing appropriate instruction from children's backgrounds. Otuya noted that evaluative data are clearly inconclusive, because, to date, it is unknown whether subject-matter competency combined with pedagogical training or subject-matter competency without pedagogical training determines effective instruction. Other researchers concurred regarding the call for adequate evaluation (Buechler & Fulford, 1992) and for individual attention to the goals and needs of each program (Shulman, 1992).

Natriello (1992) asserted that although the debate over alternative teacher certification has created "more heat than light," it has provided at least four elements of a broader strategic vision of teacher preparation: (1) "a new role for state and local education agencies in the management of the supply of teachers" (2) "greater attention to the role of selection processes in the quest for quality," (3) "careful examination of the content of teacher education," and (4) "another look at the role of schools in the education of teachers" (p. 8). Attinasi and Schoon (1992) attempted to defuse the "alternative teacher certification time bomb" by promoting as essential to any "wave of future teacher education": (1) "joint authority, (2) content combined with pedagogy, (3) resources to guide interns," and (4) "a clear and substantive evaluation plan" (p. 10). Apparently some concepts were coming into focus from the wide varieties of unrelated studies already completed. Researchers understood that some very talented individuals wishing to teach simply did not, because of commitments to work or family. They have access to teacher education and certificate programs that the colleges offered but that were often useless in the marketplace, whereas certificate programs schools needed often went vacant. Researchers also grasped the value of teacher education and pointed out the needs of the students who most frequently lack properly credentialed teachers: the poor, urban, special needs, and language-different students.

The Role of Alternative Certification in Educating Teachers for Children in Poverty

Haberman (1992b) continued to elaborate on themes of the debate on the appropriateness and effectiveness of alternative teacher certification throughout the early 1990s. Much of his approach was based on the assumption that teaching children in poverty is not the same thing as teaching children who are broadly advantaged. The author stated:

The best way to improve urban schools is to get better teachers. The best way to get better teachers is to recruit educated adults who closely resemble the star teachers already effective in urban schools. The best

way to train these recruits is by having them actually teach and be coached on-the-job by star urban teachers. (p. 125)

Teachers need subject-matter content as well as teaching strategies, but these are not enough; the "component which is vital for urban, multicultural teachers, and which must be the organizing theme for all other forms of know-how, is an ideology—a set of ideas that reflect the social needs and aspirations of a people" (p. 126). Haberman's star teachers of children in poverty work to build, more than test scores or achievement, "good people—people with character who are to some degree inner-directed by reflection and commitments, not merely by impulse" (p. 126). Decidedly a "moral craft," the star urban teacher believes it is his or her responsibility to "help students see meaning in knowledge, integrate and apply it to their lives and remain permanently affected by this learning" (p. 126). Guidance for the daily decisions they make is not obtainable, Haberman reasoned, from professors; discovering what "should be" is a highly articulated ideology worked out in a multicultural, multilingual setting and shared among colleagues as they practice their craft. Novice teachers become stars in the same way that star teachers teach—by sharing the sources of their learning, by practicing making decisions, by reflecting and asking why, by setting their own direction, and by being inner directed. Such teachers, Haberman averred, are not likely to be graduates of traditional teacher education programs.

Inappropriate teacher education, said Haberman (1992a) in a special edition of *Teacher Education and Practice* dedicated in part to the alternative certification debate, foists on children already at a disadvantage the added burden of being taught by teachers "who are in the process of failing" (p. 17). Noting that 50% of regularly trained beginners are gone in 3 years, the author also added that this attrition rate is based on the low numbers of traditional graduates who make it to the classroom for even 1 year after receiving their certification. Alternative teacher certification, Haberman posited, will "stop the exploitation of low-income children by traditionally prepared beginners who are 'finding themselves' at the expense of poor children" (p. 18).

What, Haberman further probed, would have to be changed in order for traditional programs of teacher education to succeed in preparing teachers for children in poverty? The clients would have to be the children and parents in the schoolhouse, working back from their interests toward an appropriate training program to generate the model needed. The "ultimate values to be preserved are not (the) present forms of teacher training" (p. 20). College courses, further, do not offer a valid picture of the teacher's day or work, nor do established syllabi that are independent of each student's need. Also needing change are the assumptions about the learners in the teacher education curriculum, which should be based on "some vision of the adult learner" (p. 21). Use of technology that transcends media "literacy" is also essential, as is a carefully thought-out selection process. Selection, Haberman contended, is "at the heart of the matter" because education courses are not so powerful that they can change "fearful or passive bigots with good social skills and high GPAs" into successful teachers of poor students (p. 22). Haberman then recommended focusing the preparation program on multiculturalism and urbanness, on the specific needs of children in poverty, on ways that children in poverty are different from advantaged children, and on the mitigating effects of culture, income, gender, and physical and emotional health. Located in professional development schools, the program would be taught by high numbers of full-time classroom teachers coteaching with professors.

Haberman included a number of other recommendations, the most critical of which is that "There can be no program of American teacher education without an undergirding ideology" (p. 26). This ideology is the cultural mortar with which all decisions are built; the idea that ideals are inconsequential damages children. Haberman concluded, "Stars and failures have different commitments, different roles for themselves as teachers, and different goals for schools. . . . Until traditional programs of teacher education make serious structural and content changes, they will continue to be irrelevant to the schooling of children in poverty" (p. 27).

Further Evaluation Needed The U.S. Department of Education noted the growing phenomenon of alternative teacher certification programs that, between 1990 and 1993, produced some 40,000 teachers (National Center for Education Statistics, 1993). The authors of the report cited federal plans to monitor alternative teacher certification programs beginning in 1994 to discern how the program changes over time as well as to gather information about the characteristics and qualifications of teachers thus certified. Growing numbers of alternative teacher certification programs spawned additional research on the outcomes they support.

Sandlin, Young, and Karge (1992–1993) challenged the appropriateness of such a large-scale effort to overcome personnel shortages in states like California. The authors asserted "many beginning teachers suffer numerous problems and varied amounts of stress during the transition period (into the classroom). In turn, the quality of instruction for many youngsters may be less than it should be" (p. 16). The authors arranged for site visits—blind reviews—of classroom activity on 16 items. By the end of the year, the two groups showed no significant differences across any of the categories. In a survey of teacher concerns, beginning teachers showed higher levels of concern about all elements of the teaching task; interpretations of what such a finding signify varied. Sandlin, Young, and Karge concluded that, "It is crucial that institutions of higher education structure their programs to ensure beginners have an adequate knowledge and experiential base before they take on full-time responsibility for students" (p. 22).

Birrell (1993) concurred that initial support is critical. He compared the influence of prior experiences on traditional and nontraditional novices and found that nontraditional candidates would benefit from added support and patience while being inducted into the profession. Bryant and Nichols (1993) compared 4-year traditional students to fifth-year master's-level students on success rate in student teaching, differences in content and strategies of thinking, choice of urban or nonurban teaching environment, and overall readiness to teach. The authors found no significant differences in the two groups on any measure but concluded that the master's-level fifth-year program in fact provided an effective alternative certification route for "the stu-

dent who holds a bachelor's degree, has work experience and has a strong desire to become a teacher" (p. 8).

In another study, external reviewers used statewide program standards similar to those used to evaluate a university intern program to review a district-based alternative teacher preparation program in the Los Angeles Independent School District (Salley, 1993). The program met 26 of the 30 standards fully; reviewers found the program to be "marginal" on the remaining four standards. "Commendations" cited program design, multicultural and district orientation, intern popularity and demand, program recruiting and screening, limited English proficiency (LEP) and bilingual instruction components, orientation to state goals and documents, program personnel expertise, cohort and site coordinator expertise, and thematic unit development as strengths of the district-offered teacher preparation program. External reviewers recommended the addition of publicity regarding the transportability of the credential granted, the opportunity for anonymous evaluation, greater care in timing and hiring, closer collaboration with mentor teacher networks, broadening of the authentic assessment for novices to include the affective realm, and greater integration of theory and practice to improve the program.

In November 1993, a full issue of *Education and Urban Society* was devoted to alternative teacher certification (Dial & Stevens, 1993). Observing a number of historical dynamics that have led to the development of alternative routes to teacher certification, Dial and Stevens focused on the willingness of alternative teacher certification interns to teach in the inner city. For that reason, urban educators are quite interested in the viability of these programs. Stoddart (1993) examined the assumption that, in recruiting from a different candidate pool than do traditional colleges of education, alternative certification programs attracted those willing to teach in urban schools. Stoddart found that the alternative program she examined at Michigan State University did indeed attract higher percentages of minority students. Further, alternative interns demonstrated a greater willingness to teach in urban environments and more uniform levels of high expectations for both poor and advantaged learners. Alternative route interns were also more responsible for their students' progress and less likely to think of students as difficult to teach. Stoddart further demonstrated that interns with similar life experiences or views as the students taught tended not to categorize students' potential on the basis of race or wealth. Rather, these teachers empowered student learning by affirming the value of their ethnicity, the usefulness of diverse student backgrounds to aid in learning, student creativity in overcoming hardship, and the ability of many students to show leadership. In concluding the study, Stoddart found teacher dispositions to be critical to student success. About the more successful practices of the alternative teacher certification interns, she noted their superior ability to trade a "cultural deficit" model for a model that affirmed urban realities as building blocks for growth.

Natriello and Zumwalt (1993) surveyed traditional teacher education candidates and alternative teacher certification interns regarding the types of places where they had lived, urban, suburban/urban, small town, rural, and so on. Like Stoddart, Natriello and Zumwalt found alternate route teachers more willing to teach urban students and larger percentages willing to teach disadvantaged students. They discovered that alternate route teachers were "more likely to report having lived in an urban community" (22.7%) than college-prepared elementary teachers (13.6%) (p. 53). Alternate routes also provided more minority individuals than did traditional routes and more individuals with language diversity, although the majority of both groups spoke only English. The authors concluded that the Provisional Teacher Program was indeed "an important addition to the pool of urban teachers" (p. 59). Because alternate route teachers tended to become teachers for disadvantaged students in greater numbers than do nonalternate route teachers, the authors cautioned that, "Policy makers and program managers should redouble their efforts to improve the quality of instruction offered to alternate route candidates" (p. 61).

Themes of Alternative Teacher Certification Remain Controversial

Qualitative studies of alternative teacher certification candidates further showed that, with the possible exception of *Teach for America* interns, new teachers did not come into schools via alternate routes from unemployment to get a job (Dial & Stevens, 1993). Teachers interviewed reported that their new careers held more meaning for them and that they left other jobs because they were making an intentional commitment to youth. A study in the same issue of *Education and Urban Society* by Houston, Marshall, and McDavid (1993) found, as did previous studies in the volume, alternative certification interns to be more racially and ethnically diverse than certified teachers, more likely to be male, and more often married than were traditionally certified teachers. Surveyed on three issues—perceived problems, assistance by mentors, and confidence, satisfaction, and plans to continue teaching—respondents demonstrated different growth cycles and changes but ultimately ended up in equivalent places. The authors concluded, "The debate about alternative certification continues. The results of this study support those who indicate that there are no differences between those who have spent 2 or more years completing a traditional certification program and those who have spent a few weeks preparing for their first job in the classroom. Indeed, after 8 months of teaching, there were no differences between alternatively certified teachers and traditionally prepared teachers" (p. 88).

Is route to certification a significant factor in teacher retention? That topic concluded the issue of *Education and Urban Society* dedicated to alternative teacher certification (Adams & Dial, 1993). Do certain candidate pools stay longer? Adams and Dial concluded that men are less likely to leave the district than are women and that women older than 40 years of age are less likely to leave than are their younger counterparts. Whites were more likely to leave than were blacks or Hispanics; teachers with only a bachelor's degree were 68% more likely to leave the school than teachers with a graduate degree. Finally, the authors concluded that "Traditionally certified teachers were approximately 19% more likely to leave the district than alternatively certified teachers" (p. 97). Several cautions, the authors added, are in order. Resigners may not necessarily have left teaching; they simply left the urban district being studied. Fur-

ther, traditionally certified teachers may be more mobile because they have more education coursework on their transcripts. Finally, the important covariates of sex, ethnicity, education, and certification route may act as "proxies for other underlying causes of teacher turnover in the district" (p. 98). In any case, the authors concluded, understanding the factors that increase the likelihood of turnover will help administrators hire as stable a work force as possible.

Further explorations of numerous aspects and possibilities of alternative teacher certification occurred in a 1994 theme issue of *The Educational Forum* (Edelfelt, 1994). This volume developed the implications, however unsynthetic, of expanding alternative teacher certification initiatives. The objective of those in that potential teacher pool who sought to teach was a central concern for Steffensen (1994), who summarized teacher education reform initiatives from the early 1980s to 1994. Steffensen focused on alternative teacher certification as one of numerous "parochial" reforms—like choice, Teach for America, home-based schools, systemic reform, and more. Seeing alternative teacher certification as a "diversion" away from the crucial issue of adequate federal support for education, Steffensen reviewed the few successful reform efforts he felt have emerged from the nation's capitol since the 1900s and was clear that alternative teacher certification is not numbered among them.

Feistritzer (1994) saw the alternative teacher certification movement as a direct response to projected teacher shortages first discussed in the 1980s. She articulated that history for *The Educational Forum*. Feistritzer analyzed why the shortage never occurred and further why states pursued alternative routes nonetheless; they wanted to find a better way to prepare teachers than the traditional college programs. Citing New Jersey's 1984 initiative to attract liberal arts majors into teaching, she noted the growth of alternative programs nationwide, now numbering 68 programs in 41 states. Twenty-five programs appeared in Texas alone. Feistritzer observed that the shortage agenda has receded and that "true alternative certification" programs now facilitated the entry into teaching of individuals with liberal arts degrees and "considerable life experience" (p. 135). Feistritzer found that out of the 140,500 total certifications issued during 1989–1990, about 50,000 were alternative teacher certifications; these data reflected a growth in interest in the teaching profession including mid-career switchers, teachers returning to the profession, and military retirees. Across the board, Feistritzer noted, surveys revealed that interest in teaching as a career was high and that alternative teacher certification models rode that crest of interest to bring to the nation's classrooms "large numbers of highly qualified, talented, and enthusiastic individuals," (p. 137).

Rather more critical in his assessment, Wise (1994) conceptualized alternative teacher certification as essentially a choice between professionalism and amateurism. Defining "alternative certification" as a "process in which the state licenses a person who has not completed a typical state-approved or equivalent program of studies designed to prepare individuals to teach," Wise advocated quality control of those entering the profession through the mechanisms of licensing, accreditation, and advanced certification. Wise noted that the Council of Chief State School Officers (CSSO) has developed core licensure standards; the NCATE has begun restructuring of schools of education;

and the National Board for Professional Teaching Standards (NBPTS) has begun board certification of advanced teachers. All these initiatives were undermined by alternative teacher certification. Asserting that proponents of alternative teacher certification loosened the standards in order to solve the teacher shortage, Wise concluded with four recommendations for all involved in teacher preparation: (1) graduation from an accredited teacher education institution, (2) state licensing systems that are based on performance measures, (3) state-level policy support for improved preservice education and high-quality alternate routes to licensure, and (4) funding for graduate programs for nontraditional candidates.

Dill (1994) noted in "Teacher Education in Texas: A New Paradigm" that even though alternative teacher certification programs in Texas began in order to address shortages, the programs eventually served other purposes as well. They became not a "quick-fix" or shortened proposal in a state where 18 hours of college credit is the maximum allowed undergraduates, but an alternative mode of learning more than the equivalent to 18 credit hours while learning and doing simultaneously (Dill, 1994; Dill & Stafford, 1994). Regional service centers and independent school districts themselves can develop alternative teacher certification programs, providing an arena for rich innovation and systemic reform in teacher education. Dill described program development as collaborative, while rigorous applicant screening sought to ensure that individuals who were admitted to the "hands-on" program had ideals and could use them, and were problem solvers and lifelong learners. These individuals, Dill wrote, are often of a distinctly different personality and demographic profile than typical undergraduate teacher education majors. So dramatically different is the Texas model from most other teacher education initiatives that it should be seen as a catalyst for innovation more than as a model to be strictly followed. However, certain aspects of that innovation became very compelling: Models must be developed that enhance minority recruitment and facilitate the smooth transition into the profession for mid-career switchers. It has become apparent, Dill asserted, that the higher education model favors the young and the advantaged and holds inherent bias against a demographically representative teaching force. Although not a panacea, the bold Texas experiment is a lesson from which educators nationwide could draw some insight.

Calling such experimentation not alternative teacher certification but "alternative preparation," Howey and Zimpher (1994) maintained that preparation of educators outside the college or university setting jeopardized the intellectual sophistication and scientific rigor of the profession (p. 156). Noting that "'real-world' experience *alone* can be, and often is, a wretched teacher" (p. 156), the authors asserted that nonshortcut alternative programming can nevertheless achieve improved quality of teacher education in cost-effective ways, bring access to teacher education for special populations and can simultaneously lead to improvement of both teacher and student education. Howey and Zimpher claimed that collaboration demands awareness of how differently various subjects are learned and taught. Teachers cannot be expected to teach all subjects equally well; they must be able to collaborate and cooperate. The authors further affirmed the essential nature of teamwork and Pre-K-through-teacher-preparation interdepen-

dence required new roles for all involved, as well as appropriate settings in which to learn these evolving roles.

Kaplan (1994) specifically addressed the role of higher education in teacher education reform. The author recalled that, "The preparation of teachers and the qualifications of those who prepare them are currently scrutinized in a manner unparalleled in the history of American education" (p. 171). Kaplan then detailed the response of the ATE to this scrutiny and concluded that, despite legitimate critique, higher education faculty have a unique role in and responsibility for the nurturing of new professionals.

Several authors soundly disagreed with the assertion that higher education is uniquely able to educate new teachers. Willis (1994) criticized most alternative teacher education programs as seeking primarily to increase the number of new teachers through improved access or affordability; one exception was Teach For America (TFA). TFA responded more expeditiously to the ever-changing needs of school cultures than any institution of higher education could, Willis declared. University rigidity results from tradition, faculty tenure, and local board practices that slow reform in schools and in teacher education, inhibiting helpful risk taking. Reform at all levels must occur simultaneously. Willis noted that innovations such as shared staff, adjunct relationships, and sophisticated uses of technology need to support overall teacher education reform that is based more on the particular strengths of teachers and less on a certain age or grade of the targeted population to be taught. Citing the important role that private funding can play in supporting risky innovations in teacher education, Willis concluded that schools of the future will have to develop professionals in such a way that risk becomes institutionwide learning and change.

Like Willis, Haberman (1994) explored his own doubts about whether or not the traditional model of teacher education could be salvaged; he likened the traditional model to "catalogues of spare parts for machines that have never been built" (p. 162). Focusing on the unmet needs of students in urban schools for excellent teachers, Haberman recalled that having students in teacher education programs—even a surplus of each prospective teachers—does not guarantee that urban shortages will be met. In fact, few, if any, graduates of traditional programs are willing to teach in urban vacancies or would succeed if they were willing. Wholesale neglect of urban schools pointed not to nuances in a delivery model or to convenience or cost, but to ideology, Haberman averred. Why has traditional teacher education failed so thoroughly to meet the needs of urban students?

Variety in the types of abilities, skills, and types of knowledge as opposed to a uniform "knowledge base"; lack of targeted teacher education that supports teachers for a specific population they will teach, such as urban or rural; inability of professors to teach "what they don't know"; irrelevant selection criteria such as GPA; and the inappropriateness of late adolescents entering the teaching force, especially in urban settings, doom the attempt, said Haberman (1994, p. 163). He recalled the centrality of a good public school education to the success of children who often have little else in their lives that builds their success. On these most needy students, graduates from traditional programs "learn" to teach, often fail, and then quit or go to the suburbs. Detailing the selection process, the "principles of excellence that should define the expertise of faculty" who educate teachers, the content (which defines teaching as a "moral craft"), principles of coaching and evaluation, Haberman posited that all factors point to the unmet needs of urban students for dramatically different forms of teacher education. Regardless of the role of the university in this process, collaboration and attention to the specific skills and characteristics of successful urban teachers should be recognized. This would be best accomplished by, at least, certification as a teacher of urban youth.

Several specific alternative teacher certification programs, each unique and not related to one another, demonstrated the variety of reasons for their inception throughout their implementation. Keltner (1994) detailed a series of collaboratively developed programs in Texas that facilitate the certification of former Army personnel for classroom teaching. Kopp (1994), who founded TFA, outlined that organization's mission to recruit undergraduates who had not majored in teacher education and support them in their careers as teachers. Like Willis, Kopp (1994) articulated the need for highly personalized, self-initiated, and self-implemented professional development models. Advocating that teachers should demonstrate excellent performance through portfolio assessment prior to certification, Kopp agreed with others in the volume that paradigm shifts, collaborative restructuring, and new ways to enter the profession are sorely needed. Stafford and Barrow (1994), in describing the Houston Independent School District (HISD) model, cited four components to the district-driven program that are vital to the success of all: (1) screening, (2) training, (3) supervision, and (4) support. A detailed program description and flowcharts described the many faceted preparation program. Maintaining that their program is "no longer just an avenue to overcome teacher shortages in critical areas," the authors saw the HISD model as "a philosophy and a system of beliefs" as well (pp. 199–200).

McKibben and Ray (1994) not only described California's programs of alternative teacher certification but sought to provide a "template for the refinement of AC programs" (p. 201). The template had four elements: (1) conditions, (2) dispositions, (3) responses, and (4) outcomes. After defining and describing each of these four elements in detail, the authors conceptualized the state department's approach and activities not as competitive with traditional teacher education but as a way to allow "economically disadvantaged teacher candidates and work-seasoned, second-career persons" to enter the teaching profession (p. 208). Noting the pivotal role of ongoing support and mentoring, the authors added, "To be effective, program administrators should follow programs for two to five years after they have completed the program. By documenting the extent to which successful teachers remained in the program and were awarded gainful employment, administrators can better identify specific ways to improve the preparation of teachers, the learning that occurs within classrooms, and the overall satisfaction of the community with its school" (p. 207).

Can we individualize teacher education to meet the unique needs of education students in the way teacher educators teach curriculum modification? Knauth (1994) described such an individualized approach with an analysis of "Teachers for Chicago," a graduate-level collaborative effort of the Chicago Public

Schools, the Chicago Teachers Union, the Council of Chicago Area Deans of Education, and the Golden Apple Foundation for Excellence in Teaching. Aware of diversity in school environments, university cultures, interns' needs, and mentoring styles, the program mentors resisted a "cookie cutter" approach and concentrated the first year on classroom management and discipline. The second year focused more on instructional methodologies. As interns progressed toward the master's degree that would signify the completion of the program, stronger collegial networks and forms of cooperation relieved these novices of the isolation new teachers often feel. Mentors served as adjunct faculty to local universities, occasionally increasing university–school partnership opportunities. Knauth reported that university faculty as well as public school mentors worked together to modify and to restructure certain parts of the standard education curriculum at the college, but that only time will show if closer relationships can result in widespread public school partnerships and innovation.

In "Final Thoughts on Alternative Certification," Edelfelt (1994) discussed what has been achieved through the establishment of a variety of types and definitions of alternative teacher certification, what types(s) of knowledge have been gained, areas remaining critical on the research agenda, the impact on traditional teacher education, and the future of these endeavors. Edelfelt noted that minority gains have been palpable; some shortages have been relieved; the needs of minority and urban youth may be better served by alternative teacher certification interns, and clearly, hands-on instruction of those with greater maturity points to a need for traditional systems to increase access to teacher education. Impacts on traditional teacher education nationwide appeared to be few. Asserting that alternative teacher certification is more "than tinkering with the periphery," Edelfelt saw the many challenges to the traditional ways of educating teachers posed by alternative teacher certification as true innovation and progress.

CONCLUSION

Edelfelt (1994) affirmed the value of a systemic redesign of teacher education, although the variety of experiments alternative programs represent remain largely confined to urban models and are seldom externally evaluated. Calls for more complete data on the effectiveness of teachers variously certified, cost analyses, retention issues, and restructuring implications go largely unanswered. Traditional forms of teacher education prevail, and the urgent summons for comprehensive evaluative data go mainly unheeded. Teacher training designed to meet the specific needs of urban and rural youth in poverty remain a low national priority. Clearly, the burgeoning populations of poor, minority, and language diverse public school students and their growing numbers of misassigned and emergency permit teachers have not pressed universities into radically addressing systemic restructuring of the status quo, further outlining a largely unresponsive teacher preparation monolith. What questions did the "variety of context-specific naturally occurring experiments" in teacher preparation leave unanswered (Zumwalt, 1991, p. 84)? Among possible responses:

1. Is selection more important than preparation? What is the relative value of these two dynamics? If candidates shown to be excellent teachers could be selected from a wide pool prior to certification training, what individual modifications would be appropriate for the preparation phase? What type of program provides maximum flexibility to respond to individual K–12 and prospective teacher preparation needs?

2. At what psychological developmental level should a teacher perform? Should a teacher be an adult or a late adolescent? Does it matter?

3. Are altered forms of certification needed to meet the needs of restructured schools? Should certification be student population, not content centered? Should certification specify whether teachers are prepared to deal with students in at-risk situations, in poverty, language-diverse, or extremely rural or urban environments? Students so prepared may be able to teach suburban and advantaged students, but the reverse may not necessarily be true.

4. Are traditional forms of teacher education, in which student teaching culminates the field experiences, as effective as internships or extensive "hands-on" experience, in which novices assume major if not sole responsibility for a class? Which form of field experience best prepares teachers to deal with racism, gangs, poverty, violence, sexual and drug abuse, low motivation, and chronic unemployment, and so on as normal responses to urban and other socioeconomically disadvantaged environments?

5. What is the role of belief and ideology in a system that is forbidden to discriminate along ideological lines? How should traditional certification programs deal with or screen out students who do not believe that all children can learn? How are the philosophy and beliefs of practicing teachers who are consistently successful with children in poverty, where most vacancies occur, best taught to novices prior to certification? Who should teach novices?

6. Alternative forms of teacher certification yield more demographically representative populations of teachers. Precisely why is this true? What insight about accessibility might be available to leaders of traditional models?

7. When should teacher educators address development of theory-to-practice abilities? During applicant screening? During appropriate coursework? During an internship? During the first 5 years of teaching? All of the above?

8. Should credit-driven systems such as institutions of higher education be eased into becoming vacancy-driven systems? Until vacancies in classrooms and the unmet needs of public school students concretely inspire higher education to meet those needs, urban and at-risk students will lack teachers and college of education graduates will lack jobs.

9. How can changes be made in traditional and alternative teacher preparation that resonate with exemplary pedagogy, such as flexible programs based on needs assessment, student strengths, multiage environments, learner style, and target audience?

10. How can all forms of teacher preparation provide models of learning communities that prepare graduates for the twenty-first, not the nineteenth century—valuing and using cultural diversity concretely in curriculum; linking needed social services to learners regardless of age or stage in schooling; providing models of consensus, dispute resolution, and prosocial goals for students of education as well as in the K–12 system; and nurturing educators who will be student advocates and reformers, not managers or supporters of the status quo?

11. What changes occur to the preparation program if teacher educators view public school students and not college students as the recipients of their efforts—their clients—and their evaluators?

12. How might programs that do not use internships, and hence cannot see how their students actually teach a class the way they eventually will, evaluate the outcomes of the program offered?

Clearly, alternative teacher certification has done more than moderate between the arts and science faculties who would advocate primarily for more content coursework for novices and the practitioners who would suggest simplistically that "hands-on" training is all that is needed (Roth & Pipho, 1990). By providing a rich continuum of models, both unilateral and collaborative, the concept of alternative teacher certification now suggests a variety of strategies for developing content and pedagogical skills in novice teachers who themselves deserve more than a "cookie cutter" preparation. Despite vocal opposition from unions and traditionalists, alternative teacher certification programs appear to be an experiment increasingly worthy of credible consideration; reformers are no longer blithely dismissing well-constructed alternative programs as oxymorons or "back-door" access (Birckbichler, 1994). In some cases, alternative certification programs have become so broadly recognized as successful innovations in education that they have encroached on traditional turf and suffered the type of setbacks reserved only for genuine threats to established bureaucracies. In other cases, as models proliferate, lines may blur between what was formerly a universally defined "traditional" model and its distinct "alternatives." Choice of a model of teacher certification will be truly insignificant when the goal is reached—when all students, both advantaged and in poverty, diverse and homogeneous, majority and minority, have teachers who want to be with them, who are well prepared to serve their needs, and whose teaching results in student and community success.

References

Adams, G. J., & Dial, M. (1993, November). Teacher survival: A Cox regression model. *Education and Urban Society, 26*(1), 90–99.

American Association of Colleges for Teacher Education (AACTE). (1989). *Alternative preparation for licensure.* Policy statement. Washington, DC: Author.

Ashton, P. (Ed.). (1991, March–April). Alternative approaches to teacher education. *Journal of Teacher Education, 42*(2), 82.

Association of Teacher Educators (ATE), Commission on Alternative Certification. (1989). *Alternatives, yes. Lower standards, no! Minimum standards for alternative teacher certification programs.* Reston, VA: Author.

Attinasi, J., & Schoon, K. (1992). *Danger: Explosive! Defusing the alternative certification controversy*. Policy briefs, 17. Oak Brook, IL: North Central Regional Educational Laboratory.

Baird, A. W. (1991a). *Alternative teacher certification programs*. Washington, DC: U.S. Department of Education, Office of Intergovernmental and Interagency Affairs.

Baird, A. W. (1991b). *Remarks prepared for delivery before the Federal Interagency Committee on Education*. Washington, DC: U.S. Department of Education, Office of Intergovernmental and Interagency Affairs.

Ball, D. L., & Wilson, S. M. (1990, April). *Knowing the subject and learning to teach it: Examining assumptions about becoming a mathematics teacher*. Paper presented at the annual meeting of the American Educational Research Association, Boston.

Banks, S. R., & Necco, E. G. (1990, Spring–Summer). The alternative certification controversy. *Teacher Education and Practice, 6*(1), 23–28.

Barnes, S., Salmon, J., & Wale, W. (1990, Spring–Summer). Alternative teacher certification in Texas: A look at initial results. *Teacher Education and Practice, 6*(1), 29–34.

Bell, D., & Roach, P. (1989, October). *Alternative certification: Pathway to success or blind alley in the teacher shortage*. Paper presented at the meeting of the Association of Teacher Educators (ATE) Mid-America Conference, Kingston/Durant, OK.

Bennett, C. (1991, March–April). The teacher as decision maker program: An alternative for career-change preservice teachers. *Journal of Teacher Education, 42*(2), 119–130.

Birchbichler, D. (1994, March). Foreign language policy and teacher education. In R. D. Lambert (Ed.), *The annals of the American Academy of Political and Social Science: Vol. 532. Foreign language policy: An agenda for change* (pp. 177–188). Baltimore: Johns Hopkins University.

Birrell, J. R. (1993, February). *The influence of prior experiences on teaching schemata of traditional and nontraditional elementary preservice teachers*. Paper presented at the annual meeting of the Association of Teacher Educators (ATE), Los Angeles.

Bliss, T. (1990, Spring). Alternate certification in Connecticut: Implications for the improvement of teaching. In W. D. Hawley (Ed.), *Peabody Journal of Education, 67*(3), 35–54.

Brown, D., Edington, E., Spencer, D. A., & Tinafero, J. (1989). A comparison of alternative certification, traditionally trained, and emergency permit teachers. *Teacher Education & Practice, 5*(2), 21–23.

Bryant, G. W., & Nichols, M. L. (1993, February). *Comparing master of arts in teaching graduates with four year graduates in teaching education: What are the differences in preparation and the student teaching experience?* Paper presented at the annual meeting of the Association of Teacher Educators (ATE), Los Angeles.

Buechler, M., & Fulford, N. (1992). *Alternative teacher certification. Policy briefs, 17*. Oak Brook, IL: North Central Regional Educational Laboratory.

Buttery, T. J., Haberman, M., & Houston, W. R. (1990, Summer). First annual ATE survey of critical issues in teacher education. *Action in Teacher Education, 12*(2), 1–7.

Cochran-Smith, M. (1991, March–April). Reinventing student teaching. *Journal of Teacher Education, 42*(2), 104–118.

Cooperman, S., & Klagholz, L. (1985, June). New Jersey's alternate route to certification. *Phi Delta Kappan, 66*(10), 691–695.

Cornett, L. (1990). Alternative certification: State policies in the SREB states. In W. D. Hawley (Ed.), *Peabody Journal of Education, 67*(3), 55–83.

Culver, V., Eicher, B. K., & Sacks, A. (1986, Summer). Confronting the teacher shortage: Are alternative certification programs the answer? *Action in Teacher Education, 8*(2), 19–24.

Darling-Hammond, L. (1990, Spring). Teaching and knowledge: Policy issues posed by alternate certification for teachers. In W. D. Hawley (Ed.), *Peabody Journal of Education, 67*(3), 123–154.

Darling-Hammond, L., Hudson, L., & Kirby, S. N. (1989, Fall). Nontraditional recruits to mathematics and science teaching. *Educational Evaluation and Policy Analysis, 11*(3), 301–323.

Day, L. M. (1989, Summer). Yes, there is another way! An alternative post-baccalaureate licensure program. *Kappa Delta Pi Record, 25*(4), 112–116.

Denton, J., & Morris, J. (1991). Recruitment and selection of mathematics and science teaching candidates for an alternative teacher certification program. *Action in Teacher Education, 13*(2), 10–19.

Denton, J., & Smith, N. (1983). *Alternative teacher preparation programs: A cost-effectiveness comparison* (No. 86). Portland, OR: Northwest Regional Educational Laboratory.

Dial, M., & Stevens, C. J. (Eds.). (1993, November). Alternative teacher certification [Special Issue]. *Education and Urban Society, 26*(1).

Dill, V. (1990, November). Support for the "unsupportable." *Phi Delta Kappan, 72*(3), 198–199.

Dill, V. (1994, Winter). Teacher education in Texas: A new paradigm. In R. A. Edelfelt (Ed.), *Educational Forum, 58*(2), 147–154.

Dill, V., & Stafford, D. (1994, April). School-based teacher education. *Phi Delta Kappan, 75*(8), 620–623.

Edelfelt, R. (1986). Managing teacher supply and demand. *Action in Teacher Education, 8*(2), 31–37.

Edelfelt, R. (1994, Winter). Editorial: Final thoughts on alternative certification. *Educational Forum, 58*(2), 220–223.

Eubanks, E., & Parish, R. (1990). Why does the status quo persist? *Phi Delta Kappan, 72*(3), 196–197.

Evertson, C., Hawley, W., & Zlotnik, M. (1985). Making a difference in educational quality through teacher education. *Journal of Teacher Education, 35*(3), 2–10.

Feistritzer, C. E. (1990a). *Profile of teachers in the U.S.— 1990*. Washington, DC: National Center for Education Information.

Feistritzer, C. E. (1990b). Special report: Alternative teacher certification in Texas. *Teacher Education Reports, 12*(2), 1–8.

Feistritzer, C. E. (1992). *Who wants to teach?* Washington, DC: National Center for Education Information.

Feistritzer, C. E. (1994, Winter). The evolution of alternative teacher certification. In R. A. Edelfelt, (Ed.), *The Educational Forum 58*(2), 132–138.

Feistritzer, C. E., & Chester, D. (1991). *Alternative teacher certification: A state by state analysis*. Washington, DC: National Center for Education Information.

Fenstermacher, G. (1990, Spring). The place of alternative certification in the education of teachers. In W. D. Hawley (Ed.), *Peabody Journal of Education, 67*(3), 155–185.

Florida Department of Education. (1988). *Teachers for Florida's classrooms: The Experimental Alternative Certification Program for Secondary Teachers*. Tallahassee: Florida State Department of Education. (ERIC Document Reproduction Service No. ED 337 439).

Franke, D. (1991, November). The alternate route: Testimonial from a Texas teacher. *Educational Leadership, 49*(3), 34–35.

Galen, H., & Kardon, B. (1986). Accepting the challenge: A partnership model for teacher education. *Action in Teacher Education, 8*(2), 45–50.

Galluzzo, G., & Ritter, D. (1986). Identifying standards for evaluating alternative route programs. *Action in Teacher Education, 8*(2), 59–64.

Goebel, S. D. (1986). *Alternative certification program final report*. Austin: Texas Education Agency State Board of Education Minutes. Based on a preliminary report presented to the Houston Independent School District Administration May 20, 1986, and brought before the State Board of Education, January 9, 1987.

Goebel, S. D., & Ronacher, K. (1989). *Alternative certification program final report. Texas Education Agency State Board of Education final report, 1988–1989*. Houston: Houston Independent School District.

Goodlad, J. (1990, November). Better teachers for our nation's schools. *Phi Delta Kappan, 72*(3), 185–194.

Graham, P. (1989). The other certification: More benefits than risks? *NEA Today, 7*(6), 75–79.

Gursky, D. (1989). Looking for a short cut. *Teacher Magazine, 1*(3), 43–49.

Guyton, E., Fox, M. C., & Sisk, K. S. (1991). Comparison of teaching attitudes, teacher efficacy, and teacher performance of first year teachers prepared by alternative and traditional teacher education programs. *Action in Teacher Education, 13*(2), 1–9.

Haberman, M. (Ed.). (1986). Alternative teacher certification. *Action in Teacher Education, 8*(2), 13–18.

Haberman, M. (1991a, November 6). Catching up with reform in teacher education. *Education Week, 11*(10), 29–36.

Haberman, M. (1991b). *The dimensions of excellence in teacher education*. Washington, DC: Office of Governmental Affairs, U.S. Department of Education.

Haberman, M. (1992a, Spring–Summer). Alternative certification: Can the problems of urban education be resolved by traditional teacher education? *Teacher Education and Practice, 8*(1), 13–27.

Haberman, M. (1992b, Spring). The ideology of star teachers of children in poverty. *Educational Horizons, 70*(3), 125–129.

Haberman, M. (1994, Winter). Preparing teachers for the real world of urban schools. In R. A. Edelfelt (Ed.), *Educational Forum, 58*(2), 162–168.

Hassard, J. (1989). *Alternative certification of secondary foreign language, mathematics, and science teachers*. Report No. 141. Atlanta: Georgia State University. (ERIC Document Reproduction Service No. ED 317 493)

Hawk, P. & Schmidt, M. (1989). Teacher preparation: A comparison of traditional and alternative programs. *Journal of Teacher Education, 40*(5), 53–58.

Hawley, W. D. (1990, Spring). The theory and practice of alternative certification: Implications for the improvement of teaching. *Peabody Journal of Education, 67*(3), 3–34.

Hawley, W. D. (Ed.). (1992). *The alternative certification of teachers*. Teacher Education Monograph: No. 14. Washington, DC: ERIC Clearinghouse on Teacher Education.

Hazlett, J. S. (1984, Fall). Alternative certification. *Contemporary Education, 56*(1), 46–48.

Hines, P. (1992, January 10). From the armed forces to the teaching force. *The Wall Street Journal*, p. 8.

Hodge, C. (1991, Spring–Summer). Teacher education and NCATE: An interview with Art Wise. *Teacher Education and Practice, 7*(1), 7–12.

Howey, K., & Zimpher, N. (1994, Winter). Nontraditional contexts for learning to teach. In R. A. Edelfelt (Ed.), *The Educational Forum, 58*(2), 155–161.

Houston, W. R., Marshall, F., & McDavid, T. (1993, November). Problems of traditionally prepared and alternatively certified teachers. *Education and Urban Society, 26*(1), 78–89.

Huling-Austin, L. (1986). Factors to consider in alternative certification programs: What can be learned from teacher induction research? *Action in Teacher Education, 8*(2), 51–58.

Huling-Austin, L., Odell, S., Ishler, P., Kay, R., & Edelfelt, R. (1989). *Assisting the beginning teacher*. Reston, VA: Association of Teacher Educators.

Hutton, J. B. (1987). *Alternative teacher certification: Its policy implications for classroom and personnel practice*. Monograph Number 5. Commerce, TX: Center for Policy Studies and Research in Elementary and Secondary Education. (ERIC Reproduction Service No. ED 286 264)

Irons, J., & Wale, B. (1988, November). *An evaluative study of the Texas Alternative Teacher Certification Program*. Austin, TX: Texas Education Agency Division of Teacher Education.

Ishler, R. (1988). Teacher education Texas style. *Action in Teacher Education, 10*(3), 46–49.

Kaplan, L. (1994, Winter). Teacher certification: Collaborative reform. In R. A. Edelfelt (Ed.), *Educational Forum, 58*(2), 168–172.

Keltner, D. (1994, Winter). Troops to teachers: Alternative certification and the military. In R. A. Edelfelt (Ed.), *Educational Forum, 58*(20), 182–186.

Knauth, W. (1994, Winter). Teachers for Chicago: Changing the connections. In R. A. Edelfelt (Ed.), *Educational Forum, 58*(2), 209–213.

Knight, S., Owens, E., & Waxman, H. (Winter, 1990–1991). Comparing the classroom learning environments of traditionally and alternatively certified teachers. *Action in Teacher Education, 12*(4), 29–34.

Kopp, W. (1994, Winter). Teach for America: Moving beyond the debate. In R. A. Edelfelt (Ed.), *Educational Forum, 58*(2), 187–192.

Leslie, C., & Lewis, S. (1990, October). The failure of teacher education. *Newsweek*, pp. 58–60.

Littleton, M., Beach, D., Larmer, B., & Calahan, A. (1991). An effective university-based alternative certification program: The essential components. *Teacher Education and Practice, 7*(1), 37–43.

Marchant, G. J. (1990, February). *Alternative certification and the knowledge base for teachers*. Paper presented at the annual meeting of the American Association of Colleges for Teacher Education, Chicago.

McDiarmid, G. W., & Wilson, S. M. (1991, March–April). An exploration of the subject matter knowledge of alternate route teachers: Can we assume they know their subject? *Journal of Teacher Education, 42*(2), 93–103.

McKibben, M. (1988a, Summer). Alternative certification in California. *Teacher Education Quarterly, 15*(3), 49–59.

McKibben, M. (1988b). Alternative teacher certification programs. *Educational Leadership, 46*(3), 32–35.

McKibben, M. (1991, April). *University internship programs in California*. Paper presented at the annual meeting of the American Educational Research Association, Chicago.

McKibben, M., & Ray, L. (1994, Winter). A guide for alternative certification program improvement. In R. A. Edelfelt (Ed.), *Educational Forum, 58*(2), 201–208.

Million, S. (1987, November). *Maintaining academic integrity in the midst of educational reform: An alternative certification program*. (Report No. 141). Paper presented at the meeting of the annual national conference of the National Council of States on Inservice Education, San Diego.

Murnane, R. J., Singer, J. D., Willett, J. B., Kemple, J. J., & Olsen, R. J. (1991). *Who will teach?* Cambridge, MA: Harvard University Press.

National Education Association. (1990). *Ensuring high standards in nontraditional routes to licensure*. Washington, DC: Author. Standing Committee on Instruction and Professional Development.

National Center for Education Statistics. (1993). *America's teachers: Profile of a profession*. NCES Publication No. 93-025. Washington, DC: U.S. Government Printing Office.

Natriello, G. (1992). *Toward the strategic use of alternative routes to teaching*. Policy briefs, 17. Oak Brook, IL: North Central Regional Educational Laboratory.

Natriello, G., & Zumwalt, K. (1992). Challenges to an alternative route for teacher education. In A. Lieberman (Ed.), *The 91st yearbook of the Society for the Study of Education* (Part I, pp. 59–78). Chicago: University of Chicago Press.

Natriello, G., & Zumwalt, K. (1993). New teachers for urban schools? The contribution of the provisional teacher program in New Jersey. *Education and Urban Society, 26*(1), 49–62.

Oliver, B., & McKibben, M. (1985). Teacher trainees: Alternative credentialing in California. *Journal of Teacher Education, 36*(3), 20–23.

Otuya, E. (1992, November). Alternative teacher certification—An update. *ERIC Digest, 91*(6), unpaginated.

Parramore, B. (1986). The impact of deregulation on the partnership in teacher certification. *Action in Teacher Education, 8*(2), 7–12.

Rosiek, J. (1990, May 4). Training subversives as teachers. *The New York Times, 139*(48), p. 225.

Roth, R. A. (1986a). Alternate and alternative certification: Purposes, assumptions, implications. *Action in Teacher Education, 8*(2), 1–6.

Roth, R. A. (1986b). Emergency certificates, misassignment of teachers, and other 'dirty little secrets.' *Phi Delta Kappan, 67*(10), 725–727.

Roth, R. A. (1988). California contradictions: Creating your own crisis. *Action in Teacher Education, 10*(3), 41–45.

Roth, R. A. (1989). The teacher education program: An endangered species? *Phi Delta Kappan, 71*(4), 319–323.

Roth, R. A., & Lutz, P. B. (1986, November). *Alternative certification: Issues and perspectives.* Charleston, WV: Appalachia Educational Laboratory.

Roth, R., & Pipho, C. (1990). Teacher education standards. In W. Houston (Ed.), *Handbook of research on teacher education* (pp. 119–135). New York: Macmillan.

Rumberger, R. (1985). The shortage of mathematics and science teachers: A review of the evidence. *Educational Evaluation and Policy Analysis, 7*(4), 355–369.

Salley, R. L. (1993, June). *Review of the district intern program in Los Angeles Unified School District.* Sacramento: Commission on Teacher Credentialing.

Sandlin, R. A., Young, B. L., & Karge, B. D. (1992–1993, Winter). Regularly and alternatively credentialed beginning teachers: Comparison and contrast of their development. *Action in Teacher Education, 14*(4), 16–23.

Schlechty, P., & Vance, V. (1983). Recruitment, selection, and retention: The shape of the teaching force. *The Elementary School Journal, 83*(4), 469–487.

Schussler, E., & Testa, R. (1984, November). *How does the issue of changing teacher education and certification affect staff development?* Orlando: National Council of States on Inservice Education.

Shulman, D. (1992). *Alternative routes to certification: Are we on the right track?* Policy Briefs, 17. Oak Brook, IL: North Central Regional Educational Laboratory.

Shulman, J. H. (1989, September–October). Blue freeways: Traveling the alternate route with big-city teacher trainees. *Journal of Teacher Education, 40*(5), 2–8.

Smith, J. M. (1991, November). The alternate route: Flaws in the New Jersey plan. *Educational Leadership, 49*(3), 32–36.

Stafford, D., & Barrow, G. (1994, Winter). Houston's alternative certification program. In R. A. Edelfelt (Ed.), *The Educational Forum, 58*(2), 193–200.

Steffensen, J. (1994, Winter). Certification: The past as prelude. In R. A. Edelfelt (Ed.), *The Educational Forum, 58*(2), 126–131.

Stoddart, T. (1990, Spring). Los Angeles Unified School District Intern Program: Recruiting and preparing teachers for an urban context. In W. D. Hawley (Ed.), *Peabody Journal of Education, 67*(3), 84–122.

Stoddart, T. (1993, November). Who is prepared to teach in urban schools? *Education and Urban Society, 26*(1), 29–48.

Suydam, M. (1986). Alternative certification for teachers. (ERIC Document Reproduction Service No. ED 266 137)

Texas Education Agency. (1990). *Alternative teacher certification in Texas, 1991–1992.* Austin: Texas Education Agency No. GE161102-R1.

Texas Education Agency. (1993a). *Alternative teacher certification in Texas, 1992–1993.* Austin: Texas Education Agency, No. GE342001.

Texas Education Agency. (January, 1993b). Professional educator preparation policy development in Texas. *Policy Research.* Austin: Texas Education Agency, No. GE341005.

Watts, D. (1986). Alternate routes to teacher certification: A dangerous trend. *Action in Teacher Education, 8*(2), 25–29.

Willis, P. (1994, Winter). Staffing our schools. In R. A. Edelfelt (Ed.), *The Educational Forum, 58*(2), 173–179.

Wise, A. (1994, Winter). Choosing between professionalism and amateurism. In R. A. Edelfelt (Ed.), *The Educational Forum, 58*(2), 139–146.

Wise, A. E., & Darling-Hammond, L. (1991, September 4). Alternative certification is an oxymoron. *Education Week,* 46–56.

Wisniewski, R. (1986). Alternative programs and the reform of teacher education. *Action in Teacher Education, 8*(2), 37–44.

Zumwalt, K. (1991). Alternate routes to teaching: Three alternative approaches. *Journal of Teacher Education, 42*(2), 83–92.

·44·

IMPROVING RURAL TEACHER EDUCATION

Weldon Beckner

WAYLAND BAPTIST UNIVERSITY

One of the major problems encountered in the field of rural education historically has been the notion that rural schools should be modeled after good urban or suburban schools, and the same situation has confronted rural teacher education. "A teacher is a teacher, is a teacher, is a teacher" is now seen to be an inadequate concept because of the numerous differences among people of the world today.

Those directly involved in teacher education, particularly field experience and student teaching, support the position that, just as the small schools typically found in sparsely populated areas must be unique to fit the needs of the constituency, so should the preparation of teachers for those schools be unique to prepare those teachers for effective service to the communities, their schools and the students attending those schools (Easton, 1985; Jones, 1985; Stone, 1990). However, few institutions offer special programs for students aspiring to teach in rural schools (Stone, 1990). Of the teachers surveyed in nine Western states, 80% reported that they received no specific preparation for service in a rural setting (Reece, 1984).

Research relative to education in rural schools and preparation of teachers to serve in those schools are not matters of little consequence. More than 38% of the students enrolled in American schools during 1989–1990 attended schools in less populated areas. Those attending schools classified as "rural" (places with a population of 2,500 or less) made up 16.5% of the total, while those in "small towns" (less than 25,000 population) included 21.8% of the school population (Stern, 1992). No other equally large segment of our nation has received so little attention relative to its special needs and potential.

There are recognized advantages of growing up in rural areas and going to typically small schools. Unfortunately, these natural advantages are often lost in the tendencies of teachers and school administrators to follow tradition, convention, or habits that have been developed in larger population centers and larger schools. There are also some obvious disadvantages of being schooled in rural areas, and teachers for those schools also need preparation in how best to alleviate those disadvantages.

This chapter reviews the characteristics of small schools in general (including their strengths and weaknesses), and effective small schools in particular, before exploring implications for both preservice and in-service preparation of teachers for those schools.

It must be noted at this point that research on rural education, and particularly on the preparation of rural teachers, is meager and often lacks sophistication (DeYoung, 1987). Research supporting some of the conclusions expressed in this chapter was conducted in the mid-1980s, and, except for the seminal work of authors such as Bloom (1976), Nachtigal (1982), and Sher (1977), these citations have not been included because they are old.

Much of what is presented in the literature is, at best, informed opinion or conclusions drawn from very limited experience, although some notable experts may have expressed those opinions or conclusions. Generalizations from individual or small numbers of cases and personal experiences have at times been the best evidence available relative to critical questions and issues in rural education. Educational research itself is relatively new, and much of the effort to this point has been aimed at particular policy or finance matters (DeYoung, 1987). Hopefully, this chapter inspires new research to support the obvious needs in rural teacher preparation and the sincere efforts of those engaged in that endeavor.

DEFINITION AND CHARACTERISTICS OF RURAL SCHOOLS

What is meant by "rural" or "small"? The variations in how these two words are defined has been a serious problem in research efforts and support programs aimed at the schools they describe. There has been little consistency, particularly in the earlier years of research, directed at rural education, so it is difficult to generalize about the results of these research efforts.

Defining "rural" is more than an academic concern, as noted by Stern (1992). "Funding eligibility and policy issues are frequently linked to a school's or school district's rurality—usually measured in terms of sparse settlement, isolation from a population center, or both" (p. 72). State statutes vary in their definitions of rural, and various federal statutes are no more consistent. The Census Bureau, for instance, in its decennial survey defines rural in a manner inconsistent with its own monthly Current Population Survey.

As inexact as it may be, to define rural we must simply fall back on what seems to be common sense and the most general practice, with a dictionary definition as our basic guide. Rural is defined as "of, pertaining to, or characteristic of the country, country life, or country people" (Flexner, 1987, p. 1,684), and that general concept will be followed in this discussion of rural education and how to prepare teachers for service in rural schools.

Describing rural schools is just as difficult as defining them. They are as diverse as the geography within which they are found, and the students attending them are similarly diverse. "There is no typical rural area, nor is there any longer a typical rural employment pattern" (Stern, 1992, p. 72). This diversity would seem to dictate appropriate variations in organization and instruction, but this is not usually the case.

Problems of poverty and other "disadvantages" exist in both urban and rural areas, and a common assumption has been that treatment of those problems should be similar in all schools. Questions of efficiency have been confused with those of effectiveness, usually to the detriment of rural school funding and programs. Organizational and financial arrangements for rural schools, such as state funding formulas and class size requirements, have usually been dictated by urban practices, regardless of their appropriateness for rural communities and rural schools.

Challenges to rural educators have many origins (Carroll, 1990), including demographic shifts, economic changes, technological improvements in education, increased demand for reform in curriculum and classroom management, teacher shortages, low educational attainment, financial support, and federal and state rural education policies. "Low wages, unemployment, outmigration by the younger and the more highly trained, high poverty rates, and the existence of a sizable group 'disconnected from society' have serious implications for . . . children" (Stern, 1992). Historically, states have taken responsibility for education, with the federal government acting to ensure equal opportunity and to disseminate new approaches, but both levels of government have tended to neglect the specific needs of rural schools and their students.

Perhaps the general characteristics of rural schools can best be described in terms of their advantages and disadvantages. Any such generalization is subject to considerable error, of course, but there is probably "more truth than fiction" in the conclusions. Both advantages and disadvantages are discussed briefly under the same general headings.

Community Relationships and Control

Rural schools are an integral part of the community—and the community is part of the school. Without the schools, many rural communities would have very little in the way of social or community activity. There tends to be strong support from parents and other community members and close working rela-

tionships between the staff and members of the community. There also tends to be more parental involvement in the schools. The community exerts more direct control over the school and thus sees that the school serves the specific needs of the community.

The other side of the coin relative to community involvement in rural schools results from the typically very conservative nature of rural communities and their reluctance to change to meet the changing needs of students and the larger society. Cultural impoverishment and parochialism may be evident, especially if the community is isolated. Combining this with close community ties often results in an overbearing influence by the community on the school, particularly on values and customs. Many small communities are relatively homogeneous and provide students with little opportunity to increase their knowledge of the diversity in people and cultures that exists in our world today. In addition, small communities often seem to develop inferiority complexes toward their city counterparts, and this may affect the morale and aspirations of their young people.

Teachers

One of the major advantages claimed by those associated with rural schools is their close teacher–student relations, and there is considerable justification for this claim. Teachers must assume a variety of roles in a rural school, and they unavoidably are in regular contact with most of the students in the school. Teachers are more likely to be respected as valuable members of the community, and because they are usually a part of various community activities, they are more likely to understand and adapt to rural community life. Teacher–student ratios are usually smaller, and because they usually must be generalists to some extent, rural teachers are often more receptive to cooperative program planning and promising innovations such as continuous progress organization, site-based decision making, cooperative learning, and interdisciplinary programs.

On the negative side, attracting and keeping quality teachers is one of the greatest difficulties faced by rural schools, especially those in economically disadvantaged areas. As mentioned, teachers and others in rural schools may suffer from an inferiority complex about their school and their professional effectiveness. Unless they are well established in the community, social life and the development of satisfactory personal relationships are difficult for rural teachers, particularly those who are young and unmarried. Rural teachers are frequently isolated from colleagues in their special field, and there are usually limited opportunities for professional interaction and development. The limited number of teachers may mean that some are required to teach outside their field of professional strength. Multiple lesson preparations are usually necessary, and supportive services to help teachers provide for students with various disadvantages or personal problems are often inadequate. Academic freedom is often curtailed by the conservative attitudes of the community and of the local school board, again limiting learning opportunities for students.

Students

Students in rural schools are the ultimate beneficiaries of the closer relationships usually existing among parents, teachers, administrators, and the community at large. With good school and community leadership, community and school morale may be higher than typical in urban areas, resulting in improved student conduct, less alienation, and improved pride in their community, their school, and themselves. Students are more likely to approach teachers and other school personnel with individual needs and concerns, and a much larger percentage of students is usually involved in student activity programs. This makes such programs better learning experiences for more students rather than a stage for stellar performers, and they have more opportunities for developing individual identity and potential.

Disadvantages for rural school students are related primarily to fewer choices of course offerings and teachers and fewer provisions for students needing special attention or support services. Without good school and community leadership, students may pick up community feelings of inadequacy or inferiority, which may inhibit their adaptation and success in larger communities and universities. A lack of ethnic and cultural diversity in the community may limit student exposure to the varied ethnic, socioeconomic, and cultural groups.

Curriculum and Instruction

Although curriculum and instruction in rural schools are often considered weaknesses, rural schools are more likely to be learner-centered, and the smaller organization provides some advantages relative to curriculum change and instructional improvement. Scheduling and other logistical problems are usually less complex. If the inherent advantages of smaller teacher–student ratios and smaller class sizes are realized, improved teaching and learning will result.

However, rural schools tend to mimic larger schools in organizing their curriculum and in teaching methodology. Possible instructional improvement through more use of community resources is often lost in the emphasis on traditional curriculum programs and instructional practices.

Finance and Administration

Financing rural schools is usually considered a problem area, because smaller enrollments are thought to be inherently uneconomical. This may be true if enrollments are exceptionally small, but with good management, rural schools can be adequately funded without undue strain on the local community, if state and federal governments assume their fair share of school costs. However, as federal and state legislatures become more and more dominated by urban constituencies, school finance laws tend to favor those schools, to the detriment of rural school districts.

Although they typically carry an exceptionally heavy load of responsibilities and time commitments, with inadequate secretarial service, rural school administrators tend to work closely with classroom teachers and with students. There is usually less bureaucracy and red tape and fewer regulations to complicate the lives of teachers and students (Beckner, 1983).

CHARACTERISTICS OF EFFECTIVE RURAL SCHOOLS

The search for "effective schools" has dominated the field of education and educational research in recent years, and this search has been no less directed toward rural schools than those in urban settings. Unfortunately, assumptions have been common that an effective school has the same characteristics in all settings and circumstances. A few essential characteristics are usually present in effective schools, but we are now learning that effective schools are recognized by their results as well as by their characteristics. This is a particularly important matter for rural schools, because their individual situations are so varied. The practices that produce good results may be played on a common theme, but they have many special melodies.

Organization

Organizational aspects of effective rural schools are different not so much in structure as in tone. Most rural schools have a rather traditional organizational structure, but within this traditional structure, effective rural schools show a marked emphasis on teaching, learning, curriculum organization, and cooperative decision making.

A significant rural school deviation from effective organizational aspects of urban schools is seen in the critically important role of the superintendent, paralleling the role of the principal for effective inner-city schools (Jacobson, 1986). It is possible for an individual urban school to achieve exceptional effectiveness in an otherwise less than effective school district, because of the principal and the autonomy given to the principal and the school. This is highly unlikely in a rural school district because of the close relationships between all administrators, teachers, and community members.

One of the organizational advantages of rural school districts revolves around smaller size and more freedom from bureaucracy and organizational rigidity. This advantage is useless, however, if the school and community leaders do not move to institute effective organizational changes. Individual leadership by principals, and particularly by superintendents, is absolutely essential to significant improvement in educational outcomes.

One of the more effective organizational changes for all schools, and particularly rural schools, is guided by the research of Bloom (1976). This research emphasizes the conclusion that cognitive and affective entry behaviors of students account for about 75% of differences in student learning outcomes. Therefore, improving instructional quality has little chance of overcoming the effects of inadequate entry behaviors unless the instruction takes into account cognitive and affective deficiencies. This calls for some form of "continuous progress" or "mastery learning" organization and for changing grade reporting and other practices to see that students feel successful in school and in individual classes. It also calls for various kinds of cooperative teaching and learning, where the teachers become learning facilitators rather than custodians and dispensers of knowledge.

Because of fewer human resources, teachers in rural schools must assume a larger responsibility for their own curriculum development than do most teachers in city schools. There is, therefore, a need for curriculum specialists to get into a situation, to assess the problem, and to solve the problem quickly in order to move to another problem. In rural schools, classroom teachers must often become that curriculum specialist, and they must evaluate their curriculum development work by its effect in their classrooms. Pehrsson and Mook (1983) point out that this is a generic principle in curriculum development, but it is a principle that assumes a critical role in rural school curriculum development.

Teachers, particularly in rural school districts, need proof of the effectiveness of curriculum development (they must see a change in student behavior or learning). They must then decide what is best and what is effective within the context of their own classroom. To do this, teachers need more guidance initially, but they need to work toward independence by learning how to learn from their students.

Rural schools may be directly linked to community development in rural areas by emphasizing a community-based curriculum that teaches cooperation, the role of citizens, and leadership development (Raftery & Mulkey, 1991). This concept follows a larger perspective of the school curriculum that views it in community context. The curriculum thus encompasses the community, and the community becomes a major part of the curriculum.

Instruction

Quality instruction is important for a school to become effective, but it must build on other required qualities of the total school program, as discussed (Beckner, 1987; Bloom, 1976; Lee, 1991). In recent years, almost all of the effort that has gone into improving schools, both urban and rural, has been to improve instruction. This kind of effort is worthwhile, but it has tended to take attention and effort away from other perhaps more important needs for organizational and administrative change in our school systems.

A variety of systems and programs have been developed and extensively promoted throughout the country to improve instruction, and they are applicable to both urban and rural schools, if properly adapted. Those advocated by Madeline Hunter (1976), or modeled after her recommendations, have probably been the most common. Just how successful these efforts have been in improving learning is subject to debate. Many of them have been linked to teacher evaluation and merit pay programs, and this has severely limited their effectiveness.

Effective rural schools show evidence of attention to teaching and learning improvement, and they usually make use of one or more of the programs currently in fashion. They also use various kinds of student testing to measure student learning and to validate instructional processes. They are usually careful, however, to avoid allowing improving test scores to become an end in itself (DeYoung, 1987).

Many effective rural schools give special attention to linking the instructional program to development of vocational and professional skills. Nachtigal (1992b), among others, has shown that school development and community development may be

part of the same effort in rural communities, with significant benefit to both the students and the economic well-being of the community (Versteeg, 1993; Wigginton, 1985). Projects developed and conducted throughout the country by Sher (1977) and DeLargy (1992), whereby students actually operate their own businesses, have been particularly impressive in developing the personal and business skills of students while improving the economic well-being of the community.

For many years, effective educators have stressed the importance of real-life and "hands-on" instruction. Effective rural schools use these techniques extensively, along with other complementary methods, such as independent study and self-paced instruction. Cooperative learning and peer instruction also have long been significant parts of rural education, especially in very small schools where two or more grade levels or subjects may be taught at the same time in the same room and by the same teacher.

Recent developments in what is now commonly referred to as "distance learning" is producing much excitement and optimism among rural educators because of its potential for overcoming many of the inherent disadvantages related to instruction in rural schools. The most recent developments in two-way audio and video communication via telephone lines has opened the way to sharing of teachers, materials, and expertise among cooperating schools and school districts in much more effective fashion than has been possible in the past with use of satellite and less effective telephone technology. Effective rural schools of the present and future must make as much use of this technology as possible (Followhill & Andersen, 1991; Withrow, 1990).

In addition to distance learning, technological development, particularly computer and CD-ROM technology, has made it possible for rural schools to overcome the normally severe shortages of learning resources that result from isolation and lack of finances. Teachers and students in the most remote parts of the country may now make use of data bases and other resources previously available only to those with access to the largest libraries and metropolitan learning resources (Barker, 1991; Beckner & Barker, 1994).

School–Community Relations

As has already been noted, school–community relations may provide one of the most important rural school advantages. However, many problems and disadvantages may come from poor community–school relations as well. The school and the community will almost inevitably be closer than in most urban areas. The critical question is, What does this closeness produce?

The success of rural school improvement efforts depends on how well they fit local community needs and local educational needs. Schooling in rural America is still very much the community's business, and school effectiveness depends on community support and involvement in the school and its efforts. In communities where the education level of the general population is modest and expectations for the education of young people are low, for instance, basic community values may tend to be a deterrent to support of schools and teachers because of a prevailing attitude that "what was good enough for me is good enough for my kids."

Gregory and Smith (1987) expressed the fear that in the typical American high school "any reasonable sense of community has been lost" (p. 23). A similar fear could reasonably be expressed about most elementary schools of this country, particularly the larger ones. Outmoded authoritarian leadership practices, tracking, overuse of competition, and excessive use of standardized tests (among other things) have tended to produce an atmosphere of fear and oppression rather than one of security, cooperation, and mutual support necessary for a strong and productive sense of community.

Effective rural schools "fit" the community. They are consistent with the facts of rural life and preparation of young people of the community for futures in the community and elsewhere. There is local "ownership" of the school and its programs, but day-to-day operation of the school is left to the professional teachers and administrators.

IMPLICATIONS FOR RURAL TEACHER PRESERVICE EDUCATION

Much of the preparation needed for rural school teachers is similar, or even identical, to that needed for other teachers, and the following discussion does not dwell on these common needs. The major focus is on preparation needs that require special attention if we expect beginning teachers to do well in rural schools.

Recruitment, Selection, and Retention

Few would disagree with the statement that the most important ingredient of good instruction is well-qualified and dedicated teachers (Matthes, 1987; Wollman, 1990–1991). Good teachers must have basic skills and talents for teaching, along with the desire to teach and good preparation. Recruitment, selection, and retention, then, become the most important parts of teacher preparation and other efforts to produce good instruction.

Rural schools have difficulty recruiting and retaining teachers. A 1987–1988 survey of school administrators revealed that over 38% of the administrators in rural and small-city schools reported that they had difficulty in finding qualified applicants (Choy et al., 1993). This may be due to some extent to lower salaries, as 1987–1988 data also indicated that the scheduled salaries of rural and small-city teachers averaged $737 per year less than the national average and $2,432 less than those in districts of 10,000 or more students (Choy et al., 1993).

The national teacher turnover rate is 6% annually, but in rural areas it reaches 30% to 50% (Stone, 1990). Salaries may affect turnover as well as recruitment, but rural teachers often leave because of social, cultural, geographic, and professional isolation. They are often unprepared for rural realities that demand knowledge in multiple subjects and know-how in conducting a range of school activities (Luft, 1992–1993; Stone, 1990).

In rural schools, vacancies tend to occur on a regular basis for the same positions. Teachers tend to be either permanent or short-term. Those who are permanent live in the community, and because of family ties or ties to the community they are unlikely to leave or quit teaching until retirement. Those who are short-term are usually fresh out of college, perhaps planning on teaching only until they get married or have children, or planning to move on to a more desirable location within 2 or 3 years. This creates a situation where schools are constantly recruiting for the same positions (Muse & Thomas, 1992).

The first step in recruiting new teachers involves knowing something about current rural teachers. Where do they come from? What characteristics should one recruiting rural teachers look for? Why do teachers choose to teach in rural schools? Answers to these questions will guide successful recruiting efforts.

Those individuals most likely to teach successfully in rural schools tend to have grown up in rural communities and to have attended rural schools. Many times they are teaching in the same community where they grew up. Others may take a position in a rural school until something becomes available in a larger community, but they are not likely to become permanent and contributing members of the rural school and community (Hare, 1991; Muse & Thomas, 1992).

Realistic marketing is the key to obtaining and keeping good teachers in rural schools. Emphasis should be given to the real benefits; such as few discipline problems, less red tape, more personal contact, and greater chance for leadership (Stone, 1990). Cost of living is often less in rural areas, and provision of housing or other special fringe benefits helps attract good teachers. Developing good recruitment materials in the form of videotapes and attractive brochures that emphasize the positive aspects of living in the community may be effectively used at job fairs and with presentations to future teachers.

Effective teacher recruitment is an ongoing activity, not just a frantic effort when a teaching vacancy occurs. It involves encouraging and assisting students growing up in the community to become teachers and to return to the community and staying in touch with former students who are preparing to teach. Scholarships may be offered to local students to go to college in return for specified years of service to the school district.

Quality attracts quality, so building and publicizing the reputation of the school is important to teacher recruiting. Current students, parents, concerned citizens, former students going to college, alumni, and staff may all be enlisted to help with attracting teachers to the community.

Arranging for teacher education students to do their student teaching in the district on a regular basis, if possible, and maintaining contact with key personnel at various teacher preparation institutions provides personal contacts that may attract new teachers. Outstanding teachers in larger districts who were raised and educated in smaller schools may be identified and recruited by being reminded of the many benefits they received while growing up in a small-town atmosphere. Emphasizing the benefits of raising children in a smaller town becomes more and more attractive as the social and economic problems of urban areas continue to grow.

Attractive financial and working conditions are obviously essential to attracting and holding good teachers. Providing good salaries, various fringe benefits such as health and life insurance, investments for retirement, attractive and less expensive housing, personal and professional leave provisions, and support for graduate study will help attract and hold good teachers to rural schools. Businesses in the community may help by providing employment for spouses and for teachers during the summer (Hare, 1991; Muse & Thomas, 1992).

School districts, either urban or rural, that are most successful in recruiting and keeping good teachers, follow a careful and thorough plan for selection, in addition to aggressive recruiting, just as do the more successful organizations in business and industry (Pesek, 1993). Such a plan relies on a separate teacher selection committee for each vacancy that occurs. This committee is made up primarily of teachers, chaired by a well-qualified and respected teacher, and it is given the responsibility and authority to select the person to fill the position. The superintendent, or his designee, provides assistance to the search and selection committee, but the selection decision is left to the committee. The principal of the school involved is usually a member of the committee, but there is no attempt on the part of the principal to dominate or overly to influence the selection decision.

One of the major differences in the way things are best done in rural schools as contrasted to city schools is in the selection of teachers. Conventional wisdom among those involved in selection of teachers says that the person best qualified according to academic criteria should be selected. Selection of teachers for rural schools may need to give equal, and perhaps more, attention to other factors. They include the following:

- Certification and ability to teach in more than one subject area or grade level.
- Ability to teach students with a wide range of achievement in the same classroom.
- Ability and willingness to enjoy living in a rural area and teaching in a smaller school.
- Ability and willingness to supervise extracurricular activities.
- Ability to adjust to cultural differences of students and help them overcome cultural biases and challenges.
- Potential for being content living in a rural community and teaching in a rural school for a reasonable time. (Hare, 1991)

The task of considering these various aspects of teacher qualifications is usually made even more difficult by the fact that the pool of candidates is likely to be much smaller than would be the case in a more urban setting.

Selecting the most appropriate candidate for a rural teaching position has much to do with retention in the system for a reasonable time and with the probable success of efforts to help the teacher become an effective teacher and an otherwise valuable member of the community. Because most induction activities take place after the teacher is employed and on the job, this aspect of the personnel function in rural schools is discussed more fully in the section of this chapter that deals with professional development (in-service) efforts.

Content Knowledge

Mention was made in the introduction to this chapter that one of the major problems in preparing teachers for rural schools was the notion that competent teachers are similar, no matter where or what they teach, and that no special preparation is necessary to prepare teachers for service in rural schools. Early research in rural education refuted this and recommended that special preparation programs be developed for teachers planning to teach in rural schools (Barker 1986; Guenther & Weible, 1983; Jones, 1985; Miller, 1988). Such special preparation extends into all aspects of preservice teacher preparation.

Special preparation of teachers for rural schools must give attention to the cultural context of a rural setting, which may produce both a feeling of professional isolation and loss of personal privacy. Teachers must be prepared as adequately as possible before beginning to teach, because in-service training is usually inadequate, even though teachers are usually assigned to more subjects, more grade levels, and more extracurricular activities. Financial limitations often dictate lower budgets and salaries, inadequate teaching materials, and fewer opportunities for special student learning experiences. Even some of the advantages found in rural schools, such as a less pressured environment, greater cooperation from parents and the community, more student involvement, and more interaction among students, parents, and staff require special preparation for teachers if they are to maximize these natural opportunities (Barker, 1986; Miller, 1988).

Content knowledge needed by those preparing to teach in rural schools is not so much different as it is broader, conducive to versatility, and adapted to the realities of rural society (Horn, Davis, & Hilt, 1985; Matthes, 1987; Parker, 1985). Breadth and versatility may be developed through composite majors, compressed and integrated courses, preparation in two or more recognized teaching fields, both elementary and secondary endorsement, special education training, and participation in extracurricular activities. However, to do this while avoiding unreasonably long teacher certification programs, requires adaptations in most state laws relative to teacher preparation and changes in the typical university practices for organizing subject matter and courses. A certain degree of depth in content knowledge must be sacrificed to gain the breadth and versatility needed by teachers in rural schools. University academic departments have tended to be very reluctant to make such changes.

Content knowledge needed by rural teachers also includes aspects of community life and the social context of rural education. Living and teaching in rural communities requires a willingness to be more a part of the community and a contributor to various community activities. Social interactions, conventions, and customs vary from those in urban communities, and they vary from community to community.

The knowledge of human development required to teach successfully in a rural school needs to be broader, just as with subject areas, because of the fact that teachers must usually be responsible for a larger age range of students. This is often true for elementary teachers and almost universally so for secondary teachers.

Human development occurs in somewhat different fashion in rural communities, due in large part to closer family ties and broader based community life. Many students tend to be more involved in family businesses, particularly farming, and more interested in various community activities. Students may be less involved, because of the limited opportunities and the fewer number of community activities. Social and cultural activities are usually very limited. Development of social skills and other aspects of human development, may thus occur faster in some students, slower in others, and differently in ways other than would be the case in more urban settings.

Pedagogical Knowledge and Experience

Pedagogical training for all teachers is undergoing reform as school restructuring gains momentum across the United States. As this process continues, teacher preparation and school restructuring must support and enhance each other (Frazier, 1993). For instance, site-based decision making requires that teachers become more professional and more competent in making good organizational and classroom decisions. Concepts such as mastery learning, whole-language instruction, continuous progress, and cooperative learning require that teachers see themselves more as facilitators and resource persons, rather than instructors, classroom directors, or dispensers of information. Rural teachers, just as others, need to be prepared for these revised roles and revitalized ways of organizing and facilitating student learning. This is discussed elsewhere in this handbook, so only unique preparation needs of rural teachers are discussed here.

The need for special pedagogical preparation for rural teachers is caused by a variety of rural realities that have been documented by many writers, including Galbraith (1992), Miller (1988), and Schmuck and Schmuck (1992). These realities include:

- Small enrollments, resulting in classes with multiage students and students studying more than one subject
- Small numbers of teachers, resulting in assignment to teaching subjects for which the teacher is inadequately prepared
- Multiple preparations to provide adequate breadth of curriculum
- Overexposure of students to individual teachers
- Inadequate support services
- Inadequate information and resource materials
- Inadequate equipment and supplies
- Multiple assignments to extracurricular and other duties
- Inadequate professional development opportunities
- Inadequate definition of policies and procedures
- Combination of elementary and secondary classrooms in one building
- Unique sociocultural situations
- Lack of privacy and personal freedom
- Expanded community involvement
- Geographic, and sometimes linguistic, isolation
- Inadequate housing
- Personal isolation and loneliness

Observations and specific examples given by Schmuck and Schmuck (1992) serve to illustrate the need for special pedagogical preparation of rural teachers.

Of the 30 secondary classes we observed, 22 were clearly controlled almost constantly by the teacher. We saw teachers standing in front lecturing to rows of students with only occasional student talk as a response to the teachers' questions. That was as true in a class of 12 as it was in a class of 26. (p. 24)

Students were busy with extracurricular activities, but it was rare for students to tell us they were enthusiastic about schoolwork. (p. 7)

About 30% of teachers made school boring for most students, and at times their behavior added stress to the students' lives. (p. 21)

The need for special preparation in "how to teach" may be met in a variety of ways. The basic principles of this preparation are the same for elementary and secondary teachers, but the application of these principles differs to meet the age and maturity differences of the students.

One of the major deterrents to effective pedagogical preparation of rural teachers is the tendency in recent reform movements to identify a "one best method" of teaching. This works against the needs for versatility and breadth required to teach effectively in rural settings where there may be multiage classrooms and a broader spectrum of student and community needs. Rural teachers must be trained to evaluate and plan for curriculum organization and teaching so as best to accommodate the range of student needs in the classroom and community needs.

To achieve the required competencies, those preparing to teach in rural schools need training programs that have some special characteristics. Some of these have somewhat different applications, depending on whether the teacher is working in an elementary or secondary school, but for the most part they are very similar in practice as well as in principle. From the recommendations of various writers, including Galbraith (1992), Guenther and Weible (1983), Kleinfeld, McDiarmid, and Parrett (1992), Miller (1988), Parker (1985), and Wigginton (1985), it may be concluded that preservice preparation programs for rural teachers should:

- Provide experiences in classroom organization for a broad range of student abilities and competencies
- Provide extensive field experience in rural settings, dealing with special problems of teaching in those settings
- Give special attention to becoming aware of community culture, sociology, and economics and how to adapt the curriculum and lesson planning to those realities
- Develop understanding and competency in providing for rural students with special learning and physical needs, including available resources
- Provide elementary teachers with at least a minimum level of ability to teach art, music, and other special subjects
- Develop understanding of the need for service to the community and how to be appropriately involved in community service
- Develop skill in teaching methods that incorporate principles of cooperation, student interaction with the teacher and with other students, experiential learning in a community context, practical applications of subject matter, developing student initiative and independence, and use of community resources
- Develop understanding and teaching skills relative to multicultural education and global understanding

- Develop broad skill in the use of technology and distance learning opportunities
- Develop understanding of challenges presented by at-risk students in rural communities and ways to meet them
- Develop counseling and career guidance skills; provide practical understanding of rural living, including both advantages and disadvantages
- Develop skill in using the commuinty and other resources for enriching student experiences
- Develop skill in using tutorials, peer teaching, independent study, and other individualized teaching techniques and resources
- Develop skill in teaching problem solving, critical thinking, and entrepreneurial skills in rural settings
- Provide secondary teachers with the knowledge and skill to teach in two or more subject areas
- Develop ability to teach without adequate resources, such as an elementary gymnasium, formal science lab, curriculum guide, or teaching materials
- Particularly for secondary teachers, develop the understanding and ability needed to support extensively student extracurricular activities
- Develop special subject specialists (art, music, etc.) able to teach throughout the K–12 system

Use of Technology

Recent advances in communication technology, particularly its "distance learning" aspect, provide the means to alleviate greatly many of the typical difficulties associated with rural education and with preparing teachers for rural schools. Computers, if used to their full potential, provide numerous ways to enhance teaching and learning in rural schools (Robson, Routcliffe, & Fitzgerald, 1992; Templeton & Paden, 1991). Unfortunately, computer use in most schools is still limited to word processing, local data base creation, and basic spreadsheet applications. Adding CD-ROM capabilities allows enrichment of basic lesson material with materials of various kinds, such as simulation, educational games, and access to various data bases. Linking with videodiscs allows multimedia applications of various kinds. More and better computer software is now available to use for drill and practice, tutorials, and materials supplementation.

As telephone service to rural communities advances to include modern lines and cable, good two-way audio and video instruction is becoming available. This vastly expands opportunities for the sharing of teacher expertise, resource materials, and student cooperation between schools and school districts.

Far too many rural schools are failing to access the vast telecommunications resources and services available through use of computers and modems. Through services and data bases such as Internet, both teachers and students may overcome many of the problems of rural education created by limited financial and educational resources. The major deterrents are usually lack of teacher expertise and access to dedicated telephone lines and modern telephone systems.

If rural teachers are to make good use of computers and various forms of distance learning, they must receive considerable special preparation. Most college graduates now are required to show a modest degree of computer literacy, but rural teachers need a much larger amount of training and experience in computer use for electronic field trips, learning resources access, and networking of classrooms to share teachers and to allow students from two or more schools to interact with each other (Beckner & Barker, 1994; Knapczyk, Brush, Champion, Hubbard, & Rodes, 1992; Swick, 1988).

Collegial and Community Relations

Those who study life in rural areas and the development of those areas, whether economic, educational, or some other aspect, almost universally stress the concept of community as a way both to understand and to improve rural life. Schmuck and Schmuck (1992), for instance, wrote at some length about the involvement of students, parents, and other community members in the various aspects of community life, particularly those related to the school as an entertainment center, location for other kinds of community activity, and general conveyer of community culture:

Although some particular small district may not bring together diverse American subcultures, it always offers a common culture, regardless of where you go, for 5- to 18-year-olds in American society. And small districts, perhaps more than their large urban and suburban counterparts, do more than that; they bring citizens together to enhance a feeling of community identity. (p. 10)

The concept of community seems simple enough, but it is not easily defined. Drawing from a number of sources, Galbraith (1992) stated that it includes "social interaction, common ties, relationships within places; commonalities in interests, and locational criteria" (p. 9). His conclusion is that community may be defined as "the combination and interrelationship of geographic, locational, and non-locational units, systems, and characteristics that provide relevance and growth to individuals, groups, and organizations" (p. 10).

Current images of "rural community," particularly as portrayed by advertisers, tend to be inaccurate in a number of ways (Hobbs, 1992).

The images of country, as exemplified in the marketing of products from blue jeans to music to suburban housing developments, tend to cast country as escape from the constraints, pressures, and fast-paced life of the cities.

But the commercialized images of country tend to be at substantial variance with current facts concerning rural America and its communities. Images persist which portray rural America as the bastion of hard work and tradition, of simple lifestyles, and communities where people know and care about each other. Rural people are seldom portrayed as wealthy, but nevertheless are thought to be enjoying the good life. Current facts portray a different picture. Urban income is 36 percent greater than rural and growing more rapidly. The poverty rate in nonmetro areas is 35 percent higher than metro. Unemployment is 25 percent higher in rural areas, but underemployment is a more serious problem.

Times have blurred what were once clear distinctions between rural and urban America. The extremes are still easy to find and classify as either urban or rural, but most Americans now live somewhere between those extremes. Over the past several decades American society has been transformed into a mass society dominated by urban lifestyles, economic activity, and institutions which have extended into and engulfed the country. (pp. 21–22)

An interesting perspective (probably subject to question in many modern-day rural communities) on rural values and sense of community has been described by McFaul (1989) in terms of what he calls "peasant philosophy." The concept is not intended to be negative in any way, nor does it refer to an occupation or a measure of influence. It is defined as an old system of beliefs among people who are rooted to the land, drawing their sense of pride and purpose from hard physical work. Peasant philosophy is conservative and traditional. It does not change much from place to place, and those who subscribe to it are loyal to their home territory. There tends to be a general mistrust of far-away, official sources of power. It should probably not be concluded that this "peasant philosophy" pervades all rural communities, but the notion is useful in analyzing common difficulties of understanding and communicating with many rural citizens.

Developing and preserving a sense of community is becoming more and more difficult with "the emergence of new rural trade and service areas and the replacement of proximity by social space" (Hobbs, 1992, p. 32). Many residents of declining communities develop a sense of fatalism and resign themselves to continued decline, but those in developing areas may face the task of integrating new community members into the "history and fiction" of the old community or developing a new and revised sense of community.

Changes originating outside the community may also produce conflicts and potential loss of community. They make it even more difficult for a community consensus to survive and for the community to move ahead with economic and educational development.

Education, broadly defined, is likely to have more to do with economic development and other determinants of the future well-being of rural communities than any other aspect of the community. Rural America needs knowledge-based economic and community development to thrive, either economically or socially, and a variety of educational and training services will be needed to support this development. However, the education services needed will require tailoring to meet the varying local needs and circumstances found in different rural communities, contrasted with the traditional standardization of educational services. Providers must be prepared to work collaboratively, not only among various providers of education and training but also with a broader spectrum of community groups, agencies, and organizations, to identify needs and how they can be met best (Hobbs, 1992).

The school, as the formal educational unit, is a large part of the effort to establish community identity through education. However, as indicated, connecting education and community also includes various forms of nonformal and informal education. Nonformal education occurs through organizations and agencies that use education as a secondary or allied part of their mission, such as the YMCA, cooperative extension, religious institutions, service clubs, and other voluntary organizations.

Informal education, which make up most of the education that takes place within community structures, involves interaction between human and material resources, such as conversations, recreation, listening to mass media, or reading (Galbraith, 1992). Those who plan to teach in rural schools must be prepared to work through all of these education providers to achieve the educational goals of the community and the larger society.

A common human need of people making up a community is that of belonging—the deep need for long-term, close, and personal relationships. Teachers in rural schools often indicate this need as the primary reason they live and teach in rural communities, and most of those who study and write about rural communities express this aspect of rural life as universal and essential to a sense of community and personal well-being. This feeling of belonging leads teachers to believe that they can influence more readily the lives of students and life in the community than they could in a city or large school district (Galbraith, 1992; Gregory & Smith, 1987; Schmuck & Schmuck, 1992).

To facilitate this sense of belonging and of community requires a different approach to school organization and structure than the traditional model, particularly among high schools. As Gregory and Smith (1987) emphasized, schools need to be organized so that teachers and students develop closer relationships; they should feel a sense of belonging and self-worth; and parents and other community members should become vital parts of the school and its efforts. The isolation created between teachers and students, teachers and teachers, and teachers and administrators by separated classrooms, isolated offices, and hierarchical decision making must end (Schmuck & Schmuck, 1992). Smaller schools inherently have the basic attribute needed for this type of school structure. Large schools will have to be divided or organized into smaller operational units in the same building to have a chance of achieving the structure and cohesiveness required to develop the kind of schools needed.

A change in the structure of the school must be accompanied by a change in the basic relationships between teachers, students, and administrators if significant school improvement is to be achieved. After their extensive study of rural America and its schools, Schmuck and Schmuck (1992) supported this need with the observation that "small districts, like their urban and suburban counterparts, fostered I–It transactions" (p. 11). Taken from Buber (1958) and other sociologists, this concept describes situations where people relate to each other in terms of a category or function. Teachers think mainly of their students' level of competence or motivation, categorizing them as "hard workers," "troublemakers," and "jocks," for example. Students are judged by their skills in mathematics, reading, social studies, art, or athletics. This whole approach to relationships creates psychological distance between teachers and students, and even between teachers and teachers, that works against achieving the desired results in schools. Rather, there develops a lack of interpersonal openness, an absence of mutual understanding, and a modicum of collaboration and cooperation in classrooms and schools. Consequently, there is little excitement and enthusiasm about teaching and learning.

Adequate attention is seldom given in teacher education programs to providing rural teacher candidates with appropriate knowledge, experience, and understanding that is directly related to the life and culture of rural schools and communities. This need is difficult to fill for a variety of reasons, the most obvious one of which is the fact that there is great diversity in salient aspects of rural life across the country. Values, customs, and expectations related to rural education show similar diversity. Those preparing to teach in rural schools must become aware of the various aspects of rural community, how they are changing, and how educational efforts must be adapted to the unique needs and goals of the individual community.

The diversity evident in many aspects of rural life requires that teacher education efforts be designed so that the acquired knowledge and understanding of the school setting where teacher candidates will serve are appropriate to the particular community. Knowledge of the academic content to be taught is not so different from that expected in city schools, but knowledge and understanding of the school setting and pedagogical implications are varied and are often less than obvious to most observers.

An understanding of the aspects of rural community life makes it possible for rural teachers to become a part of the community. This, in turn, facilitates use of community resources, both human and physical, as teachers develop plans and procedures for their classes. They gain respect and support from parents and other community members that will also allow them to be more effective in the classroom and other educational activities of the community.

Field Experience

The importance of field experience in preparing teachers for rural schools has already been stated, but it cannot be overemphasized. Neither is it adequately attended to in most teacher education programs.

Ideally, field experiences of several kinds should begin with the first year in college. It should be part of most coursework, as well as a separate and intensive program during the final phases of the teacher education program. Beginning with short-term focused observations, adequate field experience will proceed through more long-term and general observations, to working in tutorial fashion with individual students, providing small-group teaching and leadership, assuming progressively greater responsibility for teaching an entire class, and culminating with a true internship during which the student experiences the full range of activities and responsibilities required of a classroom teacher. Throughout these experiences, there should be close correlation with classroom studies and extensive feedback to the student by university personnel and supervising classroom teachers.

So far, the description of recommended field experiences would fit students preparing for service either in city or rural schools. As with academic and pedagogical aspects of the preparation program, this common preparation should be made relevant and applicable to the rural setting in appropriate fashion—particularly by placing the field experiences in rural settings. Techniques from applied sociology and anthropology to help focus student observations and experiences have been found effective throughout field experience programs.

To provide good field experiences for prospective rural teachers requires extensive collaboration between university and school district personnel. Various community, school, and classroom projects may provide realistic experiences living and teaching in a rural community. A true internship, where students live in the community for up to a year, provides invaluable experience and opportunity to develop understanding of teaching and living in rural areas (Cross & Murphy, 1988; Martin & Wood, 1984; Murphy, 1984; Williams & Cross, 1985).

The field experience will be more valuable to students if there is adequate structure to the program. Some orientation to the specific community in which the experience will occur, review of appropriate materials and methods of instruction in the specific anticipated setting for the field experience, adequate supervision and feedback to the student (perhaps using a clinical supervision model), and training of collaborating teachers will help ensure that students receive the best experience possible (Koury, Ludlow, & Wienke, 1991).

Field experiences appropriate and adequate to provide good preparation for rural teachers are expensive in time and effort for the students and for their university and local school supervisors. Consequently, to this point in our history of teacher preparation, they have not been as good for most teacher education students as they should be.

IMPLICATIONS FOR RURAL TEACHER PROFESSIONAL DEVELOPMENT

One of the greatest weaknesses of American education in general, and rural education in particular, is the failure adequately to assist teachers with their professional development after they begin teaching. Most persons responsible for support and implementation of educational efforts seem to believe that most teachers are willing and able to assume responsibility for maintaining and improving their professional knowledge and skills. Again, research on the subject is scant about rural teachers, but there are several understandings from the available literature and authoritative beliefs about the professional development of rural teachers that may be accepted with considerable confidence.

As discussed in the preservice preparation section of this chapter, programs and program content designed to prepare teacher education students for the specific needs of rural schools and students are scarce and usually inadequate. Reece (1984) reported, for example, that 80% of teachers and 75% of principals had no specific preparation for service in a rural setting. As a result, the professional development of rural teachers is particularly needed.

The educational reform movement in most states has resulted in increased requirements that must be considered by rural educators, administrators, and board members. Although these mandates set parameters, local communities may adapt goals and practices relative to content, standards, and expectations, time allotments, and local preferences molded by custom and culture (Campbell, 1985).

The basic principles and, to some extent, the specifics of effective professional development are very similar for all teachers. However, adaptations must be made in rural settings to fit the specific needs and community situations of individual schools and teachers within those schools. The most obvious of these needs are caused by population sparsity, very limited resources, and local expectations. How these needs may be met through appropriate local adaptations for professional development of teachers will be reviewed as related to new teacher induction, principles to observe, typical stages of professional development and professional development programs, organization to achieve desired results, program delivery, and leadership.

Induction of New Teachers

Perhaps no aspect of teacher preparation and retention is so neglected in the typical school district in this country as is the induction of new teachers, and it tends to be even more neglected in rural schools (Brulle & Allred, 1991; Lemke, 1989, 1991). Skilled craftsmen are required to go through an extended period of apprenticeship before they are allowed to work independently. Medical doctors complete at least 3 years of residency programs under the close supervision of experienced doctors, during which time they gradually assume the responsibility and independence of a licensed doctor. Lawyers go through clerkships to gain experience and guidance. What do most school districts do for those fresh graduates of teacher education programs? In most cases, very little, in spite of the fact that their basic training to obtain a baccalaureate degree and a teaching license generally requires no more than a part-time experience for one semester in a classroom situation under the direct supervision and guidance of experienced teachers. We should not be surprised that so many of our beginning teachers quit after 1 year.

Most of the studies and recommendations about teacher preparation that have come out since the 1940s have included something about helping beginning teachers. One of the more recent ones, sponsored by the Education Commission of the States, makes the induction period the subject of one of its major recommendations (Frazier, 1993):

The State should see the beginning teacher's induction period as an integral part of the teacher preparation sequence. The state should express its expectation that the same collaborative effort involving arts and sciences faculty, pedagogical experts and school district personnel begun in the early stages of the teacher preparation program be continued through at least the first year of teaching. (p. 19)

Frazier (1993) and others further propose that an induction experience should include provisions such as:

1. Opportunities for acquiring additional knowledge (both academic and pedagogical) and instructional skill
2. Mentoring by one or more experienced and skillful colleagues
3. Seminars and group discussions by beginning teachers, led by mentors and/or other experienced teachers
4. Visits and supplementary instruction by educators who were involved in the initial preparation program
5. Opportunities for developing attitudes that foster effective teaching and community membership

6. Assistance with recognizing the effects of isolation and how to help students overcome them
7. Assistance with compensating for disadvantages found in rural schools and for making the most of their natural advantages
8. Assistance with becoming integrated into the school district and the community
9. Requirement by the state that full certification be withheld until the new teacher has completed 1 to 3 years of successful teaching under the guidance of mentor teachers
10. Requirement by the state that first-year teachers undergo more extensive evaluation and professional development than successful experienced teachers

These recommendations apply to teachers in most settings. Appropriate adaptations are needed for special circumstances, such as those existing in rural schools, as described.

Through whatever means may be utilized to help them during their first years of teaching, teachers must develop a sense of professional efficacy related to student achievement. Nurturing this sense of efficacy requires getting involved in the planning process, fostering a sense of openness and collaboration with other teachers and with administrators and parents (Matthes, 1987; Stone, 1990).

Principles of Effective Professional Development for Rural Teachers

Many of the specifics of effective professional development efforts for rural teachers vary, but the guiding principles for those efforts are well established in the general literature on professional development of teachers and the small amount of literature available that deals specifically with rural teachers. They do not all apply to every situation, but most of them are important to providing good education in rural schools. The following listing comes from a variety of sources and includes those that seem to be most important. Some adaptations are needed, consistent with the special needs of rural schools and their communities, as discussed (Campbell 1985; Frazier, 1993; Helge, 1985; Reece, 1984, Searl, Rand, & Struck, 1991; Vaughan, Foster, Morris, & Bernal, 1990):

1. The district and school mission and goals statements must form the basis for planning and implementing teacher professional development.
2. Beginning teachers should be given only temporary certification to teach. Recertification requirements should be related to individual teacher needs and to individual school needs.
3. Individual teacher needs must be determined on the basis of regular evaluation procedures that focus on specific teacher behaviors.
4. Teachers with similar needs and interests should work together to improve their professional skills.
5. Rural cultural issues must be a significant part of rural teacher professional development.
6. Professional development must emphasize the student diversity that rural teachers encounter.

7. Much attention must be given to improving skills in organizing classes and materials appropriate to the wide range of student abilities and interests and the multiple teaching responsibilities faced by rural teachers.
8. Teachers must be directly involved and make the major decisions relative to curriculum development.
9. Frequent observation of teachers in the classroom should be performed by more than one supervisor or teacher colleague.
10. Adequate training and time are available for teachers to work collaboratively, using clinical supervision and coaching procedures.
11. A variety of resources are used in professional development, including the community itself, nonprofessional staff, business and industry, and shared teaching activities.
12. Distinctive staff development needs include obtaining specialized teaching resources, mastering the use of applicable technology, integrating rural-focused content into the curriculum and the classroom, securing funding, involving the community, relating to parents, peers, and community members, and meeting the needs of special students.
13. Both short-term and long-term needs must be addressed in planning and implementing professional development.
14. There must be adequate incentive in the form of monetary support for special training, provision of time during the normal workday, professional recognition, and increased pay.
15. Both teachers and administrators need training in planning, directing, and implementing in-service programs.

Stages of Staff Development in Rural Schools

Although there is no magic formula to follow to achieve effective staff development in rural schools, it has been well established that there are some general stages that characterize good programs (Sly, Everett, McQuarrie, & Wood, 1990; Wood & Kleine, 1987). Most current research does not differentiate between city and rural schools, and it seems that these stages would apply to both (Wood & Kleine, 1987).

The five stages of staff development identified through the work of Wood, Thompson, & Russell (1981) are widely accepted. They are arranged in sequential, cyclical stages and may be briefly described as follows:

Stage I, Readiness, emphasizes selection and understanding of, and commitment to, new behaviors by a school staff or group of educators. In Stage II, Planning, the specific plans for an inservice program (to be implemented over three to five years) are developed to achieve the desired changes or professional practices selected in Stage I. In the Training Stage, III, the plans are translated into practice. The Implementation Stage, IV, focuses on insuring professional behavior of teachers and administrators in their own work setting. Stage V, Maintenance, begins as new behaviors are integrated into daily practice. The aim of this final stage is to ensure that once a change in performance is operational, it will continue over time. (Wood et al., 1981, p. 64)

There is some evidence that these stages are appropriate for use in rural schools (Sly et al., 1990). Within the five stages of Readiness, Planning, Training, Implementation, and Maintenance, 38 practices were subjected to review by Oklahoma rural school administrators, staff development committee chairs, and classroom teachers to examine their perceived degree of use and the degree to which the practices were valued:

The Oklahoma rural school personnel surveyed indicated that the level of implementation of these practices was higher in the Readiness and the Planning stages than in the Training, Implementation and the Maintenance stages. With the exception of four practices the principals indicated higher implementation of the practices than did the teachers. (Sly et al., 1990, p. 12)

The item that received the highest perception of use was "The school has a written list of goals for the improvement of school programs during the next three to five years." The lowest was "The leaders of staff development activities visit the job setting, when needed, to help the inservice participants refine or review previous learning" (pp. 12–16). The mean response relative to implementation of the practices was 59%.

The responses concerning to what extent the practices should be employed when planning and implementing staff development in rural schools were consistently positive for all of the practices included in the survey (Sly et al., 1990, p. 17).

The responses from administrators and teachers differed somewhat relative to both the value and use of the various professional development practices. The general tendency seemed to be that the administrators favored and perceived more use for practices that placed more responsibility and influence with the administrators, and the teachers leaned toward more teacher involvement and influence. This was consistent with conclusions that teachers had little or no involvement in many aspects of staff development. An additional disturbing finding was that two thirds of the teachers indicated that practices such as peer support, small-group learning, and experiential learning were not employed in their staff development, even though over two thirds of them stated that these practices should be included in staff development training (Sly et al., 1990, pp. 17–18).

Conclusions drawn from the Oklahoma study are probably very similar to those that would result from similar studies of rural schools in other states. Schools have long-range improvement goals to guide staff development, but objectives have not been written and specific activities have not been planned:

This seems to suggest that districts are taking care of the long-range abstract steps related to staff development (establishing goals), but are not attending to the long-range concrete steps (writing specific objectives and planning specific activities). By doing this, these schools appear to be aborting their staff development efforts before there is a chance for success. (Sly et al., 1990, p. 18)

Organization and Delivery

The purposes and principles for effective staff development are basically the same for all schools. However, with distance and resource availability providing major challenges, significant adjustments must be made in rural areas relative to organization and delivery of these programs. Three categories encompass the more common efforts—collaboration of various kinds, use of technology for distance learning, and arrangements for advanced formal study.

Collaboration facilitates the use of the expertise available in the area for the joint benefit of several schools or school districts. This expertise may exist in nearby university staff, regional service centers, "institutes" or "centers" organized to encourage collaboration, or local leadership teams of various kinds.

Universities have traditionally waited for students to come to the campus for formal coursework. This practice does not encourage most rural teachers to benefit from the expertise available on university campuses, because they often are not required to seek additional formal education and they do not see enough benefit to justify the cost, time, or effort. Examples from universities that have decided to reach out to rural areas with special programs for rural teacher in-service training show that these programs have multiple benefits, for both the rural teachers and the university faculty members who broaden their vision and skills by getting out in "the real world" of rural schools (Gray, 1989; Knapczyk, Rodes, Brush, Champion, & Hubbard, 1991; Martinez & Mossman, 1989).

Regional service centers, most of which receive funding from the state, provide a variety of training opportunities for rural school personnel. This is done by staff from the service center or by teachers and administrators from local schools who are selected and their work coordinated by service center staff. Less formal, "free-standing" forms of organization separate from universities and regional service centers have been formed by individual school districts and by two or more cooperating districts to develop various kinds of skill improvement experiences such as peer coaching, clinical supervision practices, and special program training. Many schools and teachers have benefited from these services, although sometimes there has been a tendency to neglect sufficient consideration of local and individual needs in selecting and providing services (Flanagan & Trueblood, 1986; Killian & Byrd, 1988; Phelps & Wright, 1986).

Technology, used in various forms of "distance learning" projects, provides a new and attractive form of professional development for rural teachers. It may be, in fact, that there is a tendency to overlook other more traditional ways of providing these services because of the "space age" aura that tends to surround modern technology. Earlier efforts (primarily by means of satellite transmission) were sometimes disappointing because of the natural limitations imposed by less than true two-way audio and video capabilities, the difficulty of matching individual needs, and technical problems. Current technological advances in true two-way audio and video service via computers and telephone lines seem to open a vastly improved opportunity for both teaching and professional development in rural areas (Barker, 1991; Beckner & Barker, 1994; Borchers, Shroyer, & Enochs, 1992; Knapczyk, 1991; Stevens, 1993).

More formal and traditional opportunities are available through university graduate courses, sometimes offered in special formats and time frames. Tuition reduction provisions and other forms of expense reduction have been effective in encouraging teachers to avail themselves of these opportunities (Dobson & Dobson, 1985; Killian & Byrd, 1988). Professional leaves continue to be a viable, although little used, option (Muse & Thomas, 1992). Recertification and advanced forms of certification requiring formal credits are proposed as an additional way to promote rural teacher professional development (Frazier, 1993).

Leadership

Leadership related to the professional development of rural schools is one of the most difficult tasks for administrators. Rural school administrators share the necessity of being generalists, responsible for a multitude of tasks, and sometimes conflicting roles. Most rural school districts are not large enough to justify or afford more than a minimum number of administrators—usually a superintendent and perhaps one principal (who also often teaches) for each school. Many times a principal will be responsible for more than one school, and even the superintendents of the smaller districts serve part-time as principals or even teachers or coaches.

The rural school superintendent is responsible for the same plethora of state and federal regulations and reports that plagues city superintendents, with very little help to meet their demands. The organization may not be as complex or the numbers as large, but the overall task is daunting, to say the least, and it makes any significant attempt at instructional or staff leadership difficult.

The principal is the building manager, personnel director, program developer, public relations director, student disciplinarian, and sometime custodian and bus driver, which leaves little time or energy for instructional or professional development leadership. In addition, the typical culture of rural communities, coupled with custom and general expectations of students, teachers, parents, and townspeople, makes it very difficult for teachers and administrators to develop the kind of rapport and working relationship that organizational research tells us is most effective today. Underneath the informal, congenial, and cooperative relationships that seem to exist between school administrators and teachers, there is typically an undercurrent of authoritarianism, top-down decision making, and basic lack of trust that is detrimental to effective staff and program development (Muse & Thomas, 1992; Nachtigal, 1992a; Schmuck & Schmuck, 1992).

SUMMARY AND RESEARCH RECOMMENDATIONS

The educational system of this country developed its roots in rural areas and small towns. The value systems and positive attitudes toward education that have grown from these roots into modern educational systems and practices still may be found in rural schools. But these schools have been largely left to tradition and to emulation of urban practices as they attempt to meet the educational needs of today's young people who live in these areas. No other minority population has had so little attention given to its unique needs and potential as have the students of our rural schools.

There is general agreement among those who study education, and particularly education in rural areas and small schools, that these schools and their students have special needs. There are different kinds of constraints, as well as similar ones, to the same extent that there are different kinds of geography, ethnicity, and culture. Socioeconomic conditions range from the most advantaged to the most disadvantaged. Population sparsity and the resulting isolation present developmental and social challenges to young people and their teachers. These challenges are quite different from those found in our cities and larger towns. Funding inequities are well documented, with differences of shameful proportions.

Relationships between the schools in rural areas and the community, and rural development in general, are important. The same is true in urban areas, but the circumstances and forces that shape effective community–school relationships and community development are vastly different, both in kind and in magnitude. Equitable and adequate school finance takes on some unique qualities, and the changing economic and social landscape affects schools and teaching both inside and outside the classroom. All of this helps determine what is required to prepare successful rural teachers.

Miller (1988) skillfully summarized the factors that develop as a result of the varied forces impacting rural life, rural schools, and rural teaching. Preparation programs for those who will teach in rural schools must give more adequate attention to these factors if the results of education in rural schools are to be as our nation and society require. His list could be expanded or revised in various ways, but it seems to describe fairly adequately the basic challenge faced by those responsible for preparing teachers for rural schools:

Classroom Factors

Classes are often made up of more than one grade level.
Often the student–teacher ratio is smaller.
Teachers typically have three to five different preparations daily.
Teachers often teach classes in areas in which they are not prepared.
Limited and/or dated equipment, instructional materials and supplies are available.
Limited informational resources for student use (media and library related) are available.
Lack of support for dealing with special needs children is common.

School Factors

Teachers are often responsible for extensive administrative, supervisory, extracurricular, and maintenance responsibilities.
Junior and senior high schools are often combined.
Limited resources, supplies, and materials are often outdated.
Teachers are more isolated from ongoing staff development.
Little or no in-service support is present.
Little professional development information is available.
Fewer defined policies (a more informal administrative style) are in evidence.
Lower salaries are paid.

Sociocultural Factors

Difficulty in finding adequate housing is common.
Difficulty in buying and selling property is common.
Private lives are more open to scrutiny.

Cultural and geographical isolation and/or cultural/linguistic isolation is in evidence.
Services such as medical and shopping may be quite distant.
High parental expectations for involvement in community activities are common.
Greater emphasis is placed on informal and personal communications.
Loneliness and difficulty fitting into an often close-knit community are common.
Adjustment to extreme weather conditions is frequent.

Organizing a teacher preparation program to provide adequately for the circumstances described may be done in various ways. Many have advocated a completely separate and distinct program, but this seems unlikely to occur in most universities. There have been more efforts to prepare rural teachers by following a plan that adjusts and adapts various parts of a standard program, and these efforts seem to have a better chance of success and longevity. A proposal by Horn et al. (1985) is typical of this program adjustment approach. They called it "the substitution/addition option."

This "substitution/addition option" maintains all basic elements of a traditional teacher education program (general education, teaching specialty, and professional education):

General Education: Use electives for courses that relate to the rural environment and substitute courses where possible, i.e., rural sociology for "introduction" to sociology, agricultural economics for "principles" of economics, etc.
Teaching Specialty: Choose more generalized or comprehensive major, i.e., social studies rather than history, physical science rather than physics, etc.; qualify for multiple teaching endorsements, with particular emphasis on unrelated areas, i.e., biology and English, a foreign language and social studies, etc.
Professional Education: Early and continuous field experiences in rural/small schools; additional field experiences during college vacation time, i.e., early January, spring break, and late May; methods courses focused on techniques for small groups, independent study, use of technology and curriculum development, using local resources; foundations courses, particularly educational sociology, including case studies of rural communities and/or independent study projects on rural community organizations and dynamics; extended resident student teaching experience in a rural community. (p. 33)

Studies to identify and recommend an agenda for rural education research and development have shown that virtually every topic discussed in this chapter is a field "ripe unto harvest" and is in dire need of further study (Barker & Stephens, 1985; Department of Education, 1991; DeYoung, 1987). Recommendations included in the Department of Education (1991) brochure, which were developed and disseminated through the collaborative efforts of the Office of Vocational and Adult Education, The Office of Educational Research and Improvement, The Office of Intergovernmental and Interagency Affairs, and the National Rural Education Association, summarized the various recommendations and research questions that have been made about the preparation of rural teachers.

• Researchers should clearly define the factors that describe and affect the rural community being studied, such as geography isolation; economy of scale; and variability in culture, economy, and social environment.

- Serious curricular concerns have been raised over needs assessment, individualized instruction, design and implementation, cooperation with private-sector development, access, and adult literacy improvement.
- Research on school and community relationships should describe the environment within which learning occurs.
- Research on rural school personnel should be focused on recruitment, retention, professional development, administration, and supervision.
- The learning outcomes achieved from each new technological advance need to be studied—individually and comparatively.
- Research should focus on the effects of school aid financial distribution formulas used by the states and the federal government, the impact of school consolidation, and issues of education standards and quality. (Department of Education, 1991)

Because of the dedication of rural teachers and administrators, supported by the relatively recent increase in efforts to understand the needs of rural education and how to better provide for those needs, good progress is evident to maximize natural advantages and to minimize disadvantages. To continue this progress successfully will require that much more attention be given to preparing teachers for the unique challenges and opportunities of teaching in rural schools. The opportunity and the hope are well stated by one of the pioneers in rural education research and development (Nachtigal, 1992a):

Given existing quality standards and our assessment procedures, rural schools are not public education's proverbial country cousin. Size is certainly not necessarily the determining factor for quality. Rural schools have strengths, which if capitalized on, can be made to compensate for perceived weaknesses which result from overlaying an urban-oriented, industrial model of schooling on rural society. In fact, freed from the constraints of this system, rural and small-town schools might well lead the way in redesigning the kinds of schools needed for the twenty-first century. (p. 69)

Those concerned with preparing our young people for a largely unknown and somewhat frightening twenty-first century place supreme importance on recruiting and preparing dedicated and competent teachers—rightfully so. In the process, we must not overlook or give inadequate attention to the special preparation requirements of those who will serve in rural America.

References

Barker, B. O. (1986, January). *Efforts to improve the preparation of teachers for rural schools.* Paper presented at the annual conference of the Southwest Educational Research Association, Houston, TX. (ERIC Document Reproduction Service No. ED 265 993)

Barker, B. O. (1991). Technological delivery systems and applications for K–12 instruction in rural schools. In A. J. De Young (Ed.), *Rural education issues and practice* (pp. 203–238). New York: Garland.

Barker, B. O., & Stephens, E. R. (1985, May). *National rural education research agenda.* Unpublished manuscript, Rural Education Association, Colorado State University, Fort Collins.

Beckner, W. E. (1983). *The case for the smaller school.* Bloomington, IN: Phi Delta Kappa Educational Foundation.

Beckner, W. E. (1987). *Effective rural schools: Where are we? Where are we going? How do we get there?* Paper presented at the National Rural Education Research Forum, Lake Placid, NY. (ERIC Document Reproduction Service No. ED 301 366)

Beckner, W. E., & Barker, B. O. (1994). *Modern use of technology in rural education.* Bloomington, IN: Phi Delta Kappa Educational Foundation.

Bloom, B. S. (1976). *Human characteristics and school learning.* New York: McGraw-Hill.

Borchers, C. A., Shroyer, M. G., & Enochs, L. G. (1992). A staff development model to encourage the use of microcomputers in science teaching in rural schools. *School Science and Mathematics, 92*(7), 384–391.

Brulle, A. R., & Allred, K. (1991). Teacher education in rural areas: A challenge for all. In M. Lee (Ed.), *Reaching our potential: Rural education in the 90's* (pp. 470–476). Conference proceedings, Rural Education Symposium, Nashville, TN. Bellingham: National Rural Development Institute, Western Washington University. (ERIC Document Reproduction Service No. ED 334 082)

Buber, M. (1958). *I and thou.* New York: Scribner.

Campbell, A. (1985, August). *Components of rural education excellence.* Paper presented at the National Rural Education Research Forum, Kansas City, MO. (ERIC Document Reproduction Service No. ED 258 783)

Carroll, S. E. (1990). *Rural education problems: Current status and future focus.* Unpublished manuscript, Louisiana College, Pineville. (ERIC Document Reproduction Service No. ED 321 935)

Choy, S. P., Bobbitt, S. A., Henke, R. R., Medrich, E. A., Horn, L. J., & Lieberman, J. (1993). *America's teachers: Profile of a profession.* Washington, DC: National Center for Education Statistics, U.S. Department of Education.

Cross, W. K., & Murphy, P. J. (1988). *A new Canadian teacher education programme for rural teachers.* Unpublished manuscript, University of Victoria, British Columbia. (ERIC Document Reproduction Service No. ED 302 377)

DeLargy, P. (Ed.). (1992, Winter). *The REAL story.* Chapel Hill, NC: REAL Enterprises, Inc.

Department of Education. (1991, May). *An agenda for research and development on rural education.* Washington, DC: U.S. Government Printing Office.

DeYoung, A. J. (1987). The status of American rural education research: An integrated review and commentary. *Review of Educational Research, 57*(2), 123–148.

Dobson, R. L., & Dobson, J. E. (1985, October). *CE/MORE: A rural staff development model.* Paper presented at the annual conference of the National Rural Education Association, Bellingham, WA. (ERIC Document Reproduction Service No. ED 279 484)

Easton, S. E. (1985, October). *Social studies and citizenship education in rural America: Process and product.* Paper presented at the National Conference on Rural Teacher Education, Bellingham, WA. (ERIC Document Reproduction Service No. ED 261 847)

Flanagan, K. R., & Trueblood, C. R. (1986, October). *Designing effective rural school staff development programs.* Paper presented at the annual conference of the National Rural Education Association, Little Rock, AR. (ERIC Document Reproduction Service No. ED 275 467)

Flexner, S. B. (Ed.). (1987). *The Random House dictionary of the English language, unabridged* (2nd ed.). New York: Random House.

Followill, R. W., & Andersen, R. J. (1991, July 15). Distance learning in the Arizona sun. *Telephony, 221,* 32–34.

Frazier, C. M. (1993). *Policy recommendations for linking teacher education to school reform.* ECS Report No. TE-93-2. Denver: Education Commission of the States.

Galbraith, M. W. (1992). Lifelong education and community. In M. W. Galbraith (Ed.), *Education in the rural American community* (pp. 3–19). Malabar, FL: Krieger.

Gray, J. B., Jr. (1989). Rural teaching effectiveness network. In *Education and the changing rural community: anticipating the 21st century.* Proceedings of the 1989 ACRES/NRSSC Symposium, Nashville, TN. (ERIC Document Reproduction Service No. ED 315 237)

Gregory, T. B., & Smith, G. R. (1987). *High schools as communities: The small school reconsidered.* Bloomington IN: Phi Delta Kappa Educational Foundation.

Guenther, J., & Weible, T. (1983). Preparing teachers for rural schools. *Research in Rural Education, 1*(2), 59–61.

Hare, D. (1991). Identifying, recruiting, selecting, inducting, and supervising rural teachers. In A. J. DeYoung (Ed.), *Rural education issues and practice* (pp. 149–175). New York: Garland.

Helge, D. (1985). *Planning staff development programs for rural teachers.* Unpublished manuscript. (ERIC Document Reproduction Service No. ED 260 874)

Hobbs, D. (1992). *The rural context for education: Adjusting the images.* In M. E. Galbraith (Ed.), *Education in the rural American community* (pp. 21–41). Malabar, FL: Krieger.

Horn, J. G., Davis, P., & Hilt, R. (1985). Importance of areas of preparation for teaching in rural/small schools. *Research in Rural Education, 3*(1), 23–29.

Hunter, M. C. (1976). *Rx improved instruction.* El Segundo, CA: TIP Publications.

Jacobson, S. L. (1986). *Administrative leadership and effective small-rural schools: A comparative case study.* Ithaca: Cornell University. (ERIC Document Reproduction Service No. ED 276 548)

Jones, B. J. (1985). *Preservice programs for teaching in a rural environment: Survey of selected states and recommendations.* Unpublished manuscript. (ERIC Document Reproduction Service No. ED 261 826)

Killian, J. E., & Byrd, D. M. (1988). A cooperative staff development model that taps the strengths of rural schools. *Journal of Staff Development, 9*(4), 34–37.

Kleinfeld, J., McDiarmid, G. W., & Parrett, W. H. (1992). *Inventive teaching: The heart of the small school.* Fairbanks: Center for Cross-Cultural Studies, University of Alaska.

Knapczyk, D. R. (1991). Collaborative teacher training using distance education and technology. In M. Lee (Ed.), *Reaching our potential: Rural education in the 90's* (pp. 804–810). Conference proceedings, Rural Education Symposium, Nashville, TN. Bellingham: National Rural Development Institute, Western Washington University. (ERIC Document Reproduction Service No. ED 342 521)

Knapczyk, D. R., Brush, T., Champion, M. A., Hubbard, L., & Rodes, P. (1992). Going the distance for staff development. *Educational Horizons, 70*(2), 88–91.

Knapczyk, D. R., Rodes, P., Brush, T., Champion, M. A., & Hubbard, L. (1991). *Improving staff development in rural communities.* Unpublished manuscript. (ERIC Document Reproduction Service No. ED 345 890)

Koury, K. A., Ludlow, B. L., & Wienke, C. (1991). A collaborative approach to on-the-job practicum supervision of rural teachers. In M. Lee (Ed.), *Reaching our potential: Rural education in the 90's* (pp. 266–270). Conference proceedings, Rural Education Symposium, Nashville, TN. Bellingham: National Rural Development Institute, Western Washington University. (ERIC Document Reproduction Service No. ED 334 082)

Lee, M. (Ed.). (1991). *Reaching our potential: Rural education in the 90's.* Conference proceedings, Rural Education Symposium, Nashville, TN. Bellingham, WA: National Rural Development Institute, Western Washington University. (ERIC Document Reproduction Service No. ED 334 082)

Lemke, J. C. (1989). Supporting beginning teachers in rural and small schools. In *Education and the changing rural community: Anticipating the 21st century.* Conference proceedings of the 1989 ACRES/NRSSC Symposium, Nashville, TN. (ERIC Document Reproduction Service No. ED 315 235)

Lemke, J. C. (1991). How to recruit and retain teachers in rural or small schools: Why administrators need to know. In M. Lee (Ed.), *Reaching our potential: Rural education in the 90's* (pp. 542–544). Conference proceedings, Rural Education Symposium, Nashville, TN. Bellingham: National Rural Development Institute, Western Washington University. (ERIC Document Reproduction Service No. ED 334 082)

Luft, V. D. (1992–1993). Teacher recruitment and retention practices in rural school districts. *The Rural Educator, 14*(2), 20–24.

Martin, R. E., Jr., & Wood, G. H. (1984). The preparation of rural teachers. *The Small School Forum, 6*(1), 27–28.

Martinez, K., & Mossman, S. (1989). A staff renewal center for rural education. *The Rural Educator, 11*(1), 23–25.

Mattes, W. A. (1987). *School effectiveness: The teacher's perspective.* Paper presented at the National Rural Education Research Forum, Lake Placid, NY. (ERIC Document Reproduction Service No. ED 301 367)

McFaul, J. (1989). *Traditional values and rural education (peasant philosophy).* Paper presented at the annual conference of the Society for the Provision of Education in Rural Australia, Canberra, Australia. (ERIC Document Reproduction Service No. ED 352 221)

Miller, B. A. (1988). *Teacher preparation for rural schools.* Portland: Northwest Regional Educational Laboratory.

Murphy, P. J. (1984). Rural schools in British Columbia. *The Rural Educator, 6*(1), 6–8.

Muse, I. D., & Thomas, G. J. (1992). Elementary education. In M. W. Galbraith (Ed.), *Education in the rural American community* (pp. 45–72). Malabar, FL: Krieger.

Nachtigal, P. M. (Ed.). (1982). *Rural education: In search of a better way.* Boulder, CO: Westview.

Nachtigal, P. M. (1992a). Rural schooling: Obsolete or harbinger of the future? *Educational Horizons, 70*(2), 66–70.

Nachtigal, P. M. (1992b). Secondary education. In M. W. Galbraith (Ed.), *Education in the rural American community* (pp. 73–89). Malabar, FL: Krieger.

Parker, R. (1985). *Rural school/small college collaboration.* Paper presented at the annual conference of the National Rural Education Association, Bellingham, WA. (ERIC Document Reproduction Service No. ED 266 910)

Pehrsson, R. S., & Mook, J. E. (1983). *A model of curriculum development in rural schools.* Unpublished manuscript. (ERIC Document Reproduction Service No. ED 230 361)

Pesek, J. G. (1993). Recruiting and retaining teachers in Pennsylvania's rural school districts. *The Rural Educator, 14*(3), 25–30.

Phelps, M. S., & Wright, J. D. (1986). *Peer coaching—A staff development strategy for rural teachers.* Unpublished manuscript. (ERIC Document Reproduction Service No. ED 277 513)

Raftery, S. R., & Mulkey, D. (Eds.). (1991). *A working regional conference: The role of education in rural community development, September 1989.* Proceedings of a conference conducted at Roanoke, VA. (ERIC Document Reproduction Service No. ED 330 536)

Reece, J. L. (1984). *Inservice needs: Perceptions of rural teachers, principals, and school board members—A nine state study.* Paper presented at the annual meeting of the American Education Research

Association, New Orleans. (ERIC Document Reproduction Service No. ED 252 332)

Robson, J., Routcliffe, P., & Fitzgerald, R. (1992). Remote schooling and information technology: Comments on a recent survey. *Education in Rural Australia, 2*(2), 33–36.

Schmuck, R. A., & Schmuck, P. A. (1992). *Small districts, big problems.* Newbury Park, CA: Corwin Press.

Searl, J., Rand, D., & Struck, J. (1991). Developing a training program for early childhood inservice personnel preparation: A rural approach. In M. Lee (Ed.), *Reaching our potential: Rural education in the 90's* (pp. 255–264). Conference proceedings, Rural Education Symposium, Nashville. Bellingham: National Rural Development Institute, Western Washington University. (ERIC Document Reproduction Service No. ED 334 082)

Sher, J. P. (1977). *Education in rural America: A reassessment of conventional wisdom.* Boulder: Westview Press.

Sly, G., Everett, R., McQuarrie, F. O., Jr., & Wood, F. H. (1990). The shadowed face of staff development: Rural schools. *Research in Rural Education, 6*(3), 11–19.

Stern, J. D. (1992). How demographic trends for the eighties affect rural and small-town schools. *Educational Horizons, 70*(2), 71–77.

Stevens, K. (1993). New communication technologies for teacher development in small rural schools. *The Rural Educator, 15*(1), 11–13.

Stone, D. (1990). *Recruiting and retaining teachers in rural schools.* Far West Laboratory Knowledge Brief. Number Four. San Francisco: Far West Laboratory for Educational Research and Development. (ERIC Document Reproduction Service No. ED 328 383)

Swick, K. (1988). Rural teachers integrate technology into early childhood education. *The Rural Educator, 10*(1), 19–23.

Templeton, C. J., & Paden, R. A. (1991). Enhancing curriculum through technology in the rural school. In M. Lee (Ed.), *Reaching our potential: Rural education in the 90's* (pp. 144–147). Conference proceedings, Rural Education symposium, Nashville. Bellingham: National Rural Development Institute, Western Washington University. (ERIC Document Reproduction Service No. ED 334 082)

Vaughan, M., Foster, D., Morris, P. B., & Bernal, J. (1990). *Patterns for country stars: Systematic staff development for rural, small schools.* Austin: Southwest Educational Development Laboratory.

Versteeg, D. (1993). The rural high school as community resource. *Educational Leadership, 50*(7), 54–55.

Wigginton, E. (1985). *Sometimes a shining moment: The Foxfire experience.* Garden City, NY: Anchor Press/Doubleday.

Williams, R. L., & Cross, W. K. (1985, October). *Early field experience: A recipe for rural teacher retention.* Paper presented at the annual National Rural and Small Schools Conference, Bellingham, WA. (ERIC Document Reproduction Service No. ED 284 700)

Withrow, F. (1990). Star schools distance learning: The promise. *Technological Horizons in Education Journal, 17,* 62–64.

Wollman, D. P. (1990–1991), Teacher recruitment and selection, *The Rural Educator, 12*(2), 24–26.

Wood, F., & Kleine, P. F. (1987, October). *Staff development research and rural schools: A critical appraisal.* Paper presented at the National Rural Education Research Forum, Lake Placid, NY. (ERIC Document Reproduction Service No. ED 301 368)

Wood, F. H., Thompson, S. R., & Russell, F. (1981). Designing effective staff development programs. In B. Dillon-Peterson (Ed.), *Staff development/organizational development* (pp. 24–64). Alexandria, VA: Association for Supervision and Curriculum Development.

·45·

INFORMATION TECHNOLOGY
AND TEACHER EDUCATION

Jerry W. Willis

UNIVERSITY OF HOUSTON

Howard D. Mehlinger

INDIANA UNIVERSITY

This review looks at the literature on the use of information technology (IT) in teacher education with an emphasis on publications since 1987. Although the literature on this topic is scattered over many sources, there is a substantial and growing base of scholarship. For this review the literature has been divided into broad categories. The following section looks at current conditions in teacher education. The section begins with a review of the available surveys on the current status of information technology in teacher education. It also considers the theoretical underpinnings of IT in teacher education. The next section looks at research and practice in the different areas of teacher education—from stand-alone educational computing courses to technology use in student teaching. The review concludes with sections on critical issues in information technology and teacher education (ITTE) and research agendas for the future.

Much of the literature on information technology and teacher education could be summarized in one sentence: Most preservice teachers know very little about effective use of technology in education and leaders believe there is a pressing need to increase substantially the amount and quality of instruction teachers receive about technology. The idea may be expressed aggressively, assertively, or in more subtle forms, but the virtually universal conclusion is that teacher education, particularly preservice, is not preparing educators to work in a technology-enriched classroom. Consider, for example, these quotes:

Educators and educational researchers consistently cite one factor as central to the full development of technology's use in the schools—the classroom teachers. (Office of Technology Assessment, 1988, p. 87)

By and large our colleges of education are doing a miserable job of preparing teachers to deal with the Information Age. (Moursund, 1989, p. 9)

The teachers now coming out of schools of education have almost zero acquaintance with computers, because very few schools of education anywhere in the world are in a position to deal with this question adequately. (Bork, 1991, p. 359)

The vast majority of today's teachers have had little or no training on how to apply computers in teaching. Recent reports suggest that only about one-third of all K–12 teachers have had even 10 hours of computer training. (Office of Technology Assessment, 1988, p. 98)

The results of work to date have been conclusive: the potential of the new information and communication technologies for improving learning and teaching will not be realised unless teachers are well trained and retrained in their pedagogical use in the classroom. . . . Yet, in only a few countries is such training a compulsory part of the teachers programme. This is a very serious problem as these teachers . . . will be, sooner or later, confronted by the need to use technologies with their students. (Organisation for Economic Co-Operation and Development, 1992)

The authors would like to express their appreciation to John Sikula and Tom Buttery for their thoughtful and useful critiques of early drafts of this chapter.

Teachers are emerging from their preservice training to become part of the problem of integrating technology into the classroom rather than part of the solution. (Lawson, 1988, p. 1)

Countries such as Sweden, France and the Netherlands have comprehensive policies [about teacher education and information technology], but in 1986 only 9 out of 24 OECD countries [OECD, 1992] included any teacher training in their programmes for introducing the new information technologies. Its importance is now recognized, but nowhere is it sufficient to meet demand or need, however. Most programmes only give teachers the basic skills in using a computer, leaving them to develop its use in the classroom. Only the Netherlands seems to have had a programme of training of headteachers and heads of departments and then rather belatedly. . . . The position of initial teacher training is even worse, with almost no thought being given to it. Even if this were corrected there remains a need for some kind of semi-permanent training function, and certainly one of [e.g., one time or local] schemes are inadequate. . . . Sadly, teacher training is often curtailed, reducing the effectiveness of any adoption of new information technologies. (McCormick, 1992, pp. 34–35)

Classrooms of today resemble their ancestors of 50 and 100 years ago much more closely than do today's hospital operating rooms, business offices, manufacturing plants, or scientific labs. . . . Despite the desire of most teachers to use computers and other interactive technologies in their teaching, most have not received sufficient or appropriate education and training to enable them to use technology effectively. (Fulton, 1989, p. 12)

Finally, perhaps the single most important factor of all: If teacher preparation programs are to offer effective training in technology utilization, university faculty must themselves understand, use, and be able to teach about technology applications. The reality is that the bulk of faculty currently engaged in teacher preparation were themselves not prepared to use technologies, nor have most kept current with technology developments. . . . For most faculty in teacher education . . . technology is a bother, a mystery, a blur, a largely incomprehensible phenomenon. (Gooler, 1989, p. 20)

If technology is to be widely used, teachers and administrators need training. Training to use technology must be a part of every entry-level teacher's preparation and should continue throughout a teacher's career so that he or she can keep abreast of developing technologies. The most effective training is accomplished within the curricular area in which the technology is to be used. (National Governors' Association, 1991, p. 37)

These quotations, drawn from the literature of several countries and written by authors in many different fields, illustrate the general conclusion that teachers need training on the use of technology in education. There is virtually universal agreement on that. There is not, however, universal agreement on *what* teachers should be taught or *how* they should be prepared. As a new, emerging field of scholarship, ITTE is influenced by, and reflective of, many trends, theories, and perspectives from the social sciences and education.

TECHNOLOGY IN TEACHER EDUCATION: CURRENT CONDITIONS

One way the current status of technology in teacher education can be approached is through analysis of the surveys of current

practice that have been published. A second is through an analysis of the theoretical frameworks that guide practice today. Both approaches are used here.

Surveys of Current Practice and Conditions

A number of surveys have been conducted since the mid-1980s on various aspects of technology and education. The surveys of current school practices by Becker (1984, 1984–1985) at Johns Hopkins University, for example, are well known. The status of computer technology in K–12 schools has even been surveyed by popular computer magazines. Much of the September 1992 issue of *MacWorld* was devoted to what the editors called "America's shame—the growing national embarrassment: Our record of implementing personal computers in primary and secondary schools" (Borrel, 1992, p. 25). In a scathing series of articles *MacWorld* writers took virtually every aspect of educational computing to task. Equity issues, poor-quality software, antiquated equipment in poor repair, and outmoded models of instruction were all cited as major problems (Branscum, 1992). However, the most vociferous criticism was aimed at the federal government:

Sadly, our overall record on computer implementation in schools is perhaps most appropriately compared to the mismanagement of savings and loan associations over the last decade. No wonder government officials, school administrators, and legislators prefer to cite their public exhortations rather than the realities. (Borrell, 1992, p. 25)

Government agencies such as the Office of Education Research and Improvement (OERI) in the Department of Education were criticized for a "scandalous lack of leadership . . . regarding education and technology . . . Educators I interviewed say there is a crying need for a consistent, well-implemented, nationally-led research effort" (Branscum, 1992, p. 86). In the same issue Kondracke (1992), a senior editor for *New Republic,* was critical of the Bush administration, especially Secretary of Education Lamar Alexander and Diane Ravitch, Department of Education assistant secretary for research, for a failure to provide leadership and support for technology initiatives in education, including the training of teachers. Kondracke argued that politics had slowed, even stopped, progress in diffusing technology into the education system. That view is shared by Congressional leaders quoted in the *MacWorld* special issue:

Congressman George Brown, D-Calif., at 14 terms one of our most experienced legislators and one of the key developers of policy on technology in education, says that both [parties] seize upon this issue in an effort to secure political advantages for their party . . . preventing improvement and creating a stalemate. (Borrell, 1992, p. 26)

Studies and personnel of the Office of Technology Assessment, a support agency for the U.S. Congress, were also quoted extensively in support of the proposition that efforts to increase the use of technology in schools have fallen woefully short:

Despite good intentions, the best information, and the hopes of planners, we have at most established demonstration centers for what might be. Linda Roberts, project director of the Office of Technology Assessment (OTA) landmark study *Power On!*, confirms this. We have demonstrations of what is possible, but if you go to a typical school, you will see that we're hardly using [computers] at all. We're good at innovation, but where we fall down is [implementation] because we are not a controlled education system, like foreign educational systems. There is no similar use and implementation of technology here. (Borrell, 1992, p. 28)

Although most of the available surveys deal primarily with the use of technology in K–12 education, several have specifically addressed technology and teacher education. For example, Kennedy (1987) evaluated a selected sample of 1985 university catalogs and found that only 20% listed a course on educational computing. Handler and Pigott (1994) surveyed teacher education students in the Midwest 1 year after graduation and found that only 16% felt adequately prepared by their teacher education program to use computers as instructional tools. In an Australian study Oliver (in press) reported that 41% of recent graduates felt they were "poorly" or "very poorly" prepared to use technology in the classroom. There are also studies of attitudes, use of technology by teacher education students, and technology in teacher education programs.

Attitude Studies

The attitudes of preservice and in-service teachers have been studied far more than any other aspect of the topic. (For an analysis of scales used to study computer attitudes see Woodrow, 1991.) Attitudes certainly influence usage, but the emphasis on attitudes is not necessarily due to their importance relative to other factors. Attitudes are convenient, and the research strategies used to study them are easily implemented even when it would be very difficult or impossible to conduct other types of research.

That typical teacher education students are somewhat anxious about computers, feel unprepared to use them, but want to learn about computers is relatively well established at this point (Blythe & Nuttall, 1992; Johnson & Hoot, 1986; Lichtman, 1979; Mueller, Husband, Christou, & Sun, 1991). Some studies have reported that many teacher education students are not anxious about computers (Beers, Orzech, & Parsons, 1992; Hunt & Bohlin, 1992), but even in these studies a sizable portion of the sample does report some concern.

Relationships between attitudes and other variables have been the focus of several studies. Brownell, Zirkler, and Brownell (1991), for example, found that teacher education students see computer users in other fields as more comfortable with computers than teachers and more likely to become competent using the technology.

At San Diego State University (Mathison, 1986) most of the teacher education students (85) in a study rated computer-related skills as important, but only 10% felt that the training they received in the teacher education program was adequate. A University of Northern Iowa study (Fratianni, Decker, & Korver-Baum, 1990) found only 19% of the students in their student teaching semester felt that they were adequately prepared to use technology in their classrooms, and 67% felt that a course of educational computing should be required. An interesting

pattern of comfort levels emerged that may have significant implications for planning technology experiences in preservice programs. Although there were no gender-related differences, "students majoring in science, math, and home economics felt more comfortable using technology than those majoring in language arts, social science, music and physical education" (pp. 17, 19). "No respondents from the science, math, and home economics disciplines indicated that they were very uncomfortable with the use of technology as a teaching tool. No respondents in the language arts, social science, music and physical education disciplines indicated a very high level of comfort with the use of technology" (p. 19).

A national study reported results similar to those found in local studies. In 1987 the American Association of Colleges for Teacher Education (AACTE) conducted a survey of teacher educators and student teachers. They were asked to evaluate the effectiveness of various components of their teacher education program, including preparation in planning instruction, evaluating learning, managing classrooms, developing materials, and teaching with computers. In every category except one, at least 60% of the teacher education faculty surveyed felt that their graduates were adequately prepared. And in all except one category, the ratings of the student teachers surveyed closely approximated those of the faculty. The one area in which less than 60% of the faculty felt students were prepared was teach with computers. Only 58% of the faculty felt that students were prepared in this area. Teach with computers was also the only area where student ratings were substantially lower than faculty ratings. Only 29% of the students felt that they were prepared to teach with computers.

Teacher education studies also report that completing a course on educational computing improves attitudes toward technology in the classroom of in-service teachers (Baird, Ellis, & Kuerbis, 1989; Berger & Carlson, 1988a; Madsen & Sebastiani, 1987) and preservice teachers (Anderson, 1991; Huppert & Lazarowitz, 1991). Savenye, Davidson, and Orr (1992) found that a preservice educational computing course produced more positive attitudes and also lowered computer anxiety.

Surveys of Teacher Education Students and Novice Teachers in Schools

Davis and Coles (1992) surveyed the information technology experiences of entering teacher education students in the United Kingdom. They reported that entering students have a wide range of experiences and skills: 63% had used a computer, 86% wanted to use technology in their classrooms when they graduated, but 25% doubted they could learn to use technology effectively. Similar results were reported in another U.K. survey (Blackmore et al., 1992).

As more and more teacher education programs adopt site-based models or develop collaborative programs that involve professional development schools, the role of technology in the schools where teacher education students practice will become increasingly important. Several studies of this aspect of ITTE have been published. For example, Blackmore (1992) surveyed teacher education students at Liverpool Polytechnic concerning the computer experiences they had while completing block school experiences in their second and third year. Liverpool Polytechnic requires students to spend 100 days in a school and makes a concerted effort to place students in settings where technology is regularly used in classrooms. However, in spite of that effort only 36% of the students reported using computers with children while working in their assigned school, and much of the use was occasional or only once. Questions about confidence using the computer, personally and with children, indicated that most of the teacher education students were not confident. Access to computers was a problem in many schools as were teachers who could not effectively help because they were not confident users themselves. One interesting finding was a discrepancy between the reports by supervisors and students. Whereas 36% of the students said that they used computers while working in schools, their university supervisors said that 48% of the students were using them. This difference suggests surveys completed by someone who is not directly involved in an activity and may be overly optimistic about usage levels.

After summarizing the survey results as well as interviews with students and supervisors, Blackmore (1992) concluded:

The present survey . . . has demonstrated that for the majority of students computer access was not too much of a problem. So, if the equipment is in schools why are students not using computers whilst teaching children? Some students (and they are in a minority), have no problems using computers with children and are clearly confident to continue to do so. But what of the less confident majority? Their courses have failed to equip them with the skills, knowledge and attitudes necessary to meet the demands of the National Curriculum regarding Information Technology. This clearly is an aspect of initial teacher education which requires critical examination. (p. 55)

Blackmore ends her paper with a series of suggestions about how teacher education programs can prepare students to use technology in the classroom better.

Blackmore's observation that reports from supervisors and students did not always agree highlights the need to pay attention to the type of data used to draw conclusions about classroom use of computers. Copley's (1992b) review of the literature convincingly makes the point that even self-reports of computer use in the classroom are often higher than observed use.

In the United States Novak (1991) studied the ways in which beginning elementary teachers in Michigan used computers in their classrooms. In this qualitative study Novak used in-depth, focused interviews, classroom observations, and logs kept by the teachers. She found that these teachers, like most first-year teachers, felt overwhelmed by the demands of the classroom in their first months of work. By October or November, however, they began to use the computer in their rooms. The initial uses were not complicated. They included introducing students to the operation of the computer, word processing, and drill and practice activities. Novak felt that they selected drill and practice activities because they were similar to the "workbook" style of teaching these teachers used in other subjects. A typical pattern of computer use involved a whole-group lesson taught by the teacher with follow-up work on the computer. Even this approach was problematic because only one computer was available in the classroom and it was difficult to provide time for all the children to use it. Novak found that the teachers did not know about the many instructional strategies for using a computer for whole-group instruction and they did not know about the software packages that supported those strategies. The teachers were, in fact,

unfamiliar with most software and had difficulty in locating programs to truly meet their instructional needs. In most cases, they selected drill-and-practice programs—often weakly designed programs—which reinforced basic academic skills that the majority of the class had already mastered. (p. 266)

Novak related the problems first-year teachers had to both *what* they are taught about technology in teacher education programs and *how* they are taught. She recommended that case studies be developed for use in teacher education programs that illustrate the different ways in which technology can be integrated into the classroom. In addition, she suggested that field experiences such as student teaching include opportunities to work with experienced computer-using teachers and that developing and teaching computer-supported lessons be a requirement. Novak noted that several topics were not covered in their preservice program that would be very useful to the beginning teacher. They included educational telecommunications, coverage of the various instructional methods that can be supported by computers, and selection and evaluation of educational software. She also recommended that methods courses include more coverage of technology and that teacher education faculty "move away from the traditional lecture mode of instruction to include other methods, including those incorporating the computer" (p. 267).

Another study of how teachers use computers (Carey, 1991b) compared the behaviors of teachers in two contexts, their regular classroom and the school computer lab. Carey found that behavior patterns were essentially the same across the two contexts. In her opinion, the widely held assumption that teachers will automatically take on different roles that involve more facilitative behavior when computers are involved is not necessarily accurate.

Surveys of Teacher Education Programs

A rare type of survey research in this field is a study that looks at what is currently happening in the teacher education programs across the country relative to technology. Although this type of information would be very helpful, only a few surveys of this sort have been published. In 1986 Cobb and Horn surveyed programs that prepare special education teachers and concluded that students were not being taught about the powerful new technologies available for use in special education. Another 1986 survey (Lehman, 1986) found that only 66% of the programs preparing science teachers taught them about using computers in the teaching of science, and only 25% of the programs required students to take an educational computing course. A 1990 survey by Blythe and Nuttall (1992) of teacher educators at Chester College in England found that only a few instructors felt competent and comfortable about helping their students work with information technology in classrooms. More recently, Wetzel (1993) surveyed education faculty at a new university, Arizona State University West Campus, and found that less than 5% required students to evaluate software in the courses they taught and less than 10% demonstrated the use of educational software in their courses. A 1994 study of Florida teacher education programs (Roblyer & Barron, 1993) found that many faculty were aware of the need to increase coverage of technology in the courses they taught, but lack of time and availablity of equipment were barriers.

The lack of computer experiences and training in preservice teacher education was pointed out in the Office of Technology Assessment (OTA) study in the mid-80s. The OTA report, *Power On!* was published in 1988:

Only about one-third of all K–12 teachers have had even 10 hours of computer training, much of which was at the introduction or computer literacy level. This remains a serious problem and is reflected in the fact that, despite the presence of computers in almost all K–12 schools nationwide, only half of the nation's teachers reported ever using computers in their instruction. (p. 98)

Fulton's (1988, 1989) explications of the OTA study also emphasized the crucial nature of teacher training and offered a number of suggestions about how to integrate technology into teacher education. A similar perspective was taken by Bruder (1988, 1989) in her analysis of teacher education and technology. After analyzing an *Electronic Learning* survey and interviewing a number of teacher educators, she concluded that technology is not being incorporated into teacher education for three main reasons: (1) The curriculum is already very crowded and it is difficult to find time for technology, (2) faculty in colleges of education are resistant to the idea of incorporating technology into their areas of teaching, and (3) the competency requirements of states are many and some do not include knowledge of technology in their list.

Resources are a crucial aspect of any effort to provide instruction about technology, and Parker (1989–1990) studied the resources available in colleges of education (COE). She reported that most COE had at least a computer lab for student use and at least some educational software. It is difficult, however, to interpret Parker's data because information relating resources to the population of students was not available for most questions and no systematic effort was made to evaluate the quality of the computers available. Quantity is not always the best indicator of technology resources. A school with 150 Commodore 64 computers with cassette tape storage systems would generally be considered in worse shape than a school with 75 Macintosh Quadra systems with large hard disk drives.

Another study that looked at resources did attempt to tie the amount and type of resources to the amount and type needed. As part of a statewide effort (Michigan State Board of Education, 1988) to improve preservice technology preparation for teacher education students, Carr, Novak, and Berger (1992) surveyed the teacher education programs in Michigan that were participants in the Michigan State Board of Education's Preservice Technology Project. Surveys were completed by the institution's representative to the Preservice Technology Project. Detailed coverage of this survey is presented in the *Handbook for Preservice Technology Training* (Michigan State Board of Education, 1990). The survey asked what resources were needed to do the job as well as the resources that were available at the institution. Three major barriers to integration of tech-

nology into the preservice curriculum emerged: (1) adequate funding from the state and institution to support 2 and 3 below, (2) incentives to encourage faculty to increase their knowledge about and experience with educational technology, and (3) enough up-to-date equipment and software to serve the faculty and students in the program. The survey found many teacher education programs had less equipment and more antiquated hardware than schools in the surrounding region. A sizable increase in funding for hardware and software would be required to bring many programs up to minimally adequate levels. Similar conclusions were drawn from a U.K. survey (ITTE, 1991) of teacher education programs. The second barrier was based on the conclusion that many teacher education faculty simply do not have the background, experience, expertise, or interest to integrate technology into their courses.

Detailed analysis in the *Handbook for Preservice Technology Training* indicated that the average school/college/department of education had 29 computers available for student use and there was a significant disparity between public and private schools. Private institutions had 1 computer for every 12.5 teacher education students, whereas public programs had 1 for every 50 students. Some of the data suggested that teacher education programs at public colleges and universities received less than their proportional share of the computer funds and that funding at private colleges and universities is more in line with the size of the program relative to the size of the institution.

This survey found that 95% of the institutions offered some computer training to teacher education students and 40% required the training for at least some teacher education majors. A fourth of the institutions required it for all teacher education students. The Michigan survey also calls into question the theory that faculty who shift from typewriters to word processors will soon begin incorporating technology into their teaching. About 70% of the faculty surveyed were using technology for professional applications such as word processing, statistical analysis, or preparation of overheads for a presentation. Less than 30%, however, were using technology in the courses they taught. The problem of faculty interest and competence was cited as one reason why many programs that wanted to integrate coverage across the teacher education curriculum elected to add a stand-alone course instead. "The primary reason for adding courses on technology, rather than integrating technology into existing methods and other courses, has been the reluctance of faculty members to use new technology with students" (I-33).

A study much like the Michigan research was conducted in five upper midwestern states by Peterson (1989) for her dissertation at the University of South Dakota. Peterson mailed a survey about computers in elementary education certification programs to deans and directors of teacher education in South Dakota, North Dakota, Iowa, Nebraska, and Minnesota. Of the 93 surveys mailed 79 were completed and returned. Just over half the programs (51%) had a separate educational computing course. A more detailed analysis indicated that 65% of the public institutions had a separate course, whereas only 45% of the private schools did.

Only 27% of the respondents said that their state required a computer course for certification but a course was required by 54% of the programs, which is a bit difficult to interpret considering that only 51% reported having such a course. The seeming contradiction is explained by replies to another question that indicated that only 60% of the courses on computing were taught by education faculty. The rest were taught primarily by faculty in computer science and math departments. This suggests that deans and directors responding to this survey counted general computer literacy and perhaps even programming courses as courses for elementary education majors. The actual number of colleges and universities offering a true educational computing course may be much lower than the 51% reported.

Insufficient faculty interest was cited as a major or moderate barrier to expanding use of computers by 27% of the private schools and 55% of the public schools. In contrast, only 19% of the private and 22% of the public institutions rated lack of student interest as a moderate barrier and none reported student interest was a major problem. However, only 45% of the programs reported they considered backgrounds, interests, or experience in computer technology when recruiting new faculty, whereas 55% said that a shortage of trained faculty was a major or moderate barrier to expanding use of computers.

About 68% of the programs offered at least one in-service program on computers for faculty. However, when asked who provided the training the results showed that 65% of the training was provided by the central computer services group, computer science faculty, business faculty, or math faculty. Only 19% of the in-service training was provided by a teacher education faculty member. This pattern suggests that the topics covered were more likely to be general computer literacy or programming instead of educational computing. Data from the survey confirm that pattern. In-service training was most often provided on word processing and introduction to computers. Only 14% of the in-service provided dealt with integrating computer coverage into teacher education courses. General computer literacy, standard applications such as word processing and data bases, and programming accounted for 61% of the topics covered by in-service programs.

Although the Michigan study and the Peterson study pointed out several areas of concern, the source of the data was not a random sample of individual teacher educators. In Michigan one teacher educator at each institution, the institutional representative to a statewide task force on technology, was asked to complete the survey. Peterson mailed surveys to deans and directors of education. The use of a selected rather than random sample of teacher educators brings up the question of whether the responses reflect the reality of what is happening in teacher education. When asked to describe what is happening in an entire program, leaders may not be close enough to the "action" to answer accurately. Are needs over- or underemphasized? Are resources under- or overreported?

One way of considering these questions is to look at the results of a comprehensive survey by Leite (1990) of teacher educators in the Delaware Valley of Pennsylvania. Leite sent a survey to every teacher educator teaching a course in elementary and secondary certification programs at the 18 colleges and universities in the valley. Faculty indicated that only 21% of all teacher education courses incorporated the use of computers in any way. When asked why computers were not used, two common reasons given were that computers were not necessary in the course (29%) and computers were part of other courses (20%). Lack of access to hardware and software was listed by only 5% of the respondents, and lack of appropriate software was listed by 11%. Of the small number of courses that did use computers, 70% required use, but it was optional in the rest.

If those who reported optional use are eliminated, the percentage of courses in which computers are used would drop from 21% to 14%. In a typical program that includes 11 different teacher education courses, 14% would translate into 1.5 courses where computers are used. Leite's data indicate that in 60% of the courses that do cover topics related to computers, the time spent on the topic is between 1 to 5 hours of work. In 26% of the courses the time spent on computers is 6 to 10 hours. If we extrapolate from an average of 1.5 courses that deal with computers and select 6 hours as the typical amount of time per course spent on computers, the resulting 9 hours per student during the entire teacher education program is quite discouraging. When Leite looked at the types of computer activities used in the courses, the results were again discouraging. Individual activity was the main way in which computers were incorporated into the course (41%), followed by watching a teacher demonstration (30%). Small-group activities accounted for 23% of use, which suggests that students rarely taught lessons using technology or participated in microteaching activities that included technology.

If the responses that report that 61% to 100% of the course was computer related (suggesting that this was probably a media or educational computing course) are removed from the data, then 35% of the computer integration involved watching an instructor demonstration. Individual activities accounted for 33%, small-group activities accounted for 26% of the use, and large-group work for 7%.

The results discussed thus far from Leite's study dealt with teaching about technology in teacher education courses. She also asked about using technology to teach other topics. Of the 198 instructors who returned the survey only, 20 (10%) said they used computers to teach some of the content of the course they taught. When these 20 faculty were asked how they used computers to deliver content, 23% selected the answer option "to expand students knowledge," which is very difficult to interpret. About 17% said they used the computers for drill and practice, 16% for simulations, 14% for problem solving, and 13% for gaming. Other answers such as programming, data bases, spreadsheets, graphics, and desktop publishing were all 6% or below.

When the results of the Michigan, Peterson, and Leite studies are compared it is clear that the studies completed by one individual such as the dean or director report more encouraging data than the study that obtained data from individual faculty members. It appears that either individual faculty members answer more negatively than respondents who speak for the entire teacher education program or that the Delaware Valley of Pennsylvania is far behind Michigan and the upper Midwest in technology integration. Stowe's (1992) national survey of deans and directors also reports very optimistic replies about what is happening in technology and teacher education, a pattern that contradicts much of the research reported later in this section. This pattern suggests that upper-level administrators, and perhaps individuals who are heavily invested in technology and teacher education, may overestimate the quality and amount of coverage in the programs at their schools. That explanation is supported by Beaver's (1990) study of the computer experiences of junior and senior elementary education majors at a New York University. When asked if they had used a computer in *any* college course, 68% of the 1989 group reported that computers were not a part of any of their courses. Beaver also found, as have many other studies, that teacher education students value computers in schools and want to learn. However 53% of them rated their ability to use a computer as a productivity tool as "low" or "nonexistent." Similar results were reported in a large California survey of school uses of technology (Main & Roberts, 1990), at a regional university in Pennsylvania (Sheffield, 1994), and at several universities in the South (Huang, 1994). Only 27% of the teachers Main and Roberts surveyed reported that training in the use of technology was part of their degree work. Teacher education was cited far less often than continuing education (50%), on-the-job training (70%), and in-service training (78%). Again it appears that the closer the respondent is to the event, the more disappointing the data.

The Michigan survey of teacher education programs also conducted a survey of teacher education students nearing the end of their programs (Michigan State Board of Education, 1990). In general the results indicated that many students (64%) entered the program with some computer experience and that 92% had used a computer during their program. About a fourth of students said that they owned a computer, had positive attitudes toward computers, and planned to use computers in their classrooms when they graduated (80%). A more detailed analysis indicated that students in "this sample of preservice teachers . . . do not use the computer on a regular basis, and their primary use of it is for word processing" (p. 1-14). Only 55% of the students said they had used even one piece of educational software "in any of your college educational experiences." That figure is much lower than might be expected from the institutional report that 95% of the programs have opportunities for computer-related experiences. The survey also indicated that "most preservice teachers do not have experiences using data bases, spreadsheets, telecommunications, and educational programs" (p. 1-15). One very interesting comparison in this study involves two questions on an attitude survey. About 90% of the students agreed (that is, marked "strongly agree" or "agree") with the statement "I want more experience using computers," and 80% agreed with the statement "I intend to use computers in my teaching." However, when asked if they agreed with the statement "Most teachers use computers in their classrooms," only 16% did, and when asked whether "teacher training will prepare [them] to use computers in teaching," only 23% agreed. Teacher education students in this survey were thus very optimistic about computers in schools, but they did not see that computers were being used by practicing teachers, and they did not believe that their preservice teacher education programs were preparing them to use computers.

Although the data on any question varies from report to report, it seems clear from a consideration of all the available literature that teacher education students are not being taught to use technology in teaching and that data gathered directly from students about *their* experiences or from teacher educators about what they do in *their* courses, paints a rather bleak picture of current practices. In general, the field is still in the stage of trying to get any coverage of technology into most aspects of teacher education. The issue of quality and effectiveness has not even been addressed in most surveys because there is so little, good or bad, that is happening in the average teacher education program. Data from deans and directors and leaders are somewhat more optimistic but are probably not as accurate as information provided by students and faculty. There is, however, a major proviso to the bleak picture painted in this section. That is the date of many of the surveys. Technology is a fast-changing field, and the data for most of the major surveys reviewed in this section were gathered between 1985 and 1989. Substantial changes could have occurred since those surveys were conducted, but the results of a more recent survey at one university (Beaver, 1990) supports a negative assessment of progress to date.

The ITTE Current Status Surveys

During the 1980s one of the most influential expressions of federal interest in educational technology was the OTA's study of technology use in schools. The OTA is a branch of the U.S. Congress that conducts studies of technology for the legislature. In 1988 OTA produced *Power On! New Tools for Teaching and Learning,* which detailed the current status of technology in schools (very limited use) and suggested ways of increasing effective use of technology. It is still frequently cited in the literature. OTA found that both preservice and in-service teachers received very little training on the use of technology in classrooms and identified teacher preparation as critically important if U.S. schools are to use technology effectively. In fact, because teacher preparation is so important OTA began another Power On-style study in 1993 that focuses specifically on technology and teacher education. The OTA report was due to be published in 1995. Some of the studies commissioned by OTA for the report are already available, and one will be summarized here. Willis, Austin, and Willis (1994) completed a survey of the current status of technology in teacher education for OTA. The study included random surveys of teacher education faculty and recent teacher education graduates in the United States and the United Kingdom (under the direction of Niki Davis at Exeter University). In-depth interviews of teacher educators and K–12 school administrators were also conducted. The complete report, which is several hundred pages long, is available on the Teacher Education Internet Server, which is discussed later in this chapter. A summary of the results is provided here. Two general conclusions stand out. The first is that teacher educators generally feel that information technology is an important element of both K–12 education and teacher education. In addition, they are interested in using more technology themselves. The second general conclusion is that although teacher educators use computers for word processing and other routine tasks, very few teach with or teach about technology. The study found that teacher education programs are, on average, short on equipment and software for integrating information technology and that both faculty time and support are limited on many campuses. Where support is available it is often for routine applications such as statistical analysis and word processing rather than integration into courses and student teaching. Limited faculty knowledge and faculty anxiety were seen as barriers to wider use by many respondents.

When recent graduates were asked about their experiences they reported even lower rates of information technology integration than did faculty. The great majority said that technology was not a factor in student teaching placements, and less than one in four were required to teach even one lesson that incorporated technology. When asked to rate the preparation they received for using technology in the classroom, more than half said they were "Not prepared at all" or "Poorly prepared." About one in four said that he or she was "Minimally prepared." Only 20% said that they were "Adequately prepared," "Well prepared," or "Very well prepared."

Faculty in the United Kingdom were more likely than U.S. faculty to incorporate technology into their courses. Only 25% of the British faculty sample said they did not use information technology in any way in their courses, compared to 66% of the U.S. sample. Most of the areas where U.S. faculty seemed to be more prepared related to traditional uses such as drill and practice software and computer-managed instruction. The British faculty seemed to have better access to hardware and software, and they reported that more teacher-education-specific training was available to them. The British sample of recent teacher education graduates also reported a higher level of technology integration in their programs. Whereas 33% of the U.S. sample respondents said that they were "Not prepared at all," the corresponding British figure was 5%.

The differences between U.S. and U.K. teacher education may be related to the U.K. government's decision in the 1980s to require coverage and use of information technology in both K–12 education and teacher education. Several government initiatives and a number of regulations encourage or require information technology to be included in the teacher education curriculum (Davis, 1992). However, even though the U.K. data are more encouraging than the U.S. data, they are not exemplary. In both the United States and the United Kingdom most teacher education students do not receive extensive training on the use of technology and they do not routinely use technology in their classrooms after they graduate.

THEORETICAL PERSPECTIVES

Over the past 100 years, advocates of technology in education have marched under many different banners. In the early 1900s the museum movement, or visual education advocates, lobbied for increased use of tangible items such as photographs, illustrations, graphs, maps, and models in classrooms. The first school museum opened in St. Louis in 1905 and it had much in common with today's learning resources and media centers (Reiser, 1987). Later, between the two world wars, the term *audio visual* came into vogue as technologies for recording, transmitting, and reproducing sound and images were increasingly used in schools. Today some teacher education programs still require students to complete an "AV" course that introduces students to technical tasks such as threading a 16-mm projector,

laminating reusable print materials, and creating homemade 35-mm slides.

Since World War II the term *instructional technology* (IT) has generally replaced audiovisual education. In some cases, the evolution in terms reflects a shift in emphasis—from operating equipment to designing effective instruction. Many IT leaders felt that the tendency to equate IT with equipment was inappropriate. They urged practitioners and researchers to focus instead on theories, instructional models, and teaching strategies that enhanced instructional effectiveness. Since 1950 many IT programs have adopted this new approach to IT. Others changed the names of courses, departments, and programs but maintained the focus on equipment. The equipment versus concepts and theories focus is also reflected in the current literature on ITTE. The equipment focus began with lantern slides, maps, and pictures and progressed through film, radio, television, and programmed learning machines. Today the equipment focus is on computers, telecommunications, CD-ROMs, and laser discs. Putting the equipment of instruction in the foreground hides foundation issues that are critical to the future of technology in education and ITTE. Those issues relate to concepts and theories that guide practice.

Information technology in teacher education was not a separate field when the first of three post-1960 educational technology equipment booms occurred. Programmed instruction (PI), based on Skinner's version of behaviorism, flourished for a few years in the 1970s and then faded. During that time thousands of programmed instruction books and many models of mechanical teaching machines were sold to schools, industry, and the military. Although much of the literature during that era focused on the machines for teaching, it seems quite clear today that the machinery was being used to support a behavioral model of teaching and learning. The next boom was the personal computer. With the arrival of inexpensive personal computers in the mid-1970s, computer-assisted instruction, in its many forms, became a phenomenon in education. Between 1975 and 1985 schools gradually acquired personal computers and, even more gradually, began to use them for instruction. Most of the educational software available was tutorial or drill and practice programs based on a behavior model of learning. The major exception was the LOGO programming language, which was often taught from a Piagetian constructivist perspective. The third post-1960 equipment boom was multimedia. Equipment limitations restricted most programmed instruction and early educational computing programs to text and simple graphics. With the arrival of multimedia computers in the late 1980s the possibilities expanded exponentially. Equipment such as sound cards, music synthesizer chips, CD-ROMs, laser disk players, and video compression cards gave instructional designers many more options. Sound, video, computer graphics, animation, and virtual environments are all incorporated into instructional packages today. Some multimedia packages are based on behavioral theories and are essentially little more than teacher-centered direct instruction. However, a growing number of packages are based on different theories. Most hypermedia programs, with their nonlinear approach to creating an information landscape, use cognitive theories of learning.

Although people tend to associate educational uses of technology with the "hard" sciences, the pattern of development actually has much more in common with the "soft" sciences and with fields such as philosophy. In physics, for example, one theory tends to replace another. To cite just one example, Einstein's theory of relativity largely replaced Newtonian theories. This stands in sharp contrast to philosophy and the social sciences. The epistemological positions espoused by Plato and Aristotle, for example, are still discussed today as viable alternatives in ways that Plato's and Aristotle's theories of physics would not. Plato's concept of Truth, which involves universal, abstract *Ideas* or *Forms* that "exist in a pure realm outside everyday experience and are only imperfectly manifested in concrete individuals" (Kohl, 1992, p. 109), is quite similar to Piaget's concept of schemes, schemata, or mother structures. When Piaget proponent Seymour Papert (1988) discusses in detail Piaget's concept of "mother structures" that form the cognitive foundation for learning, much of what he advocates is quite compatible with Plato's position in *Meno,* where he suggests "we are born already in possession of knowledge of which we are not conscious but which we will readily recollect if carefully prompted" (Flew, 1984, p. 271). *Meno,* a story about an illiterate slave boy, who, when asked a series of questions, is shown to already know a foundation principle of geometry illustrates the idea of innate ideas or forms. There is much in common with Plato's questioning strategies that help the student uncover or "discover" knowledge and the concept of computer-supported "microworlds" such as LOGO that children explore and with which, in the process, they construct knowledge.

Plato has much in common with Piagetian theory and both the constructivist and constructionist approaches to technology in education (Papert, 1993), but Aristotle's thought has much in common with behavioral theories. "To be an Aristotelian is to favor the concrete . . . it is to be more concerned with gathering knowledge of actual things than with the logical unification of knowledge" (Lavine, 1984, p. 70). "Aristotle is an empiricist. His injunctions against an overly-theoretical approach are as militant as those of the 'scientific' empiricists of the 17th and 18th centuries" (Feyerabend, 1988, p. 113). For Aristotle reality was to be found in experience rather than abstract ideas or forms. Aristotle thus provides some of the foundations for an objective, behavioral science of human behavior.

Over the centuries philosophy, education, and the social sciences have more often revived and renewed old concepts than introduced new, revolutionary theories that integrate several existing theories. The results are fields where many theories, which have conflicting assumptions and explanations, compete with one another for the minds of theoreticians and practitioners alike. This also reflects, to a great extent, the current status of instructional technology. Thousands of instructional packages are offered to teachers today, from traditional tutorial software to multimedia and hypermedia packages that come on CD-ROMs and laserdiscs. Virtually every major theory of learning has been used as a guide for the development of technology-supported instruction. In the 1990s there is no single defining "core" that summarizes how technology is used in schools, no particular type of equipment that is almost always associated with use in schools, no single underlying theory that dominates the field. In one school district, multimedia computers may be put to work running powerful integrated

learning systems that are the leading edge of behaviorism. In another district the same equipment may be clustered in the back of classrooms where they support constructivist approaches to teaching and learning. And in yet another district, there may be very few computers but an abundance of laserdisc players and satellite-delivered distance education. Today there is no dominant hardware or theoretical *core* at the center of all educational uses of technology.

In this fast-changing and somewhat eclectic context, it is not surprising that approaches to preparing teachers to use IT in their classrooms varies drastically from program to program. There are differences in both *what* teacher education students are taught about information technologies as well as *how* they are taught. The variation is not, however, necessarily random or unplanned. Much of it is related to theories with ancestries that go back at least as far as the ancient Greeks.

Alternatives to traditional lecture/discussion methods to teach professional skills are important aspects of several teacher education movements. Risko (1991), for example, makes the point that leaders have since the 1960s (e.g., Sarason, Davidson, & Blatt, 1962) been critical of teacher education programs because graduates typically have difficulty connecting information learned in teacher preparation programs to information needed for evaluating and responding to problems and unexpected situations in the classroom (Risko, 1991, p. 121). She uses the term *inert* to describe formalized knowledge taught out of the context in which it will be used. Carey (1991a) addressed the same problem in her educational computing course when she reduced the university-based work by 30% in exchange for extensive observations and interactions in the classrooms of computer-using teachers.

Goodlad (1990) concluded almost 30 years after the problems were pointed out, that teacher education still does not do a very good job of preparing student teachers for the complex world of the classroom. Some new approaches to teacher education are reactions to the behaviorally oriented skills-based programs, known as competency-based teacher education, that were popular in the 1970s and early 1980s. In the competency-based approach, teachers became professionals when they demonstrated that they could give the correct answers to tests after completing modules of instruction (usually packets of readings). In this view teaching is a well-structured task with clear-cut answers or solutions to the problems and issues a teacher must handle in the classroom. The task of teacher education is to teach the answers. Within this framework computers might be put to work teaching students appropriate ways to respond to a variety of classroom situations. The classroom management and classroom discipline simulations developed at the University of Alberta (which are discussed in detail later in the chapter) are good examples of how technology can be used in a competency-based program. In one of the Alberta programs, a student watches a video from a laser disc and then selects one of several alternatives for handling a discipline problem. After the choice is made, the video shows the results of the decision and a professor comes on screen to congratulate you on making a good decision (or to explain why you have made the situation worse). This is quite different from the way technology might be used in more cognitively oriented approaches to teacher education based on the belief that teaching is a complex cognitive skill and . . . teaching, occurring in relatively ill-defined environments, requires not only knowledge about what to do but the ability to know when and how to use this information when confronted with problems and unexpected situations. (Risko, 1991, p. 121)

For many teacher educators, teaching occurs in a complex, fast-moving environment in which teachers must make decisions about ill-defined, fuzzy problems that are not susceptible to simple stimulus–solution matches (Harrington, 1992; Schön, 1991). The next generation of teachers will not, therefore, become competent practitioners by memorizing correct responses to simple classroom situations. In fact, several authors have argued that the declarative or factual knowledge that is the focus of many teacher education courses is not an appropriate foundation for professional practice.

There are clearly two broad approaches to teacher education today, one based on behavioral theories and one based on cognitive/constructivist theories. The rhetoric of the debate generally pits these two approaches against each other in an either/or fashion; however, it is likely that even if one dominates the 1990s, both will contribute fruitfully to the development of more effective teacher education programs.

Behavioral Instructional Strategies

At the bottom of the two approaches is a difference in the way teaching is perceived. The uses of technology in teacher education clearly reflect those differences. The *behaviorally* based model that views teaching as a well-defined, structured activity that can be taught as a set of skills is the foundation for a number of innovations.

One of the best examples of behaviorally based instruction (also referred to as a *technical-rational* approach) is Strang's series of studies on the use of computer simulations to teach classroom management skills (Strang, Hoffman, & Abide, 1992; Strang, Landrum, & Ulmer, 1991; Strang, Vekiari, & Tankersley, 1991). Strang's (1992) computer simulation, *Teaching Worlds,* presents student teachers with a class of 12 students who are represented on the computer screen by graphic images of their heads. The task of the teacher education student is to deliver instruction to the students and to handle any behavior problems that occur. The students can be programmed to represent many types of classes, from one in which all the students are prepared for the lesson and are well behaved, to the "class from hell" in which very few of the students are prepared and most are major discipline problems. Strang based the underlying model of this simulation on the research on classroom management and instruction. When students use instructional and management strategies judged to be effective, the class performs better. When strategies judged to be ineffective are used the performance is poorer. At the end of the simulation students can receive a printout that analyzes their performance in the simulation.

Strang's simulations are some of the best technology-supported behavioral instructional packages in teacher education, but there are a number of others. D. Willis and J. Willis (1991), for example, describe a simulation designed to teach teacher education students to administer and score an informal reading inventory (IRI). The simulation assumes that students have read the manual for the IRI and requires players to make decisions as a simulated child responds to the various elements of the test. If the student administering the IRI makes a minor error, the simulation explains the error and gives the student another chance. A major error that would upset the pupil or result in incorrect scores ends the simulation, and the player is told to restudy the IRI manual and to try the simulation again. Another simulation of teacher diagnostic work was reported by Nason (1991). He developed PRODIGY, a simulation of the task of diagnosing student errors on addition of fractions. The theoretical foundation for PRODIGY is a variant of behaviorism, systems theory that assumes that all problems are well structured and are amenable to technical-rational solutions. When students run PRODIGY, they are presented with a simulated learner who makes errors when adding fractions. They observe the simulated learner solving additional problems and then develop hypotheses about the underlying causes of the error pattern they observe. Then they give the student additional fraction problems to solve to test their hypotheses and propose a remedial program that would eliminate the underlying cause of the errors.

The simulations of Strang, Willis, and Willis and of Nason use computer graphics but not video. They have the advantage of running on inexpensive computers with modest capabilities. A number of teacher education packages based on a behavioral model take advantage of the power of video as well as the computer. One example is *Essential Teaching Skills* from Ferranti Educational Systems (1987). This is another tutorial package with supporting material on videodisc. It might better be thought of as a lecture on laserdisc supported by many good video clips from a range of classrooms. The basic format of the package involves working through a series of modules that deliver tutorial instruction on the traditional topics of teaching practice: instructional strategies such as questioning techniques, learning styles, lesson plans, classroom management, and student assessment. All the modules use a standard format. The topic is presented through an introductory video, then some computer-assisted instruction follows. Each module ends with a summary and an opportunity to practice what has been learned.

When selecting multimedia instructional materials the goal is often little more than finding a multimedia package designed for a particular course. *Essential Teaching Skills (ETS)* highlights the importance of also considering carefully both the *content* and the *instructional strategies* used by the multimedia material. The content of *ETS* will please some teacher educators and offend others. For example, the first module is on learning styles. Teacher educators who have serious doubts about the whole learning styles movement will not be impressed with the fact that about one sixth of the ETS package is devoted to learning styles. The same can be said for the material on teaching strategies and instructional approaches. It presents four teaching strategies: memory development, concept development, advance organizer, and group investigation. In fact, most of the modules clearly emphasize some theories and approaches while ignoring others.

Any effective instructional package on teaching skills will undoubtedly have to make choices, but that fact is sometimes forgotten in efforts to expose teacher education students to more educational applications of technology. Overall, the content of *ETS* will be more appealing to a teacher educator who leans toward a behavioral model. The instructional strategies used and the overall design of *ETS* also reflect a behavioral model. Students log in with their own ID, and the package keeps track of progress through the course. In an unfortunate choice of terms *ETS* provides "Forward Page Turner" and "Backward Page Turner," commands that let the students move back and forth through the material on the screen. ETS has excellent graphics and video, but it uses a traditional tutorial model of instruction.

If *ETS* is an example of traditional behavioral content and instructional strategies enhanced with multimedia, then a series of packages developed by the Instructional Technology Centre at the University of Alberta illustrate traditional behavioral content and innovative instructional strategies. The Alberta videodiscs range in price from $125 to $225 and were created between 1984 and 1991. (For additional information on the Alberta videodiscs see Campbell-Bonar & Grisdale, 1991; or contact the Instructional Technology Centre, University of Alberta, Edmonton, Alberta, Canada; Tel: (403) 492-3667.) An example of the Alberta materials is *Classroom Discipline: A Simulation*. It requires a special "level II" laserdisc player and monitor but not a computer. After a video lecture introduces the concept of classroom management, students, who can work individually or in small groups, view scenarios that depict four very common types of discipline problems (student coming in late, student refusal in class, student not completing class work, and a noisy classroom). The scenarios were taped in ninth-grade classrooms in Edmonton, Alberta.

After viewing the beginning of a problem teacher education students are presented with a set of choices. They make a choice, view the student response, and then have another opportunity to choose. The procedure of choosing a response, viewing student response, and then making another choice continues through several levels. If the teacher education students make a good choice in the beginning, the scenario unfolds in a very different way from what it does when poor choices are made. For that reason, students are encouraged to work through the simulations several times and to make different choices to see what happens. At the end of each sequence of choices the narrator comments on the choices the students have made and makes suggestions, if needed.

The simulation gives students much more of the "feel" of making management decisions in the classroom, but students can practice making those decisions in a safe environment where the world stops while they think about what to do. Most student teachers have probably wished at one time or another that they could stop the ongoing rush of activity in the classroom while they thought about what to do next. The simulation fills that chasm between reading about something and trying to practice it in a real classroom.

As with the other packages from the University of Alberta this is a Level II laserdisc, which means you must use a particular type of videodisc player produced by Sony. This is a limitation because few teacher education programs have the Sony player. The Center for Information Technology in Education at the University of Houston has created software that will convert the Alberta laserdiscs to Level III, which means they can be used with any Macintosh or IBM-compatible computer that can be connected to a standard laserdisc player (Center for Information Technology in Education, 1994).

Another Alberta program is *Do I Ask Effective Questions?* The objectives relate to teaching students how to frame and ask effective questions in the classroom. Topics covered include wait time and latency, the cognitive level (à la Bloom's taxonomy) of a question, questions in direct and indirect instruction, question framing, effective feedback, and types of ineffective questioning strategies.

This package uses several instructional strategies. There are reading assignments, for example, from the 100+ pages of printed material supplied with the laserdisc. The student material can be duplicated for distribution. It can also be used as a presentation/discussion guide when material on questioning is part of a class lecture. After students work through the student guide, practice sessions based on the material require them to demonstrate mastery by paper-and-pencil tasks such as labeling teacher comments as Introduction, Instruction, Practice, or Closure or identifying student and teacher comments in terms of the lesson component they represent (such as set, modeling, guided practice, independent practice, or closure).

The material on the two-sided videodisc parallels the printed material. It includes introductory lecture material interspersed with good and bad examples of the concepts and principles covered. At many points students are asked to observe a video clip for a particular behavior such as appropriate wait time. As they work through the program students frequently view a clip and then decide whether the questioning technique used by the teacher was appropriate or not. The choice they make determines what students view next.

This package has several nice innovations. For example, some of the video clips from classrooms have two audio tracks. One track is the audio from the classroom. The other contains the teacher's comments and reflections on what is happening in the classroom.

Overall this package has much to recommend it. It is well designed, students are actively involved in several different ways, and there is flexibility in the way it can be used. It combines well-developed print materials, a good collection of overhead masters that can be used for lectures/discussions, two games that can cap the work on questioning strategies, and a two-sided laserdisc that includes several types of instructional activities. However, *Do I Ask Effective Questions?* is clearly in the mainstream of behavioral instruction with an emphasis on assessing the situation effectively and then making the appropriate response as teacher.

Another simulation, which was developed by Bosworth and Welsh (1992), is behavioral, but it is clearly a borderline product that has behavioral as well as cognitive characteristics. The simulation, *Teaching with Groups!*, requires a videodisc player and a Macintosh computer, but it takes advantage of the power of interactive video. *Teaching With Groups!* is designed for use in teacher education courses where students will learn to use a range of group methods. It fits into the behavioral category because it is based on Bandura's (1972) social learning theory and the Dreyfus and Dreyfus (1985) five-stage model of skills acquisition. Aspects of the way it is used, however, reflect cognitive models of instruction, and many of the group techniques taught emphasize student-centered learning rather than teacher-centered instruction. It covers both group leadership skills such as attending and initiating and specific group approaches such as brainstorming, small groups, and role playing. Students can view several examples of teachers using a particular group method (or doing things like building rapport in the group). They can also listen to teachers reflect on their performance in the classroom as well as the observations of experts such as supervisors.

Videodisc-based instructional packages like *Teaching With Groups!* appear to have considerable potential, but their development is not a trivial task. Two institutions, Vanderbilt University, which will be discussed later, and Cleveland State University (CSU), have developed a series of interactive videodisc programs for teacher education. At CSU Ronald Abate (1992) used an Ohio state grant to develop multimedia packages requested by teacher education faculty. His description of the development process (Abate, 1992, 1993) is an excellent guide for others considering similar projects. The CSU group developed a series of six videodisc packages that deal with different teaching strategies for reading in the elementary school. Topics include the language experience approach, using big books, and using games for language arts. All the packages share the same design. A HyperCard-like program displays options on the screen. Students can pull down menus and read about the theories that support the instructional strategy, read a short summary of the lesson demonstrated on the videodisc, and click icons to see the video that supports points made in the electronic text. They can also look at a detailed lesson plan and click icons to see video from that part of the lesson. The text students read is also hypertext. It has hot words that can be clicked for more information as well as video icons to run clips from the laserdisc. A student who wants to see how the teacher on the video closed the lesson can click an icon and immediately see that part of the lesson. The support software also includes a feature instructors can use to queue up specific segments of the video to show as they make a presentation. The software also allows instructors to create their own play list of video segments, give them a name, and then click the name to play that segment. Cleveland State faculty have also developed computer-controlled instructional video for a mathematics methods course (Atkins, 1994) and for teaching students to observe in a classroom using a special observation form (Benghiat & Abate, 1994).

To summarize, several packages have been developed within the behavioral framework for teacher education. Although they vary considerably in terms of instructional strategy, content, and type of technology used, they all have in common the assumption that teaching is a process of identifying problems clearly and applying the appropriate solutions. Teachers work in well-structured problem domains that lend themselves to preconceived solutions that have emerged from the relevant empirical research. Schön (1991) refers to this as the "technical-rational" approach to preparing professionals.

A Conceptual Error: Equating Educational Computing With Behaviorism

All the instructional programs described so far use a behavioral model (or a generally compatible theory), and it is not surprising that most of them deal with teacher behaviors for which there are generally agreed-upon right and wrong alternatives.

Although behavioral models are well represented in the literature on technology and teacher education, there is a growing body of scholarship that uses constructivist theory as a foundation. These models may, in fact, become the dominant ones in both teacher education and educational computing over this decade. During much of the 1980s behavioral theories dominated many aspects of educational computing. Tutorial as well as drill and practice programs were the result and represent a logical extension of the programmed learning movement of the 1960s and early 1970s. As color graphics, multimedia, and sound became first possible and then affordable on personal computers, developers incorporated those features into K–12 software products. The *Where Is Carmen San Diego?* series of programs from Broderbund (for more information see McCartney, 1990, and Robinson & Schonborn, 1991) is a good example of software based on behavioral principles that make good use of features such as color graphics and animation. Teacher education was also dominated by the behavioral model, often in the form of competency-based programs. This is not to say that everything was done from a behavioral perspective, however. There was work framed within other theoretical perspectives even during the heyday of behaviorally based educational computing and teacher education. LOGO, for example, which was very popular in many schools throughout the 1980s, is based on Piagetian cognitive-developmental theory.

By the end of the 1980s a cognitive revolution had gained a foothold in many colleges of education, and a significant percentage of the more innovative educational computer programs were also based on cognitive theories of teaching and learning. The face of educational software changed dramatically. Linear instruction with branches to correct errors, frames that divided information into hundreds of small bits, tell-and-test sequences, and long lists of behavioral objectives lost some of its luster. Many innovative programs today are nonlinear, use metaphors, emphasize graphic organizers, use visual representations of semantic webs, and are designed with the information landscape and cognitive load in mind. In teacher education, competency-based programs gave way to programs based on the reflective practitioner model (Schön, 1983, 1987, 1991) that makes radically different assumptions about how teachers should be prepared for their professional roles. The reflective practitioner model is a constructivist approach to teacher education that assumes that students cannot be told how to become professional educators; they must build or construct their own knowledge base, and their own professional skills, instead of being given the knowledge of someone else. Within this framework professional development occurs most effectively in environments where students can practice and then reflect on their work under the guidance of an instructor or mentor who understands the process and is a master practitioner. The goal is not to develop teachers who know all the correct answers. The classroom is not a well-structured, simple environment where preformed answers are available for every contingency. Most of the important decisions must be made on the fly in complex, unique situations that do not lend themselves to "recipes." The goal of teacher education, therefore, is to develop teachers who are in touch with what is happening in the classroom and who regularly and continuously reflect on their decisions with an eye to improving their professional practice. This approach is not accomplished by assigning readings and then assessing student mastery via objective tests, and it is not accomplished in lecture or discussion courses on theories of learning or classroom management. This difference in the context of professional practice—a well-structured environment that is amenable to technical-rational solutions versus an ill-structured environment that is full of fuzzy problems for which there are no prepared solutions—is viewed by Papert (1993) as a critical difference between behavioral and constructivist approaches to instructional technology. He describes a debate between himself and Patrick Suppes, the founder of drill-and-practice and tutorial software modes, in which Suppes says he "would rather be precisely wrong than vaguely right" (p. 167).

Constructivist models have emerged from the work of developmental theorists such as Piaget (1970) and Vygotsky (Moll, 1992; Vygotsky, 1978, 1987; Wertsch, 1985). There are, however, three major strands of the cognitive or constructivist perspective. One strand might be called cognitive-constructivist and adopts the epistemology of Piaget as a foundation for practice. In this theory children construct their own knowledge of the world through assimilation and accommodation. Within the field of educational computing, the best known cognitive-constructivist theoretician is Papert (1993) who characterizes behavioral approaches as "clean" teaching and constructivist approaches as "dirty" teaching. The contrast emphasizes the difference between approaches that isolate and break down knowledge to be learned (clean) versus approaches that are wholistic and integrative (dirty). Papert illustrated the differences between behavioral and constructivist teaching by contrasting the way Baby learned to dance in the movie *Dirty Dancing* with the traditional method:

Clean learning reduces dance to formulas describing steps, and clean learning reduces math to formulas describing procedures to manipulate symbols. The formula for the fox-trot box step is strictly analogous to the formula for adding fractions or solving equations. (Papert, 1993, p. 135)

Dirty learning, by contrast, is emotional, complex, and intertwined with the learner's social, cultural, and cognitive context.

Another cognitive psychologist, Lev Vygotsky, shares many of Piaget's assumptions about how children learn, but he places much more emphasis on the social context of learning. Piaget's cognitive theories have been used as the foundation for discovery learning models in which the teacher plays a limited role. Vygotsky's cognitive theory, which can be called social constructivism, leaves much more room for an active, involved teacher. "Psychologists such as Piaget . . . have emphasized biological maturity as an inevitable condition for learning. Vygotsky disagreed, holding that the development process was towed by the learning process and any pedagogy that did not respect this fact was sterile" (Blanck, 1992, p. 50). For Vygotsky the culture gives the child the cognitive tools needed for development. The type and quality of those tools determines, to a much greater extent than they do in Piaget's theory, the pattern and rate of development. Adults such as parents and teachers are conduits for the tools of the culture, including language. Vygotsky (1978) emphasizes his belief that learning is fundamentally a socially mediated activity. Thinking and problem-solving skills can, according to Vygotsky, be placed in three categories. Some can be performed independently by the child, and some cannot be performed even with help. Between these two extremes are skills the child can perform with help from others. Those skills are in the zone of proximal development. If a child uses these cognitive processes with the help of others such as teachers, parents, and fellow students, they will become skills that can be independently practiced. As Vygotsky put it, "What the child is able to do in collaboration today he will be able to do independently tomorrow" (1987, p. 211). Whereas an extreme interpretation of Piaget can lead to the conclusion that teachers teach best who get out of the way and let a naturally unfolding development take its natural course, Vygotsky's theory requires an active, involved teacher who is an active participant, and guide, for students.

Although Vygotsky died at the age of 37 in 1934, most of his publications did not appear in English until after 1960. Some did not even appear in Russian until the 1950s because of the Stalinist repression of intellectuals. A number of his publications are still not available in English. A number of educators have, however, reported the development of Vygotskian approaches to the use of technology. Martin (1992) applied Vygotskian theory to the use of technology in education with an emphasis on helping teachers use the technology effectively. She worked with elementary teachers who taught a science lesson developed by the researcher that linked the everyday questions of children to scientific or systematic thinking—an important concept in Vygotsky's theory. The teachers used a segment of *Voyage of the Mimi* distributed by Sunburst (for additional information see Bank Street College of Education, 1989; Colasanti & Follo, 1992; Gibbon & Hooper, 1986; and Johns, 1988), a multimedia simulation that uses laserdisc video materials. In essence, students become the crew of a ship that travels to different parts of the world on scientific expeditions. The lessons the teachers taught were videotaped and analyzed. The data showed that one critical factor in the way the lesson was taught was the teacher's own working assumptions about everyday and scientific problems. One teacher separated the two completely and led the class in separate explorations of the two, even though the goal of the lesson was to bring them together cognitively. Vygotsky's theory, which emphasizes the importance of help and guidance as students work on cognitive tasks in their zone of proximal development, is very helpful in analyzing the role of the teacher using technology-supported classrooms.

In some books, Vygotsky's theories are presented as an alternative to Piaget that puts more emphasis on the social and cultural foundations of teaching and learning (e.g., Moll, 1992). Thus Vygotsky represents social constructivism and Piaget is the foundation for cognitive constructivism. In other publications, Vygotsky is treated as another supporter of the political and economic theories of Marxism. In fact, a third variant of the cognitive alternatives to behaviorism is based on the most widely adopted form of modern Marxism. Critical theory, also known as the Frankfurt School or neo-Marxism, has been used by a number of scholars to analyze the way in which information technology is used in education. Some critical theorists who write about technology cite Vygotsky as a foundation for their work along with the work of Habermas and other members of the Frankfurt School (Geuss, 1981). Critical theory argues that all knowledge is socially and culturally contextual and must be understood as such. Knowledge or truth is thus not a reflection of some external Reality. It is, instead, a perspective developed by a particular culture, social group, or economic interest. Critical theory also argues that information technology, or technology in general, is not value free. "I see IT [information technology] as another means of production and as such it has to be viewed in the context of the political, ideological and cultural assumptions of the society that has given rise to it" (Cooley, 1992, p. 17). Technology, when introduced into education, brings with it a set of values and assumptions that, however implicit, are nevertheless influential. In this chapter this alternative to behaviorism will be referred to as *political constructivism* because it emphasizes the importance of the social and political organization of a culture. Over the past few years a number of papers have been published that analyze educational computing from the political constructivist perspective. Scott, Cole, and Engle (1992), for example, published a paper titled *Computers and Education: A Cultural Constructivist Perspective* in the AERA *Review of Research in Education*. Although there is much in this article that is inaccurate and the authors are sometimes very selective in their literature review (perhaps to make a cherished point), it does provide a very good overview of the way a sociohistorical constructivist views educational computing. The authors, who tend to prefer Vygotsky's emphasis on the social factors in cognitive development, use the term *cultural constructivist* to distinguish themselves from cognitive or Piagetian constructivists who emphasize that children learn by constructing knowledge as they interact with their environment. Scott, Cole, and Engle trace cultural constructivist models of learning to Vygotsky's (1978) brand of developmental theory, often referred to as the *cultural-historical school of psychology* or *sociohistorical psychology* (Moll, 1992) that puts a heavy emphasis on the child's interaction with adults and the culture as a source of tools that facilitate cognitive development. Using this framework Scott et al. (1992) argue that any consideration of educational computing must consider the historical and social context of use as well as the cultural implications of what is taught. The view of Scott, Cole, and Engle could also be called political constructivism and may have more solid connections to Marxist and neo-Marxist scholarship in curriculum theory and educational philosophy (Apple, 1991; Friere, 1985) than to Vygotsky. It interprets the use of technology in the schools through a filter of concern about the purpose and function of all social institutions with a particular emphasis on social class issues and questions of control and power. Scott et al. (1992), for example, begin their history of educational computing in the United States by asserting that the use of electronic computers began in the military establishment and that the military remains the most important organization promoting research in computer-based education (p. 193). They conclude that "Our own view is that one needs to be suspicious of educational technology that embodies presupposed fixed tasks and goals and a restricted range of social arrangements of a top-down, authoritarian nature" (p. 193). In their review the authors deal with many questions that also concern scholars who work from other theoretical perspectives: equity issues, gender issues, the

definition of computer literacy, differences in the type of computer experiences offered poor and well-to-do children, overblown promises that cannot possibly be fulfilled, and the undue influence of commercial vendors on school curriculum through sales of integrated learning systems.

Unfortunately, this recent review is typical of many Marxist and neo-Marxist critiques of educational technology in that it deals with genuine concerns and issues, but the effort often seems to be focused on making reality fit the perspective instead of reflecting and analyzing reality. For example, they review the use of computing in English and mathematics selectively to concentrate on drill and practice as an historically significant approach, giving somewhat less space to the other modes of interaction (p. 197). That selective review allows them to make their points much more strongly than a more balanced review would. Striebel (1991) in his influential analysis of the use of computers in education used the same general theoretical perspective (critical theory) and made many of the same mistakes.

Striebel's most serious error in analyzing computers in education is also a common one. He equates use of the equipment with the acceptance and use of one theoretical framework. To do this he limits his analysis to three ways computers can be used in education: "the drill-and-practice approach, the tutorial approach, and the simulation and programming approach" (p. 283). Then he concludes that a common framework "runs throughout the three approaches." The common framework is based on logical positivism and behavioral learning theory. All Striebel's arguments against using computers in education relate to the three uses he selected. Drill-and-practice programs "represent a very one-dimensional form of education because they restrict the goal structures, reward structures, and meaning structures of educational events to the domain of educational productivity . . . [and] therefore constitute a deterministic form of behavioral technology" (pp. 289–291). Computer-based tutorial programs "are biased against experiential learning (outside of the technological framework), quantum leaps in learning, and reflective thinking. Their value in education is therefore very limited" (p. 314). In commenting on programming and simulations Striebel believes:

> Computers tend to *legitimize* those types of knowledge that fit into their framework and delegitimize other types of knowledge. . . . Hence, computers tend to legitimize the following characteristics of knowledge . . . rule-governed order, objective systematicity, explicit clarity, non-ambiguity, non-redundancy, internal consistency, non-contradiction (i.e., logic of the excluded middle), and quantitative aspects. They also tend to legitimize deduction and induction as the only acceptable epistemological methods. . . . By way of contrast, computers tend to *delegitimize* the following characteristics of knowledge . . . emergent goals, self-constructed order, organic systematicity, connotation and tacitness, ambiguity, redundancy, dialectical rationality, simultaneity of multiple logics, and qualitative aspects. And finally, they tend to delegitimize the following epistemological methods: abduction, interpretation, intuition, introspection, and dialectical synthesis of multiple and contradictory realities. (p. 317)

Apple (1991) makes a similar argument when he concludes that:

> Currently, considerable pressure is building to have teaching and school curricula be totally prespecified and tightly controlled for the purposes

of "efficiency," "cost effectiveness," and "accountability." . . . Given these pressures, what will happen to teachers if the new technology is accepted uncritically? One of the major effects of the current (over) emphasis on computers in the classroom may be the deskilling and depowering of a considerable number of teachers. (p. 67)

The tendency to equate computer use with a behavioral approach to teaching and learning is a primary characteristic of most critiques from the philosophical left. Unfortunately, many replies to such critiques take the same tact. In replies to Striebel both Heinich (1991) and Damarin (1991) seem to accept his characterization of computers in education as drill-and-practice, tutorial, and simulation/programming. They then go on to defend in various ways the use of these three approaches. Heinich, for example, argued that drill-and-practice exercises helped him learn Chinese and that when he was in John Dewey's class the great pragmatist taught pragmatism and progressive education theory by lecture without any of the "trappings of progressive education."

In this debate one side defines educational computing as a way of imposing a behavioral model on education and argues against computers in schools because one is opposed to behavioral models. Many of the chapters in the edited book, *Understanding the New Information Technologies in Education* (Bigum & Green, 1992), take a similar tack. The other side, which is more in sympathy with behavioral approaches, argues that computers have an important role in education, in part because they support behavioral approaches to education. Neither side points out that computers are being used in many schools to support Piagetian and Vygotskian models of teaching and learning.

Ambron and Hooper's (1990) book, *Learning with Interactive Multimedia: Developing and Using Multimedia Tools in Education,* describes many educational uses of computer technology that are based on cognitive constructivist theories rather than behavioral approaches. Toomey, Mahon, and Thalathoti (1993), in fact, argue that the way teachers will use multimedia technologies will be substantially determined by their views of education. The authors note that Australia has recently begun a "reconceptualisation" of teacher education that "places a fresh emphasis on pedagogy" (p. 301). Toomey et al. (1993) divide approaches to teaching into "interventionist" and "interactionist" categories that roughly correspond to the behavioral and constructivist stands. In analyzing a series of case studies the authors suggest that the role of technology in the classroom is determined in part by the instructor's approach to teaching. They conclude that multimedia technologies are a better fit with interactionist (constructivist) teaching strategies than interventionist (behavioral) approaches.

That technology can support more than one theoretical perspective is the point of Australian teacher educators Logan and Sachs (1992):

We argue that the use of information technology (IT) in teacher education programmes can have a dual function. On the one hand, it can reinforce technicist practice by imposing the dominant educational beliefs on all students to the extent that cultural and personal differences are denied. On the other hand, IT can initiate social and cultural reflexivity so that student background and experience stand at the core of the conceptualisation and delivery of the programme. (p. 189)

Logan and Sachs (1992) go on to describe a program for integrating technology into a program to prepare teachers for rural schools that emphasizes a critical theory approach. A number of other teacher educators have also developed nonbehavioral approaches to using technology in teacher education. For example, Harrington (1992) described ways teleconferencing can be used in an educational foundations course to support and model reflection and critical analysis of issues. Martin's (1992) analysis of the way technology was integrated into the curriculum, and her analysis of the teachers' roles, used a solid Vygotskian framework. Perhaps in an effort to distinguish her application of technology from behavioral approaches, she used the term "good technology" to describe her use and concluded the multimedia aspect of the instructional package (*Voyage of the Mimi*) facilitated the teachers' efforts to integrate the package into the curriculum in ways that supported a Vygotskian perspective. She also noted that integration efforts are not inevitably successful; that is, they do not always result in instruction that matches the model promoted by the designers of the instructional material. They depend on the teacher. The *Mimi* materials could, in the hands of a teacher who takes a behavioral perspective, be used to support that approach.

To summarize, using technology in education is not equivalent to adopting a behavioral model. To characterize the situation in that manner obscures and confounds fundamental issues that should be addressed directly. In teacher education the question is not whether students are taught with and about technology; the question is how can technology support and enhance the approach to preparing teachers that you and your colleagues have adopted. The answers will be different from one group of teacher educators to another because they will work from different assumptions and theories. This perspective reflects the reality of the classroom suggested by the research of Niederhauser and Stoddart (1994) who studied the relationship between teacher's perspectives on instruction and the ways they used computers in the classroom. Using factor analysis techniques the authors found that teachers could be classified as having constructivist perspective ("computers are tools that students use in collecting, analyzing and presenting information" [p. 55]) or transmission perspective ("computers are machines that can be used to present information, give immediate reinforcement and track student progress" [p. 55]). The students of constructivist teachers were less likely to use drill-and-practice software and more likely to use word processors, graphics and design software, data bases, spreadsheets, exploration tools such as simulations and microworlds, authoring programs, and programming languages. They were also more likely to make class presentations supported by technology and to access computer bulletin boards.

Cognitive Constructivist Approaches

The constructivist perspective, which is perhaps best represented by the cognitive constructivist theory of Piaget and the social constructivist theory of Vygotsky, offers a conceptual model that has considerable appeal to many teacher educators. Within that framework, Copley (1992a) has outlined a constructivist approach to integrating technology into teacher education.

She contrasts two approaches to instruction: didactic (behavioral) and constructivist:

The didactic approach, one of information transmission, views teachers as masters of particular knowledge domains, whose job is to transmit expertise to students primarily by lectures and recitation. In the didactic class, students memorize facts and concepts of the domain, practice skills until they have mastered them, and demonstrate mastery on appropriate tests. Using the didactic perspective as a frame for a model of technology and teacher education integration, teacher educators would spend most of their time explaining kinds of software, demonstrating the use of technology in education, and training teachers to work with different types of hardware. (p. 617)

Copley's description of a constructivist approach is quite different:

The constructivist model, one of facilitating learning, views teachers as facilitators whose main function is to help students become active participants in their learning and make meaningful connections between prior knowledge, new knowledge and the processes involved in learning. The role of students from this perspective is to construct their own understandings and capabilities in carrying out challenging tasks. The most important component of instruction in the constructivist model is the modeling of the learning process. When the integration of technology and teacher education is viewed from a constructivist framework, instructors of teachers would need to model teaching and learning with technology. The instructors would design experiences that require teachers to make connections between prior knowledge, new knowledge and the processes of technology use. Furthermore, and most importantly, teachers involved in teacher education classes would be required to construct their knowledge of the subject content and technology in the role of students constructing their own understandings. (p. 681)

Copley (1992a) outlines a general constructivist model for integrating technology into teacher education and provides a detailed description of her work in math education.

The generally negative review of technology in education by Scott et al. (1992) does highlight several promising research and development projects and all of them are focused on creating computer-supported social learning environments based on cognitive theories of learning. One example of this approach is the work of the Cognition and Technology Group at Vanderbilt University. The group, which includes John Bransford, Victoria Risko, Elizabeth Goldman, Charles Kinzer, and several others, has developed a number of products based on the constructivist concept of anchored instruction:

The major goal of anchored instruction is to overcome the inert knowledge problem. We attempt to do so by creating environments that permit sustained exploration by students and teachers and enable them to understand the kinds of problems and opportunities that experts in various areas encounter and the knowledge that these experts use as tools. We also attempt to help students experience the value of exploring the same setting from multiple perspectives (e.g., as scientist or historian). (Cognition and Technology Group, 1990, p. 3)

The Vanderbilt University group is a good example of how cognitive constructivist theory can be applied to both teacher education and K–12 education. Members have been especially active in developing conceptual models as well as practical products based on a more cognitively based model of teacher education (Bransford, Franks, Vye, & Sherwood, 1989). A basic assumption of the Vanderbilt projects is that teachers cannot be *told* how to practice professionally. This assumption severely limits the role of both professional readings and lectures. As Risko (1991) put it:

College courses are dominated by ineffectual methodologies, such as lectures and use of examples that narrowly constrain representations of larger problems. . . . Too often instruction for future teachers follows a pattern in which students are simply *told* what experts know (facts) or how experts solve classroom dilemmas (procedures). Lecture-based instruction is ineffectual because it does not enable students to learn how to analyze the effects of situational and classroom contexts on a classroom teacher's choice of method. . . . Teacher education programs may be producing teachers who know *what* to do but who do not know *when* or *why* procedures are most appropriately applied. . . . Learning to translate knowledge into action may require immersing prospective teachers in problem-solving contexts that produce knowledge that interacts with the particular context and classroom situation in which the knowledge is transformed into action. (p. 123)

The Vanderbilt group has developed a number of instructional packages that reflect their assumptions about teacher education. The packages generally involve students actively in an information-rich problem-solving environment (situated cognition). Within that environment they have the opportunity to explore the problem from several perspectives and they must make many different decisions. Learning activities thus focus on a problem or situation students must deal with, but that situation provides a framework within which students have the opportunity to learn many things (anchored instruction). The Vanderbilt group has developed several "environments" that are computer-supported videodisc simulations or cases. For example, Risko (1991) and Yount, McAllister, and Risko (1991) describe a series of three videodisc-based cases used in an undergraduate course on remedial reading. Each case includes at least 30 minutes of classroom video stored on a videodisc and computer software that facilitates convenient access to the video clips. Students can explore many aspects of the cases including assessment and background information as well as performance in remedial instruction. Students access the cases through a HyperCard program that helps them locate and view the information they want. Risko believes a computer-controlled, videodisc-based case has many advantages over traditional written cases, but she views this type of instruction as a bridging activity rather than a replacement for real-world experiences. These videodisc cases cannot substitute for the vital learning that occurs during actual teaching experiences, but they have the potential for greatly enriching preteaching experiences and for helping prospective teachers develop contextual and situational knowledge needed for taking action in new settings (p. 124). Risko's use of technology introduces teacher education students to educational computing technology by modeling effective use in a teacher education course (Risko & Kinzer, 1986). This approach offers a double benefit because instruction on another topic is enhanced through the use of technology *and* students see effective use of technology modeled in their teacher education courses.

Elizabeth Goldman (Goldman & Barron, 1990) is another member of the Vanderbilt group who has developed interactive video packages for teacher education. She is concerned about the difficulty of supporting an active, inquiry-oriented approach to teacher education courses. Her work is based on the assumption that expert teachers are skilled in "predicting how students will think and err. . . . This diagnostic ability is tied to the expert's special understanding of the subject . . . and is undoubtedly derived from multiple opportunities to teach the same content. . . . A number of researchers have suggested that preservice teachers need opportunities to analyze and dissect lessons or lesson incidents presented in a case format" (Goldman & Barron, 1990). Goldman and her colleagues have developed several case-based instructional packages that help the student develop the classroom observation skills they frequently lack. The cases also deal with crucial decision making related to instructional and management activities in the classroom. Goldman's interactive cases use HyperCard stacks to control exploration of a classroom video case. One case, for example, uses a video of a preservice teacher and the supervising teacher as they teach the same fourth-grade lesson on measurement. The disk includes the preservice teacher's analysis of her lesson. The HyperCard stack provides information on research and theories related to the focus of the case. For this case the stack allows students to look at contrasts between the way the two teachers handled things like questioning techniques and directions. In one use of this case in a methods course Goldman shows students video of the preservice and experienced teachers giving directions for measuring objects at stations around the room. Then she asks them to predict what will happen. Once they have made their predictions she shows the outcome of the two sets of directions. The preservice teacher's directions confuse the children and they are not sure what to do next whereas the experienced teacher's directions produce smooth transitions from one station to another. In another context, Goldman uses the same case to illustrate and encourage self-analysis of teaching. In a comparison of math methods classes that used the videodisc cases versus classes that did not, Goldman and Barron (1990) analyzed videotapes of the students' teaching lessons. They found significant differences in favor of the video case group on four teaching performance categories: basic skills development, development of higher order cognitive and problem-solving skills, management practices, and development of positive attitudes toward mathematics.

The Vanderbilt group has also developed interactive cases on teaching fractions (Whitherspoon, Barron, & Goldman, 1991), secondary instructional methods (Randolph, Smithey, & Evertson, 1991) and elementary science instructional strategies (Marsh, Hofwolt, & Sherwood, 1991). Morgan, Rule, Salzburg, and Fodor-Davis (1991) used a similar approach to developing a videodisc program on teaching students with learning problems. At the University of Houston, Schick and Walker de Felix (1992) used the Vanderbilt model to develop materials to support training of teachers who will work with students with limited English proficiency. At Drake University, Merideth and Lotfipour (1992) developed a multimedia package named *IC Models, Interactive Computer-Based Models of Instruction,* for use in methods courses.

In their current work the Vanderbilt group, which is housed in the Peabody College of Education, has gone beyond work on individual videodisc packages that can be integrated into a methods course. They are now creating a metaphorical Peabody Professional Development School (Barron, 1993; Bowers, Barron, & Goldman, 1994), which is actually a hypermedia environment that uses a school as the metaphor for the user interface. Students see a graphical representation of the school floor plan on their computer screens, and they can explore different aspects of the school by clicking different objects on the screen. After entering the metaphorical school by signing in at the office (log in) they can, for example, go to the Demonstration Classroom and view videos of math and science lessons. They can also open a file cabinet icon in the Demonstration Classroom and view everything from pupil records to detailed lesson plans. If they move on to the Conference Room they have access to comments by Vanderbilt methods faculty. The Peabody Professional Development School is a cutting-edge attempt to create an electronic representation of "school" that can be conveniently explored by novice teacher education students. It may possibly be the forerunner of something that is still over the horizon but predictable: a virtual reality school where students can observe teachers and students as if they were right in the room with them. A virtual reality school would also allow teacher education students to take over a class themselves and try to teach "students" who exist only in the three-dimensional graphical environment of the computer system.

Although the cognitive constructivist work at Vanderbilt University is the most extensive, several other research programs use the paradigm. For example, the perspective has also been used by a group at the University of California to develop a series of hypermedia cases for courses about teaching remedial reading and writing (Reilly, Hull, & Greenleaf, 1992). The authors describe their cases as Virtual Portfolios that include collections of students' writing as well as interviews with students and teachers presented in sound-and-text formats. The Virtual Portfolios also include video clips of classroom interaction, student–teacher conferences, and individual reading and writing performances. The authors argue that technology supports the case method and that cases, which have been used for years to prepare business and law professionals, are an excellent way to develop professional teaching skills as well.

While Reilly, Hull, and Greenleaf (1992) are developing cases based on some of the same cognitive-constructivist assumptions as the Vanderbilt group, they actually represent another cognitive-constructivist movement that has had an impact on teacher education, reflective practice. Many teacher education programs, for example, have recently adopted the reflective practitioner model (Schön, 1991) that emphasizes the need to shift the instructional focus of programs away from lecture and discussion and toward experiences that more closely resemble the real world of the classroom. Yan, Anderson, and Nelson (1994) designed an E-mail system for student teachers to support reflective thinking.

Schön's theories are also part of the foundation for work at the National Center for Research on Teacher Education at Michigan State University. In a paper describing their approach to developing hypermedia instructional materials for teacher education, Lampert and Ball (1990) outlined a coherent theory of pedagogy for teacher education that emphasizes the roles technology can play. They argue that standard field experiences in regular classrooms as well as conventionally taught foundations and methods courses do not have much impact on the way novice teachers teach when they graduate. Lampert and Ball take the position that changing the way novice teachers teach requires a radical reformulation of teacher education's content, method, and setting. They conclude that teaching involves work in an ill-structured domain and the dominant pedagogy of teacher education takes neither that nor what we know about teaching adults into consideration. Teaching theories that simplify the decisions teachers make in the classroom reduce the usefulness of the information taught and make transfer difficult if not impossible. That is especially true when they are taught in a context well removed from the reality of a classroom. An alternative approach is authentic or situated instruction that deals with teaching within the context of a complex, active classroom. It is, however, difficult to place teacher education students in a real classroom where they can stop the teacher at any time and ask what that teacher was thinking before doing this or that. Real classrooms cannot be frozen in time while teacher education students discuss the current situation and predict what will happen next, or propose alternatives to dealing with the situation. However, it is just this type of situation that Lampert and Ball say is needed to allow students to "explore the terrain of teaching and learning" in the "messy contexts of real classrooms." They believe this approach "turns the conventional pedagogy of teacher education on its head" because:

Prospective teachers will learn new ways of thinking about the teaching and learning of mathematics as well as new ways to learn about practice *from* practice. By changing the ways in which knowledge about teaching and learning is produced and delivered, we hope to challenge novices to formulate ideas about good practice founded on the interplay of students' and teachers' confusion and enlightenment, boredom and engagement, communication and miscommunication. (p. 3)

This approach, which puts students in regular contact with an ongoing classroom, would be impossible without technology. With technology, however, it is quite possible. Lampert and Ball are currently developing a hypermedia-based instructional package that provides students organized access to an entire year of teaching in two mathematics classrooms via videodiscs. This work, like the work at Vanderbilt and other universities, involves heavy reliance on technology and a radical change in the underlying theories and traditional practices of teacher education. In many ways these projects attempt to bring the school classroom into the university lecture hall with the support of technology. They are also efforts to change the traditional theory first-then practice model of teacher education and bring students more frequently and more thoughtfully in contact with the classroom.

To summarize this section of the review, critical theorists (political constructivists) are correct when they say that the use of technology in education is not value neutral. They are incorrect, however, when they correlate technology use with a particular theory of learning or instruction. In teacher education, as in K–12 education, technology can be used to support instruction that expresses different theoretical frameworks. Strang's (1992) *Teaching Worlds,* for example, is clearly based on a behavioral or technical-rational model of teacher education. The Vanderbilt multimedia cases, on the other hand, were created for use in a teacher education program based on cognitive-constructivist principles. Technology does take on the theoretical values and concepts of the developers (although enterprising faculty can often adapt a package to uses the developers never considered appropriate, and any effort to increase the use of technology in teacher education should recognize that fact). A constructivist teacher educator who refuses even to consider using *Teaching Worlds* may do so because it does not fit with his or her conceptual model of what teacher education should be. The same can be said of a competency-based teacher educator who refuses to use the Vanderbilt multimedia cases on the grounds that they take too much time from other content and do not seem to increase students' knowledge enough to justify their use. The competency-based teacher educator might also object that many of the teachers on the Vanderbilt videos are not outstanding teachers; they make many mistakes and sometimes do not do the "correct" thing. The Vanderbilt group, particularly Charles Kinzer, might respond that the criticism assumes that the classroom video is to be used as examples of good practice students can emulate but that, in fact, they are cases, not examples. Cases help create a context in which students explore the concepts, issues, and problems of professional practice. As a case, the work of an imperfect teacher may provide a rich context within which to explore professional issues.

The theoretical and conceptual framework within which a teacher educator practices is the foreground on which the technological background is displayed.

INFORMATION TECHNOLOGY USES ACROSS TEACHER EDUCATION

If the theoretical perspectives of the previous section provide a clean, if oversimplified, framework for considering the roles of technology in teacher education, then this section covers the same territory in a dirty, close-to-the-ground way. It reviews the available literature on each of the major components of teacher education. There are, in fact, a great many publications that describe courses, projects, and programs that teach preservice teachers about technology. Unfortunately, much of this literature has a very short useful shelf life because the information and solutions are very situation specific. There is, however, a growing body of professional practice knowledge, as well as qualitative and quantitative research, on the use of IT in the various phases of teacher education.

The Stand-Alone Educational Computing Course

The content of stand-alone courses will be discussed later in this chapter. In this section the focus will be on organizational and management strategies for stand-alone educational computing courses. Most of the strategies that have been described are based on a behavioral model. For example, Frisbie, Harless, and Brunson (1991) described the organization of the required educational computing course at Texas Tech University that

600 students a semester complete. With only three instructors assigned to the course, the authors decided to use the Personalized System of Instruction model. They divided the course into modules students could complete independently and then receive credit for by successfully passing an objective test or, in the case of hands-on work, by handing in an assignment. Students who did not pass the test the first time could restudy the material and take another version of the test. Up to four retakes were allowed. Objective tests were administered on a VAX computer that also kept track of the student's performance. This approach, which placed a heavy emphasis on readings and hands-on assignments in the college's computer labs, probably did a very good job of teaching declarative knowledge about educational computing and the procedural knowledge of basic computer literacy. Mastery, even at a novice level, of instructional strategies that incorporate computers and related technologies, is not likely to be accomplished in such a system (and probably would not be accomplished in a methods course that had 600 students and two instructors).

With fewer students to serve and considerably more resources Troutman and White (1991) developed a model for their stand-alone course at the University of South Florida that included several innovations. Using a differentiated staffing model they divided the responsibilities for the course among a lead professor, a course administrator, a laboratory leader, and a curriculum team. They also adapted and renovated several rooms to meet the needs of different aspects of the course, and they used several grouping arrangements including large groups, small groups, and individual assignments. To reduce the instructional load on the team, some good lectures and demonstrations were captured on video and made available to students in lieu of live activities. Finally, objective assessments of student performance were computerized as were record-keeping functions.

An interesting strategy for connecting teaching with technology to learning basic computer literacy skills was reported by Frisbie (1991). In his educational computing course, which included hands-on work with Microsoft Works, students were required to use one of the Works tools (word processor, spreadsheet, data base, telecommunications program) to create an instructional product for the subject they planned to teach. The quality and inventiveness of the products developed by the students indicated they had both mastered Works and developed useful classroom tools.

Although the literature relating to educational computing courses is sparse, most of the innovations reported in the literature are clearly based on behavioral models. For those who wish to teach these courses from a constructivist or reflective practice perspective, few models or examples are available. However, Burson and Willis (1994) described the transformation of a required, multisection educational computing course for undergraduate teacher education students from a computer literacy course to one that emphasized integration of technology into the curriculum. The focus of the transformation involved reducing the number of general computer literacy requirements and replacing them with a series of microteaching activities that involve creating a lesson and then teaching a short segment that incorporates technology. Students were required to complete four microteaching activities in which they took the role

of teacher. Each student also observed or took the role of student in at least 10 more microteaching activities.

Technology and the Methods Courses

In programs where coverage of educational computing topics has been restricted to a stand-alone course, the next logical step is to begin integrating technology topics into methods courses. Papers on this topic were rare in the 1980s. Now a small but encouraging number of methods faculty are writing about their efforts to integrate technology. For example, Schmidt, Merkley, Strong, and Thompson (1994) described how a collaborative team that included technology faculty and methods faculty worked on integrating technology into the reading and language arts courses at Iowa State University.

In contrast to the literature on stand-alone computer courses, the underlying theory for methods courses integration is more likely to be constructivist. White (1991), for example, described his efforts to integrate educational applications of simulations and data bases in a social studies method course. One aspect of his integration effort requires students to develop and then microteach two lesson plans that incorporate technology. In a more recent description of the work at George Mason University, White (1994b) described a sequence of experiences that include an introductory course, technology-infused methods courses, and work with mentor teachers in professional development schools (PDS). A promising aspect of White's work is the collaboration between university faculty and PDS teachers. For example, methods faculty were paired with teachers in area schools. Half the methods faculty took advantage of this opportunity and participating teachers were paid a stipend. The result was increased coverage of technology in the methods courses. For example, a reading teacher provided opportunities for students in the language arts methods course to work with students using the *Children's Writing and Publishing Center*. In the secondary social studies methods course, a teacher discussed and demonstrated the use of data bases and interactive video. White (1994b) describes the "scheme to pair technology-able classroom teachers with methods faculty" as a "small first step" (p. 125), but it may well be an effective way of breaking down the theory/practice divide that often separates the course from classroom practice while increasing coverage of technology in the courses. Collaboration between PDS teachers and university faculty was also a critical factor in work at the University of Massachusetts–Lowell (McDevitt, 1994) that includes collaborative planning of lessons PDS teachers will teach that demonstrate pedagogical theories. The lessons are transmitted back to the university where they can be viewed by students and faculty. And, because the system provides two-way video and audio, university students and faculty can participate in discussions with the teacher. The system is also used to transmit lessons taught by student teachers back to the university. McDevitt (1994) discusses the type of research that needs to be conducted on this type of instruction in teacher education. (For a detailed analysis of the issues to consider when integrating technology into social studies methods courses see White, 1994a.)

Social studies and science methods courses were the focus of work by Ford, Whelan, Zink, and Goellner (1992). They developed model lessons that incorporated technology such as videodiscs and hypermedia software that were presented to teacher education students as demonstrations to stimulate discussion. Flake (1993), using a reflective practice model, described how she integrated reflective journal writing into a math methods course that focused on problem solving and computers.

In one of the most comprehensive efforts to integrate technology into a methods course, a University of British Columbia teacher educator, Janice Woodrow (1992, 1994), both modeled and taught students to use technology in three ways in her science methods course:

1. To support lectures (e.g., teaching materials, standard overheads and electronic nonlinear or hypermedia overheads produced as HyperCard stacks and displayed using a projection panel, lesson plans, unit plans, exams, and answer sheets)
2. To support instruction in a physics classroom (e.g., CAI software, hypermedia/multimedia programs, computer-controlled lab devices and computer simulations of lab devices and experiments)
3. As a professional tool (e.g., word processor, data base, teacher utilities)

Another comprehensive and innovative approach to integrating coverage of technology into methods courses was described by Steen and Taylor (1993), who developed the working conference approach to instruction. They have used the model at Columbia University and in Poland and Czechoslovakia to prepare teachers to use computers in mathematics education. Steen and Taylor criticize traditional educational computer training because it consists of "hardware and sofware demonstrations and a view of sample lessons" (p. 150). They believe that that type of passive training is not effective and suggest instead a *working conference* model. It involves dividing students into small groups who must thoroughly and thoughtfully evaluate a range of instructional software, demonstrate the software, and defend the evaluations to the whole group, and then create lessons involving selected software. Components of the lessons created are "taught" to the whole group, and all the lessons as well as the evaluations are duplicated and distributed to each student. Steen and Taylor's working conference model is a promising approach to moving students in methods courses from passive observation of technology to active involvement with it.

In a remedial reading methods course, French and Araujo (1991) thoroughly infused technology. Students used word processing, as well as charting/graphics programs, spreadsheets, and data base software, to complete assessment and progress reports; they used a variety of programs, including desktop publishing software in remedial work and to create custom materials, and they used a variety of educational software in their work with remedial students in the university reading center.

Videodisc technology was the basis for educational software developed by Sandra Stroot and her colleagues at Ohio State University (O'Sullivan, Stroot, Tannehill, & Chou, 1989; Stroot, Tannehill, & O'Sullivan, 1991). They developed sophisticated

computer-controlled, interactive videodisc packages to teach students how to analyze athletic performance. In a general methods course Berry (1994) used *Critical Incidents in Discipline,* a set of videodisc-based cases created by Evans, Cupp, and Kinsvatter (1987), to help preservice teachers think through and practice handling common classroom discipline problems. In an interesting research study that included both in-service and preservice teachers, Berry (1994) analyzed the approaches and perspectives used by teachers to make decisions as they progressed through the videocases. It is no surprise that experienced teachers were more successful than preservice teachers. Strang (1994) has reported many differences favoring experienced teachers in studies involving his classroom simulation. Another result reported by Berry is, however, quite interesting: "Less successful inservice teachers employed emotional and authoritarian strategies most and the less successful preservice subjects relied upon canned strategies and emotional or authoritarian evaluation of the situation" (p. 84).

An unusual approach to methods instruction was reported by Maury (1992). Early in their program all preservice elementary education students at the University of Wisconsin–Superior take a course on problem solving. The course requires students to use computers with a variety of software, including Logo-Writer. Students also spend some time teaching elementary children mathematics lessons using LogoWriter. The course thus develops some general computer literacy skills as well as concepts and hands-on practice using one type of educational software with students.

The Changing Role of Foundations Courses

In the early 1970s the purpose of many foundations courses was to deliver "facts" about the philosophical, psychological, social, and cultural foundations of education (Beyer & Zeichner, 1982; Spaulding, 1988). The foundations faculty member was, in many cases a spokesperson who represented the interests and views of both the dominant culture and the education profession (Finkelstein, 1984). That this approach to foundations fell into disfavor during the 1980s is indicated by the titles of some of the articles about these courses: Teacher Training and Educational Foundations: A Plea for Discontent (Beyer & Zeichner, 1982); What Went Wrong with the Foundations and Other Off Center Questions? (Warren, 1982); In Praise of the Anarchism to Be Found in Foundations (If You Had a Mind To) (Eisenstein, 1988); On the Eroding Foundations of Teacher Education (Sirotnik, 1990); and In Search of the Distinctive Contributions of the Social Foundations of Education to the Preparation of Teachers (Bauer, 1992). A number of articles have addressed the charge that foundations courses are irrelevant to teaching (Spaulding, 1988), have no widely accepted purpose and format (Bartos & Souter, 1982), or play only a marginal, relatively unimportant role in teacher education (Nash & Agne, 1982).

At many universities the role of the foundations course changed significantly during the 1980s. Today the purpose, content, and instructional methods in foundations courses are in flux. These courses increasingly take a critical perspective on both social and educational issues (Finkelstein, 1984) and call for students to thoughtfully consider a number of alternative perspectives on issues. The issues discussed include global perspectives (D. Johnson, 1993), racial and gender equity (Titus, 1993), multiculturalism (Marshall, 1992), feminist theory (Maher & Rathbone, 1986), world peace, and the duty of dissent (Jones-Wilson, 1986).

Although the changes in methods courses could be couched in terms of content, most are actually changes in perspective. A number of authors have criticized modernist, empirical, technical-rational approaches to foundations and have offered alternatives based on critical theory, postmodernism, or decon-structionist theory (McHoul & Luke, 1988). Beyer and Zeichner (1982) discussed the changes in terms of a move away from foundations as a neutral presentation of information needed for practice of the vocation of teaching. The shift was to a much more controversial and contentious examination of the ideological and political issues that frame education in our culture. Instead of mastering declarative or "content" information that could be evaluated on multiple-choice tests, many foundations courses now emphasize goals such as empowerment, alternative perspectives, critical thought, and reflection (Bauer, 1992).

As content, and to a greater extent, perspective, in methods courses has changed, so too have instructional strategies. Even though the instructor-centered lecture/discussion approach still dominates most foundation courses, the new perspectives often bring new approaches to instruction. Eisenstein (1988), for example, has argued for increased use of instructional methods that engage the student in both the complexities of concepts and practical implications of foundations issues. A few authors such as Griffiths and Tann (1992) recommended the creative use of media to support the new types of foundations courses. There is, however, a tendency to view technology as just one more expression of the older approaches that are being abandoned. For example, Bauer (1990) lamented that foundations of education were being ignored in the rush toward a more mechanistic, technological approach to education that influences both the way we think about education and the way we practice as professional educators. Although there are many ways in which technology can support the emerging approaches to foundations courses, very few articles have been published in this area. Instructional strategies that involve cases, simulations, and critical issues discussions can all contribute to redesigned foundations courses, and these strategies can all be supported with various forms of information technology. Video cases and computer-supported simulations, for example, may be more engaging than text-only materials (Connell, 1993). Midkiff (1991) recommends a variety of approaches, including cooperative learning activities, effective integration of video, and computer-supported instruction in foundations courses, but very little information is available on the use of these technologies in foundations courses. There are, however, a few promising reports. Strang (1992) developed a computer-based classroom simulation for his educational psychology course. At Hunter College in New York, Picciano (1993) developed a laserdisc for his social foundations course that was based on a commercial videotape about riots that occurred in New York in 1857. The goal was to help students develop an understanding of multicultural issues in an urban environment. They take the role of reporters for the *New York Daily Tribune* in 1857

and receive the assignment to write a feature article on the real causes of the riots. Resources available include a multimedia laserdisc package that includes photographs, maps, charts, eye-witness accounts, reports of the riots, and sketches of the areas where the riots occurred.

Pugh (1993) used two pieces of software, *Electronic Classroom* and *RoundTable*, to facilitate dialectical thinking ("ability to understand and reason from multiple viewpoints") in teacher education students. The course focused on two cases. One dealt with a high school English teacher who found himself in the middle of a controversy when he organized a class research project on whether the original Communion used wine or grape juice. The other case involves a first-year teacher who follows the directions of her department chair on grading policies and faces criticisms from students and parents who say she is too hard. Then, after changing to a system she developed that involves negotiations for grades, she faces complaints from other teachers. Pugh describes how students used the *Electronic Classroom* and *RoundTable* software to discuss and analyze issues and perspectives. She concluded that "the programs" facilitated the kinds of analyses and interactions that led students to practice dialectical thinking, develop a reasonably complex understanding of its principles and implications, and project applications of this concept to their own teaching" (p. 38).

Finally, in an article titled "Fostering critical reflection through technology" Harrington (1992) described the use of a structured computer conferencing system in an introductory education course. Operating within the reflective practitioner model Harrington (1991) suggests ways in which technology can contribute to the development of teachers who are critical inquirers. She recommends activities such as structured tele-conferences designed to encourage students to reflect and analyze issues, concept mapping software such as *Learning Tool,* and the computer-assisted *Diverse Perspectives Exercise* (Anderson & Bair, 1991; Bair & Anderson, 1991) that can support teacher education programs that are more cognitive, more learner centered, and more critically reflective than programs have been in the past (Harrington, 1991, p. 339). At the University of Michigan, Harrington (1992) used the computer conferencing system in her Teaching in the Elementary School course to support reflective analysis and discussion of fundamental issues in teaching. She concluded that the activity provided students with opportunities to become "aware of their own taken-for-granted assumptions, acknowledge the validity of perspectives different from their own, and reflect on the consequences of the choices they make" (p. 67). The work of Harrington, Picciano, and Strang illustrate some of the possibilities in foundations courses. There are many more, as yet untapped, opportunities for foundations faculty to harness the power of technology to support new approaches to foundations courses.

Student Teaching and Support of Practicing Teachers

Some of the ways in which technology can support teacher education as a tool rather than a topic have already been mentioned. One major use that has not been discussed is telecommunications. The pioneering work of Glen Bull and Tim Sigmon at the University of Virginia (Bull, Harris, Lloyd, & Short, 1989; Bull, Sigmon, & Shidisky, 1991) illustrates how telecommunications can be used as a link between student teachers, university faculty, and supervising teachers. The model developed at Virginia uses a distributed network of fast personal computers connected to the Internet. It supports electronic mail, conferencing, and local and international interest groups and provides access to a number of electronic databases as well as the resources available over the Internet. The Virginia model has been adopted in other states as well as other countries and is one of the more mature technologies for teacher education. Harris and Anderson (1991) provide some background on the organizational and social efforts required to establish such a network and make a number of important suggestions about the ways training and support should be provided. Bull, Cothern, and Stout (1992), in collaboration with the Consortium for School Networking (CoSN), have proposed a model for K–12 networks that would tie those networks into the National Research and Education Network (NREN) and thus make it easier for K–12 and university educators (and students) to communicate.

Telecommunications services also have been developed at a number of other colleges of education. At the University of Northern Iowa (UNI) (Waggoner, 1992; Waggoner & Switzer, 1991) an electronic mail and conferencing system connects faculty, student teachers, first-year teachers, and mentor teachers in UNI's far-flung student teaching program that covers the state. The primary goal of UNI's network and of a similar project at California State University, Long Beach (Casey, 1992), is efficient communication between students and instructors with an emphasis on communication between the university and student teaching sites around the state. Other programs have created networks, usually via Bitnet or Internet, for other purposes, including access to the resources of the Internet (Kearsley & Lynch, 1992, at George Washington University); linking novice teachers and teacher education faculty (Eskridge & Langer, 1992, at University of the Pacific); linking students in an educational computing course to practicing teachers, administrators, and elementary school students (Schneiderman, 1992, at Long Island University); serving the needs of external graduate students (Mizell, Marcus, Hesser, & Hogan, 1992, at Nova University); serving as a conduit for the exchange of information on technology and education (Wilson & Wilson, 1992); delivering a course on educational telecommunications (Schrum, 1992, at the University of Oregon); and connecting students in a methods course to elementary school students (Erickson & Mountain, 1992, at the University of Houston).

Other technologies have also been used to support student teaching. For example, faculty at LaSalle University (Bednar, Ryan, & Sweeder, 1994) created a multimodal orientation to student teaching that included a printed handbook, group presentations, and a short videotape on the professional year for teacher education students.

Using technology to support student teaching experiences is one aspect of the technology–student teaching question. Another is the amount of technology students should experience in the classrooms where they student teach. Anecdotal reports and some research (Huang, 1994; Hunt, 1994) suggest that students see very little technology in student teaching. Hunt's (1994) follow-up of students who had completed a relatively strong educational computing course found that

the impact of this coursework has not been as widespread and deeply embedded into instruction as we might like. . . . The elementary school student computer use [in classes taught by teachers who had an educational computing course] is mostly limited to wordprocessing and drill and practice software and their teachers' use of computers is typically limited to the clerical chores of teaching. (p. 40)

Hunt made three recommendations for improving the technology-related coursework preservice teachers complete: (1) discuss the issues related to managing a classroom that has technology, (2) visit model K–12 classrooms (in person or through videotapes) where computers are being used for more than drill and practice, and (3) include activities in which teacher education students envision themselves using technology in the classroom. Even with these changes, however, Hunt does not believe that separate courses will produce computerusing teachers:

Seeing technology used in a single course in educational computing, or even with several university courses, is not sufficient for preparing teachers to effectively use information technologies. Students must have many models of effective technology use, and they typically do not see advanced technologies used in their own K–12 education or in their postsecondary experience. The sites selected for preservice field experiences must give students multiple opportunities to observe and practice teaching with technology. (p. 41)

Efforts to Integrate Technology Coverage Across the Curriculum

Most teacher educators agree that a stand-alone "technology for teachers" course is of limited value if it is isolated from the rest of the teacher education curriculum. Some believe that the stand-alone course should be eliminated in favor of integration across the entire curriculum (Callister & Burbles, 1990) because the approach does not model how technology should be used in education. Others argue that a "fundamentals" course can be the foundation for integration in other courses (Downs, 1992; Wetzel, 1993). Regardless of the perspective on introductory courses, most experts agree that more is needed. Unless students see the use of technology modeled in their other courses, unless they have an opportunity to make the connection between technology and instruction in the subject or level they will teach, unless they have an opportunity to see effective use of technology modeled by teachers in classrooms and have an opportunity to use it themselves under the guidance and mentorship of experienced practitioners, they are likely to graduate with limited professional skills in this area and harbor a questionable attitude toward the use of technology in education (Collis, 1994; Wetzel, 1993; White, 1994b). In an interesting study of teacher education graduates 1 year after graduation, Handler and Pigott (1994) found that "students who felt prepared [to use technology in the classroom] reported more experiences in their methods classes and during student teaching" (p. 2). Of the teachers who felt "prepared" to use technology in the classroom 58% had at least one methods course where an instructor modeled the use of computers compared to only 27% of the teachers who felt unprepared.

Every teacher who felt prepared had evaluated software in a methods course compared to 69% of the unprepared group. The percentages reported by prepared and unprepared teachers for several other types of experiences were also quite different (pp. 9–10): often or consistently observed the computer or other technology used in instructional settings during their preclinical experience: 46% versus 18%; had a chance to use the computer in an instructional setting during preclinical experiences: 39% versus 7%; observed the computer used often or consistently during student teaching: 52% versus 31%. Few in either group had an opportunity to use technology themselves in their student teaching: 39% versus 23%.

The research reported by Handler and Pigott strongly supports the position of Wetzel (1993) and Hess (1992) who argued that we must integrate technology across the entire teacher education curriculum to be effective. "We cannot assume that the mere presentation or demonstration of technology-related instruction by a Techie will be sufficient" (Hess, 1992, p. 147). However, Collis (1994) believes that the separate histories of teacher education and educational technology present a barrier. She summed up the current state of affairs this way: "The majority of teacher education makes little or no reference to computer related technology, and . . . much computer related teacher education is stimulated and delivered by persons without an academic background in teacher education" (p. 8). Collis points out that the educational technology profession emerged during and after World War II. Since then educational technology and teacher education have generally been "proceeding in isolated and parallel paths" (p. 11). The emergence of educational computing in the 1960s and 1970s generally followed this pattern. As other fields such as business, health care, and the government enthusiastically adopted computer technologies, it would have been logical for both practicing teachers and teacher educators to develop computer-based approaches to instruction. However, in her analysis of the situation since the mid-1960s, Collis points out that the tidal wave of interest in "computers in education" was "generally launched by persons and pressures outside the mainstream of teacher education, with little or no reference to the existing educational technology or teacher education communities" (p. 13). Even when plans involved teacher training initiatives, "teacher educators were not typically among the major architects of the composite national plans" (p. 13). Collis points out that teacher education has generally adapted to pressures to use technologies by making room in the curriculum for separate courses. Today some programs have an audiovisual course and an educational computing course, each taught by a different specialist. With the emergence of multimedia technologies and educational telecommunications in the 1990s, the traditional response could be new "Multimedia and HyperMedia in Education" and "Educational Telecommunications" courses each taught by yet another specialist. Collis points out that there is a finite limit to the number of additional courses that can be added to the curriculum and suggests that all the professionals involved— teacher educators, educational technologists, multimedia specialists, and educational computing experts—should work toward "better integration of computer related teacher education with more general courses in mainstream teacher education" (p. 21). Fortunately, a number of teacher educators have recog-

nized this problem and have made some progress. Some approaches represent evolutionary variations on the stand-alone course, and others are revolutionary approaches to diffusing technology across the teacher education curriculum.

One evolutionary approach was reported by Kelly, Harris, and Shelton (1990). At California State University, Fresno, they decided that a single course that covered the same material, regardless of the level or subject area the students planned to teach, was not effective. Instead they developed a course for each of the three certification areas offered at the university: early childhood, elementary, and secondary education. All of the courses covered core content topics such as curricular integration, creating individual education plans with a word processor, and equity, ethics, and legal issues related to computer use. However, even those topics are dealt with in the context of the level the students will teach. Beyond those basics the courses deal with content related to the students' teaching area. Early childhood education students, for example, might look at ways programs like *Bank Street Storybook* (for more information, see ICCE, 1985) and *Gertrude's Secrets* (for more information, see ICCE, 1985) can be used in language arts, science, or social studies experiences. Secondary students might look at ways of using desktop publishing programs and social studies or science simulations such as *Immigrant* (for more information, see Hoelscher, 1988; Morrison & Walters, 1985) or *Odell Lake* (for more information, see NWREL, 1982). Downs (1992) described a similar effort to customize the standard educational computing course for early childhood majors at Georgia Southern University, as did Dunn and Ridgway (1994) in England. Brownell and Brownell (1994) also divided the traditional educational computer course at the Bowling Green State University into elementary and secondary education courses.

Customizing educational computing courses is certainly an improvement over standard one-size-fits-all courses, but several authors (Bitter & Yohe, 1989; Bruder 1989) have argued that integration across the teacher education curriculum is necessary. Bitter and Yohe (1989) presented a general outline for permeation across the curriculum. Few would disagree that this is needed, but the sparse number of reports that describe successful efforts to do that is an indication of just how difficult that task is. Several papers, however, have been published on this topic. Nelson, Andris, and Keefe (1991), for example, described initial efforts at integration at Southern Illinois University at Edwardsville. With strong leadership from their dean, and a grant from IBM for equipment and software, the authors worked with teacher education faculty to increase the use of technology across the curriculum. They divided the content to be taught into four categories: computer literacy, integrated software applications, teaching with computers, and content-area software. The diffusion model developed deals with basic computer literacy skills through introductory courses that require students to complete projects using software such as a word processor. Eight contact hours on computer literacy skills are included in the Introduction to Education course. The skills students learn in the early courses are reinforced throughout the program as they are required to complete assignments that involve using the computer. Additional coverage of technology is provided in other courses. For example, the educational psychology course covers learning with computers, computer-based testing, interactive simulations of teaching, and teacher utilities such as grading programs. Methods courses teach computer-supported instructional strategies and software relevant to particular subjects and levels. In their student teaching experiences students are required to demonstrate effective use of technology in the lessons they teach.

A similar effort to diffuse technology across the teacher education curriculum in a small liberal arts university, Stetson, was reported by Dershimer and Dershimer (1991). Like the Southern Illinois effort, technology was integrated into all the teacher education courses as well as student teaching. The same is true of a comprehensive integration project at Marietta College in Ohio (Erb & Golden, 1994). The Erb and Golden article is rich in the details of how different uses of technology are begun in a course at the college and then transferred to and applied in field experiences. For example, students in the Foundations of Reading course study popular CD-ROM–based books such as *Arthur's Teacher Trouble,* which is distributed by Broderbund. Then they can create lessons that use the CD as a stimulus for reader response and interdisciplinary activities. Those lessons are actually used during field placements. In a secondary methods course, students are required to create a 2-week unit plan that includes 10 daily lessons. At least one of the daily lessons must include the use of technology such as a laserdisc or computer. Instead of writing the plan as a text document, students create a hypermedia document using HyperStudio, a hypermedia authoring program distributed by Roger Wagner Productions, Marietta Colleges.

Indiana University's QUEST (Quality University Elementary Science Teaching) program deals only with elementary education students who have elected the science concentration (Gabel & Boone, 1993). It is, however, one of the few programs that integrates both technology use and technology instruction across both methods courses and subject-matter courses. Students take a required educational computing course in their second year and then complete four science courses, a science methods course, and student teaching. Across these experiences students used technology in many ways, from collecting and analyzing data in the Introduction to Scientific Inquiry course and using HyperCard stacks in the biology course to student teaching in the classrooms of computer-using mentor teachers.

Like QUEST the TECH (Technology in Early Childhood Habitats) program at the University of Delaware prepares teachers in a particular field (Caruso, Trottier, & Shade, 1994). TECH is based on a constructivist theoretical foundation and supports a range of experiences, including preservice and in-service courses and workshops. In TECH training there is "a complementary balance of theory and practice" (p. 342). For example, in a summer training program that lasts 5 days, approximately half of each day involves direct instruction on the theory that frames computer use with young children (Bruner, Erikson, Papert, Piaget, & Vygotsky) and the remaining time is spent on hands-on exploration, technical training, and software evaluation. Participants apply what they learn in the intensive 5-day program when they complete a practicum in one of the university's programs for young children.

Ryan (1992), then dean of the College of Education at Illinois State University (ISU), provided a detailed description of the efforts at a large state university of over 3,000 education students

to diffuse technology throughout the college. He describes successful efforts to obtain computing equipment for the college and work with interested faculty to increase research, development, and curricular integration. The ISU approach emphasized building external partnerships and relationships with business and industry. Substantial support from IBM, for example, helped the college enhance its computer labs and a multimedia development center. However, because resources were still limited, the college computing committee accepted proposals from faculty for projects that would enhance instruction. Several excellent, course-specific instructional packages were developed through this program, and a number of products created by education faculty are now distributed commercially.

The efforts to infuse a program with technology discussed thus far involve efforts to work essentially within existing structures and frameworks. Some programs have taken a more revolutionary approach, however, and added technology to a radically reformed or entirely new program. For example, the University of Houston, funded by a grant from AT&T, and the University of Utah are both experimenting with technology-supported teacher education programs that put the students in professional development schools for much of their preservice training. The Houston project is a collaborative effort between the university and selected schools. Most of the teacher education program is delivered at the school, and teachers at the school are major partners in the program (D. Willis, 1992). At the University of Utah, teacher education faculty spend a significant percentage of their time in K–12 schools working with technology-using teachers as well as teacher education students (Niederhauser & Stoddart, 1992). These two programs, which are not yet mature efforts, may reflect a direction that will be taken by many future innovations involving technology integration.

The proposition that deans play a crucial role in most extensive reformation and technology diffusion projects is supported by the fact that the deans at Illinois State, Houston, and Utah are all strong supporters of technology in teacher education. The same is true of another university with a well-deserved reputation for pioneering work in this area, the University of South Alabama (Uhlig, 1992).

Even though the relatively few efforts to integrate technology across the teacher education curriculum are encouraging, thus far most efforts to go beyond the educational computing and methods courses have targeted another course in the curriculum. For example, Sullivan (1991) at the University of Michigan–Flint developed computer-supported cases on legal issues in education for a social foundations course.

Another aspect of teacher education that has a significant impact on the content of courses is textbooks. Unfortunately, in her review of the content of several texts used in teacher education Padron (1992) found "woefully inadequate" coverage of technology topics in introduction to education and educational psychology textbooks.

GENERAL ISSUES IN INFORMATION TECHNOLOGY AND TEACHER EDUCATION

A number of issues in the field of information technology and teacher education relate specifically to particular components of teacher education such as foundations courses, student teaching, or technology courses. There is also a set of issues, questions, and problems that are relevant across all areas of IT use in teacher education. One such issue, theoretical foundations, has already been discussed. In this section, others are discussed: (1) guidelines and standards, (2) what should be taught, (3) state, national, and international initiatives, (4) technology diffusion and organization change, and (5) gender, equity, and cultural issues.

Guidelines and Standards

A number of groups, organizations, and states have gone beyond the assertion that we need more and better technology preparation for teachers. Several sets of guidelines, in fact, have been created over the past 15 years. The guidelines fall roughly into three distinct groups. Some treated educational computing as a subdiscipline in computer science. Others viewed the educational uses of computers, and other forms of information technology, as part of the larger field of education. A third perspective, which is emerging now, tends to view technology as a way of promoting innovations that come from other areas of education, such as curriculum theory, instructional design, or any of a number of content or learning theories.

Educational Computing as Junior Computer Science One of the earliest efforts to set guidelines for the preparation of teachers was sponsored by the Education Board of the Association for Computing Machinery (ACM) and two of its special interest groups, the Special Interest Group for Computer Science Education and the Special Interest Group for Computer Using Educators. In a publication (edited by Rogers & Moursund, 1983), several proposals on what and how preservice teachers should be taught about technology were presented. As might be expected of a publication sponsored by the ACM, a number of the proposals for teacher education were little more than revisions of courses already taught in computer science departments. A two-stage model, for example, suggested that all teacher education students be required to complete an existing course in computer science such as computer literacy or computers in society that included the following topics: What Computers Are and How They Work, A Brief History of Computers and Technology, An Introduction to Programming, A Survey of the Application of Computers in Society, A Discussion of Social Issues in Computing (Rogers & Moursund, 1983, p. 2). As an alternative the group proposed that colleges develop a special course to be offered either through the computer science department or the college of education. It would be a teacher-oriented version of the computer literacy course. The second stage of the proposed program was instruction about the computer as a tool for teaching and learning, and the group recommended that this topic be covered in existing teacher education courses.

The 1983 ACM guidelines, especially the proposals for the separate course, could be characterized as an effort to define educational computing as a subset of computer science, a sort of junior computer science for teachers. That characterization certainly fits an interesting effort that evolved from the ACM project. Kenneth Kennedy's dissertation at the University of Tennessee carries a 1987 date, but it has much in common with the 1983 ACM guidelines. That is not surprising because Kennedy used the ACM publication to design a computer education program for teacher education colleges, and he used the list of participants at the back of the ACM report to recruit a national group of experts who provided input and suggestions for revisions. At the end of his review of the literature Kennedy (1987) concluded that:

The following computer skills [are] necessary for teacher education students:

1. familiarity with machine instructions and assembly language as well as knowledge of a high level language
2. knowledge of computer assisted instruction languages and list process languages
3. programming competence to write, debug, and test programs
4. knowledge of the system facilities
5. recognition of computer applications for a variety of group and individual activities . . .
6. ability to recognize and use available support services
7. ability to evaluate hardware and software
8. ability to adapt available software to a variety of subject areas (p. 49)

Kennedy's definition of what teachers should be taught about computers is an extreme example of the junior computer science model. Fortunately, the future of educational computing will not be created in that mold. A University of South Carolina dissertation, completed 2 years before Kennedy's on virtually the same topic, came to very different conclusions. S. Johnson (1985) developed a survey instrument that asked about the topics all secondary teachers should know about as well as topics high school computer literacy teachers should know. The topics were divided into four broad categories: general computer literacy, education and the microcomputer, programming, and society and the microcomputer. He sent the survey to a novice group and an expert group and used the responses to develop his own set of guidelines. The novice group was a sample of teachers in South Carolina who were known to be regular users of technology. The expert group was a sample of individuals who regularly published, presented, or consulted on the topic of educational computing. The suggestions of the novice and expert group were almost identical, and his final set of guidelines did not include any type of programming for all teachers (Pascal and BASIC were recommended for computer literacy teachers). Johnson's set of suggestions is, in fact, similar to the next two sets to be discussed.

Information Technology as a Subspecialty in Education In 1985 the North Carolina Department of Public Instruction published *Computer Competencies for All Educators in North Carolina Public Schools*. Although the North Carolina guidelines came only 2 years after the ACM publication, they are quite different. There is, for example, not a single mention of programming in the requirements for all teachers. North Carolina divided requirements into three levels. Level I specified computer competencies for all educators. Level II dealt with competencies in specific content areas such as art education, social studies education, and science education. Level III defined minimum competencies for educators who serve as technology coordinators in the schools.

North Carolina's guidelines were developed by Department of Public Instruction staff and a task force composed of K–12 educators, university faculty, and technology leaders. Four Level I competencies, which are required of all teachers, reflect the shift from ACM's computer-science-in-schools focus to an emphasis on instructional uses of technology:

1. Understanding of and ability to use computer hardware and software
2. Demonstrated knowledge of the capabilities and limitations of computers in society with a particular emphasis on the use of computers as instructional tools
3. Ability to discuss the effects of computers on society including ethical use issues
4. Demonstrated ability to use the computer for instruction, including ability to select and evaluate appropriate courseware, select and develop effective teaching strategies that incorporate computer technology, classroom use of tool software as well as traditional CMI and CAI such as drill and practice, simulations/games/models, tutorials, and problem-solving software

Level II competencies were developed for 14 different subject areas. Most of the Level II competencies, however, are the same across most of the subject areas. They emphasize the ability to use standard hardware and software (e.g., performing computer operations: on-off sequence, loading/execute/saving/copying programs, and identifying, evaluating, and selecting software programs appropriate for instructional purposes). North Carolina's requirements, which are representative of many state-level requirements developed during the mid-1980s, are an improvement over the 1983 ACM guidelines because they begin to recognize that educational computing is separate and distinct from computer science. They are only a beginning, however, because they still focus on hardware and software usage and on the selection of educational software. Very little attention is paid to curricular integration. In addition, the North Carolina requirements emphasize procedural or how-to knowledge when it comes to computer literacy skills, but the teaching skills discussed are generally stated as declarative knowledge rather than professional practice skills.

The approach taken in the North Carolina guidelines was reinforced in 1986 when Secretary of Education Terrel Bell's National Task Force on Educational Technology issued its final report (Ridley & Hull, 1986). The group made many recommendations about the use of technology in K–12 education, but two recommendations spoke to teacher education:

The Task Force recommends that all units responsible for pre-service and in-service teacher education design and implement effective programs to prepare teachers to use technology optimally for instruction and instructional management.

Higher education institutions should redesign pre-service teacher education to include the effective uses of technology, including its uses in

teaching for subject-matter mastery and ensure that teacher educators themselves are fully competent in applying technology to education. (pp. 13, 21)

The shift toward more education in educational computing received another boost when, in 1988, the ACM published another document on technology and teacher education. It was a special issue of *Outlook*, the publication for the Special Interest Group on Computer Uses in Education, titled *Preservice Education in Educational Computing*. Eighteen invited contributors dealt with a wide range of topics, from the stand-alone educational computing course to teaching students how to use data bases in the classroom. This collection of papers reflects a perspective that has much more in common with the North Carolina guidelines than the earlier ACM publication. In several papers the authors go beyond the declarative and procedural knowledge of basic computer literacy to discuss crucial instructional and integrative issues that are at the heart of current discussions. For example, M. Watt (1988) deals with issues such as the need to model a range of instructional strategies in an educational computing course and to give students experiences they can build on when they use computers in their own classes. Watt also requires students to spend some time in a real school where computers are being used. Students finish their course with a portfolio of projects they can use when they graduate. Biglan (1992) goes even further. In her educational computing course college faculty teach fundamental concepts from learning theory and instructional design. Almost half the course, however, is taught in a local school by a teacher from that school. Berger and Carlson (1988b) argue that most educational computing courses have concentrated on technical information about the computer, rather than "methods of integrating computers into instruction" (p. 32). They propose a preservice course that concentrates on the integration of computers into the curriculum with a heavy emphasis on making the connection between computer-supported instructional strategies and the theories of learning and instruction.

A number of authors in the 1988 ACM publication were still concerned about the role of programming in courses. R. Taylor (1988), for example, offered five training maxims including Training Maxim Two: "Don't give up on teaching programming just because teaching it so far has not worked too well" (p. 4). D. Watt (1988) explained how concentrating on LOGO can accomplish many of the general objectives in an educational computing course, and Welch's (1988) description of an undergraduate educational computing course allocates 20% of the course to LOGO. Taken as a whole, however, this publication represented a step forward. Teaching about educational computing in preservice education is, for the most part, treated as an important, complex, multifaceted educational task. Authors consider topics such as equity and ethical issues (Jacobs, 1988; Segal & Marciano, 1988) and the importance of experimental learning in educational computing courses (M. Watt, 1988). In contrast to the earlier ACM report and the North Carolina guidelines, several papers discuss the specific needs of teachers in content areas such as English composition (Heeber, 1988) and mathematics (Ayers & Bitter, 1988). Although much of the emphasis is still on hardware and software mastery and programming as a mind-building exercise is still proposed, this publication supports the perspective that educational computing is a separate discipline *in education* with its own set of issues, problems, agendas, and initiatives.

Three years later, in 1991, the break with computer science as a parent discipline was again emphasized when the International Society for Technology in Education (ISTE) published *Curriculum Guidelines for Accreditation of Educational Computing and Technology Programs*. The ISTE became a constitutent member of the National Council for Accreditation of Teacher Education (NCATE), and through a committee chaired by Dr. Lajean Thomas at Louisiana Tech University it developed a set of guidelines (Thomas, 1991). Every institution applying for NCATE accreditation will respond to these guidelines in the first stage of the accreditation process. ISTE's Foundation Standards actually includes two sets of standards, one for all teacher education students and one for Educational Computing and Leadership that applies primarily to graduate programs preparing students for positions as technology coordinators. (A third set of standards was developed for programs preparing high school computer science teachers.) The standards for all teachers include 13 items that are summarized as follows:

1. Operate a computer and use a range of software.
2. Evaluate and use computers and related technologies for instruction.
3. Apply current knowledge about instruction and assessment to the use of instructional technologies.
4. Critically evaluate and use applications software and instructional packages that include the use of technology.
5. Demonstrate knowledge of the use of computers for problem solving, data collection and management, communications, presentations, and decision support.
6/7. Design and develop a range of learning activities that effectively integrate technology-based learning activities. These skills should be demonstrated in the students' subject matter or level specialty and should include a range of student grouping strategies and meet the needs of a diverse student population.
8. Demonstrate knowledge of the ways multimedia, hypermedia, and telecommunications can support instruction.
9. Demonstrate the ability to use productivity tools such as word processors, data bases, spreadsheets, and print/graphic utilities with students and for the teacher's professional use.
10. Demonstrate knowledge of ethical, legal, and equity implications of information technologies in society and model appropriate use of these technologies.
11. Find and use the resources needed to remain current in the educational uses of information technologies.
12. Use information technologies to enhance personal and professional productivity.
13. Use information technologies to facilitate the emerging roles of students and educators.

The ISTE standards are the only nationally adopted guidelines for what should be taught about technology in teacher education. They represent current thinking, and because they are a part of the NCATE accreditation process, they are likely to have more impact on the field than any previous set of standards. Hess (1992) has used them as a basis for a plan to infuse coverage of technology throughout the various components of teacher education (foundation level, professional skills level, and field level). He organized the content to be taught by level and by type of instruction (direct instruction, guided application, independent application, or demonstration).

It is interesting to compare the relative emphasis on different topics in the short executive summary versions of the 1983 ACM, 1985 North Carolina, and 1991 ISTE guidelines (Table 45.1) Using only the short summaries of each set of guidelines or standards enhances the differences between them, but there is a striking transition from 1983 to 1991 away from general computer literacy topics such as the basics of operating a computer system and toward the instructional applications of computers. Programming in traditional languages, a standard component of many educational computing courses in the early 1980s, does not appear in the 1985 or 1991 lists. However, the use of computers for instruction was not on the 1983 ACM short list, but it accounted for 25% of the 1985 North Carolina list and a whopping 73% of the 1991 ISTE list. The shift suggests that what was called *educational computing* in the early 1980s was largely a subset of computer science. What is called *educational computing* today is a specialty with a great deal of connection to educational fields such as curriculum and instruction, educational psychology, instructional design, and instructional technology. The general tenor of the ISTE standards is also reflected in the topics public school teachers, technology coordinators, and curriculum coordinators believed should be taught in teacher education programs (Niess, 1990, 1991).

The shift that has occurred in the United States has also occurred in the United Kingdom (Davis, 1992), Denmark (Bollerslev, 1988), France (Gardner & Salters, 1990; Grandbastein, 1993), and Australia (Bigum, 1990). However, some evidence suggests that the ISTE standards may represent the ideal rather than the average perspective. Some efforts over the past few years to develop model courses based on input from surveys of practicing educators do not reflect the ISTE model. Unfortunately, most of these attempts are based on surveys of teacher educators. One project to develop a model 13-week preservice teacher education course (summarized in Bruder, 1989) used input from an advisory group with a sizable majority of teacher educators. The course outline included:

1. Getting started—1 week
2. Problem solving—2 weeks
3. Teacher utilities I—1 week
4. Computers and communication—3 weeks
5. Teacher utilities II—1 week
6. Programming—2 weeks

This model is more like the second ACM proposal than the 1991 ISTE proposal. That is not surprising because two of ACM's SIGs were cosponsors of the project along with Teachers College of Columbia University and the predecessor to ISTE.

Another survey of teacher educators was conducted by Brownell (1990) in connection with a revision of his educational computing textbook. He asked a national sample of teacher educators who taught educational computing courses what topics they considered important. The topics they rated highly

TABLE 45.1. ACM, North Carolina, and ISTE Guidelines

Topic	Source of Guidelines		
	1983 ACM (%)	1985 NCª (%)	1991 ISTE (%)
General computer literacy	40	25	19
Social and ethical issues	40	50	08
Programming	20	00	00
Use of computers for instruction	00	25	73

ª Level I standards only

indicated they were interested in both traditional computer literacy and more modern educational computing subjects. They rated word processing as the second most important topic out of 16 and put LOGO, graphics, telecommunications, and interactive videodiscs at the bottom of the list. Computers and problem solving and methods of integrating computers into content areas were ranked first and third.

In their survey of members of the ISTE special interest group on teacher education, Lintner et al. (1991) asked about the content of the educational computing course respondents taught. Only 13% did not deal with programming at all while 65% covered LOGO and 45% covered BASIC. Approximately 87% still included at least some programming instruction. Although innovative applications, such as hypermedia, and subject-specific software were not part of the survey, simulations were covered in most courses (88%), as was drill-and-practice software (80%). Computer literacy topics were also well represented, including hardware (88%), word processing (98%), spreadsheets (78%), and data bases (80%). However, integrating computer activities into the curriculum was a topic in only 68% of the courses. Only half the faculty allowed students to work with educational software outside scheduled class time, and the most common instructional method was presentation by the instructor. Interactive video was used in 25% of the courses, and CD-ROM technology was covered in 13%. Some of the results of this survey are somewhat discouraging, but the small number of people who returned the survey may not have been representative of the total membership of the organization. There are, however, other relatively recent papers that continue to advocate the need to teach teachers to program. Yoder and Moursund (1993), for example, conclude that "all teachers should receive some instruction in computer programming and computer science" (p. 21).

Although some of the more recently developed guidelines do not reflect the ISTE model, most do. The emphasis on the use of technology for instruction in the ISTE guidelines is also reflected in the guidelines published in 1989 by the Council for Accreditation of Teacher Education (CATE) in the United Kingdom (DES, 1989). The CATE, which in the United Kingdom occupies a position similar to the NCATE in the United States, listed four technology-related objectives in their standards, and all of them were related to instructional uses of technology. Unfortunately, when CATE published drastically revised guidelines in 1992 (DES, 1992), references to technology were reduced to little more than a mention: "Demonstrate ability to select and use appropriate resources including Information Technology" (p. 12).

The shifts in topics considered essential in educational computing courses since the mid-1980s reflect a change in perspective on the part of those who have selected technology and teacher education as one of their scholarly interests, but they also reflect trends in the general field of personal computing. Computers and operating systems have become much more reliable and much easier to use. Thus the effort needed to learn how to use a computer is significantly reduced. More effective and interesting software is now available, which means that schools can do more with them than teach students the BASIC programming language that came with the system. And finally, although ethical and social issues are still important, the explosion of ways in which to use computers in schools effectively calls for much more attention in courses than was warranted a few years ago. The increasing range and quality of educational software has stimulated subject-specific groups to consider what teachers trained to teach a particular subject should be taught about technology.

Information Technology as a Tool for Reform Although organizations that focus on some aspect of technology in education have been the most active in developing guidelines and standards, other groups have also addressed this topic. For example, in 1989 the National Council of Teachers of English published *Computers in English and Language Arts: The Challenge of Teacher Education* (Selfe, Rodrigues, & Oates, 1989). This book presents model teacher education programs and provides detailed information on what and how English teacher education students should be taught about computers. Professional skills English teachers should master in preservice teacher education programs include how to set up a program that uses computer technology, creating prewriting activities that rely on computer support, creating and using activities that involve a word processor, networking, and using data bases in the classroom. In a follow-up on the NCTE guidelines, Kiefer (1991) argues that the guidelines, although good, do not deal with some key issues that will be crucial for training teachers in the 1990s (p. 120). Her points deal mainly with the question of whether computers will be integrated into current practices and thus support the models of instruction that dominate the English classroom now or whether they will become the basis for a fundamental change in how students are taught in English classes.

Kiefer's work (1991), and that of Owston (1993), is probably an indication of the future of educational computing in two ways. First, her perspective on educational computing is unique to a particular subject area, English composition. Although there is certainly overlap in the way computers are used in other areas such as mathematics, science, or social studies, much of what Kiefer has to say is specific to her subject area. The shift in the 1980s that made educational computing a discipline within education, instead of within computer science, may be followed by a shift in the 1990s that reduces the universal core of educational computing and increases the subject- and level-specific content significantly. If this shift does occur, the role and importance of generic educational computing courses will change significantly, and integrating coverage of technology into methods courses and student teaching will be even more critical. Second, Keifer ties the use of computers and related technologies to fundamental curriculum and instructional strategy issues in her field. For her, using computers in the classroom is not enough. They must be used in ways that support the curriculum model and instructional strategies she believes are the future of English composition instruction. This approach reflects a maturing perspective on educational computing. It does not treat all uses of computers in the classroom as equal as did so many of the research reviews published in the 1980s. In addition, it does not treat educational computing as something separate from other aspects of the classroom such as the curriculum, lesson plans, and instructional strategies. This close linkage is likely to become a standard perspective in the 1970s, and, although this is very desirable, it will make discussions about computers in the classroom much more complex.

These two issues, subject-specific questions in educational computing and the close linkage of educational computing to other aspects of the education process, are but two of the ones that will frame the discussions and debates of the 1990s. The next section, which deals with the question of what teacher education students should be taught about information technology, reflects the practical application of answers to these two questions. The type of standards that appeal to you (junior computer scientist, educational computing as a part of education, or information technology as a tool for reform) help determine what you think teacher education students should learn. So too does your view of how subject-specific coverage of computing and related technologies should be and how closely that coverage should be linked to specific theories of teaching and learning.

What Should Be Taught?

Knupfer (1991) expressed concern that the demand for more teacher preparation related to the use of computers might focus on the hardware and software currently available at the expense of the broader issues such as what should be in the school curriculum and how technology can support the goals and objectives of the school:

Many programs currently used in educational computing do not fully utilize instructional strategies to best facilitate learning. . . . It is imperative that computers do not determine curriculum, but that schools formulate their curriculum first and then consider how computers can best serve the instructional objectives and activities of that curriculum. (p. 334)

Knupfer argues that with the current generation of hardware a teacher education program that emphasize understanding how to use a complicated machine is undesirable because the machines are much easier to understand and use today. She argues that training must focus on the connection between computers and the curriculum. That focus then leads to an increased emphasis on the general changes in the roles teachers will play in a classroom where technology is effectively used:

Even the most traditional teachers who use computers effectively in their classrooms are finding that once they become secure with their ability to implement the technology, the very structure of their teaching changes. Instead of being the source of information, the teacher becomes the facilitator of information, guiding the student in the direction

of a solution and perhaps encountering larger issues along the way. In solving the steps of a problem, the students often become more knowledgeable about the topic than the teacher. In order to be successful at this method, the teacher must be willing to release the control of learning to the students, and feel secure in a different role. In such a role there is potential for the students and teacher to learn together, to learn by discovery, to access information beyond the intent of the original lesson plan, and to explore new types of projects. (Knupfer, 1991, p. 337)

Knupfer's concerns are also part of Bork's (1991) discussion of the history of educational computing. He believes that the initial stage of educational computing that emphasized hardware acquisition with little concern about how technology, once acquired, would be used, was a failure. The life of the typical student was hardly affected. In Bork's view the two stages that followed, *Let's Teach Languages* (especially BASIC) and *Let's Teach Computer Literacy,* were also failures. Bork argues that teaching everyone to program a computer in a traditional language does not provide benefits that are empirically supported:

And while computer literacy is still a popular concept, computer literacy is like motherhood in that most people are in favor of it. But unlike motherhood, it does not have a clear and precise definition [some might argue that cultural changes and advances in medical technology make it much more difficult to define motherhood today]. People agree that they like computer literacy only because they do not explore carefully what it is that they have in mind by the term computer literacy. (Bork, 1991, p. 358)

In each phase of education computing, Bork points out that there has been an emphasis on the need to train teachers. The type of training provided has varied, however, with the stage. In the initial stages teachers might learn much about the hardware and operating systems of a particular personal computer. Later, when the hardware and operating system software were a bit more understandable and reliable, thousands of teachers completed courses in programming BASIC or LOGO or, later, Pascal. It follows that if a stage of educational computing were a failure, then the training provided teachers that matched that stage also failed. Like Knupfer, Bork believes teacher training must be tied to a curricular model. He adds the requirement that we will also need something else that is lacking at present—"good materials for training the teachers to use these technology-based courses" (p. 360).

Bork and Knupfer are both specialists in educational technologies and their concerns reflect that focus. In essence, they believe that much of what is taught today about computers in teacher education misses the mark because it does not deal with the powerful ideas, concepts, and procedures that underpin innovative, effective use of technology in the classroom. That view is shared by Sherwood (1992), an Australian teacher educator who conducted a survey of technology uses and needs in Australian education. She concluded: "Most teachers have gone beyond the "nuts and bolts" stage. They want in-service training . . . to be more directed at the classroom" (p. 178). That same concern is shared by teacher educators who specialize in the various subject areas. Kiefer (1991), for example, argues that English teachers are often taught to view the computer as just another transcription device that allows writers to capture words just as quills, pens, pencils, and typewriters do, and even in ways similar to stenographers or dictating machines (p. 121). This assumption, Kiefer suggests, allows teacher educators to take the position that:

Computers are simply tools and need not become the object of particular attention, or else we probably ought to train teachers how to have students use pencils most productively. . . . Many teachers feel that the computer is simply an expensive gadget that should well go the way of overhead projectors—nice to have around when needed but not to be used every day because computers take so much time to work with. . . . If the computer is seen as no more than an alternative transcription tool, then it can be integrated in only limited ways within teaching and writing contexts. (p. 122)

Kiefer's vision of how computers will be used in English composition classes is quite different. For her the computer is the foundation for fashioning a radically different composition course that is cross disciplinary and uses a wide range of electronic services such as one-to-one and one-to-many electronic mail, electronic assignment distribution, computer conferencing, and collaborative writing. Much of the work in the class will be via networked computers that allow prewriting, draft, and revision work to be shared and critiqued by the composition teacher, the students' other teachers, and classmates. The writing activities would be supported by electronic data bases, bulletin boards, and peer group support centers on the network. Many of these electronic supports would focus on the school, but some would provide electronic links to the outside world. Keifer believes that:

the traditional teacher-education curriculum guarantees that only the most innovative teachers—or perhaps the most bored—will ever move beyond seeing the computer as a transcription tool, the occasional locus of writing, rather than as the spark for critical thinking and writing and the medium for learning and teaching that it can become. Teacher education must refocus its energies to equip all teachers with the theory and practice of writing as learning . . . and include in those practices not just our current writing-across the curriculum pedagogy but a full understanding of how an electronic writing medium enhances each learner's growth in writing and thinking. . . . In short, as we see that computers fundamentally change writing, and as writing assumes a more dominant role in critical thinking in all disciplines, we must revise the teacher-education curriculum to reflect the importance of the computer for writers and thinkers. (p. 125)

As noted, Keifer's approach to teaching about technology ties what teacher education students learn about technology very closely to curriculum and instructional strategy issues. This approach is placed in a broader perspective by Owen (1992), a U.K. teacher educator. He analyzed the common approaches to in-service teacher education about technology and organized them into six different categories. Although Owen's analysis is based on his in-service work, aspects are also relevant to preservice programs. Several of his categories are quite similar to Bork's hardware, languages, and literacy phases. Owen found that a *hardware centred model* was common in the early 1980s but failed because, "This model clearly had little vision of how teachers were meant to operate in the classroom" (p. 128). Instruction in BASIC programming was a common component of instruction using this model. Owen believes that another model, the *software centred model,* is still popular in the United Kingdom, especially in short courses and workshops:

Such courses are often given titles like The use of DTP or Getting to know Spreadsheet X. The vision of the teacher is very similar to the hardware centred model, however the content has changed to operation and specific features of software packages, which are usually commercial tools or educational developments of them, such as word processors or information retrieval software. The software may be given some context, but often the audience is heterogeneous so no clear focus can be given. (p. 129)

Owen found that a third model, the *curriculum centered model,* is the dominant one today in U.K. teacher education. He describes this approach as an adaptation of a familiar model of curriculum development: "develop, trial [test out], and then disseminate as published materials" (p. 129). Owen does not believe that this approach will be entirely successful because it requires considerable effort on the part of the teacher. "The vision of a teacher, having read or acquired materials, or having been on a course, or been visited by an advisory teacher and then being able to change teaching styles and methods, gain access to appropriate resources and styles of school organisation and to sustain the development seems to be problematic" (p. 129). Another model, the *child-* or *classroom-centered model,* also places heavy demands on the teacher. It generally involves a teacher in a detailed study of the way a child learns and requires the teacher to try out a number of computer-supported learning strategies with the child in an effort to locate the most effective strategy for the child. Owen points out that this approach is used primarily in graduate programs where the teacher is meeting requirements in a course on information technology in education.

Owen is more optimistic about two additional models. The *whole-school-centered model* provides training and support as part of an effort to change the entire school rather than what a particular teacher does in his or her classroom. This approach includes dealing with issues such as resource allocation, curriculum development, preliminary training, and ongoing support.

This is one of Owen's preferred in-service training models, and he proposes that practicing teachers are more likely to profit from other forms of training if they are part of a whole-school–centered model. This model also seems appropriate to teacher education programs as many of the same issues must be handled if technology diffusion is to be successful. His final model is also for in-service training, but it is applicable in preservice programs as well. *A teacher focused model* is based in part on the concerns-based adoption model of Hall and Loucks (1978) that proposes that training and support be tied to the stage of concern of the teacher. In the beginning stages the teacher is concerned with basics such as the fundamentals of implementing the innovation with as few problems and embarrassments as possible. In later stages the teacher is concerned with issues such as how the innovation is helping the students and how it could be improved or even replaced with something better. Owen and his team found that two types of instructional materials were most effective in a teacher-focused model of training: case studies that were directly relevant to the teachers' areas of interest and planning guides that provided a structured, detailed plan for making decisions about how information technology could be incorporated into the curriculum. Although the planning guides were relevant to individual teachers, they were designed to be used by groups of teachers or departments and included activities to encourage the development of a shared vision of the direction the group or department would take. Again this model, although designed for in-service training, has major implications both for how preservice educational computing experiences are designed and sequenced and for how the task of involving more of the teacher education faculty at an institution is approached. In one of the few systematic applications of the concerns-based adoption model to ITTE, the teacher education faculty at one university integrated technology into all 11 of the required courses in the programs for elementary and secondary education students (Todd, 1993).

In summary, what teacher education students should be taught about technology is now a complex question that can be approached from many different viewpoints. One of the more sophisticated frameworks for considering the issue is Owen's models of training. They allow us to step back from the details of an instructional plan and analyze it in ways that tie the content to the goals and to the context in which the innovations will be initiated. Owen's teacher-focused model is the only one that includes a detailed consideration of the concerns of the teacher or teacher education student. His models also include some consideration of *how,* as well as *what,* should be taught.

Information Technology Diffusion Efforts in Teacher Education

Although there have been many state and national efforts to study, encourage, and support increased use of technology in schools, the number of initiatives that have focused on teacher education—either preservice or in-service—is much smaller. A few larger projects have, however, focused on the preparation of technology-using teachers. They are discussed in this section.

State-Level Telecommunications Networks for Teachers
Several states, including Virginia, Florida, Texas, and California, have funded statewide telecommunications networks for education. The first major effort to develop such a network was based on the "academical-village" model developed by Glen Bull and his colleagues at the University of Virginia (Bull, Harris, Lloyd, & Short, 1989). The name, academical village, is a term Thomas Jefferson applied to his concept of the University of Virginia. He designed the campus to support his idea of a village that encourages free and open exchange of ideas. Bull and his colleagues saw telecommunications as a way to create a virtual or electronic village for students and educators. With a grant from IBM, the University of Virginia developers created an electronic academical village named Teacher-LINK that linked educators at the University of Virginia with student teachers in area schools as well as with K–12 students and practicing educators. Teacher-LINK supported standard services such as E-mail, file exchange, data bases of information, and forums or conferences where participants can discuss a topic of interest. Teacher-LINK was very successful and was then used by the state of Virginia to develop the Public Education Network (PEN), which is an electronic network that all teachers in Virginia can access by dialing a local or a toll-free phone number. The only items required for access are a telephone line, a computer with communications software, and a modem. Virginia's PEN has become a major channel of communication for educators, students, and teacher educators. All teachers in the state and all teacher education students can obtain an ID for the network and use it without charge. The system is supported and managed by the Virginia state education agency, and there is no charge for IDs or use. PEN is part of the Internet and consists of a set of local nodes connected to the Virgina component of the Internet, which is supported by Virginia colleges and universities. The Texas Education Network (TENET) was based, in part, on PEN and has similar services and resources. TENET charges teachers $5 a year for an ID and teacher educators pay $25 a year. Bull et al. (1991) laid out a set of design principles they felt designers of educational networks should consider:

1. Create networks that are compatible with the Internet, and thus provide access to all the resources on the Internet.
2. Use a distributed computing architecture that has a number of small mail servers that form nodes on the network instead of concentrating all the computer resources in one place.
3. Provide "universal" access. This means that teachers and students with different brands of computers should be able to use the network.
4. Use a common, easy-to-understand, interface throughout the system.
5. Provide equal access for students and teachers in rich and poor school districts, rural and urban settings. Everyone should have access through either a local call or a toll-free number.

Although these five principles eliminate many alternatives and require networks that are more expensive than some alternatives, a surprising number of the state networks for education meet most of the guidelines. The networks in Florida (FIRN), Georgia (GCEduNet), Texas (TENET), Virginia (PEN), and California are all on the Internet. They all, in fact, use the regional Internet to connect the state's educators. Most are available at no cost to educators, and most use a distributed model that avoids concentrating all the computing overhead on one cluster of centrally located machines.

Corporate Initiatives Until the late 1980s computer manufacturers like Tandy/Radio Shack, Apple, and IBM routinely gave large numbers of computers to both K–12 schools and colleges of education. Aside from the general goal of contributing to the improvement of American education, manufacturers generally hoped that the donated equipment would be very useful and the result would be increased sales in education. As the computer market became more competitive and the profits of manufacturers declined, and then disappeared in some cases, the era of general largesse disappeared. Most of the major manufacturers still have grant programs, but they are much smaller and more tightly controlled than they were a few years ago.

Equipment donations were not very successful as a way of bringing about systematic change in education. Many teachers and teacher educators who had access to equipment either used it to do the same things they had been doing all along or did not use it at all for instruction. Manufacturers realized that training and support were critical elements of successful technology diffusion efforts. In the late 1980s both Apple and IBM developed grant programs that included significant training and support. They also involved teacher education. Both companies required grant applications, considerable collaboration between university faculty, consultants, and company representatives. Two related projects of Apple Computer, the Apple Classroom of Tomorrow (ACOT), and the Christopher Columbus Consortium (CCC), emphasized partnerships between colleges of education, K–12 schools, Apple Computer, and business (Burnett, 1992). The Christopher Columbus Consortium, for example, has 37 sites around the world. The general focus has been on "teacher and faculty member empowerment" (Burnett, 1992, p. 214), but the actual activities of the sites has included "research, development, evaluation, dissemination, implementation, and training to test technological innovations in learning and instruction" (p. 214). The consortium supports communication between sites through electronic communication systems and regular conferences. An important aspect of ACOT/CCC has been research on the way teachers begin to use technology. In their research on ACOT/CCC teachers, for example, Dwyer, Ringstaff, and Sandholtz (1990) identified five phases teachers pass through as they begin to think about and then use technology. The phases are Entry, Adoption, Adaptation, Appropriation, and Invention. Much of the work of the ACOT/CCC projects has involved efforts to increase the rate of adoption (Burnett, 1992). These projects have also tended to emphasize the creation of instructional materials using HyperCard, Apple's authoring environment for the Macintosh.

Apple's major grant programs have emphasized K–12 education but with significant interest in and attention to teacher education. IBM's emphasis has been the opposite. Their teacher education grants program, which began in 1988, was aimed toward teacher education programs with some going to affiliated K–12 schools. Like Apple, IBM provided training and support to the grant recipients. Much of the training related to hardware and software use. The typical teacher education program received about $225,000 of IBM hardware and software, including a networked lab of computers. Although IBM's centralized hardware and network training (in Atlanta) of the key people from each grant site was effective, the support provided by regional and local IBM staff was not always outstanding. In addition, the changes at IBM during this period meant the IBM staff assigned to support grant schools changed often. Many of the grant sites did not, however, have the expertise needed to make the most effective use of the hardware and software provided. In 1990 IBM divided the country into nine regions and selected "lead institutions" in each region. Those institutions, with extra funding and equipment, provided support to the other grant sites in the region. The deans of the lead institutions were also organized into a National Education Advisory Board that works with IBM staff to develop effective approaches to diffusing technology into teacher education.

State Initiatives to Support Teacher Education and Technology Michigan, Florida, Texas, and California have all created state-level programs to support the integration of technology into teacher education. Although the goal of all the state initiatives was essentially the same, the approaches used were quite different from state to state. One early effort was a multiyear project of the Michigan State Board of Education. Between 1986 and 1990 the Board funded a comprehensive project that included a statewide Preservice Technology Training Task Force, several surveys, and a number of support projects. Much of this work was led by Carl Berger, then dean of the School of Education at the University of Michigan. In 1988 the Board published *Technology Training for Michigan's Preservice Teachers,* which reviews the work of the task force and offers a comprehensive set of suggestions about how technology should be incorporated into preservice teacher education. Many of the suggestions are somewhat general, but the thrust of the effort was to develop a collaborative group tht includes teacher educators, students, administrators, and K–12 representatives who work on an integration plan. Plans should include ways of developing interest and competency on the part of teacher educators. Three delivery options were addressed: one or more stand-alone courses, integration into existing courses, and field experiences. The content suggested in the report included the normal topics of operating the equipment, learning to use some productivity and educational software, and learning to use technology for classroom instruction. The report did make one somewhat unique and important suggestion. It suggested that preservice teachers need to see the use of computers within the broader context of "models of teaching." Technology then becomes one aspect of the decisions a teacher makes about how to accomplish instructional objectives. If this approach were used, the content of many courses with names like Computer Literacy for Teachers and Educational Computing would shift from basic computer literacy, productivity software, and educational software to classroom instructional strategies that incorporate the use of various forms of technology. In many ways the difference would be similar to the difference between an educational psychology course that emphasizes general theories and a methods course that includes theories and principles but focuses on learning to select and use different instructional strategies. Most educational computing courses today are probably taught like the traditional educational psychology course, but that same course may need to be taught as a methods course in the future.

Michigan's efforts to enhance the quality and breadth of technology preparation preservice teachers receive emphasized developing policies, support materials, and a collaborative network of teacher educators. Florida's approach emphasized direct training and the development of instructional materials for teachers. For example, White and VanDeventer (1990) described @*Micro,* an electronic data base of software reviews developed for the Florida Department of Education by the Florida Center for Instructional Computing at the University of South Florida. @*Micro* is available electronically over the Florida education network and on disk as a searchable data base. The Florida Department of Education also supports the Instructional Technology Resource Center at the University of Central Florida (UCF) (Baumbach & Barron, 1990). Baumbach and her colleagues at UCF have developed brochures, booklets, computer software, and videos for Florida teachers. The materials are available free of charge from the center, and they can be duplicated by local school districts for distribution to teachers. The center also publishes a newsletter. Both centers offer a series of workshops for teachers each year and support conferences in Florida on the use of technology in education.

Florida's efforts at the state level have emphasized supporting teachers already in the schools. Baumbach, Bird, and Brewer (1994) describe in some detail the work of the Instructional Technology Resource Center at the University of South Florida that has been operating for 14 years with funds from the Florida Department of Education. California, however, has invested considerable effort in both preservice and in-service education. In 1988 California changed its certification regulations to include a requirement that teachers must be prepared to teach with technology before they can be fully certified (Bullock, 1991). California appropriated millions of dollars to support both in-service teacher training and the infusion of technology into California schools. Through an initiative called the California Technology Project (Blurton, 1989) and the related Association of State Technology Using Teacher Educators (ASTUTE), the California State University system organized workshops, sponsored a statewide organization for teacher educators, developed materials for use in teacher education, and produced several publications on the integration of technology into teacher education.

The final state to be discussed is Texas. Since 1988 the Texas Education Agency (TEA) has supported a most comprehensive set of initiatives related to technology and teacher education. In 1988 TEA published the *Long-Range Plan for Technology of the Texas State Board of Education: 1988–2000.* This document was developed after an extensive study that included open hearings and reports from a series of committees. The long-range plan was an effort to rally support around a comprehensive plan for increasing the use of technology in Texas schools. The plan included 13 initiatives that required action by the Texas legislature. (Eight initiatives required funds.) Twelve of the 13 initiatives were passed. For example, the plan called for the legislature to appropriate $50 per year per pupil for technology with annual increases. Beginning in 1992–1993 the legislature appropriated $30 and has not increased it, but that annual commitment currently means that $113 million is allocated specifically for technology in Texas. Approximately $100 million is transferred directly to local school districts who can spend the funds for training and support of teachers as well as for hardware and software. The remaining $13 million is retained by TEA to support initiatives that grew out of the long-range plan. Several of these initiatives have already been mentioned. The state telecommunications network, TENET, for example, currently receives $2.5 million a year of these funds and uses a substantial amount to support training of teachers to use TENET and Internet resources available to them over TENET.

TEA also created the Texas Center for Educational Technology at the University of North Texas to conduct research, development, and training projects that support the integration of technology into education. Currently it allocates $400,000 per year to the center. A total of $6 million a year is allocated to the 20 Regional Education Service Centers (RESCs) that provide support to school districts in their area. The services vary from region to region, but most deliver in-service training programs for teachers and administrators, provide consultation to school districts, and support regional conferences and workshops. At least one person must be employed specifically for technology support to districts. Each RESC has significant flexibility in the way funds are used, but several activities are expected: (1) Maintain a technology preview center where district personnel can "investigate and select technologies appropriate to meet local needs" (TEA, 1988, p. 58), (2) assist districts in training teachers, administrators, and other staff on technology-related topics, (3) "train induction-year teachers in technology use" (TEA, 1988, p. 66). The centers are also expected to disseminate materials from the Texas Center for Educational Technology. The RESCs also distribute the electronic version of *The Educational Software Selector (TESS). TESS* is an electronic data base of several thousand educational software reviews. It can be searched in several ways, including topic and grade level. The full package takes up 11 diskettes but a CD-ROM version will be available soon. TEA purchased a TESS site license for the state of Texas and RESCs distribute the product for the cost of duplication.

The major TEA (1993) initiative to reform teacher education is a grant program to establish centers for professional development and technology in the public and private institutions that have teacher education programs. Developed in response to problems in both traditional and alternative certification programs, this initiative has two stages of funding. A $25,000 planning grant was awarded to virtually any teacher education program that submitted a proposal. With planning grant funds the college or university developed a comprehensive proposal for reform. The essential requirements all programs were to meet included:

1. Much of the preparation must be site-based in professional development schools that have established cooperative relationships with the university.
2. Students must be prepared to use technology in the classroom.
3. The plan must be created by a collaborative group in which teachers have the largest number of representatives.
4. The collaborative group must also represent the cultural diversity of the state.

Although colleges and universities were not required to participate in the project, they were offered several incentives. One was financial. Successful proposals were funded for at least 2 years. For example, a program might receive $800,000 the first year and $350,000 the next. State colleges and universities were also exempted from the "18-hour rule" that limited the number of education courses students could take. In addition, all courses taught in the professional development schools would be credited for funding at the level of student teaching courses rather than regular lecture course rates.

During the first year of operation (1991–1992) eight proposals were funded from 30 submitted. Six additional proposals were funded the next year. Texas has thus far spent $67 million on the centers for professional development and technology (CPDTs) and plans to continue the grants for additional years if the legislature appropriates funds.

It may be too early to evaluate the success of this effort to reform teacher education systematically, but it is one of a very small number of state-funded efforts at reform that makes technology a primary emphasis. The grants helped initiate serious discussions between universities and school districts about a systematic plan for preparing teachers. In many areas, this was the first time these groups had worked collaboratively on a plan. An issue that is of considerable concern to TEA at present is the question of how CPDT projects will be continued after grant funds end. From TEA's perspective the grants were a way to help universities develop innovative CPDT programs and then replace existing programs with the CPDT model. A condition of awarding the grant was that the universities plan for and support the new model of teacher education after 2 years of grant support. A commitment was required, but the grants did not have to include detailed explanations of how that would be accomplished. If the CPDT projects are successful, and if they produce better qualified teachers, the question of how to continue the programs after grant funding ends is a significant barrier that must be overcome.

Technology Diffusion Efforts in the United Kingdom The teacher education programs, and education in general, in the United Kingdom are subject to much more central government control than is typical of the United States. That has been especially true since 1980. Robinson (1992) and Davis (1992) have analyzed the changing role of technology in teacher education in the United Kingdom and the role government mandates play in the process of change. Robinson, who oversees information technology in education courses at Cambridge University, has described the ways national policy can influence such efforts. In 1984 the U.K. government published statutory regulations of teacher education. After a discouraging report (often called the Trotter Report) from Her Majesty's Inspectorate (Department of Education and Science, 1988), the criteria were revised in 1989 to specify much more precisely how information technology should be covered in teacher education programs. The 1989 regulations require that:

all courses should contain compulsory and clearly identifiable elements which enable students to make effective use of information technology (IT) in the classroom and provide a sound basis for their subsequent development in this field. They should be trained to be able to:

1. make confident use of a range of software packages and information technology devices appropriate to their subject specialism and age range;
2. review critically the relevance of software packages and information technology devices appropriate to their subject specialism and age range and judge the potential value of these in the classroom;
3. make constructive use of information technology in their teaching and in particular prepare and put into effect schemes of work incorporating appropriate uses of information technology;
4. evaluate the ways in which the use of information technology changes the nature of teaching and learning. (Department of Education and Science, 1989, Para. 6.6)

Robinson points out that integrating technology into teacher education programs is not an option in the United Kingdom, it is a government requirement. That has not, however, naturally led to widespread, effective integration of technology. The U.K. ITTE was established in 1986 and has sponsored a number of meetings on the topic. ITTE has dealt with many of the same issues and problems as have teacher educators in the United

States (Davis, 1992). For example, members of the association have regularly discussed the issue of whether coverage of information technology should be integrated across the curriculum or whether separate courses should be required of all students. The United Kingdom has less than 100 teacher education programs, and in 1986 Her Majesty's Inspectors of Schools visited 22 of them and found that the integration of technology across the teacher education curriculum was spotty and inadequate. One area singled out for concern was a tendency to focus on the technical aspects of the hardware and software at the expense of educational and curricular issues. The report (Her Majesty's Inspectorate, 1988) concluded that many programs had tried to move to a permeated model of curricular integration prematurely. For a variety of reasons, including lack of preparation on the part of teacher educators, many of the programs had tried out and then abandoned the integration model. Many returned to stand-alone courses. The experience of U.K. programs highlights the need to take the current state of a program into consideration when deciding how to integrate technology into the curriculum. It is more a *process* of development than it is a single decision.

Robinson (1992) also shows how complex the issue of technology can be. In 1988 the U.K. government published a National Curriculum that specifies the content of courses taught in state schools in England and Wales. The curriculum is very detailed, and some aspect of information technology content is included in virtually all of the subject areas. In addition, the curriculum suggests the use of specific computer-supported instructional strategies in courses. Some courses, for example, should involve students in producing desktop-published papers; in others students are to communicate via E-mail. The diverse and comprehensive way information technology is to be infused into the curriculum must be supported by a plan developed by each school. Robinson refers to this as a total permeation model, and U.K. teacher education programs were thus faced with the need to prepare teachers in all subject areas to teach their students some information technology skills. At Cambridge University the requirement was handled by assigning some of the IT instructors to serve as consultants, supporters, and co-teachers for other teacher education faculty. The training thus occurs in other courses within the teacher education program, but the faculty who teach these courses receive considerable support. Robinson (1992) points out that this approach does not always extend to the schools where students do their observations and student teaching:

Many schools are still having difficulty in meeting the information technology requirements of the National Curriculum and a significant number of students do not gain the experiences with children we hope for—and which the Government's teacher education criteria require teacher educators to provide. For students, school based training in information technology can be an experience limited by the deficiencies of today rather than the good practice of tomorrow which the government's legislation demands and teacher educators work towards. For teacher educators, school based technological education is difficult to manage, hard to monitor, problematic to assess and expensive in time. (p. 16)

Robinson's perspective is supported by a survey (ITTE, 1987) of IT coordinators who estimated that less than 10% of the teacher education students used IT in their student teaching. A more recent survey (Dunn & Ridgway, 1991) reported that 40% of the early childhood student teachers tried to use a computer at least once during their student teaching. More recently, in a description of efforts to increase the use of IT at one U.K. university, Wild and Hodgkinson (1992) reported that 70% of their students used technology during student teaching.

The problem of schools that are not yet approaching the permeation goals set by the government became even more serious for U.K. teacher education programs when the government issued guidelines requiring approximately 60% of the program be based in schools rather than the university. Some efforts to develop ongoing, mutually supportive relationships between university-based teacher educators and schools have been reported (C. Taylor, 1992), and they are likely to increase as U.K. teacher education programs deal with the new regulations about school-based instruction. As with projects at Exeter University (C. Taylor, 1992), the effort is likely to involve working with current teachers to develop their IT skills.

One recent article (Dunn & Ridgway, 1994) is encouraging in that students who completed a British teacher education program that had been revised to meet new government criteria concerning information technology reported higher rates of technology use in school-based experiences than students before the revision. However, Dunn and Ridgway's data, which were gathered over the 4-year program, suggests that students may require 4 years (or more) of experience and training before they are confident that they can use technology effectively. Only 60% of the students felt confident about their ability to use technology at the end of the program. The authors also noted that very few of the teacher educators helped students with IT uses in their school placements and that the mentor teachers were not always helpful. The question of how effectively mentor teachers support teacher education students as they try to use technology in schools was an issue for Hodgkinson and Wild (1994). In exploring the reasons why many of their students seemed well-prepared to use IT in their university courses but rarely, if ever, used IT in their school placements, the authors concluded that "a major factor is the failure of some school placement teachers to provide encouragement to their teaching practice students" (p. 101). A similar conclusion was reached by Her Majesty's Inspectorate, "A student with a low level of confidence working with a class teacher who was unenthusiastic about IT too often tended to make only minimal use of the computer" (DES, 1992, p. 7). Tearle and Davis (1992) described one approach to the problem of poorly prepared mentor teachers (and schools that lack computer resources) that has been used at Exeter University: bringing public school students into the computer labs of the university's teacher education program where preservice teachers can work with the children under the mentorship of knowledgeable faculty.

Other State and National Projects The ITTE Association in the United Kingdom holds an annual conference in July, conducts surveys and development projects with funding from U.K. granting agencies, publishes occasional papers, and began publishing the *Journal of Information Technology for Teacher Edu-*

cation in 1992. In the United States the Society for Information Technology in Teacher Education (SITTE, formerly the Society for Technology and Teacher Education, or STATE) holds an annual conference in March, publishes the *Technology and Teacher Education Annual* (which contains the papers presented at the annual conference and is available from Allyn & Bacon as a printed document and on microfiche through the ERIC system), a series of monographs on information technology and teacher education, and the *Journal of Technology and Teacher Education*. At the University of Virginia the Society also sponsors the Teacher Education Internet Server (TEIS), which can be accessed from anywhere in the world via the Internet and associated networks (Robin, Bull, Larsen, & Mitchell, 1994). The Telnet address of the STATE server is teach.virginia.edu. Telnet access is through a "text only" but functional interface. However, TEIS is also a "gopher" service that supports a graphical user interface. Most university computing services can assist anyone who wants gopher access to TEIS. The server supports conferences, a paper archive, and a data base of downloadable instructional modules (J. Willis, 1992a). The development and distribution of modules was undertaken because many teacher educators would like to incorporate or expand coverage of technology in the courses they teach but lack the time or expertise to develop the necessary support materials. The society is publishing the materials in monographs to allow developers scholarly credit for their work and is making the software and documents available in electronic form so they can be downloaded and customized to local needs.

Another organization active in the field the Special Interest Group on Teacher Education (SIG-TE) of the International Society for Technology and Education, which publishes the *Journal of Computers in Teacher Education,* hosts sessions at the National Educational Computing Conference and the Technology and Teacher Education Conference, and supports a Bitnet list (SIGTE-L) for the discussion of issues related to technology and teacher education.

There are now three journals, two annual conferences, and two electronic resources that deal specifically with information technology and teacher education. The emergence of these channels of communication, none of which is more than 8 years old, suggests that the field of information technology and teacher education is now developing as a field of scholarly inquiry. In contrast, publications about technology in K–12 schools are considerably older. The *Journal of Research on Computing in Education* began publishing in 1967, *The Computing Teacher* has been publishing since 1973, and *Computers in the Schools* began in 1983. The creation of organizations and publications that concentrate on ITTE is, however, part of a general trend toward more specialized and focused support for research and professional practice that involve educational uses of IT. Publications like the *Journal of Computing in Childhood Education,* the *Journal of Educational Multimedia and Hypermedia,* and the *Social Science Computer Review* are all relatively young publications, as are the associations and organizations that sponsor them.

Technology Diffusion and Organizational Change The creation of specialty groups and publications in the field of ITTE presents both opportunities and potential problems. As teacher education faculty associate more with colleagues who share an intense interest in IT, their own practice and research may improve, but their influence on other faculty could actually decrease. The emergence of specialty organizations and publications could lead to the creation of a small "techno-ghetto" in teacher education that has limited interaction with or influence on the rest of teacher education. And, by the same token, if members of the techno-ghetto do not have regular interaction with the rest of teacher education, their scholarly and professional work is not likely to be as effective or as relevant as it could be.

The question of organizational change and technology diffusion has been addressed in a number of ways in the literature on ITTE. The conceptual framework most often used is the concerns-based adoption model (CBAM) of Hall and Hord (1987), in which change in schools is viewed as progression through a series of stages. Teachers or university faculty can progress through those stages faster or with less difficulty if they receive support. However, the type of support needed differs with the stage. A workshop, for example, may be very effective with participants who are at one stage, but it may actually impede progress if participants are at another. Intervention must, therefore, be matched to the stage of participants, which means that a facilitator or consultant must constantly be gathering information on the progress of the project. Two progressions, Stages of Concern and Levels of Use, guide facilitators as they work with projects. There are seven stages of concern. Potential adopters begin at the Awareness stage where learning about the innovation is the focus and proceed through a series of stages: Informational, Personal, Management, Consequence, Collaboration, and Refocusing. The early stages (Personal, Management, and Consequence) focus on the impact of the innovation on the teacher. Questions such as, "Will I be able to do this?" and "How do I organize my class for this work?" predominate. Interventions such as workshops, demonstrations, and guided practice are helpful. Later focus is on the impact of the innovation and on how to improve the innovation by collaborating with others. Questions such as "How will it help my students?" and "How can I get in touch with other teachers who are doing this?" are more common. In these phases interventions such as electronic or face-to-face "interest groups" that facilitate communication between teachers are helpful. The final stage of concern, Refocusing, is dominated by questions such as "Is there something better I could be doing?" and "I think this new approach may be even better than the innovation." The stages in level of use (Nonuse, Orientation, Preparation, Mechanical Use, Routine Use, Refinement, Integration, Renewal) are essentially the "action" counterparts of the stages of concern. The CBAM model has been used to organize school-based efforts to encourage and support the use of technology in classrooms (Corda, 1991; Panyan, McPherson, Steeves, & Hummel, in press) and as a framework for organizing efforts to encourage technology diffusion in education (Freeouf & Flank, 1994; J. Willis, 1992b, 1993b). For other case studies of technology diffusion in colleges of education, see Andris, Nelson, and Smith (1994); Beacham (1994); Benavides and Surry (1994); Erb and Golden (1994), and Thompson, Schmidt, and Topp (1993).

Gender, Equity, and Cultural Issues

The question of whether technology in schools is "culture neutral" or is actually an expression of a particular culture, or subculture, already has been discussed. Neo-Marxist curriculum theorists have been particularly attentive to this issue. Apple (1991) cogently argues for this point in a paper that suggests much of the push toward bringing technology into the classroom is based on the need of capitalists for a work force with specific skills and perspectives:

> The debate about the role of the new technology in society and in schools must not be just about the technical correctness of what computers can and cannot do. These may be the least important questions. At the very core of the debate are the ideological and ethical issues concerning what schools should be about, and whose interests they should serve. The question of interests is very important currently since, because of the severe problems currently besetting economies like our own, a restructuring of what schools are *for* has reached a rather advanced stage.
>
> Thus, while there has always been a relatively close connection between the two, there is now an even closer relationship between the curriculum in our schools and corporate needs. . . . Economic and ideological pressures have become rather intense and often very overt. The language of efficiency, production, standards, cost effectiveness, job skills, work discipline, and so on—all defined by powerful groups and always threatening to become the dominant way we think about schooling—has begun to push aside concerns for a democratic curriculum, teacher autonomy, and class, gender, and race equality. (p. 61)

Apple also argued that the tendency for private schools and public schools in affluent areas to have more and better technology may put poor and minority children at a disadvantage when applying for jobs and for college admission. Knupfer (1993) has also addressed the issue of equity access. Both Apple and Knupfer, among others, have also discussed gender and culture biases in both educational software and ways computers are used in schools. In her review of the literature, Skeele (1993) concluded that computer use in education is related to gender, socioeconomic status, race, ability level, and exceptionality. She offers a series of suggestions for addressing these issues in education including the admonition that, "we must raise the consciousness of pre-service teachers and encourage them to recognize and take action when they discover technological inequities in schools. . . . We must prepare teachers who are capable of providing equal educational opportunities to all students regardless of sex, race, SES, ability level, or exceptionalities" (p. 17). The Computer Equity Expert Project (Armitage, 1993) has been particularly active in developing programs, including extensive teacher training, to improve the use of computers by females.

INFORMATION TECHNOLOGY AND THE FUTURE OF TEACHER EDUCATION

This section describes an imaginary college of education—imaginary but not fanciful. All of the activities described below are technologically possible today; all are practiced to one degree or another somewhere in the United States. In short, they can all be done now if the will and the resources to support them are employed. The following paragraphs provide a glimpse of what a college of education might become in the future.

Ben King checked his watch. "Only 10 minutes left before I meet with the Teacher Education Advisory Committee," he thought. He looked forward to these monthly meetings; they afforded him his best opportunity to review achievements, identify problems, and plan for new technology applications in collaboration with the teacher education faculty. This month, like most other months, he had much to report that would please the committee. He also knew that members would have ideas for new programs that would challenge both his budget and staff.

At least the meetings now were much more interesting than when he had become coordinator for Technology Services in the College of Education 4 years before. Then, most of the discussion focused on such dreary topics as whether the required "Computer Literacy Course for Teachers" should carry 2 or 3 hours of credit, whether the network would support multiple platforms, and whether technology was "inhuman" and might destroy the "soul" of education. "Thank God," he thought, "we now have more interesting problems to debate."

Ben was the first person to be named coordinator of Technology Services in the college. His position was created by Dean Smith after it was decided that the college had to make tremendous strides in technology use if it were to maintain its reputation as a national leader in teacher education. Furthermore, Dean Smith had become weary of the criticism from area school superintendents who wondered why they should be obligated to provide basic instruction in technology to beginning teachers who were recent graduates of the College of Education. Dean Smith recruited Ben to be coordinator and told him to bring the college into the modern age.

During Ben's first year, he devoted his energy to conducting a faculty and staff needs assessment, designing training programs, and writing specifications for equipment purchases. Now, most of his time is spent responding to faculty requests for instructional applications of technology.

He glanced at the agenda and mentally rehearsed what he would say and what others were likely to ask:

Agenda

1. Report of early experience experiment
2. Subcommittee report on collaborative learning
3. Proposals for faculty training
4. Request from the Placement Bureau

1. Report of Early Experience Experiment

Ben's report on the use of both two-way, interactive video and videodisc cases for "early experience" would be well received. For years, the College of Education had met NCATE requirements for "early expereince" by boarding students on buses and transporting them to schools throughout the state. Because the university was located in a relatively small town, the only way to expose undergraduates to urban schools was to bus them 60 miles away to the nearest city. The program was expensive; it was also inconvenient and disruptive for the schools they visited and for the teacher education students. Worst of all, it was an activity that seemed *tacked on to,* rather than fully integrated into, the curriculum, because few of the faculty accompanied students on their visits.

With the completion of the fiber-optic "highway" that had recently connected schools and colleges throughout the state, it was now a relatively simple matter to pipe a classroom from any one of several schools into any College of Education classroom. Most days each college faculty member had several choices among school classrooms he or

she could observe. Often, a session was taped so that it could be edited later to make tapes of "critical teaching moments." The equipment also allowed a faculty member or a teacher education student to control the school's classroom camera remotely in order to pick out and zoom in on the teacher or individual pupils, even though they were hundreds of miles away. Now, methods, multicultural, and educational psychology instructors had substituted video visits for bus trips as a normal and regular part of their instruction. An unanticipated, but beneficial, result was that close working relationships had been established among some of the best teachers throughout the state and the teacher education faculty. This collaboration had led Dean Smith to coin the term, *virtual professional development school* to describe her enthusiasm for what had been accomplished. Observing classrooms live over the fiber-optic connection had gradually been integrated into the teacher education courses. First to use it were the Introduction to Education faculty and a few of the methods faculty. Then more methods faculty and the educational psychology professors began using the video. When faculty noted that some class sessions were much more useful than others and that it was often difficult to find a class that "fit" the weekly topic of dicussion in methods courses, Ben's staff had worked with faculty to develop video cases. The videotapes of particularly useful classroom sessions were edited and pressed on to a laserdisc. The staff then developed hypermedia software that let faculty play relevant video clips from any of more than 50 video cases. Topics such as inquiry learning, questioning strategies, teacher-focused instruction, collaborative learning, and much more could be supported with video cases.

2. Subcommittee Report on Collaborative Learning

This subcommittee had gone beyond its original mission. The initial idea had been to use technology to give teacher education students experience working as members of a team. Even though teams were to be formed within classes, communication among team members would be encouraged between class session by E-mail. Then, one student suggested a search of the Internet to learn if other people were working on similar topics. To their surprise, not only did they discover students and faculty in other colleges eager to join their discussions, but also several classroom teachers from across the country now participate. One of the topics has become an ongoing seminar on the Internet. What had begun as a classroom exercise became an "authentic task" attracting participation of many others, leading students to understand, perhaps for the first time, what teamwork in education could become. Furthermore, promoting dialogue among students and between students and faculty outside of classes had led to more powerful instruction within class sessions.

3. Proposals for Faculty Training

One of Ben's responsibilities is to provide for faculty development opportunities in technology application. Because an underlying assumption is that the faculty cannot (should not) "teach technology" to students as if it were a separate subject, they communicate what students need to know, as well as promote supporting attitudes, by modeling the use of technology as a fundamental aspect of professional life. This makes it necessary to stretch the faculty continuously so that they can become ever better role models.

The Subcommittee on Faculty Development wants to provide faculty with training in the use of a new presentation software that operates easily from laptop computers. An obvious way for faculty members to demonstrate the use of technology is when they stand before their classes. A year earlier, each faculty member was given a laptop computer. Some use their laptops to connect to the ceiling-mounted video projectors found in each classroom, but few faculty members are taking full advantage of the computer power available to them. Further faculty training on the use of laptop computers will have payoff in more effective classroom presentations. In keeping with a move toward more student-centered instruction, workshops are planned on the use of technology to support problem-based learning strategies in many of the teacher education courses. However, Ben knows that workshops will not be enough to facilitate this change. Making a significant, meaningful change in a course is a difficult, time-consuming task. After faculty learn about several approaches to technology-supported, problem-based learning, volunteers will develop proposals to try out some of the new approaches in selected classes. Several of those proposals will be funded with equipment and staff time. The results will be reported at faculty meetings and retreats. Then, if the experiments are successful and other faculty propose innovations, the cycle will begin again with another group.

4. Request from the Placement Bureau
The director of the Placement Bureau will appear near the end of the meeting. He is seeking funds to support a series of video conferences with school officials who employ teachers for large urban school districts. In the past, it was common for recruiters from large cities to make annual visits to the College of Education. However, in the last year or so, with budget cuts as well as political pressure to include faculty and parents on recruitment committees, an increasing number of potential employers want to conduct interviews remotely. The Placement Director will propose that the cost of each candidate interview be shared among the prospective school employer, the interviewee, and the college.

Ben is certain that the committee will approve the request. The college is already using two-way video conferencing to screen applicants for its own faculty positions. It also uses video conferences occasionally to conduct doctoral dissertation defenses. Both applications are driven by the college's need to reduce cost and to save faculty time.

"Well, it is time to go," Ben thought. "This should be an easy meeting; there is no controversy in these topics."

Essential Technology Architecture for Colleges of Education

What is required of colleges of education to perform as in the scenario, and why should they try? Answers to "what" are complex and somewhat indeterminate; "why" is easier to answer but may bear a greater threat for some colleges.

Suppose that the topic were medical colleges rather than colleges of education. Would a medical college be providing medical students with the kind of education they need if the students were deprived of opportunities to experience the kind of equipment available in community hospitals where most would practice? One reason medical colleges are expensive to operate is that they must give those preparing to become doctors training in advanced techniques and practices. To do less would threaten the college's standing and accreditation. The same logic applies to programs designed to prepare chemists, engineers, and business college students.

Colleges of education should not accept lower standards. Yet, some elementary and secondary schools today are better equipped than the colleges of education from which they employ their teachers. Some elementary and secondary school teachers use modern electronic technology to a degree that should shame some teacher education programs. No teacher education program should continue to be accredited by state or national bodies if its training programs are behind the standards achieved by the schools they serve. The answer to why colleges of education should become leaders in applications of technology is easy: If they do not do so, they will miseducate teachers for careers in a profession where technology is a leading reform element.

Deciding what colleges of education must possess to be judged adequate is not so simple because technology is changing rapidly. What may seem adequate today will appear insufficient tomorrow. Instead of considering what specific kinds of technology tools or the ratio of computers to students ought to be maintained, it may be more productive to consider the underlying architecture a well-equipped college of education should provide and the needs of faculty and students that should be addressed.

First, the college needs a fully integrated, networked, and switched voice, data, and video system that provides full capability and connectivity to all classrooms and offices within the building and to other locations throughout the world. The building's infrastructure must be sufficiently robust to meet current requirements, while designed to grow to satisfy future demands. The architecture needs to be compatible with many vendor's products so that various tools can be added as needed and made fully functional. The individual user should have as much control as possible, with limits imposed only for purposes of security and cost of particular services.

Faculty offices should be equipped to send and receive voice, data, and video. Each member of the faculty and staff should have access to electronic and voice mail; each department or administrative unit must have fax and hard copy capabilities. Students must have access to clusters of computers and printers that are available throughout the day and evening to support their work. In addition, the library should have network connections for laptop computers in study carrels.

All classrooms require projection systems that support a variety of applications, including the ability to deliver interactive video real time by lecturers from distant locations and computer-based presentation systems that contain data, graphics, slides, and CD-ROM. These systems should be easy to manage so that all faculty members need to do is plug their portable laptops into the classroom connector and find that all of their presentation requirements are satisfied. Future classrooms will be expected to accommodate wireless communication that provides links among students and faculty within the classroom and connectivity to others beyond the classroom.

A college of education needs laboratories for course and lesson design and development, a place where high-end equipment and authoring tools are available to assist the faculty and students to design their own instructional materials. Until now, instructors have been either dependent on prepackaged courseware or were forced to become expert in arcane programming languages. In the future, it will be possible for teachers at all levels to become "authors" without first becoming programmers. The building must also have studios to support distance learning applications employing both audiographics and compressed as well as full-motion, two-way video. It should also have rooms where students can microteach technology-supported lessons.

The library should contain collections of high-quality courseware used in schools and other teacher education programs along with the machines necessary for previewing these instructional products. The library should model electronic search tools that provide access to information and data sources worldwide. It should also store faculty-generated products so that students can study them at their leisure. Examples are CD-ROM programs on critical teaching moments, videotapes of guest lecturers, and courseware.

All administrative services should make full use of the technology provided by the college. For example, academic counselors should employ counseling software that informs student clients of license and graduation requirements. Students and faculty should be able to secure up-to-date information on job openings when they wish and dispatch applications and credentials at an instant's notice to prospective employers. Admission information and student records should be immediately accessible to administrators and faculty.

Faculty should be able to gain access to their voice mail, electronic mail, and office computers from their homes. Students and faculty should be able to conduct library searches and gain access to on-line data sources from their dormitory rooms or from their homes, respectively.

In order for these systems to be fully effective, colleges of education must invest much greater portions of their budgets on technology support and faculty/staff development than most have done in the past. Colleges of education must employ technical experts who are capable of selecting, installing, operating, and maintaining sophisticated voice/data/video systems. They will also have to budget substantially more money to pay for warranties, software and hardware purchases, and replacement parts. Adding technology to colleges of education may lead to greater faculty productivity and perhaps reductions in staff but little savings in money.

Faculty and staff development will also acquire higher priority. Until recently, a person who had received a doctoral degree was judged to be "fully educated." Any further education that might be needed was considered to be a matter of individual choice. Thus, college faculty read journals and books, attended conferences, and pursued research or acquired further training during sabbatical leaves, but the idea that a college of education would provide skills and knowledge-building activities for groups of faculty and staff was largely a foreign concept.

Modern technology has shattered the traditional way of thinking about faculty development. Nearly all faculty require help in integrating various media into courses. Learning to use electronic conferencing, library search packages, and the Internet effectively are not accomplished easily through independent study; instruction is required. Nor can one simply transfer a teaching style used in classrooms to meet the requirements of distance learning. Teaching to students at a distance, whether through one-way video, two-way interactive video, or audiographics forces professors to consider their pedagogical techniques more seriously than many have for a long time. The same is true of innovative approaches to teacher education that emphasize cases, problems, reflective practice, or professional development schools. Many faculty require pedagogical training in order to use new methods and new media effectively.

Colleges, either on their own or in partnership with other academic units, are finding it necessary to employ trainers and instructional developers to support the training needs of their faculty and staff.

The Ideal Is Real

What has been described in the preceding section may seem ideal, but unreal, to readers who are familiar with teacher educa-tion programs in the United States. Teacher education is typically among the least funded professional programs in higher education, comparing badly with programs that prepare doctors, lawyers, and engineers. It is rarely assumed that teacher education requires specialized laboratories, computers, and modern telecommunications equipment found in other professional training programs. And those who would be shocked if told that medical schools were preparing doctors using equipment and procedures that lagged behind those found in community hospitals seem unconcerned that some public schools are better equipped than the colleges where their teachers were trained.

The preceding section provided a scenario about how technology might be employed in the future and a prescription for the technology infrastructure and support services needed to provide a sound teacher education. The scenario and the prescription were necessarily future-oriented because nearly all schools, colleges, and departments of education currently fall short of what is required. But this does not mean that what may seem unreal is impossible today. Indeed, both the preceding scenario and the prescription drew heavily on an existing facility that meets or surpasses the technology infrastructure suggested earlier.

In 1992 the Indiana University School of Education began the fall semester in a new, state-of-the-art facility designed to support professional education with all of the latest tools of the information age. This facility, called the Wendell W. Wright Education Building, houses the School of Education, the Center for Excellence in Education (a research and development center), and the Education Library. The entire project—building construction, equipment, faculty and staff training, and research and development support—cost approximately $30 million, raised in roughly equal parts from the federal government, state government, and the private sector, especially AT&T. The goal was to create a facility that would not only support the School of Education as it went about its regular tasks of providing professional education for teachers, counselors, and administrators but also serve as a national demonstration center in order to show others how technology can be used appropriately for teaching and learning.

The entire facility is served by AT&T's SYSTIMAX^R Premises Distribution System, an integrated, networked, comprehensive cabling system that handles all communications—voice, video, and data—within the building as well as between the building and other distant locations. The communications infrastructure employs single and multimode fiber-optic cable and unshielded twisted pair copper cable leading to 646 information outlets that connect all of the building's electronic devices. The wiring system supports classrooms, conference rooms, computer labs, offices, and electronic information kiosks. Each classroom is equipped to receive and send video, data, and voice; each office is equipped with computers to connect the faculty to data sources within the building, across the campus, and beyond; each telephone provides multiple capabilities, including "voice mail" that can be accessed from anywhere.

A unique capability is a video distribution system that can carry up to 60 channels of video throughout the building. Some channels are dedicated and are accessible only for specific purposes or at specific locations (e.g., counseling psychology faculty who wish to observe clinical sessions remotely from their offices); other channels carry programs throughout the building and are open to any who wish to watch (e.g., CNN News or a special program in professional education). Faculty can originate video programs from any of the information outlets that are found in the offices and classrooms, using a variety of delivery modes ranging from 112-Kb compressed digital signals over telephone lines to full-motion video carried by dedicated fiber-optic lines or satellite transmission.

The School of Education provides computer classrooms for teacher training on both Apple and MSDOS machines; an open computer lab is available throughout the day, evenings, and weekends where students can work at their convenience; the Education Library has 64 desktop computers and each of the study carrels permits students to plug portable computers into the building's communication system. A high-end computer support lab provides special equipment for faculty and students to create instructional products. Electronic kiosks provide information to visitors about the location of offices and services within the building and about the campus. The kiosks are also used to exhibit CD-ROMs and other products developed by faculty and students.

Education faculty, staff, and students are supported by the Office of Education Technology Services (ETS). The ETS has 10 full-time-equivalent staff and four part-time graduate student employees. One staff member is required full-time to maintain telephone services; a second is needed to maintain and repair computer equipment; a third supports the faculty in their use of video; a fourth provides training for faculty and staff on the use of new software applications. Others bear overall responsibility for technology planning and overseeing equipment and software purchases; still others support faculty in their classroom uses of multimedia or in the delivery of distance learning courses by means of interactive video. The ETS exists to make certain that no faculty member is discouraged from using technology because of lack of experience. It also serves to inspire and lead faculty to experiment with technology applications that were previously unknown to them.

The Indiana University School of Education quickly recognized that obtaining equipment and a "state-of-the-art" facility would not by itself yield desirable results without an adequate support system. Thus, the School of Education invests substantial amounts of its operating budget in providing support services to faculty and staff in order to make their work as easy as possible by taking optimum advantage of the facility's capabilities.

The results of these investments are programs that were inconceivable in IU's Education faculty just a few years ago. Faculty deliver graduate courses into Indiana schools using interactive video; they bring guest lecturers into their classrooms by means of live video projection; they are connected to their students by means of electronic conferences; they conduct faculty business across multiple campus sites by both video and audio conferencing; and they electronically connect schools throughout the world to ongoing research and development projects. The administration of the School of Education is increasingly "paperless"; most communication occurs electronically, and records are maintained electronically. Increasingly, students are expected to sustain electronic communication with their peers and instructors.

Faculty and staff at the IU School of Education have not yet exhausted the capabilities embedded in their new building. Furthermore, some faculty are far ahead of their colleagues in exploiting the available electronic resources. Yet, all have been affected by the new building and its information infrastructure. In Bloomington teacher education can never again be what it was before.

Visitors come from throughout the nation, as well as from abroad, to study the facility and how it is being used. Faculty from other Indiana University colleges and departments schedule special events in the Wright Building so as to take advantage of technology resources that are not generally available throughout the University. The School of Education is now perceived to have the best facilities for teaching on the Bloomington campus, a decided change from the past.

Professional Development

Technology will affect the continuing education of teachers and school administrators in at least three ways: (1) Increase the demand for continuing education, (2) affect its content; and (3) influence its means of delivery. The need for continuing education for teachers and administrators has usually been greater than school boards were willing to satisfy. Although preservice teacher education has been able to provide new teachers with essential foundation knowledge and basic skills, specific training to meet the demands of individual school employees calls for special training and orientation for new teachers. What is occurring today is that important assumptions on which schooling has been based are changing, leaving nearly all teachers in need for further training. Site-based decision making, authentic assessment, cooperative learning, meeting national standards, curriculum integration, these are but a few of the phrases that signal changes in the way schools do their business. Each of these has implications for the use of technology. In addition, the dominant roles of the textbook and the teacher as content authorities are being challenged more than ever before. "Student as knowledge worker; teacher as coach" signals a different relationship among teachers, students, and knowledge sources. Technology not only challenges the old role descriptions but also provides the means for the new roles to be fulfilled.

In the future, teachers will feel the need for constant retooling more than they did in the past. Colleges of education have typically provided only limited responses to the demand for continuing education. They have offered courses for graduate credit that lead to masters, specialists, and doctoral degrees. Teachers have taken these courses not only to meet requirements to maintain their teacher licenses but also to become eligible for new positions. Colleges also have offered workshops and special seminars, usually for graduate credit, at times convenient to their faculty and usually coinciding with school vacations.

Many of the large school corporations have employed staff to satisfy the professional development needs of their teachers. Either the professional development staff provided instruction directly through teacher centers and other institutional devices or they contracted with professional associations, independent firms, regional service agencies, or university faculty acting as private entrepreneurs to provide needed training. For the most part, colleges of education have not attempted to market training services to schools designed to meet their special needs. College faculty want time to develop their courses, and having developed them, they wish to capitalize their investment by repeating them. They are reluctant to respond swiftly to a particular school demand. College administrators face problems in finding ways to balance faculty loads, in deciding whether or not to offer graduate credit for short courses, and in possibly competing with their own faculty who wish to offer training privately for extra income.

Today, computer vendors, software developers, and private consulting firms are more likely to offer the customized training teachers require than are colleges of education. But there is a market ready to be filled by those colleges willing to take advantage of it. The continuing education market will also be influenced by new means of delivery. In the past, faculty have expected teachers and administrators to come to the college campus to receive continuing education. As schools acquire communications technology such as video teleconferencing and audiographics (a combination of audio and computer graphics), this creates opportunities for college faculty to deliver programs to teachers at their places of work. Desktop video in offices enable faculty to provide instruction and consultation at a time convenient to everyone without leaving their offices. In the future teachers will also be able to obtain professional education at home as a result of the enhanced capacity fiber-optic cable/telephone services will provide.

The rising costs of conference attendance and cuts in school budgets, leading to downsizing of professional development staff, open up opportunities for colleges of education to provide client-centered, continuing education at a distance to all who need and want it.

New Roles for Education

Technology is creating new career roles within schools and colleges; it is causing some traditional roles to be redefined; it is provoking a demand for new kinds of services. These changes create opportunities for colleges of education. More and more school districts employ technology coordinators who are responsible for leading efforts to integrate a range of technologies into the classroom. In the future, highly trained technology coordinators will be in demand.

Another new role, probably more distant in the future, is that of instructional designer. The plasticity of multimedia and hypermedia resources provides an opportunity to tailor instruction to fit the requirements of individual schools. That will create a demand for people who combine the skills of a good teacher with the ability to integrate multiple media. As teachers work more as members of teams, the opportunity to employ instructional designers as members of such teams will become obvious and natural.

Technology is also forcing redefinitions of existing roles. One example is the school librarian. The training school librarians once received is no longer adequate for their new roles as "information specialists" for the schools where they work. Students are not limited to the information available in their school libraries; they can search the world's libraries and receive documents electronically. Librarians who merely know their own collection are no longer adequate to the task; they must know how to obtain information from many sources. Increasingly, the school library is where collections of multimedia-based teaching resources are maintained; libraries also provide the electronic source of delivery to each classroom. Thus, librarians must become proficient in the use of technology to meet their expanded responsibilities.

Colleges of education can have an enormous impact on the development of these career roles; they might also be in a favored position to provide schools with services they need in order to take maximum advantage of technology. One of these services is strategic planning.

Currently, school officials have few choices among consultants who can help them plan for technology. If they are about to build a new building, they can employ architects, but few architects understand the pedagogical impact of new technology. Vendors are eager to consult, but their advice is rarely neutral; it is inevitably linked to sales. Schools prefer assistance from experts who are vendor neutral and willing to tailor advice to their needs.

In order to become a source of credible consultants, colleges of education must first make their own programs worthy of emulation. Once this has occurred, colleges can provide valuable professional services and generate substantial income by offering high-quality professional advice on how schools can best employ technology for enhancing student learning and faculty productivity. Advice could range across curriculum issues, staff development, and long-term budgeting. The decision by a school district to become a major aggressive user of technology is not a trivial one; expert knowledge is needed to make good choices and colleges of education could provide valuable assistance.

However, whether these, or any other useful services, are provided, first depends on what vision a college of education has about the future of American education. If a college believes that schools of the future are likely to remain very much like schools of the past century, there is little incentive to change. If, however, colleges decide that the power and influence of modern, electronic information technology is an inevitable component of education's future, there is no choice if they are to survive. They will either be leaders in the application of technology in education or they will be left behind.

A RESEARCH AGENDA FOR THE FUTURE

Much of the research in education is based on a model that was developed and nurtured in the social sciences. One of the chapter authors (J. Willis, 1993b) has called it "research-to-support theory." The purpose of this model is to generate empirical support for a theory. The theory is then used to guide practice. This approach, which has its roots in logical positivism, has a number of assumptions that do not always fit the context or the purpose of educational research. First, to use the model as a guide for conducting research you must eliminate confounding variables and vary only one factor between control and experimental groups. The approach thus assumes useful educational variables can be isolated, but in reality most innovations are combinations of many different "active ingredients."

For example, Risko (1991) has described her approach to re-forming remedial reading courses at Vanderbilt University. Put simply, Risko and her colleagues use video clips of teachers in the classroom as the focus of remedial reading methods courses. However, the approach is not simple. It involves many concepts and theories, including anchored instruction, case method, knowledge representation and transformation models, situated cognition, mediated learning, coaching, problem solving, multiple perspectives, and student-centered discourse. All these ideas rest on a body of research literature that supports their use. However, in her own research Risko is not contributing to any of those bodies of scholarship. Her research, which suggests that students think in more complex and sophisticated ways about teaching when they complete courses based on video cases, is "confounded" because many variables distinguish treatment from control.

A traditional alternative to research-to-support theory is summative evaluation. Summative evaluation essentially demonstrates the effectiveness of a particular instructional package. For example, the research on Risko's video cases and Strang's *Teaching Worlds* (1992) could be treated as summative evaluation of a particular product. However, in the traditional research model, studies of a simulation like *Teaching Worlds* or cases like Risko's have been considered the foundation for broader conclusions. If Strang's simulation works, for example, then the conclusion is that simulations work and should be used more often in teacher education. This approach ignores the complexity of both the instructional strategies discussed and the instructional context in which they are used. In his discussion of comparisons between computer-based instruction (CBI) and traditional instruction (TI), Cunningham (1986) put it this way: "There is no such thing as 'the truth of the matter' that CBI is better than TI or vice versa. The relative effectiveness of those methods is dependent upon an enormous number of other factors, so great a number that they could never be accommodated within any single study or even within any group of studies" (p. 5). Cunningham, and many others, including Scarr (1985), argue that we must not think of research as a process of discovering knowledge. It is, instead, a process of constructing knowledge. However, the knowledge constructed is not Truth, which, once discovered, remains true forever. "Knowledge is a construction of the human mind and 'facts' that are invented within the context of one theoretical perspective become different 'facts' within another theoretical perspective" (Cunningham, 1986, p. 5). Within Cunningham's model of research on instructional technology the goal of research is localized:

Our inquiry will never produce laws that generalize across all possible circumstances. We will never be able to say that CBI is better or worse than TI without embedding that statement within particular interpretive contexts (social, historical, cultural. . . . Let's invest our energies in exploring the potential utility of as many instructional techniques as we can think of rather than pitting them against one another. Is CBI better than TI? Since the question cannot be answered, why don't we simply try to do as good a job of each as we can. The result might even be good instruction. (pp. 6–7)

At this stage in the development of the scholarly field of information technology and teacher education, the need is for more field-tested, effective instructional materials. We need many more video cases, some based on approaches other than the one used by Risko and her colleagues at Vanderbilt University. We need more simulations, some based on models other than the behavioral model used by Strang at the University of Virginia. In general, we need instructional materials that have been developed to high standards. Traditional research-to-support theory scholarship can provide some helpful context for such development work, but it is not an appropriate model for that work. Traditional summative evaluation research can tell us whether a new package is better than "traditional instruction," however that is defined. But summative evaluation comes at the wrong time. It comes at the end of development after the instructional material has already been created. Another alternative, formative evaluation, is much more critical to the development of high-quality materials because formative evaluation, in the form of expert appraisal and tryouts with students, occurs during the process of development. Developers can use feedback from expert evaluators and from students who try out the material to revise and refine the package. This process, which is recursive and nonlinear, is probably more critical to the field now than either research-to-support theory or summative evaluation because it will enhance the quality of instructional materials available to teacher educators.

The end result of formative research is a useful product. Such products are much needed in teacher education, and, fortunately, there is a small but growing number of teacher educators who are concentrating on developing effective, technology-supported materials for teacher education. The work being conducted at Vanderbilt University and at Cleveland State University has already been mentioned. Three other centers of development for both K–12 and teacher education products are Northern Micromedia at the University of Northumbria in England; UltraLab, which is directed by Stephen Heppell at the University of East Anglia; and the Center for Information Technology in Teacher Education, which is directed by Jerry Willis at the University of Houston. Other examples include Barron and Ivers's (1994) work on creating materials (booklets, quick reference guides, brochures, and computer tutorials/simulations) to teach educators how to use telecommunications services; Abate and Hannah's (1994) creation of "video presenter" software for faculty who want to show clips of video from a laserdisc; Abell, Cennamo and Campbell's (1994) project to create videodisc-based cases on science instruction in the elementary grades; Brent's (in press) work on a "First Day of School" simulation; Matthew and Williams's (1994) HyperCard stack on the stages of writing development; and Willis and Brent's (1994) computer-based tutorial for novice preservice teacher education students on writing lesson plans. The work of these developers represents a good start, but much more is needed.

CONCLUSION

What do we know about technology in preservice teacher education? Actually we know quite a bit. We can say with confidence that teacher education students believe that computers are important in education and they want to learn to use them in their preservice programs. We can also say with some confidence that students are not learning to use technology in their programs and without significant changes in teacher education programs, that will continue to be the case.

We can point with pride to a few institutions where students do learn to use technology effectively. These tend, however, to be the leading-edge schools where at least a few faculty have selected technology and teacher education as an area of scholarly focus. These centers of interest produce research on the topic and develop instructional packages and procedures that could be used elsewhere. Unfortunately, the emphasis is on *could be used* because most of the materials developed thus far are not even distributed nationally, much less widely adopted and used.

When it comes to the details of what is happening in teacher education today, most surveys conducted thus far simply do not ask about them. Many ask about attitudes and the amount of equipment and software available. When use of technology is addressed, the surveys often ask threshold questions to students and faculty such as "Do you use technology in the course you teach?" or "In your preservice program did you ever use a computer in class?" Although these thresholds are important, we need to know much more about *what* is taught in *which* classes using *what* methods.

There are many reasons for the slow uptake of technology in teacher education programs, including lack of funds, equipment, software, and support, but the literature also clearly points to another barrier, lack of expertise on the part of teacher education faculty. There may also be a lack of interest on the part of teacher education faculty, but that is not clear at this point because faculty, in general, were not trained to use technology during their undergraduate or graduate school work. They did not see its use modeled by the faculty who taught them, and they have not received much in-service training or support at the institutions where they teach. Unfortunately, much of the in-service training that has been provided concentrates on computer literacy topics rather than on methods of using technology to support instruction in a college or university. Providing encouragement, support, and training to teacher education faculty will be a prerequisite to any effort to move beyond stand-alone courses and to diffuse technology throughout the teacher education curriculum.

Technology in teacher education has evolved through a number of phases, but the process did not involve replacing one phase with another. It appears that the "trailing edge" of the field today is still in the phase that emphasizes programming and basic computer operation. The "current" programs are offering educational computing courses that teach students a combination of topics such as word processing, data bases, and educational uses of technology. Just slightly ahead of these are programs that offer educational computing courses that emphasize curricular inte-

gration and technology-supported instructional strategies. The cutting-edge programs are actively exploring integrating technology into methods courses and student-teaching activities. Programs that have planned for and integrated technology across the curriculum are so rare that perhaps they should not even be called cutting edge at this point because "edge" implies something behind it, as in "on the edge of the oasis."

The present situation is also complicated by the increasing diversification of the field called educational computing. As it has moved away from computer science, it has become more and more a part of fields like curriculum and instruction and instructional technology. However, it has also developed much more specialization relative to subject areas. The cutting-edge uses of information technology for an English composition teacher today are quite different from many of the cutting-edge uses available to a chemistry teacher. There is certainly some overlap, but that overlap is much less than it was even a few years ago. This trend has major implications for how technology should be integrated into teacher education.

A further complication is the fact that as the use of information technology for education has matured, it has become both more content-area specific and more theory laden. Many content areas, such as reading and language arts, have a number of competing theories that guide both research and practice. And, of course, the major theories that underlie other instructional strategies in the classroom are now the basis for different computer applications and usage patterns. One point of contention is whether technology should be used to support the dominant models or serve reformation efforts. The direction information technology should take in teacher education is thus tied to debates about school and teacher education reform. In the past the general idea of "computers in education" was often proposed as a reform in itself. We are well past the stage when computers in education are some sort of monolithic entity. Several sections of this chapter have highlighted the influence of behavioral, constructivist, and critical theories on instructional technology as well as the increasing relevance of subject-specific theories.

Efforts to increase the diffusion of technology into teacher education must thus deal with a wide range of theoretical and practical issues that are currently in a state of flux themselves. In many teacher education programs today both the faculty and the content of educational computing live in a sort of "techno-ghetto" that is cut off from the rest of teacher education. In the next phase of development both the content and the faculty must be brought into the mainstream of teacher education, with all its confusion, conflicts, and theoretical debates. In the terms of developmental psychology, it is time technology and teacher education moved from parallel play to cooperative play.

References

Abate, R. (1992). The development of multimedia in teacher education. In D. Carey, R. Carey, D. Willis, & J. Willis (Eds.), *Technology and teacher education annual—1992* (pp. 271–275). Charlottesville, VA: Association for the Advancement of Computing in Education.

Abate, R. (1993). The development of multimedia instructional materials in teacher education. *Journal of Technology and Teacher Education, 1*(2), 169–180.

Abate, R., & Hannah, C. (1994). Experiences with a videodisc presentation utility. In J. Willis, B. Robin, & D. Willis (Eds.), *Technology and teacher education annual—1994* (pp. 445–447). Charlottesville, VA: Association for the Advancement of Computing in Education.

Abell, S., Cennamo, K., & Campbell, L. (1994, February). *The development of interactive video cases for use in elementary science methods courses*. Paper presented at the 74th annual meeting of the Association of Teacher Educators, Atlanta.

Ambron, S., & Hooper, K. (1990). *Learning with interactive multimedia: Developing and using multimedia tools in education*. Redmond, WA: Microsoft Press.

American Association of Colleges for Teacher Education. (1987). *Teaching teachers: Facts and figures*. Washington, DC: Author.

Anderson, D., & Bair, D. (1991). Interactive communications and simulations: The global classroom. In D. Carey, R. Carey, D. Willis, & J. Willis (Eds.), *Technology and teacher education annual—1991* (pp. 125–129). Charlottesville, VA: Association for the Advancement of Computing in Education.

Anderson, S. (1991). Computer attitudes, experience, and usage of computer conferencing by preservice educators. In D. Carey, R. Carey, D. Willis, & J. Willis (Eds.), *Technology and teacher education annual—1991* (pp. 120–123). Charlottesville, VA: Association for the Advancement of Computing in Education.

Andris, J., Nelson, W., & Smith, R. (1994). LEAPINGS into the future: Using instructional design to develop an integrated preservice teacher education computer curriculum. In J. Willis, B. Robin, & D. Willis (Eds.), *Technology and teacher education annual—1994* (pp. 161–164). Charlottesville, VA: Association for the Advancement of Computing in Education.

Apple, M. (1991). The new technology: Is it part of the solution or part of the problem in education? *Computers in the Schools, 8*(1/2/3), 59–81.

Armitage, D. (1993). Where are the girls? Increasing female participation in computer, math, and science education. In D. Carey, R. Carey, D. Willis, & J. Willis (Eds.), *Technology and teacher education annual—1993* (pp. 19–24). Charlottesville, VA: Association for the Advancement of Computing in Education.

Association for Computing Machinery. (1988). Preservice education in educational computing [special issue]. *Outlook, 20*(1).

Atkins, S. (1994). Creating images of model elementary school mathematics programs. In J. Willis, B. Robin, & D. Willis (Eds.), *Technology and teacher education annual—1994* (pp. 448–450). Charlottesville, VA: Association for the Advancement of Computing in Education.

Ayers, S., & Bitter, G. (1988). Using computers to enhance the mathematics classroom. *Outlook, 20*(1), 115–130.

Bair, D., & Anderson, D. (1991). Diverse perspectives on education: Connecting theory and practice in teacher education. In D. Carey, R. Carey, D. Willis, & J. Willis (Eds.), *Technology and teacher education annual—1991* (pp. 344–349). Charlottesville, VA: Association for the Advancement of Computing in Education.

Baird, W., Ellis, J., & Kuerbis, P. (1989). Enlist micros: Training science teachers to use microcomputers. *Journal of Research in Science Teaching, 26*(7), 567–598.

Bandura. A. (1972). Modeling theory: Some traditions, trends, and disputes. In R. D. Parke (Ed.), *Recent trends in social learning theory* (pp. 35–61). New York: Academic Press.

Bank Street College of Education. (1989). *The second voyage of the Mimi*. Pleasantville, NY: Sunburst Communications. (ERIC Document Reproduction Service No. ED 324 223)

Barron, A. (1993). *Using cases as a pedagogical technique in an elementary mathematics methods course: An example using integrated media technology*. Paper presented at the annual meeting of the American Educational Research Association, Atlanta.

Barron, A., & Ivers, K. (1994). Training materials for telecommunications: Eliminating "Teleconfusion." *Journal of Technology and Teacher Education, 2*(2), 129–142.

Bartos, R., & Souter, F. (1982). What are we teaching in educational foundations? *Journal of Teacher Education, 33*(2), 45–47.

Bauer, N. (1990, April). *Pedagogy and the "other" dimension of teacher preparation: A trend and a response*. Paper presented at the spring conference of the Confederated Organizations of Teacher Education, Syracuse. (ERIC Document Reproduction Service No. ED 323 176)

Bauer, N. (1992, November). *In search of the distinctive contributions of the social foundations of education to the preparation of teachers*. Paper presented at the annual meeting of the American Educational Studies Association, Pittsburgh. (ERIC Document Reproduction Service No. ED 353 222)

Baumbach, D., & Barron, A. (1990). Technologies for education: Getting the good news to teachers. *Computers in the Schools, 8*(1/2/3), 327–328.

Baumbach, D., Bird, M., & Brewer, S. (1994) Doing more with less: A cooperative model that works. In J. Willis, B. Robin, & D. Willis (Eds.), *Technology and teacher education annual—1994* (pp. 323–327). Charlottesville, VA: Association for the Advancement of Computing in Education.

Beacham, B. (1994). Making connections: Transforming ivory towers and little red schoolhouses. In J. Willis, B. Robin, & D. Willis (Eds.), *Technology and teacher education annual—1994* (pp. 742–744). Charlottesville, VA: Association for the Advancement of Computing in Education.

Beaver, J. (1990). *A profile of undergraduate educational technology (in) competencies: Are we preparing today's education graduates for teaching in the 1990's?* (ERIC Document Reproduction Service No. 332 985)

Becker, H. (1984, Fall). School uses of microcomputers: Report #5 from a national survey. *Journal of Computers in Mathematics and Science Teaching, 4*(1), 38–42.

Becker, H. (1984–1985, Winter). School uses of microcomputers: Report #6 from a national survey. *Journal of Computers in Mathematics and Science Teaching, 4*(2), 42–49.

Bednar, M., Ryan, F., & Sweeder, J. (1994). Did video really work? An analysis of student teachers' perceptions. In J. Willis, B. Robin, & D. Willis (Eds.), *Technology and teacher education annual—1994* (pp. 86–90). Charlottesville, VA: Association for the Advancement of Computing in Education.

Beers, M., Orzech, M., & Parsons, A. (1992). Computing in the education curriculum: Moving towards tomorrow's classroom. In D. Carey, R. Carey, D. Willis, & J. Willis (Eds.), *Technology and teacher education annual—1992* (pp. 156–157). Charlottesville, VA: Association for the Advancement of Computing in Education.

Benavides, O., & Surry, D. (1994). Train the trainer: A model for faculty development. In J. Willis, B. Robin, & D. Willis (Eds.), *Technology and teacher education annual—1994* (pp. 337–340). Charlottesville, VA: Association for the Advancement of Computing in Education.

Benghiat, K., & Abate, R. (1994). Planning and implementing a videodisc-based observation program. In J. Willis, B. Robin, & D. Willis (Eds.), *Technology and teacher education annual—1994* (pp. 451–453). Charlottesville, VA: Association for the Advancement of Computing in Education.

Berger, C., & Carlson, E. (1988a). Measuring computer literacy of teacher trainers. *Journal of Educational Computing Research, 4*(3), 247–253.

Berger, C., & Carlson, E. (1988b). A model for incorporating learning theories into preservice computer training. *Outlook, 20*(1), 32–46.

Berry, L. (1994). Interactive video simulations: Factors related to promoting teacher effectiveness. In J. Willis, B. Robin, & D. Willis (Eds.), *Technology and teacher education annual—1994* (pp. 82–85). Charlottesville, VA: Association for the Advancement of Computing in Education.

Beyer, L., & Zeichner, K. (1982). Teacher training and educational foundations: A plea for discontent. *Journal of Teacher Education, 33*(3), 18–23.

Biglan, B. (1992). Preservice instructional technology: The old, the new and the future. In D. Carey, R. Carey, D. Willis, & J. Willis (Eds.), *Technology and teacher education annual—1992* (pp. 313–314). Charlottesville, VA: Association for the Advancement of Computing in Education.

Bigum, C. (1990). Situated computing in pre-service teacher education. In A. McDougall & C. Dowling (Eds.), *Computers and education* (pp. 477–482). North Holland: Elsevier.

Bigum, C., & Green, B. (Eds.). (1992). *Understanding the new information technologies in education.* Geelong, Australia: Center for Studies in Information Technologies and Education, Deakin University.

Bitter, G., & Yohe, R. (1989). Preparing teachers for the information age. *Educational Technology, 29*(1), 22–25.

Blackmore, M. (1992). The Liverpool scene—students' experiences of information technology whilst on block school experience. *Developing Information Technology in Teacher Education, 3,* 45–59.

Blackmore, M., Stanley, N., Coles, D., Hodgkinson, K., Taylor, C., & Vaughan, G. (1992). A preliminary view of students' information technology experience across UK initial teacher training institutions. *Journal of Information Technology for Teacher Education, 1*(2), 241–254.

Blanck, G. (1992). Vygotsky: The man and his cause. In L. Moll (Ed.), *Vygotsky and education* (pp. 31–58). Cambridge: Cambridge University Press.

Blurton, C. (1989). The California Technology Project. *California Technology Project Quarterly, 1*(1), 22, 37.

Blythe, K., & Nuttall, W. (1992, April). Reflections on the impact of an information technology development programme upon the planned curriculum of an institution engaged in initial teacher training. *Developing Information Technology in Teacher Education, 2,* 3–50.

Bollerslev, P. (1988). Denmark's program for teacher informatics education. *Technological Horizons in Education, 15*(9), 73–77.

Bork, A. (1991). The history of technology and education. In N. Knupfer et al. (Eds.), *Educational computing social foundations: A symposium* (pp. 350–380). (ERIC Document Reproduction Service No. ED 334 990)

Borrell, J. (1992, September). America's shame: How we've abandoned our children's future. *MacWorld,* 25–30.

Bosworth, K., & Welsh, T. (1992). Teaching with groups: An interactive multimedia program for teacher education. In D. Carey, R. Carey, D. Willis, & J. Willis (Eds.), *Technology and teacher education annual—1992* (pp. 261–265). Charlottesville, VA: Association for the Advancement of Computing in Education.

Bowers, J., Barron, L., & Goldman, E. (1994). An interactive media environment to enhance mathematics teacher education. In J. Willis, B. Robin, & D. Willis (Eds.), *Technology and teacher education annual—1994* (pp. 515–519). Charlottesville, VA: Association for the Advancement of Computing in Education.

Branscum, D. (1992, September). Educators need support to make computing meaningful. *MacWorld,* 83–88.

Bransford, J., Franks, J., Vye, N., & Sherwood, R. (1989). New approaches to instruction: Because wisdom can't be told. In S. Vosniadou & A. Artony (Eds.), *Similarity and analogical reasoning* (pp. 470–497). New York: Cambridge University Press.

Brent, R. (in press). First day of school simulation [computer software]. Charlottesville, VA: Association for the Advancement of Computing in Education.

Brownell, G. (1990). The first course in computer education: A survey. *Journal of Computing in Teacher Education, 7*(2), 15–19.

Brownell, G., & Brownell, N. (1994). A technology course for secondary preservice teachers. In J. Willis, B. Robin, & D. Willis (Eds.), *Technology and teacher education annual—1994* (pp. 431–434). Charlottesville, VA: Association for the Advancement of Computing in Education.

Brownell, G., Zirkler, D., & Brownell, N. (1991). Preservice teachers' perceptions of teachers as computer users. In D. Carey, R. Carey, D. Willis, & J. Willis (Eds.), *Technology and teacher education annual—1991* (pp. 288–292). Charlottesville, VA: Association for the Advancement of Computing in Education.

Bruder, I. (1988). Ed schools: Literacy requirements stagnant, but more offer degrees. *Electronic Learning, 7,* 18–19.

Bruder, I. (1989). Future teachers: Are they prepared? *Electronic Learning, 8,* 32–39.

Bull, G., Cothern, H., & Stout, C. (1992). Models for a national public school computing network. In D. Carey, R. Carey, D. Willis, & J. Willis (Eds.), *Technology and teacher education annual—1992* (pp. 473–478). Charlottesville, VA: Association for the Advancement of Computing in Education.

Bull, G., Harris, J., Loyd, J., & Short, J. (1989). The electronic academical village. *Journal of Teacher Education, 40*(4), 27–31.

Bull, G., Sigmon, T., & Shidisky, C. (1991). Specifications for computer networks for support of cooperative ventures between universities and public schools. *Computers in the Schools, 8*(1/2/3), 183–185.

Bullock, D. (1991). California's teacher pre-service computer education requirements: Are they enough for the state and the nation? *Computers in the Schools, 8*(1/2/3), 111–114.

Burnett, T. (1992). The Christopher Columbus Consortium Partnership. In R. Carey, D. Carey, D. Willis, & J. Willis (Eds.), *Technology and teacher education annual—1992* (pp. 214–215). Charlottesville, VA: Association for the Advancement of Computing in Education.

Burson, J., & Willis, J. (1994). Profession-specific computer literacy: Microteaching in an educational computing course. In J. Willis, B. Robin, & D. Willis (Eds.), *Technology and teacher education annual—1994* (pp. 427–430). Charlottesville, VA: Association for the Advancement of Computing in Education.

Callister, T., & Burbles, N. (1990). Computer literacy programs in teacher education: What teachers really need to learn. *Computers & Education, 14*(1), 3–7.

Campbell-Bonar, K., & Grisdale, L. (1991). Applying principles of collaboration to videodisc design: Profile of a successful project. *Canadian Journal of Educational Communication, 20*(3), 189–203.

Carey, D. (1991a). Classroom experience in preservice computer education. In D. Carey, R. Carey, D. Willis, & J. Willis (Eds.), *Technology and teacher education annual—1991* (pp. 53–58). Charlottesville, VA: Association for the Advancement of Computing in Education.

Carey, D. (1991b). Teacher posture in the computing environment. In D. Carey, R. Carey, D. Willis, & J. Willis (Eds.), *Technology and teacher education annual—1991* (pp. 315–319). Charlottesville, VA: Association for the Advancement of Computing in Education.

Carr, L., Novak, D., & Berger, C. (1992). Integrating technology into preservice education: Determining the necessary resources. *Journal of Computing in Teacher Education 9*(1), 20–24.

Caruso, B., Trottier, C., & Shade, D. (1994). Computers and crayons: Training teachers in developmentally appropriate computer use. In J. Willis, B. Robin, & D. Willis (Eds.), *Technology and teacher education annual—1994* (pp. 341–345). Charlottesville, VA: Association for the Advancement of Computing in Education.

Casey, J. (1992). TeacherNet: Student teachers form a community of teachers. In D. Carey, R. Carey, D. Willis, & J. Willis (Eds.), *Technology and teacher education annual—1992* (pp. 491–492). Charlottesville, VA: Association for the Advancement of Computing in Education.

CATE. (1992). *Initial teacher training (secondary phase)*. Circular No. 9/92. London: Department of Education.

Center for Information Technology in Education. (1994). Software to support the Alberta Teacher Education Videodiscs [computer software]. Houston: University of Houston, College of Education.

Cobb, H., & Horn, C. (1986). Planned change in special education technology. *Journal of Special Education Technology, 8*(2), 18–27.

Cognition and Technology Group. (1990). Anchored instruction and its relationship to situated cognition. *Educational Researcher, 19*(6), 2–10.

Colasanti, A., & Follo, E. (1992). *Effectiveness of thematic teaching in curriculum design and implementation in a third grade classroom, including a planning process model using the Michigan Model Core Curriculum* (ERIC Document Reproduction Service No. ED 355 189)

Collis, B. (1994). A reflection on the relationship between technology and teacher education: Synergy or separate entities? *Journal of Information Technology for Teacher Education, 3*(1), 7–25.

Connell, M. (1993). Technology enhanced cases. In R. Carey, D. Carey, D. Willis, & J. Willis (Eds.), *Technology and teacher education annual—1993* (pp. 345–349). Charlottesville, VA: Association for the Advancement of Computing in Education.

Cooley, M. (1992). Human-centered education. In C. Bigum & B. Green (Eds.), *Understanding the new information technologies in education*. Geelong, Australia: Centre for Studies in Information Technologies and Education, Deakin University.

Copley, J. (1992a). The integration of teacher education and technology: A constructivist model. In D. Carey, R. Carey, D. Willis, & J. Willis (Eds.), *Technology and teacher education annual—1992* (pp. 617–622). Charlottesville, VA: Association for the Advancement of Computing in Education.

Copley, J. (1992b). The use of classroom observations in technology and education research. In D. Carey, R. Carey, D. Willis, & J. Willis (Eds.), *Technology and teacher education annual—1992* (pp. 381–385). Charlottesville, VA: Association for the Advancement of Computing in Education.

Corda, S. (1991). Implementing technology in schools: The change agent's environment. *Connections, 8*(1), 3–8.

Cunningham, D. (1986). Good guys and bad guys. *Educational Communication and Technology Journal, 34*(1), 3–7.

Damarin, S. (1991). Recontextualizing computers in education: A response to Streibel. In D. Hlynka & J. Belland (Eds.), *Paradigms regained* (pp. 341–350). Englewood Cliffs, NJ: Educational Technology Publications.

Davis, N. (1992). Information technology in United Kingdom initial teacher education, 1982–1992. *Journal of Information Technology for Teacher Education, 1*(1), 7–21.

Davis, N., & Coles, D. (1992). *Students' IT experience and related data across the UK on entry to initial teacher education*. Croydon, UK: Information Technology in Teacher Education Association.

Department of Education and Science (DES). (1988). *Information technology and initial teacher training: Report of the expert working group*. London: Her Majesty's Stationery Office.

Department of Education and Science (DES). (1989). *Circular 24/89 initial teacher training: Approval of courses*. London: Author.

Department of Education and Science (DES). (1992). *Information technology in initial teacher training: Two years after Trotter*. London: Her Majesty's Stationery Office.

Dershimer, E., & Dershimer, W. (1991). Technology in preservice teacher education. In D. Carey, R. Carey, D. Willis, & J. Willis (Eds.), *Technology and teacher education annual—1991* (pp. 24–26).

Charlottesville, VA: Association for the Advancement of Computing in Education.

Downs, E. (1992). Integrating technology into teacher education. In D. Carey, R. Carey, D. Willis, & J. Willis (Eds.), *Technology and teacher education annual—1992* (pp. 83–85). Charlottesville, VA: Association for the Advancement of Computing in Education.

Dreyfus, H., & Dreyfus, L. (1985). Putting computers in their proper place: Analysis versus intuition in the classroom. In D. Sloan (Ed.), *The computer in education: A critical perspective* (pp. 40–63). New York: Teachers College Press.

Dunn, S., & Ridgway, J. (1991). Computer use during primary school teaching practice: A survey. *Journal of Computer Assisted Learning, 7*(1), 7–17.

Dunn, S., & Ridgway, J. (1994). What CATE did: An exploration of the effects of the CATE criteria on students' use of information technology during teaching practice. *Journal of Information Technology for Teacher Education, 3*(1), 39–50.

Dwyer, D., Ringstaff, C., & Sandholtz, J. (1990). *Teacher beliefs and practices. Apple classrooms of tomorrow report No. 8*. Cupertino, CA: Apple Classrooms of Tomorrow.

Eisenstein, H. (1988). In praise of the anarchism to be found in foundations (If you had a mind to). *Teacher Education Quarterly, 15*(3), 61–80.

Erb, D., & Golden, C. (1994). The Marietta College model: Integration of content, methods, materials, and technology. In J. Willis, B. Robin, & D. Willis (Eds.), *Technology and teacher education annual—1994* (pp. 165–168). Charlottesville, VA: Association for the Advancement of Computing in Education.

Erickson, B., & Mountain, L. (1992). Graduate students and fourth graders, connected at home on a commercial telecommunications service. In D. Carey, R. Carey, D. Willis, & J. Willis (Eds.), *Technology and teacher education annual—1992* (pp. 527–533). Charlottesville, VA: Association for the Advancement of Computing in Education.

Eskridge, S., & Langer, M. (1992). Pacific-LINK: Supporting new teachers through electronic conferencing. In D. Carey, R. Carey, D. Willis, & J. Willis (Eds.), *Technology and teacher education annual—1992* (pp. 485–490). Charlottesville, VA: Association for the Advancement of Computing in Education.

Evans, A., Cupp, G., & Kinsvatter, R. (1987). *Critical incidents in discipline* (interactive videodisc). Kent, OH: Kent State University College of Education.

Ferranti Educational Systems. (1987). *Essential teaching skills* (multimedia package). Lancaster, PA: Author.

Feyerabend, P. (1988). *Against method*. New York: Verso.

Finkelstein, B. (1984). Servants, critics, skeptics: The place of foundations faculties in professional education. *Teacher Education Quarterly, 11*(2), 14–21.

Flake, J. (1993). Reflections on reflective learning in a computer environment. *Journal of Technology and Teacher Education, 1*(4), 373–391.

Flew, A. (1984). *A dictionary of philosophy* (Rev. 2nd ed.). New York: St. Martin's Press.

Ford, M., Whelan, C., Zink, F., & Goellner, E. (1992). Using interactive media in elementary social studies and science classes. In D. Carey, R. Carey, D. Willis, & J. Willis (Eds.), *Technology and teacher education annual—1992* (pp. 86–89). Charlottesville, VA: Association for the Advancement of Computing in Education.

Fratianni, J., Decker, R., & Korver-Baum, B. (1990). Technology: Are future teachers being prepared for the 21st century? *Journal of Computing in Teacher Education, 6*(4), 15–23.

Freeouf, B., & Flank, S. (1994). Preparing teacher educators to integrate technology into required courses: W.T.E.G. In J. Willis, B. Robin, & D. Willis (Eds.), *Technology and teacher education annual—1994* (pp. 172–177). Charlottesville, VA: Association for the Advancement of Computing in Education.

French, M., & Araujo, E. (1991). Integrating microcomputers in the graduate reading practicum: Activities from the Bowling Green State University Reading Center. *Computers in the Schools, 8*(1/2/3), 163–165.

Friere, P. (1985). *The politics of education: Culture, power and liberation* (D. Macedo, Trans.). South Hadley, MA: Bergin & Garvey.

Frisbie, A. (1991). Using integrated software as a courseware prototyping and delivery tool. In D. Carey, R. Carey, D. Willis, & J. Willis (Eds.), *Technology and teacher education annual—1991* (pp. 248–253). Charlottesville, VA: Association for the Advancement of Computing in Education.

Frisbie, A., Harless, R., & Brunson, G. (1991). Computer managed instruction in a large undergraduate teacher education course. *Computers in the Schools, 8*(1/2/3), 135–138.

Fulton, K. (1988, October). Preservice and inservice: What must be done in both. *Electronic Learning, 7,* 32–36.

Fulton, K. (1989). Technology training for teachers: A federal perspective. *Educational Technology, 29*(3), 12–19.

Gabel, D., & Boone, W. (1993). The preparation of prospective elementary science teachers in the use of technology. *Journal of Technology and Teacher Education, 1*(2), 195–207.

Gardner, J., & Salters, J. (1990). Information technology in education and teacher education in France. *European Journal of Teacher Education, 13*(3), 161–172.

Geuss, R. (1981). *The idea of a critical theory: Habermas and the Frankfurt School.* Cambridge: Cambridge University Press.

Gibbon, S., & Hooper, K. (1986, Spring). The voyage of the Mimi. *Learning tomorrow: Journal of the Apple Education Advisory Council, 3,* 195–207. (ERIC Document Reproduction Service No. ED 302 188)

Goldman, E., & Barron, L. (1990). Using hypermedia to improve the preparation of elementary teachers. *Journal of Teacher Education, 41*(3), 12–20.

Goodlad, J. (1990). Better teachers for our nation's schools. *Phi Delta Kappan, 72,* 184–194.

Gooler, D. (1989). Preparing teachers to use technologies: Can universities meet the challenge? *Educational Technology, 29*(3), 18–21.

Grandbastein, M. (1993). Informatique pour tous: A case study of information technology in teacher education in France. *Journal of Information Technology for Teacher Education, 2*(2), 219–228.

Griffiths, M., & Tann, S. (1992). Using reflective practice to link personal and public theories. *Journal of Education for Teaching, 18*(1), 69–84.

Hall, G., & Hord, S. (1987). *Change in schools: Facilitating the process.* Albany: State University of New York Press.

Hall, G., & Loucks, L. (1978). Teacher concerns as a basis for facilitating and personalizing staff development. *Teachers College Record, 80*(1), 36–53.

Handler, M., & Pigott, T. (1994, April). *Schools of education and technology preparation: Are we doing our job?* Paper presented at the annual meeting of the American Educational Research Association, New Orleans.

Harrington, H. (1991). Using technology in teacher education: Facilitating development or maintaining the status quo? In D. Carey, R. Carey, D. Willis, & J. Willis (Eds.), *Technology and teacher education annual—1991* (pp. 338–343). Charlottesville, VA: Association for the Advancement of Computing in Education.

Harrington, H. (1992). Fostering critical reflection through technology: Preparing prospective teachers for a changing society. *Journal of Information Technology for Teacher Education, 1*(1), 67–82.

Harris, J., & Anderson, S. (1991). Cultivating teacher telecommunications networks from the grass roots up: The electronic academical village at Virginia. *Computers in the Schools, 8*(1/2/3), 191–202.

Heeber, A. (1988). Integrating word processing with writing instruction: A review of research and practice. *Outlook, 20*(1), 55–64.

Heinich, R. (1991). The use of computers in education: A response to Streibel. In D. Hlynka & J. Belland (Eds.), *Paradigms regained* (pp. 335–339). Englewood Cliffs, NJ: Educational Technology Publications.

Her Majesty's Inspectorate. (1988). *A survey of information technology within initial teacher training.* London: Department of Education and Science.

Hess, R. (1992). A new model of computers and technology in education. In D. Carey, R. Carey, D. Willis, & J. Willis (Eds.), *Technology and teacher education annual—1992* (pp. 144–147). Charlottesville, VA: Association for the Advancement of Computing in Education.

Hodgkinson, K., & Wild, P. (1994). Tracking the development of student information technology capability: IT in a primary postgraduate certificate of education course over three years. *Journal of Information Technology for Teacher Education, 3*(1), 101–114.

Hoelscher, K. (1988). Making it in America. *Computers in the Schools, 5*(1/2), 179–185.

Huang, S. (1994). Prospective teachers' use and perception of the value of technology. In J. Willis, B. Robin, & D. Willis (Eds.), *Technology and teacher education annual—1994* (pp. 61–65). Charlottesville, VA: Association for the Advancement of Computing in Education.

Hunt, N. (1994). Intentions and implementations: The impact of technology coursework in elementary classrooms. In J. Willis, B. Robin, & D. Willis (Eds.), *Technology and teacher education annual—1994* (pp. 38–41). Charlottesville, VA: Association for the Advancement of Computing in Education.

Hunt, N., & Bohlin, R. (1992). Instructional implications of teacher education students' attitudes toward using computers. In D. Carey, R. Carey, D. Willis, & J. Willis (Eds.), *Technology and teacher education annual—1992* (pp. 389–392). Charlottesville, VA: Association for the Advancement of Computing in Education.

Huppert, J., & Lazarowitz, R. (1991). Student teachers' attitudes toward computer use in science classrooms. *Journal of Computing in Teacher Education, 7*(3), 12–16.

International Council for Computers in Education. (1985). *Software reviews reprinted from The Computing Teacher, March 1983—May 1985.* Eugene, OR: Author. (ERIC Document Reproduction Service No. ED 262 762)

Information Technology for Teacher Education Association. (1987). *Information technology in teacher education.* Croydon, U.K.: Author.

Information Technology for Teacher Education Association. (1991). *IT resources in initial teacher training.* Croydon, U.K.: Author.

International Society for Technology in Education. (1991). *Curriculum guidelines for accreditation of educational computing and technology programs.* Eugene, OR: Author.

Jacobs, J. (1988). Social implications of computers: Ethical and equity issues. *Outlook, 20*(1), 100–114.

Johns, K. (1988). A curriculum review: The voyage of the Mimi. *Teacher Education Quarterly, 15*(1), 88–91.

Johnson, D. (1993). Academic and intellectual foundations of teacher education in global perspectives. *Theory into Practice, 32*(1), 3–13.

Johnson, M., & Hoot, J. (1986). Computers and the elementary teacher. *Educational Horizons, 62,* 73–75.

Johnson, S. (1985). *An investigation of microcomputer literacy skills for public secondary school teachers in South Carolina.* Unpublished doctoral dissertation, University of South Carolina.

Jones-Wilson, F. C. (1986). The role of the foundations scholar with respect to three critical issues (AESA Presidential Address—1985). *Educational Studies, 17*(2), 171–183.

Kearsley, G., & Lynch, W. (1992). Teacher training and telecommunications: From bulletin boards to Internet. In D. Carey, R. Carey, D. Willis, & J. Willis (Eds.), *Technology and teacher education annual—1992* (pp. 479–481). Charlottesville, VA: Association for the Advancement of Computing in Education.

Kelly, M., Harris, S., & Shelton, M. (1990). Computer-based technologies and teacher education: Implementing California legislation (AB 1681). *Journal of Computing in Teacher Education, 6*(3), 13–20.

Kennedy, K. (1987). *A program design for computer education for teacher education colleges.* Unpublished doctoral dissertation, University of Tennessee. (University Microfilms No. 8810368.)

Kiefer, K. (1991). Computers and teacher education in the 1990s and beyond. In G. Hawisher & C. Selfe (Eds.), *Evolving perspectives on computers and composition studies: Questions for the 1990s* (pp. 117–131). Urbana, IL: National Council of Teachers of English. (ERIC Document Reproduction Service No. ED 331 088)

Knupfer, N. (1991). Educational computing and teachers: Changing roles, changing pedagogy. In N. Knupfer, R. Muffoletto, M. McIsaac, A. Bork, R. Koetting, & A. Yeaman (Eds.), *Educational computing social foundations: A symposium* (pp. 332–342). (ERIC Document Reproduction Service No. ED 334 990)

Knupfer, N. (1993). Teachers and educational computing: Changing roles and changing pedagogy. In R. Muffoletto & N. Knupfer (Eds.), *Computers in education: Social, political and historical perspectives* (pp. 163–179). Cresskill, NJ: Hampton Press.

Kohl, H. (1992). *From archetype to zeitgeist.* Boston: Little, Brown.

Kondracke, M. (1992, September). The official world: How our government views the use of computers in schools. *MacWorld,* 232–236.

Kosko, B. (1993). *Fuzzy thinking: The new science of fuzzy logic.* New York: Hyperion.

Lampert, M., & Ball, D. (1990). *Using hypermedia technology to support a new pedagogy of teacher education,* Issue Paper 90-5. East Lansing: National Center for Research on Teacher Education, College of Education, Michigan State University. (ERIC Document Reproduction Service No. ED 323 209)

Lavine, T. (1984). *From Socrates to Sartre: The philosophic quest.* New York: Bantam.

Lawson, J. (1988). Chair's message. *Outlook, 20*(1), 1–2.

Lehman, J. (1986). Microcomputer offerings in science teaching training. *School Science and Mathematics, 86*(2), 119–125.

Leite, L. (1990). *A survey of computers in undergraduate teacher education certification programs in the Delaware Valley.* Unpublished doctoral dissertation, Temple University.

Lichtman, D. (1979, January). Survey of educators' attitudes toward computers. *Creative Computing,* 48–50.

Lintner, M., Moore, P., Friske, J., Mlynarczyk, C., Thomas, L., & Wiebe, J. (1991). The required computer course for education majors: A national perspective. *Journal of Computing in Teacher Education, 7*(3), 17–23.

Logan, L., & Sachs, J. (1992). Changing teacher education through technology: A study of the Remote Area Teacher Education Project. *Journal of Information Technology for Teacher Education, 1*(2), 189–200.

Madsen, J., & Sebastiani, L. (1987). The effect of computer literacy instruction on teachers' knowledge of and attitudes toward microcomputers. *Journal of Computer-Based Instruction, 14*(2), 68–72.

Maher, F., & Rathbone, C. (1986). Teacher education and feminist theory: Some implications for practice. *American Journal of Education, 94*(2), 214–235.

Main, R., & Roberts, L. (1990). Educational technology in the California public schools: A statewide survey. *Educational Technology, 30*(12), 7–19.

Marsh, E., Hofwolt, C., & Sherwood, R. (1991). Instructional contrasts in elementary science teaching. In D. Carey, R. Carey, D. Willis, & J. Willis (Eds.), *Technology and teacher education annual—1991* (pp. 93–94). Charlottesville, VA: Association for the Advancement of Computing in Education.

Marshall, P. (1992, November). *Toward a theoretical framework for the design of multicultural education in teacher education programs.* Paper presented at the 72 annual meeting of the National Council for the Social Studies, Detroit, MI. (ERIC Document Reproduction Service No. ED 353 246)

Martin, L. (1992). Detecting and defining science problems: A study of video-mediated lessons. In L. Moll (Eds.), *Vygotsky and education: Instructional implications and applications of sociohistorical psychology* (pp. 372–402). Cambridge: Cambridge University Press.

Mathison, C. (1986). Teacher training in educational technology: What student teachers want to know. *Action in Teacher Education, 8*(3), 79–83.

Matthew, K., & Williams, N. (1994). Authentic uses of technology for curriculum planning within a language arts curriculum. In J. Willis, B. Robin, & D. Willis (Eds.), *Technology and teacher education annual—1994* (pp. 611–614). Charlottesville, VA: Association for the Advancement of Computing in Education.

Maury, K. (1992). A required problem solving course for undergraduate preservice teachers. In D. Carey, R. Carey, D. Willis, & J. Willis (Eds.), *Technology and teacher education annual—1991* (pp. 341–343). Charlottesville, VA: Association for the Advancement of Computing in Education.

McCartney, P. (1990). Writing with Carmen. *Writing Notebook: Creative Word Processing in the Classroom, 8*(2) 8–10.

McCormick, R. (1992). Curriculum development and new information technology. *Journal of Information Technology for Teacher Education, 1*(1), 23–50.

McDevitt, M. (1994). Two-way television: Linking preservice teachers to real world schools. In J. Willis, B. Robin, & D. Willis (Eds.), *Technology and teacher education annual—1994* (pp. 216–220). Charlottesville, VA: Association for the Advancement of Computing in Education.

McHoul, A., & Luke, A. (1988). Epistemological groundings of educational studies: A critique. *Journal of Educational Thought, 22*(3), 178–189.

Merideth, E., & Lotfipour, S. (1992). Reflecting through technology: A computer-laserdisc model of cooperative learning. *In* D. Carey, R. Carey, D. Willis, & J. Willis (Eds.), *Technology and teacher education annual—1992* (pp. 266–270). Charlottesville, VA: Association for the Advancement of Computing in Education.

Michigan State Board of Education. (1988). *Technology training for Michigan's preservice teachers.* Lansing: Michigan Department of Education.

Michigan State Board of Education. (1990). *Handbook for preservice technology training.* Lansing: Michigan Department of Education.

Midkiff, R. (1991). Techniques for motivating students in foundations of American education: Practicing what we preach. *Action in Teacher Education, 13*(2), 60–66.

Mizell, A., Marcus, D., Hesser, L., & Hogan, R. (1992). Distance teacher education: E > the whole. In D. Carey, R. Carey, D. Willis, & J. Willis (Eds.), *Technology and teacher education annual—1992* (pp. 498–505). Charlottesville, VA: Association for the Advancement of Computing in Education.

Moll, L. (Ed.). (1992). *Vygotsky and education: Instructional implications and applications of sociohistorical psychology.* Cambridge: Cambridge University Press.

Morgan, R., Rule, S., Salzberg, C., & Fodor-Davis, J. (1991). Videodisc-assisted courseware to prepare teachers to serve students who have learning problems. In D. Carey, R. Carey, D. Willis, & J. Willis (Eds.), *Technology and teacher education annual—1991* (pp. 74–79).

Charlottesville, VA: Association for the Advancement of Computing in Education.

Morrison, D., & Walters, J. (1985). *Immigrant: A social studies unit for AppleWorks*. Cambridge, MA: Harvard Graduate School of Education, Educational Technology Center.

Moursund, D. (1989). Why are our colleges of education continuing to graduate computer illiterate teachers? *The Computing Teacher, 16*, 9.

Mueller, R., Husband, T., Christou, C., & Sun, A. (1991). Preservice teacher attitudes towards computer technology. A log-linear analysis. *Mid-Western Educational Researcher, 4*(2), 23–27.

Nash, R., & Agne, R. (1982). Beyond marginality: A new role for foundations of education. *Journal of Teacher Education, 33*(3), 2–7.

Nason, R. (1991). PRODIGY: An intelligent computer-based system for developing teachers expertise in the diagnosis and remediation of common error patterns in the domain of common fractions. In *Proceedings of the Information Technology for Training and Education Conference* (pp. 117–123). Brisbane, Australia: (ERIC Document Reproduction Service No. ED 339 366)

National Governors' Association. (1991). *The Governors' 1991 Report on Education: Results on education 1990.* Washington, DC: Author. (ERIC Document Reproduction Service No. ED 327 969)

Nelson, W., Andris, J., & Keefe, D. (1991). Technology where they least expect it: A computer-intensive teacher education curriculum. *Computers in the Schools, 8*(1/2/3), 103–109.

Niederhauser, D., & Stoddart, T. (1992). Integrating technology with elementary mathematics: Effects of training and support. In D. Carey, R. Carey, D. Willis, & J. Willis (Eds.), *Technology and teacher education annual—1992* (pp. 430–434). Charlottesville, VA: Association for the Advancement of Computing in Education.

Niederhauser, D., & Stoddart, T. (1994). The relationship between teachers' beliefs about computer assisted instruction and their practice. In J. Willis, B. Robin, & D. Willis (Eds.), *Technology and teacher education annual—1994* (pp. 52–56). Charlottesville, VA: Association for the Advancement of Computing in Education.

Niess, M. (1990). Preparing computer-using educators for the 90s. *Journal of Computing in Teacher Education, 7*(2), 11–14.

Niess, M. (1991). Computer-using teachers in a new decade. *Education & Computing, 7*(2), 151–156.

North Carolina Department of Public Instruction (NCDPI). (1985). *Computer competencies for all educators in North Carolina public schools.* Raleigh, NC: Author.

Novak, D. (1991). An exploration of computer use by beginning elementary teachers. In D. Carey, R. Carey, D. Willis, & J. Willis (Eds.), *Technology and teacher education annual—1991* (pp. 264–267). Charlottesville, VA: Association for the Advancement of Computing in Education.

Northwest Regional Educational Laboratory. (1982). Odell Lake. MicroSIFT courseware evaluation. Portland, OR: Author. (ERIC Document Reproduction Service No. ED 232 638)

Office of Technology Assessment (OTA). (1988). *Power on! New tools for teaching and learning.* Washington, DC: United States Government Printing Office. (ERIC Document Reproduction Service No. ED 295 677)

Oliver, R. (in press). Factors influencing beginning teachers' uptake of computers. *Journal of Technology and Teacher Education.*

Organisation for Economic Co-Operation and Development (OECD), Center for Educational Research and Innovation. (1992). *Education and new information technologies teacher training and research.* Paris: Author.

O'Sullivan, M., Stroot, S., Tannehill, D., & Chou, C. (1989). Interactive video technology in teacher education. *Journal of Teacher Education, 40*(4), 20–24.

Owen, M. (1992). A teacher-centered model of development in the educational use of computers. *Journal of Information Technology for Teacher Education, 1*(1), 127–138.

Owston, R. (1993). Computers and the teaching of writing: Implications for teacher development. *Journal of Information Technology for Teacher Education, 2*(2), 239–250.

Padron, Y. (1992). A content analysis of technology coverage in teacher education books. In D. Carey, R. Carey, D. Willis, & J. Willis (Eds.), *Technology and teacher education annual—1992* (pp. 423–426). Charlottesville, VA: Association for the Advancement of Computing in Education.

Panyan, M., McPherson, S., Steeves, J., & Hummel, J. (in press). An evaluation of the technology integration enhancement model. *Journal of Technology and Teacher Education.*

Papert, S. (1988). The conservation of Piaget: The computer as grist to the constructivist mill. In G. Forman & P. Pufall (Eds.), *Constructivism in the computer age* (pp. 3–13). Hillsdale, NJ: Lawrence Erlbaum Associates.

Papert, S. (1993). *The children's machine: Rethinking school in the age of the computer.* New York: Basic Books.

Parker, J. (1989–1990). Computer facilities in colleges of education. *Journal of Computers in Teacher Education, 6*(2), 9–13.

Peterson, A. (1989). *The integration of microcomputers into teacher education programs for elementary education majors.* Unpublished doctoral dissertation, University of South Dakota.

Piaget, J. (1970). Science of education and the psychology of the child. New York: Viking.

Picciano, A. (1993). Using multimedia to teach social foundations in an urban teacher preparation program. In R. Carey, D. Carey, D. Willis, & J. Willis (Eds.), *Technology and teacher education annual—1993* (pp. 36–40). Charlottesville, VA: Association for the Advancement of Computing in Education.

Pugh, S. (1993). Using case studies and collaborative computer-assisted communication to support conceptual learning in a teacher-education course on critical reading. *Educational Technology, 33*(11), 30–38.

Randolph, C., Smithey, M., & Evertson, C. (1991). Observing in secondary classrooms: Piloting a videodisc and HyperCard stack for secondary methods students. In D. Carey, R. Carey, D. Willis, & J. Willis (Eds.), *Technology and teacher education annual—1991* (pp. 84–87). Charlottesville, VA: Association for the Advancement of Computing in Education.

Reilly, B., Hull, G., & Greenleaf, C. (1992). Using hypermedia cases in teacher education. In D. Carey, R. Carey, D. Willis, & J. Willis (Eds.), *Technology and teacher education annual—1992* (pp. 28–33). Charlottesville, VA: Association for the Advancement of Computing in Education.

Reiser, R. (1987). Introduction. In R. Gagne (Ed.), *Instructional technology: Foundations* (pp. 11–48). Hillsdale, NJ: Lawrence Erlbaum Associates.

Ridley, W., & Hull, M. (1986). Transforming American education: Reducing the risk to the nation. *Tech Trends, 31*(4), 12–24, 35.

Risko, V. (1991). Videodisc-based case methodology: A design for enhancing preservice teachers problem-solving abilities. *American Reading Forum, 11*, 121–137. (ERIC Document Reproduction Service No. ED 340 002)

Risko, V., & Kinzer, C. (1986). *Macrocontexts to facilitate learning* (Grant No. 6008710018). Washington, DC: U.S. Department of Education.

Robin, B., Bull, G., Larsen, V., & Mitchell, J. (1994). The teacher education Internet server: A new information technology resource. In J. Willis, B. Robin, & D. Willis (Eds.), *Technology and teacher education annual—1994* (pp. 631–636). Charlottesville, VA: Association for the Advancement of Computing in Education.

Robinson, B. (1992). The English national curriculum and the information technology curriculum for teacher education. In D. Carey, R. Carey, D. Willis, & J. Willis (Eds.), *Technology and teacher education annual—1992* (pp. 12–17). Charlottesville, VA: Association for the Advancement of Computing in Education.

Robinson, M., & Schonborn, A. (1991). Three instructional approaches to "Carmen Sandiego" software series. *Social-Education, 55*(6), 353–354.

Roblyer, M., & Barron, A. (1993). Technology in teacher education: A Florida study. In D. Carey, R. Carey, D. Willis, & J. Willis (Eds.), *Technology and teacher education annual—1992* (pp. 536–541). Charlottesville, VA: Association for the Advancement of Computing in Education.

Rogers, J., & Moursund, D. (1983). *Topics: Computer education for colleges of education.* New York: Association for Computing Machinery.

Ryan, T. (1992). Using technology: A college of education's experience. In D. Carey, R. Carey, D. Willis, & J. Willis (Eds.), *Technology and teacher education annual—1992* (pp. 1–11). Charlottesville, VA: Association for the Advancement of Computing in Education.

Sarason, S., Davidson, K., & Blatt, B. (1962). *The preparation of teachers: An unstudied problem in education.* New York: Wiley.

Savenye, W., Davidson, G., & Orr, K. (1992). Effects of an educational computing course on preservice teachers' attitudes and anxiety toward computers. *Journal of Computing in Childhood Education, 3*(1), 31–41.

Scarr, S. (1985). Constructing psychology: Making facts and fables for our times. *American Psychologist, 40*(5), 499–512.

Schick, J., & Walker de Felix, J. (1992). Using technology to assist language-minority students and preservice teachers. In D. Carey, R. Carey, D. Willis, & J. Willis (Eds.), *Technology and teacher education annual—1992* (pp. 255–260). Charlottesville, VA: Association for the Advancement of Computing in Education.

Schmidt, D., Merkley, D., Strong, M., & Thompson, A. (1994). An approach to technology integration for reading/language arts teacher education faculty. In J. Willis, B. Robin, & D. Willis (Eds.), *Technology and teacher education annual—1994* (pp. 773–778). Charlottesville, VA: Association for the Advancement of Computing in Education.

Schneiderman, B. (1992). Making connections beyond the classroom walls: Linking teachers and learners. In D. Carey, R. Carey, D. Willis, & J. Willis (Eds.), *Technology and teacher education annual—1992* (pp. 493–497). Charlottesville, VA: Association for the Advancement of Computing in Education.

Schön, D. (1983). *The reflective practitioner.* New York: Basic Books.

Schön, D. (1987). *Educating the reflective practitioner.* San Francisco: Jossey-Bass.

Schön, D. (Ed.). (1991). *The reflective turn. Case studies in and on educational practice.* New York: Teachers College Press.

Schrum, L. (1992). Information age innovations: Online teacher enhancement. In D. Carey, R. Carey, D. Willis, & J. Willis (Eds.), *Technology and teacher education annual—1992* (pp. 516–523). Charlottesville, VA: Association for the Advancement of Computing in Education.

Scott, T., Cole, M., & Engle, M. (1992). Computers and education: A cultural constructivist perspective. In G. Grant (Ed.), *Review of Research in Education. 18,* 191–251. Washington, DC: American Educational Research Association.

Segal, G., & Marciano, V. (1988). Issues of equivalent access to computer technology for the disabled student in the classroom. *Outlook, 20*(1), 131–140.

Selfe, C., Rodrigues, D., & Oates, W. (1989). *Computers in English and language arts: The challenge of teacher education.* Urbana, IL: National Council of Teachers of English.

Sheffield, C. (1994). Are your students like mine? Preservice students' entering technology skills. In J. Willis, B. Robin, & D. Willis (Eds.), *Technology and teacher education annual—1994* (pp. 67–71).

Charlottesville, VA: Association for the Advancement of Computing in Education.

Sherwood, C. (1992). Australian experiences with the effective classroom integration of information technology: Implications for teacher education. *Journal of Information Technology for Teacher Education, 2*(2), 167–179.

Sirotnik, K. (1990). On the eroding foundations of teacher education. *Phi Delta Kappan, 71*(9), 10–16.

Skeele, R. (1993). Technology and diversity: Resolving computer equity issues through multicultural education. In R. Carey, D. Carey, D. Willis, & J. Willis (Eds.), *Technology and teacher education annual—1993* (pp. 14–18). Charlottesville, VA: Association for the Advancement of Computing in Education.

Spaulding, C. (1988). Addressing the charges of anti-intellectualism and irrelevancy in teacher education. *Teacher Educator, 24*(1), 2–9.

Steen, F., & Taylor, R. (1993). Using the computers to teach mathematics: A working conference for teachers. *Journal of Technology and Teacher Education, 1*(2), 149–167.

Stowe, R. (1992). Teacher-preparedness for the information age. In D. Carey, R. Carey, D. Willis, & J. Willis (Eds.), *Technology and teacher education annual—1992* (pp. 357–361). Charlottesville, VA: Association for the Advancement of Computing in Education.

Strang, H. (1992). Teaching worlds [computer program]. Boston: Allyn & Bacon.

Strang, H. (1994). Assessing teaching styles in experienced teachers via a microcomputer simulation. In J. Willis, B. Robin, & D. Willis (Eds.), *Technology and teacher education annual—1994* (pp. 305–308). Charlottesville, VA: Association for the Advancement of Computing in Education.

Strang, H., Hoffman, M., & Abide, M. (1992). Cooperative participation in a computer-based teaching simulation. In D. Carey, R. Carey, D. Willis, & J. Willis (Eds.), *Technology and teacher education annual—1992* (pp. 629–633). Charlottesville, VA: Association for the Advancement of Computing in Education.

Strang, H., Landrum, M., & Ulmer, C. (1991). A self-administered simulation for training basic classroom skills. *Computers in the Schools, 8*(1/2/3), 229–243.

Strang, H., Vekiari, K., & Tankersley, M. (1991). The Curry Teaching Simulation: A window on effective teaching skills? In D. Carey, R. Carey, D. Willis, & J. Willis (Eds.), *Technology and teacher education annual—1991* (pp. 226–231). Charlottesville, VA: Association for the Advancement of Computing in Education.

Striebel, M. (1991). A critical analysis of the use of computers in education. In D. Hlynka & J. Belland (Eds.), *Paradigms regained* (pp. 283–334). Englewood Cliffs, NJ: Educational Technology Publications.

Stroot, S., Tannehill, D., & O'Sullivan, M. (1991). Skill analysis utilizing videodisc technology. *Computers in the Schools, 8*(1/2/3), 271–291.

Sullivan, G. (1991). The case-study method and computer assisted instruction in teacher education. In D. Carey, R. Carey, D. Willis, & J. Willis (Eds.), *Technology and teacher education annual—1991* (pp. 336–337). Charlottesville, VA: Association for the Advancement of Computing in Education.

Taylor, C. (1992). A case study of collaboration between university and students using IT on school practice. In *Developing IT in Teacher Education #3.* Conventry, UK: National Council for Educational Technology.

Taylor, R. (1988). A single course for preservice teachers. *Outlook, 20*(1), 3–5.

Tearle, P., & Davis, N. (1992). Bringing children, students, and IT together in the primary base at Exeter University. *Developing Information Technology in Teacher Education, 4,* 5–15.

Texas Education Agency (TEA). (1988). *Long-range plan for technology of the Texas State Board of Education: 1988–2000.* Austin: Author.

Texas Education Agency (TEA). (1993). *Request for application: Projects for educational technology.* Austin: Author.

Thomas, L. (1991). Promoting technology in teacher preparation: ISTE accreditation initiatives. *Journal of Computing in Teacher Education, 7*(3), 31–32.

Thompson, A., Schmidt, D., & Topp, N. (1993). The development and implementation of an instructional computing program for preservice teachers. In D. Carey, R. Carey, D. Willis, & J. Willis (Eds.), *Technology and teacher education annual—1993* (pp. 130–132). Charlottesville, VA: Association for the Advancement of Computing in Education.

Titus, J. (1993). Gender messages in education foundation textbooks. *Journal of Teacher-Education, 44*(1), 38–44.

Todd, N. (1993). A curriculum model for integrating technology in teacher education courses. *Journal of Computing in Teacher Education, 9*(3), 5–11.

Toomey, R., Mahon, L., & Thalathoti, V. (1993). The Linkwest Project: Comparative case studies in computer enhanced teaching and learning. *Journal of Technology and Teacher Education, 1*(3), 299–313.

Troutman, A., & White, J. (1991). Using computer technology to effectively model for prospective teachers the use of computer technology to deliver, enhance and manage instruction. *Computers in the Schools, 8*(1/2/3), 131–133.

Uhlig, G. (1992). Preparing a college of education for the 21st century. In D. Carey, R. Carey, D. Willis, & J. Willis (Eds.), *Technology and teacher education annual—1992* (pp. 365–369). Charlottesville, VA: Association for the Advancement of Computing in Education.

Vygotsky, L. (1978). *Mind in society: The development of higher psychological processes.* (M. Cole, V. John-Steiner, & E. Souberman, Eds.). Cambridge: Harvard University Press.

Vygotsky, L. (1987). Thinking and speech. In L. S. Vygotsky. *Collected works* (Vol. 1, pp. 39–285, R. Rieber & A. Carton, Eds., N. Minick, Trans.). New York: Plenum.

Waggoner, M. (1992). Planning for the use of computer conferencing in collaborative learning. In D. Carey, R. Carey, D. Willis, & J. Willis (Eds.), *Technology and teacher education annual—1992* (pp. 556–561). Charlottesville, VA: Association for the Advancement of Computing in Education.

Waggoner, M., & Switzer, T. (1991). Using computer communication to enhance teacher education. In D. Carey, R. Carey, D. Willis, & J. Willis (Eds.), *Technology and teacher education annual—1991* (pp. 135–139). Charlottesville, VA: Association for the Advancement of Computing in Education.

Warren, D. (1982). What went wrong with the foundations and other off center questions? *Journal of Teacher Education, 33*(3), 28–30.

Watt, D. (1988). The computer as microworld and microworld maker: A rationale and plan for the inclusion of Logo in an introductory, preservice course on educational computing. *Outlook, 20*(1), 81–89.

Watt, M. (1988). Experiential learning: Elements to consider in designing a preservice course in educational computing. *Outlook, 20*(1), 25–31.

Welch, F. (1988). Preparing future teachers to use computers: A course at the College of Charleston. *Outlook, 20*(1), 146–153.

Wertsch, J. V. (Ed.). (1985). *Culture, communication, and cognition: Vygotskian perspectives.* Cambridge: Cambridge University Press.

Wetzel, K. (1993). Teacher educators' uses of computers in teaching. *Journal of Technology and Teacher Education, 1*(4), 350–352.

White, C. (1991). Information technology in the preservice social studies methods course. *Computers in the Schools, 8*(1/2/3), 159–161.

White, C. (1994a). Making social studies teacher education relevant: Integrating technology into methods courses. In J. Willis, B. Robin, & D. Willis (Eds.), *Technology and teacher education annual—1994*

(pp. 230–233). Charlottesville, VA: Association for the Advancement of Computing in Education.

White, C. (1994b). Technology in restructured preservice education: School/university linkages. *Journal of Technology and Teacher Education, 2*(2), 119–129.

White, J., & VanDeventer, S. (1990). A successful model for software evaluation. *Computers in the Schools, 8*(1/2/3), 323–327.

Whitherspoon, M., Barron, L., & Goldman, E. (1991). Teaching fractions: Using hypermedia contexts to prepare elementary school teachers. In D. Carey, R. Carey, D. Willis, & J. Willis (Eds.), *Technology and teacher education annual—1991* (pp. 70–73). Charlottesville, VA: Association for the Advancement of Computing in Education.

Wild, P., & Hodgkinson, K. (1992). IT capability in primary initial teacher training. *Journal of Computer Assisted Learning, 8*(2), 79–89.

Willis, D. (1992, July). *A site-based teacher education program.* Unpublished paper presented at the annual meeting of the Information Technology for Teacher Education Association, Newcastle upon Tyne, U.K.

Willis, D., & Brent, R. (1994). Differentiated use of a lesson planning simulation. In J. Willis, B. Robin, & D. Willis (Eds.), *Technology and teacher education annual—1994* (pp. 317–319). Charlottesville, VA: Association for the Advancement of Computing in Education.

Willis, D., & Willis, J. (1991). IRIS: A training simulation for the Informal Reading Inventory. *Computers in the Schools, 8*(1/2/3), 245–248.

Willis, J. (1992a). TEACH IT Modules: Reducing the barriers to wider use of technology in education. In D. Carey, R. Carey, D. Willis, & J. Willis (Eds.), *Technology and teacher education annual—1992* (pp. 107–112). Charlottesville, VA: Association for the Advancement of Computing in Education.

Willis, J. (1992b). Technology diffusion in the "Soft Disciplines." Using social technology to support information technology. *Computers in the Schools, 9*(1), 81–105.

Willis, J. (1993a). Technology and teacher education: A research and development agenda. In H. Waxman & G. Bright (Eds.), *Approaches to research on teacher education and technology.* Charlottesville, VA: Association for the Advancement of Computing in Education.

Willis, J. (1993b). What conditions encourage technology use? It depends on the context. *Computers in the Schools, 9*(4), 13–32.

Willis, J., Austin, L., & Willis, D. (1994). *Information technology in teacher education: Surveys of the current status.* A report prepared for the Office of Technology Assessment. Houston, TX: University of Houston, College of Education.

Wilson, N., & Wilson, R. (1992). National education technology information exchange. In D. Carey, R. Carey, D. Willis, & J. Willis (Eds.), *Technology and teacher education annual—1992* (pp. 506–507). Charlottesville, VA: Association for the Advancement of Computing in Education.

Woodrow, J. (1991). A comparison of four computer attitude scales. *Journal of Educational Computing Research, 7*(2), 165–187.

Woodrow, J. (1992). A computer-based curriculum and instruction course. In D. Carey, R. Carey, D. Willis, & J. Willis (Eds.), *Technology and teacher education annual—1992* (pp. 94–98). Charlottesville, VA: Association for the Advancement of Computing in Education.

Woodrow, J. (1994). A computer-based multimedia science education course. In J. Willis, B. Robin, & D. Willis (Eds.), *Technology and teacher education annual—1994* (pp. 579–584). Charlottesville, VA: Association for the Advancement of Computing in Education.

Yan, W., Anderson, M., & Nelson, J. (1994). Facilitating reflective thinking in student teachers through electronic mail. In J. Willis, B. Robin, & D. Willis (Eds.), *Technology and teacher education an-*

nual—1994 (pp. 657–660). Charlottesville, VA: Association for the Advancement of Computing in Education.

Yoder, S., & Moursund, D. (1993). Do teachers need to know about computer programming? *Journal of Computing in Teacher Education, 9*(3), 21–26.

Yount, D., McAllister, D., & Risko, V. (1991). Improving remedial reading instruction using video-based case analysis. In D. Carey, R. Carey, D. Willis, & J. Willis (Eds.), *Technology and teacher education annual—1991* (pp. 101–104). Charlottesville, VA: Association for the Advancement of Computing in Education.

·46·

NEEDED RESEARCH IN TEACHER EDUCATION

Edward R. Ducharme

DRAKE UNIVERSITY

Mary K. Ducharme

DRAKE UNIVERSITY

We begin this chapter with a question: Of teacher education matters and issues either largely unknown or only partially known, what do teacher educators *want* to know, *need* to know, and have the capacity to discover, learn and *act upon?* Surely there are myriad things the profession might *like* to know, but about which it could do little by knowing more. For example, further research studies might provide more comprehensive data on the percentage of teacher education students obtaining teaching positions after graduation, but the profession probably could not do much with the data, interesting though they might be. Such data, unrelated to other relevant matters, are of minor importance. In this chapter we indicate areas of inquiry that need investigation; suggest why they need further investigation; and, inasmuch as the interrelationships among research inquiries are often as important as the inquiries themselves, show some critical interrelationships among areas of inquiry.

This chapter is organized in the following manner: commentary on changing practices in and views of teacher education research, a series of questions, followed by a commentary for each question and suggestions for needed research related to the question. The chapter includes sections on preservice students and programs, practicing teachers, and teacher educators with major emphasis on the first. Where appropriate, we cite references to the work of scholars on given topics. Our questions about needed research in teacher education are those we believe require initial or further exploration. Some of the topics of our questions are in the research literature; however, we believe more is needed.

TEACHER EDUCATION RESEARCH: PRACTICES AND VIEWS

Houston, Haberman, and Sikula, editors of the first edition of *Handbook of Research on Teacher Education* (1990), assert that "the research base for such important work as educating the nation's teachers is still extremely thin," and that "There is a tradition in teacher education . . . that each teacher-preparing institution rediscovers its own best way of educating teachers with little or no attention to either other institutions or the research literature" (p. ix). Others contend that educational research has had a profound effect on views of teacher preparation. Darling-Hammond (1990), for example, argues:

Since the late 1960s, educational research has exploded the myths that any teaching is as effective as any other and equally trained and experienced teachers are equally advantageous to students. Those who are well prepared to teach do indeed teach more effectively. . . . Much of this research also demonstrates the importance of teacher education for the acquisition of knowledge and skills that, when used in the classroom, improve the caliber of instruction and the success of student learning. (p. 287)

Writing of the teaching knowledge base, Palincsar and McPhail (1993) are not sanguine about the possibility of its being woven together so as to be a shared commodity:

For example, what one experiences at the macro level does not necessarily reflect what is true at the molecular level. Nonetheless, the dis-

We express our gratitude and respect to our primary reviewers, Professor Greta Morine-Dershimer of the University of Virginia and Professor Thomas Lasley of the University of Dayton, each of whom rendered thoughtful and helpful critiques. We also thank Professor Thomas Buttery and Professor John Sikula for their considerable editorial assistance and encouragement.

parate parts of science are linked together in a comprehensible whole through the lingua franca of mathematics. One must doubt whether sophisticated statistical analyses can ever weave together the multiple parts of school-based learning into a similar shared knowledge base. (p. 327)

We wonder if a similar sentiment applies to the teacher education knowledge base.

Teacher education research in the mid-1990s is somewhere between these views; further research in the United States and elsewhere is critical. Calderhead (1993), writing from an international perspective, suggests that teacher educators lack both a language and a precise description of what they do; he notes:

In several countries it seems that teacher education is not only being called more fully to account for itself, but policies are being drafted which impose particular views of professional development on the way teachers are trained, with the effect of reducing the "academic" demands of training and promoting the immediately "practical." The relatively easy imposition of these views, and their receptive, even enthusiastic, support in the media, may well highlight the fact that teacher education is not widely understood, and teacher educators themselves, although they may have an intuitive understanding of good practice, are hampered in defence of their work by the absence of any coherent theoretical account or even precise language, for describing what they do. It appears, in fact, to be extremely difficult to articulate the basis of good practice in teacher education, and extremely difficult to defend good practice in the face of a simple, dominant ideology. (p. 12)

Elliott (1993), observing the lack of dialog between those who criticize teacher education from the outside and those who do so from the inside, calls for a bringing together of some of the seemingly disparate views:

It is indeed ironic that there has been virtually no dialogue between the external and internal critics of the traditional pattern of teacher education, because they both agree on what is wrong with it; namely, that its theory driven character is inadequate as a basis for competent professional practice. What they disagree about is their view of what constitutes "competent professional practice." Some may feel that the differences between the "social market" and "teachers as researchers" perspectives are so radical that there is little point in dialogue: only in confrontation and opposition. I would disagree and claim that dialogue resulting in a degree of mutual understanding, tolerance, and accommodation of the different perspectives is possible. (p. 66)

Nichol (1993) points out that theories of teacher preparation have historically passed through four stages: (1) the apprenticeship model, (2) the theory into practice model, (3) the atheoretical pragmatic adaptation model, and (4) the practice intertwined into theory model (p. 307). He notes:

The novice repertoire is based upon inchoate knowledge rooted in personal experience and memory of his or her own schooling, folk lore and extra educational experience. The development, enrichment, and application of a new repertoire to replace novice with expert knowledge has practical activity dealing with actual classroom teaching situations at its core. Such practice is implicitly linked to theory. (pp. 307–308)

Teacher education remains rife with controversy. Despite years of discussion on what teachers should know, countless articles on the topic, and study after study, agreement on most things is elusive. Watts (1989), writing of what teachers need to know, observes that:

Basically what is being said is that teachers need knowledge of the disciplines and also, of course, of how that knowledge may be translated as appropriate to the developmental levels of students; teachers need psychological knowledge; they need knowledge of the societal context. Linked with that knowledge, and without which that knowledge is dysfunctional, we believe there is a set of values which teachers must have; we would emphasize at least a valuing of learning, a valuing of excellence and a valuing of all students. (p. 44)

Some contend that both knowledge and application of the findings of extant research as well as further research would be useful, but others question this view. Kaestle (1993) has serious reservations about the capacity of research to affect the field: "Even if improvements are made in how we supply research-based knowledge about education, there will remain a problem of limited demand from practitioners" (p. 27). Even though Kaestle was writing about classroom teachers, his remarks apply equally well to teacher educators. Berliner (1985), Lasley (1992), and Clifford and Guthrie (1988) point out the low utilization of research in teacher education and in schools of education. Howey and Zimpher (1989), in their largely positive study of teacher education on several campuses, did not report high research utilization among teacher education faculty. Zimpher and Ashburn (1985) question the knowledge base:

We believe there is considerable confusion about what constitutes the knowledge base in teacher education. A knowledge base is emerging regarding the study of teaching, but that is not synonymous with a knowledge base for teacher education. The meager research that does exist regarding teacher education is random, chaotic, and directionless. The formulation of matrices and models creates an assumed order that fails to reflect sufficiently the essential diversity of questions about the complex practice of teacher education. (p. 20)

Singer (1993), commenting on the question of how students learn and asking what educators have learned over the years about that question, aptly states the dilemma accompanying attempts to determine how people learn things.

How do students learn? What facilitates or impedes learning? Of the myriad potentially important factors, which ones are the most important? These questions, at once deceptively simple and perilously complex, lie at the heart of much educational research. A universal answer has eluded scholars and philosophers for centuries and remains, for some, the holy grail of educational research today. Does the persistence of these questions suggest that we, as a community of scholars, have learned nothing in our decades of study? Or is the inquiry into student learning a perpetual search destined never to end? (p. 353)

By substituting the word *teachers* for *students* in Singer's first sentence, one senses the applicability to teacher education of his wise observation. What *do* we know and *how* do we use what we know?

Brown and McIntyre (1993), commenting on the limited application of research findings, note:

This part [ordinary, everyday teaching] is communicated to beginning teachers only to a very limited extent, and the wheels of teaching have to be reinvented by each new generation. Furthermore, when professional teacher educators are designing their courses, it is very difficult for them to take any detailed account of what their students may learn from teachers in schools. If teachers could be helped and persuaded to make explicit the knowledge which they implicitly use in their day-to-day work, teacher education could begin to achieve something of the practical relevance and theory-practice integration which it is still accused of lacking. (p. 14)

Data on many teacher education subjects exist: number and types of institutions preparing teachers; number of teacher educators, including information about their race, ethnicity, and gender; length of time for program completion; percentages of graduates who go into teaching; and the like. These matters are countable items; they form the data that the American Association of Colleges for Teacher Education (AACTE) has gathered in recent years through its research activities known as the RATE (Research About Teacher Education) studies (AACTE, 1987, 1988, 1989, 1990, 1991). Although the RATE studies have recently gathered data on the opinions of faculty and students, their emphasis has been much on what the title of the annual RATE monographs suggests: facts and figures about teacher education with necessarily limited interpretation.

Interrelated Inquiries

Scholars have studied and written about many aspects of teacher education; however, that they have done so does not mean that the profession has answers to its critical questions. The questions persist; what exists in many cases is a series of tentative answers, perhaps hypotheses to test. Further, there is little of what we term *interrelated inquiries*. Yarger and Smith (1990) in their chapter, "Issues in Research in Teacher Education," refer to what they call "linking studies," which they define as "those that tie together or link one of the three aforementioned domains of research on teacher education" (p. 26).

The concepts of wait time and teacher preparation are good examples of interrelated inquiries worthy of further study. Considerable writing exists on the topic of *wait time* (Rowe, 1986), but relatively little exists on its empirical, long-term value to learners or on ways to instruct novice teachers to acquire the skill of using wait time in their teaching. Berliner (1985) notes that despite the presence of "20 or 30 studies on the wait-time topic . . . the behavior [wait-time] is not in the repertoire of most teachers" (p. 4). Erickson (1986) contends that "Teachers can be trained . . . to pause for a longer 'wait-time,' yet after a few months they go back to using shorter wait-time in lesson dialogue with students" (p. 132). Why do teachers prepared in the concepts of wait time not use them? Matters such as the effect of the use of wait time in the various secondary school disciplines remain largely unexplored (White & Tisher, 1986). Is wait time good for all students? What are the effects of wait time versus a staccatolike pattern of questioning? What is the difference between the use of wait time versus Professor Kingsfield's questioning manner in the long-running television series *The Paper Chase?* The profession should study such interrelated matters in educational research.

Teacher educators have historically not effectively interrelated research knowledge and practice. Galluzzo and Craig

(1990), commenting on the research on teacher attitudes, note that "There is precedence for linking knowledge, teaching behaviors, dispositions, and attitudes in teacher education. . . . However, studies of teacher preparation have neglected to link these distinct sets of criterion variables" (p. 609). Some suggest that teacher educators *act* as though things occur in some interrelated way, that actions, learnings, and activities have specific effects on teachers. Kelchtermans (1993) observes that "We assume that the professional experiences of teachers result in a sense of professional self and a subjective educational theory" (p. 199), while Pope (1993) notes that "Much of teacher thinking is tacit—i.e. know-how gained through experience and not usually articulated" (p. 25).

But some scholars caution about linkages between theory and practice. Calderhead (1993) argues that the view of research and practice is too simplistic and unworkable:

If we take a simple view of research and practice and the relationship between them, there is an apparent easy solution to the problem. Research tells us how experienced teachers plan, student teachers do not know how to plan, therefore we can tell them about the research and the problem will be solved. Such an approach has generally not been found to be effective either . . . the relationship between research and practice in teacher education has tended in the past to be characterized by fairly insular conceptions of both research and practice and a tendency to view research purely as a means of supporting and informing practice rather than in terms of a reciprocal questioning and exploration. (pp. 15 and 17)

After reviewing commentary about the teaching knowledge base, Kerdman and Phillips (1993) are uncertain of its value:

Recognizing, however, that there is no one right way to promote successful practice, it becomes incumbent on us to reassess these assumptions. And clearly, as we discuss these matters and try to forge educational policies and educational practices, our findings—the findings of researchers—must be taken into account. But rather than constituting a knowledge base that contains directions for practice, research findings serve as a resource—one resource among, perhaps many that can be put to diverse uses by the various participants in the conversations about education. (p. 312)

It is clear that if a jury exists on these matters it is still out.

Changing Views of Research on Teacher Education

Views of acceptable research on teacher education and teaching have undergone considerable change since 1983 when Johnston and Ryan wrote: "In this brief section of the chapter we examine *nonresearch* professional literature published on the beginning teacher in the United States from 1930 to the present" (p. 138, emphasis original). In their *nonresearch* section they included such items as reflective interpretations of beginning teachers' experiences and scholarly essays about the beginning teacher and the process of beginning to teach. While debate about what constitutes quality research continues, many scholars in the 1990s would recognize such areas of inquiry as legitimate forms and subjects of *research* and would not term them *nonresearch*. In his 1975 overview of research on teacher education, Turner has 37 references in his 25 footnotes, 19 of which refer to doctoral studies rather than publications, a condition suggesting that, as far as Turner was concerned, much of research of note was occurring in doctoral work. The topics include matter such as the *social background and the preparation of secondary school social studies in Ohio: 1967–68,* a topic highly suitable for publishable research in the 1990s.

The Emergence of Qualitative Research

Quantitative research is a staple in educational research and will continue to be so. Perusal of the programs of Division K of the American Educational Research Association (AERA) reveals that researchers are increasingly reporting on qualitative studies, frequently on topics that Johnston and Ryan's dictum would have placed beyond the pale. Yet these studies are not without their controversial aspects. Britzman (1991) acknowledges the importance of telling the stories of teachers' lives— an important component in many recent studies—yet calls attention to the potential dangers in such research:

This type of knowledge production requires the researcher to be sensitive to representing the voices of those experiencing educational life as sources of knowledge, and to be committed to preserving their dignity and struggle. . . . Finally, attending to the voice of teachers attempts to remedy the traditionally imposed silences of research subjects as primarily spoken about but rarely speaking for themselves. . . . As similar and disparate themes across participants are identified and analyzed, collections of life histories are likely to allow the development of a grounded theory of teaching experience. A fundamental assumption, then, of research that attempts to renovate theory is that examined life is educative. The act of simultaneously recounting and re-creating one's cumulative experiences should provide critical insight into lived lives. Likewise, in reading about others, we may learn something about ourselves and come to value our own struggle for voice. . . . Unless the narrations of practices are read through theories of discourse— that is, as representing particular ideological interests, orientations, and meanings, and of deploying relations of power—there remains the danger of viewing personal knowledge as unencumbered by authoritative discourse and as unmediated by the relations of power and authority that work through every teaching and research practice. (pp. 51–53)

Richardson (1996) writes about *practical inquiry* under which she includes *reflective practice,* and *action research* and *formal research,* under which she includes what is "generally written about in research and research methodology chapters and is often broken down by methodological types: experimental, correlational, survey, case study, qualitative, evaluation, etc." She goes on to describe the varied techniques and applications of her categories of research, often providing examples from the literature.

Huberman (1993) makes a compelling argument for interactive research as a way of effecting transfer of knowledge:

Users [of research] are not construed simply as "targets" but as actors who will transform the knowledge base in line with their own representation of the problem. Also, the process of knowledge transfer is seen as a series of transactions, in which study findings are "negotiated" between the two parties. (p. 37)

The value to practitioners [of research] has always been obvious: access to new, potentially powerful ideas and tools. The values to researchers have been less clear. If it turns out, however, that interactive

modes of dissemination are a booster to conceptual progression, as depicted in my fictitious example, the "payoff" within the research community may be far greater. One would then work through one's findings with a group of experienced practitioners not for reasons of altruism nor of activism, but rather to empower or to refine the conceptual tools with which we researchers ply our trade. Doing it this way, in fact, may often be more beneficial than replicating a study or engaging with colleagues at professional meetings. One might, literally, change one's mind. In other words, if we researchers are interested in changing our minds, we need to take our findings out into the field and observe very carefully how they hold up under duress. (p. 51)

For many, the research controversy centers on real or perceived differences between quantitative and qualitative research studies. For others, arguing that good research necessitates both, the distinction is arbitrary or frivolous. Still, differences linger for some in the profession, perhaps described in the simplistic statement that one contingent argues that if something cannot be quantified, its meaning remains irrelevant or inapplicable while the other broadly defined contingent contends that it is the particulars of each thing counted that matter. Happily—as a reading of current journal articles and attendance at American Educational Research Association Division K presentations indicate—most teacher educators appear to have embraced a fusion.

Much recently published research relies heavily on interviews with elementary, secondary, and higher education faculty, a great deal of it requiring that interviewees look retrospectively at their professional and private lives. Acker (1989) notes:

Large-scale surveys of teachers seem increasingly rare, and sample size no longer seems to matter in view of the depth of insight generated by intensive interviewing and observation, even with a few individuals. Ethnographic investigations, life-history or career-history data, and to a lesser extent personal reflection have been the methods of choice in recent work. (p. 9)

Such research places tremendous responsibility for objectivity, clarity, and interpretation on the researcher. Interviewees are often very willing to talk, and the researcher has the responsibility of selecting and analyzing what he or she determines to be of worth. Kelchtermans (1993) comments:

But it remains striking how quickly teachers were willing to talk about themselves very openly. . . . If teachers get the chance to talk about themselves as a teacher to an interested, non-evaluative listener, it seems they take that chance with pleasure and commitment. This doesn't however, absolve the researcher from taking into account the motives of the respondent, while analyzing and interpreting autobiographical materials. (p. 214)

Brown and McIntyre (1993) affirm that researchers should inquire of teachers and their work, that there are justifications for looking at the world from teachers' perspectives:

There are, therefore, powerful arguments to be made, from the perspective of teacher education, for investigations in the ways in which experienced teachers conceptualize their own teaching, the criteria they use in evaluating their own performance, and how they achieve the things which they do well. But there are other kinds of justifications for research which attempt to make sense of teaching in this way. One of these justifications arises from the concerns of curriculum justification. (p. 14)

Ducharme (1993) comments on the difficulty in ascertaining elusive truth from interviewees: "when people tell their own stories there is never total reliability. Individuals may often select what they want to say, forget things or choose to omit them for whatever reason, exaggerate what happened, and so forth" (p. 15).

The profession requires quality research of all kinds. Our preference is that researchers, either singly or in tandem, investigate the topics we suggest and other important ones from a variety of perspectives. Richardson's list (1996) is a good benchmark for the delineation of research methodological types; her ensuing explanations are artful and appropriate. We turn now to the questions we believe need additional research.

QUESTIONS FOR FURTHER RESEARCH

In this section we comment on the preservice aspects of teacher education, an area of work consuming much of the energy and time of most teacher educators. Questions about the preparation of teachers, what is effective and what is not, what teachers should know and be able to do persist despite many efforts to analyze problems and propose solutions.

Question *What psychological traits of applicants for teacher education are likely to be predictive of success in teaching?*

Commentary There is much in the literature on teacher education about the importance of the "best and the brightest," the best informed, the most socially committed, and the most whatever else the particular writer may think appropriate for teachers. Literature and scholarship exist in a variety of fields to suggest that the psychological makeup of individuals may have a great effect on present and future performance. For example, prospective astronauts undergo intensive testing prior to acceptance into the program. We wonder: would analysis of teachers deemed successful by peers, students, supervisors, and community reveal particular characteristics that present in prospective teachers would augur well for their future success? The literature reveals that others have studied this problem, but they have studied it from the perspective of simply learning what characteristics effective teachers possess.

Nias (1989) observes that:

This stress upon personality is encouraged by allegiance to philosophical traditions which see the personal relationship between teacher and learner as central to the educational process. . . . Teachers socialized in this tradition tend to identify with their classes, talk of themselves in relationship to their pupils as "we." Indeed many teachers derive intense satisfaction from feeling "natural" and "whole" in their relationship with children, and from creating a sense of community within classes and schools. (pp. 156–157)

Elliott (1989) indicates that determining excellence and effectiveness is an international issue. Demonstrating that the concerns for emerging competencies in teachers is international

among teacher educators, the English scholar Wilson (1985), writing of teachers whom students saw as highly acceptable, noted that the students valued teachers who had the qualities of "warmth and understanding, vitality, personal autonomy and ability to communicate in a range of settings" (p. 146) and rejected teachers who "are impersonal and non-caring, by their impatience create tensions, are biased, dogmatic and political, show signs of becoming stale and burnt out" (p. 146). Elliott (1989) also reported that, according to Watts (1987),

a Board claimed that the relevant competencies for entry to teacher education programmes include autonomy, initiative, resourcefulness; adaptability and flexibility; creativity; genuine concern for children and appropriate attitudes to all children; ability to relate well to others; and capacity for empathy; valuing of excellence and learning. (pp. 146–147)

Elliott (1989) further notes that the contexts in which teachers teach may be critical in determining their effectiveness:

A further difficulty is that effectiveness in teaching is often in the nature of the school and its students. One teacher located in a socially or economically depressed inner city school may be highly effective but find difficulty in a single-teacher, remote, rural school. The point here is that teaching is an extremely diverse profession because of the range of clientele and settings, and to conceptualize effectiveness as a single dimensioned aspect is impossible. For selection criteria this implies an attempt to identify a range of qualities in applicants from a more expansive list. For this reason, problems of reliability and validity must abound in the process. (p. 147)

Elliott (1989) goes on to report that:

The National Inquiry into Teacher Education (Auchmuty, 1980) received a large number of submissions from teacher, parents and community groups arguing from the use of personal criteria such as patience, commitment and maturity in teacher selection, on the grounds that the profession would be enhanced if teachers exhibited higher levels of such qualities which were unlikely to be capable of development within preservice courses. (p. 145)

Needed Research Writing of the research agenda appropriate for assessing teacher competencies, Wilson and Thomson (1989) note:

The second priority is follow-up studies of predictive validity of these assessment decisions. Without criterion validity there is no basis for getting beyond hunch in how we assess candidates and in fine tuning of the process. . . . A variety of studies in different educational contexts, national and international, would serve to illuminate the extent to which the skills of teaching, and the teacher's role, are context specific or universal. (p. 214)

They further observe that:

No issue could be more central to the quality of the education service, or to the capacity of the service to provide children and adolescents with challenging intellectual, personal and social experiences at the most vital formative part of their development. The status, indeed the survival, of the public education service depends on investigating these issues fully, and applying the findings to the identification and development of people to staff schools and colleges. (p. 215)

As mentioned, Elliott (1989) lists the qualities a group of teachers saw as appropriate for future teachers—"warmth and understanding, vitality, personal autonomy, and ability to communicate in a range of settings" (p. 146). He further observed that answers to the question of what qualities characterize quality teachers may be a ways off:

Answers to these types of empirical problems can only be found in longitudinal studies of teachers which begin gathering data at the point of selection. In teacher education, claims are made that our level of knowledge is not sufficient for us to proceed with selection strategies based on well defined multiple criteria (including personal characteristics). The irony is that it is probably in beginning to pursue such strategies that we can build up and refine our knowledge base in the area and so justify their use. We will be more knowledgeable about the criteria we use for selection and the methods we employ only if we begin to develop and implement these. Our failure to do so will mean that future enquiries into teaching and teacher education will inevitably continue to receive submissions asserting that "research evidence was lacking" or assuming that "qualities typically mentioned are at a fluid stage of development among school leavers." (pp. 149–150)

Longitudinal studies are costly and difficult, but teacher education would profit greatly from such studies. Bullough (1989, 1993), in his ongoing study of Kerrie, provides an example of such useful studies.

Questions *What are the optimal times for prospective and practicing teachers to learn and acquire specific knowledge and skills? Are they different for different kinds of students?*

Commentary Despite imperatives from such powerful groups as the Holmes Group (1986) and the Carnegie Forum on Education and the Economy (1986) urging the abolishment of undergraduate teacher preparation programs, teacher education remains largely the province of undergraduate programs; and the majority of teachers come from undergraduate studies directly into teaching. Teacher educators teach a wide variety of content and skills to people in their late teens and early twenties, forced by circumstance and custom to act as though students between 18 and 22 are at an optimum age to learn necessary knowledge, skills, and attitudes for teaching. Faculty continue to write and publish articles in teacher education journals about their successful undergraduate programs. That the vast majority of teachers, both successful and unsuccessful, prepared at the undergraduate level should not deter us from asking questions about the optimum ages for different individuals to learn different things.

However much teacher educators claim that their preparation programs accomplish, some continue to argue that preservice preparation is largely irrelevant, that teachers learn about their craft when they begin to teach. Yinger and Hendricks-Lee (1993) ask compelling questions:

For example, why is it that most graduates of teacher education programs still have most of their learning to do? Why do teachers point to their first few years of teaching as the place where they really learned to teach? Why has the theory–practice split been of such great concern to teacher educators? Why all the recent attention to different types of knowledge that practitioners need? (p. 100)

Despite the energy and time that teacher educators spend with teacher preparation students, the students continue to indicate on graduation and placement within the schools that their preparation was inadequate. Why? That is a compelling question.

Most teacher education programs devote considerable energy to providing their students with the knowledge and skill for the preparation of lesson plans. Yet Brown and McIntyre (1993) contend that:

Student teachers soon become aware that despite the emphasis in their college courses on detailed lesson plans and learning objectives, experienced teachers seem to manage well without them. This is not to suggest that the objectives model is not useful and important. It does point, nevertheless, to a discontinuity between that way of viewing teaching and the actual craft of the job. (p. 18)

Zeichner and Tabachnick (1981) wonder about the effects of the school climate on the teacher education student during student teaching and beyond. They speculate that the school climate may wash out the effects of teacher preparation.

Tickle (1989) argues that prospective teachers are consumed with how-to-do-it matters, with acquiring what he calls "secrets of the trade," and that they acquire professional competence as they work with teachers:

I have shown in my work with undergraduate student teachers how the initial encounters with classroom practice were concerned with learning the "secrets of the trade." There was a commitment among students to doing the things which teachers do—including the menial tasks. The way to learn what teachers do, for those students, was to work with teachers and take responsibility for doing their work . . . the work was interactive, as the students adjusted to the professional expectations for becoming a teacher: as they came to know the context of the schools and communities in which they worked; as they mastered subject knowledge within the demands of teaching; as they acquired knowledge within the demands of teaching; as they acquired instructional strategies and classroom management skills; and, as they developed professional attitudes and perspectives. (pp. 97–98)

Brown and McIntyre (1993) point out that this acquired-in-the-field knowledge is of great importance to prospective teachers, that experienced teachers have acquired much pragmatic knowledge that they pass on to those entering the profession:

Most of us, and particularly teacher educators, acknowledge that student teachers can and should learn a great deal from the experienced teachers they observe in schools. Underlying this approach is an acceptance that over a period of time experienced teachers have acquired substantial practical knowledge about teaching, largely through their classroom experience rather than their formal training. It is this knowledge which is reflected in the ways they go about their routine day-to-day teaching, and it is clear that student teachers also need to acquire such knowledge. (p. 12)

In studying the careers of several teachers, Cohen (1991) found considerable distaste for the preparation they had had at the university. One of them observed that "The basic problem with these ed courses . . . is overkill. . . . The whole master's program could have been condensed into a couple of courses" (p. 65). Teacher education would not believe such to be the case; why do graduates often perceive it to be the case?

Needed Research We suggest that researchers consider what portions of professional study and skill that undergraduates can profitably study and acquire. For example, most preparation programs teach one version or another of an educational foundations course, a custom practice honors and accrediting bodies approve of. Although we recognize that there are many courses that teacher preparation students have in common, we focus on only one in order to raise some questions about appropriateness. We recognize that other courses or experiences in teacher preparation could illustrate our points perhaps equally well. Borman (1990) contends, based on two studies by Birkel in 1983 of the attitudes toward foundations courses of approximately 1,000 students at Ball State University, a 1984 survey by Dawson, Mazurek, and DeYoung of 615 students at two universities, and examination of syllabi and student course reviews at American Educational Studies Association (AESA) annual meetings that "Such courses, especially when their contents highlight current social issues and sociological concepts, are seen as particularly informative and valuable" (p. 398). Titus (1993) argues, based on his analyses of the most widely used foundations textbooks, that "While the overt content of the textbooks may not be sexist, unspoken messages exist in the texts' selective inattention to gender and ambivalence in the coverage of sexism and female oppression that define such issues as insignificant and unimportant" (p. 42). It appears to us that "current social issues" and "selective inattention to gender" in education foundations textbooks are interrelated matters, and that researchers could profitably study their relationship. We wonder if the age of 19 or so is the optimum time in students' lives to learn about the history of education in American life, various educational philosophies and philosophers, the federal role in education, and the host of other topics the typical educational foundations texts cover (Arends, 1991; Ornstein & Levine, 1989).

What would the profession learn about the perceived value of such courses by studies of traditional college-age students and nontraditional, older students enrolling in preservice programs or returning to study for advanced work? What would the profession learn about how education foundations professors send a message different from what the textbooks convey? Does the different message, if it exists, counter prospective teachers' negative perceptions of ethnic and gender differences that Avery and Walker (1993) find? Would readings such as Trueba's (1993) chapter on castification in America help prospective teachers understand the others' lives better and teach differently? Liston and Zeichner (1990) observe that:

Most teacher education programs give little attention to the social, political, and cultural context of schooling. Most programs are much too narrowly focused. This sort of narrow focus is not unusual in the educational community. Commentators have noted the tendency of educational scholars and teachers (and some might add, the general population) to examine situations within narrow rather than wider purviews. (p. 611)

Further studies should demonstrate or fail to demonstrate Liston and Zeichner's conclusions. More important, studies could help determine if, in those programs in which faculty teach the "right" material, students learn from and apply the materials of the courses in their student teaching and subsequent careers.

Multicultural education, which has entered the curricula of most teacher education programs, requires research. Numerous articles and texts exist purporting to show how and what to teach (Banks, 1991; Diaz, 1992; Heid, 1988; Jacob & Jordan, 1993); numerous pronouncements exist promoting its importance (Grant & Secada, 1990; Sleeter & Grant, 1987). We wonder: To what degree does multicultural education permeate teacher preparation? What is the effect of this work in the day-to-day, year-after-year lives of teachers? Do teachers grasp and apply the importance of the significant differences occurring in their own lives and in the lives of the students whom they teach because of where they were born, the color of their skin, the cultural backgrounds, and other related matters? Do they understand the varying perspectives that individuals within the teaching profession take? Liston and Zeichner (1990) believe that:

A crucial aspect of our social reconstructionist orientation is a concern for altering, through education, relations of domination and subordination. It is difficult to deny that in today's world being Black and living in a large metropolitan area greatly increase the odds that one will receive an inferior education and most probably experience a life of subordination. (p. 620)

Questions What are the similarities and differences between older, nontraditional, and traditional, college-age prospective teachers? Are the special programs for nontraditional students that some institutions have appropriate for them? How do students react to these programs?

Commentary Since the mid-1980s, individuals have entered teaching from careers in the military, government, business, and other fields. Some institutions have assembled special programs for them; others have entered them as individuals in ongoing programs with traditional students. Guyton, Fox, and Sisk (1991) find little significantly different in the profiles of nontraditional teacher preparation students whom they studied from those of traditional students. They did find, however, that they had a larger retention rate—83% versus "as low as 25% for others" (p. 7).

Needed Research Guyton et al.'s (1991) study suggests that nontraditional teaching candidates stay in teaching at a higher rate than do traditionally aged students, but their study fails to illuminate whether they are better, worse, or equal as teachers. There are clearly some age and experience differences between 19-year olds preparing to teach and a 47-year-old veteran of military service preparing to teach. Which ones are relevant to the preparation of teachers? Common sense might suggest that they will behave differently in the classrooms, but we do not know that to be the case. Is it good or bad that nontraditional teachers stay in the classroom longer than do traditional, college-age teachers? Which kinds of teachers, in the main, serve the schools and the children better?

Questions What are the implications of the largely female population of teachers vis-à-vis the largely male population of teacher education faculty and elementary and secondary school administrators? Why do so few males enter elementary teaching?

Commentary Nearly every data-gathering exercise since the 1960s focusing on those currently teaching and those preparing to teach in elementary and secondary schools includes a common conclusion: The profession is overwhelmingly female (National Center for Education Statistics, 1992; see also AACTE, 1987, 1988, 1989, 1990, 1991). The percentage of females was 68.7 in 1961; 65.7 in 1971; and 68.8 in 1986 (National Center for Educational Statistics, 1992). That is a "finding" that tells interested parties something about the makeup of the profession but nothing about what the condition means to teachers, children, parents, and preparation programs. What are the verifiable consequences of this condition? Commenting on what they perceive as the relatively low status of the teacher education faculty, Katz and Raths (1985) ask, "Does the fact that most candidates [teacher education students] are females act as a low status characteristic to compound this problem in some way?" (p. 11). Liston and Zeichner (1990), remarking on their own experience as males in elementary education, note:

Many of our prospective women teachers express surprise that a man would want to be an elementary teacher. Many of our male college mentors thought we should choose more appropriate careers. And, more recently, many of our male colleagues have advised us to focus on matters other than teacher education (p. 630). Few prospective teachers initially question the gendered nature of the division of labor in schools, the possibility of a gender bias in the elementary, secondary, or university curriculum, or the probable effect of a teaching career on their personal and professional lives. Committed as we are to nondiscriminatory and nonrepressive educational agenda, the strong possibility that gender dynamics in schools and society may contribute to antidemocratic biases seems good enough reason to examine gender relations. (p. 631)

It is interesting that Liston and Zeichner are as much, if not more, concerned with the problem as it affects them and others' perceptions of them as they are about the effect it has on the women in the profession. Black (1989) contends that division of labor by gender is more dramatic in higher education than in schools, where many think it is rampant.

Data on the public schools indicate that approximately 75% of principals in elementary and secondary schools are male (National Center for Education Statistics, 1992). Still other data indicate that even though approximately three quarters of those currently preparing to teach are female, the teacher educator population is largely male (American Association of Colleges for Teacher Education, 1987, 1988, 1989, 1990, 1991; NCES, 1990). No research study investigates these conditions from an interrelated perspective; that is, no one has carefully studied the condition and its effects on the largely female population of elementary school teachers teaching in schools with male principals after having completed programs in which most of the faculty were male. Hargreaves (1994) sees the gender issues as extremely important:

The world of the school, and of the elementary school in particular, is a world where a predominantly female teaching force comes into contact with a predominantly male administration. . . . The control, administration, and supervision of elementary teachers' work is, in this respect, overwhelmingly a process whereby supervising men manage the working lives of women. This heavily gendered process in the administration of teachers' work has important implications for the relationship of time to teachers' work and educational change. (p. 104)

Grant (1989), suggesting that these conditions transcend national borders, observes from the United Kingdom that:

We also need to know more about the characteristics which may combine with gender to increase or depress women's chances of promotion. So far existing surveys have paid little attention to charting either differential career routes or opportunity structures available to women teachers from different class, ethnic or other groups; this is clearly a direction for future research.

The acknowledged pattern of "career" followed by women needs to be acknowledged and legitimized by those with power to promote. This would have far-reaching consequences, requiring a revision of present employment practices as well as questioning the roles currently played by advisers, headteachers and governors. But it might also result in an equal representation of women in management posts in schools and all the ensuing benefits that would bring. (p. 48)

The effect on salary is pernicious. Adelman (1991), in data based on the intensive study of high school graduates of 1972, notes that 22.3% of the men with bachelor's degrees in education earned advanced degrees, whereas only 20.1% of women with bachelor's degrees did so; he further observes that of education majors who reported full-time employment of more than 5 full years between July 1979 and December 1985, all men reported a mean 5.84 years of employment and average salary of $21,651; women without children, 5.8 years and $18,544; and women with children, 5.55 years and $17,524.

Knowing the conditions just described does not provide the knowledge required to change the situations, even if the profession or society wanted to. There simply is no way to alter the conditions significantly. So is this knowledge about which the profession can do nothing? We think not. The profession could move beyond the data to ask the questions indicated and a few others. The effects of these conditions on female preservice students *could* be almost anything, ranging from no awareness, to an ingrained subservience, to anger, to developing father figure relationships. There simply is very little knowledge of the effects of the conditions on female prospective and practicing teachers. Nor do we know the effects of these conditions on male preservice elementary education students. It could range from no effect to latent sexism, early ambition to be an administrator to withdrawal from the profession. Do these prospective teachers perpetuate habits they will extend into the schools when they begin to teach? Again, the point is that there simply is very little knowledge.

Needed Research We suggest that researchers explore further: What are the effects on the female teachers and would-be teachers of these conditions? What are the effects on the male teachers and would-be teachers of these conditions? How do male teacher education faculty feel about teaching largely female classes? Is the climate reported in elementary and secondary schools a function of the gender makeup of administration and staff? Liston and Zeichner (1990) report:

When teachers do interact, there tends to be a norm against asking one another for help: to do so admits failure. In their interactions with administrators, teachers tend to see themselves in an ambiguous position. Teachers desire little interference from the principal in their classroom activities but at the same time they want the principal to act as a buffer between themselves and the outside world. (p. 617)

Is gender difference a cause of this relationship in which female teachers see the principals as the ones who keep the outside world from interfering with their work?

Do professors of education continue the gender biases in the questions they direct toward female and male students that they likely experienced in their earlier education (Acker, 1989)? McAninch (1993) contends that the largely female population of teacher education students will, based on the work of Belenky, Clinchy, Goldberger, and Tarule (1986), "be intuitive, prize personal experience, and, on the basis of their firsthand experience, reject the texts and words of scholars" (p. 36). Is such the case? If it is, what is needed to assist teachers to become the divergent thinkers needed to work with the divergent populations?

Acker (1989) noted:

We can also question whether the cards will always be stacked against women teachers by a patriarchal society, or whether social change, feminist activity and informed sociological scholarship can reshuffle the pack. (p. 7)

Taking gender seriously need not de-emphasize the social divisions which cut across it, nor suggest a hierarchy of oppression. What it does make clear is that many possible questions about teachers' careers and experiences have not yet been answered, or even asked, because the dominant model has limited the scope of our collective imagination. For example, what is the impact on teachers of working in a school catering for a particular social class, religious or ethnic mix, or a single-sex school? Are these effects different for teachers who themselves possess different characteristics? (p. 18)

We will subsequently comment on gender issues in needed research about the teacher education professoriate, but it is important to note here the effect it may have on promotion and tenure. This is clearly an area of interrelated research.

Question How should prospective teachers and practicing teachers demonstrate what they know and can do?

Commentary This question addresses the controversial matter of teacher assessment, one dominant in much of the national discourse. Discussion over what teachers should know and be able to do is eternal; issues over how they can demonstrate what they know and can do are myriad. Teacher educators have a particular interest in being able to demonstrate the efficacy of their teaching. Assessments of teacher performance or alleged assessments of teacher performances have been frequently present in the public mind (Cuban, 1984). National curriculum guidelines argue for particular areas of knowledge (e.g., math) as part of teacher preparation; best-selling critics of education contend that a cultural vacuum has emerged (Bennett, 1993) and argue that the content in schools must change; the National Board for Professional Teaching Standards is developing varied ways of determining teacher performance and awarding national certification to select teachers.

Needed Research Studies are necessary in such areas as the relationships, if any, between preparation program emphases

and actual teaching; relationships between results of whatever assessments or tests are used and performance; degrees to which national testing emphases are driving teacher preparation programs; and emerging texts for use in teacher preparation and assessment and testing emphases. Studies are necessary to determine the distinctions between rhetoric and performance.

Questions Are there distinctive teacher preparation programs in the United States? What are their indicators? In relationship to what? What is their life cycle? What are the characteristics that can be related to their distinctiveness? Are any of these applicable or able to be emulated by other institutions? What is the place of alternative teacher certification in teacher education?

Commentary Some literature exists that suggests what the hallmark of effective teacher education programs is; little exists to determine the most distinctive programs. Howey and Zimpher (1989) describe effective components and people in a limited number of programs. Clifford and Guthrie (1988), Goodlad, Soder, and Sirotnik (1990), the Holmes Group (1986), and others call for reform or describe what they believe should be. Tyson (1994) notes what she believes to be appropriate directions for teacher education. Arguments include more liberal arts, ever earlier field experiences, mentoring, release from perceived cumbersome certification requirements allowing holders of bachelor's degrees to teach as in Teach for America, rigorous testing of candidates, and so forth. Despite the presence of these and other works, knowledge remains limited. The results of such studies might interest practitioners, policymakers, and other concerned groups.

The emergence of alternative teacher preparation programs includes teacher education in the schools managed by school personnel, free-standing programs, totally off-campus programs, and school–higher education collaboratives. In 1990, 48 states had alternative certification of one kind or another (AACTE, 1990); some states have organized offices to assist individuals to obtain alternate certification.

Needed Research Programs in teacher education exist in many different types of institutions with variable resources; for example, in comprehensive universities, in 4-year colleges, in masters-level universities. There are 4-year programs, fifth-year programs, extended degree programs, postbaccalaureate programs, and alternative programs for nontraditional students. All of them graduate and recommend for certification candidates, many of whom become teachers. Teacher education needs research to consider, given differing contexts, and the need for the best utilization of resources. Teacher educators must learn the degree to which phrases like "reflective practitioner" go beyond glib descriptors for programs. They need to learn appropriate mixes between theory and practice for different kinds of candidates. Are there programs that systematically and consistently produce teachers of extraordinarily high quality? If so, do these programs have other characteristics in common that may contribute to that high quality? Clearly, no answers suiting all places and all candidates will emerge, but some enlightenment should and could ensue. The profession would profit from a study of why there is so much interest in alternative certification beyond rhetoric.

Question What differences should characterize the preparation of teachers for urban environments?

Commentary Brookhart and Rusnak (1993) describe what they believe to be a successful preparation program for urban teachers, but they do not first demonstrate that a need exists for significantly different preparation. Haberman (1991) describes eleven conditions that he believes should characterize urban teachers, including such matters as their being involved with planning their activities, applying fairness and equity, and questioning assumptions. These, of course, are what many believe should characterize all teachers; Haberman (1991) and others (Brophy, 1982; Knapp & Shields, 1990) are eloquent on exhortation on what should be but do not demonstrate that what they propose and advocate will make things better for urban children. Weiner (1993) provides insightful commentary on her years of teaching in urban schools and raises provocative questions.

Needed Research Advocacy and invention have led to many developments in education. Where would American elementary and secondary education be if Horace Mann had not advocated for the common school? The development of the normal schools was a function of the documented need for bodies in front of children to instruct them, but there was no research base for establishment of the kind of normal school that ensued and the types of preparation they promoted. Currently there is a similar documented need for teachers in urban schools, but beyond anecdotal stories in Sunday supplements about effective teachers, the basis for particular preparation is weak. We acknowledge that research in this area would be extremely complex, but the profession must assume the responsibility.

Question What are the values of teacher education students keeping journals?

Commentary Calderhead (1993) raises provocative questions about journals.

For instance, work on narratives and journal writing has been used to justify reflective practices in some programs and also to provide a methodology, but the use of such practices in teacher education itself raises many questions that are important to explore our understanding of professional development. For instance, how does journal writing contribute to students' professional development—is it inspiring confidence through valuing the person? Is it making educational values and assumptions explicit and therefore more amenable to critical scrutiny? Is it essentially cathartic in alleviating anxiety about classroom experiences? Does it promote greater autonomy and self-direction in professional development by thrusting greater responsibility upon the students themselves? Does it facilitate problem-solving by helping teachers make their problems explicit? Both for teacher education and for research, it is important to pursue these questions so that the processes of professional development are more fully understood and so that the ways in which professional development can be structured and facilitated can also be appreciated, leading perhaps, in turn, to other practices in teacher education and to other questions for research. (pp. 16–17)

Holly and Mcloughlin (1989) argue that:

Writing about teaching [journaling], we suggest, is a powerful method for documenting and learning from experience. (p. 259)

Keeping a personal-professional journal is both a way to record the journey of teaching and growing, and to experience the processes purposely and sensitively. (p. 281)

Like so many things in the profession, journaling *seems* like a good thing to do. Questions persist: What precisely do prospective teachers gain from journaling? Are the advantages or disadvantages of journaling spread equally across students, or do some students profit while others gain little, perhaps even have negative effects? Are journaling effects visible in teaching? If so, what are they?

Needed Research Feiman-Nemser (1990), writing of the teacher preparation program at the University of Wisconsin simply notes that "Journals, the fourth component, encourage student teachers to reflect systematically on their own development and their actions in the classroom" (p. 227). So runs the argument. Because teacher education researchers (Curtiss, 1993) are increasingly using the journals of teacher education students in their scholarly work, we can conclude that the student journals are helpful in *their* research, but the broader questions of how they do or do not help or otherwise affect the prospective teachers remains to be answered.

Question What are the discernible effects of the uses of cases in teacher education?

Commentary Since the late 1980s some teacher educators have advocated the use of cases in teacher preparation, both for preservice and for practicing teachers. There has been rapid growth in the use of cases in teacher education as an instructional strategy and in the development of case studies as a research method (Bullough, 1989, 1993; Valli, 1993). Grossman (1989) notes that, "The case study approach to research on teacher knowledge represents an attempt to gather in-depth data on the content and organization of an individual's knowledge" (p. 25). Cooper (1994), Grossman (1990), McAninch (1993), Merseth (1991a, 1991b), J. Shulman (1992a, 1992b), Wasserman (1993), and others have either authored or edited texts and monographs on the uses of cases in teacher education. Recent teacher education literature is rife with exhortations for the use of cases in teacher education, description of cases and suggested applications, and compendia of cases. L. Shulman (1992) argues that:

In all forms of professional education, there lurks an overarching goal: to teach the neophyte "to think like" a member of the profession. Learning to think like a lawyer, a teacher, a physician, or an anthropologist involves many aspects of practice. (p. 9)

Lieberman and Miller (1992) offer brief case studies at the end of each of their chapters in their text for school improvement. Bullough's (1989) *First-Year Teacher: A Case Study* effectively presents the dilemmas and joys of first-year teaching. Witherell and Noddings (1991) tellingly communicate the power of stories in explaining people's lives, a view not lost on researchers doing case studies. Clandinin, Davies, Hogan, and Kennard

(1993) present a series of stories in teacher education that they believe lead to a richer program and teacher development. Merseth and Lacey (1993) contend that, "very little empirical data" (p. 287) exist to support optimism about the potential for case studies to enhance teacher education.

Needed Research Although some contend that little exists to support the use of case studies to enhance teacher education, teacher educators persist in writing and using them (Bullough, 1993; McAninch, 1993; Merseth, 1991a, 1991b; Valli, 1992). Yarger and Smith (1990) indicate that case studies "can provide the consumer with an in-depth description of some teacher education phenomenon" (p. 31). But toward what end? L. Shulman (1992) warns educators:

Beware of references to *the* case method. Those who use cases in teaching become strong advocates of their own approach, zealous in defense of a particular way of building a lesson or unit of instruction around a case. Yet there are several ways to think about cases as occasions for teaching. (p. 10)

What purpose(s) beyond human interest do case studies serve in the preparation of teachers? Novels and stories may instruct us about life in various cultures, but do they change our beliefs and practices? The potentially rich field of case studies and the application to teacher growth and development beg exploration. If only because of the proliferation of materials and strong advocacy, teacher education needs research on the effects of the method, both short and long term.

Question *What results of early field experiences in teacher preparation can be demonstrated empirically? What are the benefits of yearlong internships prior to full-time teaching? What are the liabilities?*

Commentary Advocacy for early field experiences preceding student teaching has been long and, ultimately, successful (Ducharme & Ducharme, 1993; McIntyre, 1983). Most programs now require it; many state certification processes demand it. The rhetoric and the anecdotal evidence purporting its value are considerable; the research demonstrating effect or outcomes, negligible. Waxman and Walberg (1986) see little that is conclusive about early experience:

The contradictions and conflicting interpretations of the research as well as the shortage of experimental and longitudinal studies in this area constitute a serious national concern, especially in light of proposed reductions in the number of pedagogy courses offered in teacher education programs and increase the number of field experiences for prospective teachers in several states . . . some educators challenge the widespread belief that field experiences help prospective teachers become more effective teachers. While they maintain that they may give future teachers a taste of reality, they also claim that they can foster bad habits and narrow vision. (p. 166)

Using a combination of research-based citations and informal cases, Feiman-Nemser and Buchmann (1986) raise the question of whether or not "experience is as good a teacher of teachers as most people think" (p. 62). They conclude that, "At best, field experience in teacher preparation means learning things that are only part of the job of teaching" (p. 71).

Advocacy for yearlong internships prior to full-time teaching has a similar history. Limited research exists to suggest that those in internships become effective, valued teachers, but other studies suggest that teachers from 4-year programs also become effective, valued teachers. There is little research that looks at and comments on differences between those who enroll in programs with yearlong internships and those in conventional programs, leaving open the question of whether the alleged effectiveness of yearlong internships is a function of the programs or of the kinds of individuals who enroll in them.

Needed Research Teacher education may not be much further along than it was when Waxman and Walberg (1986) contended that,

Research workers must retain both openmindedness and skepticism about the research on early field experiences, because there is a limited knowledge base regarding the effectiveness of our teacher education practices. More empirical studies and research syntheses are needed to help us understand the impact of early field experiences for prospective teachers. Teacher education institutions need information on how a variety of educational factors interact with early field experiences and subsequently on how they affect prospective teachers. (p. 179)

Zeichner (1987) points out in his review of research on field experiences in teacher education that three specific elements are necessary in studies of field experiences: "(1) the structure and content of the field experience program, (2) the characteristics of placement sites, and (3) the characteristics, dispositions, and abilities of individual students and their significant others" (p. 112).

What do students in early field experiences actually do? Do they engage with students? Are they assistant clerks in the classrooms? Do they learn "true" and useful things in early experience? Is any experience better than none? Because early field experiences are so common now, one would be hardpressed to study differences between those who have them and those who do not. But this condition should not preclude studying the effects on students and the classrooms in which they have their early experiences. Research regarding the amount and value of teacher education faculty time invested in the development and maintenance of early field experiences is critical in determining the use of resources, utilization of faculty, and well-being of students.

Questions *What effect does supervision by a tenure-line faculty member, a graduate student, or part-time supervisor have on the performance of student teachers or interns? What are student teacher views of this matter?*

Commentary Although some contend that student teachers are best served by having "regular," tenure-line faculty as supervisors, the common practice in many institutions is for almost anyone but tenure-line faculty to supervise student teachers, such as in-school professionals, graduate students, part-time faculty, retired public school administrators and teachers, or faculty from academic departments. Beyond advocacy for the involvement of full-time faculty in supervision, little exists in the literature indicating what best serves the development of student teachers.

Needed Research The issue is simple, but the answer is no doubt complicated. Aside from the urgings of well-meaning writers, NCATE, and state and regional accrediting agencies, little research exists supporting the contention that primarily tenure-line faculty should supervise student teachers and interns. There are, to be sure, studies (AACTE, 1988) indicating that graduate students often supervise student teachers and interns, but that fact does not demonstrate whether the students are better or worse served by part-time graduate students than they would be by tenure-track faculty. Although the research would be enormously complicated, the profession would profit from a series of studies indicating the relative effects of part-time and tenure-track supervisors. What is the best investment of time and money? What point is served by utilizing full-time faculty, part-time faculty, and graduate students in supervision?

Question *What is the value of teacher education faculty assuming teaching roles in elementary and secondary schools?*

Commentary Much is made of the alleged need for teacher educators to "return" to the schools and spend prolonged time in them and perhaps thus become savvy about contemporary conditions and able to provide more relevant education for prospective teachers.

Katz and Raths (1985) ask a question similar to ours:

Critics of teacher education programs suggest that one of the causes of weakness is that staff members have had little recent school teaching experience. In what ways would teacher educators change as a consequence of being required to work in schools? (p. 12)

Bruckerhoff (1991) provides a stirring account of his time in a high school during which he "posed" as a secondary school teacher. Neither Bruckerhoff nor others who have written about time spent in the schools have indicated changes for better or worse as a consequence of working in schools, beyond vague remarks about understanding the schools better or perhaps altering their own practices. Little documentation exists.

The emergence of professional development schools (PDSs), a much heralded consequence in part of the Holmes Group (1986) work and the Carnegie Forum on Education and the Economy (1986), increasingly places teacher education faculty in schools as resources, occasional teachers of elementary and secondary students, instructors of on-site undergraduate and graduate courses, and researchers. Stallings and Kowalski (1990) contend that PDSs have as their goal "partnerships that join teachers, administrators, and college faculties in an effort to restructure the induction of teachers into the teaching profession" (p. 256). They conclude with the observation that "evaluations must be planned and carried out if there is to develop a body of knowledge about teacher preparation through professional development schools" (p. 262).

Professional Development Schools (Abdal-Haqq, 1992), a publication sponsored by the AACTE through its Clinical Schools Clearinghouse, provides capsule descriptions of some 80 schools more or less identified as PDSs. Although indicating that "over 90% of PDSs are tailored to preservice and beginning teachers and approximately that 75% include in-service teacher education components," the writers provide no evidence of the efficacy of the efforts to assist either pre- or in-service teachers.

Darling-Hammond's (1994) book contains many stories of how colleges and universities have cooperated in developing some of these schools. The key to the work lies in a subtopic of the introductory chapter: "Possibilities of Professional Development Schools" (p. 8). The profession will invest thousands of person hours in the development, operation, and maintenance of PDSs, but because of a lack of sustained research over time, teacher education will profit little.

Needed Research Teacher education must go beyond descriptions of the organization of PDSs, the schedule changes made in higher education and in the elementary and secondary schools, and counting of contact hours. These issues relate to all school activities of teacher educators. How do these efforts relate to promotion and tenure, to salary advancement in higher education? Stallings and Kowalski (1990) noted in their review of professional development schools that:

In the 1980s there were many conceptualizations of professional development schools, and at the time of this writing, only a few have been implemented. Only 3 could be found to have collected systematic qualitative and/or quantitative baseline data, so that they could estimate changes resulting from model intervention. Such evaluations must be planned and carried out if there is to develop a body of knowledge about teacher preparation through professional development schools. (p. 262)

The task remains.

Question *What changes in pedagogy, attitude toward learners, and self-concepts occur in teachers as they age and mature?*

Commentary Prospective teachers enter and exit from the preparation programs, generally completing undergraduate programs within 4 to 5 years and completing graduate certification programs such as Master of Arts in Teaching within 2 years, including an internship. Those acquiring teaching positions and remaining long term in teaching may spend 25 to 35 years in the schools. Many teacher educators spend energy and resources working with teachers in in-service efforts. The combination of incomplete preparation programs, new expectations such as mainstreaming, changes in state standards, personal desires for professional mobility requiring additional certification such as school administration, and a general desire on teachers' parts to continue to learn and to grow provide an environment in which teacher educators can interact with in-place professionals for a portion of their careers. Much remains to be learned about teachers and their lives, the role of university-provided in-service work in their careers, and long-term implications of work with teachers and schools for the teacher education professoriate.

Long-term studies of teachers are beginning to emerge. Lasley (1992) provides a valuable guide for the study of teachers' lives through the application of the concepts of stages. He relates this approach to be an enhancement of teacher reflection and suggests that "staff developers must be able to both identify a teacher's stage of pedagogical orientation and have some understanding of the psychological orientation of the teacher in the context of the school setting" (p. 24).

Studies often focus on the development of teachers with respect to professional practice as they age and mature, rarely on their changes in self-concept, their socialization patterns, or their attitudes toward the curriculum. Are Brekelmans and Creton (1993) right when they claim that teachers lose much of their zest as they age?

As their careers progress teachers become less cooperative and their enthusiasm seems to dwindle at the hands of routine and stress. They may gradually distance themselves from students, and their norms and values may change. They can also become increasingly tired, impatient, and demanding with students. (p. 101)

Studies could inform the preparation of teacher education students, giving them insights into the careers they are considering. Goodson (1992) contends:

For it remains clear that, in the accounts they give about life in schools, teachers constantly refer to personal and biographical factors. From their point of view, it would seem that professional practices are embedded in wider life concerns. We need to listen closely to their views on the relationship between "school life" and "whole life" for in that dialectic crucial tales about careers and commitments will be told. (p. 16)

For some this kind of knowledge for students prior to beginning their teaching is problematic. Liston and Zeichner (1990) comment:

Examining the working conditions of teachers allows prospective teachers insight into the institutional context of their work and how it affects their ability to teach. Initial reactions to the idea that such content should be included in teacher education curricula usually border on skepticism and disbelief. Analyzing teachers' work and the conditions of their work will, the skeptics argue, only result in cynicism, despair, and the abandonment of teaching. The realities are considered a bit too harsh for a neophyte. (p. 619)

We would prefer to believe, along with Liston and Zeichner and others, that teacher preparation students are stronger than the skeptics believe they are.

Floden (1993), commenting on the uses of case studies in the education of teachers, raises some largely unanswered questions that relate to teachers' preparation and professional lives: "Who are the students of teacher education? What is known about how these students learn? What learning is most important at each point in a teacher's career" (p. ix)? Sikes, Measor, and Woods (1985) studied teachers in different age cohorts, but their study depended heavily on teacher recall of events in their past lives. Spencer (1986) similarly relied on teacher memory. What do teachers value as they mature? Is much of their meaning derived from their students' achievements and learnings as Lortie (1975) and others have asserted? Jackson (1968) found that teachers obtained higher meaning from the interest and involvement of their students, not simply from their achievements.

Studies of the careers of teachers are yielding insights into their lives. Brown and McIntyre (1993) in *Making Sense of Teaching* provide a guide into understanding the day-to-day lives of teachers. They describe, in considerable detail, how teachers talk about their work and how researchers can effectively go about asking about that work. Brekelmans and Creton

(1993) remark on the difficulty of following teachers throughout their careers:

Throughout their careers teachers often experience periods of growth and decline. These peaks and valleys may affect teacher-communication style. To adequately describe these changes, researchers would have to collect data from career beginning to end. This, of course, is clearly a daunting task. (p. 81)

Hargreaves (1994), in his wide-ranging study of teaching, speculates about how and why teachers change:

How *do* teachers change—at this moment or any other? What makes teachers change in the face of change and what makes them dig in their heels and resist? Questions such as these concern what is commonly referred to as the *change process:* the practices and the procedures, the rules and relationships, the sociological and psychological mechanisms which shape the destiny of any change, whatever its content, and which lead it to prosper or fail. (p. 10)

Bruckerhoff (1991), in his study of the daily lives of the 16 members of the social studies department, divides them into the Academic Clique and the Coaches' Clique. Bruckerhoff's study provides those who educate teachers with clearly drawn episodes from daily lives. The question is what would teacher educators do with the information and insights? Should teacher preparation and in-service teacher education look different?

Some teachers continue to find it difficult to define precisely what they do and how they do it. Brown and McIntyre (1993) suggest the difficulty inherent in understanding the work of skilled teachers:

Unfortunately, it is the case that the more skillful is the teaching the more difficult it is to understand how success is being achieved. Many student teachers have the experience of observing a class where the teacher seems effortlessly to have the pupils "eating out of her hand"; the next day the student may take the same class and find the pupils uncontrollable. In general, it seems that while we recognize that there are those with mastery of some aspects of teaching, we have no coherent account of what they are master of and how they achieve what they achieve. The effect of this has been to limit the value of school-based elements of teacher education programmes, despite the fact that elements are important components of pre-service teacher education throughout the world. (pp. 12–13)

Goodson (1992) and his colleagues point out the importance of studying teachers' lives and the varied ways of doing so.

Needed Research What does the work of Bruckerhoff (1991), Cusick (1981), Peshkin (1986), Sizer (1985), and others say about the preparation of teachers? Have the excitement, the ennui, the joy, the frustration, the anomie, and the other qualities attributed to the teacher participants in these and similar studies affected how teachers are prepared? Do prospective teachers read these works, and, if they do, to what end? Researchers might study the implications for and effects on practicing teachers who might read such material. Teacher growth in skill and knowledge is a career-long matter, and one wonders about the effects of reading about other teachers and their lives.

Questions *What changes in pedagogy, attitude toward learners, and self-concepts occur in teacher educators as they age*

and mature? What is known about the preparation of teacher educators?

Commentary As recently as the mid-1980s, Troyer (1986) noted the limited knowledge of teacher educators and professors of education. Although some writing existed, most of it was descriptive and anecdotal, and little was analytic. The situation has changed considerably since then, as researchers have begun to study the professoriate.

Clifford and Guthrie (1988), Ducharme (1993), Ducharme and Ducharme (in press), Howey and Zimpher (1989), Judge (1982), Lanier and Little (1986), Popkewitz (1987), Wisniewski and Ducharme (1989), and others have recently contributed to the field, but many questions persist. In describing how others perceived education faculty, Katz and Raths (1985) note that:

Students and school teachers tend to dismiss teacher educators as high-minded, impractical, idealistic, excessively theoretical, and even too scientific. On the other hand, colleagues on campus seem to attribute opposite characteristics to them, faulting them for being too practical, atheoretical, and non empirical. In both cases, the attributions were pejorative. (p. 11)

Considerable demographic data are presently available on teacher educators (for example, AACTE, 1987, 1988, 1989, 1990, 1991; Ducharme & Agne, 1982). Studies on the meaning of the data, although growing in number, are less plentiful. Hall and Koehler (undated) argue that:

Research on *teacher eductors as practitioners* should be undertaken. Specific study focus might be: Clearer identification of the target (characteristics, training received versus that needed, skills developed versus those needed); clearer conceptualization of the role (how and what training is carried out by the teacher educator and what roles accrue to them); study of effects (on students, on sex and racial bias, and in different contexts). A heavier emphasis should be placed on *descriptive research* (to understand a phenomenon) as a complement to *improvement research* (designed with intended impact on practice) in order to provide a sufficient base for conceptual and theoretical work. (pp. iii and iv, original emphasis)

Britzman (1991), in her story of the life of Professor Joe Probe, has epitomized the dilemmas of teacher educators with a sense of social mission that they attempt to invest in their students. Probe has a high level of frustration in making his views known. As valuable and interesting as this portrait is, it also points to the need for more in-depth studies of teacher educator attitudes.

Needed Research Ducharme (1993) presents teacher educators at various age and professional levels, but his study does not provide an ongoing long-term description of the faculty. Teacher education needs the kinds of studies that are emerging about teachers: long-term, life studies, shadow descriptions, and a variety of other approaches. Teacher educators develop, grow, and change, but the literature on them fails to reflect these conditions.

Question Are there differences that relate to teacher performance between teaching graduates of NCATE member institu-

tions and graduates of nonmember institutions otherwise similar in size, type, and scope?

Commentary Chief claims for national accreditation in any profession are that standards for admission will be higher, the graduates will perform better in their work, and there will be a higher level of public trust. The contention is that the clients fare better when dealing with professionals from nationally accredited institutions. Little research exists either to demonstrate or disprove the contention. Katz and Raths asked a similar question in 1985:

Are graduates of NCATE accredited institutions better teachers, on the average, than graduates from non accredited institutions? Is the content of NCATE approved teacher education programs different from those which are not NCATE approved? (p. 13)

Despite over a decade of heightened attention to and development of accreditation practices and programs, Katz and Raths's questions remain unanswered. Wise (1993–1994) comments that, "Graduation from an NCATE-accredited school equips a teacher with the tools he or she needs to accept the challenges faced by educators today" (p. 1). What are the tools? Are graduates from nonaccredited schools not in possession of the same "tools"? The matter of the precise differences between those from accredited institutions and those from nonaccredited institutions remains vague. Are there discernible differences in content knowledge, rapport with students, social commitment, methods of instruction, and/or effectiveness in multicultural settings?

Needed Research The topic of local, regional, and national accreditation remains of interest and controversy. We suggest that researchers study the *effects* of accreditation, not the *perceived professional need.* This would be an enormous but immensely valuable task. We suggest that researchers develop strategies and methods to study what, if any, results accrue to students in elementary and secondary schools that relate to their being taught by individuals from either accredited or nonaccredited programs. Teacher education would also profit from analyses of the various accreditation processes of regional higher education reviews and profession-specific reviews. Realistic and rigorous cost analyses would also be helpful. Valuable research would move from the rhetoric of the asserted professional responsibility for institutional membership in much current literature (i.e., Gideonse et al., 1993) to the demonstrable value for teacher education graduates, the schools in which they teach, and the youth whom they teach.

CONCLUSION

Several months ago we began this chapter excited about the possibilities of delineating some of the research needed by the profession in which we have spent our professional lives. We end it in the same mood. As coeditors of the *Journal of Teacher Education*, we see on an almost daily basis the fruits of the research efforts of some of our colleagues. After reading a submission, we often say to ourselves something like, "Hmm, there's an interesting topic that is worthy of publication but clearly needs more research." We suspect that readers of this chapter will similarly say, "Hmm, they hit on some interesting topics, but what about . . . ?"

Each week brings a new journal or text to our attention. Often there is a new insight, a novel observation about the research. The writing of such a chapter could go on forever. For many teacher educators, the writing of this chapter does go on forever, as they read and learn of new things and alter or reflect on what they do.

Yet the quest for certainty bedevils all, certainty eludes us all. We are reminded of words from the seventeenth-century poetry of John Donne (1962), a quotation rich in meaning for all of us who seek the resolution of complex questions in simple solutions.

On a huge hill,
Cragged and steep, Truth stands, and he that will
Reach her, about and about must go,
And what the hill's suddenness resists, win so.
Yet strive so that before age, death's twilight,
Thy soul rest, for none can work in that night.
To will implies delay; therefore now do.

Donne counsels both knowledge and action. Truth in teacher education, the object of research, either stands on a cragged and steep hill or lies in a pocked and deep hole. Either way, the profession must go beyond *will* and *do*.

References

Abdal-Haqq, I. (1992). *Professional development schools: A directory of projects in the United States.* Washington, DC: American Association of Colleges for Teacher Education.

Acker, S. (Ed.). (1989). *Teachers, gender and careers.* New York: Falmer.

Adelman, C. (1991). *Women at thirty-something: Paradoxes of attainment.* Washington, DC: U.S. Department of Education, Office of Educational Research and Improvement.

American Association of Colleges for Teacher Education. (1990). *Teacher education policy in the states: A 50-state survey of legislative and administrative actions.* Washington, DC: Author.

American Association of Colleges for Teacher Education. (1987, 1988, 1989, 1990, 1991). *Teaching teachers: Facts and figures.* Washington, DC: Author.

Arends, R. I. (1991). *Learning to teach* (2nd ed.). New York: McGraw-Hill.

Auchmuty, J. (1980). *National inquiry into teacher education.* Canberra, Australia: Australian Publishing Service.

Avery, P. G., & Walker, C. (1993). Prospective teachers' perceptions of ethnic and gender differences. *Journal of Teacher Education, 44*(1), 27–37.

Banks, J. A. (1991). *Teaching strategies for ethnic studies* (5th Ed.) Boston: Allyn & Bacon.

Belenky, M. F., Clinchy, B. M., Goldberger, N. R., & Tarule, J. (1986). *Women's ways of knowing.* New York: Basic Books.

Bennett, W. (1993). *The book of virtues.* New York: Simon & Schuster.

Berliner, D. C. (1985). Laboratory settings and the study of teacher education. *Journal of Teacher Education, 36*(6), 2–8.

Birkel, L. (1983). How students view foundational studies in education. *Teacher Education, 5,* 79–87.

Black, E. (1989). Women's work in a man's world: Training in a college of further education. In S. Acker (Ed.), *Teachers, gender & careers* (pp. 139–150). New York: Falmer.

Borman, K. M. (1990). Foundations of education in teacher education. In R. Houston (Ed.), *Handbook of research on teacher education* (pp. 393–402). New York: Macmillan.

Brekelmans, M., & Creton, H. (1993). Interpersonal teacher behavior throughout the career. In T. Wubbels & J. Levy. (Eds.), *Do you know what you look like? Interpersonal relationships in education* (pp. 81–102). New York: Falmer.

Britzman, D. P. (1991). *Practice makes practice: A critical study of learning to teach.* Albany: State University of New York Press.

Brookhart, S. M., & Rusnak, T. G. (1993). A pedagogy of enrichment, not poverty: Successful lessons of exemplary urban teachers. *Journal of Teacher Education, 44*(1), 17–26.

Brophy, J. E. (1982). Successful teaching strategies for the inner-city child. *Phi Delta Kappan, 63,* 527–530.

Brown, S., & McIntyre, D. J. (1993). *Making sense of teaching.* Philadelphia: Open University Press.

Bruckerhoff, C. E. (1991). *Between classes: Faculty life at Truman High.* New York: Teachers College Press.

Bullough, R. V., Jr. (1989). *First year teacher: A case study.* New York: Teachers College Press.

Bullough, R. V., Jr. (with Baughman, K.). (1993). Continuity and change in teacher development: First year teacher after five years. *Journal of Teacher Education, 44*(2), 86–95.

Calderhead, J. (1993). The contribution of research on teachers thinking to the professional development of teachers. In C. Day, J. Calderhead, & P. Denicolo, (Eds.), *Research on teacher thinking: Understanding professional development* (pp. 11–18). Washington, DC: Falmer.

Carnegie Forum on Education and the Economy. (1986). *A nation prepared: Teachers for the 21st century.* New York: Author.

Clandinin, D., Davies, A., Hogan, P., & Kennard, B. (Eds.). (1993). *Learning to teach, teaching to learn.* New York: Teachers College Press.

Clifford, G., & Guthrie, J. (1988). *Ed school.* Chicago: University of Chicago Press.

Cohen, R. M. (1991). *A lifetime of teaching: Portraits of five veteran high school teachers.* New York: Teachers College Press.

Cooper, J. M. (Ed.). (1994). *Teachers' problem solving: A casebook of award-winning cases.* Boston: Allyn & Bacon.

Cuban, L. (1984). *How teachers taught: Constancy and change in American classrooms, 1890–1980.* New York: Longman.

Curtiss, P. K. M. (1993). Perceptions of human technologies in teaching: A pedagogical methods course in the extended elementary teacher education program. *Journal of Teacher Education, 44*(2), 139–148.

Cusick, P. A. (1981). *The egalitarian ideal and the American high school.* New York: Holt, Rinehart, & Winston.

Darling-Hammond, L. (1990). Teachers and teaching: Signs of a changing profession. In R. Houston (Ed.), *Handbook of research on teacher education* (pp. 267–290). New York: Macmillan.

Darling-Hammond, L. (1994). *Professional development schools.* New York: Teachers College Press.

Dawson, D., Mazurek, K., & De Young, A. J. (1984). Courses in the social foundations of teaching: The students' view. *Journal of Education for Teaching, 10*(3), 242–248.

Diaz, C. (Ed.). (1992). *Multicultural education for the 21st century.* Washington, DC: National Education Association.

Donne, J. (1962). Satire on religion. In M. Abrams, E. Donaldson, H. Smith, R. Adams, S. Monk, G. Ford, & D. Daiches (Eds.), *The Norton anthology of English literature* (pp. 368–371). New York: Norton.

Ducharme, E. R. (1993). *The lives of teacher educators.* New York: Teachers College Press.

Ducharme, E. R., & Agne, R. M. (1982). The education professoriate: A research based perspective. *Journal of Teacher Education, 33*(6), 30–36.

Ducharme, E. R., & Ducharme, M. K. (in press). Development of the teacher education professoriate. In F. Murray (Ed.), *Knowledge base for teacher educators.* San Francisco: Jossey-Bass.

Ducharme, M. K., & Ducharme, E. R. (1993). School-based teacher education in the United States: An uneven evolution. *Australian Journal of Teacher Education, 18*(2), 15–22.

Elliott, J. (1993). Professional education and the idea of a practical educational science. In J. Elliott (Ed.), *Reconstructing teacher education: Teacher development* (pp. 65–85). Washington, DC: Falmer.

Elliott, R. (1989). Selecting better teachers: Some possibilities. In J. D. Wilson, G. O. B. Thomson, R. E. Millward, & T. Keenan (Eds.), *Assessments for teacher development* (pp. 144–152). New York: Falmer.

Erickson, F. (1986). Qualitative methods in research on teaching. In M. Wittrock (Ed.), *Handbook of research on teaching* (3rd ed., pp. 119–161). New York: Macmillan.

Feiman-Nemser, S. (1990). Teacher preparation: Structural and conceptual alternatives. In R. Houston (Ed.), *Handbook of research on teacher education* (pp. 212–233). New York: Macmillan.

Feiman-Nemser, S., & Buchmann, M. (1986). Pitfalls of experience in teacher preparation. In J. Raths & L. Katz (Eds.), *Advances in teacher education* (vol. 2, pp. 61–73). Norwood, NJ: Ablex.

Floden, R. E. (1993). Foreword. In A. R., McAninch, *Teacher thinking and the case method: Theory and future directions.* New York: Teachers College Press.

Galluzzo, G. R., & Craig, J. R. (1990). In R. Houston (Ed.), *Handbook of research on teacher education* (pp. 599–616). New York: Macmillan.

Gideonse, E. H., Ducharme, M. K., Ducharme, D., Gollnick, M. S., Lilly, E. L., Schelke, & Smith, P. (1993). *Capturing the vision: Reflections on NCATE's redesign five years after.* Washington, DC: American Association of Colleges for Teacher Education.

Goodlad, J. I., Soder, R., & Sirotnik (Eds.). (1990). *Places where teachers are taught.* San Francisco: Jossey-Bass.

Goodson, I. (1992). *Studying teachers' lives.* New York: Teachers College Press.

Grant, C. A., & Secada, W. G. (1990). Preparing teachers for diversity. In R. Houston (Ed.), *Handbook of research on teacher education* (pp. 403–422). New York: Macmillan.

Grant, R. (1989). Women teachers' careers pathways: Towards an alternative model of "career." In S. Aker (Ed.), *Teachers, gender and careers* (pp. 35–50). New York: Falmer.

Grossman, P. (1989). A study in contrast: Sources of pedagogical content knowledge for secondary English. *Journal of Teacher Education, 40*(5), 24–31.

Grossman, P. (1990). *The making of a teacher: Teacher knowledge and teacher education.* New York: Teachers College Press.

Guyton, E., Fox, M., & Sisk, K. (1991). Comparison of teaching attitudes, teacher efficacy, and teacher performance of first year teachers prepared by alternative and traditional teacher education programs. *Action in Teacher Education, 13*(2), 1–9.

Haberman, M. (1991). The pedagogy of poverty versus good teaching. *Phi Delta Kappan, 73,* 290–294.

Hall, G. E., & Koehler, V. R. (n.d.). *A national agenda for research and development in teacher education.* Austin: Research and Development Center for Teacher Education, University of Texas at Austin.

Hargreaves, A. (1994). *Changing teachers, changing times: Teachers' work and culture in the postmodern age.* New York: Teachers College Press.

Heid, C. A. (Ed.). (1988). *Multicultural education: Knowledge and perceptions.* Bloomington: Indiana University Press.

Holly, M. L., & Mcloughlin, C. S. (1989). Professional development and journal writing. In M. L. Holly & C. S. Mcloughlin (Eds.), *Perspectives on teacher professional development* (pp. 259–284). New York: Falmer.

Holmes Group. (1986). *Tomorrow's teachers: A report of the Holmes Group.* East Lansing, MI: Author.

Houston, W. R., Haberman, M., & Sikula, J. (1990). Preface. In R. Houston (Ed.) *Handbook of research on teacher education* (pp. ix–xi). New York: Macmillan.

Howey, K. R., & Zimpher, N. L. (1989). *Profiles of preservice teacher education: Inquiry into the nature of programs.* Albany: State University of New York Press.

Huberman, M. (1993). Changing minds: The dissemination of research and its effects on practice and theory. In C. Day, J. Calderhead, & P. Denicolo, (Eds.), *Research on teacher thinking: Understanding professional development* (pp. 34–52). Washington, DC: Falmer.

Jackson, P. W. (1968). *Life in classrooms.* New York: Holt, Rinehart, and Winston.

Jacob, E., & Jordan, C. (Eds.). (1993). *Minority education: Anthropological perspectives.* Norwood, NJ: Ablex.

Johnston, R., & Ryan, K. (1983). Research on the beginning teacher: Implications for teacher education. In K. Howey & W. Gardner (Eds.), *The education of teachers: A look ahead* (pp. 120–141). New York: Longman.

Judge, H. (1982). *American graduate schools of education: A view from abroad.* New York: Ford Foundation.

Kaestle, C. D. (1993). The awful reputation of education research. *Educational Researcher, 22*(1), 23–31.

Katz, L., & Raths, J. D. (1985). A framework for research on teacher education programs. *Journal of Teacher Education, 36*(6), 9–15.

Kelchtermans, G. (1993). Teachers and their career story: A biographical perspective on professional development. In C. Day, J. Calderhead, & P. Denicolo, (Eds.), *Research on teacher thinking: Understanding professional development* (pp. 198–220). Washington, DC: Falmer.

Kerdman, D., & Phillips, D. C. (1993). Empiricism and the knowledge base of educational practice. *Review of Educational Research, 63*(3), 305–313.

Knapp, M. S., & Shields, P. M. (1990). Reconceiving academic instruction for the children of poverty. *Phi Delta Kappan, 71,* 752–758.

Lanier, J. E., & Little, J. W. (1986). Research on teacher education. In M. C. Whittrock (Ed.), *Handbook of research on teaching* (3rd ed., pp. 527–569). New York: Macmillan.

Lasley, T. J. (1992). Promoting teacher reflection. *Journal of Staff Development, 13*(1), 24–29.

Lieberman, A., & Miller, L. (1992). *Teachers: Their world and their work.* New York: Teachers College Press.

Liston, D. P., & Zeichner, K. M. (1990). Teacher education and the social context: Issues for curriculum development. *American Educational Research Journal, 27*(4), 610–636.

Lortie, D. C. (1975). *Schoolteacher: A sociological study.* Chicago: University of Chicago Press.

McAninch, A. R. (1993). *Teacher thinking and the case method: Theory and future directions.* New York: Teachers College Press.

McIntyre, D. J. (1983). *Field experiences in teacher education: From student to teacher.* Washington, DC: Foundation for Excellence in Teacher Education and the ERIC Clearinghouse on Teacher Education.

Merseth, K. (1991a). *The case for cases in teacher education*. Washington, DC: American Association of Higher Education and the American Association of Colleges for Teacher Education.

Merseth, K. (1991b). The early history of case-based instruction: Insights for teacher education today. *Journal of Teacher Education, 42*(4), 243–249.

Merseth, K., & Lacey, C. (1993). Weaving stronger fabric: The pedagogical promise of hypermedia and case methods in teacher education. *Teaching and Teacher Education, 9*(3), 283–299.

National Center for Education Statistics. (1990). *Faculty in higher education institutions, 1988*. Washington, DC: U.S. Government Printing Office.

National Center for Education Statistics. (1992). *Digest of education statistics: 1992*. Washington, DC: U.S. Government Printing Office.

Nias, J. (1989). Teaching and the self. In M. L. Holly & C. S. Mcloughlin (Eds.), *Perspectives on teacher professional development* (pp. 155–172). New York: Falmer.

Nichol, J. (1993). The Exeter school-based PGCE: An alternative teacher training model. *Journal of Education for Teaching, 19*(3), 303–324.

Ornstein, A. C., & Levine, D. U. (1989). *Foundations of education* (4th ed.). Boston: Houghton Mifflin.

Palincsar, A. S., & McPhail, J. C. (1993). A critique of the metaphor of distillation in "Toward a knowledge base for school learning." *Review of Educational Research, 63*(3), 327–334.

Peshkin, A. (1986). *God's choice*. Chicago: University of Chicago Press.

Pope, M. (1993). Anticipating teacher thinking. In C. Day, J. Calderhead, & P. Denicolo, (Eds.), *Research on teacher thinking: Understanding professional development* (pp. 19–33). Washington, DC: Falmer.

Popkewitz, T. (Ed.). (1987). *Critical studies in teacher education: Its folklore, theory, and practice*. New York: Falmer.

Richardson, V. (1996). The case for formal research and practical inquiry in teacher education. In F. Murray (Ed.), *Knowledge base for teacher educators*. San Francisco: Jossey-Bass.

Rowe, M. B. (1986). Wait time: Slowing down may be a way of speeding up! *Journal of Teacher Education, 37*(1) 43–50.

Shulman, J. H. (Ed.) (1992a). *Case studies in teacher education*. New York: Teachers College Press.

Shulman, J. H. (Ed.) (1992b). *Learning to think like a teacher: The study of cases*. New York: Teachers College Press.

Shulman, L. (1992). Toward a pedagogy of cases. In J. Shulman (Ed.), *Case methods in teacher education* (pp. 1–32). New York: Teachers College Press.

Sikes, P., Measor, L., & Woods, P. (1985). *Teacher careers: Crises and continuities*. London: Falmer.

Singer, J. D. (1993). On faith and microscopes: Methodological lenses for learning about learning. *Review of Educational Research, 63*(3), 353–364.

Sizer, T. J. (1985). *Horace's compromise*. Boston: Houghton Mifflin.

Sleeter, C. E., & Grant, C. (1987). An analysis of multicultural education in the United States. *Harvard Educational Review, 57,* 421–444.

Spencer, D. A. (1986). *Contemporary women teachers: Balancing school and home*. New York: Longman.

Stallings, J. A., & Kowalski, T. J. (1990). Research on professional development schools. In W. R. Houston (Ed.), *Handbook of research on teacher education* (pp. 251–263). New York: Macmillan.

Tickle, L. (1989). New teachers and the development of professionalism. In M. L. Holly & C. S. Mcloughlin (Eds.), *Perspectives on teacher professional development* (pp. 93–118). New York: Falmer.

Titus, J. J. (1993). Gender messages in education foundations textbooks. *Journal of Teacher Education, 44*(1), 38–44.

Troyer, M. (1986). A synthesis of research of the characteristics of teacher educators. *Journal of Teacher Education, 37*(5), 6–11.

Trueba, H. T. (1993). Castification in multicultural America. In H. T. Trueba, C. Rodriguez, Y. Zou, & J. Cintron (Eds.), *Healing multicultural America: Mexican immigrants rise to power in rural California* (pp. 29–51). Washington, DC: Falmer.

Turner, R. L. (1975). An overview of research in teacher education. In K. Ryan (Ed.), *Teacher education* (74th yearbook of the National Society for the Study of Education, pt. 2, pp. 87–110). Chicago: University of Chicago Press.

Tyson, H. (1994). *Who will teach the children: Progress and resistance in teacher education*. San Francisco: Jossey-Bass.

Valli, L. (Ed.) (1992). *Reflective teacher education: Cases and critiques*. Albany: State University of New York Press.

Valli, L. (with Agastinetti, A.). (1993). Teaching before and after professional preparation: The story of a high school mathematics teacher. *Journal of Teacher Education, 44*(2), 107–118.

Wasserman, S. (1993). *Getting down to cases*. New York: Teachers College Press.

Watts, B. (1989). Project 21: Teachers for the twenty-first century. In J. D. Wilson, G. O. B. Thomson, R. E. Millward, & T. Keenan (Eds.), *Assessments for teacher development* (pp. 41–52). New York: Falmer.

Waxman, H. C., & Walberg, H. J. (1986). Effects of early field experiences. In J. Raths & L. Katz (Eds.), *Advances in teacher education* (vol. 2, pp. 165–184). Norwood, NJ: Ablex.

Weiner, L. (1993). *Preparing teachers for urban schools*. New York: Teachers College Press.

White, R. T., & Tisher, R. P. (1986). Research on natural sciences. In M. C. Wittrock (Ed.). *Handbook of research on teaching* (3rd ed., pp. 874–905). New York: Macmillan.

Wilson, J. D. (1985). *Judgments of quality: Assessing candidates for entry into initial teacher training in Scotland*. Final report of Criteria for Teacher Selection Project, Scotland: Moray House College of Education.

Wilson, J. D., & Thomson, G. O. (1989). Conclusions and the research agenda. In J. D. Wilson, G. O. B. Thomson, R. E. Millward, & T. Keenan (Eds.), *Assessments for teacher development* (pp. 207–218). New York: Falmer.

Wise, A. (1993–1994). Preface. *Teacher education: A guide to NCATE-accredited colleges and institutions*. Washington, DC: National Council for Accreditation of Teacher Education.

Wisniewski, R., & Ducharme, E. R. (Eds.). (1989). *The professors of teaching: An inquiry*. Albany: State University of New York Press.

Witherell, C. S., & Noddings, N. (Eds.). (1991). *Stories lives tell: Narrative and dialogue in education*. New York: Teachers College Press.

Yarger, S. J., & Smith, P. L. (1990). Issues in research in teacher education. In R. Houston (Ed.), *Handbook of research on teacher education* (pp. 25–39). New York: Macmillan.

Yinger, R., & Hendricks-Lee, M. (1993). Working knowledge in teaching. In C. Day, J. Calderhead, & P. Denicolo, (Eds.), *Research on teacher thinking: Understanding professional development* (pp. 100–123). Washington, DC: The Falmer Press.

Zeichner, K. M. (1987). The ecology of field experiences: Toward an understanding of field experiences in teacher development. In M. Haberman & J. M. Backus (Eds.). *Advances in teacher education* (Vol. 3) (pp. 92–117). Norwood, NJ: Ablex.

Zeichner, K. M., & Tabachnick, B. R. (1981). Are the effects of university teacher education 'washed out' by school experiences? *Journal of Teacher Education, 32*(3), 7–13.

Zimpher, N. L., & Ashburn, E. (1985). Studying the professional development of teachers: How conceptions of the world inform the research agenda. *Journal of Teacher Education, 36*(6), 16–26.

· 47 ·

TEACHER EDUCATION RESEARCH
IN INTERNATIONAL SETTINGS

B. Bradley West
MICHIGAN STATE UNIVERSITY

Elaine Jarchow
TEXAS TECH UNIVERSITY

Nancy L. Quisenberry
SOUTHERN ILLINOIS UNIVERSITY–CARBONDALE

This chapter might be aptly titled, "International Teacher Education Research: Work in Progress" because there is literally no end to the complex and overwhelming task of discovering, reporting, summarizing, analyzing, and critiquing the corpus of teacher education research conducted in nations outside the United States. Such a task is probably suitable to an encyclopedia or perhaps a book dedicated to the topic. However, by limiting the chapter goals, the reference time span, methodology, and communication techniques, a report on teacher education research in other parts of the world is at least somewhat feasible.

The authors think of a handbook as different from a usual book in which an author is thorough in a treatment of the subject (a typical handbook chapter is about 17 pages), different from a collection of teacher education monographs, and different from a collection of journal manuscripts. A handbook has

a reference and a pragmatic quality. Thus, an important goal of the chapter is to provide information that readers may find useful. The authors understand our readers to be teacher educators, not those who generally subscribe to publications such as the *International Journal of Education Research,* the educational research journals of Britain, Scandinavia, Zimbabwe, or the *Indian Educational Review* published in New Delhi.

Why should American teacher educators have an interest in teacher education research in other nations? Some suggest that because the cultural contexts are sometimes so widely different, there is no particular reason to be interested, for example, in knowing the details of a teacher education study in China. But that in itself is a compelling reason—*because* the cultural contexts are different. Simply put, knowing and understanding teacher education research in other lands clarify and deepen insight into our own ability to ask pivotal questions about our

The authors wish to thank the author correspondents (see Table 47.1) for their splendid country reports. Most courageously wrote in English—their second, third, and even fourth language, in some cases. We acknowledge, especially in the initial stages, the ideas and reviews of Professor Harry Judge, Oxford University; Professor Christopher Clark, Michigan State University; and Professor Marco Todeschini, Editor of the European *Journal of Teacher Education.* Professor Thérèse Tchombe of the University of Yaounde I (Cameroon) and Professor Bamrung Torut, Silpakorn University (Thailand), were instrumental in identifying studies that would have escaped our investigation. Throughout our journey, we were most ably assisted by Ms. Barbara Reeves, Department of Teacher Education at Michigan State University, who volunteered her time and expertise in the technical preparation of this chapter. Thanks are also due to typist Ms. Katrina Switalski, College of Education at the University of Nevada, Las Vegas, for her contributions to the project.

own practice. Schwille (1993), addressing the South East Asian Research Review International Conference in Brunei, put it this way: "Teacher education is entering an era in which comparative international inquiry can provide more insight than heretofore into mainstream areas of schooling and help improve practice in these areas." If one knows and understands the *raison d'être* of a given educational practice in America, but not how the practice is considered in other parts of the globe, one could get the idea that the practice is important throughout the world. If actually so, this understanding contributes to a personal knowledge of a rather universal practice in teacher education. If not actually so, one develops some understanding of how and why the practice is culturally specific.

These considerations, then, and the idea that behavior (i.e., what researchers research) illustrates what is valued in teacher education in a given country led us to decide that the primary goal of the chapter is to provide some answer to the question, "What teacher education research is being done in (country name)?" Recognizing that research is reported not only in national publications but also in a myriad of other institutional, provincial, and regional publications, we decided that a good way to identify teacher education research in any given country is to contact a noted researcher in that country.

Armed with an extensive list of personal and professional contacts throughout the world, we began nominating and communicating with colleague researchers with whom we could collaborate. Eventually several dozen "author correspondents" were identified, many of whom sent reports of teacher education research in their respective countries (see Table 47.1). Not all colleagues contacted were able to participate in a timely fashion, and so this chapter consists of those reports received by the publisher's and editors' deadline.

Research questions in the developing world, although often similar to those in industrial nations, may be answered by researchers who do not have access to scholarly journals. The author correspondent list affords readers some opportunity to obtain additional information on the studies cited for the author correspondent's country. Particularly in the developing world, full citations and information on findings may not have been available to the author correspondents. However, we decided to include as much information as is known about the reference for a given bibliographic citation, even though it may be incomplete and without a report of findings. World political, economic, communication, and resource situations change rapidly and without warning, thus affecting standards of scholarly inquiry.

Another goal of this chapter is to identify some teacher education research being done in the United States that involves international populations, themes, or content. This goal adds a complementary dimension to research conducted in foreign countries.

Two other decisions also guided the work: the time frame of the research and the method of reporting the findings. The research reports were usually limited to those that have been published since the mid-1980s, and the chapter was organized by country and then usually by content within each country (there are some exceptions, notably, Belarus and Switzerland). "Content" is defined as the topical areas within each section of this handbook: (1) teacher education as a field of study;

(2) recruitment, selection, and initial preparation; (3) contextual influences on teacher education; (4) teacher education curriculum; (5) continuing professional growth, development, and assessment; (6) diversity and equity issues; and (7) emerging directions in teacher education.

Generally, readers can locate with relative ease teacher education research in content areas ("admission standards" for example) but cannot easily come to an idea of the breadth of research in a given country. To provide a sense of what is being researched in a given country is our main goal. If each chapter in this handbook had an international section, however, one could locate international research by topic, and perhaps future editions might take this approach.

In an innovative move, a final decision was made to impart a dynamic interactive quality to the chapter by providing references and even contacts for readers to begin or advance their own internationalization of research in teacher education. The end-of-chapter appendix provides a list of selected educational international organizations with brief annotations on the work of each group. Readers are invited to contact the organizations directly for further information.

During the search for international teacher education research studies, two sources were especially helpful. The first is the Carfax Publishing Company (Graham Hobbs, Carfax Information Systems, P.O. Box 25, Abington, Oxfordshire OX14 3UE, United Kingdom; phone: 44 (0) 235-521 154). Carfax publishes about 110 professional journals, including the *British Educational Research Journal, Compare: A Journal of Comparative Education, Contents Pages in Education, European Journal of Teacher Education, Journal of Education for Teaching, Scandinavian Journal of Educational Research,* and the *South Pacific Journal of Teacher Education. Contents Pages in Education* is a particularly rich source of information. It is a computer-based, international current awareness service that publishes the contents pages of more than 700 of the world's education journals. Contents pages are arranged alphabetically by journal title and are reset to a standardized format. Some of the included journals are *Action in Teacher Education, Alberta Journal of Educational Research, American Educational Research Journal, Australian Journal of Teacher Education, Teaching and Teacher Education: An International Journal of Research and Studies,* and the *Zimbabwe Journal of Educational Research.* Carfax may also be contacted for subscriptions and other information (P.O. Box 2025, Dunnellon, FL 34430-2025; Fax (904) 489-6996).

The second resource is *Research in Teacher Education: International Perspectives* edited by Richard P. Tisher and Marvin F. Wideen (1990). This book originated from an international research symposium at the annual meeting of the American Educational Research Association in 1987. There were 15 international author contributors to the book (see Table 47.1) and 4 from the United States. The book looks at the part played by research in the ongoing challenge of providing the best education possible for those who teach our children. Those writing about teacher education in many countries described it as badly underfunded, uncomfortable where housed, and out of touch with the schools for which the teachers are being prepared. The book is a contribution toward the improvement of teacher education through an examination of the research

TABLE 47.1. Author Correspondents[a]

Country	Name	Affiliation
Belarus	Larisa Kirilyuk	Senior lecturer, Pedagogical Department, Belarusian State Pedagogical University, Minsk, Belarus
Brazil	A. M. Monjardim	Universidad de Federal Do Espirito Santo
	H. B. Passamai	Chefe do Departament, Universidad Federal Do Espirito Santo
Brunei Darussalam	Sim Wong-Kooi	Professor of Education, Universiti Brunei Darussalam
Burkina Faso	Martial Dembélé	Ph.D. candidate in Curriculum, Teaching and Education Policy, Michigan State University, East Lansing, Michigan
Canada	Marvin Wideen[b]	Professor in Faculty of Education, Simon Fraser University, Burnaby, British Columbia, Canada
Province of Quebec	Mack St-Louis	Université du Québec à Trois-Rivières, Quebec, Canada
China	Jian Wang	Department of Teacher Education, Michigan State University, East Lansing, Michigan
Finland	Hannele Rousi	Vocational Teacher Education, College of Finland
	Hannele Niemi	Professor of Education, University of Tampere, Finland
Great Britain	David McNamara[b]	Professor of Primary Education and Chairman, School of Education, University of Durham
India	R. Govinda[b]	Senior Fellow, National Institute of Educational Planning and Administration
	M. B. Buch[b]	Chairman, Society for Educational Research and Development, University of Baroda
Ireland	John Heywood	University of Dublin, Trinity College, Dublin, Ireland
Israel	Miriam Ben-Peretz[b]	Dean, School of Education, University of Haifa
	Esther Yankelvitch	College of Education, University of Haifa
Netherlands	Eric De Vreede	Rijks Universiteit, Groningen, Netherlands
	Frans K. Kieviet[b]	Department of Educational Sciences, University of Leiden, Leiden, Netherlands
	Fred A. Korthagen	Rijks Universiteit Utrecht, Utrecht, Netherlands
New Zealand	Hugh Barr	Senior Lecturer, School of Education, University of Waikata, Hamilton, New Zealand
Scotland	Ronnie Mackay	Head of Primary Education Department, University of Strathclyde, Glasgow, Scotland
Senegal (Africa)	Pai Obanya	Director, Regional Office for Education in Africa, Daka, Senegal
Singapore	Ho Wah Kam[b]	Head of the Educational Research Unit, Institute of Education, Singapore
Slovenia	Cveta Razdevsek-Pucko	Faculty of Education, University of Ljubljana
Spain	Joana Noguera	Professor of Education and Psychology, University of Rovira I Virgili, Tarragona, Spain
Sweden	Bertil Gran[b]	Associate Professor of Education, University of Lund, Sweden
Switzerland	Rolf Dubs	Institute for the Teaching of Economics and Business Administration, University of St. Gall, St. Gallen, Switzerland
United States	Christopher Knight	Graduate Research Assistant, College of Education, University of Toledo, Toledo, Ohio, USA
Germany	Hans Gerhard Klinzing[b]	Professor, School of Education, University of Tübingen
Zimbabwe	Ann Schneller	International Networks in Education and Development, College of Education, Michigan State University, East Lansing, Michigan

[a] If an author correspondent is not listed for a country, the report was prepared by one of this chapter's authors.

[b] = Indicates author of country chapter in Tischer, R. P. & Wideen, M. F. (Eds.). (1990). *Research in teacher education: International perspectives*. London: Falmer. This information is abstracted into the respective country report in this chapter.

taking place in some different countries around the world. The authors take stock of past research, identify what can be learned from it, determine how it can be characterized, assess what contributions have already been made, and propose where they should go in the future. Some of the reports and summaries from the foreign contributors in the book are also reported in this chapter.

Other references were also helpful. Dunkin (1987) edited the *International Encyclopedia of Teaching and Teacher Education,* which is designed to enable readers to obtain authoritative statements concerning specific topics in teaching and teacher education. The reference work is organized conceptually and not by country. The Teacher Education Pre-service Section, for example, has entries on laboratory schools, student teaching, supervision of student teachers, lesson analysis studies, skills related to teaching, and other relevant topics.

The comprehensive *International Encyclopedia of Education,* edited by Husen and Postelthwaite (1989), contains background information on the system of education in approximately 134 countries and is thus invaluable in understanding the setting of teacher education in these countries.

There are also four relatively recent professional journal issues that are particularly relevant to teacher education in international settings:

1. *Action in Teacher Education* (1991, Fall). *Teacher Education: Perspectives from Abroad, XIII*(3). This volume was edited by G. A. Churkuian and C. Kissock and consisted of 14 articles about teacher education in Africa, the Asia-Pacific region, Australia, Brazil, Taiwan, the Council of Europe, Czechoslovakia, India, New Zealand, Russia, Slovenia, Turkey, the United Kingdom, and Zimbabwe.

2. *Journal of Teacher Education* (1991, January–February). *Educating for a Global Society, 42*(1). This volume has three articles focused on global perspectives:
   a. Global Perspectives for Teachers: An Urgent Priority, by J. L. Tucker and P. L. Cistone.
   b. Preparing American Secondary Social Studies Teachers to Teach with a Global Perspective, by M. Merryfield.
   c. Developing a Global Perspective: Strategies for Teacher Education Programs, by M. Bruce (former editor of the *European Journal of Teacher Education*), R. Podemski, and C. Anderson.
3. *Journal of Teacher Education* (1991, November–December). *Comparative Teacher Education, 42*(5), in which the following can be found:
   a. Worldwide Issues and Problems in Teacher Education, by H. Leavitt.
   b. Beyond Dogma: Teacher Education in the USSR, by S. Keer.
   c. Teacher Education in Countries Around the World: Studies in the ERIC Data Base, by D. Stewart.
4. *Teacher Development Outside the United States: A Selected Annotated Bibliography* (1994). This work was compiled by M. B. Maline and published by the Office of Research, U.S. Department of Education (ISBN 0-16-045140-X). The selected publications in this volume came from many sources and more than 38 countries, including research from Chile, Columbia, Costa Rica, Ecuador, Mauritius, Nigeria, and Taiwan. Content areas are country specific but generally are classified into preservice training, professional development (in-service training), innovations and reform, policy, and other content specific topics such as science teaching and learning. The hope is that these research reports, currently being held by the U.S. Department of Education's National Education Library at 555 New Jersey Avenue, NW, Washington, DC 20208, can soon be shared via the Internet.

Finally, we know that there are serious omissions from this chapter. In an undertaking this broad, it would be miraculous to have missed only a dozen. Hence, we invite readers to alert us to sources of information and studies that have escaped our detection and that can be subsequently noted in future editions.

What now follows are the teacher education reports by country provided by country author correspondent and/or abstracted from the country reports in Tisher and Wideen's (1990) *Research in Teacher Education: International Perspectives*. The chapter concludes with a comprehensive reference list. As noted, full citations are given when known. The authors decided it was better to report what was known rather than omit the entry entirely because of lack of a page number, volume number, or other missing information.

The U.S. Agency for International Development (USAID) is extensively involved in teacher training projects in developing nations. A number of project summaries describe efforts undertaken since 1988. Each project's ISN is noted in the text and in the bibliography and can be used to order more information (Agency for International Development, Center for Development Information and Evaluation, Development Information Division, Washington, DC 20523-1802).

ARMENIA

Recruitment, Selection, and Initial Preparation

Edoyan (1992) in "The Organizing of Teaching Under Extreme Conditions" explored the organization of preservice and inservice teacher education after a devastating earthquake. Tents and movable laboratories proved to be effective.

AUSTRALIA

Teacher Education as a Field of Study

W. Crebbin (1992) in "Beginning to Make a Difference: Learning to Question Schooling Through Student-Teachers' Personal Theories and Critical Reflection," discussed a teacher education program designed to help students become aware of the theories that inform their practice and to reflect critically on how schooling has been structured.

Recruitment, Selection, and Initial Preparation

The notion of teacher education as a socialization process emphasizes the more covert aspects of professional development, such as self-esteem and confidence. This suggests a new approach to evaluation in teacher training programs. Lindop (1987) in *Evaluating Effectiveness in Teacher Education* investigated how to measure student teachers' professional self-perception. The subjects were second-year students in a 3-year elementary education program in Australia. A semantic differential instrument that gives insights into student teachers' self-perceptions, such as orderliness, clarity, enthusiasm, creativity, warmth and supportiveness, and satisfaction and conformity, was used in data collection. Findings indicated that at the initial round of practice teaching, high achievers showed much more positive experiences than the others on all dimensions. Middle achievers indicated a less positive pattern, and low achievers presented a more negative experience. At the final round of teaching, high achievers gained in all dimensions except satisfaction, and middle achievers maintained on the dimension of warmth, orderliness, and clarity, indicating the overall satisfaction with the course. The results revealed that the instrument was an effective means of evaluating course effectiveness in the teacher training program.

In "Relating Theory to Practice in Teacher Education," Lowell, Pope, and Sherman (1992) investigated the importance of agreement with pedagogical theory in training prospective teachers in a teacher education program in Australia. A recent review of literature in teacher education indicated disagreement in pedagogical values, particularly on the values of theories of learning to the practice of teaching. The subjects were 58 postgraduate students enrolled for the Diploma in Education at the University of Adelaide, Australia. The subjects were asked to evaluate whether the inclusion of theory in courses offered in the teacher training program had a positive influence on actual practice. The results supported the beliefs that the teaching theory had practical value. Theory-based psychology courses were found to be rated much more positively in terms of being practical and in building professional skills and confidence than the theory courses in philosophy, history, and sociology.

Hogben and Lawson (1983) in "Attitudes of Secondary School Teacher Trainees and Their Practice Teaching Supervisors" investigated 21 students enrolled in a 1-year postgraduate Diploma in Education program for secondary teachers at the Flinders University of South Australia. The 21 supervising teachers who participated in the study were regular classroom teachers who supervised the student teachers during their teaching practice period. An attitude scale (a semantic differential instrument comprised of 31 concepts) was used in gathering data. The attitudes were measured three times during the year. The teachers' attitudes were scaled one time on the assumption that the experienced teachers' attitudes were unlikely to change significantly during the year. The results revealed that students' attitudes were practically oriented and did not consider theory highly. Their attitude patterns were closely similar to a group of teachers with whom they were closely associated while doing practice teaching. In general, students' attitudes toward teacher education declined from the beginning of the year, although not significantly. The results of the study revealed that the students' attitudes shifted closely to those of their supervising teachers after a period of teaching practice in schools. The similarity between the attitudes of the students and of the teachers supports the belief that the students developed attitudes similar to those of the teachers during the long exposure to the teachers over many years of schooling.

Hogben and Lawson (1984a) examined the stability and change in attitudes of teacher trainees and beginning teachers toward issues in education and schooling. The subjects were four Diploma in Education students who became full-time classroom teachers. The four subjects were high school teachers of different school subjects in different schools in Southern Australia. The subjects' attitudes were measured five separate times during the 2-year period. The attitude scale, a semantic differential instrument, was used in gathering the data. The authors also interviewed the subjects at their school. The results revealed that there was a great degree of change in attitudes toward certain concepts and that there was a stability of attitudes toward other concepts. The direction of the change is largely distinctive, depending on the individual's situation. The most important factor that influenced the change in the study was the attitude toward practices adopted by the school in welcoming the new teacher. The beginning teachers' experience was influenced by the support provided by the school community.

Carpenter and Foster (1979) found that many preservice teachers enter teaching by default, with no clear commitment and that only less than half enter because they are interested in it, desire security and recognition, or are influenced by their teachers.

Ryan et al. (1982) in *Perceptions of Teaching as a Career* found that at least one third of graduating high school students believe that teaching is poor employment.

Teacher Education Curriculum

Wilson (1990) examined the preparedness of Australian preservice teachers for computer applications (knowledge, experi-

ence, and attitude toward computers). The subjects were 65 first-year education students, University of Tasmania, in the 1989 academic year. A questionnaire was designed to collect data. The results revealed that the majority of the students showed positive attitudes toward taking advantage of computers but were poorly prepared to use them. Thirty-four percent of the students indicated very little or no knowledge of computers. A number of prospective teachers reported that they were nervous and showed anxiety in using computers.

Carter and Hacker (1987) reported an exploratory study of changes in the intellectual behaviors occurring in the classrooms of 29 student teachers of social studies during teaching practice. The purpose of the study was to quantify changes in prospective teachers' behaviors as the teaching practicum progressed and to compare student teachers' performance with that of experienced teachers of social studies. Student teachers with no previous teaching experience at a university in western Australia were observed teaching secondary school classes for three teaching practice periods. The findings showed that there were changes in the interactions of student teachers across the first two periods of teaching practicum. There was an increase in the proportion of teacher talk from 66% to 81% of the interaction. There was an increase on interactions regarding transmitting factual information from 27% to 49%. However, on the third practicum, the proportion dealing with factual transmission dropped to 30%. On comparing these behaviors with those of experienced teachers, it was found that students engaged in less intellectual activities, and more on conveying factual information.

Hewitson (1979) in *Research Into Teacher Education: The Practical Teaching Skills* concluded that trainees like skill development and microteaching courses, and Thompson and Levis (1980) concluded that when explicit objectives, criterion-referenced assessment, controlled experience, and mastery criteria were included, competency-based programs were effective.

Continuing Professional Growth, Development, and Assessment

Carpenter and Byde (1986) in "The Meaning of Commitment to Teaching: The Views of Beginning Teachers" reported that for some beginning teachers commitment was related to the extrinsic rewards associated with teaching, whereas for others it was interwoven with what they saw as the intrinsic rewards, variety, contact with young people, and the satisfaction of assisting pupils to achieve.

Diamond (1985) in "Becoming a Teacher: An Altering Eye" asked teachers to model teaching characteristics that were slightly different from their own. The teachers later exhibited positive changes with respect to keeping pupils and with classroom routines.

McArthur (1981) in *"The First Five Years of Teaching"* concluded that for most new teachers there is a strengthening in commitment during the first 5 years of teaching.

Sachs and Logan (1990) in "Control or Development? A Study of Inservice Education" maintained that Australian inservice education policies have unintentionally controlled and deskilled teachers. The focus is on Queensland, Australia, from 1973 to 1986. The government's need to preserve the status quo is seen as the reason for emphasis on teachers' managerial skills over curricular and instructional skills. Teachers' professional development is affected negatively.

Traill (1992) in "A Study of the Career Patterns and Professional Problems of Teacher Education Graduates" analyzed beginning teacher questionnaires and found that more than one half of the respondents would choose teacher education again as a career. Comparisons with international data showed differences in the areas of classroom discipline, motivating students, and relationships with parents. Implications for the teacher education curriculum were in the areas of in-service education, support structures, and preservice courses.

In 1990 Mackay completed a study aimed at making contact with teacher graduates of Armidale College of Advanced Education in New South Wales in order to gain an understanding of where graduates were living, their employment profile, their perceptions of their initial training, and how the college could assist them further in their careers. A literature search identified few published studies on this topic, although obviously institutions produce in-house documents and surveys conducted by government departments and national graduate organizations for planning purposes. These data, however, are not in the public domain. Therefore, this study was undertaken in order to extend the information available. The survey indicated that graduates have taken the initiative in searching for and finding jobs at a time of uncertainty and limited employment within the New South Wales Education Department. There has been some "brain drain," particularly "male drain" from the potential pool of teachers to the nongovernment sector and interstate. This should be of concern to the department especially when it is combined with the image that many graduate teachers have of the department as bureaucratic and uncaring in comparison to other education systems. Clearly, the department needs to give further thought to providing support and incentives for future teachers.

Armidale College was perceived in a very positive light, but some areas in the preservice program need attention, not just in specific areas such as programming or specialization. The college also faces a problem in accessing more schools for regular teaching and demonstrations and must deal with financial and demographic constraints. There are some matters over which the college has control and some over which it does not. Graduates reported a deep concern about the nexus between theory and practice. Initial graduates, returning for upgrading courses, believed that a master's degree should be freely available for classroom teachers. The author concluded that new methods of contact with graduates and the Department of Education need to be explored and that areas of specialization available to students need to be broadened to give greater flexibility in a tight employment market.

Diversity and Equity Issues

Hickling-Hudson and McMeniman (1993) investigated the extent to which Australian teacher education institutions have reponded to multicultural issues in their curriculum. A majority of Australia's present-day population consists of a mix of origi-

nal migrant groups as well as Australian aborigines. In large-scale national studies reviewed by Campbell and McMeniman (1985), the researchers found that the preservice and in-service preparation of teachers was inadequate for responding to culturally and linguistically different students. Thirty-four institutions participated in the most recent study. It was found that 7 had no specific subjects dedicated to multicultural issues, whereas 27 institutions provide between them 93 specialist multicultural subjects. Of these subjects, 59 are electives taken by relatively few students. Thirty-four of the subjects were compulsory. Nine of the universities provide subjects that fall within the category "education for a multicultural society." Fifteen universities offer subjects that explore issues in aboriginal education. Eight provide subjects that investigate multicultural teaching methods, 9 offer subjects in the teaching of English as a second language, and 4 have training in foreign language pedagogy. Sixteen of the 34 institutions provide general education subjects that include only a small component relating to multicultural issues. There are significantly more compulsory than elective subjects from this latter category.

A second part of the data analysis identified the extent to which there was a multicultural emphasis in different teacher education programs. This analysis showed that programs ranged from those in which multiculturalism permeates the entire teacher education program to those in which the multicultural component was little more than a token.

Emerging Directions in Teacher Education

Brady et al. (1992) in "The Implications of the Remote Area Teacher Education Program (RATEP) for Tertiary Distance Education" described an interactive computer-assisted learning program to deliver teacher education courses to aboriginal and Torres Strait islander students living in remote communities. Elliott (1992) in "Moving From Domestication to Internationalization: Teacher Education in Papua, New Guinea," described a 5-year project designed to develop the competence of teacher educators. For further details on some of these studies, the reader is referred to Chapter 5 in Tisher and Wideen (1990).

BELARUS

National interest in teacher education in the Republic of Belarus is just emerging. Before the proclamation of the independence and sovereignty of Belarus in 1991 there was a Scientific and Research Institute of Teacher Education within the USSR Academy of Pedagogical Sciences, which existed for about a year. However, study during this short period did not bring any perceptible results. Besides, all studies of this institute were considerably influenced by the Russian researchers and were of minor importance.

From 1992 until now a series of studies have focused on teacher education in the Republic of Belarus. Matskevich (1993) in "What Should We Teach Teachers" in the book *Polemical Sketches and Education* emphasized teacher education content of epistemology, semiotic, logic, rhetoric, theory of activity, hermeneutic, psychology, anthropology, and sociology. In this chapter, the author also discussed mechanisms of phenomenology and modern forms of teacher education.

The problem of philosophical grounds of teacher education was illustrated in the study *A Concept of National School of Belarus,* carried out by a group of Belarusian scientists, including philosophers, psychologists, teachers, sociologists, and linguists under the head of Gusakovsky (1993). The authors suggested a teacher education philosophy that shifts the content focus from science to culture. They want learning to become a new educational paradigm for teachers wherein a teacher assumes the position of a mediator between student and culture. Starting in 1992 a Belarusia monthly magazine, *Education and Training,* has been regularly publishing articles on teacher education problems. An article by Kochetov (1992), *Pedagogical Creation: Thoughts and Search,* is also related to philosophical considerations.

Peresypkin (1993) in "Will We Dare to?" considers two different views of teacher education: training of pedagogical staff and teacher education itself. As the author pointed out, the process of transition from one educational paradigm to another is very complicated, and at the moment this is not being developed in Belarus.

Kirilyuk and Krouchinin (1992) in their article "Paradox of Knowledge: Attempt of Solution," offered an algorithm of joint work of a teacher and students in applied pedagogic workshops in teacher educational institutions. In another article about teacher education in the Republic of Belarus, Kirilyuk, and Krouchinky (1994) suggested their own model of teacher education, made an excursion into the history of teacher education in Belarus, and described their experience in implementing the proposed model.

Kharlamov (1992), author of the textbook *Pedagogies,* examined in an article (1994) the basic organizational problems in teacher education formation in Belarus.

Finally, there are a series of studies and articles by young researchers in the field of pedagogy and pedagogical psychology in Belarus, published in *Psychological Science and Public Practice.* These include: "Reflexive and Situational Pattern of Pedagogical Professional Development" by Krasnova, Krasnova, and Polopnnikov (1993); "About Pedagogical Reflexion" by Krouchinin (1993); and "Joint Creative Work as a Special Regime of Pedagogical Activity" by Kremer (1993).

BELIZE

Rosado (1990), in a doctoral dissertation completed at Boston College, studied the perceptions of selected elementary school teachers who were trained in Belize between 1976 and 1987 about the adequacy and utility of the training they received.

BOTSWANA

Teacher Education as a Field of Study

Audit of Botswana Junior Secondary Education Improvement (1991; ISN 71403) described 27 participants, against a target of 18, who were sent for long-term training to the United States.

Of these participants, 26 completed their studies and, as of November 1990, had returned to Botswana working in the Ministry of Education as intended.

Continuing Professional Growth, Development, and Assessment

Primary Education Improvement Project in Botswana (1989; ISN 60547) summarized the interim evaluation of a project to strengthen the capacity of Botswana's Ministry of Education and the University of Botswana to improve preservice and in-service training of primary school teachers. Several lessons were learned. Staff training and localization of leadership are important components of effective institution building. Prior to undertaking a decentralized in-service training model, a careful cost–benefit analysis should be conducted.

Project Assistance Completion Report: Primary Education Improvement Project in Botswana (1989; ISN 61920) described a project to upgrade primary education in Botswana by establishing preservice training programs with the University of Botswana and in-service programs with the Ministry of Education. To provide in-service teacher education, advisors cooperated with staff to offer a network of workshops for about 120 teachers and education officers per year. These workshops, which focused on reading, math/science, and English as a second language, proved effective and worthwhile, especially because many participants conducted follow-up workshops in their districts.

BRAZIL

Recruitment, Selection, and Initial Preparation

Feldens and Duncan (1988) in "Brazilians Speak Out About Their Schools: Implications for Teacher Education" reported on the results of a large-scale study examining beliefs of teachers, students, and parents regarding desirable schooling and teaching in Brazil. Implications of their beliefs for teacher education are discussed.

Teacher Education Curriculum

Castro, Jesus, Schneider, and Ferreira (1986) in *Special Education Services in the State of Espirito Santo, Brazil: A Diagnosis* analyzed a series of questionnaires to follow up on teacher training graduates and to improve both the preservice and in-service curriculum.

Castro, Sodre, Passamai, and Pessott (1989) in *Diagnosis of Educational Administration in the State of Espirito Santo* analyzed questionnaires completed by high school principals to determine teacher education curricular needs.

Continuing Professional Growth, Development, and Assessment

Passamai (1983) in *Interdependence Between Salary Differentials, Function, and Academic Background—Empirical Study of the Egresses from the Administration, Economics, and Peda-*

gogy Courses in the State of Espirito Santo used a statistical analysis of questionnaires to determine that in-service training improves the salary differentials that exist among education personnel. These differentials result from individual academic background, graduate courses, length of time since graduation, and number of working years.

Diversity and Equity Issues

Mian (1993) in *Learning of German/Pomeranian Immigrant Descendants in Espirito Santo, Brazil* used an ethnographic approach to investigate the relationship of state-assigned teachers to the learning processes of German/Pomeranian immigrants in Espirito Santo, Brazil. Because the students do not master Portuguese and the teacher does not master the Pomeranian dialect, the linguistic barrier prohibits communication and learning.

BRUNEI DARUSSALAM

Teacher Education as a Field of Study

Welsh (1992), in *Student Perceptions of the "Qualities of a Good Teacher": Some Implications for the Design of the Teacher Education Curriculum,* described a study concerned with student constructs of a model of good teaching in a Southeast Asian context. Differences in perception were found to be related to age, gender, previous experience of teaching, and subject specialization. Factor analysis revealed that the social role of the teacher is most important.

Recruitment, Selection, and Initial Preparation

McMurray (1992) conducted a study on beliefs, values, and levels of self-confidence of University of Brunei Darussalam teacher education students. This study involved a survey of 326 students who were enrolled in four programs offered by the University of Brunei Darussalam for the training of generalist primary and secondary teachers. The results showed that students in all four programs believe that the focus of schooling is and should continue to be the promotion of academic development. On the question of sources of pupil failure and success, the students ranked first the teachers' failure to use effective teaching methods. They ranked last the students' lack of intellectual ability.

In terms of sources of teaching success, the data showed that the teachers' ability to communicate at a level the pupils understand was seen as paramount, with somewhat less importance attached to acknowledging differences in the academic, social, and cultural backgrounds of individual students. Regarding the students' beliefs about education, high levels of agreement were found on items concerned with "teacher characteristics." The students also were in general agreement and had a high regard for process whereby knowing how to teach was seen as more important than what to teach. Students believed that exceptional children should be accommodated in special settings. There was a high level of

disagreement among students that indicated that they do not subscribe to the notion of streaming students based on ability or accept the fact that some students are incapable of learning the basic skills in reading and mathematics. They do concur that learning occurs in groups and that it can be fun. The students appeared evenly divided on the question of whether persistently disruptive pupils should be removed from the classroom.

When the four programs were studied, some clear differences emerged between the primary and secondary education students. A change also occurs across years of study in the program. A clear majority of the students begin their training believing the classroom to be largely teacher centered. By the third year, as many as 60% acknowledged that pupil needs, not the syllabus, should occupy the bulk of teacher attention. Further differences were revealed among the students in the four programs in beliefs about the ability of the students to learn difficult concepts such as science and mathematics and between groups who support the idea of a fixed curriculum and those who do not. One secondary program regards the development of work-related skills as paramount, whereas no one in two other secondary groups adopts this as a priority. The students were also asked to respond and to rate 10 sources of professional knowledge. The students had a tendency to assign importance to almost all the sources of professional knowledge. However, significantly more importance was attached to teaching practice along with content and methods courses compared with other academic sources such as books and personal education courses. Students were also measured on their level of confidence. The highest areas of confidence were in the most general roles such as establishing a friendly atmosphere, planning lessons, and assessing both one's own teaching and pupil learning.

BURKINA FASO

Dembèlè (1991) in *Political Instability, Economic Hardships and the Preservice Education of Secondary Teachers in Burkina Faso: 1960–1990* aimed at tracing the various institutional arrangements for preparing secondary teachers in Burkina Faso (formerly Upper Volta) from 1960 until 1990. Using a multidimensional conceptual framework, including economic, social, political, and educational realities, the author explored why particular institutions or programs were created and then phased out at particular times; why they operated the way they did; why some remained on paper; and the conditions for the sustainability of the most recent effort to systematize and centralize development since independence. The policy of access to secondary teaching was found to have largely shaped the development of preservice secondary teacher education. These factors were found to interact with the country's socioeconomic and educational realities, the career choices and opportunities of university graduates, and the low level of expectation that policymakers seem to have had for secondary teaching. All these factors contributed to making teaching an unattractive profession, and the education of secondary teachers a low-profile, low-priority enterprise.

CANADA

Teacher Education as a Field of Study

Fullan, Wideen, and Estabrook (1983) published *A Study of Teacher Training Institutions in Anglophone Canada: Volume 1: Current Perspectives on Teacher Training in Canada: An Overview of Faculty and Student Perceptions*. Data collected from 10 faculties of education in Canada had two main objectives: (1) to analyze the process of change in teacher training institutions based on information from administrators, faculty, and students, and (2) to study the impact of the data feedback process on each of the institutions. This is the first in a five-volume report. Other volumes examine organizational development in faculties of education, research in Canadian teacher training, change in Canadian teacher training, and an executive summary that presents procedures and results for a general audience.

Recruitment, Selection, and Initial Preparation

Ricord (1986) examined the development of the "teaching self" of student teachers during their teaching practicum at the University of Alberta, Canada. The subjects were nine student teachers who were practice-teaching. The student teachers were interviewed at the beginning of their teaching practice and again at the end of the field experience program. The students were asked questions regarding themselves as teachers, teaching in general, and themselves in teaching. The results revealed that they felt positive about themselves before they began teaching, were confident with their self-image, and were emotionally mature. The student teachers' main concern was their academic impact on the pupils and their self-growth. During the teaching practicum their personality factors were vitally important in influencing their teaching perspectives. Preservice teachers who were authoritative, emphatic, and controlled had fewer problems in adjusting to the teaching role than those who were not. Eight of the nine preservice teachers studied had dilemmas in regard to personal versus school goals, thoughts versus actions, and the ideal versus ideology. The author recommended that because conflict was an important factor of the students' personality during their teaching practicum, the university should have a facilitator to help interpret the meaning of their experiences to bridge the wide discrepancies before and after the teaching practicum. That person should have a role of facilitator, instead of an evaluator.

Dawson, Mazurek, and Deyoung (1984) investigated preservice teachers' perceptions of the social foundations component of a bachelor of education program. The subjects were 615 second-, third-, and fourth-year student teachers who were enrolled in teacher education programs in two universities. Using results from a questionnaire, the researchers found that more than 62% of the students agreed that educational foundations courses provided them with novel and important perspectives for viewing education. About 62% of the respondents stated that foundations courses helped them have a better understanding of modern education. About 66% agreed that foundations courses were valuable to preservice teachers. Sixty-

five percent viewed foundational courses as a necessary and desirable element in the teacher training program. Students' attitudes in elementary and secondary programs were not significantly different. In addition, there were no significant differences in attitudes among the students who were seeking a bachelor's degree in education as their first degree course and those who were seeking it as an after-degree course. The findings of the study indicated that preservice teachers recognized the importance and usefulness of the social foundations courses in their teacher training program.

Taylor and Miller (1985) examined the relationship between performance in both professional coursework and in the practicum in a teacher training program for prospective elementary teachers in "Professional Coursework and the Practicum: Do Good Students Make Good Teachers?" The subjects were 107 students in elementary education at the University of Alberta, Canada. The academic performance of the students was based on final grades in the following professional courses: educational administration, educational foundations, educational psychology, and educational curriculum and instruction. The students' practicum performance was ascertained utilizing the progress report completed by both cooperating teachers and faculty consultants. The data analysis showed significantly that there was little relationship between theoretical coursework and student teaching performance (less than .20). The R-square indicating the proportion of variance in student teaching performance explained by academic performance was less than 10%.

Housego (1992) reported on a study of elementary teacher education students' feelings of preparedness to teach and teacher efficacy. The results revealed that students' feelings of preparedness to teach significantly increased in the first 3 terms but did not increase in the fourth and final terms. Female students felt significantly more prepared to teach than male students. The feelings of preparedness did not increase significantly for multicultural education students. Teacher efficacy scores did not increase significantly in any term, although female students significantly showed higher scores on personal and teacher efficacy than males. Borys et al. (1991) in "An Alternative Model for Rural Preservice Practicum Supervision" reported on a model that grew out of the need to prepare teachers who were willing and able to teach in rural settings as well as to deal with declining resources at universities. The collaboration for this model took place between Port Vermilion School Division and the University of Alberta's faculty of education. Students were selected for their strong academic records. Front planning took place with the supervising teachers, and students were provided stipends to help cover room and board during the time they were placed in the school district. The initial response to the use of the model has been very positive and was judged to be generally successful by all participants.

Fullan, Connelly, Watson, Heller, and Scane (1990) in "Teacher Education in Ontario: Current Practice and Options for the Future" described the events that led up to the report and the methodology used. Main pressures for educational reform in teacher education are identified both internationally and in Ontario. Chapter 2 offers a brief history of preservice teacher education as background to a description of present teacher education in Ontario and presents preliminary analysis of the major issues. Chapter 3 sets out a perspective for thinking about teacher education. In-service teacher education is emphasized in a section on the importance and characteristics of schools as places of professional development. The final chapter sets forth proposals for change and includes an assessment of each recommendation.

Murphy and Cross (1990) in "Preparing Teachers for Rural Schools: A Canadian Approach" reported on the 5-year rural elementary teacher education program at the University of Victoria, British Columbia. This program features extended field experience in remote rural schools and communities and the program seeks to provide preservice elementary teachers with a realistic awareness of the rural teacher's work life.

Russell (1986) reported findings from a study of beginning teachers' development of knowledge-in-action (a term for the knowledge that is apparent in a professional's day-to-day actions). The study involved candidates in a bachelor of education program at Queen's University, Kingston, Ontario. Participants in the study were observed and interviewed at frequent intervals during their practice teaching placements. Transcriptions of lessons and interviews were prepared for analysis, providing a data base for comparisons over time and across participants.

Geddis (1990) presented a report, "The Role of the Practicum in Development of Reflective Teachers," to the Joint Centre for Teacher Development Invitational Conference, Stoney Lake, Ontario. This paper considered the role that the preservice practicum can play in developing reflective teachers. The practicum has been regarded as a kind of apprenticeship in which the student teacher observes and then emulates the practices of the master teacher. Such a view is rooted in a craft conception of teaching in which student teachers are more concerned with the acquisition of a relatively well-defined set of techniques and strategies than with the development of the skills necessary for critical reflection. As the focus of teacher education shifts to the development of critically reflective practitioners, it becomes essential that the role of the preservice practicum be rethought. The author looks initially at Dewey's conception of reflective thinking, and then at Schoen's extension of Dewey's ideas into the concept of a reflective practitioner. With this as a backdrop, the author then reviews the literature on the practicum as it is presently constituted and then articulates a number of issues that need to be addressed in the preservice practicum if it is to make a significant contribution to the development of critically reflective teachers.

Turner-Muecke, Russell, and Bowyer (1986) in "Reflection-in-action: Case study of a clinical supervisor" reported an analysis of a series of conferences between a student teacher and supervisor in which the supervisor attempted to follow the principles of clinical supervision. Clinial supervision seeks to develop a teacher's own skills of analysis of teaching, with many similarities to what Schoen has termed "reflection-in-action." This paper focused on a clinical supervisor's reflection of her or his own professional behavior over a series of conferences that spanned 2 months. The inquiry explored the premise that the supervisor's own reflection-in-action is just as important as the reflection that the supervision attempts to foster in the teacher being supervised.

Contextual Influences on Teacher Education

Wideen and Holborn (1986a) in "Change and Survival in Faculties of Education" identified major changes occurring in teacher education in Anglophone Canada since the mid-1950s. The authors analyzed these changes and identified a set of conditions necessary for effective program development in faculties of education to occur.

Teacher Education Curriculum

Young (1991–1992) examined ways in which prospective teachers of a bachelor of education program made curriculum decisions in elementary school classrooms. The subjects were 43 prospective teachers in their fourth year in a teacher training program of a university in western Canada. The students were asked to plan a unit of study for a sixth-grade classroom. The students' discussions were taperecorded and transcribed for content analysis. The findings revealed three distinctive major approaches to integration. The first approach showed a low degree of integration. The school subjects were taught separately, although there was a common theme among the subjects. The purpose of schooling for this group was the transmission of knowledge from the teacher to the student. Emphasis was placed more on teaching than learning. The second approach integrated an intermediate degree of integration. The lesson unit consisted of separate subjects that shared a common theme, but the subjects lost their identity. The purpose of the schools according to this group was the acquisition of knowledge by children. The emphasis shifted from teaching to learning. The third approach showed a high degree of integration. The lesson unit did not focus on a particular subject, but instead many subjects were drawn upon as needed. The subjects lost their identity. For this group, the purpose of schooling was to assist children to construct their own knowledge from their experience. The teacher's role was as facilitator, guide, and co-learner with the children. The findings of this study indicated that preservice teachers need a strong knowledge base in both integration and the subjects taught in elementary schools.

Holborn (1983) in "Integrating Theory and Practice From the Student Teacher's Perspective" emphasized that little consideration has been given to the student teacher as an active participant in teacher education. Within the framework of the student as an active participant, the author followed eight students through a 16-week teacher education program in which a combination of campus and field experiences were used to bring the two components together. The following generalizations emerged from the study: The process of integration is personal and individual, the interactive process is recursive, it incorporates feedback from others, it involves reflection as well as cognitive levels of experience, it can facilitate a closed relationship between theoretical and practical components, and it can occur at different levels of abstraction. Holborn found that the timetable, the clustering of students, and the use of reflective journals facilitated the program.

In "A Collaborative Approach to Help Novice Science Teachers Reflect on Changes in Their Construction of the Role of Science Teacher" Shapiro (1991) described an approach to the study of growth and change in student teachers' views about science teaching as they gain experience and practice in the field. Views about the thought and activities of science teaching were assessed prior to students' university teacher methods courses, then again following their classroom practicum teaching experiences. Student teachers provided linguistic categories (constructs) for various science teaching experiences, then collaborated with interviewers to convey their ideas about the reasons for changes that occurred in the application of these objective (survey) and subjective (interview) data. Analysis of the types of personal construct changes that occurred allowed the delineation of categories of change as students became socialized in the role of teacher. Excerpts from individual case study reports illustrate the outcomes of the study and are the basis for considering the implications of incorporating student views in the design of teacher education programs.

Munby and Russell (1990) in "Reframing the Nature of Subject Matter: A Case Study in the Development of Professional Knowledge" paid special attention to changes in the earliest years of teaching.

MacKinnon (1989) discussed a particular view of the reflection process in the supervision of student teachers of science. He attempted to make explicit underlying assumptions regarding the nature of what comes to be known through reflection, its outcomes, and the activities or conditions that seem to evoke reflection among student teachers. Although the context of the orientation is that of science teaching, the issues addressed are clearly generalizable to other disciplines and areas of teacher education. The agenda may suggest to some minds that it begs a prior question: What is reflection about teaching? More fundamentally, what is it about teacher education that requires student teachers to be reflective? Four brief scenarios provided a context for developing answers to these questions.

Moon, Mayer-Smith, and Wideen (1993) reported on learning to teach science. The report reviewed 15 recent studies in which researchers followed beginning teachers through selected aspects of their teacher preparation. The review examined how such research informed practice, how programs affect students' learning to teach, and how beginning teachers gain and use knowledge. The authors conceptualized the study around teacher development, constructivism, and knowledge utilization. Each study was analyzed from a holistic viewpoint to gain a sense of the methods and also from an analytical perspective to identify the areas to which each study contributed. As a line of research, learning to teach in science is characterized by variability and complexity; those involved are typically close to the subjects being studied. Program implications were limited and the research did not deal with knowledge and strangely had little to say about how beginners learn to teach. Constructivism provided the conceptual framework in 13 of the 15 studies reviewed. The review found many of the studies problematic and, consequently the paper takes a critical stance.

Dolbec (1992) described an action research project that allowed university researchers to train three teacher educators in research methodology, curriculum, and pedagogical supervision.

Continuing Professional Growth, Development, and Assessment

Wideen and Hopkins (1984) examined the effects associated with a university on the professional growth of cooperating teachers. The authors identified three factors that emerged to optimize professional growth among teachers: (1) involvement, (2) philosophical compatibility, and (3) source of influence. Student teachers were also found to be an influential source on the teachers.

Birch and Neufeld (1984) in "Innovation in Distance Education Applied to the Professional Development of Teachers: A Canadian Perspective" reported on a distance learning inservice program in British Columbia. In an evaluation of the program, television instruction was adjudicated inferior to direct classroom instruction in 2 out of 10 categories, student-to-student interaction and student-to-instructor interaction. Other categories that were measured included attention or alertness, rate of presentation or pacing, ease of note taking, use of visual aids, motivation to work, attitude toward learning, physical comfort, and stress. In each of these categories, student attitudes were significantly more positive toward distance education using television than toward direct instruction in the classroom. The authors concluded that when all factors were taken together, it was clear that television instruction was an acceptable alternative to direct instruction. The advantage of television instruction is the ability to present a variety of classroom demonstrations to students in support of instructional theory. In the category of visual aids, 96% of the students rated television instruction superior to classroom instruction, 85% of the students reported that they were more alert, 86% were more motivated, and 95% reported they had a more positive attitude toward television instruction than toward traditional classroom instruction. Although the live, interactive television component of this program was eliminated because of scarce air time, the reaction of the students indicated that the elimination of this live, interactive segment may have been a step backward. Although only 27% of the students phoned the studios during the television program, this was explained as a function of the fact that teachers videotaped the presentations and watched at their leisure at home. Thus, they were unavailable to respond to or interact with the television studio. Finally, students submitted higher ratings favoring the design and organization of the telecourses on assignments, examinations, courseload, and registration routines.

Grimmett and Ratzlaff (1986) cited research in both Canada and the United States to support two consistent findings about cooperating teachers and expectations: The role of the cooperating teacher is poorly defined and teachers are unprepared for the task of student teaching supervision. They found no Canadian study that investigated the expectations for the cooperating teachers. This study identified the specific expectations held for the role of cooperating teacher by student teachers, university superintendents, and students. A 166-item questionnaire was distributed to 75 universities, 950 students, and 1,375 cooperating teachers at the University of British Columbia. The study produced a high level of consensus around the functions, orientation, planning/instruction, evaluation, and professional development of cooperating teachers. All agreed to the need for cooperating teachers to have a more active role in professional socialization. These results differed from those in the United States. The research concludes with a discussion of why the findings are different from those in the United States.

Housego and Grimmett (1985) edited *Teaching and Teacher Education: Generating and Utilizing Valid Knowledge for Professional Socialization*. The book is the outcome of a national conference (1984), hosted by the Centre for the Study of Teacher Education at the University of British Columbia and reported research on teaching and teacher education. The book begins by sketching some of the research-based possibilities such as: (1) viewing teaching as a complex decision-making process in a dynamic social environment, (2) seeing future teacher educators as careful utilizers of research, and (3) regarding teacher education as a powerful means of professional socialization. A variety of topics are then discussed by chapter authors.

School-based teacher development by Wideen (1989) described a study of a single school where significant change had occurred. As a result of this innovation, a school once considered nearly dysfunctional in terms of teacher growth became a center in the community where teachers felt confident enough to display their programs to the public at large. Wideen visited the school regularly over a 3-year period, observing classrooms, interviewing teachers, the principal, and others in the teaching of language arts, which moved from basal readers to a writing process. Other aspects of teaching became affected over the period. The author identified the role of the principal, the power of group process, the innovation itself, the availability and use of knowledge, and district support as the contributing factors. Teacher development carried a close relationship to the school improvement project that allowed highly varied and independent perspectives to be taken by the teachers. Wideen stressed the central role of teachers in the process, and he questioned systems that seek to impose a collegial atmosphere in the school.

MacKinnon and Grunau (1991) in "Teacher Development Through Reflection, Community, and Discourse" dealt with a community of student teachers and their discourse patterns during an innovative school-based program at the University of Toronto. The theoretical underpinning of the paper comes from a constructivist view of knowledge, considerations of the reflective practitioner, and ideas on the role of the individual and of society on human development. Students were provided with forums to enable them to take on the role of the teacher, to "frame" their experiences as teachers do, and to develop "intellectual empathy" with the students being taught. How Mead's concept of the generalized other can be used in group work is also discussed. A detailed discussion of the program (specifically the teaching of forensic science) is included. A new perspective in envisioning teacher education programs is presented.

In 1989 Russell in "Studying Teaching With a Colleague as a Mode of Professional Development" analyzed four cases in which teachers discuss their practice with a colleague. Experiences of the four groups varied in terms of areas examined, depth achieved, data collection and analysis, and levels of insights. For all the groups, the collaborative experience appeared satisfying, and the author suggested that such collaboration

can contribute in powerful and unusual ways to a teacher's professional development.

In "Teacher Educators as Researchers: Cultivating Conditions for Reflective Practice in Teacher Preparation" Grimmett (1988) suggested a way in which teacher educators can emerge as action researchers as they fulfill the necessary obligations attributed to the important role of educating preservice teachers. Through an examination of the research literature in teacher education and staff development, the author derived implications for certain processes and contexts in the teacher education program. Central to the paper is the question of whether these reflective processes and contexts are best framed according to a developmental conceptualization of teacher education or whether they are more effectively attained by beginning at the outset with an inquiry-based approach frequently accompanied in student teachers by mystery and confusion. This choice represents the teacher education dilemma.

McNay and Cole (1989) in "Induction Programs in Ontario Schools: Current Views and Directions for the Future" reported views expressed by Ontario educators in response to an earlier article on teacher induction programs. The need and rationale for induction programs, their funding and governance, professional status issues, enabling factors, the role of mentor teachers, and program evaluation are discussed.

Diversity and Equity Issues

In "Multicultural Education in Alberta's Teacher Training Institutions" VanBalkom (1991) examined multicultural education courses offered by the faculties of education in various teacher training institutions in Alberta, Canada. The results revealed that, with the exception of one institution, faculties of education offered some courses dealing with multiculturalism, minority education, cross-cultural communications, and the like. Of the 15 courses offered, one was at the graduate level and seven courses were noncompulsory undergraduate courses in the bachelor of education program or a certificate program. English as a second language (ESL) departments offered multicultural education courses with a special emphasis. No universities offered multicultural education courses as compulsory undergraduate courses. The authors concluded that faculties of education were doing little to provide multicultural education in their teacher training programs.

Emerging Directions in Teacher Education

Cramm and Kelleher (1992) described the development of parallel "cases" of four outstanding teachers in Canada and Great Britain as they planned and taught the same curriculum unit/topic to their classes of 10-year-old pupils. The authors analyzed the use and impact of such comparative international cases of teaching in preservice teacher education.

Wideen and Holborn (1986b) published a summative article that is a critical review of reported research in Canada on teacher education. One hundred and two research papers were reviewed that dealt with practicum, student characteristics, or program effectiveness. The authors summarized the research and made suggestions on how to improve the research in Canada. A central suggestion was that researchers need to understand better the context of teacher education and to use methods of research that are less from an empirical-analytical paradigm.

In "Trends and Developments in Teacher Education: A Synopsis of Reports and Major Works," Wideen (1987) summarized the recommendations contained within recent Canadian, British, and American reports on proposed teacher education reform. In particular, the paper concentrated on the historical changes that have occurred within the Canadian context of teacher education. The author discussed the pluralistic, often irreconcilable, principles or beliefs that have led to the development of teacher preparation programs that conflict in terms of both overriding philosophy and prescriptions for practice. In addition, the paper examined certain unresolved issues within teacher education (issues such as who should control teacher training programs and how theory and practice can best be blended). Wideen concluded by delineating eight directions for future teacher education programs. This article would be of interest to those seeking a brief, generalized account of the historical factors that have both helped determine teacher education reform movement and continue to influence debate concerning the ideal preservice education for teachers.

In *Research in Teacher Education: Current Problems and Future Prospects in Canada,* Grimmett (1984) offered 18 papers in seven sections. The seven sections are: (1) what is teacher education: a conceptualization; (2) Where is teacher education: a contextualization; (3) problems in evaluating teacher education programs; (4) teacher education programs and research on teaching; (5) current research; (6) research priorities; and (7) future prospects.

For further details on some of these studies and others the reader is referred to Chapter 2 in Tisher and Wideen (1990).

CANADA, PROVINCE OF QUEBEC

Teacher Education as a Field of Study

In 1993 Van Der Maren wrote about knowledge needed by future teachers to attain the status and be perceived as a professional. After identifying the type of knowledge underlying the practices and the status of a professional, the author asked several questions: Who are the repositories of this knowledge, how can this knowledge be expanded, and what are the most efficient means for transmitting this knowledge? The development of proposals must take into consideration a double social objective, which may on its own create a paradox: the problem of making teaching more professional while teaching personnel are by definition accountable to the state and, also, to provide a university type and level of training while their task is described as the transmission of knowledge that is socially specified and determined.

Lessard and Mathurin (1989) traced the major evolutionary trends of the Quebec teacher group at the primary and secondary levels, from the Quiet Revolution to the present. The socio-historical approach presented the internal structure of the teacher group and its parameters of integration, differentiation, and segmentation. The authors also described the dominant concepts of the teacher's function and its evolution. Specifically,

they pointed out the university as one instance of the professional legitimacy of teachers. At the theoretical level, the paper discussed the concept of professionalization-proletarization as a way to integrate the teacher group within the dominant social structure.

Recruitment, Selection, and Initial Preparation

In 1992, Des Lièvres, Pelletier, and Demers described the results of a survey of attitudes about science and primary-level teacher trainees. Five themes were examined: science and health, science and environment, science and moral behavior, science and scientists, and the various sciences. Respondents to a questionnaire were 322 females and 25 males enrolled in teacher training for primary level at three Quebec universities. The authors noted significant differences in the results obtained and discussed didactic implications.

Portugais and Lévèsques (1991) in "The Transfer of High-Cognitive-Level Questioning Ability During Initial Teacher Training" reported on a study of the transfer of two components of questioning ability: the asking of high–cognitive-level questions and wait time after questioning. The results from 12 future high school mathematics teachers were subjected to both quantitative and qualitative analyses. The findings tend to show that, for the majority of students, there is no transfer of the ability to ask high-cognitive-level questions following the first practicum. A discussion of these results led the authors to suggest hypotheses regarding the conditions of transfer.

Continuing Professional Growth, Development, and Assessment

Bujold, Coté, Paré, and Chevrette (1994) conducted a needs assessment in training student teacher supervisors. Students from Quebec's Laval University Faculty of Education who plan to teach primary school must first complete a 3-month teaching practicum in a regular class during the senior year of the bachelor program. During this practicum, the student teacher is supervised and supported by a university associated teacher. An experienced teacher, partly relieved from teaching duties, coordinates the associated teacher's training work and actively participates in the supervision of the student teacher. Each supervisor is responsible for 10 trainees, observing each of them in class on four occasions during the practicum. Both supervisors and associated teachers are responsible for the evaluation of the trainees at the end of the practicum. Within the scope of a higher education degree in educational psychology, the faculty of education offers a particular field of study to associated teachers and supervisors in educational supervision. To adjust the program and its courses to the needs of the users, a needs assessment survey was conducted with associated teachers, supervisors, and student teachers. A first survey using seven questions was conducted with more than 20 associated teachers and supervisors. A second survey was answered by 30 student teachers. The data collected were analyzed using quantitative and qualitative methods. This report presented the research problematics, methodology, results, a comparative study of literature, and proposals for further research on training teaching practicum supervisors.

Hivon, Beauchesne, Lavoie, and Tétreault (1994) conducted a 4-year action research study to create a partnership among the parties involved in the supervision of student teachers in three fields of basic teacher training: remedial, elementary, and high school teaching. Designing and implementing a program to improve supervision competence revealed many aspects of the complexities of the supervision process within a partnership. The result confirmed just how important such a program is to improving reflective and feedback skills in supervision. The study also demonstrated that cooperating teachers, highly valued by the students themselves, do not give very specific feedback during the student teaching experience. However, meetings with the university supervisor focus primarily on tasks related to the university curriculum. Results showed that both parties foster student teachers' self-confidence and certain reflective and practical teaching knowledge. This study strongly emphasized the importance of the triad (student teacher, cooperating teacher, and university supervisor) in creating a university–school partnership for learning to teach.

St-Louis (1994) conducted research focused on beginning teacher induction programs and studied the criteria for choosing a good mentor and the characteristics of effective mentor relationships.

Brunelle et al. (1994) conducted a research project aimed at understanding how preservice teachers can progressively integrate an interactive pedagogy to prevent or solve discipline problems in secondary physical education classes. The concept of interactive pedagogy allows for a reconciliation between the teachers' assertiveness and their openness to students' needs. The teacher education model tested in this research program differs from the traditional "knowledge then application"; it includes three types of activities: (1) preparatory (learning theoretical frameworks as a basis of reflective practice), (2) insertion (experimenting teaching strategies and reflecting on one's action), and (3) integration (the future teachers ask for complementary knowledge and skills according to their needs).

Lévèsque and Gervais (1994) studied first-year teacher induction. In Quebec, teacher education reform has led to a number of research projects involving partnerships between universities' faculties, school boards, and the provincial departments of education. Some exploratory studies on teacher induction are presently being funded by the Quebec Department of Education (MEQ) to define the conditions of meaningful teacher induction and monitoring practices. Working with three important school boards, the authors' purposes were to: (1) identify criteria for mentors' recruitment, (2) explore ways of training mentor teachers, and (3) experiment with meaningful mentoring activities. Administrative aspects are also considered.

Charbonneau (1993) in "Current Training Models and Professionalization of Teaching: A Critical Analysis of the North American Tendencies" pointed out that for some, the way to remediate various weaknesses and to give new spirit to the school is through professionalization. A necessary condition in attaining this objective is to accentuate the professional character of initial teacher training. This analysis examined the legitimacy of the professionalization movement, criticized the relation between this and current training models and emerging

approaches, and finally suggested a profile of various components for future professional practices.

Valentina and Cassidy (1983) researched teachers' perceptions on intermediate-level teacher preparation in Ontario. This study was a doctoral dissertation completed at the State University of New York, Buffalo.

Teacher Education Curriculum

Jutras (1994) researched student teachers' pedagogical ideas and values in high school education. Considering that teachers are consistently required to refer to their personal conception of education, student teacher professors must help gear their students' pedagogical ideas in order for them to develop a clear educational position. This study was based on data that consist of symbols, values, and ideas about education and teaching provided by student teachers. The results revealed what these students think and believe about teaching. The analysis showed how important it is for professors in high school teacher education programs to take into consideration these beliefs and build on them to help the students reorganize and strengthen their pedagogical views.

Gauthier and Tardif (in press) studied the different types of professional knowledge transmitted by teacher training programs in Quebec to compare them with those forming the basis of professional knowledge in teaching. They made suggestions to improve teachers' training programs and elaborated on basic professional knowledge attributed to the field of teaching.

Hensler (1992) studied the development of an integrated approach to learning strategy instruction and teacher education. This research was conducted according to an approach using conceptual clarification, critical analysis, and the integration of findings derived from theoretical studies as well as empirical work in the area of learning strategies and instruction. The results are presented as heuristic models rather than prescriptions for pedagogical action. The first model presented a multifaceted approach to learning strategy instruction. The second presented a frame of reference for teacher education in the domain of learning strategy instruction: the definition of goals and priorities, the selection and organization of content, teaching methodology, the types of learning opportunities, as well as the method of evaluation. This research raised several questions about the manner in which conclusions drawn from research in education are being conveyed to students in teacher education programs.

Guilbert (1990) attempted to verify the applicability of case studies in an inquiry teaching approach toward the practical training at the university level. The author explored the pertinence of this approach in investigating reflective processes of future teachers and in the development of professional knowledge. The methodology for this investigation included an opinion questionnaire and qualitative analyses of workshop discussions. These results showed both the applicability and the pertinence of this approach.

In "Teacher Training in Computer-Based Education: Assessment and Tendencies" (1989), Farine and Hupper of the University of Montreal described the state of teacher training in microcomputers in Quebec. The authors presented various types of training programs and their content, as well as a critique of each. Word processing was presented as an ideal method for training teachers in computer-based education. The authors presented several recommendations for teacher training.

CHINA

Teacher education research in the People's Republic of China began in the early 1950s soon after the Communist Party came to power and was mainly influenced by the former Soviet Union. But during 1966–1976, the "Cultural Revolution" caused a suspension of teacher education research and other kinds of educational research. After the Cultural Revolution, however, teacher education research in China began to revive and to develop in accordance with the government's reform and open-door policies.

From 1983 to 1994, teacher research can be generally divided into: (1) surveys supported or carried out by national and local educational administrations; and (2) research studies by individual researchers and teachers. Although Chinese teacher education research covers both preservice and in-service teacher education, most of the research is focused on teacher education structure and curriculum.

Teacher Education as a Field of Study

Tan and Mingshuim (1984) studied reform in teacher education in China and reported that the different levels of teacher education institutions have lengthened their course of study. The secondary teacher school program has been increased from 3 to 4 years and, in some teacher colleges, 4 to 5 years. Curricular offerings and the content of training programs and methods of teaching have also been reformed. To strengthen professional training, the tendency is to increase the teaching hours of educational theory and educational practice, to encourage more frequent contacts between teachers, colleges, and secondary schools, and to give more attention to training and teaching abilities and techniques. Reform has been directed toward strengthening the study of the foundations of educational theory and techniques, renewing the system of scientific knowledge, compressing the content of classical material in order to enrich the content with new achievements of scientific research, and stressing the combination of theory with practice, especially with actual situations in schools. In reforming the methods of teaching, all levels of teacher education in China have emphasized China's experience and the successful teaching achievements from abroad. New technologies have been introduced into classroom teaching, and the development of self-study abilities, logical thinking abilities, organizational and administrative abilities, and skills in oral expression and scientific research have been stressed. In the early 1980s, the Central Institute of Educational Research was rebuilt to become the National Center. About 16 province and 37 teacher colleges and universities were organized into institutes of educational research. Twenty-eight provinces have organized educational societies, and 15 national societies of education were established. A nationwide network of educational research agencies

was set up, and by 1994 many had started research on the theoretical and practical problems of education with some encouraging results.

Recruitment, Selection, and Initial Preparation

Paine (1990) explored the conceptual basis of teaching in China through the metaphor of teacher as virtuoso performer, with teaching considered as an art. Field research results on teacher preparation and elementary and secondary teaching practice are discussed. Shortcomings of this teaching model and implications for educational reform are considered.

Weiping (1992) in "Issues and Trends in Current Developments of Teacher Education in China" discussed the effects of low salaries on admission to teacher training programs.

The Student Department of the National Educational Commission (1990), a group of researchers, studied two problems in student enrollment at the normal universities: (1) Why were fewer students applying for admission? (2) Why did they seem to be of lesser ability? The research discovered several reasons for the problems: The lower socioeconomic status of secondary school teachers; their heavy workload and housing problems; reduced opportunities for mobility and a narrower road for employment; lower financial support for the students in teacher education; lower funding for basic education; the value changes among young people; and improper ways of enrollment. Several suggestions were provided to solve the problems: higher salaries for teachers to raise their living standards; more financial support for students in teacher education; more investment in the elementary and secondary schools to improve the physical teaching environments; and changes in the ways of recruiting students to teacher education programs.

"Preliminary Thoughts on Improving Instruction of Teaching Methodology in Higher Teacher Education Institutions," an essay by Weixiang (1983), pointed out that in the normal colleges and universities, students had less training and education in teaching and teaching research. This problem was reflected in outmoded textbooks of teaching and teaching research, lack of qualified professors for teacher training courses, and less chances for the students to understand the real world of schools. Suggestions for improving the situation were to recruit better teachers to the normal universities to teach teaching and research courses; provide more time for the teacher training courses in teacher education programs; pay more attention to developing students' teaching ability; and centralize the syllabus and textbooks of teaching and teaching research at the national level. Shuming (1987) studied the different structures of secondary normal schools, which are mainly responsible for training elementary teachers. By comparing the existing structures the author concluded that a new structure of secondary normal schools should be established to better satisfy the needs of elementary schools. Anbang (1989) discovered that although China's schools needed teachers of foreign languages, biology, history and politics, arts, music, and physical education, the normal colleges and universities were training the teachers according to their tradition and not to meet the school needs. This mismatch made the problem of lack of teachers in these areas even worse. So it was quite necessary to reform the structure of programs of normal universities and to increase the adapatability of these normal institutions to meet the needs of secondary schools.

Contextual Influences on Teacher Education

Zhongxiu (1989) researched the relationship between the government's outward economy policy and the reform of higher teacher education. The author learned that under the influences of outward economy policy, teacher education should change to emphasize a guiding ideology of higher teacher education; ways of managing higher teacher education institutions; conceptions of the good teacher education student; and types of teachers in the institutions. Youtang (1988) studied aspects of the *Necessity of Higher Normal Education to Suit the Needs of Economic Development and Rural Secondary School* and found that as traditional agriculture changed to modern agriculture, teacher education should evolve accordingly in order to satisfy the changing needs of the rural secondary school. More and more teachers with the knowledge and technology of modern agricultural production are needed for the rural secondary schools and higher teacher education should take the training responsibility.

Teacher Education Curriculum

Tianxiang et al. (1989) researched restructuring of the curriculum system for higher normal education and identified two major weaknesses of the curriculum: (1) improper ratios between general knowledge and special knowledge courses and subject matter and teaching courses; required and optional courses, time for teaching practice and time for main courses; and (2) an outmoded, narrow and impractical curriculum content. The author developed a strategy of restructuring the curriculum in higher normal universities. Yinquan's (1989) study also focused on the issue of restructuring curriculum in the secondary normal school. By comparing the contemporary curriculum with that of the last 30 years and those of the other countries, the author found that (1) teaching training courses took less hours than seemed appropriate in the secondary normal schools, (2) teaching courses themselves were unbalanced and unrelated, and (3) the knowledge base in the teaching courses was outmoded and impractical. These three weaknesses of the curriculum also partially explain the lower quality of secondary normal education.

Yanping (1991) studied reform of science education in secondary teacher schools. This study concluded that the hour reduction of science education courses in secondary normal schools by the government made it necessary to reform the science education in the schools. The author pointed out that the focus of this reform should be on building a proper relationship between science training and teacher training. Laifu and Zhonglai (1989) studied explorations in specialized curriculum of mathematics in Chinese institutions of teacher education. The study sample included hundreds of math students in the eight normal universities. The investigation discovered that different mathematics courses functioned differently in developing students' varied abilities. Suggestions for designing a proper math program for math students in the normal universities were provided.

Continuing Professional Development, Growth, and Assessment

In his research on preservice and in-service teacher education in China, Wang (1987) reported on 290 institutions at the provincial and municipal levels and 2,174 at the county level that organized in-service programs for school administrators and teachers. This research identified how in-service teacher education played a role in remedying teachers who were (1) unqualified or had failed in qualifying examinations set by local authorities, and/or (2) basically qualified, but without a corresponding educational background. Wenxing (1990) analyzed the life and work of teachers in 20 schools in Sichuan Province by surveying 400 teachers and discovered that (1) the lower economic status and living standard of teachers provide no motivation to teach well, (2) too much work and less spare time had a great negative impact on their health, and (3) the lower socioeconomic status of teachers discouraged young people from considering teaching as a career. The author concluded that the key to improving the quality of teaching is to raise teachers' socioeconomic status, increase professionalism in teaching, and emphasize better management of teachers.

For further details on some of these studies, and others, the reader is referred to Chapter 13 in Tischer and Wideen (1990).

CZECH REPUBLIC

Continuing Professional Growth, Development, and Assessment

In 1988 the European Information Centre for Further Education of Teachers published *Selected Aspects in Inservice Education of Teachers in the Eighties*. This report analyzed aspects and trends of in-service teacher education and developed recommendations for improvement. The personality of contemporary teachers, their dominant activities, and their problems were also discussed. The conclusions of three major research activities on in-service teacher education in the 1980s were analyzed in detail: The Organization for Economic Cooperation and Development Project, directed toward general optimalization of such training; the project of the Council for Mutual Economic Assistance (socialist countries), devoted to the main trends in research; and the United Nations Educational, Scientific, and Cultural Organization Project, oriented toward the characteristics of models. The second section of this report focuses on the Information Centre for Further Education of Teachers from 1983 to 1986 and on profiles of the users.

EGYPT

Teacher Education Curriculum

Zeitoun (1987) assessed the competencies of preservice Egyptian biology teachers in identifying and correcting misconceptions about photosynthesis in a written answer. He examined the relationship between competency and four factors: (1) background knowledge about photosynthesis, (2) field-independent/ field-dependent cognitive style, (3) previous teaching practice with photosynthesis, and (4) previous experience in scoring students' writing. The findings in general suggested a need for developing training programs that increase preservice teachers' competencies in diagnosing and correcting students' misconceptions.

Continuing Professional Growth, Development, and Assessment

El-Meligi (1992) in *Perceptions of Our Future World: An Imperative for Today's Teacher Education Programs* reported the results of a questionnaire administered to in-service teachers to detect their awareness of current and future world changes, role expectations and role conception, their probable acceptance or refusal of role changes, and the impact of these variables on role performance. His findings have impacted the in-service teacher education curriculum in the area of current issues. Cochran and Miller (1984) conducted a 2-year study to identify specific competencies of teachers whose students achieved above-average scores on a standard proficiency test and reported the results in *Teacher Competence as Determined by Student Achievement.* Thirty-one elementary school teachers in Cairo, Egypt, whose classes have the highest and the lowest averages on an English proficiency test were observed. The data were collected by using a competency-based observation instrument. The data analysis revealed that there was no significant relationship between the nine areas of teacher competence and high or low average student performance.

Kotb (1984) reported in "Innovations in Inservice Teacher Education in Egypt" on a program developed in 1983 for 10,000 primary school teachers to attend 13 centers in the governance of Cairo and Giza to enhance their skills. Because teachers have difficulty studying on a full-time basis and traveling to learning centers, materials are delivered to the teachers during the school year. Teachers adopt a self-study system that uses multimedia, including books, manuals, television, and radio programs. Whenever they are free, teachers come to study centers to meet with the teaching staff and to discuss the program material. Teachers attend regular classes for 2 months during summer vacation to study subjects that require practical or language drills. It was anticipated that this experimental teacher education program would continue.

EL SALVADOR

Lemke (1989) in *Present, Past, and Future of Training Teachers in El Salvador* (ISN 67193) provided a background description of preservice and in-service training of early childhood and primary school teachers in El Salvador in the late 1980s, presented within the context of a country torn by internal strife and war for over a decade.

FINLAND

Teacher Education as a Field of Study

Niemi (1990) in *The Significance of Research in Developing of Teacher Education* concluded that more research should focus on different aspects of teacher education and that research on teaching should be more closely integrated with teacher education programs and research components in teacher education.

Recruitment, Selection, and Initial Preparation

Kari (1993) in *Teacher Orientation in the Early Stages of Teacher Education* concluded that student teachers have a good decision-making process. Their attitudes toward the teacher profession are mainly realistic.

Teacher Education Curriculum

Etelapelto (1992) in "Reflectivity and Self-Awareness in the Development of Expertise" focused on work orientation and its significance in the development of expertise. The concept of reflection was first defined and critically reviewed. This was followed by the question of how reflectivity can be promoted in working and learning activities.

Halaka (1992) in *Development of Scientific Thinking in the Training of Class Teachers,* concluded that students who are at the final stage of their training are reasonably well aware of the importance of studying education, but they would like to perceive more connections between education and the related disciplines. The majority of students claim that the material taught in education is conveyed in a form inappropriate for practical applications. However, students at the final stage of their studies regarded project work (thesis writing) as a meaningful form of study.

Hamalainen (1993) presented a social pedagogical model of teacher education for social work. Social pedagogical orientation in social work, in education for social work, and in vocational teacher education for social work, is based on the link between the social and the pedagogical.

Kalaoja (1992), Kalaoja and Pikkarainen (1993), and Pikkarainen (1992) used action research and concluded that reflection and professional skills can be remarkably promoted with adult and distance learning methods and by connecting the teaching to real contexts. However, some problems with new methods were found.

Korpinen (1992) in *Quantity and Quality-Education and Growth. The Evaluation of Class Teachers' Training at the Department of Teacher Education at the Jyvaskyla University in 1979–1992.* The author presented the evaluation process model of teacher training and suggested that to form unified teacher education, which is student centered, the emphasis should be on student teachers' professional self-image and on a deep teacher–student relationship that aims for teacher development and growth in teaching.

Niemi (1984a, 1984b, 1988, 1992a, 1992b) used surveys and interviews to conclude that successful secondary teacher education is based on the interaction between student teachers' personal qualities (e.g., commitment to teaching profession, high self-esteem, and self-confidence to work as an educator); the quality of cognitive processes activated by teacher education programs (e.g., integration theory and practice, demanding cognitive challenges); and support of student teachers' professional development (e.g., reflective supervision, which aims towards teachers' autonomy and responsibility).

Niikko (1993) examined the factors that influenced the practical knowledge of 11 student teachers in the social and health care branches. Their views about the need to develop themselves professionally and their ideas about their development during the advanced studies in teacher education were examined. The correlation between the actual development and the students' own goals for development was also considered. Metaphors and images were used in the analysis, and the material was gathered from the essays written in three stages by the student teachers. The results were analyzed phenomographically, and the content categories were analyzed.

Ojanen (1991) in *Reflective, Professional Supervision, a Critical Analysis of Supervisory Approach on Scientific Basis* concluded that supervisors' professional identity seems to be related to their own knowledge and ability to self-analyze. Their ability to relate theory and practice is still evolving as they realize the intent of their work. Only a small number of supervisors use a holistic approach when they analyze their students' professional growth process.

Ojanen (1992) in *Researching Reflective Style on the Supervision of Teaching Practice and Professional Identity of the Supervisors* examined how the supervisors operationalized their aims and intentions in the supervision of the practice teaching. The following features characterize the aims: (1) They are unclear, (2) not evaluated, and (3) not clearly conceptualized. In implementing the supervision, becoming aware of oneself stimulates the supervisor to reflect. The more the reflective process was linked to the learning situation, the more creative it was. Using oneself as an instrument resulted in a coordination of insight and cognitive learning of the supervisor. Positive reflection is also closely connected to strong professional identity.

Rasanen (1993) used action research to develop a course on ethics for teacher education. A model of moral dimensions was developed, and students' consciousness of the moral dimensions was widened and deepened.

Rousi (1991) described the teacher training model for social work, with built-in structures for developing training and action research. The aim of the educational/training process is to allow the continuous development of being aware of one's own thinking, understanding and actions, concerning both the trainees and the teacher educators.

Rousi (1993) discussed the pedagogical view on which the curriculum of vocational teacher education is based. The article draws on pedgagogical applications of critical theory and experimental learning theory in which the teacher is seen as the facilitator of learning.

Suojanen (1992) in *Action Research—A Way for Teachers to Develop Their Profession* compared an action research group and control group in textile and clothing courses in a vocational teacher education program using journals, tape recordings, diagnostic and summative tests, and evaluation of products. The author concluded that action research helped achieve the objectives and made it easier to organize the structure of knowledge hierarchically.

Continuing Professional Growth, Development, and Assessment

Jarvinen (1991, 1992a, 1992b) used phenomenography and qualitative methods in a series of studies on reflection. The author concluded that the objects of reflection are professional personality, teaching and learning process, content of teaching and the curriculum, and the relationship between the educational institution and society. The levels of reflection are: technical competence, reflective practice, and its theoretical basis and critical awareness. There was great individual variation in reflective thinking during education. The transition phase from the preservice to in-service period was very problematic.

Kohonen (1992) in *Restructuring School Learning as Learner Education: Towards a Collegial School Culture and Learning,* used interviews and action research to conclude that pre- and in-service teacher education needs a major paradigm shift from the transmission model of teaching based on behavioristic learning theory toward experiential learning, which is based on constructivist and humanistic theories of learning. Teacher educators can be involved as partners and facilitators in the process by helping teachers access the necessary knowledge and by providing opportunities for continuing in-service education.

Laine (1992a, 1992b, 1993) concluded that the conceptions of education, teaching, and learning of beginning teacher education students were still at the superficial stage of everyday thinking. The conceptions of the students, however, developed clearly during the training, and students were well aware of their conceptual development during training.

Niemi (1992c) in *Teachers' Professional Development* used the results of questionnaires and interviews and concluded that new elementary and secondary school teachers from Finnish teacher education programs in universities value the research component connected with their training. They have good professional skills for teaching in classrooms. Teachers, however, lack collegial collaboration, community, and social dimensions in their education.

Ropo (1987) in *Teachers' Conceptions of Teaching and Teaching Behavior: Some Differences Between Expert and Novice Teachers* analyzed what student teachers of mathematics and English think of various issues in learning and teaching. He concluded that the theoretical and methodological starting points of the study provided useful information for future research. The structure of knowledge differs between experts and novices in terms of hierarchy and organization.

Snellman (1988, 1989) used free written descriptions and explanations, thematic interviews, and account analyses to study education students' images of the child and concluded that the student teachers' conceptions are idealistic. The child is seen as a being with no connection to time and place. The conceptions of the child do not change during teacher training. Instead, the conceptions of teaching and the teacher change.

Uljens (1992a, 1992b, 1992c) used phenomenology and phenomenography to describe student teachers' conceptions of learning and focused on learning as a change process.

Diversity and Equity Issues

Liikanen (1990) in *Fairy Tale as a Model of Identity and Life Position* used transactional analysis and script analysis to conclude that the cultural script model can be used as a basis for developing meaningful study units for teacher education. Transactional analysis enables one to study the script messages that have been mediated during early childhood. In addition, it is possible to study the script messages that are mediated by the favorite fairy tales of early childhood. The favorite fairy tales of early childhood described by the student teacher belong mainly to the Western fairy-tale tradition.

Sunnari (1990) in *Hidden Structures and Educational Perspectives in the School and in Teacher Education, Particularly Gender Agenda* used process observation, interviews, document analyses, and developmental research to conclude that hidden structures according to gender look the same in the school and in the teacher education department. People *interpret* each other so that gender is one important element, although these same people think themselves to be neutral. Those hidden structures are difficult to change, especially so at the individual level.

Emerging Directions in Teacher Education

Niemi (1993) in *Teachers' Orientation Towards the Future* used data gathered in interviews to conclude that anticipating the future and creating it will require more of teachers than present teacher education programs offer. Teacher need an ability to anticipate the future. Prerequisites for future orientation are that pre- and inservice teacher education programs emphasize three elements in professional growth: (1) rationality, (2) intuitive thinking, and (3) morality.

FRANCE

Gardner and Salters (1990) studied the development of information technology in education and teacher education in France. This paper concerned the use of information technology in education in France and is presented in two parts. The first part provided a brief survey of the development of information technology in education, and the second presents the authors' observations of the current situation, made during a recent series of visits to educational institutions in France. The report provided a broad overview of the development of industrial technology in education in France with a focus on the authors' particular interest: the nature and organization of teacher education for information technology development.

GREAT BRITAIN

Recruitment, Selection, and Initial Preparation

In "Developing a Programme for Selecting Primary Teachers" Wilson and Mitchell (1985) studied selection procedures for student teachers. They used a team of trained assessors who observed potential students in a variety of situations. Seventy candidates in a 4-year bachelor of education course were interviewed, and data were collected on their personal qualities, intellectual abilities, and attitudes. These candidates were then observed in leaderless discussion groups, given simulated

teaching tasks and a traditional employment type of interview. The authors found that it was feasible to establish a viable selection program but that quality could be improved.

McNamara (1986) studied the factor of the institutions' prospectus as an influence on student choice in "Prospectus for Teaching: A Misleading Image." He did a content analysis of the pictorial information contained in the prospectus of initial teacher training institutions. He found that the image of teaching conveyed by the prospectuses, which were designed to recruit applicants into teacher training courses, was at variance with primary school practice as described by available survey evidence. He suggested that teacher training institutions should include in their prospectuses pictorial information that showed something of the huge variety and diversity of approaches used in primary practice and the challenges that would be faced by teachers in today's schools.

Bullock and Scott (1990) in "Enterprise Awareness in Teacher Education (EATE): The Evaluation of an Innovation in Initial Teacher Education" reported that the Enterprise Awareness in Teacher Education program incorporates enterprise, economic, and industrial issues into all preservice teacher education in England, Scotland, and Wales through an extensive program of faculty development.

Craft (1990) discussed changes in British teacher education since the 1960s, noting the impact of the 1988 Education Reform Act. Qualitative changes include rigorous national accreditation structures, an all-graduate teacher population, and in-service education of teachers.

Wright and Dillon (1990) described the use of interactive video (IV) in initial teacher training in the United Kingdom. Five types of learner control of IV use are highlighted: (1) as a presentation system; (2) for independent structure learning, (3) as a resource for students in teaching practice, (4) as an information source, and (5) as a surrogate tutor. Twenty-six references are included.

Kyriacou and Cheng (1993) studied the attitudes of 109 student teachers at the University of York toward the humanistic approach to teaching and learning in schools. In the first phase of the study, all the student teachers completed a 20-item questionnaire characterizing the humanistic approach. In the second phase of the study, 16 student teachers were interviewed during their block teaching practice in order to further explore their responses to the questionnaire and also to explore their descriptions of teachers they had been taught by as pupils whom they remember with respect and affection, and those remembered with dislike or even hatred. The findings indicated that the student teachers generally held positive attitudes toward the humanistic approach but that ideals were difficult to relate to realities of classroom life.

Contextual Influence on Teacher Education

McNamara (1990) reported that the Education Reform Act passed in 1988 should create significant changes in Britain's teacher training institutions, and thus far, it has had a profound impact. Institutions are now mandated as to how they should prepare both student teachers and practicing teachers to deliver the national curriculum, which is legislated in the Education Reform Act. McNamara reported that the secretary of state for education outlined a scenario in 1989 in which local education authorities (which employ teachers and manage the education systems at the local level) will have a more prominent role in the initial and in-service training of teachers, which will become more school-based and will draw on, rather than rely on, the services of the teacher training institution. McNamara further reported that there has been a dramatic shift since 1984 in that the government has sought not only to control both the numbers and the distribution of student teacher training places within higher education but also to proscribe the content of the teacher training courses. With the establishment of the Council for the Accreditation of Teacher Education, the Department of Education and Science (DES) was able to establish criteria by which teacher training programs could be judged prior to their formal approval by the secretary of state for education. The same government that had set more than 30 criteria for the initial teacher training programs is now advocating routes into teaching that do not require conventional forms of training.

Sharpe (1983) studied planning and control of teacher education in England and Wales in a doctoral dissertation completed at Harvard University.

Teacher Education Curriculum

Meighan and Harber (1986) reported a case study of students in a postgraduate certificate program who were given an opportunity to opt for different approaches to their learning. In this study, students could select one of the following approaches for their methods course: the authoritarian expert, the authoritarian consultative, or the democratic. The authors reported experience in implementing and evaluating the democratic approach. Both students and tutors were required to adjust to different models of learning. The evaluation suggested that students did not regret having chosen the democratic mode. They reported that they felt confident and learned to develop their existing skills and to acquire new ones. They developed confidence in their own thinking and were highly motivated. These students also were able to cope with teaching in the authoritarian schools that were typically encountered, and through this methodology, acquired a vision of possible alternatives.

In "Working With Children in Trouble: An Interprofessional Approach to the Training of Teachers and Social Workers" Russell-Gebbett (1984) sought to expand the professional contacts of postgraduate student teachers. The course was also attended by trainee social workers. Russell-Gebbett's rationale was that social workers and school teachers seldom communicate effectively with one another while working with the same children. The course was evaluated using attitude tests. Through the challenge of critical argument and problem solving, the evidence indicated that the workshop encouraged training teachers to assess more realistically their roles in handling children in trouble and to see that their work complements that of others in the field. The course also gave individuals entering the two different professions an opportunity to meet and exchange views.

Calderhead and Miller (1986) undertook detailed case studies of eight students to explore the process whereby subject-matter knowledge informed their classroom practice. They found that students themselves valued their own high-level subject-matter knowledge and made use of it in their lesson planning. Their practical teaching, however, was based more on direct practical experience and observation of and discussion with other teachers and was hardly influenced by subject knowledge. Calderhead conducted two additional studies with students in their field experience. The first, which focused on the quality of reflection in student teachers' professional learning (1987), followed 10 students through their field experiences during their training year. He found that the students' capacity to think reflectively about practice quickly reached a plateau and that situational factors in the classroom constrained their practice. The second study (1988) investigated what 27 student teachers learned from their introductory school experience. Even though tutors and teachers tried to structure and to standardize the school experience for all students, it took different forms that offered qualitatively different types of professional learning.

In "Patchwork Pedagogy: A Case Study of Supervisors' Emphasis on Pedagogy in Post-Lesson Conference" Mansfield (1986) looked at the supervisor's role during school practice. Previous knowledge of the institution in question had indicated that there was a disjunction between supervisors' aims and what students actually practice in the schools, so this study encouraged supervisors to become more involved with students and joint teaching. However, student supervisors were constrained by the lack of clear frameworks for developing students' pedagogical skills, and their efforts were hampered by the difficulties of presenting students with critical information in the emotionally charged situation of the practice classroom.

Continuing Professional Growth, Development, and Assessment

Halpin, Croll, and Redman (1990) in "Teachers' Perceptions of the Effects of Inservice Education" presented results of a British study of nearly 200 teachers who attended in-service education and training (INSET) courses at four British universities. Teachers who believed that their skills improved also reported improvements in student attainment. This study found INSET to be more effective in improving individual teachers' attitudes and in increasing their knowledge than in improving school organization and policy.

Lynch and Burns (1984) compared teachers who did or did not attend in-service courses. Teachers indicated that the main reasons why they were not prepared to attend in-service courses were that they did not wish to give up their own time, they had little opportunity for doing so, it was too tiring after school, they lacked financial support or time, and there was no incentive or encouragement. A large number of teachers claimed that they did not need in-service education. The main reasons given for attending in-service courses were to improve promotion prospects, a desire to improve knowledge or enhance self-esteem, to improve teaching skills, and financial motivation.

Diversity and Equity Issues

In "A Study of Gender Discrimination in a Primary Program of Teacher Training" Skelton (1987) learned that initial teacher training programs do little to promote student teachers' awareness of discriminatory practices in the classroom. Based on research with a primary postgraduate certificate in education course, the author found that student teachers tended to absorb messages that actually promoted views about gender discrimination through the hidden curriculum. Student teachers learn that they should expect to find differences in the capabilities, attitudes, and behaviors of boys and girls in the primary classroom. This study showed why gender discrimination continues to be a feature of primary education.

Jayne (1987) undertook the challenge of describing how one college aimed to make teachers in training more knowledgeable and skilled in providing equal education opportunities for boys and girls at the classroom level. The college rewrote a primary teacher training program to focus on increasing awareness skills and practices concerning sexual equality. The task involved changing course syllabi, implementing a program of staff development, and investigating how change could be brought about within teacher training courses. Evaluation suggested that the initiative was worthwhile and involved staff as well as students in new learning experiences.

Lawes (1987b) conducted a study on student teachers' awareness of pupils' nonverbal responses. In this investigation, 57 student teachers decoded pupil's nonverbal signals displayed on a video. Analysis of the data indicated that student teachers whose teaching competence was rated as low also tended to be those who were poor at decoding a pupil's nonverbal signals. In a second study focused on the relationship between nonverbal awareness of self and teaching competence in student teachers, Lawes (1987a) investigated 81 students' beliefs about nonverbal activity in the classroom and their awareness of their own nonverbal behavior. Lawes found that the student teachers rated as competent were more aware of the importance of pupils' nonverbal activity and their own nonverbal behavior. On this same theme, St. J. Neill, Fitzgerald, and Jones (1983) compared 92 student teachers' and 90 practitioner teachers' awareness of nonverbal communications in the classroom. Teachers who were rated as effective were more likely to mention the importance of nonverbal communication, and probationer teachers were more aware of the importance of nonverbal communication than were students.

Emerging Directions in Teacher Education

Cashdan (1992) in "New Partnership—Initial Teacher Training in the U.K." discussed the implications of placing the major responsibility for teacher training in the hands of secondary school headmasters. Cashdan noted that the secretary of state for education planned to increase the school-based element of initial preservice teacher training to 80% of students' time. The paper discussed the implications of this proposal for the professional training and status of teachers, as well as for a partnership in the Sheffield area.

For further details on some of these studies and others the reader is referred to Chapter 8 in Tischer and Wideen (1990).

HONG KONG

Recruitment, Selection, and Initial Preparation

Cooke and Pang (1992) conducted a study on entry characteristics of trained and untrained beginning teachers in which 129 secondary teachers in art, science, and English from the University of Hong Kong were surveyed. The study also included a survey of principals who were to identify their perceptions of the problems and needs of beginning teachers as well as the availability and nature of school-based induction provision in local secondary schools. The results of the study showed that teaching in the first year is not easy, with 45% of the beginning teachers in the whole group considering their first year experience difficult or extremely difficult. The interviews indicated that most teachers were busy, felt tired, and had little social life in the earlier part of the year. Over one half of the teachers found some discrepancy between their expectations and reality. These discrepancies were mostly about workload and students (low learning incentive, poor discipline, unexpected attitudes and behaviors). The major problems of beginning teachers lay in the areas of teaching and lesson preparation. This study differentiated between the trained, partially trained, and untrained teachers. The partially trained and untrained teachers had a wider range of problems than the trained group. These problems included the area of discipline (management and control) and, to some degree, syllabus, administration, and personal areas as well. The partially trained group had the widest range, and the trained group had the narrowest. The top 10 major problems were to manage the class in good order; to handle disruptive students in class; to deal with individual differences in learning abilities with mixed-ability classes and with slow learners and low motivation of incentive of students to learn; to arouse student interest in the subject matter; to be aware of students' previous learning; to know their own teaching effectiveness; and to deal with inadequate time for lesson preparation, inadequate facilities and equipment, low English standards of students, and coping with the fast pace of examination classes. The authors noted that many of these problems are not simple and are not easy to solve, even for more experienced teachers.

The survey of principals indicated that their views on novice problems were very consistent with the beginners' own perceptions. Student discipline and teaching were considered major problems of beginners. Other problems of beginners perceived as major problems by principals included personal problems, administrative problems, and problems related to the syllabus. Findings also indicate that the beginning teachers were not given much help or support. System-based induction provision was minimal. Out of a possible list of 27 induction activities, only four were received by more than half of the teachers. Most of these were those offered at the beginning of the first term and were more or less familiarization and orientation-type activities. Results of the principals surveyed also indicated that only beginning-of-the-term activities were used for induction proposes. In looking at job adjustment at both mid-year and end-of-year surveys, trained teachers were doing better than the untrained and partially trained teachers. In an analysis of job satisfaction, it was found that the partially trained and untrained groups were dissatisfied with a wider range of aspects than the trained group. Of the whole group, 46% of the teachers indicated that they wished to change schools, and 24% intended to leave the profession at the end of the year. Percentages were higher for the partially trained and untrained groups than for the trained group.

Continuing Professional Growth, Development, and Assessment

Cheng (1992) studied the relationship of teachers' professional ethics to school organizational characteristics such as leadership, social norms, and organizational structures and found that principals' leadership seems to be the critical predictor of teachers' professional ethics.

INDIA

More than 670,000 primary schools and about 65,000 secondary schools are served by the teacher education system in India. There are about 1,200 primary teacher education institutions and about 500 secondary teacher education institutions throughout the country. These institutions are not uniformly placed and create a surplus in some areas and shortages in others. The secondary teacher education institutions are primarily tied to universities. Of nearly 150 studies on teacher education that have been conducted since the mid-1980s, more than four fifths of these were at the secondary level.

Recruitment, Selection, and Initial Preparation

Pillai and Mohan (1985) conducted a large-scale survey of why graduates chose to teach. Responses to the questionnaire were guided more by concern for social acceptability than by real intentions. Gopalacharyulu (1984) reported in *A Study of Relationship Between Certain Psychological Factors and Achievement of Student Teachers in Teacher Training Institutes of Andhra Pradesh* that the academic performance of student teachers was significantly influenced by socioeconomic status and attitude toward the teaching profession. Personality did not have an impact on achievement. Goyal, Sabharwal, and Tewari (1984) in *Developing Tools for Admission to Secondary Teacher Training Institutions in India* surveyed the characteristics of 749 student teachers. Using multiple regression analysis, they reported that intelligence, attitude, and personality factors were effective predictors of achievement. The authors found no significant correlation between previous teaching experience and achievement. In another study, Patil (1984) found a significant correlation between academic performance of student teachers and their intelligence, attitude, and interest. In *Personality Traits and Attainment of Skills Through Microteaching* Katiyar (1982) used a 16-personality factor questionnaire and found that skill acquisition through microteaching had a significant positive correlation with ego strength, shrewdness, conservatism, and dependence. In *A Study of the Adjustment of Trainees of Teachers Training Colleges of Gujarat*, Donga

(1987) found that adjustment level depended on socioeconomic status, length of teaching experience, and gender of the student teacher. More difficulties were experienced in adjustment the longer the teaching experience was. Females were better adjusted than their male counterparts. Adjustment level, however, had no relationship with academic achievement.

Contextual Influences on Teacher Education

To understand the various dimensions of teaching practice programs, their organization, and the problems involved, Rai (1982) conducted *A Survey of the Problems of Teachers' Training Colleges With Regard to Practicing Schools;* Mohanty (1984) conducted *A Study of Student Teaching Programmes in Colleges of Education with Special Reference to Innovation;* Raj (1984) conducted *A Study of the Organization and Administration of Student Teaching Programs in the Secondary Teacher Education Institutions;* and Shah (1986) conducted "A Survey of Management of Student Teaching in India." Considerable variations across the country in the organization of teaching practice was found. Three main models were being followed. Some institutions had adopted block teaching practice of the internship model for organizing the teacher practice program. In the block model, student teachers were attached to particular schools on a full-time basis for a period ranging from 2 to 6 weeks. During this time they were required to participate in all the activities of the school along with their practice classes. A second model had the student teachers attending theory classes, receiving guidance from their supervisors at the teacher training colleges, and participating in teaching practice at the school on alternate days. A small number of institutions had adopted a third approach. Here, student teachers spent half of the day with their supervisors on the college campus and the remaining half at the practicing schools. Two problems were found to be generally affecting the teaching practice: (1) inadequate guidance and supervision by the teacher educators, and (2) lack of cooperation and coordination among the school and college authorities. Mohanty (1984) found that the stress in the teaching practice program was only on the delivery of a prescribed number of lessons. It was not on providing feedback to student teachers for improving the quality of performance.

Teacher Education Curriculum

A very important study was conducted by Singh (1985) on comparisons of integrated and traditional methods in terms of attitude toward teaching, teaching competence, and role performance. In this study students who had completed the 4-year integrated program of teacher training for the secondary level were compared with the traditional model of 1-year training following a basic bachelor's degree. Although no significant difference was found in the attitude of the teachers who had undergone the two different models of training, teachers who had undergone training through the integrated model achieved higher scores in their teaching competence and in role performance. Subject analysis showed that science students benefited significantly more by the integrated training approach than their counterparts from the social science subjects.

In the development of teaching skills, microteaching was a subject of interest of Khan (1985). He conducted experiments that compared microteaching with a conventional approach and concluded that microteaching proved to be more effective in terms of performance of learners on achievement tests. He also focused on improvements in general teaching competence.

Another study on microteaching, *A Critical Study of Microteaching Techniques With a View to Suggest Improvement in Its Implementation in Colleges of Education,* was conducted by Oak (1986). This study was conducted in a context of three subjects: science, mathematics, and mother tongue. Relevant skills were identified that were based on student teacher perceptions and on direct observations. It was concluded that the subject is an important variable in the process of teaching skills development through microteaching. A study conducted by Prabhune, Marathe, and Cohani (1984), *An Experimental Study to Measure the Effect of Microteaching Skills and Different Strategies of Feedback on the Student Teachers' Performance With Respect to Teaching,* reported that three variations used in the study did not have any significant impact on the general teaching competence of the student teachers: self-feedback through audio cassette, peer feedback, and supervisor's feedback.

Having established the use of microteaching in a teacher education program, Ekbote (1987) studied how it evolved in *Development of a Strategy for Integration of Skills in Teacher Training.* Carried out in the normal conditions of a teacher training institution, this study was developmental as well as experimental in nature. The study resulted in a package of instructional material for integration of teaching skills through microteaching. Dave (1987) studied the relative effectiveness of microteaching using a summative model of integration versus a miniteaching model in terms of general teaching competence, teacher attitude toward teaching, and student liking and achievement. The miniteaching model was found to be more effective in terms of student achievement as well as attitudes toward teaching.

Continuing Professional Growth, Development, and Assessment

A study by Kalyanpurkar (1986), *The Effect of Microteaching on the Teaching Competence of Inservice Teachers and Its Impact on Pupils' Attainment and Pupils' Liking* reported a positive impact of training and microteaching on the use of teaching skills and also on student learning. This study was conducted on a large scale involving 36 teachers and 720 pupils. The purpose was to explore the efficacy of microteaching as a tool for developing teaching skills in in-service teachers. It focused on four teaching skills: probing skills, reinforcement, explaining with examples, and stimulus variation.

Butala (1987) conducted an extensive survey that found that the majority of teachers were not covered under any in-service program. The in-service programs mainly concentrated on knowledge of grading in school subjects, except for a few that dealt with such aspects as educational technology and educational management. The teachers felt that the programs were generally useful for their professional growth and that

participation in such in-service training programs should be given due consideration in their promotion to higher posts.

Sinha (1982) conducted a study of teacher education in Bihar that confirmed earlier findings that trained teachers were superior to untrained ones in almost all aspects of their professional work. The author also found that untrained teachers were more prone to purely content-oriented interactions in their approach to teaching.

For further details on some of these studies and others, the reader is referred to Chapter 9 in Tischer and Wideen (1990).

INDONESIA

Teacher Education as a Field of Study

Nielsen et al. (1990) wrote a study entitled *Cost-Effectiveness of Distance and Conventional Approaches to Teacher Education in Indonesia: Executive Summary and Recommendations* (ISN 71445).

Sulistiorini and Nielsen (1990) investigated a related topic in *Private Costs of Teacher Training Through Distance Education in Indonesia* (ISN 71439).

IRELAND

Recruitment, Selection, and Initial Preparation

Barry (1992) in "Comparative Ratings of Teacher Image by Preservice Teachers in the United States and Ireland" studied 453 Irish and U.S. preservice teachers to determine their attitudes toward the profession and occupational prestige. Significant differences were found in the way participants evaluated teaching. Gender was a factor. Overall results indicated that the mean attitude score of U.S. subjects was significantly higher. Also, based on a significant interaction effect, Irish males tended to have more positive attitudes toward teaching than did Irish females. The reverse was true for U.S. participants. Differences were also found on how subjects ranked teaching on a list of 15 occupational classifications.

Lowe (1991) studied Ireland and its teachers. This article provided an overview of the role education plays in Ireland, the value placed on education and educators by the Irish society, and concluded with views educators hold about their standing and profession. The author concluded that education is a national priority and is highly regarded.

Teacher Education as a Field of Study

Ryan and Cremin (1993) in "Developing the European Dimension in Teacher Education: A Case Study in European Teacher Education" described a joint Irish–UK project to train 19 students over a period of 4 weeks in European dimensions. Eleven tutors from 10 institutions in seven countries participated.

Continuing Professional Growth, Development, and Assessment

"The Recognition of Conjunctive and Identity Needs in Teacher Development: Their Implications for the Planning of Inservice Training" was described by Fitzgibbon and Heywood in 1986. The lessons of in-company training are applied to teacher in-service programs. The constraints of identity, experience, and security, and, therefore, of the relevance of particular in-service programs are discussed. The lack of recognition that many needs are conjunctive lead to unnecessary duplication in course design. The potential of communal course spiral structures for the effective utilization of resources was illustrated.

Heywood and Fitzgibbon (1980) also wrote "The Role of Self-Assessment in the Design and Evaluation of Short Courses for the Training of Head Teachers in Management." There is little research on the impact that in-service training programs have on subsequent job performance. Reasons for this are advanced, including a section of the training of teachers in the design of public examinations and assessments. Their implementation and evaluation indicated the amount of training required for such activities as well as the trade-offs that have to be made.

Martin (1992) wrote "The Application of Research on Classroom Management to an Inservice Program for Teachers." The impetus for the program was triggered by a perception of malaise among Irish teachers arising from increasing levels of stress and other complexities that their role has acquired. This course was designed to help them with their classroom management. Teachers in the experimental group were compared with a control group. The results were encouraging. Teachers were enabled to make sense of their existing practices in terms of research and fine-tune and extend their existing skills.

The following four reports are all concerned with the same activity, namely, a course designed to show the relationship between theory and practice in the classroom through a series of replicatory research activities. The course approximates one eighth of a 1-year program for the training of graduates to become secondary teachers. Over the year, they are asked to undertake six activities in which they replicate research relating to instructional theories within their normal teaching practice problems. Various aspects of the course are described in contributions one and two. Students' attitudes toward the course are given in two; some comments relating to the staff perspective are included. Because the course began in 1985, the student reports relating to these activities have been retained—some 4,000 in all. They have been the subject of meta-analyses to see if they can contribute to an understanding of the relationships between instruction and learning in the classroom. Contributions three and four are reports on these meta-analyses. The reports are: (1) Heywood (1991), "Student Teachers as Researchers of Instruction in the Classroom"; (2) Fitzgibbon, Heywood, and Cameron (1991), "The Matching of Learning Styles to Teaching During Teacher Education: A Preliminary Study in Experience Versus Theory in Teacher Education"; (3) Heywood, Fitzgibbon, and Cameron (1991), "Experience Versus Theory in Teacher Education: Student Teachers as Researchers"; and (4) Heywood and Heywood (1993), "The Training of Student Teachers in Discovery Methods of Instruction and Learning."

ISRAEL

This overview relates to research carried out in Israel since the mid-1980s and focuses especially on the 1990–1995 period. The overview covers papers published mainly in local journals that are based in teacher education institutions or the Ministry of Education. This phenomenon reflects the importance assigned to the study of programs to share their experiences and insights and to disseminate this knowledge among colleagues. The Ministry of Education supports and funds these studies.

Teacher Education as a Field of Study

Stahl (1991) dealt with the problem of bridging the gap between research and teacher education by turning an evaluation report into a textbook of didactics and adapting it for use in staff development. Dror (1992), in "Between Academization and Personal Development—Teacher Education in Israel Between 1980–1990" addressed a central dilemma of teacher education in Israel, namely, the tension between the "academization" of the process, through emphasizing scientific disciplines, as opposed to focusing on the personal development of student teachers.

Recruitment, Selection, and Initial Preparation

Schechtman (1990) examined a validation of a group assessment procedure for the selection of teacher education candidates, particularly for its ability to predict success in a teacher education program. The study involved 141 Israeli student teachers and suggested that a group assessment procedure is a better alternative than individual interviews for predicting success in a teacher education program, because group assessment assesses the personality factors related to teacher success more effectively.

Peretz et al. (1992) in "Evaluation of a One-Year Internship Program for Student-Teachers (Interns) at Ben-Gurion University of the Negev," assessed the patterns of interaction between mentors and interns and found that efficient supervision is based on good communication between mentors and interns and that the longer the training period, the better the intern will be prepared for teaching.

Kremer-Hayon and Wubbels (1992) used a survey questionnaire to study the relation between Israeli student teachers' perceptions of the supervision climate and their satisfaction with supervision. The authors also studied their cooperating teachers. They concluded that cooperative styles of supervision are positively related to student teacher satisfaction, whereas oppositional ones (including uncertain and strict) are negatively related. Both directive and nondirective styles produced high levels of satisfaction.

Contextual Influences on Teacher Education

Klebanov (1990) studied the "Problems and Difficulties of Beginning Teachers as Related to Personal and Contextual Features." Other authors and titles include the following: Halwitz (1990), "Becoming a Teacher: Professional Socialization in Teacher Education Institutes in Israel"; and Zmora (1990), "Changes in Attitudes and Professional Behavior Throughout the Process of Teacher Education." These studies link institutional contexts and professional development.

Teacher Education Curriculum

In "Teacher Education in Israel: A Present Situation," Lamm (1986) examined teacher education programs in various Israeli institutions and discussed the role of ideological concepts, religious beliefs, and political reform in shaping the different programs. Porat (1993) evaluated the curriculum of pedagogical studies as perceived by students in a teacher education college. Scherf (1992) focused on the practicum in a teacher education college and reported on the construction and use of an assessment instrument. In a study of practical experiences in teacher education, Ziv (1989) discussed the inherent difficulties encountered in implementing a practicum for student teachers. Her article focused on problems concerning the structure of the school system and the nature of the actual experiences. Schonberg and Cornbleth (1988) described and analyzed ways and means for introducing reflective thinking models in the curriculum of teacher education programs. The basic orientation of curriculum studies in the context of teacher education in Israel is an evaluative one, with major importance assigned to students' viewpoints. Ariav (1992) in "Beit Berl College, 1980–1990: A Case Study of the Professionalization of Teacher Education in Israel" studied the 10-year process of professionalizing teacher education in Israel in the areas of practicum, school–college partnerships, internal evaluation, collaborative research, and networking.

Continuing Professional Growth, Development, and Assessment

Zuzovsky (1992) wrote "A Model of Teachers' Professional Development and Its Application to Teacher Education." Katz (1990) published "Personal Constructs in the Perception of Students by Student-Teachers in a Teacher Education College." Lewy (1992) in "Evaluation Results as Input for Improving the Quality of Inservice Programs: Using Responses to Open-Ended Questions" suggested ways of using evaluation results to improve the quality of in-service programs. Zellermayer (1990) in "Teachers' Development Towards the Reflective Teaching of Writing: An Action Research" reported results from a longitudinal study of 18 teachers' development in writing instruction. Two approaches to writing instruction were contrasted: technical rationality and reflection-in-action. This four-phase action research study was carried out in the context of a 1-year in-service training program to prepare writing teacher trainers in Israel. The author concluded that the teachers needed additional support beyond the 1-year workshop to maintain and practice the ideas learned in the workshop.

All these researchers are interested in continuing professional growth. Zuzovsky used a theoretical frame for this purpose, and Lewy proposed a more contextualized approach,

relying on actual data collected from participants and deriving recommendations from its analysis. Other researchers who analyze data concerning teacher education programs and their implications for teacher development are Silberstein and Karinsky (1992) in "Perspectives of Expert-Teacher Studies in Teacher Education" and Mor (1993) in "Continuing Education for Teachers in Teacher Education Colleges."

Kremer-Hayon's (1992) "Teachers' Professional Development—An Elaboration of the Concept" article is a theoretical elaboration of the concept of teachers' professional development, and Keiny (1994) reported on teachers' professional development and emphasized that the establishment of a collaborative framework between universities or colleges of education is a prerequisite for teachers' professional development or conceptual change.

Diversity and Equity Issues

As Israel is an immigration country, researchers turn their attention to issues of diversity and equity. An example of such work is the study of Weintraub (1993), which focused on the process of retraining immigrant teachers. The article discussed problems of prejudice and resentment, external demands, and pressures experienced by immigrant teachers.

Emerging Directions in Teacher Education

Guri-Rozenblit (1992) in "The Interactive Model of the Open University and Teacher Education Colleges in the Israeli Teacher Education System" analyzes an innovative teacher education model based on a program that integrates studies at the open University of Israel and colleges of teacher education.

Silberstein (1993) proposed a new approach for teacher education in curriculum development and reported on the development of curriculum modules reflecting this approach.

Gottlieb (1991) examined teacher education reform in Israel in "Global Rhetoric, Local Policy: Teacher Training Reform in Israeli Education." This research focused on educational reform documents analyzed by applying methods from poetics and intellectual history. The analysis demonstrated how global reform rhetoric has been used to negotiate a new construct somewhere between the "ideal model" of teacher professionalism imported from pace-setting countries and the local situation.

The field of studies of teacher education in Israel is dynamic and versatile; it reflects societal concerns about education and strives to facilitate the advancement of teacher education programs.

For further details on some of these studies and others, the reader is referred to Chapter 12 in Tischer and Wideen (1990).

JAMAICA

Harriott (1987) investigated institutional innovations in teacher training colleges in Jamaica, West Indies, in a doctoral dissertation completed at Fordham University.

JAPAN

Many problems were found in the elementary and secondary schools of Japan in the 1980s and were attributed to the lack of confidence among teachers. Thus, national advisory groups made improvement of the teacher force a main theme for educational reform in Japan. This concern led to a focus on research in teacher education that became one of the most noteworthy fields in education. Academic societies came together to hold symposia on reform of teacher education, and this theme was featured in their journals.

Recruitment, Selection, and Initial Preparation

Collins (1989) in "The Development of Teacher Education in Japan, 1868–1980s" examined the introduction of teacher education into Japan, the manner in which foreign, governmental, and industrial influences have affected the development of teacher education, and the nature of current educational reforms. The National Institute for Educational Research (1989) in *Teacher Training in Japan,* provided statistical information on the current status of teacher education in Japan. Data were given on the number of universities, junior colleges, and appointed teacher education institutions; number of graduates who obtained teacher certification; percentage distribution of teachers by educational attainment; minimum number of credits required for teacher certification (education-related subjects and kinds of certificates); major subject studies required for the lower secondary school teacher certificate; and minimum requirements for new teacher certificates, revised in 1989–1990. Teacher education reform is discussed briefly.

Yaosaka and Ushiwata (1988) administered a questionnaire to 499 college teachers of foundations courses and found that many college teachers wanted to stress fundamental and theoretical aspects rather than practical ones in preservice education. A similar study by Matsudaira (1982) found that beginning teachers considered their preservice education to be weak in practical knowledge and technique and also that a big gap exists between school teachers and college teachers regarding the role of preservice education. Maki et al. (1980) conducted a developmental study on foundations of education as a required subject for certification. They studied the content and methods used at the teacher preparation institutions through a survey of the staff that asked about the titles and credits of courses and the conditions for study. They also examined textbook content. They found a vagueness in the character of the foundations of education as a professional subject.

A very comprehensive study of student teaching was conducted by Fujieda, Maejima, and Shirai (1980) and Fujieda and Shirai (1981) in a "Study on the Improvement of Student Teaching (the Second and Third Interim Reports)." In this study 41 national and private universities and colleges were surveyed through a questionnaire. Case studies of six of the universities and colleges were followed by interviews. The researchers also surveyed primary and secondary schools attached to national universities and colleges, and finally they surveyed college student teacher candidates through questionnaires. A huge gap existed between universities and colleges and between primary and secondary schools regarding the significance and role of student teaching in preservice education.

Another area of interest in Japanese research is student attitudes. Akiyama (1981) surveyed student teachers' aspirations for teaching by using a questionnaire that the author gave before and after student teaching. Of those surveyed, 27% strengthened their aspiration for teaching as a result of their student teaching experience, and 20% weakened their aspiration for teaching because they became aware that they were inadequate for the teaching profession. Another study by Suzuki and others (1983), entitled "Effect of Student Teaching Practice on Personal Desire to Be a Teacher," conducted a similar survey with results comparable to those of Fujieda. Sato (1979) found a positive relationship between the grades given to student teachers and their level of education, empathy, and experience. A study by Inoue (1979) found a high correlation between student teachers' self-esteem and their student teaching experiences.

In 1982 Matsuo completed "A Study on Teachers: College Students' Consciousness About Becoming a Teacher." The author surveyed freshmen of Fukoka Teachers College five times during a 10-year period. During that time, the college students' aspiration for teaching grew. Among 18 different jobs, they ranked teaching, especially primary teaching, as the first vocational preference. Only half of those, however, thought that they were adequate to be teachers. Ito (1980) conducted a study that showed that students who had a high aspiration for teaching when they applied for admission had decided to become teachers when they were young. This decision remained and developed through preservice education, for he found that 91.9% of them wanted to become teachers when they graduated from college. Only 67.5% of those who had no aspiration for teaching when they applied for admission wanted to become teachers. A study by Hayashi (1986), *Students' Aspiration for the Teaching Profession: An Analytical Study of Students' Self-Evaluation of Their Teaching Aptitude,* also focused on the development of a professional orientation for teaching among college students. The results of his study showed a relationship between the students' aspirations for teaching, eligibility for teaching, leadership, and emotional stability.

Tsuchiya (1987), writing in "What Will Change With the Establishment of the System of Inservice Education for Beginning Teachers?" quoted the results of the investigation done by the Japan Senior High School Teachers Union. He pointed out that the freedom of thought and religion of applicants were violated through interviews during teacher selection. In another study (1981) he also found that in the qualifications for taking the examinations for teacher selection, there was discrimination against age and nationality. Maejima (1981) also cited problems of unfairness in teacher selection. The study, entitled "A Study on the Teacher Selection and Appointment System," showed that 21.6% of the teachers surveyed heard of or experienced unfair selections that were influenced by personal considerations or through a relative. Suzuki in 1986 studied selection and appointment of teachers and found that the proportion of women was higher than that of men when the number of examination applicants to the number hired was compared.

Examinations play a major role in Japanese education. Maejima (1987) in "The Problem of Selection of Teachers and Formation of Teacher Competencies" found that some lectures were a collection of questions from past examinations and became a textbook where students memorized a lot of words to pass the teacher selection examination instead of trying to understand and think deeply on the subject. Students' attitudes toward and interest in teacher selection were studied by Horiuchi and Mizumoto (1986) who administered a questionnaire to college students and found that 80% of the students began to prepare for examinations a half year in advance and one third prepared for 3 months. They found that almost all of the students surveyed crammed for the teacher selection examination using collections of questionnaires on the market. Their study showed that students did not find their college education helpful in preparing them for the examination.

Supervisors and principals were surveyed by Ueda and others (1987) who found that the supervisors and principals wanted diversified but accurate selection methods and that they wanted new teachers with natural dispositions for teaching, knowledge, and techniques that could work, as well as experienced teachers immediately after entry to teaching.

Continuing Professional Growth, Development, and Assessment

Since the 1970s research in the studies of in-service education has increased dramatically in Japan. "Systematization" of in-service education was proposed by the National Advisory Committee on Education. Kishimoto, Okatoo, Hayashi, and Koyama (1981) conducted "A Study of the Teachers' Professional Development Model (II): A Factor Analysis of Teaching Competencies" and identified the actual conditions related to the professional development of teachers and therefore established a professional growth and developmental model as the foundation of the systematization. They designed a questionnaire to obtain a score on a set of competency items, the degree of importance attributed to those items, and to identify the competency items that teachers felt they need to learn. They administered the questionnaire to 1,040 teachers and found that in 36 of 48 teacher competency items, teachers' age and length of experience played a central role in explaining the score patterns. Ojima (1982) administered a questionnaire to teachers who were in their twenties, thirties, and over 40, as well as to chiefs of the research and instruction departments and assistant principals and principals. The author asked about the content of in-service education provided. Findings showed that the routes of teacher development and the needs of in-service education were many and varied. A study by Haitani (1981) found that some administrative agencies enforced the systematization in-service education on teachers without any consideration of their needs of volunteerism. The problems of in-service education are further elaborated on by Ueda et al. (1987). These researchers surveyed administrative agencies and found that 71.6% of the school supervisors who prepared and provided in-service education to teachers thought it met with good results. However, only 28.6% of the teachers agreed. The findings are controversial, though, as noted in a study by Izuno, Yoshida, Enomoto, and Ueno (1981). They found that teachers differed among themselves regarding the type of school in-service they wanted. Teachers in their twenties and thirties liked informal,

spontaneous, and individual in-service education in the schools. Teachers in their forties and fifties liked formal, planned, and collaborative in-service in the schools. The Japanese way of life also enters into this controversy as described by a study by Amagasa (1981). Amagasa analyzed the elements of organization climate that promote the group-oriented behavior pattern; they found a combination of professional competitive and stable elements in the school and teaching professions.

Since the 1980s attention has been paid to in-service education for young teachers and new teachers. Studies by Ojima (1980) and Ojima, Nagai, and Amagasa (1981) attempted to clarify young teachers' awareness of their teaching ability, to identify the factors contributing to mature teaching, and to assess teachers' morale to participate in several kinds of in-service training. The studies demonstrated that one of the main factors used in helping young teachers grow was on-the-job training by their experienced colleagues during daily school life. Ojima (1983) further described the needs of first-year teachers. He found that young teachers need support from their colleagues because they are extremely unprepared for teaching and because of the poor independence of youth in Japanese society. Minamimoto (1986) found that in-service education in schools had an effect on young teachers because they modeled themselves after experienced teachers. But he also found that sizeable differences in conditions in each school influenced the upgrading of the qualification of young teachers.

For further details on some of these studies and others, the reader is referred to Chapter 3 in Tischer and Wideen (1990).

KOREA

Teacher Education as a Field of Study

Chianghan (1992) in "The Current Status and Future Directions of Teacher Education in Korea" studied the current status of teacher education in the areas of recruitment, curriculum, and quality.

Song (1983) studied the present status of the education of elementary school teachers in Korea and developed recommendations for alternative approaches in a doctoral dissertation completed at Vanderbilt University.

KUWAIT

Al-Jassar (1991) conducted a study of the perceived adequacy of teaching competencies included in an intermediate and secondary teacher preparation program in the College of Education at Kuwait University. This was a doctoral dissertation completed at the University of Pittsburgh.

LIBERIA

McDowell and Moulton (1990) wrote *Final Impact Evaluation of the PEP Pilot Radio Broadcasts in Liberia* (ISN 71580). The Liberian Primary Education Program is an instructional system adopted by the Ministry of Education as the national program for primary education in Liberia. It was designed to overcome a shortage of adequately trained primary school teachers, textbooks, and other educational materials. The purpose of the evaluation was to determine the programs' impact on the administrative performance of school principals and the teaching performance of second- and fifth-grade teachers. It was found that the radio programs alone (after removing the impact of inservice supervision visits) did indeed help to improve about one third of the skills that were measured. The results of the evaluation indicate that radio and supervision play an important role in improving the performance of those teachers and principals whose skills are not up to the standard of the group.

Kromer and Fanslow (1990) in *Liberian Primary Education Project (PEP): Final Report* (ISN 71578) provided a final contractor report on a project to assist Liberia's Ministry of Education in reforming its primary education system. Training was also provided to 2,010 teachers and principals in the use of the new materials and methods and to 214 supervisors.

Walety and Williams-Lamptez (1990) studied teacher training and a resource center for adult education in Liberia, including the curriculum and organization of the center in a doctoral dissertation completed at Columbia University.

LITHUANIA

Teacher Education Curriculum

Razma (1992) described a Lithuanian attempt to train a new generation of teachers free of Bolshevik constraints. The new teacher education curricula will be free of ideology and will emphasize contemporary teaching structures. It will be humanitarian and will make use of the history of the nation, its ethnic culture, traditions, and understandings.

MALAYSIA

Recruitment, Selection, and Initial Preparation

Lourdusamy and Ghani (1990) reported on 206 third-year students in the "Student Teachers' Personal Conception of Teaching." These students were enrolled in the bachelor of arts with education and the bachelor of science with education programs. Only two characteristics of teaching marked by the students were viewed negatively, enjoyment and creativity. These student teachers did not conceive of the activities of teaching as enjoyable or creative. More than 15% of the students also viewed teaching as static, conservative, conforming, passive, disorganized, and stereotyped in nature. A factor analysis also showed that the subjects viewed teaching from three different perspectives: (1) a noble and desirable social activity, (2) an altruistic activity, and (3) an activity that requires adaptability on the part of the teacher. Gender differences were found when the subgroup analysis was completed. Female student teachers saw teaching as a social activity that is respected, liked, and productive, successful, consistent, useful, and creative in nature, more so than the male student teachers. A significant difference existed between the male and female subjects on factor two, which related to the perspective of teaching as an altruistic activity. The female student teachers considered teaching as an activity requiring the teachers to be caring, encouraging, and systematic. When the academic program was considered, the humanities students viewed teaching as a respected profession, more so than the science student teachers.

Seng (1990) conducted a study of creative thinking abilities of 165 third- and fourth-year bachelor of science education degree students at the University of Malaysia. Using the Torrence Test of Creative Thinking, he found that the mean score for the group for originality was 63.12; for fluency the mean was 54.78; and in terms of raw scores, elaboration was the highest score and flexibility the lowest score. The correlations in analysis indicated that originality, fluency, and flexibility of these teachers were more closely related to each other than to elaboration. It appeared from the study that teachers who are more original are also more fluent in their thinking and more flexible. Results indicated that teachers who are able to exhibit elaboration may not necessarily be original, fluent, and flexible in their thinking. Chi-square analysis related to gender differences in creativity indicated that there were significantly more males among the more creative groups and more females among the less creative groups.

Teacher Education Curriculum

Concern for the preparation of teachers of chemistry led to a study by Loke (1990), *Perceptions of Chemistry Teacher Trainees and Teacher Educators Concerning a Training Programme for Malaysian Teachers in Chemistry With Particular Reference to Classroom Behavior*. The study evaluated the perceptions of former chemistry teacher trainees from the University of Malaysia concerning their professional preparation. Two hundred and eighty-six former chemistry teacher trainees and eight science teacher educators of the Faculty of Education, University of Malaysia, comprised the study. Two hundred and twenty-one were experienced teachers and 65 were inexperienced teachers. Thirty-six classroom behaviors were rated, and the respondents rated most of the groupings as highly desirable. The science education faculty members, however, had perceived most of these classroom behaviors as more desirable than the experienced chemistry teachers or the inexperienced chemistry teachers. All three groups perceived the teaching of metric system, measurement and calculations, and the maintenance of a safe and orderly laboratory environment as the most important classroom behaviors. They also believed they should serve as important models for students' attitude development in science. All of the respondents were skeptical in considering the community environment to be an extension of the science classroom and did not perceive it as a teaching or learning resource. Most of the respondents did not show much inclination to classroom behavior that required teachers to be proficient in transferring their knowledge of and practice in science research methods to efficient and effective pedagogical practices or to take an active participation in national curriculum development. The chemistry teachers considered the classroom behavior that required them to provide experiences that emphasized the interrelatedness of science technology and humanities as one of the least important, and the science education faculty perceived the demonstration of in-depth knowledge of concepts and processes in at least one science area as least desirable. The chemistry teachers favored most of the desired classroom behavior that required classroom field settings for evaluation. However, the science education faculty members showed higher desirability for classroom behaviors that were dependent on classroom settings. All three groups, however, agreed that a majority of the classroom behavior that did not require a classroom setting should be regarded as the least important. The study discusses in great detail the analysis of the various behavior responses.

Continuing Professional Growth, Development, and Assessment

Rahman et al. (1992) in "Teachers in Rural Schools: The "Extra" They Need" studied teachers and principals in a rural Malaysian district and found that teachers were satisfied, challenged, and committed but constrained by the lack of parental involvement, low motivation among pupils, inadequate residential facilities, and poor teaching aids. They perceived their teaching preparation as generally adequate but indicated that more needs to be done in the areas of rural preservice teaching practice and to produce instructional materials for rural areas.

MEXICO

Continuing Professional Growth, Development, and Assessment

Magallanes et al. (1992) in "Training for Research and Development of Teaching" described the achievements of a program designed to create research abilities in kindergarten and primary school teachers.

NAMIBIA

Continuing Professional Growth, Development, and Assessment

The relationship between teacher competence and learner progress was the focus of a 1993 study by Mkandawire and Marira. The subject of "The Evaluation of Teacher Professional Competencies in Former Non-white Namibian Schools" has attracted widespread attention in Namibia, especially after independence, because it has been suggested that teachers, particularly in former black schools, are ineffective and encourage rote learning and little thinking. The national examination low pass rates continue to be an area of great concern. With the examination reforms currently under way in the country, in which continuous assessment will play a major role in evaluation, concern has been raised regarding teacher competence in assessing students. The study discussed the integration of theory and practice by teachers in former nonwhite schools and the impact this has on the evaluation of their professional competencies in teaching and assessing of their students.

NEPAL

In 1990 the Academy for Educational Development prepared a final report on radio education teacher training in Nepal. This report is available from the U.S. Agency for International Development (ISN 72905).

NETHERLANDS

Teaching Education as a Field of Study

Coonen (1987) studied teacher educators in training institutes for primary education. Expert teacher educators were interviewed, and a questionnaire survey was conducted (Likert-type scale) among a representative sample of 489 lecturers in the training institutes for primary education. The overall conclusion was that the institutes for primary education were facing very serious problems in such a way that the conditions for innovations were highly unfavorable.

De Frankrijker and Kieviet (1991) in "Examining the Research on Practice Teaching in Teacher Education: A Review Especially Focused on the Persons Involved," analyzed scientific Dutch and international journals on research findings of empirical research on individuals involved in the school practicum. They concluded that the diversity of the selected studies is most striking. Partly because of this diversity theory on the potential role of teaching practice is poor.

Kieviet (1984) surveyed specific research themes in the field of teacher education in the Netherlands and abroad and found a need for a framework for programming the research in this field.

Tillema (1988) in "Coping With New Challenges in Teacher Education" used a survey study and questionnaire for teachers in primary education. Teachers felt most competent in the areas closest to their daily classroom activity and least competent in subject-matter presentation and diagnosis. Competencies required outside the classroom are less valued by teachers and cause uncertainty in their professional status.

Recruitment, Selection, and Initial Preparation

Olgers and Risenkamp (1980) concluded that teachers in training institutes favored a sound theoretical and educational basis for the teaching profession, whereas the teaching in secondary education tended more to the practical needs in everyday teaching. Students tended toward theoretical, educational aspects of the profession.

Aziv (1993) in *Integrating Knowledge and Beliefs: Stimulating Learning to Teach in Student Teachers,* concluded that there are a number of promising approaches to teacher preparation that help student teachers in making sense of their practice teaching experiences, and these approaches are worthwhile and effective in bringing about lasting changes in the student teacher's cognitive repertoire and beliefs about teaching.

Borgmans (1991) researched arguments for enrollment of students in teacher education with a special emphasis on developments in the labor market for teachers in primary education, which is fluctuating heavily. Attention was paid to various elements in the demand for teachers and to how such fluctuations could be lessened.

De Frankrijker (1990) in "The Training of Primary Education Teachers in the Netherlands: Discrepancies Between Supply and Demand, 1920–1990" analyzed statistics and state reports to conclude that in the Netherlands there have been alternating periods of teacher shortages and oversupply. The Dutch government adopts primarily reactive policies in response to changing demographic factors, economic recessions, and internal educational processes.

Tillema and Veenman (1985) in *Problem Survey of Teacher Training* and Tillema (1986) in *Teacher Training at University* concluded that the following problems existed with training: relations between teacher training institutes and the external environment; the input and output of teacher training; the quality of teacher education; student practice teaching; and in-service education.

Veenman (1990) reviewed the Dutch literature on the recruitment, selection, and training of school leaders. School leaders are recruited from the ranks of teachers. In most appointment procedures the roles of the selectors have not been prescribed in advance. Women are underrepresented in principalships. The professional development of those wishing to become school leaders is ad hoc, and no formal certification is required. The mainstream of management programs for the principalship is carried out in in-service programs (with non–award-bearing certificates).

Contextual Influences on Teacher Education

Borger and Tillema (1993) in "Transferring Knowledge to Classroom Teaching: Putting Knowledge Into Action" used a field experiment in which the utilization of acquired knowledge was tested in teaching practice situations. Two methods of presenting educational knowledge to student teachers were tested, according to an embedding and an immersion approach. The model that stresses active, metacognitive involvement with materials produced better results in the transfer of knowledge to practice situations.

Teacher Education Curriculum

Oddens (1992) in "Professionalization, Status, and Career: Results of 10 Year Integrated Teacher Training for Technical Subjects" surveyed 335 graduates of a teacher training program for teachers of technical subjects. The author concluded that only 32% of the groups were employed in schools and that industry offered strong incentive to the graduates.

Boschhuizen and Brinkman (1991) developed "A Proposal for a Teaching Strategy Based on Pre-instructional Ideas of Pupils. Environmental Education: The Use of Pupils' Ideas About Cycles of Nature and Health." Much research has been done on pupils' ideas, but little has been done on strategies that make use of these ideas in teaching, especially in biology education. Moreover little research, up until now, concentrates on concepts regarding environmental education. For environmental education the concepts of "cycles" and "health" are

important. In this paper pupils' ideas on these concepts were assessed and represented, and common pupil ideas between the two concepts are discussed. A teaching strategy based on pupils' ideas was elaborated.

Koetsier, Wubbels, and Driel (1992) in "An Investigation Into Careful Supervision of Student Teaching" compared the results of the Independent Final Teaching Period (IFTP), which had to do with carefully supervised student teaching with a selection of recent authoritative English-language studies considered representative of the existing scientific body of knowledge on the preparation of teachers. The comparison with the literature produced a number of conditions for carefully supervised student teaching. In some cases the results of the IFTP project served to refine descriptions in the literature, and in other cases the results built on the literature to produce more specific strategies for implementing those conditions.

Korthagen (1992) in "Techniques for Stimulating Reflection in Teacher Education Seminars" described four techniques (wall, columns, repertory grid, and arrows) that can be used in seminars to stimulate student teachers to reflect on their teaching practice and to promote cognitive change and investigated effects of the techniques in a group of 18 student teachers at a Dutch university. Favorable effects were demonstrated, although cognitions of prospective teachers about educational goals seem to be resistant to change. The process of restructuring cognition was promoted by students' reflecting on the relationships in teaching.

Lang (1990) in "Does Psychology Contribute Anything to Education?" discussed the importance of psychology in training and supporting teachers and provides reasons for the decline in interest in psychology among educators. Psychological knowledge and research are of vital importance for teachers in helping them to deal with their students. The author maintained that psychologists have concentrated too heavily on theoretical research and have neglected practical application of their knowledge to specific teaching situations.

Out (1986) in *Problem Oriented Teacher Training* studied primary education student teachers and teacher educators in a preservice program and evaluated eight different groups of students at three training institutes during 3 years using nine modules, in which the problem-oriented strategy had been elaborated. A variety of observation instruments were used. Generally speaking, the strategy strengthened the relation between the achievement of the objectives by the student and the completion of the student activities.

Roelofs, Raemaekers, and Veenman (1991), in "Improving Instructional and Classroom Management Skills: Effects of a Staff Development Program and Coaching" considered the effects of a staff development program conducted by teacher trainers and school counselors for teachers in mixed-age classes. They found a significant treatment effect for pupils' time-on-task levels in mixed-age classrooms of trained teachers and for teachers' instructional and classroom management skills. On two aspects of instructional and classroom management skills, larger gains were found for coached teachers: organizing effective instruction, and dealing with disturbances. Time-on-task levels improved more strongly in classes of coached teachers.

Tillema, De Jong, and Mathijssen (1990) used a field experiment with experienced teachers to conclude that providing clear and essential concepts that are fundamental to skill acquisition enhances knowledge acquisition and to a lesser degree performance as compared with a training model that stresses practice alone.

Vedder (1984) in *Teaching Profession, an Orientation* and Vedder and Bannick (1988) in *The Development of Practical Skills and Reflection at the Beginning Teacher Training* evaluated "one-to-one" lessons and noted that the method contributed especially to contacts the teacher-to-be made with pupils and subject matter to be taught.

Korthagen (1982) described how secondary math education students used reflective teaching. The students set goals and used self-improvement techniques. The phases included action, looking back on the action, awareness of essential aspects, and creating alternative methods of action. Some students preferred external steering to reflection. In "The influence of learning orientations on the development of reflective teaching" (1988), he continued to investigate whether persons are directed by internal or external orientations, and he expanded upon Korthagen and Verkuyl's *Supply and Demand: Learning Conceptions and Their Importance for Teacher Education Programs* (1987) and concluded that no difference in the preference for learning by means of reflection can be found. In 1988 Korthagen and Wubbels studied training for reflection to determine readiness for innovation and job satisfaction. No differences were found in the disposition to reflect, but reflective preservice teachers seemed to have more positive self-images.

Veenman, Leenders, Meyer, and Sanders (1993) considered the effects of a preservice training course on effective instruction. They used a quasi-experimental, treatment-control group investigation, to study classroom observation of student teachers' teaching behaviors regarding effective instruction and student engagement rates. Ratings from supervising teachers showed that trained student teachers used the recommended instructional skills after completion of the course significantly better than prior to the course.

Verloop (1989) in *Interactive Cognition of Student Teachers: An Intervention Study* studied student teachers for primary and secondary education in a preservice program. The methodology included a comparison of three experimental groups: One group studied the educational theory and worked through the treatment videotape; one group only studied the educational theory verbally, and one group followed the normal program. The major instruments included stimulated recall and specially developed observation instruments. The superior value of the video treatment with regard to the number of interactive cognitions as well as the number of interactive behaviors was confirmed. Moreover, with the video group not only was the theory more fully employed but also this employment was steered more by relevant cognition.

Wubbels, Crèton, and Hermans (1993) asked what lessons from research on teacher communication styles can be useful in teacher education. They reviewed studies on teacher–student communication with the Leary Model and concluded that preservice teacher education student teachers should be trained to show dominant behavior. In in-service education cooperative behavior should be the focus of attention. Cognitive and behavioral approaches should be used to develop an adequate behavioral repertoire for teachers.

Continuing Professional Growth, Development, and Assessment

Brandsma and De Jong (1991) reported on research into the efficacy of practice-oriented in-service courses for teachers in vocational training. The emphasis was on the extent to which the course led to changes in the daily practice of teachers.

Brekelmans and Crèton (1993) in "Interpersonal Teacher Behavior Through the Career" combined cross-sectional, longitudinal, and case-study design and used QUIT (questionnaire on interpersonal teacher behavior) and open-ended interviews. Data were gathered about perceptions of both students and teachers on the actual behavior of teachers and about the way teachers themselves perceive the changes during their career. According to both teachers themselves and their students, changes were mainly found in dominant behavior, which intensifies toward the teacher ideal during the first 10 years of the career. After this point dominance stabilizes. Cooperative behavior, however, basically remained consistent throughout the entire teaching career, and there is no shift toward the teacher ideal.

Bruining and Van Der Vegt (1987) described the considerations in the design and final construction of an in-service course for school directors of kindergarten and primary schoolsl (who were merging at that time) in the Netherlands. The course was based on theories on innovation and management of change processes and had to support the merging of the two school kinds into the "basic school."

Casismir (1988) described the in-service training within their framework of the NIVO project (new information technology in secondary education). Target groups, teachers of the course, approaches, results, and problems of the project are described.

Corporaal (1991) in "Repertory Grid Research Into the Cognition of Prospective Primary School Teachers" studied student teachers in primary education using a repertory grid interview with 117 first- and third-year students from 12 different teacher training institutes. From the data four main dimensions of respondents' cognition could be distinguished: (1) businesslike versus personal and social, (2) teaching situation versus matters surrounding the teaching situation, (3) ends versus means and (4) individual versus group.

Corporaal, Boei, and Kieviet (1993) studied student teachers in primary education by conducting an in-depth study using a longitudinal research design. The number of concepts at the disposal of the student teachers increased significantly during the first year. Significant changes also appeared in the way student teachers related the concepts to each other.

Creemers (1986) reviewed the current situation with regard to the relation between educational reform, educational research, and in-service training of teachers in the Netherlands. The author concluded that the three have gone their own ways and have made little use of the others' questions and research outcomes.

Crèton and Wubbels (1984) in *Problems of Classroom Discipline With Beginning Teachers* considered a study of possibilities to find a solution for these problems through guidance.

Crèton, Wubbels, and Hooymayers (1989) in "Escalated Disorderly Situations in the Classroom and the Improvement of

These Situations" used case study observations, interviews with teachers, students, and school mentors, and an action research component in counseling the beginning teacher to study the effect of the student's or the teacher's first mother tongue in secondary education.

De Jong, Matthijssen, and Tillema (1988) in *The Effects of Training and Coaching of Teachers* investigated the effects of different proportions of time spent on explanation and practice. Coaching by a tutor appeared to strengthen student teachers' knowledge level.

De Jong, Matthijssen, and Tillema (1987) in "Characteristics of Inservice Training Course" concluded that a significant difference exists between what is known about effective training components and what is offered in in-service courses.

The recent interest and need for teacher professional development calls for the clarification of the concept of professional development. In 1991, Kremer-Hayon published *Teacher professional development—The elaboration of a concept*. The study focuses on the analysis of concepts of development, in general, and of teacher developmental stages, in particular, of professions and of professional knowledge as the basis for a systematic composition of the concept of professional development. This systematic attempt calls for the juxtaposition of these two concepts—profession and development—and for an integration of the relationships among them. This may be obtained, the authors suggest, with the aid of a mapping sequence (Gutman, 1954) that hosts five facets. Each facet consists of its constituent elements. Mapping sentences are derived from theoretical rationales and provide conceptual frameworks from which paradigms and hypotheses may be derived. In view of the varying conceptions mentioned in the study with regard to development and profession, the authors disclose the way in which these conceptions co-exist and whether any concept structure may be detected. The authors suggest that a mapping sentence provides a conceptual framework for this purpose.

Professional development may be viewed:

Facet A
   with perception of development according to the model of
• stability
• ordered change
• flexibility

Facet B
   at a stage of
• preservice sand induction
• competency building
• growth and enthusiasm
• career wind down and exit

Facet C
   with a view of teaching as
• bureaucratic
• autonomous

Facet D
   with a perception of profession as
• monolithic
• pluralistic

Facet E
   and of knowledge as
• practical rationality
• epistemology of practice

Practically, the study may guide teacher developers in planning various programs to suit varying conceptions of professional development.

Korthagen (1993) in "The Role of Reflection in Teachers' Professional Development" compared the effects of two different programs on the developmental processes in student teachers. The major instruments included interviews, the IEO test (internal/external learning orientation), and the QTI (questionnaire on teacher interaction). The author concluded that the program has positive effects on reflectivity but that a mismatch between program approach and the learning orientation of less reflective student teachers occurs. Graduates of a program aiming at the promotion of reflection show better interpersonal behavior, a more adequate self-image, and more job satisfaction. These effects were stronger more than 2 years after graduation.

Tillema and Veenman (1987) used conceptual analysis of recent training studies in teacher education and concluded that a cognitive orientation to training has provided the profession with different criteria and solutions for studying teacher's acquisition of competence.

Tillema (1992) in "Supporting Teaching—Effects of Delivery Factors in Teacher Support Programs" used causal modeling to study teachers in primary education. Usability, quality of products, and dissemination strategy are factors with the largest impact on teacher's conceptual and actual use of products.

Van Tulder, Roelofs, Veenman, and Voeten (1992) studied the extent to which various types of supplementary training for teachers actually influenced the classroom activities of teachers.

Van Tulder, Veenman, and Sieben (1988) in "Features of Effective In-service Activities: Results of a Delphi-Study," convened a panel of Dutch experts in the field of in-service education. After reviewing studies on effective in-service education and educational implementation, a list of statements of effective in-service characteristics was reviewed in three rounds by experts using a modified Delphi technique. The Delphi study resulted in a list of 34 statements that reflect appropriate and important features of effective in-service teacher education.

Van Tulder and Veenman (1991) in "Characteristics of Effective Inservice Programs and Activities: Results of a Dutch Survey" carried out a survey among teachers, principals, teacher educators, and school counselors. In spite of extensive criticism about the value of in-service education, most participants were positive about the design and execution of the activities. However, in-service education has been closely watched for effectiveness, especially where it concerns applicability and functionality, which are generally judged to be insufficient.

Van Tulder, Van Der Vegt, and Veenman (1993) in "Inservice Education in Innovating Schools: A Multi-Case Study" used techniques of informal and structured interviewing, incidental nonparticipant observation, and document review to gather data. In the complex process of realizing change by means of a basically well-designed in-service education program, great demands are made on the schools. In the implementation process three factors appeared to be crucial: the instrumental capacity of the school, the structuring of the school organization for implementation, and the steering and coordination of the process by the school leader.

Vonk (1984) used the case study approach to produce a comparison of 21 qualitative in-depth case studies of first-year students. Vonk elaborated on the problems beginning teachers face during induction and on coping strategies.

Vonk and Schras (1987) in "From Beginning to Experienced Teacher: A Study of the Professional Development of Teachers During Their First Four Years of Service" used semi-structured retrospective interviews of 20 teachers during their second to fifth year of teaching and provided analysis of the characteristics of teachers' professional development during that period.

Vonk (1993b) in "Teacher Induction: The Great Omission in Education" produced a qualitative, in-depth study of first-year teachers and overviewed the outcomes of a long-term study of the professional development of beginning teachers.

Vonk (1993a) in *The Knowledge Base for Mentors of Beginning Teachers* studied mentors of beginning teachers and proposed a theoretical scheme for mentoring beginning teachers and an overview of mentor knowledge and skills.

Wubbels and Korthagen (1990) in "The Effects of a Preservice Teacher Education Program for the Preparation of Reflective Teachers" asked student teachers in secondary mathematics education whether a reflective teacher education program works. He concluded that graduates from the reflective teacher education program show better interpersonal relationships with students, feel more job satisfaction, and have more adequate self-perception, especially after 3 or more years after graduation.

Wubbels, Brekelmans, and Crèton (1993) in "Interpersonal Teacher Behavior, Changes and Improvements" combined a cross-sectional and longitudinal design and used QUIT to study perceptions of students, perceptions of teachers of their own behavior, and teachers' perceptions of ideal behavior. In the first 4 years of a teaching career there is a dramatic increase in leadership behavior. At some moment between 5 years and 10 years of experience, relations with students become more conducive to attaining high outcomes, both cognitive and affective. Afterward there is a slow deterioration of cooperative behavior.

Diversity and Equity Issues

De Frankrijker (1993) in "Multicultural Education at Teacher Training Institutes for Primary Education in the Netherlands" conducted a literature review concerning multicultural activities in Dutch teacher training institutes compared with findings of a telephone survey of 57 representatives of teacher training colleges and related data to general findings in other Western countries. He concluded that most teacher training colleges in Western countries have made little progress in preparing their students for teaching in a multicultural and multiethnic society.

De Frankrijker and Lie (1993) in *Expert Beliefs About Teacher Training in Multicultural Perspective: The Multicultural Competent Teacher in the Netherlands* used a Delphi study of two rounds to value 25 items on a scale of 5. Box plots were used to inform the panel experts on average and personal scores of Delphi round I. The panel as a whole did agree about most of the issues: the more important the item, the higher the consen-

sus. Items concerning attitudes and skills were perceived as more important than knowledge of items. Competencies referring to a flexible and open mind, positive attitudes toward mother tongue language and culture, sensitiveness to acts of racism and discrimination were judged as most important.

De Frankrijker and De Wit (1993) in "Teaching Practice and the Preparation of Primary Schoolteachers for a Multicultural Society" assembled a Delphi research panel of 48 educational experts who were questioned about the desired and realized role of teaching practice in a multicultural perspective. The study concluded that compulsory teaching practice in general and in Dutch as a second language has been considered as very important to the preparation of teachers for cultural and ethnic diversity.

Emerging Directions in Teacher Education

In teacher training it is necessary to take into account the practical knowledge student teachers have about teaching. In 1993 Buitink in "Research on Teacher Thinking and Implications for Teacher Training" concluded that student teachers should have the opportunity of integrating theories that are being taught with their own practical knowledge. This can only happen if the student teacher recognizes the theories as being relevant to teaching practice. To facilitate and to stimulate such an integration process, teacher trainers need to have insight in the content and the development of the practical knowledge of teaching.

Veenman (1987) in "Teacher for Tomorrow and the Day After Tomorrow" compared U.S. reports on teacher education: *Tomorrow's Teachers* from The Holmes Group (1986) and *A Nation Prepared: Teachers for the 21st Century* from the Carnegie Task Force on Teaching as a Profession (1986). The relevance of the findings for the Dutch situation is discussed in relation to Dutch plans for educational reform and teacher education.

Wubbels (1986) in "Research at and Into the Training of Teachers" reported a sketch of perspectives for further research based on results of recent research of education and teacher education with an emphasis on fundamental research. Wubbels made a plea for research into preferences of teachers in teaching; the relation between reflectivity and routine in teaching behavior; specific aspects of various school subjects in the teaching and learning process; learning processes in adults; and training programs and their outcomes.

Wubbels (1992) studied teacher education and the universities in the Netherlands. This case study outlines the relation between the Dutch universities and teacher education in a historical context and introduced the various types of primary and secondary education in the Netherlands along with the teacher education for these school types. Also mentioned were some characteristics of universities and higher vocational institutes. Important issues in the changing relationship between universities and teacher preparation are reviewed briefly.

For further details on some of these studies and others, the reader is referred to Chapter 4 in Tischer and Widden (1990).

NEW ZEALAND

Teacher Education as a Field of Study

Clift (1983a, 1983b) completed two studies investigating the institutional evaluations and reviews carried out in New Zealand colleges of teacher education between 1978 and 1983. Four review exercises were described and comment is made on the influence of the process on college programs and college faculty. The material was gathered by interview, questionnaire, and documentation. Each case study concluded with a list of specific suggestions as to how the impact of the evaluations could have been enhanced.

Recruitment, Selection, and Initial Preparation

Davies (1991) and Nicholl (1992) in *The Selection and Recruitment of Teacher Trainees* published annual reports that analyzed national teacher recruitment policies and their application in colleges of education and universities. They provided a statistical breakdown of applicants for teacher education in terms of age, gender, education, and ethnicity.

Teacher Education Curriculum

A nationwide research project aimed at ascertaining the policies, practices, and problems of in-school training of student teachers in New Zealand colleges of teacher education was undertaken by Battersby and Ramsay (1988). The research design consisted of case studies of two colleges and a general review of in-school training policies at another three. The final report pointed out marked similarities among institutions in terms of official policies on school-based experiences, most undertaken in series of blocked sections. There was a variety of ways of organizing these blocks. All institutions required teaching faculty to supervise students placed in schools. Students were required to cover all primary school curriculum areas and to take responsibility for periods of full classroom control and management. The final report commented on the need for national links and liaison between colleges of teacher education and the advantages of common policies and procedures. The researchers argued that the gap between theory and practice is not really met under the present system. They advocated more training for placement teachers and for supervising staff. They pointed out the difficulty of precise assessment of student teacher practica. The final report argued for a collaborative teacher education program involving students, colleges of education faculty, and tutor teachers. The program should be individualized as much as possible. Ideally, the present programs need to be expanded to become 6-year programs with teacher education courses following the attainment of a liberal bachelors degree.

Harding (1991) studied the career intentions of a group of students enrolled at the Palmerston North College of Teacher Education. Many students expressed dissatisfaction with their student teaching experience in child care centers and ranked kindergartens more highly. A small majority indicated that they would only work in kindergartens after graduating.

Renwick (1990) undertook a longitudinal study of graduate student teachers preparing to teach in New Zealand primary and intermediate schools between 1988 and 1992. The author considered the attitudes and perceptions of students from these institutions at their time of selection for teacher education and in each subsequent year of their study program. Initial data were obtained through postal questionnaires; later material was obtained from interviews and student records. The research concluded

that colleges need to recognize prior experiences and to emphasize the practical components of teacher education.

Crabtree (1990) outlined the policies and procedures used to develop a new early childhood education curriculum at a college of education. The curriculum was designed to provide an active commitment to nondiscriminatory attitudes and practices and to use an andrological approach to teaching based on pragmatic, developmental views of education.

Jarchow (1992) analyzed the use of case studies in New Zealand's teacher education curriculum and suggested that sociologists and teacher educators should collaborate on the writing and analysis of cases, teacher educators should extend the range of analytical methods used in the discussion of cases, and case authors should strive for validity checks on the cases that they write. Massey (1989) outlined problems associated with teaching practice procedures in New Zealand and discussed the nature of an effective teaching practice curriculum.

O'Brien (1991) reported that New Zealand's Hutt Valley outpost experimental teacher training model was established in 1969 on a local high school campus following problems recruiting secondary teacher trainees. By offering local training, researchers found that students more often sought local positions when they graduated.

Renwick (1983) emphasized the need for colleges of teacher education in New Zealand to respond to changes caused by recent curriculum and administrative developments in New Zealand education. These changes include increased autonomy for colleges of education, responsibility for teacher support services, closer affiliation with universities, and revisions and changes in the content of teacher education programs. Examples were drawn from the six colleges of education in New Zealand.

Diversity and Equity Issues

Irwin (1991) published a critical analysis of Maori education that outlines changes in policy and administration and considers teacher education as it applies to Maori students and schooling. The author provided samples of current programs offered in national teacher education programs.

Renwick (1989) in *Some Student Views on Equity Issues* surveyed the attitudes of student teachers to gender equity and ethnic issues.

Harrison (1986) described programs for training teachers for cross-cultural classrooms in Alaska and compared these with similar programs operating for Maori students in New Zealand.

Cazden (1990) in "Differential Treatment in New Zealand: Reflections on Research in Minority Education" discussed the treatment of Maori children in the first year of school, the research documenting this problem, and an attempted in-service intervention with New Zealand junior class teachers. Two successful school models were noted, and the complex issues in minority education were considered.

Emerging Directions in Teacher Education

Harvey and Green (1984) in *Attitudes of New Zealand Teachers, Teachers in Training and Non-Teachers Toward Mainstreaming* surveyed students in their first and final years of elementary school teacher education at Wellington College of Teacher Education, students in the first and second year of early childhood education at the same institution, and a random sample of elementary school teachers in the Wellington district. All took a 40-item survey. The survey asked respondents about their experiences in special education and with children with special abilities. The variable that showed the strongest association to mainstreaming was whether or not respondents had completed a teacher education program in special education.

MacAlpine (1993) in "Some Contemporary Issues in the Education of Children With Special Abilities" noted that recent changes to New Zealand curricula and school administration procedures have influenced education of the gifted in New Zealand schools. The author argued that attitudes toward children with special abilities are directly related to teaching experience. The period of initial teacher education is an important part of this process. This survey of New Zealand student teachers assessed their attitudes about "seven myths" regarding education of the gifted and determined how well they considered their teacher education program had prepared them to teach children with special needs.

Renwick (1985) in *Student Teachers and Parents* surveyed 364 student teachers and asked students their opinion of the role of parents in junior elementary school and kindergarten classrooms and the extent to which their program of teacher education had helped them to relate to parents in this situation. One hundred of the students were interviewed again 1 year after their graduation.

NIGERIA

Recruitment, Selection, and Initial Preparation

Akpe (1987) evaluated an elementary teacher program in Nigeria to determine the degree of congruence among the perceptions of major groups involved in the teacher training program at Rivers State College of Education, Nigeria. The subjects were 21 program lecturers, 106 students, 162 graduates, and 51 employers. Some of the major findings were: (1) The respondents agreed that the program was achieving its objectives, (2) all interest groups agreed that the program provided a sufficient foundation for advancement in elementary education, (3) the respondents agreed that previous teaching experience should be included as a compulsory admission requirement, (4) the respondents agreed that graduates were qualified to teach and supervise instruction in the elementary school, and (5) all interest groups agreed that it was premature for students to select teaching subjects at the end of the first year in the education program. However, there were some disagreements among the respondents in certain areas, such as the program graduates' competence to teach in school, the qualities of the graduates, and the public image of the program.

Akpe (1991) examined factors influencing the choice of teaching subjects in preservice teacher education in Nigeria for 119 final-year students in an elementary teacher education program of a college of education. The subjects wrote biodata composed of their educational background, choice of subject combination, and reasons for such choices. The results revealed that there was an imbalance of choice in teaching subjects. The language arts/social studies were favored by both males and females. A high number of students with previous training and background selected a science and mathematics combination, a number greater than that of those students with only a secondary school background. Important factors influencing students' choice of subjects was their level of performance during the first 2 years in the college of education, opportunities for further education, and finding jobs.

Onocha and Okpala (1987) investigated reasoning ability and the relationship between reasoning ability, gender, and age of student teachers in an elementary education program in Nigeria. The Test of Logical Thinking was used to assess students' formal reasoning. The results revealed that 52% of the prospective teachers were able to use reasoning ability to solve problems presented in the test. However, 72% were unable to give correct answers and justification for the probability reasoning mode. Eighty-eight percent provided correct answers for the correlational reasoning mode, and 72% were able to utilize combinational reasoning to solve problems in the reasoning test. The data in general indicated that preservice teachers had limitations in formal reasoning ability. The authors suggested that there was a need to include a course on science teaching and the development of reasoning in teacher training programs in Nigeria. It was hoped that the course would promote the development of formal reasoning ability in preservice teachers in the education programs.

Akpe (1988) conducted a study "Using Consumer Evaluation to Improve College Curricula in Nigerian Teacher Training." He examined 114 Nigerian students' impression of the bachelor's of education program in a college of education during the academic year 1985–1986. Some of the questionnaire's findings revealed that female students were more satisfied with the program than males. Students with a teaching experience background were more satisfied than those who had never taught before entering into the program. Students for whom education was their first choice when applying for college entrance were more pleased with the program than those for whom education was their second or third choice. The students considered methodology courses most useful for their future teaching careers. Sociology of education, history of education, and philosphy of education were considered least useful for students' future careers. The data analysis revealed students' dissatisfaction with the general organization of the bachelor of education program, the poor facilities, and staffing for carrying out the program.

Continuing Professional Growth, Development, and Assessment

A study entitled "Problems of Universalizing Access and Promoting Equity in Primary Education for the Rural Dwellers of Ondo State: Challenges of Teacher Education in Rural Areas" by Adelabu (1991) has some relevance for teacher education. This study surveyed 220 teachers in Ondo State in Nigeria and found that 71.4% of the teachers were from the same local environment, thus maintaining a local perception of students' habits and attitudes; 87.3% of the teachers confirmed that the teaching learning facilities of their schools were not satisfactory and therefore inadequate; 87.33% reported poor job satisfaction; 82.7% of the respondents indicated that their social status as villager rural teachers was not satisfactory; and 88.3% of the teachers were not satisfied with prospects for in-service training or staff development. The nature of the rural area in which they teach was the basic reason for frequent demands for transfer, resignation, dropout, and teacher absenteeism in the schools. Teachers miss pipe-borne water, electricity, good roads, health facilities, post offices, good secondary schools for their own children, good accommodations, telephones, and recreation centers. Of the respondents in this survey, 83.6% indicated that their preparation was not relevant to the needs of the rural dwellers. They therefore found it difficult to cope with the rural situations they faced and could not adapt their training to these situations.

Adejumo and Alao in "Effectiveness of Teacher Preparation Programmes in Nigerian Universities: Universities and Secondary School Teachers' Perspectives" (1991) studied sampled graduates of teacher preparation programs as well as university teacher educators of teacher preparation programs. Both groups agreed that preparation for recordkeeping was ineffective. Forty-two percent of the teacher graduates indicated that the teaching of recordkeeping was barely adequate to inadequate. Of the teacher education faculty, 50% indicated that their faculty's record in school recordkeeping was barely adequate or inadequate. A second area that was rated low in the effectiveness of teacher preparation was school administration. About 24% of the graduates of the teacher programs found their preparation barely adequate or inadequate, and 40% of the university teacher educators found the preparation barely adequate. Much higher ratings were given by both groups for instructional techniques, foundations of education, school interpersonal relations, and subject specialization. The study found no significant variations in the ratings of the graduate teachers from the different universities, which indicates that teacher training programs in Nigerian universities are fairly comparable in terms of how former students rate them.

Orby and Onvbogu (1993) researched alternative teacher certification routes in Nigeria in a doctoral dissertation study completed at the University of Toledo.

PAKISTAN

Ahmad (1990) compiled *Comparative Study of the Effects of P.T.C. (Primary Teaching Certificate) Training by A.I.O.U. (Allama Iqbal Open University) Teacher Training Colleges and School (i.e., Schools) on Teaching Styles and Student Achievement in Science and Mathematics in Primary Schools in Pakistan* (ISN 72693).

Farooq (1988) in *Training of Primary School Teachers in Pakistan: Different Models* (ISN 64770) described current teacher training models and presented the background for upcoming research on instructional practices in Pakistani primary schools that will be conducted collaboratively by the Academy of Education Planning and Management, Islamabad, and BRIDGES (Basic Research and Implementation in Developing Education Systems). At present there are three major types of preservice training offered the aspiring teacher: (1) the Traditional Teacher Training Program, (2) the Field-Based Teacher

Training Program, and (3) the Distance Teacher Training Program; and four kinds of inservice training: (1) the Educational Extension Centers' Programs, (2) the R.T.C. Program, (3) the P.T.O.C. Program of Allama Iqba Open University, and (4) the Learning Modules Training of the P.N.E. wing of the ministry of education. Together these programs prepare the teacher for beginning and continuing service in the wide variety of primary schools existing in Pakistan today.

Qaisrani (1990) published *Effect of Teacher Level and Quality of Formal Schooling and Professional Training on Students' Achievement in Primary Schools in Pakistan* (ISN 72697).

Qureshi (1990) wrote *Impact of Preservice Teacher Training on Classroom Practices in Primary Schools of Pakistan* (ISN 72698).

POLAND

Continuing Professional Growth, Development, and Assessment

Potulicka (1988) examined the elements and functions of Poland's Radio and Television University for Teachers (NURT), a didactic research unit of the Institute of Teacher Training, in relation to in-service teacher education. Efforts to modify the NURT teaching system were discussed along with teachers' assessments of NURT's methods.

SAUDI ARABIA

Recruitment, Selection, and Initial Preparation

Sharpes (1986) examined the United Nations Educational, Scientific, and Cultural Organization (UNESCO) data in "Teacher Training and Higher Education in Selected Islamic Countries." He reported that there was a high percentage of teacher education students in Saudi Arabia compared with other Islamic countries—namely, Algeria, Bangladesh, Indonesia, Lebanon, Libya, Malaysia, Morocco, and Pakistan. Even though the enrollment of teacher education in Saudi Arabia was high, it was insufficient to service the expanding school enrollment of the country. Schools in Saudi Arabia had to import large numbers of teachers to teach all subjects. In secondary schools in the late 1970s there were no Saudi teachers in teacher training colleges in Arabic, English, math, or science. In 1980 there were about 8,000 intermediate and secondary school teachers, of which only 10% were Saudi graduates. The number indicated the low production of teacher graduates in Saudi Arabia, which was not enough to maintain expanding school growth.

SCOTLAND

Research on teacher education issues in Scotland covers a wide range of topics. Although some of the issues are dealt with through research in other parts of the United Kingdom, many of them relate to distinctive features of the educational system and of teacher education in Scotland. Please contact the author correspondent, Mr. Ronnie Mackay (see Table 47.1) for further information concerning any of the following studies.

Recruitment, Selection, and Initial Preparation

In *Criteria of Teacher Selection Project (C.A.T.S.)* (1985), Barclay et al. aimed to (1) document and describe the current policies and procedures used by Scottish colleges of education to select students for preservice primary and secondary teacher training courses, (2) collect evidence about selection methods used by other agencies engaged in people-centered employment, (3) obtain student perceptions of professional competence, and (4) develop and evaluate a model for selection.

In *School Experience in Initial Primary School Teacher Training* (1993) Stark studied the current school experience of students in the fourth year of the bachelor of education degree at Jordanhill and, in particular, the role of the school and teachers who receive students during school placements.

Continuing Professional Growth, Development, and Assessment

In *The Qualities of Teachers: Building on Craft Knowledge*, Brown, McIntyre, and McAlpine (1988) sought to understand how teachers conceptualize and what they value in their teaching. The idea for the project came out of a recognition of the well-documented gap between the theory and the practice of teaching that all too often educational innovations take little account of what is actually happening in the classroom and that much in-service teacher education is based on a "deficit" rather than a "building on strengths" model. The first stage of the project involved 16 teachers (12 secondary and 4 primary). The subject specialties of the secondary teachers covered the typical range of subjects in secondary school curriculum. With each teacher, the method adopted was to observe and record each teaching a number of lessons. Each lesson was followed by an interview, in which the teachers were asked to report on what they thought they had done well. The secondary stage of the research involved extended work with five of the teachers from the first stage. The aim of this part of the study was to understand how teachers did the things they do well. It attempted to unravel the routines that experienced teachers use in their day-to-day teaching. The third stage of the research involved experiments in preservice teacher education. The aim of this stage was to explore how to help student teachers gain access to the craft knowledge of teachers through observation and interview. In the final stage of the project, findings are being used to inform an initiative in the P.G.C.E. (Post Graduate Certificate in Education) at the University of Oxford. The project has moved, therefore, from a piece of fundamental research exploring the nature of teaching to an applied approach where the aim is to help students gain access to the knowledge of experienced teachers.

Cameron-Jones, Skinner, and McIntosh in *Focus on Teaching: Staff Development in Primary Schools* (1985) studied a development project based in primary schools. Its objective was to increase teachers' critical awareness, use, and modification of pedagogical concepts in the course of their own day-to-day work

in classrooms. Six primary schools in Borders, Fife, and Lothian contributed to the project. At first the work centered on means for eliciting and facilitating teachers' analyses of their current classroom practice. The project then progressed to a concern with the ways in which teachers effected, reflected on, and described classroom change. From the exploratory studies, the project moved on to work with teachers in producing materials to support a fully developed teacher-as-researcher approach to school-based staff development in the area of pedagogy.

The Practice of Staff Development in Secondary Schools, Phase Two by Cumming, Kidd, Melver, and Wight (1985) (1) identified and portrayed the variety of existing approaches to staff development, (2) analyzed these approaches and identified key issues, and (3) disseminated the findings to schools through written and personal communications.

The Qualities of Teachers: Building on Experience by Brown, McAlpine, McIntyre, and Munn (1988) generated new understanding of the professional craft knowledge and expertise of the experienced teacher. It explored the possibilities of using these understandings as a basis for new resources and strategies for in-service or preservice teacher education and educational innovation. The research (1) investigated the qualities that experienced teachers value in their own teaching and that students value in their teachers, (2) attempted to articulate the nature of the skills and strategies used by teachers when manifesting such valued qualities, (3) explored ideas on how to facilitate the articulation and sharing of teachers' professional craft knowledge and expertise, and (4) formulated and tested strategies for such sharing in in-service or other contexts.

In *The Role of the Schools and Colleges in the Training and Assessment of Primary School Teachers* Elder (1986) investigated the roles of the college and school in the training and assessing of primary school teachers. The project: (1) negotiated shared and agreed-upon aims of teaching practice between school and college, (2) developed profiles for use with student teachers that assess teaching practice on dimensions acceptable to college, school, and students; and (3) identified and quantified the college and school contribution for both training and assessing student teachers.

The first phase of the project consisted of a detailed examination using data from questionnaires and interviews about the understandings of class teachers, students, and tutors on the main aims of teaching practice. In light of the information received, additional documentation for schools on student assessment in first year was produced. The second phase of the project involved narrowing the focus of the research to investigate the essential links and relationships involved in effective student training and reliable assessment. Several closely observed case studies were undertaken in order to examine what actually takes place in a classroom when a student is on teaching practice. The third phase of the research developed and utilized self-evaluation procedures with final-year students to be used in cooperative consultation with their class teachers and college tutors. It is hoped that the development of such self-evaluation procedures will draw teacher, student, and tutor together so that each provides a potent contribution to the assessment of the student as a potential teacher. This approach will subsequently be evaluated using interview and questionnaire. The final trial of all developed materials, negotiation procedures, and assessment schedules led to a number of recommendations about the essential nature of the relationship and conditions that must exist between college and school for a successful student school experience.

Students and Probationers in Transition by Draper (1988) examined the relationship between students' experience of the college course and probationers' experience of teaching and identified predictors of difficulties both on the course and during the probationary period.

In *A Study of Probationers* (1991) Draper, Fraser, and Taylor investigated the support provided for probationer-teachers by schools and education authorities, the criteria used in making recommendations to the General Teaching Council regarding fee registration, and the collecting and analyzing of probationers' views concerning the relevance of their initial training. The study included both primary and secondary probationers and identified good practices with respect to the induction, support, and assessment of probationer-teachers.

Black, Hall, and Martin (1990) studied *Teaching, Learning, and Assessment in the National Certificate* by investigating teaching methods, learning strategies, assessment procedures, and their interaction in the national certificate. Particular attention was given to the changes in teaching methodology attributable to the national certificate and to similarities and differences in the perceptions of staff, students, and employers. The research utilized structural interviews, observation of practice, and questionnaires aimed at each target group.

In *Returners to Teaching,* MacDonald, Munn, and Robinson (1991) researched the factors affecting the career choices of different groups of nonpracticing teachers and assessed whether there are practical measures that could be adopted to encourage these groups to return to teaching.

Diversity and Equity Issues

In *Ethnic Monitoring of the Training of Teachers* Corner (1988) (1) surveyed colleges and departments of education in Scotland to ascertain the extent of current participation by ethnic and linguistic minorities, (2) reviewed their current policies and the extent and ways in which they encourage equality of opportunity, and (3) obtained evidence about the extent of multicultural education courses within colleges and departments of education.

SINGAPORE

Although teacher education research in Singapore has a longer history than expected, much of the work is hardly known outside of a small circle of researchers, and in contrast to other countries, most of the research is focused on preservice teacher education.

Recruitment, Selection, and Initial Preparation

In *An Experimental Study of Inter-Rater Reliability of Teaching Practice Supervision* Yeap et al. (1985) researched whether supervisor interrater reliability could be improved through group interaction after supervisors watched videotaped teaching lessons. A group of supervisors (experimental) discussed the lesson and their ratings among themselves after viewing a videotaped lesson, whereas a control group did not. Although

the variance within the experimental group was only slightly reduced, all supervisors were more consistent when rating different aspects of the same lesson a second time. The "Feasibility of the Minnesota Teacher Attitude Inventory (MTAI) as a Selection Instrument for Pre-Service Teacher Education" by Eng et al. (1983) presented a study on representative of a general class of selection studies (selection as an event is important in Far Eastern cultures and commands more research attention than might be otherwise expected). The MTAI and similar instruments showed moderate success in differentiating among effective and less effective trainees on such criteria as coursework and teaching practice. In a report published in the *Singapore Journal of Education,* "Additional Selection Criteria Research Project: Selection and Performance of 1983 Diploma in Education Students at the Institute of Education" Tay-Koay (1985) confirmed that emotionally stable, intelligent, and less anxious students do well in teacher education programs.

Lau (1968) researched motives for choosing teaching as a career and identified two major reasons: an opportunity to (1) render service to society, and (2) help educate the younger generation. Elementary entrants (mostly women) mentioned: (1) fondness for children, and (2) teaching being suitable as a career for women. In contrast, in a later study in 1983 Soh discovered some changes: The 1981 sample saw teaching as a realization of their potential and ambition through working with children and did not enter teaching simply because it was a noble occupation.

Chang (1990) reported that Singapore has attempted to use school-based intervention studies as a vital feedback system in developing a more viable and sensitive preservice curriculum. The Institute of Education (IE), the sole trainer of teachers in Singapore, is conducting research that aims at assessing the effectiveness of teaching methods used to foster the development of learning strategies and metacognitive skills in English and mathematics studies among students of various background characteristics. Data from two concurrent studies provide information on IE students' and secondary school students' learning strategies and academic ability. A sample of differential student learning behaviors from three ability streams is presented: special, express, and normal. Findings from a questionnaire submitted to teachers indicated that the teachers' perceptions of effective strategies did not seem to match the students' experiences with the strategies, but the students' ability seemed to influence the teachers' perception of the effectiveness of the strategies. Preservice teachers need to know that all pupils, regardless of ability, should be taught effective learning strategies.

Continuing Professional Growth, Development, and Assessment

In *Survey on Teacher Education Objectives: The Views of Full Time Diploma-in-Education Students in Institute of Education* (Mosbergen et al., 1982) respondents gave top priority to the knowledge and skills needed for classroom teaching; medium priority to supportive activities such as selection of resource materials; and low priority to teaching aids and administrative duties. Ng (1987) conducted *An Inquiry Into the Use of Clinical Supervision With Student Teachers* and found that the clinical supervision method worked well with students who were motivated, intelligent, and mature and less so with students who sought a judgmental supervision method. The use of pair teaching to improve the practicum experience in preservice teacher education was studied by Chen and Skuja (1988). Ths method of supervision, the authors reported, was seen as less of a hierarchial and judgmental method of supervision than one-on-one supervision and appeared to work well with students who were pupil-centered as compared to those who had a proclivity toward self-development and self-achievement.

In *Teaching Practice Supervision: What Are Supervisors After?* Soh, Lam, and Poh (1985) found that supervisors were looking for evidence of thorough planning and the orchestration of learning activities, especially in the beginning of practice teaching. Subsequently, supervisors gave emphasis to the development of instructional strategies and reinforcement of learning.

Ho et al. (1983) conducted a study representative of a class of induction studies in Singapore that reported that although most teachers found their preparation to be "adequate," some thought that it was rather idealistic. In ranking "problems" in the same study, behavior/discipline problems emerged as the primary concern. Using an interview technique Skuja and Lim-Quek (1984) studied the experiences of beginning teachers, and although the focus was on "problems" similar to those identified in earlier studies, the teachers reported enjoying teaching and felt prepared to adapt to changing classroom situations.

In a study of the experiences and perceptions of graduate teachers after 1 year of full-time teaching, Lim-Quek and Tay-Koay (1987) found that graduates generally viewed their training as adequate, although some reported some lack of confidence in maintaining discipline and dealing effectively with behavior problems. This study also reported a relationship between performing well in student teaching and feeling competent in teaching.

In a study of the influence of training on the performance of teacher supervisors, Chew-Goh (1986) concluded that supervision seminars and workshops do have an impact on the supervision skills of teacher educators, particularly workshops that are well organized and task oriented.

For further details on these as well as other studies on Singapore the reader is referred to Chapter 7 in Tischer and Wideen (1990).

SLOVENIA

The author correspondent for Slovenia (see Table 47.1) advises that there are five major publications on education in Slovenia:

1. *Sodobna Pedagogika*—SP (Contemporary Pedagogic). The leading educational review in Slovenia, abstracts in English, five double issues yearly, ISSN 0038-0474.
2. *Vzgoja In Izobrazevanje* (Education). Review on innovations and management in education, abstracts in English, six issues yearly, ISSN 0350-5065.
3. *Pedagoska Obzorja* (Educational Horizons). Journal for general and special didactics questions, abstracts in English, four issues yearly, ISSN 0353-1392.
4. *Educa*. Journal for topics about preschool and early school years, abstracts in English, six issues yearly, ISSN 0353-9369.

5. *The School Field*. International journal of theory and research in the field of education, published twice a year, in English, ISSN 0350-6807.

Dr. Cveta Razdevsek-Pucko (1983a, 1983b, 1983c, 1984, 1988a, 1988b, 1990, 1991, 1992a, 1992b) author-correspondent for Slovenia, identified the following studies as the basis for her summative report but has not incorporated author names into the summary. For further information, contact Dr. Razdevsek-Pucko directly (see Table 47.1). These authors are Cagran (1988, 1989), Golli (1980), Hederih (1992), Inthar (1991), Juasovec (1988), Marentic-Pozarnik (1981), Papotnik (1988), Plestenjak (1980), Skerbinek (1987), Tomic (1990), Valencic (1991), and Vogrinc (1982).

Recruitment, Selection, and Initial Preparation

Researchers in Slovenia have used questionnaires; interviews; case studies; experimental microteaching with analysis of videotapes; analysis of students' diaries; and personality, intelligence, and creativity tests in teacher education research. Studies have found that convergent as well as divergent aptitudes have low impact on student teachers' study success, and student teachers are sociable, adaptable, cooperative, expressive, and emotionally warm. They are tolerant, noncompetitive, and function better in a group. They are moderate and cautious, oppose changes, and tend to be traditional. Student teachers are not satisfied with the extent of teaching practice (field practice).

Student teachers ranked the impact of the feedback from videotapes and from their students first and the comments of mentors and experts in special didactics second. They ranked cooperation with colleagues and writing a diary as the less important aspects for their professional growth during block practice in schools.

Teaching strategies are important for "the art" of teaching; some elements (questioning, moderating discussions) of microteaching should prove to be very useful for developing effective teaching strategies.

Teacher Education Curriculum

Researchers used questionnaires, analysis of graduates' diploma theses, and analysis of the teacher education curriculum to study aspects of curriculum. Major findings suggested that the interdisciplinary diploma theses are very successful; the students working on theses are better students, and they receive higher exam grades. Student teachers preferred subjects that are more directive and are designed to offer a body of knowledge needed for exams. They do not like those subjects that broaden their knowledge, where more independent work is expected of them, without a direct connection with exams or with teaching practice.

The consecutive model of teacher education for some types of secondary school teachers was evaluated, and the results suggest an increased sensitivity toward self-reflection of their own work. They now pay more attention to student needs. Teachers also reported better communication with parents.

In an evaluation study on the faculty level of primary teacher education the graduates emphasized the main gains to be more knowledge, more time for personal and professional growth, and a higher self-esteem. The student teacher and graduates as well agreed that the development of teacher education was absolutely necessary and meaningful, but they are not really satisfied with the proficiency level of the program. Nearly all graduates stressed the need for more practical knowledge and for more field practice.

Continuing Professional Growth, Development, and Assessment

State exams showed that teachers do not have enough practical knowledge and make mistakes throughout all phases of school work. Headmasters are more satisfied with teachers with higher grades in the practical part of their studies. When comparing their salaries with salaries in other professions, teachers are not satisfied with the emphasis placed on their level of education. If they had a chance, more than half of them would leave the teaching profession.

Young teachers are critical about their teacher education program as well as about their experienced colleagues in school, who were not helpful enough at the time they were novice teachers. They would like to have more opportunity for in-service. Teachers do not like being active participants in educational research; they prefer a passive role—being respondents only. Teachers, especially those with many years of practice, do not feel much need for in-service; they prefer being directed about their in-service; they like less specific topics, yet prefer active methods of in-service. Teachers with more intensive needs for in-service activities have a less directive style of work, and their pupils are more motivated for school work.

Novice teachers do not feel well enough prepared for independent work nor are they satisfied with the organization of their initiation period; neither are their mentors satisfied with the organization of the initiation period: They complain about a shortage of time, and they do not feel well enough prepared for work with novice teachers either.

The opportunity of experiencing school initiation wherein a young novice teacher works together (in the same classroom) with an experienced teacher was appreciated by all the participants. The experienced teachers felt that they benefited through new, fresh ideas of young teachers, and the young beginners stressed the smooth beginning of their school career, positive experiences, and less frustration. They liked the combination of help (when needed) on one hand and independence on the other hand. The model was assessed as a benefit for the children and for the professional development of the young teachers.

Emerging Directions in Teacher Education

Researchers used questionnaires and comparative analyses of teacher education programs to study the field of teacher education. In comparison with European Community and Council of Europe countries, Slovenia has developed a high standard of teacher education, regarding the faculty level and the level of academization. The problem remains in the field of the practical part of teacher education, resulting from the conflict between subject-oriented teacher education on the one hand and student-oriented teacher education on the other. The directions for further development of teacher education have been set, especially in the field of the initiation period of the teaching profession. The model of a second teacher (teacher assistant) in the classroom is suggested as a successful way of uniting the higher theoretical knowledge of those who finished a faculty level of teacher education with the successful practice of experienced teachers.

SOUTH AFRICA

Recruitment, Selection, and Initial Preparation

De Kock (1992) in "An intensive communication training programme (ICTP) for preservice teachers" studied 32 students in their final preservice training year who were selected for this study based on identified communication problems, such as lack of self-confidence, timidness, poor eye contact, and voice projection linked with a negative self-concept. The attitude of the selected group of students at the beginning of the program could be described as negative and, at times, aggressive. A number of students who were excellent communicators also were selected to take part in the program. Findings, using the Emotions Profile Index (EPI), indicated a positive outcome of the ICTP. Following the training program, the most notable changes were in the acceptance of others, spontaneity, and socializing. To examine the effect of the program further, a follow-up study was conducted with 180 students, 90 in the experimental group and 90 in the control group. The results were statistically significant.

Emerging Directions in Teacher Education

Murphy and Naidu (1992) in *The Development of New Inservice and Further Education Programmes in an Era of Changing Social and Political Conditions—A Case Study of Natal/Kwazulu (South Africa)* explored new ways of delivering information to teacher educators and of empowering them through the pursuit of the democratization of education.

FORMER SOVIET UNION

Recruitment, Selection, and Initial Preparation

Evans, Ferrucci, and Cyr (1989) in *Mathematics Teacher Preparation: USA Versus USSR* reported that the vast majority of mathematics graduates in the former Soviet Union are female, primarily because most mathematics graduates will become teachers, and most males do not want to teach because of low salaries and lack of respect for teachers, problems shared by the United States. In the former Soviet Union, mathematics majors take the equivalent of approximately 146 U.S. credit hours of mathematics during their 5-year program compared to the 45 to 50 credits that students take at U.S. institutions. General education is emphasized in U.S. schools; in Soviet schools very little, if any, emphasis is placed on general education because so much is done at earlier levels. It is apparent that Soviet educators of grades 1–10 are better prepared in mathematics than their U.S. counterparts. This lack of preparation of U.S. teachers could be one of the factors that leads to the discouraging results of comparisons between the achievement of U.S. students and that of students of other nationalities.

SPAIN

Recruitment, Selection, and Initial Preparation

Fernandez, Gonzalez, and Subirats (1988) in "The Tutor's Role in Teaching Practice in Initial Teacher Training" described different types of teaching practices used in the University of Barcelona's teacher education college, the function of the teacher as a tutor, and teacher/tutor's relationship with student teachers and experienced classroom teachers. The authors also introduced a model of teacher educators' practices and discussed the qualifications needed by teachers/tutors.

Noguera et al. (1985) in *Methods of Selection and Teacher Training* used observation and experimentation to conclude that an integrated group of nine instruments offer assistance in selecting teachers and assessing their knowledge of the basic skills.

Teacher Education Curriculum

Angulo (1986) in *Microsupervision: A Technique to Train Supervisors* investigated methodologies better to train tutor teachers who supervise practice teachers. He emphasized the nature of transactions in supervisory interviews.

SRI LANKA

Effectiveness and Costs of Three Approaches to Train Elementary School Teachers in Sri Lanka (1990) emphasized a cost-effectiveness approach to educating elementary teachers (ISN 71434).

Rugh (1990) wrote *Improving Teacher Effectiveness in the Classroom in Sri Lanka* (ISN 71444).

Nielsen et al. (1991) in *Cost-effectiveness of Distance Education in Teacher Training in Sri Lanka and Indonesia* (ISN 71380) focused on an alternative, economical method for in-service teacher training. The results of the study reported here (examining teacher education programs in Sri Lanka and Indonesia) indicated that there was a relatively inexpensive way for governments to increase the effectiveness of their teaching force. The most effective distance education methods relied on cooperative or collaborative learning, in which groups of teacher trainees met to discuss their lessons and the difficulties they were having with them. These meetings helped sustain the motivation to study and partially substituted for the presence of a teacher. The network of relationships established during the training program continued after it was finished and helped to maintain the teachers' morale and motivation when they were back in their classrooms.

SWAZILAND

Swaziland Teacher Training Project: Final Impact Evaluation (1991; ISN 71725) summarized the final evaluation of the Swaziland Teacher Training Project to improve the pedagogical abilities of primary school teachers. The major findings of the team were that the project had a significant impact on curriculum revision, the quality of teacher training, the quality of teacher performance, the government of Swaziland's awareness of the significance of primary school education, and the Ministry of Education's dedication to primary education.

Teacher Training Project in Swaziland (1987; ISN 60818) summarized the interim evaluation of a project to improve Swaziland's capacity to train primary school teachers. It expanded preservice programs from a 2-year Primary Teaching Certificate program to a 3-year Primary Teaching Certificate. Doing so has achieved uniformity in primary teacher training. New topics such as special education, ecology, guidance, environmental education, and curriculum development have also been added to existing preservice courses. In-service teacher education workshops have been a major contribution and have qualitatively far exceeded projected numbers; more than 3,000 teachers will benefit by the end of the project.

SWEDEN

During the 1960s and 1970s under the auspices of the Swedish governmental committees, high priority was given to research on teacher training and much research occurred. From 1977 to 1987, the situation changed drastically, and no exhaustive research projects were carried out. Resources were allocated for minor research and development projects covering most of the teacher training institutions. Since 1990, a new interest has occurred that could have important effects on teacher training in the future.

Recruitment, Selection, and Initial Preparation

Studies in the early 1980s have tended to look at the effect of the 1970s reform findings. Gran (1982) in a study of the relationship between research and basic teacher training, found that more teacher educators than previously were engaging in research and development. He also found that local conditions were being affected, personal competencies were fostered more than general knowledge, and student involvement in local activities was low.

In Sweden a large proportion (at least 1 1/2 years) of the teacher training program is, by tradition, practice teaching. Angel (1974) in "Practical Teacher Training for Class Teachers: A Study of Personality and Attitude Development During the Training Period" studied the teacher training part of professional socialization. Angel's study showed that the process gave rise to more authoritarian and less child-centered attitudes, which are contrary to the aims of teacher education. Angel's findings emphasized the importance of the tutoring process in practice teaching, the close coordination between teaching practice and theoretical studies, and the follow-up on trainees' experiences after the practice period.

Jonsson and Ahlström (1988) studied educational belief systems among teacher educators. They examined the content of the tutoring process and what is treated in discussion with the student in training. The individual teacher educators' belief systems were studied by observing their visits to the classroom. Researchers recorded and analyzed the discussions between the teacher educators and the student teachers and found that varying supervising styles emerged. These discussions, along with specific episodes from lessons, were examined in a series of interviews with each tutor, and an individual profile constructed for each one that was also discussed in a second interview. These studies showed that lecturers from the school of education stressed the specialized rather than the common and general aspects of teaching and therefore developed a more technocratic than integrated professional role. The students learned a rather traditional teaching role that emphasized the cognitive aims of the school with little regard to more global goals such as democracy, equal opportunities, internationalism, and preparedness for the future.

Continuing Professional Growth, Development, and Assessment

Gran (1985) in *Is Inservice Training of Teachers a Good Means to Improve the School?* found that values and norms of parliament and government, although easily transferrable to the local community level and to school leaders, did not easily transfer to teachers. The teachers had other priorities concerning the needs for in-service training than those of the school leaders. The problems as determined by the National Board of Education were not necessarily the same as those that teachers believed needed to be addressed. The study showed that success in in-service training is only partly due to the content of the program. The structure of the schools or the "receiving apparatus" is of the utmost importance. The author also found that in-service training has to be carried out close to the practical teaching situation and through teamwork with teachers.

Ekholm (1988) described an overview of in-service teacher education in Sweden that focuses on the role of in-service education of teachers in the local school. The term *INSET* refers to short-cycle nature (e.g., social development, working methods in the classroom, or cooperation between teachers). This summary is based on research reports and reviews of various publications produced in this field within the major international joint bodies. The functions of INSET in Finland, Denmark, and Norway are also described. The document reviewed the literature and discussed the role of action research focused on improvements that have occurred at local school levels. Recommendations for new initiatives on the part of local schools are discussed, and 52 references are included.

Emerging Directions in Teacher Education

Carlson and Stenmalm-Sjoblom (1992) in "Improving Teacher Education Through International Cooperation and Partnership: Sweden and the United States" described collaborative teacher education research projects between Vaxjo University, Sweden, and the University of Minnesota, Duluth. Findings indicated a more inner-directed, group-oriented approach to teacher education in Sweden compared to a more outer-directed, individualistic approach in the United States.

For further details on some of these studies and others, the reader is referred to Chapter 11 in Tischer and Wideen (1990).

SWITZERLAND

Teacher education research in Switzerland does not have a long tradition or many studies for three reasons. First, the education in Teachers Institutes (so called Lehrerseminar, grades 10–14) prepares elementary school teachers only for practical teaching and is not research oriented. This situation is expected to change in the coming years when the Teachers Institutes will become Teachers Colleges (Pädagogische Hochschulen) with a focus on research and teacher education. Second, the universities are responsible for the preparation of secondary school teachers (grades 9–12). The departments of education within the university have only a few research institutes, and these, mostly for financial reasons, are small and concentrate on other research topics. This is partly because the organization and implementation of teacher education is primarily seen as a political question and the decisions are taken by the state in collaboration with teachers, which results in less regard for research. Third, the Swiss school system is very decentralized. Therefore, each state (Kanton) holds strongly to their local traditions and political views on teacher education. Also the political authorities are not strongly interested in research results on teacher education. Most books, studies, and articles on teacher education in Switzerland are concerned with programmatic principles and organizational questions of teacher education and propose new models without much research orientation.

The Swiss Coordination Center for Research in Education, located in Aarau, Switzerland, deals with educational research at the national level and is officially charged with establishing and maintaining contacts at the international level. It does not carry out research projects itself but promotes cooperation in educational research, provides information services, and offers retrieval, publishing, and other services in the field of educational research in Switzerland. The index of the Swiss Coordination Center for Research in Education, however, mentions 19 titles of research projects on teacher education for the period 1987–1993 that can be divided in the following general topics: aptitude and motivation for becoming a teacher, evaluation of teacher education, evaluation and coaching of teachers, and organization of teacher education.

Aptitude and Motivation for Becoming a Teacher

Eugster (1988) studied two types of teacher education that have been discussed in Switzerland for many years: the traditional ("unsplitted") way in a specialized Teachers Institute, and the "splitted" way with a general education and succeeding specialization in a teachers institute. Eugster hypothesized that two types of teacher education (actual situation in Switzerland) are only justified if the students in each organization differ in personality, attitudes, and motivation concerning the profession of teaching. If there are no differences, the expensive two-way system can be reduced to one way. He found significant differences in the personality, attitudes, and motivation between the two groups of students and proposed to maintain the traditional "unsplitted" way of the teachers' institution.

In 1992 Luethy studied the testing systems for admission to teachers institutes. Although all institutes tested for achievement potential, 11 of 21 also tested psychological makeup, creativity, and communication skills. Luethy also studied combinations of psychological tests in the institutes but could not draw any conclusions about the validity of the best combination of tests because of the lack of a workable definition of a good teacher.

Evaluation of Teacher Education

Frey and Frey (1988) studied the preparation of mathematics and science teachers by asking teacher educators, teacher supervisors and future teachers what their study needs are. The three most frequently mentioned needs were: (1) selection of content/lesson planning, (2) teaching methods, and (3) teacher personality. Forty-nine percent of the answers were concerned with at least one of these three topics. Aerne (1990) studied the implementation of the teaching model at the University of St. Gallen. He observed the preparation of lessons as teachers talked about what they were preparing and then the teaching of the lesson in actual classrooms by 16 teachers. It is important to note in this study that these teachers had 2 to 5 years of practical experience after their teacher training with this model at the University. He found that those teachers who evaluated the teacher training program favorably and who earned higher final grades at the university used more elements of the model than those with a less positive opinion and poorer final grades. It appeared, however, that each teacher gradually constructed his or her own approach to teaching because they gauged the model presented at St. Gallen as too complex. The main activities taken from the model and applied in their own teaching were selection of content, lesson planning, and media. In contrast, the most neglected activities were thoughts about the students in class and interpretation of the curriculum and objectives.

Evaluation and Coaching of Teachers

For many years questions about the effectiveness of evaluating or coaching teachers by politically elected laymen have been discussed. In 1981 a study by Olibeth demonstrated that laymen can be trained for teacher supervision. Teachers were asked to evaluate the quality of the coaching before and after the training, and neutral scientists evaluated written reports about observed lessons before and after training. In both cases significant improvements of the evaluative work and the coaching of the layman were found. Recently several states decided to introduce a system of teacher appraisal and merit pay, a decision which is in considerable dispute. Two research projects are therefore in progress.

In 1992 Frey studied a system in which the school principal agreed with each teacher to evaluate 5 out of 25 behaviors and aptitudes each year. Dubs (1990) studied a system of teacher-prepared portfolios. These are assessed by a schoolboard member (layman) and two specially trained teachers. The portfolio includes documents of planning and thoughts about the teaching of classes, presentation of all tests used and grading practice; and information about extracurricular work and videotaped lessons.

Evaluation of Different Forms of Teacher Training

The professional teacher education literature in Switzerland is not without many articles on good practice and innovative ideas. Most of these articles are based on questioning, observation sheets, and the like but are not within a systematic research design. Therefore, they remain speculative.

THAILAND

Continuing Professional Growth, Development, and Assessment

Ligons (1990) reviewed key innovations in in-service education in Thailand since 1980 (ISN 72469) and in "Preschool teacher training in Finland, Hong Kong, Italy, and Thailand" Olmstead and Hoas (1989) reported on findings from the International Association for the Evaluation of Educational Achievement (Project IEA). In reviewing information regarding teacher education on Thailand for preschool education, they reported that the training of preschool teachers in Thailand is primarily the responsibility of the government and takes place in teacher training colleges where a diploma can be earned after a 2-year, postsecondary program. Bachelor's degrees are offered in 14 teacher training colleges and in three universities. Master's degree programs are offered at two universities; however, the level of qualified preschool personnel is low. In a 1984 survey of child care centers, 38% of the workers (people with little initial training) reported no in-service training despite the government directive to increase this type of training to meet its needs for expansion.

In a doctoral dissertation completed at North Texas State University, Naowarath (1989) researched developing and administering a nonmetropolitan teacher education program in northeast Thailand. Isra-Pavirat (1982) completed a study of educators' perceptions concerning teacher education in selected institutions in Thailand as a doctoral dissertation at Oklahoma State University.

TURKEY

Recruitment, Selection, and Initial Preparation

Aydin (1990) in "Mathematics teacher preparation in Turkey today" described the transfer of teacher education into the university system in Turkey. The author also discussed the need to develop a new model of student assessment and to select and attract more capable and committed individuals into teaching.

UNITED STATES

Special Topics, Overseas Teaching

The following reports are in a U.S. classification because the studies, although USA based, are focused on international teacher education research.

Mahan and Stachowski (1987) analyzed feedback from British and Irish educators for improving overseas teaching experiences. The authors reported the observations and beliefs of educators in Great Britain, Scotland, and the Republic of Ireland pertaining to the performance of U.S. student teachers in the schools of these nations. The authors also provided recommendations to student participants and U.S. teacher educators for the improvement of overseas teaching experiences.

Mahan and Stachowski (1989) summarized instructional suggestions concerning overseas teaching. Interviews with 32 British and Irish supervisors of U.S. student teachers produced several suggestions for improving the preparation component of overseas practicum placements. The suggestions were related to planning and preparation for teaching, basic teacher preparation courses, cultural preparation, content, arrangements and logistics, and teacher image and style.

In 1989 Mahan and Stachowski (1988–1989) also reported data gathered from 200 participants in a successful overseas student teaching program conducted by Indiana University. The data suggested how stateside student teaching helps or hinders subsequent teaching practicum experiences in overseas nations. Steps are suggested that can eliminate or minimize difficulties encountered by student teachers abroad.

Mahan and Stachowski (1990) in "New Horizons: Student Teaching Abroad to Enrich Understanding of Diversity" compared learning reported by novice teachers in conventional, state-side student teaching assignments and learning reported by students who did student teaching overseas. Overseas participants acquired more learning than did their counterparts, exhibited broader perspectives in the context of their learning, and acknowledged a greater variety of learning sources.

Vall and Tennison (1991–1992) in *International Student Teaching: Stimulus for Developing Reflective Teachers* discussed how culture shock (implicit in a cross-cultural student teaching experience) necessitates that participants think critically and reflect about teaching. The article described an international student teaching component at two Minnesota colleges. After 7 weeks of student teaching in the United States, participants spend 6 weeks in British primary (K–6) classrooms.

West (1985) analyzed *The State of the Profession: International Field/Student Teaching Experiences in Undergraduate Teacher Preparation: Images for the Near Future* and discussed five viable models for the conduct of overseas student teaching programs.

WEST GERMANY

In this West German report, titles of studies, with one exception, are not incorporated into the text because of translation difficulties (i.e., some concepts have no direct or understandable parallel in English).

Klinzing (1990) reviewed over 200 empirical analytical studies published since the 1970s. He reported that research on teacher education in West Germany is conducted primarily by individuals from universities and teacher training institutions. The studies are mostly short-term projects with the exception of long-term projects at the University of Konstanz on teacher attitudes and projects on laboratory training at the University of Tübingen. Publications from the institutions are mostly of a theoretical nature. Empirical analytical research is relatively rare. He reported that *Geisteswissenschaftlich*-oriented educationalists have dominated since World War II and that they maintain their resistance to empirical research. Only about 10% of all publications on teacher education and training have involved empirical analytical studies.

Recruitment, Selection, and Initial Preparation

Zachmann-Hintermeier and Treiber (1986) and Heller and Wichterlich (1982) evaluated content-oriented courses on mastery of teaching. Their studies indicated that student teachers gain basic knowledge, value the content and form of the program, and become positive in their attitudes toward education. Lindemann (1984) studied the teacher practicum and found that student teachers felt that they were insufficiently prepared. They desired more praxis-related courses before the practicum and criticized the insufficient supervision by college supervisors and mentors. In a study by Roth (1981), the effects of spending the first 6 months of college in schools as an introductory practicum were compared to those from traditional courses supplemented by protocol material. There were no significant differences between groups, but the prospective elementary and Hauptschul teachers became more permissive, were more pupil-oriented and nondirective, and accepted the dominant role of the teacher to a greater degree and the teachers' role to diagnose and cope with people's learning difficulties to a lesser degree.

Roth's (1981) research on video and films produced mixed results about the attitude of trainees to video demonstrations and the perceived benefits and impact on trainees. Brunner (1985) found that in the 1980s about 50% of teacher training colleges and universities in West Germany were using teaching laboratories for preparing teachers. He also found that direct teaching is used by the majority of the institutions with teaching laboratories. Klinzing and Klinzing-Eurich (1988) reviewed teaching laboratory research. They found that about 25% of the research dealt with indirect programs that attempt to change personality and characteristics and promote learner-supportive attitudes, improve abilities, improvise, and foster assertiveness through case studies, play simulation, group encounters, and exercises in reacting to and interpreting educational situations. They found that researchers used a variety of criterion measures including attribute tests, personality inventory, self-concept and attitude scales, and tests of performance that showed that generally the programs were favorably received. Trainees stated that they learned a great deal and were able to write satisfactory solutions to hypothetical critical incidents in the classroom. They also noted that the research is not without difficulties and has no clear findings regarding changes and variables, such as attitudes, personality characteristics, and performance.

Other studies were concerned with direct programs of training in laboratory research. Langthaler, Schultz, and Elsinghorst (1986) indicated that this kind of training was rated very favorably and that knowledge was acquired successfully. Klinzing, Leuteritz, Schiefer, and Steiger (1986) found that verbal and nonverbal perceptiveness were enhanced. Tennstädt (1987) found that the reactions of trainees to hypothetical discipline problems were improved and that the quantity and quality of teacher classroom behaviors were improved in the skill areas previously mentioned. Klinzing, Klinzing-Eurich, and Floden (1989) looked beyond judgment of training effectiveness in terms of merely their enhancement of the frequency of target skills and found that the trainees learned not only the use of skills but also when and how to use them appropriately.

Kolstad, Coker, and Edelhoff (1989) examined teacher education in Germany. This article provided an overview of the teacher education program offered in Germany. The authors suggested many aspects worth considering for implementation in the United States.

Contextual Influences on Teacher Education

Preuss and Hofsass (1991) studied experiences related to professional identity and strategies of teacher training in Berlin. School organization is changing in respect of social integration since integrating handicapped pupils was introduced from 1975. Three basic models are being implemented: differentiating instructional objects, peripatetic teacher systems, and cooperative schools. The concepts of professionalization in pre- and in-service teacher training focus on the teachers as key persons of the social environment as well as of the learning process; this results in a change of professional identity for teachers.

Continuing Professional Growth, Development, and Assessment

Neubauer (1983) in a study of beginning teachers supported other research that showed that during intense periods of praxis in the second stage of teacher education and during induction, trainee and beginning teachers became more conservative, dominant, and concerned about academic progress and classroom control than they did earlier in their teacher education. Studies such as Roth (1981), showed that trainees tend to become more conservative, conforming, dominating, and concerned about classroom control as they progress through their second stage of teacher education and enter the profession. Dann, Müller-Fohrbrodt, and Cloetta (1981), in a longitudinal study, suggested that elementary and Hauptschul teachers continue to become more conservative and authoritarian during their final stages of teacher education and first 3 years of teaching.

Gorny (1991) in "Fundamental Informatics in Teacher Education in West Germany" discussed the introduction of information science and technology into West German schools and focused on the teacher education system, computer hardware and software, and approaches to in-service teacher training.

For further details on some of these studies and others, the reader is referred to Chapter 6 in Tischer and Wideen (1990).

ZIMBABWE

Recruitment, Selection, and Initial Preparation

Dzvimbo (1989) appraised the dilemmas encountered by the ministries of education and teachers' colleges responsible for implementing Zimbabwe's 1980–1987 teacher education reform and noted that struggles in Zimbabwe's political economy are related to conflict in the teacher education system. Suggestions for policy are presented.

Siyakwazi and Nyarwaranda (1993) studied a sample of 264 student teachers and learned that both primary and secondary student teachers prefer being deployed (assigned) in urban rather than rural schools. In the case of rural areas, the student teachers show preference for mission rather than council schools. Where mission schools are well-equipped, however, have facilities, and proper accommodations, and are easily accessible, student teachers report that they can perform well.

In 1990 Chivore conducted a study to identify major issues related to people's perceptions of attitudes toward teaching as a profession in developed and developing countries. These issues included teaching in other professions, socioeconomic status, class structures, gender, rural/urban factors, and others. By comparing attitudes in developed and developing countries on these factors, the author hoped that educationists in developing countries would appreciate the deficiencies as challenges and would carry out research in their own countries, especially African countries.

In 1986 Disabanda reported on Zimbabwe's integrated teacher education course (ZINTE) as an example of how a government can cope with the problem of recruiting sufficient teachers to meet educational objectives. When the country became independent, the introduction of free education created an unprecedented rise in primary school enrollments in Zimbabwe. Primary school enrollments increased from 800,000 in 1980 to over two million in 1982. To meet the demand, the teaching force was increased from 21,000 to 54,000, but about 15,000 were untrained. To cope with the situation, a 4-year sandwich program was introduced to expand and train this teaching force rapidly. Students attended a 16-week residential course followed by 10 terms of teaching, and finished with another 16-week residential course. During the period of on-the-job training, teachers continued their studies through correspondence courses and were assessed in class by visiting monitors. The program emphasized nonfinancial incentives. During the outplacement period, students were deployed in clusters of three or more per school in order to encourage their interaction, to maintain their enthusiasm, and to facilitate school-based tutorials. The course curriculum emphasized community projects that help the teacher play a pivotal role in community affairs.

In a doctoral dissertation completed at Iowa State University, Zvacke (1989) studied distributive education in the teacher education program in Zimbabwe.

MULTICOUNTRY REPORTS

The following reports include more than one country and are thus classified in a separate section.

Teacher Education as a Field of Study

Kooi and Sim (1992) in *Reflective Review of Teacher Education in "ASEAN" Countries in an Era of Global Change* examined state-of-the-art reviews of teacher education in five ASEAN countries and suggested the need to develop innovative teacher education strategies that are surface, structural, substantive, and systemic.

Recruitment, Selection, and Initial Preparation

Bruce (1989) in *Teacher Education and the ERASMUS Program* reported on teacher education participation in the programs of the ERASMUS Bureau and its Inter-University Cooperation Program, which is designed to promote European awareness among European higher education institutions.

Continuing Professional Growth, Development, and Assessment

Coldevin and Naidu (1989) in *Inservice Teacher Education at a Distance: Trends in Third World Development* reported that education resources in most developing countries are experiencing pressure from spiraling population growth, government policies to achieve universal primary education, attempts to reduce teacher–pupil ratios, and the shortage of professionally trained and/or academically qualified teachers. Strategies that have been adopted to remedy teacher shortages include the use of double shifts with increasing teacher–pupil ratios; expatriate teachers; more female teachers; home or community-based school equivalency programs; in-school equivalency programs; school broadcasts; and in-service teacher education through distance teaching. Efforts by universities in Kenya, Fiji, and the West Indies are noted. Distance education programs are recommended as effective parallel systems to traditional training patterns.

Farah and Tarvin (1989) reported on how curricular changes have affected the nature and types of in-service teacher education programs in developing South Asian countries in the 1980s. They make projections on trends that may ensure that in-service teacher education programs will continue to be an important means of initiating changes in curriculum in these countries.

Savoie-Zajc (1992) examined the effect of in-service training as a change strategy through the comparative analysis of two externally designed in-service programs for teacher trainees in Haiti and Brazil.

Veenman (1984) produced a metaanalysis including 83 studies from different countries concerning problems of beginning teachers. The eight problems perceived most by beginning teachers are classroom discipline, motivating students, dealing with individual differences, assessing students' work, relationships with parents, organization of class work, insufficient and/or inadequate teaching materials and supplies, and dealing with problems of individual students.

Emerging Directions in Teacher Education

Aston and Fakhro (1992) used case studies to explore the relationship of the new information technologies to preservice and in-service education in developing countries, the Middle East, and Europe.

Doornekamp and Van Kesteren (1991) studied primary school teacher training in the European Community. The colleges of education for primary school teachers in the Netherlands have gone through several mergers in the space of just a few years. Many colleges of education became part of a polytechnic. The authors studied how the specific characteristics of the education of primary school teachers can show to full advantage in a large institute of higher vocational education. In the Dutch situation as well as that of the other countries of the European Community (Great Britain and the Federal Republic of Germany in particular) the phenomena of "integration" and "differentiation" have been studied. The authors concluded that mergers of primary school teacher training colleges can be a serious threat to the educational identity of teacher training as a whole.

Hughes (1988) in *Future Directions for Teacher Education, Trends, Needs, and Alternatives Relating to Inclusion of New Content Areas in Teacher Education* offered a comprehensive, global view of future directions for teacher education. In the first section, factors indicating the need for change are discussed. Education is seen as an agent of social change with various national approaches sharing common concerns and facing similar key issues to be resolved. In the second section changes in teacher education responsive to societal concerns are considered. Major issues include the need for new approaches to teacher education, the career development of teachers, and the need for support services. Teacher recruitment and selection, initial preparation, and continuing professional development are seen as key factors in improving education at all levels. The third section deals with the means of response to the need for change in pre- and in-service training, with a focus on the importance of an interdisciplinary approach to teacher education. Incentives and barriers in in-service education are considered along with different modes of training. In the final section the importance of evaluation for program improvement, accountability, and the selection and promotion of teachers is discussed.

The International Council on Education for Teaching (ICET) (1988) in *Progress and Promise in Teacher Education* addressed in a world conference assembly of preservice and in-service teacher education multicultural education, reflective teaching, instructional improvement, curriculum models, educational change, beginning teacher induction, collaboration, teacher and student teacher supervision, educational objectives, moral responsibility, physical education, student assessment, student attitudes and motivation, non- and limited-English-proficient students, and the future of teacher education.

Obanya (1992) in "The African Teacher of the 21st Century" attempted to answer the following questions about the African teacher in the 21st Century: What types of teachers will be needed? How will they be selected? What curricula will best train them?

Ratteree (1992) in "The ILO/UNESCO Recommendation Concerning the Status of Teachers" *ICET 1992 Yearbook,* examined the only international normative instrument for the teaching profession and its 146 clauses adopted by UNESCO and the International Xx Office in 1966.

Vonk (1991) in "Some Trends in the Development of Curricula for the Professional Preparation of Primary and Secondary School Teachers in Europe: A Comparative Study" used a comparison of representative documents to describe and analyze trends in the professional preparation of primary and secondary school teachers in Europe.

References

Academy for Educational Development. (1990). *RETT (Radio education teacher training) II: Final report in Nepal*. USAID. (ISN 72905) (Nepal)

Adejumo, D., & Alao, K. (1991). Effectiveness of teacher preparation programs in Nigerian universities: Universities and secondary school teachers' perspectives. In *ICET International Yearbook on Teacher Education, 1991* (pp. 386–397). (Nigeria)

Adelabu, M. (1991). Problems of universalizing access and promoting equity in primary education for the rural dwellers of Ondo State: Challenges of teacher education in rural areas. In *ICET International Yearbook on Teacher Education, 1991* (pp. 210–221). (Nigeria)

Aerne, P. (1990). *Die Unterrichtsvorbereitung von Handelslehrern in der Alltagspraxis* (The preparation of lessons of teachers in economics and business administration in everyday practice). Unpublished doctoral dissertation, St. Gallen. (Switzerland)

Ahmad, I. (1990). *Comparative study of the effects of P.T.C. (primary teaching certificate) training by A.I.O.U. (Allama Iqbal Open University) teacher training colleges and school (i.e., schools) on teaching styles and student achievement in science and mathematics in primary schools in Pakistan*. USAID. ISN 72693. (Pakistan)

Akiyama, M. (1981). A study on the changes of student-teachers' attitudes (2): Changes in their attitudes toward teaching profession and the analysis of their factors. *Journal of the Faculty of Education, Saga University, 29*(1), 53–71. (Japan)

Akpe, C. S. (1987). The evaluation of a Nigerian primary teacher education program. *Journal of Education for Teaching, 13*(3), 277–284. (Nigeria)

Akpe, C. S. (1988). Using consumer evaluation to improve college curricula in Nigerian teacher training. *Journal of Education for Teaching, 14*(1), 85–90. (Nigeria)

Akpe, C. S. (1991). Choice of teaching subjects in preservice teacher education in Nigeria. *Journal of Education for Teaching, 17*(2), 213–219. (Nigeria)

Al-Jassar, S. (1991). *A study of perceived adequacy of teaching competencies included in an intermediate and secondary teacher preparation program in the College of Education at Kuwait University*. Unpublished doctoral dissertation, University of Pittsburgh, Pittsburgh, PA. (Kuwait/USA)

Amagasa, S. (1981). The fundamental study on the organizational climate in the in-service education of teachers. *Bulletin of Japan Educational Administration Society, 7*, 115–128. (Japan)

Anbang, X. (1989, January). Adjusting college training program, improving students' social adaptability, *Teacher Education Research*. (China)

Angel, B. (1974). Praktikterminin i lågstadierlärarut-bildningen: En undersörändringar under utbildningstiden (Practical teacher training for class teachers: A study of personality and attitude development during the training period). *Pedagogisk-psykologiska problem, 257*. Malmö, School of Education. (Sweden)

Angulo, L. (1986). *Microsupervision: A technique to train supervisors*. (Spain)

Ariav, T. (1992). Beit Berl College, 1980–1990: A case study of the professionalization of teacher education in Israel. In *Teacher education in an era of global change*. Arlington, VA: International Council on Education for Teaching. (Israel)

Aston, M., & Fakhro, S. (1992). Implications for change in teacher education strategies offered by the new information technologies. In *Teacher education in an era of global change*. Arlington, VA: International Council on Education for Teaching. (General)

Audit of Botswana junior secondary education improvement. (1991). USAID. (ISN 71403). (Botswana)

Aydin, Y. (1990). Mathematics teacher preparation in Turkey today. *Educational Studies in Mathematics, 21,* 471–478. (Turkey)

Aziv, D. (ed). (1993). *Integrating knowledge and beliefs: Stimulating learning to teach in student teachers. From practice to theory*. Paper presented at the International Conference on Teacher Education, Tel Aviv, Israel. (Netherlands)

Barclay, A., Jenkins, D., McKay, B., Mitchell, L., Turner, D., Wilson, J. D., & Young, J. (1985). *Criteria of teacher selection project (C.A.T.S.)*. (Scotland)

Barry, G. (1992). Comparative ratings of teacher image by preservice teachers in the United States and Ireland. In *Teacher education in an era of global change*. Arlington, VA: International Council on Education for Teaching. (Ireland)

Battersby, D., & Ramsay, P. D. K. (1988). *The study of in-school training for division "A" student teachers project*. Unpublished manuscript. Palmerston North, Massey University; Hamilton, University of Waikato. (New Zealand)

Birch, D., & Neufeld, R. (1984). Innovations in distance education applied to the professional development of teachers: A Canadian perspective. In *ICET Yearbook* (pp. 93–110). Arlington, VA: International Council on Education for Teaching. (Canada)

Black, H. D., Hall, J., & Martin, S. (1990). *Teaching, learning, and assessment in the national certificate*. (Scotland)

Borger, H., & Tillema, H. H. (1993). Transferring knowledge to classroom teaching: Putting knowledge into action. In C. Day, J. Calderhead, & P. Denicolo (Eds.), *Research on teacher thinking, towards understanding professional development* (pp. 185–197). London: Falmer. (Netherlands)

Borgmans, L. (1991). *Occupational choice: the market for primary school teachers*. Maastricht: Research for students in the work market, Faculty of Economics, State University at Limburg. (Netherlands)

Borys, A., Wilgosh, L., Lefèbvre, V., Kisilevich, B., Samireden, W., Olson, A., & Ware, R. (1991). An alternative model for rural preservice practicum supervision. *Education Canada*, Winter, 4–7. (Canada)

Boschhuizen, R., & Brinkman, F. G. (1991). A proposal for a teaching strategy based on pre-instructional ideas of pupils. Environmental education: The use of pupils' ideas about cycles of nature and health. *European Journal on Teacher Education, 14*(1), 45–56. (Netherlands)

Brady, P., et al. (1992). The implications of the remote area teacher education program (RATEP) for tertiary distance education. In *Teacher education in an era of global change*. Arlington, VA: International Council on Education in Teaching. (Australia)

Brandsma, H. P., & De Jong, R. (1991). *Praktijkgerichte nascholing en onderwijsverandering: een exploratief onderzoek* (Practice oriented inservice training and education change: An exploring survey). Groningen: RION. (Netherlands)

Brekelmans, M., & Creton, H. A. (1993). Interpersonal teacher behavior throughout the career. In Th. Wubbels & J. Levy (Eds.), *Do you know what you look like?* (pp. 81–102). London: Falmer. (Netherlands)

Brown, S. A., McAlpine, A., McIntyre, D. J., & Munn, P. (1988). *The qualities of teachers: Building on experience*. (Scotland)

Brown, S. A., McIntyre, D. J., & McAlpine, A. (1988). *The qualities of teachers: Building on craft knowledge.* (Scotland)

Bruce, M. (1989). Teacher education and the ERASMUS program. *European Journal of Teacher Education, 12,* 197–228. (General)

Bruce, M., Podemski, R., & Anderson, C. (1991). Developing a global perspective: Strategies for teacher education programs. *Journal of Teacher Education, 42*(1), 21–27. (General)

Bruining, G. R. P., & Van Der Vegt, R. (1987). Implementing complex innovations: Design considerations for an educational intervention. In K. A. Leithwood, W. Rutherford, & R. Van Der Vegt (Eds.), *Preparing school leaders for educational improvement* (pp. 155–183). London: Croom Helm. (Netherlands)

Brunelle, J., Tousignant, M., Gagnon, J., Brunelle, J. P., Martel, D., Spallanzani, C., Sarazin, J., & Goyette, R. (1994). *Learning to integrate a more interactive pedagogy to prevent discipline problems through a reflective practice.* (Canada)

Brunner, R. (1985). Der Einsatz praxisorientierter Verfahren in der Lehrerausbildung an den Hochschulen der Bundesrepublik Deutschland (Concerning the amount of exercise-oriented methods in teacher training at the colleges of the Federal Republic of Germany). *Unterrichtswissenschaft, 13*(2), 169–181. (West Germany)

Buitink, J. (1993). Research on teacher thinking and implications for teacher training. *European Journal of Teacher Education, 16*(3), 195–203. (Netherlands)

Bujold, N., Coté, E., Paré, A., & Chevrette, Y. (1994). *Needs assessment in training student teacher supervisors.* Université Laval. (Canada)

Bullock, K. M., & Scott, W. A. H. (1990). Enterprise Awareness in Teacher Education (EATE): The evaluation of an innovation in initial teacher education. *Assessment and Evaluation in Higher Education, 15,* 232–240. (Great Britain)

Butala, M. (1987). *A critical inquiry into inservice educational programs conducted by secondary teachers training colleges of Gujarat State.* Unpublished doctoral dissertation, Gujarat University. (India)

Cagran, B. (1988). Pedagogical methodology and teacher education. *Sodobna Pedagogika, 39*(9–10), 449–452. [Contact Slovenia author correspondent.]

Cagran, B. (1989). Teachers and empirical educational research. *Sodobna Pedagogika, 40*(7–8), 340–344. [Contact Slovenia author correspondent.]

Calderhead, J. (1987). The quality of reflection in student teachers' professional learning. *European Journal of Teacher Education, 10*(3), 269–278. (Great Britain)

Calderhead, J. (1988). Learning from introductory school experience. *Journal of Education for Teaching, 14*(1), 75–83. (Great Britain)

Calderhead, J., & Miller, E. (1986). *The integration of subject matter knowledge in student teachers' classroom practice.* Research Monograph Series. Lancaster: University of Lancaster, School of Education. (Great Britain)

Cameron-Jones, M., Skinner, D., & McIntosh, A. (1985). *Focus on teaching: Staff development in primary schools.* (Scotland)

Campbell, J., & McMeniman, M. (1985). *The English as a second language (ESL) factors and index study.* Canberra: Commonwealth Schools Commission. (Australia)

Carlson, H., & Stenmalm-Sjoblom. (1992). Improving teacher education through international cooperation and partnership: Sweden and the United States. In *Teacher education in an era of global change.* Arlington, VA: International Council on Education for Teaching. (Sweden)

Carnegie Task Force on Teaching as a Profession. (1986). *A nation prepared: Teachers for the 21st century.* New York: Author. (United States)

Carpenter, P., & Byde, P. (1986). The meaning of commitment to teaching: The views of beginning teachers. *The South Pacific Journal of Teacher Education, 14*(1), 13–25. (Australia)

Carpenter, P., & Foster, W. (1979). Deciding to teach. *Australian Journal of Education, 23,* 121–131. (Australia)

Carter, D. S. G., & Hacker, R. G. (1987). A longitudinal study of the classroom behaviors of student teachers of social studies. *Journal of Education for Teaching, 13*(3), 251–256. (Australia)

Cashdan, A. (1992). New partnership—Initial teacher training in the U.K. *Teacher education in an era of global change.* Arlington, VA: International Council on Education for Teaching. (Great Britain)

Casismir, G. (1988). Inservice training in the NIVO-project in The Netherlands. *European Journal of Education. Research, Development and Policies, 23*(4), 315–321. (Netherlands)

Castro, R., Jesus, D., Schneider, M., & Ferreira, M. (1986). *Special education services in the state of Espirito Santo, Brazil: A diagnosis.* (contact H. B. Passamai). (Brazil)

Castro, R. A., Sodre, M., Passamai, H., & Pessott. (1989). *Diagnosis of educational administration in the state of Espirito Santo.* (Contact H. B. Passamai). (Brazil)

Cazden, C. B. (1990). Differential treatment in New Zealand: Reflections on research in minority education. *Teaching and Teacher Education, 6,* 291–303. (New Zealand)

Chang, A. S. C. (1990). *School-based intervention and preservice training in effective learning strategies.* Paper presented at the World Assembly of the International Council on Education for Teaching, Singapore. (ERIC Document Reproduction Service No. ED 324 279) (Singapore)

Charbonneau, M. (1993). *Current training models and professionalization of teaching: A critical analysis of the North American tendencies.* Unpublished manuscript, University of Montréal. (Canada)

Chen, A. Y., & Skuja, R. (1988). *The use of pair teaching to improve the practicum experience in pre-service teacher education.* Unpublished paper, Institute of Education, Singapore. (Singapore)

Cheng, Y. C. (1992). Teachers' professional ethics as related to students' educational outcomes and organizational characteristics. In *Teacher education in an era of global change.* Arlington, VA: International Council on Education for Teaching. (Hong Kong)

Chew-Goh, G. E. (1986). *The influence of training on the performance of teacher supervisors.* Unpublished master's dissertation, National University of Singapore. (Singapore)

Chianghan, L. (1992). The current status and future directions of teacher education in Korea. In *Teacher education in an era of global change.* Arlington, VA: International Council on Education for Teaching. (Korea)

Chivore, B. (1990). A comparative analysis of attitudes towards and perceptions of the teaching profession. *Zimbabwe Journal of Educational Research, 2*(2), 135–163. (Zimbabwe)

Churkuian, G. A., & Kissock, C. (Eds.). (1991). Teacher education: Perspectives from abroad. *Action in Teacher Education, 13*(3). (United States)

Clift, J. C. (1983a). *Improving the utilization of information gained through evaluation.* Wellington, Victoria: University of Wellington. (New Zealand)

Clift, J. C. (1983b). *Meta evaluation of institutional reviews.* Wellington, Victoria: University of Wellington. (New Zealand)

Cochran, J., & Miller, C. (1984). *Teacher competence as determined by student achievement.* (ERIC Document Reproduction Service No. ED 246 645). (Egypt)

Coldevin, G., & Naidu, S. (1989). Inservice teacher education at a distance: Trends in Third World development. *Open Learning, 4*(1), 9–15. (General)

Collins, K. A. (1989). The development of teacher education in Japan, 1968–1980s. *Teacher and Teacher Education, 5*(6), 217–228. (Japan)

Cooke, B. L., & Pang, K. C. (1992). Entry characteristics of trained and untrained beginning teachers. In Ho Wah Kam & Ruth Y. L. Wong (Eds.), *Improving the quality of the teaching profession: An interna-*

tional perspective (pp. 19–44). Singapore: International Council on Education for Teaching. (Singapore)

Coonen, H. W. A. M. (1987). *De opleiding van leraren basisonderwijs* (Teacher education for primary schools). Unpublished doctoral dissertation (with English summary), Leiden University. Den Bosch: Katholiek Pedagogisch Centrum. (Netherlands)

Corner, T. (1988). *Ethnic monitoring of the training of teachers.* (Scotland)

Corporaal, A. H. (1991). Repertory grid research into the cognitions of prospective primary school teachers. *Teaching and Teacher Education, 7,* 315–329. (Netherlands)

Corporaal, A. H., Boei, F., & Kieviet, F. K. (1993). Reflections upon five years of repertory grid research into declarative schemata of prospective teachers. *Journal of Structural Learning, 11*(4), 333–348. (Netherlands)

Crabtree, B. (1990). Knowledge and curriculum planning in a college of education. Palmerston North, Delta. *The Journal of the Education Department of Massey University, 43,* 49–56. (New Zealand)

Craft, M. (1990). Charting the changes in teacher education. *Cambridge Journal of Education, 20*(1), 73–78. (Great Britain)

Cramm, F., & Kelleher, R. (1992). The development and use of parallel international cases of teaching. In *Teacher education in an era of global change.* Arlington, VA: International Council on Education for Teaching. (Canada)

Crebbin, W. (1992). Beginning to make a difference: Learning to question schooling through student-teachers' personal theories and critical reflection. In *Teacher education in an era of global change.* Arlington, VA: International Council on Education for Teaching. (Australia)

Creemers, B. P. M. (1986). Relationships between research on teaching, educational innovation, and teaching: The case of the Netherlands. *Teaching and Teacher Education, 2*(2), 105–113. (Netherlands)

Crèton, H. A., & Wubbels, T. (1984). *Ordeproblemen bij beginnende leraren; een analyse van de ordeproblemen bij beginnende leraren in het voortgezet onderwijs en een studie naar de mogelijkeden om via begeleiding een oplossing voor deze problemen te viden. (Problems of classroom discipline with beginning teachers and a study of possibilities to find a solution for these problems through guidance).* Doctoral thesis, Rijksuniversiteit Utrecht. Utrecht: WCC. (Netherlands)

Crèton, H. A., Wubbels, T., & Hooymayers, H. P. (1989). Escalated disorderly situations in the classroom and the improvement of these situations. *Teaching and Teacher Education, 5*(3), 205–216. (Netherlands)

Cumming, C. I., Kidd, J. M., Melver, J. M., & Wight, J. R. (1985). *The practice of staff development in secondary schools, phase two.* (Scotland)

Dann, H. D., Müller-Fohrbrodt, B., & Cloetta, B. (1981). Sozialisation junger Lehrer im Beruf: "Praxisschock" drei Jahre später (Socialization of young teachers in the business: "Practice shock" three years later). *Zeitschrift für entwicklungspsychologie und Pädagogische Psychologie, 13*(3), 251–262. (West Germany)

Dave, C. S. (1987). *Relative effectiveness of microteaching having summative model of integration versus miniteaching model in terms of general teaching competence, teacher attitude towards teaching, pupil liking and pupil achievement.* Unpublished doctoral dissertation, Devi Ahilya Vishwa Vidyalay. (India)

Davies, L. (1991). *The selection and recruitment of teacher trainees for 1991.* Wellington: Research and Statistics Decision, Ministry of Education, *4,* 16–37. (New Zealand)

Dawson, D., Mazurek, K., & Deyoung, A. J. (1984). Courses in the social foundations of education: The students' view. *Journal of Education for Teaching, 10*(3), 242–248. (Canada)

De Frankrijker, H. (1990). The training of primary education teachers in the Netherlands: Discrepancies between supply and demand, 1920–1990. In J. T. Voorbach & L. G. M. Prick (Eds.), *Research and developments on teacher education in the Netherlands* (pp. 99–111). Amsterdam/Lisse: Sets & Zeitlinger. (Netherlands)

De Frankrijker, H. (1993). Multicultural education at teacher training institutes for primary education in the Netherlands. In G. Verma (Ed.), *Inequality and teacher education: An international perspective* (pp. 121–133). London: Falmer. (Netherlands)

De Frankrijker, H., & De Wit, W. (1993). Teaching practice and the preparation of primary schoolteachers for a multicultural society. In J. T. Voorbach (Ed.), *Teacher Education 9. Research and developments on teacher education in the Netherlands* (pp. 5–15). De Lier: Academic Book Centre. (Netherlands)

De Frankrijker, H., & Kieviet, F. K. (1991). Examining the research on practice teaching in teacher education: A review especially focused on the persons involved. In H. Voorbach & L. Prick (Eds.), *Teacher Education 8. Research and developments on teacher education in the Netherlands* (pp. 146–159). Amsterdam/Lisse: Swets & Zeitlinger. (Netherlands)

De Frankrijker, H., & Lie, R. (1993). *Expert beliefs about teacher training in multicultural perspective: The multicultural competent teacher in the Netherlands.* Paper presented at the 18th ATEE conference, Lisbon, Portugal. In J. T. Voorbach (Ed.), *Teacher Education 10. Research and developments on teacher education in the Netherlands.* De Lier: Academic Book Centre. (Netherlands)

De Jong, R., Matthijssen, C., & Tillema, H. H. (1987). Kenmerken van nascholingscursussen (Characteristics of inservice training course). In J. J. Peters & H. H. Tillema (Eds.), *Schooling in onderwijs en bedrijf* (Schooling in Education and Industry). Lisse: Swets & Zeitlinger. (Netherlands)

De Jong, R., Matthijssen, C., & Tillema, H. H. (1988). *The effects of training and coaching of teachers.* Paper presented at the annual convention of the Dutch Association for Educational Research (ORD), Leuven. (Netherlands)

De Kock, D. (1992). An intensive communication training programme (ICTP) for preservice teachers. In H. W. K. Wong & R. Y. L. Wong (Eds.), *Improving the quality of the teaching profession: An international perspective* (pp. 167–176). Singapore: International Council on Education for Teaching. (South Africa)

Dembèlè, M. (1991). *Political instability, economic hardships and the preservice education of secondary teachers in Burkina Faso: 1960–1990.* Unpublished doctoral dissertation, Michigan State University. (Burkina Faso)

Des Lièvres, T., Pelletier, M. L., & Demers, M. (1992). *Attitudes toward science in teacher training for primary level.* Laval University, Montreal. (Canada)

Diamond, C. T. P. (1985). Becoming a teacher: An altering eye. In D. Bannister (Ed.), *Issues and approaches in personal construct theory.* London: Academic Press. (Australia)

Disabanda. (1986). *Zimbabwe's integrated teacher education course (ZINTE).* (Zimbabwe)

Dolbec, A. (1992). Action research as a partnership strategy in the training of teachers: Report of an experience. In *Teacher education in an era of global change* (p. 142). Arlington, VA: International Council on Education for Teaching. (Canada)

Donga, N. S. (1987). *A study of the adjustment of trainees of teachers training colleges of Gujarat.* Unpublished doctoral dissertation, Saurashtra University. (India)

Doornekamp, B. G., & van Kesteren, B. J. (1991). Primary school teacher training in the European community: An overview of recent developments. *European Journal of Teacher Education, 14*(3), 241–251. (General)

Draper, J. (1988). *Students and probationers in transition.* (Scotland)

Draper, J., Fraser, H., & Taylor, W. B. (1991). *A study of probationers.* (Scotland)

Dror, Y. (1992). Between academization and personal development—teacher education in Israel between 1980–1990. *Direction in Teacher Education—A Journal of Research in Teacher Education and Inservice Training, 1,* 11–37. (Hebrew) (Israel)

Dubs, R. (1990). Qualifikationen fur Lehrkrafte. Ziele, Probleme, Grenzen und Möglichkeiten (Qualifications of teachers' aims, problems, limitations and possibilities). *Schweizerische Zeitschrift für kaufmannisches Bildungswesen, 84,* 115–140. (Switzerland)

Dunkin, M. (Ed.). (1987). *International encyclopedia of teaching and teacher education.* Oxford, England. (United States).

Dzvimbo, K. P. (1989). The dilemmas of teacher education reform in Zimbabwe. *Interchange, 20*(4), 16–31. (Zimbabwe)

Edoyan, R. (1992). The organizing of teaching under extreme conditions. In *Teacher education in an era of global change,* (p. 82). Arlington, VA: International Council on Education for Teaching. (Armenia)

Effectiveness and costs of three approaches to train elementary school teachers in Sri Lanka. (1990). USAID. (ISN 71434) (Sri Lanka)

Ekbote, E. R. (1987). *Development of a strategy for integration of skills in teacher training.* Unpublished doctoral dissertation, University of Baroda. (India)

Ekholm, M. (1988). *Inservice teacher education and school development.* Stockholm: National Swedish Board of Education. (ERIC Document Reproduction Service No. ED 306 199) (Sweden)

Elder, R. J. (1986). *The role of the schools and colleges in the training and assessment of primary school teachers.* (Scotland)

Elliott, R. (1992). Moving from domestication to internationalization: Teacher education in Papua, New Guinea. In *Teacher education in an era of global change* (p. 142). Arlington, VA: International Council on Education for Teaching. (Australia)

El-Meligi, M. H. (1992). Perceptions of our future world: An imperative for today's teacher education programs. In *Teacher education in an era of global change* (p. 108). Arlington, VA: International Council on Education for Teaching. (Egypt)

Eng, S. P. et al. (1983). Feasibility of the MTAI as a selection instrument for pre-service teacher education: A pilot project. *Singapore Journal of Education, 5*(2), 20–42. (Singapore)

Etelapelto, A. (1992). *Reflectivity and self-awareness in the development of expertise.* Reports from the Vocational Teacher Education University of Jyvaskyla, 3. (Finland)

Eugster, W. (1988). *Eignung und Motivation für den Lehrerberuf: Eine empirische Untersuchung über persönlichkeitsmerkmale von Lehramtskandidaten (Aptitude and motivation for the profession of teaching: An empirical study about personality traits of student teachers).* Unpublished doctoral dissertation, University of Zurich. (Switzerland)

European Information Centre for Further Education of Teachers. (1988). *Selected aspects of inservice education of teachers in the eighties (Further education of teachers series, 6).* Prague, Czechoslovakia: Charles University. (ERIC Document Reproduction Service No. ED 309 139) (Czech Republic)

Evans, R. C., Ferrucci, B. J., & Cyr, V. (1989). *Mathematics teacher preparation: USA versus USSR.* (ERIC Document Reproduction Series No. ED 322 089) (Soviet Union)

Farah, A. H., & Tarvin, W. L. (1989). Curricular change and in-service teacher training programs in developing South Asian countries. *Journal of Curriculum Studies, 21,* 567–571. (General)

Farine, A., & Hupper, C. (1989). *Teacher training in computer-based education: Assessment and tendencies.* University of Montreal. (Canada)

Farooq, R. A. (1988). *Training of primary school teachers in Pakistan: Different models.* USAID. (ISN 64770) (Pakistan)

Feldens, M. D. G. F., & Duncan, J. K. (1988). Brazilians speak out about their schools: Implications for teacher education. *Journal of Education for Teaching, 14,* 105–123. (Brazil)

Fernandez, M., Gonzalez, R., & Subirats, A. (1988). The tutor's role in teaching practice in initial teacher training. *European Journal of Teacher Education, 11,* 123–130. (Spain)

Fitzgibbon, A., & Heywood, J. (1986). The recognition of conjunctive and identity needs in teacher development: Their implications for the planning of inservice training. *European Journal of Teacher Education, 9*(3), 271–286. (Ireland)

Fitzgibbon, A., Heywood, J., & Cameron, L. A. (1991). The matching of learning styles to teaching during teacher education. A preliminary study in experience versus theory in teacher education. In C. L. Callaghan (Eds.), *Learning styles in the classroom* (pp. 1–21). Monographs of the department of teacher education (Vol. 2). Dublin, Ireland: University of Dublin. (Ireland)

Frey, K. (1992). *Qualifizieren von Lehrerinnen und Lehrern an höheren Bildungseinrichtungen (Qualification of teachers at high schools).* Zurich: Zentrum fuer Weiterbildung. (Switzerland)

Frey, K., & Frey, A. (1988). *Anforderungen an die allgemeine Didaktik: Eine erhebung bei den Fachdidaktikern, Praktikumslehrern und studenten der ETH (Prerequisites for the construction of a course in didactics: An inquiry with teacher trainers, mentors, and students).* Zurich: ETH, Institut für Verhältenswissenschaft. (Switzerland)

Fujieda, S., Maejima, Y., & Shirai, M. (1980). Study on the improvement of student teaching (the second interim report). Japanese Society for the Study of Education, Study Committee on Teacher Education. *A study on the practical strategies for the improvement of teacher education, 2,* 34–103. (Japan)

Fujieda, S., & Shirai, M. (1981). Study on the improvement of student teaching (the third interim report). Japanese Society for the Study of Education, Study Committee on Teacher Education. *A study on the practical strategies for the improvement of teacher education, 3,* 28–58. (Japan)

Fullan, M. G., Connelly, F. M., Watson, N., Heller, M., & Scane, J. (1990). *Teacher education in Ontario: Current practice and options for the future.* Toronto, Canada: Ontario Department of Education, Ontario Ministry of Colleges and Universities. (ERIC Document Reproductive Service No. ED 319 697). (Canada)

Fullan, M., Wideen, M., & Estabrook, G. (1983). *A study of teacher training institutions in Anglophone Canada, Volume I: Current perspectives on teacher training in Canada, an overview of faculty and student perceptions.* Report prepared for the Social Sciences and Humanities Council (Grant# 410–77-0459-21). Vancouver: Simon Fraser University. (Canada)

Gardner, J., & Salters, J. (1990). Information technology in education and teacher education in France. *European Journal of Teacher Education, 13* (3), 161–172. (France)

Gauthier, C., & Tardif, M. (in press). Types of knowledge in the teachers' training programs in Quebec, at the primary education level. Laval University. (Canada)

Geddis, A. N. (1990, May). *The role of the practicum in development of reflective teachers.* Paper presented at the Joint Centre for Teacher Development Invitational Conference, D Lake, Ontario. (Canada)

Golli, D. (1980). Uniting theory with practice in teacher training. *Sodobna Pedagogika, 34*(5–6), 184–194. [Contact Slovenia author correspondent.]

Gopalacharyulu, R. V. V. (1984). *A study of relationship between certain psychological factors and achievement of student teachers in teacher training institutes of Andhra Pradesh.* Unpublished doctoral dissertation, Sri Venkateshwara University. (India)

Gorny, P. (1991). Fundamental informatics in teacher education in West Germany. *Computers and Education, 16,* 37–42. (West Germany)

Gottlieb, E. (1991). Global rhetoric, local policy: Teacher training reform in Israeli education. *Educational Policy, 5*(2), 178–192. (Israel)

Goyal, J. C., Sabharwal, N., & Tewari, A. D. (1984). *Developing tools for admission to secondary teacher training institutions in India.* New Delhi: NCERT. (India)

Gran, B. (1982). *The relationship between research and basic teacher training*. Rapport från Styrelsen för Lund/Malmo högskoleregion, Nr 9. Lund: Regionstyrelsen. (Sweden)

Gran, B. (1985). *Is inservice training of teachers a good means to improve the school?* Stockholm, Sweden: Skolöverstyrelsen. (Sweden)

Grimmett, P. P. (Ed.). (1984). *Research in teacher education: Current problems and future prospects in Canada*. (Vancouver: Vancouver Centre for the Study of Education, University of British Columbia. (Canada)

Grimmett, P. P. (1988, June). *Teacher educators as researchers: Cultivating conditions for reflective practice in teacher preparation*. Paper presented at the CATE-Invitational Pre-Conference, Windsor, Ontario. (Canada)

Grimmett, P. P., & Ratzlaff, H. C. (1986). Expectations for the cooperating teacher. *Teacher Education, 37*(6), 41–50. (Canada)

Guilbert, L. (1990). *A case study within the framework of an inquiry teaching approach and practical teacher training*. Laval University. (Canada)

Guri-Rozenblit, S. (1992). The integrative model of the open university and teacher education colleges in the Israeli teacher education system. *Directions in Teacher Education—A Journal of Research in Teacher Education and Inservice Training, 1*, 151–165. (Israel)

Gusakovsky, M. (1993). *A concept of a national school of Belarus*. Minsk. [Contact Belarus author-correspondent for further details.] (Belarus)

Gutman, L. (1954). A new approach to factor analysis: The tadex. In D. F. Lazarshfeld (Ed.), *Mathematical thinking in social sciences*. (pp. 216–348). Glenco, IL: Free Press.

Haitani, J. (1981). A study of the systemization of inservice education for teachers. *Bulletin of the Japan Educational Administration Society, 7*, 37–50. (Japan)

Halaka, J. (1992). *Development of scientific thinking in the training of class teachers. An analysis of the attainment of the goals of advanced studies in education in the light of phenomenological approach*. (Finland)

Halpin, D., Croll, P., & Redman, K. (1990). Teachers' perceptions of the effects of inservice education. *British Educational Research Journal, 16*, 163–177. (Great Britain)

Halwitz, M. (1990). Becoming a teacher: Professional socialization in teacher education institutes in Israel. *Studies in Teacher Education*, 107–122. (Hebrew) (Israel)

Hamalainen, J. (1993). *Social pedagogic orientation in the vocational teacher education of social work*. Reports from the Vocational Teacher Education College of Jyvaskyla, 5. (Finland)

Harding, J. (1991). *A study of career intentions: 1990 intake diploma of teaching (early childhood) students*. Conference proceedings, Fifth Early Childhood Convention, Dunedin. (New Zealand)

Harriott, M. (1987). *Institutional innovations in teacher training colleges in Jamaica, West Indies*. Unpublished doctoral dissertation, Fordham University. (Jamaica)

Harrison, B. (1986). Preparing teachers for bicultural classrooms: Alaskan parallels. Palmerston North, Delta. *The Journal of the Education Department of Massey University, 38*, 36–44. (New Zealand)

Harvey, D., & Green, C. (1984). Attitudes of New Zealand teachers, teachers in training and non-teachers toward mainstreaming. Wellington. *New Zealand Journal of Educational Studies, 19*(1), 34–44. (New Zealand)

Hayashi, T. (1986). Students' aspiration for the teaching profession: An analytical study of students' self-evaluation of their teaching aptitude. *Technical Bulletin of Tokushima Bunri University, 31*, 21–41. (Japan)

Hederih, D. (1992). Features of personality structure of students at the faculty of pedagogy maribor. *Sodobna Pedagogika 43*(5–6), 285–292. [Contact Slovenia author correspondent.]

Heller, K. A., & Wichterlich, H. (1982). Evaluation des DIFF—Fernstudienlehrgangs "Ausbildung zum Beratungslehrer" (Evaluation of the DIFF—distance education course of study "Improvement of the cooperating teacher"). *Psychologie in Erziehung und Unterricht, 30*, 22–26. (West Germany)

Hensler, H. (1992). *Development of an integrated approach to learning strategy instruction and teacher education*. Quebec: Sherbrooke University. (Canada)

Hewitson, M. (Ed.) (1979). *Research into teacher education: The practical teaching skills*. ERDC Report No. 19. Canberra: Australian Government Publishing Service. (Australia)

Heywood, J. (1991). Student teachers as researchers of instruction in the classroom. In J. H. C. Vonk & H. J. van Heiden (Eds.), *New prospects for teacher education in Europe*. Amsterdam/Brussels: Universitaire Leranenoplciding Vrje Universiteit. Association for Teacher Education in Europe. (Ireland)

Heywood, J., & Fitzgibbon, A. (1980). The role of self-assessment in the design and evaluation of short courses for the training of head teachers in management. In J. Heywood, S. McGuinness, & D. E. Murphy (Eds.), *Final report of the public examination project to the Minister of Education*. Dublin: School of Education, University of Dublin. (Ireland)

Heywood, J., Fitzgibbon, A., & Cameron, L. A. (1991). Experience versus theory in teacher education. Student teachers as researchers. In P. Carroll (Ed.), *An investigation of the learning styles inventory during student teaching in German* (Monographs of the Department of Teacher Education, 2). Dublin, Ireland: University of Dublin. (Ireland)

Heywood, J., & Heywood, S. (1993). The training of student teachers in discovery methods of instruction and learning. In A. L. Leino et al. (Eds.), *Integration of technology and reflection in teaching: A challenge for European teacher education*. Helsinki: ATEE Conference Proceedings, University of Helsinki. (Ireland)

Hickling-Hudson, A., & McMeniman, M. (1993). Curricular responses to multiculturalism: An overview of teacher education courses in Australia. *Teacher & Teacher Education, 9*(3), 243–252. (Australia)

Hivon, R., Beauchesne, A., Lavoie, M., & Tétreault, R. (1994). *A university-school partnership for the supervision of student teachers*. Quebec: Sherbrooke University. (Canada)

Ho, W. K. et al. (1983). Continuity and discontinuity between training and school experience: Follow-up studies of former students of the Institute of Education. *Singapore Journal of Education, 5*(2), 49–63. (Singapore)

Hogben, D., & Lawson, M. J. (1983). Attitudes of secondary school teacher trainees and their practice teaching supervisors. *Journal of Education for Teaching, 9*(3), 249–263. (Australia)

Hogben, D., & Lawson, M. J. (1984a). Attitude stability and change during teacher training. *The South Pacific Journal of Teacher Education, 12*(2), 34–44. (Australia)

Hogben, D., & Lawson, M. J. (1984b). Trainee and beginning teacher attitude stability and change: Four case studies. *Journal of Education for Teaching, 10*(2), 135–153. (Australia)

Holborn, P. (1983). *Integrating theory and practice from the student teacher's perspective*. Paper presented at the annual meeting of the American Educational Research Association, Montreal. (Canada)

Holmes Group. (1986). *Tomorrow's teachers*. East Lansing, MI: Author. (United States)

Horiuchi, T., & Mizumoto, N. (1986). Students' attitudes toward and interests in teacher selection. *Bulletin of Kyoto University of Education, 69*, 11–35. (Japan)

Housego, B. (1992). Monitoring student teachers' feelings of preparedness to teach and teacher efficacy in a new elementary teacher education program. *Journal of Education for Teaching, 18*(3), 259–272. (Canada)

Housego, I. E., & Grimmett, P. P. (Eds.). (1985). *Teaching and teacher education: Generating and utilizing valid knowledge for professional socialization.* Canada: Wedge Press, University of British Columbia. (Canada)

Hughes, P. (1988). *Future directions for teacher education. Trends, needs, and alternatives relating to inclusion of new content areas in teacher education.* Paris: UNESCO, Department of Higher Education and Training of Educational Personnel Report No. ED/C/14.1; ED/HEP/TEP. (ERIC Document Reproduction Service No. ED 327 540) (General)

Husen, T., & Postethwaite, T. N. (Eds.). (1987/supplement, 1989). *International Encyclopedia of Education.* New York: Pergamon Press. (United States)

Inoue, S. (1979). Effects of self-esteem level in student teaching. *Bulletin of School of Education, Okayama University, 52,* 185–198. (Japan)

Inthar, D. (1991). Mentor-teacher and novice-teacher in elementary school. *Sodobna Pedagogika, 42*(9–10), 568–578. [Contact Slovenia author correspondent].

International Council on Education for Teaching (ICET). (1988). *Progress and promise in teacher education.* Papers of the conference of the South Pacific Association and ICET, Sydney, Australia. (ERIC Document Reproduction Service No. ED 310 091). (United States)

Irwin, K. (1991). Maori education in 1991: A review. *New Zealand Annual Review of Education.* Wellington: New Zealand.

Isra-Pavirat, S. (1982). *Study of educators' perceptions concerning teacher education in selected institutions in Thailand.* Unpublished doctoral dissertation, Oklahoma State University. (Thailand)

Ito, K. (1980). Developmental process of professional orientation of students of the faculty of education. *Bulletin of the Faculty of Education, Shizuoka University, Liberal Arts and Social Sciences, 31,* 115–128. (Japan)

Izuno, T., Yoshida, H., Enomoto, K., & Ueno, K. (1981). A study on the elements making for leadership in teachers. *Bulletin of the Japan Educational Administration Society, 7,* 129–143. (Japan)

Jarchow, E. (1992). The case method in teacher education: Six lessons from New Zealand. *Education, 112*(4), 624–630. (New Zealand)

Jarvinen, A. (1991). Development of reflective thinking during teacher education. In M. Carretero et al. (Eds.), *Learning and instruction. European research in an international context: Vol. 111* (pp. 527–538). Oxford: Pergamon Press. (Finland)

Jarvinen, A. (1992a). Development of reflection during high-level professional education. In *Quality and communication for improvement. Proceedings* (pp. 93–109). Twelfth European AIR Forum, Lyon 1990. Utrecht: Lemma. (Finland)

Jarvinen, A. (1992b). Development of reflective thinking from student teaching to beginning teaching. In S. Ojanen (Ed.), *Nordic teacher training congress: Challenges for teacher's profession in the 21st century* (pp. 60–72). University of Joensuu, Finland. Research Reports of the Faculty of Education, no. 44. (Finland)

Jayne, E. (1987). A case study of implementing equal opportunities: Sex equity. *Journal of Education for Teaching, 13*(2), 155–162. (Great Britain)

Jonsson, M., & Ahlström, K-G. (1988). *Educational belief systems among teacher educators,* Uppsala: Uppsala University, Department of Education. (Sweden)

Juasovec, N. (1988). Creative students and study success. *Sodobna Pedagogika, 39*(7–8), 374–381. [Contact Slovenia author correspondent.]

Jutras, F. (1994). *Student teachers' pedagogical ideas and values in high school education.* Quebec: Sherbrooke University. (Canada)

Kalaoja, E. (1992, July). Teacher training innovations from a rural point of view: The Haave project in Oulu. In *Developing rural schools—A key to community growth.* Interskola Conference 1992 in Bodo, Norway. (Finland)

Kalaoja, E., & Pikkarainen, E. (1993, August). Innovative teacher education: A reflective, contextual and decentralized model in Leino. *Integration of technology and reflection in teaching: A challenge for European teacher education.* The seventeenth conference of the Association for Teacher Education in Europe, Lahti, Finland. (Finland)

Kalyanpurkar, S. (1986). *The effect of microteaching on the teaching competence of inservice teachers and its impact on pupils' attainment and pupils' liking.* Unpublished doctoral dissertation, Devi Ahilya Vishwa Vidyalay. (India)

Kari, J. (1993, August). *Teacher orientation in the early stages of teacher education.* Paper presented at the sixth ISATT conference, 10 Gothenburg, Finland. (Finland)

Katiyar, B. L. (1982). *Personality traits and attainment of skills through microteaching.* Unpublished doctoral dissertation, Banaras Hindu University. (India)

Katz, S. (1990). Personal constructs in the perception of students by student-teachers in a teacher education college. *Students in Teacher Education,* 107–122. (Hebrew) (Israel)

Keer, S. (1991, November–December). Beyond dogma: Teacher education in the USSR. *Journal of Teacher Education, 42*(5), 332–349. (United States)

Keiny, S. (1994). Teachers' professional development: A dialogue between universities and schools. *Theory into Practice in Curriculum Planning, 9.* Israeli Ministry of Education, Department of Curriculum. (Hebrew) (Israel)

Khan, A. H. (1985). *Effectiveness of microteaching technique in terms of student achievement.* Unpublished doctoral dissertation, Avadh University. (India)

Kharlamov, I. (1992). *Pedagogics.* [Contact Belarus author correspondent for further information.] (Belarus)

Kharlamov, I. (1994). Improvement of textbooks and teaching pedagogics. *Education and training, 5,* 103–113. [Contact Belarus author correspondent for further information.] (Belarus)

Kieviet, F. K. (1984). Opleiding onderwijsgevenden: Trends in onderwijskundig onderzoek (Teacher education: Trends in educational research). *VOR-Bulletin, 8*(1), 6–13. (Netherlands)

Kirilyuk, L., & Krouchinin, S. (1992). Paradox of knowledge: Attempt of solution. *Education and training, 5,* 64–69. [Contact Belarus author correspondent for further information.] (Belarus)

Kirilyuk, L., & Krouchinin, S. (1994). About teacher education in the Republic of Belarus. *Education and training, 7,* 17–29. [Contact Belarus author correspondent for further information.] (Belarus)

Kishimoto, K., Okatoo, T., Hayashi, T., & Koyama, E. (1981). A study of the teachers' professional development model (II): A factor analysis of teaching competencies. *Bulletin of Faculty of Education, University of Hiroshima, 30,* 119–129. (Japan)

Klebanov, A. (1990). Problems and difficulties of beginning teachers as related to personal and contextual features. *Studies in Teacher Education,* 53–71. (Israel)

Klinzing, H. G. (1990). Research on teacher education in West Germany. In R. P. Tisher & M. F. Wideen (Eds.), *Research in teacher education: International perspectives* (pp. 89–104). Bristol, PA: Falmer. (West Germany)

Klinzing, H. G., & Klinzing-Eurich, G. (1988). Lehrerausbildung im Laboratorium: Ein Überblick über die forschung in der Bundesrepublik Deutschland (Teacher improvement in the laboratory: An overview of the research in the Federal Republic of Germany). In A. Leuteritz, C. Weisbach, & T. Helle (Eds.), *Konkrete Pädogik: Festschrift für Walther Zifreund zum 60. Geburtstag* (pp. 121–140). Tübingen: Attempto. (West Germany)

Klinzing, H. G., Klinzing-Eurich, G., & Floden, R. E. (1989, April). *Integrating the functions of laboratory practice: Skill acquisition and reflection-based decision making in improving expository teaching.* Paper presented at the annual meeting of the American Educational Research Association, San Francisco. (West Germany)

Klinzing, H. G., Leuteritz, A., Schiefer, H. J., & Steiger, S. (1986). Auswirkungen von "direktem" und "indirektem" Training auf nichtverbale Sensitivität und nichtverbale Ausdruksdraft (Effects of "direct" and "indirect" training on nonverbal expressions). In W. Langhthaler & H. Schneider (Eds.), *Video-rückmeldung und verhaltenstraining* (pp. 145–194). Münster: Maks Publishers. (West Germany)

Kochetov, A. (1992). *Pedagogical creation: Thoughts and search,* Nos. 1–4. [Contact Belarus author correspondent for further information.] (Belarus)

Koetsier, C. P., Wubbels, T., & Driel, C. (1992). An investigation into careful supervision of student teaching. In J. H. C. Vonk, J. H. G. J. Giesbers, J. J. Peters, & T. Wubbels (Eds.), *New prospects for teacher education in Europe II: Conference proceedings* (pp. 245–254). Utrecht: WCC. (Netherlands)

Kohonen, V. (1992, August). *Restructuring school learning as learner education: Towards a collegial school culture and learning.* Paper presented at the Nordic teacher training congress challenges for teachers' profession in the 21st century, Lahti. University of Joensuu, Research Reports of the Faculty of Education, 44(92), 36–59. (Finland)

Kolstad, R. K., Coker, D. R., & Elelhoff, C. (1989, January). Teacher education in Germany: An alternative method for the U.S. *The Clearing House, 62*(5), 233–235. (West Germany)

Kooi, S. W., & Sim, W. K. (1992). Reflective review of teacher education in "Asean" countries in an era of global change. In *Teacher education in an era of global change.* Arlington, VA: International Council on Education for Teaching. (Asia)

Korpinen, E. (1992). *Quantity and quality-education and growth. The evaluation of class teachers' training at the department of teacher education at the Jyvaskyla University in 1979–1992.* (Finland)

Korthagen, F. A. J. (1982). *Learning to reflect as a basis for teacher training.* Unpublished doctoral dissertation with English summary, Gravenhage (The Hague) (Netherlands)

Korthagen, F. A. J. (1987). Internally and externally steered teaching in the training of teachers. In J. J. Peters & H. H. Tillema (Eds.), *Schooling in education and industry.* Lisse: Swets and Zeitlinger. (Netherlands)

Korthagen, F. A. J. (1988). The influence of learning orientations on the development of reflective teaching. In J. Calderhead (Ed.), *Teachers' professional learning.* Lewes: Falmer. (Netherlands)

Korthagen, F. A. J. (1992). Techniques for stimulating reflection in teacher education seminars. *Teaching and Teacher Education, 8*(3), 265–274. (Netherlands)

Korthagen, F. A. J. (1993). The role of reflection in teachers' professional development. In L. Kremer-Hayon, H. C. Vonk, & R. Fessler (Eds.), *Teacher professional development: A multiple perspective approach* (133–145). Amsterdam/Lisse: Swets & Zeitlinger. (Netherlands)

Korthagen, F. A. J., & Verkuyl, H. S. (1987, April). *Supply and demand: Learning conceptions and their importance for teacher education programs.* Paper presented at the annual meeting of the American Educational Research Association, Washington. (Netherlands)

Korthagen, F. A. J., & Wubbels, T. (1988). *The effects of a training that aims at teaching prospective teachers to reflect.* Paper presented at the annual convention of the Dutch Association for Educational Research (ORD), Leuven. (Netherlands)

Kotb, U. S. E. (1984). Innovations in inservice teacher education in Egypt. *ICET Yearbook, 1984* (pp. 57–64). (Egypt)

Krasnova, T., Krasnova, Y., & Polopnnikov, A. (1993). Reflexive and situational pattern of pedagogical professional development. *Psychological science and public practice,* 23–26. (Belarus)

Kremer, E. (1993). Joint creative work as a special regime of pedagogical activity. *Psychological Science and Public Practice* (pp. 195–197). (Belarus)

Kremer-Hayon, L. (1991). Teacher professional development—The elaboration of a concept. *European Journal of Teacher Education, 14*(1), 79–85. (Israel)

Kremer-Hayon, L. (1992). Teachers' professional development—An elaboration of the concept. *Studies in Education 57/58,* 145–156. (Hebrew, Published by the University of Haifa) (Israel)

Kremer-Hayon, L., & Wubbels, T. (1992). Interpersonal relationships of cooperating teachers and student teachers' satisfaction with supervision. *Journal of Classroom Interaction, 27*(1), 31–38. (Israel)

Kromer, W., & Fanslow, W. (1990). *Liberian primary education project (PEP): Final report.* USAID. (ISN 71578) (Liberia)

Krouchinin, S. (1993). About pedagogical reflexion. *Psychological science and public practice,* 23–26. (Belarus)

Kyriacou, C., & Cheng, H. (1993). Student teachers' attitudes toward the humanistic approach to teaching and learning in schools. *European Journal of Teacher Education, 16*(2), 163–168. (Great Britain)

Laifu, L., & Zhonglai, L. (1989). *Explorations in specialized curriculum of mathematics in Chinese institutions of teacher education.* Teacher Education Research. (China)

Laine, K. (1992a). *The students' conceptions of education, teaching and learning I: Describing the conceptions of students becoming nursery school, class and subject teachers.* University of Turku, Faculty of Education. (Finland)

Laine, K. (1992b). *The students' conceptions of education, teaching and learning II: Conceptions of students becoming nursery school, class and subject teachers at the beginning of training.* University of Turku, Faculty of Education. (Finland)

Laine, K. (1993). *The students' conceptions of education, teaching and learning III: Changes in the conceptions held by students becoming nursery school and class teachers during their training.* University of Turku, Faculty of Education. (Finland)

Lamm, Z. (1986). Teacher education in Israel: A present situation. *European Journal of Teacher Education, 9*(3), 233–245. (Israel)

Lang, G. (1990). Draagt de psychologie iets bij aan het onderwijs? (Does psychology contribute anything to education?) *Psycholoog, 25*(1), 6–9. (Netherlands)

Langthaler, W., Schultz, R., & Elsinghorst, J. (1986). Effekte eines Lehr-Labor-Training "Lob und Tadel" (Effects of a teaching-laboratory-training "commendation and criticism") *Unterrichtswissenschaft, 3,* 291–302. (West Germany)

Lau, W. H., et al. (1968). *Why teach?: A study of motives for choosing teaching as a career.* Singapore: Teachers Training College. (Singapore)

Lawes, J. S. (1987a). The relationship between non-verbal awareness of self and teaching competence in student teachers. *Journal of Education for Teaching, 13*(2), 147–154. (Great Britain)

Lawes, J. S. (1987b). Student teachers' awareness of pupils' non-verbal responses. *Journal of Education for Teaching, 13*(3), 257–266. (Great Britain)

Leavitt, H. (1991, November–December). Worldwide issues and problems in teacher education. *Journal of Teacher Education, 42*(5), 323–331. (United States)

Lemke, D. A. (1989, October). *Present, past, and future of training teachers in El Salvador.* USAID. (ISN 67193) (El Salvador)

Lessard, C., & Mathurin, C. (1989). *Evolutionary trends of the Quebec teacher group at the primary and secondary levels: 1960–1986.* University of Montreal. (Canada)

Lévèsque, M., & Gervais, C. (1994). *First year teacher induction.* (Université de Montréal. (Canada)

Lewy, A. (1992). Evaluation results as input for improving the quality of inservice programs: Using responses to open-ended questions. *Directions in teacher education—A journal of research in teacher education and in-service training, 1,* 105–120. (Hebrew) (Israel)

Ligons, C. M. (1990). *Inservice education in Thailand: Key innovations since 1980.* USAID. (ISN 72469) (Thailand)

Liikanen, P. (1990). *Fairy tale as a model of identity and life position.* University of Jyvaskyla, Department of Teacher Education. (Finland)

Lim-Quek, M., & Tay-Koay, S. L. (1987). *The experiences and perceptions of graduate teachers after one year of full-time teaching: A follow-up study.* Unpublished report, Institute of Education. (Singapore)

Lindemann, H. (1984). Schulpraxis in der lehrerausbildung: Eine Untersuchung bei Lehramtsstudenten des Faches Chemie (School practice in teacher training: An investigation of student teachers in a chemistry department). *Naturwissenschaft im Unterricht—Physik/Chemie, 32,* 318–322. (West Germany)

Lindop, C. (1987). Evaluating effectiveness in teacher education. *Journal of Education for Teaching, 11*(2), 165–176. (Australia)

Loke, S. H. (1990). Perceptions of chemistry teacher trainees and teacher educators concerning a training programme for Malaysian teachers in chemistry with particular reference to classroom behavior. In H. W. Kam & R. Y. L. Wong (Eds.), *Improving the quality of the teaching profession: An international perspective* (pp. 227–240). Singapore: International Council on Education for Teaching. (Malaysia)

Lourdusamy, A., & Ghani, Z. (1990). Student teachers' personal conception of teaching. In H. W. Kam & R. Y. L. Wong (Eds.), *Improving the quality of the teaching profession: An international perspective* (pp. 103–114). Singapore: International Council on Education for Teaching. (Malaysia)

Lowe, J. (1991, April–May). Ireland and its teachers. *OECD Observer.* (Ireland)

Lowell, J. A., Pope, S., & Sherman, B. F. (1992). Relating theory to practice in teacher education. *Journal of Education for Teaching, 18*(2), 159–172. (Australia)

Luethy, R. (1992). *Eignungsabklärung in der Lehrerbildung (Aptitude testing in teacher training institutes).* Bern: EDK. (Switzerland)

Lynch, J. & Burns, B. (1984). Non-attenders of INSET functions: Some comparison with attenders. *Journal of Education for Teaching, 10*(2), 164–177. (Great Britain)

MacAlpine, D. (1993). *Some contemporary issues in the education of children with special abilities, Palmerston North.* Proceedings of the conference of the New Zealand Council for Gifted Education, Guiding the Gifted Conference. (New Zealand)

MacDonald, C., Munn, P., & Robinson, R. (1991). *Returners to teaching.* (Scotland)

Mackay, G. (1990). Graduate survey of teachers from the Armidale College of Advanced Education. *South Pacific Journal of Teacher Education, 18*(1), 55–64. (Australia)

MacKinnon, A. (1989, March). *Reflection in a science teaching practicum.* Paper presented at the annual meeting of the American Educational Research Association, San Francisco. (Canada)

MacKinnon, A., & Grunau, H. (1991, April). *Teacher development through reflection, community, and discourse.* Paper presented at the annual meeting of the American Educational Research Association, Chicago. (Canada)

Maejima, Y. (1981). A study on the teacher selection and appointment system. *Bulletin of the Educational Administration, Tokyo University, 2,* 104–116. (Japan)

Maejima, Y. (1987). The problem of selection of teachers and formation of teacher competencies. *Bulletin of the Japanese Society of Education Law, 16,* 48–61. (Japan)

Magallanes, L., et al. (1992). Training for research and development of teaching. In *Teacher education in an era of global change.* Arlington, VA: International Council on Education for Teaching. (Mexico)

Mahan, J. M., & Stachowski, L. L. (1987). Feedback from British and Irish educators for improving overseas teaching experiences. *Journal of Education for Teaching, 13*(1), 29–47. (United States)

Mahan, J. M., & Stachowski, L. L. (1988–1989, Winter). Positive and negative influences of prerequisite stateside student teaching on overseas student teaching candidates. *Action in Teacher Education, X*(4), 32–41. (United States)

Mahan, J. M., & Stachowski, L. L. (1989, November–December). Instructional suggestions from abroad concerning overseas teaching. *Journal of Teacher Education, 12*(3), 13–21. (United States)

Mahan, J. M., & Stachowski, L. L. (1990, Fall). New horizons: student teaching abroad to enrich understanding of diversity. *Action in Teacher Education, XII*(3), 13–21. (United States)

Maki, M., et al. (1980). A developmental study on "foundation of education" as a required subject for teacher certification. *Bulletin of the National Institute for Educational Research, 97,* (Japan)

Maline, M. B. (Compiler). (1994, April). *Teacher development outside the United States: A selected annotated bibliography.* Washington, DC: U.S. Department of Education, Office of Research. (United States)

Mansfield, P. A. (1986). Patchwork pedagogy: A case study of supervisors' emphasis on pedagogy in post-lesson conference. *Journal of Education for Teaching, 12*(3), 259–271. (Great Britain)

Marentic-Pozarnik, B. (1981). New approaches to uniting theory with practice in developing teaching skills of prospective teachers. *Sodobna Pedagogika, 32*(5–6), 235–250, 354–369, 436–448. [Contact Slovenia author correspondent.]

Martin, M. (1992). The application of research on classroom management to an inservice program for teachers. *Irish Educational Studies, 11,* 207–223. (Ireland)

Massey, L. (1989, December). *A teaching practice curriculum, Heretaunga.* New Zealand Association for Research in Education, Conference Report. (New Zealand)

Matskevich, V. (1993). What should we teach teachers? In *Polemical sketches and education.* (Belarus)

Matsudaira, N. (1982). Education in the universities and colleges perceived by beginning teachers: The evaluation of teacher education in universities and colleges. Japanese Society for the Study of Education, Study Committee on Teacher Education. *A Study of the Practical Strategies on the Improvement of Teacher Education, 4,* 130–144. (Japan)

Matsuo, Y. (1982). A study on teachers: College students' consciousness about becoming a teacher. *Bulletin of Fukuoka University of Education, 32,* 169–175. (Japan)

McArthur, J. T. (1981). *The first five years of teaching.* [ERDC Report No. 30.] Canberra: Australian Government Publishing Service. (Australia)

McDowell, J., & Moulton, J. (1990). *Final impact evaluation of the PEP pilot radio broadcasts in Liberia.* USAID. (ISN 71580) (Liberia)

McMurray, D. (1992). An analysis of the beliefs, values and levels of self-confidence of Universiti Brunei Darussalam teacher education students. In H. W. Kam & R. Y. L. Wong (Eds.), *Improving the quality of the teaching profession: An international perspective* (pp. 115–122). Singapore: International Council on Education for Teaching. (Brunei Darussalam)

McNamara, D. (1986). Prospectus for teaching: A misleading image. *Journal of Education for Teaching, 11*(1), 25–33. (Great Britain)

McNamara, D. (1990). Research on teacher training in a changing society: The case of Britain in the late 1980s. In R. P. Tisher & M. F. Wideen (Eds.), *Research in teacher education: International perspectives* (pp. 121–140). Bristol, PA: Falmer. (Great Britain)

McNay, M., & Cole, A. L. (1989). Induction programs in Ontario schools: Current views and directions for the future. *Education Canada, 28*(4), 4–11, 44–45. (Canada)

Meighan, R., & Harber, C. (1986). Democratic learning in teacher education: A review of experience at one institution. *Journal of Education for Teaching, 12*(2), 163–172. (Great Britain)

Merryfield, M. (1991, January–February). Preparing American secondary social studies teachers to teach with a global perspective. *Journal of Teacher Education, 42*(1), 11–20. (United States)

Mian, B. E. (1993). *Learning of German/Pomeranian immigrant descendants in Espirito Santo, Brazil.* (Brazil)

Minamimoto, O. (1986). A study on the young primary school teacher's competence perceived by school leaders. *Journal of the Japanese Association for the Study of Educational Administration, 23,* 79–94. (Japan)

Mkandawire, D. S. J., & Marira, C. (1993). The evaluation of teacher professional competencies in former non-white Namibian schools. *Zimbabwe Journal of Educational Research, 5*(2), 124–153. (Namibia)

Mohanty, S. B. (1984). *A study of student teaching programs in colleges of education with special reference to innovation.* Unpublished master's dissertation, University of Baroda. (India)

Moon, B. J., Mayer-Smith, J. A., & Wideen, M. F. (1993, April). *Recent research on learning to teach science: A critical review.* (Canada)

Mor, D. (1993). Continuing education for teachers in teacher education colleges. *Dapim, 17* (Hebrew) (Israel)

Mosbergen, R., et al. (1982). *Survey on teacher education objectives: The views of full-time diploma-in-education students in Institute of Education.* Singapore: Institute of Education. (Singapore)

Munby, H., & Russell, T. (1990, May). *Reframing the nature of subject matter: A case study in the development of professional knowledge.* Paper presented at the Invitational Conference of the Joint Centre for Teacher Development, D. Lake, Ontario. (Canada)

Murphy, J. G., & Naidu, R. A. (1992). The development of new inservice and further education programmes in an era of changing social and political conditions—a case study of Natal/Kwazulu (South Africa). In *Teacher education in an era of global change* (p. 89). Arlington, VA: International Council on Education for Teaching. (South Africa)

Murphy, P., & Cross, W. (1990). Preparing teachers for rural schools: A Canadian approach. *Rural Educator, 11*(3), 10–11. (Canada)

Naowarath, Y. (1989). *Developing and administering a nonmetropolitan teacher education program in northeast Thailand.* Unpublished doctoral dissertation, North Texas State University. (Thailand)

National Institute for Educational Research (NIER). (1989). *Teacher training in Japan.* (NIER Occasional Paper 03/89). Tokyo: NIER. (ERIC Document Reproduction Service No. ED 313 360) (Japan)

Neubauer, W. (1983). Dimensionale Struktur der impliziten Führungstheorie bei Lehrern und Lehrerstudenten. *Psychologie in Erziehung und Unterricht, 30,* 183–191. (West Germany)

Ng, M. (1987). *An inquiry into the use of clinical supervision with student teachers.* Unpublished masters' dissertation, National University of Singapore. (Singapore)

Nicholl, K. (1992). *The selection and recruitment of teacher trainees for 1992.* Wellington: Research and Statistics Division, Ministry of Education. (New Zealand)

Nielsen, H. D., Djalil, A., et al. (1990). *Cost-effectiveness of distance and conventional approaches to teacher education in Indonesia: Executive summary and recommendations.* USAID. (ISN 71445) (Indonesia)

Nielsen, H. D., Tatto, M. T., et al. (1991). *Cost-effectiveness of distance education in teacher training in Sri Lanka and Indonesia.* USAID. (ISN 71380) (Indonesia)

Niemi, H. (1984a). *Personality and interaction attitudes of secondary school student teachers.* (Research Report 19). Helsinki: University of Helsinki, Department of Teacher Education. (Finnish) (Finland)

Niemi, H. (1984b). *Secondary school student teachers' difficulties in teaching, internalizing the conflicts and their evaluation of teacher education and its development.* (Research Report 20). Helsinki: University of Helsinki, Department of Teacher Education. (Finnish) (Finland)

Niemi, H. (1988). *Is teaching also a moral craft for secondary school teachers? Cognitive and emotional processes of student teachers in professional development during teacher education.* (Research Report 61). Helsinki: University of Helsinki, Department of Teacher Education. (Finland)

Niemi, H. (1990). *The significance of research in developing of teacher education. The dimensions of renewing teacher education.* (Report 24.) University of Jyvaskyla, Department of Teacher Education. (Finnish) (Finland)

Niemi, H. (1992a, April). *Gearing master thesis to promote critical thinking in preservice teacher education.* Paper presented as a part of the Finnish project Educating Critical Professionals at the annual meeting of the American Educational Research Association, San Francisco. (Finland)

Niemi, H. (1992b, August). *The moral nature of teaching among young teachers—How to support and help them in the beginning of teaching careers.* (Paper presented at the Nordic Teacher Training Congress challenges for teachers' profession in the 21st century, Lahti (Finland)

Niemi, H. (1992c). *Teachers' professional development, Part 1: Scientific thesis as part of studies, development as teachers and the future. Theoretical frame of reference for the research project and empirical results on teachers' professional development.* (Reports 87/1992). University of Oulu, Faculty of Education. (Finnish, Summary in English) (Finland)

Niemi, H. (1993). *Teachers' orientation towards the future. Integration of technology and reflection in teaching: A challenge for European teacher education.* In A. L. Leino et al. (Eds.), *ATEE Conference Proceedings 1992* (pp. 91–102). Helsinki: University of Helsinki. (Finland)

Niikko, A. (1993). *On student teachers' practical knowledge and on transformation of this knowledge in the advanced stages of teacher education.* (Finland)

Noguera, J., et al. (1985). *Methods of selection and teacher training.* (contact J. Noguera). (Spain)

Oak, A. W. (1986). *A critical study of microteaching techniques with a view to suggest improvement in its implementation in colleges of education.* SNDT University, Department of Post-Graduate Education and Research. (India)

Obanya, P. (1992). The African teacher of the 21st century. In *Teacher education in an era of global change.* Arlington, VA: International Council on Education for Teaching. (General)

O'Brien, R. B. (1991). Outpost models of teacher training in New Zealand. *Action in Teacher Education, XIII*(3), 40–42. (New Zealand)

Oddens, D. A. M. (1992). Professionalization, status, and career: Results of 10 year integrated teacher training for technical subjects. In *Teacher education in an era of global change.* Arlington, VA: International Council on Education for Teaching. (Netherlands)

Ojanen, S. (1991). *Reflective, professional supervision, a critical analysis of supervisory approach on scientific basis.* (Research Reports of the Faculty of Education. Education No. 42). University of Joensuu. (New Zealand)

Ojanen, S. (1992). *Researching reflective style on the supervision of teaching practice and professional identity of the supervisors.* (Research Reports of the Faculty of Education. Education No. 44). University of Joensuu. (General)

Ojima, H. (1980). The "self-analysis" of teachers under five years' experience of teaching. *Journal of the Japanese Association of Educational Administration, 22,* 1–13. (Japan)

Ojima, H. (1982). Improvement of the quality of the teaching profession and the systematization of content of in-service education. In Japan Educational Administration Society, Special Committee on Supervision, *A comprehensive study on the improvement of the quality of teaching profession and supervision.* Tsukuba City: Japan Educational Administration Society (Japan)

Ojima, H. (1983). A study on the characteristics of competence improvement in "junior teachers" through an opinion survey of INSET.

Bulletin of Institute of Education, the University of Tsukuba, 7, 17–47. (Japan)

Ojima, H., Nagai, S., & Amagasa, S. (1981). An empirical study of young teachers' teaching ability and their demand for in-service training. *Bulletin of Institute of Education, the University of Tsukuba, 5,* 71–110. (Japan)

Olgers, A., & Risenkamp, J. (1980). *De onderwijskundige voorbereiding van aanstaande leraren (The educational preparation of prospective teachers).* Unpublished doctoral dissertation with English summary. The Hague: Startsuitgeverij. (Netherlands)

Olibeth, N. (1981). *Fach-oder Laieninspektorat? Ein Vergleich und eine empirische Untersuchung (Mentoring by specialists or laymen: A comparison and an empirical study).* Unpublished doctoral dissertation, St. Gallen. (Switzerland)

Olmsted, P., & Hoas, H. (1989). Preschool teacher training in Finland, Hong Kong, Italy and Thailand. (Accounts from the IEA pre-primary project). *Early Childhood Education, 65*(5), 283–287. (Thailand)

Onocha, C. O., & Okpala, P. N. (1987). Reasoning ability of a group of Nigerian preservice primary teachers. *Journal of Education for Teaching, 13*(1), 79–80. (Nigeria)

Orby, L., & Onvbogu, O. (1993). *Alternative teacher certification routes: Applications to professional education in Nigeria.* Unpublished doctoral dissertation, University of Toledo. (Nigeria)

Out, T. J. (1986). *Probleemgericht opleiden* (Problem oriented teacher training). Unpublished doctoral dissertation (with English summary), Leiden University. The Hague: SVO. (Netherlands)

Paine, L. W. (1990). The teacher as virtuoso: A Chinese model for teaching. *Teachers College Record, 92,* 49–81. (China)

Papotnik, A. (1988). *Quality teacher training—A prerequisite for renovation in education.* Papers presented at the conference at 30th Anniversary of Common 8-year Elementary School in Slovenia, Ljubljana. [Contact Slovenia author correspondent.]

Passamai, H. B. (1983). *Interdependence between salary differentials, function, and academic background—Empirical study of the egresses from the administration, economics, and pedagogy courses in the state of Espirito Santo.* (Brazil)

Patil, G. G. (1984). *A differential study of intelligence, interest and attitudes of the BEd college students as contributory factors towards their achievement in the compulsory subjects.* Unpublished doctoral dissertation, Nagpur University. (India)

Peresypkin, A. (1993). Will we dare to? *Education and training, 6,* 37–45. (Belarus)

Peretz, A. et al. (1992). Evaluation of a one-year internship program for student-teachers (interns) at Ben-Gurion University of the Negev. In *Teacher education in an era of global change* (p. 115). Arlington, VA: International Council on Education for Teaching. (Israel)

Pikkarainen, E. (1992). Distance education and the new media in the decentralized teacher training experiment: The Haave project. In *Developing rural schools—A key to community growth.* (Interskola Conference in Bodo, Norway). Bodo: Nordland County Director of Education. (Finland)

Pillai, J. K., & Mohan, S. (1985). *Why graduates choose to teach: A survey.* Madurai Kamaraj University, Department of Education. (India)

Plestenjak, M. (1980). Dissatisfaction of primary school teachers due to the way their educational level is evaluated. *Sodobna Pedagogika, 31*(9–10), 396–408. [Contact Slovenia author correspondent.]

Porat, N. (1993). The curriculum of pedagogic studies as perceived by students. *Dapim, 17,* (Hebrew) (Israel)

Portugais, J., & Lévèsques, M. (1991). *The transfer of high-cognitive-level questioning ability during initial teacher training.* Université de Montréal. (Canada)

Potulicka, E. (1988). Poland: The radio and television university for teachers. *Prospects, 18,* 207–215. (Poland)

Prabhune, P. P., Marathe, A. H., & Cohani, G. R. (1984). *An experimental study to measure the effect of microteaching skills and different strategies of feedback on the student: Teachers' performance with respect to teaching.* Pune: State Institute Education. (India)

Preuss, E., & Hofsass, T. (1991). Integration in the Federal Republic of Germany: Experiences related to professional identity and strategies of teacher training in Berlin. *European Journal of Teacher Education, 14*(2), 131–137. (West Germany)

Primary education improvement project in Botswana. (1989). USAID. (ISN 60547) (Botswana)

Project Assistance completion report: Primary education improvement in Botswana. (1989). USAID. (ISN 61920) (Botswana)

Qaisrani, M. N. (1990). *Effect of teacher level and quality of formal schooling and professional training on students' achievement in primary schools in Pakistan.* USAID. (ISN 72697) (Pakistan)

Qureshi, M. I. (1990). *Impact of preservice teacher training on classroom practices in primary schools of Pakistan.* USAID. (ISN 72698) (Pakistan)

Rahman, A. et al. (1992). Teachers in rural schools: The "extra" they need. In *Teacher education in an era of global change* (p. 90). Arlington, VA: International Council on Education for Teaching. (Malaysia)

Rai, V. K. (1982). *A survey of the problems of teachers' training colleges with regard to practicing schools.* Unpublished doctoral dissertation, Gujarat University. (India)

Raj, T. (1984). *A study of the organization and administration of student teaching programs in the secondary teacher education institutions.* Unpublished doctoral dissertation, Agra University. (India)

Rasanen, R. (1993, September). *From words to action in teachers' professional ethics: Education and research.* Paper presented at the Association for Teacher Education in Europe, Lisbon, Portugal. (Finland)

Ratteree, B. (1992). The ILO/UNESCO recommendation concerning the status of teachers. In *Teacher education in an era of global change* (p. 116). Arlington, VA: International Council on Education for Teaching. (General)

Razdevsek-Pucko, C. (1983a). *Certain psychological and socioeconomical factors influencing study success, duration of studies and professional efficiency of students from pedagogical academy in Ljubljana.* Master's theses, University in Ljubljana, Faculty of Philosophical Sciences. (Slovenia)

Razdevsek-Pucko, C. (1983b). *Efficiency of graduates from pedagogical secondary school during their studies at the pedagogical academy in Ljubljana and in teaching practice.* Papers from the conference of Slovene Psychological Academy, Ljubljana, Slovenia. (Slovenia)

Razdevsek-Pucko, C. (1983c). *The opinions about the initial teacher education programme.* Paper presented at the AACTE eighteenth annual conference, Lisbon, Portugal. (Slovenia)

Razdevsek-Pucko, C. (1984). Efficiency of teachers—Graduates from pedagogical academy in Ljubljana. *Revija za psihologiju* (Journal of the Yugoslav Psychological Association, ISSN 0352-1605), *15*(102), 89–95. (Slovenia)

Razdevsek-Pucko, C. (1988a). Inter-disciplinary diploma theses—New quality in teacher education. *Sodobna Pedagogika, 39*(5–6), 242–245. (Slovenia)

Razdevsek-Pucko, C. (1988b). *Motivation of primary school teachers for inservice training.* Paper presented at the conference at 30th Anniversary of Common 8-Year Elementary School in Slovenia, Ljubljana. (Slovenia)

Razdevsek-Pucko, C. (1990). *The influence of teachers' motivation for INSET on teacher-pupil interactions.* Paper presented at the ATEE fifteenth annual conference, Limerick, Ireland. (Slovenia)

Razdevsek-Pucko, C. (1991). Contemporary trends in teacher education. *Vzgoja in izobrazevanje* (Education), *22*(4), 9–13. (Slovenia)

Razdevsek-Pucko, C. (1992a). *Support teacher: A double role at the beginning of the school career.* Paper presented at the ATEE seventeenth annual conference, Lahti, Finland. (Slovenia)

Razdevsek-Pucko, C. (1992b). *Teacher education—from theory to practice or from practice to theory*. Paper presented at the conference on Teacher Education: What Do We Want and What Are We Able to Do, Ljubljana. (Slovenia)

Razma, S. (1992). The system of teacher training in Lithuania reborn: Ways and conditions of democratization and modernization. In *Teacher education in an era of global change, 1990*. Arlington, VA: International Council on Education for Teaching. (Lithuania)

Renwick, M. (1983). *Innovations in teacher education*. Wellington: New Zealand Council for Educational Research. (New Zealand)

Renwick, M. (1985). *Student teachers and parents*. Wellington: New Zealand Council for Educational Research. (New Zealand)

Renwick, M. (1989). *Some student views on equity issues*. Wellington: New Zealand Council for Educational Research. (New Zealand)

Renwick, M. (1990). *Windows on teacher education*. Wellington: New Zealand Council for Educational Research. (New Zealand)

Ricord, O. (1986). A developmental study of the "teaching self" in student teaching. *Journal of Education for Teaching, 12*(1), 65–76. (Canada)

Roelofs, E., Raemaekers, J., & Veenman, S. (1991). Improving instructional and classroom management skills: Effects of a staff development programme and coaching. *Schooling Effectiveness and School Improvement, 2*(3), 192–212. (Netherlands)

Ropo, E. (1987, April). *Teachers' conceptions of teaching and teaching behavior: Some differences between expert and novice teacher*. Paper presented at the annual meeting of the AERA, Washington, DC. (Finland)

Rosado, J. A. (1990). *A study of perceptions of selected elementary school teachers who were trained in Belize 1976–1987 as to the adequacy and utility of the training they received*. Unpublished doctoral dissertation, Boston College. (Belize)

Roth, J. H. (1981). Veränderung Berufsrelevanter Einstellungen von Lehrer-studenten (Changing student teachers' attitudes about the relevance of the profession). *Psychologie in Erziehung und Unterricht, 28*, 344–350. (West Germany)

Rousi, H. (1991). *A review of the theoretical premises of teacher training as applied to teacher training for social work*. (Reports from Vocational Teacher Education). University of Jyvaskyla 1. (Finland)

Rousi, H. (1993). *On the foundations of vocational teacher education*. (Reports from Vocational Teacher Education). University of Jyvaskyla 5. (Finland)

Rugh, A. B. (1990). *Improving teacher effectiveness in the classroom in Sri Lanka*. USAID. (ISN 71444) (Sri Lanka)

Russell, T. (1986). *Beginning teachers development of knowledge—In action*. Paper presented at the annual meeting of the AERA, April 1986, San Francisco. (United States)

Russell, T. (1989). *Studying teaching with a colleague as a mode of professional development*. Paper presented at the annual conference of the Canadian Society for the Study of Education, Quebec City. (Canada)

Russell-Gebbett, J. (1984). Working with children in trouble: An interprofessional approach to the training of teachers and social workers. *Journal of Education for Teaching, 10*(1), 73–81. (Great Britain)

Ryan, A. S., Reynolds, P., & collaborators. (1982). *Perceptions of teaching as a career: Report no. 1, survey of year, 12 students*. (Report of a joint project by Western Australian College of Advanced Education and the Western Australian Institute of Technology). (Australia)

Ryan, C., & Cremin, P. (1993). Developing the European dimension in teacher education: A case study in European teacher education. In A. L. Leino, et al. (Eds.), *Integration of technology and reflection in teaching. A challenge for European teacher education*. ATEE Proceedings. Helsinki: University of Helsinki. (Finland)

Sachs, J., & Logan, L. (1990). Control or development? A study of inservice education. *Journal of Curriculum Studies, 22*, 473–481. (Australia)

Sato, S. (1979). A psychological study of student teaching (iii): Grades received and education experience. *Memoirs of the Faculty of Education, Kumamoto University, 28*, 219–229. (Japan)

Savoie-Zajc, L. (1992). External assistance in inservice training of teachers: The Haitian and the Brazilian experiences. In *Teacher education in an era of global change*, (p. 118). Arlington, VA: International Council on Education for Teaching. (General)

Schechtman, Z. (1990). Validation of group-assessment procedure for the selection of the teacher-education candidate. *Studies in Education, 53/54*, 129–138. (Hebrew) (Israel)

Scherf, S. (1992). The practicum in a teacher education college. *Dapim, 14*. (Hebrew) (Israel)

Schonberg, S., & Cornbleth, I. (1988). Reflective processes in teacher education. *Issues in Education, 23–26* (Hebrew) (Israel)

Schwille, J. (1993). *The promise of comparative inquiry in teacher education and teacher development: Lessons to be learned from non-Western countries*. Paper prepared for the international conference, "Towards Education for All," Brunei. (United States)

Seng, L. Y. M. (1990). A study of the creative thinking abilities of Malaysian preservice teachers. In H. W. Kam & R. Y. L. Wong (Eds.), *Improving the quality of the teaching profession: An international perspective* (pp. 198–206). Singapore: International Council on Education for Teaching. (Malaysia)

Shah, M. M. (1986). *A survey of management of student teaching in India*. Unpublished manuscript, University of Baroda, Centre of Advanced Study in Education. (India)

Shapiro, B. L. (1991). A collaborative approach to help novice science teachers reflect on changes in their construction of the role of science teacher. *Educational Research, 137*(2), 119–132. (Canada)

Sharpe, D. R. (1983). *Planning and control of teacher education in England and Wales*. Unpublished doctoral dissertation, Harvard University. (Great Britain)

Sharpes, D. K. (1986). Teacher training and higher education in selected Islamic countries. *Journal of Education for Teaching, 12*(3), 245–258. (Saudi Arabia)

Shuming, Y. (1987). *More thoughts on secondary normal school system*. Educational Research. (China)

Silberstein, M. (1993). A new conceptual approach to teacher education in the curriculum domain. *Dapim, 17*, 27–37. (Hebrew) (Israel)

Silberstein, M., & Karinsky, A. (1992). Perspectives of expert-teacher studies in teacher education. *Studies in Education, 57/58*, 157–178. (Hebrew) (Israel)

Singh, N. (1985). *A comparative study of teachers trained through integrated and traditional methods in terms of attitude towards teaching, teaching competence and role performance*. Unpublished doctoral dissertation, Banaras Hindu University. (India)

Sinha, P. (1982). *An evaluative study of teacher education in Bihar*. Unpublished doctoral dissertation, Patna University. (India)

Siyakwazi, P., & Nyarwaranda, V. (1993). Student teachers' perceptions of and attitudes towards teaching practice deployment in Zimbabwe. *Zimbabwe Journal of Educational Research, 5*(1), 90–106. (Zimbabwe)

Skelton, C. (1987). A study of gender discrimination in a primary program of teacher training. *Journal of Educational Review, 57*(1), 1–22. (Great Britain)

Skerbinek, M. (1987). How teachers from Ljubljana evaluate their higher or university education. *Sodobna Pedagogika, 38*(1–2), 37–48. [Contact Slovenia author correspondent.]

Skuja, R., & Lim-Quek, M. (1984). *The experiences of beginning teachers: A follow-up study report based on interview data*. Unpublished report, Institute of Education, (Singapore)

Snellman, L. (1988). Opiskelijoiden Kasityksia lapsesta opettajaopintojensa alkaessa (The image of the child in the minds of education students). *Joensuun yliopisto. Kasvatustieteiden Tiedekunnan Selosteita, 21*, (Finland)

Snellman, L. (1989, March). *Did their ideas change? Education tutors evaluate junior and senior students' ideas on education*. Paper presented at the NFPF Congress, Uppsala. Sweden. (Finland)

Soh, K. C. (1983). *Student teachers' backgrounds and motives for teaching: A 1968–1981 comparison*. (Occasional Paper 11). Singapore: Institute of Education. (Singapore)

Soh, K. C., Lam, T. L., & Poh, S. H. (1985). *Teaching practice supervision: What are supervisors after?* Singapore: Institute of Education. (Singapore)

Song, B. J. (1983). *Education of elementary school teachers in Korea: Present status and proposal for alternative approach*. Unpublished doctoral dissertation, Vanderbilt University. (Korea)

Stahl, A. (1991). Bridging the gap between research and teacher education. *Journal of Education for Teachers, 17*(3), 293–299. (Israel)

Stark, R. (1993). *School experience in initial primary school teacher training*. (Scotland)

Stewart, D. (1991, November–December). Teacher education in countries around the world: Studies in the ERIC data base. *Journal of Teacher Education, 42*(5), 350–356. (United States)

St. J. Neill, S. R., Fitzgerald, J. M., & Jones, R. (1983). The relation between reported awareness of non-verbal communication and rated effectiveness in probationer and student teacher. *Journal of Education for Teaching, 9*(1), 16–29. (Great Britain)

St-Louis, M. (1994). *Professional insertion: Indicators for effective mentors programs*. University of Quebec in Trois-Rivières. (Canada)

Student Department of the National Educational Commission. (1990). *An investigation report on the enrollment situation of normal universities*. Educational Research. (China)

Sulistiorini, R., & Nielsen, H. D. (1990). *Private costs of teacher training through distance education in Indonesia*. USAID. (ISN 71439) (Indonesia)

Sunnari, V. (1990). *Hidden structures and educational perspectives in the school and in teacher education, particularly gender agenda*. (Finland)

Suojanen, U. (1992, August). Action research—A way for teachers to develop their profession. Nordic teacher training congress challenges for teachers' profession in the 21st century, Lahti. *University of Joensuu, Research Reports of the Faculty of Education, 44*(92), 109–112.

Suzuki, M. et al. (1983). Effect of student teaching practice on personal desire to be a teacher (II). *Bulletin of the Faculty of Education, Kobe University, 71*, 245–277. (Japan)

Suzuki, S. (1986). Selection and appointment of teachers. In M. Shinbori (Ed.), *Re-examination of preservice education*. Tokyo: Kyoiku Kaihatsu Kenkyusho. (Japan)

Swaziland teacher training project: Final impact evaluation. (1991). USAID. (ISN 71725) (Swaziland)

Tan, R. M., & Mingshuim, Z. (1984). Recent innovations of China's teacher education. In *Innovations in teacher education: The pursuit of excellence. International yearbook on teacher education* (pp. 27–38). (China)

Tay-Koay, S. L. (1985). Additional selection criteria research project: Selection and performance of 1983 diploma in education students at the Institute of Education. *Singapore Journal of Education, 7*(2), 65–70. (Singapore)

Taylor, G. D., & Miller, P. J. (1985). Professional course work and the practicum: Do good students make good teachers? *Canadian Journal of Education, 10*(2), 105–120. (Canada)

Teacher training project in Swaziland. (1987). USAID. (ISN 60818) (Swaziland)

Tennstädt, K. C. (1987). Das konstanzer Trainingsmodell (KTM): Einführung und ausgewählte Ergebnisse einer ersten Evaluation (The stable training model: Introduction and selected results of a first evaluation). In J. Schlee & D. Wahl (Eds.), *Veränderungen subjektiver*

Theorien von Lehrern (pp. 206–235). Oldenburg: Oldenburg University (West Germany)

Thompson, H., & Levis, D. (1980). An experimental evaluation of competency-based teacher education. *The South Pacific Journal of Teacher Education, 8*(1), 38–48. (Australia)

Tianxiang, X., et al. (1989). *On the restructuring of curriculum system in high normal education*. Educational Research. (China)

Tillema, H. H. (1986). *De universitaire lerarenopleiding: Een aanvullende probleemverkenning ten behoeve van de SVO programalijn opleiding onderwijsgevenden* (Teacher training at university: A supplementary survey of problems on behalf of the SVO program on teacher training). Gravenhage: SVO. (Netherlands)

Tillema, H. H. (1988). Coping with new challenges in teacher education. In A. McAlpine, S. Brown, et al. (Eds.), *New challenges for teachers and teacher education* (pp. 61–73). Lisse: Swets & Zeitlinger. (Netherlands)

Tillema, H. H. (1992). Supporting teaching—Effects of delivery factors in teacher support programs. In H. Voorbach (Ed.), *Teacher education* (8) (pp. 189–194). De Lier: ABC. (Netherlands)

Tillema, H. H., De Jong, R., & Mathijssen, C. (1990). Conceptual or experience based learning of teachers. *Teaching and teacher education, 6*(2), 165–172. (Netherlands)

Tillema, H. H., & Veenman, S. A. M. (1985). *Probleemverkenning opleiding onderwijsgevenden* (Problem survey of teacher training). 's-Gravenhage: SVO. (Netherlands)

Tillema, H. H., & Veenman, S. (1987). Conceptualizing training methods in teacher education. *International Journal of Educational Research, 11*(5), 519–529. (Netherlands)

Tischer, R. P., & Wideen, M. F. (Eds.). (1990). *Research in teacher education: International perspectives*. Philadelphia: Falmer. (Netherlands)

Tomic, A. (1990). Teacher education for some professional-theoretical subjects on secondary level—The consecutive model. *Sodobna Pedagogika, 41*(9–10), 506–518. [Contact Slovenia author correspondent.]

Traill, R. (1992). A study of the career patterns and professional problems of teacher education graduates. In *Teacher education in an era of global change* (p. 120). Arlington, VA: International Council on Education for Teaching. (Australia)

Tsuchiya, M. (1981). Some problems concerning teacher selection and appointment. Japanese Society for the Study of Education, Study Committee on Teacher Education, *A Study on the Practical Strategies for the Improvement of Teacher Education, 3*, 194–206. (Japan)

Tsuchiya, M. (1987). What will change with the establishment of the system of inservice education for beginning teachers? In relation to the selection of teachers. In Yamada & Tsucherja (Eds.), *What will change with the establishment of the system of inservice education for beginning teachers*. Tokyo: Kyoiku Shiryo Shuppankai. (Japan)

Tucker, J. L., & Cistone, P. L. (1991). Global perspectives for teachers: An urgent priority. *Journal of Teacher Education, 42*(3), 3–10. (United States)

Turner-Muecke, L. A., Russell, T., & Bowyer, J. (1986). Reflection-in-action: Case study of a clinical supervisor. *Journal of Curriculum and Supervision, 2*(1), 40–49. (Canada)

Ueda, M., et al. (1987). The actual figures and problems of teacher-selection procedure and inservice training. *Bulletin of the Japan Educational Administration Society, 13*, 159–184. (Japan)

Uljens, M. (1992a). *Phenomenological features of phenomenography*. (Report no 1992:03). Göteborg: University of Göteborg, Department of Education and Educational Research. (Finland)

Uljens, M. (1992b). What is learning a change of? In R. Mykletun, (Ed.), *Kogressrapport fra den 20. nordiske kogress for pedagogisk forskning* (pp. 91–108). Stavanger: Rogalandsforskning. (Finland)

Uljens, M. (1992c). *What is learning a change of?* (Report no. 1992:01). Göteborg: Department of Education and Educational Research, University of Göteborg. (Finland)

Valencic, M. (1991). *Contribution of the block preservice teaching practice to the student-teachers' professionalization.* [Contact Slovenia author correspondent.]

Valentina, A., & Cassidy, G. (1983). *Teacher perspectives on intermediate level teacher preparation in Ontario.* Unpublished doctoral dissertation, State University of New York at Buffalo. (Canada)

Vall, G. N., & Tennison, J. M. (1991–1992). International student teaching: Stimulus for developing reflective teachers. *Action in Teacher Education, 13*(4), 31–36. (United States)

VanBalkom, W. D. (1991). Multicultural education in Alberta's teacher training Institutions. *Education Canada,* Autumn, 46–48. (Canada)

Van Der Maren, J. M. (1993). *Knowledge needed by future teachers to attain the status and be perceived as a professional.* Université de Montréal. (Canada)

Van Tulder, M., Roelofs, E., Veenman, S., & Voeten, M. (1992). Effecten van nascholing op het ondervijsgedrag van leraren. (The impact of inservice education on teacher behavior in classrooms). *Pedagogicshe-Studien, 69*(2), 99–111. (Netherlands)

Van Tulder, M., Van Der Vegt, R., & Veenman, S. (1993). In-service education in innovating schools: A multi-case study. *International Journal of Qualitative Studies in Education, 6*(2), 129–142. (Netherlands)

Van Tulder, M., & Veenman, S. (1991). Characteristics of effective inservice programmes and activities: Results of a Dutch survey. *Educational Studies, 17*(1), 25–48. (Netherlands)

Van Tulder, M., Veenman, S., & Sieben, J. (1988). Features of effective in-service activities: Results of a delphi-study. *Educational Studies, 14*(2), 209–223. (Netherlands)

Vedder, J. (1984). *Orientatie op het beroep van leraar: Praktische vorming en reflecteren aan het begin van de lerarenopleiding* (Teaching profession, an orientation: Practical training and reflecting at the start of teacher training). Unpublished doctoral dissertation, with English summary. Lisse: Swets & Zeitlinger. (Netherlands)

Vedder, J., & Bannink, P. (1988). The development of practical skills and reflection at the beginning teacher training. In J. T. Voorbach & L. G. M. Prick (Eds.), *Teacher education 4, research and developments on teacher education in the Netherlands.* The Hague: SVO/ATEE. (Netherlands)

Veenman, S. A. M. (1984). Perceived problems of beginning teachers. *Review of Educational Research, 54,* 143–178. (Netherlands)

Veenman, S. A. M. (1987). Leraren voor morgen en overmorgen (Teacher for tomorrow and the day after tomorrow). *Pedagogische Studien, 64*(12), 508–510. (Netherlands)

Veenman, S. (1990). *Recruitment, selection, and training of school leaders in the Netherlands.* Report prepared for Universidad del Deusto, Bilbao/Basque Government, Vittoria-Gasteiz. (ERIC Document Reproduction Service No. ED 317 503) (Netherlands)

Veenman, S., Leenders, Y., Meyer, P., & Sanders, M. (1993). Effects of a preservice teacher preparation programme on effective instruction. *Education Studies, 19*(1), 3–18. (Netherlands)

Verloop, N. (1989). *Interactive cognitions of student teachers: An intervention study.* Unpublished doctoral dissertation, Leiden University/CITO, Leiden/Arnhem. (Netherlands)

Vogrinc, J. (1982). State exams for teachers Sodobna *Pedagogika, 33*(9–10), 415–424. (Contact Slovenia author correspondent.)

Vonk, J. H. C. (1984). *Teacher education and teacher practice.* Amsterdam: Free University Press. (Netherlands)

Vonk, J. H. C. (1991). Some trends in the development of curricula for the professional preparation of primary and secondary school teachers in Europe: A comparative study. *British Journal of Educational Studies, 39*(2), 117–137. (Netherlands)

Vonk, J. H. C. (1993a). *The knowledge base for mentors of beginning teachers.* Paper presented at the annual meeting of the American Educational Research Association, Atlanta. (Netherlands)

Vonk, J. H. C. (1993b). Teacher induction: The great omission in education. In M. Galton & B. Moon (Eds.), *Handbook of Teacher Education in Europe.* London: David Foulton/Council of Europe. (Netherlands)

Vonk, J. H. C., & Schras, G. A. (1987). From beginning to experienced teacher: A study of the professional development of teachers during their first four years of service. *European Journal of Teacher Education, 10*(1), 95–111. (Netherlands)

Walety, F., & Williams-Lamptez. (1990). *Teacher training and resource center for adult education in Liberia: curriculum and organization.* Unpublished doctoral dissertation, Columbia University. (Liberia)

Wang, C. (1987). Pre-service and in-service teacher education in China. *Canadian and International Education, 16*(1), 133–143. (China)

Weintraub, E. (1993). The retraining of immigrant teachers. *English Teacher's Journal—Israel, 46,* 73–77. (Israel)

Weiping, S. (1992). Issues and trends in current developments of teacher education in China. In *Teacher education in an era of global change.* Arlington, VA: International Council on Education for Teaching. (China)

Weixiang, P. (1983). *Preliminary thoughts on improving instruction of teaching methodology in higher teacher education institutions.* Educational Research. (China)

Welsh, J. (1992). Student perceptions of the "qualities of a good teacher": Some implications for the design of the teacher education curriculum. In *Teacher education in an era of global change* (p. 121). Arlington, VA: International Council on Education for Teaching. (Brunei Darussalem)

Wenxing, C. (1990). *An analysis of life and work of teachers in 20 schools in Sichuan Province.* Educational Research. (China)

West, B. B. (1985). *The state of the profession: International field/student teaching experiences in undergraduate teacher preparation, images for the near future.* Paper prepared for the international teacher education guidelines of the American Association of Colleges for Teacher Education, April 1985, Michigan State University, East Lansing. (United States)

Wideen, M. F. (1987). *Trends and developments in teacher education: A synopsis of reports and major works.* Burnaby, British Columbia: Simon Fraser University. (Canada)

Wideen, M. F. (1989). *School based teacher development.* Paper based on research supported by the Social Science and Humanities Research Council and Seed Grants from Simon Fraser University and the Prince Rupert School District, Burnaby, British Columbia. (Canada)

Wideen, M. F., & Holborn, P. (1986a). Change and survival in faculties of education. *Interchange, 17*(1), 33–47. (Canada)

Wideen, M. F., & Holborn, P. (1986b). Research in Canadian teacher education: Promises and problems. *Canadian Journal of Education, 11*(4), 557–583. (Canada)

Wideen, M. F., & Hopkins, D. (1984). Professional renewal through teacher education at York University. *Alberta Journal of Education Research, 30*(1), 26–37. (Canada)

Wilson, B. (1990). The preparedness of teacher trainees for computer utilization: The Australian and British experiences. *Journal of Education for Teaching, 16*(2), 161–171. (Australia)

Wilson, J. D., & Mitchell, L. (1985). Developing a programme for selecting primary teachers. *Journal of Education for Teaching, 11*(3), 264–280. (Great Britain)

Wright, B., & Dillon, P. (1990). Some applications of interactive video in initial teacher training. *Educational Technology, 27*(1), 43–50. (Great Britain)

Wubbels, T. (1986). Onderzoek aan en voor de opleiding van onderwijsgevenden (Research at and into the training of teachers). In N. A. J. Lagerwij & T. Wubbels (Eds.), *Onderwijsverbetering als opdracht (Improvement of education as a mission)* (pp. 88–98). Lisse, Netherlands: Swets en Zeitlinger. (Netherlands)

Wubbels, T. (1992). Teacher education and the universities in the Netherlands. *European Journal of Teacher Education, 15*(3), 157–172. (Netherlands)

Wubbels, T., Brekelmans, M., & Crèton, H. A. (1993). Interpersonal teacher behavior, changes and improvements. In L. Kremer, H. Vonk, & R. Fessler (Eds.), *Professional development of teachers* (pp. 147–166). Lisse, Netherlands: Swets & Zeitlinger. (Netherlands)

Wubbels, T., Crèton, H., & Hermans, J. (1993). Teacher education program. In T. Wubbels & J. Levy (Eds.), *Do you know what you look like?* (pp. 146–161). London: Falmer. (Netherlands)

Wubbels, T., & Korthagen, F. A. J. (1990). The effects of a preservice teacher education program for the preparation of reflective teachers. *Journal of Education for Teaching, 16*(1), 29–43. (Netherlands)

Yanping, L. (1991). *About reform of science education in secondary teacher schools.* Educational Research. (China)

Yaosaka, O., & Ushiwata, J. (1988). The consciousness of the college teacher on the improvement of teacher education concerning student guidance. *Research Bulletin of the National Institute for Educational Research, 17,* 13–34. (Japan)

Yeap, L. L., Khor, P., Lui, E., Lam, T. L., Poh, S. H., & Soh, K. C. (1985). *An experimental study of inter-rater reliability of teaching practice supervision (a pilot study).* Singapore: Institute of Education. (Singapore)

Yinquan, J. (1989). *More thoughts on reform of curriculum in secondary normal school.* Educational Research. (China)

Young, J. H. (1991–1992). Curriculum integration: Perceptions of preservice teachers. *Action in Teacher Education, 13*(4), 1–9. (Canada)

Youtang, J. (1988). *Necessity of higher normal education to suit the needs of economic development and rural secondary school.* Educational Research. (China)

Zachmann-Hintermeier, U., & Treiber, B. (1986). Zielerreichendes Unterrichten: Erprobung eines Lehrertrainingsprogramms (Objective-rich teaching: Testing of a teacher training program). *Psychologie in Erziehung und Unterricht, 33,* 220–228. (West Germany)

Zeitoun, H. H. (1987). *The competencies of preservice Egyptian biology teachers in identifying and correcting misconceptions about photosynthesis in a written answer: An evaluative and correlational study.* (ERIC Document Reproduction Service No. 290 628) (Egypt)

Zellermayer, M. (1990). Teachers' development towards the reflective teaching of writing: An action research. *Teaching and Teacher Education, 6,* 337–354. (Israel)

Zhongxiu, Y. (1989). *Outward economy and reform of higher teacher education.* Teacher Education Research. (China)

Ziv, S. (1989). Practical experiences in teacher education. *Dapim, 10,* 25–43. (Hebrew) (Israel)

Zmora, D. (1990). Changes in attitudes and professional behavior throughout the process of teacher education. *Studies in Teacher Education,* 73–95. (Hebrew) (Israel)

Zuzovsky, R. (1992). A model of teachers' professional development and its application to teacher education. *Direction in Teacher Education—A Journal of Research in Teacher Education and Inservice Training, 1,* 105–120. (Hebrew) (Israel)

Zvacke, S. M. (1989). *Distributive education in the teacher education program in Zimbabwe.* Unpublished doctoral dissertation, Iowa State University. (Zimbabwe)

Appendix

ATE Council for International Affairs
Council Headquarters
c/o Dr. Brad West
116 Erickson Hall
College of Education
Michigan State University
East Lansing, MI 48824
Tel: (517) 353-0632; Fax: (517) 432-2795; E-mail: BradWest@MSU.EDU
Administration of general Council business.

ATE Council for International Affairs
Committee for International Research
c/o Dr. Nancy Quisenberry
College of Education
Southern Illinois University–Carbondale
Carbondale, IL 62901
Tel: (618) 453-2415; Fax: (618) 453-1646; E-mail: GE1140@SIUCVMB.SIU.EDU

Promotes networking among USA and international teacher education researchers to share findings, collaborate in studies, inform members of governmental teacher education research projects such as those funded by UNESCO, the World Bank, or USAID. Facilitates ATE members' involvement in such agencies and assists in ATE member procurement of grant Request for Proposals (RFPs) and resources for conducting international teacher education research projects.

ATE Council for International Affairs
Committee for International Service
c/o Dr. Elaine Jarchow
Dean, College of Education
Box 441071
Texas Tech University

Lubbock, TX 89154
Tel: (806) 742-2377; Fax: (806) 742-2179; E-mail: J2ELA@TTACS.TTU.EDU

A clearinghouse of information on international teacher organizations (ICET, SIETAR, WCCI, ISTI, Consortia) and funding grant opportunities to develop international teacher education activities. Works cooperatively with Committees on Teaching and Research to internationalize the teacher education curricula, utilize locally available international resources, and promote consulting opportunities for teacher education faculties.

ATE Council for International Affairs
Committee for International Teaching
c/o Dr. Sharon Brennan
College of Education
1008 Taylor Building
University of Kentucky
Lexington, KY 40506-0001
Tel: (606) 257-1857; Fax: (606) 258-1045; E-mail: CPD434@UKCC.UKY.EDU

This committee of the Council is a clearinghouse of information on international student teaching programs and stateside "international" experiences for preservice teachers. Programs are aimed at sharing ideas about curriculum development and instructional practices with educators in countries outside the United States through on-site visits and computer networks.

Association for Teacher Education in Europe
Ms. M. L. Kotterman, Executive Director
60 Rue de la Concorde
B-1050 Brussels, Belgium
Tel: 32-2-540 9781; Fax: 32-2-514 11.72

Publishes bimonthly newsletter with English translations; holds regional and annual meetings similar to those of the ATE. Membership information available from ATE Council for International Affairs.

American Forum for Global Education
45 John Street, Suite 908
New York, NY 10038
Tel: (212) 732-8606; Fax: (212) 791-4132
Publishes resource books. Examples include *International Studies Funding and Resources Book; Group Portrait: Internationalizing the Disciplines; The New Global Yellow Pages,* a resource directory listing 172 organizations that provide services related to international and global education. Provides fundamental literature (such as *Internationalizing Your School*) and curriculum materials from the National Clearinghouse on Development Education. Holds annual conferences and other meetings.

American Council on the Teaching of Foreign Languages
6 Executive Boulevard
Yonkers, NY
Tel: (914) 963-8830; Fax (914): 963-1275

Cooperative Projects in International Education
The Stanley Foundation
216 Sycamore Street, Suite 800
Muscatine, IA 52761
Tel: (319) 264-1500; Fax: (319) 264-0864

Council on International Exchange of Scholars
3007 Tilden Street, NW, Suite 5M
Washington, DC 20008-3009
Tel: (202) 686-6232
Fulbright Scholar, Teacher Exchange, and Scholar in Residence Programs

Council on International Educational Exchange
205 East 42nd Street
New York, NY 10017
Tel: (212) 661-1414; Fax: (212) 972-3231
Facilitates international education and youth/study travel through a variety of overseas travel, study, and work opportunities.

Institute of International Education
809 United Nations Plaza
New York, NY 10017
Tel: (212) 838-8200; Fax: (212) 984-5452
Educational and cultural exchanges

International Council on Education for Teaching
2009 N. 14th Street, Suite 609
Arlington, VA 22201
Tel: (703) 525-5253; Fax: (703) 351-9381
The International Council on Education for Teaching is an international organization dedicated to the improvement of teacher education

throughout the world. Each year the Council sponsors a World Assembly that provides special opportunities for participants to share their expertise, ideas, and research findings with one another to improve the quality of educational personnel.

National Association for Foreign Student Affairs
1875 Connecticut Avenue, NW, Suite 1000
Washington, DC 20009
Tel: (202) 462-4811; Fax: (202) 667-3419
Promotes exchanges as educational resources to develop knowledge and appreciations. Comprehensive newsletter and international publications.

People to People
501 East Armor Boulevard
Kansas City, MO 64109
Tel: (816) 421-6343
Voluntary effort of private citizens to advance the cause of international friendship.

U.S. Department of Education
Center for International Education
600 Independence Avenue, SW
Washington, DC 20202
Tel: (202) 401-9798

This center administers many programs: (1) the International Visitors Program; (2) the International Studies Branch—this includes Fulbright-Hays Programs such as Group Projects Abroad and Seminars Abroad and Bilateral Projects and Title VI–Higher Education Act Programs such as the Undergraduate International Studies and Foreign Language Program and the Centers for International Business Education and Business and International Education; (3) the Advanced Training and Research Branch includes Fulbright-Hays Programs such as Doctoral Dissertation Research Abroad and Faculty Research Abroad and Title VI–Higher Education Act Programs such as International Research and Studies and Language Resource Centers and National Resource Centers and Foreign Language and Area Studies Fellowships.

World Council for Curriculum and Instruction
c/o Estela Matriano
College of Education
University of Cincinnati
Cincinnati, OH 45221-0002
Tel: (513) 556-3573; Fax: (513) 556-2483

World Learning
P.O. Box 676
Brattleboro, VT 05302
Tel: (802) 257-7751; Fax: (802) 258-3248
Promotes intercultural exchange programs. The School for International Training has undergraduate and graduate programs in intercultural management, overseas refugee, and community development and training programs.

A FUTURE FOR TEACHER EDUCATION
DEVELOPING A STRONG SENSE
OF PROFESSIONALISM

Thomas Barone
ARIZONA STATE UNIVERSITY

David C. Berliner
ARIZONA STATE UNIVERSITY

Jay Blanchard
ARIZONA STATE UNIVERSITY

Ursula Casanova
ARIZONA STATE UNIVERSITY

Thomas McGowan
ARIZONA STATE UNIVERSITY

Because of demographic imperatives the future of teacher education is bright. First, the school-age population is increasing from an enrollment of about 45 million students in the early 1990s to an enrollment of about 53 million students in the early years of the new century (Recruiting New Teachers, Inc., 1993). Second, the median age of teachers in the work force has increased from about 34 years of age in 1976, to about 43 years of age in 1991, with large numbers of the nation's teachers now more than 50 years of age (Recruiting New Teachers, Inc., 1993). Demographics such as these ensure a heightened demand for classroom teachers throughout the nation because, over the next decade or so, student enrollment will increase by about 10% and teacher retirement rates will soar. So the bright side is an immediate future where there will be a strong demand for professionals to staff the classrooms of the nation. But what will those persons be like?

Some other social forces at work, however, suggest that the future of teacher education is gloomy. Added to the consistently poor funding of teacher education on college campuses throughout the nation, say in comparison to the biological sciences, engineering, or business (Ebmeier, Twombly, & Teeter, 1991), is the precarious funding of the states. The outlook over the next decade, and beyond, is that on the collection side states will have revenue problems, while on the spending side pressing social needs such as medical care, law enforcement, and incarceration will compete with education for increasingly scarce state funds. Therefore, university budgets will be reduced or cut (House, 1994), and in that environment education at the universities will probably do more poorly vis-à-vis other areas than it usually does. Furthermore, and perhaps most important, there is the widespread perception that too many of today's programs of teacher education are inadequate—too costly of time and money, too removed from practice, too easy to get through, and of unknown effectiveness. Worse, many of the criticisms of teacher education come from those who best know these programs, those within the profession itself. So there is reason to be gloomy about our future, too.

Criticism, however, can be used to redesign programs, not just abandon them, as some have suggested. And that is what we have done, for we believe that the extant criticisms of teacher education can be used to improve the enterprise markedly. We have suggestions about *a* future for teacher education (not *the* future), based on the feedback we have received from student and veteran teachers over the years and on our own reflections about what they have said. For some time now we have engaged pre- and in-service educators in conversations about teaching and the journeys they have taken to understand their craft and their role in the educational system. Our dialog has centered on related questions: What has your teacher education program enabled you to value, to know, and to do as a professional? In what ways did your preparation program encourage you to grow as an educator?

In their responses, most teachers recall finishing a form of educational "basic training" rather than initiating a process of becoming professional educators. Our conversations imply new directions for American teacher education that would substantively change most programs that prepare and repair educators for contemporary classroom life. To capture and convey their recollections and opinions, we have assembled two fictitious professional life histories that represent our many conversations with teachers. Virginia, termed an *expert* by supervisors and peers, is described first. The thoughts of Greg, a *novice,* who will be teaching far into the future, are described next. Following these composite life histories, we offer our reflections about a future for American teacher education that would provide the Virginias and Gregs of the next generation with a different story to tell.

PROFESSIONAL PROFILES

Virginia's Story: Professionalism Lost and Found

Virginia completed a "really traditional" training program at a small state teachers college in the midwestern United States. Right after graduation, she taught science in the middle grades for about 15 years, relying heavily on a blend of print materials, expository instruction, and pencil-and-paper assessment. After her fifth year at the same junior high school, she sought and assumed leadership positions with the local teachers' association to bridge a growing gap between her life as a classroom teacher and her professional aspirations.

Three years ago, "acting on an impulse," Virginia applied for a master teacher position at her district's professional development school (PDS). Her selection revived and redirected her teaching career. Regular interaction with school administrators and university partners have induced a quest for strong professionalism that absorbs increasing amounts of her time and effort. Virginia reserves part of her schedule for reflection and self-examination. Almost daily, she records her thoughts in a journal, attempting to describe the nature of her work with children so she might better understand and articulate her craft. She

intentionally extends the parameters that once defined her classroom practice, reaching farther and farther afield for insights and inspiration. Moreover, Virginia seeks opportunities to share knowledge with parents, community leaders, and other educators, negotiating ways to reshape the learning environments in her classroom and school. She is particularly seeking ways to work with children, who, because of poverty and family difficulties, are harder to teach than others more socially and economically advantaged.

But Virginia is bitter. She characterizes her preservice training as an obstacle to professional growth. She attributes much of her delay in seeking professionalism's promised land to the incoherence of her teacher education program. Virginia spent 4 years "getting out of the way" a lengthy series of general studies requirements, educational foundations courses, and a methods block, followed by the chance to student-teach. Her program seemed disconnected without and within, and elements of the program were largely unrelated. In the methods block, particularly, the courses were discrete and independent. In a rapid-fire sequence, Virginia took diagnostic reading, curriculum development, a survey of teaching approaches generally appropriate for secondary school–bound students, and a science-specific methods course. In one foundation course, educational psychology, she studied learning theory, classroom management, instructional planning, then assessment, all disconnected from each other. Within each course she was warned of the "problems" inherent in teaching children who were different from her— African-American, Hispanic, and Asian—but no one could tell her why this was a problem. Classroom and community contexts rarely entered the courses. After finishing her coursework, she was dispatched to a 12-week practicum placement in a junior high school, and, with few exceptions, rarely thought much about the university-based segments of her program. With only an occasional exception, they seemed artificial and contrived, so distant from the real world of children and the complexity of the classroom.

For Virginia, the fragmentation that marked her professional training remains its most disturbing quality. Only recently, and despite the best efforts of her teacher education, has she begun to believe strongly that teaching and learning constitute an interactive, organic process. Compared to her earlier attempts to deliver science content to children, she now experiments with teaching approaches that invite young scientists to investigate their world. She struggles to avoid dispensing bits of information in isolation, and cannot imagine that she learned to teach science that way. She uses the term *teacher education* quite loosely and laments that her program reduced the art and craft of teaching to a pseudoscience of tactical decision making. She wonders aloud why professors rarely accounted for the classroom contexts that should inform almost every option for practice.

Even more troubling, Virginia emerged from "ed. school" without much sense of what it takes to operate as a professional and without the knowledge, skills, and dispositions to seek professional status. As a preservice student, she seldom asked questions, made meaning, or found opportunities for thoughtfulness; instead, she wrote furiously in a notebook while professors dictated five-step planning models and outlined theoretical positions. Virginia cannot remember translating knowledge into classroom action, formulating a position that supported her instructional choices, or defending her beliefs about teaching in professional dialog. For Virginia, her teacher training seemed terrifyingly mindless and antagonistic to the rich professional life that she now tries so hard to generate. Virginia labels ed. school "just a waste of my time," an opportunity for professional growth that was forever lost.

Greg's Story: A University-Dominated "Field-Based" Program

After college, apprenticeship, and 10 years as a journeyman pipe fitter, Greg entered a postbaccalaureate teacher preparation program to redirect his career path, raising his young family's social position and his sons' professional aspirations in the process. Although strongly motivated to succeed, his family situation and job obligations forced him to move slowly, and so the certification requirements were stretched over a 5-year period. After some soul searching and financial sacrifice, Greg student-taught in the elementary school where he now teaches fifth grade. The sprawling campus-style facility serves almost 1,000 children from a suburban, middle-class neighborhood, where "the nice families live." Greg's students seem to learn readily and thoroughly; they attained most State Essential Skills for math, language arts, and reading, while approaching the scores that were desired for science and social studies. Greg displays little doubt that his teaching career has begun in a promising fashion.

Yet, as a first-year teacher, Greg spends too many moments worrying about his inability to demonstrate pedagogical essential skills and to conceptualize teaching's "big picture." He grows concerned, at times even angered, that he completed more than 50 credit hours of coursework without realizing the magnitude or complexity of the learning process and acquiring the abilities to identify appropriate practices for particular contexts. Asked to describe his teacher education, Greg recites a laundry list of courses taken: two required classes in child development, two in "basic" mathematics, two in "remedial fine arts" (i.e., to eliminate his deficiencies in music and art appreciation), one in computer education, one in classroom management, three in developmental reading, one in the history of American education, one in curriculum development, and four in methodologies specific to particular subject areas (e.g., math, social studies, science, and communication arts). Program guidelines, moreover, permitted him to take these courses in almost random order, fitting them into his work schedule whenever possible.

Professors and classmates provided Greg with "terrific handouts" that explicate "dynamite lesson ideas" and list important works of children's literature. He soaked up great quantities of information about instructional strategists, child developmentalists, and educational theorists that he knows he should remember but cannot. He became acquainted with some interesting people who showed promise as professional colleagues. But, for all the providing, soaking up, and acquainting that occurred, Greg found few opportunities for clarifying his emerging perceptions about children and schools

and for developing them into some sort of educational platform that might guide his practice. He concluded his professional preparation program confused about what his craft entails and finds it most unsettling that he can elaborate the "what and why" of the pipe-fitting trade but cannot articulate a pedagogical rationale.

After 9 months of teaching, Greg struggles to identify student needs and place them in any broader context. He admits that he "pretty much flies by the seat of his pants," operating his classroom on a day-to-day basis and confessing that "long-range planning means knowing what I'll do this afternoon." In a programmatic or curricular sense, Greg reveals a sketchy-at-best notion of what he intends to accomplish, how he might approach his many tasks, and why he should tackle them. He acknowledges that "there's never enough time in a day to teach all that I have to teach" but cannot find connecting points among the myriad outcomes that fill district curriculum guides for each subject area. He finds it curious that he cannot formulate a clear and concise response to the question: What do you believe about teaching and learning?

Searching for an instructional direction, Greg wants to develop thematic units that integrate content and present related knowledge, skills, and dispositions in meaningful packages, preferably using some of the new technology in which his school has invested heavily. Yet, he resists taking the necessary design time because he cannot establish a coherent, appropriate course of study that might inform his choice of unit topics. Instead, Greg makes a few hesitant attempts to inject a little math into a science lesson or to select books for silent reading that treat social studies–related issues. Given time to reflect, Greg might characterize his teacher education program as a university-dominated, weak "field-based" program—a thoughtless rush of coursework, disconnected from classroom practice and context, without a theoretical framework or set of beliefs about teaching that might inform and focus his efforts to resolve the problems that confront most first-year teachers.

The Unifying Vision: A Strong Professional

Let us now look at some dimensions of a possible teacher education program, a design that has accommodated the mistakes of the past and might be spoken about much more favorably by the next Virginia and Greg to enter the teaching profession. This one out of a number of possible futures for teacher education focuses on five key dimensions that every teacher preparation program struggles with. All desire that their teachers: (1) develop an educational ideology for interpreting curricula, (2) acquire teaching methods, (3) understand the general pedagogical knowledge base, (4) be responsive to a multicultural student body, and (5) understand technology. Although there is much more to a teacher education program than these five dimensions, they are central to contemporary programs of teacher education. In each domain we note problems and use these to discuss alternatives, sketching broad outlines of how teachers in a future program of teacher education might form the beliefs, gain the knowledge, and be able to do the things they must do to create enriching lives for themselves and their students. Accompanying this assemblage of ideas are speculations about the kind of curricular changes that colleges of teacher education must make in order to move these visions of the future toward reality. The visions all revolve around one pervasive image, an image that is simultaneously fuzzy and powerful, hard to define, and yet holding all the elements of a teacher education program together. This is the image of the teacher as a certain kind of professional. A *strong professional*. A future for teacher education can be built around this unifying image.

DEVELOPING AN EDUCATIONAL IDEOLOGY FOR INTERPRETING CURRICULUM

Three Elements of Strong Professionalism

The stories of Virginia and Greg are not meant to represent the stories of all teachers who have passed through teacher preparation programs. We do suggest, however, that many program deficiencies identified by these two teachers are common. Broadly speaking, these stories highlight a failure on the part of preparation programs to promote a coherent ideology that would allow for a robust sort of professionalism. Now, the reader may think that she or he has already fathomed the meaning of the term *professional,* for it is bandied about with relish and frequency, its meaning often taken for granted. But because the image of the professional teacher in our particular vision does not precisely match any of the usual ones, its own definition must be stipulated. In this chapter educational professionalism is defined in terms of three critical elements. These elements are the *articulative,* the *operational,* and the *political* dimensions of teaching. These elements, in turn, can be found in several dimensions in a program of teacher education that takes as its charge the development of teachers who can be described as *strong* professionals. We will now examine each of these elements of professionalism and suggest how teacher education programs of the future might attend to them.

The Articulative Dimension of Strong Professionalism

The first element of strong professionalism is the *articulative* dimension. Professionals are said to be strong insofar as they are largely free and able to articulate—and hence to *profess*—what they hold to be beneficial and effective within their particular field of endeavor. Schoolteachers who are strong professionals engage in the kind of critical reflection that enables them to make and express informed judgments about a variety of curricular and educational phenomena. Like many other teachers, Greg and Virginia are struggling to engage in this kind of creative thinking, having had little practice doing so in their formal preparatory experiences.

The educational ideas and practices about which strong educational professionals make judgments reside partially within the realm of the theoretical. These professionals are able to formulate cogent positions related to broad, classic, philosophical questions such as "what should I teach to whom and why?" and "what knowledge is of most worth?"

(or as recently amended, "*whose* knowledge—teacher's, student's, testmaker's, etc.—is of most worth?"). A professional teacher's set of beliefs about what constitutes good education does not, however, remain entirely at a decontextualized, abstract, theoretical level. A strong professional educator is also able to do what Greg, for example, says he often cannot: articulate positions concerning the wisdom of particular practices situated within specific historical and cultural contexts. For example, is it wise to provide curricular and instructional tracking for particular students under this particular set of circumstances? Why or why not? For these second-grade Hispanic students, should the content used in teaching them to read arise from within their own experiences and culture? Should an hour each day be set aside to teach study skills to this Appalachian ninth grader who is intent on leaving school?

But the defense of one's answers to just these few localized questions must, in turn, draw on a wider, more generalized set of ideas about what constitutes good educational practice. A strong professional educator thus engages in a dialectical process of critical reflection: She or he can make informed theoretical judgments about the quality of particular practices while abstracting from examples of practice to formulate defensible theoretical positions.

Of course, each informed judgment implies a value position. Each requires of the teacher the presence of a curriculum platform (Walker, 1971), an idea of what is, and a vision of what ought to be. A curriculum platform serves to guide the curriculum developer in determining what one should do to realize a vision. The presence of a well-defined platform means that the teacher has grounded his or her judgment in empirical observations and reflections about the nature of educational virtue. In other words, an articulated curriculum platform embodies a clear sense of what kinds of schooling experiences can wisely be called *educational.*

Now, the metaphor of a curriculum platform may be insufficient insofar as it conveys an image of a fixed, enduring structure, rather than what it usually is: a fragile nexus of often vague attitudes, tentative beliefs, complex dispositions, and incomplete understandings. Moreover, a platform is not a pure product of dispassionate rational reflection; to the contrary, central educational beliefs and values are somewhat shaped by profound and pervasive life experiences, as for example, those beliefs and values imprinted within an "apprenticeship-of-observation" during one's time as a youngster in school (Lortie, 1975). Intuition and insight are also important contributors to a curriculum platform. But a mature educational professional has, by whatever means, acquired a more or less coherent constellation of ideas about what constitutes educational virtuousness. This integrated system of beliefs, or, if you will, set of platform planks, is the content of an educational ideology. And if certain neopragmatist philosophers are correct in asserting that one is what one believes, then the attachment to this ideological content can be said to constitute who one *is* as an educator. The professing of that dearly held, carefully considered nexus of beliefs constitutes the articulation of an educational identity, the creation of a professional self.

Virginia and Greg can testify to the fact that the creation of professional selves often does not happen in a school of education. Moreover, teachers have usually not been encouraged on the job to articulate for themselves a personal stance about curricular and educational matters. Although teachers tend to play a prominent role in implementing the curriculum, members of other educational constituencies have assumed greater responsibility for creating curriculum content and setting educational priorities. Because teachers lack the power to generate, initiate, and prioritize curriculum content, a set of personal or professional guidelines for engaging in such decision making has been made to appear superfluous. At least two categories of usurpers of teacher responsibility over curriculum creation and prioritization can be identified. The first are the professional knowledge makers, especially university academics. The second can be described as political agents of a democratic populace and a capitalistic marketplace.

Teaching is often seen as a profession in the sense of a modern technological field like agricultural engineering or physical therapy (Friedson, 1986). An important attribute common to workers in those fields is their ability to employ specialized knowledge and technical skills for the benefit of the larger public. But this knowledge and these skills are largely generated by workers in other professions, especially natural and social scientists, and other academic subject-matter specialists. As scholarly professionals, these other workers derive their power from the larger culture that has legitimated their claims to expert knowledge (Barone, 1987). This "objectified," purportedly value-free, expert knowledge is thereby placed safely beyond the pale of personal preference or subjective judgment.

For teachers curriculum content has rarely been presented as arising out of personal experience, or out of negotiations with students. Instead, the subject matter of learning has been generated and selected by others, such as professors in colleges of education and employees of organizations who create standardized examinations. It has been packaged in the form of standardized exams, textbooks, and instructional programs, and shipped to classrooms from publishing houses. The teacher, as a modern technological professional, has typically been discouraged, in and out of schools of education, from thinking of such imported, "privileged" knowledge as itself a product of human judgment that is inevitably value based, and therefore vulnerable to challenge and critique.

A second source of the usurpation of teacher prerogative over curriculum initiation is more directly related to issues of economic and political control. This source relates to the role of the teacher within an institution organized to serve a capitalist economy. An enduring and familiar metaphor of the school is that of a factory or business designed to process students efficiently through the stages of an educational assembly line. As conceived by adherents to the scientific management approach, the contours of the finished product (i.e., the ideal graduate) should match those of a carefully designed prototype. The prototype is designed using the criteria of the marketplace (Callahan, 1962). In educational terms, this means that economic forces within the larger culture influence the curriculum content expected to be acquired by the marketable finished product—the certificated graduate.

Political forces also operate to constrain curriculum leadership on the part of the teacher. Curriculum priorities may be politicized at the national level by, for example, commissions and task forces. At the state level, legislators, heads of education departments, and governmental agencies attempt to establish and reinforce their own priorities. Local school boards are also the sites of political struggles for determining what will be taught. Each of these governmental bodies acts on behalf of the general populace and/or special interest groups within the political marketplace. Each also presses curricular demands that drain the autonomy of the teacher over matters of curriculum choice. When teachers are encouraged to view themselves as servile respondents to various political forces rather than curriculum leaders, or as molders of raw materials rather than educators of human beings, then personal visions of educational virtue come to be regarded as annoying distractions rather than as sources of professional inspiration.

The Operational Dimension of Strong Professionalism

As many commentators have noted, influence over the curriculum by agents external to the classroom, always present to some degree, has become stronger and more pervasive since the 1970s (Aronowitz & Giroux, 1985). Since that time teachers such as Greg and Virginia have increasingly been imagined as conduits of mandated curriculum content rather than as creative practitioners who are capable of developing original material and activities. The increased separation of the conceptualization of the curriculum from those who teach it has indeed resulted in the disenfranchisement of teachers, in the diminished sense of ownership of their craft (Goodman, 1988).

But the external curriculum control that has developed since the 1970s has not only become more pervasive. It has also shifted in character. Once aiming primarily to promote general goals at the level of the ideal curriculum (Goodlad, 1984), outside forces are now more determined to have those goals enacted. Especially at the level of the states, attempts have been made to align the various elements of the curriculum (textbooks, examinations, district curriculum guides [recall Greg's story], and other teaching materials) with mandated program goals and aims. This more intrusive approach extends curriculum control beyond the articulative dimension to the operational dimension of professionalism. That is, teachers are not merely discouraged from imagining their own desired educational outcomes, but also if they do generate a personal vision, they are prevented from realizing the ideals implicit in their pedagogical preferences.

This move toward curriculum alignment is understandable in terms of the scientific management approach that supports the metaphor of school as factory or business. The teacher is, in this scheme, a "semiprofessional functionary" locked into a top-down bureaucratic organizational arrangement (Foster, 1986; Henderson, 1992). The teacher, separated into egg-crate classrooms and isolated by packed teaching schedules, is expected to behave in accordance with predetermined administrative policy designed to heighten efficiency, that is, to maximize output (student learning) at minimum cost (Darling-Hammond, 1988). Teacher accountability procedures are designed to ensure that teachers are indeed functioning efficiently in accordance with administration directives.

Such procedures also deny teachers possession and realization of a professional ideology. Teachers such as Virginia who are (however slowly) becoming stronger at the articulative level do indeed possess an increasingly clear sense of preferred ideological content or beliefs and interpretations that purport to be true and valid. But ideologies have not only content but also *functions,* and ideologies function in the production and consumption, as well as the representation of behavior (Giroux, 1988). The *actions* that teachers undertake are, therefore, as ideologically based as the platforms they articulate. Deprofessionalization at the operational level means a curtailment of freedom to *practice* one's profession in a preferred manner.

Whereas ideological content exists at the reflective discourse level, ideology may *function* at the level of either consciousness or unconsciousness. Teachers are often not aware of the ideological functions of certain practices in which they engage. But whatever their ideological proclivities, a strong professional *is* more fully aware of need for congruence between platform and practice. Neither technical skill nor deep affection for a particular planning or teaching approach will, alone, suffice for the operational dimension of strong professionalism. Both must be present. Thus, a teacher who is skilled at designing and administering teacher-made tests is operationally strong only when she or he also values and can intelligently defend the purposes, processes, and outcomes of that preferred form of evaluation practice over available alternatives (Cherry-Holmes, 1988, p. 4). If she or he cannot, then an external mandate eliminating exams in favor of portfolios violates no professional prerogatives. On the other hand, a teacher who is talented at creating circumstances in the classroom that promote vocabulary building without lists of random words may be able to express an elaborate rationale undergirding her practice, one based, perhaps, on an ideology of whole language. When that teacher is required to administer a weekly vocabulary exam on specified word lists, the operational element of professionalism is constricted. She or he is prevented from exercising (and further developing) a talent for educating in a manner that is consonant with a well-articulated personal platform.

The Political Dimension of Strong Professionalism

Judge (1988, pp. 229–230) made an important distinction between profession*alism* and profession*ism*. The former is oriented to an ideal of service to others, and the latter consists of "self-serving efforts of privileged groups to preserve a mystique, to delineate a monopoly, to resist access to their ranks, to resist external controls." Does curriculum or educational leadership on the part of teachers necessarily imply a professionistic disregard of the voices of students and members of other constituencies with a stake in the future of our democratic society? The answer is: clearly not.

Professional teachers are principals rather than simply agents for others. They have a distinctive code of ethics that focuses on the interest of clients. That code of ethics can be seen as an ideal of service. Teachers must, however, always be mindful that they live and work within a democratic culture, a culture in which power must be shared rather than hoarded and lorded

over others. No matter how caring their ethic, how elaborate their platform, teachers become professionistic when they assume that professional autonomy means a cavalier disregard for the judgments of members of other educational constituencies.

But despite a "second wave" of school reform that has emphasized their empowerment (Lieberman, 1988), teachers in present-day America are in greater danger of remaining the kinds of quasi-professional functionaries implied within the accountability movement and exemplified by Virginia and Greg, than of wallowing in a selfish mode of professionism. For that reason teachers who are curriculum leaders must partake of a third element of professionalism, the political element.

Recall that strong professional teachers will have acquired, first, an ability to articulate a personal perspective on educational matters, and, second, the talents to operationalize their platform within a classroom setting. But what about teachers who experience *critical dissonance* (Cochran-Smith, 1991), an incongruity between their own perspectives on what is educationally virtuous and the constraints (implicit or explicit) within ideologically hostile educational surroundings? What are they to do? As strong professionals, they must struggle to alter those surroundings. Indeed, the third element of strong professionalism concerns the political efforts of teachers toward the creation of the professional space needed to implement their ethically based curriculum platforms.

The sources of constraint on platform implementation are as numerous as the educational constituencies that exist in a democratic society. These constituencies include those already mentioned (state legislators, school boards, textbook and test publishers, external and plant administrators), and others such as parents, fellow teachers, students, and even maintenance personnel who refuse to rearrange furniture for alternative teaching modes. Teachers who are forced to assume subordinate positions within a top-down organizational arrangement are in special need of an arsenal of strategies for resisting the constraints on their professional prerogatives. Our vision is of strong professionals who possess such strategies and who are adept at using them.

Educating Teachers for Strong Professionalism

Visions, like dreams, are often misunderstood to be ethereal entities that are devoid of worldly characteristics, unrelated to gritty empirical realities. They are, in fact, often media of discovery in which the commonplace phenomena of mundane existence are recast into useful new forms. (One example among many literally "dreamt up" scientific "discoveries" is the German chemist Kekule's late-night vision of a coiled snake that led to an awareness of the circular nature of the molecular structure of the benzene ring.) In addition, the realignment of minutiae in dreams can sometimes yield powerful moral visions; visions of this sort adumbrate a more ethical and appropriate order of existence. This kind of visionary is burdened with the task of shaping reality to fit the dream.

Ours is this kind of vision. Here we will imagine a re-formed teacher education program, one that incorporates the elements of curriculum leadership and teacher professionalism described earlier. But just as Kekule's vision was not cut out of whole cloth, neither is ours. Many of its individual elements can be found in existing teacher education programs that are themselves former visions that have recently reshaped reality. We intend to recast these elements into a single imaginary form, the form of a preservice program that we see as a harbinger of what is to come in the rapidly approaching twenty-first century. It is the kind of program that the Virginias and Gregs of the future might see as a blessing.

Educating for the Articulative Dimension of Professionalism

At the heart of the articulative dimension of professionalism is platform growth and refinement. This growth occurs within a process of critical reflection (Beyer, 1984) and deliberation that enables students to see deeply into and to make sense of seemingly superficial and disparate educational phenomena. Students of education must, that is, construct an educational platform that rests on an educational ideology. An educational ideology, as we have stated, is a set of organized, ethically and politically relevant beliefs about the practice of curriculum and teaching, including what is worth teaching to whom and how it should be taught.

Many educational ideologies may be identified. We will mention four that are familiar to American educationists. One is that of *holistic progressivism* as reflected in the works of John Dewey, Boyd Bode, John L. Childs, R. Bruce Rapp, Herbert Kohl, and Charles Silberman. Another is the overtly political ideology of *reconstructionism/critical theory* that can be traced back to Plato's *Republic* and Comenius's *Great Didactic,* through the work of political progressivist George S. Counts, to the 1950s reconstructionist ideas of Harold Rugg, B. Othanel Smith, and Theodore Brameld, up to today's activist educational scholarship by the likes of Apple, Giroux, and Freire. Third is an ideology that emphasizes the classical canon of Western civilization and a curriculum that teaches the "traditional values" contained within those works. This is the ideology of *academic rationalism* (Eisner & Vallance, 1974) as espoused by educational essentialists such as Robert Maynard Hutchins, Mortimer Adler, Allan Bloom, and William Bennett. And fourth is the (already mentioned) ideology that often sees itself as levitating high above the messy political battlefield, the ideology of *scientific management.*

Prospective teachers must be able to examine the central notions in each of these (*and/or other*) educational ideologies in order to gain a sense of their own professional identity. This examination can be fostered through contact with at least three kinds of texts—texts of educational theory, case studies of various sorts, and the "texts" of actual classroom life.

At various points throughout their preparatory program, future teachers will confront classical texts that articulate prominent theoretical viewpoints on curricular issues. Examples will include Dewey's *Education and Experience* (1963), Freire's *Pedagogy of the Oppressed* (1970), and Adler's *The Paideia Proposal* (1982). Of course, read in isolation of the world of practice, these abstract statements will appear rather detached from the life experiences of preservice teachers. Their lofty theory needs grounding, and so these texts must be augmented

with observational experience in real classroom and vicarious experience in storied ones. How so?

Recent thinking on the nature of case studies has identified a link with storytelling (Carter, 1993). Case studies that portray in story form the nuances of classroom practice engaged in by fully developed teacher characters achieve an important aspiration of literature, that of providing vicarious access to the lived-in world of its protagonists (Barone & Eisner, in press). Although some such case studies already exist, there need to be many more. The creation of case studies by education students themselves will be one way of filling this gap.

Of course, many existing works of literature (fictional and nonfictional, and of varying aesthetic quality) portray curriculum and teaching activities from particular ideological slants. Some represent apologias for a preferred approach (e.g., *Marva Collins' Way,* Collins & Tamarkin, 1982), and others offer stringent critiques (as in Dickens' depiction of Mr. Gradgrind's harsh utilitarianism in *Hard Times,* 1969). Each of these stories represents a case of contextualized educational theory; they illustrate ideologies in use and can help students visualize the real-world underpinnings of various educational ideologies.

Whenever feasible, the kind of vicarious participation offered to students through stories and case studies should be complemented by field-based activities in community schools. The earliest of these should take place in a variety of schools, each of which evidences an alternative ideology in action. These experiences should move beyond nonfocused observation to the practice of inquiry, enabling students, with guidance from university faculty, to begin their careers as teacher researchers. Students will learn to engage in multicase ethnographic research as they compare and contrast the various features of different forms of curriculum and pedagogy. They will tease out the meanings brought to daily experiences by the players in the classroom scene, assess significance in terms of their platforms under construction, and reach tentative conclusions about their ideological preferences.

Confrontations with theoretical and storied texts and field-based ethnographic inquiry are the sources of perplexities that prompt students into a kind of critical deliberation. Reflective equilibrium begins with the confrontation of newly apprehended, disturbingly persuasive, conceptions of theory in practice that transgress against already held, comfortable, and taken-for-granted ideas, beliefs, and ethical ends. An ethical disequilibrium having been created between old ideas or values and new ones, negotiations ensue. The critical deliberator goes back and forth, modifying and pruning old beliefs and new imperatives until a state of equilibrium is once again achieved (Liston, 1986; Nielson, 1985).

Opportunities for critical deliberation, and the ensuing platform refinement, will be offered throughout teacher education programs of the future. They will occur not just on lonely occasions in which students wrestle privately with the kinds of texts mentioned. Imagine also the quest for an ethical equilibrium as a group activity in seminar discussions. Imagine reflective writing about platform struggles in journals to be shared with university faculty, "cooperating teachers" in the field, and fellow students. Imagine consultation sessions with university faculty about the nature of each student's personal struggles toward sense making about the shape of the platform articulation process that is resulting in ever stronger professionalism.

Educating for the Operational Dimension of Professionalism

One difference between the articulative and operational dimensions of professionalism is suggested by the distinction between "knowing that" and "knowing how" (Ryle, 1949). The former involves "cognitive repertoires," the latter is concerned with "competencies."

Within the operational dimension of professionalism are located three genera of performance competencies. These are the competencies involved in knowing *how to plan,* knowing *how to teach,* and knowing *how to inquire.* In the planning of the curriculum, in executing those plans, and even in research strategies, ideologies function at both the conscious and unconscious levels. Strong professionals, however, operationalize with some degree of awareness of broader ideological considerations. They are, remember, talented at planning, teaching, and researching in a manner that resonates with their own deeply held notions of educational virtue. They know *how* to plan, teach, and inquire in a manner that will further conscious aims *that* they know (believe) are worthwhile.

Teacher education programs of the future that foster operational talents will necessarily possess strong field-based components. After stretches of ethnographic observation in classrooms, students will move to a planning and teaching phase. Because their platforms may still be poorly defined during these early program activities, students will be required to plan and teach for short periods in at least two classroom settings, each of which represents different educational ideologies. Students who teach briefly in, say, a Waldorf school, with its distinctly holistic approach to education, and subsequently, in a highly regimented, traditionalist, "back-to-basics" school will gain practical experience in contrasting (even conflicting) ideological settings. Articulative as well as operational outcomes should result: Students should also be in a better position to intelligently compare facets of their experiences in light of widely divergent ends in view.

With the gradual growth of a personal educational belief system a student can move on to the final phase of a preservice program. This is student teaching for an extended time under the guidance of a cooperating teacher whose ideological preferences resonate with those of the student teacher. University faculty will work closely, in the field and in university meeting rooms, with both cooperating teachers and student teachers, serving not as "supervisors" (insofar as that term suggests a hierarchical, top-down, factory metaphor of schools), but as critics, coaches, and resource persons. Faculty members will ensure that the practical activities are enfolded in the ongoing critical deliberation activities described earlier. They will also demonstrate within their own university-based courses teaching practices that are consonant with the various ideologies about which they are teaching.

One final element in the operational dimension of the making of strong educational professionals needs mentioning—the research element. Ethnographic research accompanies the articulative dimension, and within the operational dimension the student continues to engage in the kind of field-based inquiry that is characteristic of all strong professional teachers. Now, however, the student is no longer merely observing but also operationalizing the activities of planning and teaching. Therefore, in the final phases of the student-teaching experience, students will become critical (Carr & Kemmis, 1986), engaging in forms of teacher-generated "action research" that enable them to enhance the quality of their ideologically based practice.

Many valuable metalessons can be learned through such research activity. One is that research is not an esoteric activity that has little to do with daily classroom concerns. Action researchers learn to assume ownership over their own inquiry by doing their own research on their own questions that result in changes in their own behavior. As a result they can learn that teacher research can be an important agency for change (Goswami & Stillman, 1987).

Educating for the Political Dimension of Professionalism

It is one thing to possess a potential for teaching in the direction toward which one's professional compass points, but it is quite another to know how to realize that potential in an institutional setting with its own ideological imperatives. Accomplishing the latter requires competence in the *politics of teaching.* The political dimension of teaching has long been ignored by teacher education programs (Goodlad, 1990a, 1990b). In our vision it is not.

Beginning teachers who have been assisted in developing a strong professional identity and who have acquired a degree of competence in operationalizing their deeply held beliefs can still be denied the power to be who they are and to plan and teach in a manner they consider educationally virtuous. Indeed, restrictions on autonomy will be present in even the most empowering school environment. Pressures from a variety of sources (both internal and external to the classroom) will inevitably require some negotiation of educational aims and practices. Ensuing compromises should not, however, be automatically regarded as undesirable. Indeed, lest a teacher resort to the kind of arrogant professionism described earlier, opposing views of others with legitimate claims on the education of the child—parents, community members, and others—must be respected. Still, the strong professional will move to persuade and educate those who harbor ideologically contrary notions about curriculum and pedagogy. In order to maximize their potential for educational leadership, strong professional teachers must possess a host of political skills and competencies.

It can be argued that the teachers who are most in need of political finesse are activists of a reconstructionist or critical theory bent. Teacher educators sympathetic to this philosophy have suggested that much standard school policy and practice remain profoundly antidemocratic in their tendency to perpetuate inequalities based on race, class, and gender and that prospective teachers need to learn how to replace, not replicate, these unfortunate policies and practices (Barone, 1987; Beyer,

1984; Goodman, 1986). They must, that is, learn how to "teach against the grain" (Cochran-Smith, 1991).

But being politically savvy is important for a teacher regardless of ideological leanings. For example, the space of a traditionalist teacher is encroached on when a school district's "whole-language" policy mandates threaten the professional privileges of a passionate and thoughtful advocate of phonics. That teacher, too, may need *environmental competence*—the ability of a citizen-teacher to move beyond merely coping with life conditions and to exert effectively, as an ethical agent of change, influence on public affairs in accordance with a carefully constructed platform (Newmann, 1975).

An "against-the-grain" teacher education curriculum will include several elements that foster environmental competence. These elements will pervade the entire program. One is seminar-style exposure to practicing classroom teachers who discuss their personal experiences in dealing with dissonance between their platforms and contrarian pressures from parents, administrators, fellow teachers, and so on. A second element is found in university course content that directly treats the politics of teaching; readings of case studies of activist teachers (Goodman, 1992) will be combined with theoretical analyses of the nature of school change (Fullan, 1982, 1991; Sarason, 1982). Third, the possibilities for curriculum change and the mechanisms of educational leadership can be the focus of action research projects by students. But perhaps the most important program element for teaching how to teach against the grain will be the field-based component.

Student perspectives on teaching are much more likely to be altered as a result of field-based experiences than formal, university classroom activities. It is in the field that students acquire the culture of the profession as they learn to think and behave like experienced teachers. Because of the formative power of these field experiences, wise placement of students is critical.

Three criteria seem crucial for determining student teaching field placements that result in strong professionalism at the political level. First, student teachers will be assigned to teachers with whom they resonate ideologically. Second, these teachers should, whenever possible, be located within an educational setting that is not totally compatible with their own ideological proclivities. (For example, a progressivist student will work with a progressivist teacher who is not teaching in a homogeneously progressivist school.) Third, the experienced teachers will demonstrate competence in "teaching against the grain" within their school setting. When the goal of a teacher education program is to create educational leaders, then it is indeed important that students find themselves in the company of teachers who model elements of educational leadership in ideologically challenging situations.

The talents of educational leadership in such situations include competence at negotiating for space in which to pursue one's own educational ends. Goodman (1986) described specific examples of negotiations between some preservice teachers and administrators, other school staff, and parents:

Some [student teachers] bargain for time. While they teach the regular curriculum, they are given a certain amount of time each day to teach their [own] units. Others must follow the school's curriculum, but sig-

nificantly alter it. For example, many pre-service teachers have taught units on state history, but beyond this directive they have negotiated the freedom to develop their own content, materials, and activities. In this manner, individuals get practical experience, to some degree, at being change agents in their practicum site. (p. 196)

At the heart of successful negotiations by a strong professional is the capacity for exerting influence on the affairs of his or her teaching community through persuasion. For, persuasion is the quintessence of public life (Bernstein, 1986). Moreover, persuasion need not be accomplished exclusively through verbal acts; the strong professional has also learned to persuade others of an ethical vision through exemplar, by living that set of beliefs.

Summary

A beginning teacher who is a strong professional is, therefore, one who, after carefully examining several paths to educational virtue, has acquired the ability to articulate an educational platform, one who has developed competence in inquiring, planning, and teaching in accordance with that platform, and finally, one who through word and practice is able to inspire—and persuade—others to respect that ethically grounded set of beliefs and practices.

This, then, is one vision of strong professional teachers, and the kind of teacher education program that will bring them into being. As Virginia and Greg have reminded us, many teacher preparation programs in the last part of the twentieth century have been mired in a process of training weak professionals, scatterbrained practitioners who cannot formulate a coherent vision of their professional selves. Although they perhaps gain a degree of technical competence, these teachers-to-be were nevertheless taught to leave curriculum decision making to those presumably wiser, or at least more powerful, in the taken-for-granted modern political and organizational scheme of things. Current trends, including trends toward the implementation of many program elements described in this chapter, suggest that the future of teacher education will be different. This may be because these trends are fueled by the determination of those of us who share a vision of strong professional teachers to redouble our efforts at persuading our fellow teacher educators to adopt such a vision. This is a determination to become, ourselves, through word and deed, strong professional educators of teachers.

THE ACQUISITION OF TEACHING METHODS

Methods courses focus on the teaching and learning of subject matter and on conveying the tools for thoughtful, effective, and purposeful classroom practice in that subject-matter area. Such courses have long occupied a central place in programs for the education of prospective classroom teachers. In terms of sequence, preservice students typically encounter a *methods block* midway through a three-step training cycle (i.e., foundations, then methods, then student teaching). In terms of quantity, methods courses are also central to most teacher education programs. Foundations courses and practicum experiences account for roughly 60% of the credit hours required for graduation or certification, with methods consuming the remaining 40%. In terms of time frame, traditional teacher education programs typically last four to six semesters, with methods coursework extending across two or three of them. Arguably, such emphasis is most appropriate. Teacher education programs, after all, exist primarily to produce articulate, capable, and inspired professionals who can facilitate learning in our nation's classrooms.

Our vision of programs designed to generate strong professional educators places particular emphasis on a powerful methods component, one designed from the start to be transformational (Jackson, 1987). As they plan, teach, assess, and inquire, strong professional teachers investigate their craft, construct a pedagogical belief system from their findings, and base classroom decisions on these values. They understand what children should learn and can articulate why young people should make meaning from this content. Strong professionals continually demonstrate the ability to engage children in productive learning experiences that yield important knowledge, skills, and dispositions. And last, but never least, strong teachers must represent their professional judgments and beliefs to students, parents, peers, community leaders, and instructional supervisors. Methods courses must be designed to contribute to the process through which teachers learn the articulative, operational, and political dimensions that distinguish true *artisans* of the teaching craft (Casey, 1993).

The Problem with Methods Courses

Despite its promise as a transformational vehicle, the traditional methods component seems more likely to inhibit movement toward strong professionalism than to enhance it. The disjointed quality of most methods coursework renders the formulation and articulation of an instructional vision problematic at best. Methods courses hardly complement the other segments of a teacher education program (Goodlad, 1990a). Rather than *increasing* levels of curiosity, inquiry, and potential resistance to the pedagogical status quo, methods courses often force students to abandon reflective and articulative pursuits in favor of mastering and replicating long-accepted practice (Goodman, 1986). Even in methods blocks that encourage critical reflection, the learnings that students do acquire are too often contradicted, diminished, even eliminated during student teaching (Zeichner & Tabachnick, 1981).

Within the methods block, discrete courses compete for students' attention (Goodlad, 1990a). Most blocks include overviews of generic strategies applicable to a variety of instructional settings and appropriate for a range of student needs. These courses typically adopt *function* as an organizational theme, surveying methods and materials for instructional design, management, curriculum development, or assessment across the curriculum. Additional courses feature approaches and resources for planning, teaching, and assessment that are specific to particular subject areas (e.g., math, language arts, social studies, or science methods).

Whether generic or specific, each course operates independently from other offerings, with only occasional references to apparently related teaching functions or subject areas. Students frequently repeat identical assignments for multiple professors (e.g., developing a thematic unit, preparing a test, interviewing a classroom teacher), often becoming frustrated by tasks that seem repetitive and meaningless. No belief system informs the arrangement or content of the methods block; no platforms emanate from its daily routines and required assignments. Collectively, these courses present theory that is not only separate from practice but also generated without thoughtfulness. They suggest that teaching can be practiced without rationale. Professors seem to dodge the question of pedagogical virtue, offering only rare opportunities to judge teaching in terms of truth, goodness, and beauty.

Indeed, most methods blocks introduce and reinforce teaching competencies in such isolated and random fashion that preservice students cannot formulate an educational platform that might make these skills truly operational. Preservice students such as Virginia and Greg too frequently planned lessons they never taught, managed, or assessed. They developed thematic units for imaginary classrooms, without regard for the abilities or prior knowledge that real children might possess. They designed learning experiences for a subject area such as history without incorporating mathematical, scientific, and/or geographic content. By repeating similar assignments, preservice students lose the chance to master the uses of complex and powerful teaching practices. Like Virginia and Greg, they eventually grow tired and disaffected. Or, they voice frustration that they cannot consider particular methodological trees in terms of a surrounding forest.

Furthermore, traditional methods courses force preservice teachers to construct educational platforms independently. For one thing, education professors award letter grades that force most methods students to compete against peers rather than to dialog and collaborate with them. Traditional methods classes, moreover, often have such large enrollments that interaction is inhibited or even prevented. Students are taught lecture and recitation style, further discouraging meaningful conversation. They rarely hone their belief systems through meaningful conversations and negotiations that might introduce alternative viewpoints and reconcile unfamiliar information. An intellectual vacuum is a difficult environment in which to build an educational platform.

Perhaps most significant, preservice students seem insulated, almost protected from audiences that they should regularly contact. They rarely venture into classrooms in diverse, urban neighborhoods or attend community events. They seldom encounter parents or talk with teachers, except for scheduled meetings that occur in clinical settings. Traveling alone (although rarely at night), methods students drop into schools, participant-observe a single classroom setting, and withdraw to the university. Because professors almost never accompany students on these expeditions, practicum experiences rarely inform class discussions or serve as laboratories for testing theory. It is not particularly reassuring to note that the faults of the methods block are also the faults of much university teaching. Criticisms like these hold for the programs of study in sociology, psychology, literature, science, and a host of university majors. Nevertheless, from these critical descriptions comes a vision of a future.

Seeking an Alternative Model

Looking at the Old to Develop the New Traditional methods courses mitigate against strong professionalism because they reflect a conception of subject-area teaching that has long been visible and popular, but outdated and unproductive as well. The typical methods block perpetuates instruction that seems overly didactic and relentlessly separative. Preservice students learn how to teach through a pedagogy that isolates knowledge by field and discipline. They enjoy few opportunities to construct understandings that might generate meaningful classroom practice. In course after methods course, students witness a reductionist pedagogy in which teaching is something trivial, mechanical, and manipulative rather than an expansionist pedagogy in which teaching becomes something true, just, and good.

Admittedly, most methods blocks include coursework in generic approaches to instructional design, classroom management, and assessment that applies across content areas. Yet, methods students spend the majority of their time learning to teach the elementary curriculum subject by subject or acquiring the tools to focus their instructional efforts on one secondary discipline. Methods coursework emulates what Beauchamp (1981) labeled a *separate subjects* or *discipline-centered* scheme of curricular organization. He acknowledged this model, but hardly advocated it. In fact, he cautioned that "little or no attention is given [in a discipline-centered curriculum] to the interrelationships among the various subjects, nor do the designers give evidence of realizing that a curriculum is something that has to characterize a whole school program" (p. 118). That methods coursework would perpetuate such a restrictive curricular design seems curious, at best.

Methods professors, moreover, seem to view pedagogical knowledge, skills, and dispositions as commodities to be dispensed or delivered. Using expository instruction almost exclusively, they feed course content in great spoonfuls, reinforcing the stereotype that students should sit, listen, and record important information in a notebook so it can be memorized, then recalled for a test. Long lists of course requirements convince preservice teachers that school work should be completed in great quantity and at a pace that does not permit high quality. They see clearly that students should be almost exclusively linguistic and logical or mathematical; there just are not enough hours in the school day for spatial, musical, bodily/kinesthetic, interpersonal, or intrapersonal ways of knowing (Gardner, 1983).

Finally, methods students are inculcated in a simplistic, linear framework for making instructional decisions. In most methods courses, participants follow a syllabus specifying a list of predetermined objectives to guide instruction as well as the instruments used to assess these outcomes. Instruction usually occurs through a three-step procedure: Content is introduced, developed, or practiced through a series of activities, then brought to closure. Preservice teachers watch as their instructors personify a range of pedagogical catch words, including: *mastery, test item, competency-based, effective, discipline, logically sequenced activities, managed instruction, expectations and consequences, reteaching,* and *evaluation*. Methods classrooms seldom exemplify such alternative phrases as: *holistic, inquiry, caring, aesthetic, reflection, social activism, authentic, flexibil-ity, problem solving,* and *dialog*. The absence of these terms seems unfortunate, as their presence might indicate a learning environment in which strong professionalism could emerge and mature.

Traditionalists might respond to this critique by noting that such reductionist pedagogy prevails beyond the walls of most methods classrooms. They might even ask: What's the fuss? Methods coursework resembles the objectives-driven, assessment-led instruction so common across the elementary and secondary grades. Admittedly, most methods professors champion an alternative pedagogy that contrasts markedly with the structured, textbook-dominated, direct instruction practiced in the schools. Yet, their actions rarely speak as loudly as their words. Typically, they transmit their visions for teaching through methods and materials no better than the vehicles used by most classroom teachers. Methods courses, despite their insistence on ideal practice, are taught in ways that mirror the real instruction in our nation's schools. Methods students, in all probability, are conditioned to practice instructional universals that have characterized American classrooms for decades and will continue to do so for years to come. So, what *is* the problem?

Developing the New The problem surfaces only when classroom teachers like Virginia and Greg refuse to accept an instructional status quo that limits the potential growth of *all* young learners. The problem takes form when classroom teachers develop a coherent educational platform and therefore question whether back-to-basic methods and materials can serve the learning needs of contemporary youth, particularly an increasingly diverse and economically deprived school population. The problem screams for attention when teachers attempt to articulate visions of what good teaching should be, try to operate in ways that reflect these pedagogical platforms, and work collaboratively to spread these conceptions of virtuous teaching to other classrooms. Simply put, the problem arises and refuses to disappear when teachers become strong professionals, obligated to think, feel, and act in ways that they believe are best for the children in their charge.

Fortunately, we need not travel far to find a pedagogy in which the subject areas become integrative sources of knowledge rather than distinct repositories of information, in which young people are encouraged to construct meaning rather than accumulate content. In recent years, educators from school, university, and research laboratories have assembled to create profiles of good teaching across a range of fields and disciplines. Detailed pedagogical visions for social studies, science, mathematics, the arts, the language arts, geography, history, political science, and economics have emerged. These documents are distinctive in their particulars, but, when examined closely and collectively, they reveal a coherent, consistent, and enlightened sense of what teaching should be. Teaching should be noble and purposeful, integrative and holistic, constructivist in nature, and active and engaging. In the future, teacher education programs must be consistent with these ideals.

A Noble and Purposeful Pedagogy

First and foremost, in our vision of a strong professional, teaching should reflect lofty ideals and noble purposes. The strong professional educators we envision expect to transform young people, to inspire them to think, to feel, and to take social action as citizens in a democratic society (Colton & Sparks-Langer, 1993). They declare their teaching purpose with broad goals that target information processing and problem solving rather than narrow objectives that specify the degree to which discrete skills and bits of information must be mastered. Their teaching radiates a moral tone, a conviction that children should become more virtuous people for having the opportunity to learn (Fenstermacher, 1990). As they take classroom action, these strong professionals regularly display a profound concern for young people's present and future welfare.

Social studies educators, for example, are dedicated to enabling young people to "assume with integrity 'the office of citizen' in our democratic republic . . . [and] participate in shaping the future to sustain and improve our democratic republic in an interdependent world" (National Council for the Social Studies [NCSS], 1994, p. 1). They envision social studies as "a liberating force in the life of every citizen" and challenge educators to develop not only competent but also caring citizens who "believe in and work for the common good of the nation and humanity" (NCSS, 1994, pp. 5–6). Social studies as a field only becomes powerful when it is value based, involving the ethical dimensions of topics and addressing controversial issues (NCSS, 1993). Teachers must challenge young citizens, demanding "well-reasoned arguments rather than opinions voiced without thought or commitment" (NCSS, 1993). Every participant in the continual dialog that characterizes good social studies teaching must think reflectively and make informed decisions as classroom events unfold (NCSS, 1993).

Similarly, mathematics educators express their pedagogical vision "for the benefit of [their] students, as well as for [their] social and economic future" (National Council of Teachers of Mathematics [NCTM], 1989, p. 12). Across the grade levels, the math education community shows far more concern for children's ability to communicate, reason, and connect mathematical ideas than for the quantity of basic skills they acquire (NCTM, 1989). Conceptually oriented curricula allow children to make sense of mathematical concepts and perceive how these ideas interrelate meaningfully. In turn, such understandings support the development of problem solving ability, apparently the "bottom line" for mathematics educators (NCTM, 1989). The products of mathematics teaching are young citizens who can explore, justify, represent, solve, construct, discuss, use, investigate, describe, develop, and predict in a world where mathematics is increasingly applied across diverse fields (NCTM, 1989). School mathematics must ensure that today's students are prepared to live in the twenty-first century (NCTM, 1989).

Science educators aim for nothing less than universal scientific literacy, the essential understandings and habits of mind required for citizenship in an increasingly technological society (Project 2061, 1989). As the means to this end, they have identified a common core of science learnings based on five criteria: (1) utility, (2) social responsibility, (3) the intrinsic value of knowledge, (4) philosophical value, and (5) childhood enrichment (Project 2061, 1989). Science teachers must believe that the scientifically literate citizen appreciates the diversity and unity that characterizes the natural world and can apply scientific learnings to meet individual and social purposes (Project 2061, 1989). Scientific literacy equips young citizens "to participate thoughtfully with fellow citizens in building and protecting a society that is open, decent, and vital" (Project 2061, 1989, p. 12).

An Integrative and Holistic Pedagogy

Second, our vision of teaching assumes that learning best occurs across disciplinary boundaries rather than being confined within them. Studying the academic disciplines (and the school subject areas that draw on their content) certainly opens young people to important knowledge, skills, dispositions, and habits of mind that have been advanced, tested, and explicated over generations of systematic inquiry. Yet, meaningful learning must ultimately transcend these content sources. Students should reach into multiple fields to formulate and weigh important generalizations; they should examine issues from alternative disciplinary perspectives. Focusing on the subject areas too narrowly or in isolation limits the degree to which young people comprehend an issue being decided. Only by perceiving interrelationships among knowledge, dispositions, and processes can a learner achieve real understanding (Griffin, 1988).

Social studies curriculum standards, for example, assert that social studies should be "the integrated study of the social sciences and humanities to promote civic competence" (NCSS, 1994, p. 1). As learners pursue coordinated, systematic investigation of civic themes, they draw on varied disciplines and fields (e.g., archeology, economics, geography, history, law, religion, sociology) as well as "appropriate content from the humanities, mathematics and natural sciences" (NCSS, 1994, p. 1). Developers of these standards compare the teaching and learning of civic competence to an orchestral performance. To satisfy the composer's thematic intent, certain instruments take the lead while others play supporting roles; at other times, the full ensemble plays together. Like a musical ensemble, the disciplines interact and unite to ensure that students "learn connected networks of knowledge, skills, beliefs, and dispositions that they will find useful both in and out of school" (NCSS, 1994, p. 14).

What all students should know and be able to do in science, at the end of selected grade levels, is provided in *Benchmarks for Science Literacy* (Project 2061, 1993). This curricular tool, moreover, illustrates the connections between science and other disciplines as it emphasizes K–12 continuity across the curriculum. Reform-minded science educators seem convinced that young people do not acquire essential knowledge, skills, and attitudes only in science class. They argue that scientific literacy comes as a result of the "total school experience from kindergarten through high school" (Project 2061, 1989, p. 3). They sketch broad themes and interdisciplinary relationships that might help young citizens contribute to the welfare of a free society. Their pedagogical vision departs from past conceptions of science teaching and learning because "boundaries between traditional subject matter categories are softened and connections are emphasized" (Project 2061, 1989, p. 4).

Mathematics educators present curriculum and evaluation standards as integrative and encompassing as the proposals offered by their social studies and science colleagues. They insist that the shift to an information society has expanded the influence of mathematics almost exponentially, so that it touches diverse fields in various applications (NCTM, 1989). To gain mathematical literacy, learners must appreciate the role of mathematics across our complex society and "explore relationships among mathematics and the disciplines it serves: the physical and life sciences, the social sciences, and the humanities" (NCTM, 1989, p. 5). The mathematics curriculum must afford all students opportunities to acquire tools for data analysis and problem solving that are applicable to many disciplines (NCTM, 1989). Above all, teachers must design lessons that "include deliberate attempts, through specific instructional activities, to connect ideas and procedures both among different mathematical topics and with other content areas" (NCTM, 1989, p. 11).

A Constructivist Pedagogy

Third, this pedagogical vision insists that learning is constructed by the student, not delivered by the teacher. The term *cover* drops from the professional lexicon. Teachers no longer *go over the material* or *get information to students*. Instead, they target depth of understanding, refinement of skills, and application of knowledge (Goodlad, 1990b; Griffin, 1986). Teachers help young people make meaning from classroom (as well as out-of-school) experiences. What children learn depends on a range of internal and external variables both within and outside the teacher's sphere of influence. As a result, the teacher cannot control the learning process, but she or he can prompt, facilitate, guide, energize, enrich, and assess its progress. Even more crucial than encouraging new understandings, the teacher must allow students to employ these learnings as they reflect, make decisions, and solve problems. Because such activities consume more time than expository instruction, the number of curricular topics shrinks so students can do more things with less content.

Mathematics reformers, for example, aim to restore the "belief that learning mathematics is a sense-making experience" (NCTM, 1989, p. 15). Young people must pursue mathematical literacy along a path that involves, yet ultimately transcends, arithmetic operations and geometric theorems (NCTM, 1989). Reformers advocate a conceptually oriented curriculum that enables children to acquire mathematical literacy "by constructing meaning in the context of physical situations" and allows "mathematical abstractions to emerge from empirical experience" (NCTM, 1989, p. 17). They insist that the mathematics classroom become a society populated by "active individuals who construct, modify, and integrate ideas" (NCTM, 1989, p. 17). Yet, reformers acknowledge that solving (and formulating) intriguing, open-ended problems often involves cooperative work and can absorb hours, days, and even weeks of class time. Emphasizing mathematical concepts and relationships requires pruning and focusing the curriculum so teachers can increase the time spent developing particular understandings.

Science educators also base curricular revisions on a "less-is-more" philosophy that assumes that teachers need more time to teach key ideas and skills more thoroughly and intensively (Project 2061, 1993). They have attempted to formulate a core curriculum of essential ideas for scientific literacy, emphasizing "ideas and thinking skills . . . at the expense of specialized

vocabulary and memorized procedures" (Project 2061, 1989, p. 4). In this approach, children consider less material, but understand it better, gaining a greater grasp of how science works in the process. They reference these complex learnings as they address current social issues (Project 2061, 1993). In the visionary science classroom, young people explore questions rather than acquire predetermined answers; they interact and argue rather than sit and recite; they *do* rather than read and listen (Project 2061, 1989).

Social educators also embrace constructivist pedagogy, offering a version that reflects a citizenship tone. Classroom experiences should engage young people in social inquiry, enabling them to construct *knowledge,* practice *skills,* and commit to the civic *values* that characterize a democratic society (NCSS, 1994). As they build civic competence, children search for information and manipulate data; they develop and present arguments and stories; they participate in groups and make social choices (NCSS, 1993). Social studies classrooms are *places of learning* that "foster aesthetics, civility, ethics, openness, conversation, security, stewardship, craftsmanship, and individual liberty" (NCSS, 1994, p. 13). Because citizenship lessons involve "sustained examination of a few important topics rather than superficial coverage of many," the social studies curriculum incorporates selected, important ideas that can be taught for "understanding, appreciation, and life application" (NCSS, 1994, p. 15).

An Active, Engaging Pedagogy

Fourth, the strong professionals in our vision believe that learning is an active, engaging process, and they teach accordingly. They promote dialog among all participants in the classroom community, acting on the premise that young people should interact and transact social business as they construct new learnings (Moll, 1990). They encourage student conversations, movement around the classroom, and manipulation of varied resources. Strong teachers enable children to gather and use information as they solve problems that seem purposeful and authentic. They recognize that active, experiential learning is vitally important for *all* students regardless of cultural background or academic ability (Bennett, 1990). Their teaching arises from meaningful social contexts, emphasizes the functions of learning, and acknowledges children's needs and interests (Au, 1993).

Emerging standards for science education assert that effective teaching derives from research-tested learning principles, classroom-tested craft experience, and respect for the spirit of scientific inquiry (Project 2061, 1989). Thus, lessons should open with questions about phenomena rather than answers to be committed to memory. As learning experiences continue, young people form hypotheses, collect data, and analyze their findings. They design investigations and processes, raising levels of curiosity and creativity in the process (Project 2061, 1989). Young scientists, not their teacher, determine the question for investigation and develop a research design. With teacher guidance, they select appropriate apparatus and identify data-collection procedures, presenting their findings for review by other investigators. If they cannot justify results, students recast their experiments and try again (Project 2061, 1993). Simply put, children *do* science, conducting investigations and explaining their findings (Project 2061, 1993).

Social studies teaching becomes *powerful* when learning is active and activist (NCSS, 1993). As lessons unfold, teachers and learners think reflectively and make informed decisions. Important social understandings result from a "process of active construction of knowledge" that features interactive discourse among all learners (NCSS, 1994, p. 16). Teachers gradually, but intentionally, move from direct instructional strategies (e.g., modeling, explaining, supplying information) to less directive approaches that force students to become independent and self-regulated learners (NCSS, 1993). Powerful social studies teaching involves authentic activities that "call for real-life application using the skills and content of the field" (NCSS, 1994, p. 16). Teachers help students "construct an accurate and positive view of citizenship and become citizens able to address persisting issues, promote civic ideals and practices, and improve our democratic republic" (NCSS, 1994, p. 18).

Ideally, mathematics teaching reflects the principle: "*Knowing* mathematics is *doing* mathematics" (NCTM, 1989, p. 6). Teachers should create an environment that encourages children to explore, develop, test, discuss, and apply ideas so they can construct mathematical understandings (NCTM, 1989). Young people should define, set up, approach, and solve problems using a repertoire of techniques. They should uncover the underlying mathematical features of a topic, issue, or situation. To facilitate such active learning, classrooms (particularly those in the primary grades) should be "equipped with a wide variety of physical materials and supplies" (NCTM, 1989, p. 17). Because mathematics learning is a collaborative as well as an active process, students should interact not only with varied teaching materials and the physical world but also with classmates and community people (NCTM, 1989).

Clearly, recent efforts have produced a visionary pedagogy that might redefine and revitalize teaching in the fields and disciplines. Four characteristics distinguish this pedagogy from more traditional approaches to instruction. Visionary classroom practice is: noble and purposeful, integrative and holistic, constructivist and meaningful, and active and engaging. Only strong professional teachers can shape and articulate this vision, make it operational in the classroom, and negotiate its implications with the audiences concerned. Such a vision can guide strong professionals as they plan learning experiences, teach them with young people, assess their effects, and inquire about their relative truth, goodness, and virtue.

Designing Visionary Methods Courses

Formulating a visionary methods block might seem a straightforward and fairly simple task. After all, the disciplines have spoken, explicating a pedagogical vision that seems informed, thorough and promising. University curriculum committees need only categorize and compartmentalize the pedagogical content revealed in the various manifestos for classroom reform. The resulting package of knowledge, skills, and dispositions can be dispensed in three-credit pieces over four to six semesters. After a quick overview of salient learning theories and all-purpose strategies, preservice teachers can dig into math, social studies, science, language arts, and reading methods as appro-

priate, armed with handbooks supplied by the professional associations. Methods professors can tell preservice students what they need to do and assign them in-class and practicum tasks in which they can practice doing it.

Although this course of action seems temptingly straightforward, it also seems hopelessly misguided, an approach to methods *training* for the past, not the future. If we believe that the vision for strong professionalism has merit, we understand that we must do far more than inform preservice students about what they need to do in the classroom. Simply put, the methods courses themselves must become noble and purposeful, integrative and holistic, constructivist and meaningful, and active and engaging. Their content must reflect a pedagogical vision, but it is more imperative that the ways in which we structure, sequence, and teach methods exemplify the artistry of teaching. To become strong professionals, methods students must encounter many examples of quality teaching as it is judged by individuals with different views of quality, construct a pedagogical platform from these experiences, operate this platform in diverse contexts, and illustrate its worth in school settings.

Although we insist that the time for transforming methods courses has arrived, we cannot provide blueprints specifying a form they should take. The nature of a teacher education program depends on situations and circumstances at a particular institution and in surrounding school districts. Prescribing program and course content, moreover, clashes with the notion of strong professionalism that we advance. The nature of methods coursework must be articulated, operationalized, and negotiated by program participants. We cannot dictate, but we will share four guiding principles that teacher educators might reference as they design and implement a methods block for the future. These principles underly strong, visionary teaching and can shape methods experiences that encourage preservice students to lead a strong professional life.

Noble and Purposeful Instruction Clearly, teachers who articulate a visionary pedagogy, practice it in their classrooms, and negotiate its continued vitality stand for something greater than professional (or personal) survival. Their teaching, after all, reflects a moral tone. They expect to transform and inspire young people, nurturing social decision makers who can exert positive influences on our nation's welfare (Fenstermacher, 1990). Strong teachers care about their students and aspire to an ideal of public service. Methods instructors can do no less if they wish to contribute meaningfully to the professional development of preservice teachers.

Strong methods professors, like their classroom counterparts, must take a stand and *profess* what teaching should be. Mastery of the subject matter is not a sufficient credential for assuming the role of teacher educator. Strong professors "live" in schools, know classroom life, and appreciate the needs, wants, and abilities of today's children. Given the diversity and complexity that characterize so many of our nation's schools, they must themselves gain the practical experience and theoretical knowledge to determine methodologies and materials that seem good, just, and true. They can articulate, demonstrate, and negotiate these choices in their college classrooms.

In our vision, perhaps in any vision, of what a strong methods professor would be like, we expect demonstrations of concern for the personal and professional welfare of their preservice charges. As silly as it sounds, they are expected to recognize students by name and ask how classes are going. They are available for conversations about teaching and informal discussion of issues facing educators today. Strong methods professors conduct their classes at a leisurely pace and in a relaxed, informal atmosphere. They digress from the daily schedule whenever appropriate. Yet, their courses are purposeful and focused. Broad goals are clearly communicated to students and assignments are well understood. Class sessions feature a dialog that is continual and inclusive. Strong professors prompt, guide, enrich, but often simply observe student conversation. Participants in a methods course relate as colleagues. Members of the instructional team (e.g., professors, graduate students, and classroom teachers) interact spontaneously and without regard for titles or formalities. They demonstrate their mutual respect by listening carefully to each other, sharing the classroom stage and planning, teaching, assessing, and inquiring collaboratively. They afford their students similar courtesy and expect that it will be returned. Teaching of this type is rarely found anywhere in the large contemporary university, and this is a shame. But such teaching is needed even more in programs of teacher preparation than elsewhere in the university because what is modeled is as important as what is transmitted. And novice teachers need models of respectful instruction.

The methods block should be organized to encourage such a collegial tone. Class sizes are small by past standards, never exceeding 25 students. Preservice teachers experience the methods block in cohort groups that persist throughout their teacher education program. If possible, a group receives all methods instruction from the same faculty team. As students are assigned to particular groups, selection is more systematic than random, influenced by such variables as location, compatibility, and student interests.

In a collegial learning environment, the lines between researcher and practitioner are blurred, never drawn. Traditionally, when teachers and professors work together, university people assume responsibility for theoretical issues and concerns, calling on school personnel periodically for infusions of "real life." Even the teacher-as-researcher is usually asked to keep a tight focus on the mundane, reducing issues of classroom practice to the routine and trivial in the process (Goodson, 1994). Yet, true colleagues address pedagogical concerns from both theoretical and practical perspectives, regardless of rank or pedigree. Preservice students can only benefit from interacting with practitioners about the ideal world of research and with theorists about the real world of the classroom.

Finally, the noble and purposeful methods block must have a central and powerful political dimension. Preservice students cannot construct a vision of good teaching in professional isolation. As prerequisites for the methods block, they should complete coursework that helps them appreciate diversity issues and study a foreign language. As part of their methods preparation, they must venture far beyond university halls and walls to determine what constitutes pedagogical virtue, immersing themselves in community life on a regular basis. They should wander through a street fair, take tickets at a school carnival, and attend school board meetings. In small groups (and with methods instructors, if possible), they should visit school neigh-

borhoods after school hours. Students only develop a commitment to educational service outside a college classroom. Methods courses should be housed in school communities where opportunities to contribute to the public good are rich and prevalent. Methods instructors should require service work in the neighborhood as well as practicum work in the school. At the same time, methods students must assume responsibility for initiating and finalizing service commitments.

Integrative and Holistic Instruction Typically, preservice students are exposed to pedagogical methods and materials in random and piecemeal fashion. Some attention is given to function as pedagogical tools are introduced and reviewed (e.g., instruments for assessment, techniques for management, models for planning). Still, teaching strategies and resources are typically categorized and examined by subject area or discipline. Students examine the ways to teach reading, mathematics, or music, a process that ensures that pedagogical content remains incoherent and repetitive.

Examining teaching practice discipline by discipline renders the construction of a pedagogical platform an almost impossible undertaking. We must remember a fundamental assumption of the vision of teaching reviewed previously: All complex forms of learning (including learning to teach) best occur across disciplinary boundaries rather than confined within them. Only by perceiving relationships among knowledge, dispositions, and processes can any learner achieve real understanding (Griffin, 1988). More to the point, grouping instructional methods by subject area badly misdirects the emphasis, distracting methods students from what deserves their undivided attention. They are forced to view teaching in terms of disciplinary products rather than the learning process. Crucially important variables (e.g., knowledge/power relationships; children's needs/abilities) are sublimated when pedagogical choices are made primarily in a disciplinary context.

Although epistemological concerns certainly influence teaching practice, disciplinary restrictions on the utility of particular teaching strategies often seem more contrived than real. Examining how to teach certain elements of historical knowledge, for example, has far less significance than exploring the varied uses and effects of simulation or literature-based instruction across history, geography, mathematics, science, and the arts. Even more vital, methods students should investigate the ways in which knowledge, skills, and dispositions from one field might enrich students' understanding of another (e.g., examining a historical period from an aesthetic perspective; applying mathematical processes to study demographic trends; investigating the geopolitical effects of selected scientific or technological breakthroughs).

Methods instruction should feature the planning, teaching, assessing, and inquiring that constitute teaching, not the subject areas that comprise the school curriculum. Disciplinary concerns should influence the ways we teach, not dictate our instructional choices. Preservice students should learn to conceptualize teaching in terms of student learning and classroom contexts. They should search for ways to help children construct patterns of understanding that transcend subject areas. They should discover methodologies that help children generalize from data and perceive the relationships among ideas. They should connect related instructional approaches, not separate them by discipline or field.

The methods block needs restructuring before preservice students can experience teaching in a holistic, integrative manner. As a first step, courses like Teaching Elementary School Mathematics should be replaced with such offerings as Designing Thematic Units or Teaching in Urban Settings or Engaging All Learners in Reflective Inquiry. We should abandon the all-purpose, three-credit course with more specialized and flexible offerings that target particular topics or themes (e.g., a series of one-credit modules examining techniques for gathering information about young learners; a five-credit offering that treats the rationale, function, and implications of indirect instructional models).

In addition, we should block coursework, creating extended sessions in which students can examine teaching methods and materials in depth. If courses met daily in schools (or at least near them) for 4 to 5 hours at a time, methods instructors could integrate coursework with practicum experiences. For example, preservice students could consider classroom management, venture into classrooms to try selected strategies, and then discuss their findings with expert teachers from the instructional team. Or, during a course on assessing student learning, they might exit a class session, help develop and administer a test in a middle-level classroom, then return and enrich discussion of measurement techniques with their experiences. In such methods courses, theory and practice might actually merge, enabling students to experience and exercise the full effect of the articulative, operational, and political dimensions of strong professionalism.

Constructivist and Meaningful Instruction As we have seen, visionary teachers support the learning process, encouraging young people to make meaning from classroom experiences. They teach for depth of understanding, refinement of skills, and application of knowledge (Goodlad, 1990b; Griffin, 1986). Strong methods instructors should follow these leaders, affording their students many opportunities to make pedagogical decisions and solve learning problems. And, they should allow ample time for reflection and critical analysis after instructional choices are made. Strong professionalism can only emerge after preservice students articulate, operate, and negotiate meaning from many opportunities to plan, teach, assess, and inquire.

As a first step toward methods experiences that are constructivist and meaningful, participants need to ask the right questions and dialog about possible responses. Typically, methods students have focused considerable energy on formulating individual responses to some pretty basic pedagogical questions. What strategy works most effectively? How should it be implemented? When should the test be given? Where should potential troublemakers be seated? Such queries delimit class discussion and force preservice teachers to accept a scientific management view of teaching. If methods students are to articulate a pedagogical vision, they must ask and be asked much deeper and better questions. What are you trying to accomplish with this group of learners? What characterizes the ways in which these students learn? Which strategy will work best with them? Would that strategy work better with a different group of learners? Why or why not? What might be the strategy's benefits and

shortcomings? Who might benefit the most and least? Does the room arrangement enhance or limit the strategy's effects? Why? When would you know if the strategy is working? How would you tell?

As a second step, methods courses should become more democratic in the ways in which power is assumed, held, and exercised. Power now rests solely with the methods professor. She or he has sole authority and responsibility for long- and short-term planning, teaching daily activities, arranging practica, assessing student progress, and directing inquiry about the learning process. Shifting course responsibility from a single professor to an instructional team of professors, graduate students, and teachers will necessitate a considerable transfer of power. But, methods course governance, like school governance, should become even more inclusive. Preservice students should design assignments as well as complete them. They should self-direct learning experiences and self-assess their progress. They must negotiate course business with members of the instructional team. Preservice teachers will never articulate, operate, assess, and inquire without learning how to take responsibility for their own professional growth.

As methods coursework proceeds, preservice students should negotiate procedural matters and instructional issues with an expanding cast of educational players. Simply put, they must explore the uses and abuses of power in political arenas beyond their methods block. Their attendance at regular meetings of school staff, school administrators, and the school board should be mandatory. They should dialog with parents and parent groups. As they work with teachers, they should be encouraged to probe beyond the surface of classroom procedures and routines. Of course, they should ask: What is happening here? They also might raise the questions: Why is it happening *that* way? Is there a better way to do that? Teachers involved as teacher educators cannot have "thin skins." They need to realize that methods students must occasionally rock the boat, not just sit in it, if they are to strengthen their grip on the tools for strong professional practice.

In any learning experience, students make meaning from varied texts. In a constructivist and meaningful methods block, preservice students require at least three types of text: attempts to explicate educational theory; case studies of various sorts; and the emerging narrative of classroom life. Since they serve complementary roles in nurturing professional growth, all three should inform learning activities throughout the methods block.

As students articulate their teaching platforms, they should confront texts that communicate educational theories and ideologies and contrast these viewpoints through personal deliberation and interpersonal conversation. Students will also require case studies and repeated exposure to living, breathing classrooms to ground these ideas. As they construct the operational talents to realize their visions, students clearly must reference case studies and reside in multiple school settings, exploring and testing instructional approaches that seem compatible with their emerging platforms. They will also need to revisit familiar theorists and encounter new thinkers to check the fit between the operational and the articulative. As they enter the political world of negotiation, confrontation, and compromise, methods students must investigate a rich case study literature so that the rough-and-tumble of political life neither shocks nor surprises them. They must also draw on multiple practicum experiences to construct the knowledge, finesse, and dispositions to accommodate and preserve their platform in a possibly hostile political environment. Before departing the methods block, they must continue to consult theoretical texts to make sense of (and perhaps gain reassurance about) what they have encountered and accomplished.

Much of the reason why these three types of text complement one another so well and contribute so powerfully to the development of strong professionalism is their common reliance on story. In the best examples of the narrative form, information unfolds in a natural progression that preservice students can follow with relative ease. Numerous examples support important ideas, rendering them familiar and understandable. As Egan (1986) has indicated, telling a story affords the learner clearer access to material and greater engagement with it. Using story as text for methods coursework allows preservice students to establish both cognitive and affective meaning, affording broader and deeper understanding of the teaching act (Egan, 1986). More traditional, expository methods texts emphasize the informational at the expense of the emotional, limiting students' abilities to assume a strong professional stance.

Stories, moreover, "call" to preservice professionals (Coles, 1989). Stories are "renderings of life" that not only comfort prospective teachers or lawyers or doctors, "but admonish us, point us in new directions, or give us the courage to stay a given course" (Coles, 1989, p. 159). As preservice students articulate a vision, make it operational, and represent it to a political world, stories introduce them to "spiritual companions," characters "however 'imaginary' in nature who give us pause and help us in the private moments when we try to find our bearings" (Coles, 1989, p. 160). More crucial, stories beget stories. Hearing "the call of stories" (Coles, 1989) often inspires us to call back, to tell our own stories in return. When methods students listen to stories, their learning is stimulated in powerful ways. When they have opportunities to tell stories back, whether in journals or lesson summaries or position papers, their learning grows significantly.

Constructivist and meaningful teaching, although productive and powerful, consumes more time and effort than more expository approaches to methods instruction. Arrangements must be made and materials assembled. Activities that encourage dialog and reflection literally eat up the clock. Like science, mathematics, and social studies visionaries that we encountered earlier, methods instructors must do more with less content. Preservice students need more than a passing acquaintance with Vygotsky, Piaget, Bruner, and the cognitive psychologists. They must examine a theory or strategy, investigate its ramifications, then test its validity with different children in multiple contexts. This is how the articulate dimension of professionalism develops. With opportunities for such intensive inquiry, fewer topics does indeed generate more meaningful learning.

Active and Engaging Instruction If methods instruction is noble and purposeful, integrative and holistic, and constructivist and meaningful, it must inevitably become active and engaging as well. Methods instructors who intend to develop strong professional teachers must enable them to make decisions that

seem purposeful and authentic in settings that seem realistic and replicable. Preservice students must experience teaching that arises from meaningful social contexts, emphasizes the functions of learning, and acknowledges the learner's needs and interests (Au, 1993).

In our judgment, the greater the distance between a teacher education program and real schools inhabited by real teachers and children, the lesser the likelihood that active and engaging methods instruction will occur. We strongly advocate methods coursework that abandons past dichotomies between practice and theory. To achieve this merger, we would end distinctions between college-bound courses and field-based practicum work. In essence, the methods block becomes an extended internship, with the ratio of practice teaching to coursework increasing steadily. Presently, preservice students are university based, dropping into placement situations with increasing frequency as their teacher education programs progress. Their professional preparation often is only field-based during the culminating, student-teaching semester. In the future, methods coursework would be site-based from the outset, with students dropping into scheduled class sessions with decreasing frequency. These meetings should be held at the school in which a cohort group is interning.

Admittedly, some institutions might find it impossible to conduct the major portion of a teacher education program in the field. Even with teaching teams composed largely of graduate students and classroom teachers, an entirely field-based methods block might not prove "cost-effective." In that case, we insist that methods coursework involve as much practicum work as possible and that practica be closely integrated with other program elements (e.g., teacher-mentors chosen for their understanding of and resonance with program philosophy or course requirements developed with mentors' input).

Wherever a methods block is located, we would insist that the university-based elements of the methods block incorporate laboratory settings as much as possible. Various pedagogical technologies (e.g., complex instruction, cooperative learning) as well as existing hard technology (e.g., computers, interactive video) afford methods instructors considerable power to engage and empower their preservice learners. "Early returns" indicate that both pedagogical and hard technology transform traditional instructor and student roles to a considerable degree. At the very least, these approaches make it much more difficult for the methods professor to stand near the chalkboard and talk while about 40 preservice teachers sit and listen.

Finally, the political dimension of strong professionalism requires that methods coursework be not only active but also activist. To be sure, students must interact, think critically, solve problems, simulate, learn cooperatively, and participate in sophisticated pedagogical technologies. At the same time, their actions must hold real and readily apparent benefits for young as well as older learners. They must not only take action but also provide service to an educational constituency in need. Their pedagogical exercises, in short, must accomplish more than satisfying methods course requirements. Preservice students must plan, teach, and assess lessons that contribute meaningfully to children's learning. They must not only attend but also help conduct parent conferences. They should design and implement school functions that reach into the surrounding community (e.g., a multicultural fair, a book festival). A strong professional educator would strive for nothing less.

Summary

Changing methods coursework as dramatically as we have proposed seems a daunting task. Many logistical and attitudinal barriers stand in the way of such a transformation. For some, we may resemble Don Quixote on his quest for virtue. Like the good Don, we feel pure and true and good. And just like him, we may have trouble being taken seriously.

Dismissing our designs for the methods courses of the future may seem the sensible response to a costly, impractical vision that will prove difficult to implement. Such negativism is certainly an anticipated reaction, for methods coursework has resisted substantive change for many years. In defense of our proposals for the future, we turn attention back to schools and teacher preparation programs in the present. We remember Virginia and Greg, struggling to realize educational dreams without collegial support and sufficient professional preparation. We recall their ambitions and frustrations, their hopes and disappointments, their desires to do good things for children, and their suspicions that they will somehow fail. Most vividly, we cannot forget their sense that their teacher education programs trained them to be weak technicians, not strong professionals.

Realizing our visions for methods coursework may be a daunting task, but it is a worthy one. Our schools need educators who believe that teaching should be noble and purposeful, integrative and holistic, constructivist and meaningful, and active and engaging. Our classrooms need educators who have experienced such a vision during teacher education. Our teachers need colleagues who have learned to articulate an educational platform, can take action to make this ideal a classroom reality, and, by example, can inspire others to do the same. The nation is in need of strong professional teachers, for our children deserve nothing less.

UNDERSTANDING THE GENERAL PEDAGOGICAL KNOWLEDGE BASE

A strong professional must be able to articulate and operationalize the knowledge base that exists for teaching. But of course, what constitutes the appropriate knowledge base cannot be decided without controversy. Here we will talk about just one of the many legitimate sources of knowledge about teaching and learning, the knowledge that is arrived at from traditional "scientific" methods, now in some need of defense in the postmodern world, an era marked by much antiscientific rhetoric in education. We make no claim here that this is the only kind of knowledge that is needed in a program of teacher education; in fact, we would claim just the opposite. As we noted in the preceding section on teaching methods, we think that an exemplary teacher education program must ensure that its participants reflect on experience and understand educational contexts. But we also believe that the scientific knowledge generated in sociology, educational psychology, anthropology,

economics, and research on teaching, to name a few of the scientific areas contributing to the knowledge base, provide a rich, legitimate, and potentially useful source of knowledge for prospective teachers. How will the school of education of the future teach that knowledge base?

Honesty, Integrity, Thoroughness, Ethics, and Contemporaneity in Teacher Education

First we are compelled to note that an *honest* program of teacher education must find the time to present different perspectives on what constitutes knowledge for a prospective teacher. Honesty demands exposure to ideas that are counter to one's own. In this case honesty demands inclusion of the more radical critical analyses of schools and a critique of the "technical" or "scientific" approach to teaching. The knowledge base that is chosen to be of value in a program of teacher education should be learned by preservice teachers because it is perceived to be a valuable guide for practice. It should not be learned merely because it is prescribed by the directors of the program of teacher education. The critics and the promoters of scientifically derived knowledge about education must each be read and discussed so that the teacher education program has a chance at developing strong professional teachers and teacher educators, each of whom can articulate an educational platform that allows him or her to incorporate or reject the knowledge base that is offered.

A program of teacher education with *integrity* must also find a way to teach the knowledge derived from this research tradition in a way that is compatible with mindfulness, not foster simple technical use of that research. The simple transmission of the knowledge base to prospective teachers cannot be our goal if we value the image of a strong professional. More concern about the means of instruction in teacher education programs is needed. We argue, for example, that a preservice or in-service teacher who simply learns how to use cooperative learning techniques because there is replicable scientific evidence that it has worked well in certain situations is acting in a mindless way. Research about the effects of cooperative learning is certainly compelling, but to use it appropriately requires at the least: understanding of the traditional power and authority relations in classrooms and the changes in the role of the teacher that occur when cooperative learning is instituted; a genuine belief in the competency of youngsters to direct more of their own learning; a move away from rewarding individualistic and competitive efforts and a move toward rewarding group efforts in some way that is equitable for all the members of the group; having as much concern for the democratic processes by means of which a group functions as for the content of what is being learned; and so forth. To prevent mindless implementation by faithful and committed converts, one must provide teacher education students access to information about many aspects of innovation in teaching. In the case of cooperative learning, this means studying reports of the negative aspects of cooperative learning, the resistance by many parents to teaching by means of these methods, and the fact that cooperative learning does not work in some settings or among some groups of students (McCaslin and Good, 1996).

Thorough programs of teacher education will find ways to teach the limits as well as the substance of our knowledge. Knowledge derived from the social sciences cannot be taught as if it is stable or as if it can generalize across contexts. Social facts change by decades, a problem that physicists, chemists, and others from the natural science rarely face. The speed of sound in a vacuum does not change as the decades go by, but we may have perfectly replicable social scientific findings that no longer hold true because the times we live in have changed. For example, all the scientific data on female motivational patterns and school achievement collected before, say, 1960, is no longer applicable. The changed view of women in our society, as a function of the feminist revolution, has simply made obsolete a number of "facts" that the research community once thought it had nailed down. Furthermore, what we purport to call knowledge rarely can be employed without thinking about context and side effects.

Few social science findings hold up over all educational contexts. A program that works in an Eastern urban area may not work in a rural Western setting, and vice versa. So prospective teachers need to be taught tentativeness about the application of scientific educational research at their school site, and they need to check what is predicted to happen against what is actually experienced during implementation. The choice of one pedagogical technique always has implications that are not obvious, and these must be made manifest. A teacher misunderstands educational research if she or he believes that the decision to use a mastery learning model of instruction, a particular homework policy, a cooperative learning strategy, or a particular testing format can be based on the research evidence alone. It is quite rare that a technical solution can be found to the common problems of education without generating still other problems. So a *thorough* program of teacher education designed to develop strong articulate professionals must ensure that the research base be thought about in light of personal and community values and goals, the possible side effects and cost-effectiveness, and the merit and worth of particular actions.

An *ethical* program of teacher education makes it clear that what we call knowledge is rarely, if ever, really neutral. The questions of "Who's knowledge is it?," "How was it obtained?," and "Toward what ends will it be used?" are legitimate questions to ask throughout a program of teacher education. The development of a political sense among teachers requires an understanding of these issues.

A *contemporary* program of teacher education must go beyond the guidelines that the National Council for Acreditation of Teacher Education (1987) suggests when it requires that a teacher education program have a formal knowledge base to teach (Galluzzo & Pankratz, 1990). Perhaps possessing a knowledge base is enough for an auto mechanic, but in our eyes it is not enough for a teacher. The design of an exemplary program of teacher education would take the articulative, operational, and political dimensions of a teaching platform more seriously and ensure that its graduates not only know the extant scientific knowledge base but also why that knowledge can be useful to teachers and why critics argue that this is not so. The graduates should also know that such knowledge is limited by time and by context, that it has unintended side effects, and that it is political both in terms of its creation and its use. From

the funding of the original study to its implementation in the classroom, there is nothing neutral about pedagogical knowledge, and the teacher education programs of the future must develop that understanding among faculty as well as its students.

To teach the knowledge base and *not* teach these other factors is to ensure the development of weak professionals. We expect that the educational platform adopted by a teacher will be heavily influenced by research; however, it will provide no advantage to the profession if research is communicated as formulae to follow instead of ideas to think seriously about. For too long those that have taught the knowledge base in methods and foundations courses have abrogated their responsibility to teach prospective teachers to think mindfully about that research. Such an approach is demeaning of the kind of professional teacher we imagine and whose image we use to guide the development of the teacher education program of the future.

What Knowledge Shall We Emphasize?

Just like any other scientific field, educational researchers have discovered some simple *findings,* invented some complex instructional *technology,* described some generative *concepts,* and developed some full-blown *theories* that are useful for understanding and improving education.

To ignore these theories, concepts, technologies, and findings, as is sometimes the case, is churlish. To make too much out of them, however, would be ill-conceived. We believe that it is perfectly appropriate to take those theories, concepts, technologies, and findings quite seriously in a teacher education program, to have their effects on practice openly examined or to inform the debate about practice. A beginning teacher must be guided to understand that a lot of expensive data have been collected. Whether in the form of findings, technology, concepts, or theories, such hard-won information from hardworking, committed, researchers should be treated quite seriously in developing an educational platform. Let us look then at the theories, concepts, technology, and findings that can inform a beginning teacher and explore how to promote these ideas in a serious but not authoritative way.

Theories to Think With By *theory* we mean something like the formal and mathematically specifiable model of school learning first proposed by John Carroll (1963). The broad characteristics of this model have been verified in a few hundred empirical studies (Carroll, 1985) and by common sense as well. Other less well-specified, but no less well-developed, theories exist, for example, the contemporary constructivist model of learning. This is a model of learning *and* motivation that has direct implications for curriculum, instruction, and assessment. We have also Vygotskian perspectives on the social nature of knowledge, with their many implications for schooling. And we have mature and well-validated theories about achievement and attributions about achievement that are associated with competitive versus personal goal structures in classroom learning. In fact, the entire field of motivation is influenced by and has verified the importance of the Expectancy × Value theory of motivation first proposed decades ago (Feather, 1982). The teacher education program of the future that does not communi-cate these theories would be as negligent as the medical school that failed to teach homeostasis or the relationship between nutrition and health.

We understand that targeted and useful theories to guide instruction are hard to come by. But the Division of Educational Psychology of the American Psychological Association has made one such attempt (with the Presidential Task Force on Psychology in Education and the American Psychological Asso-ciation, 1993). Its synthesis of contemporary learning theory, motivation, and individual differences can be used as a heuristic for developing both a platform with which to educate students in the public schools and to design a program of teacher educa-tion. What follows is a synthesis of contemporary theory:

1. *On the nature of the learning process.* Learning is a natural process of pursuing personally meaningful goals; it is active, volitional, and intentionally mediated; it is a process of discovering and constructing meaning from information and experience, filtered through the learner's own percep-tions, thoughts, and feelings.
2. *On the goals of the learning process.* The learner seeks to create meaningful, coherent representations of knowledge regardless of the quantity and quality of data available.
3. *On the construction of knowledge.* The learner links new information with existing and future-oriented knowledge in uniquely meaningful ways.
4. *On developing higher order thinking.* Higher order strate-gies for "thinking about thinking" for overseeing and moni-toring mental operations facilitate creative and critical think-ing and the development of expertise.
5. *On motivational influences on learning.* The depth and breadth of information processed and what and how much is learned and remembered are influenced by: (1) self-awareness and belief about personal control, competence, and ability, (2) clarity and saliency of personal values, inter-ests, and goals, (3) personal expectations for success or failure, and (4) the resulting motivation to learn.
6. *On intrinsic motivation to learn.* Individuals are naturally curious and enjoy learning, but intense negative cognitions and emotions (e.g., feeling insecure, worrying about failure, being self-conscious or shy, and fearing corporal punish-ment, ridicule, or stigmatizing labels) thwart this enthu-siasm.
7. *On the characteristics of motivation-enhancing tasks.* Curi-osity, creativity, and higher order thinking are stimulated by relevant, authentic learning tasks of optimal difficulty and novelty for each student.
8. *On the constraints and opportunities offered by develop-ment.* Individuals progress through stages of physical, intel-lectual, emotional, and social development that are a func-tion of unique genetic and environmental factors.
9. *On social and cultural diversity.* Learning is facilitated by social interactions and communication with others in flexi-ble, diverse (in age, culture, family background, etc.), and adaptive instructional settings.
10. *On social acceptance, self-esteem, and learning.* Learning and self-esteem are heightened when individuals are in respectful and caring relationships with others who see

their potential, genuinely appreciate their unique talents, and accept them as individuals.
11. *On individual differences in learning.* Although basic prin-ciples of learning, motivation, and effective instruction apply to all learners (regardless of ethnicity, race, gender, physical ability, religion, or socioeconomic status), learners have different capabilities and preferences for learning mode and strategies. These differences are a function of the environment (what is learned and communicated in different cultures or other social groups) and heredity (what occurs naturally as a function of genetic influences).
12. *On individual constructions of reality.* Personal beliefs, thoughts, and understandings resulting from prior learning and interpretations become the individual's basis for con-structing reality and interpreting life experiences.

These contemporary principles of psychology are vastly dif-ferent from those that used to guide education and teacher education. Programs of teacher education that do not acknowl-edge these changes are old-fashioned, if not wrong-headed and harmful! Teacher education programs of the future will adopt (no doubt) modified versions of these heuristics for teach-ing and learning and be judged deficient if their programs and the products of their programs have violated the spirit and the substance of these principles about human learning.

Concepts to Classify With By *concepts* we mean the terms and ideas that help us label and identify aspects of classrooms and schools in order to make them more understandable. These concepts are developed from both analytic and empirical work. They are used to describe phenomena that might not be at-tended to as readily if we could not name and describe them. For example, educational research has given us such rich and useful concepts as curriculum alignment, academic learning time, withitness, grade surety, buggy algorithm, multiple intelli-gences, zone of proximal development, accommodation and assimilation, authentic assessment, transparent assessment, dis-tributed intelligence, situated cognition, and so forth. The list of potentially useful concepts has grown enormously, while the time to teach what we know in teacher preparation pro-grams has been cut dramatically. But the teacher education curriculum of the future will have to find the time to teach such concepts in a respectful manner or admit they are denying teacher education students important pedagogical information on which to build their platform.

A strong professional needs experiences that teach that the language of education is "loaded." Because the concepts we use to describe the phenomena we are interested in often have hidden meanings, (e.g., "learning disabled," "economically de-prived," "culturally different") and we socially construct our world through the concepts that we have, classrooms are not nearly as objectively described as are steel ingots. It is therefore important that the major concepts of the various subfields that make up education be fully explored, not merely learned so that their definition is understood, but genuinely analyzed. If it is not clear how important this exercise is in a program of teacher education, think about the concept of "intelligence." Why was it supposed to be a property of an individual and not a group? That is, why is not intelligence shared or distributed among the members of groups? How is it that intelligence would be viewed as something shared by a community under the situative theory of learning (Greeno, Collins, & Resnick, 1996) but would not be viewed that way from a behavioral or cognitive theory of learning? These are issues of great importance that require conceptual analysis, not just concept learning, in programs of teacher preparation.

Pedagogical Technology for Augmenting Instruction By *pedagogical technology* we mean systems of instruction such as cooperative learning (Slavin, 1990), complex instruction (Cohen, 1994), reciprocal teaching (Palincsar & Brown, 1984), the Missouri Mathematics project (Good & Grouws, 1979), the well-verified claims about enhancement of achievement and attitudes toward schooling associated with cross-age and peer tutoring projects (Cohen, Kulik, & Kulik, 1982), or the reading recovery program (Anderson & Armbruster, 1990; Clay, 1985). We are not discussing here the hard technologies of computers or interactive videos and the like that ought to be adjuncts to our teacher education program (see last section). Here we note that there are alternatives to frontal teaching and that these alternatives are pedagogical technologies of considerable power. These are technologies as much as is a new pump and water purification system that is delivered to a tribe in a remote village in the Andes. When such new technology brings water to a village it changes the work and the roles of the adults and children in the village. As the rates of disease and health change, and the life expectancy of members of the village changes, adjustments are needed in the ways that allow for the distribution of scarce food resources and the role expectations for elders in the group.

Each of the large-scale instructional systems that has been mentioned previously requires no less. The roles of teachers and students change in, say, classrooms with a good deal of cooperative learning or where cross-age tutoring takes place. And as the achievement and attitude of the students change as a result of such systems, so does the need for change by other people in the system, for example, counselors, special education personnel, and parents. New technology almost always results in changes, sometimes dramatic ones, in the ways that people behave, whether in a tribe or classroom. The teacher education program of the future will have to find ways to give pre- and in-service teachers opportunities to practice with these new technologies, for merely talking about them is the least efficient way to get them examined seriously by classroom teachers.

Findings to Check Out The individual pieces of replicable data that are not necessarily well embedded in elaborate theory constitute the *findings* of the research community. Every field has these kind of findings. For example, medicine had findings about aspirin over 80 years before they learned some of the mechanisms involved in its use. In our field we have findings associated with wait time, which have been found in over a dozen studies to increase the quality of the instructional conversations in the classroom and to improve academic achievement as well (Tobin, 1987). We also have a coherent set of findings about retention in grade that is not embedded in or greatly influenced by a grand theory (Shepard & Smith, 1989). We have

replicable findings about the use of advance organizers, the provision of academic feedback to students, the use of higher order questions in recitations, the provision of verbal markers of importance in lectures, the use of student summaries at the end of lessons, the distress caused by high-stakes testing, the power of the project method of teaching, and many others (see Gage & Berliner, 1992, and other texts that present contemporary scientific findings). The theoretical ties associated with these findings are not obvious and sometimes seem to be forced, but their empirical status cannot be questioned. Each finding has been replicated in a research study or verified with teacher collaborators. The teacher education program of the future must turn out teachers who: (1) know about and (2) understand the usefulness of these findings. Again, to do less, as is now often the case, is to admit our complicity in denying teacher education students important pedagogical information on which to build their platform.

The question we must struggle with is why the theories, concepts, technology, and findings of educational research are not well taught today, and how we must make them well taught in the education schools of the future. We seem to miss opportunities to communicate our research to teachers in ways that would have them remember more of it. Some thoughts on remediating that situation follow.

How Should We Communicate Our Findings, Technology, Concepts, and Theories?

If a future program of teacher education wishes to take seriously the teaching of scientific knowledge of the type we have described it must: (1) infuse the preservice teacher education program with sensible introductions to the research findings, technologies, concepts and theories that we have; (2) develop respect for research at the preservice level; (3) improve the quality of the in-service education of teachers; and (4) embed the findings of educational research in the life of classrooms. We touch briefly on each of these topics, and as we do so, we use the term *findings* as a generic term, referring to findings, concepts, technology, and theory.

Infusing Preservice Teacher Education with the Scientific Knowledge Base A fundamental rule of professional preparation is to turn out people that will do no harm. That is true for licensure in cosmetology as well as teaching. Do we ensure that the teachers we turn out of preservice programs operationalize their understanding that communication of low expectations to a child is often causally related to decrements in performance? Do we ensure that every teacher we turn out articulates that retention in grade is the wrong decision for the vast majority of the children for whom such decisions are made and who can operationalize that belief and demonstrate the political know-how to resist those forces that want to do otherwise? Do we ensure that every graduate acts in ways that reflect the fact that measured IQ is malleable and subject to change as environments change? How do we ensure that in teacher preparation programs our candidates know, at a level deeper than that revealed by a response to a multiple-choice item, that positive reinforcement is better than punishment? Or that punishment 2 is superior to punishment 1? Or that time-management skills are among the most important skills a teacher can learn? Or that bilingual children are not starting with a deficit but instead have cognitive advantages over monolingual children? How do we ensure that novice teachers learn the simple notion that "grade level" does not mean what a lay person supposes it to mean, because a child who is in second grade and tests at the fourth grade is not expected to do fourth-grade work at all. These are all findings that could lead to harm if not well understood, and so the teacher education program of the future must ensure that its graduates understand these issues and, at the least, do no harm.

But the research community has given us more findings than those. We have numerous findings that provide decided advantages for a teacher who uses them over one who does not. For example, we must ensure that all our graduates of teacher education programs can create advance organizers; can form higher order questions; have practiced invoking the relevant schema at the start of an instructional episode; have experience in cooperative learning activities; have at least 1 week's experience managing a peer or cross-age tutoring program; have created rubrics and have practiced holistic scoring of essay examinations; or have taught a child a cognitive strategy that facilitates learning. These examples are taken primarily from the discipline of educational psychology. But the list of empirically verifiable findings can go on for a long time if we include other social science disciplines.

Too many educational scholars condemn educational research by confusing its inherent usefulness with the patently ineffective delivery system used during preservice education. We run terribly cheap teacher education programs throughout the United States and therefore never get a good test of what might happen were we funded like, say, a military or industrial training program, a medical school, or a school of engineering.

Pedagogical Laboratories for Learning the Usefulness of Educational Research

Imagine the difference in our ability to transmit knowledge if we had a pedagogical laboratory where every candidate had practice in teaching real students and also had competent mentors to critique their performance (Berliner, 1984). In such a setting we would see microteaching over long periods so that novices learn and judge the effectiveness of interactive teaching skills or novices managing, at least for a short time, a real cross-age tutorial program. We would see simulated parent–teacher interviews, where practice would be gained in explaining student performance; constructivist lessons developed, taught, and analyzed; or cognitive strategies being practiced. We would have a library of exemplary tapes to see and analyze the brilliant lessons of expert pedagogues teaching lessons that every teacher will have to teach—the rain cycle, the rotation and revolution of the earth, quadratic equations. Videotaped models of master performances illustrating the metaphors and analogies and other devices to explain and contextualize knowledge would be commonplace and the source materials for hours of analysis. Creative alternative assessment instruments appro-

priate to such lessons would be available to study. As we let our imaginations go we wonder what we could accomplish in pedagogical learning laboratories if we had the same per capita funding of a medical or engineering school or if we spent the same amount on teachers in training as we spent on pilots in training.

It is unfortunate that during the 1970s throughout America state legislatures took away hours and hours of time in teacher preparation programs. Their reasoning was partially correct, namely, that much of what we taught was commonsensical craft knowledge perhaps learned better on the job. But as teacher education coursework was reduced, the research community was creating the largest, most reliable, and usable empirical data base that has ever existed in education. And now we cannot ensure that such knowledge is taught and learned in ways that either help our teachers to do no harm or give them advantages over those that have not been in teacher education programs. Lack of funds (see Sikula's preface to this handbook) and of time conspire to make us miss an opportunity to teach our research findings.

If this situation were to change we would need to redesign preservice coursework and infuse it with funds to provide high-quality laboratory experiences at the preservice level. The invention of the laboratory as a teaching setting in the 1820s in chemistry spread rapidly to the other sciences, notably biology and physics. The rationale for this much more expensive form of instruction was that the knowledge learned in books was no longer enough to become a competent physicist, chemist, or biologist. What was needed in addition to book knowledge, said the scientists, was experimentation in a laboratory setting where supervision and safety allow the findings, concepts, technologies, and theories of the field to be rendered not just *more* understandable but also understandable at a *deeper* level. These are precisely the reasons why the development of expensive, time-consuming, labor-intensive, pedagogical laboratories for learning how to teach is overdue in preservice teacher education. Without them, we will continue to miss the opportunity to demonstrate the usefulness of our research.

Development of Respect for Scientific Research at the Preservice Level The teacher preparation programs at many institutions are designed in ways that usually do not promote respect for educational researchers and educational research. One reason for this is due to the design of many programs of teacher education. It is not unusual for foundation courses to be deliberately separated from methods courses, and then often those courses are kept separate from the student-teaching or classroom experiences. Inherent in the design of most teacher education programs is separation, not integration of praxis and theoria. Such designs keep the novice focused on the workplace and on survival skills training. This marginalizes learning how to think about research-based practices that might increase the possibility for more effective teaching and learning. Educational research can earn little respect in a system designed to separate, not integrate, what we do from the needs of student teachers. The preceding section also discusses this problem. The school of the future needs to experiment with novel ways to blend praxis and theoria.

A second factor that promotes disrespect for educational research in preservice education is the long-standing distrust of research by practical people, particularly teachers and administrators. Each school day these people must negotiate a complex set of school and classroom problems about which research can say little that is specific. Thus, they disdain researchers and ignore their findings, preferring to rely on their experience and craft knowledge rather than the abstract findings of research. And this distrust is communicated to the novice teacher. But the complexity and uncertainty of practice do not automatically mean that educational research is incapable of illuminating the decisions that must be made, even those that are made on the run. Both Virginia and Greg, old pro and novice, are each faced with myriad problems, but some of their dilemmas have already been illuminated by research, even though because of their training they do not know that.

Educational research gains the respect of practitioners when those who teach it admit that research will rarely provide straightforward prescriptions for practice. We believe that the findings of educational research will be more useful to practitioners if taught to them with a little more tentativeness and a little less arrogance. When research is presented to a practitioner as a guide, requiring adaptations to local circumstances, we are more honest about what it is capable of doing. Under these conditions research findings will garner more respect than if we try to pass them off as revealed truth. John Dewey once talked about psychological findings as simply "working hypotheses," and William James discussed the lack of relationship between knowing the findings of research and good teaching. If we are to garner respect for educational research in the teacher education programs of the future, this more modest attitude about research in education needs to be integral to the design of the program (Berliner, 1993).

In many efforts to disseminate the scientific knowledge base we overpromise what can be delivered, or research findings get confused with normative standards, requiring teachers to behave in accordance with the findings. We should instead be promoting our research as no more and no less than a way to illuminate possibilities and certainly as less generalizable and more subject to variations due to local contexts than we once thought.

Dewey asked 100 years ago "Can a teacher receive from another a statement of the means by which he is to reach his ends, and not become hopelessly servile in his attitude?" (Dewey 1900, p. 110). In the long run, our heavy-handedness in communicating research to pre- and in-service teachers has resulted in resentment, and educational platforms had few planks derived from the findings of the scientific community. Thus, the education school of the future needs a faculty that demonstrates modesty about the accomplishments of the scientific community and the usefulness of scientific findings for practitioners. This may be the only way that teachers will allow the research findings to influence the platforms that they build.

Improve the Quality of In-service Education for Teachers In-service teacher education throughout the nation is a scandal. Its many shortcomings include the short duration of the in-service programs, the lack of any follow-up, the "stuff-it-in-the-head" style of learning that is often the means by which

something is communicated, and so forth (Fenstermacher & Berliner, 1985). Worse, however, is the passing on of unwarranted knowledge, a problem in both preservice and in-service education.

The daylong in-service workshop on learning styles that pays a consultant a small fortune is one type of dissemination of unwarranted knowledge. The left-brain/right-brain special consultants that "pop in, pop off, and pop out of town" provide another type. The disciplinarians, the outcome-based sales force, the Madeline Hunterites, the year-rounders, and others are active in-service providers and their "knowledge" may be taught in preservice courses as well. But there is little or *no* warrant for their message. The research base supporting their beliefs is shoddy. Educational research often gets a bad name from the phony educational research that is sold at in-service workshops and promulgated in some preservice courses. Pre- and in-service teacher education programs of the future must separate out the acceptable scientific findings of a community of scholars from the conjecture of others, some of which is flimflam. This conservatism is to be used only when the research is to be taught, not when alternative views of education are taught. For example, we know of no reason not to discuss seriously the pros and cons of year-round education, but we know of little in the way of scientific research that would support these programs. As far as we know, such high-quality research has yet to be done and we do not think that the programs of teacher education in the future should confuse these two issues—promoting the innovative new idea versus scientific research or rigorous program evaluation.

When warranted research is presented in a respectful manner, as an in-service program for teachers, by teachers, it has had enormous success in changing practice. The AFT Educational Research and Dissemination Program (Billups, 1984) can point to a decade of such success. Derived from the educational research base that some say is of little use, thousands of teachers who have participated in the program found their practice enhanced. This program demonstrates that it is the method by which we communicate our findings, more than anything inherent in the findings of educational research, that is our problem.

Embed the Findings of Educational Research in the Reality of Classrooms Everyday life is not filled with propositions of the type that educational psychology and the other sciences are good at deducing. Rather, it is comprised of cases, episodes, emotional relationships, and filled with personal meaning. In short, life is lived and recalled in a narrative form as story, not as propositions. There is even evidence that the brain stores propositions and episodes in different ways (Squire, 1987).

People who acquire their knowledge in context learn that knowledge is a tool, a means to achieve something, not an end in itself, a point made by Dewey throughout his long career. If what we learn is out of context, like so much of mathematics and language learned in school, it becomes inert. To this day most of what we teach as educational research findings is taught like phonics and vocabulary in reading or like logarithms and geometry in mathematics; that is, it is taught in a decontextualized manner. Perhaps much of our research lies fallow because we often fail to give it the quality of a tool. We fail to embed it in meaningful contexts, we fail to embed it in stories that teachers and policymakers can use.

We note the importance of this way of communicating in the preceding section. But those who wish to promote the research base have not, as a rule, learned to provide sensible and trustworthy stories for teachers to think about and act upon. We believe that such stories need to become a part of teacher education programs. The teachers of America are primarily practical people, unlikely to interpret the regression equations in a research study on their own. We miss an opportunity to convey our research in a usable form when we fail to tell stories that are faithful to the data that were collected. And because much of teaching is rightly thought of as decision making in an ambiguous public setting, with little time for contemplation, cases are needed to illustrate the ways the knowledge base can be used (Shulman, 1991; Silverman, Welty, & Lyon, 1994). Case studies of grading practices, learning, and motivation problems in particular students, disruptive behavior, and cheating all illuminate the knowledge base on assessment, constructivism, discipline, and moral behavior. The research base when disseminated, in part through stories, and taught, in part through cases, makes the abstract and objective knowledge of pedagogy concrete and personally meaningful. Thus teacher preparation programs need much more time devoted to instruction that emphasizes the applicability of research to the realities of classroom life. Reality may be glimpsed through movies, novels, stories, cases, and personal experiences. Whatever the genre, the goal is the same, namely, the grounding in reality of the ideas generated by research.

When Should We Teach the Pedagogical Knowledge Base?

Virtually all programs of teacher preparation have ignored developmental views of learning to teach. As far as we know, in almost all programs of teacher preparation the responsibility of the university for education and supervision ends with the graduation of the novice teacher—ending the teacher–student relationship at precisely the time that the most learning about teaching will take place. This is of course nonsensical. The first few years on the job are crucial in the development of teaching skills, and researchers now have some ideas about how that developmental process takes place (Berliner, 1994; Borko & Putnam, 1995). Berliner's model suggests the five following stages.

Stage 1: Novice Level For the novice the commonplaces of an environment need to be discriminated, the elements of the tasks to be performed need to be labeled and learned, and the novice must be given a set of context-free rules for action. In learning to drive an automobile, for example, one is taught the meaning of the "yield" sign (a commonplace), and to shift from first gear at 12 miles an hour (a context-free rule that gives the novice guidance even if it is an inadequate rule for driving on hills, slippery roads, etc., and that suffices until more experience is gained). There are similarities to these situations in learning to teach. The novice teacher is taught the meaning of terms such as higher order questions, reinforcement, and learning disabled. Novices are taught context-free rules such as "give praise for right an-

swers," "wait 3 seconds after asking a higher order question," and "never criticize a student." Understanding of the commonplaces and some context-free rules are what is needed to begin to teach. The behavior of the novice, whether automobile driver, chess player, or teacher is usually rational, relatively inflexible, and tends to conform to whatever rules and procedures they were told to follow. Only minimal skill at the tasks of driving, chess playing, or teaching should really be expected of a novice. This is a stage for learning the objective facts and features of situations, for gaining experience. It is the stage at which real world experience appears to the learner to be far more important than verbal information, as attested to by generations of drivers, chess players, and student teachers. Student teachers and many first-year teachers may be considered novices.

Stage 2: Advanced Beginner Level As experience is gained, the novice becomes an advanced beginner (see Bullough, 1989, for a case study of a teacher in transition from a novice to an advanced beginner). Many second- and third-year teachers are likely to be in this developmental stage. This is the stage when experience can become melded with verbal knowledge and when episodic and case knowledge are built up and complement the propositional knowledge that is learned in our programs of teacher preparation. This is a crucial point. The know-how to run a class cannot be taught, it is learned through episodes (personally meaningful, emotionally loaded events such as the death of a student, or the overcoming of a reading problem) and cases (successful ways to handle the type of student who will not do homework or will not share). So much of what is needed to succeed as a teacher is learned while being a teacher, and the university will have to help moderate that learning or let it occur without any input—which is silly.

Without meaningful past episodes and cases to relate the experience of the present to, individuals are unsure of themselves, they do not know what to do or what not to do. This is true of learning to drive a car, when the advanced beginner is suddenly confronted with fog, ice, or a traffic jam. In education we see advanced beginners having difficulty knowing what to do when a student challenges the teacher's authority, neurotically seeks the teacher's attention, or boasts of her or his "A" performance. Such incidents in driving or teaching are understood better after the second and third time they happen. Strategic knowledge—when to ignore or break rules and when to follow them—is also developed in this stage as context begins to guide behavior. For example, in learning to teach you learn that praise does not always have the desired effect, as when a low-ability student interprets it as communicating low expectations. You learn that criticism after a bad performance by a usually good student can be quite motivating. Experience is affecting behavior, but the advanced beginner may still have no sense of what is important. Mentoring by a knowledgeable other is likely to be particularly important during this time. The mentor can mediate the environment for the novice, helping the novice to learn what is and is not important.

The novice and the advanced beginner, although intensely involved in the learning process, often fail to take full responsibility for their actions. This occurs because they are labeling and describing events, following rules, recognizing and classifying contexts, but not yet actively determining through personal agency what is happening. The acceptance of full personal responsibility for classroom instruction occurs when one develops a sense of personal agency, willfully choosing what to do. This occurs in the next stage of development.

Stage 3: Competent Level With further experience and some motivation to succeed most of the advanced beginners become competent performers of the skills needed in their domain of interest. Not all advanced beginners, however, are likely to reach this level. Evidence exists that some teachers remain "fixed" at a less than competent level of performance (Borko, 1992; Eisenhart & Jones, 1992). And we all have muttered at drivers who, though experienced, are not in our judgment competent. Nevertheless, it is believed that many third- and fourth-year teachers, as well as more experienced teachers, reach a level of performance that we consider to be competent. Two characteristics distinguish the competent performers of a skill. First, they make conscious choices about what they are going to do. They set priorities and decide on plans. They have rational goals and choose sensible means for reaching the ends they have in mind. Second, while enacting their skill, they can determine what is and what is not important. From their experience they know what to attend to and what to ignore. This is the stage in which teachers learn not to make timing and targeting errors, because they have learned through experience what to attend to and what to ignore in the classroom. This is when teachers learn to make curriculum and instruction decisions, such as when to stay with a topic and when to move on based on a particular teaching context and a particular group of students.

Because they are more personally in control of the events around them, following their own plans, and responding only to the information that they choose to, teachers at the competent stage tend to feel more responsibility for what happens. They are not detached. Thus, they often feel emotional about success and failure in their area in a way that is different and more intense from novices or advanced beginners. And they have more vivid memories of their successes and failures as well. But the competent performer is not yet very fast, fluid, or flexible in behavior. These are characteristics of the last two stages in the development of expertise.

Stage 4: Proficient Level About the fifth year, a modest number of teachers move into the proficient stage of development. This is the stage at which intuition or know-how becomes prominent. Out of the wealth of experience that the proficient individual has accumulated comes a holistic way of viewing the situations they encounter. They recognize similarities among events that the novice fails to see—that is the residue of experience. For example, the proficient teacher may notice without conscious effort that today's mathematics lesson is bogging down for the same reason that last week's spelling lesson bombed. At some higher level of pattern categorization, the similarities between disparate events are understood. This holistic recognition of patterns as similar allows proficient individuals to predict events more precisely, because they see more things as alike and therefore as having been experienced before. Their rich case knowledge can be brought to bear on the problem. Chess masters, bridge masters, expert

air traffic controllers, and expert radiologists rely heavily on this ability. The proficient performer, however, while intuitive in pattern recognition and in ways of knowing, is still likely to be analytic and deliberative in deciding what to do. The proficient stage is the stage of most tournament chess and bridge players. But the grand masters are those few who move to a stage higher, to the expert level.

Stage 5: Expert Level If the novice is deliberate, the advanced beginner insightful, the competent performer rational, and the proficient performer intuitive, we might categorize the expert as often being arational. Experts have both an intuitive grasp of the situation and seem to sense in nonanalytic and nondeliberative ways the appropriate response to be made. They show fluid performance, they seem able to respond to their environment in an effortless manner. The expert safety in football, the expert martial artist in combat, the expert chess master, and the expert teacher in classroom recitations all seem to know where to be or what to do at the right time.

Experts engage in performance in a qualitatively different way from the novice or the competent performer. The experts are not consciously choosing what to attend to and what to do. They are acting effortlessly, fluidly, and in a way that seems irrational because it is not easily described as deductive or analytic behavior. Although it is beyond the usual meaning of rational, because neither calculation or deliberative thought are involved, the behavior of the expert is certainly not irrational. Insight into the behavior of the expert can be obtained from the writings of Schön (1983), as he discusses knowledge-in-action, and from the work of Polya (1954), in his discussion of the role played by tacit knowledge in problem solving.

This theory of development is reasonably well supported by data and has heuristic value for thinking about the education of teachers. The empirical research in this area has yielded many reliable findings about the differences between experts and novices. For example, compared to the novices, the experts have better pattern recognition skills, are more responsive to student needs, and are more concerned about students taking responsibility for their work. Experts make more valid inferences about what is going on in classrooms, engage in more principled reasoning, represent problems in richer ways, have more routines to accomplish the work of the class, are more work oriented, and are more flexible in their teaching. These findings suggest that a good deal of preservice teacher education needs to be rethought.

At best, the beginning graduates of teacher preparation programs will do little harm, and if their education was remarkably successful, they will be capable of learning much from their first year of experience. But having just completed a program of teacher education, the novice teacher must be recognized as not yet very competent. This should not be surprising because teaching is a very complicated social activity, and it ought to take a relatively long time to master. So we anticipate that the teacher preparation programs of the future would continue obligations to graduates into the field: to remind them of the methods that they had intended to try; to keep before them the knowledge base that could help them interpret events in their classroom; and perhaps, most important of all, to help the novice remain true to the ideology underlying curricula platforms. The norms of the workplace are very powerful. If the teachers we educate at the university are to show the effects of that education, then those teachers should not be abandoned when they start their careers.

Basic routines—the automatization of some aspects of performance—were found to be an important part of the experts' performance, for it frees their minds for tackling more important issues. This suggests that in the future, along with all the other suggestions we have, programs of preservice teacher education should deliberately train novices in the common routines of classroom life. These include taking attendance, giving and receiving homework, conducting an opening homework review, getting activities started and stopped, and so forth. Furthermore, because experts demonstrate far more flexibility in their teaching than novices do, some of the creative new pedagogy we recommended earlier in this chapter may not be possible until later in a teacher's career. We may do novices a disservice by promoting complicated instructional procedures and grouping patterns that may be beyond their developmental level. Some simpler forms of pedagogy may be appropriate while episodic, case and strategic knowledge are acquired. Moreover, because experts possess better pattern-recognition capability, can reason better about classroom phenomena, make more valid inferences about classroom processes, and so forth, the entire curriculum of the preservice program needs to be reorganized to recognize that such differences exist and that they impact what can be learned early in one's career. We believe that the future calls for a greater involvement in the early years of a teacher's career by teacher educators because the research on teacher development and common sense both agree on the importance of these years in the development of a strong professional identity.

Who Should Teach the Pedagogical Knowledge Base?

The emphasis on a future that calls for a more longitudinal approach to teacher education suggests that the university faculty have to share the educational responsibilities with field-based personnel. These are the competent, proficient, and expert teachers who are articulate about teaching and can serve as mentors for novice teachers as they grow in their abilities to teach. Virginia may be one of these mentors. Greg could profit from her understandings of teaching as he struggles with his first teaching assignment. The mentors will themselves need to be genuine members of the university programs, understanding the need to help young teachers find ways to articulate and operationalize what universities have to offer them *at developmentally appropriate times.* The development of a strong professional teacher begins in the preservice programs of teacher education, but the preservice program of teacher preparation of the future will recognize that it *only begins there,* that it is a careerlong process, and that the primary determinant of the strength of professionalism that teachers ultimately display lies in the community of fellow teachers of which they are a part.

It is there, in a community of teachers, administrators, students, and their parents that the political knowledge of a strong professional is acquired. Virginia's personal history shows her seeking a community in which to be active politically. It probably takes a certain amount of experience to understand the politics of pedagogical decision making. For example, the research base for pedagogy may suggest that cooperative and collaborative teaching methods be tried, but some parents will find that to be objectionable, claiming that it destroys the basic competitive spirit that makes the economy move; the research may suggest trying out a more thinking-skills oriented program, but some members of the fundamentalist religious community may object; the research may suggest new forms of assessment, but the school board may want to impose even more standardized norm-referenced tests; and so forth. There is nothing neutral about educational decisions; each is a political act, and each has repercussions that a novice teacher must learn to anticipate if she or he is to develop successfully into a strong professional educator, one who can operationalize a curricular ideology in which she or he believes. Mentors who themselves are strong professionals can do that.

Summary

The pedagogical knowledge that teachers need to be able to articulate and operationalize is not taught well now. The teacher preparation programs of the future that are compatible with the vision we sketch here would teach the knowledge base in ways that are honest, ethical, thorough, and contemporary. In essence, this means that our knowledge should be taught as rich ideas for thinking about instruction, not as prescriptions for how to behave in classrooms. The research has yielded theories, concepts, technology, and findings that can inform a beginning teacher like Greg. But to teach what the educational research community has to offer in a way that will actually affect what teachers do requires incorporating pedagogical laboratories into preservice instruction so that pedagogical knowledge can be turned into pedagogical skills, so that "knowing that" is melded with "knowing how" (see the first section). The entire preservice teacher education program needs to be infused with research that can be put into practice so the operational dimension of professionalism is developed. The teacher education program needs to respect research rather than disdaining it. And the program must help teachers distinguish the difference between substantiated, warranted research and testimonials of sales people and missionaries. Finally, the research findings need to be embedded in the life of classrooms.

The research base is not easy to comprehend or apply until after experience has taught novice teachers its lessons. Teachers ordinarily develop their abilities over time, progressing from novice, to advanced beginner, to competent in a few years. After about 5 years some competent teachers will develop further, becoming proficient or expert in their teaching. The differences between expert and novice teachers suggests that much important learning takes place during the first few years of teaching, requiring the development of programs of teacher education that are longitudinal in nature and that extend into the first few years of a novice teacher's career. The university and carefully selected site-based mentors must share the responsibility for educating the new teacher in articulating and operationalizing the research, and in understanding the political implications of each pedagogical act.

RESPONSIVENESS TO A MULTICULTURAL STUDENT BODY

Increasing diversity among students, contrasted with the continuing homogeneity of those who would educate them, places a large responsibility on those who are to prepare teachers for the classrooms of the future. If present trends continue, by the year 2000 only about 5% of the national teaching force will be teachers of color, while demographic projections indicate continued increases in the diversity of the school attending population. This demographic discrepancy requires increases in the diversity of the teaching cohort through more intense and successful recruitment efforts among minority students. But it also makes clear the need for increased attention to the preparation of all teachers for classrooms where diversity is the norm rather than the exception.

Imagine, if you will, urban classrooms filled with brown and black children representing a variety of ethnicities and languages. They will be facing teachers who are not like them physically and are probably also monolingual English speakers, and of a higher socioeconomic status. The increased isolation of the social classes in our urban communities ensures that few of those teachers will have had the sorts of experiences that engender the empathy necessary to understand their students' lives or the barriers they might face. Even less likely is the possibility that they will see potential to be released, rather than disadvantage to be compensated for, among their students. In fact, using their uninformed professional judgment, these teachers may themselves create hurdles through the use of commonly accepted but dysfunctional practices such as tracking (Oakes, 1985) and language immersion (Cummins, 1986). The results of these popular, yet discredited, pedagogical strategies are already apparent in the failures of the urban and rural poor, yet the reasons for the students' lack of success is seldom connected to deficiencies in the teachers' practices. Those practices are often learned in the teacher preparation program.

Teacher education programs have traditionally been based on the assumed homogeneity of the school population. Little attention has been paid to the ways in which students differ on the basis of gender, ethnicity, language, or regional variations. The only differences expected and planned for seem to be those related to grade level, the most artificial of differences, or on measured intellectual ability, the most biased of measures. Thus, although much attention is devoted to what is appropriate for third graders or for the "fast" and "slow" students, the appropriateness of a given strategy for girls or boys, or for urban African-Americans and rural, white midwesterners, is hardly ever discussed. When it is discussed, the focus tends to be not on the cultural influences on human ways of knowing but rather on the need for remedial instructional assistance for unsuccessful students. In most of today's teacher education programs difference tends to become confused with disadvantage and failure.

One reason for this confusion is the predominance of what Bowers and Flinders (1990) call "the management paradigm." This approach to the problems of teaching and learning has been the basis for a large body of research in education that has contributed much to our understanding of classrooms.

However, because it is based primarily on behaviorist theory, this approach tends to see the individual as an independent agent unaffected by the forces of culture and emotions. Teachers trained within that tradition tend to value power and control over their students while considering variance from expected norms as a deficiency.

Only recently has awareness of the cultural and class discrepancies between teachers and students and their relationship to student outcomes gained the attention of teacher educators. This attention has resulted in the current interest in "multicultural education." Although this overdue interest in "multicultural education" is welcome, the topic is most often addressed, if at all, in short presentations that tend to emphasize cultural peculiarities rather than the pervasive problems of racism, oppression, and power relationships. The naive beliefs of teachers in training are never confronted. Thus, newly trained teachers often enter their classrooms with their preconceptions intact and their values unchallenged (Sleeter, 1992). This approach contributes little to the educational well-being of all our students, who, whether majority or minority, midwestern white, or urban poor, must be nurtured in an atmosphere that makes visible the differences that divide us as well as the commonalities that unite us. They also need to understand the historical inequities that have distorted the outcomes of schooling for many of them.

Overcoming long-standing assumptions nurtured by stereotypes repeatedly reinforced by the media is a difficult task, especially when the trainees are adults. Even well-designed, long-term programs have only limited success in effecting the cognitive and affective changes that are necessary for those who would teach in unfamiliar situations (Sleeter, 1992).

Preparing teachers to be strong professionals in classrooms populated by heterogeneous groups of students also entails paying attention to the three essential elements described in the introduction to this chapter: the articulative, operational, and political. These key dimensions will be used here as well to describe the manifestations of cultural responsiveness that will be expected from strong professionals. It should be understood that because these dimensions are overlapping and interdependent, they are not likely to exist in isolation.

The Articulative Dimension

A staunch belief in the "American dream" is deeply embedded within the psyche of the nation. It is commonly accepted that hard work is rewarded and that talent and effort invested in education will inevitably lead us to the realization of our dreams. As a graduate student in educational administration commented in her journal: "I was taught, and the educational system supported, my belief that achievement was both a product of ability and effort" (Anonymous, 1994). These beliefs are so pervasive that even those who fail to realize their dreams often blame only themselves for their failure. An African-American high school student demonstrated his readiness to accept that responsibility when he spoke about his future: "I think the only thing that's holding me back from getting a good education might be me. I just have to be ready to accept it" (Nieto, 1992, p. 56). This may appear to be an admirable stance for such a young person to assume, but by his trust in the system he is ignoring structural factors such as tracking, low expectations, and "dumbed-down" curriculum that are likely to raise barriers along the way.

The unexamined national belief in the "American dream" is challenged by the existence of populations that remain marginalized from the social mainstream. Most of them are urban and minority, but many are also rural and are as likely to be white as to be people of color. Some speak a language other than English, others speak local variations of English that are just as unwelcome in the school.

Members of these marginalized groups are often unsuccessful in school. They fill the unemployment rolls and, when employed, occupy the lowest rungs of the ladder. They own little, suffer poor health, and their survival often depends on minimal government subsidies. They have not achieved the "American dream." And their children are often quickly categorized as "at-risk" (Donmoyer & Kos, 1993; Richardson, Casanova, Placier, & Guilfoyle, 1989).

The teachers assigned to teach the children of these communities, whether majority or minority, are likely to have been successful students. Sometimes they were the first ones in their families to graduate from college. They are the embodiment of the "American dream." They have worked hard, they have achieved, they have made it. They "know" that hard work is rewarded. As one school principal noted in a class journal recently: "I don't know what it's like to work hard and not have it pay off for you" (Anonymous, 1994). Given such deeply held and reinforced beliefs, these teachers reasonably assume that lack of success is evidence of laziness, lack of talent, or both. But they are not unkind people. Their choice of teaching as a career is often based on their "love of children." Sometimes they demonstrate an almost missionary zeal in their interest in "helping" children. But their view of the students in their classroom is permeated with their unexamined cultural assumptions. They will assume incompetence and lower their expectations; they will tend to see individual failure where there is social failure, even when faced with contrary evidence (Spencer, 1994; Richardson et al., 1989). They will tend to blame parents and the students themselves for their lack of success.

The challenge for the future is to ensure that those who aspire to teach in tomorrow's classrooms can transcend cultural barriers that limit their perceptions of students. Teachers need to be able to articulate a view of childhood that promotes children, all children, as the holders of potential waiting to be tapped. Strong professionals must come face to face with the unexamined beliefs promoted by the culture. They must be helped to understand the limitations of their own experiences.

To become strong professionals beginning teachers need to make evident and articulate the role that racism, oppression, and power have played in their lives as well as in the lives of their students. In the future, programs of teacher preparation will require that novice teachers study their own life stories so that they can begin to understand how their experiences were affected by sociohistorical conditions. And they will need to connect those conditions with their consequences in order to understand how different life stories and different sociohistorical conditions might have different consequences for others.

Strong professionals in increasingly diverse classrooms will need to understand the varieties of human knowledge and recognize the explicit and implicit assumptions that determine what is valued in the school. Increased appreciation of the knowledge that exists beyond the school and its usefulness when incorporated into the classroom must be understood by these teachers. They must be able to define and articulate different criteria for determining the worth of various forms of knowing. And they must be able to do this not only within their pedagogical settings but also beyond the classrooms, within the communities they serve.

Teachers who are strong professionals in a diverse society will value all forms of human communication. This means that vernacular languages, whether oral, written, or signed, will be accepted as legitimate forms of expression, not because school standard English is unimportant, but because children's native knowledge also must be valued while their repertoires are expanded. As Betances (1990) has noted in remembering a teacher who insisted he must forget his native Spanish language in order to learn English, teaching should never be about *unlearning* anything, it should always be about learning *more*.

The distinctiveness and peculiarities of cultural characteristics and inclinations should not be ignored, but neither should they become the focus of attention. Teachers who are strong professionals must be sensitive to the generalities of cultural behavior without surrendering to stereotypes that limit individual potential. It is important to avoid misunderstandings based on erroneous cultural assumptions. Strong professionals must seek to be sensitive to that possibility by reserving judgment and seeking clarification when they encounter unfamiliar situations. They must be advocates for their students, acting as cultural brokers for them when the need arises.

Above all, strong professionals in diverse classrooms must learn to articulate their belief in the benefits of diversity to the social system. They must be able to be confident in their ability to balance the individual and communal good. They must relish, rather than fear, the consequences of difference. In the vision we have for the future of teacher education, conflict in a teachers' classroom will be seen as a pedagogical opportunity for further learning rather than as a social problem to be controlled.

The Operational Dimension

What will be the operational characteristics of strong professionals in diverse classrooms? Teachers in tomorrow's classrooms will need to put into operation student-based pedagogical approaches. One-size-fits-all strategies will not do anymore, if they ever did. Strong professionals will display the confidence necessary to implement a curriculum that begins and ends with the student. The skills that enable a teacher to draw from a students' knowledge base to bridge over into unexplored territory will need to be a part of the strong professional's inventory. Rather than seeing the students as vessels for a finite amount of information, tomorrow's teachers will need to see their students as knowledgeable, if novice, learners who will extend their knowledge and intellectual growth by connecting what they already know to new information. This theme runs through the first two sections of this chapter.

Strong professionals will insist that they know their students well enough to be able to guide them in studying topics of personal interest and significance. In the Bronx Middle School

Collaborative, for example, a teacher and researcher have taught sixth graders to be ethnographers in their own communities. These students are encouraged to learn from their peers, their parents, and other members of the community. Not surprisingly, the students have chosen to study topics such as drugs, teen pregnancy, homelessness, and others that reflect their lived experiences. Through this process these children are eagerly learning the same skills they might reject if taught through traditionally impersonal textbooks and workbooks (Beck & Newman, 1992).

Although students' individual interests and knowledge will initiate the quest for new knowledge, the process will need to be carried out in collaboration with others who bring their skills and knowledge to bear on the problem. Serving the social needs of a heterogeneous participatory democracy will require genuine cooperation. Strong professionals seeking to educate tomorrow's citizens will need to promote and teach *collaborative* strategies that help their students to develop the skills necessary for successfully working in groups to solve the problems of a diverse society. They will also need to model those strategies within their own professional lives.

Closing the classroom door to colleagues will need to give way to collaborative arrangements that allow for the aggregation and utilization of diverse knowledge. Diversity among the student population will require first of all diversity among the instructional staff. Strong professionals will need to demand that diversity whenever the opportunity arises. That change will require all teachers to model for their students the social skills they may now demand only of them. That is, they will need to learn how to work with colleagues, who, having different sociohistorical experiences, hold different values and demonstrate different skills. That is not an easy task.

In recounting changes in her own thinking as a result of working closely with Korean and Latino colleagues, a principal described how she had initially been frustrated about differences in the task orientation between herself, a Euro-American, and her colleagues. She had been most concerned with efficiency and solving problems, whereas they had focused their attention on those affected by the problems. For her colleagues, spending time with concerned parents and children took precedence over a tight schedule. She realized the importance of their contribution when she noticed that, although she was getting the paperwork done, students and their parents would seek her colleagues out for help (Beck & Newman, 1992).

Tomorrow's strong professionals will need to develop a variety of pedagogical approaches far exceeding the knowledge base of individual teachers. A faculty that reflects the diversity of the students is likely to include teachers who can serve as cultural brokers to the school. They can act as bridges between a community's cultural knowledge and the school's pedagogical approaches. Collegiality will, therefore, become a necessity rather than a desirable option for tomorrow's strong professionals. And collegiality will need to extend beyond the school to the academic institutions where researchers seek to improve their understanding of teaching and learning.

Strong professionals always have to be knowledge seekers. They can do this through reading and studying, but they can also do this through collaborative partnerships with those who devote their professional lives to the process of inquiry. This will prove to be especially valuable for those teachers and researchers who are bewildered by the demands posed by an increasing diverse school population. Researchers in education have become more cognizant of the need to work jointly with practitioners as they seek a better understanding of the educational process. The strong professionals of tomorrow will be eager participants in such partnerships not only to learn from, but also to teach, the academicians. The mutual advantages that result from those relationships have been amply documented (Díaz, Moll, & Mehan, 1986; Heath, 1983; Torres-Guzmán, Mercado, Quintero, & Rivera-Viera, 1994). In such relationships the theoreticians, as well as the practitioners, often learn new ways to describe and make sense of the school environment while they pay attention to the needs of a diverse student body.

Strong professionals in the classroom will need to be alert to change in order to keep pace with their students. Their search for knowledge and understanding cannot be limited to traditional sources such as encyclopedias and museums. Our students are increasingly at the mercy of popular media where stereotypical notions about people's behavior are left unexamined. Tomorrow's teachers need to consider that influence on their students. They will need to be aware of those media messages and to help their students to become informed and critical viewers and listeners. "By ignoring the cultural and social forms that are authorized by youth and simultaneously empower or disempower them, educators risk complicitly silencing and negating their students" (Giroux & Simon, 1989, p. 3).

Strong professionals will also seek to broaden their linguistic repertoire. Fluency in languages other than English will become a necessity for teachers who want to provide the best instruction for their students. As celebrated Mexican author Carlos Fuentes noted: "Monolingualism is a curable disease." But in the absence of linguistic knowledge on their part, teachers will also want to put into practice alternative pedagogical strategies that facilitate learning for students who are not fluent in English (Lucas, 1993; Milk, 1993).

The operational activities of strong professionals will not end in the classroom or the school building. Public schools have generally ignored the strategic and cultural resources that households in low socioeconomic communities contain. These useful assets have been termed "funds of knowledge" by Vélez-Ibañez and Greenberg (1992) who have found that social exchange in these communities continues to provide individual access to historic funds of knowledge. This knowledge also provides the cultural matrix for incorporating new understandings and relationships in a manner compatible with the community's traditions. These anthropologists argue that "grasping the social relationships in which children are ensconced and the broad features of learning generated in the home are key if we are to understand the construction of cultural identity and the emergence of cultural personality" (p. 313).

Teachers in Arizona, working closely with researchers, followed up Vélez-Ibañez & Greenberg's funds of knowledge theory by conducting analyses of households and how they function through their social ties and networks. The extent of knowledge found in these communities was evidence of the strengths and resources available. After identifying some of those resources, teachers invited parents as experts on topics related to themes being studied in their classrooms. The researchers and the teachers worked closely with parents and community members to create situations where these funds of knowledge would become legitimate resources for teaching and learning (Moll, Amanti, Neff, & González, 1992).

The teachers in this project became convinced that valuable knowledge—knowledge that could be mobilized for academic learning—existed beyond the classroom. These collective funds of knowledge became part of the "core" curriculum. In these activities the teachers became facilitators who mediated the students' interactions with text as well as with the social resources available in their communities.

Moll (1992) argues that the role of the teachers in this process is critical and that it is also demanding and laborious work that requires collaboration. He believes that maintaining supportive contexts where teachers can collaborate with other colleagues, including researchers and parents, is an indispensible component for obtaining positive change in education (Moll, 1992). Goldenberg and Gallimore (1991) have noted that the possibility for reforming schools "depends on a better understanding of the interplay between research knowledge and local knowledge." They claim that it is only through a better understanding of this interplay that research can have a significant effect on the schools. Thus the skills necessary to work cooperatively with disparate groups will need to be a part of the basic knowledge of tomorrow's strong professionals. And success in these endeavors will also call for a political approach.

The Political Dimension

Teachers have often thought of themselves as apolitical. Education cannot be tainted by politics, they feel, without losing its neutrality. These beliefs have diluted teacher participation in the national, state, and local political processes. In spite of the size of this "interest group" whose interest is the welfare of children, its weight has never been very effectively felt at the seats of power. For example, teachers, as a group, have been conspicuously absent among the advocates for poor and minority children.

This is not surprising given that the education of teachers in the United States has been dominated by a view of teaching as an "applied science" and of the teacher as a passive recipient of professional knowledge developed by "experts." Teacher training has emphasized what works most efficiently rather than the critical analysis of the school curricula. Within this behavioristic model teachers are expected to be obedient civil servants dedicated to carrying out the dictates of others (Aronowitz & Giroux, 1985). The difference between teacher "training" and teacher "education" becomes crucial here, and it is the latter that needs to be stressed.

Teacher training is presently conceived as a problem of management rather than an intellectual endeavor. It follows that the notion that teachers should be involved in the production of curricular materials appropriate to the social and cultural contexts in which they teach becomes irrelevant. When excellence is purely a quality demonstrated through higher scores in reading and mathematics, teacher autonomy and control are seen as hindrances to school administrators interested solely in efficient management.

Aronowitz and Giroux (1985) propose viewing teachers as intellectuals who ". . . must take active responsibility for raising serious questions about what they teach, how they are to teach it, and what the larger goals are for which they are striving" (p. 31). These authors apply to teachers Kohl's (1983) definition of the intellectual as " . . . someone who knows about his or her field, has a wide breadth of knowledge about other aspects of the world . . . uses experience to develop theory and questions theory on the basis of further experience . . . [and who] also . . . has the courage to question authority and . . . refuses to act counter to his or her . . . experience and judgment." Their position describes a program that is educative of teachers, not one that trains teachers. That is the proper way to prepare teachers for politically active lives.

This perception of teachers as intellectuals challenges the notion of value-free discourse that supposedly ensures the objectivity and detachment of intellectuals. Instead, Aronowitz and Giroux promote a view of teachers as "transformative intellectuals" who can make the political more pedagogical and the pedagogical more political. That is, teachers need to bring education into the political sphere where the struggle for meaning as well as for power relations needs to be fought. They must also make the pedagogical more political utilizing approaches that make knowledge meaningful, critical, and emancipatory. This approach presupposes a view of schooling where critical reflection and action help students overcome injustices and change themselves. Transformative intellectuals encourage students to take an active voice in their learning experiences (Aronowitz & Giroux, 1985).

Cummins (1986) also called for the emancipation or empowerment of minority students. He argues that these students are disempowered educationally in much the same way their communities are. Instead, minority students should be empowered as a result of their interactions with educators in the schools. But genuine incorporation of students' experiences, that is, their cultures, into the curriculum can happen only when educators abandon pedagogical assumptions that focus primarily on predetermined knowledge and skills (Cummins, 1988).

The strong professionals of tomorrow must be prepared to assume a more politically mature stance than their predecessors. They can only do that if they succeed in setting aside a professional history that has gradually eroded their autonomy and knowledge. Our strong professionals will need to be knowledgeable, wise users of experience, and ready to stand up for what they believe is right.

Summary

How then should we prepare our students, given the many expectations set out in this section for the teachers of tomorrow? We need to understand that we must change our content as well as our methods. We will not develop the strong professionals described here from the graduates of courses filled with passive note takers who dutifully fulfill their requirements for the desired grade. We will also not succeed in developing the skills needed by future strong professionals from courses that prescribe approaches in the absence of a context or from students who have had limited experiences with the diversity they will find in their schools when they become teachers.

The strong professionals we envision will only come about as a result of changes in the academic environments that seek to prepare them. We must foster environments that challenge students to think critically, to question the status quo, and to develop their confidence as intellectuals. Teacher preparation classes ought to provide the liveliest forums for discussion where pedagogical theories are critically examined to make their ideological roots transparent. Future teachers must participate in critical analyses that take place in environments that encourage collegiality not only among teachers but also between teachers and researchers as well as parents and members of the communities served by the schools.

We must also broaden the content of teacher preparation programs. The traditional psychological approach must be broadened to incorporate anthropological and sociological perspectives that can help students understand the demographic and cultural changes they will encounter in the schools. But learning about "the other" in the safety of a university classroom is not enough. Our students must be nudged into situations that force them to come face to face with themselves through encounters with the other. We need to stop believing that the students who enter our classrooms are no different from those they will later meet in their own classrooms. Focusing only on differences may be a sign of racism, but ignoring those differences is equally offensive. Strong professionals cannot ignore differences, they need to accept them without judging them to be deficient. They can only do so if they are comfortable with who they are and have an understanding of their students that comes not from reading the records but from getting to know them and their families through observation and conversation.

This seems like a large order, and it is. More than anything else the community of teacher educators needs to accept its own complicity in the current inadequacies of classroom teachers to develop successfully the potential of so many of our young people. The poor and minority students who reject what the schools have to offer and slowly but surely leave that painful environment, are our responsibility too. That is why we must determine to change ourselves before we demand changes in the schools.

TECHNOLOGY

Technology is one of the most fascinating and modern aspects of life today. Its relentless and almost frighteningly innovative spirit has placed it everywhere. Regardless of the community or culture where it is used, technology seems to have the same vitality and forceful attention-gathering effects. Most people like it. They respond to it. They soon depend on it. For them technology seems to have few limitations and almost magical strengths. Unfortunately, these magical strengths exist in few classrooms. Despite the absence from the classroom, technology is in the daily lives of everyone, including students, teachers, and teacher educators. Most of today's K–12 and higher education classrooms are filled with students

who have spent the greater portion of their lives staring at tubes of one kind or another. Television, Nintendo, MTV, and computers are

for this generation the primary medium of cultural transmission. From the playpen to early adulthood, the 13-inch screen, not the printed page, offers the dominant learning environment. (Winner, 1994, p. 66)

By the fall of 1994, 26% of American homes had personal computers, and most had TVs and VCRs. As a result, technological transformations have resulted in cultural ones. Technology has become not only a vehicle for the transmission of cultural information but also a means by which people define themselves and the world around them. It has become so important that diverse and quarrelsome groups like school boards, national, state, and local government officials, administrators, teachers, and parents have reached an unusual agreement: Technology needs to be incorporated into education. This is understandable. Historically the response by societies to change has been to teach the young about change. Unfortunately, these diverse groups have yet to reach agreement on what is meant by the terms *technology* and *incorporated!* In fact, some have ignored more fundamental questions such as, What kind of learning does it permit? What are the intellectual tendencies it encourages? What sort of culture does it produce (Ellel, 1964; McLuhan, 1964; Postman, 1985)?

Many years ago Thoreau warned that inventions are but an improved means to an unimproved end. Technology may be the educational innovation of the twentieth century, but in order for Virginia, Greg, and other teachers, as well as teacher educators, to sort out some of the hyperbole and oversell associated with it, they must engage in the kind of critical reflection that enables them to make and express informed judgments about what aspects of the human condition known as teaching will be improved by using technology. Perhaps a few lines from the science fiction short story, *The Fun They Had* (Asimov, 1974) might point out the need for critical reflection and informed judgments. The year is 2157, and there are no schools—everyone is taught at home with mechanical teachers. Margie, a school-age youngster, speculates about how it must have been when people were teachers.

Margie went into the schoolroom. It was right next to her bedroom, and the mechanical teacher was on and waiting for her. It was always on at the same time every day except Saturday and Sunday. The screen lit up, and it said: "Today's arithmetic lesson is on addition of proper fractions. Please insert yesterday's homework in the proper slot." Margie did so with a sigh. She was thinking about the old schools they had when her grandfather's grandfather was a little boy. All the kids from the whole neighborhood came, laughing and shouting in the schoolyard, sitting together in the schoolroom, going home together at the end of the day. They learned the same things, so they could help one another in the homework and talk about it. And the teachers were people. (p. 155)

The New Prometheus?

Like it or not, modern technology is seen by many as the new Prometheus: The creator of a new order for both higher education and K–12 education. Technology, once in the background of modern culture is now in the foreground. There seems to be a collective enthusiasm and belief among many that technology offers solutions to complex social and educational challenges such as single-parent families, child abuse, gangs, poverty, crime, the widening gap between the rich and poor, racial inequality, guns, drugs, AIDS, and endangered environments—to name a few. But before technology can solve these challenges and create a new order, it needs to accomplish a variety of simpler tasks under some very difficult conditions. Technobabble, chatter, and slogans will not suffice as solutions. Virginia and Greg already know that technology will not be a panacea for the challenges faced by teaching and teacher education. They have already figured out what technology can do and cannot do for them. They are developing and beginning to articulate what they believe are technology's answers to the challenges in their classrooms. For Virginia and Greg technology is seen as an effective, efficient, and creative teaching tool. It is also a tool that provides new teaching and learning opportunities (Brooks & Kopp, 1989) and that leads to different forms of thinking, and different forms of thinking can lead to different kinds of meaning (Eisner, 1993). The success of technology to do all of this requires that Virginia and Greg, as well as other teachers and teacher educators, clearly decide what they want technology to do and how they want it to do it! As noted, this means that teachers and teacher educators must develop and articulate clear views of what technology experiences can be called educational and operationalize these views in their classrooms. They must also represent—and perhaps defend—their professional judgments and beliefs about technology to students, parents, peers, and community leaders. Virginia and Greg have already figured out that technology will not subdue the endless enemies of the strong professional educator.

How Can Technology Help?

Trying to articulate and operationalize the roles of technology in teaching and teacher education necessarily means deciding what technology can do for each. Today, there are few indications this is happening. There are no indications it happened in the past. For instance, there is no evidence that teacher education contributed in any way to the technological successes of the 1980s, namely, calculators, distance learning, computer-assisted instruction (CAI), and desktop publishing and word processing (Honey & Henriquez, 1993). It seems worth noting at this point that technology cuts right through two large, ever-changing landscapes: higher education and K–12 education. This situation contributes to the malaise and bewilderment that surrounds attempts to define and operationalize the roles of technology in teaching and teacher education. For example, consider teacher educators. On the one hand, they will be expected to use technology to teach their academic specializations. On the other, they will be expected to introduce preservice and in-service teachers to technology that can be used with their K–12 students. These are distinct and separate applications of technology, neither of which currently supports the other. In the future, teacher educators will find themselves struggling to figure out not only what technology can do for teacher education in higher education classrooms but also what technology can do in K–12 classrooms.

Today, modern technology is available in most K–12 classrooms and teacher education classrooms but only in the form of TVs, VCRs, and videotapes. Beyond these, technology is not having a widespread impact on teaching or teacher education (Bennett & Bennett, 1994; Kline, 1994; Strudler, 1994; U.S. Congress, Office of Technology Assessment, 1988, 1995; Waxman & Huang, 1993). (See also Willis & Mehlinger, Chap. 45, this volume.) More than a few critics of technology have noted that technology has produced no notable or worthwhile changes in teaching or learning (Cuban, 1989; Hannafin & Savenye, 1993; Hill, 1994; LaFrenz & Friedman, 1989; *MacWorld*, 1992; Papert, 1993; Perelman, 1992; Pillar, 1992; Postman, 1992; Scrimshaw, 1993; Selby, 1993). Higher education may be in worse shape than K–12 education (Greene, 1991). According to Kline (1994), technology in teacher education classes at institutions of higher education are lagging behind other academic specializations. In a review of technology applications in higher education journals and periodicals, Kline (1994) found a handful of articles about the use of technology in education and no articles about technology in teacher education. This suggested that although technology is being used in some higher education academic specializations, it is not being used to educate teachers. In surveys, Strudler (1994) and Strudler and Gall (1988) came to the same conclusions but found that teacher educators would like to use technology—but are not.

The Future: Trying to Figure It Out!

Pundits, columnists, and commentators aside, as Virginia, Greg, and other educators struggle to articulate and operationalize views of technology in their classrooms, they will notice little agreement among themselves in views or actions. Some will seek to implement instruction and learning anchored by technology. Others will see technology leading to "different forms of thinking [that] lead to different forms of meaning" (Eisner, 1993, p. 6). Some will use technology to minimize weaknesses of classroom practices, while, they hope, maximizing the strengths. Others will use technology as an almost unnoticed tool incorporated naturally into teaching and learning much like paper, pencils, and erasers. Finally, some teachers will use technology to do the same things they have always done— perhaps more efficiently and effectively.

Today and in the future, teacher educators will have to grapple with technology issues not only in their own academic specializations but also in K–12 classrooms (see Carey, Carey, Willis, & Willis, 1993; Willis, Robin, & Willis, 1994, for a number of articles on these issues, and see also U.S. Department of Education, Office of Research, Using Technology to Support Education Reform, 1993). As noted, these are separate issues, but each share common principles. (1) Integration of technology throughout the curriculum is advantageous for teaching and learning, and (2) teacher education classes that involve integrated technology practices will enhance classroom teachers' efforts to integrate technology with their own students.

If teacher education programs accept these two principles, and assuming appropriate technologies are available and supported, it seems to follow that they will set as a goal the integration of technology into all phases of teacher education programs. Having set that goal, though, teacher education programs will have to consider how to meet it.

Currently most teacher education programs claim some degree of emphasis on technology. Typically, they offer two general types of courses where teachers might have an opportunity to discuss and perhaps use technology. The first may be an introductory course on educational technology and media. The second may be an academic specialization course dealing with subjects such as language arts or mathematics education where technology may be included (Dunfey, 1989; French, Landretti, & Tutolo, 1993; Honey & Moeller, 1990; Humphreys, 1989; O'Donnell, 1991; Sommer & Collins, 1989). Good intentions aside, most of these educational technology and academic specialization courses only "introduce" students to technology. Classroom modeling, observation, and teaching experiences with technology in K–12 schools where students and teachers are actually using technology generally are not included (Handler, 1993; Newren & Lasher, 1993; Newren, Waggener, & Kopp, 1991; Novak & Knowles, 1991).

Despite claims by teacher education institutions that technology is an important part of the curriculum, preservice teachers report they received little technology education and as a result feel unprepared to use technology in K–12 classrooms and probably feel as if their students know more about technology than they do (Handler, 1993; Hunt, 1994; Kraus, Hoffman, Oughton, & Rosenbluth, 1994; Kromhout & Butzin, 1993; Topp, Thompson, & Schmidt, 1994; U.S. Congress, Office of Technology Assessment, 1988, 1995). Several years ago, Shiengold (1991) noted that instructors in teacher education programs must be able to help teachers use technology in their classroom practices. Courses on only hardware and software are not enough. In addition, instructors must move away from isolated examples of technology removed from any relationship to the curriculum and any meaningful classroom contexts (Finkel, 1993). Teachers need help developing classroom environments that support technology integration. As Carey (1994) noted, teacher education programs must deal with models of instruction, curriculum, and learning with technology. If technology is to have any chance of success, teachers must be comfortable with it and see it as a resource that enables rather than interferes with daily teaching.

In-service or graduate teacher education does not fare much better. Three recent surveys report that teachers in the United States had little or no education on how to apply technology to teaching and learning (International Association for the Evaluation of Educational Achievement, 1992; U.S. Congress, Office of Technology Assessment, 1988, 1995; see also Brooks & Kopp, 1989; Carey et al., 1993; Willis et al., 1994). The consequences are obvious. To cite just one example: In 1989 the San Francisco, California, public schools installed 17 multimedia systems along with social studies and history software developed by the National Geographic Society. No teacher in-service education was provided. By the end of the school year most of the systems were idle. Only after teachers were given training in how to integrate the multimedia content into their lesson plans did teachers start using the systems (Yoder, 1991). Of course, this example points out the fallacy of purchasing hardware and software and ignoring teacher education (Stoddart & Niederhauser, 1994).

What should the programs of the future look like? Or perhaps put more simply, what technology skills should teacher educators emphasize either in the support of their academic specializations or K–12 applications? The International Society for Technology in Education (ISTE, 1992) has provided some suggestions. To meet the technology needs of the next century, ISTE maintains that teachers should be able to:

1. Operate a computer system in order to use software successfully
2. Evaluate and use computers and related technologies to support the instructional process
3. Apply current instructional principles, research, and appropriate assessment practices to the use of computers and related technologies
4. Explore, evaluate, and use computer technology–based materials
5. Demonstrate knowledge of uses of computers for problem solving, data collection, information management, communications, presentations, and decision making
6. Design and develop student learning activities that integrate computing and technology for a variety of student grouping strategies and for diverse student populations
7. Evaluate, select, and integrate computer technology–based instruction in one's own subject area(s) and/or grade level(s)
8. Demonstrate knowledge of multimedia, hypermedia, and telecommunications activities to support instruction
9. Demonstrate skill in using productivity tools for professional and personal use, including word processing, data base, spreadsheet, and print/graphic utilities
10. Demonstrate knowledge of equity, ethical, legal, and human issues of computing and technology
11. Identify resources for staying current in applications of computing and related technologies in education
12. Use computer-based technologies to access information to enhance personal and professional productivity
13. Apply computers and related technologies to facilitate emerging roles of the learner and the educator

The ideal way to incorporate these ISTE suggestions into teacher education programs is for instructors to model technology use in their classrooms (Handler, 1993; Munday, Windham, & Stamper, 1991). To this statement must be added the requirement that for K–12 applications, the modeling should take place in "real" classrooms with teachers and students in as rich a contextual environment as possible. This is especially important for preservice teachers who lack the experience-based contexts that make technology demonstrations meaningful. Instructors must demonstrate that technology can be educationally useful and contribute in some way to the learning process (Bork, 1985). Unfortunately, to provide courses with modeling requires instructors with expertise in academic specializations, an understanding of K–12 applications, and an understanding of school culture.

In summary, probably every teacher educator would like to broaden the roles of technology in both academic specialization and K–12 applications. Unfortunately, these ever-broadening roles make enormous requirements of technologies as well as teacher educators. Above all else, teacher educators must articulate and operationalize what they want technology to do and how they want it to do it (Robinson, 1993). Perhaps they need to begin with just one class or perhaps even one teacher.

Swan and Mitrani (1993) found that behavior changing interactions between individual teachers and students involving technology happen at a very basic level, that is, one student and one teacher, not with teachers and groups of students.

Three Technologies for the Future

As Virginia, Greg, and other educators struggle to articulate and operationalize views of technology in their classrooms, they can center their efforts around three technologies that can provide immediate help for their students: telecommunications, desktop publishing and word processing, and multimedia.

Telecommunication This is the decade of the Infobahn, the I-highway (information), and the Internet. These communication technologies are bringing together people and information at a speed unimaginable in the past. As a result immense shifts in the structure of communications have brought explosive growth to the telecommunication industries. It has not gone unnoticed by Virginia and Greg—and most others—that telecommunication has the potential to alter teaching and learning (National Research Council, 1994). Rosy predictions abound! Slogans are solutions! We have within our grasp the technological means to construct learning environments that have the informational density of the Library of Congress, the pedagogical skill of Socrates, and the excitement and holding power of a video game. Learners in these new networked environments are able to marshall colleagues, faculty, libraries, laboratories, and other resources from around the world at their own pace, according to their own schedule, in a setting of their own choosing, and in close contact and cooperation with others. But there are questions. Changing the way people communicate can be both good and bad. Steinberg (1994) recently suggested that despite the enormous potential of telecommunication, at least one component is not meeting more lofty expectations, namely, E-mail and bulletin boards. This asynchronous media has exposed the weakness of humans to idle chatter and gossip. "When a message can be sent in a matter of seconds at virtually no cost to the sender and has a life span of only a few weeks, there is little incentive to spend much time on its content" (p. 25).

TELECOMMUNICATIONS DEFINED. Telecommunication has historically meant simply communication across distances, but more recently it has come to mean "electronic" or "digital" communication across distances. Its ultimate goal is to create individual networks that allow the flow of information widely and with little resistance from individual to individual.

Today, at its most basic level, telecommunication involves four technologies: (1) a computer, (2) a modem, (3) a phone line, and (4) networks. More advanced telecommunication involves television, cable television (including interactive multimedia software), narrowcasting, videotape, compact and laser disc, satellite, and the latest in high-bandwidth fiber optics. These technologies, individually or as a group, do not automatically allow teachers and students electronic communication or broadcast rights and capabilities. Instead, they must be linked or networked for these rights to be obtained. Once linked or networked, telecommunication technologies can provide for:

(1) communication—forums, bulletin boards, E-mail, (2) instruction and instructional resources management, (3) curriculum and staff development, (4) administration, (5) library management, and (6) information processing.

The opportunities for telecommunication networks to support educators are almost limitless. In the United States alone, an educators telecommunication network could contain 80,000 K–12 schools, 15,000 school districts, 7 million teachers and teaching staff, 45 million students, and several thousand colleges of education and educational agencies—quite a network! Already there are dozens of commercial and noncommercial networks for teachers and students (e.g., Internet, Compuserve, America Online, eWorld, Prodigy, National Geographic Kids Network, Kidsnet, FrEdMail, Learning Link, NASA Space Link, NREN-National Research Education Network). Many teachers and students are already avid telecommunication users. A recent nationwide survey of K–12 teachers that used telecommunication networks regularly in their classrooms found that (1) communication and (2) reference searches were the major applications (Honey & Henriquez, 1993).

It is possible to suggest that telecommunication networks have the potential to change some of the ways teachers and their students interact, communicate, and learn from one another. Through telecommunication networks teachers and students have an opportunity to affect what people think and feel by influencing those with whom they communicate by changing perceptions and opinions (Kurshan & Dawson, 1992; MacKenthun, 1992; Marcus, 1990). The emergence of telecommunication networks can allow teachers and students to create worldwide classrooms, in essence tapping into a global mind that metaphorically exists as students, teachers, and computers come together through telecommunications. Students and teachers can become global information artists by combining multimedia techniques to disseminate their work locally, nationally, and worldwide. To this end, Rogers (1986) has suggested that telecommunications can provide a substitute for transportation: Instead of moving people to information and ideas, telecommunication networks move information and ideas to people.

Although telecommunication uses are at present limited to a few schools, in the near future many classrooms will regularly be using it for teacher and student projects, teacher and student networking, and bringing new resources into classrooms.

THE FUTURE OF TELECOMMUNICATIONS. What will classroom telecommunication (including networks) look like? The U.S. government has officially termed telecommunication (networks) the National Information Infrastructure (NII). Despite the title, the NII has no ownership or management. It is defined and influenced by the environment in which it is used. As a result, many diverse groups have suggestions on how the NII should look. For example, a government-sponsored group, the National Coordinating Committee and FORUM on Technology in Education and Training (1994) has suggested the following: The NII should be (1) ubiquitous and extend throughout all segments of society; (2) permit the high-speed transmission of voice, video, data, and multimedia; (3) provide seamless interconnection among all relevant information networks and services; (4) have a comprehensive directory of users, resources, and services; (5) be user friendly; (6) support interaction among users; (7) possess adequate measures to ensure the security of resources on the network; (8) coordinate NII related-education and training activities conducted by federal departments and identify and disseminate to regional, state, and local agencies those applications that are successful; and (9) integrate the NII and related technologies into national and state plans for education and training.

What demands will classroom telecommunication (NII) place on teachers and teacher educators? No one knows yet! But, teachers and teacher educators will need to define areas of responsibility and accountability. Teachers interested in telecommunications, like Virginia and Greg as well as teacher educators, will need to make explicit the benefits for students. All educators will need to accept responsibility for the development of a framework for telecommunication standards. Educators will need to acquire technical expertise to use telecommunications, especially to retrieve, evaluate, shape, and manipulate information. Educators will need to develop a research and development agenda aimed at documenting the advantages and disadvantages of telecommunications for themselves and their students.

Still another issue concerns the "look and feel" of classroom telecommunication. Will it end up looking like a TV? A computer? A video game? A telephone? A movie? or something else? Although what we are presenting is an oversimplification of many complex issues, the "look and feel" issue is more important than one might think because it determines who will control the *format* and *content* of classroom telecommunications. There are fundamental differences between communication, entertainment, and computer industries on many issues that will affect teaching and teacher education. For example, will classrooms have access to quality programming or reruns of commercial shows? Will classrooms become another market for advertisement? Who will have access to telecommunications? At what costs? Will the rich schools get telecommunications and the poor schools TVs and videotapes? As teachers and teacher educators struggle to articulate and operationalize their views on telecommunications, these and many more questions need answers. Teachers like Virginia and Greg are especially concerned with questions about teaching and learning. How can telecommunications lead to more learning and understanding? Can these opportunities be universal? Will the I-highway also be the E-highway (education)? Will the much-heralded claims of "expanded areas of communication" and "easier flows of information" come true—and to whose benefit? What will the students learn? What will it mean? How will they use that information? How can strong professionals develop a curricula platform in the midst of so much uncertainty? These questions and many more plague educators (Pearlman, 1994). In the final analysis, the I-Highway may contain all the problems encountered by its metaphorical parent with cracks, holes, ruts, poor signs, wrecks, off-ramps at the wrong places, inconsiderate motorists—and drive-by shootings.

Desktop Publishing and Word Processing

Desktop publishing and word processing technologies have changed the way some people communicate. All aspects of society have felt the impact of these technologies, and teaching and teacher education are not exceptions.

DESKTOP PUBLISHING AND WORD PROCESSING DEFINED. Very simply put, word processing programs allow writers to create and manipulate language through additions and deletions, cutting and pasting of text, and any number of other text or graphic arrangements or formats. Many programs include editing aids such as spelling checkers, grammar checkers, and thesauruses. Once word processing documents have been created, desktop publishing programs allow the writers to become printers, creating print and pictorial documents through features that include editing and formatting. (How the document looks!) In addition, desktop publishing and word processing programs can be networked to other electronic information systems such as data bases and on-line libraries for even more applications. This diversity of applications was found in a recent study of 600 K–12 teachers who considered themselves technology users. Teachers reported using an average of 14 to 15 different applications in their classrooms. Word processing was the most common application, and the most common uses for word processing revolved around student projects such as reports and newsletters (Brady, 1991).

THE FUTURE OF DESKTOP PUBLISHING AND WORD PROCESSING. Several issues surround how teachers and teacher educators will use technology to write and publish in meaningful and productive ways. Discussions about these issues have just begun to appear in the literature (Lewis, 1991; Ornstein, 1992; see also Carey et al., 1993; Willis et al., 1994). A particular issue will continue to be the type of desktop publishing and word processing technologies used in the classroom. There are a wide variety of old and new technologies available. So, what are Virginia, Greg, other teachers, and teacher educators to do with the mismatch of desktop and word processing technologies? What about the newest technologies and the ones who had their moment of glory but are now left behind? For instance, what is Virginia to do with the educational technology laboratory that has desktop publishing and word processing technologies that have been outdated for years? There are no easy answers. But, teachers and teacher educators should insist that students complete assignments (when appropriate), using up-to-date desktop publishing and word processing technologies. Obviously, as schools, parents, teachers, and teacher educators begin to adopt newer forms of desktop publishing and word processing, these forms have greater potential for enhancing teaching and learning processes than do technologies of the past (Ornstein, 1992).

Another issue is which desktop publishing and word processing technologies work best? With which students? Under which conditions (Joram, Woodruff, Bryson, & Lindsay, 1992; Kean & Kean, 1992; Levin, 1991)? In addition, just because teachers and teacher educators place technologies in their classroom (or make them available) does not mean that students will use them. Moreover, it must be pointed out that technology tools like word processors do not guarantee success. Success for teachers and teacher education will come from *why* their students write, *what* they write, and *whom* they write to.

In the final analysis, desktop publishing and word processing probably have more potential to support teaching and teacher education than any of the other current technologies. Research seems to support the notion that these technologies have positive effects on K–12 teaching and learning (Cochran-Smith, 1991; Hawisher, 1989; Kozma, 1991; Macarthur, 1988). Anecdotal accounts would seem to confirm the value of desktop publishing and word processing not only for education but also throughout the culture. One anecdotal example might reinforce the point. The poem below was written by a man only identified as Ed. He had ALS (amyotrophic lateral sclerosis—Lou Gehrig's disease). He was bedridden, and the only movement he could control was his eyes. The poem below was written with a computer that recorded the movement of his eyelids with infrared sensors. It was featured in an article by Bill Machrone (1994) in *PC Magazine*.

> Every morning in Africa, a gazelle wakes up.
> It knows it must run faster than the fastest lion,
> Or it will be killed.
>
> Every morning in Africa, a lion wakes up,
> It knows that it must outrun the slowest
>   gazelle,
> Or it will starve to death.
>
> It doesn't matter whether you're a lion or a
>   gazelle,
> When the Sun comes up in the morning, you'd
>   better be running!

Multimedia Multimedia technologies have burgeoned. They are intended to be simply ways of exchanging or communicating information, but, they have become much more!

At the beginning of the twentieth century, multimedia meant blackboards and white chalk and a limited variety of books, paper, and pencils. By the midpoint of the twentieth century teachers had green boards and yellow chalk, television, radio, film projectors and films, filmstrip projectors and filmstrips, record players and records, overhead projectors and transparencies, audio tape recorders and audio tapes, as well as books, paper, and pencils in a wide variety of sizes, shapes, and colors. Today, exchanging information includes white boards and "magic markers," computers, cameras, videotape players and tapes, compact disc players and discs, videodisc (laserdisc) players and discs, interactive cable television, as well as telecommunication networks both ground and satellite based. For the future, what all this means is that the sprawl of information and the diversity of digital media that mark the end of the twentieth century present colossal changes and challenges for teachers and teacher educators.

MULTIMEDIA DEFINED. Multimedia applications "can best be defined as various combinations of text, graphics, sound, video, and animation that are controlled, coordinated and delivered by the computer" (Lynch, 1992, p. 2). These applications tie together any number of audio, video, and textual resources (i.e., compact disc, videodisc, films, records, microphones, audiotapes and recorders, videotapes and recorders, cameras, photographs, television, radio, telephone, printed text). At present and for the near future, to use state-of-the-art multimedia means that teacher educators must have computers that are powerful and fast. Computers with large internal and external

data storage and high-resolution color screens are needed. Computers with stereo sound and the ability to add, subtract, or mix sound, are common today. Finally, the computers need "plug and play" or "built-in" compact disk and/or videodisc (laserdisc) players. These multimedia computers also need internal computer programs that can provide the cohesiveness necessary to retrieve and guide video and audio information from its internal and external sources.

In K–12 classrooms and teacher education multimedia applications can be used for lecture/presentations, collaborative learning, individualized learning, and just about any other methodology imaginable. There is enough variety and versatility in multimedia that virtually any educator can use it in a classroom. For the immediate future, most multimedia applications will come in two varieties: "ready-to-use" (prepackaged) or "construct-your-own."

READY-TO-USE MULTIMEDIA. For the near future the most complex, advanced, and powerful multimedia application commercially available will continue to be IBM/EduQuest Illuminated Books and Manuscripts (including a related product entitled Columbus: A Journey to Discovery). Each of these titles (i.e., Letter From Birmingham Jail, Black Elk Speaks, Hamlet, Declaration of Independence, Ulysses) allows teachers and students to read and research literary works supported by a number of educational resources that include dictionaries, film, animation, speeches, discussions, still photographs—all of which help explore relationships between the literary works and other disciplines. Illuminated Books and Manuscripts has been described as a text augmentation system with a variety of audio and video enhancements. It provides an example that can inform teachers, students, and parents about what the future holds for multimedia and teaching.

CONSTRUCT-YOUR-OWN MULTIMEDIA. The construct-your-own or do-it-yourself applications provide tools that allow teacher educators and teachers to manipulate video and audio information and create their own multimedia programs. Technologically, these applications generally require multimedia personal computers, scanners, video/audio digitizers, CD-ROMs, videodiscs and cameras (still and videotape), printers, as well as authoring programs. So far, few examples have appeared in the literature documenting teacher educators' use of construct-your-own multimedia applications. However, as entertainment and technology companies continue to add easy-to-use digital audio and video to personal computers, teacher educators will begin to adopt the technology.

THE FUTURE OF MULTIMEDIA. One issue revolves around the complex alliances of businesses that have emerged to create and deliver multimedia worldwide. These businesses are primarily interested in offices, factories, and living rooms, not in classrooms. Educators will not find the diversity of multimedia applications available to the business and entertainment markets in their classrooms—at least not yet.

A second issue is cost. The proliferation of newer and better multimedia technologies makes it difficult to mix and match technologies as well as keep up with seemingly endless advancements. With limited funds, educators have a legitimate worry about locking in multimedia technologies and then watching something newer and better come along—as they inevitably will. Also, construct-your-own applications require special training as well as administrative and technical support.

A third issue is inherent in the very nature of multimedia. The media can become the message, and for many students the messages must be entertaining. It would seem almost a certainty that as the power and popularity of multimedia increase, so will the chances for misuse. As seems the case with many of the twentieth-century's most innovative technologies, the uses of multimedia are as powerful as they are troubling.

Despite these and other issues, teachers and teacher educators must remember that classroom uses of computer-based multimedia for teacher education are just beginning. Much remains to be determined, but one thing is certain: In the near future the dazzling array of multimedia sights and sounds that have been reserved for buying and selling, entertaining, and advertising, will be available to teacher educators courtesy of the multimedia.

Summary

In the future, technology will find more ways to help Virginia and Greg than they will find ways to help technology. What this means is that technology is not gently nudging teachers like Virginia and Greg toward the future; instead, it is constantly pressuring them and others. Teachers and teacher educators will be expected to use technology to provide educational alternatives and choices that expand and stretch opportunities for learning. And given ever-limiting education budgets, teachers will be expected to use technology to provide low-cost, inexpensive instructional resources. Teachers will also be expected to use technology to help students organize and structure complex tasks while providing access to real-life phenomena. For example, multimedia simulations delivered by telecommunications can provide teachers and students with learning situations that involve complex or previously unavailable phenomena such as real-time classroom demonstrations. Teachers will be expected to help students use resource-rich informational environments through electronic libraries and bulletin board systems via computer networks and satellite telecommunications. These telecommunication tools can promote collaboration between teachers and students across the street and around the globe. Finally, teachers and teacher educators will be expected to help with technology applications students who require individualized learning opportunities. The research of Swan and Mitrani (1993) seems particularly revealing about the future for technology in teaching and teacher education. They suggest that technology seems to be having a greater effect on educational practice than simply providing for the efficient delivery of instruction. Technology seems to be having the kind of effects that McLuhan (1964) maintained communications media would have on those who used them—that the defining properties of the media are internalized by the users, who then incorporate those properties into their thinking. The defining property of technology may well be interactivity. And it may well be that technology's interactivity will be reflected in more equal control of the student–teacher interac-

tion and greater individualization of learning. Students will expect interactive technologies at school and to use them at a pace that mirrors their applications in entertainment and business.

But as severe as these pressures will be, little can happen unless there are sufficient financial resources coupled with technology planning that features strong professional educators deciding what they want technology to do and how they want it to do it (Finkel, 1993; Honey & Moeller, 1990; MacCarthy, 1993; Mahmood & Hirt, 1992; Ritchie & Wiburg, 1993; Shiengold & Hadley, 1990; Whitaker, Schwartz, & Vockell, 1989; Wiburg, 1994). Without resources and planning, technology use in teaching and teacher education will develop not by design but by accretion. It will not resemble anything but a large amorphous protoplasmic organism, growing without a recognizable form and floating around willy-nilly.

One final story seems to illustrate some of the dilemmas faced by teachers and teacher educators in the struggle to use technology. In the short story *And madly teach* (Biggle, 1976) there are no longer schools on earth, and all students are taught at home through television. Students have 9,999 courses to choose from, courtesy of television. Teacher education is based on an educational philosophy entitled The New Education, and the accompanying textbook, *Techniques and Procedures of TV Teaching*. The philosophy features no evaluation of students' learning, no assignments, just evaluation of teachers. These evaluations are based on the number of TVs tuned to a particular lesson and how long the lesson is tuned in. A teacher's TV audience is sampled once every 2 weeks. One teacher, Miss Boltz, a new arrival from a traditional school on another planet, objects to New Education and TV teaching. A conversation between her and Mr. Stewart, one of the experienced TV physics teachers, reveals her misgivings:

[Miss Boltz:] I miss the students. It worries me, not being able to know them or to check on their progress.

[Mr. Stewart:] The New Education looks at it this way: We expose the child to the proper subject matter. The exposure takes place in his own home, which is the natural environment for him. He will absorb whatever his individual capacity permits, and more than that we have no right to expect.

[Miss Boltz:] The child has no sense of accomplishment—no incentive to learn.

[Mr. Stewart:] More irrelevant abstractions. What the New Education strives for is the technique that has made advertising such an important factor in our economy. Hold the people's attention, make them buy in spite of themselves. Or hold the student's attention and make him learn whether he wants to or not.

[Miss Boltz:] But, the student learns no social values!

[Mr. Stewart:] On the other hand, the school has no discipline problems. No extracurricular activities to supervise. No problem of transporting children to school and home again. You aren't convinced?

[Miss Boltz:] Certainly not!

[Mr. Stewart:] Keep it to yourself. And just between us, I'll tell you the most potent factor in this philosophy of the New Education. It's money. Instead of a fortune invested in buildings and real estate, with thousands of schools to maintain, we have one TV studio. We save another fortune in teachers' salaries by having one teacher for a good many thousands of students instead of one for maybe twenty or thirty. The bright kids will learn no matter how badly they're taught, and that's all our civilization needs—a few bright people to build a lot of bright machines. (p. 9)

CONCLUSION

We started this chapter by stating that the teacher of the future will have to be a strong professional. This was what Virginia sought and what Greg seeks to be. That fuzzy concept now has some substantive and moral shape.

The development of an articulate teacher who can operationalize beliefs and engage in politics to promote those beliefs is neither a lucky outcome nor merely a desirable outcome of a teacher education program. The development of such a teacher is the result of a deliberate program of teacher education. Moreover, teachers of this kind are required, not simply desirable, if our profession and our nation are to flourish. Public education is the linchpin of our democracy. Throughout most of the early decades of American education the goal of the schools was to have students so in touch with the practical world that upon graduation they could plant both feet firmly on the ground. Eventually less practical and more romantic and abstract goals for education were formulated, and some critics said that this ensured a situation where upon graduation students had both feet planted firmly in the air. In this complex postmodern world, where scholars of all fields are involved with the deconstruction and reinterpretation of knowledge, it appears that the students

of today will have both of their feet firmly planted on banana peels! Such precarious times call for the most personally integrated professional teachers—teachers that have strong (not fixed, but strong) educational platforms from which to operate. Through its teaching of the methods courses and the research base, through its introduction to the issues and needs of a multicultural and technological society, programs of teacher preparation must provide novice teachers the means to build coherent and compassionate curriculum platforms.

Clearly we have indicated an exciting future for teacher education, although one that is hard to realize. Aspects of our vision will only become common if the leaders of teacher preparation programs can:

- Demand the hours necessary for teacher education students to learn to teach and to assume the responsibilities of an educator, because it takes time to acquire such complex knowledge, skill, and moral sensitivity
- Find mechanisms to continue a formal involvement with the graduates of teacher preparation programs during their first few years on the job, for learning to teach is a developmental process
- Find the resources necessary to conduct high-quality teacher preparation programs, because the education of strong professionals requires at least as much financial support as is given to other less lofty professions

References

Adler, M. (1982). *The Paideia Proposal: An educational manifesto*. New York: Macmillan.

Anderson, R. C., & Armbruster, B. B. (1990). *Some maxims for learning and instruction*. (Technical report No. 491). Urbana, IL: Center for the Study of Reading, University of Illinois.

Anonymous. (1994). *Verbatim quotes extracted from journals collected from doctoral students as part of a class on cultural diversity for aspiring school administrators*. Tempe, AZ: Arizona State University.

Aronowitz, S., & Giroux, H. A. (1985). *Education under siege: The conservative, liberal, and radical debate over schooling*. South Hadley, MA: Bergin & Garvey.

Asimov, I. (1974). *The best of Isaac Asimov*. New York: Doubleday.

Au, K. H. (1993). *Literacy instruction in multicultural settings*. Fort Worth: Harcourt Brace Jovanovich.

Barone, T. (1987). Educational platforms, teacher selection, and school reform: Issues emanating from a biographical case study. *Journal of Teacher Education. 38*(2), 13–18.

Barone, T., & Eisner, E. (in press). Arts-based educational research. In R. M. Jaeger (Ed.), *Complementary methods for research in education* (2nd ed.). Washington, DC: American Educational Research Association.

Beauchamp, G. A. (1981). *Curriculum theory* (4th ed.). Itasca, IL: Peacock Publishers.

Beck, L., & Newman, R. (1992, October). *Caring in contexts of diversity: Notes from the field*. Paper presented at the annual meeting of the University Council for Educational Administration, Philadelphia, PA.

Bennett, C. I. (1990). *Comprehensive multicultural education: Theory and practice*. Boston: Allyn & Bacon.

Bennett, C., & Bennett, J. (1994). United we stand: A portrait of teachers and technology in rural America. In J. Willis, B. Robin, & D. Willis (Eds.), *Technology and teacher education annual* (pp. 725–729).

Charlottesville, VA: Association for the Advancement of Computing in Education.

Berliner, D. C. (1984). Making the right changes in preservice teacher education. *Phi Delta Kappan, 66,* 94–96.

Berliner, D. C. (1993). The 100-year journey of educational psychology: From interest, to disdain, to respect for practice. In T. K. Fagen & G. R. VanderBos (Eds.), *Exploring applied psychology: Origins and critical analyses*. Washington, DC: American Psychological Association.

Berliner, D. C. (1994). The wonders of exemplary performances. In J. N. Mangieri & C. C. Block (Eds.), *Creating powerful thinking in teachers and students*. Fort Worth, TX: Harcourt Brace.

Bernstein, R. (1986). *Philosophical profiles*. Philadelphia: University of Pennsylvania Press.

Betances, S. (1990). Understanding the dimensions of the problem. In J. G. Bain & J. L. Herman (Eds.), *Making schools work for underachieving students*. New York: Greenwood.

Beyer, L. (1984). Field experience, ideology, and the development of critical reflectivity. *Journal of Teacher Education, 35*(3), 121–136.

Biggle, L. (1976). *A galaxy of strangers*. New York: Doubleday.

Billups, L. H. (1984). The American Education of Teachers educational research and dissemination program. In J. R. Egbert & M. M. Kluender (Eds.), *Using research to improve teacher education*. Lincoln: The Nebraska Consortium, College of Education, University of Nebraska.

Bork, A. (1985). *Personal computers in education*. New York: Harper & Row.

Borko, H. (1992, April). *Patterns across the profiles: A critical look at theories of learning to teach*. Paper presented at the annual meeting of the American Educational Research Association, San Francisco.

Borko, H., & Putnam, R. (1996). Learning to teach. In D. C. Berliner & R. C. Calfee (Eds.), *Handbook of educational psychology*. New York: Macmillan.

Bowers, C. A., & Flinders, D. J. (1990). *Responsive teaching: An ecological approach to classroom patterns of language, culture and thought*. New York: Teachers College Press.

Brady, H. (1991). New survey summarizes what top technology teachers have learned. *Technology and Learning, 11*(4), 38.

Brooks, D., & Kopp, T. (1989). Technology in teacher education. *Journal of Teacher Education, 40,* 2–8.

Bullough, R. (1989). *First year teacher: A case study*. New York: Teachers College Press.

Callahan, R. (1962). *Education and the cult of efficiency*. Chicago: University of Chicago Press.

Carey, D. (1994). Teacher roles and technology integration: Moving from teacher as director to teacher as facilitator. *Computers in the Schools, 9*(2/3), 105–118.

Carey, D., Carey, R., Willis, D., & Willis, J. (Eds.). (1993). *Technology and Teacher Education Annual—1993*. Charlottesville, VA: Association for the Advancement of Computing in Education.

Carr, W., & Kemmis, S. (1986). *Becoming critical: Education, knowledge, and action research*. London: Falmer.

Carroll, J. B. (1963). A model of school learning. *Teachers College Record, 64,* 723–733.

Carroll, J. B. (1985). The model of school learning: Progress of an idea. In C. W. Fisher & D. C. Berliner (Eds.), *Perspectives on instructional time*. New York: Longman.

Carter, K. (1993). The place of story in the study of teaching and teacher education. *Educational Researcher, 22*(1), 5–12, 18.

Casey, K. (1993). *I answer with my life: Life histories of women teachers working for social change*. New York: Routledge.

Cherry-Holmes, C. (1988). *Power and criticism: Poststructuralist investigations in education*. New York: Teachers College Press.

Clay, M. M. (1985). *The early detection of reading difficulties*. Portsmouth, NH: Heinemann.

Cochran-Smith, M. (1991). Learning to teach against the grain. *Harvard Educational Review, 61*(3), 279–310.

Cohen, E. G. (1994). *Designing groupwork: Strategies for the heterogenous classroom*. New York: Teachers College Press.

Cohen, P., Kulik, J. A., & Kulik, C. C. (1982). Educational outcomes of tutoring. *American Educational Research Journal, 19,* 237–248.

Coles, R. (1989). *The call of stories: Teaching and the moral imagination*. Boston: Houghton Mifflin.

Collins, M., & Tamarkin, C. (1982). *Marva Collins' way*. New York: St. Martin's Press.

Colton, A., & Sparks-Langer, G. (1993). A conceptual framework to guide the development of teacher education and decision making. *Journal of Teacher Education, 44*(1), 45–54.

Cuban, L. (1989). Neoprogressive visions and organizational realities. *Harvard Educational Review, 59*(2), 217–222.

Cummings, J. (1986). Empowering minority students: A framework for intervention. *Harvard Educational Review, 56*(12), 18–36.

Cummins, J. (1988). From multicultural to anti-racist education: An analysis of programmes and policies in Ontario. In T. Skutnabb-Kangas & J. Cummins (Eds.), *Minority education: From shame to struggle*. Clevendon: Multilingual Matters.

Darling-Hammond, L. (1988). Accountability and teacher professionalism. *American Educator, 12*(4), 8–13, 38–43.

Dewey, J. (1963). *Experience and education*. New York: Collier Books.

Díaz, S., Moll, L. C., & Mehan, H. (1986). Sociocultural resources in instruction: A context-specific approach. In *Beyond language: Social and cultural factors in schooling language minority students*. Los Angeles: Office of Bilingual Education, California State Department of Education, Evaluation, Dissemination and Assessment Center.

Dickens, C. (1969). *Hard times for these times*. Harmondsworth: Penguin.

Donmoyer, R., & Kos, R. (1993). *At-risk students: Portraits, policies, programs and practices*. Albany: State University of New York Press.

Dunfey. (1989). Integrating computers into the language arts curriculum at Lesley College. In C. Selfe, D. Rodrigues, & W. Oates (Eds.), *Computer in English and the Language Arts* (pp. 17–26). Urbana, IL: National Council of Teachers of English.

Ebmeier, H., Twombly, S., & Teeter, D. J. (1991, April). *The comparability and adequacy of financial support for schools of education*. Paper presented at the annual meeting of the American Educational Research Association, Chicago.

Egan, K. (1986). *Teaching as story telling*, Chicago: The University of Chicago Press.

Eisenhart, M., & Jones, D. (1992, April). *Developing teacher expertise: Two theories and a study*, Paper presented at the annual meeting of the American Educational Research Association, San Francisco.

Eisner, E. (1993). Forms of understanding and the future of educational research. *Educational Researcher, 22*(7), 5–11.

Eisner, E., & Vallance, E. (1974). *Conflicting conceptions of curriculum*. Berkeley: McCutchan.

Ellel, J. (1964). *The technological society*. New York: Knopf.

Feather, N. (Ed.). (1982). *Expectations and actions*. Hillsdale, NJ: Erlbaum.

Fenstermacher, G. D. (1990). Some moral considerations on teaching as a profession. In J. D. Goodlad, R. Soder, & K. A. Sirotnik (Eds.), *The moral dimensions of teaching* (pp. 130–151). San Francisco: Jossey-Bass.

Fenstermacher, G. D., & Berliner, D. C. (1985). A conceptual framework for evaluating staff development. *Elementary School Journal, 85,* 281–314.

Finkel, L. (1993). Moving your district toward technology. In T. Cannings & L. Finkel (Eds.), *The technology age classroom* (pp. 254–256). Wilsonville, OR: Franklin, Beedle & Associates.

Foster, W. (1986). *Paradigms and promises: New approaches to educational administration*. Buffalo, NY: Prometheus Books.

Freire, P. (1970). *Pedagogy of the oppressed*. (M. B. Ramos, Trans.) New York: Seabury.

French, M., Landretti, A., & Tutolo, D. (1993). Enhancing use of computer technology in an integrated reading/language arts methods class. In D. Carey, R. Carey, D. Willis, & J. Willis (Eds.), *Technology and Teacher Education Annual* (pp. 117–121), Charlottsville, VA: Association for the Advancement of Computing in Education.

Friedson, E. (1986). *Professional powers*. Chicago: University of Chicago Press.

Fullan, M. (1982). *The meaning of educational change*. New York: Teachers College Press.

Fullan, M. G. (1991). *The new meaning of educational change*. New York: Teachers College Press.

Gage, N. L., & Berliner, D. C. (1992). *Educational Psychology* (5th ed.). Boston: Houghton Mifflin.

Galluzzo, G. R., & Pankratz, R. S. (1990, September–October). Five attributes of a teacher education program knowledge base. *Journal of Teacher Education, 41*(4), 7–14.

Gardner, H. (1983). *Frames of mind*. New York: Basic Books.

Giroux, H. (1988). *Schooling and the struggle for public life*. Minneapolis: University of Minnesota Press.

Giroux, H. A., Simon, R. I., & contributors. (1989). *Popular culture: Schooling and everyday life*. Toronto: Ontario Institute for Studies in Education.

Goldenberg, C., & Gallimore, R. (1991). Local knowledge, research knowledge, and educational change: A case study of first-grade Spanish reading improvement. *Educational Researcher, 29*(8), 2–14.

Good, T. L., & Grouws, D. A. (1979). The Missouri mathematics effectiveness project. *Journal of Educational Psychology, 71,* 355–362.

Goodlad, J. (1984). *A place called school.* New York: McGraw-Hill.

Goodlad, J. I. (1990a). Studying the education of educators: From conception to findings. *Phi Delta Kappan, 71,* 698–701.

Goodlad, J. I. (1990b). *Teachers for our nation's schools.* San Francisco: Jossey-Bass.

Goodman, J. (1986). Teaching preservice teachers a critical approach to curriculum design: A descriptive account. *Curriculum Inquiry, 16*(2), 179–201.

Goodman, J. (1988). The political tactics and teaching strategies of reflective, active preservice teachers. *The Elementary School Journal, 89*(1), 23–41.

Goodman, J. (1992). *Elementary schooling for critical democracy.* Albany: State University of New York Press.

Goodson, I. (1994). Studying the teacher's life and work. *Teaching & Teacher Education, 10*(1), 29–37.

Goswami, D., & Stillman, P. (Eds.). (1987). *Reclaiming the classroom: Teacher research as an agency for change.* Philadelphia: Falmer.

Greene, B. (1991). A survey of computer integration into college courses. *Educational Technology, 31*(6), 37–47.

Greeno, J. G., Collins, A., & Resnick, L. B. (1996). Cognition and learning. In D. C. Berliner & R. C. Calfee (Eds.), *Handbook of educational psychology.* New York: Macmillan.

Griffin, G. A. (1986, October). *Teaching as a profession: The reform agenda for teacher education.* Thirteenth annual Finkelstein Memorial Lecture, University of Rhode Island, Kingston, RI.

Griffin, G. A. (1988). Leadership for curriculum improvement: The school administrator's role. In L. N. Tanner (Ed.), *Critical issues in curriculum: Eighty-seventh yearbook of the National Society for the Study of Education* (pp. 244–266). Chicago: The University of Chicago Press.

Handler, M. (1993). Preparing new teachers to use computer technology: Perceptions and suggestions for teacher education. *Computers in Education, 20*(2), 147–156.

Hannafin, R., & Savenye, W. (1993). Technology in the classroom: The teacher's new role and resistance to it. *Educational Technology, 33*(6), 26–31.

Hawisher, G. (1989). Research and recommendations for computers and composition. In G. Hawisher & C. Selfe (Eds.), *Critical perspectives on computers and composition instruction* (pp. 44–69). New York: Teachers College Press.

Heath, S. B. (1983). *Ways with words.* New York: Cambridge University Press.

Henderson, J. (1992). *Reflective teaching: Becoming an inquiring educator.* New York: Macmillan.

Hill, D. (1994, January). Professor Papert and his learning machine. *Teacher,* 16–19.

Honey, M., & Henriquez, A. (1993). *Telecommunications and K–12 educators: Findings from a national survey.* New York: Center for Technology in Education, Bank Street College of Education.

Honey, M., & Moeller, B. (1990). *Teachers' beliefs about technology integration: Different values, different understandings.* (ERIC Document Reproduction Service No. ED 326 203)

House, E. R. (1994). Policy and productivity in higher education. *Educational Researcher, 23*(5), 27–32.

Humphreys, D. (1989). *A computer-training program for English teachers: Cuyahoga Community College and the urban initiatives action program.* In C. Selfe, D. Rodrigues, & W. Oates (Eds.), *Computer in English and the Language Arts* (pp. 3–16). Urbana, IL: National Council of Teachers of English.

Hunt, N. (1994). Intentions and implementations: The impact of technology coursework in elementary classrooms. In J. Willis, B. Robin, & D. Willis (Eds.), *Technology and Teacher Education Annual* (pp.

38–41). Charlottesville, VA: Association for the Advancement of Computing in Education.

International Association for the Evaluation of Educational Achievement. (1992). *Computers in American schools, 1992: An overview.* Minneapolis: International Association for the Evaluation of Educational Achievement. (Available from IEA, Computers in Education Study, University of Minnesota, 909 Social Sciences, 267 19th Ave., South, Minneapolis, MN, 55455–0412)

International Society for Technology in Education. (1992). *Curriculum guidelines for accreditation of educational computing and technology programs.* Eugene, OR: Author.

Jackson, P. (1987). On the place of narration in teaching. In D. C. Berliner and B. Rosenshine (Eds.), *Talks to teachers.* New York: Random House.

Joram, E., Woodruff, E., Bryson, M., & Lindsay, P. (1992). The effects of revising with a word processor on written composition. *Research in the Teaching of English, 26,* 167–193.

Judge, H. (1988). Afterword. In A. Lieberman (Ed.), *Building a professional culture in schools.* New York: Teachers College Press.

Kean, D. M., & Kean, D. K. (1992). Using model technology. *Middle School Journal, 23,* 44–45.

Kline, F. (1994). Multimedia in teacher education: Coping with the human element. In J. Willis, B. Robin, & D. Willis (Eds.), *Technology and Teacher Education Annual* (pp. 759–763). Charlottesville, VA: Association for the Advancement of Computing in Education.

Kohl, H. (1983, August). Examining closely what we do. *Learning, 29.*

Kozma, R. (1991). Learning with media. *Review of Educatonal Research, 61,* 179–211.

Kraus, L., Hoffman, N., Oughton, J., & Rosenbluth, G. (1994). Student teachers' perceptions of technology in the schools. In J. Willis, B. Robin, & D. Willis (Eds.), *Technology and Teacher Education Annual* (pp. 42–45). Charlottesville, VA: Association for the Advancement of Computing in Education.

Kromhout, O., & Butzin, S. (1993). Integrating computers into the elementary school curriculum: An evaluation of nine Project CHILD model schools. *Journal of Research on Computing in Education, 26*(1), 55–69.

Kurshan, T., & Dawson, B. (1992). The global classroom: Reaching beyond the walls of the school building. *Teaching and Learning, 12,* 48–51.

LaFrenz, D., & Friedman, J. (1989). Computers don't change education, teachers do! *Harvard Educational Review, 59*(2), 222–225.

Levin, J. (1991). You can't just plug it in: integrating the computer into the curriculum (CAI). *Dissertation Abstracts International, 51/12A,* 4096-A.

Lewis, P. H. (1991). The technology of tomorrow. *Principal, 71,* 6–7.

Lieberman, A. (Ed.). (1988). *Building a professional culture in schools.* New York: Teachers College Press.

Liston, D. P. (1986). *Moral deliberation and reflective teacher action.* Paper presented at the annual meeeting of the American Educational Research Association, San Francisco, CA.

Lortie, D. C. (1975). *School teacher: A sociological study.* Chicago: University of Chicago Press.

Lucas, T. (1993). Secondary schooling for students becoming bilingual. In M. B. Arias & U. Casanova (Eds.), *Bilingual education: Politics, practice, and research.* Ninety-second Yearbook of the National Society for the Study of Education (Part 2). Chicago: University of Chicago Press.

Lynch, P. (1992). Teaching with multimedia. *Syllabus, 22,* 2–5.

Macarthur, C. (1988). The impact of computers on the writing process. *Exceptional Children, 54,* 536–542.

MacCarthy, R. (1993). Making the future work: The road to curriculum integration. In T. Cannings & L. Finkel (Eds.), *The technology age classroom* (pp. 246–253). Wilsonville, OR: Franklin, Beedle & Associates.

Machrone, B. (1994, June 28). Eyes on the Prize. *PC Magazine,* 87–88.

MacKenthun, C. (1992). Linking students in global communications. *Momentum, 23,* 44–46.

MacWorld (Staff). (1992, September 9). America's shame: Personal computers in education. *MacWorld,* 25–29.

Mahmood, M., & Hirt, S. (1992). *Evaluating a technology integration causal model for the K–12 public school curriculum: A LISREL analysis.* (ERIC Document Reproduction Service No. ED 346 847)

Marcus, S. (1990). Computers in the language arts: From pioneers to settlers. *Language Arts, 67,* 519–524.

McCaslin, M., & Good, T. L. (1996). The informal curriculum. In D. C. Berliner & R. C. Calfee (Eds.), *Handbook of educational psychology.* New York: Macmillan.

McLuhan, M. (1964). *Understanding media.* New York: McGraw-Hill.

Milk, R. D. (1993). Bilingual education and English as a second language: The elementary school. In M. B. Arias & U. Casanova (Eds.), *Bilingual education: Politics, practice, and research.* Ninety-second Yearbook of the National Society for the Study of Education (Part 2). Chicago: University of Chicago Press.

Moll, L. C. (Ed.). (1990). *Vygotsky and education: Instructional implications and applications of sociohistorical psychology.* New York: Cambridge University Press.

Moll, L. C. (1992, March). Bilingual classroom study and community analysis: Some recent trends. *Educational Researcher, 21*(2), 20–24.

Moll, L. C., Amanti, C., Neff, D., & González, N. (1992). Funds of knowledge for teaching: Using a qualitative approach to connect homes and classrooms. *Theory Into Practice, 31,* 132–141.

Munday, R., Windham, R., & Stamper, J. (1991). Technology for learning: Are teachers being prepared? *Educational Technology, 31*(3), 29–32.

National Coordinating Committee and FORUM on Technology in Education and Training. (1994). *NCC-TET National Policy Subcommittee Memorandum of January 18, 1994.* Alexandria, VA: ISTE.

National Council for Accreditation of Teacher Education (1987). *Standards, procedures and policies for the accreditation of professional education units.* Washington, DC: Author.

National Council for the Social Studies. (1993). A vision of powerful teaching and learning in the social studies: Building understanding and civic efficacy. *Social Education, 57*(5), 213–223.

National Council for the Social Studies. (1994). *Curriculum standards for the social studies* [Excerpted Draft]. Washington, DC: Author.

National Council of Teachers of Mathematics. (1989). *Curriculum and evaluation standards for school mathematics.* Reston, VA: Author.

National Research Council. (1994). *Realizing the information future.* National Research Council of the National Academy of Sciences. New York: National Academy Press.

Neilson, K. (1985). *Equality and liberty.* Totowa, NJ: Rowman and Allenheld.

Newmann, F. (1975). *Education for citizen action.* Berkeley: McCutchan.

Newren, E., & Lasher, E. (1993). The basic instructional media course for teacher education. *International Journal of Instructional Media, 20*(3), 251–262.

Newren, E., Waggener, J., & Kopp, T. (1991). Media and technology for preservice teachers: Design, development, and implementation of a basic course. *Educational Technology, 31*(12), 7–14.

Nieto, S. (1992). *Affirming diversity: The sociopolitical context of multicultural education.* White Plains, NY: Longman.

Novak, D., & Knowles, J. (1991). Beginning elementary teachers' use of computers in classroom instruction. *Action in Teacher Education, 13*(2), 43–51.

Oakes, J. (1985). *Keeping track: How schools structure inequality.* New Haven: Yale University Press.

O'Donnell, E. (1991). Teacher perceptions of their personal computer needs to integrate computers into their classroom instruction. *Dissertation Abstracts International,* 42A(10).

Ornstein, A. (1992). Making effective use of computer technology. *NASSP Bulletin: The Journal for Middle Level and High School Administrators, 76,* 27–33.

Palincsar, A. S., & Brown, A. L. (1984). Reciprocal teaching of comprehension fostering and comprehension monitoring activities. *Cognition and Instruction, 2,* 117–175.

Papert, S. (1993). *The children's machine: Rethinking school in the age of the computer.* New York: Basic Books.

Pearlman, R. (1994, May 25). Can K–12 education drive on the information superhighway? *Education Week,* 38, 48.

Perelman, L. (1992). *School's out: Hyper learning, the new technology, and the end of education.* New York: Morrow.

Pillar, C. (1992, September 9). Separate realities. *MacWorld,* 218–239.

Polya, G. (1954). *How to solve it.* Princeton: Princeton University Press.

Postman, N. (1985). *Amusing ourselves to death: Public discourse in the Age of Show Business.* New York: Penguin.

Postman, N. (1992). *Technology.* New York: Knopf.

Presidential Task Force on Psychology in Education/American Psychological Association. (1993). *Learner-centered psychological principles: Guidelines for school redesign and reform.* Washington, DC: American Psychological Association.

Project 2061, American Association for the Advancement of Science. (1989). *Science for all Americans: A Project 2061 report on literacy goals in science, mathematics, and technology.* Washington, DC: Author.

Project 2061, American Association for the Advancement of Science. (1993). *Benchmarks for science literacy.* New York: Oxford University Press.

Recruiting New Teachers, Inc. (1993). *State policies to improve the teacher workforce.* Belmont, MA: Author.

Richardson, V. K., Casanova, U., Placier, P., & Gilfoyle, K. (1989). *Schoolchildren at-risk.* London: Falmer.

Ritchie, D., & Wiburg, K. (1993). Integrating technologies into the curriculum: Why has it been so slow and how can we speed it up? In D. Carey, R. Carey, D. Willis, & J. Willis (Eds.), *Technology and Teacher Education Annual—1993* (pp. 268–272). Charlottesville, VA: Association for the Advancement of Computing in Education.

Robinson, B. (1993). The politics of technology in education and the role of teacher educators. In D. Carey, R. Carey, D. Willis, & J. Willis (Eds.), *Technology and Teacher Education Annual—1993* (pp. 9–13). Charlottesville, VA: Association for the Advancement of Computing in Education.

Rogers, E. (1986). *Communication technology: The new media in society.* New York: Free Press.

Ryle, G. (1949). *The concept of mind.* New York: Barnes & Noble.

Sarason, S. (1982). *The culture of school and the problem of change.* Boston: Allyn & Bacon.

Schön, D. (1983). *The reflective practitioner.* New York: Basic Books.

Scrimshaw, P. (Ed.). (1993). *Language, classrooms & computers.* London: Routledge.

Selby, C. (1993). Technology: From myths to realities. *Phi Delta Kappan, 74*(9), 684–689.

Shepard, L. A., & Smith, M. L. (Eds.) (1989). *Flunking grades: Research and policies on retention.* Philadelphia: Falmer.

Shiengold, K. (1991). Restructuring for learning with technology: The potential for synergy. *Phi Delta Kappan, 73*(1), 17–27.

Shiengold, K., & Hadley, M. (1990). *Accomplished teachers: Integrated computers into classroom practice.* New York: Teachers College Press.

Shulman, J. (1991). Classroom casebooks. *Educational Leadership, 49*(3), 28–31.

Silverman, R., Welty, W. M., & Lyon, S. (1994). *Educational psychology cases for teacher problem solving.* New York: McGraw-Hill.

Slavin, R. E. (1990). *Cooperative learning: Theory, research and practice.* Englewood Cliffs, NJ: Prentice-Hall.

Sleeter, C. E. (1992). *Keepers of the American dream: A study of staff development and multicultural education.* London: Falmer.

Sommer, E., & Collins, J. (1989). English teachers and the potential of microcomputers as instructional resources at the State University of Buffalo. In C. Selfe, D. Rodrigues, & W. Oates (Eds.), *Computer in English and the Language Arts* (pp. 27–42). Urbana, IL: National Council of Teachers of English.

Spencer, D. A. (1994). *Final report of the South Mountain High School research project.* Tempe: College of Education, Arizona State University.

Squire, L. R. (1987). *Memory and brain.* New York: Oxford University Press.

Steinberg, S. (1994, July). Travels on the Net. *Technology Review,* 20–31.

Stoddart, T., & Neiderhauser, D. (1994). Technology and educational change. *Computers in the Schools, 9*(2/3), 5–22.

Strudler, N. (1994). A tale of computer use at three elementary schools: Implications for teacher educators. In J. Willis, B. Robin, & D. Willis (Eds.), *Technology and Teacher Education Annual—1994* (pp. 756–758). Charlottesville, VA: Association for the Advancement of Computing in Education.

Strudler, N., & Gall, M. (1988). *Overcoming impediments to microcomputer implementation in the classroom.* (ERIC Document Reproduction Service No. ED 298 938)

Swan, K., & Mitrani, M. (1993). The changing nature of teaching and learning in computer-based classrooms. *Journal of Research on Computing in Education, 26*(1), 40–54.

Tobin, K. G. (1987). The role of wait-time in higher cognitive-level learning. *Review of Educational Research, 57,* 69–95.

Topp, N., Thompson, A., & Schmidt, D. (1994). Teacher preservice experiences and classroom computer use of recent college graduates. In J. Willis, B. Robin, & D. Willis (Eds.), *Technology and Teacher Education Annual—1994* (pp. 46–51). Charlottesville, VA: Association for the Advancement of Computing in Education.

Torres-Guzmán, M. E., Mercado, C. I., Quintero, A. H., & Rivera-Viera, D. (1994). Teaching and learning in Puerto Rican/Latino collaboratives: Implications for teacher education. In E. R. Hollins, J. E. King, & W. C. Hayman (Eds.), *Teaching diverse populations: Formulating a knowledge base.* Albany: State University of New York Press.

U.S. Congress, Office of Technology Assessment. (1988). *Power on!* Washington, DC: U.S. Government Printing Office.

U.S. Congress, Office of Technology Assessment. (1995). *Untitled.* (Report to be released in 1995) Washington, DC: U.S. Government Printing Office.

U.S. Department of Education, Office of Research. (1993). *Using technology to support education reform.* Washington, DC: U.S. Government Printing Office.

Vélez-Ibañez, C. G., & Greenberg, J. B. (1992, December). Formation and transformation of funds of knowledge among U.S.-Mexican households. *Anthropology & Education Quarterly, 23,* 313–335.

Walker, D. (1971). A naturalistic model for curriculum development. *School Review, 80,* 1–24.

Waxman, H., & Huang, S. (1993). Investigating computer use in elementary and middle school inner-city classrooms. In D. Carey, R. Carey, D. Willis, & J. Willis (Eds.), *Technology and Teacher Education Annual—1993* (pp. 524–527). Charlottesville, VA: Association for the Advancement of Computing in Education.

Whitaker, B., Schwartz, E., & Vockell, E. (1989). *The computer in the reading curriculum.* Watsonville, CA: Mitchell.

Wiburg, K. (1994). Integrating technologies into schools: Why has it been so slow? *The Computing Teacher, 21*(5), 6–8.

Willis, J., Robin, B., & Willis, D. (Eds.). (1994). *Technology and Teacher Education Annual—1994* Charlottesville, VA: Association for the Advancement of Computing in Education.

Winner, L. (1994, May–June). The virtually educated. *Technology Review, 66.*

Yoder, S. (1991, October 21). Readin', writin' and multimedia. *The Wall Street Journal,* p. R-12.

Zeichner, K. M., & Tabachnick, B. R. (1981). Are the effects of university teacher education "washed-out" by school experience? *Journal of Teacher Education, 32*(3), 7–11.

AUTHOR INDEX

SUBJECT INDEX